Noah's ark and the building of the Cities of Argos and Athens, from Jean de Courcy's
Chronicle of Bouquechardiere, *1450.*
(© Gianni Dagli Orti/CORBIS)

NEW
CATHOLIC
ENCYCLOPEDIA

NEW CATHOLIC ENCYCLOPEDIA

SECOND EDITION

10
Mos–Pat

Detroit • New York • San Diego • San Francisco • Cleveland • New Haven, Conn. • Waterville, Maine • London • Munich

in association with

THE CATHOLIC UNIVERSITY OF AMERICA • WASHINGTON, D.C.

The New Catholic Encyclopedia, Second Edition

Project Editors
Thomas Carson, Joann Cerrito

Editorial
Erin Bealmear, Jim Craddock, Stephen Cusack,
Miranda Ferrara, Kristin Hart, Melissa Hill,
Margaret Mazurkiewicz, Carol Schwartz,
Christine Tomassini, Michael J. Tyrkus

Permissions
Edna Hedblad, Shalice Shah-Caldwell

Imaging and Multimedia
Randy Bassett, Dean Dauphinais, Robert
Duncan, Leitha Etheridge-Sims, Mary K.
Grimes, Lezlie Light, Dan Newell, David G.
Oblender, Christine O'Bryan, Luke
Rademacher, Pamela Reed

Product Design
Michelle DiMercurio

Data Capture
Civie Green

Manufacturing
Rhonda Williams

Indexing
Victoria Agee, Victoria Baker, Francine
Cronshaw, Lynne Maday, Do Mi Stauber,
Amy Suchowski

© 2003 by The Catholic University of America.
Published by Gale. Gale is an imprint of The
Gale Group, Inc., a division of Thomson
Learning, Inc.

Gale and Design™ and Thomson Learning™
are trademarks used herein under license.

For more information, contact
The Gale Group, Inc.
27500 Drake Rd.
Farmington Hills, MI 48331-3535
Or you can visit our Internet site at
http://www.gale.com

While every effort has been made to ensure
the reliability of the information presented in
this publication, The Gale Group, Inc. does
not guarantee the accuracy of the data contained herein. The Gale Group, Inc. accepts
no payment for listing; and inclusion in the
publication of any organization, agency, institution, publication, service, or individual does
not imply endorsement of the editors or publisher. Errors brought to the attention of the
publisher and verified to the satisfaction of
the publisher will be corrected in future editions.

LIBRARY OF CONGRESS CATALOGING-IN-PUBLICATION DATA

New Catholic encyclopedia.—2nd ed.
    p. cm.
        Includes bibliographical references and indexes.
        ISBN 0-7876-4004-2
        1. Catholic Church—Encyclopedias. I. Catholic University of America.
BX841 .N44 2002
282' .03—dc21
        2002000924

ISBN: 0-7876-4004-2 (set)
0-7876-4005-0 (v. 1)
0-7876-4006-9 (v. 2)
0-7876-4007-7 (v. 3)
0-7876-4008-5 (v. 4)

0-7876-4009-3 (v. 5)
0-7876-4010-7 (v. 6)
0-7876-4011-5 (v. 7)
0-7876-4012-3 (v. 8)
0-7876-4013-1 (v. 9)

0-7876-4014-x (v. 10)
0-7876-4015-8 (v. 11)
0-7876-4016-6 (v. 12)
0-7876-4017-4 (v. 13)
0-7876-4018-2 (v. 14)
0-7876-4019-0 (v. 15)

Printed in the United States of America
10 9 8 7 6 5 4 3

West Hills College Coalinga
Fitch Library
300 Cherry Lane
Coalinga, CA 93210

For The Catholic University of America Press

EDITORIAL STAFF

Executive Editor
Berard L. Marthaler, O.F.M.Conv., S.T.D., Ph.D.

Associate Editor
Gregory F. LaNave, Ph.D.

Assistant Editors
Jonathan Y. Tan, Ph.D.
Richard E. McCarron, Ph.D.

Editorial Assistant
Denis J. Obermeyer

**Director of The Catholic University of
America Press**
David J. McGonagle, Ph.D.

CONTRIBUTING EDITORS

John Borelli, Ph.D., Associate Director of Secretariat for Ecumenical and Interreligious Affairs, United States Conference of Catholic Bishops, Washington, D.C.

Drew Christiansen, S.J., Ph.D., Senior Fellow, Woodstock Theological Center, Washington, D.C.

Anne M. Clifford, C.S.J., Ph.D., Associate Professor of Theology, Duquesne University, Pittsburgh, Pennsylvania

Raymond F. Collins, M.A., S.T.D., Professor of New Testament, The Catholic University of America, Washington, D.C.

Cyprian Davis, O.S.B., S.T.L., Ph.D., Professor of Church History, Saint Meinrad School of Theology, Saint Meinrad, Indiana

Dennis M. Doyle, Ph.D., Associate Professor of Religious Studies, University of Dayton, Dayton, Ohio

Angelyn Dries, O.S.F., Ph.D., Associate Professor of Religious Studies, Cardinal Stritch University, Milwaukee, Wisconsin

Arthur Espelage, O.F.M., J.C.D., Executive Coordinator, Canon Law Society of America, Washington, D.C.

Eugene J. Fisher, Ph.D., Associate Director of Secretariat for Ecumenical and Interreligious Affairs, United States Conference of Catholic Bishops, Washington, D.C.

Edward J. Furton, Ph.D., Editor-in-Chief, The National Catholic Bioethics Quarterly, Brighton, Massachusetts

James F. Garneau, Ph.D., Academic Dean, The Pontifical College Josephinum, Columbus, Ohio

J. A. Wayne Hellmann, O.F.M.Conv., Dr. Theol., Professor of Theological Studies, St. Louis University, St. Louis, Missouri

Joseph T. Kelley, Ph.D., D.Min., Director of the Center for Augustinian Study, Merrimack College, North Andover, Massachusetts

Judith M. Kubicki, C.S.S.F., Ph.D., Assistant Professor of Theology, Fordham University, Bronx, New York

William P. Loewe, Ph.D., Associate Professor of Religion and Religious Education, The Catholic University of America, Washington, D.C.

Rose M. McDermott, S.S.J., J.C.D., Associate Professor of Canon Law, The Catholic University of America, Washington, D.C.

R. Bruce Miller, M.S.L.S., Head, Theology/Philosophy, Canon Law Libraries, The Catholic University of America, Washington, D.C.

Francis J. Moloney, S.D.B., S.T.L., S.S.L., D.Phil., Professor of Biblical Studies, The Catholic University of America, Washington, D.C.

Katherine I. Rabenstein, B.S.F.S., Senior Credentialing Specialist, American Nurses Association, Washington, D.C.

Joel Rippinger, O.S.B., M.A., S.T.L., Subprior, Marmion Abbey, Aurora, Illinois

Foreword

This revised edition of the *New Catholic Encyclopedia* represents a third generation in the evolution of the text that traces its lineage back to the *Catholic Encyclopedia* published from 1907 to 1912. In 1967, sixty years after the first volume of the original set appeared, The Catholic University of America and the McGraw-Hill Book Company joined together in organizing a small army of editors and scholars to produce the *New Catholic Encyclopedia*. Although planning for the *NCE* had begun before the Second Vatican Council and most of the 17,000 entries were written before Council ended, Vatican II enhanced the encyclopedia's value and importance. The research and the scholarship that went into the articles witnessed to the continuity and richness of the Catholic Tradition given fresh expression by Council. In order to keep the *NCE* current, supplementary volumes were published in 1972, 1978, 1988, and 1995. Now, at the beginning of the third millennium, The Catholic University of America is proud to join with The Gale Group in presenting a new edition of the *New Catholic Encyclopedia*. It updates and incorporates the many articles from the 1967 edition and its supplements that have stood the test of time and adds hundreds of new entries.

As the president of The Catholic University of America, I cannot but be pleased at the reception the *NCE* has received. It has come to be recognized as an authoritative reference work in the field of religious studies and is praised for its comprehensive coverage of the Church's history and institutions. Although Canon Law no longer requires encyclopedias and reference works of this kind to receive an *imprimatur* before publication, I am confident that this new edition, like the original, reports accurate information about Catholic beliefs and practices. The editorial staff and their consultants were careful to present official Church teachings in a straightforward manner, and in areas where there are legitimate disputes over fact and differences in interpretation of events, they made every effort to insure a fair and balanced presentation of the issues.

The way for this revised edition was prepared by the publication, in 2000, of a Jubilee volume of the *NCE*, heralding the beginning of the new millennium. In my foreword to that volume I quoted Pope John Paul II's encyclical on Faith and Human Reason in which he wrote that history is "the arena where we see what God does for humanity." The *New Catholic Encyclopedia* describes that arena. It reports events, people, and ideas—"the things we know best and can verify most easily, the things of our everyday life, apart from which we cannot understand ourselves" (*Fides et ratio,* 12).

Finally, I want to express appreciation on my own behalf and on the behalf of the readers of these volumes to everyone who helped make this revision a reality. We are all indebted to The Gale Group and the staff of The Catholic University of America Press for their dedication and the alacrity with which they produced it.

Very Reverend David M. O'Connell, C.M., J.C.D.
President
The Catholic University of America

Preface to the Revised Edition

When first published in 1967 the *New Catholic Encyclopedia* was greeted with enthusiasm by librarians, researchers, and general readers interested in Catholicism. In the United States the *NCE* has been recognized as the standard reference work on matters of special interest to Catholics. In an effort to keep the encyclopedia current, supplementary volumes were published in 1972, 1978, 1988, and 1995. However, it became increasingly apparent that further supplements would not be adequate to this task. The publishers subsequently decided to undertake a thorough revision of the *NCE,* beginning with the publication of a Jubilee volume at the start of the new millennium.

Like the biblical scribe who brings from his store room of knowledge both the new and the old, this revised edition of the *New Catholic Encyclopedia* incorporates material from the 15-volume original edition and the supplement volumes. Entries that have withstood the test of time have been edited, and some have been amended to include the latest information and research. Hundreds of new entries have been added. For all practical purposes, it is an entirely new edition intended to serve as a comprehensive and authoritative work of reference reporting on the movements and interests that have shaped Christianity in general and Catholicism in particular over two millennia.

SCOPE

The title reflects its outlook and breadth. It is the *New Catholic Encyclopedia,* not merely a new encyclopedia of Catholicism. In addition to providing information on the doctrine, organization, and history of Christianity over the centuries, it includes information about persons, institutions, cultural phenomena, religions, philosophies, and social movements that have affected the Catholic Church from within and without. Accordingly, the *NCE* attends to the history and particular traditions of the Eastern Churches and the Churches of the Protestant Reformation, and other ecclesial communities. Christianity cannot be understood without exploring its roots in ancient Israel and Judaism, nor can the history of the medieval and modern Church be understood apart from its relationship with Islam. Interfaith dialogue requires an appreciation of Buddhism and other world religions, as well as some knowledge of the history of religion in general.

On the assumption that most readers and researchers who use the *NCE* are individuals interested in Catholicism in general and the Church in North America in particular, its editorial content gives priority to the Western Church, while not neglecting the churches in the East; to Roman Catholicism, acknowledging much common history with Protestantism; and to Catholicism in the United States, recognizing that it represents only a small part of the universal Church.

Scripture, Theology, Patrology, Liturgy. The many and varied articles dealing with Sacred Scripture and specific books of the Bible reflect contemporary biblical scholarship and its concerns. The *NCE* highlights official church teachings as expressed by the Church's magisterium. It reports developments in theology, explains issues and introduces ecclesiastical writers from the early Church Fathers to present-day theologians whose works exercise major influence on the development of Christian thought. The *NCE* traces the evolution of the Church's worship with special emphasis on rites and rituals consequent to the liturgical reforms and renewal initiated by the Second Vatican Council.

Church History. From its inception Christianity has been shaped by historical circumstances and itself has become a historical force. The *NCE* presents the Church's history from a number of points of view against the background of general political and cultural history. The revised edition reports in some detail the Church's missionary activity as it grew from a small community in Jerusalem to the worldwide phenomenon it is today. Some entries, such as those dealing with the Middle Ages, the Reformation, and the Enlightenment, focus on major time-periods and movements that cut across geographical boundaries. Other articles describe the history and structure of the Church in specific areas, countries, and regions. There are separate entries for many dioceses and monasteries which by reason of antiquity, size, or influence are of special importance in ecclesiastical history, as there are for religious orders and congregations. The *NCE* rounds out its comprehensive history of the Church with articles on religious movements and biographies of individuals.

Canon and Civil Law. The Church inherited and has safeguarded the precious legacy of ancient Rome, described by Virgil, "to rule people under law, [and] to establish the way of peace." The *NCE* deals with issues of ecclesiastical jurisprudence and outlines the development of legislation governing communal practices and individual obligations, taking care to incorporate and reference the 1983 *Code of Canon Law* throughout and, where appropriate, the *Code of Canons for the Eastern Churches.* It deals with issues of Church-State relations and with civil law as it impacts on the Church and Church's teaching regarding human rights and freedoms.

Philosophy. The Catholic tradition from its earliest years has investigated the relationship between faith and reason. The *NCE* considers at some length the many and varied schools of ancient, medieval, and modern philosophy with emphasis, when appropriate, on their relationship to theological positions. It pays particular attention to the scholastic tradition, particularly Thomism, which is prominent in Catholic intellectual history. Articles on many major and lesser philosophers contribute to a comprehensive survey of philosophy from pre-Christian times to the present.

Biography and Hagiography. The *NCE,* making an exception for the reigning pope, leaves to other reference works biographical information about living persons. This revised edition presents biographical sketches of hundreds of men and women, Christian and non-Christian, saints and sinners, because of their significance for the Church. They include: Old and New Testament figures; the Fathers of the Church and ecclesiastical writers; pagan and Christian emperors; medieval and modern kings; heads of state and other political figures; heretics and champions of orthodoxy; major and minor figures in the Reformation and Counter Reformation; popes, bishops, and priests; founders and members of religious orders and congregations; lay men and lay women; scholars, authors, composers, and artists. The *NCE* includes biographies of most saints whose feasts were once celebrated or are currently celebrated by the universal church. The revised edition relies on Butler's *Lives of the Saints* and similar reference works to give accounts of many saints, but the *NCE* also

provides biographical information about recently canonized and beatified individuals who are, for one reason or another, of special interest to the English-speaking world.

Social Sciences. Social sciences came into their own in the twentieth century. Many articles in the *NCE* rely on data drawn from anthropology, economics, psychology and sociology for a better understanding of religious structures and behaviors. Papal encyclicals and pastoral letters of episcopal conferences are the source of principles and norms for Christian attitudes and practice in the field of social action and legislation. The *NCE* draws attention to the Church's organized activities in pursuit of peace and justice, social welfare and human rights. The growth of the role of the laity in the work of the Church also receives thorough coverage.

ARRANGEMENT OF ENTRIES

The articles in the *NCE* are arranged alphabetically by the first substantive word using the word-by-word method of alphabetization; thus "New Zealand" precedes "Newman, John Henry," and "Old Testament Literature" precedes "Oldcastle, Sir John." Monarchs, patriarchs, popes, and others who share a Christian name and are differentiated by a title and numerical designation are alphabetized by their title and then arranged numerically. Thus, entries for Byzantine emperors Leo I through IV precede those for popes of the same name, while "Henry VIII, King of England" precedes "Henry IV, King of France."

Maps, Charts, and Illustrations. The *New Catholic Encyclopedia* contains nearly 3,000 illustrations, including photographs, maps, and tables. Entries focusing on the Church in specific countries contain a map of the country as well as easy-to-read tables giving statistical data and, where helpful, lists of archdioceses and dioceses. Entries on the Church in U.S. states also contain tables listing archdioceses and dioceses where appropriate. The numerous photographs appearing in the *New Catholic Encyclopedia* help to illustrate the history of the Church, its role in modern societies, and the many magnificent works of art it has inspired.

SPECIAL FEATURES

Subject Overview Articles. For the convenience and guidance of the reader, the *New Catholic Encyclopedia* contains several brief articles outlining the scope of major fields: "Theology, Articles on," "Liturgy, Articles on," "Jesus Christ, Articles on," etc.

Cross-References. The cross-reference system in the *NCE* serves to direct the reader to related material in other articles. The appearance of a name or term in small capital letters in text indicates that there is an article of that title elsewhere in the encyclopedia. In some cases, the name of the related article has been inserted at the appropriate point as a *see* reference: (*see* THOMAS AQUINAS, ST.). When a further aspect of the subject is treated under another title, a *see also* reference is placed at the end of the article. In addition to this extensive cross-reference system, the comprehensive index in volume 15 will greatly increase the reader's ability to access the wealth of information contained in the encyclopedia.

Abbreviations List. Following common practice, books and versions of the Bible as well as other standard works by selected authors have been abbreviated throughout the text. A guide to these abbreviations follows this preface.

The Editors

Abbreviations

The system of abbreviations used for the works of Plato, Aristotle, St. Augustine, and St. Thomas Aquinas is as follows: Plato is cited by book and Stephanus number only, e.g., Phaedo 79B; Rep. 480A. Aristotle is cited by book and Bekker number only, e.g., Anal. post. 72b 8–12; Anim. 430a 18. St. Augustine is cited as in the Thesaurus Linguae Latinae, e.g., C. acad. 3.20.45; Conf. 13.38.53, with capitalization of the first word of the title. St. Thomas is cited as in scholarly journals, but using Arabic numerals. In addition, the following abbreviations have been used throughout the encyclopedia for biblical books and versions of the Bible.

Books

Acts	Acts of the Apostles
Am	Amos
Bar	Baruch
1–2 Chr	1 and 2 Chronicles (1 and 2 Paralipomenon in Septuagint and Vulgate)
Col	Colossians
1–2 Cor	1 and 2 Corinthians
Dn	Daniel
Dt	Deuteronomy
Eccl	Ecclesiastes
Eph	Ephesians
Est	Esther
Ex	Exodus
Ez	Ezekiel
Ezr	Ezra (Esdras B in Septuagint; 1 Esdras in Vulgate)
Gal	Galatians
Gn	Genesis
Hb	Habakkuk
Heb	Hebrews
Hg	Haggai
Hos	Hosea
Is	Isaiah
Jas	James
Jb	Job
Jdt	Judith
Jer	Jeremiah
Jgs	Judges
Jl	Joel
Jn	John
1–3 Jn	1, 2, and 3 John
Jon	Jonah
Jos	Joshua
Jude	Jude
1–2 Kgs	1 and 2 Kings (3 and 4 Kings in Septuagint and Vulgate)
Lam	Lamentations
Lk	Luke
Lv	Leviticus
Mal	Malachi (Malachias in Vulgate)
1–2 Mc	1 and 2 Maccabees
Mi	Micah
Mk	Mark
Mt	Matthew
Na	Nahum
Neh	Nehemiah (2 Esdras in Septuagint and Vulgate)
Nm	Numbers
Ob	Obadiah
Phil	Philippians
Phlm	Philemon
Prv	Proverbs
Ps	Psalms
1–2 Pt	1 and 2 Peter
Rom	Romans
Ru	Ruth
Rv	Revelation (Apocalypse in Vulgate)
Sg	Song of Songs
Sir	Sirach (Wisdom of Ben Sira; Ecclesiasticus in Septuagint and Vulgate)
1–2 Sm	1 and 2 Samuel (1 and 2 Kings in Septuagint and Vulgate)
Tb	Tobit
1–2 Thes	1 and 2 Thessalonians
Ti	Titus
1–2 Tm	1 and 2 Timothy
Wis	Wisdom
Zec	Zechariah
Zep	Zephaniah

Versions

Apoc	Apocrypha
ARV	American Standard Revised Version
ARVm	American Standard Revised Version, margin
AT	American Translation
AV	Authorized Version (King James)
CCD	Confraternity of Christian Doctrine
DV	Douay-Challoner Version

ERV	English Revised Version	NJB	New Jerusalem Bible
ERVm	English Revised Version, margin	NRSV	New Revised Standard Version
EV	English Version(s) of the Bible	NT	New Testament
JB	Jerusalem Bible	OT	Old Testament
LXX	Septuagint	RSV	Revised Standard Version
MT	Masoretic Text	RV	Revised Version
NAB	New American Bible	RVm	Revised Version, margin
NEB	New English Bible	Syr	Syriac
NIV	New International Version	Vulg	Vulgate

M

MOSAICS

Pictures or patterns formed by closely spaced polychrome or monochrome stones (tesserae) of near uniform size, natural or artificial, embedded in a binder, such as cement. In its use as architectural revetment and pavement surfacing, mosaic combines decorative qualities with a high resistance to humidity and wear. These qualities mosaic shares with related media, such as glazed tile, stone incrustation, and inlay. The latter differ from mosaic in that their units are larger and of varying sizes and shapes. The employment of these media began very early in history. An inlay depicting animal fables decorates an early dynastic harp from Ur (Museum of the University of Pennsylvania, Philadelphia). Glazed tile is found in the funerary precinct of Pharao Zoser of the Third Dynasty in Old Kingdom Egypt. It is noteworthy that the extensive and refined use of stone incrustation parallels that of mosaic during the late Roman and early Byzantine periods.

Terminology. The term ''mosaic'' seems borrowed from the Greek μοῦσα. In its present meaning it is of late antique origin (Spartian, *Pesc. Nig.* 6.8: ''pictum de musio''; Trebellius Pollio, *Trig. Tyr.* 25.4: ''pictura est de museo''; Augustine, *Civ.* 16.1.1: ''quac musivo picta sunt''). The term seems to have been applied at first only to wall and vault decoration and not to pavements. A list of artisans in a decree of A.D. 337 (*Cod. Theod.* 13.4.2) includes both *tessellarii* who laid mosaic pavements and *musivarii,* makers of wall and vault mosaics. The comprehensive use of the term to include both kinds of mosaic became established gradually in the post-antique period.

Early History. The earliest recorded use of mosaic is found in Sumer. A temple façade in Warka (Biblical Erech), dating from the protoliterate period before 3000 B.C., was covered with geometric designs formed by colored cones of fired clay embedded in the walls. Luxury objects and jewelry decorated with a mosaic inlay of costly materials were produced in ancient Mesopotamia,

Crete, and Egypt. However, a continuity of mosaic production on a large scale can be observed only since ancient Greece. Beyond the boundaries of European civilization the Aztecs and Mayans had developed an independent production of turquoise mosaics used on armor and luxury articles.

Ancient Greece and Rome. In ancient Greece figural scenes composed of polychrome pebbles have been found on pavements dating from the late 5th and early 4th centuries B.C. These pebble mosaics were popular in the early Hellenistic period. Some examples of rare quality have been excavated at Olynthus and Pella. Polychrome pebble pavements of decorative design were used during the archaic period. The earliest pebble mosaic is of the late 8th century; it was discovered at Gordion in Asia Minor and consists of geometric designs distributed in a blue and red pattern on a white ground.

It seems likely that the rounded shapes of pebbles and their limited polychromy as found in nature induced the Greeks to stress silhouette and outline in the design of their figured pebble mosaics. Nonetheless, certain of these display a considerable degree of modeling in the round, notably the ''Stag Hunt'' by Gnosis excavated at Pella.

During the Hellenistic period the development of the practice of cutting stones into small pieces of deliberate shape, called tesserae, allowed for an increase of sophistication in pictorial design akin to painting, with which the pebble mosaics had not been able to compete. An example of this technique is a panel by Sophilos depicting Alexandria personified found at Thmuis in Egypt.

Other tessellated pavements of the 3d century B.C. have been found in Morgantina. By the 2d century before Christ tessellated pavements achieved an extreme refinement in technique and pictorial conventions. Mosaics found in the palace of the Attalids at Pergamon, dating from the period before the annexation of the city by the Romans (133 B.C.), are among the finest Hellenistic pavements known. They are notable for the extremely small

Mosaic showing the "Death of the Virgin" by Michele Giambono, mid-15th century.

size of their tesserae and particularly for their rich polychromy intensified by the appearance—the earliest recorded on pavements—of glass tesserae in colors not available in natural stone. The development of a brilliant mosaic art during the Hellenistic period, attested by a limited number of originals, is corroborated by Roman copies and texts. The luxurious boats of Hellenistic rulers were decorated with mosaics. Sosos, a Pergamene mosaicist, is credited by Pliny with the invention of "the unswept floor," a subject often repeated on Roman mosaic pavements (*Nat. Hist.* 36.184). Roman reflections of sophisticated pictorial conventions developed in Hellenistic mosaic are found in the mosaics located in the lower sanctuary of Fortuna at Palestrina, from the period of Sulla (82–79 B.C.). One depicts a panoramic Nilotic landscape filled with human figures, architecture, and the fauna of Egypt. The other portrays a sanctuary of Neptune beneath the sea filled with fish and encompassed by a shore. The many abrupt changes in scale and orientation evident in the composition of this mosaic are in accord with its pavement location, which excludes the possibility of a consistent spatial vision on the part of the viewer.

The widespread use of mosaics in the decoration of the Hellenistic home is illustrated by the mosaic pavements located in middle-class houses in Delos of the 2d

century B.C. During this century the Romans came into intimate contact with the Hellenistic world, and the Roman patricians soon adopted the practice of decorating homes with mosaic. The wealthy Campanian houses, buried by the eruption of Vesuvius in A.D. 79, were amply decorated with mosaics. In the House of the Faun in Pompeii were found pavements dating from the latter part of the 2d century B.C. (Naples Museum). Most famous is the large panel depicting the victory of Alexander over Darius at Issus. It copies a Hellenistic painting, most likely by Philoxenos of Eretria. Judging from the recorded names of mosaicists on signed pavements, the artists were mainly of Greek origin.

During the period of the Roman Republic and the early Empire decorative mosaics were a popular means of pavement surfacing. Their tesserae were large, of relatively constant shape and size, and evenly laid. These decorative mosaics, whose production required no unusual talent, were called *opus tessellatum* by the Romans, who distinguished between them and the much finer *opus vermiculatum* (wormlike workmanship) comprising smaller figural panels made of much finer stones, irregularly disposed. Such smaller panels were capable of great refinements in pictorial modeling and landscape space. A number of the finest *emblemata* from Campanian houses, notably the Dioskurides panel from the House of the Faun, were mounted on plaques. The mounting indicates that they had been produced in specialized workshops and were then acquired for insertion in the pavements.

Occasionally mosaics in the towns buried by Vesuvius were used on the surfaces of walls and columns. In a small court of a house in Herculaneum an entire wall that contained a fountain and niches was decorated with mosaic. Sparkling glass tesserae depicted hounds chasing deer and vine branches and festoons set against a dark ground. On an adjacent wall appeared a panel portraying Neptune and Amphitrite. The resistance of mosaic surfaces to humidity led to their application on the walls and vaults of baths and *nymphaea*. However, the use of mosaic on a large scale can be traced only from the 2d century A.D. Remains of vault mosaics appear in the baths of the *Sette Sapienti* in Ostia and in the *canopus* of Hadrian's villa in Tivoli.

During the later Roman Empire the mosaic emblem of limited size containing figural subjects was gradually replaced by a more extensive pictorial design. This tendency involved changes toward simplification in technique and composition; it is evident in the black and white pavements popular in Italy during the 2d and 3d centuries A.D. These pavements allowed for a graphic clarity in the discernment of an expansive subject matter presented on a neutral white ground. The reduced mosaic style of late antiquity yielded masterpieces, for example, the polychrome mosaic of the Glorification of Hercules in the Tetrarchial villa at Piazza Armerina in Sicily.

Mosaic pavements were used widely in private homes and public buildings throughout the Empire. A particularly rich tradition of polychrome pavements in North Africa extends from the 1st century A.D. until after the Vandal conquest. An early North African pavement of unusual refinement was found in a villa at Zliten, dating from the later 1st century A.D. It depicts a plant scroll with various birds and animals distributed among the volutes. The extreme fineness of the work in the figured parts is indicated by the mean count of 40 to 50 tesserae per square centimeter.

Excavations that have been made at Antioch, in Asia Minor, have given evidence of a continuous mosaic production extending from the middle Empire into the early Byzantine period. A pavement showing the Seasons from the Constantinian villa in Antioch is square and sectioned into geometric fields disposed around a common center; this symmetrical mode of composition lent itself to the design of ceilings and domes.

Early Christian, Medieval, and Byzantine Mosaics. The development of mosaic as the preferred monumental art extends from early Christianity through the entire course of the Byzantine Empire. In the medieval West its use was centered in Italy and was dependent on the presence and influence of early Christian sources, as well as on the influence of Byzantium. Northern Christian Europe was acquainted with architectural mosaic until the Carolingian revival as witnessed by the original mosaic decoration of Charlemagne's Palatine chapel at Aachen. However, in the later Middle Ages mosaic as the preferred architectural decoration was replaced by sculpture, fresco, and stained glass.

The earliest extant vault mosaic in good condition is located in a modest Christian tomb beneath St. Peter's in Rome. Christ-Helios in a quadriga occupies the apex of the vault. A radiant halo surrounds the head, and the figure is displayed against a gold ground. A grapevine spreads over the golden vault, which preceded by a short period of time the construction of the church above it.

The intense polychromatic effect achieved in large interiors by the use of mosaic revetment, and especially by gold tesserae, is evident in Hagios Georgios in Thessalonica, whose mosaics date probably from the later 4th century. The most impressive of all must have been the interior of Hagia Sophia in Constantinople (532–537; 557 and after) judging by descriptions contemporary with its construction. The gold mosaic surfacing of its vaults produced a radiance that was intended to transform the expe-

"The Battle of Raphida," mosaic, c. 432 to 440.

rience of the architectural interior into a vision of God's heaven: "The dome covers the church like the radiant heavens" (Paulus Silentiarius).

In centralized domed buildings with mosaic interiors, churches or baptisteries, the main subject is located in the center of the dome with subordinate subjects grouped around it. In the Baptistery of the Arians in Ravenna (c. 500) the Baptism of Christ is so situated. In the zone around the Baptism appear the Twelve Apostles. The dome of the Baptistery of the Orthodox (449–452) has a third zone that shows, in alternation, the four Gospel books set on altars and four ornate empty thrones (Ap 22.1–4).

The longitudinal basilica was decorated at times with mosaic on its façade. During the Middle Ages the façade of Old St. Peter's in Rome depicted the 24 Elders adoring the Holy Lamb (Ap 4.4–11). Mosaics were distributed around the interior of the basilica. The mosaics on the nave walls of S. Maria Maggiore in Rome (432–440) depict Old Testament scenes, and along the nave walls of Sant'Apollinare Nuovo in Ravenna (6th century) processions of saints move in the direction of the apse. A striking apse mosaic is preserved in Sant'Apollinare in Classe (dedicated 549). In the center of the apse St. Apollinaris spreads his arms apart in the *orans* gesture. He is flanked by 12 lambs denoting the Apostles. Above the saint is depicted a Transfiguration rendered in symbolic terms. Christ appears in the shape of a cross enclosed in a *mandorla* that encloses a starry sky. A small bust of Christ is located at the center point of the cross. The three sheep beneath the *mandorla* symbolize the Apostles present at the Transfiguration. Elijah and Moses appear in the sky above. The mosaic decoration of the Christian sanctuary presented the illiterate devout with visual sermons whose beauty was intended to deepen the experience of faith. The mosaic panel in San Vitale in Ravenna depicting Justinian and his court illustrates an ability to represent succinct resemblances with reduced means.

In the later Byzantine period refined workmanship was particularly stressed, for instance, in the carefully modeled figures of the Deësis mosaic in Hagia Sophia in Constantinople (late 12th or 13th century). This tendency reached a peak in the portable mosaics of late Byzantium composed of extremely fine stones. Two such panels depict the 12 main feasts of the liturgical year (14th century; Opera del Duomo, Florence). The concern for the thematic distribution of mosaics within centralized interiors culminates in the decoration of the post-iconoclast cross-in-square church. In the church at Daphni (*c.* 1100) a severe Christ Pantocrator dominates the center of the dome and turns His eyes upon the devout beneath. Around Him are the 12 Apostles, and further below appear scenes from the life of Christ; the Virgin and Child occupy the eastern apse.

During the course of the Middle Ages the influence of Byzantine mosaics often reached far beyond the geographical boundaries of Byzantium. The mosaics of the Ummayad mosque at Damascus (8th century) depict landscapes with villas, derived from ancient Roman and classicizing Byzantine sources and transmitted by Byzantine mosaicists working for Muslim patrons.

Byzantine influence in medieval Italy is reflected in the flourishing mosaic activity in the Veneto and Norman Sicily. The Norman kings employed Byzantine artists for the mosaic decoration of their cathedrals at Monreale and Cefalù (12th century). St. Mark's Cathedral in Venice (1063 and after), which was copied after the Church of the Holy Apostles in Constantinople, offers with its vast mosaic program perhaps the most cogent visual reflection of the interior decoration of the large churches of the Byzantine capital. The Virgin and Child in the apse of the basilica at Torcello (12th century), floating on a sea of gold, is perhaps the most striking example of Byzantine mosaic style in the West.

Rome, with its heritage of early Christian mosaics, remained an active center of mosaic production until the advent of the Renaissance. GIOTTO's most monumental pictorial work was the Navicella, a mosaic 52 feet wide and 33 feet high, located on the entrance tower facing the atrium of Old St. Peter's in Rome. This mosaic may well have imitated an early Christian model. A major artistic achievement of the 13th century in Tuscany was the vast mosaic decoration of the dome of the baptistery of Florence.

From the Renaissance until Modern Times. With the advent of the Italian Renaissance and the fall of Byzantium to the Turks mosaic ceased to be a primary artistic medium. From the 15th century onward it relied mainly on conventions established by the painters. The ''Death of the Virgin'' in the Mascoli Chapel in St. Mark's in Venice, perhaps the finest mosaic of its period (mid-15th century), illustrates this attitude. Its perspective depth explains, as in Renaissance painting, the natural spatial relationships within the panel itself; but its deep space is totally unrelated to the shape of the vault on which the panel rests. RAPHAEL supplied the cartoons for Luigi di Pace's mosaics in the dome of the Chigi Chapel in S. Maria del Popolo in Rome (1516). The reliance of the mosaicist on the painter can be traced in St. Mark's, Venice, during the following centuries. The 18th-century ''Arrival of the Body of St. Mark'' by Leopoldo del Pozzo, situated over the north door of the facade, is based on a cartoon by Sebastiano Ricci. The same situation prevailed elsewhere in Italy. During this period mosaicists had little interest in medieval work. Orazio Manenti's thorough reconstruction of Giotto's Navicella (1673–75), relocated in the narthex of St. Peter's in Rome, follows Giotto only in the general features of the composition.

In the later 18th century the renewal of interest in classical, early Christian, and medieval mosaics resulted in a growth of mosaic production throughout Europe; the renewal also reached America. This revival reflected in many ways the eclecticism of the period. Early Christian mosaics were carelessly restored, as in the case of the apse mosaic of San Michele in Affricisco in Ravenna, acquired by Prussia in 1844 and transferred to Berlin. Early Christian subject matter was rendered in an unrelated contemporary style, as in Burne-Jones's pre-Raphaelite ''Christ Enthroned Flanked by Angels'' in the American Church in Rome. The classical pavements discovered in the excavations of the Roman towns in Campania influenced the activity of the Belloni workshop in Paris during the early 19th century.

During the 19th and the early 20th centuries churches received extensive mosaic decoration. St. Paul's in London was partially decorated with mosaics after designs by G. F. Watts and Alfred Stevens. In Paris, the apse of the Panthéon was covered with a mosaic depicting "Christ Revealing to the Angel of France the Destinies of her People," and Magne and Merson depicted in Sacré Coeur (1912–23) a Christ in Glory, the Virgin, St. Michael, and Joan of Arc. The new cathedral in St. Louis, Mo. (dedicated in 1914) is decorated largely with mosaics designed by Albert Oerken. On the whole, the style of all these mosaics is eclectic and mechanical.

At the present time mosaic is used widely as an adjunct to architecture and as an independent art. But its importance is not clearly established. The preference in contemporary art for composite media has blurred the role of mosaic as an independent medium. The recent mosaics of Jeanne Reynal, consisting of tesserae scattered here and there on rough panels of colored cement, illustrate this tendency. Around the turn of the century Gaudí used mosaic together with glazed tile and other materials in the revetment of his *art nouveau* architecture in Barcelona.

In recent church architecture, because of the increased awareness of the medieval heritage of Christian mosaics, frequent use is made of mosaic for the decoration of central areas in the sanctuary. On the whole, however, the influence of the architecture of the International Style on recent churches and buildings in general, with its emphasis on clean wall surfaces and spatial clarity, seems to have impeded a broader role for architectural mosaic. A notable recent exception is the university library in Mexico City, designed and decorated by Juan O'Gorman. The exterior of the library is wholly covered with mosaics depicting scenes from the history of Mexico. In the bright sun these mosaics sheathe the building in a blaze of color.

Bibliography: E. ALFÖLDI-ROSENBAUM and J. WARD-PERKINS, *Justinianic Mosaic Pavements in Cyrenaican Churches* (Rome 1980). J. BALTY, *Mosaïques antiques de syrie* (Brussels 1977). M. VAN BERCHEM and E. CLOUZET, *Mosaïques chrétiennes du Ive au Xe siècle* (Geneva 1924). W.A. DASZEWSKI and D. MICHAELIDES, *Mosaic Floors in Cyprus* (Ravenna, 1988). F.W. DEICHMANN, *Frühchristliche Bauten und Mosaiken von Ravenna* (Weisbaden 1958). O. DEMUS, *Byzantine Mosaic Decoration: Aspects of Monumental Art in Byzantium* (London 1948; reprint New York 1976); *The Mosaics of Norman Sicily* (London 1950); *The Mosaics of San Marco in Venice*, 2 v. (Chicago 1984). E. DIEZ and O. DEMUS, *Byzantine Mosaics in Greece: Hosios Lucas and Daphni* (Cambridge, Mass. 1931). K. M. D. DUNBABIN, *The Mosaics of Roman North Africa* (Oxford 1978). E. KITZINGER, "The Mosaics of the Cappella Palatina in Palermo," *Art Bulletin* 31 (1949): 269–92. V. LAZAREV, *Old Russian Murals and Mosaics from the XI to the XVI Century* (London 1966). D. LEVI, *Antioch Mosaic Pavements*, 2 v. (Princeton 1947). D. MOURIKI, *The Mosaics of Nea Moni on Chios*, 2 v. (Athens 1985). W. OAKESHOTT, *The Mosaics of Rome from the Third to the Fourteenth Century* (London 1967). M. PICCIRILLO, *The Mosaics of Jordan* (Amman 1993). M. SPIRO, *Critical Corpus of the Mosaic Pavements on the Greek Mainland, Fourth–Sixth Centuries* (New York 1978). W. F. VOLBACH, *Early Christian Mosaics from the Fourth to the Seventh Centuries Rome, Naples, Milan, Ravenna*

(New York 1946). T. WHITTEMORE, *The Mosaics of Haghia Sophia at Istanbul, 1933–34. The Mosaics of the Southern Vestibule* (Oxford 1936); *The Mosaics of Haghia Sophia at Istanbul. Third Preliminary Report* (Oxford 1942).

[J. POLZER]

MOSCATI, GIUSEPPE MARIO CAROLO ALPHONSE, ST.

Lay physician; b. Benevento, Italy, July 25, 1880; d. Naples, Italy, April 12, 1927. Giuseppe Moscati was seventh of the nine children of Francesco Moscati (d. Dec. 21, 1897), a magistrate, and his wife Rosa (d. Nov. 25, 1914). The family moved to Naples when his father was appointed (1884) president of the court. Following his graduation from secondary school with honors (1897), Giuseppe studied medicine at the University of Naples. He earned his degree with first-class honors (Aug. 14, 1903) by his thesis on hepatic urogenesis.

At age twenty-three Giuseppe began his career at the Santa Maria del Populo Hospital for the Incurables in Naples. When Vesuvius erupted (April 1906), Moscati rushed to the hospital at Torre del Greco to help evacuate patients before the roof collapsed. Similarly, in 1911, he assisted in containing a cholera outbreak. That same year he finished his scientific preparation, passed the medical boards, was appointed to a university chair in biochemistry, and began lecturing on applied research and clinical research, as well as clinical medicine. He became known as one of the most outstanding researchers in his field.

In addition to his educational and scientific contributions, Giuseppe was a practicing physician and an administrator. In the course of time he was appointed director of military hospitals during World War I with the rank of major (1915), director of the Hospital for Incurables (July 16, 1919), coadjutor ordinary, medical director of the United Hospitals, director of the department of tuberculosis, and associate of the Royal Academy of Surgery.

Giuseppe Moscati is honored by the Church for the manner in which he practiced medicine. He required no payment from the poor, the homeless, religious, or priests, and, in fact, paid for their prescriptions himself. He used his time with patients to speak to them about the faith, often healing wounded souls as well as bodies. Moscati dedicated himself to the sacraments and prayer for his patients. He died peacefully of a stroke at age forty-seven. Three years later, his relics were translated to the church of Gesù Nuovo.

Moscati was declared venerable in 1973, beatified by Paul VI in 1975, and canonized by John Paul II, Oct. 25, 1987. Patron of bachelors.

Feast: Nov. 16.

Bibliography: *Acta Apostolicae Sedis* (1976): 259–62. *Giuseppe Moscati nel ricordo dei suoi contemporanei* (Naples 1967). *L'Osservatore Romano,* Eng. Ed. 48 (1975): 5–7; 45 (1987): 10,12. A. MARRANZINI, *Giuseppe Moscati, modello del laico cristiano di oggi* (Rome 1989). F. D'ONOFRIO, *Joseph Moscati as Seen by a Medical Doctor* (Messina 1991). G. PAPÁSOGLI, *Giuseppe Moscati: vita di un medico santo* (2nd ed. Rome 1975). D. PARRELLA, *St. Joseph Moscati: The Holy Doctor of Naples* (Naples 1987). A. TRIPODORO, *Preghiere in onore di S. Giuseppe Moscati* (3rd ed., Naples 1994); *Giuseppe Moscati, il medico santo di Napoli* (2nd ed., Naples 1999).

[K. I. RABENSTEIN]

MOSCHUS, JOHN

Seventh-century Byzantine monk and scriptural writer (also known as *Eucratas*); d. 619 or 620. He was a monk and traveler, known for his collection of vivid monastic tales titled *Leimon* or *Neos Paradeisos* (in Latin, *Pratum Spirituale*). Moschus began his monastic life at St. Theodosius' near Jerusalem in the third quarter of the sixth century. He made sojourns elsewhere in Palestine, Egypt, Sinai, Cyprus, Antioch, Egypt again, and finally Rome (614), usually accompanied by his disciple SOPHRONIUS the Sophist, later patriarch of Jerusalem.

Toward the end of his life, John set down over 300 tales of edifying incidents, replete with details of the life and beliefs of the times. These are dedicated to Sophronius, but the preface indicates that Sophronius saw to their publication after John's death in Rome and his burial at the monastery of St. Theodosius. Their circulation was widespread. There are translations in Old Slavonic and Arabic; in Latin, a partial translation of the ninth and eleventh centuries; in Italian, first printed in 1475; and in the Latin of AMBROSE TRAVERSARI (1423–24), published by Lippomano in 1558 and reprinted many times.

The Greek text was first printed by Fronton du Duc (1624), more completely by Cotelier (1686). French translations appeared in 1599, in 1653 by Arnauld d'Andilly, and in 1946 by M. J. Rouët de Journel. There seems to be no English translation. It is a neglected source of social and religious history, and a critical edition is needed. Sophronius and Moschus also composed a life of John the Almsgiver, Patriarch of Alexandria, of which only a portion has survived.

Bibliography: J. P. MIGNE, ed. *Patrologia Graeca,* 161 v. (Paris 1857–66) 87.3:2851–3112; *Patrologia latina,* 217 v. (Paris 1878–90) 74:119–122. H. G. BECK, *Kirche und theologische Literatur im byzantinischen Reich* (Munich 1959) 412. H. LECLERCQ, *Dictionnaire d'archéologie chrétienne et de liturgie,* 15 v. (Paris 1907–53) 7.2:2190–2196. O. BARDENHEWER, *Geschichte der Altkirchlichen Literatur,* 5 v. (Freiburg 1914–32) 5:131–135. H. USENER, ed., *Der heiligen Tychon* (Leipzig 1907). T. NISSEN, "Unbekannte Erzählungen aus dem Pratum Spirituale," *Byzantinische Zeitschrift* 38 (1938): 351–376. E. MIONI, *Orientalia Christiana periodica* 17 (1951): 61–94, MSS; *Studi bizantini* 8 (1953): 29–36. F. HALKIN, ed., *Bibliotheca hagiographica graeca,* 3 v. (Brussels 1957) 3:1440z–1442tb. I. ABULADZE, ed., *John Moschus, Pratum Spirituale* (Tiflis 1960), in Georgian. H. GELZER, ed., *Leben des heiligen Johannes des Barmherzigen* (Leipzig 1893) 108–112. N. H. BAYNES and E. A. S. DAWES, trs., *Three Byzantine Saints* (Oxford 1948) 199–206. N. H. BAYNES, "The Pratum Spirituale," *Orientalia Christiana periodica* 13 (1947): 404–414, reprinted in his *Byzantine Studies and Other Essays* (New York 1955) 261–270.

[P. SHERWOOD]

MOSES

Leader of the Israelites in their exodus from Egypt and their mediator in their COVENANT with Yahweh at Mt. Sinai. Little is known with historical exactitude about this key figure in the history of Israel through whose efforts the motley Hebrews became a tribal confederacy and, ultimately, a monarchy. Although his existence is no longer denied by scholars, arriving at the historical substance of Moses has been made complex by authors and editors of the Pentateuch. Factual details have long been obscured in the oral and written traditions of the cult epic celebrating the historical deeds of Yahweh.

Life. The name Moses (Heb. *mōšeh*) is of Egyptian origin (*mes, mesu,* born), perhaps originally connected with the name of an Egyptian god (as in the names Thutmose, Ahmose, etc.) that was later omitted under the influence of Israelite monotheism. A popular Hebrew etymology is offered in Ex 2.10 connecting *mōšeh* with *māšâ* [to draw forth (out of water)]. Moses was born apparently at the beginning of the 13th century B.C., the son (Ex 2.1–4; 7.7; Nm 26.59) of Hebrew parents Amram and Jochabed (Ex 6.20), with an older sister Miriam and a younger (?) brother AARON. The account of his birth parallels the legendary story of King Sargon I of Akkad, who, deposited in a basket boat and rescued, achieved great prominence. As a ward of the Pharaoh's daughter, Moses doubtless pursued the academic program of an Egyptian scribe (cf. Acts 7.22). The Biblical narrative, a composite of oral and perhaps even written traditions, portrays Moses as fleeing to Midian after killing an Egyptian in defense of a countryman (Ex 2.11–15). There he again exercised his role of champion in the cause of the seven daughters of the Kenite Jethro, a Midian priest, in whose household he then resided (2.16–21). Moses married Zipporah, a daughter of Jethro, who bore him two children, Gershom (2.22) and Eliezer (18.4). On Mt. SINAI (HOREB) Moses the shepherd experienced a theophany in the event of the burning bush. Commissioning Moses to deliver the Hebrews from Egypt, Yahweh entrusted him with the credentials of the revelation of His identity as

Yahweh, the God of Abraham, Isaac, and Jacob (3.6), together with the power to perform miraculous signs (4.1–9). In a scene somewhat inconsistent with his personality and education, Moses pleaded his ineptness for the task. Yahweh assigned a coadjutor role to Aaron (4.14–16). Before Pharaoh, Moses and Aaron presented in vain the case for the Hebrews, so that Yahweh punished Pharaoh with the ten PLAGUES OF EGYPT (7.14–12.30). Finally Moses led the Hebrews from Egypt after the ceremonial of a Passover meal. The journey to freedom became a flight from captors as Pharaoh's army attempted to recover his laborers. Moses was forced to lead the people through the only avenue of escape, the RED SEA, into the desert. Arriving at Mt. Sinai, the people through Moses entered formally into the covenant relationship with Yahweh (Ex 19 and 24; Dt 5), the terms of which are codified in the Decalogue (Ex 20.1–17; Dt 5.6–21) and the BOOK OF THE COVENANT (Ex 21–23). At Cades Moses guided the Israelite tribes through the difficult period of development. His mission accomplished, he died at Mt. Nebo without entering the promised land of Canaan (Nm 20).

Though the name of Moses has always been connected with the Pentateuch, his personal contribution to Israel was long overlooked. Outside the Pentateuch the oldest references to the Exodus make no mention of Moses. Reference is seldom made to him among the Prophets. Perhaps this is due to the Israelite mentality of eliminating instrumental causes and attributing events to the direct intervention of Yahweh. The picture that Israelite tradition created is reflected in his subordinate characterization by later authors as the servant of God (2 Kgs 21.8; Ps 105.26; Mal 3.22; Bar 2.28), God's chosen one (Ps 106.23), priest (Ps 98[99].6), prophet (Hos 23.13; Wis 11.1), and man of God (1Chr 23.14). In the NT, where he is the most frequently mentioned OT personality, he appears primarily as the lawgiver (Mt 8.4; Mk 7.10; Jn 1.17) who communicates God's law to man. For this reason Jesus met opposition in attempting to bring the law of Moses to final realization. As Moses proclaimed the Old Law from Mt. Sinai, the Gospel writers similarly situated Jesus on a mountain for the revelation of the New Law. The typological prefigurement of Jesus by Moses in the Exodus events is solidly founded. Jesus used him to witness His approaching suffering and death (Mt 17.1–8; Mk 9.1–8; Lk 9.28–36). Moses is a model of faith for all Christians (Heb 11.23–29).

Iconography. Although Moses is portrayed as the father type in the Sistine Chapel, elsewhere he is more often represented in the role of savior and legislator. The striking of the rock and the revelation of the Law were the two predominant scenes until the 5th century, when other themes were introduced. The Christian community

A memorial to Moses, situated on the mountain where he was said to have died after surveying the promised land, Mount Nebo, Syria. Photograph by John R. Jones. (©Papilio/CORBIS)

forged detailed comparisons between the activities of Moses and those of Jesus, some founded in Scripture, others in the creative imagination: e.g., between the burning bush and the virginal birth of Jesus, between the crossing of the Red Sea and Baptism (1 Cor 10.1–2), between the brazen serpent and the Crucified (Jn 3.14–15), between the manna and the Eucharist (1 Cor 10.3–4), between the striking of the rock and the piercing of the side of Christ. As a result of a misunderstanding of Ex 34.29–35 Moses was often portrayed with two horns (instead of rays) on his forehead (cf. 2 Cor 3.7).

Bibliography: M. BUBER, *Moses, the Revelation and the Covenant* (Oxford 1946; Torchbooks, New York 1958). R. MELLINKOFF, *The Horned Moses in Medieval Art and Thought* (Berkeley, Calif. 1970). D. DAICHES, *Moses: The Man and His Vision* (New York 1975). J. COHEN, *The Origins and Evolution of the Moses Nativity Story* (Leiden 1993). G. W. COATS, *The Moses Tradition* (Sheffield, Eng. 1993). J. VAN SETERS, *The Life of Moses: The Yahwist as Historian in Exodus-Numbers* (Louisville, Ky. 1994).

[E. ROESSLER/EDS.]

MOSES THE BLACK, ST.

Monk; b. *c.* 330; d. *c.* 405. Ethiopian by race, Moses was one of the most picturesque of the DESERT FATHERS.

"Moses and the Burning Bush," painting by Raphael, early 16th Century, the Vatican, Rome. (©David Lees/CORBIS)

First a servant or slave of an Egyptian official, he was dismissed for his immoral conduct and continual thefts, and he took to brigandage and soon gathered a gang that terrorized the district. His strength and ferocity became legendary. The details of his conversion are not known. It is thought that he took refuge from the law with some monks and was overwhelmed by their example, for he next appears at the monastery of Petra in the Desert of Scete. He found it hard to control his violence, but he was encouraged by Abbot St. Isidore of Alexandria. Finally, through physical labor, mortification, and prayer, he succeeded in overcoming himself. THEOPHILUS OF ALEXANDRIA heard of his virtue and ordained him a priest. When the Berbers threatened his monastery, he remained with seven companions; all but one perished. He was buried at the monastery of Dair al–Baramus, which still stands.

Feast: Aug. 28.

Bibliography: A. BUTLER, *The Lives of the Saints* (New York 1956) 3:435–436. *Acta Sanctorum* Aug. 6:199–212.

[E. D. CARTER]

MOSQUE

Islamic place of worship. The Arabic word *masjid*, literally, a place of worship, is derived from the verb *sajada*, to prostrate one's self; the term is to be compared with Nabataean *msgd'*, a votive STELE, and with Ethiopic *mesgad*, a church or temple. In Islam the mosque is also called *muṣallā*, a place where one prays (*ṣallā*) and more commonly, *jāmi'* (pl. *jāwāmi'*), a gathering place.

Plan of the Mosque. The normal mosque consists fundamentally of a large open, quadrangular court (*ṣaḥn*) surrounded by a colonnaded portico (*muġaṭṭā*) supported by several (often many) rows of columns, the passages between which are called *riwāq* (pl. *'arwiqa*). In the center of the court stands a large basin (*mīḍa'a*) with a fountain for making ablutions (*wuḍū'*). The covered hall on the side facing MECCA is generally much deeper, and in the wall on this side is a large ornamented niche called the *miḥrāb*, which indicates the *qibla* or direction in which one is oriented during prayer; in front of this the IMĀM stands while leading the prayer. In larger mosques there may be several *miḥrābs* used by different ''rites'' (*madhāhib; see* ISLAMIC LAW). Near the *miḥrāb* stands the *minbar*, an elevated seat from which the Friday sermon (*khuṭba*) is preached; this was originally a kind of throne from which the ruler or governor might address the people and was therefore reserved, in the earliest period, for only the chief mosques. Attached to the outside wall of the building, often on the corners, stands one or more towers or minarets (*manāra, ma'dhana, mi'dhana*), from which the call to prayer is first sounded by the muezzin (Arabic, *mu'adhdhin*), within some larger mosques there is also a raised platform (*dakka*), near the *minbar*. From here he repeats the call at two specified points during the Friday service. There is also a seat (*kursī*) with a desk for the recitation of the QUR'AN by the *qāri'* (or *qāṣṣ*). Within the *riwāq* along the *qibla* side there is in some principal mosques an enclosure (*maqṣūra*) near the *miḥrāb*, reserved for the ruler, where he may pray free from any danger of attack. In larger mosques there are a number of apartments (called also *riwāq*, or *zāwiya*), built within the extended *riwāq* or in subsidiary buildings, set aside for various purposes. These serve for study and teaching, or as living quarters for Qur'ān readers and other personnel of the mosque, or frequently for students and those making a retreat (*i'tikāf*), whether simply during the last ten days of RAMAḌĀN or on a more or less permanent basis.

Early Mosques. The most important shrine in Islam is the Holy Mosque (*al-masjid al-ḥarām*) of MECCA that contains in its enclosure the Ka'aba, a rectangular building 40 feet by 35 feet and some 50 feet high, oriented at its corners toward the cardinal points of the compass and containing in its eastern corner the Black Stone, which has been an object of particular cult from ancient times. Around the Ka'aba is a paved area (*maṭāf*) where the *ṭawāf* (*see* HAJJ) is made. The Ka'aba was destroyed during a siege in 64/684 (i.e., A.H. 64=A.D. 684), at which time it was already a reconstructed edifice, dating from 608, of alternating courses of stone and wood; the replacement, entirely of stone, was built by 'Abdallāh ibn al-Zubayr.

The earliest mosques of Islam were little more than open quadrangles. The house of the Prophet in MEDINA, where his followers gathered for prayer, consisted of an open court surrounded by mud-brick walls; against the north wall was a roofed portico (*zulla*) supported by palm

Moses, holding the tablets of the Ten Commandments.

stems; along the east wall there were built, over a period of time, nine little huts for MUHAMMAD's wives. Where preexisting buildings were not simply taken over, as was the case in Damascus, Homs, and elsewhere, the first mosques were no more than quadrangles marked off next to the governor's or commander's residence (*dār al-'imāra*) to which walls were later added, as in Baṣra (founded 14/635) and Kūfa (founded 17/638). In Fusṭāṭ, the original mosque was built (21/642) by 'Amr ibn al-'Aṣ as a simple walled quadrangle with some kind of roof, possibly a *zulla*. (On the development of the mosque, *see* ISLAMIC ART.)

The Mosque and Worship. The mosque was, at the beginning, the center of all aspects of the community life of Islam; thus the first mosques of Medina, Baṣra, Kūfa, Damascus, and Fusṭāṭ were built immediately adjacent to the *dār al-'imāra* and the *dīwān* or government offices. The caliph or provincial governor received his investiture in the mosque and there acted as *imām* and *khaṭīb*, his *khuṭba*, or discourse, often consisting in orders for battle, etc., while the faithful were exhorted by the preaching of the *qāṣṣ* (pl. *quṣṣāṣ*). Outside the capital prayers were recited in the mosque for the Caliph or ruler as a kind of oath of loyalty; often it was in the mosque that revolutions were begun, the first open sign thereof being the substitution of another name for that of the ruler. Al-

Mosque of the Sultan Hassan, Cairo, Egypt.

though it was from the outset a place in which people gathered for many purposes, the mosque rapidly took on the character of a sanctuary and came to be called, as in the most ancient Semitic usage regarding sacred shrines, the House of God (*bayt Allāh*), a name originally applied in Islam only to the Ka'aba. A particular holiness was, of course, attached to the Mosque of Medina, where the Prophet was buried; also to that of Qubā, just outside Medina, where he stopped and prayed immediately before entering the city in September 622 (*see* HIJRA). Prayer in the mosque and the recitation there of the Qur'ān, especially in the mosque of Medina or those associated with some renowned saint, is considered particularly meritorious. A special holiness too is associated by some with the *miḥrāb* and the *minbar*, and visitors or pilgrims will often touch them hoping to receive a blessing (*baraka*).

The Friday or congregational mosque (*al-masjid al-jāmi'*) is specifically designated within a community for the common Friday service that every male Muslim who has reached the age of reason is obliged to attend. Originally it was a community function in which the ruler led the prayer and preached the *khuṭba;* for this reason the number of congregational mosques (early called *dhât manābir*, i.e., having a *minbar*) was restricted. According to some authorities there should be no more than one in a particular town; in fact, according to others there should

be no congregational mosque save in the chief cities. With the great increase in the number of Muslims, however, and the universal need that was felt for the weekly community service, there came to be Friday mosques even in the villages; the larger centers may have several, often of considerable size. From the beginning there were many mosques besides the congregational mosques. Numerous local and tribal mosques formed the center of both the religious and political activities of particular groups.

Again, following the ancient Arabian custom of honoring the graves of ancestors and important chiefs and the Christian veneration of the saints, a great number of mosques were built as sanctuaries over the tombs of various saints and heroes of Islam, distinguished for their piety, learning, etc., even though the association of a place of prayer with a tomb was frowned upon by many authorities. Numerous mosques were built in Hijaz in association with events in the life of the Prophet; there and elsewhere other mosques arose in particular commemoration of 'ALĪ and his descendants. The site of the temple of Solomon in Jerusalem, where the Dome of the Rock now stands, is linked both by Muslim tradition and by the name given its congregational mosque, *al-Masjid al-'Aqṣā* (the Furthermost Mosque), with a reference in the Qur'ān and with the life of Muḥammad.

While originally the building of mosques and their maintenance were taken as responsibilities of the government, later many were built and endowed by private individuals as pious works. As a result, the number of mosques reported to have existed at certain times in various major cities, even allowing for considerable exaggeration on the part of the sources, is truly astounding.

The Mosque and Education. Teaching in Islam has always been associated with the mosque, as the primary sciences (*'ulūm*) of Islam are concerned with the Qur'ān, the *ḥadīth* [*see* ISLAMIC TRADITIONS (HADITH)] and the law (*fiqh*). From early times mention is made of the *majlis* or *ḥalqa* (circle) of those who came to hear and receive the instruction of learned men and ascetics who taught and preached there. Teaching was done in all the important mosques, several of which had extensive libraries, and in many of the smaller ones, so that finally the term *jāmi'* became the equivalent of *madrasa* (school) and *riwāq* came to mean a student's living quarters. The 'Azhar Mosque was built in Cairo in 361/972, and in 378/988 the Fatimid Caliph, al'Azīz, endowed 35 chairs of learning; the lecturers not only received ample salaries, but also were housed in rooms adjacent to the mosque. Scholars were attached likewise to the mosques of 'Amr and Ibn Ṭûlûn, also in Cairo, and to most of the important mosques throughout Islam. In many of these, stipends (some quite high) were available for students who were given lodging in or near the mosque.

Bibliography: J. PEDERSEN, *Encyclopedia of Islam,* ed. B. LEWIS et al. (2d ed. Leiden 1954–) 3:362–428. For further bibliog., *see* ISLAMIC ART.

[R. M. FRANK/EDS.]

MOSQUERA, MANUEL JOSÉ

Archbishop of Bogotá, staunch opponent of regalism; b. Popayán, 1800; d. Marseilles, France, 1853. He was a member of a distinguished family. He studied in Popayán and Quito. After being ordained, he held several posts in Popayán: rector of the University of Cauca, canon, and vicar-general. Selected archbishop of Bogotá by the congress of 1834, his selection was confirmed by the Pope, and he took over his see in 1835. From the start, he worked for the sanctification of his clergy. To this end he reorganized the seminary and made it a model for others in Spanish America; he organized the Spiritual Exercises for the priests and issued important decrees on ecclesiastical discipline. He visited all of his extensive diocese and endeavored to provide for the Christian education of youth. For this purpose he opened a secondary school run by the Jesuits; he adapted the catechism to the needs of the people of his diocese; and he helped to establish elementary schools. Mosquera tried to support the legitimate government in times of revolution, and this made many enemies for him. Since the government considered itself the heir of the Spanish crown in the exercise of patronage, the congress of 1851 passed a series of laws on religious matters that amounted to serious interference in the discipline of the Church. The archbishop of Bogotá addressed respectful but forceful messages to the congress and to the president, requesting the repeal of these laws and stating that in good conscience he could not comply with them. He asked his suffragans to work to the same end. The congress of 1852 took him to court for disobeying the laws and inciting others to do so, and he was condemned to exile and deprived of his salary. Pope Pius IX on several occasions formally approved the archbishop's conduct. Mosquera traveled to the United States, where he was given a warm demonstration by the Catholics of New York. He continued to France and was en route to Rome to see the pope when he died.

Bibliography: M. M. DE MOSQUERA, *Documentos para la biografía e historia del espicopado del . . . Manuel José Mosquera,* 3 v. (Paris 1858).

[J. RESTREPO POSADA]

MOTA Y ESCOBAR, ALONSO DE LA

Mexican bishop; b. Mexico City, 1556; d. Puebla, April 15, 1625. He was educated at the Dominican convent in Mexico City, earning a doctorate in theology. After serving as a curate in Chiapas, he was sent to Spain by the University of Mexico; there he eventually became tutor to the future King Philip II. After receiving his degree in canon law from the University of Salamanca, he returned to Mexico to become dean successively of Michoacán, Tlaxcala, and Mexico City. He twice refused appointment as bishop (of Nicaragua and later of Panama) before accepting the See of Guadalajara in 1597. His work among the indigenous people earned him considerable fame, particularly during the rebellion in the Serranía of Topía in 1601. Preaching to the rebels in their own language, he exhorted them to remain obedient. Through a policy of care, gentleness, and justice he succeeded in pacifying them while at the same time he won the Spaniards over to better treatment of the indigenous tribes. One result of his labors was the baptism of five important caciques. In 1608, Bishop Mota y Escobar was transferred to the see of Puebla de los Angeles, where he founded several hospitals, the Colegio de la Compañía de Jesús, the convent of Trinidad, the monastery of Carmen y Santa Ines, and several chapels.

Bibliography: M. CUEVAS, *Historia de la Iglesia en México,* 5 v. (5th ed. Mexico City 1946–47).

[E. J. GOODMAN]

MOTET

A musical term of French origin, generally applied to a vocal, or vocal and instrumental, work with a Latin text intended for church use. In the Middle Ages and Renaissance, secular and political motets also were extensively cultivated, and the term fell somewhat into disrepute, though not disuse, for titles such as *Sacrae cantiones vulgo motecta appellatae* are occasionally encountered. In its earliest stages the motet was a verbal trope of the clausula (the short melisma in the chant Gradual or Alleluia)—words (*mots*) carefully underlaid to the hitherto vocalized *duplum* (second voice part). The *duplum* later changed its name to *motetus.* When a third or fourth voice was added to the existing tenor and *duplum,* it might sing the same text as the *motetus* (conductus-motet), or each voice might have a separate text. Two or three texts could be sung simultaneously without incurring practical or aesthetic objections, since the various texts were usually related to each other as well as to the feast for which the composition was intended. The tenor, whose rhythm was usually less lively than that of the

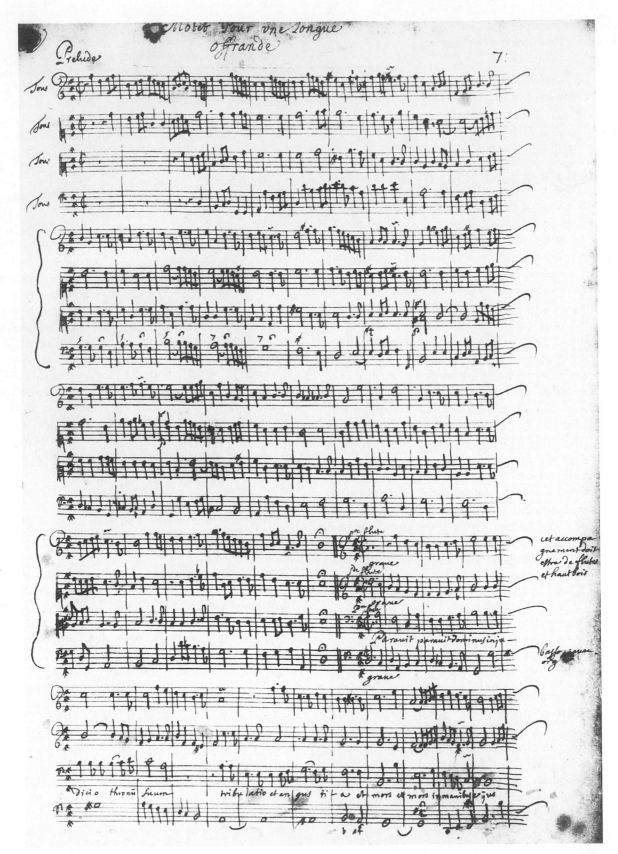

Manuscript page of sheet music, opening of prelude to "Motet for a Long Offertory," a choral-orchestral piece by Marc Antoine Charpentier.

upper parts, was often provided with a syllable or word indicating the source of the chant, and therefore the organum as a whole.

Although in the 13th century the early motet was at its peak as a genuine and expressive embellishment of the liturgy, it was then also that the substitution of French secular texts for the Latin took place. By mid-century the top voice part tended to predominate because of its deliberately attractive melodic interest (Franconian style), showing the way for the more advanced methods of Petrus de Cruce, Philippe de Vitry, and Guillaume de Machaut, all of whom wrote political as well as liturgical motets. From the short-winded *ordines,* or rhythmic schemes for the tenor, the concept of *isorhythm* slowly developed, reaching a perfect, though by no means final, stage of technique in the motets of Machaut. Originally applied to the tenor only, isorhythm later pervaded all voice parts in certain motets, so that they were melodically independent but rhythmically bound to a recurring pattern called *talea.* Some relaxing of this strict compositional discipline came with the motets of Guillaume Dufay and John Dunstable, whose example was influential for a considerable part of the 15th century. At this time it was not unusual to find the plainsong, skillfully decorated, in the highest voice, supported by two independent instrumental parts.

The growth of choral polyphony caused a further change in the career of the motet. Texture became much richer, progressing from density to radiance in the works of Ockeghem, Obrecht, and Desprez. Their music, known throughout Europe, set a standard of taste and technique that was to usher in the greatest era of the choral motet, culminating in the vast production of Lasso, Palestrina, Byrd, Victoria, and their contemporaries. Most of their texts were still liturgical, but some composers preferred psalm verses and other Biblical texts occasionally brought together for special reasons. Ceremonial motets for great occasions of church and state continued to emerge from time to time, and a growing interest in instrumental support can be sensed toward the end of the 16th century. The Roman composers remained faithful to the unaccompanied choral motet well into the baroque era, while the Venetians (notably G. Gabrieli and Monteverdi) were boldly experimenting in instrumentation, spatial separation of choirs, and new effects of every kind (*stile concitato*). Lully, Charpentier, and Couperin brought the choralorchestral motet to its zenith in France; Schütz, Buxtehude, and Bach gave to Germany a rich heritage of solo and choral motets. From the 17th century onwards, the term motet came to be applied mainly to non-liturgical musical settings of religious texts. With the end of the Baroque period, the motet became less prominent as a distinctive genre of church music.

Bibliography: M. BUKOFZER, *Studies in Medieval and Renaissance Music* (New York 1950). F. L. HARRISON, *Music in Medieval Britain* (New York 1958).

[D. STEVENS/EDS.]

MOTHER OF GOD

That Mary is the mother of God (see THEOTOKOS) is a revealed fact so closely linked to Christ's salvific plan for the human race that since the Council of Ephesus in 431 its recognition has been the touchstone of Christian orthodoxy. If Mary is not truly the mother of God, then Christ is not true God as well as true man, and he is not the Redeemer of the whole of humanity.

What makes Mary's motherhood essentially different from purely human motherhood is not the fact that she did something more or something different in conceiving her child, but that her child is a Divine Person. St. Ignatius of Antioch writes that God Our Lord Jesus Christ was born of Mary, who was from the seed of David. Opponents to this teaching sprang up in the early Church. GNOSTICISM, which taught a redemption from the flesh through knowledge, considered the flesh an evil thing utterly beneath God's dignity. DOCETISM held that Christ's body was a mere phantom. VALENTINUS erroneously taught that Christ's real body was a celestial body that merely passed through Mary's body as through a channel. In his version of the New Testament, MARCION has Christ appear as a full-grown man. These false teachings were ably refuted by St. Ignatius of Antioch, St. Justin, St. Irenaeus, Hippolytus, and Tertullian, but others continued to challenge this key doctrine.

Faustus of Mileve, the champion of MANICHAEISM, affirmed that the virgin whom the Holy Spirit overshadowed was the earth itself and not Mary, and that later the mortal Christ became divine when He was baptized in the Jordan. In rebuttal St. Augustine speaks in his sermons of Mary as God's mother and clearly distinguishes between Mary's conceiving and that of her cousin Elizabeth.

ARIANISM and NESTORIANISM did not deny that Mary is the real mother of Christ, but did deny that Christ is God. In denying this primitive belief that the Incarnate Word is the uncreated Son of the Father, coequal to the Father, the Arians refused to accept Christ's divinity and as a consequence Mary's divine motherhood.

St. ATHANASIUS, ARIUS's opponent, proclaimed Mary the mother of God (θεοτόκος, THEOTOKOS) and buttressed the doctrine theologically by giving the first explanation of the interchange of properties known in theology as the COMMUNICATION OF IDIOMS. The early

4th-century prayer, the earliest known Marian prayer, begins with the words: "We fly to thy patronage, holy Mother of God."

The denial of Mary's divine motherhood by NESTO-RIUS led to the General Council of EPHESUS. Nestorius, Patriarch of Constantinople, was a disciple of Bishop THE-ODORE OF MOPSUESTIA, who was in turn the disciple of DIODORE, Bishop of Tarsus. As representatives of the AN-TIOCH SCHOOL of theology, these three saw two persons in Christ, and the Son of God was distinct from the Son of David. Mary was for them the mother of Christ in whom the Word dwelt substantially.

When St. CYRIL OF ALEXANDRIA heard that Nestorius was preaching that Mary was christotoko (χριστοτόκος, mother of Christ) but not theotokos (mother of God), he took Nestorius to task in letters, sermons, and writings that defended the INCARNATION and the divine maternity. In the midst of a flurry of letters with charges and countercharges showered upon Pope CELESTINE I by both St. Cyril and Nestorius, the Emperor THEODOSIUS II convoked the General Council of Ephesus.

At the first session, on June 22, 431, the Council fathers unanimously approved one of St. Cyril's doctrinal letters and deposed Nestorius (H. Denzinger, *Enchiridion symbolorum* ed. A. Schönmetzer, 250–53). The enthusiastic crowds surged through the streets of the city, shouting "Holy Mary, Mother of God." The official approval of the doctrine contained in St. Cyril's letter was in effect the equivalent of a definition. Theotokos became the chant of the Christian, and the commemoration of "the glorious and ever virgin Mary, Mother of God," found its way into the liturgy of the Eucharist in the Christian East and West.

Mystery of the Motherhood. To restore the human race into his own image, the heavenly Father willed to put his own Son into the very materials of his creation in such a way that the eternal Word would restore harmony in the universe of matter and spirit and between the human and divine orders. The Son of God would become a Son of Adam, and a daughter of Adam's race would become the mother of God's own Son. St. Irenaeus develops this parallelism between the fallen angel and the disobedient virgin in Eden and the loyal angel and the obedient virgin at Nazareth, between the first Adam and the tree in paradise and the Second Adam and the Tree on Calvary.

Since divine motherhood involves the human conception of a preexistent Person, the relation of divine motherhood might even exist from the first instant of Mary's own existence, because of her predestination as mother of God. St. Peter Chrysologus asks why Mary, who was a virgin after Christ's birth, could not be his

mother before his conception? Sylvester de Saavedra, studying the likeness between the virgin mother and the eternal Father, claimed that the root and perfection of the mother-Son relation of Mary to Christ is a grace infused into Mary's body preceding in nature Mary's generative action.

M. J. Scheeben looked rather to the relationship of the mother's union with the divine Word. The mutual giving of the Person of the Word and Mary to each other in mutual consent is a kind of divine marriage. These divine nuptials (*matrimonium ratum*) by a special grace in her soul virtually and radically bestow upon Mary the bride the divine motherhood front the first instant of her existence. Mary's divine brideship is completed (*matrimonium consummatum*) at the Incarnation. This theory has no support in Scripture or patristic tradition.

M. J. Nicolás finds the essence of Mary's motherhood not in a relationship of union but rather in a relationship of origin and even of opposition. The proper effect of generation is separation, since the human flesh substantially sanctified is no longer Mary's flesh in the very instant in which the HYPOSTATIC UNION is realized. This resulting relation of origin forms a supernatural reality that stands between the hypostatic union and the accidental union caused by sanctifying GRACE.

Theologians commonly agree that Mary's transient generative activity is the proper foundation of her relationship to her Son. St. Thomas Aquinas affirms that some relations are founded upon what remains in the agent from the action performed (*In 3 sent.* 8.5). Nicolás explains the kind of perfection left in a mother because of her generative action.

As the divine Word assumed a nature perfect in its humanity, he accepted Mary's generative act as a perfect human act—virginal, conscious, voluntary. What remains in the agent after the transient generative action is a permanent disposition or habit, drawing the mother to her child as an immediately connatural object of knowledge and love. As the human generative act was composed of a spiritual and a material element, so does the resulting habit possess composite elements. And just as human nature is raised to the supernatural order by sharing in the divine nature Mary's human motherhood is raised to the hypostatic order by sharing in the relationship of the eternal Father to the Son. Thus Mary's maternal perfection is a unique relationship, a formal image of the relationship which the eternal Father has to the same divine Son. Only the Father and Mary have generated the same eternal Person, he according to his divine nature, she according to his human nature.

From his patristic studies, Joseph Bover concludes that the mother of God would have to be a virginal moth-

er and that only the mother of God could be a virginal mother. Aquinas bases his theology of Mary's virginity upon her assimilation to the Father in virtue of her divine motherhood (*see* VIRGIN BIRTH).

J. M. Alonso finds in the Church Fathers the thesis that the divine motherhood is a formal participation in the fecundity of the Father. He holds that the three Divine Persons in the order of efficient causality keep their distinct functions in the identity of operations and impress their personal characters on the effect produced. The supernatural form effected in Mary by the Trinitarian relation of the Father is called her personal maternal being, and is the only sanctifying form she possesses. Alonso's thesis seems to disregard papal teaching that all the divine activities that sanctify the human race are common to the Trinity.

De la Taille holds that what gives a divine gift a strictly supernatural quality is the relation of union between created OBEDIENTIAL POTENCY and uncreated act. Just as the Word elevated and substantially united his human nature to his Person by actuating it with his divine act of existence, so by analogy in the accidental order the Father communicates his fecundity, elevating and assimilating to himself the foundation of Mary's human motherhood.

[P. C. HOELLE/C. W. FIELDS/EDS.]

Liturgical Feast. First introduced toward the end of the 4th century, the Feast of Mary, Mother of God is the oldest Marian feast in the Roman liturgical calendar. In the latter part of the 5th century, especially after the Council of Ephesus (431), the liturgical commemoration of the Mother of God appeared in many places. Its date varied, but generally it was close to Christmas: December 18 in Spain, January 18 in Gaul, and January 1, the octave of Christmas in Rome. Thus, the first Marian feast was a feast of the divine maternity of Mary and it concluded the Christmas Octave in the Roman calendar. Until the middle of the 7th century, the Christian West did not seem to have known any other feast other than the feast of Mary, Mother of God. When other Marian feasts were introduced from the 7th century onward, the feast of Mary, Mother of God declined in importance and was replaced by the feast of Circumcision of Christ. The 1969 revision of the Roman liturgical calendar revived the celebration of the feast of Mary, Mother of God on January 1, thereby restoring the octave of Christmas to its original Marian character.

Bibliography: R. LAURENTIN, *Queen of Heaven,* tr. G. SMITH (New York 1956). H. M. MANTEAU-BONAMY, *Maternité divine et l'Incarnation* (*Bibliothèque Thomiste* 27; Paris 1949). M. J. NI-COLÁS, ''Le Concept intégral et maternité divine,'' *Revue thomiste* 42–43 (1937) 58–93, 230–72. W. J. BURGHARDT, ''Theotokos: The Mother of God,'' E. D. O'CONNOR, ed., *The Mystery of the Woman* (Notre Dame, Indiana 1956) 5–33. C. FECKES, *The Mystery of the Divine Motherhood,* tr. G. SMITH (New York 1941) 13–82, M. D. PHILIPPE, ''Le Mystère de la maternité divine de Marie,'' H. DU MANOIR DE JUAYE, ed., *Maria: Études sur la Sainte Vierge,* 6 v. (Paris 1949–61) 6:367–416, with extensive bibliography. M. SCH-MAUS, *Katholische Dogmatik,* 5 v. in 8 (5th ed. Munich 1953–59; 6th ed. 1960–) 5:62–114. G. VAN ACKEREN, ''Mary's Divine Motherhood,'' Carol Mariol 2:177–227. A. VONIER, *The Divine Motherhood,* in *Collected Works,* 3 v. (rev. ed. Westminster, Maryland 1952–53) 1:327–75. J. M. ALONSO, ''Hacia una Mariología trinitaria: dos escuelas,'' *Estudios Marianos* 10 (1950) 141–91; 12 (1952) 237–67. J. M. BOVER, ''Cómo conciben los Santos Padres el misterio de la divina maternidad. La virginidad, clave de la maternidad divina,'' *ibid.* 8 (1949) 185–256. J. M. DELGADO VARELA, ''Fr. Silvestre de Saavedra y su concepto de maternidad divina,'' *ibid.* 4 (1945) 521–58. S. MEO, *La Maternitá divina di Maria nel Concilio Ecumenico di Efeso* (Rome 1959). C. SPICQ, *Ce que Jésus doit à sa mère selon la théologie bibliqu et d'après les théologiens médiévaux* (Montreal 1959).

[C. W. FIELDS/EDS.]

Mother Teresa of Calcutta. (AP/Wide World Photos)

MOTHER TERESA OF CALCUTTA

Founder of Missionaries of Charity, teacher, social worker, Nobel Peace Prize Laureate; b. Aug. 26, 1910, Shkup, Albania, in the Ottoman Empire (now Skopje, the capital of the Republic of Macedonia); d. Sept. 5, 1997,

Calcutta, India. Baptized Gonxha (in English, Agnes) Bojaxhiu, she was one of five children of a middle-class family. Her father Nikola, a grocer, died in 1919, and her mother, Dronda, in 1968. At the age of 18, Gonxha joined the Sisters of Loreto with the intention of serving in the missions. En route to India she spent two months in Ireland, studying English. When she entered the novitiate in 1929 at Darjeeling in the foothills of the Himalayas, she became known as Sister Teresa. Professed in 1931, she was sent to teach at St Mary's School for Girls in Calcutta. On Sept. 10, 1946, while riding the train to Darjeeling, Sister Teresa experienced "a second calling," a vocation to serve the poor of Calcutta. In August 1948, she left the sisters of Loreto with the blessing of her superiors and the permission of the archbishop of Calcutta to live in the slums of Matizhil. She donned the sari and applied for citizenship in her adopted country. Teresa's initial effort was to organize dispensaries and outdoor schools where she fed, clothed, and taught poor children. The women, including some of her former students, whom she enlisted as volunteers to assist in the work became the nucleus of the Missionaries of Charity. In 1950 the order received canonical approval from church authorities.

In 1952 Mother Teresa opened the first of many hospices for the dying. In 1957 she founded a leper colony called Shanti Nagar (Town of Peace) near Asansol, India. Under her guidance the Missionaries of Charity established numerous centers where they ministered to the aged, lepers, cripples, AIDS victims, and the dying. In 1963 the Indian government awarded her the Padmashri ("Lord of the Lotus") for her services. As the Missionaries of Charity expanded their ministry to other countries, Mother Teresa's reputation spread throughout the world. In recognition of her work Pope Paul VI awarded her the first Pope John XXIII Peace Prize in 1971, and she received the Nobel Prize for Peace in 1979. Upon accepting the Nobel honor she said, "I choose the poverty of our poor people. But I am grateful to receive [the Nobel] in the name of the hungry, the naked, the homeless, of the crippled, of the blind, of the lepers, of all those people who feel unwanted, unloved, uncared-for throughout society, people that have become a burden to society and are shunned by everyone."

The sisters continued every six years to reelect her as major superior until early 1997 when, because of her rapidly failing health, they acceded to her wish to step down. In March they elected Nepal-born Sister Nirmala to head the order. Surrounded by sisters of the community Mother Teresa died peacefully on Sept. 5, 1997. On September 13, they buried her in a simple white marble tomb in the mother house of the Missionaries of Charity. In reminiscing about Mother Teresa some weeks after her death Pope John Paul II who had met with her on several occasions said, "I hope she will be a saint." Eighteen months later, he dispensed with the normal five-year waiting period and allowed the archbishop of Calcutta to initiate the formal process for beatification.

See Also: MISSIONARIES OF CHARITY.

Bibliography: E. EGAN and K. EGAN, eds., *Mother Teresa and the Beatitudes* (San Francisco 1992). C. FELDMAN, *Mother Teresa: Love Stays,* tr. P. HEINEGG (New York 1998). M. MUGGERIDGE, *Something Beautiful for God,* 2d ed. (San Francisco 1986).

[B. L. MARTHALER]

MOTION

Motion (Gr. κίνησις, Lat. *motus*) can be taken in a wide and in a strict sense. In the wide sense it stands for any CHANGE, for any transition from one state or condition to another. In a strict sense it means successive and continuous change, usually spoken of as movement. Aristotle held that it is unnecessary to prove the existence of motion, since the fact is evident. This notwithstanding, motion constitutes the first and enduring problem of philosophy, and through the study of it philosophers come to significant insights into material being and into the nature of being itself. It is also of interest to psychologists, for the perception of motion—examined in scholastic and modern psychology alike—has given rise to several theories on this subject. Accordingly, the present article treats motion under two aspects, the first part dealing with it from the standpoint of philosophy, the second from that of psychology.

Motion In Philosophy

Originating among the early Greeks, the philosophical analysis of motion reached its fullest development in the thought of Aristotle and the scholastics. This analysis forms the conceptual background against which the characteristic approach of modern science, as well as further contributions by modern philosophers, are most easily discussed.

Early Greeks. Since the early Greek philosophers lacked precise concepts of the different kinds of being, they reduced all changes to the simplest type of motion, local motion or change of place. From the beginning they spoke of the process of becoming in this terminology: things came into being by being "separated" from an original mass, by condensation and rarefaction, or by a downward and upward path. The only philosophers to deny the possibility of change were PARMENIDES and his Eleatic school. The famous paradoxes of ZENO OF ELEA, for example, purported to disprove the intelligibility of local motion. Because his concept of being was absolute,

Parmenides himself denied that anything could come to be. The subsequent atomists were one in denying the possibility of absolute coming into being. They reduced all change to local motion, that is, to the redistribution of atoms in space (*see* ATOMISM; GREEK PHILOSOPHY).

PLATO distinguished motion from becoming (γένεσις; *Theaetetus* 152D–153E), although he usually understood motion as local motion (*Laws* 893B–894A). In *Theaetetus* (181C–182A), however, he introduced the concept of qualitative change or alteration (ἀλλοίωσιν) as one of the two types of motion. He also defined soul as "the motion which can move itself" (*Laws* 896A), and he listed psychic operations as examples of motion (*Laws* 897A). Yet he was constrained to think even of the movement of reason as similar to the local motion of a sphere and its relatively immobile central point (*Laws* 898A; cf. *Tim.* 33B–34A).

Aristotelian concept. It remained for ARISTOTLE to give the first reasonably complete analysis (*Physics* 200b 12–231a 20; 250b 11–267b 26). In this he was followed by St. THOMAS AQUINAS, whose commentary on Aristotle's *Physics* is the fullest account of a philosophy of motion. Beause of his historical milieu, Aristotle had first to justify the possibility of motion by assigning principles that would account for motion in the face of the Eleatic denial. The possibility of change he saved by distinguishing being into ten categories and into actual and potential being. For Aristotle motion was the proper formality from which to study nature and natural phenomena. No other formality, such as being or extension, can in his view reveal the nature and explain the sensible properties of matter. He maintained it necessary, however, to distinguish motions that are natural from motions that result from art, chance, or compulsion. The first kind is of fundamental relevance to his scientific study of the world.

In Book 3 of the *Physics* the famous definition of motion is given. Aristotle begins by stating the concepts to be used in its definition. Since motion spans several CATEGORIES OF BEING, the elements of the definition must also transcend the categories; the only available prior concepts for defining motion are POTENCY AND ACT. Motion must be situated midway between potentiality and full actuality. When a body is only in potency, it is not yet in motion; when it has been fully actualized, the motion has ceased. Therefore, motion consists of imperfect ACT. But since imperfect act can be the termination of a motion or the starting point of a new motion, it is necessary to indicate motion as the act of a being in potency precisely as still in potency to more of the same act. Hence, motion is defined as "the fulfilment [act] of what exists in potency in so far as it is in potency" (201a, 10).

Types of motion. Plato had adumbrated various types of motion, but Aristotle put the classification on a scientific basis. Motions are distinguished by the goal or *terminus ad quem* (*Physics* 224b 7). Motion does not of itself belong in the categories of being, since it is not BEING, but BECOMING; however, it is reduced to the category of the being in which it terminates.

Local Motion. The first, most obvious, and easiest motion to observe is change of PLACE, or local motion. It is divided into circular, straight, and mixed, as well as into uniform and accelerated. The nature of motion is most easily seen in local motion, and even the terms one uses to describe other types are terms applied primarily to local motion. Local motion clearly goes from term to term, from a point of departure to one of arrival. These two terms are opposed and incompatible, but admit intermediary states: thus, they are called contraries. The motion between them is continuous, or unbroken and successive, that is, traversing the intervening positions. It is divisible by reason of the extension crossed. Since an instant is not divisible, motion cannot be instantaneous, but takes TIME. Likewise, motion properly speaking belongs only to bodies, since only they have the divisibility essential to motion. Local motion of some sort is involved in all other motions, and other motions are called such by analogy with local motion.

Alteration. Qualitative motion is called alteration. It is realized only in the third species of QUALITY, namely, sensible qualities. Only these fit the definition of motion as continuing and successive actualization of potency. Changes occurring in the vital or psychic orders are not motions in the same sense as local change and change of sensible qualities. One speaks of the mind as "proceeding" from known to unknown, of discursive REASONING; this, however, is only by analogy with local motion. Vital and psychic operations are not acts of beings in potency, but of beings already proximately determined to act; these operations are not the fulfillment of potentialities, but the products of potentialities already actualized (cf. St. Thomas, *Summa theologiae* 1a, 18.3 ad 1). Further, in psychic acts there is not the successiveness characteristic of motion, nor the contrariety between the terms of the process. In SENSATION the preliminary stimulation of the sensory organs is a qualitative change, but the determination of the faculty itself is not a gradual reception of act and thus is not motion. In the sensitive appetite there is motion, insofar as there is a physical accompaniment to the psychic act; the motion may be qualitative or local. Changes of moral disposition, although gradual, are not truly motions, but rather one or a series of instantaneous changes. Substantial changes are preceeded by alterations that dispose matter toward becoming a new being, but the actual generation of a new substance and destruction of the old are instantaneous, and are thereby not classified as motions in the strict sense. (*See* SUBSTANTIAL CHANGE.)

Augmentation and Diminution. Motion in the category of QUANTITY is called augmentation or growth and diminution or decrease. Augmentation does not consist of mere addition of distinct quantities to form an aggregation; such would reduce to local motion and would be augmentative, but not the motion of augmentation. The motion of augmentation must take place within the unity of a single SUBSTANCE. This happens only in living beings. By nutrition these assimilate their food into their own substance and consequently achieve growth. This is a true motion. It involves some local motion, as a growing body extends spatially. It is gradual, ordinarily so slow as to escape observation. It passes through successive stages, from the smallest one-cell stage to the full measure of growth determined by the specific nature. It also goes from contrary to contrary, from one positive state to another in the order of quantity. Such a motion is obviously immanent operation on the part of the living subject as agent, but it is true motion on the part of the subject as receptive of a new perfection. The opposite of augmentation is diminution or decrease.

Other Categories. The two categories of ACTION and passion do not constitute separate types of motion, for they are really identified with motion. Action is motion considered as being *from* the agent. Passion is the same motion considered *in* the patient. There is no motion in the category of "when" (*quando*), since time itself is the measure of motion. Nor is there motion in the category of RELATION. A new relation arises as a result of a change in some other category; for instance, by reason of a change of place, a relation of proximity arises, and from change of quality in one being, a relation of similarity or dissimilarity results in another being. A mutual relation can come into being and cease to be without any change in one of the related members. Hence, change is merely incidental to relation. The categories of SITUATION (*situs*) and condition or vestition (*habitus*) are constituted by relations, and so do not found separate types of motion.

Reality of motion. The objective reality of motion is known through a recognition of the various stages of actualization from the beginning to the ultimate termination of motion, even though these stages are not identified with motion. Fundamentally, each one has immediate experience of his own motions, particularly local (see below, Motion in Psychology). The paradoxes of Zeno, while purporting to disprove the reality of local motion, can be solved by an analysis of the CONTINUUM and of the infinite (cf. *Physics* 239b 5–240a 18). Though directed against the intelligibility of motion, they do not overturn the immediate EVIDENCE of the fact of motion.

The reality of motion is further confirmed by the need of an efficient cause or mover. Motion is an emergence from a state of potentiality to one of actuality. This is possible only under the influence of some being in act. Even vital movement requires that one part of a living being function as agent and another part as patient; otherwise the same being would be in potency and act together. The mover must be distinct from the moved and must be proportioned to the motion produced. There must be contact, at least mediate; there is no action at a distance. In a series of movers that are themselves moved, there is no ultimate explanation for the motion unless there be a first unmoved mover, a first cause of motion (*see* MOTION, FIRST CAUSE OF).

Motion in modern science. The Aristotelian requirement of a mover in act as necessary to account for motion was not easily satisfied; this was particularly the case in assigning the cause of projectile motion, such as of a stone thrown upward. Aristotle had explained the motion of the projectile after it left contact with the mover by supposing that the agent moves not only the stone, but also the surrounding air, giving the air motive power to continue projecting the stone. In the 6th century, JOHN PHILOPONUS of Alexandria criticized the Aristotelian theory and proposed the theory of IMPETUS in its stead: the mover imparts a "motive power" or energy to the projectile itself. In the 14th century JOHN BURIDAN spoke of the impetus as a qualitative power given to the body by the mover. He suggested that impetus theory could explain the motion of the heavenly bodies, once God had put them in motion. His doctrine has been assimilated into Aristotelianism and scholasticism, where impetus is explained as a quality or an instrumental power communicated by the mover. It is usually not thought to be an efficient cause of motion, but rather it is seen as analogous to the internal principle of natural motion.

Ockhamist Critique. WILLIAM OF OCKHAM reduced all physical being to the two categories of substance and quality, the only two that denoted distinct realities. The reality of local motion and position in place were thus denied, and there was no longer need to find a cause for the continuance of projectile motion. Accordingly, Ockham could deny both the original Aristotelian and the impetus theory.

Galileo's Contribution. Galileo GALILEI initiated a radical departure from such theory and study of motion. Confining himself to local motion, he stated that he had discovered by experiment certain properties of motion not hitherto observed or demonstrated. He set himself to study these properties through the method of measurement and correlation. Motion, for him, gave way to momentum, the product of the quantity of matter and velocity. Galileo identified momentum with impetus, and this became no longer an instrument or principle of motion, but a property of motion. He was not interested in an efficient cause for the continuance of motion, but in a measurable external cause of the acceleration or retardation of motion. Therefore, observing that a velocity once imparted to a body is accelerated or retarded according to the slope of the plane along which the motion takes place, he inferred that frictionless motion along a horizontal plane is uniform and perpetual. However, since in the real world this horizontal plane is circular—the surface of the sea, the path of the heavenly bodies—then the motion of bodies continues in a circular path, rather than in a straight line. Thus did Galileo give partial formulation to the principle of inertia.

Newton and Mechanism. Sir Isaac Newton correctly stated the principle of inertia as the first of his axioms, or laws of motion: "Every body continues in its state of rest, or of uniform motion in a straight line, unless it is compelled to change that state by forces impressed on it." From this and other axioms, Newton developed the science of mechanics, discovering in the process a formula of gravitation that is applicable to celestial as well as terrestrial phenomena. He also studied the properties of light according to principles of motion, and in his *Optics* he proposed a science of nature guided and inspired by mechanics. Newton's successors thereupon extended mechanics into every region of science, into acoustics, hydrodynamics, magnetism, electricity, heat, even into biology, psychology, economics, and sociology, at the expense of denying all that is not reducible to matter and motion (*see* MECHANISM).

Recent Physics. The use of mechanical principles as ultimate explanations of physical reality ran into difficulties in the 20th century with the advent of relativity and quantum theory. The Heisenberg principle of uncertainty, according to which it is impossible in principle to measure both the position and velocity of a particle, makes it impossible to construct a mechanical model of the world. Moreover, the concept of quantum jumps is interpreted by some to involve a denial of the continuity of motion.

Motion in modern philosophy. René DESCARTES recalled the common doctrine that NATURE is the principle of motion and rest, but he could conceive of motion only as local motion. Therefore, he attempted an explanation of all material reality from a mechanical point of view, i.e., in terms of matter and local motion. He held that all that man can know of external objects are their figure, magnitudes, and motions—all modes of extension. Color, odor, taste, and other sensible qualities, in this view, are not objective. Descartes also taught that in the beginning God created a definite quantity of motion, which remains constant. Not interested in the Aristotelian or qualitative definition of motion, which he never understood, he concentrated instead on the quantity of motion, or momentum. Motion became, for him, an actual and measurable state of a body, without consideration of a potential state that is being further actualized (cf. *Principles of Philosophy* 2.24–36).

Leibniz and Kant. LEIBNIZ objected to Descartes's idea that the quantity of motion in the universe remains constant; this, for Leibniz, is true rather of force (*Discourse on Metaphysics* 17–18). Likewise, he denied that extension is a clear and distinct idea. Extension, together with size, figure, and motion, are subjective phenomena, no less than the other sensible qualities the mechanists had rejected. Accordingly, he formulated his monadology, a doctrine in which bodies are composed of simple forces, psychic in character (*see* MONAD). The DYNAMISM of the system did not prevent Leibniz from interpreting bodily actions mechanically, even though they do not act upon one another. Bodies are divine machines or natural automatons (*The Monadology* 64). The motions of bodies, however, are regulated by their preestablished harmony with one another and with souls, which act according to final causality and the divine plan of the best possible world.

Immanuel KANT, in his precritical days, developed the monadology of Leibniz. In his definitive philosophy he defined motion as "actuation in space" (*Critique of Pure Reason* B291). Motion is an empirical concept, since experience apprises one of something moving in space and time. But there is also a subjective element to it: the two forms of sensibility, space and time, organize the successive determinations of a movable object.

Bergson's Critique. The most searching criticism of such views was that of Henri BERGSON, who held that the scientific mind cannot grasp the reality of motion. The intellect makes static, snapshot views of various stages of a transition, thereby solidifying into discontinuous images the fluid continuity of the real. Just as a movie projector, by reason of the movement of the apparatus, reconstitutes the motion that had been immobilized in a series of still pictures, so does the mind string snapshots of reality upon an abstract "becoming" contributed by the mind itself. The mechanism of ordinary knowledge is "cinematographical." In order to grasp reality, which is duration or change itself, one must escape from the cinematographical mechanism and employ a metaphysical intuition. Since change is the essence of reality, there is no underlying subject of change; movement does not imply a mobile [see *Creative Evolution* (New York

1911); *The Creative Mind* (New York 1946)]. The mobile continuity of the real, or concrete duration, is for Bergson the subject of metaphysics. If Bergson's critique accomplishes nothing else, it at least intimates that modern thinkers, by reducing motion to a state, have allowed reality in flux to escape them.

See Also: PHILOSOPHY OF NATURE; MATTER AND FORM; SCIENCE (IN THE MIDDLE AGES).

Bibliography: ARISTOTLE, *Physics,* tr. R. P. HARDIE and P. K. GAYE, v. 2 of *The Works of Aristotle,* ed. W. D. ROSS, 12 v. (Oxford 1908–52). THOMAS AQUINAS, *Commentary on Aristotle's "Physics,"* tr. R. J. BLACKWELL et al. (New Haven, Conn. 1963). M. J. ADLER, ed. *The Great Ideas: A Syntopicon of Great Books of the Western World* (Chicago, Ill. 1952) 1:193–217; 2:80–112. J. A. WEISHEIPL, *Nature and Gravitation* (River Forest, Ill. 1955). J. TONQUÉDEC, *La Philosophie de la nature* (Paris 1956) 1.3. C. MAZZANTINI, *Enciclopedia filosofica* (Venice-Rome 1957) 1:1676–87. S. CARAMELLA, *Enciclopedia filosofica* (Venice-Rome 1957) 3:750–758.

[M. A. GLUTZ]

Motion in Psychology

The study of motion in psychology has a long and interesting history. Once it was realized that motion could be experienced when there was no physical movement and that actual physical motion might not be experienced as such, the investigation of just how man perceives movement captured the interest of psychologists. To explain these illusions, most psychologists relied upon some type of logical analysis in terms of space and time, until the significant research of Max Wertheimer on apparent movement showed that a new phenomenological approach was needed.

Perception of Movement. Current investigation of the perception of movement may be classified under the following headings: induced movement; autokinetic movement; direction, speed, and causality of movement; and apparent movement.

Induced Movement. In induced movement one object is displaced in relation to another, but the subject is not able to perceive which has moved. He may, for example, see the object move when in reality it is the frame that has moved. The tendency is to interpret the figure as moving rather than the background. Also the meaning of the stimulus for the particular subject can determine which of two stimuli the subject perceives as moving.

Autokinetic Movement. Another interesting illusion of movement is the autokinetic effect, in which a stationary point of light is perceived as moving in a completely dark room. This phenomenon is explained largely in terms of nystagmus eye movements, but it is influenced also by the posture of the body, and kinesthetic sensations from the muscles. Moreover the autokinetic phenomenon is greatly influenced by social suggestibility of the subject. In both induced and autokinetic movement, the experienced movement cannot be differentiated from real movement.

Direction, Speed, and Causality. More recently it has been discovered that both direction and speed of movement depend upon the organizational factors present. It appears that the speed of movement is apprehended independently of distance or time. One peculiarity of directional movement is the trapezoidal illusion, in which a rotating trapezoid is perceived as oscillating because of the conflict in cues. Another interesting piece of research by A. E. Michotte (1881–1965) indicates that movement can have more complex attributes such as causality. The simulated appearance of one ball striking another is perceived as the first ball causing the second to move, even though there is no actual contact.

Apparent Movement. Of great importance is the study of the perception of movement. To illustrate this phenomenon two lights are mounted side by side. First one, then the other, is turned on and off. By varying the time between the turning on of the two lights, one induces three different perceptual experiences. If the time interval is long, the first light is perceived simultaneously. If the time interval is just right, one light is perceived as moving from position *A* to position *B*. A light is seen as moving when in fact there is no movement at all, and across a space where there is no stimulus present. The same phenomenon of apparent movement has also been reported for skin sensitivity of two successive stimuli, and for the hearing of two successive clicks.

The conditions governing the occurrence of the phi-phenomenon were investigated by Korte (1915). He found that the threshold was determined by distance between stimuli, the time interval of the succession, and the intensity of the stimuli. Moreover, the direction of the apparent movement was determined by the grouping laws of proximity and similarity. Finally the spatial arrangement of the successive stimuli may direct the apparent movement.

Theories of Perception. On the basis of the phi-phenomenon, field theorists maintain that movement is a primary sensory phenomenon not reducible to sensory attributes or to space or time. On the other hand the sensory-tonic theory of H. Werner and S. Wapner stresses the role of muscle activity in enhancing the autokinetic effect of apparent movement. The transactional functionalism theory of Ames's group and the probabilist theory of Brunswick attempt to explain the illusion of movement in terms of the cues of position, size, distance, and past experience, maintaining that these operate immediately and unconsciously.

The explanation offered by Thomistic psychologists is that movement is a *per accidens* sensible known through the operation of the internal senses, operating simultaneously in conjunction with the external senses and through physiological and psychological cues. The IMAGINATION is the faculty that supplies the sense of movement in conjunction with the work of the senses; thus the phenomenon of apparent movement results from the work of the imagination. This faculty fuses together the successive sense impressions, e.g., moving pictures, and at the same time relates this information to the past experience of actual moving things to give an experience of movement. Such a Thomistic view can give a rational explanation of all the phenomena of movement reported in experimental psychology; yet it should be noted that what it subjects to complex analysis is in reality a spontaneous and frequently an unconscious process.

See Also: SENSATION; SENSE KNOWLEDGE; SENSES.

Bibliography: F. H. ALLPORT, *Theories of Perception and the Concept of Structure* (New York 1955). A. AMES, *Visual Perception and the Rotating Trapezoidal Window* (Psychological Monographs: General and Applied 65.7; Washington 1951). S. H. BARTLEY, *Principles of Perception* (New York 1958). E. G. BORING, *Sensational and Perception in the History of Experimental Psychology* (New York 1942). D. KRECH and R. S. CRUTCHFIELD, *Elements of Psychology* (New York 1958).

[J. H. VOOR]

MOTION, FIRST CAUSE OF

Experience shows that some things in the world are in motion, whereas others are at rest, and that things pass from rest to motion and from motion to rest. In view of these facts, the question arises whether each and every thing is so constituted as to be capable of both motion and rest, capable of being either a mover or something moved, or whether besides things of this sort, something exists that is a mover, but is itself unmoved by any other. Is there an unmoved mover that is the primal source or first cause of motion? Scholastic philosophers commonly answer this question in the affirmative.

Existence of an Unmoved Mover

The scholastic proofs for the existence of a first unmoved mover are based upon an argument first proposed by ARISTOTLE (*Phys.* 241b 24–267b 27) and subsequently commented upon by St. THOMAS AQUINAS (*In 7 phys.* 1–9; *In 8 phys.* 1–23) in the context of their natural philosophy. In what follows, the concepts and distinctions presupposed to this argument are first explained, then the argument itself is exposed, and some observations made on the place of such a proof in natural philosophy and its relevance to traditional proofs for the existence of God.

Presuppositions. By MOTION is meant the act or process of change. This is not a disembodied energy, nor something purely and simply actual, but an actual determination of a natural body precisely as this is capable of further actuation. Motion thus conceived requires a mobile or potential subject that remains the self-same throughout the change, but becomes different from the way in which it was before the change. When a body passes from REST to MOTION, motion itself begins to be in this mobile subject. Whatever begins to be does not spring from mere nothing, nor does it produce itself, but depends for its being on some active principle, called the efficient cause. The efficient cause is the mover, or active source of motion, whereas motion is an effect produced in the moved or mobile subject. Each kind of motion requires a mobile subject capable of being moved with that motion, as well as a mover able to produce the motion.

Atemporal Aspect. If the supposition is made that motion had a beginning in time and has not existed from eternity, then it is manifest that there must be a first efficient cause of motion, because anything that begins to be requires an efficient cause from which it originates. However, since it is not clear from human experience or scientific reasoning that motion did have a beginning in time, the present discussion does not assume this.

Accidental vs. Essential. In order to prove by reasoning that there is a first cause of motion, a distinction should be made between motion that is caused or possessed accidentally and motion that is caused or possessed essentially. Motion is accidental when it is associated with something that merely belongs to something moved, as a color belongs to an animal and is moved accidentally when the animal moves. Motion is also accidental to something contained as a part in a whole; when the whole is moved, the part shares the motion of the whole, as a man in a boat is moved with the boat. On the other hand, motion is essential to something that is moved of itself, and not merely as part of another. Thus the motion of a stick moved by the hand, or of a thrown stone, is essential motion. Accidental motion presupposes and requires essential motion, and to the latter the argument is confined.

Mover and Moved. Several conditions must be fulfilled in order for essential motion to occur. First of all there must be a distinction between the mover and the moved: whatever is moved is moved by something else. The distinction between the mover and the moved appears by way of induction from sensory experience, and by reasoning from effect to cause. Among the things that have essential motion, some derive their motion from themselves, and others from something else; in some cases the motion is natural, whereas in other cases it is mechanical, that is, by impressed force.

It is manifest that things moved mechanically, by art or by violence, are moved by something else, that is, by a mover distinct from the moved. On the other hand, living things have in themselves an active principle or efficient cause of their own motion, by which they move themselves in different ways. They are also composed of heterogeneous parts; the part that causes motion is distinct from the part moved, as the nerves and muscles are distinct from the bones. Organisms thus move themselves by means of their parts, with the part in motion being moved by another part that is an active cause of motion. Nonliving bodies do not appear to move themselves, or to have in themselves an efficient cause of their own motion; thus they are moved by some cause that is distinct from themselves.

Reason also aids in understanding that whatever is in motion is moved by something else. Motion itself is an effect requiring both an efficient cause and a subject capable of being moved. If something is in motion and does not have the efficient cause of its motion within itself, then it is moved by something other than itself. If it does have the cause of motion within itself, then it moves itself by means of its parts, and these are related as mover and moved. In all cases, whatever is in motion is divisible and has parts, and the whole depends upon the parts, both for its existence and for its motion, whether it is moved by something else or moves itself.

Contact and Simultaneity. The second condition required for motion is that the mover and the moved must be together. Experience shows that some things are capable of causing motion and yet sometimes are not causing it, and that some things are capable of motion, but sometimes are at rest. Motion requires not only a distinction between the mover and the moved, but also that mover and moved be together in place and time. The need for contact between the mover and the moved may be understood inductively, by considering the various kinds of motion, whether according to place or quality or quantity, and by reasoning in terms of cause and effect.

Local Motion. In regard to local motion, everything that is moved locally is moved either by itself or by something else. Something that moves itself has the cause of motion in itself, and so in this case it is clear that the mover and the moved are together as parts of one and the same whole. A body can be moved locally by something else in various ways, namely, by pushing, pulling, carrying, etc. Yet all these are reducible to some kind of combining or separating, because by local motion things are either brought together or separated.

Both experience and reason show that combining or separating require contact between the mover and the moved. The reason lies in the fact that the mover is the principle and cause from which the motion proceeds and begins to exist in the moved. Without contact the mover would have nothing on which to act. Since mover and moved are together and, as it were, one by contact, they share one and the same motion in different ways: the mover as efficient cause and the moved as patient or subject. Just as an effect cannot come from nothing, so it cannot come to be without some contact with its source. (*See* ACTION AT A DISTANCE.)

Alteration and Augmentation. In cases of change in quality, whatever causes alteration and whatever is altered are in contact with each other. This is clear in regard to sensory qualities and the organs of sense. For sensations of touch, taste, or smell to take place, something with the peculiar sensible quality must contact the proper organ of sense to act on it and cause the sensation, which is a kind of alteration. Sight and hearing also require contact with the appropriate sense, although in these cases the distant object first causes an alteration in the medium, and then, through the medium, causes an alteration in the sense. Likewise, when the condition of contact is fulfilled, natural bodies interact through their physical and chemical qualities and cause alterations in each other. In change of quantity also, whether increase or decrease, there is contact between the organism and the parts that are added or lost.

Together in Time. Furthermore, mover and moved are together in time as well as in place; that is, they are simultaneous. At the same time as the mover causes motion, the moved is in motion. This is seen in the example of the hand moving the pen. The motion of the pen requires the hand as mover and contact of the hand with the pen; when, and only when the hand moves the pen, the pen is moved by the hand. Mover and moved are together in place and time because they are parts of one system, and the motion is the act of both mover and moved, although in different ways: it is actively from the mover and passively in the moved (*see* ACTION AND PASSION).

Argument for a First Cause. Although man has no experimental knowledge of the prime mover, he can reason from sensible effects to the first cause of motion. It is evident from experience that something can be moved by something else in two ways. The proximate mover may itself be the source of motion, or this mover may depend upon something else. A mover that is itself the source of motion may cause the motion either directly and immediately, or through one or more intermediates, as a man can move a stone either immediately or by means of a stick in his hand. In such a case the stone is moved principally by the man, and only instrumentally by the stick, because the man moves the stick, but the stick does not move the man, nor does it move the stone unless it is moved by the man.

With facts and distinctions such as these in mind, one can propose a general argument. Many things in the world are in motion, but everything in motion is moved by something else, and mover and moved are together in place and time. The mover, in turn, is either moved by something else or it is not. In either case there must be a first mover that is not moved by anything else, but is itself as unmoved mover and the first cause of motion. Motion requires an efficient cause, and every cause that is a moved mover requires another efficient cause. Every moved mover, regardless of how many there may be in any given series, is an intermediate cause dependent upon another cause. Such a series of movers moved by something else cannot be infinite, but must terminate in a first cause of motion that is not moved by any other. If there were no unmoved mover, there would be no first cause of motion nor any other cause, and hence no motion, which is contrary to fact.

This argument may be stated briefly in another way. Where there is motion, there must be a moved and a mover, distinct and yet together in place and time. There may also be an intermediate mover or instrument of motion. Motion is in the moved; the intermediate mover moves something and is moved by something; there must also be a first cause of motion that is unmoved by anything else, because the effect cannot be without such a cause. If anything is a mover and yet incapable of causing motion by itself, but only as moved by something else, and this in turn by something else, then such a series of moved movers cannot be infinite. It must be limited, in the sense that an unmoved mover must be the first cause of motion. Besides all the movers moved by something else, however many they may be, or of whatever kind, there must be a first cause of motion that imparts motion by itself and is an unmoved mover, independent of every other.

Role in Natural Philosophy. Questions concerning the first cause of motion may arise either in natural philosophy, or in metaphysics, or in natural and sacred theology. In natural philosophy the first cause of motion is considered only insofar as is necessary to understand motion in natural things and to determine whether the primary source of motion is or is not a natural body (*see* PHILOSOPHY OF NATURE). A body is something extended and divisible in parts that are in it and thus compose the whole. A body or extended whole is not an independent being, but depends upon its own parts for its being. A body is dependent upon its parts for being moved, because motion requires a subject that is extended and divisible into parts, but the first cause of motion is completely independent in action, and hence also in being, because operation follows being, and the manner of acting is consequent upon the manner of being. There

fore, the first cause of motion is not a body, and does not have parts on which it depends for its being and acting. It is not composed of matter and form, nor of potency and act. It is not capable of being moved or having motion, either by itself or by something else, but is the unmoved mover of other things. Because it is unmoved, it is not a temporal being but eternal. Because it is unmoved and incorporeal, it does not cause motion mechanically, as one body moves another from without, but rather as mind or intelligence moves a body with a higher order of action. It may be true that there are many kinds of spiritual beings who are intermediate movers, in the sense that they cause motion only insofar as they are themselves moved by another mover in a way different from the movements to which material things are subject. If this is the case, however, these spiritual beings are not the first cause of motion whose existence has been proved, but are themselves moved by it.

To account for motion in the world, it is sufficient for the purposes of natural philosophy to admit one first cause of motion. One mover entirely unmoved suffices to cause motion in all things that are moved—not indeed as the only mover, but as the only first and unmoved mover—because it acts with complete independence, whereas everything that is moved in any way whatever is dependent upon an unmoved mover. Moreover, the first cause of motion is eternal and acts without detriment to itself, and so is capable of being the first cause of all motions in the world. Furthermore, the unity and the order of the world indicate that the first cause of motion is one and unique, somewhat as the orderly motion of an army indicates that there is one in command (*see* UNIVERSE, ORDER OF). To treat of the first cause more profoundly and in greater detail pertains to metaphysics and theology (*see* GOD, PROOFS FOR THE EXISTENCE OF).

First Mover and God. It is sometimes questioned whether the first cause of motion proved in natural philosophy is the being whom men call God, and whether the existence of God can be discussed or proved with the concepts and principles that pertain to natural philosophy. Although the considerations of this branch of philosophy are limited, and the first cause of motion is not included within the proper subject of natural science, yet Aristotle touched upon these ultimate problems in his *Physics,* and both St. Thomas Aquinas and Sir Isaac Newton maintained that in natural science one should seek the first cause of motion, and treat of God inasmuch as He can be known as the cause of motion in the world. Moreover, as has been shown in the argument above, one can prove the existence of the first cause of motion through the data of experience and the principles of ordinary understanding and can show that this cause is not a natural body but an incorporeal and unmoved mover, entirely independent in action and being, and so reasonably identified with the being that men call God.

This proof from matter and motion, suggested by Aristotle and pursued by St. Thomas, has many advantages. From ordinary experience and consciousness men are aware not only of sensible motions in the world, but also of activities such as sensation, thought, and volition in themselves. Although these last are not motions in the strict sense of the term, nevertheless they are motions in the broad sense of alterations or qualitative dispositions. Sensations are initiated by sensible motions, and thoughts and volitions are in some ways dependent upon sensible motions, as they are also causes of sensible motion in man and in other things. Even thoughts and volitions are dependent on a first cause of motion, because every passing from potency to act requires a mover and ultimately an unmoved mover. It is the proper business of the natural philosopher to seek the causes of motion in natural bodies, and in order to understand his subject he must not rest content with some intermediate mover, nor with all intermediate movers—supposing that they could all be determined—but must seek the first cause of motion. Furthermore, it is only after one knows, through the study of nature, that there exists a kind of being that is not mobile or corporeal, but immobile and incorporeal (including the unmoved mover and spiritual substances) and that he can show the need for a science, beyond natural philosophy, called METAPHYSICS (*see* BEING).

See Also: GOD; EFFICIENT CAUSALITY.

Bibliography: E. A. SILLEM, *Ways of Thinking About God* (New York 1961). V. E. SMITH, *General Science of Nature* (Milwaukee 1958). W. A. WALLACE, ''Newtonian Antinomies against the *Prima Via*,'' *The Thomist* 19 (1956) 151–192. M. J. ADLER, ed., *The Great Ideas: A Syntopicon of Great Books of the Western World* (Chicago 1952) 1:179–192, 543–604.

[W. H. KANE]

MOTIVE

Whatever moves the human WILL, or the sufficient explanation for the act of willing in man. This article investigates the elements that move the rational APPETITE from a state of potential willing to that of actually willing. The investigation, which is propaedeutic to all moral science, can be treated in two ways: the philosopher pursues the broad principles that necessarily cover and are applicable to the quasi-infinite variety of human operations, whereas the psychologist considers the same human actions in their more particular existential framework of environment, heredity, biochemistry, etc. The former's conclusions are universal, certain, and ''confused,'' in the sense that all particular differences are fused into a broad unity. The latter's approach gives a more detailed and comparatively clearer, though less certain, picture of human acts in their concrete setting. The two methodologies, though distinct, are, however, complementary; for it is only by their dual process that any integral and sure knowledge of human actions can be gleaned.

This article limits itself to the philosophical analysis of the will's motivation. To ensure completeness, it first considers the fact of the will's motion and its causes, then the mode of freedom in which the will is moved.

Motion of the Will. To discern the cause of the will's motion, it is necessary to distinguish between the two moments of any MOTION, that is, that which physically produces the motion and that which determines it by way of OBJECT, or term. This distinction concerns itself with efficient causality in the order of exercise, namely, to will or not, and with final causality in the order of specification, namely, to will this or that; in other words, with what moves the will as agent and with what moves it as providing its object.

The first conclusion to be seen is that in the actual execution of properly human activity, the will holds the place of first mover in man and so is itself unmoved in this order by any other human faculty. The reason is not hard to discover. Every action is by nature directed toward an object that is its END and GOOD. Now, by comparison, one can see that the object of the will is a more universal end and good than the objects of man's other powers; for the will seeks the good of the whole individual, while all other potencies are inclined only to their particular perfection. Thus man is conscious that he ponders, eats, walks, etc., as he wills. The proper object of the will alone is the total good of the one willing, which is integrated by the partial goods of thinking, eating, walking, etc.

In the order of specification, however, the will cannot but be moved by other faculties. The observation that one cannot love what he does not know is here pertinent. The rational appetite is indeed thrust toward goods, but this drive must be elicited by knowledge of what is good and convenient. If a person is to be open to being and goodness, he must first be aware of reality. Certainly, man's emotional states depend on his consciousness, no matter how dim or clouded, of the pleasurable and the painful. So too, a truly human response to good (and conversely evil) must be governed to some degree at least by an intellectual insight into the goodness of things. In short, if one is to will any particular good, he must first have seen it in the light of what he has conceived as his perfection. Thus the will can operate only inasmuch as it is moved by the intellect presenting a possible good to be desired and attained.

Yet the acts of the intellect and will are exercised in the concrete existential order. Men are not subsistent spiritual faculties operating outside of the spatiotemporal dimension. It is always the will of this individual that seeks what he, as a person, wants here and now. The integral conception of a human act, then, demands recognition of man's emotional states as somewhat determinative of his will-acts. Experientially, one is aware of willing to do things precisely because of his emotional condition, of fear, desire, hate, etc. Words spoken in anger are often regretted when wrath has subsided; what was then viewed as good is now regarded with remorse. The sensitive appetites therefore have their dispositive role in shaping the will-act by molding the man willing to the present desirability of this or that particular good (*see* EMOTION [MORAL ASPECT]).

Cause of Will's Motion. Within man, then, the will is the prime mover in the executing of his actions, while the will in turn is moved by way of object by the INTELLECT presenting and the passions disposing. A question remains, however, regarding the will's primacy in moving man. Here experience seems to furnish the answer. The will simply moves itself. Everyone is conscious that he wills to do and to have solely because it is his will. And, let it be added, man is not aware of any exterior force moving him physically; dispositively yes, but not as if it were compelling him to act. This appears true from the very nature of the will, because any particular good that one opts for here and now is always sought in relation to and pursuant of an all-embracive fulfillment. As the will-power is actualized in regard to all-good, it is not inconsistent that it move itself here and now to any particular good. Always the particular is contained in the universal; the commander who can order an army into battle has the power of moving a battalion into action.

While experience testifies to the self-motion of the will, reason is constrained to seek a further explanation. Granting that the will moves itself in terms of particular goods sought, because it is already actualized in regard to its universal function of being open to all-being and good, yet this primary inclination must be accounted for. The will at one time had to pass from the mere capability to the actual willing of this end. As the will is unmoved efficiently by anything within man, clearly the source of its motion must be sought in a mover exterior to himself.

The history of man testifies to the validity of this quest. Cassius might protest that "the fault, dear Brutus, lies not in our stars," but the human race has ever looked upon the celestial luminaries as forces of its destiny. Such has been a constant belief from man's primitive religious persuasions to the more sophisticated theories associated with an ever-expanding universe. Despite its popularity, however, careful study has as constantly rejected this opinion as impossible. That the heavens, atmospheric conditions, etc., have an influence on human affairs is an undeniable fact. But to dispose a man objectively in his willing is in the order of specification, and reason rightly rejects the thesis that the grossly material can efficiently actuate the spiritual, or that the inferior can activate the superior. To hold the contrary is in effect to deny the spiritual nature of man's vital principle; it is to reduce the human to the merely animal.

Indeed, the search for the necessary mover of man's will can be successfully terminated neither in the material order of nature nor even in a world of limited and finite being. The principle of SUFFICIENT REASON is here invoked. A cause, limited in itself, cannot suffice to explain an infinite effect. But man's will is unlimited in its yearning for consummation; there is no finite determination in its inclination to embrace all-being and all-good. The cause, then, of this infinite thirst, this openness to being as such, can be only what is itself unlimited, the infinite and uncaused source of all being, "to which everyone gives the name of God."

Freedom of Motion. This conclusion, of course, poses a problem in regard to the FREEDOM with which the will is traditionally endowed. It seems that if man is not his own first mover, then the ultimate responsibility for his actions must lie in another. It is necessary, therefore, to inspect more closely the manner, or mode, in which the will is moved, i.e., to discover whether it is activated necessarily or freely.

Specification. In the order of specification, the will-act, like all motion, is constituted formally and finally by its proper object. Moreover, the primary limitation of its action must come from its natural determination, that is, from the object that specifies it. This object is the good, or that which is convenient to the one willing. But this good, as has been seen, is presented to the will under the universal competency of the intellect. This means that the proper and adequate object of the will, naturally determining it, will be what is universally good containing within its ambit whatever possesses in any way the aspect of being and goodness. As the eye is for seeing and the hand for manipulating, so too is the will for the real possession of unlimited being and goodness. To this object the will is necessitated by the force of its nature. Whatever a man wills as his good may not be truly good, but it must be sought as constituting or contributing to his perfection. "All men seek happiness," and though at times it may be sought in the ultimate flight from the absurdity of existence, yet in the main man necessarily wills his life and his thought as necessary conditions to his fulfillment.

But beyond this basic determination to HAPPINESS, the will remains free to choose or reject any particular good. It is true that a psychological determinism as old as Socrates posits that the will must always choose the better good. More than a trace of this theory underlies educational systems that expect the more educated person to be necessarily the better person.

Yet such a position inevitably defeats its own idealistic aim, for it limits the horizons of man by curtailing his freedom. The human mind with its universal power of penetration is apprehensive not only of being and goodness in things, but also of the imperfection and limitation native to this finite world of reality. Always the particular good presented to the will can be shown as possessing goodness, and so being desirable, or as lacking in being, and so being undesirable. The will, determined only to the universal good, is not then irresistibly drawn to anything that lacks this universal appeal. Even an abstract consideration of a being necessarily possessive of all being would not perforce move the will, since the very concept of such a being is itself contingent and so unable to move necessarily. Therefore, although the will is determined to goodness, under which aspect alone it may operate, yet, confronted by any particular object lacking a totality of goodness, it remains free.

Again, the question of man's freedom in the light of his emotional reactions has always been a matter of dispute. There are those who, conceiving man as a highly organized type of animal life, contend that, given a certain degree of emotional intensity, he must react in a determined way. There are many who delimit the extent of human liberty in the face of social and physiological factors, all of which influence man by way of emotional stimulation.

But a philosophical consideration of the principles of human action, gained not in an a priori hypothesis but through observation of human nature, ineluctably refutes any such determination of the sensitive order, while at the same time admitting its dispositive influence. For if man's powers of apprehension and appetition are really distinguished into the rational and the animal, the intellectual and the sensitive, his activity will be likewise characterized. Since it is the PERSON who operates by his various faculties, it is possible that his action may be threefold. His activity may be solely on the intellectual plane, as is evidenced when he is so fully integrated as to arrive at the state of maturity in which his rational nature completely controls his sensitive activity. Again, his action may be purely emotional, in which case all rational vitality is lacking, as in the child or mentally retarded adult. Still a third state is possible, that is, when his voluntary movement runs counter to his animal inclinations. In this more common state, reason and will, though experiencing the impact of passion, are yet free to repel its influence and to hold themselves aloof from its tensions. Thus—as is implicitly affirmed in traditional social and legal thought—whenever there is properly human activity, man is free and capable of restraining the demands of sensitive nature.

Exercise. The problem of the will's freedom in the order of exercise must finally be faced. The will, as any other potential agent, must derive its actualization from a being that is itself unmoved since it is PURE ACT (*see* MOTION, FIRST CAUSE OF). Since subsistent activity would by nature be an irresistible mover, it seems clear that a will so moved could hardly retain the capacity of not moving. The will then would be necessarily moved to execution and its so-called liberty would become impossible.

In principle, the problem is solved by considering the efficacy of the First CAUSE whose power extends not only to the production of all things (including the will-act) but also to the mode or manner in which such things are effected. If one is not to fall back into a discredited OCCASIONALISM, one must grant true causality to things. Experience, moreover, is the best proof that the will is an agent that acts freely. As secondary cause, it is indeed moved to its proper operation according to the nature of its being as a participation of Being itself. Since its nature is to operate freely, it is moved freely by the sole cause of its nature. To hold otherwise, for a deistic determinism, would be to place an impossible limitation on providence. But here the human mind reaches the mystery of infinity. Conscious of its own limitation, the human intellect strives in vain to understand how subsistent motion can be composed with liberty of CHOICE. Reason can demonstrate the truth of each principle, but their correspondence remains shrouded in the transcendence of the First Cause.

See Also: CAUSALITY, DIVINE; FREE WILL; HUMAN ACT; PREMOTION, PHYSICAL.

Bibliography: THOMAS AQUINAS, *Summa theologiae* 1a2ae. 8, 9, 10. R. E. BRENNAN, *General Psychology* (rev. ed. New York 1952); *Thomistic Psychology* (New York 1956). H. B. VEATCH, *Rational Man: A Modern Interpretation of Aristotelian Ethics* (Bloomington, Ind. 1962).

[T. K. CONNOLLY]

MOTIVE, UNCONSCIOUS

In discussion of the influence of an unconscious or hidden motive upon the morality of human action, the term has been applied to two quite different situations, sometimes with no clear recognition that between them there is a difference that is, from the moral point of view, one not only of degree but also of kind. Sometimes the hidden motive is understood to be more or less deliberately or culpably excluded from consciousness by a kind of self-deception; at other times it indicates a motive that an automatic psychic mechanism has buried deeply in the unconscious, where it is inaccessible under ordinary circumstances to the conscious mind but exercises a notable influence upon an individual's conscious behavior.

Self-Deception. This is common enough in human experience. "It is a common and often repeated conviction of the ascetical writers through the ages that human beings are all too apt to allow their behavior to be determined by motives quite other than those which they think to be operative; and unless that assumption is accepted, all the warnings of the ascetical writers against self-deception become meaningless" (Vann 118). In this kind of situation the hidden motive is the true end for which the agent acts, and the motive that is consciously asserted is no more than a fabrication invented by the individual to permit himself to appear in his own eyes and in those of others in a more creditable light. The motive he invents is not in any true sense the cause of his acting as he does, but is simply the excuse with which he attempts to justify his action. His inadvertence to his true motive is voluntary and culpable, and it does not in any way prevent his action from being attributable to the motive that is truly operative. In this type of case, therefore, there is no question of double motivation in any proper sense of the term. There is one true motive, and the other is falsely pretexted and asserted by the conscious mind. One cannot generalize, however, and say that wherever there is self-deception that is in any degree culpable, the hidden predisposition to act in a particular way always constitutes a true end or motive in the sense in which the moralist understands the term. But it can be reasonably said that if a person does in fact act for an end that he culpably excludes from consciousness, then the camouflaged objective is the real motive of the action. There is no theoretical difficulty in harmonizing such a falsification of motivation with the teaching of Catholic moral theology regarding the structure of the human act. It is a possibility of which moralists and ascetical writers have always been aware.

Strictly Unconscious Motive. The difficulty lies rather in integrating into the traditional concept of the human act the motive that is alleged by depth psychologists to lie in some cases more deeply buried in the unconscious through the operation of nonvoluntary psychic mechanisms. The existence of such motivation has not been established beyond doubt, but it is assumed by many and, indeed, is asserted to be a common if not indeed a normal phenomenon and one by no means reserved to those suffering from psychic disorder. It may appear difficult, however, to reconcile this assumption with the view of the human act taken in traditional Christian moral thought, according to which a man is normally capable of knowing and indeed of choosing the ends for which he acts.

To avoid equivocation, a distinction must be made between the meaning given to motivation by the psychologist and by the moral theologian. The moralist generally uses the term in the sense of an end, or *causa finalis,* to which human action is directed, whereas for the psychologist a motive is more likely to signify a drive, a tendency, an urge, or an impulse to act—a meaning that is, incidentally, nearer to that given the term by St. Thomas Aquinas, for whom a *causa motiva,* or a *principium movens,* or simply a *motivum,* was identified with efficiency rather than finality. This distinction makes it possible to see that the operation of an unconscious motive (psychological) does not necessarily invalidate, or contradict, or make unreal the motive (moral) asserted by the conscious mind. The two can coexist, each contributing in a different order of causality to the same human activity but without negating the reality of the influence of the other (see Ford and Kelly 1:126).

If there exists a kind of knowledge or volition below the level of consciousness, this cannot be sufficient to account for proper human motivation or the finalization of the human act in the full sense of the word. The unconscious desire, if it exercises any influence at all, must do so in the form of impulses or urges toward activities in conformity with its bent. Impulses or urges, however, account for one's feeling like doing something, but they do not at all account for why he does it.

In the past the vagaries of individual impulse were regarded as mysterious, and it was considered sufficient for moral judgment to evaluate an act simply in the light of what appears in the conscious mind. Modern depth psychology has not essentially altered this situation. If its assumptions are valid, these simply make clearer the causes of the predispositions and inclinations that precede moral decision. That these influenced moral decision in some cases was not a thing unknown to the older theologians or even to the ancient philosophers. But from the fact of influence it cannot be inferred that they normally dominate or control human behavior. The conscious mind, aware of an urge or an impulse to something though unaware of its cause, evaluates what one is attracted to and considers whether it can be harmonized with one's interests as these are consciously recognized, whether it can be integrated into a pattern of life one consciously wants to realize. This rational deliberation leads to the acceptance or the repudiation of the impulse. If it is accepted, its satisfaction becomes a human motive and end; if it is rejected, it does not. The rejected impulse may continue to be felt, but its satisfaction is desired only on a level below that of deliberate volition. If it is so strong that it cannot be resisted, the hidden motive does actually dominate and control behavior, but what one does in such a case is neither human nor moral, and so has no human end or goal. But where deliberation is not frustrated, the hidden motive will do no more than account for something seeming desirable. It may explain desire on the level of sense, or perhaps even velleity in the will, but it does not account for actual choice. This must be explained in terms of the end to which one's activity is consciously directed.

Rationalization. Unconscious motivation is sometimes expounded in such a way as to make the deliberation of the conscious mind appear simply a rationalization. The conscious mind looks for and finds acceptable pretexts for doing what the unconscious wants for different and less creditable reasons, the mind's deliberation being simply a bit of stage play to hoodwink the conscience. This, however, is an unfounded assumption. The conscious mind not only finds justifying reasons to act upon some impulses, but it also finds cause to reject others. A man does not live in blind submission to his impulses and urges, whatever their source. Consider, for example, a man who has an unconscious desire to dominate and subdue others and experiences in consequence consciously felt impulses to aggressive behavior of one kind or another. Sometimes he may yield to these impulses because he judges aggression to be appropriate and reasonable in the circumstances, as well it may be; but at other times he will reject them because he sees that aggression would be unreasonable and would serve no good end. That such judgment can be sound and honest is plentifully evident from human experience.

Nevertheless, one should grant the possibility of unconsciously motivated impulses being rationalized by the conscious mind in an objectionable sense of the term. It is possible for a person to deceive himself more or less culpably in thinking that his activities are directed to the good end he alleges. But when such is the case, the spurious character of the pretexted motivation should be perceptible to the conscious mind, however deeply in the unconscious the source of the impulses may be hidden; a good examination of conscience should bring to light the fact that one's behavior is not reasonably related to the lofty ends one claims to serve.

It may also be granted that the existence of an unconscious motive can predispose an individual to rationalize his behavior in an objectionable sense. Before the time of modern psychology it was well known that men incline to find reasons to justify what they feel inclined to do. A strong unconscious motive may therefore prove an obstacle to sound moral judgment and rectitude of will, but it does not follow that these are normally made impossible.

Bibliography: J. C. FORD and G. A. KELLY, *Contemporary Moral Theology,* 2 v. (Westminster, Md. 1958–63) 1:174–200. A. PLÉ, "L'Acte moral et la *pseudo-morale* de l'inconscient," *La Vie spirituelle* suppl. 40 (1957) 24–68. E. TESSON, "Moral Conscience and Psychiatry" *New Problems in Medical Ethics,* ed. P. FLOOD, v. 3 (Westminster, Md. 1957) 85–102. C. H. NODET, "Psychoanalysis and Morality," *ibid.* 103–117. C. ODIER, *Les Deux sources consciente et inconsciente de la vie morale* (2d ed. Neuchâtel 1947). G. VANN, "Unconscious Motivation and Pseudo-Virtue," *Homiletic and Pastoral Review* 57 (1956) 115–123. J. C. FORD, "Reply to Father Vann," *ibid.* 124–127. K. RAHNER, "Uber die gute Meinung," *Geist und Leben* 28 (1955) 281–298.

[P. K. MEAGHER]

MOTOLINÍA, TORIBIO DE BENAVENTE

Franciscan missionary, one of the "Twelve Apostles" in Mexico; b. Benavente, León, Spain, *c.* 1495; d. Mexico City, probably in 1565. As a young man he became a Franciscan, joining the strict reformed section of the Province of Santiago. In 1523 Martín de VALENCIA was instructed by the Franciscan minister general to choose 12 friars from the province for the first formal Franciscan mission to Mexico. Father Toribio was one of those chosen. Upon arriving in Mexico in May of 1524, he took for his name the first word he learned in the Tlaxcalan tongue, *motolinía,* meaning "poverty." In June of 1524, when the friars formed the Custody of the Holy Gospel, he was appointed the first superior of the Friary of San Francisco in Mexico City. In spite of the municipal officials, he maintained the authority of the Franciscan *custos* as head of the Church in Mexico. In 1525 he was appointed superior of Huejotzingo, and in 1527 he went to Honduras and Nicaragua, returning in 1529. That year he gained the enmity of the civil authorities by granting asylum in Huejotzingo to native leaders who had complained of heavy taxations. From 1530 to 1533 he was guardian in Tlaxcala, and he traveled widely among the native people west and north of Mexico City, helping to found the Spanish town of Puebla. In 1534 he was once more sent to Guatemala. Returning after a year or so, he was stationed as a missionary in Tlaxcala.

When the Custody of the Holy Gospel was made a province, Motolonía was appointed guardian of Tlaxcala and was instructed to write an account of the life and beliefs of the native people in pre-Spanish times and a history of the work of the Franciscans among them. From this came his *Historia de los indios de Nueva España,* completed in 1541, his most important work. Later he wrote a related volume entitled *Memoriales.* In 1543 he was again sent to Guatemala as *custos* of a band of 24 friars. When conflicts arose with the Dominicans and several Franciscans asked to leave, he resigned his office in 1545 and returned to Mexico. In 1546 he became acting provincial in Mexico when the provincial was lost at sea; later he was made provincial by election (1548–51). Little is known of his later work. In 1555 he wrote a scathing attack on the exaggerations in Las Casas' *Brevísima relación*. His last years were spent in retirement in the friary of Mexico City.

Bibliography: I. P. FERNÁNDEZ, *Fray Toribio Motolinía, O.F.M., frente a Fray Bartolomé de las Casas, O.P.: Estudio y edición crítica de la carta de Motolinía al emperador (Tlaxcala, a 2 de enero de 1555)* (Salamanca 1989). T. MOTOLINÍA, *Memoriales e Historia de los indios de la Nueva Espanã. Estudio preliminar por Fidel de Lejarza* (Madrid 1970); *History of the Indians of New Spain,* tr. and ed., F. B. STECK (Washington 1951).

[F. B. WARREN]

MOTRIL, MARTYRS OF, BB.

The Martyrs of Motril, also known as Vicente Soler and Companions, Augustinian Recollect Martyrs of Spain; d. July 25–26 and Aug. 15, 1936, near Motril, Granada, Spain; beatified by John Paul II, March 7, 1999.

This group of seven Augustinian Recollects and a parish priest of Motril represent a small fraction of the 7,000 priests and religious killed for their faith during the Spanish Civil War (1936–39). One week after the war began, revolutionaries attacked (July 25, 1936) the Augustinian monastery, forced five priests out, and shot them in the street when they refused to renounce their faith. The next day two priests sought refuge in prayer in the Church of the Divine Shepherd next to the monastery. They were found and killed in the church courtyard. The final priest was captured later. All eight were decreed martyrs on March 8, 1997. In his beatification homily Pope John Paul II stressed that they "did not die for an ideology, but freely gave their lives for Someone who had already died for them. They gave back to Christ the gift they had received from him." The blesseds include:

Diez, José Ricardo; Augustinian priest, d. July 25, 1936 in the streets of Motril.

Inchausti, Leon, Augustinian priest, d. July 25, 1936 in the streets of Motril.

Martin Sierra, Manuel, parish priest at the Church of the Divine Shepherd in Motril; d. July 26, 1936.

Moreno, Julian Benigno, Augustinian priest, d. July 25, 1936 in the streets of Motril.

Palacios, Deogracias, Augustinian priest, d. July 25, 1936 in the streets of Motril.

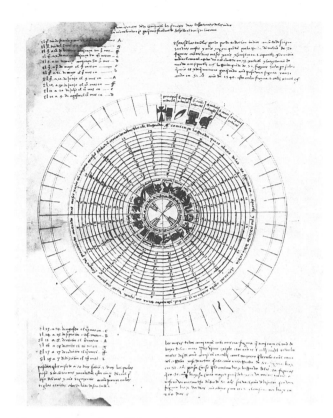

Manuscript page from "Memoriales," an Aztec calendar, by Toribio De Benavente Motolinía.

Pinilla, Vicente, Augustinian priest, d. July 26, 1936 with Father Manuel Martin in the church courtyard after praying in the parish church.

Rada, José, Augustinian priest, d. July 25, 1936 in the streets of Motril.

Soler, Vicente, Augustinian priest, b. 1867, Malon near Saragossa, Spain; d. Aug. 15, 1936. He had been a missionary in the Philippines, provincial in Spain, and superior general of the order for seven months in 1926. He had been in the choir when five of his brothers were arrested and shot. He escaped but was caught and imprisoned on July 29, 1936. Throughout his incarceration he ministered to other prisoners and lead them in a Marian novena in the days before his death. He offered his life in exchange for that of a father of eight children, but the offer was declined. He was shot with 16 others. One of the 18 survived to relate the story of Vicente's martyrdom.

Bibliography: V. CÁRCEL ORTÍ, *Martires españoles del siglo XX* (Madrid 1995). W. H. CARROLL, *The Last Crusade* (Front Royal, Va. 1996). J. PÉREZ DE URBEL, *Catholic Martyrs of the Spanish Civil War,* tr. M. F. INGRAMS (Kansas City, Mo. 1993). *Acta Apostolicae Sedis* 310–12.

[K. I. RABENSTEIN]

John R. Mott.

MOTT, JOHN RALEIGH

YOUNG MEN'S CHRISTIAN ASSOCIATION (YMCA) official, evangelical missionary, and leader in the WORLD COUNCIL OF CHURCHES (WCC); b. Livingston Manor, N.Y., May 25, 1865; d. Orlando, Fla., Jan. 31, 1955. He was the son of John S. and Elmira (Dodge) Mott. After graduating (1888) from Cornell University, Ithaca, N.Y., he married (1891) Leila White and became chairman of the executive committee of the Student Volunteer Movement and student secretary of the International Committee of the YMCA. In 1895 he helped to organize the World Student Christian Federation to coordinate youth groups for Christian unity, and he was its general secretary (1895–1920) and chairman (1920–28). From 1900 to 1914 he repeatedly toured the world, especially the Far East, to organize Christian youth and student movements, becoming one of the chief proponents of ecumenical Christianity. After heading the first preparatory commission for the Edinburgh World Missionary Conference (1910), he was chairman of its continuing committee until 1920, when it became the International Missionary Council with him as chairman to 1942. Meanwhile he continued his work for the YMCA, becoming (1915) secretary of its International Committee and also of the National Council of the YMCA in the United States. During World War I he was general secretary for the National War Work Council of the YMCA and worked with the Allied armies and among prisoners of war in Europe. From 1926 to 1946 he was president of the YMCA's World's Committee and World's Alliance. He received France's Legion of Honor, America's Distinguished Service Medal, and Norway's Nobel Peace Prize (1946).

Mott exercised an important influence on the ECUMENICAL movement of the early 20th century. According to C. Howard Hopkins, *History of the Y.M.C.A. in North America* (1951), "the most obvious contribution of the Y.M.C.A. to the world-wide movement that eventuated in the World Council of Churches was the person and influence of John R. Mott." He spent 50 years exemplifying the slogan adopted by the World's Alliance in 1881: that they may be one. His work with the International Missionary Council was permeated by this spirit and contributed to the formation of the World Council of Churches. In 1937 he presided over the first Faith and Order Conference at Oxford, England; a year later at Utrecht, Netherlands, he acted as vice chairman of the provisional committee to plan the projected world council. This project was delayed by war, but was crowned with success at Amsterdam in 1948, where he served as one of the presidents. Recognition of his enormous contribution to ecumenicism was given him there, when he was made lifetime honorary president of the WCC. His 16 books dealt mainly with world evangelism.

Bibliography: J. R. MOTT, *Address and Papers,* 6 v. (New York 1946–47). G. M. FISHER, J. R. MOTT, *Architect of Cooperation and Unity* (New York 1952). C. H. HOPKINS, *John R. Mott, 1865–1955: A Biography* (Grand Rapids, Mich. 1980). R. MACKIE, *Layman Extraordinary: John R. Mott 1865–1955* (New York 1955). B. MATTHEWS, *John R. Mott. World Citizen* (New York 1934).

[D. J. BOWMAN]

MOUNIER, EMMANUEL

Founder of a philosophy of PERSONALISM; b. Grenoble, April 1, 1905; d. Paris, March 22, 1950. Mounier began his active career as a professor of philosophy at St. Omer. In October 1932 he founded the journal *Esprit,* in which he applied his philosophy of personalism to the contemporary social, political, and cultural problems of the France of his day. During World War II he was a member of the Lyons resistance; was arrested (1941) but later released as a result of a hunger strike; and spent the occupation near Beauvillon, where he was a member of the *dromois maquis*. He resumed the editorship of *Esprit* after the war. Three of his works that have appeared in English translation are *A Personalist Manifesto* (New York 1938), *Personalism* (London 1952), and *Be Not Afraid: Studies in Personalist Sociology* (New York 1954).

Mounier's personalism was based on belief in the person as a spiritual being, maintaining his existence by adhering to a hierarchy of values freely adopted and assimilated. The person lives by his own responsible activity and interior development, unifies all his activity in freedom, and by creative acts develops his individuality and vocation. The person freely involves himself in the world while maintaining a spiritual detachment from, and transcendence over, the material aspects of civilization. Personalism means "engagement in action" in contemporary civilization. Real communion is also a demand of the person; the need for it leads to neither individualism nor communism, but to a personalist communitarian society in which each person would achieve his vocation in the totality, and in which the communion of the totality would be the result of the efforts of each person.

Mounier applied this philosophy to contemporary society. For him, the capitalist economic order subordinated the person to a system of production because of the profit motive. A personalist economic order would regulate the economy according to service rendered to the members of society. This would mean in practice a type of socialism involving elimination of the primacy of the profit motive, socialization of certain sectors of industry, development of cooperative life, the priority of labor over capital, the abolition of class distinctions based on division of labor or wealth, and the priority of personal responsibility over organizations.

In Mounier's thought, a personalist political order would be based upon a pluralistic society. The resulting democracy would be limited by the spiritual person and the rights of the natural societies that compose the nation. Such a democracy would be based upon autonomous societies exercising authority in their own spheres of influence and freely cooperating for national projects; it would result in a decentralization of authority and the personalization of the political order.

Bibliography: *Emmanuel Mounier: 1905–1950* (Paris 1950), also in *Esprit* 18 (1950): 721–1080. C. MOIX, *La Pensée d'Emmanuel Mounier* (Paris 1960). D. WOLF, "Emmanuel Mounier: A Catholic of the Left," *Review of Politics* 22 (1960): 324–344.

[D. WOLF]

MOUNT ATHOS, MONASTIC REPUBLIC OF

The Monastic Republic of Mount Athos is unique in being a theocratic republic whose principal inhabitants are multi-ethnic Orthodox monks from Greece, Turkey and the Slavic countries. Although it is within the physical boundaries of Greece, the Greek Constitution recognizes its administrative autonomy. Ecclesiastically, it is subject to the jurisdiction of the Ecumenical Patriarchate of CONSTANTINOPLE rather than the Greek Orthodox Church.

History. Mount Athos is the outside promontory of the three-pronged peninsula in northern Greece called Chalcidice that extends about 35 miles into the Aegean Sea and is named after a pyramid-like peak that rises to 6,760 feet. Before the arrival of Christian monks the site contained several cities dating from pre-Christian antiquity. Legend places a sanctuary of Zeus or Jupiter on the peninsula. Even today the traces can be seen of the canal, 3,950 feet long, that Xerxes constructed on the isthmus in his attempt to invade Greece in 480 B.C. without having to undergo the dangers of rounding the cape of the peninsula.

Although there were individual hermits inhabiting the Holy Mountain earlier, the first documentary records of Christian hermitages are from the 9th century when fugitives from the persecutions of ICONOCLASM increased the hermit population. Organized monastic life began there in 963, when Saint ATHANASIUS the Athonite built the first cenobitic monastery, known as the Great Lavra. His Rule derived chiefly from that of Saint BASIL the Great and Saint THEODORE THE STUDITE. Despite opposition to the innovations of organized community monasticism on Mount Athos, and with the support of the Byzantine Emperors Nicephorus Phocas and John I Tzimisces, the Rule of Saint Athanasius was accepted as a model; cenobitic life was imposed upon the hermits and Athanasius became the abbot, ruling 58 monasteries.

Under the constitution approved by the Emperor Constantine Monomachus, the famous law excluding women and female animals from the holy mount was enacted in 1045. In the 11th century other Christian nations began to send representatives to Mount Athos, and princes of the Balkan peninsula and of the northern Slav countries (especially Russia) endowed monasteries, thus making the peninsula pan-Orthodox in its representation. Even after the Eastern Schism (*c.* 1054), Benedictine monks of Amalfi, Italy, maintained a Catholic monastery there.

The monks turned to Pope INNOCENT III for protection against the Latin Crusaders and Catalan invaders in the 13th century; but when the Turks captured Salonica in 1430, the monks broke off all contact with Rome and submitted to their Turkish rulers.

Monasteries. Today Mount Athos exists as a republic under the Greek government, but enjoys self-rule. Internal government is centered in the holy *Koinotis* (central governing body) made up of 20 members chosen from the 20 monasteries that have the sole voting power. From these 20 members, a committee of four called the *epistatae* is chosen to form the executive branch. A president elected for one year presides over the sessions, which are held in the capital of Karyes, the seat of government since the 10th century. Of the 20 monasteries with voting power, 17 are Greek, one Bulgarian, one Russian, and one Serbian; these are: the Great Lavra (the oldest), Vatopedi, Saint Panteleimon (Russian), Hilandari (Serbian), Xeropotamou, Xenophontos, Docheiariou, Kastamonitou, Zographou (Bulgarian), Esphigmenou, Pantokratoros, Iviron, Koutlomousiou, Philotheou, Karakallou, Saint Paul's, Dionysiou, Gregoriou, Simopetra, and Stavroniketa (the last built, in 1545). Historically some of the monasteries adopted the idiorrhythmic monastic life, while others adopted the cenobitic monastic life. Under the cenobitic system, monks give a great degree of obedience to an abbot (*higoumenos*) chosen for life, perform all liturgical services in common, and submit to a stricter discipline in regard to food and property. In contrast, the idiorythmic (literally, one's own rhythm) model allowed the individual monk to set his own pace. The idiorythmic model came under much criticism for its propensity to tolerate abuses and laxity among the monks. By 1992, all 20 principal monasteries became cenobitic, when the Pantokratoros officially adopted the cenobitic model, being the last to do so.

Besides the 20 main monasteries, there are others, called sketes, some of which are even larger than the 20 main monasteries. These sketes, or clusters of ascetics living together, are also divided into the cenobitic and idiorrhythmic types. The cenobitic sketes differ externally from the main cenobitic monasteries, only in that rather than an abbot, a superior (*dikaios*) rules and is subject to the abbot of the main monastery to which the skete belongs. The idorrhythmic sketes are groups of small huts with three of four monks living together in each hut. In the midst of these clusters of huts there is the central church (*kyriakon*), so called because the monks come to common liturgical services only on Sunday, the day of the Lord (*Kyrios*). An elder rules the hut or hermitage, while the whole group of huts comes under the rule of a superior chosen by the main monastery to which the skete is attached. Observance in the idiorrhythmic skete, unlike the idiorrhythmic life in the main monasteries, is usually conducive to strict discipline and fervor in religious life.

Scattered throughout the rugged terrain of Mount Athos there are independent hermitages, called *kalyves.* The hermits who inhabit the southernmost tip of the peninsula (called *Karoulia* meaning pulleys), live one to a hut or in very small groups; each hermitage is independent and directly under one of the main monasteries. There are also *kellia,* separated houses ruled by an elder and dependent only upon the main monasteries, but in which the ascetical rule is not so austere as that practiced in the *kalyves.* Thus one finds a great deal of variety in monastic rule and observance, with much left to individual preference.

Architecture, Art, Libraries. Because of the ravages of time, earthquakes, plundering by pirates and the coming of Latin Crusaders, little of the architecture and art work dates back further than the 16th century; yet because of the utter conservatism, all that is found exactly reflects the Byzantine architecture and art of the 10th to 14th centuries. All the large monasteries follow an identical architectural plan and have fortified walls on the outside and on the inside a quadrangle, where the central church (*katholikon*) is found. The walls of the church and the numerous cupolas are frescoed; along with the art work of icons painted on wood, the metal work, and the *iconastasis,* the frescoes reflect very well the style of medieval Byzantine religious art.

Many of the libraries, such as those in the monasteries of Saint Paul and Simopetra, have been destroyed by fire; some were ravaged by the Turks during the War of Greek Independence (1821–29); and others were depleted by the neglect or even the vandalism of monks. Many ancient manuscripts were sold to libraries and museums in Russia and France; but about 11,000 remain, dealing mostly with theological and ecclesiastical subjects. Since contemplation rather than intellectual culture has characterized the monks of Mount Athos, little research has been done on these manuscripts. There has been a steady movement to give the monks a better education, and aspirants now spend five years training at the Athonias school in Karyes before they are attached to a monastery.

Mount Athos is unique as the last outpost where Byzantine religious culture and the spirituality of HESYCHASM are preserved in contemporary times.

Bibliography: *Le Millénaire du mont Athos, 963–1963,* 2 v. (Chevetogne, Belgium 1963–64) R. M. DAWKINS, *The Monks of Athos* (New York 1936). F. W. HASLUCK, *Athos and Its Monasteries* (New York 1924). S. LOCH, *Athos: The Holy Mountain* (New York 1959). C. KARAMBELAS, *Contemporary Ascetics of Mount Athos* (Platina, California 1991). S. KADAS, *Mount Athos: An Illustrated Guide to the Monasteries and Their History* (Athens 1993). R. GOTHÓNI, *Tales and Truth: Pilgrrimage on Mount Athos Past an Present* (Helsinki 1994). A. GOLITZIN, *The Living Witness of the Holy Mountain: Contemporary Voices from Mount Athos* (South

Canaan, Pennsylvania 1996). A. BRYER and M. CUNNINGHAM, eds. *Mount Athos and Byzantine Monasticism: Papers from the Twenty-eighth Spring Symposium of Byzantine Studies, Birmingham, March 1994* (Brookfield, Vermont 1996). R. ROBERSON, *The Eastern Christian Churches: A Brief Survey* (6th ed. Rome 1999). X. ZIMBARDO and B. UNSWORTH, *Monks of Dust: The Holy Men of Mount Athos* (New York 2001).

[G. A. MALONEY/EDS.]

MOUNT MELLERAY ABBEY

Monastery of Cistercian contemplatives of the strict observance or TRAPPISTS, Cappoquin, County Waterford, Ireland. It was founded in 1832 by 64 monks expelled from the abbey of MELLERAY, France, after the revolution of 1830. The monks, mostly Irish, a few English, were under the leadership of Dom Vincent M. Ryan (1778–1845) a native of Waterford City, and former prior of the French abbey. They obtained refuge on a farm in Kerry until 1832 when Sir Richard Keane of Cappoquin offered them 500 acres of unreclaimed moorland. Nearly 10,000 volunteers from neighboring parishes helped to erect a temporary house, to fence the land and to begin its reclamation. In 1838 the Church was consecrated, but the monks lived in poverty—yet during the Great Famine of 1847 and its aftermath they aided starving thousands. The following monasteries have been founded by Mount Melleray: 1835, Mount St. Bernard, Leicestershire, England; 1849, New Melleray, Iowa; 1878, Mount St. Joseph, Roscrea, Ireland: 1938, MELLIFONT ABBEY, County Louth, Ireland; 1948, Portglenone, County Antrim, Ireland; 1954, Kopua, Hawke's Bay, New Zealand.

Bibliography: L. H. COTTINEAU, *Répertoire topobibliographique des abbayes et prieurés*, 2 v. (Mâcon 1935–39) 2:1999. A. J. LUDDY, *The Story of Mount Melleray* (Dublin 1946).

[K. J. WALSH]

MOUNT OF OLIVES

The Mount of Olives lies east of the city of JERUSALEM. A long ridge, running north and south for about two miles, separated from Jerusalem by the Kidron Valley, it is slightly higher in elevation than the city itself. The hill is part of the central Judean range that falls off sharply to the Jordan Valley on the east and more gradually to the Mediterranean Sea on the west. The term "Mount of Olives" refers most properly to the southernmost of the ridge's three sections. The northernmost section is known as Mt. Scopus. The middle section is probably the site of the Old Testament Nob (1 Sm 21.1). The southern section, directly east of the Temple area, now called Jebel et-Tur, is, properly, the Mount of Olives, the traditional site of Jesus' Ascension into heaven. The village Kefr et-Tur, on the eastern slope, is believed to be the site of Bethphage, while farther down the southeastern end of the slope stood Bethany.

In the Old Testament. The Mount of Olives is mentioned only once in the Old Testament and only in a rather late post-exilic book, the Apocalypse of Zechariah (Zec 14.4), but it must be the same hill that was the scene of David's flight from Absalom (2 Sm 15.23). In Ez 11.23, the hill to the east of the city on which "the glory of the Lord . . . took a stand" after leaving the Temple must also have been the Mount of Olives. In Zec 14.4, on the day of the Lord's return to Jerusalem, ". . . his feet shall rest upon the Mount of Olives, which is opposite Jerusalem to the east. The Mount of Olives shall be cleft in two from east to west by a very deep valley, and half the mountain shall move to the north and half to the south."

In the New Testament. The Mount of Olives is mentioned frequently in the Gospels, either as τὸ ὄρος τῶν ἐλαιῶν (the mountain of the olive trees) or τὸ ὄρος τὸ καλούμενον Ἐλαιών (the hill called "The Olive Grove"). The vicinity of the hill was frequented by Jesus whenever He visited Jerusalem. The road from Jericho to Jerusalem passed over this ridge. It was along this road that His triumphal entry into Jerusalem took place (Lk 19.37). When He came over the brow of the hill and saw the city, He wept because of the suffering in store for it (Lk 19.41–44). Jesus delivered his eschatological discourse while sitting on the Mount of Olives (Mt 24.3; Mk 13.3). He spent the last nights before His death on the Mount (Lk 21.37), at Bethany, or Bethphage, or in the Garden of Gethsemani just across the Kidron (Jn 18.1) at the foot of the Mount. The Ascension of Jesus into heaven took place from the Mount of Olives, according to Acts 1.12.

Shrines and Archeology. The Mount of Olives is dotted with Christian shrines commemorating these events in Our Lord's life. Evidence of shrines and literary witnesses go back to very early times. The pilgrim Etheria, shortly before 400, mentioned that she took part in the liturgical services at Eleona, a church erected by the Empress Helena, to commemorate the spot where Our Lord taught; she mentions the place whence Our Lord ascended to heaven; she also mentions Gethsemani and Bethany. Today a modern basilica at Gethsemani is built upon the foundations of earlier churches. Halfway up the hill is a small chapel commemorating Our Lord's weeping over Jerusalem. In his excavations there B. Bagatti has found numerous OSSUARIES dating from early Christianity. Farther up the hill is the church and convent of Carmelite nuns, called the Pater Noster Monastery in

The Mount of Olives, a hill opposite Jerusalem where many of the events surrounding the Crucifixion of Christ are believed to have taken place. (Michael Maslan Historic Photographs/CORBIS)

memory of Luke's account of the Lord's Prayer (Lk 11.1–4). On top of the hill are the restored remains of an octagonal church, now in the possession of Muslims, and believed to occupy the spot from which Jesus ascended into heaven.

Bibliography: L. HEIDET, *Dictionnaire de la Bible*, ed. F. VIGOUROUX (Paris 1895–1912) 4.2:1779–93. B. BAGATTI, *Dictionnaire de la Bible*, suppl. ed. L. PIROT, et al. (Paris 1928–) 6:688–699. H. VINCENT and F. M. ABEL, *Jérusalem Nouvelle*, v.2 of *Jérusalem: Recherches de topographie, d'archéologie et d'histoire*, 2 v. (Paris 1912–26).

[S. MUSHOLT]

MOUNT ST. MARY'S COLLEGE AND SEMINARY

Founded in 1808 by Father John Dubois, Mount Saint Mary's comprises the second-oldest Catholic college and the second-oldest Catholic seminary in the United States [preceded, respectively, by Georgetown University (1789) and St. Mary's Seminary, Baltimore (1791)]. It is located near Emmitsburg, Maryland, about 70 miles north of Washington, D.C. Dubois, a refugee from revolutionary France, bought a tract of land on the side of a mountain already known as Saint Mary's Mountain. He built a church there in 1806, and in 1808 established a college as a preparatory seminary for Saint Mary's in Baltimore. Later in 1808, he became associated with the Society of St. Sulpice, who operated St. Mary's, and in 1811 control of the Mount was formally transferred to the Sulpicians. In 1812 Dubois was joined by Father Simon Gabriel Bruté de Remur, who came to be known as the Mount's "second founding father." Except for 1815–18, Bruté remained at the Mount, teaching theology and philosophy and exercising a strong hand in institutional governance, until 1834, when he was made bishop of Vincennes, Indiana.

In 1809, St. Elizabeth Anne Seton came to Mount St. Mary's. Dubois lent her his cabin while she awaited the completion of her own settlement in St. Joseph Valley, two miles away. He served as her religious superior and was instrumental in her community's adoption of a modified version of the rule of the Daughters of Charity, with whom he had been familiar in France. Bruté later served as her spiritual director. One of Mother Seton's sons, William, is buried in the cemetery on the Mount campus.

Though founded as a preparatory seminary, the college needed the income provided by young men who did not intend to study for priesthood, and was a "mixed" institution at least from 1811. Also for reasons of economy, Dubois initiated a system in which older students taught younger ones (a system which persisted into the twentieth century). This required some students to remain at the Mount beyond the point at which they could have entered Saint Mary's. Eventually, in 1820, Dubois obtained permission to introduce a full program in theology for study toward priesthood. Thus, by 1820 the institution included something like the college and seminary as they now exist, though what was then the college later divided into a high school or "preparatory school," which closed in 1936, and a college in the modern sense.

By 1826, financial difficulties and competition between St. Mary's and the Mount as major seminaries had led to a formal separation of the Mount—and of Dubois and Bruté personally—from the Sulpicians, who ceded control of the Mount back to Dubois. Upon his appointment that year as bishop of New York, Dubois sought unsuccessfully to give Mount Saint Mary's to the Jesuits at Georgetown but eventually deeded it to two diocesan priests. Together with Bruté, they formed the nucleus of the College Council, which became the institution's official owner and governing body when it was chartered in 1830 by the state of Maryland. With this charter, the institution's official name became Mount Saint Mary's College, whereas previously it had been called Mount Saint Mary's Seminary.

The College Council, composed of diocesan priests, was self-perpetuating and elected from its own members the president and other officers of the college. In 1930, a separate administration, headed by a rector, was established for the seminary, under the president and the council. Previously, the president of the college had served as seminary rector. In 1967 the council dissolved itself and the college was re-incorporated under a Board of Trustees. In 1971 Dr. John J. Dillon became the Mount's first lay president. While in 1967 priests comprised nearly half the faculty, by 2001 most remaining priest faculty were in the seminary and only one taught full-time in the college.

The Civil War threatened the college's survival, as enrollment dropped substantially and afterward many southern families were unable to pay their debts to the college. The resulting financial difficulties led to the college's being placed in receivership in 1881, but it was rescued in 1882 after a fund-raising effort led by James Cardinal Gibbons. Over the next several decades, it expanded its enrollment and physical plant. World War II shrank the student population once again, but the college remained open to train naval officers. After the closing of nearby St. Joseph's College, operated by the Daughters of Charity, at the end of the 1971–72 school year, Mount Saint Mary's became co-educational (1972). Today a slight majority of its undergraduate students are women.

The college offers degrees of Bachelor of Arts and Bachelor of Science in 24 fields. An integrated and sequenced liberal arts core curriculum, established by the faculty in 1988, is the centerpiece of Mount undergraduate education. The seminary offers the degrees of Master of Divinity and Master of Arts. A graduate program in business, leading to a degree of Master of Business Administration, and a Master of Education program were established in the college in 1975 and 1992 respectively. In 2001, the full-time equivalent enrollment, graduate and undergraduate, in the college was more than 1500, while the seminary enrolled approximately 150. The campus includes the National Shrine Grotto of Our Lady of Lourdes. The mountainside site dates from the time of Dubois and Mother Seton as a place of private meditation. In 1879, a replica of the Lourdes Grotto in France was added. After 1958, the centenary of the Lourdes apparitions, the grotto was expanded and opened to the wider public. As many as 100,000 people visit it each year.

In the nineteenth century Mount Saint Mary's came to be known as the "Cradle of Bishops," having given the church 29 bishops, including John J. Hughes (first archbishop of New York), John McCloskey (first American cardinal), and John B. Purcell (first archbishop of Cincinnati). Twentieth-century alumni have included Bishop James E. Walsh of Maryknoll (imprisoned for 12 years by the Chinese Communists), Archbishop Harry J. Flynn of Minneapolis-St. Paul, Monsignor Geno Baroni (civil rights activist and Undersecretary of Housing and Urban Development under President Carter), and Father Stanley Rother, assassinated in Guatemala in 1984 as a result of his work on behalf of the rural poor. Lay alumni have included the nineteenth-century artist John LaFarge and poet George Henry Miles.

Bibliography: M. M. MELINE and E. F. MCSWEENEY, *The Story of the Mountain* (Emmitsburg, Md. 1911). D. C. NUSBAUM, "The Lengthened Shadow: The Beginnings of Mount Saint Mary's,"

Celebrational Works: Essays Honoring the One Hundred Seventy-Fifth Anniversary of the Founding of Mount Saint Mary's, ed. M. J. NUSBAUM (Emmitsburg, Md. 1984), 13–45. A. H. LEDOUX, "Mount Saint Mary's College and Seminary," *Encyclopedia of American Catholic History,* 983–4. J. M. WHITE, *The Diocesan Seminary in the United States: A History from the 1780s to the Present* (South Bend, Ind. 1989).

[W. J. COLLINGE]

MOURRET, FERNAND

Ecclesiastical historian; b. Eygalières (Bouche-du-Rhône), France, Dec. 3, 1854; d. Paris, May 28, 1938. Fernand Maria Émile Mourret completed his classical education and studied law at Aix-en-Provence. After the obligatory military service, he practiced law for a short time and in 1879 entered the seminary of St. Sulpice at Issy, near Paris. In 1883 he joined the SULPICIANS and was sent to study in Rome, where he was ordained on Dec. 22, 1883. Severe illness forced him to interrupt his graduate studies in Rome after one year. Too frail for seminary work, he devoted the next ten years to less arduous tasks. He taught in the major seminary in Avignon (1894–96) and was then appointed to teach philosophy in the seminary of St. Sulpice in Issy. In 1898 he was transferred to the Sulpician theological school on the Rue de Regard, Paris, where he taught apologetics, dogmatic theology, and sacred eloquence. In 1902 he began to teach ecclesiastical history, the subject with which his name remains associated. His principal works, all published in Paris, are *La Vénérable Marie Rivier* (1898); *Leçons sur l'art de prêcher* (1909); *Le Mouvement catholique en France de 1830 à 1850* (1917); *Les Directions politiques, intellectuelles et sociales de Léon XIII* (1920); and *La papauté* (1929). *Le Concile du Vatican, d'après des documents inédits* (1919) made use of the papers of M. Icard, former superior of St. Sulpice. In conjunction with J. Carreyre, Mourret published *Précis d'histoire de l'Église* (3 v. 1924). Mourret's best-known work is *Histoire générale de l'Église* (9 v. 1914–27), written to provide his students with an up-to-date textbook. Essentially it represents the history courses conducted by Mourret, but for the contemporary period it constitutes an original work that remains authoritative, especially for French history. The first eight volumes (to 1878) have been translated into English by Newton Thompson as *A History of the Catholic Church* (1931–57). Mourret was an eminent professor, noted for his extensive knowledge, vivacity, and clarity, and he won renown, too, as a professor of homiletics and a spiritual director. He was extraordinarily kind and accessible.

Bibliography: *Bulletin Trimestriel des Anciens Elèves de S. Sulpice* (Paris 1903).

[E. JARRY]

MOVEMENT FOR A BETTER WORLD

An international movement to infuse in individuals and groups the spirit of mutual charity and unity that provides the basis for the social presence of Jesus: "For where two or three are gathered together for my sake, there am I in the midst of them" (Mt 18.20). The movement was inaugurated by Pius XII. In a radio message Feb. 10, 1952, Pope Pius called himself the "herald of a better world willed by God" and asked for a renewal of the structures of society [*Dal Nostro cuore Acta Apostolicae Sedis* 44 (1952) 158–162]. The founder and first international director, Riccardo Lombardi, SJ, of Rocca di Papa, Italy, answered the plea. Since 1952, through Father Lombardi's initiative, promoting groups of the movement have been established on every continent. The promoting group consists of specially trained clergy, religious and laity who strive to promote international collaboration and the quest for the common good and peace in the strife-torn world. To this end, the movement works closely with other international organizations at all levels, including the United Nations. Within parishes, the movement seeks to promote renewal of parish life, and a deeper awareness of and consequence sense of responsibility and commitment for reaching out to others.

Bibliography: R. LOMBARDI, *Towards a New World* (New York 1958); *Esercitazioni per un mondo Migliore* (Rome 1958), Eng. in prep., outline and format of the Better World Retreats; *The Salvation of the Unbeliever,* tr. D. M. WHITE (Westminster, Md. 1956); *Rifare il mondo* (2d ed. Rocca di Papa 1959); *Orientamenti fondamentali* (11th ed. Rome 1957); *La dottrina marxista: esposizione e discussione* (3d ed. Rome 1956); *La storia e il suo protagonista* (3d ed. Rome 1947).

[R. L. BENNETT/P. M. HARTIGAN/EDS.]

MOWINCKEL, SIGMUND

Old Testament scholar; b. Lutheran manse of Kjerringöy, Norway, Aug. 4, 1884; d. Oslo, June 4, 1965. In 1917 he began his academic career at the University of Oslo, where he had matriculated the previous year. He was ordained in 1940. His most important works are *Psalmenstudien* 1–6 (1921–24) and *The Psalms in Israel's Worship* 1–2 (1951, tr. 1962). While following in the footsteps of his former teacher at Giessen, H. Gunkel, he went beyond him and established the cultic character of nearly all Psalms. He associated many Psalms with the autumn harvest festival of the New Year, in which Yahweh was ritually enthroned. Other insights of his are the role of the king (the communal "I" in the Psalms), and the eventual democratization of the Psalms, whereby they became a vehicle of prayer for the average worshiper. Also important is *He That Cometh* (1951, tr. 1956), a basic study of Old Testament messianism and eschatology (the latter would have risen out of the disappointment of the exile).

His expertise ranged throughout the Old Testament: *Tetrateuch-Pentateuch-Hexateuch* (1964), *La religion et la culte* (1957), *Prophecy and Tradition* (1946), and *Le décalogue* (1927). He combined intellectual brilliance with a warm faith in *The Old Testament as the Word of God* (1938, tr. 1959).

Bibliography: D. R. AP-THOMAS, "An Appreciation of Sigmund Mowinckel's Contribution to Biblical Studies," *Journal of Biblical Literature* 75 (1966) 315–335. A. S. KAPELRUD, "Sigmund Mowinckel and Old Testament Study," *Annual of the Swedish Theological Institute* 5 (1967) 4–29. D. KVALE and D. RIAN, eds., *Sigmund Mowinckel's Life and Works: A Bibliography* (Oslo 1984).

[R. E. MURPHY]

MOYË, JOHN MARTIN, BL.

Founder of religious congregations of women and missionary to China; b. Cutting, Lorraine, France, January 27, 1730; d. Trier, Germany, May 4, 1793. John, the sixth of 13 children born to John Moyë and Catherine Demange, was educated at the Collège of Pont-à-Mousson, the Jesuit College of Strasbourg, and the Seminary of Saint-Simon in Metz. After his ordination in 1754, Father Moyë devoted himself as vicar to pastoral work in the Diocese of Metz for 17 years. To secure free education for village children, he founded the Congregation of the Sisters of Divine Providence in 1762. He was appointed superior of the Seminary of Saint-Dié in 1767, but two years later he asked to join the PARIS FOREIGN MISSIONARY SOCIETY. On March 28, 1773, he arrived in Chengdu, the capital of Sichuan in southwestern China, to work under Bp. François Pottier, the vicar apostolic. His missionary field covered half of Sichuan and the province of Guizhou. He worked there for ten years with tireless and inventive zeal, baptizing native children in danger of death, writing books of devotion, and organizing exercises of piety. In 1782 he established an Institute of Christian Virgins to care for the sick and to give Christian instruction to Chinese women and children in their homes.

Physical exhaustion and the opposition to his apostolic methods manifested by his five co-workers caused him to ask to return to France in 1784. Lorraine again became the field of his apostolate and the Sisters of Divine Providence his special care. Within the decade, the French Revolution created grave religious problems. Father Moyë gave counsel and generous help to the persecuted nonjuring priests and the religious forced from their cloisters. To save the congregation he had founded, he moved the Sisters of Divine Providence to Trier in 1791. The advance of the French army, however, caused its suppression the next year. Restored in 1816, the congregation numbered 116 convents by the end of the century, and in 1866 the Sisters made a foundation in San Antonio, Texas. Father Moyë died in the typhus epidemic that spread to Trier. LEO XIII approved the introduction of his cause, January 14, 1891. The heroicity of his virtue was proclaimed May 21, 1945, and he was beatified Dec. 27, 1954, by PIUS XII.

Feast: May 4.

Bibliography: *Acta Apostolicae Sedis* 38 (1946) 287–290; 46 (1954) 734–737,739–740; 47 (1955) 33–39. J. MARCHAL, *Vie de M. l'abbé Moyë de la Société des Missions Étrangères, fondateur de la Congrégation des Soeurs de la Providence en Lorraine* . . . (Paris 1872). G. GOYAU, *Un Devancier de l'oeuvre de la Sainte-Enfance: Jean-Martin Moyë, missionaire on Chine, 1772–1783* (Paris 1937). R. PLUS, *J. M. Moyë* . . . *des Missions Étrangères: fondateur des Soeurs de la Providence* (Paris 1947). M. G. CALLAHAN, *The Life of Blessed John Martin Moyë* (Milwaukee 1964). J. GUENNOU, *Le Bienheureux Jean-Martin Moye* (Paris 1970). M. KERNEL, *De l'Insécurité: le projet de vie des Soeurs de la Providence selon le "Directoire" de Jean-Martin Moyë* (Paris 1976). G. H. TAVARD, *L'expérience de Jean-Martin Moye: mystique et mission* (Paris 1978); *Lorsque Dieu fait tout: la doctrine spirituelle du bienheureux Jean-Martin Moye* (Paris 1984).

[G. M. GRAY]

MOYENMOUTIER, ABBEY OF

Former Benedictine monastery located in the Vosges Mountains on the upper Meurthe River in eastern France. It was founded toward the end of the 7th century by St. HIDULF, a monk at Saint-Miximin and auxiliary bishop of Trier, who, having left Trier, settled as a hermit on the site that was to become Moyenmoutier. Others joined him and formed a small monastery situated midway between five others, consequently known as *medianum monasterium* or Moyenmoutier. In its long history (11 centuries) Moyenmoutier was influenced by reform movements emanating from the Abbey of GORZE, and later, from CLUNY. One of its outstanding sons was HUMBERT OF SILVA CANDIDA. To counteract the evils brought by the system of commendatory abbots, it joined (1601) with the Abbey of Saint-Vanne at Verdun in forming the great Congregation of Saint-Vanne et Saint-Hydulphe, which was suppressed by the French Revolution in 1790.

Bibliography: *Monumenta Germaniae Historica: Scriptores* (Berlin 1826–) 4:87–92. L. H. COTTINEAU, *Répertoire topobibliographique des abbayes et prieurés*, 2 v. (Mâcon 1935–39) 2:2008–09. A. POTTHAST, *Bibliotheca historica medii aevi* (2d ed. 1896; repr. Graz 1954) 1:733. *Gallia Christiana* (Paris 1715–85) 13:1398–1407. G. ALLEMANG, *Lexikon für Theologie und Kirche*,

NEW CATHOLIC ENCYCLOPEDIA

37

ed. J. HOFER and K. RAHNER, 10 v. (2d, new ed. Freiburg 1957–65) 7:666. H. LECLERCQ, *Dictionnaire d'archéologie chrétienne et de liturgie,* ed. F. CABROL, H. LECLERCQ, and H. I. MARROU, 15 v. (Paris 1907–53) 12.1:380–390, on its foundation and early abbots.

[C. DAVIS]

MOZAMBIQUE, THE CATHOLIC CHURCH IN

Capital: Maputo (formerly Lournenço Marques).
Size: 297,730 sq. miles.
Population: 19,104,700 in 2000.
Languages: Portuguese; indigenous dialects are spoken in various regions.
Religions: 4,585,130 Catholics (24%), 3,855,000 Muslims (20%), 4,250,300 Protestants (22%), 6,414,270 adhere to indigenous beliefs or do not practice a religion.

The Republic of Mozambique is located in southeastern AFRICA and is bordered by the Indian Ocean on the east, the Republic of South Africa and Swaziland on the south and southeast, Zimbabwe and Zambia on the west, Malawi on the northwest and Tanzania on the north. The region, with its tropical climate, contains a low coastal region that rises to central uplands, with high plateaus in the northwest and mountains at its western border. Natural resources include coal, titanium, natural gas and hydropower, while agricultural products consist of cotton, cashew nuts, sugar cane, tea, copra, coconuts and citrus.

After its discovery by Vasco da Gama in 1498, Mozambique served as a way station for the Portuguese en route to India around the Cape of Good Hope. Later it was a source of slaves for Brazil. Its boundaries were definitely established only in 1891. In 1951 it became an overseas province of Portugal and in 1975 gained full independence. The massive emigration of the Portuguese elite, a drought and civil war resulted in the region being considered one of the poorest nations in Africa by the early 1990s. However, the fall of Mozambique's Marxist government, Great Britain's decision to cancel some of the Mozambique's debt and the privatization of industry bolstered the sagging economy, attracting foreign investments. Despite increasing economic stability, the high illiteracy rate and the human toll from AIDS caused the standard of living to suffer; by 2000 the average life expectancy of a Mozambican was 37 years of age.

Early History. Portuguese Jesuits initiated mission activity in the 16th century, and Gonçalo da SILVEIRA, SJ, was martyred in 1561 after baptizing the rulers of Monomotapa and 300 persons in the court. Portuguese territories in the region were attached to the See of GOA in India, until 1612 when they formed a separate prelature *nullius*. The Dominicans, who had entered the area in 1577, evangelized the Monomotapa region, whose king was baptized in 1652. After many isolated efforts, a sustained missionary presence was established in the 17th century when the Dominicans, the Jesuits and the Augustinians worked on the southern coast and up the Zambezi. Quelimane, Sena and Tete developed into important centers; even Zumbo, near the Zambian border, was reached and maintained well into the 19th century. A decline of the mission during the 18th century was accelerated by the anti-Jesuit policies of the Marquis de POMBAL. Portugal's suppression of religious orders in 1834 made the situation worse and by 1855 no missionaries remained.

A change for the better occurred in 1881 when the Jesuits resumed their work. They were joined by the Franciscans in 1898, and by 1910 there were 71 missionaries, mostly Portuguese. The mission again suffered from the extreme anticlericalism of Portuguese regimes between 1910 and 1925, but the Concordat and the Missionary Statute with the Holy See in 1940 resulted in progress and the creation of the hierarchy. The number of Catholics rose from 4,000 in 1900 to 60,000 in 1936, and to 850,000 in 1960. Archbishop Teódosio de Gouveia of Lourenço Marques received the red hat in 1940, the first prelate south of the Sahara ever to be named cardinal.

The 1940 concordat, while strengthening the Church, did little to extricate the Church from the repressions of colonialism. Missions were funded by the state to the degree to which they served colonial interests. Generous financial help for religious orders, including the payment of salaries, free overseas passages, special status for bishops who enjoyed privileges similar to state governors and authority for all primary education were some of the rewards for the Church's subservience to Portugal's "civilizing mission." Internally, the Mozambican Church appeared very much as a faithful copy of religion as practiced and organized in Portugal. Many a missionary never bothered to learn a local African language. Small efforts were made to inculturate the liturgy, catechetics and pastoral methods (*see* INCULTURATION, THEOLOGY OF). The Church's leadership remained decidedly Portuguese. The first Mozambican Catholic priest of the modern period was not ordained until 1953, and native clergy in the year of independence numbered only 38 against 478 foreign priests.

The period 1940 to 1970 was one of great expansion as churches, missions, schools and clinics were constructed, among them the catechetical center Nazaré, founded in 1968 near Beira and run by the White Fathers. However, the Church remained unaware of the growing unrest among the native population. As late as 1970, in the pastoral letter ''A Christian Message for the Ordering of Right Relations in Mozambique,'' the bishops, all Portuguese, noted ''the total absence of racial discrimination in Portuguese laws,'' condemned ''every kind of guerrilla action (*terrorismo*)'' and expressed the wish that social inequalities be resolved gradually. With the notable exception of Bishop Sebastião Soares Resende of Beira (d. 1967) and later of Bishop Vieira Pinto of Nampula, the hierarchy supported the colonial status quo, remained silent in the face of repression and injustices, and even defended the colonial war waged in the name of Christian civilization.

The conformist attitude of the hierarchy was increasingly rejected by many missionaries. In May of 1971, 48 White Fathers from Beira and Tete left Mozambique in order not to be ''accomplices of an official support which even the bishops . . . seem to give to a regime that shrewdly uses the Church to consolidate and perpetuate in Africa an anachronistic situation.'' This missionary exodus had repercussions on other congregations, especially those of the Burgos, Consolata and Comboni Fathers. In the meantime, local violence escalated and local priests began to confront bishops with reports of civilian massacres. While the hierarchy protested to the governor general, its protest was ineffective. In July of 1973 a report on the violence by the Burgos Fathers found its way to the international press via the *London Times* (July 10, 1973). As protests multiplied, so did deportations; nearly 100 missionaries, including Bishop Pinto of Nampula, were expelled prior to the coup that overthrew the Portuguese government on April 25, 1974.

The Church after Independence. On June 25, 1975 Mozambique gained political independence as the People's Republic of Mozambique, resulting in a radical change in Church-State relations. While the liberation government, FRELIMO, appreciated the efforts of some priests to promote the struggle for independence, it remained critical of the Church as a whole. The government of President Samora Machel nationalized church assets and stopped all subsidies. Clergy were turned out of their residences, seminaries shut and schools and hospitals taken over by the state. Radio Pax, founded in 1953 in Beira, was shut down. Four bishops resigned and hundreds of church personnel left the country by the end of 1976 as a result of the radical disestablishment of the Church. Under the new constitution, Mozambique became a secular state, although the freedom to practice one's faith was guaranteed. The socialist government's attitude toward the Church eventually softened into a growing appreciation of the Church's role in charity, particularly in the face of the civil war that would follow. A perceptible thaw in Church-state relations occurred in

Archdioceses	Suffragans
Beira	Chimoio, Gurué, Quelimane, Tete
Maputo	Inhambane, Xai-Xai (formerly João Belo)
Nampula	Lichinga (formerly Vila Cabral; 1963), Nacala, Pemba (formerly Porto Amelia; 1957).

1982 when some buildings were returned for Church use, and seminaries were allowed to reopen. Prior to his death in a plane crash in 1986, President Machel told Church leaders: ''Let us cooperate in dialogue without prejudice on either side. Let us argue, if necessary, but not about subjects of secondary importance.'' The state eventually decreed that all nationalized church institutions be returned.

A New Pastoral Vision. Church leaders created a new vision of missionary and pastoral work. A document by Nampula's bishop published in July of 1975 reflected this vision by stating that the colonial and bourgeois mentality should shift to an awareness and solidarity with native people, and that the Church should not defend its material interests over its main interest, the salvation of the people. In March of 1975 the country's first two native bishops were ordained. Two years later the first National Pastoral Assembly developed practical programs for change that stressed lay ministries; the second Assembly, held in 1991, would review these programs in the light of the traumatic civil war and add recognition of the dignity of the human being and social justice by means of reconciliation and re-evangelization.

After the government released to the Church those buildings confiscated immediately after independence, it raised a new issue. While some Catholics advocated a return to the highly institutionalized infrastructure of the pre-civil war era, others called for an approach rooted in small, local Christian communities, with a respect for native languages and cultures and meaningful enculturation of the faith.

When Pope John Paul II visited the region in September of 1988, the civil war had created over two million refugees while tens of thousands had been killed. The pope appealed for a national dialogue asserting that the Church would help by every possible means, and denounced all terror in the strongest terms, confirming the local bishops in their indefatigable appeals for peace and reconciliation. Alexandre Cardinal dos Santos of Maputo and Archbishop Jaime Gonçalves of Beira played an im-

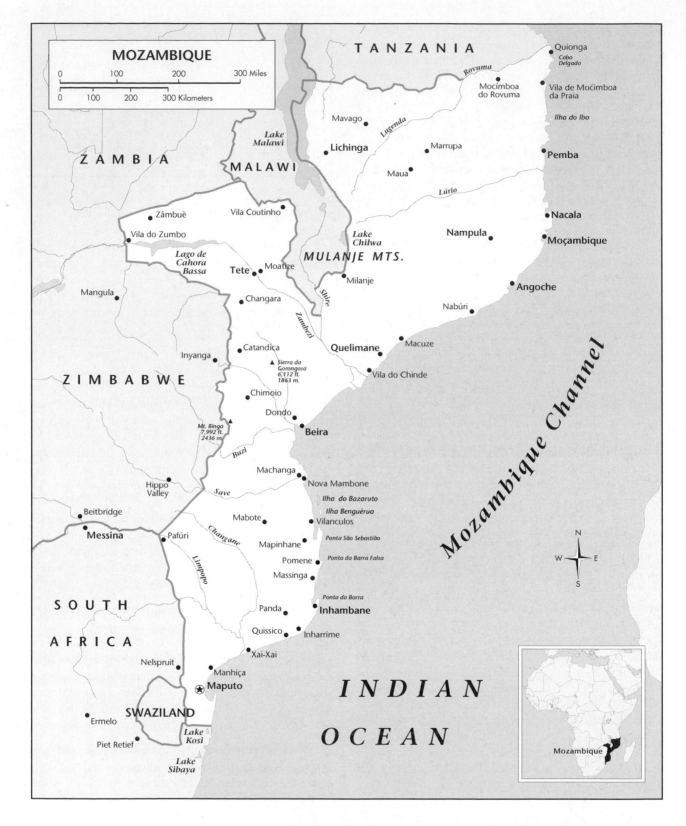

MOZAMBIQUE

portant role during the four years of strenuous negotiations between the warring factions FRELIMO and RENAMO, finally leading to the Rome Peace Accord of Oct. 4 1992. The first multiparty elections were held in 1994 and a year later Mozambique became the first non-British colony admitted to the Commonwealth of Nations. Diplomatic relations with the Holy See were established in 1995.

Into the 21st Century. By 2000 the Church in Mozambique had 277 active parishes tended by 88 diocesan and 328 religious priests. Other religious included approximately 90 brothers and 890 sisters, many of whom worked in the country's 217 primary and 32 secondary Catholic schools. Responding to an increasing need for Church personnel to support a growing Catholic community, churches in Brazil, Nigeria and Zimbabwe sent priests and others, while a renewed commitment was made by orders and congregations formerly active in the country. The Comboni Missionaries reopened their famous Technical Training School in Nampula and a Catholic University was planned for Beira. Most Catholics resided in the central provinces, while a growing Muslim population could be found in the north and along the coast. In response to the severe flooding experienced in the region by cyclone Eline in March of 2000, the pope donated $150,000 from his private charity, Cor Unum, to aid in the relieve efforts led by Caritas Mozambique.

Bibliography: F. CORREIA, *O método missionário dos Jesuitas em Moçambique 1881–1910* (Braga 1992). L. DA COSTA FERREIRA, *Igreja Ministerial em Moçambique* (Lisboa 1987). A. HASTINGS, *Wiriyamu* (London 1974). IDOC DOCUMENTATION SERVICE, *The Church in Mozambique. Minutes of a Discussion between the Roman Catholic Bishops and the Government of Mozambique* (Rome 1979). F. LOPES, *Missões Franciscanas em Moçambique: 1898—1970* (Braga 1972). *Mozambique: A Church in a Socialist State in a Time of Radical Change,* Pro Mundi Vita Dossier (Brussels 1977). O. PERESSINI, *Mozambico: Una Chiesa tra i marxisti* (Bologna 1980). P. SCHEBESTA, *Portugals Konquistamission in Südost-Afrika* (Siegburg 1967). M. VAN LAY, *Kirche im Entkolonisierungskonflict: eine Fallstudie zum Krieg um die Entkolonisierung Mozambiks 1964–1974* (Munich 1981). F. DE ALMEIDA, *História da Igreja em Portugal,* 4 v. (Coimbra 1910–22). L. KILGER, *Die erste Mission unter den Bantustämmen Ostafrikas* (Münster 1917). M. DE OLIVEIRA, *História eclesiástica de Portugal* (2d ed. Lisbon 1948). A. BRASIO, *Monumenta missionaria africana,* 7 v. (Lisbon 1952–56). R. WENZEL, *Portugal und der Heilige Stuhl* (Lisbon 1958). R. PATTEE, *Portugal na África contemporâanea* (Coimbra 1959). J. DUFFY, *Portuguese Africa* (Cambridge, MA 1959); *Portugal in Africa* (Cambridge, MA 1962). A. DA SILVA REGO, *Llções de missionologia* (Estudos de ciências políticas e sociais 56; Lisbon 1961). *Bilan du Monde,* 2:619–622. *Annuario Pontificio* has annual data on all dioceses.

[R. PATTEE/A. PLANGGER/EDS.]

MOZARABIC CHANT

The repertory of chant used in the Mozarabic (Visigothic) liturgy of the medieval Church in Spain. This chant style burgeoned and came to full bloom between 550 and 650 and was firmly fixed at the time of the Arab invasion (771). It is called Mozarabic because the term

Chants of Mozarabic Rite.

describes a Christian living under Arab or Islamic domination (711–1085), and because its principal MSS date from this period. The principal surviving musical codices of the Visigothic-Mozarabic liturgy are preserved in the cathedral of Toledo; in San Domingo Abbey, Silos; in San Millán Abbey, Cogolla; in the cathedral of León; and in the University of Santiago de Compostela. These codices, copied in the 10th and 11th centuries, contain an almost complete musical repertory of the Visigothic Church of Toledo that dates back to the 6th, 7th, and early 8th centuries. The most precious of them is the Antiphonary of León. According to some scholars, this is an early 10th-century copy of an original MS of King Wamba written for the Toledo parish of St. Leocadia in 672. It begins with the feast of St. Ascisclus (November 17) and contains the Office and the Mass for the entire ecclesiastical year.

Notation. Mozarabic chant had its own musical notation, but the notation of these codices is illegible for the reason that there is not a single musical codex of the Mozarabic period that is copied upon lines of the musical staff. When in the 11th century the Gregorian codices without lines were transcribed into codices with lines, Spanish musicians did not do the same for their own melodies. As a consequence, the Visigothic-Mozarabic neumes are legible only to the extent of the number of their notes. There is no means of determining the relations of tonal height within the notes of a neume, nor its melodic connection with the preceding and following neumes. The melodic treasury incased within the neumes is undecipherable without the help of a later diastematic notation. Such notation was found for 20 or so of the actual melodies preserved. In 12 folios of the MS of the *Liber Ordinum* of the Monastery of San Millan an Aquitainian superimposed system was substituted for erased Mozarabic neumes. The comparison of these folios with the Mozarabic neumatic notation of the same pieces in the MS of the *Liber Ordinum* of the San Domingo monastery of Silos served as a key to decipher the existing melodies. These melodies show that Mozarabic chant was monodic and of a free rhythm and modality equal to that of Gregorian chant. They exemplify syllabic, neumatic, and melismatic styles.

There are two classes of script in Mozarabic notation: the horizontal and the vertical. The horizontal script pertains exclusively to the codices of Toledo and to a very fragmentary Portuguese codex of Coimbra. In these codices the neumes incline to the right. The codex of Silos and the Antiphonary of León are in vertical scripts. Both the horizontal and vertical scripts originated, however, in the scriptoria of Toledo.

Diffusion. Through the efforts of CHARLEMAGNE and the promulgation of the *Lex Romana,* France sacrificed her own liturgy and chant for the liturgy and chant of Rome. The effect of this edict in Spain paralleled the success of the reconquest. The *Lex Romana* did not triumph in Aragon until 1071 and became successful in Navarre, Castille, and Leon only in 1076. The Spanish Mozarabic rite was finally suppressed by Pope GREGORY VII in 1089, except for six parishes in Toledo where it was allowed to continue. Here it struggled along with much difficulty and became almost extinct until Cardinal XIMÉNES DE CISNEROS became archbishop of Toledo. He received a concession from Pope Julius II in 1508 to found the Mozarabic chapel of Corpus Christi in the cathedral church of Toledo. The service books edited by him include a missal in 1500 and a breviary in 1502. They preserve some Mozarabic melodies in an altered form of the older, non-diastematic sources.

See Also: MOZARABIC RITE.

Bibliography: C. ROJO and G. PRADO, *El canto mozárabe* (Barcelona 1929). G. PRADO, ''Mozarabic Melodics,'' *Speculum* 3 (1928) 218–239. H. ANGLÈS, *La música española* (Barcelona 1941); P. WAGNER, ''Der Mozarabische Kirchengesang,'' *Gesammelte Aufsätze zur Kulturgeschichte Spaniens* 1 (Spanische Forschungen der Görresgesellschaft 1; Münster 1928) 102–141. A. M. MUNDÓ, ''La datación de los códices litúrgicos visigóticos toledanos,'' *Hispania sacra, 18* (1965), 1–25. C. W. BROCKETT, *Antiphons, Responsories and Other Chants of the Mozarabic Rite* (Brooklyn, NY, 1968). D. M. RANDEL, ''Responsorial Psalmody in the Mozarabic Rite,'' *Etudes gregoriennes* 10 (1969), 87–116. D. M. RANDEL *The Responsorial Psalm Tones for the Mozarabic Office* (Princeton, NJ, 1969). J. PINELL, ''El problema de las dos tradiciones del antiguo rito hispánico,'' *Liturgia y música mozárabes* [Toledo 1975] (Toledo, 1978), 3–44. M. C. DÍAZ Y DÍAZ, ''Literary Aspects of the Visigothic Liturgy,'' *Visigothic Spain: New Approaches*, ed. E. JAMES (Oxford, 1980), 61–76. D. M. RANDEL, ''Antiphonal Psalmody in the Mozarabic Rite,'' *International Musicological Society: Congress Report 12* [Berkeley 1977], ed. D. HEARTZ and B. WADE (Kassel, 1981), 414–22. K. LEVY, ''Old-Hispanic Chant in its European Context,'' *España en la música de occidente* [Salamanca 1985], ed. E. CASARES RODICIO, I. FERNÁNDEZ DE LA CUESTA and J. LÓPEZ-CALO (Madrid, 1987), vol. 1, 3–14. M. HUGLO, ''Recherches sur les tons psalmodiques de l'ancienne liturgie hispanique,'' *Revista de musicologia* 16 (1993), 477–90. K. LEVY, ''The Iberian Peninsula and the Formation of Early Western Chant,'' *Revista de musicologia* 16 (1993), 435–7. D. M. RANDEL, ''The Old Hispanic Rite as Evidence for the Earliest Forms of the Western Christian Liturgies,'' *Revista de musicologia* 16 (1993), 491–6.

[I. WORTMAN/EDS.]

MOZARABIC RITE

The name that designates the autochthonous liturgical system celebrated by Christians in Spain. The rite has been variously called the *Visigothic* or *Gothic* rite because of its greatest development under Visigothic rule beginning in the 5th century, and the Mozarabic rite because of its celebration by Christians in areas under Islamic control from 711 to 1492. These Christians were called *mozárabes* (''like Arabs'' or ''Arabicized''). The rite is also referred to as the Old Spanish rite or the Hispanic rite. With its official reestablishment in 1988, the rite was renamed the Hispano-Mozarabic rite in order to designate its origin, Hispania, and to honor the ethnic Mozarabs who have continued to celebrate it over the centuries.

History. The Hispano-Mozarabic rite is one of several Latin language liturgical systems developed in the West after Christianity had been implanted and began to spread throughout the Roman empire in the first centuries of the Church. Only three Western rites have survived to this day, namely the Roman, the Milanese (Ambrosian), and the Spanish.

The rite has experienced various vicissitudes as well as periodic renewals throughout the course of its history. A charge of Adoptionism stemming from the Council of Frankfurt (794), the Europeanizing efforts of Alfonso VI (1065–1109), and the program of liturgical unification of Gregory VII (1073–1085) contributed to the rite's suppression in 1080 by the Council of Burgos. However, when Toledo was retaken from Islamic control in 1085, Christians there were permitted to retain their rite solely in the then-existing six parishes. Only two of these parishes survive today, namely Santa Eulalia y San Marcos and Santas Justa y Rufina. The ancient liturgy of Spain has been celebrated in these two parishes on a continuous though limited basis. After the Roman rite was decreed for Spain, the Hispano-Mozarabic rite began a long period of decline. This decline was partially stemmed by the humanist Cardinal Francisco XIMÉNEZ DE CISNEROS (1436–1517) after he became Archbishop of Toledo (1495). He saw the rite as part of the ancient Spanish heritage stemming from the classical Roman era. In order to save this heritage he had editions of the Missal and Breviary prepared. Furthermore, he founded a cadre of Mozarabic chaplains and installed them in the Corpus Christi chapel of Toledo's Cathedral, where the rite is celebrated on a daily basis. The publication of liturgical books and the establishment of a chaplaincy helped to conserve and perpetuate the rite. The rite is also celebrated once or twice a year at the Talavera chapel in Salamanca and on special occasions at other sites throughout Spain. Even so, only the Eucharist and the Divine Office in the Hispano-Mozarabic rite tend to be celebrated outside of Toledo. Baptism, Confirmation, and Marriage are celebrated on a periodic basis in the Mozarabic parishes of Toledo. The other sacraments are yet to be revived. At an unofficial level, elements of the Hispano-Mozarabic rite survived in popular devotions.

Renewal. Vatican Council II, in its call for the reform of the liturgy in the Constitution *Sacrosanctum Concilium*, paid particular attention to liturgy's pastoral aspect. The need for adaptation of the liturgy was especially accentuated. Instead of rigid uniformity in the celebration of liturgy throughout the Catholic world, room was made for legitimate differences. As a facet of this, the Council explicitly fostered diversity in the celebration of the liturgy by calling for the incorporation of the genius and talent of the various peoples who comprise the Catholic Church. Behind this principle is the perception that diversity in the celebration of the liturgy in no way harms unity but instead displays the universality of the Church. As a consequence, all the rites celebrated by Catholics in East or West are recognized as enjoying the same dignity and privileges as the Roman rite. Therefore, the ancient Spanish rite enjoys renewed status and life.

Prior to its renewal, the rite was subjected to the same principles and norms of reform as the Roman rite. Thus, the Spanish church undertook efforts to revitalize its ancient rite by studying the available liturgical sources. In this way the church preserved the rite's authentic structure and content to the extent possible. The "masses" or sets of eleven variable prayers used in the celebration of the Eucharist underwent a careful theological review and were revised as needed according to the Church's doctrine. The prayers are the *Oratio Post*

Manuscript folio from "Orationale Gothicum," prayers for non-Eucharistic Mozarabic services, 9th century, found in monastery of San Domingo de Silos, Burgos, Spain (Add. MS 30.852, fol. 16v).

Gloriam, Oratio Admonitionis, Alia, Oratio Post Nomina, Oratio Ad Pacem, Illatio, Oratio Post Sanctus, Oratio Post Pridie, Ad Orationem Dominicam, Benedictio, and *Completuria.* Cardinal Marcelo González Martín established a commission of fourteen members in 1982 for the purpose of reforming the rite's liturgical celebrations. The Commission prepared the new *Ordo Missae* for the Eucharist and published it in 1985. The *Ordo* was approved by the Spanish Episcopal Conference in 1986 and received confirmation *ad interim* from the Congregation for Divine Worship and the Discipline of the Sacraments in 1988. That same year the restored rite became an optional liturgy for Spain under certain stipulations. The official Latin text of the *Ordo Missae iuxta ritum Hispano-Mozarabicum* appears in the new *Missale Hispano-Mozarabicum* of 1991. In January 1992 Cardinal González Martín decreed the obligatory use of the *Missale* for use at Eucharist in the Hispano-Mozarabic rite. In addition, an *ad experimentum* Spanish translation of the texts has been made for use in Toledo.

Sources. The extant manuscripts date from the 8th to the 14th centuries. Dom Jordi Pinell, OSB (1921–1997), considered the premier expert on the rite during its restoration, catalogued 250 liturgical texts emanating from this era. The recovery and study of the ancient manuscripts have led scholars to identify two distinct traditions, simply named A and B. Tradition A comprises the majority of the recovered texts, dated to the 8th through 12th centuries; these have been linked to the ancient Roman provinces of Tarraconensis and Carthaginensis and include the cities of Narbonne and Toledo. This group of manuscripts were conserved primarily by the parish of Santa Eulalia. Tradition B texts are later and are as late as the 14th century; they are associated with the Roman province of Betica and its capital Seville. These manuscripts were conserved by the parish of Santas Justa y Rufina. Nonetheless, in Pinell's assessment the Tradition B texts contain the more ancient elements. The frequent indications of the authors of hymns and liturgical texts are an interesting feature of the Hispano-Mozarabic manuscripts. These include the brothers Leander (d. 600) and Isidore of Seville (d. 636) as well as Ildephonse (d. 667) and Julian of Toledo (d. 690).

Pinell and other members of the Commission relied heavily on the previous work of Marius FÉROTIN. Interest in the Mozarabic codices in the contemporary era was initiated at the end of the 19th century. Through his work on ancient Spanish sources discovered at Silos and San Millán de la Cogolla (near Burgos), Férotin was able to identify two codices of a ritual entitled the *Liber Ordinum*. He produced the first critical edition in 1904. Férotin produced in 1912 a critical edition of ancient manuscripts found in various places in Toledo that he compiled and identified as the *Liber Mozarabicus Sacramentorum*. His ground-breaking work aided further analysis of the textual sources, which resulted in clarifications as to their origin, purpose and transmission. José Janini, in his analysis of the texts of the *Liber Ordinum*, for example, was able to make distinctions between them that Férotin did not make and thus identified Codex A as destined for episcopal use and Codex B for presbyteral use. Janini updated the critical edition of Codex A and called it the *Liber Ordinum Episcopal*. Other critical editions have been published as well. These include the *Sacramentary of Vich*, the *Office*, which represents the oldest extant text of the office of the Hispano-Mozarabic liturgy, and, an updated critical edition of the *Liber Missarum*. In addition, Janini published a critical edition of the *Liber Misticus* for Lent and Easter in 1980.

The texts used by the parishes of Santas Justa y Rufina and of Santa Eulalia were continuously recopied until the beginning of the 14th century. However, due to the movement of peoples as well as the eventual blending of the Mozarabic community with the Castillians and Franks, and the limited number of clergy and parishioners who knew how to celebrate the rite, it was in danger of

disappearing by the 15th century. Cardinal Cisneros assigned Alfonso Ortiz, a canon of the cathedral, the task of preparing an edition of the missal and breviary, which appeared in 1500 and 1502 respectively. The missal was reedited in Rome in 1755 along with a commentary by Alexander Lesley. Cardinal Francisco Antonio Lorenzana reedited the breviary in Madrid in 1775 and published a corrected version of the missal in Rome in 1804.

Based on the publication of the extant sources in critical editions and the work of Cisneros and Lorenzana, the new *Missale Hispano-Mozarabicum* for the Eucharist appeared in 1991. Published to date are the two volume *Missale* (sacramentary), two volume *Liber Commicus* (lectionary), the *Liber Offerentium* (the book of the altar containing the *Ordo Missae* published in a Latin version and a Spanish translation), the General Calendar, and a bilingual (Spanish-Latin) worship aid for the assembly.

Eucharist. The eucharist reflects a tripartite structure of proclamation of the Word, anaphora, and communion. These are elements common to other Western and Eastern rites. How these are executed, however, distinguishes the rite from others. Two distinctive features of the eucharistic celebration are the initial rites or prayers and actions of the liturgy, and the transition from the proclamation of the Word to the beginning of the anaphora. The two Hispano-Mozarabic traditions, identified by Pinell, reveal an important difference in how the eucharistic celebration commenced. Probably in the second half of the 7th century, an introductory section was added to the structure of the Mass, apparently due to the influence of other rites. Tradition A (Toledo) maintained this addition for Mass throughout the year. Tradition B (Seville), however, omitted this introductory part on ferial days and on the Sundays of Lent. Tradition B provides the core of the restored rite though augmented by Tradition A.

When the Mass begins with the introductory rites they consist of an antiphon called *Praelegendum*, the hymn *Gloria in excelsis*, and an *Oratio Post Gloriam*. In addition, on solemnities the *Trisagion* is sung between the *Gloria* and the oration. The last part of the introductory rites is the prayer *Oratio Post Gloriam*. This prayer roughly corresponds to the Roman collect (opening prayer). A characteristic aspect of Hispano-Mozarabic prayers is that they tend to echo preceding texts. The *Oratio Post Gloriam* does this by reiterating themes from the *Gloria*, the *Trisagion* or from both. Consequently, the *Oratio Post Gloriam* completes the introductory rites rather than initiates the Liturgy of the Word. The restored rite follows the practice of Tradition B (Seville) during ferial days and the Sundays of Lent. On these occasions the *Praelegendum*, the *Gloria*, the *Trisagion*, and the

Oratio Post Gloriam are omitted. When this occurs, the priest enters, kisses the altar, bows to say a private preparatory prayer, goes to the chair, and greets the people. The Liturgy of the Word then commences.

An ancient feature of the Hispano-Mozarabic Liturgy of the Word is the proclamation of three scriptural pericopes during the Ordinary Sundays of the year. There are two distinct distributions of readings and chants for most of the solemnities and some liturgical seasons. Nevertheless, the readings may be chosen from either cycle during certain times of the year. Some of the pericopes for the eucharist are marked by *centonization* rather than the *lectio continua* of the Roman rite. *Centonization* is the practice of putting together a variety of passages drawn from different parts of the Bible and assembled into one reading.

The first reading is titled *Prophetia* and is taken from the Prophets or the Law. It is replaced by a reading from the Wisdom books and an additional reading from the Historical books during Lent, resulting in four readings during this season. During Eastertide, the *Prophetia* reading may be substituted by a reading from Revelation. After the first reading, the *Psallendum* is sung. This is the name given to the repertoire of psalm texts used as a response to the reading. The *Threni* are chanted in place of the *Psallendum* on the Wednesdays and Fridays of the first five weeks of Lent in the Hispano-Mozarabic calendar. The *Threni* texts are penitential in character and dramatically express the Church's repentance as well as recount the suffering of Christ. The texts are based on various passages from Lamentations, Job, and Isaiah.

The second reading is called *Apostolus* and refers to the readings from the epistles, both Pauline and catholic. The *Apostolus* may be preceded by a reading from the Acts of the Martyrs on the feast day of a martyr. Therefore, on these days, there are four readings. After the reading from the martyr's life, a portion of the *Bendictiones* or Canticle of the Three Children from the Book of Daniel (Dn 3:51–90) is sung and leads to the *Apostolus*.

The *Evangelium*, a reading from the Gospel, completes the scriptural readings. This is marked off from the others by the greeting *Dominus sit semper vobiscum* as in the Roman rite. The Liturgy of the Word is concluded by the *Laudes*, an antiphon of praise which includes singing the *Alleluia*, except in Lent. This is always chanted after the Gospel, never before. In addition, if there is a homily, *Laudes* follows it.

The prayers and actions that take place between the Liturgy of the Word and the anaphora are a second distinctive feature of the Hispano-Mozarabic Eucharist.

These consist of the Offering, Diptychs, and Sign of Peace, three elements that are linked together by four variable prayers, namely the *Oratio Admonitionis, Alia, Oratio Post Nomina*, and *Oratio Ad Pacem*. Throughout this intermediary ritual, the prayers are divided among the presider, the deacon, and the assembly. The usual interjection of the assembly is *Amen* but also included are phrases that echo what has been said before. The intermediary ritual begins with the *Sacrificium*, an antiphon that recalls the sacrifices of Old Testament figures such as Abel, Abraham and Melchizedek. It accompanies the offering, which consists of the preparation of the bread and wine as well as their placement on the altar by the ministers. *Sacrificium*, with its theme of sacrificial offering, sets the tone for what follows. After the antiphon, the priest prays the *Oratio Admonitionis*, a unique prayer in that it is addressed to the assembly. It also reflects the motif of the feast or liturgical season being celebrated. This prayer is followed by the admonition *Oremus*, the first of only two times this appears. The choir or assembly responds by singing or reciting *Hagios, Hagios, Hagios, Domine Deus, Rex aeterne, tibi laudes et gratias*.

The Diptychs or Solemn Intercessions are the next element in the celebration. The title refers to a litany of intercessions for the needs of the Church and of humanity in the course of which the names of the living and the dead are introduced. They assume the character of a solemn profession of unity in faith and love with the universal Church which encompasses the clergy, the faithful, the saints, and the faithful departed. They also include petitions for temporal needs such as for the ill, prisoners, and travelers. Two of the four variable prayers comprising the intermediary ritual occur in the midst of this formal supplication: the *Alia* and the *Oratio Post Nomina*. The *Alia* echoes the earlier offering by asking God to accept the gifts of the Church, the bread and wine, as well as what they signify, namely the submission of the Christian community to God's saving action. At the same time the intercessions are joined to the bread and wine as part of the offering. The *Oratio Post Nomina* concludes the Diptychs by reiterating their content. The text of the oration frequently relates the proclamation of the names in ordinary prayer to their inscription in the heavenly Book of Life. The last phase of this intermediary ritual consists in the fourth variable prayer, the *Oratio Ad Pacem*, as well as a Trinitarian blessing, the Sign of Peace, and the antiphon *Pacem meam do vobis*.

Upon completion of the intermediary ritual, the Liturgy of the Eucharist commences with the anaphora. The anaphora follows a fixed structure consisting of Dialogue, *Illatio, Sanctus, Oratio Post Sanctus*, Institution Narrative, *Oratio Post Pridie*, Doxology, and *Amen*. It should be noted that there is no set content to the prayers of the anaphora *per se* in the Hispano-Mozarabic liturgy. That is, they vary in content, length, and subject of address, seemingly according to the specific season or feast being celebrated. The underlying motive for the difference in length and content appears to be the principle of variability. This principle allows for the articulation of different themes by means of Mass-sets, that is, groups of prayer formulas destined for specific celebrations. Only the Dialogue, *Sanctus*, Institution Narrative, and *Amen* have invariable content. The anaphora begins with a Dialogue between presider and assembly which is very similar to the Roman Preface Dialogue. The Hispano-Mozarabic Dialogue begins with *Introibo ad altare Dei*. The incipit is identical to the antiphon from Psalm 43:4 used in the entrance rites of the Roman rite. The next element in the eucharistic prayer, the *Illatio*, is equivalent to the Preface of the Roman rite and like it, is variable in content. Even so, its focus tends to be thanksgiving for salvation. The *Illatio* is directed to both the Father and Son though this can vary according to the main idea expressed in the body of the prayer.

The heavenly hymn as found in Isaiah 6:3 with its Christian modification now follows. This element is invariable, but unlike the Roman *Sanctus*, the Spanish version adapts the conclusion of the second phrase from "full of your glory" to "full of your glorious majesty." As for the third, fourth, and fifth phrases, a unique feature of the Hispano-Mozarabic version is its dependence on the Vulgate Matthew 21:9 which says: *Hosanna filio David. Benedictus, qui venit in nomine Domini. Hosanna in altissimis*. In the Hispano-Mozarabic version, *in excelsis* replaces *in altissimis* in the last acclamation. Finally, the *Sanctus* concludes with the Greek version of the opening acclamation: *Hagios, Hagios, Hagios, Kyrie O Theos*. This is the second time *Hagios* is used in the Spanish liturgy as a regular congregational response in the revised celebration; it also occurs in the midst of the Diptychs. The *Trisagion* also incorporates *Hagios* during the opening rituals when it is chanted by the choir.

The *Oratio Post Sanctus* is the next element in the Spanish liturgy. It is a prayer that varies in length and content according to the liturgical season or particular feast being celebrated. The prayer's main function is to transition from the *Sanctus* to the Institution Narrative. The Institution Narrative of the Hispano-Mozarabic liturgy is taken almost literally from 1 Cor 11:23–26 with minor adaptations to the incipit and the Pauline gloss at the conclusion. The use of the Pauline version distinguishes the Institution Narrative from other Catholic rites both in East and West. Also, distinctive is the use of *Amen* as the congregational response to two of the three sections of the Narrative. The next variable prayer, the *Oratio Post Pridie*, corresponds to the anamnesis and epi-

clesis of the Roman rite though its content rarely elaborates remembrance or the invocation of the Spirit. Instead the prayer tends to be addressed directly to Christ and makes explicit the object of memory: his saving work and life-giving power. The anaphora concludes with a doxology. As can be expected, the text is variable with only the first few words and the *saecula saeculorum* leading to the *Amen* fixed.

The Hispano-Mozarabic liturgy commences communion with four distinct elements of preparation including the Creed, Fraction Rite, Lord's Prayer, and Blessing. The two Spanish traditions ordered these elements differently. Tradition A began with the Fraction Rite and then followed with the Creed and the Lord's Prayer, whereas Tradition B began with the Creed followed by the Fraction Rite and then the Lord's Prayer. The reformed rite of 1988 has opted for the order of Tradition B. A sacerdotal admonition, *Fidem, quam corde credimus, ore autem dicamus* initiates the communal recitation of the Creed in unison by the community. In this way a link is made between the *Sic credimus* which follows the Institution Narrative and the reception of communion. The Spanish liturgy was the first in the West to introduce into the eucharist a version of the Creed following the form of Nicaea I (325) as amended by Constantinople I (381). This was done in 589 shortly after the conversion of the VISIGOTHS to Catholicism and was dictated for the churches under their jurisdiction, including those in Gaul. The text used in the liturgy today is the version promulgated by Toledo III (589). The recitation of the Creed is followed by the Fraction Rite during which the host is broken into nine pieces. The fraction is accompanied by a very brief acclamation. Upon being broken, the pieces are arranged on the paten in the form of a cross. As the presider places them on the paten, he names the nine mysteries of Christ celebrated throughout the Hispano-Mozarabic liturgical year: *Corporatio, Nativitas, Circumcisio, Apparitio, Passio, Mors, Resurrectio, Gloria*, and *Regnum*. After a variable introduction, the presider begins the prayer with *Oremus* and then divides the Lord's Prayer into eight petitions. After each petition, the assembly responds with *Amen*. This is the second and last time *Oremus* is used in the Eucharist. The Lord's Prayer and its responses are usually chanted. An embolism, similar to the current Roman version though lengthier, follows the Lord's Prayer. An important difference though is that the assembly responds *Amen* to the embolism instead of a doxology.

The presider then elevates the paten and chalice declaring *Sancta sanctis* (Holy things for holy people). This is the only elevation in the ritual. Afterwards the presider takes the ninth particle, titled *Regnum*, and deposits it into the chalice saying a prayer that refers to the reconciliation wrought by the Body and Blood of Christ. Before the presider consumes the various particles, the deacon instructs those present to bow their heads for the blessing. The assembly responds *Deo gratias* to the instruction. The presider then invokes the blessing. It is a unique prayer, though, in that it consists of three variable verses generally directed to those present; they respond *Amen* to each verse. A stereotyped formula referring to God in the third person follows. Toledo IV (633) fixed the position of the blessing prior to communion.

Communion takes place under both species and is accompanied by the *Cantus Ad Accedentes*, an antiphon based on Psalm 33:6. After the distribution, another antiphon is sung expressing thanksgiving. The *Post Communionem* antiphon is followed by a final oration titled *Completuria*. The celebration is finalized with a greeting by the presider and dismissal by the deacon.

Church Building. The earliest type of church buildings identified as Mozarabic give evidence of Visigothic influence with their distinctive horseshoe arches, compartmentalized spaces, and columns with carved capitals decorated with animal and plant motifs. The building is usually divided into three naves. The apse at the end of the center nave is often separated from the nave by a low wall forming a type of iconostasis. Illuminations indicate that a curtain was also used to separate the sanctuary-apse from the nave. Some buildings follow a Greek cross floor plan with a rectangular sanctuary while others follow a basilical plan. Later Mozarabic church buildings show evidence of distinctive Arabic influences such as inlaid ceilings and merlons on roof lines. The use of richly ornamented frescoes and plaster decorative elements influenced by Islamic practice are also evident. Mozarabic architecture is associated with this "mixed style" of Visigothic and Islamic elements.

Bibliography: Archdiocese of Toledo, *Missale Hispano-Mozarabicum* (2 vols.) (1991); *Ordo Missae-Liber Offerentium*, (1991); *Ordinario de la Misa del Rito Hispano-Mozarabe-Oferencio* (1991); *Liber Commicus* (2 v.) (1994); *Rito Hispano-Mozarabe Ordinario de la Misa* (1996). X. BARRAL I ALTET, *The Early Middle Ages: From Late Antiquity to A.D. 1000* (Taschen's World Architecture series; Cologne 1997). H. LECLERQ, *Dictionnaire d'archéologie chrétienne et de liturgie* 12.1:309–491. M. FÉROTIN, *Le Liber ordinum en usage dans l'église Wisigothique et Mozarabe d'Espagne du Ve au IXe siècle* (*Monumenta Ecclesiae Liturgica* 5; Paris 1904); *Le Liber Mozarabicus sacramentorum et les manuscrits mozarabs* (ibid. 6; Paris 1912). J. JANINI, *Liber Missarum de Toledo* (2 v.) (*Serie Liturgica Fuentes* III; Toledo 1982). J. PINELL, *Liturgia hispánica* (*Biblioteca Litúrgica* 9; Barcelona 1998). Vatican II documents: *Sacrosanctum Concilium* (1963), DOL 1; *Orientalium Ecclesiarum* (1964), DOL 5; *Instruction (First) Inter Oecumenici* (1964), DOL 23; G. RAMIS, "Pervivencia y actualidad del Rito Hispano-Mozarabe" *Notitiae* 20 (1983) 282–6; G. RAMIS, "Liturgia Hispano-Mozarabe. Boletín Bibliográfico (1993–1998)" *Ecclesia Orans* (1999) 123–131; V. A. LENTI,

Wolfgang Amadeus Mozart.

"Liturgical reform and the Ambrosian and Mozarabic Rites" *Worship* 68 (1994) 417–426.

[R. GOMEZ]

MOZART, WOLFGANG AMADEUS

A principal composer of the classical period and of all time; b. Salzburg, Austria, Jan. 27, 1756 (baptized Johannes Chrysostomus Wolfgang Theophilus); d. Vienna, Dec. 5, 1791. Mozart's father, Leopold, had been a respected composer and violinist in the employ of the archiepiscopal court of Salzburg. As a small boy, Mozart already displayed amazing talents as violinist and harpsichordist, even as composer. In 1769 he entered Archbishop Colloredo's service. There, he had frequent opportunities for writing sacred music, yet he resented increasingly the confining environment of a small ecclesiastical state, and this resentment was aggravated by travels to important musical centers throughout Europe. The inevitable break between the archbishop and the young musician occurred in 1781. Mozart then settled in Vienna, always hoping for a desirable court position. As late as 1790 he applied for an appointment to the Austrian court, stating in his application that "from my childhood on I have been familiar with the church style." The desired appointment did not materialize. That Mozart wrote virtually no sacred music after leaving Salzburg is attributed in part to this failure, but also to the curtailment of church music during the age of JOSEPHINISM.

Mozart was essentially a believing and practicing Catholic, as seems certain from many of his letters (Einstein, *Mozart: His Character, His Life, His Work* 77–81). He saw no conflict between his religious beliefs and Freemasonry in which he became involved in 1784, taking an active part in its affairs and providing a number of compositions for Masonic occasions—e.g., Cantatas K. 429, 471, 623; *Masonic Funeral Music*, K. 477. The "Masonic virtues" of tolerance, brotherly love, steadfastness, and silence also figure in the libretto of *The Magic Flute*, an opera generally interpreted as a Masonic allegory. Objections against liturgical use of Mozart's sacred compositions have often been voiced, in the 19th century and today, chiefly because of their allegedly "worldly" or "operatic" nature. Such a view can largely be explained by the fact that his operas and his instrumental music have always been more widely known. Many features that simply represent Mozart's own style, and that of his period, when encountered in his sacred works remind some listeners of his secular music. To this day, however, his church music regularly receives liturgical performances in Austria and Southern Germany.

Sacred Works. Both individual Mass movements and complete Masses from Mozart's childhood and adolescence have been preserved, e.g., the *Kyrie*, K. 33 (1766), and the *Missa Brevis*, K. 49 (1768). Many early works (e.g., the incomplete *Missa Brevis*, K. 115) indicate that he had studied the sacred music of Eberlin and Michael HAYDN, especially their works in strict (contrapuntal) style; yet few of his own compositions are consistently in this style. Strict contrapuntal writing (the *stile antico* of which Padre Martini was considered a master) represented a challenge to the young composer but was in Mozart's idiom united with other elements, especially the prevailing Italian church style—the *stile moderno*, in which one melodic line was prominent, and often quite florid, with orchestral accompaniment.

Masses. The *Missa Solemnis,* K. 139, a substantial early work, has a large orchestra with timpani and four trumpets. Other important settings include the *Missa in honorem SSmae Trinitatis*, K. 167, in which there is no vocal solo writing; the *Missa Brevis* in C, K. 220, in an essentially homophonic style; K. 257, the "Credo Mass" (so-called because of the recurring exclamation "Credo, credo"); the "Coronation Mass," K. 317, written for a small pilgrimage church near Salzburg; and the great but incomplete Mass in C-minor, K. 427 (1783). Some portions of this last, especially the *Laudamus te* with its florid solo passages in Neapolitan style, have been cited as evidence of the "operatic" quality of his sacred music. Other sections, however, are severely contrapuntal, some in five- or eight-part choral writing. Much of the music is serious, full of dramatic tension, expressing the sacred text with eloquence and sincerity. The unfinished Requiem, K. 626, completed by his pupil Franz Süssmayer, has become his best-known sacred work. During his last years Mozart thought often of death; he seems to have felt that the Requiem, commissioned under rather mysterious circumstances, was to be his own funeral Mass, and the setting is consistently in keeping with the text.

Other Liturgical Music. Among other extended sacred works are two settings of Vesper Psalms and Magnificat, K. 321 and 339, and several litanies, K. 109, 125, 195, 243. His smaller sacred works, especially the motets, show great variety. The Introit *Cibavit eos*, K. 44 (Bologna 1770), is a study in the *stile antico*, based on a Gregorian CANTUS FIRMUS. Other motets, e.g., the Offertory *Inter natos mulierum*, K. 72, reflect the musical idiom of the young composer's home environment. Motets in the purely soloistic Italian style were written when an occasion called for them. One such, *Exsultate, jubilate*, K. 165, composed for the *castrato* Rauzzini, consists of three arias, ending with the well-known *Alleluia*. His last motet, *Ave verum corpus*, K. 618 (1791), scored for four voices, strings, and organ, still appeals widely because of its simplicity and sincerity. There are also 17 church or "Epistle" sonatas, short compositions for strings and organ, with wind and timpani parts added in some instances. In the Salzburg cathedral these compositions were traditionally performed between the Epistle and the Gospel (*see* ORGAN MUSIC).

Style. Many stylistic characteristics of Mozart's sacred works are found also in his secular music. Some Mass movements are in sonata form (suggested especially by the *Kyrie-Christe-Kyrie* text). Characteristic themes may recur throughout a movement. Melodic structure, the harmonies, and instrumentation found in Mass and Offertory frequently resemble those of symphony and opera. No more than in J. S. BACH's age did composers of Mozart's draw rigid distinctions between sacred and secular style, though counterpoint (the "Palestrina style") was considered especially suitable for the church, particularly during Advent and Lent. Mozart's style developed and matured along similar lines in sacred and secular works. Thus, parallel prominence is given to wind instruments and use of chromaticism in Mozart's later sacred works (C-minor Mass, *Requiem*) and in symphonies and concertos from the same period. Skillful counterpoint distinguishes many of his later works, especially after 1782, when his acquaintance with Baron Swieten led to renewed interest in the music of Bach and HANDEL. While he impressed his own style characteristics on his sacred music, Mozart did observe many conventions found in liturgical music of his age, among them the use of a figured bass (by then largely obsolete in secular music), and the traditional fugal endings of Gloria (*Cum Sancto Spiritu*) and *Credo* (*Et vitam venturi saeculi*).

Bibliography: *Werke: Kristisch durchgesehene Gesammtausgabe*, 74 v. in 69 (Leipzig 1877–1905; repr. Ann Arbor 1951–). *Neue Ausgabe sämtlicher Werke* (Kassel 1955–), edition of the Internationale Stiftung Mozarteum in Salzburg. *The Letters of Mozart and His Family*, ed. and tr. E. ANDERSON, 3 v. (London 1938). Literature. O. E. DEUTSCH, *Mozart: A Documentary Biography*, tr. E. BLOM et al. (Stanford 1965). A. EINSTEIN, *Mozart: His Character, His Life, His Work*, tr. A. MENDEL and N. BRODER (New York 1945). E. BLOM, *Mozart* (London 1935). K. G. FELLERER, *Mozarts Kirchenmusik* (Salzburg 1955). K. G. FELLERER, *The History of Catholic Church Music*, tr. F. A. BRUNNER (Baltimore 1961). R. G. PAULY, *Music in the Classic Period* (New York 1965). K. GEIRINGER, ''The Church Music,'' *The Mozart Companion*, ed. H. C. R. LANDON and D. MITCHELL (New York 1956) 361–376. L. VON KÖCHEL, *Chronologisch-thematisches Verzeichnis . . . Mozarts*, ed. F. GIEGLING et al. (6th ed. Wiesbaden 1964), the basis, since 1862, of ''K numbers'' or ''Köchel listing'' universally adopted in place of opus numbers (which Mozart rarely used) for identification purposes. F. LIPPMANN, *Die Musik in Geschichte und Gegenwart*, ed. F. BLUME (Kassel-Basel 1949–) 9:699–839. W. HUMMEL, ''Mozart Gesellschaften,'' *ibid.* 839–842, includes Mozarteum. S. DURANT, ''The Chronology of Mozart's *La clemenza di Tito* Reconsidered,'' *Music and Letters* 80 (1999) 560–594. C. EISEN, ''Another Look at the 'Corrupt Passage' in Mozart's G Minor Symphony, K.550: Its Sources, 'Solutions, and Implications for the Composition of the Final Trilogy,'' *Early Music* 25 (1997), 373–380. F. GONIN, ''Mozart et le Padre Martini: histoire d'une légende?,'' *Revue de Musicologie* 85 (1999) 277–295. S. P. KEEFE, ''Dramatic Dialogue in Mozart's Viennese Piano Concertos: A Study of Competition and Cooperation in Three First Movements,'' *The Musical Quarterly* 83 (1999) 169–204. H. KOWAR, ''*Die Zauberflöte*: ein tantrisches Ritual?,'' *Studien zur Musikwissenschaft* 42 (1993) 167–180. M. LATCHAM, ''Mozart and the Pianos of Gabriel Anton Walter,'' *Early Music* 25 (1997) 382–400. R. MAUNDER, and D. ROWLAND, ''Mozart's pedal piano,'' *Early Music* 23 (1995) 287–296. B. SIMKIN, ''The Case for Mozart's Affliction with Tourette Syndrome,'' *Journal of the Conductors' Guild* 12 (1991) 50–64.

[R. G. PAULY]

MOZI

Chinese philosopher also transliterated as Mo Tzu, Mo Ti; and political theorist. He holds a unique place in the history of Chinese thought for his logical method, deep religious faith, and his doctrine and practice of universal love (*chien ai*). He disagreed with the Confucians of his time on certain fundamental points, and singly condemned their skepticism about Heaven and ghosts, fatalism, and preoccupation with ritual and music.

In Moist philosophy, as seen in the *Mozi* (''Master Mo''), the concepts of achievement and benefit are the standards for judging whether a theory is right or wrong, beneficial or harmful. A theory is right and beneficial if it is patterned on the deeds of the sage kings of old, if it is borne out by the experience of the common people, and if it is applied to government with proven benefits to the country and the people. The wealth and populousness of a country are its greatest benefits. Whatever does not further these two ends or tends to injure them must be discarded. Thus, lavish funerals, prolonged mourning, extravagant entertainment, elaborate ritual and music, and costly government should be abandoned. But the greatest harm is done by the incessant struggle of man against man, state against state. Its cause lies in the failure of men to love one another. Men, being partial in their love, hate and injure others. Their partiality must be replaced by universality, which is obtained when everyone loves others as he loves himself and regards the state, city, family, and possessions of others as he regards his own; when he feeds the hungry, clothes the cold, serves the sick, and buries the dead. The calamities of the world all come from men's failure to love one another, and may be prevented or remedied only by the practice of universal love.

The motive for universal love is the Lord on High, or Heaven (*Shangdi, Tian*). Heaven wills righteousness and imparts the standard of right to the Son of Heaven (*Tianzi:* the emperor), who in turn communicates it to the people. All men must follow the Will of Heaven, yet only the Son of Heaven can identify himself with Heaven. Representing Heaven on earth, the Son of Heaven issues orders, and the people have but to fulfill them. The emperor thus becomes the absolute arbiter of men's ideas and actions.

In its early centuries, Moism flourished, and it appears to have been a principal rival of Confucianism until about the 1st century B.C., when it went into decline and eventual extinction.

Bibliography: *Ethical and Political Works of Motse,* tr. Y. P. MEI (London 1929). Y. P. MEI, *Motse, the Neglected Rival of Confucius* (London 1934). Y. L. FUNG, *A History of Chinese Philosophy,* 2 v. (Princeton 1952) v.1. H. G. CREEL, *Chinese Thought from Confucius to Mao Tse–tung* (Chicago 1953). W. T. DE BARY et al., eds., *Sources of Chinese Tradition* (Records of Civilization: Sources and Studies 55; New York 1960).

[A. S. ROSSO]

MRAK, IGNATIUS

Second bishop of Marquette, MI; b. Hotovle, Carniola, Austria, Oct. 16, 1818; d. Marquette, Feb. 1, 1901. After education at the Royal Gymnasium and the Seminary of Laibach (Ljubiljana), he was ordained there on

Aug. 3, 1837. Influenced by the work of his countryman Frederic BARAGA, Mrak sought admission (1845) to the Diocese of Detroit, Michigan. Upon arriving there, in October of 1845, he was immediately sent to assist another countryman, Rev. Francis PIERZ, at Arbre Croche (Harbor Springs). Two years later Mrak was given his own mission at La Croix (Cross Village) with Middletown (Good Hart), Castor Island (Beaver Island), and Manistee (Manistique) included. Here and later at Grande Traverse the missionary spent 13 years ministering to the indigenous people of the lakelands. Much to his dismay, Mrak was chosen (1868) to succeed Baraga as bishop of Sault Ste. Marie and Marquette. He was consecrated in the metropolitan cathedral at Cincinnati, Ohio, on Feb. 7, 1869, wearing secondhand regalia.

Devoted to a life of simplicity, Mrak continued his work among the Native Americans and struggled to meet the pioneer needs of the Catholic Church in northern Michigan. He made special efforts to improve the caliber and education of his missionary clergy and opened Catholic schools wherever possible. He also organized elected lay boards to assist pastors in the material administration of their parishes. Because of a painful rheumatic condition, he resigned his see (1878), which then had 20 priests serving 27 churches with missions and a Catholic population of 20,000. Appointed titular bishop of Antinoe, Mrak returned to his beloved missions. During the last nine years of his life he remained at Marquette, where he performed chaplain duties at St. Mary's Hospital. Mentally alert to the end, the old missionary made his last public appearance in August of 1899 at the consecration of Marquette's fourth bishop, Frederick Eis, whom he had ordained.

Bibliography: Archives, Diocese of Marquette, Mrak Papers. A. I. REZEK, *History of the Diocese of Sault Ste. Marie and Marquette,* 2 v. (Houghton, MI 1906–07).

[C. J. CARMODY]

MUARD, MARIE JEAN BAPTISTE

Founder of the Society of ST. EDMUND; b. Vireaux (Yonne), France, April 24, 1809; d. La Pierre-qui-Vire (Yonne), France, June 19, 1854. After studies at the major seminary in Sens, he was ordained (1834) and spent the next six years in parochial ministries. He was eager to become a missionary, but his bishop refused him permission to go to China. In 1843 he founded at the ancient Cistercian monastery in Pontigny (Yonne) a group of diocesan missionary priests, known originally as Prêtres Auxiliaires, Missionaires de St. Edmond, and later as the Society of St. Edmund. Muard remained at Pontigny until 1848. During this period he gave stability to the

community and composed its rule. After sojourning in Rome and Subiaco he returned to France and in 1850 founded the monastery of Sainte Marie de La Pierrequi-Vire near Avallon (Yonne). This community, which belongs to the Benedictine congregation of Subiaco, became an abbey in 1884. Muard continued an active apostolate until he fell ill after preaching a mission at Saint-Étienne. He died a few days later. His process for beatification opened in Rome in 1928.

Bibliography: *The Life of Jean Baptiste Muard,* v. 9 of *Library of Religious Biography,* ed. E. H. THOMPSON, 9 v. (London 1867–86). L. BRULÉE, *Life of the Rev. Mary John Baptist Muard,* tr. I. ROBOT (New York 1882). J. BOUCHARD, *Vie du R. P. Muard,* 2 v. (Paris 1893). L. VEUILLOT, *Le R. P. Muard* (Paris 1901). D. HUERRE, *Jean-Baptiste Muard* (Saint-Léger-Vauban, Yonne 1950). G. BERNOVILLE, *Le Père Muard* (Paris 1942). V. F. NICOLLE, *Historical Sketch of the Society of St. Edmund* (Burlington, VT 1943). P. LOUSIN, *Revue Mabillon* 51 (1961): 179–191.

[G. E. DUPONT]

MUENCH, ALOISIUS JOSEPH

Cardinal and diplomat; b. Milwaukee, WI, Feb. 18, 1889; d. Rome, Italy, Feb. 15, 1962. He was the oldest of six children of immigrant German parents. After studies at St. Francis Seminary, Milwaukee, he was ordained on June 8, 1913, and served as assistant at St. Michael's Church, Milwaukee, and at the University Chapel, Madison. He received a master's degree (1919) from the University of Wisconsin and studied at the University of Fribourg, Switzerland, receiving his doctor's degree *summa cum laude* in the social sciences. Before returning to the United States, he spent a year auditing classes at Louvain, Cambridge, Oxford, London, and the Sorbonne. In 1922 he was appointed to St. Francis Seminary, Milwaukee, where he served as professor of dogma and as rector. On Aug. 10, 1935, he was named third bishop of FARGO, North Dakota, and on Oct. 15, 1935, he was consecrated in the Gesu Church in Milwaukee by Archbishop Amleto Cicognani, apostolic delegate to the United States.

Assuming his new duties at the height of the Depression, Muench proved himself an able administrator. He organized the Catholic Church Expansion Fund to save many mortgaged and indebted parishes and to provide capital funds for future expansion. He founded a diocesan newspaper, established diocesan seminary scholarships, organized a priests' mutual aid fund, convoked the first synod in the diocese, and published a synodal book of diocesan legislation. Active in many social conferences and organizations, he was a staunch supporter of the Catholic Central Union and was prominent in the National Catholic Rural Life Conference, serving two terms as its president. With two priests of the Fargo diocese, William T. Mulloy and Vincent J. Ryan (both later bishops), Muench edited a sociological work, *Manifesto on Rural Life*. He was a member of the pontifical commission for the Catholic University of America, Washington, D.C., and of the episcopal Commission for Peace among Peoples, as well as of the international organization Pax Romana. Throughout his 23 years as bishop of Fargo he wrote an annual Lenten pastoral letter for distribution among his flock. The most famous of these, ''One World in Charity'' (1946), was a plea for just treatment of our former enemies, and it condemned the Morgenthau plan of restricting Germany to a rural economy. A translation of this letter found wide distribution in Germany.

In February of 1946 Pope Pius XII appointed Muench apostolic visitator to Germany; shortly thereafter Secretary of War Robert P. Patterson named him liaison consultant for religious affairs to the military governor of Germany. In this capacity he was advisor to General Lucius Clay and his successors on matters involving the Catholic Church and the American Army of Occupation. He also functioned as administrator of the Vatican mission established by the Pope to provide for the spiritual and material needs of the refugees, expellees, and displaced persons in Germany. The National Catholic Welfare Conference also appointed Muench to serve as military vicar delegate for the Catholics serving in the American Armed Forces in Germany. In November of 1949, in anticipation of Germany's independence and sovereignty, Pope Pius XII named Muench regent of the apostolic nunciature in Germany, and a year later granted him the personal title of archbishop. On March 6, 1951, when Germany became sovereign, Muench as papal nuncio was the first diplomat to present his credentials to the West German government; he was named dean of the diplomatic corps. In gratitude for his varied and signal services to the German people, Theodore Heuss, President of the West German Republic, conferred upon Muench Germany's highest honor, the Grand Cross of the Order of Merit on Dec. 20, 1957.

On Dec. 9, 1959, Pope John XXIII made Muench a member of the College of Cardinals with the title of St. Bernard at the Baths. He was the first American to serve actively as a cardinal in the Roman Curia. He was a member of the Sacred Congregations of Religious, Rites, and Extraordinary Affairs, as well as protector of a number of religious communities. He died in Rome at Villa Salvator Mundi, after receiving personally the apostolic blessing of Pope John XXIII; his remains were interred in St. Mary's Cemetery, Fargo.

[G. M. WEBER]

MUḤAMMAD

Founder of the religion of ISLAM; b. Mecca, *c.* A.D. 570; d. Medina, Arabia, 632. His life is generally divided into three periods: (1) his early life, the period of about 40 years before he received his ''prophetic call'' (2) his first or ''Meccan'' period as prophet of Islam, dated from his first ''revelations'' and public appearances declaring his message about 610 and extending to 622, the date of his flight from MECCA to MEDINA (known as the *HIJRA*, ''emigration''); and (3) his second or ''Medinese'' period as prophet, during which he firmly established Islam as a religion and state, between 622 and his death in 632.

Early Life. Muḥammad's father died before his birth, and at age six he lost his mother. During his earliest years he was entrusted to the care of his grandfather 'Abd-al-Muṭṭalib, and later came under the protection of his uncle Abū Ṭālib. The Hāshim family into which he was born was a part of the Quraysh tribe, then prominent in Mecca; it was in fact among the most important constituents of the Quraysh, though clearly below the two leading families of Makhzūm and 'Umayyah. In spite of their social prominence, however, the Hāshimites had grown relatively poor just before Muḥammad's birth, and indications are that his early years as an orphan were spent under conditions rather miserable even for the times. Little reliable information concerning his youth has come down in the ISLAMIC TRADITIONS (ḤADĪTH), since, in the view of early Muslims, the period of the *Jāhiliyyah* (ignorance) before Islam, even as regards Muḥammad himself, was of scant interest. Later traditions supplied the need and embellished this portion of the biography with tales such as the famous BAHIRA LEGEND, some of them with fairly evident Biblical parallels and a few containing elements with a modicum of plausibility. It is certain at least that Muḥammad engaged in commerce and trade, perhaps to the extent of participating in trade caravans to Syria, and that his financial situation improved substantially when, at the age of about 25, he married a rich merchant's widow named Khadījah. By her he had seven children, four daughters, who lived to maturity, and three sons, who died in infancy or early youth. Mecca at this time was no mere desert oasis but a bustling and prosperous center of commerce on the major north-south trade route and its sanctuaries were places of religious pilgrimage for many neighboring tribes.

Attitude to Paganism. Muḥammad began by following the idolatrous beliefs and practices that were commonly adhered to by his tribe, by most of the citizens of Mecca, and by much of Arabia generally (*see* ARABIA). So deeply ingrained were his early religious experiences, in fact, that later, as the prophet of Islam, he occasionally made extraordinary concessions to Meccan paganism, attempting no doubt to harmonize some of its elements in order to render Islam more appealing to the Meccans. The principal example is the later incorporation of the ritual at the Ka'aba in Mecca, where a black stone was worshipped by the pagans, into Islam as the center of worship and direction of prayer (Arabic *qiblah*). It is also likely that he had early acquired a familiarity with and possibly even penchant for the special rhymed prose (called *saj'*) used by the Arab soothsayers in their wild utterances, choosing it later as the style of his own "recitation" (Arabic *qur'ān*), the QUR'ĀN.

It is a matter of general agreement, however, that what Muḥammad retained of his early paganism was slight indeed by comparison with his single-minded conviction that as a system it had to be overthrown. A case has been made that mere economic gain was the inspiration for Muḥammad's religious revolution. That case does not suit the facts as they are known. Muḥammad must gradually have been appalled at the absurdities of pagan worship and the low level of pagan morals around him—for instance, the live burial of female infants.

Attitude to Judaism and Christianity. Neither Arabian Jews nor Arabian Christians, unfortunately, were to be classed among the better representatives of their faiths at the time. The Jews had lived in comparative isolation possibly since the middle of the first millenium B.C., although they had been mildly successful in proselytism. Of the two, Muḥammad evidently preferred the former, though there is one later Qur'ānic verse (5.85) that may indicate that he came eventually to regret that early preference.

Relations with "the Pure Ones." Most important of all, Muḥammad was associated with a small group of men, which included his wife's cousin Waraqa ibn-Nawfal, who thought of themselves as *ḥunafā'*, "the pure ones," and who favored a monotheism of a somewhat syncretistic nature that tended toward neither Judaism nor Christianity. Three out of four of the most famous *ḥunafā'* later became Christians. As for Muḥammad, the essential simplicity and the syncretistic quality of the *ḥanīf* views must have impressed him deeply and evoked a firm conviction, for he withdrew into solitude more and more frequently in order to meditate on them. For this purpose he developed a habit of going up late at night to a cave on Ḥirā', a mountain near the city. It was there that he had an experience one night that completely changed his own life and profoundly affected human history.

Meccan Period. Although the Islamic "traditions" are usually highly problematical, they remain our unique sources for Muḥammad's life and can be made to yield important insights. In the light of the general account they present of Muḥammad's "prophetic call" and of his activities immediately thereafter, it is not sensible to doubt the man's basic sincerity at this point or to assert that he fabricated that and all subsequent experiences of "revelation." It is preferable, though of course far more difficult, to explain these highly colored but often remarkably plausible accounts in other ways. Apparently Muḥammad had been confused and despondent just before his first revelation, one source (no less reliable than the others) going so far as to insist that he had been contemplating suicide at the precise moment it occurred. However that may have been, his claim was to have seen a personal vision that commanded him, "Recite!" He replied, "What shall I recite?" [or, according to later interpretations concerned with proving him illiterate and thereby establishing more firmly the credibility of the Qur'ān, "I cannot recite (*or*, read)"]. There followed the revelation of the first part of Qur'ān 96 or, according to other versions of the tradition, 68, 74, or 93.

Effect of First Revelation. Muḥammad himself was frightened, incredulous, and unsure of the meaning of the experience. It required persuasion from his wife and friends before he was convinced and believed that he had actually received a revelation from God. From the Medinese period on, Muslims have confidently asserted that all of the revelations of the Qur'ān were delivered to Muḥammad through the medium of the Archangel Gabriel and that he memorized, but never wrote, them for his disciples. But there is no mention of Gabriel until the revelations of the Medinese period, and indications are that Muḥammad was first persuaded that he was receiving the revelations from God Himself, or from "the Spirit," most likely to be identified with the Holy Spirit. In any case, it is necessary to recognize that after his first doubts he himself never again questioned that his revelations were in a literal sense the word of God. As it worked itself out in his own mind, with assistance from the revelations themselves in the Muslim view, he was not to be considered inspired, let alone divine, but rather the vehicle through whom God and His angel were dictating a final revelation, a redaction of previous revelations whose authenticity he never challenged, to the Arabs and to all mankind. That dictation came in parts (Arabic *'āyāt,* used for "verses") from a heavenly archetype. He was a messenger (*rasûl*) and a prophet (*nabi*), indeed the last of the prophets, as he was ultimately compelled to assert.

Early Chapters of the Qur'ān. The temper of the first chapters (Arabic *sūra*) of the Qur'ān is simple and fiery, unobjectionable and even appealing to a Christian. The nature of Muḥammad's message as therein conveyed is mainly a warning to men of their sins, more particularly to the Meccans against polytheism. One supreme God (*Allāh,* best understood, as it must have been to not a few contemporaries, as *'ilāh,* "god," with the definite article), whose attributes and statements identified Him as the God of the Jews and the Christians, demanded surrender of men's wills to Himself. He commanded men to become converted, reform, purify their actions, and unify in faith. He reminded some (and told most for the first time) that there is an afterlife in which, after judgment, men will continue forever in a state of punishment or pleasure. These eschatological passages in the Qur'ān, primitive as they are, are not only the best from a literary standpoint but also the most endearing and vindicating from a Christian standpoint. During these years they clearly were not regarded by Muḥammad as the basis of a new religion but rather as a "proof" and continuation of an old religion within which the Arabs, too, had a noble destiny as the sons of Abraham. He was called *'ummî* in the Qur'ān, which does not mean (as his followers needlessly contended) that he was an "illiterate" prophet, but rather that he was a prophet to a "people without a (sacred) book," an apostle to the Gentiles.

Opposition at Mecca. Unfortunately for all concerned, but chiefly for Muḥammad himself, his message and claims were met either with indifference and scoffing or with general, swift, and powerful opposition. The pagan Meccans, including his well-to-do relatives, took his "warning" very much to heart, but not as he intended. They immediately set about organizing resistance to Muḥammad and planning the elimination of his tiny group of followers (Arabic *muslimûn,* hence Muslims, "those who have surrendered"). It must be granted that their reaction was justifiable inasmuch as the growth of a religious sect in Mecca with principles such as Muḥammad's constituted a serious threat to the basis of the main source of wealth for Mecca's leading families, its pilgrimage trade. Even worse for Muḥammad, in consideration of the results, was the refusal of neighboring Jews and Christians to recognize in him a true prophet in the line of their common tradition. Moreover, small as it was, the community of Islam was already experiencing apostasy induced by pagan intrigues and Jewish and Christian skepticism.

Concessions to Paganism. At this point interesting new material was introduced into the more recent chapters of the Qur'ān, much of it aimed at, or conveniently coincidental with, coming to terms with the opposition. The Meccans were treated to sermons against trust in wealth, which leads only to pride and hinders man from realizing his dependence upon God. On the other hand, the goddesses (al-Lāt, worshiped at Ṭā'if; al-'Uzzā, worshiped at Nakhlah; and Manāt, whose shrine lay between Mecca and Medina) were acknowledged to be venerable "daughters of Allah" (Qur'ān 22.51) whose cults might therefore be expected to continue without hindrance. These devices neither convinced nor placated the Meccans, and Muḥammad was soon to regret such revelations and declare them "Satanic suggestions" rather than God's revelation. Ultimately a good many verses in the Qur'ān were "abrogated" in this fashion. For the benefit of Jews and Christians the revelations embarked upon fuller statements embodying items in their creeds and references to, even a few tentative narrations of, their Biblical sources. Whether this latter attempt produced more concrete results or merely promised a more fruitful line of development for Islam is impossible to determine. At any rate, it lasted well into the Medinese period.

At the same time Muḥammad sent about 80 Muslims to Ethiopia to seek refuge with the Christian Negus. Surface indications are that the increasing persecution of the Meccans alone prompted this action, but closer scrutiny suggests that Muḥammad may have been troubled over sharp differences within his community. He hoped to prevent apostasy by entrusting one group with a mission to attempt to win sympathy from the Negus, perhaps also the promise of military assistance or at least trade relations. The Negus was understandably perplexed, but permitted the Muslims to remain. Some of them did not return to Arabia until seven years after the Hijra.

Muḥammad was obviously losing ground in Mecca. There were planned attacks during his public preaching and economic boycotts against his followers. About 619 he lost both the stabilizing presence of his wife Khadījah and the protective presence of his guardian Abū Ṭālib, who as chief of the Hāshim clan had warded off more violent steps toward destroying Muḥammad. He seemed to be faced now with a single set of alternatives, either to abandon his cause and community altogether, or to find a different site in which to settle them. Reports from the Ethiopian diaspora had evidently not raised hopes of possibilities in that direction. Then a highly fortuitous opportunity presented itself.

First Followers at Medina. On occasion Muḥammad had had among his audience in Mecca various tribesmen from other parts of Arabia, and had already asserted in clear terms that Islam was destined to unify the Arab tribes. To members of two tribes of the Banū Qaylah in Medina, the Aws and the Khazraj, such an idea had a very immediate and practical interest. They were tribes of Judaized Arabs who had been feuding with one another for many years. Some of their constituents, who had come to regard the feud as mutually debilitating and had heard (or heard of) Muḥammad, thought that he would be an ideal mediator, since there were religious disputes involved in the feud that Islam seemed capable of harmonizing. In 620 and 621, when Muḥammad's fortunes at Mecca were at their lowest ebb, he made an encouragingly steady number of converts from Medina. Accordingly, arrangements were made for his followers to leave Mecca unobtrusively in small groups and, finally, for his own departure.

Medinese Period. The first day of the Arabian lunar year in which the Hijra took place, July 16, 622, was later chosen as the beginning of the Islamic era. It might at first appear strange that that date was selected in preference to that of Muḥammad's birth or first revelation, but the selection was a natural one after the fact. Islam as a state was born with the Hijra. Scholars have tended to exaggerate somewhat the difference in Muḥammad's character after the Hijra. Difference there was, but far greater was the difference in the community of Islam itself as it was transformed into a conquering state at Medina.

Results of the Hijra. That transformation did not take place at once. Change was neither rapid nor general at first, for the Hijra had not by any means solved all of Muḥammad's problems. Although this early period of trial in Medina was eased by the fact that so many of the Medinese (later called the *Anṣār,* helpers) accepted Islam, he still encountered strong opposition to his presence and his message and was not able to halt the feuding of the Aws and Khazraj immediately. However, Muḥammad took two particular steps at this time aimed at a bold solution of the major problems. First, he integrated as far as possible the *Muhājirūn,* the ''emigrants'' who had come from Mecca, with the native population of Medina by means of employment, intermarriage, and a system of assumption of fraternal relationship. Then he attempted to win the unqualified support of the Jewish communities in and around the city. Apparently he thought he could achieve this end with relative ease simply by incorporating into Islam various forms of Jewish ritual and law. His optimism on this score was, however, misguided, since most of the Jews resented what they regarded as his rewriting of their Scriptures and completely rejected his claims to prophethood. The final period in the development of the Islamic faith under Muḥammad can be understood only in the light of this formidable opposition of the Jewish communities. Ultimately the wholesale incorporation of Jewish elements ceased and Islam assumed its own direction of prayer, Mecca, and its own month of fasting, Ramaḍān.

First ''Holy War.'' Before that, however, Muḥammad proved himself to be a shrewd and eminently practical political leader as well as prophet to his community. For economic and social reasons he now openly sanctioned warfare, preached *jihād* (holy war) against unbelievers, and himself led expeditions against trading caravans and neighboring Bedouin tribes. It seems quite clear that these expeditions were part of a more general scheme whereby Muḥammad hoped to blockade his most formidable enemies, the Meccans, into surrendering to his authority, while impressing the rest of the Arabs with the growing force of his religious state. In 624 the Muslims won their first major military victory at Badr. The opposition had been accustomed to attack and assembled an army of approximately 1,000 men. Muḥammad with a force of only about 300 ambushed the army and greatly elevated Islamic morale and his own position in the eyes of the enemy and neutral forces. But the battle of Badr did not secure an unshakable footing for Muḥammad or his followers. In the next year, for instance, the Muslims were badly defeated at Uḥud, and Muḥammad himself was wounded. Yet the only major Meccan effort against Muḥammad, a siege of Medina, ended in failure, and meanwhile Muḥammad was enjoying even greater successes in the realm of conversion. He won over some prominent persons by force of his personality and several tribes by means of alliance—frequently marriage alliance, which so swelled his own harem that it was necessary to receive a special revelation permitting himself more than the usual four wives.

Winning of Mecca. In 628 Muḥammad won one of his major victories by sheer stratagem. He announced his intention of coming to Mecca with his followers for the peaceful purpose of making the pilgrimage to the Ka'aba. The confused Meccans were forced to conclude a treaty at al-Ḥudaybiyah allowing for an annual pilgrimage of Muslims under terms of complete truce between the two forces. Muḥammad then turned toward unifying the Arab tribes north of Medina. So successful was this effort during the following 22 months that in 630 Muḥammad was able to return to Mecca and enter it against only token resistance. Victory had to be consolidated, however, and Muḥammad spent much of his time during the remaining two years of his life in seeking solutions to the complicated problem of tribal allegiances. His efforts met with considerable success in 631, the ''Year of Delegations (of Arab tribal shaykhs)'' of early Islamic historiography.

Consolidation of His Triumphs. Not all his time was occupied in warfare and secular activities during the Medinese period. The bulk of Qur'ānic revelation in these years far outweighs that from Mecca. In these chapters the rhymed style of *saj'* remained, but there was little left of the imagery, succinctness, and fire that characterized the Meccan chapters. They were ponderous relations of Biblical stories and legislative detail. At Mecca Muḥammad had proclaimed a new religion that was rather bare. At Medina he clothed it and set it up as a community embodying a radical reform of the Arabian social structure. He succeeded in replacing Arab tribalism with a notion of *'ummah,* a brotherhood of true believers under God destined for dominion in this world and enjoyment in the next.

Muḥammad had experienced bitter disappointment in the failure of Jews and Christians to accept Islam. When he was able, he retaliated by forcing Khaybar and other Jewish colonies to submit to his rule. But he was too respectful of the prophetic tradition in which he saw himself, and too economically canny, to fail to single out the *ahl-al-kitāb* (people of the Scripture, hence Jews and Christians) from others. Those who were willing to accept Islamic rule could retain their faiths under certain conditions, chief among which was the payment of a larger tax. Those who refused were to be treated like others, to be subjugated or killed. Draconian system as it no doubt was, it was still better than what pagans, including his own relatives, received at his hands.

Muḥammad did not return to Mecca to make the pilgrimage in 631. Instead he sent Abū Bakr to proclaim that henceforth pagans were not to participate in the pilgrimage. They were given four months to be converted to Islam or face extinction. In the following year Muḥammad made his ''Farewell Pilgrimage,'' solely in the company of his believing Muslims. His war against Meccan idolatry had been so crowned with victory that it no longer made any great difference that a Meccan idol now lay at the pivot of a dynamic, virtually irrepressible force soon to make its indelible marks upon the world outside Arabia. A few months later in 632, after a short illness, Muḥammad died. Abū Bakr, the father of his favorite wife 'Ā'ishah, succeeded him as his first CALIPH (Arabic *khalīfah,* ''successor'').

See Also: ISLAM; QUR'ĀN.

Bibliography: T. ANDRAE, *Mohammed: The Man and His Faith* (New York 1936). F. P. BUHL, *Das Leben Muḥammeds* (Leipzig 1930). E. DERMENGHEM, *Muḥammad and the Islamic Tradition* (New York 1958). A. GUILLAUME, *New Light on the Life of Muḥammad* (Manchester 1960). M. HAMIDULLAH, *Le Prophète de l'Islam,* 2 v. (Paris 1959). M. IBN ISHÂQ, *Sîrat Rasûl Allâh* (*The Life of Muhammad*), tr. A. GUILLAUME (London 1955). D. S. MARGOLIOUTH, *Mohammad and the Rise of Islam* (New York 1905). W. MUIR, *The Life of Mohammed* (rev. ed. Edinburgh 1923). W. M. WATT, *Muḥammad at Mecca* (New York 1953); *Muḥammad at Medina* (New York 1956); *Muḥammad, Prophet and Statesman* (New York 1961). A. J. WENSINCK, *Mohammed en de Joden te Medina* (Leiden 1928).

[J. KRITZECK/EDS.]

MÜHLENBERG, HENRY MELCHIOR

Organizer of the Lutheran Church in Colonial America; b. Einbeck, Hanover, Germany, Sept. 6, 1711; d. Trappe, PA, Oct. 7, 1787. Educated under the influence of PIETISM at Göttingen University, in Hanover, Muhlenberg was sent to America in 1742 in response to appeals from Lutheran colonists.

Despite the fact that the center of Muhlenberg's activity was in southeastern Pennsylvania, his travels and correspondence extended his influence to the entire Atlantic seaboard. He strengthened existing congregations and helped to organize new ones, secured additional clergymen from Europe and began to train a native ministry, united ministers and congregations in a synodical organization (1748), and through his reports to Europe (the so-called Halle Reports) secured financial and other assistance. Mühlenberg's three sons achieved prominence: Peter (1746–1807) was brigadier general in the American Revolution; Frederick (1750–1801) was first speaker of the U.S. Congress; and Henry Ernest (1753–1815) was a botanist as well as a clergyman.

Bibliography: *The Journals of Henry Melchior Muhlenberg,* tr. T. G. TAPPERT and J. W. DOBERSTEIN, 3 v. (Philadelphia 1942–58). P. A. W. WALLACE, *The Muhlenbergs of Pennsylvania* (Philadelphia 1950), bibliog. 321–342.

[T. G. TAPPERT]

MULDOON, PETER JAMES

Bishop; b. Columbia, CA, Oct. 10, 1862; d. Rockford, IL, Oct. 8, 1927. He was the eldest son of Irish immigrant parents, John and Catherine (Coughlin) Muldoon. After attending the public schools of Stockton, Calif., he continued his studies at St. Mary's College, St. Mary, Kentucky. In 1881, he entered St. Mary's Seminary, Baltimore, Maryland, for his philosophical and theological training. He was ordained for the Archdiocese of Chicago by Bishop John Loughlin of Brooklyn, New York, on Dec. 18, 1886. A favorite of Archbishop P. A. FEEHAN, he acted as his chancellor and secretary from 1888 to 1895, when he was appointed pastor of St. Charles Borromeo Church, Chicago. The recognition accorded the young American-born priest was resented by some of the Irish-born clergy of the archdiocese, and a few vented their hostility on him and flouted the authority of the archbishop.

When Archbishop Patrick A. Feehan and his auxiliary, Alexander J. McGavick, declined in health, Muldoon was consecrated titular bishop of Tamassus and auxiliary of Chicago in Holy Name Cathedral on July 25, 1901, by Cardinal Sebastian Martinelli, apostolic delegate to the United States. Martinelli's presence was construed as Rome's approbation of the young bishop and an admonition to his detractors. Six days after his consecration he was appointed vicar-general of the archdiocese.

Feehan died on July 12, 1902, and Muldoon, the administrator, was one of the candidates for the vacant see. However, in January of 1903, Rome transferred Bishop James E. Quigley of Buffalo to Chicago. Five years later, the Diocese of Rockford was erected from territory of the Archdiocese of Chicago, and Muldoon was named bishop of the new see. He was a candidate for the See of CHICAGO when Quigley died in July of 1915, but Rome appointed George W. Mundelein, auxiliary bishop of Brooklyn. In December of 1916, Muldoon was consulted about accepting the vacant See of Monterey-Los Angeles, California, but he expressed his preference for remaining in Rockford. There followed five months of confusion and frustration. The appointment of Muldoon to the West was made, the bulls were issued, and the wire services informed, but the bishop refused to act until an answer was received from Rome on his recent petition to remain in Rockford. In May of 1917, Rome finally acquiesced, and Muldoon remained in his diocese.

During his years as a bishop in Chicago and Rockford, Muldoon played a prominent role in the movement for social reform, gaining a reputation as a friend of labor and a defender of labor unions. When the American Federation of Catholic Societies, under the inspiration of Peter E. Dietz, a prominent labor priest, established a social service commission in 1911, Muldoon was appointed chairman. As chairman of the National Catholic War Council (1917–18), he became a nationally known figure. This organization, designed to coordinate all Catholic activities in furthering the war effort, brought Muldoon into close association with members of other religious groups and governmental agencies. His forcefulness and diplomacy ensured the success of the council and prompted Cardinal James Gibbons to propose a peacetime organization comparable to it. Muldoon, as one of the new committee members, submitted a program to the hierarchy at their meeting in September of 1919. It was approved, though not unanimously.

Rome at first viewed the new organization favorably, but when dissatisfied American bishops complained to the pope, the original approbation was qualified and then revoked. On his ad limina visit in 1920, Muldoon pleaded the case of the National Catholic Welfare Council; later Bishop Joseph Schrembs of Cleveland, Ohio, was dispatched to Rome to defend the new organization. The Holy See finally gave unqualified approbation, and the new agency was continued under the title of National Catholic Welfare Conference (NCWC).

During the formative years of the NCWC Muldoon was chairman of its Social Action Department and commanded attention locally and nationally in the social reform movement. Muldoon's death in 1927 came after an illness of several months.

Bibliography: A. I. ABELL, *American Catholicism and Social Action: A Search for Social Justice, 1869–1950* (New York 1960). M. WILLIAMS, *American Catholics in the War* (New York 1921). F. G. MCMANAMIN, "Peter J. Muldoon, First Bishop of Rockford, 1862–1927," *American Historical Review* 48 (1962): 365–378.

[F. G. MC MANAMIN]

MULHERIN, MARY GABRIELLA

Maryknoll Sister, missionary to Korea, co-founder of the Korean Credit Union in 1960, b. Scranton, Penn., 1900; d. Maryknoll, N.Y., 1993. Worked as a legal secretary for several years after high school. After she heard Maryknoll co-founder, Thomas F. PRICE, preach, she decided to enter the MARYKNOLL SISTERS in 1923, and was sent as a missionary to Korea. Between 1926 and 1941, Mulherin directed the Industry Department in Yeung Yu, was later was a language teacher in the same city, and served in several other towns, including the capital of Korea, Pyongyang. When World War II erupted, she returned to the United States to work as the secretary for the Maryknoll Superior General, Bishop James Edward WALSH. She returned to a war-torn and divided Korea in 1952, chagrined at the plight of the people. As part of the reconstruction of the social agencies of the country, Mulherin and Maryknoll Father George M. Carroll founded the Korean Association of Voluntary Associations in order to coordinate the many volunteer groups which had arisen after the Korean conflict. Because the war left many widows who did not have a source of income, Mulherin organized art and craft schools to teach them and other young women, who were without sources of income, how to lead economically independent lives.

In 1960, amidst a student revolution and the collapse of the Syngman Rhee government, Mulherin inaugurated a leadership training program for thirty workers, as the foundation for a voluntary Credit Union Movement. On May 1, 1960, twenty-eight members formed the first union on the Maryknoll Sisters' compound in Pusan. The movement was based on the principles Mulherin learned in Nova Scotia under the tutelage of Monsignor Moses M. Coady. The leadership training of the Antigonish Movement was based on democratic values and developed trust and self-responsibility among the members. After the first year as the director of the Credit Union, Mulherin turned over the leadership to two Korean leaders. When the Korean government honored her in 1988, the organization numbered 1.3 million members. She retired in 1967 and returned to Maryknoll, N.Y., where she continued her interest in the unions through conversations with visiting Koreans until her death in 1993.

Bibliography: SR. G. MULHERIN, *Brief History of the Maryknoll Sisters in North Korea, October, 1924 to October, 1950*

(Maryknoll, NY 1959), typescript. SR. G. MULHERIN, "The Role of Korean Woman in Christian Development," in *Fourth Apostolic Workshop on Social Justice* (Maryknoll, NY 1967).

[A. DRIES]

MULLANY, AZARIAS OF THE CROSS, BROTHER

Educator, author; b. near Killenaule, County Tipperary, Ireland, June 29, 1847; d. Plattsburg, NY, Aug. 20, 1893. Patrick Francis Mullany immigrated to Deerfield, New York, in 1857. While attending Assumption Academy, Utica, New York, he chose the vocation of his teachers, the Brothers of the Christian Schools; he was professed in 1862. He was assigned in 1866 to Rock Hill College, Ellicott City, Maryland, as a teacher of mathematics. He was president of the college (1879–86) and worked with such educators as Daniel Coit Gilman, Herbert Baxter Adams, and Andrew D. White. He moved to De La Salle Institute, New York City, in 1888, where his lectures and writings made him one of the best-known Catholic religious in America. He helped to organize Catholic reading circles and was a founder of the Catholic Summer School of America at Plattsburg. Although limited by ill health and inadequate formal education, he mastered nine languages and became a specialist in varied fields of knowledge, notably literature and philosophy. A frequent contributor to Catholic periodicals and the *International Journal of Ethics,* his chief writings were *An Essay Contributing to the Philosophy of Literature* (1874), *The Development of Old English Thought* (1879), *Aristotle and the Christian Church* (1888), *Books and Reading* (1889), and *Phases of Thought and Criticism* (1892). Posthumously, many of his articles and reviews were compiled as *Essays Educational, Essays Philosophical, Essays Miscellaneous* (1896).

[B. R. WEITEKAMP]

MULRY, THOMAS MAURICE

First president of the Superior Council of the U.S. Society of ST. VINCENT DE PAUL, and businessman; b. New York City, Feb. 13, 1855; d. there, March 10, 1916. Of Irish–Dutch extraction, he was the second of 14 children born to Thomas Mulry and Parthenia (Crolius) Mulry, of New York City. He was educated in parochial schools and at De La Salle Academy and as a young man took night classes at old Cooper Union. In 1872, after the family's second brief venture into farming in Wisconsin, he became associated with his father as an excavation contractor in the firm of Mulry and Son, New York. In

1880 Mulry married Mary E. Gallagher, a Hunter College graduate and teacher in New York public schools. The couple had 13 children; four of them joined the Society of Jesus, and one became a Sister of Charity. The contracting business of Mulry and Son prospered, with the younger Mulry eventually taking over active management. As a moderately successful businessman, he expanded his interests to include banking, insurance, and real estate, becoming president of the Emigrant Industrial Savings Bank in 1906.

After becoming a member of the Society of St. Vincent de Paul at 17, Mulry continued throughout his life to exercise this layman's charitable vocation, accepting offices from the presidency of St. Bernard's Parish Conference, 1880, to the presidency of the Superior Council of the U.S., 1915. Under his leadership, Vincentians relinquished an earlier position of aloofness and entered into cooperative effort with other public and private welfare agencies. Mulry permanently influenced the Catholic charities movement in the U.S. He fought the abuses inherent in almshouse care of dependent children and, notably, succeeded in improving conditions and standards of placement care. His plea for moderation all but ended the long controversy between advocates of institutional care and proponents of foster home care. *The Government in Charity* (1912), his principal publication, vigorously affirmed the state's responsibility to encourage and work cooperatively with private charitable agencies, but opposed excessive secularization of social welfare work. Under his direction special programs were initiated: summer outings and camps for needy boys and girls; the Catholic Home Bureau, which stimulated Catholic home placement programs; and the Catholic Boys' Club movement. National unification of the St. Vincent de Paul Society, attributable in part to Mulry's leadership, was achieved with the establishment of the Superior Council of the U.S. in 1915.

Although principally identified with the Vincentian organization, Mulry achieved recognition in the broader welfare community. He was among the founders and served as a vice president of the National Conference of Catholic Charities, helped establish the Fordham School of Social Service, founded St. Elizabeth's Home for Convalescent Women and Girls, and was a member of the Board of Governors of the New York Catholic Protectory. In 1907 he was elected president of the National Conference of Charities and Correction. U.S. President Theodore Roosevelt named him to be one of a committee of three to organize the first White House Conference on Children (1909).

Bibliography: J. W. HELMES, *Thomas M. Mulry: A Volunteer's Contribution to Social Work* (Washington 1938). D. T. MC-COLGAN, *A Century of Charity,* 2 v. (Milwaukee 1951).

[D. BAKER]

MULTITUDE

Considered absolutely and in the broadest sense of the term, unspecified plurality, hence intelligible only as opposed to some kind of UNITY. Often usage connotes, in addition to mere plurality, a collectivity or superior kind of unification embracing a plurality of more ultimate units, as when one speaks of "a multitude." The more properly metaphysical notion refers to a non-numerable plurality. This article discusses the origin of the notion, its various analogies, and its uses in philosophy and theology.

Origin. In the order of development of the various analogical uses of this term, the first refers to the kind of plurality that is grasped in immediate sense experience, such a rudimentary and ultimate experience that no further analysis seems capable of altering the basic content or interpretation. Prior to any notion of number, this plurality of material things is available to the sense of touch, to sight, and to hearing. The ability to grasp such a plurality as a collective set is sometimes referred to as number sense, but this precedes the formation of the number concept since number, taken concretely, is a measured material multitude. This prime analogate of multitude, pertaining to material entities only, manifests finer distinctions within it. Thus some pluralities are not perfect in the sense that their parts cannot be perfectly distinguished, e.g., the fingers of the hand, distinct yet joined. Again, some multitudes are irreducible, e.g., a group of men, whereas others are not, e.g., several pieces of wax that can be melted together to form one. This latter instance indicates that plurality is due to materiality, to quantity, and not to formal differences that characterize the individual members who constitute the multitude.

Analogies. Plurality requires some kind of distinction, for without distinction there is simple IDENTITY under which only unity can be found. Confining one's thought to perceptible, physical multitude, it makes little difference whether the elements of the collection be substantial individuals or mere parts, whether they be of the same type or species or simply diverse in kind. Almost any degree of physical separation or any kind of actual separation will suffice to found such a multitude, but some sort of dividedness based on the distinctions proper to quantified matter is required. Since distinction itself is based on some mode of opposition that sets one element over against another, the ultimate foundation of physical multitude can be found in the fact that in extended matter one part is not the other: "this here" is not "that there." This opposition, a difference in QUANTITY, is sometimes called SITUATION (*situs*). The parts of such a quantitative multitude can be understood as units; and when the collection is compared to a representative unit, the number, or relative measure, of the collection can be determined. This kind of multitude is opposed to, and yet, in some way, composed of, units that can be signified by the numeral "1."

Following a somewhat similar line of development, it is possible to conceive of multitude in another, analogous, sense based on some mode of formal OPPOSITION. Consequent upon opposition, formal distinctions can be made, and thus DIVISION and plurality or multitude in a formal sense. This notion of multitude is often called transcendental and is opposed to transcendental unity or unity of BEING itself, since form is the principle of entitative unity. Aristotle distinguished four modes of formal opposition: contradiction, contrariety, privation, and relation. Any of these may found a formal distinction and hence transcendental multitude—"transcendental" because not limited to any category but analogically common, as the term being is common. Clearly the notion of multitude changes as the basis of opposition changes, but in any case the correlative unity is a kind of nondividedness in being itself and hence not a standard for quantitative measure or enumeration. A formal, or transcendental, multitude cannot be counted in any sense of the term, whereas material, or quantitative, multitude is the proper subject of enumeration.

Philosophy and Theology. In philosophical thought the opposition between unity and multiplicity appears in many guises. The problem of the one and the many is one of the most fundamental metaphysical issues: how can being be one, i.e., common to all that is, and yet be the obvious multitude that it is? The Eleatics tended to regard multiplicity as an illusion of the senses (*see* GREEK PHILOSOPHY). PLATO found a unity in the transcendent Idea in which the sensible multitude participates, and Aristotle resorted to a theory of ANALOGY to preserve both undeniable facts. The solution of I. KANT, unique in its time, required a synthesizing activity of the mind that alone could attain intelligible unity in phenomenal multiplicity by the imposition of its own categories and connectives. The same issue reappears in epistemology as a dispute between NOMINALISM and REALISM, in the philosophy of logic as the problem of UNIVERSALS, in the philosophy of nature as the problem of MONISM versus pluralism, and in philosophical theology as PANTHEISM versus monotheism. Even in the philosophical considerations of mathematics, which seems to concern itself with quantitative plurality, there is a reflection of the problem in questions about the formation of the number concept.

In theology the concept of transcendental multitude is quite important inasmuch as all distinction and hence plurality of nonmaterial being must be formal. Any speculation about the pluralities of ANGELS involves transcendental multitude, and each angelic individual can be understood as formally distinguished from all others. Likewise, in Trinitarian theology, the divine Persons are distinguished by a relational opposition that is itself transcendental and so the multiplicity in the Persons must be analogically transcendental. Apparently the image-making power of the human mind and the necessity for material signification create the impression that such multiplicity is subject to counting.

Bibliography: D. J. B. HAWKINS, *Being and Becoming* (New York 1954), ch. 7. F. SLADECZEK, "Die spekulative Auffassung vom Wesen der Einheit in ihrer Auswirkung auf Philosophie und Theologie," *Scholastik* 25 (1950) 361–88. D. GARCIA, "De Metaphysica multitudinis ordinatione et de tribus simpliciter diversis specibus ejusdem secundum divi Thomae principia," *Divus Thomas*, 3d series 31 (1928) 83–109, 607–38; 32 (1929) 43–56.

[C. F. WEIHER]

MUNDELEIN, GEORGE WILLIAM

Cardinal, third archbishop of Chicago, Ill., archdiocese; b. New York City, July 2, 1872; d. Chicago, Oct. 2, 1939. He was the only son of Francis and Mary (Goetz) Mundelein, who sent him to St. Nicholas parochial school on Manhattan's lower East Side. Because his family had only modest means, friends helped him through De La Salle Institute and Manhattan College, New York City, from which he received a B.A. degree in 1889. A fellow Classmate, Patrick J. Hayes, and he decided to study for the priesthood. It is not altogether clear why he decided to study for the neighboring Diocese of Brooklyn, N.Y. He spent three years at St. Vincent's Seminary in Beatty, Pa., and completed his training at the Propaganda College, Rome. He was ordained in Rome by Bishop Charles McDonnell of Brooklyn on June 8, 1895, and celebrated his first Mass at St. Peter's Tomb.

On his return to Brooklyn, he was appointed McDonnell's associate secretary and administrator of the Lithuanian Church at Williamsburg. In December of 1897 he became diocesan chancellor, and nine years later was made a domestic prelate, an unusual distinction in those days. The Arcadia, a group of Catholic scholars known for their literary attainments, elected him to membership on April 20, 1907. At the request of McDonnell, Mundelein was named titular bishop of Loryma and auxiliary bishop of Brooklyn and consecrated on Sept. 21,

George William Mundelein.

1909, in St. James Procathedral. He resigned as chancellor to become rector of the Cathedral Chapel of Queen of All Saints, where he supervised the building of a church, school, and rectory, combined in one Gothic structure. He also directed the erection of Cathedral College of the Immaculate Conception, the preparatory seminary.

Archbishop of Chicago. On Dec. 9, 1915, Mundelein was chosen to be the third archbishop of CHICAGO. Only 43 years old, he was the youngest archbishop in the United States. His enthronement in Holy Name Cathedral took place on Feb. 9, 1916, with the apostolic delegate, Archbishop Giovanni Bonzano, presiding. A civic reception followed at the Auditorium Theatre on February 13 at which the new archbishop spoke, promising to bring the name of his predecessor Archbishop James E. Quigley "permanently and prominently before every man, woman, and child in the diocese." This pledge was fulfilled three months later when a pastoral letter of May 14, 1916, announced the building of Quigley Preparatory Seminary, a project the clergy and people enthusiastically supported. While this building was under construction, Mundelein planned a major seminary, which the archdiocese had needed since August of 1868 when the seminary department of the University of St. Mary of the Lake had been closed. A site was found near Area, Ill., and when the diamond jubilee of the archdiocese and the silver jubilee of the archbishop's ordination were celebrated in April 1920, the project for a new major seminary was announced. The purse given to the archbishop for his jubilee was used to begin construction of the philosophy buildings. During the next 14 years St. Mary of the Lake Seminary added 14 buildings in Georgian architecture to its plant on the shores of Lake Eara in Lake County. In 1924 the town of Area changed its name to Mundelein, and the school became known as Mundelein Seminary. Ten years later, the Congregation of Seminaries and Universities recognized St. Mary of the Lake Seminary as a pontifical faculty of theology with the privilege of conferring the doctorate in theology. Mundelein always took special interest in the seminary and collected rare books, manuscripts, autographs, coins, vestments, chalices, and pictures for its museum, library, and chapels.

Another of Mundelein's notable accomplishments was the organization of Catholic Charities in March of 1918, by which he united the diverse charitable activities of the archdiocese and prompted support for them. He never forgot that he had been a poor boy and always expressed affection for the underprivileged. Each year at Christmas he personally paid for a complete outfit of clothing and shoes for 100 needy children. Toward the end of his life he said to the members of the Holy Name Society: "The trouble with us in the past has been that we were too often allied or drawn into an alliance with the wrong side. Selfish employers of labor have flattered the Church by calling it a great conservative force, and then called upon it to act as a police force when they paid but a pittance of wages to those who worked for them. I hope that day is gone by. Our place is beside the poor, behind the working man."

Cardinal. All Chicago rejoiced at the news on March 2, 1924, that its archbishop would be elevated to the College of Cardinals in the consistory of March 24. When Mundelein was in Rome to receive the red hat, he began preparations to hold the 28th International Eucharistic Congress in Chicago from June 20 to 24, 1926. More than a million Catholics, including 12 cardinals, 64 archbishops, 309 bishops, 500 monsignors, and 8,000 priests made this congress one of the greatest religious demonstrations ever witnessed in the United States. In 1928, when Pope Pius XI appealed for help in building the new Propaganda College in Rome, Mundelein responded with a check for $1,500,000, underwritten by the generous mission contributions of his priests and people.

In 1934 he celebrated his episcopal silver jubilee in Rome, where he purchased a building for the Collegio S. Maria del Lago, a house for postgraduate students. Three years later on May 18, 1937, he condemned the religious persecution undertaken by Hitler and the Nazi party. His description of the Fuehrer as "an Austrian paperhanger" brought protests at the Vatican and Washington.

A personal friendship developed between Mundelein and president Franklin D. Roosevelt. When the new Outer Drive Bridge, Chicago, was dedicated on Oct. 5, 1937, the President was his luncheon guest. In October of 1938 Mundelein served as papal legate to the eighth national Eucharistic Congress in New Orleans, La. While in Rome to report to Pope Pius XI, he celebrated the beatification Mass for Frances Xavier CABRINI, whose funeral Mass he had offered in Chicago in 1917. After the death of Pope Pius XI in February of 1939, Mundelein participated in the conclave that elected Cardinal Eugenio Pacelli as Pope Pius XII on March 2, 1939. Seven months later Cardinal Mundelein died suddenly of a coronary thrombosis and was buried in a crypt behind the main altar in the seminary that bears his name.

Bibliography: P. R. MARTIN, comp., *The First Cardinal of the West* (Chicago 1934). E. T. REGAN, *One Hundred Years: The History of the Church of the Holy Name* (Chicago 1949). G. W. MUNDELEIN, *Letters of a Bishop to His Flock* (New York 1927).

[H. C. KOENIG]

MUNDWILER, FINTAN

Second abbot of ST. MEINRAD, Ind.; b. Dietikon, Zurich, Switzerland, July 12, 1835; d. St. Meinrad, Feb. 14, 1898. He studied at the claustral school at EINSIEDELN, entered that monastery in 1854, and was ordained in 1859. With Martin MARTY, later abbot and bishop, Mundwiler was sent (1859) to the newly founded monastery of St. Meinrad, where he served as rector of the school and first prior (1870). Upon Marty's nomination as vicar apostolic of the Dakota Territory, Mundwiler was elected second abbot of St. Meinrad on Feb. 3, 1880. During his term of office St. Meinrad experienced many difficulties, including the destructive fire of 1887, the struggles to rebuild, and certain internal dissensions. With tact and moderation Abbot Fintan brought about a renewal in observance, the reconstruction of the abbey, and an increase in school enrollment. Under him St. Meinrad's daughterhouse, New Subiaco in Arkansas, was made an abbey (1891), and St. Joseph's Abbey in Louisiana was founded (1889). He was the first president (1881) of the Swiss-American Congregation of BENEDICTINES, and he composed the congregation's first statutes.

Bibliography: Archives, St. Meinrad Archabbey, Einsiedeln, Conception Abbey, St. Joseph's Abbey, and New Subiaco Abbey.

A. KLEBER, *History of St. Meinrad Archabbey, 1854–1954* (St. Meinrad, IN 1954).

[C. DAVIS]

MUNGUÍA, CLEMENTE DE JESÚS

Mexican prelate and scholar, active in the defense of the Church during the Liberal reform and the period of Emperor Maximilian; b. Los Reyes, Michoacán, Nov. 21, 1810; d. Rome, Dec. 14, 1868. He graduated in law and practiced the profession in Morelia and Mexico City from 1838 to 1841, when he was ordained to the priesthood. He then served in various ecclesiastical posts of the Diocese of Morelia, including those of vicar-general and vicar of the curia. In 1843 he was named rector of the seminary, where he had taught, and he brought this institution to a high level of academic and scientific activity. Munguía was elevated to the bishopric of Michoacán in 1850. In 1853 he was named president of the council of state by the dictator Santa Anna. With the victory of the Ayutla revolution, he vigorously defended the Church against the Liberal reformers and was exiled in 1856 by President Comonfort. Returning to his diocese the following year, he declared himself in favor of the Plan of Tacubaya, which called for the derogation of the liberal constitution of 1857 and set in motion the War of the Reform. At the conclusion of the war in 1861, which resulted in victory for the Reform party under Benito Juárez, he was again sent into exile. With the beginning of the French invasion of Mexico, he returned to Morelia in 1863 as its first archbishop. He soon incurred the enmity of Emperor Maximilian because of his outspoken views on the rights of the Church. He was one of the prelates who signed the Manifest of Dec. 29, 1864, urging the government not to legislate in religious matters without a previous concordat with the pope. He also protested against the Law of Religious Tolerance; but disillusioned in his hopes under the emperor, he went into exile again in 1865 and spent his last days in Rome. A prolific writer, he left 14 volumes, ranging from a course in universal jurisprudence (1844) to a synthesis of the philosophy of thought and expression (1852), in addition to numerous essays and addresses.

Bibliography: E. VALVERDE TÉLLEZ, *Bio-bibliografía eclesiástica mexicana, 1821–1943,* 3 v. (Mexico City 1949).

[J. A. MAGNER]

MUNICH METHOD IN CATECHETICS

An adaptation to catechetics of the psychological steps of learning and teaching, developed by J. F. Herbart and T. Ziller. The Munich catechists formulated their method in six principal and secondary steps: presentation, explanation, application and preparation, aim, and synthesis. The primary steps in the teaching procedure correspond to three steps in learning on the part of the pupil (viz., perception, understanding, and practice). Furthermore, there is direct appeal to the cognitive and appetitive powers of the learner: to the senses and imagination in the ''presentation,'' to the intellect in the ''explanation,'' and to the will and emotions in the ''application.'' These principles of learning have their roots in the psychology of Aristotle and were formulated by St. Thomas Aquinas as the bases for all learning and teaching. A story, usually from the Bible, containing a doctrinal or moral truth is presented by the teacher; explanation of the religious elements to be learned is followed by practical application to daily living. The inductive process of teaching from the known to the unknown, from the concrete to the abstract, was a major improvement over the hitherto prevailing word analysis of the catechism answers.

Bibliography: H. W. OFFELE, *Geschichte und Grundanliegen der sogenannten Münchener katechetischen Methode* (Munich 1961). For more complete bibliographical data see L. LENTNER et al., eds., *Katechetisches Wörterbuch* (Freiburg 1961).

[J. B. COLLINS]

MUNIFICENTISSIMUS DEUS

On Nov. 1, 1950, Pope Pius XII defined the Church's doctrine of the ASSUMPTION OF MARY into heaven. The phrase *Munificentissimus Deus* (Most Bountiful God) both entitles and begins the document of definition, an apostolic constitution.

Apart from its survey of various descriptions and defenses of the Assumption, and the definition itself, this papal bull has established itself as a milestone in the history of MARIOLOGY for: (1) the capital significance which the Pope gives to the universal contemporary belief in the Assumption as evidenced by the almost unanimous concurrence of the bishops of the world when he asked their opinion: ''This outstanding agreement of the Catholic prelates and the faithful by itself and in a way altogether certain and free of all errors, manifested this privilege as a truth revealed by God and contained in that divine deposit which Christ has delivered to His Spouse to be guarded faithfully and to be taught infallibly''; (2) the lack of systematic appeal to Holy Scripture as basis for the proclamation. The Pope states that all the ''proofs and considerations of the Fathers and theologians are based on the Scriptures as their ultimate foundation,'' but he does not analyze individual texts (as did Pius IX in *Ineffa-*

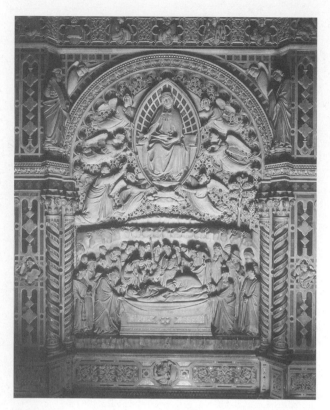

Relief sculpture of the death and assumption of the Virgin Mary, from the church of Or San Michelle, Florence, Italy. (©David Lees/CORBIS)

bilis Deus, the definition of the IMMACULATE CONCEPTION). It is noteworthy that (1), despite the long history of differences on the meaning of the PROTO-EVANGELIUM (Gn. 3.15), he forthrightly applies the text to Mary; (2) without any exegetic reservation he alludes to "theologians and preachers who, following in the footsteps of the Fathers, have been rather free in their use of events and expressions taken from Sacred Scripture''; (3) with approval he refers to St. Bonaventure who applied to Mary "in a kind of accommodated sense" words of the Canticle (8.5) which helped to justify, in the original sermon, belief in the Assumption.

Then, after drawing practical moral consequences from this belief, the document concludes with the solemn statement: "We pronounce, declare, and define it to be a divinely revealed dogma that the Immaculate Mother of God, the ever Virgin Mary, having completed the course of her earthly life, was assumed body and soul into heavenly glory.''

Bibliography: PIUS XII, "Munificentissimus Deus," *Acta Apostolicae Sedis* 42 (1950) 753–771; Eng. *Catholic Mind* 49 (Jan. 1951) 65–78. B. CAPELLE, "Théologic de l'Assumption d'après la bulle 'Munificentissimus Deus.'" *Nouvelle revue théologique* 72 (1950) 1009–27. *Sacrae theologiae summa* 2:2.201–223.

[J. W. LANGLINAIS]

MUÑOZ, VICENTE

Franciscan architect; b. Seville, Spain, 1699; d. Salta, Argentina, Sept. 8, 1784. He entered the convent of Buenos Aires as a Franciscan novice on July 7, 1741. Muñoz directed the building of the church of San Francisco in Buenos Aires, begun in 1730 with plans formulated by Andrés Blanqui, SJ. Since the church was not inaugurated until 1754, Muñoz probably carried out the major part of the work. Years later, when the convent was rebuilt, he again acted as builder and director. Muñoz also directed the work on the chapel of Terciarios de San Roque in Buenos Aires. Muñoz, called to Córdoba to complete work on the cathedral (begun in 1690 by architect José González Merguelte and continued in 1729 by Blanqui), probably designed its majestic dome, equalled in beauty by few works in all America. In 1759 he moved to Salta to direct the work of the new Franciscan church. Although there is no documentary proof that the plans were by Muñoz, the similarity of the dome to that of the cathedral of Córdoba suggests that he was the author. In 1882 the forward part of this church was completely remodeled by Luis Giorgi, and at present Muñoz is credited with the design of San Francisco de Salta only from the transept back. Although there is no proof that he planned the buildings mentioned above, it is certain that he was their builder, a fact that attests to the exceptional quality of his skills as a technician.

Bibliography: G. FURLONG, *Arquitectos argentinos durante la dominación hispánica* (Buenos Aires 1946). M. J. BUSCHIAZZO, *Historia de la arquitectura colonial en Iberoamérica* (Buenos Aires 1961).

[M. J. BUSCHIAZZO]

MÜNZER, THOMAS

Revolutionary sixteenth-century Anabaptist leader who fatefully influenced the Catholic and Protestant attitude toward the Anabaptist movement; b. Stolberg, Germany, before 1490 (1468?); d. Mühlhausen, Germany, May 27, 1525. After studying at universities in Leipzig and Frankfurt an der Oder, he was ordained and served for a time as convent chaplain. At the Leipzig Disputation in 1519 he met Luther, who recommended that Münzer serve a church in Zwickau (1520). In this socially unstable environment Münzer came under the influence of Nicolaus Storch and his Zwickau prophets, which led him to accept direct communication with God, rejecting Luther's reliance on the written word. Expelled from Zwickau (1521), he wandered about Central Europe until he was invited in 1523 to serve a church in Allsted in Electoral Saxony. Münzer proved to be a successful and eloquent preacher. He produced the first complete German liturgy, which anticipated Luther and influenced liturgical development. Involved in agitation against local authorities, Münzer organized a secret confederation consisting of peasants and miners from neighboring Mansfeld. In a command performance sermon preached on July 13, 1524, he vainly attempted to win John of Saxony, brother of Frederick the Wise, to his plan to establish a theocratic state. Opposed by Luther and forbidden to preach, Münzer fled to Mühlhausen, where he aided Heinrich Pfeiffer in making the city a center of the peasant revolt. He soon joined a roving, undisciplined, and poorly equipped army of peasants whom he encouraged with his apocalyptic preaching. Captured and tortured after their rout at Frankenhausen (1525), he recanted his political and religious views before execution. Replacing Luther's justification by faith with justification by suffering and Luther's distinction between the two kingdoms with theocratic millennial hopes, Münzer obtained religious certainty through dreams and visions. When these proved to be delusions he collapsed. Erroneously considered the typical Anabaptist by the Protestant reformers and the typical chaotic consequence of the Reformation by Catholics, Münzer became a symbol, distorting both Protestant and Catholic interpretations of the Reformation. His later popularity among Marxists as an early communist is based upon a misinterpretation of the records.

Bibliography: *Werke,* ed. G. FRANZ (Gütersloh). G. W. FORELL, ''Thomas Münzer, Symbol and Reality,'' *Dialog* 2 (1963): 12–33. C. HINRICHS, *Luther und Müntzer* (Berlin 1952). M. M. SMIRIN, *Die Volksreformation des Thomas Münzer und der Grosse Bauernkrieg,* tr. H. NICHTWEISS (2d ed. Berlin 1956). G. H. WILLIAMS, ed., *Spiritual and Anabaptist Writers* (Philadelphia 1957). G. FRANZ, *Die Religion in Geschichte und Gegenwart,* 6 v. (Tübingen 1957–63) 4:1183–1184. E. ISERLOH, *Lexicon für Theologie und Kirche,* 10 v. (Freiburg 1957–65) 7:689–690.

[G. W. FORELL]

MURATORI, LODOVICO ANTONIO

Italian historian; b. Vignola, Italy, Oct. 21, 1672; d. Modena, Jan. 23, 1750. He began his brilliant scholarly career in 1695 as Doctor of the Bibliotheca Ambrosiana in Milan. Declining other offers, such as that of Victor Amadeus II who wanted him for the University of Turin, Muratori returned to Modena in 1700 as ducal archivist. There he devoted himself to the history of the political life of the ESTE family; his work *Antichità estensi* (2 v., Modena 1717, 1740), the basis of his fame as a historian, grew out of his several studies on the current legal struggle between Pope CLEMENT XI and Emperor Joseph I for possession of the city of Comacchio. At the suggestion of Apostolo Zeno, Muratori began collecting the works

Thomas Münzer. (Archive Photos)

of historians of the Italian Middle Ages, *Rerum Italicarum scriptores* (27 v., Modena 1723–38; v. 28 posthumously pub. in 1751; 2d ed., Città di Castello 1900). This work, together with his other publications of sources, *Antiquitates Italicae medii aevi* (6 v., Milan 1738–43) and *Novus thesaurus veterum inscriptionum* (6 v., Milan 1739–43), marked Muratori as the founder and initiator of modern Italian historiography. In his 12-volume *Annali d'Italia* (Milan 1744–49), deliberately patterned on MABILLON's annals of the Benedictine Order, Muratori did not succeed in really elaborating his source material, but his *Annali* do represent the first large-scale attempt at a unified view of Italian history. A conscientious priest as well as a historian, Muratori was unswerving in his recognition of ecclesiastical authority in purely theological questions, but he consistently and trenchantly held that historical criticism should be brought to bear on the secular phenomena of the Church. This brought him into conflict with current ecclesiastical opinion in regard to the power of the PAPACY and the cult of the saints (*see* HAGIOGRAPHY). His moderate reformist ideas, especially his demand for freedom of science and scholarship, even in questions of religion, mark him as a representative advocate of ''enlightened Catholicism'' [see especially his work *De ingeniorum moderatione in religionibus negotio* (Paris 1714)].

Bibliography: Works. *Opere,* 36 v. (Arezzo 1767–80; 2d ed. in 48 v. Venice 1790–1800); *Scritti inediti di L. A. M.* (Bologna 1872; 2d ed. 1880); *Epistolario di L. A. M.,* ed. M. CAMPORI, 14 v. (Modena 1901–22); *Corrispondenza tra L. A. M. e G. G. Leibniz,* ed. M. CAMPORI (Modena 1892). **Literature.** G. F. SOLI MURATORI, *Vita del proposto L. A. M.* (Venice 1756). É. AMANN, *Dictionnaire de théologie catholique,* 15 v. (Paris 1903–50)10.2:2547–2556. T. SORBELLI, *Bibliografia Muratoriana,* 2 v. (Modena 1943–44). S. BERTELLI, *Erudizione e storia in L. A. M.* (Naples 1960). E. COCHRANE, "M.: The Vocation of a Historian," *American Catholic Historical Review* 51 (1965): 153–172.

[H. RUMPLER]

MURATORIAN CANON

Discovered by L. A. MURATORI in the Ambrosian Library at Milan in 1740, the Muratorian fragment is the oldest known canon of the New Testament. The Milan copy, which seems to have come from Bobbio, is hardly older than the eighth century. Mutilated at both ends, it contains 85 lines. Four fragments, probably of the 11th and 12th centuries, were found at Monte Cassino.

The date of composition is clear from lines 74–77: "Very recently [*nuperrime*], in our times, Hermas wrote the *Shepherd,* when his brother, Bishop Pius, was sitting in the chair of the Church of the City of Rome" (*see* HERMAS, SHEPHERD OF). The pontificate of Pius I was about A.D. 142–155.

The poor Latin suggests that the original was Greek. Additionally, the neuter plural subject with singular verb (*alia plura . . . recipi non potest:* lines 65–67) is normal in Greek, but barbarous in Latin. Most of the literature of the Roman Church at this time was in Greek, but Latin was also in use by the end of the second century, and there were at that time Latin translations of at least part of Scripture. Moreover, the play on words in lines 67–68, *fel cum melle misceri non congruit,* could not be made in Greek. Perhaps the translator substituted a current Latin saying for a different original.

It is uncertain who composed this canon. Clement of Alexandria, Melito of Sardes, Polycrates of Ephesus, Pope Victor, Pope St. Zephyrinus, and St. Hippolytus have been suggested as possible authors. The last, the first antipope, is the most favored. From the way it speaks of the city, the canon seems to have been written at Rome. It uses a tone of authority, which would accord with one who claimed to be pope; e.g., it says firmly that some works attributed to St. Paul "cannot be received in the Catholic Church," and, "We receive only the Apocalypses of John and Peter." Moreover, the canon strongly argues, against the Roman priest Caius, that St. John the Apostle wrote both the fourth Gospel and the Apocalypse. The arguments used are thought to come from Hippolytus. M. J. Lagrange [*Revue biblique* 42 (1933) 182] cites Denys bar-Salibi, a 12th–century Syrian: "Hippolytus says that John, writing . . . 13 Epistles, wrote them to seven churches" (cf. lines 48–50 of the canon). Yet these arguments are not conclusive; the author might be merely citing general belief or decisions of authority. Nor would Hippolytus have used a tone of authority before *c.* 217, when he laid claim to the papacy, but that was not soon after the papacy of Pius I (cf. lines 74–77). For the contents, *see* CANON, BIBLICAL 3.

Bibliography: J. QUASTEN, *Patrology* (Westminster, Maryland 1950–) 2:207–210. B. ALTANER, *Patrology,* tr. H. GRAEF (New York 1960) 158–160. H. LECLERCQ, *Dictionnaire d'archéologie chrétienne et de liturgie,* ed. F. CABROL, H. LECLERCQ and H. I. MARROU (Paris 1907–53) 12.1:543–560. M. J. LAGRANGE, *Histoire ancienne du Canon du N.T.,* pt. 1, *Introduction à l'étude du N.T.* (pts. 1, 2, 4, Paris 1933–37); "L'Auteur du Canon de Muratori," *Revue biblique* 35 (1926) 83–88; "Le Canon d'Hippolyte et le Fragment de Muratori," *Revue biblique* 42 (1933) 161–186.

[W. G. MOST]

MURBACH, ABBEY OF

Former Benedictine abbey in Upper Alsace, near Colmar, France, on the Murbach River; one of the most important German abbeys of the Middle Ages. It was founded a little before 728 by Count Eberhard, and St. PIRMIN of Reichenau. It soon received great prerogatives: vast possessions, EXEMPTION from episcopal jurisdiction, and autonomy under the Holy See. Murbach enjoyed its finest era in Carolingian times, when it had an important community, schools, and a rich library. Deserted in the 11th century during the INVESTITURE STRUGGLE, it was quickly reestablished during the 12th century; its beautiful church, of which some parts still remain, was built at that time. During the 13th century the abbot ranked among the princes of the empire, and Murbach was imperial territory. But at the end of that century the abbey suffered a decline—a decline even more pronounced in the 14th century when the abbey would accept only noblemen. Common life was abandoned in the 15th century. From the 14th century the prince abbots of Murbach were also the abbots of Lure, in the Diocese of Besançon; and in 1560 Pius IV permanently united the two monasteries, both then held in COMMENDATION. The affiliation of Murbach with the Swiss Benedictines in 1666 and then with the congregation of Strasbourg in 1715 proved to be vain attempts at restoring the common life. In 1764 the monks obtained the right to become secular clerics and moved to the neighboring town of Guebwiller. A riot on July 26 and 27, 1789, destroyed this chapter of CANONS composed exclusively of noblemen.

Bibliography: A. GATRIO, *Die Abtei Murbach im Elsass,* 2 v. (Strasbourg 1895). M. BARTH, *Handbuch der elsässischen Kirchen* *im Mittelalter,* v.2 (Archives de l'Église d'Alsace 12; Strasbourg 1961) 519–1190, esp. 886–897, with bibliog. O. FELD, *Lexikon für Theologie und Kirche,* ed. J. HOFER and K. RAHNER, 10 v. (2d, new ed. Freiburg 1957–65) 7:693–694.

[J. CHOUX]

MURI, ABBEY OF

Benedictine abbey, formerly in Aargau, Diocese of Basel, Switzerland; since 1845 in the former Augustinian monastery of Gries in Bolzano, Italy. It was founded in 1027 by the Hapsburgs as a family cloister and settled from EINSIEDELN. The first prior, Reginbold (1032–55), built the convent. The church, a Romanesque three-nave, flat-roof basilica with two towers, was consecrated in 1064; and in 1065 the provost became an abbot. In 1082, as the customary of FRUTTUARIA was introduced from SANKT BLASIEN, Muri was detached from the Hapsburgs, who became *advocati.* The abbey came under imperial (1114) and papal (1139) protection. The *Acta Murensia,* begun c. 1150, offer data on the early Hapsburgs. In the 14th century fire damaged the abbey twice; in 1431 the right of *advocatus* went to the Swiss Confederation. Pontifical privileges were granted to the abbots in 1507. The Reformation brought Muri, which had accumulated extensive possessions, to the brink of ruin; but Abbot Johann Jodokus Singeisen (1596–1644) applied Tridentine reforms, helped found the Swiss Benedictine Congregation (1602), and raised Muri to new heights. In 1622 the abbey became exempt from the bishop of Constance. Placidus Zurlauben (1684–1723) was made a prince of the empire (1701) after he acquired new lands, making Muri the richest abbey in Switzerland. Decline began with restrictions by the Helvetic Republic, and secularization by Aargau occurred in 1841. Austria offered a refuge to the monks in Gries; the abbot, however, retains his title of Muri. Since 1841 the abbey has cared for the Swiss Gymnasium in Sarnen. The buildings in Muri now house a mental institution; and the church, which was rebuilt (1694–97), now serves a parish. The stained-glass windows, as well as the library went to Aargau.

Bibliography: M. KIEM, *Geschichte der Benediktiner-Abtei Muri-Gries,* 2 v. (Stans 1881–91). H. STEINACKER, "Die ältesten Geschichtsquellen des habsburgischen Hausklosters Muri," *Zeitschrift für die Geschichte des Oberrheins,* NS 23 (Heidelberg 1908) 387–420. O. HUNKELER, *Abt J. J. Singeisen* (Diss. Fribourg 1951). R. AMSCHWAND, *Abt A. Regli und die Aufhebung des Klosters Muri* (Diss. Fribourg 1956); *Lexikon für Theologie und Kirche,* ed. J. HOFER and K. RAHNER, 10 v. (2d, new ed. Freiburg 1957 65) 7:694. *Sarnen Jahresbericht* (1955–56). O. L. KAPSNER, *A Benedictine Bibliography: An Author-Subject Union List,* 2 v. (2d ed. Collegeville, Minn. 1962) 2:242. L. H. COTTINEAU, *Répertoire topobibliographique des abbayes et prieurés,* 2 v. (Mâcon 1935–39) 2:2020–22.

[A. MAISSEN]

MURIALDO, LEONARDO, BL.

Founder of the Congregation of St. Joseph (Turin); b. Turin, Italy, Oct. 26, 1828; d. Turin, March 30, 1900. Murialdo studied theology in the university of Turin, where he obtained a doctorate (1850) and was ordained (1851). He then devoted himself to the education of poor boys, and in 1857 he became director of the oratory of San Luigi, offered to him by St. John BOSCO. To improve his pedagogical talents and to familiarize himself with the French school of spirituality, Murialdo attended the seminary of St. Sulpice in Paris (1865–66). Upon returning to Turin he was named rector of the Collegio Artigianelli, which aimed to supply poor youths between the ages of 8 and 24 with Christian education and training in a trade. Under Murialdo's leadership the school gained a high reputation for its modern methods of vocational guidance and for its superior teaching staff.

In 1873 Murialdo founded the Pious Congregation of St. Joseph (Turin) and became its superior general. As one of the first in Italy to promote the Catholic worker movement, he established Catholic workers' unions (Unioni Operaie Cattoliche, 1871) in Turin and began the weekly publication *La Voce dell'Operaio.* To effect the Christian renewal of society and win liberty for the Church, Murialdo participated actively in the Opera dei Congressi, served on Catholic committees, and initiated many Catholic associations. At the sixth Catholic Congress in Naples (1883), he established a national federation of societies to improve the press and founded the monthly *La buona stampa.* In beatifying him (Nov. 3, 1963), Paul VI remarked that the Church was exalting not only his personal virtues, but also "the social force that these virtues clothe." Murialdo's remains are venerated in the church of St. Barbara in Turin.

Bibliography: E. REFFO, *Il teologo L. Murialdo* (Turin 1903; 6th ed. Rome 1964). G. VERCELLUNO, *Vita e spirito del Servo di Dio teologo L. Murialdo* (Bergamo 1941). J. COTTINO, *Il beato L. Murialdo* (Pignerol 1963). F. BEA, *Beato L. Murialdo* (Rome 1963). A. MARENGO, *Contributi per uno studio su L. Murialdo educatore* (Rome 1964).

[G. MILONE]

MURIEL, DOMINGO

Jesuit philosopher and canonist; b. Tamanes, near Salamanca, Spain, 1718; d. Faenza, Italy, Jan. 23, 1795. He entered the Society of Jesus in 1734, and was sent to Rio de la Plata in 1748. As professor of philosophy in Córdoba, he introduced the "new or Cartesian philosophy." He was subsequently a professor of moral theology and canon law, rector of the Colegio of Monserrat, and secretary to the provincial. In 1762 he was selected as procurator at the courts of Madrid and Rome; he was in Spain at the time of the expulsion of the Jesuits in 1767. During his exile in the Papal States, he was rector and provincial of the province of Paraguay with headquarters in Faenza. The general opinion of his holiness was such that the cause of his beatification was initiated soon after his death. No less distinguished for his knowledge than for his sanctity, he wrote the *Fasti novi orbis et ordinationum apostolicarum ad Indias pertinentium breviarium* (Venice 1786), and *Rudimenta Juris Naturae et Gentium* (Venice 1791), as well as several unpublished writings in the archives of Italy and Spain, such as the "Collectanea dogmática de saeculo XVIII" and "Monumenta historica, chronologica, dogmática ab anno 1776 ad annum 1780." Among Muriel's published writings that do not, however, bear his name is his *Lettre à l'auteur de l'article jésuite dans le Dictionnaire Encyclopédique* (1766). He also wrote the *Breve noticia de las misiones vivas de la Compañía de Jesús en la provincia del Paraguay* (1766).

Bibliography: G. FURLONG, *Domingo Muriel* (Buenos Aires 1934); *Domingo Muriel, S.J., y su Relación de las misiones* (Buenos Aires 1955).

[G. FURLONG]

MURILLO, BARTOLOMÉ ESTEBAN

Bartolomé Esteban Murillo.

Painter of the "golden age" of Spanish baroque; b. Seville, 1617 (baptized Jan. 1, 1618); d. Seville, April 3, 1682. He was a devout man who for a time aspired to the priesthood; his daughter became a Dominican and his son a Franciscan. Orphaned at an early age, he earned a livelihood by painting cheap religious pictures until he studied (1642–45) at the royal galleries in Madrid under Velázquez, from whom he learned a great deal. Murillo then became the favorite artist of Seville's aristocratic class and the universally popular interpreter of the Immaculate Conception. His first effort on this theme resembles the earlier Ribera in grandiosity; such works, at Aranjuez and the Prado (Madrid), adumbrate the rococo. Among Murillo's other renowned works are *The Angels' Kitchen, St. Elizabeth Healing the Sick, St. Francis with the Crucified Christ,* and the *Vision of St. Anthony.* His religious work is distinctively baroque in its brilliant coloring and preference for beauty that tends toward intimacy and prettiness, and away from classical perfection and the spiritual realities (the *estilo vaporoso*). This same spirit marks his paintings of childhood, such as *Children with a Shell* and *Little St. John,* and his secular subjects are unique in Spanish painting as clearly foretelling the spontaneity of composition, lightness of movement, and decorativeness of the eighteenth century. The best of these is the charming genre piece, *The Women at the Window* or *The Duenna.*

Bibliography: G. C. WILLIAMSON, *Murillo* (London 1902). A. F. CALVERT, *Murillo* (London 1908). A. MUÑOZ, ed., *Murillo* (Leipzig 1943). A. L. MAYER, *Murillo* (Klassiker der Kunst in Gesamtausgaben 22; 2d ed. Stuttgart 1923); U. THIEME and F. BECKER, eds., *Allgemeines Lexikon der bildenden Künstler von der Antike bis zur Gegenwart* (Leipzig 1907–38) 25: 285–287. G. KUBLER and M. SORIA, *Art and Architecture in Spain and Portugal and Their American Dominions, 1500 to 1800* (*Pelican History of Art*, ed. N. PEVSNER (Baltimore 1953–) Z17; 1959). O. F. L. HAGEN, *Patterns and Principles of Spanish Art* (Madison 1943). G. JEDLICKA, *Spanish Painting,* tr. J. M. BROWN JOHN (New York 1964).

[R. J. VEROSTKO]

MURNER, THOMAS

Satirist and vigorous foe of Luther; b. Oberehnheim, Alsace, Dec. 24, 1475; d. Oberehnheim, Aug. 22, 1537. Murner entered the Order of Friars Minor Conventual at the age of 15 and was ordained when he was 19. Between

1495 and 1502 he traveled in France, Germany, and Poland, studying at Freiburg, and receiving the M.A. degree at Paris, and the Th.B. at Cracow. He returned to Strassburg in 1502. In 1506 Emperor Maximilian I made him poet laureate. He criticized in satire the abuses of the Church, and welcomed the reformers until they attacked dogmas and tradition. From this time he became the champion of Catholicism at Strassburg against Lutheranism and at Lucerne against Zwinglianism. The Peace of Zurich in 1529 stipulated that Murner be brought to trial before judges of the Protestant cantons, but he fled to the Palatinate. In 1530 he returned to Oberehnheim, where he remained until his death. Murner represents the contrasts of his age. He was ardent for reform, yet crude in his writings; passionate for novelties, but an advocate of tradition; frivolous and grave, restless and tormented with the contradictions of the time.

Murner's works include *Chartiludium logicae* (Cracow 1507); *Ludus studentum Friburgensium* (Frankfort 1512); *Arma patientiae, Germania nova, Narrenbeschwörung* (Strassburg, 1519); *Der lutherischen evangelischen Kirchendieb und Ketzerkalender* (Lucerne 1526); translation of the *Defense of the Seven Sacraments* by Henry VIII (Strassburg 1522); and *Causa helvetica orthodoxae fidei* (Lucerne 1528).

Bibliography: L. GAUS, ''Thomas Murner,'' in *German Writers of the Renaissance and Reformation 1280–1580* (Detroit 1997) 184–97, bibliography. I. BACKUS, ''Augustine and Jerome in Thomas Murner's De Augustiniana Hieronymianaque Refomatione Peotarum,'' in *Autoritas Patrum II* (Mainz 1998) 13–25. A. BERGER, *Satirische Feldzuge wider die Reformation: Thomas Murner, Daniel von Soest* (Darmstadt 1967).

[R. J. BARTMAN]

MURPHY, JOHN

Spiritual director, preacher; b. Dublin, Dec. 29, 1710; d. Dublin, July 3, 1753. He was the son of Bryan Murphy, tallow chandler of Thomas Street, Dublin, and Alice McMahon. Bryan, deprived of his father by the Williamite wars, through apprenticeship had been brought up a Presbyterian, but returned to the Church on his deathbed. John showed early promise, was sent to Santiago in 1727, and then went to Salamanca, where his brilliance, linguistic ability, and ascetic spirit made a notable impression. Ill health compelled his return to Dublin, where he was ordained. His priestly ministry was remarkable for charity, preaching that attracted many non-Catholics, and extraordinary influence with the crowds in a time of many riots. Tireless in counteracting the effects of the Charter Schools, in providing for orphans, in caring for the wayward, he undermined a weak constitution by his unremitting apostolate in Dean Swift's Dublin, coupled with his self-mortification. Though a canon, he remained always an assistant priest in his native parish of St. Catherine. In 1750 he visited Rome to solicit help in the struggle against the Charter Schools and received the Doctory of Divinity degree. His funeral evoked an extraordinary manifestation of public grief, noted by the Protestant press of the day.

Bibliography: *An Account of the Life . . . of Rev. John Murphy, D.D.* (Dublin 1753).

[J. J. MEAGHER]

MURPHY, JOHN JOSEPH

Publisher and printer; b. County Tyrone, Ireland, March 12, 1812; d. Baltimore, MD, May 27, 1880. His parents, Bernard and Mary (McCullough) Murphy, immigrated to Delaware when John was ten years old. After attending New Castle Academy, Delaware, he learned printing in Philadelphia and about 1835 moved to Baltimore where he established a book and stationery store. He married Margaret E. O'Donnoghue (1852), who died in 1869; they had seven children. During his publishing career, which began in 1836, he issued 1,458 editions of 817 titles, the peak year being 1860 with 91 imprints. Spiritual reading and devotional works constituted the largest category with 100 entries, the most famous being Cardinal Gibbons's *The Faith of Our Fathers,* which sold more than two million copies. As the publisher of documents pertaining to the dogma of the Immaculate Conception he was awarded a papal gold medal in 1855; for the *Acta et Decreta* of the Second Plenary Council of Baltimore (*see* BALTIMORE, COUNCILS OF), he was given the title of ''Typographer of the Holy See.'' In the field of serials, he published the *U.S. Catholic Magazine* (1842–49), later absorbed by the *Catholic Mirror.* He launched one of the earliest Catholic juveniles, the *Catholic Youth Magazine* (1857–61), and was the publisher (1859–61) of the *Metropolitan Catholic Almanac and Laity's Directory,* begun (1833) as the *U.S. Catholic Almanac.* The Murphy imprint appeared on many speeches, especially of those of congressmen, on five by Jefferson Davis, for example, and on several by Stephen Douglas. For a quarter of a century he published for the Maryland Historical Society of which he was a member. The Murphy firm was dissolved in 1943 and the New York firm of P. J. Kenedy took over the assets.

[E. P. WILLGING]

MURRAY, DANIEL

Archbishop of Dublin; b. near Arklow, County Wicklow, April 18, 1768; d. Dublin, Feb. 26, 1852. After studies at the Irish College in Salamanca, Spain, he was ordained (1792) and then served as a curate in Dublin and Arklow. At the request of the aged Archbishop John TROY of Dublin, Murray was consecrated his coadjutor bishop with the right of succession (1809). A man of gentle manner and moderate views, Murray was active at a critical time for the Church in Ireland. He was president of St. Patrick's College, Maynooth (1812–13). His deep involvement in the veto controversy caused him to visit Rome in 1814 and again in 1815 to oppose granting the British government a veto over Irish ecclesiastical appointments. Largely because of Irish opposition, the veto proposal was dropped. As archbishop of Dublin (1823–52), Murray devoted much attention to providing schools and hospitals, especially for the poor. With Mary AIKENHEAD he founded the Irish Sisters of Charity (1811). Under his patronage Catherine MCAULEY introduced the Sisters of Mercy in Ireland, and Frances BALL established the Ladies of Loretto in Dublin. Murray encouraged the Irish Christian Brothers to work in his diocese. During the struggle for Catholic EMANCIPATION, Murray was an active supporter of the Catholic Association. His political views were always Whig rather than nationalist. Usually he avoided political controversy, but he did not hesitate to oppose Daniel O'CONNELL during the agitation to repeal Ireland's legislative union with England. Murray cooperated with the government in establishing the Commission for Charitable Donations and Bequests (1844–45), despite O'Connell's opposition. Murray also upheld the government's program for higher education (the so-called godless colleges) against O'Connell, Archbishop John MacHale, and the majority of the bishops. Successive British governments sought Murray's advice on matters concerning Catholics.

Bibliography: W. MEAGHER, *Notices of Life and Character of . . . Murray, Late Roman Catholic Archbishop of Dublin . . .* (Dublin 1853). J. T. GILBERT, *Dictionary of National Biography from the Earliest Times to 1900,* 63 v. (London 1885–1900) 13:1249. P. BOYLAN, *Souvenir of the Centenary of the Death of Most Rev. Daniel Murray* (Dublin 1952).

[K. B. NOWLAN]

MURRAY, JOHN COURTNEY

Jesuit theologian and expert on Church-state relations; b. New York City, Sept. 12, 1904; d. New York City, Aug. 16, 1967; the son of Michael John and Margaret Courtney Murray; entered the Society of Jesus in 1920; ordained June 25, 1933. Murray was educated at Weston College (B.A., 1926), Boston College (M.A., 1927), Woodstock College in Maryland (S.T.L., 1934), and the Gregorian University in Rome (S.T.D., 1937). Upon completing his studies at the Gregorian University,

he was appointed professor of dogmatic theology at Woodstock, the Jesuit theological seminary for the Maryland province, where he remained on the staff until his death. He was one of the chief editors of the scholarly quarterly, *Theological Studies* (1941–1967); visiting professor of Medieval Philosophy and Culture at Yale (1951–52); and noted peritus at Vatican Council II. He also served as director of the John La Farge Institute in New York City, a center for the interreligious and interracial dialogue that was Murray's life-long commitment.

Murray first gained prominence through a series of literary debates on the questions of ecumenical cooperation, religious freedom, and the Church-state relationship. Convinced that the Catholic Church could not accomplish a redemptive purpose in society and history on its own, he began to promote what was then known as "inter-religious cooperation." This led to several bishops and theologians accusing him of promoting indifferentism. At the same time, many Jews and Protestants were equally suspicious of Catholic motives in "inter-religious cooperation," fearing that the Catholic Church would infringe on the religious freedom of non-Catholics. Writing in *Theological Studies* along with two other prominent Jesuits, John La Farge and Wilfried Parsons, Murray defended his view on Church-state relations and religious freedom against the attacks of several conservative theologians, notably Francis CONNELL C.Ss.R., Joseph Clifford FENTON and George Shea, writing in the *American Ecclesiastical Review.* The discussion continued in the two journals for more than eight years, and attracted national and international attention. In the debates, Murray strongly insisted that the American system of Church-state relations was in fact the most desirable form and should be acknowledged as such by the Vatican.

Murray's view attracted the criticism of Cardinal Ottaviani, secretary of the Holy Office, who denounced Murray's stance without naming him in a lecture on the duties of a Catholic state toward religion on March 5, 1953. After being assured by PIUS XII'S private secretary, Robert Leiber, S.J. that Ottaviani's views were his own, and by other sources that Pius XII's subsequent speech in December 1953 on tolerance was a diplomatic repudiation of Ottaviani, Murray delivered a lecture at THE CATHOLIC UNIVERSITY OF AMERICA in March 1954 where he publicly stated that Pius XII had repudiated the position of Ottaviani on church-state relations. After learning of this, Ottaviani initiated a formal investigation into Murray's views. At a session on July 7, 1954, the Holy Office held that Murray's views, summarized in four propositions, were condemned as "erroneous." These were communicated to Murray by the Jesuit Father General in 1954. The Holy Office also attempted, without success, to halt the publication of a book by the University of Notre Dame Press that contained an essay of Murray's that was deemed objectionable. In October 1954, Murray's chief critics, Fenton and Connell, were given copies of the four propositions against Murray and informed of the measures against him, but they were told that these measures were to be kept under wraps.

Under pressure from the Holy Office, Murray's Jesuit superiors in Rome requested that he stop speaking and writing on the topic. When his 1955 essay to clarify and defend his position was rejected by the Roman censor, Murray was advised by his Jesuit superiors to withdraw from this area of enquiry. After another attempt in 1958 to clarify his stance was refused permission, Murray turned to what he called a "public philosophy," a set of principles derived from natural law that could serve as the foundation of a pluralistic society, providing the criteria for addressing social-ethical issues. In 1960, a selection of his many essays on this issue was published as *We Hold These Truths: Reflections on the American Proposition,* which subsequently earned him a place on the cover of *Time* magazine.

During the second session of Vatican Council II, Murray became one of the most influential and best known periti from the United States. Notwithstanding the repudiation of his views in the Theological Commission's first draft on Church and state, Cardinal Spellman secured Murray's appointment as a peritus, enabling him to be the U.S. bishops' chief adviser on Church-state matters. Murray was entrusted by Cardinal BEA and his committee with the task of rewriting the Declaration on Religious Freedom (*Dignitatis humanae*), following the suggestions of the Council fathers in the second session. The final draft of the document, promulgated in 1965, adheres for the most part to the language and reasoning of Murray. In addition, his many appearances before various national groups of bishops contributed to the successful acceptance of his ideas on religious freedom by the Council. He spent the final two years of his life writing and lecturing on the Declaration on Religious Freedom.

In addition to many periodical articles, Murray is the author of the following books: *We Hold These Truths* (1961), *The Problem of God* (1963), *Yesterday and Today* (1963), *Problems of Religious Freedom* (1965), and editor of *Religious Liberty, An End and A Beginning* (1966). A selection of Murray's important writings may be found in J. C. Murray, *Bridging the Sacred and the Secular: Selected Writings*, ed. J. L. Hooper (Washington, DC 1994).

Bibliography: D. PELOTTE, *John Courtney Murray: Theologian In Conflict* (New York 1976). D. GONNET, *La liberté religieuse à Vatican II: La contribution de John Courtney Murray* (Paris 1994). J. L. HOOPER, *The Ethics of Discourse: The Social Philosophy of John Courtney Murray* (Washington, DC 1986). R. MCELROY, *The Search for an American Public Theology: The Contribution of John Courtney Murray* (New York 1989).

[C. P. MICHAEL/J. M. KOMONCHAK]

MURRAY, PATRICK

Theologian; b. Clones, County Monaghan, Ireland, Nov. 18, 1811; d. Maynooth, Nov. 15, 1882. He entered Maynooth in 1829 and was elected a Dunboyne scholar, which meant three years of graduate study. He was appointed to a chair in theology and occupied it until his death. His major theological work, *De Ecclesia Christi* (3 v. Dublin 1860–66), was long a source book for Catholic controversialists. He was intensely interested in the theological education of the laity and wrote four volumes of *Essays, Chiefly Theological* (Dublin 1850–53) for this purpose. At his death he was prefect of the Dunboyne Establishment, revered for his kindliness as a professor, for his holiness of life and for his intellectual gifts.

Bibliography: D. COGHLAN, C. G. HERBERMANN, ed., *The Catholic Encyclopedia,* 16 v. (New York 1907–14) 10:646–647.

[A. ROCK]

MURRI, ROMOLO

Italian priest, sociologist, politician, publicist, Modernist; b. Montesampietrangeli (Ascoli Piceno), Aug. 27, 1870; d. Rome, March 12, 1944. After ordination (1893) he studied at the University of Rome, founded the Catholic periodical *Vita nuova,* participated in the origins of the Federazione universitaria cattolica italiana, and adhered enthusiastically to the Catholic social movement and to Christian Democracy. *Cultura sociale,* a periodical begun by him in 1898, advocated a new political and social direction for Catholic activity. Soon he came into conflict with the leadership of the Opera dei Congressi and its president, Giambattista Paganuzzi, and guided a group, composed mostly of young persons, that was eager for independence and for predominance in the entire Catholic movement. Murri was unable to reach an understanding even with the second (social) group of the Opera dei Congressi, the one most open and disposed to collaborate, because of the ever more direct intervention of the Holy See in the Catholic social movement during the last years of Pope Leo XIII. The widening of the conflict induced Pope Pius X to suppress the Opera dei Congressi and to reorganize on other bases Italian CATHOLIC ACTION. Murri became discontented, partly because he was not placed in charge, and founded the Lega democratica nazionale, condemned by Pope Pius X in 1906. Passing from the political to the doctrinal field, Murri showed himself favorable to philosophico-theological modernism, in rebellion against the hierarchy. In 1907 Murri was suspended *a divinis,* and in 1909 he was excommunicated. Some of his best disciples then abandoned him. He continued his conflict in the new *Rivista di cultura,* the organ of the Lega democratica nazionale. Turning again to political life, he was elected a deputy (1909) and joined the extreme left. After losing all his political influence, he devoted himself to writing for the liberal press. Murri was a very talented man and a prolific author who could arouse enthusiasm, but who was incapable of directing a movement or collaborating with one. He returned to the Church in 1943.

Bibliography: P. SCOPPOLA, ''R. Murri e la prima democrazia cristiana,'' *Il Mulino* 6 (1957): 99–115; ''Il modernismo politico in Italia: La Lega democratica nazionale,'' *Rivista storica italiana* 69 (1957): 61–109; *Dal Neoguelfismo alla Democrazia cristiana* (2d ed. Rome 1961); *Crisi modernista e rinnovamento cattolico in Italia* (Bologna 1961). B. BROGI, *La Lega democratica nazionale* (Rome 1959).

[A. MARTINI]

MUSIC (PHILOSOPHY)

Initially music (Lat. *musica,* Gr. μουσική [τέχνη]) was employed in a broad sense to signify any human art over which the nine Muses presided. It was then gradually restricted in meaning to signify the fine art of combining vocal and instrumental sounds into rhythmic, melodic, and harmonic structure. It is generally regarded as the most moving emotionally of all the arts. Since the concern of philosophers with music is summarized in their attempts to arrive at ever more precise definitions, this article explores in a summary fashion the positions of a number of philosophers on the nature of music.

Greek Thought. Among available documents, the fragments of the Pythagoreans are the oldest. Their principal interest in music was to discern the mysterious role of number in the physicomathematical order. By means of this investigation, they discovered three important truths about music: (1) tonal intervals can be described by fixed numerical relations: (2) harmony is produced by contraries (namely, high and low sounds); and (3) an analogy exists between geometric and musical harmony inasmuch as (*a*) musical harmony has a continuity similar to the continuity of various geometric figures and solids, and (*b*) musical harmonies can involve inverted proportions. (*See* PYTHAGORAS AND PYTHAGOREANS.)

Plato. The divine origin of harmony and rhythm was emphasized by PLATO. Thus God has produced in man the natural inclination to produce harmony and rhythm, not at random, but ultimately in imitation of spiritual harmony (*Ion* 534D, E). Mathematics, according to Plato, is of considerable help in making a clear delineation of rhythms and harmonies (*Rep.* 400). In the *Laws* (812C), he describes music as ''the movement of melodies imitating the soul agitated by the passions.''

Aristotle. In general, ARISTOTLE accepts what his predecessors have said about music (*Pol.* 1340a 14–19; 1340b 5–10; 1341b 8–15, 23–40). In his extended consideration of music in the *Politics* (1339a 11–1342b 33), he discusses the role of music in the education of youth, and in this context manifests certain formalities about music not previously recognized or made explicit. Aristotle agrees with the common view that music imitates the movement of human emotions (*Poet.* 1447a 20–25; *Pol.* 1340a 19–1340b 10). But since human emotions are related to human action, music imitates artistically human action as well, and therefore should first be examined in a general consideration of all the arts (*Poet.* 1447a 14–17).

In the extant writings of Aristotle there is not much treatment of music distinctively as an art form. In some agreement with Plato, Aristotle recognizes that the formal principles for disposing musical matter are derived from mathematics; arithmetic provides number, which ensures proportion within and among rhythms and harmonies, and geometry serves as the foundation for conceiving and achieving musical coherence (cf. *Phys.* 194a 8: *Meta.* 1004a 6–8). Because of this special relation between music and mathematics, music is a distinct science and art (*Anal. post.* 76a 9–15, 23–25). Yet music has something in common with the arts of epic, tragedy, comedy, dithryambic poetry, dancing, and painting (*Poet.* 1447a 20–1447b 15; 1448a 1–18; 1449a 1–12). From the general science of poetics, music derives the distinction of meters and their capacity for mutual order with a view to signifying epic, tragic, or comic action (*ibid.*). In this way, music can be understood to signify the order of human emotions as related particularly to these three types of action.

Since man is naturally inclined to be iambic in speech, Aristotle maintains that the iamb is the natural meter (*ibid.* 1449a 24–27). The external use of the iamb, however, is traceable to the human inclination to resolve problems; and the iamb contains the sign of indecisiveness (the ''arsis'' or light measure) as its first part, the sign of decisiveness (the ''thesis'' or weighty measure) as its second part. Thus iambic music, or music wherein the iamb is the architectonic and regulating meter, is especially apt to help man develop his natural propensity to speak and move decisively, and, indirectly, to judge

"Parnassus," fresco by Raphael, detail showing Apollo as the symbol of music, playing the viola da braccio, surrounded by the Muses, in the Stanza della Segnatura, Vatican Palace; fresco completed in 1510.

decisively (*Pol.* 1340a 16–19; 1340a 40–1340b 14; 1341a 3–9).

Aristotle goes on to discuss the musical "modes," which are established by the proportion of harmony to rhythm (*Pol.* 1341a 17–1342b 17). Thus the Doric mode is the best for the training of young persons because the Doric harmonies have the best proportion to iambic meter, whereas the proportion of the Lydian harmonies to the iamb is not very clear and is, therefore, more suitable for very young children and elderly persons (*Pol.* 1342a 1–1342b 30).

Plotinus and the Prescholastic Tradition. PLOTI-NUS starts his examination of music by observing that its ulterior purpose is to bear the listener beyond nature, to the highest beauty, whereby the soul, being beautified, becomes like God (*Enneads* 1.6.6). More generally, however (and here Plotinus makes explicit a truth generally presupposed in Aristotle's discussions), music has the

poetic purpose of making man attentive to some truth that should be examined (*ibid.* 4.4.40). This it accomplishes by binding his irrational appetites. As regards the signification of the meters, Plotinus notes that the art concerning sounds is analogous to "intelligible rhythm" (*ibid.* 5.9.11).

The contributions of St. AUGUSTINE to traditional doctrine on music are considerable. Observing the proportion between musical continuity and the muscular control exercised by the singer, he describes music as "the science of good modulation." Since this proportion has a similar effect upon the listener, he goes on to say that music is the science moving man "by the preserved dimensions of tempi and intervals" (*Musica* 1.2–3). On the basis of the foregoing, music is a principle whereby man can know, analogously, the harmony of God's government (*Epist.* 166.5.13); and, from the knowledge of the immutable numbers in music, one can analogize to immutable Truth (*Musica* 6; *Retract.* 1.11).

In addition to his extensive consideration of the relation between mathematics and music, BOETHIUS distinguishes three types of music: (1) mundane, found especially in the phenomena of the heavens; (2) human, which gives the incorporeal vivacity of reason to the body and reconciles the rational and irrational parts of the soul; and (3) that which enables instruments to serve melody (*De instit. mus.* 1. 2). According to his description of "human" music, then, one purpose of music is to counteract sluggishness in the body and its faculties (*ibid.* 5.2).

Whether Boethius arrived at this conclusion on his own or because of his close friendship with CASSIODORUS is hard to discern. One of the best read and most extensive writers on music during the early Middle Ages, Cassiodorus was more interested in proportion and harmony as achieved in musical works than under their strictly mathematical aspects. He describes music as "the discipline which examines the differences and accords among mutually congruous things, that is, sounds" (*Comm. in Ps.* 97). The suggested analogous supposition of the term "sounds" is confirmed by his tenet that sonorous music is the symbol of all physical and moral harmony (*Epist. ad Boeth.*). This harmony is readily discerned in the first-accomplished, although nonprimary, effect of music, namely, pleasure in the experience of bodily well-being and of the soul's love for the body. Indeed, there is a mysterious bond between musical pleasure and supreme happiness, because aesthetic joy is a symbol of happiness in heaven; the satisfaction of the soul in music is especially analogous to the beatific vision because of the similarity in the respective effortless acts of the intellect (*De anima* 12).

Within its own scope, music frees man from the cares of life, distracts him from his occupations and preoccupations, and raises him to fully interesting activities (*Epist. ad Boeth.*). Cassiodorus held that, by promoting fortitude, the Dorian mode promotes also modesty and chastity. By the use of harmonies of a range lower than those employed by the Greeks, the Phrygian mode can animate the soul to fight against evil, while the Lydian mode comforts the person who feels defeated (*ibid.*). According to Cassiodorus there are three parts of music, namely, harmony, rhythm, and meter (*ibid.*). Vocal music should observe the notes, pauses, accents, pedal melody, and "composition" of the phrase (*ibid.*). Finally, he mentions the fact that natural overtones and natural undertones are contained in the human voice as focused on distinct mid-range tones, and that this fact constitutes the basic meaning of "symphony" (or "sounding together").

High Scholasticism and Grosseteste. Most of St. ALBERT THE GREAT's important observations on music are contained in his *Commentary on Aristotle's Politics* (bk. 8). In addition to his many references to Aristotle's doctrine on music. St. THOMAS AQUINAS made a theological application of the Aristotelian summation, with further analyses, in his *Commentary on Psalm 32*.

The coherence of the tradition concerning music up to and including Aquinas is rather clear. ROBERT GROSSETESTE, however, introduced a subtle confusion that served to obscure this solid tradition for at least 6 centuries. As summarized by De Bruyne (*Études d'Esthétique médiévale* 3: 139–148), Grosseteste teaches that there are five fundamental proportionalities, identically repeated in a whole, from which is derived "all beauty, that is, all 'concord,' whatever the magnitudes may be." This fundamental, universal, metaphysical principle is as true of plastic beauty as it is of sonic beauty (*De luce* 59). The five proportionalities are at the basis of harmony in the musical arts: music, dancing, and poetry (*ibid.*). Both sonic and visible forms can be represented by simple figures (*De gen. sonorum* 8). All these forms are reduced to movements, which can be measured and ordered according to the principles of spatial proportionality, as well as by time measures (*De artibus liberalibus* 2). One and the same discipline concerns the proportions in singing and in the movements of the body (*ibid.* 3). All artistic compositions, however, are regulated by the number ten and the simple relations that it contains, and the ethical effects of music are based upon the concordance between the proportionality in the soul and the proportionality of sensible nature (*ibid.*).

THOMAS OF YORK and ROGER BACON extend Grosseteste's position, Bacon holding that music is the fundamental art, since, without it, grammar and the other arts of the trivium cannot possibly be learned with any thoroughness (*Opus majus* 4).

Here one has an attempted philosophical justification of formalistic music, that is, music without pulsation (or genuine modulation). The truths partially contained in Grosseteste's position are that the proportions established by number do regulate artistic production; that geometry is a discipline that enables the artist to establish coherence (taken in its full analogous meaning) in the work he produces; and that what is directly imitated is natural movement (especially human motion). But by reducing all these truths to mathematical proportions, Grosseteste tends to destroy the hierarchy of artistic signification.

Renaissance and Modern Developments. A reaction against this position was manifested early in the RENAISSANCE by M. FICINO, who held that "love is the master of all the arts," including music. Later G. VICO taught that, like poetry, music has divine and heroic characteristics; it is the expression of "the most violent passions of the nascent human race," and that, therefore, music is the first expression of man, coming before words and the reflections of the "pure mind" (*Scienza nuova*). Apparently, then, Vico was restoring the analogous signification of music; yet his dialectical language prevents one from establishing this point with certainty. He arrived at Roger Bacon's cited position, yet based upon another principle.

For G. W. LEIBNIZ, music is "a hidden arithmetical exercise of the mind not knowing how to number itself" (*Epist.* 154). According to Immanuel KANT, music is "a charming game concerned with the sensations of hearing" (*The Critique of Judgment* 1). He doubts whether it is truly an art, since it is "the pleasure which culture incites [the game of thoughts being the effect of a quasi-mechanical association] and, judged by reason, it has less value than any of the other *beaux-arts*" (*ibid.*). Finally, music is "a continuous commotion and excitation of the soul" (*ibid.*).

Friedrich Schlegel seems to revive Vico's position by holding that, since music expresses the most profound sentiments, it is analogous to philosophy. Arthur SCHOPENHAUER expands this doctrine by teaching that music has an absolute primacy over the other arts because of its inconfutably metaphysical character. Unlike the other arts, music represents the will, rather than ideas. It is an immediate objectivization. Richard WAGNER rejects Schopenhauer's conclusions, but agrees with him in his general position that music manifests the profound essence of things, especially the tragic aspect of human existence. Friedrich NIETZSCHE carries the implicit pessimism of these tenets to its logical extreme by holding that, since music is a Dionysian rather than a plastic-Apollinean art, it is concerned with the world of drunkenness and dreaming.

Recognizing that the foregoing positions involve almost a complete denial of music as a discipline, Eduard Hanslick maintains that the expression of sentiments does not constitute the content of music, and that specifically musical beauty consists only in sounds and their artistic arrangement. Paul Hindemith and Igor Stravinsky have espoused Hanslick's theory as accenting the most important aspect in the act of composing.

The Nature of Music. As is evident from the foregoing, direct contributions to an essential definition of music seem to have ended with the propagation of Grosseteste's ultimate reduction of music to mathematics. From his predecessors, however, one can glean its basic elements and say that music is the art which, through the use of modulation and the mathematical de-lineation of rhythms and harmonies (and, possibly, with the aid of established modes), imitates human emotions as engaged in epic or dramatic action, with the direct aim of recreational contemplation, which indirectly promotes man in the moral good. This definition corresponds with the general position taken by critics and others on the nature of music.

Mention should finally be made of scholars and composers who have developed the science of music under its mathematical and acoustical aspects. In fact, a knowledge of this development, together with a thorough acquaintance with the works representing the whole history of music, and a knowledge of contemporary acoustical research, are all needed for a full appreciation of the philosophical tradition concerned with this subject.

See Also: ART (PHILOSOPHY); LIBERAL ARTS.

Bibliography: J. PORTNOY, *The Philosopher and Music: A Historical Outline* (New York 1955). E. DE BRUYNE, *Études d'esthétique médiévale,* 3 v. (Bruges 1946). A. M. MOSCHETTI, *Enciclopedia filosofica,* 4 v. (Venice-Rome 1957) 3:770–779. R. EISLER, *Wörterbuch der philosophischen Begriffe,* 3 v. (4th ed. Berlin 1927–30) 2:190–191. W. D. ALLEN, *Philosophies of Music History* (New York 1939, repr. 1962). *History of Music in Sound,* ed. G. ABRAHAM et al., 10 v. (New York 1953–59). O. THOMPSON, ed., *The International Cyclopedia of Music and Musicians,* rev. N. SLONIMSKY (5th ed. New York 1949).

[F. C. LEHNER]

MUSSO, CORNELIUS

Theologian; b. Piacenza, April 16, 1511; d. Rome, Jan. 9, 1574. He joined the Conventual Franciscans at Piacenza, studied at the University of Padua, and taught metaphysics at the University of Pavia and theology at the University of Bologna. He was consecrated bishop of Bertinoro in 1541, and was transferred to Bitonto in 1544. Musso gave the inaugural address at the Council of TRENT, and thereafter played a considerable role in the procedural sessions. He took a particularly active part in the discussions on the sources of revelation, original sin, justification, and the Sacraments. At the end of the council, he returned to his diocese to begin the work of reform. Opposition from the court of Naples forced him to give up this work and resign his see in 1572. His sermons fill eight volumes. Musso is faithful to BONAVENTURE and DUNS SCOTUS in theology; his chief works are: the *De Deo Uno et Trino* (Venice 1585), *Commentaria in b. Pauli Epistolam ad Romanos* (Venice 1588), and *De Divina Historia Libri III* (Venice 1585, 1587).

Bibliography: C. E. NORMAN, *Humanist Taste and Franciscan Values: Cornelio Musso and Catholic Preaching in Sixteenth-Century Italy* (New York 1998). G. DE ROSA, "Il Francescano Cornelio Musso dal Concilio di Trento al Dioceso di Bitonto,'' *Rivista di storia della Chiesa in Italia 40* (1986) 55–91. R. J. BARTMAN, ''Cornelius Musso, Tridentine Theologian and Orator,'' *Franciscan Studies* 5 (1945) 247–276. G. ODOARDI, ''Fra Cornelio Musso, O. F. M. Conv. Padre, oratore e teologo al Concilio di Trento,'' *Miscellanea Francescana* 48 (1948) 223–242, 450–478; 49 (1949) 36–71.

[P. FEHLNER]

MU'TAZILITES

The earliest important theological school of ISLAM. The name (Arabic *mu'tazila*) is derived from the verb *i'tazala,* meaning ''to separate oneself from.'' The first Mu'tazilites were political, those who ''separated themselves from'' both 'ALĪ and his opponents in the quarrel over the legitimacy of his succession to the caliphate. Later the term indicated the position that the Muslim grave sinner was neither believer, unbeliever, nor hypocrite, but simply a sinner (*fāsiq*).

History. The founders of the Mu'tazilite school were Wāṣil ibn 'Aṭā' (d. 748) and 'Amr ibn 'Ubayd (d. 762), both of Baṣra. But Abu'l-Hudhayl al-'Allāf (d. 840) was the true founder of Mu'tazilite dogmatics. Other prominent members of the Baṣra school were Mu'ammar, Hishām al-Fuwaṭī al-Aṣamm, and al-Naẓẓām. The Baghdad school was founded by Bishr ibn al-Mu'tamir (d. 826), and included such men as Thumāma ibn Ashras and Ibn Abī Du'ād. Under the Caliphs Ma'mūn, Mu'taṣim, and Wāthiq, Mu'tazilism was the state theology, and its teaching that the QUR'ĀN was created was enforced by a kind of inquisition (*miḥna*). The Caliph Mutawakkil was hostile to the Mu'tazilites, and from his time on the school gradually declined, though it long maintained centers in the eastern part of the empire. After the Mongol invasions it survived mainly among the Zaydites of YEMEN, where it still exists.

Teachings. There are divergencies in doctrine among the many Mu'tazilite doctors, yet nearly all have held the fundamental position expressed in the five basic principles commonly attributed to the Mu'tazilites. The first, pure monotheism (*tawḥid*), is the most important principle of Mu'tazilism, since it is the source of almost all its doctrines. God is one in the strictest sense. Anthropomorphisms are to be denied, or, when they occur in the Qur'ān, are to be interpreted symbolically. The attributes commonly assigned to God have only a figurative meaning and are in no way realities in or distinct from the divine essence. The Qur'ān is created. There is no beatific vision. Several solutions are proposed to the problems of creation and of God's relation to the created world.

The second principle concerns divine justice (*'adl*). God is supremely just. He always does what is best for His creation. He cannot will evil; hence man is personally responsible for his own moral acts. The Mu'tazilites insisted strongly on man's free will, a position that was practically rejected by later ''orthodox'' Muslim theology. The third principle, called ''the promise and the threat'' (*al-wa'd wa'l-wa'īd*), begot discussions concerning the final lot of the believer, sinner, and infidel; the nature of faith and unbelief; grave and light sins; legal questions in general; and the authenticity of traditions. The fourth was the intermediate state of the grave sinner (*al-manzila bayna'l-manzilatayn*). This is not clearly distinct from the two preceding principles. But the discussion of the grave sinner's state involved lengthy consideration of the caliphate and of the legitimacy of the first four caliphs. The fifth principle dealt with commanding good and forbidding evil. The expression is Qur'ānic (e.g., 3.106, 110). Disapproval of evil must be by word and deed, and even by the use of the sword. This was little discussed as time went on. The general framework of these five principles left much room for refinement and difference of opinion, and later discussions often developed into philosophical disputes.

Significance. The Mu'tazilites have sometimes been called rationalists, freethinkers, or liberals of Islam. They were rationalists only in the sense that they used rational argument in their teaching. To this they were forced by the necessity of defending Islam against the dualists (Manichaeans) and the followers of other religions, many of whom became halfhearted converts to Islam. It later became the practice of ''orthodox'' writers to vilify the Mu'tazilites in every possible way. Their writings were destroyed, so that the only surviving Mu'tazilite manuscript, apart from works preserved in Yemen, is the *Kitab al-Intiṣār,* edited by Nyberg in 1925. Certain Zaydite manuscripts in Yemen may lead to a better knowledge of the Mu'tazilites and their teaching. By their polemic they certainly saved Islam from its early adversaries, and by their use of reasoning and philosophy they founded the science of KALĀM. They also contributed much to the development of the sciences of Qur'ān exegesis, jurisprudence, and tradition. Far from being liberal, they showed much intolerance when themselves protected by the state. They played an important role in the development of Muslim theology and profoundly influenced many of the ''orthodox'' theologians. Since the time of Muḥammad 'Abduh, the great Egyptian reformer (d. 1905), there have been indications of a revival of interest in the Mu'tazilites among Muslim thinkers, and even of a return to some of their principal theses. This ''neo-Mu'tazilism'' could have far-reaching effects on the development and direction of modern Islam.

Bibliography: H. S. NYBERG, *Encyclopedia of Islam,* ed. B. LEWIS et al. (2d ed. Leiden 1954–)¹ 3:841–847; *The Shorter Encyclopedia of Islam* (Leiden 1953) 421–427. A. N. NADER, *Le Système philosophique des Mu'tazila* (Beirut 1956). *Kitāb-al-Intiṣār (Le Livre du triomphe et de la réfutation d'lbn al Rawandi l'hérétique),* Arabic text and French translation of Nyberg's 1925 edition referred to in the text. R. CASPAR, "Le Renouveau du Mo'tazalisme," *Mélanges de l'Institut Dominicain d'Études Orientales du Caire* 4 (1957) 141–202. *See also* the relevant bibliographies under ASH'ARĪ, AL-; KALĀM. M. A. COOK, *Commanding Right and Forbidding Wrong in Islamic Thought* (Cambridge, England 2000)

[R. J. MCCARTHY]

MUTH, CARL

Journalist; b. Worms am Rhein, Jan. 31, 1867; d. Reichenhall (Bavaria), Nov. 15, 1944. His parents were devout Catholics, and his father's occupation as church painter brought young Carl early into contact with the problems of art and religion. Muth took six years of his gymnasium studies in Algiers, where the whole spiritual and intellectual ferment of French Catholicism was revealed to him under the influence of Cardinal Charles LAVIGERIE. Muth abandoned early plans for mission work to devote himself to the study of political science and German philology in Giessen, Berlin, and Strassburg. During this time he contributed to the *Mainzer Journal,* was editor (1893–95) of the daily *Der Elsässer* (Strassburg), and published the family magazine *Alte und Neue Welt,* in which he concerned himself principally with the problem of modern literature. In an article "Wem gehört die Zukunft" (1893), he opposed the superstitious belief in progress inherent in materialism and began considering for the first time the possibilities of overcoming the "literary inferiority" of the Catholics in Germany, so as to liberate church and theology from their isolation.

With his polemical works published under the pseudonym of Veremundus (*Steht die katholische Belletristik auf der Höhe der Zeit?,* and *Die literarischen Aufgaben der deutschen Katholiken,* 1899), he launched the "Catholic literary controversy" in which he had to fight on two fronts, against the intellectually unambitious in his own camp and against the "Enlighteners" hostile to the Church. He was severely critical of the literary backwardness of Catholic writers and critics, whom he reproached for "apathy and unconcern for the general artistic endeavors of the nation," denominational prejudice, moral and pedagogical narrowmindedness, and "a positively unbelievable prudery." Simultaneously Muth opposed modernism and its naturalistic and materialistic aberrations, proposing instead an idealistic philosophy. He won the debate with his key work, *Wiedergeburt der Dichtung aus dem religiösen Erlebnis* (1909), directed particularly against his principal opponent, Richard von Kralik and Viennese neoromanticism ("The Gral").

A stay in Paris brought Muth into contact with the *renouveau catholique;* this contact was crucial for his later development. The magazine *Hochland* (a monthly publication "for all fields of knowledge, literature, and art"), which he founded in 1903 to cope with the grave perils and difficulties besetting German Catholic literature, aimed at a "new encounter between Church and culture." Until World War I, *Hochland*'s interests were mainly literary; only in 1916 did the magazine begin to devote attention to political and social problems. Muth became a champion of the concept of democracy within the still predominantly monarchically minded German Catholicism of those days. The essay "Res publica" (1926) typifies his political stand; it is a call to Catholics to become aware of their political responsibility and to cooperate actively in the fashioning of the new social order.

Muth believed that Europe's survival was dependent on the solution of the social question, on whether it would be possible to imbue social democracy with the sentiments and impulses of Christian brotherliness. He made an urgent appeal to all Christians (in "Die Stunde des Bürgertums," 1930) to abandon their antisocialist prejudices and to the socialists to get rid of their anti-Christian resentments. Muth was forthright in his opposition to the rising tide of national socialism (in *Das dritte Reich und die Sturmvögel des Nationalsozialismus,* 1931). *Hochland* maintained its stand even after Hitler had come to power and was banned only in 1941. It resumed publication in 1946 and remained in publication in Munich, under the direction of Muth's long-time associate Karl Schaezler.

Bibliography: K. ACKERMANN, *Der Widerstand der Monatsschrift Hochland gegen den Nationalsozialismus* (Munich 1965), with bibliog. *Wiederbegegnung von Kirche und Kultur in Deutschland: Festschrift für Karl Muth* (Munich 1927).

[O. B. ROEGELE]

MUTTATHUPANDATU, ALPHONSA, BL.

Baptized Anna and called Annakutty, also known as Sister Alphonsa of India, Alphonsa of the Immaculate Conception, Alphonsa of Bharananganam; mystic, virgin of the Syro-Malabar Poor Clares; b. Aug.19, 1910, Arpukara, India; d. July 28, 1946, Bharananganam, India. The fourth child of Joseph Muttahupadathu and his wife Mary, who died shortly after her birth; her family ensured Annakutty was well educated in preparation for a good marriage. Recognizing her vocation to religious life, Annakutty rejected her suitors and disfigured herself with fire so that she would be unmarriageable. Thereafter she was permitted to join the tertiary Clarist sisters in their convent at Bharananganam (Pentecost 1927). With the veil of the postulant she received the name Alphonsa of the Immaculate Conception (Aug. 2, 1928). She became a novice on August 12, 1935 and made final vows the following year. Throughout her life she endured repeated illness and physical pain, but received the consolation of mystical union. She possessed the gift of prophecy and experienced a vision of Saint Thérèse of Lisieux. Alphonsa's death after a prolonged illness went almost unnoticed. However, when miracles were granted to Alphonsa's beloved school children through her intercession, her tomb at Bharananganam became a pilgrimage site. The diocesan process for her beatification began, Dec. 2, 1953, and a miracle wrought through Alphonsa's intercession was approved, July 6, 1985. She and Blessed Kuriokose Chavara became the first Indians raised to the altars, when they were beatified at Kottayam, Archdiocese of Changanacherry, Kerala, India, by John Paul II, Feb. 8, 1986.

Feast: Feb. 8.

Bibliography: K. C. CHACKO, *The Spirituality of Blessed Alphonsa* (Ernakulam 1986). C. G. DEMPSEY, *Kerala Christian Sainthood: Collisions of Culture and Worldview in South India* (Oxford 2001). *Acta Apostolicae Sedis* (1986): 306. *L'Osservatore Romano,* Eng. ed. 7 (1986): 6–7.

[K. I. RABENSTEIN]

MUZI, GIOVANNI

Bishop of Città di Castello and first papal representative to come to the Americas; b. Rome, 1772; d. Spoleto, 1849. With independence, it became necessary for the Spanish-American republics to conduct their own ecclesiastical affairs with the Holy See. In 1822 a Chilean envoy, Archdean José Ignacio CIENFUEGOS, arrived in Rome and requested that a nuncio be sent to Chile with ample power to settle the many critical problems of the Church there. Since Chile was not yet recognized as an independent country, it was decided to send an apostolic vicar, or non-diplomatic representative of the Holy See. Muzi, auditor of Nuncio Pablo Leardi in Vienna since 1817 and a former theology professor of the Roman College, was chosen for the mission. He was named titular archbishop of Filipos and was given faculties for Chile and for all Spanish American countries. These faculties included the naming and consecrating of bishops without further recourse to Rome.

The Muzi Mission, as it became known, left Genoa on Oct. 5, 1823, with Gian Maria Mastai, later Pope Pius IX, as chaplain to the archbishop, and Giuseppe Sallusti, who wrote a history of the mission, as secretary. Muzi's

reception and later expulsion from Buenos Aires, his eight-month stay in Santiago, and his visit to Montevideo belong to the church history of these countries. Before returning to Genoa, where he arrived June 25, 1825, Muzi wrote a *Carta apologética* (Córdoba 1825) defending his mission against his many critics. In Rome the archbishop gave the first detailed report on the condition of the Church in the various countries he visited.

After the personal failure of his mission, he retired from the papal diplomatic service and accepted the bishopric of Città di Castello, where he published an important work of local history, *Memorie ecclesiastichi e civili di Città di Castello* (7 v. 1842–44). He was consulted regularly on Spanish-American Church problems by the Congregation of Extraordinary Ecclesiastical Affairs. A special report he had compiled on his mission to America was lost until recently, but it has been located in the Vatican Archives.

Bibliography: P. LETURIA, *Relaciones entre la Santa Sede e Hispanoamérica,* 3 v. (Rome 1959–60). P. LETURIA and M. BATLLORI, "La primera misión Pontificia a Hispanoamérica, 1823–1825" *Studi e Testi* 229 (1964).

[W. J. COLEMAN]

MYCONIUS, FRIEDRICH

One of the leading Protestant reformers in central Germany; b. Lichtenfels am Main, Dec. 25, 1490; d. Gotha, April 7, 1546. While attending Latin school in Annaberg, Myconius (also called Mecum) encountered Johann TETZEL, the indulgence preacher, and was offended by him. Myconius joined the Franciscan Order, but he failed to find assurance of God's grace in the monastic way of life. In 1524 he fled to Electoral Saxony. He was active as an evangelical preacher in Zwickau and Buchholz and in August 1524 went to Gotha. He reformed the church order, participated in the official church and school visitations in Thuringia in 1527 and 1533, attended the Marburg Colloquy in 1529, contributed to the Nuremberg Concord of 1536, and helped in the negotiations at Schmalkalden in 1537, Frankfurt and Nuremberg in 1539, and Hagenau in 1540. In Melanchthon's place he made a trip to England in 1538 for union efforts with the English Church. He helped to introduce the Reformation in Annaberg and Leipzig in 1539 upon the death of Duke George.

Bibliography: F. MYCONIUS, *Geschichte der Reformation,* ed. O. CLEMEN (Leipzig 1914); *Der Briefwechsel des Friedrich Mykonius, 1524–1546,* ed. H. U. DELIUS (Tübingen 1960). P. SCHERFFIG, *Friedrich Mekum von Lichtenfels: Ein Lebensbild aus dem Reformationszeitalter* (Leipzig 1909). R. JAUERNIG, *Die Religion in Geschichte und Gegenwart,* 6 v. (Tübingen 1957–63) 4:1229–1230.

[L. W. SPITZ]

MYCONIUS, OSWALD

Swiss humanist and reformer: b. Lucerne, Switzerland, 1488; d. Basel, Oct.14, 1552. Myconius (originally Geisshäusler) was educated at Rottweil, Bern, and at the University of Basel (1510–14). He came to Zürich as a teacher in 1516. In 1518 his influence was decisive in securing the election of his friend Huldrych ZWINGLI as people's priest of Great Minster. He began intensive study of the Bible in 1520 and went to Lucerne in that same year to teach. His departure in 1522 was occasioned by his open espousal of the Reformation. After a brief sojourn in Einsiedeln, he returned to Zürich in 1523 to assist Zwingli in his reform of the city. In 1531 he moved to Basel, there to succeed OECOLAMPADIUS as antistes of the city in August 1532. In addition to writing commentaries on several books of the Bible, he wrote a brief biography of Zwingli in 1532, prepared the Basel Confession of 1534, and contributed to the formulation of the First Helvetic Confession of 1536 (*see* CONFESSIONS OF FAITH, II: PROTESTANT CONFESSIONS OF FAITH).

Bibliography: K. R. HAGENBACH, *Johann Oekolampad und Oswald Myconius* (Leben und ausgewählte Schriften der Väter und Begründer der reformirten Kirche 2; Elberfeld 1859) 309–462. O. E. STRASSER, *Die Religion in Geschichte und Gegenwart*, 7 v. (3d ed. Tübingen 1957–65) 4:1230.

[C. GARSIDE, JR.]

MYSTAGOGY

Mystagogy ("interpretation of mystery") is the final period of the initiation of adults (*Rite of Christian Initiation of Adults* [Study Edition, Chicago 1988] 37). During this period the meaning of the Sacraments is explained to those who have newly received them. When Baptisms take place at the Easter Vigil, the mystagogy are held at the Sunday Masses of the Easter season (ibid. 40). No specific ceremonies are prescribed for this period, save that the neophytes maintain a special place among the faithful and are mentioned in the homily and the General Intercessions (ibid. 236). The purpose of the mystagogy is to enable the newly baptized to draw from their sacramental experience a new sense of the faith, the Church, and the world (ibid. 38). The families of the neophytes, their godparents, and the entire congregation share in this experience with them, but a heavy responsibility must fall upon the "mystagogue," the person (normally the pastor) who opens to them the mysteries of faith.

The practice of mystagogy emerged in the early Church, where the term "Mystagogical Catechesis" (*Katecheseis Mystagogikai*) referred to the postbaptismal catechesis of the neophytes. Sources indicate that this period of postbaptismal catechesis lasted anywhere from five to seven days during Easter week. Its purpose was to explain to the neophytes the significance of the various rituals, signs, and symbols that they experienced at their initiation at the Easter Vigil. In contrast to the didactic orientation of prebaptismal catechesis, which focused on the communication of the foundational creedal tenets of the Christian faith, postbaptismal catechesis explored rituals, metaphors, symbols, images, and stories to reveal the deeper significance of the initiation experience.

It was at the mystagogy that St. AMBROSE, St. CYRIL OF JERUSALEM, and other Church Fathers preached their classic homilies on the Christian Sacraments, opening their meaning to those who were newly frequenting them. It is here that the Church has traditionally taught the meaning of the sacramental life in Christ. These postbaptismal homilies represent some of the richest sources of patristic sacramental theology.

With the decline of adult baptism and the corresponding rise in infant baptism in the Middle Ages, the period of mystagogy, together with the CATECHUMENATE process, fell into disuse. It was reintroduced in 1972, with the promulgation of the *Rite of Christian Initiation of Adults*. For the Church today the period remains one of great importance both pastorally and pedagogically. It requires the active participation not only of the newly baptized and the pastor, but of the whole congregation, for it incorporates the newly baptized into the community of the faithful and places instruction in the meaning of the Sacraments in the context of their frequent reception. In this way the newly baptized can deepen and enrich their own experience of the Sacraments by a clear exposition of the Sacraments' inner meaning for their own lives and that of the whole Church and a showing forth of that meaning in the actual community life of the Church.

Bibliography: *Rite of Christian Initiation of Adults* (Study Edition, Chicago 1988). H. RILEY, *Christian Initiation: A Comparative Study* (Washington, D.C. 1974). F. J. YARNOLD, *The Awe-Inspiring Rites of Initiation* (Edinburgh and Collegeville 1994). M. E. JOHNSON, *The Rites of Christian Initiation: Their Evolution and Interpretation* (Collegeville 1999).

[L. L. MITCHELL/EDS.]

MYSTERIUM FIDEI

Encyclical letter, "Mystery of the Faith," promulgated by Pope Paul VI on Sept. 3, 1965. In light of the initiative of the Second Vatican Council to reform the sacred liturgy of the Church, *Mysterium fidei* provides clarification and direction concerning the doctrine and worship of the Eucharist.

The introduction establishes that when treating the reform of the liturgy, Vatican II "considered nothing to be more important than urging the faithful to participate actively and with sound faith and with utmost devotion in the celebration of this most holy mystery; to offer it with the priest to God as a sacrifice for their own salvation and for that of the whole world, and to find in it spiritual nourishment'' (no. 2). Following these points, the pope affirms, ''the mystery of the Eucharist is at the heart and center of the liturgy itself'' (no. 3). He explains that with regard to the Eucharist the council ''wished to make evident the indissoluble relationship between faith and devotion'' (no. 4).

In part 2, ''Reasons for Pastoral Concern and Anxiety,'' Paul VI registers alarm at ''opinions'' about the Mystery of the Eucharist that circulate ''in written or spoken word'' (no. 10). As a corrective to these judgments, he decrees that the following interpretations are ''not allowable'': ''to emphasize . . . the Mass 'of the community' to the extent of disparaging Masses celebrated in private; or to stress the sign value of the sacrament as if the symbolism . . . expresses fully and exhaustively the meaning of Christ's presence; or to discuss the mystery of transubstantiation without mentioning the changing of the . . . bread . . . and wine . . . as stated by the Council of Trent; or finally, to propose and to act on the opinion according to which Christ the Lord is no longer present in the consecrated hosts left after the celebration of the sacrifice of the Mass'' (no. 11).

Part 3, ''The Holy Eucharist Is a Mystery of Faith,'' highlights the concept of *mystery*: the Eucharist is a ''very great mystery'' and a ''Mystery of Faith'' (no. 15). Believers must approach the Eucharistic mystery with ''humble respect, not following human [rational] arguments . . . but adhering firmly to divine revelation'' (no. 16). Investigations of this unparalleled mystery should be guided by ''the magisterium of the Church'' (no. 22). In addition to ''safeguarding'' the integrity of the Eucharistic mystery itself, its ''proper mode of expression'' (no. 23) must also be safeguarded. Thus, the Church has established a ''rule of language,'' which it has ''confirmed . . . with the authority of the councils'' (no. 24).

In part 4, ''The Mystery of the Eucharist Is Verified in the Sacrifice of the Mass,'' the pope reviews traditional Catholic doctrine related to the Mass. Here, he indicates that ''the whole Church . . . in union with Christ in His role as Priest and Victim, offers the Sacrifice of the Mass and is offered in it.'' He also underscores, ''the distinction between the universal priesthood and the hierarchical priesthood is one of essence and not merely one of degree'' (no. 31). Explaining the ''public and social nature of every Mass,'' the pope says, ''Mass is not something private; it is an act of Christ and of the Church.'' As such, ''every Mass is offered not for the salvation of ourselves alone, but also for that of the whole world'' (no. 32).

In part 5, ''In the Sacrifice of the Mass Christ Is Made Sacramentally Present,'' the pope teaches that ''sacrifice and Sacrament pertain inseparably to the same mystery.'' The foundational principle of this instruction is that ''in an unbloody representation of the Sacrifice of the Cross and in application of its saving power, in the Sacrifice of the Mass the Lord is immolated when, through the words of consecration, He begins to be present in a sacramental form under the appearances of bread and wine'' (no. 34). Of the various ways Christ is present in the Church, the Sacrament of the Eucharist ''surpasses all the others.'' To refer to Christ's presence in the Eucharist as ''real'' does not ''exclude all other types of presence as if they could not be 'real' too,'' but is ''presence in the fullest sense,'' that is, ''it is the substantial presence by which Christ, the God-man, is wholly and entirely present.'' It is ''wrong to explain this presence by . . . recourse to the 'spiritual' nature . . . of the Glorified Body of Christ . . . or by reducing it to a kind of symbolism'' (no. 39).

Part 6, ''Christ Our Lord Is Present in the Sacrament of the Eucharist by Transubstantiation,'' reiterates Catholic teaching on transubstantiation: ''the voice of the teaching and praying Church. . . . assures us that the way Christ is made present in this Sacrament is none other than by the change of the whole substance of the bread into His Body, and of the whole substance of the wine into His Blood, and that this . . . change the Catholic Church rightly calls transubstantiation.'' As a consequence of this substantial change, ''the species of bread and wine . . . take on new meaning and a new finality, for they no longer remain ordinary bread and ordinary wine, but become the sign of something sacred, the sign of a spiritual food.'' Thus, transformed bread and wine ''contain a new 'reality' which we may justly term ontological.'' Transubstantiation alters the ''objective reality'' of the bread and wine, ''since after the change of the substance or nature of the bread and wine into the Body and Blood of Christ, nothing remains of the bread and wine but the appearances, under which Christ, whole and entire, in His physical 'reality' is bodily present'' (no. 46).

Part 7, ''Latreutic Worship of the Sacrament of the Eucharist,'' recalls that the Catholic Church ''has always offered and still offers the cult of *Latria* to the Sacrament of the Eucharist, not only during Mass, but also outside of it, reserving Consecrated Hosts . . . exposing them to solemn veneration, and carrying them processionally'' (no. 56). The pope highlights the feast of Corpus Christi as a testimony to this veneration, which continues to give rise to inspirational Eucharistic pieties. Through them, the Catholic Church strives ''to do homage to Christ . . . to thank Him . . . and to implore his mercy'' (no. 63).

The concluding section, "Exhortation to Promote the Cult of the Eucharist," exhorts persons entrusted with the care of believers "to preserve this faith in its purity and integrity" and to "promote the cult of the Eucharist" (no. 64).

[K. GODFREY]

MYSTERY (IN THE BIBLE)

Exegetes of the "History of Religions" school (e.g., W. Bousset and R. Reitzenstein) have suggested that the Pauline use of μυστήριον (Gr. for "mystery") to refer to salvation in Jesus Christ was a borrowing from the pagan mystery religions as part of an attempt to make Christianity understandable to the Greek world (*see* MYSTERY RELIGIONS, GRECO-ORIENTAL). Today, however, it is more widely recognized that "mystery" was an ancient Hebrew theological term that was current in Jewish circles at the time of Christ. This article explains the concept of mystery in the Old Testament, in non-Biblical Jewish thought, and in the New Testament.

In the Old Testament. In the Septuagint (LXX) the word μυστήριον occurs some 21 times; it appears only in the postexilic books (Tobit; Judith; Daniel; Sirach; 2 Maccabees), normally translating the Hebrew word *rāz* (borrowed through Aramaic from Old Persian), which is generally in the plural. There are other Greek synonyms for mystery in these late books, including κρύπτα and ἀπόκρυφα, "secrets, hidden things." In tracing the idea of mystery, one must begin long before the postexilic period with the Hebrew concept of *sôd*, a word which is never translated by μυστήριον. This Hebrew word seems to have originally meant "council, assembly"; but ultimately it came to designate what was decided in a council, namely, "counsel," particularly "secret counsel," and thus "mystery."

Preexilic Period. One of the early theological uses for *sôd* was in reference to the heavenly council. H. W. Robinson, F. Cross, and others have shown that there was a common Semitic belief in an assembly of heavenly beings that decided the fate of the world. In pagan thought it was an assembly of the gods; in Hebrew thought it was an assembly of angels presided over by Yahweh who had the dominant role in making the decision [Jb 1.612; Ps 81(82).1]. There is probably a reference to the heavenly assembly in Gn 1.26, "Let us make man in our image and likeness"; and in Is 40.1 Yahweh's imperative is addressed to the angelic court.

The power of the heavenly *sôd* to enact decrees concerning men gave it practical importance in Hebrew life. The decisions on high were made known to the people by the prophet who was introduced through visions into the sessions of the heavenly assembly. Isaiah's call consists of his seeing the heavenly assembly where God is asking the angels, "Whom shall I send?" (Is 6.8). When Micaiah, son of Imlah, is asked by the King of Israel to prophesy, he answers by telling what he saw in the heavenly assembly (1 Kgs 22.19–22). Amos announces almost as a proverb that God will surely not do anything "until He has revealed his *sôd* to His servants the prophets" (Am 3.7). To know the heavenly *sôd* (council, counsel) became the criterion for distinguishing a true prophet from a false prophet. Jeremiah says scornfully of the false prophets, "For which of them has stood in the *sôd* of Yahweh and seen and heard His word?" (Jer 23.18; see also Jb 15.8).

Postexilic Period. This concept of a prophet's being introduced into the heavenly council and its mysterious counsels was the basis for the importance attributed to heavenly secrets in postexilic Judaism. The Persian loanword *rāz* made its way into Aramaic and Hebrew, alongside *sôd*, to express the concept of mystery. The number of individuals who claimed to have seen the heavenly mysteries increased, as did the types of mysteries that were reported.

In Daniel ch. 2 *rāz* (μυστήριον in the LXX) is used eight times to refer to Nebuchadnezzar's dream and its symbolic contents. No wise man can unravel such mysteries, but only God in heaven who reveals mysteries can make known what shall be. Here "mystery" is employed in what shall become a very frequent usage: a vision of the future given to man by God, in symbols. In apocalyptic literature it will often be an angel who interprets this mystery for the chosen seer, but sometimes God Himself speaks.

The Book of Sirach says that God's secrets, like the vicissitudes of life and the working of providence, are beyond human knowledge (Sir 11.4) and it warns man not to investigate such things (3.21–22). Occasionally, to the humble, God will reveal His secrets [4.18;42.18–19; 3.19 (Hebrew)], as He did in the past to Isaiah (48.24–25). It is in Sir 4.18 that one meets, for the first time, Wisdom as God's agent in revealing mysteries. Besides God's plan for men, mysteries in Sirach include astronomical and meteorological phenomena (43.32) and the secret actions of men, often evil (1.28–29). One way for men to come to a knowledge of mysteries is through a study of ancient traditions found in the Law, and in the teaching of the wise men and the prophets (39.7; 47.15–17).

In the Hellenistic outlook of the Book of Wisdom, the mysteries of God include His plans for the afterlife (Wis 2.22). The origins of Wisdom are classified as mysteries (6.22), and Wisdom herself is initiated into the knowledge of God (8.4). Some of the language of the mystery religions appears in this book (12.5; 14.15) but chiefly by way of attack on these religions. Solomon is pictured as the example of a man to whom God has given true knowledge of a variety of mysteries (7.17–21).

In Non-Biblical Jewish Thought. There are important uses of mystery in extra-Biblical literature. In investigating these it will be useful to distinguish between apocryphal writings in general and the Dead Sea Scrolls in particular.

Apocrypha. The sobriety of the mystery passages in the canonical literature is appreciated when one studies the noncanonical literature. Dating from the 2d century B.C., Enoch presents a fascinating variety of mysteries: (1) evil mysteries (9.6–8; 10.7; 16.3), such as those taught to women by the evil angels—an echo of Gn 6.1–4; (2) cosmic mysteries and their relation to men (41.3; 60.11–22)—an angelic guide introduces Enoch to these astrological secrets; (3) mysteries of God's will and human actions (63.3; 83.7; 84.3)—a special mystery is the judgment God will render on man's deeds (103.2; 68.5); and (4) the mystery of the Son of Man, the Elect One, hidden in God's presence before creation (48.6; 62.7), who shall be revealed on the day of judgment (62.1) to pour forth the secrets of wisdom and counsel that God has entrusted to him (53.1; 62.2).

From A.D. 60 to 150 a series of apocalypses (2 Baruch; 3 Baruch; 4 Ezra) gives witness to the last Jewish developments in the use of "mystery" parallel to the usage of the New Testament. In 2 Baruch are described the visions accorded to Baruch amid the ruins of Jerusalem after the city had fallen to the Babylonians. The term "mysteries" is used for these visions and for their interpretation. The mysteries include cosmic phenomena (48.2–3; see also 3 Baruch 1.8), as well as the happenings of the last time (2 Baruch 81.4; 85.8).

In 4 Ezra are found the visions of Ezra about the fall and rise of Jerusalem. Throughout his life, Ezra had received revelations of the mysteries of God pertaining to the future in store for Jerusalem and the world (6.32–33; 10.38); and in this he was privileged like Moses who also saw "the secrets of the times" (14.5). Some of these mysteries revealed to Ezra are to be kept secret (12.36–37; 14.6 for Moses).

The Dead Sea Scrolls. In the Qumran DEAD SEA Scrolls (DSS) also, one finds mysteries playing an important role. The Hebrew word most frequently used is *rāz,* sometimes occurring in parallelism with *sôd; nistōrôt* (hidden things) also occurs.

The first type of mystery we may distinguish in the DSS concerns God's providence as it affects angels, men, and the future of Israel. In 1QM 14.14 God's "marvelous mysteries" concern the elevating and casting down of the angels. Evil persons are under the dominion of the Angel of Darkness "according to the mysteries of God until the final time set by Him" (1QS 3.20–23; 4.18). On a more personal level the author of 1QH (9.23–24) says to God, "You have chastised me in the mystery of your wisdom." The death of the just in the final war against evil will be according to the mysteries of God to test the eagerness of others (1QM 16.11; 17.8–9). To the Teacher of Righteousness have been revealed secrets concerning the future found in the words of OT prophets (1QpHb 7.1–5); it is perhaps this figure who speaks in 1QS 11.3–4, "He made my eye contemplate His wonders; and the light of my heart, the mystery to be."

A second set of mysteries in the DSS concerns the community's own interpretation of the Law. If we remember that the Qumran community thought of itself as an assembly or council, this use of "mystery" may be related to the origins of the term as the secret counsel of a council. The ideal of intimate union between the sectarians and the angels is a theme of the DSS, and the community's council on earth was considered to be a reflection of the angelic council in heaven (1QS 11.8). Thus, in 11.5–7 one initiated into the community comes to know God's marvelous mysteries, a wisdom hidden from wise men, a fountain of glory hidden from any worldly assembly. In CDC 3.12–14 we hear that to faithful Israelites God revealed the hidden things in which all Israel had gone astray, and then by a process of historical selection the Qumran community became God's final repository of those hidden commands whose observance is necessary for eternal life (3.18–20). Those who are fully accepted as members are to be made "wise in the marvelous and true mysteries amidst the men of the community" (1QS 9.18–19), but they must keep these hidden from the noninitiated (4.6; 1QH 5.25–26). The author of the hymns seems to have a special role: "You have set me up . . . as the interpreter of knowledge in your marvelous mysteries to test the seekers of truth and to try the lovers of discipline" (1QH 2.13–14).

Thirdly, the cosmic and meteorological mysteries are also mentioned in the DSS (1QH 1.11–12, 21; 12.11–13).

Fourthly, there are evil mysteries. BELIAL has his own evil *sôd* (1QS 4.1), his own hostile mysteries (1QM 14.9); and according to these "mysteries of iniquity" men deform the works of God in their guilt (1QH 5.36). However, all this is doomed to perish. On the trumpets that will give the signal in the great war against evil will be written: "The mysteries of God for the destruction of evil" (1QM 3.8–9). (*See* APOCRYPHA 1, 2.)

In the New Testament. Because of the special use St. Paul makes of mystery, it will be useful to study his epistles separately, after having investigated the use of the term in the rest of the New Testament.

Outside the Pauline Writings. The word μυστή ριον occurs in one logion in the Gospels, a parallel passage in Mk 4.10–12; Mt 13.10–13; Lk 8.9–10, which is found between the parable of the sower and its explanation. The setting of this logion is not original, but it does concern parables: "To you is granted the mystery ["mysteries" in Matthew and Luke] of the kingdom of God; but to those who are outside everything is in parables." The fluctuation between the singular and the plural reminds us of the fluctuation in Hebrew between the use in singular of *sôd* and the use in the plural of *rāz*. This use of "the mystery of the kingdom of God" is to be associated with the use seen above where divine providence and its working for the salvation of men comes under the rubric of God's marvelous mysteries. It is to be noted that Enoch 41.1 speaks of "the mysteries of the heavens and how the kingdom is divided." That only the specially selected are given to know the mysteries is consonant with the whole history of the concept of mystery. (*See* PARABLES OF JESUS.)

In Rv 1.20 mention is made of the mystery of the seven stars seen in the right hand of Alpha and Omega; and in 17.5–6 the prostitute astride the scarlet beast is a mystery, as is her name. As said above, in Daniel and in the Jewish apocalypses "mystery" was often used to characterize symbolic visions and their interpretation. In particular, mystery as applied to the symbol of the stars may be an echo of the cosmic mysteries. In Enoch 43.1–4 the mysteries of heaven include the stars, which have names given them by God. The names of the stars are the names of the saints on earth, just as the stars of the Revelation stand for the ANGELS OF THE CHURCHES. A parallel to Rv 17.5–6 may be found in Enoch 60.10 where the explanation of LEVIATHAN and Behemoth is called a mystery; and in 3 Baruch, 3 one of the "mysteries of God" is the DRAGON of evil.

It is said in Rv 10.7 that with the trumpet of the seventh angel God's mystery will be completed, as He announced to His servants the Prophets. The last clause echoes the use of *sôd* in Am 3.7 (see also 1QpHb 7.1–5). As previously mentioned, the secret will of God concerning the end of time was one of the standard mysteries.

Pauline Writings. The earliest occurrence is in 2 Thes 2.7 where, in reference to the signs of the last times and the appearance of the man of lawlessness, it is said, "The mystery of lawlessness is already at work." This is a reference to the economy of evil. While mention is made of evil mysteries in Sirach and Enoch, the best par-

allel is in the DSS where the evil spirit is permitted to function until the end time-according to the mysteries of God. The very expression "mystery of iniquity" (i.e., lawlessness) occurs in the DSS.

Next, there are five (or six) occurrences of "mystery" in 1 Corinthians, and here the Pauline doctrine of salvific mystery is beginning to take shape. In 1 Cor 2.7 Paul speaks of "a hidden wisdom of God in a mystery, a wisdom which God predetermined before the ages for our glory, which no one of the rulers of this world had known." The emphasis is on the wisdom of God hidden in a mystery, and this wisdom is God's plan for man's salvation in Jesus. As Pauline thought and theological vocabulary progresses, the emphasis will pass over to the mystery, and wisdom will become an attribute of mystery. Connections between wisdom and mystery have been seen in the Old Testament. In 1 Cor 2.10 Paul says that this wisdom hidden in a mystery has been revealed to us through the Spirit. In both Sir 48.24–25 and Dn 4.6 God's mystery is revealed through the workings of His spirit.

Paul refers to himself as one of the "stewards of the mysteries of God" in 1 Cor 4.1. The context does not clarify this use of mystery. "Mysteries of God" is a frequent expression in the DSS; and in 1Q 36.16 mention is made of "men in custody of Your mysteries."

In contrasting various gifts with the gift of charity, Paul mentions in 1 Cor 13.2 the gift of being "acquainted with all the mysteries and all knowledge." (*See* CHARISM.) When Enoch receives a revelation, it is frequently said, "He showed me all the mysteries of . . ." (Enoch 41.1; 52.2; etc.). Thus Paul is speaking of a gift of revelation given to special figures like apocalyptic seers.

In 1 Cor 14.2 Paul says that he who speaks in a tongue is not understood, but through the Spirit he utters mysteries. It is difficult to decide whether "mysteries" here means unintelligible language or hidden truths. In 1 Cor 15.51 Paul announces the resurrection of the dead at the last trumpet as a mystery. It has been shown that mystery was connected with judgment in Enoch and connected with the afterlife in Wisdom.

There is, finally, a dubious occurrence of mystery in 1 Cor 2.1 where Paul describes how he came preaching the μυστήριον or μαρτύριον (witness) of God. The textual evidence is divided between the two readings, and it is not possible to decide with certainty which is correct.

The word mystery occurs twice in Romans. In Rom 11.25 Paul reveals the mystery that Israel has been blinded until all the nations come to believe in Jesus, but ultimately all Israel will be saved. Once again mystery is applied to the divine economy of salvation. We recall that in 4 Ezra the vision of the ultimate redemption of Jerusalem was described as a mystery. In Rom 16.25 Paul speaks of his preaching of Jesus Christ in terms of a mystery kept secret for long ages but now brought into the open and by means of the prophetic writings made known to the Gentiles. Whether this final salutation of Romans is authentic has been questioned. If it is genuinely Pauline, this is the first of Paul's equation of the mystery with Jesus Christ, an equation that is a specification of the larger mystery of God's plan of salvation. Paul mentions the prophetic foreknowledge of the mystery, a feature that has been seen as part of the most ancient Hebrew concept of mystery.

It is in the Captivity Epistles, Colossians and Ephesians, that the Pauline mystery finds its fullest expression. The equation of the mystery with Christ, seen in Romans, becomes standard: in Col 1.26–27 the mystery is identified as "Christ among you, the hope of glory"; in Col 2.2–3 Paul speaks of "the mystery of God, Christ, in whom are hidden all the treasures of wisdom and knowledge"; and in Col 4.3 and Eph 3.4 he speaks of "the mystery of Christ." Once again it is said that this mystery, which in previous generations was not made known to men, has been revealed to the Apostles and Prophets in the Spirit. Perhaps the closest parallel for this is in Enoch 48.6; 51.3; 62.7, where it is said that the Elect One, the Son of Man, was chosen and hidden in God's presence before creation to be revealed to the elect in the end time. There are good Qumran parallels for the expressions in these Epistles connecting knowledge and wisdom with mystery. One notices that Paul, who began with "wisdom hidden in a mystery" (1 Col 2.7), has come around to a mystery in which wisdom is hidden.

The special characteristic of the mystery in Ephesians is the collective aspect of the salvific plan in Christ, as in Eph 1.9–10: "the mystery of His will . . . to gather all things in Christ, both heavenly and earthly in him." This includes the subjection of the hostile angelic powers to Christ. The three references to "mystery" in Eph 3.2–11 constitute the longest single Pauline treatment of the topic, and pull together most of the themes that have already been pointed out.

A special use of "mystery" is found in Eph 5.32, where Paul cites Gn 2.24 and says, "This is a profound mystery, and I interpret it as referring to Christ and his Church." "Mystery" is used here, as by 2d-century Christian writers, especially Justin, to refer to a deeper meaning of a Scripture passage. In Sir 39.2–7 and 1QpHb 7.1–5 the theory that the hidden things of God can be found in the ancient Scriptures is propounded.

In Eph 6.19 mention is made of "the mystery of the gospel," which is but a variant of the mystery of Christ, since the gospel announces salvation for all in Christ.

In the Pastoral Epistles "mystery" is found in 1 Tm 3.9 and 16: "the mystery of faith" and "the mystery of religion." What is meant is the doctrinal content of faith or religion which involves, as 3.16 indicates, a belief in Christ from His Incarnation to His glorification. Thus, the mystery in 1 Timothy is once more God's plan of salvation for men effected in Jesus Christ.

In summation, the New Testament and Pauline use of mystery is varied with many of the same modalities found in the pre-Christian Semitic use of mystery. The predominant use concerns God's salvific plan for men in Jesus [see REVELATION, CONCEPT OF (IN THE BIBLE)], even as the origin of mystery in the Old Testament seems to have been the divine plan for men as formulated in the heavenly council. Once granted the uniqueness of Paul's concept of Jesus, there is nothing in the Pauline mystery passages by way of vocabulary and thought pattern that cannot be explained from the Jewish background without recourse to the pagan mystery religions.

Bibliography: H. A. A. KENNEDY, *St. Paul and the Mystery Religions* (London 1913). D. DEDEN, "Le 'Mystère' paulinien," *Ephemerides theologicae Lovanienses* 13 (1936) 403–442. H. RAHNER, "Christian Mysteries and Pagan Mysteries," *Greek Myths and Christian Mystery,* tr. B. BATTERSHAW (New York 1963) 3–45. K. PRÜMM, *Dictionnaire de la Bible,* suppl. ed. L. PIROT, et al. (Paris 1928–) 6:10–225. R. E. BROWN, "The Pre-Christian Semitic Concept of 'Mystery'," *Catholic Biblical Quarterly* 20 (1958) 417–443; "The Semitic Background of the New Testament *Mysterion,*" *Biblica* 39 (1958) 426–448; 40 (1959) 70–87.

[R. E. BROWN]

MYSTERY (IN THEOLOGY)

A hidden reality or secret. More specifically, in the theology of revelation, a truth that human beings cannot discover except from revelation and that, even after revelation, exceeds their comprehension. In addition to this primary meaning, which will be discussed in the present article, the term has other connected meanings that should be kept in mind: (1) in soteriology, the great redemptive acts of God in history, especially in Jesus Christ; (2) in the theology of worship, the sacramental re-enactment of the redemptive deeds of Christ (see SACRAMENTAL THEOLOGY).

History of the notion. While the complete history of the term has yet to be written, the following high points may be noted.

Greek Fathers. The term μυστήριον is used by the Greek Fathers in many senses. They include the following: 1. The salvific counsels of God, hidden from all eternity in the divine mind, but partly manifested through His Prophets and especially through Christ. 2. The great salutary interventions of God in history, whereby He executes His salvific designs, including especially the decisive events of the Incarnation, Passion, and Resurrection of Christ. 3. The hidden senses of Scripture, especially the typological sense of the Old Testament, which looks forward to Christ and the Church. 4. The Sacraments, as ritual continuations of God's salvific actions in Christ. This sacramental use of the term μυστήριον did not become established until the fourth century, when the mystery religions were no longer serious competitors of Christianity. 5. The pagan cults and rites, for example, those of Eleusis, Attis, Osiris, Cybele, and Mithra (*see* MYSTERY RELIGIONS, GRECO-ORIENTAL). 6. In some of the Alexandrian writers (notably Clement), certain esoteric doctrines that, for fear of profanation, should be restricted to an elite among the faithful. 7. In Gregory of Nyssa, objects of mystical knowledge, such as were revealed to Moses and Paul in their ecstasies. 8. Especially in the fourth-century Fathers (Gregory of Nazianzus, Gregory of Nyssa, Chrysostom, etc.), a revealed truth that even to faithful and educated Christians remains obscure by reason of its sublimity.

This last use of the term is particularly important in view of the later development of the notion. The theme of God's incomprehensibility, already set forth by Philo Judaeus in the first century, was strongly emphasized by the orthodox Fathers of the fourth century in opposition to the Eunomians, who maintained that God had so revealed Himself that the Christian believer could fully understand His essence. The anti-Eunomian Fathers developed a markedly negative (or "apophatic") theology, insisting on the total otherness and immeasurable majesty of God. As Rudolf Otto noted in his work, *The Idea of the Holy* [tr. J. W. Harvey (2d ed. New York 1958)], Chrysostom provides some of the finest expressions of the sense of the "numinous" in ancient Christian literature. With apt illustrations from the Bible, Chrysostom shows how the mysterious presence of the revealing God gives rise to sentiments of consternation, mental disarray, and trembling due to a combination of fear and delight.

In the sixth century, Pseudo-Dionysius the Areopagite made effective use of the vocabulary, of the mystery religions to inculcate a sense of holy awe. His mystical works, translated into Latin by John Scotus Erigena (*c.* 850), were to influence the great scholastics, including THOMAS AQUINAS.

Latin Fathers and Doctors. In the West the Greek term μυστήριον, especially where it referred to Christian sacred rites, was generally translated by *sacramentum.* But *mysterium* was also used, both to designate the pagan mystery cults and to signify hidden truths, including the hidden meanings of Scripture. St. AUGUSTINE uses *sacramentum* and *mysterium* almost interchangeably, but with slightly different connotations. *Sacramentum* refers primarily to the outwardly visible rite or symbol; *mysterium* refers to the hidden meaning behind it.

The medieval tradition was, on the whole, quite faithful to Augustine in its handling of the terms. Often *mysterium* was used to denote the spiritual or allegorical significance of Scripture.

St. Thomas Aquinas, relying on the etymology of the word, takes note of hiddenness or secrecy as fundamental to mystery (*In Isaiam,* prol.). In his theology, the *divina mysteria* are truths hidden in God, knowable to man only under the veils of FAITH. Very frequently in Thomas's writings *mysterium* occurs as the object of the verb *credere.* Following the biblical practice, he normally applies the term "mystery" not to the inner being of God, but to His redemptive counsels, whether already executed or still to be accomplished in eschatological times. Only on rare occasions does he call the Trinity a mystery, and then principally in connection with the Incarnation, which he terms "the most excellent of all mysteries" (*Summa Theologiae* 1a, 57.5 obj. 1). For example, in *Summa Theologiae* 1a2ae, 1.8 he distinguishes between the "secret of the Godhead" (*occultum divinitatis,* i.e., the Trinity) and the "mystery of Christ's humanity." Except in passages referring to the Eucharist, Thomas practically never calls the Sacraments mysteries. The consecrated wine, he says, is rightly called "mystery of faith" (*mysterium fidei*) because the blood of Christ is not apparent to the senses (*ibid.* 3a, 78.3 ad 5).

Nineteenth Century. During the controversies with various rationalistic movements, mystery gradually emerged as a technical term in the Catholic theology of revelation. The semirationalists maintained that human reason, at least when sufficiently schooled under the tutelage of revelation, was in principle capable of comprehending and demonstrating all the dogmas of faith. From this it would follow that faith, in the sense of an assent to testimony, would not be required on the part of those who had reached full intellectual maturity. The doctrines of the leading semirationalists were severally condemned (H. Denzinger, *Enchiridion symbolorum* [Freiburg 1963] 2738–2740, 2828–2831, 2850–2861). The Syllabus of Errors, reaffirming this stand, rejected the fundamental tenets of semirationalism (*ibid.* 2909–2914).

Vatican Council I, climaxing this development, solemnly defined that there are "true mysteries properly so called," that is, dogmas of faith that cannot be "understood and demonstrated by a properly cultivated mind from natural principles" (H. Denzinger, *Enchiridion symbolorum* [Freiburg 1963] 3041). In the chapter corresponding to this definition, the council explained that by strict mysteries it meant truths "hidden in God that cannot be known unless divinely revealed" (*ibid.* 3015) and that "by their nature so transcend a created mind that even when communicated by revelation and accepted in faith, they remain covered by the veil of faith itself and as it were shrouded in obscurity, so long as in this mortal life 'we are exiled from the Lord, for we walk by faith and not by sight'" (*ibid.* 3016; cf. 2 Cor 5.6–7).

The council, in the passage just quoted, seems to imply that there will be no more mysteries in heaven, when the light of glory replaces the dimmer light of faith. This classical position of Catholic theology—which is also that of St. Thomas (*In 1 epist. ad Cor.* 2 lect. 1)—is supported by various biblical texts in addition to the one cited by the council (e.g., 1 Cor 13.9–12; 1 Jn 3.2). Nevertheless, it is well to note, as K. Rahner has several times insisted, that no created intellect can be elevated to the point where it will have absolutely comprehensive knowledge of God (cf. H. Denzinger, *Enchiridion symbolorum* [Freiburg 1963] 3001). Not even in heaven will God be appropriated as an object by the dynamism of the human *ratio*.

While stressing the negative note of incomprehensibility, Vatican I took pains to point out that "reason, enlightened by faith, when it diligently, reverently, and modestly inquires, by the gift of God, attains some understanding of mysteries, and that a most profitable one" (*ibid.* 3016). Such understanding is achieved by comparison of mysteries with things naturally known, with one another, and with the final destiny of man. In this way one may perceive the harmony between the natural and supernatural orders, the mutual coherence among the truths of faith, and the meaningfulness of the mysteries for man in his earthly pilgrimage. Although the concepts by which one knows mysteries are only remotely similar to the realities for which they stand, they afford a knowledge that is fully valid so far as it goes. Indeed, the contemplation of mysteries in this life can provide a kind of faint anticipation of the eternal vision enjoyed by the blessed.

Further speculation. In the struggle against rationalistic tendencies in the nineteenth century, the notion of mystery was gradually modified. Whereas the Fathers and medieval Doctors, thinking of mystery as something hidden within a sacramental presence, were inclined to regard the Incarnation as the supreme mystery, the nineteenth-century theologians, concentrating on the features of transcendence and obscurity, more frequently held with M. Scheeben that the Blessed Trinity is the "mystery of mysteries." In line with this tendency, Leo XIII referred to the dogma of the Trinity as "the greatest of all mysteries, since it is the fountain and origin of all"

[*Divinum illud munus; Acta Sanctae Sedis* 29 (1897) 645].

In current Catholic teaching, three classes of divine mystery are commonly recognized. These are discussed below in the order of ascending sublimity.

Natural Mysteries. Naturally knowable truths that remain obscure because we lack proper and positive concepts of the realities involved are natural mysteries. While such mysteries may be found in the created order (e.g., animal instinct, human free will), they are preeminently verified in God, by reason of the extreme deficiency of the created analogies by which we know Him. For example, the divine freedom is far more a mystery than human freedom, for our experience affords no clue as to how freedom can be present in an immutable subject.

Supernatural Mysteries in the Wide Sense. Truths concerning the created order that are not knowable without revelation but that, once revealed, are free from any special obscurity are supernatural mysteries in the wide sense; for example, the primacy of the Roman pontiff in the Church. Such a fact, being dependent on God's free disposition, could not be known without revelation, but after being revealed it has an intelligibility comparable to that of other juridical notions.

Supernatural Mysteries in the Strict Sense. Those truths that cannot be known without revelation and that, even after revelation, remain obscure to us by reason of the sublimity of their object are supernatural mysteries in the strict sense. Three principal mysteries are normally recognized as belonging to this class: (1) the Trinity (H. Denzinger, *Enchiridion symbolorum* [Freiburg 1963] 3225), which is the mystery of the communication of divine life within the Godhead; (2) the Incarnation (*ibid.* 2851), which is the supreme supernatural communication of the divine life to a created nature; and (3) the elevation of finite persons to share, through grace or glory, in the divine life (*ibid.* 2854). All other supernatural mysteries (e.g., original sin, the Eucharist, the Church as a supernatural communion, predestination) are commonly held to be reducible to the three central mysteries just named.

Supernatural mysteries in the strict sense, since they concern realities of the divine order, are beyond the comprehension of any created intellect. Their special obscurity comes from the fact that they have to do with God, not merely under those aspects in which He is directly mirrored by creatures (as, for instance, His goodness is reflected in the goodness of creatures), but precisely under those aspects wherein, thanks to His immeasurable transcendence, created analogies break down (*see* ANALOGY, THEOLOGICAL USE OF). Because the generation of living creatures only remotely resembles generation within the

Godhead, we cannot reason from the former to the latter. Even after revelation, we cannot see the inner grounds that account for the fact. Revelation tells us that there are three Persons in God, that one of them has become man, and that men are called to be sharers of God's inner life. But it does not explain how such things can be.

During the early part of the twentieth century, a controversy arose as to whether we could know without revelation that there are any strict mysteries in God. Many competent theologians (e.g., C. Pesch, I. Ottiger, H. Dieckmann) replied in the negative, but others (e.g., R. Garrigou-Lagrange, M. D. Roland-Gosselin) held that we can definitely establish that there must be in God perfections that lack any counterpart in the created order, so that we could not learn them without revelation or, even after revelation, understand their internal possibility.

Apologetical considerations. Apologetics must show that the Christian notion of strict mystery is meaningful and credible. This task is necessary, for modern rationalism and scientism have sometimes claimed that in view of the unlimited possibilities of rational and scientific progress, all truths of revelation can eventually be reduced to strictly demonstrative knowledge.

To this object one may reply, with K. Rahner, that the human mind is so structured that it necessarily grasps particular limited objects against the horizon of the unconditioned and indefinable, the Absolute. Since this Absolute is the ground of all intelligibility, the human mind, even before it is the faculty of comprehension, is the faculty of mystery. The revealed mysteries of Christianity enrich our knowledge of the Absolute by certifying that God can communicate His divine life and draw near in grace without compromising His utter transcendence. But because all these truths have reference to the inner being of the Absolute, which outstrips objective concepts, the Christian mysteries can never be rationally or scientifically demonstrated.

Religious phenomenology, by showing that the notion of mystery is a constant feature of human religion, has underscored the value of mystery. All vital religions, as R. Otto recognized, live off a numinous experience of the divine presence, which arouses sentiments of awe and fascination. Men have always suspected that if God communicates with us, He must do so in a mysterious way, imparting deep and inscrutable secrets. Scheeben was therefore able to argue that the mysteries of the Christian faith, far from making it incredible, support its claim to be God's supreme self-revelation. If Christianity were devoid of mystery, he added, it could not stir and hold men as it does.

Approaching the question from another point of view, modern personalistic philosophers (such as M.

Scheler, G. Marcel, and J. Lacroix) have shown that an element of mystery is inseparable from genuinely personal knowledge. Spirit as such is never deductively proved or experimentally verified; it is normally discerned through the signs by which it freely manifests itself. When a man reveals himself to a friend, he opens up something of the mystery of his own being. If God wishes to reveal Himself and draw human beings into friendship, He must share with them His own inner mystery. The human relationship of personal intercommunion therefore provides a fruitful analogy by which to approach the revealed mystery of our SUPERNATURAL communion with God. In this perspective, mystery appears less as a particular datum of revelation than as a dimension in which the entire relationship of revelation and faith unfolds.

See Also: REVELATION, THEOLOGY OF; SYMBOL IN REVELATION; APOLOGETICS; DOGMATIC THEOLOGY; FIDEISM; HERMESIANISM; METHODOLOGY (THEOLOGY); SEMIRATIONALISM; THEOLOGY; TRADITIONALISM.

Bibliography: General. A. MICHEL, *Dictionnaire de théologie catholique,* 15 v. (Paris 1903–65) 10:2–2585; Eng. tr., C. J. MOELL, *Mystery and Prophecy* (West Baden Springs, Ind. 1954). K. RAHNER, ''The Concept of Mystery in Catholic Theology,'' *Theological Investigations* 4 (Baltimore 1966) 36–73. M. J. SCHEEBEN, *The Mysteries of Christianity,* tr. C. VOLLERT (St. Louis 1946). *Le Mystère: Semaine des intellectuals catholiques,* Paris, Nov. 18–25, 1959 (Paris 1960). J. MACQUARRIE, *Mystery and Truth* (Milwuakee 1973). History of the notion. B. NEUNHEUSER, *Lexikon für Theologie und Kirche,* 10 v. (Freiburg 1957–65) 7:729–731, with literature. F. CAVALLERA and J. DANIELOU, Introduction to J. CHRYSTOSTOME, *Sur l'incompréhensibilité de Dieu* (Sources chrétiennes 28; Paris 1951). H. RAHNER, *Greek Myths and Christian Mystery,* tr. B. BATTERSHAW (New York 1963). P. VISENTIN, ''*Mysterium-sacramentum* dai padri alla scolastica,'' *Studia Patavina* 4 (1957) 394–414, with literature. A. M. HOFFMANN, ''Der Begriff des Mysteriums bei Thomas von Aquin,'' *Divus Thomas* 17 (Fribourg 1939) 30–60. M. A. VACANT, *Études théologiques sur les constitutions du concile du Vatican,* 2 v. (Paris 1895).

[A. DULLES]

MYSTERY RELIGIONS, GRECO-ORIENTAL

The word ''mysteries,'' as used in this article, signifies the secret cults of Greco-Roman antiquity permeated by Orientalism. They form two groups. (1) Autochthonous Greek cults; in Roman times only those of Eleusis and of Dionysus—with Orphism as a branch of the latter—were still important. (2) Oriental cults; only the Phrygian and Egyptian cults developed into the complete form of a mystery religion, whereas the Syrian Adonis cult did not reach this stage. The mysteries of Mithras

Lovatelli Urn, close-up showing detail of the initiation at Eleusis. (Alinari–Art Reference/Art Resource, NY.)

have their own ideology and their own history. Therefore, they are treated separately near the end of the article.

A first question is whether the mysteries, in respect to origin, can be thought of as a whole. The answer must be affirmative, except for Orphism and Mithraism, both of which were artificial creations. The three Oriental cults, along with the Eleusinian mysteries of Demeter, belong to the same eastern Mediterranean group and have a prehistoric origin. Their unifying principle is their fertility aspect, typical of the cults of agricultural populations. Occupying a central place is a female figure, fertility personified; closely connected with her is another figure, fecundity, i.e., actual fertility or its products. This second figure, her partner, undergoes in his own person the dramatic change of the seasons in nature from yearly birth to yearly death. In Eleusis this partner is a young woman; in the Oriental types of this religion, a young man.

Chief Focal Areas. Four great focal points of fertility religion may be distinguished: ancient Crete, North Anatolia (Phrygia), Syria, and Egypt. This fourfold grouping contains many secondary focal points that are omitted in this article for the sake of brevity. The form of the fertility rite found in Syria goes back to the Sumero-Babylonian cult of Ishtar and the myth of Du-muzi-Tammuz, the existence of which is already attested for the 3d millennium B.C.

Ancient Crete. The copious data furnished by archeological excavation on Creto-Mycenean civilization show that, while the phenomenon of life stood in the forefront of thought and feeling, there are only very few traces of those excesses (e.g., the reaper vase of Knossos) such as are often connected with living fertility religions. According to present knowledge it seems that all religion here is dominated by an apparently single female deity ruling simultaneously three realms: the kingdom of animals and plants (better perhaps, of all growth), the abode of the dead, and the domain of war. The last function may be a part or a concomitant function of her role as goddess of the royal palaces and of the kings themselves. Images on seals depict religious dances of priestesses. They express a belief in the epiphany of the goddess and her male partner. At her entrance all vegetative life starts moving ecstatically. The sarcophagus of Hagia Triada shows a death cult combined with the veneration of a fertility and earth goddess. The name of Dionysus has been deciphered on one of the tablets in Linear Script B as part of a theophoric cognomen. It is, however, uncertain whether this member of the old Cretan pantheon already possessed the essential traits of the classical Dionysus and also, whether he may be considered the partner of the great goddess of nature. Neither of the two hypotheses can be wholly rejected. In any case, the Eleusinian Demeter, goddess of the fertility of the earth, is one of the most important descendants of the ancient Cretan nature goddess. The dramatic element characterizing the Eleusinian cult has its prototype in the partly ecstatic cult of ancient Crete. This assumption, which is more or less the opinion of M. P. Nilsson (*The Minoan-Mycenaean Religion and Its Survival* [2d ed. Lund 1950]), revives an old thesis of P. Foucart. Further research of the Minoan tablets may be expected to clarify ancient Cretan correlations, for both Eleusis and Dionysus, though for the latter the correlation Asia Minor—Thrace—seems to be the more important.

North Anatolia. In the culture cycle of North Anatolia, rock carvings in the vicinity of the old Hittite capital (near Ankara) depict two deities that, on account of the flowers they offer each other, were formerly dubbed god and goddess of spring and considered as prototypes of the later couple Cybele-Attis. These Hittite deities are now recognized as complex in nature, representing the sun goddess of Arinna and the Hittite representative of the Hurrian weather god Teshub. Nevertheless, there remains the motif of a "sacred marriage," which often points to a fertility cult, and in the numerous train of one of the two deities a direct ancestor of the later Cybele has been recognized. The orgiastic element, characteristic for the pair

Attis and Cybele at an early date, may have been present at this early stage of the Anatolian cult; but the Phrygian invaders of Asia Minor from Thrace certainly strengthened it. The Artemis of Ephesus is but an offshoot of this Anatolian mother. She was worshiped only incidentally and in secret rites. Their details are not known.

The goddess Anahita, is in reality an East Anatolian deity whom the Persians worshiped. Her cult in Asia Minor spread westward at an early date and she appears in company with Mithras. The similarity between Cybele and Anahita—the two were often interchanged—led at times even to a local fusion of the concomitant figures of both Attis and Mithras, although they had nothing in common with each other (cf. W. Wüst, ''Mithras'' in *Paulys Realenzyklopädie der klassischen Altertumswissenschaft,* ed. G. Wissowa et al. [Stuttgart 1893–] 15.2 [1932] 2135–).

Syria. The Syrian fertility goddess bears different names in different places of worship. Especially important is the goddess called in Greek the consort of Adonis of Byblos (likewise Aphrodite), and the Dea *Syria* of Hierapolis, also called Bambyce, Atargatis (i.e., the Atar of Attis). Conformities in ceremonial, particularly the emasculation of male followers, prove that the principal figure of this cult kept much of the nature of the old Anatolian goddess. Likewise, the old Mesopotamian Ishtar lives on in the Syrian Astarte, as is evident also from the close correspondence between Adonis of Byblos and the old Mesopotamian Dumuzi-Tammuz. Since, in the final development of the Egyptian myth, Isis finds the body of Osiris in Byblos, the clear mythological connection between the Syrian and Egyptian pair of vegetation deities is thereby indisputably confirmed.

Egypt. In Egypt the fertility aspect is found not only in Isis but, considering the connection between gods and animals, also in Hathor. The latter was represented as a horned cow or else—a case of incompleted iconographic anthropomorphism—with a cow's head. But in Egypt itself, and especially in the Egyptian component of Hellenism, Isis and her partner Osiris were destined to have a far greater influence.

Mythicoritual Development of the Basic Vegetation Duality. A mother goddess does not occupy the supreme role in cult, as she did in Crete, among any of the Near Eastern peoples where such a female divinity is found. Everywhere male deities have the leading place. Thus, in Mesopotamia several great gods, e.g., Anu, Enlil, Ea, Marduk, and Ashur, tower above the goddess Ishtar, notwithstanding her position as mistress of life, who appears now as virgin, now as wife and mother, while her lover Dumuzi-Tammuz shares the tragic fate of all nature heroes. In Syria at Bambyce, beside the god-

Fresco in the Villa of the Mysteries, detail depicting a girl undergoing the ordeal and bacchante, c. 50 B.C., Pompeii.

dess one finds the god designated as Attis—and as the superior figure. The whole ritual as represented on coins shows that he is not conceived as having a secondary position, as the Phrygian Attis and the later Adonis of Byblos had. Lucian's description in his *De Dea Syria* makes this clear.

The same is true of the female successor of the North Anatolian mother goddess, named usually after the many individual mountains in the forests of which she was thought to roam, but less frequently after towns. The invasion of the Phrygians, a people related to the Greeks, brought her into contact with a religious sphere that assigned the chief role to a male deity. And the mountain mother surely had to take a subordinate position herself wherever the Greek colonists of Asia Minor seized power. Thus, in Homer the Idaean Mother—the ''Mother of Mt. Ida'' of the Trojans—is represented as being closely connected with Zeus, but as subject to him. Copious archaeological evidence from the mountain dominating Ephesus, of later date but clearly pre-Christian, has confirmed the different relative positions of mistress of nature and high god. A whole row of reliefs depict the triad Zeus, with beard; the Great Mother, with tympanon and other emblems and flanked by lions; and the youth Attis. One of the inscriptions of Ephesus expressly mentions Zeus as the autochthonous, or ancestral god. Hence, it may be concluded that the Greeks did not favor the elevation of Attis to the status of a true god, as is to be noted here and there in Phrygia as a result of his assimilation to Men, the moon god; nor did they favor the loose relationship of Attis and Cybele, which will be discussed below.

In the chief centers of population the cult of the Great Mother had extensive temple possessions and was under the control of a hierarchic priesthood that often politically administered the temple territory. It is sufficient to mention the temple-states of Ma (i.e., mother), Commagene, Bambyce, Hierapolis Castabala, and also the theocratic state of Ephesia. But the fact that a supreme deity of the stature of Zeus was being recognized at the same time proves that these fertility cults were not to be regarded as the total expression of religion but rather as elements in the whole religious complex of the area. That is very important for the understanding of their precise nature after their expansion westward, especially in the Roman Empire. The individual Oriental cults could not, and probably did not, wish, of their own accord at least, to compete with Christianity. They were part of the total potential of paganism that under imperial leadership wished to prevent Christianity from conquering souls.

Common Elements in the Mystery Cults. Their original structural likeness was not lost in later development, although naturally the cults emanating from a single point of departure came to differ considerably in details. The similar course of historical evolution makes it possible to sketch the nature of this group of Oriental cults together, at least with regard to their main features.

It is appropriate to start with the myth, since it contains so many common elements. In every case there is a basic pair of deities dissimilar in rank. Of these two, the female figure embodies fertility itself, whereas her male companion (who is intended to portray fecundity, the result of fertility, i.e., the abundant growth of plants and animals) is represented sometimes as her son, sometimes as her lover, and hence exhibits a peculiar hybrid character. This basic personification opened the road for further mythology, and it was a road that could not help leading into many byways.

O. Kern has given the following explanation. In the subtropical regions that are regarded as the home of the mysteries, namely, Asia Minor, Egypt, and the Aegean area, the change from the winter stagnation of nature into sprouting vegetation and the still greater change seen in the decline of growth in summer as a result of heat and drought usually occur abruptly and are full of contrasts. These contrasts, with their very disquieting effects on the feelings, found expression in emotional outbursts, and the

more so as men pictured to themselves the proximate cause of the death, assumed as real, that the mythological being representing biological life was destined to undergo. Typical for Phrygia is the legend of the death of Attis, circulating with many variations; he emasculates himself out of remorse for his unfaithfulness toward his mistress, the Great Mother. In Syria, Adonis dies during the hunt, killed by a wild boar. In Egypt, Osiris succumbs to the snares of Seth, who symbolizes the hot desert wind that is so dangerous to most plants.

When once this stage was reached in the construction of the myth, a psychologically simpler motivation followed. A double set of feasts, often gathered in a cycle, mourning the disappearance of vegetation and again hailing its reappearance, was established. Instead of a merely mild, sympathetic feeling for the impersonal decay of nature, one could now abandon himself to personal grief at the tragic death of a being regarded as a youthful and handsome person. This personal relation gave a new emphasis to the joyous feast that belonged to the whole series of religious celebrations. These expressions of religious emotion were publicized by mass actions and not by individuals. In this way primitive celebrations honoring demigods of vegetation became great public festivals in their area of origin.

Intense excitement, however, could easily lead in two directions to sexual excesses. Cruelty and lust are passions that are psychologically closely related. It seems that in prehistoric times it was considered a service to the community to give to the Mistress of Nature the sacrifice of sexual power through emasculation. This may be compared to sacred prostitution, which represented an offering to the powers of fertility, and was often regarded as a magic act. Research has confirmed for many of these cults the emasculation of priests even of the highest class, although it is difficult to ascertain how widespread this practice actually was in later historical times. In many places, e.g., in the service of the Magna Mater of Pessinus, the emasculated high priest was called Attis and therefore as such was the companion or attendant of the goddess. This peculiar fact has led to the opinion that the emasculation of cult personnel, long practiced as a fertility sacrifice, was transferred to the myth of the god, thus providing the mythical αἴτιον (explanation) for the ancient rite.

The Element of Secrecy. All the cultic phenomena mentioned have been postulated on fairly solid ground for the early part of the 1st millennium B.C., and for the areas of origin of the Oriental group of the later Hellenistic mysteries. If the god occupying the primary position in the pair of vegetation divinities in northwestern Asia Minor is called Zeus, the insertion "Homeric religion" on the table is justified. The Indo-European tribes that fused with the original inhabitants of the Aegean area and founded the Greek people looked upon these ecstatic fertility rites as foreign and strange. The knightly and warlike class of nobles of the archaic and legendary period immortalized by Homer gave a tone to the religious sphere and kept itself aloof from the whole world of chthonic cults. Hence, since the older religious element was pushed into the background in Greece, it was in Greece itself that psychological necessity gradually led to secrecy. The autochthonic population, keeping strictly to the ancient forms of worship (e.g., in Eleusis) came to practice them apart and surrounded them with a wall of silence.

But even in Greece it is not likely that this esoteric factor, necessitated by circumstances, was the sole reason for the origin of secrecy. An added reason may have been that the rites had a partly sexual character, as is obvious from the pronounced biological mentality from which they derived their origin. This is also why many women's cults (e.g., the Thesmophoria at Athens and the cult of the Bona Dea at Rome) were closed to men. Some authors, K. Kerényi, e.g., have tried with much insight to show that male societies were at the root of the ancient secret cults. This hypothesis is manifestly untenable in the case of the most important cults (e.g., that of Eleusis), since they were open to both sexes from the outset, although their priestly functions were in the hands of women. Lastly, wherever eschatological hopes came to be connected with the performance of the rites, a certain awe for the latter, which were said to conceal something sublime, tended to encourage the practice of secrecy on the part of all. At Eleusis, it is true, this hope itself is not part of the secret but only the ritual way for becoming a sharer in it.

The Eleusinian Mysteries

The early Christian writers, especially CLEMENT OF ALEXANDRIA, are severe in their criticism of the Eleusinian Mysteries (see Clement of Alexandria, *Protrept.* 2.21.2).

General Characterization and Early History. This cult may claim a detailed treatment because of the long tradition of supporting evidence and its important role in the classical period. It seems very probable that, at the beginning of the 3d century B.C., the Hellenistic form of the Egyptian mysteries was fashioned on the Eleusinian by Timotheus, a member of the Eleusinian priestly family of the Eumolpids, and that a similar imitation may be assumed in the case of the final elaboration of the cult of the Magna Mater and Attis under the early Roman principate.

Thus the Eleusinian ritual may be regarded as a typical and historical Greco-Oriental mystery religion. It includes the Dionysiac mysteries, the second mystery cult rooted in early Greek religion. Specialists such as U. von Wilamowitz-Moellendorff hold that the latter was not merely the only mystery cult still active in imperial times, but that it was very important. The discoveries in the Roman cemetery under St. Peter's at Rome have shown that in the later years of the 2d century A.D. Dionysian emblems had replaced Egyptian ones. Although this fact may be explained as a matter of fashion, it tends to reveal in any event a newly awakened interest in Dionysus as a porter god and god of the netherworld—aspects of the deity that were stressed in the mysteries.

The Eleusinian mysteries belong to a cycle of feasts performed in two stages, a year apart, or even in three stages, thus requiring a total period of three years if performed according to rule. The three stages are: initiation (μύησις), dedication (τελετή), and full revelation of the mystery (ἐπόπτεια). A person could take part in these ceremonies only once, but it was not a civic duty to participate. It is not certain whether famous Athenians, who were deeply interested in ancestral beliefs, such as the tragedian Aeschylus, were mystai of Eleusis. Yet the Eleusinian celebrations were considered to have an importance and to bring honor to the city. Eleusis, originally, was not connected with Athens; it was an independent and significant place, the residence of a king. The foundations of the citadel reach back partly to the beginning of the 1st millennium B.C. The place of worship was structurally connected with the royal stronghold situated on the top of the adjacent height.

By the early 7th century B.C., Eleusis had lost its independence to Athens. As a result, the administration of the cult passed into the hands of Athenian officials, who respected the old customs, as ancient religious sentiment demanded. Thus, they permitted the old Eleusinian families, among which certain ritualistic functions were hereditary, to retain their rights and privileges, reserving for themselves, however, the power of appointing the high priest.

The Celebration of the Mysteries. The celebration of the mysteries was connected with Athens in the following manner. The preliminary ceremonies were held in Athens and were somewhat modified. But the second and third stage of the ceremonies, which took place in September (Boedromion) and could be held only in Eleusis, began with a solemn procession from Athens to Eleusis.

The dominant theme of the myth is the mother love of Demeter for her daughter Kore—this generic name being apparently older than the individualized name Persephone. Many who might be indifferent to other features of this myth could still appreciate this beautiful human motif. Everywhere else the core of the myth is not mother love but sexual love between man and woman, and only in the Egyptian mysteries is this sexual love the love between husband and wife (Isis and Osiris). In Egypt a child, the boy Horus, is added to this couple, but that is only a side aspect of the myth and does not affect it in any essential way, as it does in part at Eleusis. Actually, however, as regards the symbolism of the Eleusinian Kore, the dominant feature is her relationship to Pluto, the god of death. Kore, the bride whom he captures, represents the final destiny of all vegetative life, indeed of all earthly life, and thus can portray human death in an allegorical manner. The other associations with her and her mother, intended and aroused by the mysteries, become more meaningful only when both become mediators of a better life after death.

The Eleusinian hope is the high point of the so-called Homeric *Hymn to Demeter,* where in 5.479–481 the lot of the initiated in the hereafter is pictured as more pleasant than that of the noninitiated. Several verses later, they are called the blessed on whom the pair of exalted and chaste goddesses bestow their loving care. The same word blessed (ὄλβιος) describing the lot of the initiates is used by Pindar (Frg. 137, ed. Bergk) and Sophocles (Turchi, no. 152). The word ὄλβιος has about the same sense as the word μακάριος used in the two accounts of the Sermon on the Mount (Mt 5:3– ; Lk 6:20–). But whereas this word, as used by the Evangelists, praises as blessed the way of life made possible by the New Covenant, the sole title to Eleusinian blessedness is initiation. There is no question of atonement. Only the worst criminals were excluded from initiation, a point severely criticized already in antiquity.

Opinions differ respecting the performance of the rites in the second and third stages and also respecting the precise arrangement of the interior of the sacred building. Benches for spectators, cut out of rock and still recognizable today, prove that participants in the cult engaged in liturgic actions that were visible to all. Literary allusions to emotions of fear manifested by the spectators, and likewise the express mentioning of a descent (καταβάσιον) by Asterius (*Hom.* 10; *Patrologia Graeca,* ed. J. P. Migne, 161 v. [Paris 1857–66] 40:324B) suggest the dramatic performance of the moving legend of the rape of Persephone by Pluto. Clement of Alexandria (*Protrept.* 2.21) has preserved for us the so-called password (σύνθημα) of Eleusis. It is a formula to be repeated by the candidate for final admission, who had to show thereby that he had passed the intermediate stage. Thus one learns the main actions. The formula runs: "I have fasted, I have drunk of the sacred cup [κυκεών], I have taken [the things] from the sacred chest, having tasted thereof

I have placed them into the basket and again from the basket into the chest." The fasting and drinking from a ritualistic container evidently aim to imitate ceremonially the fasting of Demeter out of sorrow for the disappearance of her daughter, as related in the legend, and also the drink with which she refreshed herself after having been cheered by the indecent jests of her maid Baubo.

Fertility Aspects of the Rites. In his account, Clement of Alexandria puts the Baubo scene before the cultic action and criticizes it harshly. The handling of the anonymous things (ἀπόρρητα) suggests that they were symbols of female and male sexuality. The dual containers, differentiated by the names "chest" and "basket," seem also to confirm this view. This assumption seems logical and is confirmed by other intimations of the Church Fathers.

This explanation of the last act of the *synthema,* or password ceremony, which is described in such cryptic language, seems sound for intrinsic and extrinsic reasons. (1) Such an act is in keeping with a fertility cult. Other secondary Eleusinian rites contain this feature, as the call to the earth: ὕε, χύε, "rain, conceive" (Proclus, *In Tim.* 40E). (2) This action is appropriate to the second stage of the rites. (3) Certain finds in the temple of Demeter at Priene, a kind of affiliate of Eleusis, similar to the one established especially in Alexandria, show a marked sexual emphasis. These finds suggest directly the use of the female sexual symbols as a means of initiation. The simultaneous use of the male symbol is the more easily explained, since the latter plays a central role in the Hellenistic mystery rites that exhibit a more or less close dependence on Eleusis.

The procedure at the third stage, revelation (ἐπόπτεια), is known through independent and credible assertions of early ecclesiastical writers and Fathers. Two acts are mentioned. The first is the "hierogamy," or sacred marriage between the high priest (hierophant) and priestess (cf. Gregory of Nazianzus and Proclus; Turchi, nos. 32–). It was probably intended to symbolize the mythical nuptials of Demeter and Iasion on the thrice-plowed field (Hesiod, *Theog.* 969–972), itself the mythical symbol of the sacred marriage of heaven and earth. Hippolytus furnishes important additional information. The priest raised a freshly cut ear of wheat—obviously the fruit of this sacred marriage—with the loud cry: "The exalted goddess bore a holy boy, the strong one bore a strong child" (Turchi, no. 130). As a confirmation of the prehistoric age of this rite and of the relation of the nucleus of the Eleusinian cult actions to the early farming stage of culture, it is to be noted that the same rite has been found in North Africa and in the period preceding the spread of the Indo-European culture in the West (cf. D. J. Wölfel in König, *Christus,* 1:340–).

Thus, one sees that at Eleusis hope in a better life to come and improvement of material welfare, which is so dependent on the fruits of the earth, are closely connected. St. Paul has pointed out an association of ideas between wheat and the hereafter (1 Cor 15.37). Eleusinian eschatology, however, did not embrace precisely what for Paul was the symbolism of the sprouting seed, namely, bodily resurrection. The quasi-official formulation of the Eleusinian hope in the Homeric *Hymn* is remarkably modest. It does not look beyond a life in the lower world, and even for this it dares to promise the initiates, as opposed to noninitiates, only a gradual improvement in their lot.

Evaluation and Later History. Yet these rites gave their initiates the consolation that there was at least one form of divine worship that showed some interest in the great question of the beyond. The official cults of the Greek states ignored this problem. The Olympians enjoyed their own blessedness without caring for the future lot of men. M. J. Lagrange has given the noblest interpretation of the Eleusinian Mysteries; one should not speak blindly of magic here, but should regard the whole procedure as an act of trust in the power of the "august goddesses." But despite the consolation furnished by the rites and the veneration they enjoyed from age itself, they could not withstand critical examination. The comfort could be only as real as the persons of the divinities themselves.

Later classic times and especially the Hellenistic age, however, recognized fully the symbolic-mythical values contained in the rites. Not only in Athenian but in all ancient literature, Eleusis was renowned as an inalienable jewel of the city of Athens, a symbol of its cultural contributions, the first and most basic of which was the raising of cereals. Even after the mysteries had lost all credence in ancient Greece, including Attica itself, they were still celebrated with pomp as old folk customs, with a feeling for history and with a treasuring of the past for its own sake. During the several revivals of Greek culture, beginning with the great efforts of Hadrian, the mysteries' power of attraction was proved again and again, especially in the case of the Romans who took pleasure in becoming initiates. Alaric destroyed a great part of the sanctuary in A.D. 395, and the celebration of the rites was forbidden by the laws of Theodosius the Great in the same period.

The Cult of the Great Mother, or Magna Mater

Within a limited space it is not possible to cover all vegetation or fertility cults that have mystery elements. The cult of the Great Mother, however, deserves formal treatment, being both so representative and so important.

The early Greeks were already familiar with the mother of Zeus (Μήτηρ ʽΡέα), simply as mother of the gods, a figure undoubtedly related to the mother goddess of Asia Minor. But this Greek Rhea has no partner of such dubious and uncertain status as Cybele's partner Attis. When, therefore, the Phrygian goddess with her companion Attis asked for admission, as was inevitable in a commercial town such as Athens as a result of the influx of immigrants from Asia Minor, the new mother goddess was not identified simply with Rhea but had to be satisfied, like all foreign cults, with a place outside the city walls.

But apparently, already before the Persian wars, some traits of the Asian form of the mother cult had been introduced into the Greek worship of Rhea. This has psychological probability in its favor, since Pindar praises the venerable Asian Mother in one of his Olympic odes (on Hiero). In the Hellenistic Age, the worship of the Magna Mater is conducted at the Peiraeus in full Asiatic style by the ὀργεῶνες (i.e., men who celebrate the *orgia*) with the assistance of a special cult personnel. There is mention of a priestess of Attis and a couch (κλίνη) that she must prepare for the god. This act may represent the mourning over the dead Attis, who previously seems to have been honored by joyous dances around a throne. Plato was familiar with the exotic ritual of enthronement (ἐνθρονισμός) as part of the initiation of the followers of the Magna Mater, the corybantes (*Euthyd.* 429D).

Eight hundred years after Plato, in the 4th century A.D., when *taurobolia* were celebrated in Athens in honor of the Magna Mater, the Asian Mother definitely entered the Greek pantheon and had Demeter and Kore beside her as companion goddesses—a situation that would have been unthinkable in early times.

The Cult of Magna Mater in the Roman Period. The Romans knew Adonis at an early time in their history, partly through the Greeks of south Italy, and partly through the Etruscans. In 205 B.C., in the crisis of the Second Punic War, they introduced the cult of the Asian Mother from Pessinus in Galatia. The Phrygian cult was given a place on the Palatine, opposite the later house of Livia, but the astute heads of the Roman state allowed only one annual public celebration: the lustration of the image of the Magna Mater in the Almo stream, which had no connection with the fate of Attis. The cult, in the form given it by the emperor Claudius, who was interested in religious antiquities, is known through its incorporation in the Roman religious calendar as well as through archeological representations, e.g., on a sarcophagus in *S. Lorenzo fuori le mura*. In order to understand the performance of the cult in this later and elaborated form, one must remember the personality of Attis as the representation of the nature cycle and also the basic structure of his myth as outlined earlier in this article. A pine tree, which was intended to represent the hero, profusely decorated as a tree of spring and adorned with an image of Attis, was carried in procession (Firmicus Maternus, *De errore prof. rel.* 22). At the same time, the tree, since it was an evergreen, may have symbolized his ostensibly newly assumed life, though the myth says nothing about this. Then the procession with the image of the Magna Mater was carried out with much greater pomp. Quite apart from these public ceremonies, secret rites were also performed. As in Eleusis, these were obviously based on ritualistic imitation of events in the myth. Firmicus Maternus mentions a ceremony of mourning the dead (*ibid.* 23), probably but not necessarily referring to Attis, and an anointing of the throat of the candidates with oil, with the accompanying words: "Take courage, mystae, you belong to a god who has been saved, and he will also be your salvation from toil." Even more valuable is the formula reported in common by both Firmicus Maternus and Clement of Alexandria: "I have eaten from the *tympanon* [drum], I drank from the *kymbalon* [cymbal]"—both are instruments employed in the worship of the goddess. Whereas in Firmicus the words "I became a mystes of Attis" follow immediately, Clement mentions (*Protr.* 2.15) two more mystic acts: "I carried the *kernos,* I slipped into the bridal chamber." The *kernos,* a container having several parts and found already in ancient worship, was employed as something intended obviously to produce its effect as an archaic rite. The last statement quoted gives a key at least to the general meaning.

Evaluation and Later History. Obviously the rite was intended to impress upon the mystai the subjective certainty of having been united in a special way with the goddess, as in a mystic marriage or, on a more modest plane, as Lagrange has proposed, as a personal servant of the Great Mother. It seems clear that the strong motivation of hope present in this cult, a hope in harmony with the religious interests of the Greco-Roman period, probably served as a foundation for a belief in a higher and better life beyond the grave. It would thus be in the line of the Eleusinian ideology. The rhetorical vehemence with which Firmicus, the chief source, criticizes such rites must be understood in the light of the times. But the Christian polemist is right in reminding the believers in these mysteries that the whole activity has no real value or meaning, since it is based entirely on myth. In form and content the sacred formulas are essentially an imitation of the Eleusinian "symbol." Formally they are a synopsis of the rites that the candidate for membership had to undergo before he could be admitted to the final initiation. In content these rites are modeled on the myth, as the containers chosen for food and drink are the drum and the cymbal. These instruments were said to have been used by the goddess on her mythical journey through the mountains of Asia Minor and hence were employed also in the public processions in honor of Cybele.

Something original, something as yet without analogy in any Greek cult, is mentioned by Prudentius (*Peristeph*). In some 80 verses he describes the ceremony of the *TAUROBOLIUM* in the cult of the Magna Mater. It deserves notice here because the rebirth mentioned in the pertinent inscriptions as the expected effect has often been compared with the rebirth that is promised as an effect of baptism (Ti 3:5). But the *taurobolium* aimed at a restoration of physical forces only through the blood of a bull. The general atmosphere of the rite is not one of spiritual hopes, and it is occasionally taken over as a rite beneficial for the common good (*pro salute Caesaris*). All the Western evidence dates from the 2d century A.D. on.

The Mysteries of Dionysus

Between the Eleusian and the Dionysian mysteries there are several important differences. The cult of Eleusis keeps its external structure unchanged, primarily because it is bound to a definite locality, but the cult of Dionysus varies considerably in place and time. The significance of the two Eleusinian divinities is already evident from the Homeric poems; and in addition to the data furnished by archeology, a considerable body of relatively clear information is found in early Christian literature.

As regards the secret worship of Dionysus (i.e., mystery rites that go back to the pre-Hellenic period), the evidence comes in part from widely separated places and is difficult to correlate. Furthermore, the evidence is open to serious question on the historical side and refers to markedly different periods. Yet Dionysus is a divinity who is clearly the object of a mystery cult. This is evident from his local origin and his myth, scanty as it is, as well as from the nature of the god as revealed by the sum of all available data—and especially by the data preserved in the form of his cult.

According to Greek legend, Dionysus came to Greece from Thrace (as in Euripides's *Bacchae*) and also by sea (as is recalled in the role of the vehicle in the form of a ship employed in the Athenian Dionysia). The recently established connection of this god with ancient Cretan religion tends to confirm that he was not out of harmony with the Greek fertility worship and was integrated into it at an early date. The restriction of the domain of Dionysus to wine, and more specifically to viticulture, is found in certain ancient writers, e.g., Diodorus, who have spun out long myths on Dionysus as the god of wine. Relying on this evidence, H. Jeanmaire thinks he can clarify more sharply the particular function of this god and his cult. The difficulty is that among the late mythographers it is hard to distinguish between earlier and later myths. The Orphics elaborated the saga of the birth of the god into a confused pattern of stories in order to obtain a foundation for their profound speculation. The older saga tells of the tragic death of the god's mother, Semele, and it is highly suggestive that this name means earth, as P. Kretschmer has established. The desire to see Zeus cost her her life.

The myth relates matters that normally belong to child rearing, but with this difference, that the people engaged in this task are naturally mythical persons. Thus Hermes entrusts the care of the child to the nymphs, but it soon escapes from its nurses. This incident provides the Boeotian cult of Dionysus, at least in the later period, with the motif of a search in the mountains for Dionysus by the Thyads. The latter are but other names for the frenzied female attendants of the god, the Maenads, who personify in the cult the nymphs assigned to the care of the child by Hermes.

The birth of a god who, like Dionysus, is so closely connected with vegetation and belongs to the old pair of fertility divinities, must be followed by a death. Accordingly, Philochorus, a specialist in the history of religion writing in the early Hellenistic age, mentions a tomb of Dionysus within the temple precinct of Delphi. The ceremonies devoted to the awakening of the god to a new birth took place, however, only every third year. This was a very awkward situation, since Dionysus was regarded as being temporarily in residence at Delphi, substituting for Apollo, who was thought to spend the winter with the Hyperboreans.

The love affair between Dionysus and Ariadne is typical of the vegetation myth: Ariadne's early death is the counterpart of the disappearance of Persephone. The myth, which in the elaborate literary form given it by poets such as Nonnus (5th century A.D.) tells of Dionysus's journey to India, is very late. It is merely a reflection of Alexander's Indian campaign.

Spread of the Cult and Its Special Features. The older myths of the journeys of Dionysus reflect the early propagation and the peculiar nature of the cult. This cult, manifestly an ecstatic one from the outset and under the strong influence of women, was spread successfully despite the opposition of political authorities, as indicated in the story of the revenge of Dionysus on the Theban king Pentheus. Euripides in his *Bacchae* describes this revenge in detail. Bacchus (Dionysus) induces Pentheus to search for the Maenads who are roving about Mt. Parnassus, but they take him for an animal and tear him to pieces. This is, at the same time, one of the earliest accounts of the rite of omophagy. During the winter and early spring, female worshipers of Dionysus used to roam about Parnassus, hunting down wild animals, tearing them apart, and eating their raw flesh.

Phrygia furnishes more convincing evidence than does central Greece for the ceremony of the awakening of Dionysus. Here he passes for a god hibernating in the realm of Persephone—a slight mitigation only of the idea of the death of the vegetation god, who in spring is brought in with great pomp at the feast of the *Katagogia* (cf. Wilamowitz-Moellendorff, *Die Religion der Griechen* [Leipzig 1932] 2:373–). In the Hellenistic period there is mention of a state-controlled cult of Dionysus at Miletus, in which raw flesh was eaten, evidently a civilized continuance of ancient savage customs, but subsequently placed under state control (*ibid.* 372). The mad celebrations in the Parnassus region, which were intended also to awaken the god Dionysus, did not exclude men completely but were the special privilege of women. In this respect, because of the esoteric tendency present, the celebrations in question fall within the general framework of the mystery cult.

The time after Alexander witnessed a general revival of Dionysian worship. For Egypt, there is proof for the spread of secret Dionysian rites in the fact that Ptolemy Philopator took measures to bring even the privately conducted rites of Dionysus under his control. A royal decree ordered those in possession of initiation formulas to register them in person with the government; obviously the government feared excesses. About the same time this cult, which for a long time had been prevalent in southern Italy, exhibited a new development, characterized by violence, sexual excesses, and even murder; and it spread to Rome itself. Therefore the Roman Senate took prompt and severe action, as is recorded in the extant inscription on bronze, the *Senatus consultum de Bacchanalibus* and by the historian Livy (39.14.1).

The Pompeian Evidence. Nevertheless, more moderate forms of the rite were allowed to continue, as is proved by the series of paintings in one of the halls of the so-called Villa dei Mysteri (also called the Villa Item). The connection with the cult of Dionysus is certain, since in this cycle of paintings Dionysus, with his familiar attribute the *thyrsus,* or staff, and reposing on the bosom of his beloved Ariadne, occupies the commanding place. This obviously mythical scene may be considered as expressing the inner meaning of the mystery that is to be dramatically presented. As the precise portraiture indicates, the actors include not only definite persons, such as the mistress of the house, but also, along with them and without sharp distinction, mythical beings such as Silenus and Pan. A winged form, whether a mythical figure or a personification of the mystic rite (τελετή), lays the lash upon the back of a woman. This scene is framed first by the unveiling of the phallus, the initiation proper, and secondly by the solo dance of a woman. If it was intended to symbolize the joys of the hereafter to be expected from participation in the initiation, this dance, not perhaps positively licentious and yet not especially exalted in character, bears witness to the typically pagan concept of the future life. In any case, the series of scenes in the Villa Item, whether representing an initiation into a mystery or simply a bridal ceremony, is characteristic of a Greco-Roman Dionysian ritual, with an emphasis on sensation and surprise.

This set of paintings of the Villa Item, notably the initiation rite proper (i.e., the unveiling of the phallus), is paralleled by a series of so-called Campanian reliefs, and M. I. Rostovtzeff has interpreted the paintings of the Casa Omerica in Pompeii as having much the same content. Accordingly, it seems assured that some kind of mystery cult of Dionysus flourished in the vicinity of Naples in the 1st century A.D. Whether the inscription of Agripinilla describes genuine Dionysiac worship or refers to more or less licentious revels under the cloak of mystery rites is not clear (see M. P. Nilsson, *Geschichte der griechischen Religion,* 2 v. [2d ed. Munich 1955–61] 2:343–344). By this time the Hellenistic mystery religion had developed a kind of "common liturgical language" with fixed formulas.

Problems of Interpretation. The real secret seems to be the sexual element, but sublimated as a symbol of all fertility. The striving to come into closer contact with the mystery divinities, however, is difficult to explain, especially in the case of Dionysus, when one looks for the precise reason why Dionysus should be a particularly fitting mediator of hopes for the hereafter. Heraclitus of Ephesus, reflecting on the riotous scenes during the Dionysia in his city in the 5th century B.C., states in one of his customary obscure utterances: "They celebrate the grape feast in honor of Hades." But he says this as one who sees more deeply than the common man, and he says it with pensive melancholy in the light of the contrast between festive joy and the frailty of all vegetative and earthly life. In any case, the cycle of Dionysian myths, while to a limited degree symbolizing growth, offers far less expectation of salvation than is the case in the Oriental group.

A ritualistic drama commemorating the annual awakening and passing of vegetation, as mentioned earlier, maintained itself in a few places only, e.g., in Delphi and in Phrygia. Even this fact would hardly be known, unless historians such as Plutarch with antiquarian interests had reported it. Dionysus was surnamed from the outset Lyseus as a symbolic personification of or as the mythical giver of wine. All that ancient speculation itself associated with this title exhibits an attempt at a theological interpretation of this metaphor, which has interest chiefly because, beneath the play of legend, it reveals the religious aspirations and longing for salvation on the part of pagan souls.

Orphism

The myth of the child Dionysus already pointed in the direction of the Dionysus of Orphism. The latter figure, it is true, has received a highly complex elaboration and is overladen with fantastic myths that cannot be told here in detail. And yet Orphism is so important that some attention must be given it in this article. It was certainly a combination of opposites and had a bad name in antiquity because of its practice of licentious rites and its strange manner of life. Orphism, the origins of which continue to be warmly debated, alone among the mystery religions—except perhaps Mithraism and the Egyptian mysteries because of their emphasis on eschatology—possessed a complete system of doctrine, and was concerned with the dissemination of knowledge. All other mysteries, being essentially forms of worship, aimed only at producing certain dispositions of mind and vague hopes.

Earlier History. In the modern investigation of mystery religions, Orphism has long occupied a special place through the importance assigned to it by Plato. Whether the latter agrees with the opinions he introduces from Orphism is not always clear from his words. It is to be assumed rather that he wishes merely to praise the general character and line of thought that he quotes in support of his own doctrines, e.g., the belief in retribution in the hereafter and therefore in the meaning of human life as involving moral responsibility.

In support of such a view of life Orphism created a profound myth. It can be traced back to an origin in single individuals and in the first place to Onomacritus, who lived in the age of the Pisistratids (6th–5th century B.C.). The lot of man is viewed as a miserable result of an original sin, yet one not committed by man but by his mythical ancestors. According to Orphic teaching men are formed out of the ashes of the Titans, sons of Uranus and Gaia, therefore, of a pre-Olympian race of gods. They had been destroyed by the lightning of Zeus because they had committed the outrage of tearing to pieces and devouring his child Dionysus, all except his heart. Athena brought the heart to Zeus, who in turn swallowed it and produced another Dionysus, namely, the Dionysus of Orphism. The Papyrus Smily, also called the Papyrus Gurob after its place of discovery in Egypt (Kern, *Orph. Frg.* 31), dates from the 3d century B.C. and confirms the earlier myth.

In mentioning the playthings of the child Dionysus, it tells of the Titans tearing him to pieces. They fell upon him while he was playing a child's game, amusing himself with the apples of the Hesperides. This tends to prove its existence at an earlier date in the Greek area, the sole source for its spread to Egypt. It is very interesting to note that writers under the early empire are the first to tell that the Titans had devoured the limbs of the child.

Orphism, in keeping with the formal, artificial character of its origins, left free scope for further development and personal transformation. But as opposed to the view of I. M. Linforth, it must be maintained that closed Orphic associations, therefore societies of mystai, existed already in classical Greek times. In the Hellenistic age, the Papyrus Gurob—perhaps because it was the cult legend of one of the Dionysian societies that by order of Ptolemy Philopator was required to turn over religious documents—appears to confirm the existence of mysteries under Orphic influence. Orphism in this period, however, seems to have been the object of scholarly study rather than a living and active cult.

Later History and Evaluation. An Orphic book of hymns dating from the early imperial age seems to be the work of certain societies, especially in the city of Pergamon, where a shrine has been discovered in which deities praised in the hymns were worshiped. But the manner of worship that the book indicates has nothing to do with a mystery religion so far as almost all external rites described are concerned. The cosmogony of Orphism—which is intended to include its theogony and anthropogony—was fully elaborated apparently only at a late date and is known exclusively from Neoplatonic sources. It gives an important place to the primitive cosmic egg. This motif is not a mythical Greek fabrication but belongs to the earliest mythological cosmogony and can be traced back to very early prehistoric cultures. In the Roman imperial age it was connected with the figure of Aion. The Aion of Modena is of the greatest value historically. It is a figure so loaded with attributes as to leave an unaesthetic impression; but to the men of late antiquity, to which it belongs, it served as a symbol of the esoteric wisdom underlying the outward representation. The so-called Orphic passports for the dead, found in Crete and south Italy, contain instructions for a confession of innocence similar to those with which the ancient Egyptians provided themselves for their meeting with the judge of the dead in the other world. Connection with Egypt, accordingly, has been suggested for this Orphic phenomenon (see Prümm, *Dictionnaire de la Bible*, suppl. ed. L. Pirot et al. [Paris 1928–] 6:72).

Mithraism and Other Oriental Mysteries

At the outset, it may be stated that there are certain analogies with Orphism. These analogies are found in the form of its origin and in its emphasis on doctrinal content. Mithraism, like Orphism, was founded by specific individuals. Magi, Persian priests from north and east Persia and from the highlands of Cappadocia, consciously influenced by the tendencies toward a union of Greek and Oriental religious elements, created this cult in the 4th—3d century B.C. The Oriental basis was primarily Persian popular religion and not Persian Zoroastrianism. Zoroaster had condemned all gods of the popular religion without being able to extirpate them. The Magi put the Indo-Persian deity Mitra, conceived as a noble figure and given certain features of the Babylonian sun-god Shamash, in the center of a theogonic and cosmogonic myth. The name Mitra means truth, faithfulness, or contract. (*See* MITHRAS AND MITHRAISM.)

Sources of Mithraism. In the absence of literary sources, the myth must be interpreted essentially from the monuments, a relatively large number of which have been preserved. The fairly copious monumental evidence is to be explained in part from the nature of the places of worship. The latter were artificial grottoes, imitations of natural caves, which were low and small and could accommodate only a few dozen worshipers. No Mithraic association had more than 100 members, and most of them had a much smaller number. Since the worshipers were mostly soldiers, the *Mithraea,* or shrines of the cult, have been found especially on the frontiers—hence, in Britain, along the Rhenish and Danubian Limes, and in Africa and Asia. Dura-Europos on the Euphrates was a flourishing center of Mithraism. After the abandonment of the military frontiers under various pressures, these shrines, often wholly or partly subterranean, no longer occasioned special interest, and thus much of their content was left intact. Obviously Rome as a military center and world capital with a large percentage of foreigners in its population has revealed many Mithraic shrines, though these may not have been used simultaneously. Archeological investigation has identified more than 50. Ostia, possibly more Orientalized than Rome, has yielded 18 *Mithraea,* a relatively large number, even if they are usually small.

The Mithraic Myth. The doctrine of Mithraism, a combination of Greek theogony and an Iranian myth, is concerned with the origin of fertility from a celestial bull. The god, born out of a rock, who enters an already existing pantheon of the Greek type, brings this bull from the kingdom of the moon and kills him. This triumph of youthful force was given a typical iconographic form by a great artist and this form was never changed: a representation of Nike bringing a sacrifice of thanksgiving after victory. This achievement of Mithras made Mithraism an appropriate religion for soldiers. Further mythical scenes beside the main picture show another battle of Mithras, this time with the Sun (*Sol, Helios*), who finally receives him in friendship and takes him to heaven in his chariot. The last scene undoubtedly embodies the hope that is impressed in seven ceremonial stages (Raven, Nymph, Soldier, Lion, Persian, Sun-runner, Father): an expectation of an afterlife in the sky, which gained ground under the empire, because an underworld hereafter came to be felt as gloomy and repulsive.

Mithraic Ritual. The whole interior of the Mithraic shrine is arranged for holding a meal in the ancient way, with participants reclining on couches—hence the bench-like structures along the side walls. The meal consisted of bread and water. But neither the meal nor the Mithraic baptism—exclusively a form of purification as found in many religions—was the essential element of Mithraic ritual. The all-important feature was the tests of courage required for admission to the higher degrees. They are represented in formidable fashion in the *Mithraeum* of Capua and partially also in that found under the church of St. Prisca in Rome. An inscription from the latter mentions a *cauterisatio,* the branding with the sign of the god, a ceremony that Tertullian compares with confirmation. A *Mithraeum* discovered at San Marino (Castelli Romani) exhibits beautiful cultic scenes.

For the higher speculations associated with Mithraism, the *Borysthenic* discourse of the famous Sophist Dio Chrysostom (b. *c.* A.D. 40; d. after 112), is repeatedly cited. He describes a cosmogony and an anthropogony, including a kind of original sin of man, in the sense of Plato's *Phaedrus,* but with emphasis on the Stoic doctrine of universal conflagration. It is not known, however, to what extent this is his own personal doctrine (cf. M. P. Nilsson, *Geschichte der griechischen Religion,* 2:688). The age and origin of the figure of Aion, which is often represented separately along with the bull scene and which resembles the Orphic Aion of Modena, are doubtful. The opinion of F. Cumont, who would have Aion dominate the whole pantheon, has lost ground. The figure is now identified rather with Ahriman himself, the evil principle of Mazdaism, and it seems that a place was found for this worship in Mithraism.

Other Oriental Mysteries. It is not necessary here to deal in detail with the cult of Adonis—which never became a fully developed mystery religion—and with the Egyptian mysteries, since their more important aspects were covered earlier in the article and in particular in the treatment of the Mysteries of Eleusis. Attention was called also to the possibility of connecting the congratula-

tion of the mystai on "the god that has been saved," which is directed perhaps to the mystae of the Magna Mater, with the mystae of Osiris. Since the various mysteries had so much in common, it is very much to the point to refer to a passage in the *Metamorphoses* of Apuleius. It makes a journey to the elements or the stars the core of the mysteries of Isis. This journey was probably intended to be an actual anticipation of the eventually expected real journey to the stars (see *Metamorphoses* 11.23).

Relations with Christianity

The question of the relations between the mystery religions and Christianity arose in the 19th century as a result of the simultaneous operation of two factors, namely, the systematic scholarly investigation of the history of the mystery religions by classical philology and archeology and the decline in the belief in the historical reliability of the New Testament revelation as a consequence of so-called liberal and historical exegesis. Within the limits of this article, only the high points concerning the question of relationship can be treated. For detailed coverage, see the bibliography following this article.

New Testament Evidence and Its Interpretation. In contrast to the Old Testament, where a specific warning is given against Adonis worship, the Gospels mention the Magi; and this in itself might well be interpreted as containing an allusion to a mystery cult, namely, that of the Persian Mithras (cf. Matthew ch. 2). On the basis of the copious evidence for the employment of Semitic equivalents in the Qumran texts for the Greek *mysterion,* it is clear that the mere use of the term *mysterion* does not mean that St. Paul consciously wished to imply a connection between Christian and pagan use of the term, to say nothing of any positive approval of any Christian connection with pagan mysteries whether in their forms of worship or in their literary or written presentations. Paul uses the word *mysterion* nearly always in the singular, while by contrast the pagan mysteries are nearly always mentioned in the plural. The following point is more significant. Paul employs the singular form *mysterion* in the sense of the secret, hidden design of God in its totality. There is no emphasis on the cult aspect.

Christian Mystery and Pagan Mystery. Forms of worship, namely, the Sacraments, may be included in the term *mysteria* as found in 1 Cor 4.1; but in that case, as incorporated into the plan of salvation as a unity and in subordination to the Apostles' mission of serving as ambassadors of Christ (2 Cor 5.19, 20).

Even among Catholics, a certain school of exegesis has maintained that Paul saw the tragic experiences of the heroes of the mysteries as a divine pedagogy for the pagans to prepare them for the message of salvation, and from that point of view intended to represent, as opposed to the pagan mystery cults, the real and true mystery. This is unlikely, however, for several reasons. The ancient mysteries do not represent a historical fact, but a regularly recurring annual rhythm. In Christian worship "representation" is not a theatrical and mimic one in a series of separate acts, but is centered as one single moment, the redemptive and decisive act of the Lord on the cross. Finally, in Christian worship this remembrance of a fact is not connected with specific seasons (at least in apostolic times), but takes place every Sunday, and continues to be observed even after the institution of the main liturgical feasts with Easter as their center.

The Apostles' various admonitions against revels, banquets, etc., cannot be interpreted as referring specifically and literally to the mysteries; at most they are concerned with the excesses occasioned by the public and private worship of Dionysus (Rom 13.13; Eph 5.18). Some exegetes suspect an implied condemnation of the mysteries in the reminiscence in 1 Cor 12.1 of a "magic urge" on the part of hearers to certain cults. Such scholars adopt this view because they believe that Paul, with the idea of the "dumb idols" vividly in mind, is perhaps thinking of those divinities whose emotional worship presents a certain resemblance to excesses connected with phenomena at Corinth. A more likely reference to pagan mysteries is to be found in the heresy of Colossae (see *Dictionnaire de la Bible,* suppl. ed. L. Pirot et al. [Paris 1928–] 6 [1960] 218–222).

Bibliography: The literature on the mystery religions is voluminous and, given the difficulties presented by the sources, on many points there is no unanimity among scholars. The older literature in this field, furthermore, is dominated, in general, by a tendency to regard Christianity as largely, if not exclusively, an adaptation of the pagan mysteries. General works. N. TURCHI, *Fontes historian mysteriorum aevi hellenistici* (Rome 1923). R. FOLLET and K. PRÜMM, "Mystères," *Dictionnaire de la Bible,* suppl. ed. L. PIROT et al. (Paris 1928–) 6 (1960) 1–225; *Religionsgeschichtliches Handbuch* (new ed. Rome 1954) esp. 213–356 and 843–846. (These comprehensive studies by the contributor give full details and furnish copious bibliography). O. KERN and T. HOPFNER, "Mysterien," *Paulys Realenzyklopädie der klassischen Altertumswissenschaft,* ed. G. WISSOWA et al. (Stuttgart 1893–) 16. 2 (1935) 1209–1350. U. VON WILAMOWITZ-MOELLENDORFF, *Der Glaube der Hellenen,* 2 v. (Berlin 1931–32). M. P. NILSSON, *Geschichte der griechischen Religion,* 2 v. (2d ed. Munich 1955–61). (The contents of these last two standard, comprehensive works can be easily controlled through the excellent indexes.) F. CUMONT, *Lux perpetua* (Paris 1949). Special works. P. FOUCART, *Les Mystères d'Éleusis* (Paris 1914). G. MYLONAS, *Eleusis and the Eleusinian Mysteries* (Princeton 1961), with good bibliog.; he rejects, however, interpretations given by a number of other scholars. M. P. NILSSON, *The Dionysiac Mysteries of the Hellenistic Age* (Lund 1957). M. I. ROSTOVTZEFF, *Mystic Italy* (New York 1927). H. JEANMAIRE, *Histoire du culte du Bacchus* (Paris 1959). A. BRUHL, *Liber Pater. Origine et expansion du culte dionysiaque à Rome et dans le monde romain* (Paris 1953). O. KERN, *Orphicorum fragmenta* (Berlin 1922). I. M. LINFORTH, *The Arts of Orpheus* (Berkeley 1941). W. K. C. GUTHRIE, *Orpheus and Greek Religion* (2d ed. London 1952). J. CARCOPINO, *Aspects mystiques de la Rome païenne* (Paris 1941). H. GRAILLOT, *Le Culte de Cybèle Mère de Dieu, à Rome et dans l'Empire romain* (Paris 1912). M. J. LAGRANGE, "Attis et le Cristianisme," *Revue biblique* 28 (1919) 419–480. G. NAGEL, "Les Mystères d'Osiris dans l'ancienne Égypte," *Eranos-Jahrbuch* 11 (1944) 145–166. A. J. FESTUGIÈRE, *Personal Religion among the Greeks* (Berkeley 1960). M. P. NILSSON, "The Syncretistic Relief of Modena," *Symbolae Osloenses* 24 (1945) 1ff. On the relations of the mystery religions and Christianity, in addition to K. PRÜMM, "Mystères," 173–225 *op. cit.,* see H. PINARD DE LA BOULLAYE, *L'Étude comparée des religions,* 3 v. (5th ed. Paris 1929) 1:361–544. K. PRÜMM, *Der christliche Glaube und die altheidnische Welt,* 2 v. (Leipzig 1935). L. DE GRANDMAISON, *Jesus Christ: His Person, His Message, His Credentials,* 3 v. (New York 1935–37) v. 3, esp. 349–377. M. J. LAGRANGE, *Introduction à l'étude du Nouveau Testament,* pt. 4, *Critique historique,* pt. 4.1, *Les Mystères: L'Orphisme* (2d ed. Paris 1937) esp. 187–224. C. COLPE, *Die religionsgeschichtliche Schule: Darstellung und Kritik ihres Bildes vom gnostlischen Erlösermythus* (Göttingen 1961). C. VAGAGGINI, *Il senso teologico della liturgia* (2d ed. Rome 1958); Eng. *Theological Dimensions of the Liturgy,* tr. I. I. DOYLE (Collegeville, Minn. 1959).

[K. PRÜMM]

MYSTERY THEOLOGY

The doctrine proposed by O. CASEL concerning the active presence of Christ's redeeming action in the Sacraments, especially in the Eucharist.

Casel's Theory. In more than 100 articles, letters, and works from 1918 to 1941, Casel never ceased to develop, to clarify, and to defend a doctrine that he deemed adequate to express the teachings of the Fathers and the most ancient liturgies and that he based on the notion of *mysterium.* The most explicit exposition of this doctrine can be found in his work *The Mystery of Christian Worship* (Westminster, Md. 1962; originally published in German in 1932). He says: "The mystery means three things and one. First of all it is God considered in Himself as the infinitely distant, holy, unapproachable, to whom no man may draw near and live. . . . And this all-holy one reveals His mystery, comes down to His creatures and reveals Himself to them; yet once again *in mysterio,* that is to say, in a revelation by grace to those whom He has chosen, the humble, the pure of heart" (5). "For St. Paul μυστήριον is the marvellous revelation of God in Christ. . . . Christ is the mystery in person, because He shows the invisible Godhead in the flesh" (6). "Since Christ is no longer visible among us, in St. Leo the Great's words, 'What was visible in the Lord has passed over into the mysteries.' We meet His person, His saving deeds, the working of His grace in the mysteries of His worship. ST. AMBROSE writes: 'I find you in your mysteries'" (7). "The content of the mystery of Christ is, therefore, the person of the God-man and His redeeming act for the salvation of the Church; it is through this act that the Church is integrated into the mystery" (12).

It is precisely in the mystery of worship that this integration of the Church in the mystery of Christ takes place. "As a participation in the life and truth of God, this divine reality infinitely surpasses all abstract teaching. It could not be encompassed in a doctrine; it had to find expression in symbols. Cultic symbols, then, are necessary modes of expression; they do not have a purely pedagogical value, but are bearers of divine salvation. Thus the mystery of Christ finds its necessary incarnation in the mystery of worship" ["Glaube, Gnosis und Mysterium," *Jahrbuch für Liturgieqissenschaft* 15 (1941) 276]. "The [cultic] mysteries are a working out and an application of Christ's mystery. God, who revealed Himself in the man Christ, continues after the Ascension of Christ to act on earth through Christ the high priest according to the ordinary economy of communicating grace in the Church, namely, the mystery of worship, which is nothing else but the prolongation of the God-man's action on earth" (*The Mystery of Christian Worship* 27).

Although essentially in conformity with the best tradition explicated in PIUS XII'S *Mediator Dei* and Vatican Council II's *Constitution on the Sacred Liturgy,* Casel's teaching comprised two elements that in time gave rise to violent controversies. These controversies at least have gradually shown what in Casel's position was of passing value and what represented a permanent theological acquisition.

Pagan Mysteries. Casel placed his teaching against the perspective of the mystery cults of the ancient Hellenic Mediterranean world. He certainly did not claim that the pagan mysteries exercised a direct influence on the organization of Christian worship. He nonetheless insisted that the use of the same terms by both indicated a fundamental analogy, not indeed on the level of objects, but on that of ways of expression. "The language of the ancient mysteries was used unhesitatingly to express to some extent the unfathomable content of what she [the Church] possessed; indeed many ancient forms and customs were taken over to enrich and adorn the simplicity of the Christian ritual" (*The Mystery of Christian Worship* 34).

This aspect of Casel's theory was subjected to lively attack, notably by K. Prümm and J. M. Hanssens, who rejected any influence of pagan mystery terminology in Christian liturgy and believed the Christian use of the term mystery had to be interpreted solely in accordance with its Biblical meaning: a divine secret communicated by revelation. One may say that Casel's theory has been greatly undermined by subsequent research done on the mystery cults. It seems well established that the latter contained no precise doctrine on the participation of the mysteries in the divine life, even less on the intervention of savior-gods. On the contrary, D. Deden and G. Söhngen appear to have solidly proved the continuity of the Christian doctrine of mystery with the Biblical tradition, notably the Pauline texts.

Presence of the Redemptive Act. Casel, however, put the accent on the active reality of the mystery of salvation to the point that the very presence of the saving act becomes reactualized in the liturgy. He based the necessity for this reactualization on the fact—to him indisputable—that tradition understands man's participation in the mystery of salvation as implying and demanding a real but mystical participation in the life and death of Christ. It demands a life and a death of Christ in the very sacramental act; this is how we share in His act of salvation. Some of Casel's expressions seem to imply a reactualization of even the historical aspect of the redemptive act. Despite his lack of precision, his thought was very firm on this point. He did not insist on such historical contingencies, but his fear of seeing the realism of the mystery-presence reduced, and his inability to use a more conceptual way of thinking prevented him from accepting the approach of other theologians, even of those who were less distant from his own conception than he recognized. However, his disciples, notably V. Warnach and B. Neunheuser, thought they were able to be faithful to him and yet propose explanations with more delicate nuances and more in conformity with classical theological modes of expression.

Controversy and Progress. Both aspects of Casel's doctrine came in for criticism; his harshest critics were J. B. Umberg and Prümm, who rejected not only his theory of the Christian mystery's relationship to the pagan mystery cults, but also his conception of the mystery presence.

The traditional character of Casel's doctrine and its conformity with patristic teaching have also been the object of discussions. It can now be considered as established (L. Monden, E. Schillebeeckx, and J. Betz) that the Fathers

> . . . regard sacramental grace as an ontological participation in the glorified existence of Christ by means of a real configuration to the mystery of His passion and death. In particular, they hold the Mass to be the reactualization, the representation (in the etymological sense of the word) of the sacrificial act of Christ on the cross for His Mystical Body. They therefore clearly and indubitably affirm the *fact* of a presence of Christ's death as a saving act in the mystery of Christian worship. Beyond this they do not go. One does not find in

their writings a speculatively elaborated theory of the Sacraments; they do not provide any indications as to the *how* of the mystery presence. [Monden 188]

The compatibility of Casel's doctrine with St. THOMAS AQUINAS'S theology was also discussed. Casel himself did not seem certain that his teaching was in accord with Thomas. Söhngen, the first theologian to attempt the integration of a modified Caselian doctrine in the perspective of classical theology, considered Casel's thought at least foreign to Thomas's teaching.

Such was not the opinion of E. Schillebeeckx, who took up and deepened the views of A. Vonier and E. Masure. Because of the hypostatic union, all that Christ's humanity experienced was assumed by the Divine Person whose acts do not suffer the limits of duration. Consequently, the effect of each act will be realized when the Divine Will, eternally actual, determines that it should be realized. It is primarily through the Sacraments and the other mysteries of worship instituted by the Church that the redemptive mystery is brought to us according to the will of Christ. Summarizing Schillebeeckx's thought, J. Gaillard writes (541):

> In the liturgical mysteries we have, at one and the same time, the actual presence of the transcendent element and the virtual presence of the total act (passion, resurrection, etc.) always acting, though its transitory elements belong definitively to the past. The historical salvific act is thus attained by the mysteries, either in itself as far as its permanent element is concerned, or by divine power as far as its purely temporal element is concerned. Liturgical mysteries are truly the celebration and manifestation of the historical redeeming act, even though their actual content is only the *mysterium*, i.e., the permanent element and the instrumental power.

Moreover, the Thomistic teaching on the sacramental character as a participation in the priesthood of Christ ensures "the real foundation for this unity [of the various liturgical mysteries] and therefore occupies a key position in Catholic sacramentalism. Because of the sacramental character, the symbolic worship of the Church becomes a *mysterium;* by this *mysterium* the Sacraments are Christ's own actions in and through the Church" (Schillebeeckx 670).

Bibliography: A complete list of Casel's works (211 nos.) may be found in A. MAYER et al., eds., *Vom christlichen Mysterium* (Düsseldorf 1951). For the study of the various controversies, the essential work remains T. FILTHAUT, *Die Kontroverse uber die Mysterienlehre* (Warendorf 1947), Fr. *La Théologie des mystères* (Paris 1955). G. SÖHNGEN, *Symbol und Wirklichkeit im Kultmysterium* (Bonn 1937): *Der Wesensaufbau des Mysteriums* (Bonn 1938). V. WARNACH, "Zum Problem der Mysteriengegenwart," *Liturgis-ches Leben* 5 (1938) 9–39. B. NEUNHEUSER, "Mysteriengegenwart: Ein Theologumenon inmitten des Gesprächs," *Archiv Für Liturgiewissenschaft* 3 (1953) 104–133; "Ende des Gesprächs um die Mysteriengegenwart?" *ibid.* 4 (1956) 316–324; "Dom Odo Casel and Latest Research," *Downside Review* 76 (1958) 266–273. L. MONDEN, *Het Misoffer als Mysterie* (Roermond 1948). J. BETZ, *Die Eucharistie in der Zeit der griechischen Väter* (Freiburg 1955–61) v.1.1. E. MASURE, *The Sacrifice of the Mystical Body,* tr. A. THOROLD (London 1954). A. VONIER, *A Key to the Doctrine of the Eucharist* (1925; reprint Westminster, Md. 1956). E. H. SCHILLEBEECKX, *De sacramentele heilseconomie* (Antwerp 1952). C. DAVIS, "Dom Odo Casel and the Theology of Mysteries," *Worship* 34 (1960) 428–438; *Liturgy and Doctrine* (New York 1960). D. DEDEN, "Le 'Mystère' paulinien," *Ephemerides theologicae Lovanienses* 13 (1936) 405–442. J. UMBERG, "Mysterien Frömmigkeit?" *Zeitschrift für Aszese und Mystik* 1 (1926) 351–356; "Die These von der Mysteriengegenwart," *Zeitschrift für katholische Theologie* 52 (1928) 357–400; "Sacramenta efficiunt quod significant," *ibid.* 54 (1930) 92–105. J. M. HANSSENS, "Estne Liturgia cultus mystericus?" *Periodica de re morali canonica liturgica* 23 (1934) 112–132, 137–160. K. PRÜMM, *Der christliche Glaube und die altheidnische Welt,* 2 v. (Leipzig 1935); *Christentum als Neuheitserlebnis* (Freiburg 1939). J. GAILLARD, "La Théologie des Mystères," *Revue thomiste* 57 (1957) 510–551. A. SCHILSON, *Theologie als Sakramententheologie: Die Mysterientheologie Odo Casels,* 2nd ed. (Mainz 1987). A. SCHILSON, "Die Gegenwart des Ursprungs: Überlegungen zur bleibenden Aktualität der Mysterientheologie Odo Casels," *Liturgisches Jahrbuch* 43 (1993) 6–29. M.-J. KRAHE, *"Der Herr ist der Geist": Studien zur Theologie Odo Casels,* 2 vols. (St. Ottilien 1986). A. A. HÄUSSLING, "Odo Casel – noch von Aktualität? Eine Rückschau in eigener Sache aus Anlaß des hundertsten Geburtstages des ersten Herausgebers," *Archiv für Liturgiewissenschaft* 28 (1986) 357–387. A. GROZIER, *Odo Casel – Künder des Christusmysteriums,* ed. Abt-Herwegen-Institut der Abtei Maria Laach (Regensburg 1986).

[I. H. DALMAIS/EDS.]

MYSTICAL BODY OF CHRIST

The phrase "Body of Christ," as applied to the Church, is both Pauline and patristic, but the adjectival modifier "mystical" is neither. As far as known, the phrase "*Mystical* Body" is first used to designate the militant Church in Latin theological writings of the second half of the 12th century; and the first official document using it is Boniface VIII's bull *Unam Sanctam* (Nov. 18, 1302, H. Denzinger, *Enchiridion symbolorum* 870–75). From the time of the Eucharistic controversies in the 9th century until c. 1150, the Latin phrase *Corpus mysticum* occurs frequently, but it always means Christ's Eucharistic Body. In this Eucharistic meaning there is at work a profound awareness, chiefly Augustinian in inspiration, of the intimate link between Christ's Eucharistic (i.e., mystical) Body, and his Church Body, often called at this time Christ's true Body (*verum Corpus*). The connection is this: the mystical Eucharistic Body, as a sacramental mystery, both signifies and realizes the "true" or Church-Body of Christ. From c. 1150 onward, BEREN-

GARIUS's errors touching Christ's Eucharistic Presence occasioned by way of reaction such an emphasis on the identity of Christ's Eucharistic Body with his "physical" Body (see *Enchiridion symbolorum* 700), that the Eucharist began to be called Christ's "true" Body (*verum Corpus*); and, by a gradual inversion of the two earlier formulas, Christ's Church-Body began to be called his Mystical Body to distinguish it from his true physical Body present in the Eucharist. At first, the qualifier "mystical," applied to the Church-Body, kept its traditional Eucharistic resonances; the Church-Body is thought of as a "mystically" or sacramentally signified and realized Body. With the passage of time, however, this Eucharistic sense of the qualifier "mystical" gradually disappeared. In St. Thomas this dissociation of the adjective "mystical" from its Eucharistic context seems already well begun (see *Summa theologiae* 3, 8.1 and 8.3); and by the time of the Reformation the Eucharistic connection was wholly lost. For the meaning attached to the term in the early 20th century, see Pius XII's encyclical MYSTICI CORPORIS, par. 58.

St. Paul. Exegetes are not wholly agreed (1) on the origin and meaning of the Pauline theme "Body of Christ;" (2) on the relation between 1 Cor and Rom, where the theme occurs only occasionally, and later epistles such as Col and Eph, where the theme is central and combined with the new themes of "Head" and "fullness."

Origin of Theme. Some exegetes see its origin in the popular Stoic commonplace likening the cosmos or the state to an organism (see 1 Cor 12.12–30; Rom 12.4–5), while others prefer to appeal to the Gnostic myth-motif of the Primal Heavenly Man. Still the most distinctively important elements of the Pauline Body of Christ theme are to be found within the resources of Christian revelation and life, and within the framework of Judaic habits of thought and of expression.

In his presentation of SALVATION HISTORY St. Paul sees Christ as the countertype of ADAM. Just as "the first man, Adam" (1 Cor 15.45) was the head of humankind in its catastrophic fall, so Christ, "the last Adam, became a life-giving spirit" (*ibid.*) to the new humankind, restored according to "the likeness of the heavenly man" (1 Cor 15.49; see Rom 8.29. See in general 1 Cor 15.20–28; 45–49; Rom 5.12–21). Because Christ, risen and glorified after the victory in his own Body-Person over sin and death, is "the beginning" (Col 1.18; 1 Cor 15.20, 23), i.e., not merely a fresh start in time, but a total fontal beginning of new life, he is the Head of the new humanity in whom all live anew.

In this Adam-Christ parallel St. Paul is using a Hebraic category of thought, namely, the so-called "corpo-rate or inclusive personality." To the Hebraic mind the father-head of a family or nation is looked on as fulfilling a real-representative role compassing and including all his issue; he acts in their name and stead and holds their destiny in his own person and work. His descendants in turn are their forefather, in the sense that his destiny unfolds itself in their lives. This conceptual framework enabled the Hebrew to pass in thought and language from the One to the Many in him, and vice versa. Such inclusiveness, when applied to Christ's Person and work, supposes his oneness with human flesh and blood, but is grounded primarily in his mission, held from his Father, to be the one who is the beginning of the new age and the new creation; whose saving acts, once done in history's center, have meaning and make destiny for the Many compassed in his Body-Person; and whose Spirit-filled Humanity is now in glory qualified to invest sacramentally the Many, as they appear in the unfolding of time, with the new life which is his once and forever.

To appreciate the realism of St. Paul's SOTERIOLOGY, one must recognize how forcefully he stresses the role of the human being Jesus in salvation history (see Rom 5.15; 1 Cor 15.21; 15.47; 1 Timothy 2.5). To St. Paul SALVATION in Christ is neither Greek nor Gnostic in aiming at any final emancipation from the body; rather it presses for the integral renewal of the "old man" in totality. This is possible only through union with the human being Jesus and with his saving work, wrought in his Body-Person; this is possible only through a sharing in his passage from his lowly Body of death, wholly like (sin apart) the human being's own natural style of existence, to his new Body of life in glory. In Christ's own life the Body of sin and death, which he took on himself at his Father's behest, was broken in death (see Rom 8.3), and in a critical reversal of the old world's momentum this same Body, now "spiritual" and "life-giving" (1 Cor 15.44–58), is endowed with all the newness of life through the Spirit (Rom 1.4). To be saved one must share in Christ's way and level of life; one must be wholly conformed to "the body of his glory" (Phil 3.21; see 2 Cor 3.18); one must "bear the likeness of the heavenly man" (1 Cor 15.49). The Body of Jesus, the living Body-Person, has then the decisive role in the work of the salvation of humans; and it is into that Body, passing and passed from death to glorious life, that Christians are baptized (see Rom 6.3–11; Gal 3.27; 1 Cor 1.13–15) in a union the reality of which belongs to a new final order that in this present world is still hidden (Col 3.3) and only beginning. By Baptism in faith the whole Christian, as a body-person, begins sharing in the new life of the human being Jesus, and this sacramental union, inaugurated in Baptism and consummated in the Eucharist, tends right from the start, even in this world, toward the "spiritual

West Hills College Coalinga
Fitch Library
300 Cherry Lane
Coalinga, CA 93210

body'' that will transform the human being's ''natural body'' (1 Cor 15.44; see Rom 6.8; 8.11).

The Pauline theme of the Body of Christ has thus primarily a soteriological provenience and meaning. It always involves a reference to the individual Body of Christ, i.e., to him who has borne death up in his own Body onto the cross, and who enters into heaven to become the bearer of new life in his glorious Body. The mode of this most unique of unions by which the glorious Christ compasses in himself all Christians as his members is something St. Paul is not much concerned with. What he does stress is: (1) the tremendous reality and intimacy of this inward-outward union, without prejudice to the distinct personalities, divine or human; (2) the prime ground of the union in the dead and risen Savior, the human being Jesus (see Col 2.17); (3) the wholeness of the term of the union, i.e., the individual member is a body-person; and (4) the many members who are Body together, or ''fellow members of the same body'' (Eph 3.6).

Relation of Great Epistles to Col and Eph. The main lines of the development of the theme in Rom and 1 Cor (1 Cor 6.12–20; 10.17; 12.12–30; Rom 12.4–5) are substantially continued in later epistles (Col 2.11–13, compared with 1.22; 3.9–11; Eph 2.14–16; 4.4–6). These letters are clearly within the tradition of Paul, though their direct authorship is debatable. They combine new traits with the earlier Body of Christ theme, thus enriching it with a fusion of new elements. The new emphases in Col are the following: (1) the Body is now personified and practically identified with the universal Church; (2) the glorified Christ appears as the Head of the Church-Body and is thus clearly distinguished from it; and (3) the Body theme is associated with a more cosmic dimension of salvation, a development that is manifested by its linkage with the term ''fullness.'' Eph includes these themes and contributes further: (1) a focus on the hierarchical structure of the Body of Christ; and (2) the image of the Church as the ''Bride of Christ,'' which stresses its distinctiveness from Christ more than its identity. The Body of Christ now designates the object of Christ's redemptive love; He is the ''savior of the body'' (Eph 5.23), of which Christians are ''the members'' (5.30). This Body is a living organism, holding together all Christians and which ''attains a growth which is of God'' (Col 2.19; see Eph 4.16). This Body is ''the Church'' (Col 1.18, 24; Eph 1.22–23; 5.23–33); Christians are its ''members'' (Eph 4.25); and Christ is its ''Head'' (Col 1.18; 2.19; Eph 1.22; 4.15–16; 5.23). Lastly, this Body is associated with the theme of ''fullness'' (Col 1.18–2.3; 2.9; Eph 1.23; 4.13–16).

In the Head-Body combination, the term Head is used in a twofold metaphorical sense: (1) superior authority or leader (Col 1.18; Eph 1.22; 5.23); (2) source of the energies of life and growth (Col 2.19; Eph 4.15–16). The origin of this thematic combination is not easy to discern. However, the term Head, meaning superior authority, is a Biblical metaphor, which St. Paul applies to Christ, apart from the Body theme, first in 1 Cor 11.3, and then later in Col 2.10. In the latter case St. Paul calls Christ the Head of the cosmic ''Powers,'' thus countering certain false speculations, current at Colossae, that placed Christ on a level with these ''Powers.'' Once Christ is thus thought of as Head in this sense, the metaphor could be conveniently combined with the Body theme, with Christ becoming the authoritative Head, the glorious Lord, ruling his Body the Church. The Head-Body combination once thus made, could admit a further metaphorical coloration with the use of the term Head to signify the vital principle of nurture and of growth in a living body, a usage which St. Paul could have taken over from his Hellenistic milieu, especially from the Stoics or from contemporary medical language.

The splendid passage in Eph 5.22–32 is a synthesis of all the ideas on the Church as Body and Christ as Head, with the exception of the Head understood as principle of the Body's life and growth.

Members of the Body. For St. Paul the baptized faithful are members of the Body. He emphasizes the charismatic diversity in unity of the various members of Christ's Body in his one Spirit (1 Cor 12; Rom 12.3–8). The faithful are ''fellow-members of the same body'' (Eph 3.6), not in spite of their differing CHARISMS, but because of them. The member's various gifts (see 1 Cor 12.7) are meant to conspire under the one Spirit, their author and mover (1 Cor 12.7–11; see Eph 4.7), to serve and adorn the whole Body (Rom 12.3–8; 1 Cor 12.7; 14.12, 26). This unity in diversity is a permanent characteristic of the structure and life of Christ's Body (1 Cor 12; Rom 12.3–8).

Spirit and Body. That Christ's Body is intimately joined to the Spirit is clear from the way St. Paul coordinates ''one body and one Spirit'' (Eph 4.4; see Eph 2.16, 18). The Spirit that is the life principle of the new economy is the Spirit of the Father who quickens the Body of the risen Christ, and through Him, the Christian (1 Cor 15.44–49; see 1 Cor 6.17). The Spirit of Christ (Rom 8.9; Gal 4.6; Phil 1.19; see 2 Cor 3.17) is the inward life-giving principle, sovereignly building up and forming the Church as the living Body of Christ (1 Cor 12.3–11, 13). The Spirit is given in Baptism (1 Cor 6.11; Tit 3.5).

Fathers. The mystery of the Church as Christ's Body found congenial expression in the Fathers (notably Origen, Hilary, Athanasius, Chrysostom, Cyril of Alexandria, and Augustine), although often they treat it less in itself than in the elaboration of other doctrinal themes, e.g., the INCARNATION, the REDEMPTION, the divinization of the Christian, and the Eucharist. Here only certain general patristic orientations will be indicated.

(1) St. Ignatius of Antioch touched the heart of this mystery when he urged the faithful of the Church of Magnesia to "a union both according to the flesh and according to the spirit" (*To the Magnesians*, 1.2; see *To the Smyrnaeans*, 12.2). The key patristic belief that Ignatius expresses here is this: that the empiric Church-Body that the Fathers knew so well as churchmen and as faithful is Christ's Spirit-quickened Body; that the great mystery that the Father had in mind since eternity is now being realized, with a beginning finality, in the continuing work of Christ in his Body, the present Church. In the early Church "the appeal to the Church's holiness was born of the fact that men took the visible Church seriously" (J. Ratzinger, *Volk und Haus Gottes in Augustins Lehre von der Kirche*, München 1954, 65). The grace of the new economy is profoundly incarnational, an embodied grace, because the Church's "beginning and first-fruits is the flesh of Christ" (Augustine, *In epist. Ioh.* 2.2, *Patrologia Latina*, ed. J. P Migne, 35:1990). The principle that the Fathers used in their reflections on the mystery of the visible Church is "the sacramental principle, which marks the necessary union between the visible sign and the hidden reality, . . . a principle as dear to the West as to the East" (J. DANIÉLOU, "Μία Ἐκκλησία chez les Pères grecs des premiers siécles," in *1054–1954: L'Église et les Églises*, Chevetogne 1954, 1.139).

(2) A second patristic constant is this: "the great and glorious Body of Christ" (Irenaeus, *Adversus haereses* 4.33.7, *Patrologia Graeca*, ed. J. P. Migne, 7:1076) is the one sphere of Christ's Spirit ever "realizing the will of the Father in human beings and renewing them from their old way into the newness of Christ" (*ibid.* 3.17.1, *Patrologia Graeca* 7:929). "For," says Paul, "God has established in the Church Apostles, prophets, teachers,—and all the other effects of the Spirit's working, in which those who do not come together in the Church, have no share. . . . Where the Church is, there is the Spirit of God; and where the Spirit of God is, there is the Church and all grace. And the Spirit is truth. Wherefore those who have no share in the Spirit . . . do not drink of the shining water flowing from the Body of Christ . . . "(*ibid.* 3.24.1, *Patrologia Graeca* 7:966). It is to "Christ's own Spirit" (Cyril of Alexandria, *In Ioh. Evang.* 17.20–21, *Patrologia Graeca* 74:561) that is primarily due the varied and total inward-outward life of Christ's Body, in which each member has his proper energies and role suiting him to serve the interplay of faith and hope and love in the communion of the saints; it is to the Spirit likewise that is due the Body's splendid holiness. These patristic convictions are condensed in an Augustinian formula still current: "What the soul is to the body of a human being, that the Holy Spirit is to Christ's Body which is the Church" (*Serm.* 267.4, *Patrologia Latina* 38:1231). Indeed these patristic affirmations were so urgent and so massive that they opened up genuine problems. Faced with certain heterodox puritan movements such as MONTANISM and DONATISM, the Fathers were challenged to save not merely the appearances, but the reality of the "Una Sancta," the One Holy Body of Christ. Among the troublesome problems that they thus had to grapple with were these: (a) how is the grave sinner, especially a heresiarch, to be thought of as having place and role within the glorious Body of Christ; (b) in what measure is the Spirit, with his grace, at work outside the Church's frontiers, particularly in the Sacraments of the schismatic and Heretic?

(3) Another significant orientation is the indissoluble association that the Fathers proclaimed between Christ's Eucharistic Body and his Church-Body, with the Eucharist being the supreme symbol and the chief realization of the inward-outward unity of the Church-Body. To the Fathers it was unthinkable to accord the Eucharist a kind of independent treatment apart from its chief effect, which is the in- and con-corporation of Christ's members in his one Body. To partake of the Eucharist meant to be embodied into the Church. Communion in the sacred "things" or elements of the Eucharist (*communio sanctorum* in the real-sacramental sense) meant communion with Christ and with the saints who are his members (*communio sanctorum* in the masculine-personal sense). For St. Augustine, writes Ratzinger, "what makes the essence of the concrete Church is this: that she celebrates and is the Body of Christ" ("Herkunft und Sinn der Civitas-Lehre Augustins," in *Augustinus Magister*, Paris 1954, 2.978). Augustine, who here, as elsewhere, dominates the whole development of medieval ECCLESIOLOGY, says: "If then you are the Body of Christ and his members, your mystery is laid on the Lord's table; you are receiving your own mystery. . . . Be what you see, and receive what you are" (*Serm.* 272, *Patrologia Latina* 38:1247–48).

(4) One last patristic orientation. At times some Fathers give the term "Body of Christ" a meaning and an extension different from that of the Pauline letters, in which Christ's Body is a visible Body, sacramentally and hierarchically structured, and composed of baptized Christians as its members. St. Augustine, e.g., more than once makes the Body of Christ comprehend all the saints "who are to be born and to believe in Christ from Abel himself until the end of time" (*In Psalm. 90 serm.* 2.1, *Patrologia Latina* 37:1159). The Church-Body thus understood as reaching out and comprising in a solidarity

of Christian faith all the saints of both covenants, old and new, is a theological construct, due mainly to the Latin Fathers. St. Augustine and St. Gregory the Great were deeply influential in impressing this development on later Western ecclesiology.

Although the Fathers found it useful to express in this way the continuing unity of the whole historical economy of salvation, nevertheless they had a deep sense of the newness and originality of Christianity and held that the Church of the Old Testament was but an imperfect, preparatory stage, a kind of childhood minority with respect to the adult Church of the New Testament. But in their effort to stress the overall economy of salvation in the one Christ, what held their attention, at least from St. Augustine onward, was rather the invisible line of inward Christian grace; whereas the continuing embodiment, itself a grace, of that same inward grace in both the Old Testament and the New Testament, was much less satisfactorily integrated into a balanced synthesis. This orientation tended to view the mystery of salvation from a metahistorical and an asocial plane. In affirming that the Old Testament saints, by their faith in the Christ to come, were really Christians and members of his Body, St. Augustine explained that "the times have changed, but not the faith . . . the signs have varied, but the faith abides" (In evang. Ioh. 45.9, Patrologia Latina 35:1722, 1723). This Augustinian orientation occasioned in subsequent Western theology a bias toward an un-Pauline disembodiment of Christ's Body, toward a one-sided view of Christ's Body as an interior community of grace with Christ, whose headship is thus limited to an invisible inpouring of grace. The question left unanswered is this: what has the fullness of the times (Heb 1.1–2) brought to the fullness of the mystery; and wherein lies the fulfillment within the acknowledged continuity (Col 2.17)?

Medieval Period. St. Augustine's authority dominates the ecclesiology of the early and high scholastic periods. As in the patristic age, so too here there are no formal treatises of ecclesiology. The pertinent matter is distributed piecemeal, not only in the various questions of the summists (see SENTENCES AND SUMMAE), but also in liturgical, homiletic, and exegetical writings.

In the 12th century the dominant description of the Church is the Body of Christ. This designation, although allowing a variety of meaning and extension as in the Fathers, still has its central reference and focus in the visible Catholic Church. However, the elaboration of the theme "Body of Christ" commonly emphasizes the inward community of grace in Christ, without any special effort to integrate the socio-juridic aspect of the Church into the Body of Christ. Such a one-sided concern marks an inchoative dissociation of sensibility and interest with respect to the total mystery, i.e., the theandric reality of the Body of Christ. The reasons for this practical dissociation are the following: (1) the patronage of the Augustinian tradition in ecclesiology; (2) the then visible Church as a reality, peacefully forming and framing life, unchallenged by any significant heresies; (3) the beginnings of Canon Law as a separate discipline, with socio-juridic questions in ecclesiology falling gradually to its purview, while the more inward elements of the Church were appropriated to speculative dogma.

The 13th century does not fundamentally alter the orientations and emphases of the 12th. The scholastics of this period, beyond doubt, had a sound sense of the theandric nature of the Body of Christ (see, e.g., St. Thomas, Summa theologiae 1a2ae, 108.1; 3a, 60.6; 3a, 62.6). This fact is discernible, for instance, in the physico-instrumental causality assigned by St. Thomas to Christ the Head in his humanity (Summa theologiae 3a, 8.1 ad 1), a role that Augustine never attributed to the human being Jesus (see G. Philips, "L'influence du Christ Chef sur son corps mystique suivant s. Augustin," in Augustinus Magister, Paris 1954, 2.805–15); it is perceptible, too, in the strongly affirmed ecclesial dimension of the Eucharist, which is "the Sacrament of Church unity" (St. Thomas, Summa theologiae 3a, 67.2), and whose reality is "the unity of the Mystical Body" (Summa theologiae 3a, 73.3), or "the Mystical Body of Christ which is the society of the saints" (Summa theologiae 3a, 80.4).

It is clear enough, however, that in practice the 13th-century theologians were more interested in the inward grace of the Christian Body than in the Christian embodiment, itself a grace, of that inward grace. What commanded their attention was the inwardness of grace. This fact is discernible in various ways:

1. In the Augustinian view that "the ancient Fathers belonged to the same Body of the Church as we do" (St. Thomas, Summa theologiae 3a, 8.3 ad 3). Citing the Aristotelean dictum that "each thing appears to be that which preponderates in it" (Summa theologiae 1a2ae, 106.1), and rightly holding that "the grace of the Holy Spirit" (ibid.) is the chief element in the New Covenant, St. Thomas concludes that the saints of the Old Covenant "in this respect belonged to the New Testament" (ibid., ad 3). This theological construct uses "Body" in a quite un-Pauline way.

2. In the treatment of Christ's Headship—and of the correlative membership or incorporation of the faithful—principally from the viewpoint of the Head's invisible inpouring of interior grace (St. Thomas, Summa theologiae 3a, 8.3 corp. and ad 3) and of the member's inward adhesion to the Head through faith and love.

3. In the tendency to look on the heavenly Church in a way analogous to the Augustinian consideration of the Church of the New Alliance, i.e., to attend to what is "principal" in it, namely, the soul's vision of the Triune God, without a firm enough evangelical emphasis on what is "secondary," i.e., the whole human being, according to the Biblical anthropology, gloriously sharing in one's risen body in the new life with one's fellows (see St. Thomas, *In 3 Sent.* 26.2.5, sols. 1–2 compared with *Summa theologiae* 1a2ae, 106.1 corp. and ad 1; 1a2ae, 107.1 ad 3).

14th to the 19th Century. The 14th and 15th centuries mark the beginnings of a separate treatise on the Church, often the work of canonists and arising chiefly under the sign of controversy. The 16th-century Reformers, with their dissociation of any empirical Church from the true Church of the saints or the predestined, led the Catholic controversialists to counter by stressing the visible Church as the social means of salvation and by deemphasizing some of the older Augustinian themes judged less useful to mark the visible reality of the New Testament Church. BELLARMINE, e.g., distinguishing between the "body" and the "soul" of the Church, and between the various ways of pertaining to them, singly and jointly, (see *De Eccl. Mil.*, ch. 2), gives a value to the element "body" in which, at the rare extreme, the visible elements, i.e., "the external profession of the faith and sharing in the sacraments" (*ibid.*), seem to acquire almost a consistency by themselves. The Church, which is "a society, not of angels, nor of souls, but of human beings" (*ibid.* ch. 12), has for "its form, not interior faith, . . . but exterior, i.e., the confession of faith"(*ibid.* ch. 10). In this Bellarminian emphasis, which admittedly considers only very extreme cases, the meaning of "body" becomes almost the opposite of what that term so often stressed in the medieval scholastics, i.e., the inward grace-filled company of the Christian saints. At the same time the older Augustinian ecclesiology continued its way unflaggingly, chiefly in more speculative theological writing.

It is symptomatic that neither orientation was very successful with the theological problem of the grave sinner's place in Christ's Body; and that often the solution, phrased in embarrassed language, resulted in a partial dissociation of the visible Church and the Mystical Body.

19th Century. J. A. MÖHLER (1796 to 1838) contributed decisively to a recentering of the theology of the Mystical Body, though his early and later works stand somewhat in tension with each other. In *Die Einheit in der Kirche* (1825) Möhler rather romantically describes the Body of the Church as "the concentration of love" (no. 64), thus assigning a dynamism to grace that is in-

ward-outward in its orientation; "the whole social structure of the Church is nothing else but the embodied love" (*ibid.* of the community of the faithful, itsel fashioned by the Spirit of the Lord. In *Symbolik* (5th ed. 1838), however, Möhler resolutely makes the redemptive Incarnation the guiding principle of his ecclesiology. The visible Body of the Church is presented as a theandric mystery, patterned on Christ as its paradigm (*see* THEANDRIC ACTS OF CHRIST), and charged with continuing his work and his way among human beings until he come. Möhler thus establishes a fruitful and harmonious interplay of life between the Church as the bearer of salvation and the Church as the company of the saints; under both aspects—that of the saving energies of Christian grace and that of the new life of salvation in Christian grace—the Church is an embodied grace, both sacramental and social.

Möhler's later orientations were usefully elaborated by several theologians who in one way or another underwent his influence and who had an affinity of spirit with him. They are Carlo PASSAGLIA (1812 to 1887), Klemens SCHRADER (1820 to 1875), J. B. FRANZELIN (1816 to 1886), and the celebrated M. J. SCHEEBEN (1835 to 1888). The work of the first three of these, although today not well known, was solid and influential. Themes from Möhler's early and later works continue to stand in tension in contemporary ecclesiology.

20th Century. Pius XII's *Mystici Corporis* (1943) used the Mystical Body of Christ to tie together the Church understood as a social institution with the Church of grace and love imbued with the Holy Spirit. In that encyclical, he explicitly identified the Mystical Body of Christ with the Roman Catholic Church. Many theologians whose work was to be influential at the Second Vatican Council, such as Yves Congar and Charles Journet, developed the mystical body as a major theme. Vatican II's *Lumen gentium* also used the Mystical Body of Christ as a prominent image. It complemented it, however, with other important images of the Church, such as the People of God, the Pilgrim Church, the Communion of Saints, and the Church as Leaven in the World. Also, although *Mystici Corporis* was not lacking in ecumenical sensitivity, in *Lumen Gentium* the identification of the Mystical Body with the Catholic Church was expressed in a yet more ecumenically sensitive manner: "this church of Christ . . . subsists in the Catholic Church. . . . Nevertheless, many elements of sanctification and of truth are found outside its visible confines." (8) The Mystical Body of Christ continues to function in official church documents as well as the work of theologians as a primary and indispensable image of the Church.

See Also: BROTHER IN CHRIST; INCORPORATION IN CHRIST; SOUL OF THE CHURCH; COMMUNION OF

SAINTS; OFFICE, ECCLESIASTICAL; PAUL, APOSTLE, ST.; CHURCH, ARTICLES ON.

Bibliography: P. BENOIT, ''Corps, tête et plérôme dans les épîtres de la captivité,'' *Revue biblique* 63 (1956) 5–44. L. CERFAUX, *The Church in the Theology of St. Paul,* tr. G. WEBB and A. WALKER (New York 1959). J. A. T. ROBINSON, *The Body: A Study in Pauline Theology* (London 1952). F. MALMBERG, *Ein Leib - Ein Geist* (Freiburg 1960). S. TROMP, *Corpus Christi quod est ecclesia,* 3 v. (Rome 1960). H. DE LUBAC, *Corpus Mysticum: L'Eucharistie et l'église au moyen-âge* (2d ed. Paris 1949). M. SCHMAUS, *Die Lehre von der Kirche,* v.3.1 of *Katholische Dogmatik* (5th ed. Munich 1955–58). É. MERSCH, *The Whole Christ,* tr. J. R. KELLEY (Milwaukee 1938; London 1949). V. BRANICK, *Understanding the New Testament and Its New Testament and Its Message* (New York 1998). M. HIMES, *Ongoing Incarnation: Johann Adam Möhler and the Beginnings of Modern Ecclesiology* (New York 1997).

[F. X. LAWLOR/D. M. DOYLE]

MYSTICAL MARRIAGE

Mystical marriage or spiritual marriage (also espousal to Christ) is a figure used to denote the state of a human soul living intimately united to God through grace and love. In a broad sense, mystical marriage is applicable to all unions of souls loved by God and drawn to Him, as in the case of virgins solemnly consecrated, religious in vows, and all other souls espoused to Christ (2 Cor 11.2). More properly, and in a more restricted sense, mystical marriage refers to what is recognized in mystical theology as a ''transforming'' union between a soul and God, requiring extraordinary graces, and to which God calls only a few particularly privileged persons, e.g., SS. John of the Cross and Teresa of Avila. The latter (*Interior Castle,* 7 Mansions, ch. 2) and the former (*Spir. Cant.,* stanzas 12–27) recognize the ''transforming'' (permanent) union as distinct from and higher than mere spiritual bethrothal (transitory). Mystical marriage constitutes a consummate union of love; a total possession, a fusion of ''lives''—the soul is made one with God, made divine, by participation, without losing its identity. It is a total union involving the transformation of the substance of the soul by sanctifying grace, and the transformation of the faculties by divine light and love (*Ascent of Mt. Carmel* 2, 5, 6). The initiative in this matter and the choice of souls to whom this union is granted belong to Christ. It is permeated with His transcendence; its action and effects are of the Holy Spirit. Though this union is not of its own will, the soul ''adheres to Christ with all its strength; lives for Him; allows itself to be ruled by Him,'' according to St. Bernard of Clairvaux (*In Cant. Serm.* 85, 12).

It is a union that comprises the elements of a certain continuous awareness of the presence of the Divine Spouse; a consciousness of His assistance in the higher operation of intellect and will. These and other characteristics notwithstanding, we find St. Teresa admitting that she did not know with what to compare it—since it is so sublime a favor and brings the soul such great delight (7 *Mansions*).

The model of mystical marriage is the union of the Humanity of Christ with the Verbum—a union perfect in charity and absolute in continuity. Mary, the Bride of Christ par excellence, is its greatest exemplar in this life.

The figure of marriage significantly portrays that intimate union of a completely dedicated soul (bride) to Christ (Bridegroom). Its basis is found in Holy Scripture, e.g., marriage was a common image of the union of Yahweh and His people Israel (Hos 2.19). It was a figure familiar to the Fathers of the Church. St. Ambrose referred to consecrated virgins as ''married to God'' (*De Virg.,* I, c.8, n.52). Jesus called Himself the ''Bridegroom'' (Mt 9.15); and St. Paul writes: ''For I betrothed you to one spouse'' [Christ] (2 Cor 11.2).

Mystical marriage is always related to the mystery of Redemption, which was accomplished objectively through the Redeemer, Christ the Bridegroom; and is realized subjectively in the soul-bride, through Baptism and sanctification. Redemption enters into the very essence of mystical marriage; it gives it a salvific value. In this life, it bestows upon the soul in ''transforming'' union, a ''taste'' of the joy of consummated love with her Divine Bridegroom in the Beatific Vision (Rv 21.2).

Bibliography: *Dictionnaire de spiritualité ascétique et mystique,* ed. M. VILLER et al. 2.2:1643–2193 (Paris 1932). P. LEJEUNE, *Dictionnaire de théologie catholique* 2.2:1616–31 (Paris 1903–50). TERESA OF ÁVILA, *Obras completas,* new rev. ed. E. DE LA MADRE DE DIOS, 3 v. (*Biblioteca de autores cristianos* 74, 120, 189; 51–59) v. 2; *Complete Works,* ed. SILVERIO DE SANTA TERESA and E. A. PEERS, 3 v. (New York 1946) v. 2, ''Interior Castle.'' JOHN OF THE CROSS, *Complete Works,* ed. SILVERIO DE SANTA TERESA and E. A. PEERS, 3 v. (Westminster, Md. 1963) ''Ascent of Mount Carmel'' and ''A Spiritual Canticle of the Soul.'' J. J. MCMAHON, *The Divine Union in the Subida del monte Carmelo and the Noche oscura of Saint John of the Cross* (Washington 1941). BERNARD OF CLAIRVAUX, *Opera,* ed. J. LECLERCQ (Rome 1957) 2 v. to date. C. MARMION, *Sponsa Verbi: The Virgin Consecrated to Chris,* tr. F. IZARD (St. Louis 1925). P. KETTER, *Christ and Womankind,* tr. I. MCHUGH (2nd ed. rev. and enl.; Westminster, Md. 1952).

[A. A. BIALAS]

MYSTICAL PHENOMENA

In popular usage, the term mystical phenomena is sometimes used to embrace all those unusual and mysterious phenomena that surpass the known, normal powers of the human soul and imply the operation of some being superior to the soul or of some unfamiliar factor within the human soul. So understood, the subject would belong to the field of parapsychology, which investigates phenomena of this kind in religion and mysticism, spiritualism, occultism, diabolism, psychology, physiology, physics, and chemistry (Omez, 11–17).

In Christian spirituality, however, the term is taken in a stricter sense and includes only: (1) those internal and external manifestations that ordinarily proceed from the authentic mystical activity of a soul (concomitant mystical phenomena); and (2) the extraordinary graces, charisms, or miracles that sometimes accompany mystical activity but are not essentially related to mystical operations as such (charismatic mystical phenomena). Concomitant mystical phenomena are called ordinary mystical phenomena and are supernatural *quoad substantiam;* charismatic mystical phenomena are called extraordinary and are supernatural *quoad modum* [R. Garrigou-Lagrange, *Christian Perfection and Contemplation* (St. Louis 1937) 235–238].

From the point of view of Christian spirituality an authentic mystical contemplation of the purely natural order is a contradiction in terms, and an intimate experience of God can occur only through grace (J. Maritain, *Les Degrés du savoir,* 4th French ed., 534). However it would seem that an authentic mystical experience and the concomitant phenomena are possible among non-Christians who possess a high degree of sanctifying grace and sufficient intensity of charity. Moreover, it is possible that certain persons, psychologically so gifted, may enjoy a profound awareness of God that although less intense than authentic mystical experience, is yet beyond the religious experience of the average believer. Into this latter category would fall numerous Buddhist, Hindu, and other non-Christian ''mystics'' whose experiences are tentatively explained by some parapsychologists as a *psi*-function of the human soul [Omez, 20–26; H. Brémond, *Prière et Poesie* (Paris 1926); A. Wiesenger, 3–96].

The present treatment of mystical phenomena is restricted to those manifestations that ordinarily proceed from authentic mystical activity (concomitant mystical phenomena) and those extraordinary psychosomatic manifestations that sometimes occur in authentic mystics (charismatic mystical phenomena).

Concomitant Mystical Phenomena. The concomitant phenomena vary with the degree of intensity of mystical activity and serve as an indication of the soul's progress in the mystical life, although each soul does not necessarily experience all the concomitant phenomena or even all the phenomena proper to a given stage, for mystical activity is the work of God, who can lead souls as He will. Moreover, mystical activity is possible in the life of a person who is not in the mystical state. Theologians

commonly agree that mystical activity is essentially an experience of God, more or less intensely felt through the operation of the gifts of the Holy Spirit; and since the gifts themselves pertain to the supernatural organism of the spiritual life, whatever proceeds from the activity of the gifts should be classified as concomitant and ordinary phenomena.

The division of concomitant mystical phenomena given by St. Teresa of Avila (cf. *Interior Castle,* 4th–7th *Mansions*) has been adopted by most theologians since her time. She lists the mystical phenomena in connection with the various grades of mystical prayer, and the same approach is used by St. John of the Cross and St. Francis de Sales (cf. *Treatise on the Love of God* ch. 6–7). [For the mystical activity of the active life, see John of St. Thomas, *The Gifts of the Holy Ghost* (New York 1951); G. G. Carluccio, *The Seven Steps to Spiritual Perfection* (Ottawa, Canada 1949); and J. Maritain, *Prayer and Intelligence* (London 1928).]

The following are the principal and concomitant mystical phenomena, from the beginning to the end of the mystical state: 1. An intuition of God or divine things, as distinct from discursive knowledge, with a profound penetration of divine mysteries. 2. An experimental or quasi-experimental knowledge of God or divine things. This is the essential phenomenon of the mystical life and is usually accompanied by spiritual joy, interior absorption in God, disdain for wordly pleasures, and a desire for greater perfection (cf. Poulain, 2, 5–6; Arintero, 2, 3). 3. Passive purification of the senses, which presupposes the active purgations of senses and spirit (*see* PURIFICATION, SPIRITUAL). 4. Continued awareness of the presence of God, accompanied by ''sleep'' or suspension of the faculties, filial fear of God, love of suffering, divine touches, spiritual sensations, flights of the spirit leading to ecstasy, wounds of love, and interior communications (see St. Teresa, *Interior Castle,* 5th–6th *Mansions*; Arintero, 2:4, 7). 5. Passive purgation of the spirit (see St. John of the Cross, *Dark Night*; Arintero, 2:184–204). 6. Total death to self, heroism in the practice of virtue, joy in persecution, zeal for the salvation of souls, and relative confirmation in grace.

Charismatic Mystical Phenomena. Extraordinary mystical phenomena do not occur in the normal development of the spiritual life, but proceed from a supernatural cause distinct from sanctifying grace, the virtues, and the gifts of the Holy Spirit. Therefore they are classified as charisms (*gratiae gratis datae*) and since charisms neither presuppose grace in the soul of the individual nor flow from sanctifying grace, they are no proof of the sanctity of the individual. Some charisms are true miracles; others are supernatural in cause but do not necessarily surpass the powers of created nature and thus are called "epiphenomena" of the mystical life and are "paranormal" in relation to mystical activity (cf. the charisms listed in 1 Cor 12.4, which pertain to the apostolate).

Considered exclusively as paranormal, extraordinary phenomena could be attributed to one of three possible causes: God, occult natural powers, or diabolical influence. Hence the rule established by Pope Benedict XIV in *De Beatificatione et Canonizatione Servorum Dei:* No phenomenon is to be attributed to a supernatural power until all possible natural or diabolical explanation has been investigated and excluded. The difficulty involved in discerning the cause of paranormal mystical phenomena is that the psychosomatic structure can react to stimuli in a limited number of ways. Sometimes the same psychic or bodily reaction will occur in a seizure of hysteria as in a true mystical ecstasy (e.g., visions, locutions, or revelations). In many instances the most that can be concluded is that a phenomenon could have proceeded from God, from some occult natural power, or from a diabolic influence. In view of the foregoing, the following statements serve as rules of discernment concerning paranormal phenomena: 1. No extraordinary phenomenon may be attributed to a supernatural, i.e., divine, cause as long as a natural or diabolical explanation is possible. 2. The extraordinary phenomenon is not of itself an indication of the sanctity of the individual, for God could grant charisms to a person in mortal sin and even work miracles through such persons. 3. Normally it would be temerarious to petition God for charisms or miracles, since none of these phenomena flow from sanctifying grace, the virtues, and the gifts of the Holy Spirit; and privileges of this kind could in fact be damaging to the spiritual life of an individual. 4. No extraordinary phenomenon is necessary for the attainment of sanctity. 5. The extraordinary phenomena, when they come from God, are generally classified as *gratiae gratis datae,* and are primarily for the good of the faithful and not for the one who receives them, although accidentally the individual may benefit from them. 6. Because of the impossibility of identifying the cause of some of the extraordinary phenomena, the investigator should consider primarily the effects of the phenomena on the life of the individual who has experienced them. (For the signs of the spirit of God, the diabolic spirit, and the human spirit see Arintero, 2:7; Royo-Aumann, 28.)

Is it possible that a person could be subject to the influence of several of these spirits at the same time? Or in other words, could a true mystic be subject to diabolical influence at the same time that he is acting under the impulses of the gift of the Holy Spirit? Or is it possible for a person to be acted upon by a gift of the Holy Spirit (a truly mystical operation) and at the same time suffer from a pathological mental or organic condition? The answer to these questions can best be stated in a series of conclusions: 1. Any deliberately willed phenomenon that involves a defect in any virtue is incompatible with the perfection of charity that constitutes Christian perfection and sanctity. 2. Any phenomenon that flows from the weakness of the individual or from any other cause that is not deliberately willed may coexist with mystical phenomena, so that a genuine mystic may exhibit truly neurotic or psychotic symptoms. 3. It is possible that a true mystic may, with God's permission, be given over to the influence and power of the devil (diabolical obsession). 4. Any person, even one in mortal sin, could be the recipient of any of the *gratiae gratis datae* or be the instrument of God in working a miracle.

Since grace does not destroy nature, but perfects it (cf. St. Thomas Aquinas, *Summa theologiae* 1a, 1.8 ad 2), and since each person is unique, certain individuals will be better or worse disposed for the perfection of virtue by reason of temperament and other characteristics that influence the workings of grace. Because of these predispositions, certain types will be more inclined to manifest paranormal phenomena, charisms, or truly mystical phenomena. Thus, the choleric and the melancholic temperaments are more receptive to ecstasy, trance, visions, raptures, revelations, and locutions (see St. Teresa, *Book of Foundations,* ch. 7); the sanguine temperament is more disposed to interior touches, caresses, consoling visions, or any phenomenon of the affective order. The history of spirituality shows that women are more prone to illusion than men, and more women among the saints have been remarkable for extraordinary phenomena. Other factors that dispose for extraordinary phenomena are a vivid imagination, uncontrolled emotions, badly regulated mental prayer, exhausting mental labor, and excessive austerities.

Charismatic Phenomena. The following are the principal charismatic phenomena.

Visions. By visions we mean the perception of an object that is naturally invisible to man. Visions can be divided into corporeal (perception by bodily eyes), imaginative (result of a phantasm in the imagination), or intellectual (result of intelligible species impressed on the intellect); (*see* SPECIES, INTENTIONAL). Corporeal and imaginative visions may be caused by some natural power or by the devil, and therefore such possibilities must be investigated. The intellectual vision could not be caused immediately by the devil, who has no direct access to the human intellect, but it could proceed from a natural or a supernatural cause (*see* VISIONS).

Locutions. These are interior illuminations by means of words or statements, sometimes accompanied by a vision and seeming to proceed from the object represented. They can be divided into auricular (words heard with the bodily ear), imaginative (words perceived in the imagination), and intellectual (concepts perceived immediately by the intellect). Unlike prophecy, locutions are generally for the consolation or enlightenment of the one who receives them and thus differ from *gratiae gratis datae* in the strict definition. Auricular or imaginative locutions could proceed from any one of three causes: natural, diabolical, or supernatural; intellectual locutions could proceed from natural or supernatural causes (*see* LOCUTIONS).

Revelations. These are manifestations of hidden truths that are not normally accessible to man. Truly mystical revelation is usually accompanied by the gift of prophecy and its interpretation requires the gift of DISCERNMENT of spirits. Revelations may be absolute (simple statement of a truth or mystery), conditioned (usually a threat or promise based on some condition), or denunciatory (a condemnation or threat of punishment). Private revelations may proceed from a natural, a diabolical, or a supernatural source, and even if the revelation is supernatural in origin, the seer may unwittingly distort its meaning (*see* REVELATIONS, PRIVATE).

Reading of Hearts. The knowledge of the secret thoughts of others or of their internal state without communication is known as reading of hearts. The certain knowledge of the secret thoughts of others is truly supernatural, since the devil has no access to the spiritual faculties of men and no human being can know the mind of another unless it is in some way communicated. But knowledge of the secrets of another's heart may be conjectured by the devil and transmitted to a person, or they may be surmised by a deluded individual who takes his conjectures to be supernatural illuminations.

Hierognosis. This is the ability to recognize a person or object as holy or blessed and to distinguish what is genuinely so from what is not. A similar phenomenon with regard to holy objects is sometimes found in sinners and therefore the phenomenon is not necessarily supernatural but could also proceed from a diabolical power.

Flames of Love. These are burning sensations in the body without apparent cause. They admit of degrees: simple interior heat (usually a sensation around the heart, which gradually extends to other parts of the body), intense ardors (when the heat becomes unbearable and cold applications must be used), and material burning (when the heat reaches the point of scorching the clothing or blistering the skin, especially around the heart). This phenomenon could be caused by the devil or some pathological condition and therefore is not necessarily to be attributed to a supernatural cause.

Stigmata. These phenomena are the spontaneous appearance of wounds and bleeding that resemble the wounds of Christ. Sometimes the entire body is covered with wounds, as if from a scourging, or the forehead is punctured as if by thorns. These wounds usually appear during ecstasy and the wounds do not become inflamed or infected. Stigmatization could be produced by natural causes (autosuggestion, hypnosis, fraud), by the devil, or by supernatural power (*see* STIGMATIZATION).

Tears of Blood and Bloody Sweat (Hematidrosis). The effusion of blood from the eyes, as in weeping, or from the pores of the skin, as in perspiring, could be caused by the devil or it could be the effect of some physical or psychic pathology.

Exchange of Hearts. The substitution of the heart of the mystic for the symbolic heart of Christ, or the bestowal of a ring to designate the mystical espousal or MYSTICAL MARRIAGE, could also be effected in an imaginative vision.

Bilocation. This phenomenon is the simultaneous presence of a material body in two distinct places at the same time. It is physically impossible that a physical body can be in two places at the same time by a circumscriptive presence, although this is denied by Leibniz, Suárez (*De Eucharistia*, 48.5.4), and Bellarmine (*De Sacramento Eucharist.*, 3.3.662). True bilocation with circumscriptive presence could not occur even by a miracle. What is miraculous in this phenomenon is that while the physical body is circumscriptively present in a given place, the same body is present by a sensible representation in a distinct place.

Agility. This is evidenced in the instantaneous movement of a material body from one place to another without passing through the intervening space. The agility could only be apparent if the movement were not instantaneous, but simply faster than the human eye could follow.

Levitation. This is the elevation of the human body above the ground without visible cause and its suspension in the air without natural support. It may also appear in the form of ecstatic flight or ecstatic walk. True levitation cannot as yet be naturally explained. Apparent levitation has been witnessed at spiritualistic séances and in certain cases of psychosomatic pathology (see Thurston).

Compenetration of Bodies. This occurs when one material body appears to pass through another material body. It is generally held to be philosophically impossible although much remains to be learned concerning the quantity, weight, and distribution of parts in a body. In the apparent compenetration of bodies, one of the bodies could be an immaterial representation of a body; or it is possible that a body might enjoy the anticipated quality of subtlety that is characteristic of a glorified body.

Bodily Incombustibility. This is the ability of bodies to withstand the natural laws of combustibility. It may be due to some occult natural cause or to the devil. If mystical, it could be interpreted as a testimony of the holiness of the individual or, in cases of a test by fire, of the truth of doctrine.

Bodily Elongation or Shrinking. Sudden reduction or increase in size of the body may occur for no apparent reason. This is said to have occurred in spiritualistic séances (see Thurston, 192–208) and could also be caused by occult natural powers or by the intervention of the devil. It is not generally accepted as a mystical phenomenon because of its morbidity and apparent lack of purpose.

Inedia. This is an absolute and total abstinence from all nourishment beyond the limits of nature. Some investigators are not convinced that inedia is necessarily miraculous.

Mystical Aureoles and Illuminations. Resplendent light may emanate from the body of an individual, especially during ecstasy or contemplation. It is considered an anticipation of the radiant splendor of a glorified body. Illumination and phosphorescence have been verified of certain plants and animals.

Sweet Odors. These have been noted as emanating from the living or dead body of a person. They are classified as miraculous by Benedict XIV, although the phenomenon could be caused by the devil or by autosuggestion. If it is a true mystical phenomenon, it is interpreted as the sign of the sweet odor of glory and a testimony to the holiness of an individual.

Blood Prodigies, Bodily Incorruptibility, and Absence of Rigor Mortis. These phenomena are well attested in the lives of the saints. Many cases could possibly have a natural explanation or be caused by diabolical power. Some are accepted as true mystical phenomena and testimonies from God concerning the holiness of an individual; others seem to be purely morbid and serve no spiritual purpose.

Bibliography: BENEDICT XIV, *Doctrinam de servorum Dei beatificatione et beatorum canonizatione* (Rome 1757). A. FONCK, *Dictionnaire de théologie catholique,* ed. A. VACANT, 15 v. (Paris 1903–50; Tables générales 1951–) 10.2:2599–2674. JOHN OF THE CROSS, *Complete Works,* ed. SILVERIO DE SANTA TERESA and E. A. PEERS, 3 v. (Westminster, MD 1953). TERESA OF ÁVILA, *Complete Works,* ed. SILVERIO DE SANTA TERESA and E. A. PEERS, 3 v. (New York 1946). A. F. POULAIN, *The Graces of Interior Prayer,* tr. L. L. YORKE SMITH (6th ed. St. Louis 1950). A. SAUDREAU, *The Degrees of Spiritual Life,* tr. B. CAMM, 2 v. (New York 1907); *The Mystical State* (New York 1924). J. MARÉCHAL, *Studies in the Psychology of the Mystics,* tr. A. THOROLD (London 1927). A. FARGES, *Mystical Phenomena Compared with Their Human and Diabolical Counterfeits,* tr. S. P. JACQUES (2d ed. London 1926). J. G. ARINTERO, *The Mystical Evolution in the Development and Vitality of the Church,* tr. J. AUMANN, 2 v. (St. Louis 1949–51). A. ROYO, *The Theology of Christian Perfection,* tr. J. AUMANN (Dubuque 1962). R. GARRIGOU-LAGRANGE, *The Three Ages of Interior Life,* tr. T. DOYLE, 2 v. (St. Louis 1947–48). A. TANQUEREY, *The Spiritual Life* (Westminster, MD 1945). H. THURSTON, *The Physical Phenomena of Mysticism* (Chicago 1952). A. WIESINGER, *Occult Phenomena in the Light of Theology* (Westminster, MD 1957). E. UNDERHILL, *Mysticism* (12th ed. rev., New York 1960). Z. ARADI, *The Book of Miracles* (New York 1956). R. OMEZ, *Psychical Phenomena* (Twentieth Century Encyclopedia of Catholicism 36; New York 1959). J. MARITAIN, *Distinguish to Unite or the Degrees of Knowledge,* tr. G. B. PHELAN, from 4th French ed. (New York 1959).

[J. AUMANN]

MYSTICAL UNION

Mystical union may be described as the relationship between a person and God in the highest degrees of the mystical life. Ordinarily, mystical union is said to have three stages: prayer of union, prayer of ecstatic union, and prayer of transforming union (MYSTICAL MARRIAGE).

In the prayer of union the soul is deeply aware of God's presence. All the internal powers of the soul, including the memory and imagination, are captivated and occupied with God. This union, usually of short duration, is marked by the absence of distractions, and the certainty of being deeply united to God.

The prayer of ecstatic union differs from the prayer of union in that the external senses are also suspended or captivated. As the intensity of the mystical union grows, it becomes so great that the body cannot withstand it and so falls into ecstasy. In this union the Holy Spirit, acting through His gifts, so intimately and ardently unites the soul to God that the natural weakness of the subject cannot withstand the intensity of the light and love communicated. The soul falls into ecstasy, and this causes the body to experience an alienation of the senses.

In the prayer of transforming union (mystical marriage) there is a complete transformation of the soul into the Beloved. God gives Himself to the soul and the soul gives itself to God in a certain consummation of divine love, so that the soul shares in God's life as fully as is possible in this life. This union is more or less permanent; the soul is more conscious than ever of the Blessed Trinity. The soul is absorbed in seeking the honor of God, eagerly desiring to undertake anything or suffer anything that God may will.

Bibliography: TERESA OF AVILA, *Interior Castle; in Complete Works,* ed. SILVERIO DE SANTA TERESA and E. A. PEERS, 3 v.

(New York 1946) v. 2. JOHN OF THE CROSS, *The Living Flame of Love,* tr. D. LEWIS (New York 1912). A. ROYO, *The Theology of Christian Perfection,* tr. and ed. J. AUMANN (Dubuque 1962).

[N. LOHKAMP]

MYSTICI CORPORIS

Pius XII issued the encyclical *Mystici corporis* [*Acta Apostolicae Sedis* 35 (1943) 193–248] on June 29, 1943. The encyclical was in part a reaction against a vague and diffuse tendency discernible in some quarters of Catholic theology, especially in the years between the two world wars, toward what has been labeled a romantic vitalism or biologism in ECCLESIOLOGY. Nonetheless the encyclical is primarily a positive document, designed to present a doctrinal view of the militant Church as the Body of Christ (pars. 11, 90). Its obvious effort to synthesize the achievements of the past, both theological and magisterial, around the theme of the Body of Christ supports the view that the document's chief concern is not merely terminological exactitude but doctrinal formation.

Among the chief orientations found in the encyclical the following deserve notice: (1) there is a decisive turning away from a non-Incarnational and asocial concept of Christian GRACE, which tends to regard grace's outward dimension as a purely provisional and transient reality; (2) hence the socio-sacramental reality of the Church as the communal life of grace is itself a true component of the total Christian grace, and thus Christ's Church Body cannot be the anomaly of a nonbody in which the vital relationships between Head and members tend to be unchurched; (3) this theandric ecclesiology is grounded on a pneumatology in which the role of Christ's Spirit, insofar as He is at once immanent in and transcendent to Christ's Church Body, is analogous to His role in Christ's physical Body, i.e., He is sent to invest Christ's Church, in whole and in its parts, with Christ's own life and energies, and thus to assimilate it, Body and members, to Christ, its paradigm and Head; (4) Christ is the "sustainer" of His Body (51–52), its HYPOSTASIS in some mysterious sense, without prejudice to His own transcendence or to the distinct personalities of His many members.

Against this larger background it is easier to situate the following positions of the encyclical: (1) the identification of the Roman Catholic Church with the MYSTICAL BODY OF CHRIST on earth; (2) the delineation of the inward-outward grace of membership in a way clearly affirming the outward factors, without, however, any unilateralism; (3) the refusal to admit any basic dislocation between the Church of law and the Church of love, indeed the affirmation of the complementariness of the pneumatic and the juridic missions in the Church; (4) finally, the strong sense of Christian communion, or of the total common life of the Church, conceived as an inward-outward total grace, with a variety of members gifted in Christ, comprising both the lowly and the exalted, each serving together in his way the upbuilding of the Body in Christian love.

Mystici Corporis's direct identification of the Church of Christ as the Roman Catholic Church has been qualified by the ecumenical position expressed in Vatican II's *Lumen gentium* that "the unique Church of Christ . . . subsists in the Catholic Church, which is governed by the successor of Peter and by the bishops in communion with him. Nevertheless, many elements of sanctification and of truth are found outside its visible confines."

The encyclical concerns itself chiefly with the NT "militant Church" (1); hence it does not stress the OT ἐκκλησία as the forerunner of the NT Church Body of Christ, nor is any special relief given to the heavenly Jerusalem as the final realization of the Church's earthly pilgrimage. The encyclical does not attend to the question whether the NT "Body" theme has, over and above its assured metaphorical sense, a prior realistic sense, related to Christ's real Body, dead to sin on the cross, risen again to new life, and now gloriously reigning in heaven. The profound nexus between Christ's Eucharistic Body and His Church Body, though by no means passed over (81–84, 18), is not as centrally placed in the encyclical as, e.g., in patristic ecclesiology. The question is left open whether the Holy Spirit may be considered the soul of the Mystical Body in any proper sense (*see* SOUL OF THE CHURCH).

It has been noted that the encyclical omits the Biblical theme of the Church as the PEOPLE OF GOD and to that extent constricts the overall viewpoint from which the mystery of the Church can profitably be regarded. The metaphorical theme of God's people is proposed as a useful complement to the Body theme, particularly advantageous in that it enables the theologian to reflect better on the historical continuity between the two covenants, old and new, and between the two covenant peoples, according to God's total plan of SALVATION. Any effort, however, to invest the Biblical theme of the Body of Christ with theological disfavor, as an infratheological construct, or to dislodge it from its notable place among the many Biblical themes or images cumulatively employed and required to draw out that measure of fruitful understanding that man may reach in this life of the mystery of Christ's Church, is a disservice marked for failure.

Bibliography: J. HAMER, "Signification et Portée del'Encyclique *Mystici Corporis,*" *L'Église est une communion* (Paris 1962) 11–34. F. MALMBERG, "Die Enzyklika Mystici Corporis:

Dogmatischer Wert und innere Struktur,'' *Ein Leib-Ein Geist* (Freiburg 1960) 43–54. A. MICHEL, *Dictionnaire de théologie catholique, Tables générales* ed. A. VACANT et al. (Paris 1951) 1: 1116–18. W. BARTZ, *Lexicon für Theologie und Kirche*, ed. J. HOFER and K. RAHNER (Freiburg 1957–65) 7:731–732.

[F. X. LAWLOR/D. M. DOYLE]

MYSTICISM

A term used to cover a literally bewildering variety of states of mind. Perhaps the most useful definition is that given by Jean GERSON: ''Theologia mystica est experimentalis cognitio habita de Deo per amoris unitivi complexum'' (Mystical theology is knowledge of God by experience, arrived at through the embrace of unifying love). There are three points to notice: (1) the use of the term mystical theology (which was traditional in the Church until comparatively modern times) associates the mystical state with, while distinguishing it from, natural theology, which enables man to arrive at some knowledge of God by natural reason: also from dogmatic theology, which treats of the knowledge of God arrived at by revelation. (2) We do come to know God through mystical theology. (3) This knowledge is obtained not by intellectual processes but by the more direct experience implied in the term ''unifying love.''

Non-Christian mysticism. This article is concerned primarily with Catholic mysticism, but it is necessary to recognize that Catholics and Christians in general have no monopoly on mysticism. Indeed, every religious tradition has its mystical aspect, and we cannot do adequate justice to the subject of Catholic mysticism without seeing something of the background from which it sprang. Just as in the realm of Biblical scholarship, exegetes have come to recognize that we cannot isolate the Jewish experience from the larger context of Egyptian and Babylonian religion, so we have to see the whole development of Christian mysticism in the light of a common human striving.

Thus, within the remote world of China an early teaching maintained that man's highest purpose was the quest of *Dao* (*see* DAOISM), which was regarded as the Ultimate Reality, source of all that is, pervading and harmonizing all natural phenomena. Hence, for man, *Dao* is the exemplar of conduct and man can find himself only by some kind of identification with it.

The process by which this identification is achieved bears a remarkable resemblance to the traditional teaching of Christian mysticism. First comes a process of purgation. In the words of LAOZI: ''Only one who is eternally free from earthly passions can apprehend the spiritual essence of *Dao*.'' After this stage comes the condition in which the achievement of virtue is not a self-conscious, self-regarding effort but rather a connatural state. The final stage is reached when harmony with *Dao* is fully realized. In this condition, man is the unresisting vehicle of *Dao*, so that he is able to rise above the limitations of matter and the laws of the physical universe.

On the other hand, it must be insisted that in much Chinese speculation, especially in the writings of Laozi, there is no idea of ''religion'' as we understand the term, no sense of a personal relationship with God, or of obligations to him. In fact, the end of the mystical way for the Daoist might well seem to be an absorption into some pantheistic system (*see* PANTHEISM). It is hardly surprising that, to all intents and purposes, Daoism became amalgamated with BUDDHISM.

Of HINDUISM it is unnecessary to speak here, except to mention the possible influence that Indian ideas had on the Greek tradition through Pythagoras, and hence on Plato and NEOPLATONISM. Neoplatonic influence on the Christian tradition through PLOTINUS and PROCLUS is undeniable. It was recognized that nothing made life more worth living than to look upon Beauty, not just in its partial and imperfect realizations, but in itself.

There is a kind of universal tradition embracing a metaphysics ''that recognizes a divine reality, substantial to the world of things and lives and minds; and a psychology that finds in the soul something similar or even identical with divine reality; and an ethic that places man's final end in the imminent and transcendent Ground of all being.'' (See A. Huxley, *The Perennial Philosophy*, introduction.)

Is mystical experience open to all? Yet, if the foregoing were true, the problem at once arises, why is the recognition of this universal reality so partial and fragmentary? What is it about the mystics that enables them to pierce through the veil that conceals from so many others the essential truth and goodness and beauty of God Himself? In the words of one of the mystics quoted by Huxley (*ibid.*):

> O my God, how does it happen in this poor world that thou art so great and yet nobody finds thee, that thou callest so loudly and nobody hears thee, that thou art so near and nobody feels thee, that thou givest thyself to everybody and nobody knows thy name? Men flee from thee and say they cannot find thee; they turn their backs on thee and say they cannot see thee; they stop their ears and say they cannot hear thee.

There has been much debate whether the full mystical experience is possible for all men or whether it is open only to those of a certain temperament. Dom Cuthbert Butler, a recognized authority, argued that the traditional

Christian view, which had been lost to sight during the 18th and 19th centuries, is that all men are called to a specifically mystical way of knowing and loving God. In favor of this view he quoted Bishop John Hedley, who argued that contemplation is the chief act of the heart of man, for the heart flowers in the act of charity, and contemplation is charity that is actual, pure, and flowering under the movement of the Holy Spirit. It differs from ordinary prayer, yet is not extraordinary in the sense that humble souls cannot aspire to it. It is not a miraculous activity, but is simply the perfection of supernatural prayer, ordinarily given by God to those who remove obstacles to it and avail themselves of the requisite means.

R. Garrigou-Lagrange protested against the view that there are two ways of perfection: an ordinary way, intended for all, and an extraordinary one of prayer and mystical life, to which all fervent souls are not called by God. On the contrary, there is only one unitive way, not of its nature extraordinary, to which, by docility to the Holy Spirit, generous souls are led to perfection. Nevertheless, it must be acknowledged that because of a lack of proper guidance or because of other unfavorable circumstances, or because particular individuals are strongly inclined to exterior activities, some generous souls may not arrive at the mystic life during the span of an ordinary lifetime. This, however, Garrigou-Lagrange considered to be accidental.

Accidental or not, Abbot Butler recognized the situation to be so common that, through no fault of the individual concerned, the circumstances of life may, and often do, render the experience of mystical union all but impossible. He cited St. Gregory's complaint that by becoming pope he had lost the gift of contemplation he had enjoyed in the monastery, and concluded there is much to be said for the view that there are not one or two ''unitive ways'' but many, just as there are many mansions in our Father's house.

One of the problems raised by much mystical literature is that far too many authors seem anxious to achieve a basic classification of states into which, like some bed of Procrustes, the diversified experiences of a whole host of highly individualized personalities must be made to fit. The all but infinite variety of physiological conditions, intellectual endowments, social background, educational equipment, and the like, render it unlikely a priori that the way to God will be precisely the same even for any two persons, let alone for a whole mass of people. It seems desirable, therefore, to maintain flexibility of mind in trying to evaluate the accounts that different mystics give of their experiences, even while we recognize that, as the fundamental qualities of human nature remain unchanged, so there is likely to be a rough parallelism between any two sets of experience.

The role of grace. Certainly an absolutely essential starting point for all is the desire to arrive at whatever the goal may be and a consequent willingness to undertake whatever steps may be required to attain that goal. Yet even this starting point itself implies some faint recognition of what the goal is. ''You would not be looking for me if you had not found me,'' as Pascal expressed it. Already the process of turning away from what is not God in order to come to God has begun; already God is ''drawing'' the soul to Himself. It is here that we begin to encounter what is probably the crucial problem in any discussion of mysticism—the cooperation between the soul and God. This is, of course, only a specialized form of a larger problem (*see* GRACE AND NATURE), but it calls for particular treatment here.

Without going into the question of the possibility of genuine mystical experiences for those who do not belong in any external sense to Christianity (though the modern view tends to be that such grace may be more widely available than was once thought), all Christian writers agree that where genuine mystical experiences occur they are the direct result not of any efforts of the mystics themselves but of a special grace over and above the ordinary graces available to all Christians.

Some chosen souls appear to enjoy more than the ordinary gift of faith and the power to love and serve God. They seem to enjoy a supernatural knowledge and love beyond that of other generous souls, as though in some manner they participated more fully in God's own knowledge and love of Himself, and thus shared more intimately in the life of the Blessed Trinity and of the blessed in heaven. In their case, grace appears to do more than cooperate with their human effort. It is as if God produces in them a knowledge and love that exceeds all that can be felt or expressed by the faculties, although it is experienced by the soul.

The whole mystery of the relationship between any human soul and its Creator, at any phase and therefore especially at the stage of mystical union, springs from the nature of man's being. Dependent as he is on the creative act of an eternal Creator, an act that is described in its temporal effects as an act of conservation, man's whole conscious life is passed in a space-time world; yet he is more than a ''pilgrim of eternity.'' The roots of his being, at a level deeper than consciousness, are to be found in the very Being of God Himself. Because of original sin the consciousness of God that would seem to be connatural to man has become fitful and obscure. It can be restored only by a rigid process of ''purgation,'' a deliberate effort to turn away from this space-time world of everyday experience to concentrate on the eternal reality of God.

Precisely because so much of our conscious life is inextricably bound up with this world of sense, the process of purgation is a painful one. Hence follows the dark night of the senses, then the dark night of the soul, in the course of which the personality is detached from that absorption in temporal, material reality that has become connatural to man. Hence comes, too, the traditional insistence on the *via negativa*, the attainment to some knowledge of God by seeing Him as the denial of all that is commonly thought and felt by human beings through the ordinary channels. In this "cloud of unknowing," the mystic learns God by unlearning, so to speak, everything that is not God. Moreover, unlike the objects of ordinary knowing, God is not the passive object of the mystic's contemplation. Rather is He the active inspiration, an overwhelming Power to whom the mystic submits freely and therefore not inertly. The surrender becomes an immense enrichment, simply because the knowledge and love of God is the consummation of man's purpose.

The mystic's knowledge of God. St. Thomas Aquinas developed what has come to be accepted as the classic explanation of what we may call the mechanics of the intellectual communication implicit in the experience of mystical union. Human knowledge begins with some sense of awareness. On this raw material—the colored shapes, the sounds and feelings, the scents and tastes produced by physical and chemical interaction between an external object and the sense organ—the intellect works to "abstract" the idea or concept that is the specific object of normal, human rational activity. Out of changeable phenomena is derived the changeless concept. By linking together these abstract ideas the mind makes judgments; it reasons and infers. Ordinarily in the act of thinking the concept is never entirely free of a penumbra of images or phantasms, be they no more than the words in which we normally clothe our ideas. (Yet we do distinguish between the word and the idea, as is shown by those occasions when, as we say, we are trying to find the right word to express what is in our minds.)

In the highest forms of intellectual activity, it does seem that the image becomes less and less helpful and can indeed be a positive nuisance. The most obvious example is provided by mathematical reasoning. The geometrical figure, the algrebraic formulas are necessary to begin the process; but the stage is reached sooner or later when what we are thinking of bears only the remotest relation to what can be pictured: the curve is replaced by the formula, which is seen to bear less relation to what it purports to describe than do the stenographer's notes to the rhetorical cadences of the speaker, or the notes of a musical score to the symphony or sonata as it is created by the composer or performed by the orchestra.

Perhaps there was some way of knowing that began with an immediate activity of intellect without any previous stage of sensation and abstraction. Since any created nature is finite and liable to imperfection, only by special divine help would human nature be able to abide permanently in the enjoyment of a situation calling for the complete integration and subordination of all its faculties to the purposes of the spiritual side of its being. Having lost that preternatural endowment, man, of himself, is no longer capable of that intellectual awareness of God which, if awareness is to be adequate, must obviously be free from the distorting effects of imagery. God is pure spirit and is therefore not to be described in language drawn from sense experience.

But there seems to be no reason in the nature of things why, in some cases and for special reasons, God should not confer a grace that might restore a person temporarily to that condition of perfection that man enjoyed before the Fall. We may presume that whereas in an unfallen state man's preternatural endowments would enable him to enjoy such an immediate awareness of God while still retaining his normal consciousness, direct awareness is not possible in the fallen state except at the price of a suspension of normal consciousness. In St. Thomas's words:

> In contemplation, God is seen by a medium which is the light of wisdom elevating the mind to discern the divine. . .; and thus the divine is seen by the contemplative by means of grace after sin, though more perfectly in the state of innocence. [*De ver.* 18.1 ad 4.]

The foregoing remains no more than a theory, but as far as it goes, it is a coherent explanation and serves as at least a useful working hypothesis. It helps us also to understand why the mystic, after his experience, is invariably incapable of describing what happened or even, it would seem, of remembering anything at all except that something did happen. Thus St. Augustine says:

> Thy invisible things, understood by those that are made, I saw indeed, but was not able to fix my gaze thereon; my weakness was beaten back, and I was reduced to my ordinary experience (*Conf.* 7.23).

Moreover, as F. L. Mascall says (*Christ, the Christian and the Church*, 61):

> When the soul tries to describe this object to itself, when it tries to relate this knowledge to knowledge obtained by normal means, and above all when it tries to tell other people about it, it is faced with an enormous problem of translation and interpretation.

A. F. Poulain, in an exhaustive treatise on this subject, includes examples of some remarkable ways in which mystics interpreted their experiences. Thus St. Mechtild apparently declared that Christ had told her in a vision that the virtue of patience was especially dear to Him because *patientia* combines *pax* and *scientia;* St. Catherine of Siena claimed to have had a vision in which Our Lady revealed that she was *not* conceived immaculate! In individual cases, of course, it is possible to doubt whether any genuine mystical experience did in fact occur; but it is equally possible to suppose that, in attempting to translate into normal language and thought the contents of some mystical illumination, even a saint must be reduced to an ordinary way of thinking.

Validity of mystical experience. At this point, the question may well be asked, by both the skeptic and the sincere believer, whether there may not be some validity in R. A. Vaughan's unkind definition: "Mysticism is that form of error which mistakes for a divine manifestation operations of a merely human faculty." How can the mystics be said to "know" something that cannot be expressed in words and communicated to others, or rendered explicit by the mystics even to the mystics themselves? Perhaps it must be admitted that mystical experiences cannot be "justified" or authenticated by and in themselves. But this is not to say that there is no answer to the question raised here.

There is danger of concentrating too closely on mystical experience as an isolated phenomenon, dissecting the statements of this or that individual mystic, and so losing sight of the whole history of the subject. For in the words of William James: "There is about mystical utterances an eternal unanimity which ought to make a critic stop and think."

First, there is the general background of the long line of Christian mystics to be considered. The intellectual equipment, temperamental qualities, and educational opportunities of such men and women as SS. John, Paul, Augustine, the Pseudo-Dionysius, SS. Gregory, Bernard, Teresa of Avila, and John of the Cross, to say nothing of the English and German mystics, were so vastly different that one might expect differing approaches to mystical activity and widely dissimilar consequences. Yet, despite immense difference in detail, there is an almost monotonous sameness about their general attitudes to the basic matters of moral conduct and religious beliefs. If mystical experience were no more than a self-induced trance, and if the alleged intuition of a divine reality were sheer hallucination, it is remarkable that these baseless and purely subjective phenomena should be under the control of a persisting framework of ideas and beliefs.

Forgetting for the moment the specific problem of the authenticity of mystical experiences, one might look at normal Christian belief and practice. We believe that this world of material substance and rational and moral activity is but the surface of an unfathomed abyss of energy, eternally operative and effective.

"The weariness, the fever and the fret" that make up the conscious content of normal human experience cannot be understood save in relation to an external existence, which is the deepest reality. From that deepest reality man has come to live out his little day, realizing, as best he may with the help of God, the perfection for which he was made. Even apart from the assurance of revelation, there is what is described by Dean Inge as "the raw material of all religion, and perhaps of all philosophy and art as well, namely that dim consciousness of the *beyond*, which is part of our nature as human beings." At the heart of the Christian message is the doctrine that the world of man and the world of God, time and eternity, meet and blend in the Incarnate Word. Our reasons for believing this have nothing to do with mysticism.

Mysticism, on the other hand, has a history of experience in which the mystic claims to have been in immediate contact with the Ground of Being, known in an intellectual way that is free from imaginative content and incapable of normal conceptualization. Further, the result of the total experience is not so much a deepening of understanding as a sort of fusing of personalities. Hence the prevalence of language and imagery drawn from the common experience of human love, an experience leading to physical union in which the lovers seek to express an identification of interests, desires, joys, and delights as symbolizing a longing for union of personality. It is not given to mortals to achieve such union; but, from the accounts the mystics have left, it would seem that somehow it is achieved in the highest form of their experience, sometimes even described as a "mystical marriage." Now human love is a powerful revealer of personality. Through love one comes to know another in a profounder way than by the ordinary exchange of social contact. (It is not without significance that we speak of a man's "knowing" a woman in sexual intercourse.) The difference between God's self-revelation in what may be called the ordinary ways—through the Prophets, the teaching Church—and what is given to the mystic in his special experiences may well be that, in the latter, there is a fusing of will and intellect in one act, analogous to but immeasurably fuller than the communion of souls that is experienced in human love.

Recalling Gerson's definition—"knowledge of God arrived at through the embrace of unifying love"—we might suggest that, in the mystic's experience, there is a complete coordination of both intellect and will, directed toward God, who is the perfect and adequate end of their activity. Hence, it can be seen why the effect of mystical contemplation is not merely, not even primarily, an illumination of the intellect but chiefly a deepening of the whole personality, an enriching of character, a development of virtue. It is this fact that, in the end, is the guarantee of the mystic's claim. For in the authentic mystic, we have a man or woman who is invariably distinguished for integrity, candor, and sensitivity of conscience. At the state of ordinary awareness, he shares our ideals, our beliefs, our principles of conduct. It is conceivable that, in some cases, the mystic's alleging of his experience of God is a piece of self-deception, hallucination, hysteria, megalomania, and the like. But it is absurd to suggest that all the mystics are so deceived all the time. Once it is admitted that some of the mystics may be right sometimes, that some of them genuinely "experience God" in an act wherein the whole of their spiritual nature, will, and intellect is operating at the highest level attainable by man (and then only with the special assistance of God), there is sufficient ground for claiming the mystics as witnesses, in a sense eyewitnesses, to the ultimate truth after which the rest of us are dimly groping.

Modern interest. Current interest in mysticism is both theoretical and practical, is not limited to the educated or initiated, and is ecumenical or cross-cultural in its orientation. An adequate assessment of the current situation needs to consider more than the spectacular or exotic features, which, in the long view of Christian history, suggest the déjà vu rather than innovation. Particular notice should be taken of new directions in Christian spirituality, presaged by current mystical language and symbolism. Furthermore, its rather broad theoretical base adds a dimension to the contemporary renascence of mysticism which prompts more serious reflection and indicates that Christian spirituality may be in the process of significant modification.

Scholarly or theoretical interest in mysticism has been steady and fruitful, even if not intense, throughout the present century. William James' chapter "Mysticism" in his *Varieties of Religious Experience* (1902), with its observation that mysticism discloses a realm of consciousness beyond the rational, gave an unremitting impetus to the study of mysticism by the behavioral and social sciences and to the continuing dialogue within and among these disciplines. The comparative study of religions has considerably improved the comprehension of a notoriously elusive subject. Even the well-known experimental attempts to induce mystical experiences by means of drugs have led to meaningful distinctions between the religious goal of spiritual endeavor and its occasional exotic sensory accompaniments. Reasonable facsimiles of the latter can be artificially stimulated, and this fact, itself well known for centuries, has reempha-

sized the age-old cautions of the spiritual masters against overvaluation of emotional states.

Interest in mysticism as experiential also follows behavioral science's concerns with the role and function of emotion generally, especially in its capacity to add richness and depth to life. Proliferation of sensitivity clinics and awareness institutes of indescribable variety is some indication of a general search for emotional fulfillment, a datum which corroborates theoretical observations. The successful quest for more intense feelings of personal intimacy as well as for a closer relationship with nature and life generally, has made the so-called peak experience, described by Abraham Maslow, less extraordinary.

Developments in theology. In the theological sphere of theory, modern Christian theologians, unlike their medieval predecessors, have not given much attention to the mystical emphasis. Post-Tridentine Catholic theology, with its defensive stress on ritual efficacy and ecclesiastical authority, felt compelled to relegate mysticism to the exotic realm inhabited by a few "chosen souls" on the way to "infused contemplation." Mainline Protestant theology had little need for mystical vision because "this worldly," mundane activity was not seen to have any causal relationship to salvation and hence did not need to be transcended. Protestantism represented a "this-worldly asceticism" rather than an "other-worldly mysticism" in Max Weber's categories. The antimysticism of Karl Barth and Emile Brunner reflect this emphasis.

Current theological interest in mysticism owes much to ecumenical developments. Mystical traditions within the major religions seem to share so much common ground that ecumenical endeavor frequently appears superfluous. Recent exponents of the view that at their highest, mystical levels, the world religions are, in reality, one religion (e.g. A. Huxley, F. Schuon, and S. Radakrishnan) have understandably been criticized for glossing over precious and essential distinctions, but their positions do highlight areas of almost ready-made religious unity. Conceptions of the Absolute and, even more so, descriptions of ineffable experience, tend linguistically to converge as they approach what they perceive to be their respective goals.

In its ecumenical concerns Christian theology has begun what promises to be an enormously fruitful discussion with comparative-religions studies. Mystical worldviews as well as mystical practices are three major preoccupations among comparative-religions scholars which have already stimulated some development in Christian mystical theology. Jungian psychology has also proved to be an important partner to this multileveled conversation. William Johnston's works on Zen and

Christian mysticism offer a distinguished example of the theological enrichment available from such comparative studies. Robert Zaehner's comparative studies of Hindu, Muslim, and Christian mysticism have also made an enormous contribution, not only by way of generating scholarly interest in the subject but also by reason of his clarification of similarities and differences.

Some support is given scholarly concerns by widespread popular interest in Zen and Yoga. The faddish nature of the popular brands is often obvious, but the very fact of concern or curiosity, and especially its breadth, could signal substantial readjustment in overall religious orientation. At the very least it indicates a dissatisfaction with religious resources traditionally available in the Christian West. Even though such forms as Yoga and techniques as Transcendental Meditation assert their nonreligious nature and are allegedly compatible with the traditional faiths, it is apparent that all but the merely physical (''Yoga as exercise'') do clash in some way with traditional Christianity (*see* YOGA).

Significance for Christian spirituality. From the two distinguishing and mutually inseparable marks of the mystical phenomenon, namely its experiential emphasis and its unitive worldview, several observations relative to contemporary Christian spirituality suggest themselves. To some extent these two marks or characteristics correspond to the correlative symbols Self and Universe, and any decided enlargement of consciousness in either area would elicit a corresponding reaction toward maintaining intimacy and cohesion between the two. Historical periods witnessing significant world expansion and its corresponding threat to intellectual and psychological cosmos are invariably accompanied by a rise in mystical experience and a more comprehensive religious worldview.

The mystical vision of Teilhard de Chardin accommodates an impressive range of recent world-expanding discovery, stretching from paleontology's substantial revisions regarding human origins all the way to nuclear theory and space travel. With the affirmation characteristic of the mystic and an imminentism at times nearly indistinguishable from pantheism, he offers a spirituality in his *The Divine Milieu*, which meshes with contemporary valuations of nature, science, and technology and which, in its cosmic sweep, is little disturbed by the hairsplitting details that exercised traditional dogmatic and moral theology. His vision offers Christians, both Protestant and Catholic, an affirmative valuation of work and invention, of learning and recreation. For Teilhard, as well as for his kindred spirit in India, Sri Aurobindo Ghose, all these activities are inherently religious and need no ritual blessing or specific intention to make them so. Matter itself is raised to the plane of the spiritual and this *coincidentia oppositorum* finds resonance in the social sphere where the mystical and the prophetic become one in the cause of social reform.

Contrary to many popular images, the mystical religious mode is not extraordinary and is not for reclusive types. As James and others have asserted, there is a mystical dimension in all serious and sincere religion. Contemporary religion's emphasis on social problems, its deemphasis of institutional and clerical prerogatives, its diminished enthusiasm for laws, forms, and ritual all bear upon the current interest in mysticism. Even rather ordinary or commonplace religious experience can be personally transforming and authoritative and, because of its immediacy, tends to reduce dependence on institutional structures and to call into question their very relevance. This helps explain the apparent inner freedom as well as the specific orientation of such famous innovators and reformers as Paul, Bernard, Catherine of Siena, Eckhart, and Cusanus.

Teilhard's is by no means the only mystical vision influencing contemporary spirituality. An approach that can be thought of as a personalist emphasis forming a salutary counterbalance to Teilhard's universalism is the I-Thou religious vision of Martin Buber. Despite Buber's demurrer, his spiritual approach bears all the necessary marks of the mystical mode: it is experiential, comprehensive, immediate, and transforming. Buber's influence upon Catholic spirituality continues to be both deep and broad. Thomas Merton's life and example have been influential in sustaining an interest in contemplative spirituality, and he himself embodied the cross-cultural emphasis mentioned above. His last days were spent in Asia pursuing the mystic ideal. He is significant not so much for the power of his vision as for the orientation and persistence of his quest. Finally, mention should be made of Simone Weil, a mystic of powerful and awe-inspiring conviction, whose importance for the spirituality of the future should not be minimized. As visionaries all of these shared a deep engagement in the world and helped set the tone for a spirituality of personalism and human concern, global in its orientation and resource, affirmative in its assessment of nature and action.

Bibliography: From an almost limitless selection, the following brief list gives a representative picture. W. R. INGE, *Christian Mysticism* (London 1899). A. THOROLD, *An Essay in Aid of the Better Appreciation of Catholic Mysticism* (London 1900). W. JAMES, *The Varieties of Religious Experience* (New York 1902). R. M. JONES, *Studies in Mystical Religion* (London 1909). A. F. POULAIN, *The Graces of Interior Prayer*, tr. L. L. YORKE SMITH (St. Louis 1950). A. B. SHARPE, *Mysticism: Its True Nature and Value* (St. Louis 1910). E. UNDERHILL, *Mysticism* (12th ed. rev. New York 1960); *The Essentials of Mysticism . . .* (New York 1920). E. C. BUTLER, *Western Mysticism* (London 1922). F. VON HÜGEL, *The*

Mystical Element of Religion, 2 v. (2d ed. London 1923). R. OTTO, *Mysticism East and West*, tr. B. L. BRACEY (New York 1932). J. CHAPMAN, *The Spiritual Letters . . .* , ed. R. HUDLESTON (2d ed. London 1935). R. A. KNOX, *Enthusiasm* (New York 1961). D. KNOWLES, *The English Mystical Tradition* (New York 1961). S. SPENCER, *Mysticism in World Religion* (Baltimore 1963). F. C. HAPPOLD, *Mysticism: A Study and an Anthology* (Baltimore 1963), excellent bibliog. M. L. FURSE, *Mysticism: Window on a World View* (Nashville 1977). G. HARKNESS, *Mysticism: Its Meaning and Message* (Nashville 1973). W. JOHNSTON, *The Still Point: Reflections on Zen and Christian Mysticism* (New York 1977).

[T. CORBISHLEY/J. E. BIECHLER]

MYSTICISM IN LITERATURE

A consideration of the place of mysticism in literature poses some initial difficulties in the matter of definition (for the characteristics of mysticism, properly so called, *see* MYSTICISM). It should therefore be these qualities that imbue works that can properly be called both literary and mystical. The habit is quite current, unfortunately, for any literary work to be called "mystical" as long as it manifests a deep religious attitude or experience, deals with the supernatural or even the preternatural, or sees nature as a veil that at once conceals and reveals the Absolute. In the strictest sense, mysticism is the direct, intuitional experience of God through unifying love. There have been and are mystics in this strict sense outside the Catholic Church, even among non-Christians (e.g., Muslims or pagan Greeks). Such experiences, however, are difficult to identify. When absorptions in the Soul of the universe or in some universal Mind are described, it is difficult to determine whether these are an experience of a personal God in charity. Oftentimes there is question only of a religious experience in the realm of ideas and feelings. Without prejudging the mystical quality in this strict sense in the writings of Blake, Huysmans, Emerson, or Goethe (to take these as representatives of different literatures), it seems possible and even necessary to distinguish their vague and often pantheistic-tinged absorption from the more effective union with a personal God that gives depth and fire to the writings of such mystics as ST. JOHN OF THE CROSS, St. FRANCIS OF ASSISI, and St. CATHERINE OF SIENA.

It may not be an oversimplification to say that the first type of mysticism is an "I-It" relationship, the second an "I-Thou" realization, and that consequently from this second more intimate confrontation a more profound, moving, and universally significant literature would be expected to arise. This expectation is largely fulfilled in the writings of the "I-Thou" mystics; the frustration that so often hampers the efforts of these mystics to state their experiences arises from the very fact that their union with God in intuitive love has been so intimate, so unique, so literally ineffable that it defies capture in human words.

Manuscript page from "The Cloud of Unknowing," 14th century, introductory prayer before prologue (MS Harl. 674, fol. 17v).

"I-It" Mystics. The whole course of world literature has been definitely shaped by those who wrote what may be called mysticism in a broad sense. This mysticism is specified by an intense realization of the difference between things of this world and the great otherworldly spiritual realities. Since many of these writers receive separate treatment in this encyclopedia, they cannot be singled out here for extensive consideration. To give but a sampling, and restricting mention to those who are of acknowledged literary importance, there are from ancient times and up to the 12th century PLATO and PLOTINUS, PHILO JUDAEUS, AVICEBRON (Ibn Gabirol), and MAIMONIDES (Moses ben Maimon); in later times, Samuel COLERIDGE and BLAKE in England, Jonathan EDWARDS and EMERSON in the United States, Johann HERDER and Klopstock in Germany, and the Symbolists in France. Many more, without being clearly Christian, have spoken eloquently of a world beyond sense, and their collective testimony to these invisible realities has been a force constantly and powerfully working against the materialistic and positivistic influences that always threaten to infiltrate a literature written by sense-fettered and earthbound men.

"I-Thou" Mystics. It is, however, with mystics in the strictest sense of the word that one enters the realm of a literature that is unique in its intrinsic beauty and significance. The Epistles of St. Paul and St. John and the Revelation open the way to the subsequent attempts of Christian mystics to recount in human language the sublimity of their experience of direct knowledge of God. St. Paul distills the literary difficulty that all Christian mystics have faced when he states (almost in complaint) that he was "caught up into paradise, and heard secret words, which it is not granted to man to utter" (2 Cor 12.3). His account of his raptures and visions is nevertheless magnificent prose. St. Augustine hints at something of the same difficulty in expressing the ineffable when he says: "Thee when first I saw, Thou liftedst me up, that I might see there was something which I might see, and that as yet I was not the man to see it" (*Confessions,* tr. Watts [London 1912] 1.373). But Augustine overleaped the barrier of expression to give the world in the *Confessions,* and indeed in much of his other work, abiding literary masterpieces. The influence of NEOPLATONISM gave a distinct literary quality to the work of Dionysius the Areopagite (*see* PSEUDO-DIONYSIUS), one of the great shapers of subsequent Christian mysticism.

The Middle Ages saw a great flowering of mysticism. Most of the accounts of mystical experience are superb in the fervent tenderness and modesty that make them gems of affective literature. Such, for example, is St. BERNARD OF CLAIRVAUX's sermon on the Song of Songs:

> I confess, then, though I say it in my foolishness, that the Word visited me, and even very often. But although He very frequently entered into my soul, I have never at any time been sensible of the precise moment of His coming. I have felt that he was present. . . . You will ask, then, how, since the ways of His access are thus incapable of being traced, I could know that He was present? But he is living and full of energy, and as soon as He has entered into me He has quickened my sleeping soul, has aroused and softened and goaded my heart, which was in a state of torpor, and hard as a stone. He has begun to pluck up and destroy, to plant and to build, to water the dry places, to illuminate the gloomy spots, to throw open those which were shut close, to inflame with warmth those which were cold, as also to strengthen its crooked paths and make its rough places smooth, so that my soul might bless the Lord, and all that is within me praise His holy Name. (*Life and Works,* ed. J. Mabillon [London 1896] 4.457.)

Others whose prose possesses this literary charm were RICHARD OF SAINT-VICTOR, St. BONAVENTURE, and St. DOMINIC; there were also mystics who were great poets, such as St. THOMAS AQUINAS, whose majestic hymns (e.g., *Pange lingua* and *Sacris solemniis juncta*

sunt gaudia) are obviously the fruit of his own mystical prayer.

The literary qualities of the English MYSTICS have often been adverted to. There is a simplicity and charm to their recounting of their experiences, which recalls the Franciscan influence that stemmed so largely from St. Francis of Assisi himself (*see* FIORETTI, THE) and from the *Laudi* of his followers. But there is much Augustinian influence at work, too, as may be seen in the anonymous *The Cloud of Unknowing* (between 1345 and 1386). Other true masterpieces of the English school are Walter Hilton's *The Scale of Perfection,* JULIAN OF NORWICH's *Revelations of Divine Love,* and Richard Rolle's poems.

On the Continent, Jan van RUYSBROECK introduced a superb symbolism in his *The Book of the Sparkling Stone* and spoke with great ardor in *The Adornment of the Spiritual Marriage.* The same intimate fervor is manifest in the works of St. BRIDGET OF SWEDEN and St. CATHERINE OF SIENA. The great German mystics, such as MECHTILD OF MAGDEBURG and St. HILDEGARD OF BINGEN, had profound literary influence. But it is to Spain that one looks for the greatest mystical literature, beginning with the Catalan, Raymond LULL, and culminating in the rich prose of St. TERESA OF AVILA and the sublime poetry of St. John of the Cross.

One of the seminal literary achievements of the mystics was in developing and deepening (if not in originating) various symbolical "frames" for the account of their experiences. Such, for example, are the symbols of the ladder, the pilgrimage, and, with particular influence, the bold symbols of earthly wooing, love, and marriage as analogues of the divine union. But even more fruitful for deeply affective and intimately moving revelation has been the mystics' constant meditation on the Passion of Christ. It has been *this* intimacy that has given the "I-Thou" mystics the source of the superb literature produced by them. They, like (but how much more profoundly than) their paler "I-It" counterparts, speak in a chorus of loving testimony to the reality (in truth, a *personal* reality) of the God with whom they had achieved direct, intuitive knowledge through unifying love. That they were not able to speak of this experience more often in what are called the accents of literature lay in the fact, as Julian of Norwich said in her *Revelations of Divine Love,* that "Ah, hard and grievous was His pain . . . for which pains I saw that all is too little that I can say; for it may not be told."

[H. C. GARDINER/E. E. LARKIN]

MYSTICS, ENGLISH

The great flowering of English mysticism was in the 14th century, with such writers as Walter HILTON, JULIAN OF NORWICH, Richard Rolle (*see* ROLLE DE HAMPOLE, RICHARD), and the nameless author of *The CLOUD OF UNKNOWING*. It was the full and final growth of a tradition of devotion and speculation that had begun soon after the Christianization of England with Bede; in many of his homilies and commentaries we find his learning in the Scriptures and the Fathers expressing itself in an affective prose that tells of a progress through prayer and contemplation to an immediate perception of God's nature. In Bede's writings we find the germ of the devotions to the Sacred Heart, to the Passion and to the mysteries of Our Lady, for which later medieval England was to become famous.

Development. From the earliest days of the Anglo-Saxon Church, contacts with Ireland, though not always amicable, had existed. No doubt the Irish contributed to the growth of the body of highly individual prayers, especially those to the crucified Savior, found in such pre-Conquest compilations as the Books of Cerne and Nunnaminster. *The Dream of the Rood,* a much earlier composition, is beyond question the finest contribution of Old English literature to Christian devotional writing. One further circumstance in the religious life of the times, a trait shared with Ireland, helped to mold the forms and the thought fully expressed only centuries later: England became celebrated for its great numbers of hermits and anchorites. It may be that the Norman Conquest, which for a time excluded most Englishmen from ecclesiastical preferment, gave impetus to the solitary life of contemplation. Certainly in the 11th century and onward, we have much evidence to show that this life was pursued by many.

In the simple illiterate hermit Godric of Finchale, poet of the love of Christ and His Mother, we have a successor to the great tradition of Caedmon. Godric's contemporary, Christina of Markyate, though she wrote nothing, survives in her biography as an intrepid seeker for graces which she gained only by a total denial of the world. Some of the greatest figures in the English Church of this time wrote treatises which became standard among those vowed to anchoritic contemplation. Special mention must be made of St. Anselm's Latin *Meditations,* St. Aelred's Latin *Mirror of Love* and St. Edmund's French *Mirror of Holy Church.* Their fruitfulness is witnessed by the speed with which they were turned into English, and the wide circulation such translations gained. In the early 13th century there appeared a wholly original English work, the ANCRENE RIWLE, in which the traditions of vernacular prose writing were given new life. The *Riwle* is only one of a number of contemporary guides to the solitary life of contemplation. The "Katherine Group" of English spiritual writings show that the author of the *Riwle* was not alone in his revival of English prose. Until the very end of organized religious life in the mid-16th century, the *Riwle* continued to be read, adapted, copied, and quoted. Many works which gained an independent fame in the 14th and 15th centuries, such as *The Chastising of God's Children, The Poor Caitiff* and *Disce Mori,* derive inspiration from it; and its study is today essential to those who would understand the individual genius of the spiritual thought of the age.

Religious Poetry. The religious life of medieval England is, indeed, singular in the West for the huge body of vernacular religious poetry, almost all of it anonymous, which has come down to us. It is still fashionable to regard much of it, the poems of love for Our Lady in particular, as derivative alike in language and inspiration from profane songs of courtly love; but this view is objectionable in many ways. It is equally arguable that courtly literature owes much of its inspiration to religious models, and the evidence, in England alone, provided by such very early lyrics as those of Godric and the evocative quatrain upon the Crucifixion quoted by St. Edmund in the *Mirror,* shows that the Franciscans were far from being the first to make popular songs about the love of God. Even before Richard Rolle we have such poems as Thomas of Hales's *Love Rune* to witness to the survival of long-established traditions. In Rolle, though we may think his reputation as a contemplative exaggerated, in his own times and ours, we find an unrivaled poet of the sweetness of divine love. The author of the *Cloud* and Walter Hilton both make adverse criticisms of the type of devotion which Rolle popularized, showing that it could lead to a superstitious veneration of "consolations," real or imagined, for their own sake; but they were themselves in some respects Rolle's debtors. He helped to preserve and adapt the style in which they wrote, and there are few who study the *Cloud* and *The Scale of Perfection* without having first known Rolle's *Incendium Amoris* and his English treatises and poems. Who the author of the *Cloud* was we do not know, nor is his identity important. His teachings, partly inspired by Pseudo-Dionysius and Richard of Saint-Victor, on the steps in contemplation and prayer that will lead to an immediate union with God, to "deification," aroused hostility. Doctrinally, the *Cloud* and its constellation of minor treatises, *Privy Counsel* and the rest, resemble principally John Ruysbroeck among Western mystics. Walter Hilton, the solitary turned Augustinian canon, is more sober, more academic, less original in his manner of presentation; nonetheless his writings established themselves in the 15th century as authoritative guides to contemplative prayer.

Ecstatic Mysticism. Quite apart from these two is their contemporary, Julian, the anchorite of Norwich whose *Revelations* show her to have been England's one great ecstatic mystic. This she does not claim for herself: her book merely records a series of mysterious visions, granted to her over a short period early in life, and the doctrine she drew from them after long pondering. What she teaches of the Incarnation, the Passion, Redemption, and damnation, makes comparison of her with Hadewijch, Mechtild of Magdeburg, and Catherine of Siena not inappropriate.

Until the ruin of organized Catholic life, and afterwards, these mystics continued deeply to influence the country's life and thought, as St. Thomas More and Augustine Baker, among many others, show us; but they had written for an age which had died, and it was not until the 19th century revived men's reverence for the medieval world that they were able again to show students of spiritual life the paths towards God which they, no less than the saints of the Counter Reformation, had followed to their goal.

Bibliography: D. KNOWLES, *English Mystics* (London 1927); *The English Mystical Tradition* (New York 1961). W. R. INGE, *Studies of English Mystics* (London 1906), St. Margaret's lectures for 1905–06; to be read with caution. M. WARD, ed., *The English Way: Studies in English Sanctity from St. Bede to Newman* (New York 1933). E. COLLEDGE, *Medieval Mystics of England* (New York 1961).

[E. COLLEDGE]

MYTH, LITERARY

The investigation of "literary" myth is not limited to those forms that are found in highly developed civilizations with a written literature. As a matter of fact, it is essential for an exact understanding of myth to give special importance to primitive and archaic cultures because the more sophisticated forms of the so-called high civilizations frequently conceal or cloud myth's true nature and function.

DEFINITION

In a very general way, myth can be defined as a story about the holy. Already in the oldest Greek texts where the word occurs, it is used—though not exclusively—for narrative or story, and at an early period it became the technical expression for the traditional stories about the gods. The evolution of the concept of myth, partly of a merely semantic nature, and partly caused by a changing religious consciousness or attitude, is very instructive with regard to the present confusion in the use of the term.

The Greek term μῦθος, which means word, is derived from the Indo-European root *meudh* or *mudh,* i.e.,

to reflect, to think over, to consider. This seems to indicate an original stress upon the deeper content of the word, the definitive and final expression of a reality. However, the opposition between μῦθος and λόγος, introduced by the SOPHISTS, who disbelieved—or misunderstood—the stories about the gods, gave later on a rather pejorative connotation to μῦθος. Xenophanes made a radical criticism of the mythologies as related by Homer and Hesiod. Theagenes of Rhegion interpreted them allegorically, whereas Euhemerus invented a pseudohistorical explanation of myth, which, to this day, continues to be called after him (EUHEMERISM). Plato repeatedly equated myth with legend or fairy tale, although he himself used myths as appropriate means to convey a mystery. Aristotle regarded myth as a product of fancy and fabulation. All these authors, to be sure, knew myths mainly through the literary transformations of the poets, where legendary and etiological elements are plentiful. In Lucian μυθολογεῖν means to lie, to tell tall stories. This Hellenistic conception is typical also for the Judeo-Christian tradition: myths were discredited fictional narratives and were rejected as absurdities and falsehoods, if not as abominations and diabolical inventions.

RENEWED INTEREST SINCE THE RENAISSANCE

With the revival of classical antiquity, the Renaissance renewed the interest in myth. Natalis Comes considered myth to be a symbolical or allegorical expression of philosophical speculations. VICO, a remarkably independent figure in an era of rationalism, interpreted myth as a spontaneous reaction of primitive man to natural phenomena, but also as a poetic expression of historical events. His interpretation combined allegorical explanation and historical reductionism. The Romantic movement gave much emphasis to the religious factor in myth, e.g., J. G. HERDER and especially SCHELLING, who saw myth as a necessary stage in the self-revelation of the Absolute. In the second half of the 19th century, the systematic and comparative study of religions, then first established as a science, although naturally interested in myth, still largely shared the old prejudices of the ENLIGHTENMENT. Max Müller's (1823–1900) ingenious and widely popular, but rather extravagant, thesis about myth as a disease of language is well known, but even Frazer, an arduous and rather well-informed student of religions, regarded myths as mistaken explanations of human or natural phenomena. RATIONALISM called myth everything that did not agree with its own concept of reality. For W. Wundt (1832–1920) it was a product of imagination; for L. Lévy-Bruhl (1857–1939), of a prelogic, a primitive mentality.

The neo-Kantian philosopher CASSIRER attempted to evaluate the mythical function in the structure of human consciousness. He rejected the allegorical interpretation and stressed the autonomy of myth as a symbolic form and an interpretation of reality: it was the primitive intuition of the cosmic solidarity of life. Freud, JUNG, and their psychoanalytical schools gave a new impetus to the study of myth by pointing out the striking similarities between their content and the universe of the unconscious. Their error, all too often, was to reduce myth altogether to the dynamics of the unconscious.

20TH-CENTURY DEVELOPMENTS

In the mid-1960s, philosophers such as K. JASPERS (1883–1969) and P. RICOEUR (1913–) gave a very positive evaluation of myth as an expression, or as a cipher, of the transcendent, a language of being. It was, however, the diligent study of primitive religions, where myths exist in a more or less unadulterated form as living and functional religious values, that proved to be the determining factor in the new understanding of myth. Although, in the common acceptance of the word, myth still belongs more or less to the world of imagination, there was a growing awareness of the fact that myth is par excellence the language of religion. Anthropology, ethnology, phenomenology, and the history of religions, completing the insights of sociology, psychology, philosophy, and folklore, were instrumental in the 20th-century revalorization of myth.

From the works of scholars such as J. Baumann (1837–1916), A. E. Jensen (1899–1965), and M. ELIADE (1908–1986), it was easy to extract a synthetic view of myth, although not so easy to define or to describe it in such a way as to take care of the variety of forms and types of myths resulting from its intricate development. Fundamentally, myth is the sacred story of a primordial event that constitutes and inaugurates a reality and hence determines man's existential situation in the cosmos as a sacred world. Myths deal with the so-called limit-situations of man, as expressed in the great mysterious moments of his existence: birth, death, initiation. But they make such limitations transparent for their sacred meaning, referring them to a divine prototype that happened in mythical time, or, rather, mythical no-time.

RECOGNITION OF SACRED CHARACTER

It is this sacred character that distinguishes myth from related literary types: saga, legend, and fairy tale, although, in fact, it is rather difficult to discover pure myths. Most myths, by the time they are recorded, appear as hybrid literary types, and it is not always simple to make out where myth ends and legend begins. Sagas, and to a certain extent also legends, are founded on something that really, or at least supposedly, happened in time, whereas myths deal with metahistorical events. Fairy tales, however, have no fundamental relation whatsoever to time or reality. But myth has this relation in an eminent way because it founds reality, brings a reality into time. Moreover, as Eliade, among others, convincingly shown, fairy tales and legends are often secularized myths. There is no doubt that myths are primary; no longer understood, they ceased to be revelations of a mystery or expressions of a mode of being in the world, but became diversions told for entertainment. However, their initiatory character very often can still be recognized. One could say, in a certain sense, that myth becomes less and less myth when it becomes more and more literature, because it enters a process of secularization in which it is blended and embellished with many nonmythical elements. But even in its highly sophisticated forms as a literary work, myth cannot be understood unless its religious nature is first recognized.

R. Pettazzoni gave due importance to the fact that the Pawnee and other North American Indian tribes make a distinction between true and false stories. According to this distinction, which can easily be substantiated and corroborated with evidence from archaic peoples all over the world, myths are true stories that deal with the holy and the supernatural, whereas false stories, those that have a profane content, are just make-believe.

It is important, however, to stress the difference between the truth of myth and its historical veracity. Myth, of its very nature, repels historicity, because the event it relates happened before history began, in an eternal instant. Myth, therefore, is not some sort of garbled history; it tells what really happened, not in time, but in the beginning, in the era of the gods. It is the story of a primordial event that accounts for the way a reality came into existence, i.e., began to exist in time. If myth is true, it is because it deals with what is real par excellence, because it deals with the reality that accounts for what exists in time and space. It reveals the true nature and structure of the *hic et nunc* realities by relating them to a metaempirical reality. It reveals the deeper, authentic meaning of life by showing how this particular mode of being in the world came about. In general one might say that the etiological concept, and consequently the etiological criticism of myth, misses the point, because it misunderstands the true nature of myth. Myth does not explain as much as it reveals and is unconcerned about apparent contradictions, because such contradictions exist in the empirical realm only. Historical and logical precision are irrelevant in the world of myth, because myth expresses not an erudition but a consciousness of a reality. It expresses what, in the religious consciousness of the believer, is true and valid.

The distinction between true and false stories in archaic cultures is also a distinction between sacred and profane. Myth is holy because its protagonists are gods or superhuman beings who intervene in the universe and establish it as an ordered cosmos. Myth is holy also because of the sacredness it makes present. Already the mere recitation of the myth results in the supernatural being present *hic et nunc,* and in this way mediates to those who hear it an insight into the holy ground of empirical or phenomenological reality. Usually this recitation is restricted to certain periods of sacred time. Frequently it is performed in the course of cult ceremonies, in which the myth is then the ἱερὸς λόγος, by certain authorized members of the community only, priests or elders. There may be certain taboos involved with the recitation too, e.g., the presence of women. Myth is not common property; one has to be initiated into it. Usually the stories about the gods are known thoroughly to certain experts only, who have the task of initiating the boys coming of age into the sacred traditions of the tribe.

EXEMPLARY CHARACTER

Another fundamental characteristic of myth is its exemplarity. The intervention of the gods in this world, related in the myths, is paradigmatic and normative for man's behavior, ritual as well as social. One could say that myth prescribes for man the mode of being in the world, which it reveals to him: his place in time and space, his participation in the world of animals and plants as well as in the society of men, his cosmic dimension, the laws that govern the specific nature of his human existence, etc. The order the gods established, because it is powerful and holy, because it is reality, has to be safeguarded. Their deeds, because they constitute reality, life, salvation, have to be faithfully repeated, and therefore they become models for all significant human activities. This explains why archaic man is fundamentally imitative and traditional: he wants to secure the power of his actions and gestures by patterning them after the powerful deeds and gestures of the gods. The order of the cosmos and the regularity of its phenomena are reflected in the sacred norms that determine social relations and ethical behavior, as well as ritual procedure. Moreover, since the model is no part of the temporal, but some sort of an eternal instant, it remains paradigmatic and can be repeated over and over again in time. For archaic man, reality is a function of the imitation of a mythical archetype.

MYTH AND RITUAL

The exemplary nature of myth is most evident in the ritual reenactment of a holy, primordial event. As suggested above, the recitation of a myth is in itself already some sort of a ritual because of the solemnity connected with the recitation: "Der rezitierte Mythus ist immer ein Schöpfungswort" (G. van der Leeuw). Very often, however, the recitation of the myth is accompanied by a dra-

matic representation of the event that it relates. The ritual execution of the myth makes the primordial creative event infinitely repeatable and hence continuously present in time. By reenacting the deeds of the gods that brought about reality, life, fecundity, etc., man is able effectively to maintain or renew them. Ritual projects man into the era of the gods, makes him contemporary with them, and lets him share in their creative work.

This close association between myth and ritual gave origin, beginning with the work of W. Robertson Smith (1846–1894), to widely opposed theories about the nature of their mutual relationship. Is myth the offshoot or description of the corresponding ritual, or is it, on the contrary, some sort of libretto or script for the dramatic representation in ritual? Both theories found very articulate defenders. The first one, in particular, was brilliantly proposed and widely popularized by the English myth and ritual school (S. H. Hooke) and the Scandinavian school of Uppsala (Mowinckel). However, they did not always escape successfully the pitfall of some sort of pan-ritualism, which attempts to reduce almost everything to a ritual origin. In a certain sense the opposing theories carried on a sterile discussion, because, historically speaking, it is impossible to substantiate any linear or genealogical evolution from ritual to myth, or vice versa. All agreed that one can find examples of primary rituals as well as of primary myths, but nothing allows one to project this present situation into the origin. True enough, at a certain stage of the development of religious consciousness it is possible to find the awareness that a myth sanctions a rite. But since myth, as B. K. Malinowski (1884–1942) put it, vouches for the efficiency of a rite, this awareness may very well be an a posteriori etiological interpretation. It would be hazardous to conclude from this to the chronological priority of the ritual. Myth certainly is not fundamentally an etiological explanation of a ritual or a rationalization of an existing custom. It would be wrong to reject the possibility, or even the fact, that in the later development of both myth and ritual the former assumed the function of explaining or justifying obscured aspects of the latter, but to accept as the origin of myth a rite that has to be explained would leave no alternative to the shaky theory of the magical origin of religion. (*See* RELIGION; RELIGION IN PRIMITIVE CULTURE.)

Neither myth nor ritual really explains anything; rather, they express in parallel, more often intertwined, and always mutually complementary ways the fundamental religious experience of archaic man in a cosmos that reveals the creative presence of the gods. It does not make too much sense, for example, to say that the recitation of the *ENUMA ELISH* by the Babylonian priests at the Akitu festival served the purpose of explaining the ceremonies. Rather, it is the presence, within its temporal reenactment, of the ideal, eternal model. The mystery of creation is expressed simultaneously in word and in imitation. The ritual in the strict sense of the term presents the event, and the myth relates this presentation to its transcendental model and meaning. The concomitant myth, in a certain sense, identifies the ritual reenactment with its divine prototype, and, by so doing, intrinsically determines or prescribes the process to be followed.

The dichotomy of myth and ritual seems to be a recent phenomenon. For primitive man they were not two things brought together, but two aspects of one reality, one experience expressed in the two fundamental forms of human expression: word and gesture, each one clarifying, complementing, and requesting the other. Really primary is the divine model or archetype as it is revealed in the reality of the cosmos and of life. "We must do what the gods did in the beginning," says the Śatapatha Brāhmana, and this old Indian adage is valid all over the world. Even where myth, because its justifying or etiological character is obvious, can be proved to be chronologically secondary to the rite, it would still be imperative to distinguish between the formulation and the content of the myth. Myth and ritual are not to be separated; where they are, myth enters a process of secularization and ritual becomes superstition.

TYPES OF MYTH

Myths are usually classified according to their subject matter: cosmogonic, theogonic, and anthropogonic myths, Paradise myths, myths of Fall and Flood, soteriological or eschatological myths. The various types can, of course, be further subdivided typologically; the cosmogonic myth, for example, could be further divided into myths of emergence, of the earth-diving type, of struggle with the primordial dragon, of dismemberment of a primordial being, etc. Such divisions have their practical usefulness but are quite artificial, and there would be a good case for reducing all myths, if not to a single type, at least to one prototype. Indeed, all myths have a very definite common denominator: they deal with the beginnings of realities—the origins of the world and of humankind, of life and death, of the animal and vegetable species, of culture and civilization, of worship and initiation, of society, its leaders and institutions. The only apparent exception, the eschatological myth, in fact also deals with the restitution of creation in its original purity and integrity. Because it reveals how the totality of the real came into being, the cosmogonic creation myth is the prototypical one, continued and completed by the other myths.

MYTH AND THE BIBLE

Where the word myth is mentioned in the Bible, almost exclusively in the NT, it is invariably in the pejorative sense of fiction, old wives' tale, lie, or error. Typical is the well-known text of 2 Tm 4.4: "They will stop their ears to truth, and turn to myth." It is obvious, however, that this negative attitude is nothing more than a conformity with the prevalent use of the term, together with a rather exclusivistic religious absolutism. Foreign religious traditions are not false because they are myths; they are called myths because they are, or are supposed to be, false. This does not necessarily imply a fundamental incongruity between Holy Scripture and myth, as myth is understood. The incongruity is not between Bible and myth, but between Bible and falsity.

It is evident that the narratives of Genesis about the creation of the world and of man, about Eden and the Fall, etc., are not really history in the ordinary sense of the word, but very much stories about events that took place "in the beginning," events that constituted the cosmos as a reality, and about man in his specific mode of being in the world, his existential situation as a created, mortal, sexed, and cultural being. If it could be substantiated that the story of Genesis ch. 1 was recited at the Hebrew New Year's festival, this association between the creation myth and the annual ritual of cosmic renewal would be a further confirmation of its mythic character. Other examples of this association between narrative and ritual—with the essential difference that the mythical archetype is replaced by an historical prototype—are the Exodus story, reenacted in the Passover ceremony, and the mystery of Christ's redemptive sacrifice and Resurrection, renewed in the Eucharistic celebration of the Mass.

The Bible, as a literary work, has a tradition that includes myth as a literary genre and does not reject mythical patterns from other civilizations. This is not surprising; what is surprising is the remarkable restraint Israel used in this regard. One could say that, in a certain sense, the authors of the Bible demythologized to a great extent whatever myth they used. In the cultural and civilizational context of the Bible, the use of mythical language in order to express the supernatural and transcendental content of a religious message is self-evident. Because myth reveals in a dramatic way what philosophy and theology try to express conceptually and dialectically, it adapts itself naturally to the expression of an active divine presence in the cosmos. Because myth is not limited by the laws of logic, it expresses naturally the divine reality as something that transcends thought in a *coincidentia oppositorum*. Because myth takes place in a nontemporal era, it presents naturally a transtemporal or metahistorical event that never happened, but always is, *ab origine*.

With regard to the mythical outlook of religious man, there is, however, in the Judeo-Christian tradition a totally new factor. Although mythical patterns remain discernible, the decisive events are no longer extratemporal, but, in a very real sense, historical: God intervenes effectively in human history. Myth reveals the existence of the gods as the ground of all created reality, but the Bible reveals God's activity on the scene of time. In myth, as in Platonism, time is but the moving image of unmoving eternity, a never ceasing repetition of creation through a process of periodical regeneration. But in the Judeo-Christian tradition time is creation itself in the act of being accomplished. Historical events have a value in themselves because they mark God's interventions in time. They do not mark a recurrence of archetypes, but a new, unique, and decisive moment in an irreversible process. The message of the Prophets, for example, is much more about these interventions of God in history than about His presence in the cosmos. As a matter of fact, one could very well, with Tresmontant, define the *nabi* (prophet) as one who has the understanding of the sense of history. Here again there is an implicit demythologization in the Bible.

Creation, Fall, and Flood can be said to be events of the beginning, but not the Exodus, the passage of the Red Sea, the crossing of the Jordan, the invasion of Canaan. These are historical events. Again, the mythical pattern is discernible in the ritual repetition of creation of those events as well as in the liturgical year that periodically repeats the events of the Nativity, life, death, and Resurrection of Jesus. But, although the reactualization is obvious, especially in the Sacraments, this repetition is nevertheless, in the awareness of the believers, a remembrance of an historical fact, an *ephapax* that already achieved its soteriological end "once and for all." In 2 Pt 1.16–18 one can see the importance given to this historical aspect by early Christianity, and again it is in opposition to myth: "We were not following fictitious tales when we made known to you . . . Jesus Christ, but we had been eyewitnesses. . . . We ourselves heard. . . . We were with him."

After STRAUSS, RENAN, and others in the 19th century, Rudolf BULTMANN (1884–1976) stressed the mythical character of the NT and the need to demythologize the Christian kerygma, i.e., to strip it from its obsolete, mythological elements, caused mainly by Hellenistic gnosticism and Jewish apocalyptic ideas, in order then to interpret it anthropologically or existentially. Since this question is extensively dealt with in other articles, a few general remarks will suffice here (*see* DEMYTHOLOGIZING; FORM CRITICISM, BIBLICAL). Sometimes demythologization really stands for deliteralization, a nonliteral interpretation or understanding of an imagery that became inappropriate because it was based on an outdated, mistaken, or incomplete knowledge, e.g., an erroneous cos-

mology. This is, of course, what respectable theology did throughout the ages, and it is imperative as long as the message is not evacuated with its expression. Insofar as myth, for Bultmann, is to conceive and to express the divine in terms of human life, the only alternative to some sort of *re*-mythologization seems to be complete silence. Finally, demythologization sometimes stands for an effort to salvage in the narratives of the NT the historical kernel from its so-called "mythical husk." To assess critically what is strictly historical and what is not is certainly to be commended. But to distinguish does not mean to separate or to oppose. What is denounced as mythical garb may be a necessary or at least a convenient instrument to reveal the historical event as a theophany. To eliminate myth in this sense would be disastrous because both myth and fact are demanded by—and coinstrumental in—the revelation of divine presence in history. As such they validate each other.

See Also: MYTH AND MYTHOLOGY; MYTH AND MYTHOLOGY (IN THE BIBLE).

Bibliography: J. DE VRIES, *Forschungsgeschichte der Mythologie* (Freiburg 1961). M. ELIADE, *Patterns in Comparative Religion,* tr. R. SHEED (New York 1958); *Myths, Dreams, and Mysteries* (New York 1961); *Myth and Reality* (New York 1963). T. J. SEBEOK, ed., *Myth: A Symposium* (Bloomington, Ind. 1958). H. A. MURRAY, ed., *Myth and Mythmaking* (New York 1960). R. CAILLOIS, *Le Mythe et l'homme* (Paris 1938). B. MALINOWSKI, *The Myth in Primitive Psychology* (London 1926). A. E. JENSEN, *Myth and Cult among Primitive Peoples,* tr. M. T. CHOLDIN and W. WEISSLEDER (Chicago 1963); ed., *Mythe, Mensch und Umwelt* (Bamberg 1950). W. NESTLÉ, *Vom Mythos zum Logos* (Stuttgart 1940). E. CASSIRER, *Philosophy of Symbolic Forms,* tr. R. MANHEIM (New Haven 1953–57) v.2. H. M. and N. K. CHADWICK, *The Growth of Literature,* 3 v. (Cambridge, Eng. 1932–40). C. G. JUNG and C. KERÉNYI, *Einführung in das Wesen der Mythologie* (Amsterdam 1941). R. QUENEAU, ed., *Histoire des littératures* (Encyclopédie de la Pléiade 1, 3, 7; Paris 1955–58) v.1. R. PETTAZZONI, *Essays on the History of Religions,* tr. H. J. ROSE (Leiden 1954). H. BAUMANN, "Mythos in ethnologischer Sicht," *Studium generale* 12 (1959) 1–17. G. VAN RIET, "Mythe et vérité," in his *Problèmes d'épistémologie* (Paris 1960).

[F. DE GRAEVE]

MYTH AND MYTHOLOGY

The myth is a narrative that portrays an event. What marks the narrative as a myth are both the characters appearing in it and the influence of the event on the structure and order of the existence or life assumed. The time in which the mythical event takes place is therefore of basic meaning for every other time.

Precise Definition

If attention is concentrated on the characters appearing in myth, there is a tendency to define myth simply as a narrative or story concerned with gods. However, such a definition needs certain qualifications. Myth, it is true, usually deals with gods or divine beings (daemons, angels, and others), but a story about gods in itself is by no means necessarily a myth. The territory of genuine mythical literature is abandoned as soon as a people has reached the cultural stage in which, through its love of stories, it creates ever new and more exciting tales about its favorite gods, ascribing unusual traits or features to them and furnishing details concerning their complicated adventures or escapades. Such stories about gods lead to creative literary art and serve merely for entertainment.

The genuine myth deals with incidents and actions, with struggles and afflictions, with death and resurrection, with defeat and victory, in which the god endures his lot and reveals his nature. The myth, therefore, is not a divine biography. While in biography the essential and the unessential are combined, the myth is concerned in its narrative exclusively with the character and range of activity of the god, focusing attention on his relation to the cosmos and to man. If the myth, for example, tells of a divine child, this is not to be understood as the beginning of a continuing story, which later covers his full growth and development. The divine child is identical with the god himself, and his activity corresponds to the activity that the god carries out according to his nature.

The nature of the myth is revealed in Kerényi's definition of it as the "story of beginnings." The myth tells about a god and, in so doing, gives an account of origins. In the mythical event a condition or an order is introduced and is realized in a foundation. The myth as such adduces in etiological fashion the reason that the condition or order exhibits the precise form that it has and not another. Yet it should be emphasized that the reason intended is to be regarded first as ἀρχή (beginnings) and then as αἴτιον (cause). The relation between the mythical event and the consequent order connected with it has not occurred by chance or in any external way, but order itself has sprung from the content of the event in the process of its happening.

MYTH AND TIME

There is a correspondence between the original character of the myth and the kind of time in which the mythical event takes place. The myth is thought of as true insofar as no doubt is present that the mythical event actually took place. However, it did not happen in the real time in which the history of the given people has developed. The time of the myth transcends historical time. Its time is not prehistoric time, but primeval time, and, in respect to eschatological myths, not the future but the last days, the end of time.

Primeval time comes before all other time; although the time of origins, it has the peculiarity that it can never be actual past. In a certain measure it is constantly present, since the organization and form of existence is rooted in it. If one lives as a hunter or as a farmer in harmony with the changing rhythm of nature or lives within the given social order and condition, he is firmly moored in the primitiveness that the mythical events of the primeval time have established. If one wishes to understand the conditions of existence, he must, consequently, put himself back directly; he cannot proceed to understanding solely through analysis. Explanation is always found in what is behind, in the primeval time that is immediately accessible through myth.

MYTH AND CULT

The dialectic inherent in the circumstance that the mythical happening is always found before every time, and yet is likewise present in every time, forms the background for the proper function of myth, namely, its participation as λεγόμενα (things said) in cult. There can be myths without connection with cult, having become completely detached from cult and given a continued life as stories only. Nevertheless myth, not only in most cases, but also by virtue of its nature as the narrative or history of origins, is so closely connected with cult that its function in cult belongs to its definition. In the cultic action the original event becomes present, and primeval time becomes the now or lives again through repetition. The god performs anew his order-founding act, he fulfills anew his destiny, or takes on anew his sphere of existence.

There is much to justify the view that cult is earlier than myth and that therefore, ordinarily, cult does not form around myth; conversely, myth derives its origin from cult. However, in that case it is impossible to know how the thought, without which the whole cult action is connected, originated. In any event, this special kind of cultural form goes far back in human history, and it may be assumed that it belongs to a time in which man was able to express himself better by other means than language, namely, by dance, gestures, attitudes, and primitive types of music. Therefore, the basic events and experiences that created society were not preserved through linguistic formulations or in memory, but were passed on through a repeatedly new enactment in the institution of cult. When man then attained a cultural level that enabled him, with the help of language, to construct connected formulations of his thought, spoken elements received a constantly increasing role in cultic action. A ἱερὸς λόγος was created. While it participates in a sense in the cult action, the function of the ἱερὸς λόγος is not to inform or to explain, but rather to put an action into operation. It is only at this stage that a meaningful narrative is composed, which, in etiological fashion, explains the individual parts in the cultic action. As the λεγόμενα (things said), it is a parallel structure that accompanies and harmonizes with the δρώμενα (things done) in cult.

Myth, Saga, Legend, and Märchen

Myth, as a special kind of primitive narrative, must be distinguished from other similar narrative forms. However, the distinction can be made only in a general way, for it must be emphasized that the boundary lines cannot always be sharply drawn. The narrative can slip over easily from one form into another, and the same motifs can be found in the different forms. Nevertheless, distinction contributes to better understanding.

SAGA

While the myth is primitive history and is concerned with establishing order in the structure of existence, saga is more closely bound to a locale and is connected with definite historical events and places. The time in which the saga events take place is in the past of the given people, and the persons portrayed are for the most part heroic figures who ostensibly have played a decisive role in great events. Often, but by no means always, an actual historical event underlies the saga, but it is then so embellished or forced to fit such fixed schemata that the separation of what is strictly historical in the content is hardly possible.

If a cult develops around the hero of the saga, he becomes the object of religious worship or his actions are magnified into the deeds of a savior. Saga is thus transformed into myth. In another respect also the creative possibilities of saga are freer than those of myth. Thus, without losing its character as saga, it can be enriched with new features and expanded into a whole saga cycle. It is not connected with cult, but in general serves rather as a form of entertainment; and in this respect it admits additional elements and alterations.

Like myth, saga often has etiological meaning, but the explanation that it gives, in contrast to that of myth, is actually an αἴτιον (cause), and its object is usually a local phenomenon: the giving of a name, a custom connected with a place, a geographical feature, and similar things. The etiological factor, however, is rarely the main concern of saga; it is introduced rather as a supplementary observation of an explanatory addition.

LEGEND

The term legend comes from the period of the early Church when it was customary, especially in monastic communities, to read accounts of the saints or martyrs at divine service or on their feast days. Hence it is clear that legend, as well as saga, is a narrative that is based on historical events and persons, but that enriches and embellishes its material through the free play of the imagination. Hence the special tone of the legend is also clear of itself. Legend is religious in character and is intended in a special way to have an edifying effect. Its characters, accordingly, are always figures ideal in piety, models worthy of reverence, who inspire admiration and imitation.

Accordingly, it is not strange that the various legends have common traits. The similar kind of piety, the same examples of god-fearing actions, holy renunciation, and martyrlike pathos recur in legend after legend. Legend as a kind of narrative is not restricted to Christianity in antiquity and the Middle Ages. A legendary literature was created universally around great religious personalities, and their image was transmitted to later times in the form of the legendary biography (cf. the legendary life of Buddha). Finally, given the religious character of a legend, it can appear also in forms that approach the myth. Furthermore, terminology in this respect is not sharply fixed, and one can employ the expression cult-legend as a synonymous designation for the word myth.

MÄRCHEN

The root of *Märchen* is entirely different. In contrast to all other kinds of narratives it is not concerned with real persons or events, but establishes its own world and its own time. The *Märchen*' setting is an indefinite place—"east of the sun and west of the moon"—and its events occur at an indefinite time—"there was once." It has no relation to the world or time in which actuality is the characteristic feature.

Consequently, it operates under other laws than those of the real world. Everything is quite different, yet the *Märchen* does not abandon itself to confusion and caprice. On the contrary, its happenings are subject to inflexible laws. This fixity finds expression also in its style. The structure of the *Märchen* is strict, and it is dominated throughout by schematic features, as, for example, repetition, triple groupings, suspense, and similar devices. However, the *Märchen* and the myth are closely related in their origin. In both forms of narrative the same primitive view of the world and of life is clearly present. But what in the myth takes place in the sphere of reality is, in the *Märchen*, consciously elevated into the realm of fantasy and its regulated play. Accordingly, the *Märchen* of its nature is fundamentally harmless, although the most horrible things can transpire in it.

At the risk of oversimplification, it may be said that, while all four narrative forms operate with the same motifs, each operates in a wholly different manner, and in one peculiar to itself in each case. In the saga, the theme is handled usually in tragic fashion; in the legend, to serve the purpose of edification, and in the *Märchen,* primarily to give pleasure. The myth alone understands its theme to be origin and foundation.

Classification of Myths

The classification of myths can be attempted only in broad lines, and the assignment of specific myths to specific categories is often open to question. Nevertheless, the setting up of a scheme of classification is indispensable if one wishes to get a concrete and clear understanding of myth.

COSMOGONIC MYTH

By definition, this type of myth deals with origins, and by its nature it is always cosmic in scope. The cosmogonic category of myths is the basic group with which the remaining groups are combined in various ways. The cosmogonic myth tells of the origin of the cosmos either through a direct act on the part of the creator or through emanation from a primeval being or nature. The act of creation can be carried out by the High God alone or in cooperation with other mythical beings—or sometimes with the primeval man or with an evil adversary. However, the High God can also withdraw into the background, either because he is outside the myth or because, after his primitive act of creation, he leaves the further work of creation to be accomplished by other powers.

The process of creation can be represented as an intellectual act whereby God alone, through his thought, word, or will calls the world into existence, or it can be conceived also as a craftsman's shaping of preexistent matter. If, on the other hand, the origin of the world is thought of as an emanation process, the cosmogonic myth then speaks usually of a long and highly imaginative development in which a primeval being is divided or split up to constitute a multiform world.

THEOGONIC MYTHS

The creation of the gods is the theme of special myths. These describe how the polytheistic world of the gods originated as a creation of a High God, or how a first divine pair became the ancestors of the subsequent world of the gods. Accordingly, the theogonic myths can be regarded also as a part of a cosmogony, the *Theogony* of Hesiod being the best known example. The appearance of the gods is itself a part of the general development of the cosmos, and generations of gods can arise that replace each other—often in dramatic ways. The relation of the High God to the world of gods that he has created is never a hostile one. On the contrary, the High God has withdrawn into his heavenly realms, in which he has an un-

troubled existence, while other divinities, who may be characterized in some respects as intermediate beings, must preserve and guard the created cosmos.

ANTHROPOGONIC MYTHS

The origin of men frequently plays an important role in mythology. The cosmogonic and theogonic myths then form only the prologue to an anthropogony. But the opposite type of myth is also found, in which the entrance of men into the world does not play even the slightest role and is therefore insignificant. Again, in many other myths, man is portrayed as a special or unique being, either in the form of a powerful primeval man who helped the creator god in his further work, or as a central figure of divine origin who was created to rule over the cosmos. Anthropogony can be emphasized also in a more naturalistic fashion: man, like the plants, has grown out of the earth or has been born of stone, or formed as a figure from clay. In the Orphic myths man sprang from the ashes of the Titans as a dualistic unity of soul and body. Universally, anthropogonic myth, with inventive imagination, depicts the contemporary view of the nature and function of man.

MYTHS OF THE PRIMITIVE STATE OF THE COSMOS AND MAN

Myths dealing with this theme not only describe the original state of the cosmos, but are intended especially to furnish information on the processes that led to subsequent and present conditions. Many myths tell how death came into the world. This happened through a chance event, through disobedience, through some clumsiness or carelessness, or because a command was not observed. With death, evil also came into the world. Man must suffer and work hard; he has fallen from his primitive happy state into evil snares and has become subject to stern conditions. The various cultural spheres have their origin also in events of the mythical primeval time. The structure of society is to be traced back to primeval happenings, the present laws are of divine origin, and the great bearers of civilization founded the patterns and regulations of the various professions, even when they often had to overcome in decisive battles powers threatening them.

SAVIOR MYTHS

The myth of the savior-god is closely connected especially with the mystery cults and is often a further development of earlier agricultural myths. Underlying all differentiating details, there is an extraordinarily widespread and strikingly uniform schema. The god is the object of an evil attack on the part of evil powers and is put to death in tragic circumstances. The good powers, however, inaugurate countermeasures and the god is restored to new life, often in connection with his conquest or dominion over the kingdom of the dead.

ESCHATOLOGICAL MYTHS

Eschatological myths have a much less extensive distribution. They postulate a definite conception of the nature of history and occupy themselves with speculations on its end. They usually portray the final time as a period of dramatic cosmic events that point to the coming of the hero-god and in which judgment will be rendered on good and evil. The events of the final time lead to a new creation and to the establishment of a state of bliss, which is often conceived as the restoration of the happy condition lost in primeval time.

MYTHOLOGICAL SYSTEMS

In origin, myths are short, limited narratives that, according to the occasion, relate an appropriate mythical event. However, if the myth-forming period of a people is approaching its end and the store of myths has become so rich that even contradictory traits or elements are present, theological speculation begins to operate. An effort is made to combine the myths into a system of homogeneous character, and to remove aberrations or disharmonies, in order to give the total myth complex the appearance of a theologically consistent whole. This development is often accompanied by a somewhat depreciatory attitude to the original ''naive'' form, and the mythological system subjects the content of the individual myths to thorough allegorical interpretation.

The systematization of myth, therefore, is an indication that the myth has lost its proper character. People no longer believe in the literal reality of the myth, but regard it as the expression of ''eternal'' truths. The myth is transformed into a philosophical theorem; its personal and active forces are now only the cloak for abstract, metaphysical concepts; and the views on the nature of existence and on the nature of man have actually become nonmythical. The realities of existence are no longer ascribed to primeval events. Accordingly, the appropriate form of expression, namely, the visualizing dramatic narrative of myth, is lost also, and its place is taken by metaphysical definition and philosophical argument. In other words, the mythological system is the transitional stage from true myth to metaphysical speculation.

The Origin and Development of Mythology

D. HUME (1711–1766) made the study of myths a field of scientific investigation. As opposed to the Deistic ideas of a ''natural religion,'' he maintained that mythological concepts are a kind of primitive explanation of nature and that their origin is to be sought in the sphere of the emotions. Hope and especially fear are the factors that impel people to formulate mythico-religious concepts.

INFLUENCE OF IDEALISM AND ROMANTICISM

German Idealism and Romanticism, as a reaction against the Enlightenment, rediscovered myths and evaluated them primarily from an aesthetic point of view as poetical or literary creations. The mythical composition was regarded as an independent product of intellectual life, an independent contribution of the creative imagination. On the speculative-philosophical plane, F. W. SCHELLING (1775–1854), especially, raised myths to a position of central importance. The principles that are found in the mind of God as a unity penetrate human consciousness by a kind of metaphysical process. They split apart in opposition and tension, and at this stage they are best called myths.

WUNDT, OTTO, CASSIRER, AND TILLICH

The Religio-Historical School in the second half of the 19th century, under the leadership of H. Usener (1834–1905), went back to the ideas of Hume. W. Wundt (1832–1920), however, made a new advance in the investigation of myths. He regarded the emotions as the sources of myths. But the possibility of the emotions' leading to mythical ideas is to be ultimately ascribed to the imagination. Through the apperception of things as persons, it is possible for man to objectify his emotional states. Wundt, nevertheless, did not yet have clearly in view the specific elements in the feelings and imagination that produce myths.

In this regard R. OTTO (1869–1937) made a supplementary contribution. His description of the emotional states, by which man is affected in the presence of the numinous, is characterized especially by his view that religious feeling is something specific. The primary thing is the emotional state. The myths merely cluster about it as creations of the imagination. Moreover, at the same time, they are by-products that can harden into a shell, and the shell can prevent the development of a genuine religious attitude or disposition.

E. CASSIRER (1874–1945) investigated the phenomena of myths more from an epistemological than from a psychological point of view. According to his conception, the myth has its own nature; and beside art, language, and science it constitutes one of the symbolic forms of intellectual life. It builds its world according to its own laws and derives its specific value from the association of meaning inherent in itself. On the other hand, for Cassirer, the symbolism of the myth remained a kind of primitive understanding of life that gave rise to scientific knowledge and its development.

Here P. TILLICH opposed Cassirer. Myth, according to Tillich, falls in the category of the unconditioned or of the being other-worldly to which the religious act is directed. The myth chooses its own objects, which it sets up as symbols of the unconditioned. Insofar as the unconditioned is a reality, the myth in its symbolic orientation to the unconditioned is also real. Tillich emphasizes that the myth does not select its symbols arbitrarily. The creation of symbols is governed by the law that the symbol itself participates in what it is to symbolize.

FREUD AND JUNG

Finally psychoanalysis made important contributions to the understanding of the myth. S. Freud (1836–1939) considered myths the expression of suppressed desires. He enunciated a psychological law according to which suppressions precipitate themselves in a symbolic expression, a discovery that has served as a basis for the psychoanalysis of the meaning of dreams. Of considerable influence also has been Freud's idea of the origin of civilization out of primeval events, and of primeval sin, the permanent consequence of which he called the Oedipus complex.

Symbol formations, understood and evaluated on a purely individual basis, are interpreted by C. G. JUNG (1875–1961) as an authentic expression of superindividual truths of life, the starting point for the life of the individual ego. With the help of his concept of the collective unconscious and of archetypes as the forms under which it makes its appearance, Jung attempted to break through the barriers of individual psychology and to make dreams and myths function as the symbols in which hidden transcendence as such manifests itself in the world of human consciousness. Jung's ideas have had fruitful influence on contemporary mythological research.

Bibliography: G. LANCZKOWSKI, *Lexikon für Theologie und Kirche*, ed. J. HOFER and K. RAHNER, (2d new ed. Freiburg 1957–65) 7:746–750. J. SLØK et al., *Die Religion in Geschichte und Gegenwart*, 7 v. (3d ed. Tübingen 1957–65) 4:1263–78, with bibliog. H. J. ROSE, *A Handbook of Greek Mythology* (6th ed. New York 1958) 1–16. H. USENER, *Götternamen* (3d ed. Bonn 1948). W. WUNDT, *Völkerpsychologie* (3d and 4th ed. Leipzig 1923–26) v. 4–6. S. FREUD, *The Interpretation of Dreams* (1900–01) in *Standard Edition of the Complete Psychological Works*, ed. J. STRACHEY, 24 v. (London 1953–) v. 4–5; *Das Unbehagen in der Kultur* (Vienna 1930), tr. J. RIVIÈRE; *Civilization and Its Discontents* (London 1930). B. MALINOWSKI, *The Myth in Primitive Psychology* (London 1926). R. OTTO, *The Idea of the Holy*, tr. J. W. HARVEY (2d ed. New York 1958). E. CASSIRER, *Mythical Thought*, v. 2 of *The Philosophy of Symbolic Forms*, tr. R. MANHEIM, 3 v. (New Haven 1953–57). C. KLUCKHOHN, "Myths and Rituals: A General Theory," *Harvard Theological Review* 35 (Cambridge, Mass. 1942) 45–79. M. ELIADE, *The Myth of the Eternal Return*, tr. W. R. TRASK (Bollingen Ser. 46; New York 1954); *Myths, Dreams, and Mysteries*, tr. P. MAIRET (New York 1960). D. BIDNEY, "The Concept of Myth and the Problem of Psychocultural Evolution," *American Anthropologist* 52 (1950) 16–26. H. ABRAHAMSSON, *The Origin of Death* (Uppsala 1951). C. G. JUNG and K. KERÉNYI, *Einführung in das Wesen der Mythologie* (4th ed. Zurich 1951). W. F. OTTO, *Gesetz, Urbild und Mythos* (Stuttgart 1951). E. BUESS, *Die Geschichte des mythischen Erkennens* (Munich 1953). J. L. SEIFERT, *Sinndeutung des Mythos* (Vienna 1954). H. KNITTERMEYER, *Das Problem des Mythos* (Wilhelmshaven 1955). W. BASCOM, "The Myth Ritual Theory," *Journal of American Folklore* 70 (1957) 103–114. T. J. SEBEOK, ed., *Myth: A Symposium* (Bloomington, Ind. 1958). R. T. CHRISTIANSEN, *The Migratory Legends* (Helsinki 1958).

[J. SLØK]

MYTH AND MYTHOLOGY (IN THE BIBLE)

The affirmation of the presence or absence of myth in the Bible depends largely on the definition of myth. In the light of modern Biblical research, if the term is correctly understood, there is no reason why it could not be legitimately used in reference to the interpretation of a number of Biblical passages. On the definition and nature of myth, *see* MYTH AND MYTHOLOGY above.

In the Septuagint the Greek word μῦθος (myth) occurs only in Sir 20.19, where, however, it has the meaning of proverb. The NT condemns myths (μῦθοι) as so many "fables" (1 Tm 1.4), "old wives' tales" (1 Tm 4.7), "commandments of men," incompatible with the truth (2 Tm 4.4; Ti 1.14), and "fictitious tales" (2 Pt 1.16). Consequently, until recently scholars generally tended to exclude myth from the Bible. It was alleged that Israel's staunch monotheism was incompatible with the polytheism essential to myth, that its linear approach to historical phenomena ran counter to the cyclic pattern of myth. Biblical authors had, indeed, sometimes utilized mythical motifs for the sake of poetic ornamentation (Is 14.12–15; Ez 28.12–19); one might even grant that occasional myths had found their way into the Bible together with something of the mythical mentality that had inspired them (e.g., in Gn 2.4b–3.24), but these had been so purged and transformed in the process that they hardly deserved the name of myth.

With a reappraisal of the nature of myth, however, and a growing tendency to consider polytheistic elements as accidental to mythopoeic mentality, more and more authors have begun to affirm the presence of myth, or something akin to myth, in the Bible. They refer to passages such as the YAHWIST's CREATION STORY and his account of PARADISE and the FALL OF MAN, of the DELUGE, and of the TOWER OF BABEL, the many references to Yahweh's slaughter of, or domination over, the primeval sea monster, etc. (*See* ABYSS; CHAOS; LEVIATHAN; DRAGON.) These passages, it is argued, are neither historical (i.e., derived from human testimony based on direct observation of the events) nor properly theological (i.e., deduced by discursive reasoning process). They take place in primeval times; their main actors share many of the charac-

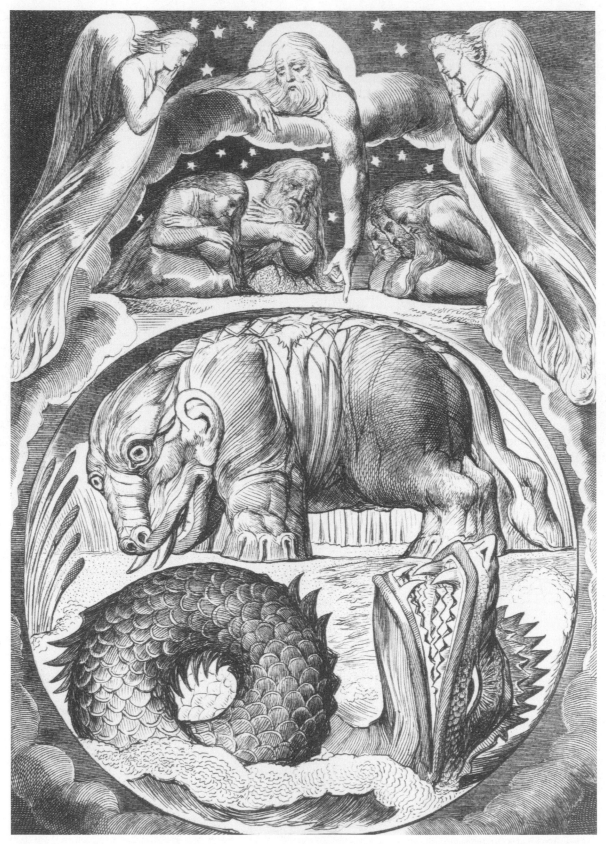

"Behemoth and Leviathan," engraving by William Blake from his book *"Inventions to the Book of Job,"* 1820–1826. (©Corbis)

teristics of mythical personages; and they constitute an attempt to explain contemporary phenomena. Yet one hesitates to apply, without reservation, the term myth to these passages because of the important differences between them and their counterparts outside Israel. There is no doubt that the purging of all polytheistic traits (and consequently of all theogonies and theomachies) and the incorporation of these narratives into a basically historical pattern make myth in the Bible something quite unique. Furthermore, the existence of a religious festival in Israel that might have served as the cultic context for the reenactment of these myths is doubtful. Recent efforts on the part of the Scandinavian School to make of the Hebrew Feast of the NEW YEAR and the Feast of BOOTHS (Tabernacles) the occasion for the recitation of Biblical myths [see S. Mowinckel, *Psalmenstudien* (v.2 Kristiania 1922)] have not found general acceptance. However, whether or not one admits the presence of myth in the Bible depends largely on how one defines it. If myth is taken to mean no more than a popular explanation in figurative language of certain natural phenomena, there is no reason why the term cannot be applied to a number of Biblical passages.

See Also: DEMYTHOLOGIZING.

Bibliography: *Encyclopedic Dictionary of the Bible*, tr. and adap. by L. HARTMAN (New York 1963) 1584–88. H. CAZELLES and R. MARLÉ, *Dictionnaire de la Bible* suppl. ed. L. PIROT et al. (Paris 1928–) 6:246–268. G. LANCKOWSKI and H. FRIES, *Lexikon für Theologie und Kirche*, ed. J. HOFER and K. RAHNER, 10 v. (2d new ed. Freiburg 1957–65) 7:746–752. S. MOWINCKEL and R. BULTMANN, *Die Religion in Geschichte und Gegenwart*, 7 v. (3d ed. Tübingen 1957–65) 4:1274–82. G. STÄHLIN and G. KITTEL, *Theologisches Wörterbuch zum Neuen Testament* (Stuttgart 1935–) 4:769–803. H. FRANKFORT et al., *The Intellectual Adventure of Ancient Man* (Chicago 1946), later pub. as *Before Philosophy* (pa. Baltimore 1959). C. HARTLICH and W. SACHS, *Der Ursprung des Mythosbegriffes in der modernen Bibelwissenschaft* (Tübingen 1952). E. O. JAMES, *Myth and Ritual in the Ancient Near East* (New York 1958). B. S. CHILDS, *Myth and Reality in the O.T.* (Naperville, Ill. 1960). J. BARR, ''The Meaning of *Mythology* in Relation to the O.T.,'' *Vetus Testamentum* 9 (1959) 1–10. J. L. MCKENZIE, ''Myth and the O.T.,'' *Catholic Biblical Quarterly* 21 (1959) 265–282.

[L. F. HARTMAN]

MYTH AND REFLECTIVE THOUGHT

Myths as concrete, graphic narratives of the divine and its world are a religiohistorical phenomenon, reflecting also a morphological aspect of cultural development. In their actual existence they point to a datum that must be considered fundamental for solving the general problem of the nature of man.

Although in very different ways, the narratives generally designated as myths furnish basically information on the world as a whole, on the ultimate questions of human existence, on the meaning and end of life, in short, on matters to which only the most concentrated application of reflection gives access. However, the general experience of investigators is ''that all questioning of the Primitives for information in respect to reflective thinking is wont to be unsuccessful'' [P. Schebesta, *Die Negrito Asiens* (Vienna 1957) 2.2:35]. Do the myths, then, represent a preliminary form of an, as yet, nonreflective and immediate CONSCIOUSNESS in relation to the world as a whole, to a world view? And if so, to what extent and in what way is this possible?

If one begins with an actual phenomenon, something similar confronts him. In his conscience he chooses the good, that which accords with man in relation to the whole. The concept of the good and the whole is therefore essentially proper to conscience. This means, however, that the concepts proper to conscience, which are revealed in their characteristic content by reflection, are those that presuppose a relation to a whole that is itself first discerned only by reflection. The reality of conscience can be said to refer, therefore, to a spiritual dimension within man, even before reflective thought becomes occupied with a full elaboration of its content and thus makes its reality evident. In this way the possibility arises for a nonanalogical, graphic form of discourse, viz, myth, to become actual. Accordingly, myth is nothing but the immediate consciousness, expressed by language in a state that is still vague and imprecise, of ultimate relations or, in a total way, of human existence as conditioned in matter, life, society, and culture. This grounding of reflective thought in conscience gives the answer to that open and persistent aporia in philosophy regarding the possibility, in respect to content, of the basic relationship or connection that becomes evident in the thinking of thinking, i.e., of the problem that has entered the history of philosophy under the heading of INNATISM (*ideae innatae*). Mythical thinking reveals itself as a constituent factor of thinking in general.

This indication of the mythical structure of man, however, raises the question of the truth and the manner of appearance of myth. One can examine the truth of the myth directly from the basic data of conscience and indirectly by means of a morphological investigation of the material of the myth's content. Accordingly, the truth in the myth dealing with origins consists in this, that man, whether in nonreflective speech or in silence (silence, insofar as it is of the same origin as speech), possesses the consciousness of his divine origin and of the divine character of the world, mankind, and history as derived from that same origin. However, myth is untrue and defective if its mythical elements are separated from their whole and are made independent—a process that can be discerned by cultural and religio-morphological study of the polytheistic forms of religion and their myths.

Myth as the constituent element of theory immediately connected with consciousness, arising out of the attitude or reaction to the world, is therefore in its truth or untruth—the transitions, at times, are necessarily fluid since there are no obvious boundaries in the defining consciousness—of decisive meaning for every age. For since man has his being in the mythical structure, the given myth is not only decisive for the possibility and truth of theory (the world view interpreted as world outlook) but also for the application that in weal or woe determines history. In fact, one might even say that man always has a world view that cannot be demythologized. In this sense reflection has before it a twofold task: (1) to investigate in what way, being mythically determined and established itself, it can find the true myth and translate it into its reality as a recognition of truth; (2) to discover in what forms myths, withdrawing into veiled silence, brought, and bring, truth and untruth to actuality in history and in the present age.

Bibliography: E. CASSIRER, *Philosophy of Symbolic Forms* 3 v. (New York 1953–57) v.2. W. DUPRÉ, ''Die methodologische Bedeutung von Sprache und Mythos und das Weltbild der Bambuti,'' *Festschrift Paul Schebesta* (Vienna 1963). M. ELIADE, *Aspects du mythe* (Paris 1963). A. ANDWANDER. *Zum Probleme des Mythos* (Vienna 1964), with copious bibliog.

[W. DUPRÉ]

N

NACCHIANTI, GIACOMO (NACLANTUS)

Theologian; b. Florence, *c.* 1500; d. Chioggia, March 6, 1569. In 1518 he joined the Dominican Order and in 1544 was named bishop of Chioggia. During the first phase of the Council of TRENT he intervened vehemently, although not always opportunely. Besides opposing the privileges accorded by the council to mitred abbots, he attacked the propositions of those council fathers who wanted to place simple tradition on a plane with inspired Scripture, describing them as impious. Three days later he submitted with exemplary humility to the final decree. For a time his teaching remained suspect, and an inquiry was conducted in Nacchianti's diocese in 1548 and 1549. After the favorable outcome of the inquiry, Nacchianti played an important role in the 1562 session of the council. He contributed to the disciplinary discussion on the question of bishops' residing in their dioceses and the doctrinal discussion on the Last Supper as a sacrifice. When he returned to his diocese after the council, he applied its decrees zealously. His principal works, printed originally in Venice (1567), are the *Ennarrationes in Epist. ad Ephesios, Ennarrationes in Epist. ad Romanos, Sacrae Scripturae medulla,* and the *Tractationes XVIII theologales variae.* Though faithful to St. Thomas, Nacchianti nonetheless fused abundant scriptural material into a synthesis of his own.

Bibliography: J. QUÉTIF and J. ÉCHARD, *Scriptores Ordinis Praedicatorum,* 5 v. (Paris 1719–23) 2.1:202–203. M. M. GORCE, *Dictionnaire de théologie catholique,* ed. A. VACANT et al., 15 v. (Paris 1903–50; Tables générales 1951–) 11.1:2–3.

[W. D. HUGHES]

NADAL, GERÓNIMO

Jesuit theologian, special emissary of St. IGNATIUS LOYOLA in promulgating the Constitutions of the Society of Jesus throughout Europe; b. Palma, Majorca, Aug. 11, 1507; d. Rome, April 3, 1580.

Nadal studied with Ignatius at Alcalá in 1526 and again at Paris from 1532 to 1535, but refused to make the *Spiritual Exercises.* He was ordained at Avignon, received his doctorate in theology, and in 1538 returned to Majorca, where he taught theology. In 1542, after reading a letter written by Francis Xavier from India, he began to think about the society in Rome and finally joined Ignatius there in 1545. He entered the society on November 29 of that year. He became so closely associated with Ignatius that he is variously referred to by authors as Ignatius's "voice and soul," "heart," "arm," "second mind," "alter ego," and the "second founder of the Jesuits."

Nadal became the first rector of the first Jesuit college, that of Messina in Sicily, in 1548. His educational program there led eventually to the development of the RATIO STUDIORUM. In 1552, he began a life of travel from one end of Europe to the other, under four successive generals, promulgating the newly written constitutions of the society, acting as vicar-general, assistant, visitor, and peacemaker. Twice rector of the Roman College, he took part in the Diet of Augsburg and was a papal theologian at the Council of TRENT.

Although unknown among spiritual writers, Nadal breathes throughout his many works, in great part unpublished, the special spirit of the Society of Jesus. His teaching on prayer is especially illuminating, particularly on the relationship between prayer and action.

Bibliography: G. NADAL, *Epistolae,* 4 v. (*Monumenta historica Societatis Jesu*; 1905). M. NICOLAU, *Jeronimo Nadal, S.J. 1507–1580: Sus obras y doctrinas espirituales* (Madrid 1949). J. F. CONWELL, *Contemplation in Action: A Study in Ignatian Prayer* (Spokane 1957). J. BRODRICK, *The Progress of the Jesuits, 1556–79* (New York 1947).

[J. F. CONWELL]

NAGLE, NANO HONORIA

Educator, foundress of the Presentation Sisters; b. Ballygriffin, near Mallow, County Cork, Ireland, *c.* 1718;

d. Cork, April 26, 1784. She was the eldest of seven children of Garret Nagle and Ann Mathew, members of the remnant of the dispossessed Catholic landowners and JACOBITES in politics. During an unexplained change in family fortunes (*c.* 1728), she was sent to France. On her father's death (*c.* 1746), she returned to Dublin with her mother and sister, Ann. Since 1733, Dublin Catholics in addition to struggling against the disabling penal laws had had to contend against a new threat to the faith, the heavily endowed government-supported exploitation of poverty, contrived through the Charter Schools and their proselytizing institutions. The discovery that her sister, Ann, had disposed of a dress-length of silk—Nano liked to be fashionable—to help the poor, followed shortly afterward by Ann's death, fired her determination to devote the remainder of her life to God in the service of the poor. The first step was a return to the family home to begin her apostolate in the immediate district. However, overwhelmed by the immensity of the problem compounded of poverty and ignorance, she entered a convent in France, but not for long. Solemnly advised by her Jesuit director, she returned to begin a school in a mud cabin in Cove Lane, Cork, *c.* 1754 or 1755. In nine months, at a time when Catholic schools were illegal, 200 girls were attending. In 1757 she was aided by a considerable inheritance, and within two years she was conducting seven schools, five for girls and two for boys, that provided a rudimentary secular education, religious instruction, and an assiduous preparation for the encounter with Christ in the Sacraments. To expand and make permanent this apostolic work for the poor, she introduced the Ursuline nuns in 1771, at great cost to herself. But her heart was set on the specific needs of the Irish apostolate, and so she founded in 1775, with a very few companions, the Society of the Charitable Instruction, "which excluded every exercise of charity, which was not in favour of the poor" (Walsh, *Nano Nagle and the Presentation Sisters* 1959), and which, after her death, grew into the famous Presentation Order. An inspiration to the men of her time, this small, physically weak woman radiated a Pauline energy in her zeal for the Christian education of youth.

Bibliography: T. J. WALSH, *Nano Nagle and the Presentation Sisters* (Dublin 1959). M. R. O'CALLAGHAN, *Flame of Love: Life of Nano Nagle* (Milwaukee 1960).

[J. J. MEAGHER]

NAGLE, URBAN

Also known as Edward J., dramatist, orator, pioneer in the apostolate of the theater; b. Providence, Rhode Island, Sept. 10, 1905; d. Cincinnati, Ohio, March 11, 1965. After public and parochial schooling, Nagle gradu-

ated from La Salle Academy and Providence College and received a Ph.D. (1934) from The Catholic University of America, Washington, D.C. He was professed as a Dominican friar on Aug. 19, 1925, and ordained on June 15, 1931. Subsequently he served as a professor at Providence College, the editor of the *Holy Name Journal,* and chaplain for the Dominican Sisters' motherhouse at St. Mary of the Springs, Columbus, Ohio.

Nagle devoted the first 20 years of his priestly life to the drama, while fulfilling other assignments. In 1932, with Thomas F. Carey, OP, he founded the Blackfriars Guild. Five years later they established the Blackfriar Institute of Dramatic Arts at Catholic University that later became the Speech and Drama Department. As one of the cofounders of the Catholic Theatre Conference (1937), Nagle served for 25 years on its board of governors and was honored in 1961 with its Father Dineen Award. From 1940 to 1951 he was the moderator of the Blackfriars Guild in New York City, which operates the oldest off-Broadway theater.

Nagle's principal dramas were *Barter* (1929), a Longmans Green prize play; *Catherine the Valiant* (1931); *Savonarola* (1938), selected as one of the Ten Best Plays of the 1941–42 season by the New York *Herald-Tribune; Lady of Fatima* (1948); and *City of Kings* (1949), a Christopher prize play.

Bibliography: W. ROMIG, ed., *The Book of Catholic Authors,* 5th ser. (Grosse Pointe 1957).

[J. B. LARNEN]

NAGOT, FRANCIS CHARLES

Religious superior; b. Tours, France, April 19, 1734; d. Emmitsburg, MD, April 9, 1816. He made his classical studies at the Jesuit college in his native city. In 1753 he entered the Little Community of Saint-Sulpice, Paris. He was accepted as a candidate for the Society of St. Sulpice, and ordained on May 31, 1760. In 1760 he was appointed to teach theology at the major seminary in Nantes, and he earned his doctorate in theology from the University of Nantes, with which the seminary was affiliated. In 1768 he was recalled to Paris and made superior of the Little Company. Two years later he became superior of the Little Seminary of Saint-Sulpice. In 1789 he was appointed vice rector of the Grand Seminary of Saint-Sulpice and named one of the 12 assistants of the superior general. He was sent to London in 1790 to arrange with Bp. John CARROLL for the foundation of a seminary in the new Diocese of BALTIMORE, MD. Nagot, having been designated superior of the group, arrived in Baltimore with three Sulpician priests and five students. On July 18,

1791, they occupied One-Mile Tavern at North Paca Street, on the site of the present St. Mary's Seminary, the first Catholic seminary in the U.S. In 1806 Nagot opened a minor seminary at Pigeon Hill, PA, but in 1809 this seminary closed and the students were transferred to Mt. St. Mary's, Emmitsburg, MD. Shortly after observing his sacerdotal golden jubilee, Nagot resigned as superior of Mt. St. Mary's. He continued to live at the seminary until his death. The best known of his five published works is the *Vie de M. Olier* (1818).

Bibliography: L. BERTRAND, *Bibliothèque sulpicienne*, 3 v. (Paris 1900) v.2.

[C. J. NOONAN]

NAHMANIDES (MOSES BEN NAHMAN)

Talmudist, Biblical commentator; b. Gerona, Kingdom of Aragon, Spain, *c.* 1195, d. Acre, Palestine, *c.* 1270. According to the acrostic formed by his title and name, Rabbi Moses ben Nahman, he was called "the RaMBaN," in official non-Jewish documents, "Maestre Bonastrug de Porta," and "Gerondi" from his birthplace.

Life. In addition to his rabbinical duties, first at Gerona and then at Barcelona, Nahmanides seems to have practiced medicine. He was the father of a family that included, besides his daughters, a son who died early in life, a son named Solomon, and another named Nahmān. The most noteworthy episodes in his career were his unsuccessful attempt, *c.* 1232, to conciliate the factions that warred over MAIMONIDES' *Guide for the Perplexed,* and his celebrated disputation in 1263 at Barcelona with Pablo Cristiá, OP, often styled erroneously "Pablo Christiani."

Fray Pablo, a convert from Judaism, had undertaken to demonstrate the truth of Christianity from Jewish sources and had enlisted the authority of Jaime I of Aragon to arrange a disputation with Nahmanides. Freedom of speech was stipulated for this debate, but both sides published accounts claiming victory. Nahmanides' account gave such offense that he was arraigned, sentenced to two years' banishment, and his pamphlet was burned. Attempts were made to increase this sentence; Pope Clement IV intervened on the side of severity, although he forbade the execution or mutilation of Nahmanides.

On Sept. 2, 1267, Nahmanides arrived in Jerusalem where he spent his remaining years in exile; he died, probably at Acre, and was buried at Haifa, close to the grave of Jehiel of Paris.

Writings. At 15 Nahmanides began to write supplements to the Code of Rabbi Isaac Alfāsī and soon followed these with writings intended to defend that master against Rabbi Zerahiah ha-Levi Gerondi and Rabbi Abraham ben David. Nahmanides is the author of glosses on a long list of Talmudic treatises and of at least three works of halakah. As he had defended Alfāsī in his youth, so in his maturity Nahmanides defended the 9th-century "Laws of the Ancients" against Maimonides, although, in a letter to the conservative rabbis of France, he praised the merits of Maimonides. His "Letter on the Sanctity [of Marriage]" opposed the disdain for human impulse which, he felt, Maimonides had adopted from "that Greek," Aristotle. Nahmanides wrote commentaries on the Canticle of Canticles, on the Book of Job, and, in exile, on the Pentateuch; he published a sermon preached in the presence of the King of Castile. Three letters written during his exile have survived. He commented on the *Book of Yehirah* and possibly on other cabalistic texts. He wrote also liturgical poems and prayers.

Exegetical Postulates. As early as his defense of Alfāsī, Nahmanides set down in his "Wars of the Lord" a principle Aristotle would not have disavowed: "There is in the art [of commenting] no such certain demonstration as in mathematics or astronomy" (Schechter, 112). The authority of the ancient rabbis, he held, deserved respect: "Though their words are not quite evident to us, we submit to them." Despite his "desire and delight to be the disciple of the earlier authorities," even the "pure wine of their wisdom" must give way to evidence. He was unwilling to be "a donkey carrying books." Hence, "when their views are inconceivable to my thoughts, I will plead in all modesty, but shall judge according to the sight of my eyes" (*ibid.,* 111, 112). One instance of such independence is his rejection of the dictum of Rabbi Simlai that there are 614 precepts in the Law. "How to number the commandments," wrote Nahmanides, "is a matter on which I suspect all of us [are mistaken] and the truth must be left to Him who will solve all doubts" (*ibid.,* 112). Since Rabbi Simlai's text is merely "homiletical," the solution given is optional—a line of argument to which he had recourse in his disputation with Fray Pablo. Another crucial assertion of Nahmanides in the course of that debate is that the date of the appearance of the Messiah has less importance for Jews than Christians imagine. In his *Date of the Redemption* Nahmanides argued that to be faithful to the Mosaic Law under Christian rule is more difficult, and thus more meritorious, than in the days of the Messiah.

Theological Opinions. Nahmanides was content to enumerate three basic Jewish dogmas: the world has been created, God exercises providence, and God possesses a knowledge that is also foreknowledge and omniscience. But Nahmanides' thought is rich in unconventional solutions. God, identical with His Glory and Presence, is the author not only of conspicuous miracles such as the ten plagues of Egypt, but also of miracles so frequent and constant that they escape all notice. The Torah (Mosaic Law) knows that all things are miraculous and attributes "nothing to nature or to the order of the world" (Schechter, 119–120). Apart from the Torah "there would be no difference between man and the lower animate species"; even Christians and Muslims, thanks to translations, are "heirs of the Torah" and this is why they too are civilized (*ibid.*, 122). The soul of man exists before its life in the material body and a soul can animate successively more than one body. Thus in a levirate marriage a child can inherit the soul of his actual father's deceased brother; and it is with justice that the iniquity of the father falls on his children in whom his guilty soul lives anew (*ibid.*, 118).

Naḥmanides deplored his exile in moving terms: "I am banished from my table, far removed from friend and kinsman . . . with the sweet and dear children whom I have brought up on my knees, I left also my soul." But he knew the solace of the Psalmist too: "The loss of all this and of every other glory my eyes saw is compensated by having now the joy of being a day in thy courts [O Jerusalem]!" (*ibid.*, 109, 110).

Bibliography: S. SCHECHTER, *Studies in Judaism* (1st ser. Philadelphia 1920), On the disputation between M. Naḥmanides and P. Cristiá, see C. ROTH, "The Disputation of Barcelona (1263)," *Harvard Theological Review* 43 (1950) 117–144. G. VAJDA, *Introduction à la pensée juive du moyen âge* (Paris 1947) 110, 152, 153, 165, 210, 232, 233.

[E. A. SYNAN]

NAHUM, BOOK OF

A collection of oracles exulting over the fall of NINE-VEH, capital of Assyria, enemy of Yahweh and His people.

Division and Content. The book consists of five literary units, as follows: (1) An alphabetic psalm (1.2–10). The acrostic, however, is incomplete and the order somewhat disturbed. It describes a theophany of Yahweh, destroying His enemies and protecting those who trust in Him. The form and content of this section differ from the rest of the book. Many scholars, accordingly, hold that it is not Nahum's work; it may be earlier or later. The editor who collected Nahum's oracles and who is responsible for the present book probably inserted this psalm. As an introductory poem, it provides the proper light for viewing Nineveh's fall. (2) An oracle of doom against an Assyrian king, probably Sennacherib who invaded the land in 701 B.C. (1.11, 14). (3) An oracle of consolation for Juda (1.12–13; 2.1, 3). The theme common to these

Illumination from the Book of Nahum in the "Great Bible of Demeter Neksei-Lipocz" (Pre. Acc. MS 1, v. 2, folio 189), God speaking to Nahum and his disciple, c. 1350.

verses is hope and comfort for Judah; she will no longer suffer from Assyria. Some scholars regard these verses as additions to Nahum's poetry. The evidence for this view is not very forceful. (4) Two poems on Nineveh's fall (2.2, 4–14:3.1–3). The first is a vivid war song that describes with great effectiveness the storming and plundering of Nineveh and the flight of her people. The second poem opens with a cry of woe for Nineveh. The description of the confusion of the stricken city is remarkably effective. (5) Two short satires on Nineveh's fall. The first (3.4–7) depicts Nineveh as a harlot; she will receive the punishment imposed on a harlot. The second satire (3.8–19) recalls the fate of Thebes (Noh), the ancient Egyptian capital. Nineveh is no better; a similar destruction awaits her. Assurbanipal, the Assyrian king, captured Thebes in 663 B.C. Nineveh fell to the Babylonians and Medes in the late summer (July-August) of 612 B.C.

Composition, Date, and Teaching. The Book of Nahum is a collection of oracles, edited like the other PRO-PHETIC BOOKS OF THE OLD TESTAMENT. Nahum's oral preaching probably took place during the period 626–612 B.C. Some modern authors have proposed a different view of the book; they consider Nahum a cultic work, a thanksgiving liturgy over the accomplished fall of Nineveh or a rogation liturgy praying for its fall. It is likely that Nahum was a temple prophet and perhaps associated with Josiah in the work of reform. But the textual evidence for these interpretations is scant.

Nahum is a thoroughgoing Israelite, a patriot who proclaims Yahweh's fidelity to His vine (2.3). More than once he affirms Yahweh's universal lordship of history. He always relates Nineveh's punishment to the sins of Assyria. Nahum's prophesying coincided with Josiah's reign, the period of great Deuteronomic reform. This may explain the absence of any reference to Israel's sins. Another explanation may simply be that not all of Nahum's oracles have been preserved.

Bibliography: A. GEORGE, *Dictionnaire de la Bible,* suppl. ed. L. PIROT, et al. (Paris 1928–) 6:291–301. *Encyclopedic Dictionary of the Bible,* translated and adapted by L. HARTMAN (New York 1963) 1601–02. B. VAWTER, *The Conscience of Israel* (New York 1961) 219–221. J. P. HYATT, ''Nahum,'' *Peake's Commentary on the Bible,* ed. M. BLACK and H. H. ROWLEY (New York 1962) 635–636.

[J. MORIARITY]

NAILS, HOLY

A term used to designate the nails with which the Roman soldiers fastened Jesus to the cross. Although their history and present location are uncertain, the holy nails are regarded with veneration by Christians because of their connection with the CRUCIFIXION of Jesus.

The Roman manner of crucifixion was by means of ropes or nails or both together. The narratives of the PASSION OF CHRIST in the Bible, with their bare statement of the event, do not specify whether ropes or nails were used in the Crucifixion of Jesus. More informative are the accounts of the resurrected Christ; that of John explicitly states that Jesus' hands carried the mark of the nails (Jn 20.25, 27), while that of Luke, according to the commonly accepted text, states that the feet, too, carried such marks (Lk 24.39). The Septuagint translation of Ps 21 (22).17 (traditionally taken as a messianic psalm) as ''They have dug [ὤρυξαν] my hands and my feet'' helped to establish the view that the feet of Jesus were also nailed to the cross.

In regard to the feet, the iconography of Christian tradition shows three successive stages: the earliest representations of Jesus on the cross (on the carved door of Santa Sabina, Rome, and the CRUCIFIX in St. Martin's cathedral, Lucca, Italy—both from the fifth century) show only the hands of Jesus nailed to the cross; from the sixth to the 12th century each foot is represented as nailed sep-

arately to the cross; from the 13th century onward the image of Jesus on the cross is generally depicted with only one nail piercing both feet, with one foot on top of the other. Yet the witness of iconography, far removed from the actual event, has followed custom based on uncertain traditions. The Holy SHROUD OF TURIN indicates that the feet of Jesus were nailed, but it does not give clear evidence whether they were nailed separately or together. However, it would have been difficult for executioners to pierce both feet of a condemned man with a single nail; hence it seems probable that Jesus' feet were nailed separately.

The history of the holy nails is less certain than their number. St. HELENA is credited with having found the holy nails when she discovered the true cross of Jesus. According to St. GREGORY OF TOURS (*Patrologia Latina,* ed. J. P. Migne [Paris 1878–90] 71:710) two of the nails were used to make a bit for the bridle of Constantine's horse, and another was used to decorate his statue. At present some 30 nails, each purporting to be one of the original holy nails, are venerated throughout the world. Which, if any, of these is authentic will probably never be determined because of the maze of devotion and emotion that has accumulated around them.

Bibliography: J. W. HEWITT, ''The Use of Nails in the Crucifixion,'' *Harvard Theological Review* (Cambridge, Ma. 1908–) 25 (1932) 29–45. L. H. GRONDIJS, *L'Iconographie byzantine du Crucifié mort sur la croix* (2d ed. Brussels 1947). C. E. POCKNEE, *Cross and Crucifix in Christian Worship and Devotion* (London 1962). J. BLINZLER, *The Trial of Jesus,* tr. I. and F. MCHUGH (Westminster, Md. 1959) 264–265. P. BARBET, *A Doctor at Calvary,* (New York 1954). W. BULST, *The Shroud of Turin,* tr. S. MCKENNA and J. J. GALVIN (Milwaukee 1957) 38, 49, 62.

[M. W. SCHOENBERG]

NAJRAN, MARTYRS OF

Fifth- and sixth-century Christians put to death in South Arabia. St. Arethas and his companions were martyred in Najran, a town in northern YEMEN and a center of South Arabian Christianity. Before 520 the South Arabian Prince DHŪ NUWĀS MASRUK (Dunaan), a convert to Judaism, revolted against the Aksumite Ethiopians who ruled the Arabs and Jews of Yemen. He seized the capital, Zafar, massacred the garrison and clergy, and turned the church into a synagogue. In 523 (or late 524) he blockaded Najran, but impatient of a long siege, he offered an amnesty in return for capitulation. Despite the warnings of the aged Prince Arethas, the people agreed. Dhū Nuwās pillaged the Christians, exhumed and burned the corpse of Bishop Paul, set fire to the church, cast 427 priests and deacons, monks and consecrated virgins into a furnace at the bottom of a ravine, decapitated Arethas

"*Christ Removed from the Cross,*" by Annibal Carracci, 1507. (©Historical Picture Archive/CORBIS)

and 200 (or 340) others among the chiefs and nobility, and massacred more than 4,000 of the common people who refused to declare that "Christ is a man and not a God." The atrocities were halted when the Aksumite king Elesbaan and his army defeated the forces of Dhū Nuwās and annihilated the power of the Yemenite Jews; unfortunately he used barbaric cruelty in the process. Though the Najran martyrs were undoubtedly Christians, it is not clear to what extent they may have unwittingly been Monophysites.

Feast: Oct. 24 (Roman martyrology).

Bibliography: *Bibliotheca hagiographica orientalis* (Brussels 1910) 99–106. *Acta Sanctorum* Oct. 10:661–762, 919–920. J. PÉRIER, *Dictionnaire d'histoire et de géographie ecclésiastiques,* ed. A. BAUDRILLART et al. (Paris 1912–) 3:1650–53, brief critical appraisal of the sources. J. RYCKMANS, *La Persécution des chrétiens himyarites au sixième siècle* (Istanbul 1956).

[W. J. BURGHARDT]

NAMES, CHRISTIAN

A person's Christian name is usually the given name added to the family, tribal, or local designation to distinguish one from the other members of the family. The custom of distinguishing a person's first name from the family name is late in development, though many Romans had two or three names paralleling the family name. Ancient and early medieval man usually had one name, and was distinguished from others by reference to his father or to his town or place of origin. Among ancient peoples, generally, a name was considered the identification of the essence, nature, or function of an individual, rather than merely a distinguishing appellation. This is true of biblical names and of those found among non-Hebrew nations. It is exemplified in the name given to Christ by divine order: "You shall call His name Jesus, for He will save His people from their sins" (Mt 1.21); and to Simon, son of Jonah, by Christ: "You are Peter and upon this rock [*petra*] I will build my Church" (Mt 20.18). This relation between a name and the function or significance of the bearer is illustrated by the use of the word "name" itself to signify the presence or the power of God, whose nature or inner being was unknowable (Ps 20.2; Jer 6.10; Mal 1.6, 11, 14; 2.5), as well as of Christ as the Son of God (Mc 9.38–39; Mt 7.22).

Early Christian Names. There is no evidence that the primitive or early Christians changed their names on receiving baptism; in general they had the names of the people or nation among whom they were born, and in the New Testament there are many names of converts derived from those of the pagan gods or Greco-Roman cult. This fact is further borne out by the Christian names discovered on inscriptions found in the catacombs and cemeteries of Rome and elsewhere, down to the 4th and 5th centuries, and is true likewise of the martyrs, confessors, and bishops mentioned in early Church history.

The first certain evidence of a change of name inspired by Christian belief is supplied by Ignatius of Antioch (d. *c.* 110), who refers to himself as "also called Theophorus," or the God-bearer (*Epistle ad Ephesus*). The claim of Pope Damasus I (366–384) on an epigram (7) that the Apostle to the Gentiles had changed his name from Saul to Paul at baptism is not substantiated by Acts, where he is called Paul in 11.18; but the name Saul is still used in 13.9. CYPRIAN of Carthage (d. 258) speaks of two bishops and a confessor who had changed their names respectively to Peter, Paul, and Moses; and DIONYSIUS OF ALEXANDRIA (d. 264) says that many Christians took the names of Peter and Paul, and particularly of John, the well-beloved disciple, out of veneration for the Apostles (Eusebius, *Ecclesiastical History* 7.25.14). Eusebius further witnesses to the fact that in Palestine five Egyptian martyrs rejected their pagan names out of hatred for idolatry and called themselves Elijah, Jeremiah, Isaiah, Samuel, and Daniel (*On the martyrs of Palestine* 11.8). Cyprian of Carthage added Caecilianus to his name in honor of the priest who converted him; and Eusebius of Caesarea, that of the martyr PAMPHILUS, who had been his friend and mentor. Inscriptional evidence shows that this custom was common.

Early Baptismal Names. It is not known when Christians generally began to give their infants Christian names at baptism. The people of Antioch are said to have called their children after Bp. Meletius of Antioch (360–381); but AMBROSE of Milan (*On Virgins* 3) and JOHN CHRYSOSTOM at the close of the 4th century complained that Christians were giving their children names haphazardly, and suggested that they consider giving them names of illustrious men and women who had earned credit with God (*Patrologia Graeca*, 50:515). THEODORET OF CYR witnesses to the fact that people gave children the names of martyrs to provide them with protectors (*Graecarum affectionum curatio* 8.67). The Arabic canon 30 of the Council of Nicaea I (325), however, is a much later falsification; and evidence for a change of name such as that of the martyr St. Balsamus to the name Peter, as recorded in his vita, is questionable.

The name of Mary found in St. Paul's Epistle to the Romans (16.6) and in several early catacomb inscriptions is probably the feminine of the Roman Marius, and does not seem to have been in general usage among early Christians, probably out of special reverence. This seems true also of Joseph. John is found frequently in Italy after the 4th century, but is rare in Gaul and almost unknown during this period in Germany and Spain. Peter and Paul were used widely as Christian names after the 3d century. Gradually, with the recognition of Christianity as the religion of the empire, names connected with the doctrines of the faith, such as Anastasius (resurrection); Athanasius (immortality); Redempta, Reparatus, and Renatus (redemption, rebirth in baptism); and Salutia and Soteris (salvation) appear regularly in Christian inscriptions on tombs and monuments. Likewise, names connected with the Christian feasts are common, such as Epiphanius, Natalio, Pascasius, Pentecoste, Quadragesima, and Sabbatius (H. Leclercq, *Dictionnaire d'archéologie chrétienne et de liturgie,* 12.2:1513). The name Martyrius appears in the 4th century and is widespread in both Greek and Latin.

Names are taken from Christian ideas, such as Quodvultdeus (God's will); Theodulus (God's servant); Deusdona, Deusdedit, and Adeodatus (God's gift); as well as from virtues, such as Agape (love); Pistis and Fides (faith); and Elpis and Spes (hope); many imitate the names of the martyrs and confessors indicating Christian attitudes as well, such as Irene (peace), Victor and Victoria, Vincentius, Gaudentius and Hilarius, Caelestinus and Felicissimus. Nevertheless, in the lists of bishops attending the early councils and synods, along with specifically Christian names, there are still many pagan names, even those of the gods, indicating that there was no uniformity of practice or tradition in the adoption of Christian names. The continuance of the use of pagan names in late antiquity was based on local usage that included dignified names such as Aequitas, Probitas, Pietas, Melite, Hedone, Jucundus, and Elegans, as well as such inelegant names as Alogius, Fugitivus, Importunus, Calumniosus, Malus, Foedula, Stercus, and Stercorius—in the past opprobrious names given to Christians by pagans in the period of persecution.

Evidence of the changing of names on conversion is clear in the 5th century. For example, Acacius, bishop of Constantinople, changed the name of Athenaïs to Eudocia on her baptism before she married the young emperor Theodosius II (421). St. Euthymius, the 6th-century Palestine monk, changed the name of barbarian chieftain Aspebet to Peter, and Bp. Innocent of Tortona had changed his name from Quintus on becoming bishop. Also, Bede speaks of King Cedwalla being baptized as Peter (*Ecclesiastical History* 5.7).

Christian Gaul. In Gaul to the end of the 4th century, Christian inscriptions record only Greek and Latin names, but between the 5th and 7th century there is a gradual ascendancy of Germanic names. The historian Gregory of Tours (538–594) illustrates the intermixture of Greco-Latin and barbarian names: his grandparents were George and Leocadia; his parents, Florentius and Armentaria; his brother was Peter, and his sister was married to a Justinus; his uncle was Gondolfus; and his nieces, Eustenia and Justina. The clergy in general seem to have been recruited from Gallo-Roman families and had Roman names, as did many of the officials and administrators under the MEROVINGIANS, since they were allowed to live under Roman law by a constitution of Clothaire (*tit.* 58. *lex* 1) attested by the Council of Tours (567). Germanic names prevailed even though at baptism such barbarian princes as Hermegild and Caedual were given the names of Peter and John. Waldo took the name of Berchtramnus, and Favo became Allowinus (Gregory of Tours, *Historia Francorum,* 5.39; 8.32).

With the conquest of the various parts of Europe and North Africa, the barbarian names gradually took preponderance, although among princes and the educated, some Roman and many hybrid names persisted. In the royal families of the Visigoths, Burgundians, Ostrogoths and Franks, Saxons, and Celts similar-sounding names were handed down from one generation to another. Thus in the family of King CLOVIS and the Burgundian princess Clothilde, the first syllable Gund was repeated in the names Guntharius, Gundovaldus, and Guntchramnus; and Chlodo was echoed in Chlodebaudus, Chlotharius, Chlodomerus, and Chlodovaldus; while feminine names ran to Chlodobergis and Chlodesinda, Theodovaldus, and Theodechildis.

Saxons, Celts, and Slavs. In Anglo-Saxon England the prefix ''Aethel'' in names such as Aethelstane, Aethelbald, Aethelfrith, and Aethelheard is common among bishops and princes, as are the names Aelfred, Aelfhere, and Aelfric; princes and abbesses are Aelfled and Aethelflaed. Aldfrith and Aldgisil vie with Ceolfrith, Ceolnoth, Ceolred, and Ceowulf. Similar combinations are evidenced by Eadbald, Eadbert, Eadburga, and Osgar, Osmund, Oswald, and Wulfhelm, Wulfric, and Wulstan. Saxon names are reflected also among freedmen and serfs, and the changeover to Norman names (11th–12th century) was a political issue.

Although the pagan names were retained among the Celts in Ireland, an attempt was made to reconcile them with similar-sounding Latin names. Thus the pagan Diarmaid became the Latin Jeremias; Seanachan was biblicized into Jonathan; but names such as Brigid, Ita, and Deirdre were soon Christianized by belonging to native saints. Mary was originally brought into Gaelic as Muirē; but when the Normans came in the 11th century, there was a transfer from Marie to Moira or Maureen. A similar metamorphosis overtook John, which had become Eoin or Owen in Gaelic, but became Sean when the Norman form Jean was introduced, while Sheila was the Irish equivalent Julie.

Among the Slavs similar developments are met after the 7th century when the king of Bosnia, Rudoslav, married a Roman princess and called their son Petroslav, who in turn had a son Paulimir. Byzantine names continued the Greco-Roman tradition and affected contiguous nations as they became Christian. Other Eastern peoples reflect in their first names the Christian names current in the ambience of the apostles who converted them.

Saints' Names at Baptism. Insistence on the giving of a Christian name at baptism was not regularized before the councils and rituals of the 14th century, when the names in the martyrologies, legends of the saints, translations of relics, pilgrimages, romances and histories of the Crusades, and the morality plays popularized Old and New Testament names as well as those of the martyrs and saints of the early Church. In northern Europe in the 15th century, the names of Joseph and Mary came into common use; in Spain and Greece people had not hesitated to employ the names Jesus and Christ.

With the Renaissance in Europe there was a return to pagan names, and a similar phenomenon is noticeable in the Byzantine world among scholars. The emphasis on Christian names received impetus from the Council of Trent (sess. 25) which insisted on the orthodoxy of the veneration of saints against Protestant denial. The Roman catechism of the council and the Roman Ritual of 1614 strongly urged priests not to allow parents to give their children strange, laughable, obscene, or idolatrous names. The 1917 Code of Canon Law instructed the parish priest to persuade people to give children a saint's name, and if they refused, to enter both the given name and that of a saint in the baptismal register (c. 761). The *Catechism of the Catholic Church* (CCC) notes the significance of a person receiving a name in Church at the time of baptism. According to the CCC it can be the name of a saint who ''provides a model of Christian charity,'' or the baptismal name can ''express a Christian mystery or Christian virtue'' (CCC, 2156). The CCC quotes the 1983 Code of Canon Law that states, ''parents, sponsors, and the pastor are to see that a name is not given which is foreign to Christian sentiment'' (c. 855).

Title Churches and Guilds. Roman title churches took their names originally from the donors or the locations; in the late 4th and 5th centuries these names were canonized as those of saints. Nevertheless, churches that preserved the relics of a saint or in which there was a special connection with a martyr or Christian truth were named after that subject, though the church itself was dedicated to God. Thus churches of the Anastasia or Resurrection, of the Savior, and of the Cross were erected in Jerusalem; and, with some confusion, churches in other cities were given similar names.

Later Christian antiquity and the early Middle Ages saw churches dedicated in honor of the great figures of the Old Testament, of the Apostles, or of other holy persons of the New Testament, usually with a legendary connection such as those of SS. Lazarus, Mary Magdalen, Dionysius (French, Denis). The translation of relics, pilgrimages to Rome and the Holy Land, and the legends of the saints also influenced the selection of patrons for guilds and brotherhoods, as well as the cultivation of special saints by religious orders, such as Mary Magdalen and Peter among the Cluniacs; the Blessed Virgin among the Premonstratensians and Cistercians; John the Baptist by the Templars and Hospitallers; and among the knightly orders appeared the names Lawrence, Ulrich, Vitus, Aegidius, Michael, George, Nicholas, Catherine of Alexandria, Barbara, and Margaret of Antioch. With the regularized process for the canonization of saints, countries, cities, and dioceses, as well as princes, bishops, and republics selected their particular patron saints. Since 1630 most of these patrons have been acknowledged with rescripts by the Congregation of Rites.

In the second half of the 19th century a systematic collection and historical evaluation of patron saints was begun, but in the selection of patrons for particular activities or assistance, both historical fact and legend still played a part. In contemporary times the popes have appointed certain saints as universal patrons; thus St. Joseph, as the Patron of the Universal Church and of the Laborer; Aloysius Gonzaga, for students; Camillus of Lellis and John of God, for the sick, doctors, and nurses; Paschal Baylon, for Eucharistic societies and sacramental brotherhoods; the Curé d'Ars, for pastors; John Chrysostom, for preachers; Alphonsus Liguori, for confessors and moral theologians; Vincent de Paul, for charitable works; Francis of Assisi, for Catholic Action; Francis de Sales, for the press; Theresa of Lisieux, for world missions; Frances of Rome, for fliers; and Christopher, for automobile drivers. Popular selection still honors St. Barbara for vocations; the Three Kings, for travelers; Margaret of Antioch and Gerard Majella, for the pregnant; Gallus and Sigismund of Burgundy, against fevers; and Lucy of Syracuse and Clare of Assisi, for eye diseases. The universal recourse, however, to patron saints in every aspect of life that pervaded the Middle Ages was destroyed with the Protestant Reformation.

Papal Names. There is no evidence for the change of name on the part of a new pope before JOHN II (533–535), whose original name was Mercurius. Both Roman and Greek names appear almost indiscriminately in the early list of popes. John XII (955–963) changed from Octavian; Gregory V (996–999), from Bruno; Sylvester II (999–1003), from Gerbert; Peter of Pavia took the name John XIV (983–984); and Peter of Albano, Sergius IV (1009–1012). After that, it became the custom for the pope to take a new name, although Adrian VI (1522–23) and Marcellus II (1555), retained their original names.

Religious Names. There is evidence that, from at least the 6th century, aspirants for the monastic way of life changed their names on entrance into religious life. In the Eastern Church, the custom grew of taking the name of a saint whose first initial was the same as one's given name; thus Basil would take the name of St. BESSARION. During his probationary period or novitiate, the candidate would write the life of his patron saint for his menologion, in order to be able to imitate the saint more perfectly. Behind the change of name was the determination to cut oneself off from one's worldly identification and one's former way of life, as well as a complete dedication of the new man to the service of Christ. This custom seems to have influenced the papal change of name, which became the rule in the 11th century.

Bibliography: H. LECLERCQ, *Dictionnaire d'archéologie chrétienne et de liturgie,* ed. F. CABROL, H. LECLERCQ, and H. I. MARROU, 15 v. (Paris 1907–53) 12.2:1482–1553. J. GEWIESS et al., *Lexikon für Theologie und Kirche,* ed. J. HOFER and K. RAHNER, 10 v. (2d, new ed. Freiburg 1957–65) 7:780–783. W. DÜRIG, *ibid.* 784. J. B. LEHNER and W. DÜRIG, *ibid.* 8:187–192, patron saints. H. LESÊTRE, *Dictionnaire de la Bible,* ed. F. VIGOUROUX, 5 v. (Paris 1895–1912) 4.2:1669–77. H. USENER, *Götternamen* (3d ed. Bonn 1948). E. SCHLENKER, *Die Lehre von den göttlichen Namen* (Freiburg 1938). W. DÜRIG, *Geburtstag und Namenstag* (Munich 1954). F. BOND, *Dedications and Patron Saints of English Churches* (London 1914). H. DELEHAYE, *Les Origines du culte des martyrs* (2d ed. Brussels 1933). H. SCHAUERTE, *Die volkstümliche Heiligenverehrung* (Münster 1948). R. L. POOLE, ''The Names and Numbers of Medieval Popes,'' *English Historical Review* 32 (1917) 465–478. P. RABIKAUSKAS, ''Papstnamen und Ordnungszahl,'' *Römische Quartalschrift für christliche Altertumskunde und für Kirchengeschichte* 51 (1956) 1–15. F. KRÄMER, *ibid.* 148–188. F. BOCK, *Die Religion in Geschichte und Gegenwart,* 7 v. (3d ed. Tübingen 1957–65) 5:49–50. J. JUNGMANN, *Liturgisches Jahrbuch* 4 (1954) 130–148. T. KLAUSER, *Christlicher Märtyrerkult, heidnischer Heroenkult und spätjüdische Heiligenverehrung* (Cologne 1960). F. G. HOLWECK, *A Biographical Dictionary of the Saints* (St. Louis

1924). P. WOULFE, *Irish Names and Surnames* (Dublin 1923). *National Catholic Almanac* (Paterson, N.J. 1965).

[F. X. MURPHY/EDS.]

NAMES, MEDIEVAL

The last traces of the Roman system of personal nomenclature scarcely outlasted the 6th century in the West. Under the empire the "three names" (*praenomen, nomen,* and *cognomen*) that had earlier sufficed to designate the citizen were often swelled by the multiplication of *cognomina* to an unconscionable number. Reaction to this extravagance created a welcome for the principle observed by the barbarian invaders, that the individual had but one name. Even in thoroughly Romanized areas this name itself was, from the 5th century onward, increasingly likely to be of Germanic origin: in Gaul the proportion of Germanic to other names—1 to 3 in the 5th century—had become 3 to 1 by the 7th century, and four centuries later the few Greek and Roman names in use were almost all those of scriptural saints. Though vernacular forms naturally differed from language to language and though local popularity, such as that of *Alan* in Brittany, *Baldwin* in Flanders, and *Edward* in England, might affect distribution, the dominant names were then common to most of the countries of Christian Europe. Their universality was further emphasized by the fact that in written documents the same standard Latin forms translated them everywhere.

Various circumstances combined to restrict the number of names in general use during the Middle Ages. The sources of Germanic name formation had dried up by *c.* 850, and resistance to other innovating influences was protracted; e.g., the Church generally favored only names with religious associations. Of the names actually current at any given time, fashion concentrated popularity on relatively few: more than half the Englishmen named in 13th-century records are called *John, William, Robert, Richard,* or *Henry.* Once a name had gained favor, its success was prolonged by the custom, copiously attested for the English landowning classes but almost certainly not peculiar to them, whereby the name given to a child at Baptism was that of one of the godparents, unless long-standing family tradition or devotion to a particular saint dictated another choice. The continued vogue of the five names mentioned above actually raised to nearly two-thirds the proportion of 14th-century Englishmen bearing one or another of them.

In everyday life people who had received the same name at Baptism might be known by differing hypocoristic or diminutive forms of it, and this must generally have been the case when, as often happened in the later Middle Ages, the same baptismal name was borne by two or more living children of the same parents. However, in documents in which the same Latin form rendered both the baptismal name itself and all the variant hypocoristics, confusion between namesakes could be avoided only by the addition of identifying particulars, or surnames.

Surnames, as thus defined, appear in French documents toward the close of the 10th century. At first they were used only occasionally and as a means of separating persons of the same name mentioned in the same instrument; later they occurred in contexts in which no such need for differentiation is apparent. They fall into four main classes. The first, which identify the bearer by reference to his parentage, are often collectively described as patronymics (a term that does not exclude metronymics); the second class indicate the individual's occupation, status, or nationality; the third are toponymics, or locality names, taken from his place of abode or origin; and the fourth are sobriquets alluding to his personal characteristics, physical or moral.

Early surnames are essentially personal and are by no means constant. The same person might be known at different times and in different places by different surnames, and scribes seem sometimes to have deliberately selected the one that was most apt in the circumstances of the transaction they were recording. The name par excellence of the individual was that he had received at Baptism; it remained fixed throughout his life except in the very rare cases in which it was changed by the bishop at Confirmation.

The processes by which surnames became hereditary are obscure, and generalization is not easy. It seems to be agreed that in all countries a tendency in this direction is observed among the nobility before the humbler classes; in the southern parts of individual countries before the northern; in town before country; and in France (early in the 11th century) and England (among the Norman invaders) before Germany. But one must wait until 1267 for a London jury to declare of a convicted felon, variously known as Cantebrigge and Derby, that he "ought, as they understand, to have his father's surname and thus to be called Roger de Cantebrigge."

It was certainly very slowly that surnames came to be conventionally regarded as hereditary; and in all countries there were long periods of transition during which some members of society had hereditary surnames, some had personal surnames, and some had no surnames at all. The stages in the transition are very roughly marked by changes in scribal practice. At their first appearance surnames are subjected in Latin documents to such Latinization as they will admit; but later there is a growing tendency to leave them in the vernacular. The significance of this, so far as patronymic surnames are concerned, may be deduced from 13th-century decisions of the English court of Common Pleas that *Gilbertus filius Stephani* and *Johannes filius Walteri* were inadmissible ways of naming Gilbert Fitz Estevene and John Fitz Wauter, whose respective fathers were not named Stephen and Walter.

Bibliography: E. W. FÖRSTEMANN, *Altdeutsches Namenbuch,* 2 v. in 3 (v.1, 2d ed., v.2, 3d ed. 1900–16), v.1, *Personennamen.* G. E. COKAYNE, *The Complete Peerage . . . ,* ed. V. GIBBS et al., v.3 (London 1913), app. C. E. G. WITHYCOMBE, *The Oxford Dictionary of English Christian Names* (2d ed. Oxford 1950). A. DAUZAT, *Dictionnaire étymologique des noms de famille et prénoms de France* (Paris 1951). P. H. REANEY, *Dictionary of British Surnames* (London 1958).

[L. C. HECTOR]

NAMIBIA, THE CATHOLIC CHURCH IN

Located in southern Africa, the Republic of Namibia is bound on the west by the Atlantic Ocean, on the north by Angola and Zambia, on the east by Botswana, and on the west and south by the Republic of South Africa. A long, thin strip of land, the Caprivi Strip, extends the northern border of Namibia east between Angola and Botswana to Zambia. With a terrain consisting of high plateau, the climate is hot and dry, and rain is infrequent. The Namib Desert stretches along the western coast, while in the east is the Kalahari. Namibia is predominantly agricultural, with its main crops millet, sorghum and peanuts, but a large percentage of its income comes from diamonds, other minerals and fish products. Natural resources include copper, uranium, gold, lead, tin, lithium, Zinc and natural gas, as well as unexplored coal, oil and iron ore deposits.

From 1884 until 1920, as Sud-West Africa, Namibia was a German colony, and from 1920 to 1988 it was administered by the Republic of South Africa as a mandate of the League of Nations. In 1966 Marxist revolutionaries began a rebellion and renamed the region, although South Africa fought to retain the territory until the United Nations intervened. Namibia became an independent republic in 1990. Rich in natural resources, it is the fifth-largest uranium producer in the world, although its climate forces it to import much of its food. Most of the country's wealth passes to foreign investors, leaving half the population in poverty, dependent on subsistence agriculture for their survival. The life expectancy of the average Namibian is 42.5 years, in part due to the spread of HIV/AIDS; 38 percent were literate in 2000.

History. The region was originally inhabited by Khoikhoi (Hottentot), San and Herero tribes. Christianity

---

Capital: Windhoek.
Size: 317,725 sq. miles.
Population: 1,771,325 in 2000.
Languages: English, Afrikaans, German; indigenous languages are spoken in various regions.
Religions: 336,550 Catholics (19%), 903,375 Lutherans (51%), 106,270 Dutch Reformed (6%), 99,765 Anglican (5%), 325,364 practice indigenous faiths.
Archdiocese: Windhoek, with suffragan Keetmanshoop. An apostolic vicariate is located at Rundu.

---

made its first appearance in 1486, when Portuguese navigators under Bartholomew DIAS landed briefly at Cape Cross and Angra Pequena (Luderitzbucht) and planted crosses. Lutheran missionaries from Germany arrived in 1850. In 1878 Father Duparquest of the HOLY GHOST FATHERS came from Angola and traversed the territory by ox wagon. The Prefecture Apostolic of Cimbebasia was erected in 1879 and entrusted to his congregation. When the Prefecture of Lower Cimbebasia was created in 1892, it was confided to the OBLATES OF MARY IMMACULATE (OMI). The region became a German protectorate in 1884, and in 1896 the new government granted these religious a site overlooking the town of Windhoek that was later termed Roman Hill because of the cathedral, rectory, hospital convent and high school erected there. The OBLATES OF ST. FRANCIS DE SALES, who had charge of the Orange River vicariate since 1884, were entrusted in 1909 with the Great Namaqualand, which became a vicariate in 1930; its name was changed to Keetmanshoop in 1949. The second vicariate, which embraces the northern part of the country, is Windhoek, erected in 1926 and confided to the OMI.

Namibia endured a period of violence beginning shortly after the turn of the 20th century. From 1904 to 1907 German forces almost exterminated the Herero and Nama tribes, killing around 80,000 Africans in the aftermath of an uprising against the intruding colonialists. Namibia was captured by South Africa during World War I, and in 1919 the mandate was transferred from Germany to South Africa by the League of Nations. After the demise of the league, the United Nations assumed trusteeship, but this was not recognized by South Africa, which continued its occupation and control of Namibia. The UN continued to demand that South Africa withdraw and the demand was confirmed by a series of World Court rulings. In 1966, the UN General Assembly terminated South Africa's mandate and declared Namibia to be the direct responsibility of the UN.

Independence. A 1971 High Court of Justice at the Hague determined South Africa's occupation of the region illegal; instead the black nationalist South West Africa Peoples' Organization (SWAPO) was deemed the true representative of the Namibian people. SWAPO members were predominately Ovambo people of the north, with fewer members of the Herero tribe. The South African government, responding to the UN declaration and the threat of SWAPO and rejecting a 1979 UN-supervised transition to independence, resorted to Draconian emergency regulations: most public meetings were prohibited; police had complete freedom to detain suspects indefinitely for interrogation; arrests, torture and execution were routine methods of discouraging opposition to South African rule.

The Church, together with the Lutheran church and leaders of other Christian faiths, were involved in the push for independence, repeatedly calling for a change in South African policy and the restoration of freedom and human rights. Several religious leaders were expelled from the country because of their efforts on behalf of justice. In 1988 the UN convinced South African leaders to negotiate with SWAPO leader Samuel Nujoma, a Marxist who won the presidency in November of 1989, after South Africa relinquished is claims to all but Walvis Bay. An important port, Walvis Bay was returned to Namibia in 1994.

Namibia promulgated a new constitution on March 12, 1990 that guaranteed freedom of religion to all citizens, although no denomination was subsidized by the state. In 1994 the church hierarchy was established when Windhoek became the archdiocese for the country. While sporadic acts of violence in the country did involve the Church on occasion, such violence resulted from tribal rather than religious conflicts. In 1998 the German government sent a formal apology to the Herero people, calling the 1904 massacres of men, women and children "a particularly dark chapter in our bilateral relations."

Into the 21st Century. By 2000 Namibia had 66 parishes, tended by 13 diocesan and 58 religious priests, although more were needed. Other religious included approximately 36 brothers and 285 sisters. Most of the native children in the country attended the Catholic-run schools, which numbered 27 primary and eight secondary schools by 2000. Many of the country's hospitals, dispensaries, orphanages and hostels were also left to Church care, as the region continued to battle the spread of AIDS. By 2000 one out of every four Namibians were infected with the HIV virus. Church evangelization efforts were enhanced by the publication of an Afrikaans Sacrametary and Lectionary begun in south Africa in the late 1980s by the Afrikaans Apostolate.

Bibliography: J. E. BRADY, *Trekking for Souls* (Cedara, Natal 1952) *Bilan du Monde,* 2:801–803. *The Catholic Directory of South Africa* (Capetown 1917–). M. GILBERT, *A History of the 20th Century,* v. 3 (New York 1999). *Annuario Pontificio* has information on all diocese.

[J. E. BRADY/EDS.]

NANETTI, CLELIA, ST.

In religion Maria Chiara (Eng.: Mary Clare); martyr, religious of the Franciscan Missionaries of Mary; b. Jan. 9, 1872, Santa Maria Maddalena, Rovigo, Italy; d. July 9, 1900, Taiyüan, China. Impulsive, intelligent Clelia was born into a loving family of means. Although pious (one brother, Barnabé, was a Franciscan), her parents objected to her religious vocation. She joined the Franciscan Missionaries of Mary on Jan. 24, 1892 and began her novitiate three months later. She was sent to China soon after making her profession, arriving in Shanxi on May 4, 1899. When the Boxers threatened the mission, the bishop prepared to evacuate the orphanage, where Sr. Clelia was working. Clelia and the orphans returned when they found their escape route blocked. She was killed by the sword as she said, "Always forward!" She was beatified with her religious sisters by Pope Pius XII, Nov. 24, 1946, and canonized, Oct. 1, 2000, by Pope John Paul II with Augustine Zhao Rong and companions.

Feast: July 4.

Bibliography: G. GOYAU, *Valiant Women: Mother Mary of the Passion and the Franciscan Missionaries of Mary,* tr. G. TELFORD (London 1936). M. T. DE BLARER, *Les Bse Marie Hermine de Jésus et ses compagnes, franciscaines missionnaires de Marie, massacrées le 9 juillet 1900 à Tai–Yuan–Fou, Chine* (Paris 1947). L. M. BALCONI, *Le Martiri di Taiyuen* (Milan 1945). *Acta Apostolica Sedis* 47 (1955) 381–388. *L'Osservatore Romano,* Eng. Ed. 40 (2000): 1–2, 10.

[K. I. RABENSTEIN]

NANTES, EDICT OF

A proclamation issued by HENRY IV of France, April 13, 1598, providing a measure of toleration, civil rights and liberties, and security for French HUGUENOTS. It contained 92 general articles signed by the king April 3, 1598, 56 particular or secret articles signed May 3, and three brevets. The first brevet gave an endowment of 45,000 crowns annually for the support of the clergy and churches of the Reformed Church; the second gave 180,000 crowns a year for the upkeep of garrisons in the fortified towns; the third distributed 23,000 crowns to certain Huguenot leaders. According to the general and particular articles: Roman Catholicism was restored and reestablished where it had previously been practiced, and any interference with divine service was forbidden; members of the Reformed religion were permitted to live without restriction anywhere in France and were allowed freedom of religious worship wherever they had been permitted to worship publicly by the edicts of 1577, 1596, and 1597, and in two towns in every bailiwick; they could not conduct services within five leagues of Paris, but services could be held in the homes of Huguenot nobles; they were granted complete civil liberties, including the right to hold public office and attend colleges and academies; they were permitted to hold synods and political meetings; special tribunals were authorized to settle disputes between Catholics and Huguenots, the one in the Parlement of Paris to consist of ten Catholics and six Protestants, the provincial parlements to have an equal number of Protestants and Catholics; the salaries of Protestant ministers were paid and some financial aid was provided for their colleges; the Huguenots were given 100 security areas or towns for eight years, the king was to pay the cost of the garrisons, and the governors of these towns were to be nominated by the king with the consent of the churches. The edict was registered in Paris and Grenoble in 1599; in Dijon, Toulouse, Bordeaux, Aix, and Rennes in 1600; but not until 1609 in Rouen.

The edict was a compromise only. The "Politiques," who were particularly responsible for it, asserted that religious toleration was a matter of expediency rather than a matter of principle. The Catholic clergy opposed the granting to the Huguenots of freedom of conscience, civil liberty, the right to ecclesiastical assemblies, and state subsidies for the Protestant Church. The Protestants were unhappy about limitations imposed upon them, and fearful that the edict would be violated after Henry's death. The lease on the fortified towns was renewed in 1611 and thrice more until 1624, but soon after Henry's assassination (1610) there were violations of the edict: discrimination against Huguenots in employment, their exclusion from some professional schools, restrictions on public worship, destruction of some Protestant churches. An uneasy truce developed into open conflict. After the fall of La Rochelle in 1628, Louis XIII, on the advice of RICHELIEU, issued the Edict of Alais (1629), depriving the Huguenots of all political rights and razing fortifications, but preserving religious liberties. After the peace of Alais, however, there was a gradual deterioration of the Huguenot religious position. Restrictions against them were more open under LOUIS XIV, who revoked the edict on Oct. 18, 1685.

Bibliography: J. VIÉNOT, *Histoire de la réforme française,* 2 v. (Paris 1926–34). J. FAUREY, *L'Édit de Nantes et la question de la tolérance* (Paris 1929). J. ORCIBAL, *Louis XIV et les protestants* (Paris 1951). W. J. STANKIEWICZ, *Politics and Religion in Seventeenth-Century France* (Berkeley 1960). L. PASTOR, *The History of the Popes from the Close of the Middle Ages,* 40 v. (London-St. Louis 1938–61) 23:157–164.

[D. R. PENN]

Napoleon I.

NAPOLEON I

French general, emperor; b. Ajaccio, Corsica, Aug. 5, 1769; d. Saint Helena, May 5, 1821.

Early Years. Napoleon was the son of Charles and Laetitia (Ramolino) Bonaparte. His father was thriftless and fickle, but his mother was economical, orderly, morally austere, religious in the Corsican manner, and very severe. The maternal influence over the Christian upbringing of her unruly, taciturn son seems not to have been profound. In 1780 Napoleon received chastisements from his mother when he refused to attend Mass, but this did not increase his devoutness. His great-uncle Lucien, an archdeacon, was more adept in conciliating wisdom with thrift than in preaching fervor. At the military school in Brienne, which he entered in April 1779, the boy was industrious and avid to learn, but quarrelsome and increasingly aloof. He remained attached to Father Charles, who prepared him for First Communion, but was much less edified by the other Minims who taught him and who celebrated Mass in 10 minutes, according to him. In 1784 he transferred to a military school in Paris where the technical training was first class, but the religious formation revolved too much around external practices imposed by school discipline and reflected the 18th-century spirit that penetrated the institution. The young cadet had to attend Mass each weekday and high Mass, Vespers, and catechism class on Sunday; he had to receive Holy Communion bimonthly and go to confession monthly. His independent spirit and his already weakened faith found this conformism irritating. The crisis that caused Napoleon's detachment from the Church was intellectual rather than moral. Pleasure did not attract him. His meager income reduced him to a poor, austere mode of life. On his own testimony books were his sole debauchery; so enticing were they that he often deprived himself of food to purchase them. He nourished himself on the ancient classics and still more on such modern authors as Rousseau, Voltaire, Montesquieu, Mably, and Reynald. As a result the rationalism of the ENLIGHTENMENT penetrated his spirit and displaced his weakly rooted Christian beliefs. During his stay at the artillery school of La Fère, he ceased to approach the Sacraments and received them no more until his deathbed. He subscribed to the principles of 1789 and sided with the FRENCH REVOLUTION.

Napoleon continued to regard Corsica as his true homeland. He reserved for it the first display of his revolutionary fervor in order to install there the new revolutionary regime, which his family supported. His brother Joseph Bonaparte was elected a member of the Directory, and his uncle Joseph FESCH took the oath upholding the CIVIL CONSTITUTION OF THE CLERGY in order to become vicar to Bishop Guasco; but Napoleon himself failed to obtain a military command. The Bonapartes came into conflict with Pascal Paoli, who opposed the Revolution, and had to flee to France (June 1793).

From 1793 to 1799. The uprising in southern France in favor of the Girondins supplied the young artillery captain with an opportunity to reveal his military genius. Toulon, which had fallen into English hands, was reconquered thanks to a plan devised by Napoleon. This success won him the favor of ROBESPIERRE, the rank of general at the age of 22, and the command of the artillery in the French army in Italy. After July 27, 1794 (9 Thermidor), Napoleon was branded as a follower of Robespierre, stripped of his rank, and arrested. He then offered his services to Paul Barras and subdued the royalist insurrection (October 1795). As a reward Barras named him general of a division and commandant of the army of Paris. Barras, however, distrusted the savior of the Republic and tried to control Napoleon by turning over to him his mistress, the widow Josephine de Beauharnais. Bonaparte became passionately attached to this woman and entered a civil marriage with her (March 9, 1796)

once he had been made general in charge of the army in Italy. Both of them could have had recourse to either the refractory or the constitutional priests, but neither of them troubled to do so. Josephine continued to attend the sermons of the constitutional Bishop Belmas at St. Étienne du Mont; yet this woman of fashion regarded morality lightly. Her religion was nothing but vague sentimentality.

Italian Campaign. During the war in Italy Napoleon learned from experience the social realities that he must take into account in formulating his political policies and military strategy. Despite his limited resources he confronted an offensive by new Austrian armies. To protect his rear he had to win the support of Italian Jacobins and at the same time to placate the Catholic populace, which threatened to rise against the French Revolutionary troops. Napoleon was so much impressed by the attachment of the Italians to the Church that he refused to obey the Directory's orders to march on Rome and "smash the throne of stupidity." After a first campaign in Romagna he stopped at Bologna and there signed with the Holy See an armistice guaranteeing papal neutrality while assuring himself of a war contribution of 21 million francs (June 20, 1797). After negotiations at Paris failed to effect definitive peace, a second campaign conquered Romagna and the Legations, but Bonaparte refrained from proceeding farther and informed PIUS VI that he could remain undisturbed in Rome. Napoleon promised also to provide protection for the pope and the Church, because "it is my special concern that no one make any change in the religion of our fathers." On his own initiative General Bonaparte reopened negotiations and concluded the Treaty of Tolentino (Feb. 19, 1797) without conforming to the Directory's instructions. This pact severed from the STATES OF THE CHURCH only the Legations, Ancona, and Avignon. The pope retained sovereignty over the rest of his territories, but paid 33 million francs as war indemnity, which was "equivalent to ten times Rome." This consoled the French government for these territorial concessions.

Religious Policy. No question arose concerning a bull retracting papal condemnations of the Civil Constitution of the Clergy and requiring Catholic support of the revolutionary regime. Napoleon declared that he had not spoken about religion. He was convinced that an agreement on this point could not be reached with the basically anticlerical Directory. On this subject he had already framed his basic policies of inviting priests to preach obedience to the government, consolidating the new constitution, reconciling the constitutional with the refractory clergy, and leading the majority of Frenchmen back to religion. At that moment, however, the situation did not seem to him propitious to put his ideas into operation.

Napoleon's project for Italian unification encountered Catholic opposition because the Jacobins with whom he dealt to create the Cispadine Republic and then the Cisalpine Republic practiced an anti-religious policy contrary to his views. The general sought unsuccessfully to moderate the Cisalpine government and the regional commissioners. But after his departure these men followed their own wishes. The discontent provoked by their anti-Christian action contributed largely to the uprising of 1799, which caused the collapse of a regime imposed by the French invader. Bonaparte heeded the lessons taught by this experience. It was not Catholicism as such that he intended to respect, but popular sentiment. His policy in the Egyptian campaign, during which he favored Islam, was inspired by the same selfish and realistic outlook.

Religious Restoration in France. Religion counted for naught in the *coup d'état* of Brumaire (Nov. 9, 1799), contrived by Sieyès for financial and political motives. But Bonaparte, whose military cooperation had seemed indispensable for the success of this operation, asserted himself as head of the consular government and gave to it a personal orientation. For reasons of domestic and foreign policy he intended to regulate the religious question. Before he could start a campaign to terminate the war then raging, he had of necessity to pacify the Vendée region. Thanks to BERNIER, he succeeded by granting to the Vendeans religious liberty in the Treaty of Montfaucon. Logic dictated that the same freedom should extend to the whole nation. The decree of 28 Nivôse (Jan. 17, 1799) provided it and yet demanded from priests no more than fidelity to the constitution. On the other hand, another decree (Dec. 30, 1799) sought to dissipate the bias against the French Revolution in the papal conclave then meeting in Venice and to combat Austrian influence in the conclave by prescribing exceptional honors for the remains of Pius VI. For the moment these half measures had to suffice, because the First Consul was not yet firmly established in power. He preferred to wait until further military victory strengthened his authority before putting into effect his full program. His discourse to the clergy in Milan (June 5, 1800), which became widely known, indicated that he would discuss with the pope a complete reconciliation between France and the Church. Not until the victory at Marengo, however, did he reveal the plan already matured in his mind and charge Cardinal Carlo Martiniana of Vercelli to transmit his proposals to PIUS VII.

Religious Outlook. Napoleon was undoubtedly more eager to promote his own policy than the interests of the Church, but the extent to which his policy corresponded with his personal dispositions toward Catholicism is disputed. From this time until his exile to Saint Helena, his contradictory statements can be invoked in opposite senses; but since these utterances varied according to the circumstances and the questioners and the effect Napoleon wished to obtain, they cannot be taken literally or interpreted as proof of his religious disquiet. Napoleon was basically an enlightened despot in the 18th-century style, nourished by the philosophers of that period. Like Voltaire, he judged religion necessary for the populace. His Deism, his belief in the immortality of the soul, and his religious sentimentality came from Rousseau and Robespierre. He did not believe in Catholicism as the one true religion. For him all religions possessed some value; all should be admitted in places where they exist; and all should be utilized for the good of the state. He believed in controlling religion but not in imposing it on others. As a son of the French Revolution he was faithful to the principles of 1789. At the same time he was willing to derive from GALLICANISM other principles that permitted the ruler to limit papal interventions. His religious practice remained external, official, and restricted to attendance at Sunday Mass, an obligation from which he excused himself in the army, because the army, which idolized him, had no need of cult or chaplains (*see* CATECHISM, IMPERIAL).

Concordat of 1801. Napoleon's plan of religious restoration was part of his plan for a general restoration in France. Since the population as a whole clung to Catholicism, he sought to satisfy it while utilizing its religion. He believed that public opinion did not demand the restitution of ecclesiastical goods alienated during the Revolution. As for the clergy, he considered that a subsistence salary would be sufficient compensation. Napoleon judged also that national unity required ending the schism caused by the Civil Constitution of the Clergy. His policy of reconciliation aimed to produce neither victor nor vanquished and obliged him to maintain a balance between the bishops of the *ancien régime* and the constitutional bishops by forcing both groups to resign. Thereupon the First Consul would name the entire new hierarchy. In doing so he planned to select some bishops from the *ancien régime* prelates and some from the constitutional hierarchy and to amalgamate them with new elements. He wanted to retain from the Revolution the division of dioceses according to civil districts, or departments, while reducing the number of dioceses lest the budget become too burdensome and disaffect the public. The same realism that dictated all these measures obliged Napoleon to have recourse to the pope in order to disavow the error committed by the Civil Constitution in 1790 and to prevent the reappearance of religious divisions. Therefore he recognized Pius VII's authority, but on the condition that the pope recognize the legitimacy of Napoleon's government. He admitted also the pope's authority to remove bishops and to appoint others in their stead. In accordance with the principles of 1789, however, he insisted that all cults must enjoy liberty and that Catholicism must not be the state religion. His plan envisioned finally that the liberty accorded Catholic public cult should be submitted to such police regulations as deemed necessary.

After laborious negotiations Pius VII and Napoleon reached agreement in the CONCORDAT OF 1801. But this text masked rather than dissolved their differences. Quickly the First Consul incorporated the Organic Articles into the Concordat, severely restricting its scope.

Conflict with Pius VII. Much graver than the causes of conflict to which the application of the Concordat gave rise was the fundamental opposition between Napoleon Bonaparte and the pope. The former lacked a spiritual sense; the latter was essentially a spiritual man. Despite their mutual sympathy, even affection, the two men were bound to come into conflict. Conciliating though he was, the Holy Father would not compromise his principles even when his independence was jeopardized. Napoleon perceived this at the time of his coronation as emperor (Dec. 2, 1804). The pope, fortified only by vague promises, agreed to come from Rome to Paris and to allow modifications in the traditional ceremony. On the eve of the event Josephine, who wanted an indissoluble religious marriage lest she be later repudiated, explained to the pope the details of the couple's civil marriage. Pius VII then insisted that this irregular situation be rectified immediately if he were to participate in the coronation the next day. Napoleon had to consent to have his union blessed by the Church, but did so only on condition that Cardinal Fesch, his uncle, officiate at the marriage without witnesses and that this matter be kept shrouded in secrecy similar to that of the confessional. Pius VII returned from his journey to France without obtaining any of the religious advantages he sought, except for some secondary ones.

To the difficulties presented by the French concordat were added those caused by the Italian concordat (1803). In some respects the latter was more favorable to the Church, since it recognized Catholicism as the state religion; but this good feature was offset by the Melzi decrees. Napoleon's coronation as king of Italy (1805) speeded the introduction into northern Italy of French laws and institutions that were inspired by the spirit of the French Revolution. Moreover, Pius VII refused to conclude the German concordat proposed by the Emperor Napoleon for the ecclesiastical reorganization of Germany.

The extension of the French Empire and the resultant wars hastened the crisis, which became acute after 1810, between the pope and the ruler who wanted to be the successor of Caesar and Charlemagne. Although Napoleon invoked his "system," neither his foreign nor his religious policies conformed to fixed, preconceived notions. Instead his ideas were in continual flux and were modified according to the needs of the moment. It was not his ill-defined system that guided Napoleon but the "force of things." At the same time his military victories and the ever-widening scope of his conflicts accentuated his autocracy. In his policy and strategy Italy played a key role. He was attached to the peninsula also because to it he owed his start toward fame and because the memories of imperial Rome were always dear to his heart. The debarcation of the allied forces at Naples previous to the battle of Austerlitz obliged him to hold Italy to protect his rear. Therefore in 1806 he integrated Naples, Venice, and the duchies with the Kingdom of Italy and extended to these regions the provisions of the Italian concordat and the French legal code. This provoked Pius VII's protests.

Imprisonment of Pius VII. Up to this point Napoleon had not occupied the remaining States of the Church. Now he demanded that the pope expel foreign agents and close his ports to the allies. So tense did the situation become that Fesch was recalled from Rome and Consalvi resigned as papal secretary of state (June 17, 1806). Once Napoleon had crushed Prussia and concluded peace with Russia at Tilsit, he increased his demands on the pope. To prevent any opening in the Continental Blockade, whose aim was to ruin England's economy and force its capitulation, Napoleon ordered Pius VII to close his ports to the British. He even asked the pope for military aid against the heretics, "our common enemies." As father to all Christians Pius VII repulsed this ultimatum. Bayane's attempt at negotiation failed. Napoleon then ordered Gen. François de Miollis to occupy Rome (Feb. 21, 1808). He decreed the annexation of the States of the Church to the French Empire (May 16, 1809); and when Pius VII retaliated by excommunicating the perpetrators of this sacrilege, he ordered General Radet in July to remove the pope from Rome and then to conduct him as a prisoner to Savona, in northern Italy.

One last step that remained was to bring the Supreme Pontiff to Paris to make him pope of the Great Empire. But nothing could weaken Pius VII's resistance. When he was deprived of his liberty and his advisers, he refused to exercise his papal powers or to institute bishops canonically. Thenceforth the struggle centered on this last point. As vacant sees multiplied, Napoleon tried vainly to end this impasse by turning to the French episcopate. An ecclesiastical committee was convened in 1809 to find a solution, but it disappointed him.

Second Marriage. To complicate matters still more, Napoleon sought to assure himself a male heir by ridding himself of Josephine and marrying a girl with royal blood. Two decisions of the Parisian diocesan and metropolitan ecclesiastical officials, which were correctly rendered, declared Napoleon's marriage on the eve of coronation null. The first decision was based on defect of form; the second was based on defect of form and also on Napoleon's merely simulated consent to the marriage contract. A controversy followed concerning the competence of these diocesan tribunals. Among the Roman cardinals then in Paris one group was convinced that the solution of this case pertained to the pope and refused to assist at the emperor's marriage to Archduchess Marie Louise of Austria (April 1810). The reprisals against these "black" cardinals did not in any way promote the success of the mission of Cardinals Giuseppe SPINA and Carlo Caselli, who were sent to Savona to work out a settlement with Pius VII.

Institution of Bishops. To circumvent the difficulties caused by Pius VII's refusal to give canonical institution to newly named bishops, Napoleon nominated to the See of Paris Jean MAURY and caused the diocesan chapter to confer on him the powers of vicar capitular. Pius VII ruined this scheme by sending secretly to Paris a brief that declared Maury's powers null. In his fury the emperor ordered the pope kept in closer confinement and began a police persecution against clerical resistance.

The emotion roused by the Maury affair convinced Napoleon of the need to solve the problem. He appointed a second committee to find a solution, but it had recourse to subterfuges. At a solemn gathering (March 11, 1811) Monsieur ÉMERY defended papal authority so courageously that the emperor displayed his admiration. A delegation of bishops to Savona shook Pius VII's resolve for a short time, but it had no lasting result because the pope revoked his concessions concerning canonical institution by a metropolitan. Napoleon then resigned himself to convoking the imperial council of 1811. There the bishops as a group resisted him, but individually they bowed to his will. When another delegation went to Savona, Pius VII conceded to the metropolitan, acting in the pope's name, the power of instituting bishops after six months. Napoleon demanded a change in this last point, but Pius VII refused. The situation thus had arrived at a new deadlock.

Concordat of Fontainebleau. Napoleon had the pope transferred to Fontainebleau, near Paris (June 1812), in the expectation that a victorious military campaign in Russia would permit him to overcome finally the resistance of the "old imbecile." After returning from the disastrous Russian expedition, the emperor was more determined than ever to succeed by extracting from the Holy Father a new concordat. Pius VII signed the so-called CONCORDAT OF FONTAINEBLEAU, but this text was intended only as a preliminary one that would serve as the basis for a later definitive agreement, provided everything were kept secret. When Napoleon in bad faith published this document as if it were a concluded concordat, Pius VII withdrew the concessions envisaged by him as the basis of the accord. As military defeat overwhelmed him, Napoleon freed the pope (Jan. 21, 1814). During the Hundred Days he tried vainly to regain the Holy See's friendship; but Waterloo rendered Msgr. Izoard's mission useless.

Last Years. In writing about Napoleon's religious attitude during his exile at Saint Helena (1815–21), Las Cases, Gourgaud, Bertrand, and Marchand have contradicted one another. Their accounts leave a mixed impression. In his last testament the emperor expressed a desire to die in the Catholic religion that he had inherited from his forebears and to receive before death Viaticum, Extreme Unction, and whatever else was customary in similar cases. According to Bertrand he was motivated solely by a belief that this would "promote public morality." Not all historians accept this interpretation. Napoleon died on May 5, 1821, after receiving the ministrations of Abbé Vignali on May 1. Pius VII was the one responsible for sending a chaplain to Saint Helena after the European powers refused to heed the papal request to mitigate Napoleon's sufferings. The pope had not forgotten that Napoleon had reestablished religion in France. Because of the "pious and courageous effort of 1801," Pius VII had long since forgiven the subsequent wrongs at Savona and Fontainebleau, which he described as mere errors of a spirit carried away by human ambition, whereas the Concordat was a Christian, heroic, and beneficial action.

Bibliography: J. LEFLON, *La Crise révolutionnaire, 1789–1846* (Fliche–Martin 20; 1949). A. LATREILLE, *L'Église catholique et la révolution française,* 2 v. (Paris 1946–50); *Napoléon et le Saint–Siège, 1803–1808* (Paris 1935). V. BINDEL, *Histoire religieuse de Napoléon,* 2 v. (Paris 1941). L. MADELIN, *Histoire du Consulat et de l'Empire,* 16 v. (Paris 1937–54). A. DANSETTE, *Religious History of Modern France,* trans. by J. DINGLE (New York 1961) v.1. E. E. Y. HALES, *The Emperor and the Pope* (New York 1961). S. DELACROIX, *La Réorganisation de l'Église de France après la Révolution* (Paris 1962–). J. SCHMIDLIN, *Papstgeschichte der neuesten Zeit,* 1800–1939 (Munich 1933–39) v.1. A. THEINER, *Histoire des deux concordats de la république française et de la république cisalpine conclus en 1801 et 1803,* 2 v. (Bar–le–Duc 1869). A. BOULAY DE LA MEURTHE, *Histoire de la négociation du Concordat de 1801* (Tours 1920); *Histoire du rétablissement du culte en France 1802–05* (Tours 1925). M. ROBERTI, *Milano capitale napoleonica,* 3 v. (Milan 1946–47) v.1. A. FUGIER, *Napoléon et l'Italie* (Paris 1947). L. GRÉGOIRE, *Le Divorce de Napoléon et de l'Impératrice Joséphine: Étude du dossier canonique* (Paris 1957). G. GOURGAUD and C. J. F. T. DE MONTHOLON, *Mémoirs pour servir à l'histoire de France sous Napoléon. écrits à Sainte Hélène, par les généraux qui ont partagé sa captivité, et publiés sur les manuscrits entièrement corrigés de la main de Napoléon,* 8 v. (Paris 1823–25); ed. D. LANCROIX, 5 v. (new ed. Paris 1905). M. J. E. A. D. DE LAS CASES, *Mémorial de Sainte–Hélène,* 4 v. in 8 (London 1823), separate Eng. and Fr. eds. with same title and format;

Napoleon III.

ed. J. PRÉVOST, 2 v. (Paris 1935). H. G. BERTRAND, *Cahiers de Sainte–Hélène, janvier–mai 1821,* ed. P. FLEURIOT DE LANGLE (Paris 1949).

[J. LEFLON]

NAPOLEON III

Emperor of France; b. Paris, April 20, 1808; d. Chislehurst, England, Jan. 9, 1873. He was baptized Charles Louis and was the third son of Louis and Hortense Bonaparte (then king and queen of Holland) and the nephew of Napoleon Bonaparte. He was forced by the Congress of Vienna to spend his early manhood in exile. Educated in a Bavarian Gymnasium, he acquired Swiss citizenship. As a member of the CARBONARI he took part in a local Italian revolution (1830–31) against the Austrian Hapsburgs. The combined efforts of his mother and Cardinal Mastai (later Pius IX) were required to rescue him from capture and possible execution. He afterward attempted two ill-fated *coups d'état* against the bourgeois government of the Orleanist King Louis Philippe. Pardoned after the failure of his coup of 1832 at Strasbourg, Louis Napoleon visited Boston, MA (1836–37), before going to England to await the death of his mother. The attempted coup of 1840 at Boulogne led to his imprisonment at the Ham fortress near the Belgian border. With the help of Dr. Henru Conneau, he escaped (1846) to England, where he established important political and social connections. In 1848 he served as a constable in London during the Chartist demonstration.

As an intellectual, Louis Napoleon was influenced by the socialist ideology of SAINT-SIMON. He wrote several treatises, two of which foreshadowed his political and socioeconomic policies, which would place him among the first rulers to cope with problems emerging from the industrial revolution. His *Napoleonic Ideas* advanced a constructive social and economic program for the French people. In *The Extinction of Pauperism* he advocated a regulated economy and social hierarchy, ideas that led later critics to label him a protofascist.

In 1848 the February and June Revolutions in France spelled the permanent end of monarchy and ushered in the Second French Republic. A constitution was adopted in November, and, assisted by the Napoleonic legend, his own versatile appeal and program, and the fear of socialism, Louis Napoleon was elected president for a terminal four-year term. He had won Catholic support by promising, after negotiations with MONTALEMBERT, to protect religion, grant the Church freedom of education, and guarantee the freedom and authority of the pope, then in exile at Gaeta. As president, he dispatched troops to occupy Rome and permit the return of Pius IX, and he recommended the Falloux Law on education. The constitution enabled the conservative Legislative Assembly to control the executive, but imprudent decisions in limiting the suffrage and in granting presidential power to appoint army and police chiefs made possible Louis's coups of 1851 and 1852. The first coup granted Louis sweeping powers to revise the constitution, while the coup of 1852 established the Second Empire. Montalembert broke with him, but Louis VEUILLOT and Bishop MARET led most Catholics to support his imperial claims. Republican opposition was subdued, and in 1853 the emperor married the beautiful Spanish countess, Eugenie de Teba. Three years later the prince imperial, Louis Napoleon (1856–79), was born, assuring succession to the throne.

The domestic policy of Napoleon III stimulated the progress of the industrial revolution. A network of railroads and a banking system contributed to national unity, while the economy was bolstered by government credit at home and in imperial territory. Banking developed with great vigor. Government banks (the Crédit Foncier and the Crédit Agricole) and the private Crédit Mobilier encouraged industrialization, commerce, urban development, and agricultural growth. The Bank of France centralized the banking structure. The Cobden Treaty of 1860 with England committed France to a policy of free trade. It was less remunerative than expected, but a public works program averted economic dislocation and made possible the prefect G. E. Haussmann's beautification of Paris. In 1864 the government permitted the rise of labor unions with rights of strike and bargaining.

Relative peace and prosperity were conducive to the growth of French culture and the contributions of L. PASTEUR in science, F. M. de Lesseps in engineering, C. P. Baudelaire and G. Flaubert in literature, J. Offenbach and G. Courbet in the arts, and J. Garnier in architecture. Catholicism flourished despite the growing differences between Liberal Catholics and the ultramontanists (*see* ULTRAMONTANISM). Numerous religious congregations of women were authorized, and French missionaries labored in many parts of the world, especially in southeast Asia. LOURDES became an international shrine of pilgrimage.

Ambitious overextension in the field of foreign affairs led France to disaster. Among Napoleon's imperial ventures, the Crimean War was particularly expensive in lives and money and brought questionable diplomatic gain. The War of Italian Liberation (1859–60) revealed that France alone could not control the balance of power. Theoretically committed to the *RISORGIMENTO*, Napoleon was fearful of alienating Catholic support, and consequently his maintenance of French troops in Rome deprived the United Italian armies of their most desired prize. Only with the withdrawal of these troops in 1870 was the last remnant of the STATES OF THE CHURCH occupied. The Mexican expedition (1861–67) terminated in the execution of ''Emperor'' Maximilian, the withdrawal of French troops, and loss of prestige. Imperial expansion into Indochina and Algeria led to a century of tension and eventual expulsion. In 1863–64 Polish patriots waited in vain for French help. Only Romania, which achieved autonomy, profited from Napoleon's idealistic belief that he could act as the arbiter of European destiny. Overconfidence and preoccupation with unsound foreign ventures blinded him to the rise of a powerful Prussia. The French defeat in the Franco-Prussian War (1870–71) resulted in the capture and exile of the emperor and the humiliating Treaty of Frankfurt. France never wholly regained the prestige attained by Napoleon during his 22 years of rule.

Bibliography: A. L. GUÉRARD, *Napoleon III* (Cambridge, MA 1943). *Oeuvres de Napoleon III*, 5 v. (Paris 1854–69). P. GUÉRIOT, *Napoleon III*, 2 v. (Paris 1933–34). P. DE LA GORCE, *Histoire du Second Empire*, 7 v. (Paris 1894–1905). J. MAURAIN, *La Politique ecclésiastique du Second Empire de 1852 à 1869* (Paris 1930). É. OLLIVIER, *L'Empire libéral: Études, récits, souvenirs*, 18 v. (Paris 1894–1918). A. DANSETTE, *Religious History of Modern France*, tr. J. DINGLE v.1 (New York 1961). R. W. COLLINS, *Catholicism and the Second French Republic* (New York 1923).

[R. J. MARAS]

NAPPER, GEORGE, BL.

Priest, martyr; b. Holywell Manor, Oxford, England, 1550; d. hanged, drawn, and quartered at Oxford, Nov. 9, 1610. George was the son of Edward Napper (d. 1558) and his second wife, Anne Peto of Chesterton, Warwickshire (the niece of William Cardinal Peto). George endured many things because of his Catholic faith, including expulsion from Corpus Christi College, Oxford (1568). He visited the English College at Rheims (Aug. 24, 1579) for which he was imprisoned the following year at the Wood Street Counter in London (December 1580 until June 1589). Upon acknowledging the royal supremacy, he was released. In 1596, he began seminary studies at Douai. Following his ordination, he set off for the English mission (1603), where he lived with his brother William in the family home. George was found carrying a pyx with two consecrated Hosts and a reliquary when he was arrested at Kirtlington near Woodstock (July 19, 1610). The next day he was sent to Oxford Castle. Soon thereafter he was indicted under 27 Eliz., c. 2 for being a priest, condemned, but reprieved. In prison he reconciled a condemned felon, which added the crime of persuasion to popery. Even then it was expected that he would be banished rather than executed. His refusal to take the oath of supremacy settled the matter. He was permitted to say Mass prior to his death. Some of Napper's relics were retrieved by the faithful and buried in the former chapel of Sanford manor, which later became a preceptory of Knights Templar. Napper was beatified by Pius XI on Dec. 15, 1929.

Feast of the English Martyrs: May 4 (England).

See Also: ENGLAND, SCOTLAND, AND WALES, MARTYRS OF.

Bibliography: R. CHALLONER, *Memoirs of Missionary Priests*, ed. J. H. POLLEN (rev. ed. London 1924; repr. Farnborough 1969). J. H. POLLEN, *Acts of English Martyrs* (London 1891).

[K. I. RABENSTEIN]

NARRATIVE THEOLOGY

Narrative theology adopts the hermeneutical principle that the key to the meaning of a text is found in its literary genre and style. Narrative theology's own genre, as it has come to be understood by practitioners in the late 20th century, is that of story or *narratio*. As old as religious literature itself, and used as a clearly defined form in classical rhetoric, *narratio* has become the subject of recent efforts at analysis and systemization. Appreciation of the usefulness of story as a vehicle for theology has grown apace with modern hermeneutical theory (*see* HERMENEUTICS; HERMENEUTICS, BIBLICAL).

In narrative theology, Biblical stories are commonly held up as paradigms. Though they vary from fully developed scenes with dialogue to brief and sometimes cryptic summaries, Biblical narratives center on action and movement, making verbal forms very prominent. Description (nouns, adjectives) plays a subordinate part in Biblical narrative; nothing, whether character, inner feelings or scenery which does not contribute to the action has a place in the story, and in this the Biblical style differs from the Homeric. The narrator—not an actor in the drama—tells the story from an outsider's point of view; thus he appears as a reliable, authoritative and objective interpreter of events, able to provide the reader access to privileged information and a correct interpretation of their meaning.

This relatively new approach to theological exploration has proven to be a fruitful endeavor on several counts: first, it challenges head on the traditional view that religious truths are necessarily best expressed in propositional form; second, it lends force to the claim that religion can never be a purely personal quest; and third, it promises to make theology far more accessible to the laity than it has been heretofore. Advocates of narrative theology argue that not only is the Church's faith fundamentally narrative in structure, but that human experience itself reflects a "storied" character. It therefore follows that full participation in the ecclesial community and the formation of Christian identity assumes access to and knowledge of the Church's own "story" of salvation.

Narrative Theology. Few if any art forms can be considered more ancient or satisfying than that of the craft of good narrative, but scholarly interest in it seems to wax and wane with the currents of culture. The present very positive attention it is receiving as an important theological category appears to be due to a number of converging cultural and academic factors, particularly a resurgence of interest in Biblical studies, disenchantment with rationalistic and abstract forms of thought, and a corresponding renewed interest in subjectivity, symbol, imagination, and the arts. A further and perhaps even more significant factor has been an increased awareness of historical RELATIVISM. A growing historical awareness and sophistication has resulted in the recognition that narrative structure is an appropriate form for expressing an historically-rooted faith such as Christianity. Narrative permits us to understand "truth" in existential rather than absolute terms. The telling of a story, in effect, suggests a confessional commitment and not (necessarily) universal truth claims.

Interest in narrative theology has blossomed in the last two decades. A general understanding of its special contribution to theology can be indicated by mention of a few seminal works. H. Richard NIEBUHR's *The Meaning of Revelation* (1941) is often cited as having provided the initial conceptual groundwork for narrative theology. Niebuhr distinguished between history proper as a factual, potentially verifiable account of events, and a subjective "internal" history—by which he meant personal identity. Niebuhr claimed that in the encounter with the Church's story, an individual's "internal" history underwent reinterpretation.

Thirty years later religious philosopher Steven Crites produced a brilliant essay that proved seminal to the development of this approach. In "The Narrative Quality of Experience" (1971) Crites claimed that, far from being ephemeral, cultural forms of expression are neither historical accidents, products of culture, nor the consequence of individual ingenuity. While it is true that cultural forms are still culturally *particular,* certain persistent cultural forms, such as language, are the mark of what it means to be human and serve as the necessary condition of historical existence. He maintained therefore that in speaking of experience one speaks of a movement through time. Human consciousness grasps its objects in an inherently temporal way insofar as it anticipates the future, attends to the present, and remembers the past. For this reason narrative is not a contrived or foreign form imposed on human experience but an accurate reflection or symbol of the time-bound nature of that experience. This means that stories are not just a human possibility; they are a human *inevitability.*

Uniquely important experiences occasion the holding of festal celebrations and the telling of "sacred" stories (myths) which are in fact world-creating, i.e., in the first instance they shape consciousness; in the second, they function "not like monuments that men behold, but like dwelling places. People live in them" (Crites 1971). In written form, such stories function as "Scripture."

Roman Catholic scholar John Shea makes the same point when he observes that the "ambition of myth is not to be one more interesting but forgettable account but to become the structure of consciousness through which human situations will be appropriated" (Shea 1978). The question, according to Shea, is not whether we, as humans, "have" myths but always *what kind of myths do we have?* A careful probing of autobiographies always reveals a root metaphor that gives unity and coherence to a person's life. The arguments of Crites and Shea about the fundamental power of myth to shape consciousness and world view lend credence to the claim of narrative theologians that the individual self is best understood as a "story"—a story which must be interpreted by and ultimately "owned" by the community of faith and its Scripture.

The Communal Story. Given the claims made about the inherently narrative structure of human experience and consciousness, it follows that the essential identity of a human community must necessarily be a kind of narration. A connected narrative is at once the most efficient and effective way of remembering; and this common memory is essential to the continued existence of any historical community, including the Church. Theologian George Stroup explains the vital function of narrative in the life of the individual believer and the Christian community. In an ecclesial context, the story of salvation functions as a kind of "glue": To be a true participant, one must be able to recite the community's stories and allow those stories to shape personal identity.

The Church has always been concerned to tell its story, first in the context of catechetical instruction, as a means of inviting and inducting newcomers into the community, and second, in liturgical celebration as a means of sustaining Christian identity and faithful witness to God's word. One of the tasks of narrative theology is to understand the process by which the community's story is grasped and appropriated by individuals. At what point does the Christian narrative shape consciousness and construct or reconstruct personal history? And does "knowing" the story entail living it? Is it possible for the individual to claim a living faith and not know the community's story? Stroup argues that the genre of narrative is indispensible to the communication, explication, and personal appropriation of the Christian faith.

Christians have learned the significance of story and its personal appropriation from the Jewish tradition and the Hebrew Scriptures. As an historical, time-bound faith, Christianity has often been referred to as a "religion of the Book." This is true not only because Scripture contains the authoritative versions of the Church's sacred stories of origin; it is also true in the sense that Scripture provides the normative model for *how, when, and why* the stories are to be retold. According to contemporary Biblical scholars, the earliest expressions of Hebrew worship entailed the retelling or recital of past events—events that witness to a history of deliverance and blessing.

This ritual of remembering was not simply a matter of promoting conservative interests or maintaining a romanticized, heroic vision of the past. For Israel, to recount the mighty acts of God was to invoke that same redemptive power as a transforming force in the lives of those who remember. The ritual recital in effect "contemporized" the saving event for each new generation: "The LORD our God made a covenant with us in Horeb. *Not with our fathers* did the LORD make this covenant, but *with us*, who are all of us here alive today . . ." (Dt 5:2–3). For centuries Jews celebrating the Passover have reminded themselves that it was *they* and not merely their ancestors who were delivered at the sea by the mighty hand of Yahweh.

This direct and dramatic form of appropriating the communal story (which scholars term "actualization") implies a release of power and is therefore best understood as a *sacramental* action. The Christian Eucharist is likewise a ritual remembering in which a new generation is permitted to participate in the definitive "saving" event, and today the Church is seeking to recover the narrative structure of worship and doctrinal formulations. For example, the category of "story" has become particularly attractive to political and liberation theologians who see in the plight of the Third World and other marginalized classes all the elements of the Exodus drama (*see* LIBERATION THEOLOGY). They recognize that Biblical narrative is really the only form of theology that is accessible and therefore compelling to the unlettered.

Furthermore, the abstraction of Biblical narrative into formal doctrine blunts the "bite" of these stories. The effect (inevitably) is to rob the Gospel of its potential power to subvert long-established, institutionalized injustices. German theologian, Johann Baptist Metz (1980) argues that all doctrine should have an obvious narrative and "practical" structure. Recognizing that stories, like Sacraments, are "efficacious" and thus able to transform the hearer, he warns against repeated abstractions that eviscerate the performative power of the Church's stories of salvation. The Church must consciously begin to stress the narrative quality of the Sacraments, to recognize that what Sacraments signify are stories, and that these saving stories reveal truths that would otherwise not be known. The Church, therefore, does not tell stories in order to teach doctrine. The real function of doctrine is to "protect the narrative memory of salvation in a scientific world, to allow it to be at stake and to prepare a way for a renewal of this narrative, without which the experience of salvation is silenced" (Metz 213).

Biography as Theology. The Church's story is told in yet another context, indirectly yet powerfully, and that is in the lives of faithful Christians. The lives of the saints (hagiography) has always been a popular narrative genre for communicating the faith. The current resurgence of interest in personal life histories as a form of theologizing presents more than a subjectivist preoccupation with psychology and psychotherapy. It is probably best understood as a new variety of hagiography. Liberation theologians such as James Cone (1975) or Robert McAfee Brown (1975) claim that oppressed people have "true" stories to tell and that giving voice to these stories is a form of empowerment. Feminists maintain that as the faith experience of women is not popularly recognized, the Church's story has not yet been fully told. Theologians such as George Stroup (1981) and James W. McClendon (1974), on the other hand, are more interested in linking theological and ethical themes with the genre of biography and attendant hermeneutical issues. They want to know what happens when an individual life story intersects or "collides" with the communal story. In what sense are people's lives governed by root metaphors supplied by Christian tradition? Do the lives of holy people modify or enlarge our understanding of traditional doctrines? Whose story changes and how?

Implications for Liturgy and Catechesis. Although some argue that narrative theologians are not really saying anything new, their message carries a force by virtue of the technical support supplied by their study of literary criticism, linguistics, the philosophy of history, depth psychology, ethics, and social criticism. What this relatively untested enterprise lacks in precision, it more than makes up for in energy and enthusiasm. If what it says about the formative power of the Church's communal narrative is taken seriously, there are several obvious implications for liturgical and catechetical practice.

First, narrative should form the core of both preaching and teaching. Biblical and traditional materials are most effectively presented in narrative rather than propositional form.

Second, the Church has the responsibility to preserve the story *faithfully*. Faithful preservation implies that the full, and not an idealized, truncated or emasculated version of the Church's story should be told. Biblical material should not be watered down or mercilessly clipped as a strategy for protecting the community from its own mortifying failures or its great successes. Faithfulness further implies that the Bible be permitted to address the community as an objective, history-like story. To allow the Biblical stories to mean whatever the reader wants them to mean is poor Biblical stewardship. It becomes a form of domestication which robs Biblical narrative of its efficacy and transformative power.

Third, the Church needs to recognize and respect the sacramental efficacy of its own narrative. Stewards of the word—preachers, teachers, and theologians—need to tell these stories as expectantly as they pray, and to teach them as intentionally as they teach the Christian creed which itself tells the story of creation and salvation. Stories are channels of power and grace, the rock on which sound doctrine rests.

Fourth and finally, the Church needs to become much more adept and consciously active in the task of supporting the telling or revisioning of personal faith his-

tories. Clergy and laity alike need help in developing the skills necessary to reinterpret the experiences of daily life in terms of the Church's collective story of salvation.

Bibliography: E. AUERBACH, *Mimesis* (Princeton, N.J. 1957). R. MCA. BROWN, "My Story and 'The Story'." *Theology Today* 32 (1975) 166–173. J. H. CONE, "The Story Context of Black Theology," *Theology Today* 32 (1975) 144–150. S. CRITES, "The Narrative Quality of Experience," *Journal of the American Academy of Religion* 34 (1971) 219–311, J. CROSSAN, *The Dark Interval* (Niles, Ill. 1976). G. FACKRE, *The Christian Story* (Grand Rapids, Mich. 1978). H. FREI, *The Eclipse of Biblical Narrative* (New Haven 1974). M. GOLDBERG, *Jews and Christians: Getting Our Stories Straight* (Nashville 1985); *Theology and Narrative* (Nashville 1981). J. B. METZ, *Faith in History and Society* (New York 1980). J. W. MCCLENDON, *Biography as Theology* (Nashville 1974). J. NAVONE and T. COOPER, *Tellers of the Word* (New York 1981). H. R. NIEBUHR, *The Meaning of Revelation* (New York 1941). P. RICOEUR, *Time and Narrative* (Chicago 1984). J. SHEA, *Stories of God* (Chicago 1978). G. STROUP, *The Promise of Narrative Theology* (Atlanta, Ga. 1981).

[R. MAAS]

NARY, CORNELIUS

Priest, controversialist, translator; b. near Naas, Co. Kildare, Ireland, *c.* 1660; d. Dublin, March 3, 1738. After being educated locally, he was ordained in Kilkenny in 1684, went to Irish College, Paris, graduated doctor of laws from the University of Paris, and became tutor in London to the Earl of Antrim. He was appointed parish priest of St. Michan's, Dublin, *c.* 1700, and composed a catechism for the use of his parish (1705), to which he introduced the Dominican and Poor Clare nuns. In 1717 he translated the New Testament with practical liturgical intent. He wrote a "powerful memorial" (Lecky) on the subject of the oath of abjuration, called *The Case of the Catholics of Ireland* (1724). Nary's literary activity included an ambitious *New History of the World* (Dublin 1720); translations from the French; writings on UNIGENITUS; and, among others, replies to one George Synge, *Charitable Address to All Who Are of the Communion of Rome* (1728). An active member of the diocesan chapter, he figured in domestic controversies.

Bibliography: J. WARE, *Works,* ed. and tr. W. HARRIS, 3 v. (Dublin 1739–64) 2:299. N. DONNELLY, *History of Dublin Parishes* (Dublin n.d.) 3:50–55. W. E. H. LECKY, *History of Ireland in the 18th Century,* 5 v. (London 1893).

[J. J. MEAGHER]

NASCIMBENI, GIUSEPPE, BL.

Priest, founder of the Little Sisters of the Holy Family (*Piccole Suore della Sacra Famiglia*); b. March 22, 1851, Torri del Benaco, Italy; d. Jan. 21, 1922, Castelletto del Garda, northern Italy.

Giuseppe, the son of Antonio Nascimbeni and Amidaea Sartori, completed his seminary training at Verona, Venetia. Following his ordination in 1874, he taught and served as priest in the parish of San Pietro di Lavagno. On Nov. 2, 1877, Nascimbeni was sent to the small village of Castelletto, where he remained the rest of his life as a teacher and associate, then as pastor.

He was an exemplary parish priest, created protonotary apostolic by Pius X in 1911, who was active in advancing modernization in the area. He helped establish the local bank and post office, promoted the olive oil industry, urged the installation of modern utilities, and oversaw the construction of the parish church (1905–08), an oratory, a nursery school, an orphanage, and a nursing home.

After trying and failing to persuade several congregations to send nuns to the area, on the advice of his bishop, Cardinal Bartolomeo Bacilieri, he founded (Nov. 6, 1892) the institute of Little Sisters of the Holy Family with four sisters, including Maria Mantovani. The congregation works in hundreds of institutes in Italy and abroad training girls, caring for the elderly, and teaching.

Nascimbeni, who cared for his flock spiritually and materially, died after a stroke (1916) and long illness. His mausoleum is in the chapel of the institute at Castelletto. Pope John Paul II, praising Father Giuseppe as a pastor of consummate charity and virtue, beatified him at Verona, April 17, 1988.

Feast: Jan. 20.

Bibliography: A. PRONZATO, *Il diritto di chiamarsi padre: profilo di mons. Giuseppe Nascimbeni, fondatore delle Piccole suore della Sacra Famiglia* (Turin 1980). *Acta Apostolicae Sedis* (1988) 586. *L'Osservatore Romano,* English edition, 15 (1988) 2, 5.

[K. I. RABENSTEIN]

NATHAN

The name of a prophet in the days of DAVID and SOLOMON; the name also of one of David's sons. The prophet Nathan [Heb. *nātān,* shortened form of a theophoric compound, such as *nātan-'ēl,* "God has given (a son)"] dissuaded David from building a temple and gave him the important oracle that promised perpetuity to the Davidic Dynasty (2 Sm 7.1–29). He reproved David for his adultery and murder of Uriah (2 Sm 12.1–15). According to the Biblical CHRONICLER, it was with Nathan's concurrence that David arranged the musical service for the sanctuary (2 Chr 29.25). Nathan supported Solomon in his bid for the throne (1 Kgs 1.10–45). According to 1 Chr 29.29 and 2 Chr 9.29 Nathan wrote a history of David and Solomon.

Nathan, son of David (2 Sm 5.14), is probably the ancestor of the family mentioned in Zec 12.12. St. Luke (3.31) traces the lineage of Jesus through this Nathan rather than through Solomon.

[F. BUCK]

NATIONAL APOSTOLATE FOR INCLUSION MINISTRY (NAFIM)

The National Apostolate for Inclusion Ministry (NAfIM), formerly the National Apostolate for the Mentally Retarded (NAMR), is an organization dedicated to including mentally challenged persons in ecclesial life. The new designation took effect in 1997. In the 1960s society at large began to observe a changing consciousness toward those with mental disabilities. Catholics began forging an idea for a national support network. In 1961, interested parties gathering at an Inter-American CCD Congress in Dallas, Texas, formed a core group and, after a series of meetings, a constitution was later approved in West Hartford, Connecticut (1967). In August 1970, also in West Hartford, the first NAMR conference took place. The first president was Reverend Matthew M. Pasaniello of New Jersey.

During the 1970s, NAMR incorporated, established an office at Trinity College, Washington, D.C., and was included in the Official Catholic Directory. It also changed its name in 1974 to the National Apostolate with Mentally Retarded Persons (NAMRP), a name it kept until 1992, when it was renamed as the National Apostolate with People with Mental Retardation (NAPMR). Meanwhile, the organization endeavored to create inclusive ministry across the country by collaborating with like-minded groups.

In accordance with the United States Bishops' pastoral letters on people with disabilities, NAfIM seeks to witness "to the Good News that all persons are created in God's image and likeness" and that the mentally retarded share "virtues like courage, patience, perseverence, compassion, and sensitivity that should serve as an inspiration to all Christians." Therefore, the principle purposes of the NAfIM are: (1) to promote the full incorporation of persons with mental retardation within the life of the Church; (2) to enhance the growth of persons with mental retardation and the entire Church through the prophetic role of persons with mental retardation; (3) to take steps in both the Church and the community at large, on a national and local level, to bring before the public the spiritual, interpersonal, and communal gifts of persons with mental retardation; (4) to foster quality evangelization, catechesis, sacramental preparation, and participa-

Nathan Berating David, c. 17th century. (©Historical Picture Archive/CORBIS)

tion, and ongoing spiritual development of persons with mental retardation; and (5) to provide a forum for those involved in direct ministry with persons with mental retardation.

At the level of education, NafIM has sought to develop appropriate curriculum materials with the goal of mainstreaming children with mental disabilities into Catholic school settings.

Annually, there is a membership conference in various sections of the United States. The members—parents, teachers, chaplains, nurses, administrators, DREs, volunteers, and professionals from other areas—attend workshops, liturgies, and lectures which highlight key areas and future trends in the field of catechesis and mental retardation. All who participate in the spiritual, mental, or physical development of the mentally retarded are eligible for membership. NAfIM publishes a quarterly newsletter and provides consulting services. The NAfIM is presently based in Riverdale, Maryland.

Bibliography: R. BARON and D. SENIOR, *Opening Hearts, Minds, and Doors: Embodying the Inclusive and Vulnerable Love of God* (Chicago 1999). NATIONAL COUNCIL OF CATHOLIC BISHOPS, *Guidelines for the Celebration of the Sacraments with Persons with Disabilities* (Washington, D.C. 1995); *Welcome and Justice for Persons with Disabilities: A Framework of Access and Inclusion* (Washington, D.C. 1999).

[P. J. HAYES/J. MOLONEY]

NATIONAL ASSOCIATION OF EVANGELICALS

A voluntary association of American Protestant evangelical churches, schools, organizations, and individuals who are united without executive or legislative control on the basis of a commonly accepted statement of faith. The purpose of the Association is to provide national identification for evangelicals, fellowship in cooperative witness, and service in every major field of evangelical concern. The occasion for the foundation of the Association was dissatisfaction among evangelical Protestants with the then Federal Council of Churches of Christ in America (1905–50; *see* NATIONAL COUNCIL OF THE CHURCHES OF CHRIST IN THE U.S.A.). They objected that the Council had admitted to its membership a large number of "liberals" who, in their philosophy and theology, were un-Biblical and even anti-Biblical; that it had deliberately omitted or purposely neglected to include provisions for the preservation of all the values inherent in historic Protestantism; and that it had forced evangelicals to take protective measures to ensure their liberty in preaching the Gospel and in carrying out their church programs.

The first organized effort of evangelicals to unite among themselves was the formation in 1929 of the regional New England Fellowship. Its success led to a meeting of evangelical leaders in Chicago, Illinois, Oct. 27–28, 1941, and the unanimous decision to call a national conference in St. Louis, Missouri, April 7–9, 1942. Representatives from approximately 40 denominations agreed at the St. Louis meeting "to organize an Association which shall give articulation and united voice to our faith and purposes." In May of 1943 at Chicago, a constitutional convention worked out a statement of faith that was built on the Bible as the supreme authority in all matters of belief and conduct. With this creedal basis, the convention then adopted a permanent constitution. The national office is located in Los Angeles, California. Central to the Association is the Office of Governmental Affairs in Washington, D.C., which keeps a watch on legislation, the infringement of religious liberties, religious persecutions, and other matters of evangelical interest. The monthly magazine, *United Evangelical Action,* is the official publication of the Association.

Bibliography: J. D. MURCH, *Cooperation without Compromise* (Grand Rapids 1956).

[R. MATZERATH/EDS.]

NATIONAL ASSOCIATION OF PASTORAL MUSICIANS

A national membership organization primarily composed of musicians, musician-liturgists, clergy, and other leaders of prayer devoted to serving the life and mission of the Church through fostering the art of musical liturgy in Roman Catholic worshiping communities in the United States of America. Founded July 1, 1976, NPM has a unique interest in the practical issues facing the practicing musician and the parish clergy. As an association of musicians and clergy, its stated purposes are: (1) to pro-

vide support for practicing parish musicians through improved repertoire, through increased knowledge of the role of music in the liturgy, through practical helps for effective participation in parish liturgical–committee planning of music; (2) to provide a forum for advocating musical excellence in liturgical celebrations; (3) to provide a vehicle for disseminating evaluations of new and current musical selections; and (4) to assist diocesan and parish level efforts in improving the quality of and interest in parish music.

Membership is provided for Directors of Music Ministries, Catholic Music Educators, as well as special interest sections for choir directors, cantors, clergy, organists, campus ministers, ensemble musicians, musicians in the military, youth, seminary music educators, eastern Church musicians, and musicians serving Hispanic, African American and other ethnic communities.

Publications include *Pastoral Music, Pastoral Music Notebook, Catholic Music Educator, Praxis, NPM clergy Update, The Liturgical Singer, NPM Organists,* and *NPM Publications.* Additional services include Conventions, Schools and Institutes, and NPM Hotline which assists musicians seeking positions and parishes looking for musicians. NPM is affliated with the United States Conference of Catholic Bishops. Its head office is located in Washington, DC.

[V. FUNK]

NATIONAL BLACK SISTERS' CONFERENCE

Established in August 1968, the National Black Sisters' Conference (NBSC) seeks to provide ongoing support on the formation, education, and support of African-American women religious; to develop resources for the deepening of spirituality and promotion of unity and solidarity among African-American women religious; to facilitate the development of religious education from an African-American perspective; to stimulate the growth of African-American spirituality; to highlight the racism, powerlessness, poverty, and the distorted self-image of victimized African-American people; to promote knowledge and appreciation of the beauty of African-American cultural-religious heritage; to encourage the growth of African-American religious leadership within the church and in religious communities; and to articulate a cohesive African-American identity for African-American women religious. The NBSC holds annual meetings and organizes annual joint conferences with the National Black Catholic Clergy Caucus and the National Black Catholic Seminarian Association. It also provides a ministry clearinghouse for African-American women religious who want to minister within the African-American community, and a resource center for statistical research of African-American women religious throughout the United States. Its regular publications include *Signs of Soul* and *"Tell It like It Is"—Catechetics from the Black Perspective*. Its headquarters is in Washington, D.C.

[P. CHAPPELL]

NATIONAL CATHOLIC COALITION FOR RESPONSIBLE INVESTMENT

The National Catholic Coalition for Responsible Investment (NCCRI) was begun in February 1973 as a joint project of the National Federation of Priests Councils, the Leadership Conference of Women Religious, the Conference of Major Superiors of Men, the National Assembly of Women Religious, the Catholic Committee of Urban Ministry, and the National Catholic Conference for Interracial Justice. Coordinators of NCCRI since its foundation have been Reverends Eugene Boyle, Donald Bargen, OMI, and Michael Crosby, OFM Cap. NCCRI has a twofold purpose: to educate Catholic institutions about the desirability and manner of becoming involved in corporate social responsibility; and to facilitate the effort of Catholic institutions in their involvement.

The educational component of NCCRI was given in over 500 Catholic dioceses, religious congregations, schools, and health-care centers in 17 regional meetings since 1973. As a result of most of these seminars, regional coalitions were formed to achieve the second goal of NCCRI, the active effort of Catholic institutions in the corporate responsibility movement. By 1978 ten regions, comprising over 150 portfolio-holding Catholic institutions, became actively involved through membership in the Interfaith Center on Corporate Responsibility (ICCR) in New York, a joint project of both NCCRI-related organizations and major Protestant denominations and agencies. In 1977, Sister Regina Murphy, SC, was elected the first Catholic chairperson of ICCR. In 2001, ICCR had over 275 Catholic, Protestant, and Jewish institutions that used their investments in the marketplace to promote social change.

[M. CROSBY/P. HAYES]

NATIONAL CATHOLIC CONFERENCE FOR INTERRACIAL JUSTICE (NCCIJ)

Founded in 1959–1960 at Chicago as a federation of Catholic Interracial Councils, NCCIJ now has its national office at the Josephite Seminary in Washington, DC. It implements the teaching of the Catholic Church on cultural and racial justice and serves to further the Church's vision of multicultural and multiracial understanding. Bridge-building between the white and black populations was the original rationale for Catholic Interracial Councils (CIC), a movement begun in the 1930s, under the guidance of John LAFARGE, SJ (1880–1963). Both personally and as editor for the Jesuit weekly *America*, LaFarge hammered home to U.S. Catholics that racism was a sin. The pioneer effort in the New York City area, launched on June 6, 1934 (Pentecost Sunday), led to imitation elsewhere, until a CIC was to be found in almost every large urban area. The NCCIJ wasestablished to coordinate the effort of the Councils, although each maintains its independence. For many years, the New York CIC published the *Interracial Review*, which reported on items of interest to African-Americans. NCCIJ continues to publish a newsletter, *Commitment*.

On Aug. 28, 1958, the first National Catholic Conference for Interracial Justice was held at Loyola University in Chicago. The leaders of the Chicago CIC had orchestrated this meeting. As a result of this, the NCCIJ sprung up the following year. Shortly thereafter, the American bishops issued a pastoral letter, "Discrimination and Christian Conscience" (Nov. 14, 1958), which said, "The heart of the race question is religious and moral." No other previous statement of the American hierarchy had described the problem in this way.

Varied and intensive governmental programs, together with the emergence of the Black Power movement of the 1960s, led to less emphasis on maintaining private interracial coalitions of volunteer members and consequently to fewer Catholic interracial councils. During the 1960s, NCCIJ served as catalyst and secretariat for the first National Conference on Religion and Race (Chicago 1963) and for Catholic participation in the widespread demonstrations and other programs designed to achieve the federal Civil Rights acts of 1964 and 1968. In the late 1970s, the Conference's major areas of concern included full, fair and equal opportunity employment, and Catholic school integration. Special emphasis was put on efforts to have the Church's own practices conform to the principles of social justice that Catholics accept and proclaim. In 1990, the NCCIJ began its *Creating an Inclusive Church* program "to assist the Church in addressing the increasing diversity of its membership with justice, unity, and love." It seeks to address under-representation of minorities in diocesan offices, purchasing, and ministry. The *Plan for Parish Action* (1992) focuses on building bridges between races and cultures and ensuring that all activities of the parish include all races and cultures. The

Conference makes its services available to all, regardless of race, color, religion, or national origin.

NCCIJ is supported by contributions from individual and organization members, general appeals, and foundation grants. The Conference includes bishops, religious, and laity on its policy-making board, but it is an autonomous body, although approved by official Catholic leadership. At the national level, NCCIJ strives to be effective, by itself and in coalition with other civil rights and community groups (esp. NAACP, the National Office of Black Catholics, and those involved in the Spanish-speaking apostolate), in assuring the passage and enforcement of federal legislation guaranteeing equal rights and opportunities for all people, regardless of race, color, or national origin, in the areas of employment, housing, education, welfare, and health care. Two perspectives are aggressively maintained: (1) racial justice is a moral issue, transcending economics and politics; (2) the ministry to achieve interracial justice is not limited to a particular group, but is an obligation shared by all, with special responsibilities on Christians who recognize the universality of redemption and brotherhood in Jesus Christ.

Bibliography: J. LAFARGE, *Interracial Justice* (New York 1937; rev. ed., *The Race Question* [London 1943]); idem., *No Postponement* (London 1951); M. A. ZIELINSKI, *"Doing the Truth": The Catholic Interracial Council of New York, 1945–1965* (Ph.D. dissertation, Catholic University of America, 1989). Some archival materials for the NCCIJ may be found at Marquette University as well as among the papers of John LaFarge, SJ, at Georgetown University. The archives for the CIC-NY are located at the Catholic University of America.

[P. J. HAYES/A. J. WELSH]

NATIONAL CATHOLIC DEVELOPMENT CONFERENCE

The National Catholic Development Conference, Inc. (NCDC) was founded in 1968 to assist its members in developing ethical and successful methods of fund raising. Rev. Richarch Drabik, MIC, was the first president. Voting membership is open to those Catholic institutions listed in the *Official Catholic Directory*. Nonvoting associate and corporate membership is open to those individuals and institutions who are not eligible for active membership. In 2001, it was the largest development organization and included dioceses, religious orders and provinces, hospitals, and educational institutions.

The professional beginnings of the NCDC can be traced back to 1955 when a group of mission procurators and development directors began meeting under the aegis of the Mission Secretariat in Washington, D.C. In the early 1960s members of the Catholic Press Association (CPA) with fund-raising concerns began to hold annual meetings. They called themselves the Catholic Fund-Raising Conference and met in conjunction with the CPA convention. Directly out of this group the NCDC was formed. It was incorporated in New York State, March 5, 1968. The year following its incorporation, the NCDC drew up its *Precepts of Stewardship*, a set of ethical guidelines for fund raising. Originally nine in number (now six), these include the requirement of official church approval, good stewardship practices, integrity in business associations, and the good taste and sound theology which must be associated with religious fund raising. Conditions for membership include adherence to these *Precepts* and to the 1977 NCCB *Principles and Guidelines for Fund Raising in the United States*. The annual highlight of the Conference's activities is its development convention, held usually in September, which attracts several hundred attendees. The Conference's services to members include a continuing education program, a development resource library, and a public-information program, "Giving is an Act of Faith," established to compile and disseminate material on fund-raising institutions and their programs. The NCDC has established six regional planning groups that serve religious fund-raising professionals in designated areas of the U.S. It also offers a Planned Giving Professionals Mentoring Program for its members who have limited experience in planned giving. The Conference also tracks pertinent legislation relevant to development professionals.

The NCDC maintains a liaison with the episcopal and religious conferences of the U.S., and it represents its members on postal-affairs committees and before regulatory and legislative groups. It publishes the periodical called *Dimensions*, and issues a report called *The Monitor*, which trackes postal legislation.

See Also: INTERNATIONAL CATHOLIC STEWARDSHIP COUNCIL.

[P. J. HAYES/E. DILL]

NATIONAL CATHOLIC EDUCATIONAL ASSOCIATION (NCEA)

The largest professional education association in the world, comprising institutional members and educators serving at all levels of Catholic education. Founded in 1904 as the Catholic Educational Association of the U.S. (CEA), it united three separate organizations: the Education Conference of Catholic Seminary Faculties (1897);

Second-grade students at a Catholic school. (©David H. Wells/CORBIS)

the Association of Catholic Colleges (1898); and the Parish School Conference (1902). In 1927, the CEA changed its name to the National Catholic Educational Association (NCEA).

Much of the inspiration and organization are attributed to Rt. Rev. Msgr. Thomas J. CONATY, rector of The CATHOLIC UNIVERSITY OF AMERICA, and Rev. Francis W. HOWARD of Columbus, Ohio. Conaty became bishop of Los Angeles in 1903, and his successor at The Catholic University, Most Rev. Denis J. O'CONNELL, became the NCEA's first president general and served from 1904 to 1908.

The following goals characterize the work of NCEA: to promote and encourage the principles and ideals of Christian education and formation; to encourage and provide means whereby Catholic educators and their institutions can work cooperatively and effectively for professional growth; to promote and interpret the Catho-

lic educational endeavor in its contribution to the total national educational enterprise and to the general welfare of the nation; and to seek and foster cooperation nationally and internationally between Catholic educational institutions and agencies which promote the general education of society.

In the beginning, the CEA had only three departments: for seminaries, colleges, and parish schools. These three departments expanded over the decades into the present seven constitutive departments: Association of Catholic Colleges and Universities (ACCU); Chief Administrators of Catholic Education (CACE); Elementary Schools; Secondary Schools; National Association of Boards of Catholic Education (NABE); Religious Education; and Seminary.

The NCEA strives to be a meaningful service organization for all Catholic education. It encourages creative new designs for educational programs and it features

160

strong efforts to assist decision-makers who are charged with keeping Catholic education a vital force. In addition to its publications, it sponsors an annual convention to bring together all Catholic educators.

Since 1929, the headquarters of the association has been located in Washington, DC.

[M. IRWIN/J. F. MEYERS/C. A. KOOB/EDS.]

NATIONAL CATHOLIC PHARMACISTS GUILD OF THE U.S.

An association of Catholic pharmacists organized in 1962. Before that date there were some diocesan associations of Catholic pharmacists in various parts of the U.S. One of these, the Catholic Pharmacists Guild of St. James of the Diocese of Fall River, MA, presented to its bishop, the Most Rev. James L. Connolly, a plan for a national pharmacists' organization. With the bishop's approval, and with the cooperation of officers of other diocesan guilds, the St. James Guild sponsored a national membership campaign that resulted in an organizational meeting in New York City on Sept. 19, 1962, with 21 diocesan representatives present. The decision was reached to form a national guild. Today the Guild is based in St. Louis, Mo. The group focuses on ethics, morals, medical missions, and drug donations. Its members periodically contribute to public policy advocacy, especially with respect to pharmaco-therapies and vaccine development.

[T. P. KEATING/P. J. HAYES]

NATIONAL CATHOLIC STUDENT COALITION (NCSC)

NCSC was chartered in 1982 by 40 college and university students from around the United States. The group is a successor to the National Newman Club Federation (1908–1968) and the National Federation of Catholic College Students (1938–1968). Where the former was responsible to the Catholic student population at non-Catholic colleges and universities, the latter worked on behalf of only Catholic institutions of higher learning. Today, NCSC is a movement for lay undergraduate students in all U.S. colleges and universities and embraces and serves some four million Catholic college students. Students affiliate with the NCSC through student government organizations on the various campuses, usually through campus ministries. As of June 2000, NCSC had a membership of 150 (120 organization/campus ministry memberships, 30 individual student and alumni members). It is the U.S. constituent member of Pax Romana-

International Movement of Catholic Students (IMCS) and it is through the IMCS that NCSC has a voice as a non-governmental organization at the United Nations. IMCS also represents its affiliates to the Pontifical Council of the Laity.

According to its constitution approved for 2001, the NCSC's mission is to form students in the faith, form the Christian conscience, educate for justice, facilitate personal development, and train future leaders. The organization is established to be a voice for Catholic college students in the U.S.; to provide them with resources for information and leadership development; to partner with local campus ministries and other national and international movements; and to provide a network of campus ministry groups and contact persons. It is comprised of an executive board and several regional boards and committees.

The old NFCCS had its first meeting at Manhattanville College in New York City in 1938. The following year it joined the Newman Federation in becoming U.S. members of the International Movement of Catholic Students (IMCS), which had been instituted by the Holy See in 1921. Also in 1939, the two groups hosted the World Congress of Pax Romana-IMCS on the campuses of Fordham University, Manhattanville College, and the Catholic University of America. During their meetings, where participants heard Dorothy Day among others, the second world war broke out, stranding many European delegates in the United States. The Pax Romana-IMCS remained in the U.S. for the duration of the war under the direction of Edward Kirchner, a collaborator of John Courtney Murray, SJ. By the mid-1960s, NFCCS had a membership of 100,000 students in more than 125 Catholic colleges and universities throughout 15 regions. However, upon the dissolution of the Newman Federation and NFCCS in 1968, the reorganization and downgrading of the old National Catholic Welfare Conference's Youth Department after the Second Vatican Council, and a cultural and attitudinal shift that occurred in the 1960s with respect to student movements generally, the Catholic student was left without formal organizational ties. This changed in 1980, when Joseph Kirchner, the son of Edward Kirchner, and Linda Wirth of the IMCS, rallied college students across the country to re-organize. In March 1982, the NCSC was founded in New York City. Each year since 1985, the NCSC has hosted a leadership conference that traditionally draws several hundred student participants.

Today, communications among the various regions are facilitated through the NCSC's official newspaper, *The Catholic Collegian*. NCSC is also involved in World Youth Days.

Bibliography: J. W. EVANS, *The Newman Movement: Roman Catholics in American Higher Education, 1883–1971* (Notre Dame 1980). Archival materials for NFCCS may be found in the holdings of the Youth Department of the NCWC for the years 1941–1968 and similarly for the Newman movements for the years 1929–1971, both at the Catholic University of America.

[P. J. HAYES]

NATIONAL CONFERENCE FOR COMMUNITY AND JUSTICE (NCCJ)

Formerly known as the National Conference for Christians and Jews—an organization founded in 1927 to promote cooperation in the social order between Jews and Christians—the National Conference for Community and Justice mirrors its heritage by broadening its mission to combat all forms of social bigotry. The new designation took effect in 1997. The old NCCJ was an attempt to counteract the religious intolerance that marked the 1920s in the U.S. In 1928 the presidential campaign, with its anti-Catholic prejudice, induced members of the Federal Council of Churches to form a committee that later became the National Conference of Christians and Jews. Judge and former Secretary of War Newton D. Baker, financier Roger Williams Straus, and Carlton J. H. Hayes, of Columbia University and a former ambassador to Spain, were the founding co-chairmen; Dr. Everett R. Clinchy was the first executive director.

Some members of the Catholic hierarchy, particularly Archbishop John T. McNicholas of Cincinnati, remained reticent during the 1930s and 1940s, following an interpretation of a letter of Pope Leo XIII that held that intercredal cooperation was a form of syncretism or religious indifferentism. Not all bishops saw the matter in these terms and Archbishop Edward Hanna of San Francisco publicly endorsed NCCJ. In its first decade, many priests, including J. Elliot Ross and T. Lawrason Riggs, worked vigorously on its behalf.

The NCCJ has never been an interfaith movement. As a civic organization of religiously motivated people, it promotes civic good will of all religious, ethnic, gender, and racial groups without compromise of religious beliefs. Its basic philosophy stems from the Judeo-Christian ethic of the equality of all people, while its technique is educational penetration of many heterogeneous groups to bring about better understanding and cooperation in matters of common social concern.

In the 1990s, NCCJ began to sponsor a nationally telecast discussion known as *The National Conversation on Race, Ethnicity, and Culture*, which became a model for civil conversation for issues such as the impact of race on public education and regional economic development, immigration, affirmative action, and welfare reform.

While headquartered in New York City, NCCJ has offices or affiliates in several dozen major U.S. cities where workshops and symposia are sponsored. Recent programs have included Seminarians Interacting, which brings future religious leaders into contact with one another to learn about their counterparts in other faith traditions. SI also includes Muslim students. Other educational work of the conference has been carried on primarily through up linked workshops and discussion groups.

Bibliography: J. E. PITT, *Adventures in Brotherhood* (New York 1955). E. R. CLINCHY, *All in the Name of God* (New York 1934). P. J. HAYES, ''J. Elliot Ross and the National Conference for Christians and Jews: A Catholic Contribution to Tolerance in America,'' *Journal of Ecumenical Studies* 37:3/4 (2000). C. E. SILCOX, ''Protestant-Catholic-Jewish Relations: A Seminar at Columbia University,'' *Religious Education* 24 (1929) 207–249. C. SILCOX and G. M. FISHER, *Catholics, Jews, and Protestants: A Study of Relationships in the United States and Canada* (repr. Westport, Conn. 1979). The NCCJ papers are located in the Social Welfare History Archive at the University of Minnesota.

[J. M. EAGAN/P. J. HAYES]

NATIONAL CONFERENCE OF CATECHETICAL LEADERSHIP

The National Conference of Catechetical Leadership (NCCL), which has as its mission to enrich and strengthen the ministry of catechesis in the United States, traces its roots to 1934 when diocesan directors of the Confraternity of Christian Doctrine (CCD) were first convened by Bishop Edwin O'Hara of Great Falls, Montana. The directors successfully petitioned the bishops to establish both an episcopal committee and a national center for the Confraternity of Christian Doctrine. The episcopal committee was formed in November of that same year, and the national center was established in 1935. In 1936, the directors began to meet annually under the aegis of the National Center.

When the directors gathered in New Orleans for their thirtieth annual meeting in April 1966, they decided to form their own organization, independent of the National Center. Episcopal approval for the move was sought and given in September of that year by the Bishops' Committee for CCD meeting in Pittsburgh for the Twelfth National Catechetical Congress. The National Conference of Diocesan Directors of Religious Education/CCD (NCDD) was formally launched in January 1967. NCDD was organized around the ecclesiastical provinces in the United States with the board of directors consisting of elected officers and a representative from each province.

In 1991, the organization changed its bylaws, structure, and governance to widen its membership and to facilitate decision-making and governance processes. In addition to diocesan directors and their staffs, membership was expanded to include academicians, parish directors of religious education, publishers, and affiliated organizations.

Governance of the NCCL is exercised primarily through two bodies: a Representative Council and a Board of Directors. The Representative Council includes representation from the ecclesiastical provinces and the various membership constituencies. The Council's basic functions are to elect the board of directors, entertain matters affecting the state and direction of religious education/catechesis, and to articulate the values of the Conference. The smaller board of directors supervises, regulates, and directs the affairs of the Conference. Both bodies meet in the fall and spring. The officers of the Conference are elected by the general membership.

The Conference publishes a journal, *Catechetical Leadership*, five times a year and quarterly update reports. The Conference holds *ex officio* status on the Bishops' Subcommittee on Catechesis and their Committee on Education. The national offices are located in Washington, DC.

[N. A. PARENT]

NATIONAL COUNCIL OF CATHOLIC MEN (NCCM)

A national federation of organizations of Catholic laymen (NCCM), established in 1920 under the National Catholic Welfare Conference (NCWC) and mandated by the American hierarchy to promote and service the development of the lay apostolate and Catholic Action. NCCM celebrated its golden anniversary in 1970 and was briefly merged with the National Conference of Catholic Women (NCCW) to form the National Council of Catholic Laity (NCCL), before both NCCM and NCCL became inactive in 1975.

Membership and Government. The NCCM's member organizations included parish societies, interparochial societies, state-wide organizations, diocesan federations, and national organizations. The majority of NCCM's programs and services were channeled to its affiliated organizations through diocesan and deanery councils. Approximately 10,000 men's organizations with a total membership of nearly nine million were affiliated with the NCCM.

The NCCM was governed by a general assembly consisting of the presidents of diocesan councils and national organizations, who in turn elected an executive

board composed of 16 members. From the beginning of Vatican Council II, the NCCM's policies were related to the major areas of renewal in the Church's life, namely, liturgy, Scripture, ecumenism, catechetics, and social action.

Objectives and Activities. The major objectives of the NCCM were to federate Catholic men's organizations into a common agency; to develop, promote, and service programs of apostolic action related to contemporary issues; to serve as an informational service link between the NCWC and laymen's organizations; to be a central clearinghouse for information on Catholic laymen's activities; to promote and coordinate lay cooperation in national matters affecting the Church; to help existing Catholic men's organizations to work more effectively in their own localities; to cooperate in furthering the aims of all approved movements in the interest of the Church and society in general; to participate in national and international movements related to its goal; and to bring about a better appreciation of Catholic principles and ideals in the social, economic, educational, and civic life of the U.S.

The major areas of the NCCM's apostolate included: (1) religious activities, such as spiritual and apostolic formation, pastoral assistance, liturgy, and retreats; (2) communications—by means of parish libraries, promotion of the NCCM's radio and television programs, and cooperation with the Legion of Decency and the National Office for Decent Literature (both now defunct); (3) civic and social action—in areas of race relations, migratory labor, employment and problems of the "dropout," urban redevelopment, rural life, cooperation in community affairs, and educational programs on the Church's social encyclicals; (4) legislation—local, state, and national laws relating to current issues such as civil rights, education, the aged, social welfare, labor, and agriculture; (5) family life—family retreats, Cana conferences, family-life institutes, and religious practices and instructions in the home; (6) youth—cooperation with diocesan and parish youth directors, sponsorship of youth leadership training courses, and promotion of recreational and educational facilities; (7) public relations—internal news letters; bulletins; and press, radio, and television releases on organizational programs; (8) international affairs—the fostering of foreign students and visitors; educational programs on the United Nations; study clubs; and meetings on foreign affairs, missions, underdeveloped countries, and world peace; (9) organization and development—training through the NCCM's leaders' course in the lay apostolate in affiliated organizations, and through the speakers' bureau and membership drives.

Four regular publications supplied continuous service to the NCCM's affiliated organizations: *Alert Catho-*

lic Men, Program and Training, Executive Newsletter, and *Highlights.* In its program of leadership training and weekend retreats, the NCCM provided intensive study and training in the lay apostolate for a small group of lay leaders in an atmosphere of prayer, combined with liturgical and scriptural services. The NCCM maintained a library of Catholic films and was responsible also for all regularly scheduled national Catholic network radio and television programs, the best known of which is the National Broadcasting Company's "Catholic Hour," instituted in 1930.

[M. H. WORK/EDS.]

NATIONAL COUNCIL OF CATHOLIC WOMEN (NCCW)

A federation of some 6,000 Catholic women's organizations representing millions of Catholic women across the United States. The NCCW was founded in 1920 at the request of the United States Catholic bishops who had seen the work accomplished by the many separate Catholic women's groups during World War I and urged them to unite their efforts by forming a federation. The NCCW eventually was a constituent member of the Lay Organization Department of the National Catholic Welfare Conference. The NCCW is composed of affiliated parish or area women's groups, and diocesan and national organizations, as well as supporting members. The organization acts through these affiliates to support, educate, and empower all Catholic women in spirituality, leadership, and service.

In 1920 when the NCWC's Department of Lay Organizations was divided into the National Council of Catholic Men (NCCM) and the National Council of Catholic Women, the NCCW had only 90 affiliated organizations. In its early days, the NCCW managed the National Catholic School of Social Service (NCSSS), 1921–1947, for women, prior to its merger with the School of Social Work, for men, at The Catholic University of America. From 1948–1977, Margaret Mealey led the organization as Executive Director. In January 1963, at the invitation of Pres. John F. Kennedy, NCCW representatives met with interdenominational leaders to examine the role of churches and synagogues in eliminating racial discrimination from their own institutions and communities. The NCCW responded by conducting leadership institutes throughout the U.S. to address the race problem. Since 1982, NCCW's respite program has trained over 1,300 volunteers in 15 states to act as temporary surrogate caregivers for people who are caring for elderly or disabled relatives in their homes. There are programs that assist at-risk women and children, as well as women in prison, and children in foster care. The NCCW's interreligious endeavors include working with Jewish women on environmental concerns in several states. Initiatives have included resolutions to ban human embryo stem cell research, to install internet filtering devices in schools, to reject a nuclear missile defense program, and to increase public awareness of the plight of the world's refugees.

As a federation of existing organizations, the NCCW is designed to unite Catholic women's organizations and individual Catholic women throughout the United States; provide a medium for Catholic women to speak and act upon matters of mutual interest; support social action efforts and train Catholic women to become leaders in many areas of life; represent U. S. Catholic women in national and international organizations and programs; collaborate with other organizations and agencies on issues of common concern; and assist Catholic women to act upon current issues in the Church and society.

The NCCW is a service agency. Its programs are implemented through six commissions: Church, Family Concerns, Community Concerns, International Concerns, Legislation, and Organization. These programs reach national audiences as well as those attached to dioceses and deaneries, parishes and local groups. Special cooperation is afforded the CONFRATERNITY OF CHRISTIAN DOCTRINE, CATHOLIC CHARITIES, Catholic Relief Services, National Catholic Rural Life Conference.

The NCCW represents U.S. Catholic women at national and international meetings of government and non-government agencies concerned with the welfare of women or the moral and religious welfare of humanity. The NCCW holds membership in World Union of Catholic Women's Organizations (WUCWO) and Women in Community Services (WICS). It is a member of the United States Catholic Conference. Its publications vary, but since 1975, NCCW has published the bi-monthly magazine *Catholic Woman.* The NCCW is required by its constitution to meet in convention biennially to conduct its business and elect its governing board. In alternate years, regional leadership training institutes are held in strategic areas to give women from all 50 states an opportunity to attend.

Bibliography: Archival material for the NCCW is located at The Catholic University of America (1920–1999). *Catholic Woman* (1975—). R. L. O'HALLORAN, *Organized Catholic Laywomen: The National Council of Catholic Women, 1920–1995* (Ph.D. dissertation, Catholic University of America, 1996).

[P. J. HAYES]

NATIONAL COUNCIL OF THE CHURCHES OF CHRIST IN THE U.S.A.

Established in 1950 and headquartered in New York City, the National Council of the Churches of Christ in the U.S.A. (NCCC-USA) is a federation of 36 mainline Protestant, Anglican, and Eastern Orthodox churches. Its preamble reads, ''The NCCC-USA is a cooperative agency of Christian communions seeking to fulfill the mission to which God calls them. The member communions, responding to the Gospel revealed in the Scriptures, confess Jesus, the Incarnate Son of God, as Saviour and Lord. Relying on the transforming power of the Holy Spirit, the Council works to bring churches into a life-giving fellowship, an independent witness, study and action to the glory of God and in service to all creation.''

The NCCC-USA was formed by uniting into one body 12 interdenominational agencies that had hitherto been carrying on cooperative programs among the churches: the Federal Council of Churches (1908), the Foreign Missions Conference of North America (1803 and 1911); the Home Missions Council of North America (1908); the International Council of Religious Education (1922), actually an outgrowth of a national Sunday School Convention (1832); the Missionary Education Movement of the U.S. and Canada (1902); the National Protestant Council on Higher Education (1911); the United Council of Church Women (1940); the United Stewardship Council (1920); Church World Service (1946); Interseminary Committee (1880); the Protestant Film Commission (1947); and the Protestant Radio Commission (1947).

Historical Development. The American counterpart of the world ECUMENICAL movement had two phases: the formation of new churches through organic merger and the cooperative federation of many denominations for the sake of greater efficiency. Since 1900 the principal denominational cooperatives have been the Federal Council of Churches, organized in 1908, and the National Council of Churches, which succeeded the Federal Council in 1950. Among the contributing factors that helped to shape the National Council was the growing interest in social studies, which showed that American denominationalism was often less doctrinal than cultural and ethnic. Its divisiveness, therefore, could be resolved at least partially by active collaboration in the externals of church life without infringing on the creedal autonomy of the different churches.

When the Federal Council was formed in 1908, its 28 member churches included BAPTISTS, METHODISTS, and PRESBYTERIANS, but the number was only a fraction of the total Protestant population. Its basis of union was modeled on the principles of American democracy. According to its constitution, the Federal Council was to express the fellowship and catholic unity of the Protestant denominations, with a view to bringing them into united service for Christ and the world. Although the largest, the Federal Council was only one of several like agencies that sought to bridge the denominational differences in American Protestantism. They had all been founded to make their work more effective, but this was not enough. As the agencies evolved their programs, they found they had overlapping responsibilities in various areas. Closer cooperative action was needed. Further study and negotiation were finally terminated in 1941 at an historic Atlantic City, N.J., conference that recommended ''creation of a single cooperative agency to succeed all of the existing national councils.'' This met with enthusiastic acceptance, and after nine years of planning, the National Council of Churches was established in Cleveland, Ohio, Nov. 28 to Dec. 1, 1950. Delegates of 29 Protestant and Orthodox bodies joined forces to express their common faith and witness of cooperation with one another.

The preamble of the constitution they adopted stated, ''In the providence of God, the time has come when it seems fitting more fully to manifest oneness in Jesus Christ as Divine Lord and Savior, by the creation of an inclusive cooperative agency of the Christian Churches in the United States of America.''

Eleven purposes were specified in the 1950 constitution, of which the most important is to continue and extend the functions of the original merging societies, along with the STUDENT VOLUNTEER MOVEMENT and the United Student Christian Council that joined after 1950. Each of the other ten aims was directed to the more general scope of the Christian religion:

1. To manifest more fully the oneness of the Church of Christ according to the Scriptures and to further the efforts of the member churches in proclaiming the Gospel of Jesus Christ to the end that all men may believe in Him

2. To encourage the study and use of the Bible

3. To carry on programs for and with the churches by which the life of the Church may be renewed and the mission of the Church may be fulfilled

4. To foster and encourage cooperation, fellowship, and mutual counsel among the churches for the purposes set forth in this Constitution

5. To assist the churches in self-examination of their life and witness in accordance with their understanding of the will of God and of the Lordship of Jesus Christ as Divine Head of the Church

6. To further works of Christian love and service throughout the nation and the world

7. To study and to speak and act on conditions and issues in the nation and the world which involve moral, ethical, and spiritual principles inherent in the Christian Gospel

8. To encourage cooperation among local churches and to further the development of councils and other organizations in agreement with the Preamble of this Constitution, and to maintain cooperative relationships with such bodies

9. To establish and maintain consultative and cooperative relationships with the World Council of Churches; other international, regional, and national ecumenical organizations; and agencies related to the churches in the United States

10. To establish specific objectives and to carry forward programs and activities for achieving the purposes herein stated

One passage in the certificate of incorporation reveals the Council's concern not to infringe on the freedom of its constituency. "It shall have no authority or administrative control," the document reads, "over the communions or churches which become its members or its affiliated or co-operating bodies. It shall have no authority to prescribe a common creed, or form of church government, or form of worship, or to limit the autonomy of such communions or churches."

At the beginning of the 21st century, the NCCC-USA comprises 36 member churches from the Protestant, Anglican, and Orthodox traditions:

African Methodist Episcopal Church
African Methodist Episcopal Zion Church
Alliance of Baptists
American Baptist Churches in the USA
The Antiochian Orthodox Christian Archdiocese of North America
Diocese of the Armenian Church of America
Christian Church (Disciples of Christ)
Christian Methodist Episcopal Church
Church of the Brethren
The Coptic Orthodox Church in North America
The Episcopal Church
Evangelical Lutheran Church in America
Friends United Meeting
Greek Orthodox Archdiocese of America
Hungarian Reformed Church in America
International Council of Community Churches
Korean Presbyterian Church in America
Malankara Orthodox Syrian Church
Mar Thoma Church
Moravian Church in America Northern Province and Southern Province
National Baptist Convention of America
National Baptist Convention, U.S.A., Inc.
National Missionary Baptist Convention of America

Orthodox Church in America
Patriarchal Parishes of the Russian Orthodox Church in the USA
Philadelphia Yearly Meeting of the Religious Society of Friends
Polish National Catholic Church of America
Presbyterian Church (U.S.A.)
Progressive National Baptist Convention, Inc.
Reformed Church in America
Serbian Orthodox Church in the U.S.A. and Canada
The Swedenborgian Church
Syrian Orthodox Church of Antioch
Ukrainian Orthodox Church of America
United Church of Christ
The United Methodist Church

The NCCC-USA is actively involved in the scholarly research of the Bible. It sponsored the Revised Standard Version and its successor, the New Revised Standard Version of the Bible. Through the Church World Service (CWS), it carries out relief work in more than 80 countries. Its Washington, D.C. office deals with public policy issues, testifying on the moral, ethical, and other theological implications of proposed legislative enactments and other policy decisions. The NCCC-USA is also actively involved in many ecumenical and interreligious organizations at the local, national and international levels.

Since Vatican Council II there has been a steadily increasing cooperation between the NCCC-USA and the Roman Catholic Church. A Joint Working Committee, made up of designated representatives of the NCCC-USA and the National Conference of Catholic Bishops, meets at regular intervals for exchange of information as to plans and projects and for the furthering of mutual understanding. There are Roman Catholic participants in several of the Council's program units, including full membership in the Commission on Faith and Order.

Bibliography: Triennial Reports, National Council of the Churches of Christ in the U.S.A. (New York 1966–1969, 1969–1972). S. MCC. CAVERT, *Church Cooperation and Unity in America: A Historical Review, 1900–1970* (New York 1970). "Report on Possible Roman Catholic Membership in the National Council of Churches" (U.S. Catholic Conference 1972).

[J. A. HARDON/S. MCC. CAVERT/D. J. BOWMAN/EDS.]

NATIONAL ORGANIZATION FOR CONTINUING EDUCATION OF ROMAN CATHOLIC CLERGY (NOCERCC)

A network of diocesan and religious directors of presbyteral continuing education/formation that attempts to educate and motivate clergy for more effective ministry in the Church. It frequently serves as a consultant to the Committee on Priestly Life and Ministry of the U.S. Conference of Catholic Bishops. In 2001, there were 257 dioceses, one Ukrainian diocese, and 62 religious congregations and provinces as full members. Full membership is limited to dioceses and religious provinces; affiliate membership comprises universities and agencies offering resources in continuing education.

NOCERCC was founded in 1973 at a meeting of directors of continuing education of priests convened by the National Federation of Priests' Councils. During this meeting at the university of Notre Dame, a Board of Directors was named with representation from each of the twelve (now thirteen) episcopal regions, and the first president was elected. The first representative for men religious was elected to the Board in 1974. There are now two places on the board for representatives from religious congregations. An advisory council is comprised of lay people and clergy. In October 1979, NOCERCC established its national office in Chicago where it remains to this day.

NOCERCC promotes continuing education of priests through current research, resources, and training for continuing education directors of dioceses and religious communities and to committees of the USCCB; encourages supradiocesan and regional cooperation of directors of continuing education; acts as liaison with ecumenical groups; and sponsors an annual convention. NOCERCC has funded research projects and developed programs in: priestly spirituality, preaching, policies on alcoholism, social justice, management and leadership styles, shared ministry, sexuality, seminary training, and models of parish planning. NOCERCC works closely with the Catholic Coalition on Preaching. It also publishes a bimonthly newsletter, *News Notes*.

Bibliography: E. E. LARKIN, and G. T. BROCCOLO, eds., *Spiritual Renewal of the American Priesthood* (Washington, DC 1972). D. HOGE, ''Expressed Needs and Attitudes of Newly Ordained Priests'' (Chicago 1999). NOCERCC, *Handbook for the Continuing Formation of Priests* (Chicago n.d.); Convention *Proceedings* (1991–1994, 1997). J. M. WHITE, *A Work Never Finished: The First Twenty-Five Years of the National Organization for Continuing Education of Roman Catholic Clergy (NOCERCC), 1973–1998* (Chicago 1998). United States Conference of Catholic Bishops, *The Basic Plan for the Ongoing Formation of Priests* (Washington, DC 2001); National Conference of Catholic Bishops, *Program for Priestly Formation* (Washington, DC 1992).

[J. B. DUNNING/P. J. HAYES]

National Shrine of the Immaculate Conception Church in 1959. (©Bettmann/CORBIS)

NATIONAL SHRINE OF THE IMMACULATE CONCEPTION

The Basilica of the National Shrine of the Immaculate Conception is the largest Catholic church in the United States and among the largest churches in the world. Located in Washington, D.C., adjacent to the campus of The CATHOLIC UNIVERSITY OF AMERICA, it honors the Blessed Virgin Mary who, under the title of the Immaculate Conception, was named patroness of the United States by the bishops at the Sixth Provincial Council of Baltimore (1846). Pope John Paul II bestowed on it the honorific distinction of minor basilica.

Bishop Thomas SHAHAN, fourth rector of The Catholic University, conceived the idea of a national shrine, and in 1914 with the approval of Pope Pius X work went forward. The architects under the direction of Charles Maginnis (1867–1955) sought to create a structure that was distinctively American. They settled on a design that was contemporary and original but in the spirit of Byzantine and Romanesque architecture. Eugene F. Kennedy Jr. designed the superstructure.

James Cardinal Gibbons laid the cornerstone on Sept. 23, 1920, and by 1931 the crypt church and some of the crypt areas had been completed. After a period of inactivity, building was resumed at the urging of the newly appointed archbishop of Washington, Patrick O'Boyle, and Bishop John Noll of Fort Wayne. In the years 1954 to 1959 the exterior of the upper church was built, and 10 of the 11 planned chapels added. It was dedicated by Francis Cardinal Spellman of New York, Nov. 20, 1959, while work on the interior continued.

The edifice is in the form of a Latin cross, 459 feet long, 240 feet wide at the transepts. The height is 120 feet to the peak of the roof, 237 feet to the top of the dome, and 329 feet to the top of the bell tower. The seating capacity is 3,500; total capacity is 6,000. It was built without structural steel, entirely of masonry. The Knights Tower (bell tower) adds a strong vertical accent to the overall composition of the shrine. On the tiled dome, huge gold symbols of Our Lady appear against a blue background. The sculpture of the east wall of the exterior illustrates the theme of faith; that of the west wall, charity. The north wall features contemplatives, and the art of the facade centers around Christ and Our Lady. Notable among the 137 separate pieces of sculpture on the exterior are two figures by Ivan Městrović.

The interior walls of the main (upper) church are covered with Botticino and Travertine marble decorated with bas-reliefs. The entire south wall above the entrance is covered by a large mosaic depicting the "Universal Call to Holiness." On each side of the upper church there is a long row of high Roman arches leading to the sanctuary. A 3,500 square-foot mosaic of Christ in Majesty by John de Rosen adorns the north apse (interior of the cupola/dome), and two smaller domes above the sanctuary have mosaics depicting the Lamb of God and the descent of the Holy Spirit. The flanking east and west apses have images honoring Mary and Joseph, and below are altars dedicated to the 15 mysteries of the rosary decorated with marble and brilliant mosaics. The 176 stained-glass windows include three rosette windows.

The crypt church is a low, vaulted room with massive arches focusing attention upon the main altar, an isolated block of golden Algerian onyx. The crypt's marbles, golden mosaics, and ceramic tiles, rich in doctrinal and historical meaning, emphasize Marian themes. More than 30 devotional and liturgical areas as well as a gift shop, bookstore, and cafeteria are located on the crypt level. The National Shrine is under the direction of a Board of Trustees appointed by the National Conference of Catholic Bishops.

Bibliography: F. R. DIFREDERICO, *The Mosaics of the National Shrine of the Immaculate Conception* (Washington, D.C. 1980). W. P. KENNEDY, *The National Shrine of the Immaculate Conception* (Washington 1922). B. A. MCKENNA, *Memoirs of the First Director* (Washington 1959). T. J. GRADY, *American Ecclesiastical Review* 136 (1957):145–154; 137 (1957): 400–409; 141 (1959): 217–231.

[T. J. GRADY/P. SONSKI]

NATIVISM, AMERICAN

Described by its historian (J. Higham, 4) as "intense opposition to an internal minority on the ground of its foreign (i.e. "un-American") connections." Major nativistic traditions in the United States include anti-Catholicism, antiradicalism, and the cult of Anglo-Saxon superiority; its major historical contribution has been the restriction of immigration.

Historical Beginnings. The ideological elements in U.S. nativism, which account in part for its anti-Catholic tradition, include the Protestant origins of 12 of the colonies; Protestant hostility to early Catholic rulers in Maryland; and the secularist ideology animating revolutionary leaders, most of whom regarded Catholicism as outmoded European obscurantism. Antiradicalism was stimulated by conservative horror at European upheavals, especially the French Revolutions of 1789 and 1870 and the Russian Revolution of 1917, and the resultant desire to preserve the United States from similar disturbances. Belief in Anglo-Saxon superiority was heightened by fear of loss of power through the growth of immigrant political strength.

The economic and social aspects of nativism include ethnic rivalries; resentment of immigrant competition for labor rewards; anxiety of older immigrants to increase their standing as Americans by discrimination against newer groups; business fear of unionization, countered by business benefits from immigrant labor; and political expediency, directly through exploitation of popular causes or through readiness to employ any weapon for the destruction of dangerous antagonists, and indirectly, by fabricating nativist issues to divert attention from real and disruptive questions (as the Know-Nothing uproar was used to distract the public from the slavery controversy; *see* KNOW-NOTHINGISM).

Sectionally, nativism assumed different forms. Easterners in a comparatively rigid social structure both opposed the rise of alien elements and feared immigrant conquest of the cities. The prewar South feared European subversion of American institutions, notably slavery, by English abolitionists and by Catholics who might be expected to obey the renewed papal condemnation of slavery by Gregory XVI. J. L. Chapman's *Americanism versus Romanism* (1856) is typical of the latter nativist school. The immigrant was welcomed in the West and post–Civil War South, particularly where communities were rapidly expanding or not fully formed, but as the frontier situation disappeared, competition bred hostility. Frustrated agrarian crusaders tended to seek a simple cause for their failure and found in Catholic, Jew, or immigrant a convenient scapegoat as their fears focused on an alien, depraved Europe and the seemingly foreign-dominated East [see, e.g., C. Vann Woodward, *Tom Watson* (1938)]. Orientals offering cheap labor inspired Pacific coast nativist riots, leading to a 10-year Chinese exclusion act (1882, reenacted 1894, made permanent 1904), the effective commencement of immigration exclusion.

Major Periods of Prevalence. Increasing tensions with revolutionary France, including the expectation of war, led to the imposition of security measures by the Alien and Sedition Acts of 1798. These included the Naturalization Act, extending the prenaturalization period from five to 14 years (the old system was restored in 1802); the Alien Act, authorizing the president to expel aliens merely on suspicion of treasonable inclinations or belief in their being a threat to the public safety (this expired in 1802); and the Alien Enemies Act, empowering the president in wartime to imprison or deport enemy subjects. Aimed at Pres. John Adams's Francophile Jeffersonian critics, many of whom were of alien origin, the acts endangered Irish exiles in particular, since their forcible return to British dominions could result in their destruction for United Irishmen affiliations. Although the main struggle and prosecutions took place under the Sedition Act, the Federalist regime remained strongly hostile to Irish radicals, and its minister to London, Rufus King, sought to prevent their coming to the United States. The identification of John Adams with restrictionist measures was the more tragic in view of his previous history of friendship for Irish patriotic aspirations (see his *Novanglus*), but the violent, incendiary tones of the journalists of the day, coupled with his fear of a Paris-style uprising, led him to become one of the champions of alien repression.

1830 to 1860. The swift economic and territorial expansion of the United States brought with it a certain rootlessness and the craving for simple moral solutions. The intellectual simplicity of the religious revivalism that swayed Jacksonian America made for a firmness of moral standard, but it also carried the seeds of intolerance toward faiths alien to itself. The same spirit looked for clear-cut issues in the problems of the day and led to a rapid growth of American conspiracy consciousness that continued for more than a century. The secrecy of Masonic proceedings and of the Catholic confessional became prime targets for the conspiracy seeker, and the anti-Catholicism of the revivalist preachers exacerbated the tendency to see in the Church an anti-American men-

First page of "Protestant Vindicator," Aug. 28, 1834.

ace. Thus the mob burning of the Ursuline Convent at Charlestown, Mass., on Aug. 11, 1834, was the sequel to three violently anti-Catholic sermons delivered in Boston the previous day by the Presbyterian clergyman Lyman BEECHER.

Anti-Masonry first emerged following the unaccountable disappearance of William Morgan (September 1826), a renegade Mason who proposed to publish the secrets of the order. Anti-Masonry forces organized a political party in New York State (1830) and contested the next presidential election under the banner of William Wirt, who carried only Vermont. Ambitious politicians (W. H. Seward, Thurlow Weed, Thaddeus Stevens) used the party in their own interest and abruptly deserted it when voters lost interest in the issue. After 1836 the party disappeared. The European origins of Masonry were among the aspects of the order under attack, but it was chiefly its role as precursor of nativistic parties that won anti-Masonry its significance in U.S. history.

Even movements of purely American origin, such as Mormonism, suffered persecution at the hands of their neighbors for divergence from the American religious norm and for economic discrimination against "Gentiles" during these years, but the most bitter hostility was reserved for Catholicism. The 1830s saw the emergence of a stream of anti-Catholic propaganda in magazines, newspapers, pamphlets, and books. These included pleas for curbing Catholic immigration, opposition to Catholic schools and officeholders [e.g., "Brutus" (Samuel F. B. Morse), "Foreign Conspiracy against the Liberties of the United States" (1834)], and organs avowedly seeking the conversion of Catholics, of which the *American Protestant Vindicator* (1834–42), edited by Rev. W. C. Brownlee proclaimed itself the champion. Brownlee and his followers maintained they could save the "wretchedly deluded votaries" of Catholicism only by a zealous exposure of the alleged iniquities of that religion. Such exposés wasted little space on purely doctrinal controversy, but were devoted to revelations of plots hatched in Austria and elsewhere for the enslavement or mass murder of American Protestants by immigrant Catholic hordes, agitation against Catholic schools then becoming popular among many non-Catholics, and allegations respecting the sexual morals of nuns and clerics.

Some anti-Catholic crusaders sought to the best of their ability to keep such charges as they made within the realm of the verifiable, but in popularity and number they were far outstripped by the myth-makers. A craving for pornography without attendant guilt feelings was satisfied by a perusal of many anti-Catholic tracts that in their efforts to attract an audience were an easy prey to the temptation for bawdy improvisation on the themes of convent and confessional, as exploited by priests for purposes of sexual outlet. The most celebrated of these publications, the *Awful Disclosures of the Hotel Dieu Nunnery of Montreal* (1836) and its sequel, both allegedly the work of an ex-inmate, Maria Monk, branded the institution in question as a nest of debauchery, infanticide, murder, and rape, all described in detail and profusely illustrated. Actually, Maria Monk was an impostor of apparently deranged mind, whose persuasively written work was probably the offspring of overzealous Protestant ministers into whose hands she fell. Her charges were extensively examined and refuted by public-spirited Protestant writers, notably Col. William L. Stone, no friend to Catholicism. But the book, even after the lapse of Maria Monk into drunkenness, prostitution, and theft (she died in prison in 1849), was reprinted many times for dissemination in anti-Catholic crusades.

Clashes between Protestant and Catholic mobs fanned the flames, as did the American renewal of Orange-Catholic hostility originating in Ireland. Catholic protests against reading the King James Bible in public school, and demands for public aid to parochial schools also added fuel to the controversy. Chief areas of anti-Catholic sentiment in this phase were New York City and Philadelphia, Pa., where in the summer of 1844, 20 died and 100 were injured in Orange-Catholic riots. The Irish Great Famine (1845–52) sent 1,250,000 starving Irish immigrants to the United States between 1845 and 1855. Since their destitution prevented migration to the West, they choked the Eastern cities, radically and suddenly altering them. Native American opinion, while philanthropically disposed to assist the impoverished in Ireland, was dismayed at the hitherto unparalleled experience of a pauper immigration on such a scale, and as the political bosses sought to make capital from the new arrivals, anger mounted. The Native American party (founded 1845) and its successor (the Know-Nothing, or American, party of the 1850s) called for drastic changes in naturalization laws. Know-Nothingism reached its greatest strength in 1855, but it split on the slavery issue, with the Southern forces left in control. Former President Millard Fillmore, the party candidate in 1856, carried Maryland alone, after which the party declined. The Civil War, in which many immigrants distinguished themselves, destroyed nativism for a time; war hysteria was turned against "Copperheads."

The nativistic character of Know-Nothingism was revealingly illustrated by the fact that the Know-Nothings specifically exempted Louisiana Catholic Creoles (some of whom joined the party) from charges of participation in the Catholic conspiracy against the United States. Because the Creoles, unlike Maryland Catholics, had maintained a separate identity in the face of Catholic immigration, their "American-ness"—of which, on the slavery issue, they gave proof—was therefore unquestioned. On the other hand, descendants of English or Irish colonial settlers attracted suspicion because they permitted themselves to be the summit of a Catholic social ladder of which the pauper Irish immigrants were the base.

1886 to 1896. Increased immigration, intensification of the labor-capital struggle, and concern over the strength of Catholic political bosses contributed to a renewal of nativism in the late 1880s. Antiradicalism and anti-Catholicism joined in protest against Cardinal James Gibbons's championship of the KNIGHTS OF LABOR, which, led by the Catholic Terence V. Powderly, reached its zenith in membership in 1886. The Haymarket bomb-throwing in Chicago, Ill. (May 1, 1886), unleashed a tide of antilabor sentiment not restricted to the anarchists associated with the incident. Foreign-born leadership in labor and socialist and anarchist movements became the focus of protest, while the AMERICAN PROTECTIVE ASSOCIATION (APA) revived the anti-Catholic issue, utilizing the old methods of propaganda and issues of attack as well as enmity to the Knights of Labor. The APA declined after 1896. Meanwhile, labor unions themselves were swinging toward immigration restriction in their opposition to the challenge of foreign labor. In 1897 the

American Federation of Labor (AFL) officially endorsed the demand for a literacy test, thereby joining hands with Boston intellectuals banded together in the Immigration Restriction League, whose most vociferous spokesperson in Congress was Sen. Henry Cabot Lodge. Pres. Grover Cleveland's veto of a bill embodying the literacy provision (February 1897) frustrated their efforts, and nativism suffered a setback following the return of prosperity and the redirectioning of nationalism by the Spanish-American War and its attendant climate of expansionism.

1905 to 1930. Nativism in the late 19th and early 20th century was marked by a more sophisticated intellectual racism than the earlier crude glorification of the Anglo-Saxon. Social Darwinism was adapted to assign to the immigrant the role of unfittest in his native country; eugenics was employed to assail "degenerate breeding-stocks"; and anthropology, classifying the races under Nordic (fair longhead), Alpine (roundhead), etc., rather than national categories, was pressed into service as part of the nativist's intellectual equipment. Glorification of the Nordic race and lamentation for the corruption introduced by immigrants of "inferior" racial origin were the themes of Madison Grant's *The Passing of the Great Race* (1916) that, largely ignored at first publication, became widely influential after the war. Such ideas, filtered through to the political world, led to a new departure in nativist attitudes as they were renewed; henceforth hostility was turned chiefly against the Mediterranean peoples, who had been immigrating in substantially increasing numbers in recent years. Ironically, those most bitterly assailed as factors liable to cause degeneration of the American people included Southeast European Jews, Southern Italians, and Greeks, whose ancestors had laid the foundations of western Judeo-Christian civilization.

Anti-Catholicism was kept alive, notably in the South, by such journals as *Tom Watson's Magazine* and the *Menace* (whose circulation reached a peak of 1,500,000 in 1915). Aggressive nationalism mounted during the war years against the hitherto largely unassailed German-Americans, and later against pacifists, socialists, anarchists, and radicals of all kinds. In the high tide of retreat from internationalism after the war, the great red scare of 1919 [see Robert K. Murray, *Red Scare* (1955)] included both a widespread deportation of Soviet sympathizers by Attorney General A. Mitchell Palmer and violent physical assaults on left-wing groups, notably the Industrial Workers of the World (IWW), by such nativist elements as the American Legion. In 1920, writes Higham (p. 263), "while the redemption of the alien ebbed . . . , the old drive for the rejection of the immigrant passed all previous bounds."

Anti-Semitism, supplanting anti-Catholicism in the nativist response to the radical challenge, found expression in the widely disseminated and fraudulent "Protocols of the Elders of Zion," which laid the Bolshevist successes in Russia at the door of the Jews. The *Dearborn Independent* (1919–27) was perhaps the spearhead of the anti-Jewish attack. The revived KU KLUX KLAN, however, was undiscriminating in its nativism; African Americans, Jews, Catholics, and the foreign-born of all kinds came literally under its lash. The new motion picture industry gave assistance to the Klan by a production glorifying its predecessor of Reconstruction days based on Thomas Dixon's *The Clansman* (1905) and entitled *Birth of a Nation* (released 1915). The anti-Catholic aspect of the Klan first came to prominence in 1920 and flourished thereafter. Its power flowed far beyond the South to the Middle West and Far West, and membership at its apogee reached five million (Indiana and Oregon being areas of outstanding strength). Scandals tore it asunder after 1925; in its heyday the outrages charged against it, including murder, had come to an impressive figure.

This national fever of xenophobia received congressional acknowledgment in the revival of immigration restriction. The AFL, its nativism aggravated by reaction to the IWW challenge, continued to agitate in this cause. Congressmen who enjoyed labor support tried to catch the immigrant vote as well, but rural nativist forces, led by the anti-IWW, anti-Japanese Congressman Albert Johnson of Washington, demanded suspension of immigration. A compromise measure, restricting immigrants to three percent of each nationality in the population according to the 1910 census, became law (May 19, 1921). Thus was born the quota system, a feature of all subsequent restrictionist legislation. The literacy test had been embodied in legislation passed over Pres. Woodrow Wilson's veto in 1917.

The quota was altered to two percent of the 1890 census for each nationality group, and the maximum quota halved from 357,000 (1924); the maximum quota was further reduced to 150,000 a year with apportionment by nationality on the basis of the national population situation in 1920 (a provision of the 1924 law, but not actually effected until 1929). Satiated by this revolutionary alteration in U.S. immigration policy, nativism (or 100 percent Americanism, as it called itself) waned in this postwar phase. The nomination of Gov. Alfred E. Smith of New York by the Democrats for the 1928 presidential election rekindled some of the flames, but without significant effect; the administration candidate, Herbert Hoover, was invincible regardless of his opponent. Smith's nomination was in itself testimony to nativism's losses.

After 1930. Sporadic outbreaks of nativism accompanied the Depression years, notably as an American accompaniment to the rise of European Fascism. The anti-Semitic campaigns of Rev. Charles E. COUGHLIN, whose radio addresses led his superiors to silence him, had their Protestant equivalent in the diatribes of Rev. Gerald L. K. Smith, former follower of Louisiana demagogue Huey Long. An undercurrent of racism was kept alive by the agitators in the South, notably Sen. Theodore G. Bilbo of Mississippi. Publisher William Randolph Hearst, Elizabeth Dilling, and others sought to foment a second red scare in 1934–35, and the sensitive area of education once more became the focus of witch-hunts against alleged seduction of the innocent [see Walter Metzger, *Academic Freedom in the Age of the University* (1955)]. Meanwhile, the American Civil Liberties Union recorded the greatest "variety and number of serious violations of civil liberties" since the war. Seven state legislatures enacted teachers' oath statutes, but this was a measure of the failure to fulfill nativist promise, as far more had been debated. The crusade, fascist in character, identifying mild liberals with Communists, proved immediately ugly but ultimately it was somewhat harmless.

World War II destroyed anti-Semitism as a political force in American life, but brought with it much injustice to Japanese Americans, interned for the duration. In a Supreme Court decision [*Korematsu v. U.S.* (1944)] Japanese exclusion from the West Coast was upheld. The burden of proof of loyalty was thrust upon the unfortunate Japanese Americans, although the court, in *Ex parte Endo* (1944), denied that a person of proved loyalty could be detained. Many innocent Americans of Japanese extraction suffered socially, as well as from the danger of internment. The House Committee on Un-American Activities, an instrument of nativism by definition, was given permanent status in 1945.

With the advent of the Cold War, nativism obtained a fresh lease on life. The Communist ideology of America's chief antagonist, the U.S.S.R., offered easy rewards to the superpatriot who chose to confine himself to fighting the Cold War at home. The third red scare shook America to its foundations and culminated in the McCarthy hearings. Sen. Joseph McCarthy of Wisconsin attracted perhaps the greatest body of support and opprobrium for his exploitation of the disloyalty issue; the better entrenched Sen. Patrick McCarran of Nevada employed the scare for the preparation of nativist legislation that would outlast it. The Internal Security (McCarran) Act of 1951 forced Communists and Communist-front bodies to register as agents of a foreign power, dedicated to overthrow the U.S. government by violence, thus rendering them liable to imprisonment under the Alien Registration (Smith) Act of 1940. The Smith and McCarran Acts tightened control on aliens, the latter measure excluding from the United States any member or foreign member of a totalitarian organization (in practice this has not been employed against Fascists). The McCarran-Walter Act (1952) codified existing immigration laws, increasing their rigidity; screening measures were introduced to weed out subversives. Both McCarran bills became law over presidential veto.

The destruction of many innocent reputations through congressional investigation and the demoralization of the diplomatic and military arms of government through the same process ultimately brought about McCarthy's overthrow (1954). The ensuing revulsion and McCarran's death (1953) ended the most violent phase of latter-day nativism. Many political and social legacies remained, however, and small Fascist organizations (e.g., the John Birch Society) continued to manifest extreme nativism. Anti-Catholic propaganda declined during the Cold War, except among a small, though much publicized, minority. The most celebrated of these was Paul Blanshard, who sought to identify the Kremlin with the Vatican in the public mind. Blanshard's liberal origins, combined with the antilibertarian aspects of Catholicism cited by him, placed an attractive gloss on what was merely a reassertion of the old charge that Catholicism was un-American; his works fostered a suspicion of Catholics among liberals of shallow mind. Blanshard avoided the usual charges of clerical immorality and Catholic conspiracy for the mass murder of Protestants; this concession to modern standards of objectivity was not imitated by the anti-Catholicism evoked by the Democratic nomination for the presidency of another Catholic, John F. Kennedy. Although nativism may have accounted for some votes against Kennedy, his election and subsequent assassination probably destroyed anti-Catholicism as a force in American life. By the national character of his appeal, in life and after death, Kennedy offered proof of what nativists had so long denied, namely, that a descendant of pauper, "undesirable" immigrants could prove himself a representative and patriotic American.

Effects on the United States. The nativism written on the statute books since 1921 did much to isolate the United States from currents of world opinion and the realities of foreign situations, a particularly perilous contribution in terms of the country's international responsibilities. It constituted a denial of the freedom and receptivity of American society, two traits whereby the United States came to enjoy her role as a leader in the spread of democracy and liberty. It fostered a negative nationalism, founded on hatred, that continued to corrode a true patriotism; it became an ally of the cause of discrimination against, and segregation of, African American citizens. By making conformity a virtue, nativism immeasurably eroded the force of one of the traditions that had built America—a constant readiness to respond to the challenge of the unknown.

Effects on Catholicism in the United States. Although few Catholics were driven from their faith by nativist outbreaks, a heavily nativist climate probably had more corrosive effects, notably in the South and parts of the West where Catholics lacked numbers to give one another moral reassurance. The Catholic response to nativist attack at times lacked wisdom, but seldom courage. It also had less pleasant features. Thus Catholics failed to unite with other minority groups under attack, e.g., African Americans and Jews, but rather tended, especially in the 20th century, to welcome the turning aside of nativist wrath in other directions. Intergroup hostility among immigrants themselves abetted this tendency. Ultimately, it is to be feared that nativism fostered in American Catholicism an intense zeal to cleanse itself of the un-American stigma at all costs. During the slavery crisis, Catholics, regardless of Gregory XVI's teachings, temporized on the slavery issue and strongly denounced the un-Americanism of the abolitionists. A century later, Catholics had so readily identified themselves with the prevailing impulse to conform to the American attitude, that, for instance, "the American Church," in Richard Hofstadter's phrase, "absorbed little of the impressive scholarship of German Catholicism or the questioning intellectualism of the French Church" [*Anti-Intellectualism in American Life* (1963), 138]. Moreover, the Protestant nativist, who clamored for further restriction of immigration and saw in every liberal academic a Communist incendiary, found allies among the Catholics, who had formerly been targets for his most bitter bigotry. The tragedy lies in the fact that nativism, taken at its word, was confounded with truly American patriotism even by its former victims.

Bibliography: R. A. BILLINGTON, *The Protestant Crusade, 1800–1860* (New York 1938). C. J. BARRY et al., "Symposium on Nativism" in *American Catholic Historical Review* 44 (Washington 1958) 137–164. O. HANDLIN, *Race and Nationality in American Life* (Boston 1957). M. A. JONES, *American Immigration* (Chicago 1960). M. L. HANSEN, *The Immigrant in American History* (Cambridge, Mass. 1940). M. A. RAY, *American Opinion of Roman Catholicism in the 18th Century* (New York 1936). J. HIGHAM, *Strangers in the Land: Patterns of American Nativism, 1860–1925* (New Brunswick, N.J. 1955).

[O. D. EDWARDS]

NATIVITY OF CHRIST

The date of the birth of JESUS CHRIST can be calculated only approximately; the most probable date seems to be about the year 7 or 6 B.C. It is well known that the calculations of DIONYSIUS EXIGUUS upon which the system of determining the year of Christ's birth is based are in error. Matthew 2.1 says that the birth of Christ took place in the days of King HEROD (THE GREAT). It is known from JOSEPHUS that Herod died in the spring of the year 4 B.C. In the 15th year of Tiberius, Jesus was about 30 years old (Lk 3.23); this would be the year A.D. 28–29.

One may date Christ's birth more precisely from the information given by Lk 2.2, that the birth took place at the time of the census under Cyrinus. Cyrinus was Publius Sulpicius Quirinius, who was governor of the province of Syria. During his administration a census took place in Judea previous to the incorporation of that kingdom into the province of Syria upon the deposition of Archelaus in A.D. 6. This census took place while Caesar Augustus was ruling the Roman Empire (30 B.C.–A.D. 14). The relationship of the census under Quirinius to the imperial census is a matter of perplexity for historians. Perhaps Quirinius inaugurated the census under a special commission in 6 or 7 B.C. after his first term as governor and completed it by a better known census during his second term, A.D. 6 to 12. No further precision of the date can be made, since the date of December 25 does not correspond to Christ's birth, but to the feast of the *Natalis Solis Invicti,* the Roman sun festival at the solstice.

According to Matthew and Luke, Jesus Christ was born in Bethlehem, a village in Judea about six miles south of Jerusalem, slightly to the west. The place is mentioned in the Gospel account to show Christ's Davidic ancestry, since Bethlehem is the city of David. The fact of the birth at Bethlehem is not stated anywhere else in the New Testament; the account in Jn 7.40–42 implies the ignorance of the people regarding the birth of Christ in Bethlehem. There was no apologetic reason for the Gospel writers to invent the Bethlehem birthplace merely to confirm Christ's Davidic origin, since the popular belief at the time did not suppose that the Messiah would come from Bethlehem. There is no written evidence in Jewish tradition for the Bethlehem birthplace of the Messiah before the third century A.D. The popular thought in Our Lord's time was that the birthplace of the Messiah was unknown, and that when He came, He would present Himself in such a way that no one would know where He came from. Since it would have served no useful purpose for the early Christians to invent Christ's birth in Bethlehem, one must conclude that He was actually born there. Mi 5.1 is obscure.

Bibliography: J. BLINZLER, *Lexikon für Theologie und Kirche,* ed. J. HOFER and K. RAHNER (Freiberg 1957–65) 2:422–425. A. BEA and U. HOLZMEISTER, *Chronologia vitae Christi* (Rome 1933). H. U. INSTINSKY, *Das Jahr der Geburt Christi* (Munich 1957). B. BOTTE, *Les Origines de la Noël et de l'Épiphanie* (Louvain 1932).

[R. L. FOLEY]

"The Nativity of Jesus Christ," 15th-century fresco painting, Italian nativity by Fra Angelico, cell number five in the convent of San Marco, Florence, Italy, c. 1436–1445. (©Massimo Listri/CORBIS)

Scenes from the early life of Christ and the Madonna, 13th century. (©Archivo Iconografico, S.A./CORBIS)

NATIVITY OF MARY

Sacred Scripture mentions nothing specifically about Mary's conception and birth. What is known of her nativity derives principally from the Apocrypha—books that are generally unreliable historically, but that sometimes incorporate genuine traditions, some of which have found their way into the Church's liturgy.

In the Apocrypha. The oldest (*c.* A.D. 150) and basic Apocryphon referring to Mary's nativity is entitled Birth of Mary: Revelation of James [Papyrus Bodmer V] or, more popularly (since Postel, 1552), Protoevangelium of James. Its anonymous and probably Judeo-Christian author, indignant at anti-Marian calumnies of the time, glorified the Virgin MOTHER OF GOD in what amounts to a primitive Mariology. The opening five chapters of the work describe the miraculous, though not necessarily ''immaculate,'' conception and birth of Mary. Joachim and Anne, a wealthy couple elderly and childless, beseech God to remove the humiliation of sterility and grant them a child. Each is assured separately by an angel that their prayers had been heard, and Mary is born after seven [nine] months. Some versions and recensions of the Protoevangelium, understanding the angel's assurance to Joachim in a past tense, suggest a virginal conception in

Anne's womb. Later pertinent Apocrypha (Gospel of Pseudo-Matthew, probably 8th-9th centuries; Gospel of the Birth of Mary, a shortened form of Pseudo-Matthew; a Syriac-Armenian Infancy Gospel; and some Coptic Lives of the Virgin) all rest on and repeat evidence of the Protoevangelium.

Mary's Birthplace and Davidic Descent. According to Lk 1.26 Mary was living at NAZARETH when she conceived her divine Son. In the absence of further scriptural data, some presume that Nazareth would have been her own birthplace. In much later Apocrypha (e.g., Gospel of the Birth of Mary), Nazareth is given as the home of Joachim and Anne. The Protoevangelium of James supposes that Mary was conceived and born in Jerusalem, a tradition supported by later writers and by remnants of a small oratory (*c.* A.D. 300) in Jerusalem, above which the fifth-century basilica of St. Anne was built.

It is still disputed whether Mary, like Joseph, was of David's line. Some see the genealogies in Matthew ch. 1 and Luke ch. 3 as referring only to Joseph's forebears, not Mary's. They point out that Elizabeth, Mary's relative, was of Aaronitic descent (Lk 1.5), which might indicate that Mary too was of a priestly family. However, a tradition going as far back as Ignatius of Antioch (*Eph.*

18.2; 20.2; *Rom.* 7.3; *Smyrn.* 1.1) and Justin Martyr (1 *Apol.* 32; *Dial.* 43.45, 100, 120), based on New Testament texts that seem to refer to Christ's descent from David according to the flesh [Lk 1. (27), 32, 69; Rom 1.3], testify to Mary's Davidic lineage; cf. also Tertullian *De carne Christi* 22; Augustine *Cons. Evang.* 2.2.4; Pseudo-James; and Pseudo-Matthew. More probably, then, Mary's parents were descendants of David, and Mary's Son was the Son of David according to the flesh, not merely legally through the putative fatherhood of Joseph.

See Also: ANNE AND JOACHIM, SS.; IMMACULATE CONCEPTION; MARY, BLESSED VIRGIN, ARTICLES ON.

Bibliography: M. LINDGREN-TRIDELL, "Der Stammbaum Maria aus Anna und Joachim," *Marburger Jahrbuch für Kunstwissenschaft* 11–12 (1938–39) 289–308. A. MERK, "Das Marienbild des Neuen Bundes," in *Katholische Marienkunde,* ed. P. STRÄTER, 3 v. (Paderborn 1947–51) 1:44–84. O. CULLMANN, "Infancy Gospels," in *New Testament Apocrypha,* ed. E. HENNECKE et al. (Philadelphia 1963–) 1:363–. A. RUSH, "Mary in the Apocrypha of the N.T.," J. B. CAROL ed., *Mariology* 3 v. (Milwaukee 1954–61) 1:156–184. *Dictionnaire de la Bible,* suppl. ed. L. PIROT, et al. (Paris 1928–) 4:780–781.

[E. MAY]

NATURAL FAMILY PLANNING

Natural family planning (NFP) is a generalized term that refers to methods of self-monitoring natural biological signs and symptoms of fertility. The purpose of NFP is to identify the days of fertility and infertility during a woman's menstrual cycle. Knowing this information enables a couple to either avoid or achieve a pregnancy. Inherent in the use of NFP is that couples abstain from intercourse during the times of fertility if they wish to avoid pregnancy. Natural family planning has also been referred to as "periodic abstinence," "rhythm," and "fertility awareness."

History. Although many previous scientific studies contributed to the development of natural methods of family planing, it was not until the late 1920s that two physician scientists discovered a key ingredient that led to the formulation of the first reliable method of natural birth regulation. Experiments by Dr. Kyusako Ogino from Japan and Dr. Herman Knaus from Germany provided them with information to estimate the approximate time of ovulation in a woman's menstrual cycle and to determine that once a woman ovulates there will be approximately 14 days until her next menses. From this information (and knowing the approximate life span of the woman's egg and man's sperm), they independently developed formulas for estimating the fertile times in a woman's menstrual cycle. These formulas are called the "calendar method" and later simply "rhythm" as adapted from the title of a popular book written on the method by Leo Latz, M.D. (1946) an American physician.

Reproductive scientists have known since the early part of the twentieth century that a woman's body temperature rises about 2 to 4 degrees after ovulation. However, it was not until the mid-1930s that a Catholic parish priest (Fr. Wilhelm Hillebrand from Germany) first applied this knowledge to the use of natural birth regulation. A number of his parishioners became pregnant after using the rhythm method to avoid pregnancy. Concerned about these pregnancies, Fr. Hillebrand instructed women to take their daily waking temperatures along with the calendar formulas to determine their fertile period. This method of natural birth control was later called the basal body temperature method or "BBT."

As early as the ninth century a number of physicians and scientists speculated that the fertile time of a woman's menstrual cycle occurred around the time a watery cervical-vaginal fluid was secreted. However, it was not until the 1930s and 1940s that scientists were able to correlate this stretchy, watery, slippery mucus with ovulation. A few physicians subsequently applied this knowledge as a means of monitoring fertility along with calendar formulas, changes in body temperature, and cervical changes. These methods collectively have been called the Sympto-Thermal methods, "STM" for short (or in Europe the double check or multiple index method).

In the 1960s, a husband-wife physician team from Australia, Drs. John and Evelyn Billings, discovered that monitoring the sensations and changes in cervical-vaginal fluids throughout the menstrual cycle was a simple and accurate means of determining the fertile and infertile times of the cycle. A large five-country study of the Billings Method or what is now called the Ovulation Method (OM) was conducted in the late 1970s by the World Health Organization. The WHO study confirmed the simplicity, accuracy, and effectiveness of the OM.

During the 1970s a number of variations and standardized forms of the sympto-thermal and cervical mucus (only) methods were developed. Most notable in the United States were the Creighton Model (cervical mucus only) system developed by Thomas Hilgers, M.D. (Hilgers 1995) and colleagues; the Family of the Americas cervical mucus only system developed by Mercedes Wilson (Wilson 1998); and the teaching system of the sympto-thermal method developed by John Kippley (Kippley 1996) (in conjunction with Konald Prem, M.D. at the University of Minnesota).

Since Ogino and Knaus developed the calendar formulas, technological devices have also been available to aid women and couples in monitoring their fertility. Such simple devices as beads, fertility wheels, and thermometers continue to be used as simple tracking systems. Recent scientific discoveries now allow women to track their fertility through computers, Internet programs, and with electronic hormonal fertility monitors. Newer methods of NFP that incorporate this modern technology are now being developed and tested.

Scientific Foundations. Recent reproductive research has confirmed that women have a six-day window of fertility during their menstrual cycle, namely, the day of ovulation and the five previous days. Determining the beginning and end of these six days and the peak of fertility is the goal of modern NFP. A woman's fertility begins when an egg (or ovum) in her ovaries starts to ripen in a small vessel called a follicle. The follicle produces a female hormone called estrogen that stimulates cells along the opening of her cervix to produce mucus. The mucus at first appears sticky, tacky, and cloudy but progresses to a very watery, stretchy, and slippery consistency at peak. Once a woman ovulates and the ovum is released from the follicle, the cells of the follicle change and produce another hormone called progesterone. Progesterone heats up the woman's body and causes the mucus to dry up at the cervix. After ovulation, the egg only lives from 12 to 24 hours. Therefore, once a woman reaches her peak fertility and ovulates, she is at the beginning of the end of her fertile window. The reason that a woman's fertility is about six days is because the sperm from a man can live in good cervical mucus for three to five days. If a couple has intercourse when the egg is ripening and the follicle is stimulating good cervical mucus, then the sperm can survive to fertilize the egg three to five days later.

There are a number of natural biological markers used in modern methods of NFP to help couples determine the beginning and end of their fertile period. The most common biological indicators are (1) changes in the characteristics of cervical mucus, (2) changes in the cervix, (3) changes in the daily waking body temperature, and (4) changes in female reproductive hormones. Some modern methods of NFP also continue to use "rhythm" formulas to determine the beginning and end of fertility.

One or more of the following fertility markers indicates the beginning of the fertile time in a woman's menstrual cycle: a change of sensation at the vulva from dry to sticky, tacky or moist; the presence of cervical mucus; the cervix starts to soften and rise; rising levels of estrogen as detected in the urine; and the length of the shortest of the last 6 cycles minus 20 days.

The peak of fertility (i.e., the estimated time of ovulation) is indicated by one or more of the following biological indicators: the last day of clear, watery, stretchy, slippery mucus and/or lubricative sensation; a rise in the resting body temperature of 2 to 4 degrees; the cervix is soft, open, and high in the vagina; peak levels of luteinizing hormone (LH) detected in the urine; rising levels of progesterone detected in the urine.

The end of fertility is determined by counting three (and sometimes four) days after the above biological markers are recorded. The end of fertility can also be determined by the length of the longest of the last 6 to 12 cycles minus 10 days. A more accurate and scientific determination comes from detecting urinary metabolites of the rising levels of the hormone progesterone, confirming that ovulation has taken place. There are many other biological indicators such as salivary or vaginal electrical resistance, salivary ferning, glucose levels, vaginal-cervical mucus volume, and others that have been and continue to be tested as possible self-monitored signs of fertility.

Most of the above self-detected biological indicators of fertility have been tested to validate their accuracy in detecting ovulation and the peak of fertility. The current gold standard of validating the day of ovulation is through the use of serial ultrasound to detect the growing and collapsed follicle. Based on the correlation with this gold standard, the most accurate self-indicators of ovulation are measures of urinary metabolites of LH, estrogen, and progesterone through the use of electronic fertility monitors and urinary (chemical assay) type test strips. Research also indicates that the peak day in cervical mucus (i.e., the last day of clear, stretchy, slippery mucus and/or lubricative sensation) varies around the day of ovulation plus or minus three days 99% of the time. Hence the instruction to count three days after the peak day as the end of fertility.

There have been numerous studies to determine the effectiveness of the various systems of NFP to avoid pregnancy. When systems of NFP are taught and used correctly, they range in effectiveness to avoid pregnancy (based on 100 women over 12 months of use) from 85% with calendar formulas to close to 99% with double indicator methods. The effectiveness in typical use drops to a range of about 75 to 90% largely due to the lack of compliance in following basic instructions. There have been few comparative studies on the effectiveness of the various systems of NFP.

Church teaching. The morality of this method of avoiding conception must be judged within the total context of the modern couple's marriage vocation, in relation to which the practice of NFP constitutes a means to an end.

Morally indifferent means. Considered in itself, the practice of NFP does not constitute a deviation from right moral order in the use of sex. PIUS XI, in the encyclical *CASTI CONNUBII*, stated that having intercourse during the infertile times to avoid pregnancy is not an act against nature. This teaching was echoed by PAUL VI in the encyclical *HUMANAE VITAE*. Marriage does not oblige couples to engage in conjugal relations at any specific time. Neither avoidance of intercourse during the fertile period of a cycle nor restriction of its use to sterile periods violates the integrity of the marital act. Profiting from their knowledge of the normal functioning of the female reproductive system, couples may restrict intercourse to those periods that are considered most favorable for either the avoidance or the promotion of pregnancy. In contrast to contraception, which constitutes a deliberate attempt directly to inhibit or impede the normal progress of the physiological process of reproduction voluntarily initiated by the couple when they engage in marital relations, the practice of NFP fully respects the intrinsic natural structure of the conjugal act and in this regard must be considered a morally indifferent means for regulating family size.

Requisite conditions. Because the practice of NFP involves the deliberate restriction of marital relations to limited periods during the menstrual cycle, the conditions required for its morally licit use are determined by the demands of marriage. First, both partners must freely agree to the practice. Second, both partners must be capable of bearing the possible tension and strain that may result from the use of this practice. If the restriction of marital relations to limited periods seriously threatens the growth of mutual love and harmony between husband and wife, the couple must seek adequate means to modify the situation or cease the practice. Third, couples must have sufficient reason for employing this practice. As PIUS XII pointed out in an address to the Italian Catholic Union of Midwives on October 29, 1951 (*Vegliare con sollecitudine*), marriage is a state of life that confers certain rights and also imposes the fulfillment of a positive work, namely, to provide for the conservation of the human race. This obligation is serious, though in the case of a given couple special circumstances or conditions of a medical, eugenical, economic, or social nature may render its fulfillment inopportune or unreasonable either for a time or throughout marriage. Hence, although it would be seriously sinful for a childless couple to employ NFP throughout marriage without a serious excusing reason, couples who generously accept their obligation to have children may licitly make use of this practice both for spacing pregnancies and for regulating family size in accord with a reasonable estimate of their parental capacities.

Common objections. The practice of NFP has been subjected to criticism on various grounds. In addition to those who reject the Church's traditional teaching regarding the morally licit means of regulating family size, some object to the practice because they judge that its use implies lack of trust in PROVIDENCE and will lead to a "contraceptive mentality." Yet authentic trust in Providence does not free couples from personal responsibility, but requires that they exercise prudent judgment in fulfilling their procreative mission. Granting that the temptation to selfishness is perennial, couples who are serious enough about their vocation to follow the Church's teaching regarding contraception are not likely to reject the privilege of parenthood.

A further set of objections stems from the belief that NFP creates undue anxiety and seriously inhibits the spontaneous expression of marital love. Like all other methods of family regulation short of absolute continence, the practice of NFP does involve some uncertainty and requires consistent foresight and care, though well-motivated couples apparently find this no insurmountable obstacle. The required restriction of intercourse to limited periods obviously inhibits spontaneity in expressing this form of marital love, yet one must carefully distinguish between spontaneity of sexual expression and spontaneity in expressing love. The former is necessarily curbed by the demands of justice and charity as well as by the normal exigencies of social life; NFP inhibits the latter only if the couple has developed no alternate means of expressing love. Acquiring the disciplined control required by NFP does involve personal sacrifice, but marital relations can retain their significance as authentic expressions of love only if they foster the couple's integral development as Christian partners and parents.

Relationship to the vocation of marriage. Like all authentic vocations, marriage is designed to provide for the Christian's full development and sanctification in the service of Christ. It differs specifically from other vocations in its special mission, which is to provide for the couple's mutual, complementary fulfillment in a procreative union. Although all marriage partners accept an enduring commitment to foster their mutual happiness and perfection in Christ by dedicating themselves to the service of life, individual couples may differ widely in regard to both their parental abilities and the conditions or circumstances under which they must live. Because there exists no necessary relationship between procreative capacity and the ability to raise a family, many couples find it difficult to reconcile their normal expressions of marital love with the demands of the moral law. It is precisely in this context that the practice of NFP assumes primary significance. Provided they generously dedicate themselves to having a family, couples now have available a morally licit, reliable means of spacing pregnancies and regulating family size. The method requires sacrifice and self-mastery, yet these traits characterize all authentic expressions of love and are not beyond the strength of couples who have recourse to prayer and the Sacraments.

Prompted by the writings of Pope JOHN PAUL II, the Church in recent years has frequently articulated its understanding of human sexuality in terms of a "theology of the body." The conjugal act is an act of total reciprocal self-giving of husband and wife. When a couple uses contraception, they no longer are totally giving of themselves but rather are conditional in their love-making. The contraceptive act is in a sense a living "lie" or falsification of the inner truth of the conjugal act. In the 1982 apostolic exhortation, *Familiaris consortio*, Pope John Paul II reiterated that the differences between artificial contraception and methods of natural birth regulation were irreconcilable. The teachings in *Familiaris consortio* are reflected in the *Catholic Catechism of the Catholic Church*, which says "periodic continence, that is, the methods of birth regulation based on self-observation and the use of infertile periods, is in conformity with the objective criteria of morality. These methods respect the bodies of the spouses, encourage tenderness between them, and favor the education of an authentic freedom" (2370). In the 1995 encyclical *EVANGELIUM VITAE*, John Paul II encouraged all married couples to learn NFP and called for the promotion of centers of NFP as a means to build a culture of life.

Bibliography: E. L. BILLINGS, J. J. BILLINGS, and M. CATERINICH, *Billings Atlas of the Ovulation Method* (Melbourne, Australia 1989). European Society of Human Reproduction and Embryology (ESHRE), "Optimal Use of Infertility Diagnostic Tests and Treatments," *Human Reproduction* 15 (2000): 723–732. R. J. FEHRING, "New Technology in Natural Family Planning," *Journal of Obstetric, Gynecologic, and Neonatal Nursing* 20 (1991): 199–205; "Review and Analysis of the Peak Day," *Current Medical Research: A Supplement of NFP Forum* 10 (1999): 9–16. R. J. FEHRING and A. SCHLIDT, "Trends in Contraceptive Use among Catholics in the United States," *Linacre Quarterly* (2001). T. W. HILGERS, *The Scientific Foundations of the Ovulation Method* (Omaha 1995). R. KAMBIC, "The Effectiveness of Natural Family Planning," *Current Medical Research. A Supplement of NFP Forum* 11 (2000): 11–16. J. KIPPLEY, *The Art of Natural Family Planning* (Cincinnati 1996). H. KNAUS, *Periodic Fertility and Sterility in Women. A Natural Method of Birth Control* (Vienna 1934). L. LATZ, *The Rhythm of Sterility and Fertility in Women* (Chicago 1946). K. OGINO, *Conception Period of Women* (Harrisburg, Penn. 1934). A. J. WILCOX, C. R. WEINBERG, and D. D. BAIRD, "Timing of Sexual Intercourse in Relation to Ovulation: Effects of the Probability of Conception, Survival of the Pregnancy, and Sex of the Baby," *New England Journal of Medicine* 333 (1995): 1517–1521. M. WILSON, *Love and Fertility* (Dunkirk, Md. 1998). World Health Organization (WHO), "A Prospective Multicentre Trial of the Ovulation Methods of Natural Family Planning. II. The Effectiveness Phase," *Fertility and Sterilization* 36 (1981): 591–598. R. F. VOLLMAN, "Wilhelm Hillebrand, The First Teacher of the STM,"

in A. ZIMMERMAN, ed., *Natural Family Planning, Nature's Way—God's Way* (Milwaukee 1980).

[R. J. FEHRING/J. L. THOMAS]

NATURAL LAW

A LAW or rule of action that is implicit in the very nature of things. The term is sometimes used in the plural form to designate laws that regulate the activities of nature in both the organic and the inorganic realm. Properly speaking, however, it is exclusively applied to man and designates a prescriptive rule of conduct naturally received by and measuring human reason which enables human reason rightly to measure human action. For St. THOMAS AQUINAS, "natural law is nothing other than the participation of eternal law in rational creatures" (*Summa theologiae* 1a2ae, 91.2); thus Aquinas conceives it as the imprint of God's providential plan on man's natural reason. This article is divided into three main sections. The first treats of the historical development of the concept of natural law; the second provides a Thomistic analysis of the concept; and the third discusses the place of the concept in contemporary theology and philosophy. (For specific applications of the concept, *see* NATURAL LAW AND JURISPRUDENCE; NATURAL LAW IN POLITICAL THOUGHT.)

HISTORICAL DEVELOPMENT

Although natural law has always been perceived in its basic content by human beings, its concept has been formalized, elaborated, articulated, and systematized only with the growth and development of philosophy. The historical evolution of this doctrine may be conveniently traced through six periods: (1) the pagan period, corresponding to that of the Greco-Roman world and extending from HERACLITUS to St. Paul; (2) the Catholic and scholastic period, extending from St. Paul to Hugo GROTIUS; (3) the Protestant and post-scholastic period, extending from Grotius and S. von Pufendorf (1632–94) to J. Bentham; (4) the period of decline, corresponding to the rise of positivism and extending from BENTHAM and D. HUME to F. Gény (1861–1959) and R. Stammler (1856–1938); (5) the contemporary period of revival, extending from Gény and Stammler to the mid-1960s; and (6) the debates of the late 20th century.

Greco-Roman Period. There is evidence of the idea of a universal divine law binding on man in Oriental literature, such as that of China, long before the rise of philosophy in the West. But the origin of a natural-law doctrine, with its elaboration as an unbroken, continuous development, is first to be found among the ancient Greek poets and historians. Thus Sophocles (c. 497–406 B.C.), Thucydides (*c.* 460–400 B.C.), and Xenophon (*c.* 427–355 B.C.) presented a concept of the natural law that is divine, universal, and known to all.

Greek Philosophers. A development of this early Greek notion appears in the writings of Heraclitus, who held that the natural law is eternal and immutable, the foundation of human laws (*Fragments* 102, 112–116). Other Greek philosophers, such as PLATO, elucidated this doctrine (*Laws* 715, 884–910; *Rep.* 419–445). It was left to Plato's student ARISTOTLE, however, to clarify the distinction between natural law and law that is humanly enacted (*Eth. Nic.* 1134b 18–1136a 9; *Rhet.* 1373b 1–18). Such Greek philosophers used observation and experience to discover an order in the universe that they associated with a predictable, regular recurrence of events. Traceable to the activity of animate and inanimate matter, this recurrence is in response to an ordering principle or law that rules the cosmos. But man also is part of the cosmos and hence subject to an ordering law, which in his case is the right or just by nature. Morals and human law, for the Greeks, thus have their foundation in the harmony of nature or the natural law. This law exists independently of human will and has universal validity. It provides objective principles and ideals to which human beings must conform, by their very nature, as part of the cosmos. Functionally, therefore, natural law affords a measure for the wise, the good, the just, the prudent, and the happy man. It provides too a basis for an idealized political and social order. It also makes possible the distinction between the category of divine, universal, and unchangeable law and that of human, politically enacted, and variable law.

Whereas Aristotle does not thematize the theological and metaphysical element the definitory relation to eternal law—so strongly as do either earlier figures such as Heraclitus, later authors such as Cicero, or in the Christian era Boethius, Augustine, or St. Thomas Aquinas, it is nonetheless clear that the naturally just and virtuous is a function of conforming to natural order that is derived from its divine origin, and whose entailments in virtue are analogously "divine." The ordering of human nature to a hierarchy of perfective ends prior to choice is essential to his teaching; hence his strong emphasis upon the truth that strictly speaking the end is not directly a matter of choice. Man is by nature ordered to happiness as his final end, and that which by nature constitutes this happiness is a function of the teleological order of man to contemplation of God and the virtues appropriate to the active life.

Nonetheless, the idea of natural law at this stage of its evolution tends to subordinate the individual to the Greek city-state. Even for Aristotle, individual man achieves the perfection of his human nature through law only in the good order of the city-state, which is analogous to the cosmic order (*Pol.* 1252a 1 1253a 38). The doctrine of natural law reached its highest development in the PAGAN world within STOICISM, the philosophical movement founded by Zeno of Citium (*c.* 336–*c.* 264 B.C.). Characteristic of Zeno's teaching and that of other Stoic philosophers, such as Chrysippus (*c.* 280 B.C.), was the thesis that man is a citizen of the world. Thus emphasis was placed on the nature of man as such and not merely as related to political society. A broader society consequently results from human nature itself, which is subject to the law of right reason. The individual thus comes to be recognized as a moral unit who is governed by universal law, which prescribes a pattern of conduct that is discoverable by reason. In this way, law and justice are seen as transcending the confines of the city-state.

Roman Thought. After the military conquest of Greece by Rome *c.* 146 B.C., the Stoic idea of natural law began to infiltrate the Roman world. CICERO played an important role in interpreting and disseminating this idea. For him, natural law is the highest reason implanted in nature, transcending space and time; it is eternal and unchangeable, the same in Rome as in Athens. Coming from God, it commands what is to be done and forbids what is to be avoided. It precedes written law and the state. More specifically, it embodies basic principles (e.g., the right of self-defense against aggression), regulates justice (giving to each his due), and promotes the common good. It also forbids fraud and theft. Among the Romans, natural law came to be chiefly related to the juridical and legal orders. The natural right, or the just by nature, therefore became the *ius naturale* of the Roman jurists, i.e., a speculative body of universal moral ideas and principles.

The *ius civile,* or body of legal precepts, was applied exclusively to Roman citizens. But eventually, after Rome became a great maritime and trading center, it became necessary to supplement the *ius civile* with the *ius gentium,* or body of law for foreigners. As positive law, the *ius gentium* was constructed from the common denominator of principles obtaining in the various legal systems of countries from which foreigners came. The policy of using this common denominator was rationalized on the grounds that it was only the implementation of the *ius naturale,* the expression of universal reason. By the end of the classical age of Roman jurisprudence, i.e., about 300 years after the death of Cicero, hundreds of texts had referred to *ius naturale, naturalis ratio,* and *rerum natura.* Thus Ulpian (d. A.D. 228), the great Roman jurist, stated that insofar as the *ius civile* is concerned, slaves are not regarded as persons; nevertheless, this is not true under natural law because under that law all men are equal (*Digest* 50.17.32). Ulpian was obviously referring to the natural law when he wrote that the precepts of the law are to live honestly, to harm no one, and to render each his own (*Institutes* 1.1.3; *Digest* 1.1.10). Most Roman jurists, such as Gaius (2d century A.D.), oriented the legal order toward the natural law primarily by following the standard of objective right reason as manifested in experience (*Institutes* 1.156, 158).

Catholic and Scholastic Period. Although the Fathers of the early Christian Church understandably emphasized the ''new law'' of revelation rather than simply the natural law, nonetheless the conception of natural law was integral to their theology. Among those authors in whom this is clearest are St. PAUL, St. JOHN CHRYSOSTOM, St. AUGUSTINE, and St. ISIDORE OF SEVILLE, all of whom borrowed Stoic ideas in describing the interrelationship between natural and supernatural laws. The Stoics had been equivocal as to whether the ultimate source of natural law was personal and divine or whether divinity was immanent in nature in the sense of a monist PANTHEISM. It was impossible for them to synthesize natural law with the myths of the pagan religions of their time. In this area, the Fathers of the Church, and later the scholastics, were able to supply new insights based on supernatural revelation.

Early Christianity. St. Paul, the Apostle of the Gentiles, wrote that the natural law is inscribed in the hearts of all men, even though all do not have the Law (of Sinai) of divine revelation (Rom 2.12 16). St. John Chrysostom taught that the natural law is promulgated through man's conscience, which supplies the basis of human law (*Ad pop. ant.* 12). According to St. Augustine, the *ius naturale* comes from a personal, all-wise, and all-powerful God, the same God who has authored the Christian Scriptures; hence natural law is not derived from nature in the pantheistic sense (*Civ* 11.4.2). St. Isidore of Seville held that all laws are either divine or human and that *ius naturale* is the law observed everywhere by the instinct of nature, such as that ordaining the marriage of man and woman, the procreation and rearing of children, and the like. It is not human positive law (*On Laws* 4).

Canonists. The canonists, especially as seen in the *Decretum* of GRATIAN, were chiefly responsible for transmitting the interrelationship between natural and supernatural law that had been worked out by the Fathers to the golden age of scholastic philosophy. According to Gratian, all justice is founded on natural law, which is of divine origin (*Decretum* 1). This law goes back to the beginning of mankind; its content is to be found in the Ten Commandments and the Gospel, which dictates the golden rule of doing to others what one wishes done to oneself. A decade after Gratian, the canonist RUFINUS referred to the natural law as the divine power that nature implants in man, impelling him to do good and avoid evil (*Summa Decretorum*).

Thomistic Concept. But it remained for St. Thomas Aquinas to perfect the idea of natural law. This he did by distinguishing in the natural law of the Stoics and in the *ius naturale* of the Romans the *lex aeterna* and the *lex naturalis*. The eternal law is the plan of the divine providence governing the cosmos, man, and matter, both animate and inanimate. It is the ordering wisdom of God. Natural law is that part of the eternal law that is properly applicable to man alone, although it may be spoken of lower creatures by a kind of analogy. All creatures—including human creatures—passively receive their being, natures, and natural ordering to perfective ends from God. But man's creation as a rational being enables him to receive this ordering of his nature as providing *reasons* to act and not to act. Human reason takes its measure from the objective ordering of human nature to the order of ends that perfects it.

Natural law is in accord with man's nature (*Summa theologiae* 1a2ae, 91.2 4). Subrational creatures and inanimate matter must obey the eternal law, but man can disobey it because he has freedom as to moral choice. However, he ought to obey the natural law, for otherwise he violates his nature. Thus did Aquinas correct the error of Ulpian, who is quoted in Justinian's *Digest* (6th century A.D.) as having declared that the law of nature is not peculiar to the human race but belongs to all creatures (1.1.1 4). Ulpian had made the natural law (a part) identical with the eternal law (the whole).

According to Aquinas, *ius naturale* is encompassed within *lex naturalis* insofar as it relates to man. By this semantic change he gave rationally discovered law a statutory connotation, while insisting that natural law has the same source as supernatural law. But Aquinas did not destroy the rational basis of the pagan, Aristotelian-Stoic doctrine of natural law by substituting the authority of supernatural law, in the sense of truth revealed in the Bible, in its place. Rather, to use a metaphor, he taught that the single coin of divine law is stamped on one side by the supernatural law of Judeo-Christian theology, accepted on faith, through grace, as the word of God, and on the other side by the natural law, perceived by reason. Inasmuch as both laws emanate from a single source, they can never be in conflict. Precisely because man is called to an end surpassing nature, a law higher than the natural law is required to direct him to this end, but the ''new law'' of grace elevates and perfects nature rather than destroying it. According to Aquinas, natural law is nothing other than a participation in the eternal law. Gradually the emphasis would shift to nature, and then finally collapse into the solitary emphasis upon what law is known first.

Later Thought. In the 14th century, the Thomistic view of natural law was challenged by some. Thus, DUNS SCOTUS wrote that *lex naturalis* has no intrinsic connection with the essence of God and hence can be different from what it happens to be (*Op. Oxon.* 1.8.5. 22–23). WILLIAM OF OCKHAM held that natural law is wholly the product of divine will; it is divine positive law, or supernatural law, since God is primarily absolute and omnipotent will (*Quodl.* 1.10.3; 1.13). Both deviated, therefore, from the Thomistic idea of natural law by eliminating intellect and reason from its authoritative basis. But in the 16th century, reason was restored to the doctrine of natural law by Spanish jurist-theologians such as Domingo de SOTO (*De iustitia et iure* 1.5.2) and Francisco SUÁREZ (*A Treatise on Law and God the Lawgiver* 2.6.5). These thinkers affirmed that the ultimate source of the natural law is in the divine will and intellect; and its proximate principle, in the essence of man. They also emphasized a historical-analytical and comparative-empirical approach that gave content to natural law, particularly in the field of international relations.

Protestant and Postscholastic Period. The outbreak of the Reformation in the 16th century initiated a new period in the history of the doctrine of natural law. The term ''natural law'' had been so long embedded in the thinking of the Western world that philosophers and jurists continued to use it after the Reformation, although they attributed to it an essentially new and heterogeneous content. Insofar as the theology of the Reformation affirmed the private interpretation of the Scriptures, it led to the rejection of the idea of objective truth in the areas of both supernatural and natural law. The conscience of the individual became more than the source of personal moral responsibility; it became the measure of truth in all matters of right and wrong, good and evil. Subjective theories of natural law, detached from the element of experience, began to postulate the existence of a state or condition of nature in which man lived before he constructed politically organized society. In this state of nature, there was a ''law of nature.'' This myth of the natural state often was a ''counter'' to the theological account of Eden and the fall of man. Moral and social disorder would be traced, not to original and actual sin, but to natural dynamisms which condition and to some extent war against social order. Unlike the natural law, the law of nature was not related chiefly to conduct in general nor to the legal and theological orders, but rather to political order. This emphasis accompanied the rise of political problems ensuing from *cuius regio eius religio* (the religion of the state is that of whoever reigns), i.e., the emergence and growth of national states and churches.

Law of Nature School. According to the law of nature school, man perceives the natural law by his subjective faculty of reason, which contemplates human nature as an abstract essence existing in a vacuum, apart from time and place. Man determines the content of the law of nature not by induction but by a purely deductive process. (The scholastics had made use of induction here, studying the standard of right reason in relation to historical and contemporary experience.) The law of nature school exalted the autonomy of the individual faculty of reason; that this led to an excessive subjectivism is evidenced by the basic disagreement within the school over the state of nature, the content of the law of nature in this aboriginal condition, and its fate once man established politically and legally organized society by a social contract.

Grotius. The contributions of Hugo Grotius effected the transition between the scholastic and the law of nature concepts of natural law. Like the scholastics, Grotius believed in the existence of objective right reason, with resulting immutable principles, and in God as the highest source of natural law (*De iure belli ac pacis* 1.1). Unlike them, he held that the natural law could exist even without a personal and divine Law-Giver, since it had a sufficient basis in reason alone. He also stressed individualism, RATIONALISM, and the social aspect of rational human nature in reference to natural law (*ibid.* 1.3.8). But he did not go so far as to hold that the social nature of man is the sole source of natural law. Grotius erred in believing that man once lived in a state of nature under a law of nature that could be derived from man's essence. He taught that it was possible to deduce by strict logic a complete system of principles with universal validity and from these to develop an all-sufficient code of legal rules (*ibid.* prol.). He thus failed to distinguish the immutable aspects of the natural law, the mutable conclusions that result from the application of immutable principles to changing factors, and the positive law that implements both types of principles. Under his law of nature doctrine, therefore, natural law lost the flexibility and dynamism it had enjoyed in the prior periods.

Pufendorf. Samuel von Pufendorf first articulated the concept of the law of nature in its pure or classical form. For him, the *ius naturale* is related to God's will, not to His essence. It is not a rational participation in the eternal law, as Aquinas taught, but is identified wholly with the human impulse toward sociability. The sociable capacity of man is the sole proximate source of natural law, the starting point of speculation in this sphere (*De iure naturae et gentium* 2.3). Pufendorf considered reason so autonomous that in effect civil law, both substantive and procedural, became natural law, even though in theory he distinguished between natural law and positive law. For him, natural law is only a model law, advisory but not mandatory. Hence the state enacts positive law so that the natural law may be obeyed (*ibid.*).

Hobbes and Locke. The great divergence among the various adherents of the law of nature school may be seen by comparing the views of T. HOBBES with those of J. LOCKE. Hobbes saw the state of nature as a state of war of all against all, in which the life of man is solitary, poor, nasty, brutish, and short. The basic norm is self-preservation, springing from natural law, which is a dictate of right reason regarding things to be done or omitted for the preservation of life and limb. The first fundamental law of nature is that peace be sought, and all other natural laws are derived from this. Morality is rooted, therefore, in peace; this is the reason why agreements must be kept (*Leviathan* 13). According to Hobbes, the law of nature prescribes that man should form the civil state in order to preserve the fundamental right to life. In establishing the state, however, man surrendered his freedom, equality, and the right to everything he had enjoyed in the state of nature, physical survival alone excepted. This was done by a covenant. The will of the resulting omnipotent state is based on the fundamental principle that agreements must be kept. Man may not morally resist the state because its enactments are natural law. Indeed the state, as the authoritative interpreter of both natural and supernatural law, was transformed into a mortal god in a literal sense. If there is a conflict between a command of the state and the private moral judgment of the individual, Hobbes advises the latter to go to Christ by martyrdom (*ibid.* 18). But for Locke, contrary to Hobbes, the historical state of nature was a condition of peace, good will, and mutual cooperation. Man enjoyed the right of freedom and equality, as well as the right to work and own property. The law of nature dictated justice, but the authority of civil society was necessary to enforce it. Politically organized society resulted from a SOCIAL CONTRACT, but the continuing obligation of obedience on the part of the people depends on the proper observance of that contract by the sovereign (*Second Treatise on Civil Government* 19). For Locke man is not, in the strict sense, under any obligation of law prior to the convening of the state, nor is man obligated to convene such a state. Rather, Locke sees natural law as a dictate of practical common sense a nominalistic symbol for the rights of the individual, reflecting his self-interest. These rights do not emanate from the natural law by intrinsic necessity; rather, they limit the political sovereign and should be enforced by human positive law (*ibid.* 9).

Others. Conceptions of the state of nature and the law of nature found therein were expressed by J. J. ROUSSEAU (*The Social Contract* 1.8, 2.6, 4.2), C. Thomasius (*Fundamenta iuris naturae et gentium*), C. WOLFF (*Institutiones iuris naturae et gentium* 2), and others. The term "law of nature" became so ambiguous that it was used to justify such divergent theories as enlightened despotism, state absolutism, and the omnipotence of the democratic state. The ultimate position was that each individual's reasoning faculty manufactures natural law, rather than discovers it. These accounts, for the most part, do not situate natural law within a wider metaphysical and theological context.

Kant. The tendency to separate natural law from the foci of eternal law and nature is brought to its consummation in the doctrine of I. KANT, who introduced a new doctrine of objective right which is only equivocally related to classical natural law. He argued that the state of nature was only a historical fiction to explain the foundation of the civil state, since man had always lived in a social state (in this narrow regard, his doctrine shares something with Aristotelian and Thomistic teaching). However, he also maintained that man cannot reach the ideal, or perfect, law by a process of pure reason (*The Philosophy of Law* 1; *Introduction to the Metaphysics of Morals* 4.24). Kant argued that the formal, subjective elements of the reasoning process do not come from experience, and that they are valid only insofar as they are referred to some possible experience. Hence Kant denied the very possibility of metaphysical truth, since on his account first principles are not derived from the mind's initial contact with being, but are rather pure emanations of universal human subjectivity. What remains is human experience understood as shaped by universal subjective categories which on the Kantian view cannot be known to pertain to reality as such. Hence causal knowledge of the reality of God, the reasoned understanding of the nature of human freedom as a corollary of the nature of the human intellect, and the proofs for the immortality of the human soul are set aside and become mere subjective *postulates* of practical reason. Likewise, Kant reduces the ordering of nature to perfective ends to a mere empirical datum that in no way defines moral duty and may even serve as a motive for immoral breach of duty.

Kant projected an individualist idea of natural right. Freedom of will became the ultimate, supreme, immutable value, a natural inborn right that included all natural rights. He reconciled the conflict between the equally free wills of the various individuals in society by a CATEGORICAL IMPERATIVE, a universal law directing that each individual should so act that the free exercise of his will would enable him to live without interfering with the like freedom of others. Under this theory, natural law is not a part of an eternal law, although the natural law supplies the immutable ideal of freedom upon which the categorical imperative is constructed. The categorical imperative is imposed by a necessity inherent in the very idea of freedom.

Period of Decline. The Enlightenment accounts of natural law shorn of metaphysics and theology and progressively reduced to immanent nature and finally to Kant's formalism of pure right reached a high degree of prestige at the end of the 18th century, but it gave way in the 19th century to POSITIVISM, which held the authority of the state to be supreme in every sense. The reasons for this decline may be enumerated as follows. First, even before the dawn of the 19th century, D. Hume laid the groundwork for the widespread assault on natural-law doctrine. A skeptic, he proclaimed that the human mind can never attain the essences of things and that it cannot determine what is intrinsically morally good or evil. Morality is not a matter of idealism but is determined by the sentiment of approval, itself related to the useful. According to Hume, the moral law has no basis in the rational and social nature of man and has no connection with immutable truth. Second, positivism was promoted by individualist utilitarians, such as J. Bentham (*Treatise on Legislation* 13). In place of idealism, Bentham substituted the notion of utility as measured by the greatest good or by the happiness of the greatest number, taking happiness in the sense of personal satisfaction and advantage. Bentham sought consciously to build a new body of law. He was the forerunner of John Austin (1790–1859), who created the analytical school of jurisprudence, a school widely influential among Anglo-American jurists. Third, the historical school, founded by F. K. von Savigny, contributed indirectly to the rise of positivism. It maintained that natural, or ideal, law springs spontaneously from the spirit of a people and is reflected in custom. It is a higher law, found and not made. For this school, customary law, like natural law, limited the authority of the political sovereign to make law. Yet the historical school was positivist in its ultimate philosophy, for it believed that customary law was the result of the will of the people yielding to non-rational impulses and responding to historical necessity rather than to right reason. Fourth, positivism was advanced by the newly emerging science of sociology, which had its origin in the writings of positivist philosophers such as A. COMTE. Assuming a mechanistic view of the physical universe based on mathematically demonstrable laws that control the activity of nature, it regarded moral and social laws as analogous to the law of gravitation. Sociological jurisprudence later abandoned this approach.

Correctives to the Law of Nature. From the viewpoint of the scholastic doctrine of natural law, it is understandable, however, why the analytical, historical, and sociological schools were able to attract a following. Each of these schools in its own way corrected a deficiency of the pseudoconcept of natural law that had been developed in the 17th and 18th centuries. Whereas Aquinas had visualized man as a rational and social animal who relies on both reason and experience and needs a legal order enforced by a temporal sovereign, the law of nature school overemphasized subjective reason in its analysis. These reactions against the law of nature school were therefore quite legitimate, even though they had little to do with the natural-law doctrine of Aquinas. The analytical school focused attention on legal analysis and the logical interdependence of legal rules and precepts; it stressed the fact that law is in the external forum and should be enforced by the sovereign. The historical school restored the factor of experience. The sociological school reintroduced the element of the social status of man and the means-ends aspect of law, as maintained by Aquinas. Each of these schools erred, however, by concentrating on one factor to the exclusion of others and by refusing to accept any immutable moral value, such as the dignity of the individual. Other factors that contributed to the rise of positivism included the search for an explanation to justify absolute political sovereignty in both domestic and foreign affairs, the thrust of moral RELATIVISM related to anthropological studies, the rejection of a priori postulates by the physical sciences, and mistaken ideas about human EVOLUTION, EMPIRICISM, pragmatism, and materialistic psychiatry.

Period of Revival. A reaction against the sterility and ineffectiveness of positivism began with a revival of natural law doctrine. This revival was led by F. Gény, a neoscholastic, and R. Stammler, a neo-Kantian. Both scholars emphasized the sociological aspects of the natural law, an emphasis that has continued throughout the contemporary period. Gény began the revival in France by considering the social life of the individual as a moral phenomenon governed by the natural law as understood by Aquinas. He used the Thomistic doctrine of natural law to provide a much-needed equitable and sociological interpretation for European codes. Gény's notions received great encouragement from Pope Leo XIII, especially through his encyclicals relating to political and social matters, such as *LIBERTAS* (1888) and *RERUM NOVARUM* (1891), and by succeeding popes (*see* SCHOLASTICISM, 3). Renewed interest in the scholastic doctrine of natural law as this relates to the legal and social orders began in the United States in the 1920s and 1930s. Law reviews sponsored by such universities as Fordham, Detroit, Marquette, Georgetown, and Notre Dame became channels for an ever-growing literature. The American Catholic Philosophical Association established a committee on the philosophy of law in the early 1930s that arranged an annual forum for the presentation of papers relating to natural law and the solution of legal and social problems. These bodies expanded further the body of natural-law literature. The revival of natural-law doctrine was enormously accelerated by the experience of two world wars. European emigrés contributed much on the

North American continent to the renascence of natural-law teaching. Jacques MARITAIN, Yves SIMON, Heinrich Rommen, and others, made cogent argument in behalf of the tradition of natural law given classical articulation by St. Thomas Aquinas. Many legal philosophers, recoiling from the horrors of untrammeled state power after the Nazi experience, took up with interest the consideration of a higher law than the positive law of the state. After World War II, it was manifest that such a doctrine alone could provide an authoritative basis for upholding the intrinsic dignity of the individual against ruthless dictatorship. The quest for political and legal justice resulted in the rediscovery that there is a moral order springing from an authority beyond the human will. The theological/metaphysical aspect of the tradition was rekindled in the consideration of the theonomic character of natural law, while concern for the legal/juridic/moral implications of the natural law also intensified. Interest in the doctrine of the natural law was evidenced in the United States by the *Journal of the American Bar Association,* the *Natural Law Forum of the University of Notre Dame,* and the *Catholic Lawyer,* published by the St. Thomas More Institute for Legal Research of St. John's University, New York. Southern Methodist University, Dallas, sponsors an annual symposium on natural law; and Loyola University, New Orleans, houses an institute on natural law as related to the solution of some contemporary social problem. The revival of natural-law doctrine has been widespread in Latin America, especially in Argentina and Mexico; in Europe it flourishes particularly in Italy, Germany, France, and Spain; and it is evident in the Orient.

Nonscholastic Circles. Stammler initiated a revival of the NEO-KANTIAN doctrine of natural right. For him, the content of the natural law is wholly changeable and changing, dependent upon the social ideals and conditions of a particular time and place. Through natural law, all possible individual goals of the community of freely willing men are to be harmonized. He thus reconciled the idea of natural law with the notions of evolution and utility. A later neo-Kantian development in the field of legal philosophy was led by Giorgio del Vecchio. His position is closer to the Thomistic than that of Stammler. Indeed, the position of Del Vecchio represents the tendency to minimize the speculative aspect of natural law theory so as to avoid the antimetaphysical criticisms flowing from Kant and Hume. He admits the existence of a divine Law-Giver who has given man a supernatural law by revelation, but he does not relate this Law-Giver to the natural law. He derives the elements of transcendence and immutability for his juridical idealism from the essence of man rather than deriving them from the divine will and intellect. Other nonscholastic doctrines that deploy the terminology of "natural law" have rejected any immutable,

transcendental, objective ideal of conduct to which man should conform his behavior. Exponents of this type of natural-law doctrine, such as M. R. Cohen (1880–1947), accept the existence only of relative ideals for human conduct. But these ideals do exist a priori in an objective order and do not arise solely from facts. For such authors as well as for the neo-Kantians, the "ought" stands in juxtaposition to the "is." This is to say that these theorists embrace a pronounced dichotomy of nature and the good, divorcing practical knowledge from its speculative roots along Humean lines. Other natural-law writers, such as L. L. Fuller and Jerome Hall, deviate more markedly from the scholastic idea of natural law. They believe that there are ideals for the evaluation of man's conduct, but that these are principally generalizations of what will best advance the social interest.

Late 20th Century. The late 20th century has seen substantial work and controversy within all the major areas of natural-law theory, from theology and metaphysics, to natural ontology, to epistemology, to law and jurisprudence. This all-encompassing controversy and research is attributable to four distinct historical influences. First, it is in part due to the engagement of natural lawyers with radical theological pluralism following the Second VATICAN COUNCIL; second, it also flows from reactions against proportionalism on the one hand, and even more fundamentally against Humean and Kantian anti-metaphysical tendencies, on the other; third, it is a result of legal and political pressures and the growing volatility on the North American continent of Church-state legal issues, about all of which the tradition of natural law provides an important context for understanding; and fourth, the general encroachment of such reductionist methods as historicism, relativism, and scientism entails a proportionate response at every level of reasoning (see Pope JOHN PAUL II, *FIDES ET RATIO*). Out of this dense weaving and interweaving of themes and controversies, three points are clear: the renascence of natural-law theory, especially in Thomism but also in competing and contrasting accounts such as the new natural-law theory championed by Grisez and Finnis; the special impetus given to the metaphysically founded Thomistic natural-law reasoning by the encyclicals *VERITATIS SPLENDOR* and *Fides et ratio*; and the importance of work done regarding both the significance of a normative conception of nature for theology, and of work applying natural law reasoning to jurisprudence and politics.

The New Natural-Law Theorists. During this period of time, the "new natural-law theory" propounded by and John Finnis has gained adherents while undergoing serious criticism from proponents of more traditional Thomistic natural-law theory. Grisez's influential work, *The Way of the Lord Jesus,* has brought this account to the foreground. Grisez and Finnis argue for a methodological and, as it were, temporary epistemic separation of the precepts of natural law from their speculative context, insisting that the prime precepts of the natural law are in no way derived from speculative truths. They also argue that basic moral goods are simply incomparable and do not exemplify any morally significant order amongst one another prior to human choice—what is called the "incommensurability thesis." Arguing for the existence of universal moral norms, including negative norms, these authors strongly criticize proportionalism, while also denying the claims of more traditional Aristotelians and Thomists that moral goods or ends exemplify a teleological hierarchy that is morally significant prior to choice.

Thomistic and Aristotelian Natural-Law Theorists. An important school of Aristotelian and Thomistic philosophers has argued that although the transition from knowledge of nature to preceptive norms is not simply a function of definition, nonetheless it is impossible even temporarily to detach epistemic awareness of the natural law from its ontological foundation. Ralph McInerny has extensively criticized the new natural-law theorists' account of the first precept of law, as well as their denial of the ethical significance of natural teleology. Henry Veatch engaged in a lengthy and lucid discussion with theorists of the analytic tradition, seeking to vindicate natural teleology within ethics from essentially Humean and Kantian criticisms. Russell Hittinger, in particular, has argued that the method of the new natural-law theorists tends toward fideism insofar as it separates natural-law duties to God from the speculative natural knowledge of the reality of God. He has set forth a strong argument that natural law is unequivocally "law"—that, as St. Thomas writes in the prologue to his treatise on law in the *Summa theologiae,* law is indeed an "extrinsic" principle, since ontologically the law and that of which the law is the norm are not one and the same.

Other Theorists. In addition to the well-delineated Thomistic and New Natural-Law Theory schools, a variety of other prominent authors have persisted in contributing important analyses and discussions. Most prominently, Martin Rhonheimer has set forth an interpretation of Aquinas on the natural law in *Natural Law and Practical Reason* (New York 2000). Rhonheimer argues, against the general weight of the Thomistic school, that man's reason is the formal promulgator of the natural law. Like the New Natural-Law Theorists, he seeks to rescue natural law from the claims that it is physicalistic or merely naturalistic, which places his work at the very crossroads of the dispute of the Thomistic School with the New Natural-Law Theorists.

Bibliography: B. F. BROWN, ed., *The Natural Law Reader* (New York 1960). G. DEL VECCHIO, *Philosophy of Law,* tr. T. O. MARTIN (Washington, D.C. 1953). A. PASSERIN D'ENTRÉVES, *Natural Law* (London 1951). D. FITZGERALD, "The State of Nature: Theories of the 17th and 18th Centuries and Natural Law," *American Catholic Philosophical Association, Proceedings of the Annual Meeting* 32 (1958) 161–172. J. F. GARCÊA, "The Natural Law," *ibid.* 22 (1947) 1–18. C. A. HART, "Metaphysical Foundations of the Natural Law," *ibid.* 24 (1950) 18–28. J. MARITAIN, *The Rights of Man and Natural Law,* tr. D. C. ANSON (New York 1943); *Man and the State* (Chicago, Ill. 1951). Notre Dame Univ., Natural Law Institute: *Proceedings* 1:5 (1947–1951). R. POUND, "The Revival of Natural Law," *Notre Dame Lawyer* 17 (1941–42) 287–372. H. A. ROMMEN, *The Natural Law,* tr. T. A. HANLEY (St. Louis 1947). Y. SIMON, *The Tradition of Natural Law,* tr. V. KUIC and R. J. THOMPSON (New York 1992). J. FINNIS, *Natural Law and Natural Right* (Oxford 1980); *Aquinas, Moral, Political, and Legal Theory* (Oxford 1998). G. GRISEZ, *The Way of the Lord Jesus,* 3 v. (Chicago 1983–1997). R. MCINERNY, *Ethica Thomistica* (Washington, D.C. rev. ed. 1997). R. HITTINGER, "Natural Law and Catholic Moral Theology," in *A Preserving Grace,* ed. M. CROMARTIE (Washington, D.C. 1997); "Natural Law as Law," *American Journal of Jurisprudence* 39 (1994) 1–32; *A Critique of the New Natural Law Theory* (Notre Dame, Ind. 1987). H. VEATCH, *For an Ontology of Morals* (Evanston, Ill. 1971). L. DEWAN, "St. Thomas, Our Natural Lights, and the Moral Order," *Angelicum* 67 (1990) 283–307; "St. Thomas, John Finnis, and the Political Common Good," *The Thomist* 64 (2000) 337–374; S. A. LONG, "St. Thomas Aquinas Through the Analytic Looking Glass," *ibid.* 65 (2001) 259–300. S. PINCKAERS, *The Sources of Christian Ethics,* tr. M. T. NOBLE (Washington, D.C. 1995). R. CESSARIO, *The Moral Virtues and Theological Ethics* (Notre Dame, Ind. 1992); *Introduction to Moral Theology* (Washington, D.C. 2001).

[B. F. BROWN/S. A. LONG]

THOMISTIC ANALYSIS

Natural law, as can be seen from its history, has been the subject of much controversy. A partial explanation for this is that advocates of natural law have frequently ignored its ontological basis and adopted as their starting point what they considered the distinctive characteristic of human nature. As each proponent had his own concept of human nature, it was inevitable that each would have his own peculiar philosophy of natural law. Yet when viewed in isolation from its ontological origin, human nature itself furnishes norms that have little more than psychological validity. CONFUCIUS and his early disciples recognized this. Thus the opening sentence of the Confucian classic, *The Unvarying Mean,* reads: "What is ordained of Heaven is called the essential nature of man; the following of this essential nature is called the natural law; the cultivation and refinement of this natural law is called culture." The Confucian view is close to that of St. Thomas Aquinas, who held that natural law is a participation of the eternal law in man, and that positive law consists in variable determinations of immutable fundamental principles as these are applied to the varying conditions and circumstances of social life. For both Aquinas and Confucius, positive law, itself an integral part of culture, is a development and implementation of the God-given natural law that man bears within him. This part of the article presents an analysis of the concept of natural law based on the philosophy of St. Thomas Aquinas. It discusses the relation of natural law to eternal law and positive law, the essentials of natural-law doctrine, the effects of natural law, man's awareness of the law, and its various confirmations in divine revelation and in papal teaching. More recent philosophical positions that are relevant to contemporary developments in theology are discussed in the third part of the article.

Relation to Eternal Law and Positive Law. Eternal law, natural law, and positive law, though distinct from one another, form a continuous series that may be compared to a tree. The eternal law is its hidden root; the natural law is its main trunk; and the different systems of positive law are its branches. All systems of human law contain, in varying proportions, natural principles and positive rules. The former are not made but are merely declared by human authority; therefore they may not be abrogated. In the words of Pope LEO XIII:

> Of the laws enacted by men, some are concerned with what is good or bad by its very nature; and they command men to follow after what is right and to shun what is wrong, adding at the same time a suitable sanction. But such laws by no means derive their origin from civil society; because just as civil society did not create human nature, so neither can it be said to be the author of the good which befits human nature, or of the evil which is contrary to it. Laws come before men live together in society and have their origin in the natural, and consequently in the eternal, law. The precepts, therefore, of the natural law, contained bodily in the laws of men, have not merely the force of human law, but they possess that higher and more august sanction which belongs to the law of nature and the eternal law. (*Libertas praestantissimum*, June 20, 1888)

Of the positive rules of law, the same Pontiff said:

> Now there are other enactments of the civil authority, which do not follow directly, but somewhat remotely, from the natural law, and decide many points which the law of nature treats only in a general and indefinite way. For instance, though nature commands all to contribute to the public peace and prosperity, still whatever belongs to the manner and circumstances, and conditions under which such service is to be rendered must be determined by the wisdom of men and not by Nature herself." (*ibid.*)

Thus, positive law is nothing more than an implementation of the natural law that must vary with the changing circumstances and conditions of social life.

Essentials of Natural-Law Doctrine. The eternal law is the plan of the divine providence governing the cosmos, man, and matter, both animate and inanimate. It is the ordering wisdom of God. Natural law is said by Thomas to be "nothing else" than a rational participation of this divine ordering wisdom. This is to say that natural law is defined by its metaphysical and theological character. The preceptive commands of the natural law derive their normativity from being rooted in the perfect being, good, and truth of God which are not admixed or limited by any potency or imperfection whatsoever. For St. Thomas "command" is an act of the intellect; thus, the precepts of the natural law while willed by God always are conformed to the divine wisdom and goodness. Natural law is that part of the eternal law that is properly applicable to man alone, although it may be spoken of lower creatures by a kind of analogy—by "participation and similitude."

Human reason is a "measured measure": it takes its measure from the objective ordering of human nature to the order of ends that perfects it, and thus consequently reason is enabled to be the rule and measure of right action. Yet the natural law is promulgated by God through instilling it in man's mind so as to be known—it is not "self-promulgated" by our knowing, but rather is promulgated by its being divinely instilled in the rational nature of man so as to be naturally known. Hence the natural law meets the requisites of law generally: it is promulgated by God who has authority over the commonwealth of being, and is for the sake of the common good (God being the extrinsic common good of the whole universe). Natural law is natural in several important senses. First, it is said to be natural because we are naturally subject to it, quite apart from any choice. The end, and indeed the whole hierarchy of ends, which perfects human nature is not among those things that are subject to human dominion. We may affect our motion to the end by our choice of means, but we can neither alter our natural ordination to happiness, nor alter that in which this happiness naturally consists. Second, the law is called natural because our initial awareness of the law—as an epistemic matter—derives from our awareness of our natural ordering to ends. For example, we do not choose to be creatures who thirst in the desert, who are lonely when lacking friends, who are confused when lacking truth: we simply *are* such creatures, and the initial awareness of the ordering of human nature to the whole hierarchy of ends is natural rather than received merely by book learning, or by oral tradition. Third, the natural law is said to be natural as contrasted with the *lex nova* of supernatural grace that governs the higher ordering of human nature to an end that transcends any natural end, namely, the essentially supernatural beatific vision of God.

Also fundamental to St. Thomas's philosophy of natural law is the distinction between the speculative reason and practical reason (*see* COGNITION, SPECULATIVE-PRACTICAL). Speculative knowledge pertains to that which cannot change and is sought for the sake of knowing itself, whereas practical knowledge pertains to the changeable (objects of deliberation) and is sought for the sake of action. Yet practical knowledge presupposes prior speculative adequation toward the ends of human living. Though virtuous action is conformed to right appetite, right appetite itself presupposes knowledge of the end. The natural sciences are the work of the speculative reason; natural law, on the other hand, is a "dictate of the practical reason." "The precepts of the natural law are to the practical reason what the first principles of demonstrations are to the speculative reason, because both are self-evident principles" (*Summa theologiae* 1a2ae, 94.2). Just as being is what first falls under the apprehension of the speculative reason, so good is what first falls under the apprehension of the practical reason. The practical reason is directed to action, and every agent acts for an end that it regards as good. Hence the first principle of the natural law is that good is to be done and evil is to be avoided. "All other precepts of the natural law are based upon this: so that whatever the practical reason naturally apprehends as man's good or evil belongs to the precepts of the natural law as something to be done or avoided" (*ibid.*).

Both the speculative and the practical reason attain the same degree of certainty with regard to first principles, but not with regard to the conclusions drawn from these principles. St. Thomas makes a point of this difference: "For, since the speculative reason is concerned chiefly with necessary things, which cannot be otherwise than they are, its proper conclusions, like universal principles, are true without fail. The practical reason, on the other hand, is concerned with contingent matters, which are human actions; consequently, although there is some necessity in its general principles, the more we descend to matters of detail the more frequently we encounter defects" (*Summa theologiae* 1a2ae, 94.4). Thus, for St. Thomas, it is vain to expect the same certainty in judicial decisions as in the physical sciences, but it would be rash to deny altogether the existence of universal principles that constitute the natural law.

Content of Natural Law. St. Thomas defines the natural law as the participation of the eternal law in the rational creature (*ibid.* 1a2ae, 91.2). It should be noted, however, that the participation to which he refers is limited and defective. "Human reason cannot have a full participation of the dictate of the Divine Reason, but according to its own mode, and imperfectly" (91.3 ad 1). In other words, man's natural participation of the eternal

law consists in the knowledge of certain general principles, not of every particular decision relating to an individual case. Since generality admits of infinite degrees, the precepts of natural law cannot be numbered exactly. All such precepts are instantiations of the primary precept that good is to be done and evil avoided. They are not simply deduced from the first precept of law (*primum preceptis legis*) that good is to be done and pursued and evil to be avoided, because this first premise is insufficiently determinate to serve such a role. This first precept of law embraces the whole dynamic ordering of man to the good and to the entire hierarchy of ends. Thus the natural law is made effective through virtues, the various *habitus* whereby one acts promptly, joyfully, and well, with respect to the end. As conclusions from the natural law become more and more remote, they shade off into the sphere of human law; therefore, there can be no clear-cut borderline between natural and human law. That is why St. Thomas maintains that the natural law can be changed by way of addition and is capable of unlimited growth (94.5).

For St. Thomas all the moral precepts of the Old Law pertain to the natural law in the sense that all are consonant with reason, although all do not pertain to natural law in the same way (100.1). Of the Ten Commandments the first three (according to the enumeration in common use among Catholics) pertain also to divine positive law inasmuch as man needs instruction by God to enable him to perceive their consonance with reason (it is a matter of natural justice that man owes public worship to God, and hence acceptance of whatever divine revelation dictates may be said to be commanded by the natural law as well as by the divine law). The remaining seven precepts pertain to the natural law not only in the sense that they are consonant with reason, but also inasmuch as this consonance does not require revelation to be known. The latter precepts are among the most proximate conclusions from the primary principles. "Honor thy father and thy mother" is a concretization of "good is to be done," and the remaining six Commandments are concretizations of "evil is to be avoided." All are among those things "that the natural reason of every man, of his own accord and at once, judges should be done or avoided" (*ibid.*). Other precepts of the Old Law pertain also to natural law, even though their rightness is not immediately apparent. An example is "Honor the person of the aged man" (*ibid.*), which is among the more remote conclusions. For St. Thomas, the two most immediate conclusions deducible from the primary precept are: "Thou shalt love the Lord thy God" and "Thou shalt love thy neighbor"; all the precepts of the Decalogue are referred to these (100.3 ad 1).

Besides moral precepts, St. Thomas mentions two other types, namely, the ceremonial and the judicial (or juridical). The ceremonial precepts are determinations of the natural law whereby man is directed to God, whereas the juridical precepts are determinations of the natural law whereby man is directed to his neighbor. Unlike conclusions, determinations belong not to the integral body of the natural law but to positive law, whether divine or human. There is no question that the ceremonial precepts, which deal with the ways and forms of worship, belong to divine positive law. As to the judicial or juridical precepts, although most are determinations of the natural law, some may be conclusions (however remote) of the natural law, and therefore constitute an integral part of it.

Determination vs. Conclusion. The distinction between a conclusion and a determination is clearly expressed by St. Thomas: "The law of nature has it that the evildoer should be punished; but that he be punished in this or that way, is a determination of the natural law" (*Summa theologiae* 1a2ae, 95.2). Similarly, it is a conclusion of the natural law that he who injures another should compensate him; but exactly how to compensate him is a determination that can be laid down by positive law and is subject to change. For instance, the following law is found in Exodus: "When a man steals an ox or a sheep and slaughters or sells it, he shall restore five oxen for the one ox, and four sheep for the one sheep" (21.37). Such a prescription is certainly not a part of the natural law because it is not evident to natural reason. The case is different with the following: "You shall not molest or oppress an alien, for you were once aliens yourselves in the land of Egypt" (Ex 22.21). "You shall not wrong any widow or orphan" (22.22). "The innocent and the just you shall not put to death" (23.7). "Never take a bribe, for a bribe blinds even the most clear-sighted and twists the words even of the just" (23.8). Whether these are referred to as moral or juridical precepts, they are conclusions of the natural law whose rectitude is apparent to man's reason.

While determinations form no part of the natural law, their proper function is to implement the natural law. An instance of this is found in the modern law of restitution. The natural law demands that one who is unjustly enriched at the expense of another should restore whatever benefits he has derived from his unjust act. In order to implement this dictate of natural reason, American judges have invented the fiction of "constructive trust." As Justice B. N. Cardozo has put it, "When property has been acquired in such circumstances that the holder of the legal title may not in good conscience retain the beneficial interest, equity converts him into a trustee" (225 N.Y. 380, 386). Judge C. S. Desmond has said that "a constructive trust will be erected whenever necessary to satisfy the demands of justice. Since a constructive trust

is merely 'the formula through which the conscience of equity finds expression,' its applicability is limited only by the inventiveness of men who find new ways to enrich themselves by grasping what should not belong to them" (299 N.Y. 27). Here positive law serves the natural law as a faithful and efficient handmaid.

The cases of constructive trust also furnish an apt illustration of the function of SYNDERESIS, CONSCIENCE, and PRUDENCE and their mutual workings with respect to natural law. It is the role of synderesis to perceive the principles of natural law: the principles here involved are that no one should enrich himself unjustly at the expense of another and that, if he does, he should be required to restore the benefits to the latter. It is the role of conscience to recognize that, in this or that particular case, a particular party is unjustly enriched. Finally, it is the role of prudence to devise or choose the best means of implementing the demands of justice. The interworkings of these functions in the jurist are seen at their best in the courts of equity, which had their origins in the English chancellor, who was at the same time "the keeper of the king's conscience." No doubt many of the chancellors were steeped in the Christian tradition of the natural law.

Effects of Natural Law. Among the principal effects of the natural law are its obligation and its sanction. The obligation of natural law arises from two sources: (1) primarily, the ordering wisdom of God; (2) secondarily, the essential order of things as naturally measuring the human reason, which reason is then fitted to be the measure of human acts. Of all creatures, man alone is endowed with a moral law and with reason to discern its obligations. He is aware that it is precisely this ingrained moral law that distinguishes him from the lower animals. It is the badge of his natural nobility. To obey the dictates of this moral law is to be true to his own nature. To play false to his nature, on the other hand, is to fall lower than brute animals, who, although devoid of rationality and a sense of obligation, follow instinctively the laws of their nature.

Regarding the provenance of law's obligation from God, Immanuel Kant observed: "Two things I contemplate with ceaseless awe; The stars of heaven, and man's sense of law." This expresses more than a cosmic emotion that springs from the feeling of harmony between macrocosm and microcosm; the awe of which Kant speaks comes also from an awareness, at least implicit, of God the Supreme Lawgiver. When one is aware that the same God who established the order of the universe also instituted the internal order of man's nature, his vision is like that of David, who saw the whole universe radiant with the glory of God (Ps 18.24). The laws that the Lord has written in man's heart, however, convey more than Kant's categorical imperatives; they are also a perennial delight. This high vision defies all human expression and imagination; yet one sure effect of it is that man's desire and will are "revolved, like a wheel which is moved evenly, by the love which moves the sun and the other stars" (Dante, *Paradiso*, 33.142).

Sanction. Only a portion of the natural law can be adopted and enforced by human law with its external sanctions. To take a simple instance, human law can forbid adultery with penal and civil sanctions. But Christ said that "anyone who so much as looks with lust at a woman has already committed adultery with her in his heart" (Mt 5.28). This, too, belongs to the natural law; but human law is too clumsy of an instrument to take cognizance of such cases. Does this mean that the natural law is without a sanction of its own? If so, it would be ineffectual. In fact, however, natural law is more effective than human law. In the first place, virtue is its own reward; and vice, its own punishment. One simply cannot be virtuous without being happy, nor can one sin without being miserable.

The end proportioned to man's nature is fulfillment through practical and speculative virtue, although in this ordering of creation, nature is further ordered to the beatific end and hence all natural ends are further ordered to beatitude. Natural law entails being entirely true to the actual ordering of human nature. VIRTUE promotes this cause, whereas VICE frustrates it. As a Chinese proverb has it, "there is no happiness like that of doing good." And it is equally true that there is no hell like sinning. Herein lies the intrinsic sanction of the natural law. Again, natural law is sanctioned by the law of spiritual causality: one reaps what one sows. "Do men gather grapes from thorns, or figs from thistles? Even so, every good tree bears good fruit, but the bad tree bears bad fruit" (Mt 7.16–17). In saying this, Christ merely restated part of the natural law. For it does not take a special revelation to know that "God's mill grinds slowly but surely," as the Greeks observed. Lao Tze put the same truth in this way: "Vast is Heaven's net; / Sparse-meshed it is, and yet / Nothing can slip through it." Finally, since God is supremely just, real virtue (especially when hidden) will not go unrewarded any more than deliberate and unrepented viciousness will go unpunished. The Christian law of mercy does not abolish this fundamental law of divine justice: on the contrary, it reveals the nature of this justice more fully, gives man a chance to begin anew, calls him to repentance, and enables him to meet its obligations. Christ did not come to destroy the natural law, but to fulfill it (cf. Mt 5.17). As a consequence of His coming, the Christian's obligation to fulfill the law has increased immeasurably. For unless his justice exceeds that of those who know not Christ, he shall not enter the kingdom of heaven.

Awareness of Natural Law. It has already been stated that our inceptive knowledge of the natural law proceeds not merely by book learning or custom, but from natural awareness of the ordering of human nature itself. Its primary precept of pursuing good and avoiding evil and its immediate conclusions are indemonstrable; yet they are self-evident principles of the practical reason. Thus it is not merely or primarily by logical or empirical reasoning that the first precepts of the natural law are known, but by the natural habitus called "synderesis." Synderesis is a habit of the reason; it is not an all-purpose moral intuitionism along the lines of G. E. Moore, but rather a habitus of moral light through whose act nature inclines to good and warns from evil. Its act presupposes that knowledge required for the intelligibility of the precepts involved. Conscience, on the other hand, is the act that applies this general knowledge to a particular situation. If, for instance, a person sees a little child crawling into a well, he sees immediately that it is his duty to hold the child back and save its life, no matter whose child it may happen to be. This awareness is the working of conscience. If, moreover, one fails to rescue the child and it is drowned in the well, he feels remorse. This, too, is the working of conscience, which, having given the command in the first instance, applies its sanction for failure to carry it out. Synderesis is the natural habit whereby we are disposed to know the law, and conscience is the act of its application to particular cases.

Since the elementary principles of the natural law are innate in human nature, evidences of it appear even in primitive law. Yet there is a growth in the content of natural law with the progress of civilization. As the human mind becomes more and more enlightened, it becomes capable of devising new and more effective methods of ascertaining the truth and implementing the natural law. Similarly, the human heart, refined by the developments of arts and letters, grows in sensitivity to new values and needs of humanity; as a consequence, it prompts legislators and judges to draw new conclusions from the first principles of the natural law. In this way, our awareness of naturally just claims has been enhanced in the course of history, as the justice of these claims is recognized but not made by human law. One example is the development of moral consensus regarding the evil of the institution of chattel slavery. Another is the growing moral awareness of the evils that may ensue upon the new technology of biological cloning technologies that applied to man deny the dignity of the human person.

Divine Revelation and Papal Teaching. The natural law is independent of any divine revelation. Its first principles are common to all men and are not the exclusive possession of the Judeo-Christian tradition. However, there can be no question that Christian writers have been greatly aided by revelation in their discovery of the natural law and natural rights. This point was brought out clearly by Chancellor James Kent in *Wightman v Wightman* (Chancery Court of New York, 1820. 4 Johnson Ch. 343). Pronouncing the nullity of the marriage of a lunatic, Chancellor Kent said: "That such a marriage is criminal and void by the Law of Nature, is a point universally conceded. And, by the Law of Nature, I understand those fit and just rules of conduct which the Creator has prescribed to Man, as a dependent and social being; and which are to be ascertained from the deductions of right reason, though they may be more precisely known, and more explicitly declared by Divine Revelation."

It is truly characteristic of her catholicity that the Church has persistently "affirmed the value of what is human and is in conformity with nature," notwithstanding her teaching on original sin. PIUS XII, the greatest jurist among the modern popes, never tired of speaking of the natural law. In his address to members of the International Convention of Humanistic Studies (1949), he observed: "She [the Church] does not admit that in the sight of God man is mere corruption and sin. On the contrary, in the eyes of the Church, original sin did not intimately affect man's aptitudes and strength, and has left essentially intact the natural light of his intelligence and his freedom. Man endowed with this nature is undoubtedly injured and weakened by the heavy inheritance of a fallen nature, deprived of supernatural and preternatural gifts. He must make an effort to observe the natural law—this with the powerful assistance of the Grace of Christ—so that he can live as the honor of God and his dignity as man require." Starting from the essential nobility of human nature, the pope went on to say:

> The natural law here is the foundation on which the social doctrine of the Church rests. It is precisely her Christian conception of the world which has inspired and sustained the Church in building up this doctrine on such a foundation. When she struggles to win and defend her own freedom, she is actually doing this for the true freedom and for the fundamental rights of man. In her eyes these essential rights are so inviolable that no argument of State and no pretext of the common good can prevail against them. . . . It cannot touch these rights for they constitute what is most precious in the common good.

Pius XII saw that the chief source of confusion and disorder in the 20th century lay in the deliberate abandonment of the natural law. In his very first encyclical, *Summi Pontificatus*, he asserted: "One leading mistake We may single out, as the fountainhead, deeply hidden, from which the evils of the modern state derive their origin. Both in private life and in the state itself, and moreover in the mutual relations of race with race, of country with country, the one universal standard of morality is set aside; by which We mean the natural law, now buried away under a mass of destructive criticism and of neglect." This has become possible because in some states, at least, the pernicious doctrine of state absolutism has prevailed, with the result that the state has actually usurped the position of God. When the Author of the natural law is set aside, there can be no room for the natural law, which, as Pius XII insisted, "reposes, as upon its foundation, on the notion of God, the Almighty Creator and Father of us all, the Supreme and Perfect Law-giver, the wise and just Rewarder of human conduct."

Bibliography: J. C. H. WU, *Fountain of Justice* (New York 1955). J. MESSNER, *Social Ethics: Natural Law in the Modern World,* tr. J. J. DOHERTY (new ed. St. Louis, Mo. 1964). M. T. ROONEY, *Lawlessness, Law, Sanction* (Washington, D.C. 1937). Notre Dame Univ., *Natural Law Institute: Proceedings* v. 1–5 (1947–51). J. D. WILD, *Plato's Modern Enemies and the Theory of Natural Law* (Chicago, Ill. 1953). P. J. STANLIS, *Edmund Burke and the Natural Law* (Ann Arbor, Mich. 1958). A. G. CICOGNANI, *Canon Law,* tr. J. O'HARA and F. BRENNAN (2d ed. Westminster, Md. 1947; repr. 1949). J. MARITAIN, *Man and the State* (Chicago, Ill. 1951); *An Introduction to the Basic Problems of Moral Philosophy,* tr. C. N. BORGERHOFF (Albany, N.Y. 1990). Y. SIMON, *The Tradition of Natural Law,* tr. V. KUIC and R. J. THOMPSON (New York 1992). R. MCINERNY, *Ethica Thomistica* (Washington, D.C. 1997); *Aquinas on Human Action: A Theory of Practice* (Washington, D.C. 1992). R. HITTINGER, "Natural Law and Catholic Moral Theology," in *A Preserving Grace,* ed. M. CROMARTIE (Washington, D.C. 1997); "Natural Law as Law," *American Journal of Jurisprudence* 39 (1994) 1–32.

[J. C. H. WU/S. A. LONG]

CONTEMPORARY THEOLOGY AND PHILOSOPHY

One distinction that is indispensable for understanding the place of natural law in contemporary theology and philosophy is that between the ontology of natural law, or its existence, and the epistemology of natural law, or the knowledge of principles that may be said to constitute it. It seems from the dissent that takes place in contemporary discussions of natural law that there is more disagreement over the epistemology than there is over the ontology.

Protestant Criticisms. S. E. Stumpf suggests such a distinction when he asserts that contemporary Protestant thought is fundamentally critical of natural-law theory, although it does not repudiate the theory completely. For the Protestant, the disagreement arises from a philosophy that is based on the accessibility of nature to man's rational powers, an accessibility that he is unwilling to admit. For him the "Catholic" natural law is associated with the Thomistic notion of the analogy of being, according to which the natural law is defined in terms of the eternal law that exists in God. The promulgation of this law, as has been explained above, is made in the rational nature of man. The application of its principles, whether primary, secondary, or tertiary, to contingent situations is made by the consciences of men in their practical prudential judgments. For many Protestants, this explanation places too much importance on stable natures and rational powers, and not enough upon the ambiguity in every moral situation. Reinhold NIEBUHR's criticism of what he calls "classical, catholic, and modern natural law concepts" proceeds along these very lines. He insists that these concepts do not allow for the historical character of human existence because they are radicated in a classical rationalism that did not understand history. These concepts, for Niebuhr, do not appreciate the uniqueness of the historical situation or the accretions that came into the definition of natural law through history. The general principles are too inflexible, and the definitions of these general principles are too historically conditioned. Niebuhr does not deny an "essential" nature of man, but the profoundest problem for him is the historical elaboration of man's essential human nature, on the one hand, and the historical biases that have insinuated themselves into the definition of that essential human nature, on the other.

A second criticism, for Niebuhr, is the tendency in the classical theory to make the law of love an addition to the law of obligation, with the result that the one deals with the determinate possibilities and the other the indeterminate possibilities of good. In his view, clear lines between determinate and indeterminate possibilities cannot and should not be drawn. Niebuhr illustrates this by saying that justice is an application of the law of love for which the rules are not absolute but relative. All such rules are applications of the law of love and do not have independence apart from it. They would be autonomous only if they were based upon an "essential" social structure, and there is no definition of such an essential structure of community, except the law of love. Stumpf makes this the cardinal point of criticism between the Protestant and Catholic conceptions of natural law. The ground of ethics is love even for the natural man and such love is the fulfillment and completion of the law. Love and grace are not dimensions of the supernatural order only, but justice is infused and transfigured by love. The Protestant conception, then, is fundamentally the confrontation of man with the God of judgment and love commanding him, not through the mediation of abstract primary, secondary, and tertiary principles, but subjecting him to the single imperative of an undifferentiated and naturally indefinable love. No law mediates between man and God— only love—and this love is the natural law for the very reason that love is the law of man's essential human nature, which passes otherwise undefined. The metaphysical structure of reality, and the teleological structure of nature, are each set aside as at best merely provisional and awaiting reformulation in the new law.

Different Views of Reason. It should be seen at once that all Catholic and many Protestant theologians would admit an essential human nature, but even there the word "essential" demands quotation marks and precise refinements of meaning. R. E. Fitch, dean of the Pacific School of Religion, is quoted in a footnote of an article by A. R. Jonsen "Arguing Ethics" (*Homiletic and Pastoral Review* [Jan. 1964] 302), in which reference is made to two entirely different views of reason that are possible in any discussion of natural law. For the Catholic, the stress is on the reason that is Aristotelian, classical, ordered, and universal; for the Protestant, the emphasis is on the reason that is individualistic, inquiring, and experimental. Fitch says that both are needed, and no one will question that conclusion. The combination of the two stresses might be assisted by the suggestive use of the phrase "prismatic analysis" in connection with the formation of the practical prudential judgments of the individual conscience. It can readily be seen how the most general principles of law passing through this individual human prism receive all the colorations, the ambiguities, the obstacles, and the helps from the particular existential historical moment of their passage. For the person who leans toward a somewhat complete situationalism, no law passes through the human prism but the law of love; anything else that he might designate as law is not exigent and obligatory, but guiding and tentative, provisional and contingent. The position of the moderate situationalist is one that appreciates both the imperative of obligation and the imperative of love, while giving full validity to all the contingent factors in the ambiguous ethical situation. Between the divine transcendence and the ever-changing human situation, J. C. Bennett places the "middle axioms," which seem to be employed to mediate between more general norms and the unique structural situation. Niebuhr speaks of "enduring structures of meaning and value" that must be assured a valid role in the ethical choice. Will Herberg finds some clarification of these conceptions of the "enduring structures of meaning and value" of Niebuhr and the "middle axioms" of Bennett by citing Edmund BURKE, who has this to say about natural rights:

> These metaphysical rights, entering into common life, like rays of light which pierce into a dense medium, are . . . refracted from a straight line . . . [and] undergo such a variety of refractions and reflections that it becomes absurd to speak of them as if they continued in the simplicity of their original direction. ("Conservatives, Liberals and

the Natural Law, II," *National Review,* June 19, 1962)

Philosophical Presuppositions. The fundamental disagreement on natural-law theory, therefore, is rooted in philosophical presuppositions on the nature of law, on the nature of man, on the very meaning of "natural." The signification of a theory of natural law for the Roman Catholic, the Protestant, and the secular humanist will be conditioned from the very start by these philosophical presuppositions. In fact, many theological disagreements find their ultimate sources of division in philosophical premises. To those inclined to regard metaphysical knowledge as not so respectable a knowledge as that of the empiro-logical sciences, the intelligibility of nature, of man, of law, and of God will be regarded with increasing skepticism. All these obstacles that are profoundly philosophical will make difficult the acceptance even of the existence of natural law at its barest minimum. When, in addition to the difference in philosophical presuppositions, the differences in theology concerning the nature of original sin and its consequences for the nature of man are studied, it can be more clearly seen why natural law for the Catholic has been a dialectical tool. It stands to reason that he can employ this tool effectively only if he constantly appreciates these philosophical and theological differences.

Catholic Theology. Natural law has understandably been of interest to the Catholic theologian, who has always interested himself in the mutual relation of reason and faith and is convinced that God operates in history through the natures of things and especially through the nature of man. He presumes that man's nature has not been totally deformed by original sin and that his intellect and will are capable of constructing a natural theology and a moral philosophy that are valid and complemented by supernatural theology and a moral theology. In light of this judgment, he does not hesitate to study the essential ordering of human nature and to discover certain conformities and deformities with respect to it. Unfortunately, the principal obstacle to the acceptance of natural law in modern times is the mistaken notion that this law belongs to the Catholic Church and no other. Yet it is undeniably true that the Catholic Church has been the most vigorous defender of natural-law theory in areas ranging from property rights to contraception and from the problems of medical ethics to those of nuclear warfare.

With the gradual lowering of moral standards, however, the Church has given more of her magisterial attention to the claims of nature and justice. J. FUCHS, in *Lex Naturae zur Theologie des Naturrechts* (Düsseldorf 1955, 9–12), shows that since the reign of Pius IX the term "natural law" has been employed with increasing frequency in the documents of the Church. The term was constantly mentioned in the allocutions and discourses of Pius XII on the issues of peace and war, on political organizations, and on the obligations of the many professions, especially medicine and law. Yet the fact that the Church has been concerned with defending the natural and to relate it to the supernatural does not make the natural itself supernatural. The natural law is the basis and foundation for the supernatural code of ethics found in moral theology, whereas the additional evidence for certain forms of ethical conduct derives from biblical sources and from tradition. At times the papal documents refer to elevated human nature, to human nature supernaturalized by grace; where this is done, however, the texts are clear, and such citations do not permit a reader to conclude that the argument from reason has been so substantially undermined that only Catholic faith provides a valid and cogent ground for ethical conduct. The interrelation between faith and reason on the precise question of the probative value of evidence from natural law is most certainly ground for debate among Catholic theologians, but no one of them would deny completely all probative value and all cogency to a natural-law argument.

This issue has received heightened attention as a result of the discussions of the normative relation of nature and grace ensuing after the publication of Henri de LUBAC's famous *Surnaturel* (Paris 1946). The issue is whether the integrity of the natural order does not require a natural end for man (granted that this end is no longer actually the ultimate end, and that in the order of divine providence that this end is further ordered to the beatific *finis ultimus*). De Lubac argued the impossibility of any natural end for man proportioned to human nature itself. This denial has seemed to many Thomists to constitute a denial of the relative integrity and autonomy of the natural order. St. Thomas Aquinas expressly held that man could have been created in a purely natural state, (e.g., *Quod.* I, q. 4, a.3, resp.) and that if man had been so created, the deprivation of supernatural beatitude would not constitute a punishment as now it does (*De malo,* q.1, art. 5, ad 15). This clearly implies in St. Thomas's teaching that there is a felicity or end proportionate to man's nature, distinct from the further ordering in grace to which man is now actually called and toward which natural ends are now ordered. In the years following *Surnaturel,* the works of Hans Urs von BALTHASAR and those by thinkers of the *COMMUNIO* school who radicalize this position of de Lubac (e.g., David Schindler), as well as of some by Greek Orthodox theologians (John Zizioulas) have brought these questions further into the foreground. The Thomistic teaching persists in exerting a powerful influence over the formulation and understanding of the issue of natural law within Catholic theology.

Charge of Vagueness and Ambiguity. A fundamental criticism, especially from circles outside the Church, points to the difficulties in the presentation of the natural law; the presentation seems to be indeterminate and unsatisfactory, at least as its defenders formulate it. Again, the evidence that the defenders of natural law adduce may not be cogent in the light of differences in moral beliefs and practices at different times and places. N. Bobbio, in "Quelques arguments contre le droit naturel" [*Le droit naturel* (Paris 1959) 175–190], suggests this criticism when he remarks that philosophers are inclined to deny that the natural law is natural, whereas legal scholars tend to deny that it is a law. The response for the Thomistic supporters of natural law is that it is both natural and genuinely a law, that it is verifiable as natural and valid in an authentic meaning of law. Robert Gordis points out the dilemma of those who stand outside the dominant tradition of natural law but are sympathetic to its value. He refers to Robert M. Hutchins's observation that natural law appears to many to be "a body of doctrine that is so vague as to be useless or so biased as to be menacing." For such persons the vagueness and ambiguity of terms such as "nature" and "natural" have always been a part of the history of ideas. For them the opinion of Leslie Stephens may not be the cynical exaggeration that it is for others: "Nature is a word contrived in order to introduce as many equivocations as possible into all theories, political, legal, artistic or literary, into which it enters." Critics of natural law are ready to add to the catalog of meanings given to "nature." D. G. Ritchie, in *Natural Rights* (2d ed. [London 1903] 20 47), has a chapter "On the History of the Idea of Nature in Law and Politics"; Erik Wolf's *Das Problem der Naturrechtslehre* (Karlsruhe 1955) gives nine meanings for "nature" in the context of natural law alone; and Philippe Delhaye's *Permanence du droit naturel* ([Louvain 1960] 9–21) has an introduction that explains at least 20 meanings of "nature."

This testimony to the vagueness and ambiguity of the term "nature" was not unknown to the proponents of natural law from their examinations of its meaning for the Stoics, John Duns Scotus, Bishop J. Butler, Hume, and Rousseau. Yves Simon commented on this difficulty in *The Tradition of Natural Law*. He considers the confusion of ideological aspiration with philosophic contemplation of the natural law to have led to the tendency to suppose that natural law can decide "with the universality proper to essences, incomparably more issues than it is actually able to decide." He notes the tendency of certain teachers to treat as matters of natural law issues that demand "treatment in terms of prudence" and contends that such exaggerated claims in behalf of natural law will tend to engender "disappointment and skepticism" as well as that contempt naturally felt for sophistry (*The Tradition of Natural Law* [New York 1992] 23–24).

Yet the proponent of natural law does insist that human rational nature is subject to a normative order in which may be verified the essential features of law: it is promulgated by God from creation, it is prescriptive and preceptive insofar as providing reasons to do and not to do, and it is for the sake of the common good, issued by the One who is the governor of the entire commonwealth of being. That in the order of knowing we are aware of moral truths prior to being aware of these as being law merely establishes a distinction between the order of discovery and the order of being. Accusations of ambiguity arguably betray a deontological tendency that would obviate the role of virtue in the prudential articulation of the implications of the natural law. The study of the human virtues and natural law are essentially complementary, for in its classical formulation natural law is made effective in and through human virtues—active potencies or dispositions for acting strongly and joyfully toward the good.

Contributions of Anthropology. As helps in this analysis, tradition, revelation, and authority are implied by the actual further ordering of nature to grace, as well as by the purely natural calling of human persons to the extrinsic common good of the universe (God), of justice and truth, of the political state, and even of the family. The traditional elaboration of natural law must also be supplemented by materials from cultural anthropology and from all the sciences insofar as they do not stray from their formal objects. Thomistic ethicians have an important function in the incorporation of these contributions. In "Human Evolution: A Challenge to Thomistic Ethics" [*International Philosophical Quarterly* 2 (1962) 50–80], Charles Fay shows how some of the changes resulting from man's biocultural evolution may so transform the relation between man and nature (e.g., atomic energy, polymer chemistry) that certain acts may receive a different moral evaluation. R. H. Beis, in "Some Contributions of Anthropology to Ethics" [*Thomist* 28 (1964) 174–224], considers the several advantages that a knowledge of anthropology holds for the ethician and discounts the anxiety of those who consider that anthropology supports only ethical relativity. In fact, Beis finds contradictions in the position of anthropological ethical relativity when it attempts to assume values of its own.

The philosopher-theologian, interested in a firm foundation for his natural-law position, is not unconscious of the advances in the contributions of anthropology to ethics. He is encouraged to recognize that anthropology does not scientifically establish ethical relativity. However, it is appropriate to the study of natural law to clarify the distinction between what is universal and invariable in human nature and what is conditioned by the circumstances of cultural development.

Other Disciplines. It may be overly optimistic and naïve to consider that there can be more fruitful agreement on natural law by further clarification of the two aspects of human nature, the absolute and invariable, and the relative and conditioned. If the former has been emphasized in the past, the latter is not being ignored in the present. This is especially so in contemporary discussions of natural-law jurisprudence.

Again, the modern ethician and theologian who introduces references to natural law in medical morality or in sexual ethics does not ignore scientific facts that are relevant. The discussion of the licit use of ANOVULANTS in certain pathological conditions raises many questions for whose answer the ethician is ready to accept all the scientific help he can get. The modern ethician and theologian of natural law takes into account all relevant scientific data and frequently finds the lack of consensus not among ethicians and theologians, but among scientists themselves. Where lack of consensus among practitioners of the sciences flows from an inadequate philosophy of nature that generates confusion about and obscures natural teleology, substantial nature, or other essentially philosophic elements, such lack of consensus implies only that those in question should educate themselves. But where genuine differences within a field itself—as opposed to precursory differences—are at issue, the natural lawyer must await clarification. One necessity thus revealed is that of distinguishing ideologically driven errors and confusions flowing from scientism from the more limited methods of positive science.

Role of the Church. To avoid such confusion, the Catholic Church has always maintained that the natural law is an object of its teaching authority and that its guidance is necessary for an adequate knowledge of the natural law. This is not merely a pragmatic decision, but a clear mandate implied by the further ordering of all natural ends to the beatific finality. Just as the natural law governs man's normative ordering toward the ends proportionate to his nature, so divine law governs the order toward that supernatural end which is disproportionate to any finite nature. Gerald Kelly, SJ, refers to the moral (not physical) necessity of revelation in this regard. In other words, the guidance of the Church is a practical, or moral, necessity for obtaining an adequate knowledge of the natural law. When it is considered that the natural law is sufficiently promulgated, according to its proponents, if there is promulgation of its primary and secondary precepts in such a way that no one can be invincibly ignorant of these, this alone might be thought to leave so much to be discovered by man himself that, without the assistance of some guide and authority, his search would not be very satisfactory. Of course, this by itself might only indicate that the further implications of the natural law are not effortlessly known by all, which is indeed true even of the natural order of the physical cosmos, and hence is all the more true of man's participation in the eternal law. The need for grace is not unique to this area of human striving, either—any integrally right use of human capacities will require grace to be ordered to the due end of beatific finality. Nonetheless, the harm done to human affectivity and inclination by sin, and the higher ordering of all natural ends to the beatific finality, alike indicate the need for guidance from the custodian of divine revelation to assure correct understanding of the natural law.

St. Thomas makes clear (*Summa theologiae* I-II, q. 85, a. 1, resp.) that nature is, in part, destroyed by original sin. He identifies three senses of human nature: 1) the principles and properties of human nature; 2) the natural inclination to virtue; and 3) that gift of original justice conferred upon the first parents of the human race. He states that the third (the gift of original justice) is destroyed by sin; the second (the natural inclination to virtue) is diminished (but not utterly destroyed) by sin; and the first (the principles and properties of human nature) is neither destroyed nor diminished by sin. Because the root of our natural inclination to virtue is the rational nature, this inclination cannot be wholly extinguished. Knowledge of the natural law and its implications is always in principle naturally possible. The natural tendency of the rational creature to God cannot wholly be eradicated. But because the natural inclination to virtue is diminished by sin, full knowledge of—and robust conformity to—the natural law implies the aid of revelation and grace. This is especially so inasmuch as the diminishment of natural inclination by sin implies diminished natural vigor in the pursuit of the good—whereas it is those who vigorously strain toward the good who are most able to discern its implications.

See Also: NATURE; MAN; LAW; LAW, PHILOSOPHY OF.

Bibliography: C. W. KEGLEY and R. W. BRETALL, eds., *Reinhold Niebuhr: His Religious, Social and Political Thought* (New York 1956). *Handbook of Christian Theology,* ed. M. HALVERSON and A. H. COHEN (New York 1958). J. COGLEY et al., *Natural Law and Modern Society* (Cleveland, O.H. 1963). L. R. WARD, "Natural Law in Contemporary Legal Philosophy" *Proceedings of the American Catholic Philosophical Association* 33 (1959) 137–143. S. BERTKE, *The Possibility of Invincible Ignorance of the Natural Law* (Catholic University of America Studies in Sacred Theology 58; Washington, D.C. 1941). R. D. LUMB, "Law, Reason and Will," *Philosophical Studies* 10 (1960) 179–189. G. P. GRANT, *Philosophy in the Mass Age* (New York 1960). J. MARITAIN, *Science and Wis-*

dom,* tr. B. WALL (London 1940); *An Introduction to the Basic Problems of Moral Philosophy,* tr. C. N. BORGERHOFF (Albany, N.Y. 1990). Y. SIMON, *The Tradition of Natural Law,* tr. V. KUIC and R. J. THOMPSON (New York 1992). R. MCINERNY, *Ethica Thomistica,* rev. ed. (Washington, D.C. 1997); *Aquinas on Human Action: A Theory of Practice* (Washington, D.C. 1992); *The Question of Christian Ethics* (Washington, D.C. 1990). R. HITTINGER, ''Natural Law and Catholic Moral Theology,'' in *A Preserving Grace,* ed. M. CROMARTIE (Washington, D.C. 1997); also, ''Natural Law as Law,'' *American Journal of Jurisprudence* 39 (1994) 1–32.

[T. A. WASSMER/S. A. LONG]

NATURAL LAW AND JURISPRUDENCE

The philosophy of the NATURAL LAW is predicated upon the existence of an objective moral order, within the scope of human intelligence and the capacity of human virtue, upon which the peace and happiness of personal, national, and international life depend, and to which all human beings, civil societies, and voting majorities are bound in conscience to conform.

According to this philosophy human beings are endowed by their Creator with certain natural rights and obligations to enable them to attain in human dignity their divine destiny. These natural rights and obligations are inalienable precisely because they are God-given. They are antecedent, both in logic and in nature, to the formation of civil societies and the casting of ballots. They are not granted by the beneficence of the state, democratic or otherwise; consequently the tyranny of the state, democratic or otherwise, cannot destroy them. In fact it is the moral responsibility of the state, through the instrumentality of its civil law, to acknowledge their existence and protect their exercise, to foster and facilitate their enjoyment by the wise and scientific implementation of the natural law with a practical and consonant code of civil rights and obligations.

Search for Objectivity. The construction and maintenance of a *corpus juris* adequately implementing the natural law is a monumental and perpetual task demanding the constant devotion, the clearest intelligence, and the most mature scholarship of the legal profession. For the fundamental principles of the natural law, universal and immutable as the human nature from which they derive, require rational application to the constantly changing political, social, economic, and technological conditions of dynamic civil society.

The application of the natural law postulates change since the circumstances of human existence necessarily change. It is inconsistent with unquestioning complacency in the *status quo*. It demands a reasoned acceptance of the good and a rejection of the bad, in all that is new, and advocates a critical search for the better. It postulates constant scrutiny of the data of history, sociology, politics, economics, psychology, biology, medicine, and other pertinent human knowledge. It insists that effort toward improvement of the *corpus juris* be made in the light of the origin, dignity, and destiny of man and in the knowledge of the origin, nature, and purpose of the state.

The relationship between natural law and civil law or, as it is popularly denominated, between morals and law, is the prime problem of jurisprudence. It is a particularly difficult and delicate problem in a society such as the pluralistic American society in which large groups of citizens sincerely differ, theologically and philosophically, about the morality of many activities and institutions and about the proper public policy of the state concerning them.

Americans were once divided upon the moral and legal issues of human slavery. They were later divided upon the moral and legal issues of racial discrimination. They have been divided over the moral and legal issues concerning capital and labor, compulsory military service and thermonuclear weapons, loyalty oaths and flag salutes, prize fighting and gambling, Bible reading and prayers in public schools, the equal treatment of children in private schools, the use of alcoholic beverages, the control of obscenity, and many other moral-legal questions.

Despite their shared reverence for the sanctity of human LIFE, for the sacredness of MARRIAGE, for the holiness of the marriage act, for the dignity of children, the fact is that Americans have been divided over civil laws and public policy respecting marriage and divorce, monogamy and polygamy, adultery and fornication, prostitution and homosexuality, artificial contraception and insemination, abortion and sterilization, the adoption of children, suicide and euthanasia, capital punishment, and even the questions of blood transfusions or medical aid to sick or dying children.

Possibly some of the differences will never be solved to the satisfaction of all, but will be determined from time to time merely by majority vote. Nevertheless the peace and good order of a pluralistic society demand that it sincerely strive to resolve its differences, as best it can, with civil dialogue and mutual respect, on sound moral and legal principles.

Law and Morality. Americans desire a civil society and a legal system founded upon valid principles of morality. The philosophy of the Declaration of Independence epitomizes and expresses this desire. It appeals in express terms to God, the Creator, the Supreme Judge of the World, and expressly commits the young American nation to His divine providence, basing its claim to freedom upon inalienable rights bestowed by God.

Morality Influencing Law. The moral law comes from God. The civil order depends upon the moral order. The good society cannot be based upon police power alone. For it is MORALITY that imposes the obligation in conscience to obey civil law. Without such obedience the enforcement of civil law, the administration of justice, and the preservation of liberty would be impossible. It is a fact of human experience that the majority of people, in the majority of their actions, habitually obey the law of the land, not out of fear of police sanctions, but because they recognize that they are morally bound to do so. The moral obligation to obey civil law is the foundation of a decent and free society.

Civil law, accordingly, must respect the natural law. Man-made law cannot validly command the violation of any God-given obligation, nor can it validly prohibit the exercise of any God-given right. Law must be just. An unjust law cannot, of itself, bind the human conscience. An unjust law is, in reality, no law at all, but merely an act of governmental violence and a species of immoral force. At various times and places men have been forced to submit to immoral laws. For almost 100 years in America the abomination of human slavery was enforced by law. An immoral law contradicts CONSCIENCE. Conscience and the natural law repudiate immoral civil laws.

This is not to say that each individual is sufficient unto himself to determine arbitrarily which laws he will obey and which he will disregard. In cases of genuine doubt, it is reasonable to presume that civil laws, enacted under the safeguards of constitutional processes, are consonant with the natural law. Nevertheless, a palpably immoral law cannot bind the human conscience. There is a moral right to disregard it. There may be a moral obligation to resist it to the death. In the face of a clear and irreconcilable conflict between the natural and the civil law, between morals and law, we must obey God rather than man.

The great body of American law is based upon the natural law. The incorporation of sound moral principles has been the most conspicuous factor in the development and refinement of American common and constitutional law. A simple example is seen in the fundamental axiom of criminal law: that, except for reasonable minor exceptions, the overt act does not make a criminal unless his mental state is criminal—*actus non facit reum nisi mens sit rea*—which was a principle of moral theology long before its adoption by criminal law. Similarly, with understandable exceptions, the moral principle of personal responsibility, based upon the premise of freedom of the will, constitutes the foundation and determines the superstructure of all of American criminal and civil law. The legality of American free society is essentially predicated upon morality.

The refining influence of morals upon American law is evident in the development of equity; in the evolution of the law of contracts and torts; in the explication of the law of theft, from larceny through embezzlement to false pretenses; in the law of sales, from the crude *caveat emptor* to decent dealing; in the law of agency, from mere authority to fiduciary obligations; in the law of property, from raw power to social duties; in the law of industrial relations, from laissez-faire rugged individualism to fraternal responsibilities; in American constitutional law, from allowance of human slavery to the statutes initiating freedom and equality; in the law of equal protection, from maintenance of racial segregation to the legislation upholding human dignity; in the law of procedural and substantive due process; and so with many other principles and precepts of American common and constitutional law.

Law Encouraging Morality. But the moral order depends upon the legal order also. Civil laws are necessary for the recognition and the implementation of morals in organized society. Without the support and the sanction of civil law, many moral obligations could not be fulfilled, and many moral rights could not be protected against the encroachments of the unscrupulous and the machinations of the malicious. The law and the police power of the state are necessary to protect the vast majority of the people in their fixed intention and obligation to observe the precepts of the moral order.

Furthermore, the law must do more than protect those obvious moral rights and obligations upon which all men easily agree. It must do more than enforce the immediately evident principles of the natural law about which there is a general consensus. The law has an educative as well as a coercive function. The law cannot escape the perplexing task of advancing from the immediately evident and universally conceded principles of morality to the derivative principles that depend upon mediate and empirical evidence. Law is a practical and progressive science. It must specify and apply particular principles of morality by enacting specific and particular rules and standards that do not bask in the sunlight of universal agreement. The law is frequently relegated to the dimmer light of argument and controversy; sometimes, unfortunately, to the semidarkness of strident partisanship and bitter emotionalism. In light or in darkness, the law must relentlessly express, as best it can, the public morality and the common good of society. Moral sensitivity must characterize public opinion, objectivity must prevail in the legislative process, and scholarly wisdom in the judicial process.

Public Morality. Fundamental to the concept and purpose of civil law is the fact that legality and morality, while interrelated and interdependent, are not identical. Their respective fields overlap, but they are not coextensive. Many crimes are sins, and many sins are crimes, but crime and sin are not the same thing. Certain crimes, such as the so-called public-welfare offenses that are penalized as overt acts regardless of the mental state, can be committed without sin; certain sins, such as simple lying or solitary masturbation, can be committed without crime. But lying that involves fraud or libel or masturbation that involves public indecency are both sins and crimes. They are sins because they are immoral. They are crimes because they offend that aspect of the common good of civil society that is properly called public morality. It is not the purpose or function of civil law to prohibit or penalize an immoral act simply because it is immoral. The end or purpose of civil law is the public or common good of civil society. In the field of morals, therefore, the scope of civil law is not the area of purely private morality, but of public morality.

It is not easy to delineate with precision the specific fields of public and private morality. It is difficult to draw a sharp line that will clearly and satisfactorily distinguish those moral actions that properly fall within the legislative competence of the state and those that are properly beyond it. In such a task reasonable men may differ, and their opinions may vary from time to time and from culture to culture. The distinction is certainly not the difference between publicity and secrecy. The publicized lie is not a crime. The secret murder is. The distinction is between those actions that primarily concern the actor as an individual, and those actions that concern the neighbor or the community in such a way as to affect substantially the common good of civil society.

The field of public morality is by no means confined to criminal law; it embraces also the areas of civil law, such as contracts, torts, property, equity, commercial and industrial rights, and especially constitutional law. It is helpful for understanding of public morality to consider a number of obviously immoral actions punished as crimes by mature and civilized states.

Murder, manslaughter, rape, mayhem, assault and battery violate the personal rights of others to life and bodily integrity; kidnapping and false imprisonment violate the personal rights of others to liberty and locomotion; robbery, larceny, embezzlement, and false pretenses violate the personal rights of others to property; arson and burglary violate the personal rights of others to habitation and enclosure; libel violates the personal rights of others

to reputation; bribery and perjury pervert the administration of justice and obstruct the preservation of liberty; commercialized vice corrupts the citizenry and offends the public decency; riots disrupt the public peace and order; treason invades the security of law itself. All the above rights and values are essential to a just and ordered liberty, that is, to the common good of organized civil society. All immoral actions, therefore, that militate against such rights and values are in the field of public morality and properly subject to state legislative power.

Private Morality. It is a misleading half-truth to say that the state cannot legislate morality. Every state can, should, and does in fact legislate in the field of public morality. Society could not exist without such legislation. The whole of American law is witness to the fact. But the state should not, and usually cannot, legislate in the field of purely private morality.

Purely internal acts of virtue and of vice constitute a large part of the field of morality, of the good or evil human life, but the state is utterly incompetent to legislate concerning purely internal acts of virtue or of vice and seldom attempts it. Moreover, apart from purely internal acts, the state should not attempt to legislate concerning those overt acts that are in the field of purely private morality. The nature of the state indicates that its legislative competence extends only to that part of morality that affects the common good of civil society and that is properly called public morality. In view of this limitation, and in this sense only, it may be said that it is not the state's business to legislate morality.

The stability of the marriage bond, many rights and obligations of the married, the care of legitimate and illegitimate children, the rights of the unborn, the protection of youth from corruption, the prevention of sexual promiscuity and venereal disease, the curtailing of alcoholism and drug addiction, the safeguarding of the poor from fleecing by gambling syndicates, and the general condition of fundamental socio-moral standards are matters that clearly affect the public or common good of society. For that reason they are properly within the scope of civil law and public policy.

Nevertheless the American states differ substantially in their laws and public policies concerning marriage, divorce, separation, abortion, adoption, adultery, fornication, prostitution, homosexuality, contraception, gambling, alcohol, narcotics, capital punishment, etc. It is submitted that these differences reflect disagreement on one or more of the following three questions: whether the given activity is immoral; if immoral, whether it is in the field of private or public morality; if in the field of public morality, whether this or that public policy is the proper or prudential way to handle the immoral activity.

Inalienable Human Rights. The philosophy of the natural law postulates a number of fundamental human rights and obligations that are absolute and inalienable and that must be protected by civil law. Among such rights are those to life, worship, marriage, property, labor, speech, locomotion, assembly, and reputation. The "absolute" character of such rights creates a difficulty for those who do not understand natural-law philosophy.

Such rights are absolute in the sense that they derive from human nature. They are not mere gifts from the state. The state is bound to protect them and cannot destroy them even though, at times, states have physically prevented their exercise. Legalized human slavery prevented the exercise of these fundamental human rights, but it did not destroy the rights themselves.

Limited. Fundamental human rights are not absolute in the sense that they are unlimited in scope. It is commonplace in the philosophy of natural law that human rights, even the most fundamental, are limited. They are limited in the sense that they are subject to specification, qualification, expansion and contraction, and even forfeiture of exercise, as the equal rights of others and the requirements of the common good reasonably indicate.

Some typical limitations upon the scope of the fundamental human rights enumerated above are as follows. Life may be forfeited upon just conviction of a capital crime (*see* CAPITAL PUNISHMENT). The right to it is qualified by the right of others to legitimate self-defense, is subject to the right of the state to reasonable prevention of crime, and may be endangered in the waging of a just WAR. The right to worship may be qualified by reasonable restrictions as to time, place, and circumstance; and hence, e.g., prayer meetings may be prohibited at high noon in the middle of Times Square. That to marriage may be specified and qualified by reasonable restrictions as to age and consanguinity—but not by so-called miscegenation statutes that conflict with the essential right. The right to property may be qualified, contracted, or expanded, by reasonable zoning laws, antitrust legislation, wage and hour and safety regulations. The right to labor may be specified and qualified by reasonable licensing requirements, sanitary regulations, wage and hour and safety regulations. Speech may be restricted by reasonable laws concerning incitement to crime, libel and slander, obscenity, and the divulgence of information to the enemy in time of war. Locomotion may be qualified by reasonable passport rules and immigration laws. The right of assembly may be qualified by reasonable requirements in the interest of public health, safety, and order. The right to reputation may be qualified by reasonable laws requiring testimony in public trials, allowing fair comment on public affairs and officials, requiring the dis-

closure or reporting of embarrassing contagious diseases. These are simply random examples of typical limitations upon the scope of a few obvious, natural and inalienable rights. All such rights are subject to similar limitations.

If the scope of natural rights were subject to unreasonable or arbitrary limitation, either by the fiat of a dictator or a democratic majority vote, then they would be subject to simple extinction and could not be said to be absolute. If, however, the scope of natural rights is subject only to reasonable limitation for the sake of the common good, then indeed they are not subject to simple extinction and can properly be said to be absolute. Reasonable limitation of scope is a proper condition of natural and inalienable rights.

The human person, in his essential nature, is not merely an individual being. He is also a social being living with his fellows in an organized society that is subject to political, economic, technological, and social change. His natural rights—and corresponding obligations to respect the natural rights of others—are both individual and social. To consider him solely as an individual would lead to anarchy. To consider him solely as a social unit would lead to totalitarianism. But his individual-social nature, adequately considered, leads inevitably to the conclusion that his natural rights are absolute, in the sense explained, because he is an individual for whose rights good governments are instituted. Reasonable reflection leads also to the compatible conclusion that his natural rights are limited in scope, in the sense explained, because he is also a social person obliged by nature to contribute to the common good of human society.

Immutable. Confusion is created also by the universal and immutable character of fundamental principles of natural law. Such principles are as universal and immutable as the human nature from which they are derived. When properly understood, they suffer no exceptions.

The four monosyllables, "Thou shalt not kill," are sometimes used to express a fundamental secondary principle of the natural law. If these four words were to be taken in simplistic literalness, they would not indicate a universal and immutable principle, because there are circumstances in which killing is obviously permissible.

The quoted words merely indicate the natural law principle that is adequately expressed as, "Thou shalt not kill or inflict bodily harm upon any human being *unjustly.*" This principle is universal and immutable. In its negative aspect, it prohibits the immoral killing or inflicting of bodily harm upon self or other human beings. In its positive aspect, it commands a reasonable preservation of life and bodily integrity. Therefore, acts of legitimate self-defense, defense of others, warfare, executions for crime, corporal punishment, surgery, vaccination, anesthesia, and strenuous sports are relevant to the principle if they are justifiable.

The justification of such acts will depend upon the norm of morality, i.e., conformity with or difformity from human nature individually and socially considered, upon the nature of the act, the circumstances of the action, and the motives of the actor. But the principle "Thou shalt not kill or inflict bodily harm upon any human being unjustly" remains universal and immutable.

This is not to say that the determination of such moral and legal justification is automatic or without difficulty. A particular question of the justifiability of self-defense may be extremely difficult in regard to both morals and law, without the slightest doubt being cast upon the universality or immutability of the principle. The solution of such problems gives rise to the sciences of morality and lawmaking.

A principle of morality or of law is not without value because its application to particular cases is difficult. The American constitutional phrase "due process of law" indicates a legal principle (declaring and enforcing a principle of natural law) that has taxed the judicial mind for centuries. And the development of the legal concept of due process of law has occasioned influences of natural law on jurisprudence. The natural law, which says that a human being may not be deprived of his life unjustly, is recognized and enforced by the civil law, which says that a human being may not be deprived of his life without due process of law. In close cases, moralists and legalists of reasonable but finite mentalities may differ about the application of justice and due process. General principles alone do not decide particular cases; but particular cases cannot be decided without them.

Conclusion. Difficulty is sometimes engendered by a failure to distinguish between a principle of the natural law and a rule of the civil law. The former is universal and immutable, the latter is not. A principle of natural law can be known by man, because he can know his nature and essential relationships; but a principle of the natural law cannot be made, changed, or destroyed by man because he cannot make, change, or destroy his essential nature. Conversely a rule of the civil law must be made and may be amended or repealed by man's legislative or judicial process. Thus a rule of the civil law lacks the universality and immutability of a principle of the natural law. This is the precise reason why rules of civil law, as they are enacted, amended, and formulated from time to time and from circumstance to circumstance, should always be consonant with the principles of natural law. It is why the natural law constitutes the general norm to measure the justice or injustice of civil law.

Among the changeable and changing rules of civil law are: the rule of consideration in contracts, the rule of hearsay in evidence, the rule of recording in property, the rule of witnesses in wills, the rule of strict liability in torts, the rule of "retreating to the wall" in crimes, and hundreds of others, from the rules governing statutes of limitations to traffic rules and minor procedural regulations. As rules, they have a certain generality, but they are subject to exceptions, and they require change, gradual or drastic, as time, circumstance, and wisdom demand. They are practical and subsidiary means whereby the civil law, more or less efficiently, applies the principles of the natural law to human beings living in the constantly changing political, economic, technological, and social conditions of civil society.

Three factors have contributed to the confusion and misunderstanding concerning the impact of natural law upon civil law. First, the misuse of natural law terminology, in the 19th and early 20th centuries, in support of laissez-faire rugged individualism—seen in many old Supreme Court decisions that piously exalted property and contractual rights to the detriment of other basic human rights and the genuine needs of the COMMON GOOD. Second, the lack of familiarity of members of the legal profession with the writings of the natural law philosophers and reliance upon secondary, unscholarly sources of information. Third, an unfortunate propensity, on the part of enthusiasts of natural law, to claim too much for their philosophy. The naive proposition "All we have to do to solve our practical problems is to apply natural law" is similar to the false panacea "All we have to do is to apply the Constitution."

The natural law itself is inadequate to solve the complex problems of a dynamic human society. It requires implementation by civil law; and such implementation involves not merely argumentation and research, but validation even by trial and error. The search is for the best civil laws to act for the personal and the common good.

See Also: LAW, PHILOSOPHY OF.

Bibliography: R. F. BÉGIN, *Natural Law and Positive Law* (Catholic University of America Canon Law Studies 393; Washington 1959). J. ELLUL, *The Theological Foundation of Law,* tr. M. WIESER (Garden City, NY 1960). Center for the Study of Democratic Institutions, *Natural Law and Modern Society* (Cleveland 1963). A. L. HARDING, ed., *Natural Law and Natural Rights* (Dallas 1955). F. S. C. NORTHROP, "Philosophical Issues in Contemporary Law," *Natural Law Forum* 2 (1957) 41–63. M. T. ROONEY, *Lawlessness, Law, and Sanction* (Washington 1937). L. STRAUSS, *Natural Right and History* (Chicago 1953). J. C. H. WU, *Fountain of Justice* (New York 1955).

[W. J. KENEALY]

NATURAL LAW IN POLITICAL THOUGHT

NATURAL LAW has been a perennial theme for political philosophers; and even in mid-20th century, after 150 years of critical analysis, it retains an interest and vitality. The concept of natural law originated in the classical period, reached its highest development in late medieval and early modern times, and continues to be significant, especially in legal theory and in the ideology of Christian democracy and other movements of Catholic inspiration. In the course of 2,500 years, the appeal to certain fixed universal principles that can be perceived in NATURE and in human nature has taken a variety of forms and served a number of functions; but as long as men have sought justifications for the political order beyond those of tradition and revelation, the appeal to nature and natural law has remained an element in political thought (*see* STATE).

Classical Period. It was the breakdown of the traditional order in the period following the Persian Wars and the immediate confrontation of widely varying political systems that first gave rise to the appeal to nature in ancient Greece. In the search for an ethical and legal standard, the participants in the political discussions of 5th-century Athens made use of the concept of nature (*physis*) that had been used in earlier scientific speculation to explain the ultimate constituent elements of the universe. In Thucydides's history of the Peloponnesian Wars and in the opening pages of Plato's *Republic,* there are images of the then current Sophist doctrine that by a natural law the strong do and should rule the weak. Surviving fragments of Sophist writings also indicate that some argued that all men were equal by nature and that social as well as moral distinctions were purely conventional. In his *Republic* PLATO attempted to respond to both these criticisms, arguing for a natural order of reason over the passions in the individual and of the more rational over the less intelligent in society. ARISTOTLE based his defense of slavery on a natural inequality among men and appealed to the nature of man as the basis for government and private property. Equally important for the history of the theory was Aristotle's teleological method, his attribution of an inherent purposiveness and intelligibility to nature. Yet neither Plato nor Aristotle developed a full-fledged natural law theory as such. For Plato law was associated with the rigid and inadequate legal rules of the contemporary Greek city-state; it appeared to be a second-best compromise when the rule of the wise could not be assured. In his *Nicomachean Ethics* Aristotle wrote of a natural justice invariable among gods but variable among men (1134b); in the *Politics* he described law as "reason free from passion" (1287a), and in the *Rhetoric* he alluded to a universal or common law "in accordance with nature" (1373b). Yet it is only in the writings of the Stoics that the term "law of nature" was used, and a systematic theory of a higher law based on nature developed.

Emerging in Greece after the breakdown of the Greek city-state and the triumph of the Macedonian Empire, STOICISM became the dominant philosophy of the ruling classes of the Roman Empire and profoundly influenced the formulation of ROMAN LAW. According to Stoic thought man participated in divine Reason, which permeated the universe; and it was in the common possession of reason, considered both as a moral and intellectual faculty, that all men were equal by nature. Stoic thought on natural law thus departed in theory from the elitism of Plato and Aristotle, although in practice CICERO, whose *De republica* and *De legibus* are the principal sources for Stoic natural law theories, rejected democracy and argued for the rule of a rational elite. A similar hesitancy to apply the practical consequences of the theory characterized the attitude of Cicero and the Roman lawyers toward a possible conflict between the natural law and existing legal institutions, such as slavery, that were viewed as contrary to the natural equality of all mankind.

Christian Development. Christianity gave a different basis to the doctrine of equality—the moral responsibility of every man to God—and a different appeal as the basis of political legitimacy—the will of God. Christianity had a higher law, but it was not the law of nature; it was that of divine revelation (*see* REVELATION, THEOLOGY OF). The early Christian attitude toward nature was ambiguous. On the one hand, nature (and especially human nature) had been corrupted by ORIGINAL SIN. The pagan philosophers without the guidance of revelation were steeped in sin, which would adversely affect their ability to attain moral truth. As Tertullian put it, "not Athens, but Jerusalem" (*De praescriptione haereticorum,* ch. 7). On the other hand, nature was created by God, who as a purposive and intelligent Being had established an ordered universe. Moreover, St. Paul, who was familiar with Stoic thought, had written, "When the Gentiles who have no law do by nature what the Law prescribes, these having no law are a law unto themselves. They show the work of the Law written in their hearts" (Rom 2.14–15).

In their confrontation with classical culture, the Fathers of the Church ultimately adopted the latter attitude and incorporated the natural-law doctrine as part of the Christian tradition. St. AUGUSTINE himself, despite his emphasis on the opposition of nature and grace, often referred to the natural law in his writings. However, the Stoic teaching about the original equality of all men received a different formulation in Christian teaching. The Fathers saw equality as the condition in the Garden of

Eden and attributed all forms of domination and government, property, and slavery to man's fall from grace. As this instance demonstrates, the relation of natural law to revelation was not clear in early Christian writings; and as late as the writings of the canon lawyers of the 12th and 13th centuries, the natural and the divine law tended to be equated.

It was the genius of St. THOMAS AQUINAS in the 13th century to distinguish divine law, in the sense of revelation, from natural law, in the sense of those moral imperatives that man can perceive with his reason in an ordered universe created by God. Aquinas drew on Aristotle to affirm the natural character of government and to relate Aristotelian teleology to the natural law in a hierarchy of ends and inclinations in human nature corresponding to the principal precepts of the natural law. In a famous passage (*Summa theologiae* 1a2ae, 94.2) he described these as existence; self-preservation; the family; and education, society, and (natural) religion.

The appeal to the natural law had more force in the Middle Ages when it was associated directly with God's will than in Roman times when it was simply a philosophic theory. Yet despite Aquinas's argument that human laws contrary to natural law are null and void (ST 1a2ae, 95.2.), it was not widely used for the purpose of invalidating existing laws or practices. Laws were sometimes opposed by referring to natural and divine law (retaining the canonist confusion of the two), but the most common appeals were to the positive law of the Church or to traditional feudal rights. The natural law decreed human equality, but there was no demand for the abolition of slavery; and the belief in a hierarchical universe, derived ultimately from Neoplatonist sources, tended to justify a hierarchical social order as a part of the nature of things. Yet in the late Middle Ages the doctrine of the original natural equality of all mankind was also cited to reinforce the development of representative institutions in both Church and State, and appeals were made in both canon and civil law to the principle that all those affected by governmental decisions have a natural-law right to give their consent, either through representatives or (more often) tacitly.

Modern Period. Aquinas had asserted the limits of human reason and the importance of the divine law as a guide and a supplement to the natural law; but at the same time, in emphasizing the rational character of the moral law and the powers of the human reason to attain truth, he had helped to lay open the possibility of the assertion of a naturalist and rationalist morality without recourse to revelation, or for that matter, to God. The late scholastics had asked whether the natural law was so firmly based in reason that even God himself could not change

it, and GROTIUS (1583–1645), the first of the modern theorists of international law, argued in 1625 that the natural law would still exist "even if we should concede that which cannot be conceded without the utmost wickedness, that there is no God" (*De Jure Belli ac Pacis,* prolegomena). Although one can exaggerate the secularism of early modern theories of natural law, there is no doubt that the medieval link between the natural and the divine law was broken once there was disagreement after the Reformation as to the content of revelation. In fact, it appeared for a time that the reformers' suspicion of reason and the natural man would end all reference to the natural law by Christian writers. However, the need for a common standard in a religiously divided Christendom compelled those who wrote works of political theory to appeal to it and to develop theories as to its origin and content that were less specifically religious than those of the Middle Ages.

In the works of Thomas HOBBES (1588–1679) the term natural law was used to describe a set of maxims for self-preservation, and a hypothetical state of nature replaced the Judeo-Christian Garden of Eden. God entered only as the enforcing sovereign of revealed law, not as the eternal reason of Thomism. John LOCKE (1632–1704) borrowed the state of nature from Hobbes, but combined it with a theory of natural law that was derived from St. Thomas by way of the Anglican divine Thomas HOOKER (1553–1600). Although there are problems in relating Locke's theory of natural law to the empiricism of his *Essay Concerning Human Understanding,* the recent discovery of a manuscript copy of his *Essays on the Law of Nature* makes it clear that his theory of natural law was more traditional than Hobbesian. A novel element, however, was his strong emphasis on the right of private property as decreed by the natural law.

In the 17th-century theories, the natural law served the important function of providing a ground for legitimacy in a political theory. For Grotius the requirements of the social nature of man were the source of the binding force of international law. For Hobbes, man's drive to preserve himself made obedience to the sovereign a moral obligation. For Locke, the natural rights of man provided the basis for consent to government and the limits upon the exercise of power. In all three cases, too, the natural law was seen as prescribing a fundamental equality among men that was not simply a characteristic of some earlier lost state—although in Hobbes's theory, this equality was more physical than moral. In the same century, new scientific advances undermined whatever arguments for hierarchy could be drawn from analogy to the structure of the universe. Natural law arguments were drawn from human nature, not from nature in general.

It was as a theory of consent and equality that natural law, as transformed by Locke into natural rights, achieved its most widespread acceptance in the 18th century. In the Declaration of Independence (1776) and the Declaration of the Rights of Man (1789), it became a central feature of the ideologies of the American and French Revolutions; and subsequently it provided the intellectual background for the early court decisions that established the American doctrine of judicial review.

Yet at the very time that it attained its greatest influence the theory of the law of nature was subjected to a series of attacks that led to a rapid decline in its influence. In England David HUME (1711–76) in his *Treatise of Human Nature* (1740) took issue with the notion that any values could be derived from the facts of nature or human nature, while the utilitarians such as Jeremy BENTHAM (1748–1832) argued that moral and legal principles were better derived from their effects on society than from anything inherent in nature. On the Continent, Immanuel KANT (1724–1804) posited a sharp dichotomy between the facts of nature and the realm of moral obligation, and attempted to draw conclusions about law and morality from the nature of legal and moral obligation rather than from the nature of man. In the 19th century, the positivists attempted to separate legality and morality to the detriment of natural-law theory, which had considered them as closely related (*see* POSITIVISM IN JURISPRUDENCE). The theory of evolution and new anthropological research also revealed that the nature of man was not as fixed and unchanging as the defenders of natural law had assumed. By the end of the 19th century, the only political theory that made use of natural law was that contained in the papal social and political encyclicals, which continued to speak in terms of Thomistic natural-law theory (*see* SOCIAL THOUGHT, PAPAL).

Natural Law Revival. In the 20th century, particularly since the 1930s, there has been a marked revival of interest in natural law as it relates to political theory. A variety of different factors account for this. The excesses of the Nazi regime suggested the need for a higher standard beyond that of the positive law, and after World War II the UN Declaration of Human Rights was justified by some as an attempt to set down natural law obligations binding on governments. The neo-Thomist revival, and especially the writings of Jacques MARITAIN (1882–1973), modernized the theory of Aquinas and placed greater emphasis on the development in history of new insights into the implications of the natural law, thus partially coming to terms with the evolutionist critique. In terms of practical effect, the most important development was the organization of Christian Democratic parties in Europe and more recently in Latin America, whose programs are couched in natural-law terms borrowed from the papal encyclicals and the writings of Maritain. Proposals such as family allowances, worker participation in management, guarantees of the right to organize trade unions, and, more recently, religious freedom and a nuclear test ban treaty have been advocated as conclusions from the natural law. In the area of personal morality with implications for public policy, artificial birth control, sterilization, and divorce have been opposed as prohibited by the same law. Among the areas currently in dispute among natural-law theorists of Thomist inspiration are the extent of the limits on property rights that may be imposed by the state, and the morality of nuclear warfare.

Aside from legal theorists, there are few non-Thomist political philosophers who use the vocabulary of natural law. Yet much of the writing about politics and morals is based on an implicit or explicit conception of the nature of man and the prerequisites for the full expression of human potentialities. To speak about the dignity of man or the necessity of human freedom is to assert a goal for society and the political order that is related to certain universal and constant values inherent in the nature of man. That these moral and legal conceptions vary in different societies proves only that the perception and application of these goals and the choice among them in the common situation of conflict of one with another remains difficult. Ultimately the problem remains the one that puzzled the Greeks: how to find the one in the many, a constant principle in a world of change, a measure that is neither too rigid nor too vague to provide a standard for positive law and government and a basis for political obligation. The answer that the Greeks first conceived—a law of nature—continues to appeal to political theorists, among them many who are not aware of the type of argument they are using.

Bibliography: A. PASSERIN D'ENTRÈVES, *Natural Law: An Introduction to Legal Philosophy* (New York 1951), the best general survey of the topic with an excellent bibliog. Center for the Study of Democratic Institutions, *Natural Law and Modern Society* (Cleveland 1963). E. S. CORWIN, *The "Higher Law" Background of American Constitutional Law* (Ithaca, NY 1955). J. MARITAIN, *Man and the State* (Chicago 1951); *The Rights of Man and Natural Law,* tr. D. C. ANSON (New York 1943). H. A. ROMMEN, *The Natural Law,* tr. T. P. HANLEY (St. Louis 1947). L. STRAUSS, *Natural Right and History* (Chicago 1953).

[P. E. SIGMUND]

NATURAL ORDER

The terms natural and natural order have been used extensively in modern theology to distinguish as sharply as possible what is meant by supernatural and supernatural order. While this contrast and correlation has had a long history in Catholic theology, its modern usage and emphasis appear to stem from the middle of the 19th century. Confronted with the spread of philosophical naturalism as well as various theories of natural religion, the theologians began to make the notion of the supernatural a fundamental category of systematic theology. As used in this context the notions natural and natural order serve to underline clearly the transcendent character of the divine order and the gratuitous character of the order of grace, which they incorporate into the notion of the absolute supernatural. The natural order, therefore, would be defined as a created order in which man would be directed to an end or destiny that is strictly proportionate to his capacities, powers, and exigencies. This end would be God as known through reason. In contrast the absolutely supernatural would be that which completely transcends the capacities, powers, and exigencies of created or creatable nature. The notion of the natural order played a very important role in the systematic treatment of such areas as apologetics, revelation, and grace. It enabled the theologian to bring out clearly the transcendence of the divine order and the gratuity of man's call to the beatific vision as well as his elevation by God's grace.

In recent years, however, there has been considerable questioning and debate over the exact content of this theological notion of natural as contrasted with supernatural. The basis of the criticism lies in the fact that the usage is built upon a more precise, specific, and detailed definition of natural than is legitimately possible. It is argued that historical man is a reality whose total actual nature can be known only through revelation. Revelation helps us to discern some elements proper to the natural order. Rational analysis discloses other elements. Hence while nature and grace are clearly distinct, nothing can be defined in such specific detail that a kind of clear and proven horizontal line could be drawn between the natural and the supernatural.

The theological opinion that gave rise to this critique began with the fact that God has called historical man to the BEATIFIC VISION. From this fact it is argued that this divinely given vocation is not something merely logical awaiting some future actualization. Rather it is a fact; it is real and must have an impact on man that influences the very structure of his nature. Hence the supernatural, while gratuitous, is rooted in man from the very beginning of his existence. By reason of this he has a tendency to the beatific vision and a resonance of it in his very being. It is this situation that Karl RAHNER describes as ''the SUPERNATURAL EXISTENTIAL.'' If, therefore, the supernatural is already present in man in the sense described, there is no element of his nature that is not in some way touched by it. Hence the difficulty or even impossibility of saying what precisely is natural and so belongs to the natural order. In all this it should be noted that the protagonists of this position do not reject the possibility that God could create intelligent beings and not call them to the beatific vision.

Bibliography: S. OTTO, ''Natur,'' H. FRIES, ed., *Handbuch theologischer Grundbegriffe,* 2 v. (Munich 1962–63) 2:217–219. H. DE LUBAC, *Surnaturel: Études historiques* (Paris 1946) 325–395. M. J. SCHEEBEN, *Nature and Grace,* tr. C. VOLLERT (St. Louis 1954). K. RAHNER, ''Concerning the Relationship between Nature and Grace,'' *Theological Investigations,* v.1, tr. C. ERNST (Baltimore 1961) 297–317. J. P. KENNY, ''Reflections of Human Nature and the Supernatural,'' *Theological Studies* 14 (1953) 280–287.

[E. M. BURKE]

NATURALISM

A movement within American philosophy affirming that nature is the whole of reality; that man has his origin growth, and decay within nature; and that nature—defined as that which is amenable to scientific investigation—is self-explanatory. The term is used also (1) for an ethical doctrine teaching that MORALITY consists in living according to nature or to biological impulse; (2) for the aesthetic doctrine holding that art must imitate nature (*see* AESTHETICS); and (3) for the religious belief that identifies nature with the Godhead (*see* PANTHEISM). This article is concerned with the philosophical position known as American naturalism, treating of its history and its salient characteristics, and concluding with a critique from the viewpoint of theistic realism.

History. As a philosophical attitude, naturalism is not indigenous to America. Its European roots are evident in British EMPIRICISM and in the POSITIVISM and sociologism of August COMTE and Ernst Mach. Nowhere but in the United States, however, has the term naturalism been commonly used to designate a particular set of philosophical views. Yet naturalism arrived relatively late on the American scene. It arose as an alternative to the IDEALISM dominant in American thought during the last quarter of the 19th century and influential during the first two decades of the 30th. By the 1930s, naturalism had clearly replaced idealism as the predominant trend in American philosophical thinking.

The first major expression of the naturalistic temper in the United States is to be found in the *Life of Reason* (5 v., New York 1905–06) of George SANTAYANA. Other systematic expressions are subsequently to be found in Roy Wood Sellars' *Evolutionary Naturalism* (Chicago 1921), Frederick J. E. Woodbridge's *Nature and Mind* (New York 1937), and James B. Pratt's *Naturalism* (New York 1938). Contributions that also must be mentioned are those of Morris R. Cohen (*Reason and Nature,* New York 1931), Clarence I. Lewis (*Mind and World Order,* New York 1929), and William P. Montague (*The Ways of Things,* New York 1940).

Of American naturalists, however, John Dewey is the most important, not only because of his significant contribution to the doctrinal development of naturalism but also because through him naturalism has come to exert a strong influence on public education and consequently on the American mind generally. The history of American naturalism is strikingly reflected in Dewey's own intellectual development as he moved from an early defense of idealism, confident that the new discoveries in biology and psychology could be incorporated into an idealistic framework, to an outright naturalism, presented as the only outlook compatible with the modern scientific world view. The mature naturalism of Dewey not only is apparent in his later works such as *Experience and Nature* (Chicago 1925) and *The Quest for Certainty* (New York 1929), but it is reflected also in the writings of his disciples, particularly in the articles of his co-contributors to the platform volumes, *American Philosophy Today and Tomorrow* (ed. H. M. Kallen and S. Hook, New York 1935) and *Naturalism and the Human Spirit* (ed. Y. H. Krikorian, New York 1944). Many of the contributors to these two volumes subsequently developed themes first presented there. Although American naturalism is not to be identified with the authors represented in these symposia, it is evident that they well represent this tendency in 20th-century American thought. Of the contributors to these volumes, three of Dewey's disciples may be singled out as representative of the naturalistic interest and temperament, viz, S. Hook, E. Nagel, and J. H. Randall, Jr.

Sidney Hook (1902–1989), long associated with the Washington Square College of New York University, wrote extensively on social questions. His works include: *John Dewey: An Intellectual Portrait* (New York 1939), *Reason, Social Myths, and Democracy* (New York 1940), *Education for Modern Man* (New York 1950), and *The Quest for Being* (New York) 1961). Ernest Nagel (1901–1985), who taught at Columbia University after 1930, wrote principally in the philosophy of science and did much to refine the naturalist's concept of science. His important works are: *Sovereign Reason* (New York 1954), *Logic without Metaphysics* (New York 1957), *The Structure of Science* (New York 1961). John Herman Randall, Jr. (1899–1980), lectured at Columbia after 1925. Randall was notably influenced by Woodbridge as well as by Dewey. A historian of philosophy and perhaps more metaphysically inclined than most naturalists, Randall's major contributions to naturalism are his volumes *Nature and Historical Experience* (New York 1958) and *The Role of Knowledge in Western Religion* (Boston 1958).

At the beginning of the 21st century the naturalistic temperament dominates the American academic scene, representing an unchallenged view of reality. Few philosophers may call themselves "naturalist" or publish works with that term in the title. The idealism to which it was counterpoised in the early decades of the 20th century has long ago disappeared. Most in the naturalistic tradition adhere to a materialism in the order of being and to an agnosticism with respect to the existence of God. Two prominent American philosophers in the tradition of Dewey may be taken as representative of the naturalism of a previous generation: John Rawls (1921–) and Richard Rorty (1931–). Rawl's *A Theory of Justice* (1971) is mandatory reading for graduate students in philosophy, not only in America but also in Europe. Rorty's *Philosophy and the Mirror of Nature* (1979) has been influential in literary as well as philosophical circles, advancing a subjectivism that denies that truth can be achieved.

Characteristics. The principal notions that underlie naturalism may be explained by sketching its characteristic teachings, i.e., its method, epistemology, anthropology, pragmatism, empiricism, ethics, and philosophy of value.

Method. Most of the proponents of naturalism present it as a tendency, an outlook, or a frame of mind, rather than as a system. Two basic theses underlie all naturalistic investigation. The first affirms that whatever happens in nature is dependent in some fundamental way on the organization of bodies located in space and time, and the second insists that the "scientific method" is the only means of obtaining reliable knowledge. Naturalists, on the whole, are found to be rather ambiguous in stating the nature of scientific method, but most would admit of its analogical predication. In a broad sense, scientific method is regarded as nothing more than the use of "critical intelligence." Hence the disciplines of sociology and economics, as well as history in some of its phases, are regarded by the naturalist as genuinely scientific.

Epistemology. Epistemologically the naturalist must be considered to be a realist, in the sense that he holds that the objects of knowledge are extramental and that they exist as they are perceived to be, although nominalistic and Kantian tendencies can at times be discerned in some naturalists. Metaphysically, the naturalist presents himself as antidualistic, objecting to the distinctions between the natural and supernatural, between man and nature, mind and body, and appearance and reality. He will accept the designation "materialist" if he is allowed to distinguish between reductive materialism and his own. Reductive materialism, or naturalism, affirms merely that every mental event is contingent upon the organization of certain physical events. The naturalist is careful to avoid suggesting that an idea is nothing but "a potential or tentative muscular response" or that pain and the occurrence of physiological manifestations is a contingent or causal one. As to the existence of God, immortality, separated souls or spirits, cosmic purpose or design, these are denied by the naturalist "for the same generic reasons that he denies the existence of fairies, elves, leprechauns, and an invisible satellite revolving between earth and moon." There is no evidence for any of them.

Anthropology. As to his teaching on man, the naturalist grants that man is unique among animals in ability and accomplishment but denies that he occupies a special place in nature. Between man and his animal ancestors there is only a difference of degree, not one of kind. Consciousness, like the other phenomena, can be described empirically, at least in its effects, and accounted for in terms of matter and the organization of matter. Presupposed by the naturalist is a theory of biological evolution according to which nature in its evolutionary process regularly gives rise to operations and functions on newer and higher levels. Consciousness and thought are regarded as two such higher operations. They have their sole cause in the organism in which they appear. Admittedly, thought and consciousness are distinct from any previous products of an evolving nature, but the factors from which they arose are no different, except for their particular organization, from the factors whence physical, chemical, and biological processes arose.

Pragmatism. By temperament the naturalist is oriented toward the practical. With the pragmatist he agrees that knowledge, if it is to be considered meaningful, must have practical consequences. But whereas C. S. PEIRCE and W. James would be reluctant to identify pragmatism with any one method, the naturalist, particularly in the INSTRUMENTALISM of John Dewey, identifies experimental science as the perfect example of the intimate connection between theory and practice, between knowing and doing. For the naturalist, mind or intelligence exists as a problem-solving power, and this function is regarded as more important than its theoretical employment. Science, insofar as it is the most perfect form of intelligence, takes on the status of instrument par excellence.

Concerned with the application of critical intelligence to the social, political, and economic problems of the times, the naturalist is contemptuous of fixed codes theologically or philosophically derived. He regards religion and traditional philosophy as impediments rather than as aids to social progress. Although he looks upon belief in God as a dangerous drain on social energies, he does not deny a certain sociological value to religion. But he does deny that it produces knowledge that can be subjected to rigorous criticism. What is valuable in religious witness, the naturalist asserts, can be derived from other sources.

Empiricism. Although the naturalist by disposition eschews systems, he has nevertheless, by adopting an empiricist attitude toward the problems of substance, efficient causality, and final causality, produced a consistent metaphysics with consequences in the moral and civic orders. By defining substance as a logical category, as that segment of the process called reality upon which man chooses to fasten his attention, and by adopting D. Hume's analysis of causality, the naturalist has ruled out the question of the origin of the universe. Because situations are always encountered as particular, concrete, and determinable, once can never experience anything that might be called "the Universe." The Universe, or Nature, has no meaning except in the sense that it might be considered a locus for all processes. The meaning of any process, according to the naturalist, is the way it functions in its context. Now what has no context can have no function and hence no meaning. The Universe has no discoverable context, since one experiences it neither as a whole nor as coming to be. Hence the question of its origin is a meaningless question.

Ethics. The implications for ethics are apparent. Since, according to the naturalist, there is no transcendent end for man, values must be found within the social context. As Krikorian has written, "the source of motivation for humanity must be found within the natural setting of its existence . . . rather than in something which is neither verifiable no approachable." Values are relative because the most one can determine is "how best" he can do something under a particular set of circumstances. What is best absolutely is beyond one's knowledge. Man cannot determine what is best in the ultimate context, because the ultimate context is beyond discovery. Hence the good of a situation has to be determined on the basis of the defeat to be rectified. Each situation will give rise to its own good. There will be no fixed absolutes as the supernaturalist would suppose. The imposition of fixed or transcendent ends is simply a sign of an emotional grappling for certainty where certainty is impossible.

Values. In the realm of values the naturalist has been primarily a philosopher of ethics or an epistemologist, rather than a moral philosopher in the traditional sense. His concern has been with the question of how values ought to be determined. Although all naturalists are agreed that scientific procedure ought to be employed in ethics, there is no general agreement as to what constitutes scientific procedure. The naturalist recognizes that normative propositions cannot be determined by the same procedure employed in verifying questions of fact. He admits also that the use of data derived from the physical and behavioral sciences does not constitute an ethics as scientific. Most naturalists find the problem of how to determine values scientifically a particularly vexing one. Confronted with the problem, many fall back on custom or inclination as a guide in determining what is morally best or resort to some form of utilitarianism. But most naturalist admit that custom or inclination is not a sure guide; the whole point of the naturalist's concern with morals has been to get away from subjectivism. Utilitarianism is likewise found unsatisfactory, because it begs the question as to which of the ends and relationships human beings naturally cherish, or which of the values they normally institute, are desirable in the long run; it also fails to take into account the empirically discernible fact that man acts out of motives of duty. Admittedly naturalistic ethics is incomplete.

Critique. In evaluating the work of the American naturalist, the validity of many of his insights must be acknowledged: for example, his insistence on starting with experience, his interest in social and political questions, his concerns for an enlightened and critical morality, his emphasis on clarity and the useful function that linguistic analysis can perform in achieving clarity, and his demand that the philosopher shun any special witness, such as that which might be provided by intuition or religious faith. The naturalist's attack on idealism, his repudiation of the Cartesian dichotomy between mind and body, his criticism of some prevailing ethical and religious conceptions of nature are features that are not reserved to naturalism but are part of a common REALISM and can therefore be accepted.

But what cannot be accepted is the naturalist's principal thesis that the boundaries of scientific knowledge are the boundaries of certain knowledge. Nowhere does the scientist himself proclaim that his method is the only one productive of reliable knowledge. Science includes no such treatment of epistemology or values as one finds them in naturalism. The naturalist's defense of his position is not a scientific defense but is based on an appeal to common sense and to the data of history.

The naturalist rightly attempts to rule out anything that has no claim to genuine knowledge, but in doing so he has assumed that philosophy has produced no certain knowledge. Also, he has implicitly denied that there is truth or falsity in philosophical knowledge. Again, the naturalist's employment of history is selective. The history of philosophy is not merely a record of discord. It also discloses amid the diversity of opinion and the prevalence of conflict a core of common philosophical experience that exhibits a remarkable unity. Étienne GILSON has clearly shown in his *Unity of Philosophical Experience* (New York 1937) that similar approaches to perennial problems yield strikingly similar results. It seems, therefore, that the task of "critical intelligence" is not the wholesale repudiation of philosophy but the sifting of diverse opinions to determine what is valuable in them.

The naturalist's thesis that traditional philosophy and theology, especially during their period of ascendancy in the Middle Ages, have exercised a retarding influence on science is belied by developments in the history of evidence, accumulated since the pioneer work of P. Duhem and L. Thorndike, to show that medieval philosophy and theology, far from impeding the development of science and technology, actually laid the groundwork, through discussions of science and scientific method, for the so-called scientific renaissance of the 17th century. Also indefensible is the assumption that the distinction between God and nature inevitably leads to an antagonism in which man's temporal ends are slighted. Although theism in some of its forms may result in a neglect of temporal values, the history of Christianity, in every age, is replete with examples of concern for specifically human ends (*see* MAN, NATURAL END OF).

From an epistemological point of view, the naturalist's delimitation of reality to nature is a consequence of an uncritically assumed empiricism. In adopting the empiricist's solution to the problems of SUBSTANCE and CAUSALITY, the naturalist has automatically ruled out the possibility of reasoning to a transcendent cause of nature or of recognizing the spiritual component of man. By following Hume, the naturalist opens himself to the same charges that are brought against that 18th-century philosopher, namely, that in atomizing experience he falsifies the fact that things are not given in isolation but in a dynamic interrelation with other things, both conferring and receiving action. Against the naturalist it can be argued that a respect for the empirical origins of knowledge does not oblige one to turn his back upon the generic traits of existence that can be discovered through reflection and by means of inference. Nor does an acknowledgment of the contingent and novel blind one to the unity and connectedness that also are features of nature. Finally, the naturalist's commitment to empiricism has rendered him impotent in precisely the area I which he has most wanted to succeed, the area of values. Naturalistic ethics as yet remains a program rather than an accomplishment. In a certain sense, this last remark can be made of the whole of naturalism, which in its positive character at times seems to be saying no more than "Let us be scientific!"

See Also: RATIONALISM.

Bibliography: P. ROMANELL, *Toward a Critical Naturalism* (New York 1958). J. D. COLLINS, *Three Paths in Philosophy* (Chicago 1962), a critique of naturalism from the standpoint of a theistic realism. R. RORTY, *Consequences of Pragmatism* (Minneapolis 1982); *Achieving Our Country: Leftist Thought in Twentieth-Century America* (Cambridge 1998). J. NIZNIK and J. SANDERS, eds., *Debating the State of Philosophy: Habermas, Rorty, and Kolakowski* (Westport, Connecticut 1996). H. J. SAATKAMP, ed., *Rorty and Pragmatism* (New Haven 1986).

[J. P. DOUGHERTY]

NATURE (IN PHILOSOPHY)

From the Latin *natura* (Gr. φύσις), a term with many related meanings in philosophy and with extensive applications in theology. Among philosophers it is commonly taken to mean the essence of a thing as this is the source of its properties or operations; more strictly, however, it is a primary and per se principle of motion and rest that is found in natural things as opposed to artifacts. It is sometimes used in the more restricted sense of human nature, for which meaning *see* MAN. Theologians use the term in opposition to grace or to supernature, particularly when discussing human nature, and in opposition to person, particularly in Trinitarian theology and Christology.

Since nature is the proper subject of the PHILOSOPHY OF NATURE, the major emphasis in this article is on nature as studied in natural philosophy. Topics treated include the primary meanings of the concept, its development among the Greeks, modifications in it occasioned by the rise of modern science, an Aristotelian analysis of its meaning in natural philosophy, and various secondary meanings.

Primary Meanings. On Nature (Περὶ φύσεως) is the title under which the writings of the pre-Socratics have been handed down to posterity. Some doubt exists as to what precisely was the first meaning, but it is generally admitted that at least an early and important use of the term φύσις was to designate the primordial stuff or underlying substratum persisting through all CHANGE. It is likely that the early Ionian philosophers imagined the world as developing in an orderly fashion from within, somewhat as a living being, and hence the primary substance would have been viewed, though indistinctly, as a source of activity. Thus φύσις was an intrinsic principle that accounted for the ceaseless change or BECOMING of things. Moreover, the very process of becoming, it seems, was itself called φύσις, a term that is etymologically related to φύω, to grow (cf. Lat. *natura* and *nascor*). Finally, at some later date the term was applied to the changing things themselves taken in their totality. This is possibly the most common sense of nature in modern usage and was probably the meaning of φύσις intended in the title Περί φύσεως. (For Aristotle's account of the etymology and the meanings of φύσις, see *Meta.* 1014b 16–1015a 19.)

Greek Development. The attempt of the Ionians of the 6th century B.C. to explain all becoming in terms of one material principle (e.g., water or air or fire) reached its logical conclusion in PARMENIDES with the very denial of nature as process. For Parmenides all being must be one and exclude all nonbeing; as such it is perfectly immutable, and only as such is it knowable; all change is but sensory illusion. After Parmenides, there was an attempt to reconcile BEING, stable object of intellect, with the becoming of sensory experience. Fundamental reality remained immutable; it was, however, multiple: the four elements of EMPEDOCLES; the "seeds," infinite in number, of ANAXAGORAS; the atoms of Leucippus and DEMOCRITUS. These particles, in motion, combined and separated, and as such were principles of change and of a multiplicity of changing compounds. The atomists, with their homogeneous particles differing only in size and shape, interpreted all change in terms of movement in space ("void") and all sensible qualities, such as color, in terms of quantitative differences (*see* ATOMISM). They have been considered as forerunners to modern science. So too have the Pythagoreans, who, from the 6th century B.C., had been seeking to explain the world in the light of numbers.

The claim to find the ultimate explanation of reality in the random motions of corporeal elements, i.e., in nature and chance, was strongly opposed by PLATO. If nature means the primary source of becoming, what is truly nature, for him, could only be what is really first, and that is intelligence and art. Thus, with Plato, nature in the commonly accepted sense gave way to divine soul, and chance to divine direction (*Laws* 888E–899D). Finality, introduced as conscious design, was lodged in a principle (soul) distinct from the purely corporeal. Likewise, the intelligibility of sensible bodies was to be sought beyond them, in the changeless, purely intelligible Ideas, of which they are imperfect imitations (*Phaedo; Rep.* 449–540). The order of the sensible world could be seen, too, in terms of the a priori principles of pure number. As for the changing imitations considered in themselves, of these there could be no science, but only a likely account.

Nature was reinstated as a true principle and a real source of explanation within the material universe by ARISTOTLE, who thus restored the philosophy of nature to the rank of a SCIENCE (*SCIENTIA*). Aristotle continued the naturalist tradition of the pre-Socratics, his science being qualitative rather than mathematical, empirical rather than rationalist. It was far from being a mere return, however. After Plato there was form to be reckoned with. In Aristotle the natural world becomes intelligible in itself only because nature is identified with form in matter—with form now seen as the actuality of matter—even more properly than with matter itself (*see* MATTER AND FORM). This form becomes the origin of activity, and matter, considered in itself, is reduced to a principle of mere passivity and receptivity. The realization of form in matter is the goal of natural activity, and although there are various combinations and separations of elements, it is always for the sake of a form; hence, the teleological view, as opposed to the mechanistic, remains dominant. But purpose is now found in the unconscious workings of form as well as in the conscious activities of rational soul. Although Aristotle conceived the natural universe as impregnated with and illuminated by form, for the ultimate explanation he too reached beyond nature. It is the desire to imitate the fully actual reality of Pure Form that, in the final analysis, explains all the ceaseless processes of nature.

Later Modifications. Both the Platonist and the Aristotelian view of nature extended into the Middle Ages. The early period was largely Neoplatonist, but in the 13th century the commentaries of St. ALBERT THE GREAT and especially of St. THOMAS AQUINAS brought the Aristotelian doctrine of nature into the foreground.

In the 16th and 17th centuries, the rapid development of the new empirico-mathematical science was accompanied by an emphatic rejection of teleology: the conception of natures tending to ends. At first, change was Platonistically explained by an inherent, creative principle (*natura naturans*) animating and directing the world of nature (*natura naturata*)—terms that go back to the Latin translation of AVERROËS. *See* WORLD SOUL (ANIMA MUNDI). Before long, however, under the influence of F. BACON, J. KEPLER, G. GALILEI, R. DESCARTES, I. Newton, and others, the account became thoroughly mechanistic. With the rejection of the geocentric astronomy and the adoption of the universal law of gravitation, the qualitatively differentiated world of Aristotle gave place to a totally homogeneous universe. Purely qualitative differences, such as color, were considered to be functions of quantitative structure, and were soon dismissed as mere appearances to a sentient mind. Matter as potency was replaced by matter as mass and extension. All change was reduced to the motion of smallest parts in space; all causality, to prior events, i.e., to prior motions, identical causes being followed by identical effects. The spontaneous activity of bodies gave way to the idea of force (impact, attraction) and the impulse toward ends was displaced by inertia, the disposition to remain always the same. Nature thus became, for the scientist and the philosopher of nature alike, a mechanical system of inert, homogeneous mass-bodies, situated in space and time, moved by external forces, and utterly devoid of all but quantitative properties. (*See* MECHANISM.)

In the 20th century, the adequacy of purely mechanistic principles of explanation has been seriously questioned for the biological and psychological sciences. Further, the scientific theories of evolution along with the physicist's conception of matter as energy have made more generally acceptable a view that was already to some degree in evidence in the philosophies of G. W. LEIBNIZ and G. W. F. HEGEL, viz, the idea of nature as internally active and engaged in process. This concep-

tion, to which in some instances has been added the idea of aim, has found philosophical expression in the works of such thinkers as H. BERGSON, S. ALEXANDER, and A. N. WHITEHEAD.

Aristotelian Analysis. A fuller presentation of the Aristotelian concept of nature, which has been generally adopted by scholastic thinkers, entails considering his definition of nature, nature as passive, nature as active, end as nature, and related concepts.

Definition of Nature. Aristotle (*Phys.* 192b 8–32) reached his definition of nature by way of a comparison of the things that exist by nature (viz, animals and their parts, plants and simple bodies) with those that exist by other causes, in particular by art. The former are seen to have within them a tendency to move, i.e., to change. The artifact as such has no such tendency. It has an inclination to change only accidentally insofar as it is made of a natural substance. Nature, then, concluded Aristotle, is the principle or cause of being moved and being at rest in that in which it is primarily, by reason of itself and not accidentally.

"Being moved" implies passivity. Strictly speaking, the principle that constitutes a thing as a mover is a nature only when the mover by its activity is itself moved. Also, MOTION here includes any kind of corporeal change, accidental or substantial; it excludes, however, spiritual operations, such as intellection. "Rest" implies the attainment of the end to which the movement was directed. The phrase "by reason of itself and not accidentally" excludes such cases as the doctor who cures himself. The art of medicine is, in this case, intrinsic but accidental to the one who is being cured, considered as such.

Nature as Passive. Nature, thus defined, was identified by Aristotle first (*Phys.* 193a 10–30) with MATTER taken as the substratum of change, i.e., as the passive, potential principle of being moved. In opposition to the pre-Socratics, Aristotle conceived of the ultimate material principle (primary matter) as being of itself bereft of all form, purely passive, pure potentiality. The matter, however, from which becoming proceeds, taken in its concrete existence, is always determined matter. The substantial form currently possessed, determining the matter in a particular way, always limits and defines matter's immediate potentialities. This is true both for the potency of primary matter for new substantial forms and more obviously for the accidental receptivities characteristic of any given being. Furthermore, since the form already possessed by the matter can be the source of certain activities as well, the matter on which a natural agent operates, just as it is never pure potency, need not be entirely passive. Its activity, in fact, may run contrary to the aim of the agent.

Nature as Active. It is especially with FORM, however, that Aristotle is concerned to identify nature (*Phys.* 193a 30-b 19). The ancients, not distinguishing the two principles of matter and form, had conceived of their primordial stuff as already determined and capable of activity. Once substantial form is disassociated from matter and recognized as principle of essential determination, source of activity, and end of generation, it becomes obvious that form more than matter deserves to be called nature. Nature, then, as active principle of movement, is substantial form. (Note that, although one says "Nature acts," strictly speaking it is the composite substance that acts in virtue of its nature.)

Form is the source of two different types of activity in nature. First and more obviously, form is the intrinsic source of the vital activities of the living body. As such, it is known as SOUL. And as such it is a nature, since, by these activities, the living being is itself moved. The soul, in fact, is the primary source of activity whereby one part of the heterogeneous composite moves another part. Moreover, all the vital activities are either movements themselves (e.g., growth) or essentially connected with movements (e.g., sensation) or they pre-suppose movements (e.g., intellection). The soul, however, is also the principle of generation, an activity that is essentially directed to another substance. But even as such, it is a nature, insofar as the movement takes place within the same species, if not within the same individual (*Meta.* 1032a 15–26).

Second, form is the intrinsic source of the spontaneous activities characteristic of a given body, e.g., a chemical element (*Gen. et cor.* 323b 2–324b 25). Inanimate bodies, not having differentiated parts, do not move themselves. Their activities, on the contrary, are directed to other bodies that in turn may affect them. The forms, in this case, satisfy the requirement of interiority in the definition of nature insofar as they are parts within a system of interrelated active and passive potencies.

In Aristotle's cosmology, however, there are certain movements of bodies that do arise from an intrinsic source (*Phys.* 254b 33–255b 31), as in his example of a body falling to the ground—a movement that does not appear to require an external agent (*see* MOTION, FIRST CAUSE OF). In this case, however, nature functions as a principle of activity without constituting the thing as a mover. The body, in fact, does not move itself, part moving part, as does the living thing. For Aristotle, rather, the movement arises spontaneously from the impulse of the form toward what is appropriate to it, which, in this instance, is a suitable environment. (For a study of this conception in conjunction with the theories of gravity and relativity, see J. A. Weisheipl.)

End as Nature. Whether a movement is natural or not cannot always be determined by sole reference to the active and passive principles. The determining factor is ultimately the END of becoming, and this too is nature (*Phys.* 193b 13–19, 194a 27–32).

Nature, in one sense, has been identified with the receptive and determinable principle. There are, however, in the world of nature, potencies that are not natural: the capacity of a natural body to take on an artificial form, or the capacity to be altered by some violent action. The natural potency differs from these in that it is a positive inclination to an act that perfects or fulfills the being so inclined, or else contributes to the good of the species or even to the good of the universe as a whole. The passive principle in nature, moreover, is normally related to a natural AGENT, through the activity of which it is brought to act. The activity of natural agents is accounted for by the tendency of the form in nature to actualize and bring to completion what is potential either within the same individual or beyond. The natural agent, then, actively tends to that good or perfection to which the potential principle is passively inclined. Furthermore, the natural agent, fixed in its species by its form, is also determined by this same principle with respect to specific goals, which it attains for the most part. Thus the acts to which it naturally directs matter by its activity are determinate acts. It is in this sense that a nature is said to act for an end. (Obviously, the end as a good is more easily recognized in the activity of living beings than it is in the workings of the inanimate world.) Consequently, it is the act or form, considered as the end to which a natural being tends either actively or passively, that determines whether a process is or is not in accordance with nature. And in those cases where the good of the whole is in opposition to the good of the individual (as in the case of corruption), it is the former that takes precedence as a determining principle. (*See* FINALITY, PRINCIPLE OF.)

The form considered as end, furthermore, is itself properly called nature. It is a principle of becoming, and one that, in the essential order of things, is prior even to the passive and active principles as such. It is also intrinsic, insofar as natural movements are for the sake of the form (*finis cui*) from which they spring. In fact, the natural form seeks its own preservation and development within the individual; it tends by generation to its own continuance, as a specific form, in other individuals; and ultimately, by realizing its specific ends, it contributes to the order and preservation of the universe, i.e., to the good of the whole of which it is a part.

Related Concepts. Art, VIOLENCE, and CHANCE are all active principles that presuppose nature but operate outside the order of natural finality. *See* ART (PHILOSOPHY).

Secondary Meanings. From nature meaning the form or essence that is the end of generation, the word has been extended to signify any essence whatsoever without reference at all to becoming (see Thomas Aquinas, *In 5 meta.* 5.822–823). This sense, as applicable to any being, material or immaterial, is frequently conveyed by the terms definition and quiddity. A meaning somewhat closer to the original is that of essence as the source of any activity, whether of physical movement or of spiritual operation (*De ente* 1). This sense, too, is sometimes conveyed by the term substance. For a fuller discussion of these concepts, *see* ESSENCE; FORM; DEFINITION; QUIDDITY; SUBSTANCE. For a treatment of laws of nature, *see* PHYSICAL LAWS; NATURAL LAW; and for the principle of the uniformity of nature on which such laws are based, *see* UNIFORMITY.

Bibliography: M. J. ADLER, ed., *The Great Ideas: A Syntopicon of Great Books of the Western World,* 2 v. (Chicago 1952); v.2, 3 of *Great Books of the Western World* 2:225–250. A. GUZZO and V. MATHIEU, *Enciclopedia filosofica,* 4 v. (Venice-Rome 1957) 3:789–811. J. B. METZ, *Lexikon für Theologie und Kirche,* ed. J. HOFER and K. RAHNER, 10 v. (2d, new ed. Freiburg 1957–65) 7:805–808. R. G. COLLINGWOOD, *The Idea of Nature* (New York 1960). A. N. WHITEHEAD, *The Concept of Nature* (Cambridge, England 1920; repr. 1930). J. A. WEISHEIPL, *Nature and Gravitation* (River Forest, IL 1955). A. MANSION, *Introduction à la physique aristotélicienne* (2d ed. Louvain 1946). S. O'FLYNN BRENNAN, "Physis: The Meaning of Nature in the Aristotelian Philosophy of Nature," *Thomist* 24 (1961) 383–401.

[S. O'FLYNN BRENNAN]

NATURE (IN THEOLOGY)

Clarification of the concept nature has enriched the development of theology and the understanding of the Christian faith. It has given a more accurate understanding and depth to the theology of the Trinity, Incarnation, Redemption, Mystical Body, the Church, Mary, and man. Historically, the notion of nature has been focal in every era: from the Trinitarian-Christological controversies of Christian antiquity, through the grace disputes of Pelagianism and Protestantism, to Modernism and existentialism. The term nature is not met in the Old Testament nor does the concrete mentality of the Semites lend itself to an abstract and transcendental concept of nature, predicable of God, angels, man, and irrational creation. Though the word nature, φύσις, is used in the New Testament, its meaning must be determined in each instance from the context. St. AUGUSTINE was hampered in his efforts to preserve the supernaturality of grace by his notion of nature in its primary etymological sense of *natus,* born. Although he maintained man's condition prior to the Fall to be "natural," the Doctor of Grace is not calling into question the supernaturality of that condition but is af-

firming the "original" characteristic of that state. In the decrees of the Councils of Ephesus and Chalcedon and in the writings of the contemporary Fathers there is a gradual precisional evolution of the term nature. St. Thomas Aquinas made a major contribution to Catholic theology by clearly distinguishing between GRACE and nature, fixing the boundaries of the NATURAL ORDER and the SUPERNATURAL ORDER. The contribution of current theologians would be their emphasis on the concrete, historical, and social aspects of nature.

In contemporary theology the term nature is used in two senses. (1) In a general sense, nature refers to the created universe (rational or irrational or both) with determined laws of interdependence and God as its source and end. (2) In a specific sense, nature includes not only the philosophical definition as that which determines a being's species and proper activity but a deeper understanding from revelation of the concrete nature of man, angel, and God. The following consideration of nature in theology is divided according to these two senses of the term.

Nature in a Specific Sense. The philosophical understanding of nature has already been treated extensively in the previous article; we may now proceed to a consideration of the contribution of revelation and theology.

Human Nature. Humanity does not know precisely just what human nature is or exactly how far it extends. Philosophy through experience and reflection gives certain definite concepts about nature, but humanity never knows exactly when too much or too little has been included in any concept. Theology goes beyond philosophy and sees nature as being from God and directed to God in special ways, as including SUPERNATURAL and grace-qualified factors, and as being in a historical-social situation where new experiences in humanity's process of realization leads to an understanding of its essence and what is contingent. Humanity is always historically becoming, and therefore the understanding of concrete nature is also permanently *in via.* Philosophy, then, can give a well-grounded concept of the nature of humanity, but it is for theology with revelation to further consider humanity's nature in its supernatural context.

Three major constants appear in Catholic theological understanding of human nature. (1) Humanity is the IMAGE OF GOD. Because of its special similarity to God, human nature has an immediate ordination to Him. Human nature itself, therefore, will ever constitute a moral principle for judging human behavior. (2) Humankind is one: it has not only an essential unity by human nature but an even greater unity in Adam and Christ. Therefore, the previously mentioned conformity-with-nature moral principle must be understood not merely of the individual but also of all humanity as one. Moreover, this oneness of humankind offers the natural foundation for the law of love of neighbor and has important consequences for the Church's social teaching. (3) The unity of human nature is one of the most distinctive characteristics of the Judeo-Christian conception of humanity, combining the two apparently heterogeneous worlds of matter and of spirit. History has shown that Christian insistence on humankind's fundamental unity is the sole effective remedy for monism, whether in the form of an idealistic spiritualism or of an empirical materialism. Even the Christian has not found it easy to avoid tendencies that overemphasize now one and now another aspect of humanity's enigmatic nature.

Humanity, in its capacity of incarnate spirit, has a place in the divine plan that surpasses its nature. Even though this human nature considered abstractly is not altered by its history, it must ever be borne in mind that abstract human nature never did nor does exist. The whole spiritual and cultural history of humanity testifies that it continually experiences new modes of realization and understanding of its nature. Theological consideration of human nature must never stop with an examination of human nature as such, but must always include concrete human nature with its history centered in its ELEVATION in Christ.

Angelic Nature. Theology confirms philosophy's stand that human nature, incarnate spirit, crowns the material universe. However, above human nature is the angelic nature: "You have made him [man] a little less than the angels" (Ps 8.6). The existence of created beings of a purely spiritual nature is unknown to philosophy. In fact, the very concept carries with it the connotation of the unreal and the unrealizable to modern thinkers. Catholic theology, seeing the wonderful completion of the material universe in the manifold degrees of perfection, confirms the becomingness of a similar gradation in the spiritual universe. Humanity occupies the lowest place in this universe of spiritual beings, having a more perfect nature than what is purely material but still partially dependent upon matter. In accordance with the general providence of God, governing the inferior through the superior, angels have definite roles to fulfill in the lives of men and in the ordering of the whole material universe (*see* ANGELS).

Theology of the Trinity and Incarnation. In expressing its belief in supernatural realities, the Church does not bind itself to any particular philosophical system. This is brought out most clearly when it presents its two most fundamental mysteries, the Trinity and the Incarnation, in terms of nature and person. In the formulation of these mysteries, these terms are analogies to be understood only in the light of the revealed reality. The foundation for the analogical application of the terms nature and person to these mysteries rests on a minimal number of philosophical presuppositions. Nature simply refers to that which constitutes the internal unity of anything. Person says nothing more than separateness from everyone and everything else—hence INCOMMUNICABILITY. The precise meaning of these terms in the dogmatic formulas is grasped by the Church only by reflection on the very mysteries of the Trinity and the Incarnation. Because of the necessarily partial character of any expression of a supernatural reality, faith seeking understanding has always sought, and eventually used, other analogies to complement the nature-person analogy, e.g., those based on mutual relations, human mind, and human love.

The mystery of the Incarnation reveals a concrete, individual, human nature without a human personality. In the presence of this mystery, Catholic theology has been perennially confronted with the yet unanswered question of the relation of nature and person. Philosophy is usually content with the identification of the concrete, individual, existing nature and the person. Some contemporary trends in theology suggest a reexamination of this philosophical position, not only on an ontological, but also on a psychological plane.

Nature in a General Sense. Two questions are raised in theology by nature in a general sense: (1) concerning the relation between the natural and supernatural orders, and (2) concerning the different states of nature.

Natural and Supernatural Orders. By the natural order is meant the natural disposition and relationship of creatures among themselves and to God, the extrinsic author and end of everything within the order. Humanity with its natural faculties seeks to attain a perfect, mediate possession of God. This end could be attained by human activity in the material universe in accordance with the norm of the order—the natural law. By the supernatural order is meant the supernatural disposition and relationship of creatures among themselves and to God, the extrinsic author and end of everything within the order. Jesus Christ, His human nature elevated by the HYPOSTATIC UNION and sanctifying grace, beatific vision and love, is the one mediator between God and humankind and is therefore the intrinsic author and end of everything in this order. Humanity is elevated by a sharing in the divine nature (sanctifying grace) and in the infused divine powers (theological virtues). By union with Christ and corresponding activity in accordance with the norm of the order—the divine positive law—humanity can attain an immediate possession of God through beatific vision and love.

Though the natural order is not a de facto order, still theology is concerned with that order because of its manner of elevation. The supernatural does not imply the suppression of the natural but rather its supereminent realization. Hence the adages: "The supernatural is not opposed to but above nature"; "Grace does not destroy but perfects nature." These principles must, however, be carefully understood, for they contain a certain equivocation. The supernatural is not a perfection of nature within the order of nature. The Christian humanist is often tempted to view the supernatural as though it were simply a supreme realization of natural perfection. Central to the Christian message is the absolute incapability of nature to attain to the supernatural, for the supernatural is a perfection of a higher order than the natural. The supernatural, to be sure, is the full realization of nature but in a perfection that transcends the natural order completely. The Christian way of death-resurrection is one not merely of removing sin but also of transcending the natural for a greater openness to the supernatural received as grace—pure gift. Supernatural grace, therefore, is not some superstructure, imposing itself on human nature and disturbing the order of pure nature. Grace, it is true, is unexacted by humankind's nature, but God created humankind so that it *could* receive this gift and receive it as such: as an unexpected, unexacted gift.

The point of contact between the natural and supernatural orders is human nature, for only humanity, abstracting from the angels, is capable of being elevated to the supernatural order. This capacity in human nature is referred to as OBEDIENTIAL POTENCY. Theology clearly distinguishes this capacity in human nature for the supernatural, which God alone can fulfill, from all of humankind's other natural capabilities, which humanity itself can carry out. The existence of such an obediential potency in human nature is known only through revelation of the fact of actual supernatural elevation. Still this openness of the human spirit for the supernatural indicates not only a nonrepugnance but even a becomingness for the supernatural elevation. The conception, then, of obediential potency is not to be seen in its purely negative aspect as freeing humankind from the contradiction of a supernatural-natural union, but more positively as an inner, conditional ordination to the supernatural. This openness of spirit is central for the understanding of the scriptural doctrine that man is made in the image and likeness of God.

States of Nature. Even though, historically, nature never existed without the supernatural elevation, nature connotes a perfection complete in itself and hence could exist in a purely natural state. Theologians distinguish five different possible states of nature: (1) PURE NATURE, with no PRETERNATURAL or supernatural elevation; (2)

integral nature, with preternatural endowments; (3) elevated nature (the original state of man prior to the Fall), with preternatural and supernatural gifts; (4) fallen unredeemed nature, incapable of attaining its end because of sin; (5) redeemed nature, superabundantly restored to its original elevated state by the REDEMPTION of Jesus Christ. Even though the last is the only actual state of human nature known, there would seem to be no intrinsic impossibility for the actual existence of the other states. In fact, some theologians see a certain appropriate completeness of the universe in positing the actual existence of these other states of nature on planets other than the earth.

God's Glory. "God saw that all He had made was very good" (Gn 1.31). Only the whole of God's creation contains the divinely intended manifestation of His goodness [*see* GLORY OF GOD (END OF CREATION)]. Every area of human endeavor contributes its proper insight into the glory of God discovered in nature. The scientist encounters the beauty of nature in its manifold variation, generous richness, and prodigious creativity. The philosopher discovers in nature an underlying permanence and unity that preserve a most wonderful order in the whole. Only theology attains to the ultimate harmonization of nature's multiplicity and unity in its Creator, who has revealed Himself to be one in nature and triune in personality. This triune Deity has, moreover, offered to share with all created nature His own harmonious multiplicity in unity. This properly divine beauty is shared in immediately by the more excellent angelic and, through Christ, human natures, mediately by all nature "because creation itself also will be delivered from its slavery to corruption into the freedom of the glory of the sons of God" (Rom 8.21).

See Also: BAIUS AND BAIANISM; DESTINY, SUPERNATURAL; PERSON (IN PHILOSOPHY); PERSON (IN THEOLOGY); SUPERNATURAL EXISTENTIAL; TRINITY, HOLY.

Bibliography: Y. E. MASSON, *Dictionnaire de théologie catholique,* ed. A. VACANT et al. (Paris 1903–50) 11.1:36–44. J. ALFARO, *Lexikon für Theologie und Kirche,* ed. J. HOFER and K. RAHNER (Freiburg 1957–65) 7:809–810, 830–835. H. LESÈTRE, *Dictionnaire de la Bible,* ed. F. VIGOUROUX, 5 v. (Paris 1895–1912) 4:1488–90. H. KUHN and S. OTTO, *Handbuch theologischer Grundbegriffe,* ed. H. FRIES, 2 v. (Munich 1962–63) 2:211–221. I. M. DALMAU, *Sacrae theologiae summa* (BAC 2.2; Madrid 1958). I. SOLANO, *ibid.* 3.1. R. LE TROQUER, *What Is Man?* tr. E. E. SMITH (New York 1961). K. RAHNER, *God, Christ, Mary and Grace,* tr. C. ERNST (his *Theological Investigations* 1; Baltimore 1961). J. B. HAWKINS, "On Nature and Person in Speculative Theology," *Downside Review* 80 (1962) 1–11.

[M. J. DORENKEMPER]

NAUCLERUS, JOHN

German humanist and historian; b. probably in Württemberg, *c.* 1425–30; d. Tübingen, Jan. 5, 1510. Nauclerus (properly Verge or Vergenhans) acted as tutor and counselor for the future Duke Eberhard V of Württemberg from 1450 to 1459, serving also as pastor and canon of Brackenheim. He was provost of Stuttgart (1465–72) and possibly was active at the Universities of Paris and Basel. Nauclerus was instrumental in the founding of the University of TÜBINGEN (1477) and taught Canon Law there, functioning also as rector and then, from 1483 to 1509, as chancellor and provost.

Around 1504 he wrote *Memorabilium omnis aetatis et omnium gentium chronici commentarii,* covering the years from the creation of the world to his day. The work divides history into ages and counts 63 generations to the birth of Christ and 51 from Christ to 1501. Written in annalistic style, Nauclerus's history reflects the spiritual attitude of the Middle Ages, unaffected by the humanistic spirit of his own age. It shows a strong predisposition for affairs in his homeland, for Church matters and papal proceedings, but it is a valuable resource for the contemporary period. Unpublished until after Nauclerus's death, the history was edited by MELANCHTHON and printed in Tübingen in 1516. It had such great success that nine editions were printed before 1617. Besides his administrative work and his literary undertakings, Nauclerus was a canon lawyer and sought a compromise between local custom and Canon Law.

Bibliography: Works. *De Symonia* (Tübingen 1500); *Memorabilium . . . commentarii,* 2 v. (Tübingen 1516). Literature. P. JOACHIMSEN, *Geschichtsauffassung und Geschichtschreibung in Deutschland unter dem Einfluss des Humanismus* (Leipzig 1910) 1:91–104. J. W. THOMPSON and B. J. HOLM, *History of Historical Writing,* 2 v. (New York 1942) 1:426. H. TÜCHLE, *Lexikon für Theologie und Kirche,* ed. J. HOFER and K. RAHNER (Freiberg 1957–65) 7:845.

[C. R. BYERLY]

NAUSEA, FRIEDRICH (GRAU)

Theologian; b. Waischenfeld (hence he is called Blancicampianus), Upper Franconia, *c.* 1490; d. Trent, Feb. 6, 1552. He studied at Leipzig (1514); Pavia (1518); Padua, where he obtained the doctorate in law (1523); and Siena. He interrupted his theological studies to accompany Cardinal L. CAMPEGGIO on his trip as legate to combat heresy in Germany. On the way, Nausea tried at Bretten to win P. Melanchthon back to the Catholic faith. Named pastor at Frankfurt in 1525, Nausea had to withdraw because of Protestant pressure, and from 1526 until 1533 he labored fruitfully at Mainz as cathedral preacher

and as a writer (*Centuriae IV homiliarum* [Cologne 1530]). Ferdinand I called him to Vienna in 1534 and made him court preacher. There he became coadjutor in 1538 and successor in 1541 of Bp. J. Fabri. In 1540 and 1541 he took part in the religious discussions at Hagenau and Worms. By word and in writing Nausea worked against the spread of the Reformation and sought the reform of the Church, above all through the renewal of the bishops and priests. He ordered the visitation of his parishes (*Pastorialium inquisitionum elenchi tres* [Vienna 1547]), sought a better training of future priests (*Isagogicon de clericis ordinandis* [Vienna 1548]), and looked after the catechizing of the people (*Catechismus Catholicus* [Vienna 1543]). By means of suggestions for reform and an extensive literary and personal activity, he paved the way for the Council of Trent, in which he participated for the first time in 1551. At the council he argued in favor of COMMUNION under both species and marriage of the clergy. Unfortunately, death soon ended Nausea's reforming influence.

Bibliography: É. AMANN, *Dictionnaire de théologie catholique,* ed. A. VACANT et al., 15 v. (Paris 1903–50; Tables générales 1951–) 11.1:45–51. H. GOLLOB, *Friedrich Nausea: Probleme der Gegenreformation* (Vienna 1952). H. JEDIN, "Das konziliare Reformprogramm Friedrich Nauseas," *Historisches Jahrbuch der Görres-Gesellschaft* 77 (1958) 229–253. R. BÄUMER, *Lexikon für Theologie und Kirche,* ed. J. HOFER and K. RAHNER, 10 v. (2d, new ed. Freiburg 1957–65) 7:847.

[E. ISERLOH]

NAVAL GIRBES, JOSEFA, BL.

Lay craftsperson, mystic, member of the Third Order Secular of Our Lady of Mount Carmel and St. Teresa of Jesus; b. Dec.11, 1820, Algemesi (near Valencia), Spain; d. Feb. 24, 1893, Algemesi. Following the death of her mother (1833), Josefa took over the running of her family's household. Five years later, she made a personal vow of perpetual chastity and became a Carmelite tertiary. To provide instruction for girls and young women, she started an embroidery workshop in her home (1850). While teaching them her art, she was able to evangelize her entourage. Josefa reinvigorated the spiritual life of those around her and actively encouraged vocations to religious life. In the course of her ministry to the terminally ill, Josefa display heroic courage during the cholera epidemic of 1885. She achieved mystical union with God at 55. Her mortal remains are enshrined in her parish church, Saint James in Algemesi. She was beatified by Pope John Paul II, Sept. 25, 1988.

Feast: Nov. 6 (Carmelites).

Bibliography: *Acta Apostolicae Sedis* (1988): 1092.

[K. I. RABENSTEIN]

NAVARRE, UNIVERSITY OF

Established in Pamplona, Spain, by OPUS DEI—now the Prelature of the Holy Cross and Opus Dei—as a center for higher studies, the university was officially inaugurated with the opening of the Law School in 1952. Other schools soon followed: Medicine and Nursing (1954), Humanities (1955), Sciences (1957), Journalism (1958), and Engineering (1960), the last located in the neighboring city of San Sebastian. The Canon Law department opened in 1959. The IESE Business School, located in Barcelona, was incorporated in 1958.

In August 1960, in accordance with the 1953 Spanish Concordat, the university was erected as a Catholic university by the Holy See under the title it bears today, The University of Navarre. The Spanish government, due partly to the establishment of this new university, signed an agreement with the Holy See on April 5, 1962, stating the conditions for the accreditation of degrees by ecclesiastical universities. On Sept. 8, 1962 recognition was granted to all the existing departments. Thus the University of Navarre inaugurated a new era of freedom in education in Spain, bringing an end to the state monopoly in effect since the nineteenth century.

After its recognition as a university, the schools of pharmacy and architecture and the institutes of liberal arts and modern languages were begun. Although the curriculum closely followed other Spanish universities, the board of directors tried to incorporate the best university traditions of other countries.

The grand chancellor of the University of Navarre, who is the prelate of Opus Dei, works closely with the board of governors in supervising the direction of the university. The governing board comprises the president, several vice-presidents, a secretary general, an administrator and the various deans. Each faculty is governed by a board made up of the dean, assistant dean, secretary, and professors; student representatives are also present on the board. The university is financed by student tuition, research contracts, and the contributions from the Association of Friends of the University. It does not receive any funding from the Spanish government.

The university publishes journals on archaeology, architecture, family studies, public relations, law, Canon Law, philosophy, history of the Church, literature, theology and current events. The university press publishes numerous books each year. Departmental libraries have been set up for the humanities, geography, social sciences, medicine, and biology. The schools of medicine, sciences, and pharmacy share departmental offices and work in conjunction the Clínica Universitaria, a highly specialized teaching hospital that has become world-renowned in medical science.

[J. A. PANIAGUA/R. PELLITERO]

NAVARRETE, DOMINGO FERNÁNDEZ

Dominican missionary, polemicist, archbishop, and primate of the West Indies; b. Castrogeriz, Spain, 1618; d. Santo Domingo (Hispaniola), Feb. 16, 1686. After religious profession at Peñafiel on Dec. 8, 1635, and higher studies at Valladolid, Navarrete volunteered for the Philippines, and arrived there on June 23, 1648. A decade later he transferred to the China field (Macau, July 14, 1658), working in Fujian and Zhejiang provinces until the outbreak, in 1665, of the disastrous Regency persecution. Internment of the mission personnel at Canton (March 25, 1666) made possible a collective conference to adopt uniform directives of pastoral action for the China Church, a program in 42 articles. In an interchange of argumentative briefs with the Jesuit apologists through 1668 and 1669, Navarrete opposed implementation of Alexander VII's permissive ruling of 1656 for the Rites (art. 41), but in the end gave written adherence to an earlier text of the Jesuit practices (Sept. 29, 1669). Three months later, however, he secretly left Canton and set out for Europe, arriving at Lisbon on March 19, 1672. While mission procurator at Madrid, he began composition of a massive trilogy dealing with the culture, peoples, and Christian penetration of the Chinese Empire and characterized by trenchant strictures on Jesuit methods there. Besides its controversial chapters, the first volume, *Tratados historicos, politicos, ethnicos y religiosos* (Madrid 1676), contains a spirited account of the missionary's travels and adventures (Eng. tr., Churchill, 1704); the second, *Controversias antiguas y modernas*, more combative in spirit, was suppressed by the Inquisition in 1679. Two years earlier its author had left for the Spanish Indies (July 17, 1677), having been nominated to the archiepiscopal See of Santo Domingo. Consecrated on April 4, 1682, he spent the remaining four years of his life in an embattled effort to raise the standard of colonial morals, aided in this struggle for reform by the local Jesuits, whose zeal he praised in successive reports to the Crown. (*See* CHINESE RITES CONTROVERSY.)

Bibliography: *The Travels and Controversies of Friar Domingo Navarrete 1618–1686,* ed. J. S. CUMMINS, 2 v. (London 1962). *Scriptores Ordinis* 2.2:720–723.

[F. A. ROULEAU]

NAVARRO MIGUEL, CARLO (CHARLES), BL.

Martyr, priest of the Order of Poor Clerics Regular of the Mother of God of the Pious Schools (Piarists); b. Feb. 11, 1911 in Torrente, Valencia, Spain; d. Sept. 22, 1936. Carlos was ordained to the priesthood in 1935 and served in Albacete. He sought refuge at his parent's home as the violence against religious increased during the Spanish Civil War. On September 12, soldiers seized him and imprisoned him. Early on September 22 he was shot along with two other priests of the town. He was beatified on Oct. 1, 1995 by Pope John Paul II together with 12 other Piarists (*see* PAMPLONA, DIONISIO AND COMPANIONS, BB.).

Feast: Sept. 22.

Bibliography: "Decreto Super Martyrio," *Acta Apostolicae Sedis* (1995): 651–656. *La Documentation Catholique* 2125 (Nov. 5, 1995): 924.

[L. GENDERNALIK/EDS]

NAYA, FLORENTÍN FELIPE, BL.

Martyr, lay brother of the Order of Poor Clerics Regular of the Mother of God of the Pious Schools (Piarists); b. Oct. 10, 1856 in Alquézar, Huesca, Spain; d. Aug. 9, 1936. Felipe lived under house arrest with his confreres for two weeks. Partially blind and in ill health in his advanced age, he devoted himself to constant prayer. Four kilometers from Peralta, on a hill about ten meters from the side of the road, he and Faustino OTEIZA SEGURA were gunned down by anticlerical revolutionaries. He was beatified on Oct. 1, 1995 by Pope John Paul II together with 12 other Piarists (*see* PAMPLONA, DIONISIO AND COMPANIONS, BB.).

Feast: Sept. 22.

Bibliography: "Decreto Super Martyrio," *Acta Apostolicae Sedis* (1995): 651–656. *La Documentation Catholique* 2125 (Nov. 5, 1995): 924.

[L. GENDERNALIK/EDS]

NAZARENES (BROTHERHOOD OF ST. LUKE)

A group of 19th-century German painters inspired by Christian faith and German nationalism to paint in imitation of the Italian Quattrocento masters. Although they predated the full Romantic movement, their spirit is one of studied return to another age as an ideal, with the additional sentimental confusion of religio-ethical and aesthetic values. The leader of the Brotherhood was Johann Friedrich Overbeck (1789–1869), who as a disciple of Friedrich SCHLEGEL was converted to Catholicism (1813). Protesting the academic instruction at the Vienna Academy, Overbeck, with Franz Pforr and Ludwig Vogel, left Germany for Rome in 1810, intending to revive Christian fresco painting in the "simple and pure" style of PERUGINO and Raphael. They lived a communal life in the convent of San Isidoro, where they were joined by other disciples: W. von Schadow, the Veit brothers, J. D. Passavant, J. Führich, Schnorr von Carolsfeld, and Peter von Cornelius (1783–1867). As a group they produced two murals: a "Joseph in Egypt" cycle (Casa Bartoldi 1816), and a "Dante and Tasso" cycle (Villa Massimi 1817–27). Overbeck and Cornelius are known also for their individual works, e.g., Overbeck's fresco in the Portiuncula, Assisi. Although these two later renounced the ideals of the brotherhood, its spirit lived on in English Pre-Raphaelitism.

Bibliography: G. DEHIO, *Geschichte der deutschen Kunst,* 4 v. (Berlin 1934) v.4. H. FOCILLON, *Le Peinture aux XIXᵉ et XXᵉ siècles du réalisme à nos jours* (Paris 1928). M. HOWITT, *Friedrich Overbeck,* 2 v. (Freiburg 1886). A. KUHN, *Peter Cornelius und die geistigen Strömungen seiner Zeit* (Berlin 1921). H. GELLER, *Die Bildnisse der deutschen Künstler in Rom 1800–1830* (Berlin 1952). K. SIMON, U. THIEME, and F. BECKER, eds., *Allgemeines Lexikon der bildenden Künstler von der Antike bis zur Gegenwart,* 37 v. (Leipzig 1907–38) 7:432–438. P. F. SCHMIDT, *ibid.,* 26:104–106.

[M. M. MICHELS]

NAZARETH

City nestled among the hills of Galilee. It is not mentioned in the Old Testament literature, or in the Talmud, or by Josephus. It is referred to frequently, however, in the New Testament because Jesus came from that city and was known as the Nazarene. Although it is called a city, it is quite small. The name is spelled in different ways in the New Testament. Most frequently it is Ναζαρέτ or Ναζαρέθ, but it occurs also as Ναζαρά, Ναζαράτ, or Ναζαράθ.

It was at Nazareth that the angel Gabriel brought to Mary the message that she was to be the mother of the Savior (Lk 1.26). Mary and Joseph left there to go to Bethlehem, where Jesus was born. Then the Holy Family returned to Nazareth after their flight into Egypt (Mt 2.23). There Jesus spent the years of His hidden life (Mt 2.23; Lk 2.39, 51). During His public life Jesus seldom visited Nazareth because He was not well received there (Lk 4.16–30). That Nazareth was not highly regarded may be inferred from the question of Nathaniel, from neighboring Cana, "Can anything good come out of Nazareth?" (Jn 1.46).

During the 1st century Nazareth was inhabited not only by Jews, but also by Christians, some of whom, it seems, were relatives of Our Lord. In the early 4th century Joseph of Tiberias had been commissioned by Constantine to build churches for Christians in the Jewish towns and villages of Galilee. We may suppose that he built a church at Nazareth because of the town's intimate connection with Jesus. In 634 the Muslims occupied Nazareth and made life difficult for its Christians. In the 12th century the Crusaders made Nazareth into an episcopal city, but it did not remain so for long, because the city soon fell back into the hands of the Muslims. The Franciscans established a convent in the city in 1390, but only since 1620 have they been able to remain there permanently. Since 1948 Nazareth has been within the confines of the State of Israel.

Of the many shrines commemorating events of the New Testament, the two most important are the House of St Joseph and the Sanctuary of the Annunciation. In the preparations for constructing a new basilica over the spot where the Annunciation took place, a systematic excavation was conducted by B. Bagatti. He has shown that here, underneath the church built in 1730 by the Franciscans, which had been removed to give place to the new basilica, there was a church built by the Crusaders. Earlier than this, there was a 5th-century church that in turn had been preceded by a Christian structure from as early as A.D. 200. Numerous graffiti were found on the plaster walls and on the plastered surfaces of loose stones, made by early Judeo-Christians. Of special interest is one of the graffiti containing, in Greek, the opening words of the angelic salutation, "Hail, Mary."

Bibliography: *Encyclopedic Dictionary of the Bible,* translated and adapted by L. HARTMAN (New York, 1963) 1616–18. B. BAGATTI, "Ritrovamenti nella Nazaret evangelica," *Stud. Bibl. Franc. Liber Annuus* 5 (Jerusalem 1954–55) 5–44; *Dictionnaire de la Bible,* suppl. ed. L. PIROT, et al. (Paris 1928–) 6:318–333. S. SALLER, "Recent Work at the Shrine of the Annunciation at Nazareth," *The Catholic Biblical Quarterly* 25 (Washington, DC 1963) 348–353. C. KOPP, *The Holy Places of the Gospels,* tr. R. WALLS (New York 1963) 49–86.

[S. MUSHOLT]

NAZARIUS OF LÉRINS, ST.

Abbot; b. *c.* 584; d. *c.* 629. He appears in the abbatial list as 14th abbot of LÉRINS. Little is known about him. Like his predecessors at Lérins, Nazarius labored to root out the remaining vestiges of pagan worship into which the district frequently lapsed. He is said to have despoiled a sanctuary of Venus near the monastery and to have established there a convent for women that flourished until the Saracen raids of the eighth century. His name is inscribed in the Gallican calendar of saints.

Statue of the Holy Family, Church of Saint Joseph, Nazareth, Israel. (©Dave Bartruff/CORBIS)

Feast: Nov. 18.

Bibliography: *Gallia Christiana* 3:1193. P. MEYER, "La Vie latine de saint Honorat et Raimon Féraut," *Romania* 8 (1879) 481–508. U. CHEVALIER, *Répertoire des sources historiques du moyen-age* 2:3291.

[B. F. SCHERER]

NAZIRITES

Nazirites are persons consecrated to God through a special vow. The basic text concerning the Nazirites (Heb. *nāzîr,* from the root *nzr,* to separate, closely related to *ndr,* to vow) is Nm 6.1–21, according to which they have a threefold obligation: to abstain from wine and all fermented drink (*see* Rechabites: Jer 35.5–8), to leave their hair uncut, and to avoid all contact with dead bodies. The first provision seems to be a reaction of Israel's nomad background against the agricultural life adopted in Canaan, seen as a corrupting influence, and the third is connected with ritual purity; the second provision is undoubtedly a very ancient practice, but one to which it is difficult to assign an explanation.

Although Nm 6.1–21 belongs to the priestly tradition (*see* PRIESTLY WRITERS, PENTATEUCHAL), and is, therefore, a recent text, it is certain that it codifies a very ancient custom. The vow of the Nazirites is mentioned in several historical and prophetical texts of the Bible and seems to have taken different forms in the course of time. The earliest texts that speak of it, Jgs 13.4–5, 7, 13–14; 16.17 (Samson), 1 Sm 1.11 (Samuel), and Am 2.11–12, present the consecration of the Nazirites as lifelong, and as resulting from a divine call. Of the three obligations of the Nazirites given in Nm 6.1–21 only the one concerning the hair is mentioned in the cases of Samuel (1 Sm 1.11) and Samson (Jgs 13.5)—though abstinence from wine is imposed on Samson's mother—and only the one concerning wine in Am 2.11–12. The practice of the Nazirite vow was certainly still known in the later period of the Old Testament (1 Mc 3.49–51) and in New Testament times; and it is mentioned in Josephus and in the Talmud. St. Paul made a vow of this kind at Cenchrae (Acts 18.18) and offered the prescribed sacrifices along with four others, at the Temple of Jerusalem (Acts 21.23–24). Some think that St. John the Baptist was also a Nazirite (Lk 1.15).

Nazirites are found, therefore, throughout Biblical history. One must see in this practice a particular manifestation of religious asceticism, and also, in the early period of Hebrew history, a symptom of the reaction of Yahwism against the Canaanite influence.

Bibliography: M. JASTROW, "The *Nazir* Legislation," *Journal of Biblical Literature* 33 (1914) 266–285. R. DE VAUX, *Ancient Israel, Its Life and Institutions,* tr. J. MCHUGH (New York 1961) 466–467. *Encyclopedic Dictionary of the Bible,* tr. and adap. by L. HARTMAN (New York 1963), from A. VAN DEN BORN, *Bijbels Woordenboek* (1618).

[A. L. BARBIERI]

NE TEMERE

The words *Ne Temere* (lest perhaps) are the opening words of a decree concerning the juridical form of marriage. After consultation with the commission of cardinals, assigned the task of codifying the law of the Church, the decree was issued by Pope PIUS X through the Congregation of the Council on Aug. 2, 1907, to take effect on Easter Sunday, April 19, 1908 (P. Gasparri and I. Serédi, *Codicis iuris canonici fontes* 1917 n. 4340).

The *TAMETSI* decree (Nov. 11, 1563) of the 24th session of the Council of Trent had already established a juridical form necessary for the validity of marriage. *Tametsi* stated: "Those who shall attempt to contract marriage otherwise than in the presence of the parish priest or of another priest authorized by the parish priest or by the Ordinary and in the presence of two or three witnesses, the Holy Council renders absolutely incapable of

thus contracting marriage and declares such contracts invalid and null, as by the present decree it invalidates and annuls them."

Despite the *Tametsi* decree, and despite further clarifications from the Roman congregations and the wide faculties given to ordinaries and their delegates, there still remained great need for further amplification and legislation in the Church with regard to the form of marriage.

Clandestine marriages continued to be contracted. This often condemned practice presented many moral as well as legal problems. The decree *Tametsi,* however, had not been published everywhere so that it had not become effective throughout the universal Church. Where it had been published doubts remained concerning the proper pastor before whom a marriage was to be contracted. Finally, the *Tametsi* decree had made no exemption from the law for baptized non-Catholics. The last difficulty had been somewhat alleviated by the decree *Matrimonia quae in locis* of Benedict XIV, which exempted baptized non-Catholics from the juridical form of marriage (Nov. 4, 1741). This decree was issued originally for Belgium and Holland only, but was later extended to other parts of the world and then applied to all places where the *Tametsi* decree had been promulgated.

In his declaration, Benedict XIV referred to the widespread doubts and anxieties that troubled bishops, pastors, and missionaries concerning the validity of non-Catholic and mixed marriages. To settle the various difficulties once and for all while abolishing any contrary law or custom, the *Ne Temere* decree made the following provisions: (1) All Latin-rite Catholics were bound to the juridical form of marriage when they married Catholics; (2) Non-Catholics were exempted when they married among themselves; (3) The "communication of privilege" admitted by Benedict's declaration was henceforth abolished, so Catholics were bound to the juridical form when they married non-Catholics, except in Germany and Hungary as a result of the constitution *Provida* given by Pope Pius X to Germany and later extended to Hungary; (4) The juridical form required the presence of the local ordinary or pastor or a priest delegated by either. These ministers could validly assist at all marriages within the territorial limits of their respective jurisdictions. The presence of at least two other witnesses was required; (5) In imminent danger of death, if neither the ordinary nor pastor nor a delegate of one of these could be present, marriage could be contracted validly before any priest and two witnesses for the sake of peace of conscience or the legitimation of offspring; (6) In places where the local ordinary, pastor, or delegate could not be present and the absence had endured for at least a month, marriage could be contracted before two witnesses without the presence of a priest. Moreover, the *Ne Temere* decree, in the interest of good order, determined that marriages ought to be celebrated in the parish of the bride.

The legislation on the canonical form of marriage as laid down by the decree *Ne Temere* was later substantially adopted by the Code of Canon Law, which went into effect on May 19, 1918. The one major difference between the legislation of the Code of Canon Law and the legislation contained in the *Ne Temere* concerned persons who had been baptized in the Catholic Church but who later lost their identification with the Church. The *Ne Temere* decree made no exception for these persons with regard to the canonical form of marriage. The Code of Canon Law provided for them in canon 1099.2, exempting non-Catholics who had been baptized in the Catholic Church provided one or both of their parents were non-Catholics and provided they were raised from infancy outside the Catholic Church.

Finally, on Aug. 1, 1948, Pope Pius XII eliminated the exemption afforded by the latter part of the above-mentioned canon 1099.2. This final ruling concerning the form of marriage became effective on Jan. 1, 1949.

Bibliography: E. FUS, *The Extraordinary Form of Marriage according to Canon 1098* (Catholic University of America Canon Law Studies 348; Washington 1954). J. CARBERRY, *The Juridical Form of Marriage* (Catholic University of America Canon Law Studies 84; Washington 1934). W. BOUDREAUX, *The "ab acatholicis nati" of Canon 1099.2* (Catholic University of America Canon Law Studies 227; Washington 1946). A. MARX, *The Declaration of Nullity of Marriages Contracted outside the Church* (Catholic University of America Canon Law Studies 182; Washington 1943).

[W. VAN OMMEREN]

NEALE, LEONARD

Second archbishop of the BALTIMORE, Maryland Archdiocese, president of Georgetown College, Washington, D.C.; b. Port Tobacco, Maryland, Oct. 15, 1746; d. Baltimore, June 18, 1817. Neale was born of an old Maryland family, son of William and Anne Neale. At about the age of 12, he was sent to Europe to obtain his education under Catholic auspices, a privilege he could not enjoy in the colony. After his course at St. Omer's in French Flanders, he entered the Society of Jesus on Sept. 7, 1767. At the time of the suppression of the Society in 1773 he was a priest and still engaged in the study of theology. He then went to England and from there to Demarara in British Guiana as a missionary.

In 1783, Neale returned to Maryland and was assigned to the mission of Port Tobacco. When the yellow fever plague of 1793 in Philadelphia took the lives of Lorenz Graessel, who had been named coadjutor bishop of Baltimore, and Francis Anthony Fleming, OP, Neale went to Philadelphia and was soon named its vicar-general by Bp. John CARROLL. During Neale's ministry in that city, he met Miss Alice Lalor and helped her to found the first community of Visitation Nuns in the U.S.

In 1798, Carroll called Neale to the presidency of Georgetown College. While retaining this post, he was selected as Carroll's coadjutor and was consecrated bishop of Gortyna in the procathedral of St. Peter's in Baltimore on Dec. 7, 1800, the first time this ceremony was performed in the U.S. Neale joined Carroll in 1803 in writing to Gabriel Gruber, superior of the Jesuits in Russia, to present the petition of the former Jesuits to be joined with the Society of Jesus still existing in White Russia. Moreover, Neale's support of this project continued until the viva voce restoration was effected in 1806. He likewise rejoiced with the Jesuits at their final and complete restoration throughout the world in 1814.

On the death of Carroll, Dec. 3, 1815, Neale succeeded to the metropolitan See of Baltimore, receiving the pallium from Pius VII the following year. One of his first acts was to request from the Holy See the formal approval of the Visitation community at Georgetown. His episcopate was sorely tried by schisms in Philadelphia and Charleston, South Carolina. Burdened by these troubles, he sought a coadjutor and selected the Sulpician, Ambrose Maréchal. The latter's appointment as titular bishop of Stauropolis on July 24, 1817, came about a month after the archbishop's death. Neale is buried in a crypt beneath the altar of the convent chapel of the Visitation Convent in Georgetown, Washington, D.C.

Bibliography: M. BRISLEN, "The Episcopacy of Leonard Neale," *Historical Records and Studies of the U. S. Catholic Historical Society of New York* 34 (1945) 20–111. P. K. GUILDAY, *The Life and Times of John Carroll, Archbishop of Baltimore, 1735–1818* 2 v. (Westminster, Md. 1954). A. M. MELVILLE, *John Carroll of Baltimore* (New York 1955).

[J. M. DALEY]

NEAMTU, ABBEY OF

Fourteenth-century Romanian monastery, outside the town of Targu Neamt, northeast Romania, in Moldavia. Targu Neamt was once an important fortress, built in 1210. Later, Neamtu Abbey was founded at the site of a hermitage there. The monastery became one of the largest, richest, and most famous monastic foundations in ROMANIA. During its golden age it had two churches, ten towers, and more than 600 monks. It was enlarged and enriched by Stephen the Great, Prince of Moldavia (1457–1503) and became a center for pilgrims and tourists.

Bibliography: I. CRĂCIUNAȘ, "The Monastery of Neamt, the Center of Monasticism in Moldavia," *Mitropolia Moldovei și Sucevei,* 38 (1962) 343–353, in Romanian. S. PORCESCU, "Cultural Activity of Neamt in the 15th Century, *ibid.* 477–506, in Romanian.

[J. PAPIN]

NEBO (NABU)

Nebu (Nabu) is one of the more important minor deities of the Babylonian–Assyrian pantheon. The god Nebo (Akkadian Nabû, "the called") appears in the Code of HAMMURABI in the early 2nd millennium B.C. as son of the national god MARDUK and tutelary deity of the city Borsippa (to the south of the city of BABYLON) and of its temple Ezida. In later documents he is characterized as the divine scribe, writer, and bearer of the "tablets of destiny" that enshrine the decrees of the gods. In accordance with this role, he was considered patron of the scribal art and of human learning.

The cult of Nebo originated and remained strong in BABYLONIA, where it played an important part in the annual New Year Festival at Babylon; during this time, his statue was borne from Borsippa to Babylon, where it was honored together with that of Marduk. It is to this festival that the satirical words of Is 46.1 refer: "BEL [i.e., Marduk] bows down, Nebo stoops, their idols are upon beasts and cattle." Though the worship of Nebo was adopted in ASSYRIA, the intermittent anti–Babylonian feeling there prevented his attaining the prominence he enjoyed in Babylonia.

The name of the god is found in the Old Testament as a theophoric element in several Babylonian proper names of the period preceding and during the Exile: Nebuchednezzar (Nebo, protect the son, Jer 21.2 and *passim*), Nabu zaradan (Nebo gave offspring, Jer 39.9 and *passim*), Nabu–sezban (Nebo, save me! Jer 39.13), and—in a form altered by the piety of Biblical scribes—Abdenago (Servant of Nebo, Dn 1.7 and *passim*).

See Also: MESOPOTAMIA, ANCIENT, 3.

Bibliography: *Encyclopedic Dictionary of the Bible,* tr. and adap. by L. HARTMAN (New York 1963), from A. VAN DEN BORN, *Bijels Woordenboek* (1619). F. NÖTSCHER, *Lexikon für Theologie und Kirche*[2], ed. J. HOFER and K. RAHNER (Frieburg 1957–65); suppl., *Das Zweite Vatikanische Konzil: Dokumente und Kommentare,* ed. H. S. BRECHTER et al., pt. 1 (1966) 7: 755–756. A. DEIMEL, *Pantheon Babylonicum* (Rome 1914), s.v. Nabû. K. L. TALLQVIST, *Akkadische Götterepitheta* (Helsingfors 1938) s.v. Nabû. J. B. PRICHARD, *Ancient Near Eastern Texts Relating to the Old Testament* (Princeton 1955) 331–334.

[R. I. CAPLICE]

NEBRASKA, CATHOLIC CHURCH IN

Nebraska, a largely agrarian Midwestern state situated near the center of the contiguous 48 states, is bounded on the north by South Dakota, on the West by Wyoming, in its southwestern corner by Colorado, and on the south by Kansas. On the east, the Missouri River separates the state from Iowa and the northwestern corner of Missouri. The Platte River flows throughout the state from west to east, separating the Diocese of Lincoln in the south from the two sees to the north—the Archdiocese of OMAHA in the northeast and the Diocese of Grand Island in the northwest.

Nebraska first fell under Catholic ecclesiastical jurisdiction in 1493 when Spain laid claim to North America. France took control of the area in 1682, putting the region under the authority of the bishop of Quebec. Native populations in what would later become Nebraska included the Omaha, Oto, Pawnee, Ponca, and Sioux. The first European Catholics made their appearance in the area in 1720, when Lieutenant Colonel Pedro de Villasur entered with a party of over a hundred, including Friar Juan Mingues, a Franciscan chaplain to the group. The Pawnee attacked their camp near the fork of the Platte and the present-day city of North Platte, killing Villasur, Mingues, and many others. French-Canadian brothers Pierre and Paul Mallet explored and crossed the region in 1739 in search of a passage to New Mexico. For nearly a century thereafter, francophone fur trading developed in the area, particularly near the confluence of the Platte and the Missouri Rivers close to the future towns of Bellevue and Omaha. Many of the fur traders took native women as brides, and their offspring were among the first Catholics in the area to be baptized by later missionaries.

Ecclesiastical authority shifted between the Spanish and the French as often as political control changed, until the United States secured the area as part of the Louisiana Purchase in 1803, when the region thus became the pastoral responsibility of the bishop of Baltimore. The Lewis and Clark expedition, which camped on the west bank of the Missouri near present-day Fort Calhoun in the summer of 1804, opened the region to more intensive fur-trading activities. Among the most prominent and successful of the traders were Manuel Lisa, Lucien Fontanelle, and Peter Sarpy, the latter two of whom befriended and supported missionaries to the region. In 1846, the Mormon peoples on their way to Utah made camp for about a year at Florence, north of present-day Omaha. Ecclesiastically, the region was assigned to the jurisdiction of the bishop of New Orleans in 1815, and then of the bishop of St. Louis in 1827.

In 1827, three Jesuits, Fr. Felix Verreydt, Bro. Andrew Mazella, and Fr. Peter Jean DESMET, established the

St. Joseph Mission in what is now the city of Council Bluffs, Iowa, in order to minister to the Potowatami. Missionary service to the future Nebraska area commenced when Fr. DeSmet crossed the Missouri River to baptize two Oto infants, Elizabeth Loise and Julia Tayon, in Bellevue on July 6, 1838. These were the first documented baptisms in what would later become the state of Nebraska.

DeSmet's subsequent travels took him to the Great Plains Council, which took place 35 miles down the Platte from Fort Laramie, Wyoming, just inside the current Nebraska border, in 1851. The Council gathered about 10,000 native Americans of various tribes to whom the government offered indemnity for future white incursions through their territories. DeSmet performed the first documented Mass in Nebraska at the Council on September 14. Eleven days later, DeSmet witnessed the first documented Catholic marriage in the area, between Louis Vasquez and Narcissa, at Fort Kearney.

In 1850, Pope Pius IX established the Vicariate Apostolic of the Territory East of the Rocky Mountains (also known as "of Indian Territory"), which included the present-day states of Nebraska, Kansas, and Oklahoma, and those parts of the present-day states of South Dakota, North Dakota, Wyoming, and Colorado which lay between the Missouri River and the Rocky Mountains. Jean Baptist MIÈGE, S.J., appointed vicar apostolic, was consecrated a bishop and began his ministries to the region in 1851. Miège faced the immense difficulty of administering a huge territory with very few priests. A few offered assistance from the Diocese of Dubuque, and a tiny number of Jesuit missionaries ministered to the western parts of the area. In 1854, the Kansas-Nebraska Bill divided the political region into two distinct territories along the fortieth parallel, and opened the area to white American settlement, meaning that Miège would have to minister to a growing number of whites as well as the native populations. And in 1855, Congress called for the construction of military and wagon roads westward, with Omaha as the eastern terminus, ensuring the town's future as a transportation hub.

In August of 1856, at Eighth and Harney Streets in Omaha, Miège and area Catholics dedicated St. Mary's, the first church building of any denomination in the future state of Nebraska. Many non-Catholics contributed to its construction, in part to attract immigration and to raise real estate values in the city. Fr. Jeremiah TRECY (1824–88), a priest of the Diocese of Dubuque and an advocate of Catholic colonization efforts, led a group of Irish immigrants into present-day Dakota County to found St. John's City, the first all-Catholic settlement in Nebraska. The colony failed within a few years, largely

Archdiocese/Diocese	Year Created
Archdiocese of Omaha	1945
Diocese of Grand Island	1917
Diocese of Lincoln	1887

because of a destructive tornado in 1860. Most of the settlers sought their fortunes as miners in the West, but several relocated to the nearby town of Franklin (which was later renamed Jackson) or retained their farming claims. Daniel Sheehan, archbishop of Omaha from 1969 to 1993, descended from one of the original Dakota County families.

In 1855, frustrated by his inability to minister to such a vast region, Miège asked that a second vicariate be carved out of his territory. The Holy See announced the creation of the Vicariate of Nebraska on Feb. 17, 1857, in a division coinciding with the 1854 political settlement, with the understanding that Miège would govern both vicariates for the time being. In response to his continued pleas, on Jan. 28, 1859, James Myles O'Gorman, a Trappist monk from New Melleray Abbey in Dubuque, was named a bishop and first vicar apostolic of Nebraska. The first communities of religious women in the state were the Sisters of Mercy, who arrived in 1864, and the Benedictine Sisters, who came in 1865.

O'Gorman established Omaha as his see city and shortly thereafter, on June 25, 1859, ordained the first priest of the vicariate, Fr. William Kelly. During O'Gorman's tenure, several factors brought about significant growth in the future state of Nebraska and the town of Omaha. The Civil War closed off other routes west, funneling the traffic to mines in California, the Black Hills, and especially Colorado, where gold had been discovered in 1850, through Nebraska. Irish Catholics among the freighters and outfitters bolstered Church numbers in the Omaha area. After the war, the Union Pacific built its transcontinental railroad, with Omaha as one of its major centers. Becoming a transportation center also served to boost the state's agricultural economy. The Irish immigrants attracted by the availability of railroad construction work swelled the state's Catholic population. Nebraska gained sufficient population to become the 37th state on March 1, 1867.

However, O'Gorman still struggled with the problem of how to administer such a large area with so few priests. By the end of 1860, O'Gorman had only four priests and a Jesuit brother to assist him in ministry, and only nine priests in 1864 to minister to an estimated 50,000 Catholics. O'Gorman oversaw the building of a modest Gothic cathedral at Ninth and Howard Streets, St.

Philomena's, financed in part by Edward and Mary Lucretia Creighton. But because the area's Catholics were often too poor to support their clergy or to build churches, O'Gorman depended significantly on financial support from the Society for the Propagation of the Faith in Lyons, France, as well as the occasional aid of the Leopoldine Society of Vienna and the Ludwig Missionsverein of Munich.

Fr. Emmanuel Hartig, O.S.B., of the Atchison, Kansas, Benedictine priory, was assigned to minister to Catholics in Nebraska City. On July 11, 1862, he dedicated St. Benedict's Church, the oldest standing church in the state of Nebraska. However, Nebraska City also occasioned the earliest ethnic infighting in the Church in Nebraska, as English-speaking Irish Catholics chafed at attending German-speaking services. Such tensions became a greater problem as increased numbers of German immigrants, fleeing the KULTURKAMPF, streamed into the area, and waves of aspiring Bohemian farmers entered the state, in the 1870s. About one of every eight Bohemians living in the United States prior to World War I lived in Nebraska. The majority of these, about 5,000 families, resided on farms in Butler, Colfax, Saline, and Saunders County. Meanwhile, in the 1870s, Irish Catholics continued to establish colonies at O'Neill in Holt County and Greeley in Greeley County. John Fitzgerald, a contractor of the Burlington railroad who moved to Lincoln in the early 1870s, established himself as that city's first millionaire. He financed a convent and an orphanage in Lincoln while at the same time drawing national attention as president of the American branch of Charles Stewart Parnell's Land League, the Irish National League.

O'Gorman died on July 4, 1874. Fr. John IRELAND, pastor of the cathedral of St. Paul, Minnesota, was appointed to succeed him on Feb. 12, 1875, but his ordinary, Bishop Thomas Grace of St. Paul, successfully requested that the appointment be revoked so that Ireland could remain in Minnesota and become his coadjutor. At long last, O'Gorman's successor, James O'Connor, was consecrated as vicar apostolic on Aug. 10, 1876. O'Connor is especially remembered for having been the spiritual director who guided St. Katharine DREXEL, foundress of the Sisters of the Blessed Sacrament for the Indian and Colored Peoples, to pursue religious life and missionary work. Drexel founded St. Augustine's Indian School in Winnebago in Thurston County in 1908. St. Augustine's remains the prime educational facility for Native Americans in Nebraska. In 2000, a delegation of Winnebago students and parishioners attended Drexel's canonization in Rome. It was also O'Connor who invited the Jesuits to direct Creighton University, founded in 1878 with the proceeds of a generous bequest of Edward and Mary Lucretia Creighton.

O'Connor's ecclesiastical territory diminished in geographical size over the course of his episcopate, beginning with the creation of the Vicariate of Dakota in 1880, and the Vicariate of Montana in 1883. Omaha was erected a diocese consisting of the states of Nebraska and Wyoming on Oct. 2, 1885, with O'Connor as its first ordinary. Soon thereafter, on Aug. 2, 1887, the Holy See also established the Diocese of Cheyenne, consisting of the entire state of Wyoming, and the Diocese of Lincoln, consisting of all of Nebraska south of the Platte River, all of which was territory formerly assigned to Omaha. During this period, Italian, Polish, Hungarian, and Ukrainian immigrants joined the Catholic communities in the city of Omaha and in the Nebraska countryside.

Thomas Bonacum, the first bishop of the Diocese of Lincoln (1887–1911), inherited 32 priests, 29 parishes, 74 missions, and 23,160 Catholic faithful. His successors were J. Henry Tihen (1911–17), Charles O'Reilly (1918–23), Francis Beckman (1924–30), Louis B. Kucera (1930–57), James V. Casey (1957–67), Glennon P. Flavin (1967–92), and Fabian W. Bruskewitz (1992–). On Aug. 18, 1965, the Apostolic Delegate, Archbishop Egidio Vagnozzi, presided at the dedication of Lincoln's new Cathedral of the Risen Christ, of distinctly modern design.

O'Connor died on May 27, 1890, and was succeeded by Richard Scannell (1891–1916), whose episcopate was characterized by the economic struggles of the 1890s, poor health, and the commissioning of St. Cecilia's Cathedral, designed by Thomas Kimball. On Oct. 6, 1907, Scannell blessed the cornerstone of this Spanish Renaissance structure, which remains one of the ten largest cathedrals in the country. The cathedral was restored in 2000 to reflect Kimball's original designs for the interior.

On March 8, 1912, the Holy See again divided the territory of the Diocese of Omaha, erecting the Diocese of Kearney out of its western portion and appointing James A. Duffy as its first bishop. The Kearney Diocese, two-and-a-half times the size of the Omaha diocese, featured approximately 40,000 sparsely-populated square miles, including ranch lands, the desolate Sand Hills, and the Scottsbluff National Monument. The assignment of the more populous and prosperous counties of Hall, Howard, Greeley, and Wheeler, on the western edge of the Omaha diocese, however, remained in dispute, until May 13, 1916, when these counties were officially transferred to the Kearney diocese. Subsequently, the see city was transferred to Grand Island in Hall County on April 11, 1917. Duffy resigned in 1931, and was succeeded by Stanislaus V. Bona (1931–45), Edward J. Hunkeler (1945–51), John L. Paschang (1951–78), and Lawrence J. McNamara (1978–). At the time of his death, at the age of 103, on March 21, 1999, retired Bishop Paschang was the world's oldest bishop.

In December 1917, Fr. Edward FLANAGAN, an Irish immigrant priest, housed 12 homeless boys, and founded what would later be known as Boys Town. He attracted substantial philanthropic support with his plan to provide homeless and abandoned youth with vocational and academic education under a program of gentle discipline. A building program in the 1920s marked the creation of a large community to the west of Omaha in order to serve a growing number of young men. During the 1980s and 1990s, the city of Omaha grew around Boys Town's main campus. In 2001, the institution served 2,130 boys and girls, with 18 satellite sites in 15 states serving a total of 35,410 young people. Boys Town began to offer services to girls in 1979, and in August 2000, based upon a referendum of the community's residents, its name was changed to Girls and Boys Town.

Omaha witnessed a succession of notable ordinaries; Jeremiah Harty (1916–27) came to Omaha after 13 years as archbishop of Manila, and Joseph RUMMEL (1928–35) later became the Archbishop of New Orleans, where he courageously desegregated the Catholic school system in the face of bitter opposition. In September of 1930, during Rummel's episcopate, Omaha hosted the Sixth National Eucharistic Congress, a public gathering of thousands of the local faithful, and prelates from across the nation. James Hugh RYAN (1935–47) was transferred to Omaha following his controversial rectorship of the CATHOLIC UNIVERSITY OF AMERICA, where he had tried to reform and improve the academic programs. During his episcopacy, on Aug. 10, 1945, Omaha was elevated to an archdiocese, with Lincoln and Grand Island assigned as its suffragan sees. Archbishop Gerald T. Bergan (1948–69) presided over a program of copious institutional expansion. Archbishop Daniel Sheehan (1969–93), a native of the Omaha archdiocese, worked hard to preserve Catholic education while carrying out the decrees of the Second Vatican Council.

In the postconciliar decades, declining birthrates among farm families, the corporatization of agriculture, and the shift of population from rural to urban areas led to smaller rural congregations. Rather than closing parishes, all three dioceses in the state instituted the modern equivalent of clerical circuit riding whereby a pastor serves up to three parishes or missions.

In the 1990s, economic prosperity in the state brought change to Nebraska Catholicism. In the city of Omaha, the arrival and growth of the communications and agribusiness industries engendered significant suburban expansion. Gigantic megaparishes emerged on the southern and especially the western sides of the metro-

politan area to accommodate the abundant growth of Catholic populations there. Low unemployment and needy job markets, particularly in the meat-packing industry, led to a boom in the number of Hispanic immigrants entering the area, especially in the latter half of the decade. The state's Hispanic population grew from 36,969 in 1990 to 94,425 in 2000. Although many of these immigrants could be described as migrant workers, an increasing number of Hispanics began to establish roots in the state by purchasing houses or starting small businesses. As of 2001, 12 parishes in the Archdiocese of Omaha and eight each in the Grand Island and Lincoln dioceses provided Spanish Mass and some form of Hispanic ministry, while Church-based services for immigrants emerged in each of the dioceses. Meanwhile, a growing need arose for Hmong and Vietnamese ministry. Several Nebraska parishes have sponsored refugees in the wake of the Vietnam War, and continued immigration swelled their numbers.

The African American Catholic population in the state has remained small, and is largely concentrated at St. Benedict the Moor and Sacred Heart Parishes in Omaha. Fr. John Markoe, S.J., founded the DePorres Club at Creighton University in 1947 to work toward racial justice. During the 1950s and 1960s, Archbishop Bergan spoke out in support of equal treatment for blacks in education, employment, and housing.

Religious communities of men represented in Nebraska include the JESUITS, with communities at Creighton University and Creighton Preparatory School in Omaha, the BENEDICTINES, who run the Mount Michael High School near Elkhorn, and the COLUMBAN FATHERS, whose national headquarters are in Bellevue. Women's congregations present include the SISTERS OF MERCY, who founded the College of St. Mary for women in Omaha in 1923, the Dominican Sisters, the SERVANTS OF MARY, the POOR CLARES, NOTRE DAME SISTERS, and the Society of the Sacred Heart, who operated Duchesne College prior to its closing.

By the start of the new millennium, the Diocese of Lincoln garnered an international reputation as a diocese with particularly conservative policies and programs. In the mid-1990s, Lincoln was one of two dioceses in the country forbidding the use of female altar servers. In 1996, Bishop Bruskewitz excommunicated Catholic members of 12 organizations whose teachings and policies he judged to be incompatible with the Catholic faith. In 1997, the diocese established St. Gregory the Great Seminary for collegians, the first freestanding diocesan seminary to open in the United States in several decades. The seminary served 19 Lincoln seminarians during the 2000–01 school year, and hoped to welcome seminarians from other dioceses in subsequent years. In 1998, construction began in Denton, Nebraska, on Our Lady of Guadalupe Seminary, the house of formation for English-speaking members of the Priestly Fraternity of St. Peter, a group dedicated to providing the preconciliar Latin Mass and other sacraments for the faithful. Also in the 1990s, the diocese welcomed a group of Holy Family Sisters of the Needy from Nigeria and a group of Discalced Carmelite Sisters, who established a new monastery in Agnew in 1999.

Meanwhile, in the Archdiocese of Omaha, a new community of men and women, the Intercessors of the Lamb, was granted the canonical status of a public association of the faithful in 1998. In 1985, groundbreaking began in Omaha on the Pope Paul VI Institute for the Study of Human Reproduction. The Institute has gained national and international recognition for its Catholic research and education on matters of human reproduction, especially Natural Family Planning. On Jan. 9, 1999, lay Catholics in Omaha began broadcasts from radio station KVSS, which featured material from EWTN and St. Joseph Radio as well as local church programming.

In 2000, the state's three bishops—Bruskewitz, Omaha's Curtiss, and Grand Island's McNamara—united successfully to support a proposed "Defense of Marriage" referendum, which established in state law that marriage could only be contracted between a man and a woman. They also voted to ensure that the ecclesiastical Province of Omaha would remain the only province in the nation outside of the East Coast to maintain the traditional day (i.e., 40 days after Easter) for the celebration of Ascension Thursday rather than moving it to the subsequent Sunday. The bishops' unified efforts reflect a common vision within an increasingly diverse Catholic population in the state of Nebraska.

> Total population in 2000 according to Catholic records: 1,634,699.
> Catholic population: 364,733. 22.3 percent of total.
> Omaha Catholics: 220,179 out of total: 827,608. 26.6 percent of total.
> Lincoln Catholics: 89,107 out of total: 516,662. 17.2 percent of total.
> Grand Island Catholics: 55,447 out of total: 290,429. 19.1 percent of total.

Bibliography: H. W. CASPER, S.J., *History of the Catholic Church in Nebraska* (Milwaukee 1960–66); Vol. I: *The Church on the Northern Plains,* 1960; Vol. II: *The Church on the Fading Frontier,* 1966; Vol. III: *Catholic Chapters in Nebraska Immigration,* 1966. W. E. RAMSEY and B. D. SHRIER, *A Gentle Shepherd: The Life and Times of Archbishop Daniel E. Sheehan* (Omaha 1999). SISTER LORETTA, C.P.P.S., *History of the Catholic Church in the Diocese of Lincoln, Nebraska, 1887–1987* (Lincoln 1986). S. SZMREC-SANYI, *History of the Catholic Church in Northeast Nebraska* (Omaha 1983).

[S. A. WEIDNER]

NEBUCHADNEZZAR, KING OF BABYLON

Reigned Sept. 7, 605, to 562 B.C. On the 1st of Elul, upon the death of his father, Nabopolassar, Nebuchadnezzar II ascended the throne of the Neo-Babylonian Empire. The spelling of his name as Nabuchodonosor in the Vulgate and Douai Version has its basis in the Septuagint spelling, Ναβουχοδονοσόρ, which has the vowels of the original name approximately correct but incorrectly has an "n" for an "r" as the third last consonant. The original Akkadian name is *Nabū-kuduruṣur* [O Nabu, protect the border (or, the heir?)]. (*See* NEBO (NABU).) The Hebrew Masoretic Text has the name either as *nᵉbukadreṣṣer* (so usually in Jeremiah) or less correctly as *nᵉbukadneṣṣer* (so elsewhere).

The Old Testament and several ancient historians, such as Josephus, mention Nebuchadnezzar, as do many dedicatory inscriptions of his buildings; but the details of his reign were unknown until the recent publication of the Babylonian Chronicle by the British Museum. In 608–607 B.C., Nabopolassar and Nebuchadnezzar (then Crown Prince) led the Babylonian forces against the mountainous country north of northwestern Mesopotamia. The next year saw another Babylonian invasion of southern Armenia and of the cities in the vicinity of Carchemish, the city on the Euphrates where Pharao NECO had established himself after defeating King Josiah of Judah at MEGIDDO (see 2 Kgs 23.29) and invading Syria. In the late spring of 605, after Nabopolassar had returned to Babylon, Nebuchadnezzar defeated Neco at Carchemish and again at Hamath on the Orontes. Just as Syria lay open to the Babylonian advance, Nabopolassar died in Babylon on the 8th of Ab (August 15), and Nebuchadnezzar returned to the capital city. The following year he was back in Syria, where he subdued Ashkelon and began to make inroads into Judah. An unsuccessful invasion of Egypt in late 601 forced Nebuchadnezzar to return to Babylon to recoup his strength.

At this point King Joachim of Judah (609–598), who had paid tribute to Babylon for three years, rebelled and thus committed a fatal error. After conquering northern Arabia, the Babylonians advanced against Jerusalem in 598–597. Joachim died soon after the siege began, and his 18-year-old son, Joachin, inherited the crown. After three months Jerusalem fell (March 16, 597), and its new king was taken to Babylon. Joachim's brother Sedecia was elevated to the throne by Nebuchadnezzar. His ten-year reign (597–587) was marked by continual agitation and sedition. By 589, inflamed with fierce patriotism and bolstered by promises of Egyptian support, Judah had pushed itself into open and irrevocable revolt. Nebuchadnezzar immediately reacted and besieged Jerusalem in late 588 or early 587. On the 9th of Tammuz (July 30), 587, the city fell. Shortly afterward, it was completely destroyed, and its inhabitants were deported to Babylonia. Judah was organized into the provincial system of the empire, and its population of poor peasants was governed by Godolia (Gedalia), a former chief minister of Sedecia.

Although there is a gap in the Babylonian Chronicle extending from the 11th year of Nebuchadnezzar's reign (594–593) to the 3d year of Neriglissar's (557–556), it is known from an inscription that Nebuchadnezzar led his armies in an unsuccessful invasion of Egypt in 568. Nebuchadnezzar's long reign saw Babylonia rise to its zenith as a world power. Temples, public buildings, palaces, and canals were built not only in Babylonia itself, but in the other cities of the realm. The German archeologists of the "Deutsch-Orient Gesellschaft," headed by Dr. R. Koldewey, began excavating the site of the city of BABYLON in 1899. The careful method employed yielded the ruins of the city that was once the capital of a world empire. After a reign of 43 years, Nebuchadnezzar was succeeded by his son Evil-Merodach. No historical value is to be attached to the Nebuchadnezzar of the Book of Daniel or that of Judith.

Bibliography: *Encyclopedic Dictionary of the Bible,* translated and adapted by L. HARTMAN (New York 1963) 1595–98. M. LEIBOVICI, *Dictionnaire de la Bible,* suppl. ed. L. PIROT, et al. (Paris 1928–) 6:286–291. F. GÖSSMANN, *Lexikon für Theologie und Kirche,* ed. J. HOFER and K. RAHNER, 10 v. (2d, new ed. Freiburg 1957–65); suppl., *Das Zweite Vatikanische Konzil: Dokumente und kommentare,* ed. H. S. BRECHTER et al., pt. 1 (1966) 7:861–862. D. J. WISEMAN, *Chronicles of Chaldean Kings, 626–556 B.C., in the British Museum* (London 1956). W. F. ALBRIGHT, "The Nebuchadnezzar and Neriglissar Chronicles," *The Bulletin of the American Schools of Oriental Research* 143 (1956) 28–33. D. N. FREEDMAN, "The Babylonian Chronicle," *The Biblical Archaeologist* 19 (1956) 50–60. J. BRIGHT, *A History of Israel* (Philadelphia 1959) 304–311, 324–326. M. NOTH, *The History of Israel,* tr. P. R. ACKROYD (2d ed. New York 1960) 280–294.

[D. L. MAGNETTI]

NECESSITY

Necessity signifies something fixed or determined that must be, or be so, and cannot be otherwise. Man cannot think that to be is the same as not to be, nor can he at once both affirm and deny the same of the same. Thus some awareness of necessity is included in the FIRST PRINCIPLES of human thought. However, a more distinct knowledge of necessity and its diverse kinds is attained with the notion of CAUSALITY. A cause is something that influences the being of another, or upon which something must follow with dependence in being. To know in the full sense of genuine understanding is, by common consent, to know the proper cause or necessary reason of being, on account of which something is, or is so, and cannot be otherwise.

When necessity is considered in regard to being or that which is, it is opposed to CONTINGENCY or corruptibility. A changeable thing, as such, is not a necessary being. Considered in relation to knowledge, necessity is opposed to OPINION or PROBABILITY, whereas in action it is opposed to FREEDOM.

Origins in Aristotle. In order to explain the meaning of necessity, ARISTOTLE lists examples according to the different kinds of causes (*Meta.* 1015a 20–1015b 16). Something may be necessary as a concurrent cause of being and life, as respiration is necessary for an organism. Furthermore, something may be necessary for the attaining of a good or the avoiding of an evil, as a journey may be necessary, or the taking of medicine. Again, force or violence have necessity, and also whatever is effected by force or violence. In general, that is necessary which cannot be otherwise, whether by reason of an intrinsic cause, such as matter or form or intrinsic nature, or by reason of an extrinsic cause, whether final or efficient. Just as in logical demonstrations necessary conclusions follow from necessary premises, so that which is necessary may be either an effect having a necessary cause, or a cause that is necessary of itself and not dependent upon another cause. In ancient times the heavenly bodies were thought to be necessary beings of incorruptible nature, yet dependent upon another cause. The first cause of all is itself uncaused. This is the strictly necessary being, the one that is purely actual and immutable.

Scholastic Doctrine. Considerations such as these, together with many others, were elaborated in the works of the medieval scholastics, among which the teaching of St. THOMAS AQUINAS is most representative. They taught that God is the only necessary being not dependent upon any other cause. God is subsistent being and intelligence. In Him being and essence, or nature, are identical, and so He is, or exists, with the most absolute necessity (*Summa theologiae* 1a, 3.4).

Necessity in Creatures. Furthermore, the scholastics taught that God created the world of bodies and intelligent spirits by the free exercise of His omnipotence, not from eternity but at the beginning of time, and not by necessity of His nature, or out of need for them, but out of generosity and benevolence (ST 1a, 19.3; 44.1). Hence the world is contingent upon God's good pleasure, and constantly depends in being on the Creator, without whose conserving act it would cease to be. Nevertheless, even in contingent beings there is something necessary, and there is nothing so contingent that it does not have necessary aspects (ST 1a, 86.3). Speaking of creatures as they are according to their own being and natures, spiritual beings together with their essential properties are strictly necessary and cannot be otherwise by any power within themselves. Material beings also are strictly necessary as regards matter and motion in general. Although particular bodies are contingent and corruptible, still in the course of nature they do not come from nothing, nor do they pass into nothing, but the corruption of one is the generation of another. Matter as the primary subject of change can be neither generated nor corrupted, nor can the general principles of motion cease to operate by any defect in themselves. The course of nature is neither chaotic nor perfectly regular; it includes many kinds of events and products that occur with regularity, as well as many that are incidental and accidental. Events and products that occur with regularity have determined efficient and material causes, and they share the necessity of their causes. Incidental and accidental occurrences, although undetermined or casual in particular, are necessary concomitants in the world order. (Cf. *C. gent.* 2.30.)

Natural Necessity. Because the course of nature is not perfectly regular, and because in particular cases the materials required for a process might be lacking or indisposed, or the agent might be prevented from producing its regular effect, the question was raised about the possibility of a philosophy or science of nature (*see* PHILOSOPHY OF NATURE). Do natural things have principles, causes, or elements that can be discovered and by which they can be explained scientifically? This question was answered in the affirmative from two points of view. In the first place, it was thought that the various species of natural things are distinguishable empirically by differences that are distinct and irreducible and that occur with sufficient regularity to manifest the definable natures with their consequent properties. These natures are changeable and corruptible as they are found in individuals, but when understood abstractly and according to their essential principles, they are necessary and universal. In the second place, the orderly processes of nature attain great natural advantages that are regularly produced and that are the ends or goals of natural activity. If one supposes that the natural end which is usually attained will in fact be attained, then certain other things are necessary, namely, certain materials to be determined or actualized by certain agents. To this there is no exception, and therefore it was maintained that from this point of view natural science is possible. It was thought that man can attain knowledge of natural things that is necessary and univer-

sal, not merely in regard to the general aspects of nature, but also in regard to the distinct species with their parts and interrelations. In order to attain a more detailed knowledge of nature, the scholastics undertook some experimentation and measurement, but progress was slow and few appreciated the importance of quantitative considerations. What was more characteristic of their thought was that while acknowledging that matter and motion are necessary, they sought a reason for this necessity in the end or final cause, which they admitted to be only conditionally or hypothetically necessary. Their cardinal point was that if the end is, or is to be, then the antecedents must be, without exception, in the order of nature. (Cf. *In 2 phys.* 15.)

Mathematical Necessity. Necessity in the objects of mathematics was held to be clearer and stronger than that in physical things (*see* MATHEMATICS, PHILOSOPHY OF). The mathematician abstracted from sensible matter and motion, and considered quantitative beings merely as they are imaginable and intelligible. Mathematical numbers and figures were considered as existing only in the mind of the mathematician, and were constructed in the mind out of their known principles and elements. Hence they were regarded as more clearly and certainly known than physical things, and it was thought that many of their properties could be demonstrated as necessary. For many centuries mathematics was regarded as the paradigm of necessary and universal knowledge. (Cf. *In Boeth. de Trin.* 5.2; 6.1.)

However, the scholastics did not admit that in either physics or mathematics one considers forms or essences absolutely, according to their strictest necessity. This is the business of the metaphysician, who relates effects to their ultimate causes, whether of being or of truth and goodness, and tries to explain all things in relation to their strictly necessary cause, namely, God. (*See* METAPHYSICS.)

Moral Necessity. The scholastics pointed out a likeness between the necessity found in physical processes and that found in moral actions (*see* ETHICS). In a physical process there is unconditioned or absolute necessity on the part of the matter and the agent, and conditioned or hypothetical necessity on the part of the goal that is or is to be attained by determined means. So also in moral action there is absolute necessity in the principle that each man desires to be humanly happy, and hypothetical necessity to choose the reasonable good and avoid evil in order to achieve genuine happiness. The desire for GOOD is naturally determined, not free, but together with reason it is the principle of free CHOICE of the means to happiness. Yet freedom of choice might be impeded or lessened by ignorance and emotion. (Cf. *In 6 eth.* 3.1142–52.)

Logical Necessity. Necessity was admitted also in the purely logical order of mental operations. The mind begins to function and so must first apprehend its own object, called BEING, and then something opposed to being, which might be NONBEING or this as opposed to that. Then with natural necessity man judges that being is not nonbeing, or this is not that. Thus he attains the first principle of thought, called the principle of CONTRADICTION, which is not a supposition but an axiom, that is, a necessary, self-grounded, or self-evident principle. Likewise, after one knows whole and part, he must judge with natural necessity that the whole is greater than the part. In regard to these primitive concepts and principles the mind is naturally determined by the clearest EVIDENCE, and so error is here impossible. From principles that are known to be true and necessary, one can by valid reasoning draw conclusions that are also true and necessary (*see* DEMONSTRATION). In formal logic it is sufficient that the consequence or logical connection between the principles and the conclusion be valid and necessary, according to the laws of reasoning based on the axioms or postulates of the system. The necessity in this case is not absolute but hypothetical: if a valid conclusion is to be reached, the premises must be thus or so; and if the premises are thus or so, this conclusion must follow because it is the only one permitted by the axioms, all others being excluded. (Cf. *In 1 anal. post.* 13; *In 2 anal. post.* 7.)

Nonscholastic Thought. During the scholastic period there were many thinkers, both Platonists and nominalists, who rejected the moderate REALISM of Aristotle and his medieval followers. Nominalists emphasized the contingencies in sensory experience, and neglected or denied the intelligible necessities of being, with its necessary reasons and causes. Platonists did not look for intelligibility in the sensible world, but rather in the world of transcendent ideas and spiritual realities. (*See* NOMINALISM; PLATONISM.)

Cartesianism. At the beginning of the modern period, R. DESCARTES endeavored to make a complete break from the methods and principles of ordinary thought and traditional philosophy. He chose to proceed not from knowledge of something that is necessary and universal, such as the principle of contradiction, but from the particular fact of his own thought, which he identified with his own being. Thereafter, he went step by step from one clear and distinct idea to another, without seeking in all cases a rational or intelligible connection between his ideas.

The method and teachings of Descartes resulted in opposing tendencies of RATIONALISM and EMPIRICISM, and of IDEALISM and MATERIALISM, with attempts to unite both tendencies in various forms of MONISM.

Rationalism and Empiricism. B. SPINOZA and G. W. LEIBNIZ developed the rationalist tendencies into a deterministic view of God and the world. According to these thinkers, necessity was opposed to freedom only when it resulted from external domination or compulsion, not from internal determination. God is free because He is self-determined, and all nature is determined by God. Hence everything is necessary and nothing contingent, nor is there genuine freedom of choice in God or man.

T. HOBBES, J. LOCKE, and D. HUME also defined freedom as lack of external compulsion. Hume maintained that everything has a cause, and denied CHANCE, but held that man does not know necessary causes in nature. Kant saw that this restriction of human knowledge to PHENOMENA threatened the validity of physical science as developed particularly by I. Newton. Hence, in order to defend this kind of science, Kant attributed the elements of necessity and universality to the structure of the mind that knows, rather than to the thing known. He held that the mind has necessary ways of knowing, antecedent to all experience of particular things, and maintained that the essences of things and their necessary causes are speculatively unknowable. However, he admitted that the acknowledgement of God and freedom, morality, and immortality are practically necessary for a good life.

Idealism and Materialism. This strain of subjectivism was further developed into idealism by J. G. FICHTE, F. SCHELLING, and G. W. F. HEGEL to the point where the inner necessity of the idea was identified with the outer necessity of historical fact. Communists now interpret the Hegelian dialectic as a determined order of materialistic evolution that eventually and inevitably will favor themselves.

Formalism. Many contemporary logicians and mathematicians profess to have no interest in principles that are true and necessary. They employ terms that are defined only by the postulates of the AXIOMATIC SYSTEM they freely invent, and frankly acknowledge that one cannot know whether the systems in actual use are either complete or self-consistent.

Critique. This brief account shows that modern ways of philosophical thought are far removed from the natural realism of Aristotle and the scholastics. Nevertheless, universality and consistency remain the goals of thought, and these necessarily exclude self-contradiction. It appears impossible to doubt the necessity of the principle of contradiction, or the ability of the human mind to know TRUTH, and to discover in some cases, at least, the necessary reasons and causes of being, without which things cannot be as they are or as they ought to be. In such knowledge of the necessary reasons and causes of being, genuine SCIENCE, PHILOSOPHY, and WISDOM are commonly thought to consist.

See Also: CONTINGENCY; POSSIBILITY.

Bibliography: G. JALBERT, *Nécessité et contingence chez saint Thomas d'Aquin et chez ses prédécesseurs* (Ottawa 1961). J. CHEVALIER, *La Notion du nécessaire chez Aristote et chez ses prédécesseurs* (Paris 1915). J. MARITAIN, ''Réflexions sur la nécessité et la contingence,'' *Angelicum* 14 (1937) 281–295. M. J. ADLER, ed., *The Great Ideas: A Syntopicon of Great Books of the Western World,* 2 v. (Chicago 1952); v.2, 3 of *Great Books of the Western World* 2:251–269. A. GUZZO and V. MATHIEU, *Enciclopedia filosofica,* 4 v. (Venice-Rome 1957) 3:828–837. R. EISLER, *Wörterbuch der philosophischen Begriffe,* 3 v. (4th ed. Berlin 1927–30) 2:259–271.

[W. H. KANE]

NECESSITY OF MEANS

Something is said to be necessary with the necessity of means when it fulfills the function of *means* to an end; hence it is intrinsically related to the nature of the subject necessitating it. This necessity belongs to the ontological order.

Necessity of means can be absolute or relative. It is *absolute* when it excludes the possibility of being supplied by something else; e.g., sanctifying grace is necessary for the beatific vision by absolute necessity of means. Absolute necessity of means is also called metaphysical necessity.

Necessity of means is *relative* when it does not exclude the possibility of being supplied by something else. Thus Baptism of water is necessary for salvation by a relative necessity of means; in fact, under certain conditions, Baptism of desire (*in voto*) can remit original sin. Similarly the Church is necessary for salvation by absolute necessity of means, but membership in the Church is necessary only by relative necessity of means, because, if one is invincibly ignorant of the Church and at the same time, through the Church's invisible mediation, one possesses faith and sanctifying grace, one can be saved without being a formal member. Relative necessity of means is also called physical necessity.

In more theological language, absolute necessity of means demands the presence of a thing that is the means in its full reality (*in re*), whereas relative necessity can be satisfied by the desire for it or *VOTUM* (*IN VOTO*).

See Also: NECESSITY OF PRECEPT; SALVATION, NECESSITY OF THE CHURCH FOR.

Bibliography: F. LAKNER, *Lexikon für Theologie und Kirche*[2], ed. J. HOFER and K. RAHNER (Freiburg 1957–65); suppl., *Das Zweite Vatikanische Konzil: Dokumente und Kommentare,* ed. H. S. BRECHTER et al., pt. 1 (1966) 7:862–863.

[M. EMINYAN]

NECESSITY OF PRECEPT

Something is said to be necessary by necessity of precept when it is required by a positive will of the superior or legislator. Hence the quality or entity in question is not intrinsically related to the nature of the subject requiring it, but only extrinsically, i.e., by the free determination of another subject.

This necessity belongs to the *moral* order, and not to the metaphysical order; hence it ceases to urge when it is physically or morally impossible to satisfy it. Thus, to hear Mass on Sunday, being imposed by a positive law of the Church under pain of mortal sin, is necessary by necessity of precept. If a dispensation is obtained from the legitimate authority, or if the law cannot be fulfilled except with grave inconvenience, or if it is physically impossible to fulfill it, the law ceases to urge.

The Catholic Church, for instance, is said to be necessary for SALVATION, not only by necessity of means, but also by necessity of precept. Christ set up the kingdom of God on earth, which is the Church, and entrusted it to the Apostles and their successors. All must have the Gospel of the kingdom preached to them and be baptized in order to form part of this kingdom, and those who refuse cannot be saved (Mk 16.16). Similarly Baptism is necessary for salvation, not only by necessity of means, but also by necessity of precept, namely, by the positive will of Christ and by the law of the Church.

See Also: NECESSITY OF MEANS; SALVATION, NECESSITY OF THE CHURCH FOR; VOTUM.

Bibliography: J. SCHMID and F. LAKNER, *Lexikon für Theologie und Kirche,* ed. J. HOFER and K. RAHNER (Freiberg 1957–65) 7:1056–59. É. AMANN, *Dictionnaire de théologie catholique,* ed. A. VACANT et al. (Paris 1903—50) 11.1:55–56.

[M. EMINYAN]

NECROLOGY

A list or register in which the names of dead members, associates, and benefactors of religious communities or capitular and collegial bodies were inscribed so that prayers might be offered for their souls on the anniversary of their death.

Though the necrology eventually assumed its own proper form and use, it originated in the DIPTYCHS from which were read the names of those to be commemorated during Mass. In the 7th century the list of the dead, by then become impossibly long, began to be limited to those directly related to the community and was arranged according to the day of death. At first these lists were inserted in liturgical books already in existence, in Sacramentaries, calendars, and MARTYROLOGIES. Then, as the necrology became longer, it was drawn up as an independent register following the plan of a calendar with obits arranged according to the day of the month. This form began to be used late in the 8th century. Eventually the list of the dead was read with the martyrology during the canonical hour of Prime. It is probably for this reason that the register was often called *martyrologium* in the Middle Ages. Other common names were *liber obituum, liber defunctorum, necrologium,* and *obituarius.* In a few cases the name *liber vitae* was used, though this term usually referred to the living. In its final form, attained by about 1100, the necrology included the names of deceased members of the community, the deceased of communities that had entered a fellowship of prayer, servants, and benefactors.

Of somewhat different form were the *Annales necrologici,* in which the names of the dead were noted year by year, either as part of the annual notice in a chronicle or in a register especially given to this purpose, e.g., the Fulda Annals 779–1065 (*Monumenta Germaniae Historica: Scriptores,* 13:161–215).

The necrologies of the Middle Ages have proved a useful source for the historian and the philologist. They are still in use by some religious orders and various charitable societies that commemorate the anniversaries of deceased members.

Bibliography: Sources. Description. W. WATTENBACH, *Deutschlands Geschichtsquellen im Mittelalter bis zur Mitte des 13. Jh.,* v.1 (7th ed. Stuttgart-Berlin 1904) 1:437–460. A. POTTHAST, *Bibliotheca historica medii aevi* (2d ed. 1896; repr. Graz 1954) 2:807–842. *Inventaire des obituaires belges* (Brussels 1899), suppl. by U. BERLIÉRE in *Bulletin de l'Académie royale des sciences, de lettres et des beaux-arts de Belgique, commission royale d'histoire* 72 (1903) lxxxiii–cxii. W. WATTENBACH, *Deutschlands Geschichtsquellen im Mittelalter. Vorzeit und Karolinger,* Hefte 1–4, ed. W. LEVISON and H. LÖWE (Weimar 1952–63) 1:64–67. Editions. *Monumenta Germaniae Historica: Necrologia* (Berlin 1826–) 1–5. *Necrologi e libri affini della provincia Romana,* ed. P. EGIDI, 2 v. (Fonti per la storia d'Italia 44–45; Rome 1908–14). *Necrologio del Liber confratrum di S. Matteo di Salerno,* ed. C. A. GARUFI (*ibid.* 56; 1922). *I necrologie Cassinesi,* ed. M. INGUANEZ (*ibid.* 83; 1941–). *Recueil des historiens de la France, Obituaires,* ed. G. GUIGUE et al., 5 v. (Paris 1902–33). Literature. F. X. WEGELE, *Zur Literatur und Kritik der fränkischen Nekrologien* (Nördlingen 1864). E. EBNER, *Die klösterlichen Gebets-Verbrüderungen bis zum Ausgange des karolingischen Zeitalters* (Regensburg 1890). A. MOLINIER, *Les Obituaires français au moyen âge* (Paris 1890). H. LECLERCQ, *Dictionnaire d'archéologie chrétienne et de liturgie,* ed. F. CABROL, H. LECLERCQ, and H. I. MARROU, 15 v. (Paris 1907–53) 12.2:1834–57. A. FRANZEN, "L'Obituaire de St.-Victor de Xanten," *Revue d'histoire ecclésiastique* (Louvain 1900–) 61 (1961) 36–41. F. ZOEPFL, *Lexikon für Theologie und Kirche,* ed. J. HOFER and K. RAHNER, 10 v. (2d, new ed. 1957–65) 7:873–874.

[M. M. SHEEHAN]

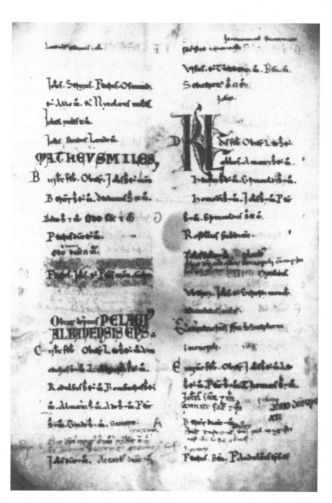

Manuscript folio from 12th-century necrology, inscribed with names of deceased persons to be commemorated between January 29 and February 2.

NECROMANCY

A form of magic employed for calling up the spirits of the dead, or demons, to foretell the future or to accomplish some other act in the natural world that would otherwise be impossible. The practitioners from ancient times to the present have usually belonged to a special class of priests or seers. Necromancy, in various forms, has had a worldwide distribution. It had an important place in the Assyro-Babylonian and Egyptian civilizations, and a well-known example is found in the Old Testament. The Greeks were familiar with it, as is indicated by the elaborate ritual used by Odysseus in calling up the spirits of the dead (*Odyssey,* 11.23–332), and by the role assigned to the departed in temple medicine. It was current also among the Etruscans and Romans. Although necromancy was severely condemned by the Church, repeated references are made to the practice in the Middle Ages and the Renaissance, and a considerable body of writings on the subject is extant. The traditional necromancy was made famous by the Faust legend and its literary treatment by Marlowe and Goethe.

See Also: DIVINATION; MAGIC

Bibliography: H. J. ROSE, J. HASTINGS, ed., *Encyclopedia of Religion and Ethics,* 13 v. (Edinburgh 1908–27) 4:775–780, esp. 778. K. PRÜMM, *Religionsgeschichtliches Handbuch für den Raum der altchristlichen Umwelt* (2d ed. Rome 1954) 380–383. T. HOPFNER, *Paulys Realenzyklopädie der klassischen Altertumswissenschaft,* ed. G. WISSOWA et al. (1935) 16.2:2218–33. J. HASTINGS, ed., *Encyclopedia of Religion and Ethics,* 13 v. (Edinburgh 1908–27), index volume, see ''necromancy.'' L. THORNDIKE, *A History of Magic and Experimental Science,* 8 v. (New York 1923–58), see index in each volume.

[T. A. BRADY]

NEERCASSEL, JOANNES VAN

Bishop of Castoria *in partibus,* and sixth vicar apostolic of the Dutch Mission; b. Gorcum, 1623; d. Zwolle, June 6, 1686. After studies in Cuyck, Louvain, and Paris, where he joined the Congregation of the Oratory, he was ordained in 1648. He became vicar-general of the archbishopric of Utrecht in 1653, coadjutor of Vicars Zacharias de Metz in 1661 and Balduinus Cats in 1662. He succeeded Cats in the next year. His was a brilliant, somewhat capricious personality, formed in the Berullian school and inclined toward Jansenistic rigorism. Of his writings, *Amor poenitens* (1683) was censured by the Index in 1690; the *Tractatus de sanctorum. . . cultu* (1675) was criticized for disparaging the cult of the saints; and the *Tractatus de lectione Scripturarum* (1677) was reproved for allowing the reading of the Bible in the vernacular. Though he signed the anti-Jansenist formula of Alexander VII without restriction, he had relations with the Abbey of PORT-ROYAL and invited Antoine ARNAULD to settle down at Delft.

Bibliography: R. R. POST, ed., *Romeinsche bronnen* (The Hague 1941—). L. J. ROGIER, *Geschiedenis van het katholicisme in Noord-Nederland,* 3 v. (Amsterdam 1945–47) v. 2.

[P. POLMAN]

NEHEMIAH

Jewish governor of Judea under the Persians. He succeeded in having the fallen walls of Jerusalem rebuilt. Before he was governor, Nehemiah (Heb. *nᵉhemyâ*) was an official at the court of the Persian king, Artaxerxes I (465–424 B.C.). The conditions under which the Palestinian Jews then lived were far from ideal. The defenses of the capital, Jerusalem, lay in ruins and the Jews, themselves, were subject to harassment and oppression by their predatory neighbors. Hearing of these conditions and moved by pity for his people, Nehemiah obtained credentials from the king and set out in the 20th year of Artaxerxes for Jerusalem, where he remained for 12 years (445–433 B.C.) as governor (*pehâ* in Neh 5.14, 15, 18; 12.26; *tiršātā'* in Neh 8.9; 10.2; Neh 2.1–8; 5.14).

His first major accomplishment was to rebuild the wall of Jerusalem, despite the threats and various stratagems of the neighboring governors, Sanballat of Samaria, Tobiah the Ammonite, and Geshem the Arab, who accused him of rebellion against the king (Neh 2.10, 19; ch. 4; ch. 6). In Neh 7.15 it is said the wall was completed in 52 days, but the period of two years and four months that Josephus (*Ant.* 11.5.8) allows for is a much more plausible length of time.

During this time, famine and usurious exactions of the upper classes brought the poorer people crying to Nehemiah for relief (Neh 5.1–5). Prompt action by the governor—his request to the assembled leaders, with pointed reference to his own unselfish example—led to the restoration of lands and houses to the indigent (Neh 5.6–13; 5.14–19). Next, Nehemiah resettled a tenth of Judea's population, moving them into the newly fortified Jerusalem (Neh 7.4–5; 11.1–2). The dedication of the city's wall is described (in the Chronicler's style) in Neh 12.27–43.

In 433 B.C., Nehemiah returned to Artaxerxes (Neh 13.6). Sometime after that, but before the king's death in 424, Nehemiah came again to Jerusalem as governor. This time he was noted principally for correcting abuses. He drove Tobiah from a room that had formerly served as a temple storeroom but had been given to Tobiah for his personal use (Neh 13.4–9); reinstated the practice of tithing for the support of the Levites (Neh 13.10–14); enforced observance of the Sabbath (Neh 13.15–22); and prohibited marriages with foreigners, to prevent such marriages from leading the Jews into idolatrous practices (Neh 13.23–27). He also expelled the son-in-law of Sanballat from the Jerusalemite priesthood (Neh 13.28–29).

Comparatively little else is known of Nehemiah. According to Neh 7.2 he placed his brother, Hanani, in charge of Jerusalem. In Sir 49.13 he is praised for restoring Jerusalem's defenses. The ''memories of Nehemiah'' cited in 2 Mc 1.36 associate him with a discovery of fire-producing νεφθαρ (naphtha), and in 2 Mc 2.13 it is said that he founded a library and collected various books: (1) about kings (the Old Testament books of Joshua through Kings?), (2) Prophets, (3) David's writings (Psalms), and (4) royal letters (of the Persian kings) concerning votive offerings. One Talmudic reference identifies him (incorrectly) with Zerubbabel (*Sanhedrin* 38a), and another credits him (wrongly) with the completion of the book of

Chronicles (*Baba Bathra* 15a). For the Book of Nehemiah, *see* CHRONICLER, BIBLICAL.

Bibliography: *Encyclopedic Dictionary of the Bible* tr. and adap. by L. HARTMAN (New York 1963) 1626–27. H. SCHNEIDER, *Lexikon für Theologie und Kirche*, ed. J. HOFER and K. RAHNER (Freiburg 1957–65) 7:868–869. K. GALLING, *Die Religion in Geschichte und Gegenwart* (Tübingen 1957–65) 4:1395–96. H. H. ROWLEY, "Nehemiah's Mission and Its Background," *The Bulletin of the John Rylands Library* 37 (Manchester 1955) 528–561. A. FERNÁNDEZ, *Un hombre de carácter: Nehemías* (Jerusalem 1940).

[N. J. MCELENEY]

NEHEMIAH, BOOK OF

A biblical book whose principal narratives relate: (1) the return of Nehemiah, an official (cupbearer) at the court of the Persian king Artaxerxes I (464–423 B.C.) to the province of Judah; (2) the work of Nehemiah and the Jewish people in rebuilding the walls of Jerusalem, despite economic difficulties and the opposition of the Samaritan governor Sanaballat and others; (3) the reading of the Law by the priest-scribe Ezra and the renewal of the covenant with God by the Jewish community; (4) the rehabitation of Jerusalem; and (5) the return of Nehemiah to Jerusalem after an interval at the Persian court and his correction of abuses discovered upon his return. (For a more complete treatment of this book, *see* CHRONICLER, BIBLICAL.)

[N. J. MCELENEY]

NEILL, STEPHEN CHARLES

Anglican missionary bishop, missiology and ecumenist, b. Edinburgh, 1900; d. 1984. Born into a missionary family, he experienced a conversion while in college and followed his missionary parents to India, where he was ordained a deacon. Later, his dissertation at Trinity College, Cambridge, compared Plotinus' writings with those of Gregory of Nyssa and Gregory of Nazianzen, a work which served as his introduction to Hindu monism. He left the academic life and became a member of the Church Missionary Society in India, where he served for 22 years, evangelizing, traveling, and teaching Indian students in the Tamil language. He eventually learned 14 languages and was a pioneer in teaching theology in the vernacular, both in India and later in Africa. In 1939, he was made bishop of Tinnevelly, India, and remained there through World War II, but after a psychological breakdown in 1945, Neill left the country.

From his early years Neill strove toward reconciliation among Christians, first in a united Church in South India, as the associate general secretary at the International Missionary Council and World Council of Churches from 1948 to 1951, and as general editor of World Christian Books for the next ten years. His gift for speaking and writing often appealed to a variety of Protestant groups. Neill was appointed professor of missions and ecumenical theology at the University of Hamburg (1962–1967) and professor of religious studies at the University of Nairobi (1929–1973). He was a prolific writer with over 100 works he edited or authored, many of them related to ecumenism and mission.

Bibliography: S. NEILL and R. ROUSE, eds., *The History of the Ecumenical Movement 1517–1948* (London 1954). S. NEILL, *Christian Faith and Other Faiths* (London 1961). S. NEILL, *A History of the Christian Missions* (London 1964). G. H. ANDERSON, J. GOODWIN, and S. NEILL, eds., *Dictionary of World Mission* (London 1970). F. JACKSON, *God's Apprentice: The Autobiography of Bishop Stephen Neill* (London 1991).

[A. DRIES]

NELSON, JOHN, BL.

Jesuit priest and martyr; b. Skelton, Yorkshire, England, *c.* 1534–35; d. hanged, drawn, and quartered at Tyburn (London), Feb. 3, 1578. Three of the five sons of Sir Nicholas Nelson—John, Martin, and Thomas—became priests. John began his seminary studies at Douai in 1573 at about age 40. He was ordained (June 11, 1576) by Abp. Louis de Berlaymont of Cambrai at Bynche, Hainault. Five months later he departed the Continent with four other newly ordained priests to enter the English mission. He labored in London for about a year before his arrest (Dec. 1, 1577) and commitment to Newgate Prison. During his examination by the High Commissioners a few days later, he adamantly denied the authority of the queen in spiritual matters and described Elizabeth as a heretic and schismatic. He repeated these statements at his trial, Feb. 1, 1578. For this he was found guilty of high treason and condemned to execution. Thereafter he was thrown into the Pit of the Tower of London—an underground dungeon, where he prepared for death.

During his imprisonment at Newgate, he wrote to the French Jesuits seeking admission to the Society. Permission was granted; thus, Nelson is recognized as a Jesuit martyr.

On the gallows he witnessed powerfully to the faith for which he was dying. Praying common prayers in Latin, asking and granting pardon for offenses, and seeking the intercession of the faithful. He said: "I die in the unity of the Catholic Church; and for that unity do now most willingly suffer my blood to be shed; therefore, I beseech God . . . to make you, and all others that are not such already, true Catholic men, and both to live and die in the unity of our Holy Mother, the Catholic Roman Church.'' His last words as his disembowelment began: ''I forgive the queen and all the authors of my death.''

He was beatified by Pope Leo XIII on Dec. 9, 1886.

Feast of the English Martyrs: May 4 (England); Dec. 1 (Jesuits).

See Also: ENGLAND, SCOTLAND, AND WALES, MARTYRS OF.

Bibliography: B. CAMM, ed., *Lives of the English Martyrs,* (New York 1905), II, 223. R. CHALLONER, *Memoirs of Missionary Priests,* ed. J. H. POLLEN (rev. ed. London 1924; repr. Farnborough 1969). J. H. POLLEN, *Acts of English Martyrs* (London 1891). J. N. TYLENDA, *Jesuit Saints & Martyrs* (Chicago 1998), 30–32.

[K. I. RABENSTEIN]

NEMESIUS OF EMESA

Bishop of Emesa (now Homs), early Christian psychologist; fl. *c.* 390–400. Apart from his treatise *On the Nature of Man,* nothing is known of his life, but there is no reason for identifying him with Nemesius, pagan governor of Cappadocia (*c.* 383 to 389), the friend and correspondent of St. GREGORY OF NAZIANZUS. Several Greek manuscripts of his work and excerpts quoted by MAXIMUS THE CONFESSOR call him a bishop. Nemesius, a man of considerable culture, was acquainted with philosophical and medical literature, and was critical and independent in his judgment of doctrines. Although Origen, Basil the Great, and especially Gregory of Nyssa had written of man and the soul, Nemesius composed the first *summa* of Christian psychology in the East. The work is a compilation, with extensive borrowings from Galen and the philosophers; but the material is assessed from a Christian viewpoint before being admitted into a remarkable synthesis that is neither Platonic nor Aristotelian, but Christian in character.

The opening chapter criticizes the concepts of man advanced by Plotinus and Apollinaris, Aristotle, and Plato, and then emphasizes the place of man in the plan of creation. Since man bridges the spiritual and the material worlds, he occupies a privileged place and has a corresponding obligation to live up to the dignity God has given him. This requires a correct concept of what the soul is (ch. 2). Here neither Plato nor Aristotle provides an adequate doctrine: one making the soul too independent of the body, the other reducing the soul to little more than a quality of the body. Nemesius concludes that the soul is an incorporeal entity, subsistent in itself, immortal, and yet designed for union with the body, and discovers in Ammonius Saccas and Porphyry the best

explanation of that union (ch. 3): the soul is not changed in the union nor does it become corruptible with or through the body, and yet it makes one being with the body. A certain parallel for such a unique union Nemesius finds in the union of the Divine Word and the human nature in the Incarnation. He has no clear statement on the origin of the soul, and seems to believe in a species of pre-existence totally devoid of Platonic myth or of the errors of ORIGEN.

After a detailed study of the powers of the soul, based on Galen's divisions of the brain, and on anthropological doctrines of the Stoics, Aristotle, and others (chapters through which the scholastics became acquainted with much ancient tradition), Nemesius lays the foundation for a Christian philosophy of free will and human acts. Although he depends on Aristotle's *Nicomachean Ethics* for many details, such as the classification of human acts (ch. 29–), the power of choice (ch. 33–), Nemesius establishes, as a specifically Christian approach, the fact that free will is a concomitant of reason: ''If the creature is endowed with reason, it is master of what it does, or else the power to deliberate and choose is pointless; and if it is master of its actions, it must by all means possess free will'' (ch. 41). Changeableness, also, is a mark of the creature, even in its rational nature. The psychology of the human act propounded by Nemesius was perfected by Maximus the Confessor (580–662); as passed on by the Syrian Mose bar Kepha, ANASTASIUS SINAITA, and JOHN DAMASCENE, it became an important part of scholastic doctrine [cf. *Recherches de théologie ancienne et médiévale* 21 (1954) 51–100; and O. Lottin, *Psychologie et morale aux XIIe et XIIIe siècles,* v.1 (Gembloux 1957) 393–424].

The treatise came to be ascribed to St. Gregory of Nyssa (who had written a work ''On the Making of Man''), and was known under his name to the Western scholastics in the Latin translations of ALPHANUS OF SALERNO (d. 1085) and Burgundio of Pisa (*c.* 1160), although some sentences were also known to the scholastics under the name of Remigius.

Bibliography: É. H. GILSON, *History of Christian Philosophy in the Middle Ages* (New York 1955). J. QUASTEN, ed. *Patrology,* 3 v. (Westminster, Md. 1950) 3:351–355. W. TELFER, *Cyril of Jerusalem and Nemesius of Emesa* (Philadelphia 1955). É. AMANN, *Dictionnaire de théologie catholique,* ed. A. VACANT et al., 15 v. (Paris 1903–50; Tables générales 1951–) 11.1:62–67. E. SKARO, *Paulys Realenzyklopädie der klassischen Altertumswissenschaft* 7 (1940) 562–566. I. BRADY, ''Remigius Nemesius,'' *Franciscan Studies* 8 (1948) 275–284.

[I. BRADY]

NENGAPETE, MARIE-CLÉMENTINE ANUARITE, BL.

Baptized Anuarite (Anawarite or Alphonsine), martyr of the Congregation of the Holy Family; b. Dec. 29, 1939, Matali, Wamba, Belgian Congo, Africa; d. Dec. 1, 1964, Isiro near Kisangani, Zaire. Anuarite was baptized with her mother and sister. In 1954 at the age of fifteen, she entered the Congregation of the Holy Family at Bafwabaka and was professed (Aug. 5, 1959) as Sister Marie-Clémentine. Ten years later the Congo, which had gained its independence four years earlier, was in turmoil. General Olenga's rebels, who had assassinated Bishop Wittehois of Wamba (Nov. 26, 1964), arrived at the convent on Nov. 29, 1964, to conduct the nuns and orphans to Isiro for safety. Soon after their arrival, Sisters Marie-Clémentine and Bokuma were separated from the rest for the pleasure of two colonels. When Mother Kasima protested, Colonel Yuma Deo threatened to kill all thirty-four women and children. Sister Marie-Clémentine offered herself as the victim, but refused the advances of Colonel Olombe. After being brutalized, she was shot in the chest but lingered in pain for another day. She was immediately revered as a virgin martyr and formally beatified at Kinshasa, Zaire (now the Democratic Republic of the Congo), by John Paul II, Aug. 15, 1985.

Bibliography: N. L. M. MALAMBA, *Dix propos autour d'une béatification* (Lubumbashi 1987). *Acta Apostolicae Sedis* (1985): 923. *L'Osservatore Romano*, Eng. ed. 36 (1985): 7–8.

[K. I. RABENSTEIN]

NEOCAESAREA

Three bishoprics bear the name Neocaesarea in the early Church.

Neocaesarea in Bithynia. The exact location is uncertain, but it was probably in the western part of Bithynia mentioned in 1 Peter 1.1. Two of its bishops attended synods in Constantinople: Olympius (*c.* 381) and Cyriacus (518).

Neocaesarea in Pontus Polemoniacus. Here Origen's distinguished student, St. GREGORY THAUMATURGUS, was bishop *c.* 240 to 270. According to St. GREGORY OF NYSSA, the Church in Pontus suffered persecution under emperors DECIUS and Galerius. When peace was restored, Gregory Thaumaturgus christianized pagan festivals, gathered the relics of martyrs, fixed days for commemorating their triumphs, and inspired his flock to erect churches. An important synod between 314 and 325 enacted legislation that affected the catechumenate for many years and barred the *clinici* from the priesthood on the ground that they had received baptism more from fear of death and judgment than from dedication to Christ. Some ruins, fragments of inscriptions, and sculptures remain as witnesses to the once flourishing church.

Neocaesarea on the Euphrates in Northern Syria. This was a military garrison in Augusta Euphratensis, whose fortifications were strengthened under JUSTINIAN I. THEODORET OF CYR (*Die griechischen christlichen Schriftsteller der ersten drei Jahrhunderte*, 44:31) mentions Paul, bishop of Neocaesarea, who had suffered for the faith, as being present at the Council of NICAEA I.

Bibliography: W. RUGE, *Paulys Realenzyklopädie der klassischen Altertumswissenschaft*, ed. G. WISSOWA et al. (Stuttgart 1935) 16.2:2409–13. W. M. RAMSAY, *The Historical Geography of Asia Minor* (London 1890). A. VON HARNACK, *Die Mission und Ausbreitung*, v.2 (Leipzig 1906). H. LECLERCQ, *Dictionnaire d'archéologie chrétienne et de liturgie* (Paris 1907–53) 4.2:2298; 12.1:1103. A. KREUZ, *Lexikon für Theologie und Kirche*, ed. J. HOFER and K. RAHNER (Freiburg 1957–65) 7:876.

[H. DRESSLER]

NEOCATECHUMENAL WAY

The Neocatechumenal Way, or the Neocatechumenate, is a loosely organized Catholic renewal and catechetical apostolate founded in 1962 in the Palomeras slums of Madrid by Kiko Argüello, who serves as a chief catechist of the movement and is currently a consultor to the Pontifical Council on the Laity. From the start, the Neocatechumenate received the approval and support of the bishop of Madrid at the time, Casimiro Morcillo.

In 1974 Pope PAUL VI welcomed members of Neocatechumenal communities in a general audience and declared that this "way" after baptism would "renew in today's Christian communities those effects of maturity and deepening that, in the primitive Church, were realized by the period of preparation for baptism." Twenty-five years later, in 1990, Pope JOHN PAUL II officially recognized the Neocatechumenal Way as "an itinerary of catholic formation, valid for our society and for our times," and encouraged bishops and priests in the Church to "value and support this work for the new evangelization." Again in 1994, Pope John Paul II praised the Neocatechumenal Way for showing that "the small community, sustained by the Word of God and by the dominical Eucharist, becomes a place of communion, where the family recovers the sense and the joy of its fundamental mission to transmit both natural and supernatural life." In 1997 Pope John Paul II encouraged members of the Neocatechumenal Way in their effort to draft stautes for ecclesiastical recognition.

With the encouragement of Pope Paul VI and Pope John Paul II, the Neocatechumenal Way has spread to dioceses whose bishops welcome it and in parishes whose pastors are committed to it. There are about 200,000 members in more than 100 countries, organized in 300 small communities in 80 dioceses. Giuseppe Gennarini brought the Neocatechumenal Way to the United States in 1975; they are represented in the archdioceses of Denver, Newark, New York, and Washington, as well as on the West Coast and Texas.

Explicitly avoiding the appellations "movement" or "association," the Neocatechumenal Way is a self-styled program or apostolate of Christian formation. With its stress on exclusive fellowship, intense personal commitment, simplicity of life, communal sharing, and apostolic zeal, the Neocatechumenal Way takes its inspiration from the structure and ethos of the first Christian communities who were known as adherents of "the Way." The program seeks to recover and replicate the early Christian catechumenal pattern of KERYGMA, conversion, and liturgy as a phased or progressive formation of new Christians: the announcement of salvation that calls for moral decision and thus changes the lives of its hearers and is sealed by participation in the sacramental life of the Church. Proponents of the Neocatechumenal program offer it to Christians who are already baptized but who lack adequate formation in the faith and are thus "quasi-catechumens." It appeals to committed Catholics who want to deepen their faith and to fallen-away Catholics who want to rediscover it.

Service to Local Church. Although the Neocatechumenate is fundamentally a lay movement, the commitment and leadership of the diocesan bishop and the local pastors are crucial to its organization and activities. The founders and leaders of the Neocatechumenate stress its role as a service to the local church. The Eucharist, celebrated by the pastor with great reverence in homes or in small groups, is the anchor of the Neocatechumenal Way. Participants in the seven-year-long formation program are called "catechumens" in order to signal the fact that even the baptized person may not yet have attained a sufficient level of conversion and knowledge in the life of the faith. While continuing to live at home, catechumens participate in this formation as members of communities of 15 to 30 members who meet at least twice a week for catechesis and to celebrate the Eucharist. Day-long meetings are held monthly, as well as occasional social gatherings and regular "scrutinies" and liturgies to mark the transition to a new stage of formation. Eventually, some members become "itinerants" and move on in order to establish Neocatechumenal communities elsewhere.

Another important aspect of the Neocatechumenate is its dedication to the cultivation of religious and priestly vocations and to the foundation of "missionary seminaries" with formation programs patterned on the principles of the Neocatechumenal Way. The best known of these seminaries is the Redemptoris Mater in Rome. Others have been founded in Madrid, Warsaw, Bangalore, Newark, Medellín, Bogotá, Callao (Peru), and Takamatsu (Japan). The seminaries are distinguished by their combination of Christian initiation and formation for the presbyterate.

In 1990 Pope John Paul II assigned to Bishop Paul Josef Cordes, now president of the Pontifical Council Cor Unum, responsibility *ad personam* for the apostolate of the Way.

Bibliography: G. GENNARINI, "The Role of the Christian Family in Announcing the Gospel in Today's World," *L'Osservatore Romano,* English edition (Oct. 19, 1987) 18–19. JOHN PAUL II, "Address to Itinerant Catechists," *L'Osservatore Romano,* English edition (Feb. 2, 1994) 10–11. *Ibid.,* "Address to Members of the Neocatechumenal Way," *L'Osservatore Romano,* English edition (Feb. 5, 1997) 9. "Epistola R.P.D. Paulo Iosepho Cordes, episcopo tit. Naissitano, Delegato *in persona* ad Communitates Novi Catechumenatus," *Acta Apostolicae Sedis* 82 (1990) 1513–1515. PAUL VI, "Address to Neocatechumenal Communities," *Notitiae* 95–96 (1974) 230.

[J. A. DINOIA]

NEO-GUELFISM

The program of Italian Catholic liberals during the RISORGIMENTO who stressed the relation between the Church and civilization and led the reform-unification movement from 1843 to 1848. Some Italians used the term Neo-Guelfism in derision, but its followers accepted it. These opponents, the Neo-Ghibellines, thought the temporal power of the papacy a hindrance to Italian unification. They were fewer in number and less noted than the Neo-Guelfs, whose ranks included such scholars and writers as Balbo, Capponi, Manzoni, TOSTI, and Carlo Troya.

The leading Neo-Guelf was Vincenzo GIOBERTI. In his most famous book, *Del Primato Morale e Civile degli Italiani* (1843), he reminded his countrymen of their former greatness, proposed liberal reforms, and a unification plan that envisioned a federation of the independent states of the peninsula with the pope as president and the king of Sardinia as military defender. The book was popular and influential. It appealed to moderates who disapproved of Mazzini. The book also inspired Balbo to write *Le Speranze d'Italia.* The future PIUS IX discussed both books with friends. Soon after his elevation to the papacy (1846), he began a series of reforms in the STATES OF THE CHURCH that attracted much attention, and helped the progress of reform in other Italian states.

The effectiveness of Neo-Guelfism quickly subsided after the revolution of 1848, and very little interest was shown thereafter in federation. Even in 1843 not all Neo-Guelfs accepted Gioberti's main notion of the pope as president of Italy. Balbo and others preferred Charles Albert as king. When Pius IX proposed a customs union and a federation with Tuscany and Piedmont, Charles Albert proposed a defensive league, which conflicted with the Pope's position as a spiritual leader. After the decline of Neo-Guelfism, Italians turned to the leadership of Piedmont for the unification of Italy.

Bibliography: G. F. H. and J. BERKELEY, *Italy in the Making*, 3 v. (Cambridge, Eng. 1932–40). B. CROCE, *History of Europe in the Nineteenth Century*, tr. H. FURST (New York 1933); *Storia della storiografia italiana nel secolo decimonono*, 2 v. (3d rev. ed., Bari 1947) v.1.

[M. L. SHAY]

NEO-KANTIANISM

A term employed in the history of philosophy to designate the sustained attempt, by a number of groups and from different points of view, to reconstitute the thought of Immanuel KANT as the basis for a philosophy that would meet the problematic and speculative exigencies of the second half of the 19th century. It was primarily a German movement, with centers at a number of German universities; it was not exclusively so, however, for its influence was felt in England, France, Italy, and, with the emigration of Ernst CASSIRER, one of the last great representatives of the movement, in the U.S. Otto Liebmann (1840–1912), in his work *Kant und die Epigonen* (Stuttgart 1865), is credited both with the decisive initiation of the current and with the coining of its rubric, "back to Kant," for he concluded the studies of the work of J. G. FICHTE, F. W. J. SCHELLING, G. W. F. HEGEL, A. SCHOPENHAUER, etc., which comprise the book, with this phrase. The rubric cannot be taken, however, as indicating a single unitary movement, for there existed a great diversity of opinion as to the doctrines of Kant to which return should be made. Moreover, even when some degree of consent was achieved on this point, various interpretations of the favored doctrines were offered. These interpretations were not always wholly self-consistent or consistent with each other; nor, finally, were they authentic interpretations of Kant that realized all the potentialities of his thought. On the whole, the cultural pressure of POSITIVISM tended to make the Neo-Kantians place an excessively narrow interpretation on Kant's philosophy.

Historical Background. The historical background of the Neo-Kantian movement is provided by positivism, toward which Neo-Kantianism exhibits an ambivalent at-

Wilhelm Dilthey. (©Bettmann/CORBIS)

titude. On the one hand, its central motive is a rejection of the positivist claims; on the other, it exhibits the influence of positivism in many facets of its doctrines and methods. Thus, it repudiates the attitudes of positivism as dogmatic and antiphilosophical; at the same time, it accepts the central thesis of positivism, i.e., that physicomathematical science provides the paradigm of all valid forms of knowledge. In accordance with this view, it conceives the philosophical task as the critical investigation of the conditions that make this kind of knowledge possible and valid. This conception of the task of philosophy constitutes the real point of contact and reference between Neo-Kantianism and Kant; for Kant had conceived philosophy as the critical examination and determination of the a priori principles and structures that render experience of the physical world and action in the moral sphere possible and provide the basis for scientific, ethical, and preferential discourse. At the same time, Neo-Kantianism devotes considerable attention to the tradition of Romanticism, which it criticized and rejected far more forcibly than it did positivism (*see* ROMANTICISM, PHILOSOPHICAL). Romanticism had directed sharp criticism against physicomathematical science on the basis of the abstractness intrinsic to it; it had proposed instead a conception of philosophy as concrete knowledge, free from and unlimited by such abstractness. Romanticism had, in its own way, claimed Kant as progenitor; Neo-Kantianism rejected this claim as spurious, pointing out that the essence of Kantian method was scientific rigor, a quality conspicuously lacking among the Romantic philosophers. Its return to Kant was an effort to preserve the positivist ideal of a philosophy as scientifically rigorous as a physico-mathematical discipline and, with this, the Kantian transcendental values. The historical development of the movement is determined by its efforts to realize this ideal in the various areas of speculative interest.

Principal Currents. The principal currents comprising the Neo-Kantian movement, or at least conventionally allied with it, are (1) the realist current, whose principal exponent was A. Riehl; (2) the psychological current, represented by L. Nelson, the follower of the psychologist J. F. Fries; (3) the metaphysical current, a chief representative of which was the same Leibmann who is credited with originating the Neo-Kantian motto; (4) the logical current, called the School of Marburg because its center was at that university, led by H. Cohen and counting as its chief figures P. Natorp and E. Cassirer; (5) the value theory current, called also the School of Baden, including among its adherents such distinguished figures as H. Rickert, W. Windelband, H. Münsterburg, and, by a looser connection, W. Dilthey; and finally, for the sake of completeness, (6) the physiological current, associated with the researches of H. A. von Humboldt and the relativistic current of G. Simmel. The important figure of Bruno BAUCH was dominant in the movement for many years; though formed in the School of Baden and always devoted chiefly to its theoretical interests, he exercised, through his editorship of the important journal *Kantstudien*, a guiding influence over all the currents of the movement. From the point of view of theoretical interest, clarity of development, and distinction of achievement, the logical School of Marburg and the value-theory oriented School of Baden are the outstanding elements of the Neo-Kantian movement.

Alois Riehl. The realistic current found its chief exponent in Alois Riehl (1844–1924), whose chief work, *Der philosophische Kritizismus* (2 v. Leipzig 1876–87), was the basic document of the movement. Riehl strikes a characteristic note of all Neo-Kantians by his resolute rejection of metaphysics as a philosophical science. Philosophy, for him, is a science of experience and what does not fall within experience can find no expression in philosophical discourse. At the same time, he rejects, *en bloc*, all the idealistic and Romantic interpretations of Kant; these assign an exclusive role to the subject, which, in Hegel's phrase, takes the world onto itself. Riehl returns rather to Kant's original distinction and insists that from the subject can be derived only the form of knowledge; the content of knowledge must come from experi-

ence, and ultimately from sense experience. It must be noted that, while returning to this original Kantian distinction, Riehl tends to overlook the many difficulties to which it had given rise and the efforts made, in the idealistic tradition, to meet these difficulties. Riehl is one of those who was forced by the cultural pressure of positivism to impose an excessively narrow interpretation on Kantian thought. For Riehl, the Kant of the *Critique of Pure Reason* is very nearly the only Kant, and philosophy becomes identical with the theory of knowledge and its adjunct problems. He remains strictly faithful to Kant in that he conceives the theory of knowledge in gnoseological, and never in psychological, terms.

Leonard Nelson. The last-mentioned attitude sets Riehl in contrast with the psychological current, the chief exponent of which was Leonard Nelson (1882–1927). Nelson, professor at Göttingen from 1919 until his death and founder of the Neo-Friesian School, proposed, on the model of Jakob Friedrich Fries (1773–1843), to develop the critical GNOSEOLOGY of Kant on psychological bases and in accord with a strict psychological method. The author of many studies and editor of the journal of the Neo-Friesian School (*Abhandlungen der Friesschen Schule*) for a number of years, Nelson is best known, perhaps, for his contributions to this journal questioning the possibility of the theory of knowledge—in much the same sense as Riehl had proposed to make such a theory the exclusive concern of philosophy. Nelson's criticism is based on the fact that this theory would presume to offer a criterion for determining the validity of knowledge, while the status of such a criterion would be entirely ambiguous. On the one hand, it could not itself be knowledge; nor, on the other hand, could it fall outside the sphere of knowledge, since a criterion, to be used, must be known. His solution was to return to the simpler and immediate elements of consciousness that could become the object of psychological treatment. The entire process of the Kantian critiques was thus recast in psychologically descriptive terms—and not only the processes of knowledge but such ethical principles as the categorical imperative as well. Nelson enjoyed a considerable influence, but this waned rapidly during the period between World War I and World War II.

Otto Liebmann. The metaphysical current of Neo-Kantianism found its chief exponent in Liebmann. The fame of his early work *Kant und die Epigonen* tends to place in the shade his more positive and constructive work, precisely the work that establishes him as the leading figure of the metaphysical current of Neo-Kantianism. His avowed purpose was to develop the basic problems of Kantianism in such a manner as to achieve a synthesis between the demands of criticism and those of metaphysics. It might also be said that he sought to carry criticism beyond the point where Kant had left it to build a systematic metaphysics that would be faithful to the conditions laid down by the critical philosophy. An idea of what he meant by metaphysics may be gathered by his assertion that, whereas physics deducts facts from laws, the role of metaphysics is to determine the why of all that happens in nature and experience. Metaphysics in this sense is possible only if it is at the same time critical, by which he meant that it proceeds by a hypothetical consideration of the essence of things. Yet his would be a metaphysics relative to the human mind, since the critical attitude demands that, at every point in the construction of that metaphysics, the conditions of human understanding be taken as limits and terms of reference. Liebmann made a like condition for the unity of ethical theory and the critical attitude. There are no absolute values, since values are relative to the valuing subject; yet, with constant reference to that subject, it is still possible to achieve an ethics of transcendental value.

Marburg School. Equally adamant in its opposition to the "psychologization" of Kant and inclined in an antimetaphysical direction was the School of Marburg, perhaps the most distinguished of the Neo-Kantian groups. It was a school in a very true sense, for it had a physical location, identifiable personnel in constant and explicit communication with each other, and a commonly accepted goal and method. Founded by Hermann Cohen (1843–1918), it retained during its entire career the stamp of his personality and the direction he imparted to it. Cohen also attracted men of high caliber both in their formation and scholarship and in their theoretical capacity. The most eminent of these were Paul Natorp (1854–1924) and Ernst Cassirer (1874–1945), the last-named bringing international prestige to the group by his masterly historical work and his well-researched and carefully articulated speculative efforts. An excellent account of the school and its work is provided by Natorp in his essay "Kant und die Marburger Schule," *Kantstudien* 17 (1912) 193–221.

The direction given by Cohen and characteristic of the school throughout its career is logical and methodological; its main link with Kant is the *Critique of Pure Reason*. The chief concern is the determination of the logical-transcendental conditions of science. Among these, it assigns a prominence to the logical structures that condition experience, tending to dissolve INTUITION into the logical processes and no longer assigning it an autonomous position and function; it thus truncates a goodly portion of the *Critique of Pure Reason*. The diminishing of the elements of immediacy in experience tends to throw into clearer relief the controlled methodological procedures of science and to reveal science as less and less dependent on the "given" element in expe-

rience. The logical processes of thought tend more and more to determine the object completely, though never, in keeping with the notion of the "thing-in-itself," entirely encompassing it.

Though concentrated in the area of science and pure reason, the attention of the Marburg School also embraced the areas of ethics and aesthetics, achieving notable insights in both. It tended to absorb the phenomenon of religion into the ethical area, a tendency already perceptible in Kant, though not explicit in his intention. The ethical field, in turn, was largely socialized by both Cohen and Natorp and, subsequently, by other members and adherents of the school.

Another notable characteristic of the Marburg School was its constant interrelation of theoretical and historical interests. Its theoretical works exhibit a high degree of erudition and historical sense, and its historical works are distinguished by the way in which they are related to, and made to serve, the clarification of theoretical problems of philosophy. Cassirer especially distinguished himself in this way.

Baden School. No less eminent in its personnel and achievements was the School of Baden. This current of Neo-Kantianism numbered among its representatives the historian of philosophy W. Windelband (1848–1912), the theoretician of value H. Rickert (1863–1936), and the incomparable W. DILTHEY (1833–1911), whose work was predominantly in the theory of history and of culture. In justice to Dilthey, it should be noted that his achievement places him outside the limits of any school and establishes him as an original thinker in his own right.

The general character of the School of Baden may best be indicated by contrasting it with that of the Marburg School. The Baden School was convinced of the necessity of a critical study of culture and values at least as philosophical as that sought for the sciences of nature in the Marburg School. It was convinced, moreover, that the instruments necessary for such a work were present in the critical philosophy of Kant, and especially in the *Critique of Judgment*. Windelband's reflections on history and his contraposition of history to the natural sciences as equal areas of knowledge and investigation led him to establish a classification of the sciences into nomothetical and idiographic. The natural sciences are defined as nomothetic because they seek to establish the laws of nature; the sciences of culture are called, by contrast, idiographic because they seek the form of cultures. The natural, or nomothetic, sciences generalize particular facts that are considered typical instances of a single species, whereas the idiographic sciences are individualizing, seeking the form of a particular culture or expressive work.

Windelband's student Rickert continued this line of thought, seeking to advance beyond his teacher by establishing the difference between natural and cultural sciences on a more formal basis; this formal basis was the reference of the sciences of culture to value in the sense in which R. H. Lotze (1817–81) had defined that term. The cultural sciences have value as their formal object. On this basis, Rickert undertook the elaboration of a general theory of value.

This tendency was carried to its culmination by Dilthey both in theory and in practice. For Dilthey the ''sciences of the spirit'' (i.e., of value, culture, and history) are gnoseologically anterior to the sciences of nature; indeed, all science is a product of historical experience and expression. Dilthey developed a psychological basis for the sciences of the spirit that involved a subtle theory of the hermeneutics of the historical document. He applied his theories with great perception in such works as his *Leben Schleiermachers* (2 v. Berlin 1867–70), which revealed the potential of biography in the history of ideas and offered a new conception of cultural biography.

Influence. The influence of Neo-Kantianism may be seen in every major figure in German thought to the end of the 19th century. In England a ''return to Kant'' movement is to be found in Robert Adamson (1852–1902), in France in C. B. Renouvier (1815–1903), and in Italy in Francesco Fiorentino (1834–94).

See Also: KANTIANISM; CRITICISM, PHILOSOPHICAL.

Bibliography: G. VARET, *Manuel de bibliographie philosophique*, 2 v. (Paris 1956) 1:476–490. I. M. BOCHEŃSKI, *Contemporary European Philosophy*, tr. D. NICHOLL and K. ASCHENBRENNER (Berkeley 1956). F. C. COPLESTON, *History of Philosophy* (Westminster, MD 1946–) v.7. H. LÜBBE, *Lexikon für Theologie und Kirche*, ed. J. HOFER and K. RAHNER, 10 v. (2d, new ed. Freiburg 1957–65); suppl., *Das Zweite Vatikanische Konzil: Dokumente und kommentare*, ed. H. S. BRECHTER et al., pt. 1 (1966)2 7:911–913; *Die Religion in Geschichte und Gegenwart,* 7 v. (3d ed. Tübingen 1957–65) 4:1421–25. K. VORLÄNDER, *Kant und sein Einfluss auf das deutsche Denken* (2d ed. Bielefeld 1922). A. DENEFFE, *Kant und die katholische Wahrheit* (Freiburg 1922).

[A. R. CAPONIGRI]

NEO-ORTHODOXY

A Protestant theological movement, originating in the dissent of such men as Karl BARTH from the liberal Protestant view of religion. To Barth and his associates, to whose thought the name dialectical, or crisis, theology was first given, religion based on experience is no religion at all. Against the religion of experience, therefore, they invoked those tenets of the Reformation that tend to make the qualitative distance between God and man appear infinite and not susceptible of being overcome.

The ''orthodoxy'' of these positions, then, consists in adherence to themes such as the incompetence of human reason in attaining knowledge of God. In fact, this noetic armature of the doctrine of man's depravity is the rallying point of this school of thought, with a correlative, the absolute need of divine grace for man's salvation. Theologians of this persuasion emphasize also the inflexibility of God's judgment against sin.

The ''new'' factors of what typifies neo-orthodoxy consist in methods and emphases either not available to or eschewed by Protestant orthodoxy of the 17th and 18th centuries. Adherents of the latter tended to be fundamentalist in their view of the Biblical text, in contrast to the neo-orthodox, who avail themselves of the benefits of modern criticism in their use of the Bible. Even in strictly doctrinal matters the new school could be called ''impressionistic,'' in the sense that some doctrines of the Reformation receive an entirely personal treatment at their hands, e.g., predestination according to Barth. Neo-orthodoxy, essentially a protest against the humanistic elements that had, to the mind of its proponents, spoiled Protestantism and made it ''liberal,'' is unintelligible outside this context. This accounts, for example, for the tendency among these theologians habitually to express the attributes of God in such a way that every ''Yes'' is balanced off by an equally emphatic ''No.''

If reaction against creeping ANTHROPOMORPHISM, thought by the neo-orthodox to be the malady of liberal Protestantism, is the point of the movement's origin, it is, paradoxically, also the factor of cohesion—for neo-orthodoxy is by no means a single, carefully articulated thought system. Certain names are, to be sure, identified with it, but not with the rigor of a species to its genus. Each of the two major branches of the Reformation is represented among the neo-orthodox. Among the Calvinists, Barth is most characteristically so. In fact, in the spectrum of neo-orthodoxy Barth holds a place quite clearly distinguishable. Distrust of natural theology as a possible path to God and the correlative suspicion of the theological relevance of the analogy of being were epitomized in his thought. The critical freedom with which the neo-orthodox viewed their progenitors in the Reformation came to a climax in him too, for it was evident throughout his *Church Dogmatics* that only the Scriptures were, in principle, to be accepted as normative—and this to the exclusion even of the authority of John Calvin. In Barth the transcendent majesty of God and the lightning power of his word were trumpeted to the extent that his critics questioned the possibility of his putting into true focus the doctrines of reconciliation (JUSTIFICATION) and redemption (the term he uses for the final liberation of man in God).

G. Aulén made the most systematic case for neo-orthodoxy outside the Lutheran tradition (he himself belonged to the school of Lund). What Barth shouted from rooftops, however, Aulén, together with others such as E. Brunner, recited in a lower register. The touchstone is the attitude toward the use of reason in gaining knowledge about God. Aulén was not so absolute as Barth; neither was he enamored, however, of any mixing of theology and metaphysics.

P. TILLICH and R. NIEBUHR were sometimes called neo-orthodox; it appears, however, that the United States may not have the right climate for purebred orthodoxy. These two theologians, though they evolved with and in the same direction as Barth for some time, finally came to adopt a position whereby theology was seen as exercising a mediating function between the church and the world. In this case it would have to accord reason an important function in the verifying of theological data.

Bibliography: W. M. HORTON, *Christian Theology, an Ecumenical Approach* (rev. and enl. ed. New York 1958). J. MACQUARRIE, *Twentieth-Century Religious Thought* (New York 1963)

[M. B. SCHEPERS]

NEOPHYTE

From the Greek νεόφυτος, meaning newly planted, a term found once in the New Testament (1 Tm 3.6). It came into use in the Church to designate those newly converted from paganism or from any non-Christian sect, and later, by extension, was applied to those recently admitted to the religious or clerical states. The term in its earlier use contained an obvious allusion to the new planting or engrafting of the convert by baptism into the Mystical Body of Christ. The use of the word was extended later to describe those newly admitted to the clerical or monastic life (Gregory I, *Patrologia Latina: Epistles*; 77:784); and in both senses it passed into *Corpus iuris canonici* (D.48.1.2). It is also used more generally to refer to someone newly engaged in a particular work or career.

St. Paul cautioned against the laying of hands on neophytes to make them bishops, lest their lack of experience in the faith render them arrogant or deficient; and the Council of NICAEA I (325) formally condemned the ordination or consecration of a neophyte as an abuse that encouraged clerical ambition or promoted the vanity of the people who desired to have a prominent personage as their bishop. JEROME (*Patrologia Latina: Ad Oceanum*, 22:663); GREGORY OF NAZIANZUS (*Patrologia Graeca*, 35:1090); and GREGORY I (*Patrologia Latina*, 77:1030–37) also inveighed against this practice, although during the 4th and 5th centuries there were nota-

ble exceptions, such as Ambrose of Milan, Augustine of Hippo, Synesius of Cyrene, and Nestorius of Constantinople.

In the 4th century the term covered catechumens who had put off the reception of baptism until adulthood and upon being baptized, usually on the vigil of Easter or Pentecost, were clothed in white garments for eight days, given the *traditio legis Christi*, the kiss of peace (*osculum pacis*), anointed for confirmation, and admitted to reception of the Eucharist.

During the Middle Ages special care was paid to converts who through their change in religion were frequently deprived of position. Richard, the prior of Bermondsey, founded a hospital of converts in 1213; this was imitated by the Dominicans at Oxford, and Henry III established a *domus conversorum* in London for catechumens and neophyte Jews. The Council of BASEL in 1431 prescribed a manner of procedure for neophytes (J. D. Mansi, *Sacrorum Concilliorum nova et amplissima collectio* 29:99–101). St. IGNATIUS OF LOYOLA occasioned the erection of a *casa dei neofiti* at Rome in 1543, and GREGORY XIII built the house still standing near the Church of the Madonna dei Monti for the same purpose (May 20, 1580).

Local councils in the New World prescribed that after their baptism converts should be given special instructions including the four prayers *Pater, Ave, Credo,* and *Salve Regina* (Conc. of Mexico, 1555, c. 1; Synod of Quito, 1570). While the first political junta in Mexico (1524) had apparently forbidden the giving of the Eucharist to native neophytes even as Viaticum, PAUL III declared that the natives were true human beings endowed with reason and should be admitted to the Sacraments (*Veritas ipsa*, June 2, 1537), and in 1567 the Council of Lima prescribed the giving of Paschal Communion and Viaticum to the neophytes. A similar problem in India was settled by ALEXANDER VII (Jan. 18, 1658). In 1645 and 1656 Propaganda declared that the Chinese neophytes were obliged to observe the Church's law concerning the reception of the Sacraments and fasting. In modern missionary work, special care is given to the postbaptismal formation of neophytes.

In the development of Canon Law the status of a neophyte was considered an irregularity (*ex defectu fidei*) for the reception of orders; but the Code treated it as merely a simple impediment (1917 *Codex Iuris Canonicis* cc.987n6, 542n2).

Bibliography: H. LECLERCQ, *Dictionnaire d'archéologie chrétienne et de liturgie* (Paris 1907–53) 12.1:1103–07. R. NAZ, *Dictionnaire de droit canonique*, v.6 (Paris 1935–65) 997. J. SCHMIDLIN, *Catholic Mission Theory*, tr. M. BRAUN (Techny, Ill. 1931).

[P. K. MEAGHER/J. BEAUDRY]

NEOPLATONISM

In the strict sense, Neoplatonism designates the particular form that PLATONISM took on at the end of the ancient era, from the 3d to the 6th centuries after Christ. In a broad sense, it designates the currents of thought before or after this period that offer some analogy with one or other of the characteristics of Platonism at the end of the ancient era. The treatment in this article discusses the place of Neoplatonism in the history of ancient thought, the history of Neoplatonism, and the relationships between Neoplatonism and Christianity.

Characteristics of Neoplatonism. Neoplatonism, taken in the strict sense, exhibits three principal characteristics. First it is an exegesis of Plato's *Dialogues*, coupled with an attempt to systematize even disparate texts by appealing to a hierarchy among levels of reality. Then it is a method of spiritual life. Finally, and notably in the case of PROCLUS, it is a pagan theology seeking to systematize, and attain a rational grasp of, the revelations of the gods.

Recent historical studies seem to conclude that these characteristics are not new and that Neoplatonism existed already at the time of ancient Platonism, indeed even during Plato's life. The interpretations of Plato proposed by A. J. Festugière and Léon Robin authorize such a view. Following W. Theiler's discovery of a form of Neoplatonism deriving from Antiochus of Ascalon and Posidonius, C. J. de Vogel and Philip Merlan found in the ancient Academy, i.e., in the works of Aristotle and of Plato himself, the existence of a hierarchy among the levels of reality and the modes of knowledge (the good, the ideas, souls, nature, and matter). Again, the history of allegorical interpretation has shown that pagan theology was also very traditional. Thus what is called Neoplatonism would quite simply be identified with Platonic scholasticism.

Although this view merits serious consideration, it should not obfuscate what is new and irreducible in late Platonism as compared with ancient Platonism, namely, the desire to arrive at complete systematization and absolute internal coherence. During the 2d century, immediately before PLOTINUS's work, the philosophical tradition was overburdened with heteroclite and incoherent elements. Even Antiochus of Ascalon added doctrinal elements, borrowed from ARISTOTELIANISM and STOICISM, to Platonic teaching. Moreover, there was a tendency to merge philosophical syncretism with a religious syncretism that made equal acknowledgement of all revelations capable of providing salvation for the soul. This was the epoch of pagan, Christian, and Jewish GNOSTICISM.

Reacting against such a confusion, Plotinus invited man to interior simplification and unification. In this he was heir to Stoicism, which proposed the attainment of spiritual coherence by way of recollection and conversion to the divine Word, immanent in man, as well as in all other things. The immanence of the Word was assured by a total blending or complete interpenetration of the Word and matter.

Neoplatonism thus transferred the spirit of Stoicism to the Platonic universe. Everything is in all: each level of the hierarchy of things contains the whole of possible reality, but under a different aspect. The One contains all things, as do also the Intellect, the Soul, or the sensible world, but each hypostasis contains the whole of reality in its own way. In the One, all things are potentially present; in the Intellect they are compenetrated in an immediate intuition; in the Soul they are unfolded as in rational discourse; in the sensible world, they are mutually exterior, like sensations. The conversion, then, consists in reascending to a mode of knowledge that is even more unitive, in such a way as to arrive at a coincidence, in mystical ecstasy, with the Absolute from which these levels of reality and these modes of knowledge proceed. The system of things and the life of the soul are animated with the same movement of procession and conversion, unfolding and concentration.

History of Neoplatonism. At the beginning of the 3d century, at Alexandria, Plotinus had pursued the courses of Ammonius Saccas, who was the teacher also of ORIGEN, the Father of the Church. Plotinus was strongly influenced by his teacher and later, in Rome, taught "according to the spirit of Ammonius." In default of precise knowledge of the doctrines professed by Ammonius, Plotinus must remain for us the founder of Neoplatonism, i.e., the movement for interior unification just described.

Porphyry's Influence. With PORPHYRY, a disciple of Plotinus and his successor at Rome, a decisive turning point was reached. While preserving the purely Platonic message of his teacher, Porphyry returned to the earlier traditions and held that religious revelations, too, could make the way of salvation known. He is the first known philosopher to comment upon the *Chaldaic Oracles,* a long poem composed during the era of Marcus Aurelius. This pretended to expound a divine revelation that, beside theurgic practices aimed at leading the soul to the heavenly world, proposed a theological system inspired by Platonism and Pythagoreanism. It taught that after a supreme, transcendent God, endowed with intellect and will, came a second God, the Demiurge, and a whole hierarchy of astral divinities. Because of Porphyry's influence, these *Oracles* were to become the bible of Neoplatonism. However, taken literally, their teachings were hardly compatible with the doctrine of Plotinus.

Iamblichus and Proclus. All later Neoplatonism can be defined as an attempt to achieve a systematization among Plotinianism, the *Chaldaic Oracles,* and the *Orphic Hymns.* In opposition to Porphyry, with a view to safeguarding the transcendency of the One (strongly maintained by Plotinus), and by taking account of even the smallest details in the text of the *Oracles,* his successors multiplied the intermediary hypostases and the levels of reality. At the beginning of the 4th century, the Syrian, IAMBLICHUS, became the initiator of this new exegetical method. Although he taught in Syria, after his death (*c.* 330) the greater part of his disciples formed a group at Pergamum in Mysia. From this school came the writings of Emperor Julian and the treatise of Sallust entitled *On the Gods and the World.* The tradition of Iamblichus seems to have been introduced at Athens during the second half of the 4th century.

At the beginning of the 5th century, Syrianus and Proclus, the representatives of this tendency, constructed a vast system which brought Platonism, Chaldeanism, and ORPHISM into unison. Two basic principles dominate this synthesis. The first is the principle of analogy: while developing the unity represented by the immediately higher level of reality, each level of reality imitates this unity; everything is in all, according to more or less unified modes. The second principle is that of mediation: to imitate transcendent unity, each level of reality is endowed with a ternary structure, which, departing from unity, unfolds itself and goes on to return to unity because of conversion; to become itself, it must leave itself. In 529, the Emperor Justinian decided to bring an end to the school at Athens, the last bastion of paganism in the Christian empire. The head of the school, Damascius, then took refuge with his disciples near King Chosroes in Persia.

Damascius was the last great Neoplatonist. His *Questions and Solutions Concerning First Principles* constitute a profound criticism of Neoplatonism. The notion of the Absolute is for him very problematic. If the Absolute does not have any relation with anything else, it can no longer be the Principle. By the very claim that the Absolute is utterly unknowable and undefinable, the relation of other things to the Absolute is undefinable, and the whole metaphysical edifice of Neoplatonism comes in danger of crumbling.

Effect in the West. If the East was dominated by the tradition of Iamblichus, the Latin West knew only the tradition of Porphyry and Plotinus. This is true of pagan authors—Firmicus Maternus, MACROBIUS, and Martianus Capella—as well as of Christian writers—Marius Victorinus, Ambrose, Augustine, CALCIDIUS, and Claudianus Mamertus. BOETHIUS alone, who wrote at the beginning of the 6th century, came under the influence of the schools at Athens and Alexandria. Even at Alexandria,

the influence of Iamblichus's tradition was disseminated slowly and in moderate form. At the beginning of the 5th century, Hypatias and Synesius knew only Plotinus and Porphyry. Only at a later date did Hierocles, Hermias, Ammonius, Olympidorus, and Simplicius follow courses given at the school in Athens; and the Neoplatonism that they professed was always more sober, of a more moral character, and more scientific than that professed by their teachers: Syrianus, Proclus, or Damascius. Moreover, from the 6th century onward, the school became predominantly Aristotelian and Christian.

Neoplatonism and Christianity. From Plotinus to Damascius, Neoplatonism was always anti-Christian. Attacking the Christian Gnostics, Plotinus simultaneously combatted specifically Christian notions, as, for example, that of creation. Porphyry and the Emperor Julian wrote treatises against the Christians that provoked refutations from Eusebius of Cesarea and Cyril of Alexandria.

From the middle of the 4th century onward, however, Christian thought was strongly influenced by Neoplatonic philosophy and mysticism. In the East, Basil of Cesarea, Gregory of Nyssa, Synesius of Cyrene, and NEMESIUS OF EMESA, and, in the West, Marius Victorinus, Ambrose, and Augustine, made abundant use of Plotinus or Porphyry, frequently without citing them. In the 5th century, PSEUDO-DIONYSIUS borrowed his hierarchical universe from Proclus. In the East, this direct influence of Neoplatonism continued throughout the Byzantine period, notably up to Psellus (11th century), Michael Italicos (12th century), Nicephoros Gregoras (14th century), and Gemistos Plethon (15th century). Plethon played a role in restoring Neoplatonism to the West in the course of the Italian Renaissance, at the court of the Medici. In the West, from the high period of the Middle Ages onward, Neoplatonism was accepted through the works of Ambrose, Augustine, Boethius, Calcidius, and Macrobius. In the 9th century, JOHN SCOTUS ERIGENA translated the writings of pseudo-Dionysius and Maximus the Confessor, and, in his *De divisione naturae,* combined the Proclan Neoplatonism of pseudo-Dionysius with the Porphyrian Neoplatonism of Augustine.

Arabian Thought. From the 12th century onward, Neoplatonism entered the medieval West by another route, namely, that of ARABIAN PHILOSOPHY. In fact, the texts of the Greek philosophers had been translated into Syriac by Nestorian Christians at the school of Edessa (431–439), and once they had been propagated in Persia, they were translated into Arabic during the 9th century, after the establishment of Baghdad. Under the influence of these translations, Arabian philosophy became a Neoplatonic interpretation of the works of Aristotle. Once it came into Spain during the 12th century, this Arabian philosophy placed Christian thought into renewed contact with Neoplatonism.

From the 12th century onward, Latin translations from Arabic or Greek gave Christian theologians a direct knowledge of Neoplatonic works, namely, the LIBER DE CAUSIS (translated during the 12th century), the *Theology of Aristotle,* the *Elements of Theology* by Proclus, and Proclus's commentary on the *Parmenides*, translated by William of Moerbeke in the 13th century. Having received a strongly Platonized thought from the Christian tradition, certain theologians of this era, reading these Neoplatonic texts, regarded Platonism as naturally Christian.

Later Mysticism. The influence of Neoplatonism reached its apogee, at the end of the 13th century, in the writings of certain German Dominicans, all disciples of ALBERT THE GREAT, namely, THEODORIC OF FREIBERG, Berthold of Mosburg, NICHOLAS OF STRASSBURG, and especially Meister ECKHART. Under the influence of this current, mysticism in the Rhine region developed also through the writings of HENRY SUSO, TAULER, and RUYSBROECK. This German Neoplatonism was to become one of the sources of modern thought through the work of NICHOLAS OF CUSA, who transformed the metaphysics of Proclus into a method of knowledge that sought an ever deeper vision of the unity of the universe.

All these Byzantine, Latin, Arabian, or Germanic currents of Neoplatonism were united in the Italian Renaissance, which produced the great attempts at religious and philosophical unity by Giordano BRUNO and Tommaso CAMPANELLA. During the modern era, the Platonic tradition was to be perpetuated both in England by the CAMBRIDGE PLATONISTS and in the *Siris* of Berkeley (1744), and in Germany by the IDEALISM of SCHELLING and HEGEL.

Evaluation. The encounter between Neoplatonism and Christianity thus conditions the entire history of Western philosophy. During the patristic period, it provided an apt vocabulary for theology. The Trinitarian theology of Marius Victorinus, Basil of Cesarea, Augustine, and Synesius borrowed formulas from Porphyry, enabling it to express the unity of substance in the Trinity of hypostases. The Porphyrian expressions concerning the union of the soul and the body were of equal service in the formulation of the dogma concerning the hypostatic union, that is, a union without confusion of natures. In this regard, Nemesius has been a most valuable witness.

Yet, from the patristic era onward, Neoplatonism has had an influence on Christian teachings concerning the spiritual life that is highly disputable. The ancient tradition went from the humanity of Christ to the knowledge of the Father; it took ecclesiastical experience, i.e., the effect of the Holy Spirit in the Church, as its point of departure to attain God. Neoplatonism, on the contrary, pretended that an immediate and experimental knowledge of the transcendent God is possible. While making the necessary corrections in this matter, St. Augustine and St. Gregory of Nyssa were led to a like doctrine. From this there would result, in teachings on mysticism, a disequilibrium between the doctrine on union with God and the doctrine on the mediation of the Incarnate Christ. Pushed to the extreme, the danger makes its appearance in such writings as those of Meister Eckhart, who held that "the uncreated spark" of the soul is co-eternal with the Ineffable.

Bibliography: T. WHITTAKER, *The Neo-Platonists: A Study in the History of Hellenism* (2d ed. Cambridge, England 1928). A. H. ARMSTRONG, *An Introduction to Ancient Philosophy* (3d ed. London 1957). P. HENRY, *Plotin et l'Occident* (Louvain 1934). P. P. COURCELLE, *Les Lettres grecques en Occident* (new rev. ed. Paris 1948). A. J. FESTUGIÈRE, *Contemplation et vie contemplative selon Platon* (Paris 1936). L. ROBIN, *Les Rapports de l'être et de la connaissance d'après Platon* (Paris 1957). W. THEILER, *Die Vorbereitung des Neuplatonismus* (Berlin 1930); *Die chaldäischen Orakel und die Hymnen des Synesios* (Halle 1942). C. J. DE VOGEL, "On the Neoplatonic Character of Platonism and the Platonic Character of Neoplatonism," *Mind* 62 (1953) 43–64. P. MERLAN, *From Platonism to Neoplatonism* (2d ed. The Hague 1953). Fondation Hardt, pour l'études de l'antiquité classique, v.5, *Les Sources de Plotin* (Geneva 1960). H. LEWY, *Chaldaean Oracles and Theurgy* (Cairo 1956). C. SALLUST, *Concerning the Gods and the Universe*, tr. A. D. NOCK (New York 1926). DAMASCIUS LE DIADOQUE, *Dubitationes et solutiones de primis principiis*, ed. C. E. RUELLE (Paris 1889). R. ARNOU, *Dictionnaire de théologie catholique,* ed. A. VACANT, 15 v. (Paris 1903–50; Tables générales 1951–) 12.2:2258–2392. P. SHOREY, *Platonism, Ancient and Modern* (Berkeley 1938). W. D. GEOGHEGAN, *Platonism in Recent Religious Thought* (New York 1958).

[P. HADOT]

NEO-PYTHAGOREANISM

The Pythagorean school of philosophy became extinct in the 4th century B.C., but there continued to be "exoteric" Pythagoreans who cultivated an ascetic way of life modeled on the supposed practice of Pythagoras himself. References to them are found in Middle Comedy (in H. Diels, *Die Fragmente der Vorsokratiker: Griechisch und Deutsch*, ed. W. Kranz, 1, no. 58E), and the moralizing tractates preserved in Stobaeus [ed. F. G. A. Mullach, *Fragmenta Philosophorum Graecorum* 2 (Paris 1867) 1–129]. Pythagoreanism had been originally perpetuated only by oral teaching, and the succession was broken in the 4th century. Therefore, when the school was revived in the 1st century B.C., especially at Alexandria and Rome, it became eclectic, drawing on the doctrines of various schools. Thus, Sextus Empiricus gives two accounts of the Neo-Pythagorean number doctrine, the first of which (10.261–281) is Platonic, and the second (10.281–284), Stoic. Diogenes Laërtius (8.24–33) preserves a good, though brief, statement of Neo-Pythagorean tenets quoted from Alexander Polyhistor. Alexander discusses number symbolism, teachings on souls and *daimones,* the structure of the world, the kinship of man with gods and animals, and rewards and punishments in a future life. He does not mention transmigration of souls, but this doctrine is attested elsewhere.

Number Symbolism. Number symbolism is characteristic of Neo-Pythagorean thought. Some members of the sect used only the monad (Stoic), while others also introduced the undefined dyad (Platonic). In this and other respects, Neo-Pythagoreanism was not unified in doctrine. It was a movement rather than a well-defined school, and it is therefore not always easy to tell who was a Neo-Pythagorean and who was not. For instance, the work of Pseudo-Timaeus of Locri contains nothing specifically Pythagorean, and Ocellus Lucanus could as easily be regarded as a Peripatetic.

Moral Precepts and Practices. After number symbolism, moral precepts are the most characteristic mark of Neo-Pythagorean writings [e.g., Iamblichus, "Golden Verses," *Vita Pythagorae,* ed. A. Nauck (Leipzig 1884)]. The doctrine that all living things—gods, men, animals—are akin led to many practices: abstinence from meat and fish, the use of linen rather than woolen clothing, the cultivation of self-control and friendship, and the careful observance of piety toward the gods. Some members of the school believed that the air was full of souls and divine spirits (*daimones*), that dreams are a reality, and that burial rites are very important [see F. Cumont, *Recherches sur le symbolisme funéraire des Romains* (Paris 1942)]. Some advocated an examination of conscience every evening. Agatharchides mentions three ways in which men become better: by making themselves as like the gods as possible; by doing good deeds; and by death, which frees the soul from bodily contamination. It is not surprising that such men looked down upon others with less high ideals and that, like the contemporary early Christians, they were regarded with suspicion, particularly in Rome, where all foreign religions were mistrusted.

Some Neo-Pythagoreans also practiced magic or worse, at least in popular opinion. P. Nigidius Figulus, whose piety Cicero extolled (*Ad Fam.* 4.13), used boys as mediums in the recovery of treasure (Apuleius, *Apol.* 42); and Vatinius, whom Cicero accused of sacrificing boys to the Manes (*In Vat.* 14, and *Schol. Bob.* ad 1), was a member of Nigidius's circle.

Apollonius of Tyana. The best-known Neo-Pythagorean is APOLLONIUS OF TYANA, born about the beginning of the Christian Era. According to his biographer Philostratus, he substituted hymns and prayers for blood offerings, forbade the use of meat and wine, ate vegetables, wore linen, never bathed or cut his hair, practiced holy silence and sexual purity, and thus was united to the gods. He acquired magic powers as well as knowledge of the future and the past, including that of his own previous incarnation (Philostratus, *Vita Apoll.* 3.23; 6.21). The letters ascribed to him reveal Apollonius as he seemed to his immediate followers before the time of Philostratus. Apollonius was clearly a powerful personality living in a believing age, and he appealed to the learned as well as to the simple. Even some Christians respected him, for Sidonius Apollinaris (c. A.D. 432–80), Bishop of Clermont, transcribed for a friend a revised version of a Latin translation of Apollonius's biography (*Epist.* 8.3). There were undoubtedly other similar Neo-Pythagorean teachers of whom we know nothing.

Evaluation of Neo-Pythagoreanism. There is little philosophy in all this. Neo-Pythagoreanism was most conspicuously a religious movement, as its general character and concerns make clear. The Neo-Pythagoreans were often at odds with contemporary society, but, at the same time, the movement embodied several characteristic features of the religious life of the Empire: mysticism and occultism, belief in miracles, asceticism, stern morality, and the close union of the believers within their own group.

Neo-Pythagoreanism was absorbed into Neoplatonism, as is evident from the writings of Numenius (c. A.D. 150–250), who regarded the teachings of Pythagoras and Plato as practically identical, and from the lives of Pythagoras by Iamblichus and Porphyry. At an earlier date, it certainly influenced Philo Judaeus's terminology and it affected Christian thought through Clement of Alexandria. The latter often mentions Pythagoras, but largely as he was known through the Neo-Pythagorean writings.

See Also: ASCETICISM; GREEK PHILOSOPHY (RELIGIOUS ASPECTS); NEOPLATONISM; PYTHAGORAS AND PYTHAGOREANS.

Bibliography: Sources. *Ocellus Lucanus,* ed. R. HARDER (Berlin 1926). *P. Nigidii Figuli operum reliquia,* ed. A. SWOBODA (Vienna 1889). E. A. LEEMANS, *Studie over den wijsgeer Numenius van Apamia mit uitgave der fragmenten* (Brussels 1937). Other works. F. UEBERWEG, *Grundiss der Geschichte der Philosophie,* ed. K. PRAECHTER et al., 5 v. (11th, 12th ed. Berlin 1923–28) 1:513–24. R. DODDS, *The Oxford Classical Dictionary,* ed. M. CARY et al. (Oxford 1949) 603. R. BEUTLER, *Paulys Realenzyklopädie der klassischen Altertumswissenschaft,* ed. G. WISSOWA et al. (1937) 17.2:2361–80. M.P. NILSSON, *Geschichte der griechischen Religion* (2d ed. Munich 1955–) 2:396–407. A. SCHMEKEL, *Die Philosophie* *der Mittleren Stoa* (Berlin 1892). A. DELATTE, *Études sur la littérature pythagorienne* (Paris 1915).

[H. S. LONG]

NEOSCHOLASTICISM AND NEOTHOMISM

Neoscholasticism and neothomism are terms frequently used to designate the revival of THOMISM in the 19th and 20th centuries (*see* SCHOLASTICISM, 3). Even before AETERNI PATRIS of LEO XIII Catholic scholars eager to promote a CHRISTIAN philosophy tended to identify scholasticism with Thomism and vice versa. The historical studies of M. DE WULF revealed some differences among 13th-century scholastics, but these he dismissed in order to obtain a common body of philosophical teachings, which he and others called *philosophia perennis.* For De Wulf, *philosophia perennis,* "elaborated by the Greeks and brought to perfection by the great medieval teachers, has never ceased to exist even in modern times." Recognizing that Thomism was too narrow a term to designate a perennial philosophy, he preferred to speak of scholasticism and neoscholasticism. For him, neoscholasticism eliminated false or useless notions in 13th-century scholasticism, such as celestial movers, the incorruptibility of celestial bodies, their influence on terrestrial events, the diffusion of sensible "species" throughout a medium and their introduction into the organs of sense. The generally accepted view of neoscholasticism was expressed by De Wulf in his *Scholasticism Old and New,* tr. P. Coffey (Dublin 1907). It is retained in the titles of certain Catholic philosophical journals, e.g., *The New Scholasticism, Revue néo-scholastique* (1894–1909), *Revue néo-scholastique de philosophie* (1910–45), and *Rivista di filosofia neoscolastica.*

Later historical studies, notably by P. MANDONNET and by É. Gilson, revealed profound differences among medieval scholastics that could not be dismissed. Moreover, a single body of philosophical thought called *philosophia perennis* could not be found to exist among the Greeks, medieval scholastics, and contemporary scholastics. The view of De Wulf and the Louvain school was discredited by Gilson and others. Neoscholastic and Neothomistic thought were frozen in safe manuals during the crisis of Modernism. Instead of using scholastic and Thomistic principles to solve modern problems, as was the wish of Leo XIII, neoscholastic manuals were, for the most part, content to provide a philosophical foundation for the study of theology. Narrowness and lack of vitality helped to give a pejorative sense to the terms neoscholasticism and neothomism.

More profound studies of the texts of St. THOMAS AQUINAS frequently revealed discrepancies between the authentic teaching of St. Thomas and views presented as neothomistic. Thus many Thomists felt that the prefix "neo" could be understood as a negation of true Thomism. For this reason, J. MARITAIN wrote: "I am not a neo–Thomist. All in all, I would rather be a paleo–Thomist than a neo–Thomist. I am, or at least I hope I am, a Thomist" [*Existence and the Existent,* tr. L. Galantière and G. Phelan (New York 1948) 1].

Neothomism, like Thomism itself, is only one philosophical and theological school within the whole of scholasticism. Moreover, both terms have been used in a favorable and in an unfavorable sense. In a pejorative sense they signify a type of modern thought that is narrow, irrelevant, or unfaithful to the true mind and spirit of the great thinkers of the Middle Ages. In a favorable sense they signify living thought that is both faithful to the great masters of the Middle Ages and relevant to modern problems.

See Also: SCHOLASTICISM, 3.

Bibliography: M. DE WULF, *The Catholic Encyclopedia,* ed. C. G. HERBERMANN et al., 16 v. (New York 1907–14; suppl. 1922) 10:746–749. P. DEZZA and G. SANTINELLO, *Enciclopedia filosofica,* 4 v. (Venice–Rome 1957) 3:874–880.

[J. A. WEISHEIPL]

NEOT, ST.

Monk, hermit; d. *c.* 900. After ordination he moved from GLASTONBURY ABBEY to Cornwall in western England where he lived as a hermit. According to legend he became the friend of ALFRED THE GREAT; the story of the burned cakes and Alfred is first found in a history of the Shrine of St. Neot in Cornwall. He went on a pilgrimage to Rome to pray for Alfred's victory over the Danes. Neot was buried in Cornwall, but later his body was moved to St. Neot's in Huntingdonshire. It is possible that there were actually two saints of the same name, one a Celt from Cornwall, the other an Anglo-Saxon.

Feast: July 31.

Bibliography: *Acta Sanctorum* July 7:325–340. *Bibliotheca hagiographica latina antiquae et mediae aetatis* 2:6052–56. R. WUELCKER, "Ein angelsaechsisches Leben des Neot," *Anglia* 3 (1880) 102–114. J. ASSER, *Life of King Alfred, together with the Annals of Saint Neot Erroneously Ascribed to Asser,* ed. W. H. STEVENSON (Oxford 1904) 256–258, 296–299. F. WORMALD, ed., *English Kalendars before A.D. 1100* (London 1934–). A. M. ZIMMERMANN, *Kalendarium Benedictinum: Die Heiligen und Seligen des Benediktinerorderns und seiner Zweige* (Metten 1933–38) 2:518–521.

[R. T. MEYER]

NEPAL, THE CATHOLIC CHURCH IN

Located in the Himalayas, between India and Tibet, Nepal has four distinct geographical areas: a strip of low lying land along the Indian border, the ''mid-hills'' (up to 10,000 ft.), the Himalayan Range, and in the northwest, a mountainous area which is part of the Tibetan marginal mountains. Climatic zones range from the subtropical to the arctic conditions of the Himalayan Range. Nepal is a constitutional monarchy with a parliamentary form of government and a two-house legislature. The king is the constitutional head of state. It is the only officially Hindu country in the world, and the king must be a Hindu. Nepal is also one of the least economically developed countries in the world, with almost half of the population under the absolute poverty line. Average life expectancy is only about 55 years and few people outside of the urban areas have access to modern health care. The economy is primarily rural and agriculture-based, but few farmers have sufficient land to yield more than bare subsistence. Unemployment is high and underemployment is common with about half of the entire work force working for less than 40 hours a week.

The Catholic Church in Nepal. Christianity first entered Nepal when Jesuit missionaries passed through the country from 1628 onward. In 1703 Nepal became a part of the Italian Capuchin Mission to Tibet. The first Capuchins arrived in Kathmandu in 1715. From 1715 to 1769 the Capuchins were active in the three cities of the Kathmandu Valley: Kathmandu, Patan and Bhaktapur. At that time the present area of Nepal comprised many tiny independent kingdoms across the hills. In 1742 the King of Gorkha, to the west of Kathmandu, united these small kingdoms into a larger country. He conquered the three kingdoms of the Kathmandu Valley in 1769. During that period, the Capuchins faced severe difficulties arising from the closure of their mission in Tibet, a severe shortage of resources, and a hostile Gorkhali king who accused them of being in league with the British who had sided with the former kings of the Valley. Hence, the Capuchins withdrew from Nepal for India with a small group of converts, who settled in the village of Chuhari in north Bihar. In 1786, the Capuchins returned to Nepal. Over the next several years they had a sporadic presence in Nepal. The last Capuchin died in Kathmandu in 1810 and no others were assigned.

In 1814 Nepal fought and lost the war with the British East India Company. As a result, Nepal was forced to accept a treaty which specified, among other things, that no foreigners were permitted to enter Nepal without the specific permission of the governor general in Calcutta, a permission that was seldom granted and only for short visits. This treaty remained in force until 1951 and

Capital: Kathmandu
Size: 54,362 sq. miles.
Population: 25,284,463 (in 2001). Known as "the ethnic turntable of Asia," Nepal's population is racially diverse, comprising Newars, Indians, Tibetans, Gurungs, Magars, Tamangs, Bhotias, Rais, Limbus and Sherpas, all of whom have settled in the region over the last 2,000 years.
Languages: Nepali (official; spoken by 90% of the population), about a dozen other languages and about 30 major dialects. English is also widely spoken.
Religions: Nepal is the only official Hindu state in the world. More than 90% of its population are Hindus, about 5% are Buddhists, Muslims number about 3%, and Christians are less than 1%. The Constitution permits Nepalese to practice their traditional religions without hindrance. Conversion from Hinduism to any other religion is prohibited by law and subject to a penalty of three years of imprisonment.
See: Nepal is a Prefecture Apostolic.

effectively closed Nepal to any missionary activity. By 1951 there was no trace left in Nepal of the Capuchin mission. From 1846 to 1951 Nepal was governed by a family of autocratic, hereditary prime ministers, the Ranas. With the overthrow of the Rana regime in 1951 and the return of power to the king, things changed. A new treaty was signed with the now independent government of India, and Nepal opened up to the international community. In 1951 the JESUITS from Patna in Bihar, India, were invited to open a school for boys in Nepal. They were followed in 1954 by the IBVM (Loretto) sisters who opened a school for girls.

Ecclesiastically Nepal was placed under the jurisdiction of the Vicariate Apostolic of Tibet and Hindustan in 1784 and from 1808 was under various Indian jurisdictions. In 1919 Nepal was incorporated into the newly created diocese of Patna, Bihar. In 1984, Nepal established diplomatic relations with the Holy See. Nepal became a *Missio Sui Iuris,* and was subsequently raised to an Prefecture Apostolic in 1997. Since the opening of Nepal in 1951 various religious groups, both Protestant and Catholic, have been invited to Nepal to help the country in the fields of education, health, social welfare and general development. The Jesuits in Nepal have expanded their work to include four schools, one college and a research center. They also have an extensive social ministry in cooperation with the development efforts of the Nepal government. In addition to the Jesuits there are now four other orders of men and 15 orders of religious women working in Nepal. Their efforts are concentrated primarily in education but also in social work, including a center for women afflicted with HIV, a drug rehabilitation center and non-formal education. The personnel of these religious orders are mainly from India.

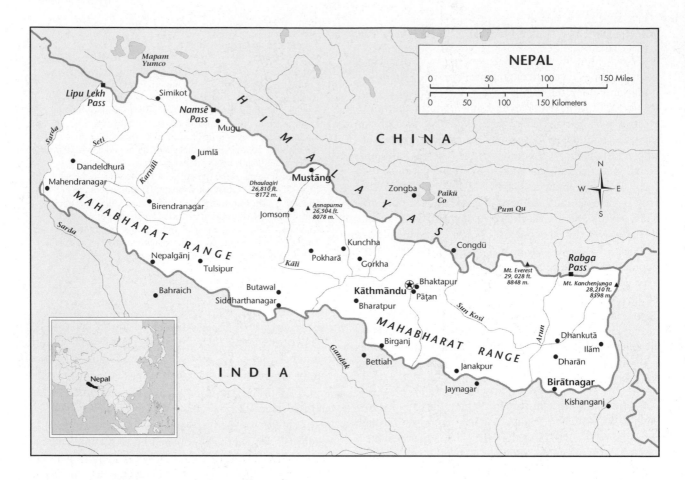

Protestant Churches in Nepal. Protestant efforts in Nepal began in 1953 when two American missionary families, Methodist and Presbyterian, were invited to open a hospital. They sought the cooperation of other Protestant groups, and in 1954 founded the United Mission to Nepal (UMN), an inter-denominational organization which functions as the main organ of Protestant efforts. Today UMN has 33 member bodies and 20 affiliated members from various Christian churches that contribute personnel and support. UMN is the largest missionary body with expatriate personnel working in various parts of the country and engaged in a variety of health, educational and developmental works. In addition to the UMN, the SEVENTH DAY ADVENTISTS opened a hospital in 1957, the Evangelical Alliance Mission carries out medical work, and the International Nepal Fellowship is engaged in working with victims of Hansen's disease. There are several native Protestant communities throughout the country. Except for one community affiliated to the Assembly of God, all of these communities are independent with no denominational affiliation. The number of native Protestants considerably exceeds that of Catholics.

Bibliography: G. FLETCHER, *The Fabulous Flemings of Kathmandu* (USA 1964). J. LINDELL, *Nepal and the Gospel of God* (Kathmandu 1979). L. PETECH, *Il Nuovo Ramusio*, v. 2, *I Missionari Italiani Nel Tibet E. Nel Nepal,* Parts 1-4 (Rome 1952). F. VANNINI, *Christian Settlements in Nepal during the Eighteenth Century* (New Delhi 1976). UMN, *Introducing Nepal and the UMN* (Kathmandu 1986).

[J. K. LOCKE]

NEPOS OF ARSINOË

Third-century Millenarianist and bishop of Arsinoë (modern Medinet El Faiyûm, Egypt); author of liturgical hymns and of a Judaizing view of the Apocalypse called a *Refutation of the Allegorists.* Though lost, this book is described by Eusebius of Caesarea (*Hist. eccl.,* 7.24, 25) as having been refuted by Bp. DIONYSIUS OF ALEXANDRIA (d. 265) in a two-volume tract, *On Promises.* Nepos propounded a Millenaristic viewpoint in which he interpreted the promises made to the saints in the Scriptures as due to be fulfilled on this earth during a 1,000-year reign of the just, in which man's physical powers would be given full satisfaction. Dionysius first held a three-day conference to dispel the effects of this doctrine among the Egyptian bishops, then wrote his refutation. But the disciples of Nepos apparently initiated several schismatic movements that explain the Church's generally reticent attitude toward allegorical interpretation of the Scripture. Nepos's views also witness to the continuance of Judaistic tendencies in the Church of the third century.

Bibliography: J. KIRCHMEYER, *Lexikon für Theologie und Kirche,* ed. J. HOFER and K. RAHNER, 10 v. (2d, new ed. Freiburg 1957–65) 7:878. É. AMANN, *Dictionnaire de théologie catholique,* ed. A. VACANT et al., 15 v. (Paris 1903–50; Tables générales 1951–) 11.1:68–69. J. QUASTEN, *Patrology,* 3 v. (Westminster, Md. 1950–) 2:103–104. L. GRY, *Le Millénarisme* (Paris 1904) 101–107. C. L. FELTOE, ed., *The Letters of Dionysius of Alexandria* (Cambridge, Eng. 1904) 106–126.

[J. BENTIVEGNA]

NEPOTISM

The practice of popes and other ecclesiastics (and hence of any person in a position of authority) of showing special favor to relatives or other interested parties. It is associated particularly with certain popes, some of whom understandably placed their relatives in positions of trust in times of crisis. First-degree papal nepotism, or the selecting of a nephew or relative for curial office, goes back to Pope Adrian I (722–795), who made a nephew *primicerius,* or senior "Judge Palatine." Examples occur more thickly from the 10th century onward; thus Innocent III (1198–1216) turned to his own family, particularly to his brother Richard, in order to bring the fractious Roman commune to heel. Dante (*Inf.* 19.31) characterized Pope Nicholas III (1277–80) as "greedily advancing" the ORSINI family; more justifiably, perhaps, he also attacked (*Inf.* 19.52–81; 27.85–129) Pope Boniface VIII (1294–1303), since Boniface's pontificate was notably preoccupied with the aggrandizement of the GAETANI family and the relentless harrying of the rival Colonna family. Thus in early 1295 he made his favorite nephew Benedetto Gaetani a Cardinal, at the end of the year honoring similarly two other nephews, Giacomo Gaetani Tommasini, a Franciscan, and Francesco Gaetani, a married man separated from his wife, as well as another relative, the curial poet JAMES GAETANI STEFANESCHI. The Avignon cardinals and popes, particularly Clement V and Clement VI, consolidated the tradition [see B. Guillemain, *La Cour pontificale d'Avignon* (Paris 1962) 156–164, 171–175], to the great disgust of Petrarch [*Epistulae sine nomine* 11, ed. P. Piur, *Petrarcas Buch ohne Namen und die päpstliche Kurie* (Halle 1925)]. However, if the development of papal PROVISION aided the popes in beneficing relatives, it must be remembered that one of the less well-known complaints against the system was that it cut across "episcopal nepotism"; as Bp. Grandison of Exeter (1328–69) put it, "I have for many years been unable to provide for my nephews and

retainers" [A. J. Bannister, *The Cathedral Church of Hereford* (London 1924) 182 n.2]. The golden age of nepotism came with the Renaissance popes: Callistus III (1455–58) called the BORGIAS from Spain; Sixtus IV (1471–84) spread his favors among DELLA ROVERE, Sansoni, Bassi, and RIARIO relatives; the Borgia, Alexander VI (1492–1503), made his son Cesare chancellor of the Church and sought to carve for him a hereditary state in central Italy; Leo X (1513–21) impoverished the Church in attempting to conquer Urbino for his nephew Lorenzo de' MEDICI. The trend was stemmed to some extent by the bull *Admonet nos of* Pius V (1567), but second-degree nepotism, or the conferring of favors instead of offices, was to continue until the constitution *Romanum decet pontificem* (1692) put an end to its grosser aspects; in the meantime papal families such as the ALDOBRANDINI, BORGHESE, BARBERINI, and Pamphili had benefited hugely.

Bibliography: P. FERRARIS, A. MERCATI, and A. PELZER, *Dizionario ecclesiastico,* 3 v. (Turin 1954–58) 2:1123. G. SCHWAIGER, *Lexikon für Theologie und Kirche,* ed. J. HOFER and K. RAHNER, 10 v. (2d, new ed. Freiburg 1957–65) 7:878–879.

[L. E. BOYLE]

NERESHEIM, ABBEY OF

In Württemberg, south Germany; its patrons are SS. ULRICH and AFRA of AUGSBURG. Founded for canons by Count Hartmann of Dillingen (1095), it was settled by Benedictines from PETERSHAUSEN (1106) and ZWIEFALTEN (1119). In 1497 it joined the MELK reform and in 1685 the Augsburg Congregation of the Holy Ghost. In the 17th and 18th centuries it had close ties with the Jesuit University of Dillingen and sent professors to the lyceum in Freising and the University of Salzburg, while it had its own school of philosophy and theology and a gymnasium (to 1806). Secularized in 1803 and awarded to the princes of Thurn and Taxis, it was restored as an abbey in 1920. The baroque cloister (1694–1714) has rich stucco-work; the church (1745–98), B. Neumann's most mature work, has cupola frescoes by Martin Knoller (1769–75). The humanist Abbot Benedikt Maria Angehrn (1755–87), cousin of Prince-abbot Beda Angehrn of SANKT GALLEN (1767–96) and imperial administrator of SANKT ULRICH in Augsburg (1778–82), was opposed by the monk Benedikt Maria Werkmeister (b. 1745; d. 1823), a talented scholar who championed the Catholic Enlightenment and had ties with I. H. von WESSENBERG. The monk K. Nack wrote a history of the abbey (Neresheim 1792).

St. Philip Neri. (Archive Photos)

Bibliography: P. WEISSENBERGER, *Lexikon für Theologie und Kirche,* ed. J. HOFER and K. RAHNER, 10 v. (2d, new ed. Freiburg 1957–65) 7:879–880.

[P. WEISSENBERGER]

NERI, PHILIP, ST.

Catholic reformer and founder of the Oratorians; b. Florence, July 21, 1515; d. Rome, May 26, 1595. Philip, son of Francesco, a Florentine lawyer, and his wife Lucrezia da Mosciano (d. 1520), grew up with his two sisters, Caterina and Elizabetta, in the care of a loving stepmother. He was both popular and pious as a boy, and was found often with the Dominicans at St. Mark's, where he talked with the friars and learned to revere SAVONAROLA, who was executed in Florence in 1498.

Apostle of Rome. Philip's family sent him, at 17, to his uncle, Romolo, a merchant of San Germano (now Cassino), who was willing to take Philip into his business and eventually to leave it to him. The prospect of a prosperous commercial career repelled Philip, who wished by then to give his life directly to God. With this intention, he left for Rome (1533), where he lodged with a Florentine, Galeotto del Caccia, whose two small sons he tutored. Already Philip was eating and sleeping little, and

praying much. From 1535 until 1538 he followed courses in philosophy at the Sapienza University and in theology at Sant' Agostino, earning high praise as a student. Instead of becoming a priest, as expected, Philip abandoned his studies, and for 13 years followed what was, for that time, an unusual, even idiosyncratic, vocation—that of a layman, entirely on his own, devoting himself exclusively to prayer and the Christian apostolate. He meditated on the Gospels; he prayed, sometimes, it seems, in ecstasy; he frequented the Catacombs (a reflection of his interest in the primitive Church); he persuaded friends and acquaintances to turn to Christ. In 1548 under the spiritual direction of Persiano Rosa, he organized some laymen into the Confraternitá di SS. Trinitá to assist poor and convalescent pilgrims. This grew into the celebrated hospital of S. Trinitá dei Pellegrini. The background of this activity must be remembered: corruption in the Church at Rome, an indifferent clergy, a people paganized by the Renaissance, a Reformation movement in the North attracting the loyalty of whole nations, and a reforming council just convening at Trent.

Father Rosa urged that he could serve the Church better as a priest, and on May 23, 1551, Philip was ordained. He lived for some years at the church of S. Girolamo della Carità with other priests and exercised a distinctive apostolate in the confessional. For the further instruction and sanctification of his penitents he arranged, in the afternoons, informal talks, discussions, and prayers in a room above the church. He also led excursions to other churches, often with music and a picnic on the way. In 1559, his "Pilgrimage to the Seven Churches" brought censure from Paul IV and the temporary suspension of all Philip's works. He aroused jealousy, and he was represented as encouraging plots against Paul IV, fomenting a sect, and holding "conventicles," The more moderate reformer Pius IV succeeded in this same year (1559), and Philip was back in favor.

Development of the Oratory. Several of Philip's followers became priests and from 1564 they lived as a community at the church of S. Giovanni dei Fiorentini, where they prayed and ate together (but took no religious vows) and celebrated the Eucharist and preached regularly. This was the beginning of the Oratory, as it is now known. Its distinctive feature was the popular daily afternoon service of four informal talks, interspersed with vernacular prayers and hymns. The talks concerned the spiritual life, Scripture, church history, and the study of a saint's life. PALESTRINA, one of Philip's followers, contributed musical settings for scriptural readings, hymns, motets, and *laudi spirituali* (hence the term Oratorio). The multivolume *Annales Ecclesiastici* of Caesar Baronius, whose standard of critical scholarship was high for his times, grew from his regular talks in the Oratory.

Persecution reoccurred in 1567 when it was reported to Pius V that the Oratory was an assemblage of heretics, where laymen preached and sang vernacular hymns. But the intervention of Cardinal Charles BORROMEO saved the Oratory. In 1575 Pope Gregory XIII, a friend to Philip, formally approved the new "Congregation of the Oratory," as a group of priests living in community without vows, for prayer and preaching. The small, dilapidated church of S. Maria in Vallicella was given to the congregation, and on the site was built a large new one, which has continued to be known as the Chiesa Nuova, and to be the church of the Roman Oratory. Philip was the first provost (superior); he was succeeded by Baronius.

Until Philip died, his advice was continually sought. Visitors, including many cardinals, thronged his room, and (SS.) IGNATIUS OF LOYOLA, CAMILLUS DE LELLIS, John LEONARDI, Charles Borromeo, FELIX OF CANTALICE, and FRANCIS DE SALES delighted in his friendship. As an influence in the Counter Reformation Philip has been justly counted with the Jesuits and the Council of Trent, on the grounds that as the "Apostle of Rome" he was foremost in converting to personal holiness many of those most influential in the central government of the Church. Philip has been considered an eccentric buffoon studying to mortify himself and proud Renaissance gentlemen into humility; a suspect leader of an evangelical reform movement; a saint around whom miracles were constantly occurring; a holy founder of 45 oratories now in existence; and an exponent of real, living, personal faith. Invariably Philip's humility, his gaiety, his personal attractiveness, and his fervent attachment to the Person of Christ have been noticed.

John Henry NEWMAN felt his attractiveness, joined the Oratory, and founded the first English-speaking house (Birmingham). Philip was beatified by Paul V (1615) and canonized by Gregory XV (May 12, 1622).

Feast: May 26.

Bibliography: A. BUTLER, *The Lives of the Saints*, ed. H. THURSTON and D. ATTWATER (New York 1956) 2:395–399. R. BÄUMER, *Lexicon für Theologie und Kirche*, ed. J. HOFER and K. RAHNER (Freiburg 1957–65)[2] 7:881. C. GASBARRI, *Filippo Neri, santo romano* (2d ed. Rome 1944). L. PONNELLE and L. BORDET, *St. Philip Neri and the Roman Society of His Times*, tr. R. F. KERR (New York 1933), list and discussion of sources. A. CAPECELATRO, *The Life of Saint Philip Neri . . .*, tr. T. A. POPE, 2 v. (new ed. New York 1926). G. INCISA DELLA ROCHETTA et al., eds., *Il primo processo per san Filippo Neri*, 3 v. (Studi e Testi 191, 196, 205; 1957–60). A. BAUDRILLART, *Saint Philippe Néri, 1515–1595* (Paris 1939). P. G. BACCI, *Vita di Sto Filippo Neri* (Verona 1624); Eng. *Life of St. Philip Neri*, ed. F. I. ANTROBUS, 2 v. (rev. ed. St. Louis 1903). V. J. MATTHEWS, *St. Philip Neri* (London 1934). L. BOUYER, *The Roman Socrates*, tr. M. DAY (Westminster, Md. 1958). F.W. FABER, ed., *The School of St. Philip Neri* (London 1850). F. W. FABER, ed., *If God Be with Us: The Maxims of St. Philip Neri* (Herefordshire 1994). R. ADDINTON, *The Idea of the Oratory* (London 1996). L. BOUYER, *St. Philip Neri: A Portrait* (Herefordshire 1995). P. TURKS, *Philip Neri: The Fire of Joy* (New York 1995).

[J. CHALLENOR]

NERINCKX, CHARLES

Frontier missionary, founder of the Sisters of Loretto; b. Herffelingen, Belgium, Oct. 2, 1761; d. Ste. Genevieve, Missouri, Aug. 12, 1824. The son of Sebastian, a successful physician, and Petronilla (Langendries) Nerinckx, Nerinckx was the eldest of seven sons and seven daughters, many of whom entered religious orders. He studied philosophy at the University of Louvain, Belgium, and was ordained Nov. 1, 1785. After a decade as parish priest in Mechlin and Meerbeek, he spent ten years administering the Sacraments from various hiding places, notwithstanding the rigors of the French Revolution.

In September 1803, through Princess Amalia GALLITZIN, he offered his services to Bp. John Carroll, arriving in Baltimore in November of 1804. He was sent to Georgetown College (now University), Washington, D.C. to study, then to Kentucky to join Stephen T. BADIN, until that time the only priest in that vast mission field. Nerinckx arrived at Bardstown, Kentucky in July of 1805; he worked for the next seven years with Badin, then alone in various parishes. During his 19 years in the state he built 14 churches. In 1809 he organized the first Holy Name Society in Kentucky, and in 1812, with two young women, founded the Sisters of LORETTO, the first native American community.

Nerinckx made two trips to Europe, returning with valuable paintings and religious supplies. He also brought over the first Jesuits to work in the West, among them Pierre Jean DE SMET. Disagreement with Bp. Guy Chabrat over the rule of the Sisters of Loretto prompted him to withdraw to Missouri in 1824, where death overtook him before he could realize his hope of working with the Indians. In 1833 his remains were returned to the motherhouse he had established at Loretto, Kentucky.

Nerinckx was noted for his great strength and his devotion to duty. Because it took six weeks to cover his mission stations, he spent his days in the saddle and his nights in the woods, often in physical danger. Although regarded as stern, he was gentle when instructing children and slaves. His uncompromising stand against the evil practices of the frontier caused friction, and later critics mistakenly accused him of being prone to Jansenistic tendencies. Several Latin manuscripts indicative of his scholarship and hundreds of his letters have been discovered in the Mechlin diocesan archives; many other letters are preserved in the Baltimore archdiocesan archives.

Nero, Emperor of Rome. (©Michael Nicholson/CORBIS)

Bibliography: W. J. HOWLETT, *Life of Rev. Charles Nerinckx* (Techny, Ill. 1915). C. P. MAES, *Life of Rev. Charles Nerinckx* (Cincinnati 1880). H. MAGARET, *Giant in the Wilderness* (Milwaukee 1952). J. H. SCHAUINGER, *Stephen T. Badin* (Milwaukee 1956). R. J. PURCELL, *Dictionary of American Biography*, ed. A. JOHNSON and D. MALONE. (New York 1926–36) 13:428–429. M. J. SPALDING, *Sketches of the Early Catholic Missions of Kentucky, 1787–1827* (Louisville 1844). A. C. MINOGUE, *Loretto Annals of the Century* (New York 1912).

[J. H. SCHAUINGER]

NERO, ROMAN EMPEROR

Reigned A.D. 54 to 68; b. Anzio, Dec. 15, 37; d. Rome, June 9, 68. He was adopted in 50 by the Emperor Claudius, who had married his own niece, Agrippina, Nero's mother. In 53 Nero married Octavia, the daughter of Claudius. When Claudius was poisoned in 54 on the orders of Agrippina, Nero was presented to the soldiers as the new emperor. For the first five years his reign was popular, owing to the careful guidance of SENECA and Burrus. In 55 when Agrippina threatened to side with Britannicus, the son of Claudius, against him, Nero had him poisoned, and in 59, weary of his mother's demands, he had her murdered. In 62 he divorced Octavia and married his mistress. In this same year Burrus died and Seneca re-

tired; their place was taken by Ofonius Tigellinus, who converted the last years of Nero's rule into a reign of terror. Nero the Hellenophile surrounded himself with Greeks and Orientals; he was also an enthusiast for the arts and extravagant spectacles, which together with his tendency to autocracy cost him the support of conservative Romans. Despite the relief measures he provided for those left destitute, he was blamed for the fire of July 18, 64, that broke out in the Circus Maximus and destroyed half of Rome. Nero turned the blame on the Christians, according to TACITUS, and many of them were put to death by cruel tortures. Peter and Paul were martyred in Rome under Nero, but the year of their death is uncertain. A conspiracy against Nero in 65 under Calpurnius Piso failed, but in 68 the armies under Julius Vindex at Lyons and Servius Sulpicius Galba in Spain revolted. Deserted by the pretorian guards and condemned to death by the senate, Nero killed himself.

Bibliography: A. MOMIGLIANO, *The Cambridge Ancient History* 10:702–742. M. A. LEVI, *Nerone e suoi tempi* (Milan 1949). E. HOHL, *Paulys Realenzyklopädie der klassischen Altertumswissenschaft* Suppl 3:349–394. H. U. INSTINSKY, *Lexikon für Theologie und Kirche*[2] 7:881–882.

[M. J. COSTELLOE]

NERSES

The name of many Armenian churchmen and officials, five of whom are discussed in this article.

Nerses the Great, St., 4th-century Armenian catholicos or patriarch; b. Cappadocia, 333 or 337; d. Khakh, on the Euphrates, 373 (feast, Monday after the 4th Sunday after Pentecost). Nerses was the son of Athanakines and Bambish, the sister of King Diran, and a close relative of St. GREGORY THE ILLUMINATOR. He was educated in Cappadocia and married a Mamikonian princess, who bore him a son, Isaac the Great, and died a few years later. In the early years of the reign of King Arshak II, he returned to Armenia, served as a royal counselor and custodian of the royal sword, and was chosen the catholicos by popular acclamation after the death of Patriarch Shahak. He was consecrated at Caesarea in Cappadocia, the metropolitan see for ARMENIA, by Eusebius (or possibly Dianos) in 353, and he initiated a reform of the Armenian church with a synod held at Ashtishat. He promulgated decrees prohibiting marriages between close relatives, denounced pagan practices, and introduced positive legislation regarding fasting and monastic life. He also erected schools, convents, hospitals, asylums, and churches in imitation of Cappadocian ecclesiastical activities. King Arshak deposed him for condemning the scandals of the court, and from 360 to

362 he appealed for aid in Constantinople. He returned to Armenia (364 or 368) and was restored as catholicos by King Pap after Arshak had been betrayed to the Persians by members of his entourage. Nerses rebuilt the churches destroyed by the Persians. In 372 he took part in a synod at Caesarea, but he was apparently poisoned at the king's command for denouncing the royal family's evil ways. His career is described by Faustus of Byzantium (*History*), whose narrative must be used with caution.

Nerses II Astaraketzi, Armenian catholicos from 548 to 557. He called the Synod of Dwin (554–555) at which 18 bishops participated and condemned the Khoujik sect imported into Armenia by merchants infected with both Nestorianism and Manichaeism. The 38 canons of the synod are important for the development of Armenian teaching on the Sacraments and monastic life.

Nerses III, Armenian catholicos from 642 to 661. Endowed with a Byzantine education, Nerses built the patriarchal palace and the church of St. Gregory in Vagarshapat and received the title *Schinogh* or builder. He attempted to win the Armenian Church to the Chalcedonian viewpoint on the question of the two natures in Christ, but he had to cede before the opposition of Theodore Rschtuni and returned to his original bishopric at Taykh.

Nerses of Lambron, St., bishop of Tarsus in Cilicia; b. Lambron, Cilicia, 1153; d. Tarsus, July 14, 1198 (feast, Monday after 3d Sunday after Assumption). The son of Oshin II (d. 1168), prince of Lambron, Nerses was educated in the Armenian monasteries of Skewra and Siav-Liarn, and spoke Armenian, Greek, Latin, and Syrian. His granduncle Nerses IV ordained him in Hromkla, and he changed his name from Smbat to Nerses and retired to a solitude. At the request of Gregory IV Tegha, he accepted the archbishopric of Tarsus in 1175; he was selected as an ambassador by King Leo II to greet Frederick Barbarossa. Upon Frederick's death in the river Saleph (1190), he took the young Prince Frederick under his protection. He participated in reunion efforts with Rome and Byzantium, gave the opening discourses at the Synods of Hromkla (1179) and Tarsus (1196), and undertook an embassy to Constantinople in 1197. Of his 33 preserved writings, those devoted to the liturgy, biblical commentaries, preaching, and Church discipline are the most significant. He also translated into Armenian a number of patristic works, including the Rule of St. Benedict, the Dialogues of Gregory the Great, and the Ekthesis of Epiphanius of Constantia, as well as the Syro-Roman legal code. Some of his works have been edited and translated into German by Max zu Sachsen, K. Bruns, E. Sachau, and F. Finck.

Bibliography: V. INGLISIAN and M. VAN DEN OUDENRIJN, *Lexikon für Theologie und Kirche*, ed. J. HOFER and K. RAHNER (Freiburg 1957–65) 7:882–884. H. G. BECK, *Die Religion in Geschichte und Gegenwart* (Tübingen 1957–65) 4:1403, Nerses IV. H. F. TOURNEBIZE, *Histoire politique et religieuse de l'Arménie* (Paris 1910); *Dictionnaire d'histoire et de géographie ecclésiastiques*, ed. A. BAUDRILLART et al. (Paris 1912–) 4:297–298. J. B. EMINE. tr., in *Collection des historiens anciens et modernes de l'Arménie*. ed. V. LANGLOIS et al., 2 v. (Paris 1867–69). R. GROUSSET, *Histoire de l'Arménie* (Paris 1947). É. AMANN, *Dictionnaire de théologie catholique*, ed. A. VACANT et al. (Paris 1903–50) 15.1: 538–540. J. MARQUART, *Philologus* 55 (1896) 213–227. N. AKINIAN, *Analecta Bollandiana* 67 (1949) 74–86, Nerses the Great. G. CAPULETTI, *Sancti Nersetis Clajensis opera*, 2 v. (Venice 1833). F. NÈVE, *L'Arménie chrétienne et sa littérature* (Louvain 1886). A. TERMIKELIAN, *Die armenische Kirche in ihren Beziehungen zur byzantischen* (Jena 1892). P. DZOULIKIAN, *Proche-Orient chrétien* 11 (1961) 36–43, Nerses IV and Nerses of Lambron. P. TEKEYAN, *Controverses christologiques en Arméno-Cilicie* (*Orientalia Christiana Analecta* 124; 1939).

[N. M. SETIAN]

NERSES GRATIOSUS (ŠNORHALI)

Archbishop (Catholicos) 1166–73, saint in the Armenian Church; b. Cilicia, 1102; d. Hromkla, 1173. Nerses IV Klayeci, called Šnorhali or "the Gracious," was educated by his uncle Catholicos Gregory II and the great Armenian doctor Stephen Manuk. Nerses succeeded his brother, Gregory III Pahlavuni, as catholicos and had his residence at Hromkla, on the Euphrates. He was a competent theologian and worked (1170–72) with Manuel I Comnenus for the reunion of the Byzantine and the Armenian Churches. Manuel sent the Byzantine theologian Theorianus to Hromkla for theological conferences at which Nerses and several bishops accepted the Chalcedonian formula concerning the two natures in Christ, despite the opposition of Syrian delegates. Nerses also accepted the Byzantine calendar for the main ecclesiastical feasts to convince Patriarch MICHAEL III ANCHIALUS (1170–78) of his orthodoxy.

Nerses became an ardent defender of the traditional doctrines of the Armenian Church against MONOPHYSITISM and was quoted in this context by Pius XII in the encyclical *Sempiternus Christus rex* (1951). He was one of the early leaders in the Armenian literary renaissance. Among his writings are a complaint about the fall of Edessa (1144), Biblical commentaries, and encyclical letters treating of canonical matters. He was noted as a poet and writer of sacred hymns. His *Twenty-four Hour Prayers* (the daily prayers of St. Nerses) was translated into 32 languages of the Christian world. Before he died, he named the younger of his two nephews, both bishops, to succeed him. The elder, however, imprisoned his cousin and had himself consecrated catholicos under the name Gregory IV Tegha (For bibliography, *see* NERSES).

Charter of protection granted to Nestorian Church by Caliph Muktafi II of Baghdad, 1138.

Feast: Aug. 3.

[J. M. BUCKLEY]

NESTORIANISM

A development of the Antiochene theology as it had been formulated by Eustathius of Sebaste, Diodore of Tarsus, and THEODORE OF MOPSUESTIA in reaction to Arianism and Apollinarianism. It is clearly dyophysitic (*duo physeis,* or two natures in Christ), in contrast with the explanations of Saint CYRIL OF ALEXANDRIA, who held that in Christ there was one nature (*mia physis*), in which teaching Cyril's opponents detected Apollinarian echoes.

Nestorian Teaching. The doctrine of Nestorius is known through fragments of his letters and sermons preserved in the Acts of the Council of EPHESUS, frequent citations in the works of Saint Cyril of Alexandria, fragments of a personal apology (*Tragoedia*) composed after

his deposition but before 439, and through the text of another apology, *The Bazaar of Heracleides,* written toward the end of his life and preserved in an interpolated Syrian version. Further information is offered by such opponents as John CASSIAN (*De Incarnatione Domini contra Nestorium* of 429–30) and Saint Cyril (*Adv. Nestorii Blasphemias* of 430), who convinced their contemporaries and posterity that Nestorius was a heretic.

Some modern historians, such as A. Harnack, F. Loofs, J. Bethune-Baker, and L. Duchesne, have sought to reestablish Nestorius's good name, saying that he was not necessarily a Nestorian; and A. Grillmeier believes that underlying the Nestorian formulas, even though these are contestable or plainly heterodox, there are valuable theological suppositions.

Christology. The Christological thought of Nestorius is dominated by Cappadocian theology and is affected by Stoic thought. Although it was not devoid of speculative value, nevertheless, in its attempt to avoid ARIANISM and Apollinarianism, Nestorianism did not reflect the true tradition of the Church. This fact was recognized by the early historians, such as Socrates (*Ecclesiastical History* 8.29.30); for in his *Bazaar of Heracleides,* Nestorius asserted that the key word THEOTOKOS had not been used by the Fathers.

Nestorius never spoke of "two sons," nor did he consider Christ as simply a man (*purus homo*); hence it was improper on the part of Eusebius of Doryleum to accuse him of the ADOPTIONISM of Paul of Samosata, a theology that saw Christ as a man who through his sufferings and virtues attained the dignity of a Son of God (Bewährungstheologie).

Cyril spoke of one sole nature (*mia physis*) in Christ, a nature that could be understood in the way that Cyril intended: as a concrete, existent subject. But Nestorius defined a nature in the sense of *ousia,* or substance, and distinguished precisely between the human nature and the divine nature, applying in his Christology the distinction between nature (*ousia*) and person (*hypostasis*), which was currently in use in the trinitarian theology. Remarking that "wherever the Scriptures mention the economy [of salvation in the Incarnation] of the Lord," they attribute His birth and Passion not to the divinity but to humanity, Nestorius refused to attribute to the divine nature the human acts and sufferings of Jesus (*Epist. ad Cyrillum*). This statement represents the crux of the disagreement between Cyril and Nestorius; it makes it probable that if their ideas and vocabulary could have been neatly clarified and defined, the argument as well as the schism could have been avoided.

The Theotokos. Nestorius refused to call Mary the *Theotokos* (God bearer), which proved to be the starting point for the whole quarrel. He held that to call Mary the Mother of God would be in effect to say that the divine nature had been born of a woman; Mary had begotten only a man, to whom the Word of God was united. Nestorius would agree to say *Theotokos* (Mother of God) only on the condition that one said at the same time *anthropotokos* (mother of man); for him the right word was *christotokos* (mother of Christ).

While distinguishing between the natures, Nestorius still affirmed their union. He would not consent to speak of "two sons"; but he spoke of a conjunction, a voluntary union, or one of accommodation, and gave the impression of believing in a union in the psychological or moral order rather than that of a metaphysical nature. This would be an extrinsic union like that of a temple with the divinity inhabiting it, of clothing and the wearer, or of an instrument (*organon*) and the user. Certain of these examples, such as that of the temple, are found in the Scriptures and in tradition.

Nestorius affirmed the close union and conjunction of a concrete human nature with the divinity, and the termination of that union is the *prosopon* or person of Christ, God and man. This involves a central point of difference between the theology of Nestorius and that of Cyril as well as that which the Church made its own at the Council of EPHESUS and in subsequent tradition.

Saint Cyril. For Cyril, who justly drew support from the Creed of Nicaea, the unique subject is the Word (*Logos*) incarnate, become man in such fashion that it can be said that it is the Word that is born, lives, suffers, and dies in the flesh; there is no distinguishing between the Word and Christ. Nestorius on the other hand made a distinction between the *Logos* (the divine nature) and Christ (the Son, the Lord), which he saw as a result of the union of the divine nature and the human nature. Christ for him was like the total of two natures or the expression of their union, rather than the unique divine subject of the Incarnation. Nestorius spoke likewise of a "*prosopon* of union," the result of the union of the two *prosopa*, the divine and the human.

There is no doubt that Nestorius used the term *prosopon* (which meant originally the mask or representation of a person in the Greek theater) in expressions that recall the "communication of idioms," and he used formulas that Cyril might have employed; but the metaphysical foundation behind this use of "nature" and "person" was insufficient to protect the personal unity represented by the "*Word Incarnate.*"

According to É. Amann, Nestorius could not imagine a nature without its own subsistence, or which was not a concrete hypostasis or personality. He did not clearly comprehend the distinction between the concept of real existence and that of independent subsistence. According to G. Prestige, Nestorius was not able to reduce to a unique, clearly differentiated person the two natures of Christ, which he nevertheless distinguished with such admirable realism.

The Nestorian Church. After the Council of Ephesus a strong Nestorian party existed in eastern Syria around the theological school of Ibas of Edessa, who was apparently a convinced Nestorian. After the theological peace achieved in the agreement of 433 between Cyril of Alexandria and John of Antioch, a number of bishops who rejected that agreement drew closer to the Syrian Church of Persia, which officially adopted Nestorianism at the Synod of Seleucia in 486. The Nestorians were expelled from Edessa in 489 by the Emperor Zeno and emigrated to Persia. It was thus that the Nestorian Church broke away from the faith of the Church of Constantinople and the Byzantine Empire.

The Nestorianism of the Persian Church was greatly strengthened at the synod of 612 when it adopted the heterodox principles of the catholicos, Babai the Great: two natures, two *hypostaseis,* one sole *prosopon;* the term *theotokos* was formally excluded. This Church continued to flourish in spite of periods of persecution under the Sassanids, and even after the invasions of the Turks and Mongols. Its strength is witnessed by its theological schools at Seleucia and NISIBIS; its monasticism; and missionary expansion in Arabia, India (Malabar), Turkistan, Tibet, and even in China, where the bilingual inscription (in Syrian and Chinese) of Si-ngan-fu attests its presence in 781. The invasion and bloody persecution by Tamerlane (1380) almost destroyed the Nestorian Church, which today is greatly reduced in size in Iraq, Iran, and Syria and has a number of congregations in the United States.

A reunion of the Nestorians of Cyprus with Rome took place in 1445. In 1553 the Nestorian patriarch John Sulaqua professed the Catholic faith at Rome and was recognized as patriarch of Mosul. The union thus achieved continues today. Since 1696 the Chaldean patriarch has the title patriarch of Babylon. The Chaldeans number about 180,000 adherents. The Nestorians of Malabar, reunited with Rome in 1599, have some 1,300,000 communicants and use the old Syrian liturgy of Addai and Mari (*see* SYRO-MALABAR LITURGY).

Bibliography: NESTORIUS, *Nestoriana*, ed. F. LOOFS et al. (Halle 1905); *Le Livre d'Héraclide de Damas*, tr. and ed. F. NAU et al. (Paris 1910), Eng. tr. *The Bazaar of Heracleides*, tr. and ed. G. R. DRIVER and L. HODGSON (Oxford 1925). J. F. B. BAKER, *Nestorius and His Teaching* (Cambridge, England 1908). F. LOOFS, *Nestorius and His Place in the History of the Christian Doctrine* (Cambridge, England 1914). É. AMANN, *Dictionnaire de théologie* *catholique,* ed. A. VACANT et al., 15 v. (Paris 1903–50) 11.1:76–157. A. GRILLMEIER and H. BACHT, *Das Konzil von Chalkedon: Geschichte und Gegenwart,* 3 v. (Würzburg 1951–54) 1:120–202; "Das Scandalum oecumenicum des Nestorius," *Scholastik* 36 (1961) 321–56. P. T. CAMELOT, *Das Konzil von Chalkedon: Geschichte und Gegenwart* 1:213–42; *Éphèse et Chalcédoine,* v.2 of *Histoire des conciles oecuméniques* (Paris 1962). L. I. SCIPIONI, *Ricerche sulla Cristologia del Libro di Eraclide di Nestorio* (Fribourg 1956). F. NAU, *L'Expansion nestorienne en Asie* (Paris 1914). E. TISSERANT, *Dictionnaire de théologie catholique* 11.1:157–323. K. S. LATOURETTE, *A History of the Expansion of Christianity,* 7 v. (New York 1937–45) 2. W. C. EMHARDT and G. M. LAMSA, *The Oldest Christian People; A Brief Account of the History and Traditions of the Assyrian People and the Fateful History of the Nestorian Church,* introduction by J. G. MURRAY (New York 1970). J. JOSEPH, *The Modern Assyrians of the Middle East: Encounters with Western Christian Missions, Archaeologists, and Colonial Powers* (Leiden and Boston 2000). S. P. BROCK, "The Christology of the Church in the East in the Synods in the Fifth to Early Seventh Centuries," in *Aksum-Thyateira* (Athens 1985) 125–42.

[P. T. CAMELOT]

NESTORIUS

Patriarch of Constantinople and heresiarch; b. Germanicia in Euphratesian Syria, after A.D. 381; d. Libya, after 451. Of Persian parenthood, Nestorius studied in Antioch and entered the monastery of Euprepios, where he was ordained. He penetrated deeply into the Antiochene theology, although it is doubtful that he became a disciple of THEODORE OF MOPSUESTIA. An orator, he was selected by THEODOSIUS II to succeed Sisinnius as bishop of Constantinople and was consecrated April 10, 428. A zealous opponent of ARIANISM and PELAGIANISM, he corresponded with Pope CELESTINE I on the Pelagianism of JULIAN OF ECLANUM, then residing in Constantinople.

Nestorius inaugurated a vast theological quarrel by preaching against the title THEOTOKOS, or Mother of God, given to the Virgin Mary, claiming she should be called rather the Mother of Christ. His doctrine was challenged by Eusebius of Doryleum, still a layman, who posted a *contestatio,* or rebuttal, on the doors of HAGIA SOPHIA in Constantinople, charging Nestorius with the errors of PAUL OF SAMOSATA. Nestorius wrote to Pope Celestine to explain his teaching on the Christotokos, and Eusebius sent the pope copies of the bishop's sermons. Meanwhile CYRIL OF ALEXANDRIA, disturbed by agitation on the part of Egyptian monks, sent two letters to Nestorius warning him of the heretical implications in calling Mary only the Mother of Christ and not the Mother of God. Cyril finally sent a dossier of the argument to Celestine, who in a Roman synod (August 430) summoned Nestorius to retract within ten days and charged Cyril with executing this sentence. After a synod at Alexandria in which Nes-

torius' teaching was condemned (November 430), Cyril wrote a third letter to Nestorius to which he adjoined 12 anathemas (*capitula*) requesting Nestorius's acquiescence and signature. Nestorius in turn charged Cyril with APOLLINARIANISM and called upon the Emperor Theodosius II to convoke a council to settle the matter. The Council of EPHESUS met in June 431, but Nestorius refused to appear before it when Cyril, charged by Pope Celestine with acting as his legate, took over the presidency. In a session on June 22, 431, Nestorius was condemned as a heretic and despite charges of irregularity in the Council's proceedings, Theodosius deposed Nestorius and relegated him to a monastery from which, at the insistence of JOHN OF ANTIOCH, he was sent into exile to Petra in Arabia (436) and finally to the Great Oasis in Libya, where he died.

In 435 Theodosius ordered the writings of Nestorius to be burnt; hence only fragments of his sermons, letters, and treatises have been preserved. They were edited by F. LOOFS in 1905. His *Bazaar of Heraclides,* discovered in 1895 in a Syrian translation, is an autobiographical defense of his teaching in which he claims that his doctrine was identical with that of Pope LEO I and FLAVIAN OF CONSTANTINOPLE. Its literary form attests Nestorius' eloquence, and its plea for charity and forgiveness have caused a reestimate of his guilt as a heretic, although the doctrine known as NESTORIANISM took its rise from his preaching. A fragment of an earlier defense, known as the *Tragedy* of Nestorius, written probably between 431 and 435, has been preserved in Greek, Latin, and Syriac, and a number of his letters and sermons have been published in the literature dealing with the Council of Ephesus.

Bibliography: NESTORIUS, *Nestoriana: Fragmente,* tr. and ed. F. LOOFS et al. (Halle 1905). É. AMANN, *Dictionnaire de théologie catholique,* ed. A. VACANT et al., 15 v. (Paris 1903–50; Tables Générales 1951–) 11.1:76–157. I. RUCHER, *Paulys Realenzyklopädie der klassischen Altertumswissenschaft,* ed. G. WISSOWA et al. 17.1:126–137. J. QUASTEN, *Patrology,* 3 v. (Westminster, Md. 1950–) 3:514–519. *Acta conciliorum oecumenicorum* (Berlin 1914–) 1.1.1–6. J. F. BETHUNE-BAKER, *Nestorius and His Teaching* (Cambridge, Eng. 1908). R. V. SELLERS, *Two Ancient Christologies* (London 1940). P. GALTIER, "Nestorius mal compris, mal traduit," *Gregorianum* 34 (1953). 427–433.

[P. T. CAMELOT]

NETHERLANDS, THE CATHOLIC CHURCH IN

The Kingdom of the Netherlands, also known as Holland, is one of the Low Countries in northwestern Europe, along with Belgium and Luxembourg. Bound on the west and north by the North Sea, on the east by Germany and on the south by Belgium, the Netherlands has traditionally boasted the highest population density in the world. Since 1815 the government has been a constitutional monarchy and has been noted for its socialist policies; it also led the world as one of the founding member nations of NATO in the mid-twentieth century.

The Middle Ages to 1559

During the early Christian era Batavian and other Germanic tribes inhabited the Low Countries, although regions south of the Rhine, including Maastricht and Heerlen and points to the south and west of the North Sea, were under Roman control. Christianity may have been introduced in the 2nd and 3rd centuries by soldiers, officials, merchants and slaves, but not in any systematic way. The first bishop appeared only in the 4th century: the Armenian St. Servatius (Sarbatios) had his see at Tongeren (*c.* 346–359) and was buried at Maastricht in the Church of St. Servaas. At the Council of Rimini (359) Servatius was a defender of orthodoxy. However, inroads made by Saxon invaders and the 5th century Frankish occupation and colonization of superficially Romanized frontier regions halted all expressions of Christianity there.

Missions before Charlemagne. Missionary activity in the Low Countries started anew after the baptism of King Clovis in 496 at Reims. Bishop VEDAST (VAAST) labored in the Artois; Falco, in Tongeren; and Eleutherus, in Tournai. Further to the north, St. AMANDUS was the first missionary bishop; he became bishop of Maastricht (*c.* 649), to which town the bishops of Tongeren, already before Monulphus (558), had moved their residence. From then on Irish, Anglo-Saxon and Frankish missionaries established themselves in newly founded monasteries and devoted themselves to the mission of the north. Between 625 and 730, 21 new monasteries were founded, mostly in the Romanized south. From Maastricht St. LAMBERT (670–705) and, after the translation of the residence, from Liège St. HUBERT (705–727) preached the gospel in Brabant. Christianity did not penetrate Frisia, the region north of the Rhine and the Meuse, before conquest by the Franks between 689 and 719. The isolated efforts of the Anglo-Saxons, St. WILFRID OF YORK (678) and Wicbert (688–689) failed because of the Frisian-Frankish war. However, the Northumbrian St. WILLIBRORD (d. 739) and his companions had started systematic evangelization by 690. Five years later Willibrord was appointed bishop of Utrecht by King Pepin II and was approved and consecrated by Pope Sergius I.

Many Anglo-Saxon missionaries crossed the North Sea, including St. BONIFACE, who became the second bishop of Utrecht (753) before he was murdered by the Frisians at Dokkum on June 5, 754; St. WILLEHAD, who

was later bishop of Bremen; Liudger; and St. LEBUINUS. These men were supported in their efforts by the then-dwindling Frankish royal power and were aided by monks already in the region. By *c.* 800 the Low Countries were fully Christianized. Utrecht became the most important diocese and, like Liège, was a suffragan of the Archdiocese of Cologne. To the north and the east, parts of the newly won territories were brought under the supervision of the Dioceses of Münster and Osnabrück. The southern regions belonged to the Archdiocese of Reims and to the Dioceses of Noyon-Tournai, Cambrai and Terwaan (Thérouanne).

The 9th Century. During his reign CHARLEMAGNE contributed greatly to the growth of the territorial, juridical and financial independence of the Sees of Utrecht and Liège by extending and reinforcing their rights of immunity. The raids of the Normans (810, 834–837, 880–882) wrought wholesale destruction of churches (Utrecht before 858) and monasteries, including EGMOND and Maastricht. Bishops Hunger (854–866), Odilbold (870–899) and RADBOD (900–917) had to live in exile in Odilienberg near Roermond and in Deventer. Bishop Balderik (918–976) was finally able to rebuild the cathedral, chapter-houses and the monastery in the ruined town of Utrecht.

Bishops Gain Secular Power. By 870 most of the Low Country region had come under the political control of Germany, and from 925 constituted a dependency of the Kingdom of Lotharingia. In conformity with the German (Ottonian-Salic) system, during the 10th and 11th centuries the bishops of Utrecht and Liège found themselves endowed with secular rights and privileges; they were even entrusted with the civil rule of counties. These bishops became princes of the empire, trustworthy defenders of the king's power against disgruntled counts and dukes striving to free themselves from royal control. Thus in Utrecht Bishop Ansfried of Hoey (995–1010) received royal territory and judicial rights; Bishop Adalbold (1010–26) a county in Drente and Teisterbant; and Bishop Bernold (Bernulfus; 1027–54) two more counties,

---

Capital: Amsterdam; the Hague is the seat of government.
Size: 14,140 sq. miles.
Population: 15,892,237 in 2000.
Language: Dutch.
Religions: 5,403,369 Catholics (34%), 476,760 Muslim (3%), 3,973,059 Protestants (25%), 317,844 Jews (2%), 5,721,205 without religious affiliations.
Archdiocese: Utrecht, with suffragans Breda, Haarlem, Roermond, 's-Hertogenbosch, Groningen, and Rotterdam (the last two erected in 1955). The country also contains one Military Ordinariate for military personnel and their families.

THE NETHERLANDS

0   25   50 Miles

0   25   50 Kilometers

East Frisian Islands

West Frisian Islands

Terschelling

Ameland

Schiermonnikoog

Emden

Vlieland

Leeuwarden

Princess Margriet Canal

Groningen

Texel

Waddenzee

Veendam

Den Helder

Dam with locks

Heerenveen

Assen

IJsselmeer

Emmen

Northeast Polder

Hoogereen

Meppen

Alkmaar

Emlichheim

Noordzee-kanaal

Lelystad

Zwolle

Zaanstad

Flevoland Polder

Haarlem

Roalte

Rheine

Amsterdam

IJssel

Enschede

Leiden

Apeldoorn

The Hague

Amersfoort

Delft

Utrecht

Hengelo

Amsterdam-Rijnkanaal

Nederrijn

Arnhem

Winterswijk

Rotterdam

Lek

Waal

Nijmegen

Borken

Dordrecht

Maas

's-Hertogenbosch

GERMANY

Oosterschelde

Wilhelminakanaal

Zuid-Willemskanaal

Rhein

Breda

Middelburg

Tilburg

Westerschelde

Eindhoven

Maas

Düsseldorf

Antwerp

Mönchengladbach

Gent

BELGIUM

Schelde

Heerlen

Brussels

Maastricht

Aachen

Liege

FRANCE

North Sea

The Netherlands

demesnes and regalian rights. The secular territories gradually bestowed upon the bishops of Utrecht up to 1054, the so-called ''Sticht,'' together with all pertinent judicial, political and military rights, were transferred as part of a deliberate imperial program designed to create ecclesiastical secular territories that would serve as powerful institutional counterparts in the political balance of the German empire. Liège arrived at the same stage under Bishop NOTKER (972–1008). In return, several monasteries, such as Thorn and Elten, also became political entities, directly subjected to the empire.

Their increasingly political position forced the bishops to resort to military action against rebellious imperial vassals, such as the prefect Balderik or Count Diederik III of Holland. The interweaving of ecclesiastical and secular interests profoundly influenced the spiritual orientation not only of the bishops, but also of the higher clergy, monks, nuns, common people and nobility. Personal relations to God were now affected by the same political, feudal, juridical and hierarchical factors that dominated everyday life.

Gregorian Reform. Utrecht was one of the acknowledged strongholds of the imperialists during the INVESTITURE STRUGGLE which sought to unite the Christian West under the leadership of the pope. Bishop William (1054–76) signed, as the third important man, the act of deposition of Pope GREGORY VII. Bishop Conrad (1076–99) was as closely connected with the old imperial system as were his Liège confrères Henry of Verdun (1075–91) and Otbert (1091–1119). The abbots of St. Paul's Abbey in Utrecht and of Egmond Abbey, who had not been influenced by the spirit of the CLUNIAC REFORM in its implementation by Pope Gregory VII, were firm supporters of the imperial cause. Egmond was not transferred into the possession of the Holy See by the owner of the monastery, Count Diederick VI of Holland, before 1140.

The northern Low Countries were more interested in the moral rather than the political aspects of the GREGORIAN REFORM. Everywhere a strong enthusiasm was in evidence for the newly discovered evangelical ideals of apostolic life (poverty and preaching). Among the chief promoters of this spiritual renewal was St. NORBERT OF XANTEN (c. 1080–1134), founder of the PREMONSTRATENSIANS. The Canons Regular of St. Augustine (at Rolduc from 1112) and the Benedictines also attracted numerous new members. While there had once been only three monasteries in the northern regions, from this period they multiplied rapidly and effected an enthusiasm for the Christian life among the laity. The heretical preaching of the layman TANCHELM (c. 1100) near Antwerp advocated an extreme moral reform, extending to revolt against the clergy, the liturgy, tithes and the administration of Sacraments by unworthy priests.

Only after 1100 did the archbishops of Utrecht begin to move slowly in the Gregorian direction. Godebold (1114–27), the first to leave the imperial party, wholeheartedly approved the Concordat of WORMS (1122). The concordat, as applied to Utrecht, meant that there would be no more foreigners in the see, no more imperial nominations, but instead free election by the five chapters of Utrecht and by the cathedral chapter of Liège of native candidates, such as Andreas of Cuyk (1127–39) and Harbert (1139–50) for Utrecht, and of natives of Namur, Louvain, Jülich, Leien and other towns of the area for Liège. The rise of new powers was manifested in the ardent struggle among the princes of Holland, Guelders and Cleves and the chapters and the municipal communities of Utrecht and Deventer at the election of Herman of Hoorn (1150–56).

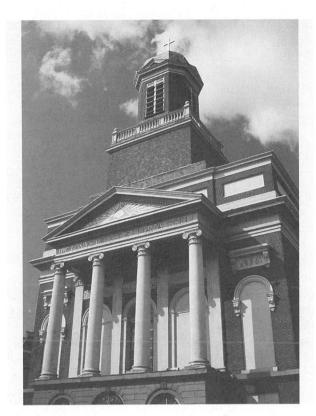

The Roman Catholic Hartebrugkerk Church, built in 1835, Leiden, Zuid, Holland Province, Netherlands. (©Michael John Kielty/CORBIS)

In other respects, however, the period after the Concordat of Worms was not sharply distinguished from the preceding one. The spread of monasteries in the Low Countries continued in a more concentrated form. The Benedictines, for example, founded 17 monasteries between 1122 and 1215. The transition to monasteries with a more severe rule (Canons Regular, Norbertines, Benedictines) indicated an intense interest in monastic life. The 14 CISTERCIAN convents for nuns that were established within 50 years demonstrated the important role of women in this movement. The newly created double MONASTERIES for men and women eventually became independent foundations.

Third Crusade to Western Schism. The religious zeal inspired by the Crusades of the 11th through the 14th centuries led to the birth and spread of new military orders. The Knights of MALTA, the TEUTONIC KNIGHTS and the TEMPLARS founded their own houses in the Low Countries, mostly in the years 1240 to 1260.

In the Low Countries several leading lords, as well as the populace, took an active part in the CRUSADES: Dirk VI of Holland (1139), Floris III of Holland and his son William, and Otto of Guelders were in the army of FREDERICK I, BARBAROSSA (1184). Bishop Otto

(1216–27) and his men, and Count William of Holland, together with the Frisians, fought the Muslims at Damietta (1217). But the crusaders were diverted at times to serve secular purposes, as when the Frisian crusaders were employed to fight the rebellious Stedingers, who did not wish to pay tithes to the archbishop of Bremen (1234). Crusaders were also used to capture (1248) the town of Aachen, site of imperial coronations, for the Roman king, William IV of Holland.

Holy Roman Emperor Frederick Barbarossa again appointed bishops (Geoffrey of Rhenen, 1156–78; Baldwin of Holland, 1178–96) who would support his battles against the pope and against the lay nobles. At the time of the double election in Germany (1198), the bishops of Utrecht and Liège, like their Rhenish colleagues, supported the Guelph candidate opposing the German emperor, until finally FREDERICK II was eliminated as a determining factor in ecclesiastical policy. The electoral chapters, however, were to find the emperor's place taken increasingly by the neighboring territorial princes of Holland and Guelders, and later by the popes during the Avignon period. Many secular considerations, such as conflicting international or territorial political interests, now determined the election, appointment, deposition or translation of bishops.

Synodal records and statutes, nevertheless, reveal a continuing interest in liturgy, discipline, administration of Sacraments, celebration of feasts, ecclesiastical organization and monastic life. Around 1350 there were 100 days that were celebrated as solemnly as Sundays, an anomaly in a world which was steadily becoming urbanized and commercialized. The MENDICANT ORDERS began c. 1230 to come to the new towns in Holland, Brabant and Utrecht, and provided residents with appropriate spiritual care. The rise of the BEGUINES reflected the interplay of religious and social factors (a surplus of women). Among the important spiritual phenomena in this period were the Eucharistic miracle at Amsterdam (1345), the hysterical preoccupation with death by the Flagellants and the Dancers (1347), the observantist movement in the convents and the DEVOTIO MODERNA, which at the end of the 14th century found a promoter of European significance in Gerard GROOTE of Deventer (1340–84) (see BRETHREN OF THE COMMON LIFE; WINDESHEIM; THOMAS À KEMPIS; IMITATION OF CHRIST; SPIRITUALITY OF THE LOW COUNTRIES).

During the Middle Ages the Low Countries produced no theologians or philosophers of world fame, but they did supply many scholars who played important roles at the universities of Paris, Cologne, Louvain and Heidelberg. Included among them were MARSILIUS OF INGHEN (d. 1396), HENRY OF GORKUM (d. 1431) and Heymericus de Campo (d. 1460). Only Wessel GANSFORT (1419–89) acquired international importance; his treatises later won the admiration of Martin Luther.

1378 to 1559. During the WESTERN SCHISM the Low Countries supported URBAN VI and the Roman line of claimants against the Clement VII and the French claims, apart from a short period of neutrality at Liège dictated by Philip of Burgundy. The concordat of Pope Martin V with the German nation (1418) following the schism meant, for the Low Countries, a considerable restriction in papal PROVISION and appointments. The estates of Utrecht, the chapters, the nobility and the citizens of the towns of the Sticht thereafter played a primary role in the election of the bishop of Utrecht, their spiritual and temporal lord.

Political differences were the main cause of the first Utrecht schism (1423–1433–1449), in which the western part of the diocese (Nedersticht) supported the cause of the papal appointee Zweder of Kuilenburg, while the eastern districts (Oversticht) followed their elected candidate Rudolf of Diepholt. The whole conflict was essentially a Burgundian affair, since Duke Philip of Burgundy was pushing into the northern territories. Burgundian influence kept growing stronger through the centralization initiated by the duke. His illegitimate son David received the See of Utrecht (1457–96), and his nephew Louis of Bourbon the See of Liège (1455–82). Eventually nearly all the northern regions came under Philip of Burgundy's control. In the same way Frederick of Baden (1496–1517), a grandnephew of Philip the Fair, Duke of Burgundy, was appointed for Utrecht by his uncle the Roman Emperor Maximilian I, who on this occasion received a papal privilege of free appointment. But the Burgundian-Hapsburg family abandoned Frederick when he compromised himself by negotiating with France, and the see was given to another Burgundian protégé, Philip of Burgundy (1517–24). Henry of Bavaria, the next bishop, was not even consecrated. Unable to resist Burgundian pressure, he surrendered in 1528 to Emperor Charles V the temporal territories and rights held by the See of Utrecht since 1054. This marked the end of the Middle Ages in the Netherlands.

From a religious viewpoint the close of the Middle Ages was occasioned by the progress of the REFORMATION. The evangelical, dogmatic-moral orientation of northern HUMANISM supported by the practical mentality of the Devotio Moderna, the aversion against quibbling scholasticism, and the increasing criticisms of ecclesiastical abuses prepared the way for the new doctrines. The new critical philological method of Erasmian theology manifested itself in a series of vehement attacks on the old scholastic system and met with severe resistance at the University of Louvain. Precisely because of his personalistic humanism, Desiderius ERASMUS of Rotterdam (1469–1536) was not the man to reconcile the doctrinal controversies of his age.

The specifically Dutch form of the new theology was not Lutheranism but Sacramentarianism (Hinne Rode, Cornelis Hoen); but the popular spiritualistic movement of the ANABAPTISTS attracted many of the lower classes. Government repression, however, quelled the revolutionary excesses and forced Anabaptism to cease its involvement in public activity (Quiet Baptists; MENNONITES). It was French CALVINISM that caused the separation of more than half the population from the Church by identifying the cause of reformed religion with the struggle for political independence and for the preservation of national rights against the dominating policy of Spain.

1559 to 1795

The most obvious sign of the centralizing, absolutist Hapsburg policy that would eventually culminate in the unification of the Netherlands under Charles V, was the concordat of 1559, which King PHILIP II OF SPAIN, ruler of the Netherlands, extorted from Pope PAUL IV. Already at the secularization of Utrecht, Charles V had acquired an obvious right of episcopal nomination, and Bishops William of Enckenvoirt and George of Egmond were no longer regarded as significant authorities. True power and jurisdiction rested with the higher clergy and the chapters. Since the spread of Lutheranism was not restrained by imperial edict, a more efficient ecclesiastical organization was needed. By the bull *Super universas* (May 12, 1599) the Holy See created three new ecclesiastical provinces: CAMBRAI (with Arras, Tournai, Namur and St. Omer as suffragans); Mechelen (with Ypres, Ghent, Bruges, Antwerp, Bois-le-Duc and Roermond); and Utrecht (with Haarlem, Deventer, Middelburg, Groningen and Leeuwarden). The nominees of Philip II were far from ideal; the only bishops outstanding for ability and virtue were Nicolas de Castro of Middelburg, Cunerus Petri of Leeuwarden and Wilhelm Lindanus of Roermond.

Origins and Spread of Protestantism. The Netherlands region needed reformation urgently. The number of priests increased considerably in the 15th century. By the end of this century there were about 6,000 secular and 3,000 religious priests with 1,600 parishes and 75 collegiate churches with 1,200 canons; but 25 percent of these priests did not observe the law of celibacy, and most of them had received poor theological training. As a result the parish priests and the regular clergy were unable either to effectively refute the arguments for Lutheranism and Calvinism to hold their flocks together. Young priests

with the training advocated by the Council of Trent were lacking everywhere in the Low Countries because of the absence of seminaries there.

Chapters and magistrates, opposed as they were to the new organization of dioceses, delayed the holding of a council of the Archdiocese of Utrecht until 1565. Prelates and chapters accepted the Tridentine doctrinal decrees, but not until 1568 did they submit to the disciplinary measures that would curtail their jurisdiction. The projected new seminary was not erected.

In this unfavorable situation all plans for Catholic reform came to naught even before the rebellious Calvinist minorities invaded Holland and Gelderland in 1572 and in the name of freedom and of reformed religion cut short all organized Catholic life. Subsequently the Calvinists won by military force the remaining northern provinces in which the reformed religion was sometimes introduced with violence (Martyrs of GORKUM and of Alkmaar). In Utrecht Catholicism was liquidated between 1579 and 1580; with the death of Archbishop Schenck (Aug. 25, 1580) the hierarchy in this ecclesiastical province came to an end. The worthy Bishop Govert van Mierlo of Haarlem (d. 1587) had to flee from the Calvinistic terror in May of 1578 and was never able to return to his see. His cathedral chapter continued his work, however, and was an important center of missionary activity as late as 1703. The bishop of Middelburg died in May of 1573; the bishop of Groningen, in October of 1576 and the bishop of Deventer died in May of 1577. Cunerus Petri of Leeuwarden was banished in April of 1578. Philip II nominated others in their places, but these nominees did not receive papal confirmation and were therefore of no importance in the regions where Calvinists were preponderant. Brabant and Limburg did not belong to the rebellious Calvinistic federation until *c.* 1630. The hierarchy was preserved at Bois-le-Duc until 1632 and at Roermond until 1801. In these two dioceses the Tridentine reforms were introduced with such ease and success that Catholicism has remained strong in these regions to the present time.

Catholic Reform. A solution for the inadequate ecclesiastical organization was found when Sasbout Vosmeer (d. 1614), a secular priest belonging to a patrician family of Delft, was appointed vicar-general for Utrecht (1583) and for Middelburg (1584). In his administration Vosmeer was subject to the newly erected nunciature at Cologne until 1596 and after that, to the nunciature at Brussels. In 1592 Vosmeer became vicar apostolic; he received episcopal consecration in 1602. This appointment indicated clearly that the Holland mission was directly under Roman control. From 1622 until 1908 it was under the Congregation for the Propagation of the Faith. Vosmeer's good example stimulated a handful of young priests to devote themselves under very difficult circumstances to missionary work around Delft. Willem Coopal, vicar of the chapter in Haarlem from 1592, was the soul of the missionary activity in northern Holland. Utrecht and Oldenzaal later became important regional missionary centers. As a result of this missionary endeavor many predominately Catholic villages exist today even in regions that are almost entirely Protestant. However, the great shortage of zealous priests allowed regions such as Drente, Groningen and Friesland to become almost completely Protestant. The regular clergy could fill the need only partially; until 1614, for example, there were only 15 Jesuits in the Dutch mission. The situation changed for the better a few years later. By 1630 there were nearly 100 religious and 300 secular priests at work. The increase was due to the newly founded seminaries at Cologne (1602) and Louvain (1617). Later priests also came from Douai. The Vicars Apostolic Philippus ROVENIUS (1614–51) and Johannes NEERCASSEL (1663–86) distinguished themselves by concentrating all their forces on pastoral activity. Rivalry between regular and secular clergy adversely affected the results.

Restrictions on Catholics. The Netherlands has never been subjected to the imposition of Protestantism by force, nor was the Reformed Church an officially established one (*see* REFORMED CHURCHES). As a religious minority Catholics were excluded from political offices, magistracies and guilds, but judicial officers in nearly every town allowed Catholics to hold religious services in private homes, garrets and barns for a financial consideration. Despite such obstacles, important Catholic artists contributed to the glory of the Dutch golden age: convert and poet Joost van den Vondel, painter Jan Steen, architect Hendrik de Keyser and musician Joannes Stalpaert van der Wielen are only the most famous among a great number. The 17th century was not dominated by a Calvinistic cultural hegemony, but the official repression, the exclusion from social life and from certain forms of trade and industry affected the personal and collective honor and vitality of Catholics more and more. Under the circumstances it is not surprising that Catholicism in the Netherlands declined until it comprised only a third of the population by 1726. Around 1700 the leading merchants, industrialists and intellectuals were Protestants, and the gentry were on the verge of converting to Calvinism (the poverty-stricken and the proletariat had done so from the very beginning). Catholics were to be found in the middle class, among the shopkeepers and artisans. Only in the 18th and 19th centuries did immigration from Westphalia change this pattern. The distilling of gin, the preparation of tobacco and other products, and, later, the manufacture of textiles enabled these Catholic immigrants to acquire enough wealth to position them in the upper classes of Dutch society.

In view of the unfavorable position of Catholicism in the Netherlands, the division in Catholic ranks caused by the Schism of UTRECHT is all the more regrettable. After 1702 the Estates of Holland no longer permitted the presence of a vicar apostolic appointed by Rome. This left Catholics without a legitimate leader. No new bishops were appointed, the Sacrament of Confirmation was not administered, churches were not consecrated and there was only a perfunctory supervision from Brussels by an Italian nuncio acting as vice-superior of the Dutch mission. After the death in 1727 of the vicar apostolic J. van Bijleveldt the only form of ecclesiastical organization was that of nine archpresbyterates: Holland, Zeeland, Friesland, West Friesland, Utrecht, Gelderland, Twent, Salland and Groningen. This organization remained unchanged until 1853.

The Rise of the Modern Church: 1795 to World War I

After Dutch patriots, inspired by the spirit of the French Revolution, turned the Netherlands into the Batavian Republic (1795–1806), the religious situation changed. A decree of the Batavian National Assembly (Aug. 5, 1796) ended the extremely close union of the State with the privileged Reformed Church. In succeeding years the country, once a commercial superpower, would come increasingly under the sway of Napoleonic France, while many of its colonies were lost to Great Britain.

1795 to 1853. The introduction of the principles of the FRENCH REVOLUTION into the Netherlands legally emancipated the suppressed Catholics and gave them the opportunity to become magistrates. In the National Assembly (March of 1796) 25 percent of the members were Catholics. Brabant was admitted to the Batavian Republic, but Limburg and Zeeuws-Vlaanderen were annexed to France. This resulted in the abolition in 1801 of the Diocese of Roermond, the territory of which was divided between Aachen and Liège. The Vicariate Apostolic of Breda was created in 1803. This new freedom profited Catholics. Churches were restored, and new ones could be built. Priests were no longer required to seek government permission in order to function. The construction of seminaries in Breda, Bois-le-Duc, Warmond and 's-Heerenberg (1798–99) made it possible to educate the clergy of the Netherlands on native soil.

King Louis Bonaparte (1806–10), appointed by his brother, the Emperor Napoleon, changed this freedom into a new kind of Gallican servitude by creating a department of cult and by demanding control over such ecclesiastical affairs as the education and payment of the clergy, the administration of churches and the projected reestablishment of the hierarchy. The annexation of the Kingdom of Holland to France (1810–13) was only a brief interlude. During it the Diocese of 's-Hertogenbosch was reestablished, but its bishop could not take possession of his see because of opposition from the local clergy. Breda was annexed to the See of Mechelen. Van Maanen, Goubeau and Van Gobbelschroy, who served as advisers to King William I (1813–39) in a newly independent Holland, learned the ideas of Louis Napoleon and maintained in practice the provisions of the French CONCORDAT OF 1801 and the ORGANIC ARTICLES. P. G. van Ghert, influenced by the philosophy of HEGEL regarding the state, aimed to form a national Church under governmental supervision. To this end he created the college of philosophy at Louvain (1825), where seminarians would imbibe the spirit of FEBRONIANISM before studying theology. These projects caused such a serious conflict that King William I asked for a new concordat (1827). This document abolished the concordat of 1801 for Limburg and established on paper the organization of dioceses. But it was not put into effect fully because Protestants and anticlericals opposed it and because the Catholic clergy disliked any agreement that gave the crown preponderant influence in the nomination of bishops and canons. The northern Netherlands remained a missionary district, the subject of a power struggle among political factions.

King William II (1840–49), who was strongly influenced by Johannes Zwijsen, a priest in Tilburg, favored the Catholic desire to found new monasteries and to start Catholic schools and social care; but he did not succeed in putting the concordat of 1827 into effect. As a result of the secession of Belgium (1830) from the Netherlands the Vicariate Apostolic of Limburg was separated from Liège (1840), Zeeuws-Flanders was annexed to the Vicariate Apostolic of Breda (1841) and the vicars apostolic of Breda, Bois-le-Duc and Roermond received the episcopal dignity (1842). The reestablishment of the Catholic hierarchy had to await the constitution of 1848, which granted freedom of education and of ecclesiastical organization under the country's new parliamentary government.

Catholics cooperated with liberals for the principles of unrestricted political freedom. For a generation the Catholic laity had been stimulated by the publications of J. Le Sage ten Broek, whose periodical *De Godsdienstvriend,* begun in 1818, was influenced by Hugues Félicité de LAMENNAIS in its ultramontane outlook. Also influential were Professors Cornelis Broere and Franciscus van Vree of Warmond, who strove for a Catholic cultural revival by founding *De Katholiek* (1842) and the Catholic daily *De Tijd* (1845). Differences in politico-ecclesiastical thought brought into being two groups of Catholic laymen. A conservative group, Gallican in spirit, centered around the department of cult and favored government influence in ecclesiastical affairs. A second group, composed of younger persons, gathered around *De Tijd* and strove for complete separation of church and state. The latter group received the support of most of the professors at Warmond and of Bishop Zwijsen, the vicar apostolic of Bois-le-Duc.

The conservatives requested the reestablishment of the hierarchy, but the progressives and liberals actually obtained it in 1853 as a logical consequence of the principles of freedom contained in the constitution of 1848. The ideas formulated by Bishop C. A. von Bommel of Liège influenced the papal bull *Ex qua die arcano,* in which Pius IX restored the hierarchical organization of 1559. The Archdiocese of Utrecht was made the metropolitan see. Its archbishop, Johannes Zwijsen, was made administrator of Bois-le-Duc. Suffragan to Utrecht were the Dioceses of Haarlem, Breda and Roermond. The Vicariates of Megen and Grave, erected in 1801 for the Netherlands sections of the suppressed Dioceses of Roermond and Liège, were associated with Bois-le-Duc.

Protestants joined with conservatives who opposed the Liberal premier Jan Thorbecke. Their vehement reaction caused the fall of Thorbecke (1853) and led to the promulgation of an innocuous decree requiring a bishop to ask for official admission before taking up residence in his see.

1853 to World War I. During the last half of the 19th century Dutch Catholics tended to dwell in cultural isolation. A common past as a religious minority, the increasing centralization of ecclesiastical authority in Rome, and Pius IX's teachings in QUANTA CURA and in the SYLLABUS OF ERRORS (1864) promoted among these Catholics an attitude of separation from the world, modeled on the outlook of the French publications *L'Univers* and *La Croix.* Ultramontanism found strong support in the Netherlands. With the exception of Bishop Franciscus van Vree of Haarlem, the hierarchy concerned itself with ecclesiastical administration and pastoral works, and it did not engage in scientific or theological discussions. Original scholarly productions were few. The most important ones were those of Cornelis Broere in theology, W. Nuyens in history, J. A. ALBERDINGK THYM in literature and T. Borret in archeology. Catholics played a more important role in music, architecture and sculpture because of the work of Pierre Cuypers, Louis Royer and the three Strackés.

The Catholic alliance with the Liberals in politics bore good fruit, but it did not endure because of the disinclination of the Liberals to put into effect the results of 1848 and to grant to Catholics complete freedom and government subsidies for Catholic elementary schools (1857, 1878). Hermann Schaepman (1844–1903), priest, poet and politician, was mainly responsible for the conservative direction taken by Catholics. In 1880 he became a member of the second chamber of the Estates-General, and he published *Proeve van een Program* (1883), which provided the basis for the political organization of Catholics in *Rooms Katholieke Staatspartij* (1896). In conjunction with Abraham Kuyper, the Protestant political leader, Schaepman established a Catholic-Protestant coalition to oppose the influences of liberalism. By combining the struggle for widening the suffrage with the school issue at the time when the constitution was revised (1887), Schaepman discovered the road that led to the granting of general suffrage and to the equating of public and private education in the distribution of public funds (1917). In his later years Schaepman followed the directives of Pope Leo XIII concerning social problems and collaboration with non-Catholics. Alfons Ariëns, the pupil of Schaepman, founded the Association of Catholic Laborers (*R. K. Werkliedenvereniging*), which formed the nucleus of the present-day *Katholieke Arbeiders Beweging*. Henri Poels strove after 1910 for the social emancipation of the workers in Limburg.

After Leo XIII's death (1903) there was in the Netherlands, as elsewhere in the Church, a reaction against appeasement, free scientific research and irenic spirituality. The concentration on purely spiritual matters gave rise to a very intense Eucharistic life and interest in the liturgy. At the same time the reaction against MODERNISM promoted INTEGRALISM. The eager vigilance of Integralists, such as M. A. Thompson, a priest who edited the Rotterdam Catholic daily newspaper *De Maasbode* (1897–1912), stigmatized all efforts for parliamentary and social democracy and all ecumenical and irenic colloquies as traitorous collaboration with a libertine world.

The 20th Century and Beyond

Since the revolt of 1830 decided the future of Belgium as an independent state, the United Kingdom of the Netherlands has remained under a constitutional form of government. Neutral during World War I, the country relinquished control over several of its remaining colonies during the first part of the 20th century; in 1954 the islands comprising the Netherlands Antilles were granted full partnership in the Kingdom of the Netherlands, and as late as 1975 Suriname was granted political independence. Like many other nations, in addition to political realignments, the Netherlands also experienced a resurgent interest in Catholicism during the century.

The first decades of the 20th century witnessed a remarkable development of efficient Catholic organizations in the spiritual and secular spheres. Throughout the Netherlands parishes were created and churches built. The foundation of the Catholic University of Nijmegen (1923) and of the Catholic School of Economics in Tilburg (1927) were the most outstanding events in the progress of Catholic higher education. Several monasteries were also built, while Catholic hospitals and other charitable works increased in number. Missionary zeal intensified. The apostolate of Christian culture gained a wide following.

This organized Catholicism drew serious criticisms from younger intellectuals, among them Willem Asselbergs (alias Anton van Duinkerken), who fought as hard against the "heresies" of humanism and vitalism as against Catholic attitudes of self-sufficiency and triumph. The generation after Schaepman was so willing to continue his policy of political alliance with Protestants that a Catholic, Charles Ruys de Beerenbrouck, was prime minister in three cabinets (1918–22, 1922–25, 1929–33). To an increasing degree Catholics also sought closer relations with the country's socialist leaders following World War I, blaming other Catholic politicians for conformism to traditional principles that did not offer any solution for mounting economic and social problems at the national and international levels. The decline of effective democracy led some Catholics to look with favor on Italian Fascism and, to a lesser extent, on German National Socialism, and to form *De Nieuwe Gemeenschap* and *Zwart Front*.

World War II reunited all elements in a common resistance to the German occupation of the country. Johannes de JONG, Archbishop of Utrecht and later cardinal (1945), was recognized universally as the leader in the resistance to the ideology of National Socialism. In 1941 membership in the *National-Socialistische Beweging* was forbidden. It was during the German occupation that Catholics and Protestants began the colloquies that would eventually effect a healthful change in the spiritual climate and promote the ECUMENICAL MOVEMENT. The ideals of political cooperation after World War II tried to break through the bastions of confessional parties and formulate a comprehensive national policy. The Catholic bishops, however, while preferring to retain existing Catholic organizations, also revealed an awareness of the shortcomings of isolationism (*Episcopal Mandate,* 1954).

An ecumenical spirit began to grow within the country during the early 1950s, as Catholics became more active participants in national, political and cultural life. Religious discrimination began to decline. Important historical syntheses by L. J. Rogier destroyed the remnants of the former ghetto mentality and stimulated Dutch Catholicism to a self-conscious thought and action described as "progressive." At Vatican Council II Cardinal Bernardus Alfrink and others gave evidence of the vigor and forward-looking outlook that would be characteristic of Netherlands Catholicism during the second half of the 20th century. However, a synod held in Rome in January of 1980 yielded little progress in improving the internal stability of the Church in the Netherlands.

Moving into the New Millennium. By the 1990s the influence of religion on secular life was continuing its downward trend, the Netherlands' socialist political policies often running counter to Church doctrine. As had been predicted at Vatican Council II, Dutch Catholics were becoming polarized over both religious and social issues. Ministries for women and celibacy among priests were among those Church-related issues that found Catholics on both sides, while other concerns, such as assisted suicide and sexual morality, were debated in the political arena as well as in the Church. In 1995 the Katholiek Politieke Partij (K-P-P) was founded as a means to provide like-minded Catholics with a conservative voice in social policy issues, such as abortion, divorce, drug use, euthanasia, immigration and others. The *Katholiek Niewsblad* (newspaper) was also established to serve Catholic interests.

Within one of the most politically liberal nations in the world, a strong, united Catholic presence remains crucial if Church doctrine is have an effect on Dutch social policies. Such organizations as the Federation of Catholic and Protestant Employers Associations and other trade unions representing Catholic workers have actively lobbied the nation's First and Second Chamber representatives. The 1998 Dutch Bishops' conference ended with a pastoral letter calling on Catholics to lobby the government to stop turning away asylum-seekers from countries such as Iran, citing as "a particular responsibility for churches, politicians, and others" to change existing closed-door immigration policies. In September of 2000 the Dutch parliament's approval of same-sex marriage legislation prompted the Vatican to dub the policy "a insult to reason," a criticism in line with Pope John Paul II's stated objection to such legislation.

The Catholic Presence. In 1650 nearly half the population of the Netherlands was Catholic, but in 1726 that number had dropped to about one-third. According to the 1809 census, 38.1 percent were Catholics, that number holding relatively steady into the 21st century.

Like other parts of Europe, the Netherlands received an influx of Muslims from Morocco, Turkey and Indonesia beginning in the 1960s, resulting in the construction of over 300 mosques throughout the country. In contrast, by 2000 there were 1,683 parishes, 1,664 secular and 2,599 religious priests, 214 major seminarians, 1,712 religious men and 13,216 religious women administering to the Catholic faith.

Catholic elementary and secondary schools, which receive financial support from the government, account for 35 percent of all schools at these levels and enrolled 40 percent of all students. The pontifical Catholic University of Nijmegen and the School of Economics at Tilburg continued with student enrollments in the thousands. The nation's 120 Catholic hospitals had over 25,000 beds, while Catholics presses published over 20 newspapers appearing at least once a week and numerous books and periodicals of a religious, cultural or scientific character.

Bibliography: A. G. WEILER et al., *Geschiedenis van de Kerk in Nederland* (2d ed. Utrecht-Antwerp 1963). R. R. POST, *Kerkelijke verhoudingen vóór de Reformatie van c. 1500 tot c. 1580* (Utrecht 1954); *Kerkgeschiedenis van Nederland in de Middeleeuwen,* 2 v. (Utrecht 1957). S. AXTERS, *Geschiedenis van de vroomheid in de Nederlanden,* 4 v. (Antwerp 1950–60). L. J. ROGIER, *Geschiedenis van het katholicisme in Noord-Nederland,* 3 v. (Amsterdam 1945–47). P. GEYL, *The Revolt of the Netherlands, 1555–1609* (London 1932; 2d ed. New York 1958); *The Netherlands in the 17th Century,* 2 v. (New York 1961–64). L. J. ROGIER and N. DE ROOY, *In vrijheid herboren: Katholiek Nederland, 1853–1953* (The Hague 1953), revised as, L. J. ROGIER, *Katholieke herleving* (2d ed. The Hague 1962). K. S. LATOURETTE, *Christianity in a Revolutionary Age: A History of Christianity in the Nineteenth and Twentieth Centuries,* 5 v. (New York 1958–62) v.1, 2, 4. É. DE MOREAU, *Dictionnaire d'histoire et de géographie ecclésiastiques,* ed. A. BAUDRILLART et al. (Paris 1912–) 7: 519–756. J. A. DE KOK, *Nederland op de breuklijn Rome-Reformatie: Numerieke aspecten van protestantisering en katholieke herleving in de Noordelijke Nederlanden, 1580–1880* (Assen 1964), with summary in Eng. G. BROM, *Dictionnaire de théologie catholique,* ed. A. VACANT et al., 15 v. (Paris 1903–50) 12.1:79–96. S. VAN DER LINDE et al., *Die Religion in Geschichte und Gegenwart,* 7 v. (3d ed. Tübingen 1957–65) 4:1460–71. P. H. WINKELMANN, *Lexikon für Theologie und Kirche* eds., J. HOFER and K. RAHNER, 10 v. (2d, new ed. Freiburg 1957–65) 7:952–955. *Bilan du Monde* 2:676–687. *Annuario Pontificio* has annual data on all dioceses.

[A. G. WEILER/EDS.]

NETHERLANDS REFORMED CHURCH

The Calvinistic Reformed Church in the Netherlands, *Nederlandse Hervormde Kerk* (NHK), came into existence at a general synod convened by King William I in 1816 shortly after the political restoration of the country. The roots of this Church go back, however, to the 16th-century Reformation. Synods between 1571 and 1619 established the doctrinal alignment and discipline of the Reformed Church in Holland. Accordingly the

NHK inherited as its confessional literature the *Confessio Belgica* (1561), the Heidelberg Catechism (1563), and the canons of Dordrecht on predestination (1619). *See* CONFESSIONS OF FAITH, PROTESTANT. At this time the NHK adopted a presbyterian form of ecclesiastical government, with an annual synod to enact legislation. Synodal decrees had to be submitted to the monarch for approval. Greater autonomy was granted in 1852, and all controls were removed in 1876.

Internal troubles, which plagued the NHK from its inception, corresponded to some extent to the current political controversies between liberals and conservatives. Thus, in reaction to the liberal interpretation of the binding force of confessions, a revival movement arose in the 1830s. Under Hendrik de Cock (1801–42) a group of these revivalists separated in 1834 from the NHK and formed the Christian Reformed Church, *Christlijke Gereformeerde Kerk* (CGK). Much more serious was the break that resulted from a long-standing controversy between the "modernist" and "orthodox" parties. The latter group, led by Abraham Kuyper, professed fidelity to the original tenets of the Calvinist reformation and protested the corruption of these beliefs by the "freethinkers." Kuyper founded the Free University of Amsterdam (1880) and formed, with his disciples, the Reformed Mourning Church, *Gereformeerde Kerk* (1886). When many of the CGK joined Kuyper's movement in 1892, the Reformed Churches in the Netherlands, *Gereformeerde Kerke in Nederland* (GKN), originated. Within the NHK, meanwhile, tensions between the "ethical" party under A. J. T. Jonker and the "free-thinking" party of Niemeyer led to further divisions. All efforts to achieve real unity before World War II proved fruitless, but the shared experiences during the Nazi occupation created an *entente* that culminated in a new church order (1951).

In 1965 the NHK had some three million members, about one-third of the country's population. The GKN, with somewhat less than 700,000 followers, represented about seven percent of the inhabitants. The CGK had about 60,000 adherents. All three groups are Calvinist in theology and are organized in the traditional synodal manner. Each congregation elects a consistory composed of elders and deacons, and each local congregation has the right to call a minister to serve it. Synods are of three kinds: (1) synods of various classes, (2) provincial synods, and (3) general or national synods. There are also committees to coordinate the missionary, social, and other activities of the Churches. BARTHIANISM had a great impact, especially in the NHK.

See Also: REFORMED CHURCHES; REFORMED CHURCHES IN NORTH AMERICA.

Bibliography: W. F. DANKBAAR, *Evangelisches Kirchenlexicon: Kirchlich-theologisches Handwörterbuch,* ed. H. BRUNOTTE and O. WEBER 2:1589–96. S. VAN DER LINDE and K. H. MISKOTTE, *Die Religion in Geschichte und Gegenwart,* 7 v. (3d ed. Tübingen 1957–65) 4:1465–67, 1469–71. W. SCHATZ, *Lexikon für Theologie und Kirche,* ed. J. HOFER and K. RAHNER, 10 v. (2d, new ed. Freiburg 1957–65); suppl., *Das ZweiteVatikanische Konzil: Dokumente und kommentare,* ed. H. S. BRECHTER et al., pt. 1 (1966) 7:864. F. THŸSSEN, *ibid.* 2:1149.

[M. B. SCHEPERS]

NETTER, THOMAS

Carmelite theologian, generally known as Thomas Netter of Walden; b. Saffron Walden, Essex, England, *c.* 1370; d. Rouen, France, Nov. 2, 1430. At an early age he entered the CARMELITE order at London where he was ordained in 1396. His subsequent studies at Oxford brought him into contact with Wyclifite teaching, the logic of which at first attracted him. He soon discovered, however, that J. WYCLIF was "an open counterfeiter of Scripture" and devoted much of his energy to refuting Wyclif and eliminating Lollardy. His main work on this subject, *Doctrinale fidei catholicae contra Wiclevistas et Hussitas,* was written *c.* 1421 at the request of Henry V. He was present at the trials of J. Oldcastle and other LOLLARDS and is reputed to have criticized Henry V for not proceeding more vigorously against Lollards; the same issues led him into controversy with Peter PAYNE at Oxford. At the councils of PISA and CONSTANCE he served as a delegate for his order, of which he was elected provincial for England in 1414. In 1419 he was sent by Henry V as envoy to Vladislav, King of Poland; Alexander, Duke of Lithuania; and Michael, Grand Master of the Teutonic Knights. Three years later he attended Henry V on his deathbed and preached the sermon at his funeral. Appointed confessor to the young Henry VI, Netter accompanied the king to France in 1430, and died in Rouen, where he was buried. Though Netter is notorious in English tradition as the hammer of the Lollards, he is remembered among the Carmelites as a distinguished scholar and restorer of the order's discipline.

Bibliography: B. ZIMMERMAN, ed., "Epistolae Waldensis," in *Mon. Hist. Carmelitana* (Lerins 1907) 444–482. J. MERCIER, *Dictionnaire de théologie catholique,* ed. A. VACANT et al., 15 v. (Paris 1903–50; Tables générales 1951–) 15.2:3505–06. D. KNOWLES, *The Religious Orders in England,* 3 v. (Cambridge, Eng. 1948–60) 2:146–148. A. B. EMDEN, *A Biographical Register of the University of Oxford to A.D. 1500,* 3 v. (Oxford 1957–59) 2:1343–44. J. A. ROBSON, *Wyclif and the Oxford Schools* (Cambridge, Eng. 1961).

[D. NICHOLL]

NEUMANN, JOHN NEPOMUCENE, ST.

Bishop; b. Prachatitz, Bohemia, March 28, 1811; d. Philadelphia, Pa., Jan. 5, 1860. He was the son of Philip and Agnes (Lebis) Neumann. He was educated in Budweis, Bohemia, at the gymnasium of the Pious Workers, and entered the diocesan seminary in 1831. Two years later he transferred to the school of theology at the Charles Ferdinand University, Prague, Bohemia. Upon completing his seminary studies in 1835, he was not immediately ordained because the Diocese of Budweis was sufficiently staffed with priests. Having resolved to become a missionary in the U.S., he decided to set out even before ordination. He landed in New York with but one suit of clothes and a dollar; he was accepted into the Diocese of New York and ordained by Bishop John Dubois June 25, 1836. After serving four years in the region of Buffalo, N.Y., Neumann entered the Congregation of the Most Holy Redeemer and took his vows at Baltimore, Md., on Jan. 16, 1842. He was the first Redemptorist to be professed in America. Following appointments as assistant parish priest in Baltimore and pastor of St. Philomena's parish in Pittsburgh, Pa., he was named viceregent, and later vice provincial, of all Redemptorists in the U.S. During his two years in these posts (1847–49), he placed the Redemptorists in the forefront of the parochial school movement. He subsequently served as consultor to the vice provincial and pastor of St. Alphonsus parish, Baltimore.

Neumann was named bishop of Philadelphia by Pius IX, and was consecrated in Baltimore by Abp. Francis Patrick Kenrick on March 28, 1852. During Neumann's episcopacy, over 80 churches were constructed in the diocese. He organized the parochial schools into a diocesan system and increased the number of pupils almost twentyfold within a few years. He established the Forty Hours devotion on a diocesan basis and made yearly visitations that took him into every parish and mission station. Among the teaching orders he introduced into his diocese were the Holy Cross Sisters, the Holy Cross Brothers, the Sisters of Notre Dame de Namur, the Immaculate Heart Sisters, and the Christian Brothers. He founded the Sisters of the Third Order of St. Francis in Philadelphia and the preparatory seminary at Glen Riddle, Pa. The construction of SS. Peter and Paul Cathedral, Philadelphia, was begun by him. Neumann wrote many articles for Catholic newspapers and periodicals but did not always sign his writings. Among his published works were *Kleiner Katechismus* (1846), the larger *Katholischer Katechismus* (1846), and *Biblische Geschichte des Alten und Neuen Testamentes zum Gebrauch der katolischen Schulen* (1849). His heavy burden led Pius IX to give him a coadjutor, Bp. James F. Wood, in 1857.

Neumann, small of stature and humble in manner, possessed organizing ability and a knowledge of six modern languages. Many openly admired his saintliness during his lifetime. After his death, stories of his hidden virtues and of favors obtained through his intercession led the Philadelphia diocesan authorities to examine his life history. This ordinary process was succeeded by the apostolic process in 1897. On Dec. 11, 1921, Benedict XV solemnly declared the heroicity of Neumann's virtues. On Oct. 13, 1963, Neumann became the first American bishop to be beatified.

Bibliography: *The Autobiography of Saint John Neumann*, tr. A. C. RUSH (Boston 1977). T. E. BYERLEY, *Saint John Neumann: Wonder-Worker of Philadelphia: Recent Miracles, 1961–1991* (Philadelphia, 1992). A. R. CALLAGHAN, *The Tridentine Model of the Bishop and His Jurisdictional Authority and Pastoral Concern as Regards the Sacrament of Orders and the Episcopacy of John Nepomucene Neumann* (Rome 1978). M. J. CURLEY, *Venerable John Neumann, CSSR, Fourth Bishop of Philadelphia* (Washington 1952). P. DOUGLAS, *Saint of Philadelphia: The Life of Bishop John Neumann* (Cambridge, Mass. 1977). P. DWAN, *Saint John Neumann* (London 1977). *Funeral Obsequies of Right Reverend John Nepomucene Neumann . . .* (Philadelphia 1860). BROTHER FLAVIUS, *The House on Logan Square; A Story of Blessed John Neumann* (Notre Dame, Ind., 1964). W. FREAN, *Blessed John Neumann, the Helper of the Afflicted* (Ballarat, Australia 1963). J. J. GALVIN, *In Journeyings Often; Blessed John Nepomucene Neumann* (Rome 1963); *Blessed John Neumann, Bishop of Philadelphia* (Baltimore 1964). J. F. HINDMAN, *An Ordinary Saint* (New York 1977). T. LANGAN, *John Neumann: Harvester of Souls* (Huntington, Ind. 1976). M. P. LITKOWSKI, *Friend to All* (Battle Creek, Mich. 1987). J. A. MANTON and F. A. NOVAK, *Venerable Bishop John Nepomucene Neumann* (St. Paul 1960). F. X. MURPHY, *John Nepomucene Neumann, Saint* (South Hackensack, N.J. 1977). R. H. WILSON, *St. John Neumann* (Philadelphia 1977).

[M. J. CURLEY]

NEUMANN, THERESA

Mystic and stigmatic; b. Konnersreuth, Bavaria, April 9, 1898; d. there, Sept. 18, 1962. Her parents were simple country folk, who gave their daughter a thoroughly Christian education. Father Naber, the pastor of Konnersreuth and her spiritual guide, noticed nothing remarkable about her in childhood. In her early years she suffered an illness that left her somewhat irritable and nervous, and she was, moreover, subject to frequent attacks of vertigo. After completing her elementary schooling, she was employed in 1912 as a servant by a neighbor, Max Neumann. On March 10, 1918, a fire broke out on the adjacent farm. This terrified Theresa, but she was capable of taking part in the activity organized by Neumann to keep the flames away from his home. For two hours she handed up pail after pail of water to dampen the buildings. Then a pail suddenly slipped from her hand. She could "do no more." Her legs became numb; in her

Theresa Neumann.

back she felt a pain as if something had pinched her. This condition continued so that she was able to undertake only lighter tasks on the farm. However, in April she was compelled by her employer to resume heavier work. While she was mounting the stairs of a cellar, carrying a sack of potatoes, her legs suddenly gave way and she fell backward, striking her head against a stone ledge. Unfit for strenuous labor, she returned to her mother's home, where she helped with the housework.

Her sufferings, however, did not cease, and at this time her character underwent transformation, and she became melancholy and irritable. Everything seemed to annoy her, and she was frequently provoked to such fits of temper that she became unbearable to her family. In April 1918 she entered the hospital at Waldsassen, but she left after a stay of seven weeks without showing any improvement. On the contrary, her symptoms were noticeably aggravated; her violent spasms became stronger and more frequent. Her sight weakened until May 17, 1919, when she found upon emerging from a severe convulsive attack that she was "blind." About this time Theresa also suffered anaesthesia of the entire left side of her body, and was deaf in her left ear. For three months she was subject to paralytic attacks in her left arm. Toward Christmas 1922 she experienced a violent pain in her throat that made it impossible for her to swallow solid

food. After October 1918, when she became bedridden, her body was often covered with sores and abscesses. In November 1925, she had appendicitis, and a year later, pneumonia. From all these illnesses she was cured without medical help, a circumstance that she and her friends attributed to the miraculous help of God.

Phenomena. The Lent of 1926 marked a new stage in Theresa's life. At that time she began to have "Friday ecstasies" in which she saw in vision the Passion of Christ, with many details not mentioned in the Gospel. This vision did not constitute a continuous spectacle, but was broken down into about 50 separate episodes (stations). The duration of these varied from two to 15 minutes. In the intervals between particular stations she would fall first into a state of "absorption," in which her mind resembled that of an infant and the simplest notions were unintelligible to her. This was regularly followed by a state of "exalted repose," in which Theresa might speak, perhaps using unaccustomed turns of phrase, or she might communicate Christ's counsels and orders to others or announce future events. The Friday ecstasies were associated with the stigmata on her hands and feet and left side.

Interpretation. The cause of the strange phenomena in Theresa's life can be discussed without calling into question the possibility of her sanctity, and there has, in fact, been a long and heated controversy on the subject.

Theresa's marvelous recoveries from her various illnesses could have been miraculous, but the certain judgment that they were seems unwarranted, especially if they are considered in the light of the principles followed by the Congregation of Rites in examining miracles. There is insufficient evidence either that alleged organic illnesses existed or that their cure could not have been effected by natural forces. Regarding her Friday ecstasies, their supernatural character cannot be confidently affirmed according to the rules laid down by Benedict XIV and by mystical authorities such as SS. TERESA OF AVILA and JOHN OF THE CROSS. It is for this reason that a number of ascetical theologians, such as Professor Westermayr, Dom Mager, OSB, Father Bruno, OCD, and others, have vigorously opposed what they called the mysticism of Konnersreuth.

Again, stigmatization carries with it no guarantee of its miraculous origin. It could well have been, it seems, a natural effect of her "ecstatic emotion." The first appearance of her stigmata, their gradual slow evolution, their changing shape, their strict dependence upon the emotion, the manner in which Theresa treated them, etc., all seem to favor this theory. Moreover, an impressive number of modern theologians believe that STIGMATIZATION as such can be explained without a direct miraculous intervention on the part of God. Her visions also are susceptible of a natural psychological explanation, and indeed there are elements in their content that give rise to theological objections to attributing a divine origin to them.

Her prolonged fasting provides a greater difficulty. It is claimed that from September 1927 until her death she took no nourishment. Unfortunately, Theresa's family never allowed the thorough examination of this point that the Catholic hierarchy insistently demanded. The refusal to cooperate with the Church on this decisive point created serious suspicions. The observation of Theresa's fasting by four Franciscan nuns for a two-week period during July 1927 was accomplished in conditions that make it impossible to regard it as a guarantee that Theresa's fast was absolute.

Bibliography: R. BIOT, *L'Énigme des stigmatisés* (Paris 1955). J. DEUTSCH, *Ärzliche Kritik an Konnersreuth: Wunder oder Hysterie?* (Lippstadt 1938). H. HEERMANN, "Um Konnersreuth," *Theologie und Glaube* 24 (1932) 215–228. H. C. GRAEF, *The Case of Therese Neumann* (Westminster, Md. 1951). F. VON LAMA, *Therese Neumann: A Stigmatist of Our Days,* tr. A. P. SCHIMBERG (Milwaukee 1929). P. MANSION, "Thérèse Neumann et autres stigmatisés," *Saint-Luc médical* (1933) 387ff. N. G. MCCLUSKEY, "Darkness and Light over Konnersreuth," *Priest* 10 (1954) 764–774. B. PORAY-MADEYSKI, *Le Cas de la visionnaire stigmatisée Thérèse Neumann* (Paris 1940). F. L. SCHLEYER, *Die Stigmatisation mit den Blutmalen* (Hannover 1950). P. SIWEK, *The Riddle of Konnersreuth,* tr. I. MCCORMICK (Milwaukee 1953); "Why Write Theresa Neumann?" *Priest* 12 (1956) 725–733; "Konnersreuth Again," *ibid.* 13 (1957) 506–511; "Some Mystical Phenomena," *ibid.* 14 (1958) 488–493, 590–598, 664–672; "The Two Stigmatists Padre Pio and Theresa Neumann," *Revue de l'Université d'Ottawa* 28 (1958) 105–129. J. TEODOROWICZ, *Mystical Phenomena in the Life of Theresa Neumann,* tr. R. KRAUS (St. Louis 1940). L. WITT, *Konnersreuth in Lichte der Religion und Wissenschaft* (Waldsassen 1927). F. GERLICH, *Die stigmatisierte Therese Neumann von Konnersreuth,* 2 v. (Munich 1929).

[P. SIWEK]

NEURURER, OTTO, BL.

First priest martyred by the Nazis; b. March 25, 1882, Piller, Oberinntal, Austria; d. May 30, 1940 at Buchenwald concentration camp near Weimar. Otto, the youngest of twelve children of peasants, attended the Vincentian minor seminary and diocesan major seminary in Brixen (Bressanone), South Tyrol. He was ordained priest on June 29, 1907 by Archbishop Altenweisel. His first assignment was in Urdens (Zillertal), then he served in parishes in Fiß (Oberinntal), Kappl (Paznautal), and Innsbruck, among others.

During Neururer's final assignment at SS. Peter and Paul in Götzens, the Nazis occupied Tyrol and subjected the Church to persecution. Neururer was arrested for interfering with a "German marriage" after he advised a girl against marrying a dissolute, divorced man who was a friend of the Tyrolean *Gauleiter,* the highest local Nazi official. He was tortured in Dachau concentration camp, then sent to Buchenwald, where he catechized other inmates, despite severe prohibition. A camp spy reported the priest's actions, and Neururer was hanged by his ankles.

His cremated remains are enshrined under the altar of his parish church at Götzens. In his beatification homily (Nov. 24, 1996), Pope John Paul II praised Neururer for "defending the sanctity of Christian marriage in the most difficult and dangerous circumstances." He is the patron of preachers, marriage, and priestly service.

Feast: May 30.

Bibliography: J. GELMI, *Kirchengeschichte Tirols* (Innsbruck 1986): 198, 257, 260. H. TSCHOL, *Pfarrer Neururer-Priester und Blutzeuge* (Innsbruck 1963); *Otto Neururer* (Innsbruck 1982). *L'Osservatore Romano,* English edition, no. 48 (1996): 1–3.

[K. I. RABENSTEIN]

NEVADA, CATHOLIC CHURCH IN

The formal beginning of Roman Catholicism in the territory that would eventually become the State of Nevada dates back to Aug. 16, 1860, when Archbishop Joseph Sadoc ALEMANY of San Francisco sent the Reverend Hugh GALLAGHER to establish a mission at Carson Valley. There is inconclusive evidence, however, that Franciscan missionary explorers Atanasio Dominguez and Silvestre de Escalante passed through the area in 1776 seeking a new route from Santa Fe, New Mexico to Monterey, California. Another Franciscan, Fray Francisco Garcas, following the Colorado River, is credited with having said the first Mass near what became Laughlin, Nevada, that same year.

The whole region was nominally a part of Mexico, but the Mexican government did little to colonize or govern it because it seemingly had little economic value. During the first decades of the 1800s, American trappers and explorers began to enter the area. The Old Spanish Trail was opened through Las Vegas in the 1830s. In 1848 the Treaty of Guadalupe Hidalgo was signed and Mexico formally ceded to the United States the territory that included what are now the states of California, Nevada and Utah, most of Arizona as well as parts of New Mexico, Colorado and Wyoming.

Thousands of emigrants traveled through the deserts of the Great Basin en route to California, but the first per-

Pope John Paul II (center) celebrating Mass in St. Peter's Basilica at the beatification ceremony in honor of Otto Neururer (on tapestry) and Jakob Gapp, who also died in a Nazi concentration camp.

manent settlements in the Nevada territory date from 1851 when both Mormon Station (Genoa) and Gold Canyon (Dayton) were established. In 1854 Carson County was created in Western Utah Territory. By 1857 the residents of Carson County were petitioning the federal government to allow them to create their own government as Nevada Territory. The Nevada Territory was established in 1861, and three years later in 1864 it was admitted to the Union as the 36th state. Nevada might not have come into existence so soon had it not been for the discovery of silver. The Sierra passes had been explored prior to the Gold Rush, and after 1848 the Humboldt River route, long known to trappers, became a highway for gold seekers journeying to California. Rich silver deposits were discovered during the following decade leading to the famous Comstock bonanza of 1859.

In 1866 the eastern boundary of Nevada was moved one degree of longitude east giving Nevada additional territory from Utah. The final change in the state's territory came in 1867 when land was taken from Arizona Territory and added to Lincoln County in southern Nevada.

Shifting Boundaries. The shifting of political and ecclesiastical boundaries impacted on the development of the Church. The Nevada territory was a part of the diocese of Sonora, Mexico, until 1840 when it was placed under the jurisdiction of the bishop of the Two Californias, GARCIA DIEGO Y MORENO. After occupation by Americans, it became necessary to bring the territory into the diocesan structure of the United States. The territory of Upper California, including Nevada, was placed under the jurisdiction of the newly created diocese of Monterey, California. Three years later, in 1853, Nevada was transferred to the archdiocese of San Francisco when Bishop Joseph Sadoc Alemany became the first prelate of that new archdiocese. During this time the population was sparse and care of souls in this vast territory was of little concern, nor was there any missionary outreach to the native peoples who lived in the area. The discovery of the valuable mineral deposits brought about a dramatic change to the territory in general and to the Church.

In 1858, given the increase in numbers of people, Archbishop Alemany sent the brothers Joseph and Hugh Gallagher, the first priests assigned to Carson County. Father Joseph Gallagher (1821–87) began service in Genoa, Carson City and Virginia City in 1858 but probably traveled from Bodie, California. His brother Hugh (1815–87), later settled in the territory and built churches in the town of Genoa in 1860, in Carson City, and in Virginia City, the last directly on the Comstock Lode, center of Nevada's mining riches.

In 1860 when the Vicariate Apostolic of Marysville, California, was created it included Carson County. All the territory from the Pacific Ocean to the Western Boundary of Utah and north of the 39th degree of latitude was assigned to the new Vicariate Apostolic under the jurisdiction of Right Rev. Eugene O'Connell who was consecrated bishop Feb. 3, 1861. All the territory in Nevada south of the 39th degree of latitude was left in the archdiocese of San Francisco. At this time the population of Nevada was centered mostly around the area of Carson County. The division of the territory of the State of Nevada between two ecclesiastical jurisdictions was to continue for 70 years.

In 1862 Bishop O'Connell sent newly ordained Patrick MANOGUE, a former miner, to serve the Church in Nevada. From the time of his arrival at the end of June 1862 until 1884 when he became the bishop of Grass Valley, Patrick Manogue was the driving force of the growth of the Catholic Church in Northern Nevada. His parish was all of the Nevada territory north of the 39th parallel, and St. Mary's in the Mountains in Virginia City became the center of Catholic life in Western Nevada. The parish church that Manogue built in 1877 continues in use.

With substantial support from Mr. and Mrs. John Mackay, Comstock mine-owners, in 1864 Manogue constructed a school and orphanage. The Daughters of Charity led by Sister Frederica McGrath came from San Francisco to staff these institutions. In 1875, again with financial support from the Mackay family and the Miners Union, he began construction of a hospital. The Daughters of Charity operated the hospital until 1897 when it was sold to Storey County and the sisters left.

Alone at first, and later with the aid of assistants, Manogue was responsible for ministering to the Catholics in the far-flung mining camps and ranches. Little by little new parishes were cut off from the parish of St. Mary's in the Mountains. Divide and Gold Hill were established in 1863; Austin, 1864; Carson, 1865; Reno, 1871; Eureka, 1872; and so on through the years. Manogue was made coadjutor bishop of the Diocese of Grass Valley, California in 1881 but he spent a great deal of time in Virginia City until he succeeded to the see in 1884. With the erection of the Diocese of Sacramento (1886), eight counties of the state of Nevada were included in the California diocese.

The rise and fall of the mining camps shaped the early formation of the Church in Nevada. The coming of the railroads helped to stabilize some portions of the population. Among the early immigrants who came into the state were Italians and Basque peoples from the Pyrenees Mountains. Many Italians first came to Northern Nevada to work for the railroad but soon began to purchase land and focus on truck farming and ranching. Nevada's geography lent itself to sheep herding. The Basque people were first brought to Nevada as shepherds, a trade for which they were noted. These two groups along with the Irish who originally came to the mines made up the bulk of the early Catholic population of northern Nevada.

The southern portion of the state developed more slowly. The territory below the 39th parallel remained under the jurisdiction of the Archdiocese of San Francisco until 1887 when it was detached and ceded to the Vicariate of Salt Lake. Father Lawrence SCANLAN whom Archbishop Alemany had sent to establish a parish in Pioche in 1870 was appointed the first Vicar Apostolic of Utah and Nevada. At the time that Salt Lake City became a diocese in 1891, the ecclesiastical jurisdictions of Nevada were again reorganized. It was more practical to divide the state along a north-south line rather than the previous east-west line. The eastern and southern counties of Elko, Lander, Eureka, White Pine, Nye, Lincoln and eventually, Clark, were attached to Salt Lake. The western counties of Washoe, Humboldt, Storey, Ormsby, Douglas, Churchill, Lyon, Mineral, Esmeralda and later, Pershing were assigned to Sacramento.

By 1871 the little town of Reno located along the banks of the Truckee River had grown sufficiently to support a parish that became the center for the Washoe County Missions. St. Mary's parish included much of northern Nevada up to the Oregon border and parts of eastern California as well. In 1879 a group of Dominican nuns from Delaware opened Mt. St. Mary's Academy for young ladies. It flourished for 10 years, but by the turn of the nineties as the mines began to fail it fell on hard times. Two of the sisters stayed on in Reno and as their number grew they opened a small hospital. In 1912 on the advice of Bishop Thomas Grace, they affiliated with the Congregation of the Most Holy Name of Jesus in San Rafael, California. The coming of the sisters from California was a milestone in hospital care in Reno. St. Mary's Hospital received full accreditation in 1922, and in 1930 a more modern facility was built.

Meanwhile in 1904 the Southern Pacific Railroad moved their shops and divisional headquarters from Wadsworth to a site four miles east of Reno. A new town came into being almost overnight, and the parish of the Immaculate Conception was founded.

An Eventful Year. In 1931 two events occurred that were to shape the future of the Church in the state of Nevada, the one directly and the other indirectly. On March 27, 1931, the Holy See detached all the territory within the State of Nevada from the dioceses of Sacramento and Salt Lake and created the diocese of Reno. It was the first time the Catholics of the state of Nevada were contained in one ecclesiastical jurisdiction. Rev. Thomas K. Gorman, a priest of the diocese of Los Angeles, was installed as the first Bishop of Reno on Aug. 19, 1931. The creation of the diocese was occasioned almost by chance. Chicago's Cardinal George Mundelein during a train ride through Nevada en route to San Francisco asked who served as bishop of this vast expanse. He was astonished to learn that of all the 48 states, Nevada was the only one without its own bishop. Upon his return to the archdiocese of Chicago, Cardinal Mundelein took steps to rectify the situation.

From the time of Bishop Patrick Manogue to the formation of the diocese of Reno, the part of Nevada belonging to the diocese of Sacramento had been governed by Bishop Thomas Grace from 1896 to 1921; by Bishop Patrick Keane from 1922 to 1928; and by Bishop Robert Armstrong from 1929 to 1931. The portion of Nevada within the jurisdiction of Salt Lake had, since the death of Bishop Scanlan in 1915, been governed by Bishop Joseph Glass, 1915 to 1926, and by Bishop John MITTY from 1926 to 1931.

Las Vegas. Even as Bishop Gorman began to structure the new Diocese of Reno, another event occurred that would radically change Nevada. In 1931 the Nevada legislature legalized gambling, and the first casino opened on Fremont Street in Las Vegas.

The history of Las Vegas was much like that of other dusty, desert towns in Nevada. Because it had an artesian well, however, it was a regular stop for travelers. Sometime between 1830 and 1848, Vegas ("meadows") as shown on the maps was changed to Las Vegas. Mormon settlers had come to the area in 1855, but they abandoned the valley in 1858. By 1890 railroad developers had decided that this water rich valley would be a prime location for a railroad stop facility and town. By 1904 a tent city had sprung up to support the construction of the first railroad grade into Las Vegas. In 1905 the San Pedro, Los Angeles and Salt Lake Railroad made its inaugural run from California to points east. That same year the Union Pacific auctioned off 1,200 lots in a single day in an area that today is known as Glitter Gulch: Fremont Street in Las Vegas. In 1908 Bishop Scanlan of Salt Lake established St. Joan of Arc Parish, the lone Catholic parish in Las Vegas for the next 34 years.

The Las Vegas economy was only slightly effected by the Depression. The construction of Hoover Dam, begun in 1930, gave rise to Boulder City and the parish of St. Andrew (1931). The development of the Union Pacific Railroad and legal gambling ensured a fairly steady stream of income. With World War II the federal government found sites in Nevada attractive for military and other uses. Nellis Air Force Base expanded, and a major titanium plant was built in Henderson. The well-known Area 51, the secret flight testing base, was in mid-Nevada as was Mercury Test Site, used for atomic weapons. Casinos, though often small and simple, were to be found in every city, town and hamlet throughout the state, but it was after World War II that the state began its amazing development.

When Bishop Gorman was transferred to the diocese of Dallas-Fort Worth as coadjutor bishop in 1952, his successor was Robert J. Dwyer, the rector of the Cathedral of the Madeleine in Salt Lake City. Nevada was experiencing great growth particularly in the Las Vegas area, and Bishop Dwyer continued the task of providing parishes and schools. He convened the first Diocesan Synod in 1957. In an effort to support the missions, newly developing parishes, and to build schools, he developed the *Frontier of the Faith* newsletter and traveled extensively throughout the country to raise funds. He invited sisters from Ireland, Cuba and the Philippines who joined with American religious to staff the schools.

At the time Bishop Dwyer arrived in Nevada the total population was about 160,000 including about 25,000 Catholics. By 1960 the population of the state had risen to slightly more than 285,000, and the Catholic population more than doubled. Much of the growth occurred in southern Nevada and was indicative of a trend that continued to the end of the century.

Bishop Dwyer was appointed Archbishop of Portland, Oregon, in December, 1966, and Bishop Joseph Green, auxiliary bishop in Lansing, Michigan, became the third Bishop of Reno. Installed in May of 1967, Bishop Green's main task was the implementation of the reforms of Vatican Council II. He instituted the Catholic Services Appeal to provide support for the necessary diocesan programs that served parishes statewide. He also traveled extensively to encourage vocations to the service of the Church in Nevada and fostered a spirit of ecumenism toward other religious groups. Even as the population boomed, Bishop Green maintained a steady focus on renovating and upgrading existing parishes and the development of the Church as envisioned by the Fathers of Vatican II. A series of illnesses, aggravated by a severe financial crisis, caused Bishop Green to retire in 1974.

Bishop Norman F. McFarland, auxiliary in San Francisco, who first came to Nevada as Apostolic Administrator in 1974 was appointed Bishop of the Diocese of Reno in February, 1976. With the collegial assistance of the American hierarchy, McFarland managed to put the diocese on a firm financial footing. The same year he was appointed bishop of the diocese, McFarland petitioned and Pope Paul VI agreed to redesignate it as the Diocese of Reno-Las Vegas with Guardian Angel Shrine in Las Vegas as the co-cathedral. In the midst of the financial crisis, the growth of the diocese continued unabated.

In August 1987 Bishop Daniel F. Walsh, auxiliary of San Francisco, succeeded McFarland who had been named bishop of Orange, California. His installation was celebrated at Guardian Angel Cathedral in Las Vegas where he would also establish a Chancery Office and a residence in order to be more available to the needs of the Church in southern Nevada where 58 percent of the Catholic population now lived. Las Vegas had become a major destination city for people from all around the world. The thousands of visitors to the mega-resorts, entertainment and convention centers required the services of the Church. Bishop Walsh put an increased focus on ministry to the Hispanic population in the state.

The need to minister to the Catholic community scattered across 110,800 square miles of desert and the travel between Reno and Las Vegas, almost 500 miles apart, taxed the health and stamina of Bishop Walsh as it had Bishop Green. It became increasingly clear that this could not continue. By 1995, the population of Nevada had risen to nearly 1.5 million people with nearly 450,000 Catholics. Recognizing the situation, the Holy See announced on March 21, 1995, the division of the Diocese of Reno-Las Vegas into two separate dioceses. The Diocese of Reno was to consist of 12 northern counties with 25 parishes and 11 missions. The newly created Diocese of Las Vegas was to consist of five southern counties with 23 parishes and eight missions. Bishop Phillip F. Straling of San Bernardino, California was appointed sixth Bishop of Reno and Bishop Daniel F. Walsh was appointed first Bishop of Las Vegas.

In May 2000, Bishop Daniel Walsh was installed as Bishop of Santa Rosa, California. Monsignor Joseph A. Pepe, a priest of the Archdiocese of Philadelphia serving in Santa Fe, was appointed the second Bishop of Las Vegas. He was installed at Guardian Angel Cathedral on May 31, 2001.

The story of the Church in Nevada in the 20th century comprises a history of growth. Despite their small numbers in a heavily unchurched state, Catholics were visible and successful in a variety of political, economic and community endeavors. They held elective offices on both the state and national levels and were very active in every aspect of the civic life. At the beginning of the 21st century the Church's charitable outreach is without equal in the state. In small communities across Nevada the faith is lived out much as it has been for many years, but in the larger cities there is an urgent need to assimilate newcomers made more difficult by the shortage of priests. Being without priests is not a new experience in Nevada. In the formative days of the Church small communities were visited by a priest on an infrequent basis. It is the laity, assisted by a small cadre of zealous clergy and religious, who will be responsible for keeping the faith strong in the years ahead as was so often the case in Nevada history.

Bibliography: T. K. GORMAN, *Seventy-Five Years of Catholic Life in Nevada* (Reno 1935). E. M. MACK and B. W. SAWYER, *Here Is Nevada* (Sparks, Nev. 1965). *Inventory of the Church Archives of Nevada; Roman Catholic Church.* Historical Records Survey, Division of Professional and Service Projects; Work Projects Administration. The Historical Records Survey, Reno, NV, 1939. K. M. FRANKS, ed., *Strength of Our Roots, Faith and Our Vision, 1850–2000* (Dominican Sisters of San Rafael 2000).

[M. CUNNINGHAM]

NEVIN, JOHN WILLIAMSON

American Protestant theologian; b. Upper Strasburg, Pa., Feb. 20, 1803; d. Lancaster, Pa., June 6, 1886. He graduated from Union College, Schenectady, N.Y. (1821), and entered Princeton Theological Seminary, N.J., where he studied under Archibald Alexander and Charles Hodge. Through Hodge he became interested in the works of August Neander and began the study of German. In 1830 Nevin became professor of biblical literature at Western Theological Seminary, Pittsburgh, Pa., where he was noted as an extreme abolitionist. Differences with the administration led to his resignation in 1840 to accept a professorship at the German Reformed Seminary, Mercersburg, Pa. Nevin's historical studies and sympathy for the German tradition, as well as his Old School background, made him a champion of the doctrine and liturgy of the Heidelburg Catechism against the "new measures" of revivalists. In 1844 he published *The Anxious Bench*, the first appeal of the Mercersburg theology, which emphasized the heritage of the Reformed Church from Catholicism. The following year he and Philip Schaff were codefendants before the Synod of Pennsylvania on charges of Puseyism. In 1846 Nevin published his best-known book, *The Mystical Presence*, an attempt to restore the traditional Reformed understanding of the Lord's Supper against prevailing Zwinglian views. His important works on *The History and Genius of the Heidelburg Catechism* and on *The Church* followed in 1847. With Schaff he founded in 1849 the *Mercersburg Review*, which became the chief organ of their movement. Nevin established a tradition of doctrinal loyalty, liturgical renewal, and ecumenism; but the Mercersburg movement was never wholly accepted by his church. In 1861 he left the seminary to become a professor at Franklin and Marshall College, Lancaster, Pa.; he served as its president from 1866 to 1876.

Bibliography: T. APPEL, *The Life and Work of John Williamson Nevin* (Philadelphia 1889). J. H. NICHOLS, *Romanticism in American Theology* (Chicago 1961). D. DUNN, *A History of the Evangelical and Reformed Church* (Philadelphia 1961).

[R. K. MACMASTER]

NEW ABBEY (SWEETHEART)

Former Cistercian abbey, situated seven miles south of Dumfries, Scotland, in the Diocese of Galloway. It was founded April 10, 1273, by Dervorgilla, the widow of John de Balliol, and dedicated to St. Mary, and was the last CISTERCIAN abbey to be built in Scotland until 1946. The monks called it Sweetheart (or *Dulce Cor*) because the foundress, a grandniece of two Scottish kings and the mother of another (John Balliol 1292–96), had her husband's heart embalmed after his death and kept in her presence; and this, following her own death in 1289, was buried with her in the new abbey she had founded. The abbey was colonized from DUNDRENNAN, and like its nearby motherhouse, suffered badly in the Anglo-Scottish wars of independence (1296–1306). After the disaster of Flodden in 1513, the monks placed themselves and their property under the protection of Lord Maxwell, which action undoubtedly saved the buildings from destruction by the reformers in 1559–60. Its last abbot, Gilbert Broun, was forced into exile when the abbey with its revenues was annexed to the crown in 1587, but he returned twice to defend the old religion, was finally arrested, and died in exile in 1612. In 1624 the abbey was erected into a temporal lordship for Robert Spottiswoode, who styled himself Lord New Abbey. It is now a ruin.

Bibliography: J. M. CANIVEZ, ed., *Statuta capitulorum generalium ordinis cisterciensis ab anno 1116 ad annum 1786,* 8 v. (Louvain 1933–41) 3:91, 201; 6:690. J. S. RICHARDSON, *The Abbey of Sweetheart* (2d ed. Edinburgh 1951). S. CRUDEN, *Scottish Abbeys* (Edinburgh 1960) 73–74.

[L. MACFARLANE]

NEW AGE MOVEMENT

The New Age (NA) Movement is a variegated cultural phenomenon. In its broadest sense, the term refers to a configuration of Eastern and Western esoteric psychologies, philosophies, and religious traditions that have been brought into convergence with new paradigms in science and modern psychology. The New Age Movement has links with the Eastern and Western occult and mystical/metaphysical traditions. In the United States, the movement is the inheritor of the Aquarian "new religious consciousness" of the 1960s and 1970s.

New Age cultural referents include health food stores, parapsychology research organizations, psychic

The remains of Sweetheart Abbey, Dumfries and Galloway. (©Polypix; Eye Ubiquitous/CORBIS)

development groups; interest in REINCARNATION, AS-TROLOGY, WITCHCRAFT, tarot cards, the I Ching, out-of-body experience, channeling, and in the "healing powers" of crystals and pyramids; "transformational" techniques ranging from MEDITATION to martial arts; alternative or "holistic" medicine, body therapies, and a melange of other "consciousness raising" techniques.

While there is no hard-line NA gospel *per se,* nor unanimity of NA beliefs, the conviction that humanity is on the threshold of a radical spiritual transformation is a central motif. New Age thinking also embraces eclectic and syncretistic healing strategies and spiritual disciplines, reasserts various forms of supernaturalism and sacramentalism, and promotes the full realization of human potential. Themes of "transformation," "consciousness raising," "self-realization," "higher self," the "god within," and "global unity" are standard NA parlance. New Age thinking also animates elements of

the contemporary environmental movement, notably in relation to ECO-FEMINISM and creation theology.

Growth of the Movement. The spread of NA thinking in modern society has been propagated through movement literature and through a multitude of seminars and training programs focused on human potential and self improvement. Various teachers, empowerment practitioners, and assorted SHAMANS have facilitated such programs. These include cultural celebrities as diverse as Baba Ram Dass (Richard Alpert), a former professor of psychology at Harvard; the actress Shirley MacLaine; and David Spangler, formerly a co-director of a Scottish community at Findhorn and author of *Revelation, The Birth of a New Age* (1976). New Age perspectives have also been popularized by Marilyn Ferguson's book, *The Aquarian Conspiracy: Personal and Social Transformation in the 1980s,* an impassioned discussion of the need to create a new society based on a "turnabout in con-

New Age visionary dressed as a Native American spirit, Mount Shasta, California, 1994. (©Catherine Karnow/CORBIS)

sciousness'' and a vastly enlarged concept of human potential.

Cultural historians have emphasized the continuity between current NA ideas and earlier American interest in metaphysical, occult, and non-Western spiritual traditions (viz., TRANSCENDENTALISM, SPIRITUALISM, THEOSOPHY, NEW THOUGHT). They have also pointed to NA affinities with the long-standing American utopian tradition and the quintessential American dream of transcending one's background by reinventing one's self.

Social and behavioral science perspectives link the appeal of the NA to the cultural crisis of post-1950s America. From this perspective, the NA is a cultural response to the weakening of structures and institutions that integrate society. The contradictions of late capitalism's commodity culture and the spiritual poverty of the technocratic state, characterized by massive bureaucracy, depersonalization, aesthetic sterility, and the dominance of instrumental rationality compounded this crisis. Other factors facilitating the spread of NA thinking include the decline of mainline religions, the expansion of comparative religion courses, the increase in Asian immigration, and mass marketing techniques by NA spiritual entrepreneurs. The high media visibility of Hollywood celebrities promoting NA concepts and theories also contributed to the cultural visibility of the movement.

During the last four decades, a large part of the recruiting ground for religious and spiritual experiment has been among the relatively privileged and social elites. In this context, the spread of the NA Movement is attributable, in part, to structural characteristics of demographic and generational shifts associated with an emerging cohort of ''baby boomers'' whose affluence and greater discretionary time have freed them for diverse spiritual and cultural pursuits.

Criticism of the Movement. Criticism of NA therapies and philosophies comes from two main sources: left-leaning cultural critics and academics and conservative Christians. Cultural critics and academics censure the movement for its assault on the heritage of the ENLIGHTENMENT and for sowing doubt about the trustworthiness of rational thought. Accordingly, NA devotees promote alchemist-like spirituality, superstition, pseudoscience, incipient totalitarianism, a dangerous ahistoricism, and, in some cases, outright fraud.

Cultural critics also asserted that exotic NA interests such as crystal gazing and ''harmonic convergence'' are contrived, artificial phenomena that actually point to the triviality of spiritual matters in modern society. From a psychological perspective, some NA devotees manifest narcissistic and obsessive self-fixation traits that mirror the powerlessness, alienation, and atomistic individualism endemic in society. New Age ''higher consciousness'' is, therefore, little more than a misguided initiative to rescue the modern American ''minimal self.'' In addition, NA practitioners have been accused of mimicking liberalism's idioms of globalism, cooperation, and tolerance. However, because some currents in the movement reject or minimize reformist political struggle, they implicitly promote apolitical escapism and reinforce the status quo.

The most aggressive assault on NA thinking comes from fundamentalist and conservative Christians who link NA spiritual effervescence with exotic ''cults,'' with secular HUMANISM, and with the emergence of a ''false'' and ''one world'' religion. ''Bible believing'' Christians denounce NA apologists for distorting and/or rejecting the Bible's message of sin and salvation, for promoting the ''occult'' and ''demonic,'' and for contaminating the Christian tradition with false spiritual ideas. The New Age Movement is construed as the shadow of the anti-Christ and another cultural barometer of the apostate age.

More moderate Christian critics point to the latent GNOSTICISM in much NA thought and to the movement's promotion of magic-like ritualization and its co-option of traditional religious symbolism. These critics have also reproached the NA Movement for failing to address the reality of evil (or for viewing social and structural oppression as merely a state of mind), for failing to link "self-realization" with moral guidance, and for extolling forms of self-exploration that too readily degenerate into self-promotion. In addition, both secular and religious critics criticize certain NA currents for amoralism, for the degradation and blatant commercialization of piety, and for the tendency to reduce religion to psychology.

The spread of New Age thinking has also been interpreted in more positive ways. First, the phenomenon shows that people do not respond to new social and cultural problems by abandoning religion as much as by developing new religious innovations and orientations on the ruins of the old. What is "new" about much NA thinking is not the content, *per se*, but the unexpected spread of such ideas in the face of assumptions regarding the alleged inexorable triumph of secularization.

Second, the NA Movement points to the continuing problem of the bifurcation of religious and scientific orientations that has long afflicted Western civilization. In response to this situation, people often compartmentalize their meaning systems. The privatization of religion is one aspect of this; the idolatry of technique another. New Age thinking with its call for "holistic" and "integrated" living is both symptomatic of this cultural problem and a creative and contemporary response to it.

Third, while the spread of NA theories and practices can be seen as an indictment of organized religion's failure to respond in creative and dynamic ways to new cultural trends, the movement has also stimulated a renewed interest in mysticism, meditation, and spiritual renewal within the Christian tradition. New Age ideals have also converged with a new stress on eclectic approaches to spirituality in many mainline churches.

The most positive aspects of NA ideals are those that encourage consensus decision making, integrated living, the emphasis on freedom for positive growth, creative action, and the call for human solidarity. Certain NA motifs are also highly relevant to aspects of the emerging ecological ethos and for the need for a new cosmology relevant to environmental concerns.

In its overall composition and visibility, the NA Movement gives expression to the dynamic and ongoing realignment of religion and culture. In reference to the Christian tradition, the NA Movement provides another opportunity for both spiritual revitalization within the tradition and for a new and creative discernment of the vibrant relationship between the Gospel and culture.

Bibliography: J. A. SALIBA, *Christian Responses to the New Age Movement* (London 1999). F. M. BORDEWICH, "Colorado's Thriving Cults," *The New York Times Magazine* (May 1, 1988): 37–44. W. D. DINGES, "Aquarian Spirituality: The New Age Movement in America," *The Catholic World* (May/June 1989): 137–142. M. FERGUSON, *The Aquarian Conspiracy: Personal and Social Transformation in the 1980s* (Los Angeles 1980). C. LASCH, *The Minimal Self; Psychic Survival in Troubled Times* (New York 1984). J. R. LEWIS and J. G. MELTON, *Perspectives on the New Age* (Albany 1992). T. PETERS, *The Cosmic Self* (San Francisco 1991).

[W. D. DINGES]

NEW AMERICAN BIBLE

The origins of the *New American Bible* (NAB), which was first published in 1970, began with what was previously called the Confraternity Version.

Confraternity Revisions Catholics were becoming increasingly aware of the need of revising the Douay-Rheims-Challoner Bible. There were discrepancies in its numerous editions introduced by private typographers and publishers; there were instances of lack of identification of the ecclesiastical authority approving the editions. The need of revision was intensified by the Confraternity of Christian Doctrine's (CCD) promotion of Bible instructions and study clubs throughout the U.S. Accordingly on Jan. 18, 1936, the chairman of the Bishops Committee of the CCD, Edwin V. O'Hara, proposed to Biblical scholars meeting at the Sulpician Seminary in Washington a revision of the Douay-Rheims-Challoner Bible. The meeting resulted in a twofold decision: to undertake the revision of the Catholic English Bible in use and to form an association of Catholic Biblical scholars that would promote scientific and popular Scripture studies and publications. The Bishops' Committee of the CCD offered its patronage to the association and its work. Oct. 3, 1936, was the founding date.

New Testament. At this time the principles of revision for the NT were drawn up. It was agreed to adhere to the Latin Clementine Vulgate and to render its sense exactly and in clear and simple English. Recourse to the Greek was made for the sense of the Latin but not for deviation from the VULGATE. Variants between Latin and Greek were treated in footnotes. Diction, style, and rhythm of the current text were retained as far as possible; mistakes were corrected; obsolete words modernized; and words introduced for sense were italicized. "Thee" and "thou" were retained; first words of sentences, rather than of verses, were capitalized; long and involved sentences were broken up without detriment to sense. The text was arranged in paragraph form; chapter and verse numbers were indicated in the margin. Cross-references were placed between the text and footnotes; poetic passages were printed in verse form. Divisions, subdivisions, and boxed paragraph headings enhanced the format and readability of the text. The names of the revisers and editors appeared on the final page.

The NT revision was completed in 1941. It was published by the St. Anthony Guild Press of Paterson, N.J. The Holy Name Society undertook the task of distribution. More than one million copies were sold in the first year. Though the work had been planned as a revision, the amount of independent translation was such that it was aptly regarded as a new translation.

Old Testament. The revision of the OT Vulgate presented its own special problems. Not all the books were translated by St. Jerome from the original languages into a uniform Latin version. The Psalter of the Vulgate is Jerome's revision of the Old Latin version from the LXX. Sirach, Baruch, Wisdom, and 1 and 2 Maccabees are from the revised Old Latin. The principles governing the revision of the OT [see *Catholic Biblical Quarterly* 1 (1939) 267–269] followed those for the revision of the NT as far as they could be applied. Proper names translated by St. Jerome were restored.

Sample portions of the OT revision were printed, not published; e.g., the minor Prophets and the first 40 Psalms. Though the OT revision was well under way by 1944, the project was abruptly terminated in favor of a complete change of plan, as explained in the following section.

Confraternity Version. A response of the PONTIFICAL BIBLICAL COMMISSION (Aug. 22, 1943) favored translation of the Bible from the original into modern languages [*Acta Apostolicae Sedis* 35 (1943) 270]. The encyclical of Pius XII *DIVINO AFFLANTE SPIRITU* (1943) urged the study of Oriental languages and literatures and recourse to the original texts. These directives caused the committees for the OT and NT translations to choose the original texts of Hebrew, Aramaic, and Greek as the basis of an entirely new translation called the Confraternity Version (CV). The Bishops' Committee of the CCD was in agreement with this. Edward Arbez, SS, notified the Catholic hierarchy of the change in a letter dated April 22, 1944.

Old Testament. The new principles of translation of the OT [see *Catholic Biblical Quarterly* 6 (1944) 363–364] prescribed the use of the Kittel-Kahle edition of the Hebrew and Aramaic texts for translating the protocanonical books and the Swete edition of the OT in Greek for the deuterocanonical books except for the parts of Sirach that have been preserved in Hebrew. Textual corrections were made on the basis of the ancient versions. Conjectural emendations were kept to the minimum. St. Anthony Guild was the publisher. The final board of editors consisted of Louis F. Hartman, CSSR,

Msgr. Patrick W. Skehan, and Stephen J. Hartdegen, OFM, all members of the Catholic Biblical Association. These were authorized to pass final judgment on all the OT books. In harmony with the ecumenical spirit of VATICAN COUNCIL II, some outstanding non-Catholic scholars were engaged to edit 1 and 2 Samuel (F. M. Cross) and 2 Kings (J. A. Sanders) and to revise Genesis (D. N. Freedman). In the interest of uniform Bible usage, the completed OT adopted the Hebrew name forms instead of the Vulgate forms previously used.

New Testament. The CV NT, translated from the original Greek, was entrusted to a separate committee headed by Msgr. Myles M. Bourke, assisted by R. E. BROWN, SS; D. Stanley, SJ; J. A. Fitzmyer, SJ; R. Kugelman, CP; T. Halton; E. F. Siegman, CPPS; B. Vawter, CM, J. Quinn, and the Protestant scholars W. D. Davies and John Knox. The first portions appeared in the form of scriptural readings in the Roman Missal. The OT translation principles also guided the NT translation as far as applicable. The same applied to its external form. Confronted with the variety of style of the various books, the translators strove to reflect this variety and to render the text faithfully, even in its informal, conversational, and derogatory nuances. Before publication of the entire NT, the work was submitted to the critical examination and judgment of a literary editor.

The final volume of the CV OT appeared in 1969. The following year saw the completion of the NT, translated by a separate group of scholars. After some revision of the OT, both were published together in 1970 under the name *New American Bible* (NAB).

The New American Bible Revised. A project to revise the *New American Bible* began with the New Testament books. In 1978 a five-member steering committee chaired by Rev. F. T. Gignac, SJ, undertook to formulate principles to guide the revision, assembled collaborators, and subsequently served as the editorial board. About a dozen translators submitted initial drafts of revised translations together with introductions, notes, and cross references. The editorial board devoted six years to a careful review of this material to insure consistency and accuracy, in dialogue with the translators, other consultants, and an episcopal committee chaired by the Most Rev. John F. Whealon. The revised NT was approved both for publication and for liturgical use in 1986 and was issued early in 1987 by several publishers.

In reality, this thorough revision constitutes a new translation. The introductions, notes, and cross references are almost all new, and are much more extensive and consistent than in the first edition. The original threefold purpose of the NAB (liturgical use, private reading, and study) was maintained, but special attention was given to its suitability for public proclamation. The revision is more literal than the first edition, reflecting an approach to translation that tends more to formal equivalence. The language is more traditional, seeking a dignified level of speech appropriate to liturgical usage, though without archaisms. The editors were concerned to maintain lexical consistency wherever appropriate, thus responding to a frequent criticism of the 1970 version, especially in regard to parallel passages in the Synoptic Gospels.

The revised NAB NT takes a moderate approach to the contemporary concern about discriminatory language. Care was exercised to avoid expressions in English that could be taken as tendentious or offensive to any minority. The editors tried to render gender-inclusive expressions by similar terms in English to the extent that this could be done without violation of other principles.

In 1986 a project was initiated within the Catholic Biblical Association of America to produce a translation of the psalter more suitable for liturgical use. The revision committee finished the project in 1991. After some changes recommended by the episcopal committee, the translation was approved by the Administrative Conference of the National Conference of Catholic Bishops (NCCB) in September 1991 and was approved for liturgical use by the full body of the NCCB at the November 1991 meeting. In May 1992, the lectionary which included the revised psalter was approved and sent to Rome, where its approval was confirmed by the Congregation for Divine Worship. But the confirmation was revoked by the same congregation in June 1994 because of concerns over inclusive language.

In 1990 the Catholic Biblical Association of America passed a resolution to produce a revision of the rest of the Old Testament of the *New American Bible*. The reasons for this were the length of time since the Confraternity version was originally completed (1952–69), the fact that the notes were very sparse in the Old Testament sections and often in need of complete rewriting, the list of inaccuracies noted in the Old Testament translation, the discovery of new Hebrew texts for many of the individual Old Testament books, and a concern for the integrity of the version in view of the revised New Testament translation and the recent revision of the psalter. It was noted that the *New American Bible* represents a significantly different version from other translations such as the New *Revised Standard Version* (which remained rooted in the tradition ultimately of the King James Version). As a fresh translation from the original languages into contemporary English, it represents a cross between formal and dynamic equivalency. And as the only American Old Testament translation done exclusively under Catholic auspices, it allows the Catholic Church in the United

States to have a translation of its own. The project was formally approved by the Administrative Conference of the NCCB in 1993.

Bibliography: J. BARR, "After Five Years: A Retrospect on Two Major Translations of the Bible," *Heythrop Journal* 15 (1974) 381–405. W. HARRELSON, "The New American Bible," *Duke Divinity School Review* 44 (1979) 124–136; repr. L. R. BAILEY, *The Word of God: A Guide to English Versions of the Bible* (Atlanta 1982). S. KUBO and W. F. SPECHT, *So Many Versions?* (rev. ed. Grand Rapids 1983) 213–221.

[S. J. HARTDEGEN/C. J. PEIFER/F. T. GIGNAC]

NEW APOSTOLIC CHURCH

Created in 1863 as the result of a schism within the CATHOLIC APOSTOLIC CHURCH. About four-fifths of its members lived in Germany, but there were also members in England, Canada, Switzerland, Holland, France, Australia, South Africa, the U. S., and South America.

Some members of the Catholic Apostolic Church in North Germany began to be concerned about the survival of the church when six of its 12 apostles had died by 1860. They rallied around Heinrich Geyer, who believed that the deceased apostles should be replaced by new ones; when he began to choose such successors, he was excommunicated by the parent body. The dissenters organized the Universal Christian Apostolic Mission whose name was changed to the New Apostolic Church in 1906. The leading role in the new sect was soon filled by F. W. Schwartz, who supplanted Geyer as head of the organization in 1878. Influenced by the CALVINISM of the Dutch Reformed Church, Schwartz reversed the Catholic tendencies of the original Catholic Apostolic Church. His successor, Fritz Krebs, appointed himself chief apostle (*Stamm-apostel*) and reduced the authority of the other apostles. He chose his own successor, Hermann Niehaus, who served as chief apostle for 25 years after Kreb's death in 1905. The sect sent missionaries throughout the world and reported 300,000 members by 1932. The number of apostles was increased beyond 12 so that there would be one apostle for each administrative area. J. G. Bischoff became chief apostle after the death of Niehaus, and despite some schisms, the New Apostolic Church almost doubled its membership during his administration. He died in 1960 and immediately after his death 27 apostles elected Walter Schmidt chief apostle.

The New Apostolic local congregations are tightly organized through a hierarchy headed by the chief apostle. In addition there are apostles, bishops, district elders, and local pastors and evangelists. As in Mormonism, the New Apostolic Church allows the reception of baptism, communion, and sealing by proxy for the dead. Only an apostle can confer the sacrament of "sealing," which is known also as the baptism of fire. Those who are sealed can share in the first resurrection and participate in the rule by Christ during the millennium. Worship services in the New Apostolic Church are austere and resemble the Calvinist order of worship. Almost all traces of the Catholic liturgical emphasis of the parent body have disappeared. The church is adventist, authoritarian, and aggressively mission-minded. A schism by 11 apostles in 1956 claimed 50,000 adherents. These dissenters reject baptism for the dead and have tried to restore a more Catholic liturgy. There are several smaller dissenting groups, such as the Apostolate of Jesus Christ and the Dutch *Apostolisch Genootschap*.

Bibliography: K. ALGERMISSEN, *Christian Sects,* tr. J. R. FOSTER (New York 1962) 25–34.

[W. J. WHALEN/EDS.]

NEW HAMPSHIRE, CATHOLIC CHURCH IN

One of the Thirteen Colonies, New Hampshire was admitted to the Union (1788) as the ninth state. It is bounded on the north by Canada, on the east by Maine and the Atlantic Ocean, on the south by Massachusetts, and on the west by the Connecticut River and Vermont. Concord is the state capital; and Manchester, the largest city, is the episcopal seat of the only diocese in the state. In 2001 there were 477,997 Catholics, about 27 percent of the state's population of 1.2 million. Manchester is a suffragan see of the Archdiocese of Boston.

Early History. Originally a dissenting offshoot of the Massachusetts Bay colony, New Hampshire became a separate royal colony in 1680 and in the aftermath of the Revolutionary War established itself as a sovereign state, always retaining its Protestant bent. Under the revised constitution of 1784, the state imposed a religious test that excluded Catholics from the major offices in the state government. The constitution also authorized towns to support "public Protestant teachers of piety, religion, and morality" (art. 6).

Abenaki natives, converted by Jesuit missionaries from Quebec, were the first Catholics of New Hampshire. The first Catholic Masses in New Hampshire were celebrated in July 1694 by a pair of French Jesuit priests who had accompanied a war party that raided an European settlement at Oyster River near Durham. During the colonial wars they were forced back into Maine and eventually into Canada. Beginning with the last decade of the 18th century, missionaries, including Francis A. Matignon and Jean A. Cheverus, stopped in New Hampshire, particular-

ly at Portsmouth, on their way to and from Maine, a far more promising mission field. When Boston became a diocese (1808), Bishop Cheverus was given jurisdiction over all New England, including about 100 Catholics in New Hampshire. In 1816 Virgil BARBER, an Episcopalian minister from Claremont, NH, entered the Catholic Church with his wife and five children. Later he became a Jesuit, was ordained in 1822, and founded a church and an academy at Claremont, the first Catholic institutions in the state. Financial and family problems forced his removal in 1827, causing the abandonment of about 100 converts, who for the most part lapsed from the faith.

The first parish was founded at Dover in 1828 by Rev. Charles French; two years later Michael Healy was established as resident pastor. Also serving the area were itinerant missionaries, such as John B. Daly, OFM, who spent 19 years there. By 1835 there were 387 Catholics, two churches, and two priests in New Hampshire. The number of Catholics in the state remained negligible until the influx of Irish settlers in the wake of the famines of the mid-1840s. Their presence was resented; in 1855 Gov. Ralph Metcalf, elected by the Know-Nothing (nativist) party, made a vigorous anti-Catholic speech to the legislature. But the agitation died down quickly, and the Know-Nothings quietly disappeared as the newly founded Republican party solidified its ranks for the election of 1860. In 1877 constitutional changes abolished substantially all the religious qualifications for public office.

In 1853 Maine and New Hampshire were separated from the Boston diocese to form the new Diocese of Portland. At the time the only three parishes in New Hampshire were at Dover, Claremont, and Manchester. By 1858 increased immigration led William McDonald, pastor of St. Anne's, Manchester, to invite the Sisters of Mercy to open the first Catholic grammar school. From 1863 to 1869 the municipal school board took complete financial responsibility for this institution. After the Civil War, French-Canadian immigration predominated, resulting in the creation in 1871 of the first national parishes—St. Augustin at Manchester and St. Aloysius of Gonzaga at Nashua. In 1884 New Hampshire was split off from the Diocese of Portland, ME, and Manchester became the seat of the new diocese.

Manchester Diocese. After Manchester became a separate diocese in 1884, the Most Reverend Denis M. BRADLEY who, though Irish-born had grown up in Manchester, was named the first bishop (1884–1903). Bradley increased the number of churches, chapels, mission stations, and parish schools. The Catholic population swelled from 45,000 to over 100,000, the clergy from 40 to 107, and the children in Catholic schools from 3,000 to 12,000. Bradley's successor, John B. Delany, served only 21 months before succumbing to appendicitis. He was followed by George A. Guertin (1907–32), a native of Nashua of French-Canadian descent.

Bishop Guertin, who stressed the building of parochial schools, had to contend with the nationalistic controversies of the 1920s. A segment of the French-Canadian clergy and faithful opposed certain policies of the bishop as being contrary to their "national" rights and interests, which led to deep divisions among the clergy. Bishop Guertin, because of his heritage and his position as bishop, found himself squarely in the middle of the controversy. Elsewhere in the state, Polish congregations where experiencing similar types of conflict that led to the establishment of the Polish National Catholic Church. The stress of these controversies, plus a nine-month strike at the Amoskeag Mills, the major employer in Manchester, and the onset of the Depression led to Guertin's retirement to a sanitarium in New Jersey in 1931. He died a few months later at the age of 62, and was succeeded by John B. PETERSON (1932–44), who had been an auxiliary bishop in Boston. The fourth bishop of Manchester proved himself a skilled administrator by guiding the diocese through the Depression and maintaining harmony in the diocese by establishing a balance between English-speaking and non-English-speaking clergy and administrators.

The Catholic Church in New Hampshire experienced considerable growth in the years immediately following World War II. Bishop Matthew F. BRADY (1944–59) established 30 new parishes, built 17 churches, and added 11 elementary schools, 14 convents, five high schools, three homes for the aged, and two large summer camps for children. Early in 1959 the newly elected Pope John XXIII called for an ecumenical council. Bishop Brady, who was suffering from heart problems, did not live to participate. He died on Sept. 20, 1959 and on December 2, Bishop Ernest Primeau was named as his successor.

Bishop Primeau (1960–74) was known in Rome from his time as rector of the residence for Chicago priests working the curia. During the preparatory period (1960–62), he was a member of the Commission for the Discipline of the Clergy and Faithful. Later in Rome, Bishop Primeau played an active role in the Council itself, serving as a U.S. representative on the International Committee of Bishops and in the Secretariat for Promoting Christian Unity. Back in New Hampshire, Bishop Primeau took steps to implement the directives of the Council. He began by convoking a diocesan synod. The first general session opened on Nov. 3, 1965 at Immaculata High School in Manchester, and three years later, the synodal acts were promulgated after a Mass at

LaSalette Shrine, near Enfield, New Hampshire. (©Phil Schermeister/CORBIS)

the Cathedral on June 3, 1968. On the administrative side, the diocese consolidated all of its departments into a new administration building, which was dedicated on Aug. 9, 1964.

Bishop Primeau resigned in January 1974 (died June 15, 1989) and was succeeded the following year by Bishop Odore Gendron (1975–90). Gendron was a native of Manchester and served as pastor of a number of prominent ethnic French parishes. It was during this period that a shift began in the state's Catholic population. As the state's ethnic population assimilated, loyalty to the ethnic churches decreased. This led to the decline of ethnic parishes in the cities. At the same time, population growth in the southern part of the state, which is less than one hour from Boston, resulted in new parishes being established in southern suburban locations.

In the world that followed the Second Vatican Council, changes in the Catholic Church and new opportunities for women in the secular world led to a significant decrease in the number of women religious in the state. In the decade that followed, the loss of these women, many of whom staffed the state's Catholic schools, led to the consolidation and closure of many schools throughout New Hampshire.

By 1990, when Bishop Gendron retired and was replaced by Bishop Leo E. O'Neil, the situation was exacerbated by the declining number of priests available to serve as pastors. Bishop O'Neil began a system of "twinning," whereby two small parishes share the same pastor. Bishop O'Neil also sought to invigorate older parishes by assigning new immigrant groups to them as a home parish. Two examples are St. Louis Gonzaga Church in Nashua, which had been predominantly French, and St. Anne Church in Manchester, which was Irish. Both churches are now home parishes for Hispanic and Vietnamese Catholics. Other recent immigrant groups include Portuguese, Sudanese, Bosnian and Croatian.

Upon his death in 1998, Bishop O'Neil was succeeded by Bishop John B. McCormack. McCormack was born and raised in Massachusetts and served both as a pastor and administrator for the Archdiocese of Boston before coming to New Hampshire. Bishop McCormack continues to oversee the consolidation of older parishes in the cities and the construction of new ones in the suburbs. For example, in 2000 four parishes in Berlin, NH, an industrial city in the northern part of the state, were combined to create one new parish. At the same time suburban communities in the southeastern part of the state have found themselves in the position of building larger churches or establishing new parishes.

Education. Catholic institutions of higher learning in New Hampshire include St. Anselm's College, founded (1887) in Manchester by the Benedictines, Notre Dame College in Manchester (sponsored by the Sisters of the Holy Cross), and Rivier College in Nashua (sponsored by the Sisters of the Presentation of Mary).

Bibliography: R. H. LORD et al., *History of the Archdiocese of Boston . . . 1604–1943*, 3 v. (New York 1944). M. ST. L. KEGRESSE, *A History of Catholic Education in New Hampshire* (Doctoral diss. unpub. Boston U. 1955). R. B. DISHMAN and D. C. KNAPP, *A New Constitution for New Hampshire* (Durham, NH 1956). J. D. SQUIRES, *Granite State of the United States*, 4 v. (New York 1956); *New Hampshire Revised Statutes Annotated, 1955* (Rochester, NY 1955); *West's New Hampshire Digest, 1760 to Date* (Boston 1951–).

[F. L. BRODERICK/W. H. PARADIS/C. S. STAUB]

NEW HAVEN THEOLOGY

Also known as Taylorism, refers to the 19th-century New England theological system that originated with Nathaniel William TAYLOR, professor at Yale Divinity School, New Haven, Conn. (1822–58). An exposition of Puritan theology, it was the most influential and controversial since that of Jonathan EDWARDS. Using rational philosophy, Taylor devised a system that dealt with human responsibility and featured freedom of the will. Taylor, called "the Pelagianist" by some Calvinists, taught that there is a native sinlessness in man, an ability in him to renovate his own soul, and self-love, or the desire for happiness, is the source of all voluntary action. Although he considered himself to be in the Edwards tradition, Taylor's views represented a serious departure from strict Puritan Calvinism (*see* GREAT AWAKENING). His teaching that man's acts are not necessitated, but free, because man may act "in a contrary way at all times," was interpreted by many as a denial of Calvinism's cardinal tenet on the absolute sovereignty of God. Moreover, his belief that man may be motivated to a conversion of life seemed contrary to the Calvinist doctrine on "Divine Benevolence." When resistance to these ideas mounted, a fellow Congregationalist, Bennett Tyler, led the opposition, founding a new divinity school in Hartford, Conn., to teach "traditional Puritanism."

In addition, Presbyterian opposition was strong and even more consequential. Charles Hodge of Princeton Divinity School wrote vehement attacks against "the novelties of New England Theology"; those who agreed with him became known as the "Old School" within Presbyterianism. Many younger clergymen and revivalists who found Taylor's teachings appealing and useful in their work were referred to as the "New School." The two groups exchanged accusations of heresy; disagreements on other issues arose frequently, especially on the missions where cooperation with the Congregationalists was fostered and a plan of eventual union drawn up. Here the Old School charged that the New School and Congregationalist influences had subverted Presbyterian order and that innovations had crept into their worship. By 1837, when a general assembly was held in Philadelphia, Pa., the controversy had reached its peak. The Old School dissolved completely the plan of union with the Congregationalists and cut off several New York New School synods. When these asked for readmittance and were refused, they formed their own assembly, to which all the New School group affiliated themselves, causing a schism that lasted 32 years. By 1880 Taylor's views were generally rejected by all. However, his insistence that divine governance must be understood in a way that includes man's moral responsibility paved the way for the later transition from rigid Calvinism to "Liberal Orthodoxy" in America.

Bibliography: F. H. FOSTER, *A Genetic History of the New England Theology* (New York 1963). S. E. MEAD, *Nathaniel William Taylor, 1786–1858: A Connecticut Liberal* (Chicago 1942).

[T. HORGAN]

Archdiocese/Diocese	Year Created
Archdiocese of Newark	1937
Diocese of Camden	1937
Diocese of Metuchen	1981
Diocese of Paterson	1937
Diocese of Trenton	1881

NEW JERSEY, CATHOLIC CHURCH IN

A Middle Atlantic state, one of the Thirteen Colonies, admitted to the Union as the third state on Dec. 18, 1787. Bordering on New York, Pennsylvania, Delaware, and the Atlantic Ocean, New Jersey is heavily urbanized and the most densely populated of the states. Newark is the largest city, and Trenton is the capital. The population in 2001 was 7.6 million, of whom 3.4 million, about 44 percent, were Catholic. They are served by the Archdiocese of Newark and its four suffragan sees, Camden, Metuchen, Paterson, and Trenton.

Catholicism in the Colonial Period. After the English assumed control from the Dutch in 1664, New Jersey was divided into West Jersey, a Quaker stronghold, and East Jersey, whose fortunes were tied to New York City. Proprietary government ended in 1702, when the Jerseys were united as a royal colony. In 1738, New Jersey was established as a separate legal entity under Lewis Morris, the first Royal Governor. Its geographic position and large Tory population gave it a leading role in the American Revolution, and it was an important defender of the small states in the Federal Constitutional Convention of 1787.

For much of New Jersey's early history, Catholics were neither numerous nor significant. Catholic immigration was discouraged by legal and social conditions. In 1668, the first general assembly of the Province of East Jersey was held in Elizabeth. William Douglas of Bergen, who had been elected, was refused his seat because, as a Catholic, he was not able to take the required oath.

The first known Catholic resident of West Jersey seems to have been John Tatham, also known as John Gray, a former monk of Douai Abbey in England, who left the monastery (possibly absconding with some funds in the process) and settled first in Pennsylvania and then in the area of Trenton in New Jersey. The inventory of his estate shows that he possessed a number of Catholic books, and items for the celebration of the Eucharist. There is some evidence that he served as Governor of West Jersey for a time.

In 1683, the Catholic King James I appointed an Irish governor of New York, Thomas Dongan, who brought with him a Catholic priest, later to be joined by two more, who occasionally would go to Elizabeth and Woodbridge to administer the sacraments. When James was overthrown, the anti-Catholic sentiment returned.

In 1698, the East Jersey Assembly promised religious tolerance, but not for those of the "Romish" religion. When New Jersey became a Royal Colony in 1702, Queen Anne, writing to her representative, Lord Cornbury, said that he should give liberty to all "except Papists." She went on to express fear of the "dangers which may happen from popish recusants." Under George II, an oath was administered to civil and military officers, which contained anti-Catholic sentiments. In 1758, religious toleration for all "except papists" was again reiterated.

Meanwhile Catholic settlers came to New Jersey in some numbers, especially as the glass and iron industries were developed, and their settlements were tended by Jesuit missionaries working out of St. Joseph's Church in Philadelphia and "riding the circuit" through New Jersey. Theodore Schneider, S.J., cared for the spiritual needs of Catholics in New Jersey, especially in Salem County, where a number of Catholics had settled. He was followed by Ferdinand Steinmeyer, who adopted the English name FARMER. Farmer made twice-yearly trips through New Jersey to visit the communities of Catholics. His mission stations included Ringwood, Basking Ridge, Charlottenburg, Pilesgrove, Cohansey, Long Pond, Mount Hope, and Springfield. Catholics had come to Ringwood in 1764 to work in the mines. Farmer spent a total of 21 years ministering to the scattered Catholics of New Jersey. His registers include Irish, English, German and French names. While New Jersey officially remained anti-Catholic, the ministrations of the Jesuits from Philadelphia, which were frequent enough surely to bring notice, were tolerated, although Farmer did report some instances of anti-Catholic prejudice.

Another known Catholic of the period, Patrick Colvin, who operated a ferry on the Delaware river near Trenton, is said to have supplied some of the boats that George Washington used to ferry his troops from Pennsylvania on Christmas Eve, 1776, when he was on his way to attack the British troops at Trenton. A number of Catholic officers from France who had come to help the cause of the revolution, settled at war's end in Madison.

They were soon joined by other French Catholics who fled the French Revolution. Although these Catholics worshiped in the Presbyterian Church because of the lack of a Catholic Church, they remained staunch Catholics, and their descendants were among the founders of Saint Vincent Martyr Church in Madison.

This anti-Catholic atmosphere continued in New Jersey into the post-colonial period. The state constitution, adopted in 1776, excluded an established church and guaranteed to everyone "the inestimable privilege of worshipping Almighty God in a manner agreeable to the dictates of his own conscience," but it guaranteed only that "no protestant inhabitant . . .be denied the enjoyment of any civil right merely on account of his religious principles"and that "all persons professing a belief in the faith of any protestant sect . . .shall be capable of being elected into any office of profitor trust or being a member of either branch of the legislature." These provisions were not removed until a new constitution was drafted in 1844.

Nineteenth-Century Growth. The ecclesiastical status of New Jersey changed several times in the 19th century. When the Diocese of Baltimore was erected in 1789, the state was included in its jurisdiction, and there is a record of a visit paid to Trenton by Bp. John CARROLL in September 1803. When the Dioceses of Philadelphia and New York were established in 1808, New Jersey was divided between them. Belonging to New York was "the eastern part of the province of New Jersey closest to" it. Attached to Philadelphia was "the western and southern part of the province of New Jersey." Following the recommendation of the Second Provincial Council of Baltimore (1833), the Holy See, on June 18,1834, redefined the boundaries of all the dioceses in the U.S.; New Jersey, however, remained divided between New York and Philadelphia.

The years following the War of 1812 were a time of rapid industrial and commercial development in New Jersey. Catholic immigration, especially from Ireland and Germany, increased with the railroad and canal building that began in the 1830s. By 1814 the number of Catholics in Trenton had increased sufficiently to build a small church, which was dedicated to St. Francis by Michael Egan, first bishop of Philadelphia. In 1820 the Catholic community in Paterson received its first pastor, Rev. Richard Bulger. Newark's first parish, St. John's, was established in 1826, and its church dedicated in 1828.

When NEWARK became a diocese in 1853, encompassing the whole state, James Roosevelt BAYLEY, a former Episcopalian, and nephew of Mother Seton, was named first bishop. At the time, the city of Newark had three churches, the original St. John's; St. Mary's, for the Germans; and the new St. Patrick's. In Trenton there were two: St. John's and St. Francis of Assisi (the original St. Francis) for the Germans. In the entire state there were 30 churches, with at least as many mission stations, all tended by 30 priests.

The rapid growth of the foreign Catholic population caused concern among the mostly Protestant population and gave rise to a new wave of anti-Catholic sentiment. The Know-Nothings were particularly prominent in New Jersey. The trouble culminated in an attack on St. Mary's Catholic Church on Shipman Street in Newark, which was a German ethnic parish. Tension had been building up ever since a fire in the nearby Halsey and Taylor factory, whose workers were mainly Irish and German immigrants, was ignored by the Protestant fire brigades nearby. During an Orangemen parade in September, 1854, an exchange of words and rocks led to a riot that destroyed the church and led to the deaths of two Irishmen "at the hands of persons unknown" according to the coroner's report, but who had certainly been shot by some of the marchers.

Despite opposition, the number of Catholics in New Jersey continued to grow. In July 1881, Pope Leo XIII divided the diocese of Newark. Fourteen counties in central and southern New Jersey were split off to form the diocese of Trenton. The Most Reverend Michael J. O'Farrell of New York was named the first bishop.

Twentieth Century. Immigrants continued to come. Their numbers and place of origin changed the composition of New Jersey Catholicism. Italians came in large numbers at the end of the19th century, and eastern Europeans came in the first quarter of the 20th century. In order to address their religious and cultural needs the bishops created national parishes, notably in urban areas. The national parishes were also a source of tensions when their members felt their customs and practices were not understood or appreciated. Sometimes the tension was a question of authority pitting clergy against the bishop. In a few cases it led to the establishment of independent church bodies as among the Poles in 1987, and the Ruthenians in 1936.

In 1937 the Holy See once again rearranged the ecclesiastical map of the state. The counties of Passaic, Morris, and Sussex were separated from Newark to form the Diocese of Paterson. Bishop Thomas H. McLaughlin, to that point an auxiliary bishop in Newark, was named Paterson's first bishop. The counties of Camden, Atlantic, Cape May, Cumberland, Gloucester and Salem were split from Trenton to form the Diocese of Camden. Most Reverend Bartholomew Eustace of New York was named its first ordinary. Newark was raised to the rank of archdiocese with the new dioceses as its suffragan sees. In 1981 the Holy See again divided the Diocese of Trenton forming the counties of Warren, Hunterdon, Sommerset, and Middlesex into the Diocese of Metuchen with Most Reverend Theodore McCarrick who had been an auxiliary in New York its first bishop. Bishop McCarrick served in Metuchen until 1986 when he was promoted to the archdiocese of Newark.

New Jersey has a goodly number of Eastern Catholics and is the home of two of eparchies of the Eastern Churches. The Eparchy of Passaic, embracing Byzantine-Ruthenian Catholics living in New Jesey and eastern Pennsylvania, was established in 1963. More recently, the Eparchy of Our Lady of Deliverance of Newark for Syrian Catholics was established in 1995.

New Jersey is home to six Catholic institutions of higher learning, the most prominent of which is Seton Hall University, founded in 1856 in Madison as Seton Hall College, and now located in South Orange. It is a diocesan university, staffed by the priests of the Archdiocese of Newark. The major seminary for the Archdiocese of Newark, Immaculate Conception Seminary, serves as Seton Hall's graduate school of theology. The minor seminary, Saint Andrew's, is also part of Seton Hall. Other Catholic colleges in the state include Caldwell College (sponsored by the Sisters of Dominic), St. Peter's College in Jersey City (sponsored by the Jesuits), Georgian Court College in Lakewood (sponsored by the Sisters of Mercy), Felician College (sponsored by the Felician Sisters), and College of St. Elizabeth in Morristown (sponsored by the Sisters of Charity of St. Elizabeth).

Bibliography: J. M. FLYNN, *The Catholic Church in New Jersey* (Morristown, N.J. 1904). W. T. LEAHY, *The Catholic Church of the Diocese of Trenton* (Princeton 1907). C. J. GIGLIO, ed., *Building God's Kingdom. A History of the Diocese of Camden.* (South Orange 1981). R. J. KUPKE, *Living Stones: A History of the Catholic Church in the Diocese of Paterson* (Clifton 1987). J. C. SHENROCK, ed. *Upon the Rock: A New History of the Diocese of Trenton* (Trenton 1993). NEW JERSEY CATHOLIC HISTORICAL COMMISSION, *The Bishops of Newark, 1855–1978* (South Orange 1978).

[J. H. BRADY/A. CURLEY]

NEW JERUSALEM CHURCH

Known also as the New Church or the Swedenborgian Church, organized in London, England, in 1787 by students of the theological writings of Emanuel SWEDENBORG (1688–1772). Swedenborg himself never organized a church or even a group. The first organizer in London was Robert Hindmarsh, a Methodist. Subsequently ministers were ordained and other groups recognized; in 1789 the first general conference of the New Church met in the chapel at Great Eastcheap.

Swedenborgian doctrine was introduced into the U.S. in 1784; the first congregation was organized in Baltimore, Md., in 1792. By 1817 the number of existing societies was sufficient to form a General Convention of the New Jerusalem, which met that year in Philadelphia. A separate body of Swedenborgians was formed in 1890, and in 1897 took the name of the General Church of the New Jerusalem with headquarters in Bryn Athyn, Pennsylvania. This group considers itself more faithful to the ideas of Swedenborg, has its own school system, and in government is similar to the EPISCOPAL CHURCH. The General Convention churches are more liberal in doctrine, more active in ecumenical cooperation, and are congregational in church polity.

A distinctive characteristic of the Swedenborgian churches is their unusual doctrine on God: He is One and is "the Lord and Savior Jesus Christ, in whom is the Father, Son and Holy Spirit" (*Adoramus,* a non-creedal formula used in many churches). This seems to be a Trinity of Person, not of Persons. Other distinctive doctrines are derived from Swedenborg's spiritual writings, although local option determines the selection for any individual congregation. Some consider him the heaven-sent revealer of the true spiritual meaning of Scripture; others look upon him much as Lutherans consider Martin Luther or Roman Catholics regard the Greek Fathers. Swedenborgian doctrines more commonly held include the belief that Sacred Scripture is God's Word, revealing Jesus Christ as the "Divine Human" by faith, in whom humanity is saved; the New Jerusalem is a symbol of a new spiritual era, heralded by Swedenborg's spiritual interpretation of the Word; and humans are free spirits temporarily clothed with a material body; death releases them into the world of God and angels, where they make their final free choice of heaven or hell.

Thus a Swedenborgian is a Christian who finds in the writings of Swedenborg a meaning of life that points the way to growth of mind and spirit, resulting in a life of loving service to others. Membership in a Swedenborgian congregation is by baptism or confirmation, or simply with a letter of transfer from another Christian church. Many Swedenborgians enroll in other local churches where no local Swedenborgian church exists.

Bibliography: M. BLOCK, *The New Church in the New World* (New York 1932). W. WUNSCH, *An Outline of New Church Teaching* (New York 1926). H. KELLER, *My Religion* (New York 1964).

[D. J. BOWMAN/EDS.]

Archdiocese/Diocese	Year Created
Archdiocese of Santa Fe	1875
Diocese of Gallup	1939
Diocese of Las Cruces	1980

NEW MEXICO, CATHOLIC CHURCH IN

New Mexico, located in southwestern United States, was admitted to the Union in 1912. Bordered by Arizona on the west, Colorado on the north, Oklahoma and Texas on the east, and the Mexican states of Chihuahua and Sonora on the south, New Mexico is a "triadic" state — three geographic areas, three cultures, three flags, three congressional districts, three dioceses. The land area of 121,364 square miles (5th largest) is roughly divided into the Great Plains in the east, the Rocky Mountains in the center, and high plateau in the west. The state is bisected by the Rio Grande, known in Spanish times as the Rio Bravo del Norte, which is a major source of irrigation. The state's major cities are Albuquerque (448,607) a major transportation and commercial hub of the Southwest; Las Cruces (74,267) the major city in the southern part of the state; and Santa Fe (62,203) the capital.

In 2001 New Mexico's population numbered 1,935,430 (37th largest) of which is 40.7 percent claimed Hispanic ancestry (highest proportion in the U.S.) and 9.5 percent Native American (highest after Alaska). The Hispanic population ranges from families who have been present in the state for nearly four centuries to recent immigrants. The Native American population includes the Pueblo people, whose historic villages dot the Rio Grande valley, and the Navajos, whose enormous reservation occupies much of northwestern New Mexico into Arizona. The 473,107 Catholics, about 24 percent of the state's population, are served by the Archdiocese of SANTA FE, and the dioceses of Gallup and Las Cruces. The Province of Santa Fe also includes the dioceses of Tucson and Phoenix in Arizona.

New Mexico is a study in contrasts. Acoma Pueblo is the oldest occupied town in the United States, dating perhaps 1,000 years before the English settlement at Jamestown. Santa Fe is the oldest capital city in the country, the Palace of the Governors the oldest public building, and San Miguel in Santa Fe the oldest continuously functioning church in the United States. But in the 20th century New Mexico ushered in the atomic age. The Manhattan Project which developed the first atom bomb was housed at the government laboratories at Los Ala-

mos, and the first bomb was detonated at Trinity Site on the White Sands National Monument near Alamogordo.

The Colonial Period. Early attempts at exploration and evangelization went hand in hand under the Spanish. A Franciscan friar, Marcos de NIZA (c. 1495–1558), assisted by a Moorish survivor of a previous expedition under Cabeza de Vaca, led a small expedition north from Mexico in 1539. The Moor was killed by the inhabitants of Zuni Pueblo, and the friar retreated south. Fueled by the friar's descriptions of Zuni, coupled with legends of the wealthy "seven cities of Cibola," a major expedition was mounted in 1540 under Francisco Vasquez de Coronado. For two years Coronado explored the present American Southwest, wintering twice along the Rio Grande. Although it failed to locate any wealthy cities, Coronado's expedition, wandering from the Grand Canyon to the Kansas plains, added immeasurably to the geographic knowledge of the Southwest.

When Coronado withdrew in 1542, several of the FRANCISCANS stayed behind and established a mission on the Rio Grande. All were eventually killed. Fray Juan de PADILLA (c. 1500–1544), the protomartyr of the United States, was probably killed somewhere in western Kansas. Fray Juan de la Cruz became the first martyr of New Mexico. Over the next half-century New Mexico languished on the back burner of the Spanish colonial empire. Religiously, there were forays into the area by several Franciscans, moved both by a missionary spirit and a sense of the millennial possibilities of the area. In political and geographic minds, the area began to take shape as the frontier against possible southern expansion by the English.

Finally in 1598, a serious colonizing expedition was mounted under Don Juan de Onate. Initially Onate established his capital at a pueblo called Ohkay Owingeh on the east bank of the Rio Grande which he christened San Juan de los Caballeros. Two years later the capital was moved to a new settlement named San Gabriel on the west bank of the Rio Grande at its confluence with the Rio Chama. In 1608 Onate resigned the governorship under pressure, and was replaced by Pedro de Peralta. In 1610 Peralta supervised the establishment of a new capital, La Villa Real de la Santa Fe de San Francisco de Asis, some 30 miles southeast of San Gabriel.

The early Franciscan missionaries were members of the Province of the Holy Gospel in Mexico, and although thinly spread among a growing number of missions, they were, by and large, dedicated, and in some cases talented, missionaries. Nonetheless, the friars were hampered by difficulties of personnel and resources. In addition, the reliance of the friars on presenting Christianity in the terms of a western European cultural milieu often placed them

Shrine at the Sanctuary of Chimayo, New Mexico. (©G. John Renard)

at odds with the neophytes, especially in the areas of language, societal relations, and cosmology.

After the departure of Onate, the friars moved their headquarters from San Gabriel to the more centrally located pueblo of Santo Domingo. In 1616, New Mexico was designated a semi-autonomous Franciscan ''custody'' of the Conversion of Saint Paul. Fray Estevan Perea, the first *custos,* reported 11 missions, 20 friars, and some 10,000 Christianized natives. The needs of the missions were provided for by a triennial supply train from Mexico. Significant among the friars in this period was Fray Alonso de BENAVIDES (*c.* 1580–1636), appointed *custos* in 1623. He arrived in Santa Fe late in 1625 bearing with him the image of the Blessed Virgin Mary, still venerated today in the Santa Fe Cathedral as *La Conquistadora,* Our Lady of Peace, the oldest Marian image in the country. Returning to Spain in 1630, he wrote a ''Memorial'' to the king and the Franciscan minister general, detailing the state of the province and the missions, and asking for the appointment of a bishop for New Mexico.

Isolated at the very edge of the Spanish colonial empire, the early years of the New Mexico colony were neither prosperous nor peaceful. The colony failed to produce much material wealth either for the colonists on the scene, or for the governments in Mexico City and Madrid. In most times the friars were at odds with the governors over the support of the missions and the treatment of the natives. When the friars and the governors were in agreement, it was often at the expense of the native peoples.

On Aug. 10, 1680 the pent-up rage among the Pueblo people, coupled with several years of agricultural failure, erupted in a full-scale revolt, remarkable for its ferocity and for the unity it produced, albeit temporarily, among the Pueblos. Under the leadership of a man named Po-pe, from San Juan Pueblo, the natives mounted a successful coordinated offensive despite language barriers. The missions were desecrated, 21 friars and 400 Spaniards were killed, and the rest took shelter at Santa Fe, which soon came under siege. On August 21, under the watchful eyes of the natives who were content to see them go, the Spaniards abandoned Santa Fe and trekked southward to El Paso, where they remained for the next dozen years.

In 1692, concerned about an unprotected border, and about the bad example the revolt presented to other natives, Spain commissioned Don Diego de Vargas to reconquer the province for Spain. Leading a contingent of friars, soldiers, and colonists north from El Paso de Vargas re-entered Santa Fe on Dec. 16, 1693. The pueblos were, for the most part, peaceably restored to Spanish and Christian hegemony—but with a difference. The cultural and religious sensibilities of the natives were treated with more respect than previously, and gradually a more authentically New Mexican spirituality began to emerge from the convergence of cultures. During the next century this spirituality flowered in several areas. Creating the only truly American form of religious architecture, the New Mexicans constructed churches of adobe and woodwork which seemed to blend in with the landscape. Native *santeros* developed an indigenous religious devotional art, both primitive and highly evocative. Finally, devotional sites, pilgrimages, celebrations, and confraternities, such as *La Fraternidad Piadosa de Nuestro Padre Jesus Nazareno* (better known as the *Penitentes*), evolved which combined aspects of the different cultures present in the province.

For almost the entire colonial period, New Mexico theoretically came under the jurisdiction of the vast Diocese of Durango, founded in 1620, which was for many years the largest diocese in New Spain. But at a distance of 1,500 miles from Durango, Santa Fe only experienced an episcopal visitation a handful of times over the course of two Spanish centuries, notably by Bishop Benito Crespo in 1730. In reality, the Franciscans were in almost exclusive control of the New Mexican church. However, they were not assiduous in developing native vocations in the province, relying instead on missionaries from Spain and Mexico.

Santiago Roybal (1694–1744), ordained a secular priest in Durango around 1730, was the first in a thin line of native New Mexicans, who, at considerable difficulty, left the province to be educated and ordained in Mexico, and then returned to serve as priests in the northern kingdom. Born near present-day San Ildefonso Pueblo, Roybal is presumably the first native of what is now the United States to be ordained a priest. During his priestly ministry he was the bishop's *vicario* in Santa Fe, but also the sole non-Franciscan in the province.

Nineteenth Century. The early 19th century was, in general, a time of decline for church structures in New Mexico. The emergence of independence movements in various areas of Spanish America diverted funds from the missions which were still supported by the Spanish crown. Once Mexico achieved independence from Spain in 1821, New Mexico was theoretically no longer as remote from the national government. But in reality, the struggling newly independent government was even less likely to be generous with remote ecclesiastical outposts, and indeed was seeking money from the Church. In addition, the Mexican Congress ordered the expulsion of all

Spanish citizens from the country with the result that by 1848 there were no friars left in New Mexico. And finally, Mexican Independence was not immediately recognized by the Holy See, resulting in a standoff over appointments to vacant sees. By 1827, there were no bishops in Mexico, resulting in no ordinations.

This combination of a lack of leadership, clergy and money was most painfully felt in New Mexico, at the fringe of the newly independent country. At the beginning of the 19th century, there were subsidized provisions for 22 priests in New Mexico. In the first three decades of the century, the Spanish settlements grew more numerous and more widespread, and the population itself grew in size and diversity as trade routes opened up with Missouri to the northeast. At the same time the bishops in Durango began to secularize the larger Spanish parishes beginning in 1816. But the changes brought by independence were quickly felt, and by 1829 there were only 12 priests in the province, mostly native New Mexicans, caring for a growing population with dwindling resources. As a result of these conditions, many churches fell into disrepair and ruin, and the sacraments were celebrated in the more remote missions less frequently or hardly ever. And in many of these missions the spiritual life of the mission was left to the leadership of lay groups, such as the *Penitentes*. Prominent among the New Mexican priests of this era were Juan Felipe Ortiz in Santa Fe, Jose Manuel Gallegos in Albuquerque, and Antonio Jose Martinez in Taos.

In 1832, Durango received a new bishop, Jose Antonio Laureano de Zubiria. Over the next 20 years, he would make pastoral visits to New Mexico (in 1833, 1845 and 1850). Zubiria appointed Father Ortiz in Santa Fe as his vicar for the area, and authorized Father Martinez in Taos to establish a rudimentary preparatory seminary. Over the next dozen years, a dozen young men who had initially been trained at Taos would return to serve as priests in New Mexico, raising the number of clergy in the province to 17 by 1851.

The Treaty of Guadalupe Hidalgo in 1848, ending the two-year Mexican-American War, brought New Mexico under the aegis of the United States. This change in civil control rather quickly resulted in a change in ecclesiastical government as well. The question of a bishop for New Mexico, which had been bandied about in Mexico City and Madrid for over two centuries, was decisively answered by the American bishops meeting in the Seventh Provincial Council of Baltimore in 1849. In addition to asking for new archdioceses and dioceses, the bishops requested a vicariate to be established for the vast territory between California and the Rocky Mountains recently acquired from Mexico. Pope Pius IX responded on July

19, 1850 by establishing the Vicariate Apostolic of New Mexico with the seat at Santa Fe. A few days later, the pope named Jean Baptiste LAMY (1814–1888), a French diocesan priest working in the Cincinnati Diocese, as titular Bishop of Agathonica and first Vicar Apostolic. A native of Lempdes in the French Puy-de-Dome, Lamy was serving at Covington, Ky. at the time. He was consecrated on Nov. 4, 1850 at Saint Peter in Chains Cathedral in Cincinnati, and, together with Joseph MACHEBEUF, a comrade from France, arrived in Santa Fe on Aug. 10, 1851.

Lamy's new vicariate contained, by his own count, 68,000 Catholics, 8–9,000 Catholic natives, 26 churches, 40 chapels, and 12 native priests. At its height, Lamy's jurisdiction extended to all of New Mexico, Arizona, Colorado and part of Utah. Lamy's first concern was to build up the Church in New Mexico by means of a more numerous and better educated clergy and Catholic schools. Lamy recruited the Sisters of Loretto from Kentucky (1852), the Brothers of the Christian Schools from France (1859), the Sisters of Charity of Cincinnati (1865), the Jesuit Fathers from Naples (1867), as well as numerous secular priests and seminarians from France and elsewhere. This growth was recognized by subsequent institutional development. The vicariate apostolic was erected as the Diocese of Santa Fe in 1853; Arizona and Colorado were erected as separate vicariates apostolic in 1868 with Machebeuf and another French missionary, Jean Baptiste Salpointe as first vicars; and Santa Fe was advanced to a metropolitan archdiocese in 1875.

Lamy's 35 years as bishop in New Mexico were not without difficulties. His struggle with the bishops of Durango over boundaries and jurisdiction went on for two decades. He was disappointed several times in his dealings with the U.S. Bureau of Indian Affairs over education for the natives. And his dealings with the native clergy, particularly Father Martinez of Taos, remain controversial, sometimes resulting in suspension, and, in Martinez' case, excommunication. Lamy saw these priests as poorly educated and lacking in clerical discipline, at times to the point of scandal. On their part, the priests saw his introduction of European clergy, religious, and customs as disdainful of their own indigenous culture and religiosity. The gradual rise of the walls of Lamy's new French Romanesque cathedral (1869–1884) around the existing adobe *parroquia* of Santa Fe was perhaps emblematic of their sense of Lamy's supplanting the native faith.

As leader of the established Catholic faith of the Spanish inhabitants, but at the same time having been deeply steeped in Catholic European culture and thoroughly Americanized during his decade as a missionary in Ohio and Kentucky, Lamy was an important figure in 19th-century New Mexico, helping the area to mature religiously, and to transform its self-understanding from the northern frontier of an old kingdom to a part of the great American West. Lamy was memorialized by Willa Cather in her 1927 novel *Death Comes for the Archbishop*, and by Paul Horgan in his 1975 Pulitzer-prize-winning biography, *Lamy of Santa Fe*.

Twentieth Century. Lamy was followed by a succession of French archbishops: Salpointe (1885–1894), Placide Louis Chapelle (1894–1897), Peter Thomas Bourgade (1899–1908), and Jean Baptiste Pitaval (1909–1918). Salpointe prevailed upon Katherine DREXEL to send her Sisters of the Blessed Sacrament to Santa Fe in 1894 to staff St. Catherine's Indian School. In his retirement he wrote a history of the Church in the Southwest, *Soldiers of the Cross*, often used by later historians. While Bishop of Tucson, Bourgade reintroduced the Franciscans to New Mexico, inviting the brown-robed friars of the Cincinnati Province (not the blue-robed friars of colonial times) to staff the vast Navajo Reservation. When promoted to Santa Fe, Bourgade brought the friars to Pena Blanca in 1900, and gradually from there to many of the ancient pueblos, and other parishes in the state. Bourgade also helped found the Catholic Church Extension Society, and during his episcopate St. Joseph's Hospital was established in Albuquerque.

By 1918, with the outbreak of World War I, the availability of priests from France had ended, and with that in mind, Archbishop Pitaval resigned and suggested to the Holy See that a Franciscan be named to replace him since they would have the best likelihood of securing much-needed priests for the diocese. In 1919 Rome complied with his request and appointed the pastor of Pena Blanca, Albert T. Daeger, O.F.M. (1919–1932) as archbishop. In 1929, after a draught of many years, Archbishop Daeger had the joy of ordaining three New Mexican priests.

Daeger was succeeded by Rudolph A. Gerken (1933–1943), Edwin V. Byrne (1943–1963) and James P. Davis (1964–1974). Gerken had been the first Bishop of Amarillo, Texas; Byrne and Davis had previously served as bishops in Puerto Rico. The Byrne years witnessed the tremendous post-war growth in New Mexico including the establishment of the atomic energy laboratories at Los Alamos. To meet the growth, Catholic colleges developed in Santa Fe and Albuquerque, and numerous new parishes and schools were opened, including 16 in Albuquerque alone. Byrne fostered native vocations by establishing a minor seminary at Santa Fe. Archbishop Byrne was also instrumental in the founding of three religious communities, the Servants of the Holy

Paraclete, who work with troubled priests, the Handmaids of the Precious Blood, a contemplative community, and the Little Brothers of the Good Shepherd, who care for the destitute. Archbishop Davis presided over the implementation of the Second Vatican Council decrees, and in 1967 moved the archdiocesan headquarters from Santa Fe to Albuquerque.

The growth of the Santa Fe metropolitan province is indicative of the religious, geographical, political and demographic developments in the Southwest during the past century. When Santa Fe was made a metropolitan archdiocese in 1875, it had two suffragans, the vicariates apostolic of Colorado and Arizona, which later evolved into the dioceses of Denver (1887) and Tucson (1897). A third suffragan was added in 1914, when the Tucson Diocese was divided and southern New Mexico and the West Texas Panhandle were formed into the Diocese of El Paso. The growth across the Southwest in the early decades of the 20th century was reflected in a series of ecclesial changes that affected the area in 1936–1941. In 1936 Los Angeles, Calif. was raised to a metropolitan see, and Tucson was placed in this new province. In 1939, northern Arizona was detached from Tucson and northeastern New Mexico was detached from Santa Fe, and a new diocese established at Gallup. Finally, in 1941 Denver was made a metropolitan archdiocese and at the same time divided with a new diocese at Pueblo. Thus from 1941 to 1969 Santa Fe had just two suffragans, El Paso and Gallup, and the province included New Mexico, west Texas, and northern Arizona.

In 1969, with territory taken from both Tucson and Gallup, a new diocese was created at Phoenix, Ariz. As a result of this division, Gallup lost most of its Arizona territory with the exception of the Navajo and Hopi Reservations. Since three new dioceses were created in southern California in the same decade, both the new diocese at Phoenix, as well as Tucson, were returned to the Santa Fe Province. Finally, in 1982, southern New Mexico was detached from El Paso, and a new diocese established at Las Cruces. With its territory reduced to the West Texas Panhandle, the El Paso Diocese joined the other Texas sees as part of the San Antonio Province. This marked the first time that El Paso was not ecclesiastically joined to Santa Fe since the late 16th century. Thus the Santa Fe Province today comprises all New Mexico and Arizona, with the four suffragan sees of Gallup, Las Cruces, Phoenix, and Tucson, and a Catholic population of 1.2 million.

In 1974, with the retirement of Archbishop Davis, the archdiocesan vicar general, Robert F. Sanchez, became the tenth Archbishop of Santa Fe. A native of Socorro, he was the first New Mexican to head the archdiocese. Sanchez initiated a number of programs to better preserve the ancient culture of the archdiocese, especially its churches, and to better integrate the Hispanic, Native American, and Anglo cultures present in the state. In 1992-1993, a series of scandals compromised Sanchez' ability to provide leadership for the archdiocese. He resigned in 1993, and was succeeded by the Bishop Michael J. Sheehan of Lubbock, Texas. Sheehan has successfully led the archdiocese through a time of financial and morale crisis.

On the Threshold of the Third Millennium. At the beginning of the third Christian millennium the Santa Fe Archdiocese spanned 15 and part of an additional four counties in northern and eastern New Mexico with 275,955 Catholics in 90 parishes. The Gallup Diocese covered four full and four partial counties in western New Mexico, as well as two full and one partial county in northeastern Arizona with 54,258 Catholics in 58 parishes. The territory of Las Cruces Diocese consists of New Mexico's ten southern counties, with a Catholic population of 127,370 in 45 parishes. The first bishop of Gallup was a Franciscan friar, Bernard T. Espelage, O.F.M. (1939–1969). He has been succeeded by Jerome J. Hastrich (1969–1990), and Donald E. Pelotte, S.S.S. (1990–). Bishop Pelotte, a member of Maine's Abenaki Tribe, is the first Native American bishop in the United States. The Las Cruces Diocese has been served since its inception by Bishop Ricardo Ramirez, C.S.B. (1982–).

Several religious communities are important to the fabric of religious life in New Mexico. The Benedictines have two prominent abbeys—Christ in the Desert at Abiquiu with its striking church, and Our Lady of Guadalupe at Pecos with its extensive ministry in the Charismatic Movement. The Premonstratensians, or Norbertines, also have a monastic foundation at Albuquerque at Santa Maria de la Vid Priory. Since 1985 the Franciscans once again have their own Southwest jurisdiction in the Province of Our Lady of Guadalupe headquartered in Albuquerque. Among the Franciscan ministries is Father Richard Rohr's Center for Action and Contemplation at Albuquerque. The Conventual Franciscans staff Holy Cross Retreat Center in Mesilla Park in the Las Cruces diocese. The Christian Brothers staff the College of Santa Fe, St. Michael's High School, and the Sangre de Cristo refoundation center for priests and religious at Santa Fe. The Servants of the Holy Paraclete have their headquarters at Jemez Springs, and the Augustinian Recollects have a provincial delegate house in Mesilla.

Women religious have been present in New Mexico since the advent of the Sisters of LORETTO in 1856. Originally introduced to open schools and hospitals, today sisters from many different congregations are present in the state in parochial, educational, and healthcare ministries. There are cloistered Carmelite monasteries at Santa Fe and Gallup, a Poor Clares monastery at Roswell, and a Benedictine priory at Abiquiu. The Handmaids of the Precious Blood have their motherhouse and novitiate at Jemez Springs. The Canossian Daughters of Charity have a provincialate at Albuquerque, and the Felician Sisters at Rio Rancho.

The adobe churches of New Mexico—from Cristo Rey in Santa Fe, the largest adobe structure in the country, to the small village *moradas* of the Penitentes—constitute a distinctive and cherished artistic patrimony of the state, and a significant architectural contribution to the United States. Among the most-photographed are San Estevan in Acoma Pueblo, San Jose de Gracia in Trampas, San Miguel del Vado in Ribera, San Francisco de Asis in Ranchos de Taos, and the famous pilgrimage *Santuario* of El Senor de Esquipulas in Chimayo.

Bibliography: H. W. BOWDEN, "Spanish Missions, Cultural Conflict and the Pueblo Revolt of 1680," *Church History* 44 (June 1975), 217–288. A. CHAVEZ, *But Time and Chance. The Story of Padre Martinez of Taos, 1793–1867* (Santa Fe 1983); *My Penitente Land* (Albuquerque 1974). P. HORGAN, *Great River, the Rio Grande in North American History* (New York 1968); *Lamy of Santa Fe* (New York 1975). J. KESSELL, *The Missions of New Mexico since 1776* (Albuquerque 1979). F. V. SCHOLES, *Church and State in New Mexico, 1610–1650* (Albuquerque 1937); *Troublous Times in New Mexico, 1659–1670* (Albuquerque 1942). M. J. SHEEHAN, ed., *Four Hundred Years of Faith* (Albuquerque 1998). T. J. STEELE, P. RHETTS, and B. AWALT, eds., *Seeds of Struggle/Harvest of Faith. The Papers of the Archdiocese of Santa Fe Catholic Cuarto Centennial Conference on the History of the Catholic Church in New Mexico* (Albuquerque 1998). F. A. DOMÍNGUEZ, *Missions of New Mexico, 1776*, tr. E. B. ADAMS and A. CHÁVEZ (Albuquerque 1956). J. B. SALPOINTE, *Soldiers of the Cross* (Banning, Calif. 1898). B. SEGALE, *At the End of the Santa Fe Trail* (Milwaukee 1948).

[R. J. KUPKE]

NEW-MOON FEAST, HEBREW

In ancient Israel the first day of each month, i.e., the day after the new moon was sighted, was a feast day with ordinances similar to those of the SABBATH, with which it is linked in several passages (e.g., 2 Kgs 4.23). It has not been demonstrated, however, that the two were in fact originally connected. The monthly feast is not mentioned in the festival calendars of the Pentateuch, but in Nm 28.11–15 the sacrifices for it are prescribed in detail. The antiquity of the feast is clear, however, from allusions in the Prophets (Is 1.13–14; Hos 2.13; Am 8.5), and a New–Moon dinner at the royal court, requiring ritual purity for participation, is described in 1 Sm 20.5–29. Like the Sabbath, it was a day of rest from work.

The New–Moon Day was observed throughout Old Testament times (e.g., Ezr 3.5; Neh 10.33) and in New Testament times as well (Col 2.16), but it gradually lost its importance and disappeared from Jewish life. In later Biblical times only the first of the seventh month, Tishri, retained its prominence (Lv 23.24–25; Nm 29.1–6) and was observed with special solemnity: rest, trumpet blasts, a holy convocation, and sacrifices. This solemnity may reflect an earlier time when this day was a new year's day. The much later Hebrew Feast of the NEW YEAR, Rosh ha–Shanah, retained the characteristic trumpet blast of the first day of Tishri. But the New Moon Day of Tishri is never mentioned in the Bible as a new year feast.

Bibliography: H. EISING, *Lexikon für Theologie und Kirche*[2], ed. J. HOFER and K. RAHNER (Freiburg 1957–65); suppl., *Das Zweite Vatikanische Konzil: Dokumente und Kommentare,* ed. H. S. BRECHTER et al., pt. 1 (1966), 7:916–917. R. DE VAUX, *Ancient Israel, Its Life and Institutions,* tr. J. MCHUGH (New York 1961) 469–470. K. KOHLER, *The Jewish Encyclopedia,* ed. J. SINGER, 13 v. (New York 1901–06) 9:243–244. A. CAQUOT, "Remarques sur la fête de la *néoménie* dans l'ancien Israël," *Revue de l'histoire des religions* 158 (1960) 1 18.

[G. W. MACRAE]

NEW NORCIA, ABBEY OF

A Benedictine abbey *nullius* (*Novae Nursiae*), in Western Australia, about 80 miles north of Perth, of which it is a suffragan. It was founded (1846) by a Spanish monk, Rosendo Salvado, for the evangelization of Australian aborigines. After living three years among these primitive nomads, Dom Salvado (1814–1900) visited Europe (1849) in search of missionaries. While in Rome he was appointed bishop of Port Victoria (now Darwin). Before he could return, his entire flock abandoned the region for southern goldfields, whereupon the pope permitted him to return to New Norcia. Bishop Salvado and his young Spanish community built a monastery, and cleared the land for agriculture. They established schools, built cottages for married natives, and introduced them to farming and handicrafts. In March 1867 Pius IX made the monastery an abbey *nullius* and a prefecture apostolic. On a visit to Rome (1900), Bishop Salvado arranged for its affiliation with the Spanish province of the Subiaco Congregation of BENEDICTINES. His successor, Dom Fulgentius Torres (abbot 1902–14), found a changing social situation. With the coming of European settlers and a decline in the number of natives, the abbey had to provide for the spiritual needs of a white, rather than a nonwhite, population. In the north, however, Abbot Torres established a new mission to aborigines in 1908 on the Drysdale River.

St. Louis Cathedral, New Orleans, designed by Cass Gilbert, built 1904. (©Philip Gould/CORBIS)

Bibliography: J. T. MCMAHON, *The Salvado Story* (Perth 1956). *Annuario Pontificio* 728 (1964).

[J. G. MURTAGH]

NEW ORLEANS, ARCHDIOCESE OF

(*Novae Aureliae*) Metropolitan see erected April 25, 1793, as the Diocese of Louisiana and the Floridas by Pius VI upon the application of King Charles IV of Spain. The vast territory of the original diocese, except for the area under the jurisdiction of the Diocese of Baltimore, stretched from the Rocky Mountains to the Atlantic and from Canada to the Gulf of Mexico. The territory, detached from the See of Havana, was previously part of the older Diocese of Santiago de Cuba, under whose jurisdiction the Louisiana colony had passed in 1762. Before that date, Quebec had spiritual jurisdiction over French colonial Louisiana. After the 1849 Provincial Council of Baltimore recommended additional ecclesiastical jurisdictions, Pius IX on July 19, 1850, raised New Orleans to the rank of metropolitan see. The first suffragan dioceses were those of Galveston, Tex.; Mobile, Ala.; Natchez, Miss.; and Little Rock, Ark. In 2001, the province included the Archdiocese of New Orleans and six additional Louisiana dioceses: Alexandria, Baton Rouge, Houma-Thibodaux, Lafayette, Lake Charles, and Shreveport. The archdiocese covers 4,208 square miles and includes eight civil parishes (counties), namely, Jefferson, Orleans, Plaquemines, St. Bernard, St. Charles, St. John the Baptist, St. Tammany, and Washington. The Catholic population numbers about 490,000 or 36.8% of the total population.

Early History. The parish church with the longest uninterrupted history is St. Louis Basilica, whose origin extends practically to the founding of New Orleans in 1718. The first Mass in what is now the archdiocese was offered nearly 20 years earlier, on March 3, 1699, by Rev. Anastase Douay, a Franciscan missionary, with the expedition of Pierre Le Moyne, Sieur d'Iberville, who established the power of France in the Lower Mississippi Valley. On a later expedition to Louisiana with Iberville, the Jesuit Paul Du Ru put to use his fragmentary knowledge of the tribal languages of the Bayagoula, Ouma, and Natchez tribes by preparing a rudimentary catechism for their instruction. By early spring of 1700, du Ru was supervising the construction of a small church in a native village in Iberville parish.

The Council of the Marine in 1717 recommended turning the colony over to John Law's Company of the West and its successor, the Company of the Indies (or Mississippi Company). In accordance with the charter issued by the regent, Philip II, Duke of Orleans, religious affairs were included in the activities of the Company of the West from 1717 to 1731. Occasionally priests, known as concession chaplains, were among the personnel assigned to the land grants in the colony. More important than the concessions, however, was the founding of New Orleans as the new capital of the colony by Jean Baptiste Le Moyne, Sieur de Bienville, brother of Iberville, in 1718. The plan for the city, laid by Adrien de Pauger, provided for a church and presbytery. Divine services were held in improvised and inadequate quarters until April 1727, when the first substantial St. Louis parish church was finally completed.

Carmelite, Jesuit, and Capuchin priests labored in the colony during its formative years. The first Capuchins were Bruno de Langres, who arrived in New Orleans towards the end of 1722, and Philibert de Vianden, who took charge of the district from the Chapitoulas, a few miles above the original boundaries of the city, to Pointe Coupée, including Les Allemands, the German Coast, and the intervening concessions. Les Allemands had a chapel, dedicated to St. John, on the west bank of the Mississippi as early as 1724. In April 1723, Bruno was replaced as superior of the Capuchin missions in Louisiana by Raphael de Luxembourg, who was also vicar-general of the bishop of Quebec. Raphael established, in 1725, the first school for boys in New Orleans, but it lasted only five or six years. Nicolas Ignace de Beaubois, founder of the Jesuit missions in New Orleans, induced the Ursulines of Rouen, France, to establish a military hospital and school for girls. The pioneer group of Ursulines reached New Orleans on Aug. 6, 1727, and began the educational enterprise that has continued without interruption to this day. In 1722, the Jesuits, who contributed notably to the spiritual and economic well-being of the area, undertook the spiritual jurisdiction of the native peoples of the colony, a responsibility entrusted to them by Bp. Louis Duplessis-Mornay of Quebec. Their endeavors were supported in large measure by an extensive indigo and sugar plantation adjacent to New Orleans. In July 1763, while Michael Baudouin was superior, the Jesuits were dispossessed of their property and banished from Louisiana. Their departure, some 10 years before the society was suppressed, seriously hampered and retarded the growth of the Church in colonial Louisiana.

After 1772, Church affairs in New Orleans bore a definite Spanish stamp. Cirillo de Barcelona, chaplain of the Spanish expedition against the British in West Florida, was consecrated auxiliary bishop for the Louisiana colony on March 6, 1785. Shortly before leaving for his consecration in Cuba, he appointed his assistant Antonio de SEDELLA temporary pastor of St. Louis. For decades thereafter, Sedella, known as Père Antoine, was the center of controversy in the area.

First Bishops. When the Diocese of Louisiana and the Floridas was created in 1793, Luis Ignacio de PEÑALVER Y CÁRDENAS was consecrated as first ordinary and arrived in New Orleans on July 17, 1795, marking the beginning of home government in Church affairs. Peñalver noted in a report to the Spanish government that of the 11,000 Catholics in New Orleans, only about 400 performed their Easter duty. He instituted a number of necessary reforms, combated religious indifference and Voltaireanism, and established parishes in such places as the Poste des Avoyelles, Many (Neustra Señora de Guadalupe at Bayou Scie), and Monroe. Meanwhile, the parish church in use since 1727 had been destroyed in the great fire of 1788 and a new structure, the future Cathedral of St. Louis, was completed in 1794. Renovated several times, it was elevated to a minor basilica in 1964.

In 1801 Peñalver was transferred to the Archdiocese of Guatemala and jurisdictional quarrels, interdiction, and threats of schism marked the next 15 years in New Orleans. Père Antoine was at odds with Rev. Patrick Walsh and Canon Thomas Hassett, who attempted to administer the diocese during the episcopal vacancy; the wardens of the cathedral (*marguilliers*), after assuming control of church temporalities in 1805, waxed more and more arrogant; and, to complicate matters further, Spain ceded Louisiana back to France, which, in turn, sold it to the U.S. in 1803. Aware of the territorial transfer, the Holy See decided not to send Bishop-elect Francisco Porro y Peinado to Louisiana, and on Sept. 1, 1805, placed it temporarily under the spiritual supervision of Bp. John Carroll of Baltimore, Md. Carroll in time named the chaplain of the Ursulines, Jean Olivier, his vicar-general, but the latter's authority was openly challenged by Père Antoine and the cathedral wardens. Finally, on Aug. 18, 1812, Rev. Louis William DUBOURG, president of Georgetown College and founder of St. Mary's College in Baltimore, was named administrator apostolic by Archbishop Carroll. It was Dubourg, complying with Andrew Jackson's request, who officiated at a Te Deum in St. Louis Cathedral following the U.S. victory over the British at the Battle of New Orleans on Jan. 8, 1815.

On Sept. 24, 1815, Dubourg was consecrated in Rome, and Louisiana finally had a bishop, after an interregnum of nearly 15 years. Dubourg, however, remained in Europe for the next two years, enlisting priests and seminarians, as well as the services of the Religious of the Sacred Heart, and helping in the formation of the organization that eventually became the Pontifical Society for the PROPAGATION OF THE FAITH. Upon arriving in the U.S., Dubourg went to St. Louis, Mo., and returned to New Orleans only in late 1820. The next year he called a synod, which was attended by 20 priests. On March 25, 1824, Joseph ROSATI, CM, was consecrated as Dubourg's coadjutor, but his administration of the Church in New Orleans amounted to supervision at a distance, since he resided in St. Louis. A significant event of the period was the arrival of the Sisters of Charity from Emmitsburg, Md., to staff the Poydras Asylum in New Orleans. Dubourg resigned in mid-1826 and died in 1833 as archbishop of Besancon, France.

Dubourg's resignation left the lower end of the Mississippi Valley without a resident bishop and was the signal for further disorders, which the annual visits of Rosati could not completely control. Rosati, appointed bishop of St. Louis in 1827, in time recommended a fellow Vincentian for the See of New Orleans, and Leo Raymond de Neckère was consecrated in St. Louis Cathedral on June 24, 1830. His regime was brief, for he was stricken with yellow fever and died on Sept. 5, 1833. A few months before (April 21, 1833), he had established New Orleans's second parish, St. Patrick's, to accommodate the Irish immigrants and other English-speaking people of the city. He had also invited to the diocese the Sisters of Our Lady of Mount Carmel from Tours, France, but they arrived after the bishop's death, and settled in Plattenville on Bayou Lafourche.

A remarkable period of Church expansion coincided with the growing importance of New Orleans as a center of commerce and expanding population. The city, emerging as fourth largest in the nation, increased in population from 29,737 in 1830 to 102,193 in 1840. The diocese covered the entire state, and had a total population approaching 300,000, served by 26 churches and 27 priests, when Anthony BLANC became fourth bishop, Nov. 22, 1835.

Blanc. During the 25 years Blanc administered the see, the number of churches increased to 73, and priests to 92. He established Assumption Seminary on Bayou Lafourche, two colleges, nine academies and schools, four orphanages, a hospital, and a home for girls. Under the guidance of Etienne Rousselon, vicar-general, the Sisters of the Holy Family were founded (1842) as a diocesan African-American religious congregation to teach, care for orphans, and tend to the aged of the African-American community. The cause for the canonization of their foundress, Henriette Dehille, was introduced in 1988. Blanc invited five communities of nuns to the diocese: the Sisters Marianites of Holy Cross (1848); the Sisters of St. Joseph of Bourg (1856); the School Sisters of

Notre Dame (1856); the Sisters of Our Lady of the Good Shepherd (1859); and the Dominican Sisters, who, however, did not arrive from Cabra, Ireland, until four months after his death. The Redemptorist fathers established themselves (1843) in nearby Lafayette, where German, Irish, and French immigrants had settled. The Jesuit fathers opened the College of the Immaculate Conception in 1849 on a plot of ground that had once formed part of the plantation of which they had been defrauded in 1763. The Congregation of Holy Cross came (1849) to stabilize St. Mary's Orphan Boys' Home, which had been opened by Adam Kindelon, first pastor of St. Patrick's. Rev. Cyril De la Croix organized the first conference of the Society of St. Vincent de Paul after a layman, William Blair Lancaster, brought a manual of the society to New Orleans (1852).

Blanc called two diocesan synods and two provincial councils. A long and severe struggle with the church wardens culminated in the withdrawal of the clergy from the cathedral (1843). During the recrudescence of NATIVISM, he was the target of polemics and abuse in the press, but a loyal laity, represented by the Catholic Temperance Society, rallied to his defense. In litigation with the wardens, the Louisiana supreme court upheld the position of the bishop (1844). Three years after Blanc became archbishop of New Orleans in 1850, his jurisdiction was reduced about 22,000 square miles by the erection in the upper part of the state of the Diocese of Natchitoches, but the Catholic population of the archdiocese was decreased by only 25,000. After his death on June 20, 1860, the archdiocese was administered by Father Rousselon until the arrival of Archbishop-elect Jean Marie ODIN from Galveston, Tex.

Odin. The second archbishop took possession of his see only a few days after the bombardment of Ft. Sumter on April 12, 1861, Louisiana having already seceded from the Union and joined the Confederacy. During the Civil War, the archbishop's position was an extremely delicate one, calling for infinite tact and diplomacy. The times grew more trying after the city was occupied by federal troops on May 1, 1862. Union forces wrought considerable damage on Church properties in such places as Pointe Coupée and Donaldsonville, and the war years witnessed a disruption of religious and educational work in Thibodaux, Convent, Plaquemine, Grand Coteau, and elsewhere. Reconstruction was no less trying, but Odin continued, within limitations, the expansion program of his predecessor.

During the archbishop's visit to Europe in 1863 in search of men and money for his diocese, the Marist Fathers accepted his invitation to labor in Louisiana. In 1867 the OBLATE SISTERS OF PROVIDENCE, a Baltimore community of African-American nuns, began staffing a home for dependent children. The LITTLE SISTERS OF THE POOR opened their home for the aged poor after a committee of pious women, called Les Dames de la Providence, asked for their help in maintaining a home for the aged founded in 1840. The Brothers of the Sacred Heart came to New Orleans from Mobile in 1869. The archbishop invited the SISTERS OF MERCY, who began their visits to the parish prison, city workhouse, boys' house of refuge, and the mental hospital in 1869. The first Benedictine convent in the archdiocese was opened (1870) in the German national parish of Holy Trinity, New Orleans. The nuns arrived from Covington, Ky., and later established a motherhouse in Covington, La.

After numerous request for assistance, Odin finally obtained a coadjutor with right of succession. He was Napoléon Joseph Perché, who had been chaplain of the Ursulines for many years, founder (1842) of the first Catholic newspaper in Louisiana (*Le Propagateur Catholique*), and vicar-general of the archdiocese. He was consecrated in St. Louis Cathedral on May 1, 1870, and succeeded to the see when Odin died in France, May 25, 1870.

Perché and Leray. Like his predecessors, Perché invited several communities to the archdiocese: the Sisters of Perpetual Adoration, now known as the SISTERS OF THE MOST HOLY SACRAMENT, who arrived at Waggaman in 1872; the Sisters of Christian Charity, who established themselves at St. Henry's convent, New Orleans, in 1873; and the Discalced CARMELITE Nuns, who arrived in 1877. In addition, Archbishop Perché approved the founding of a diocesan community, the Sisters of Immaculate Conception, organized on July 11, 1874, in Labadieville with Elvina Vienne as first superior. Soon after his installation as head of the see, Perché also inaugurated a costly program of church building, school construction, and parish foundations that contrasted sharply with the record of his predecessor. These expenses, plus financial aid to families impoverished by the Civil War, caused the archdiocesan debt to soar to $590,925, of which $257,080 was due European bondholders.

Weakened by age and infirmities, and overwhelmed by the tremendous debt, the archbishop asked for a coadjutor. The Holy See appointed Francis Xavier Leray of Natchitoches, who became archbishop upon Perché's death on Dec. 27, 1883. Leray's chief concern as coadjutor and as ordinary was the reduction of the archdiocesan debt, so his administration was practically without building or expansion programs. The only new community established in the archdiocese was that of the Poor Clare Nuns (1885). Upon his death on Sept. 23, 1887, Leray was succeeded by Francis Janssens, the Dutch-born bishop of Natchez.

Janssens. The new archbishop received the pallium from Cardinal James Gibbons on May 8, 1889, although he had actually taken possession of the archdiocese on Sept. 16, 1888. He invited the Benedictines of ST. MEINRAD'S ABBEY in Indiana to open a seminary for the training of priests. Luke Grüwe, OSB, established (1890) what later became St. Joseph's Abbey (St. Benedict, La.), and Janssens dedicated the seminary on Sept. 3, 1891. The archbishop welcomed Mother Frances Xavier CABRINI to New Orleans and encouraged her to establish (1892) a house primarily to assist Italians who had begun to migrate in large numbers to the city. In 1893, he asked the Sisters of the Holy Family to care for dependent or neglected African-American boys, and thus started the present Lafon Home for Boys, one of several institutions named for, and supported by, a bequest from the local black philanthropist Thomy Lafon.

Janssens was greatly esteemed throughout the archdiocese, which numbered 341,613 in the centennial year of 1893. He encouraged spiritual ministrations to patients at the leprosarium at Carville, La. When the hurricane of 1893 swept the Louisiana Gulf Coast, Janssens went among the Italian, Spanish, and Malay fishermen in the island settlements in a small boat to comfort them; he later helped them to rebuild their homes. He promoted devotion to Our Lady under the title of Prompt Succor. The corporate structure of each parish, as it exists today, was determined in 1894 when each parish was legally incorporated with the archbishop, the vicar-general, the pastor, and two lay directors as board members. Janssens was the first ordinary to promote native vocations on a large scale; his predecessors generally had depended on priests and seminarians from Europe, and had leaned heavily on religious to staff new parishes. He sponsored the Catholic Winter School, opened parochial schools, and launched a dozen new parishes. Alarmed at the defections from the faith among the African-Americans, he established St. Katherine's (1895) as a black parish, but on a temporary basis, since he did not wish to promote racial segregation. He died June 9, 1897, while en route to Europe in the interest of the archdiocese.

Chapelle. Placide Louis CHAPELLE, sixth archbishop of New Orleans, was transferred from Santa Fe., N. Mex., in February 1898. In concern over the archdiocesan debt, he ordered the annual contribution of 12 percent of the revenues of each parish for five years. This helped in the eventual liquidation of the longstanding debt, although it aroused the displeasure of some pastors. Chapelle's relations with his priests, many of them born and educated in France, were hardly improved by his extended, though necessary absences as apostolic delegate extraordinary, to Puerto Rico and Cuba, and later as apostolic delegate to the Philippine Islands. It was evident that he needed an auxiliary and one was provided when the pastor of Annunciation Church in New Orleans, Gustave Rouxel, was consecrated on April 9, 1899. In 1898 the archbishop, in his anxiety to economize, withdrew aid from the preparatory seminary at St. Benedict. On the other hand, he opened a theological seminary (1900) in an existing building next to St. Stephen's Church, New Orleans, with Fathers of the Congregation of the Mission as professors. Some 12 parishes and missions were established during Chapelle's regime and the Dominican fathers began (1903) their ministry in the archdiocese. Chapelle died a victim of yellow fever, on Aug. 9, 1905.

Blenk. The next ordinary, James Hubert Blenk, SM, was well known to the archdiocese long before his appointment on April 20, 1906. He had served as bishop of Puerto Rico, former auditor and secretary to the apostolic delegation to the West Indies, rector of Holy Name of Mary Church, and president of Jefferson College, Convent, La. Blenk, an ardent promoter of Catholic education, set up (1908) the first archdiocesan school board and appointed the first superintendent of schools. The preparatory seminary was again placed under the care of the Benedictine fathers of St. Joseph's Abbey (1908), but the theological courses were discontinued (1907) at the seminary opened by Chapelle. Most major seminarians of the archdiocese matriculated at Kenrick Seminary in St. Louis and St. Mary's Seminary in Baltimore, or studied abroad. In September 1904 the Jesuits started a small college in New Orleans, which in 1911 was amalgamated with the College of the Immaculate Conception and became Loyola University. Blenk designated (1908) St. Mary's the normal school for women religious engaged in teaching in the archdiocese. In time St. Mary's Dominican became an accredited Catholic woman's college.

French Benedictine nuns, forced to leave their country, settled (1906) in Ramsay under the guidance of Paul Schaeuble, OSB, who had become first abbot of St. Joseph's in 1903. The Sisters Servants of Mary, having left Mexico during the Carranza revolution, found refuge also in the archdiocese and inaugurated (1914) their ministrations among the sick and bedridden in the city. The sisters of the Society of St. Teresa of Jesus, likewise refugees from Mexico, began teaching at St. Louis Cathedral school in 1915. That same year, the archbishop urgently requested Mother Katharine Drexel, foundress of the Sisters of the BLESSED SACRAMENT, to undertake the education of African-American youth in New Orleans. In 1917 the sisters opened a normal school and the following year they were authorized by the state legislature to conduct colleges and confer degrees. The sisters launched XAVIER UNIVERSITY OF LOUISIANA in 1925. For further ministration to the African-American population, the archbishop solicited the services of St. Joseph's Society of the Sacred Heart (Josephites) and the Holy Ghost Fathers, assigning six parishes to the former and one to the latter. In 1911 the Brothers of Christian Schools purchased St. Paul's College, Covington, from the Benedictine Fathers. In 1912 the Ursulines, under the supervision of their chaplain, François Racine, moved from their third convent building to a new site on State Street where, 10 years later, the national shrine of Our Lady of Prompt Succor was erected.

Early in his administration, Blenk strengthened lay groups. He organized (1906) the State Board of Holy Name Societies, the Louisiana State Federation of Catholic Societies (1909), and the Federation of Catholic Societies of Women of Louisiana. He promoted the Catholic Order of Foresters, the Knights of Columbus, and the Knights of Peter Claver. The growth of the population in the archdiocese, especially in southwest Louisiana, made a division expedient. Partition was effected Jan. 11, 1918, shortly before Abp. John William Shaw was promoted to the New Orleans see. Jules Benjamin Jeanmard, administrator of the archdiocese following the death of Blenk (April 15, 1917), was named first bishop of the new Diocese of Lafayette. The area of the archdiocese was reduced by about 11,000 square miles, 40 church parishes, and a population of about 300,000.

Shaw. One of Shaw's first actions was to invite the OBLATES OF MARY IMMACULATE, with whom he had worked closely as bishop of San Antonio, Tex., to administer St. Louis Cathedral and to take charge of the churches and missions in Livingston parish. In 1919 the Sisters of Charity of the Incarnate Word, from San Antonio also, came to teach at St. Francis de Sales parochial school. In 1920 Archbishop Shaw, with his chancellor August J. Bruening, began to lay plans for a financial campaign for the erection of a major seminary. With the help of laymen, the campaign realized close to $1 million and Notre Dame Seminary, staffed by Marist Fathers, became a reality in September 1923. In Baton Rouge, the Sisters of St. Francis of Calais opened Our Lady of the Lake Hospital (1923). Franciscan fathers returned to the archdiocese on July 21, 1925, when they took charge of the newly established parish of St. Mary of the Angels in the city, and missions of the Lower Coast. The Sisters of the Holy Ghost and Mary Immaculate arrived from San Antonio in September 1926 to teach the African-American children of St. Luke's School, Thibodaux. Shaw encouraged the endeavors of Catharine Bostick and Zoe Grouchy in the establishment of the MISSIONARY SERVANTS OF THE MOST HOLY EUCHARIST of the Third Order of St. Dominic, a community intended for religious instruction of the children in public schools and for social relief work. In 1928 the Society of the Divine Word took over the mission stations on both the east and west bank of the lower

Mississippi River. In 1931 the Jesuits purchased the old Jefferson College in Convent and converted it into Manresa House for laymen's retreats.

Father (later Bishop) Maurice Schexnayder began Newman Club work in 1929 at Louisiana State University, one-third of whose student body was Catholic. Monsignor Peter M. H. Wynhoven established (1925) Hope Haven for orphaned and abandoned boys, later placed under the Salesian Fathers of St. John Bosco. Opposite Hope Haven, Madonna Manor for small boys replaced St. Mary's and St. Joseph's Orphanages. Wynhoven, in addition to many other assignments, also reorganized the social services and charities of the archdiocese by setting up (1924) Associated Catholic Charities. In 1922 Shaw convoked the sixth synod, the first in 33 years. In 1932 he launched the official diocesan paper, *Catholic Action of the South,* with Wynhoven as first editor in chief. It replaced the *Morning Star,* which had been published between 1878 and 1930.

Shaw's last years were burdened by problems of the financial depression of the 1930s. Some archdiocesan funds were frozen in local banks and several parishes found it difficult to meet the high interest due on monies borrowed during the 1920s. Nevertheless 33 new parishes were opened between 1919 and 1934. After a brief illness, Shaw died on Nov. 2, 1934, and Jean Marius Laval, who had been consecrated auxiliary (1911) to Blenk, became administrator.

Rummel. Joseph Francis RUMMEL (1876–1965) became the ninth Archbishop of New Orleans; he was born in Germany and immigrated to New York City with his parents in 1882. Rummel studied at seminaries in New Hampshire, New York and Rome, where he was ordained to the priesthood in 1902 and received his S.T.D. in 1903. He took an early interest in social problems, leading the relief work for Germans. In 1928 he was ordained Bishop of Omaha, Neb. On March 9, 1935, he was appointed Archbishop of New Orleans. Rummel guided the archdiocese during a period of rapid Catholic growth that saw the establishment of 48 new parishes and several schools.

The increasing participation of the laity in Church life became more evident during this period. The most tangible evidence of this participation was the growth and multiplication of many local units of national organizations such as the Confraternity of Christian Doctrine (1935), the Archdiocesan Council of Catholic Women (1936), the Catholic Youth Organization (1936), Christian Family Movement (1953), and Young Christian Workers (1954). The most striking example of the changing nature of Louisiana Catholicism during this period was the Eighth National Eucharistic Congress, held in New Orleans on October 17–20, 1938— the first National Eucharistic Congress to be held in the South.

With the bombing of Pearl Harbor on Dec. 7, 1941, the U.S. became a nation at war. Louisiana Catholics again entered wholeheartedly into conflict. Archbishop Rummel immediately issued "A Nation at War," urging Catholic support for the war effort. Young men and women enlisted; the local work force reoriented itself to a wartime economy; while Catholic parishes, schools, and institutions participated in the many patriotic drives to support the war effort.

After the war, the archdiocese encouraged generous support for relief efforts, worked for a temporary extension of rent control, and established a local resettlement bureau to assist (and sometimes resettle) more than 33,000 displaced persons who entered the U.S. via New Orleans between 1949 and 1952.

The post-war years were a time of rapid demographic growth and change. In 1945, the Catholic population of the archdiocese was estimated at 385,000. By 1962, the number increased to 630,000. The G. I. bill provided many with an opportunity for a college education, a better job, and a new home. Whole sections of New Orleans and its surrounding areas witnessed rapid development as new home construction boomed. Undeveloped suburban land was rapidly transformed into populated neighborhoods.

In 1935, 43,411 children were being educated in 122 Catholic elementary, secondary, and special schools. There were two Catholic universities—Loyola and Xavier—in the archdiocese. By 1965, more than 92,600 students were attending 197 Catholic elementary and secondary schools in the Archdiocese of New Orleans and the recently established Diocese of Baton Rouge. High school programs were rapidly expanding; teachers and principals were increasingly degreed and state certified; curricula were becoming more diversified as science and mathematics programs expanded; and the proportion of lay teachers grew steadily. The guiding force for much of this period was Msgr. Henry C. Bezou, who served as superintendent of archdiocesan schools from 1943 to 1968.

Rummel labored patiently for over a quarter century to create a community atmosphere conducive to full racial equality, to foster the growth of church organizations, facilities, and activities among African-American Catholics and, eventually, to achieve integration of Catholic parishes, schools, organizations, and institutions. In 1939, Xavier University in New Orleans began a Catholic Action School for African Americans. In 1951, the archdiocese's first secondary school for young black males— St. Augustine High School—was established. Many national and local black leaders received their secondary education at St. Augustine.

The 1954 Supreme Court decision in *Brown vs. the Board of Education of Topeka, Kansas,* marked the legal end to segregated public schools. Louisiana, like the other southern states, resisted desegregation. Legislative attempts to prohibit integration, even in Catholic schools, were eventually declared unconstitutional. Archbishop Rummel was the first Catholic bishop in the South to accept African-American students into his minor and major seminaries. On March 15, 1953, his pastoral letter, ''Blessed are the Peacemakers,'' ordered the desegregation of all Catholic parish activities and organizations. He suspended all Catholic services at Jesuit Bend mission (1955–1958) after an African-American priest was prevented from celebrating Mass there. In his pastoral letter of Feb. 11, 1956, he declared racial segregation morally wrong and sinful. He was also influential in preparing and gaining support for the 1958 U.S. Catholic bishops' statement condemning racism. He believed, however, that the process of integration had to proceed slowly to be successful. Not all shared his patience.

Rummel encouraged local clergy to educate their parishioners in social justice issues and consistently supported their efforts to implement social programs. In 1940, the South's first Catholic Conference on Industrial Problems was held in New Orleans. Rummel vigorously supported the rights of the working class. He publicly opposed Louisiana's right to work laws and actively supported the efforts of Louisiana agricultural workers, particularly sugar cane workers, to organize in the 1950s. He supported the unsuccessful 1953 sugar cane workers' strike.

Rummel turned over administration of the Archdiocese of New Orleans to Archbishop John P. Cody on June 1, 1962. He passed away in New Orleans on Nov. 8, 1964.

Cody. John Patrick CODY (1907–1982), a native and priest of St. Louis, was ordained in Rome in 1931, ministered in the Vatican Secretariate of State and Archdiocese of St. Louis, and served as Auxiliary Bishop of St. Louis, Coadjutor Bishop of St. Joseph, Mo., and Bishop of Kansas City-St. Joseph before his appointment as Coadjutor Archbishop of New Orleans on July 20, 1961. He was named apostolic administrator on June 1, 1962, and became archbishop on Nov. 8, 1964.

Cody oversaw the rapid expansion of parishes and schools; initiated an extensive building program, particularly for high schools; initiated new programs for the needy and handicapped; expanded programs for Catholic students in state universities and colleges; reorganized archdiocesan administration and finances; promoted greater lay participation through the Confraternity of Christian Doctrine and Family Life Bureau; and encour-

aged closer relations with Protestant and Jewish communities through Operation Understanding. Twenty-five new parishes were established during his brief tenure.

On March 27, 1962, at Cody's insistence, the desegregation of all Catholic schools for the 1962–1963 school year was announced. As Msgr. Henry Bezou later recalled, Archbishop Cody ''made it clear . . . that neither gradualism nor tokenism could remain the New Orleans policy.'' The desegregation order unleashed a storm of protest. The Catholic school in Buras was set on fire. A small, vocal group attacked archdiocesan officials in Citizen Council meetings, mimeographed sheets, newspaper advertisements, and press releases, and staged public demonstrations. Three protesters were eventually excommunicated, not for their outspoken opposition to integration, but for their public disobedience. One, Judge Leander Perez of Plaquemines parish, was later reconciled. Despite some student withdrawals, Catholic school enrollment steadily increased in the first three years of desegregation.

Cody also implemented the initial reforms of the Second Vatican Council. Changes in liturgical practices, parish administration, lay involvement, and social outreach were soon evident. He also established new archdiocesan offices to assist an increasingly complex ministry: the Vocation Office, the Family Life Office, the Cemeteries Office, and the Building Commission. In 1965, Cody was transferred to Chicago; he died in 1982.

Hannan. Philip Matthew Hannan (1913–), a native of Washington, D.C., was ordained a priest in 1939, became Auxiliary Bishop of Washington in 1956, and was named eleventh Archbishop of New Orleans on Sept. 29, 1965. In the same year, Harold R. Perry (1916–1991), a native of Lake Charles, Louisiana, and former provincial of the Society of the Divine Word, was appointed Auxiliary Bishop of New Orleans, the first 20th-century African-American Catholic bishop.

During his episcopate, the archdiocesan social services programs grew at a tremendous rate. Christopher Homes, Inc. was established in 1966 to provide safe and affordable housing. Catholic Charities sponsored a massive refugee resettlement program for the Cubans and Vietnamese. In 1983, Second Harvesters was established to distribute food to the needy. By the late 1980s, the archdiocese was the largest single private provider of social services in Louisiana.

Parish expansion continued at a rapid rate. Thirty-one new parishes were established between 1966 and 1988: eight in New Orleans and 23 in the seven surrounding civil parishes. Eastern New Orleans, St. Tammany Parish, the west bank of Jefferson Parish, and St. Charles Parish were the centers of Catholic parish growth.

Existing archdiocesan offices were expanded and new offices such as the Office of Black Ministries and Latin American Apostolate were established. The new consultative process was evident in the establishment of an archdiocesan pastoral council, a priests' council, an elected archdiocesan school board, and several other major advisory boards. A series of town hall meetings led to an archdiocesan-wide RENEW program. The Eighth Archdiocesan Synod (1987), culminating seven years of consultation and review, promulgated a new set of policies, procedures and norms to reflect the new vision of the Church and to "renew the life of the People of God by setting forth regulations accommodated to the needs of the times."

The first archdiocesan formation program for permanent deacons began in 1972; the first class was ordained two years later. By 2001, there were 192 permanent deacons in the archdiocese. Permanent deacons minister in a variety of programs in parishes, prisons, hospitals, the Stella Maris Maritime Center, Ozanam Inn, and Project Lazarus (hospice for AIDS patients) among others.

In 1975, 80,000 attended the Holy Year Celebration in the newly built Superdome. In 1984, Vatican Pavilion was part of the Louisiana World Exposition held in New Orleans. On September 12–13, 1987, Pope John Paul II made his historic visit to the city.

Schulte. Francis Bible Schulte (1926–), a native of Philadelphia, was ordained priest in 1952, ordained Auxiliary Bishop in 1981, appointed Bishop of the Diocese of Wheeling-Charleston, West Virginia, in 1985, and elevated to the twelfth Archbishop of New Orleans on Feb. 14, 1989.

Almost immediately, Archbishop Schulte undertook a comprehensive study of archdiocesan schools. The study recommended the strengthening of the office of superintendent, the establishment of a strong middle-school program, the need to subsidize needy schools, higher and uniform teachers' salaries, uniform registration and activity fees, and the development of a marketing strategy for parochial schools. In 1991, the archdiocese's many ministries, apostolates, programs, and services were reorganized. Six departments—Clergy, Religious, Christian Formation, Community Services, Financial Services, and Pastoral Services—were created to direct and coordinate the ministries of archdiocesan offices and programs. In 1992, a new mission statement was promulgated, one that emphasized the multi-cultural composition of the archdiocesan family as well as the Church's commitment to proclaim and embody the Good News of Jesus Christ, to build a peaceful kingdom, and to be a servant to all regardless of social condition or religious affiliation.

The rapid expansion of archdiocesan parishes, schools, and social programs, the centralization and growth of administration, and the resultant growth of lay employees had placed new financial demands on the archdiocese. In 1989, the archdiocese had a $12 million external debt. In 1990, a finance council of local business leaders was established. Central accounting procedures were standardized. Departmental budgeting, reporting, and accountability were put in place. Regular internal audits of parishes and schools were initiated. A decade later, the archdiocese's external debt was eliminated, despite continued, though restrained, expansion.

In 1993, the archdiocesan bicentennial celebration included a special Mass; the publication of a volume of historical essays; an exhibit at the New Orleans Museum of Art; and a capital campaign to establish a $20 million endowment for Notre Dame Seminary, needy Catholic schools, and retired and infirm priests. The campaign surpassed its goal and was the most successful in archdiocesan history.

In 1996, the archdiocese began a five-year parish re-evaluation and planning program called Catholic Life: 2000. Each parish undertook a detailed, broad-based self-study, assessing its strengths and weaknesses in worship, word, service, and resources. These were reviewed and coordinated at a deanery and then an archdiocesan level. Catholic Life: 2000 was promulgated in 2001, charting the future of parish revitalization, transformation, and restructuring to better serve the Church and the wider community with available resources.

New Orleans has always been a cosmopolitan city; the archdiocese was no different. African Americans formed the core of the city's political leadership. More than a dozen Catholic parishes were predominantly African American. Hispanic membership was increasing in many parishes. The archdiocese's fastest growing immigrant community was the Vietnamese. In 1983, the first Vietnamese parish was established; in 1995, St. Agnes Le Thi Thanh Parish for Southeast Asians was founded in Marrero. In 2001, two national parishes and three missions served the vibrant and fast-growing Vietnamese Catholic community in the archdiocese. In 2001, Hanmaum Korean Catholic Church was opened in Metairie.

Bibliography: Archives, Archdiocese of New Orleans. R. BAUDIER, *The Catholic Church in Louisiana* (New Orleans 1939; repr. 1972). T. BECNEL, *Labor, Church, and the Sugar Establishment Louisiana 1887–1976* (Baton Rouge 1980). H. BEZOU, *Metairie: A Tongue of Land to Pasture* (Gretna, La. 1973). G. CONRAD, ed., *Cross, Crozier and Crucible: A Volume Celebrating the Bicentennial of a Catholic Diocese in Louisiana* (Lafayette, La. 1993). M. CURLEY, *Church and State in the Spanish Floridas (1783–1822)* (Washington, D.C. 1940). A. KASTEEL, *Francis Janssens, 1843–1897, A Dutch-American Prelate* (Lafayette, La. 1992). D.

Hare Krishna devotee chanting, San Francisco, California, 1982. (©Vince Streano/CORBIS)

LABBÉ, *Jim Crow Comes to Church: The Establishment of Segregated Catholic Parishes in South Louisiana* (Lafayette, La. 1971). A. MELVILLE, *Louis William DuBourg: Bishop of Louisiana and the Floridas, Bishop of Montauban, and Archbishop of Besançon, 1766–1833* (Chicago 1986). E. NIEHAUS, *The Irish in New Orleans, 1800–1860* (Baton Rouge 1965). C. NOLAN, *A History of the Archdiocese of New Orleans* (Strasbourg 2000). C. NOLAN, *A Southern Catholic Heritage*, v. 1, *Colonial Period, 1704–1813* (New Orleans 1976). C. O'NEILL, *Church and State in French Colonial Louisiana: Policy and Politics to 1732.* (New Haven 1966). *Sacramental Records of the Roman Catholic Church of the Archdiocese of New Orleans, 1718–1825* (New Orleans 1987–2001), v. 1–7 ed. by E. WOODS and C. NOLAN; v. 8–16 by C. NOLAN and D. DUPONT.

[H. C. BEZOU/C. E. NOLAN]

NEW RELIGIOUS MOVEMENTS

New Religious Movements is a label covering a broad spectrum of world-wide spiritual ferment that has been especially pronounced since the 1960s. Use of the expression has partially superceded the terms ''sect'' or ''cult'' in reference to non-mainline religious movements—although the latter (more pejorative) terms are still widely used in public discourse.

The discussion of new religious movement (NRMs) in this article is restricted to North America. However, NRMs are a world-wide phenomena by no means confined to the United States. A wide variety of both indigenous and imported NRMs have flourished globally in the post–World War II era, especially in Latin America, Africa, and Japan. While it is not possible to gage accurately the total number of individuals involved in these movements, the scale on which they have emerged since the 1960s is unique.

NRMs in North America vary considerably in size, in theological and organizational characteristics, and in their spiritual techniques, therapies and rituals. They can be grouped into three broad categories:

1. Movements of a non-Christian, non-Western derivation: Buddhist groups (Zen, Nichiren Shoshu, Tantrism), HARE KRISHNA (International Society for Krishna Consciousness), TRANSCENDENTAL MEDITATION (Science of Creative Intelligence), Meher Baba, and other Hindu-derived guru groups.

2. Christian or Neo-Christian groups: Charismatics/ neo-Pentecostals, the UNIFICATION CHURCH (Moonies), groups associated with the Jesus Movement (Alamo Foundation, Children of God), the Way Ministry, the conservative/fundamentalism New Religious Right, televangelist ministries, Roman Catholic Traditionalists.

3. Religio-therapeutic self-help groups derivative of transpersonal psychology and the human potential movement that syncretistically combine traditional and eclectic elements of religious language, symbolism, and discipline (SCIENTOLOGY, est, Arica, Eckankar and various NEW AGE groups).

Aside from the above categories, NRMs have also been grouped according to leadership style, organizational characteristics, and whether or not their theologies are monistic or dualistic, world rejecting, world affirming, or world accommodating.

Although it has been common practice to refer to the above groups as "new" religious movements, many were neither new as religious phenomenon nor new to the American culture. The Hare Krishna movement was brought to the United States in 1965 by A. C. Bhaktivedanta Swami Prabhupada. The beliefs of the movement, however, derive from a *bhakti* tradition founded by Sri Caitanya in Bengal, India, in the 16th century. Other Buddhist and Hindu-derived movements popularized in the 1960s had earlier penetrated American culture through the initiatives of individuals such as Swami Vivekananda, Madame Blavatsky, Soyen Shaku, Shigetsu Sasaki, Paranahansa Yogananda, and others. Ethnic-based Eastern religions had also taken root in American society long before popular interest in these traditions surfaced during the 1960s and 1970s. The New Religious Right also had clear historical lineage in early 20th century Protestant fundamentalism.

The "new" aspects of NRMs in the 1960s and 1970s applied to their unexpected growth in the face of secularization (especially the assumption that supernaturalism was outmoded and dying); the fact that many such movements—especially the counter-culture and quasi-therapeutic groups—appealed to a youthful constituency, which was predominantly middle-class, affluent, college-educated and which had not been traditionally associated with marginal religious movements; the manner in which NRMs offered religious cosmologies with unique combinations of theological or cultural elements that in themselves were familiar; and where NRMs were based on religious forms of another culture or where they expressed a radical shift in American cultural values.

Two aspects of NRMS have received widespread attention. The first concerns assessment of the social and historical factors that facilitate the rise of such movements. The second concerns explicating the dynamics of recruitment and commitment by which NRMs form and sustain their membership.

The Rise of New Religious Movements. Religious movements seem to arise where dominant religious institutions are internally unstable, where theological innovation is possible, where charismatic leadership is present, where the socio-political climate fosters religious liberty and expressiveness, and where the normative meaning and plausibility structures of a society have been weakened.

Historians generally interpreted the proliferation of NRMs in the 1960s and 1970s as a manifestation of the religious enthusiasm that periodically alters the American religious landscape. These outbreaks of religious effervescence ("Great Awakenings") give expression to the realignment of religion and culture brought about by revitalization tendencies within religious traditions themselves, and by socio-cultural adjustments attending modernization.

The rise of NRMs has also been linked to the dynamics of secularization. According to this view, religious history is dominated by cycles rather than by a linear trend toward increasing secularity. The staying power of religion lies in the fact that individuals continue to need supernaturally based "compensators" for rewards that are scarce, inequitably distributed, or materially unattainable. Thus, most individuals do not respond to new social and cultural problems by abandoning religion, but by developing religious innovations or new religions on the ruins of the old, especially where mainline religions have moved in the direction of secularization and cultural accommodation. Viewed from this perspective, secularization is a self-limiting process that actually stimulates the rise of NRMs.

A different interpretation, more in keeping with the traditional assessment that secularization has a corrosive effect on religion, holds that NRMs are a manifestation of, rather than a response to, secularization. Counter culture and religio-therapeutic groups in particular are derided as contrived, artificial, and bizarre phenomena that point to the triviality of religion in modern society. These movements give expression to the structural differentiation of religion and to its reduction to the status of a packaged and marketed consumer item in contemporary culture. Such groups are said to manifest ritualized traits of narcissistic and obsessive self-fixation. In so doing, they mirror the powerlessness and alienation endemic in modern society. They have no formative influence on the larger culture, either because their sources of inspiration are esoteric and highly subjective, or because participants see themselves in exclusive terms and withdraw from "worldly pursuits" in an individualized quest for salvation—thus reinforcing the status quo and testifying to the waning social significance of religion in modern society. This interpretation of the rise of NRMs vis-à-vis secularization theory is not applicable, however, to movements that stress moral constraints, self-discipline, and social altruism.

Cultural Crisis. A widely accepted perspective on the rise of NRMs is the cultural crisis hypothesis. This interpretive framework focuses on the socio-cultural conditions conducive to religious change. It does not explain the appeal of particular NRMs nor differential growth rates among them.

The culture crisis hypothesis holds that NRMs flourish in response to fundamental alterations in the social and meaning structures that integrate a society. Because religious values and forms are enmeshed with the historical, cultural, and social structures through which religious self-understanding is expressed, strains and alterations in these dimensions of social reality necessarily produce strains and alterations in the religious sphere. According to this hypothesis, the rise of NRMs in the United States was functionally related to a broad value crisis and mass disaffection from the common understanding of American culture that occurred between the election of President John F. Kennedy and the collapse of the American regime in Vietnam in 1975. The trauma of the Civil Rights Movement, the atrocities in Vietnam, assassinations, and the spread of post-Watergate political cynicism, eroded core American cultural values and the structures by which they were upheld, including institutions responsible for conveying moral and spiritual values. These cultural shocks polarized Americans, delegitimized institutional authority, eroded the politico-moral ideology of American civil religion, and brought about a decisive break with the meaning of the past, especially among many idealist youth.

NRMs grew fruitfully in this cultural vacuum. In one manner or another, most NRMs emphasized the primacy of experience over creed and dogma, access to spiritual and personal empowerment, unifying values in the form of a pragmatic, success-oriented, or a syncretistic theology proposed as a new revelation, and more meaningful expressions of social solidarity and community-oriented lifestyles.

Movements such as the Unification Church and the New Religious Right responded to the culture crisis with a revitalized synthesis of political and religious themes. The "Moral Majority" and kindred groups, such as Christian Voice, Religious Roundtable, and National Christian Action Coalition, called for a restoration of moral traditionalism, a renewed sense of national order and purpose, and a reassertion of values and myths associated with the gospel of wealth, patriotic idealism, and the messianic understanding of American life and national identity.

The rapid proliferation of NRMs during the 1960s has also been interpreted as a consequence of social experimentation (not directly related to a cultural crisis) stemming from demographic and generational shifts and the new lifestyles and social arrangement flamboyantly popularized by the "hippie" counter-culture. By the 1960s, the "baby boom" and the post–World War II transformation of the American class structure had produced a burgeoning youth population whose affluence, social posture, and greater discretionary time facilitated experimentation with a wide variety of living arrangements and life styles. Widespread psychedelic drug experimentation provided an important link between the youth-oriented counter-culture and the rise of NRMs. In some instances, drug experimentation altered spiritual frames of reference and/or broke down normative perceptions of everyday reality, thereby facilitating movement into NRMs that emphasized meditative or "mystical" religious experience. In other instances (especially the Jesus Movement of the late 1960s), NRMs provided participants with a therapeutic means of kicking a drug habit.

While the precise relationship between the presence of cultural fragmentation and crisis and the rise of NRMs remains subject to debate, it is clear that the proliferation of NRMs is both stimulated and facilitated by strain in value, meaning, and plausibility structures that undergird a social order. The presence of outmoded or discredited myths, ideologies, and institutional arrangements, and the absence of meaningful community experience are key factors conducive to religious ferment.

Conversion Recruitment. Prior to the 1960s, social and behavioral science theories about participation in "sects" and "cults" focused almost exclusively on the lower-class origins of such movements and on the psycho-economic relationship between their ideology and alleged deprivations of neophytes. Sociological and anthropological studies consistently linked the rise of "sects," "revitalization movements," "cargo," and "crisis" cults to severe social and cultural dislocation. Participation in such movements was viewed as compensatory behavior that arose in response to unrest, privation, and maladjustment. Although the concept of deprivation was broadened to include social, organismic, ethical, and psychical tensions, the operating assumption continued to hold that converts to "sects" and "cults" were individuals who experienced some form of personal or cultural trauma. This assumption animates the culture crisis hypothesis discussed earlier.

Although deprivation/motivation theory remains an important insight into religious affiliation, the understanding of conversion/recruitment on the basis of the analysis of NRMs is now more nuanced, interactive, and process oriented. Deprivation/motivation has come under serious criticism because of its conceptual vagueness, reductionism, and failure to give adequate attention to the active role played by religious groups and organizations in the conversion/recruitment process. While it is true that some people will find a particular world-view more appealing than another because of their psychological or emotional state, closer attention has been drawn to issues of structural availability, to how conversion/recruitment works as a funneling process, to the role of social interaction and interpersonal bonds, to the role of participants as active seekers, and to the specific strategies by which groups mobilize resources and seek participants to achieve their objectives.

Conversion/recruitment dynamics vary across groups and among individuals. However, most studies of conversion/recruitment vis-à-vis NRMs have focused on two levels of analysis: predispositional and situational factors.

Predispositional factors are internal variables related to a convert's motivational state and prior socialization. They include the presence of "felt needs" and/or tensions in the individual, the holding of a religious problem-solving perspective, and religious-seeking incentives.

Many participants in NRMs were geographically unsettled, subjectively dissatisfied with their lives, alienated from dominant institutions, and lacking strong communal ties. Many had participated in or experimented with several NRMs before actually joining a specific one. Participants also tended to be drawn from the ranks of young adults previously socialized in mainline (and more liberal) religious traditions, but who were unchurched at the time of their NRM affiliation.

Situational factors are external variables related to the individual's interaction with the proselytizing organization. They include encountering the NRM at a "turning point" in one's life, the development (or pre-existence) of affective bonds, intensive encapsulation, and the weakening or neutralization of affective ties outside the movement.

Studies have consistently shown that NRMs that employed the establishment of affective bonds in the service of proselytizing grew more rapidly than those that did not. Movements that recruited individuals who were social isolates before joining had slower growth rates because their members failed to provide a new network for movement growth. NRMs that isolated their participants from society, or that required the severance of non-movement interpersonal ties, also grew less rapidly than those that were more fluid and open.

Studies of conversion/recruitment dynamics in NRMs also suggest that some individuals assume movement roles and participate in group activities prior to actual commitment to or knowledgeable understanding of the specific belief system. Social pressures and group encapsulation then work to intensify commitment. Conversion/recruitment under these circumstances is a socially structured event arising out of role relationships and the necessity of legitimating behavior at variance with the individual's normal social intercourse. The fact that some individuals joined NRMs quickly and with only sketchy knowledge about the group gave rise to questions about group manipulation and deception.

Other theories explain conversion to NRMs as rational choice process in which individuals assess their needs at the time and determine the balance of rewards and costs associated with a particular movement. Ambiguities over gender role identity and relationships have also been linked with NRMs involvement.

Deprogramming Controversy. Not unlike controversies surrounding new religions in earlier eras, contemporary NRMs have met with varying degrees of public hostility and opposition. Conflicts over groups such as the Children of God (The Family), the Unification Church, and the Hare Krishna movement have generally focused on allegations of financial exploitation, misrepresentation, political intrigue, authoritarian leadership, sexual impropriety, and charges that such groups utilize "brainwashing" and "mind-control" techniques both as strategies for recruitment and as a means of retaining individuals against their will. The tragic mass murder/suicide of over 900 followers of the Rev. Jim Jones in Guyana in 1978—along with other well-publicized controversies surrounding NRM leaders—stimulated anti-cult initiatives at the time.

In response to the above factors, and to youth behavior that violated parental perceptions and expectations and the cultural values of MATERIALISM, occupation competition, and achievement, anti-cult groups, such as the American Freedom Foundation, the Citizens Freedom Foundation, and the Spiritual Counterfeit Program, began forming in the early 1970s. These organizations consisted primarily of parents, NRM apostates, and professional "deprogrammers" who viewed many NRMs as dangerous expressions of intense religious commitment, zealotry, or dogmatic sectarianism.

To secure the goal of freeing individuals from "destructive cults," anti-cult organizations established informational networks, monitored NRMs, sought to educate the public through published and media material, and lobbied to gain support for their activities and legislation to curb NRM activity.

Coercive action against NRM participants was initiated under the aegis of seeking temporary guardianships and conservatorships through the legal system. More controversial extra-legal initiatives included forcible abductions and intense "deprogramming" sessions. Courts have generally been reluctant to prosecute coercive deprogramming on the grounds that such episodes involve family or parental matters.

Although anti-cult groups have had only limited success in mobilizing other institutions against new religions, they have been more successful at achieving symbolic degradation of NRMs. However, there has been little empirical evidence to show that the vast majority of NRM participants are recruited through "brainwashing" or coercive tactics, or that they were kept in movements by Orwellian-like mind-control techniques. The perception that NRMs engage in "brainwashing" has repeatedly been called in question by scholarly research and by many religious leaders. The small number of actual recruits relative to contacts and the extremely high dropout rates among groups against which such charges have been directed belie such allegations.

Religious Response to NRMs. The attitude of mainline religious bodies toward NRMs varied from active opposition, to indifference, to qualified endorsement.

Protestant conservative/fundamentalist groups took the most active role in developing a coherent and largely negative response. Literature published by these organizations assert Christian claims of exclusivism and alert individuals to the "dangers" of cults as the work of the anti-Christ.

A second approach is a more benign rejection of NRMs as a resurgence of GNOSTICISM—especially those groups that emphasize "knowledge," mystical experiences, and freeing the divine within. These NRMs are held to be incompatible with Christianity and, in the case of those Eastern-derived religions, unlikely to become socially significant outside their own cultural milieu.

A third approach looks positively on NRMs as legitimate religious phenomena, as presenting new opportunities for inter-religious dialogue, as a challenge for self-evaluation, and as a stimulus for spiritual and ecclesial renewal within mainline religions.

On May 4, 1986, the Vatican released a report on "Sects or New Religious Movements: Pastoral Challenge" in response to mounting episcopal concern over the dramatic growth of NRMs among Catholic populations. According to the document, the spread of NRMs is not to be viewed as a threat but as a stimulus for spiritual and ecclesial renewal. Such movements are to be approached with an attitude of openness and understanding

reflecting the principles of respect for the person and religious liberty laid down by Vatican II. At the same time, Catholics are cautioned against being "naively irenical." The Church's response to NRMs is acknowledged to extend beyond the "spiritual" to the social, cultural, political, and economic conditions from which NRMs draw their constituents. Community and parish patterns that are more caring and relevant are encouraged. Special attention is to be paid to the role of Holy Scripture, catechesis and evangelization. Forms of worship and ministry are to be relevant to cultural environments and life situations. Creativity in the liturgy, diversified ministries, and lay leadership are also called for in response to NRMs.

Bibliography: S. E. AHLSTROM, "National Trauma and Changing Religious Values," *Daedalus* (Winter 1978): 13–29. E. BAKER, ed., *Of God and Men: New Religious Movements in the West* (Macon, Ga. 1983). D. G. BROMLEY and P. E. HAMMOND, *The Future of New Religious Movements* (Macon, Ga. 1987). J. A. BECKFORD, *Cult Controversies: The Societal Response to New Religious Movements* (New York 1985). D. BROMLEY and J. T. RICHARDSON, eds., *The Brainwashing/Deprogramming Controversy* (Toronto 1983). R. S. ELLWOOD, *Religious and Spiritual Groups in Modern America* (Englewood Cliffs, N.J. 1973). L. P. GERLACH and V. HINE, "Five Factors Crucial to the Growth and Spread of a Modern Religious Movement," *Journal for The Scientific Study of Religion* 7 (1966) 23–40. B. WILSON, ed., *The Social Impact of the New Religions* (New York 1981). C. GLOCK and R. BELLAH, eds., *The New Religious Consciousness* (Berkeley 1976). J. NEEDLEMAN and G. BARKER, eds., *Understanding the New Religions* (New York 1978). J. T. RICHARDSON, *Conversion Careers: In and Out of the New Religions* (Beverly Hills, Calif. 1978). T. ROBBINS and D. ANTHONY, eds., *In Gods We Trust: New Patterns of Religious Pluralism in America* (New Brunswick 1981). A. D SHUPE and D. G. BROMLEY, *The New Vigilantes: Deprogrammers, Anti-Cultists and the New Religions* (Beverly Hills, Calif. 1980). R. STARK and W. S. BAINBRIDGE, *The Future of Religion: Secularization and Cult Formation* (Berkeley 1985). R. WUTHNOW, *The Consciousness Reformation* (Berkeley 1976). M. FUSS, et al., *Rethinking New Religious Movements* (Rome 1998). M. GALANTER, *Cults: Faith, Healing, and Coercion,* 2d. ed. (New York 1999). L. L. DAWSON, *Comprehending Cults: The Sociology of New Religious Movements* (Toronto 1998).

[W. D. DINGES]

NEW TESTAMENT BOOKS

The New Testament, comprising 27 books, forms a unit of literature that complements the Old Testament and completes the written record of God's revelation to mankind (*see* OLD TESTAMENT LITERATURE). The present division of New Testament writings is by no means chronological. Under the influence of the Old Testament division of historical, didactic, and prophetical works, a similar division was made in early Christendom for the New Testament writings, and this became stabilized at the Council of Trent (*Enchiridion biblicum* 59). Thus, for the historical section there are the four Gospels and Acts;

for the didactic section, the 14 Epistles of Paul, the 2 Epistles of Peter, the 3 of John, the Epistle of James, and the Epistle of Jude; and for the prophetic section, the Book of Revelation (a.k.a., the Apocalypse) of John.

See Also: The Articles on the Individual Books of the New Testament.

Bibliography: J. N. SANDERS, "The Literature and Canon of the NT," *Peake's Commentary on the Bible,* ed. M. BLACK and H. H. ROWLEY (New York 1962) 676–682. A. WIKENHAUSER, *New Testament Introduciton,* tr. J. CUNNINGHAM (New York 1958). R. E. BROWN, *An Introduction to the New Testament* (New York 1997). J. S. KSELMAN and R. D. WITHERUP in *New Jerome Biblical Commentary* 1130–1145.

[B. A. LAZOR]

NEW TESTAMENT SCHOLARSHIP

Shortly after the First World War the application of the various form-critical methods to the New Testament by Karl Ludwig Schmidt, Martin DIBELIUS and Rudolf BULTMANN led to a trend in New Testament exegesis in which particular attention was paid to the different literary genres of the 27 books of the New Testament. An intermingling of historico-literary study with philosophical and theological interpretation led some interpreters to be hesitant about adopting the new methods, but their hesitancy was generally overcome in subsequent years. Within Roman Catholicism PIUS XII'S encyclical, *DIVINO AFFLANTE SPIRITU* (1943), warmly endorsed the FORM-CRITICAL method of Biblical interpretation and supported the use of the method by Roman Catholic Biblical scholars. Shortly after World War II, within the Biblical guild itself, reservations began to be stressed about the ultimate utility of the new methods, particularly with regard to the SYNOPTIC GOSPELS where their application was most heavily concentrated.

Historicity. Some of the early form critics had suggested that the oral tradition of the Church had become so fixed and stylized that it was impossible for the traditions to say very much about the historical Jesus himself. Some of Bultmann's disciples, the so-called post-Bultmannians, also expressed a real concern for the historical Jesus. In 1953, Tübingen's Ernst Käsemann raised the issue of "the continuity of the gospel in the discontinuity of the times and the variations of the kerygma." From this concern was born a "new quest for the historical Jesus." The new quest admitted that it was virtually impossible to recover the specific details of Jesus' life and ministry, but suggested that the application of newer methods pointed to realities in his life and ministry which served as the basis for the KERYGMA, the development of the oral tradition, and subsequent theological reflection.

In addition, the radical historical skepticism of some early form critics eventually gave rise to the development of a series of criteria for determining the basic historicity of events and realities relating to the historical Jesus. The law of dual exclusion implied that the narration of events which neither served the narrow interests of the later Church nor were part of the general Jewish culture must have occurred because of historical reminiscence. The criterion of multiple attestation invoked the attestation of a tradition in different sources or in different literary forms as an indication of the essential historicity of the tradition.

Redaction Criticism. In some form-critical analyses, the stress on the formative role of tradition and the internal constraints of the literary genres themselves almost reduced the synoptists to the role of being mere collectors of community traditions. Bultmann, for example, had not included a study of the Synoptic Gospels in his classic two-volume work on the theology of the New Testament. A reaction to the potential one-sidedness of the results of form-critical study developed with the emergence of redaction criticism.

The method essentially concentrates on the role that individual authors have in shaping the oral traditions which have been handed down, as well as the editorial work done on written source material. It deals with an author's selection of material from all that is available to him, the adaptations made on the material that is used, its arrangement, as well as the material that results from an author's own creativity. Since the method concerns how an author uses material that is received, both emendation criticism and compositional analysis are part of the discipline. Its application to a given text highlights the literary uniqueness and specific thought of the text and leads to the affirmation that it was written by a person who must be considered as a real author and a true thinker (theologian).

In the study of the Synoptic Gospels, the pathfinder in the application of the new method was Willi Marxsen. His 1954 doctoral thesis, presented at the University of Kiel, Germany, examined the Gospel of MARK. Marxsen highlighted Mark's understanding of "gospel" as well as the fashion in which Mark used geographical categories (e.g., Galilee, the desert) with symbolic or theological reference. In the same year, a German professor at the University of Zurich, Switzerland, published a new study on LUKE. Translated into English, Hans Conzelmann's work had as a title *The Theology of Saint Luke,* but the literal translation of the German title was "the middle of time" (*Die Mitte der Zeit*). Conzelmann's thesis held that it was inaccurate to consider Luke, the author of the Gospel and of the ACTS OF THE APOSTLES, principally as an historian. Rather Luke should be considered as a theologian with a singular vision of history. According to this vision, JESUS CHRIST stands at the center of history, with the history of Israel as His precedent and the history of the Church unfolding in the period which follows.

Life Situation. In the study of the Gospels, the use of the tools of redaction criticism required scholars to examine three life-situations in the development of the gospel tradition: the life situation of Jesus, the life situation of the Church, and the life situation of the evangelists. The new and refined concern for the historicity of the Jesus-event led scholars to consider with particular seriousness such singular events as the Baptism and death of Jesus, as well as His typical activities, e.g., casting out demons and preaching in parables. Application and development of the form-critical method itself, along with a study of the history of traditions, further clarified the life situation of the Church as the milieu which was both conservative and formative with regard to the traditions about Jesus.

The proponents of redaction criticism concentrated their greatest attention on the life situation of the evangelists. While the Gospel writers were considered to be authors and theologians in their own right, the composition of their respective Gospels was not done in a vacuum. The situation of the local churches was the milieu in which the literary-theological works of MATTHEW, Mark, and Luke were produced. Their respective Gospels were produced within specific communities, to whose problems the Gospels responded and whose theology was reflected in them.

Since redaction criticism focused on the manner in which an evangelist worked with his tradition and edited his sources, redaction critics needed to identify the literary sources utilized by the synoptists. The basic working hypothesis, even among Roman Catholic authors, who for the most part no longer held to the traditional view that Matthew was the first of the written Gospels, was that of Markan priority. Mark's Gospel was considered to be the major extant literary source for Matthew and Luke. Both of these evangelists also made use of a collection of Jesus' sayings. Q, the Sayings Source, is no longer extant, but it can be reconstituted on the basis of a comparative study of the discourse material in Matthew and Luke. Redaction criticism's interest in the editorial process thus led to a concentration of study on the Gospel of Mark and the Q source.

Perhaps the most significant features of the results of redaction-critical analyses of the Synoptic Gospels were the attention paid to the uniqueness of each Gospel and the specific theological insights of each of the evangelists. Ruled out of consideration are homogenized narratives which group together in a single construct two or more evangelical accounts of a tradition, thereby obscuring or passing over the singularly rich witness of each evangelist. In this way the traditional designation of the Synoptic Gospels, that is, "the Gospel according to Matthew (Mark or Luke)" took on a new significance.

Although the redaction-critical method was initially developed in the academic circles of the German Lutheran tradition, it was widely adopted in the world of Biblical scholarship. Within Roman Catholicism the use of the method was essentially endorsed by *Sancta Mater ecclesia* (April 21, 1964), the Instruction of the Pontifical Biblical Commission on the Historical Truth of the Gospels. The instruction spoke of the evangelists' selection of material, its adaptation, and placement in the respective Gospels. VATICAN COUNCIL II's Dogmatic Constitution on Divine Revelation likewise endorsed the method, especially when it stated that "the sacred authors wrote the four Gospels, selecting some things from the many which had been handed on by word of mouth or in writing, reducing some of them to a synthesis, explicating some things in view of the situation of their churches . . ." (*Dei Verbum*, n. 19).

The similarities that exist among the Synoptic Gospels point to some form of literary interdependence among them and provide a context for a comparative study of traditional materials. The absence of extant sources and the relative lack of possibilities for comparative study of the other New Testament texts have resulted in the methods of redaction-critical analysis being principally applied to the Synoptic Gospels among the New Testament texts.

Acts and Paul. In principle the redaction-critical method is not lacking in possibilities for fruitful analysis of the other New Testament books. The literary and historical insights gleaned from a study of Luke provide a key for a redaction-critical analysis of Acts. The possibility of comparing New Testament epistles with Hellenistic epistolary literature have highlighted the particularity of the Pauline letter and the development of an epistolary tradition, with dependence on PAUL, within the early Church.

Redaction criticism requires scholars to be particularly sensitive to the peculiarities of an individual author's thought, style, and vocabulary. Attention to these elements in the study of the Pauline corpus (Rom, 1–2 Cor, Gal, Eph, Col, Phil, 1–2 Thes, 1–2 Tim, Ti, Phlm) has led to significant developments in regard to the authorship of the epistles. The new trend is particularly apparent in the commentaries of the 1980s. Since that time a study of various thematic, stylistic, and linguistic considerations has led the majority of scholars to consider (in declining order according to the size of the majority) 1–2 Tim, Ti, Eph, Col, and 2 Thes as pseudepigraphal compositions. The remaining seven letters (Rom, 1–2 Cor, Gal, Phil, 1 Thes, Phlm) are commonly accepted as Pauline. These Pauline *homologoumena* constitute a critical Pauline corpus within the canonical collection of Pauline writings.

John. Elements of tradition and redaction are also to be discerned in the Johannine corpus (Jn, 1–2–3 Jn, Rv). Compositional analysis has also been usefully applied to both JOHN and REVELATION. The relationship between each of these writings and their respective ecclesial situations, especially the separation between church and synagogue, has been a major focus of attention in recent scholarship.

Manuscripts and Text. Many of the recent developments in New Testament scholarship have therefore been due to refinements in the methods of literary analysis. Alongside the methods of textual criticism, source criticism, form criticism, and the history of traditions, redaction criticism is now an integral part of the historical-critical approach to the Biblical text. Further insights into the meaning of some New Testament texts, particularly John and Revelation, have come as a result of the discovery of two major groups of ancient manuscripts.

By providing scholars with significant comparative material, the discovery of manuscripts at Nag Hammadi in 1945 and of others at QUMRAN and nearby Wadi Murabba'at in 1947 to 1956 has had significant influence on the understanding of the New Testament in recent years. The Nag Hammadi finds generally shed considerable light on the early gnosticism within which early Christianity developed and suggest possibilities as to how some Christian trajectories or trends of thought tended to develop. The Palestinian finds have clarified the real diversity of the religious situation of first century Palestine and have provided scholars with significant new insights into Jewish apocalyptic thought and ESCHATOLOGICAL expectations.

Since we do not possess any autograph copies of books of the New Testament, a first task in the historical-critical approach to the New Testament is the establishment of a Greek text of the different books. Nag Hammadi's *Gospel of Thomas*, a fourth-century Coptic manuscript of a text which dates from the second century, has proved to be a significant addition as a witness to the textual development of the sayings of Jesus. Other than the publication of the Bodmer papyri in the mid-20th century, there has been no discovery and publication of a New Testament manuscript to rival Tischendorf's discovery of the *Codex Sinaiticus* in the late 19th century.

One new development with regard to the Greek text of the New Testament has been the publication of a virtually standard edition of the text. An international committee, under the leadership of Kurt Aland of the Munster Institute for Textual Research, has produced a popular edition. The editors intended that this Greek text should serve as a basis for the various translations of the New Testament into the modern languages. Originally appearing as *The Greek New Testament* (London 1966) it has since been published as the fourth revised edition of *The Greek New Testament* (London 1993) and as the 27th edition of Nestle-Aland's *Novum Testamentum Graece* (Munster 1993), with but minor changes in later printings.

The historical-critical method of New Testament interpretation is the model within which most scholars work. These interpreters seek to make an ''exegesis'' of the text. They try to determine what an author said and meant within his own context as he wrote his texts. The several different methodologies subsumed under the historical-critical rubric attempt to elucidate an author's intended meaning by studying his language, his method of writing, and the historical, cultural, and literary circumstances within which he wrote.

The PONTIFICAL BIBLICAL COMMISSION'S ''The Interpretation of the Bible in the Church'' (1993) endorsed the historical-critical method as ''the indispensable method for the scientific study of the meaning. . . . its proper understanding not only admits the use of this method but actually requires it.'' This document also offered an overview, and occasionally some criticism, of various other approaches to the study of the New Testament including the history of the interpretation of the text, its Wirkungsgeschichte.

Rhetorical Criticism. Parallel with the development of the historical-critical method is the emergence of rhetorical criticism. Depending on one's point of view, rhetorical criticism can be identified as an adjunct to the classic historical-critical method or as a particular approach within the general category of specific disciplines belonging to the historical-critical method. Rhetorical criticism is an approach that is attentive to the fact that ''it is the creative synthesis of the particular formulation of the pericope with the content that makes it the distinctive composition that it is'' (James Muilenburg). It concentrates on the ability of New Testament passages to persuade or convince.

Most New Testament texts were intended to be read aloud to an audience (see 1 Thes 5:27). In rhetorical-critical analysis, three levels of style are typically distinguished, according to the author's intention in communicating with his audience. The orator teaches in plain style, praises or condemns in a middle style, and moves the audience in a grand style. One element of style is *lexis*, the author's choice of words and his use of various figures of speech. The other element is *synthesis*, composition. This is concerned with the way that words are formed into phrases, phrases into clauses, and clauses into sentences.

Many New Testament scholars believe that rhetorical criticism is of limited value since it seems to reduce the various New Testament texts to the level of one-time events, thereby obscuring their meaning for modern readers. Proponents of the method retort that this charge can be leveled against form- and redaction-criticism as well. Their use of the categories of Hellenistic rhetoric draws attention to an element of the various literary forms used in the New Testament generally neglected by classic form-critical analysis, namely its ability to make an impact upon the audience. Rhetorical criticism is applied to both the literary micro genres [the *Magnificat,* (Lk 1:46–55), for example, can be characterized as epideictic] and the literary macro genres found in the New Testament. By the turn of the millennium, rhetorical criticism has become a sine qua non for the study of Paul's letters.

Hermeneutics. While the various form-critical methods are generally employed in academic treatments of the New Testament Scriptures, considerable reaction to the exclusive use of the historical-critical method has developed in academic and other circles. Essentially the reaction focuses on a criticism that the historical-critical method concentrates too much on the past. Its approach is diachronical, that is, it indicates how a text came into existence. It indicates what a text meant in the past, but does not indicate what a text means at the present time. Indeed there are authors who question whether it is possible to speak at all about what a text means, as if there were but a single meaning of the text, and as if this meaning were the meaning intended by the author.

This criticism is voiced, among others, by those who approach the New Testament from the standpoint of the hermeneutical theories developed by Paul RICOEUR and Hans-Georg GADAMER. There are significant differences between the hermeneutics of each of these authors, especially between Ricoeur's theory of the nature of textuality and Gadamer's dialectical hermeneutics, but there is some significant similarity in their views. Ricoeur stresses that a text enjoys a certain semantic independence, especially vis-à-vis its author. Gadamer uses the dialogue as an important analogue for the interpretation of a text.

In the view of both authors the interpretation of a text is always an historical, linguistic event. Each of them considers that a text conveys meaning insofar as it opens up a world of meaning for the reader. The understanding of a text results from the coming together of the reader's own horizon and that of the text on the basis of a shared tradition of concerns. From this point of view, the real focus of New Testament scholarship is the contemporary meaning of the text, rather than the somewhat hypothetical rediscovery of what the text meant in the past. At the very least, one must distinguish various levels of meaning of the New Testament texts.

Structural Analysis. Other critics of the exclusive use of the historical-critical methods of New Testament interpretation proposed the method of structural analysis as a useful approach to the New Testament texts. In fact "structural analysis" is an umbrella term used to cover a variety of literary methods used in an attempt to understand how a text conveys meaning. "A text does not have meaning, a text is meaningful" is the premise of the structural analytic approach.

These various methods are akin to the methods used in the contemporary study of secular literature. One stress is on the identity of a text as anything that is written. Another is on the function of language as both informative and metaphorical. Still another is the importance of paradigms as tools useful for the understanding of texts. There is no single method of structural analysis, but significant structural analytic approaches to the New Testament have been developed in France, Germany and the United States. In France, concern with the function and nature of narrative has proved helpful for an understanding of the Gospels and PARABLES OF JESUS. In the United States, the parables have frequently been studied with the aid of the newer literary methods, but Daniel Patte has demonstrated the broader applicability of the method with studies on Paul's epistles as well as the Gospel of Matthew. With the advent of the new millennium the use of structural analysis in New Testament study had receded in favor of literary approaches and various pointed readings of the text.

Narrative analysis has come to the fore as a useful method for understanding the New Testament, especially, Matthew, Mark, Luke-Acts (to be considered as a single two-part work), and John since these books are stories. As the method has been developed and used in the United States, narrative analysis draws the reader's attention to the plot, setting (time and place), and characterization that each of the New Testament authors employ. These elements serve to create a "narrative world" which the reader of the story is implicitly invited to adopt. The story conveys its meaning to the extent that a contemporary reader, the "real" reader can identify with the audience for whom the text was originally intended, the "intended" reader.

To some lesser degree narrative analysis is less fruitful for the study of the epistles, where epistolary criticism has come to the fore. Modern technology has allowed New Testament scholars to have access to many non-literary letters written about the same time as the epistles. Analysis of these letters enables scholars to better the form, function, and idiom of letters in the Hellenistic world. A. J. Malherbe's work has a major role to play in the development of epistolary criticism.

Sociological Reading. Other reactions to the historical-critical method have come from those who ask whether its presupposition that historical and literary categories provide the best entree to an understanding of the New Testament texts. Are not sociological categories equally useful? John G. Gager's *Kingdom and Community: The Social World of Early Christianity* (1975) was the first full-scale application of sociological concepts to early Christianity.

Contemporary sociological reading of the New Testament is quite different from the sociological approach to the Scriptures developed by the Chicago school during the early part of the 20th century. Elements of social theory and cultural anthropology are often incorporated into a sociological approach to the text. Some of the newer approaches are, even from the historian's viewpoint, relatively bias-free. Within this parameter can be considered the work of Gerd Theisse on Jesus and his disciples, using the sociological category of the wandering charismatic, and his social analysis of the church at Corinth, as well as Wayne Meeks' work on early urban Christians. What, for example, was the significance of the early Christian structural organization according to house churches? On the other hand, the Jesus Seminar has used sociological readings to portray what many scholars considered to be an extremely biased picture of Jesus.

Some sociological readings of the New Testament are, by design, engaged interpretations of the texts. To this category of sociological readings belong the materialistic, often Marxist, readings which point to elements of class struggle attested by the Scripture. Closely related would be the pastorally engaged reading of the text by proponents of liberation theology. Frequently this type of approach emphasizes the importance of the poor as a particularly significant group for whom the gospel of Jesus was intended.

Feminist Hermeneutics. During the 1980s, a FEMINIST HERMENEUTIC of the New Testament was developed. Drawing attention to the fact that the role of women seems to have been downplayed in the male-dominated cultural circumstances in which the New Testament was written, proponents of this approach take a variety of tacks. For some, the important thing is to develop a prophetic stance, thereby criticizing the neglect of women from within the Biblical tradition itself. For others (e.g.,

Phyllis Trible), it is a matter of drawing attention to texts overlooked or misinterpreted by male-dominated hermeneutics. A more radical, revisionist approach was taken by Elisabeth Schlusser-Fiorenza, especially in *In Memory of Her* (New York 1983). Schlusser-Fiorenza goes beyond the canon of the New Testament in an endeavor to show that the real situation of the early Christian faith allowed a greater role for women than the canonical New Testament texts seem to reflect. The most radical form of feminist hermeneutics rejects the authority of the Bible as the biased product of a patriarchal society.

Psychoanalytic Reading. From quite a different vantage point is the reading of the New Testament by those who approach the text from a psychoanalytic point of view. The psychoanalytic reading developed in French-speaking Europe in the 1970s and has remained basically confined to continental Europe since then. The underlying principle of the psychoanalytic reading is that nothing results from chance. Everything that is written proceeds from a definite motivation, even if this motivation lies at pre- and un-conscious levels.

The psychoanalytic reading essentially approaches a New Testament text with four different, but related, questions: How do the structures of an author's psyche relate to the production of the text at hand? What psychoanalytic categories are useful for portraying the characters, for example, in the narrative about Judas or that of the prodigal son? What is the relationship between a text and meaning, for example, in the passion and Resurrection narratives? Finally, how does the reader identify with the text; to which aspects of his psyche does the text appeal? Although the psychoanalytic reading of the New Testament has generally been limited to one or another relatively short pericope, some psychoanalytic readings of longer texts (e.g., Mk) have appeared.

Canonical Criticism. Yet another approach to New Testament scholarship is to be found in work of those who pronounce themselves in favor of canon criticism. The approach has principally developed in the United States, where a pioneering statement was made by Brevard Childs in *The New Testament as Canon: an Introduction* (Philadelphia 1984). The approach concentrates on a discernment of how the various materials contained in the individual books and the books themselves were rendered into Scripture. Of particular interest is a concern to deal with the effect of the canonical collection on the individual parts. It lays emphasis upon a holistic reading of the text in which the whole is the canonical collection as such.

In the hermeneutical circle of classic expositions of New Testament texts according to the historical-critical method, the whole which clarifies the parts is the entirety of an individual work or the collection of an individual author's work. In the hermeneutical circle of canonical criticism, it is the canonical collection which clarifies the significance of the parts (the individual books and their component parts). In turn, these parts help to clarify the meaning of the New Testament canon.

See Also: PASTORAL EPISTLES; CATHOLIC EPISTLES; NEW TESTAMENT LITERATURE.

Bibliography: W. A. BEARDSLEE, *Literary Criticism of the New Testament* (Philadelphia 1970). R. F. COLLINS, *Introduction to the New Testament* (Garden City 1983). W. G. DOTY, *Letters in Primitive Christianity* (Philadelphia 1973). H. Y. GAMBLE, *The New Testament Canon: Its Making and Meaning* (Philadelphia 1985). C. OSIEK, *What Are They Saying About the Social Setting of the New Testament?* (New York/Mahwah 1984). D. PATTE, *What Is Structural Analysis?* (Philadelphia 1976). N. PERRIN, *What Is Redaction Criticism?* (Philadelphia 1971). N. R. PETERSEN, *Literary Criticism for New Testament Critics* (Philadelphia 1978).

[R. F. COLLINS]

NEW THOUGHT

A movement embracing any form of modern belief in the practice of mental healing other than those associated with traditional Christianity. The name came into vogue in 1895 and was used as the title of a magazine published for a time in Melrose, Massachusetts, to describe a "new thought" about life, based on the premise that knowledge of the real world of ideas has marvelous power to relieve people of various ills.

History. The movement began with the work of Phineas P. Quimby (1802–66), of Portland, Maine, who practiced mental and spiritual healing for more than 20 years and greatly influenced Mary Baker EDDY, foundress of CHRISTIAN SCIENCE. At first Quimby practiced unqualified mesmerism; the client would sit opposite the doctor, who then held the person's hands and looked him intently in the eye. As the patient went into a mesmeric sleep, Quimby spoke to him and talked him out of his ailment, often manipulating the affected part with hands that were moistened for greater efficiency. Later, Quimby became convinced that disease was simply an error of the mind and not a real thing, so that mesmerism could be dispensed with and equal, or even better, results assured. In time he claimed that his only power consisted in the knowledge he had that sickness is illusion and in the ability to communicate this assurance to others. In a circular addressed to the sick, Quimby thus described his own system: "My practice is unlike all medical practice. I give no medicine, and make no outward applications. I tell the patient his troubles, and what he thinks is his disease; and my explanation is the cure. If I succeed in correcting his errors, I change the fluids of the system and establish *the truth, or health. The truth is the cure.* This mode of practice applies to all cases."

Quimby organized no society, but persons whom he had helped adopted his method, passing it on to others with additions and changes of their own. Two of his followers, Warren F. Evans and Julius A. Dresser, gave systematic form to his ideas; they are regarded as the intellectual founders of New Thought and its allied movements. Evans published six books on the subject, of which the most significant were *The Mental Cure* (1869), *Mental Medicine* (1872), and *Soul and Body* (1875). According to Evans, disease has its roots in wrong belief. Once that is changed, disease is cured. A devoted Swedenborgian, he had long been familiar with the writings of G. BERKELEY and other idealists (*see* SWEDENBORG, E.). His own character and personal experiences further led him to a point where he was ready to apply an extreme form of idealism to the healing of disease. Dresser, cured by Quimby in 1860, began his major work in mental healing in 1882 in Boston, where Dresser and his wife, Annetta, were competing with Mrs. Eddy. When Dresser's clients were curious to learn how they had been healed, he obliged with a series of 12 class lectures, which included a study of the divine immanence and a consideration that the spiritual life is continuous, that men already live in eternity. "To realize that our real life is spiritual was to overcome the illusions of sense-experience with its manifold bondages." Dresser's son and biographer popularized his father's teaching.

Evans and Dresser remained faithful to the memory of Quimby, whereas Mrs. Eddy disclaimed all dependence on her benefactor, whom she called "an ignorant mesmerist." Mrs. Eddy's followers became organized in a tightly knit society, the Church of Christ, Scientist; the disciples of Quimby founded numerous small groups under different names, such as Divine Science, Unity, Practical Christianity, Home of Truth, and the Church of the Higher Life. Before the turn of the century, these came to be known as New Thought and in 1894 the first national convention was held. In 1908 the name National New Thought Alliance was adopted and six years later the organization became international. Its membership was extended to all the major countries of the world.

Basic Principles. Although New Thought did not substantially change after the time of Quimby, Evans, and Dresser, there was an expansion of scope to cover a broader perspective than healing sickness. The Declaration of Principles, adopted by the International Alliance in 1917, begins by affirming "the freedom of each soul as to its choice and as to belief." Accordingly no creedal profession is necessary. "The essence of the New

Thought is Truth, and each individual must be loyal to the Truth he sees. The windows of his soul must be kept open at each moment for the higher light, and his mind must be always hospitable to each new inspiration.''

Allowing for a monistic interpretation of the universe, the declaration states, ''We affirm the new thought of God as Universal Love, Life, Truth and Joy, in whom we live, move, and have our being, and by whom we are held together; and His mind is our mind now, that realizing our oneness with Him means love, truth, peace, health, and plenty.'' In the same strain, taking monistically Christ's words about the kingdom within us, New Thought asserts that ''we are one with the Father'' (*see* MONISM).

In keeping with Quimby's theory of the mind's influence, it is held that ''Man's body is his holy temple. Every function of it, every cell of it, is intelligent, and is shaped, ruled, repaired, and controlled by mind. He whose body is full of light is full of health. Spiritual healing has existed among all races in all times. It has now become a part of the higher science and art of living the life more abundant.''

Consistent with its stress on present well-being, New Thought believes that ''Heaven is here and now, the life everlasting that becomes conscious immortality, the communion of mind with mind throughout the universe of thoughts, the nothingness of all error and negation, including death, the variety in unity that produces the individual expressions of the One-Life.'' All this is to be understood against the background of an idealism that some have traced to G. W. F. HEGEL and others to Berkeley. ''We affirm,'' the declaration concludes, ''that the universe is spiritual and we are spiritual beings.''

New Thought considers itself a form of Christianity, while denying the Trinity, original sin, and the divinity of Christ. It proposes instead a cosmic hypostatic union that reflects the Christology of David STRAUSS. ''Every man is an incarnation of God,'' New Thought teaches, ''anyone who recognizes this and lives in conscious and harmonious union with Spirit, automatically becomes Christ.''

Unlike other denominations that emphasize mental health, such as Christian Science, New Thought permits dual membership; many of its adherents are active church-goers in the more liberal Protestant denominations.

Bibliography: M. BACH, *The Unity of Life* (Englewood Cliffs, NJ 1962). H. E. CADY, *Lessons in Truth* (rev. ed. Lee's Summit, MO 1955). H. W. DRESSER, *Health and the Inner Life* (New York 1906); *A History of the New Thought Movement* (New York 1919). E. HOLMES, *New Thought Terms and Their Meanings* (New York 1942). R. PEEL, *Christian Science: Its Encounter with American Culture* (New York 1958).

[J. A. HARDON]

NEW ULM, DIOCESE OF

Established Nov. 18, 1957, the Diocese of New Ulm (*Novae Ulmae*), a suffragan see of the Archdiocese of ST. PAUL-MINNEAPOLIS, comprises a 15-county area in western Minnesota. Alphonse J. Schladweiler, the first bishop, served for 18 years from Jan. 30, 1958, until his retirement on Dec. 23, 1975. He died at the age of 93 on April 3, 1996.

The first church in New Ulm, begun in 1858, was destroyed before completion during the Sioux uprising in 1862. Alexander Berghold became the first resident pastor (January 1869). In 1870 a second edifice was blessed in honor of the Holy Trinity. Construction of the third church (later the cathedral) was begun in 1890; the Romanesque structure was blessed in 1893. The diocese is distinctly rural. Most of the parishes are in small towns with numerous farm parishioners; some parishes are totally rural. At the time it was made a diocese, the only two cities, New Ulm and Willmar, had a combined population of more than 10,000 (1960 census).

In addition to creating the foundation for the new diocese, Schladweiler was one of the first of the U.S. bishops to respond to the appeal from Pope Pius XII to establish missions in South America. Under his leadership, New Ulm assumed the responsibility for staffing the parish of San Lucas Toliman in Guatemala. Later Schladweiler participated in all the sessions of the VATICAN COUNCIL II in Rome from 1962–1965, and after the council he was active in implementing its decrees.

His successor, Raymond A. Lucker, brought with him a national reputation in the field of religious education and pastoral ministry. Born in 1927 and ordained a priest in 1952 for the Archdiocese of St. Paul, Lucker earned a doctorate in theology (S.T.D.) from the University of St. Thomas in Rome and a doctorate in education (Ph.D.) from the University of Minnesota. He served first as assistant director, then as diocesan director of the CONFRATERNITY OF CHRISTIAN DOCTRINE (1958–1969), and in 1966 he was named Superintendent of Education for the Archdiocese of St. Paul and Minneapolis. In 1969 he was named Director of the Department of Education for the United States Catholic Conference in Washington, D.C., a post he held until 1971 when he was appointed auxiliary bishop in the Archdiocese of St. Paul and Minneapolis.

In his almost 25 years as bishop of New Ulm, Lucker shaped the structures of the diocese. He shared his own vision of the modern Church through active promotion of renewal movements such as RENEW, adult faith formation, pastoral planning, and lay involvement in the life and ministry of the Church. He was the first bishop in the United States to appoint lay men and women as pastoral administrators in parishes, beginning in March, 1981. Lucker brought the diocese into the national spotlight. He attended the International Catechetical Congress in Rome in 1971, and was elected by the Bishops of the United States as a delegate to the Synod in 1977 that dealt with catechetics; he was an alternate delegate to the Synod in 1987. A pioneer in the American catechetical renewal and a strong advocate of involving laity, including women, in ministry, he was much sought after by national organizations as a speaker. He was a leader in the nationwide development of the Confraternity of Christian Doctrine and was advisor to the National Conference of Diocesan Directors (later renamed the National Conference of Catechetical Leaders). He was one of the founders of the Catechetical Forum, an association of catechetical writers, professors, directors and other leaders, and was an active member of the CATHOLIC THEOLOGICAL SOCIETY OF AMERICA. An indefatigable worker, Bishop Lucker served on the National Conference of Catholic Bishops' Administrative Committee and the committees on Latin America, Evangelization, Diaconate, Laity, Catechetical Directory, and Charismatic Renewal.

Afflicted with melanoma, Bishop Lucker resigned the see in November 2000. Less than a year later he succumbed to the disease, Sept. 1, 2001, and was buried in New Ulm.

On Aug. 6, 2001 the Most Reverend John Clayton Nienstedt, S.T.D. was installed as third bishop of the Diocese of New Ulm. Ordained a priest in 1974, he was appointed an auxiliary bishop of the Archdiocese of Detroit in 1996.

Bibliography: J. M. REARDON, *The Catholic Church in the Diocese of St. Paul* (St. Paul 1952). P. H. AHERN, ed., *Catholic Heritage in Minnesota, North Dakota, South Dakota* (St. Paul 1964).

[G. B. KUNZ/B. HUEBSCH.]

NEW YORK, ARCHDIOCESE OF

(*Neo-Eboracensis*) Metropolitan see, 4,717 square miles, comprising the boroughs of Manhattan, Bronx, and Richmond, in New York City, and the counties of Westchester, Putnam, Dutchess, Rockland, Orange, Sullivan, and Ulster. The diocese was created April 8, 1808; the archdiocese, July 19, 1850. The dioceses suffragan to New York included Albany, Brooklyn, Buffalo, Ogdens-

burg, Rochester, Rockville Centre, and Syracuse. These, along with Newark, Paterson, and part of Trenton, in New Jersey, made up the territory of the original see. In the first division (1847), the creation of the Dioceses of Albany and Buffalo cut off the northern and western sections of the state; in the second (1853), the new Sees of Brooklyn and Newark removed Long Island and New Jersey. Since 1861, when the boundary between Albany and New York was readjusted, the limits of the archdiocese, with the exception of the period from 1885 to 1932, when the Bahama Islands were under the jurisdiction of New York, have remained unchanged.

Colonial Period

From the time that Giovanni da Verrazano discovered New York Bay (1524), the area has had Catholic associations. The explorers Estevan Gomez and Samuel de Champlain preceded Henry Hudson in sailing both the southern and northern waters of the state.

Dutch. The Dutch settlement of New Amsterdam was only a year old when the Franciscan Joseph d'Aillon, probably the first priest to enter the state, visited the Niagara region (1627). Thereafter Jesuits established missions among the Iroquois. René Goupil became the first martyr within the confines of the state (1642); his companion, Isaac Jogues, suffered martyrdom in 1646, with John de Lalande, at Ossernenon (Auriesville). *See* NORTH AMERICAN MARTYRS. Fathers Claude Dablon and Pierre Chaumonot built a chapel where Syracuse now stands (1655). Two years later Father Simon Le Moyne came downriver to minister to a few Catholics, both Dutch and French, in New Amsterdam, and probably to offer Mass there, on a French ship and in the settlement.

English. Apart from the converts made by the Jesuits among the indigenous peoples, Kateri TEKAKWITHA being the most famous example (1676), very few Catholics were to be found in the colony when the Dutch ceded it to the English in 1664. The former, while establishing the Reformed Church, had been mildly tolerant; the latter, especially under the Catholic governor, Thomas Dongan (1683–88), were for a time even more generous. Dongan's Charter of Libertys and Privileges granted religious freedom, thereby enabling the Jesuits who arrived about this time—Fathers Thomas Harvey, Henry Harrison, and Charles Gage—with two lay brothers to assist them, to celebrate Mass and to set up a short-lived Latin school near the present Trinity Church.

The overthrow of King James II in England and Jacob Leisler's rebellion in New York put an end to such tolerance. Penal laws, similar to those in Britain, thereafter specifically excluded Catholics from the rights of citizenship and banned their priests from the colony under pain of perpetual imprisonment and of death upon escape and recapture. In 1709 the Jesuits were forced to abandon their missions among the Iroquois, and barely a trace of Catholics, native or white, is discernible for the rest of the colonial period. John Ury, a nonjuring Protestant clergyman, suspected of being a Catholic priest and a leader of the ''Negro Plot'' of 1741, was executed, along with several Spanish Catholic African slaves. A number of exiled French-Acadian Catholics entered New York in 1755 but were scattered through the colony under indenture and soon lost to history as Catholics. A band of Scottish Catholics settled in the Mohawk Valley (1773) under Father John MacKenna, the first resident priest since Dongan's time. As loyalists they moved to Canada in the course of the American Revolution. Probably as early as 1775 Father Ferdinand FARMER, SJ, began periodically to visit New York City to say Mass secretly for a handful of Catholics in a loft on Water Street. Father de la Motte and other French naval chaplains, one with Washington's troops on the site of the present archdiocesan seminary in Yonkers, celebrated Mass for Catholics of the area during the Revolution. It was not, however, until the state constitution of 1777 guaranteed religious liberty and the British evacuated New York that Father Farmer could openly enter the city in 1784.

In October of the same year Charles WHELAN, an Irish Capuchin, arrived in New York where he began to say Mass in the house of José Roiz Silva, a wealthy Portuguese merchant; he became the nucleus of a congregation of about 200 Catholics. In the whole state, so the prefect apostolic, John Carroll, estimated (1785), there were about 1,500 Catholics. New York was, until 1800, capital of the republic, and the small Catholic body was augmented by official representatives of Catholic European powers, in whose houses chaplains also celebrated Mass, and by the few Catholic members of Congress. Led by Hector St. John de Crèvecoeur, the French consul, and taking advantage of a state law of 1784 permitting any religious denomination to organize as a body corporate, they set up The Trustees of the Roman Catholic Church in the City of New York. Crèvecoeur, with £1,000 advanced by Thomas Stoughton, the Spanish consul general, and the latter's business partner, Dominick Lynch, bought the unexpired leases of five lots of the Trinity Church Farm. There, on Oct. 5, 1785, the Spanish ambassador, Don Diego de Gardoqui, officiated at the laying of the cornerstone of the mother church of New York, Old St. Peter's, on Barclay Street. In the very method of its establishment, St. Peter's was to be the prototype in a half century of trustee difficulties for the American Church.

With the arrival in late 1785 of another Capuchin, Andrew Nugent, the possibility of gross abuse in the system became apparent. Nugent, with a group of trustees

St. Patrick's Cathedral, built c. 1910, New York. (Photo by Irving Underhill/CORBIS)

and parishioners, soon created a faction against Whelan which, despite a hurried visit of Carroll to New York, caused the first schism in the American Church and the departure of Whelan from the city. Although Nugent had the satisfaction of opening St. Peter's on Nov. 4, 1786, he in turn antagonized the trustees and was suspended by Carroll, who made a second visit to the city in 1787. Nugent lost his post through legal action by the trustees and was succeeded by a Dominican, William O'BRIEN.

For a decade thereafter O'Brien maintained harmony. He toured Cuba and Mexico to collect funds and furnishings for the infant church. In periodic yellow fever epidemics he ministered heroically to victims. In his time a second church, St. Mary's in Albany (1798), was built. St. Peter's free school was opened (1800), the first of its kind in New York and the recipient of public funds after 1806. Elizabeth Ann Seton, later foundress of the Sisters of Charity, was received into the Church in 1805.

Diocese

On April 8, 1808, Pope Pius VII created the Diocese of New York and appointed Richard Luke Concanen, an Irish Dominican resident in Rome, first bishop.

Concanen. Concanen, destined owing to the Napoleonic Wars never to reach his see and to die in Naples

Young girls lighting votive candles in St. Patrick's Cathedral, Christmas Night, New York City, New York, 1996. (Associated Press/AP)

(June 19, 1810), empowered John Carroll, now archbishop of Baltimore, to appoint a vicar-general for New York. Thus, in October 1808, Anthony KOHLMANN, accompanied by a fellow Jesuit, Benedict FENWICK, and four scholastics, arrived from Maryland as administrator. Although the two priests found St. Peter's congregation to be composed mainly of Irish-Americans, they preached in French and German as well as in English and soon attracted a flock so numerous (14,000) that on June 8, 1809, Kohlmann laid the cornerstone of the second church in the city, St. Patrick's, intended as a cathedral for the first bishop. In the same year he founded the New York Literary Institution, a college that prospered until the recall of most of the Jesuits to Maryland in 1813. In 1812 three Ursuline nuns from Ireland opened an academy and free school. In 1813 a group of exiled French Trappists started an orphan asylum in the building vacated by the Literary Institution. Again promise was abortive: the Trappists returned to France in 1814, and the

Ursulines sailed for Ireland two years later. Meanwhile Kohlmann was recalled to Maryland (1815), two years after winning, in a celebrated case before the Court of General Sessions, a favorable decision respecting the seal of Confession which set a precedent in American law. On May 4, 1815, old St. Patrick's Cathedral, Mott Street, was dedicated by Bishop Cheverus of Boston.

Connolly. Six months later John CONNOLLY, who had been an Irish Dominican living in Rome at the time he was consecrated second bishop of New York on Nov. 6, 1814, arrived in his see. He found about 15,000 Catholics in a population of 100,000, only three churches, and four priests in a diocese covering the whole of New York State and the northern half of New Jersey. Compelled to act as bishop, parish priest, and curate, he succeeded in opening another free school in the basement of St. Patrick's (1816). He also introduced Mother Seton's Sisters of Charity to the city (1817), made long visitations of his diocese (1817 and 1820), and established nine additional churches. New York State was growing rapidly, becoming after 1820 the most populous in the Union. Construction of the Erie Canal (1817–25) attracted thousands of Irish laborers for whom the bishop could not provide priests. He had no seminary and noted sadly what he considered the repugnance of American youth to the ecclesiastical state. His problems multiplied when public aid for church schools was ended in 1824 on account of alleged misuse of funds by the Bethel Baptist Church corporation. Moreover, he lost probably his ablest assistant when Benedict Fenwick was withdrawn from New York by his Jesuit superiors (1817). He also had to contend with strained relations with some of his clergy, and especially with the trustees who controlled the churches. Fathers Charles French and Thomas Carbry, supporting the bishop, were in open and sometimes scandalous opposition to Fathers Peter Malou and William Taylor, who were on the side of the trustees. So acrimonious did the debate become that the trustees sent Taylor to Rome to complain against and possibly to supplant the ordinary. Bishop Plessis of Quebec was directed by the cardinal prefect of the Congregation of Propaganda Fide to visit New York (1820) and report on the trouble. The departure from the diocese of the priests who led both factions and the suspension of Malou brought an uneasy peace; but it further depleted the ranks of the clergy.

When Bishop Connolly died, Feb. 6, 1825, the diocese fell to the care of his vicar-general, John POWER, who, since his arrival from Ireland in 1819, by his moderation of the trustee dispute and by his ability generally, had won the affection of all parties and the expectation that he would succeed to the see. In the 21 months of his administration he reinstated Malou, founded New York's first Catholic newspaper, the *Truth Teller* (1825), built a new orphan asylum under the care of the Sisters of Charity (1826), and dedicated a third church in the city, St. Mary's (1826). The appointment, therefore, of John DUBOIS, president of Mt. St. Mary's College and Seminary in Emmitsburg, Md., as third bishop in 1826 came as a somewhat unwelcome surprise to the preponderantly Irish congregations in New York. They viewed him as a Frenchman, incapable of fluent English, and seemingly, as a former Sulpician, imposed on them by Archbishop Maréchal of Baltimore and the Sulpicians there. The new bishop's first pastoral letter (July 1827), in which he sought to refute such suspicions, got a cool reception.

Dubois. In the summer of 1828, when Dubois made a 3,000-mile tour of visitation, there were only 18 priests in his vast diocese to minister to a population of nearly 150,000 Catholics. Shortly thereafter (1829), in order to secure both priests and funds for a seminary, he journeyed to Rome and Paris. Two years later, having been unsuccessful in recruiting additions to his clergy but with about $18,000 in financial aid from the Congregation of Propaganda and the Society for the Propagation of the Faith, he was able to lay the cornerstone of a seminary at Nyack, N.Y. (1833). Within slightly more than a year the building was destroyed by fire, uninsured and a total loss. Subsequent attempts to establish a seminary in Brooklyn and in Lafargeville were equally disappointing. The trustees of the cathedral frustrated Dubois's effort (1829) to set up a school for boys under a religious brotherhood, and in 1834 they refused to accept a successor to their pastor, Thomas Levins, whom he had suspended. They even threatened to withhold the bishop's salary.

Distracted by such internal dissension, the Catholics at the same time became targets of a renascent bigotry. Already in 1824 the recently introduced Orange Society had provoked an anti-Catholic riot in Greenwich Village. Ten years later, in the same neighborhood, men of St. Joseph's Parish guarded by night the work of building their church, and in 1835 armed parishoners prevented a threatened attack on the cathedral. Editorials in the *Protestant,* the *Awful Disclosures* of Maria Monk, William Brownlee's "American Protestant Association," and Samuel Morse's "Native American Democratic Association" all fomented hatred. Bishop Dubois shunned controversy, but his priests were not so reticent. John Power and Felix Varela in the *Truth Teller,* Thomas Levins and Joseph Schneller in the *Weekly Register and Catholic Diary,* and Constantine Pise in the *Catholic Expositor* vigorously rebutted the Protestant press. In Philadelphia, Father John Hughes was making a public mark in debate with a Presbyterian minister, John Breckenridge.

In 1837 Dubois, debilitated by his struggle with the trustees, by age, and by crippling attacks of rheumatism,

accepted the appointment of this same John HUGHES as his coadjutor, with right of succession, and consecrated him in St. Patrick's Cathedral on Jan. 7, 1838. From the outset the coadjutor proved master of the situation. Long familiar with the abuses of trusteeism in Philadelphia, he successfully appealed to the congregation of the cathedral against their truculent trustees (1839) and thus dealt the system a blow from which it was never to recover in New York. In the same year Dubois resigned diocesan management to his coadjutor and entered a reluctant retirement. He died on Dec. 20, 1842. Despite the travail of his administration, the Catholic population of his diocese had risen by one-third, the number of clergy had tripled, and there had been a fourfold increase in churches. To care for German immigration, rapidly increasing after 1830, he had welcomed the Redemptorists into the diocese, encouraged the building of St. Nicholas's Church in the city, and provided a superintendent of the scattered German communities in the person of Father John Raffeiner.

Archdiocese

Under Hughes the See of New York, like the city itself, was to gain preeminence in America. In the two decades after 1840 about 70 percent of the more than four million immigrants to the U.S. entered through the port of New York. Many of them, Irish and Germans uprooted by famine and revolution, were Catholics who settled in the city or were drawn along the Hudson and Mohawk valleys to the cotton and woolen mills, iron and tanning industries, and construction on the Croton Aqueduct and the Hudson River railroad. In 1851 alone, 221,213 Irish landed in New York.

Hughes. For the protection of these immigrants, Hughes encouraged the formation of the Irish Emigrant Society, the Emigrant Industrial Savings Bank, and an immigrant commission of the state legislature. He denounced the importation of Irish secret societies, the foreignism of Young Irelanders and their radical press, as well as the too-swift Americanization advocated by such native converts as Orestes BROWNSON. He fought sectarian proselytism preying upon the immigrants' destitution, and, controversially, Catholic projects to settle them on western lands. They so swelled the population of the diocese that it was split in 1847 by the erection of the Sees of Albany and Buffalo. New York was raised to an archdiocese in 1850, and restricted again in 1853 by the creation of Brooklyn and Newark. Yet at the time of Hughes's death in 1864, the churches and chapels in this now reduced territory outnumbered by over 20 those for the whole area of 1840, and the number of priests had more than tripled. The archbishop had established St. Joseph's Seminary (1840) and St. John's College (1841), both at Fordham, N.Y., promoted the founding of the

North American College in Rome (1859), welcomed the opening of Manhattan College, New York City (1853), and planned a provincial seminary at Troy.

Bishop Hughes's reputation as a formidable controversialist, already proved in the Breckenridge debate, was further publicized in sharp and sometimes bitter exchanges with Mayor James Harper, Colonel William Stone, "Kirwan" (the Reverend Nicholas Murray), Horace Greeley, James Gordon Bennett, Senator Lewis Cass, Erastus Brooks, and Orestes Brownson. In 1840, the bishop led a campaign to regain for the eight Catholic free schools of New York City a proportionate share of the common school fund. His argument before the Common Council, while unavailing, drew attention, as did his endorsement of a slate of candidates favorable to the Catholic claims in the state election of that year, to the injustice of a situation whereby the professedly nonsectarian, but actually Protestant and privately controlled, Public School Society received state funds at the same time that Catholic schools were excluded from such benefit. Two years later the state legislature, by extending the common school system of the rest of the state to the city, spelled the eventual demise of the Society. The apparent failure of the Catholics forced them back upon their own meager resources. Led by Hughes, they established 38 new free schools and academies before the end of his episcopate.

The aggressiveness of their bishop, while inspiriting his socially inferior, largely immigrant, and hitherto rather supine flock, excited nativist alarm. A mob smashed the windows of the cathedral and of the bishop's house in 1842. Two years later, armed Catholics, with Hughes's encouragement, again had to defend the cathedral and themselves from a repetition of the nativist riots in Philadelphia. Anti-Catholic sentiment also accounted for the election in 1844 of James Harper as mayor on the Native American ticket, and for the origin in New York in 1852 of the Know-Nothing party (*see* KNOW-NOTHINGISM). The city, while fervently greeting the revolutionist Louis Kossuth in 1851, treated shamefully a papal nuncio, Archbishop BEDINI, two years later. National absorption in the issues leading to the Civil War helped to dissipate prevalent bigotry. Archbishop Hughes, who in 1846 had declined a request of President Polk that he intercede with the Catholic Mexicans at the outset of the Mexican War, readily accepted in 1861 a commission of his friend William Seward, Secretary of State, and of President Lincoln to visit Europe and there represent the Union cause. The Catholic laity of New York, largely Irish, while deprecating abolitionism, as did their archbishop, contributed impressive numbers and valorous service, particularly in New York's famous 69th Regiment, to the Union forces. Their religious communities, especially the Sisters of Charity and the Sisters of Mercy, were among the first nurses of the battlefield. Moreover, it was mainly the personal appeal of the archbishop himself, at the request of Governor Horatio Seymour, that quelled the notorious New York draft riots of 1863.

John Hughes died on Jan. 3, 1864, leaving a well-ordered archdiocese and ecclesiastical province. Improvements had been effected through the legislation of the first two New York diocesan synods (1842 and 1848) and three provincial councils (1854, 1860, 1861). Hughes had organized a diocesan chancery (1853), patronized 10 new religious communities, and rescued church property from the mismanagement of lay trustees. His flock had increased in numerical strength and by the accession of notable converts in what appeared to be an American counterpart of the Oxford movement. They had an articulate press as represented by Brownson's *Quarterly Review,* the *Freeman's Journal,* the *Metropolitan Record,* and Father Isaac HECKER's *Catholic World.* Archdiocesan charities were advanced by the founding of a pioneer conference of the Society of St. Vincent de Paul and the opening of St. Vincent's Hospital. A local branch of the Society for the Propagation of the Faith was established. The cornerstone was laid for the boldly conceived new St. Patrick's Cathedral, and the archbishop had come to be recognized as a figure of national prominence.

McCloskey. The importance of New York in the nation and in the universal Church received recognition during the next episcopate (1864–85) in the elevation of its archbishop to the cardinalate. John MCCLOSKEY—a native of New York, consecrated coadjutor to Hughes in 1844, transferred to Albany as its first bishop in 1847, and installed as fifth bishop and second archbishop of New York on Aug. 21, 1864—became America's first prince of the Church in 1875. The ceremonies of investiture of the new cardinal, and the dedication, four years later, of the new cathedral received unprecedented publicity, attesting the change in public sentiment toward the Church. This was further evidenced by the election in 1880 of William R. Grace as first Catholic mayor of the city. The cardinal, unlike his predecessor, mild-mannered and benign, stood as a public figure mainly on account of his rank. During his irenic administration the archdiocese experienced more than a double growth in the number of churches, clergy, and schools. Significantly, as immigrants raised the Catholic population of towns along and east and west of the Hudson, 58 of the 90 new churches were built outside New York City. Holy Rosary Mission was founded (1884) to minister to the large proportion of Catholics among the more than six million immigrants who debarked at Castle Garden between 1861 and 1890. To provide for Catholic Italians, arriving in steadily increasing numbers after 1880, the first church exclusively for their use was entrusted to the Pallottine Fathers (1884).

The national complexion of the clergy was also changing. Hitherto, although 107 priests had been ordained from St. Joseph's Seminary in Fordham (1840–61), a major proportion of the New York clergy was recruited in Europe, especially in Ireland. With the opening of St. Joseph's Provincial Seminary in Troy (1864–96), the 741 priests ordained there for the various dioceses of the ecclesiastical province were almost all native Americans. From 1864 to 1885 approximately 16 religious communities of priests, sisters, and brothers arrived to assist them. Charitable works increased proportionately, notably with the opening of the New York Foundling Hospital under the Sisters of Charity, the first institution of its kind in the U.S., the New York Catholic Protectory for delinquent children, Father John DRUMGOOLE's Mission of the Immaculate Virgin for homeless waifs, and a rapid multiplication of conferences of the St. Vincent de Paul Society. Elsewhere signs of confidence and maturity appeared in the founding of Hecker's Catholic Publication Society, P. J. Hickey's popular *Catholic Review,* and John Gilmary SHEA's United States Catholic Historical Society. Although the third and fourth diocesan synods (1868 and 1882) and the fourth provincial council (1883), which the cardinal convoked, did not effect all the executive reorganization and pastoral adaptation necessary in a fast-changing archdiocese, his untroubled administration stands in contrast to those of his predecessor and successor. Enfeebled in his last years, he relied increasingly upon the assistance of a coadjutor archbishop until his death on Oct. 10, 1885.

Corrigan. The coadjutor (since 1880), Michael A. CORRIGAN, immediately succeeded to the archbishopric. One of his first acts was to convoke the fifth New York diocesan synod (1886), the decrees of which, in 20 titles and 264 numbers, were so thorough and brought such efficiency into diocesan administration and discipline, that the four subsequent synods of his episcopate (1889, 1892, 1895, 1898) could add little to them. The Catholic population almost doubled during Corrigan's administration (1885–1902). Over five million immigrants entered the country between 1881 and 1890, followed by almost four million in the next decade, the majority now coming from Catholic sections of Europe. As early as 1886 the archbishop, in a report to Rome, noted among the foreign-language-speaking Catholics in New York City some 60,000 Germans, as many Bohemians, 50,000 Italians, 25,000 French, 20,000 Poles, and lesser numbers of French-Canadians, Spaniards, Greeks, and Lithuanians. By 1902 non-English-speaking Catholics in New York had the services of over 100 priests of their respective nationalities and more than 50 churches. The Italians alone,

the largest group among them, had 50 Italian priests and 20 churches and chapels, as well as the ministrations of the recently arrived Pallottine sisters, Mother Cabrini's Missionary Sisters of the Sacred Heart, the Scalabrinian fathers, and the Salesians. The Blessed Sacrament fathers came to work among the French-Canadians and the Assumptionists among the Spanish-speaking. During the same period the total number of churches and chapels again more than doubled, as did the number of diocesan and regular clergy. Eight new religious communities of men and 16 of women, two of them, the Sisters of Divine Compassion and the Dominican Sisters of St. Rose of Lima, founded in New York, began work in the archdiocese. Despite the severe depression of 1893 to 1896, a model seminary, the new St. Joseph's in Dunwoodie was built. Corrigan also inaugurated a trend toward specialization in the work of the clergy by establishing the New York Apostolate, a Confraternity of Christian Doctrine, a superintendent and an association of diocesan charities, a diocesan superintendent of schools, examining boards for teachers, and school commissioners for the various districts of the archdiocese.

Catholic education was a hotly debated issue of the day. The archbishop had the satisfaction of promulgating in his synod of 1886 the instructions of the Third Plenary Council of BALTIMORE (1884) on the necessity of parochial schools. He doubled the number of such schools within his own jurisdiction and rallied New York patronage as the main support of a national Catholic summer school (1892). He viewed with distrust, as harmful to the concept and growing system of Catholic schools, such compromise solutions as the Faribault-Stillwater experiments of Abp. John Ireland of St. Paul and the POUGHKEEPSIE PLAN in operation in his own archdiocese since 1873. His conservative position on this question, and on others such as membership of Catholics in secret societies, Irish nationalism, the Catholic University in Washington, and the prevalence of a heterodox AMERICANISM, led to disagreement with other members of the American hierarchy, particularly Archbishop Ireland, and to an ecclesiastical *cause célèbre* in New York. Edward MCGLYNN, rector of St. Stephen's Church and long an opponent of separate schools, in 1886 actively associated himself with the mayoral campaign of Henry George, to whose radical land and tax theories he publicly subscribed. Refusing to obey the archbishop's prohibition of such political engagement, McGlynn was repeatedly suspended and eventually removed from St. Stephen's. Subsequently excommunicated for failure to account in Rome for his insubordination and his adherence to the Georgian economic theories, he and his supporters bitterly denounced the archbishop and the Roman authorities. The affair, exploited by a sensational newspaper press, focused unwarranted attention on personalities and withdrew it from more substantial and positive elements of growth of the Church in New York. Despite the furor the archbishop, characteristically, held to a routine of efficient diocesan administration. He oversaw construction of the seminary in Dunwoodie, completed the spires of his cathedral and projected its Lady Chapel, and planned, before his death on May 5, 1902, a preparatory seminary.

Farley. His successor, John M. FARLEY, auxiliary bishop since 1895, was installed as fourth archbishop of New York on Oct. 5, 1902. Astutely pursuing a policy of conciliation, dramatically emphasized in his returning from Rome in 1904 with the nomination to monsignorial dignity of eight of his priests (an unprecedented number and some of them former partisans of McGlynn), he soon overcame the residue of disunion in the ranks of the clergy. The beginning of monthly days of recollection for priests in the same year, the opening of Cathedral College as a preparatory seminary in 1903, and a doubling of the number of priests of religious communities were also to add vigor and numbers to the clergy, so necessary to cope with a still mounting population. Although before the end of his administration (1918) the trend of older residents away from Manhattan toward Brooklyn and New Jersey had begun, immigration was still to account for a rise of about 200,000 in Catholic population. In a decade (1901–10) that greeted nearly 9,000,000 immigrants, of whom 1,285,349 came in 1907, the peak year in American immigration history, Italians continued to constitute the largest segment of Catholics. Only a few months after his accession the archbishop presided at a meeting of his Italian clergy to discuss the problem. Of the slightly more than 100 new churches he established, over a third were for the care of Italian-Americans. The Holy Ghost fathers began their ministry among the African Americans of Harlem, and in 1912 Mother Drexel's Sisters of the Blessed Sacrament opened their first school for black children there.

The era also saw the ebbing of debate over Catholic education. The archbishop, created a cardinal in 1911, strongly supported the rather precarious fortunes of The CATHOLIC UNIVERSITY OF AMERICA, the infant National Catholic Educational Association, and the organization of the College of New Rochelle, the first Catholic college for women in the state. While the Catholic population of the archdiocese rose by about 20 percent, church schools and their enrollments doubled in number; two priests were appointed superintendents of parochial schools. Approximately 2,000 Catholic teachers in the public schools were united in an association called The Workers for God and Country. Other signs of vitality appeared in the publication, under the auspices of Dunwoodie Seminary, of the highly respected *New York Review* (1905–08), the

first scientific Catholic theological journal in the U.S., and the *Catholic Encyclopedia* (1907–14), largely under the cardinal's patronage. These years also marked the corporate conversion of the Anglican Friars and Sisters of the Atonement, the beginning of the laymen's retreat movement, and public celebration of the centenary of the diocese. The Lady Chapel of the cathedral was completed and the entire edifice solemnly consecrated. The Catholic Foreign Mission Society of America (MARYKNOLL) established its headquarters and seminary in the archdiocese; and the local Society for the Propagation of the Faith was reconstituted and contributions to the missions rose from a few thousand dollars annually to over a quarter of a million by 1918. An attempt to coordinate all other charities of the archdiocese in an organization known as the United Catholic Works was arrested by the outbreak of World War I.

Before Cardinal Farley died, Sept. 17, 1918, the entrance of the U.S. into the war tested the resources of the archdiocese. The cardinal founded the New York Catholic War Council, which sponsored a soldiers' and sailors' club, a women's Catholic patriotic club, and a Catholic hospital for shell-shocked patients. His auxiliary bishop (since 1914), Patrick J. HAYES, was appointed by the Holy See bishop ordinary of the U.S. army and navy chaplains (1917). He so effectively recruited and organized the corps of Catholic chaplains that by the end of the war there were 1,523 priests, in five vicariates, under his jurisdiction. Of the 1,023 Catholic chaplains already commissioned by Nov. 11, 1918, the 87 from New York formed a contingent more than twice as large as that from any other diocese. Bishop Hayes also made personal appeals in behalf of the Liberty Loans and was a director of a Knights of Columbus drive that raised nearly $5 million for work among servicemen.

Hayes. On March 10, 1919, in the same year that a fellow native of New York's lower East Side, Alfred E. Smith, became the first elected Catholic governor of the state, the former auxiliary was named to the See of New York as its fifth archbishop. Five years later he received an enthusiastic reception, replete with tickertape parade from the Battery, when he returned from Rome a cardinal. During the 19 years of his administration the Catholic population of the archdiocese fell from over 1,250,000 to about 1,000,000. This was the result of the gradual decline in immigration during the 1920s and a sharp drop during the Depression years of the thirties, as well as an accelerated exodus of Catholic families to metropolitan areas beyond his jurisdiction. The number of churches, nevertheless, increased by one-sixth; schools, by one-half; and the clergy, by one-third. Charitable institutions and services had continued to multiply, often with overlapping and duplication of activity and at the expense of economy and efficiency. Three months after his accession the new archbishop announced a detailed survey of the more than 200 welfare agencies of the archdiocese, and in the following year he coordinated them all under a secretary for charities, at the head of a corporation entitled Catholic Charities of the Archdiocese of New York. The new organization was commended by the New York State Board of Charities (1920) as "the most significant and important event of the year in the field of charitable work." It quickly assumed a position of leadership among private welfare organizations throughout the country and served as a model for other dioceses. Supported by a special gifts committee of the laity and an annual parish appeal that soon netted over $1 million yearly, Catholic Charities successfully met the challenge of the severe financial depression following the stock market collapse of 1929 and earned for its founder the popular title Cardinal of Charity.

Never a dynamic public figure, the cardinal spent the last years of his life in semiretirement. He did, however, introduce the Catholic Youth Organization to the diocese (1936), patronize the literature committee that bore his name, and promote a Catholic theater movement. The heart ailment which seriously restricted his activities eventually resulted in his death, Sept. 4, 1938.

Spellman. The appointment of Francis J. SPELLMAN, the auxiliary bishop of Boston, as the sixth archbishop of New York on April 15, 1939, shattered two precedents. He was the first archbishop of New York in 100 years who had not been closely associated with his predecessor, and he was a significant figure in the American hierarchy even before his appointment to New York. As a result of his friendship with both Pope Pius XII and President Franklin D. Roosevelt, as well as his own intelligence, energy and ambition, Spellman became the most important archbishop of New York since John Hughes and the most influential American prelate since James Cardinal Gibbons. As expected, he received the Cardinal's red hat at the first postwar consistory on Feb. 18, 1946.

Once installed as archbishop on Sept. 8, 1939, Spellman moved quickly to modernize and centralize the organizational structure of the archdiocese. He immediately refinanced the diocesan debt of $28 million through bankers in New York and Boston, saving the archdiocese $500,000 per year in interest payments. In short order he introduced a central purchasing agency, a diocesan insurance office and a diocesan building commission. He also reorganized the chancery office, matrimonial tribunal and administrative offices of the archdiocese, housing them in an elegant mansion across the street from St. Patrick's Cathedral. Spellman's centralizing policies ended the autonomy that pastors had enjoyed under Hayes. Although

Spellman compensated them with a lavish bestowal of papal honors, he deliberately remained an aloof and impersonal figure to his priests. For the day-to-day administration of the archdiocese, he relied heavily on the services of James Francis McIntyre and later John Maguire, both of whom in turn were appointed coadjutor archbishops without the right of succession.

Spellman played an important role on both the national and international scene. He was instrumental in persuading President Roosevelt to appoint a "personal representative" to the Holy See on Dec. 23, 1939. Spellman's responsibilities as Military Vicar for the Armed Forces (an appointment he received on Dec. 11, 1939) increased dramatically following the entry of the United States into World War II. Thereafter the Military Ordinariate became one of the largest dioceses in the world with several million military personnel and their families and some 5,000 full- and part-time chaplains. Throughout the era of the Cold War Spellman remained an outspoken foe of Communism both at home and abroad. His ecclesiastical influence was further enhanced because New York City was the headquarters of important national agencies such as Catholic Relief Services, the Catholic Committee on Refugees, the Bishops' Resettlement Committee for Refugees, the Catholic Near East Welfare Association and the Society for the Propagation of the Faith.

The advent of World War II forestalled any large-scale building projects in the archdiocese, but, even before Pearl Harbor, Spellman managed to establish two new parishes, install a new main altar in St. Patrick's Cathedral, relocate the minor seminary and begin a system of diocesan high schools. After the war the archdiocese embarked upon a major expansion of its infrastructure. Between 1939 and 1967 enrollment in Catholic schools almost doubled on the elementary level (to 179,052) and almost tripled on the high school and college levels (to 49,842 and 27,949 respectively). Spellman spent several million dollars renovating St. Joseph's Seminary, adding a new library and gymnasium. Catholic Charities also experienced a major expansion of its 200 member agencies as well as the construction of a dozen new hospitals, homes for the aged and child-caring centers. The New York Foundling Hospital, one of Spellman's favorite charities, was moved to a modern facility, and St. Vincent's Hospital developed into a full-fledged medical center.

After declining during the 1920s and 1930s, the Catholic population of the archdiocese almost doubled during the Spellman years from c. 1,000,000 to 1,848,000. Much of the increase was due to the influx after World War II of over 600,000 Puerto Rican immigrants, who transformed many of the traditional Catholic ethnic neighborhoods into solidly Hispanic enclaves while the older residents joined the flight to the suburbs. To meet this major pastoral challenge, Spellman established an Office of Spanish Catholic Action and made a major commitment of diocesan clergy. By 1961 the archdiocese had over 200 Spanish-speaking priests and approximately one-third of the parishes were providing religious services in Spanish.

After Vatican II (1962–1965), Spellman dutifully implemented the liturgical changes although he deplored them privately as "too many and too soon." He also divided the archdiocese into six vicariates, established an elected Senate of Priests and agreed to the creation of two experimental parishes headed by a team of priests. One of Spellman's proudest moments occurred on Oct. 4, 1965, when Pope Paul VI made a one-day visit to New York City and celebrated Mass in Yankee Stadium before a crowd of 92,000 worshippers. In the fall of 1966 (at the age of 77) he offered the pope his resignation, but it was refused. During the 1960s the Civil Rights movement and the Vietnam War, together with the impact of Vatican II, led to a period of unprecedented turmoil for American Catholics. By the time of Spellman's death on Dec. 2, 1967, the successful synthesis of Catholicism and Americanism that he once epitomized no longer seemed adequate to the needs of the day.

Cooke. The appointment on March 8, 1968, of Terence J. COOKE as the seventh archbishop of New York was a surprise to many knowledgeable observers. A native New Yorker only 47 years old, Cooke was the youngest of the 10 auxiliary bishops and (with the exception of Hughes and Corrigan) the youngest ordinary ever appointed to New York. His selection was widely attributed to the influence of Spellman with whom he had been closely associated for the previous 10 years. Like Spellman, Cooke was also appointed Military Vicar for the Armed Forces (April 4, 1968) and was made a cardinal (April 28, 1969).

Cooke received his baptism of fire on the day of his installation, April 4, 1968, when the assassination of Dr. Martin Luther King, Jr., touched off riots throughout the country. That evening Cooke went to Harlem to plead for racial peace. He played little role in national or international affairs, except as chairman of the U.S. Bishops' Committee on Pro-Life Activities where he worked vigorously to combat abortion. However, he concentrated his attention on his own diocese, providing two much needed skills, managerial ability and pastoral sensitivity. An affable man who preferred conciliation to confrontation, he was also the master of the soft answer that turns away wrath but concedes nothing. A born micromanager, he used his detailed knowledge of the inner workings of the archdiocese to administer carefully the available financial resources. Critics complained that his financial expertise was not matched by long-term vision, but his non-confrontational style of leadership spared New York the ideological polarization among the clergy that occurred in some other dioceses.

During Cooke's years as archbishop, the population of the archdiocese remained virtually the same, but only because Catholic immigrants, predominantly Hispanic, continued to replace the dwindling number of middle-class white Catholics. The sacramental statistics indicated an abrupt decline in religious practice. Infant baptisms fell from 50,219 in 1967 to 32,168 in 1984, and church weddings declined from 15,511 to 10,208. For the first time in history there was a sharp drop in the number of both diocesan priests (from 1,108 to 777) and diocesan seminarians (from 501 to 238). Under Spellman the number of parishes had increased by 34; under Cooke there was a net gain of only four parishes. In order to utilize better the diminishing resources, Cooke established the Inter-Parish Finance Commission, which levied a tax on all parishes and then used the income to subsidize the poorer parishes. By 1979 the total funds disbursed amounted to a whopping $26 million. As a result only 49 of the 305 parish elementary schools were forced to close despite a massive decline in enrollment (from 179,052 in 1967 to 89,853 in 1984) and the mass exodus of 3,257 of the 4,130 sisters from the classrooms.

Cooke consolidated the administrative offices of the archdiocese in a new Catholic Center on the East Side of Manhattan, established the Office of Pastoral Research, opened the St. John Neumann Residence for seminarians, founded the Archdiocesan Catechetical Institute, and organized the Inner-City Scholarship Fund, which provided subsidies of over one million dollars per year to minority students (two-thirds of them non-Catholic) in parochial schools. Sensitive to the demographic changes in the archdiocese, he appointed the first black and Hispanic auxiliary bishops, created the Office of Black Catholics and supported the Northeast Center for Hispanics. As Military Vicar he discreetly defended U.S. involvement in the Vietnam War and also continued Spellman's practice of frequent visits to troops overseas.

Not all of the leadership in the archdiocese came from the top. In South Bronx, the poorest Congressional district in the United States, as crime, arson and the abandonment of buildings engulfed 20 square miles of the borough in the early 1970s, parish priests and religious organized community action groups and sponsored urban renewal projects to stop the decline. Jill Jonnes, the historian of the Bronx, wrote in 1986: "The Catholic Church quietly emerged as the institution most committed to preserving and resurrecting the benighted South Bronx. Not one church or Catholic school was closed.'' In 1979, when the newly-elected Pope John Paul II made a two-day visit to New York City, he overrode the security concerns of the police and stopped in both Harlem and the South Bronx before celebrating Mass in Yankee Stadium.

On Aug. 26, 1983, after a secret eight-year struggle with cancer, Cooke revealed to the public that he was terminally ill. After his death on Oct. 6, 1983, large crowds filed past his bier and attended his funeral in tribute to the inspiring way that he had faced death. The New York *Daily News* commented: ''[He] showed us all how to pass from time to eternity with courage and grace.''

O'Connor. Cooke's successor was John J. O'CONNOR, a native of Philadelphia, who was appointed the eighth archbishop of New York on Jan. 31, 1984. He had served in the Military Ordinariate as auxiliary bishop to Cooke from 1979 until 1983 when he became the bishop of Scranton. Prior to that, he had spent 27 years as a navy chaplain, rising to Chief of Chaplains with the rank of Rear Admiral. O'Connor was made a cardinal on May 25, 1958. On that same day the Military Ordinariate was separated from New York, ending a personal connection that had existed under the three previous archbishops since 1917.

Despite his 64 years, O'Connor adopted a busy schedule that he maintained almost to the end of his 16 years in New York. He preached virtually every Sunday in St. Patrick's Cathedral and made frequent pastoral visits throughout the archdiocese as well as numerous trips to Rome. Unlike Cooke, he adopted a high profile and signaled his intention to give New York the same national prominence that it had enjoyed under Spellman. Unlike Spellman, however, who relied on personal political and business connections, O'Connor made deft use of his communications skills to influence public opinion through the media. An admirer of the feisty John Hughes, the first archbishop of New York, O'Connor seemed to welcome public confrontation over controversial issues like abortion. The *New York Times,* often a critic of O'Connor, grudgingly admitted in 1998 that he was ''perhaps the one person in New York with a platform to rival that of the mayor'' and shortly before his death acknowledged him as ''the de facto leader of American Catholics.''

Between 1984 and 2000 the Catholic population of the archdiocese increased from 1,839,000 to 2,407,393, constituting 45% of the total population. However, the number of baptisms remained virtually the same and the number of marriages declined by a quarter. The ethnic, economic and social diversity of the archdiocese was remarkable. One rural parish in Dutchess County contained 50,000 acres of private land for fox hunting, while in one Bronx parish 58% of the people lived below the poverty level. Mass was celebrated in at least 22 languages every Sunday with 135 of the 413 parishes providing Mass in Spanish. Hispanic Catholics included not only Puerto Ricans, but also Dominicans, Mexicans, and natives of many Central and South American countries. A new phenomenon was the influx of Asian Catholics from Korea, China, Vietnam and the Philippines. Immigrants from Albania, Palestine, Portugal, Haiti, and even an increase in immigration from Ireland, added to the ethnic mix.

The enrollment in the 303 Catholic elementary and high schools remained steady at around 100,000, with almost half of the students (many of them non-Catholics) coming from minority groups. The archdiocese also remained a major provider of health care and social services with 17 hospitals, three health care facilities, 17 homes for the aged, 14 child-caring institutions, and 129 social agencies operated by Catholic Charities. ''They provided the best social services that were available,'' said Mayor Edward Koch. The staffing of parishes and schools became increasingly difficult since O'Connor in his later years was reluctant to close or consolidate them despite the decline in the number of diocesan priests (from 777 in 1984 to 563 in 2000), teaching sisters (from 873 to 236) and teaching brothers (from 93 to 60). On a more positive note, two new religious communities were founded, the Franciscan Friars of the Renewal and the Sisters of Life, and the number of permanent deacons increased to 310.

O'Connor offered his resignation to the pope upon reaching 75 in 1995, but it was refused. That year Pope John Paul made his second visit to New York and celebrated Mass in Central Park with 125,000 people in attendance. In late August 1999 O'Connor underwent surgery for a brain tumor from which he never recovered and died on May 3, 2000.

Egan. The appointment of Edward Egan as the ninth archbishop of New York was announced on May 11, 2000, only eight days after the death of Cardinal O'Connor. A native of Oak Park, Illinois, Egan was ordained in Rome as a priest of the archdiocese of Chicago on Dec. 15, 1957. He returned to Rome to earn a doctorate in canon law and later to serve as a judge of the Roman Rota from 1971 until 1985. In that year he was appointed auxiliary bishop of New York where he served as the Vicar for Education until his appointment as the bishop of Bridgeport on Nov. 8, 1988. He was installed as archbishop of New York in St. Patrick's Cathedral on June 19, 2000, and was made a Cardinal on Feb. 21, 2001.

The bloody event of Sept. 11, 2001 made a lasting impact on the people of New York City, when Islamist terrorists in two hijacked commercial airplanes attacked the twin towers of the World Trade Center with a tremendous loss of lives. Every parish church held impromptu services and more formal services on September 14, a national day of morning. Some parishes in New York City and the suburbs suffered the loss of dozens of parishioners and celebrated memorial Masses for victims whose bodies were never recovered. An estimated 90% of the almost 400 police officers and firefighters who lost their lives in the collapse of the twin towers were Catholics. Among them was Fr. Mychal Judge, OFM, the fire department chaplain, who was killed by falling debris while ministering to the dying. For weeks afterwards the crowded churches testified to the searing impact of the atrocity on the souls of all New Yorkers.

Like Spellman in 1939, one of Egan's main priorities was the restoration of the financial condition of the archdiocese, a task that he had already accomplished in the diocese of Bridgeport. In keeping with his goal of reducing the debt by $20 million over a two-year period, he consolidated the seminary faculties, streamlined the administrative offices of the archdiocese, closed a few ailing schools, reduced the weekly diocesan newspaper to a monthly, and gave clear indication of the need for further economies.

Bibliography: J. T. SMITH, *The Catholic Church in New York*, 2 v. (New York 1905). L. R. RYAN, *Old St. Peter's, the Mother Church of Catholic New York, 1785–1935* (United States Catholic Historical Society 15; New York 1935). M. P. CARTHY, *Old St. Patrick's, New York's First Cathedral* (New York 1947). *Historical Records and Studies of the U.S. Catholic Historical Society of New York* (1900–). J. R. HASSARD, *Life of the Most Reverend John Hughes, D.D., First Archbishop of New York* (New York 1866). J. M. FARLEY, *The Life of John Cardinal McCloskey, First Prince of the Church in America, 1810–1885* (New York 1918); *Memorial of the Most Reverend Michael Augustine Corrigan, D.D., Third Archbishop of New York* (New York 1902). R. I. GANNON, *The Cardinal Spellman Story* (New York 1962). M. E. BROWN, *Churches, Communities and Children: Italian Immigrants in the Archdiocese of New York, 1880–1945* (New York 1995). F. D. COHALAN, *A Popular History of the Archdiocese of New York* (Yonkers 1983). J. P. DOLAN, *The Immigrant Church: New York's Irish and German Catholics, 1815–1865* (Baltimore 1975). R. E. CURRAN, *Michael Augustine Corrigan and the Shaping of Conservative Catholicism in America, 1878–1902* (New York 1978). A. M. DIAZ-STEVENS, *Oxcart Catholicism on Fifth Avenue: The Impact of the Puerto Rican Migration upon the Archdiocese of New York* (Notre Dame 1993). S. DIGIOVANNI, *Archbishop Corrigan and the Italian Immigrants* (Huntington, Ind. 1994). J. C. FARLEY, *The Life of John Cardinal McCloskey* (New York 1918). B. J. GROESCHEL and T. L. WEBER, *Thy Will Be Done: A Spiritual Portrait of Terence Cardinal Cooke* (New York 1990). R. I. GANNON, *The Cardinal Spellman Story* (New York 1962). J. R. G. HASSARD, *Life of the Most Reverend John Hughes* (New York 1866). R. SHAW, *Dagger John: The Unquiet Life and Times of Archbishop John Hughes* (New York 1977). T. J. SHELLEY, *Dunwoodie: The History of St. Joseph's Seminary* (Westminster, Md. 1992); *The History of the Archdiocese of New York* (Strasbourg 1999). J. T. SMITH, *History of the Church in New York,* 2 vols. (Boston and New York 1902).

[J. A. REYNOLDS/T. J. SHELLEY]

NEW YORK, CATHOLIC CHURCH IN

The eleventh of the original 13 states to ratify the U.S. constitution (1788), New York is bounded on the north by Lake Ontario, the St. Lawrence River, and Canada; on the east by Vermont, Massachusetts, and Connecticut; on the south by New Jersey, Pennsylvania, and the Atlantic Ocean; and on the west by Pennsylvania, Lake Erie, and the Niagara River. New York's capital city is Albany; other major cities, in addition to New York City, the most populous metropolitan area, are Buffalo, Rochester, and Syracuse. In 2001 New York's population was 18,589,886, second largest in the nation, of whom 7,396,485, about 40 percent, were Catholics. There were eight dioceses. In addition to the metropolitan see of NEW YORK CITY, they were Albany and Buffalo, Brooklyn and Ogdensburg, Rochester and Rockville Centre, and Syracuse.

Early History. Long before New York became known as the Empire State, it was the home of a mighty confederacy of Native American tribes made up of the Mohawks, Oneidas, Onondagas, Cayugas, and Senecas. This union of tribes was known to the French as the Iroquois and to the English as the Five Nations (later Six when the Tuscaroras joined in 1715). Successful in dominating the other Native American tribes of the area, they also terrorized European settlers and missionaries and exercised an important influence on the colonial history of this area.

The first Europeans to come into contact with the Five Nations were the French, who occasionally sent vessels up the Hudson to trade with the Native American after the discovery in 1524 of New York Bay and the river by Giovanni da Verrazano, a Florentine in the service of Francis I of France. By July 1609 French efforts to lay the foundations of New France and to spread Christianity had penetrated to Lake Champlain, thereby arousing the hostility of the Iroquois, who for years thereafter held the balance of power between the English and the French in America.

In September 1609, Henry Hudson, an English mariner employed by the Dutch East India Company to search for a new passage to the East Indies, entered New York harbor in the *Half Moon* and followed the river that bears his name as far north as the present site of Albany. On the basis of this claim, the Dutch colony of New Netherland was founded in 1624, when the first permanent settlers consisting of about 30 families, mostly Walloon, arrived. The population had grown to 200 or more by 1626, when the government of the province was fully established with power vested mainly in a director-general and council. Soon after, Manhattan Island was purchased from the Native Americans for 60 guilders ($24), and Ft. Amsterdam was erected at its lower end and the settlement there made the seat of government. Although the charter of 1640 declared that "no other Religion shall be publicly admitted in New Netherland except the Reformed . . . ," these Dutch Calvinists were less virulent in their opposition to Catholicism than their New England brethren. In fact, Isaac Jogues, SJ, was rescued from the tortures of the Iroquois by the Dutch at Ft. Orange and brought to New Amsterdam in the fall of 1643, where he was kindly received by Gov. William Kieft (*see* NORTH AMERICAN MARTYRS). Nevertheless, the paucity of Catholic settlers—Jogues found only two in the town—continued during the entire period of Dutch rule despite the fact that the total population of the province increased from 2,000 to 10,000 between 1653 and 1664.

Colonial Period. New Netherland passed into the hands of the English when, in March 1664, Charles II erected it with additional territory into a province and awarded it to his brother, James, Duke of York, who became its lord proprietor. The conquest of the Dutch colony was completed without fighting when, on September 8, Gov. Peter Stuyvesant formally surrendered to the English. This marked the beginning of brighter prospects for Catholic settlement in the province henceforth to be known as New York. The conversion to Catholicism in 1672 of the royal proprietor, the future James II, was soon reflected in the directives he issued for the government of his American domain. In 1682 he appointed a Catholic, Col. Thomas Dongan, as governor and instructed him to accede to the long-standing demand of the colonists for a representative assembly. When the new governor arrived in New York in August 1683, his party included an English Jesuit, Thomas Harvey, who was later joined by two other priests and two lay brothers of his society.

Dongan, an administrator of considerable ability, lost no time in summoning the assembly that in October 1683 passed the bill of rights that he had proposed. This Charter of Liberties and Privileges, containing a guarantee of entire freedom in religion, placed the Catholic governor of New York with Roger WILLIAMS, the CALVERTS, and William PENN as the chief promoters of religious freedom in colonial America. During the remainder of Dongan's term of office, the various denominations had their respective houses of worship, and the little Catholic chapel in Ft. James was the first site where Mass was regularly offered in New York by the Jesuits who ministered to the relatively few Catholic settlers. It was Dongan's

Archdiocese/Diocese	Year Created
Archdiocese of New York	1850
Diocese of Albany	1847
Diocese of Brooklyn	1853
Diocese of Buffalo	1847
Diocese of Ogdensburg	1872
Diocese of Rochester	1868
Diocese of Rockville Center	1957
Diocese of Syracuse	1886

plan to counteract the influence of French missionaries by seeking additional English Jesuits to take up work among the Native Americans to the north, an area that he felt rightly belonged to the British crown. But his official career was brought to an end before the English Jesuits could carry out the policy regarding the Native Americans of New York.

After the English revolution of 1688 and the accession of William and Mary, the American colonies were thrown into a ferment of excitement. In New York, the German-born Calvinist Jacob Leisler led an armed rebellion in May 1689, which ushered in a reign of terror. The policy of religious toleration in New York was soon replaced with restrictive measures against Catholics; the former Governor Dongan was hunted as a traitor, and the Jesuits were compelled to flee the colony. With the establishment of the Church of England by law in four of the leading counties of New York in 1693, the long dark night of penal legislation descended upon the few Catholics who were courageous enough to remain in the province. Although Leisler was removed and executed in 1691, anti-Catholic legislation continued to be multiplied under Henry Sloughter, the new governor, and his successors. An act of 1700 made it a crime for a priest to be found in New York, and anyone who harbored a priest was subject to a fine of 200 pounds. Perhaps no other single incident better illustrates the intensity of colonial anti-Catholic rancor than the reception accorded the Acadians, or "French Neutrals," expelled from their homes in 1755 and distributed among the colonies from Massachusetts to Georgia. Of the quota sent to New York, the adults were bound out as indentured servants and the children assigned to Protestant families. Unquestionably this persecution and proscription of Catholics in the colony not only sufficed to keep their numbers from increasing but also tended to discourage any who might have possessed the faith from announcing the fact. These dismal conditions were to obtain until after the Revolution, and Mass was not celebrated in a public manner until offered by the chaplains of the French troops who were sent to aid the colonies in their struggle. Meanwhile, affairs in the colony generally were concerned chiefly with the de-

Cardinal Francis Spellman delivering message from Pope Pius XII at Pontifical Mass, St. Patrick's Cathedral, New York, 1946. (AP/Wide World Photos)

fense of the northern frontier and the rising disaffection of the colonists with the English government's colonial policy.

Revolutionary War. The quickening spirit of rebellion against the mother country's political and economic measures undoubtedly drew increased strength from the prejudice aroused by the passage of the QUEBEC ACT in June 1774. In colony after colony, pulpit and press warned that the ''popery act'' that secured for Canada freedom for the exercise of the Catholic religion was a serious menace to colonial Protestantism. The first colonial flag run up in New York in place of the English colors bore on one side the inscription ''George III-Rex. and the Liberties of America.—No Popery.'' It is small wonder, then, that Catholics found their position a difficult one, faced as they were with the dilemma of deciding on which side to cast their lot as the colony moved to make common cause with the revolutionists. On July 9, 1776, the delegates to the New York provincial congress adopted the Declaration of Independence and formally committed the province to the rebel cause. Undoubtedly the Catholic colonists were aware that many of the most vigorous opponents of the British policy of coercion had been the bitterest persecutors of ''papists.'' On the other

hand, their experience with the British government offered little hope for religious liberty or anything like political and social equality. In the end the greater number of Catholics chose to cast in their lot with the revolutionists and only a few of them joined the loyalist group. The patriotic part played by American Catholics in the revolutionary struggle and the aid of Catholic France and Spain marked a weakening of the anti-Catholic bias. However, when Congress advised the several states to adopt constitutions, the New York convention meeting for that purpose at Kingston on March 6, 1777, adopted an amendment to the naturalization clause, proposed by John Jay, which effectively excluded foreign-born Roman Catholics from citizenship. Not until 1806 was this offensive clause abrogated. Nevertheless, the period of Catholic proscription was drawing to a close; and when on Nov. 25, 1783, the British forces finally evacuated New York City, such Catholics as were in the city at the time began to assemble once again for the open celebration of their religion.

Institutional Growth. In the years that followed the War for Independence, and especially in the early 19th century, remarkable gains were made in the social and economic fields, the extension of agriculture, the development of manufactures, the growth of commerce and transportation, and the improvement of educational facilities. Companies that acquired land grants from the state encouraged systematic colonization of the Iroquois country, drawing settlers from Vermont, Massachusetts, Connecticut, and elsewhere in the state. The need for laborers to build the great inland waterways, the Erie and the Champlain-Hudson canals, in the time of Governor De Witt Clinton (1817–21; 1825–28), brought a flood of immigrants from Ireland, Scotland, England, and Germany. Their descendants settled the towns and cities that grew up along the canals, and in turn drew others into the region. Thus the population of the state grew from 340,120 in 1790 to almost two million in 1830, and there were a goodly number of Catholics among the new immigrants, notably the Irish.

When Baltimore was raised to the status of an archbishopric in 1808, New York was one of the new suffragan sees. Its territory included all of New York state and the upper half of New Jersey. The first division of the diocese was made in 1847 when the northern and western sections of the state were cut off to create the dioceses of Albany and Buffalo. Bishop John MCCLOSKEY, then coadjutor bishop in New York, became the first bishop of Albany (1847 to 1864 when he returned to New York City as archbishop). The Reverend John TIMON, Superior of the Congregation of the Mission (Vicentians) and sometime missionary in Texas, was named the first bishop of Buffalo. In 1850 Pope Pius IX made New York a metropolitan see and named Bishop John HUGHES as the first archbishop. Boston, Hartford, Albany, and Buffalo were its suffragans. Two more dioceses were carved out of the archdiocese of New York in 1853, Brooklyn and NEWARK, New Jersey. The Reverend John Loughlin was named the first bishop of Brooklyn, and the Reverend James Roosevelt BAYLEY (a nephew of Elizabeth Bayley Seton), the first bishop of Newark (and later, the eighth Archbishop of Baltimore). The diocese of Rochester was separated from Albany in 1868 with Bishop Bernard J. MCQUAID the first ordinary. Four years later in 1872 Ogdensburg was made a diocese. About the time that Syracuse was made a diocese in 1886, the Bahama Islands were placed under New York's jurisdiction because access was thought to be easier than from Charleston, South Carolina, which formerly had jurisdiction. The diocesan structure of the state of New York remained unchanged from 1886 until 1957, when Rockville Centre was separated from Brooklyn.

For much of the 19th century, the Church in New York depended on priests from Europe to staff the national parishes that were being established to serve different ethnic groups, but early on the bishops of New York endeavored to establish their own seminary. Bishop Dubois built a seminary at Nyack-on-Hudson in 1833, but it burned down just as it was ready to open. After several other abortive attempts, Bishop John Hughes opened St. John's Seminary in 1841 at Fordham, then a village outside the city. In 1864 the students were moved to St. Joseph's Provincial Seminary in Troy, New York. Before it closed in 1896 it educated more than 700 priests. The poor living conditions at the Troy seminary caused Bishop McQuaid to open St. Bernard's Seminary in Rochester in 1893, and in 1896 Archbishop Corrigan established St. Joseph's Seminary in the Dunwoodie section of Yonkers. The Dunwoodie seminary gained a reputation as a intellectual center of American Catholicism. From 1905 to 1908, its faculty were major contributors to the *New York Review*, the leading Catholic theological publication in the country, and to the *Catholic Encyclopedia* (1907–12).

Immigration picked up momentum again after the Civil War. Beginning in the 1880s immigrants from Italy and Slavic lands came in increasing numbers. By the turn of the century, there were an estimated 400,000 immigrants in the archdiocese of New York alone, and Buffalo had a number of large Polish parishes. French-Canadians emigrated from Quebec to settle in upstate New York around Cohoes and Plattsburg. But the flood of immigrants also stirred a new wave of anti-Catholic bigotry. In the 1850s Archbishop John Hughes openly confronted the Know-Nothing movement so that it did not have the impact in New York that it had elsewhere in the country. In 1855 the state legislature passed a statute that prohibit-

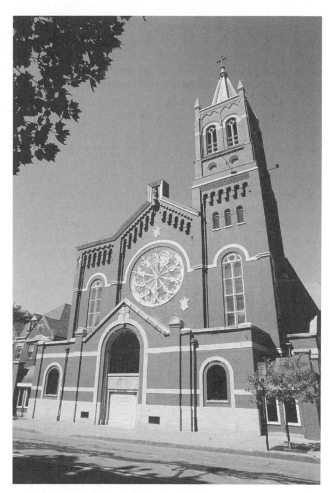

St. Mary's Church, Rochester, New York. (©The Purcell Team/ CORBIS)

ed Catholic bishops from holding title to property in trust for the churches and ecclesiastical institutions, but it was quietly repealed after the Civil War began. Later in the century, however, the National League for the Protection of American Interests (N.L.P.A.I.) made an effort to deny government funds to Catholic schools and charitable institutions.

The legacy of the N.L.P.A.I. continued. Several city and state investigative committees submitted Catholic social agencies to close scrutiny in the years before World War I. In 1916 the bishops organized the New York Catholic Conference, the first such organization in the U.S. It provides a forum for the exchange of information between dioceses on social issues and matters of concern to the Church. The Conference enables the dioceses of the state to present a unified position with regard to existing legislation and public policy. After the war Archbishop Patrick J. HAYES (1919–38) took steps to reorganize Catholic Charities and set professional standards for social welfare that were widely imitated by other dioceses.

Despite restrictive laws in the 1920s, immigration continued during the years between WWI and World War II. As Catholics increased in numbers they came more and more to exercise political influence and public policy. Alfred E. Smith, the first Catholic presidential nominee of a major party, was known for his efforts to bring about reforms during his four terms as governor of New York (1919–20; 1923–28). Catholic social agencies collaborated in welfare programs during the depression, and individual Catholics like Dorothy and John LAFARGE were prophetic voices speaking against war and racial discrimination.

In the wake of World War II, the Church experienced many changes. There was an influx of Puerto Ricans into the city of New York. The GI Bill created a whole new clientele for colleges and universities, and thus caused Catholic institutions to expand both physical plants and academic programs. The growth of the suburbs, at the expense of the size, economy, and social make-up of the urban centers, impacted on the Church in the cities. As the urban congregations dwindled in size and number, dioceses were forced to build new parishes and schools in the suburbs. The Diocese of Rockville Centre was an example of the change. The Catholic population, predominantly white middle class, almost tripled between the time it was split off from the diocese in Brooklyn in 1957 to 2001 growing from 497,000 to 1.4 million.

Catholic Education. Alongside the free elementary schools, provided as early as 1633 during the period of Dutch control, and higher education that had its beginning with the founding of King's College (Columbia) in 1754, the Church gradually developed an extensive network of elementary schools, high schools, and colleges. At the beginning of the 21st century, there were 29 Catholic universities and colleges in the state, many of which were located in the metropolitan region of New York City. Jesuit-run Fordham University (1841) was the first Catholic institution for higher education in New York, and the College of New Rochelle (established 1904 by the Ursulines) was the first Catholic college for women chartered in the state. Other prominent Catholic universities in the state include ST. BONAVENTURE UNIVERSITY (sponsored by the Franciscans), St. John's University in Jamaica, NY and Niagara University (both sponsored by the Vincentians), Manhattan College in Bronx (sponsored by the De La Salle Brothers), Iona College in New Rochelle (sponsored by the Irish Christian Brothers), and Canisius College in Buffalo (sponsored by the Jesuits).

Bibliography: J. R. BAYLEY, *Brief Sketch of the Early History of the Catholic Church on the Island of New York* (New York 1853; repr. 1870). M. J. BLOCKER, *A History of Catholic Life in the Diocese of Albany* (New York 1975). M. CARTY, *A Cathedral of Suitable Magnificence: St. Patrick's Cathedral* (Wilmington, DE 1984). F. D. COHALAN, *A Popular History of the Archdiocese of New York* (Yonkers, NY 1983). J. P. DOLAN, *The Immigrant Church: New York's Irish and German Catholics, 1815–1865* (Baltimore 1975). J. DE L. LEONARD, *Richly Blessed: The History of the Diocese of Rockville Centre* (Rockville Centre 1991). R. F. MCNAMARA, *History of the Diocese of Rochester 1868–1968* (Rochester, NY 1968). D. J. O'BRIEN, *Faith and Friendship: Catholicism in the Diocese of Syracuse, 1886–1986* (Syracuse, NY 1987). J. K. SHARP, *History of the Diocese of Brooklyn, 1853–1953*, 2 v. (New York 1954). R. SHAW, *Dagger John: The Unquiet Life and Times of Archbishop John Hughes of New York* (New York 1977). T. J. SHELLEY, *Dunwoodie: The History of St. Joseph's Seminary* (Westminster, MD 1993). M. C. TAYLOR, *A History of the Foundations of Catholicism in Northern New York* (New York 1976).

[M. P. CARTHY/EDS.]

NEW ZEALAND, THE CATHOLIC CHURCH IN

Located 1,180 miles south of Australia, New Zealand, which forms part of OCEANIA in the southwest Pacific Ocean, comprises two major islands—North Island and South Island, separated by the Cook Strait—as well as smaller islands that include Stewart, Chatham, Bounty, Antipodes, Auckland, Campbell and Kermadec islands. A mountainous region, the islands also contain areas of low plains at the coast. The climate is temperate, although conditions vary throughout the islands. Mild earthquakes are commonplace occurrences and volcanic activity infrequently occurs. Natural resources include natural gas, iron ore, coal, gold and limestone, while agricultural products consist of wheat, barley, potatoes, fruits, vegetables and wool.

The region was discovered and named by the Dutch explorer Abel Tasman in 1642. Captain James Cook visited and mapped the area from 1769. New Zealand, which became a British colony in 1840, was granted responsible government in 1856. In 1907 it became a self-governing state in the British Commonwealth. The southern sections were settled systematically from the British Isles, and in recent years the government has made efforts to address the mistreatment of Maori natives during and since the region's colonization. In 1994, the government began paying compensation to Maori tribes whose lands were seized after the Waitangi Treaty of 1840. Approximately 80 percent of the population live in urban areas.

Catholic Origins and Growth. The original people of New Zealand were the Maori, called *tangata whenua*, or "the people of the land," who inhabited the islands from 800. By the time the first British colonists arrived *c.*1800, there were some 100,000 Maori on the islands. British Protestant missionaries began working with success among the Maoris in 1814. By 1830, 1,000 Europeans, mostly of British origin, lived in the region. The Vicariate Apostolic of Western Oceania, created in 1836, included New Zealand and was entrusted to the MARIST FATHERS (SM), and Bishop Jean Pompallier became the first vicar apostolic. After Pompallier learned from Bishop John Polding of Sydney, Australia that Thomas Poynton, his family, and about 20 other Catholics were living in the far northwest of New Zealand, he traveled to Poynton's house on the Hokianga. In 1839 he transferred his headquarters to Kororareka, the chief port for whaling ships.

In February of 1840 the Treaty of Waitangi signified the agreement of 46 Maori head chiefs to recognize the suzerainty of Queen Victoria, in return for the preservation of land and tribal rights. Despite the treaty, land was illegally seized from the Maori throughout the next century, leading to the Anglo-Maori wars from 1860–72. Many Maori also lost their hunting and fishing rights, leaving them without a means of support. Meanwhile, French Marists made progress among the Maoris, and by 1843 there were 12 mission stations in the country.

The Vicariate of Western Oceania was divided in 1842 to create the Vicariate of Central Oceania, including New Zealand. In 1846 Philip Viard, SM, was consecrated coadjutor to Pompallier and laid the cornerstone of St. Patrick's Cathedral in Auckland, where Pompallier made his headquarters after Hone Heke's rebellion in the far north (1845–46). Pompallier's differences with Marist superiors led Rome to divide New Zealand in 1848 into the dioceses of Wellington and Auckland. Viard and the Marists were given Wellington, the southern region. In 1850 Pompallier returned to Auckland from Europe with ten clerics and eight Sisters of Mercy from Carlow, Ireland.

From 1859 North Island suffered from land disputes between Europeans and Maoris, followed by warfare in Taranaki and the Waikato. During and after these wars British soldiers, among them many Irish Catholics, were demobilized and settled in the country. The ensuing Hau Hau outbreaks, extending to the east coast, lasted until 1871, when they were crushed with the aid of friendly tribes. The Maori missions went into an almost total eclipse until their revival in 1881 under the Marists in the south and the MILL HILL MISSIONARIES in the north. Bishop John Luck of Auckland (1882–96), an English Benedictine, reorganized the Maori mission in his diocese.

Gold discoveries in 1861, combined with the absence of hostile Maoris, led to the rapid development of Otago and Southland. Many of the numerous immigrants were Irish miners who came from Australia. D. Moreau, SM, founded the Dunedin mission on South Island in 1861. In 1869 Otago and Southland were formed into the

Capital: Wellington.
Size: 104,000 sq. miles.
Population: 3,819,760 in 2000.
Languages: English, Maori.
Religions: 496,570 Catholics (13%), 2,521,000 Protestants (66%), 76,380 Ratana and Ringatu (Maori-Christian faiths; 2%), 725,810 other or without religious affiliation.
Metropolitan see: Archdiocese of Wellington, with suffragan sees Auckland, Christchurch, Dunedin, Hamilton, and Palmerston North. There is also a military ordinariate located in the islands. The country remains under the jurisdiction of the Congregation for the Propagation of the Faith.

Diocese of Dunedin. The first bishop was Patrick Moran (1869–96), former vicar apostolic of the Eastern District on the Cape of Good Hope, South Africa, who arrived in 1871 with a priest and ten Dominican sisters from Dublin. When Moran encountered strong anti-Catholic sentiments in heavily Presbyterian Otago, he took the offensive. During his episcopate he created a Catholic school system, began construction of a Gothic cathedral and started *The Tablet,* a Catholic weekly that flourished through the 20th century.

The diocese of Christchurch on South Island received its first resident priest c. 1840 at the French settlement of Akaroa. The town of Christchurch, colonized in 1850 as an Anglican settlement, lacked a resident priest until 1860. Catholics opened their first primary school in Auckland in 1841 and their first secondary school in Northcote, Auckland, in 1849. In 1887 the diocese of Christchurch was created; it included the provinces of Canterbury and Westland, the latter province being transformed by gold discoveries after 1865. John Grimes, an English Marist, became the first bishop (1887–1915). He was notable for his organizing ability and devotion to the liturgy. Besides establishing a good Catholic school system, he completed a new cathedral by 1905. Holy Name Seminary was opened in Christchurch in 1947.

Bibliography: J. B. F. POMPALLIER, *Early History of the Catholic Church in Oceania,* tr. A. HERMAN (Auckland 1888). P. F. MORAN, *History of the Catholic Church in Australasia* (Sydney 1897). A. MONFAT, *Les Origines de la foi catholique dans la Nouvelle Zélande* (Lyon 1896). J. J. WILSON, *The Church in New Zealand,* 2 v. (Dunedin 1910–26). F. REDWOOD, *Reminiscences of Early Days in New Zealand* (Wellington 1922). P. T. MCKEEFRY, *Fishers of Men* (Auckland 1938). K. S. LATOURETTE, *A History of the Expansion of Christianity,* 7 v. (New York 1937–45) v.5, 7. Sisters of Mercy, *Gracious Is the Time* (Auckland 1952). M. C. GOULTER, *Sons of France* (Wellington 1957). L. G. KEYS, *Life and Times of Bishop Pompallier* (Christchurch 1957). V. J. MCGLONE, *Fruits of Toil* (Carterton 1957). *Bilan du Monde,* 2:651–655. *Official Year Book of the Catholic Church of Australasia* (Sydney 1963–64), annual.

[M. MULCAHY]

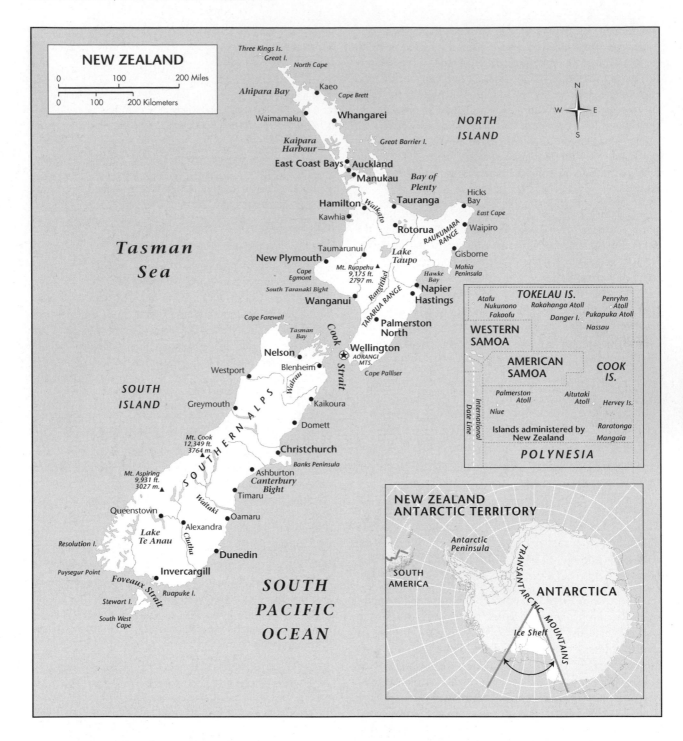

The Modern Church

On Sept. 26, 1907, New Zealand became an independent nation under the British Commonwealth. Under a series of liberal governments from 1891–1911 and again during World War II, the region became increasingly known for its socialist policies and its state-administered education and social welfare programs. In the mid-1970s the government began a program to quasi-nationalize se-

lected parochial and other private schools and in 1984 began a major economic restructuring in an effort to build a globally competitive free market economy. By the 1990s the region entered an economic downturn that resulted in social welfare cutbacks, the end of free education and the end of free socialized health care, although by the end of the 20th century New Zealand boasted a strong international market for its goods and low inflation.

Catholic Basilica viewed from cemetery, Wellington, New Zealand. (©E.O. Hoppi/CORBIS)

Since the time of its founding in the 19th century and through the 20th century, the Church experienced steady if unspectacular growth. In 1980 the dioceses of Hamilton (carved off the southern portion of Auckland Diocese) and Palmerston North (carved off the northern portion of Wellington Archdiocese) were established, thus creating five dioceses in the country. When New Zealand acquired Tokelau as an overseas territory, these Pacific islands were placed under the Archdiocese of Wellington, but were later made a mission sui juris.

The Effects of Vatican II. In the years following the Second Vatican Council (1962–65) the bishops implemented the Council's decrees. The participation of laity in programs of adult formation, including those of the National Center for Religious Studies, teaching in Catholic schools and in other social support groups, was conspicuous. On the other hand, some felt that Catholics lost a depth of devotion as a result of Vatican II, citing a decrease in Sunday Mass attendance, the lack of regular de-

votions such as the rosary and Benediction of the Blessed Sacrament, the increased number of mixed marriages and irregular unions, and the growing indifference of the New Zealand population in general. Some who feared the loss of Catholicism joined local chapters of Catholics United for the Faith, while others joined the St. Pius X Society and were served by priests of that society (*see* LEFEBVRE, MARCEL).

After Vatican II the Church entered into a theological dialogue with the National Council of Churches and worked with it on the Interchurch Commission for Immigration and Refugee Resettlement and the Ecumenical Secretariat on Development. From these flowed ecumenical endeavors, often in industrial, prison and other chaplaincies. The Church was a founding member of the new Conference of Churches of Aotearoa-New Zealand in 1987, and established bilateral dialogues with the Anglican, Presbyterian and Methodist churches, as well as annual meetings.

While some changes in the Church were responses to Vatican II, others were the result of a decrease in number of priests and religious, particularly in urban areas. Priests under age 40 were rare by the end of the 20th century and priests under 50 a significant minority. Vocations to the priesthood also fell off to a great degree. Religious shared the problems of old age and scarcity of vocations with the general clergy. Age and the integration of schools removed many from the classroom, and some turned to ministry as pastoral assistants in parishes, counselors, youth directors, visitors of the sick and other apostolates. Several Catholic hospitals closed down, but the involvement of the religious in rest homes for the elderly remained a fruitful and needed apostolate. Over 300 New Zealand missionaries, clergy, religious and lay people worked abroad helping in evangelization, working in the Pacific, as well as Asia, the Americas, and Africa.

The Church and the Maori. A national resurgence within Maoridom dating back to the early 20th century received new impetus after World War II, especially as the Maori became more urbanized and educated. The injustices suffered by the Maori since the Treaty of Waitangi were revisited, and a reinterpretation of that treaty made with the intention of righting legal wrongs, especially with regard to land and fisheries dispossession. The Church remained at the forefront of this movement through episcopal statements and peace and justice commissions, as well as in work done in conjunction with other churches.

The New Zealand bishops encouraged the appointment of the first Maori bishop, Takuira Mariu of the Society of Mary, to a Maori congregation in 1988. The bishops also established a national Maori *runanga,* or council, with representatives of Maori lay, religious and clergy. The council supported and advised the New Zealand Catholic Bishops' Conference on all matters relating to the pastoral care of Maori people.

Besides the indigenous Maori people, new immigrants added much to the New Zealand Catholic identity. Many immigrants after World War II were European Catholics. In the late 20th century an influx of Pacific Islanders, especially from Samoa, created the need for special chaplaincies similar to those required for other ethnic groups after World War II.

Evolving Church-State Relations. While New Zealand was organized in provinces, most provinces subsidized denominational schools. After the abolition of the provinces in 1876, the central government canceled this aid and organized a national system of free, secular and compulsory schools, in 1964's Education Act noting that while teaching should be of a secular character, religious instruction and observances were allowed in state schools. Under the constitution, Catholic-run primary and secondary schools received no support from the state except for a few fringe benefits. With passage of the Integration Act of 1975 the government integrated financially troubled Catholic schools into the state system, providing staff salaries, equipment, general running costs and maintenance while allowing the Church the freedom to run the schools as they chose. Much effort was put into managing the massive debts contracted to bring over 250 of the country's schools up to the maintenance standard demanded by the state before obtaining the designation of an "integrated school." In addition, lay teachers, now the majority, required formation in theology and spirituality in order to preserve the special character of Catholic schools. Financially sound Catholic schools continued to operate as before.

The government's efforts to socialize the economy and social system led to an increase in unemployment and a reduction of state pensions and resulted in the greatest disparity between rich and poor since the 1930s. In 1993 the bishops questioned the government's economic and social policy in the "Statement of Intent." In addition, the Church worked to alleviate the misery and hunger of many through social agencies and parish foodbanks.

In November of 1986, Pope John Paul II visited New Zealand, receiving a traditional Maori welcome in Auckland, and participating in an ecumenical service in Christchurch. The pope addressed the country repeatedly in the following decade, warning the New Zealand Church to avoid becoming corrupted by modern secular culture. However, the New Zealand Bishops' Conference continued its tradition of liberal positions, in 2000 advocating both contraception use for teens who insisted upon being sexually active and a government plan to grant homosexual couples the same legal rights as married couples. Both positions drew strong opposition from conservative Catholics in New Zealand, as well as from the Vatican.

Into the 21st Century. By 2000 there were 279 parishes tended by 369 diocesan and 250 religious priests. Other religious included approximately 180 brothers and 1,185 sisters, many of whom participated in operating the 192 primary and 47 secondary schools run by the Church, as well as aiding in other social service endeavors. Most numerous among male orders were the Marist Fathers, Marist Brothers, the Redemptorists and the Trappists. Women religious included the Sisters of Mercy, the Congregation of Our Lady of the Missions, and the Sisters of St. Joseph of the Sacred Heart. As the New Zealand Church looked toward the future, its major concerns included the increasing ill effects of a secular society, the incursions made by Pentecostal and other evangelist sects and the treatment of the Maori people. Despite their reported church affiliation, a poll taken in 1997 reported that one fourth of all New Zealanders admitted actively adhering to no religion.

Bibliography: L. G. KEYS, *Philip Viard, Bishop of Wellington* (Christchurch 1968). F. MCKAY, *The Life of James K. Baxter* (Auckland 1990). J. MACKEY, *The Making of a State Education System* (London 1967). E. R. SIMMONS, *A Brief History of the Catholic Church in New Zealand* (Auckland 1978); *In cruce salus; A History of the Diocese of Auckland 1948–1980* (Auckland 1982); *Pompallier—Prince of Bishops* (Auckland 1984). R. WILTGEN, *The Founding of the Roman Catholic Church in Oceania 1825–1850* (Canberra 1979).

[J. BROADBENT/EDS.]

NEWARK, ARCHDIOCESE OF

Also known as *Novarcensis;* a metropolitan see comprising Essex, Hudson, Bergen, and Union counties in the northeastern part of New Jersey. It is the smallest of all the dioceses in the 50 states (513 sq. miles). The archdiocese is divided into 235 parishes and missions. Catholics comprise about 50 percent of the total population of 2.8 million, placing Newark as the seventh largest U.S. see in population. The Province of Newark, coterminous with the state of New Jersey, includes the suffragan dioceses of Trenton, Paterson, Camden, and Metuchen.

Administration. Before the erection of Newark as a separate diocese suffragan to New York in 1853, Catholics of the northern counties of New Jersey belonged to the New York archdiocese, while the southern half of the state was included in the Diocese of Philadelphia, PA. The religious history of New Jersey in the colonial period and the early republic was largely Protestant, although small groups of Catholics were ministered to by Jesuit missionary priests, among them Ferdinand FARMER, Lorenz GRASSEL, and Leonard NEALE, and six parishes were established in various parts of the state in the period between 1814 and 1827.

With the advent of thousands of German and Irish Catholic immigrants into New Jersey towns, the Holy See erected Newark as a diocese on July 29, 1853, and included in its jurisdiction the entire state of New Jersey with its 40,000 Catholic inhabitants. In 1881, 14 central and southern counties were detached from Newark when the Diocese of Trenton was erected. On Dec. 9, 1937, Pius XI divided Trenton into the Sees of Trenton and Camden, and the two northern counties of Passaic and Morris were removed from the Newark jurisdiction and assigned to the newly erected Diocese of Paterson. The following day, December 10, Newark was raised to the status of an archdiocese.

Bayley. James Roosevelt BAYLEY, a convert to Catholicism, served as first bishop of Newark from 1853 to 1872, when he was named archbishop of Baltimore. His episcopate in Newark was devoted largely to the founding and staffing of religious institutes of every kind. The diocesan priesthood was augmented, and the beginnings of an educated Catholic laity were provided by the establishment of Seton Hall College (now University) in South Orange, NJ in 1856. This institution included the major Seminary of the Immaculate Conception from 1862 to 1927. The Benedictines, Passionists, Conventual Franciscans, and Jesuits were the earliest men's orders brought into the diocese to assist the diocesan clergy. A new community of Sisters of Charity was formed by Bayley in Newark in 1859, moving its headquarters to Convent Station the next year. Other early communities of sisters who engaged in teaching, hospital, and orphanage work were the Benedictine Sisters, the School Sisters of Notre Dame, the Sisters of Mercy, the Sisters of St. Joseph, and the Dominican and Franciscan Sisters. The Brothers of the Christian Schools entered the diocese to conduct boys' classes in a number of the parish schools.

Corrigan. The second bishop, Michael Augustine CORRIGAN, was vicar general of the diocese when he succeeded Bayley in 1873 and served until 1880, when he was transferred to New York. Faced with numerous financial problems at Seton Hall and in the parishes, Corrigan raised funds and donated large sums from his family estate. He introduced additional religious communities, including the Second Order Dominican Sisters, Sisters of the Good Shepherd, and Franciscan Brothers.

Wigger. A native of New York, Winand Michael WIGGER, was ordained for the Newark diocese and engaged in parish work until he was named third bishop of Newark in 1881, a position he retained until his death on Jan. 5, 1901. During his administration he unsuccessfully backed a school aid bill in the assembly (1892–93) to give state aid to parochial schools. Under his direction, work was begun on the new Cathedral of the Sacred Heart, on ground purchased by Bayley. By 1901 the number of Catholics had increased to 300,000 and priests totaled 265; of these 75 were religious.

John Joseph O'Connor. Having been born in Newark, June 11, 1855, and ordained in 1877, the fourth bishop taught at Seton Hall and at the seminary, and served as seminary rector, vicar general, and pastor, until his appointment to the episcopate in 1901. He headed the Diocese of Newark until his death there on May 20, 1927. During his 26-year episcopate, additional funds were raised to continue work on the new cathedral. In 1926, the major Seminary of the Immaculate Conception was moved to Darlington.

Thomas Joseph Walsh. Newark's fifth bishop and first archbishop was born Dec. 6, 1873, at Parker's Landing, PA, and was ordained for the Buffalo, NY diocese in 1900, where he was chancellor until appointed bishop of Trenton in 1918. He was transferred to Newark in 1928 and served as its first archbishop from Dec. 10, 1937 until his death on June 6, 1952. He initiated a campaign for a new seminary building and chapel at Darlington (1936), organized the Mt. Carmel Guild to supervise social work, and in 1951 founded an archdiocesan newspaper, the *Advocate*. He also began a drive in 1950 for funds to complete Sacred Heart Cathedral and initiated work on the building's interior.

Thomas Aloysius Boland. The second archbishop was born in Orange, NJ, in 1896 and ordained in 1922. He taught at Seton Hall and the Darlington seminary and served as chancellor, auxiliary bishop (1940), and bishop of Paterson (1947–53), before being installed as archbishop of Newark on Jan. 14, 1953. Under him, Mt. Carmel Guild was reorganized in 1954 and its work extended to aid the blind, the deaf, and other handicapped groups. Serra International was introduced in 1954 and the sodality movement organized on an archdiocesan level in 1957. The Cathedral of the Sacred Heart, which is French-Gothic in design, was consecrated on Oct. 19, 1954. In 1961 a development campaign was inaugurated to provide eight new high schools, four homes for the aged, and a philosophy house at the major seminary. By 1964 there were 1,177 priests, including 358 religious, serving the archdiocese, as well as 3,244 sisters and 205 brothers.

Peter Leo Gerety. Gerety was named the third archbishop on April 2, 1974. He was born in Shelton, CT in 1912; both of his parents were natives of New Jersey. He studied theology at St. Sulpice Seminary in Issy, France, and was ordained in 1939. After serving in parish and hospital ministry, he became director of an interracial social and religious center from 1942 to 1956, when the center became St. Martin de Porres parish and he was named pastor. He was involved in the Black Apostolate for 24 years, chairing the Hartford Archdiocesan Committee on Human Rights as well as the Ecumenical Commission. In 1966 he was ordained co-adjutor bishop of Portland, ME, and succeeded Bishop Feeney there in 1969. When he became archbishop of Newark in 1974, he faced the challenge of a $26 million dollar debt inherited from his predecessor. By January 1984 this debt was paid, and new structures were put into place to assure the proper administrative and financial support of the pastoral ministry in the archdiocese. Some programs begun under his leadership, such as RENEW and Ministry to Divorced and Separated Catholics, became national models. Archbishop Gerety retired in July, 1986.

Theodore E. McCarrick. McCarrick was appointed the fourth archbishop of Newark in July 1986, after serv-

ing as the founding bishop of Metuchen, NJ since 1981. He grew up in New York City and was educated at Fordham University and St. Joseph's Seminary, Dunwoodie. After his ordination in 1958, he was assigned as an assistant chaplain at Catholic University of America, where he proceeded to earn a doctorate in sociology in 1963. He became president of the University of Ponce in Puerto Rico in 1965, and returned to New York in 1969 to head the Office of Catholic Education and serve as personal secretary to Cardinal Cooke. In 1977 he was named auxiliary bishop in New York, and in 1981 he became the first bishop of the diocese of Metuchen, NJ. In 1990 he successfully conducted a $50 million dollar capital campaign which helped to endow a number of archdiocesan programs. He also invited the neocatechumenate to start Redemptoris Mater House of Formation to train seminarians for the missionary-diocesan priesthood. Most of the archdiocesan offices were brought together in a new archdiocesan center at a site across from the Sacred Heart Cathedral in Newark, which was named a basilica by Pope John Paul II at the time of his visit in October 1995. In 1999 Archbishop McCarrick launched a campaign for stewardship in every parish to encourage individuals to give their time, talent and treasure in a spirit of discipleship. The results of this campaign are being shared with needy parishes. In November 2000, Archbishop McCarrick was named archbishop of Washington, DC, and was made a cardinal by Pope John Paul II on Feb. 21, 2001.

John Joseph Myers. Myers became the fifth archbishop of Newark on Oct. 9, 2001, after serving 11 years as bishop of Peoria, IL. He was raised in the Peoria diocese and was ordained after his theological studies in Rome in December 1966. He served for a year in the United States Catholic Conference and completed his studies for a doctorate in Canon Law at Catholic University in Washington, DC. After serving in various parish and chancery ministries, he was ordained co-adjutor bishop in 1987 and acceded to the See of Peoria on Jan. 23, 1990.

Institutional Development. In addition to Seton Hall University, conducted by the archdiocesan clergy and lay faculty, the archdiocese contains St. Peter's College, Jersey City, conducted by the Jesuit Fathers, Caldwell College, conducted by the Dominican Sisters of Caldwell, and Felician College in Lodi, conducted by the Felician Sisters. Besides its main campus at South Orange, Seton Hall also operates the School of Law in Newark.

The archdiocesan major seminary was relocated from Darlington, near Ramsey, to the campus of Seton Hall University in October 1984. A pre-theology program and four years of theological studies are provided for seminarians from the archdiocese, including those in the neocatechumenate, and for several other dioceses and religious orders. The minor seminary, Seton Hall Divinity School, has been located on the South Orange campus of Seton Hall since 1862.

In 2001 there were 37 secondary schools in the archdiocese, with a total student enrollment of 16,047. Parish elementary schools numbered 132 with an enrollment of 40,474. There are eight Catholic hospitals in the archdiocese: St. James's and St. Michael's, in Newark; St. Elizabeth's Hospital, in Elizabeth; St. Mary's, in Hoboken; St. Francis's, in Jersey City; St. Vincent's, in Montclair; St. Mary's, in Orange; and Holy Name, in Teaneck. There are seven homes for the aged, and 114 health care centers.

Catholic Community Services includes among its activities the Mount Carmel Guild Behavioral Healthcare System with offices in all four counties. C.C.S. also coordinates the Apostolate with the Developmentally Disabled and the Deaf, along with the Prison Ministry and Ministry to People on the Move (Airport and Seaport Chaplaincies).

Bibliography: New Jersey Historical Records Commission, *The Bishops of Newark, 1853–1978* (South Orange, NJ 1978).

[T. IVORY]

NEWBATTLE (NEWBOTTLE), ABBEY OF

Former CISTERCIAN abbey in the county of Midlothian, old Diocese of Saint Andrews, Scotland (Neubotle, i.e., a new dwelling). It was founded by DAVID I and his son Henry, Nov. 1, 1140, and dedicated to St. Mary; it was the first daughterhouse of MELROSE. Its later acquisitions included a coal mine and a quarry, which provided the monks with a useful source of income. The abbey was badly damaged by the English in 1385, 1544, and 1548. In 1560 its abbot, Mark Ker, subscribed to the reformed religion and secured the abbey's properties for his son. The east range of the abbey is now incorporated into Newbattle Abbey College.

Bibliography: *Registrum S. Marie de Neubotle*, ed. C. INNES (Edinburgh 1849). *Royal Commission on the Ancient and Historical Monuments and Constructions of Scotland: Counties of Midlothian and West Lothian* (Edinburgh 1929). J. M. CANIVEZ, ed., *Statuta capitulorum generalium ordinis cisterciensis*, 8 v. (Louvain 1933–41), 5:750–751; 6:406, 689–690; 7:37. G. W. S. BARROW, ''Scottish Rulers and the Religious Orders, 1070–1153,'' *Transactions of the Royal Historical Society*, 5th ser. 3 (1953) 94–95. D. E. EASSON, *Medieval Religious Houses: Scotland* (London 1957) 65.

[L. MACFARLANE]

NEWDIGATE, SEBASTIAN, BL.

Carthusian priest, martyr; b. Harefield Place, Middlesex, England; d. hanged, drawn, and quartered at Tyburn (London), June 19, 1535. Sebastian was the well-born younger son of the king's sergeant John Newdigate and the heiress of John Nevill of Sutton in Lincolnshire. After completing his education at Cambridge, he joined Henry VIII's court and became an intimate of the king. After the death (1524) of his wife, he placed his daughter Amphelys in the care of others and entered the London Charterhouse of the Carthusians. On June 6, 1534, he signed the Oath of Succession with the addendum ''in as far as the law of God permits.'' He was arrested (May 25, 1535) for denying the king's supremacy, and bound in irons in a standing position for 14 days at the Marshalsea Prison. There Henry made a personal plea for Sebastian to conform in exchange for riches and honors. Following his refusal, Newdigate was brought before the Privy Council, then sent to the Tower, where Henry again visited him. After his trial (June 11), he was returned to the Tower. He was executed with BB. William EXMEW and Humphrey MIDDLEMORE. Newdigate was beatified by Pope Leo XIII on Dec. 9, 1886.

Feast of the English Martyrs: May 4 (England); May 11 (Archdiocese of Birmingham).

See Also: ENGLAND, SCOTLAND, AND WALES, MARTYRS OF.

Bibliography: R. CHALLONER, *Memoirs of Missionary Priests*, ed. J. H. POLLEN (rev. ed. London 1924; repr. Farnborough 1969). J. H. POLLEN, *Acts of English Martyrs* (London 1891).

[K. I. RABENSTEIN]

NEWMAN, JOHN HENRY

Apologist, theologian, cardinal; b. London, Feb. 21, 1801; d. Birmingham, England, Aug. 11, 1890.

Life

He was the eldest of the six children of John Newman, an unsuccessful London banker, and Jemima Fourdrinier, the daughter of a well-to-do middle-class French Protestant paper manufacturer. The other children in order of birth were Charles Robert (1802), Harriet (1803), Francis (1805), Jemima (1807), and Mary Sophia (1809). Newman entered the private boarding school at Ealing in 1808. Although his life at home had been warm and happy, in 1816 the bank with which his father was associated failed, and from then on the family was in reduced circumstances. Newman's sisters were sent to their grandmother, but he continued at Ealing. This event profoundly affected the entire family; the father died in 1824.

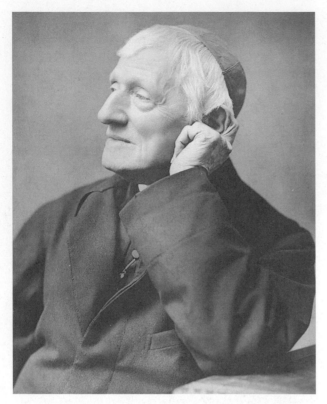

John Henry Newman. (©Hulton-Deutsch Collection/CORBIS)

As a Protestant. Newman's early religious orientation was toward Calvinism and Fundamentalism. In 1816, however, shortly after the failure of the bank and the subsequent catastrophe at home and apparently in connection with an illness that profoundly disturbed him, Newman went through a five-month period that he later referred to as conversion. At that time a friend introduced him to Thomas Scott's *The Force of Truth* and Milner's *Church History*. The first convinced him of the divinity of Christ, and the second introduced him to the Fathers of the Church of the 4th and 5th centuries. He concluded that God willed him to lead a life of celibacy. There was apparently a complete change in the vision he had of himself. The nature of this spiritual crisis is somewhat obscure, but he emerged from it as a different person. He considered the experience to have been a turning point in his career. He gained a profound awareness of the presence of God. The beginnings of an intellectual foundation for his moral convictions stem from this period. He emerged with a love for the Fathers of the Church and a fear and abhorrence of Rome and the papacy, which seem to have come from his reading of Newton's *On the Prophecies*. His new insights produced certain basic contradictions that would engage him for the next 30 years.

University Life. Newman matriculated at Trinity College, Oxford, in December 1816 and took up residence there the following June. While there, he made the acquaintance of John William Bowden, who was to be his close friend and frequent support until Bowden's death in 1844. He and Bowden undertook the publication of a literary magazine called *The Undergraduate* in 1819. Newman won a scholarship at the end of his first year and gained a reputation as a student. In the schools examination in November 1820, to the surprise of all, he failed to achieve honors in either the mathematical sciences or the classics. He retained his scholarship, however, and determined to stay on at Oxford until he would take Holy Orders.

Newman tried the schools examination at Oriel in 1822 and was elected a fellow at Oriel on April 12 of that year. It was there that he met Edward Bouverie PUSEY, Richard WHATLY, Edward Copelston, Edward Hawkins, and Thomas Arnold. He was ordained deacon on June 13, 1824. The following October his father died.

Newman accepted the curacy of St. Clement's, which he retained until his appointment as public tutor of Oriel in 1826. He was ordained as an Anglican priest May 29, 1825. He served as public examiner in classics in the B.A. degree for the university in 1827–28 and was given the vicarage of St. Mary's, the university church, in 1828. He served as the university select preacher (1831–32) and that same year relinquished his college tutorship.

When Richard Hurrell FROUDE was elected to a fellowship at Oriel in March 1826, he and Newman became close friends. In 1832 Newman accompanied him on a Mediterranean cruise needed for Froude's health. Then, while traveling alone through Europe, Newman was beset by long and dangerous illness in Sicily. During his convalescence he made several trips to Catholic shrines and churches in Europe; it was on his return to England that he wrote his famous poem "Lead Kindly Light."

Oxford Movement. Shortly after his return (July 1833) to England the question of disestablishment of the Anglican Church was introduced before Parliament. Newman, Froude, John KEBLE, and William PALMER threw themselves into the task of writing tracts and dissents of the church. The following December the *Tracts for the Times* began to appear. Of these, there were eventually 90, of which 26 were written by Newman.

The Tractarian movement, with Newman at its head, evoked considerable criticism on the part of both the bishops and the priests of the Church of England. Hurrell Froude took as active a part in the movement as he was able, suffering as he was from tuberculosis, which forced him to live away from England. Froude died in the beginning of 1836, a serious loss to Newman, who depended on him for support in the OXFORD MOVEMENT, as the Tractarian movement came to be called, as well as for his spiritual insights and warm friendship.

The next few years were a time of tremendous intellectual activity for Newman. He was engaged in writing the tracts as well as preparing the sermons he preached at St. Mary's, later published as the *Parochial and Plain Sermons*. In 1838 he became the editor of the *British Critic*, a magazine that was a platform for expression for those members of the Anglican Church who had Catholic sympathies. It was at this time too that Newman began his serious studies of the Fathers of the Church. Following his famous *Tract 90*, which was an attempt to interpret the Thirty-Nine Articles of the Church of England in a Catholic sense, he was censured by the authorities of the University of Oxford as well as by 24 bishops of the Anglican communion. As a consequence, in 1841 Newman retired to Littlemore, part of the parish of St. Mary's. Having refurbished a small stable and several outhouses, in which he and several companions lived according to a daily rule of life, he began a life of prayer and fasting for the purpose of clarifying his opinions about the Church Catholic. In 1845 he wrote his *Essay on the Development of Christian Doctrine* and made the decision to become a member of the Roman Church. He was received into the Roman Catholic Church by Dominic BARBERI, an Italian Passionist, on Oct. 9, 1845, in the small private chapel at Littlemore. Many of the companions living with him in Littlemore became Catholics at the same time, but Keble, Pusey, and Newman's own family remained members of the Church of England.

As a Catholic. Newman and his convert companions left Littlemore in February 1846. They took up residence at the old Oscott College, renamed Maryvale by Newman. It was near the residence of Bp. Nicholas P. WISEMAN, who was then living at the new Oscott College not far from Maryvale. Wiseman took on the direction of the new community, and through his encouragement Newman decided to become a priest of the Roman Catholic Church. He and Ambrose St. John, one of his Littlemore companions, left England for the College of Propaganda in Rome in September 1846. There they had their first introduction to systematic Catholic theology, which lasted for about one year. Newman was ordained priest on Trinity Sunday 1847. He offered his first Mass on the Feast of Corpus Christi 1847.

Founding the Oratory. Before returning to England, with the encouragement of several of his Roman friends and of Pope Pius IX as well, Newman and his companions went to the Oratory of St. Philip Neri at Santa Croce to learn the rule and customs of the Oratory.

After returning to England on Christmas Eve 1847, Newman established the first Oratory in England at Bir-

mingham the following February 2. His influence among the Catholics and recent Anglican converts was very great. He was joined in the Oratory by Frederick W. FABER and other converts from the Church of England. After a falling out of no great consequence, Newman encouraged Faber to open an Oratory in London. This he did in May 1849, while Newman stayed behind to undertake the instruction of the factory workers of Birmingham.

Rome's restoration of the English hierarchy in 1850 gave rise to a wave of antipapal feeling among the members of the Church of England. The no-popery campaign was assisted indirectly by the return of Wiseman to England as the cardinal archbishop of Westminster, preceded by his famous but misunderstood pastoral letter *From Out the Flaminian Gate*. Newman wrote a number of letters of explanation to newspapers under the pen name Catholicus. The ORATORIANS came under severe attack by the no-popery forces, perhaps because during this time a new house for the Birmingham Oratorians was under construction at Edgbaston. The Protestant Alliance fomented the antipopery campaign in England by providing a chapel for Giacinto Achilli, a married former Dominican priest, who came to London in 1850 after refusing to do penance for his scandalous behavior in the previous positions he occupied in Italy. He published a book, *Dealings with the Inquisition*, which was popular and widespread in the Anglican communion. In an article in the *Dublin Review*, Wiseman criticized Achilli and exposed a number of his previous sexual irregularities; he also encouraged Newman to make a more direct criticism in the sermons he was preaching in Birmingham (later gathered together as *The Present Positions of Catholics in England*). With the support of the Protestant Alliance, Achilli brought a case of criminal libel against Newman. Convicted of libel in June 1852, Newman, through his lawyer, moved for a new trial. Although the move was not granted, the delay provided time for the public's temper to cool so that Newman was released after he paid a fine of £100 plus trial expenses amounting to approximately $60,000. The costs of the trial were borne by Newman's friends in England, Europe, and America. It was a moral victory for Newman.

An Irish University. Throughout this troublesome period Newman was developing his idea on the nature of education. He delivered a series of lectures on university education in London in 1852. They were delivered to fulfill a promise he had made in 1851 to Dr. P. CULLEN, Archbishop of Armagh, and later Cardinal Archbishop of Dublin, that he would accept the rectorship of a new Catholic university that Cullen was determined upon for Ireland. Disappointed over his failures to begin the new university in Ireland, he tendered his resignation to the

Irish bishops. The university lectures that he had delivered in London six years earlier were amplified and completed during his stay in Ireland and were eventually published as his *The Idea of a University*.

Papal Authority. During his stay in Dublin there was also anxiety at home because of several differences of opinion that arose between the Oratories of London and Birmingham. Newman was accused of trying to dominate the London Oratory and thereby reduce its autonomy; his reputation suffered because of the disputes between himself and Faber. Faber became more and more identified with the ultramontane movement among English Catholics. Because of his criticism of Faber's handling of the London Oratory and of his peculiar, perhaps saccharine, attitude toward spirituality, Newman not only was accused of disapproving ULTRAMONTANISM but was held suspect of disloyalty toward the prerogatives of the pope himself.

Partly as a theological conviction and partly by way of reaction to the antipopery movements in England, a number of Catholic intellectuals expressed the belief that the temporal power of the pope was essential to the constitution of the Church. There had been an increasing centralization of authority in both disciplinary and doctrinal matters in the person of the pope during the 19th century. In the 1850s there was a growing movement in favor of a strong formal declaration of papal INFALLIBILITY. Although Newman did not publicize his grave reservations about the direction of this movement, he did refuse to participate in the demonstrations that were organized to support it.

Upon his return from Ireland in 1858 he was asked by the English hierarchy to take over the editorship of a Catholic periodical entitled *The Rambler*. Shortly after he assumed its editorship, he prepared an essay of his own entitled *On Consulting the Faithful in Matters of Doctrine*. This essay was delated to Rome, and subsequently Newman had to resign from the editorship of the magazine. The matter was not finally cleared up, nor was Newman finally exonerated, until 1867.

In 1864 Charles Kingsley attacked the Roman clergy in general and Newman in particular, alleging that both held the view that truth has no value. Newman felt the attack totally unjustified and undertook a defense of himself and the Roman clergy. Writing in weekly installments for publication in a newspaper, Newman defended his own conversion in a series of essays later published together as the *Apologia pro vita sua*. It caught the public interest and reestablished Newman's significance and importance in the religious life of England. The entire work was completed in two months.

After his plans to found a Catholic center at Oxford failed, Newman set his mind to preparing a statement on the relationship between faith and reason to be valid not only for the intellectuals but for the common man as well. His thoughts on this crucial topic were finally published as *The Grammar of Assent* (1870). It was designed to justify the faith of the ordinary man who was often unable to formulate his faith for himself.

The year that the work appeared in print VATICAN COUNCIL I was holding its sessions. There was a growing eagerness on the part of H. E. MANNING and W. G. WARD, together with the ultramontane faction in England, to see the doctrine of papal infallibility defined in the strongest possible terms. Newman's position on papal infallibility was that, before being defined, such a doctrine should be given more time to mature. He asserted that he belived in papal infallibility from the day he became a Catholic and was never opposed to the definition of the doctrine as such, but felt the definition to be inopportune. He asserted, however, that should the Council adopt a definition, he would be the first to conform.

Newman was personally invited by PIUS IX to attend the sessions of the Council, but he asked to be excused. His request to be excused was misunderstood, but it was based on his desire to remain in the Oratory and to avoid the pomp necessary to such large ecclesiastical gatherings.

The result of the Council was a definition of infallibility in precisely the way that Newman had always believed it, and far less rigoristic than was desired by Manning and Ward. Subsequent to the definition there was enormous political criticism raised by conspicuous lay members of the Anglican church. William Ewart GLADSTONE launched an aggressive attack against the dogma of infallibility as well as against the Catholic Church as a whole. It was felt that his criticism voiced the opinion of many members of the Church of England. Since Manning's defense of the dogma was unconvincing, Newman wrote one of his own, his famous *Letter to the Duke of Norfolk*, which was warmly received by both the Church of England and the Roman Church, and won the approval of Manning and Ward. A faulty translation was forwarded to Rome, however, and was misunderstood by Cardinal A. Franchi, who asked Manning to have Newman make some corrections. But Manning wrote Franchi a heated defense of Newman, which brought the two men together in friendship. After Manning's vote of confidence, Newman's prestige in Rome increased considerably.

Cardinalate. After suffering one of the most severe trials of his later years in the death of Ambrose St. John in 1875, Newman experienced one of his greatest vindications in 1879, when Bp. W. B. ULLATHORNE informed him that the new pope, Leo XIII, wished to bestow on him the dignity of cardinal and would permit him to continue to live in his Oratory. Though Newman was then 78 and in precarious health, he made the trip to Rome to receive the honor. The previous year, 1878, his old college, Trinity of Oxford, had made him its first honorary fellow. He paid another visit to Oxford as a cardinal and preached in St. Aloysius Church there.

Newman continued to live at the Oratory in the simple manner to which he had become accustomed. He suffered an illness in 1888 and was weakened by several falls. He offered his last Mass on Christmas Day 1889. Until then he was alert and shared the community life with the other fathers of the Oratory. He presided over the close of the school term of 1890. Shortly thereafter he died quietly. The words engraved on his memorial stone were of his own choosing: *Ex Umbris Et Imaginibus In Veritatem.*

Doctrine

It is not easy to characterize any one of the principal doctrines that go to form the Newman corpus. The principal contribution of Newman to religious thought is his extraordinary ability to gather insights and express them in so complete a way that no aspect of them is left untouched. His thought is developmental. He was not schooled in the traditional scholastic method, nor was he attached to pure speculative reason, which, he often feared, had a tendency to outstrip the facts on which it exercised itself. His principal orientation from his earliest days was formed mainly by his daily reading of Sacred Scripture. Later in his career, especially in the Oxford days, he developed an intense interest in the Fathers of the Church. His doctrine reflects the scattered notices of doctrine that are characteristic of both Scripture and the Fathers. Whatever systematization they enjoy in his writings is due largely to the necessity of polemics or in rare cases to his truly unified and well-articulated theory of the development of doctrine. The doctrines discussed below have been selected as perhaps more characteristic of his thought than others upon which he has made observations, but which seem to be less central to his principal religious thought.

Scripture. Apart from Tract 85 (*Holy Scripture in its Relation to the Catholic Creed*) and certain articles published in 1884, Newman's thoughts on Scripture are scattered throughout all his works. Two problems seemed to form the basis of his doctrine on Scripture: the inspiration of Scripture and its interpretation. Against the rejection of inspiration and inerrancy that characterized Anglican Scripture study after the time of A. P. Stanley

and B. Jowett (1855) and the difficulties raised by the rapidly advancing positive sciences, Newman taught (at least in 1861–63) that the Scriptures were all inspired, as were their authors. In his writings at that time (collected by J. Seynaeve from the Birmingham Oratory archives and published in 1953 as *Newman 1861–1863 Inspiration Papers*), he examined the documents of the magisterium, the internal scriptural evidence, and the testimony of the Fathers and theologians on scriptural inspiration and concluded (before Vatican Council I) that the books of Scripture are directly inspired but that there was no formal definition by the Church making their inspiration a dogma of faith. Subsequently he said that one is bound to believe in the inspiration of the sacred authors (Trent) and of the books themselves (Vatican I). For him, the Church's magisterium is the unique and infallible interpreter of the Bible. As a matter of fact, the gift of inspiration requires as its complement the gift of infallibility. Inspiration, however, pertained only to those sections dealing with faith and morals. There are some grounds for believing that there was a direct but implicit condemnation of Newman's view on this in *Providentissimus Deus,* but that Leo XIII refrained from mentioning his name out of respect for him.

Newman felt that the whole of Scripture, in all its parts (Vatican I), is inspired, but not all the elements in each of these parts (*totaliter sed non tota*). Possibly *obiter dicta* were included in the books by the human author; these may not be inspired, according to Newman. The final interpretation of Scripture and its sense, however, must be left to the Church's magisterium. Two principles seem to dominate Newman's method of exegesis: the first is the conviction that Scripture is essentially a work of religion, not of science or history; the second is his "sacramental principle" based on the belief that all the works of God are one and that less important elements of these works (the visible world) are shadows, figures, types, signs, and promises of the more important elements (the invisible world). It may be in terms of this latter principle, as a matter of fact, that he interpreted the theory of instrumental causality in the exploration of his theory of inspiration, rather than in terms of the developed scholastic notion, which he may never have fully accepted or, perhaps, understood.

Newman taught the unity of the two Testaments and the progressive fulfillment of the Old through additional revelation finally to be completed by the New, resulting in a unity founded on Christ. He preferred the mystical or allegorical interpretation of the Alexandrian Fathers to the literal interpretation of Antioch, but later in his life he found it necessary more frequently to use critico-literary methods. For him, Scripture may contain several senses, but the identification of them may not be left to the personal taste or intellectual disposition of the interpreter. He rejected polysemia, or metasemia, i.e., the theory that there may be a multiplicity of literal senses in a single text. Two scriptural senses are distinguishable in Newman's theory: the literal sense and the mystical sense. The latter, in turn, contains two other senses: the typical sense founded on the facts, events, and persons described, and the *sensus plenior* that belongs to the words themselves. Newman did not regard Scripture as a teaching instrument but rather as a standard of orthodoxy against which the catechesis of the teacher is compared and to which the apologist appeals for the proof of his doctrinal formulations.

Tradition. Newman's doctrine on tradition is developed within the theological context of the continuity of churches that he sees to exist between the pagan, Jewish, and Christian dispensations. There have been "revelations," at times to pagan poets as well as to Jewish Prophets, which are finally summed up in Christ. The initial revelations God made to mankind gradually became part of the deposit of faith and may be found within the structure of the Church Catholic. The Church is not always fully conscious of all the elements of its deposit of faith but is always under its influence by way of what might be called vacant vision. It is the vision the Church has of those aspects of its doctrine that are not completely formulated but yet exist within its life. The Christian revelation that found its summation in Christ is somewhat the same as but somewhat different from the general revelation that was given to mankind under both pagan and Jewish dispensations. Even amid the varieties of Christian traditions that now exist, it is possible to perceive the true tradition that was in existence at the beginning and still exists. The basic link that exists between the Christian and Jewish dispensation is the link of prophecy. Prophecy is uttered in the Old Testament and fulfilled in the New. The continuity between the Jewish dispensation and the Christian is so close that the one can be said to have become the other. Within the dispensations is a continuity of tradition.

Tradition is a variety of uniform custom. For Newman it is something silent but living. It is similar to a river before the rocks intercept it. There seems to be no definite shape or form given to the waters until the stream is intercepted by obstacles, at which time it comes to life. Tradition is a habit of opinion in the Church. It is something the Church reflects upon, masters, and expresses, depending on the emergency it faces. It is something that is necessarily unwritten. It is too much alive and too much part of the Church's very nature to be able to be committed entirely to writing. Tradition would seem, then, to be identified almost with the life of the church itself.

Types of Tradition. In the early Church it was unnecessary and even undesirable to formulate the elements of tradition into doctrines. As the ages of the Church followed each other, as the distance from apostolic times increased, and as the fervor and devotion of later times began to wane, there was need for a gradual and ever more sophisticated formulation of the belief of Christians. With the rise of heresies and attacks on the Church from both friends and enemies, an additional reason for the formulation of doctrine arose. It soon became necessary to develop a means of testing whether a given formulation of doctrine being spread among the Christian people was in fact part of the apostolic tradition. The test that applies to determine whether or not a given aspect of tradition is apostolic is the following: "Whatever doctrine the primitive ages unanimously attest, whether by consent of Fathers, or by Councils, or by the events of history, or by controversies, or in whatever way, whatever may fairly and reasonably be considered to be the universal belief of those ages, it is to be received as coming from the Apostles" (*Via Media* 1:50). For Newman there are two kinds of tradition: episcopal tradition and prophetical tradition. Episcopal tradition is the definite set of beliefs that have been passed on from bishop to bishop and have been called to the attention of each Christian. It is surrounded by a body of explanations of its meaning. On the other hand, prophetical tradition cannot be contained in a code or a treatise, but is rather a body of truth that pervades the entire Church like the atmosphere. Sometimes it is the same as episcopal tradition; other times it develops into legend or fable. It is partly written and partly unwritten, partly the interpretation and partly the supplement of Scripture (ibid. 1:249). The obligation to believe the content of the creed and tradition is wider than the development of the creed and tradition itself. The Christian's duty of obedience to the creed is far wider than the extension that can be given to the meaning of the creed.

True tradition is to be perceived not by purely historical methodology, since historical evidence reaches only part way in the determination of what the Church's doctrine is. It is not history that makes a person a Catholic, but rather the Church's dogmatic use of history in which the Catholic believes. The dogmatic use of history involves the use of Scripture, tradition, and the ecclesiastical sense. No doctrine can be disproved by history, but by the same token no doctrine can be proved simply by history. There is a standard of Catholic doctrine and it is to be found in the early Fathers of the Church. The ultimate test of whether or not a doctrine is apostolic is whether the early Fathers believed that it was part of the tradition of the Church in their own age. True tradition can be recognized if there is an unbroken line of testimony in its behalf from Father to Father. True tradition will be ancient tradition. The Church's use of history will show with regard to a true tradition that whenever the past ages have spoken at all they have spoken in witness to it. Tradition is not wholly identified with the creed or with Scripture but is the system of faith and ordinances each generation receives from the preceding one.

With regard to the existence of a body of doctrine separate and independent from the Scripture, i.e., the question of constitutive tradition, Newman's final belief was that there is a formulated creed that existed from the beginning apart from Scripture and that Scripture itself is part of a wider concept, which he finally came to call tradition. Scripture takes for granted certain sanctions, doctrines, and messages necessary for salvation that, if not found in Scripture, must be sought outside of it. Scripture by its structure and its own teaching presumes the existence of a tradition outside itself. Newman did not enter into the question of whether the truths that are contained outside Scripture are substantive additions or whether they are simply developments that come from the early Church's commenting on Scripture. He left open the question whether there are matters of faith contained in the extrascriptural deposit or simply matters of conduct or discipline. However, it does seem from the notes added to his published works, in the editing he did toward the end of his life, that throughout the major part of his writing career he had the belief that all revealed doctrine is contained in Scripture. It is clear from the autobiographical writings that Newman had read St. Robert BELLARMINE and had a clear notion of what theologians today call constitutive tradition. His final stance on the question of constitutive tradition was that there is a body of doctrine not contained in Scripture, not indeed opposed to it, but independent of it and separate from it.

Both the Church and tradition are considered by Newman to be interpreters of Scripture. Both tradition and Scripture, in turn, are interpreted by the infallible magisterium of the Church. Tradition, however, is not limited by Scripture or by the creed. It is wider than either, is developmental in nature, and requires an assent of faith that is coextensive with its entire developmental capacity.

There was at the beginning a definite lack of formulation of doctrine in the ante-Nicene Church. This is in no way an indication that the doctrines later formulated did not exist in the first four centuries, nor does it indicate that such doctrines were not part of the tradition or were not recognized as part of it. An explicable silence with regard to doctrine in the early Church is not an evidence either for or against the doctrine. Especially because of devices such as the *Disciplina Arcani* and the three

modes of the Economy identified by Newman it is reasonable to expect that there would be a lack of formulation of doctrine in the early Church. The modes of the Economy according to Newman are as follows: (1) in some cases, concealing the truth when it could be done without deceit; (2) in some cases, stating the truth only partially; and (3) in some cases, representing it under the nearest form possible when an inquirer could not possibly understand it exactly. The *Disciplina Arcani* is an example of the first mode of the Economy; the answer that Christians believe in only one God to the question "Do Christians believe in the Trinity" would be an example of the second mode; and the representation of angels with wings would be an instance of the third Economical mode, designed to fit the context of the knowledge of a people to whom Christianity was preached for the first time.

Newman takes notice of certain cautions to be employed in interpreting the Fathers as sources of tradition. Complexity, with the attendant possibility of misunderstanding, follows from the very nature of the Church as king, prophet, and priest. Its simultaneous exercise of this threefold function is often confusing to the uninitiated. In addition to this, one should be aware that the Fathers often speak the truth in a context of their own age and culture; one should avoid the danger of confusing actual mistakes on the part of the Fathers in interpreting Scripture with their true traditionary teaching. Newman stresses the danger of oversystematizing tradition to the point where reason exceeds the positive evidence. Finally, he cautions against the danger of reading the words and thoughts of the expositors of tradition within the context of a later age.

Sources of Apostolic Tradition. According to Newman the several sources of apostolic tradition may be divided into negative and positive sources. As negative sources, Newman singles out heresies and the influence they have had on the formulation of doctrine. He points out that an attack on an aspect of the Church's life usually results in the formulation of a doctrinal statement to display the orthodox attitude. Silence is another negative source. It is the peculiar reticence of certain past times with regard to important doctrines. The reticence must be explained, often by a later formulation.

There are several positive sources of evidence mentioned in Newman's writings: the testimony of individuals, of theologians, and of the schools, the literary expression of an age, and the testimony of the Fathers, of the bishops of the Church, of the magisterium, and finally of the popes.

The diversity of sources of information concerning tradition led Newman, in his structured thinking on tradition, to formulate what he took to be the basis of the proof from tradition. The basis of any proof from tradition, however, must be that the early Church thought that such a thing was correct, and the early Church must have known (*Discussions and Arguments* 149). The certitude possible from a study of tradition is nonhistorical certitude. One must not expect irrefragable proof for all the points of doctrine now existing in the Church, since many of these were formulated only gradually.

In the attempt to implement such a proof, Newman formulated the argument from convergence of evidence. This argument is based partly on Butler's theory of analogy. There is a significant original contribution made by Newman based in part on Butler and in part on the rule of Vincent of Lérins: *Quod semper, quod ubique, quod ab omnibus creditum est.* Although it is impossible in practice to apply the rule of Vincent of Lérins absolutely, it is possible to observe a center toward which a number of independent pieces of information gravitate. It is inconceivable that this center to which they converge could be error; it must be truth. There is a metaphysical element in the argument from convergence of evidence that transcends the elements of the argument itself. Whereas the final certitude that may be arrived at from an array of testimony is moral-historical, the convergence of independent testimonies introduces a metaphysical element into the proof. Whereas moral certitude may be gained from the facts of the case, the convergence of the facts must be explained on a metaphysical basis that is wider than the historical evidence alone.

Nature of Belief. Newman's doctrine on how Christians give reasonable belief to the doctrines of Scripture and tradition is to be found partly in the *Oxford University Sermons* and fully developed in *The Grammar of Assent.* The context within which his theory of belief was articulated was the problem raised for the large numbers of uneducated Christians, who give their assent to the doctrines of Christianity, by the theory enunciated by John Locke that the real lover of truth will not admit any proposition with greater assurance than will be warranted by the logical proofs on which it is built. Newman recognized that in practice the vast majority of Christians do not base their assurance of faith on a well-reasoned body of logical propositions or proofs. The question he asked was how the assent of faith that characterizes these Christians is a rational and therefore reasonable act of faith.

Newman gathered the factors involved in the solution to this question from a close analysis of the mental acts involved in holding propositions of any kind, including religious. He described these acts as three: doubt, which is interrogative in form and asks a question; inference, which is conclusionary in form and conditional

since it rests on premises; and assent, which is assertive in form and is categorical, since it implies the absence of conditional premises. He further distinguished between notional and real assent. Notional assent is given to propositions that are abstract and general and contain terms that refer to things that do not exist as such. Real assent, on the other hand, is given to propositions that are made up of singular nouns and of terms that stand for things that are external to man. Real assent is more vivid and forceful than notional. Notional assent is given to propositions of profession, credence, opinion, presumption, or speculation. Notional assent contemplates its own creations instead of really existing extramental realities. With regard to giving assent to dogmas, a real assent given to them results in an act of religion; a notional assent given to them results in a theological act. Every religious man is to a certain extent a theologian, and no theology can exist without the presence of religion.

The key to the understanding of Newman's theory of belief is the distinction he made between the acts of assent and of inference. Inference is conditional and is based on conditional verification. Assent, on the other hand, is to some degree independent of inference. The strength or validity of the act of assent does not depend directly on the strength or validity of the conditional inferences that precede it. This distinction establishes the possibility of a strict assent to a proposition that is not inferentially verified by correspondingly strong inferences. Assent is either simple, when it is exercised unconsciously, or complex, when it is made conscious and arrived at deliberately. Both forms, however, are to some degree independent of the inferences that precede them.

Inference deals always with comparisons of propositions so that the conclusions drawn are abstract and can be applied to concrete matters only with probability, not with certain proof. Assent, however, is unconditional and is applied unconditionally to concrete reality. The question arises how it is possible to pass from inference to assent. In this Newman depended heavily on Bp. J. BUTLER's theory of analogy. From it he established an argument that is somewhat different from Butler's and transcends it: the argument from the accumulation of probabilities that are each independent of the other and perhaps too tenuous to lead to assent separately or perhaps too subtle and circuitous to be able to be converted into syllogisms or too numerous and various for such a conversion even though it is possible to convert them. It is the unconscious working together of the various parts of a mosaic gradually taking form before one's mental eye, rather than the strict Aristotelian logical deduction characteristic of other epistemological approaches to the problem of assent. Drawing conclusions from such probabilities and giving the assent of belief to the pervading conclusion contained within them, but never consciously formulated, requires the operation of a special sense that Newman called the illative sense. It is by means of this illative sense that the ordinary uneducated man can have a real certitude of the fundamental truths of religion without demonstrative proofs. To prove that the doctrines to which Christians give assent are part of the authentic tradition of the apostolic age, it must be shown that current Christian doctrines have developed from the apostolic age in such a way that they are identical even though they have undergone change.

During his Anglican years Newman was eager to establish the identity between the Anglican communion and the Church of the first four centuries. To do this he undertook a serious historical study of the Fathers. At the time of his conversion in 1845, he was in the final page proofs of *An Essay on the Development of Christian Doctrine.* It was an attempt to explain both the fact of change in the Church and its direction as well, with the result that the Anglican Church could be identified with the ante-Nicene Church. It led Newman to quite an opposite conclusion, however: that the Anglican Church was not the same as the Church of the first four centuries, but that the Roman Church was. The *Essay* is divided into two parts, the first having to do with doctrinal developments in themselves, and the second with doctrinal developments relative to doctrinal corruptions. Newman's theory of the development of doctrine is based on his belief that it is characteristic of an important and vital idea to live in the mind that has received it and to become an active principle that leads to a number of self-reflections and applications of the idea to other ideas as they develop. He listed five kinds of development: political, logical, historical, ethical, and metaphysical. A Christian idea is no less an idea because it is Christian. There is, accordingly, an antecedent argument in favor of the development of Christian ideas and therefore of Christian doctrine. There is need for an infallible guide to determine the direction of the development, but development there must be.

The essential characteristics of true development of a doctrine within Christianity are the following: preservation of type, continuity of principles, power of assimilation, logical sequence, anticipation of its final configuration, conservative action on its past, and lasting vigor.

The significance of Newman's doctrine of development cannot be overemphasized in modern theology. Attempts at formulating theories of development of doctrine in the 20th century draw heavily on Newman's original insights. His theories on tradition and the nature of belief underlie much modern speculation in fundamental dogmatic theology. The religious insights of Newman have never been exploited fully. In the 20th century it has become possible, because of the availability of his published writings and the 20,000 or more letters he wrote during his life, to come to a better understanding of his religious genius and the meaning it has for the present time.

Bibliography: *Collected Works,* 25 v. (New York 1890–1927); *The Letters and Diaries of John Henry Newman,* ed. C. S. DESSAIN (New York 1961–); *Autobiographical Writings,* ed. H. TRISTRAM (New York 1957). G. BIEMER, *Überlieferung und Offenbarung: Die Lehre von der Tradition nach J. H. Newman* (Freiburg 1961). A. J. BOEKRAAD and H. TRISTRAM, *The Argument from Conscience to the Existence of God according to J. H. Newman* (Louvain 1961). L. BOUYER, *Newman, His Life and Spirituality,* tr. J. L. MAY (New York 1958). O. CHADWICK, *From Bossuet to Newman: The Idea of Doctrinal Development* (Cambridge, Eng. 1957). C. DAWSON, *The Spirit of the Oxford Movement* (New York 1933). R. A. DIBBLE, *John Henry Newman: The Concept of Infallible Doctrinal Authority* (Washington 1955). H. FRIES, *Die Religionsphilosophie Newmans* (Stuttgart 1948). J. GUITTON, *La Philosophie de Newman* (Paris 1933). F. KAISER, *The Concept of Conscience according to J. H. Newman* (Washington 1958). M. NÉDONCELLE, *La Philosophie religieuse de J. H. Newman* (Strasbourg 1946). J. SEYNAEVE, *Cardinal Newman's Doctrine on Holy Scripture* (Louvain 1953); *Dictionnaire de la Bible,* ed. L. PIROT, et al. (Paris 1928–) 6:427–474. M. TREVOR, *Newman: The Pillar of the Cloud* (Garden City, N.Y. 1962); *Newman: Light in Winter* (Garden City, N.Y. 1963). J. H. WALGRAVE, *Newman the Theologian,* tr. A. V. LITTLEDALE (New York 1960). W. P. WARD, *The Life of John Henry Cardinal Newman* (New York 1912). T. MERRIGAN, *Clear Heads and Holy Hearts: The Religious and Theological Ideal of John Henry Newman* (Louvain 1991). E. SULLIVAN, *Things Old and New: An Ecumenical Reflection on the Theology of John Henry Newman* (Boston 1993). G. MAGILL, *Discourse and Context: An Interdisciplinary Study of John Henry Newman* (Carbondale, IL 1993). I. T. KER, *Healing the Wound of Humanity: The Spirituality of John Henry Newman* (London 1993). J. R. GRIFFIN, *A Historical Commentary on the Major Catholic Works of Cardinal Newman* (New York 1993). J. R. PAGE, *What Will Dr Newman Do: John Henry Newman and Papal Infallibility, 1865–1875* (Collegeville, Minn. 1994). F. MCGRATH, *John Henry Newman: Universal Revelation* (Macon, Ga. 1997). I. T. KER, ed. *Newman and Conversion* (Notre Dame, Ind. 1997). S. L. JAKI, *Newman's Challenge* (Grand Rapids, Mich. 2000).

[J. P. WHALEN]

Literary Influence

Newman exercised a profound influence on the literature of the English-speaking world and on the whole Western literary community. His works not only survive; they are also actively studied. The collected edition has been reprinted often. Important single works, such as *The Idea of a University, Apologia pro vita sua,* and *The Grammar of Assent,* are available in numerous editions in many languages. New collections of his letters, memorabilia, diaries, and notes continue to appear regularly. Learned articles, monographs, and full-length studies of Newman's views on theology, philosophy, church history, education, and literature testify also to the quality of enduring vitality found in his writings.

Newman has been classified chiefly as a didactic or apologetic writer, and his specifically literary achievement is often described as the fashioning of a style perfectly suited to his rhetorical intentions. Recently, however, literary scholars have studied the aesthetic elements of the structure and style of his books and of individual sermons, essays, and poems. Thus, in the symposium *Newman's Apologia: A Classic Reconsidered* (New York 1964), it was pointed out that the *Apologia* is more than an objective history of Newman's religious opinions and a reasoned argument supporting the validity of his doctrinal claims. It is also, and just as importantly, a spiritual autobiography marked by aesthetic distance, dramatic structure, a delicate handling of perspective and tone. In short, in his *Apologia* Newman also *creates* an image of a soul working out its eternal destiny. Similar studies of *The Idea of a University* and of individual sermons such as "The Second Spring" emphasize the point that Newman's art is, in Dwight Culler's phrase, "a mediatorial form," that is, one that infuses imagination and intuition into the world of fact and reason.

Poetry and the Novel. Newman's reputation as a writer of expository prose has overshadowed his valuable contributions to poetry, the novel, and literary theory. Despite their Victorian accent, his verses and hymns, particularly "Lead Kindly Light," still appeal to the meditative reader. His long poem, *The Dream of Gerontius* (1866), is greatly admired for its fervor and sonority as well as for the accuracy with which it expresses the Christian theology of death. Newman's novels were closely related to the experiences of his own conversion. In *Loss and Gain* (1848) Charles Reding, in part at least the alter ego of the author, is shown in his pilgrimage toward the Catholic Church. Here, Newman's sensitive rendering of the Oxonian atmosphere, his unerringly accurate psychological observation, his power of dramatizing religious argument, have earned for him the distinction "of being the only eminent Victorian who could write a confessional novel of spiritual autobiography in high spirits as well as high seriousness" (Margaret Maison, *The Victorian Vision,* 1961). *Callista* (1856), a historical fiction set in 3rd-century North Africa, also explores the psychology of conversion, but with special attention to the pagan milieu. Alfred Duggan characterized *Callista* as "unique, like the mind that composed it: unique, astringent, remorseless, unforgettable," a view that sums up the book's 20th-century reputation. In both novels aspects of Newman's religious experiences that were later to be revealed more directly in the *Apologia* are encountered.

Theory of Literature. Newman's writings on literature, most of them delivered as lectures contained in *The Idea of a University* (3rd edition), offer pregnant theories about literary style and literary history in the plan of a liberal education. "Thought and speech are inseparable from each other," he wrote. "Matter and expression are parts of one: style is a thinking out into language. . . . The style really cannot be abstracted from the sense. . . ." He regarded literature as the book of man, just as science was the book of nature, and theology the book of God. Thus for Newman the study of literature was a study of natural man in his historical processes. In making this point Newman redirected Catholic higher education toward a humanistic rather than utilitarian path.

Newman's greatest influence, however, is the action of his own personality on readers and, particularly, on writers. H. Belloc and G. K. Chesterton, Graham Greene and Evelyn Waugh, Ronald Knox and Christopher Dawson, each according to his temperament, has experienced the shock of Newman's commitments and reflected the light of his intuitions.

Bibliography: R. A. COLBY, "The Poetical Structure of Newman's *Apologia pro vita sua,"* *Journal of Religion* 33 (1953) 47–57. C. F. HARROLD, *John Henry Newman: An Expository and Critical Study of His Mind, Thought and Art* (London 1945) 440–452. J. J. REILLY, *Newman as a Man of Letters* (New York 1925). A. S. RYAN, "Newman's Conception of Literature" in *Critical Studies in Arnold, Emerson and Newman* (U. of Iowa Humanistic Studies VI, No. 1; Iowa City 1942). F. TARDIVEL, *La Personalité littéraire de Newman* (Paris 1937). F. KERR and D. NICHOLLS, eds., *John Henry Newman: Reason, Rhetoric and Romanticism* (Carbondale, IL 1991) T. R. WRIGHT, "Newman on Literature: 'Thinking out into Language',"* *Literature and Theology* 5 (1991) 181–197. E. BLOCK, ed. *Critical Essays on John Henry Newman* (Victoria, British Columbia 1992). M. SUNDERMEIER and R. CHURCHILL, eds., *The Literary and Educational Effects of the Thought of John Henry Newman* (Lewiston, NY 1995).

[F. X. CONNOLLY]

NEWMAN APOSTOLATE

The work of the Church on the campuses of secular universities and colleges. While its first objective is the religious education, pastoral care, and apostolic formation of Catholic students attending secular colleges, it is deeply concerned with the presentation of Catholic thought and culture to the whole university community. This article gives a brief history of the origins and development of the Newman movement and of the national organizations that have been established to promote its growth.

Beginnings. The first Newman Club was formed at the University of Pennsylvania in Philadelphia in 1893. Timothy L. Harrington, a medical student at the university, was primarily responsible for its organization. In his undergraduate days at the University of Wisconsin in Madison, he had belonged to the Melvin Club for Catholic students. Finding no similar organization at the University of Pennsylvania, Harrington elicited the interest of others in the medical and dental schools, and after receiving the approval of P. J. Garvey, pastor of St. James Church, in whose parish the university was located, proceeded with its organization. It was Harrington who suggested the name Newman Club in honor of Cardinal John Henry NEWMAN, the English scholar and churchman who had died just three years before. Harrington became the first president of the Newman Club. Of the first officers of the Newman Club, Harrington and two others, James J. Walsh and his brother Joseph, later became men of such prominence in Catholic affairs that they were listed in the *American Catholic Who's Who.*

In addition to establishing an organization for Catholic collegians under the direction of a chaplain, these pioneers began a threefold program—religious, intellectual, and social—that still remains basic to the Newman Apostolate; they chose Cardinal Newman as their patron. The accusation has been made that Newman has been patron of this apostolate in name only. But in fact Newman's spirit, ideas, and ideals have had a continuing influence on the development of the movement; and he has often provided the one source of unity in an apostolate carried on in diverse circumstances and at differing stages of development.

For almost 50 years after this first Newman Club, the work of the Church for those attending secular colleges was carried out almost entirely within the framework of similar student organizations, more and more of which came to be called Newman Clubs. At times and in some places these clubs might not even have an officially recognized chaplain. Carlton J. H. Hayes, recalling his early days at Columbia University, observed that a classmate of his "did found a Newman Club, but it was a strictly lay organization; and what outside clerical instruction we occasionally got was bootlegged to us, so-to-speak, by a brave Jesuit and scholarly editor of the *Catholic Encyclopedia,* the late Father John Wynne." Hayes further noted that a metropolitan federation of clubs, formed by faculty advisers, was "without benefit of clergy." Usually, however, a chaplain was appointed by the bishop, though in many instances only by a casual general directive to "look after the students at the college."

The year after its foundation, the Newman Club at Pennsylvania sponsored a lecture by Bp. John J. Keane, then rector of The Catholic University of America, Washington, D.C. The lecture, "The Outcome of Philosophic Thought," was given in the university chapel to a large audience that included a professor of philosophy (an Episcopalian minister) and many of his friends. A few years later the Penn Newman Club sponsored a lecture by Cardinal James Gibbons. Then gradually the social program grew, and after the middle of the 20th century Newman Clubs were said by a national secular magazine to be noted more "for tea-dances than theology."

Early Developments. Although the Newman Club was the sole Catholic program in most places until after World War II (and still is at small schools), as far back as 1906 other patterns began to develop. In 1906 Henry C. Hengell was appointed by Abp. Sebastian G. Messner of Milwaukee to serve the Catholic students at the University of Wisconsin in Madison as full-time chaplain. That same year, Abp. Patrick W. Riordan of San Francisco asked the Paulist Fathers to provide a full-time chaplain for the University of California at Berkeley. In 1910 St. Paul's Chapel at the University of Wisconsin and Newman Hall, with its St. Thomas Chapel, at Berkeley, were built. Student organizations were maintained on both campuses and the scope of the Newman work was greatly enlarged. There was, for all practical purposes, a university parish at Wisconsin and California. The chaplain gave his full time to the Newman Apostolate and became acquainted with the university. He found some of the faculty anxious to cooperate with religious groups for the welfare of the students. He came to be viewed as the Catholic chaplain of the university, rather than as restricted to the group of students who belonged to the Newman Club.

Question of Religious Education. The appointment of full-time chaplains led to other developments. As priests came to understand better the religious needs of the campus community and developed a better perspective of the role of the Church and the Church's responsibility in this community, they saw that the apostolate was an educational one. Pastoral concern would in one sense always be first; Catholic students' salvation was to be achieved through the sacramental grace and liturgical worship of God in His Church. But their salvation and Christian perfection would normally be attained only if the knowledge and understanding of their faith was commensurate with their secular knowledge. Formal educational programs were imperative; and given the circumstances, credit courses in religion were a practical necessity if many students were to take them.

In 1915 arrangements were made by the Paulists in charge of the Newman Foundation at the University of Texas to teach Bible courses for which university credit would be received. Protestant groups at the University of Texas had been offering such courses for a number of years; and after a full-time Catholic chaplain arrived, similar arrangements were approved for a "Catholic Bible Chair."

A similar plan, developed in 1919 at the University of Illinois, was initiated by the Catholic chaplain, John A. O'Brien, in cooperation with Protestant chaplains. The university senate, petitioned to allow university credit for religion courses, gave approval, but with the stipulation that each religious foundation be chartered by the State of Illinois as a school of religion and that certain standards regarding facilities and personnel be met. Having purchased a frame house on campus with borrowed money, O'Brien obtained the charter from the state and in 1920 offered three courses for Catholic students. In his efforts to provide adequate and permanent facilities, however, he precipitated a controversy that affected the development of the Newman movement for many years to come.

Catholic Foundation Controversy. O'Brien's project for the Catholic educational foundation at the University of Illinois had the approval not only of Bp. E. M. Dunne of Peoria, the diocese in which the university is located, but also of Abp. George W. Mundelein of Chicago and the other bishops of Illinois. In an address before the state convention of the Knights of Columbus on May 12, 1925, appealing for financial help to build the Catholic foundation at the university, O'Brien stressed the educational role of the foundation as a supplement to the secular education offered by the university. A few months later (Aug. 22, 1925) appeared the first of a series of articles in the Jesuit weekly *America* that continued periodically for the next several months to attack secular education, Catholics attending secular colleges and universities, and, in a particular way, O'Brien's concept of the Catholic foundation. The attitude of *America* was perhaps summed up in an editorial comment on March 20, 1926:

> *America* has repeatedly gone on record as heartily in favor of ministering to the spiritual needs of Catholics at secular colleges and universities. What *America* opposes is undue extension of the Newman Club idea into the educational field of those institutions.

This attitude was shared by many at that time and for many years to come. Archbishop Michael J. Curley of Baltimore was particularly outspoken against the Catholic foundation plan and openly stated that those who were backing it "are waging a secret hypocritical warfare against the best interests of the Church in America. . . . The whole movement is decidedly inimical to the Church of Jesus Christ. It matters little who the authors are. Luther and Arius were both priests."

As a result, bishops who shared such an evaluation (and it seems that for years, most did) merely tolerated Newman Clubs as a necessary evil, as something purely remedial—much like prison chaplaincies—and made it clear that their only purpose was to safeguard the faith of students who should not have been at secular colleges anyway. Any efforts to provide a positive program of religious education was considered as calculated to attract to secular colleges students who would otherwise have gone to a Catholic college. The few studies made during those years had consistently shown there were three primary reasons for Catholics' attendance at secular schools: financial necessity (particularly in publicly supported institutions), proximity to home (financial considerations often entering in again), and availability of courses not offered in Catholic colleges. It could, of course, be shown that many Catholics were in secular colleges for less worthy reasons, though these were actually in the minority. Nevertheless, the conviction persisted that a Catholic foundation at a secular university would be harmful to Catholic colleges—and so they were not established until the second half of the 20th century. It is noteworthy that, except for priests directly involved in the Newman movement and an occasional layman, the Jesuit editors of *America* were the first to speak out openly to urge reversal of the stand taken by their predecessors 35 years earlier. In May of 1960 they wrote:

> Some way must be found to insure that Catholic students on secular campuses share to the greatest possible degree in the positive benefits of Catholic higher education. . . . What is required is a new kind of Newman Club, more on the scale of a Catholic Institute. This would be complete with library, lounges, study facilities, lecture halls, seminar rooms, and above all, a faculty competent to create the scholarly climate of Christian culture that attracts and challenges students.

The official acceptance of the educative role of the Newman apostolate came in 1962, when the college and university department of the National Catholic Educational Association (NCEA) amended its bylaws to provide associate membership for Newman educational centers. Since that time Newman concerns have been an integral part of the annual NCEA convention, and the Newman Apostolate is seen as an important arm of Catholic higher education.

The *America* editorial and the acceptance of Newman by the NCEA were symbolic of a more general change in attitude toward the Newman movement. Several factors brought about this change. The most obvious was the fact that every two out of three Catholics were enrolled in secular institutions, while most Catholic colleges had capacity enrollments. Other factors also played a part: bishops' awareness that many vocations were coming from the secular campus; assumption by Catholic faculty of secular colleges and former Newman students of prominent roles of lay leadership in parish and diocese; an increase in the number of priests, brothers, and sisters doing graduate work at secular universities. Each in its own way served to break down the prejudice that the secular university was totally inimical to Catholic life and values. Along with this, and perhaps even more important, was the general change that had taken place in the social status of Catholics and of the Church in America, and the resulting weakening of the earlier ghetto mentality of the Catholic community and the more positive evaluation of facets of American culture and of American institutions. Another factor was the impact of the national organizations formed to promote the Newman Apostolate. Helping in a variety of ways, these national groups helped most, perhaps, just by being national rather than local, and thus bringing the importance of the Newman Apostolate to the attention of the whole American Church. The first of these got its start in the early 20th century.

Federation of College Catholic Clubs. In the spring of 1915 representatives of five Catholic clubs from New York City colleges gathered to discuss the formation of a federation of such clubs. The clubs included the Barat Club of Hunter College, the Newman Club of the College of the City of New York, the Newman Club of Columbia College, the Craigie Club of Barnard College, and the Catholic Club of Teachers' College. The purpose of the federation was to join for mutual assistance in preserving and strengthening the Catholic faith of club members. On Oct. 28, 1915, students and faculty members of these colleges met at the New York home of Mrs. Jacob L. Phillips, formally organized the Federation of College Catholic Clubs (FCCC), and elected its first officers: president, Prof. James A. Kieran of Hunter College; vice president, Prof. Alexis I. DuPont Coleman of the College of the City of New York; and secretary, Frank W. Demuth, a graduate student at Columbia College. At the first annual conference, held the following July at the Catholic Summer School at Cliff Haven, N.Y., 50 delegates from 11 college clubs were present. In addition to the original five, there were delegates from Smith College, Northampton, Mass.; New York University; Adelphi College, Garden City, N.Y.; Brooklyn Polytechnic Institute; Princeton University, N.J.; and the University of Pennsylvania, Philadelphia. A similar federation, organized earlier (1908) at Purdue University, Lafayette, Ind., made up mostly of Catholic Clubs in the Middle West—the Catholic Students' Association of America—remained in existence until World War I. Its member clubs later joined the Federation of Catholic College Clubs.

In June of 1917, the professorial leaders of the young federation published the first issue of *Newman Quarterly*. It was intended "to hasten the growth and expansion" of the FCCC, to promote "inter-club cooperation and national unity," and to serve as "the expression of intellectual Catholicism." In 1926, *Newman News* replaced the *Newman Quarterly*. Until its demise in 1946, it supplied the clubs each month with articles and items that addressed the interests and needs of the members.

Another significant event of 1917 was the appointment of John W. KEOGH as chaplain general of the FCCC. Keogh had been the first full-time chaplain at Pennsylvania, and remained chaplain of the federation until 1935. He traveled from one end of the country to the other urging the formation of Newman Clubs and the appointment of chaplains. Where Newman Clubs were already established, he urged affiliation with the federation. He was a man of priestly integrity and orthodoxy, and his concern for the Church and the salvation of souls could never be questioned. When he relinquished the post of national chaplain, the federation had withstood its greatest period of opposition and was ready for a new period of development.

For more than 25 years after its organization, this federation of Newman Clubs had at best been tolerated by the ecclesiastical authorities. In several instances the local ordinary refused to appear at an annual convention held in his diocese. On one occasion the bishop agreed to meet the student officers at his home—and then proceeded to excoriate them for attending secular colleges. Then, in 1941, with the formation of the National Council of Catholic Youth at the behest of the Holy See, the Newman Club Federation was accepted as a full member of the college and university section, and thus finally received the formal approbation of the American bishops. Permanent headquarters were established at the National Catholic Welfare Conference (NCWC) building in Washington, D.C., and a part-time executive secretary had a desk in the NCWC Youth Department. Eventually a full-time executive secretary was engaged, and in 1952, Thomas A. Carlin, OSFS, was appointed as the first priest to direct the national office.

John Henry Cardinal Newman Honorary Society. The 1938 convention of the Newman Club Federation in Washington occasioned the formation of another national organization related to the Newman movement. For several years a special honor key for outstanding service to the Newman movement had been conferred by the federation. Now it was decided to bring these honorees into a permanent society, to form, as it were, an elite group devoted to the furthering of the Newman movement, as well as to provide local groups with a means to confer special recognition for outstanding service. After 1950 the John Henry Cardinal Newman Honorary Society brought national attention to the Newman movement by conferring annually the Cardinal Newman award on a distinguished lay Catholic. This award recognizes an individual for some special contribution to the work of the Newman Apostolate or for that individual's special exemplification of its goals and ideals. Among those who have received this award are Clare Booth Luce, Mr. and Mrs. Frank Sheed, Dr. Jerome Kerwin, Sen. Eugene McCarthy, Dr. Carlton J. H. Hayes, Dr. Helen C. White, Benjamin G. Raskob, and Dr. George Shuster.

National Newman Chaplains Association. Following World War II, the number of full-time chaplains increased rapidly. In 1950, at the Mid-Century Newman Convention held in Cleveland, eight of them organized a professional association for Newman chaplains. Recognizing the voluntary character of affiliation with this group (as with all affiliation to the national Newman movement), the association sought, in the words of its brief charter, "to set standards for educational and pastoral programs by discussion and agreement; and to implement them by mutual assistance." By 1960, over half the estimated 500 priests assigned to work with Newman Clubs belonged to the Chaplains' Association.

Through the regular meetings of the association's advisory board and executive committee, a consensus developed on a number of points regarding the basic philosophy of the Newman Apostolate. A number of publications and (since 1962) a training school for new chaplains, as well as an institute for new chaplains during the annual meeting, made it possible to assist newly appointed chaplains and to guide them by commonly accepted principles of operation. The importance of the educational function of the Newman Apostolate and the educational role of the chaplain in his work on the secular campus was stressed, but always within a framework of the basic pastoral ministry of the Newman chaplain.

Role of the National Chaplain. Following Keogh's long term as national chaplain, the tenure of this post has varied. Until 1942 voting delegates at the national convention elected the national chaplain, much the same as other officers in the federation. After the inclusion of the Newman Federation in the NCWC in 1941, the episcopal chair of the youth department appointed the episcopal moderator for the Newman Federation, and he, in turn, appointed the national chaplain. For several years, the term of office was only a year; but on petition of the Chaplains Association in 1951, it was approved that the term of office should be two years and that the Chaplains Association should present a preferential list of names to the episcopal moderator.

Over the years many outstanding priests gave leadership to the Newman movement through the office of national chaplain. Donald Cleary of Cornell University,

Ithaca, N.Y., chaplain from 1940–44, wrote the first Newman Club manual and played a key role in gaining official recognition for the Newman Federation through its affiliation with the NCWC. Edward Duncan, of the Newman Foundation at the University of Illinois, nurtured a vision for the future of the Newman Movement that earned him election as the first president of the Chaplains' Association.

During the 1950s, 11 priests who had been Newman chaplains became bishops. Three active chaplains, made bishops within 18 months, proved to be of special benefit to the movement: Leonard P. Cowley of the University of Minnesota, Minn., became auxiliary bishop of St. Paul; Paul J. Hallinan, director of Newman Clubs in Cleveland, became bishop of Charleston and was later named first archbishop of Atlanta; Robert E. Tracy of Louisiana State University, Baton Rouge, became auxiliary bishop of Lafayette, La., and later first bishop of Baton Rouge; and Maurice Schexnayder, who became the auxiliary bishop of New Orleans. They worked hard to forge closer ties between the Newman Club Federation and the Bishops' Conference.

In addition to being informal episcopal witness for the Newman Apostolate, Bishop Hallinan became episcopal moderator of the national Newman work in 1960 and gave decisive leadership to the movement for three years.

In 1965 the role played by the national chaplain was assumed largely by the priest in charge of the national office at the NCWC, when the one holding this position became assistant director of the youth department and director of the National Newman Apostolate.

National Newman Alumni Association. At least as early as 1920 Newman Alumni Clubs had been formed to offer a program of continuing religious education to its members and to support the work of the Church on campus. For many years these clubs belonged to the national federation on the same basis as the campus clubs, and their members were a strong force in the leadership of the federation. In line with the policy to make the federation truly a student organization, these alumni clubs withdrew from the federation in 1957 to form the National Newman Alumni Association as an affiliate organization to the federation. Provision was made for individual memberships in the association as well as club membership. The alumni attempted to promote the work of the apostolate, particularly by assisting in the national public relations program.

National Newman Foundation. In an effort to obtain funds for the many needs of the Newman Apostolate, to ensure responsible control of such funds for the welfare of the Church, and to prepare for the growing financial needs of the future, the Chaplains Association petitioned the bishops of the NCWC administrative board in November of 1959 to approve a plan to set up a national foundation as a nonprofit corporation. This proposal was approved and a charter for the foundation was issued by the District of Columbia in May of 1960. For several months it was directed by a temporary board of trustees made up of Newman chaplains. In December of 1962 control of the foundation was turned over to a permanent board of 20 lay Catholics and six clerics who held official positions in the National Newman Apostolate. Besides seeking funds from individuals and corporations, the National Newman Foundation also appealed for grants from other foundations to fund special projects.

National Newman Association of Faculty and Staff. Recognizing that many contributions can be made to the Newman Apostolate by the Catholic faculty members and others on the administrative staffs of our secular colleges and universities, a national association for such persons was begun in 1959, primarily as a means of communication with the Catholic faculty in secular institutions. Governed by a desire to keep organization to a minimum, the development of this segment of the apostolate has proceeded slowly, though on a local level there were many instances of strong faculty participation in the local Newman program.

National Newman Apostolate. Six national organizations were established over the years to further this work of the Church on the secular campus. Except for the special approval given to the foundation, for many years only the National Newman Club Federation had the formal approval of the American hierarchy. When the federation was first organized in 1915, it was technically a federation of student clubs. In fact, it was an organization run by faculty, alumni, and chaplains; it was not until 1938 that the federation constitution allowed an undergraduate student to hold national office and not until 1942 that a student could become president of the federation. When formally recognized by the bishops, the federation was placed in the youth department of the NCWC, and for 20 years the work of the national Newman movement was carried on under the fiction that this was an exclusively student operation. The welfare of Catholic students was indeed the principal concern of the Newman movement, but as has been seen, there were certainly other than student organizations set up to promote this apostolate.

Recognition of these developments led Abp. John F. Dearden of Detroit, as episcopal chairman of the NCWC youth department, in consultation with Bishop Hallinan, as episcopal adviser to the Newman movement, to reorganize the national Newman work under the umbrella title of the National Newman Apostolate, and to give formal approval to these six national organizations as component units of the national apostolate.

In April of 1962 this recognition was formalized by Abp. John J. Krol, who succeeded Archbishop Dearden in the youth department post, and who established the National Newman Apostolate as a full section of the youth department. Charles Albright, CSP, who served as executive secretary for the federation, became the first coordinating secretary of the national apostolate. A former student officer of the federation was named his assistant as executive secretary for the student federation.

Thus, from clubs of Catholic students, arising at the Universities of Wisconsin and Pennsylvania and similar places around 1900, and from a struggling but ever expanding federation of these clubs, a major Apostolate of the American Church developed in the 1950s and 1960s. It focused on every aspect of the secular university community and, commissioned by the Roman Catholic Bishops of the country, boldly went forth to carry out the work of the Church there: the National Newman Apostolate.

Starting around 1970, the Newman Apostolate underwent dramatic restructuring. It once again became diocese-centered and reflected a number of features from those days before 1910, when a handful of bishops set up "Catholic Halls" with full-time chaplains to celebrate Mass and to teach Catholicism on a regular basis in the university setting. Over 200 diocesan directors continued to lead the ministry with the aid of their own national organization. Meanwhile, Newman Centers and university parishes replaced Newman Clubs as the primary source of institutional Catholic identity on the secular campus. In 1969 the Newman Chaplains' Association reorganized itself into the Catholic Campus Ministry Association (CCMA). Its membership has grown to include women religious, and lay men and women. By then it had taken on many of the functions delegated to the youth and educational offices of the former NCWC. Finally, also in response to the Second Vatican Council, a new ecumenical spirit among chaplains (both men and women) and students manifested itself towards members of other religious traditions. In a similar spirit, Catholic college leaders showed a new readiness to cooperate with the Newman Apostolate.

In 1873 John Henry Newman asserted that the elementary principle of the "new philosophy" was that "in all things we must go by reason, in nothing by faith." A century later and more, those laboring in the milieu of the secular campus, who revere him as the patron and inspiration of their apostolate, faithfully continued to bring to those campuses the pastoral ministry and religious literacy that give salvific meaning to academic study.

Bibliography: W. J. WHALEN, *Catholics on Campus* (Milwaukee 1961). J. W. EVANS, *The Newman Movement: Roman Catholics in American Higher Education, 1883–1971* (Notre Dame 1980).

[C. ALBRIGHT/J. W. EVANS]

NEWTOWN MANOR SCHOOL

About 1653 Ralph Crouch, a layman, established a school at Newtown, St. Mary's County, Md. Crouch, who had been in the Novitiate of the Society of Jesus at Watten, Belgium, for some time, around 1640 came to assist the Jesuit Fathers in the Maryland Mission. The school, which opened in 1653, was made possible by a provision in the will of Edward Cotten: "I doe give all my female cattle and their increase forever to be disposed of . . . unto charitable uses . . . the stocks to be preserved and the profits to be made use of to the use of a Schooll." He expressed his desire that "if they shall think convenient . . . the Schooll [shall] be kept at Newtown" (*Maryland Land Records*, Liber 1, 46–48). In a letter dated Sept. 4, 1662, Crouch stated, "I affirme boldly alsoe that on my part I did (as appeared to all my neighbors) as much as lay in mee, fulfill the will of the deceased [Cotten], in remoueing my teaching of schoole to the New Towne: and there was ready some years to teach, eyther Protestant or Catholikes" (*Archives of Maryland*, 49, 20–22).

Crouch returned to Europe in 1659 and was readmitted into the Jesuit Novitiate at Watten as a coadjutor brother. He died at Liège Nov. 18, 1679. The school, however, was still in operation in 1662, when it was mentioned in the trial of Francis Fitzherbert, SJ, and perhaps until at least 1667, since an item in the estate of Robert Cole, of Newtown, contains provision for "the Childrens Schooling" (*Archives of Maryland*, 41, 566–567; 57, 206).

In 1668 William Bretton and his wife Temperance sold Newtown Manor to the Jesuits, who in 1677 opened a school for humanities at the site. In a 1681 letter of the English Provincial, John Warner, reference is made to a school opened four years earlier under the direction of the Jesuits Francis Pennington and Michael Forster, who were assisted by Brothers Gregory Tuberville and John Berboel. That the school was more than a "Three R's Academy" is indicated by the fact that the pupils were admitted into European colleges. Two boys sent to St. Omers, Belgium, from this school in 1681 were Robert Brooke, the first native-born Marylander to become a Jesuit, and Thomas Gardiner. Thomas Hothersall, a Jesuit scholastic who used the alias Slater in the Maryland Mission, taught grammar and humanities at the school from 1683 until his death in 1698. Although the school at Newtown Manor seems never to have fully developed, it kept alive the idea of an education under Catholic auspices and maintained, as it were, the franchise for later and fuller developments.

Bibliography: T. HUGHES, *History of the Society of Jesus in North America: Colonial and Federal,* 3 v. (New York 1907–17) v.2. J. M. DALEY, *Georgetown University: Origin and Early Years* (Washington 1957). E. W. BEITZELL, "William Bretton of Newtown Neck, St. Mary's County," *Maryland Historical Magazine* 50 (1955) 24–33; "Newtown Hundred," *ibid.* 51 (1956) 125–139.

[J. M. DALEY]

NICAEA I, COUNCIL OF

The first general council of the Christian Church, convoked by Emperor CONSTANTINE I, probably toward the close of 324, and lasted from May 20 or June 19 to *c.* Aug. 25, 325.

Background. After his victory over Licinius (September 324), Constantine, Emperor of the East, found his provinces seriously disturbed by religious controversy, spearheaded by the Alexandrian priest ARIUS and his bishop, ALEXANDER. The dissension apparently began about the year 318, or somewhat later, when Arius was publicly rebuked by Bishop Alexander for teaching that the Word was not coeternal with the Father but had a beginning of existence; otherwise, Arius said, there would be two "unbegotten" principles. If, then, the Word had a beginning, He could not be of the same nature as the Father; He must, like other creatures, have been made from nothing. Nor can He be called the true and natural Son of God; at best He is the adopted Son. It follows that the Word, as a creature, is in fact the first and most perfect of creatures and is subject to change and sin. He did save mankind, but because He was utterly faithful to God's grace. Arius seems to have denied that the Incarnate Word had a human soul. The deep roots of his doctrine are discoverable in his master, LUCIAN OF ANTIOCH, and it is understandable that Arius's fellow disciples at Antioch, called Collucianists were among the first fervid promoters of ARIANISM.

Unwilling to change his position, Arius had to appear before a synod of almost 100 bishops of Egypt and Libya convoked by Bp. Alexander *c.* 320. Remaining unmoved, he was excommunicated by the synod, as were his followers, Bps. Secundus of Ptolemaïs and Theonas of Marmarica, and some of the Alexandrian clergy and virgins. As usual, Alexander sent encyclical letters in the synod's name to the more distinguished bishops, explaining and refuting the errors of Arius, notifying them of his excommunication and requesting them to avoid communion with him. These letters affirm, especially on the basis of John ch. 1, that the Word is coeternal with the Father, truly God, God's only begotten Son.

Expelled from Alexandria, Arius went to Coelesyria to fellow disciples, prominent among whom were Paulinus of Tyre and Theonas of Laodicea. EUSEBIUS OF CAESAREA gave him a friendly welcome. In Nicomedia, whose bishop, EUSEBIUS, lent him unfailing support, he wrote the *Thalia* (Banquet), a long rhapsody, at least partly in metric form, in which he incorporated his theological ideas. With his growing number of supporters he held a synod, which issued encyclical letters against Alexander. This situation continued during the persecution waged by Licinius against the Christians (321–324) and was of serious concern to his conqueror, Constantine.

Captivated by Christianity, Constantine wanted to give it the protection of the state; for, in line with the old Roman idea, he regarded himself as Pontifex Maximus of Christianity, "bishop in matters external" (*Vita Const.* 4.24). As such, he thought it his task to settle a controversy that was upsetting the politico-religious unity of his Christian empire. Theologically incompetent despite the assistance of his adviser Bishop Hosius of Córdoba, Constantine wrote to Alexander and Arius enjoining silence in this nuanced matter, which seemed to him to have no relation to Christian dogma. Hosius, who took the emperor's letter to Alexander, returned unsuccessful. When another synod in Antioch late in 324 failed to effect the desired unity, the emperor decided to settle the controversy by a general synod of the more important bishops of the world. He hoped that such a synod would also solve the paschal controversy concerning the date of EASTER. There were still QUARTODECIMANS who followed Jewish custom; and although most of the bishops celebrated Easter on Sunday in honor of the Resurrection, even some of these, to determine the lunar cycle, consulted the Jews, who did not follow the astronomical computation as did the Christian churches. Constantine wanted to eliminate these differences by establishing the date of Easter independently of the Jews.

The Council. The council opened at Nicaea in Bithynia (modern Iznik, northwestern Turkey in Asia), in Constantine's palace, with an address by the emperor. About 300 bishops were present (the number 318 reported by AMBROSE of Milan and HILARY OF POITIERS is symbolic: cf. the 318 servants of Abraham, Gn 14.14), and almost all were from the eastern half of the empire; more than 100 came from Asia Minor, about 30 from Syria-Phoenicia, fewer than 20 from Palestine and Egypt. Prominent figures were Hosius of Córdoba (who presided with the delegates of Pope Sylvester, the Roman priests Vitus and Vincentius), Alexander of Alexandria (accompanied by his secretary and future successor, the deacon Athanasius), EUSTATHIUS OF ANTIOCH, MARCELLUS OF ANCYRA, Eusebius of Caesarea in Palestine, Leontius of Caesarea in Cappadocia, MACARIUS OF JERUSALEM, Eu-

sebius of Nicomedia, Caecilianus of Carthage, and some "confessors" who had suffered in the persecution of Licinius. In the beginning at least, Constantine was honorary president and even intervened to ensure peaceful discussion.

Doctrinal Definition. Doctrinal issues were the council's first concern. Arian-minded bishops proposed a formula of faith (contents not extant) that was indignantly rejected by the vast majority. Then Eusebius of Caesarea proposed the baptismal creed of his own Church, the oldest eastern creed now known. Its orthodoxy gained it general approval, but a majority of the bishops insisted on certain additions that would counter the Arian errors more clearly and explicitly. The first, ἐκ τῆς οὐσίας τοῦ πατρός, directly contradicted the Arian affirmation that the Son, not genuinely begotten, did not proceed from the very essence, or nature, of the Father, but only by the Father's will, like other creatures. The second addition, γεννηθέντα οὐ ποιηθένα, confronted Arius's statement that the Son is not so by nature, but is "made" by the Father. The third addition, ὁμοούσιον τῷ πατρί, comprised the most significant word of the creed, the sword of division for decades after the council.

Not a biblical word, ὁμοούσιος appears for the first time in Gnostic literature: they are ὁμοούσιοι who belong to the same category of nature. Since in strict generation the son has the same nature as his father, there is always ὁμοουσία here; this the Arians denied to the Word with understandable logic because they denied His generation. The word "ὁμοουσία" affirms that the Word is God as the Father is God, and this because He is the Father's true Son. And if this affirmation is linked with the first article of the creed, "one God Father," it is clear that the Nicene Creed proclaims numerical identity of the Father's nature and the Son's. The creed does no more than mention the Third Person, for the divinity of the Spirit was not at issue. (*See* HOMOOUSIOS.)

The Nicene Creed was the first dogmatic definition of the Christian Church and through the ages has served as a tessera of orthodoxy. Almost all the expressions used are scriptural, with the addition of certain words that are philosophical in origin. The meaning of Scripture is made clear in the light of tradition. The Son's divinity in its strict sense is defined.

Easter Question and Canons. As for Easter, the Fathers decreed (1) that all Christians should observe it on the same day, (2) that Jewish customs should not be followed, and (3) that the practice of the West, of Egypt, and of other Churches should remain in force, namely, of celebrating Easter on the Sunday following the first full moon after the vernal equinox.

Nicaea promulgated 20 disciplinary decrees (cf. *Conciliorum oecumenicorum decreta* 5–15). In later times certain Syriac and Arabic canons (*pseudonicaeni*) were falsely attributed to the council. Canons 15 and 16 forbid bishops, priests, and deacons to involve themselves in the affairs of another diocese or locality. Canon 4 orders that bishops be appointed by all the other bishops of the province, and in case of difficulty, by at least three; the appointment was to be ratified by the metropolitan bishop. Canon 5 declares that provincial synods are to be held twice a year, presumably under the metropolitan, to examine excommunications inflicted by bishops. The famous canons 6 and 7 ratify the traditional prerogatives of Eastern Churches.

The bishop of Alexandria has power over Egypt, Libya, and Pentapolis, after the fashion of Rome's quasi-patriarchal authority. Here is the seed of the patriarchate: the patriarch has under him all the metropolitans of the entire region. The age-old privileges of Antioch, Aelia (rebuilt as Jerusalem), and other Churches are ratified, but it is not clear whether the privileges in question are merely honorary.

Some canons have to do with the dignity of the clergy: the ordination of eunuchs (c.1), of those insufficiently tested since baptism or proved unworthy (c.2), of those who have denied the faith in persecution (c.10), and cohabitation of clerics with other than relatives or women beyond suspicion (c.3). Canon 13 confirms the ancient practice of giving Communion to penitents at the hour of death. A twofold criterion is set up for the admission of heretics (c.19): those who have not erred on the doctrine of the Trinity, such as the Novatians, are to be reconciled without repetition of their baptism; the followers of PAUL OF SAMOSATA, however, are to be rebaptized, since it is not clear that they confess the Trinity. Deacons are warned (c.18) to give precedence to bishops and priests. On Sundays and the days of Pentecost, the faithful are to stand for the liturgy, not kneel (c.20).

Aftermath. It is not certain how long the council lasted, though it was probably for several weeks, at the close of which Constantine bade the fathers farewell. Only two bishops, Secundus of Ptolemaïs and Theonas of Marmarica, refused to sign the creed and the accompanying anathema. With Arius, they were exiled to Illyricum. Constantine confirmed the decrees of Nicaea, proclaimed them laws of the empire, and wrote a letter to the bishops of Alexandria and other absent bishops expressing his joy that harmony in faith had been achieved. While Constantine lived, none of the friends of Arius who were dissatisfied with the doctrine of Nicaea dared to attack the Symbol directly. The Eusebians (Eusebius of Nicomedia and his supporters) maneuvered rather to remove the more influential representatives of Nicaea from the scene by political strategy; conspicuous proof of their success is discoverable in the exiling of Eustathius of Antioch and Athanasius even under Constantine.

Of the Acts of the council, there are preserved only the Symbol with the added anathema against the Arians, the disciplinary canons, lists of the bishops in attendance (extant in different languages and not always consistent), and the synodal letter notifying the Alexandrian Church of the excommunication of Arius and his followers.

Although Nicaea's judgment on Arianism was clear and conclusive, it was a sign of contradiction and cause of serious division in the East until 381, primarily because of the word "ὁμοούσιος." In their opposition to the council and to the expression, Arians and Semi-Arians were in agreement.

The so-called *Acta* of Nicaea used by Gelasius of Cyzicus (*Patrologia Graeca,* 85:1191–1360) and the Coptic Acts edited by E. Revillout, *Le concile de Nicée d'après les textes coptes et les diverses collections canoniques* (2 v. Paris 1876, 1898), are apparently spurious. The extant documents of Nicaea have been edited by H. G. Opitz, *Athanasius Werke* 3.1 (Berlin-Leipzig 1934). For the canons, see *Histoire des conciles d'après les documents originaux,* 1.2:528–620, and *Conciliorum oecumenicorum decreta* v. 5–15; for the list of bishops, H. Gelzer, H. Hilgenfeld, and O. Cuntz, *Patrum nicaenorum nomina* (Leipzig 1898), and E. Honigmann, "Une liste inédite des Pères de Nicée," *Byzantion* 20 (1950) 63–71; for the decree on Easter, *Iuris ecclesiastici graecorum historia et monumenta,* 1:435–436, and H. Leclercq, *Dictionnaire d'archéologie chrétienne et de liturgie,* 13.2:1549.

Bibliography: C. J. VON HEFELE, *Histoire des conciles d'après les documents originaux,* tr. and continued by H. LECLERCQ, 10 v. in 19 (Paris 1907–38) 1.1:335–632. G. BARDY, *Histoire de l'église depuis les origines jusqu'à nos jours,* ed. A. FLICHE and V. MARTIN (Paris 1935–) 3:69–176. M. GOEMANS, *Het algemeen concilie in de vierde eeuw* (Nijmegen 1945), ch. 2–3. I. ORTIZ DE URBINA, *Nicée et Constantinople* (Paris 1963); *El símbolo niceno* (Madrid 1947). V. C. DE CLERCQ, *Ossius of Cordova* (Washington 1954). J. N. D. KELLY, *Early Christian Creeds* (2d ed. New York 1960) 205–230. J. N. D. KELLY, "The Nicene Creed: A Turning Point," *Scottish Journal of Theology* 36 (1983) 23–39. C. LUBHEID, "The Alleged Second Session of the Council of Nicaea," *Journal of Ecclesiastical History* 34 (1983)165–174; *The Council of Nicea* (Galway, Ireland 1982). R. GREGG, ed., *Arianism* (Cambridge, Mass. 1985).

[I. ORTIZ DE URBINA]

NICAEA II, COUNCIL OF

The seventh ecumenical council of the Church, and the last to be recognized by the Eastern Church, August to October 787.

History. When Emperor Leo IV died prematurely on Sept. 8, 780, any hope of ever restoring the veneration of IMAGES—a practice forbidden in Byzantium for more than a century and a half—appeared impossible. The entire state machinery and the high offices of the Church were in the hands of men committed to ICONOCLASM; the army, which Emperor CONSTANTINE V Copronymos, the most passionate iconoclast of all, had so often led to victory, remained jealously devoted to his memory. Yet when Empress IRENE assumed power in 780 in the name of her son, Constantine VI, who was still a minor, she was determined to restore the veneration of icons throughout the Empire. A plot, vigorously repressed, enabled her to get rid of ministers and other personages hostile to inconoduly. She then contacted Pope ADRIAN I (*sacra* of Aug. 29, 784), informing him of the intention of the Byzantine government to convoke a general council and requesting him to send duly empowered representatives. Furthermore, to remove the main obstacle to such a council, Patriarch PAUL IV was replaced as patriarch by the Empress's own secretary, TARASIUS.

The order convoking the council was promulgated throughout the Eastern Empire at the beginning of 786. Rome had welcomed this step on the part of the Greeks and sent a delegation of two members of the Roman clergy: a secular cleric and a religious, namely, the archpriest Peter and the hegumen Peter of the Greek monastery of San Saba. There were no other representatives from the West. The Byzantine episcopate sent 350 of its members. On Aug. 1, 786, the Council opened in Constantinople itself, in the basilica of the Holy Apostles, in the presence of the sovereigns, but elements of the imperial guard broke into the church, forcing the Council's temporary dissolution. But Prime Minister Stavrakios transferred or disbanded all regiments that had mutinied, and the Empress transferred the Council to Nicaea in Bithynia, where it opened on Sept. 24, 787.

The sessions, eight in all, lasted three weeks, and all except the last were held at the church of Hagia Sophia in Nicaea. Patriarch Tarasius, not the papal legates, presided, but the legates signed all documents first and were always listed first.

The Council had to decide immediately about the iconoclastic bishops, of whom many were present. Could the Council recognize their right to be seated? It took the first three sessions to dispose of this burning question, for the monks—numerous and active—opposed with determination the Council's decision to recognize the iconoclasts once they had abjured their heresy before the assembly. The next two sessions (October 1 and 4) established the legitimacy of the veneration of icons through an examination of scriptural and patristic tradition. The sixth session (October 5 and 6) dealt with Rome's demand that the great synod held at Hiereia in 754 be condemned. The seventh session (October 13) climaxed debate by fixing the terms of the dogmatic decree (ὅρος) that proclaimed belief in the efficacy of the intercession of saints, in the legitimacy of the veneration of icons or statues, i.e., veneration or relative cult as opposed to the cult of latria (*see* WORSHIP) which is the highest adoration, and due God alone. Twenty-two disciplinary canons were appended to this dogmatic definition. The Empress—not without ulterior political motives—wished to associate the people of the capital city with the decisions of the Council and therefore decided to close the Council by a sort of apotheosis, having all the fathers come to Constantinople for an eighth session in the Magnaura palace itself. On October 23 all gathered before the sovereign, who addressed the assembly herself and then had the decree of faith proclaimed; she then signed it, even before her son, Constantine VI, and the Roman legates. The *Acta* of the Council became the law of the state; their strict enforcement was to assure the Byzantine Church, despite some harassment by the old heresy, a respite of some 30 years. The Council thus marked the end of the first period of iconoclasm.

Acts of the Council. Though the East was virtually restored to peace by the Council, the appearance of the *Acta* in the West caused considerable uproar. It is not very probable that the actual text of the proceedings had been submitted to Pope Adrian I for approval, even though Patriarch Tarasius had reported to him on what had transpired at the Council. The *Acta* themselves reached the Holy See in a translation containing grave errors on essential points, even going so far as to represent the fathers of Nicaea as saying the opposite of what they had actually defined. CHARLEMAGNE, kept in ignorance of what had occurred in the East and still smarting from the wound to his self-esteem caused by the rupture of the engagement of his daughter Rotrude with the young Emperor Constantine VI, submitted to the theologians of his court, including ALCUIN, the translation of the *Acta* that the Pope had sent him. The astonishment of his experts was so great that the monarch—who was more interested in condemning the Byzantine emperor, whose rank and title within Christendom he coveted—commissioned a refutation in a work called the *Capitulate de imaginibus,* or the *LIBRI CAROLINI.* Charlemagne then convened a great council at Frankfurt of 350 bishops who, in the presence of papal legates, condemned the Council of Nicaea. A special embassy brought to Rome an extract of the *Libri Carolini,* as well as a letter in which Charlemagne adjured the Pope to deny approval of the Council of Nicaea. In 794 the Pope replied in a memorandum that refuted in detail the complaints of the Frankish court, though with moderation. But the Holy See still did not give immediate approval to the *Acta* in question, for Constantinople refused to give Rome satisfaction in other matters, e.g., restitution to Rome of those Italian and Illyrian territories and patrimonies transferred to the Patriarchate of CONSTANTINOPLE by Emperor Leo III in 733. Even in the East the Council was not recognized until 843; its ecumenical status was not actually confirmed until the Council of CONSTANTINOPLE IV in 869 to 870. Moreover, the Patriarch PHOTIUS was able to complain in the synod of 879 to 880 that Rome had still not recognized its authority. However, Nicaea II was recognized almost immediately by the legates at the session of Jan. 26, 880, and soon after by Pope JOHN VIII in person, as a result of his reconciliation with Photius. The insertion of the Council of Nicaea II, after 880, into the formula of the papal profession of faith was the Western Church's seal of recognition of its ecumenical status.

Bibliography: Sources. J. D. MANSI, *Scarorum Conciliorum nova et amplissima collectio,* 31 v. (Florence-Venice 1757–98); reprinted and continued by L. PETIT and J. B. MARTIN 53 v. in 60 (Paris 1889–1927; repr. Graz 1960–) 12:991–1154; 13:1, for the Acts. *Ibid.* 12:951–90; 13:759–820, for various documents. E. JAFFÉ, *Regesta pontificum romanorum ab condita ecclesia ad annum post Christum natum 1198,* ed. P. EWALD (2d ed. Leipzig 1881–88 repr. Graz 1956) 2448, 2483, pontifical letters. *Liber pontificalis,* ed. L. DUCHESNE, v. 1–2 (Paris 1886–92) 1:486–523, for Pope Adrian I. F. DÖLGER, *Corpus der griechischen Urkunden des Mittelalters und der neueren Zeit,* series A, *Regesten* (Munich 1924–32) 341–47, 349, imperial letters. V. GRUMEL, *Les Regestes des actes du patriarcat de Constantinople* (Kadikoi-Bucharest 1932–) 351–59, patriarchal Acts. Literature. C. J. VON HEFELE, *Histoire des conciles d'après les documents originaux,* tr. and continued by H. LECLERCQ, 10 v. in 19 (Paris 1907–38) 3.2:601–798. H. LECLERCQ, *Dictionnaire d'archéologie chrétienne et de liturgie,* ed. F. CABROL, H. LECLERCQ, and H. I. MARROU, 15 v. (Paris 1907–53) 7:263–267. G. FRITZ, *Dictionnaire de théologie catholique,* ed. A. VACANT et al., 15 v. (Paris 1903–50) 11.1:417–41; *Dictionnaire de théologie catholique: Tables générales* (1951–) 665–66. G. OSTROGORSKY, "Ro und Byzanz im Kampfe um die Bilderverehrung. Papst Hadrian I. und das VII. Oekumenische Konzil von Nikäa," *Seminarium Kondakovianum* 6 (1933) 73–87. G. OSTROGORSKY, *History of the Byzantine State,* tr. J. HUSSEY from 2d German ed. (Oxford 1956); American ed. by P. CHARANIS (New Brunswick, N.J. 1957) 156–65. A. FLICHE and V. MARTIN, eds., *Histoire de l'église depuis les origines jusqu'á nos jours* (Paris 1935–) 6:107–20. E. HAMMERSCH-MIDT, "Eine Definition von *Hypostasis* und *Ousia* während des VII. Allgemeinen Konzils," *Ostkirchliche Studien* 5 (1956) 52–55. P. VAN DEN VEN, "La Patristique et l'hagiographie au concile de Nicée de 787," *Byzantion* 25–27 (1955–57) 325–62. L. USPENKIJ, "Sedmoj vselenskij sober i dogmat ob ikonopočitanii [The 7th ecumenical council and the dogma of the cult of images]," *Zurnal Moskovskoj Patriarchii* fasc. 12 (1958) 40–48, in Russian. R. BÄUMER, *Lexikon für Theologie und Kirche,* ed. J. HOFER and K. RAHNER, 10 v. (2d, new ed. Freiburg 1957–65) 7:967–68. J. M. A. SALLES-DABADIE, *Les Conciles oecuméniques dans l'histoire* (Geneva 1962). On the *Libri Carolini.* K. HAMPE, "Hadrians I. Vertheidigung der zweiten nicaenischen Synode gegen die Angriffe Karls des Grossen," *Neues Archiv der Gesellschaft für ältere deutsche Geschichtskunde* 21 (1895) 83–113. G. HOCQUARD, *Catholicisme. Hier aujourd'hui et demain,* ed. G. JACQUEMET (Paris 1947–) 2:586–88. H. SCHADE, "Die *Libri Carolini* und ihrer Stellung zum Bild," *Zeitschrift für katholische Theologie* 79 (1957) 69–78. G. HAENDLER, *Epochen karolingischer Theologie* (Theologische Arbeiten 10; Berlin 1958). K. BAUS, *Lexikon für Theologie und Kirche* 6:1020–21. A. GIAKALIS, *Images of the Divine: The Theology of Icons at the Seventh Ecumenical Council* (Leiden 1994). G. LIMOURIS, *Icons: Windows on Eternity: Theology and Spirituality in Colour* (Geneva 1990).

[V. LAURENT]

NICARAGUA, THE CATHOLIC CHURCH IN

The largest Central American country, the Republic of Nicaragua is located approximately 375 miles from the Panama Canal and 375 miles from Mexico. It is bound on the north by Honduras, on the east by the Caribbean Sea, on the south by Costa Rica and on the west by the Pacific Ocean. Nicaragua's population is concentrated along the Pacific coast; its major cities are Managua, León and Granada, and its chief port is Corinto. The climate is generally hot and humid except in the mountainous region and its Caribbean coastline has earned the name the "Mosquito Coast." Nicaragua has two great lakes and a number of rivers which flow into the Atlantic. The volcanic chain near the Pacific coast is always active but not dangerously so. Nicaragua is an agricultural and cattle-raising country whose largest exports are cotton, coffee, sugar, bananas and beef; it also has gold and copper mines.

Church History. Nicaragua was first inhabited by South American natives, who settled the coastal regions, and by the 10th century the region experienced an influx of immigrants from Mexico. Christopher Columbus, on his fourth voyage to the New World, "discovered" the Atlantic portion of Nicaragua on Sept. 12, 1502; Gil González d'Avila discovered the Pacific portion 20 years later. In 1524 the conquest of the region by Spain was accomplished by Francisco Hernández de Córdoba, who founded the cities of Granada and León; the monetary unit of the country, the cordoba, was named after him. During the colonial period Nicaragua suffered from the depredations of English pirates; in defense against them Rafaela Herrera became a national heroine.

Catholicism came to Nicaragua with Columbus and was established with the conquest by Córdoba. The first chaplain arrived with Avila in 1522, and in 1524 the first Franciscan church was founded in Granada. The first bishop for the province of Nicaragua was named in 1527. However, Fray Pedro de Zúñiga died in Cádiz before setting out for his see and was succeeded by Diego Álvarez de Osorio, who took possession of the bishopric in León in 1532. Bartolomé de LAS CASAS first visited Nicaragua in 1530 and returned in 1532 with four other Dominicans to found the convent of San Pablo at the request of Bishop Osorio. During the colonial period the JESUITS also established themselves in Nicaragua, and accomplished much of the missionary work through the 18th century.

Nicaragua remained a part of the captaincy-general of Guatemala until 1821, when along with the rest of the provinces of Central America (except Chiapas, which was annexed to Mexico), it became independent and joined the United Provinces of Central America. In 1836 that federation was dissolved, and after many vicissitudes Nicaragua became an independent republic in 1845. In 1855 it was taken over by an American buccaneer William Walker, who, after seizing the country, made himself president before being driven out by Nicaraguan and Central American troops in 1857. When his new attempt to invade Central America failed, Walker was shot in Honduras in 1860. After his death, the country enjoyed a peaceful period under conservative rule that lasted until the early 1890s.

Protestantism was introduced along the Atlantic coast in the mid-19th century by Englishmen from Jamaica. Not until the 20th century did Catholic missionaries begin intensive work in that area. Protestant sects would penetrate the Pacific area after World War I and increased their activities after World War II. The most active groups were Baptists, Evangelists, Seventh-Day Adventists, Mormons, Anglicans and Moravians.

In 1892 a military *coup d'état* brought to power General José Santos Zelaya, a man of liberal ideas, educated in Europe. Despite the beneficial reforms he introduced, Zelaya governed Nicaragua for 17 years with a dictatorial iron hand before revolutionaries ousted him with U.S. backing. Upon his fall, Nicaragua went through another convulsive period until a new armed rebellion brought the Liberals back to power in 1929. The United States played an important role in Nicaraguan politics from 1909 until the occupation forces were finally withdrawn in 1933.

The Modern Church. In 1937 Anastasio Somoza gained dictatorial power and held it until his assassination in 1956. From 1957 to the late 1970s Nicaragua continued to enjoy relative tranquility under the rule of first Somoza's son Luis (1957–63) and then his nephew, General Anastasio Debayle Somoza. During General Somoza's

Capital: Managua.
Size: 50,464 sq. miles.
Population: 4,812,569 in 2000.
Languages: Spanish; English and indigenous languages are spoken in various regions.
Religions: 3,513,175 Roman Catholics (73%), 673,766 Evangelical Protestants (15%), 240,628 other (5%); 385,000 with no religious affiliation.
Archdiocese: Managua, with suffragans Estelí, Granada, Jinotega, Juigalpa, León, and Matagalpa. There is a vicariate apostolic located in Bluefields.

regime the Sandinista guerilla group came into being, composed of landless peasantry, and over time they gained in power. Civil war broke out in 1976, and on July 17, 1979 Somoza was forced to flee the country. Nicaragua's Sandinista government quickly set about confiscating property from the wealthy classes, who retaliated by forming the Contra army.

The socialist policies of the Sandinistas—particularly with regard to land reform and redistribution of wealth—were popular with many less-affluent Catholics, while certain priests supported the regime within the context of a quasi-Marxist ''liberation'' as opposed to ''salvation'' theology that had begun to take shape at the Latin American Bishop's conference in 1968 (*see* LIBERATION THEOLOGY). During his visit to the region in 1983, Pope John Paul II surprised audiences by shaking his finger at the kneeling Father Cardenal, one of four Catholic priests who took positions in the Sandinista government in opposition to Vatican orders. More conservative Catholics sided with the former elite class in their opposition to the government and welcomed the CIA-sponsored Contra's efforts to unseat them. By the late 1990s Nicaraguan bishops advocated in favor of compromise between the socialist and U.S.-backed government factions. The nation's economy failed after the United States instituted a trade embargo in 1981; poverty increased, hand in hand with terrorism and human rights abuses, into the 21st century. The Church-supported coalition government elected in 1996 confronted an economic disaster, as well as the potential for renewed violence.

In November of 1998 another tragedy struck the region in the form of Hurricane Mitch, which left 2,500 Nicaraguans dead and many others homeless. Recognizing the people's confidence in the Church, the government allowed Catholic officials to distribute much-needed drinking water and other relief supplies to hurricane victims. Two years later the loss of crops in the outlying Eteli region threatened famine, and the Church, through Carítas, again responded with needed aid.

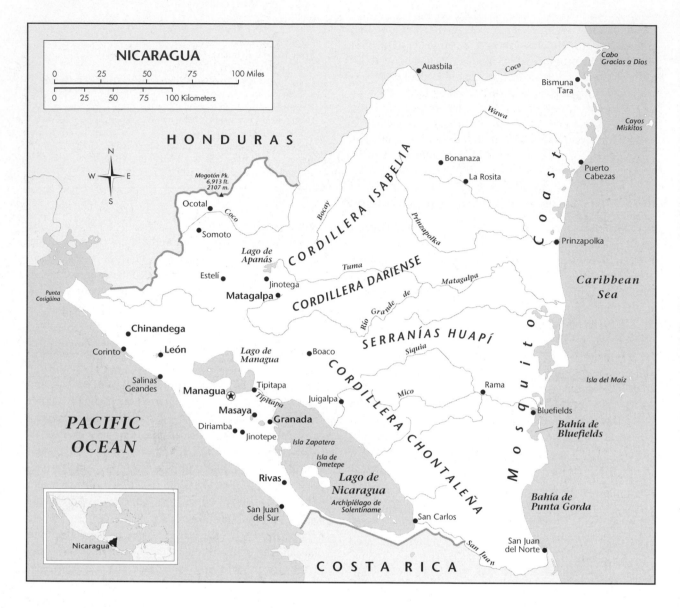

Moving into the 21st Century. At the close of the 20th century relations between Church and state remained amicable. As had been the tradition for centuries, leaders from the Church met routinely with Nicaraguan government officials and were often consulted by the government when appropriate. Pope John Paul II made his second visit to Managua in February of 1996 by encouraging Nicaraguans to revitalize their moral traditions. The pope also praised the arrival of peace, adding: "you have recovered your sovereign humanity—Christian and national." The coalition government's continued opposition to abortion and family matters was championed by the Church, although it became increasingly problematic on the international level as wealthy nations liberalized their social policies. In 2000, when financial assistance was requested from the Scandinavian nations in the wake of Hurricane Mitch, such aid was al-most denied because Nicaragua's Minister of the Family, Max Padilla, refused to acknowledge homosexual relationships as a legitimate basis of the family unit. At home, flare-ups also began to occur, as in 1998, when Sandinistan politicians tried to eliminate the teaching of the Catholic catechism in public schools. Still, the Church's role as the religion of the majority remained so entrenched by the beginning of the 21st century that evangelical Protestant leaders urged their ministers to enter the political realm, even if it meant giving up their congregations.

The Jesuit, SALESIAN, Christian Brothers and PIARIST orders continued to operate much-needed primary and secondary schools, which received government funding. In 1960 the Jesuits had founded the first Catholic university in Central America, and the Universidad Cen-

The Catholic Cathedral in downtown Managua, Nicaragua, photographed following a 1972 earthquake. (©Brian Vikander/CORBIS)

troamericana, in Managua, still maintained imposing credentials in civil engineering, electrical engineering, veterinary medicine, law and business administration. A national university was located in León, and in 1999 the Managua campus of the former Baptist University was transformed into a Catholic university through the funding of U.S. businessman Tom Monaghan. Several Catholic presses also operated in the country, and Managua was home to a Catholic-run radio station.

By 2000 Nicaragua contained 223 parishes, 235 secular and 176 religious priests, 93 brothers and 922 sisters. Among the religious orders were the Spanish Franciscans, Italian Franciscans, Dominicans, Jesuits, Capuchins, Salesians, Christian Brothers, Redemptorists, Piarists, Benedictines, Augustinian Recollects and the order of Jesús Divino Obrero, which runs a reformatory in Managua. Secular priests from Canada had charge of the national seminary, which was originally founded by the Dominicans in León and transferred to the capital in

1950. Religious orders of women included four native congregations founded after 1950: the Doctrineras, the Siervas Misioneras de Cristo Rey, the Misioneras Catequistas Lumen Criste and the Siervas de Nuestro Señor. Among the foreign congregations serving in Nicaragua were the Missionaries of the Sacred Heart, Sisters of the Assumption, Josephites, Sisters of Charity of the Blessed Virgin of Mercy, Oblate Sisters of Divine Love, Oblates of the Sacred Hearts, Franciscans and others. They served in primary and secondary schools and cared for the seminary, an orphanage, a sanitarium and almost all the hospitals located in the country. Among the charitable institutions operating in Nicaragua were Cáritas, Catholic Action and the Congregación Mariana.

Nicaragua contained a number of shrines to which pilgrimages were made: Nuestro Señor de Esquipulas in La Conquista, Carazo; San Jerónimo in Masaya; Santo Domingo de Guzmán in Managua; La Vírgen de la Inmaculada Concepción in El Viejo, Chinandega; Nuestro

Señor de Esquipulas in El Sauce, León; and La Vírgen de la Purísima Concepción in Granada.

Bibliography: *Nueva poesía nicaragüense,* ed. O. CUADRA DOWNING (Madrid 1949). J. D. GÁMEZ, *Historia de Nicaragua* (Managua 1889; 2d ed. Madrid 1955).

[E. GUTIÉRREZ/EDS.]

NICENE CREED

A profession of faith agreed upon, although with some misgivings because of its non-biblical terminology, by the bishops at NICAEA I (325) to defend the true faith against ARIANISM. It is basically a baptismal creed of Syro-Palestinian origin into which have been interpolated anti-Arian clauses, including the word HOMOOUSIOS (at the urging of Hosius of Córdoba and CONSTANTINE I), and to which have been appended four anathemas. Structurally, the creed (H. Denzinger, *Enchiridion symbolorum* 125, 126) is a brief, tripartite Trinitarian statement, stressing the CONSUBSTANTIALITY of the Son, His INCARNATION, redeeming death, and RESURRECTION. It concludes simply with "and in the Holy Spirit" followed by the anathemas that condemn typical Arian slogans oft repeated in ARIUS's *Thalia,* e.g., "There was when He was not." Though scholars previously maintained that the Creed of EUSEBIUS OF CAESAREA was the model of the Nicene, it is now generally admitted that Eusebius's creedal profession at Nicaea I was motivated by his desire for rehabilitation and was not intended to be a proposal of a basis for a conciliar creed.

The first witness to what is popularly known as the Nicene Creed, sometimes called the Niceno-Constantinople Creed (*Enchiridion symbolorum* 150), is found in the acts of the Council of CHALCEDON (451). Herein the Niceno-Constantinople Creed is attributed to the bishops of CONSTANTINOPLE I (381), whose amplification of the Nicene produced the Niceno-Constantinople. But careful literary analysis reveals the impossibility of the latter's dependence on the former. There are significant omissions in the Niceno-Constantinople, while there are also additions doctrinally insignificant in light of the errors of the day, together with minor differences in word order and sentence structure pointlessly made if the Niceno-Constantinople is the Nicene expanded. Furthermore, the Niceno-Constantinople contains longer sections on the Person of Christ and the Holy Spirit, as well as articles concerning belief in the Church, baptism, the resurrection of the dead, and eternal life. The majority of scholars until recently either denied any connection of the Niceno-Constantinople with Constantinople I or opted for a purely accidental association through supposed creedal professions made by CYRIL OF JERUSALEM or Nectarius at the Council. For those adhering to the traditional explanation of the Niceno-Constantinople Creed's connection with the second ecumenical Council, the creed found in Epiphanius of Constantia's *Ancoratus* (374) would surely be the Niceno-Constantinople's paradigm did not some scholars with good reason suppose that the Nicene, rather than the Niceno-Constantinople, stood in the text. The antinomies seem best resolved by the fact that before Chalcedon, creeds other than the Nicene were referred to as Nicene because of their basic fidelity in doctrine to the Nicene. Thus Constantinople I may be said to have adopted and promulgated the Niceno-Constantinople, already in existence in the baptismal liturgy, not as a new creed or as the Nicene literally expanded, but as the Nicene faith in substance, better adapted to combat the errors of the day.

The Niceno-Constantinople's recitation at the Eucharist began apparently at Antioch under the Monophysite Patriarch Peter the Fuller (d. 488); its use in the West dates from the third Council of TOLEDO (589), when possibly the FILIOQUE was inserted. The Niceno-Constantinople's place in the Roman liturgy is due to the efforts of Emperor HENRY II, who persuaded Pope BENEDICT VIII to enjoin its recitation on Sundays and on feasts of which mention is made in the Creed.

See Also: CREED; GENERATION OF THE WORD; LOGOS; WORD, THE.

Bibliography: I. ORTIZ DE URBINA, *Nicée et Constantinople* (Paris 1963). *El símbolo niceno* (Madrid 1947). J. N. D. KELLY, *Early Christian Creeds* (London 1972) 205–262. W. PANNENBURG and K. LEHMANN, eds., *Glaubensbekenninis und Kirchengemeinschaft: Das Modell des Konzils von Konstantinopel (381)* (Freiburg 1982). *Confessing the One Faith. An Ecumenical Explication of the Apostolic Faith as it is Confessed in the Nicene-Constantinopolitan Creed* (Faith and Order Paper No. 153; Geneva 1991).

[T. RYAN]

NICEPHORUS I, PATRIARCH OF CONSTANTINOPLE, ST.

Patriarchate April 12, 806 to March 13, 815; Byzantine theologian and historian; b. Constantinople, *c.* 758; d. in exile near Chalcedon, June 2, 828. Nicephorus stood in the forefront of the battle against ICONOCLASM. His father, Theodore, of noble lineage and an imperial secretary to Emperor CONSTANTINE V, had twice suffered torture, degradation, and banishment in defense of the veneration of images and had died in exile. Under TARASIUS, his predecessor in the patriarchate, Nicephorus became, like his father, an imperial secretary (770–80) and as such took part in the Council of NICAEA II (787). He later retired to a monastery, although he did not become a monk, possibly because he had fallen out of favor at court or wanted leisure for study. He was chosen head of the largest poorhouse in Constantinople, perhaps by Emperor Nicephorus I at his accession (802). Four years later, he was made patriarch against the advice of THEODORE THE STUDITE, but he soon joined forces with Theodore against Emperor Leo V in the controversy over iconoclasm. In 815 he was deposed and exiled near Chalcedon. He used his time to produce anti-iconoclastic treatises (*see* BYZANTINE CHURCH, HISTORY OF).

Two of his principal dogmatic works about the iconoclastic *horos* and *florilegium* of patristic texts of 815 are still unedited. His *Apologeticus major* and *minor* and three *Antirhetikoi* or Diatribes (813–820) are important because they preserve excerpts of Emperor Constantine's writings favoring iconoclasm. Nicephorus's works are important for the critique of patristic sources that he introduces into his theological arguments. He also wrote a history, the *Breviarium* or *Historia syntomos,* covering the years 602–769. The authenticity of several canonical and poetical works attached to his name is disputed.

After his death his bones were translated to Constantinople by Methodius (847) and interred in the church of the Holy Apostles on March 13.

Feast: March 13 (Latin and Greek Churches); June 2 (Greek Church).

Bibliography: *Patrologia Graeca.* ed J. P. MIGNE (Paris 1857–66) 100:201–850. C. G. DE BOOR, ed., *Nicephorus . . . opuscula historica* (New York 1975). L. OROSZ, ed., *The London Manuscript of Nicephoros ''Breviarium''* (Budapest 1948). R. P. BLAKE, *Byzantion* 14 (1939) 1–15. V. GRUMEL, *Revue des études byzantines* 17 (1959) 127–135. J. B. PITRA, *Spicilegium Solesmense* (Paris 1852–58) 1:371–503; 4:292–380. H. G. BECK, *Kirche und theologische Literatur im byzantinischen Reich* (Munich 1959) 490–491. R. JANIN, *Dictionnaire de théologie catholique,* ed. A. VACANT et al. (Paris 1903—50) 11.1:452–455. G. MORAVCSIK, *Byzantinoturcica,* 2 v. (2d ed. Berlin 1958) v.1. P. J. ALEXANDER, *The Patriarch Nicephorus of Constantinople* (Oxford 1958, repr. New York 1980). R. M. MAINKA, ''Zum Brief des Patriarchen Nikephoros I von Konstantinopel an Papst Leo III,'' *Ostkirchliche Studien* 13 (1964) 273–281. P. O'CONNELL, *The Ecclesiology of St. Nicephorus I* (Rome 1972). J. TRAVIS, *In Defense of the Faith: The Theology of Patriarch Nikephoros of Constantinople* (Brookline, Mass. 1984). K. PARRY, *Depicting the Word: Byzantine Iconophile Thought of the Eighth and Ninth Centuries* (Leiden 1996).

[M. J. HIGGINS]

NICEPHORUS BLEMMYDES

Byzantine monk, theologian, and advocate of reunion; b. Constantinople,1197; d. Emathia, near Ephesus, 1272. In 1205 he left Constantinople, soon after its fall to the Crusaders (1204). In the course of several years he acquired encyclopedic knowledge through his studies at Prusa, Nicaea, Ephesus, Smyrna, and other cities. In 1223 he became a member of the clergy of Nicaea. In 1232, at Nicaea, and in 1234, at Nymphaeum, he took part in the theological discussions with the Latin legates. He composed a tract defending the Greek position, which occasioned the failure of the negotiations then and again in 1250. He was entrusted with the education of the future Emperor Theodore II Lascaris and of George Akropolites, founded the monastery of Emathia near Ephesus (1248), and refused the bishopric of that city as well as the patriarchate of Nicaea offered to him by his former pupil Theodore. Toward 1256 he accepted the conciliatory attitude toward the Latins adopted by the emperor, apparently influenced by the *Dialogues on the Procession of the Holy Spirit* written by Nicetas of Maronia, and he interpreted the phrase ''per filium'' in an anti-Photian sense. However, in his autobiography, written in 1264, he repudiated any compromise with the Latins.

Preserved in two recensions, the autobiography is the chief work of his abundant literary production, which included two controversial tracts on the procession of the Holy Spirit, a testament for his monks ''Against the Filioque,'' commentaries, scholia on the Psalms with an interesting introduction (προοίμιον) on ecclesiastical chant, an encomion of St. John the Evangelist that is a dogmatic dissertation on Johannine theology, and several manuals of philosophy.

Bibliography: *Patrologia Graeca* 142. V. GRUMEL, *Dictionnaire de théologie catholique* 11.1:441–445; *Catholicisme* 2:85–86. H. G. BECK, *Lexikon für Theologie und Kirche*[2] 7:970. *Kirche und theologische Literatur im byzantinischen Reich* 671–673. G. MERCATI, *Bessarione* 31 (1915) 226–238; *Opere minore,* 5 v. (*Studi e Testi* 76–80; 1937–41); ''. . . Commento del Salterio,'' *Biblica* 26 (1945) 153–181. H. I. BELL, ''The Commentary on the Psalms,'' *Byzantinische Zeitschrift* 30 (1929–30) 295–300.

[I. DALMAIS]

NICETAS CHONIATES

Incorrectly called Akominatos, younger brother of Michael Choniates, theologian important Byzantine historian; b. Chonae (Phrygia), 1140; d. Nicaea, 1213. As a child, Nicetas went to Constantinople to study under the guidance of his elder brother. Entering civil service, he became governor of Philippopolis, where he witnessed the destruction caused by armies of FREDERICK I BARBAROSSA on the Third CRUSADE. He served as imperial secretary under Isaac II Angelus.

After the sack of Constantinople by the Crusaders in 1204, Nicetas fled to the court of Theodore I Lascaris in Nicaea, where he turned to writing. Nicetas proved to be one of the better theologians of the time. As a model for his "Treasury of Orthodoxy" he used the "Panoply of Dogma" by Euthymius Zigabenes. Nicetas's chief work is a Chronicle of 21 books covering the period from 1118 to 1206. In this work he used the treatise of Eustathius of Thessalonica in describing the capture of that region by NORMANS in 1185.

Because of his power of vivid description, he was considered the most brilliant historian of medieval Byzantium after Psellus; Nicetas was a fervent Greek patriot, reflecting the rising tide of Byzantine nationalism. He was unusually objective and reliable despite his experiences with the Crusaders' armies. His works helped to make the epoch of the Comneni one of the most brilliant and flourishing periods of Byzantine historiography.

Bibliography: *Patrologa Graeca,* ed. J. P. MIGNE (Paris 1857–66) 139:319–1057, 1101–1447; 140:9–282,122–145. R. CEILLIER, *Histoire générale des auteurs sacrés et ecclésiastiques* (Paris 1729–83) 14:1176–77; Table 2:208. L. PETIT, *Dictionnaire de théologie catholique,* ed. A. VACANT et al., (Paris 1903–50) 14.1:316–318; 16:20. K. KRUMBACHER, *Geschichte der byzantinischen Literatur* (Munich 1890) 281–286. H. G. BECK, *Kirche und theologische Literatur im byzantinischen Reich* (Munich 1959) 663–666. G. OSTROGORSKY, *History of the Byzantine State* tr. J. HUSSEY (Oxford 1956) 311–313.

[M. C. HILFERTY]

NICETAS DAVID

The Paphlagonian tenth-century disciple of Arethas, rhetor and prolific writer of encomia on Apostles, saints, and martyrs. Nicetas main work is the life of the Byzantine Patriarch IGNATIUS, which was probably composed in 907. In opposition to PHOTIUS, Nicetas presents his hero as a true saint who never yielded to the pressure of civil authorities or became unfaithful to his principles. Nicetas considered the patriarchs who succeeded Ignatius as unworthy because they shared Photius's lust for power: Stephen, Anthony, Nicholas, and Euthymius. He branded the last three as almost heretics because they had sanctioned the third and fourth marriages of the Emperor LEO VI.

As a radical opponent of tetragamy (fourth marriage), Nicetas composed a treatise against the Patriarch Euthymius and the Emperor and, disgusted by the fact that even his teacher Arethas had been induced to approve the tetragamy, retired to a hermitage near Media on the Bulgarian frontier. Suspected of espionage, he was arrested and brought to Constantinople. Because of his writings against the Patriarch and the Emperor, he would have been severely punished had he not been saved by the intercession of the Patriarch Euthymius, who allowed him to become a monk in his monastery of Agathos.

As a monk, Nicetas chose the name of David; he stayed in the monastery until 910. He devoted the rest of his life to the writing of homilies and encomia. These writings were attributed to another Nicetas, called the philosopher, but this attribution is wrong. Nicetas, the rhetor and philosopher, should be identified with the author of the life of Ignatius. The opinion that he was bishop of Dadybra is likewise false; this error was caused by a misinterpretation of the abridged form of his monastic name, David, in a manuscript. Nicetas seems to have written most of his compositions between 913 and 963. His life of Ignatius was later introduced into the anti–Photian collection and used by the opponents of Photius in their campaign against the second patriarchate of Photius and the repudiation of his immediate successors.

Bibliography: K. M. LOPAREV, "Zhitie," *Russkiĭ Arkheologicheskiĭ Institut: Izviestiĭa* 13 (1908) 173–181. J. D. MANSI *Sacrorum Conciliorum nova et amplissima collectio* (Florence–Venice 1757–98) 16:209–296, Vita Ignatii, 409–458, Anti–Photianist collection. *Patrologia Graeca.* ed. J. P. MIGNE (Paris 1857–66) 105:488–574, Vita Ignatii; *ibid.* 15–487, homilies and encomia. *Acta Sanctorum* April 3:ix–xvi, app., St. George. A. VOGT, ed., "Deux discours inédits de Nicétas de Paphlagonie," *Orientalia Christiana* 23 (1931) 5–97. P. KARLIN-HAYTER, ed., "Vita S. Euthymii," *Byzantion* 25–27 (1955–57) 1–172. F. DVORNIK, *The Photian Schism* (Cambridge, Eng. 1948). R. J. H. JENKINS, "A Note on Nicetas David Paphlago and the Vita Ignatii," *Dumbarton Oaks Papers.* Harvard University (Cambridge, MA 1941–) 18 (1965).

[F. DVORNIK]

NICETAS OF REMESIANA

Bishop and distinguished ecclesiastical writer; b. place and date unknown; d. after A.D. 414. Remesiana has been identified with the site of the modern Yugoslavian village of Bēla Palanka, east of Nish (the ancient Naissus). Although of Greek origin according to his name (the Latinized form of Νικητής), he was entirely Western in outlook and temperament and wrote excellent Latin. In 398 and 402 he visited his friend PAULINUS OF NOLA, and the latter's *Propempticon* (*Carmen* 17), written on the occasion of his departure following the first visit, is the chief source for his life. According to a reference preserved in St. Hilary (*Frg. hist.* 15) he was already a bishop in 366–367, and the mention of his name in the letter of Pope Innocent I to the bishops of Macedonia (Innocent I, *Epist.* 22) dated Dec. 13, 414, indicates that he was still living at that time. Gennadius (*De viris illustribus* 21) furnishes valuable data on his writings, although his account is very brief.

Nicetas's chief work, the *Competentibus ad baptismum instructionis libelli sex,* a manual of instructions for baptismal candidates, is preserved only in fragments, but, fortunately, the sections covering *De ratione fidei, De potentia Spiritus Sancti,* and *De symbolo* are rather long. Basing himself solidly on the teachings of the Council of NICAEA and making full use of the *Catecheses* of St. CYRIL OF JERUSALEM, he defended the consubstantiality of the Son against the ARIANS and the consubstantiality of the Holy Spirit against the MACEDONIANS. His commentary on the Creed employs the term *communio sanctorum* for the first time, and it has an important place in the history and exposition of the symbol.

The sermons, *De vigiliis servorum Dei* and *De psalmodiae bono* (or *De utilitate hymnorum*), were already recognized as genuine by the Maurist Luc D'Achéry in 1659. The first deals with the celebration of the vigils of Saturdays and Sundays, and the second stresses the importance of the singing of psalms or hymns at these vigils. In the second work, the *Magnificat* is assigned to St. Elizabeth (9, 11).

Nicetas is probably the author of the little treatise *De diversis appellationibus Christi,* but the arguments adduced to identify the *Ad lapsam virginem libellus,* assigned to him by Gennadius, with the pseudo-Ambrosian *De lapsu virginis consecratae* are not convincing. Paulinus of Nola praised Nicetas as a writer of hymns and said that he taught the barbarian Bessi and Scythians to glorify Christ in song, but no hymn has survived with his name. Despite the advocacy of Dom G. Morin and A. E. Burn, there is no solid evidence for making him the author of the *TE DEUM.*

Bibliography: *De vigiliis,* ed. C. H. TURNER, *Journal of Theological Studies* 22 (1920–21) 306–320; *De utilitate,* ed. C. H. TURNER, *ibid.* 24 (1922–23) 225–252. A. E. BURN, *Niceta of Remesiana: His Life and Works* (Cambridge, Eng. 1905). *Clavis Patrum latinorum,* ed. E. DEKKERS (Streenbrugge 1961) 646–652. F. L. CROSS, *The Oxford Dictionary of the Christian Church* (London 1957) 953–954, with bibliog. P. T. CAMELOT, *Lexikon für Theologie und Kirche,* ed. J. HOFER and K. RAHNER (Freiberg 1957–65) 7:974–975, with bibliog. B. ALTANER, *Patrology,* tr. H. GRAEF (New York 1960) 458–459. O. BARDENHEWER, *Geschichte der altkirchlichen Literatur,* 5 v. (Freiburg 1913–32) 3:598–605. U. MORICCA, *Storia della letteratura latina cristiana,* 3 v. in 5 (Turin 1928–34) 2.2:1148–63.

[M. R. P. MC GUIRE]

NICETAS STETHATOS

Byzantine controversialist and mystical writer; b. *c.* 1000; d. *c.* 1080. He received his epithet of *stethatos* or *pectoratus* (the lionhearted) when he openly rebuked Emperor CONSTANTINE IX Monomachus for his immorality. When Nicetas was 14 years old, he became a monk of STUDION monastery, where he became a devoted disciple of SYMEON THE NEW THEOLOGIAN. He was driven from the monastery for a time when he honored Symeon as a saint after his death. In the conflict (1053–54) between MICHAEL CERULARIUS and HUMBERT OF SILVA CANDIDA (*see* EASTERN SCHISM), Nicetas played a leading part in support of Cerularius but was forced by the emperor to an insincere recantation of his attacks against the Roman Church. Of his polemic on this occasion, the *Dialexis* and *Antidialogus* became the nucleus of a later comprehensive compilation on the azymes, or unleavened bread, and the *Synthesis against the Latins,* which attacked the FILIOQUE, was later to be included in NICETAS CHONIATES' *Thesaurus of Orthodoxy.* Stethatos' principal contribution to mysticism was his *Life of Symeon the New Theologian,* written to establish Symeon's sanctity against his detractors, but incidentally setting forth Nicetas's own ascetical and mystical views. Along this same line he published Symeon's works with an introduction, and composed *Against the Saint's* [i.e., Symeon's] *Accusers.* Independent writings on mysticism included a treatise on the soul and the *Spiritual Paradise.* These and his other essays on mysticism and miscellaneous subjects reveal an ascetical and mystical system that followed very closely that of his master.

Bibliography: Works. *Dialexis, Antidialogus, Synthesis,* v.2 of *Humbert und Kerullarios,* ed. A. MICHEL, 2 v. (Paderborn 1924–30); life of Simeon the New Theologian, in *Un Grand mystique byzantin: Vie de Syméon le Nouveau Théologien, 949–1022,* ed. with Fr. tr. by I. HAUSHERR and G. HORN (*Orientalia Christiana* 12; Rome 1928). Literature. M. T. DISDIER, *Dictionnaire de théologie catholique* 11.1:479–486. *Kirche und theologische Literatur im byzantinischen Reich* 535–536. H. G. BECK, *Byzantinische Zeitschrift* 53 (1960) 132–133.

[M. J. HIGGINS]

NICETIUS OF TRIER, ST.

Bishop; b. probably Limoges, France; d. Trier, Germany, December 5, 566. A BENEDICTINE monk and abbot, Nicetius was called to Trier *c.* 525 by the Frankish King Theodoric I (d. 534). He renewed his diocese by reform of clergy and promotion of monasticism, and by rebuilding churches that had fallen into disrepair, especially the cathedral. He is considered one of Trier's greatest bishops. Nicetius was active at several MEROVINGIAN synods, taking part in those of Clermont-Ferrand in 535, Orléans in 549, Toul in 550, and Paris in 551. He fearlessly denounced the transgressions of Kings Theodebert I (d. 547) and Clotaire I (d. 561). Clotaire banished him for his outspoken criticism in 560, but he was restored with honors the following year by King Sigebert I (d. 575). His correspondence with the Lombard Queen Clodiswind (d. 570) and the Byzantine Emperor JUSTINIAN I is evidence of his wider influence. He is buried in the church of St. Maximin in Trier.

Feast: Dec. 5.

Bibliography: J. MABILLON, *Acta sanctorum ordinis S. Benedicti* (Paris1668–1701) 1: 184–187. *Bibliotheca hagiographica latina antiquae et mediae aetatis* (Brussels 1898–1901) 2:6090–92. U. CHEVALIER, *Répertoire des sources historiques du moyen-âge* (Paris 1905–07) 2:3314. A. M. ZIMMERMANN, *Kalendarium Benedictinum: Die Heiligen und Seligen des Benediktinerorderns und seiner Zweige* (Metten 1933–38) 3:397–398.

[P. VOLK]

NICHOLAS, STUDITE ABBOT, ST.

Byzantine abbot and anti-Iconoclast; b. Kydonia, Crete. 793; d. Constantinople, 868. Nicholas joined his uncle Theophane, a Studite monk in Constantinople, at the age of ten and was sent by the Abbot Theodore (*see* THEODORE THE STUDITE, ST.) to study in a school under the jurisdiction of the monastery. He became a monk and priest, and followed his abbot into exile during the iconoclastic persecution (*see* ICONOCLASM). After being flogged and ill–treated, he was imprisoned for three years at Smyrna. In 821 he was freed, and, aided by his brother Titus, he rejoined the monastery after the invasion of Crete by the Saracens and the massacre of his family (*c.* 826).

Exiled anew in 829, he took refuge on the outskirts of Constantinople. In 846 he succeeded Naucratius as abbot and was forced out of the monastery again, but he returned to office in 853. In 858 he was among the first to oppose the depositions of the patriarch (St.) IGNATIUS and the nomination of PHOTIUS. There followed a new exile, deposition, and imprisonment. He died at the age 75, shortly after being reinstated (867).

As was the practice, his biography emphasizes the miracles he had accomplished. It was written in 916 under the fourth successor to Nicholas and is a most interesting document of the period aggravated by the later iconoclastic struggles and the affair of Photius. It is also a valuable source of precious information concerning the customs of the times.

Feast: Feb. 4.

Bibliography: F. COMBEFIS, ed., *Vita, Patrologia Graeca.* ed. J. P. MIGNE (Paris 1857–66) 105:863–926. *Acta Sanctorum* Feb. 1:544–557. T. NISSEN, *Byzantinisch-neugriechisch es Jahrbuch* 14 (1937–38) 331–339. G. DA COSTA–LOUILLET, *Byzantion* 25–27 (1955–57) 794–812. E. V. DOBSCHÜTZ, *Byzantinische Zeitschrift* 18 (1909) 70–72.

[I. DALMAIS]

NICHOLAS I, EMPEROR OF RUSSIA

B. Tsarskoe Seloe, Russia, June 25 (O.S.; July 7, N.S.), 1796; d. St. Petersburg, March 2, 1855. Nicholas, the son of Czar Paul I and Sophia Dorothea of Württemberg, succeeded his brother ALEXANDER I as ruler in December 1825. His motto during his three decades as sovereign was "Orthodoxy, Russianism, nationalism." To put his policy into effect, he sought to crush liberalism and maintained a rigid censorship and control over education. Yet these years witnessed a flowering of Russian literature, graced by the writings of Pushkin, Gogol, Dostoyevsky, Tolstoy, and others. The czar's expansion efforts won most of Armenia and the area at the mouth of the Danube, but it involved Russia eventually in the disastrous Crimean War (1853).

In his dealings with the Orthodox Church, Nicholas professed to restore harmonious relations, but he actually increased its dependence on the state. Catholics of the Latin rite who belonged to traditionally Catholic ethnic groups were tolerated, but Stanislav Siestrzencewicz-Bohucz, who had been Alexander I's chief instrument for controlling Latin Catholics, was deposed as metropolitan of Mogilev (1826). Catholics belonging to the EASTERN CHURCHES saw their union with Rome destroyed by Nicholas, who disapproved the continued existence of Catholic Ukrainians and Byelorussians. Joseph Semashko, an Eastern-rite priest, drew up the plan to incorporate his coreligionists into the Orthodox Church. After the Union of BREST was declared void (1839), the Ukrainian rite Catholics were subjected to the schismatic HOLY SYNOD.

The uprising in Poland (1830) caused Nicholas to contact GREGORY XVI, who condemned the violence of the revolution and urged Catholic Poles to be submissive to legitimate authority (February 1831). When the emperor expressed dissatisfaction with this admonition as too weak, the pope dispatched a stronger brief to the Polish bishops, *Superiori anno* (June 9, 1832). Previously Gregory XVI had complained about Russia's treatment of Catholics. In 1847 Pius IX concluded a concordat with the emperor.

Bibliography: C. DE GRUNWALD, *Tsar Nicholas I,* tr. B. PATMORE (New York 1955). A. BOUDOU, *Le St-Siège et la Russie, 1814–1883,* 2 v. (Paris 1922–25). J. SCHMIDLIN, *Papstgeschichte der neuesten Zeit, 1800–1939* (Munich 1933–39) v.1, 2. R. LEFÈVRE, "S. Sede e Russia e i colloqui dello Czar Nicolà I nei documenti vaticani." *Miscellanea historica pontificia* 14 (1948) 156–293. A. M. AMMANN, *Storia della Chiesa russa e dei paesi limitrofi* (Turin 1948). E. WINTER, *Russland und das Papsttum,* 2 v. (Berlin 1960–61) v.1. B. STASIEWSKI, *Lexikon für Theologie und Kirche,* ed. J. HOFER and K. RAHNER (Freiburg 1957–65) 7:997–998.

[R. F. BYRNES]

NICHOLAS I, PATRIARCH OF CONSTANTINOPLE

Constantinople patriarchate, March 1, 901, to February 907, and *c.* May 15, 912, to 925; b. Constantinople, 852; d. there, May 15, 925. Nicholas was born of an Italian slave on the private estates of Patriarch PHOTIUS and entered a career in the civil service; but, as a close friend of Photius, he was involved in his fall (886) and became a monk. Having been chosen as secretary (*Mysticus*) by Emperor LEO VI, he was appointed patriarch of Constantinople in 901. Nicholas's correspondence reveals the finer side of his complex character, his charity and forbearance in appeasing the strife over the emperor's four marriages, the so-called tetragamy; his prudence in dealing with abuses; and his zeal for converting the barbarians of Cis- and Trans-Caucasia. He was deposed in 907 either for opposing Leo VI's fourth marriage or for treasonable dealings with a rebel—eyewitness sources differ. Recalled either by Leo shortly before death or by Emperor Alexander (912–913), Nicholas headed the board of regency for the minor Constantine VII Porphyrogenitus, but experienced great difficulties. By taking a savage revenge on EUTHYMIUS I, who had replaced him as patriarch, he alienated many among the clergy, and he was opposed by the party in the state loyal to the Macedonian dynasty and the Queen Mother Zoë, who had been forced into a convent with Nicholas's connivance. Thus the Byzantine state was disturbed by conflict between the Nicholaites and Euthymians.

During the rise of Romanus Lecapenus (920–944), Nicholas used his position as regent to arrange a marriage between his ward, Constantine VII, and Romanus's daughter Helen, and conducted a diplomatic correspondence with the Bulgarian Czar Symeon in favor of a peace treaty. He achieved a reconciliation with Euthymius before the latter's death (917) and undertook a campaign to restore unity to the Church. In a synod (920) he issued a decree of union, settling the question of more than one marriage by legislating that a second marriage was on a par with a first, that a third was subject to stringent regulations, and that a fourth was equivalent to living in sin. However, an influential group demanded the intervention of the Holy See, and Nicholas requested the pope to send legates to reassert the original decision of Pope SERGIUS III (904–911) on Leo's fourth marriage, which, Nicholas said, had then become the decision of all (Grumel, *Regestes,* 675), namely, that a fourth marriage was against Byzantine law and the Byzantine sense of propriety, yet a dispensation was granted for the good of the state, the need of a settled succession in a legitimate heir. Pope JOHN X (914–928) complied, and thus in 923 he ended the schism between the Euthymians and Nichol-

Nicholas I, Emperor of Russia. (Archive Photos)

aites. Nicholas was canonized by the Byzantine Church. His literary remains consist of sermons on notable occasions, the decree of union, and his diplomatic letters.

Feast: May 15 (Greek Church).

Bibliography: *Patrologia Graeca,* ed. J. P. MIGNE, 161 v. (Paris 1857–66), 111:9–392. A. MAI, *Spicilegium Romanum,* 10 v. (Rome 1839–44) 10:161–440. *Cambridge Medieval History,* 8 v. (2d, new ed. London–New York 1964–) v. 4.1. H. G. BECK, *Kirche und theologische Literatur im byzantinischen Reich* (Munich 1959), 550. K. BAUS, *Lexikon für Theologie und Kirche,* ed. J. HOFER and K. RAHNER, 10 v. (2d, new ed. Frieburg 1957–65) 7:995. G. MORAVCSIK, *Byzantinoturcica,* 2 v. (2d ed. Berlin 1958), v. 1. G. OSTROGORSKY, *History of the Byzantine State,* tr. J. HUSSEY from 2d German ed. (Oxford 1956); American ed. by P. CHARANIS (New Brunswick, N.J. 1957) 190, 230–236. A. A. VASILIEV, *A History of the Byzantine Empire* (2d Eng. ed. Madison, Wis. 1952). J. DARROUZÈS, ed., *Epistoliers byzantins du Xe siècle* (Paris 1961). R. J. H. JENKINS, *Acta antiqua Academiae Scientiarum Hungaricae* 11 (1963) 145–147; ''Three Documents Concerning the *Tetragamy,*'' *Dumbarton Oaks Papers,* 16 (1962) 229–241; ''A Note on the *Letter to the Emir* of Nicholas Mysticus,'' *ibid.* 17 (1963) 399–401. P. KARLIN-HAYTER, ''La Préhistoire de la dernière volonté de Léon VI,'' *Byzantion* 33 (1963) 483–486.

[M. J. HIGGINS]

NICHOLAS III, PATRIARCH OF CONSTANTINOPLE

Reigned from 1084 to 1111. Of unknown origin, called Grammaticus, Nicholas became a monk in the urban monastery of Prodromos and in 1084 succeeded the deposed Eustratius Garridos as patriarch. His career was devoted to intense administrative and canonical activity. He attempted to regulate the difficult questions, raised by the Metropolitan Leo the Chalcedonian (1084–86), who opposed the employment of sacred objects for other than a religious purpose as a form of ICONOCLASM, including the use of the Church's jewels to supplement urgent needs of the imperial treasury as requested by Emperor Alexius I. Nicholas opposed imperial attempts to promote bishoprics to the rank of metropolitan sees, and he frequently intervened in strengthening monastic discipline, as in the case of the Wallachian shepherds on Mt. ATHOS. He condemned the monk Nilus (1094) and the Bogomil heretics of Constantinople, as well as their leader, the physician Basil (1110).

He was probably the author of a monastic *Typikon,* adapted from that of St. Sabas and attributed to Nicholas of Constantinople, and he laid down canonical responses for baptism, marriage, confession, fasting, and established a rite for the Proscomide, i.e., the preparation of the holy gifts at the beginning of the Liturgy. Despite his original antiunion convictions, in a synod held in September of 1089, and in a letter to Pope Urban, he went on record as favoring a resumption of relations with the papacy, but he proved intransigent in the controverted questions regarding the FILIOQUE, unleavened bread, and the Roman primacy.

Bibliography: *Patrologia Graeca,* ed. J. P. MIGNE, 161 v. (Paris 1857–66) 119:859–884; 127:972–984; 131:39–48; 138:937–950: J. B. PITRA, *Spicilegium Solesmense,* 4 v. (Paris 1852–58; repr. Graz 1961) 4:487–495. V. GRUMEL, *Les Regestes des actes du patriarcat de Constantinople* (Kadikoi-Bucharest 1947) 1.3:938–998. V. GRUMEL, "Un Document canonique inédit du patriarche Nicolas III," *Échos d'Orient* 39 (1940–42) 342–348. *Lexikon für Theologie und Kirche,* ed. J. HOFER and K. RAHNER, 10 v. (2d, new ed. Freiburg 1957–65) 7:986. W. HOLTZMANN, "Die Unionverhandlungen zwischen Kaiser Alexios I und Papst Urban II im Jahre 1089," *Byzantinische Zeitschrift* 28 (1928) 38–67. H. G. BECK, *Kirche und theologische Literatur im byzantinischen Reich* (Munich 1959) 660–661. R. JANIN, *Dictionnaire de théologie catholique,* ed. A. VACANT et al., 15 v. (Paris 1903–50; Tables générales 1951–) 11.1:614–615.

[I. DALMAIS]

NICHOLAS I, POPE, ST.

Pontificate: April 24, 858 to Nov. 13, 867. The son of an important Roman official, Nicholas entered the papal administration after receiving a good education. Made subdeacon by Pope SERGIUS II and deacon by Pope LEO IV, he served as chief adviser to Pope BENEDICT III. The efforts to extend the authority of the papal office made by these pontiffs, especially Leo IV, played a role in shaping Nicholas' concept of that office. His election had wide support, including that of Emperor Louis II, who was to remain a challenging presence throughout Nicholas' pontificate.

The first few years of Nicholas' reign passed quietly. But then a variety of appeals reflecting many of the tensions of the later Carolingian period began to reach Rome. Nicholas was seldom reluctant to become engaged. The result was an almost frenzied outburst of activity proceeding simultaneously on several fronts, which was to occupy Nicholas during the last five years of his pontificate.

One such case pitted Nicholas I against the eastern emperor and the patriarch of CONSTANTINOPLE in an encounter in which jurisdictional primacy in the religious realm and the relationship between church and state were at issue. That clash began when Patriarch IGNATIUS was deposed in 858 by Emperor MICHAEL III for political reasons and replaced by PHOTIUS, an experienced figure at the imperial court who, because he was a layman, was canonically ineligible for the patriarchal office. Ignatius' deposition produced two factions in Constantinople, each of which turned to Rome. Photius was first to do so, joining Michael III in requesting papal confirmation of his election. Nicholas declined to do so, partly because he received news that raised questions about Ignatius' deposition. Rather he decided to send legates to Constantinople to gain more information about that matter and to renew the papacy's claims to jurisdiction over Illyricum and to revenues from papal patrimonies in Sicily and southern Italy, both of which Emperor Leo III (717–741) had taken from the papacy. The papal legates overstepped their fact-finding commission and became parties to a synod in 861 which confirmed Ignatius' deposition. Nicholas responded in 863 by deposing Photius and declaring Ignatius restored to office. Despite the emperor's refusal to comply, Nicholas stood by his decision, letting the emperor know in strong language of the primacy of St. Peter's successor. But he left the case open by inviting the parties to present their cases once again, this time in Rome.

Perhaps Nicholas' leniency was a consequence of a new development affecting relations between Rome and Constantinople: the Christianization of Bulgaria, already in progress through the efforts of missionaries sent from Constantinople by Photius. But then the recently converted Bulgar king, Boris, irked by Photius' refusal to sanction an autonomous ecclesiastical establishment in Bulgaria, decided in 866 to turn to Rome. Welcoming the opportunity to become a party in the expansion of Christendom, Nicholas promptly summoned his own missionary party to Bulgaria along with his famous "Responses" to a series of questions Boris had posed about the conduct of Christian life; some of Nicholas' answers attacked Greek teaching and practices. The Roman newcomers immediately established themselves in Bulgaria at the expense of Greek missionaries who were expelled. Prompted by what he considered Rome's usurpation of his patriarchal jurisdiction and concerned about the threat to the Empire posed by a hostile Bulgar state allied with Rome, Photius now decided to take the offensive. He dispatched an encyclical to the eastern patriarchs summoning them to a council to be held in Constantinople in the summer of 867 to discuss Rome's intrusion into Bulgaria. At its meeting the council outlined a long list of irregularities in doctrine, liturgy, and moral usage sanctioned by the Roman Church and ended by excommunicating and deposing Nicholas, a move that posed a direct challenge to the pope's claim of primacy. Photius also took steps to rally Nicholas' many enemies in the West, including Emperor Louis II, against the pope. Although Nicholas was dead before the council's official acts reached Rome, he did have some inkling of what had happened. One of his last acts was to issue a call to western leaders to join in refuting the charges made by the Greeks against the Roman Church and its practices. While the excommunicated pope seemed to have met his match in Photius, events soon proved otherwise. Just before Nicholas' death, a palace revolt produced a new emperor, Basil I, and soon thereafter Photius was deposed and Ignatius reinstalled as patriarch of Constantinople. Nicholas' successors were left to take the necessary actions to end the Photian schism and resolve the Bulgar issue, but he had defined the principles upon which that settlement was based.

While Nicholas was engaged in the Photian affair, he became embroiled with another ruler and his subservient clergymen. This case involved King LOTHAIR II of Lotharingia, who in 860 put aside his wife, Theutberga, and sought to marry his mistress, Waldrada. While passion may have been involved, Lothair was driven by a more urgent consideration: assuring an heir to protect his realm from the clutches of his uncles, Charles the Bald and Louis the German. Theutberga was unable to produce a child, but Waldrada had already borne Lothair II a son. In order to sanction the dissolution of his marriage, Lothair enlisted the services of the Lotharingian episcopacy; under the leadership of Archbishops Gunther of Cologne and Theutgaud of Trier the bishops sitting in council accommodated the king by declaring his marriage to Theut-

Pope Nicholas I. (Archive Photos)

berga invalid on the basis of a trumped up charge of incest against Theutberga and authorized Lothair's marriage to Waldrada.

Upon receiving word of the case in the form of appeals from both Theutberga and Lothair II, Nicholas was faced with the issue of where according to canon law lay final authority in marriage cases. His first step was to announce in November 862 that a synod was to be held in the presence of papal legates to settle the issue; the synod's decisions were to be submitted to Rome for approval. In the meantime, Lothair II married Waldrada with Archbishop Gunther's blessing; in the eyes of Nicholas the king had by this act violated canon law and opened himself to ecclesiastical sanction. The synod met at Metz in June 863 with papal legates (probably bribed) present; it decreed that Theutberga was guilty and that Lothair's marriage to Waldrada was valid. Gunther and Theutgaud were commissioned to carry the synod's decisions to Rome for papal confirmation. There they received a rude shock. Nicholas summoned them before a Roman synod which not only voided the decisions taken at Metz but also excommunicated and deposed the archbishops. This unprecedented action prompted Archbishops Gunther and Theutgaud to mount a counterattack. They circulated their case widely, charging that Nicholas acted as if he were "emperor of the whole world" and urging that his tyranny be resisted. Their cause gained some support from Louis II, but little elsewhere, partly because Nicholas continued pursuing the case, writing letters to kings and major prelates seeking support for his position and to Lothair threatening him with excommunication. The pope finally decided to send another legate to enforce the papal decision. The mission, carried out in 865, succeeded in compelling Lothair to restore Theutberga as his legitimate wife and in arranging for the removal of Waldrada to Rome for judgment. But Nicholas' seeming victory was far from decisive. Waldrada fled Italy and renewed her liaison with Lothair; Nicholas responded by excommunicating her. Theutberga appealed to the pope, saying that she wished to come to Rome to have her intolerable marriage annulled; Nicholas refused her request, charging that he suspected that she had been forced to make her appeal by a husband still persisting in his defiant ways. And he continued to seek support in many quarters to bring pressure on Lothair II to abide by the papal decision. Nicholas also refused to restore the archbishops of Cologne and Trier to their sees. However, the situation remained uncertain. Only a few days before his death Nicholas wrote a series of letters indicating that he was not sure that Lothair had taken Theutberga back and insisting on canonically elected replacements for the sees of Cologne and Trier.

Nicholas' concept of the place of the papacy in the ecclesiastical hierarchy was demonstrated even more precisely in his involvement with two of the most powerful ecclesiastical figures of the era, Archbishops John VIII of Ravenna and Hincmar of Reims, both holders of metropolitan sees. As a result of the Carolingian religious reforms, metropolitan bishops steadily increased their authority over the bishops and other clergy of their provinces to the point where curbing their claims became a critical issue in the eyes of many, including the pope.

Archbishop John VIII was one of the more aggressive and capable in a long succession of prelates of Ravenna who sought by whatever means to resist submission to Rome and to carve a position of independence for their see. Immediately upon his succession in 850 John took actions that provoked many of his clerical and lay subjects to appeal to the pope for relief from his alleged tyranny. Between 861 and 863 Nicholas responded with a series of summons to John to appear in Rome, a sentence of excommunication, and a papal appearance in Ravenna. None of these measures constrained John, chiefly because he enjoyed the support of Emperor Louis

II, until the emperor finally commanded him to make peace with Rome. Nicholas then compelled John to appear before a Roman synod which restored him to communion but required him to accept conditions that severely limited his powers over his suffragans and magnified his subservient position with respect to the bishop of Rome.

A more formidable adversary was Archbishop HINCMAR OF REIMS, who after his election to that see in 845 established himself as a potent force in the religious affairs not only in his own province but also everywhere north of the Alps. Hincmar was a dedicated prelate, seriously concerned about maintaining the right order in the Church, but he was also particularly aggressive in expanding and enforcing his metropolitan authority. That effort led to a long and complex confrontation with Nicholas. The issues at stake emerged most clearly in two cases involving Hincmar's rights over clergy under his metropolitan authority.

The first centered around Bishop Rothad of Soissons who earned Hincmar's enmity by resisting what the archbishop claimed were his metropolitan rights over his suffragans. With the support of a provincial synod Hincmar finally deposed Rothad. When he learned of the case, Nicholas immediately raised the issue of Hincmar's authority in such cases. After an extended exchange with Hincmar, Nicholas finally ordered that Rothad be restored to his see, arguing that Hincmar had failed to recognize that all bishops had a right to appeal to Rome before being sentenced, that the pope had final jurisdiction over all cases involving bishops, and that the actions of all councils were subject to papal confirmation.

The second case involved a group of clerics, including a certain Wulfrad, who had been ordained by Archbishop Ebbo of Reims before his second deposition in 843. One of Hincmar's first acts as Ebbo's successor was to suspend the clerics ordained by Ebbo, a decision approved by a synod held at Soissons in 853; the synod's acts were confirmed by Pope Benedict III and by Nicholas himself. In the interval Wulfrad became a favorite of Charles the Bald and with the king's support was elected archbishop of Bourges, a move opposed by Hincmar. Wulfrad's eligibility for election hinged on whether he was a cleric or a layman, thus posing once again the question of the validity of Hincmar's deposition of the clerics ordained by Ebbo. The case eventually came to Nicholas' attention. He launched an effort to compel Hincmar to reverse his earlier decision on the clerics ordained by Ebbo. In the ensuing duel the combatants played ecclesiastical politics to secure their positions and exchanged letters, often vituperative, in which both parties sought to justify their actions in terms of their canonical rights. Their cases depended heavily on their exploitation of traditions defining the relationships between various officials in the ecclesiastical system and upon newly minted forgeries which produced texts supporting one or another cause. The most famous such forgery, known as the False Decretals of Pseudo-Isidore, consisted of a collection of pronouncements on ecclesiastical governance purportedly made by various authorities (popes, councils, Church fathers, emperors) in the distant past which sanctioned the ultimate authority of the bishop of Rome but which were actually fabricated in the mid-ninth century as a means of defining an authority that could protect the Church from intrusion into its affairs by secular authorities and their clerical supporters. Eventually Nicholas with the support of Charles the Bald was able to compel Hincmar to accept the consecration of Wulfrad as archbishop of Bourges and to admit that cases involving bishops were reserved to the pope, but the pope also accepted Hincmar's explanation of his action in deposing the clerics ordained by Ebbo. That act of reconciliation, taken just before Nicholas' death, came at a time when the pope needed the archbishop's support to rally opinion in the West against the charges brought by Photius against the Roman Church in the council held in Constantinople in 867. Nicholas had certainly not defeated the redoubtable archbishop, but his efforts had placed clear boundaries around the authority of metropolitans in the affairs of their provinces.

The dramatic encounters described above in which the extent and the nature of papal, episcopal, conciliar, and secular authority were at stake by no means occupied all of Nicholas' attention. He was actively involved in directing the activities of his own suffragans in Italy. He dealt with numerous other appeals from everywhere in the West involving a wide range of problems concerning doctrinal matters, Church governance, and discipline. He acted to promote Christian expansion not only by supporting the activity of his missionaries in Bulgaria but also that of Anskar in Scandinavia and of Cyril and Methodius among the Slavs in Moravia. He interacted constantly with the Carolingian rulers of his time, acting chiefly as an arbiter in their increasingly tangled and embittered relationships but almost never seeking a directive role in secular affairs. However, he was always quick to remind kings of their duties toward the Church and of the pope's right to judge their conduct as Christians. He maintained firm control over the governance of the Papal State and its resources, a policy that on several occasions led to confrontations with Emperor Louis II, who took seriously his rights and responsibilities as protector of the people and the lands of St. Peter. In short, through his numerous activities the papal presence was felt in a wide range of matters affecting all Christendom.

The significance of Nicholas' pontificate cannot be measured simply by a triumphant cataloging of his confrontations with various foes. In fact, his victories were limited; his death left his successors with major conflicts still unresolved. In several instances the success or failure of Nicholas' clashes depended on the support or lack of support from political leaders seeking to achieve ends that had little to do with the pope's goals. Nicholas was never reluctant to seek out the support of rulers willing to further papal causes. But after all these factors are taken into account, there still remains a distinctive and unique dimension to his pontificate that made him the most significant pope between GREGORY I THE GREAT (590–604) and GREGORY VII (1073–1085). That special feature was provided by the conceptual framework that motivated and guided his actions in the face of situations arising in the world in which he found himself.

The foundation stone of Nicholas' position was his firm conviction that all who were Christians constituted a single, God ordained body, which required a single head to guide it. Acting through Jesus, God commissioned St. Peter and his successors as bishops of Rome to fill that role. As monarch of the Christian community, the bishop of Rome was responsible before God for the spiritual welfare of every Christian and was endowed with certain powers assuring that that responsibility was met. The pope had the final say in defining what constituted true faith and right conduct. He was obligated to take whatever steps were necessary to judge and correct all whose behavior threatened orthodox belief and violated right conduct. The pope's power to serve as final judge extended over all other ecclesiastical officials, including patriarchs, metropolitans, and bishops, and over the acts of all Church councils. Papal judgments had binding power, so that in effect they became authoritative legislation defining how the affairs of the Christian community were to be conducted. Anyone, especially bishops, who felt maltreated by higher ecclesiastical officials or by the decisions of councils had a right to appeal to the bishop of Rome for judgment, but there was no appeal beyond that; only God could judge the pope's discharge of his pastoral duties. Nicholas had a place in his concept of the cosmic order for secular rulers. God had ordained separate spheres in human affairs: the spiritual and the secular, the former superior to the latter. Rulers in the secular sphere enjoyed the power to command in matters pertaining to that sphere, but they were obligated to promote the welfare of the religious community and to conduct their lives in accordance with right faith and morals as defined by spiritual authorities. If by their actions in these matters they failed to demonstrate their fitness for office, then they were subject to judgment and correction by ecclesiastical authorities, including ultimately the bishop of Rome.

Nicholas in no sense invented these concepts nor were any of them new; his position was solidly grounded in tradition. What was new was the coherence given to traditional concepts, the clarity with which they were articulated, and the relevance attached to them by the manner in which they were applied to real situations involving genuine clashes of interest. There remains the question of whether the ideas set forth so powerfully in his many letters and exemplified so dramatically in his actions were those of Nicholas himself. It has been argued, for instance, that the real mind behind his letters and actions was that of ANASTASIUS THE LIBRARIAN, a learned master of Church history, an astute ecclesiastical politician, and a highly effective writer who served as Nicholas' secretary after 862. Others have sought to demonstrate that Nicholas' ideas on papal authority were derived from a document that he knew was a forgery: the False Decretals of Pseudo-Isidore; consequently, Nicholas was little more than a dishonest manipulator of situations bent on gathering power into his own hands. Neither of these arguments has met the test of modern scholarship. Nicholas was his own man, piecing together from an almost inchoate body of traditional texts a consistent set of concepts that laid down the outlines of an ecclesiastical order that moved away from the caesaropapist and conciliar concepts that had held sway since the days of Constantine the Great toward a monarchical, hierarchical concept of ecclesiastical governance. For that reason, he found eager supporters in his own time when the unity of the Christian community was increasingly jeopardized by the fragmentation of authority, and he provided guidance for future generations of canonists and theologians in their efforts to shape the concepts of papal theocracy that so influenced the history of Western Christendom for several centuries to come.

Feast: Nov. 13.

Bibliography: Sources. *Le Liber Pontificalis,* ed. L. DUCHESNE, 3 v. (2d ed. Paris 1955–1957) 2: 151–172, Eng. tr. as *The Lives of the Ninth-Century Popes* by R. DAVIS (Liverpool 1995) 189–247. *Regesta Pontificum Romanorum ab condita ecclesia ad annum post Christum MCXCVIII,* ed. P. JAFFÉ, 2 v. (2d ed. Leipzig 1885–1888), 1: 341–368. *Nicolai I. Papae Epistolae,* ed. E. PERELS, *Monumenta Germaniae Historica, Epistolae* (Berlin 1925) 6.4: 257–690. *Epistolae ad divortium Lotharii II. regis pertinentes,* ed. E. DÜMMLER, ibid. 207–249. *Hincmari archiepiscopi Remensis Epistolae,* ed. E. PERELS, *Monumenta Germaniae Historica,* v. 8, part 1: Epistolae Karolini Aevi, v. 6, part 1 (Berlin 1939; reprinted, Munich 1985). *Hinkmar von Reims, De divortio Lotharii regis et Theutbergae reginae,* ed. L. BÖHRINGER, *Monumenta Germaniae Historica,* Leges, Sectio III: Concilia, v. 4, Supplement 1 (Hannover 1992). *Annales Bertiniani,* a. 863–867, ed. G. WAITZ, *Monumenta Germaniae Historica, Scriptores rerum Germanicarum in usum scholarum* (Hannover 1883), 61–90, Eng. tr. in *The Annals of St.-Bertin,* by J. L. NELSON (Manchester and New York 1991). *Annales Fuldenses,* a. 863–868, ed. F. KURZE, *Monumenta Germaniae Historica, Scriptores rerum Germanicarum in usum scholarum* (Hannover 1891)

56–67; Eng. tr. in *The Annals of Fulda* by T. REUTER (Manchester and New York 1992). *Flodoard von Reims, Die Geschichte der Reimser Kirche,* Liber III, ed. M. STRATMANN, *Monumenta Germaniae Historica,* Scriptores 36 (Hannover 1998) 190–363. J. D. MANSI, *Sacrorum conciliorum, nova et amplissima collectio,* 54 v. (Paris 1901–1920; repr. Graz 1960–1961) 15: 519–806. Literature. L. DUCHESNE, *The Beginnings of the Temporal Sovereignty of the Popes, A.D. 754–1073,* tr. A. H. MATTHEW (London 1908), 155–162. C. J. HEFELE, *Histoire des conciles d'après les documents originaux,* tr. H. LECLERCQ, v. 4, part 1 (Paris 1911) 237–464. E. PERELS, *Papst Nicholaus I. und Anastasius Bibliothecarius. Ein Beitrag zur Geschichte des Papsttum im neunten Jahrhunderts* (Berlin 1920). É. AMANN, "Nicolas Ier (saint)," in *Dictionnaire de théologie catholique* 11/1 (Paris 1931). F. X. SEPPELT, *Geschichte des Papsttums. Eine Geschichte der Päpste von den Anfängen bis zum Tod Pius X,* v. 2 (Leipzig 1934) 241–284. É. AMANN, *Histoire de l'Église depuis les origines jusqu'a nos jours,* ed. A. FLICHE and V. MARTIN (Paris 1947) 6: 367–395; 451–501. F. DVORNKIK, *The Photian Schism. History and Legend* (Cambridge 1948). J. HALLER, *Das Papsttum: Idee und Wirklichkeit,* v. 2: *Der Aufbau* (Basel 1951), 61–117. W. ULLMANN, *The Growth of Papal Government in the Middle Ages. A Study in the Ideological Relation of Clerical to Lay Power* (London 1955) 167–228. K. F. MORRISON, *The Two Kingdoms. Ecclesiology in Carolingian Political Thought* (Princeton, N.J. 1964), *passim,* especially 258–269. Y. M.-J. CONGAR "S. Nicholas Ier (+867): ses positions ecclésiologiques," *Rivista di storia della chiesa in Italia* 21: 393–410. I. DUJPEV, "I *Responsa* di Pape Nicoló I ai Bulgari neoconvertiti," *Aevum* 42: 403–428. J. L. WIECZYNSKI, "The Anti–Papal Conspiracy of the Patriarch Photius in 867," *Byzantine Studies* 1: 180–189. J. DEVISSE, *Hincmar, Archevêque de Reims, 845–882,* 3 v., Travaux d'histoire ethicopolitique 29 (Paris 1975–1976). R. J. BELLETZKIE, "Pope Nicholas I and John of Ravenna: The Struggle for Ecclesiastical Rights in the Ninth Century," *Church History* 49: 262–272. R. KOTTJE, "Kirchliches Recht und päpstlicher Autoritätsanspruch. Zu den Auseinandersetzungen über die Ehe Lothars II.," and K. KENNEDY, "The Permanence of an Idea: Three Ninth Century Ecclesiastics and the Authority of the Roman See," both in *Aus Kirche und Reich: Studien zu Theologie, Politik und Recht im Mittelalter. Festschrift für Friedrich Kempf zu seinem fünfundsiebzigsten Geburtstag und fünfzigjährigen Doktorjubiläum,* ed. H. MORDEK (Sigmaringen 1983) 97–103, 105–116. W. HARTMANN, *Die Synoden der Karolingerzeit im Frankenreich und in Italien,* Konziliengeschichte, ed. W. BRANDMÜLLER, (Paderborn 1989) 245–330. D. STEINON, "Interprétations, résistances et oppositions en Orient," and H. FUHRMANN, "Widerstände gegen den päpstlichen Primat im Abendland," both in *Il primato del vescovo di Roma nel primo millennio. Ricerche et testimonianze. Atti del symposium storico-teologico, Roma, 9–13 Ottobre, 1989,* ed. M. MACCARRONE (Vatican City 1991) 661–705, 707–736. K. HERBERS, "Der Konflikt Papst Nikolaus' mit Erzbishof Johannes VIII. Von Ravenna (861)," in *Diplomatische und chronologie Studien aus der Arbeit an den Regesta Imperii,* ed. P.-J. HEINIG, Forschungen zur Kaiser- und Papstgeschichte des Mittelalters: Beihefte zu J. F. Boehmer, Regesta Imperii 8 (Cologne 1991) 51–66. K. HERBERS, "Papst Nikolaus I. und Patriarch Photios. Das Bild des byzantinischen Gegners in lateinischen Quellen," in *Die Begegnung des Westens mit den Ostens. Kongressakten des 4. Symposions des Mediävistenverbandes in Köln 1991 aus Anlass des 1000. Todesjahres der Kaiserin Theophanu,* ed. O. ENGELS and P. SCHREINER (Sigmaringen 1993) 51–74. L. SIMEONOVA, *Diplomacy of the Letter and the Cross: Photios, Bulgaria and the Papacy, 860s–880s* (Amsterdam 1998).

[R. E. SULLIVAN]

NICHOLAS II, POPE

Pontificate: Dec. 6 (?), 1058 (at Siena), to July 20, 1061 (at Florence); b. Gerard in French Burgundy, date uncertain. He became bishop of Florence before 1045 with the support of Duke Godfrey III the Bearded of Lorraine, husband of Beatrice of Tuscany who was the mother of Mathilda of Canossa and Tuscany. At the urging of Hildebrand (later Pope GREGORY VII) and PETER DAMIAN, the cardinals who had fled to Siena elected Gerard to the papacy with the approval of the German imperial court. After the condemnation of Gerard's opponent BENEDICT X at a synod at Sutri, the troops of Duke Godfrey escorted Nicholas to Rome where he was solemnly enthroned and crowned in January 1059. Outstanding events of his pontificate are 1) the Easter synod of 1059 held at the Lateran in Rome and 2) the council of Melfi held in August 1059, where the Norman leaders Robert Guiscard and Richard of Capua became vassals of the Roman Church. On the latter occasion Nicholas completely reversed papal attitudes toward the Normans in southern Italy. Instead of pursuing war against the invaders, he invested them as feudal suzerain with their earlier conquests, which were thus legitimized. Moreover, he enfeoffed Robert Guiscard with territories that were still in the hands of Byzantines or Saracens. The text of Robert's oath of fealty has been preserved in the canonical collection of Cardinal Deusdedit. Robert promised to protect the papacy, to aid in future elections, to abstain from further attacks on the lands of St. Peter and to make regular census payments.

The Lateran synod of April 1059 is famous for its decree regulating the procedures for papal elections in the future by way of sanctioning the unusual circumstances of the election of Nicholas II in retrospect. Future popes were to be determined by deliberations of the Cardinal-bishops who subsequently were to consult the other cardinals and Roman clergy and laity. The ill-defined rights of the German emperors were not abrogated. The decree embodies a significant reduction of the influence of the Roman clergy below the rank of bishop as well as of the laity, in particular of the old Roman nobility who had conspired in the election of Benedict X. Other decrees issued by the synod of 1059 promoted the aims of the reform: clerical celibacy, strict prohibition of the acquisition of ecclesiastical offices and property through payments (simony), and a common life for cathedral canons. The faithful were ordered to boycott the masses celebrated by unchaste priests, a revolutionary measure designed to enforce obedience to papal decrees.

The reputation of Nicholas II in the sources as well as in historical writings has always been overshadowed by that of his powerful contemporaries, Peter Damian, HUMBERT OF SILVA CANDIDA, and Hildebrand. It is therefore impossible to determine his personal share in the major events of his reign, but there can be no doubt about its far-reaching importance. His reign ended for unknown reasons with a serious disagreement with the German court overshadowing the minority of the later Emperor Henry IV and favoring the schism of Cadalus of Parma.

Bibliography: A. AMBROSIONI, "Niccolò II," *Enciclopedia dei papi*, ed. M. BRAY (Rome 2000) 172–178. U.-R. BLUMENTHAL, "The Coronation of Pope Nicholas II," *Life, Law and Letters: Miscelánea histórica en honor de Antonio García y García*, ed. P. LINEHAN (Studia Gratiana 28, 1998) 121–132. H. E. J. COWDREY, "The Papacy, the Patarenes and the Church of Milan," *Transactions of the Royal Historical Society*, 5th Series, 18 (1968) 25–48; reprinted in *Popes, Monks and Crusaders*, no.V (London 1984). J. DEÉR, *Papsttum und Normannen: Untersuchungen zu ihren lehnsrechtlichen und kirchenpolitischen Beziehungen* (Cologne-Vienna 1972). E. GOEZ, *Beatrix von Canossa und Tuszien: Eine Untersuchung zur Geschichte des 11. Jahrhunderts* (Vorträge und Forschungen Sonderband 41, 1995). W. GOEZ, "Reformpapsttum, Adel und monastische Erneuerung in der Toscana," *Investiturstreit und Reichsverfassung*, ed. J. FLECKENSTEIN (Vorträge und Forschungen 17, 1973) 205–239. D. HÄGERMANN, "Zur Vorgeschichte des Pontifikats Nikolaus' II.," *Zeitschrift für Kirchengeschichte*, 81 (1970) 352–361. D. JASPER, *Das Papstwahldekret von 1059* (Sigmaringen 1986). H.-G. KRAUSE, *Das Papstwahldekret von 1059 und seine Rolle im Investiturstreit* (Rome 1960). J. LAUDAGE, *Priesterbild und Reformpapsttum im 11. Jahrhundert* (Cologne-Vienna 1984); "Nikolaus II," *Lexikon der Päpste und des Papsttums* (Freiburg 2001) 258. R. SCHIEFFER, *Die Entstehung des päpstlichen Investiturverbots für den deutschen König* (Stuttgart 1981); "Nikolaus II," *Lexikon des Mittelalters* 6 (1992) col. 1170. T. SCHMIDT, "Nicolas II," *Dictionnaire Historique de la Papauté*, ed. P. H. LEVILLAIN (Paris 1994) 1163. G. TELLENBACH, *The Church in Western Europe from the Tenth to the Early Twelfth Century*, tr. T. REUTER (Cambridge, Eng. 1993). C. VIOLANTE, "Il vescovo Gerardo-papa Niccolò II e le comunità canonicali nella diocesi di Firenze," *Bollettino Storico Pisano* 40–41 (1971–72) 17–22.

[U.-R. BLUMENTHAL]

NICHOLAS III, POPE

Pontificate: Nov. 25, 1277, to Aug. 22, 1280; b. Giovanni Gaetano Orsini, Rome, between 1210 and 1220; d. Soriano nel Cimino, near Viterbo. The ORSINI family was one of the most powerful Guelf dynasties in Rome. His father, Matteo Rosso, as senator of Rome, had defended the city against FREDERICK II and was a close friend of St. FRANCIS OF ASSISI, whose Third Order or Tertiares he joined in his old age. Grateful for the father's services to the Holy See, Pope INNOCENT IV appointed the son, Giovanni, cardinal-deacon of St. Nicholas in Carcere Tulliano (May 28, 1244) and provided him with benefices in York, Laon, and Soissons. In 1252 Giovanni participated in the papal mission to Florence to mediate between GUELFS AND GHIBELLINES. URBAN IV nominated him rector of Sabina and protector of the FRANCISCANS (1261) and, a year later, general inquisitor. As cardinal-deacon, he played a significant role in papal diplomacy, participating in the commission of cardinals that invested Charles of Anjou with the crown of Sicily (June 28, 1265). Giovanni also took part in the papal delegation to the German king, Rudolf I of Habsburg, which sought to negotiate the implementation of the imperial coronation and a settlement with Charles of Anjou in Sicily (1276).

Elected pope in Viterbo after a six-month vacancy, Nicholas III initiated a number of administrative reforms in the Church and the Papal States (*see* STATES OF THE CHURCH). He supported reforms in the papal curia, the most important of which concerned procedures in the chancery. He also sought to enhance the College of Cardinals, to which he appointed nine new members, among whom was his own brother, Giordano ORSINI, and his nephew, Latino Orsini. As bearer of an illustrious Roman lineage, Nicholas was eager to restore papal rule over the city, while preventing external control. To this end, he issued the *Constitutio super electione senatoris Urbis* (July 18, 1278), which forbade entrusting the government of Rome to foreign senators, a measure specifically designed to end the Angevin dominance. On a practical level, however, Nicholas refrained from renewing Angevin Charles of Anjou's rank as imperial vicar of Tuscany and senator of Rome. He further induced Rudolf I of Germany to acknowledge papal rule over Romagna (1278), a recognition endorsed by the German princes. The pope sent Cardinal Latino Orsini to take possession of the province and nominated another nephew, Berthold, Count of Romagna. Cardinal Latino Orsini also led the papal mission to Florence, which was intended to reorganize the rule of the city while terminating Angevin ascendancy (1279).

Nicholas's pontificate was marked by a number of attempts to resolve longstanding disputes. The union of churches decreed at the Second Council of Lyons (1274; *see* LYONS, COUNCILS OF) had not yet materialized because of the eastern emperor's failure to enforce its clauses (*see* EASTERN SCHISM). Nicholas demanded its strict enforcement and the use of stronger means to secure clergy obedience. The preservation of the Greek ritual was allowed only subsequent to papal approval and so long as it was not in contradiction to the unity of the faith; those prelates who opposed the union were forced to ask for absolution from the papal legates, sent to Constantinople for that purpose. The desired union, however, did not materialize, because of the great opposition it met among the Eastern Christians and the utilitarian approach of the emperor himself; furthermore, it brought about the postponement of the great crusade to the Holy Land, which never materialized.

As the spiritual leader of the Church but also because of his close links with the order, Nicholas was asked to settle the long internal struggle among the heirs of St. Francis, between Conventuals and Spirituals, who had brought the order as a whole to the verge of anarchy. The papal verdict was articulated in the decree *Exiit qui seminat* (Aug. 14, 1279), which confirmed the rule and provided the basis of Franciscan observance for the years to come. The pope revoked the concessions made by Pope Innocent IV in regard to the use of money and clarified apostolic rule over all possessions of the order, except those reserved by the donors. The papal document further declared that the religion of the Friars Minor "is founded upon the Gospel and strengthened by the teaching and life of Christ and His Apostles, rooted in poverty and humility by the gracious confessor of Christ, Francis. . . . The Rule obliges the abdication of the *jus domini* (dominion) and the retention of the *usus facti* (use)." The pope further established how this was to be observed, specifying the clothing to be worn. In the concluding paragraph, Nicholas forbade any change, interpretation, or addendum to the constitution, which was "to have perpetual validity and is to be published."

In the political sphere, Nicholas continued the policy of Pope GREGORY X, who tried to restrain the influence of Charles of Anjou in the Italian peninsula. In an attempt to end the conflict over Sicily and to restore equilibrium between the sovereign dynasties, the pope arranged a marriage treaty between the Angevin and Habsburg lineages, but was careful not to infringe upon the rights of the papacy (May 1280). The papal plans, however, proved short-lived, and the conflict broke out once again shortly after Nicholas's death. Nicholas's efforts to conclude a lasting peace between France and Castile remained futile, as well. The pope was more successful in Hungary, where King Ladislaus IV submitted to the apostolic dictates. Against the background of devastations perpetrated by the Cumani, Nicholas strengthened Christian influence in the area and appointed worthy prelates to the highest Church offices. At the request of the khan of the Mongols, he sent five Franciscans eastwards, whose mission set the first seeds of Christianity in Persia and China.

Nicholas established the permanent papal residence in the VATICAN and enlarged its palace and gardens. A political realist of great diplomatic skill, he was well known to his contemporaries for his integrity and impartiality. These characteristics were given public recognition when King LOUIS IX OF FRANCE asked for his services, as cardinal, to endorse the peace treaty that had been concluded between England and France (1258). In this regard, DANTE's accusations of simony, nepotism, and misconduct in Nicholas's dealings with Charles of Anjou (*Divine Comedy, Inferno, c.* 19) seem rather unfounded. The pope was buried in the Chapel of St. Nicholas, which he had built in St. Peter's Basilica.

Bibliography: *Les Registres de Nicolas III*, ed. J. GAY and S. VITTA, 2 v. (Paris 1898–1938). A. DEMSKI, *Papst Nikolaus III* (Münster 1903). R. STERNFELD, *Der Kardinal Johann Gaëtan Orsini* (Berlin 1905). S. RUNCIMAN, *The Sicilian Vespers* (Cambridge, Eng. 1958) 182–190. D. P. WALEY, *The Papal State in the 13th Century* (New York 1961). C. T. DAVIS, ''Roman Patriotism and Republican Propaganda: Ptolemy of Lucca and Pope Nicholas III,'' *Speculum. A Journal of Mediaeval Studies* 50:3 (1975) 411–433. A. ILARI, ''Il mandato di Nicolà III per i frati minori di Ferentino,'' *Ferentino: la diocesi e gli apporti francescani* (Frosinone 1979) 18–69. N. R. HAVELY, '''Io stava come'l frate,' the Franciscanism of *Inferno* XIX,'' *Dante Studies* 110 (1992) 95–106. P. HERDE, ''I papai tra Gregori X e Celestino V: il papato e gli Angiò,'' *Storia della Chiesa*, ed. D. QUAGLIONI, v. 11 (San Paolo 1994) 23–91.

[S. MENACHE]

NICHOLAS IV, POPE

Pontificate: Feb. 22, 1288, to April 4, 1292; b. Girolamo Masci in Ascoli in the March of Ancona, Sept. 30, 1227; d. Rome. Son of a clerk of humble origins, he joined the FRANCISCAN Order in his youth. After studying at Assisi and Perugia, Girolamo became provincial minister of the order in Dalmatia (1272) and two years later succeeded St. BONAVENTURE as minister general (1274–79). As such, he participated in a papal mission to Constantinople (1272) whose objective was to assure the participation of the Eastern clergy in the Second Council of Lyons (1274; *see* LYONS, COUNCILS OF). When he was on a peace mission to France, Pope NICHOLAS III appointed him cardinal priest of Sta. Prudenziana (1278). Three years later, Martin IV promoted him to the rank of cardinal-bishop of Palestrina, the last step before his accession to the Holy See.

Following an 11-month vacancy, Nicholas was unanimously elected pope as a compromise candidate. At first reluctant to accept, he consented to his election only after a second vote, thus becoming the first Franciscan to reach the See of Peter. The long interregnum reflects the split in the College of Cardinals between the pro- and anti-French factions, which was to worsen in the years to come. The many troubles in the city prevented the pope, though elected senator of Rome for life, from permanently residing in his see. Faced with unrest in other areas of the Papal State (*see* STATES OF THE CHURCH), as well, Nicholas allied the papacy with the powerful family of the Colonna. He appointed Pietro COLONNA cardinal and elevated other members of the family to high Church positions. Convenient as it was in the short run, Nicholas's policy submerged the papacy in the endless vendettas that affected Italian politics; contemporaries criticized it in terms of surrender and portrayed the pope as enclosed in a column (the Colonna's insignia), with only his tiara-crowned head emerging.

Nicholas left a positive mark on the administration of the papal curia, whose functions he regulated and supervised in a most proficient way. Aware of the growing importance of the College of Cardinals and the many challenges facing apostolic authority, he issued a decree, *Celestis altitudo potentie* (June 18, 1289), which assigned one-half of papal revenues to the cardinals. Nicholas's decision—the roots of which can be found in 13th-century practice—reflected the increasing importance of the college. It also encouraged the involvement of the highest members of the Church in the administration of the Papal State, which provided a large proportion of apostolic revenues. Nicholas allowed the cardinals to take part in the administration of the funds under the control of the cardinal chamberlain and to make appointments, upon papal agreement, to rectorates and other offices in the Papal State.

Like his immediate predecessors on the papal throne, Nicholas, too, attempted to find a suitable agreement in regard to the Kingdom of Sicily, where papal suzerainty had been seriously jeopardized as a result of the Sicilian Vespers (March 30, 1282). The brutal massacre of the French had led to Charles of Anjou's loss of the kingdom, the crown of which was bestowed on Peter III of Aragon as Manfred's heir. Nicholas favored the Angevin party and annulled the treaty of Champtranc (Oct. 28, 1288), which had confirmed Aragonese rule in Sicily. The pope, furthermore, crowned the destitute Charles of Salerno king of Naples and Sicily (May 29, 1289). Still, having learned the problematic lessons of Angevin influence, Nicholas forced the new king to pay him homage as overlord and to condition his obtaining any office or rank in Rome and the Papal State upon specific papal authorization. Nicholas accompanied his political gestures with generous benefices, which aimed at providing the needs of the military campaign. Notwithstanding papal efforts, however, the Angevin cause was lost in Sicily, whose destiny remained in the hands of the Aragonese kings and their affiliates.

Papal policy in Germany did not meet with much success, either: Nicholas conducted an intensive correspondence with Rudolf I of Habsburg, the emperor-elect, in order to resolve all discords between the empire and the papacy; but the king died in 1291, before his much-delayed coronation materialized. The pope also challenged the German plans in Hungary. When Rudolf appointed his son Albert to succeed Ladislaus IV of Hungary, Nicholas claimed the realm as a papal fief and conferred the crown upon Charles Martel, the son of his faithful ally, Charles II of Salerno. The pope succeeded in bringing an end to the lasting conflict between France and Aragon. After Alfonso III of Aragon acquiesced in the establishment of a triple entente with King Philip IV of France and Charles of Salerno—the main target of which was his own brother, James of Sicily—the pope annulled the excommunication of the Aragonese king. Ambitious as it was, however, the papal plan did not materialize. James of Sicily successfully attacked southern Italy and became king of Aragon himself after Alfonso's death (June 18, 1291). He then appointed his youngest brother, Frederick, as vicegerent of the island.

The crusade caused the pope still another setback. Following the sack of Tripoli (April 1289), Nicholas called for a CRUSADE and dispatched 20 ships eastwards. The papal appeal, though, did not find favor among the Christian princes, who were preoccupied with their own conflicts in Europe. Two years later, the fall of Crusader Acre (May 1291) ended the agonizing existence of the Christian strongholds *Outremer*. The appeals of Il-Khan Arghun of Persia, who asked to create a joint front against the Muslims, did not engender much interest in the West, either. Up to the end of the Middle Ages, the plans for the "Recovery of the Holy Land," though an integral part of the political agenda of Christendom, never materialized.

Nicholas was much more successful in his missionary work. Faithful to the Franciscan ideals, he enlisted the papacy in the service of the mission in the Balkans, the Near East, Persia, China, and Ethiopia. He sent the friar Giovanni da Montecorvino to the court of Kublai Khan (1289), thus establishing the first seeds of the Catholic faith among the Mongols (in 1307 Pope CLEMENT V appointed the same Giovanni the first archbishop of Beijing). In parallel, Nicholas renewed the persecution of the sect of *Apostolici* of False Apostles, whose members desired to live according to the precepts of the primitive Christian community in Jerusalem in order to effect a literal observance of continence and poverty, but in open challenge to ecclesiastical norms.

Pious and learned, a benefactor of art and architecture, Nicholas brought eminent artists to Rome, such as Arnolfo di Gambio, Pietro Cavallini, and Giacomo Torriti. This led to the restoration of the basilicas of St. Giovanni in Laterano and Sta. Maria Maggiore, where the pope was later buried and where Pope Sixtus V constructed an impressive tombstone to Nicholas's memory.

Bibliography: *Les Registres de Nicolas IV,* ed. E. LANGLOIS, 2 v. (Paris 1886–1905). O. SCHIFF, *Studien zur Geschichte Papst Nikolaus IV* (Berlin 1897). S. RUNCIMAN, *The Sicilian Vespers* (Cambridge, Eng. 1958). D. P. WALEY, *The Papal State in the 13th Century* (New York 1961). *Niccolà IV: Un pontificate tra Oriente ed Occidente,* ed. E. MENEST (Spoleto 1991). J. GARDNER, "Pope Nicholas IV and the Decoration of Santa Maria Maggiore," *Zeitschrift für Kuntsgeschichte* 36:1 (1973) 1–50. J. RYAN, "Pope Nicholas IV and the Evolution of the Eastern Missionary Effort," *Archivum Historiae Pontificiae* 19 (1981) 79–95. J. DENTON, "The Valuation of the Ecclesiastical Benefices of England and Wales in 1291–2," *Historical Research* 161:66 (1993) 231–250.

[S. MENACHE]

NICHOLAS V, POPE

Pontificate: March 6, 1447, to March 24, 1455; b. Tommaso Parentucelli, Sarzana, Nov. 15, 1397; d. Rome. Thomas, the son of a doctor, had to abandon his studies at Bologna on being orphaned. Thereupon he acted as tutor in two wealthy Florentine families, and was thus influenced by the humanistic and artistic ferment of that city. After finishing his studies at Bologna, he entered the household of Bp. Niccolò ALBERGATI OF BOLOGNA, whom he served faithfully for 20 years, accompanying him to Rome, Florence, and elsewhere, profiting by the example of his saintly patron. After Albergati's death (1443), EUGENE IV first made Parentucelli bishop of Bologna, which being in revolt refused him entry; Eugene then sent him on missions to Germany. There he successfully mitigated antipapal opposition and was made cardinal in December 1446.

On Eugene's death (1447), Parentucelli was elected pope. Proclaiming a policy of peace, he dismissed the mercenary troops; conciliated by concessions various Roman families, even allowing the rebuilding and partial refortification of Palestrina; and granted Bologna practical independence. Poland was attached to the Holy See by further concessions; Frederick III of Austria was won to Nicholas's cause by the Concordat of Vienna (1448) and a promise of imperial coronation, fulfilled in 1452. Frederick consequently withdrew his safe-conducts from the rump council of Basel, which then went to Lausanne. Nicholas agreed to extremely generous conditions for its dissolution, letting it accept the antipope Felix's resignation, "elect" Parentucelli pope, and decree its own dissolution. With the end of the council, Nicholas rehabilitated all its members in their dignities and made Felix cardinal with a pension (1449).

In 1450 Nicholas proclaimed a Jubilee, which drew pilgrims from all Western Christendom, and served at once to strengthen devotion, to reestablish the papacy as the center of the Church, and to improve both papal and Roman finances. The occasion was marred by an outbreak of plague, during which Nicholas left the city, and by a traffic disaster on the Ponte Sant'Angelo in which at least 172 people were trampled to death. The few, but worthy, cardinals he created included NICHOLAS OF CUSA, the promoter of reform in Germany.

The pope's chief claim to fame is the impulse he gave to the RENAISSANCE in Rome. He made, and in great part carried out, elaborate building plans (including a renovation of the Leonine city) in a Rome that was in ruins after more than a century of neglect. The stational churches, various palaces attached to basilicas, bridges, and roads, as well as the city's fortifications, were rebuilt, and in many parts of the Papal States fortresses were erected. To decorate his buildings he invited artists from many nations, especially from Florence. The best known was Fra Angelico, some of whose work still remains in the chapel of S. Lorenzo in the Vatican. The pope's commissions encouraged the art of tapestry, the ornamentation of rich vestments, and gold and silver work.

However, his principal interest was books. His agents searched for rare codices in many countries, an army of copyists was employed to multiply them, and some of the most celebrated humanists labored in their correction and translation. The writings of Herodotus, Thucydides, Homer, Polybius, Strabo, and other authors of Greek antiquity, as well as many works of the Greek Fathers, were rendered into Latin, and thus made available to those who did not read Greek. In his literary pursuits Nicholas spent vast sums of money and was generous to a fault to the humanists, several of them Greek refugees, who thronged to the papal court. At his death Nicholas left a library of 807 Latin and 353 Greek MSS, a very large collection for that day (*see* VATICAN LIBRARY).

The year 1453 was disastrous for the pope. In January he forestalled a plot against his life, becoming in consequence more timorous than ever; he had all the ringleaders executed. In May the Turks captured Constantinople, and the fleet of papal and Venetian ships (the latter with orders not to annoy the Turks) was too late to help. His health also deteriorated. He tried to rally Western Christians to a crusade, but the effort was ineffectual. With the same objective, he invited the Italian States to meet in Rome to arrange a treaty of peace. The meeting failed, but prepared the way for private diplomacy, leading to the peace of Lodi (1454), in which Nicholas and finally all the States acquiesced. The States, however, were not willing to risk their wealth for the protection of Christendom.

Nicholas, a man of unstained life, vivacious, but simple in manner, had the artistic spirit to appreciate all forms of art and to harmonize them, giving architecture the first place. His importance in the arts and in literature cannot be overestimated. In a deathbed speech he claimed that he had patronized the arts, not for personal fame but, by making Rome outstanding, to strengthen religious allegiance. His policy of "peace by concession" was breaking down as his reign ended, for the princes did not share his ideals.

Bibliography: Sources. VESPASIANO DA BISTICCI, *The Vespasiano Memoirs: Lives of Illustrious Men of the XVth Century,* tr. W. G. and E. WATERS (London 1926). G. GAIDA in L. A. MURATORI, *Rerum italicarum scriptores, 500–1500* ² (Milan 1723–51) 3.1:328–339. G. MANETTI, *Vita di Nicolò V,* tr. and introduction by A. MODIGLIANI (Rome 1999). Literature. L. PASTOR, *The History of the Popes From the Close of the Middle Ages,* (London–St. Louis 1938–61) 2:1–314. E. MÜNTZ, *Martin V - Pie II, 1417–1464,* v.1 of *Les Arts à la cour des papes pendant le XVᵉ et le XVI ᵉ siècle,* 3 v. (Paris 1878–82). E. MÜNTZ and P. FABRE, eds, *La Bibliothèque du Vatican au XVᵉ siècle* (Paris 1887). F. X. SEPPELT, *Geschichte der Päpste von den Anfängen bis zur Mitte des 20 Jh.,* (Munich 1956) 4:307–326, 490–493. T. MAGNUSON, *Studies in Roman Quattrocento Architecture* (Rome 1958). C. BURROUGHS, ''Below the Angel: An Urbanistic project in the Rome of Pope Nicholas V,'' *Journal of the Warburg and Courtauld Institutes* 45: 94–124. F. BONATTI and A. MANFREDI, eds., *Niccolò V nel sesto centario della nascita,* Atti del convegno internazionale di studi, Sarzana, 8–10 ottobre 1998 (Vatican City 2000).

[J. GILL]

NICHOLAS V, ANTIPOPE

May 12, 1328, to Aug. 25, 1330; b. Pietro Rainalducci, at Corvaro (Rieti), Italy; d. Avignon, Oct. 16, 1333. The details surrounding Pietro's life are scarce. He was from humble origins and was married for five years to Giovanna Mattei. He left his wife and joined the Franciscans at Aracoeli in Rome in 1310. The reports of his character are varied and range from admiration to disapprobation. On May 12, 1328, Emperor Louis IV of Bavaria had Pietro elected to the papacy as part of a campaign to dislodge the reigning Pope JOHN XXII. Using the name Nicholas V, Pietro found some popularity among Augustinian and spiritual Franciscan sympathizers. For example, in the early part of his reign Nicholas enjoyed support from such notables as William of Ockham and Michael of Cesena. When Louis IV was forced to retreat to northern Italy on April 11, 1329, however, Nicholas broke with his protector. Having also lost the support of his fellow Franciscans, Nicholas took temporary asylum in the castle of Burgaro under the care of Count Bonifacio of Doronatico. In order to keep him safe from an approaching Florentine army, Count Bonifacio secretly moved Nicholas to Pisa. Nevertheless, Pope John XXII discovered this new location and began negotiations for Nicholas' arrest. An agreement was eventually reached and on Aug. 25, 1330, Nicholas appeared in Avignon, renounced his office, and submitted to Pope John. Pietro Rainalducci received a small pension and pardon in exchange for his abdication but he was kept under house arrest until his death.

Bibliography: K. EUBEL, *Historisches Jahrbuch der Görres-Gesellschaft* 12 (Munich 1891) 277–308. *Encyclopedia of the Mid-*

dle Ages, ed. A. VAUCHEZ et al. (Chicago 2000) 2:1018. J. N. D. KELLY *Oxford Dictionary of Popes* (New York 1996) 216–217. A. MERCATI, *Studi e Testi* 134 (1947) 59–82. G. SCHWAIGER, *Lexikon für Theologie und Kirche,* ed. J. HOFER and K. RAHNER (Freiburg 1957–65) 7:979.

[J. A. SHEPPARD]

NICHOLAS HERMANSSON, ST.

Bishop, hymnographer; b. Skäninge, *c.* 1326; d. Linköping, Sweden, May 2, 1391. Having studied in Paris and Orléans, Nicholas (Nils or Nikolaus) was canon in Uppsala, Sweden, 1350; archdeacon in Linköping, 1360; and bishop of that diocese in 1374. He had educated BRIDGET OF SWEDEN's sons, and in 1384 Vadstena, the motherhouse of the Bridgettines (*see* BRIGITTINE SISTERS), was founded in his diocese. He is regarded as the greatest of the hymnographers of medieval Sweden. He was an important and stern churchman and at times opposed the royal power. The cult of St. ANSGAR became popular in Sweden through his efforts. In 1414 his canonization was attempted without result, but in 1499 Rome gave permission for his relics to be translated; the translation was carried out in 1515.

Feast: July 24.

Bibliography: *Bibliotheca hagographica latina antiquae et mediae aetatis* (Brussels 1898–1901) 2:6101–03. *Svenska män och kvinnor* (Stockholm 1942–) v.5. A. BUTLER, *The Lives of the Saints* ed. H. THURSTON and D. ATTWATER (New York 1956) 3:178–179. T. LUNDÉN, *Sankt Nikolaus av Linköping kanonisationsprocess: Processus canonizacionis beati Nicolai Lincopensis* (Stockholm 1963).

[H. BEKKER–NIELSEN]

NICHOLAS OF AARHUS, BL.

Danish ascetic; b. Jutland, *c.* 1150; d. Aarhus, Denmark, 1180. Nicholas, or Niels, was a bastard son of King Canute V Magnusson (d. 1157). He spent some years at the Danish court but later retired to his estates near Aarhus, where he led a simple and saintly life. Legend praises his chastity and charity. He was regarded as one of the patron saints of Aarhus although he was probably never formally canonized or beatified. There was an unsuccessful process initiated in Rome in 1254, and in connection with this a number of miracles were recorded.

Feast: Now unknown.

Bibliography: M. C. GERTZ, ed., *Vitae Sanctorum Danorum,* 3 v. (new ed. Copenhagen 1908–12) 3:391–408. N. HANSEN, *Vore Heigener* (Copenhagen 1917) 173–175. J. OLRIK, *Dansk biografisk Leksikon,* 27 v. (Copenhagen 1933–44) 16:615–616.

[H. BEKKER–NIELSEN]

NICHOLAS OF AUTRECOURT

Scholastic theologian; b. Autrecourt (Ultricuria), near Verdun, France, *c.* 1300; d. Metz, shortly after 1350. Having obtained his degree in arts at Paris, he became a bachelor of theology. In 1340 BENEDICT XII cited Nicholas to the papal court at Avignon on suspicion of teaching erroneous doctrines. On May 19, 1346, CLEMENT VI condemned Nicholas and ordered his works to be burned in public. His surviving writings are nine letters to Bernard of Arezzo, of which only two are complete; one letter to Giles of Medonta; a question, *Utrum visio creaturae possit naturaliter intendi;* and an important treatise, *Ad videndum an sermones Peripateticorum fuerini demonstrativi,* usually designated by the opening words, *Exigit ordo* or *Satis exigit ordo.* The complete treatise is extant in one manuscript only. In the prologue he states clearly that he does not intend to establish any positive teaching but only to examine the main Averroist doctrines and to test the validity of their demonstrations. He asks that the reader not accept as a fact the eternity of the world or atomism or any of the statements he makes in proving that the peripatetic conclusions are, at best, only probable and, at worst, quite false. He also asks that men not spend their whole life investigating the sayings of Aristotle and his commentators; rather, let them adhere to the sacred Christian law and the articles of faith. The judges at Nicholas's trial for heresy rejected such assertions as mere subterfuge (*excusatio vulpina*).

In his attack on ARISTOTELIANISM and Averroism, Nicholas began with two principles: that all knowledge comes from sensation and that there is only one valid criterion of certitude, namely, the basic principle that contradictories cannot at one and the same time be true. However, the senses do deceive man, and it is often difficult to reduce arguments to the principle of contradiction. Therefore, in most cases, one must be satisfied with probabilities. Nicholas applied these principles in criticisms of Averroist-Aristotelian physics, of the theory of knowledge, and of causality. Concerning physics, generation and corruption as described by Aristotle cannot be proved; atomism, which Aristotle rejected, is just as probable an explanation. Nicholas's method was either to prove a doctrine contrary to that held by Aristotle or to prove an Aristotelian argument to be insufficient. Concerning knowledge, Nicholas first proves that there is not a single intellect for all men (*see* INTELLECT, UNITY OF). He then shows that man is certain of his sensations, of his feelings, and of principles known by means of terms. He is aware of the objection that evidence and truth are not identical. In reply he asserts that, since the intellect desires truth, deprivation of truth would be a violation of universal goodness and man's desires would be in vain. Nicholas did not deny CAUSALITY, but he did deny its demonstrability. The doctrines expressed by Nicholas were not unique: JOHN OF MIRECOURT, a contemporary, taught many of them. It is difficult to assess the influence of Nicholas because of the condemnation of 60 of his theses in 1346 and his abjuration in 1347 (*Chartularium universitatis Parisiensis*, ed. H. Denifle and E. Chatelain, 4. v. [Paris 1889–97], 2:576–587). After his condemnation he is supposed to have fled to the court of Louis IV, the Bavarian.

Bibliography: J. R. O'DONNELL, ''Tractatus universalis magistri Nicholai de Ultricuria ad videndum an sermones Peripateticorum fuerint demonstrativi,'' *Mediaeval Studies* 1 (1939) 179–280; ''The Philosophy of Nicholas of Autrecourt and the Appraisal of Aristotle,'' *ibid.* 4 (1942) 97–125. J. LAPPE, *Nicolaus von Autrecourt: Sein Leben, seine Philosophie, seine Schriften (Beiträge zur Geschichte der Philosophie und Theologie des Mittelalters* 6.2; 1908). J. R. WEINBERG, *Nicolaus of Autrecourt* (Princeton 1948). M. DAL PRA, *Nicolà di Autrecourt* (Milan 1951); ''La fondazione del'empirismo e le sue aporie nel pensiero di Nicolà di Autrecourt,'' *Rivista critica dl storia della filosofia* 5 (1952), 389–402. E. MACCAGNOLA, ''Metafisica e gnoseologia in Nicolà d'Autrecourt,'' *Rivista di filosofia neoscolastica* 45 (1953) 36–53. W. P. SUHOW, ''Nicolaus von Autrecourt und die altgriechischen Atomisten,'' *Bibliotheca classica orientalis* 4.5, 318.

[J. R. O'DONNELL]

NICHOLAS OF BASEL

Layman, heretical Beghard; d. Vienna, *c.* 1395. Preaching in the Rhine region near Basel (*see* BEGUINES AND BEGHARDS), he proclaimed himself inspired and insisted that he was endowed with authority to govern the use of episcopal and priestly powers. He taught that submission to his direction was necessary for attaining spiritual perfection and that his followers could not sin even though they committed the worst crimes and disobeyed both Church and pope. K. Schmidt considered him the author of the *Bericht von der Bekehrung, Taulers* (ed. Strasbourg 1875), which attributed the conversion of Johannes TAULER (1300–61) to the *Gottesfreund vom Oberland* (Friend of God of the Upper Rhine), whom Schmidt identified as Nicholas of Basel. This theory has now been generally abandoned. Nicholas was burned at the stake with two of his followers.

Bibliography: H. DENIFLE, ''Der Gottesfreund vom Oberland und Nikolaus von Basel,'' *Historisch-politische Blätter für das katholische Deutschland* 75 (1875) 17–38, 93–122, 245–266, 340–354. E. W. MCDONNELL, *Beguines and Beghards in Medieval Culture* (New Brunswick, N.J. 1954). W. MÜLLER, *Lexikon für Theologie und Kirche*, ed. J. HOFER and K. RAHNER, 10 v. (2d, new ed. Freiburg 1957–65) 7:981–982.

[A. CONDIT]

NICHOLAS OF CLAMANGES

Christian humanist and theologian; b. Nicholas Poillevillain, Clamanges (Champagne, Diocese of Châlons), *c.* 1360; d. Paris, 1437. At the age of 12 he entered the College of Navarre in Paris, where he pursued literary and theological studies. He quickly won renown and made many lasting friendships in the circle of the humanists at court—John of Montreuil, James of Nouvion, Gonthier Col, and later Nicholas of Blaye; and at the papal court in Avignon, John Muret and John of Moccia. In 1393 he became rector of the University of PARIS, where his friends and colleagues included PETER OF AILLY and Jean GERSON. Urged by his friends, he went to Avignon, where in 1397 he became papal secretary under the antipope BENEDICT XIII. Having escaped death during the plague of 1398, he returned to Langres. Although he was deeply involved in the political pressures surrounding the AVIGNON PAPACY, Nicholas nevertheless seriously promoted measures for ending the WESTERN SCHISM. After Benedict's escape from Avignon, Nicholas rejoined him until the second withdrawal of obedience of 1408. He then returned to France permanently, residing in Langres, Valprofond, and Fontaine au Bois. In 1432 he returned to the College of Navarre in Paris; he engaged in writing till his death.

Above all Nicholas was a distinguished man of letters, an authentic Christian humanist. His was not a combative temperament; he never took sides directly in the factions that tore France asunder or the parties that divided the Church. It was by his letters and treatises that he intervened in the affairs of his century. Of his 151 extant letters, 138 were edited by J. Lydius, the others by A. Coville. Of his treatises, *De fructu eremi* and *De fructu rerum adversarum* were written *c.* 1408 at the time of his trials. Literary works include a tale and several poetic pieces, e.g., *Descriptio et laus urbis Januae, Deploratio calamitatis ecclesiasticae, Descriptio vitae rusticae, Descriptio vitae tyrannicae.* His other works treat of the internal strife in France (*De lapsu et reparatione justitiae* and the *Oratio ad Galliarum principes*) or deal with the Schism and the misfortunes of the Church, especially his *De ruina et reparatione ecclesiae* and *De praesulibus simoniacis.*

His vehement but justified criticism of the morals of ecclesiastics has sometimes caused Nicholas to be considered a precursor of the REFORMATION. But such was not the case. His critiques were no harsher than those of Peter of Ailly or Dietrich of NIEHEIM. He was neither a revolutionary nor a pagan. Although greatly influenced in his style and arguments by the ancient writers whom he cited abundantly, he always returned to the Scriptures and his reflections and counsels are authentically Chris-

Nicholas of Cusa, 15th century. (Archivo Iconografico, S.A./ CORBIS)

tian. Also extant are several beautiful prayers, a commentary on Isaias, *De filio prodigo, De novis festitatibus non instituendis,* and *De studio theologico,* in which he voices his deep conviction: We must not belabor the word of God; with it we must nourish our souls and give it abundantly to others.

Bibliography: *Opera omnia,* ed. J. M. LYDIUS (Leiden 1613); *Le Traité de la ruine de l'église,* ed. A. COVILLE (Paris 1936). A. COVILLE, *Recherches sur quelques écrivains du XIVᵉ et du XVᵉ siècle* (Paris 1935). J. LECLERCQ, ''*Les Prières inédites de Nicolas de Clamanges,*'' *Revue d'ascétique et de mystique* 23 (Toulouse 1947) 171–183. E. VANSTEENBERGHE, *Dictionnaire de théologie catholique,* ed. A. VACANT et al., 15 v. (Paris 1903–50; Tables générales 1951–) 11.1:597–600. G MOLLAT, *Catholicisme* 2:1165. R. BÄUMER, *Lexikon für Theologie und Kirche,* ed. J. HOFER and K. RAHNER, 10 v. (2d, new ed. Freiburg 1957–65) 7:983–984.

[P. GLORIEUX]

NICHOLAS OF CUSA

Cardinal and bishop of Brixen (Bressanone, Italy), ecclesiastical politician, philosopher, theologian, and mathematician, also known as Cusanus; b. Kues (Lat. Cusa), part of the town Bernkastel-Kues on the Moselle, Diocese of Treves (Trier), Germany, 1401; d. Todi in Umbria, Italy, Aug. 11, 1464.

Life. After studies at Heidelberg and Padua, Cusanus took the doctorate in Canon Law in 1423. He probably taught for a few years at the University of Cologne after 1425, and in 1428 and 1435 refused calls made upon him by the recently founded University of Louvain. His period of greatness began in 1432, when he went to the Council of BASEL to defend the claims of Ulrich of Manderscheid to the archdiocesan See of Trier against Bishop Raban of Speyer, who was named to the see by the pope. Although he lost the case, the publication of his work on ecclesiastical law, *De concordantia catholica,* in which he supported the superiority of the general council over the pope, caused him to become one of the most respected members of the council. In the course of the year, relations between EUGENE IV and the council became worse. Finally a break came over the question of a site for a proposed council for reunion with the Greeks. One of the presidents, Cardinal Giuliano CESARINI, led a minority group, which included Nicholas, in endorsing the pope's choice of a place in Italy; when Eugene moved the council to FERRARA, Cusa left Basel. His leaving the conciliar radicals and joining forces with the pope was a decisive point in his life. It was not, as many of his former friends claimed, a change of party based on convenience, but rather a genuine change of attitude stemming from his newly acquired understanding that the unity of the Church could be guaranteed only by the papacy.

In the winter of 1437–38, he was a member of the papal legation to Constantinople to win the Greek emperor and the hierarchy of the Greek Church over to the papal plan and to bring them to Italy. From the early summer of 1438 on, he worked so indefatigably in Germany for the cause of Pope Eugene at meetings with emperors and princes—until the concluding of the Vienna Concordat (1448)—that A. S. Piccolomini, later PIUS II, referred to him as the ''Hercules among Eugene's followers.'' In acknowledgment of his great services, Eugene's successor, NICHOLAS V, created Cusa a cardinal. In March 1450, the pope gave him (in disregard of the recently concluded concordat) the Diocese of Brixen, and himself consecrated Cusa, who had become a priest between 1436 and Oct. 11, 1440.

Toward the end of the Jubilee Year, the pope made him his legate to Germany with a threefold task: to invigorate the religious life of the people by preaching the Jubilee indulgence; to reform the religious and diocesan clergy; and to work for peace. This official journey, lasting from Dec. 30, 1450, to March 1452, was the high point of Cusa's life. The legate visited many cities and cloisters in a circle tour of Vienna, Magdeburg, Haarlem, and Trier, preached often to clergy and laity, held provincial and diocesan synods at which he published his reform decrees, made visitations, and disposed

"Cardinal Cusa with St. Peter in Chains," detail of Cusa's monument by Andrea Bregno, 15th century, Church of St. Peter in Chains, Rome (Alinari-Art Reference/Art Resource, NY)

authoritatively of questions placed before him. Utilizing competent coworkers, he conducted his journey as a gigantic parish mission (cf. J. Koch, *Nikolaus von Cues und seine Umwelt,* Heidelberg 1948, 116–148).

Around Easter, 1452, he took over his diocese, and he held office until his death. During the five years he actually reigned, he not only established the finances and holdings of the diocese on a sound basis, but strove to make it a model diocese through such measures as frequent episcopal sermons, diocesan synods, and visitations of parishes and cloisters. If he met opposition here, he encountered even more when he attempted to regain his land rights as a prince, in accordance with the medieval practice. Since Duke Sigmund of Austria, who as Count of Tyrol was protector of the Church in Brixen, would allow no encroachment on his own property rights, a conflict ensued, and the cardinal was eventually defeated. Fearing that the duke intended to kill him, Cusa fled from the episcopal city in June 1457 and took refuge in the fortress of Buchenstein in the Dolomites. In the fall of 1458 he left his diocese altogether. His attempt to return after the Congress of Mantua (1459) ended, after the duke's short siege of Cusa's castle at Bruneck in the Puster valley, with Cusa's promise to meet all his adver-

sary's demands. Pius II regarded the actions against the cardinal as an insult to the Holy See and began ecclesiastical proceedings against Sigmund. Since the latter would not relent, he was excommunicated and the province of Tyrol placed under interdict. Only after the death of Cusa and that of his papal benefactor was the long and bitter feud terminated and the papal censure finally removed.

The last years of the cardinal, however, were by no means solely occupied by this unfortunate strife, for the pope assigned him many important tasks. Without enumerating these, one may say that Nicholas was an influential adviser of Pius II. Nicholas's body was buried in his titular church of St. Peter in Chains, but his heart reposes in the hospital for the poor that he, his father, and sister built in his native Kues. According to a letter to the archbishop of Trier (Brixen, Dec. 14, 1453), in which he made known his intention to give to the poor whatever God gave him, he used the income from his benefices toward the hospital's construction, completed in 1458 (deed for the foundation: Rome, Dec. 3, 1458). Whereas much that the cardinal wrote and accomplished was short-lived, this institution endures to the present. Since the hospital contains his library, which is still priceless despite the losses it has suffered, it is a center for scholarly research.

Works. It is amazing that with all his extraordinary activity in ecclesiastical affairs Nicholas still found time to write. He had the singular gift of being able to concentrate on the tasks that confronted him and yet to be completely relaxed in his leisure, reading the Fathers, as well as contemplating philosophical, theological, and mathematical problems—often writing down his solutions with remarkable facility. Only his most important works can be mentioned here. On Feb. 12, 1440, in Kues, he finished his first philosophical work, *De DOCTA IGNORANTIA* (On Learned Ignorance). This document presupposes the Christian faith and proposes to show that man's knowledge of God is only ignorance. His second work, which was purely philosophical and was written about 1442, examines the extent of possible knowledge for man and is entitled *De coniecturis*. Since in his view an exact concept of truth is not possible for man, Nicholas calls every positive statement about truth "conjecture." In the summer vacation of 1450, Nicholas wrote four dialogues under the general title of *Idiota*—including *De sapientia* (2 books), *De mente,* and *De staticis experimentis*—and two mathematical treatises. The fall of Constantinople (1453) inspired him to write the religious treatise *De pace fidei,* and in his involuntary retreat in the castle at Buchenstein (1457–58) he wrote an essay concerning the problems of human knowledge, *De beryllo.* The works penned in Rome in the last years of his life—*De non aliud* (1462), *De venatione sapientiae* (1463), *De ludo globi* (1464), and *De apice theoriae* (1464)—reflect, for the most part, conversations in the household circle of his friends and young associates. In addition to these there are approximately 300 (mostly dated) sermon outlines and notes (1430–59). (See index by J. Koch, Cusanus-Texte I. Predigten 7. Heidelberg 1942, 48–194.) Separately handed down are the sermon the cardinal gave on June 5, 1463, at the investiture in the Benedictine convent at Monte Oliveto (Umbria, Italy), and the moving letter he wrote a few days later to the novices (G. von Bredow, "Das Vermächtnis des Nikolaus von Kues," *Sitzungsberichte der Akademie der Wissenschaften zu Heidelberg* 1955, 2 Abh.).

Thought. Nicholas's writings are, in their entire approach, non-scholastic; thus he cannot be located in any theological school of his time. He relies on the Neoplatonic Christian tradition, which originated with PROCLUS and PSEUDO-DIONYSIUS, and came down by way of JOHN SCOTUS ERIGENA and the School of Chartres to Meister ECKHART, without identifying himself with any school. Nicholas rejects the scholastic method of questions, arguments pro and con, etc., and develops a new style of philosophical essay. This itself is the expression of

Cusa's firm conviction that all human knowledge is inaccurate and that truth can be attained only by "infinitely many steps." The medieval ideal of the *Summa,* in which each question and answer has its determined place, no longer exists for him. A factor that played a decisive role in Cusa's mathematical as well as his philosophical essays was the idea—which occurred to him on his voyage from Constantinople to Venice (1437–38) and seemed to him like a "gift from above"—that contradictions will be resolved in infinity (*coincidentia oppositorum*). With the aid of this principle he believed that he, though a mathematical dilettante, could solve the twofold problem of the quadrature of the circle and the transformation of a circular arc into its length by simple construction.

Learned Ignorance. The discovery of this principle, above all, led him to his new method of "learned ignorance." Nicholas developed this first in the light of man's knowledge of God. He began with the Neoplatonic concept of God as an absolute unity. He preferred this concept to others, because the notion of the Triune is the fundamental concept of Christian theology. Absolute unity is infinite. Since no relationship between the infinite and the finite permits a comparison, and man's discursive thinking depends upon comparison, God is inaccessible to such thought. Is God so remote from man's knowledge that all statements made by Christian philosophers and theologians about Him are empty of content? According to the teaching of St. THOMAS AQUINAS, the analogy of being furnishes concepts that help man overcome the infinite chasm that separates him from God. This method Nicholas did not adopt as his own, because he did not accept its supposition, *viz,* the philosophy of being.

The method Cusa developed was a method of investigation through symbols (*symbolice investigare*). A symbol by its very nature relates to something it symbolizes. It does not represent a concept, but rather an image. Where does one get symbols? Nicholas answers: The human intellect either conceives symbols in itself or it creates them. An object is known to be as it is only when it owes its existence to the human intellect. It is for this reason that Nicholas chooses his first symbols from geometry. From a given straight line, a triangle, a circle, and a sphere are "unfolded." These are already contained potentially within the line itself. Thereupon, Nicholas asks one to make a double transcendence, i.e., a double venture beyond the finite. With the first step he arrives at the infinite straight line—there is only one—that does not contain within itself a potentiality for triangle, circle, and sphere, but rather, simultaneously, is really infinite triangle, infinite circle, and infinite sphere. This infinite geometric formulation is not only unimaginable but also beyond rationality, since the contradictions, straight and curved, are resolved in it (*coincidentia oppositorum*). In the second transcendence one must abstract from all quantity and raise himself to the absolute, simple infinity of God. He stays with this in "ignorance," but it is "learned ignorance," because, in symbols, one somehow touches God's infinity. It is as if he sees through a mirror darkly (1 Cor 13.12). The symbol points out that God's infinity in this way is unity, a unity that is simultaneously absolute fullness and that contains within itself implicitly (*complicite*) all opposites in absolute simplicity. Yet, in his *De coniecturis,* Cusa changed this doctrine by holding that God is infinitely above the coincidence of opposites.

The Cosmos. Although Cusa's development of geometric symbols is open to criticism [see M. Feigl, *Divus Thomas* 22 (1944) 321–338], symbolic theology, to which Nicholas devoted much thought to the end, is itself worthy of study. Especially profound and penetrating is the insight contained in *De ludo globi.* When God created the world He "unfolded" Himself, but in otherness, in such a way that all creatures are somehow images of God, although they have only a "contracted" being. The universe participates in God's infinity insofar as it has no given limits in space and time. It is also a unity, although not an absolute unity like God, but rather a contracted one that contains a potentially infinite variety and differentiation that is all implicitly within it. The "self-unfolding" of the universe can be seen in two ways. First, it develops step by step. This idea of a stepwise, hierarchical cosmos Nicholas could have taken from tradition. What was new was the thought, which G. W. LEIBNIZ was later to systematize, that all steps are so connected with each other that the world displays an uninterrupted continuity from the least elements to the highest spirits. The second consideration begins with the idea that everything that really exits is individually determined. If the universe is evidenced in the individual, the latter is similarly representative of the universe.

Nicholas breaks fundamentally, as one can see, with the ancient and medieval concept of the world. If the universe is infinite in space, then it has no immovable center. Earth is a planet among planets and not inferior to the others. It has a special place in that it is the habitat of man, whose nature is more perfect than that of other inhabitants of the visible world.

Man. Human nature is a world in miniature, a microcosmos—an idea first expressed in Greek natural philosophy. Nicholas, however, went further, speaking of man as a "human god" and a "second god." This is not for him the expression of a proud Renaissance consciousness, but rather the interpretation of the words God used to create man according to His own image (Gn 1.27). Nicholas sees this likeness above all in the creative power of the human intellect. Just as God is the Creator of the

real world, so is man not only the creator of his world of concepts (including mathematical concept), but also the inventor of many things for which he does not find a pattern in nature but only in his own intellect. Also, in this regard, he is like the Creator who encompasses all things within Himself. Man is finally like God in that he possesses freedom of will, although unlike God in that this freedom includes the possibility of choosing evil. Man can make of himself an angel or a beast; both are contained potentially in human nature. His moral responsibility is to develop within himself a likeness to the triune God.

Other Contributions. Nicholas was a universal thinker who illuminated and contributed to many areas of scientific endeavor without being a specialist in these fields. His contributions to astronomy and mathematics were significant. Through his "thought experiments" with the balance, he earned himself a place in the history of scientific methodology. The first geographical map of central Europe was inspired by him. So, too, can the first catechetical chart in the German language be traced to him. Above all he was an important legal historian who recognized the illegality of the DONATION OF CONSTANTINE and the Pseudo-Isidorian decrees; he wished to have the ancient sources of Germanic law compiled in a unified German law, and he was able to support his claims for the restoration of his rights as a prince-landowner through an exact knowledge of the documents in his episcopal archives concerning the development of the territory of the Church in Brixen. His all-embracing spirit set as a lifetime goal the reestablishing of a complete harmony in everything, but this grand scheme was destined to remain an unaccomplished ideal.

See Also: RENAISSANCE PHILOSOPHY.

Bibliography: Works. *Opera,* ed. J. FABER (Paris 1514: reprint Basel 1565), first, almost complete edition; *Opera omnia,* ed. E. HOFFMANN and R. KLIBANSKY, 14 v. (Leipzig 1932-), new critical edition; *Schriften des Nikolaus von Cues in deutscher Überseizung,* ed. E. HOFFMANN (Philosophischen Bibliothek: Leipzig 1936-). *The Vision of God,* tr. E. GURNEY-SALTER (New York 1928). *Oeuvres choisies de Nicolas de Cues,* tr. M. P. DE GANDILLAC (Paris 1942). Literature. F. C. COPLESTON, *History of Philosophy* 2. É. H. GILSON, *History of Christian Philosophy in the Middle Ages.* P. ROTTA, *Enciclopedia filosofica* 1:1379-84. E. VANSTEENBERGHE, *Le Cardinal Nicolas de Cues . . .* (Paris 1920). H. BETT, *Nicholas of Cusa* (London 1932). E. MEUTHEN, *Die letzten Jahre des Nikolaus von Kues* (Cologne 1958). P. MENNICKEN, *Nikolaus von Kues* (Leipzig 1932). M. P. DE GANDILLAC, *La Philosophie de Nicolas de Cues* (Paris 1941), Ger. *Nikolaus von Cues: Studien zu senier Philosophie und Philosophischen Weltanschauung* (Düsseldorf 1953). P. E. SIGMUND, *Nicholas of Cusa and Medieval Political Thought* (Cambridge, MA 1963). V. MARTIN, "The Dialectic Process in the Philosophy of Nicholas of Cusa," *Laval Théologique et Philosophique* 5 (1949) 213–268. E. MEUTHEN, *Das Trierer Schisma von 1430 auf dem Basler Konzil. Zur Lebensgeschichte des Nikolaus von Kues* (Buchreihe der Cusanus-Gesellschaft, ed. J. KOCH and R. HAUBST, 1; Münster 1964). *Mitteilungen und Forschungsberichte der Cusanus-Gesellschaft,* v.1 (Münster 1961-), v.1 contains good *Cusanus-Bibliographie,* suppls. in succeeding vols.

[J. KOCH]

NICHOLAS OF DINKELSBÜHL

German theologian; b. Dinkelsbühl, Germany, *c.* 1360; d. Vienna, Austria, March 17, 1433. He attended a good Latin school, probably in the Carmelite monastery of his native town, and in 1385 he went to the University of Vienna, which had only the preceding year been staffed with a theology faculty. He was awarded the master of arts degree and the licentiate in 1389 and began theological studies while lecturing in the arts faculty. From 1392 to 1393 and again in 1397, he was dean of the arts faculty. He received his licentiate in theology in 1408 and the degree of master of theology in 1409. For more than 40 years he lectured in Vienna; he was made rector of the university from 1405 to 1406 and was dean of the faculty of theology in 1418, 1425, and 1427. He continued brilliantly, if with little originality, the tradition of his more famous teachers HENRY HEINBUCHE OF LANGENSTEIN and Henry of Oyta. Nicholas was celebrated as the *lux ex Suevia,* and Peter of Pirchenwart (d. 1436) called him in his obituary "a veritable second founder of our University." In 1405 he became canon of St. Stephen's and in 1425, confessor to Duke Albrecht V (d. 1439) of Austria, whose ecclesiastical policy he had successfully supported. As an ambassador of the duke, Nicholas was active from 1414 to 1418 at the Council of CONSTANCE, where he greeted Emperor SIGISMUND upon his entry into the city on Dec. 24, 1414. He represented the German nation at the assembly that elected MARTIN V pope in 1417, ending the WESTERN SCHISM. In an oration addressed to Martin V, he begged especially for Martin's support of the reform movement initiated by the Abbey of MELK, a reform of which Nicholas was one of the founders and pioneers. As a member of the Holy Office, he was especially involved in the trial of JEROME OF PRAGUE. The testimonial he compiled on the "scandalous tenets" of the Dominican John of FALKENBERG nevertheless reveals Nicholas's natural disposition to be a mediator. In 1427 he was commissioned by Martin V to preach to the HUSSITES. Nicholas not only came out in favor of CONCILIARISM, as his class and rank would dictate, but he was a voluminous writer of important sermons on the subject, aside from his academic lecturing and research activity. His manuscripts have been preserved in Vienna, Munich, Melk, Klosterneuburg, Graz, and Vorau; and although they number more than 1,000, only a few have been edited. He wrote the usual commentaries on the *Sentences,* among which the *Quaestiones Mellicenses* are outstanding, and also commentaries on the Scriptures. Here he was following the scholastic tradition, which likewise set the style for his general sermons. He showed an original talent in his treatises and sermons on the ecclesiastical policy questions of his time, the Hussite heresy, and conciliarism. His *Avisamenta vel Reformationis methodus* deals with monastic reform; and another group of manuscripts includes various works, such as *De praeparatione ad missam.* Nicholas's remains are buried in the Cathedral of St. Stephen in Vienna.

Bibliography: A. MADRE, *Nikolaus von Dinkelsbühl: Leben und Schriften* (*Beiträge zur Geschichte der Philosophie und Theologie des Mittelalters* 40.4; 1965), important work for any serious study. K. BINDER, *Lexikon für Theologie und Kirche,* ed. J. HOFER and K. RAHNER, 10 v. (2d, new ed. Frieburg 1957–65) 7:984–985. A. LHOTSKY, *Quellenkunde zur mittelalterlichen Geschichte Österreichs* (Graz 1963) 331–335. G. KOLLER, *Princeps in ecclesia* (Graz-Vienna-Cologne 1964). P. UIBLEIN, *Mitteilungen des Institutes für österreichische Geschichtsforschung* 73 (1965).

[H. WOLFRAM]

NICHOLAS OF FLÜE, ST.

Farmer, politician, father of ten children and then hermit, whose influence saved Switzerland from disruption in 1481; b. at what is now Flüeli, near Sachseln, Obwalden, Switzerland, March 21?, 1417; d. in the Ranft, a nearby ravine, March 21, 1487. The first child of a devout and relatively wealthy couple, Klaus (as he was usually called) was a remarkable lad, given to praying unostentatiously, and early influencing his companions. As a youngster he fasted every Friday, and this was increased to four times a week, probably soon after a vision he had at the age of 16. This vision of a tower rising up from the Ranft deeply impressed him and made him long for a solitary life. In the fifteenth century there was already conscription among the Swiss, and Klaus was drafted into the army for the Zurich wars (1440–44) and the Thurgau War (1460). A fellow conscript recorded that Klaus "did but little harm to the enemy, but rather always went to one side, prayed, and protected the defeated enemy as best he could." During the Thurgau campaign he put a stop to the burning of the Dominican convent of St. Katharinental near Diessenhofen, where an Austrian garrison had taken refuge. Probably not long after the Zurich War, Klaus married Dorothea Wyss from Oberwilen. His longing for the life of a hermit had seemingly become quiescent, but it was still latent and caused an inner conflict that became acute about 20 years later. Owing to gaps in the Obwalden archives, most of Klaus's political and judicial activity must remain unknown, but, on his own admission, he had considerable authority as a judge and councilor. He said he did not remember ever having been unjust. Despite his obvious ability, he despised temporal honors and contrived to prevent his election as Landamman. About 1463, family life became a burden to him and, advised by a priest friend, he found temporary relief in devoting much time to meditation upon the Passion. Troubled by irremediable events, which were proving obstacles to his peace of mind, he withdrew from politics about 1465. The longing to become a hermit made itself felt ever more acutely; and, convinced that it was what God wanted of him, Klaus wrested the permission from Dorothea to leave her. Three and a half months after the birth of their fifth son, Nicholas, who was to become a priest and doctor in theology, Klaus left home, on Oct. 16, 1467. Fearing local opposition, he set off to cross the frontier, but near Liestal a seemingly supernatural intervention made him retrace his steps. His first attempt at heremetical life was made on the forsaken Klisterli Alp in the Melchtal. This came to nought, thanks to the curious, scoffing visitors who came to see him. Klaus repaired to the Ranft, to the site of the tower of his youthful vision, quite near his home. For the remaining 19 ½ years of his life, he abstained completely from food. Neighbors helped him build a log cabin; a year later, however, it was the local authorities, who, after having set guards to watch him and convince themselves that he and his fast were genuine, constructed a hermitage and an adjoining chapel. In 1469, Thomas Weldner, auxiliary bishop of Constance, came to test Klaus and to consecrate the chapel. Churchmen and politicians came to ask his advice, and people in great numbers consulted him in their troubles. Even his wife, with whom he had clearly a deep understanding, was among the visitors to the hermitage. Friendly, affectionate, and thoughtful, he had a remarkable gift for encouraging the sad and depressed. To all he was known as ''Bruder Klaus.'' Owing to his efforts, the quarrelling cantons came together at the Diet of Stans in December of 1481; and when, during the assembly, they were on the point of returning home to settle matters by arms, his advice to the delegates, transmitted by Heinrich am Grund, the parish priest, restored peace. Nicholas was buried at Sachseln, where his body still lies. He was canonized in 1947 and is venerated by Catholics and Protestants alike. His importance as a figure of peace and brotherhood can hardly be exaggerated. Owing to his unique visions and prodigious memory, he has attracted the attention of psychologists as well.

Feast: March 21; Sept. 25 (Switzerland).

Bibliography: R. DURRER, *Bruder Klaus,* 2 v. (Sarnen, Switz. 1917–21). K. VOKINGER, *Bruder Klaus: Sein Leben* (Stans, Switz. 1947). F. BLANKE, *Bruder Klaus von Flüe: Seine innere Geschichte* (Zurich 1948). M. L. VON FRANZ, *Die Visionen des Niklaus von Flüe* (Zurich 1959). G. R. LAMB, *Brother Nicholas* (New York 1955). I. LÜTHOLD-MINDER, *Bruder Klaus ich danke dir* (Sarnen 1975);

St. Nicholas of Myra. (©Bettmann/CORBIS)

Bruder Klaus: Wunder und Verehrung (Solothurn 1977). C. HÜRLI-MANN, H. KRÖMLER, and L. ELSER, *Bruder Klaus von Flue* (Zurich 1983), meditations. M. BOLLIGER, *Ein Stern am Himmel: Niklaus von Flüe* (Hitzkirch 1987). W. STOKAR, *Niklaus von Flüe* (Schaffhausen 1993). *Dorothea, die Ehefrau des hl. Niklaus von Flüe,* ed. W. T. HUBER (Freiburg, Switz. 1994). M. ZÜFLE, *Ranft: Erzählung und Erzählung der Erzählungen* (Zurich 1998).

[T. BOOS]

NICHOLAS OF MYRA, ST.

Bishop of Myra in Lycia, first half of the fourth century, but often called Nicholas of Bari (Italy). No historically trustworthy evidence of his ancestry or the events of his life exists, except for the fact of his episcopate. Legends have him born in the Lycian town of Patara, imprisoned in the Diocletian persecution, and present at the Council of Nicaea I, and fix his death date at 345 or 352. JUSTINIAN I built a church in his honor in the early sixth century (Procopius, *De aedificiis* 1.6), and Basil the Macedonian, an oratory in the imperial palace about 870. In the West, the first pope to bear his name built a basilica in his honor in the Lateran (*c.* 860). His cult was brought to Germany by the Byzantine Princess Theophano, wife of Otto II (973–983). It came to Italy with the theft in 1087 of his body by Italian soldiers and its ''translation'' to Bari. More than 2,000 churches are dedicated to him in France and Germany, and about 400 in England. Russia, Sicily, Lorraine, and Greece honor him as patron. The principal miracle-legends deal with his liberation of three unjustly imprisoned officers; his secret provision of dowries for three poor girls; and his deliverance of three innocent youths condemned to death. The oldest documentary evidence of the Nicholas legends is an eleventh-century manuscript in Karlsruhe Library. The dowry legend was combined in Germany with local folklore to make St. Nicholas into the bringer, on the eve of his feast, of secret presents for children; in the English-speaking countries his name was corrupted into Santa Claus, and the legend became associated with Christmas Eve.

Feast: Dec. 6; May 9 (translation of relics to Bari).

Bibliography: G. ANRICH, *Hagios Nikolaos,* 2 v. (Leipzig 1913–17). C. W. JONES, *The Saint Nicholas Liturgy and Its Literary Relationships* (Berkeley 1963); *Saint Nicholas of Myra, Bari, and Manhattan* (Chicago 1978). M. EBON, *Saint Nicholas: Life and Legend* (New York 1975). C. MÉCHIN, *Saint Nicholas: fêtes et traditions populaires d'hier et d'aujourd'hui* (Paris 1978). O. JODOGNE, ed., *Miracle de saint Nicolas et d'un juif* (Geneva 1982). A. VON EUW, *Sankt Nikolaus kommt auf Besuch* (Lucerne 1983), legends. N. P. SEVCENKO, *The Life of Saint Nicholas in Byzantine Art* (Turin 1983). E. G. CLARE, *St. Nicholas: His Legends and Iconography* (Florence 1985). A. ARENS, *Untersuchungen zu Jean Bodels Mirakel "Le jeu de Saint Nicolas"* (Stuttgart 1986). L. MARTINO, *Le reliquie di S. Nicola* (Bari 1987). R. GHESQUIERE, *Van Nicolaas van Myra tot Sinterklaas* (Leuven 1989). I. ANDREEV, *The Miracles of Saint Nicholas* (Sofia 1993). W. MEZGER, *Sankt Nikolaus: zwischen Kult und Klamauk* (Ostfildern 1993). A. SHEPARD, *The Baker's Dozen: A Saint Nicholas Tale* (New York 1995). E. M. TREHARNE, *The Old English Life of St Nicholas with the Old English Life of St Giles* (Leeds, UK 1997).

[A. G. GIBSON]

NICHOLAS OF PRUSSIA, BL.

Benedictine monk; b. Prussia, *c.* 1379; d. monastery of San Niccolo del Boschetto, near Genoa, Italy, Feb. 23, 1456. He made his vows on Feb. 6, 1414, under Abbot Louis Barbo (d. 1443) in the reformed monastery of Santa Giustina in Padua. Subsequently, he lived for a time in San Giorgio, Venice, and in SAN BENEDETTO DI POLIRONE near Mantua before going to Genoa, where he was made prior and novice master by 1430. He was noted for his zealous observance of the monastic rule, his holiness of life, and his gift of miracles. His relics are at San Giuliano d'Albaro, near Genoa. His cult is not approved.

Feast: Feb. 23.

Bibliography: A. M. ZIMMERMANN, *Kalendarium Benedictinum: Die Heiligen und Seligen des Benediktinerorderns und seiner Zweige* (Metten 1933–38) 1:247–249. F. G. HOLWECK, *A Biographical Dictionary of the Saints* (St. Louis 1924) 741–742.

A. ZIMMERMANN, *Lexikon für Theologie und Kirche* (Freiburg 1930–38) 7:588. J. JANUENSI, *Vita* in B. PEZ, *Thesaurus anecdotorum novissimus* (Augsburg 1721–29) 2.3:309–340.

[M. F. MCCARTHY]

NICHOLAS OF STRASSBURG

Dominican theologian and mystic; fl. 1323 to 1329. A member of the German province, he was a contemporary of JOHN OF STERNGASSEN, Gerard of Sterngassen, and Meister ECKHART. He may have studied theology in Paris. Before 1323 he wrote a *Summa philosophica* (5 bks.; MS Vat. lat 3091), in which he synthesized the doctrine of ALBERT THE GREAT and THOMAS AQUINAS. Between 1323 and 1329 he was lector at the priory in Cologne and vicar of the master general in reforming the German province. During the process against Eckhart in 1326 he defended his confrere and exonerated his doctrines. When the archbishop of Cologne renewed charges against Eckhart in 1327, Nicholas was also implicated. During the crisis he was excommunicated, possibly out of revenge, by a confrere, Hermann of Höchst; but the pope absolved him completely that same year. His best-known work is *De adventu Christi,* written about 1323. Some scholars have called it a plagiarism because it is a compilation drawn from two treatises by JOHN (QUIDORT) OF PARIS. Although he was a popular preacher, only 13 of his German sermons are extant; they reflect a practical approach and a sound theological piety.

Bibliography: M. GRABMANN, *Mittelalterliches Geistesleben,* 3 v. (Munich 1926–56) 1:392–431. E. FILTHAUT, *Lexikon für Theologie und Kirche,* ed. J. HOFER and K. RAHNER (Freiburg 1957–65) 7:998. H. DENIFLE, "Der Plagiator Nicolaus von Strassburg," *Archiv für Literatur- und Kirchengeschichte des Mittelalters,* ed. H. DENIFLE and F. EHRLE (Freiburg 1885–1900) 4:312–329. F. STEGMÜLLER, *Repertorium commentariorum in Sententias Petri Lombardi* (Würzburg 1947) 1:272.

[J. F. HINNEBUSCH]

NICHOLAS OF TOLENTINO, ST.

Augustinian friar; b. 1245, Sant'Angelo in Pontano; d. Tolentino, Sept. 10, 1305. He was named after St. Nicholas of Myra, whose shrine at Bari was visited by his parents before his birth. He entered the Augustinians around the time of the order's final stage of formation in 1256. After ordination to the priesthood, he served in various houses of the order in the region of the Marches until he received his final appointment to Tolentino around 1275. The main sources of information are a *Life* by Peter of Monterubbiano (dated 1326 by the Bollandists) and the documents collected in the investigation (1325) con-

"Death of Saint Nicholas of Tolentino," 14th-century fresco painting by Pietro da Rimini, Basilica of St. Nicholas, Tolentino, Italy. (©Archivo Iconografico, S.A./CORBIS)

ducted for his canonization. Peter presents Nicholas as a model religious, favored by God with visions, able to work miracles, combating demons, observing severe fasts, nightly vigils and strict poverty, yet compassionate towards others, living and dead. Recent studies have paid greater attention to the contemporary testimony collected in the canonical investigation. The witnesses emphasize his apostolate as a kindly confessor, a prudent counselor, an advocate and helper of the poor and sick, and a powerful intercessor before God. After many delays in the process, Pope Eugene IV canonized him in 1446. Nicholas was the first member of the Augustinians to receive this honor. Devotion to him spread in Italy, Spain, France, Belgium and Germany and later in the 16th and 17th centuries in Latin America. In the United States several parishes as well as some institutions of the Augustinians bear his name. He is revered as the patron of the souls in purgatory. He is usually represented wearing his habit with a star on his chest and holding a lily or a book. Magnifi-

cent 14th-century frescos adorn his richly decorated shrine at Tolentino.

Feast: Sept. 10.

Bibliography: Sources. *Acta sanctorum* Sept. 3:636–743. *Il processo per la canonizzazione di S. Nicola da Tolentino,* ed. N. OC-CHIONI (Rome 1984). Literature. D. GENTILE, *Un asceta e un apostolo: San Nicola da Tolentino* (2d ed.; Tolentino 1978), with extensive bibliography; *Bibliotheca sanctorum* 9:953 968. *San Nicola, Tolentino, le Marche: Contributi e ricerche sul processo (a. 1325) per la canonizzazione di San Nicola da Tolentino,* Convegno Internazionale di Studi Tolentino, 4–7 settembre 1985 (Tolentino 1985).

[K. A. GERSBACH]

NICHOLAS ORESME

French theologian and a founder of modern science and mathematics; b. Normandy, Diocese of Bayeux, *c.*

Page from a manuscript of "Nichomachean Ethics," written by Aristotle, translated by Nicholas Oresme: Oresme presenting his translation to King Charles V of France.

1320; d. Lisieux, July 11, 1382. A student of theology at Paris in 1348, he was grand master of the Collège de Navarre by 1356. In 1362 he was canon of Rouen and in 1364 dean of the cathedral. Some time before 1370 he became chaplain of King Charles V. He was consecrated bishop of Lisieux in 1378.

There are recent editions of some of his writings, but others are extant only in manuscripts and early editions. He wrote both in Latin and in French. At the request of Charles V he translated into French the *Nicomachean Ethics, Politics,* and *De caelo* of Aristotle and the pseudo-Aristotelian *Economics.* These translations were important in the development of the French language. Oresme's theological writings include *Contra astronomos judiciarios,* with a French adaptation *Livre de divinacions,* in which he argues against astrology and the magic arts, and a Christological treatise, *De communicatione idiomatum in Christo.*

Oresme is best known as a scientist, mathematician, and economist. His most original scientific ideas are contained in two French works, *Traité de la sphère* and *Livre du ciel et du monde.* Against Aristotle he held, on the ground of the omnipotence of God, the possibility of many universes and the movement of man's universe in space. He questioned the Aristotelian theory that the earth is at rest while the heavens rotate about it, pointing out that motion is relative to the observer: the heavens appear to revolve around the earth, but the opposite may appear to an observer in the heavens. He was a precursor of Copernicus in holding that the appearances are explained more simply by supposing the daily motion of the earth than the motion of the heavens. Although Oresme saw no obstacle to this theory in Scripture and answered objections to it, he did not hold it as certain; in the end he accepted the traditional opinion.

Oresme's contributions to mathematics include the notion of fractional powers and rules for operating them. He prepared the way for analytical geometry by his use of graphs and algebraic functions to represent variations in the intensity and extension of qualities, such as heat and motion. Oresme's *De origine, natura, jure, et mutationibus monetarum* was the first scientific study of the problem of money.

Bibliography: Works. *Traité de la sphère* (Paris 1508); *Tractatus de latitudinibus formarum* (Paris 1482), an abridgement of the unedited *Tractatus de figuratione potentiarum et mensurarum difformitatum; Le Livre du ciel et du monde,* ed. A. D. MENUT and A. J. DENOMY, *Mediaeval Studies,* (Toronto–London 1938–), 3 (1941) 185–280; 4 (1942) 159–297; 5 (1943) 167–333. *The De Moneta of Nicholas Oresme and English Mint Documents,* tr. C. JOHNSON (New York 1956). *Quaestiones super Geometriam Euclidis,* ed. H. L. BUSARD (Leiden 1961), tr., *Le Livre de Éthiques d'Aristote,* ed. A. D. MENUT (New York 1940). *Le Livre de Yconomique d'Aristote,* ed. A. D. MENUT (Philadelphia 1957). Studies. L. F. MEUNIER, *Essai sur la vie et les ouvrages de Nicole Oresme* (Paris 1857). P. M. M. DUHEM, *Études sur Léonard de Vinci,* 3 v. (Paris 1903–16; repr. 1955), 3:346–405. *Le Système du monde,* v.7 (Paris 1956), *passim.* A. MAIER, *Die Vorläufer Galileis im 14. Jahrhundert* (Rome 1949), *passim.* A. C. CROMBIE, *Augustine to Galileo: The History of Science, 400–1650* (Cambridge, Mass. 1953). G. W. COOPLAND, *Nicole Oresme and the Astrologers: A Study of His Livre de divinacions* (Liverpool 1952). M. CLAGETT, *The Science of Mechanics in the Middle Ages* (Madison, Wis. 1959), *passim.*

[A. MAURER]

NICHOLAS PAGLIA, BL.

Disciple of St. DOMINIC, preacher, founder of priories at Trani, Perugia, and, perhaps, Todi; b. Giovinazzo, near Bari, Italy, 1197; d. Perugia, Italy, Feb. 11, 1255. While studying law in BOLOGNA, he heard Dominic preach (1218) and joined the Dominican Order. He was twice provincial of the Roman province (1230–35 and in 1255). In 1231 GREGORY IX appointed him to reform the overly strict Benedictine monks of SANT' ANTIMO. He was present (1233) at the translation of Dominic's body. Prudent, charitable, and compassionate, especially to fellow religious, as superior he preached fraternal charity and joy and asked for willing, loving obedience. His relics repose under the high altar in Perugia. LEO XII beatified him on March 26, 1828. He is pictured, once by Fra Angelico (*see* FIESOLE, GUIDO DA), with rods (authority), a book (learning), and church models (founder).

Feast: Feb. 14.

Bibliography: B. ANDRIANI, *Il Beato Nicola Paglia da Giovinazzo* (Molfetta 1959). A. WALZ, *Lexikon für Theologie und Kirche,* ed. J. HOFER and K. RAHNER, 10 v. (2d, new ed. Freiburg 1957–65) 7:996–997. G. CAPPELLUTI, *Beato Nicola Paglia O. P. di Giovinazzo* (Molfetta 1967). D. MALDARELLI, *Maria SS. di Corsignano, Beato Nicola Paglia O. P.* (Molfetta 1968).

[B. CAVANAUGH]

NICHOLAS TREVET

Dominican theologian, historian, humanist; b. Somerset, England, *c.* 1265; d. after 1334. The son of a justice in eyre, Sir Thomas Trevet (d. 1283), he entered the DOMINICANS, studied at Oxford before 1300, and succeeded WILLIAM OF MACCLESFELD, OP, as regent master at the university (1303–07). His *Quaestiones disputatae, Quodlibeta I–V,* and commentary on Genesis and Exodus belong to this period. In 1307 the general chapter of his order at Strasbourg gave special commendation to these Biblical commentaries and the master general, Aymeric, urged him to complete his commentary on the Pentateuch. Later he wrote a commentary on Leviticus and sent it to Aymeric. Between 1307 and 1314 he lived in Paris, gathering material for his *Annales sex regum Angliae* (1135–1307), for his future Latin *Historia,* dedicated to Hugh of Angoulême, archdeacon of Canterbury, and for his last work, the *Cronycles,* written in Anglo-Norman (one version being dedicated to Princess Mary, sister of Edward II who was a nun of Amesbury Abbey). Returning to England, he resumed teaching at Oxford (1314–*c.* 1317) and developed a humanistic interest in the ancient classics. He commented on Seneca's *Declamationes* (*Controversiae*)—which he dedicated to John of Lenham, OP, confessor to Edward II (before 1314)—as well as on Boethius, Cicero, and Virgil. At the request of Nicholas of Prato, papal legate to England and dean of the College of Cardinals, he wrote a commentary on the *Tragedies* of Seneca; he was commissioned by Pope John XXII to write a commentary on Livy. He wrote also the earliest commentary on St. Augustine's *De civitate Dei,* later replaced in popularity and excellence by the work of his junior contemporary THOMAS WALEYS. In 1324 he was lector of the Dominican priory in London. He must still have been alive in 1334, since he mentions in the Anglo-Norman *Cronycles* that the reign of John XXII was 19 years.

Although not an original or speculative thinker, he was a pioneer in Biblical theology, historical accuracy, classical philology, and Christian humanism. His commentaries on Scripture revived Biblical studies in the Order of Preachers, and his interest in classical authors stimulated the renaissance of humanism in Europe. The popularity of his writings, which include approximately 30 works, is attested to by the more than 300 MSS that are extant.

Bibliography: *Il commento di Nicola Trevet al Tieste di Seneca,* ed. E. FRANCESCHINI (Milan 1938). J. QUÉTIF and J. ÉCHARD, *Scriptores Ordinis Praedicatorum* (New York 1959) 1.2: 561–565. A. B. EMDEN, *A Biographical Record of the University of Oxford from A.D. 1500* (Oxford 1957–59) 3:1902–03. D. A. CALLUS, *Lexicon für Theologie und Kirche,* ed. J. HOFER and K. RAHNER (Freiburg 1957–65) 7:999–1000. P GLORIEUX, *La littérature quodlibétique* (Kain 1925) 1:246–254. F. STEGMÜLLER, *Repertorium biblicum medii aevi* (Madrid 1949–61) 4:6032–38. F. EHRLE, "N.T., sein Leben seine *Quodlibet* und *Quaestiones ordinariae,*" *Festgabe Clemens Baeumker, Beiträge zur Geschichte der Philosophie und Theologie de Mittelalters* (1923) 1–63. R. J. DEAN, "Cultural Relations in the Middle Ages: N.T. and Nicholas of Prato," *Studies in Philology* 45 (1948) 541–564. B. SMALLEY, *English Friars and Antiquity in the Early 14th Century* (New York 1961).

[J. A. WEISHEIPL]

NICHOLS, GEORGE, BL.

Priest, martyr; b. *c.* 1550 at Oxford, England; hanged, drawn, and quartered there, July 5, 1589. George Nichols (also given as Nicolls or Nicholas) studied at Brasenose College, Oxford, then was assistant master at St. Paul's School, London. He arrived at Rheims with Bl. Thomas PILCHARD, Nov. 20, 1581, but went on to Rome. He was ordained priest (1583) at Rheims by Cardinal Louis de Guise. During his six-year ministry in and around Oxford, he was responsible for many conversions, including that of a celebrated highwayman during his confinement at Oxford Castle. After his arrest at Catherine Wheel Inn by the university officers, he proved to be a stout controversialist. Nichols was sent to Bridewell Prison, London, together with BB. Richard YAXLEY, Thomas BELSON, and Humphrey PRITCHARD. On June 30, all four were sent to Oxford for trial and were condemned. The heads of the priests were set up on the castle, and their quarters on the four city gates. They were beatified by Pope John Paul II on Nov. 22, 1987 with George Haydock and Companions.

Feast of the English Martyrs: May 4 (England).

See Also: ENGLAND, SCOTLAND, AND WALES, MARTYRS OF.

Bibliography: Harleian Society Publications, I, II (London, 1904), 1124. Oxford Historical Society Publications, XXXIX (Oxford, 1899), 109, 110; LV (Oxford, 1910), 33. R. CHALLONER, *Memoirs of Missionary Priests,* ed. J. H. POLLEN (rev. ed. London 1924), I, nos, 73–75. J. H. POLLEN, *Acts of English Martyrs* (London 1891).

[K. I. RABENSTEIN]

NICLAES, HENDRIK

Founder of the "House of Love," or NICOLAITES or Familists; b. Münster, Westphalia, 1502; d. 1580. In Münster, Niclaes (Nicholas) attended Latin school and worked in his father's business. At the age of 27, when he was suspected of Lutheran beliefs, he moved to Amsterdam, where he was under suspicion of being a "Münsterite." In 1541 he established a business at Emden, East Friesland, and gathered some followers. He was imprisoned, but escaped and went to the Netherlands, London, and Cologne. He wrote more than 50 pamphlets dealing with his prophecies and mystical pantheism and also carried on a literary dispute with David JORIS. About his relationship with the latter, an opponent said: "David George layed the egg and Henry Niclaes brought forth the chicken." He does not seem to have had any other Anabaptist connections. Niclaes emphasized an actual righteousness and holiness, which was practiced in the "House of Love." Connected with this was an attempted degree of enlightenment and divinization. He had some followers in England and the Netherlands, among whom was the printer Christoffel Plantijn of Antwerp. By the end of the 17th century the Nicolaites had disappeared.

Bibliography: F. NIPPOLD, "Heinrich Niclaes und das Haus der Liebe," *Zeitschrift für die historische Theologie* 32 (1862) 321–402. R. M. JONES, *Studies in Mystical Religion* (London 1909). G. H. WILLIAMS, *The Radical Reformation* (Philadelphia 1962). K. ALGERMISSEN, *Lexikon für Theologie und Kirche,* ed. J. HOFER and K. RAHNER, 10 v. (2d, new ed. Freiburg 1957–65) 4:21. G. B. BAREILLE, *Dictionnaire de théologie catholique,* ed. A. VACANT et al., 15 v. (Paris 1903–50; Tables générales 1951–) 5.2:2070–72.

[C. KRAHN]

NICODEMUS OF MAMMOLA, ST.

Calabrian-Greek ascetic, monastic founder; b. Cirò, *c.* 900; d. Mammola, March 25, 990. While still a youth, he became a Basilian monk in the famous monastic eparchy of the Mercurion, under the spiritual guidance of St. Fantino (d. *c.* 980), who also directed St. NILUS OF ROSSANO. Later on, he withdrew to Mt. Cellerano, where for many years he lived a strict ascetic life. His virtue attracted many disciples, so that the hermitage of Cellerano became a large monastic community. About 975 he moved to the region of Gerace. Subsequently he built in the woods near Mammola a monastery that after his death in 990 was dedicated to his memory. His relics are venerated in the principal church of Mammola, whose patron saint he has been since 1630. A life, written by the monk Nilus at the end of the 12th century, is the principal source for his biographers.

Feast: March 12.

Bibliography: A. AGRESTA, *Vita di s. Nicodemo Abbate* (Rome 1677). A. AROMOLO, *Vita di s. Nicodemo di Cirò* (Cirò 1901). V. ZAVAGLIA, *Vita del santo padre nostro Nicodemo* (Mammola 1961). V. SALETTA, *Vita inedita di s. Nicodemo di Calabria dal cod. Messan,* 30 (Rome 1964).

[M. PETTA]

NICODEMUS THE HAGIORITE

Monk; b. Naxos, 1748; d. Mt. Athos, July 14, 1809. He was baptized Nicholas; he made his studies at Smyrna and retired to Naxos in 1770 to escape Turkish reprisals. In 1775 he entered MOUNT ATHOS, where he took the name Nicodemus. An encounter with Macarius of Corinth in 1777 confirmed his scholarly aspirations and he was persuaded to prepare an augmented edition of Macarius's *Philocalia,* or collection of oriental patristic texts dealing with mental prayer. This edition had a great influence on the revival of HESYCHASM and the JESUS PRAYER. His revised edition of Macarius's work on frequent Communion was condemned by Procopius of Smyrna in 1785, but his position was accepted as orthodox by the Synod of Constantinople in 1819.

Nicodemus, a prolific writer, contributed to the development of hagiographical, liturgical, scriptural, mystical, and canonical interest in the Oriental churches. His most important work, the *Pedalion,* or *Rudder of the Ship of Knowledge,* is a commentary on Greek canon law, which manifests certain anti-Roman tendencies. These are usually attributed to interpolations by its editor, the monk Theodoritus, though Nicodemus elsewhere manifests obvious prejudices against Roman ecclesiastical institutions. Nevertheless, to stimulate the cultivation of mental prayer he published, in modern Greek, adaptations of both the *Spiritual Combat* of Lorenzo SCUPOLI and the *Spiritual Exercises* of IGNATIUS LOYOLA. His *Philocalia* (Venice 1782), or collection of writings on spiritual sobriety, and his *Enchiridion of Counsels* (Venice 1801), or doctrine of the custody of the five senses, the imagination, and the heart are of major influence in the contemporary Greek spirituality.

Nicodemus was solemnly canonized a saint of the Greek Church on May 31, 1955. A third edition of the *Philocalia* (Athens 1958) caused a considerable revival of interest in his writings.

Bibliography: V. GRUMEL, *Lexikon für Theologie und Kirche*[2] 4:1321; *Dictionnaire de théologie catholique* 11.1:486–490. P. MEYER, "Beiträge zur Kenntnis der neueren Geschichte und des gegenwärtigen Zustandes der Athosklöster," *Zeitschrift für Kirchengeschichte* 11 (1889) 395–435, 539–576. L. PETIT, "La Grand controverse des Colybes," *Échos d'Orient* 2 (1899) 321–331. M. VILLER, *Revus d'ascétique et de mystique* 5 (1924) 174–177.

[G. A. MALONEY]

NICOLA DA GESTURI, BL.

Baptized Giovanni Angelo Salvatore, called "Giovanni Medda," Capuchin; b. Aug. 5, 1882; Gesturi, Cagliari (archdiocese of Oristano, Sardegna), Italy; d. June 8, 1958, Cagliari. Giovanni Medda, the sixth child of a poor family, felt called to religious life but lacked the means to pursue it. He was raised by his eldest sister following the death of his parents, Giovanni Messa Serra and Priama Cogoni Zedda. After completing his primary education he worked on the farm. With the help of his parish priest, he entered the Capuchin convent of San Antonio Gesturi as a tertiary oblate (1911) and took the habit and name Fra Nicola (Oct. 30, 1913). He pronounced his first vows the following year on November 1 and his solemn vows on Feb. 16, 1919. During his first ten years of religious life, he served as cook in several Sardinian monasteries (Sassari, Oristano, and Sanluri). For the next 34 years (from 1924) Nicola was entrusted with collecting alms for the monastery in Cagliari and nearby Campidano. He developed an attitude of constant prayer, which animated all his actions. His spirituality and wisdom attracted others to him for counsel and comfort; however, he became most renowned as a miracle worker, especially for the sick. His body was buried in the cemetery of Bonaria. The ordinary process for his beatification was conducted from 1966 to 1971 and introduced in Rome in 1977. The declaration of Fra Nicola's heroic virtues came 18 years after his death (June 25, 1996). Pope John Paul II beatified him, Oct. 3, 1999.

Feast: June 8.

Bibliography: FILIPPO DA CAGLIARI, *Fra Nicola nel decennale della morte* (Sardinia 1968).

[K. I. RABENSTEIN]

NICOLAITES

Members of a libertine sect of the early Church, also known as Nicolaitans. John praises the church of EPHESUS for detesting "the works of the Nicolaites" (Rv 2.6); he scores the church of PERGAMUM for harboring "some who hold the teaching of the Nicolaites," and describes them as adherents of the teaching of BALAAM (Rv 2.14–15; cf. Nm 31.16 with 25.1–2; 2 Pt 2.15; Jude 11). The same tendency is doubtless meant in Ap 2.20–24: the church of Thyatira is blamed for tolerating a self-styled prophetess whom John calls Jezabel (2 Kgs 9.22), since she led Christians astray with her teachings about fornication and the eating of meat offered to idols (see Acts 15.20–29): these were two of the points on which James enjoined Gentile Christians to follow Jewish practice (see also 1 Corinthians, ch. 8–10). The Nicolaites seem, accordingly, to represent an excessively liberal or even antinomian outlook, possibly abusing the teachings of St. Paul on freedom (1 Cor 10.23), appealing to an esoteric knowledge that John sarcastically called "the deep things of Satan" (cf. 1 Cor 2.10). One of the serious problems that faced Christians at this time was precisely to what extent they might participate in the social and economic life of the Roman Empire, which involved attending sacrificial banquets and easily resulted in immoral practices (though the "fornication" of the Nicolaites might here mean metaphorically faithlessness to the true God).

There is no reason to link the Nicolaites with the deacon Nicholas (Acts 6.5), as Irenaeus (*Adv. haer.* 1.26.3; 3.11.1) and other Fathers have done; Clement of Alexandria (*Strom.* 2.20; 3.4) reports a story that a saying of Nicholas was misinterpreted by the Nicolaites in appealing to his authority. The existence of the Nicolaites (antinomian Gnostics) mentioned by these and other Fathers and their relationship to the Nicolaites of the Book of Revelation are problematic.

In the Middle Ages advocates of clerical celibacy, e.g., Cardinal Humbert (*C. Nicetam* 25), called their opponents Nicolaites.

Bibliography: É. AMANN, *Dictionnaire de théologie catholique* 11.1:499–506. J. MICHL, *Lexikon für Theologie und Kirche*[2] 7:976. G. KRETSCHMAR, *Die Religion in Geschichte und Gegenwart*[3] 4:1485–86. *Encyclopedic Dictionary of the Bible* 1638–39. A. VON HARNACK, "The Sect of the Nicolaitans and Nicolaus the Deacon in Jerusalem," *Journal of Religion* 3 (1923) 413–422.

[E. F. SIEGMAN]

NICOLANTONIO, MARIANO DA ROCCACASALE, BL.

Baptized Domenico, Franciscan lay brother; b. Jan. 14, 1778, Roccacasale (Aquila), Abruzzi, Italy; d. May 31 (Feast of Corpus Christi), 1866, Bellegra, Italy.

Mariano's life was characterized by simplicity and poverty. He was one of six children of Gabriel de Nicolantonio and Santa de Arcángelo. In tending the family flocks in the Morrone mountains as a young boy, he grew to love silence and reflection.

He entered Saint Nicholas Friary at Arischia, Abruzzi, took the name Mariano (Sept. 2, 1802) and pronounced his solemn vows the following year. For 12 years he engaged in prayer and work, as a carpenter, gardener, cook, and porter, at Arischia. In 1814, Mariano asked and received permission to transfer to the more austere Saint Francis Friary at Bellegra, where he served as porter for forty years, welcoming pilgrims, other travelers, and the poor. Among those he greeted and inspired was Diego ODDI, who later became a Franciscan in the same friary.

A miracle attributed to Blessed Mariano's intercession was approved by Pope John Paul II, April 6, 1998, opening the way for his beatification Oct. 3, 1999.

Feast: May 30 (Franciscans).

Bibliography: *Acta Apostolicae Sedis* 19 (1999): 965. *L'Osservatore Romano,* Eng. ed. 40 (1999): 1–3; 41 (1999): 2.

[K. I. RABENSTEIN]

NICOLAS, JEAN JACQUES AUGUSTE

French lay Catholic apologist; b. Bordeaux, Jan. 6, 1807; d. Versailles, Jan. 17, 1888. He was a lawyer in Poitiers and Bordeaux, then head of a division under the minister of cults Frédéric de Falloux (1849–54), inspector of public libraries (1854–60), judge in the tribunal of the Seine (1860–67), and counselor at the court in Paris (1867–77). After this he lived in retirement at Versailles until his death. Almost all his numerous writings were in the field of apologetics and were inspired by contemporary circumstances. His principal work, *Études philosophiques sur le Christianisme* (4 v., 1842–45; 26th ed., 1885), was composed to resolve the doubts of his father-in-law, who desired to return to the faith; it was very successful, brought the author to the attention of Falloux, and was honored with a letter from Pius IX. In reply to the *Méditations* by the Protestant François Guizot, Nicolas wrote *Du Protestantisme et de toutes les hérésies dans leur rapport avec le socialisme* (1852). After the cure of his daughter, which he attributed to the Blessed Virgin, he published an original work, *Nouvelles Études philosophiques sur le Christianisme* (4 v., 1855–60), whose three parts examined Mary's role in the divine plan, in the Gospels, and in the Church. When RENAN wrote his *Vie de Jésus,* Nicolas published in refutation *La Divinité de Jésus-Christ* (1864) and *L'Art de croire* (2 v., 1866). After the Franco-Prussian War he denounced the social evils of his homeland in *L'État sans Dieu* (1872). As a remedy he proposed the alliance of throne and altar in *La Révolution et l'ordre chrétien, Jésus-Christ, introduction à l'Évangile étudié et médité à l'usage des temps nouveaux* (1875), *La Raison et l'Évangile* (1876), and *Études sociales sur la Révolution* (2 v., 1890). Subsequent to a visit to Rome, he defended papal temporal sovereignty in *Rome et la papauté* (1882). His final work, *Étude historique et critique sur le P. Lacordaire,* was not at all favorable to the celebrated Dominican. The writings of Nicolas were not notable for theological profundity or critical historical sense, but their popularity made him one of the century's leading apologists.

Bibliography: P. LAPEYRE, *A. Nicolas, sa vie et ses oeuvres* (Paris 1892). E. BIRÉ, *Études et portraits* (2d ed. Paris-Lyon 1913) 289–311. J. CARREYRE, *Dictionnaire de théologie catholique,* ed. A. VACANT et al., 15 v. (Paris 1903–50; Tables générales 1951–) 11.1: 548–555.

[J. DAOUST]

NICOLE, PIERRE

Jansenist theologian; b. Chartres, Oct. 19, 1625; d. Paris, Nov. 16, 1695. Nicole studied philosophy at Paris where he took his master's degree in 1644 before turning his attention to theology. He received his baccalaureate from the Sorbonne in 1649. His relatives among the nuns at PORT-ROYAL arranged for him to join the group who shared the ideas of the recently deceased Abbé Saint-Cyran (*see* DUVERGIER DE HAURANNE, JEAN) and operated a school for boys near the convent. Nicole taught literature and formed a friendship with the brilliant Antoine Arnauld, younger brother of Mère Angélique (*see* AR-NAULD), Abbess of Port-Royal, and spiritual director of the nuns. Nicole collaborated with Arnauld on many writings, although often Arnauld's part was merely to give his approval. These writings are published among the 43 volumes of the collected works of Arnauld (Lausanne 1775–83).

Nicole was a close collaborator with Pascal and was so highly regarded as a writer that many read him despite their lack of interest in his generally religious subjects. His writings are chiefly polemical and were often published under pen names. He wrote much in defense of JANSENISM and against the Jesuits, although his posthumously published writings on grace are far from Jansenistic. Despite its good qualities, his writing against the quietists, produced at the request of Bossuet, goes to extremes in the rejection of mysticism. He also defended the position of the MAURISTS on monastic studies against A. J. de RANCÉ, founder of the Trappist reform.

Although far more moderate than most of the Jansenists, both in substance and in style, Nicole is characteristically Jansenist in his commitment to endless controversy and his love for fine distinctions. He probably originated the famous distinction between doctrine and fact with which Port-Royal tried to evade the condemnation of the five propositions from the AUGUSTINUS, which they were willing to accept as erroneous, but not as contained in the book. Although he was refused Sacred Orders by his bishop, Nicole leaped to the defense of clerics, who were not so ready with the pen, when they were attacked for rejecting the condemnation of the five propositions. He was constantly trying to enlist St. Thomas Aquinas in defense of his case, and even wrote a book titled *Conformity of the Jansenists and the Thomists concerning the Five Propositions.*

Among his numerous writings a few are especially deserving of mention. His fame was established by his Latin translation of the *Provincial Letters* of Pascal, published with notes and additions under the name of William Wendrock. He wrote extensive scholarly works against the Calvinists in defense of transubstantiation and the Real Presence, as well as a more general attack on Calvinist positions that produced a whole literature of controversy. Perhaps his greatest work is his *Essais de morale,* which first appeared in four volumes and were printed, emended, added to, and reprinted again and again until the edition of 1753 filled 14 volumes. The weakness of human nature and the incapacity of the natural man for virtue dominates his characteristic Jansenism in morality. In response to attacks on Jansenism he wrote two works that were later published together and give important details of life at Port-Royal, *Les Imaginaires et les visionnaires ou dix-huit lettres sur i'hérésie imaginaire.*

Bibliography: J. CARREYRE, *Dictionnaire de théologie catholique,* ed. A. VACANT et al. (Paris 1903—50) 11.1:634–646. H. BREMOND, *Histoire littéraire du sentiment réligieux en France depuis la fin des guerres de religion jusqu'à nos jours* (Paris 1917–36) 4:418–588. H. HURTER, *Nomenclator literarius theologiae catholicae* (Innsbruck 1903–13) 4:444–448. L. WILLAERT, *Lexikon für Theologie und Kirche,* ed. J. HOFER and K. RAHNER (Freiberg 1957–65) 7:948–949.

[A. ROCK]

NICOMEDIA

Ancient city of Bithynia in Asia Minor, modern Izmit, Turkey. From the 3rd to the 1st century B.C. it was the capital of Bithynia; later, the titular See of Bithynia Prima. Nicomedia was founded by King Zipoetes, whose son Nicomedes I made it his capital (*c.* 264 B.C.) and adorned it with numerous magnificent buildings. At the turn of the 2nd century B.C. Hannibal sought asylum at his court. Nicomedia remained the capital of Bithynia even after King Nicomedes III (or IV) willed the country to Rome (74 B.C.). PLINY THE YOUNGER in his letters to Trajan speaks of the senate house, an aqueduct that he had built, a forum, and the temple of Cybele. As capital of the province Nicomedia was one of the first cities in northern Asia Minor to be tianized. The first bishop of Nicomedia was Prochorus. Under Marcus Aurelius, Bp. DIONYSIUS OF CORINTH wrote a letter to the faithful of Nicomedia (*c.* 170) warning them against the heresies of Marcion. Origen lived there with his benefactor, Ambrose (*c.* 240); and the emperor DIOCLETIAN built there an imperial palace, a hippodrome, a mint, and an arsenal. CONSTANTINE I was brought up there; the pagan philosopher Libanius taught there; and LACTANTIUS served as tutor to the children of the emperor. There was a Christian church close to the imperial palace, that was destroyed (303) when Diocletian initiated a severe persecution of the Christians of Asia Minor and hundreds were martyred. Under Maximinus Daia, in 312 the persecution in Nicomedia took the lives of many faithful members of the clergy, among them Bishop Anthimus and the priest Lucian of Antioch.

In the mid-4th century Bp. Eusebius of Nicomedia granted asylum to Arius, thus making the city a center of ARIANISM. Two of its Arian bishops, Eudoxius and Demophilus, became archbishops of Constantinople. A Novatian sect settled in Nicomedia toward the end of the century. To the metropolitan See of Nicomedia (325) belonged the Dioceses of Chalcedon, Prusa, Apollonias, Hadrianoi, Caesarea in Bithynia, Nicaea, Chios, Neocaesarea, and Prusias; in the 7th century it was listed as seventh among the metropolitan sees of the Patriarchate of Constantinople.

During the 4th century Nicomedia suffered an invasion of the Goths and an earthquake (Aug. 24, 354), which ruined most of its buildings; fire completed the catastrophe. The city was rebuilt during the reign of JUSTINIAN I (527–565), but subsequently was destroyed by the Shah Khusru (Chosroes) II. In 711 Pope Constantine I visited the city, and in 1073 John Comnenus was proclaimed emperor there. In about 1330 the sultan Orkhan captured the city and restored its ramparts, parts of which still display the two epochs of Nicomedia's history, the Roman and the Byzantine. Nicomedia continued to be a metropolitan see until 1923; since then it has been a Latin titular bishopric.

In a journey through Asia Minor in 1555, H. Dernschwam recognized walls and foundations of the ancient city, but could not identify them [*Tagebuch einer Reise nach . . . Kleinasien,* ed. F. Babinger (Munich 1923) 154–156, 238]. No systematic excavations had been attempted at Nicomedia by the late 20th century; however, some remains of buildings and inscriptions came to light in 1937. A contemporary portrait of Diocletian is of great interest.

Bibliography: B. KOTTER and O. FELD, *Lexikon für Theologie und Kirche,* ed. J. HOFER and K. RAHNER (Freiburg 1957–65) 7:1001–02. R. JANIN, *Échos d'Orient* 20 (Paris 1921) 168–182, 301–319; *Dictionnaire d'histoire et de géographie ecclésiastiques,* ed. A. BAUDRILLART et al. (Paris 1912—) 9:20–28. V. SCHULTZE, *Altchristliche Städte und Landschaften,* (Gütersloh 1922) 2.1:244–305. H. LECLERCQ, *Dictionnaire d'archéologie chrétienne et de liturgie* (Paris 1907–53) 12.1:1236–45. W. RUGE, *Paulys Realenzyklopädie der klassischen Altertumswissenschaft,* ed. G. WISSOWA et. al, 17.1 (Stuttgart 1936) 468–492. F. K. DÖRNER,

Inschriften und Denkmäler aus Bithynien (Berlin 1941) 1–106, bibliog.

[G. LUZNYCKY]

NIDER, JOHANN

Dominican theologian, writer, diplomat, and reformer; b. Isny (Württemberg) *c.* 1380; d. Nuremberg, Aug. 13, 1438. Nider (Nyder, or Neider) entered the Order of Preachers at Colmar *c.* 1400, and under the saintly Conrad of Prussia was formed in the spirit of strict observance. Following his novitiate, he began his philosophical and theological studies at the University of Vienna and completed them at Cologne, where he was ordained. He soon became celebrated as a preacher throughout Germany and Switzerland. Nider attended the Council of CONSTANCE, participating in the debates over the doctrines of Hus. In 1423 he became professor of theology at the University of Vienna, and attracted many disciples by his reputation. He was prior of Nuremberg from 1425 to 1429. Throughout Germany he preached the reform initiated by Bl. RAYMOND OF CAPUA and furthered by Bl. John DOMINICI. Nider was prior of the convent of strict observance at Basle, 1429–36, and from 1429 to 1438 was vicar over all the reformed priories in Germany. In 1431 he went as theologian to the Council of BASLE, which sent him as legate to the Bohemian church. In Bohemia he preached against the HUSSITES and attempted to reunite those who had broken communion with Rome. He was conciliar legate in 1434 to the Diet of Ratisbon. In 1436, on completion of his term as prior of Basle, he returned to the University of Vienna, where he was elected dean of the faculty of theology.

His principal work, the *Formicarius* (5 v., 1517), was written in 1437. It is a collection of anecdotes and dialogues, a rich source for the religious history and political mind of the first part of the 15th century. It also contains long developments on diabolical activity. His other works are the *Praeceptorium divinae legis* (17 editions before 1500); *Tractatus de contractibus mercatorum* (8 editions before 1500); *Alphabeticum divini amoris,* which was later attributed to Gerson; *De modo bene vivendi,* erroneously thought to be a work of St. Bernard; and many other moral and ascetical works.

Bibliography: *Scriptores Ordinis* 1.2:792–794; 2.2:822. K. SCHIELER, *Magister Johannes Nieder, aus dem Orden der Prediger-Brüder* (Mainz 1885). M. M. GORCE, *Dictionnaire de théologie catholique* 11:851–854.

[J. F. QUIGLEY]

NIEBUHR, HELMUT RICHARD

Protestant theologian and educator: b. Wright City, Mo., Sept. 3, 1894: d. Greenfield, Mass., July 5, 1962. Niebuhr was born of Gustave and Lydia (Hosto) Niebuhr and was the younger brother of Reinhold NIEBUHR. After graduating from Eden Theological Seminary, Webster Groves, Mo., in 1915, he was ordained a year later in the Evangelical and Reformed Church. Niebuhr married Florence Marie Mittendorff on June 9, 1920. He obtained his B. D. at Yale Divinity School, New Haven, Conn., in 1923, and his Ph. D. at Yale University in 1924. In 1931 he joined the faculty of the Yale Divinity School where his major interest was the relationship of Christian faith to civilization. Although he was not as well known as his brother, his thought commanded wide attention. While acknowledging the need for the Church and Scripture, he warned against their deification ''as though the historical and visible church were the representative of God on earth, as though the Bible were the only word that God is speaking.'' He sought more of an I-Thou relation between God and man, and felt that Protestant theology could best minister to the Church by resuming ''the general line of march represented by the evangelical, empirical, and critical movements.'' Theological formulas were for him ''not the basis of faith, but only one of its expressions and that not the primary one.'' His works include *The Social Sources of Denominationalism* (1929), *The Kingdom of God in America* (1937), *The Meaning of Revelation* (1941), and *Christ and Culture* (1951).

Bibliography: ''Portrait,'' *Life* (Dec. 26, 1955) 140:39–40. ''Remembered Mentor,'' *Christian Century* (July 25, 1962) 79: 905. R. M. KEISER, *Roots of Relational Ethics: Responsibility in Origin and Maturity in H. Richard Niebuhr* (Atlanta 1996). R. MELVIN, *Recovering the Personal: Religious Language and the Post-critical Quest of H. Richard Niebuhr* (Atlanta 1988). J. W. FOWLER, *To See the Kingdom: The Theological Vision of H. Richard Niebuhr* (New York 1985). C. D. GRANT, *God the Center of Value: Value Theory in the Theology of H. Richard Niebuhr* (Fort Worth 1984). J. A. IRISH, *The Religious Thought of H. Richard Niebuhr* (Atlanta 1983). D. E. FADNER, *The Responsible God: A Study of the Christian Philosophy of H. Richard Niebuhr* (Missoula, Mont. 1975).

[E. DELANEY]

NIEBUHR, REINHOLD

Protestant ethicist and educator; b. Wright City, MO, June 21, 1892; d. Stockbridge, MA, June 1, 1971. He was the son of Gustave and Lydia (Hosto) Niebuhr and elder brother of H. Richard Niebuhr. After attending Eden Theological Seminary, Webster Groves, MO, he went to Yale University and received the B.D. in 1914 and the M.A. in 1915. He was ordained in the Evangelical Synod Church and undertook pastoral duties in Detroit, MI. The struggles of the labor movement in Detroit came to Niebuhr's attention, and his involvement in them was the basis for his later work in Christian social ethics. In 1928, Niebuhr took an academic post at Union Theological Seminary in New York City, and married Ursula Keppel-Compton in 1931.

At first an ardent pacifist, Niebuhr shared the optimism of the SOCIAL GOSPEL movement—an optimism that had its secular counterpart in the thought of John Dewey. However, by 1932, with the publication of *Moral Man and Immoral Society*, he argued against the "Social Gospel" that the law of love would never lead to social perfection and against the disciples of Dewey that expertise should never replace wisdom. An adequate social ethic needed more than moral piety or scientific intelligence. This realization led Niebuhr to a renewed appreciation of some biblical themes which had been neglected by the regnant liberal theology. In particular Niebuhr emphasized the doctrine of original sin. Human pride is everywhere at work and especially in the political order with the temptations of power. He thus supported political policies that carefully delineate the limits of power. His works include *Does Civilization Need Religion?* (1927), *The Nature and Destiny of Man*, 2 v. (1941 and 1943), and *Man's Nature and His Communities* (1965).

See Also: NIEBUHR, HELMUT RICHARD.

Bibliography: C. W. KEGLEY and R. W. BRETALL, eds., *Reinhold Niebuhr: His Religious, Social and Political Thought* (New York 1956). G. HARLAND, *The Thought of Reinhold Niebuhr* (London 1960).

[W. HAYES]

Reinhold Niebuhr.

NIEDERALTAICH, ABBEY OF

In the Bavarian Benedictine Congregation, Diocese of Passau; on the left bank of the Danube near the mouth of the Isar. Since the 12th century it has been called *Altaha inferior* to distinguish it from the nearby Abbey of Oberaltaich (*Altaha superior*). The Agilulfinger dukes founded it before 750 and settled it with monks from REICHENAU, who brought with them the Burgundian cult of St. MAURICE, patron of the church. Niederaltaich colonized and evangelized the Bavarian forest, Bohemia, Moravia, and Hungary, settling KREMSMÜNSTER (777). Ruined by the Hungarian wars, it was reduced to a group of canons by 1000. Bishops PILGRIM OF PASSAU and WOLFGANG OF REGENSBURG included it in the GORZE TRIER-REGENSBURG REFORM. Under St. GODARD (d. 1038), later bishop of Hildesheim, Niederaltaich headed a reform, settling or reviving TEGERNSEE, HERSFELD, Ossiach, Bakonybel, Ostrow (St. Iwan), Brevnov, and Olomouc

(Olmütz). St. Günther was a missionary and colonizer, and Bl. Richer became abbot of Monte Cassino; Judith was one of several women recluses at Niederaltaich. The abbey lost its free imperial status (857–1156) in the investiture controversy and was put under the bishop of Bamberg. Abbot Herman (1242–73), compiler of the *Annales Altahenses*, restored the abbey to its former prestige. Eight of Niederaltaich's monks were requested as abbots at a time when the old religious orders were in decline. Rebuilt after the ruin of the Thirty Years' War, the abbey was destroyed with its library in fires (1659, 1671). Abbot Joscio Hamberger (1700–39) revived it and had the baroque church built. The abbey was secularized (1803) but resettled from METTEN (1918) and united to the Priory of Innsbruck-Volders (1927) before it became an abbey again (1930). Its Ecumenical Institute has a leading role in the ECUMENICAL MOVEMENT.

Bibliography: G. LANG, *Die Heiligen und Seligen von Niederaltaich* (Metten 1941). R. BAUERREISS, *Lexikon für Theologie und*

Kirche, ed. J. HOFER and K. RAHNER, 10 v. (2d, new ed. Freiburg 1957–65) 7:950–951.

[E. M. HEUFELDER]

NIEDERMÜNSTER (ALSACE), CONVENT OF

Former abbey of nuns in the Diocese of Strasbourg; founded before 710 by St. ODILIA, at the foot of the hill topped by her convent of MONT SAINTE-ODILE. Gundelinde, niece of the foundress, was its first abbess. A famous relic of the true Cross was venerated at Niedermünster from Carolingian times until the 17th century, when it was transferred to the Jesuits at Molsheim. Niedermünster enjoyed its most brilliant era in the 13th century, but declined in the 14th. The abbey suffered partial destruction during the Peasants' Revolt (1525); it died out completely after a fire in 1542. Important ruins of the church, which had been consecrated in 1180, still remain.

Bibliography: M. BARTH, *Die heilige Odilia, Schutzherrin des Elsass,* 2 v. (Strasbourg 1938); *Handbuch der elsässischen Kirchen im Mittelalter,* 3 v. (Archives de l'Église d'Alsace NS 11–13; Strasbourg 1960–63).

[J. CHOUX]

NIEHEIM (NIEM), DIETRICH OF

Chancery official in the Roman Curia, publicist of the WESTERN SCHISM; b. Brakel, Westphalia, *c.* 1340; d. Maastricht, Netherlands, end of March 1418. Supported by WILLIAM OF OCKHAM, MARSILIUS OF PADUA, and Alexander of Roes, he gave the first comprehensive presentation of CONCILIARISM in his *Dialogus de schismate* (1410), in which he called for the reunion and reform of the Church. His *Avisamenta* (1414) contains the program for the Council of CONSTANCE. As a representative of the historically conservative approach to the empire, he stressed the right of the German emperors to call a general COUNCIL of the Church. He was an intimate of several Roman popes; in 1395 BONIFACE IX tried in vain to bestow upon him the bishopric of Verden (Germany). The Anima, the German hospital in Rome, claims him as its founder.

Bibliography: K. PIVEC and H. HEIMPEL, "Neue Forschungen zu Dietrich von Niem," *Nachrichten der Akademie d. Wissenschaften in Göttingen* (1951) H.4. H. HEIMPEL, *Dietrich von Niem, c. 1340–1418* (Münster 1932). *Neue deutsche Biographie* 3:691–692. J. LEUSCHNER, *Lexikon für Theologie und Kirche,* ed. J. HOFER and K. RAHNER, 10 v. (2d, new ed. Freiburg 1957–65) 3:386. E. F. JACOB, *Essays in the Conciliar Epoch* (3d ed. Notre Dame, Ind. 1963) 24–43.

[H. WOLFRAM]

NIELSEN, LAURENTIUS

Missionary to Sweden; b. Oslo, Norway, 1538; d. Vilnius (Vilna), Lithuania, May 5, 1622. Educated in the Lutheran faith, Nielsen received a master of arts degree in Copenhagen and in 1558 began studies for the Lutheran ministry in Louvain. Through contact with the Jesuits there, his interest in Catholicism grew. On Feb. 2, 1564, he was admitted into the Society of Jesus, and he was ordained to the priesthood the next year. He remained in Louvain until he was chosen for the Swedish mission by the Jesuit general, Everard Mercurian, with the hope that Nielsen's knowledge of the language and his Lutheran background would hasten the conversion of King John III.

John, partly through the influence of his Catholic wife, the Polish Catherine Jagellon, and partly through consideration of the political advantages of a role as mediator in the religious struggles in Europe, had indicated his interest in reconciliation with Rome. Nielsen arrived in Stockholm (1576), where he taught theology at the new college founded by the king and defended the king's liturgical innovations, which caused general displeasure in Lutheran Sweden. In 1577 the Jesuit Antonio POSSEVINO arrived in Stockholm to negotiate the conversion, and in May of 1578 he absolved John from schism and administered Communion.

Nielsen left Sweden in 1580 and taught theology at the colleges in Olmütz (1582), Prague (1587), and Braunseberg (Braniewo). In 1606 he founded a college in Denmark. Among his published writings are *Confessio christiana de via Domini* (Cracow 1604) and *De reformatione religionis christiana* (Cracow 1616).

Bibliography: A. THEINER, *Schweden und seine Stellung zum heiligen Stuhl unter Johann III. Sigismund III. und Karl IX.,* 2 v. (Augsburg 1838–39). I. IPARRAGUIRRE, *Lexikon für Theologie und Kirche,* ed. J. HOFER and K. RAHNER (Freiberg 1957–65) 7:959. C. SOMMERVOGEL, *Bibliothèque de la Compagnie de Jésus,* (Brussels-Paris 1890–1932) 5:1707–09. É. AMANN, *Dictionnaire de théologie catholique.* ed. A. VACANT et al. (Paris 1903–50) 11.1:497–499, with bibliog.

[E. D. MCSHANE]

NIETZSCHE, FRIEDRICH WILHELM

German philosopher and poet; b. Röcken (Prussian Saxony), Oct. 15, 1844; d. Weimar, Germany, Aug. 25, 1900.

Life. The son of a Lutheran pastor, Nietzsche was reared in a strictly religious atmosphere. After his father's death (1849), his mother moved to Naumburg; Nietzsche then attended the humanistic Gymnasium and the renowned Fürstenschule of neighboring Pforta (1858–64). He studied classical philology under F. W. Ritschl at the universities of Bonn and Leipzig (1862–67) and discovered the philosophy of A. SCHOPENHAUER. Though never endorsing Schopenhauer's metaphysical PESSIMISM, Nietzsche sensed in the emphasis on the supremacy of will as a universal principle a dynamism that appealed to his thirst for life in its plenitude. To Nietzsche's faltering Christian faith Schopenhauer seemed to offer a possibility of self-redemption.

On Ritschl's recommendation, Nietzsche, aged 24, was appointed professor of classical philology at the University of Basel in Switzerland, a chair he held from 1869 to 1879, when his steadily declining health forced his resignation. Of considerable consequence was Nietzsche's meeting and short-lived friendship with Richard WAGNER. Until 1872 Nietzsche's life was actually centered in Wagner's villa near Lucerne. He expected of Wagner's music drama a rebirth of the ancient Greek tragedy of Aeschylus and Sophocles. In defense of Wagner and attacking the "Socratic rationalism" of Euripides, Nietzsche wrote *Die Geburt der Tragödie aus dem Geiste der Musik* (Leipzig 1872). But the ambivalent love-hatred attitude that marked his relationship with Wagner led to disillusionment and eventual total estrangement.

From 1879 to 1889 Nietzsche lived alternately at Sils-Maria in the Swiss Engadine Alps, at Nice, and at Genoa, suffering from multiple physical ailments. His final mental collapse occurred in Turin in January 1889. His remaining 11 years Nietzsche lived in Jena and Weimar under the care of his sister Elisabeth. His mental disease was never accurately diagnosed, and the assumption that Nietzsche was suffering from progressive paralysis induced by syphilis remains unsubstantiated.

Thought. Nietzsche was a *Lebensphilosoph,* castigating the separation of philosophy and science from life. In his sensitive mind the spiritual crisis of the modern age appeared focalized. He was among the first to diagnose HISTORICISM and SCIENTISM as symptoms of decadence and of a nihilism that threatened the foundations of Western civilization. He called for a new beginning and a "transvaluation of all values" in order to stop such threats.

The development of Nietzsche's thought proceeded in three stages. The study of antiquity and the influence of Schopenhauer and Wagner first made Nietzsche experience the "ground of being" as a dialectic of opposites, of "Dionysian" and "Apollonian" life principles. His vision of a synthesis in Greek tragedy and in Wagnerian music was short-lived. The four *Unzeitgemässe Betrachtungen* (Leipzig 1873–76) characterize this period.

Friedrich Nietzsche. (Archive Photos)

Then, after the break with Wagner and the emancipation from Schopenhauer's "pessimism of weakness," Nietzsche applied psychological "experimentalism" to an examination of man and his world, launching a radical attack on traditional theology, metaphysics, and morality. With L. FEUERBACH, Nietzsche saw the idea of God and of absolute Truth as nothing but "projections" of man's most precious qualities into an illusory "beyond"; they must be reclaimed, he argued, for the enrichment of man and his "this-worldly" existence. The "death of God" he solemnly proclaimed and dramatically analyzed in the story of the "madman" in section 125 of *Die fröhliche Wissenschaft* (Chemnitz 1882–86). See also *Menschliches, Allzumenschliches* (Chemnitz 1878–80) and *Morgenröte* (Chemnitz 1881).

Nietzsche finally implemented his early thinking with the "deadly gospel" of biological and social Darwinism. The "world-ground" he now saw as *Wille zur Macht,* a "will-to-power" that by "sublimation" would generate the "Super-Man" (*Übermensch*). Christian "slave morality," born of the *ressentiment* of weaklings, was to be superseded by a "master morality, beyond good and evil." The future "lords of the world" were to rise above brute animality by ascetic self-discipline seasoned by suffering. See *Also sprach Zarathustra* (Chemnitz 1883–84), *Jenseits von Gut und Böse* (Leipzig 1886),

Zur Genealogie der Moral (Leipzig 1887), *Der Fall Wagners* (Leipzig 1888), *Ecce Homo* (1888; publ. Leipzig 1908), *Der Antichrist* (Leipzig 1888), and *Die Götzendämmerung* (Leipzig 1889). The ''vision'' that inspired Nietzsche's doctrine of ''the eternal recurrence'' he interpreted as the revelation of a cosmological law functioning without a divine lawgiver. An eternal cyclical movement of existence was seen as a substitute for the creative activity of a personal Deity. The certainty of the ''eternal return'' was to justify a joyous affirmation of all existence, signalizing a final victory over NIHILISM.

Appreciation. The ambivalences and self-contradictory theses in Nietzsche's thinking account for some gross misinterpretations of his philosophy. However, Nietzsche's distorted idea of Christianity bears the imprint of Luther's pessimism regarding the corruption of fallen human nature and of Schopenhauer's Buddhist-tainted view of Christian doctrine. Nietzsche's alleged anti-Semitism and chauvinism—eagerly propagated by the National Socialists—are refuted by his scathing denunciation of racism and his condemnation of the power politics and crude materialism of the German Empire. A distorted Nietzsche image was created also by his sister, who was bigoted and proved unreliable as executrix of Nietzsche's literary remains. But Nietzsche's philosophy did foster the rise of IRRATIONALISM, SUBJECTIVISM, VOLUNTARISM, and a biologism based on the *élan vital* of a naturalistic *Lebensphilosophie*. Nietzsche's philosophical influence is most conspicuous in secular HUMANISM and in EXISTENTIALISM. The hymnal musicality of his prose and poetry also influenced several literary and artistic schools and movements.

See Also: LIFE PHILOSOPHIES.

Bibliography: Works. *Gesammelte Werke,* 20 v. (Leipzig 1901–1926); *Gesammelte Werke: Musarionausgabe,* 23 v. (Munich 1920–29); *Werke und Briefe: Historisch-kritische Gesamtausgabe* (Munich 1933–), in progress; *The Complete Works,* ed. O. LEVY, 18 v. (London 1909–13); *The Philosophy of Nietzsche* (New York 1937), contains four major works; *The Portable Nietzsche,* comp., ed., and tr. W. KAUFMANN (New York 1954); *The Use and Abuse of History,* tr. A. COLLINS (2d rev. ed. New York 1957); *Joyful Wisdom,* tr. T. COMMON (New York 1960). Literature. F. COPLESTON, *Friedrich Nietzsche: Philosopher of Culture* (London 1942). H. A. REYBURN et al., *Nietzsche The Story of a Human Philosopher* (London 1948). W. KAUFMANN, *Nietzsche: Philosopher, Psychologist, Antichrist* (Princeton 1950). F. A. LEA, *The Tragic Philosopher: A Study of Friedrich Nietzsche* (New York 1957). M. HEIDEGGER, *Nietzsche,* 2 v. (Pfullingen 1961). R. J. HOLLINGDALE, *Nietzsche: The Man and His Philosophy* (New York 1999). M. CLARK, *Nietzsche on Truth and Philosophy* (Cambridge 1990). J. RICHARDSON, *Nietzsche's System* (Oxford 1996).

[K. F. REINHARDT]

NIEVES, ELÍAS DEL SOCORRO, BL.

Baptized Mateo Elías (Matthew Elijah), Augustinian martyr of Communist revolutionaries; b. Isla San Pedro, Yuriria, Guanajuato, Mexico, Sept. 21, 1882; d. near Cortazar, Mexico, March 10, 1928.

Born into a modest peasant family and baptized with urgency because he was in danger of death, Nieves had an early, strong vocation to the priesthood. However, he contracted tuberculosis and was temporarily blind (age 12). He regained his sight, and he assumed the responsibilities as head of household upon his father's death. Nevertheless, he was admitted (1904) to the Augustinian college at Yuriria. When he professed his vows (1911), Mateo took the name Elías del Socorro (Elijah of Our Lady of Succor) in acknowledgment of the help he received overcoming his hardships. He was ordained in 1916.

Nieves served in various parishes within Guanajauto until he was assigned to the poor, isolated parish of La Cañada de Caracheo in 1921, where he helped to build the church—physically and spiritually. In disobedience to governmental orders (1926) that forced priests to abandon rural areas, Nieves courageously hid in a cave in the nearby hills of La Gavia in order to continue administering the sacraments to his parishioners under the cover of darkness.

After fourteen months of clandestine ministry, he was arrested together with two campesinos, José Dolores and José de Jesús Sierra. Although he was dressed in the rags of a peasant, the hem of his habit betrayed him. He was questioned, and since he immediately admitted being a priest, he was detained. A parishioner negotiated for the freedom of the laymen, but they refused to abandon their pastor. En route under guard to the provincial capital of Cortazar, the two companions were killed. At the next resting place, Nieves was taunted and then shot. He faced death with fortitude, blessing his executioners, and witnessing to his faith in Christ.

His body has been moved to the parish church at La Cañada de Caracheo. Fr. Elías was beatified by Pope John Paul II, Oct. 12, 1997, together with another Augustinian, Mother Maria Teresa FASCE, who documented Nieves's martyrdom for her convent. He is a patron of Mexico.

Feast: Oct. 11.

Bibliography: *Acta Apostolicae Sedis,* no. 20 (1997): 999. *L'Osservatore Romano,* English edition, no. 42 (1997): 1, 2, 11, 12.

[K. I. RABENSTEIN]

NIFO, AGOSTINO

Italian philosopher; b. Sessa Aurunca, *ca.* 1470; d. Sessei Aurunca, 1538. Educated at the University of Padua, where he first began to teach. He left for Naples in 1499. His early acceptance of AVERROES' doctrine of the unity of the intellect as the true interpretation of Aristotle was replaced by rejection of that interpretation in his *De intellectu* (Venice 1503). In that work he presents excerpts from ALBERT THE GREAT's *De natura et origine animae* as the "true position" on the nature of the soul and intellect. He also borrows from Saint THOMAS AQUINAS and Marsilio Ficino to argue for the immortality of the soul. He had begun to learn Greek and to take the Greek Commentators, especially Simplicius and Themistius, as the best interpreters of Aristotle. On his return south, he taught at Naples and Salerno and was a member of the circle of the humanist Giovanni Pontano. He functioned as a physician. He taught at Rome in 1514 and at Pisa from 1519–1522 and later at Salerno. His own *De immortalitate animae* (Venice 1518) was a reply to Pietro Pomponazzi's work on the same subject. He declined an invitation from Paul III in 1535 to teach again at Rome. He wrote commentaries on most of Aristotle's works but there is no collected edition of his writings.

Bibliography: E. P. MAHONEY, *Two Aristotelians of the Italian Renaissance: Nicolletto Vernia and Agostino Nifo* (Aldershot 2000). B. NARDI, *Saggi sull'aristotelismo padovano dal secolo XIV al XVI* (Florence 1958).

[E. P. MAHONEY]

NIGER, THE CATHOLIC CHURCH IN

An arid, impoverished, and landlocked country in west-central Africa, the Republic of Niger is bordered on the north by Algeria and Libya, on the east by Chad, on the south by Nigeria, on the southwest by Burkina Faso and Benin, and on the west by Mali. The tropical southern savannah is home to most of Niger's population, while the north is charactcrized by sand dunes and desert plateau, the terrain broken by the mountainous Aïr region in its center. Peanuts, cowpeas, cotton and rice are among the nation's primary agricultural products, while natural resources include uranium, coal, iron ore, tin, gold and petroleum. Droughts, erosion, desertification and the destruction of wildlife populations due to poaching are among the problems faced by Niger, a country whose economy centers on subsistence agriculture and the export of uranium. The average life expectancy of a native Niger was 41.2 years in 2000; only 14 percent of the population was literate.

Europeans first entered Niger in the late 1700s, and missionaries arrived soon after, accessing the region via

Capital: Niamey. **Size:** 458,997 sq. miles. **Population:** 10,075,510 in 2000. **Languages:** French, Hausa, Djerma. **Religions:** 21,350 Catholics (.2%), 9,269,470 Muslims (92%), 10,675 Protestants (.13%), 774,015 practice indigenous religions. **Diocese:** Niamey, immediately subject to the Holy See.

the Niger river running south from Mali. The first Catholic mission, established in 1831 at Niamey, was entrusted to the Society of African Missions from the Vicariate of Dahomey (now Benin). In 1942 the Prefecture Apostolic of Niamey was created, with jurisdiction over northern Dahomey. When northern Dahomey was separated from this prefecture in 1948, Niger, with a portion of Upper Volta, was entrusted to the Redemptorists, but in 1949 the area of the Prefecture of Niamey was restricted to Niger. In 1961 the prefecture became the Diocese of Niamey.

Made a territory of French West Africa in 1904, Niger became an autonomous state of the French Community in 1958. It was granted full independence on Aug. 3, 1960. A military council took strict control of the government for most of the 1970s and 1980s, but in 1989 political activity was again made legal, resulting in the election of a coalition government led by Mahamane Ousmane. In 1990 Tuaregs rebels became active in the north, and violence against the government continued for five years before being resolved. In 1993 a constitution was drafted that authorized Niger's first free elections, but military coups in 1996 and again in 1999 further disrupted the nation. In 1999 a National Reconciliation Council make a further effort to establish civilian rule, and Mamadou Tandja was elected president with 60 percent of the vote. International aid, which had been suspended during the 1999 coup, resumed in 2000 as the government sought to develop Niger's struggling economy.

By 2000 Niger had 21 parishes, its faithful tended by four secular and 37 religious priests. Religious at work in the country included nine brothers and 90 sisters, who worked in the areas of health care and education, administering the country's eight primary and three secondary Catholic schools, as well as a hospital and health center in Galmi. Predominately Islamic, Niger's constitution nonetheless protected freedom of religion, and although a minority faith many followers of the Church were influential due to previous ties to the former French colonial government. Major Christian holidays were officially recognized by the state.

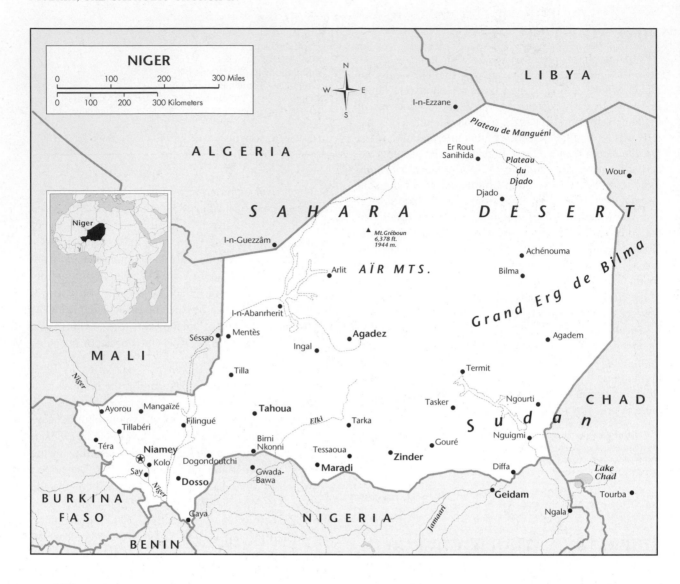

Bibliography: *Bilan du Monde,* 2:627–629. *Annuario Pontificio* has data on all diocese.

[J. BOUCHAUD/EDS.]

NIGERIA, THE CATHOLIC CHURCH IN

The Federal Republic of Nigeria is a country in West Africa, bordering Niger on the north, Chad on the northeast, Cameroon on the east, the Gulf of Guinea on the south and Benin on the west. Its coast is primarily mangrove swamp and from there the landscape rises to a plateau region, with mountains in the east and a semi-desert region to the north. Agricultural products include cocoa, soybeans, cotton, tobacco and timber, while natural resources consist of petroleum and gas reserves, coal, tin, lead, zinc and iron ore.

A largely agricultural country, Nigeria was created out of the British territories of Northern and Southern Nigeria in 1914. It received a federal constitution for three autonomous regions in 1954 and became an independent dominion in the British Commonwealth six years later. Part of the British Cameroons voted to join Nigeria in 1961. In 1963 Nigeria became a federal republic in the Commonwealth with three regions (northern, eastern and western) and the federal territory of Lagos. The most populous country in Africa, Nigeria is divided along religious lines: the Muslims that comprise half its population inhabit the north, while Christians form an important minority in the south and west. Among the region's many tribes, the Igbo are predominately Catholic.

History. Once a part of the Songhai Empire, Nigeria's coast was visited by Portuguese traders who introduced Christianity in the 15th century. While the coastal area was entrusted to the Capuchins in the 17th century, systematic evangelization did not begin until 1840, when Protestant and Catholic missionaries appeared along the coast. Ceded to Great Britain by its African king in 1861, Nigeria was administered by a succession of colonies until 1886 when it became the Colony and Protectorate of Lagos.

Nigeria became a part of the vast Vicariate Apostolic of the Two Guineas, created in 1842, but was transferred to Gabon when that vicariate was created in 1863. Priests from the Society of AFRICAN MISSIONS (SMA) arrived along with British rule in 1861. Prefectures apostolic were later formed for Upper Niger (1884) and Lower Niger (1889), after the country was briefly divided into two protectorates, the HOLY GHOST FATHERS (CSSP) sharing the missionary labor with the SMA. The Prefecture of Eastern Nigeria was created in 1911 for the more difficult missions in the Islamic north.

In 1914 the region was given the status of a single colony, and it became the Federation of Nigeria in 1954. In 1950 the hierarchy was established with two ecclesiastical provinces. Nigeria was granted its independence on Oct. 1, 1960; the same year an apostolic delegation for six countries in west-central Africa was created and headquartered in Lagos, Nigeria's capital.

In 1967 the eastern region of Biafra seceded from Nigeria, creating a state of civil war that lasted into 1970. In 1991 the capital was moved from Lagos to the central city of Abjua. By 1993 the country was ruled by General Sani Abacha, who promised to return the country to civilian rule within three years. However, his regime continued, amid charges of corruption and human rights abuses, and the imprisonment of many Nigerians on charges of insurrection, prompting Nigerian bishops to speak out in favor of democracy and the growing violence. During a March of 1998 visit by Pope John Paul II, Abacha's regime was addressed, the pope noting that "(there is) no place for intimidation and oppression of the poor and weak, for the arbitrary exclusion of individuals and groups from political life, and for the abuse of power and authority." The pope's visit was preceded by a government crackdown on dissidents.

Religious Strife Marks Transition to 21st Century. Elections were held in Nigeria in 1999, following the adoption of a new constitution based on Islamic law, English law and tribal law. President Olusegun Obasanjo, a Christian, was faced with numerous economic problems, among them broadening an economy reliant on petroleum exports and modernizing the nation's agricultural industry. Also of concern were continual flare-ups of ethnic tensions, such as the violence between Ijaw and Itsekiri in the oil-rich Delta State.

Capital: Abjua.
Size: 356,700 sq. miles.
Population: 123,337,822 in 2000.
Languages: English; Hausa, Yoruba, Igbo, and Fulani are spoken in various regions.
Religions: 16,033,916 Catholics (13%), 61,789,210 Muslims (50%), 33,301,215 Protestants (27%), 12,694,679 practice indigenous faiths (10%).

While the government did not impose a religion, it allowed states to adopt the Islamic Shari'a law as they chose. Under the strict imposition of such laws, alcohol was banned, only people with beards would be awarded government contracts, Islam became a required subject in public schools and men and women were not allowed to travel together on public transportation. Violations of law garnered such harsh punishments as public stoning and amputation. In the 1990s this prompted several northern states—among them Amfara, Kano, Niger and Sokoto—to become what critics argued were de facto Islamic states, as state governments funded the construction of mosques and otherwise supported the Islamic faith. By early 2000 northern Nigeria was wracked by ethnic violence as state governments sought to expand Shari'a into Kaduna state, which had a significant Christian population. Churches and mosques were destroyed, while thousands died in scattered riots, prompting the government to restrict some religious activity.

In February of 2000 President Obasanjo and Muslim leaders in northern Nigeria agreed that the imposition of Muslim law should cease. However, tensions continued to exist, resulting in violent flare-ups by religious extremists. In Kaduna it was reported in May of 2000 that a bounty had been placed on the head of all Catholic priests. The report came shortly after a priest in Kaduna was brutally murdered by a Muslim mob. As northern states continued to respond to the will of extremists and adopt the Shari'a criminal code, bishops increased their calls to the government to protect the rights of non-Muslims. "It is dangerous to presume that all is well simply because we are no longer burning houses or killing one another," Abuja Archbishop Onaiyekan noted publicly. "No one should expect a situation of blatant injustice to continue indefinitely without consequences."

By 2000 Nigeria had 1,528 parishes, tended by 2,494 diocesan and 640 religious priests. Within the country, 428 brothers and 2,968 sisters dedicated themselves to humanitarian efforts and the operation of the nation's 2,870 primary and 244 secondary schools. In addition to the continued religious strife in the northern states, the attention of the Church was directed towards the rising death toll resulting from the spread of AIDS within Nige-

Archdioceses	Suffragans
Abuja	Idah, Lafia, Lokoja, Makurdi, Otukpo
Benin City	Issele-Uku, Warri
Calabar	Ikot-Ekpene, Ogoja, Port Harcourt, Uyo
Ibadan	Ekiti, Ondo, Osogbo, Oyo
Jos	Jalingo, Maiduguri, Yola
Kaduna	Ilorin, Kafanchan, Kano, Minna, Sokoto, Zaria
Lagos	Abeokuta, Ijebu-Ode
Onitsha	Abakaliki, Awka, Enugu, Nnewi, Nsukka
Owerri	Aba, Ahiara, Okigwe, Orlu, Umuahia

There are apostolic vicariates at Bauchi and Bomadi and an apostolic prefecture at Kontagora.

ria's population, as well as government efforts to legalize abortion during a constitutional review in 2002.

Bibliography: *Bilan du Monde,* 2:630–638. *Annuario Pontificio* has annual data on all dioceses and prefectures.

[J. BOUCHAUD/EDS.]

NIHIL OBSTAT

The Latin expression *nihil obstat* means literally "there is nothing standing in the way." As a contemporary canonical term *nihil obstat* is employed in at least two ways: to name the kind of evaluative judgment that an ecclesiastical censor makes about a writing submitted for approval prior to publication, and to describe the form of clearance given by the Holy See to a person who is eligible for certain kinds of teaching positions in ecclesiastical faculties.

In the context of the Church's discipline on the censorship of books (cc. 823–832 in the 1983 Code of Canon Law), the local ordinary (usually the diocesan bishop) appoints a censor to review books which are submitted for the ordinary's permission to publish (*imprimatur*). The censor makes a judgment about the book by comparing it to or measuring it by "the teaching of the Church about faith and morals as it is proposed by the ecclesiastical magisterium" (c. 831). The censor grants the *nihil obstat*

if he or she perceives that the writing will not be harmful to the faith or morals of the Christian faithful. It is an essentially negative judgment: "I detect nothing harmful; I have no opposition." In making this decision censors should bear in mind the maxim which Pope John XXIII applied to this process, "In essentials unity, in debatable questions liberty, in all things charity" [*Acta Apostolicae Sedis* 51 (1959) 867].

In the context of the regulation of ecclesiastical faculties, which are those empowered by the Apostolic See to grant academic degrees having canonical effects in the Church (c. 815–821), the *nihil obstat* is required for those teachers who are to be given permanent tenure or a promotion to the highest rank of the professoriat [*Sapientia christiana* (April 15, 1979) n. 27; ActApS 71 (1979) 483]. The *nihil obstat* is granted by the Congregation for Catholic Education. No criteria for making the judgment have been published, hence the grounds for giving or withholding the *nihil obstat* are obscure. The *nihil obstat* of the Holy See is the declaration that there is nothing to impede a nomination which is proposed.

[J. A. CORIDEN]

NIHILISM

Nihilism is a 19th–century Russian intellectual movement expressed in a party program of revolutionary reform and terrorism. The word is derived from *nihil,* "nothing," and was popularized by Ivan Turgenev's novel *Fathers and Sons* (1862). Russian nihilism has little in common with what is called nihilism in the West. It was born under the czarist absolutism that evoked a powerful revulsion and antagonism in all lovers of freedom and righteousness. A movement for the liberation of human beings from any sort of enslavement found its fullest expression, especially between 1860 and 1870, in nihilism, of which the chief protagonists were Nikolai G. Chernishevsky (1828–89), Nikolai Dobrolyubov (1836–61), and Dmitry I. Pisarev (1841–68). To them the struggle for the complete emancipation of individuality was the highest value. They were extremely hostile toward everything that they termed abstract and refused to grant value to any manifestation that had no social consequences. They waged a rude and relentless war against any kind of social, political, and religious "oppression." In the concrete, they renounced God, spirit, soul, state, church, morality, nationality, and "high" culture. They were earnest in their desire for the creation of a "new man" and the destruction of the old. Their consistency and tenacity in propagating their crude materialist and utilitarian philosophy was comparable with religious endeavor. Many nihilists carried self–sacrifice so far as to

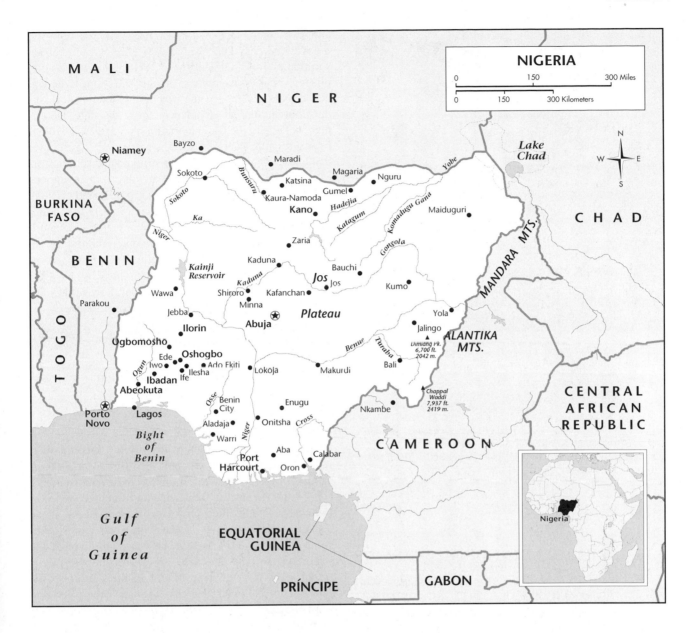

NIGERIA

0   150   300 Miles

0   150   300 Kilometers

volunteer to take the place of revolutionaries under sentence of death, lest the movement should be deprived of its leaders.

Materialism and atheism were at once preconditions and logical consequences of nihilist criticism and negation. The nihilists railed against the "unpractical" rigors of Christian morality. To them all things were lawful as long as they were useful for the individual. Their ethos was expressed in Chernishevsky's novel *What Is to Be Done?* (1863), recognized as the nihilist catechism. It emphasized love of truth; repudiated falsehood, embellishment, and exalted rhetoric; and rejected every sort of felicity that life offers. These principles were consistently followed in personal relationships and, above all, in friendship and in marriage. In nihilist circles friendship was based upon inexorable straight–forwardness, and marriage was regarded as the truest of all relationships of life.

Nihilism adopted an attitude of suspicion toward "high" culture created by a privileged class and designed only for this class. Art as a manifestation of idealism was absolutely renounced. The nihilists aimed at annihilating aesthetics either in externals or in the forms of social intercourse. They patronized the natural sciences to which they looked for the solution of all problems. In economics they propagated utopian socialism. The negation of higher authority, scientific and artistic individualism, the spirit of absolute independence, the struggle against theological and theocratic idealism, the extreme radicalism, and, to a large extent, the anarchism of the nihilists anticipated communism in Russia.

Group of boys marching at head of Catholic procession, Lagos, Nigeria. (©Paul Almasy/CORBIS)

Bibliography: T. G. MASARYK, *The Spirit of Russia,* tr. E. and C. PAUL, 2 v. (2d ed. New York 1955). H. KOHN, *The Mind of Modern Russia* (New York 1962). G. A. WETTER, *Dialectical Materialism: A Historical and Systematic Survey of Philosophy in the Soviet Union,* tr. P. HEATH (New York 1959). N. A. BERDÍAEV, *The Russian Idea,* tr. R. M. FRENCH (Boston 1962).

[C. C. GECYS]

NIKON, PATRIARCH OF MOSCOW

Patriarchate 1652–1660; b. Vel'demanovo, near Nizhniĭ Novgorod (Gorkiĭ since 1932), Russia, 1605; d. near Yaroslavl, Aug. 17, 1681. Nikon was the name in religion of Nikita Minin (or Minov), who came of peasant stock. After ordination as a Russian Orthodox priest (1625), he served in a rural parish until 1627, when he went to Moscow. After the death of his children he became a hermit on the island of Anser in the White Sea (1635) and then entered the monastery at Kozheozerskiĭ, where he became abbot (1643). In 1646 he was presented to Czar Alexis I (1645–76), whose influential counselor he became. He was appointed metropolitan of Novgorod (1646) and patriarch of Moscow (1652). Nikon was a zealous pastor, a popular preacher, and a promoter of the evangelization of Siberia. The liturgical reforms he decreed in 1653 brought the Russian liturgy to closer conformity with Greek and Ukrainian customs but suppressed numerous Russian traditional practices. Because of this he incurred the enmity of AVVAKUM and other conservatives who formed the ultranationalistic and antigovernment sect of RASKOLNIKS. Nikon's liturgical innovations paved the way for Moscow's political absorption of the Ukraine (1654–67). Once this was accomplished, Nikon's usefulness to the ambitious czar was ended. Nikon alienated the czar by his attempt to make the Church completely independent of the state. He further challenged the Russian tradition of CAESARO-PAPISM by asserting the superiority of the patriarchal dignity over that of the czar. During the czar's frequent absences from Moscow, Nikon acted as regent and did so in an authoritarian manner. The combination of religious and civil opposition led to Nikon's deposition (1660). In 1666 a synod in Moscow, attended by some of the Oriental patriarchs, exiled Nikon to the remote monastery of Belozerskiĭ-Ferapontov, but it definitively approved his liturgical reforms. He was granted amnesty by Czar Fëdor III (1676–80), but he died soon after, while journeying to his favorite monastery of Voskresenskiĭ.

Bibliography: W. PALMER, *The Patriarch and the Tsar,* 4 v. (London 1871–76). J. LEDIT, *Dictionnaire de théologie catholique* 11.1:646–655; 14.1:292–304.

[F. L. FADNER]

NILLES, NIKOLAUS

Liturgist and canonist; b. Rippweiler, Luxembourg, June 21, 1828; d. Innsbruck, Jan. 31, 1907. After his ordination in 1852 Nilles was appointed curate at Ansemberg (1853–58). He entered the Jesuits on March 20, 1858. In 1859 he was appointed professor of Canon Law at the University of Innsbruck and held the chair almost until his death; from 1870 to 1896 he was also rector of the seminary. He contributed 57 articles to the *Archiv für katholisches Kirchenrecht* and 94 to the *Zeitschrift für katholische Theologie.* He also published the following works: *Symbolae ad illustrandam historiam ecclesiae orientalis in terris coronae S. Stephani* (2 v. Innsbruck 1885), *De rationibus festorum sacratissimi Cordis Jesu et purissimi Cordis Mariae* (2 v. 5th ed. Innsbruck 1885), and *Kalendarium manuale utriusque ecclesiae orientalis et occidentalis* (2 v. 3d ed. Innsbruck 1896–97).

Bibliography: M. BLUM, *Das Collegium Germanicum zu Rom und dessen Zöglinge aus dem Luxemburger Lande* (Luxembourg 1899) 94–109. H. HURTER, *Nomenclator literarius theologiae catholicae* (Innsbruck 1903–13) 5.2:2067–69. H. LECLERCQ, *Dictionnaire d'archéologie chrétienne et de liturgie,* ed. F. CABROL, H. LECLERCQ and H. I. MARROU (Paris 1907–53) 9.2:1732–34.

[C. TESTORE]

NILUS OF ANCYRA, ST.

Abbot, ascetic writer also known as Nilus "the Elder" or "the Wise"; b. probably Ancyra (modern Ankara, Turkey), date unknown; d. Ancyra, *c.* 430. The romantic *Narrationes de caede monachorum in monte Sinae (Patrologia Graeca* 79:589–693) purports to be biography, and explains the modern misnomer, Nilus Sinaites. According to this legend, Nilus was prefect of Constantinople but left office, wife, and home to become a monk with his son Theodulus on Mt. Sinai. When the monks were attacked by barbarians, Theodulus was captured but later he was set free and reunited with Nilus, who had escaped. Impressed by their piety, the bishop of Eleusa ordained them priests and sent them back to Sinai.

Nilus's own works give more reliable biographical data. In Constantinople he esteemed JOHN CHRYSOSTOM, regarded him as his teacher, and boldly took his side against his foes. Nilus left Constantinople and became abbot of a monastery near Ancyra. His skill as a spiritual counselor is attested by his treatises on moral and ascetic subjects and by more than 1,000 letters addressed mostly to otherwise unknown recipients. Several of these are merely excerpts from his own treatises or the works of others, particularly of John Chrysostom. Many of his writings explain passages of Scripture; in these he follows the literal or historical sense but makes free use of allegorical interpretations. He refutes ARIANISM in eight letters to Gainas, general of the Goths. Other topics range from proper uses of mosaics in churches to condemnation of peculiar practices among monks, such as the STYLITES. The tracts *De oratione* and *De malignis cogitationibus,* formerly attributed to Nilus, are the work of EVAGRIUS PONTICUS.

Feast: Nov. 12.

Bibliography: *Patrologia Graeca,* ed. J. P. MIGNE, 161 v. (Paris 1857–66) v. 79. NILUS OF ANCYRA, *Narratio,* ed. F. CONCA (Leipzig 1983). K. HEUSSI, *Das Nilusproblem* (Leipzig 1921). G. T. STOKES, *A Dictionary of Christian Biography,* ed. W. SMITH and H. WACE, 4 v. (London 1877–87) 4:43–45. J. QUASTEN, *Patrology,* 4 v. (Westminster, Md. 1950–86) 3:496–504. M. T. DISDIER, *Dictionnaire de théologie catholique,* ed. A. VACANT et al., 15 v. (Paris 1903–50; Tables générales 1951–) 11.1:661–674.

[P. W. HARKINS]

NILUS OF ROSSANO, ST.

Abbot, propagator of Greek monasticism in Italy, also known as Nilus the Younger; b. Rossano, Calabria, Italy, *c.* 905; d. Abbey of Santa Agata, near Frascati, Italy, Dec. 29, 1005. After the sudden death of his wife and daughter and his own recovery from a serious illness, Nilus underwent a profound religious conversion and joined a community of Basilian monks near Mercurion, where the traditions of BASILIAN MONASTICISM in Italy had been kept alive in spite of the declining power of the Eastern Empire on the peninsula. He soon left the cloister and led a rigorously ascetic life in a secluded cave, in imitation of the fathers of the desert. But the Saracen invasions forced him *c.* 950 to found and settle down in the monastery of San Adriano near Rossano, and while abbot there he was offered, but refused, the archbishopric of his native city. Continued Muslim incursions forced his group of Basilian monks to take refuge for a while at MONTE CASSINO, the motherhouse of Benedictine monasticism. Nilus's community next settled nearby at Valleluce and fifteen years later established its LAURA at Serperi near Gaeta. It was here, *c.* 1000, that Nilus received Emperor OTTO III, who was highly impressed by the abbot's work. Although Nilus had supported Pope GREGORY V against the antipope John XVI, who was supported by the CRESCENTII, he pleaded in vain with both pope and emperor to show mercy to the usurper when he fell into their hands. Nilus also found time to write a few pieces of liturgical poetry and some letters. In 1004 he received from Gregory, count of Tusculum, a grant of land on the lower slopes of Monte Cavo, where he made a foundation that remains today the center of Greek monasticism in Italy. Although he died before work was well under way, he is still listed as the first abbot of GROTTAFERRATA. One of his successors, Bartholomew the Younger (d. *c.* 1065), wrote a Greek life of Nilus.

Feast: Sept. 26.

Bibliography: *Acta Sanctorum* 7:259–320. *Patrologia Graeca,* ed. J. P. MIGNE, 161 v. (Paris 1857–66) 120:15–165. *Analecta Bollandiana* 61 (1943) 204–206. *Bibliotheca hagiographica Graeca,* ed. F. HALKIN, 3 v. (Brussels 1957) 1370. G. MINASI, *San Nilo di Calabria* (Naples 1892). A. ROCCHI, *Vita di San Nilo abate* (Rome 1904). J. GAY, *L'Italie méridionale et l'Empire byzantin* (Paris 1904). S. GASSISI IEROMONACO, ''I Manoscritti autografti di San Nilo Juniore . . . ,'' *Oriens Christianus* 4 (1904) 308–370; *Poesie di San Nilo Juniore e di Paolo Monaco abati di Grottaferrata,* in *Oriens Christianus* 5 (1905) 26–81. A. M. ZIMMERMANN, *Kalendarium Benedictinum: Die Heiligen und Seligen des Benediktinerordens und seiner Zweige,* 4 v. (Metten 1933–38) 3:107–108. T. MINISCI, *Santa Maria di Grottaferrata . . .* (Grottaferrata 1955). H. G. BECK, *Kirche und theologische Literatur im byzantinischen Reich* (Munich 1959) 607–608. G. PENCO, *Storia del monachesimo in Italia* (Rome 1961), *passim.* B. CAPPELLI, *Il monachesimo basiliano ai confini calabro-lucania; studi e ricerche* (Naples 1963). G. PASSARELLI, *Nilo di Rossano: fiore di melograno* (Reggio Calabria 1990).

[B. J. COMASKEY]

NINA, LORENZO

Cardinal, secretary of state; b. Recanati (Marches), Italy, May 12, 1812; d. Rome, July 25, 1885. After seminary studies in Recanati and Rome, he studied law at the University of Rome and was ordained in 1834. After entering the service of the Roman CURIA, he became successively secretary of the rota; then, in the Congregation of the COUNCIL, first auditor to the secretary and later under-secretary. Pius IX named him assessor of the Holy Office and cardinal (March 1877). LEO XIII appointed him secretary of state (Aug. 9, 1878); ill health forced his retirement (Dec. 16, 1880). Although affable and prudent, he was less a diplomat than a theologian. He favored a settlement with the Kingdom of Italy. He had to deal in Belgium with the "school war" that led to the rupture of diplomatic relations (June 1880) and in France with the hostility of the Third Republic toward religious congregations. In both cases he urged Catholics to moderation. Through the nuncio to Vienna, Ludovico JACOBINI, he negotiated for a settlement of the KULTURKAMPF.

Bibliography: E. SODERINI, *Il pontificato di Leone XIII,* 3 v. (Milan 1932–33); tr. B. B. CARTER, v. 1 *The Pontificate of Leo XIII* (London 1934), v. 2 *Leo XIII, Italy and France* (1935), v. 3 not tr.

[J. M. MAYEUR]

NINEVEH

Ancient city of Assyria and its capital under the last kings of the Assyrian Empire. Its position on the eastern bank of the Tigris (opposite modern Mosul) where this river is joined by the Khosar River made the site a natural fortress, for water from the latter stream, which ran through the center of the city, could be diverted to fill the moats on the north, east, and south sides of the city. The massive walls that were erected in the last period of the city's existence (seventh century B.C.) enclosed an irregular-shaped area of *c.* 1,800 acres; the wall on the north was *c.* 7,000 feet long, on the east *c.* 3 miles long, on the south *c.* 1,000 feet long, and on the west (along the Tigris) *c.* 2 1/2 miles long. Two large mounds on the western side now stand out over the ruins of the rest of the city: that of Nebi Yūnus (the Prophet Jonah), on which is the reputed tomb of Jonah, formerly a Nestorian shrine, but now Muslim, and that of Quyunjik (little lamb).

The site of Nineveh (Akkadian *Ninua* and *Ninâ;* Heb. *nîneweh*) was occupied from at least 3800 B.C. until the time of its utter destruction by the Medes and Babylonians in 612 B.C. Although earlier Assyrian kings, who regularly resided at Assur (Asshur) or Calah (modern Khorsabad), had often used Nineveh as a secondary capital, it was only during the most glorious period of Assyrian history under the last three rulers of the Assyrian Empire—Sennacherib (705–682), Asarhaddon (681–670), and Assurbanipal (669–*c.* 633)—that Nineveh became the sole capital.

Although the native Arabic-speaking people still call this immense field of ruins Ninawa, as they have appar-

ently done for centuries, the Western world, even in Greco-Roman times, did not know where the famous city lay. The site was first clearly identified and made known to the Western world by C. J. Rich in 1821. The sacred nature of the mound of Nebi Yūnus, which covers the palace of Sennacherib, has prevented extensive excavation from being made there; but the mound of Quyunjik, with its palaces of Asarhaddon and Assurbanipal, has been subjected to repeated excavations. The earlier excavations were merely treasure hunts, which were extremely successful in sensational finds of sculptures and inscriptions; it is only in the 20th century that the site has been scientifically excavated, with careful regard for the archeological strata and the pottery so useful for chronology. Almost all of the inscriptions (especially cuneiform tablets), as well as most of the sculptures found at Nineveh, are now in the British Museum. The excavations were made here by P. E. Botta (1842), A. H. Layard (1845–47, 1849–51), H. Rawlinson (1853–55), H. Rassam (1854 and 1877–83, when he discovered Assurbanipal's great library of cuneiform tablets), G. A. Smith (1873–74), E. A. Wallis Budge (1888–89), L. W. King (1902). R. Campbell Thomson (1927–28), and the latter with M. Mallowan (1929–32).

In the Bible, Nineveh is said to have been built by Nimrod (Gn 10.11). Sennacherib returned home there after his failure to capture Jerusalem (2 Kgs 19.36; Is 37.37). ZEPHANIAH foretold the destruction of Nineveh (Zep 2.12–15), and the whole Book of NAHUM is a vivid description of its capture by the Medes and Babylonians. Jonah is said to have preached to the people of Nineveh, "the great city" (Jon 1.2; 3.1–10; 4.11), and Jesus referred to their repentance as a model for the men of His own time (Mt 12.41; Lk 11.32). TOBIT is portrayed as living in this city with his fellow exiles (Tb 1.3; 7.3; 11.1; 14.4, 15).

Bibliography: *Encyclopedic Dictionary of the Bible,* tr. and adap. by L. HARTMAN (New York 1963) 1644–45. M. RUTTEN et al., *Dictionnaire de la Bible,*, suppl. ed. L. PIROT, et al. (Paris 1928–) 6:480–506, R. C. THOMPSON and R. W. HUTCHINSON, *A Century of Exploration at Nineveh* (London 1929). A. PARROT, *Nineveh and the Old Testament,* tr. B. E. HOOKE (Studies in Biblical Archaeology 3; New York 1955; London 1956). S. A. PALLIS, *The Antiquity of Iraq* (Copenhagen 1956).

[L. A. BUSHINSKI]

NINGUARDA, FELICIANO

Italian Dominican, theologian, writer, and bishop; b. Morbegno (Sondrio), 1524; d. Como, 1595. In 1554 he was appointed vicar-general of the Order, and later professor of theology at the University of Vienna. He was invited by the Archbishop of Salzburg to be his procurator at the third session of the Council of TRENT (1562–63). Then he was entrusted with implementing the reform decrees of Trent in visitations of the religious houses of the mendicant orders in Austria, Bohemia, and Moravia. At the same time, as papal commissioner, he worked toward the reform of the Diocese of Salzburg and convoked a provincial synod in 1569. He was made bishop of Scala (Salerno) in 1577, and shortly after was appointed apostolic nuncio to Bavaria, where he served until 1583. He was transferred to the episcopal see of Santa Agata dei Goti (Benevento) in 1583, and, finally in 1588, to that of Como, his native diocese, where he died. His works include the *Defensio fidei maiorum nostrorum* (Antwerp 1575); *Manuale parochorum* (Ingolstadt 1582); *Enchiridion de censuris, irregularitate et privilegiis* (Ingolstadt 1583); and the *Manuale visitatorum* (Rome 1589).

Bibliography: J. QUÉTIF and J. ÉCHARD, *Scriptores Ordinis Praedicatorum* (New York 1959) 2:313–314. K. SCHELLHASS, *Der Dominikaner Feliciano Ninguarda und die Gegenreformation in Süddeutschland und Österreich, 1560–1583* (Rome 1930). A. WALZ, *I Domenicani al Concilio di Trento* (Rome 1961).

[A. L. REDIGONDA]

NINIAN, ST.

Early fifth-century apostle of Galloway, Scotland. Ninian, a Briton by birth, educated in the Roman rite and tradition (''regulariter'' according to BEDE, *Eccl. Hist.* 3.4), preached to the southern Picts and built in Galloway, southwest Scotland, a church of stone, called the *Candida casa,* dedicated to St. MARTIN OF TOURS. His ''converts among the Picts'' were probably the ''apostates'' referred to in the letters of St. PATRICK (*Epist.* 2, 15). His settlement, renamed Whithorn by the Anglo-Saxons, became a monastic center to which many Irish monks went for religious training in the sixth century. The inscription on his tomb, located at the *Candida casa,* was apparently interpreted in an anti-Celtic sense by Plechtelm, the first Anglo-Saxon bishop of Galloway, so that much of what Bede relates, including the dedication to St. Martin (not earlier than 500 according to P. Grosjean), is untrustworthy.

Feast: Sept. 16.

Bibliography: P. GROSJEAN, ''Les Pictes apostats dans l'Épître de S. Patrice,'' *Analecta Bollandiana* 76 (1958) 354–378. J. MACQUEEN, *St. Nynia* (London 1961). M. ANDERSON, *St. Ninian* (London 1964). AELRED, *Saint Ninian,* ed. I. MACDONALD (Edinburgh 1993). D. BROOKE, *Wild Men and Holy Places: St. Ninian, Whithorn and the Medieval Realm of Galloway* (Edinburgh 1994). P. HILL, *Whithorn and St. Ninian: The Excavation of a Monastic Town, 1984–91* (Stroud, Gloucestershire 1997).

[J. RYAN]

NIRVĀṆA

The word (in Pāli, *nibbāna*) originally meant extinction as by fire. In HĪNAYĀNA Buddhism, which denies the existence of God and soul, all beings are transitory. The craving for permanence is the cause of pain and leads to rebirth, whose process can be stopped only by achieving nirvāṇa. The visible nirvāṇa (*saṃdiṭṭhika nibbāna*), attained in the present life by an *arhat* (Pāli, *arahant*), a being perfected by enlightenment and asceticism, is extinction of lust, hatred, and ignorance producing no seed or nucleus of further rebirth. At death the *arhat* enters the invisible absolute nirvāṇa (*parinibbāna*), which is variously interpreted as: annihilation of individual personality; liberation from rebirth into an ineffable state; a state of perfect bliss; a populous and blissful heaven where personality abides.

In MAHĀYĀNA Buddhism, a *bodhisattva,* perfected by enlightened asceticism and moved by compassion, forgoes nirvāṇa to help others until all have found salvation. In AMIDISM, the oldest and most popular school, nirvāṇa is the Pure Land of Western Paradise that Amitābha, the supreme being of mercy and love, promised all those who invoked his name with faith. For the Mādhyamika school, instead, the universe exists only in the illusion of the percipient. What really exists is emptiness—the absolute truth, being, nirvāṇa, and the Body of Essence of the Buddha (*dharmakāya*). For the nihilist Vijñānavada school the universe exists only in the mind of the perceiver, and nirvāṇa is an absurd notion. In VAJRAYĀNA (DIAMOND VEHICLE), nirvāṇa is identical with the final bliss attending the union of the phenomenal Means with the noumenal Wisdom, best symbolized and effected by sexual intercourse. In China and Japan, however, these same tenets were interpreted in a way more consonant with the general belief in the survival of the individual soul and with popular idol worship.

See Also: BUDDHISM; INDIAN PHILOSOPHY.

Bibliography: L. DE LA VALLÉ POUSSIN, *Encyclopedia of Religion and Ethics,* ed. J. HASTINGS (Edinburgh 1908–27) 9:376–379; *The Way to Nirvāna* (Cambridge, Eng. 1917). T. STCHERBATSKY, *The Conception of Buddhist Nirvana* (Leningrad 1927). V. P. VARMA, ''The Philosophy of Nirvana in Early Buddhism: A Critical and Sociological Study,'' *Journal of the Bihar Research Society* 45 (1959) 226–243. W. T. DE BARY, ed., *Introduction to Oriental Civilizations,* 3 v. (Records of Civilization 54–56; New York 1958–60).

[A. S. ROSSO]

NISCH, ULRIKA FRANZISKA, BL.

Baptized Francizka, also called Francizka of Hegne, virgin of the Sisters of Mercy of the Holy Cross of Ingenbohl (*Barmherzigen Schwestern vom Heiligen Kreuz*); b. Oberdorf-Mittelbiberarch (on the Ress River near Württemberg), Schwabia, Germany, Sept. 18, 1882; d. Hegne near Rorschach am Bodensee, May 8, 1913.

Franziska was born into extreme poverty and neglected by her parents until she was seven. Her grandmother and aunt or godmother raised her until her parents took her home to assume the household duties. She became a farm servant at age twelve and in 1901 was sent to Rorschach, Switzerland, as a domestic servant. There she fell ill, was hospitalized, and was nursed by sisters of the Holy Cross of Ingenbohl, the Swiss congregation founded by Maria Theresia Scherer.

Upon her recovery and despite having no dowry, she was accepted into the order at the German provincial house at Hegne (Oct. 17, 1904), where she was professed (April 24, 1907). She served the order as cook at Bühl, then at Saint Vincent's in Baden-Baden, but later returned to Hegne. Sister Ulrika, known for her simplicity and joy, was gifted with profound mystical experiences, especially visions of the angels and saints, until 1912.

Following her death from tuberculosis at age thirty, her grave at Hegne became a pilgrimage site. Since 1991, her mortal remains have been housed in the convent church crypt at Hegne. She was beatified on Nov. 1, 1987 by Pope John Paul II.

Feast: May 8.

Bibliography: B. BAUR, *Kein Maß kennt die Liebe. Ulrika Nisch, Kreuzschwester von Hegne* (Constance 1963). W. BÜHLMANN, *Er hat auf meine Niedrigkeit geschaut: der Weg von Schwester Ulrika Nisch Kreuzschwester von Hegne, Mutterhaus Ingenbohl/Schweiz* (Beuron 1987). K. HEMMERLE, *Die leise Stimme: Ulrika Nisch ihr Weg und ihre Botschaft* (Freiburg 1987). G. MOSER, *Aus unserer Mitte: Rupert Mayer, Ulrika Nisch, Edith Stein* (Rottenburg, 1988). *Acta Apostolicae Sedis* (1987): 1117. *L'Osservatore Romano,* Eng. ed. 47 (1987): 7–8.

[K I. RABENSTEIN]

NISIBIS

Nisibis, modern Nusaybin, is a city in Turkey on the Syrian border, about 130 miles northwest of Mosul, formerly an important military and commercial center, as well as the site of a noted Nestorian theological school. The city, which is situated by the river Yaghyagha (ancient Mygdonius) as it flows through a narrow canyon from the mountains into the plains, was referred to at the beginning of the first millennium B.C. in Assyrian inscriptions under the name of Nasibina. In the 3rd century B.C. it was the capital of a rich province under the Seleucids, and was called Antiochia Mygdonia by the Greeks. For some time it was also the residence of the kings of Armenia.

Because of its strategic importance and its location on the upper trade route from Mosul to the west, the city was the scene of warfare until recent times. In 68 B.C. it was captured by Pompey but was retaken by the Persians 15 years later. In A.D. 115 its capture by Emperor Trajan earned him the title of "Parthicus." Once more lost to the Persians, it was restored to Roman rule by Septimius Severus in 297 and served as a frontier fortress. In 338, 346, and 350 it was besieged by the Persian king Shapur II; the sieges are described by St. Ephrem in his *Carmina Nisibena.* In 363 Emperor Jovian was forced to cede the city to Persia, at which time the Christians were allowed to depart. Most of the population, then, including the Christian theological school, settled in Edessa. After being taken by the Arabs in 640, the city continued to prosper well into the 10th century. Ravaged by the Mongols in 1260, Nisibis declined rapidly and by the 14th century was in ruins. By the mid-20th century it was a small town of about 3,000 inhabitants on the main railroad from Baghdad to Alep and into central Turkey.

The beginnings of Christianity in Nisibis are uncertain. According to legend, ADDAI AND MARI, two of the 72 disciples of Christ, are said to have established the church there. The first known bishop, however, was Jacob (290–338). In 410 it appears as a metropolitan see with seven suffragans, ranked immediately after Seleucia–Ctesiphon and Beth–Lapat. From the second half of the 5th century the bishops were Nestorians, and the school of NISIBIS became the theological center of the Persian Nestorian Church. There exist ruins of an ancient, two–nave church called Mar Yakub, used until very recently by the JACOBITES. Nisibis is also a Latin titular see.

Bibliography: M. LE QUIEN, *Oriens Christianus,* 3 v. (Graz 1958) 2:995–998, 1192–1204. C. PREUSSER, *Nordmesopotamische Baudenkmäler,* 2 pts. (Leipzig 1911) 40.

[G. T. DENNIS]

NISIBIS, SCHOOL OF

About the middle of the 4th century NISIBIS was known as a center of theological studies, counting among its teachers St. EPHREM. When the city came under Persian rule in 363, St. Ephrem and the school moved to Edessa within the boundaries of the Roman Empire. After the Council of Ephesus in 431 a large number of Nestorians settled in Edessa and, for a short period, took over control of the theological school. Because of imperial persecution, however, they were forced to seek refuge outside the empire and moved to Nisibis, where their opposition to the official Roman doctrine and, consequently, to the Roman emperor earned them the protection of the Persian rulers. The theological school of EDESSA was continued in Nisibis under the patronage of the Nestorian metropolitan Bar Sauma. Its foundation can be dated to about 457, the year in which its first great teacher, Narsai (Narses), who had taught in Edessa, arrived and began lecturing on theology, a task that he continued for some 40 years. For 200 years or more the school of Nisibis flourished under a succession of famous teachers, such as Abraham, the nephew of Narsai, Paul, Elias bar Sīnājā, 'ABDISHO (Ebedjesus) bar Berīkā, and others. The number of students seems to have been considerable; Abraham de beth Rabban, the second successor of Narsai and rector of the school for 60 years, had over 1,000 students. The graduates of the school filled the episcopal sees throughout the then prosperous Church in Persia, so that the entire Church in that region and in its missionary areas became Nestorian in doctrine. The foundation of another theological school about 541 by Aba Mar in Seleucia-Ctesiphon was a strong blow to Nisibis, and the establishment of the school of Baghdad about 830 led to its rapid decline.

From the beginning the theological teaching at Nisibis was based on the works of Nestorius, Diodor of Tarsus, and in particular, THEODORE OF MOPSUESTIA. In general, the instructors at Nisibis limited themselves to explaining the doctrine of Theodore, especially his commentaries on Scripture, adding very little of their own. Among the Nestorians Theodore was known as "The Commentator" par excellence. Following the pre-Chalcedonian terminology of Theodore they spoke of two natures and two hypostases with one *prosopon* in Christ. The doctrine was officially accepted by the Persian Church in a synod at Seleucia-Ctesiphon in 486 and again in 612.

The curriculum and the statutes of the school of Nisibis, undoubtedly based upon those of Edessa, have been conserved, and they probably represent the oldest statutes of any Christian theological school known to exist. The detailed regulations were revised and made stricter in 496 and again in 590. The course of studies lasted three years, and instruction was given gratuitously. The school was under the direction of a rector (Rabban) and a master who, aided by a council, was in charge of disciplinary and financial matters. There were two principal professors: the first, referred to as the Interpreter, explained Scripture according to the commentaries of Theodore of Mopsuestia; the other was known as the Master of the Lessons. The students were obliged to live in community, somewhat similar in organization to a modern seminary. They studied in a common hall where the desks differed according to students' ranks. They were forbidden to enter the Roman (Byzantine) Empire without special permission. The school was practically exempt from episcopal jurisdiction and enjoyed a number of civil privileges as well.

A description of the organization and the spirit of the school is given by a 6th-century teacher: Mar Barhadbešabba 'Arbaya, *Cause de la fondation des écoles* [ed. A. Scher, *Patrologia Orientalis,* four (Paris 1908) 317–404, Syriac text with French translation]. A history of the school and an account of the teaching of Narsai and Abraham have been given by the same author [*Patrologia Orientalis* 9 (Paris 1913) 588–631].

Bibliography: R. NELZ, *Die theologischen Schulen der morgenländischen Kirchen* (Bonn 1916) 77–110. A. BAUMSTARK, *Geschichte der syrischen Literatur* (Bonn 1922) 113–115. I. ORTIZ DE URBINA, *Patrologia syriaca* (Rome 1958) 107–111. W. DE VRIES, *Sakramententheologie bei den Nestorianern (Orientalia Christiana Analecta* [Rome 1935–] 133; 1947); *Der Kirchenbegriff der von Rom getrennten Syrer (ibid.* 145; 1955). W. F. MACOMBER, "The Christology of the Synod of Seleucia-Ctesiphon, A.D. 486," *Orientalia Christiana periodica* 24 (1958) 142–154; "The Theological Synthesis of Cyrus of Edessa, an East Syrian Theologian of the Mid-Sixth Century," *ibid.* 30 (1964) 5–38.

[G. T. DENNIS]

NIVARD, BL.

Cistercian monk; b. Fontaines-les-Dijon, Burgundy, France, *c.* 1100; d. *c.* 1150. Nivard was the youngest brother of BERNARD OF CLAIRVAUX. Following his brother's example, he joined CÎTEAUX at an early age and was later transferred to CLAIRVAUX. By order of Bernard, he participated in the foundation of a number of new Cistercian monasteries in various capacities; further details of his life, including the date and place of death, are unknown. According to unsubstantiated tradition, he was buried at Clairvaux. His cult can be traced to the 16th century but was restricted to certain Cistercian communities.

Feast: Feb. 7.

Bibliography: G. MÜLLER, "Der helige Nivard," *Cistercienser-Chronik* 8 (1896) 43–51. S. LENSSEN, *Hagiologiuim cisterciense* (Tilburg 1948–49) 1:188–189. W. W. WILLIAMS, *Saint Bernard of Clairvaux* (Westminster, MD 1952) 4–84. M. RAYMOND, *The Family That Overtook Christ* (Boston 1986) 365–413.

[L. J. LEKAI]

NIZA, MARCOS DE

Franciscan priest, discoverer of Arizona and New Mexico; b. *c.* 1495; d. Mexico City, March 25, 1558. Fray Marco was probably a native of Nice, hence a Savoyard and neither French nor Italian. He was already a priest, a member of the Friars Minor of the Regular Observance, and reputed a learned man when, in 1531, he left Europe for New Spain. Nothing is known of his earlier life.

While being detained at Hispaniola he heard about Peru, which was then being conquered, and volunteered his services for that region. Once commissioned by the commissary general of the Indies to act in his name, Fr. Marcos de Niza, as vice-commissary, became the leader of the first Franciscan friars to enter Peru, then comprising Ecuador and the present Peru. He participated in two expeditions there between 1531 and January 1535. His memorandum, executed at Santiago del Quito (Riobamba), Aug. 29, 1534, might be regarded as the official proclamation of the existence of the Custody of the Name of Jesus.

From April 20, 1535, to at least Sept. 25, 1536, Fray Marcos was in Guatemala. From there he proceeded to Mexico, arriving before April 4, 1537. In 1538 he was commissioned to explore the land north of Mexico; upon his return in August of 1539, he submitted a report, his *Relación,*

De Niza is credited with discovering present-day New Mexico. In 1540 he accompanied Coronado on his conquering expedition. From 1540 to 1543 Fray Marcos served also as provincial of the Province of the Holy Gospel in Mexico. Fray Marcos, crippled by paralysis induced by the hardships suffered during two of his later expeditions, was sent to the warmer climate of Jalapa, where Mendieta met him in 1554. Shortly before his death he asked to be brought back to Mexico City to be laid to rest.

Bibliography: A. BANDALIER, *The Discovery of New Mexico by the Franciscan Monk Friar Marcos de Niza in 1539*, trans. M. T. RODACK (Tucson 1981). C. HALLENBECK, *The Journey of Fray Marcos de Niza* (Dallas 1987).

[G. J. UNDREINER]

NIZĀRĪS

A sect of the Isma'īlī or ''Sevener'' Shī'ī division (*see* SHĪ'ITES) of Islam, headed by the Agha Khān. At the death of the Isma'īlī Fāṭimid Caliph al-Mustanṣir in A.D. 1094, the all-powerful minister al-Afḍal passed over the caliph's eldest son, Nizār, and recognized Nizār's younger brother al-Mustā'lī as IMĀM, or religious leader. The Isma'īlīs living outside Fāṭimid territory in Persia, under the leadership of Ḥasan-i Ṣabbāḥ, master of the fortress of Alamūt, maintained their loyalty to Nizār. They later claimed that their imāms were his descendants, a statement difficult to prove or disprove. Those Isma'īlīs who followed imāms of the line of Mustā'lī were, after the extinction of the Fāṭimid Caliphate by SALADIN in 1171, confined to the Yemen and the west coast of India, where they became known as Bohras.

Under Ḥasan-i Ṣabbāḥ's ''new preaching'' the Nizārī sect, from its strongholds in Persia and Syria,

passed to active struggle against the 'Abbāsid and SELJUK SUNNĪ authorities (*see* 'ABBĀSIDS; SUNNITES), seeking to establish its own version of the Islamic state. One of their most common weapons was the careful stalking and assassination of enemies of the sect, by devotees (*fidā'-īyīn*) who usually lost their lives in the act. For this, their enemies gave them the contemptuous name of *Hashshāshīn,* addicts of hashish (intoxicating hemp), thus implying that only drug-crazed men could act so recklessly. The epithet has been europeanized as ''assassin,'' and has become a name for any common murderer by violence. The act of the *fidā'ī* was regarded within the sect as heroic and meritorious.

The crusaders came in contact with a branch of the Nizārīs in Syria, where their local head was known as the Shaykh al-Jabal, the ''Old Man of the Mountain.'' The most vigorous of these leaders, Rashīd al-Dīn Sinān, played an important role in the affairs of 12th-century Syria. In 1256 the strongholds of the sect in Persia were razed by the invading Mongols of Hūlāgū Khān, and the Nizārīs entered a period of voluntary concealment (*taqīya*). In 1817 the Imām of the Nizārīs married a daughter of Fath 'Alī Shāh of Persia and was given the title of *Āghā Khān,* which his descendants have since used as their secular title. In 1840 the Agha Khan emigrated to India where Nizārī missionaries had converted numbers of Hindus, now known as Khojas, to their doctrine. The Agha Khans of the present day have become international figures, and have done much to reorganize and modernize their community.

Bibliography: M. G. S. HODGSON, *The Order of Assassins* (The Hague 1955). J. N. HOLLISTER, *The Shi'a of India* (London 1953). B. LEWIS, ''The Isma'īlīs and the Assassins,'' *The First Hundred Years,* ed. M. W. BALDWIN, v.1 of *A History of the Crusades,* ed. K. M. SETTON (Philadelphia 1955–). J. VON HAMMER-PURGSTALL, *A History of the Assassins,* tr. O. C. WOOD (London 1835).

[J. A. WILLIAMS]

NOAH

Son of Lamech and the father of Shem, Ham, and Japheth (Gn 5:28–32). In the Flood story in Genesis 6:1–9:19, God preserves Noah and his family, so that Noah is the ancestor of all humankind after the Flood. Following God's directions, Noah preserves some from each species of animals and birds to repopulate the earth in a renewed creation after the flood. Following the flood another story describes Noah as the first to plant a vineyard and make wine (Gn 9:20–28). Outside Genesis, Noah is referred to or mentioned three other places in the Old Testament, twice in the Deuterocanonical Books, and six times in the New Testament.

Noah's Ark. (©Historical Picture Archive/CORBIS)

Noah and the Flood. The account of Noah in Genesis has long been recognized as a composite woven from two of Israel's ancient oral traditions, often designated the Priestly source (P) and the YAHWIST source (J). A narrative from J in 6:1–8 has the Lord resolve to destroy all living things because of what has become of the world, but then "Noah found favor in the sight of the Lord." This is seconded by a P affirmation: "Noah was a righteous man, blameless in his generation; Noah walked with God" (v. 9). The P source continues with its account of how the sorry state of conditions on earth brings God to announce to Noah his intention to make an end of all living things (v. 11–13). But God tells Noah to build an ark, and gives specific instructions for its materials, dimensions, and layout. Noah is to enter the ark with his family and a male and female pair of all living creatures, along with appropriate food for them and the creatures. "Noah did this; he did all that God commanded him" (v. 14–22). In a section from J, the Lord commands Noah to

enter the ark with his family, "for I have seen that you alone are righteous before me in this generation." And he is to bring seven pairs of each clean animal and bird, but single pairs of the unclean creatures. "And Noah did all that the Lord had commanded him" (7:1–5). After Noah entered the ark as "God had commanded him; and the Lord shut him in" the flood came and continued forty days and nights in J or 150 days in P until all living things were dead and "only Noah was left, and those that were with him in the ark" (7:6–24). Then "God remembered Noah" and the waters began to recede. After 150 days, the ark rested on the mountains of Ararat (8:1–5). An account from J tells how Noah opened the window of the ark and sent out a raven, then three times a dove to determine when the waters had subsided (v. 6–12). The P source then tells how Noah removed the cover from the ark and saw that the earth was drying. When the earth is dry, God tells Noah to leave the ark and begin live again on the earth (vv. 13–19). From J, Noah's first act was to

"God Orders Noah to Build the Ark," by Marcantonio Raimond, c. 1500–34. (©Historical Picture Archive/CORBIS)

build an altar and to sacrifice some of the clean animals and birds. The odor pleased the Lord, who then promises never again to destroy all living creatures (v. 20–22). The P account describes Noah and his sons as the ancestors of all subsequent humanity. Like the first humans of Genesis 1:26, humans continue to have authority over animals. God repeats the blessing given to humanity in Genesis 1:28. But now, humans are permitted to eat animals, and humans are responsible for punishing the crime of murder. And God promises in a covenant with Noah and all creation, never again to destroy life and the created order (9:1–19).

Noah's Vineyard. Another story from the J source, not originally connected to the flood account, describes Noah as the first to plant a vineyard and the first to make wine. Noah's sons are not married and share Noah's tent. In the story Noah drinks the wine and becomes drunk in his tent. Noah's son Ham, the father of Canaan, then "saw the nakedness of his father, and told his two brothers outside." Shem and Japheth then respectfully cover the nakedness of their father, without seeing it. The story is thought to be a euphemistic account of how Ham or Canaan took advantage of Noah's drunkenness to sexually violate Noah's wife (see Lv 18:8). When Noah awakes and learns what has happened, he curses Canaan and blesses Shem and Japheth. The curse and blessing are the only spoken words attributed to Noah in the Bible (9:20–27).

The placement of this story after that of the flood shows how the inclination of human hearts continues to be evil after the flood (8:21). The alienation of humans, even within a family, as a consequence of sin, continues. But now it is Noah, not the Lord, who pronounces the curse because of human sin. The three sons in the original story were Shem, Japheth, and Canaan. Ham was introduced to harmonize the story with the names of Noah's sons in the previous flood account and with the account of the nations descended from Noah that follows in chapter 10.

Noah's Name. The J story of Noah's vineyard originally followed the folk etymology about Noah's name at Genesis 5:29. Lamech named his son Noah saying, "Out of the ground that the Lord has cursed this one shall bring us relief from our work and from the toil of out hands." Lamech alludes to a consequence of the first sin in Genesis 3:17 where the Lord declared that the ground is now cursed and only by "toil" and "labor" will it yield food for humans. Lamech's pun associates Noah's name *nōah* with the verb *nhm*, "to provide relief." Noah then became "a man of the soil," planted a vineyard, and produced wine that provides humans relief from their work and toil. The Septuagint, however, translated the verb in 5:29, διαναπαύσει, "he will bring rest," reflecting an understanding that Noah's name is derived from the verb *nwh*, "rest." In the various ancient Near Eastern flood stories, the heros have various names (*See* GILGAMESH EPIC). The connection of Noah from the vineyard story with the hero of Israel's version of the Flood story probably occurred during the developing oral stages behind the J source. This is reflected in several puns in the J flood story related to the concept of "rest." For example, "then the ark came to rest, *wattānah*" (8:4), "the dove found no resting place, *mānōah*" (8:9), "then the Lord smelled the pleasing (literally, 'restful'), *hannîhōah*, aroma" (8:21). In the Latin Vulgate and its derivative translations the name appears as Noe, from the Septuagint's Νῶε.

Other Biblical References to Noah. The prophet Ezekiel identified Noah, along with Daniel and Job, as righteous (Ez 14:14–20). Ben Sira included Noah among Israel's great ancestors, noting that it was Noah's righteousness that led God to preserve life on earth (Sir 44:17–18). Second Isaiah compared God's decision to no longer be angry with Israel with God's promise that "the waters of Noah should no more go over the earth" (Is 54:9). The Gospel according to Luke lists Noah among Jesus' ancestors (Lk 3:36). In the Gospel according to Matthew, the lifestyles of Jesus' contemporaries is said to be like those of Noah's contemporaries prior to the flood (Mt 24:37–38). In 2 Peter 2:5, Noah is "a herald of righteousness," while in Hebrew 11:7 Noah is "an heir of the righteousness which comes by faith" because he heeded God. God's patience while Noah was building the ark was being built is the focus of 1 Peter 3:20.

Bibliography: W. BRUEGGEMANN, *Genesis* (Atlanta 1982). A. F. CAMPBELL and M. A. O'BRIEN, *Sources of the Pentateuch: Texts, Introductions, Annotations* (Minneapolis 1993). N. COHN, *Noah's Flood: The Genesis Story in Western Thought* (New Haven 1996). A. DUNDES, ed., *The Flood Myth.* (Berkeley 1988). J. W. ROGERSON, *Genesis 1–11* (Sheffield 1991). G. J. WENHAM, *Genesis 1–15* (Waco, Texas 1987). C. WESTERMANN, *Genesis 1–11* (Minneapolis 1984).

[J. E. JENSEN]

NOAILLES, LOUIS ANTOINE DE

Cardinal archbishop of Paris; b. château of Tessières, near Aurillac, May 27, 1651; d. Paris, May 4, 1729. As the second son of Anne Jules, first duke of Noailles, he was educated in Paris and received a doctorate in theology at the Sorbonne (1676). Ordained a priest in 1675, he was made bishop of Cahors in 1679, and in June 1680, bishop of Châlons-sur-Marne, a see that conferred a peerage. In 1682 Noailles took part in the Assembly of the Clergy that adopted the four Gallican articles (*see* GALLI-

CANISM). Respect for his piety and unblemished life led to his appointment as archbishop of Paris in April 1695, an appointment supported by Mme. de Maintenon. His difficulties then began. At Châlons in 1695 he had approved Pasquier QUESNEL's *Réflexions morales*, but in 1696 he condemned a posthumous publication of the Jansenist Martin de Barcos's *Exposition de la foi . . . touchant la grâce et la prédestination* that exposed an extreme form of Augustinism. He was then attacked by an anonymous pamphlet that demanded whether one should follow Noailles the bishop of Châlons in approval of Quesnel, or Noailles the archbishop of Paris in condemning the same teachings in Barcos's book. Despite this difficulty, Noailles promoted a new edition of *Réflexions morales* (1699). He was made cardinal in 1700 at Louis XIV's solicitation. During these same years he condemned several Quietist writings (*see* QUIETISM). In so doing, he supported BOSSUET and became estranged from FÉNELON.

On July 16, 1705, Clement XI published the constitution *Vineam Domini Sabaoth*. This condemned the *Cas de conscience*, printed in 1703 and signed by 40 doctors of the Sorbonne, arguing that respectful silence concerning the five propositions of Jansenius should not debar an ecclesiastic from absolution. The cardinal had forced them to retract, the two who would not being exiled. He then acted, perhaps reluctantly, in support of *Vineam Domini*, though under his guidance the assembly of bishops who received it added a strong Gallican pronouncement as an introduction to the pontifical document. Moreover, he showed himself slow and weak on the issue of the suppression of PORT-ROYAL effected by Louis XIV in 1709. On the other hand, he turned more and more against the Jesuits, strictly controlling their faculties to preach or hear confessions in his diocese. In the same year, when the bull UNIGENITUS, condemning 101 of Quesnel's propositions, was referred to the Assembly of the Clergy, Noailles, who felt directly attacked, opposed it. These actions brought the cardinal openly into disfavor, and Louis XIV forbade his appearance at court. In 1714, with Noailles still opposing, the *Unigenitus* was registered by royal order. The king then decided to have him tried by a national council; there were also talks of his "Decardinalization." However, Louis died in 1715, and in a dramatic reversal of fate Noailles became chair of the "Ecclesiastical council" established by the Regent, the duke of Orléans. Though he was never the leader of the opposition, he continued to resist *Unigenitus*. On April 3, 1717, he joined other bishops in an appeal against the bull to a future general council, although this appeal remained secret until 1718. In August 1718 the Regent ordered acceptance of *Unigenitus* throughout France, all appeals already made being annulled. Cardinal de Noailles only formally withdrew his appeal in August 1720; he did not formally accept *Unigenitus* until October 1728. The cardinal was a good administrator of his diocese, spending generously in repairing and adorning the cathedral of Notre Dame. He was also noted for his charity. He died in 1729, leaving his property to the Hôpital Général, the Hôtel-Dieu, and the Hôpital des Enfants-Trouvés.

Bibliography: É. DE BARTHÉLEMY, *Le Cardinal de Noailles . . .* (Paris 1886). J. CARREYRE, *Le Jansénisme durant la Régence* 2 v. (Louvain 1929–33); *Dictionnaire de théologie catholique*, ed. A. VACANT et al., (Paris 1903–50) 11.1:678–681. A. LE ROY, *Le Gallicanisme au XVIIIᵉ siècle: La France et Rome de 1700 à 1715 . . .* (Paris 1892). J. F. THOMAS, *La Querelle de l'Unigenitus* (Paris 1950). C. URBAIN and E. LEVESQUE, *Les Dernières années de Bossuet* (Paris 1929). L. CEYSSENS, "Le cardinal de Noailles," in *Autour de l'Unigenitus* (Leuven 1987). P. BLET, *Le Clergé de France, Louis XIV et le Saint-Siège de 1695 à 1715* (Rome 1989). J. M. GRES-GAYER, *Théologie et pouvoir en Sorbonne* (Paris 1991). P. CHAUNU, M. FOISIL, F. DE NOIRFONTAINE, *Le basculement religieux de Paris au XVIIIe siècle* (Paris 1998). M. J. MICHEL, *Jansénisme et Paris, 1640–1730* (Paris 2000).

[D. R. CAMPBELL/J. M. GRES-GAYER]

NOAILLES, PIERRE BIENVENU

Founder of the Holy Family Sisters of Bordeaux; b. Bordeaux, France, Oct. 27, 1793; d. there, Feb. 8, 1861. After a very irreligious youth, he suddenly reformed following a visit to the Parisian church of Saint-Sulpice (1813), entered the seminary of Saint-Sulpice, and was ordained (1829). As curate in Bordeaux he took a special interest in the sick, outcasts, orphans, and peasants. To aid them he founded in 1820 the Holy Family Sisters. Until 1903, when the Holy See definitively approved the constitutions, there were seven branches of this institute, each engaged in a different type of apostolate, and bound together only by constitutions common to all of them. Since that time there have been only four branches, engaged in teaching, care of the sick, and social work, and, at one community in Bordeaux, in perpetual adoration of the Blessed Sacrament. Noailles entered into an agreement with Charles Eugène de MAZENOD whereby the spiritual direction of the sisters was confided to the OBLATES OF MARY IMMACULATE, whose superior general was also the head of the Holy Family Sisters (1858–1903). Since 1903 the sisters have had their own mother general, who resides in Talence, near Bordeaux. Despite numerous difficulties, Noailles established 124 houses. In 1961 there were 4,812 sisters, and 294 houses in 15 countries in Europe, Asia, Africa, South America (Brazil), and North America (Canada). In 1944 the cause for Noailles's beatification was introduced in Rome.

Bibliography: J. BAFFIE and P. ORTOLAN, *Vie de bon Père Pierre-Bienvenu Noailles*, 2 v. (Bordeaux 1880–81). M. HEIMBU-

CHER, *Die Orden und Kongregationen der katholischen Kirche*, 2 v. (3d ed. Paderborn 1932–34) 2:516–517. C. SALOTTI, *Acta Apostolicae Sedis* 36 (1944) 309–212.

[J. DAOUST]

NOBILI, JOHN

Missionary; b. Rome, Italy, April 8, 1812; d. Santa Clara, Calif., March 1, 1856. He entered the Jesuits in Rome on Nov. 14, 1828 and subsequently taught in the Jesuit colleges at Loretto and Fermo in Italy. After ordination in 1843, he volunteered for the missions in the Oregon Country of North America. On Aug. 5, 1844, Nobili with his Jesuit companions, Michael Accolti and Peter De Smet, arrived at Ft. Vancouver. From 1845 to 1848 he worked among the indigenous people and settlers of New Caledonia (now British Columbia). During these years, Nobili helped to establish chapels in various forts or trading posts of the Hudson's Bay Company, and his successive missionary journeys extended as far as the southern boundary of Alaska. Unexpectedly, he was recalled from his missionary work by his superior, Rev. Joseph Joset. After making his final profession as a Jesuit in May 1849, he was assigned to accompany Accolti to California. Nobili arrived in San Francisco on Dec. 8, 1849, and then assisted the Rev. Anthony Langlois in the parish of St. Francis and in the pueblo of San Jose, located 50 miles south of San Francisco. In 1850 the new bishop of Monterey, Joseph S. Alemany, OP, asked him to administer the Mission Santa Clara, several miles from San Jose, and to establish there a college for young men. Despite the secularization of the mission, Nobili established Santa Clara College, the first Jesuit and Catholic college in California. Although it was not chartered by the state of California until April 28, 1855, instruction began on March 19, 1851. Nobili served as its first president until his premature death.

Bibliography: G. J. GARRAGHAN, *Jesuits of the Middle United States*, 3 v. (New York 1938). J. W. RIORDAN, *The First Half Century of St. Ignatius Church and College* (San Francisco 1905).

[J. B. MCGLOIN]

NOBILI, ROBERTO DE

Missionary in South India and pioneer in the method of missionary adaptation; b. Rome, September 1577; d. Mylapore, India, Jan. 16, 1656. His parents, Count Pier Francesco de Nobili, a general in the Papal Army, and Clarice Cioli, a Roman lady, were both of noble birth. He was educated at the Roman College and there declared his intention of becoming a Jesuit missionary. On the death of his father (1593), his guardian and cousin Cardinal Francesco Sforza brought pressure to bear to dissuade him from this plan, and Nobili fled from Rome and put himself under the protection of the Duchess of Nocera. He completed his education in the Duchess's house; and, in 1596, with his family's reluctant consent, entered the Jesuit novitiate in Naples. In 1600 he returned to Rome for theological study, and he was ordained three years later.

Missionary Endeavors. In April of 1604 Nobili left for India. He sailed from Lisbon in a Portuguese carrack and, like all non-Portuguese missionaries, was considered a vassal of the king of Portugal, who, by his privilege of ecclesiastical patronage (the *padroado*) bore the responsibility for the evangelization of India. After suffering a shipwreck near Mozambique, Nobili arrived in Goa on May 20, 1605. He learned Tamil among the Paravas of the Fishery Coast and in November 1606 was sent by his provincial, Alberto Laerzio, to the important inland town of Madura. This was a new departure; before this the Gospel had been preached only to Indians on the coast, where missionaries could be protected by Portuguese naval guns.

Nobili's older companion in Madura was a Portuguese Jesuit, Gonçalo Fernandez, who followed the missionary method used in India throughout the 16th century. Neophytes were required to dress, eat, and behave like the Portuguese colonials. Moreover, they had to take Portuguese surnames. Conversion was, in fact, linked with cultural domination and was therefore strongly resented by the Hindus. Christian converts were, along with the Portuguese, considered as *parangis* (despised foreigners) and as such were outcastes in Indian society. The *parangis* were further despised for eating beef, drinking wine, and wearing shoes (leather was considered impure).

Nobili believed this method was mistaken, and decided to adapt himself to native customs, as Matteo RICCI had done in China. After trying vainly to persuade Fernandez to work within the framework of the caste system rather than to cut across it, Nobili decided to live separately. He adopted the saffron dress, wooden clogs, and vegetarian diet of a *sannyasi* (holy man). He marked his brow with a rectangular shape of paste to signify that he was a teacher. When the people of Madura learned that he was the son of a count, they identified him with the caste of rulers, or *Rajas*. As a *Raja sannyasi* Nobili was now free to associate with Indians of the higher castes without defiling them.

Conversion of Sivadarma. Nobili's method met with success. In the first 18 months he converted 50 people of Madura, his first convert being a Sivaite schoolteacher whom he christened Albert in honor of his provincial. In 1608 Nobili became friendly with Sivadarma, a Brahmin Sanskrit scholar, who tried to convert Nobili to the system of nondualistic Vedanta professed by most Brahmins in Madura. Through Sivadarma, Nobili became the first European to get firsthand knowledge of Sanskrit, the Vedas, and Vedanta. Meanwhile other Brahmins, jealous of Nobili's successes, tried to have him dubbed a *Parangi* and expelled. At a meeting of 800 Brahmins, Sivadarma defended Nobili and explained that even though his skin was white Nobili was a learned *sannyasi* and quite different from a *parangi*. Nobili was allowed to remain, and in 1609, he converted Sivadarma. But his baptism raised grave questions. Should Sivadarma have to discard the characteristic Brahmin thread, a triple strand of white cotton worn from the left shoulder across the breast, and the *kudumi,* or single plait of hair? On the coast Brahmin converts had been forced to do so and as a result were treated as outcastes by other Brahmins. After studying the Laws of Manu and the history of the thread and *kudumi,* Nobili drew a distinction between religious and civil signs; the thread and *kudumi* he decided belonged to the latter group. With the approval of his ordinary, Archbishop Ros of Cranganore, Nobili baptized Sivadarma on Whitsunday 1609, allowing him to retain thread and *kudumi.*

Controversy over Adaptation. Fernandez complained about Nobili's methods, including his tolerance of such Indian habits as the marking of the brow with santal and the ceremonial ablutions. In 1610 the newly appointed visitor of the provinces of Goa and Malabar, Nicolau Pimenta, censured Nobili, who promptly appealed to Rome. Claudius ACQUAVIVA, the general of the Jesuits, wrote to India suggesting modifications of Nobili's method—notably that Brahmin converts should discard the thread—but adding that "no change should be made which might compromise the existence of the mission." In a brief dated Feb. 18, 1618, Paul V ordered Archbishop de Sa and the inquisitors of Goa to hold a conference at which Nobili was to be present and to write a report on the whole affair. After Nobili had presented his case, the first inquisitor voted against his method, the second in favor of it; of the remaining 20 theologians and Indian priests only four sided with Nobili. However, when the report was forwarded to Europe, both the grand inquisitor of Portugal and the new pope, Gregory XV, in the constitution *Romanae Sedis Antistes* of Jan. 31, 1623, approved Nobili's method and decided that Brahmin converts should be allowed to retain the thread and *kudumi.*

During the years of controversy Nobili was forbidden to baptize, and spent much of his time writing, chiefly in Tamil. His most important book, *Gnanopadesam* (spiritual teaching), is virtually a *Summa theologiae.* In

1623 he was again free to baptize, and thenceforth traveled widely in South India, founding new missions. In 1640, as the result of a Portuguese war against the Nayak of Madura, Nobili and his fellow missionaries were arrested and imprisoned for about a year. In 1654 Nobili, his eyesight failing, was retired from Madura. When he had first arrived, there was not a single Christian in the hinterland of South India. When he left, the number of Christians totaled 4,183.

Nobili spent his last years in a hut outside Mylapore, still wearing his saffron clothes, living on a vegetarian diet, and dictating revised versions of his books.

Bibliography: J. BERTRAND, *La mission du Maduré d'après des documents inédits,* 4 v. (Paris 1847–54). ROBERT DE NOBILI, *Première apologie,* tr. P. DAHMEN (Paris 1931). V. CRONIN, *A Pearl to India: The Life of Roberto de Nobili* (New York 1959). P. M. D'ELIA, "L'abolizione del giuramento contro i riti Malabarici in India," *La civiltà cattolica* 91.2 (1940) 331–340, 424–431. P. DAHMEN, *Robert de Nobili* (Münster 1924); *Un Jésuite Brahme* (Bruges 1924). R. STREIT and J. DINDINGER, *Bibliotheca missionum* (Freiburg 1916) 5:40–43, 1042. *Archivum historicum Societatis Jesu* 22 (1953) 690, no. 135. C. SOMMERVOGEL et al., *Bibliothèque de la Compagnie de Jèsus* (Brussels-Paris 1890–1932) 5:1779–80. F. DE GRAEVE, "Roberto de Nobili: A Bold Attempt at Inculturation," in *Religion in the Pacific Era,* eds. F. K. FLINN and T. HENDRICKS (New York 1985). J. GALLAGHER, *Apostle of India: The Story of Roberto de Nobili* (London 1982). F. X. CLOONEY, "Roberto de Nobili, Adaptation and the Reasonable Interpretation of Religion," *Missiology* 18 (1990) 25–36. S. AROKIASAMY, *Dharma, Hindu, and Christian according to Roberto de Nobili: Analysis of Its Meaning and Its Use in Hinduism and Christianity* (Rome 1986). I. G. ZUPANOV, *Disputed Mission: Jesuit Experiments and Brahmanical Knowledge in 17th-Century India* (New York 1999).

[V. CRONIN]

NÓBREGA, MANUEL DA

Jesuit cofounder with the governor general of Portuguese authority in Brazil; b. Portugal, Oct. 18, 1517; d. Rio de Janeiro, Oct. 18, 1570. He received a degree in canon law at the University of Coimbra in 1541. He failed to win a competition for a teaching position and entered the Jesuits on Nov. 21, 1544. After serving various apostolic missions in Europe, he was appointed director of the Jesuits in America at the age of 31. He embarked for Brazil with five companions in the company of the first governor general, Tomé de Sousa. He landed there, according to tradition, carrying a cross, and his first statement to his European companions contains a sentence which is a program: "this land is our enterprise." He helped in the foundation of Salvador, capital of Bahia, and was one of the most efficient advisers of the governor. During the administration of the second governor, at odds with the first bishop, Nóbrega left Bahia for the south. He again became a principal figure in the councils of the third governor, Mere de Sá, who led Brazil for 15 years. He planned the foundation of São Paulo in 1554 and worked toward the foundation of Rio de Janeiro in 1565. He traveled as missionary and observer through all of the captaincies of Brazil, from Pernambuco to São Vicente. He was the first Jesuit superior and the first provincial of Brazil. After turning the province over to Luis da Grã, he remained superior of the southern captaincies of Espírito Santo, Rio de Janeiro, and São Vicente. He founded the Colégio de Rio de Janeiro in 1567 and was its first rector. He was appointed provincial for the second time but died before he could take over the position. He is buried in Bahia in the present cathedral, formerly the Jesuit church, beside Mem de Sá. He was an excellent priest and good administrator, and was called the "Father of the Province." Southey considered him the greatest political figure in colonial Brazil.

Bibliography: S. LEITE, *História da Companhia de Jesús no Brasil,* 10 v. (Lisbon-Rio de Janeiro 1938–50). R. SOUTHEY, *History of Brazil,* 3 v. (London 1817–22).

[A. J. LACOMBE]

NOCK, ARTHUR DARBY

Historian of ancient Greek and Roman religion; b. Feb. 22, 1902, Portsmouth, England; d. Jan. 11, 1963, Boston, Mass. Nock was educated at Trinity College, Cambridge, and attracted early notice for his masterful knowledge of Greek and Latin scholarship. His first major work was an edition of Sallustius, *On the Gods and the Universe* (Cambridge 1926). Its introductory survey of the religious and cultural background of the fourth century A. D. shows that same balance of thoughtful generalization and specific fact that was to make his chapters on Roman religious developments in the *Cambridge Ancient History* (v.10, 1934; v. 12, 1939) small masterpieces of exposition. In 1930 he became Frothingham Professor of the History of Religion at Harvard University and editor of the *Harvard Theological Review.*

His numerous articles and reviews, often as important as contributions to scholarship as the books he criticized, centered increasingly on ancient magic and religion and on Christian beginnings. His *Conversion: The Old and the New in Religion from Alexander the Great to Augustine of Hippo* (London 1933; repr. 1961) is an indispensable guide to an understanding of the religious experience of the Hellenistic and Roman age and of the coming of Christianity as it may have appeared to pagans. His little book *St. Paul* (London 1938; repr. 1963) was followed by a magisterial four-volume edition in collaboration with A. J. Festugière, OP, of the *Corpus Hermeticum* (Paris 1945–54).

Far more interested in piety and cult than in philosophy and theology, he dwelt upon the practice and the expression of the common man in antiquity, providing a sharp and detailed picture in which the literary and philosophical texts are illustrative rather than central. He had a special interest in GNOSTICISM, criticizing the view that it was a pre-Christian entity. An edition of his collected shorter writings, including a list of his publications, was in press in 1965.

Bibliography: *Arthur Darby Nock: Essays on Religion and the Ancient World,* ed. and intro. Z. STEWART, 2 v. (Cambridge, Mass. 1972); bibliography of Nock's writing.

[Z. STEWART]

NOËTUS OF SMYRNA

Monarchian heretic who taught in Smyrna, *c.* 180 to 200. His teachings are known from the antiheretical writings of HIPPOLYTUS OF ROME (d. 235). He seems to have been the first to have taught PATRIPASSIANISM, i.e., that the Father was born, suffered, and died, since the Father and the Son are only different ways (*modi*) of God's self-revelation. He admitted only an allegorical interpretation of St. John's Gospel, thus rejecting the doctrine of the Logos, and he accused his opponents of ditheism. A synod of the presbyters of Smyrna condemned him *c.* 200. One of his disciples, Epigonus, brought his doctrines to Rome.

Bibliography: HIPPOLYTUS OF ROME, *Contre les hérésies,* ed. and tr. P. NAUTIN (Paris 1949); *Philosophumena,* ed. P. WENDLAND (GCS 26; 1916) 9:3–9.3. C. H. TURNER, *Journal of Theological Studies* 23 (1921–22) 28–35. G. BARDY, *Dictionnaire de théologie catholique* 10.2:2193–2209. B. KOTTER, *Lexikon für Theologie und Kirche* 7:1018

[M. C. MCCARTHY]

NOLDIN, HIERONYMUS

Jesuit moral theologian; b. Salurn of the South Tyrol, Austria, Jan. 30, 1838; d. Vienna, Nov. 7, 1922. Ordained in 1861, Noldin entered the Society of Jesus four years later, and after ten years of study and teaching became rector of the Jesuit theologate at Innsbruck. There, in 1883, he wrote his first book, *Die Andacht zum Heiligsten Herzen Jesu* (11th German ed. 1923; first English tr. W. K. Kent, OSC, *The Devotion to the Sacred Heart of Jesus,* 1905). From 1886 to 1890 Noldin edited *Zeitschrift für Katholische Theologie* and then taught moral theology for 19 years at the University of Innsbruck. In 1902 he published his major work, *Summa Theologiae Moralis,* a three-volume Latin textbook including sections on the fundamental principles of morality, the Commandments, and the Sacraments, and two appendixes, one on the Sixth Commandment and the use of marriage, and the other on ecclesiastical penalties. This influential textbook was in its 16th edition before the author's death and enjoyed several later editions under the direction of A. Schmitt, also of the University of Innsbruck. The 33d edition appeared in 1961 under the editorship of Ġ. Heinzel. Noldin wrote three other smaller works, including *Decretum de Sponsalibus et matrimonio cum declaratione* (c. 1900) and *De iure matrimoniali iuxta codicem* (1919).

Bibliography: A. SCHMITT, *Zeitschrift für katholische Theologie* 47 (1923) 11–20. G. HEINZEL, ''Hieronymus Noldin und sein Werk,'' *ibid.,* 80 (1958) 200–210.

[J. UPTON]

NOLL, JOHN FRANCIS

Bishop and editor; b. Fort Wayne, Indiana, Jan. 25, 1875; d. Huntington, Indiana, July 31, 1956. Son of John G. and Anna (Ford) Noll. After completing his studies at St. Lawrence College, Mt. Calvary, Wisconsin, Noll attended Mt. St. Mary's Seminary in Cincinnati, Ohio. He was ordained for the Diocese of Fort Wayne by Bp. Joseph Rademacher in June 4, 1898. After two years as curate in various parishes, he became pastor at Kendallville, Indiana, in 1900, and of St. Mary's in Huntington, Indiana, in July of 1910, remaining there until he was named bishop of Fort Wayne. While pastor at Besancon, Indiana, Noll's interest in apostolic work among non-Catholics led him to publish a booklet, *Kind Words from Your Pastor,* in 1904. At Hartford City, Indiana, in 1908, he began a parish magazine that was later printed for hundreds of parishes as *The Family Digest.* In 1912, in answer to the *Menace* and other anti-Catholic papers, he began to publish a four-page paper, *Our Sunday Visitor.*

Despite his other activities, he never ceased to be a writer and editor. To inform non-Catholics, he produced *Father Smith Instructs Jackson* (1913) and *The Fairest Argument* (1914). In 1925 he founded the magazine *Acolyte,* which in 1945 became the *Priest.* His pamphlets, numbering approximately 150, embraced such titles as *The Catholic Church vs. the Federal Council of the Churches of Christ, A Catechism on Birth Control, Instructing Non-Catholics before Marriage,* and *The Parochial School, Why?* His longer books included *A Vest Pocket of Catholic Facts* (1927), *The Decline of Nations* (1940), and *Our National Enemy Number One, Education without Religion* (1942). In 1941 he added a second volume to the *History of the Diocese of Fort Wayne* begun by his predecessor, Bp. Herman J. Alerding, in 1907.

Noll was made domestic prelate in 1923, was named bishop of Fort Wayne May 12, 1925, and was consecrated by Cardinal George W. Mundelein June 30, 1925. Noll derserves credit for introducing into the diocese the Redemptorists (1927), the Capuchins (1928), the Slovak Franciscans (1929), the Oblates of Mary Immaculate (1934), the Society of the Priests of the Sacred Heart (1935), and the Crosier Fathers (1938). He reorganized Central Catholic High School, Fort Wayne, as a coeducational institution in 1938. He opened Bishop Noll High School in Hammond and St. Joseph High School in South Bend, Indiana, and established a minor seminary for the diocese at Lake Wawasee under the Crosier Fathers.

Nationally, Noll was one of the founders of the Catholic Press Association. He was one of the original members of the episcopal committee that formed the Legion of Decency to combat immorality in motion pictures, and he acted as the first chairman of the National Organization for Decent Literature. He was a member of the Board of Catholic Missions for more than 25 years. He devoted much time to the National Catholic Welfare Conference (NCWC), especially as a member of the conference's executive committee, chairman of its Department of Catholic Action, and chairman of its Committee of the Department of Lay Organizations. In this last capacity, he gave aid and direction to the National Council of Catholic Men and the National Council of Catholic Women. Among his other activities and offices was chairmanship of the National Committee on a Religious Census, which sought inclusion of religious affiliations in the Federal census. He raised $125,000, chiefly through *Our Sunday Visitor,* to erect a statue of Christ as the Light of the World at the NCWC Building in Washington, D.C. Pius XII made Noll an assistant to the papal throne March 14, 1941, and personal archbishop Sept. 2, 1953.

[T. T. MCAVOY]

NOMINALISM

A term deriving from the Latin *nomen,* meaning name, and used to designate a variety of doctrines and movements in philosophy. (1) In an ontological sense, nominalism is a doctrine according to which only individual things exist. In opposition to Platonic REALISM, which explains the similarity of individuals by saying that they share a common property or nature, i.e., by assuming the existence of UNIVERSALS that are not individuals, nominalism holds that if individuals similar to one another may be said to share anything, this can be only a spoken or written name or a mental image, i.e., something itself individual. In the strict sense nominalism is opposed also to CONCEPTUALISM, for it does not accept universals that are not individuals even as objects of thought. (2) In a polemical sense, nominalism is frequently used as an epistemological term roughly synonymous with extreme conventionalism, EMPIRICISM, or POSITIVISM. This is so because ontological nominalism has often led to a skeptical attitude concerning the objective value of intellectual knowledge. It would be wrong, however, to think that the refusal to accept universal essences must of necessity make the use of words entirely arbitrary. Ontological nominalism as such need not deny that individuals are essentially related; it merely rejects the assumption that related individuals have some namable thing that is not an individual in common. (3) Historically, "nominalism" is a term applied to philosophical and theological movements in early and late SCHOLASTICISM whose representatives were called *nominales*. Their doctrines included, among others, ontological nominalism in the broader sense, i.e., not excluding conceptualism.

Greek Origins. Even though the term "nominalism" appears much later, the doctrine can be found already in antiquity. Thus Antisthenes the Cynic is said to have objected to PLATO: "I see a horse, but I do not see horseness" (Simplicius, *In Arist. Categ.* 208,30). Aristotle defended an intermediate position between those of the CYNICS and Plato; in his view, although only individual beings with individualized natures exist in physical reality, the intellect is able to form universal concepts of such natures. This view may be referred to as a realistic conceptualism—realistic, in order to distinguish it from an idealistic conceptualism of the Kantian school.

The Stoics, who are often classified as nominalists, accepted the individuals of the material world but in addition, as an ontological foundation for logic, they postulated a special kind of universal, namely, τὸ λεκτόν, "what is said," the meaning of sentences or words. The Stoic position, therefore, amounted to an original form of conceptualism. It resembles the position of the *nominales* of scholasticism, but as yet no line of direct influence has been traced from one school to the other.

Early Scholasticism. The famous scholastic discussion of universals arose in the wake of a renaissance of Aristotelian logic or, more exactly, in connection with an argument concerning logic's place with respect to the other sciences (J. Reiners). The Neoplatonic tradition had assumed that logic was concerned with a special kind of thing, namely, with the CATEGORIES and PREDICABLES. BOETHIUS had distinguished between physics as a science of things (*res*) and logic and grammar as sciences of words (*voces*); he had stated also that the treatise on the categories dealt with words. Then, at the beginning of the 11th century, some writers asserted that predicables too could be considered not only as things but also as names.

Toward the end of the century, a controversy arose between those who taught logic in the old way as dealing with things (*in re*) and those who, like John the Sophist, the master of Roscelin, taught logic as concerned with words (*in voce*). Finally, ROSCELIN OF COMPIÈGNE explicitly denied that universals, i.e., the predicables of GENUS and SPECIES, could be things. His arguments, known from his disciple Peter ABELARD, were mainly negative, showing how Platonic realism leads to incongruous consequences. An important positive argument appealed to the authority of Aristotle, who defines a universal as "that which can be predicated of many" (*On Interpretation* 17a 39). Assuming that only words (and not things) could be predicated, it concluded that universals had to be words.

Such nominalism, however, did not exclude a realistic conceptualism (B. Geyer). It seems that Roscelin simply did not consider the problem of the CONCEPT. Abelard, however, explicitly discussed the universality of products of thought (*ficta*) and accepted the objective existence of the meanings (*dicta*) of sentences, as did the Stoics. To stress that words are not merely sounds, Abelard in his later writings preferred to say that universals were *sermones*, i.e., meaningful terms of discourse. He was convinced that there had to be an ontological justification for the use of general names: e.g., although two men do not share some "thing," man (*in homine*), they do share the status of being man (*in esse hominem*). Roscelin and Abelard continued the tradition of the earlier dialecticians by applying logical analysis to theological matters. Roscelin's incautious teachings elicited from St. ANSELM OF CANTERBURY the first-known polemics against nominalism (*De fide trin.* 2), and the nominalists' heretical formulations of the mystery of the Holy Trinity were later condemned by the Church (see H. Denzinger, *Enchiridion symbolorum* 721–739). (*See* DIALECTICS IN THE MIDDLE AGES.)

High Scholasticism. In high scholasticism the nominalist school disappeared. Everyone now taught logic as a science of meaningful words (*scientia sermocinalis*), and the new logical theories of the *consequentiae* and of the suppositions of terms, initiated by Abelard, were in full elaboration. But leading logicians, such as Peter of Spain (Pope JOHN XXI), found the acceptance of universals no longer problematical, and they did not hesitate to say that a universal term *in suppositione simplici* stood for a universal thing (*res universalis*). It was rather among Aristotelian theologians, such as St. THOMAS AQUINAS, that Abelard's criticism of Platonic realism continued to be developed.

Late Scholasticism. A new school, whose members again were called *nominales*, originated in the 14th century with WILLIAM OF OCKHAM at its head. Intending to purify Aristotelian doctrine from Avicennist-Neoplatonist corruptions (see E. A. Moody, *Logic,* 9–11), Ockham rejected the doctrine of formal distinctions proposed by John DUNS SCOTUS, according to which common natures could be distinguished in individual things. For Ockham all distinctions within a thing can be only real distinctions, and all the components distinguished are as individual as the thing itself. Like Abelard, he stressed that universals are only names or terms: two similar individuals do not agree in a common nature but only "in themselves" (*conveniunt se ipsis—In 1 sent.* 2.4EE). By denying the reality of relations he made the separation between individuals even more radical.

Ockham's Nominalism. But again this type of nominalism did not immediately exclude conceptualism. Ockham recognized not only spoken or written terms but also mental terms or concepts. In his explanations as to how concepts are to be understood, however, he was hesitant: whereas in the beginning he tended to consider them as objective products of thought (*ficta*), he later estimated that it might be sufficient to identify them simply with the subjective acts of thinking (*intellectiones*) [see Boehner, "The Realistic Conceptualism of William of Ockham"]. Since psychological acts are concrete and individual, the latter interpretation of the concepts amounts, in the terminology explained above, to ontological nominalism in the strict sense.

Ockham defended his ontological viewpoint by revising the logic of the suppositions of terms accordingly. Furthermore, he insisted that science was, properly speaking, of terms and not of things (*Philosophical Writings,* ed. and tr. P. Boehner [Indianapolis 1964] 11), since one knows propositions and these are made up of singular and universal terms. By this he did not mean to deny that one knows about real things, for in the logic of suppositions he explicitly explained how terms stood for things. His peculiar preoccupation with terms, however, explains why Ockhamist nominalists were also called terminists (*terministae*).

The above-mentioned identification of concepts and acts of thinking was in keeping with the famous principle of economy that Ockham often applied in logical analysis: "Plurality is never to be posited without necessity" (*numquam ponenda est pluralitas sine necessitate—In 1 sent.* 27.2K), or "What can be explained by fewer assumptions is vainly explained by more" (*frustra fit per plura quod potest fieri per pauciora—Summa tot.log.* 1.12). This principle, later called "Ockham's razor," can be found already before Ockham, but it characterizes very well the pragmatic aspect of nominalism. Ockham also recognized clearly the connection between ontological assumptions and linguistic formulations. For example, he explained the abstract noun humanity nominalistically by the complex phrase "man insofar as he is man" (*Summa tot.log.* 1.8). Such reformulations have gained special prominence in the contemporary discussion of nominalism (see below).

But Ockham was more than a logician. His ontological nominalism was intimately connected with his theological view of a free, all-powerful, and all-merciful God. (Distinctive of late scholastic nominalism is the fact that it included members of both the arts and theology faculties.) For Ockham, the affirmation of a real distinction in things implied that God could create one of its components without the other. In view of God's absolute power (*potentia absoluta*), the coexistence of individuals was entirely contingent; the actual order of nature and grace, moreover, was necessary only insofar as God in fact directed His power in this way (*potentia ordinata*). As a consequence, arguments depending on man's experience of the *de facto* order could lead only to probable conclusions. For Ockham, God's inner life was entirely beyond the reach of philosophical investigation. Since he admitted only real distinctions, he taught that God's nature could be only of unanalyzable simplicity, rejecting even the existence of exemplary ideas in God's mind. In his view, only theologians could attempt to formulate the mystery of Trinitarian life.

Ockhamist School. The followers of Ockham formed a new school, the *via moderna,* in opposition to the old schools of SCOTISM and THOMISM, the *via antiqua.* In England the first Ockhamists were ROBERT HOLCOT and ADAM WODHAM. In Paris the extremism of the first admirers of Ockham led in 1339 to a decree of the arts faculty prohibiting the teaching of the new doctrine (*Chartularium universitatis Parisiensis* 2:485). Apparently some participants in the scholastic art of disputation had made exaggerated use of Ockham's method of logical analysis, calling some propositions of accepted authorities, and even those of Scripture, "false according to their formulation" (*falsae de virtue sermonis*) or "simply false" (*simpliciter falsae*). The opponents of the nominalists blamed Ockham's doctrine that science was of terms and not of things for these exaggerations; thenceforth they were quick to stress that they were interested primarily in things and not in terms (*nos imus ad res, de terminis non curamus*—see Ehrle, 322).

Yet more dangerous were early accusations of heresy. Two thinkers whose doctrines were related to Ockhamism, NICHOLAS OF AUTRECOURT and JOHN OF MIRECOURT, were condemned by Pope Clement VI (see *Enchiridion symbolorum,* 1028–49). But the theological writings of Ockham himself were never condemned by the Church, and later nominalist theologians were careful not to overstep the bounds of orthodoxy.

Growth of Ockhamism. OCKHAMISM soon attracted leading personalities such as JOHN BURIDAN, NICHOLAS OF ORESME, ALBERT OF SAXONY, and MARSILIUS OF INGHEN. Although these men did not accept all of Ockham's theses, they did help the nominalist school to gain respectability. It spread to old universities, but especially to newly founded centers of learning throughout Europe. Only a few places, such as Cologne and Louvain, remained devoted exclusively to the *via antiqua.* Unfortunately, the rivalry between *antiqui* and *moderni* meant endless quarreling. Thus in Paris in 1474 the realists succeeded in curbing a strong nominalist party with the help of royal power, although in 1481 the prohibitions were abolished.

In the 14th and 15th centuries the leaders of the conciliar movement, PETER OF AILLY and Jean GERSON, belonged to the *via moderna.* (Ockham himself had already suggested the establishment of a general council to counterbalance papal power.) The nominalist school has thus been characterized as "the late medieval ecumenical movement" (H. Oberman). Its theologians intended to heal the divisions in the Church by returning to the golden age of St. BERNARD OF CLAIRVAUX and PETER LOMBARD. The quarrels of the *antiqui* about metaphysical distinctions seemed to them "to thin out the food" of true biblical revelation, and apologetical proofs based on purely philosophical reasons (*remoto Christo*) were regarded as of little use (Ockham's criticism had made their conclusions already doubtful). The influential theologian and faithful interpreter of Ockham in the late 15th century was Gabriel BIEL.

Reformation and Modern Science. There has been much debate over the relationship between the nominalist school and the Reformation. Protestants used to stress Martin LUTHER's break with the "corrupted" Catholic tradition of the late Middle Ages, whereas Catholic authors, accustomed to see in Thomism the recommended doctrine of the Church, considered the Reformation to be a consequence of the "decadent" scholasticism of the nominalists. Both views seem to be mistaken. Luther had been strongly influenced by the theology of Biel, but in his doctrine of justification he rejected the nominalist SEMI-PELAGIANISM, according to which man can do his very best by his natural power and so put himself in the proper disposition for the infusion of grace. It may also be mentioned that other Reformers, such as John WYCLIF, John HUS, and John CALVIN, were of Scotist origin and that Huldrych ZWINGLI had a Thomist background, while Johann ECK, a foremost defender of the Catholic position, belonged to the nominalist school. During the late Middle Ages, nominalism, Scotism, and Thomism were all equally accepted schools of Catholic thought. It is true that, after the Council of Trent, the nominalist semi-Pelagianism came to be antiquated and can no longer be considered compatible with Catholic belief. But, on the other hand, there are reasons to believe that Biel's teachings about Scripture and tradition and his Mariology were forerunners of the Tridentine formulations (see Oberman, 423–428).

Also prevalent is a theory to the effect that modern empirical science was a direct result of Ockham's philosophy. It is true that from his doctrine of the contingency of the world order it follows that the only adequate ground for asserting a causal relation between two phenomena is the empirical observation of regular sequence. But Ockham himself had shown no particular interest in empirical science; and although many 14th-century physicists, such as J. Buridan and N. Oresme, were associated with the *via moderna,* it must be stressed that in their physical theories they did not follow Ockham but rather continued the work of their realist predecessors (see Weisheipl).

Modern Empiricism. At Oxford the Ockhamist tradition of grammatical and logical analysis survived until far into the 17th century. T. Hobbes's logic clearly goes back to the nominalist version of the logic of terms, and, continuing up to the "ordinary language" school of philosophy of the 20th century, one finds a steady series of warnings not to be misled by the use of abstract nouns.

What characterized modern philosophy, however, was not linguistic analysis but EPISTEMOLOGY. Here the empiricist postulate to justify all knowledge by reduction to sense experience necessarily led to a strict ontological nominalism. J. LOCKE still accepted general ideas, but G. BERKELEY and D. HUME made it clear that if an idea was a picture formed by sensation or by the imagination, then it could be the picture only of something individual. There is, for example, no such thing as a picture of a triangle in general that is "neither oblique nor rectangle, neither equilateral, equicrural, nor scalenon, but all and none of these at once" (cf. Berkeley, *Principles,* Introd. 13; Hume, *Treatise* 1.1.7). The use of general names was explained psychologically by saying that a general name evoked, through habitual association, a whole chain of similar individuals. Among positivists and psychologist logicians, such views were frequently discussed throughout the 19th century, e.g., by J. S. MILL. They were later subjected to a thoroughgoing criticism by E. HUSSERL.

Contemporary Discussion. With the rise of mathematical logic, psychological questions were pushed into the background. But the problem of universals reappeared in the 20th century in a new form, consequent on the development of set theory by G. Cantor. In this theory, sets or classes are Platonic universals and are not to be confused with wholes, i.e., with "heaps" or concrete collections of individuals. A sphere, for example, is identical with the whole made up of its two halves or with the whole made up of its quarters, but in set theory the sphere, the set that has the two halves as elements, and the set made up of the quarters are three different entities. With a finite number of atomic individuals, one is able to compose only a finite number of different "heaps"; in set theory, however, the number of sets, sets of sets, etc., that can be formed from these same individuals is infinite. At first the Platonic assumption of higher and higher infinites of sets was generally accepted, and set theory became the basis of all mathematics; numbers were defined as particular sets of sets of individuals. But about 1900 various antinomies were discovered when unrestrained Platonism led to contradictions (*see* ANTINOMY). Up to the present no single way of repairing the Platonic edifice has satisfied all logicians, and some (S. Leśniewski, T. Kotarbiński, N. Goodman, W. V. O. Quine, J. H. Woodger, and R. M. Martin) have come to doubt the meaningfulness of the very notion of set. In other words, nominalism has been again resuscitated.

Yet simply to deny the existence of Platonic entities is no longer sufficient. It has become clear that a limitation of ontological assumptions implies that some logical languages are no longer meaningful. The nominalist has therefore the task of formulating everything in a suitable nominalistic language. This encounters great difficulties, and most logicians accept a limited form of Platonism. Logical positivists, such as R. Carnap, try to escape into their conventionalism: although unable to do without a Platonic language, they continue to claim that metaphysical questions are meaningless and that the issue is simply a matter of linguistic convention.

See Also: LOGICAL POSITIVISM.

Bibliography: A. CARLINI, *Enciclopedia filosofica,* 4 v. (Venice-Rome 1957) 3:927–931. J. AUER, *Lexikon für Theologie und Kirche,* ed. J. HOFER and K. RAHNER, 10 v. (2d, new ed. Freiburg 1957–65) 7:1020–23. J. KLEIN, *Die Religion in Geschichte und Gegenwart,* 7 v. (3d ed. Tübingen 1957–65) 4:1505–08. B. MATES, *Stoic Logic* (Berkeley, Calif. 1953). G. M. A. GRUBE, "Antisthenes Was No Logician," *American Philological Association, Transactions and Proceedings* 81 (1950) 16–27. P. VIGNAUX, *Dictionnaire de théologie catholique,* ed. A. VACANT et al., 15 v. (Paris 1903–50) 11.1: 717–784; *Nominalisme au XIVe Siècle* (Montreal 1948). J. REINERS, *Der Nominalismus in der Frühscholastik* (*Beiträge zur Geschichte der Philosophie und Theologie des Mittelalters* 8.5 (Münster 1910). E. A. MOODY, *The Logic of William of Ockham* (New York 1936); "Ockham, Buridan and Nicholas of Autrecourt: The Parisian Statutes of 1339 and 1340," *Franciscan Studies* 7 (1947) 113–146. P. BOEHNER, "The Realistic Conceptualism of William of Ockham," *Traditio* 4 (1946) 307–335. E. HOCHSTETTER, "Nominalismus?" *Franciscan Studies* 9 (1949) 370–403. F. EHRLE, *Der Sentenzen Kommentar Peters von Candia des Pisaner Papstes Alexanders V: Ein Beitrag zur Scheidung der Schulen in der Scholastik des vierzehnten Jahrhunderts und zur Geschichte des Wegestreites* (Franziskanische Studien Beiheft 9; Munster 1925). G. RITTER, *Studien zur Spätscholastik,* 3 v. (Sitzungsberichte der Akademie der Wissenschaften zu Heidelberg, Philos.-Hist. Klasse, v. 12.4, 13.7, 17.5; 1921–27). H. A. OBERMANN, *The Harvest of Medieval Theology: Gabriel Biel and Late Medieval Nominalism* (Cambridge, Mass. 1963). J. A. WEISHEIPL, *The Development of Physical Theory in the Middle Ages* (New York 1960). R. I. AARON, *The Theory of Universals* (Oxford 1952). E. C. LUSCHEI, *The Logical Systems of Leśniewski* (Amsterdam 1962). W. V. O. QUINE, *From a Logical Point of View* (Cambridge, Mass. 1953). N. GOODMAN, *The Structure of Appearance* (Cambridge, Mass. 1951); "A World of Individuals" in *The Problem of Universals: A Symposium* (pa. Notre Dame, Ind. 1956). R. CARNAP, *Meaning and Necessity: A Study in Semantics and Modal Logic* (2d ed. Chicago 1956). T. KOTARBIŃSKI, "Sur l'attitude réiste (ou concrètiste)," *Synthèse* 7 (1948–49) 262–273. E. HUSSERL, *Logische Untersuchungen* (2d ed. Halle 1913–21).

[G. KÜNG]

NOMOCANON

From the Greek words νόμος (law) and κανών (a rule). The word nomocanon was first used in the 11th century to indicate canonical collections that were composed of both ecclesiastical and civil laws dealing with ecclesiastical matters. The word was used later to indicate a book containing "cases of conscience," that was employed by the monks of Mt. Athos. The most popular use of the word, however, was in regard to canonical collections containing both secular and ecclesiastical laws. This type of canonical collection was proper to the Oriental Churches from the early Middle Ages and played an important role in the history of Oriental Canon Law.

From the fourth century on, an important place was accorded to ecclesiastical matters in imperial law, such as in the Theodosian Code, the Justinian collections, and the Novellae and *Bascilicae.* From the time of Constantine, civil rulers had taken on the role of protectors of the Church. As a result civil rulers became involved in matters exclusively, or at least partially, ecclesiastical; and they began to order these matters with civil laws. Collections of these imperial laws dealing with ecclesiastical matters were made and at first added to strictly canonical collections as appendices. They were later included in the main body of canonical collections, alongside strictly ecclesiastical materials, thus giving rise to a new species of canonical collection that became known as a collection of nomocanons. A "rubric" (a brief sentence indicating the subject matter) was followed by several texts that were intended to demonstrate and support the particular norm in question. These texts were drawn from both civil and ecclesiastical authorities. Frequently only a summation of the text was given, with an indication where it could be found in its entirety.

Collections of nomocanons have been among the principal sources of Oriental Canon Law since the early Middle Ages. The earliest one is the *Nomocanon L titulorum,* compiled toward the end of the sixth century. It has been falsely ascribed to Joannes Scholasticus. It underwent several revisions and was in use until the 12th century. The most important of all collections of nomocanons is the *Nomocanon XIV titulorum.* It was compiled during the reign of Emperor Heraclius, about the year 629. It is most likely the work of Enantiophanes, although it has been falsely ascribed to Photius. It consists of decrees of councils, texts of letters of the Fathers, and imperial constitutions. It underwent several revisions: a second revision in 883, which definitively placed the imperial constitutions on a par with the ecclesiastical canons; a third revision in 1198 by the celebrated canonist Theodore BALSAMON. In 928 it had been accepted by a council held at Constantinople, under the Patriarch Nicholas the Mystic, as the universal law of the Oriental Church.

Bibliography: R. NAZ *Dictionnaire de droit canonique,* ed. R. NAZ (Paris 1935–65) 6:1014. C. DE CLERCQ, *ibid.* 2: 1171–74. A. M. STICKLER, *Historia iuris canonici latini: v. 1, Historia fontium* (Turin 1950) 71–72, 407. A. VAN HOVE *Commentarium Lovaniense in Codicem iuris canonici 1* (Mechlin 1928–) 1:168–171.

[J. M. BUCKLEY]

NON EXPEDIT

This phrase, "it is not expedient," is of biblical origin (1 Cor 10.22) and has long been used by the Roman CURIA to indicate a negative reply for reasons of opportuneness. Signified here is its most famous application expressive of the Holy See's policy prohibiting Italian Catholics from participating in political elections and most other political activities of the new kingdom, which unified the peninsula by seizing the STATES OF THE CHURCH and ending the papal temporal power and whose attempt to solve the ROMAN QUESTION by the Law of GUARANTEES (1871) proved unacceptable to PIUS IX.

Origins. Giacomo MARGOTTI, a journalist in Turin, anticipated this policy when he inaugurated a widely successful propaganda campaign in 1857, urging Catholics to abstain from civil elections and coined the phrase *nè eletti nè elettori* (neither elected nor electors). Yet in 1866 Pius IX permitted Catholics who were elected deputies to take the oath of loyalty to the state provided they added: *salvis legibus divinis et ecclesiasticis* (divine and ecclesiastical laws remaining intact). The *non expedit* policy first received formal acceptance in the decree of

the Sacred Penitentiary (Sept. 10, 1874). Since numerous Catholics were uncertain whether the *non expedit* was an absolute prohibition or a recommendation, Pius IX issued a brief that declared abstention a duty and reproved attempts to entice Catholics to the polls (Jan. 29, 1877). LEO XIII renewed the prohibition on the eve of the 1880 elections, in a more solemn manner in the encyclical *Immortale Dei* (Nov. 1, 1885), and again in his approval of the Holy Office decree (June 30, 1888).

Application. Filippo Meda made the formula *nè eletti nè elettori* gradually give way to another, *preparazione nell' astensione* (preparation in abstention), which advocated that Catholics should not be mere abstentionists, but should use their civil rights, improve social and political institutions by instilling in them Christian principles, regain society to Catholicism, and terminate the hostility between Church and State. The *non expedit* did not apply to administrative elections and other forms of civic activity. Catholic participation in administrative elections was always rather sizable, and it was greeted with satisfaction by the Catholic press not as a preparation for political elections, but as an act of hostility against the revolution. Especially in the big cities of Genoa, Turin, and Naples, the administrative elections of 1878, 1879, and 1880 resulted in sensational Catholic successes; Catholics in Rome joined in the *Unione Romana* and gained control of the communal government (1879–87). In political elections, on the other hand, the *non expedit* was observed in orderly fashion by Italian Catholics, thereby causing a very notable electoral absenteeism, which created a deep chasm between the "legal country," representative of a small group of citizens who possessed and exercised the right to vote, and the "real country," constituting the vast majority, which did not possess, or refused to exercise, this right.

Disappearance. Confronted with the dangerous expansion of parties of the extreme left and with the rupture of diplomatic relations between France and the Holy See, PIUS X (1903–14) edged toward a reconciliation with Italy, whose government, headed by Giovanni Giolitti, proved to be more conciliatory. On the eve of the political elections of Nov. 13, 1904, BONOMELLI explained to the pope the risk to the social order involved in Catholic electoral abstention and the consequent victory of the extreme left, and Pius X advised Catholics to follow their consciences. This authorization abrogated the *non expedit* virtually but not formally, because the encyclical *Il fermo proposito* (June 11, 1905) confirmed the generic prohibition against participating in elections, but admitted a dispensation when bishops recognized the necessity of using the ballot for the good of souls and the supreme interests of the Church and society.

When the Universal Council (*Consiglio universale*) was established (1913), Giolitti, president of the Council of Ministers, feared a leftist victory and sought to introduce into the ministerial majority representatives of the Catholics, who were economically potent, especially in country districts and who enjoyed the veneration surrounding Catholic religious tradition. This led to the Gentiloni pact inviting Italian Catholic support of candidates who would follow the Catholic Electoral Union's religious and social ideas. With the formation of the Popular party (Jan. 19, 1919), inspired by Don STURZO, Italian Catholics finally entered the political life of Italy as an autonomous force. About this time Benedict XV abrogated the *non expedit.*

Bibliography: G. DALLA TORRE, *I cattolici e la vita pubblica italiana,* ed. G. DE ROSA, 2 v. (Rome 1962). G. DE ROSA, *Storia del movimento cattolico in Italia,* 2 v. (Bari 1966). F. OLGIATI, "Per la storia del Non expedit," *Vita e Pensiero* 33 (1950) 364–369; "La politica di S. Pio X e il conservatorismo," *ibid.* 37 (1954) 525–540. A. C. JEMOLO, *Church and State in Italy, 1850–1950,* tr. D. MOORE (Philadelphia, Pa. 1960). For additional bibliography *see* ROMAN QUESTION.

[R. MORI]

NONANTOLA, ABBEY OF

Former Benedictine monastery outside Modena, north central Italy; since 1926 an abbey *nullius* perpetually united with the archbishopric of Modena. It was founded (752) by ANSELM (d. 803), the first abbot, and endowed by the Lombard King Aistulf, receiving the relics of Pope St. Sylvester I in 756. It soon achieved political and cultural importance, and its possessions extended as far as Constantinople. It was favored and controlled by the emperors until 1083; resident abbots replaced absentee appointees in 1044. MATILDA OF TUSCANY brought the abbey to the side of the popes in the investiture controversy; the *Liber de honore ecclesiae* by Placidus (1111) defended papal rights. Nonantola was long a center of piety and learning with a famous library and scriptorium; it became an abbey in COMMENDATION (1449). Incorporation by the Cistercians (1514), reform by G. F. Bonhomini (1566), and the building of a seminary in 1567 by St. Charles BORROMEO (a commendatory abbot) did not stop the abbey's decline; and it was suppressed in 1797 by the Revolutionary government. Restored as an abbey *nullius* (1815), it was united with Modena (1821), secularized (1866), and again restored (1926). Nonantola now has its own chapter, ordinary, and minor seminary and serves 31 parishes (1964).

Bibliography: G. TIRABOSCHI, *Storia dell'augusta Badia di S. Silvestro di Nonantola,* 2 v. (Modena 1784–85). *Miscellanea di studi nonantolani* (Modena 1953). G. GULLOTTA, *Gli antichi ca-*taloghi e i codici della Abbazia di Nonantola (Vatican City 1955). J. RUYSSCHAERT, *Les Manuscrits de l'abbaye de Nonantola* (Vatican City 1955). P. GROSSI, *Le abbazie benedettine nell'alto medioevo italiano* (Florence 1957). U. CHEVALIER, *Répertoire des sources historiques du moyen-âge. Topobibliographie,* 2 v. (Paris 1894–1903) 2123. L. H. COTTINEAU, *Répertoire topobibliographique des abbayes et prieurés,* 2 v. (Mâcon 1935–39) 2:2087–88. A. VASINA, *Lexikon für Theologie und Kirche,* ed. J. HOFER and K. RAHNER, 10 v. (2d, new ed. Freiburg 1957–65) 7:1025–26.

[L. J. LEKAI]

NONBEING

Nonbeing or, in modern philosophical usage, nothing, is the negation of BEING; as such, it is to be distinguished from EVIL, which is the privation of being. Nonbeing is a being of reason, i.e., its meaning is constituted through reference to being by way of negation, which is an act of the intellect (ARISTOTLE, *Meta.* 1003b 10; 1004a 9–12; THOMAS AQUINAS, *Summa theologiae* 1a, 16.3 ad 2, 5 ad 3, 7 ad 4; *De ver.* 1.5 ad 2). Because being has many senses, nonbeing, the product of its negation, has many senses also (*Meta.* 1089a 16). Thus PLOTINUS calls the One as well as matter and evil nonbeing because they are not ESSENCE, which he identifies with being (*Enneads* 1.8.3.1–8; 3.6.7.9–13; 3.8.10.28–32; 5.2.1.1–7; 5.5.6.1–13).

Nonbeing is not independent of being, nor is being constituted by nonbeing, as G. W. F. HEGEL claimed. In its adequating and assimilating grasp of being, the intellect produces—as a by-product, as it were—that which is inadequate or unassimilated to being, viz, nonbeing. Being is evident to the intellect as not nothing. This "not nothing," however, is not that which causes being to be; rather being is not nothing simply because being *is.*

The theological truth of creation out of nothing deepens the metaphysics of nonbeing. "Out of nothing" does not mean that nothing itself is a kind of matter out of which creatures come to be. Rather, it implies that the being of creatures—as a PARTICIPATION of, and therefore a nonidentity with, the being of God—is made possible by the divine intellection of that which is simply other than God. But that which is simply other than God, the Subsisting Being, is "pure" nothing. Creatures could not exist as other than God, if before creation God did not know what is simply other than Himself. This "other" in no way measures God's knowledge, but depends upon it. The divine ideas as the exemplars of creatures are the divine essence known as able to be participated. Since participation implies difference, God must know the ways in which creatures differ from His own being (*deficiunt a vero esse;* cf. St. Thomas Aquinas, *C. gent.* 1.54)

Abbey of Nonantola. (©Vanni Archive/CORBIS)

as well as the ways in which they imitate it. But that which is simply different from, or other than, the subsisting plentitude of being (*esse*) is nothing. Such an explanation avoids PANTHEISM and explains the diversity in being without supposing matter or possibles independent of creation and without introducing real diversity into God, the source of the diversity of being. Essence, not nothing, is the intrinsic principle of the finitude of beings other than God. Nevertheless, nonbeing is the condition of the possibility of the procession of essence (as the principle limiting the *esse* of creatures) from God.

For PARMENIDES and Gorgias, nonbeing is not in any sense whatsoever. In the *Parmenides* (142A; 161E–164B) and the *Sophist* (237A–239E; 257B–259B), PLATO suggests a reality of nonbeing that grounds becoming and multiplicity (cf. Aristotle, *Phys.* 191a 23–191b 34). For Aquinas the first division or opposition is that between being and nonbeing; from this first otherness (*alteritas*) springs the plurality of beings and their

difference from each other and from the First Cause (*In Boeth. de Trin.* 4.1). For B. PASCAL, man is the mean between God and nothing, so that nothing is one of the extremes that locate man's being. For H. BERGSON, nothing is a pseudo-idea, resulting from a generalization of the displacement of one being by another. For M. HEIDEGGER, the naught is both the veil and the unveiling of the "to be," because the "to be" is not the totality of "that which is." In dread, the pathos of the naught or of the "no-*thing*-ness" of the "to be," man transcends beings or "that which is" toward the "to be" itself. For J. P. SARTRE, man is his own nothing and the being in which nothing comes into the world, because the primordial fluidity and otherness of consciousness is not held by any being-in-itself. (*See* EXISTENTIALISM)

See Also: PRIVATION (PHILOSOPHY).

Bibliography: G. KAHL-FURTHMANN, *Das Problem des Nichts* (Berlin 1934). E. PACI, *Il nulla e il problema dell'uomo* (Turin 1950). G. SIEWERTH *Der Thomismus als Identitätsystem* (2nd ed.

Frankfurt a. M. 1961). H. BERGSON, *Creative Evolution,* tr. A. MITCHELL (New York 1944). M. HEIDEGGER, *Was ist Metaphysik?* (8th ed. Frankfurt am Mainz 1960), tr. in part in *Existence and Being,* introd. W. BROCK (2nd ed. London 1957). J. P. SARTRE, *Being and Nothingness,* tr. H. E. BARNES (New York 1956).

[T. PRUFER]

NONCONFORMISTS

English Protestants who refused Anglican uniformity, also called Dissenters. In the 16th century the most important nonconformists were CONGREGATIONALISTS and Brownists; in the 17th century, PRESBYTERIANS and the RELIGIOUS SOCIETY of FRIENDS (Quakers); in the 18th and 19th, METHODISTS. All nonconformist groups before the Civil War (1638–49) were frequently called PURITANS. Today the term "Free church" is preferred.

Although the name "nonconformist" dates from 1662, actual dissent began when Protestants refused Elizabeth's Act of UNIFORMITY in 1559, objecting to bishops and Anglican liturgical usages, and advocating a "pure" (Calvinistic) Christianity. They favored local autonomy in church government, and many wished to limit the powers of the monarchy and even separate Church and State. James I therefore regarded them as a danger to the monarchy and in 1604 deprived 300 Puritan divines. Some, the Pilgrim Fathers, fled to the New World. In the reign of Charles I, Archbishop Laud's attempt to eliminate Puritan usages helped bring about the Civil War, during which nonconformist factions quarreled bitterly among themselves, united only in their opposition to Catholicism and the Anglican Establishment. After the Restoration of Charles II in 1660, the Anglican Cavalier Parliament sought to impose religious uniformity by the Clarendon Code. These harsh measures were enforced by justices of the peace eager for revenge for the oppression they had suffered under Puritans in the Civil War, and some 20 percent of the English clergy came to be deprived. James II sought nonconformist support in 1687–88 by his Declarations of Indulgence, but without success because of nonconformist suspicion of Catholics. James's Calvinist successor, William III, by the Toleration Act of 1689, granted freedom of worship to nonconformists (but not to Roman Catholics or UNITARIANS), though still excluding them from public office. Many nonconformists evaded this exclusion by taking the Anglican sacrament once a year. The restrictive legislation of 1660 to 1689 was not formally repealed, however, until 1828, the year of Catholic emancipation. Nonconformity waned during the heyday of 18th-century deism and might have died out save for the great Methodist revival.

Most 17th-century nonconformists came from the middle classes. The Whig party, organized in the 1670s, was for 150 years the champion and stronghold of Dissent. Its descendant, the Liberal party, contained most nonconformist groups of the 19th century. After 1850 nonconformists interested themselves in social questions. The rise of British socialism and the Labor party owes more to the nonconformist conscience than to Karl Marx. Among the important nonconformists were O. Cromwell, J. Milton, G. Fox, J. Bunyan, I. Watts, J. Wesley, C. Wesley, G. Whitefield, C. H. Spurgeon, R. W. Dale, and P. Forsyth.

Bibliography: T. PRICE, *The History of Protestant Nonconformity in England,* 2 v. (London 1836–38). H. S. SKEATS and C. S. MIALL, *History of the Free Churches of England* (London 1894). W. K. JORDAN, *The Development of Religious Toleration in England,* 4 v. (London 1932–40). E. ROUTLEY, *English Religious Dissent* (Cambridge, Eng. 1960). P. SCOTT, *Die Religion in Geschichte und Gegenwart,* 7 v. (3d ed. Tübingen 1957–65) 2:209. W. F. ADENEY, J. HASTINGS, ed., *Encyclopedia of Religion and Ethics,* 13 v. (Edinburgh 1908–27) 9:381–393.

[B. NORLING]

NONJURORS, ENGLISH

The name given to eight bishops and some 400 clergy of the Church of England who refused to take the oath of allegiance to William and Mary after the Glorious Revolution of 1688 out of loyalty to their previous oath to James II (*see* JAMES II, KING OF ENGLAND). Among them was Archbishop Sancroft of Canterbury. They were not notably friendly to the deposed James II and would have accepted William and Mary as regents, but not as king and queen. They were all High Churchmen, believers in passive obedience and the divine right of kings, and regarded James II as their rightful sovereign. Three days after the landing of William, George Hickes, Dean of Worcester, preached a sermon on submission to persecuting princes, citing the early Christians as examples. In February 1690, Parliament deprived the bishops of their sees and benefices and expelled them from the Anglican Church. Though reduced to poverty and persecuted by the government, they held to their claim to represent, and their duty to preserve, the true Anglican succession. They held services in secret. In 1694 the exiled James consented to nominate two new bishops, and G. Hickes and J. Wagstaffe were consecrated in secret. In 1713 Hickes, the only living nonjuring bishop, consecrated three more bishops. After the death of the Young Pretender in 1788, nonjurors largely disintegrated. The last nonjuring bishop was Charles Booth, who died in 1805.

The nonjurors found support in JACOBITE families for whom they were chaplains or tutors. Many English regarded them as apostate Anglicans or stalking horses for popery. After some time they had, in London alone, 50 chapels. Through the mediation of Peter the Great in 1716 they entered into discussions for union with four Eastern patriarchs, but by 1725 the efforts had failed. In England they sympathized with and prayed for the exiled Stuarts but were never actively disloyal to the government. In Scotland, however, where most of the Episcopal clergy were nonjurors, they took part, in accord with Episcopal disestablishment in 1689, in Jacobite uprisings in 1715 and 1745. In 1701 on the death of James II, some nonjurors accepted Queen Anne and rejoined the Anglican Church while others held that their oath to James bound them to support his descendants. In 1714 they were split over the oath to George I. They were divided also on points of theology and liturgical usage. Their secession deprived the Church of England of a group of devoted, pious, learned, and experienced churchmen whose small numbers belied their importance. They continued the tradition of the CAROLINE DIVINES and may be regarded as forerunners of the OXFORD MOVEMENT. They included T. Brett, T. Carte, J. Collier, T. Deacon, H. Dodwell, T. Hearne, T. Ken, J. Kettlewell, W. Law, C. Leslie, and R. Nelson.

Bibliography: J. H. OVERTON, *The Nonjurors* (London 1902). C. GASKOIN, J. HASTINGS, ed. *Encyclopedia of Religion and Ethics*, 13 v. (Edinburgh 1908–27) 9:394–396. N. SYKES, *Church and State in England in the XVIIIth Century* (Cambridge, Eng. 1934). F. L. CROSS, *The Oxford Dictionary of the Christian Church* (London 1957) 963–964. D. CARTER, *Die Religion in Geschichte und Gegenwart*, 7 v. (3d ed. Tübingen 1957–65) 4:1509–10.

[B. NORLING]

NONNBERG, ABBEY OF

In Salzburg, Austria; the oldest abbey of Benedictine nuns in Germany or Austria. It was founded *c.* 700 by St. RUPERT and endowed by Duke Theodo of Bavaria and his wife St. Regintrude. Until 987 Nonnberg was part of the mensal possessions of the archbishop of Salzburg. In 1043 the abbey was rebuilt in honor of St. Erentrude (d. *c.* 718), the first abbess and probably the niece of St. Rupert. The rich abbey was reserved for the nobility until the 18th century. In 1242 Abbess Gertrude of Stein received pontifical privileges, the faldstool, and a golden crown; the abbess sat with prelates in the Land-tag. After a fire in 1423 the church was rebuilt (1464–1509). Archbishop Paris Lodron introduced the Tridentine reform (1623). The abbey, which founded or restored several other convents and was never suppressed, has always been a center of learning and education.

Bibliography: M. REGINTRUDIS VON REICHLIN-MELDEGG, *Stift Nonnberg in Salzburg* (Salzburg 1953). L. H. COTTINEAU, *Répertoire topobibliographique des abbayes et prieurés*, 2 v. (Mâcon 1935–39) 2:2089. O. L. KAPSNER, *A Benedictine Bibliography: An Author-Subject Union List*, 2 v. (2d ed. Collegeville, Minn. 1962): v. 1, author part; v. 2, subject part, 2:244. F. HERMANN, *Lexikon für Theologie und Kirche*, ed. J. HOFER and K. RAHNER, 10 v. (2d, new ed. Freiburg 1957–65) 7:1026–27. H. SCHMIDINGER, *Dictionnaire d'histoire et de géographie ecclésiastiques*, ed. A. BAUDRILLART et al. (Paris 1912–) 15:697–698.

[N. BACKMUND]

NONNUS OF PANOPOLIS

Epic poet and Christian exegete; b. Panopolis, Thebaid, Egypt, *c.* 400; d. after 450. Nothing is known of the education or career of Nonnus. He is the author of an epic poem in 48 books called the *Dionysiaca* that was written at Alexandria and describes the journey of the pagan god Dionysus to India. He is also the probable author of an hexameter verse titled *Paraphrase of St. John's Gospel* because there is an obvious relationship between the two works in the language, style, and identical phraseology. Although the theme and language of the *Dionysiaca* are definitely pagan, the poem does embody Christian notions, whereas the *Paraphrase* reflects the epic form and uses pagan similes, particularly in the names of the gods. The older theory that the author wrote the *Dionysiaca* while a pagan and the *Paraphrase* after conversion has been rejected. He seems to have been steeped in the Egyptian Hellenistic tradition. In the *Paraphrase* he introduced pagan Eons as well as Monophysite theological ideas. He called Mary the THEOTOKOS and quoted Origen, Gregory Nazianzus, John Chrysostom, and Cyril of Alexandria.

Bibliography: *Patrologia Graeca*. ed. J. P. MIGNE (Paris 1857–66) 43:749–1228. A. SCHEINDLER, ed., *Nonni Panopolitani Paraphrasis* (*Bibliotheca scriptorum Graecorum et Romanorum Teubneriana*; 1881). W. H. D. ROUSE, ed. and tr., *Nonnos Dionysiaca*, 3 v. (*Loeb Classical Library*; 1940). R. KEYDELL, *Pauly Realenzyklopädie der klassischen Altertumswissenschaft*. ed. G. WISSOWA et al. 17.1 (1936) 904–921. É. AMANN, *Dictionnaire de théologie catholique*, ed. A. VACANT et al. (Paris 1903–50) 11.1:793–795. K. KUIPER, *Mnemosyne* NS 46 (1918) 225–270. L. R. LIND, *L'Antiquité classique* 7 (1938) 57–65. P. BERNARDINI MARZOLLA, *Studi italiana di filologia classica* 26 (1952) 191–209. B. ALTANER, *Patrology*, tr H. GRAEF (New York 1960) 327–328. W. BAUER, *Die Religion in Geschichte und Gegenwart* (Tübingen 1957–65) 4:1510. F. L. CROSS, *Oxford Dictionary of the Christian Church* (London 1957) 964.

[F. X. MURPHY]

NORBERT OF XANTEN, ST.

Founder of the PREMONSTRATENSIANS and archbishop of Magdeburg; b. Xanten, Duchy of Cleves, Germany,

"St. Norbert of Xanten," painting by Peter Paul Rubens, 1622. (©Burstein Collection/CORBIS)

c. 1080; d. Magdeburg, Germany, June 6, 1134. Norbert was a son of the lord of Gennep and was made a canon at nearby Xanten. He served at the courts of Frederick, archbishop of Cologne (d. 1131), and Emperor Henry V. Norbert accompanied Henry to Rome; and although he repented of his part in the humiliation of Pope PASCHAL II in 1111, he remained with the emperor. In 1115 a bolt of lightning felled Norbert from his horse, and considering it an invitation to a life of perfection, he retired to Fürstenberg, a cell near Xanten, where he spent three years (1115–1118) in a life of penance. Ordained a priest, he unsuccessfully attempted to reform the canons of Xanten, and his occasional preaching journeys caused him to be called before the Synod of Fritzlar in 1118. Norbert then distributed his possessions to the poor and, barefoot, made a trip to Saint-Gilles, where Pope Gelasius II authorized him to preach throughout the universal Church. During 1119 he wandered through northern France, Hainault, and Brabant, preaching peace and reconciliation by his life of poverty and simplicity as well as by his words. On the advice of Pope Callistus II and with the support of Bartholomew, bishop of Laon (d. 1157), Norbert established a monastery near Laon in the isolated valley of Prémontré in 1120. In the same year he assisted at the Council of Soissons, which condemned Peter ABELARD. Norbert also traveled to Cologne for relics and on his return journey made a second foundation at Floreffe near Namur. Since his itinerant preaching had attracted many followers to Prémontré, a decision on their way of life was necessary, and Norbert decided that they should follow the Rule of St. Augustine. The life was chiefly contemplative, though the ministry of preaching was not excluded, certainly not for Norbert himself. Many foundations were made throughout Europe in the next few years, and in 1125 Norbert set out for Rome, where Pope Honorius II confirmed the order.

King Lothair III was at that time defending his crown against the Hohenstaufen, and at the Diet of Speyer in 1126, Norbert preached a sermon on loyalty and obedience that won him Lothair's continuing support. At Speyer the canons of the cathedral of Magdeburg were to choose a new archbishop in Lothair's presence, thus following the form established by the Concordat of Worms (1122). They chose Norbert, whose unwillingness was overcome only by pressure from Lothair and the papal legates. In July of 1126 Norbert, still barefoot, entered Magdeburg and was consecrated. He attempted to recover the lands of the Church lost through nepotism or confiscation and also to reform the lives of the clergy, but his efforts tended only to aggravate the discontent and rebellion in his diocese.

Meanwhile, the order Norbert had left behind at Prémontré went through a crisis without his leadership. Norbert summoned the Premonstratensian leaders to Magdeburg and asked them to choose as his successor HUGH OF FOSSE, who was able to give the order direction and structure. Norbert expected to aid his reform efforts by introducing Premonstratensian canons into Magdeburg, but this as well as his other reforms resulted only in several assassination attempts and the archbishop's temporary exile.

Since the Archdiocese of Magdeburg was located on the eastern edge of the empire, part of Norbert's work as archbishop involved attempting to Christianize the Wends, who inhabited the territory east of the Elbe River. Norbert never experienced there the success that he knew from his preaching in France, Belgium, and Germany. His real accomplishment in the East was the establishment of the Premonstratensians in Magdeburg and its suffragan dioceses. These in turn were later successful in bringing about the conversion of the Wends.

In the schism of 1130, Norbert supported Innocent II's claim to the papacy and helped persuade the emperor to adhere to Innocent's cause. He accompanied Lothair's expedition to Italy (1132–33) against Anacletus II (Peter Pierleoni) and joined Bernard of Clairvaux in a vain attempt to win over Anacletus by persuasion. Although his preaching helped strengthen the resistance to imperial attempts to win back the right of investiture, Norbert continued to serve Lothair after the trip back to Germany, until illness forced him to return to Magdeburg. His fever lasted until Pentecost of 1134. He died on June 6 and was buried on June 11 at the Premonstratensian church in Magdeburg. In 1582 Gregory XIII authorized a liturgical cult for St. Norbert, and in 1627 his body was moved from Magdeburg to Strahov Abbey in Prague. In 1672 Clement X extended his feast to the universal Church.

Feast: June 6.

Bibliography: Contemporary lives are the *Vita A,* ed. R. WILMANS, *Monumenta Germaniae Historica: Scriptores,* 12:663–703, and *Vita B, Patrologia Latina,* ed. J. P. MIGNE, 217 v. (Paris 1878–90) 170:1253–1344, F. PETIT, *Norbert et l'origine des Prémontré* (Paris 1981). W. M. GRAUWEN, *Norbertus, aartsbisschop van Maagdenburg, (1126–1134)* (Brussels 1978) (German translation with revisions: *Norbert, Erzbischof von Magdeburg (1126–1134)* [Duisburg 1986]). *Analecta Praemonstratensia* has many excellent articles on Norbert by W. M. GRAUWEN, from 48 (1972) until 72 (1996). K. ELM, ed., *Norbert von Xanten, Adliger— Ordenstifter— Kirchenfürst* (Cologne 1984).

[J. R. SOMMERFELDT/T. J. ANTRY]

NORFOLK

A line of Catholic earls and dukes whose peerage dates back to the 11th century, when Ralph, a staller or constable of the court of Edward the Confessor (reign 1043–66) and a benefactor of St. Riquier's Abbey, Ponthieu, was confirmed in his lands. The earldom proper was created in 1140 or 1141 for *Hugh Bigod* (d. 1176 or 1177), who ruled East Anglia from Framlingham castle. *Roger,* fifth Bigod earl of Norfolk (1245–1306), died without heirs.

The Mowbray Line. Edward I (reign 1274–1307) revived the earldom for his son, *Thomas of Brotherton* (1300–38), who in turn died leaving no son.

Thomas de Mowbray. First duke of Norfolk; b. 1366?; d. Venice, Sept. 22, 1399. Thomas was the grandson of Thomas of Brotherton's daughter, Margaret (*c.* 1320–1400), and received the revived dukedom in 1397. He had been earl marshal at 20, and had achieved power for revealing to Richard II (reign 1377–99) the plots of the earls of Arundel and Gloucester. In 1398 he was accused of treasonable words and fled abroad.

John de Mowbray. Second duke of Norfolk; b. 1389; d. Epworth, Isle of Axholme, Oct. 19, 1432. He distin-

Thomas Howard, Duke of Norfolk. (©Bettmann/CORBIS)

guished himself in the wars with France (1417–21; 1423–24), and was restored to his father's dukedom in 1425. He was marshal at the coronation of Henry VI in 1429.

John de Mowbray. Third duke of Norfolk, hereditary earl marshal of England and fifth earl of Nottingham; b. Sept. 12, 1415; d. Nov. 6, 1461. The son of John, he supported Richard, Duke of York, in the wars for the English succession (War of the Roses, 1455–85), but changed his allegiance to the Lancastrian King Henry VI in 1459. At the second battle of St. Alban's (1461) he fled from Henry VI's camp and fought for the Yorkist Edward IV, who was crowned king of England after his victory over the Lancastrians at Towton (1461).

John de Mowbray. Fourth duke of Norfolk; b. Oct. 18, 1444; d. Framlingham, Jan. 17, 1476. He also supported the Yorkist cause, but at his death the title again lapsed. Upon the marriage of his 5-year-old daughter, Anne, to Richard, Duke of York, second son of Edward IV, on Jan. 15, 1478, the dignity was added to his titles.

The Howard Line. The illustrious house of Howard, which long stood next in blood to the sovereign, traces its lineage to John Howard of Wiggenhall St. Peter, Norfolk, whose son, William, became a judge in 1297. The Howards came to power as Yorkists.

John Howard. First duke of Norfolk; b. 1430?; d. Bosworth Field, Aug. 22, 1485. As John of Stoke Neyland he became treasurer of Edward IV's household in 1468, and was summoned to Parliament as Lord Howard. He served as captain general at sea, and was later appointed lord admiral. On June 28, 1485, 12 days after young Richard, Duke of York and Norfolk, had been sent to the Tower by his uncle Richard III (reign 1483–85), John Howard was granted the vacant dukedom; as constable of the Tower he probably was in league with the prince's murderers. At the battle of Bosworth he commanded Richard's vanguard of archers. The "Jockey of Norfolk" fell while fighting alongside his sovereign.

Thomas Howard. Second duke of Norfolk; b. 1443; d. May 21, 1524. Like his father, John Howard, he fought for the cause of Richard III at Bosworth, and after defeat spent four years in the Tower as prisoner of the new Tudor king, Henry VII (reign 1485–1509). On release he was created earl of Surrey and proved an indispensable servant of the new monarchy as lord treasurer (1501–22) and as military general on the Scottish border. He inflicted the decisive defeat on the Scots at the battle of Flodden Field on Sept. 9, 1513, and for this service was elevated to the dukedom in February 1514, and named lord admiral. He was guardian of the realm while Henry VIII (reign 1509–47) met Francis I, King of France, on the Field of the Cloth of Gold at Calais on June 7, 1520.

Thomas Howard. Third duke of Norfolk; b. 1473; d. Kenninghall, Norfolk, Aug. 25, 1554. He succeeded his father, Thomas, and also became lord treasurer. In 1495 he was married to Anne, daughter of Edward IV. A man of "very great experience in political government," as the Venetian ambassador noted, he clung to office despite the upheavals of the Reformation. He rebuilt Kenninghall Palace in the form of a letter H, and the grandeur of it and his new palace at Norwich outdid the buildings of his rival Cardinal Thomas Wolsey. Like his father he was a fearless soldier and an astute politician. He had led the vanguard at Flodden Field, and was created earl of Surrey in February 1514. At intervals he devastated the Scottish border and raided the French coast. He led the council's attack on Cardinal WOLSEY, and at the latter's fall Thomas became HENRY VIII's most trusted adviser. His position had been strengthened by the king's marriage to his niece, Anne Boleyn (1533), and by his daughter's marriage to Henry's natural son, the Duke of Richmond. His enemies hoped that Anne's trial for adultery (1536) would bring down the whole house of Howard, but Norfolk, who presided, acquiesced in her execution, and scotched a rumor that he was to be sent to the Tower by remarking that it were no more likely than "Tottenham shall turn French."

That autumn he was sent to suppress the PILGRIMAGE OF GRACE, the popular rising under Robert ASKE that was provoked by recent religious changes. At first he offered the rebels the choice of battle or submission, but at Doncaster, seeing their numbers so strong, he made a truce while their demands were forwarded to the king. In January under royal instruction he dealt with severity against the rebels, terrifying the north by his executions. In 1539 Norfolk put forward the Act of Six Articles, devised by Stephen GARDINER, which restated the doctrinal position of the Henrician Reformation. The passing of this act pointed to the decline of Thomas Cromwell's power, and it was Norfolk who in June 1540 arrested Cromwell at the council table and sent him to the Tower. In July, to consolidate his position the duke promoted the marriage of his niece Catherine Howard with Henry, but the sordid business of her trial and execution in February 1542 brought the house of Howard into disrepute. Thereafter, though far too useful to be cast aside, Norfolk remained outside the inner ring of councilors. In 1544 he defeated the Scots at Solway Moss and as general of the army in France captured Boulogne, though he was soon replaced by Edward Seymour, Earl of Hertford and Duke of Somerset (1506?–52).

As the uncle of Prince Edward, Hertford was bent on becoming regent on the accession (1547), but to achieve this meant the overthrow of the Howards. A dynastic alliance between the families, proposed by Norfolk, foundered and before the end of 1546 he was in the Tower, for his son Henry Howard, Earl of Surrey, poet and soldier of renown, had played into Hertford's hands. Surrey, it was said, devised a plan for his sister, the widowed duchess of Richmond, to become Henry's mistress. He had designs on the regency himself and was indiscreet enough to quarter the royal arms with his own. There was sufficient evidence to send him to the block on January 19 on a technical charge of treason. Old Norfolk was compromised by his son's indiscretion. On January 29 King Henry appointed commissioners to give assent to the bill of attainder against the duke, but died during the night, so Norfolk's life was saved, though he remained a prisoner of state throughout Edward VI's reign. On Mary's accession (1553) he at once returned to power, and despite his age, he prepared for the coronation as lord treasurer and earl marshal. He died full of years and honors. Though he had suppressed the Pilgrimage of Grace and shared in the scramble for monastic lands, the third duke was essentially a conservative, and it was for political and dynastic reasons that he abhorred Protestantism and despised the New Learning.

Thomas Howard. Fourth duke of Norfolk; b. March 10, 1538; d. June 2, 1572. He was the son of Henry Howard, Earl of Surrey. After a year in the custody of Sir John

Williams he was placed at Reigate (1548) under his aunt, the Duchess of Richmond, who engaged John Foxe (1516–87) as his tutor. Brought to court on Queen Mary's accession (1553) he was placed in the households successively of Bps. Stephen Gardiner and John White, who sought to eradicate the teaching of Foxe. In 1554 he became a gentleman of the chamber of the Infante, Philip of Spain, and that summer succeeded to the dukedom of his grandfather. In 1555 he married Mary Fitzalan, daughter of Henry, Earl of Arundel, but she died in childbirth in June 1557. In the first week of Elizabeth's reign (1558–1603) Thomas married Margaret Audley, widow of Lord Henry Dudley. As premier peer and sole duke he was connected by descent or alliance with most of the nobility. He was the richest landowner and his Liberty of Norfolk was the greatest private franchise in the kingdom. Despite his power as a territorial magnate that enabled him to return East Anglian and Sussex members of Parliament to Westminster, Elizabeth delayed taking him into her confidence. In December 1559 she appointed him lieutenant general in the war against the French in Scotland, which culminated in the treaty of Edinburgh, breaking the "Auld Alliance." There he came close to William Cecil (1520–98) and shared his suspicion of Robert Dudley, Earl of Leicester (1532?–88), Elizabeth's favorite; for seven years opposition to Dudley remained the basis of Norfolk's political action. On the queen's recovery from serious illness in October 1562 Dudley was made a privy councilor, and on Cecil's insistence Norfolk entered the council the same day to balance Leicester's power. Cecil, with the duke's enthusiastic support, began negotiations for Elizabeth's marriage to the Archduke Charles of Austria, which were to founder on the question of his right to a private Catholic chapel. In the Parliament of 1566 Norfolk was spokesman for the lords, insisting that Elizabeth should marry and settle the succession, and he displayed real political courage. As a result the Hapsburg negotiations were resumed, but the duke was too ill to attend the vital council meetings in the autumn of 1567 that settled the issue, and in his absence Leicester's intrigues for a French match and his stirring Protestant opinion against the Austrian alliance and its begetters wounded Norfolk.

After Margaret Audley's death Norfolk married Elizabeth, widow of Lord Thomas Dacre, in January 1567. She was a devout Catholic. Her death in childbed that autumn brought him low and it was as a widower for the third time that he began to listen to the suggestion that he should marry MARY STUART, QUEEN OF SCOTS.

Following Mary's flight to England Norfolk went as principal commissioner to York to investigate the charges brought against her in September 1568. Here William Maitland (1528?–73), Mary's secretary for foreign affairs, whispered his proposal that a match with Mary would at a stroke solve the Scottish problem and the question of the succession in England. The duke had been openly mentioned as a consort for Mary on two earlier occasions, but now that the Casket Letters had convinced him of Mary's guilt in Lord Darnley's murder (1567) he was noncommittal. Elizabeth suspected that Norfolk was not behaving impartially toward Mary and recalled him from York to an enlarged commission in London. Intrigues and the double dealing of James Stewart, Earl of Moray (1531?–70), here showed the duke in an unfavorable light and by the end of 1568 he had decided to go forward with the marriage scheme as the only avenue to power. To achieve this he made an uneasy alliance with Leicester and together they planned to get rid of William Cecil, then especially unpopular; but Elizabeth stood by her secretary and his opponents could only pursue their goal by intrigue. Other schemes were devised, such as the design of Henry FITZALAN, Earl of Arundel; John Lumley; Thomas, Earl of Northumberland; and Charles, Earl of Westmorland, for liberating Mary with Spanish arms and deposing Elizabeth. In all these schemes Norfolk's marriage with Mary was a cardinal feature.

Leicester prevaricated. He had insisted on obtaining Elizabeth's consent to the marriage himself and finally outwitted Norfolk. Elizabeth put Norfolk on his allegiance to deal no more with Mary and fearing for his life he fled from court to London and thence, on September 16, to Kenninghall. Having instructed the northern earls to call off their rising he went to Windsor to submit. The charges against him did not add up to high treason, but in the prevailing political uncertainty the Tower seemed the safest place for him, and the outbreak of the Northern Rebellion made an early release unlikely. In August 1570, after Norfolk had written a full submission, Elizabeth allowed him to go to the Charterhouse under strict supervision, on account of his health. Within weeks Roberto di Ridolfi (1531–1612), the Florentine banker, had him involved in his grand design for a Spanish invasion of England. Norfolk himself never signed the fatal letters to the Duke of Alva, Philip II, and the pope. With the unravelling of the Ridolfi conspiracy there was ample evidence to send Norfolk for trial on Jan. 16, 1572. Though he protested his innocence, his peers found him guilty. Elizabeth hesitated signing his death warrant but could not hold out indefinitely against the logic of statecraft, and the last duke of medieval creation was executed on June 2, maintaining his innocence and denying he was a Catholic. Though aloof and indecisive he remained a popular figure to the end.

The dukedom did not pass to Thomas' eldest son, Philip HOWARD, who lost the favor of Elizabeth I and was imprisoned allegedly for treason. Philip's eldest son,

Thomas (1586–1646), however, was restored to the earldom of Arundel in 1604. The friend of the antiquaries Sir Robert Cotton and Sir Henry Spelman, he formed the first notable art collection in England. Out of sympathy with the court of Charles I (reign 1625–49), he left England for Italy before the civil war, but contributed £ 54,000 to the royalist cause, in recognition of which he was created earl of Norfolk on June 6, 1644. His second son, *Henry* (1608–54), a zealous royalist, fought at Edgehill, and upon his return to his estates found that they had passed into the possession of Parliament. By a vote of the House of Commons, he was allowed to compound them for £ 6,000 in 1648. Henry's son *Thomas* (1627–77), while in exile with his grandfather, developed brain fever from which he never recovered, but at the restoration of Charles II (reign 1660–85) he became the fifth duke of Norfolk by an act of Parliament on Dec. 29, 1660. He died unmarried, and with him the earldom of Arundel descended with the dukedom. His successors for the next century play little part in public affairs: *Henry,* sixth duke (1628–84), brother of Thomas, succeeded in 1677; *Henry,* seventh duke (1655–1701), son of Henry, succeeded in 1684; *Thomas,* eighth duke (1683–1732), nephew of Henry, succeeded in 1701; *Edward,* ninth duke (1685–1777), brother of Thomas, succeeded in 1732; *Charles,* tenth duke (1720–86), descendant of the seventh duke, succeeded in 1777.

Charles Howard. Eleventh duke of Norfolk; b. March 5, 1746; d. Norfolk House, London, Dec. 16, 1815. He had been a member of Parliament for Carlisle and turned Protestant during the GORDON RIOTS. Described as a hard drinker, he, with the Prince Regent George, set the fashion for late and boisterous dinners. At a political banquet (1798) he gave a toast to ''our sovereign's health—the majesty of the people,'' which offended King George. He was dismissed from his posts. Charles took in hand the rebuilding of Arundel Castle (1791) and lived to see the completion of the new Baron's Hall (1815).

Bernard Edward Howard. Twelfth duke of Norfolk; b. Sheffield, Nov. 21, 1765; d. Norfolk House, London, March 19, 1842. The third cousin of Charles, Bernard was a Catholic and by an act of Parliament, was allowed to retain the hereditary dignity of earl marshal. He was admitted to the House of Lords after the Catholic Relief Bill (1829), and was named a privy councilor in 1830.

Bernard Edward Howard. Thirteenth duke of Norfolk; b. London, Aug. 12, 1791; d. Arundel Castle, Feb. 18, 1856. He succeeded his father, Bernard, and became the first avowed Catholic member of Parliament since 1688, being returned as member for Arundel on May 4, 1829, following the passage of Catholic Emancipation.

As a supporter of Lord John Russell (1792–1878), he voted for the anti-Catholic Ecclesiastical Titles Bill (1850) and remained little more than Catholic in name until his deathbed reconciliation.

Henry Granville Howard. Fourteenth duke of Norfolk; b. London, Nov. 7, 1815; d. Arundel Castle, Nov. 25, 1860. He changed his surname to Fitzalan-Howard in 1842. He was a Whig member of Parliament for Arundel (1837–50) when he resigned his seat on the enactment of Russell's Ecclesiastical Titles Bill and broke with the Whigs. He was renowned for his zeal as a Catholic and for his charity.

Henry Fitzalan-Howard. Fifteenth duke of Norfolk; b. London, Dec. 27, 1847; d. there, Feb. 11, 1917. He succeeded in 1860 and was the first to play a notable part in public life since the Reformation. Educated under John Henry NEWMAN at the Oratory School, he became the recognized head of the English Catholic laity, and his influence aided Newman's election to the cardinalate in 1878. He was the first lord mayor of Sheffield and first mayor of Westminster. A Unionist, he resigned the post of postmaster general in 1900 to join the Imperial Yeomanry in South Africa. As earl marshal at the coronations of Edward VII (Aug. 9, 1902) and George V (June 22, 1911) he revised several ancient usages. He built churches at Arundel and at Norwich, the latter as a thank-offering for the birth of an heir to his second wife.

Bernard Marmaduke Fitzalan-Howard. Sixteenth duke of Norfolk; b. Arundel House, May 30, 1908. He officiated as earl marshal at the coronations of George VI (May 12, 1937) and Elizabeth II (June 2, 1953). An experienced landowner, he served as joint parliamentary secretary to the Ministry of Agriculture (1941–45). His interests in sports and the countryside made him a popular figure, and in 1962 and 1963 he was manager of the English Cricket XI on its Australian tour. He also directed the state funeral of Sir Winston Churchill in 1965.

Bibliography: A. COLLINS, *The Peerage of England . . .,* enl. S.E. BRYDGES, 9 v. (London 1812). J. E. DOYLE, *The Official Baronage of England . . . 1066–1885,* 3 v. (London 1885). E. LODGE, *The Peerage and Baronetage of the British Empire as at Present Existing* (70th ed. London 1901). W. DUGDALE, *The Baronage of England . . . ,* 2 v. (London 1675–76). C. READ, ed., *Bibliography of British History: Tudor Period, 1485–1603* (2d ed. New York 1959). W. HUNT et al., *The Dictionary of National Biography From the Earliest Times to 1900,* 63 v. (London 1885–1900; repr. with corrections, 21 v., 1908–09, 1921–22, 1938; suppl. 1901–) 10:1–76, J. TAIT, *The Dictionary of National Biography From the Earliest Times to 1900,* 63 v. (London 1885–1900; repr. with corrections, 21 v., 1908–09, 1921–22, 1938; suppl. 1901–) 13:1114–35. P. HUGHES, *The Reformation in England,* 3 v. in 1 (5th, rev. ed. New York 1963). J. GILLOW, *A Literary and Biographical History or Bibliographical Dictionary of the English Catholics from 1534 to the Present time,* 5 v. (London-New York 1885–1902; repr. New York 1961) 5:184–187. L. B. SMITH, *A Tudor Tragedy:*

The Life and Times of Catherine Howard (New York 1961). N. WIL-LIAMS, *Thomas Howard, Fourth Duke of Norfolk* (London 1964).

[N. WILLIAMS]

NORIS, HENRY

Theologian and historian; b. Verona, Italy, Aug. 29, 1631; d. Rome, Feb. 23?, 1704. Noris was the son of Alessandro Noris and Caterina Manzoni. After joining the Augustinians at Rimini (1646), he served as regent of studies at Pesaro, Perugia, Florence, and Padua. He then became tutor to the son of the grand duke of Tuscany and professor of ecclesiastical history in Pisa (1674–92). Brought to Rome by Innocent XII, he was named custodian of the Vatican Library (1692), consultor to the Holy Office (1694), and cardinal (1695).

One of the leading savants of the 17th century, Noris was the primary figure in the later school of Augustinian theology (*see* AUGUSTINIANISM, THEOLOGICAL SCHOOL OF). He became involved in many controversies, especially by reason of two of his writings, *Historia pelagiana* and *Vindiciae augustinianae* (both published in Padua in 1673) that contained his interpretation of the soteriology of St. Augustine, a doctrine that he claimed was wrongly understood by both the Jansenists and their adversaries. Noris was repeatedly accused of Baianism (*see* BAIUS AND BAIANISM) and JANSENISM, but he was cleared of these charges both during his lifetime and after his death (brief of Benedict XIV, July 31, 1748). Of his numerous works (about 19 in print, 14 in MS, and many letters), the best edition is the *Opera omnia* edited by P. and G. Ballerini (v. 1–4 Verona 1729–32; v. 5 Mantua 1741).

Bibliography: F. ROJO, ''Ensayo bibliográfico de Noris, Bellelli y Berti,'' *Analecta Augustiniana* 26 (1963) 294–363. G. BRUZZONI, ''Nove lettere inedite di fra Enrico Noris,'' *Analecta Augustiniana* 62 (1999) 179–211.

[A. J. ENNIS]

NORMALITY

The condition of being in accordance with a norm. A problem relative to normality has arisen in recent times particularly in the life sciences. The difficulty of discovering normal traits has been compounded by an initial unsureness as to the way in which normality should be defined. Negatively, the normal is what is not abnormal, i.e., whatever functions at least sufficiently well to survive and to continue to function without requiring extraordinary assistance. Positively, two different norms have been proposed: the *average* norm, according to which the normal is what is characteristic of the greatest number; and the norm taken from the *best,* according to which the most perfect specimens are considered normal, all others to some extent falling short of normality. While each of the positive norms is easily reconciled with the negative, it is difficult to see how the positive norms are to be reconciled with one another, and hence to discover whether a given trait, admittedly not the best, should be considered normal or a falling short of the norm.

Types of Solution. Logically, the question of normality can arise only in a context of comparability, which involves in turn a multiplicity of similar things and also a judge to make the comparison. In a Platonic conception of the universe, the Ideas exist as the norms of all things. On any other hypothesis it is necessary to discover the norm. If the mind of the judge is taken as the sole source of the norm, either the norm is purely arbitrary, and hence of no scientific value, or the question recurs as a question about the nature of the mind itself. The source of the norm is therefore to be sought in nature as well as in judgment.

Several recent writers have noted that the question of determining the normality of anything, whether of the member of a species, the function of an organ, the mental state of an individual, or the working of a society, arises only in a context of means and end relationships.

Aristotle's *Physics* (192b 8–200b 9) supplies the elements of a solution to the problem of normality in the doctrine of CAUSALITY, particularly FINAL CAUSALITY. For Aristotle, NATURE in this regard is ''the principle and cause of motion and rest to those things, and those things only, in which she inheres primarily, as distinct from incidentally'' (192b 21–23). Each natural thing, inasmuch as it has a definite structure, has a definite function possible to it. What is definite in nature is made so by final cause. Parts are parts of a whole that specifies them by constituting their end; organs exist for the sake of the function they perform; actions are defined by the end to which they are directed. Things have definite tendencies, and the definiteness of these tendencies is explainable in terms of their final causality.

What is normal, therefore, is what performs its function well: An organ is normal if it functions in such a way as to serve the whole body; an action is normal if it attains the end such actions are directed to attain. The end may be attained perfectly or imperfectly; but if it is attained, even badly or in an extraordinary way, the function is to that extent normal. Only an act that failed to achieve the end it was directed to could be called altogether abnormal. Thus the majority, over a long period of time, can be said to be normal at least to the extent of having what is necessary for mere survival; and in this way the average is the norm. And since it belongs to the very notion of the END to be a GOOD, that which is most perfect, most in possession of its end, can also be said to be the norm. Thus the two norms, the average and the best, can be reconciled in the notion of the end.

Problems with Finality. There remains the difficulty of knowing the final causes of things. Certainly it is possible to infer from structure something of the nature of function; but no one has yet succeeded in defining even so common a natural being as a dog. The difficulty is particularly acute in the case of a human PERSON, since the person as such is unique and incapable of being defined. Negatively it may be quite clear that a person is functioning inadequately in some respect; but normality in the positive sense would seem to be impossible to determine absolutely in the case of the person. Only on the basis of actual functioning can the person be said to be normal in his personal traits; and since the potentialities of a person can never be known with complete adequacy, it is impossible to say to what extent he is realizing them. Admittedly, the natures of many things are unknown to man; but in many instances one does know what things are for; and to the extent that it is possible to discern means-end relationships, and to that extent alone, is it possible to judge the normality of anything.

Objections against the proposition that the final cause constitutes the norm in natural things are directed principally against the possibility of knowing the final cause. DESCARTES considered that on account of God's omnipotence and the weakness of the human intellect, it is impossible for man to know the final causes of natural beings, so that "what are called final causes are of no use at all in Natural Philosophy" (*Meditations,* 4). Evolutionists consider the evolution of new species an obstacle to the doctrine of natures in things. And historicity would replace human nature with history. A different objection, springing from the common confusion of final and EFFICIENT CAUSALITY, need not be considered here.

The fact of human ignorance of the purposes of many things, and particularly of "external finality" (e.g., of the purpose of a frog), does not invalidate human knowledge of many instances of "internal finality" (e.g., of the purpose of a frog's eye), especially in biology, where the notion of adaptation, or organization for an end, is fundamental. Evolution, which rests upon the chance mutations of genes and selective reproduction, logically presupposes the existence of the "matter" of the new species in the genes of the old and also the basic lawfulness of nature, which Aristotle (195b 30–200b 9) has shown must underlie CHANCE. The fact that human beings to some extent "make themselves" and make their culture argues for HABIT as "second nature" rather than against final cause. Explanation through final cause

does not eliminate the usefulness of explanation through material, formal, or efficient cause. It merely makes evident the reason for the efficient cause's forming the matter in such a way as to bring about the desired result. Deficiency on the part of the other three causes, in turn, will result in partial or total interference with the attainment of a result that could be considered in reference to what was to be expected on the basis of the usual behavior of most individuals (the average norm) or on the basis of the behavior of those recognized as the best example of a group.

See Also: PERSONALITY.

Bibliography: A. POMPEI, *Enciclopedia filosofica*, 4 v. (Venice-Rome 1957) 3:937. G. AMBROSETTI and C. NEGRO, *ibid.* 934–37. M. K. O'HARA, "Toward a Norm for Normality," *American Catholic Philosophical Association. Proceedings of the Annual Meeting* 36 (1962) 83–91. M. JAHODA, *Current Concepts of Positive Mental Health* (New York 1958). C. SMITH, *Contemporary French Philosophy: A Study in Norms and Values* (New York 1964). E. L. FACKENHEIM, *Metaphysics and Historicity* (Milwaukee 1961).

[M. K. O'HARA]

NORMANDY

Ancient province of France, originally called Neustria, bordered on the north and west by the English Channel, on the northeast by the Bresle River, which separates it from Picardy, and on the south by the region of the Vexin and the Epte River. After the French Revolution, Normandy was divided into the modern *départements* of Seine-Maritime, Eure, Orne, Calvados, and Manche.

Part of the Roman Empire after its conquest by Julius Caesar, Neustria (later called Normandy) was occupied by the FRANKS in the late fifth century and became a part of the Merovingian kingdom. In the fourth century St. Mello and St. VICTRICIUS OF ROUEN had introduced Christianity, which spread throughout the region. By the sixth century Normandy was divided into seven dioceses: Rouen, BAYEUX, Coutances, Lisieux, Avranches, Evreux, and Sées. Early Norman abbeys included SAINT-OUEN, Fontenelle, Jumièges, and Mont-Saint-Michel. After falling to the Carolingians in 751, the province remained under their rule until the ninth-century attacks of the Vikings (NORTHMEN). By the Treaty of St.-Claire-sur-Epte in 911, the Carolingian king Charles the Simple granted Rouen and its vicinity to the Norman leader Rollo, who was baptized a Christian and may have received Charles's daughter in marriage.

For a hundred years the Normans spread westward and southward from Rouen, incorporating the Bessin, the Evreçin, the Cotentin and the Avrançin in the time of Rollo's son William Longsword (930–942), who was assassinated during the expansion; and his son Richard I (942–996). Richard I married a newly-arrived Dane, Gunnor, whose descendents in the female line and their husbands came to constitute the new aristocracy of Normandy. While adopting Frankish customs and institutions, they spread their power through predatory kinship, and forged the most powerful duchy in northern France. Richard II (996–1026) married his sister Emma to King Ethelred Unraed of England, whose son EDWARD THE CONFESSOR bequeathed England to the future William the Conqueror.

During the eleventh century adventurous Normans established states in southern Italy and Sicily. In 1066 Duke William II the Bastard, later KING WILLIAM I THE CONQUEROR, defeated King HAROLD at Hastings and acquired the Anglo-Scandinavian kingdom. Upon William's death in 1087, Normandy went to his eldest son Robert Curthose and England to his second son, WILLIAM II RUFUS. HENRY I, the Conqueror's third son, gained the English crown in 1100, and conquered Normandy from his brother Curthose in 1106.

LANFRANC of Pavia arrived in Normandy about 1040, entered the abbey of BEC and became its schoolmaster and prior. ST. ANSELM arrived in the late 1050s, and when Lanfranc was appointed to the ducal abbey at Caen, Anselm became prior and later abbot of Bec. As its schoolmasters, Lanfranc and Anselm trained a whole generation of churchmen who spread throughout Northern Europe, but especially in Normandy and England. In 1070 the Conqueror brought Lanfranc to England as archbishop of Canterbury, and on Lanfranc's death Anselm succeeded him as archbishop. Together Lanfranc and Anselm populated the English church with Bec and Caen monks as abbots of English monasteries. A Bec monk, William Bona Anima, became Archbishop of Rouen. Bec monks, too, had come to rule most of the monastic houses of Normandy. Other important abbeys of Normandy included ST. EVROULT, where the Norman historian Orderic Vitalis wrote his massive history; FÉCAMP, St. Etienne, Caen, La Trinité, Caen, SAVIGNY, and SAINT-PIERRE-SUR-DIVES. Except for a brief period after Henry's death (1135), in STEPHEN'S reign (1135–54), Normandy was ruled directly by English kings until its loss by King JOHN in 1204 to the French King Philip II Augustus. The conquest of Normandy was a significant step in the formation of the French kingdom and enabled the French kings to model their institutions upon the more efficient ones that had developed in Normandy.

During the Hundred Years' War, France and England again fought over Normandy. Although conceded to England in 1359, it was returned to France in 1360 by the treaty of Brétigny. Until the invasion of Henry V in 1415, most of Normandy remained under French rule. But Henry's victories and internal French dissension led to the loss of Normandy, which was formalized by the Treaty of Troyes in 1420. Spurred by the victories and the martyrdom of JOAN OF ARC, the French mounted repeated campaigns in the years after 1431. By 1450 the English had been driven from Normandy, and it was again ruled by the French; it has remained so to the present. From the eleventh to the fifteenth century the Archdiocese of Rouen, which included all Normandy, held fourteen provincial synods. During the Wars of Religion, Normandy remained Catholic. John EUDES led the reform of the clergy there in the seventeenth century. The revolt of the Chouans was one of the factors that prompted the CONCORDAT OF 1801. Since then Normandy has included the Archdiocese of Rouen, with the Dioceses of Bayeux, Coutances, Evreux, and Sées.

Bibliography: D. C. DOUGLAS, *William the Conqueror* (Berkeley 1964). D. BATES, *Normandy Before 1066* (New York 1982). D. BATES, *William the Conqueror* (London 1989). S. N. VAUGHN, *Anselm of Bec and Robert of Meulan* (Berkeley 1981). F. M. POWICKE, *The Loss of Normandy, 1189–1204* (2nd ed.; Manchester, England 1961). É. PERROY, *The Hundred Years' War* (New York 1951). E. HALLAM, *Capetian France 987–1328* (London 1980). J. DUNBABIN, *France in the Making 843–1180* (Oxford 1985).

[S. N. VAUGHN/B. LYON]

NORMANS, THE

The Normans originated when a band of Norwegian Vikings led by the Dane Hrolf the Ganger (Rollo, in the French sources) settled in the region of the lower Seine River in the old area of Neustria, and were granted the county of Rouen, and the territory around the city of Rouen, by King Charles the Simple at the Treaty of Saint-Claire-sur-Epte in 911. Originally lumped together with the other Northmanni, or Normanni, to include Viking invaders all over Europe and stretching across the Atlantic, these Normans who settled on the Seine acquired a distinct identity separate from their Viking colleagues. Over the next hundred years, these Vikings centered in Rouen extended their control over the entire area previously known as Neustria, adding territories to the south and particularly to the west—the Bessin, the Cotentin and the Avranchin. This expansion in the west involved incorporating independent settlements of other Vikings around Bayeux and Caen, and subduing them to the rule of the count of Rouen.

Rollo was essentially still a Viking chieftain, as was his son William I Longsword, who succeeded Rollo as count in 930. Continuing in his Viking ways, in 942 William was killed in battle trying to extend his county eastward, toward Flanders. His son Richard I began the real construction of the future Duchy of Normandy. Richard's marriage to the Viking Gunnor, ''of the noblest house of the Danes,'' who had settled with others in the area around Caen began the lines of Norman aristocracy—all descended from Gunnor and her female relatives. Eleanor Searle has labeled the subsequent Norman expansion as ''Predatory Kinship.'' The Normans continued to solidify their duchy under Richard and Gunnor's son Richard II, who had gained such prestige that he was able to make a marriage alliance with England by marrying his sister Emma to King Aethelred Unraed.

Under these earliest Norman dukes the abbeys of Fécamp, Mont-St.-Michel, St. Ouen of Rouen, Fontenelle and Bernay were refounded, but the Norman counts tended to appoint their own relatives to bishoprics. The church in Normandy really began its organization under Duke William II the Bastard, who succeeded his father Robert the Magnificent as a child of seven in 1035. Shortly thereafter Lanfranc of Pavia came to Normandy and settled in as a monk of the newly-founded abbey of Bec. Abbot Herluin soon recognized his learning and appointed Lanfranc as prior. The school Lanfranc opened was the first in Normandy, and attracted both lay and clerical students from all over Europe. Duke William raised Lanfranc ''as on a watchtower'' to oversee the churches of Normandy, and Lanfranc began replacing the ducal relatives with Italian reformers as bishops. Duke William appointed Lanfranc as abbot of the new ducal foundation, St. Etienne, Caen, with its sister abbey for women, Holy Trinity, in 1060. Lanfranc chose the promising student Anselm to succeed him as Bec's schoolmaster and prior.

When William conquered England in 1066, beginning the line of Anglo-Norman kings, he brought LANFRANC to serve as Archbishop of Canterbury in 1070, and Lanfranc began replacing the abbots of England with monks of Bec, Caen, Lessay, and other abbeys under Bec's tutelage. ANSELM succeeded Herluin as abbot of Bec and Lanfranc as archbishop of Canterbury; by Anselm's death, he and Lanfranc had reformed the English church on the model of Bec's monastic ideals, while King WILLIAM I THE CONQUEROR reformulated the English government into an amalgamation of English tradition and Norman innovation, a propitious blend of both traditions, but always claiming to reconstitute the customs of his predecessor Edward the confessor. Anselm struggled with kings WILLIAM II, Rufus, and HENRY I over investitures, and persuaded the latter to abandon them despite the insistence of both kings to maintain the customs of their predecessors. Both Lanfranc and Anselm worked to hold reforming councils in England. Their espiscopates set the pattern that the English Church would follow thereafter—a pattern which survived the anarchy of the reign of the last Anglo-Norman king, Stephen.

In the time of Count Richard I of Normandy, some Normans began wandering southward and settled in southern Italy, which they viewed as a land of opportunity because of its political disunity. Many were hired as mercenaries by the LOMBARD counts and Byzantine officials, to fight against either or both, or against the invading Muslim forces from Sicily. Others made their fortune as highway robbers. Most prominent among these Normans were the 12 sons of Tancred d'Hauteville, a minor lord of the Cotentin; among them, Robert Guiscard (the crafty) emerged as the leader, who eventually carved out for himself a fief in the Apennines. Then he moved down to the plains, drove out the Greeks, supported Pope LEO IX after previously fighting against him, and finally received from Pope NICHOLAS II the investiture of the Duchies of Apulia and Calabria (1059). He also obtained license to conquer Sicily, which he and his younger brother Roger accomplished during the years 1061 to 1091. Robert Guiscard, like his contemporaries in Normandy, founded a string of abbeys, all originating with and connected to the Norman abbey of St. Evroul—St. Euphemia, Sant'Angelo at Mileto, St. Maria of Mattina, St. Maria of Camigliano, to which a number of Greek monasteries were subjected, in a manner somewhat reminiscent of the subjection of English abbeys to Bec monks. The bishoprics of southern Italy were reformed by the papacy rather than by the Normans, but Roger I the Great, in the last few years of the eleventh century, won from Pope Urban II the right to control the churches of his unified realm of Italy and Sicily. In Sicily, Roger permitted the Greek Church to remain dominant, while in Italy he subjected it to Latin rule. Although Robert Guiscard failed in his attempt to create a Sicilian-Dalmatian Empire, his brother Roger organized the new Sicilian state, and his son Bohemund distinguished himself among the leaders of the First CRUSADE, at the capture of Antioch, 1098. The same Norman line of Tancred d'Hauteville ruled, in the twelfth century, at Palermo: Roger II of Sicily was crowned king in 1130 at Antioch. Just as Canut and William the Conqueror had posed as legitimate successors of the Anglo-Saxon kings and preserved in England a number of its ancestral customs, so also the Norman kings of Sicily and the Norman princes of Antioch took on the dress of Byzantium and manifested a remarkable propensity for assimilation. Thus the organizing spirit of a handful of Normans succeeded in uniting the most dissimilar ethnic elements. Everywhere they gave birth to an original and brilliant civilization, be it Anglo-Norman, Sicilo-Norman, or Normano-Syrian.

Bibliography: DUDO OF ST. QUENTIN, *History of the Normans,* tr. E. CHRISTIANSEN (Woodbridge 1998). *The Gesta Norman-*

norum Ducum of William of Jumieges, Orderic Vitalis and Robert of Torigni, ed. and tr. E. M. C. VAN HOUTS, 2 v. (Oxford 1992–5). O. VITALIS, The Ecclesiastical History of Orderic Vitalis, ed. and tr. M. CHIBNALL, 6 v. (Oxford 1969–80). WILLIAM OF MALMESBURY, Gesta Regum Anglorum, ed. and tr. R. A. B. MYNORS; completed by R. M. THOMSON and M. WINTERBOTTOM (Oxford and New York 1998). R. H. C. DAVIS, The Normans and their Myth, (London 1976). D. BATES, Normandy Before 1066 (New York 1982). D. BATES, William the Conqueror (London 1989). D. DOUGLAS, William the Conqueror (Berkeley 1964). E. SEARLE, Predatory Kinship and the Creation of Norman Power (Berkeley 1988). F. BARLOW, William Rufus (Berkeley 1983). C. W. HOLLISTER, Henry I (New Haven 2001). G. A. LOUD, The Age of Robert Guiscard (Harlow, Eng. 2000). G. A. LOUD, Church and Society in the Norman Principality of Capus 1058–1197 (1985). H. E. J. COWDREY, The Age of Abbot Desiderius. Montecassino, the Papacy and the Normans in the Eleventh and Early Twelfth Centuries (Oxford 1983). D. MATTHEW, The Norman Kingdom of Sicily (Cambridge 1992).

[S. N. VAUGHN/R. FOREVILLE]

NORRIS, JAMES JOSEPH

Lay leader and international expert on relief, refugee, and migration problems; b. Roselle Park, N.J., Aug. 10, 1907; d. Rumson, N.J., Nov. 17, 1976. After graduating from high school in 1924, Norris joined the Missionary Servants of the Most Holy Trinity, where he collaborated closely with the order's founder, Thomas A. Judge. Leaving the order in 1934, he had a brief stint in the business world before the then Rev. Patrick O'Boyle (later the Cardinal Archbishop of Washington, D.C.) appointed him as executive assistant at the Mission of the Immaculate Virgin on Staten Island in 1936. For more than 30 years of his life, Norris was deeply committed to combatting the problems of poverty and injustice. When World War II broke out, Norris was made the assistant director (1941–42), and later executive director (1942–44) of the National Catholic Community Services. He also served with distinction as a commander in the U.S. Navy Armed Guard on active duty from 1944 to 1946.

In 1946 O'Boyle appointed Norris as the European director of War Relief Services for the National Catholic Welfare Conference, the forerunner of the Catholic Relief Services (CRS), helping in the rebuilding of the Church and national communities in Europe in the post-World War II period. From 1959 to his death he served as assistant to the executive director of CRS as that agency of the American bishops turned its energies from a recovered Europe to the third world countries, whose emergence were proving to be among the greatest challenges of the period. Norris also participated in negotiations with Mgsr. Giovanni Battista Montini (the future Paul VI), resulting in the establishment of the International Catholic Migration Commission (ICMC) in 1951. Norris became the president of ICMC (1951–74), and honorary president (1974–76). In its first 25 years of existence, the ICMC assisted more than 200,000 migrants and refugees with loans of $40 million. In both his roles as a key official in the work of CRS and the ICMC, Norris pressed church officials to utilize the strength and stability of the Church to implement Christian principles on an international level as well as to make Catholics themselves more aware of their obligations in justice and charity to the less fortunate throughout the world.

Norris was the only layman invited to address a plenary session of VATICAN COUNCIL II. On Nov. 5, 1964, Norris spoke to the assembled Council Fathers during the debate on the Pastoral Constitution on the Church in the Modern World. Speaking in Latin, he spoke on the implications and challenges of ''World Poverty and the Christian Conscience.'' One result of the address was the inclusion in the final draft of the Constitution of a proposal to establish a church agency or office which would secure full Catholic participation on social justice and world poverty (see Gaudium et spes, 90). In the ensuing years, Norris collaborated with Joseph GREMILLION, Luigi LIGUTTI, Barbara WARD, Gerald Mahon, and Arthur McCormack to lobby for the implementing of this conciliar provision. As a result of their persistent efforts, Pope Paul VI inaugurated the Pontifical Commission for Justice and Peace, Jan. 6, 1967. National justice and peace commissions were set up subsequently around the world.

A month before his death, Norris was the first American to be awarded by the UN High Commissioner for Refugees the Fridtjof Nanzen Medal, an award to persons who have distinguished themselves in helping solve problems of refugees and migrants on a world scale. Norris was the first layman to be named an official escort on Pope Paul VI's flight to Geneva in June 1966 to visit the International Labor Organization and the World Council of Churches. Pope Paul also named him a member of the Pontifical Commission for Justice and Peace and for the Pontifical Commission ''Cor Unum'' and designated him as the Vatican's representative at the funeral of Martin Luther King Jr. At the time of his death he was survived by his wife, Amanda, and four sons.

Bibliography: E. EGAN, Catholic Relief Services: The Beginning Years (Baltimore 1988). R. J. KUPKE, James J. Norris: An American Catholic Life (Ph.D. diss. Catholic University of America 1995).

[J. C. O'NEILL/EDS.]

NORTH AFRICA, EARLY CHURCH IN

The Romans conquered Carthage in 146 B.C. and turned its territory into the provincia Africana, roughly northeast Tunisia, to which Tripolitania was added later on. In 46 B.C. the Numidian kingdom of Juba was annexed (*Africa nova*) and, with *Africa vetus,* formed *Africa proconsularis.* In the year 40 Mauretania was also annexed, and two provinces were formed: Caesariensis, of which Caesarea was the capital, and Tingitana with Tingis as its capital. Numidia became a separate province in 198. Flourishing cities developed and Roman civilization reached a high peak in the second and third centuries, with famed writers, both pagan and Christian. DIOCLETIAN divided Proconsularis into three provinces: Zeugitana, Tripolitania and Byzacena. Out of eastern Mauretania Caesariensis he carved Sitifensis, making Sitifis the capital. He placed the western part of Africa, Tingitana (today Morocco), under the jurisdiction of the Diocese of Spain. Tingitana depended on the ecclesiastical province of Mauretania Caesariensis, whereas a separate ecclesiastical province corresponded to each of the other six civil provinces by the fourth century, though the civil and ecclesiastical boundaries were not quite the same.

Christianity. Apostolic origin for the African Church cannot be proved. Christianity probably came through Carthage, an important harbor, no later than the first half of the second century. The earliest dated event occurred on July 17, 180; 12 Christians of Scilli were martyred in Carthage. But as early as 197 TERTULLIAN (*Ad Scap.* 56) proudly appealed to the general Christian penetration of all ranks of society, which indicates that the evangelization had begun quite some time before. A striking fact is that the bishops were remarkably numerous, a condition explained by the fact that small dioceses were customary. By the year 225 at least 70 bishops were found in Proconsularis, and Numidia; by 411, there were 470 Catholic bishoprics and the number had grown to nearly 600 in 430. For this vast territory no metropolitan existed, except for Proconsularis, where the bishop of Carthage since the third century held metropolitan rights for all Africa. In the other provinces, the *primae sedis episcopus* was the bishop who exceeded the others by seniority.

Persecution under Decius. The Church seems to have been left in peace, until in the year 197 and especially in 202, a persecution took place, in which the most famous martyrs were PERPETUA AND FELICITY, with four companions. The recording of the events of their martyrdom is traceable possibly to Tertullian. Other works of this writer indicate that another persecution in 211–212 followed. But the greatest trial of the local church came in the persecution of DECIUS, who in 249–250 demanded of all inhabitants of the empire a certificate of sacrifice. The bishop of Carthage, CYPRIAN (249–258), testified to the large numbers of apostates (*De lapsis* 7–9). Some of these actually offered sacrifice (*sacrificati, thurificati*); others managed to obtain a false certificate to prove their compliance (*libellatici, acta facientes*). Yet, many suffered martyrdom.

After Decius' death in 251, a grave problem arose as to the treatment of the *lapsi.* Some confessors granted *libelli pacis* to the *lapsi,* but Cyprian demanded that the *sacrificati* and *thurificati* perform a lifelong penance. This occasioned a schism at Carthage, headed by the deacon Felicissimus and the priest Novatus.

Persecution under Valerian and Diocletian. St. Cyprian distinguished himself by his charitable work for those who suffered from famine and pestilence (252–254) and convoked various synods (255–256), where the question of the validity of baptism conferred by heretics was treated. Following the opinion of Tertullian (*De bapt.* 15) and many bishops of Asia, especially FIRMILIAN OF CAESAREA, Cyprian denied the validity of such baptism, thus setting a precedent for the DONATISTS. He withstood Pope STEPHEN I, who insisted on the Roman tradition, recognizing the validity of baptism conferred with the intention of doing the will of Christ. Though neither side yielded its viewpoint, no schism occurred, and the persecution of VALERIAN (257–259) claimed the pope and Cyprian as victims, along with many Africans, including those who were later called the *massa candida.*

The Emperor Gallienus restored peace to the Church, but it was rudely interrupted by the persecution of Diocletian in 295, which began in the army with the martyrdom of the young Maximilian at Theveste. Other martyrs were the veteran Typasius, the centurion Marcellus and the standard-bearer Fabius. When the persecution became general in 303, it claimed victims in Africa, including the 19 women and 30 men of Abitina near Carthage. The peace of 313 was to bring grave problems to the African Church.

Donatism. During the third century, heresy in Africa had been represented by MONTANISM, to which Tertullian adhered in his later life and MANICHAEISM (not strictly a Christian heresy). A movement arose, however, that united social and religious elements, renewed the errors of Tertullian and Cyprian, and caused havoc in the African Church for more than a century. It was known as DONATISM. The Bishop of Carthage, Mensurius, died in 311. The Archdeacon Caecilianus, his successor, had made enemies by his previous severity. These claimed that one of his Episcopal consecrators, Felix of Aptungi, had been a *traditor,* that is, guilty of the sin of having given up the sacred books during the persecution, and thus he was incapable of validly administering a Sacrament. The Church was for them a society of saints, in which authority and spiritual effectiveness depended on personal sanctity. Catholics were considered *traditores;* on conversion, freely or by force, to Donatism, baptism was repeated, and the other Sacraments given by Catholics, including the Eucharist, were treated with contempt. Donatism spread rapidly, in spite of the Emperor Constantine's persecution of the sect. Donatist doctrine was condemned first by a Roman ecclesiastical sentence in 313 and then by the council at Arles in 314.

Donatus (d. *c.* 355) was the first outstanding schismatic bishop of Carthage; under him the sect spread into other provinces, especially Numidia, which became its stronghold. In 347, a group of nomadic workers from the south, called Circumcellions, was used by Optatus, the Donatist Bishop of Bagai, against the Roman troops who tried to uproot the schism. Later, these workers adopted Donatism as a convenient ally to oppose the Roman Empire, which hindered their desire for absolute freedom from restraint.

OPTATUS OF MILEVIS and St. AUGUSTINE narrate sad details of the horrors perpetrated by the Donatists, especially the Circumcellions, against Catholic priests and monks. The sect increased so rapidly that 270 bishops attended a Donatist council of 336. After the death in exile of Donatus, he was succeeded by Parmenianus (d. 391), who not only displayed organizing activity, but wrote anti-Catholic works. Refutations by Optatus of Milevis and Augustine and efficient pastoral opposition under the Catholic Bishop of Carthage, Aurelius (392–430), took effect. The Donatists themselves split into various sects, against whom Augustine sharply pressed their inconsistencies and elaborated his theology of the Sacraments.

The Emperor Honorius aided the Catholic cause, and in 411 a meeting was held at Carthage, at which 286 Catholic and 284 Donatist bishops were in attendance. Bishops from both sides were allowed to present their viewpoints, and after a three-day discussion, the imperial representative announced the victory of the Catholics. In 412 the emperor ordered the schismatics to return to the Catholic Church, threatening the disobedient with confiscation, corporal punishment and deportation. After some hesitation Augustine admitted the wisdom of the state's intervention against the destructive activities of the Donatists and Circumcellions; when many returned to the Church, from which fear of the wild fanatics had held them, the schism was greatly weakened. Yet, even Pope GREGORY I complained in the sixth century that the error was not yet completely eradicated in Africa.

St. Augustine and Pelagianism. Augustine, himself a convert from Manichaeism, devoted a series of brilliant works as priest and bishop to a refutation of Donatism when another error called for response, namely, PELA-

GIANISM. With his collaborator Celestius, Pelagius had denied original sin and claimed that man could perform good acts and avoid sin without internal grace. Both came to Carthage in 410, but Pelagius left at once for Palestine. Paulinus of Milan attacked the errors of Celestius and upon his refusal to retract, Celestius was excommunicated by the council of Carthage in 411. Augustine saw the fundamental rejection of Christianity implied in the heresy and brought out the works that earned him the title of "Doctor of Grace." Though Pelagius was declared orthodox by the Council of Diospolis in 415, provincial councils at Carthage and Milevis in 416 renewed the condemnation of Pelagianism, and when Pope Innocent I concurred, Augustine exclaimed: *causa finita est* (*Serm.* 131.10).

Pope ZOSIMUS (417–418), on receiving professions of orthodoxy from the two heretics, blamed the African bishops for excessive zeal in condemning men who admitted the necessity of grace. The African answer was a general council at Carthage in May 418, inspired by Augustine, in which the errors of the heretics were laid bare. Zosimus then condemned Pelagianism, but the stubborn opposition of JULIAN OF ECLANUM obliged Augustine to write several further tracts dealing with marriage and grace, as well as 12 books *Contra Julianum.* In 426–427 he composed his *De gratia et libero arbitrio* and *De correptione et gratia* for the monks of Hadrumetum who challenged human liberty in relation to predestination and questioned the gift of perseverance. Thus SEMI-PELAGIANISM met its chief refutation from the African Church.

Monasticism. The monastic movement was introduced into Africa in its cenobitic form by Augustine in 388 on his return from Italy. Previously, individual monks and virgins, including Donatist sisters, had existed in Africa, but no monastery is recorded before 388. Augustine propagated the movement, as convert, priest and bishop, living with a group of ascetics. His sister became superior of a convent of nuns at Hippo, and Augustine's monastery provided ten bishops for other churches, who transplanted the monastic life to their new dioceses.

Even during the period when the VANDALS ruled in Africa (429–534) monasticism flourished in both clerical and lay circles. The life of FULGENTIUS OF RUSPE (d. *c.* 533) is witness to this, for he followed Augustine's example and practiced a monastic way of life as layman, priest and bishop. Monasteries are found as far east as Tripolitania and as far west as Mauretania Caesariensis before, during and after the Vandal occupation. These barbarians had crossed from Spain in 429, besieged Hippo in the last days of St. Augustine and captured Carthage in 439. By treaty with the Emperor VALENTINIAN III in 442 they became the recognized masters of Zeugitana, Byzacena and part of Numidia. After the death of this emperor in 455 they seized the two Mauretanias, though their control there was nominal, owing to the bellicose nature of the native Mauri.

Of the six Vandal kings, all Arians, who ruled in Africa, Geiseric, Huneric and Thrasamund persecuted the Church severely, concentrating on the higher clergy. The first two kings nearly succeeded in extirpating the Catholic bishops in favor of the ARIANS. Hence in Zeugitana under Geiseric (429–477) the number of Catholic bishops was reduced from 164 to three. Yet, in his desire to make a favorable treaty with the Emperor ZENO, Geiseric in 475 allowed the return of the Catholic exiles. His son Huneric (477–484) forced all the Catholic bishops of Africa to come to Carthage in 484 for a discussion with the Arians, after which he sent them into exile, deporting the bishops of Zeugitana to Corsica and others into the African desert. Five hundred clerics of Carthage were scourged and exiled. Later Huneric dispatched some 5,000 Catholics including many clerics to exile among the savage Mauri and tried systematically to destroy monastic life in Africa by ordering that all monasteries of men and women, together with their inhabitants, be given to the Mauri. His death put an end to the persecution, and King Gunthamund (484–496) allowed the exiled bishops to return (494). King Thrasamund (496–523) conducted the most effective persecution. No bishops could be elected, and when this decree was violated in Byzacena, 120 bishops were exiled to Sardinia, from which they returned only after his death, when King Hilderic (523–530) granted a period of peace for the Church. The last king, Gelimer, was conquered by the army of JUSTINIAN I under Belisarius in 534.

Byzantine Influence. Under the Byzantines some of the Church's ancient splendor returned; capable theologians such as Ferrandus of Carthage and FACUNDUS OF HERMIANE and frequent councils gave it a part in the affairs of the universal Church. In the dispute over the THREE CHAPTERS, the African bishops refused to subscribe to the condemnation rendered by Justinian and the Council of CONSTANTINOPLE II, and even excommunicated Pope VIGILIUS. African monks and bishops were among those who were exiled for their opposition.

Byzantine occupation, however, did not bring an enduring peace to Africa either internally or externally. The Mauri inflicted many defeats on Byzantine arms and many Christians, including 70 monks with their abbot Donatus, fled to Europe about the year 570. Internally, the corruption of civil officials went unchecked and revolts were frequent. Yet many Mauri became Christians. In the seventh century the Byzantine emperors favored MONOTHELITISM, which was rejected by many African monks under the inspiration of St. MAXIMUS THE CONFESSOR. When in 638 the Emperor HERACLIUS with his *Ecthesis* imposed Monothelitism on the whole Church, most Africans refused to sign the document and in 645 revolted against his successor Constans II.

African ecclesiastical dissension prepared the way for the Arab invasions that began with a first raid in 643. The Arabs captured Carthage in 698 and took the last Byzantine stronghold at Septem, or Ceuta, in 709. The Mohammedans gradually brought about the extinction of Christianity, first by a rapid conversion of the volatile Mauri, then by a process of attrition, reducing the number of bishoprics to three for all Africa in the time of Pope GREGORY VII. They had disappeared entirely by the 13th century.

Bibliography: A. AUDOLLENT, *Dictionnaire d'histoire et de géographie ecclésiastiques,* ed., A. BAUDRILLART et al., (Paris 1912–) 1:705–861. G. BARDY, *Catholicisme,* 1:186–191. L. DUCHESNE, *L'Église au sixième siècle* (Paris 1925). G. BARDY et al., *Histoire de l'église depuis les origines jusqu'à nos jours,* eds., A. FLICHE and V. MARTIN (Paris 1935–) v. 3, 4, 5. J. GAUDEMET, *L'Église dans l'Empire Romain* (Paris 1958). G. KRÜGER, *Lexikon für Theologie und Kirche²,* eds., J. HOFER and K. RAHNER, 10 v. (2d, new ed. Freiburg 1957–65) 1:175–176. *Histoire de l'Afrique du Nord,* eds., C. A. JULIEN and C. COURTOIS, (2d ed. Paris 1956). B. H. WARMINGTON, *The North African Provinces from Diocletian to the Vandal Conquest* (Cambridge, Eng. 1954). C. COURTOIS, *Les Vandales et l'Afrique* (Paris 1955). W. H. FREND, *Reallexikon für Antike und Christentum,* ed., T. KLAUSER [Stuttgart 1941 (1950)–] 4:128–147. J. J. GAVIGAN, *De vita monastica in Africa Septentrionali* (Turin 1962). E. L. GRASMÜCK, *Coercitio: Staat und Kirche im Donatistenstreit* (Bonn 1964).

[J. J. GAVIGAN]

NORTH AMERICAN ACADEMY OF LITURGY

The North American Academy of Liturgy (NAAL) is an ecumenical association of specialists in Christian liturgy and related arts and disciplines. The Academy's purposes are to provide channels for mutual professional assistance and for the sharing of methods and resources; to exchange technical information concerning research projects and activities of the members; to foster liturgical research, publication, and dialogue at a scholarly level; to encourage exchanges with individuals and communities of other religious traditions; and to communicate the activities of the Academy through the publication of annual proceedings.

Admission to the NAAL is restricted to persons of demonstrated competence in liturgical studies and to specialists in allied areas who contribute to the understanding of worship in a significant way. The Academy consists of members, who have established and demonstrated their competence in the fields of liturgy and related areas, and associates, who evidence a developing contribution in the field of liturgical studies and related areas.

The groundwork for the founding of the Academy was laid in December of 1973. To honor the 10th anniversary of Vatican Council II's Constitution on the Sacred Liturgy, a conference for 70 people working in the field of liturgy was sponsored by *Theological Studies* at the Franciscan Renewal Center, Scottsdale, Arizona. The conveners of the conference were Walter Burghardt, SJ, and John Gallen, SJ. Travel costs and conference expenses were underwritten by the Friends of the Franciscan Renewal Center.

At the end of this conference, the group decided to meet a year later in January of 1975, at the University of Notre Dame, South Bend, Ind., to continue its discussion and reflection and to found an official organization. At the end of the Notre Dame conference, the first officers of the Academy committee were elected: John Gallen, SJ, president, Rev. Daniel Stevick, vice-president, Dr. John Barry Ryan, secretary-treasurer, and Mary Collins, OSB, and Mr. Robert Rambusch, delegates. In 1977, the Academy was incorporated as a nonprofit organization in the state of New Jersey.

From its inception the Academy has presented the Berakah Award to honor a person who has made outstanding contributions in the field of liturgy. Published every summer, *The Proceedings of the North American Academy of Liturgy* contains papers from the annual meeting, seminar reports, and selected research essays.

Bibliography: M. COLLINS, "Liturgy in America: The Scottsdale Conference," *Worship* 48 (1974) 66–80. Papers connected with the Scottsdale Conference, *Theological Studies* 35 (1974) 233–311. Proceedings of NAAL Meetings, *Worship* 50 n. 4 (1976), 51 n. 4 (1977), 52 n. 4 (1978).

[J. B. RYAN/EDS.]

NORTH AMERICAN COLLEGE

The North American College, located in Rome, Italy, began as a residence for seminarians training for the diocesan priesthood of the U.S. In time it developed three distinct divisions, each serving a different clientele: the seminary (admitting only individuals designated by their bishops), a residence for priests pursuing advanced studies, and an Institute for Continuing Theological Education.

Foundation and History. Promising seminarians for American dioceses had been sent to Rome by their bishops as early as 1790, but they had no separate seminary until the present institution was established by Pope Pius IX, Dec. 8, 1859, on the recommendation of Abp. Gaetano BEDINI. Bedini foresaw that such a seminary would not only strengthen the theological education of the American clergy but would also bind the Church in the U.S. more closely to the Holy See. The college was housed in a former Visitandine convent on Via dell'Umiltà, near the Fontana di Treve. The Holy See loaned the property to the American bishops until 1948 when Pope Pius XII, as an "act of deference" to the U.S. hierarchy, presented it to them outright. The seminarians attended classes at the Urban College of Propaganda Fide from 1859 to 1932, when the college became affiliated with the Gregorian University.

For a quarter century after its inauguration, the American College was financially insecure. Nevertheless it quickly became the American Catholic headquarters in Rome, and its rectors assumed a role of increasing influence as spokesmen for the American Church. During Vatican Council I (1869–70), 18 archbishops and bishops from the United Stated lived and held conferences in the college. On Sept. 20, 1870, papal Rome surrendered to the invading armies of the king of Italy. A few days before the final siege 13 students from the American College proffered their services to the papal army. Pius IX gratefully refused, reminding them that they were called to a nobler warfare.

Anticlerical policies of the Kingdom of Italy directly affected the North American College. In March 1884, the Italian government moved to confiscate the college buildings, still owned by the Congregation of Propaganda Fide. Informed of this threat, Cardinal John McCloskey of New York, immediately sought the aid of the U.S. government. President Chester A. Arthur, by his prompt personal intervention, averted the peril.

On Oct. 25, 1884, Pope Leo XIII, by the brief *Ubi Primum*, decreed the long-delayed canonical establishment of the American College, and bestowed on it "pontifical" status. Increased registration obliged the college superiors to add a new wing to the property in 1901. Two years before, the handsome Villa Santa Caterina at Castel Gandolfo had been purchased as a summer residence.

World War I vexed but did not impede the College. World War II forced it to close. In May 1940, when it became apparent that Italy would enter the struggle, the students were sent home to finish their studies. During much of the war the college proper and the Villa Santa Caterina harbored exiled children of Italian colonials.

When the college finally reopened on Sept. 4, 1948, the students commuted to classes from the Villa Santa

Caterina pending the rehabilitation of the Umiltà property. Meanwhile work began on a new college near St. Peter's Basilica, in a section of the Janiculum Hill under the jurisdiction of Vatican City. Upon its completion Pius XII came in person to dedicate the new edifice on Oct. 14, 1953. The new structure, designed by Count Enrico Galeazzi, sometime governor of Vatican City, was built to house 300 occupants. Count Galeazzi is buried in the college crypt.

The Graduate Division. In 1931 with the Apostolic Constitution *Deus Scientiarum Dominius* Pope Pius XI laid the foundation for reform of programs leading to advanced degrees in ecclesiastical faculties. Two years later in 1933 the graduate division of the North American College was opened at the Casa San Giovanni on the Janiculum Hill for students already ordained. The title to this property, originally part of the 26-acre Villa Gabrielli owned by the province of Rome, had been acquired in 1924 jointly by Propaganda Fide and the U.S. hierarchy. When the seminarians moved to the new college in 1953, priests in various graduate programs occupied the old site, renamed Casa Santa Maria dell'Umiltà.

The American Bishops Office for U.S. visitors to the Vatican is also located at the Via dell'Umiltà address. It provides a service to American travelers seeking tickets for papal audiences and information about liturgical celebrations.

The Institute for Continuing Theological Education. The third division of the North American College began in 1970 as a response to the call of Vatican Council II for renewal and updating of pastoral ministers. Open to a limited number of priests each year, the institute invites lecturers and professors from the United States and the Roman theological faculties to offer classes. The institute began at Casa di Santa Maria dell'Umiltà, but was moved in 1984 to the college complex on Janiculum.

Administration. The American College is under the direction of both the Congregation for Catholic Education, representing the Holy See, and a episcopal Board of Governors, representing the United States Conference of Catholic Bishops. The pope appoints the rector from a list a list of three names proposed by the board. The following men have held this post: Bernard Smith, O.S.B. (1859–60), temporary; William George McCloskey (1860–68); Francis Silas Marean Chatard (1868–78); Louis Edward Hostlot, *né* Hasslocher (1878–84); Augustine Joseph Schulte (1884–85), temporary; Denis Joseph O'Connell (1885–95); William Henry O'Connell (1895–1901); Thomas Francis Kennedy (1901–17); Charles Aloysius O'Hern (1917–25); Eugene Francis Burke, Jr. (1925–35); Ralph Leo Hayes (1935–44); James Gerald Kealy (1945–46); Martin John O'Connor

(1946–64); Francis F. Reh (1964–68); James A. Hickey (1969–74); Harold P. Darcy (1974–79); Charles M. Murphy (1979–84); Lawrence M. Purcell (1984–89); Edwin F. O'Brien (1990–94); Timothy M. Dolan (1994–2001); and Kevin C. McCoy (2001–).

The first class in 1859 numbered 12 students from eight American dioceses. It included the grandson of St. Elizabeth Ann Seton, and Michael A. Corrigan, the future archbishop of New York. From its opening to the year 2000, close to 5000 students enrolled in the seminary and graduate divisions. Twenty-two have been named cardinals.

Bibliography: M. V. DOHERTY, *House on Humility Street* (New York 1942). R. F. MCNAMARA, *American College in Rome, 1855–1955* (Rochester, N. Y. 1956).

[R. F. MCNAMARA/R. RIEDE]

NORTH AMERICAN MARTYRS

The word martyr has a very precise meaning in ecclesiastical literature. Those who bear the name do so only when a rigorous inquiry by the Church has attested to the fact that hatred of the faith motivated those who killed them. North America honors eight martyrs; all were of European and French origin and belonged to the missions of Canada, then called New France. Six of them were priests of the Society of Jesus: Isaac Jogues, Antoine Daniel, Jean de Brébeuf, Gabriel Lalemant, Charles Garnier, and Noël Chabanel. The other two, René Goupil and Jean de la Lande, were *donnés,* lay assistants, who, without binding themselves by religious vows, worked for the Jesuit missions. Unsalaried, they received food, shelter, and help in case of illness from the fathers. All the martyrs died between Sept. 29, 1642 and Dec. 9, 1649. They were beatified on June 21, 1925, and canonized June 29, 1930; their feast day is September 26. In terms of time and place of martyrdom, they make up two groups.

First Group. This included Goupil, Jogues, and la Lande, who were martyred near Auriesville, N.Y., at Ossernenon, seat of the Mohawk tribe in the U.S.

Goupil. He was born at Anjou, France, May 13, 1608; as a youth he entered the Jesuit novitiate in Paris, but was forced to leave because of deafness. He then studied surgery at the Orléans hospital; in 1640, he arrived in Canada, where he was assigned as *donné* to the Sillery mission near Quebec. As the infirmarian at Sillery and at the Hôtel-Dieu of Quebec, he set out for Huronia. When the flotilla taking him there fell into Iroquois hands, he was captured and underwent the rigors of barbaric torture. An Iroquois killed him with an axe stroke on Sept. 29, 1642, for having made the sign of the cross over a child. The first of this group of martyrs, he is the only one whose life has been told by another martyr, Jogues. The original of this document, which was recently translated into English, is kept in the archives of the College of St. Marie of Montreal. Catholic doctors of the U.S. honor Goupil as the first of their profession to have crossed the Adirondacks.

Jogues and la Lande. Jogues was born in Orléans, France, Jan. 10, 1607. In 1636, after ordination on July 2, he arrived in Quebec and was assigned to the Huron missions. He was taken with Goupil in 1642 as he was returning to the missions after a visit to Quebec, and he was subjected to all the cruelties that the Iroquois perpetrated on their prisoners. During his captivity he baptized 60 children and in midwinter conducted his annual retreat before an outdoor cross. He was ransomed by the Dutch of Fort Orange (Albany) in 1643, and he escaped to New York and thence to France. Urban VIII granted him a dispensation to celebrate Mass, despite his mutilated left hand, saying: "It would be shameful for a martyr of Christ not to drink the blood of Christ." In Canada again in the spring of 1644, Jogues was entrusted with a brief peace mission to the Iroquois. He departed Sept. 24, 1646, for Ossernenon, but a Mohawk war party captured him; on October 18 Jogues was tomahawked and the following day his companion la Lande suffered the same fate. Jogues was known to have desired the grace of martyrdom; so when the news of the double martyrdom reached Quebec in the spring of 1647, his fellow missionaries celebrated a Mass of Thanksgiving rather than one of Requiem for the repose of his soul.

Second Group. This group—composed of Daniel, Brébeuf, Lalemant, Garnier, and Chabanel—met death within the actual confines of Canada; the first three were killed by the Iroquois, and Chabanel by a Huron apostate.

Daniel. This first martyr of Huronia was born in Dieppe, France, in 1601 and became a Jesuit novice at 20. He arrived at Cape Breton in 1632 and went to Quebec the following year. In 1634 he left for Huronia, where he remained, except for two years during which he served as director of the Huron seminary in Quebec. On July 4, 1648, he had just celebrated Mass when the mission of St. Joseph was overrun by Iroquois. After ministering to the wounded and baptizing some of them, he was struck by arrows and shot, and his trampled and desecrated body was then cast into the fire that consumed the chapel.

Brébeuf and Lalemant. Brébeuf was born at Condé-sur-Vire, Normandy, France, March 25, 1593, and had already been ordained when he arrived in Canada, June 1625. The English occupation of Quebec in 1629 necessitated his return to France, but he was able to get back to

Father Isaac Jogues, North American martyr. (Archive Photos)

his mission in 1633 and Huronia became his field of apostolate. Lalemant, born in 1610, was the nephew of Revs. Charles and Jerome Lalemant and had long dreamed of the Canadian missions. In 1646 he arrived at Quebec, but because of ill health, it was two years before he reached the Huron missions. There on March 16, 1649, an Iroquois band attacked the town of St. Ignace and captured Brébeuf and Lalemant, who were tied to stakes and underwent one of the worst martyrdoms ever recorded in history. Brébeuf suffered for three hours before dying; Lalemant died the following morning, March 17. The *Relation* states: "Before their death both their hearts were torn out through an opening made in their chest; these barbarians feasted on them inhumanly, drinking their warm blood which they drew from its source with a sacrilegious hand. While still full of life, pieces of their thighs, calves, and arms were removed by the butchers who roasted them on coals and ate them in their sight."

Garnier. He was born in Paris in 1605 and joined the Society of Jesus at 19; in 1636 he arrived in Canada, where he was assigned to the Huron mission. After devoting himself to it for 13 years, he was sent to St. Jean in 1649, when Fort St. Marie was abandoned. During an Iroquois attack on St. Jean, Garnier exhorted his faithful to flee but to keep the faith. He remained at his post and was first struck down by two bullets. Then, according to the

Relation, ''The Father received shortly thereafter two axe strokes on both temples which penetrated the brain.'' He died on Dec. 7, 1649.

Chabanel. He was born at Saugues in southern France, Feb. 7, 1613, entered the novitiate in 1630, and arrived in Canada in 1643. By education and temperament, this brilliant professor of rhetoric in France was far removed from the native ways of living and acting, and he had no aptitude for the Huron language; but in order to protect his missionary vocation, he made the vow of stability, with his superiors' permission. After serving with Garnier at St. Jean (with the Petuns?), he was on his way to Fort St. Marie II (Christian Island) when he was killed by an apostate Huron near the Nottawasaga River in Ontario, Dec. 8, 1649. He had expressed the desire to be a *martyrem in umbra,* a martyr in obscurity, unknown and forgotten. His death at first appeared to be shrouded in mystery, but in the *Relation* of 1650, Rev. Paul Ragueneau wrote: ''We learned from very reliable testimony that Father Noël Chabanel was put to death by the apostate Huron whom we suspected. He himself admitted it and added that he had committed the murder in hatred of the faith, because he saw, in his words, all the evils befalling him and his family since he had embraced the faith.''

Cult of the Martyrs. In Canada the belief that these missionaries were martyrs in the strict sense of the word led Rageneau, Jesuit superior at Quebec, to set up a dossier on the subject. This *Manuscript,* or *Mémoire,* of 1652, the original of which is kept at the College of St. Marie in Montreal, contains the text of the *Relations* and the deposition of trustworthy witnesses on the lives and circumstances of death of the martyrs. They were equally known and venerated in Europe, where the *Relations, des Jésuites* (1648–49), telling of the death of Brébeuf and Lalemant, was translated into Latin and Flemish. The *Relazione* of Rev. Francesco Bressani (Florence 1653) made them known in Italy, but events such as the society's suppression in 1773, the French Revolution in 1789, and the political changes of the times, in both Canada and the U.S., contributed to the martyrs' oblivion. Eventually, however, the cult of the martyrs, who had always had their devotees in American lands, was revived as a consequence of the Jesuit's return to Canada in 1842; of Edmund B. O'Callaghan's discovery of the *Relations,* a subsequent edition of which was published by the Canadian government in 1858 and later by R. G. Thwaites; and of the historical research of Felix Martin, John Gilmary Shea, Francis Parkman, and others. In 1912, following requests to the Holy See by the hierarchies of Canada and the U.S., the martyrs' cause was introduced; beatification followed in 1925 and canonization in 1930. Annually thousands of pilgrims visit the two sanctuaries erected in their honor: at Auriesville, the Ossernenon of old, where

Goupil, Jogues, and la Lande are venerated; and at Midland, Ontario, near the site of old Fort St. Marie of the Hurons, commemorating Daniel, Brébeuf, Lalemant, Garnier, and Chabanel.

Feast: Sept. 26.

[L. POULIOT]

NORTH CAROLINA, CATHOLIC CHURCH IN

One of the 13 original states of the United States, North Carolina was inhabited primarily by Tuscarora, Catawba, and Cherokee people when the first attempts at colonization by English settlers were begun in the 1580s. It is located on the Atlantic seaboard between Virginia and South Carolina, and bordered on the west by Tennessee. Charles II granted a charter for the territory lying between Virginia and Florida, running west to the ''South Seas,'' to eight ''absolute lords proprietors'' in 1663. North Carolina was established as a separate royal colony in 1729. In addition to the English, there were smaller groups of Scottish, Irish, Welsh, German, Swiss, and French settlers. Blacks, both slave and free, became a significant minority as the colony grew in population, and labor-intensive crops of rice, cotton, and tobacco formed an important sector of the economy.

While there is evidence that Hernando de Soto passed through the territory during his explorations of 1539 to 1543, and speculation by a few historians that some of the first colonists at Roanoke Island in the 1580s were Catholic recusants from England, the first explicit mention of Catholic residents in the colony was made by John Brickell (*The Natural History of North-Carolina*) in 1737. There was no official toleration of Catholicism in the colony until after independence, and much of the population, though Protestant, was unchurched. According to the diary of Bishop John ENGLAND of Charleston, in 1821 there were only about 150 Catholic adults in a statewide population of 650,000. The first priest on record as having resided in the state (1784–90) was a native of Ireland, Patrick Cleary, who originally came to settle his brother's estate in New Bern.

Dr. Thomas Burke of Hillsboro, elected a member of the first Provincial Congress in 1775 and later of the Continental Congress, was known to be a Catholic. In 1781 he became the state's governor, though the North Carolina Constitution of 1776 contained a test oath, barring from public office those who would deny the existence of God or ''the truth of the Protestant Religion.'' This provision stood until 1836. The most famous Catholic legislator and jurist of the period was William J. GAS-

TON of New Bern (1778–1844), who was also the first student to enroll at Georgetown College in 1791. As early as 1823 Bishop England had sought Gaston's assistance in eliminating the offensive test oath, and in the Convention of 1835, Gaston, who by that time was a state supreme court justice, contributed to the effort which eventually resulted in substituting the word ''Christian'' for ''Protestant.''

John England, a native of Ireland, was named bishop of Charleston in 1820. At that time, the diocese included both North and South Carolina, as well as Georgia. By the time of his death in 1842, there were only four Catholic churches to be found in the state: in Washington, Fayetteville, Raleigh, and New Bern, each with small congregations. The number of adult converts was small, but it included both free blacks and slaves, who worshipped together with whites when a priest was present. England himself preached throughout the state, often using courthouses and Protestant churches as venues. In addition, he promulgated a Constitution of the Diocese of Charleston, which established elected representatives of the several congregations to govern the local church and to meet in state- and diocesan-wide conventions. His successors in office quickly abandoned the system he had established.

The spirit of tolerance in the state dissipated during the antebellum period, which saw the rise of the NATIVIST and anti-Catholic KNOW-NOTHING movement. Public lectures denouncing Catholicism, and the 1852 conversion of Levi Silliman IVES (1797–1867), the second Episcopal bishop of North Carolina, to Catholicism, contributed to religious tensions and prejudice. An exception to this trend was seen in the invitation of the graduating class of 1856 at the University of North Carolina to Archbishop John J. Hughes of New York to speak at their commencement. Unable to do so that year, he was again invited and gave the address at graduation in 1860.

Pope Pius IX established the Vicariate Apostolic of North Carolina on March 3, 1868, and he named James GIBBONS of Baltimore (1834–1921) its first vicar apostolic. He was assisted by three priests to serve the estimated 700 Catholics present throughout the state. When Gibbons was named bishop of Richmond in 1872 he retained responsibility for the vicariate until 1877, when he became coadjutor archbishop of Baltimore, with the right of succession. During his administration of the vicariate, the number of Catholics in North Carolina surpassed one thousand. In addition, the Sisters of Mercy from Charleston were established at Wilmington in 1869, and Benedictine monks from Latrobe, Pennsylvania, founded a monastery (and later a college) at Garibaldi, N.C. (later Belmont), in 1876.

John J. KEANE, who succeeded Gibbons as bishop of Richmond in 1878, also inherited the responsibility for the administration of the Vicariate of North Carolina. Mark S. Gross, the vicar general, refused the appointment as vicar apostolic in 1880, and Henry P. Northrop, a native of Charleston, was then consecrated a bishop for the vicariate in 1882. The following year Northrop was named bishop of Charleston and, like Gibbons before him, was responsible for the administration of the church in North Carolina while also resident bishop of a diocese, until 1887.

The fourth vicar to be appointed was the first abbot of Maryhelp Abbey in Belmont, Leo M. HAID, O.S.B. (1849–1924), who was ordained a bishop by Gibbons in 1888. In 1891 the monastery community obtained the assignment of nine counties, which included the city of Charlotte, for a period of 50 years, to the pastoral care of abbey. During Haid's tenure, a motherhouse of the Sisters of Mercy was established in Belmont (1892); an orphanage, named Nazareth, was founded outside of Raleigh (1897); and many churches were built. Father Thomas F. PRICE (1860–1919), a native of Wilmington, N.C., and in 1911 a cofounder of the Catholic Foreign Mission Society of America (Maryknoll), had been ordained (1886). Authorized by Haid to function as an itinerant preacher in 1896, Price established a base at the orphanage, where in 1901 he founded the ''Regina Apostolorum,'' an association of secular clergy whose goal was to evangelize North Carolina and foster vocations to the priesthood there. He also founded and edited *Truth* (1897), a national monthly magazine with more than 17,000 subscribers by 1905.

Pius X, by a papal bull of June 8, 1910, erected the *abbatia nullius diocesis* of Belmont, assigning eight counties from the vicariate to the new jurisdiction. Haid, now abbot-ordinary of Belmont, remained both abbot and vicar apostolic until his death in 1924. While the monastic community found the arrangement reasonable, providing for its own security as well as the financial and pastoral stability of the vicariate, the secular clergy, including Price, strongly objected to the arrangement, especially the provision that the monastic chapter had the right to nominate all future vicars apostolic of North Carolina, and they petitioned the Holy See for the establishment of a regular diocese within the state.

It was only after Haid's death that the Diocese of Raleigh was erected by papal decree on Dec. 12, 1924, leaving the *abbatia nullius diocesis* of Belmont with its unique status, as given in 1910. In 1944 seven of its eight counties were transferred to the jurisdiction of the Bishop of Raleigh, and in 1960, Gaston County, with the exception of the monastery property, was incorporated into the

Diocese of Raleigh. Finally, in 1977, the *abbatia nullius diocesis* was suppressed by papal decree, at the request of the U.S. hierarchy.

William J. Hafey, a priest from Baltimore, was consecrated as the first bishop of Raleigh and took possession of his see in 1925. He led a small and largely scattered Catholic population, which had relatively little social, cultural, or political influence in the state. He made an intense and somewhat successful effort to secure the assistance of religious men and women in order to support his pastoral efforts. By the time he was transferred to the Diocese of Scranton in 1937, the number of religious priests working had increased from eight to 26, and the number of sisters from 84 to 199. The total number of churches had also increased from 61 to 91, and the number of ''stations'' where Mass was at least occasionally celebrated, including private homes, grew from 60 to 154. The Catholic population rose from a little more than 6,000 to over 10,000 people during a time of little immigration into the state. Efforts were made for the evangelization and conversion of the black population, especially by some of the religious congregations of men which had been recruited for this work, with some small successes.

When Eugene J. McGuinness, a priest of Philadelphia who had been working with the Catholic Church Extension Society, was named the second bishop of Raleigh in 1937, he continued much of the pastoral direction of his predecessor, and the number of religious priests serving in the diocese rose to 59. The number of secular clergy continued to climb as well, from only 23 in 1925 to 53 in 1937, and to 83 in 1944, the year in which McGuinness was made the bishop of Oklahoma City and Tulsa. The Catholic population experienced a modest rise during those years, to nearly 13,000, as conversions continued and national wartime mobilization brought greater numbers of military personnel and their families into the state.

The first southern-born bishop of the diocese was Vincent S. Waters, a native of Roanoke, Virginia, who was the ordinary from 1945 until his death in 1974. With dedicated zeal he continued in the footsteps of his two predecessors, seeking to strengthen the institutional presence of the Church throughout the state. In addition, he boldly addressed the question of racial discrimination in an era of heated controversy. In May 1953, he issued a pastoral letter condemning the sin of racism and calling for the end of all racial barriers in Catholic institutions within the diocese. He began to implement his directive by closing the ''black church'' and school in Newton Grove and ordering the integration of the larger ''white church'' and school, a move that was widely regarded as prophetic by progressive voices, nationally and beyond,

and largely decried locally. The process continued slowly, in most cases by closing churches and schools in black communities, through the 1960s.

Waters also established a diocesan paper, the *North Carolina Catholic,* as well as the North Carolina Laymen's Association, and he sought to extend the Confraternity of Christian Doctrine, along with the most contemporary teaching techniques, into all corners of the diocese. In the wake of the Second Vatican Council, having attended all the sessions, he embarked on a series of lectures and conferences, to which he invited nationally known theologians and pastors in order to educate clergy and laity on the teachings of the council. He soon encountered much opposition from some clergy and religious, however, who thought that he was impeding the pace of needed pastoral and liturgical reforms. A petition to the Holy See was formulated, seeking his removal; it was signed by several members of the diocesan clergy. Tensions were eased for some when Rome established the Diocese of Charlotte in November 1971, separating the 46 counties of western North Carolina from the Raleigh Diocese and naming the well-liked diocesan priest Michael J. Begley its first bishop.

The new diocese was made part of the Province of Atlanta, as was the Diocese of Raleigh when the former was created in 1962. Begley served from 1972 until his retirement in 1984, during a period of rapid population growth within the state and growth of Catholic Church membership. The immigration was largely from the northern states, fueled by an expanding economy, and was experienced also in the eastern part of the state. Beginning in the 1970s, and continuing throughout the following decade, another wave of immigration, bringing tens of thousands of Mexican and Central American laborers into the state, created a new pastoral reality for both dioceses, which slowly received an organized response in the form of special ministries.

The Diocese of Charlotte continued to develop its own identity under the leadership of its second bishop, John F. Donoghue, who established a separate diocesan newspaper, the *Catholic News and Herald.* This former chancellor of the Archdiocese of Washington was appointed the ordinary for Charlotte in 1984 and remained there until he was made the archbishop of Atlanta in 1993. He was succeeded by another Washingtonian, Auxiliary Bishop William F. Curlin, in 1994. At the beginning of the new millennium, the diocese counted more than 120,000 Catholics in its jurisdiction, served by 134 active priests, both secular and religious. The number of sisters involved in ministry continued to decline, from 249 in 1972 to 134, including those retired and infirm, in 2000.

In 1975, F. Joseph Gossman, an auxiliary bishop of Baltimore, took possession of the Diocese of Raleigh, committing himself to what he described as a collegial style of governance and to the ecumenical movement. Within 25 years, the population of the diocese had climbed dramatically to over 150,000 registered Catholics, which often did not include the number of Catholic Hispanics actually present. The number of religious communities who initiated a presence in the diocese also rose sharply. In 1975, 14 men religious from seven congregations served in the diocese; by 2000, there were 54 from 10 different communities. With regard to women religious, the number of congregations active also increased in that same time, from 16 to 28, but the total number of sisters working declined from 137 to 86, 10 of whom had been appointed "pastoral administrators" of parishes. The number of active diocesan priests during this quarter century failed to keep pace with the increased Catholic population, growing only by five, from 53 to 58 men.

Bibliography: P. BAUMSTEIN, *My Lord of Belmont: A Biography of Leo Haid* (Charlotte, N.C. 1985); "A Conflict of Mitres: The Diverse Politics and Cathedral Abbey of Bishop Leo Haid," *Word and Spirit* 14, (1992), 76–95. J. BRICKELL, *The Natural History of North Carolina* (Dublin 1737; Murfreesboro, N.C. 1968). J. H. SCHAUINGER, *William Gaston, Carolinian* (Milwaukee 1949). S. C. WORSLEY, "Catholicism in Antebellum North Carolina," *North Carolina Historical Review* 60 (October 1983), 399–430.

[J. F. GARNEAU]

NORTH DAKOTA, CATHOLIC CHURCH IN

It is difficult to determine exactly when Roman Catholicism entered into the Dakotas, but the Catholic population has continued to grow steadily. As of the 2000 census, the Roman Catholic population stood at 176,893, or roughly 27.5 percent of the total population of the state, in the two dioceses of Bismarck and Fargo, both suffragan sees of the Archdiocese of St. Paul, Minnesota.

French trappers and fur traders, ostensibly Catholic, had been trading with the native peoples of North Dakota—the Arikaras, the Mandans, and the Hidatsa—since the mid-18th century, but there is no evidence that they made a concerted effort to evangelize the local tribes. The first Frenchmen the North Dakota natives met were from the expedition of Sieur Pierre Gaultier de Varennes de La Verendrye, a hero of the War of Spanish Succession, in late autumn 1738. "On the morning of the 28th we arrived at the place indicated as a rendezvous for the Mandan, who arrived in the evening, one chief with 30 men and four Assiniboin," La Verendrye recorded in November 1738. "I confess I was greatly surprised, as I expect-

ed to see people quite different from the other savages according to the stories that had been told us. They did not differ from the Assiniboin, being naked except for a garment of buffalo skin carelessly worn without any breechcloth. I knew then that there was a large discount to be taken off all that had been told me." La Verendrye failed to find the Northwest Passage to the Pacific, but he put the northern Missouri River and North Dakota on the French map.

The first documented Roman Catholic presence for missionary purposes came in the summer of 1818 with the arrival of Father Severe Dumoulin at the fur trading post of Pembina, in which is now the extreme northeast corner of North Dakota. Fearing the effect of the restless and rootless fur trappers, the Bishop of Quebec, J. O. Plessis, sent Dumoulin and Father Joseph Norbert PROVENCHER, who set up a mission at Fort Douglas (later St. Boniface). The population of Pembina was composed of nearly 350 indigenous peoples and métis (peoples of Native American and European descent—mostly from Chippewa, Cree, and Assiniboin families). As the bishop had suspected, the fur trappers sold alcohol freely to the native peoples, and it was having a significantly adverse affect on the social structures and stability of the native cultures. Though unable to stop the flow of alcohol, the two priests did what they could to ameliorate the damage. In 1819, Dumoulin baptized 30 Native Americans. During his five years at Pembina, he baptized an additional 364 persons and married nearly 70 couples. Dumoulin also established a school, teaching the native and métis children to read and write French and Latin. The priest also said daily Mass (sometimes preaching in Ojibwa) and gave religious instruction to the children. Under the leadership of Dumoulin, the métis had an awakening as a new type of people. Economically, the peoples of Pembina were prospering as farmers, selling their produce to the Hudson's Bay Company (HBC). Though the métis predominated in the area, the population continued the traditional buffalo hunt every summer and fall, shortly after the respective plantings and harvests. Usually, a priest would travel with them, enforcing the Sabbath as well as ensuring that the poorer hunters had as much chance to capture the buffalo as the better hunters.

In 1823, under orders from the U.S. Government, Major Stephen H. Long surveyed the U.S.-Canadian border. The new survey line ran through the northern end of Pembina, making most of it lay in U.S. territory. The British, noting Father Dumoulin's ability to attract large numbers of indigenous peoples to Pembina, feared the Americans might use the native and métis population and the community as a base of operations against the Canadians, and so they forced the community to resettle north of the new border. The forced resettlement disrupted community life, and the population of Pembina dispersed. By 1836, Pembina was completely deserted. Upset and frustrated by the geopolitical developments and the disruption of his mission, Dumoulin departed for Quebec.

Despite Dumoulin's departure, other priests attempted to evangelize the region. The most prominent was Father George A. BELCOURT, who in 1848 established a new mission at Pembina. Unlike Dumoulin who had been driven back to Canada by the British government, Belcourt found himself exiled from Canada when he demanded that the Hudson's Bay Company give up its monopoly on the fur trade. The priest fought for the HBC to allow the non-HBC indigenous peoples to compete in a free and open market, which he considered just. The free traders lost, and as their leader, Belcourt found himself living in the Dakotas. His new mission at Pembina consisted of a log church, large garden, and a rectory. After a serious flood in 1851, Belcourt moved the mission to Walhalla, roughly 30 miles west of Pembina. There, the métis and the natives created a thriving agricultural community, despite frequent attacks by the Sioux. Belcourt continuously impressed the native peoples with his fluency in a variety of Algonquian languages. With the aid of the Sisters of the Propagation of the Faith, Belcourt also started an excellent school.

Other individual priests made their marks as well. One of the most famous missionaries to visit North Dakota was the Jesuit Father Peter John DESMET (1801–73). Though most of the Native Americans in the Dakotas greatly revered and sought the wisdom of DeSmet, he spent more of his energies among the indigenous peoples of the Pacific Northwest. Fearless and carrying no weapons of self-defense, just his breviary and flag of the Blessed Virgin Mary, DeSmet remains one of the only missionaries to have walked through the Dakotas unharmed. He attempted several times to establish a chain of Jesuit missions along the upper Missouri, but the U.S. government never consented.

At Fort Totten, Sister Mary Clapin and the Sisters of Charity established a school in 1874. As one of the chaplains at the fort, Father Jerome Hunt translated a hymnal, a prayer book, a history of the Bible, and a catechism into Lakota. In 1876, a Benedictine from St. Meinrad's in southern Indiana, Father Martin MARTY, established a mission at Fort Yates. Three years later, Pope Leo XIII declared all of Dakota Territory a vicariate and named Father Marty the first bishop.

When North Dakota became a state in late 1889, Pope Leo XIII established the region as a single diocese, naming John Shanley, a priest of Irish descent, the first diocesan bishop. Roughly 31,000 North Dakotans were Roman Catholic at the time. His 20-year reign saw considerable growth and prosperity among the Catholic population. The number and diversity of immigrants distinguished North Dakota from every other state in the Union. In 1890, almost 43 percent of its population was foreign-born. Ten years later, that percentage had only dropped to 35.4 percent. At the turn of the century, Norwegians or the children of Norwegians accounted for nearly 23 percent of the population; Germans 10.1 percent; Canadians 9.7 percent; and Germans from Russia, 7.5 percent. While most of the Norwegians were Lutheran, many of the Germans and Germans from Russia were Roman Catholic. Each ethnic group maintained allegiance to cultural patterns and traditions, and Bishop Shanley had to handle the situation delicately. To placate the more easy-going Germans from Russia, for example, Shanley recruited Swiss Benedictines whom the Germans from Russia greatly respected. They feared, however, true Germans, who they saw as harsh and oppressive. Frequently, priests would preach in a variety of languages, including Bohemian, German, and Polish. The tradition of speaking central and eastern European languages in the area continued during the Cold War when clerical refugees from Communist Europe fled to the United States.

Though homesteading reached its zenith in 1906, over 250,000 pioneers migrated to the state between 1898 and 1915. When Bishop Shanley passed away in 1909, the Holy See divided North Dakota into two dioceses, the Diocese of Bismarck and the Diocese of Fargo, reflecting the continued population growth in the state. The pope appointed a popular Benedictine, Vincent WEHRLE, as bishop of the former, and an Irishman, James O'Reilly, as head of the latter. Between 1910 and 1939, Bishop Wehrle presided over substantial growth in the diocese and fought socialism in all of its varieties, especially during the tumultuous 1920s and 1930s. Using the papal encyclicals *Aeterni Patris* and *Rerum novarum*, Wehrle especially objected to and sought to attenuate the power of the radical Non-Partisan League of North Dakota, which attempted to overturn the state constitution and implement a socialist regime in 1916 and 1917. Studious and pensive, Bishop O'Reilly also oversaw significant growth in the church during his reign. His successor in 1935 was the impressive Aloisius MUENCH of Milwaukee. In 1946 Muench became the Holy Father's personal envoy to postwar West Germany and was created a cardinal by John XXIII in 1959. Other bishops in the Diocese of Bismarck have been: Vincent J. Ryan (1940–51); Lambert A. Hoch (1952–56); Hilary B. Hacker (1956–82); John F. Kinney (1982–95); and Paul A. Zipfel (1996–). Other bishops in the Diocese of Fargo have been: Leo F. Dworschak (1947–70); Justin A. Driscoll

(1970–84); and James D. Sullivan (1985–). Samuel J. Aquila, rector of the diocesan seminary in Denver, Colorado, was named a coadjutor bishop of Fargo in 2001.

Bibliography: H. R. LAMAR, ed., *The New Encyclopedia of the American West* (New Haven, Conn. 1998). J. A. LOGAN, ed., *A Continent Defined* (Lincoln, Neb. 1997). F. LUEBKE, ed., *European Immigrants in the American West: Community Histories* (Albuquerque 1998). R. C. CARRIKER, *Father Peter John DeSmet: Jesuit in the West* (Norman, Okla. 1995). J. D. LYSENGEN and A. M. RATHKE, eds., *The Centennial Anthology of North Dakota History: Journal of the Northern Plains* (Bismarck 1996). E. B. ROBINSON, *History of North Dakota* (Lincoln, Neb. 1966). W. NUGENT, *Into the West: The Story of Its People* (New York 1999). W. H. GOETZMANN and G. WILLIAM, *The Atlas of North American Exploration: From the Norse Voyages to the Race to the Pole* (New York 1992).

[B. J. BIRZER]

NORTHERN IRELAND, THE CATHOLIC CHURCH IN

Located in the northeast part of the island of Ireland, Northern Ireland is an integral part of the United Kingdom of Great Britain and Northern Ireland. Comprised of the former Irish province of Ulster, Northern Ireland occupies the six counties of Antrim, Armagh, Down, Fermanagh, Londonderry and Tyrone as well as the boroughs of Belfast and Londonderry. Bordered on the south by the Republic of Ireland, Northern Ireland attained its present political status in 1920 by an act of the British Parliament that established two separate self-governing units within the island of Ireland. The inhabitants of Northern Ireland, within the boundaries drawn in 1920, had closer cultural and religious bonds with Great Britain and for these reasons preferred not to be part of the Irish Free State (now the Republic of Ireland). Ruled from London after a local legislature was disbanded in 1972, Northern Ireland achieved a new local government in the form of a 108-seat Assembly that was established in Belfast in 1999 to assume many of the functions formerly performed in London.

Separated from Scotland by the North Channel of the Irish Sea, Northern Ireland relies on its eastern region for much of its industry. Linen textiles and ship-building are among the region's traditional industries, although engineering, mining and chemical production has increased. Agricultural yields include barley and potatoes.

Development of Political and Religious Factions. Historically, the relationship between Northern Ireland and England extends back to the 17th century, when substantial colonies of Protestant immigrants from Scotland and England settled plantations on the greater party of the nine-county Province of Ulster. Only in this area was

Capital: Belfast.
Size: 5,462 sq. miles.
Population: 1,754,000 in 2000.
Languages: English.
Religions: 561,280 Catholics (32%), 1,175,180 Anglicans (Church of Ireland; 67%), 17,540 with other religious affiliation.
Archdiocese: Armagh, with suffragans Armagh, Clogher, Derry, Down and Connor, Dromore, Kilmore, Meath, and Raphoe; only Meath and Raphoe administer exclusively to the Republic of Ireland.

British colonization permanently effective. Paralleling the rise of the middle and working classes in Ireland's 26 Catholic counties during the 18th and 19th centuries was the rise of an Anglican and Presbyterian majority in the northeast. While Presbyterians first struggled against Anglican dominance, the two groups joined forces in the 19th century in a combined resistance against Catholic attacks on Protestant ascendancy. Failing to defeat the Home Rule movement of southern Ireland, northern Protestants accepted self-government for the six counties in which their ascendancy could be maintained. A province of Great Britain since 1920, the region maintained a remarkable stability and social conformity in which, on the whole, Presbyterians remained dominant. These two groups remained united due to the actions of the region's Catholic minority, which envisioned a unified Ireland politically distinct from Great Britain.

Beginning during the Home Rule movement of the early 1900s, and reappearing again during the Repeal movement under Daniel O' CONNELL, Belfast, Londonderry and other cities in Northern Ireland witnessed bloody faction fights. After World War I, a consistent policy discrimination against Catholic workers in the Belfast shipyards was carried out. Occasional recurrences of this bias continued, particularly in 1935, although by the late 1990s the Fair Employment Commission began to directly address religious discrimination with regard to employment. Ultimately a cold war situation took shape, as Catholic and Protestant communities remained aloof from one another to an extent unique in Western Europe. Exceptional periods of better relations existed during World War II when, in contrast to the position of neutrality adopted by the Republic of Ireland, Northern Ireland joined Great Britain in support of the Allied cause.

The Unionist party, which retained a political majority since the state was founded, at times justified discrimination against Catholics on the grounds that they were disloyal to the state, at other times on the grounds that they were anti-Protestant nationalists. In a rare break with the anti-Catholic status quo before the institution of the

Group of men gather about Catholic demonstrator killed by British Army armored vehicle during protest, 1969. (©Michael Brennan/ CORBIS)

1999 Assembly, the Northern Ireland high court had one Catholic judge appointed to its bench in 1965.

Social welfare and health programs were introduced in Great Britain following World War II, and these were also extended to Northern Ireland. While little discrimination existed in theory, Protestant majorities in local governments sometimes discriminated in such things as allocating council houses to non-Catholic workers. In a similar manner, government-sponsored secondary education was exported from England to Northern Ireland in 1947. Reflecting the northern province's demographics, the proportion of Catholic schools to Protestant was smaller and their types less varied: grammar schools were academic in their emphasis, intermediate schools more practical. This changed little through the 20th century, as substantial state support continued to be guaranteed to all schools, even those under Church control. However, discrimination against Catholics did exist in education. While education in Northern Ireland was theoretically nondenominational, in reality most of the administrative jobs within the education system were held by Protestants, giving the system a Protestant bias.

By the early 1960s repeated discrimination in housing, employment and electoral practices in favor of Prot-

estants, as well as complaints of harassment at the hands of the region's overwhelmingly Protestant police force, prompted a groundswell of protest by the Catholic minority. This protest escalated into guerilla-style violence in 1968, following police intervention in response to a group of civil rights protestors. Over the next few years the conflict hardened into war as paramilitary groups such as the nationalist Irish Republican Army (IRA) led violent attacks on opposing groups, such as the loyalist Ulster Defense Association, in an effort to abolish Northern Ireland and join the Republic. Thousands of innocent men, women and children would died in the bombings and shootings to follow. British military units had occupied Northern Ireland by 1969, and their occupation became a permanent one.

Challenges Unite all Christians. The outbreak of civil war in Northern Ireland presented churches of all denominations with a unique challenge: how to fulfill a ministry of reconciliation in a politically divided community. Unconstrained by political or geographic boundaries, churches had the unique ability to bring people from throughout the island together. However, the violence that erupted in the region after 1968 put new stresses on all faiths, as the appeals of religious leaders' efforts to compromise in the interest of peace were at odds with extremists in both factions.

Because of their inability to relate to the region's violent extremist factions, churches in Northern Ireland threw their support behind the many lay-oriented groups working for reconciliation within the divided community: the Corrymeela and Glencree centers, Peace Point Belfast and Dublin, Protestant and Catholic Encounter (PACE), Women Together, Working for Peace and many others. The Inter-Church Emergency Fund for Ireland, whose committee included official Roman Catholics as well as delegates from the Irish Council of Churches, helped many peacemaking local enterprises get started. The Reconciliation Ireland Fund, co-sponsored by the National Council of Churches of Christ in the USA Ireland Program and Pax Christi USA, channeled funds to it. By working across faiths, Northern Ireland's religious leaders set an example of transcending differences that many hoped extremist factions would follow.

Amid the violence, individual priests made their own impact. In 1972 Edward Daly succored the fatally injured after a nationalist demonstration came under fire by British troops; he subsequently became bishop of Londonderry and a strong voice for the moderate stance of many Catholics. Denis Faul of Dungannon courageously denounced IRA killings and in the same breath the official policy of interning suspected terrorists, which he held created recruits for the IRA. The Jesuits opened a house in Portadown, a Protestant-loyalist citadel, from which they issued firsthand observations on the causes of tension. Above all, the Redemptorists of Clonard Monastery, in the heart of nationalist West Belfast, maintained a liaison with extremists that prepared the ground for the IRA cease-fire announced in August 1994. These contacts did much to sustain the image of the Church in the eyes of a hard-pressed people, intimidated by one side and harassed by the other.

In 1972 the British government shut down Northern Ireland's parliament in Stormont and imposed direct rule. The actions of labor leaders such as the Protestant minister Ian Paisley, who mobilized workers in major cities, crippled efforts to build a coalition government by causing the region's economy to come to a halt. In other cases churches were burned and schools destroyed. Throughout the 1990s, while the British government, as well as representatives from the Republic of Ireland, attempted to mediate differences among factions such as Sinn Féin (the militant arm of the IRA), violence continued to break out. Regular tensions flared on an annual basis, during the Protestant celebration of the Battle of the Boyne. Fought on July 12, 1690, the battle marked the overthrow of the Catholic King James II by Protestant King William of Or-

ange; in celebration of this defeat and to provoke continued animosity, members of the Orange Order now marched through Catholic neighborhoods.

In December of 1993 Irish Prime Minister John Bruton and British Prime Minister John Major outlined the Downing Street Declaration, a peace plan accepted by both IRA and loyalist factions. While outbreaks of violence continued to erupt into the next century, they were brief, and negotiations resumed in their wake. On April 10, 1998, a peace settlement was approved between the IRA and all but the most extreme loyalist factions that was seen as capable of protecting the political and economic rights of the region's Catholic minority. Voters throughout Ireland approved the settlement by a hefty margin, and by the following year Northern Ireland had an Assembly seated in Belfast and work continued on building a coalition government that included the four political parties representing the major factions of Northern Ireland. However, it would be into the next century before guerilla groups would agree to disarm completely, and the annual Orange Order marches continued to precipitate mob-type violence.

At the time of the Downing Street Declaration, Armagh's Cardinal Daly told a parliamentary assembly at the British House of Commons that governments should not yield to the threat of terrorist violence, that unionists were entitled to the guarantee that no change would be made in the status of Northern Ireland without majority approval, and that the "validity and value" of the nationalist aspiration to achieve a united Ireland by consent should be formally recognized. Throughout the three decades of "The Troubles" the Catholic Church had taken no position that contradicted these principles. Now, following decades of violence, the Church would be faced with a different threat to life, as the newly formed North Ireland Assembly met in 2000 to consider adopting Great Britain's liberal abortion policy. Once again, Protestant and Catholic leaders were united in their opposition.

For a history of the Early Church in Northern Ireland, please *see* IRELAND, THE CATHOLIC CHURCH IN.

Bibliography: P. N. MANSERGH, *The Government of Northern Ireland: A Study in Devolution* (London 1926). A. S. QUEKETT, *The Constitution of Northern Ireland,* 3 v. (London 1928–46). A. G. DONALDSON, *Some Comparative Aspects of Irish Law* (Durham, N.C. 1957). F. H. NEWARK, *Notes on Irish Legal History* (Belfast 1960). J. J. CAMPBELL, *Catholic Schools: A Survey of a Northern Ireland Problem* (Belfast 1964). W. CORKEY, *Episodes in the History of Protestant Ulster, 1923–1947* (Belfast 1948). D. P. BARRITT and C. F. CARTER, *The Northern Ireland Problem: A Study in Group Relations* (London 1962). T. W. MOODY and J. C. BECKETT, *Queen's Belfast, 1845–1949: The History of a University,* 2 v. (London 1959); *Ulster since 1800,* ser. 1 and 2 (London 1954, 1957). British Association for Advancement of Science, *Belfast in Its Regional Setting* (London 1952). *Ulster Yearbook 1953* (Belfast 1953). *Irish*

Catholic Directory and Almanac (Dublin), annual. *Annuario Pontificio* has annual data on all dioceses. For additional bibliography, *see* IRELAND.

[R. D. EDWARDS/D. J. BOWMAN/EDS.]

NORTHMEN

A generic term used to designate the migrant people who spread by sea from the sixth to the eleventh century from Scandinavia over the whole western section of the northern hemisphere. Little is known of the Scandinavian population in the prehistoric age. There are vestiges of the Ertebølle civilization in Denmark called *Kokkenmodings* (kitchen middens or refuse heaps); the Nøstvet civilization left a few remains in Norway and Skåne. Jutland's cultivated fields are similar to those of southern England. Trade with the Roman Empire was established through Pannonia and Poland, native amber being exchanged for bronze and metals. Burial under a mound or *tumulus* (*gravhoje*), figurative inscriptions on rocks, and the first runic alphabet characterized this Nordic civilization. In spite of the semantic kinship between *Got* (GOTHS) and Götaland, one must not take literally the adage of Jordanis, "Scandinavia, the mother of all Germanic peoples," except in the case of the Cimbri, VANDALS, Angles and Burgundians, who actually were from Jutland.

The Scandinavian people undertook great migratory movements during their development: after the migration of the Heruli (third to fifth centuries), the first authentically Scandinavian raid was that made on the Frisian coast by Hygelac, Beowulf's uncle, mentioned by GREGORY OF TOURS in 520. From this time on the Vikings became, without interruption, a part of Western History, even though into the seventh century their activity was confined to waters adjoining their homeland. The unification of Sweden (sixth to ninth centuries) and the migration of the Danes after the exodus of the Angles and the Jutes to Britain gave birth to new raids.

Of the many peoples who comprised the contemporary Scandinavian population it was the *Suiones* or *Svear* who gave their name to Sweden, and the *Dani* or *Dene* to Denmark. But before the tenth century, all these groups shared a common culture, religion, and language (Old Norse), and while groups of Vikings tended to go in the direction in which their originating coastal area faced (i.e., from modern Norway across the Atlantic, from modern Sweden to modern Russia, from Denmark to the islands and coasts of Europe), any distinction between these three modern groups in the Viking age is arbitrary; for Europeans used terms such as *Dani* (sometimes transposed into *Daci*), *Northmanni*, *Normanni*, to include both those from (modern) Denmark and those from (modern) Norway together; *Dacigeni* for natives of (modern) Denmark, *Northguigigeni* for those from (modern) Norway, and *Rus* or *Varangians* for those from (modern) Sweden.

Vikings and Varangians. The term "Vikings," now used to designate all those sea raiders who sailed the Western waters in their *snekkjur*, originally applied to the function of raiding and trading, not to the people. (The etymology of the term is still uncertain: *vîkingr*, pirate; *vîk*, bay; *vising*, mariner.) Viking exploits constituted an honorable sport in Scandinavian society: on long winter evenings the skalds would transpose a Viking's narrative into poetic language. Usually it was the young men who undertook the adventurous summer voyages for raiding and trading across Europe, hoping to make their fortune. Often outlaws in exile discovered the outlying lands across the Atlantic—the Orkneys, Hebrides, Faroes and Shetlands, stepping stones to Iceland; and Greenland and Vinland, modern America. These were in turn settled by colonists, often Norwegian in origin, who brought with them their wives, children and livestock. Indeed, women could and did lead these voyages of settlement. Both Danes and Norwegians colonized Ireland, founding the first cities and kingdoms on that island. The Danes welded together the islands of the Sound, Jutland, and Skåne; the expansion of this state would propel the Danes in the ninth century to move into East Anglia and Northumbria in Britain, and into Frisia, Brittany and the river basins of the Frankish coastline.

To the east—on the Baltic and on the Volga and Dnieper Rivers—the Scandinavian invaders were known under the name of Varangians or Rus (probably from the Russian *warjag*, tradesman; *war*, merchandise; *vârar*, pledge, oath; *ruotsi*, a Finnish word for men from the north; *rousios*, a Greek word for ruddy-complected, similar to the Latin word *rufus*, and to that same word in English meaning ruddy). There, organized in merchant companies, they set up trading posts on the Baltic coastline and colonized the area around Lake Ladoga. From there they moved down the rivers, heading for the great city of Constantinople. Although the Vikings raided the relatively richer West, they used the undeveloped Slavic lands as a stepping stone to the richer Byzantine and Islamic markets in the East, which were too strong to be raided and thus subjects of trade.

At the beginning of the ninth century, Göttrick, king of Denmark, compelled the local merchants to relinquish the market of Reric on the Baltic to the town of Hedeby (Schleswig) in Jutland, thus establishing the Viking Age. Around the same time, the Varangians reestablished a junction between the Baltic and the Caspian Seas, a step toward their goal of a direct route to Baghdad. The first

Varangian route, that of the Volga, united the Baltic sea-coast, which was occupied by the Finnish tribe of the Kurs, with the shores of the Caspian Sea, then peopled by hostile tribes. But the Danes and the Swedes continued to search for a shorter route back to the West, success crowning the undertaking of Swedish King Olaf between 854 and 860, when the "great route of the Varangians to the Greeks' was opened, first by way of the Neman and the Dnieper rivers, and then by way of the Dvina and the Dnieper rivers. The Varangian chief Askold attacked the Khazars, seized Sembat, established the state of Kiev, and launched an assault on Constantinople (860). This Varangian advance into the Ukraine sometime between the departure of the AVARS and the invasion of the Patzinaks resulted in the treaty of 874, which authorized the new commercial route opening on the Black Sea. Thus the route served as a hinge in a vast trading network joining the West, by way of the Rhine and the middle Danube, to Samarkand and the Middle East. In spite of the agreements of Emperor LOUIS THE GERMAN with the Danish princes and with Byzantine Emperor Basil I, however, any benefit Western Europe derived from this route was ephemeral.

Friction between the Vikings and Western Europe began with the Frankish penetration into Frisia, Saxony, and Nordalbinga (Ditmarsh). Yet it was only c. 840—the end of the Carolingian ascendancy and contemporary to the reigns of Kings Offa of Mercia (d. 896) and Egbert of Wessex (d. 839)—that the massive Viking raids of England and the Continent began. Satisfied at first with booty and tribute, the Vikings aspired to conquer and settle after 875. The "grand army" successively attacked Britain's East Anglia, Northumbria, and Mercia, laying the foundations of the Danelaw; the resistance of the kings of Wessex, Ethelred I and ALFRED THE GREAT, and the victory at Edington over Guthrum near the Danish camp at Chippenham set the southern boundary of Danish settlement along Watling Street. Repeatedly reinforced with fresh troops from Scandinavia, the remainder of the "grand army" moved on to attack western France between the Seine and Meuse rivers; the Viking capture of prosperous Rouen (885), on the Seine, opened the route to Paris. This key city was defended by Bishop Gozelin and Odo, count of Paris, and in 886 the Frankish King Charles the Fat bribed the Vikings to retreat. But at the dawn of the tenth century, a strong detachment of *Northmanni* settled on the lower Seine and threatened the Frankish kingdom more than ever, since efforts to Christianize the Scandinavians in the West had so far ended in failure. The mission of ANSGAR in Denmark, inaugurated in 823, retreated to Frisia; the missionary archbishop of Hamburg was sacked (845); the baptism of Guthrum in England brought no subsequent Christian baptisms. Only the state of Kiev was receptive to Christianity.

Northman States. The extraordinary dynamism of the Northmen generated new political states, some unstable, but others destined to play a major role in the medieval world. As for Kiev, since the fall of the Soviet Union, Russian historians are retreating from Soviet insistence on theories of a Slavic origin and tending to acknowledge a Nordic origin to that city-state, which incorporated Slavic societies. Other Varangian states were founded on the banks of the Sea of Azov as tributaries of the Khazars, and on the shores of Lake Ladoga (Aldjborg), which were eventually subjugated by Kiev. Under Varangian influence, the word "Russian" soon came to mean a people, a state, a Christian rite, and a civilization essentially Slavic. A second Nordic state, Novgorod, developed into a Russian kingdom as well.

Norwegian expansion westward, undertaken as it was by small groups of explorers followed by warriors, remained somewhat anarchical, with the exception of a few settlements in bay areas. A viable and functioning comital government was set up in the Orkney Islands, at the northern tip of Scotland, whose independence was at times compromised by alliances with the petty Scots kings to the South and by submission to the newly forming Christian monarchy of Norway. To this day, the Orkney Islanders remain fiercely independent and firmly Scandinavian. Numerous small petty comital governments grew up on the Western Isles along the west coast of Scotland, including the Isle of Man, and these two alternated alliances with Norway, petty Scots chieftains, and kings of Norway. In Ireland, the invading Danes formed trading posts first, then petty kingdoms, which were then rivaled by petty Norse-Irish kingdoms. These foundations grew into the first cities of Ireland—Dublin, Cork, Waterford, and Limerick. They served as catalysts to the Irish kinglets to unify and drive out the Vikings—but not until many had mingled their genes with the natives. After the Battle of Clontaf (1014), Ireland remained largely Celtic. The English conquered it in 1171.

The Northwestern searoute led some audacious navigators first toward Iceland (*c.* 870), which became the refuge for outlaws, whose clans and genealogy were recorded in the *Landnâmabôk* (late twelfth century), and then toward Greenland (settled 985), not yet occupied by the Inuit. The settlement of Iceland was completed by *c.* 930, when all the arable land was taken. The settlers imported the Gulathing Law from Norway, revised it, and set up the first democracy in Europe, presided over by an elected Lawspeaker, who served for three years and recited one third of the law each year. The Legislature, *Allthing* or *Lögrétta*, composed of *Godar* (chieftain-priests), made the laws, while each of the four Quarter Courts performed the judicial functions with juries of 12 men. The Fifth Court acted as a court of appeal. This government functions to this day. In 1000, the Allthing voted to make Christianity the official religion of Iceland, with the proviso that Icelanders could practice paganism in private. Iceland thereby acquired the technology of writing, which inspired the great Icelandic saga literature of the thirteenth century. From Iceland, Eirik the Red discovered and settled Greenland, from which his son Leif Eirikson launched his settlement of Vinland in 1000—the first European settlement in America, discovered in 1965 and excavated by Helge Ingstad at L'Ans-aux-Meadows, Labrador. Leif's sister Freydis Eiriksdottir also led an expedition intended to settle the new land of Vinland, and she located and stayed in the houses her brother had built, but like her brother she was driven off by Skraelings—screamers, or Native Americans. But Greenlanders, Icelanders, and Norwegians returned to Vinland to fish the rich cod banks until about 1350, when the settlement in Greenland disappeared. But mentions of Iceland and Vinland appear as late as 1200 in the German and papal records.

Meanwhile, King Harald II Bluetooth unified Skåne, the straits, Jutland, and a part of Norway to form the kingdom Denmark, and he attempted to force Christianity on his subjects. Likewise, King Harald Fairhair unified Norway and converted his subjects, while King Olaf the Fat (later known as St. Olaf) converted and unified Sweden. Olaf became the first Norse saint upon his death at the Battle of Stiklestad in 1030. The Danelaw—a name covering the Nordic settlement in England—reflects Danish sovereignty in its organization, both military and political, but at the same time it incorporates a *sui generis* society, on whose original features scholars do not agree. It stretched from Northumbria southward almost to the Thames, and its heart was the Kingdom of York in the north, briefly unified with the Kingdom of Dublin during the height of Viking hegemony in England. This intermixing of Vikings was typical; from Dublin to York to Rouen and Novgorod, there was a never-ceasing interchange of warriors and merchants. In a world ready for expansion, Denmark and later Normandy were the catalysts. Thus it was Hrolf the Ganger (Rollo), son of Ragnald jarl of Möre, a Danish subject of Norwegian blood, who settled at the mouth of the Seine *c.* 906. The treaty of Saint-Clair-sur-Epte (911), between Frankish King Charles the Simple and Rollo, made the lower Seine a region of Nordic colonization by its surrender to the Viking band. Neustria eventually became Normandy, but only after a century of growth spreading outward from the original grant of the city of Rouen to Hrolf-Rollo and his men. The agreement required Rollo's conversion to

Christianity, and gave him King Charles' daughter in marriage. By the eleventh century Normandy comprised the seven cities of Rouen, Bayeux, Evreux, Lisieux, Sées, Coutances, and Avranches—several of which were Norman foundations.

The unity of the ANGLO-SAXONS, reestablished under the royal line of Wessex, was endangered in the period beginning in 990 by the raids of Olaf I Tryggvessøn and Sweyn I Forkbeard of Denmark. In 1016 all of England fell to Sweyn's son, King Canut of England and Denmark. Until his death in 1035, this Viking thus became the head of a land, of which England was the political, economic, cultural, and religious center. Canut converted to Christianity and became a king in the English tradition. He sent his wife Alfgifu to Norway with their son, Harald Harefoot, and married Emma of Normandy, wife of Aethelred Unraed, England's previous king, with an agreement that their sons would inherit England. To show his piety, Canut made a pilgrimage to Rome, *c.* 1025, and he made every effort to support the Church in England. His son Harold Harefoot succeeded him, only to die shortly after ascending the throne. His son by Emma, Hardacanute, then became king, but he also soon died. The Danish Earl Godwin supported Queen Emma in bringing her son by Aethelred, Edward the Confessor, to the throne. Edward married Godwin's daughter Edith, but they were childless, and his cousin William of Normandy, descendent of Rollo, eventually won England at the Battle of Hastings in 1066.

Christianization of Scandinavia. The conversion of Scandinavia was launched from several directions. The bishopric of Hamburg-Bremen sent numerous missionaries to Sweden and Norway, many of which were strenuously resisted. But Adam of Bremen gives persuasive accounts of these efforts and descriptions of the pagan religion. Viking settlement of England led many missionaries from England to travel to Norway and Denmark, especially in Canut's reign. But the conversion of all three countries was firmly linked to royal ambitions and kingdom-building by King Harald II Bluetooth of Denmark, Harold Fairhair of Norway, and St. Olaf of Sweden. Each of these kings saw the advantages of theories of Christian kingship, and they sought to construct kingdoms on the European model, as opposed to the Viking custom of small, territorial kinglets ruling limited areas. Conversion of Iceland was a practical matter: the Allthing voted to convert, probably to obtain the benefits of literacy and a European connection to offset the ambitions of King Harald Fairhair's successors to sweep Iceland into their own subjection (which one eventually did). In Normandy, the only Continental colony the Vikings successfully established, conversion took at least a century and was aided by immigrant churchmen from Italy.

LANFRANC and ANSELM, in connection with the reform papacy, reconstructed the Norman church. In Kiev and Novgorod, the Rus allied themselves with the Byzantines and converted to Orthodox Christianity. The prime decision was made by Prince Vladimir in 988, but his mother Olga, a Christian, may well have been instrumental in persuading him. Moreover, his conversion won him an imperial bride and significant trading privileges with Constantinople. But he insisted on adopting the Slavic language, not Greek, for the Russian church. And the *Russian Primary Chronicle* reports that he took away the children of the nobility and placed them in the schools he set up, so that literacy may also have been one of his motives for conversion. Even in their religion, the Vikings were a practical people.

Bibliography: ADAM OF BREMEN, *Gesta Hammaburgensis Ecclesiae Pontificum,* ed. B. SCHMEIDLER, *Scriptores rerum Germanicarum* (Hanover 1917). Tr. F. J. TSCHAN, *History of the Archbishops of Hamburg-Bremen* (New York 1959). *Anglo-Saxon Chronicle: Two of the Saxon Chronicles Parallel,* ed. C. PLUMMER and J. EARLE (Oxford 1892–99). Tr. D. WHITELOCK, D. C. DOUGLAS, and S. I. TUCKER, *The Anglo-Saxon Chronicle* (New Brunswick, NJ 1961). G. N. GARMONSWAY, *The Anglo-Saxon Chronicle,* 1950. ANSKAR, *Vita Anskarii auctore Rimberto,* ed. G. WAITZ, *Scriptores rerum Germanicarum* (Hanover 1884). ST. REMBERT, *Anskar, the Apostle of the North, 801–865,* tr. C. H. ROBINSON (London 1921). *Saxo Grammaticus, History of the Danes,* tr. P. FISHER, ed. H. E. DAVIDSON (Woodbridge, Suffolk 1979). S. STURLESON, *Heimskringla: History of the Kings of Norway,* tr. L. M. HOLLANDER (Austin, Tex. 1964). DUDO OF ST. QUENTIN, *History of the Normans,* tr. E. CHRISTIANSEN (Woodbridge, Suffolk 1998). *Russian Primary Chronicle,* trans. S. H. CROSS and O. P. SHERBOWITZ-WETZOR (Cambridge 1953). G. JONES, *A History of the Vikings* (Oxford 1984). J. JOCHENS, *Women in Old Norse Society* (Ithaca, N.Y. 1995). J. BYOCK, *Medieval Iceland* (Berkeley, Calif. 1988). J. JESCH, *Women in the Viking Age,* (Woodbridge, Suffolk 1991). G. JONES, *The Norse Atlantic Saga* (Oxford 1954). P. H. SAWYER, *The Age of the Vikings* (rev. ed. London 1971). G. VERNADSKY, *The Origins of Russia* (Oxford 1959). I. ATKINSON, *The Viking Ships* (Cambridge 1979). H. R. E. DAVIDSON, *The Viking Road to Byzantium* (London 1976). P. G. FOOTE and D. M. WILSON, *The Viking Achievement* (London 1970). S. FRANKLIN and J. SHEPHERD, *The Emergence of Rus, 760–1200* (London 1996). G. N. GARMONSWAY, *Canute and his Empire* (London 1964). M. K. LAWSON, *Cnut* (London 1993). J. MARTIN, *Medieval Russia 980–1584* (Cambridge 1995). D. O'CORRAIN, *Ireland before the Normans* (Dublin 1972). R. I. PAGE, *Chronicles of the Vikings* (London 1995). A. W. BRØGGER, *Ancient Emigrants: A History of the Norse Settlements of Scotland* (Oxford 1929). K. J. KROGH, *Viking Greenland,* with a supplement of Saga texts by G. JONES (Copenhagen 1967).

[P. D. WATKINS]

NORTON, JOHN, BL.

Lay martyr; b. in Yorkshire, England; d. Aug. 9, 1600, hanged at Durham. He was the second son of Richard Norton, who had been attainted with rebellion in 1569, and his second wife Margaret Redshaw. John Nor-

ton and his wife were arrested in their home at Laymsley, Co. Durham, for harboring an illegal priest, Bl. Thomas PALASER. They were condemned to death, but Mrs. Norton was reprieved because she was pregnant. Palaser and Norton died with their companion Bl. John TALBOT. Norton was beatified by Pope John Paul II on Nov. 22, 1987 with George Haydock and Companions.

Feast of the English Martyrs: May 4 (England).

See Also: ENGLAND, SCOTLAND, AND WALES, MARTYRS OF.

Bibliography: R. CHALLONER, *Memoirs of Missionary Priests,* ed. J. H. POLLEN (rev. ed. London 1924). J. H. POLLEN, *Acts of English Martyrs* (London 1891).

[K. I. RABENSTEIN]

NORWAY, THE CATHOLIC CHURCH IN

A northern European kingdom, Norway is located on the western coast of the Scandinavian Peninsula. It is bordered on the east by Sweden and Finland, on the south by Skagerrak, Denmark and the North Sea, on the west by the Atlantic Ocean and the North Sea, and on the north by the Arctic Ocean. A mountainous country characterized by arctic tundra in its northernmost regions, Norway contains many lakes and waterways and its irregular coastline area contains both fjords and small islands. In addition to strong timber and mining industries, Norway's economy benefited from the discovery of oil and natural gas off its coast during the mid-1900s.

The Kingdom of Norway is a constitutional monarchy. Under the political control of Denmark between 1380 and 1814, and Sweden from 1814, the country regained its independence on June 7, 1905. Its constitution dates from 1814, with modifications dating from 1884. The state church is Evangelical Lutheran.

Christianity until 1500. Christianity came to Norway mainly from England and Ireland during the reign of King Hakon the Good (935–996). It did not, however, gain a real foothold before the reigns of OLAF I TRYGGVESSØN (995–1000) and St. Olaf Haraldson (Olaf II; 1025–30; *see* OLAF II, KING OF NORWAY, ST.). Soon after being killed in the battle of Stiklestad (July 29, 1030) Olaf II was reverenced as the sainted hero of medieval Norway. His shrine at Trondheim made that town the capital of the country. The first bishops had been attached to the king's retinue, but St. Olav sent Bishop Grimkell to Bremen in northern Germany, the former bishopric of St. ANSGAR. Until 1100 Norwegian bishops, like other bishops of Scandinavia, were suffragans of the

Capital: Oslo.
Size: 125,031 sq. miles.
Population: 4,481,162 in 2000.
Languages: Norwegian; Lapp and Finnish are spoken regionally.
Religions: 40,203 Catholics (.9%), 3,853,799 Evangelical Lutherans (86%), 89,705 other (2%), 61,000 Norwegian Humanists (atheist) (1%), 436,455 without religious affiliation.
Districts: The diocese of Oslo and the prelatures of Trondheim and Tromsø.

archbishop of Bremen. In 1104 the See of LUND (in southern Sweden, but then controlled by Denmark) became the metropolitan see for all the northern regions. The pope sent Cardinal Nicholas Breakspear, an Englishman, to Norway in 1152. In cooperation with the assembly of Norwegian peers he made the See of Trondheim metropolitan for all of Norway, including Norway proper, the Orkney Islands, the Faroe Islands, the Hebrides, the Isle of Man, ICELAND and GREENLAND. Dioceses within the country from 1153 included also Bergen, Stavanger, Oslo and Hamar. Since Breakspear became the next pope, ADRIAN IV (1154–59), his ordinances received the highest respect.

As elsewhere in medieval Europe, clashes between king and hierarchy were not infrequent. The struggle of Archbishops Eystein (1161–88) and Eirik (1189–1206) with King Sverre (1177–1202) revolved mainly about royal interference in the designation of bishops and pastors and the collection of ecclesiastical tithes. Eirik went into exile in Denmark and Eystein travelled to England where he was introduced to the new Gothic style. Eystein introduced the new style into Norway when he returned and oversaw construction of the cathedral at Trondheim. Many Church-State tensions were resolved by the short-lived Union of Tönsberg (1277), by which the king granted the Church freedom in ecclesiastical nominations, while the archbishop renounced rights the Church had previously enjoyed in the appointment of kings. When the peace-loving King Magnus Lagaböter (Lawmender) died in 1280, both his sons were minors, which allowed the regents to revoke the Union of Tönsberg. Protests from Rome and Trondheim were answered with the banishment of Archbishop Jon Raude and Bishops Andrew of Oslo and Torfinn of Hamar. Jon died in Sweden (1282) and Torfinn in Flanders (1285) after visiting Rome to seek help.

When the Bubonic plague afflicted the country in 1349, it ended the flourishing period of the Church in medieval Norway. Loss of life was tremendous; out of 300 priests in the archdiocese, only 40 survived, and only one of the five bishops survived. During the next two centu-

ries no churches were built. This was evidence that the Church and the people had lost their strength.

Monastic life was introduced very early by English BENEDICTINES. The CISTERCIANS, DOMINICANS and FRANCISCANS followed (*see* DACIA) and these religious orders were likewise decimated by the plague. The Swedish-based Scandinavian order of the Bridgettines appeared in the second half of the 14th century.

The Protestant Reformation. LUTHERANISM was introduced to Norway from Copenhagen by royal decree in 1537. Since 1380 the same kings had ruled Norway and Denmark; in practice Norway had become a Danish province. As a follower of Martin LUTHER, King Christian III (1336–59) had to resort to military force to get the Norwegians to recognize his sovereignty after his election. In southern Norway, Christian was acknowledged by officeholders of Danish descent, but in Trondheim Archbishop Olav Engelbrektsson organized resistance designed to promote Norwegian independence as well as defend the Catholic faith. Olav's small forces proved ineffectual and in April of 1537 he withdrew to the Netherlands, where he died at Lier on Feb. 6, 1538. The REFORMATION came to Norway from abroad; it served the political interests of the Danish king and the magnates but did not correspond to any desire among the populace—in fact, later historians would reject the theory that Lutheranism was generally accepted in Norway before 1600. While the property of parishes was ordinarily respected, the crown confiscated all possessions of monasteries and dioceses. Lutheran beliefs and practices were introduced with great circumspection. Generally priests were allowed to continue in their posts, but when they died the royal government provided Lutheran successors. Bishop Mogens of Hamar and Bishop Hoskold of Stavanger opposed the new order; the latter was committed to prison and died at Bergen; the former was brought to Denmark, where he died at Antvortskov (1542). The See of Bergen remained vacant after 1535. Hans Rev of Oslo, born in Denmark, was the only bishop to embrace Lutheranism. He did not ordain any bishops; thus the APOSTOLIC SUCCESSION was lost in Norway, as it was in Denmark.

By the late 1500s Catholic priests were no longer admitted to Norway. By the early 17th century it became apparent that many young men of the upper classes, even sons of Lutheran ministers, were attending JESUIT schools abroad. A royal decree of 1604 excluded from any school or church office any students of these institutions. A few years later several priests of the Lutheran Diocese of Oslo were brought to public trial in Skien (1613) and forced into exile as Catholic sympathizers; the evidence against them included correspondence with Catholics abroad and

NORWAY

0   75   150 Miles

0   75   150 Kilometers

Barents Sea

Nordkapp

Hammerfest

Børselv

Kirkenes

Tana

Tromsø

Finnmarks-vidda

RUSSIA

Vesterålen

Harstad   Innset

Narvik

Lofoten

Muonio

Bodo

Torniö

Norwegian Sea

Mo i Rana

Strimasund

Hornavan

Luleå

Oulu

Kroken

Vågen

SWEDEN

Gulf of Bothnia

FINLAND

Namsos

Steinkjer

Kristiansund

Trondheim

Umeå

Ålesund   Molde

TROLL-HEIMEN

Goldhøpiggen
8,100 ft.
2469 m.

Elgå

Östersund

Storsjön

Urnes

Hersvik

Gläma

Lillehammer

Bergen

Gjøvik

Kinsarvik

Oslo

Gävle

Turku

Åland

Haugesund

Drammen

Arvika

Stockholm

Stavanger   Årdal

Skien

Fredrikstad

Baltic Sea

Egersund

Kristiansand

Vänern

Norrköping

Skagerrak

North Sea

DENMARK

Norway

a disregard of Lutheran beliefs. The influence of the Norwegian Jesuit Laurentius Nicolai Norvegus was discovered. From 1624 capital punishment threatened any Catholic priest entering the country. Even so, the secular priest John Martini Rhugius visited his native country and stayed at Larvik for three short periods (1637–41) caring for a small number of widely scattered Catholics. Improved commercial relations attracted Jesuits from the Netherlands; they stayed in Bergen for six weeks in 1648,

but enforcement of the draconian laws forced them to leave. After 1648, however, despite widely varying situations, Catholic priests continuously resided in Copenhagen, the capital and royal residence of the Danish-Norwegian kingdom. In Norway itself, which lacked a court and foreign ambassadors, it was possible for a Catholic priest to dwell only by serving as chaplain to foreign mercenaries in time of war or to foreign artisans in commercial establishments. Thus, foreign mercenaries made

Church in Bud, a fishing village near Molde, Norway.
(©Wolfgang Kaehler/CORBIS)

it possible for German Jesuits to stay in Fredrikstad (1677–91) as military chaplains to General Cicignon. The royal glassworks, begun after 1740, required skilled workers from the Catholic regions of central Europe. From time to time a priest from Denmark was permitted to visit the factories so that the workers could receive the Sacraments. After 1790 a priest, probably French, stayed some years with the French consul in Christiania, and a small, illegal Catholic congregation was tolerated. But all these instances were merely temporary arrangements and organized only for foreigners.

Reestablishment of Catholicism. The first regular Catholic parish in Norway following the Reformation was founded in 1843 in Christiania (renamed Oslo in 1925). From 1814 Norway had the same king as Sweden, due to the political negotiations of the Protestant Karl XIV Johan (1763–1844). Although the Norwegian Constitution of 1814, which declared Norway independent, did not officially change the existing draconian legislation against Catholics, it was gradually permitted to lapse. Jacob Studach, chaplain to the Catholic Princess Josephine Beauharnais, visited Norway several times. In 1833 Studach was appointed vicar apostolic of Sweden and Norway and resided in Stockholm. After Studach sent the German priest Gotfred Montz to the Norwegian

capital to baptize the French consul's child, Montz presented a petition to Karl XIV from about 60 Catholics he had met while in the capital. On March 6, 1843 provisional dispensations to celebrate Mass were granted, and on Easter Sunday, April 16, the first official Catholic service was held. The Dissenter Act of 1845 brought definitive regulations whereby religious freedom was granted to all Christians, although Lutheranism remained the official religion of the country. Austrian REDEMPTORISTS were placed in charge of the parish (1849–54) and began the construction of St. Olav's Church (the present cathedral), dedicated in 1856. The next year a small chapel was opened in Bergen, the second largest town in Norway, by the secular priest Christopher Holfeldt-Houen. In the extreme north another effort was made in 1855 when the Congregation for the Propagation of the Faith (Propaganda) created the Prefecture Apostolic of the Arctic Missions (*Poli Arctici*) comprising the northern part of the Scandinavian Peninsula, the Russian peninsula of Kola, Iceland, Greenland, the Arctic part of Canada, the Faroes and from 1860 even the Shetland Islands, the Orkneys and Caithness in the north of Scotland. The first prefect apostolic was the Russian convert Djunkowski, who returned to Russia the Orthodox Church in 1863. On Norwegian territory, stations were established at Alta (1856) and at Tromsø (1859), where a small church erected in 1860 can still be seen. The difficulty of communication within the vast Prefecture Apostolic of the North combined with a lack of priests in the south to create entirely new divisions in 1869, when Rome created a prefecture apostolic for each of the three northern countries: Norway, Sweden and Denmark. Prefect Bernard Bernard, Djunkowski's successor, administered the entire Norwegian territory, with residence in Oslo (1869–87). Norway constituted a single vicariate apostolic from 1892 until 1932, when the country was divided into three ecclesiastical territories. The southernmost territory became the Diocese of Oslo and the central region established a vicar apostolic residence in Trondheim in 1953; two years later the northern territory was elevated to a vicariate apostolic with its seat in Tromsø. The areas of Trondheim and Tromsø were entrusted to religious congregations, northern Norway to the Fathers of the Holy Family and central Norway to the Fathers of the SACRED HEART (Picpus Fathers). Secular clergy, assisted by various orders and congregations, administered the Oslo Diocese. All three bishops depended directly on Propaganda.

The Church in the 21st Century. Although in the aftermath of the Reformation, Catholicism had become a minority religion, the Church's adherents were a vital force in Norwegian society by 2000. Factors energizing the Church as it moved into the next century were increased memberships, as well as discussion within the government of revisiting the relationship between the Lutheran Church and the state, a relationship that, if altered, would allow Catholics greater latitude. As Norwegian society became increasingly secularized during the 20th century, conditions such as that requiring the king and half the Cabinet to be avowed Lutherans were viewed as vestiges of a less liberal era. The state church also provoked anger for its decision, in July of 2000, to appoint an openly homosexual clergyman in contravention to established Lutheran doctrine. This decision was opposed by a majority of Lutheran bishops and caused those seeking a more traditional basis of faith to look elsewhere for spiritual guidance.

While Church membership in 1960 was only 7,875, within four decades over 40,000 Norwegians professed Catholicism as their faith. The increase was due in large part to the immigration of refugees from Central and Eastern Europe; one estimate held that 70 percent of the country's Catholics were born abroad. In 1995 instruction in "Religious Knowledge and Education in Ethics" became compulsory in all elementary and secondary schools, replacing a previously Lutheran curriculum. The teaching of Christian ethics in an increasingly diverse culture sparked court battles brought by Muslims and members of the Norwegian Humanist Association, an atheist group, which were still underway in the courts in 2000. Like other "dissenters" Catholic pupils were exempted from participation in services or prayer outside their faith, but were required to participate in such classes. Norway's four Catholic schools, which were exempt from such curriculum requirements, received no support from the central government, although municipal subsidies were sometimes available. Catholic hospitals, which administered to all denominations, existed in nearly all of the nation's 32 parish towns by 2000 and were run by sisters of various congregations. Of the 63 priests administering to Norway's Catholics, 40 were religious and 23 were secular; they were joined in their work by 215 sisters.

Bibliography: R. KEYSER, *Den norske Kirkes historie under Katholicismen,* 2 v. (Christiania 1856–58). C. C. A. LANGE, *De norske Klostres historie I Middelalderen* (2d ed. Christiania 1856). T. B. WILSON, *History of the Church and State in Norway* (London 1903). J. METZLER, *Die apostolischen Vikariate des Nordens* (Paderborn 1919). S. UNDSET, *Saga of Saints,* tr. E. C. RAMSDEN (New York 1934). C. JOYS, *Hvad skjedde i Norge i 537* (Oslo 1937). I. H. KNUDSEN, *De relationibus inter Sanctam Sedem et Norvegiam* (Rome 1946). K. LARSEN, *A History of Norway* (Princeton, NJ 1948). E. MOLLAND, *Church Life in Norway 1800–1950,* tr. H. KAASA (Minneapolis 1957). H. RIEBER-MOHN, *Catholicism in Norway* (London 1959). G. SCHWAIGER, *Die Reformation in dem nordischen Ländern* (Munich 1962). O. GARSTEIN, *Rome and the Counter-Reformation in Scandinavia,* v.1: *1559–85* (New York 1964). *Scandinavian Churches,* ed. L. S. HUNTER (London 1965). H. HOLZAPFEL, *Lexikon für Theologie und Kirche²,* eds., J. HOFER and

Nave of Norwich Cathedral. (©Angelo Hornak/CORBIS)

K. RAHNER, 10 v. (2d, new ed. Freiburg 1957–65). E. AMDAHL, *Die Religion in Geschichte und Gegenwart,* 3 (Tübingen 1957 65) 4:1522–30. *Annuario Pontificio* (1964) 317. *St. Ansgar's Bulletin* (New York 1963).

[J. J. DUIN/P. SHELTON]

NORWICH, ANCIENT SEE OF

The Ancient See of Norwich was founded in 1095, when Herbert Losinga transferred his see there from Thetford, since Norwich had become the most important town in East Anglia. Losinga, one of the foremost men of his day, had been prior of FÉCAMP and abbot of RAMSEY, and then decided to introduce Benedictines into his cathedral. In 1096 he planned the buildings and dedicated them to the Holy Trinity; much of his work is still visible, so that Norwich remains the most purely Norman cathedral in Britain (*see* CHURCH ARCHITECTURE). Provision was made for a community of 60 monks. The wealth of the community increased during the following centuries mainly because of the appropriation of churches. Income came also from the shrine of St. WILLIAM OF NORWICH, a boy alleged to have been murdered by Jews in 1144. There were frequent disputes with the townsmen over the rights of tolls and commons. After a great affray in 1272, which resulted in the burning of the monastic buildings, the citizens had to contribute 3,000 marks toward the repairs. Bishop Percy built (*c.* 1360) a clerestory and spire to replace ones damaged in a storm, and Bishops Lyhert and Goldwell replaced the timber roof with one of stone. The diocese suffered heavily during the Bubonic plague: in one year Bishop Bateman made over about 800 institutions. In 1370 Henry DESPENSER was provided to the see; he was a military bishop, unusual in English history, who took a prominent part in the suppression of the Peasants' Revolt. The diocese was much affected by the LOLLARD heresy, and Bishop Alnwick labored hard to control the danger. The most distinguished members of the monastic community were the 14th century scholar-monks, Thomas Brinton and ADAM EASTON, both of whom spent most of their working lives at the papal Curia. The priory was dissolved in 1538, when the prior became dean and the monks were appointed canons of the new chapter.

Bibliography: E. H. CARTER, ed., *Studies in Norwich Cathedral History* (Norwich 1935). E. C. FERNIE, *Architectural History of Norwich Cathedral* (New York 1993). I. ATHERTON, *Norwich Cathedral: church, city, and diocese, 1096–1996* (London 1996). J. NICHOLLS, *The black monks' workshop: an introduction to Norwich Cathedral Cloister and Priory* (Norwich 1999).

[F. R. JOHNSTON]

NOTARY (CANON LAW)

A notary can be defined as a person legitimately constituted by ecclesiastical authority to authenticate by his or her signature ecclesiastical documents. The function of notary has its roots in the *notarius* who took notes to aid the public scribes (*tabelliones*) in drawing up documents, and in the *tabularius,* who took notes and kept the records of court proceedings in Roman law. This latter official can be found fulfilling the same function in the Church of the 5th century, and by the 12th century he had acquired the name "notary" and the right to authenticate public documents with his signature. The Fourth Lateran Council (1215) prescribed that every ecclesiastical court must have a notary.

Canon Law uses "notary" as a general term [*Codex iuris canonici* (Graz 1955) *cc.* 483, 484; *Codex canonum ecclesiarium orientalium, cc.* 253, 254] and "chancellor" as a specific type of notary [*Codex iuris canonici* (Graz 1955) *cc.* 482, 483; *Codex canonum ecclesiarium orientalium, cc.* 252, 253]. [*See* CHANCELLOR, DIOCESAN (EPARCHIAL).]

The general duties of a notary are as follows: to draft acts or documents regarding decrees, dispositions, obligations, or other things requiring their action; to record what has taken place, and to sign this record; to give access to records to those who legitimately request them;

and to declare copies of documents to be in conformity with the originals [*Codex iuris canonici* (Graz 1955) *c.* 484; *Codex canonum ecclesiarium orientalium, c.* 254].

The power of the notary may be extended to include the authentication of all ecclesiastical acts, or limited to judicial or processual documents only or to specified acts or occasions. The notary's duties are further limited to the territory in which the one appointing has jurisdiction. Lay persons may be appointed, but in matters involving the reputation of a cleric, the notary should be a priest. Although it is not required by law, knowledge of canon law is obviously of great value. Notaries can be freely removed from office by the diocesan bishop [*Codex iuris canonici* (Graz 1955) *c.* 485; *Codex canonum ecclesiarium orientalium, c.* 255].

Bibliography: R. NAZ, *Dictionnaire de droit canonique,* ed. R. NAZ, 7 v. (Paris 1935–65) 6:1015–20. G. BARRACLOUGH, *Public Notaries and the Papal Curia* (London 1934). J. C. BROWN, "The Origin and Early History of the Office of Notary," *Juridical Review* 47 (1935) 201–240, 355–417. C. J. DUERR, *The Judicial Notary* [*Catholic University of America Canon Law Studies*] 312; 1951.

[C. J. DUERR]

NOTBURGA, ST.

Maidservant; fl. ninth or tenth century; or, according to a recent version of the legend, b. Rattenberg, Tyrol, *c.* 1265; d. Sept. 14, 1313. Most of her life was spent in the service of Count Henry of Rottenburg. Pious, a diligent worker, she was noted for charity to the poor, to whom she gave food and drink. She died at Rottenburg Castle and was buried at Eben. Her relics were exhumed in 1718; ecclesiastical confirmation of her cult was given on March 27, 1862. She is an extremely popular saint among the farmers and peasants of the Tyrol, Bavaria, Slovenia, Croatia, and Istria, where numerous churches and altars are dedicated to her. Patroness of maidservants and farmers, she is invoked in cases of animal sickness and for successful childbirth. Her symbols include a sickle, a metal jug and a loaf of bread (relating to her care of the poor), and a ring of keys.

Feast: Sept. 14.

Bibliography: *Acta Sanctorum* Sept. 4:709–768. *Andenken an die Feier der Heiligsprechung der Jungfrau und Dienstmagd Notburga von Rottenburg* (Brixen-Lienz 1865). H. BACHMANN, "Die historischen Grundlagen der Notburgalegende," *Tiroler Heimat,* 24 (1960) 5–49. W. VON PFAUNDLER, *Sankt Notburga: Eine Heilige aus Tirol* (Vienna 1962), complete bibliog. 282–300.

[D. ANDREINI]

NOTES, THEOLOGICAL

Most manuals of theology before the Second Vatican Council presented their doctrine in the form of theses, and to each thesis they regularly assigned a "theological note." Thus one thesis may have been qualified as "of divine faith," another as "Catholic doctrine" or, again, "theologically certain." The system of theological notes indicated what kind of certitude the thesis involves, what kind of assent it demands. This article briefly treats the definition, author, division, and main types of theological notes.

Definition. A theological note is a judgment of the dogmatic or theological value of a proposition according to its relation with the norms of faith. The remote norms of faith are Sacred Scripture and tradition; the proximate norm is the teaching of the magisterium. [*See* TRADITION (IN THEOLOGY)]. A note presenting such an evaluative judgment is called "theological" because it makes known the theological value of a proposition. It is also called a "qualification" or "value" because it manifests the theological quality or value of the proposition.

A "theological censure" (*see* CENSURE, THEOLOGICAL) is a pejorative judgment that indicates a proposition is in some way opposed or harmful to faith or morals. If a thesis is given the theological note "of divine and Catholic faith," then a proposition that directly contradicts this thesis will be given the theological censure of "heresy."

Author. Strictly speaking, a dogmatic or theological evaluation of theses is matter for the ecclesiastical magisterium, since it alone has binding authority in the Church. But theologians can be empowered to pronounce sentence in doctrinal matters, and sometimes popes have given this power expressly to faculties of theology. Gradually it has come to be customary for theologians to pass judgment on the theological or dogmatic value of their own theses, though sometimes the Church has restricted their power and forbidden them to censure certain propositions that are still freely discussed among Catholics.

Division. There are many theological notes in use today: "divine faith," "divine and Catholic faith," "defined faith," "ecclesiastical faith," "proximate to faith"; "Catholic doctrine," "theologically certain," "common and certain doctrine"; "probable," "more probable," "common," "more common," and others.

The propositions that are qualified by these theological notes may be grouped into three or four general categories. The first embraces propositions that are in some way "of faith." The second includes propositions that are "not of faith" but are in some way "theologically certain." The third includes propositions that are "not

certain" but are more or less "probable." Many authors break the second category into two, so as to distinguish "theologically certain" propositions into those that are "Catholic doctrine" and those that are "not Catholic doctrine." The reasons for this distinction will appear presently.

Main Types. It is now possible to consider the main types of theological notes in greater detail.

Divine and Catholic Faith. The most important theological note is that of "divine and Catholic faith." It is given to truths that are dogmas of the faith and must be believed if one is not to incur the censure of heresy. Such truths demand an absolute assent, based not on intrinsic truth seen with the natural light of reason but on the authority of God revealing, who can neither deceive nor be deceived (H. Denzinger, *Enchiridion symbolorum*, ed. A. Schönmetzer, 3008).

The meaning of this note is best gathered from a dogmatic constitution of Vatican Council I: "by divine and Catholic faith everything must be believed that is contained in the written word of God or in tradition, and that is proposed by the Church as a divinely revealed object of belief either in a solemn decree or in her ordinary, universal magisterium" (*Enchiridion symbolorum* 3011).

Thus two points must be verified if a proposition is to be "of divine and Catholic faith": it must be divinely revealed and it must be proposed by the Church for belief as divinely revealed. If it is divinely revealed, or, as the Council puts it, is contained in the written word of God or in tradition, then it is "of divine faith." If it is also proposed by the Church as a divinely revealed object of belief, then it is "of divine and Catholic faith."

Such a dogma of the faith can be proposed for belief by the Church in two ways: either by a solemn decree or by her ordinary, universal magisterium. If it is proposed for belief by a solemn decree, that is, if it is solemnly defined, then its theological note is slightly changed by many theologians so as to indicate this. Instead of saying that it is "of divine and Catholic faith," they say that it is "of defined divine faith," or simply "of defined faith."

Such solemn definitions can be made by a pope speaking EX CATHEDRA, as in the definition of the Immaculate Conception by Pius IX and of the Assumption by Pius XII. Solemn definitions are also issued by ecumenical councils, such as Trent and Vatican I, in their various decrees and dogmatic constitutions.

But not only solemn definitions of the Church receive the note "of divine and Catholic faith." It is also applied to truths proposed by the Church's ordinary, universal magisterium as divinely revealed objects of belief. According to Pius IX, "that subjection which is to be made by an explicit act of divine faith must not be limited to those things which have been defined in express decrees of ecumenical councils or of Roman pontiffs; but it must also be extended to those things which, through the ordinary teaching of the whole Church throughout the world, are proposed as divinely revealed and, as a result, by universal and constant consent of Catholic theologians are held to be matters of faith" (*Enchiridion symbolorum* 2879). One finds truths of this kind in certain famous symbols, such as the so-called Athanasian Creed (*Enchiridion symbolorum* 75) or the Niceno-Constantinopolitan Creed (*Enchiridion symbolorum* 150).

There are also some particular councils whose propositions have acquired universal and irreformable value from their confirmation by a Roman pontiff and acceptance by the Church as expressions of her faith. Such are the Council of Carthage (*Enchiridion symbolorum* 222) against the Pelagians and the Second Council of Orange (*Enchiridion symbolorum* 370) against the Semi-Pelagians. From these, too, we derive propositions that are "of divine and Catholic faith" and whose denial incurs the censure of heresy.

Divine Faith. This note is used by some theologians, and more frequently in the treatise on revelation than in other treatises. They consider a truth to be "of divine faith" if it is found in the written word of God or in tradition so clearly that, even if it were not proposed by the Church for belief as divinely revealed, it would still have to be believed by divine faith. For them such truths are the divinity of Christ and His Resurrection.

Ecclesiastical Faith. This is another note occasionally encountered in manuals of theology. It is a controverted note, maintained by some theologians, rejected by others. When used, it is applied to truths that are revealed only virtually, not formally, but that are proposed by the magisterium of the Church to be held absolutely and universally. These truths are often defined, but not as dogmas of the faith. They require absolute assent because they are backed by the infallible authority of the Church. Hence they are qualified as "of ecclesiastical faith." An instance of such a truth is drawn from the Constitution of Alexander VII: "we declare and define that these five propositions taken from the book of the aforementioned Cornelius Jansen . . . were condemned in the sense intended by that same Cornelius Jansen" (*Enchiridion symbolorum* 2012).

Proximate to Faith. This frequently used not is applied to a doctrine that by almost unanimous consent is held to be revealed but is not yet expressly proposed as such by the infallible magisterium. That "God sincerely wills the salvation of all adults" is said to be such a doctrine. This note does not command absolute assent.

Catholic Doctrine. This is a common theological note but an ambiguous one. Some theologians apply it to dogmas of the faith. For others it seems to have the same meaning as "proximate to faith." By still others it is applied to one species of theologically certain propositions. Sometimes it is difficult to determine just what meaning it has.

It applies strictly to propositions that are not dogmas of the faith or strict theological conclusions from revealed truths, but yet are taught expressly and authentically by the magisterium of the Church. Such propositions, based on the authority but not the infallibility of the Church, require of the faithful a truly internal assent from a religious motive of obedience.

"Catholic doctrine" is said to extend to whatever the supreme magisterium wishes to teach expressly, without proposing it for belief, such as the chief ideas of encyclicals, propositions contrary to those that have been condemned, what is contained in the chapters of general councils without being certainly defined or what is easily deduced from these chapters, doctrinal decrees of the Roman pontiff or of Roman congregations if these have been approved and confirmed by the pope. These latter decrees are not irreformable and are of lesser weight than strictly papal precepts, but they too require an obedient assent.

Theologically Certain. This is another very common but not very satisfactory note. For it is sometimes applied only to strict THEOLOGICAL CONCLUSIONS, sometimes also to Catholic doctrine, sometimes even more widely to any common and certain doctrine of theologians. Hence "theologically certain" propositions must be carefully examined to determine just what this qualification means in each case.

In its strictest sense a proposition is called "theologically certain" if it is a certain theological conclusion from one premise that is revealed and from another that is not revealed but is naturally certain. Thus the proposition that Christ is capable of laughter is called theologically certain because it is deduced from a revealed premise (Christ is man), and from a naturally certain premise (every man is capable of laughter). (*See* ERROR, THEOLOGICAL).

In its widest sense, a "theologically certain" note is applied to propositions that theologians commonly hold as certain but that are neither strict theological conclusions from revelation nor Catholic doctrine. Many theologians qualify such propositions simply as "common and certain."

Probable. Another very common note is "probable," "more probable," etc. A thesis is termed theologically "probable" if it rests on a fallible but sufficiently grave theological motive. The Ecumenical Council of Vienne used this note: "We . . . consider the second opinion which says that in Baptism informing grace and virtues are conferred on children as well as on adults, as more probable" (*Enchiridion symbolorum* 904).

In conclusion, one may note that theologians, while they found these and other theological notes very useful, did not found a way to achieve greater uniformity in the definition and use of them.

See Also: THEOLOGICAL TERMINOLOGY.

Bibliography: H. QUILLIET, *Dictionnaire de théologie catholique*, ed. A. VACANT et al., 15 v. (Paris 1903–50) 2:2101–13. S. CARTECHINI, *De valore notarum theologicarum et de criteriis ad eas dignoscendas* (Rome 1951). J. B. FRANZELIN, *Tractatus de divina traditione et Scriptura* (4th ed. Rome 1896). L. DE GRANDMAISON, *Le Dogme chrétien: Sa nature, ses formules, son développement* (Paris 1928). J. SALAVERRI, "De valore et censura propositionum in theologia," *Estudios Ecclesiaticos* 23 (1949) 170–88.

[E. J. FORTMAN]

NOTKER BALBULUS, BL.

Poet, chronicler, Sequence writer; b. either in Heiligau (now Elgg, near Zurich) or Jonschwil (near Sankt Gallen), Switzerland, *c.* 840; d. Sankt Gallen Abbey, April 6, 912. Born of a noble Swiss family, Notker entered the Benedictine Abbey of SANKT GALLEN as a child, remained there as a student under such masters as Iso and Moengal (Marcellus) the Irishman, and stayed on to become an admired and beloved teacher, despite the speech defect that won him the sobriquet Balbulus, the "Stammerer." He was appointed librarian of the monastery in 890 and was guest master in 892 and 894, but his reputation is based on his literary activities.

Notker is now almost universally recognized as the *monachus Sangallensis* who *c.* 884 composed the anecdotal and highly imaginative *Gesta Caroli* (*Monumenta Germaniae Historica: Scriptores rerum Germanicarum* [new series] 12), based on folk tales and legends and written in colloquial Latin prose. This work, of which only the first part and some of the second are extant, won immediate and lasting popularity in the Middle Ages; its tales of CHARLEMAGNE's encounters with his Frankish bishops are chiefly responsible for the emergence of the legendary (as opposed to Einhard's historical) figure of Charlemagne in medieval literature. About 881 Notker wrote the *Breviarium regum Francorum,* a continuation of Erchanbert's chronicle. He is the author of four hymns

in honor of St. Stephen and the metrical *Vita s. Galli,* of which only fragments remain; the hymn *Media vita,* ascribed to him by a tradition that can be traced only to 1613, is probably not his. His extant letters reveal a man of spirit and wit.

It is, however, for his role in the development of the SEQUENCE that Notker is most often remembered. In the preface of his *LIBER HYMNORUM* [ed. W. von den Steinen (Bern 1960) with melodies], a collection of Sequences dedicated (*c.* 884–887) to Liutward, bishop of Vercelli and chancellor of Charles the Fat, Notker recounts that in 862 a monk from the recently sacked monastery of JUMIÈGES in France brought to Sankt Gallen an antiphonary in which a text (*prosa*) had been set to parts of the *jubilus* (the melody that prolonged the final *a* of the *Alleluia* following the Gradual of the Mass). Considering this an excellent mnemonic device for committing to memory the difficult *jubilus* melody, Notker composed a text that both imitated and improved upon the French text, the *Laudes Deo concinat.* His master Iso praised his first attempt but suggested making each syllable of the text correspond to a note of the *jubilus;* this Notker did in the *Psallat ecclesia,* a text for the dedication of a church, which won the approval of both Iso and Mocngal. Many scholars are not totally satisfied with this account of Notker's, for it only obfuscates the question that they consider crucial to a proper estimate of his traditional role as originator of the Sequence; that is, to what extent was he influenced by the earlier and much simpler French Sequences of the eighth and ninth centuries (*Analecta hymnica* [Leipzig 1886–1992] 53)? In addition, scholars are not certain how many or, in some instances, which Sequences are to be attributed to Notker. The original manuscript of the *Liber hymnorum* is not extant, and though there are eight manuscripts dating from not later than the eleventh century, no two of them are identical. Nor is Ekkehard IV's statement in the Sankt Gallen chronicle that Notker composed 50 Sequences of any help, since Ekkehard does not identify them by *incipit.* Whether or not Notker was the originator of the Sequence, there can be no doubt of his influence on German literature. His Sequences, in rhythmical prose and without rhyme, were in frequent use throughout northern Europe until the middle of the twelfth century. They are characterized by simplicity and nobility of language and style and by profundity and orthodoxy of theological content. Notker is also called the first musical composer of German stock, for he is known to have composed the music as well as the words of some of his Sequences, thus freeing the text from too great dependence upon an already existing musical composition.

Notker was beatified in 1512. Permission for a commemoration of him on April 8 was granted to the monastery of Sankt Gallen by a papal bull of Dec. 12, 1512, and

Personal note autographed by Notker Balbulus, Dec. 29, 909.

was extended to the Diocese of Constance in 1513. His relics were brought to the cathedral of Sankt Gallen in 1628. Notker's vita by Ekkehard V (*Acta sanctorum* April 1:579–595) is not altogether reliable.

Feast: April 6.

Bibliography: J. JULIAN, ed. *A Dictionary of Hymnology,* 2 v. (2d ed. London 1907 repr. New York 1957) 1:812–816. M. MANITIUS, *Geschichte der lateinischen Literatur des Mittelalters,* 3 v. (Munich 1911–31) 1:354–367, for Notker's works. S. SINGER, *Die Dichterschule von St. Gallen* (Leipzig 1922). W. VON DEN STEINEN, *Notker der Dichter und seine geistige Welt,* 2 v. (Bern 1948). F. J. E. RABY, *A History of Christian-Latin Poetry from the Beginnings to the Close of the Middle Ages* (2d ed. Oxford 1953) 211–215, brief but comprehensive survey in Eng. H. F. HAEFELE, "Studien zu Notkers *Gesta Karoli,*" *Deutsches Archiv für Erforschung des Mittelalters* 15 (1959): 358–392. W. KOSCH, *Deutsches Literatur-Lexikon,* ed. B. BERGER (Bern 1963). E. LECHNER, *Vita Notkeri Balbuli. Geistesgeschichtlicher Standort und historische Kritik* (St. Gallen 1972). R. L. CROCKER, *The Early Medieval Sequence* (Berkeley 1977). K. HALLER, *Die Legende des heiligen Notker,* ed. E.-A. KOEPPEL (Göppingen 1983). H.-J. REISCHMANN, *Die Trivialisierung des Karlsbildes der Einhard-Vita in Notkers "Gesta Karoli Magni"* (Constance 1984). P. OCHSENBEIN, *Die Notkere im Kloster Sankt Gallen* (St. Gallen 1992). J. SZÖVÉRFFY, *Die Annalen der lateinischen Hymnendichtung. Ein Handbuch,* 2 v. (Berlin 1964–65) 1:282–299.

[M. F. MCCARTHY]

NOTKER LABEO

Benedictine scholar, one of the earliest authors to translate Latin works into German, for which he was given the nickname *Teutonicus;* b. Thurgau, Switzerland, *c.* 950; d. Abbey of Sankt Gallen, June 29, 1022. Notker Labeo was one of four nephews of Abbot Ekkehard I to enter the community at SANKT GALLEN, which he joined as an OBLATE. Widely read in all branches of knowledge, he was later chosen to direct the monastic school, where one of his pupils was Ekkehard IV. In a letter (P. H. Piper, 1:859–61) to Bp. Hugh of Sion (d. 1017) Notker lists his works; of 11 translations, but only five are extant. His clear poetic style, which made him the earliest master of German prose, appears in his translations of BOETHIUS's *De consolatione philosophiae,* the two extant books of Martianus Capella's *De nuptiis Mercurii et philologiae,* the *Categories* and *Hermeneutics* of ARISTOTLE (from an earlier translation into Latin by Boethius), and in the PSALTER, perhaps Notker's most famous work (an Old High German-Latin interlinear text, MS Sankt Gallen 21, dating from *c.* 1100). No copies have been found of Notker's translations of Boethius's *De trinitate* and *Elements of Arithmetic* (?), Vergil's *Bucolica,* the DISTICHA CATONIS, Terence's *Andria,* and the *Homilia in Job* of Pope GREGORY THE GREAT, to which Notker devoted his last days.

Notker wrote an original work in German on music, about the measurement of organ pipes, among other subjects. It is the first known German work on music. He is the author of a Latin work, the *Computus,* about how to determine dates, especially that of Easter. He is credited also with a Latin textbook, *De arte rhetorica,* composed principally of excerpts from Boethius.

Notker also contributed to the development of German orthography; in the letter to Hugh of Sion he recommended accents for German words (acute for short vowels, circumflex for long). His contribution to the German vernacular may be compared to ALFRED THE GREAT's work in making Anglo-Saxon a literary language. Like Alfred, Notker translated the Latin classics to make them available to a wider audience.

Bibliography: Works. *Die Schriften Notkers und seiner Schule,* ed. P. H. PIPER, 3 v. (Freiburg 1895). *Notkers des Deutschen Werke,* ed. E. H. SEHRT and T. STARCK, 7 v. (Halle 1933–55). Literature. J. M. CLARK, *The Abbey of St. Gall as a Centre of Literature and Art* (Cambridge, Eng. 1926), *passim.* M. MANITIUS, *Geschichte der lateinischen Literatur des Mittelalters* (Munich 1911–31) 2:694–699. É. AMANN, *Dictionnaire de théologie catholique,* ed. A. VACANT et al. (Paris 1903—50) 11.1:806–807. O. A. DIETER, *The Rhetoric of Notker Labeo* (St. Louis 1940). W. VON DEN STEINEN, *Notker, der Dichter und seine geistige Welt,* 2 v. (Bern 1948). A. K. DOLCH, *Notker-Studien,* 2 v. (Borna-Leipzig 1951–52). I. SCHRÖBLER, *Notker III. von St. Gallen als Übersetzer und Commentator von Boethius . . .* (Tübingen 1953). E. H. SEHRT, *Notker-Wortschatz* (Halle 1955). F. L. CROSS, *The Oxford Dictionary of the Christian Church* (London 1957) 967. J. DUFT, *Lexikon für Theologie und Kirche,* ed. J. HOFER and K. RAHNER (Freiberg 1957–65) 7:1051.

[B. J. COMASKEY]

NOTKER OF LIÈGE, BL.

Prince bishop of Liège; b. *c.* 940; d. Liège, April 10, 1008. He came of a noble Swabian family and was a nephew of Emperor Otto I. Although he seems to have been educated at Sankt Gallen, it is unlikely that he was provost there. Made bishop of Liège in 969 and called its "second founder," he directed his energies to strengthening Church discipline, building churches, and improving the schools of his diocese. As a result of his work, the CATHEDRAL school of Saint-Lambert, divided into clerical and lay sections, was among the best in the West. He was often in the service of the Emperors Otto II, Otto III, and Henry II; and on one of his four trips to Italy, he accompanied back to Germany the body of OTTO III, whose classical notions of the empire he had enthusiastically supported. He built a cathedral in Liège after the model of Aachen, but it was destroyed by fire in 1185. He was buried in St. John's at Liège, but the present relics there are not genuine.

Feast: April 9 or 10.

Bibliography: I. HELLER, ed., *Aegidii Aureaevallensis gesta episcoporum Leodiensium, Monumenta Germaniae Scriptores* (Berlin 1825) 25:57–63. *Acta Sanctorum* April 1:58, 847. U. BERLIÈRE, "Une Biographie de l'évêque Notger au XIIᵉ siècle," *Acta Sanctorum* 8 (1891) 309–312. G. KURTH, *Notger de Liège et la civilisation au Xᵉ siècle,* 2 v. (Brussels 1905).

[W. E. WILKIE]

NOTRE DAME, SISTERS OF (SND)

The congregation of the Sisters of Notre Dame (SND, Official Catholic Directory, #2990), a pontifical institute, is devoted chiefly to education at all levels. It was founded in 1850, in Coesfeld, Germany, by two young teachers, Aldegonda Wolbring (Sr. Mary Aloysia) and Lisette Kuehling (Sr. Mary Ignatia), assisted by their spiritual director, Rev. Theodore Elting. The first members were trained by sisters from the Notre Dame Convent of Amersfoort, Netherlands, who gave them the rule that St. Marie Rose Julie BILLIART had adopted for her community. In 1900 the Holy See gave final approbation to this rule as adapted by the new congregation.

The first teacher-training school for the sisters and for other young women was opened, with government approval, in 1853 by Sr. Mary Bernarda Perger. Three years later, the Amersfoort sisters returned to their own community and the Coesfeld group elected their first superior general. Growth and expansion characterized the next 20 years until the congregation's further development was arrested by the anti-Catholic decrees of the KULTURKAMPF.

In 1874, therefore, Mother Mary Chrysostom, second superior general, welcomed the invitation of Bp. Richard Gilmour, of Cleveland, Ohio, to work in his diocese. She and eight sisters arrived in the U.S. in July 1874 and two months later they began to teach in St. Peter and St. Stephen schools in Cleveland, and the Mother of God school in Covington, Ky. Two hundred sisters were transferred to the U.S. during the next three years, and Cleveland became the administrative center of the community. In 1884 a few sisters were permitted to resume work in Germany, and when their work prospered, the motherhouse was reestablished in Muelhausen, Germany, in 1888. Over the several decades, new foundations were established in Latin America, Europe and Asia.

From the Cleveland province, other houses were established through the U.S. as the community expanded. In 1924, three new provinces were established: Covington, Ky., Toledo, Ohio, and Los Angeles, Calif. In 1947, the motherhouse was transferred to Rome, Italy.

[M. M. SMITH/EDS]

NOTRE DAME, SISTERS OF THE CONGREGATION DE

(Official Catholic Directory #2980); the Sisters of the Congregation De Notre Dame (CND) was the first religious community of women founded in North America. It was established at Montreal, Canada, by Saint Marguerite BOURGEOYS who, at the request of the governor of Montreal, opened the first school in Ville Marie, as the colony was originally called. This was in 1658, 16 years after the founding of the colony. Despite ecclesiastical opposition, she held firmly to the concept of an uncloistered congregation of simple vows, dedicated to Our Lady, following the Rule of St. Augustine, and committed to the work of education. Mother Bourgeoys' company of school mistresses of Montreal was composed of recruits from France, Canadian-born girls, two former Indian pupils, and, in 1696, Lydia Longley, the first woman from the English colonies to join their ranks. Their society acquired legal status in 1671 with letters patent from Louis XIV. On Aug. 6, 1676, they attained ecclesiastical status as the Congregation de Notre Dame of Montreal by approbation of François de Montmorency Laval, Bishop of Quebec, and on June 24, 1698, received approbation of the rule that Mother Bourgeoys had formulated. Final papal recognition of the community was granted when the constitutions were approved by Leo XIII in 1892.

The first foundation in the U.S. was made at Bourbonnais, IL, in 1860. By 1890 there were ten foundations in Illinois, Connecticut, Rhode Island, Vermont, Maine, and New York. These and subsequent foundations formed, in 1946, a U.S. province with headquarters in Staten Island, NY. The motherhouse is in Montreal, Canada.

Bibliography: *Histoire de la Congrégation de Notre Dame de Montréal,* 10.v. (Montreal 1941).

[R. M. DONAHUE/EDS.]

NOTRE DAME DE NAMUR, SISTERS OF

(S.N.D.deN., Official Catholic Directory #3000); an international congregation of pontifical right, organized into 20 provinces located in Europe, Africa, Asia, and the Americas.

Saint Marie Rose Julie BILLIART founded the congregation in Amiens, France, in 1804, in response to post-Revolutionary poverty, widespread illiteracy, and the struggle of the Roman Catholic Church in France to reestablish itself. Convinced that education was a universal right, she dedicated the congregation to the education of the poor. With the assistance of the cofoundress, Francoise Blin de Bourdon, she spent the next 12 years shaping her vision into a systematic program of formal schooling for poor girls. The success of the early schools led to a rapid expansion so that at her death in 1816, Julie Billiart had established 19 schools in five dioceses of northwest France and Belgium.

She applied her innovative spirit to the organization of the congregation, creating structures that would be adaptive and responsive to emerging apostolic opportunities. Her approach envisioned a work that would not be limited to any one diocese, that would depend upon the leadership of women in the person of a superior general, and that eliminated the distinction between choir and lay sisters. This mode of organization occasioned misunderstanding with the bishop of Amiens, John Francis Demandolx, which led to Billiart's dismissal from the diocese and the relocation of the motherhouse to Namur, Belgium, where the congregation had already established a flourishing foundation.

The second generation, under the leadership of Francoise Blin de Bourdon, faced challenges arising from the decision of the Congress of Vienna in 1815 to create the Kingdom of the Netherlands by incorporating Roman Catholic Belgium into the newly formed state ruled by the Calvinist William of Orange. Determined to minimize Roman Catholic influence in Belgium, the Dutch government launched an attack on Belgian schools through increasingly hostile regulations. Successfully meeting the demands of the new regulations, the sisters made the transition from the limited educational program Billiart had designed to a more complex one, thus hastening the professionalization of the congregation's education system. In meeting Dutch demands, the congregation

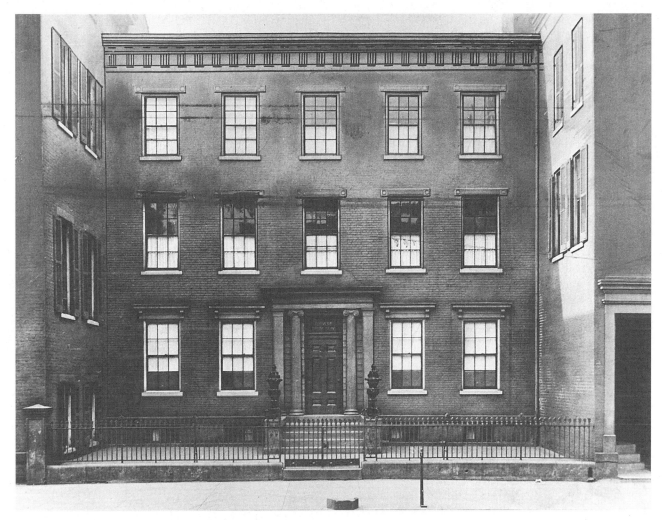

Facade of the convent of Notre Dame de Namur, Cincinnati, Ohio, the first U.S. foundation of the congregation.

implemented rigorous standards for teacher training, accepted curricular development as essential for the adaptation to changing times and local circumstances, and provided, as far as possible, the resources to maintain the financial independence of its schools.

To the United States and the World. Within this emerging system, the congregation strengthened its schools and created a flexible approach that the sisters transferred to the United States and Great Britain when the period of expansion from Belgium began in the 1840s. Accepting the invitation of Bishop John Purcell of Cincinnati, eight Belgian sisters established a foundation in his diocese in 1840 and under the leadership of Sister Louise VanDerSchrieck initiated a period of rapid movement eastward from Cincinnati to Massachusetts, Rhode Island, Pennsylvania, and Washington, D.C. In 1844, inspired by the zeal of Pierre DeSmet, S.J., another missionary group left Belgium for Oregon, where the sisters remained until being transferred to California in

1852. The first foundation in Great Britain opened at Penryn in Cornwall in 1845 and relocated to London in 1848. During the 1850s, in quick succession, foundations opened in Liverpool, Manchester, and Sheffield. In order to meet the demand for teachers in these urban areas, the sisters opened a teacher training college at Mt. Pleasant in Liverpool in 1856, directed by Sister Mary of St. Philip Lescher. By the 1890s these established provinces had developed missionary interests in Africa and in East Asia, which led to foundations in the Congo in 1894, Rhodesia (Zimbabwe) in 1899, South Africa in 1907, Japan in 1924, and China in 1929. A second wave of overseas missionary activity occurred after World War II in Africa and South America. The need for teachers in newly independent African nations resulted in foundations in Nigeria in 1963 and in Kenya in 1965. In response to the 1961 Vatican appeal to the U.S. Church to give 10 percent of its personnel to Latin America, the congregation established foundations in Brazil in 1963 and in Peru in 1970. With the exception of the Chinese houses that were suppressed in 1949, each of these former missions has become an independent unit within the congregation, responsible for the recruitment, formation, and education of its sisters, for the development of its ministries, and for its governance.

The cumulative impact of changes occurring in the second half of the 20th century created new understandings of the role of the Church in the world. The Sister Formation Movement in the United States, the consequences of World War II in Europe and in Japan, and the experience of the liberation struggles in Africa created an awareness of international and social issues that prepared sisters to be receptive to the decrees of Vatican II. In response, therefore, to *Perfectae Caritatis* (1965), the council decree calling religious communities to reform and renewal, and to *Ecclesiae Sanctae* (1966) enjoining them to convene special general chapters as agents of renewal, the Special General Chapter of 1968–1969 engaged the congregation in a lengthy period of experimentation culminating in the approved constitutions of 1989. During this 20-year period the community developed a heightened appreciation of Billiart's spirituality and recovered her emphasis on education with a preference for the poor. Sensitive to the challenge to "read the signs of the times," the congregation has supported an expansive understanding of its commitment to education that values diverse expressions of teaching and learning, all directly or indirectly in service to the poor. This new understanding has enabled sisters to enlarge the scope of their ministries and to respond to contemporary needs in a multiplicity of ways, including work in parish and diocesan religious education and liturgical programs and justice and peace programs; work with immigrants, refugees, migrants, the homeless, and the unemployed; and service in hospital ministry, in hospice care, and as chaplains and tutors in prison ministry. Sisters also serve as attorneys, canon lawyers, doctors, nurses, social workers, superintendents of schools, and vicars of religious.

Provinces continue to sponsor formal education at all levels and sisters continue to serve in diocesan school systems as teachers and administrators. The congregation also sponsors four colleges and a junior college. The oldest of its colleges in the United States, Trinity College, was chartered in 1897; Emmanuel College was founded in Boston, Massachusetts, in 1919; Notre Dame de Namur University in Belmont, California, chartered in 1868, began to offer a four-year baccalaureate program in 1951. In 1949 the Japanese province established a four-year college in Okayama that is now Notre Dame Seishin University, and in 1961 opened Notre Dame Junior College in Hiroshima. During the final decades of the 20th century, the three U.S. colleges evolved from traditional undergraduate liberal arts colleges into comprehensive universities; they have introduced programs for working adults at the undergraduate level, have strengthened and expanded their graduate programs in education, and have introduced professional programs at the graduate level ranging from pastoral ministry to health care promotion. The transformation of the colleges is also evident in the shift in administrative leadership as laywomen and laymen replace sisters of Notre Dame in these positions.

The Special General Chapter of 1969 and successive chapters have fostered the internationality of the congregation; leadership at the general level actively promotes this emphasis by sponsoring an extensive array of international meetings that touch upon every aspect of community life, including renewal programs on the spirituality of Billiart, formation, finance, and archives. Continental meetings and pre-general chapter gatherings provide corporate reflection on the emerging general chapter issues. These meetings engender a spirit of interdependence and appreciation for the diversity of cultures, lifestyles, and theologies that exist within the congregation.

Bibliography: F. BLIN, *The Memoirs of Frances Blin de Bourdon, SNDdeN,* ed. T. SULLIVAN, et al. (Westminster, Md. 1975). F. ROSNER and L. TINSLEY, eds., *The Letters of St. Julie Billiart,* 7 v. (Rome 1975). C. CLAIR, *La Bienheureuse Mere Julie Billiart* (Paris 1906). M. LINSCOTT, *Quiet Revolution* (Glasgow 1975). L. QUINET, *Vie de la Reverende Mere Julie* (Paris 1862).

[J. BLAND]

NOTRE DAME DE SION, CONGREGATION OF

(Official Catholic Directory #2950); a religious community of women founded in France in 1846 by the RATISBONNE brothers, Marie Théodore, and Marie Alphonse. It has for its aim the promotion of true understanding between Christians and Jews. This work assumes many forms. The religious strive to break down the barriers of anti-Semitism by presenting a true picture of Jews and Judaism, and by giving non-Jews a profound respect for the people from whom Christ Himself chose to come. At the same time, they try to show to the Jews the true meaning of Christianity so often distorted by misguided zeal and lack of understanding on the part of Christians. The congregation, which has its generalate in Rome, has provinces on five continents. The Sisters of Sion have been teaching in the U.S. since 1892. The American provincial headquarters is in Kansas City, MO.

[M. DOLAN/EDS.]

NOTRE DAME DU LAC, UNIVERSITY OF

Founded 1842 by the Rev. Edward F. Sorin and a small band of religious brothers, all members of the Congregation of HOLY CROSS. This congregation of priests, brothers, and sisters, with the Holy Family as their patrons, had been founded in Le Mans, France, a decade before by the Rev. Basil A. Moreau, and the Holy Cross priests, brothers, and sisters have continued to serve the university to the present. The land on which the university was founded, 524 acres in northern Indiana, 80 miles east of Chicago and 180 miles west of Detroit, had originally been purchased by the Rev. Stephen T. Badin, the first priest ordained in the United States, and had subsequently been given to the local bishop. The bishop offered the land—including two small lakes, the basis of the university's official name, Notre Dame du Lac—to Father Sorin on condition that he establish a school, and this original grant has been divided and expanded over the years into the present 1,250-acre campus.

The school made steady progress in its first decades and, by the time of Father Sorin's death in 1893, had a student enrollment of 540 and a faculty of 52 on a campus of 24 buildings. Although chartered as a university by the State of Indiana in 1844, at least half of these students were in the preparatory department or high school, another 150 in the minims department or elementary school, and approximately 35 were apprentices in the manual labor school. Six courses of study were open to the college students: the classical course (general humanities), the scientific course, the English or belles-lettres course, law, civil engineering, and the commercial course, although this last was primarily a high school program. A master of arts degree was offered as early as 1859 on completion of three years of study in philosophy and literature beyond the bachelor's degree.

To demonstrate his patriotism in face of the anti-Catholic and anti-immigrant prejudice of the 19th century, Father Sorin scheduled early graduation ceremonies for the Fourth of July and named one of his first academic buildings Washington Hall. Seven priests from Notre Dame served as chaplains in the Civil War and one of them, the Rev. William Corby, CSC, gave general absolution to New York's famed Irish Brigade before the Battle of Gettysburg, an incident commemorated to this day by a statue of the priest on that battlefield. Notre Dame claimed a number of firsts in the latter half of the 19th century: in 1869 its Law School was the first on a Catholic campus; in the 1880s it was the first American college campus to be lighted by electricity; in 1888 it became the first Catholic university to open a residence hall with individual rooms for students (Sorin Hall); and in 1899 it

was the scene of the first wireless telegraphic message sent in the United States.

In 1879, after a devastating fire, construction of the present administration building was begun, to be crowned with its famed golden dome in 1882. In 1888 the campus church, dedicated to the Sacred Heart, was completed, an impressive Gothic structure with stained-glass windows crafted by Carmelite sisters in France, murals painted by the Vatican artist Luigi Gregori, and the high altar designed by Froc-Robert of Paris. By the turn of the century, the university's most significant contributions to scholarship were probably the treatises on faith and evolution by the Rev. John A. Zahm, CSC, and the early aerodynamic studies of his younger brother, Dr. Albert Zahm.

The 20th Century. Major changes occurred in the early decades of the 20th century. The manual labor school was terminated in 1917, a summer session program was begun in 1918, the preparatory department or high school was closed in 1924, and the minims department or elementary school was eliminated in 1929, leaving Notre Dame for the first time an institution of exclusively higher education. The Rev. James A. Burns, CSC, president from 1919 to 1922, divided the college courses into five distinct colleges, each presided over by a dean. A committee on graduate study oversaw all graduate courses and degrees. With the impending loss of revenue from high school tuition, Father Burns undertook a major fund-raising campaign, completed it successfully, and organized a lay board of trustees to help manage the newly established endowment. The success of the school's football teams in the 1920s under the legendary coach Knute Rockne brought additional revenue and national fame. In the 1930s, during the presidency of the Rev. John F. O'Hara, CSC, later the cardinal-archbishop of Philadelphia, the faculty was strengthened by the addition of several European scholars fleeing Nazi domination: the mathematicians Karl Menger and Emil Artin, the physicists Arthur Haas and Eugene Guth, and the political scientists Ferdinand Hermans and Waldemar Gurian. During World War II the U.S. Navy was invited to set up V-7 and V-12 programs, and an estimated 11,000 naval officers completed their training on campus.

The Hesburgh Years. The decades following World War II were years of major growth and development, especially during the presidency of the Rev. Theodore M. Hesburgh, CSC, 1952–87. Student enrollment jumped from less than 5,000 to 9,600, the teaching and research faculty from 389 to 803, and the annual budget from $10 million to $176 million. The endowment increased from $9 million to $350 million, chiefly from several successful fund-raising drives and annual gift-giving of devoted alumni. By 1987 faculty salaries ranked in the highest quartile of the American Association of University Professors standings, and Notre Dame was consistently listed among the 25 best schools in the *US News and World Report*'s influential survey. Over 30 new buildings were constructed, including ten residence halls and 11 academic buildings, in addition to major renovations of existing buildings.

Academic life and scholarly research were enhanced with the establishment of wide-ranging institutes: the Center for the Study of Contemporary Society, the Helen Kellogg Institute for International Studies, the Center for Civil and Human Rights, the Cushwa Center for the Study of American Catholicism, the Joan B. Kroc Institute for International Peace Studies, and the Ecumenical Institute for Advanced Theological Studies in Jerusalem. The manuscript treasures of the Ambrosian Library in Milan were microfilmed for deposit at Notre Dame, as were documents pertinent to the United States in the Vatican's Propagation of the Faith Archives. A distinguished professors program was inaugurated to attract nationally and internationally renowned scholars to endowed chairs. Nine foreign study programs were begun, and a chapter of Phi Beta Kappa was installed in 1968.

In 1967 ultimate governance of the university was transferred from the Congregation of Holy Cross to a board of fellows (six Holy Cross priests and six laymen or women) and a predominantly lay board of trustees. In 1972 the university opened its doors for the first time to undergraduate women. Student unrest and anti-Vietnam War protests broke out in the late 1960s and early 1970s but on a much smaller scale than elsewhere, and the football success and national acclaim achieved by earlier coaches Knute Rockne and Frank Leahy continued under coaches Ara Parseghian in the 1960s and Lou Holtz in the 1980s.

Notre Dame at Century's End. The university continued its expansion under Father Hesburgh's successor, the Rev. Edward A. Malloy, CSC. Under the Board of Fellows and the Board of Trustees, the president is aided in guiding the university by a provost, an executive vice president, and nine other vice presidents. There were four undergraduate colleges (Arts and Letters, Science, Engineering, and Mendoza College of Business), the School of Architecture, the First Year of Studies, and the Law School. The student body at the end of the 20th century numbered 10,500. Of these, 8,000 were undergraduates, 1,500 were in graduate school, and another 1,000 were in the graduate professional programs of law, business, or divinity. Approximately 54 percent of the undergraduates were men and 46 percent women. Scholarly journals published at the university included the *American Jour-*

nal of Jurisprudence, American Midland Naturalist, American Philosophical Quarterly, Bullán, Journal of Musicology, New Scholasticism, Notre Dame Journal of Formal Logic, Review of Politics, and *U.S. Catholic Historian.* The University of Notre Dame Press remains the largest Catholic university press in the world.

Religion has retained a central place in university life. Approximately 85 percent of the undergraduates are Catholic and 50 percent of the faculty includes Holy Cross priests, brothers, and sisters, as well dedicated Catholic laypersons. The university's *Laetare Medal* is awarded each year to an outstanding American Catholic.

Bibliography: T. J. SCHLERETH, *The University of Notre Dame: A Portrait of Its History and Campus* (Notre Dame 1976). A. J. HOPE, *Notre Dame: One Hundred Years* (Notre Dame 1943). P. S. MOORE, *Academic Development, University of Notre Dame: Past, Present and Future* (Notre Dame 1960). R. P. SCHMUHL, *The University of Notre Dame: A Contemporary Portrait* (Notre Dame 1986). T. T. MCAVOY, *Father O'Hara of Notre Dame: The Cardinal-Archbishop of Philadelphia* (Notre Dame 1967); "Notre Dame, 1919–1922: The Burns Revolution," *Review of Politics* 25 (October 1963) 431–450. T. M. HESBURGH, *God, Country, Notre Dame* (New York 1990). M. O'BRIEN, *Hesburgh: A Biography* (Washington, D.C. 1998). R. E. WEBER, *Notre Dame's John Zahm* (Notre Dame 1961).

[T. E. BLANTZ]

NOTRE DAME SISTERS

Formerly known as the School Sisters de Notre Dame (ND, Official Catholic Directory #2960), a pontifical religious congregation dedicated to strengthening family life, especially through various forms of educational work in Midwestern United States. The headquarters of this American province, one of four in the congregation, is in Omaha, Nebraska. The congregation traces its origins to Loffaine, France, where in 1597 (Blessed) Alix LeClerc and (St.) Peter Fourier organized a religious congregation of women to educate young girls, specifically the poor.

Two centuries later, Fr. Gabriel Schneider (d. 1867) collaborated with M. Karoline Gerhardinger to bring a branch of the School Sisters of Notre Dame from Germany to Bohemia, again to educate the poor, especially neglected girls. When this partnership did not come to completion, Fr. Gabriel began his own congregation of the Poor School Sisters de Notre Dame on Aug. 15, 1853. After its beginnings in Hirschau, it moved its headquarters to Horazdovice, where it remained until in 1950 when communism forced the sisters to relocate to Javornik. Today the general motherhouse is located in Hradec Karlovel, in the Czech Republic.

In 1910 many bishops invited the congregation to come to the United States to care for the spiritual needs of the Czech immigrants. Mother Qualberta Krivanec led five sisters to Fenton, Missouri, to take charge of an orphanage there. As new members joined, they moved to Omaha, Nebraska, where they established their headquarters. In these early years, they assisted Fr. Edward J. FLANAGAN in the formative years of Boys Town. With continued growth they staffed schools in Nebraska, Iowa, Kansas, and South Dakota.

The Notre Dame Sisters (so called in the United States to distinguish them from the SSND groups) are called to strengthen family life through education, counseling, nursing, archdiocesan and parish work, and missionary work. They advocate for non-violence in all areas of their ministries. They also advocate for the elderly, especially through Seven Oaks of Florence, an independent living complex for low-income and frail elderly in Omaha. They are located in Iowa, Missouri, Kansas, Colorado, South Dakota, Nebraska and Honduras.

[M. HICKEY]

NOUMENA

A term used by philosophers, and mainly by Kantians, to designate objects that cannot be sensibly perceived and can only be mentally apprehended. This article sketches the pre-Kantian usages and then explains and criticizes the place of the term in KANTIANISM.

Pre-Kantian Usages. The word noumena (Gr. νοούμενα) is encountered in PLATO in several passages (Rep. 508C, 509D; *Parm.* 132C; *Tim.* 30D, 51D) and designates ideas of which it is said explicitly that they can be grasped only mentally and not sensibly (*Rep.* 507B; *Tim.* 51D). The only things accessible to sensible visualization, for Plato, are those that are subject to multiplicity and becoming; these do not exist in the full sense of the word, and form the τόπος ὁρατός (*Rep.* 532D). The Ideas, on the contrary, constitute the τόπος νοητός (Rep. 508C) and are the only true being (*Phaedrus* 247C, 249C; *Tim.* 28A), which, as such, is eternal and immutable and can be apprehended only mentally by reminiscence and dialectics. This is especially true of the original source of all ideas, of absolute goodness and absolute beauty—the beautiful and good in every respect that fully encompass all beauty and goodness (*Symp.* 210E-211D; *Rep.* 509B).

In Aristotle, the term noumena is encountered in one passage only (*Meta.* 1074b 36–1075a 5), where it is used three times; elsewhere, the term νοητά is employed in the same sense (e.g., *Anim.* 431b 20–432a 14). More specifically, Aristotle distinguishes what can be mentally comprehended from what can be sensibly perceived; on actuation, the latter coincides with sense PERCEPTION in

the same way as the former with simple APPREHENSION (Meta. 1075a 3–5; *Anim.* 431b 22–23). Contrary to Plato, Aristotle holds that what can be apprehended only mentally is not separated from sensible phenomena, but is contained in phenomena and is to be sought in them (*Anim.* 432a 3–5). Thus the mind extracts essences from visible things (*ibid.* 431b 2); the essential forms inherent in such things therefore take the place of Plato's transcending Ideas. The apprehension of the noumena, which is a kind of INTUITION in Plato, appears thus as an ABSTRACTION in Aristotle. It is perfected by a reasoning process that ascends to the highest noumena, i.e., the Divine as eternal, immovable, and separate (*Meta.* 1026a 10–30).

St. THOMAS AQUINAS, working through St. AUGUSTINE as an intermediary, effected a synthesis of Plato and Aristotle. The noumena inherent in things (*intelligibilia*) are essences, and, above all, BEING; they are grasped by abstraction. Their bases, as transcendental noumena, are the archetypal ideas of the divine intellect, which, in turn, are founded upon the archnoumenon, i.e., upon God as the subsistent being; man ascends to this conclusion by metaphysical discourse.

Kantian Notion. According to I. Kant, noumena must be distinguished from PHENOMENA; the latter are called "phenomena, in so far as they are thought as objects according to the unity of the categories" (*Critique of Pure Reason* A 248). In this text, as opposed to ordinary usage, phenomena are distinguished from appearances; the distinction, however, must be correctly understood. When one says: "The senses represent objects as they appear, the understanding as they are, the latter statement" must "be understood in the empirical meaning" (*ibid.* A 258), i.e., as objects-for-man. On the contrary, the term "noumena (*intelligibilia*)" is applied to those things "which are merely objects of understanding, and which, nevertheless, can be perceived as such by intuition, though not by sensible intuition (therefore, *coram intuitu intellectuali*)" (*ibid.* A 249). Man's concepts themselves can never determine an object; for this purpose, an intuition is needed to supplement such concepts, and for man this can only be sensible. Man has no intellectual intuition that would make possible the "transcendental use" of his concepts, i.e., a use that would reach the thing-in-itself "beyond the sphere of possible experience" (*ibid.* A 248). The noumena are ordered to this usage, which is "not contradictory" (*ibid.* A 254), since they are "merely a limiting concept" (*ibid.* A 255); one encounters them not as "intelligible objects" but merely as "a problem" (*ibid.* A 256). But they are not an "arbitrary invention" (*ibid.* A 255); on the contrary, they are "necessary" (*ibid.* A 254), although only of "negative use" (*ibid.* A 255) "in order to impose a limit upon the presumptions of sensibility'' (*ibid.*). Here, moreover, one should ''prevent sensible intuition from being extended to things in themselves,'' and one should not claim that ''sensibility is the only possible mode of intuition'' (*ibid.* A254). As a consequence, ''our understanding attains in this way a sort of negative extension, i.e., it is not limited by, but rather limits, sensibility by giving the name of noumena to things, not considered as phenomena, but as things in themselves. But our understanding imposes also limits upon itself, recognizing that it cannot know these noumena by means of the categories; hence, it is compelled to think of them merely as of an unknown something'' (*ibid.* A 256).

Beyond this usage lies that of the moral order, which shows man ''as a being endowed with internal freedom (*homo noumenon*)'' (*Metaphysik der Sitten,* Berlin Academy ed., 6:418), and which can give to his ''causality as a noumenon'' (*Critique of Practical Reason*; *ibid.* 5:50) ''for the first time objective, although only practical, reality'' (*ibid.* 48).

By way of evaluation, it may be said that Kant loses the synthesis characteristic of Aquinas by disregarding the process of abstraction that obtains the noumena, i.e., essences and being, from the phenomena. At the same time, he returns to Plato by assuming that the noumena are accessible to intellectual intuition alone, an accessibility that he justly denies to man.

See Also: CRITICISM, PHILOSOPHICAL; KNOWLEDGE, THEORIES OF

Bibliography: I. KANT, *Prolegomena,* §§32–35. R. EISLER, *Wörterbuch der philosophischen Begriffe*, 3 v. (4th ed. Berlin 1927–30) 2:271–73. F. C. COPLESTON, *History of Philosophy* (Westminster, Md. 1946–) 6:267–72. A. CARBINI, *Enciclopedia filosofica*, 4 v. (Venice-Rome 1957) 3:940–42.

[J. B. LOTZ]

NOVATIAN (ANTIPOPE) AND NOVATIANISM

Pontificate: 251. Novatian was the first, and for a long time the only, writer of the Roman Church to use Latin. The little that is known of his life is dependent on untrustworthy information supplied by his enemies. His name was certainly Novatianus, not Novatus as given by the Greeks. He must have been born *c.* 200, and received a good education in Latin, as his language attests, but he was not a Phrygian as Philostorgius asserts (*Ecclesiastical History* 8.15).

Pope Cornelius. In his letter to Bp. Fabius of Antioch, Pope CORNELIUS furnishes information on the bap-

tism, ordination, and later conduct of Novatian (Eusebius, *Ecclesiastical History* 6.43.6–22) that is at least questionable. It may be true that he received Baptism by sprinkling during a severe sickness, but it is hardly credible that his ordination was performed despite the opposition of the clergy and many of the laity or that he hid himself during a persecution, refusing to give priestly assistance to his suffering fellow Christians. If these contentions are true, it is difficult to understand how he became the *administrator* of the Roman college of priests after the martyr death of Pope FABIAN (Jan. 20, 50). As such, he wrote letters to the Church throughout the world, of which two to St. CYPRIAN OF CARTHAGE have been preserved (Cyprian, *Epistolae* 30, 36; *Corpus scriptorum ecclesiasticorum latinorum* 3:2).

Novatian as Bishop. After the election of Cornelius as the new pope in March or April of 251, Novatian had himself consecrated a bishop by three south Italian bishops, certainly not merely through foolish ambition as his enemies asserted; otherwise he would not have had the support of many clerics and contemporary confessors (Cyprian, *Epistolae* 46: Eusebius, *Ecclesiastical History* 6.43); but rather as a protest against the compliant attitude of the new pope on the question of penance.

Roman Synod. In an encyclical letter to the other bishops, Novatian announced his consecration (Cyprian, *Epistolae* 55; *Ad Novat.* 13). That same year a Roman synod of 60 bishops excommunicated him (Eusebius, *Ecclesiastical History* 6.43.2). The confessors made their peace with Pope Cornelius (Cyprian, *Epistolae* 53; *Corpus scriptorum ecclesiasticorum latinorum* [Vienna 1866–] 3), and, after some hesitation, Cyprian and the bishops of Asia Minor unanimously deserted Novatian (Sozomen, *Ecclesiastical History* 3.8). Nevertheless, he was able to propagate his church with his own bishops in every sector of the Christian world.

In the persecution under Gallus and Volusianus (251–253), Novatian had to flee Rome, and under Valerian in 258 he suffered martyrdom (Pacian, *Epistolae* 2.7), or at least became a confessor (Socrates, *Ecclesiastical History* 4.28). In 1932 a tombstone was discovered on the Via Tiburtina with the inscription: *Novatiano Beatissimo/ Martyri Gaudentius Diac[onus]/fec[it]*; however, the relationship is questionable. The MARTYROLOGY OF JEROME cites a Roman martyr named Novatianus for June 27 or 29, but without a title.

Writings. Novatian's writings do not merely show him to have been an elegant stylist, but they likewise manifest a good theological and philosophical education. Of the nine works listed by Jerome (*De vir. ill.* 70), only two have been preserved: one of them, his chief work, the *De Trinitate,* is basically apologetic in character and brings the teaching on the Trinity down to his time. In it he defends the oneness of Almighty God, and God the Creator, against the Gnostics (*see* GNOSTICISM); Christ as the Son of God the Creator, against Marcion; Christ as true man, against the Docetists; as true God, against the Adoptionists (*see* ADOPTIONISM); and as Second Person to the Father, against Sabellius (*see* SABELLIANISM); and he demonstrates, after a hymn of praise to the Holy Spirit, that despite the Godhood of Christ, there is only one God. The Holy Spirit is considered as unequal to the Father, but on this point Novatian merely reflects the consensus of Trinitarian theology of the third century.

His alleged angelology, as well as his supposed teaching on the absorption of Son in the Father, is a misunderstanding. Since he did not distinguish between the substantial attributes of the Godhood and the properties of the Persons, he could only preserve the Oneness of God through a SUBORDINATIONISM; all the more so, since he sees God not from an ontological viewpoint, but rather in the aspect of His power. Still his work is an improvement over that of Tertullian and Hippolytus

Opposition To the Church. Cause of the Strife. Novatian's dispute with the Church stemmed from the problem concerning the reception into the Church of those who had fallen in persecution. In his two letters to Cyprian, he praised Cyprian's refusal to grant a pardon to the *lapsi* before the end of the persecution, except in cases involving danger of death. Thus far one could go along with him, but as the sharpness of his first letter had caused some estrangement, so the second went beyond the limit. Novatian saw in Cyprian's temporary solution, not merely a cautionary measure, but a fundamental challenge. He thus betrayed the rigorism of an earlier period of which, at Rome, Callistus, and, in Africa, Agrippius, had broken through the first barriers. Behind Novatian's attitude there was a different conception of the Church.

If, with Cyprian, one believed that only an unconditional membership in the Church was a guarantee of eternal salvation, one would act differently than if, with Novatian, he believed the Church should be announced as a community of saints who must be kept free of all taint. While Cyprian saw in the refusal to grant pardon a prejudgment involving eternal damnation, Novatian believed that God's judgment would be compromised through pardon, since the way to God's mercy led through penance, compunction, and sorrow.

De Cibis Judaicis. This work, which has been preserved and is mentioned by Jerome, was written to Novatian's community from a distance. Here Novatian shows that the Old Testament prohibitions regarding food are to be understood in a spiritual and not in a literal sense. In particular, it is the vices symbolized by impure animals

that should be avoided. The taste of their flesh is not forbidden, but rather the flesh of sacrifice. A particular chapter is directed against the immorality of early morning drinking.

Other writings listed by Jerome are lost, but apparently Novatian is the author of two works that have been preserved under the name of Cyprian. In a *De spectaculis,* the author is dependent on Cyprian and Tertullian for his condemnation of Christian attendance at spectacles and advises his readers to meditate instead on the beauties in nature and on the word of God. In a *De bono pudicitiae,* he praises virginity, continence in marriage, and marital fidelity.

Novatianist Churches. Thanks to his animated activity (Cyprian, *Epistolae* 55.24) and his rigorism, which later led his followers to deny the forgiveness of all grave sins after Baptism (Socrates, *Ecclesiastical History* 5.22), Novatian won a large following. Marcian of Arles went over to his side; and even in Spain, Rome, and Africa, there were Novatian communities with their own bishops. On their return to the Church, a dispute over Baptism broke out in Africa.

In the East, it was above all in Phrygia, where the Montanists had prepared the way, that almost all the greater cities had Novatian bishops; Constantine I invited the Novatian Bishop of Constantinople, Acesius, to attend the Council of Nicaea (Socrates, *Ecclesiastical History* 1.10). Their acceptance of the HOMOOUSIOS and their good relations with the Catholics won them longstanding sufferance in Constantinople (Socrates, *ibid.* 5.10). Cyril fought against them in Alexandria (Socrates, *ibid.* 7.7), and in Rome, they were opposed by Popes Innocent I and Celestine I.

In the West, the Novatians gradually submitted to the larger Church, and we hear of the return of a bishop with his whole community (Leo I, *Epistolae* 12.6). In the East they held out longer. Eulogius of Alexandria directed a large work against them, but cooperation between Church and State forced them to disappear, at first in the cities and then in the country, and by the end of the seventh century the last communities were extinct.

Bibliography: É. AMANN, *Dictionnaire de théologie catholique,* ed. A. VACANT et al., (Paris 1903–50) 11.1:816–849. *Cyprianische Untersuchungen* (Bonn 1926) 403–406. M. SIMONETTI, ''Alcune osservazioni sul De Trinitate di Novaziano,'' *Studi in onore di Angelo Monteverdi,* 2 v. (Modena 1959) 2:771–783. F. SCHEIDWEILER, *Zeitschrift für Kirchengeschicte* 55 (1954–55) 126–139. C. MOHRMANN, ''Les Origines de la Latinité chrétienne à Rome,'' *Vigiliae christianae* 3 (1949) 67–106, 163–183. R. J. DISIMONE, trans. *On the Trinity* (Fathers of the Church 64; Washington, D.C. 1974). E. FERGUSON, ed., *Encyclopedia of Early Christianity* (New York 1997), 2.819–820. H. GINZLOW, *Cyprian und Novatian* (Tübingen 1974). J. N. D. KELLY, *Oxford Dictionary of Popes* (New

Worshipers caress a statue of Christ as part of a novena at Baclaran Church in the Philippines. (Catherine Karnow/CORBIS)

York 1986), 18–19. P. MATTEI, "L'anthropologie de Novatien," *Revue des Études Augustiniennes* 38 (1992), 235–239.

[P. H. WEYER]

NOVENA

Nine successive days of prayer, private or public, to obtain special favors or graces. It differs from an octave, or the eight days of prayerful celebration that follow certain feasts, because the octave has a place in the liturgy that the novena (which generally precedes a feast with which it may be associated) has not. Moreover, the octave is celebrated in a more festal spirit, whereas the novena tends to be marked by a feeling of urgent need and yearning. The novena can be considered a triple TRIDUUM, involving a more prolonged concentration of devotion and spiritual effort.

The nine days that the Apostles spent in Jerusalem at the command of the Lord as they awaited the coming of the Holy Spirit (Lk 24.49; Acts 1.4) has been suggested as a scriptural prototype of the novena, but this devotion was first introduced not as an exercise preparatory to an event of great spiritual significance but as the observance of a period of mourning. The Greeks and the Romans, as well as other peoples of antiquity, were accustomed to observe nine days of mourning (*novendialia*), with a special feast on the ninth day, after a death or burial. This practice was adopted by Christians, but with Christian rather than pagan forms of observance. Nevertheless, the pagan origin of the custom gave offense to some, and protest eventually led to the substitution of a seven-day mourning period, seven being the number of the days of the Christian week and therefore considered to have greater religious significance. However, a vestige of the earlier practice remains in the *novendialia,* or Pope's Novena, still observed after the death of a supreme pontiff. In the Middle Ages a like period was often observed after the death of other wealthy or noble individuals, but except for the novenas of Masses and prayers for the departed, this custom has fallen into disuse.

The devotional novena for the purpose of special prayers to gain some needed grace or to prepare for the celebration of some special occasion with greater solemnity made its appearance in the early Middle Ages. It began in France and Spain with a preparation of nine days for the feast of Christmas, the number nine representing the months Our Lord had spent in His mother's womb. The O ANTIPHONS that begin on December 17 are probably a vestigial survival in the liturgy of this ancient practice.

Preparatory novenas of this kind came in time to be celebrated in connection with other occasions, especially the feasts of popular saints or of Our Lady, and they were often undertaken publicly and with much external solemnity. Because Our Lady under various titles and the saints were popularly esteemed for their intercessory powers with respect to particular kinds of blessings, novenas came to be times of special supplication in which the devout sought favors such as could be hoped for through the intercession of the saints who were honored. Very often the favor sought was the recovery of health, and in times when medical science had little comfort or hope to offer those afflicted with disease it is understandable that people should turn so readily to heavenly intercessors for healing and protection.

Novenas have been attacked as superstitious, partly because of the peculiar efficacy the practice seems to attach to the number nine, and partly because of the many extraordinary and even miraculous effects with which some novenas have been credited. No doubt the possibility of superstitious abuse exists and it should be guarded against, and no other effectiveness should be attributed to novena prayers as such than is attributable to devout prayer earnestly and perseveringly undertaken in other forms. There is nothing doctrinally objectionable in the idea of a novena; on the contrary, it is a practice that can be most serviceable to true devotion and piety. Perseverance and constancy are qualities of all good prayer, and it is well that some devotional practices should give special emphasis to them by requiring repetition on successive days over a more or less extended period of time, for this manifests and stimulates the worshiper's earnestness and fervor. That one should pray more confidently and hope for special graces by the use of such means is not unreasonable.

The novena grew out of popular piety, and it was not until the 19th century that the Church recommended the practice by the granting of indulgences.

Bibliography: J. HILGERS, *The Catholic Encyclopedia*, ed. C. G. HERBERMANN et al., 16 v. (New York 1907–14) 11:141–144. F. BERINGER, *Die Ablässe, ihr Wesen und Gebrauch,* 2 v. (Paderborn 1921) 1:638–644. *Enchiridion indulgentiarum* (Rome 1952).

[P. K. MEAGHER]

NOVITIATE, CANON LAW OF

The novitiate is the required probationary period prior to profession of vows in a religious institute during which time the aspiring religious is initiated into the life of the particular institute and his or her call (*vocation*) to this institute verified. Because of the importance of novitiate for religious life, its major components and conditions are prescribed by the universal law of the Church (e.g., *Codex iuris canonicis, Codex canonum ecclesiarium orientalium,* and *Potissimum institutioni,* CICLSAL, March 2, 1990, *AAS* 82 (1990) 472–532); the proper law of each institute specifies and supplements the universal law. A period of probation is also required of candidates prior to incorporation into a secular institute or society of apostolic life; such groups, however, are not bound by the norms that follow as these groups are free to determine for themselves the manner and duration of the probationary period.

A period of probation prior to full membership has characterized religious life since its earliest expressions in the post-Apostolic era, but it was the Council of Trent (1545–63 at Sess. 24, cap. 15) that first mandated a one-year period of novitiate for all religious as a requirement for a valid subsequent profession. Current universal law for Latin rite institutes cites the minimum time as 12 months.

This article will consider the novitiate under five main headings: establishment of the novitiate, admission to the novitiate, the novitiate program, duration of the novitiate, and the termination or conclusion of the novitiate. The article will also highlight some significant differences between canonical norms governing Latin rite institutes and those governing institutes of the Eastern rites.

Establishment of Novitiate. In addition to being a period of time, the novitiate also refers to the designated place where the probationary period takes place. By means of a written decree the general or highest superior of the institute authorizes the establishment, transfer to another location, and suppression of a novitiate house. For Latin rite institutes the superior must have the consent of the council to act; for Eastern rite institutes the advice of the council suffices. If the novitiate is to be established as a new foundation, i.e., where no formally established house of the institute exists, the diocesan bishop of the place of establishment must also give written consent. Contrary to prior, more restrictive legisla-

Novices singing hymns. (©Ted Streshinsky/CORBIS)

tion, the highest superior in Latin rite institutes has authority to establish as many novitiates as are warranted, even more than one in a province if necessary. Independent monasteries, by their nature, have a right to their own novitiates. Over the last century, however, independent monasteries of similar traditions have been encouraged to form federations (Pius XII, *Sponsa Christi AAS* 43 (1951) 5–24; *Perfectae Caritatis* 22, *AAS* 58 (1966) 702–712); where such federations exist a single novitiate common to all monasteries of the given federation may be established.

The novitiate or period of probation generally takes place in a location designated by formal decree as the novitiate house. Several exceptions, however, are possible. In the first, the general superior, with consent of the council for Latin rite institutes and after consulting the council for Eastern rite institutes, may for serious reason permit an individual novice to make the novitiate in another house of the institute under the direction of another religious who assumes the role of director. The second exception, emphasizing the novitiate *community* rather than the novitiate *building,* allows for novices as a group to be assigned by the major superior (not necessarily the general superior) to another house of the institute for a

certain period. The third exception, articulated only for Latin rite institutes (*Codex iuris canonicis* 648), allows for novices in apostolic institutes whose formation program provides for apostolic experiences to reside outside the novitiate house during such assignments.

Admission to the Novitiate. Life in a religious institute begins with the novitiate and only those suitably prepared and properly disposed should be admitted. The right to admit candidates to the novitiate belongs to that major superior so designated according to the institute's proper law. For valid admission to the novitiate of a Latin rite institute it is required that a candidate be: (1) at least 17 years of age; (2) not bound by an existing marriage bond; (3) not bound by vows or other sacred bonds in another institute of consecrated life or society of apostolic life; and (4) forthcoming about, i.e, not concealing, any prior membership in another institute of consecrated life or society of apostolic life. In addition, to admit a person to the novitiate is a juridic act and the personal dispositions necessary for placing a valid juridic pertain (*Codex iuris canonicis* 125). Therefore, both the candidate seeking admission and the admitting superior must be free from constraint and admission is invalid if either party acts under force, grave fear, or malice.

Requirements for valid admission to the novitiate in an Eastern rite institute are identical to those for a Latin rite institute with the following exceptions: (1) persons under certain canonical penalty or under legitimate threat of canonical penalty are barred; (2) monastic candidates must be 18 years of age; and (3) concealing one's prior membership in another institute or society of apostolic life is not an invalidating impediment.

In addition to the requirements for validity identified in universal law, the proper law of individual institutes may establish other requirements for valid admission or other conditions. Should an invalidating impediment be detected during the screening process, either a dispensation must be obtained or the admission be refused or deferred. Also should a member of one *sui juris* rite seek admission to an institute of another rite, an indult of accommodation must first be obtained from the Apostolic See.

Superiors have wide discretion in ascertaining the suitability of candidates for their particular institute. Suitability regarding health, character, and maturity may be established through a combination of personal self-disclosure on the part of the candidate, documentary evidence and further, even secret, inquiries on the part of the superior. Before admission a candidate must present proof of baptism, confirmation, and free status. If the candidate for admission is a cleric, the superior is first to consult with the cleric's proper ordinary. If the candidate had previously been in a seminary or in another institute of consecrated life or society of apostolic life, testimony from the former seminary rector or major superior is required. Some assessment of financial solvency is also expected since those burdened by debts that they cannot repay may not be admitted. Other documentation might include medical evaluations, educational transcripts, proof of military service or immigration status, and letters of recommendation. In addition to these requirements for licit admission common to all, candidates for admission to an Eastern rite institute must also be free of family obligations (*Codex canonum ecclesiarium orientalium* 452). In seeking the necessary information to arrive at a determination about admission, superiors of Latin rite institutes are admonished to balance the demands of canon 220, avoiding damage to the good reputation of both the candidate and the institute and respecting the candidate's right to privacy.

Admission to the novitiate begins with the celebration of the Rite of Entrance for those in Latin rite institutes and with ceremonies determined in the proper law for Eastern rite institutes.

Novitiate Program. The novitiate is a probationary period, a designated place, and a process. The intense, interactive yet individualized process deepens the novice's lifelong configuration to Christ begun at baptism. The initiation that characterizes the novitiate goes far beyond simple instruction, incorporating physical, moral, intellectual, affective, and especially spiritual dimensions. (*Potissimum institutioni,* March 2, 1990, *AAS* 82 (1990) 472–532). It includes formation in the cultivation of human and Christian virtues; prayer; asceticism; liturgy; the teachings of the Church; and the history, life, and rule of the particular institute. As mature and responsible persons the novices share responsibility for their own formation and are expected to collaborate actively with the opportunities and graces of this process.

The novice director, a perpetually professed member of the institute legitimately designated according to proper law, functions directly under the authority of the major superior. The formation plan serves as a guide for the director, and for any persons assigned to assist the director, in discerning and testing the vocation of the novices and leading them gradually into the full life of the institute. The novitiate period is reserved solely for formation and, therefore, all activities in which the novices are involved should directly serve this purpose. Similarly, the novice director should be freed from other responsibilities that could interfere with this primary and critical role.

Duration of the Novitiate. For Latin rite institutes a minimum of 12 months is required for validity of the novitiate, but the institute's proper law may require up to two years. *Apostolic* institutes of the Latin rite also have the option of requiring, in addition to the minimum of 12 months in the novitiate itself, one or more apostolic experiences outside the novitiate during this probationary period. The duration of the novitiate for religious institutes belonging to the Eastern Catholic churches is similar to that of the Latin rite with the exception of Eastern rite monasteries with no temporary profession; for these monasteries a full and continuous three-year novitiate is required (*Codex canonum ecclesiarium orientalium* 457).

Absence from the novitiate is carefully regulated to protect this foundational period of formation, ensuring that the novice has sufficient freedom, accountability, and continuity to accomplish its ends. Current legislation greatly simplifies the question of absence from or interruption of the novitiate. During the basic required 12 months any absence from the designated novitiate house or community that lasts more than three months, from whatever cause, either continuous or interrupted, renders the novitiate invalid. An absence that lasts more than 15 days must be made up.

Under certain limited circumstances the minimum requirement of universal law (12 months) or of the particular institute (which may be up to two years) may be shortened. With the permission of the competent major superior, i.e., either the general superior or another major superior according to the proper law, first profession may be anticipated by up to 15 days. In the extraordinary situation of a novice in danger of death, the novice may be admitted to profession even absent the required time of novitiate. Should the novice recover the vows cease to bind and the novitiate is continued with profession being made in the usual manner.

Termination or Conclusion of the Novitiate. At any time during the novitiate a novice may freely leave the institute. Similarly, at any time during the novitiate the competent authority may freely dismiss a novice. At the completion of the prescribed novitiate one of three eventualities occurs: (1) if judged suitable, the novice may be admitted to temporary profession; (2) if judged unsuitable for profession, the novice is to be dismissed; or, (3) if there remains a question regarding suitability, the major superior has the option if the proper law permits, of extending the novitiate in a particular case for up to six additional months. For Eastern rite monastics an extension of up to one year is permitted.

[R. SMITH]

NOW

Now, in its secondary and common signification, a slice of time near the present, just gone or immediately impending. It primarily signifies the limit of the timeline or the punctiform divisor distinguishing, but linking, past and future. Because INDIVISIBLE, the now is essentially imperceptible. We conceive it directly, but implicity, when we define TIME, and by thinking away the divisibility of time, we see that the now is indivisible. A complex proportional resemblance leads to its definition. As time is related to MOTION, so the now is related to mobile being. The alternant now, the temporal correlate of mobile being, is formally other in the diverse phases of time: the now is formally alternant qual alternant. A second and similar definition reads: the now is the number of mobile being; i.e., the alternant now is the formal pluralization of the mobile along the timeline. Because invariant and formal, the now measures times as the arithmetical one measures number.

[J. M. QUINN]

NOWOGRÓDEK, MARTYRS OF, BB.

Also called Sister Maria Stella Adela Mardosewicz and ten Companions; martyrs and members of the Congregation of the Holy Family of Nazareth; S. Maria Stella, b. Ciasnówka, Nieświesk, Poland, Dec. 14, 1888; d. Nowogródek, eastern Poland (now Navahradak, Belarus), Aug. 1, 1943; beatified in Rome by John Paul II, March 5, 2000.

In 1929, Bishop Zygmunt Łoziński invited the Sisters of the Holy Family of Nazareth to undertake the education of Nowogródek's children and care for the Church of the Transfiguration (Biała Fara). There they established (1931) a school. During the Russian occupation (Sept. 1, 1939, to June 21, 1941), the sisters were barred from their convent and school. When German forces ousted the Russians, the sisters again donned their habits and returned to their ruined Convent of Christ the King.

On July 18, 1943, the Nazis arrested and sentenced 120 citizens to execution by firing squad. The sisters were dedicated to serving families and volunteered to exchange places with the fathers of children. The male hostages were released to their families, although some were interned later in German concentration camps. The second time they offered themselves in place of the only remaining priest in the region. On July 31, 1943 the Gestapo ordered S. Maria Stella and 11 of the 12 sisters (one was working in the hospital at the time of the arrest) to appear at the Gestapo headquarters. Without investigation, they were sentenced to death. The order was carried out the next day, when they were executed in the woods five kilometers from Nowogródek. Initially the martyrs were buried in a common grave. On March 19, 1945, Sister Maria Margaret Malgorzata, the only survivor of the community, oversaw the translation of their mortal remains to the Church of the Transfiguration.

Their process was officially opened in 1991. On June 28, 1999, in addition to the superior, S. Maria Stella, the following were declared martyrs: Paulina Borowik (S. Maria Felicyta, b. Rudna, Lublin, Aug. 30, 1905); Józefa Chrobot (S. Maria Kanuta, b. Raczyn, Wielun, May 22, 1896); Helena Cierpka (S. Maria Gwidona, b. Granowiec, Odalanów, Apr. 11, 1900); Eleanora Jóźwik (S. Maria Daniela, b. Poizdow, Poldlasie, Jan. 25, 1895); Anna Kokołowicz (Maria Rajmunda, b. Barwasniszk, Vilnius, Aug. 24, 1892); Eugenia Mackiewicz (Maria Kanizja, b. Suwałki, Sept. 9, 1903); Leokadia Matuszewska (Maria Heliodora, b. Stara Huta, Świecie, Feb. 8, 1906); Weronika (Veronica) Narmontowicz (Maria Boromea, b. Wiercieliszki, Grodno, Dec. 18, 1916); Julia Rapiej (Maria Sergia, b. Rogoczyn, Augustów, Aug. 18, 1900); and Jadwiga (Hedwig) Żak (Maria Imelda, b. Oświęcim, Dec. 29, 1892).

At their beatification Pope John Paul II thanked the martyrs for their witness of love, their example of Christian heroism, and their trust in the power of the Holy Spirit: ''You are the greatest inheritance of the Congregation of the Holy Family of Nazareth. You are the inheritance of the whole Church of Christ forever.'' They are patrons of Christian teaching.

Feast: August 1.

Bibliography: A. ZIENKIEWICZ, *No Greater Love* (Pulaski, Wisc. 1968). *L'Osservatore Romano,* English edition, no. 10 (8 March 2000): 3, 9.

[K. I. RABENSTEIN]

NOYES, ALFRED

English poet, critic, and biographer; b. Wolverhampton, Sept. 16, 1880; d. Isle of Wight, June 28, 1958. He was educated at Exeter College, Oxford. He married an American, Garnett Daniels, in 1907; a year after her death (1926) he married Mary Weld-Blundell. His first book of poems, *Loom of Years* (1902), appeared when he was still at Exeter, and its warm reception determined him to devote his life to poetry. He varied this career with lecturing in the U.S. (1913) and teaching at Columbia University and Princeton (1914–23), with the exception of 1916, when he served in the British Foreign Office. For some years before his death he was afflicted with blindness.

Noyes was a conservative in politics and a traditionalist in poetry. His study of English patriotism led him to devote much of his early verse to Drake and other Elizabethans (e.g., in *The Golden Hynde,* 1908), a preoccupation that gave his early work an inevitable anti-Catholic tinge. His thought soon after began to center on the need for a *philosophia perennis* as the basis of civilization, and in his poetic trilogy *Torchbearers* (1925) he showed how this philosophy had been passed along by the great thinkers of every generation. From this originally secular line of thought he came to see that the supreme expression of this philosophy was to be found in the Catholic Church. He became a Catholic in 1927. His *Unknown God* (1934) details his intellectual pilgrimage to Rome. His novel *No Other Man* (1940) was prophetic in dealing with the holocaust wrought by a secret weapon. From his numerous volumes of poetry, *Tales of the Mermaid Tavern* (1913) and *Poems of the New World* (1943) may be singled out as displaying his earlier and later styles. *Pageant of Letters* (1940), essays on English poets from Chaucer to Alice Meynell, is representative of his best literary criticism.

His biography of Voltaire (1936) was delated to the Holy Office of the Vatican and a correction was demanded; Noyes's critic was under the impression that the atheistic views commonly attributed to Voltaire were condoned by the author. Noyes had no trouble in showing that his intention had been to prove that Voltaire held no

Wall painting of St. Peter from Ramses II's temple at Wadi es-Sebua, Egypt. (©Roger Wood/CORBIS)

such views. His poetry (collected edition, New York 1947) is rather old-fashioned in style, but the wide historical perspective he brought to his work marks him as a writer of considerable stature.

Bibliography: D. STANFORD, ''Alfred Noyes 1880–1958,'' *Catholic World* 188 (1959) 297–301. J. E. TOBIN, ''Alfred Noyes: A Corrected Bibliography,'' *Catholic Library World* 15 (March 1944) 181–184, 189.

[C. HOLLIS]

NUBIA

Nubia is the section of the Nile Valley from the first cataract to the Sennar parallel. The conversion of Nubia to Christianity occurred in the 6th century, when there were close relations between the Byzantine Empire and the Christian state of Axum to the south. The region of Nubia was controlled by three kingdoms: Nobatia, in lower Nubia; Makuria, or Mukurra, in the Dongola region; and Alwa, or Alodia, with its capital near the present city of Khartoum. The inhabitants spoke Nubian, and seem to have pushed into the Nile Valley from Kordofan and Darfur a few centuries earlier. They were pagans and worshipped the gods of ancient Egypt and Meroe.

Conversion to Christianity. Christianity was brought to Nubia prior to the official conversion of the people by Monophysite refugees from Syria who had settled near Philae after the Council of CHALCEDON (451), and by a few Axumite followers of JULIAN OF HALICAR-

NASSUS, who are reported to have been living in Alwa. Most historians agree that the first missions to Nubia, and especially to Nobatia, were directed from Constantinople rather than from Egypt or Ethiopia. According to John, bishop of Ephesus, Nobatia was formally converted to Monophysite Christianity c. 543 by a mission led by Theodore, bishop of Philae, and Julian, a priest sent from Constantinople by Empress Theodora (1). Although John was a contemporary of these events, he was a Monophysite and is considered biased by some scholars; they prefer the account of Eutychius, Patriarch of Alexandria (933 to 940), who claims that Nobatia was orthodox prior to the 8th century.

According to JOHN OF BICLARO, Makuria was converted to orthodox Christianity in 569, and the same year Longinus, a Monophysite, was invited by the king of Alwa to convert his kingdom. This happened soon after the pagan temples at Philae were closed by JUSTINIAN I at the expiration of a 100-year treaty that left them open for the pagan peoples to the south. The Nubian kings seem to have accepted Christianity in part to promote good relations with Byzantium and Axum, and in part out of admiration for Byzantine culture. Pagan customs seem to have lasted until the 7th century, although Byzantine influence in art, literature, politics, and religion remained strong during the Christian period. Officials bore titles used at the imperial court and Christian names of Byzantine origin were common. Among the educated, Greek appears to have been spoken as late as the 12th century.

Muslim Invasions. In 640 Nobatia repelled a Muslim invasion led by Abdullah ibn Saad, governor of Egypt, but in 651 an Arab force reached the capital of Makuria. Because of the spirited resistance of the Nubians, the Arabs did not hold the country, but concluded a peace treaty that had important provisions concerning trade. By 710 the kingdoms of Nobatia and Makuria had been united to form a single kingdom with its capital at Old Dongola. The influence of Dongola reached as far west as Darfur, where the ruins of a Christian church appear to exist at Ain Farah.

In the 8th century, the Nubian Church was wholly Monophysite. At that time the Arabs, who preferred Coptic Christianity to the orthodox discipline of Constantinople, interfered with the appointment of new orthodox bishops. However, funerary inscriptions occurring as late as the 12th century are written in Greek and bear prayers from the Byzantine Euchologia. Between 850 and 1100 both Alwa and Dongola apparently prospered. Each country was divided into a number of bishoprics; those south of Aswan had cathedrals at Dakka, Qasr Ibrim, and Faras. Excavations in the cathedral at Faras have brought to light a list of 27 bishops who held office there, as well as a vast number of wall paintings showing kings, bishops, and religious scenes that are in an unparalleled state of preservation. Churches were common throughout the region and many are still standing.

Islamization. For a time the Nubians controlled much of upper Egypt. The presence of Christian refugees and Egyptian priests probably accounts for the prevalence of Coptic as a written language. Religious books were written also in Old Nubian. During this period, Nubians appear to have been free to settle in upper Egypt, while Muslims were free to purchase land in Nubia. By the 10th century Islam was widespread in the northern part of lower Nubia. In the 12th century Egyptian invasions and Bedouin attacks brought an end to Christian culture in most of lower Nubia, and led to the concentration of the population in fortified communities farther south. The architecture of some of the forts is said to reflect crusader influence. Christian power in Dongola was weakened by disputes over the succession to the throne, and in 1315 Kerenbes, the last Christian king, was deposed and removed to Cairo. During the rest of the century, the Beni Kanz, Hawara, and other Arab tribes rapidly introduced Islam to the Dongola region. The kingdom of Alwa was overrun by Muslims c. 1500 and the Nubian language gave way to Arabic.

Recent discoveries show that the Christian religion persisted for a time in many communities in lower Nubia, as it still does in upper Egypt. A scroll found in a bishop's tomb at Qasr Ibrim records his appointment to that office in 1372. In Ethiopia, Francisco Alvares heard reports that suggested the survival of Christianity in the Dongola region c. 1525; and a colony of Nubian Christians is said to have been living near Esna, in upper Egypt, in the 1630s. In the last century, the Nubians living at Tafa, near Aswan, took pride in their descent from the Christians of medieval Nubia.

Bibliography: U. MONNERET DE VILLARD, *Storia della Nubia cristiana* (*Orientalia Christiana Analecta,* (Rome 1935–). L. P. KIRWAN, *The Oxford University Excavations at Firka* (Oxford 1939) 49–51. G. S. MILEHAM, *Churches in Lower Nubia* (Philadelphia 1910). The UNESCO Campaign to Save the Monuments of Nubia has produced new information about Christian Nubia that appears in *Kush* (Kharloum 1953–), *The Journal of the Sudan Antiquities Service,* and in the *The Journal of Egyptian Archaeology* (London 1914–).

[B. G. TRIGGER]

NUDITY

Clothing in one form or another is universal in all but a few human societies. Nakedness among men is found, for example, among some split tribal groups in the Sudan and on the Zambezi River, in both cases as a survival of ancient Negrito practice. Even in these cases women wear an apron of leaves around the middle of their bodies, and not merely at menstruation. Where dress is normal, exhibitionist acts of nakedness often have a magical meaning. In the Norse myth of Loki and in the Japanese myth of Amaterasu, such exposure takes on a cynical aspect and is intended either to cause shock or to arouse joy. The Baubo motif among the Greeks is to be interpreted as a form of fertility magic. In the realm of magic, nakedness wards off a spell or other harmful form of magic, compels love, and gives strength to one's own practice of witchcraft and conjuring. Complete disrobing at the questioning of an oracle, in lustrations, and in temple incubation was a mark of reverence. Eschatological nakedness [see *Anthropos* 58 (1963) 579] and the ancient Arab practice of offering sacrifice naked, because of the dirt on clothes, is primarily religious in character, while the nakedness of the "air-clothed" Jainist monks is based rather on asceticism. Naked dances are connected with spirits (as in New Guinea) but also with fertility divinities.

In the Bible. In OT history the cult practice of sacred nudity does not appear as part of Israel's religion; rather, it is expressly forbidden, and exposure of one's nakedness is looked upon as shameful. In the NT, nakedness appears most significantly in a metaphorical sense in contexts commanding the Christian to clothe the "naked," i.e., the "ill-clad."

Certain pagan religions of the ancient Near East practiced sacred, ritual nakedness. Professional prophets and dervishes would work themselves into a frenzy at the shrine of a god, slashing their limbs (cf. Dt 14.1), mumbling unintelligible sounds, and whirling their naked bodies before idols in order to induce favors from the gods. There is no indisputable case of Israelite Prophets' presenting themselves stark naked before Yahweh, for the ethical spirit of the OT insisted on the personal decency of the one who was to approach Yahweh (Ex 20.26). The closest Israelite parallel to the sacred nudity of pagan prophets is that of Saul, who "stripped himself also of his garments and prophesied with the rest before Samuel and lay down naked all that day and night" (1 Sm 19.24). It is quite probable that this "nakedness" consisted in wearing only a loincloth; David is spoken of as dancing naked before the ark, even though he was girt with a linen EPHOD (2 Sm 6.14, 20). The Israelites with their high regard for personal modesty considered exposure of one's nakedness a disgrace and a shame (Gn 9.22–27), which was inflicted as punishment on prisoners of war (Is 47.3) and women guilty of adultery (Jer 13.26). Various Hebrew words for naked often mean partly clothed (Dt 28.48; Lam 4.21; 2 Chr 28.15; Ez 18.7, 16).

The Greek γυμνός means both completely naked and poorly clothed, and it is also used figuratively in the meaning of bare, exposed, and uncovered. In the episode of the young man fleeing the scene of Jesus' arrest (Mk 14.52), and perhaps in the narrative of Acts in which the evil spirit strips the Jewish exorcists (19.6), the word means "completely naked." When John writes that Peter was "stripped" while fishing (21.7), the meaning is that he was without his outer garment and was merely wearing a sleeveless blouse or smock. The Christian duty of clothing the naked refers to the obligation of helping those who are poorly clothed (Mt 25.36, 38, 43–44; Jas 2.15). In Heb 4.13 "naked" conveys the idea that all things are exposed to the eyes of God. In another sense the soul is said to be naked in the state between death and resurrection, since it is stripped of the body, which is its natural covering (2 Cor 5.3), and the "bare" grain of wheat is naked and unclothed before reaching its full growth (1 Cor 15.37). The words naked in 1 Cor 4.11 and nakedness in Rom 8.35 and 2 Cor 11.27 refer to extreme misery and destitution.

[A. CLOSS/F. J. MONTALBANO]

NUGENT, FRANCIS

Capuchin friar, agent of the Counter-Reformation, and founder of the Capuchins in Ireland and Germany; b. Ballebranagh, County Meath, Ireland, 1569; d. Charleville, France, May 18, 1635. Nugent's father was Sir Edward Nugent; his mother, Margaret O'Connor, was of the princely O'Connor Faly. At the age of 13, Nugent was sent to the Scots-Irish college at Pont-à-Mousson in Lorraine. From there he went to Louvain, secured his M.A., and in 1590 was appointed to lecture in philosophy in the University. He joined the Capuchins at Brussels on Oct. 4, 1591, the first Irishman to do so. While he was still a deacon, his preaching at Valenciennes (September 1594) brought him fame; as a result, a Capuchin friary was founded there. He became prominent in the pre-Quietist mystical movement in the Low Countries and was delated to Rome. Nugent, twice tried by the Inquisition in Rome, defended himself successfully and earned the commendation of Pope Clement VIII, who presided in August 1600 at the second trial. Nugent served in France for five years as guardian and professor of theology—Friar Joseph of Paris (François LE CLERC DU TREMBLAY) was one of his pupils.

He returned to the Low Countries (1605), where he held office continuously as guardian and definitor of the Belgian province. When in Rome as delegate for a general chapter of his order, he secured a papal brief, on May 29, 1608, from Paul V, authorizing a Capuchin mission to "England, Scotland, and Ireland." Before he could realize this project, he was appointed commissary general of the Capuchin mission to the Rhineland, Aug. 28, 1610. Under his guidance the Capuchins became a powerful religious force in Germany, particularly through his Confraternity of Our Lord's Passion. Because of internal disputes among the Capuchins, he was dismissed from his post, and in March 1615 was given a foundation at Charleville as a center for the mission to Ireland. Nugent also directed the Capuchin missionaries in England and Scotland, but in a minor capacity.

During 1623 and 1624 he negotiated with James I of England for religious toleration for English and Irish Catholics. He visited England and Ireland secretly during 1624 and 1625 and went to Rome as agent for the Irish hierarchy. A long, drawn-out dispute with the Walloon Capuchins came to a head in 1631 when he opposed a Walloon visitator sent to Charleville by the Capuchin vicar-general. Nugent was deposed from office in January 1632 and lived in retirement at Charleville until his death. Though intellectually powerful, he was primarily a man of action, founding Capuchin houses at Valenciennes (1595), Courtrai (1610), Cologne (1611), Charleville (1615), and Dublin (1624). Courageous, tenacious, and resourceful, he was a leader of men, but often too demanding; he had the defects and virtues of the pioneer.

Bibliography: Most studies have been euglogistic and uncritical. Exceptions are: A. DASSEVILLE, "Francis Nugent," *Round Table of Franciscan Research* 15 (1950) 103–117. P. HILDEBRAND, "Franciscus Nugent," *Franciscaansch Leven* 11 (1928) 21–28; 21 (1938) 301–312, 339–346; *De Kapucijnen in de Nederlanden en het prinsbisdom Luik,* 4 v. (Antwerp 1945–48) 1:146–151, 274–287; 3:13–29. F. X. MARTIN, "Sources for the History of the Irish Capuchins," *Collectanea Franciscana* 26 (1956) 67–69; *Friar Nugent* (Rome 1962). A. TEETAERT, *Dictionnaire de théologie catholique,* ed. A. VACANT et al. (Paris 1903–50) 11.1:849–850.

[F. X. MARTIN]

NUMBERS, BOOK OF

The fourth book of the Pentateuch bears the Hebrew title *bammidbār,* "in the wilderness," recalling the traditional 40 years of Israelite wandering in the desert between Egypt and the Promised Land. In English Bibles the name is derived ultimately from the title in the Septuagint (LXX), Ἀριθμοί, suggesting the book's interest in the census and other matters calling for arithmetical precision, such as the division of the land. [*See* CENSUS (IN THE BIBLE)]. This article covers the sources and literary form, authorship, and division of the book.

Sources and Literary Form. The Book of Numbers incorporates a mass of legal, statistical, and liturgical material into the historical narrative of events that took place between Sinai and the last days at Moab. Since the thrust of the account is toward the permanent establishment of norms—sanctioned by Mosaic authority—within the community, the book does not convey the absorbing concern with the acts of God in history that are found in the Deuteronomic (*see* DEUTERONOMISTS) and Yahwistic (*see* YAHWIST) traditions.

The merged Yahwistic and Elohistic (*see* ELOHIST) traditions are found in the book, but the principal source is the Priestly Tradition (*see* PRIESTLY WRITERS, PENTATEUCHAL) that has contributed almost three-quarters of the material and has given the final form and spirit to the work.

In assessing the historical value of this heterogeneous assemblage, whose origin is very complex, two extremes should be avoided: It should not be expected that the book give a detailed, purely factual, and documentary description of events; it should not be judged according to the standards and ideals of modern historical writing. On the other hand, to consider the historical events irrelevant would falsify the author's perspective. For him a religious message was important because it implied an impact of God in time and space, the irruption of God into man's history. In addition, historical and archeological studies have enormously enhanced respect for the basic historicity of the Israelite traditions in the Book of Numbers and elsewhere in the OT.

Authorship. The Book of Numbers is a compilation of material from different strata of traditions and has no clearly recognizable unity. Jewish and Christian tradition has ascribed the book to MOSES, but this must be understood only according to contemporary knowledge of what composition and authorship meant in Old Testament times. It may be said that the book was composed in the spirit of Moses and of material that in part goes back to Moses himself. In its final form, the Book of Numbers is post-Exilic.

Division. The absence of any logical and consistent plan in the arrangement of its contents makes it difficult to provide an adequate division of the book. However, selecting the geographical factor as the basis of division, the work may be divided into three parts: The first section covers the last days at Sinai (1.1–10.10). The material is from the Priestly Tradition and is concerned mostly with legal and ecclesiastical affairs. The second division concerns the journey from Sinai to Moab (10.11–22.1). This period includes the sojourn at Cades, as well as the story of Israel's abortive attempt to enter the Promised Land from the south. The last section is concerned with the events on the Plains of Moab (22.2–36.13). The BALAAM cycle dominates this section, which includes also the transfer of leadership to Josue [*see* JOSHUA, SON OF NUN], directions concerning the occupation of Canaan, and miscellaneous laws from different periods. As the book ends, the Israelites are prepared to cross the Jordan and launch the assault on Canaan.

Bibliography: H. CAZELLES, *Les Nombres* (BJ 4; Paris 1952). G. B. GRAY, *Numbers* (ICC; New York 1903). B. D. EARDMANS, ''The Composition of Numbers,'' *Oudtestamentische Studien* 6 (1949) 101–216. S. R. DRIVER, *Introduction to the Literature of the Old Testament* (New York 1905). G. E. WRIGHT and R. H. FULLER, *The Book of the Acts of God* (Garden City, N.Y. 1957). I. FRANSEN ''Du désert à la terre promise. Les plus anciens récits du livre des Nombres,'' *Bible et vie chrétienne* 5 (1954) 68–84.

[F. L. MORIARTY]

NUMEROLOGY

This article is concerned with the employment of numbers in a symbolic religious, magicoreligious, and philosophical sense. One or the other form of symbolic usage is found almost universally, but the explanation for the choice of some numbers as sacred or magical is not always clear, being lost in the remote past of the cultures involved. In practice, it is often difficult to separate the religious, magical, and philosophical usages, especially in the higher cultures or civilizations. Accordingly, it will be convenient to group the various usages under each number treated. Special attention is given to number symbolism in the ancient Near East and the Greco-Roman world.

Numbers One to Six. The number one is confined principally to religiophilosophical use. It represents the monad of the Pythagoreans and the One of Plato and the Neoplatonists.

The number two pairs or symbolizes opposites that have a clear relation with one another in ancient mythology and religion: right hand-left hand, earth-heaven, sun-moon, day-night, Ahura Mazda-Ahriman in Persian religion, *yang-yin* in Chinese thought. Whereas one is regarded as a male number, two is considered female.

The Number Three. The number three is one of the oldest and most widespread of all sacred or symbolical numbers, playing an equally important role in religion, magic, and philosophy. The divine family of father, mother, and child is already represented in the earliest strata of prehistoric Jericho and is well known from the Egyptian group of Osiris, Isis, and Horus. Divine triads—such as Indic Brahma, Vishnu, and Siva; Greek Zeus, Athena, and Apollo; Roman Jupiter, Juno, and Minerva, and Jupiter, Mars, and Quirinus—are common. Lesser divinities are likewise widely found in triads: the three Fates, the three Graces, the three Furies, and similar

groups in Teutonic and Finno-Ugric mythology. Three-headed gods are found from ancient Ireland to India. The Babylonians, Greeks, and Hindus all distinguished three worlds—Heaven, Earth, and Lower World, or Heaven, Earth, and Water. In sacrificial ritual the Romans offered a joint sacrifice of a pig, a sheep, and a bull; and in most ancient rituals there were threefold prayers, threefold invocations of the dead, and sacred festivals of three days' duration. There was a similar threefold repetition of magic formulas or incantations. The triangle was regarded by the Greeks as a perfect figure and had a central place in Greek mathematics and mystic symbolism. Time was thought of in terms of morning, midday, and evening and of past, present, and future. It should be observed also that there was a close relationship between three and nine, and groups of nine things are very often to be explained as a mere tripling of groups of three.

The Number Four. The number four was connected very early with the four phases of the moon, the four seasons, the four points of the compass, and the geometrical figure of the square. It was a symbol of completeness and perfection. Among the Greeks, four marked the birthdate of Hermes. The Ionic philosophers identified four elements, and Pythagoras adopted four as a symbol of justice. Later, four cardinal virtues were stressed by Plato; and Simonides, Plato, and Aristotle spoke of ''the four-square man.'' The Greeks, the post-Vedic literature, and the Zoroastrians all referred to four ages or periods of the world. The Romans used fourfold prayers as well as threefold ones (see Ovid, *Fasti* 4:778). The number four, especially as embodied in the square, has had an important place in the history of magic.

The Numbers Five and Six. The number five had a natural significance from the five fingers. It was the number of the Babylonian goddess Ishtar, whose symbol, the pentagram, or five-pointed star, was regarded as a magic protection against evils. The Romans offered certain sacrifices at five-year intervals, and the censor held office for a five-year term. In Manichaeism there were five Archons and five Aeons. In Chinese tradition five is a lucky number. The number six represents the macrocosm and is symbolized by the six-pointed star, a combination of two triangles.

Numbers Seven to Ten. The number seven occupies the supreme place in Babylonian religion and astrology. Its use and symbolism were disseminated widely eastward and westward from Mesopotamia. The Babylonians recognized seven planets: Jupiter, Venus, Saturn, Mars, Mercury, the Sun, and the Moon. Each day of their seven-day ''week'' was sacred to one of these celestial bodies. The four phases of the moon were comprised in a period of 4 × 7 days. The Babylonian underworld had seven divisions, and the temple towers, or ziggurats, had to have seven stories. Among the Greeks, Apollo's birthday was celebrated on the 7th of the month. In Old Persian religion there were seven Amesha Spentas, and the Rigveda speaks of seven regions and seven ponds and of the god Agni (Fire) as having seven tongues and seven wives. The tripling of seven (21) is very common in Indic literature. In Buddhism seven is as important as eight. It is to be noted that seven itself is the sum of the two sacred numbers three and four.

Numbers Eight and Nine. The number eight symbolizes perfection. The Elamites had eight heavens. Of greater importance is the use of eight in Buddhism to indicate the eightfold path that is central in its teaching. The number nine, so often used as a tripling of groups indicated by three, was much favored by the Celts, Germans, and Finno-Ugric peoples. The Greeks had nine Muses beside the three Fates and three Graces. The Chinese regarded nine as a symbol of perfection. The pagoda of nine stories was modeled on the Chinese conception of heaven.

The Number 10. The number ten, the combined total of the fingers, symbolized perfection and wisdom. In Pythagoreanism the all-important Τετρακτύς was constituted by the sum of 1+2+3+4, arranged in a series of dots with the monad forming the apex of an isosceles triangle. The number ten was significant also in the Hermetic literature. It can be resolved, furthermore, as 7+3, 6+4, and 5+5, with various symbolic meanings attached to such analyses.

Numbers 12, 40, 60, 70, 72, and Others. The number 12 is a great cosmic symbol, made up of 3×4 or 5+7. It is the number of the Zodiac in Babylonia and elsewhere, either under Babylonian influence or independently, for example, in China and in Greece. The Babylonians divided their year into 12 months and their days into 12 hours. The Greeks divided their year in the same way, worshiped a pantheon of 12 Olympian gods, and recorded 12 labors for Hercules. The Gnostics introduced 12 Aeons into their system. The Babylonians assigned the number 13 to their underworld and also to the intercalary month in their lunar calendar. It was considered unlucky because it exceeded the just and fixed number 12. There are some examples of 11's being considered as unlucky for exceeding 10. The number 14, as the double of seven, was regarded as lucky. The number 15 was the sacred number five, the symbol of Ishtar, in triple form. The numbers 25, 50, and 100 had no special significance apart from being used as round numbers in legends and stories.

The number 40, however, was important. The precise origin of its symbolic use is obscure. The tradition that the Pythagoreans transferred the germination of the bean, which took 40 days, to the human fetus and then reckoned the period of pregnancy as 7×40 (280 days) is more plausible than convincing. At any rate, 40 was used also for a period of years corresponding to a generation and then applied symbolically in various other ways. The number 60 (5×12) was fundamental in the Babylonian sexagesimal system but without special significance for religion. However, 70 (7×10) and 72 (one-fifth of the circle of 360 degrees) were both used symbolically to emphasize size and multiplicity.

The Alphabet in Numerology. The letters of the Greek alphabet were given numerical values at an early date. These letter-numbers served as the foundation for the development of an elaborate system of symbolism and divination based on the addition of the numerical values of the letters in given words and their synonyms or opposites. An example from a late Byzantine treatise (see Dornseiff 96) is sufficient to illustrate the practice:

θεός (9+5+70+200)=284; ἀγαθός (1+3+1+9+70+200) = 284; ἅγιος (1+3+10+70+200) = 284.

See Also: ASTROLOGY; DIVINATION; ABRAXAS.

Bibliography: H. J. ROSE, *The Oxford Classical Dictionary*, ed. M. CARY et al. (Oxford 1949) 614. A. SCHIMMEL and W. FUNK, *Die Religion in Geschichte und Gegenwart*, 7 v. (3d ed. Tübingen 1957–65) 6:1861–64, with bibliography. T. DAVIDSON et al., J. HASTINGS, ed., *Encyclopedia of Religion and Ethics*, 13 v. (Edinburgh 1908–27) 9:406–17. R THURNWALD, *Reallexikon der Vorgeschichte*, ed. M. EBERT, 15 v. (Berlin 1924–25) 14:459–79, with bibliography. R. MEHLEIN, ''Drei,'' *Reallexikon für Antike und Christentum*, ed. T. KLAUSER [Stuttgart 1941 (1950)–] 4:269–310, with bibliography. A. STUIBER, ''Dreieck,'' *ibid.* 310–13. E. T. BELL, *The Magic of Numbers* (London 1952). C. M. EDSMAN, ''Alphabet und Buchstabenmystik,'' *Reallexikon der Vorgeschichte* 1:246. F. DORNSEIFF, *Das Alphabet in Mystik und Magie* (2d ed. Leipzig 1925).

[M. R. P. MC GUIRE]

NUMEROLOGY (IN THE BIBLE)

Numbers may be used as simple expression of numerical values, as rhetorical expressions of the same, or as symbolic expressions of realities in some way related to numbers.

Simple Enumeration. In all existing Hebrew and Greek manuscripts of the inspired text, words expressing numbers are spelled out in full. In early times the Israelites may have used strokes or digits of some sort to express numbers, as did the Babylonians and Egyptians (e.g., in the Elephantine papyri). In later times both Jews and Greeks used the letters of their respective alphabets as numerical signs. The Masoretes indicated divisions of the Biblical text in this manner. The decimal system was basic, but traces of a duodecimal or sexagesimal system exist. (*See* WEIGHTS AND MEASURES IN THE BIBLE.) In Hebrew the digits 1 to 9 were represented by the first nine letters of the alphabet ('to *ṭ*), the decades 10 to 90 by the next nine (*y* to *ṣ*), and 100 to 400 by the last four (*q* to *t*). All other numbers were expressed as combinations of these. The abbreviation (*yh*) for the sacred name of God, Yahweh, was avoided by writing 15 as 9 plus 6 (*ṭw*) instead of 10 plus 5 (*yh*). The explanation for some apparent errors in textual transmission may lie in the similarity of certain letter numbers, especially in the primitive script; e.g., the confusion of *d* (3) with *z* (7) may explain the discrepancy in the parallel texts of 2 Sm 24.13 and 1 Chr 21.12. Erroneous transmission of the text, however, is not the only explanation of numerical discrepancies in the Bible. Biblical inspiration does not demand that every enumeration in the Bible be a direct revelation from God. Human values that are simply the vehicle for the transmission of divine truth are not made divine absolutes by the fact of inspiration, but are to be judged according to the nature of the human contingencies in which they appear.

Rhetorical Use of Numbers. Peculiar to Semitic rhetoric was the use of two numbers in sequence in order to emphasize the completeness of the enumeration. The use is frequent in numerical proverbs and oracles (Pry 30.15, 18, 21, 29; Sir 25.7, 26.5, 19; Am 1.3–2.6). Much more general and varied are what one might call round numbers. Certain numbers are used to express an indefinite amount, large or small: 1 for someone, 2 for a couple, 3 for a few, and 1000 for very many (e.g., Hos 6.2; Ex 20.6; Is 30.17). An exact number may be given for what is only an approximation. Since the superlative in Hebrew is rendered by triple repetition (Is 6.3), the number 3 signifies a certain completeness. Because of the four cosmic directions, the number 4 connotes a certain totality (in every direction). Because of the five fingers of the hand, the number 5 may signify a relatively sufficient number. Possibly because of its connection with lunar phases (approximately seven days between each quarter), the number 7 is especially significant as indicating a complete cycle or series, and multiples of 7 emphasize the extent of the series (Gn 4.15, 24; Prv 24.16; Mt 18.21–22; Mk 16.9). The number of fingers of both hands, ten, may signify all of a kind, i.e., a totality (Ex 34.28; Jb 19.3; Mt 25.1). Since it was associated with the 12 months of the solar year, the number 12 suggests a complete cycle. The number 40 is a very frequent round number and designates a rather long period the exact duration of which is not known, but the general idea is that of reaching full maturity, or perhaps more generally, any large number that could be counted but not quickly or easily (cf. the Persian word "forty–footer" meaning a centipede; see

Nm 14.34; 2 Sm 5.4; Mk 1.13). The numbers 60, 80, and 100 are sometimes found as round numbers, but 1,000 is quite frequent and evokes the idea of a large number. However, there is no real proof that it simply means "group" or "clan" and is not a real number. The rhetoric of "Saul has slain his thousands, and David his ten thousands" (1 Sm 18.7) signifies that David slew a fabulously large number (cf. Lv 26.8). In fact, many large numbers that are given as sums may actually be very rough estimates, or exorbitant exaggerations expressive of a hyperbolical intent rather than an exact summation.

Numerology. While usually classed together, a distinction can be made between symbolic and mystic numbers.

Symbolic Numbers. A symbol is something that represents an idea, sacred or otherwise, by convention or because of some association. What is important are the things symbolized, but the symbol is a rallying point that emphasizes a common aspect. The conventional and rhetorical use of numbers readily leads to symbolism through particular association, but it is often difficult to determine just where the transition begins. Moreover, the same number may have different symbolic connotations. The number 1, for example, is associated with God's uniqueness (Dt 6.4; Sir 1.6; Jn 17.11; Rom 3.30). The superlative, 3, denotes that a thing is entirely what it is said to be (e.g., dead for three days, i.e., really dead; God thrice holy, i.e., perfectly holy); it is often associated with the perfection of God's being or action (Gn 18.2). The number of cosmic totality, 4 (e.g., the four living creatures in Ez 1.5; Ap 4.6), designates comprehensiveness (four plagues, Ez 14.21; four beatitudes, Lk 6.20–22). The number 6 is associated with the creation of man and his personal efforts (six days to work), a fullness of human action but lacking the final completeness in God. The number 7 traditionally designates a complete series. Although it can designate a full complement of evil (seven devils of St. MARY MAGDALENE) as well as of good, it is particularly associated with sacred objects and with cult (week, SABBATH, feasts, sacrifices, angels, etc.). From such a concept the apocalyptic speculations of Dn 9.2,24 about the 70 weeks of years (10 jubilees of seven times seven years) lead to the DAY OF THE LORD independently of any real chronology. In general, as a number of perfection (3 plus 4), seven and its multiples, and even its half (Dn 7.25), occur frequently as symbolic numbers. As a round number of totality, ten may have some special symbolism, but it is not well defined (ten plagues of Egypt, ten commandments). Through its association with the temporal cycle, 12 seems to designate cyclic perfection or the perfection of order and government. Whether or not the division of Israel into 12 tribes arose from the monthly assignment of sanctuary care to a particular tribe cannot be ascertained, but 12 as a symbol of the people of God is found throughout the Bible—12 APOSTLES, 12 gates of the new Jerusalem, the number of the saved 144,000, i.e., 12,000 for each of the 12 tribes, etc. (Mt 19.28; Ez 48.30–34; Rv 7.4, 7.8, 21.12–14). The number 40 acquires also a certain symbolism through association with successive periods in salvation history, periods characterized by the struggle with evil from which man is ultimately saved by the power of God (Gn 7.12, 17; Dt 8.2, 9.9; 1 Kgs 19.8; Mt 4.2). The number 1,000 and its multiples, as a very large round number often without any exact numerical sense, may symbolize the perfect age. (*See* MILLENARIANISM.) The fabulous ages of the antediluvian patriarchs, quite modest alongside their Mesopotamian counterparts, probably have some special significance. However, this is scarcely discernible now (even the textual traditions do not agree on the numbers), except in the case of Henoch, the just man, who lived 365 years, the perfect number of the solar year. Perhaps there is a similar symbolism for the ages of Israel's ancestors, the census in Numbers ch. 1, the 38 years in Jn 5.5, and the 153 (sum of numbers from 1 to 17) fishes in Jn 21.11. Some numbers may be the result of gematria, the designation of a person or thing by the numerical value of the letters of a word. For example, in Matthew's genealogy of Jesus (Mt 1.1–17), where three series of 14 ancestors each are given, there may be gematria based on the name of David (in Hebrew *dwd,* i.e., 14), to show that Jesus is eminently Davidic and messianic. The interpretation of the beast's number, 666, in Ap 13.18 as Nero Caesar (written in Aramaic) is commonly accepted but not certain. Given the symbolism of 6, the triple repetition may simply designate the number of the man who refuses to enter into the designs of God and to advance to the perfection of 7.

Mystic Numbers. As distinct from a symbolic, a mystic number may be defined as a number having some hidden significance or even hidden power that only special knowledge, investigation, or supernatural enlightenment can discover and put to use. The Bible never attributes any special power to numbers, even though it recognizes that God "disposed all things by measure and number and weight" (Wis 11.20). Things are not related simply because they have the same number. Number has no special meaning apart from the thing signified. Moreover, the main purpose of inspiration is revelation, not concealment. The allegorical interpretations given to numbers by some of the Fathers of the Church, e.g., St. Augustine, must be considered as done merely by way of fanciful accommodation. While avoiding the excesses of the Pythagoreans (*see* PYTHAGORAS AND PYTHAGOREANS) and the later Cabalists (*see* CABALA), some Fathers and their audiences were fascinated by numbers and their supposed hidden meanings. The Biblical symbolism of numbers, where it really exists, is quite controlled and secondary to the more important intentions of the Biblical authors.

Bibliography: *Encyclopedic Dictionary of the Bible,* tr. and adap. by L. HARTMAN (New York 1963), from A. VAN DEN BORN, *Bijbels Woordenboek* (1649–53). W. H. BENNETT, J. HASTINGS and J. A. SELBIA, eds., *Dictionary of the Bible,* 5 v. (Edinburgh 1942–50) 701–704. O. RÜHL, G. KITTEL, *Theologisches Wöterbuch zum Neuen Testament* (Stuttgart 1935–) 1:461–464; (Eng.) 1:461–464. J. SAUER, "Zahlensymbolik," *Lexikon für Theologie und Kirche*[1], ed. M. BUCHBERGER, 10 v. (Freiburg 1930–38) 10:1025–30. X. LEON-DUFOUR, ed., *Vocabulaire du Théologie Biblique* (Paris 1962) 687–691. J. BONSIRVEN, *Vocabulaire Biblique* (Paris 1958) 110.

[H. J. SORENSEN]

NUMISMATICS

Coins of fixed weight, stamped with governmental authority and used as money for exchange of value, and also medals, frequently supply dates, depict styles of weapons, clothing, and art forms, indicate attitudes, or testify to the existence of an institution or administrative procedure otherwise not known from written or archeological sources. They thus have value for both religious and secular history. They are important not only for tracing the evolution of the Roman Empire but also for the history of the Church from antiquity to modern times. After a brief survey of the Roman imperial coinage as background, this article discusses chiefly the coins and medals of direct concern to Church history. Hebrew coinage, and Hellenistic coinage that is pertinent, are covered in other articles.

Roman Coinage from Augustus to Constantine. During the Republic, magistrates called the *tres viri auro, argento, aere flando, feriundo* (the three men for minting and striking [coins] of gold, silver, and bronze) controlled the issue of coinage under the authority of the Senate, which was indicated by the stamp S.C. for *Senatus consulto.* The obverse image gradually changed from the goddess Roma and the Dioscuri on horseback to Jupiter, to the figure of Victory, to Juno of Lanuvium in a chariot, etc., and eventually to the personal history and portraits of the magistrates. In 44 B.C. the head of Julius Caesar appeared on silver coins. Augustus permitted the Senate to coin bronze, but in practice he exercised complete control of the mints, and only the portraits of members of the imperial family were authorized. On the reverse side of the coinage political phrases were employed, such as the *signis receptis* of Augustus commemorating the recovery of the standards lost to the Parthians at the battle of Carrhae. Later Vespasian proclaimed his subjection of the Jews with the legend *Iudaea capta.* Further propaganda purposes were served by the portrayal of civic virtues,

Byzantine gold coin with Constantine VI as a youth and his mother, the Empress Irene, on obverse; reverse shows three other Eastern emperors, Leo III, Constantine V, and Leo IV.

such as *Abundantia, Concordia, Pudicitia,* and this continued almost to the end of the empire. The imperial coinage regularly records the titles of the emperors and, until the reign of Alexander Severus (d. 235), the current or last consulship of the given *princeps* and his tribunician year.

Thus the life of the Roman state is depicted on its coins: official acts of the *princeps,* his *liberalitas* in the distribution of money and bread, the arrival of the grain fleet at Ostia, the departure on a military expedition against the barbarians, the *adventus* or salute by the troops to the emperor sitting before them on horseback, the circus games and temple sacrifices, public and family religious cults and ceremonial, the association of members of a dynasty or colleagues in the rule of the empire, and the rise and fall of individual emperors. The establishment of the tetrarchy by Diocletian after 293 is depicted on medals, and the coins of Diocletian demonstrate the gradual growth of the emperor's religiopolitical consciousness of himself as the protégé of Jupiter (*Iovi conservatori Augusti*); and the coins of Maximian show him as a protégé of Hercules. The emperor gradually assumed a *maiestas divina,* as the *comes* or *numen praesens* of the godhead; he possessed the divine virtues of *pietas* and *felicitas.* This concept was already portrayed on coins that began with Aurelian's *deo et domino nato.* In solving the difficult historical problems concerned with the chronology of the tetrarchy and the reasons for its dissolution, coins play an essential part.

Constantine and Christian Coinage. In 306 CONSTANTINE I is depicted on the imperial coinage as still a protégé of Hercules in the divinely ordered Diocletian tetrarchy; but in the official speech delivered at Constantine's wedding to Fausta, the daughter of Maximian (spring 307), the latter is compared to the sun god (*Sol invictus*) rather than to the Jupiter of the tetrarchy's political theology. After 310, with the death of Maximian, Constantine's coinage no longer portrays Hercules; instead, *Mars conservator* is depicted as the protective deity accompanying the *Sol invictus.* This is a return to the tradition of Aurelian and Gallienus. Stress is placed, too, on the legitimacy of Constantine's rule, which can be traced to his lineage as the son of Constantius Chlorus. Subsequent coinage indicates the steps whereby Constantine gradually achieved full control of the empire, the year 312 being the turning point in both his religious and political thinking.

Silver coins minted at Treyes (312–313) portray Constantine as *Victor,* crowned with an ornamented helmet at whose peak is the Christian monogram CHI-RHO; and a similar portrait appears on a silver medallion at Ticinum (315) and on coins issued at Siscia (317–318). Coins in 320 carry the Vexillum with the Monogram of Christ; in 326 the Christian LABARUM appears with the legend *Spes publica.* However, as the empire was still pagan, Constantine did not interfere with the ordinary representations of the civic cult or the pagan portraiture of the emperor, and it took a century before all signs of pagan cult disappeared from the imperial coinage. Under Constantius II, Victory is depicted on a coin in the form of an angel crowning the emperor, who holds the standard of the cross. The legend reads: *Hoc signo victor eris.* During this period the Christian monogram appears frequently and is often accompanied by the alpha and omega. After a temporary revival of pagan types under Julian the Apostate, Christian-oriented coins predominate.

Byzantine and Medieval Coins. A medallion in gold commemorates the founding of Constantinople in 330 with the turreted statues of the two capitals, Rome and Constantinople, as the subject of equal veneration. After the death of Theodosius I (395) the gradual partition of the empire under Honorius (395–425) and Arcadius (395–408) is pictured on the coinage current at the time of the birth of Byzantium. Byzantine money as such begins under the Emperor ANASTASIUS I (491–518) with a new copper coinage and also a gold coin modeled on the solidus of Constantine, eventually called the bezant. It was divided into a half (the semissis) and a third (the tremissis). The main silver coin was the miliarensis, along with a small coin, the siliqua or *keration.*

Under Heraclius (610–641) the double miliarensis was first issued. Gradually the effigy of the emperor on the obverse of these coins was changed to that of the basileus in a majestic setting and clothed in hieratic vestments. Christ appears first on the reverse of a coin of A.D. 451, where He is depicted as assisting in the marriage of Marcian and Pulcheria. His next appearance, however, is much later, namely, on the coinage of Justinian II (685–695). From *c.* 900 the Virgin Mary, and eventually the saints, appear on coins, despite the difficulties over ICONOCLASM, whose history can be traced to the coinage of the period.

From the 10th century the Byzantine emperor is usually depicted in the company of a sacred personage; this is particularly true of the cup-shaped *solidi* called the *nummi scyphati,* which appear in the 11th century. In 1261 MICHAEL VIII PALAEOLOGUS issued coins with the Virgin Mary standing in the midst of the walls of Constantinople after its reconquest from the Crusaders.

The principal inscriptions on the later Byzantine coinage refer to the emperor on the obverse and to the city of minting on the reverse, along with a reference to the saint depicted and often a prayer. From the time of JUSTINIAN I profiles give way to the full face of the emperor, and the language of the inscriptions changes from Latin to Latin and Greek under Heraclius and to Greek alone under ALEXIUS I COMNENUS.

Coinage of the Medieval West. The Byzantine solidus or bezant had a widespread use in the Middle Ages and was the dominant gold coin to the 13th century. The Merovingians still imitated the golden triens of the Romans, but Charlemagne struck silver denerii in imitation of the Roman imperial types. Under the Capetians, however, the Byzantine influence is marked; the king is represented as a basileus, seated beneath a canopy, or standing with scepter in hand, or on horseback, or as a knight in battle. The legends have both a religious and a political significance: *Christus vincit, Christus regnat, Christus Imperat;* or *Karolus Dei gratia Francorum rex.* Under Henry II of England the *Ave Maria* on coins issued in his name as king of France reflects a political situation that lasted until the end of the Hundred Years' War.

The Arabs first adopted current Persian silver coins in the Orient; Byzantine copper coins in Syria and Palestine; and in Africa, the current gold coinage. Byzantine influence predominates in the Caliphite mints begun at Bashran (A.D. 660) and in the regular coinage established by Abdalmik (A.D. 695), having a gold dinar, silver dirhem, and a copper fels. The inscriptions are in Arabic and are uniformly religious. The various dynasties, such as the Omayyads and Abbasids, the Fatamids and Seljuks, continued the adaptation of Byzantine coinage, whereas the Mongols and Ottomans gradually adapted their coins to those of the Mediterranean commercial powers.

With the development of feudalism, individual suzerains as well as cities and monastic centers issued their own coinage. Although the golden solidus was the ideal coin, its large value gave way before a silver coinage under the Carolingians, and for general usage the denarius or penny of some 24 grains became almost the sole coin in circulation. The Arab silver piece, the dirhem, was worth two denier or denarii and spread with the Carolingian coinage to Germany, Italy, England, Scandinavia, Castile, and Aragon. A continuous depreciation in the value of coinage, which Gresham's (1519–79) law of bad money driving out good money would later explain, brought the denarius so low by the 12th century that it was issued in Germany as a bracteate, stamped on only one side.

Normans and Venetians. The Norman dukes in Sicily and southern Italy quickly adopted the Muslim money, but Roger II (1130–54) struck Latin coins with the legend *Dux Apuliae,* and they accordingly came to be known as ducats. Frederick II (1215–50) continued the Arab coinage but also struck Roman gold solidi and half solidi showing his bust on the obverse, as the Emperor Augustus, and the imperial eagle on the reverse side. The famous gold florin with St. John the Baptist on the obverse and the lily of Florence on the reverse was first struck in 1252 and quickly became a standard of value. Venice struck gold coins of the same weight as the florin (*c.* 1280), showing Christ standing on the obverse and the doge receiving the gonfalon from St. Mark on the reverse. Although it was at first called the ducat, it became known as the zecchino or sequin. This coinage, which was imitated by the other maritime and commercial Italian city-states, caused the Mameluke sultans of Egypt to employ the weight of the florin and sequin for their gold money in commerce between Europe and India. In the 14th century a heavy silver coin appeared called the *denarius grossus,* or groat, and in its successive types can be traced the artistic evolution that was leading into the Renaissance.

Papal Coinage. The popes began to strike money when Adrian I (772–795) issued a gold Beneventan type coin on which a crude hieratic human figure adorns the obverse, and a cross with an inscription, the reverse. The names of the popes and the Western emperors are associated on papal coins from Leo III (795–816) to Leo IX (1049) in monogrammatic inscriptions. Under John VIII (872–882) the bust of St. Peter appears; it is crowned with a conic miter in coins of Sergius III (904–911), whereas on the coins of Agapetus II (946–955) Peter is depicted with the keys and a cross. With Benedict VI (973–974) a series of papal effigies began. However, from Leo IX (1049) to Urban V (1362) no papal coins were issued. The Roman Senate struck coins after 1188 with the effigies of Peter and Paul crowned with nimbi on ducats of gold and with inscriptions, such as *S. Petrus Senator Mundi, Roma Caput Mundi,* and SPQR (*Senatus Populusque Romanus*).

Boniface VIII (1295–1303) issued a large silver coin from the mint at Ponte della Sorga bearing his portrait under a miter; he carries a key and cross in his right hand, and the whole is accompanied by the legend *Domini Bo (nifaci) Papae.* Clement V (1305–14) depicted the pope in frontal figure with miter, giving his blessing, and John XXII (1316–34) stamped the full figure of the pope on the obverse, mitred and sitting on a throne. Charles of Anjou (King of the Two Sicilies 1266–85), struck gold ducats when he was governor of Rome, and Cola di Rienzi (1347–48) did the same as tribune. Charles's coins imitate the Venetian type and show Peter giving the gonfalon

to a kneeling senator; later coins portray the coat of arms of the senator who issued the money.

Some papal issues of money were struck at Avignon between 1342 and 1700, and there were papal mints at Ancona, Bologna, Piacenza, Parma, and Ferrara. On his return to Rome, Urban V (1362–70) claimed the sole right to issue papal money; and from Martin V to Pius IX there was a continuous papal coinage on which the effigy of the popes appears in realistic and often highly artistic style. Callistus III (1455–58) struck ducats of gold and an issue of silver *grossi denarii* exhibiting the bark of Peter (or *navicella*) with full rigging surmounted by a cross and the legend *Modice fidei quare dubitetis.* Julius II (1503–13) put both Peter and Paul on the ship with a blown sail and the legend *Non prevalebunt.* This type was continued under later popes. Papal coins were struck also with Biblical scenes, representing Christ, the crib, the ark of Noa, etc., or to commemorate the architectural accomplishments of Renaissance and later popes.

Renaissance and Modern Period. With the issue of the thaler or dollar in Germany in 1518, silver money was widely used all over Europe, but it did not displace the denier since it was issued in various weights and purity by different countries. The ability to represent nature, the human portrait, and other objects had reached the zenith of accomplishment in Renaissance medallions, and the artistic style of medals influenced that of coinage. However, the requirements of rapidly expanding trade soon made the production of coins a commercial interest, and art was all but forgotten. In general trade the denier was the coin of exchange, while the solidus or German shilling was used as a gauge for money of account, and the system of librae (L), solidi (s), and denarii (d), was adopted; the pound was divided into 12 shillings and 20 pence to the shilling.

French and English Coinage. In France during the Middle Ages the common coin was the denier of the Abbey of St. Martin of Tours (*denier tournois*), while the royal coinage was known as *monnaie parisis.* St. Louis IX (1226–70) introduced the gold sou and the *gros tournois,* and thus began an important reform in the French monetary system. Fourteenth-century French coinage had considerable artistic merit, and French medallions produced during the Renaissance and the Napoleonic period exhibit the same high artistic quality.

Following the example of Pepin, Offa of Mercia (757–796) introduced the silver penny into England. Some types have the king's head or a religious symbol on the obverse and an ornament and inscription on the reverse. This coinage was imitated in the several English kingdoms and prevailed down to the late 10th century. Edward III in 1343 introduced a gold coinage that included the florin and the noble showing the picture of a rose. Edward IV (1461–70) struck a new gold coin, the angel. Henry VII brought in sovereigns worth 20 shillings and the shilling itself; his coins show a marked advance in portraiture.

Several attempts were made to introduce a copper coinage to replace the private tokens in wide, local circulation, but it was only in 1613 that John Harrington obtained a patent to produce copper farthings. The gold sovereign of James I was called a unite from the legend *Faciam eos in gentem unam.* Owing to the scarcity of gold during the civil wars, 20- and 10-shilling silver pieces were issued; but the Oxford mint put out 3-pound pieces, on one of which John Rawlins depicted the king on horseback looking over the town, and on the reverse, the heads of the "Oxford Declaration." In 1672 a true copper coinage of halfpence and farthings was introduced.

Italian and German Coinage. In Sicily and southern Italy the Normans first adopted the Arabic currency; but gradually Robert Guiscard (Duke of Apulia) and Roger I and Roller II of Sicily introduced also gold and silver coins modeled on Latin usage, while the Emperor Frederick II issued the first gold ducats or augustals. Charles of Anjou's gold coinage, already mentioned, quickly spread through the Levant. With Ferdinand I of Aragon the coinage of the Two Sicilies began to display the artistic portraiture that was characteristic of the Italian city-states all during the Renaissance.

In Germany, after Louis IV of Bavaria (1314–47), local coinage in the Low Countries, along the Moselle, and in the Rhinelands and Bavaria predominated over the imperial coinage. The introduction of the groat and the florin late in the 14th century began the modern period. From the 16th century, the thaler—first produced by the Counts of Schlick, in St. Joachimsthal in Bohemia, in 1518—became the dominant silver coin. The counts Palatine, who began coining in 1294, had mints at Heidelberg and Frankfurt. The margraves of Brandenburg minted coins in the late Middle Ages also, continuing the practice after 1701 as the kings of Prussia.

An abundance of gold in the 15th and 16th centuries is evident from the coins of Hungary and Transylvania. Early Polish coinage reflects direct English, German, and Byzantine influence, while the emerging Scandinavian states adopted the Anglo-Saxon types, using the runic alphabet for legends. During the late Middle Ages these lands drew upon the common European inheritance. In the Balkan states, both Byzantine and Venetian influences were predominant, as they employed images and legends that are entirely Christian. In Russia the Byzantine coinage held sway until Peter the Great modernized the currency. Ecclesiastical city-states, such as Cologne, Münster, Treves, Augsburg, Salzburg, and Mainz, issued their own coinage between the 11th and 18th century, as did other independent cities.

Contemporary coinage, while generally reflecting the standards of modern minting skills, suggests the vagaries of political fortunes in the various nations of the world. Moreover, it is dominated by the practical demands of trade and commerce, artistic considerations playing a secondary role. Modern metal coinage has become largely token currency; paper money takes the place of the earlier gold and silver coinages.

Numismatic Study. Collections of coins and medals are known to have existed in antiquity. On the occasion of celebrations, the Emperor Augustus gave rare or valuable coins to his entourage; and the bronze medals issued by the Antonine emperors trace the legendary history of Rome on their reverse; festive gold medals of Constantine Chlorus struck in 302 were discovered in Arras in 1922.

During the Middle Ages a number of medals were issued in commemoration of special events, such as the expulsion of the English from France at the close of the Hundred Years' War, and were distributed as gifts among the civil and ecclesiastical nobility. The main collections of coins and medals were inaugurated by the monasteries, most of which had a treasury for coins connected with the copyrooms and libraries. These monastic collections, seized by modern European governments after the French Revolution, became the foundation of many numismatic displays in public museums.

Petrarch and his circle of savants were among the first to recognize the value of coins for the interpretation and illustration of literary sources. With Cola di Rienzi, Petrarch turned to the study of numismatic evidence in an attempt to resurrect the customs of the ancient Roman republic and suggested that every library be equipped with an archive of numismatic specimens. This suggestion was honored by amateur savants and princes as well as by emerging commercial houses, such as the Fuggers, and by ecclesiastical nobles from prince-bishops to cardinals and popes. In 1553 Guillaume Rouille published a *Promptuarium,* which contained engravings of the Roman emperors obtained from coins and medals; and in 1570 Fulvio Orsini, the protégé of Pope Gregory XIII (1572–85), issued his *Imagines et elogia virorum illustrium et eruditorum.* His predecessors had been interested mainly in the iconography of the Roman rulers, but he extended his study to include a view of the past in all its achievements.

The treatise *De asse et partibus eius* by the great French classical scholar Guillaume Budé (1468–1540) was the first really systematic study on Roman coinage. Despite the increasing interest in coins and medals, the science of numismatics was founded only at the end of the 18th century by the Jesuit J. H. von ECKHEL (1737–98). Since that time the study of coins and medals has been pursued systematically and scientifically throughout the world. Owing to the progress of archeology, furthermore, large numbers of coins and medals not hitherto known are constantly being added to the earlier collections.

Bibliography: P. GRIERSON, *Coins and Medals: A Select Bibliography* (London 1954). J. BABELON, "Numismatique," *L'Histoire et ses méthodes,* ed. C. SAMARAN (Paris 1961) 329–392. H. HOCHENEGG, *Lexikon für Theologie und Kirche,* ed. J. HOFER and K. RAHNER, 10 v. (2d, new ed. Freiburg 1957–65) 7:1069–70. G. LANCZKOWSKI and W. JESSE, *Die Religion in Geschichte und Gegenwart,* 7 v. (3d ed. Tübingen 1957–65) 4:1184–87. R. S. POOLE et al., *Encyclopaedia Britannia,* 24 v. 11th ed. (New York 1911) 19:869–911. J. ECKHEL, *Doctrina numorum veterum,* 8 v. (Vienna 1792–98), v.9, *Addenda* (Leipzig 1826). J. MAURICE, *Numismatique constantinienne,* 3 v. (Paris 1908–12). P. GARDNER, *A History of Ancient Coinage* (Oxford 1918). C. SUTHERLAND, *Art in Coinage* (London 1955). H. MATTINGLY, *Roman Coins from the Earliest Times to the Fall of the Western Empire* (London 1928; rev. ed. 1960). W. WROTH, *Catalogue of the Imperial Byzantine Coins in the British Museum,* 2 v. (London 1908). B. LAUM, *Über das Wesen des Münzgeldes* (Halle 1930). C. T. SELTMAN, *Greek Coins* (2d ed. London 1955). R. SEDILLOT, *Toutes les monnaies du monde* (Paris 1954). E. BERNAREGGI, *Monete d'oro con ritratto del rinascimento italiano* (Milan 1954). M. BLOCH, *Esquisse d'une histoire monétaire de l'Europe* (Paris 1954). C. SERAFINI, in B. APOLLONI-GHETTI et al., eds., *Esplorazioni sotto la confessione di San Pietro in Vaticano,* 2 v. (Vatican City 1951), numismatic appendix.

[F. X. MURPHY]

NUN

Traditionally, in the Latin Church, the title nun was used to designate a woman who took solemn vows in a contemplative religious order. Though the distinction between solemn vows and simple vows is not made in the 1983 Code of Canon Law of the Latin Church, the term nun applies properly to members of religious orders who by tradition still profess solemn vows and who observe some form of enclosure. Even though the Code does not define the term as such, it is used throughout the postconciliar document *Ecclesiae Sanctae II* to designate religious women with solemn vows. In popular parlance, however, the term is used at present for any member of an institute of consecrated life, as well as a member of a society of apostolic life.

In the Eastern Christian tradition, monastic life is given pride of place before other forms of consecrated life since it was the prototype of all cenobitical religious life. The term nun does not appear as such, but female members of monasteries, orders and congregations are referred to by the generic term "religious."

Perfectae Caritatis, the Vatican II Decree on the Renewal of Religious Life abolished the distinction formerly made in women's institutes between choir sisters and lay sisters. "Unless circumstances do really suggest otherwise, it should be the aim to arrive at but one category of sisters in women's institutes" (*Perfectae Caritatis,* 15). It is left to the constitutions of each order to define those nuns who are bound to the choral recitation of the Divine Office. Similar norms oblige religious women in the Eastern Catholic Churches.

Bibliography: *Code of Canons of the Eastern Churches, Latin-English* (Washington, D.C. 2001). V. POSPISHIL, *Eastern Catholic Church Law,* 2nd rev. and aug. ed. (New York 1996). J. BEAL, et al, *New Commentary on the Code of Canon Law* (New York/Mahwah, NJ 2000). R. MCDERMOTT, "Two Approaches to Consecrated Life: The Code of Canons of the Eastern Churches and the Code of Canon Law" *Studia Canonica* 29 (1995) 193–239.

[C. BARTONE]

NUNC DIMITTIS (CANTICLE OF SIMEON)

Title (in Latin) of the short hymn sung by Simeon on the occasion of the presentation of Jesus in the Temple (Lk 2.29–32). Enlightened by the Holy Spirit, Simeon recognizes in the Infant presented by Mary the long-awaited "Christ of the Lord," that is, the Messiah sent by God (v.26). The Holy Infant is the embodiment of God's salvation; this salvation is universal, that is, destined for all: "prepared before the face of all peoples," Gentiles as well as Jews (v.31; cf. Is 49.6; 60.3). For the Gentiles, salvation is described as a light (cf. Is 42.6) that is revelation of divine truth (v.32). For the Jews, the Savior is "glory" (v.32), in that He is from "the Israelites . . . according to the flesh" (Rom 9.5), and brings salvation "to Jew first and then to Greek [Gentile]" (Rom 1.16). The *Nunc Dimittis* is sung daily at Compline (Night Prayer) in the Catholic Church, and as the second canticle at the Office of Evensong in the Anglican tradition.

Bibliography: R. F. TAFT, *The liturgy of the hours in East and West: the origins of the divine office and its meaning for today,* 2nd rev. ed. (Collegeville, Minn. 1993). G. GUIVER, *Company of voices: daily prayer and the people of God* (New York 1988). P. F. BRADSHAW, *Daily prayer in the early church: a study of the origin and early development of the Divine Office* (London 1981).

[A. LE HOULLIER/EDS.]

Miniature from the St. Alban Psalter illustrating "Nunc Dimittis," 12th century, in the Treasury of the Cathedral in Hildesheim, Germany.

NUNCIO, APOSTOLIC

A nuncio (from the Lat. *nuntius*, messenger) is the diplomatic representative of the APOSTOLIC SEE, that is, Rome, as well as the personal legate of the Holy Father to a civil government. In countries (usually Catholic) where the ambassador of the Holy See is automatically accorded the honorary status of dean of the diplomatic corps, the simple title "nuncio" is used. In other countries, such as the United States where the position of "dean" of the diplomatic corps rests with the ambassador with the longest tenure, the title "pro nuncio" is used. In either case, the duties are the same.

Although the duties of the papal nuncio include both diplomatic representation and internal Church matters, the latter consume a far greater portion of his time. In addition to general monitoring of the situation of the Church, other duties include the nomination and selection of bishops, review and transmission to the Holy See of official government requests, and service as the conduit for official Vatican correspondence with American Catholics and Church officials.

Early History. The history of diplomatic relations between the United States and the Holy See begins in 1779, when John Adams, writing in a nation-by-nation diplomatic survey prepared for the Confederation Congress, speculated erroneously that the Papal States would be among the last to recognize the newly independent United States, even were they to seek such recognition. "Congress," he predicted, "[would] probably never send a minister to his Holiness" because "[he could] do them no service." As for a "catholic legate or nuncio. . . or in other words an ecclesiastical tyrant," he wrote: "It is hoped the United States will be too wise ever to admit [one] into its territories." The realities of international diplomacy were soon to prove him wrong.

When the Revolutionary War ended, some of the newly independent states were under the ecclesiastical jurisdiction of the Bishop of Quebec, and the remainder were subject to that of the Vicar Apostolic in London and his vicar in New York. Both bishops had taken steps to distance themselves from the Revolution: the Bishop of Quebec because of what he considered to be the anti-Catholic views of some of the Revolution's leaders, and the Vicar Apostolic of London because of his concern that Catholics in England not be perceived as disloyal to the Crown. So it became necessary, for both political and administrative reasons, for the Holy See to revise the jurisdictional arrangement.

In 1783, an informal diplomatic contact with Benjamin Franklin, then the American minister to the French Court, was made by the Papal Nuncio at Versailles in order to determine the desires of the American government on this issue. If no suitable American candidate could be found, the nationality of the individual soon to be named as America's first Catholic bishop would present a delicate diplomatic issue. The choice of a foreigner, especially a British subject, worried Franklin, and the Vatican's diplomatic note accordingly referred to the alternative of appointing a citizen of a "friendly" nation: an obvious reference to France.

The question posed to Franklin by the Holy See was referred to a committee composed of Thomas Jefferson, Elbrige Gerry and Hugh Williamson. Although the committee declined to offer the pope the requested advice on the grounds that the federal government had no power to involve itself in religious matters, the members did note their respect for the pope as a "sovereign and a state." Mutual recognition, albeit on an informal basis, thus commenced in 1783.

Among the prelates attending the mass congregation which climaxed the annual German Catholic Conclave at Fulda were: (left to right) Cardinal Wendel, of Munich; Josef Cardinal Frings, of Cologne; and Archbishop Aloysius Muench, the Apostolic Nuncio, September, 1954. (©Bettmann/CORBIS)

Initial Relations. The first formal relationship began 14 years later in 1797 with the appointment of John B. Sartori as consul to Rome to look after American commercial affairs. This consular relationship continued without interruption until 1870 when the Papal States became a part of Italy. The Papal States sent consuls general to the United States in 1826 and 1895.

The election of Pope Pius IX in 1846 and the resulting liberalization in the government of the Papal States led to considerable debate over the issue of United States-Vatican relations in the American press. Many were opposed, but others who favored his policies, urged a closer relationship. The *New York Herald,* for example, favored the appointment of a chargé d'affairs or ambassador to the pope ''as more respectful to the pope, and more suitable to our dignity and greatness as a people.'' Thus, when President Polk recommended the creation and

funding of a diplomatic mission to the Vatican in his 1847 State of the Union message, the stage was set for formal diplomatic relations at a level short of full recognition. Jacob L. Martin was appointed as chargé d'affairs, and was later upgraded to the status of minister. The Vatican, however, did not reciprocate, and appointed no delegate during the period between 1848 and 1868.

During the Civil War, the American mission served as the locus of successful Union efforts to assure the nonrecognition of the Confederacy by the Holy See: Jefferson Davis' request for papal recognition was met with only an ambiguous reply. Official American diplomatic contact with the Vatican was suspended in 1868 as a result of rumors that American Protestants in Rome had not been permitted to practice their religion. ''America,'' said Congressman Thaddeus Stevens, had no desire to have representation ''at any Court or Government which prohibits free worship within its Jurisdiction of the Christian religion.'' Funds for the legation in Rome were cut off in 1867 to make a point—a point which would have been valid had the rumors of religious suppression been true. Diplomatic relations between the Holy See and the United States were formally terminated in 1871 when President Grant officially recognized the new government of Italy and that the Papal States had ceased to exist.

The first apostolic delegate was sent to the United States by the Holy See in 1893, but he was not accredited to the United States government, and his duties were limited to matters internal to the Church. During the period from 1871 to 1939, American relations with the Vatican were informal, but included such important contacts as the Taft mission to Rome to deal with the Philippines at the close of the Spanish-American War and the many contacts between Woodrow Wilson and Benedict XV during World War I.

Unofficial diplomatic recognition of the Vatican by the United States was reestablished at the outbreak of World War II in 1939 with the appointment of Myron Taylor (13:953c), with the rank of Ambassador, as Franklin Roosevelt's personal representative. After Taylor resigned in 1950, no replacement was named, and personal representatives were sent only for special occasions. This unofficial relationship lasted until 1970 when President Nixon resumed the practice begun by Roosevelt by naming Henry Cabot Lodge as his personal representative. Lodge served in the post from 1970–77. David Walters, appointed by President Gerald Ford, served at the post from 1977–78. President Jimmy Carter's representative was Robert Wagner, Sr., who served from 1978–81, when he was replaced by President Ronald Reagan's choice, California businessman and Catholic William Wilson.

Official Representation. In 1983, at the urging of the Reagan administration, Congress quietly repealed the 1867 ban on appropriations for a diplomatic legation to the Holy See and provided for the establishment of full diplomatic relations. President Reagan appointed William Wilson, who was then serving as the president's personal envoy, as U.S. Ambassador, and the Senate confirmed the nomination on March 7, 1984, thus reestablishing formal diplomatic relations after a lapse of 117 years. The Holy See, in turn, named Archbishop Pio Laghi, who had been serving as apostolic delegate, as pro nuncio, thus transforming the Apostolic Delegation on Massachusetts Avenue in Washington, D.C., into the Papal Nunciature or Embassy. On Oct. 15, 1986, the U.S. Senate confirmed the nomination of Frank Shakespeare, former head of CBS Television Service, as the second American ambassador at the Holy See.

The establishment of full diplomatic relations was the subject of two unsuccessful court cases filed by several religious groups and numerous individuals on the grounds that such an appointment would violate the First Amendment to the Constitution of the United States. In *Americans United for Separation of Church and State v. Reagan,* the United States Court of Appeals for the Third Circuit held that the establishment of diplomatic relations is ''one of the rare governmental decisions that the Constitution commits exclusively to the Executive Branch'' and that federal courts have no power to interfere. In *Phelps v. Reagan,* a Kansas Baptist minister alleged that diplomatic recognition of the Holy See was designed by the Reagan Administration to utilize ''the ecclesiastical machinery of a specific church. . . in carrying out its foreign policy, and. . . to advance Reagan's personal partisan agenda by currying favor with American members of a specific church in an election year.'' The United States Court of Appeals for the Tenth Circuit called the arguments ''flamboyant'' and dismissed the case because taxpayers and citizens have no standing to seek judicial oversight of the president's conduct of foreign affairs.

Bibliography: COMMITTEE ON FOREIGN RELATIONS, United States Senate, 98th Cong. 2d Sess., Hearings Nomination of William A. Wilson to be Ambassador to the Holy See (Feb. 2, 1984). AMERICANS UNITED FOR SEPARATION OF CHURCH AND STATE V. REAGAN, 786 F.2d. 194 (3d Cir 1986), *certiorari denied sub nom.* AMERICAN BAPTIST CHURCHES IN THE U.S.A. V. REAGAN, 107 S. Ct. 314 (1986). PHELPS V. REAGAN, 812 F.2d 1293 (10th Cir. 1987). S. W. BETTWY, ''United States-Vatican Recognition: Background and Issues,'' *Catholic Lawyer* 29 (1984) 225. S. W. BETTWY and M. K. SHEEHAN, ''United States Recognition Policy: The State of Vatican City,'' *California Western International Law Journal* II (1981) 1. J. AGONITO, ''Ecumenical Stirrings: Catholic-Protestant Relations During the Episcopacy of John Carroll,'' *Church History* 45 (1976) 358–373. M. MARTIN, ''United States-Vatican Relations,'' *American Catholic Historical Society Record* 69 (1958) 20–55. ''The Status of the Holy See in International Law,'' *American Journal of International Law* 46 (1952) 308. A. C. RUSH, ''Diplomatic Relations: The United States and the Papal States,'' *American Ecclesiastical Review* 126 (1952) 12–27. H. R. MARRARO, ''The Closing of the American Diplomatic Mission to the Vatican and Efforts to Revive It, 1868–1870.'' *Catholic Historical Review* 33 (1948) 423–447. L. F. STARK, ''Was the Papal Consulate in the United States Officially Ended?'' *Catholic Historical Review* 30 (1944) 165–170. W. J. LALLON, ''The Apostolic Delegation at Washington.'' *Ecclesiastical Review* 95 (1936) 576–592. P. LAGHI, ''The True Meaning of Vatican Diplomacy,'' *Origins* 13 (May 3, 1984) 769–771.

[R. A. DESTRO]

NUNES BARRETO, JOÃO

Patriarch of Abyssinia; b. Porto, Portugal, date unknown; d. Goa, India, Dec. 22, 1562. He entered the Society of Jesus as a priest in 1544 and was sent to Morocco, where he labored to redeem and care for Christian slaves. Ten years later he was called to Rome; and at the counsel of St. Ignatius Loyola and King John III of Portugal, he was named patriarch of Abyssinia by Paul IV. With Melchior Carneiro and Andrew Oviedo, chosen to be his coadjutors, he traveled to Lisbon in 1555 and after their consecration there sailed for Goa. King John, like his predecessors, dreamed of establishing communications with the descendants of PRESTER JOHN, medieval Christian monarch in Asia whose legend began in the 12th century. He also wished a firm alliance against the Muslims. Nunes sent Bishop Oviedo to win the favor of Negus (Emperor) Claudius (Calāwēdōs) of Abyssinia, but after much hardship the mission was not fruitful. In 1557 Pedro Paez, SJ, converted Negus Susenyos, but by 1633 the Jesuits were expelled due to the suspicions of Negus Fasilidas.

Bibliography: C. SOMMERVOGEL et al., *Bibliothèque de la Compagnie de Jésus,* 11 v. (Brussels-Paris 1890–1932) 5:1840–41. E. CERULLI, *Lexikon für Theologie und Kirche,* ed. J. HOFER and K RAHNER, 10 v. (2d, new ed. Freiburg 1957–65) 7:1070. P. TACCHI VENTURI, *Storia della Compagnia di Gesù* (2d ed. Rome 1950–) 2.2:559–565. L. KOCH, *Jesuiten-Lexikon: Die Gesellschaft Jesu einst und jetzt* (Paderborn 1934); photoduplicated with rev. and suppl., 2 v. (Louvain-Heverlee 1962) 1316. S. DELACROIX, ed., *Histoire universelle des missions catholiques,* 4 v. (Paris 1956–59) 1:230–231. R. STREIT and J. DINDINGER, *Bibliotheca missionum* (Freiburg 1916–) v. 15.

[E. D. MCSHANE]

NUNRAW, ABBEY OF

To date the only Cistercian monastery built in Scotland since the Reformation. It was founded in 1946 as a daughterhouse of ROSCREA (Ireland) at Haddington, East Lothian, near Edinburgh, and made an abbey in 1948. The site originally belonged to a Cistercian convent (founded 1152–58), which passed into private hands on the death of the last prioress (1563).

Bibliography: M. SHERRY, *Nunraw* (Edinburgh 1963). *Royal Commission of Ancient and Historical Monuments of Scotland: County of East Lothian* (Edinburgh 1924) xxix, xliv, xlvi, 45. W. F. GRAY and J. H. JAMIESON, *A Short History of Haddington* (Edin-

burgh 1944) 9, 22, 29–30, 41, 83, 121, 146. *Transactions of the East Lothian Antiquarian Society,* 5 (1952) 2–24; 6 (1953) 1–5. *The Catholic Directory for the Clergy and Laity of Scotland, 1964* (Glasgow 1964) 75.

[L. MACFARLANE]

NUTTER, ROBERT, BL.

Priest, martyr; *alias* Askew, Rowley; b. *c.* 1555 at Burnley, Lancashire, England; hanged, drawn, and quartered July 26, 1600 at Lancaster. Born into a wealthy family, he and his brother Bl. John Nutter (beatified 1929) studied at Brasenose College, Oxford, before being smuggled across the English Channel to enter the English College at Rheims. Robert was ordained there Dec. 21, 1581. He returned to England with Bl. George HAYDOCK using forged names and passports. The next 18 years were divided between ministerial work and imprisonment. Sentenced into exile at Boulogne with 20 other priests, but using the alias, Rowley returned to England, where he was again committed to prison at Newgate on Nov. 30, 1585. In 1587, he was transferred to the Marshalsea, then to Wisbeach Castle, Cambridgeshire (1589–90). He and several other fervent prisoners established and followed a monastic rule of life. From prison Nutter wrote to the French provincial requesting that he be admitted to the Dominican Order as a tertiary. According to the report of attorney Thomas Hesketh, he was professed a Dominican in the presence of secular priests at Wisbeach, which was certified to the provincial at Lisbon. He was beatified by Pope John Paul II on Nov. 22, 1987 with George Haydock and Companions.

Feast of the English Martyrs: May 4 (England).

See Also: ENGLAND, SCOTLAND, AND WALES, MARTYRS OF.

Bibliography: Catholic Record Society Publications I, 110; II, 248, 252, 256, 270, 273, 277, 279, 282; III, 16, 156, 384, 385, 398. R. CHALLONER, *Memoirs of Missionary Priests,* ed. J. H. POLLEN (rev. ed. London 1924), I, 120–21. M. J. DORCY, ''Ven. Robert Nutter,'' *St. Dominic's Family* (Dubuque, IA 1964), 341–342. J. H. POLLEN, *Acts of English Martyrs* (London 1891).

[K. I. RABENSTEIN]

O

O ANTIPHONS

The seven antiphons that were traditionally sung at the Magnificat in the Divine Office on the seven days before the vigil of Christmas (December 17–23), each antiphon beginning with the interjection "O." During this season the liturgical readings and chants, selected chiefly from Isaiah, announce the coming of the Messiah, and the closer the feast of Christmas approaches, the more the liturgy accentuates its call to the Savior with the cry "Come!" (*Veni*). During the Middle Ages the O antiphons enjoyed great popularity. Intonation was assigned in succession to the dignitaries of the monastery or cathedral chapter. Thus the first antiphon, *O Sapientia,* was intoned by the abbot; the next day, *O Adonai,* by the prior; *O Clavis David,* by the cellarer, and so on. The largest bell was rung throughout the singing of the O antiphon and its Magnificat.

Textual Structure and Sources. The O antiphons are all constructed on a plan similar to that of orations: first an invocation to the Messiah with a title inspired by the Old Testament (e.g., "O Emmanuel"); then an amplification stating an attribute of the Messiah and developing the invocation ("our King and our Law-giver, the one awaited by the nations, their savior"); finally, an appeal commencing always with "Come" and referring to the initial invocation ("Come to redeem us, Lord, our God"). Their sources may be either of scriptural origin or of ecclesiastical composition, the latter being a free manner of juxtaposing scriptural texts from different sources. (1) The texts of the O antiphons are virtually a mosaic of borrowings from the Prophetic and the Sapiential books: *O Sapientia* (Eccl 24.5); *O Adonai* (Ex 6.13); *O Radix Jesse* (Is 11.10); *O Claris David* (Rv 3.7; cf. Is 22.22); *O Oriens* (Zec 6.12); *O Rex Gentium* (Hg 2.8); *O Emmanuel* (Is 7.14; 8.8). These terms from the Old Testament were very early applied to Christ. Four of them (Sapientia, Rex, Emmanuel, Radix) were already employed by Pope St. Damasus (366–384) in his *Carmen de cognomentis Salvatoris* (*Patrologia Latina,* ed. J. P. Migne 103:378). None of the seven invocations, however, can be found in the *De nominibus Christi* of the Gelasian Decretal(s), sometimes attributed to the same pope [cf. Dobschütz, (*Texte und Untersuchungen* 38 1912) fasc. 4:3]. The term *Clavis David* is applied to Christ by St. Ambrose (*De institut. virg.* 9.62, *Patrologia Latina* 16:321); it was repeated in the *Pontificale romanum* in the admonition *Accipe virgam virtutis* for the consecration of a king. (2) Non-scriptural words are few and are used to link the terms borrowed from Scripture. The two pleas *Veni ad salvandum nos* (from *O Emmanuel*) and *Veni ad liberandum nos* (from *O Radix*) do not seem to be of scriptural origin. The second appears to be taken from a *Responsorium breve* of the Advent liturgy and is a very ancient text, since this appeal for liberation is found in the same words in the MOZARABIC antiphonary of Leon and is repeated at the beginning of an oration of the Mozarabic sacramentary (ed. M. Ferotin, col. 162, line 30).

Number and Origin. In inverse order the initials of each invocation (*S*apientia, *A*donai, *R*adix, *C*lavis, *O*riens, *R*ex, *E*mmanuel) constitute the acrostic ERO CRAS. This is interpreted as the response of Christ to the faithful who have called upon Him during the week: "Tomorrow I shall be there." From this acrostic we can draw two conclusions: (1) The primitive order of the antiphons was the same as that preserved today in the Roman Breviary, rather than that indicated by Amalarius (*De ordine antiphonarii,* ed. Hanssens, *Studi e Testi* 140:46) or that found in the Ambrosian antiphonary or in many Gregorian MSS. (2) The original number of the antiphons was seven. Other antiphons modeled on these seven (such as *O Thomas Didyme* or *O Virgo virginum*) are not by the same author. They do not enter into the framework of the acrostic; and, above all, they are not addressed to the Messiah. *O Thomas Didyme* was composed for the feast of St. Thomas the Apostle (December 21), always celebrated during the period when the O antiphons are sung. *O Virgo virginum,* in honor of the Virgin Mary, is probably earlier, having been cited by Amalarius, and was sometimes sung on the vigil of Christmas. Amalarius at-

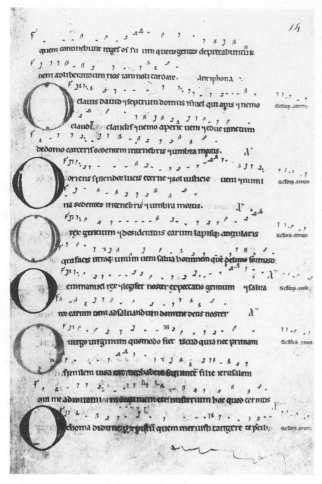

Manuscript page containing O antiphons, from 12th-century antiphony of Saint-Denis (Bib. Nat. MS lat. 17296, fol. 14r).

tributes the composition of the O antiphons to some anonymous "cantor" (*De or. antiphonarii,* ch. 13, ed. Hanssens, *Studi e Testi* 140:44), who probably lived in the eighth century, perhaps even in the seventh. All are adapted to the same melodic theme in the 2d mode. The Magnificat that follows is sung in the solemn tone as on great feasts. Both text and melody were probably composed by one and the same author.

Bibliography: C. CALLEWAERT, "De groote Adventsanti-fonen O" in his *Sacris erudiri* (Steenbrugge 1940). W. J. MCGARRY, *He Cometh* (New York 1941). "Les Grandes Antiennes," *Revue Bénédictine* 2 (1885–86) 512–516. W. APEL, *Gregorian Chant* (Bloomington IN 1958) 400.

[M. HUGLO]

O DEUS EGO AMO TE

A hymn of uncertain authorship, but attributed to St. Francis XAVIER. It is a famous Latin version of *No me*

mueve, mi Dios, an anonymous Spanish *soneto* known to have existed for many years before it was first printed in 1628. The sonnet was familiar to IGNATIUS OF LOYOLA and to Francis Xavier (d. 1552), who, in his missionary instructions, used Spanish and Portuguese versions of it. In the Latin hymn the five stanzas of irregular rhythm glow with an ardent love for the crucified Christ. The literal expression of this love has been criticized because it excludes both hope of reward and fear of punishment: *Nec amo Te ut salves me,/ Aut quia non amantes Te/ Aeterno punis igne.* English versions of the hymn are found in numerous hymnals. Another hymn, *O Deus ego amo Te/ Nam prior Tu amasti me,* paraphrases in its five stanzas the familiar prayer ascribed to Ignatius Loyola, the *Suscipe* or "Take, O Lord."

Bibliography: H. A. DANIEL, *Thesaurus hymnologicus,* 5 v. (Halle-Leipzig 1841–56) 2:335; 4:347, for text. U. CHEVALIER, *Repertorium hymnologicum* (Louvain-Brussels 1892–1921) 2:12896–98. J. JULIAN, ed., *A Dictionary of Hymnology* (New York 1957) 826, 1296. M. BRITT, ed., *The Hymns of the Breviary and Missal* (new ed. New York 1948) 193–194, for a tr. M. C. HUFF, *The Sonnet "No me mueve, mi Dios"* (Washington 1948). J. M. COOPER, "An Aspect of Perfect Love," *American Ecclesiastical Review* 115 (1946) 101–120. F. J. CONNELL, "Unselfish Love of God," *ibid.* 113 (1945) 59–61.

[G. E. CONWAY]

O FILII ET FILIAE

An Easter hymn of 12 three-line stanzas, with a triple Alleluia at the beginning and end of the hymn, and a single Alleluia after each stanza. Each verse has eight syllables and is embellished with end rhyme. The date and authorship are uncertain. Because of its simplicity it was formerly dated in the 12th century, but Julian claims 1650; others ascribe it to the Franciscan, Jean Tisserand (d. 1494). This hymn tells the story of the Resurrection: the coming of the holy women and the disciples, the message of the angel, the doubts of Thomas, and his act of faith. Numerous translations and variations exist of the text and melody.

Bibliography: F.A. MARCH, ed., *Latin Hymns* (New York 1874). P. GUÉRANGER, *The Liturgical Year* (Dublin 1868–93).

[G. E. CONWAY]

O ROMA NOBILIS

An early medieval poem in three monorhymed stanzas discovered in the early 19th century and declared the official hymn of the HOLY YEAR of 1950. The first stanza praises Christian Rome, the second invokes the aid of St. PETER, and the third, that of St. PAUL. The text is complete in only one MS (Vat. lat. 3227) from the early 12th century; a second (Monte Cassino 318) from the 11th century carries only the first strophe. The Beneventan script of both MSS suggests an origin in or near the abbey of MONTE CASSINO, probably from the late ninth or early tenth century, but TRAUBE's ascription to Verona is still prevalent. This nonliturgical poem is most frequently described, but without basis, as a medieval pilgrims' song. Its literary fame rests mainly upon the studies of B. G. Niebuhr (*editio princeps,* 1829) and L. Traube (1891). As early as 1822 the poem was being sung, in Rome and Berlin, in a choral setting by the papal choirmaster G. BAINI, who claimed to have drawn his melody from the not readily intelligible neumes of the Vatican MS. In 1909 at Fribourg, P. Wagner published the Vatican melody from the exact notation in solmization letters given in the Monte Cassino MS and demonstrated the complete inauthenticity of Baini's transcription. In both text and melody it is the matter of rhythm that largely occupies scholars today, although they are concerned also with the relation of the authentic melody of this poem to a secular piece, *O admirabile Veneris idolum.* Original settings of *O Roma nobilis* were produced by LISZT (1879) and L. Perosi (*c.* 1940). The setting in B. Reiser's *Laudes festivae* [(2d ed. Vatican City 1940) No. 97:306] is of unrecorded and doubtful origin.

Bibliography: F. J. E. RABY, ed., *Oxford Book of Medieval Latin Verse* (Oxford 1959) No. 101, text. J. SZÖVÉRFFY, *Die Annalen der lateinischen Hymnendichtung* (Berlin 1964–65) 1:383–385. Baini's transcription autograph in MS Rome Casanat. 3081. L. TRAUBE, *Abhhandlungen der Bayerischen Akademie der Wissenschaften* (Munich 1835) 19.2 (1891) 299–309 with facs. of Vat. MS. P. WAGNER, in *Kirchenmusikalisches Jahrbuch* 22 (1909) 1–16. B. M. PEEBLES, *American Benedictine Review* 1 (1950) 67–92, and in *Catholic Choirmaster* 36 (1950) 102–104, 143. I. ANGLÈS et al., in *Roma nobilis,* ed. I. CECCHETTI (Rome 1953) 1:685–689, 1183–86 (Liszt), 1187–91 (Perosi). A. MACHABEY, *Cahiers de civilisation médiévale* 2 (1959) 204. *L'Anno santo 1950 . . . a cura del Comitato centrale A. S.* (Vatican City 1952) 481, 886–887.

[B. M. PEEBLES]

OAK, SYNOD OF THE

The Synod of the Oak was a local council convoked illegally in 403 by Theophilus, Patriarch of Alexandria, in a suburb of Chalcedon called "The Oak," to depose JOHN CHRYSOSTOM from the See of Constantinople. In 401 Theophilus had excommunicated and exiled the TALL BROTHERS, and other Nitrian monks who had offended him as Origenists. They appealed to John Chrysostom, who gave them hospitality but withheld ecclesiastical communion pending final settlement of their case. They also appealed to the Emperor Arcadius, and Arcadius summoned Theophilus to appear before a synod of 40

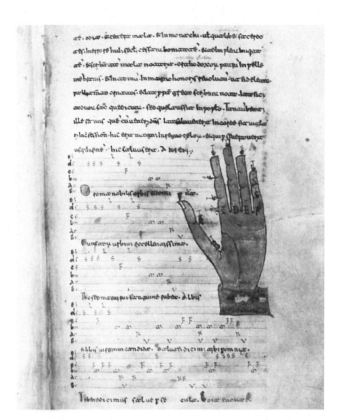

First strophe of "O Roma Nobilis," 11th century, Monte Cassino MS (MS 318, fol. 291).

bishops in Constantinople, over which Chrysostom would preside. Chrysostom protested that, canonically, Theophilus had first to be heard by a synod in his own province.

Theophilus had no such canonical qualms. On his way to the capital, he threatened that he would depose John and, on his arrival (403), connived among court and clergy to achieve that end. His plotting prospered and he moved across the Bosporus to "The Oak," where, although outside his jurisdiction, he convoked a synod of 36 bishops. Of these, at least 29 were his own Egyptian suffragans; the others were John's foes, including some Ephesian bishops whom John had deposed for simony. Two Egyptian bishops were sent to John with a curt command for him to appear before Theophilus and his synod. John refused to appear before a court whose members were at once accusers, judges, and witnesses. Next, two of John's own clergy were told to summon him. John sent back a protest citing the illegality of the synod, and the three bishops who carried this reply were manhandled by the synodal fathers. A final summons, from the emperor himself, demanded his presence. Sure of his canonical position, John again refused, and was tried *in absentia.* In 46 charges he was accused of a misuse of church funds, tyrannical treatment of his clergy, irregularities in

Titus Oates. (Archive Photos)

ritual, invasion of jurisdiction, and even high treason. All charges were frivolous, exaggerated, or totally false. Nevertheless, after 14 sessions, the synod condemned and deposed him. The charge of treason was referred to the emperor, who then ordered Chrysostom into exile.

Bibliography: C. BAUR, *John Chrysostom and His Time,* tr. M. GONZAGA, 2 v. (Westminster, Md. 1960–61) 2:237–261. C. J. VON HEFELE, *Histoire des conciles d'aprè les documents originaux,* tr. and cont. by H. LECLERCQ, 10 v. in 19 (Paris 1907–38) 2:137–154. E. VENABLES, *A Dictionary of Christian Biography,* ed. W. SMITH and H. WACE, 4 v. (London 1877–87) 1:526–528. A. BIGLMAIR, *Lexikon für Theologie und Kirche²,* ed. J. HOFER and K. RAHNER (Freiburg 1957–65); suppl. *Das Zweite Vatikanische Konzil: Dokumente und Kommentare,* ed. H. S. BRECHTER et al., pt. 1 (1966) 3:722. PHOTIUS, ''Bibliotheca, 59,'' *Patrologia Graeca,* ed. J. P. MIGNE, 161 v. (Paris 1857–66) 103:105–114. E. SCHWARTZ, *Zeitschrift für die neutestamentliche Wissenschaft und die Kunde der älteren Kirche* 36 (1937) 168–181.

[P. W. HARKINS]

OATES PLOT

The Oates Plot (or Popish Plot), named after Titus Oates (1649–1705), the principal informer, provoked the last large-scale persecution of Catholics in England. Between 1678 and 1681 more than 25 Catholics were executed in England, many more died in prison, and many hundreds were imprisoned. In what follows an account is given of (1) the political and religious background, (2) the actual outbreak of the plot, (3) its political consequences and management, and (4) some of the outstanding trials and martyrdoms.

Background. At the Restoration of Charles II in 1660, a measure of practical toleration had been accorded to Catholics and Dissenters, though fines for recusancy were still levied. The king was obviously well-disposed toward Catholics. Positive legislation in favor of toleration for Catholics was attempted immediately after the Restoration, but this was bedeviled by the rigidity of the king's adviser, Edward Hyde, Earl of Clarendon (1609–74). After the fall of Clarendon in 1667, the question of Catholicism played a part in Charles's negotiations with Louis XIV. By the Secret Treaty of Dover (1670) Charles had agreed publicly to declare himself a Catholic at such time as should appear to him most expedient. The moment never came (till his deathbed), but in 1672, as an earnest of his intentions, Charles proclaimed the Declaration of Indulgence, removing the penal laws against all Nonconformists and recusants and permitting public worship to Dissenters and private worship to recusants. The subsequent Parliament, however, introduced the Test Act, which disabled Catholics from holding public office, and Charles was compelled to re-enforce the PENAL LAWS.

Royal Succession. The next problem concerned the royal succession of James, Duke of York. Owing to the barrenness of Charles's wife, James was clearly the next in line to the throne, but his refusal in 1673 to take the Sacrament in the Church of England confirmed suspicions of his conversion to Catholicism. Parliament feared a popish successor and an inevitable alliance with France. If Charles could not be induced to divorce his infertile Catholic wife, then means had to be taken to prevent a Catholic successor. On the other hand, Louis XIV wished to stabilize his Continental conquests, to secure English neutrality while he did so, and to prevent an English alliance with the Dutch. In February 1676, therefore, Charles and Louis entered into another secret treaty, whereby, in return for financial aid, Charles promised his neutrality. But to prevent any possible agreement between Charles and Parliament, Louis also intensified his large-scale bribery of members of Parliament through his ambassadors in England. One of the agents for the distribution of parliamentary bribes was a professional newsletter writer, Edward Coleman, secretary to the Duke of York. Coleman was an overenthusiastic convert. He had come into conflict with the authorities because of his infringement of the state monopoly of licensed news, and in 1676 a French apostate, De Luzancy, accused him of dealings with a French Jesuit, Father St. Germain. From December

1676, with the knowledge of Charles II, Coleman's correspondence was being intercepted at the post office by the secretary of state.

In the year prior to the Plot, the king's chief minister, Thomas Osborne, Earl of Danby, was pursuing a difficult policy. By economic reform he was attempting to organize the treasury in such a way that Charles would be as little as possible dependent on either Parliament or Louis for his revenues. At the same time Danby was attempting to maintain a court party in Parliament on a basis of a policy of public nonalignment with France and strong Anglican safeguards for the monarchy and the constitution; but if the worst came to the worst, money from Louis was preferable to concessions to Parliament. The marriage alliance between William of Orange and the Princess Mary, daughter of James, Duke of York, in October 1677 was followed by a treaty of neutrality with the States-General. At the Congress of Nijmegen (1678) negotiations for a general European peace settlement were proceeding.

Early in 1678 the parliamentary opposition, led by the recently disgraced Anthony Ashley Cooper, Earl of Shaftesbury (1621–83), was gaining ground. The strength of the movement toward a Dutch alliance against Louis was growing, and an anti-popery scare was started in April. In the early summer Louis seemed to be ready to wreck the negotiations at Nijmegen and to be preparing for a new war. In May 1678 he signed yet another secret treaty of neutrality with Charles, but then on the strength of that Louis signed a separate peace treaty in July with the States-General of Holland. Charles thus got neither the benefit of a French subsidy nor the credit for a Dutch alliance. Danby's policy was in ruins, and he might well expect trouble from Parliament in the autumn of 1678, since he had alienated almost all support there. It is against this background that the emergence of the Popish Plot in the late summer of 1678 must be seen.

Oates and the Outbreak of the Plot. Titus Oates was born in 1649 at Oakham, Rutlandshire, son of Samuel Oates, an Anabaptist weaver. After a highly unsatisfactory career at Merchant Taylors' School, London, and at Cambridge University, he eventually succeeded in 1670 in being ordained in the Church of England. He left two clerical appointments under a cloud and was even unsuccessful as a naval chaplain. By 1676 he had already been found guilty of perjury and was strongly suspected of sodomy. He then made the acquaintance of Matthew Medburne, a Catholic actor, who introduced him into a club at the Pheasant Tavern, Fuller's Rents, London, that served as a meeting place for Catholics and Nonconformists (Richard BAXTER was a member). In 1677 Oates succeeded in being appointed as a Protestant chaplain in the household of the Catholic Duke of Norfolk at Arundel House in the Strand. About the same time he made the acquaintance of Dr. Israel Tonge (1621–80), Rector of St. Michael's, Wood Street, London. Tonge was anti-Royalist and anti-Jesuit, and was a crank. Oates found him credulous enough and offered to act as a spy on the Jesuits. On Ash Wednesday, March 3, 1677, therefore, Oates had himself received into the Catholic Church by William Berry, alias Hutchinson, a mentally unbalanced priest. In April of the same year Oates obtained an introduction to Richard Strange, Provincial of the Society of Jesus, who arranged for him to go to the English College, Valladolid. Oates arrived there in June; after four months he was expelled and returned to England. He next petitioned to be sent to the Jesuit College of Saint-Omer and arrived there in December 1677. During his stay at Saint-Omer he heard that the annual meeting of the officials of the Jesuit English province was being held in London on April 24, 1678. Oates returned to England in June and put his information at the disposal of Tonge; at the same time he attempted to blackmail the London Jesuits.

Tonge, armed with "revelations" of a Jesuit plot to assassinate the king, obtained access to Danby and to Charles. The king took little interest, but Danby saw the possibility of an anti-popish "scare" to distract public attention from the failure of his foreign policy. On August 26 Tonge warned Danby that letters concerning the plot had been sent to Rev. Thomas Downes, alias Father Bedingfield, SJ, the Duke of York's confessor at Windsor. Danby hurried to Windsor to intercept them, but Bedingfield had already collected them, had seen them to be forgeries, and had given them to the Duke of York. On September 6 Oates and Tonge approached a London magistrate, Sir Edmund Berry Godfrey, to make an affidavit concerning a deposition of 43 articles concerning a Jesuit plot, though they would not at first allow Godfrey to see the text of the deposition. Godfrey, to the chagrin of Danby, informed the Duke of York, who demanded an investigation by the Privy Council in order to expose the accusations. Oates and Tonge, therefore, with the aid of others unknown, proceeded to draft further depositions. On September 28 Tonge was summoned to attend the Council, but before the Council meeting Oates and Tonge had a plot narrative of 81 articles attested before Godfrey. Both narratives were of course a farrago of nonsense, but the development of the plot between September 6 and 28 is highly interesting. The first depositions centered on the Jesuit "consult" of April and the efforts to assassinate the king. In the later version, more names of those in Oates's immediate environment and names of those who could be arrested easily were given. The new depositions included information against Edmund Coleman; Medburne, the actor; Dr. Fogarty, Oates's physician; the Benedictines in the Savoy; and Abp. Peter TALBOT in Ireland.

There is every reason for assuming that between September 6 and 28 Oates and Tonge were being guided from another source and that that source was Danby.

The king sat with the Council on the morning of September 28 and made no attempt to disguise his disbelief in Oates, but went off in the afternoon to the races at Newmarket. Nonetheless, Oates's effrontery carried the day, and the Council adjourned in the evening having issued warrants for the arrest of the conspirators. Danby made a special point of having the Council sign a special warrant for the seizure of Coleman's papers, knowing full well the sort of correspondence that Coleman had been maintaining over the past years. Meanwhile, on the same day, Godfrey had warned Coleman of what was afoot; Coleman did not destroy his papers, but surrendered on September 30. Though not by contemporary standards treasonable, Coleman's letters were compromising and indiscreet, and he made it clear in his letters to François de LA CHAIZE, SJ, Louis XIV's confessor, that he was trying to obtain money from France to influence Parliament in favor of popery. On top of all this, on October 12, Sir Edmund Berry Godfrey disappeared and on October 17 was found strangled, with a sword through his body. Parliament met four days later.

If Danby encouraged the Oates Plot in the hopes of making it an instrument of the Anglican-Royalist wing of the court party against the papist Duke of York, there is no doubt that after the reassembly of Parliament the plot was utilized by Shaftesbury, the leader of the opposition, against the whole court party and the monarchy. Shaftesbury and the Whigs worked up mass hysteria and mob violence as a means of trying to bar the Duke of York from the succession and ultimately to drive Charles from the throne. For three years the cry of ''No popery'' was used constantly for political ends.

Political Consequences. From October 1678 to March 1681 Charles stood virtually alone against Shaftesbury and the Whig opposition. Danby was impeached in December 1678, and the court party was in ruins. Charles has been blamed for not intervening to save those Catholics condemned to death for crimes of which he knew they were innocent. But to expect Charles to have interposed the royal prerogative against the process of the courts at such a juncture is a sentimental misunderstanding of his constitutional position. On two things he stood firm: his personal honor and the succession of his brother. When Oates began to accuse Queen Catherine of treason, Charles made it clear that he would fight back with all the means in his power. Furthermore, he persuaded the unskillful Duke of York to leave the country and then, by prorogation and dissolution, frustrated successive attempts of Parliament to introduce an Exclusion Bill. For the rest he could do nothing but try to ride out the storm. Ultimately, in March 1681, he succeeded in convincing Louis XIV that the only chance for the survival of the English monarchy and the succession of the Duke of York was for the king to rule without Parliament. With a substantial subsidy from Louis in his pocket, Charles summoned his last Parliament at Oxford. On March 21 they met; on March 28 the Commons were beginning to read the Exclusion Bill when the king suddenly dissolved Parliament and for the rest of his reign ruled alone.

The king gradually reasserted his power. In April 1681 Chief Justice William Scroggs, who had conducted most of the plot trials, was removed from office. In July Shaftesbury was sent to the Tower. In November John Dryden's *Absalom and Achitophel,* a satire on Shaftesbury and the Whigs, appeared; within a year Shaftesbury fled to Holland and died. In June 1683 the ''Rye House'' Plot was discovered: this was a Whig plot to assassinate Charles on his way to Newmarket. The great Whig magnates who were implicated were prosecuted with the same vigor as the Catholics had been during the Popish Plot. As for Oates, in June 1684 the Duke of York took action against him for *scandalum magnatum,* and damages of £ 100,000 were given against him. While still in prison, Oates was indicted for perjury and came up for trial in February 1685, but the trial was deferred on account of the death of Charles. In May he was found guilty of perjury and sentenced to be pilloried and whipped annually. In 1688, on the abdication of James and the accession of William III, Oates was released from prison and became once more a government pensioner. He died in 1705.

The Trials. The first trial was obviously designed to instill terror. On Nov. 15, 1678, William Staley, a Catholic goldsmith, was arrested on the evidence of two obvious rascals and charged with having said that the king was a rogue and that he would stab the king if no one else would. He was brought to trial six days later, condemned, and executed on November 26. It was in this atmosphere that the trial of Coleman began on the following day. Seven of the jurors in Staley's case served at Coleman's trial. The most damning evidence against Coleman lay in letters written to François de la Chaize in 1675, but it is significant that the whole of Coleman's captured correspondence was not published until the end of 1680, and Coleman remained remarkably reticent about his political activities. He was condemned and executed on December 3. On Dec. 17, 1678, William Ireland, SJ, procurator of the English province; John Grove, a layman employed by the Jesuits; and Thomas Pickering, OSB, a lay brother; together with Thomas Whitebread, SJ, and John Fenwick, SJ, were tried for treason. There was only one witness against Whitebread and Fenwick, but instead of being freed, they were remanded to prison by Lord Chief Justice Scroggs. Ireland and Grove were executed on Jan. 24, 1679; Pickering was respited, probably at the instance of the queen, but was eventually executed on May 9.

On Feb. 5, 1679, three servants at Somerset House, Robert Green, Henry Berry, and Lawrence Hill, were tried and condemned for the murder of Sir Edmund Berry Godfrey on the perjured testimony of Miles Prance, a Catholic goldsmith, who had originally been arrested as a conspirator but induced to turn king's evidence. Green and Hill were executed on February 21 and Berry, a Protestant, was executed on February 28.

On Feb. 8, 1679, occurred the first acquittal. Samuel Atkins, a Protestant and a clerk of Samuel Pepys, had been arrested in November 1678 for complicity in Godfrey's murder. (The Whigs had hoped that the young man would implicate his master, Pepys, a trusted servant of the Duke of York at the Admiralty.) Fortunately, the efficient Pepys had been able to produce witnesses, all Protestants, to prove an alibi. This was doubtless a setback to the Whig plot managers, and it was not until June 13 that the next batch of major treason trials took place.

First came five Jesuits: Thomas Whitebread, the English Provincial; William Harcourt, Superior of the London district; Anthony Turner; John Fenwick; and John Gavan. Whitebread and Fenwick maintained that they could not be tried twice for the same offense, but this was overruled. Defense witnesses were produced from Saint-Omer who swore that Oates was at Saint-Omer in April 1678 and thus could not possibly have been at the Jesuit "consult" as he had claimed, but to no avail. The following day Richard Langhorne, a Catholic lawyer who had acted for the Jesuits in their business affairs, was also tried and condemned. The five Jesuits were executed on June 20 and Langhorne on July 14.

On July 10 Parliament was dissolved. On July 18 Sir George Wakeman, the queen's physician; William Marshall, OSB; William Rumley, OSB, a lay brother; and James Corker, OSB, were tried for treason and acquitted. Wakeman and Rumley were released, and retired to the Continent, but Corker and Marshall were remanded to prison to be tried for their priesthood.

Meanwhile a number of priests were put to death in the provinces on account of their priesthood. William PLESSINGTON, secular priest, was executed at Chester on July 19; Philip EVANS, SJ, and John LLOYD, secular priest, were executed at Cardiff on July 22; Nicholas Postgate, secular priest, at York on August 7; Charles MIHAN (Mahoney), OSF, an Irishman, at Ruthin, North Wales, August 12; John WALL, OSF, at Worcester, August 25; John KEMBLE, secular priest, at Hereford, also August 25; and David LEWIS, SJ, at Usk, August 27. It is noteworthy that at Stafford, Andrew Bromwich, a secular priest, though condemned to death for priesthood, was reprieved after taking the Oath of Allegiance and that Charles Carne, a secular priest, who asserted at his trial at Hereford that he had taken the Oaths of Allegiance and Supremacy was acquitted also.

On Feb. 11, 1680, Sir Thomas Gascoigne, an elderly Yorkshire baronet, was tried for treason on the evidence of two servants and was acquitted. Nevertheless his daughter Lady Tempest was sent for trial at York, together with Sir Miles Stapleton, Mary Pressicks, and a priest, Thomas Thwing. On March 17, at York assizes, they challenged so many jurors that the trial had to be held over until the summer. Eventually they were tried on July 28. Thwing was condemned and executed on October 23; the others were acquitted.

The "Meal Tub" Plot. The so-called Meal Tub Plot brings an element almost of farce into the tragic story. A Catholic midwife, Mrs. Elizabeth Cellier, a woman of extraordinary energy and fortitude, had been bringing what help she could to the Catholics in prison for the plot, and had provided for some of the defense witnesses at the trials. While visiting the jails, she met Thomas Dangerfield, imprisoned for debt, and fell, it seems, a victim to his plausible manners. She paid off his debts, and on his release he acted for her as a spy on the Whigs. He was, however, playing a double game. He gave Mrs. Cellier some papers that he claimed proved the existence of a Presbyterian plot. These Mrs. Cellier hid in a meal tub in her house. Then he made a confession to the authorities, claiming that the papers were forgeries inspired by the Catholics and that the Earl of Castlemaine, Lady Powis, and Mrs. Cellier had tried to bribe him to kill the king. Lord Castlemaine and Mrs. Cellier were tried for treason in June 1680 and acquitted. Mrs. Cellier then published her own account of her dealings with Dangerfield and of her trial. For this she was fined and condemned to stand in the pillory on September 11.

In November 1680, concurrently with its attempts to push through the Exclusion Bill, the House of Commons resolved to act against the Catholic lords who had been in the Tower since the outbreak of the plot in 1678. They chose as their first victim William Howard, Viscount Stafford. The trial of Stafford by his peers in the House of Lords took place from November 30 to December 7. If Stafford had had a jury trial, he might have been acquitted. As it was, his fate depended on a public declaration by each individual peer. Fifty-five lords found him guilty and thirty-one declared him not guilty; he was condemned to death. On December 18 Stafford, at his own request, came to the bar of the House of Lords to make a statement. He told of his efforts to obtain toleration for the Catholics at the Restoration by payment of a collective fine and went on to tell of his efforts at the time of the Test Act to secure an alliance between Shaftesbury's party and the Duke of York. At the mention of Shaftesbury he was ordered back to the Tower and was executed on December 29.

The last plot trial was that of Oliver PLUNKETT, Archbishop of Armagh. Plunkett had been arrested and brought as prisoner to Dublin Castle on Dec. 6, 1679. The reason why the Viceroy James Butler, Duke of Ormonde, had delayed so long was that, previous to the plot, Plunkett had been willing to cooperate with the authorities in the condemnation and extirpation of violence and brigandage. But by the efforts of Henry Jones, Protestant Bishop of Meath and a strong anti-Royalist, who was in close correspondence with Colonel Mansell, one of the English Whig plot managers, it was arranged that Plunkett should be brought to England to stand trial. On Oct. 30, 1680, he was brought to London and committed for trial; a host of Irish informers, mostly apostate priests, were brought over to testify against him. He was not brought to trial until May 3, 1681. By this time, after the dissolution of the Oxford Parliament in March, the plot was well on the wane. Nevertheless, Plunkett was found guilty of treason and executed on July 1, 1681. What principally told against him at his trial was the fact that the Irish prosecution witnesses were new and had not been discredited as the English informers had been. Though Plunkett was the last to be executed for the plot, many Catholics sentenced or awaiting trial remained in jail until the end of Charles II's reign.

The savagery and long persistence of the Oates Plot was attributable principally to Shaftesbury and the Whigs, it can also be partly attributed to the general cynicism and dissoluteness of the age. But a great share of the blame must be attributed to the bribery and corruption of the English Parliament by Louis XIV, the Most Christian King.

Bibliography: J. POLLOCK, *The Popish Plot* (London 1903; new ed. Cambridge, England 1944), brilliant pioneer work but unbalanced. J. LANE, *Titus Oates* (London 1949), excellent. F. S. RONALDS, *The Attempted Whig Revolution of 1674–81* (Urbana, IL 1937), thorough and detached. J. WARNER, *History of . . . the Presbyterian Plot,* ed. T. A. BIRRELL, tr. J. BLIGH, 2 v. (*Publications of the Catholic Record Society* 47, 48; 1953–55), a near contemporary account. D. OGG, *England in the Reign of Charles II,* 2 v. (2d ed. Oxford 1955; repr. pa. London 1963), excellent on political background. Besides bibliog. in the above volumes, *see* C. L. GROSE, *A Select Bibliography of British History, 1660–1760* (Chicago 1939), and suppl. in *Journal of Modern History* 12 (1940) 515–534. R. CHALLONER, *Memoirs of Missionary Priests,* ed. J. H. POLLEN (rev. ed. London 1924), invaluable martyrology. J. LINGARD, *The History of England,* 10 v. (Copyright ed. London 1883), relevant chapters are still useful. Special topics: on Coleman, Coventry MSS v.11, Longleat House, Wiltshire and Bulstrode Papers v.12, Carl H. Pforzheimer Library, New York. On Atkins, A. BRYANT, *Samuel Pepys,* 3 v. (2d ed. London 1948–49) v.2, *The Years of Peril.* On Plunkett, A. CURTAYNE, *The Trial of Oliver Plunkett* (New York 1953) and E. CURTIS, *Blessed Oliver Plunkett* (Dublin 1963), popular treatment.

[T. A. BIRRELL]

OATHS

Oaths are appeals to God in witness of the truth of statements or of the binding character of promises. The oath has been in use among all peoples; it continues to be regarded as a useful social institution and a formal guarantee of truthfulness necessary in organized society. Some (e.g., the Quakers) have interpreted Mt 5.4 to be an absolute prohibition of oaths, but Christ's words are a condemnation only of the type of trivial or profane oaths that were permitted under pharisaical casuistry (*see* OATHS IN THE BIBLE).

There was some difference of opinion among the Fathers of the Church regarding the licitness of oaths. Chrysostom regarded them as a snare of the devil to be avoided under all circumstances (*Serm. ad pop. Ant.* 15; *In Act. Apost. hom.* 8). Augustine was not concerned about a gospel prohibition, but thought that the oath should be avoided because of the danger of perjury that would arise from the frequent use of it (*In psalm.* 88.4; *De mend.* 28). Others, basing their arguments on New Testament usage, especially on the example of St. Paul, who frequently expressed himself in language indistinguishable from an oath (e.g., 1 Thes 2.5; 2 Cor 1.23; Gal 1–20; Rom 1.9), thought the taking of oaths was permissible in proper circumstances. This view prevailed in Christian times. Oaths became part of the judicial procedure; and oaths pledging fealty, fidelity, or the faithful performance of the duties of an office were recognized as having a social value. Theologians have generally held that an oath taken under proper conditions is not only licit but is also an act of the virtue of religion inasmuch as it is an expression of homage to the wisdom and power of God (St. Thomas Aquinas, *Summa Theologiae,* 2a2ae, 81.2).

By reason of the matter with which it is concerned an oath is either assertory (declaratory), that is, it calls upon God to witness that one is speaking the truth; or it is promissory, that is, it calls upon God to guarantee one's pledge to do or not to do something. In mode, an oath is either invocatory or imprecatory. In the former, one calls upon God as a witness; in the latter, one invites God's punishment if what is sworn to is false. An oath may also

bis mdulgeat p suā mīam:demēs et miseū
cors dn̄s. Jtan de tra mea ac uindiaone in sub

King Charles swearing his oath upon the Gospels, miniature in the "Coronation Book of Charles V," French, 1365 (Cotton MS Tiberius VIII, fol. 46v).

be either implicit or explicit. In the one, God is mentioned by name; in the other, the formula or gesture used is generally understood to imply the invocation of Him.

To be licit, an oath demands truthfulness, judgment (prudence), and justice (Jer 4.2). The first of these conditions requires the person who takes the oath to speak truly and, in the case of a promissory oath, to be sincere in his intention to fulfill his promise. Judgment, or prudence, requires sufficient reason for taking the oath. In an assertory oath justice demands that the statement should not be sinful (as would be the case, for example, if it were defamatory); in a promissory oath, that which is promised should be morally lawful.

In the case of the promissory oath, the object of the promise must be possible and morally good. A promise of what is impossible, evil, or vain dishonors God and has no binding force. Moreover, it is understood that one undertakes to keep the promise only so long as the fulfill-

ment remains morally possible, provided legitimate authority does not forbid it, and provided no notable change occurs in the matter of the promise, and the beneficiary of the promise does not yield his right to the fulfillment.

Because God is called to witness in an oath, the Church, as the official representative of Christ, legislates on the taking of oaths and claims the power of releasing those who are bound by promissory oaths.

See Also: PERJURY.

Bibliography: T. AQUINAS, *Summa Theologiae,* 2a2ae, 89. H. DAVIS, *Moral and Pastoral Theology,* rev. and enl. ed. by L. W. GEDDES (New York 1958) 2:44–48. H. NOLDIN, *Summa theologiae moralis,* rev. A. SCHMITT and G. HEINZEL, 3 v. (Innsbruck 1961–62); v. 1 contains complementa, *De castitate* and *De poenis ecclesiasticis,* separately paged, 2:208–223. N. IUNG, *Dictionnaire de théologie* *catholique,* ed. A. VACANT et al., 15 v. (Paris 1903–50; Tables générales 1951–) 14.2:1940–56.

[M. HERRON]

OATHS (IN THE BIBLE)

The custom of swearing, or taking oaths, that is, of putting a curse on oneself if what is asserted is not true or if a promise is not kept, has always been widespread among all people who believe either in the magical power of such self-maledictions or in the avenging justice of a deity who punishes those who swear falsely. This article is concerned with the taking of oaths as mentioned in the Bible.

In the Old Testament. Anthropomorphically, God Himself is often presented in the Old Testament as taking oaths, especially in regard to His covenant [*See* COVENANT (IN THE BIBLE)]. Thus, "he promised on oath to Abraham, Isaac, and Jacob" (Gn 50.24) to make their descendants a great nation and to give them a special land (Gn 22.16–18; 26.3–4; 35.12). He renewed this sworn promise to Moses (Dt 1.8). Later, "the Lord swore to David a firm promise" [Ps 131(132).11] of an everlasting posterity and rule [Ps 88(89).4–5, 36–37] and an eternal priesthood [Ps 109(110).4]. It is these promises that are reaffirmed by the prophets (Jer 33.21–22; Mi 7.20). Besides these oaths that promise great blessings, there are the oaths that threaten with punishment the Israelites who revolted in the desert (Nm 14.28–35).

Whether men swore by God explicitly (Gn 21.23; Jos 2.12) or implicitly (Gn 42.15; 1 Sm 1.26), an oath was a serious matter (Ex 20.7), for the oath always involved a conditional or contingent curse. Moreover, the oath was ever regarded as a sign of loyalty to God (Dt 6.13; Is 48.1), and therefore a false oath was basically a profanation of God's name (Lv 19.12; Ex 20.7). Oaths were employed both in judicial matters and in a variety of everyday affairs. Thus oaths were taken to certify the truth of an utterance and to pledge fidelity to one's word (1 Sm 14.44; 20.13; 25.22; 2 Sm 3.9; Gn 25.33; 47.31); to ascertain the guilt of a person suspected of a crime, e.g., in the trial by ORDEAL (Nm 5.16–28); and to ratify an alliance (Gn 21.24, 26, 31) or a friendship (1 Sm 20.16–17).

In the New Testament. It is only in the New Testament that the oaths made by God in the Old Testament attain their perfect fulfillment: by sending the Messiah God has been faithful to "the oath that he swore to Abraham our father" (Lk 1.73), His promise to David has been fulfilled by Christ's Resurrection (Acts 2.29–35), and it is God's solemn oath that ratifies Christ's eternal priesthood and guarantees the reality and efficacy of the New Covenant (Heb 7.21, 25).

Respect for oaths seems to have been carefully preserved by the ancient Israelites, but by the time of Christ's coming the Pharisees had distorted this traditional respect through their casuistry. Christ energetically attacked these legalistic abuses, demanding absolute sincerity of his disciples (Mk 23.16–22). He proclaimed a new ideal: "But I say to you not to swear at all" (Mt 5.34). St. James restates this teaching: "Let your yes be yes, your no, no" (Jas 5.12). Yet Christ did not absolutely abolish or condemn the use of the oath; His demand set the Christian ideal, but did not rule out the possibility of an oath on certain occasions. Thus, e.g., St. Paul often employed oath formulas in order to testify to the truth of his assertions (Rom 1.9; 9.1; 2 Cor 1.23; 11.31; Gal 1.20).

Bibliography: *Encyclopedic Dictionary of the Bible,* tr. and adap. by L. HARTMAN (New York 1963) 1656–58. J. PEDERSEN, *Der Eid bei den Semiten* (Leipzig 1914). S. H. BLANK, "The Curse, Blasphemy, the Spell, and the Oath," *Hebrew Union College Annual* 23.1 (Cincinnati 1950–51) 73–95. F. HORST, "Der Eid im AT," *Evangelische Theologie* 17 (1957) 366–384.

[J. V. MORRIS]

OATHS, ENGLISH POST-REFORMATION

From the first days of the English Reformation oaths, tests, and formal declarations were used to secure submission to the changes imposed by conformity to the Established Church. Later they were employed to penalize Catholics, and finally, as a condition of relief from legal disabilities.

Oath of Supremacy, 1534 to 1559. The early history of this oath is complicated. The statute (22 Henry VIII ch. 15) of 1530 confirmed HENRY VIII's pardon of the English clergy for unlawfully acknowledging Thomas WOLSEY's legatine authority in return for a grant of £100,000 and the Convocations' recognition (February and March 1530) that he was "of the Church and Clergy of England, [the] especial Protector, single and supreme Lord, and, as far as the law of Christ allows, even Supreme Head." The qualification, "as far as the law of Christ allows," inserted in the Convocations' declaration at the instance of St. John FISHER, was omitted in a similar acknowledgement made by Parliament after the break with Rome in the Dispensations Act, 1534 (25 Henry VIII ch. 21). Then, the first Act of Succession in 1534 (25 Henry VIII ch. 22), having recited and approved Thomas CRANMER's annulment of the king's marriage with CATHERINE OF ARAGON and Henry's marriage to Anne Boleyn, enacted that everyone "at their full ages . . . shall make a corporal oath" to keep "the whole effects and contents of this present Act." Refusal was punishable with loss of goods and life imprisonment, but no form for this oath was provided. The text of the oath taken by Lords and Commons (*Lords' Journals,* 1.82) before Parliament was prorogued in March 1534 refers, however, not only to the Act of Succession but to "all other Acts and Statutes made since the beginning of this present Parliament . . . anything therein contained," and thus to the Dispensations Act. This may have been the form of oath that was widely tendered and taken during the summer of 1534, but refused by John Fisher and Thomas MORE, among others.

In December 1534 an Act of Supremacy (26 Henry VIII ch. 1) reaffirmed that the "King is the only supreme head on earth of the Church of England called Anglicana Ecclesia," and a second Act of Succession (26 Henry VIII ch. 2) gave a form of oath said to be that intended by the earlier act. It differs from that in the *Lords' Journals* only by omitting the phrase "made since the beginning of this present Parliament," and so equally required an acknowledgement of royal supremacy. Another statute (26 Henry VIII ch. 13) made the denial of any royal title treason, so that refusal of the oath was (after Feb. 1, 1535) treason. It was for this offense that Fisher and More were convicted and executed. In July 1536 an act "For Extinguishing Papal Authority" (28 Henry VIII ch. 10) provided a new oath by which all officeholders (ecclesiastical and lay) and all who held lands of the king or took holy orders or religious vows swore they would "assist and defend" the supremacy. The Act of Succession, 1544 (35 Henry VIII ch. 1), enacted another new and very long oath that involved a profession of faith in the royal supremacy. It was to be taken by all officeholders and by anyone when required.

All legislation inconsistent with papal primacy was repealed in 1554 (1 and 2 Philip and Mary ch. 8) and most of it was revived by the first of Elizabeth I's statutes, the Act of Supremacy, 1559 (1 Elizabeth I ch. 1). This reintroduced what was substantially the 1536 oath, viz., "I, A.B., do utterly testify and declare in my conscience that the Queen's Highness is the only Supreme Governor of the Realm . . . as well as in all spiritual or ecclesiastical things or causes as temporal, and that no foreign . . . prelate . . . hath or ought to have any jurisdiction power . . . or authority ecclesiastical or spiritual within this realm." It was to be taken by the clergy and by all holding office under the Crown, and by those taking university degrees; refusal entailed disability from holding office or preferment. It appears in practice not to have been tendered in the universities or to the parochial clergy; an undertaking to use the Book of COMMON PRAYER was thought sufficient. A statute of 1563 (5 Elizabeth I ch. 1) provided that the oath could be required of schoolmasters, lawyers, and legal officials, and that refusal by anyone should be punished on the first occasion by the penalties of PRAEMUNIRE (forfeiture of lands and goods, and life imprisonment) and on a second (after the lapse of three months), as treason.

Oath of Allegiance (or Obedience), 1606. In response to a royal proclamation of November 1602, distinguishing between Jesuits and the secular clergy, and extending to the latter, in veiled language, hope of some amelioration of the laws against them, 13 secular priests on Jan. 31, 1603, submitted to Elizabeth I a *Protestation of Allegiance* in which they denounced papal sponsored plots of invasion, and bound themselves to disobey any papal decree of excommunication or deposition of the Queen. She was dying, however, and the *Protestation* had no immediate effect. After the Gunpowder Plot (1605) the persecution of Catholics was intensified, and the first of two severe statutes (3 and 4 James I ch. 4, 5) included (ch. 4 sec. 8, 9, 27) a device to create dissension among the Catholics. Although there could be no serious doubts as to Catholic loyalty, the *Protestation* and the negotiations preceding it had shown that there were differences of opinion on the pope's deposing power, which was stoutly defended by the Jesuits, among others. The following Oath of Allegiance was therefore drafted to exploit these differences and to cast doubt on that loyalty: "I, A.B., do truly and sincerely acknowledge . . . that our sovereign lord, King James, is lawful and rightful king . . . and that the pope neither of himself nor by any authority of the Church or See of Rome, or by any other means with any other, has any power to depose the king . . . or to authorise any foreign prince to invade him . . . or to give license to any to bear arms, [or] raise tumults . . . . Also I do swear that notwithstanding any sentence of excommunication or deprivation I will bear allegiance and true faith to His Majesty. . . . And I do further swear that I do from my heart abhor, detest, and abjure, as impious and heretical this damnable doctrine and position,—that princes which be excommunicated by the pope may be deposed or murdered by their subjects or by any other whatsoever. And I do believe that the pope has no power to absolve me from this oath. I do swear according to the plain and common sense and understanding of the same words." The oath became law on June 26, 1606. It could be required of anyone convicted or suspected of recusancy, and refusal entailed liability to the penalties of praemunire. After 1610 (7 James I ch. 6) it could be demanded of anyone over 18. Subscription did not, however, relieve Catholics of any of the penalties of the anti-Catholic legislation as the 1603 signatories had hoped.

On Sept. 22, 1606, Paul V condemned the oath "as it contains many things evidently contrary to faith and salvation," though he prudently refrained from enumerating them. James I replied that the oath was not meant to encroach upon anyone's conscience, and among the Catholics, minimizers maintained that the oath might be interpreted by the lawgiver's intention and might, therefore, be taken. But the Church's doctrine has always been that oaths are addressed to God Himself and must be accepted in the precise sense of the words pronounced. If James had made his subjects swear specifically "in the sense by him explained," the oath might perhaps have been endured, but when he made them "swear according to the plain and common sense and understanding of the same words" to what was injurious to Catholic consciences, this could not be tolerated. The most objectionable words were those condemning the deposing power as "impious, heretical, and damnable." The doctrine of the deposing power was, as far as practical politics went, already merely an embarrassment. But it was implied by the then-current Catholic teaching on the nature of the Church, and until the previous two or three generations it had been generally accepted as a valuable safeguard for liberty, both religious and civil. Many, including Paul V, had not realized that the power would never be in vogue again, even in Catholic countries, and they believed that it could not be denied without seriously impairing the Roman primacy. And while Robert BELLARMINE, Robert PERSONS, and several other early opponents of the oath thus went further in condemning it than later theologians have done, it is still difficult to see how a Catholic could conscientiously swear that a doctrine long maintained by the popes and by many in the Church, albeit not *de fide,* was "impious, heretical, and damnable." On its side, Rome could not allow the state to judge what was heresy or to specify the conditions under which Catholics would disobey the Holy See. Resistance to the oath was not, therefore, chiefly or solely the result of belief in the deposing power as Catholics such as Thomas PRESTON (ROGER WIDDRINGTON), who wrote in its defense, or those with Gallican leanings, such as Charles BUTLER or M. A. Tierney, have claimed. (The Sorbonne on June 30, 1681, very shortly before approving the Gallican Articles, censored the oath and found in it very little that was objectionable.) English Catholics like William BISHOP (later made a bishop by Rome) and Leander Jones, President of the English Benedictines, who explicitly rejected the deposing power, nevertheless refused the oath. Bishop was imprisoned for refusing it, while Jones consented only to an oath of his own drafting.

The archpriest George BLACKWELL, then head of the English clergy, had at first disapproved of the oath, but then in July 1606, after conferring with some of the leading clergy, allowed it. Later, after the Pope's brief, he disallowed it again, and finally, being imprisoned, he took the oath, relying on James's statement that no encroachment on conscience was intended. In a pastoral letter

Blackwell recommended the faithful to do the same. The Pope issued a new brief (Aug. 23, 1607) repeating his prohibition, and on Sept. 28, 1607, Cardinal Bellarmine wrote to Blackwell exhorting him to obey the brief. As this also proved ineffectual, a new archpriest, George Birkhead, was appointed in February 1608, and Blackwell was told that his faculties would be withdrawn if he did not retract within two months. This he refused to do, and much to James's satisfaction, continued to defend his opinion for three years before he was finally suspended. Meanwhile James himself answered the missives sent to Blackwell in an anonymous tract *Triplici Nodo, Triplex cuneus* ("A triple wedge for a triple knot," i.e., the two briefs and Bellarmine's letter). This was answered by Bellarmine, also anonymously, in *Responsio ad librum: Triplici nodo, triplex cuneus* (1608). James now dropped his anonymity and reprinted his tract with a *Premonition to Christian Princes* and an appendix on his adversaries' supposed mistakes (January 1609). Upon this Bellarmine published under his own name his *Apologia pro responsione ad librum Jacobi I* (1609). James opposed to this a treatise by a learned Scots Catholic, W. Barclay, *De porestate papae* (1609). Barclay was a decided Gallican, and Bellarmine's answer, *Tractatus de potestate summi pontificis in rebus temporalibus* (1610), gave such offense to the Gallican party that it was publicly burned in Paris by a decree of Nov. 26, 1610. A similar fate befell Francisco SUÁREZ'S answer to James, *Defensio Fidei Catholicae adversus Anglicanae sectae errores,* both in Paris and London. At every stage of the contest a host of other combatants joined the fray. On the papal side were Cardinal Du Perron, Leonard Lessius, Jakob Gretser, Thomas Fitzherbert, Martin Becanus, Caspar Scioppius, Robert Persons, N. Coeffeteau, A. Eudaemon Joannes, and Matthew Kellison. On the other side were Bp. Lancelot Andrewes, Isaac Casaubon, Paolo Sarpi, William Barlow, Robert Burhill, Pierre du Moulin, William Barrett, John Barnes, and especially the Benedictine Thomas Preston writing as Roger Widdrington. Most of the Protestant books written in Latin, together with the works of Preston and Barclay, were put on the Roman Index.

Some idea of the pressures caused by the oath may be gathered from the Acts of the Martyrs of England and Wales (*see* ENGLAND, SCOTLAND, AND WALES, MARTYRS OF) during these years. When William LAUD succeeded to Canterbury, the policy of splitting the English Catholics and driving the Jesuits from England was revived (1634), and in a new attempt to induce Catholics to take the oath another book defending it was produced, it seems by Preston, using (with his consent) the name of William Howard. An answer written in extreme terms by a young Jesuit, Edward Courtney, *vere* Leedes, led to Courtney's imprisonment, and was used to foster the impression that only Jesuit intrasigence prevented a settlement between the English government and the Catholics. Courtney was attacked also by Leander Jones who had come to England hoping that he could negotiate a *rapprochement* between Rome and Canterbury, or, failing that, toleration for the English Catholics. Jones unsuccessfully urged that Rome should withdraw its condemnation of the oath if Charles I declared it involved "nothing else but a true and natural civil obedience and loyalty" and was not "a denial of any spiritual authority belonging to His Holiness," and he attempted to devise a formula for the oath that would be acceptable to both sides. Similar proposals were mooted during the Commonwealth and after the Restoration, but none were acceptable to Rome.

Oath of Abjuration, 1643 and 1655. With the success of the Puritans in the civil wars the Oaths of Supremacy and Allegiance naturally fell into desuetude, though they were not repealed until 1650. An act of Aug. 29, 1643, provided that Catholics should forfeit two-thirds of their estates, personal and real, and that everyone should be "adjudged a papist" who refused an oath renouncing papal supremacy, transubstantiation, purgatory, and other doctrines. No Catholic could possibly take this oath. In 1655 the penalties that before 1650 attached to failure to attend the Anglican Church were, by an ordinance, attached to refusal of this oath, which was reissued in an amended (and more objectionable) form. This measure was, however, only sparingly enforced.

Test Oaths, 1672 and 1678. In 1672 after the conversion of James, then Duke of York, a Test Act compelled all holders of office under the Crown to make a short "Declaration against Transubstantiation," viz, to swear that "there is not any transubstantiation in the sacrament of the Lord's Supper . . . at or after the consecration thereof by any person whatsoever" (25 Charles II ch. 2). This test was effective: James resigned his post as Lord High Admiral. After the OATES PLOT (1678) a much longer test was devised with a further clause that "the invocation of the virgin Mary, or any saint and the Sacrifice of the Mass . . . are superstitious and idolatrous . . . and that I make this declaration without any evasion, equivocation, or mental reservation whatsoever, and without any dispensation already granted me by the pope." (30 Charles II st. 2 ch. 1). This formula later became notorious as the "King's Declaration." At the time it was appointed for officeholders and members of both Houses, except for the Duke of York.

James II largely freed himself from the obstacle to appointing Catholics to office which the Test Act imposed. He did this by exercising the prerogative dispensing power after the judges had held in *Godden v. Hales*

(1686; II State Trials 1165) that it was contrary to the principles of the constitution to deprive the Crown of the services of any of its subjects when they were needed. After the REVOLUTION OF 1688 the test was more stringently enforced; a clause was even added to the Bill of Rights requiring the sovereign himself to take the declaration (1 William and Mary sess. 2 ch. 2). Since the test was obligatory on all officeholders, the Oaths of Supremacy and Allegiance became otiose, and were therefore cut down to a line or two and joined with the Oath of Fidelity to King William (1 William and Mary sess. 1. ch. 8). This oath could be tendered to anyone by any two justices of the peace at their discretion. Persons refusing the oath were deemed popish recusants and were thereupon liable to all the penalties of the statutes punishing absence from church and were disabled from practicing as lawyers and voting at elections (7 and 8 William and Mary ch. 4; 1 George I st. 2 ch. 13).

The Irish Oath, 1774, to Emancipation, 1829. The first relaxations of the system of penal oaths were due to external pressure: the need to pacify Canada and the military demands of the war of American Independence. The Quebec Act, 1774 (14 George III ch. 83), provided that Catholics resident in the province might freely practice their religion, and should not be obliged to take the Oath of Supremacy under 1 William and Mary sess. 1 ch. 8. A simple oath of allegiance was substituted. In the same year the Irish Parliament similarly authorized an oath of allegiance to King George and rejection of the Stuart Pretender, which involved no rejection of the pope's spiritual authority or any article of faith and which could be taken by Catholic soldiers. The alleged malpractice of "no faith with heretics" was renounced; so was the deposing power, but without the objectionable words, "impious, heretical and damnable." The "temporal and civil jurisdiction of the pope, direct and indirect within the realm" was also renounced, and the promise was given that no dispensation from the oath should be considered valid. This Irish Oath was embodied in the first Catholic Relief Act, 1778 (18 George III ch. 60), which provided that English Catholics on taking it should be freed of the worst penalties of laws passed during the reign of William and Mary (11 and 12 William III ch. 4); the clergy readily took the oath.

In 1788 a committee of lay Catholics with Gallican leanings (who later formed the Cisalpine Club) were negotiating with the government for further relief. To them Lord Stanhope made it clear that if more concessions were required, more assurances should be given. A long *Protest* was accordingly drafted, which not only rejected the alleged malpractices disowned by the Irish Oath, but did so in strong and untheological language. It reintroduced, for instance, the objectionable terms "impious, heretical, and damnable'' of the 1606 oath. Nevertheless, the committee insisted (1) that the words would be understood in a broad popular way, and (2) that to obtain the Relief Act, it must be signed at once. For this reason it was freely signed by laity and clergy and by the four vicars apostolic, although two later retracted their names. When the signatures had been obtained, the new Relief Bill was brought forward by the government with an oath founded on the *Protest* (hence called the Protestation oath), which excluded from relief those who would not swear to it and accept the name of ''Protesting Catholic Dissenters.'' This bill would have divided the Catholic community. The successful opposition to it was led by John MILNER, then only a country priest, and the second Relief Act, 1791 (31 George III ch. 32) passed without any significant changes in the previous oath and without changing the name of Catholics. Even though the Emancipation Act, 1829 (10 George IV ch. 7) was eventually carried without any tests, this was not at first foreseen. The Catholic Committee continued its endeavors to disarm Protestant prejudices with proposals (like the Veto) that savored of Gallicanism. So too did the oath annexed to the bill proposed in 1813, which, from its length, was styled the ''Theological Oath.''

Repeal of the Statutory Oaths, 1867 to 1910. The Relief Acts were generally only measures of relief, leaving the old statutes, oaths, and tests on the statute book. The disused tests and oaths were repealed between 1867 and 1910. In 1867 the declaration was repealed (30 and 31 Victoria ch. 75). After this, the only person bound to pronounce the oath was the king himself at his accession. In 1871 the Promissory Oaths Act removed all the old Oaths of Allegiance (34 and 35 Victoria ch. 48). Between 1891 and 1908 five unsuccessful bills or motions were introduced into Parliament for the abolition of the king's declaration, and it was only in 1910 that this last anti-Catholic declaration was repealed by the Accession Declaration Act (10 Edward VII and 1 George V ch. 29).

Bibliography: *Statutes of the Realm,* ed. A. LUDERS et al., 12 v. (London 1810–28). *Statutes at Large* (London 1762–). *Acts and Ordinances of the Interregnum 1642–60,* ed. C. H. FIRTH and R. S. RAIT, 3 v. (London 1911). C. BUTLER, *Historical Memoirs Respecting the English, Irish, and Scottish Catholics from the Reformation to the Present Time,* 4 v. (London 1819–21). H. TOOTELL, *Dodd's Church History of England,* ed. M. A. TIERNEY, 5 v. (London 1839–43). For particular oaths: P. HUGHES, *The Reformation in England,* 3 v. in 1 (5th, rev. ed. New York 1963) v.2. R. G. USHER, *The Reconstruction of the English Church,* 2 v. (New York 1910). C. J. RYAN, ''The Jacobean Oath of Allegiance,'' *American Catholic Historical Review* 28 (1942) 159–183. G. SITWELL, ''Leander Jones's Mission to England, 1634–35,'' *Recusant History* 5 (1959–60) 132–182. T. CLANCY, ''English Catholics and the Papal Deposing Power 1570–1640,'' *ibid.* 6 (1961–62) 114–140, 205–227; 7 (1962–63) 2–10. W. K. L. WEBB, ''Thomas Preston OSB, alias Roger Widdrington 1567–1640,'' *Biographical Studies* 2 (1953–54) 216–268. W. BIRCHLEY, *The Catholiques Plea* (London 1659); *Reflections on the Oaths of Supremacy and Allegiance* (London 1661). H. THURSTON, *Titus Oates' Test* (London 1909). J. MILNER, *Supplementary Memoirs of English Catholics* (London 1820). B. N. WARD, *Dawn of the Catholic Revival in England, 1781–1803,* 2 v. (London 1909); *The Eve of Catholic Emancipation,* 3 v. (London 1911–12).

[P. R. GLAZEBROOK]

OBADIAH, BOOK OF

The fourth of the MINOR PROPHETS. The ''Vision of Obadiah,'' which is its own title (v.1), comprises only 21 verses and is thus the shortest book of the Old Testament. It falls easily into two parts: (1) the punishment of Edom on the DAY OF THE LORD because of its treachery against Judah when Jerusalem fell in 587 B.C. (1–15) and (2) Israel's victorious revenge (16–21). Verse 15b forms the closing sentence of the first part: the law of retaliation (Ex 21.23–25) will be applied to Edom. The passage in Jer 49.7–16, 22—with some differences of text and order of sentences—is similar to verses 1–14 of Obadiah, and both pieces may be dependent on a common source. Edom, a long-standing enemy of Israel, will be the object of a day of vengeance described in Is 34.1–17; 63.1–6; Ez 25.12–14; 35.1–15; Jl 4.19; and Mal 1.2–5. In Obadiah verses 11–14, vividly recall Edom's joy over Judah's calamity of 587 and its treachery on that occasion; these are the reasons for the downfall of Israel's ancient foe. The second part is eschatological; Edom's ruin is a sign of the Day of YAHWEH against all the pagan nations. Although the author was concerned primarily with Edom, the very mention of the Day of the Lord widened his horizon, and he saw the local event (judgment on Edom) as a symbol of the worldwide punishment of all Israel's enemies.

The Book of Obadiah was composed probably in the early 5th century, though it may contain material that was somewhat earlier. Edom's predicted downfall occurred before 312 B.C. (when the Nabataeans occupied Petra), and Edom was possibly already threatened *c.* 460. Thus, a reasonable date for ''Obadiah's Vision'' would be after 587 and before 460 B.C. Faith in God's fidelity toward Israel is the main theme of the book. Obadiah affirms that the day will come when oppressed Zion will become the place of salvation because of a catastrophic divine intervention ushering in a new and different order. The new order will recapture past glories, emerge in a new age beyond the divine JUDGMENT, and bring about the fulfillment of God's purpose in history. Obadiah is nationalistic in conceiving the day of Yahweh as a national restoration. The description of the new Israel (19–21) envisions the restoration of approximately the Davidic boundaries and is consistent with the aspirations of Obadiah's contemporaries.

Bibliography: *Encyclopedic Dictionary of the Bible*, tr. and adap. by L. HARTMANN (New York 1963) 3–4. M. STENZEL, *Lexikon für Theologie und Kirche*, ed. J. HOFER and K. RAHNER (Freiburg 1957–65). W. VOLLBORN, *Die Religion in Geschichte und Gegenwart* (Tübingen 1957–65) 4:1547–48. S. BULLOUGH, *Catholic Commentary on Holy Scripture*, ed. B. ORCHARD et al. (London-New York 1957) 666–668.

[J. MORIARITY]

OBAZINE (AUBAZINE), ABBEY OF

Former French abbey, Diocese of Limoges, the present Diocese of Tulle. It was founded in a forest by a group of hermits under STEPHEN OF OBAZINE, a follower of the great hermit monk, ROBERT OF ARBRISSEL. The BENEDICTINE RULE was adopted, according to the interpretation of the monks of Dalon, a neighboring community of similar background. Once it was formally organized into an abbey in 1142, it soon founded two other monasteries, La Valette and Bonnaigue, and a convent for nuns, Coyroux. Obazine merged with the CISTERCIANS in 1147. It founded four more affiliated houses (those of La Garde-Dieu, La Frenade, Grosbos, and Gourdon).

The wars and rule by commendatory abbots led to gradual decline. In 1768 it had only six monks. It was suppressed during the French Revolution. The remodeled early Gothic church (1156–90) survives as a parish church. Other monastic buildings house a community of nuns.

Bibliography: U. CHEVALIER, *Répertoire des sources historiques du moyen-âge. Topobibliographie*, 2 v. (Paris 1894–1903) 2:2165–66. G. MÜLLER, "Der Gründer der Abtei Obazine," *Cistercienser-Chronik* 40 (1928). L. H. COTTINEAU, *Répertoire topobibliographique des abbayes et prieurés*, 2 v. (Mâcon 1935–39) 2:185–186. R. GAZEAU, *Catholicisme. Hier, aujourd'hui et demain*, ed. G. JACQUEMET (Paris 1947–) 1:1006–07.

[L. J. LEKAI]

OBEDIENCE

The foundation of obedience is AUTHORITY. All true authority is ultimately divine. It is either immediately divine or, if vested proximately in men, it is derived from that of God. Authority is ordained to good, common or private. Of a number of possibilities of achieving this good, authority determines and proposes the one that is to be realized. The will of authority is expressed in Law, which is the binding rule of human action. Law, moreover, must be understood to include not only that which is written or externally manifest, but also that which the authoritative will of the Creator has implanted in the structure of created being, natural or supernatural. The adaptation of an individual's will to the authoritative will expressed in Law is obedience. By its act, the object or content of the legislator's determination is freely adopted by the obedient will and becomes a principle of initiative and action leading to the effect intended by the legislator. The subject who obeys embraces the possibility of action that the will of authority has determined should be realized. He accepts it as commanded, and renounces conflicting possibilities. Thus does he render to authority what is its due, namely, submission. A stable readiness to such submission is the virtue of obedience. This, with respect to certain determined objects, can be confirmed by VOW.

Obedience in Judeo-Christian History

A special value was attributed to obedience in both Old and New Testaments, and in later Christian history this received further emphasis through the development of the concept of religious obedience.

Old Testament. In the Old Testament, obedience to the authority of Yahweh was exercised within terms of the Covenant, whose content was embraced by the formula: "You shall be my people, and I shall be your God" (Jer 11.4; Hos 2.25; Jer 7.23; 24.7). Under the Covenant, the people assumed the obligation of fulfilling the Law. This, according to the broader concept of Deuteronomy and the Psalms, was the summit of divine revelation, considered as a norm of life. Thus the Law was the foundation of religion, of ethics, and, because of the theocratic constitution of the people, of civil life in Israel (1 Sm 8.7–9; 10.19). Hence the insistence upon a knowledge of the Law, and upon conformity of life to its demands (Ex 13.8–9; Dt 33.10; Lv 10,11; Hos 4.6; Prv 19.16; Sir 19.17; 21.11; Wis 6.18). Psalm 119 is a canticle of praise of the beauty and blessing of the Law, which is no insupportable yoke laid upon the shoulders of men (cf. Acts 15.10), but refreshment to the soul, joy to the heart, and light to the eyes (Ps 19.8–9); it is sweeter than honey (Ps 119.103); it is the theme of the song of the people in their place of exile (*ibid.* v. 54). Just as the lot of the first parents depended upon the command of Yahweh (Gn 2.16–17), so the efficacy of the Covenant and the promises attached to it depended upon the obedience of the people to the Law (Ex 19.5; Jer 11.2–5). For this reason Yahweh watched jealously over its fulfillment (Ex 20.5; Dt 28.15–19; Jer 11.2–5). Obedience is worth more than sacrifice (1 Sm 15.22; Eccl 4.12).

Obedience to Yahweh included obedience to the civil authority, which derived its power from God (Wis 6.13). The king was chosen by God (Dt 17.14; 1 Sm 8.22; 10.1; 10.24; 16.13; 2 Sm 7.18); he was the son of God (2 Sm 7.14); he was helped by God (2 Sm 7.3); was anointed by Yahweh (1 Sm 24.10; Ps 89.39); was sacrosanct (1 Sm 24.10; 2 Sm 1.14); and was to be feared as Yahweh Himself (Prv 24.21).

New Testament. The Israel of God of the New Testament is the Church-Bride (Gal 6.16), subject to Christ, her Spouse (Eph 5.21–24). Christians here upon Earth are pilgrims (Heb 11.13), seeking their own country (*ibid.* v. 14), obedient to the first leader of their journey, Christ (Heb 2.10; 12.2), and to their superiors in the Church (Heb 13.7). The Father, raising Christ from the dead, "put him above every Principality, and Power and Virtue and Domination . . . and all things he made subject under his feet, and him he gave as head over all the Church, which indeed is his body" (Eph 1.20–23). Aggregation to this body is effected by baptism (1 Cor 12.13; Rom 6.3–11; Col 2.12), by which the Christian is made a "new creation" (Gal 6.15), who ought to walk in a newness of life (Rom 6.4), living in "obedience to faith" (Rom 1.5, 16.26), living not to himself but to God (Rom 5.11, 14.7–8), under the "new covenant" (Mt 26.28; 2 Cor 3.6), under the new commandment of charity (Jn 13.34). As an all-embracing principle, this commandment contains in itself virtually the whole content of the Christian life (Mt 22.40); it includes the fulfillment of the other commandments (Gal 5.14); it sums them up (Rom 13.9); it is the fulfillment of the Law (Rom 13.10). Thus the whole of the New Testament also is, by the commandment of charity, reducible to obedience.

From the very beginning of the New Testament, in its center, which is Christ, it was permeated with obedience by the determination of the Incarnate Word to do the will of the Father (Heb 10.5–7). This purpose, hidden although present from the first instant of the Incarnation, continued through the whole life of Christ. To Him the doing of His Father's will was His food (Jn 4.34); that others might live by the same nourishment He taught them to pray, "Thy will be done" (Mt 6.10), and whoever does this will is His brother and sister and mother (Mt 12.50). This readiness to obey the Father is especially and vividly manifest in His Passion (Lk 22.42). The work of the life of Christ is a work done in obedience to the will of the Father (Jn 17.4). St. Paul expresses the obedience of Christ's life in these words: "He humbled himself, becoming obedient to death, even to death on a cross" (Phil 2.8).

In the New Testament, as well as in the Old, obedience to God includes obedience to human authority, since true human authority is from God. When the Pharisees asked whether it was lawful to give tribute to Caesar, by His answer—"Render to Caesar the things that are Caesar's, and to God the things that are God's" (Mt 22.21)—He acknowledges the rights of civil authority so long as this does not violate the rights of God (cf. Acts 4.19; Dn 3.18). According to His words to Pilate—"Thou wouldst have no power at all over me were it not given thee from above" (Jn 19.11)—God Himself grants civil authority its power, and the lot of Christ depended upon this divine grant. According to St. Paul, "Let everyone be subject to the higher authorities, for there exists no authority except from God, and those who exist have been appointed by God. Therefore who resists the authority resists the ordinance of God" (Rom 13.1–2). Since the following verses discuss rulers who are a terror not to the good but to the evil, commending the good and as God's ministers carrying the sword to execute wrath on those who do evil, it is evident that St. Paul is speaking of civil authority that does not abuse its rights. To such authority obedience must be rendered not only because of fear of punishment, but also for conscience's sake (*ibid.* v. 5). The same holds true for the relationship of Christians toward the Roman tax-gatherers (vv. 6–7). According to St. Peter, the faithful must subject themselves not only to supreme but to subordinate rulers for the sake of God (1 Pt 2.13–14). If the passages in Revelation concerning the adoration of the beast and its image (13.12–17; 14.9–11; 16.2; 20.4) are understood as referring to the Roman emperor, they do not express an attitude of hostility toward civil authority as such, but toward the paying of divine honors to the emperor. The freedom of the children of God was not to be made a pretext for rebellion against civil authority, for this freedom supposes full subjection to the will of God and to those who hold their authority from Him (Gal 5.13; Rom 6.18). Slaves were to obey their masters as they would Christ (Eph 6.5), not only the good and moderate ones, but the severe as well; harsh and unjust treatment they were to endure after the example of Christ (1 Pt 2.18–23). In marriage the woman was to be subject to the authority of the man (1 Cor 11.3; Eph 5.22–23; 1 Pt 3.1) as to that of the Lord (Eph 5.22), or "as is becoming in the Lord" (Col 3.18). The authority of the husband, however, should be exercised without harshness (Col 3.19; Eph 5.25–29). Children were to be subject to the authority of their parents (Col 3.20) in the Lord (Eph 6.1). Obedience to parents is a condition of happiness (Mt 15.4; 19.19) and is acceptable to God (Col 3.20; 1 Tm 5.4). But Christ ought to be loved more than one's parents (Mt 10.37). The authority of parents ought to be used without undue severity (Col 3.21). All human authority, in fact, ought to be exercised after the example of Christ's, who did not come to be served but to serve (Mk 10.45), and He made Himself the servant of His Disciples, although He was their Master and Lord (Jn 13.13–16). In the Christian community authority is not to be distorted into despotism, but to be considered a service (Mk 10.42; Lk 22.25). "Let him who is greatest among you become as the youngest, and him who is chief as the servant'' (Lk 22.26; Mk 10.43–45). This principle is true especially for the elders who ought to feed the flock of the Lord not under constraint, but willingly, according to God; nor yet for the sake of base gain, but eagerly; nor yet as lording it over their charges, but as becoming from the heart a pattern to the flock (1 Pt 5.2–3).

Religious Obedience. From ordinary Christian obedience, founded on the doctrine of the New Testament, the idea of religious obedience gradually emerged. The first anchorites were not drawn to their hermitages with any formal intention of subjecting themselves to the yoke of obedience to any human superior, but rather by their desire to seek the sort of annihilation proclaimed in the Gospels and the self-denial demanded by Christ, and to fulfill the obligations undertaken in baptism to renounce Satan and the world. Nevertheless, confidence in some outstanding ascetic's experience in the spiritual life inclined many individuals to submit themselves to the direction of such a person. This submission was based less upon a juridically defined authority than upon a kind of spiritual paternity of a more or less charismatic nature. The subjection was freely undertaken, was revocable, was not confirmed by vow, nor did one subject himself for life. (Cf. I. Hausherr, *Direction spirituelle en Orient autrefois* [*Orientalia Christiana Analecta* 144; Rome 1955].) Associated with an individual's confidence in the greater experience of another was his distrust of his own disordered will; this made renunciation of this will and submission to the will of a spiritual father seem good. Submission of this kind was esteemed as a great virtue among the anchorites.

The solitude of the hermits, however, though relative, seemed to provide too little opportunity for the exercise of this virtue. It was partly to provide greater scope for it that the cenobitical way of life was introduced with its hierarchical structure. Among the cenobites a new value was found in submission. They aimed at securing the spiritual welfare not only of the individual but of the community as a whole as well. Submission in a monastery meant entering upon a cloistered life under the authority of an abbot whose power was determined by rule or constitutions. Obedience was now not only, not even primarily, based upon confidence in a person but upon a foundation of juridical obligation. Not the person but the office of the religious superior was the primary consideration. Together with humility, the enemy of pride—the original sin of man—obedience took an absolute character. It left no room for questioning or judgment where commands were concerned. Apart from the rule and the will of the superior, nothing was valued as holy or prudent. There was something primitive in this attitude. The concept of obedience needed to be humanized and to be based upon a less pessimistic view of nature. It would be mitigated in time, owing to the demands of the apostolate, by a greater adaptability, a greater respect for initiative, and a more refined sense of the personal dignity of the individual. Meanwhile, the motives underlying primitive asceticism were not without value. The love of Christ, the imitation of His obedience, the practice of humility, are at the heart of all religious life. (Cf. M. Olphe-Galliard, *Histoire de l'obéissance religieuse: Des Pères du desert au cénobitisme de saint Basile et de saint Benoît,* in *L'Obéissance et la religieuse d'aujourd'hui* [Paris 1951] 29–30.) As early as St. Augustine (*Epist.* 211) and St. Caesarius of Arles (*Regula Sanctarum Virginum,* ed. G. Morin, *Florilegium Patristicum* 34) there was insistence upon the use of discretion in the exercise of authority. ''[Let the superior] be to all an example of good works; let her correct the unruly, strengthen the fainthearted, sustain the weak, bearing always in mind that she must render an account to God for them.'' Even more did St. Benedict in his *Regula Monasteriorum* (ed. B. Linderbauer, *Florilegium Patristicum* 17) strive to make provision against rigid authoritarianism and too great an insistence upon uniformity.

When religious, either as a community or as individuals, undertake missionary or cultural labors in the world, religious obedience must begin to keep in view not only the sanctification of the individual religious and the good of the community but also the demands of the apostolate. With religious engaged in work of this kind, obedience cannot ordinarily consist in doing only that which the rule or the superior commands. It would be unsuited to the apostolate, for the rule cannot make provision for all concrete circumstances, nor can a superior foresee them and by anticipatory commands chart the course to be followed in every particular case. There is frequent need for personal decision by the individual religious in accordance with the spirit of the rule and his general understanding of what his superior would want him to do. (See J. Loosen, ''Gestaltwandel im religiösen Gehorsamsideal,'' *Geist und Leben* 24 [1951] 196–209.)

The vow only gradually came to be annexed to the practice of religious obedience. The precise nature of the formula that was signed by the monks in Atripe is not known, for it has not come down to us in its entirety (J. Leipoldt, ''Schenute von Atripe und die Entstehung des nationalen agyptischen Christentums,'' *Texte und Untersuchungen zur Geschichte der altchristlichen Literatur* 25.1 [1903] 109, 195–196), but it seems to have been a true religious profession, made to God, and probably for the whole time a monk remained in the monastic state or in the monastery. There is no evidence in the part of the formula we possess, however, of a vow of religious obedience.

St. Basil seems to have exacted from those seeking admission to the cenobitic life in his monasteries a declaration, at least implicit, of obedience (*Regulae brevius tractatae* 1–2; *Patrologia Graeca* 31:1081–84). The violation of obedience was a "theft and sacrilege" (Basil, *De renunt. saec.* 4; *Patrologia Graeca* 31:633). But there is no proof of the existence of a special vow of obedience. (See D. Amand, *L'Ascèse monastique de saint Basile*, [Maredsous, Belg. 1949] 324–335.) Without doubt, however, the vow of obedience is contained in St. Benedict's *Regula Monasteriorum:* "Taken to the oratory, before all let him make the promise of stability and of conversion of life and of obedience in the presence of God and his saints" (ch. 58).

Theological Considerations

In Christianity, obedience is the concrete realization of the fundamental commitment to God to which the Christian is obliged by the fact of his baptism. By baptism he is, ontologically speaking, holy—or, in other words, consecrated through Christ to God. In correspondence with this ontological state, he ought to live not for himself but for God. But to live for God is to fulfill His will, which is the will of Supreme Authority. The will of God can be known in concrete situations by applying to them the norms of divine positive law and of natural law, and by the actual enlightenment of the Holy Spirit. Just as the whole life of Christ was one of obedience, so also should be the whole life of the Christian, since it is the formal or at least implicit fulfillment of God's authoritative will. This obedience is acceptable to God because it is realized in virtue of the obedience of Christ through the Holy Spirit who shapes the obedience of Christians, whom He moves, to the image of the obedience of Christ.

The principal divine law of Christian life is the commandment of charity. Its fulfillment is, implicitly at least, obedience as well as charity. It is obedient charity. (See B. Häring, *Das Heilige und das Gute* [Karilling vor Munchen 1950] 284–290.) This obedience is as extensive as charity itself. The commandment, as the ultimate end of the Christian life, is confined by no limits. It can be said that so much love is of precept, and that what exceeds the limits of precept is a matter of counsel. Yet everyone is commanded to love God as much as he can (Thomas Aquinas, *C. retrah. relig. ingress.* 6; cf. *Summa theologiae* 2a2ae, 184.3). The power to fulfill this commandment is the theological virtue of charity. To the limitlessness of the command there corresponds a limitlessness in the internal dynamism of the virtue. It is a universal love of benevolence that admits no limits to its desire to do good to the one who is beloved. This desire, by its own inner dynamism, with the universal laws of morality before it, as these are seen with the inner illu-

mination necessary to grasp their relevance to a present situation, seeks to express itself. For this expression, acts are necessary. These, of themselves, may be only of counsel, but they are performed, when they are necessary to the life of charity, as though they were of precept, and this because of the preceptive character of charity itself. This life of obedient charity, although it might at times be explicitly renewed, need not, however, be continuously self-conscious. When the Christian living in the state of grace does not think explicitly of God and does not move toward Him with explicit acts of charity, but conducts himself in accordance with Christian standards, his will, controlling his actions, is perfected and informed by charity, and his charity is activated, implicitly at least, in all his virtuous action. (See Thomas Aquinas, In *3 sent.* 23.3.1.1.)

Besides the law of charity there are other divine laws, each with its own content. To each there corresponds a proper fulfillment that implicitly or explicitly involves obedience. The chastity of the Christian, for example, is obedient chastity. Obedience does not take anything away from the proper nature of the virtues that it includes, any more than charity—which intrinsically informs obedience and the other virtues included in it—destroys the proper nature of those virtues or the specific distinction between them.

Obedience and Human Law. Since every human law must be included under divine law, and since human authority, whether ecclesiastical or civil, is a participation of divine authority, obedience to human law, if we consider it objectively, is ultimately given to God and in its origin is determined by charity, of which it is an expression. The direct object of the obligation of human law is indicated in the law itself. Indirectly, the law obliges one to use the means necessary for its fulfillment, to procure materials necessary for its observance, to avoid setting up obstacles, without sufficient reason, that would prevent the observance of the law, and to remove such obstacles as have been set up without sufficient reason. Human law, as preceptive, obliges to the act of obedience and to the acts of whatever other virtues may be involved in obedience. The obligation is in proportion to the importance of the object of the law to common or private welfare. The object has importance either on its own account, or dependently upon circumstances or upon the end for the sake of which the law was made. Proper fulfillment of the law supposes true interpretation of it and right application to the particular cases in which it is to be observed. In a concrete case one does not proceed simply in accordance with the words of the law, but rather in accordance with its true meaning, giving the reality of the concrete case due consideration. It belongs to EPIKEIA, as St. Thomas said, "to moderate . . . the observance of the words of the law'' (*Summa theologiae* 2a2ae, 120.2 ad 3). And epikeia is the more important part of justice (*Summa theologiae* 2a2ae, 120.2 ad 1).

Obedience and Personal Responsibility. True obedience is not a robotlike activity produced entirely by the external impulse coming from the superior. It is a personal act elicited by the subject himself, who in obedience adapts his will to the will of the superior, and it is ultimately the subject who moves himself to act. The possibility that a superior could command something objectively sinful requires the subject, even in his obedience, to keep clearheaded and to remain capable of independent thought. To obey without moral certainty of the lawfulness of what is commanded would be immoral. In his own conscience, the subject remains responsible for whatever he does even when he acts under obedience. The fact that a thing is commanded does not take away responsibility from the subject. His theoretical or speculative judgment regarding the morality of what is commanded is governed per se by the objective light of truth, not by the mind of the superior. A commanded action does not become good because the superior thinks it good, for the superior is not the cause of truth. Acting in accordance with its nature and subjecting itself to truth, the mind of the subject, even when it is in disagreement with the mind of the superior, is obedient: it yields its obedience to Him who created the intellect to act in this way, and who is the Supreme Superior.

When the morality of what is commanded is not evident, reverence, piety, and the supernatural context of the virtue of obedience will incline the speculative judgment of the subject to agreement with his superior. When the speculative judgment of the subject has no cause to see compliance as immoral, the practical judgment, which governs the doing of what is commanded, must submit itself to the command of legitimate authority acting within its proper limits. This is so even when the subject knows, from a speculative point of view, that the situation could be better dealt with otherwise, or even that the superior's command proceeds from malice. (See F. Suárez, *De religione Societatis Iesu,* lib. 4, cap. 15.) Ordinarily no long process of reasoning is required to establish the legitimacy of a command, for the supernatural enlightenment with which God assists the Christian suffices to facilitate judgment and protect him against harmful error. On the other hand, it must not be assumed that the subject's own judgment, as opposed to that of his superior, is something necessarily inordinate or worthy of contempt. The intellect, which judges, is by no means completely corrupt by reason of original sin. Indeed, in spite of the consequences of original sin, it is elevated by faith and may well be aided by the gifts of wisdom, knowledge, and understanding. Caution, however, is necessary,

for self-interest or a morbidly hypercritical spirit can dull the intellect's capacity to discern the legitimacy of a concrete command.

Obedience, therefore, does not exist for the purpose of lessening personal activity. Ultimately, even under obedience, a subject must seek the will of the Father by passing judgment upon the lawfulness of a concrete command, by personally accepting and fulfilling it, and in the fulfillment, through his own initiative, determining and realizing the necessary details undefined in the command itself.

From the fact that the superior participates in the authority of God, it does not follow that a subject, faced with a concrete command, must conduct himself as he does in accepting a matter of faith, in which he simply accepts revealed truth, relying only on the authority of God revealing. The subject ought indeed to believe that all legitimate human authority is from God, because this is a revealed truth. But he cannot accept on faith that any concrete command is legitimate, for that is something about which God has revealed nothing. The legitimacy cannot be discerned except by the personal effort of the subject, and only after this is manifest can the subject know that the concrete command expresses the will of God.

Superior and Subject. The superior who commands ought to be himself obedient even while he commands. He owes obedience to God. No one who is in command is only a superior; he is at the same time—and primarily—a subject. The whole end of obedience demands submission on the part of both subject and superior. Moreover, just as there is for the subject, simply because he is a subject, no guarantee of his right fulfillment of commands, so the superior, simply because he has legitimate authority, is not guaranteed the right use of his authority. Before God, superior and subject are redeemed children of the Father, seeking to do His will. It is the superior's duty to seek this by commanding according to the will of God; it is the subject's duty to seek it in fulfilling the legitimate commands according to the will of God. Not only is the subject to see Christ in his superior, but the superior must also see Christ in his subject, for the subject is a member of the Mystical Body of Christ. Because the superior's authority is derived from Christ, the subject has additional reason to see Christ in his superior. By the fulfillment of a legitimate command, he ought to minister to the life of the Body of Christ, and in the same way the superior in his exercise of authority should minister to that same life. But it must not be thought that God binds, moves, and illuminates the Christian to the doing of His will only through the commands of a human superior. Such an opinion is contrary to ecclesiastical tradition concerning the immediate guidance of the Holy Spirit, and it contradicts the historical fact that the life of the Church has been influenced again and again by ideas and movements that did not have their origin in obedience to a human superior but that came immediately from God.

Although the end of obedience requires obedience of both subject and superior, and although both are equal as Christians, nevertheless superior and subject, as such, do not stand on the same level. God who leads men not only immediately but also through men, by granting a participation in His authority to the superior, places him over the subject, and He gives to the superior, within the limits of his authority, the office of commanding, and He gives the subject the duty of carrying out the commands of his superior. Every effort to lower the superior within the proper ambit of his authority to the level of the subject is damaging to the essence of obedience. Such efforts cause the idea of authority and hence of true superiority to be lost to sight, and obedience fades into a dialogue that has no real power to bind the subject but leaves him free to determine for himself what he ought and what he ought not to do.

There is a certain dialectical tension between the need of obedience and the need of liberty. The goal of educating in obedience is to effect a synthesis of both elements, or, in other words, a free obedience, which will be a capacity, partly acquired and partly infused, to recognize and understand and to carry out with personal decision and a sense of responsibility the orders given by one in authority.

Orders, commands, or prohibitions that are well chosen develop respect for authority. There should be a progressive unfolding of the meaning and content of the superior's commands so that infantile forms of submission give way to others determined by objective values, particularly by religious values, which can more easily provide a solid basis for ready and free obedience.

Deviations. Distortions of obedience consist of an obsequious submission rooted in a variety of undesirable causes: egoistic ambition; a weakness with regard to the regulation of one's own life, so that obedience becomes a refuge of a person unable to make decisions or unwilling to assume responsibility; a pathological need that a person may have for a hero to admire and worship; or want of courage, or, seen from another point of view, fear of a servile kind. Genuine obedience to the will of the Father carries with it not only the submission of one's will to the command of a superior, but also, when there is abuse of authority, prudent and firm opposition.

See Also: COUNSELS, EVANGELICAL; FREEDOM; FREEDOM, SPIRITUAL; PIETY, FAMILIAL.

Bibliography: J. B. RAUS, *De sacrae obedientiae virtute et voto secundum doctrinam divi Thomae et S. Alphonsi, juxta normas ac codicem juris canonici* (Lyons 1923). F. VALENTINE, *Religious Obedience* (London 1951). R. E. REGAN, "The Exercise of Authority by Religious Superiors in Modern America," *Religious Community Life in the United States,* 2 v. (New York 1952) 1:178–185. P. K. MEAGHER, "The Spirit of Religious Obedience in America," *ibid.* 1:186–199. S. GIET, "Saint Bernard et le troisième degré d'obéissance ou la soumission de jugement," *L'Année théologique augustinienne* 7 (1946) 192–221. B. HARING, "Freiheit oder Gehorsam?" *Geist und Leben* 21 (1948) 108–121. K. ESSER, "Gehorsam und Freiheit," *Wissenschaft und Weisheit* 13 (1950) 142–150. H. MOGENET, "L'Obéissance religieuse vertu évangelique et humaine," *Revue d'ascétique et de mystique* 27 (1951) 75–95. *L'Obéissance et la religieuse d'aujourd'hui* (Paris 1951). Congressus Generalis de Statibus Perfectionis, 1950, *Acta et documenta,* 4 v. (Rome 1952) 2:396–429. J. LECLERCQ, *The Religious Vocation* (New York 1955). T. CAMELOT, "Obéissance et liberté," *La Vie spirituelle* 86 (1952) 154–168; title varies. P. PHILIPPE, "La Portée du voeu d'obéissance," *ibid.* 509–524. H. HOLSTEIN, "Le Mystère de l'obéissance," *Études* 278 (1953) 145–157. J. PÉRINELLE, *Les Voies de Dieu* (Paris 1956) 459–518. K. RAHNER, "Reflections on Obedience . . . a Basic Ignatian Concept," *Cross Currents* 10 (1960) 364–374. M. LABOURDETTE, "La Vertu d'obéissance selon saint Thomas," *Revue thomiste* 57 (1957) 626–656. K. V. TRUHLAR, *Problemata theologica de vita spirituali laicorum et religiosorum* (Collectanea spiritualia 8; Rome 1960) 81–121; *La Vie spirituelle* Suppl. 7 (1953) 249–359; *Geist und Leben* 29 (1956) 1–56; *Ciencia Tomista* 83 (1956) 219–422. P. LUMBRERAS, "La obediencia dialogada," *ibid.* 82 (1955) 65–84.

[K. V. TRUHLAR]

OBEDIENTIAL POTENCY

Obediential potency is a concept originally developed in the theology of miracles, now frequently used in the description of the NATURAL ORDER's relationship to the SUPERNATURAL. In its broadest sense obediential potency means the openness of every creature to the Creator's power to effect in it something beyond the powers of ordinary natural causes; it is the very being of an existing creature as obedient, subject, or as some hold, positively ordered to God's power to act in it. Here the term itself is first examined, then its use regarding miracles and the supernatural.

Term. It derives from two traditions: the first, going back to Ambrose (*Hex.* 1.4.13, 3.1.1) and perhaps to Scripture (Mt 8.27) or Cicero (*De leg.* 3.1.3), spoke of nature's obedience to God in creation and miracles; the second, from Augustine (*Gen. ad litt.* 9.17.32), studied the possibility in the creature of its being miraculously changed (cf. Peter Lombard, 2 *Sent.* 18.6). These traditions united in the late 12th century to produce the concept of obediential potency (Landgraf 1.1:243, fn.26). The term first appeared in the 13th century as potency of obedience (*potentia obedientiae*), e.g., in the *Summa* said to be Alexander of Hales's (1a2i:231, 469, 491; Quar. ed.

2:288, 632, 686), in Albert the Great (*In 2 sent.* 18.7; *In 4 sent.* 11.4 ad 1), Bonaventure (*In 1 sent.* 42.3 ad 1 neg.; *In 1 sent.* 42.4), and in Thomas Aquinas frequently (e.g., *De ver.* 29.3 ad 3). Obediential potency (*potentia obedientialis*) occurred in Albert (ST. THOMAS, *Summa theologiae,* 2.8.31.1.4 sed contra 1; cf. Gillon 304, fn. 3) and in Thomas (*De virt. in com.* 10 ad 13) and gradually became the usual form.

Miracles. If the laws of nature are fixed by God, how can He work a miracle without upsetting these laws and betraying a lack of wisdom? Theologians answer with the concept of obediential potency: although the creature has no positive capacity or exigency to be changed miraculously, its being is subject or obedient to what God wills to do in it beyond the activity of ordinary causes so long as no contradiction occurs. The creature is purely passive; God can do in it whatever is not repugnant to its nature. As author and governor of creatures, God includes in His providence the extraordinary interventions of His power. A miracle is thus possible. This doctrine, taught by Augustine, was formulated in terms of obediential potency by medieval theologians and has remained constant in theology.

The Supernatural. Since for Thomas Aquinas obediential potency implies pure passivity and total indetermination, he finds it inadequate to express the relationship to the supernatural of intellectual creatures; he holds instead that as IMAGE OF GOD they have a capacity for or are apt for GRACE, are ordered or habilitated to grace, have a natural DESIRE TO SEE GOD, even though the supernatural transcends their nature. Although several medieval theologians did speak of the obediential potency of nature for the supernatural, it was Cajetan who most influenced the modern use of obediential potency for this relationship. Reacting to Scotus's doctrine of man's innate desire for the supernatural and seeking to maintain the gratuity of the supernatural, he said that of itself human nature has only an obediential potency for supernatural elevation in the sense that God's elevating it is possible since this is not repugnant to human nature (In St. Thomas, *Summa theologiae,* 1.1.1.7–12; 1.12.1.9–10). (*See* ELEVATION OF MAN.) His use here of obediential potency, connoting by its origin a passive non–repugnance to miraculous change, was soon imitated by many commentators professing to follow Aquinas; they were urged to this by the need to react against M. Baius's teaching of man's exigency of the supernatural. (*See* BAIUS AND BAIANISM.) Modern followers of these commentators still retain this use of obediential potency. Some modify this position by distinguishing between the transcendental obediential potency of all things to God's intervention and the specific obediential potency to the

supernatural that is proper to intellectual creatures, since they can know universal being and good.

Many theologians today oppose this school of thought. They argue that it gives a view of the supernatural as merely juxtaposed or extrinsic to nature, furthers SECULARISM'S tenet that man can find completion solely in the natural order, makes the supernatural seem adventitious. This reaction was influenced by M. BLONDEL'S and H. de Lubac's efforts to show the intimate connection and continuity between the intellectual creature and his supernatural destiny and vocation. (*See* IMMANENCE APOLOGETICS; DESTINY, SUPERNATURAL.) Some, including those studying Aquinas by historical method, would eliminate the use of obediential potency from this area of discussion. Others, while rejecting the pure passivity of nature regarding the supernatural, still describe the relationship in terms of obediential potency but define this as the positive order or direction of nature to its fulfilment in the supernatural. Each seeks in his own way to maintain the Church's teaching that man's supernatural elevation surpasses the powers and exigencies of his nature (H. Denzinger, *ibid.,* 1921, 3005, 3891; H. Denzinger, *ibid.,* 2103).

Other particular uses of obediential potency include the obediential potency of the human intellect to infused knowledge, prophecy, etc.; of human nature for the hypostatic union; of things and words for sacramental signification and efficacy; of the whole universe to PRETERNATURAL perfection under the headship of Christ.

See Also: ANIMA NATURALITER CHRISTIANA; BEATIFIC VISION; GRACE, ARTICLES ON; MAN; MIRACLES (THEOLOGY OF); SUPERNATURAL EXISTENTIAL; SUPERNATURAL ORDER.

Bibliography: P. DUMONT, *Dictionnaire de théologie catholique,* ed. A. VACANT et al., 15 v. (Paris 1903–50; Tables générales 1951–) 14.2:2665–72, for Suárez's special doctrine of passive and active ob. pot. F. BUUCK, *Lexikon für Theologie und Kirche²,* ed. J. HOFER and K. RAHNER, 10 v. (2d, new ed. Freiburg 1957–65); suppl., *Das Zweite Vatikanische Konzil: Dokumente und Kommentare,* ed. H. S. BRECHTER et al., pt. 1 (1966) 8:646–647. G. COLOMBO, "Il problema del soprannaturale negli ultimi cinquant'anni," *Problemi e orientamenti di teologia dommatica,* 2 v. (Milan 1957) 2:545–607. A. DARMET, *Les Notions de raison séminale et de puissance obédientielle chez saint Augustin et saint Thomas d'Aquin* (Belley 1934). H. DE LUBAC, *Surnaturel: Études historiques* (Paris 1946); "Saint Thomas, *Compendium theologiae,* c. 104," *Recherches de science religieuse* 36 (1949) 300–305. R. GARRIGOU–LAGRANGE, *De revelatione,* 2 v. (5th ed. Rome 1950) 1:345–355. "Die Vorbereitung auf die Rechtfertigung und die Eingiessung der rechtfertigenden Gnade," in A. M. LANDGRAF, *Dogmengeschichte der Frühscholastik,* 4 v. (Regensburg 1952–56) 1.1:238–302. W. R. O'CONNOR, *The Eternal Quest* (New York 1947). K. RAHNER, *Nature and Grace,* tr. D. WHARTON (New York 1964). M. SCHMAUS, *Katholische Dogmatik* (6th ed. Munich 1962) 2.1:115 (pp. 217–235). B. STOECKLE, *Gratia supponit naturam: Geschichte und Analyse eines theologischen Axioms* (Studia anselmiana 49; Rome 1962) 232–263. L. CHARLIER, "Puissance passive et désir naturel selon Saint Thomas,'' *Ephemerides theologicae Lovanienses* 7 (1930) 5–28, 639–662. P. M. DE CONTENSON, ''Surnaturel,'' *Bulletin Thomiste* 8 (1947–53) 794–804, 9 (1954–56) 551–555, 10 (1957–59) 462–468. L. B. GILLON, ''Aux origines de la *puissance obédientielle*,'' *Revue thomiste* 47 (1947) 304–310. É. H. GILSON, ''Sur la problématique thomiste de la vision béatifique,'' *Archives d'histoire doctrinale et littéraire du moyen–âge* 31 (1964) 67–68. H. DE LUBAC, *Augustinisme et théologie moderne* (Paris 1965) esp. 242–251; *Le Mystère du surnaturel* (Paris 1965) esp. 87–88, 142, 179–189.

[W. H. PRINCIPE]

OBERAMMERGAU

Oberammergau is the name of a village in Upper Bavaria where a celebrated Passion play is presented by the villagers every ten years. In 1633 the villagers vowed to put on the Passion play every ten years in thanksgiving for deliverance from the plague. It may, however, have been performed before 1634. The play takes up to eight hours to perform. It was performed at ten-year interval from 1634 to 1674, and then in the decimal years from 1680 to the present with the only exceptions being in 1870 when it not performed due to the Franco-Prussian War, in 1920 because of the aftermath of World War I, and in 1940 because of World War II. Extra performances were held in 1934 and in 1985 to celebrate the 300th and 350th anniversaries. Adolf Hitler attended the 1934 performance. The text of the Passion play has been changed several times. Originally in verse, it is now in prose. The oldest text can be traced to 1600 and shows influences from the Passion plays held at St. Ulric and at St. Afra in Augsburg. For the 1985 performance the text was revised in view of charges of anti-Semitism and anti-Judaism. The Passion play of Oberammergau still occasions ecumenical concerns, particularly among Jews, for its perceived anti-Semitism and anti-Judaism.

[D. P. SHERIDAN]

OBJECT

Object is a term derived from the Latin *obiectum*, meaning what is thrown against and signifying anything that confronts another, generally a knowing SUBJECT. Among scholastics, the object is what specifies a knowing power or a science. *See* FACULTIES OF THE SOUL; SCIENCE (SCIENTIA). A distinction is commonly made between the formal object (*obiectum formale*), or the aspect under which the thing is related to the knowing power or HABIT, and the material object (*obiectum materiale*), or the THING itself abstracting from this relation; the formal object is further divided into the *obiectum formale quod,* or the precise aspect that is known, and the

obiectum formale quo, or the way in which (or the means by which) it is known. In moral science, object is frequently used to designate the goal or purpose of human action; in this meaning it becomes synonymous with END.

Among modern thinkers, object is opposed more directly to subject and thus takes on a more epistemological connotation; its main use is to designate the content or term of KNOWLEDGE. Some employ it to distinguish the content of thought from the act of thinking (L. Lavelle); others make it synonymous with the thing-in-itself as this exists independently of being known (G. Marcel). The main problem of PHENOMENOLOGY and of some forms of EXISTENTIALISM is that of bridging the gap between subject and object in the knowing process; realist philosophers provide such a bridge in the notion of INTENTIONALITY (*see* OBJECTIVITY).

Objective is a derivative of object and takes on somewhat the same connotations in different philosophical systems. In IDEALISM, something is objective if it constitutes a proper object of thought; in REALISM, and in ordinary linguistic usages, a thing is objective if it is extramental and independent of the conditions imposed by the knower. Knowledge is said to be objective if it is impersonal and universally acceptable, and a person is said to be objective if he abstracts from his particular feelings, tastes, and prejudices and restricts himself to areas of common agreement. Objectivism, when used by philosophers, is opposed to subjectivism; it may be a synonym for realism or for POSITIVISM, depending on the option of the user.

See Also: EPISTEMOLOGY; KNOWLEDGE, THEORIES OF.

Bibliography: P. FOULQUIÉ and R. SAINT–JEAN, *Dictionnaire de la langue philosophique* (Paris 1962) 485–490. A. LALANDE, *Vocabulaire technique et critique de la philosophie* (8th ed., rev. and enl. Paris 1960) 695–703. A. GUZZO and V. MATHIEU, *Enciclopedia filosofica,* 4 v. (Venice–Rome 1957) 3:990–1002. J. M. BALDWIN, *Encyclopedia of Religion and Ethics,* ed. J. HASTINGS, 13 v. (Edinburgh 1908–27) 9:440–441; ed., *Dictionary of Philosophy and Psychology,* 3 v. in 4 (New York 1901–05; repr. Gloucester 1949–57) 2:191–193. R. EISLER, *Wöterbuch der philosophischen Begriffe,* 3 v. (4th ed. Berlin 1927–30) 2:275–332.

[B. A. GENDREAU]

OBJECTIVITY

In the PHENOMENOLOGY of E. HUSSERL, the characteristic of an object of awareness, by virtue of which it can be grasped as the same by distinct acts of apprehension. By this definition, aspects of both physical bodies and essences, as well as psychological realities such as memories, are ''objectivities,'' insofar as they can be so understood. The acts of perceiving, thinking, and remembering, by which such ideas are grasped, are, on the other hand, subjective and transient. Husserl customarily distinguishes between *Gegenständlichkeit* and *Objektivität,* the former term referring to the status of things in the physical world, the latter to the meaningful aspects through which these things, as well as all other targets of awareness, are given to man. The second term, therefore, refers to a realm of objectivities that encompasses both the ''interior'' and the ''exterior'' worlds of EPISTEMOLOGY, and for this reason it is more fundamental.

Objective vs. Subjective. As it is commonly used, objectivity means not only a phenomenal, or descriptive, characteristic, but also a principle of value. Objective means that whatever the case, it is true for all subjects. In this sense it is the opposite of subjective opinions and preferences, that is, to judgments and evaluations distorted by a subject's emotions, stereotypes, biases, and the like. When used as a pejorative term, it indicates that there are factors wrongly influencing judgments and evaluations. An objective judgment or an objective evaluation is, therefore, one in which a resolution is determined essentially by the object's intrinsic meaning and value, by ''the way things are,'' rather than by the way a particular person or group (subject) thinks they are or prefers them to be.

Criteria of Objectivity. One problem, of course, is how to decide what is true for everyone. The first spontaneous criterion could be that of common consent exemplified by language or action. There may be an assumption that whatever is objective is independent of an individual's assessment; hence, that whatever idea is common to everyone is not the effect of psychological or cultural predispositions. Reference to unicorns, fairies, phlogiston, and the ether are good examples of the limitations to this criterion. To say that it has limitations, however, is not to say that it is useless when properly confined and controlled. Although common consent at a given time is clearly not sufficient ground for concluding that an idea is objective, it could be considered to be at least a necessary condition. The lack of common consent in matters of morality, however, is remarked on by many philosophers, from Socrates to the present, who nevertheless admit the possibility of objective moral norms.

In the study of nature as well, the criterion of common consent has proved to be insufficient, and has been supplemented by the controlled method of VERIFICATION, a method that attempts to minimize or eliminate the influence of subjective elements. The so-called ''scientific method,'' by reason of its success in promoting consensus among its practitioners and in extending one kind of understanding of nature, has resulted in ''scientifically established'' almost becoming a synonym for objective. In fact, some schools of philosophy have defended that synonymy, at the price of relegating secondary qualities and values to the realm of the subjective. If the rules for following the scientific method could, in fact, function as an unambiguous procedure for formulating and testing the truth of a judgment, it would constitute a necessary, if not sufficient, condition for objectivity. Here too, however, the history of scientific innovators such as L. PASTEUR, N. COPERNICUS, I. KANT, and G. Cantor shows, in retrospect, that no system of rules can prescribe the way in which the rules are to be employed. Once again, this only notes a limitation to a method of verifying objective conditions, and does not dismiss a given method as worthless.

Phenomenology's Reaction. The answer to the fundamental question regarding the objectivity of a point of view relies upon that point of view being independent of an individual attitude and therefore, at lease in principle, accessible to all; it must also be established by a fixed method. Phenomenology suggests that this is impossible and lists the reasons why these criteria are limited. Phenomenoloy's fundamental premise is that objectivity is only possible with the ''cooperation'' of the subject. That which is disclosed by experience is essentially related to the noetic attitude or INTENTIONALITY of the subject toward the world. For example, the scientific attitude is a way of understanding the meaning and being of the world that casts some things into relief and others into shadow. Other levels of meaning—the aesthetic, the religious, the social—may be rendered inaccessible if this attitude is predominant. The aim of phenomenology is, then, to describe and correlate various intentionalities, all of which are potentially revealing, some more fundamental than others, to achieve true objectivity.

In traditional terms, these observations point toward a difference between *de jure* and *de facto* objectivity, the former virtually accessible to all, the latter actually so accessible, at least to those with the requisite faculties and training. A final question is raised by those who contend that, in some instances, objectivity is accessible only to a unique individual. Gabriel Marcel has argued that this concept passes beyond the realm of the publicly verifiable, but does not lose touch with objectivity (*see* EXISTENTIALISM). Such an apparent exception tests the general rule in an important way because they can be applied to religious affirmations.

Bibliography: S. STRASSER, *Phenomenology and the Human Sciences* (Pittsburgh 1963). G. MARCEL, *The Mystery of Being,* tr. G. S. FRASER, 2 v. (Chicago 1950–51). M. POLANYI, *Personal Knowledge* (Chicago 1958). Y. SIMON, *Introduction à l'ontologie du connaître* (Paris 1933).

[F. J. CROSSON]

OBLATE

The word oblate, meaning "one offered" or "made over to God," has had various nuances in the history of the Church.

Children. From the 4th century onward the term was applied to children dedicated to a monastery by their parents. This practice, which is first found in the Eastern Church in the Rule of St. BASIL, was inspired, it appears, by the narrative of the dedication of the child Samuel by his parents (1 Sm 1.25–28): "All the days of his life he shall be lent to the Lord." Its early presence in Western monasticism is attested by the BENEDICTINE RULE, and by the Rules of CAESARIUS and AURELIAN OF ARLES. St. BENEDICT, for example, allowed in his Rule (c. 59) for infant oblation by noble parents, stating that the parents should draw up the petition on behalf of the infant, and then wrap the petition and the boy's hand in the altar cloth. For the next five centuries and more such parental oblations generally were held to bind oblate children (male and female) irrevocably to the monastic state. Any liberal readings of the prescriptions of St. Benedict's Rule that emerged were more than offset by the rigorous interpretation found in the influential *Liber de oblatione puerorum,* which RABANUS MAURUS, Abbot of Fulda, wrote to defend himself against the decision of a council at Mainz in 829. There he was charged with imposing the monastic habit by force on the later famous Saxon monk GOTTSCHALK OF ORBAIS, who at a tender age had been made an oblate by his noble father. By the 12th century, however, when in fact the practice of child oblation had almost disappeared, it was the teaching of the legal schools that a valid act of oblation or of profession could not be made before puberty; but there was no general Church legislation on the matter until the Council of Trent fixed 16 years as the minimum age of profession (cf. Session 25, *De Regularibus,* c. 15; ConOecDecr 757).

Adults. From the 7th century the term "oblate" was used also of adults who as *conversi* (lay brothers), *devoti, donati,* or *commissi,* looked after the material interests of monasteries. These oblates were never regarded fully as monks, although in the Cistercian order, unlike other monastic orders, it was recognized that "lay brothers" were committed to a life that was consecrated as that of the monks; the acceptance of lay brothers as an integral part of a religious institute occurred only with the founding of the Dominican Order in the early 13th century.

Secular Oblates. In the 13th century, also, the class known as secular oblates came into being to cover those who, while remaining in the world and retaining the usufruct of their goods, donated their possessions to a monastery and lived according to the monastic rule under the direction of the abbot. Under this heading, perhaps, should be listed the association of noble Roman ladies founded by St. FRANCES OF ROME in 1425 as the Oblates of Mary and later affiliated to the Olivetan BENEDICTINES as Oblates Regular of St. Benedict. These Oblates, who now have foundations in Switzerland and the United States, do not give up their property, nor make vows, but live in a community under a mother president to whom they make revocable vows of obedience.

Congregations of Oblates. The word oblate has also been adopted by certain religious congregations founded since the Council of Trent, the principal of which are:

1. Oblates of SS. Ambrose and Charles (*see* AMBROSIANS), a community of secular priests (originally "of St. Ambrose") founded for pastoral work in Milan in 1578 by St. Charles BORROMEO.

2. OBLATES OF MARY IMMACULATE (OMI), a missionary congregation founded in 1816 at Aix-en-Provence by Eugène de MAZENOD (later bishop of Marseilles) for the systematic reevangelization of France.

3. Oblates of the Virgin Mary (OMV), founded at Carignano, near Turin, Italy, in 1815 by Bruno Lanteri and approved in 1826.

4. Oblates of St. Charles Borromeo (of Westminister), a community of secular priests founded at Bayswater, London, in 1857 by Dr. H. E. (later cardinal) MANNING at the instigation of Cardinal WISEMAN and along the lines of the Ambrosians. The community received pontifical approval in 1877.

5. OBLATES OF ST. FRANCIS DE SALES (OSFS), founded at Troyes in 1871 by Abbè Brisson (d. 1908) for the education of the young.

6. OBLATES OF ST. JOSEPH (Guiseppini of Asti, OSJ), a congregation for the education of the poor, which Guiseppe Menello (later bishop of Acqui) founded at Asti, Italy, in 1878.

7. Oblates of the Sacred Heart of Jesus and Immaculate Heart of Mary (*see* ST. EDMUND, SOCIETY OF), founded in Burgundy, France, by Ven. M. J. B. MUARD in 1843, with headquarters at the Abbey of PONTIGNY, where St. Edmund of Canterbury was buried. Dedicated to education and the foreign missions, the congregation was approved in 1911.

Bibliography: Sources. BENEDICT, *Regula Monasteriorum,* ed. C. BUTLER (3d ed. Freiburg 1935). RABANUS MAURUS, *Liber de oblatione puerorum contra eos qui repugnant institutis b. p. Benedicti, Patrologia Latina* ed. J. P. MIGNE (Paris 1878–90) 107:419–440. Literature. L. OLIGER, "De pueris oblatis in Ordine Minorum," *Archivum Franciscanum historicum* 8 (1915) 389–447; 10 (1917) 271–288. A. LENTINI, "Note sull'oblazione dei fanciulli nella Regola di S. Benedetto,'' *Studia anselmiana* 18–19 (1947) 195–225. H. LECLERCQ, *Dictionnaire d'archéologie chrétienne et de liturgie*, ed. F. CABROL, H. LECLERCQ, and H. I. MARROU (Paris 1907–53) 12.2:1857–77. J. MARCHAL, *Le 'Droit d'oblat': Essai sur une variété de pensionnés monastiques* (Paris 1955). S. HILPISCH et al., *Lexikon für Theologie und Kirche*, ed. J. HOFER and K. RAHNER (Freiburg 1957–65) 7:1083–87.

[L. E. BOYLE]

OBLATE SISTERS OF PROVIDENCE

(OSP, Official Catholic Directory #3040); a diocesan congregation of religious women founded in 1829 at Baltimore, Md., by the French-born Sulpician Jacques Nicholas Joubert (d. 1843) for the Christian education of African-Americans. The original group included Elizabeth Lange, Marie Magdalen Balas, Rosine Boegue, and Almaide Duchemin, the first Black women in the U.S. to take religious vows. They followed a rule written for them by Joubert and received the approbation of Rome in 1831. Guided by a young Redemptorist, Thaddeus Anwander, who undertook their direction in 1857, the sisters extended their field of labor beyond the confines of Baltimore. By 1900 they were conducting schools and orphanages in rural Maryland, Washington, D.C., Missouri, Kansas, and (until 1961) Cuba. The Oblate mission field was gradually expanded to include Alabama, the Carolinas, Florida, Illinois, Louisiana, Michigan, Minnesota, Mississippi, New Jersey, New York, and Virginia. Although the education of black youth in the U.S. constitutes the congregation's special apostolate, the sisters serve wherever needed, staffing elementary and secondary schools, a junior college, and catechetical, retreat, and day-care centers. The motherhouse and novitiate are located in Baltimore.

[M. A. CHINEWORTH/EDS.]

OBLATE SISTERS OF ST. FRANCIS DE SALES

(OSFS, Official Catholic Directory #3060); a congregation with papal approbation (1911), founded in 1866 by Father Louis BRISSON and Mother Francis de Sales Aviat (d. 1914) at Troyes, France, under the inspiration of Mother Maria Salesia CHAPPUIS. The congregation is devoted to educating youth, and assisting their spiritual formation by means of catechetics, retreats, counseling, summer camps and spiritual direction. The general motherhouse is in Troyes, France. The U.S. headquarters is in Childs, Md.

Bibliography: K. BURTON, *So Much, So Soon* (New York 1953). P. DUFOUR, *Le Très Révérend Père Louis Brisson* (Paris 1937).

[H. A. PAUL]

OBLATE SISTERS OF THE MOST HOLY REDEEMER

Religious congregation (*Oblatas del Santísimo Redentor,* OSSR, Official Catholic Directory, #3030) with papal approbation whose motherhouse is in Ciempozuelos (Madrid), Spain. The institute was founded in Madrid in 1864 by Mother Antonia María de Oviedo y Schontal (d. 1898) and José Benito Serra (1810–88), a Benedictine and former missionary in Australia. Their purpose was to establish homes for wayward girls. Later, the sisters took up also other forms of social work, as well as teaching. The congregation spread from Spain to Europe (Italy), North America (U.S.), South America (Colombia, El Salvador, Guatamala) and Africa (Cameroon). The U.S. headquarters are in New York, NY.

[A. J. ENNIS]

OBLATES OF MARY IMMACULATE

(OMI, Official Catholic Directory #0910); A congregation of religious men founded at Aix-en-Provence, France, in 1816 by Charles Joseph Eugène de Mazenod. The members of this society were known first as Missionaries of Provence, then as Oblates of St. Charles (1825). Their success in parochial mission work led to a rapid expansion of the institute, and houses were established in Marseilles (1822) and Nîmes (1825). A rule, written by the founder in 1818, was approved by the first members of the congregation and received episcopal approbation in November 1818. However, by 1823 certain bishops were contesting the validity of the vows pronounced by the missionaries and were threatening to recall their subjects who had joined the society. Further hostility to the group arose when its members opposed Jansenism and showed themselves favorable to papal infallibility and ultramontanism. It became clear that the stability of the society could be ensured only by approbation higher than that of the bishops. Mazenod, therefore, went to Rome and on Feb. 17, 1826, secured the definitive approval of the Holy See for the congregation, henceforth to be known as the Oblates of Mary Immaculate.

Development. Although the first objective of the Oblates was the preaching of missions to the poor of the rural areas, it was not long before their field of work was broadened. In 1824, the congregation accepted the task of improving the clergy by the establishment of seminaries, and two years later the Oblates assumed charge of the major seminary at Marseilles. Seminary work was extended to Ajaccio, Corsica; Pittsburgh, Pa.; Buffalo, N.Y.; Frejus, Romans, and Quimper in France; and Ottawa, Canada. After the death of the founder, seminaries were accepted in Asia and Africa.

In 1831, a general chapter of the society voted to take up the work of the foreign missions. The first mission foundations were made in Canada in 1841 and a year later in the U.S. Subsequently, missions were opened in the Oregon territory (1847), Ceylon (1847), Algeria, Northwest Africa (1848–50), Natal, South Africa (1850), Australia, Japan, the Philippines, and Laos. The congregation's efforts began later in Latin America, where foundations were made in Argentina, Brazil, Bolivia, Chile, Haiti, Mexico, Paraguay, Peru, Surinam, and Uruguay.

In addition, the Oblates went to England in 1841 and later spread to Germany, Switzerland, Spain, Belgium, Holland, Italy, and Poland. Teaching was added to the original works because of the need in the mission countries. In 1848, Bishop Joseph-Eugene Guiges, OMI founded the College of Bytown which in 1866 was granted university status by the Parliament of United Canada, and in 1889 received its pontifical charter. In 1965 it became St. Paul's University and split into two entities: The University of Ottawa and St. Paul's University. St. Paul's retained the Faculties of Theology and Canon Law and related Institutes, one of which is the Ukranian Catholic Church's Skeptytsky Institute which conducts the only doctoral program of Eastern Christian Studies in the Western Hemisphere. Establishments of this kind were opened in a great number of countries in the years that followed. Parochial work, originally not considered a part of the congregation's apostolate, was included also, particularly in places like America, Africa, and Sri Lanka (formerly Ceylon), where parishes were not only accepted but also established by the Oblates.

The development of the congregation is also associated with the care of Marian shrines. The founder accepted nine of them, and this number was increased through the years. The national Marian shrine of Canada, Our Lady of the Cape, Quebec, is under the care of the Oblates. Three shrines in the U.S. are under their jurisdiction: Our Lady of Lourdes, San Antonio, Tex.; Our Lady of the Snows, Belleville, Ill.; and Our Lady of Grace, Colebrook, N.H. Under the direction of the diocesan clergy, the Oblates serve at the National Shrine of the Immaculate Conception in Washington, D.C.

Approximately 185 years after its foundation, the congregation was divided into six regions, comprising 40 provinces, 18 delegations and 15 missions. It had more than 4,600 members, of whom about 3,500 were priests, including one cardinal, ten archbishops and 33 bishops. In addition 661 scholastics were preparing for the priesthood and 540 served as coadjutor brothers. It had given to the Church three cardinals, Joseph Hippolyte Guibert (1802–86), Archbishop of Paris, and Jean Mary Rodrigue VILLENEUVE (1883–1947), Archbishop of Quebec, and Francis George, (1937–), Archbishop of Chicago. Pope John Paul II canonized the founder, Bp. Eugene de Mazenod, on Dec. 3, 1995. Two other Oblates, Fr. Joseph Gerard and Fr. Jozef Cebula, have been beatified. Preliminary steps have been taken toward the canonization of four others.

Canada. When the Oblates arrived in Montreal in December 1841, they lost no time in taking over the care of the native missions, a work that led them to the remotest regions of James Bay and Labrador. In 1845, Alexander Taché, an Oblate seminarian, went to western Canada, where eventually he became successively bishop and archbishop of Saint Boniface. The conquest of western Canada for the Church was accomplished largely by the Oblates. They preached the gospel as far as Alaska, the shores of the Arctic sea, and Hudson Bay. Ten years after their arrival they had covered the entire expanse of Canada. They were named the first bishops of almost all the episcopal sees of the West: Saint Boniface, Edmonton, Saint Albert, Prince Albert, Gravelbourg, Vancouver, New Westminster, Mackenzie, Yukon, Grouard, and Hudson Bay. They also supplied the first bishop of Ottawa, the vicars apostolic of James Bay and Labrador, bishops to Timmins and Amos, and a cardinal archbishop of Quebec.

United States. From Canada, the Oblates spread to the U.S., where they preached their first mission at Cooperville, N.Y., in 1842. In the Oregon Territory they ministered to Native American tribes and newly arrived immigrants between 1847 and 1860. While still under superiors residing in Canada, they established foundations in Pittsburgh, Pa.; Buffalo and Plattsburgh, N.Y.; Burlington, Vt.; Detroit, Mich.; St. Paul, Minn.; and Lowell, Mass. In 1849, a mission was opened in Texas. The first attempt was shortlived, but a permanent foundation was made in 1851. They established a school in Galveston and made a foundation in Brownsville. In 1858 they crossed the Rio Grande into Mexico with foundations at Matamoros, Aqualeguas, and Victoria.

The Oblates in the U.S. were members of the Canadian province until 1883, when they formed a separate American province that included all the Oblate foundations within the U.S. Father James McGrath was named first provincial, and a year later the first novitiate was established in the new province at Tewksbury, Mass. Later, other provinces were created: the Eastern, with headquarters located at Boston, Mass.; the Southern, at Houston, Tex.; the Central, at St. Paul, Minn.; the Western, at San Fernando, Calif.; and St. John the Baptist province, which is not territorial but was established for the benefit of the French-speaking population, with headquarters at Lowell, Mass. Because of dwindling numbers and in order to focus efforts in evangelization, the five American provinces merged into one in 1999. American Oblates staff missions in Brazil, Japan, the Philippines, and Haiti. Some are in the Canadian north as well as in Africa, Sri Lanka, Laos, Chile, and Brazil. There are American Oblate missionary bishops in the Philippines and Haiti. The American Oblates conduct missions also in Denmark and Greenland; one member was named bishop of Stockholm, Sweden.

In the U.S., the Oblates preach parochial missions, direct retreat houses, conduct high schools, and care for numerous parishes from coast to coast. Without counting those working in foreign fields, American Oblates in 2001 numbered 531, of whom 454 were priests, including one cardinal, one archbishop and one bishop, 36 coadjutor brothers and 41 scholastics.

Rule and Administration. In addition to the three canonical vows of poverty, chastity, and obedience, the Oblates take a vow of perseverance by which they pledge in a particular way to remain in the congregation until death, even in the event that for extrinsic reasons the members should be obliged to disperse.

Supreme authority is found in the general chapter, which is convoked by the superior general every six years to strengthen the bonds of unity and to express the members participation in the life and mission of the congregation. The ordinary governing authority is in the hands of the Superior General, elected by the general chapter for six years, with six renewable. He is assisted by a general council comprised of the councilors for the congregation's six regions of Canada, United States, Latin America, Europe, Africa and Asia/Oceania, as well as by a vicar general and two assistants general, also elected by the general chapter. A new general council is elected by the general chapter after it has elected a new superior general. A secretary general, bursar general, procurator to the Holy See and a postulator for the causes of canonization are named by the superior general with his council in plenary session.

The superior general is bound to visit the congregation, either personally or by means of his assistants or other visitors whom he chooses, every six years. The congregation is divided into six regions, 40 provinces, 18 delegations and 14 missions. Within the province, dele-

gation or mission, each local community has its superior. Provincials are appointed by the superior general in council after consulting individually the members of a province. The provincial in council appoints the superior and council of a delegation subject to confirmation by the superior general in council, while the superior of a mission is appointed by the competent major superior. The congregation receives among its members candidates for the priesthood who are trained in its novitiates and scholasticates, and frequently also in its juniorates or minor seminaries. It also receives men who, while not aspiring to the priesthood, wish to devote their technical, professional or pastoral skills, as well as the witness of their life, to the work of building up the church as brothers.

Bibliography: *Constitutions and Rules of the Congregation of the Missionary Oblates of Mary Immaculate* (Rome 2000). G. CARRIÈRE, *Histoire documentaire de la Congrégation des Missionaires Oblats de Marie Immaculée dans l'Est du Canada* (Ottawa 1957–63) 5 v. pub. J. E. CHAMPAGNE, *Les Missions catholiques dans l'Ouest canadien, 1818–1875* (Ottawa 1949). K. CRONIN, *Cross in the Wilderness* (Vancouver 1960). B. DOYON, *The Cavalry of Christ on the Rio Grande, 1849–1883* (Milwaukee 1956). *Études Oblates* J. LEFLON, *Eugène de Mazenod, Bishop of Marseilles, Founder of the Oblates of Mary Immaculate,* tr. F. D. FLANAGAN (New York 1961–). *Missions de la Congrégation des Missionaires Oblats de Marie-Immaculée* chronological compilations of official reports and personal letters. T. ORTOLAN, *Cent ans d'apostolat dans les deux hemisphères: Les Oblats de Marie Immaculée durant le premier siècle de leur existence,* 4 v. (Paris 1915–). T. RAMBERT, *Vie de Monseigneur Charles-Joseph-Eugène de Mazenod,* 2 v. (Tours 1883). A. REY, *Histoire de Monseigneur Charles-Joseph-Eugène de Mazenod,* 2 v. (Marseille 1928). G. M. WAGGETT, ''The Oblates of Mary Immaculate in the Pacific Northwest of the U.S.A. 1847–1878,'' *Études Oblates* 6 (1947) 7–88.

[G. CARRIÈRE/C. HURKES]

OBLATES OF ST. CHARLES

(OSC); an English institute of secular priests founded by Henry Edward MANNING in London (1857). The great increase in the Catholic population at that time, because of Irish immigration and conversions resulting from the Oxford Movement, led Cardinal WISEMAN to depute Manning to establish this group. Manning modeled the new institute on the Oblates of Milan, but modified their rule, composed by St. Charles BORROMEO, to suit English conditions. Pius IX approved the rule in 1877. The aim was to have diocesan priests living in communities and engaged in pastoral and domestic mission labors. Under Manning, the first superior, the Oblates established four parishes in the western section of London, built primary and secondary schools, and introduced several sisterhoods into the Westminster archdiocese to aid them. Herbert VAUGHAN, while an Oblate, founded the MILL HILL MISSIONARIES.

Bibliography: E. S. PURCELL, *Life of Cardinal Manning, Archbishop of Westminster,* 2 v. (4th ed. London 1896).

[D. WARD/EDS.]

OBLATES OF ST. FRANCIS DE SALES

A religious congregation of men, the Oblates of St. Francis de Sales, at times popularly known today as "De Sales Oblates," were founded in Troyes, France, by Reverend Louis Brisson in 1872. His early death prevented St. Francis de Sales from proceeding very far in his desire to establish a congregation of men whose spirit would be similar to that of the Order of the Visitation of Holy Mary which he had co-founded in 1610 with St. Jane de Chantal. After his death, however, St. Jane de Chantal encouraged Reverend Raymond Bonal to make a similar foundation which lasted until the early 18th century. Mother Marie de Sales Chappuis, the Superior of the Troyes Visitation Monastery, persuaded the Monastery's chaplain, Father Brisson, to make another attempt.

Early History. Father Brisson asked Father Claude Perrot, a Benedictine monk of the Abbey of Notre Dame des Ermites in Einsiedeln, Switzerland, to assist him in the formulation of constitutions for the projected congregation. Father Perrot's initial attempts, short treatises on spiritual subjects, were taken verbatim from the writings of St. Francis de Sales. In time, they were formulated into constitutions in the canonical sense. To these was added the "Spiritual Directory" which is a series of brief, insightful instructions on the right manner and disposition for performing "the actions of every day." When his bishop asked Father Brisson to take over the administration of St. Stephen's, a failing diocesan school for boys, he saw this request as the opportunity which Providence was providing him for bringing about his new foundation. In the fall of 1872, the clerical faculty members of the School, now named Saint Bernard's, began their novitiate. The congregation received its first Roman approval, the Decretum laudis, in December, 1875, and its definitive approval on Dec. 8, 1897.

Charism of the Congregation. The charism of the Oblates is the imitation of St. Francis de Sales in his own celebrated imitation of Jesus. The members of the congregation live and spread the spirit and doctrine of their Patron through sharing his spiritual legacy as found in his major works such as the *Introduction to the Devout Life* and the *Treatise on the Love of God.* For the congregation, a principal focus of Salesian spirituality is the saint's "Spiritual Directory." This masterpiece is not so much a book as it is a spiritual strategy for living the spirit of Jesuus in simple and concrete way throughout the course of each day. Its essential practices, such as the direction of intention and interior prayer, lead, in time, to a state of continual, loving union with God in heart, will, and life. This is how Scripture describes the human life of Jesus and how Oblates live Jesus themselves and teach others to do so. In this way, they participate in his saving mission today.

Imbued with the inviting spirituality of their Patron, the members of the congregation, priests and lay brothers, work to satisfy the human family's hunger for union with the Holy. They do this by showing those they serve how to observe Jesus's double commandment of love. In imitation of Jesus, they are shown how to love God with affective love, that is, in prayerful union with Him and with effective love by generously responding to His divine will for them as that will unfolds in the course of each succeeding present moment of life. They are taught how to love others by meeting their spiritual and human needs in a compassionate, concrete and caring manner; and by living the relational virtues with them: charity, humility, gentleness, patience, simplicity, and joyful optimism.

While being responsive to the Church's changing apostolic needs, the Oblates are generally involved in the Christian education of youth, parochial ministry, and foreign missions.

Expansion. In July 1882 five missionaries were sent to Pella, a small village in the region of South Africa know as Namaqualand. With later territorial additions, this region became the Apostolic Vicariate of the Orange River, which was later divided into what are now the Diocese of Keimoes-Upington, in South Africa, and the Diocese of Keetmanshoop in Namibia. Even today, Oblates continue to constitute the largest number of clergy in both dioceses. Because of political unrest and anticlerical sentiment, the Oblates who had been assigned to Brazil in 1885 were soon transferred to Montevideo, Uruguay. As soon as conditions improved, however, the congregation returned to Brazil, this time to Rio Grande do Sul. In July, 1889, the congregation established a school in Naxos, Greece, which was soon followed by one in Athens. By the end of the 19th century, European foundations had also been established in Italy, Austria, and England. Although the congregation later withdrew from England and Greece, its presence in Europe continues in Austria, France, Germany, Italy, Monaco, the Netherlands, and Switzerland.

In 1893 Father Joseph Maréchaux was assigned as chaplain to a new congregation of sisters in White Plains, New York—the Sisters of Divine Compassion. Three years later, five companions joined him, forming the original community of Oblates in the United States. Within a few years, all were assigned elsewhere, however. In the meantime, another Oblate had been sent as chaplain to the Monastery of the Visitation, then located in Wilmington, Delaware. Two other Oblates, fleeing anti-religious laws in France, joined him there in 1903. Together they established Salesianum, a private high school for boys in Wilmington, as well as a novitiate. The first provincial for the United States was appointed in 1906, the same year that the novitiate was transferred to Childs, Maryland. In 1924 the congregation established a house of studies for its scholastics near The Catholic University of America, in Washington, DC.

In 1926 the congregation accepted an invitation from the Archdiocese of Philadelphia to staff the newly established Northeast Catholic High School for boys. Rapidly following that foundation, the congregation spread throughout the United States, principally along the East Coast: Delaware, the District of Columbia, Florida, Maryland, New York, New Jersey, North Carolina, Pennsylvania, and Virginia; in the Midwest: Michigan and Ohio; and in the West: California, Oklahoma, and Utah.

Recent Developments. In 1983, after an extensive period of discernment and two exploratory visits, the congregation established a foundation in Bangalore, India. At present, there is a flourishing house of studies there, with plans underway for further expansion in India and elsewhere in Asia. In recent years, Oblates have begun small but promising ministries in Bénin, Ecuador, Ukraine, Haiti, and Mexico's Yucatan Peninsula.

The Mother House of the congregation is located in Rome. The congregation is governed by a Superior General who is elected for a six-year term, once renewable, and by four general councillors, three of whom are elected by the General Chapter while one is appointed by the Superior General. World-wide, there are 650 Oblates in ten provinces or regions. Each province or region is governed by a major superior who is either elected or appointed according to the prescriptions of particular statutes for a four-year term, twice renewable. They are assisted in governance by an elected council. The novitiate lasts one year. The perpetual profession of simple vows follows three years or more of annual vows.

Bibliography: OSFS, Official Catholic Directory #0920. P. DUFOUR, *Les Oblats de Saint François de Sales* (Paris 1938). K. BURTON, *So Much so Soon: Father Brisson, Founder of the Oblates of St. Francis de Sales* (New York 1953).

[L. S. FIORELLI]

OBLATES OF ST. JOSEPH

The Congregation of the Oblates of St. Joseph (OSJ, Official Catholic Directory #0930) was founded in 1878 by Giuseppe Marello (1844–95), Bishop of Acqui, Italy. After surviving its difficult early years, the congregation was given final approval by the Holy See April 11, 1909. The Oblates of St. Joseph are engaged in various apostolic works in parishes, schools, and foreign missions. The founder wished his followers to be ready to serve the bishops in whatever tasks were given to them. The generalate is in Rome. The congregation came to the U.S. in 1929 at the request of Thomas C. O'Reilly, Bishop of Scranton, Pa. In 1931 they opened houses in California at Madera, Santa Cruz, Sacramento, and Tomales. In the U.S. the congregation is divided into two provinces: the eastern province embraces Pennsylvania, New York, and Washington, D.C.; the western, California.

[S. CHINI/EDS.]

OBLIGATION, MORAL

Since Immanuel KANT proposed his theory of duty for duty's sake, based on his doctrine of the categorical imperative, the theme of duty or obligation has become the central one in almost all modern ethical theories. It occupies so important a place in moral reflection that in the history of philosophy moral systems are classed according as they center on the twin notions of duty and obligation or not. Kant's ethical theory, based on the notion of duty (*Pflicht*) for duty's sake, was deeply influenced by his religious background and upbringing (*see* PIETISM). Much more recently Henri BERGSON, in a truly epoch-making work (*Les deux sources de la morale et de la religion,* 1932), proposed a moral theory built around a double source of moral obligation, namely, social pressure and personal attraction (aspiration) in love and friendship. For both of these eminent thinkers, the notion of duty or obligation is fundamental in moral teaching. In contemporary thought, the English (principally Oxford) moral philosophers have devoted much energy to the semantics of moral theory in general and to the linguistic analysis of obligation in particular (Hare, Nowell-Smith, Ewing, and others). This article, however, is limited to examining the concept of obligation in the Christian ethos, or in the context of the history of salvation (*Heilsgeschichte*).

Semantics and Metaphysics of Obligation. The notion of duty and obligation is found in the sources of revelation and in sacred theology, but in a subordinate or secondary position. This is explainable by the fact that, as against the Kantian conception of things (namely, that an action or way of life is good because it presents itself as a duty or obligation through the categorical imperative), the attitude found in the sources of revelation and in theology (in fact, in most systems of moral philosophy up to the time of Kant) is just the contrary. The attitude may be expressed this way: because an action is good in itself or because it is prescribed in the law of God (see St. Thomas Aquinas, *Summa theologiae* 1a2ae, 108.1 ad 2) and as such is a manifestation of His will, it is here and now a *duty* and consequently it *obliges*. It should be carefully noted that "duty" and "obligation," although very closely related terms, are not synonymous. They are, it may be said, the twin facets of one and the same reality—duty indicating the objective reality (to be realized and put into execution) and obligation being the necessity in which one's freedom finds itself when it comes face to face with this reality. Duty is what one is bound to do by moral or legal obligation (see *Summa theologiae* 1a 2ae, 99.5 and *passim* for the distinction between moral and legal obligation and duty). The very word obligation (from *ob-ligare*) signifies the state of being bound around or enveloped by some constraint or necessity or force limiting the scope of free activity or perhaps orientating and safeguarding it (*see* FREEDOM; see also St. Thomas, *In 3 Sent.* 18. 1.2 ad 5; *De ver.* 23.1; *De malo* 16.5; *Summa theologiae* 1a, 103.8 in fine c.; *In 1 meta.* 3.58–60). One arrives at much the same notion by examining the word duty, which came into English from the French through Anglo-French (*dû, dueté*) and ultimately from the Latin *debere*, which itself is composed of *de* and *habere* meaning to have something from another, to be in possession of something that in reality belongs to another [*see* Meillet-Ernout, *Dictionnaire étymologique de la langue latine* (4th ed. Paris 1959–60) s.v. debeo].

Going just one step further from this nominal definition of obligation, one gets an insight into the metaphysical roots of obligation. For, supposing the fact of creation [St. Thomas frequently refers to the gift (*beneficium*) of creation: *C. gent.* 3.120; *Summa theologiae* 1a2ae, 100.5 ad 2; 2a2ae, 85.2; 122.4; and even once to the *right* of God based on the fact of creation (*ius creationis*): *In 3 Sent.* 9.1.1.1], it follows that all created things, sharing in or participating the being and perfections of God, are by that very fact participated being (*ens per participationem*) and as such belong (ontologically) to the Supreme Being, from whom they receive all they are and have. In this precise sense all creatures must be said to be parts of the Creator; that is, every participated being is, by definition, a part of and belongs to unparticipated, uncreated, uncaused Being, which is God. This is perhaps one of the most brilliant and profound theological insights of St. Thomas, who then proceeds to apply it in many different theological fields. He uses it, for instance, to show that the angels love God by natural love more than themselves, first of all by natural and instinctive inclination and then by conscious and voluntary ordination (cf. *Summa theologiae* 1a, 60.5; *In Dion. de div. nom.* 4.9,

10). All created things, then, from the greatest to the smallest, belong to God in their totality, not only as they come from the hands of their Maker and thus enter into being, but also, and perhaps above all, in the fullness of their being and perfection, that is, in the full self-realization brought about by their own free action and life, through which precisely they give full glory to their Creator, whose work they are (cf. *Summa theologiae* 1a, 103.2; 1a2ae, 1, 7–8; 1a2ae, 21.4 ad 3; *C. gent.* 3.16–21). This notion is of paramount importance in considering those beings that grow and develop into the perfection or fullness of their being; and above all in considering creatures whose growth into plenitude of being is under their own guidance, as is the case with human beings. Man, endowed with reason and free will, moves or guides himself into the perfection that God, the Creator, has destined for him, whether that perfection is completely proportionate to his connatural powers or corresponds rather to a gratuitous divine call and to gratuitously donated life principles (infused virtues) leading ultimately to consummation in participated divine life in the vision of heaven.

Thus, whether in the order of nature or of supernature, the metaphysical roots of all responsibility and obligation are founded in God's plan for His creation and for its ultimate consummation in and through Christ. In the Book of Sirach it is said that God, having created man from the beginning, committed him into the hands of his own counsel and at the same time gave him His law to guide him (Sirach in the Vulgate 15.14–16; *Summa theologiae* 1a, 103.5 ad 2). St. Thomas put the matter this way: just as the ship is committed by the maker or owner to the care of the captain to guide it, care for it, and bring it safely to port, so did God commit man to the care and guidance of his reason and will to bring him to the goal set by God, namely, eternal life, beatitude, and salvation (cf. *Summa theologiae* 1a2ae, 2.5; 2a2ae, 85.2).

From this theonomic notion of obligation and responsibility (based on the interpersonal relationship between the Creator and His creature), it should be immediately manifest that obligation may in no wise be conceived as something imposed from without, hampering freedom and growth, but rather as an exigency of being, and in particular as an exigency of human being in dependence of the divine Being, who wishes that His creatures come to perfection (cf. 1 Thes 4.3) and thus give Him the honor and glory that is His due. In terms of the nominal definition that was the starting point of this analysis, it can be said: man's first and fundamental duty is the perfection appointed him by God and consequently due to God, and his first and fundamental obligation is that of bringing himself to that divinely appointed consummation in being.

Obligation in the Old and New Testament. In the context of the history of salvation, it is evident that God, the Creator and Master of all things, entered into personal contact and dialogue with His creatures, with men, calling them to a special sharing in His life and friendship and entering into a covenant, or alliance, with them, and Himself established the conditions of that alliance, setting them down in brief in the Law, in the Decalogue of Sinai. The observance of the Law and the carrying out of all its prescriptions was the one guarantee of retaining the goodwill and friendship of Yahweh. Hence the reverence, devotion, and love with which the chosen people looked upon the Law. The Law and all its prescriptions, that is, the conditions of the alliance, bind or oblige them in all their doings. Of that they are fully conscious. This concentration and insistence on the Law may in no way be thought of as a kind of legalism, but rather, as a modern exegete has felicitously put it, as true nomocentrism. The voice of God came to Moses on Mt. Sinai: ''Thus shall you say to the house of Jacob; tell the Israelites: you have seen for yourselves how I treated the Egyptians and how I bore you up on eagle wings and brought you here to myself. Therefore if you hearken to my voice and keep my covenant, you shall be my special possession, dearer to me than all other people, though all the earth is mine. You shall be to me a kingdom of priests, a holy nation'' (Ex 19.3–6). When Moses told the people what the Lord had said and made known to them all the commands He had given, they answered, in the conviction than an obligation was being imposed on them: ''Everything the Lord has said, we will do'' (Ex 19.7; 24.3); and forthwith Moses committed all to writing (Ex 24.4). The observance of the Law of Yahweh brings blessing and happiness (Ex 23.20–33; Dt 28.1–14); its breach, maledictions and misfortune (Lv 26.14–.43; Dt 28.1.5–68).

The notion of obligation in the New Law and under the New Alliance remains fundamentally the same; but there are, for all that, important differences, differences not so much of content as of spirit or attitude, caused in men by the teaching and example of Christ and by His efficacious (sacramental) healing and sanctifying influence on those who believe in Him. ''God, who at sundry times and in divers manners spoke in times past to the fathers by the prophets, last of all in these days has spoken to us by His Son'' (Heb 1.1), whom when the time had matured, He sent, in order that we might receive adoption as sons, sending the spirit of His Son into our hearts, so that from being slaves and bondsmen we might, with and in Christ, become sons and heirs by the act of God (cf. Gal 4.4–7). This is the fulfillment of God's promise to enter into a new covenant with His people by transforming their hearts and renewing their spirit (cf. Ez 11.19). However, one must never forget Our Lord's constant and insistent warning that He came not to abolish the Law or the Prophets, but to fulfill them down to the minutest detail (Mt 5.17–18) by seeing that they be observed from within, from the spirit of sonship, and out of love for the person of the Lawgiver. Another warning of Christ must also be kept in mind, namely, that the sole proof of one's love for Him is the keeping of His Commandments (cf. Jn 14.15, 21;1 Jn 5.2; Jn 1.6).

In the context, then, of the New Alliance, it is evident that the roots of obligation for the new people of God are visibly and outwardly the Law and the Prophets and, in the inner being of the new creation (2 Cor 5.17), the new spirit of sonship and friendship infused into mens' hearts through and in Christ, together with mens' consciousness of this new nobility and dignity (*see* CONSCIENCE). Here it is really a question of *noblesse oblige,* and St. Paul, in the parenetic sections of his Epistles, returns to it again and again (see Eph 5.3; Col 3.12; Gal 5.22; Rom 6.22). The *Dogmatic Constitution on the Church* of Vatican Council II (ch. 2.5, 7) insistently recalls the people of God to a recognition and to a renewed consciousness of the dignity of their divine calling and of the obligations that calling imposes, echoing thereby the words of St. Leo: ''Recognize, O Christian, your dignity and having become a partaker in the divine nature, do not degrade yourself by returning to your former baseness. Remember the Head and the Body of which you are a member'' (*Serm.* 21.3; *Patrologia Latina*, ed. J. P. MIGNE [Paris 1878–90] 54:192–193).

Here a point of the greatest importance must be carefully noted. Yahweh did not conclude the alliance with individual members of the chosen people, but with the people as such, making known to them through His Prophets the terms of the alliance laid down by Him and the conditions of its observance. So it was in the course of sacred history; in the designs of divine providence, so it still is in the context of the New Alliance with the new people of God. The conditions of the alliance, it must be confessed, affect and oblige each individual, and the Spirit of God moves the minds and inspires and informs the consciences of the individual faithful (cf. Mt 10.29–33; Lk 12.6–7). To guarantee the genuineness and authenticity of such inspirations—whether in matters of faith or morals—Christ, foreseeing the ever-present danger of error and deception, endowed His Church with an infallible teaching authority vested in its pastors, who receive Christ's injunction to go teach all nations to observe all whatsoever He had commanded them (Mt 28.20), as well as the assurance that whoever listens to them listens to Him (Lk 10.16). This important matter was emphasized in a special way in Vatican Council II (cf. *loc. cit.* 2.12.2).

Obligation and Law. Before termination of the discussion on the notion of obligation in the context of the history of salvation and of the Christian ethos in particular, one final matter must be mentioned. The radical binding force of divine (and natural, which is a direct and immediate participation of divine) law, as the main source and root of obligation in the context of the history of salvation, has been examined above and need not be further expatiated. However, the question of the binding force of positive human law—whether civil, ecclesiastical, or religious—must be considered, since there is the ever-present danger of either exaggerating its binding force (*see* RIGORISM) or of so minimizing it that it no longer has any real meaning as law (*see* LAXISM). This question is all the more important in that positive law affects men more tangibly and obviously and, as man-made, appears more readily as an unwarranted curtailment of man's innate freedom. Besides, a wrong conception of things in this domain can, and indeed at times must, inevitably lead to a falsification of conscience and eventually to SCRUPULOSITY. First, the principle of St. Thomas with regard to the general binding force of positive (human) law should be carefully noted: when there is no evidence of the fact, it is a dangerous thing to lay down categorically what is or is not a mortal sin (*Quodl.* 9.7.2). Second, all positive law, if it be just and prudently made, whether civil or ecclesiastical or religious, binds in conscience and must be observed *ut in pluribus* (see *Summa theologiae* 1a2ae, 96.1 ad 3; 1a2ae, 96.6 and *passim*) under pain of sin and corresponding punishment as laid down in the law itself. Third, there is the special case of laws of constitutions that stipulate explicitly that they do not bind under sin, but oblige only to undergo the penalty attaching to their violation. This is the case, for instance, with regard to the 1932 constitutions of the Dominican Order (32.1, dating from the general chapter of Paris, 1236; *Monumenta Ordinis Fratrum Praedicatorum historica*, ed. B. M. Reichert [Rome-Stuttgart-Paris 1896–] 3.8) and, following that example, the constitutions and rules of many other orders, congregations, and confraternities. Fourth, it should be noted that therein is the source of much confusion in later moral theology. For such rules and constitutions were (and are) said to bind *sub levi* or *sub gravi,* meaning that they oblige to the acceptance of the light or grave penalty imposed by them, but in no wise insinuating that there is any question of sin: quite the contrary. In later times, and especially in post-Reformation theology, the origin of these expressions was overlooked, and they were wrongly given the meaning of obligation under light or grave sin. Hence arose the bitter discussion during the 17th century. The bitterness seems to have disappeared, but the confusion persists, and so far shows no sign of being dissipated.

Bibliography: A. MOLIEN, *Dictionnaire de théologie catholique,* ed. A. VACANT et al., (Paris 1903–50) 9.1:871–910. G. ERMECKE, *Lexikon für Theologie und Kirche,* ed. J. HOFER and K. RAHNER (Freiberg 1957–65) 8:426–428. K. E. LOGSTRUP, *Die Religion in Geschichte und Gegenwart* (Tübingen 1957–65) 5:313–317. X. LÈON-DUFOUR et al., *Vocabulaire de théologie biblique* (Paris 1962) 20–29. R. NAZ and C. LEFERVRE, *Dictionnaire de droit canonique,* ed. R. NAZ (Paris 1953–65) 6:635–677. J. TONNEAU, ''L'Obligation *ad poenam* des constitutions dominicaines,'' *Revue des sciences philosophiques et théologiques* 24 (1935) 107–115; ''Devoir et morale,'' *ibid.* 38 (1954) 233–252. W. FARRELL, ''The Roots of Obligation,'' *Thomist* 1 (1939) 14–30. L. B. GEIGER, *Le Problème de l'amour chez saint Thomas d'Aquin* (Montreal 1952). H. M. BAUMGARTNER, *Die Unbedingtheit des Sittlichen: Eine Auseinandersetzung mit Nicolai Hartmann* (Munich 1962). H. REINER, ''Wesen und Grund der sittlichen Verbindlichkeit (obligatio) bei Thomas v. Aquin'' in *Sein und Ethos: Untersuchungen zur Grundlegung der Ethik,* ed. P. ENGELHARDT (Mainz 1963) 236–266; ''Beatitudo und obligatio bei Thomas von Aquin: Antwort an P. Pinckaers,'' *ibid.* 306–328. S. PINCKAERS, ''Eudämonismus und sittliche Verbindlichkeit in der Ethik des hl. Thomas: Stellungnahme zum Beitrag Hans Reiner,'' *ibid.* 267–305. CAJETAN, ''De obligatione et observatione praeceptorum tam in religione, quam extra'' in *Opuscula omnia,* t.1, tract. 25; *Commentarii in Summa theologiae 1a2ae, 95–96; 2a2ae, 186.9.* BARTHOLOMAEUS DE MEDINA, *Expositio in Summa theologiae 1a2ae, 96.4.* G. G. MEERSSEMAN, ''La Loi purement pènale d'après les statuts de Confréries Médiévales,'' *Mélanges Joseph de Ghellinck,* 2 v. (Gembloux 1951) 2:975–1002. S. KUTTNER, *Kanonistische Schuldlehre von Gratian bis auf die Dekretalien Gregors IX.* (*Studi e Testi* 64; 1935). R. M. HARE, *The Language of Morals* (Oxford 1952).

[C. WILLIAMS]

O'BOYLE, PATRICK A.

First resident archbishop of Wash., D.C., cardinal; b. July 18, 1896, Scranton, Pa.; d. Aug. 10, 1987, Washington, D.C. He graduated from St. Thomas College (later renamed the University of Scranton), and St. Joseph's Seminary in Yonkers, N.Y. Ordained in New York's St. Patrick's Cathedral on May 21, 1921, by Patrick Cardinal HAYES, Father O'Boyle's first assignment was to St. Columba's parish in Manhattan, south of the infamous Hell's Kitchen, where he saw and experienced the urban version of the hard life.

Early Charitable Work. His work among the parish poor caught the eye of Cardinal Hayes, who gave him the first of a series of assignments concerned with the cause of the needy. In 1933, he was appointed assistant director of the Children's Division of the New York Catholic Charities; he supervised various Catholic charitable organizations and child care agencies, notably the Mission of the Immaculate Virgin on Staten Island, one of the country's largest child care institutions with more than 1,100 children enrolled. During this same period, he was a faculty member at Fordham University School of Social

Work. In 1941, he was named assistant director of New York's Catholic Charities, and in 1943, he became director of War Relief Services of the National Catholic Welfare Conference (1946–48). He served as director of Catholic Charities of New York.

Archbishop. On Nov. 15, 1947, Monsignor O'Boyle was named the first residential ordinary of the archdiocese of Washington, D.C. The Washington archdiocese had been created in 1939, but it had remained united with the archdiocese of Baltimore until Archbishop O'Boyle was appointed ordinary. (It was the first time in the United States that a priest had been named an archbishop without first serving as a bishop.)

Ordained to the episcopacy in January of 1948, O'Boyle was installed in St. Matthew's Cathedral as archbishop of Washington on Jan. 21, 1948. During his 25-year tenure as archbishop, the number of Catholics in the archdiocese more than doubled. The number of parishes increased by 50, and 317 buildings were constructed under his leadership, including schools to educate the children of the postwar baby boom; St. Ann's Infant and Maternity home for unwed mothers and their babies; Carroll Manor for the elderly; and the Lt. Joseph P. Kennedy Institute to serve the mentally handicapped.

One of his first acts as archbishop was to order the desegregation of Catholic schools and churches, an order that *The Washington Post* called ''one of the most influential acts of moral leadership in this city's history.'' The desegregation of the Catholic schools began six years before the Supreme Court outlawed segregation in the public schools in its historic *Brown v. Board of Education* decision in 1954. He also spoke out forcefully in support of racial justice and equality during the 1960s and 1970s and earned a reputation as an outspoken friend of those who were being denied basic human and civil rights.

Archbishop O'Boyle attended all the sessions of the Second VATICAN COUNCIL. He was elected to the Commission on Seminaries, Universities and Catholic Schools, where he played a significant role in shaping the Declaration of Christian Education (*Gravissimum educationis*). In a formal intervention during the final session, he urged greater sensitivity to Jewish feelings ''out of consideration of truth and charity,'' and he recommended several changes in the wording of the declaration concerning Jews and non-Christians. In the final session, as chairman of the Administrative Board of the National Catholic Welfare Conference, he spoke ''in the name of all the bishops of the United States gathered in Rome,'' urging that schema 13 (later to emerge as *Gaudium et spes*) contain a condemnation of racism and racial discrimination in all its forms.

Cardinal. He was created cardinal on June 28, 1967, by Pope PAUL VI and given his titular church, St. Nicholas in Carcere. By reason of his position as ordinary of the Archdiocese of Washington, O'Boyle was also chancellor of The Catholic University of America. Although inclined to be less involved in university affairs than previous chancellors had been, he intervened at critical periods, during the early 1960s, for example, in order to insure the success of the *New Catholic Encyclopedia,* and during the spring of 1967, when a nationally publicized protest of faculty against an action of the trustees had led to a week-long suspension of classes. He was a keen participant in the reorganization of the board of trustees and the development of new bylaws for university governance in 1968. In years of financial crisis during the late 1960s and early 1970s, he used his personal influence to obtain support for the institution.

Doctrinal Defender. Although considered by many to be a liberal on civil rights and social issues, Cardinal O'Boyle was perceived as an outspoken and unbending opponent of dissent where the Church's doctrinal or moral teachings were concerned. This was most evident in his staunch support of Pope Paul VI's 1968 encyclical, *Humanae vitae,* that upheld the Church's teaching against artificial contraception. His support of the encyclical led to a controversy involving 50 priests of the archdiocese and some priest faculty members of The Catholic University of America.

Equally outspoken on other moral issues, he opposed sterilization on grounds that it frustrates a natural right to conceive that neither the state nor an individual can take away; and he criticized government birth control programs as an intrusion into the private rights of citizens. He was critical of the Supreme Court's 1973 decision legalizing abortion; he equated abortion with murder and compared it with Hitler's slaughter of the Jews.

Cardinal O'Boyle submitted his resignation at the mandatory retirement age of 75 in 1971. His resignation was accepted in 1973. He continued to reside in Washington until his death after a short illness. He is interred in St. Matthew's Cathedral crypt. His papers from the Vatican II years are in the archives of the Mullen Library on the campus of The Catholic University of America.

Bibliography: *Washington Post* (Aug. 12, 1987) A22. V. A. YZERMANS, *American Participation in the Second Vatican Council* (New York 1967).

[J. F. DONOGHUE]

OBRECHT, JAKOB

Composer, also called Hobrecht, Obertus, etc.; b. Bergen-op-Zoom, Holland, Nov. 22, 1452; d. Ferrara,

"Salve Regina," 16th-century manuscript by Jakob Obrecht.

Italy, 1505. He was at the University of Louvain in 1470 and was ordained in 1480. In 1479 he became choir director in his native town, and from 1484 to 1485 he served at Cambrai cathedral; he was then appointed *succentor* at Bruges. On a short leave of absence in 1487 he visited Ferrara at the invitation of Duke Hercules I. From 1492 to 1496 he was a chaplain of Antwerp cathedral, but he spent his last few years at Ferrara, where he died during the plague. Composer of some 30 secular works, he first gained prominence for his Masses, some of which were inspired by (if not based upon) material by Frye, BUS-NOIS, A. Agricola, and OKEGHEM. Mostly scored for four voices, they exhibit some conservative features (rigid *cantus firmus* treatment, little melodic imitation), although harmonically they have strong tonal tendencies. His thematic material derives from a variety of sources: a German song in praise of the Virgin (*Missa Maria zart*), a Marian antiphon and other texts (*Missa Sub tuum prae-sidium*), an antiphon for Holy Thursday (*Missa Caput*);

a secular song (*Missa L'homme arm*é), a motet by anoth-er composer (*Missa Ave Regina caelorum*); it was the custom to honor past masters by borrowing their melo-dies, polyphonic textures, and structural ideas, integrat-ing them into new works with entirely different texts. In his motets, he sometimes shows an old-fashioned predi-lection for polytextuality (*Beata es, Maria; Salve crux arbor*), though his treatment of texture usually leans to-ward the clarity and fluidity of Desprez. Among his mas-terpieces are his settings of the MARIAN ANTIPHONS *SALVE REGINA, ALMA REDEMPTORIS MATER*, and *AVE REGINA CAELORUM*. A motet-Passion long ascribed to him is now known to be the work of Antoine Longueval.

Bibliography: *Werken*, ed. J. WOLF, 30 v. (Amsterdam 1908–21). *Opera Omnia*, ed. A. SMIJERS and M. VAN CREVEL (Am-sterdam 1953–). O. J. GOMBOSI, *Jacob Obrecht* (Leipzig 1925). G. REESE, *Music in the Renaissance* (rev. ed. New York 1959). B. MURRAY, "A New Light on Jacob Obrecht's Development," *Musi-cal Quarterly* (New York 1957) 43 500–516. "Jacob Obrecht's Connection with the Church of Our Lady in Antwerp," *Revue* *belge de musicologie* 11 (1957) 125–133. L. FINSCHER, *Die Musik in Geschichte und Gegenwart,* ed. F. BLUME (Kassel-Basel 1949–) 9:1814–22. *Baker's Biographical Dictionary of Musicians,* ed. N. SLONIMSKY (5th, rev. ed. New York 1958) 1175. B. J. BLACKBURN, "Obrecht's *Missa Je ne demande* and Busnoys's Chanson: An Essay in Reconstructing Lost Canons," *Tidschrift van de Koninklijke Vereniging voor Nederlandse Muziekgeschiedenis* 45 (1995), 18–32. J. M. BLOXHAM, "Plainsong and Polyphony for the Blessed Virgin: Notes on Two Masses by Jacob Obrecht," *The Journal of Musicology* 12 (1994), 51–75. D. M. RANDEL, ed., *The Harvard Biographical Dictionary of Music* (Cambridge 1996). R. D. ROSS, "The Motets of Jacob Obrecht: A Stylistic Analysis" (Ph.D. diss. University of Cincinnati, 1973). R. C. WEGMAN, *Born For the Muses: The Life and Masses of Jacob Obrecht* (Oxford: 1994.) "Agricola, Bordon, and Obrecht at Ghent: Discoveries and Revisions," *Revue Belge de Musicologie* 51 (1997), 34–48.

[D. STEVENS]

OBRECHT, M. EDMOND

Fourth abbot of Gethsemani, Ky.; b. Stotzhein, Alsace, Nov. 13, 1852; d. Gethsemani, Jan. 4, 1935. He entered La Grande Trappe, La Trappe, France, at the age of 23, intending to live all his days there in cloistered silence and anonymity. Instead, he traveled all over the globe, was known to four successive popes and many bishops, and was loved by countless people. He was ordained at Seez in 1879 and sent immediately to Rome as secretary to the procurator general of the three Trappist observances. When these amalgamated into an order in 1892, he was commissioned to collect funds in the United States for the ancient Abbey of Tre Fontane, Rome, which had become the generalate of the restored order. After four years, he returned to Rome, was sent to a struggling abbey in the French Jura, and shortly after appointed provisional superior of Gethsemani. By strong measures he saved this monastery for the United States and his order, and was elected its abbot in 1898. Exceptional administrative abilities brought him appointments as visitor to monasteries in Europe, Canada, the United States, Asia, and Africa. Obrecht was named apostolic administrator of Mariann Hill Mission in South Africa; he determined the status of these monks as missioners and not Trappists.

Bibliography: M. AMEDEUS, *Dom Edmund M. Obrecht, OCSO* (Gethsemani, Ky. 1937). M. RAYMOND, *Burnt Out Incense* (New York 1949).

[R. FLANAGAN]

OBREGONIANS (POOR INFIRMARIANS)

The popular title of the Least Brothers (*Hermanos Minimos*), founded at Madrid in 1568 by Bernardino Ob-

regón; b. near Burgos, Spain, May 20, 1540; d. Madrid, Aug. 6, 1599. Obregón, a young man of noble lineage who had begun his ecclesiastical studies, discontinued them to become an officer in the army of Philip II. Having served in several campaigns, he found himself one day at court, where a sweeper accidentally splattered his uniform with mud. Obregón angrily slapped the humble worker, who instead of retaliating, begged pardon. Heartily impressed, Obregón gave up his military career and began to nurse the sick. Soon he and some companions took over the administration of the general hospital of Madrid and spread their work to Portugal, Belgium, and the colonies. In 1594 Obregón reedited the Constitutions they had been following, and four years later his group was permitted to take the vows of religion according to the rule of the Third Order of St. Françis of Paola, adding a fourth vow of free hospitality. Paul V authorized the *Hermanos Minimos* in 1609 to wear a gray habit having a black cross on the left side as monogram. In 1592 Obregón founded an asylum for poor children in Lisbon. He also wrote an early manual on the care of the sick, *Instrucción de enfermos y verdadera practica de como se han de aplicar los remedios que enseñan los medicos* (Madrid 1607). In 1589 Obregón assisted at the deathbed of his former commander, Philip II. The Order of *Hermanos Minimos* disintegrated during the French Revolution.

Bibliography: *Enciclopedia universal illustrada Europeo-Americana* (Barcelona 1908–30, suppl. 1934–) 39:408–409.

[M. P. TRAUTH]

O'BRIEN, MATTHEW ANTHONY

Missionary; b. Nenagh, Ireland, May, 1804; d. Springfield, Ky., Jan. 15, 1871. He was the son of John and Grace (Meagher) O'Brien. In 1826, having received his early education in Ireland, he came to the United States and worked his way to Kentucky. He studied and taught at St. Mary's College, Marion County, Ky., from 1829 until he entered the Dominican Order of St. Rose Priory, near Springfield, Ky. O'Brien made his religious profession on Sept. 8, 1837 and was ordained in the summer of 1839 by Bp. Richard P. Miles, OP, of Nashville, Tenn. He completed his studies while serving as assistant novice master at St. Rose and was then transferred to St. Joseph's parish near Somerset, Ohio. There for eight years he performed missionary and pastoral duties. In 1850 O'Brien was elected provincial of the Dominican province of St. Joseph, which then consisted of only 20 missionary priests in the four states of Kentucky, Ohio, Tennessee, and Wisconsin. During his administration as provincial, he opened St. Joseph's College in Somerset,

Ohio, and preached parish missions from the Great Lakes to the Gulf of Mexico and from St. Louis east beyond the Alleghenies. From 1854 to 1857 O'Brien was prior of St. Rose in Kentucky, where he built the parish church and reopened the old College of St. Thomas, which had flourished from 1807 to 1828. In 1857 he resumed his missionary preaching, interrupting it for only two years when he was pastor of St. Peter's in London, Ontario, Canada.

Bibliography: V. F. O'DANIEL, *An American Apostle: The Very Reverend Matthew Anthony O'Brien, O.P.* (Washington 1923)

[J. B. WALKER]

O'BRIEN, TERENCE ALBERT

Bishop of Emly and martyr; b. Tower Hill Castle, Cappamore, County Limerick, 1600; d. Balls Bridge, Limerick, Oct. 31, 1651. As the son of Murtagh O'Brien and Catherine Galwey, he was related to many of the public figures of his day. His paternal uncle, Maurice O'Brien, was Protestant bishop of Killaloe (d. 1613); his grandfather, Sir Geoffrey Galwey, was recusant mayor of Limerick in the early 1600s. Terence, educated at St. Peter Martyr Priory in Toledo, Spain, was ordained there *c.* 1628. After returning to Limerick, he labored in Ireland until 1643, when he was elected provincial of the Irish Dominicans. While attending a general chapter in Rome (1644), he sought assistance for the Irish Confederation, then in revolt against the English. O'Brien, a strong supporter of the Papal Nuncio Giovanni RINUCCINI in the internal and factional struggles within Irish Catholicism, was created bishop of Emly on Rinuccini's recommendation in 1647, and consecrated at Waterford, April 2, 1648. The increasing strength of the Parliamentarians' offensive against the Irish rebels led to his eventual capture after the surrender of Limerick in October 1651. He was condemned to death ''as an original incendiary of the rebellion,'' and executed by the English; he is generally regarded as a martyr.

Bibliography: R. BAGWELL, *Dictionary of National Biography from the Earliest Times to 1900,* 63 v. (London 1885–1900) 14:773–774. M. J. HYNES, *The Mission of Rinuccini . . .* (Dublin 1932). J. O'HEYN and A. COLEMAN, *Irish Dominicans of the 17th Century* (Dundalh 1902).

[P. S. MC GARRY]

O'BRIEN, THOMAS C.

Editor, translator, liturgical scholar, teacher; b. Providence, Rhode Island, October 14, 1923; d. Chambersburg, Pennsylvania, June 18, 1991. Thomas O'Brien taught for a number of years at the Dominican House of

Studies in Washington, D.C., and became a recognized authority on the writings of St. Thomas Aquinas. In 1966, he left the Dominicans and the following year married Florence Gaudet.

Among his writings on St. Thomas was his study *Metaphysics and the Existence of God* (Thomist Press 1960). O'Brien joined the team of scholars working under the general editorship of the English Dominican Thomas Gilby in the 1960s to prepare the renowned English-Latin critical edition of the *Summa Theologiae*. He was responsible for six of the 60 volumes.

From 1966 to 1970 he worked on the editorial staff of Corpus Instrumentorum Publications in Washington, D.C., and from 1970 to 1975 he taught at the Hartford Seminary Foundation in Connecticut. While at Corpus, his projects included the *Corpus Dictionary of Western Churches* (1970), of which he was general editor. He also completed the editing of the *Encyclopedic Dictionary of Religion* (3 vols., 1979). Returning to Washington in 1977, O'Brien served as executive editor of volume 17 of the *New Catholic Encyclopedia,* a thematic and comprehensive account of how the Church had changed as a result of Vatican Council II.

From 1979 until his death in 1991, he served as editor, researcher, and translator on the staff of the International Commission on English in the Liturgy (ICEL). He was editor and translator of the *Documents on the Liturgy: Conciliar, Papal, and Curial Texts, 1963–79.* O'Brien was a major contributor to the liturgical texts produced by ICEL throughout the 1980s, particularly the *Order of Christian Funerals* (1985), the *Rite of Christian Initiation of Adults* (1986), and the *Book of Blessings* (1987).

O'Brien's principal and enduring work was as research specialist on the Latin texts of the *Missale romanum* of Paul VI. His research was an essential part of ICEL's project to revise its 1973 edition of the *Missale.* From this research he compiled ''A Lexicon of Terms in the *Missale romanum,*'' with more than 500 entries.

[J. M. SCHELLMAN]

O'BRIEN, WILLIAM VINCENT

Dominican priest; b. Dublin, Ireland, *c.* 1740; d. New York City, May 14, 1816. He became a Dominican at S. Clemente, Rome, apparently making his profession there in 1761. He completed at least part of his ecclesiastical training at the Dominican house of studies in Bologna, Italy, where he was ordained. For 17 years he preached in the Dublin area and he became preacher general of the Dominican Order. In 1787 he went to Philadelphia, Pennsylvania. While working there and in New Jersey, he supported the prefect apostolic, John CARROLL, against those who opposed the creation of a bishopric at Baltimore, Maryland. In October 1787 Carroll appointed him pastor of St. Peter's Church, Barclay Street, New York City. He organized and brought peace to that divided parish, and for 20 years he helped to keep order among Catholics in New York State. Under the auspices of Abp. Alfonso Núñez de Haro, O'Brien went to Mexico City, Mexico, about 1790, to raise funds for his church. He returned in 1792 with vestments, paintings, and money enough to install pews and erect a tower and portico. In 1800 he opened at St. Peter's the earliest free school and Catholic educational institution in New York State. During the yellow-fever epidemics of 1795 and 1798, O'Brien ministered to his people. Chronic illness forced his retirement in 1806, but he continued a limited ministry until the end of 1808.

Bibliography: V. F. O'DANIEL, *The Dominican Province of St. Joseph* (New York 1942).

[W. A. HINNEBUSCH]

O'CALLAGHAN, JEREMIAH

Writer; b. County Kerry, Ireland *c.* 1780; d. Holyoke, Mass., Feb. 23, 1861. He was ordained for the Diocese of Cloyne, Ireland, in 1805. His views on usury and his criticisms of banking alienated him from his bishop. For 11 years he was refused acceptance by various bishops, but in 1830 Bp. Benedict Fenwick of Boston, Mass., accepted him for that diocese. He was sent into Vermont, where he spent most of his remaining days as a missionary to scattered settlements of Catholics. In Burlington, Vt., he was offered five acres of land, on which he built St. Mary's Church in 1832. When it was burned to the ground by nativists in 1838, O'Callaghan rebuilt it, dedicating it to St. Peter. In his churches he permitted no pew rent or seat money, but only three voluntary offerings each year. From Vermont he traveled into the western areas of Massachusetts and the eastern regions of New York to celebrate Mass for Catholics and to administer the Sacraments. After 1837 he was aided by Rev. John B. Daly, who divided the state with him and matched his energy and zeal. The priests reported a Catholic population of 5,000 in Vermont in 1840. O'Callaghan served as procurator of the clergy at the first diocesan synod held in Boston from Aug. 21 to 26, 1842. When Burlington was made a diocese in 1853, he returned to Massachusetts and served at Northampton and at Holyoke, where he built a new church. O'Callaghan wrote pamphlets of a polemic nature during these years, explaining Catholicism to Protestants and answering the charges leveled against the Church by non-Catholic pamphlet writers and preachers. The best-known of all his works was his often reprinted *Usury or Interest* (1824), which contained an account of his early years.

Bibliography: R. H. LORD et al., *History of the Archdiocese of Boston . . . 1604–1943,* 3 v. (Boston 1945).

[T. F. CASEY]

OCCASION

(*Opportunitas agendi*) may be defined as that which affords an opportunity for a free agent to exercise its CAUSALITY. The word "free" here does not refer simply to intellectual FREEDOM, but applies analogously to sensory freedom as well; hence, the actions of a dog, as proceeding from an interior principle and as guided by knowledge, may be termed free in this wider use of the word. An occasion can provide a mere opportunity for a cognitive being to act, or it may serve as a kind of inducement for action. If the latter is the case, the occasion tends to merge with the act's final cause, making it difficult to distinguish one from the other in the concrete situation. Examples of occasions will clarify the definition. If a teacher absents herself from a room of fourth graders, she provides an occasion for her charges to become rowdy. Or again, a beautiful summer day may serve as an occasion for a family picnic.

An occasion does not strictly cause the agent to act, although it does exercise influence upon the agent. It is to be noted also that it is not absolutely necessary that a suitable occasion be present for the agent to act. The agent well may act, even when no formal occasion is presented to it; thus the schoolchildren could become rowdy whether the teacher is present or absent, and a family could go on a picnic regardless of weather conditions. Occasion pertains primarily to the AGENT, and should be distinguished from CONDITION, which pertains primarily to the patient (*see* ACTION AND PASSION).

An exaggerated emphasis has sometimes been given to occasion, particularly in the era of modern philosophy, where it has been used to deny creatural causality. Particularly associated with this movement are the post-Cartesians A. GEULINCX and N. MALEBRANCHE.

See Also: OCCASIONALISM.

Bibliography: J. M. BALDWIN, ed., *Dictionary of Philosophy and Psychology,* 3 v. in 4 (New York 1901–05; repr. Gloucester 1949–57). L. DE RAEYMAEKER, *The Philosophy of Being,* tr. E. H. ZIEGELMEYER (St. Louis 1954). B. GERRITY, *Nature, Knowledge and God* (Milwaukee 1947). T. N. HARPER, *The Metaphysics of the School,* 3 v. (London 1879–84; reprint New York 1940) esp. v.2.

[G. F. KREYCHE]

OCCASIONALISM

A philosophical doctrine with implications in both metaphysics and epistemology. In metaphysics, occasionalism teaches that there is no causal interaction between beings—their contiguity merely serves as the OCCASION for the causal influx of God; He is the only true cause. In epistemology, occasionalism teaches that the senses perceive regular sequences of events but that they do not perceive any causal interaction between these events. Thus the intellect, whose truth is measured by the evidence of the senses, can draw the conclusion that event *B* follows event *A,* but not that event *B* is caused by event *A.* One cannot, therefore, say with certitude whether there is present in nature a causal influx among beings. One cannot *know* whether things are causes. A metaphysical occasionalist denies that there *are* true causes; an epistemological occasionalist denies that man can *know* them. It is as a metaphysics that occasionalism is usually treated (*see* CAUSALITY).

History. The main points in the historical development of occasionalism can be discussed in terms of its role in Arabian philosophy and in the teachings of William of Ockham, Nicolas Malebranche, and David Hume.

Arabian Philosophy. When the Muslims were introduced to the of philosophy of Aristotle during the 9th century, there soon arose a conflict between this philosophy and some of their basic religious beliefs (*see* ARABIAN PHILOSOPHY). Aristotle taught that natures are self-contained centers of activity with substantial stability and permanence. This view seemed irreconcilable with the Islamic religious belief in the absolute power and creative activity of God. For the universe of Aristotle was sealed off from the direct, immediate, and all-pervasive power of God. Rejecting Aristotle, some Muslims fashioned a world more in keeping with their religious beliefs. According to these thinkers, known as Mutakallims, the universe is composed of discontinuous atoms; these are indivisible particles devoid of magnitude but completely homogeneous, and they are continuously created by God, who can create or annihilate them at will. No atom endures for two moments of time; each is created at every instant. God's causal efficacy as regards these atoms, and therefore all created things, is both absolute and exclusive. Atoms do nothing. But God wills the regular patterns man observes in the universe. For example, when a white garment is placed in black dye, God creates the corresponding atoms of blackness in the garment. And the same is true of all apparent human activity. Thus when a man is said to move a pen, this is the result of the direct intervention of God who creates four simultaneous accidents: the will-act of the man to move the pen; the power to move it; the movement of the hand; and the ac-

tual movement of the pen. The regular sequence of events are merely the willed occasions for God's causality.

Ockham. The occasionalism in the thought of WILLIAM OF OCKHAM may be summed up as follows. By the very fact that it is, an individual can be only itself and nothing more. Each existent is absolutely and irreducibly singular. Thus there are no relations among things. For a relation would be something that two things had in common. And since causality, as an objective factor of nature, would be a relation of dependence of one thing upon another, man can never demonstrate that one thing is the cause of another. He has only the empirical presence of sequenced events, and these he calls causes and effects. The only thing that he can affirm with certitude is that, on the occasion of this regular and repetitive sequence, the mind acquires the habit of thinking that one event really causes another. The irreducible singularity and self-identity of Ockham's existent makes any inferential transfer by the intellect to the supreme, uncaused being of God philosophically impossible. (*See* NOMINALISM; OCKHAMISM.)

Malebranche. Like the Muslim Mutakallims before him, it was in defense of religion and the divine power that Nicolas MALEBRANCHE, a Catholic priest and member of the French Oratory, taught that there is only one true cause, and it is God. This fervent and pious philosopher was convinced that the chief cause of idolatry was man's tendency to attribute to natural powers, like the sun or the rivers, the causal source of the life and fertility in the world. Malebranche held that a true cause must know not only what it does but how it does it. When a man moves his hand, he cannot tell how he does it. So he cannot be the true cause of this motion. He is only, says Malebranche, the occasional cause; the true cause, and only true cause, is God.

The occasionalism of Malebranche seems often more nominal than real. In traditional doctrine, God is said to be the first uncaused cause; it is maintained also that all other causes can cause only in actual and continued dependence upon the divine power (*see* CAUSALITY, DIVINE). At times it seems that Malebranche's occasional causes fit the definition of a true finite cause, in the sense that they are not mere passive occasions. For example, Malebranche will admit that, when one moves one's hand, one does something. This is especially true in his treatment of an act of free choice. The act is personal, and the one placing it is responsible for it; this could not be the case if one were merely a passive occasion for God to make (cause) the choice. But Malebranche's definition of a true cause is unacceptable, as demanding too much. (*See* CARTESIANISM.)

Hume. The doctrine of David HUME is similar to Ockham's. Ockham denied relations, and hence the relation of being a cause, because of his teaching on the irreducible singularity and self-identity of the existent. Hume denied CAUSALITY because it is an unknowable fact. Nothing is in the INTELLECT unless it is also somehow in the SENSES. Hume interpreted this to mean that what a man cannot sense has no meaning for his intellect. All that a man senses is a regular and repetitive sequence of events; he does not sense any causal power affecting these events. Causality is simply the anticipation of this sequence by the mind, an anticipation that has been engendered by habit. Hume was an occasionalist in the sense that he considered sequences of events to be the occasion for the engendering of the habit of anticipating their regularity, which man calls causality. (*See* EMPIRICISM.)

Philosophical Implications. The principal philosophical implications of occasionalism are those relating to the existence of God and the freedom of the human will.

Existence of God. The only valid demonstration in philosophy for the existence of God would be an intellectually seen inference from the beings of man's experience to their causal source. To deny the possibility of man's ever knowing whether causality is an objective truth actually bearing upon the being of things is to deny the possibility of an inference, intellectually grasped, of a causal source. To deny the principle of causality is to cut off any way to demonstrate the knowability of the existence of a First Cause. Occasionalism in epistemology means agnosticism in natural theology.

Freedom of the Will. If one holds in his metaphysics that only God is a true cause and creatures only the occasions on which God exercises His causality, the consequences are logically devastating for created beings. For if creatures do nothing (and what else could a mere occasion mean?), they have no end; they are not *for* anything, and so have no reason for being. In a word, occasionalism makes of a being a contradiction in terms. It also logically destroys FREE WILL; for if a person is not the true cause of his free actions, he can hardly be said to be the cause of why they are free. In a word, causality and being are so closely connected (causality is the *exercise* of being), that to empty creatures of their causality is to empty them of their being.

See Also: EFFICIENT CAUSALITY; INSTRUMENTAL CAUSALITY; METAPHYSICS, VALIDITY OF.

Bibliography: F. C. COPLESTON, *History of Philosophy* (Westminster, Md. 1946–); v.4, Descartes to Leibniz (1958). R. EISLER, *Wörterbuch der philosophischen Begriffe*, 3 v. (4th ed. Berlin 1927–30) 2:336–38. F. UEBERWEG, *Grundriss der Geschichte der Philosophie*, ed. K. PRAECHTER et al., 5 v. (11th, 12th ed. Berlin 1923–28) 3:261–69, 663–664. J. LATOUR, *Lexikon für Theologie und Kirche*, ed. J. HOFER and K. RAHNER, 10 v. (2d, new ed. Freiburg 1957–65) 7:1123–25. A. DEL NOCE, *Enciclopedia filosofica*, 4 v. (Venice-Rome 1957) 3:974–80. M. FAKHRY, *Islamic Occasionalism and Its Critiques by Averroës and Aquinas* (London 1958). M. GUEROULT, *Malebranche*, v.2.2. *L'Ordre et l'occasionalisme* (Paris 1959).

[M. R. HOLLOWAY]

OCCULTISM

A general term employed to designate all those pseudosciences or practices, such as magic, alchemy, astrology, the various forms of divination, clairvoyance, theosophy, or spiritism, which claim to have knowledge of, or even control over, the hidden mysteries or powers of nature. Modern science, and especially psychology, has gradually refuted such claims, although there are occult phenomena and practices in Asia and Africa that still require further investigation and explanation. The pseudomysticism of the devotees or practitioners of occultism should not be confused with genuine mysticism in the Christian sense, nor should occultism be confused with parapsychology or related branches of the science of psychology. The terms occultism and the occult arts are too vague to be satisfactory. Hence they have given way to specific designations, such as magic, alchemy, and astrology.

Bibliography: H. VORGRIMLER, *Lexikon für Theologie und Kirche*, ed. J. HOFER and K. RAHNER (Freiburg 1957–65) 7:1125. G. R. S. MEAD, *Encyclopedia of Religion and Ethics*, ed. J. HASTINGS (Edinburgh 1908–27) 9:444–448. A. KÖBERLE, *Die Religion in Geschichte und Gegenwart* (Tübingen 1957–65) 4:1614–19.

[P. SCHMIDT]

OCEANIA, THE CATHOLIC CHURCH IN

Oceania is a region in the central and south Pacific Ocean that contains numerous islands. It is located east of the Philippines, Indonesia, and Australia. Oceania includes Polynesia, the huge triangle formed by Hawaii, New Zealand, and Easter; Melanesia, the island groups south of the equator, north and east of Australia from Papua New Guinea to the Fijis; and Micronesia, stretching northward from the equator to the Marianas and eastward from the Palau to the Gilbert Islands. The following essay presents discussion of the development of the Catholic church in the region as a whole, followed by discussion of events in some of the island groups.

THE CHURCH IN THE REGION

Early Contacts. The Polynesians were the first group in Oceania to have extensive contacts with Europe-

Metropolitan Sees	Suffragans
Agaña (Guam)	Caroline Islands (Micronesia) and Chalan Kanoa (North Marian Islands)
Honiara (Solomon Islands)	Auki and Gizo
Nouméa (New Caledonia)	Port Vila (Vanuatu) and Wallis-Futuna
Papeete (Tahiti)	Taiohae (Marquesas Islands)
Samoa-Apia (West Samoa)	Samoa-Pago Pago (American Samoa) and Tokelau
Suva (Fiji Islands)	Rarotonga (Cook Islands) and Tarawa and Nauru (Kiribati)
In Papua New Guinea:	
Madang	Aitape, Lae, Vanimo, and Wewak
Mount Hagen	Goroka, Kundiawa, Mendi, and Wabag
Port Moresby	Alotau-Sideia, Bereina, Daru-Kiunga, and Kerema
Rabaul (New Britain)	Bougainville and Kavieng (New Ireland)

The diocese of Tonga is immediately subject to the Holy See. An apostolic prefecture is located on the Marshall Islands, and a mission sui juris is located at Funafuti, on the island of Tuvalu.

ans; they established relations with the newcomers and were fairly successful in adapting to European ways. In Melanesia, and particularly on the island of New Guinea, climate, terrain, and fierce resistance among indigenous peoples inhibited the introduction of European ideas for several centuries, and parts of Melanesia continue to practice the ancient religions of their ancestors. In Micronesia development was hindered by the multiplicity of small islands scattered over more than two million square miles. Language presented a particularly formidable obstacle to religious instruction: 12 Polynesian and 15 Micronesian tongues, and between 500 and 600 Melanesian languages or dialects were known to be spoken in the region. Before the coming of the missioners, Oceania had no written languages.

Cultural and economic patterns in Oceania varied in accordance with the broad divisions of race, the size, nature, flora and fauna of the islands, possibilities of intercommunication, and other factors. Contact with Europeans, beginning with sailors, beachcombers and missionaries, and continuing to the accelerated development occasioned by World War II, also affected culture. The economy, originally a purely subsistence one, was modified by the raising of cash crops as European contacts gave rise to new needs and the possibility of satisfying them.

Catholic Missionary Activity. The first priest known to have visited Oceania was the fleet-chaplain of Magellan in 1521. Native people occasionally met with chaplains of the Spanish ships. A Hawaiian tradition seems to indicate the presence of a priest there for some time, probably in the late 16th century. The names of many islands—Pentecost, Espiritu Santo, Asuncion—are evidence of the faith of the explorers. In 1658 Jean Paulmier de Courtonne proposed missions in "the southern land," although nothing came of this. In 1798 the Congregation for the PROPAGATION OF THE FAITH (Propaganda) entrusted the PACCANARISTS with a mission field extending from the Cape of Good Hope to Japan, Australia, and adjacent lands, including part of Oceania. Again there was no result. In 1829 Henri de Solages, appointed prefect apostolic of Réunion island, near Madagascar, proposed to extend his mission to Oceania. Propaganda confided to de Solages a prefecture extending from Easter Island to New Zealand, and from the equator to the Tropic of Capricorn, but this plan ended with his death in Madagascar in 1832. A similarly unsuccessful attempt to evangelize Tahiti was made by Spanish Franciscans who arrived from Peru in 1772–75. The first regular mission in Oceania was established in the Marianas in 1668 by Diego de Sanvitores, SJ; this mission was later staffed by the Augustinian Recollects and after by the Capuchins.

From about 1800 the Pacific area was visited by a flood of adventurers, whalers, and traders seeking profit and pleasure. It is doubtful that the Polynesians would have survived had it not been for another group who came to save them, in every sense of the word. These were the missionaries, first non-Catholics and then Catholics. Their sometimes bitter differences and petty persecutions are regrettable, but the zeal and spirit of Christian sacrifice displayed by men and women of both groups were noble. The presence of Protestants stimulated later comers and led to an astonishing Catholic expansion.

In 1825 Pierre COUDRIN, founder of the Fathers of the SACRED HEARTS, offered his group's services to the Holy See concurrent with a request of Propaganda for the establishment of a mission in Hawaii. The Prefecture Apostolic of the Sandwich Islands was established in 1825 and the first priests and brothers arrived two years later. By 1831 these priests were expelled from Hawaii and sought another mission; the prefecture made from the

Pope John Paul II during a Mass officiated inside St. Peter's Basilica at the Vatican, celebrating the Special Assembly for Oceania Synod of Bishops, Rome. (Photo by Massimo Sambucetti; AP/Wide World Photos)

Marquesas, Tuamotus, and Society Islands in 1833 was entrusted to them. This prefecture, together with the prefecture of the Sandwich Islands, formed the Vicariate Apostolic of Eastern Oceania (1833), extending from the Sandwich, or Hawaiian, Islands south to the Society Islands, and westward from Easter Island to the northern Cook Islands.

Western Oceania, a new mission, was accepted by the MARIST FATHERS. As a result, in 1836 the Vicariate of Western Oceania was erected over Melanesia and the Caroline, Marshall, and Gilbert Islands of Micronesia. The first missionaries, including St. Peter CHANEL, set out the same year. The first missions were established in Wallis and Futuna, New Zealand, and then in Tonga, New Caledonia, Samoa, and elsewhere. The following years brought tragedy as the Church attempted to establish a presence in Oceania. By 1850 the two vicariates of Eastern and Western Oceania had been divided into ten vicariates. In 1841 St. Peter Chanel was martyred at Futuna; Bishop Epalle was killed on Santa Isabel in 1845; Brother Blaise Marmoiton was killed in New Caledonia, and about the same time two priests and a brother were killed and eaten in the Solomons. The Marists lost so many men that they had to withdraw from the Solomons.

The Milan Foreign Mission Society, later called the PONTIFICAL INSTITUTE FOR FOREIGN MISSIONS, replaced the Marists but in turn withdrew after the murder of Father Mazzuconi in 1855.

In 1847 Propaganda encouraged Bishop BATAILLON to set up a seminary. In 1856 three students from Oceania entered the Propaganda College in Rome. In 1859 a minor seminary started near Sydney, Australia; it closed after some years, then reopened in 1874 on Wallis as a major seminary and produced a number of priests for Wallis, Futuna, Tonga, and Samoa.

Nearly 30 years passed before the Vicariates of Melanesia and Micronesia were confided to the SACRED HEART MISSIONARIES. In 1882 they began work in New Britain, establishing a flourishing mission under the direction of Bishop COUPPÉ. Three years later they landed in New Guinea, progressing to the Gilbert and Ellice Islands in 1888 and to the Marshalls in 1891. The Society of the DIVINE WORD was called upon to take charge of northeastern New Guinea in 1896. Countless religious—priests, brothers, and sisters who were members or associates of these two institutes—died of malaria and other diseases; others were killed by the natives. In western

New Guinea, missions were established from Indonesia. The Caroline Islands mission, begun by Jesuits in 1731, collapsed with the order's expulsion from the Spanish colonies in 1767, but began again under Spanish Capuchins when Spain's jurisdiction over the islands was established in 1886. Their effectiveness was such that after 1945 the rate of development in Papua New Guinea would require the added services of Franciscans, Capuchins, Dominicans, Passionists, Montfort Fathers and Marianhill Missionaries to staff newly formed prefectures or vicariates.

Mission Methods and Problems. When missions commenced in Oceania, anthropology and its related sciences were practically nonexistent, providing European missionaries with little or no preparation for the task of relating to the indigenous people of the region. To communicate, missionaries had to learn the language and prepare a grammar and dictionary at the same time, a task made more difficult by their failure to comprehend native cultures. Missionaries also had little or no medical training, with the result that malaria and other tropical diseases killed many, both natives and Europeans. Tragic blunders were made, the result of ignorance of native beliefs and customs, and the missions perhaps rightfully received the blame for the disintegration of native life and the death of thousands. However, this disintegration had already begun with the arrival of the whalers, beachcombers, and slavers; it likely would have been much worse but for the presence and the efforts of the missionaries. Paying for their inevitable mistakes often with their lives, missionaries were the principal force guiding the natives to the modern era: they introduced formal education, a written language, printing presses, and training in arts, crafts, and other skills. Most schools in Melanesia remained under mission control into the 20th century, though they were eventually aided and supervised by governments. Some missionaries found time to do anthropological and ethnological work of inestimable value.

Catholicism was introduced to Samoa, Tonga, Fiji, the Gilberts, and other islands with the help of natives who had been converted elsewhere. When the Solomon Islands missions were begun again in 1897, Samoan and Fijian catechists accompanied the priests. Catechists, after training, were entrusted with the care of congregations that would otherwise only receive a visit from the priests after long intervals; they taught school, conducted daily prayers and Sunday services, baptized in case of necessity, assisted the sick, and buried the dead.

The Modern Era. World War I impeded the missions in Oceania principally by interrupting the supply of personnel and income. World War II had a more direct impact, as mission stations were destroyed and missionaries interned. From 1940 to 1945, 128 priests, brothers, and sisters were killed or died of disease and starvation while in Axis captivity. In New Guinea, New Britain, the Solomons, and Micronesia, stations and staffs were almost annihilated. The interruption of regular instruction plus the demoralizing influence of wartime conditions led to a revival of pagan beliefs in some areas.

From the mid-20th century onward, conditions improved greatly. Oceanian mission schools underwent constant improvement, with many vicariates providing some form of technical education, often under the guidance of brothers. Sisters conducted schools, dispensaries, hospitals, and leprosaria, and did much to raise the status of women from their former condition of servitude in the islands. With the opening of a major seminary in New Caledonia in 1939, priests were trained for all the French language vicariates of Oceania.

Vincentians and Columban Fathers continued to be active in the region, along with Marist Brothers, Christian Brothers of Ploermel, Brothers of the Sacred Heart, and many congregations of sisters. Oceania also had a number of diocesan institutes of brothers and sisters.

Political changes altered the face of Oceania through the second half of the 20th century, as the breakup of colonial empires continued and trust territories established by the United Nations following World War II were dissolved. In 1963, the western half of the island of New Guinea, long held by the Dutch, was ceded to Indonesia as part of the Irian Jaya province; 12 years later the eastern half of the island became the independent state of Papua New Guinea. In 1970 Tonga and Fiji gained independence after a century as a British colony. In New Caledonia a nationalist movement that took shape in the 1980s lost support and the region remained under French rule. In 1986 the Federated States of Micronesia and the Republic of the Marshall Islands were both formed from the remnants of the U.N. Trust Territory of the Pacific Islands, and organized under the diocese of Caroline Islands.

By 2000 the population of Oceania was 29 percent Catholic. In 1998 an historic meeting occurred during the first Synod of Bishops for Oceania; problems addressed by the 117 bishops in attendance included increasing secularization, chronic unemployment, poverty, and sexual abuse by clergy. Issues relating to the specific ministry of the region included the shortage of priests, inculturation, religious pluralism, the rights of minorities, and geographical barriers. The Church remained steadfast in its ability to respond to the many natural disasters that affected the region; the devastation wrought by a 1998 tidal wave that swept through Papua New Guinea, destroying entire villages along the northern coast, was addressed by Catholic organizations throughout the region.

[S. J. BOURKE/EDS.]

THE CHURCH IN SPECIFIC ISLAND GROUPS

The Cook Islands. Consisting of 15 small islands stretching over 850,000 square miles, the Cook Islands are divided into two groups: the mountainous Lower Cook Islands of volcanic origin and the coral Northern Cook Islands. Captain James Cook discovered the region between 1773 and 1777. Christian evangelization began in 1821 by Protestants from the London Missionary Society; almost all the Maori population were converted to Christianity, a native clergy established, and a workable civil administration organized. The first Catholic missionaries were the Fathers of the Sacred Hearts, who arrived in 1894; they were followed by the Sisters of St. Joseph of Cluny five years later. Initially the Catholics encountered concerted opposition from local Protestant pastors and were for a time limited to their mission schools as the only practical channel of missionary activity. The Cook Islands became a British protectorate in 1888, and remained predominantly Protestant. Annexation to New Zealand in 1901 brought an ever-improving public school system that heavily taxed the resources of the missionaries to emulate. In 1922 the islands were detached ecclesiastically from the Vicariate Apostolic of Tahiti and became a prefecture apostolic; they became a vicariate apostolic in 1948 and later a diocese was established at Rarotonga. By 2000 the population of 20,407 contained 3,000 Catholics. Formal relations with the Holy See were established in April 1999.

[T. GRANNELL/EDS.]

The Fiji Islands. The Fiji Islands comprises the Fiji Archipelago and Rotuma, as well as some 100 inhabited islands. The indigenous population, Melanesian with Polynesian strains, were originally a fierce people with many brutal customs. French Marist Fathers, sent by Bishop Bataillon in 1844, began Catholic evangelization after British Wesleyan missionaries were solidly established. Finding the resultant religious and national tensions overpowering, they almost abandoned the area. As conditions slowly improved, a prefecture apostolic was created (1863) with 1,650 Catholics in three mission stations. Father Jean Baptiste Bréhéret, SM, struggled for 24 years against the increasing strength of Methodism, which, up to 1870, had won the chiefs. The vicariate (diocese in 1966) at Suva was erected in 1887 with seven stations and 4,650 Catholics. Bp. Julian Vidal, SM (1887–1922), built permanent churches, including Suva cathedral, instituted a native sisterhood (1891), and opened the famed leprosarium at Makogai (1911). He and Bishop Nicolas, SM (1922–41), introduced teaching congregations of brothers and sisters for their new schools. Beginning in 1944 Bp. Victor Foley, SM, revitalized education, beginning with teacher training, and encouraged the foundation of credit unions among the Fijians. In 2000 the population of 832,494 was predominately Protestant; the Catholic population of approximately 82,500 was divided among 34 parishes and tended by 113 priests. There were 44 primary and 18 secondary Catholic schools in operation on the islands.

[J. E. BELL/EDS.]

Kiribati. Kiribati encompasses a group of islands situated near the meeting point of the equator and the international dateline. Sixteen coral atolls, occupying 166 square miles, comprise the region, formerly the Gilbert Island colony. The region was made part of the Vicariate Apostolic of Micronesia in 1844, although missionaries were not yet at work in the region. Protestant missioners arrived in Kiribati c. 1850, followed by the first French Catholics, members of the Sacred Heart Missionaries, in 1888. Along with the Ellice Islands (now Tuvalu), the region was incorporated into the Vicariate Apostolic of the Gilbert Islands in 1897, the same year it became part of the British Commonwealth as the Gilbert and Ellice Island Colony of the Western Pacific High Commission. The vicariate spread over more than two million square miles of the Pacific Ocean. This vast distance, plus the fact that the Gilbertese are Micronesian, while the Ellice Islanders are Polynesian and their languages very dissimilar, resulted in the eventual split in the group. During World War II the mission suffered heavy losses. Through the remainder of the 20th century, education remained a major concern of the Catholic mission, which enrolled 90 percent of the children in its schools by the 1970s. After 1966 the region gained a diocese at Tarawa and Nauru that supported Kiribati's 23 parishes. Half the population of approximately 80,000 was Catholic in 2000.

French Polynesia. French Polynesia is comprised of the 11 Marquesas Islands and Tahiti, and totals 118 islands and atols. Discovered by the Spanish in 1595 and visited by Captain James Cook in 1774, they were claimed by France in 1842 though the Island of Nuku Hiva was briefly garrisoned by Americans in 1813. The unusual fierceness of the islanders, more than their geographic remoteness, hindered early evangelization. The Protestant London Missionary Society arrived in the region in 1785 but withdrew in 1825 because of these difficulties. Picpus Fathers worked in Tahiti beginning in 1831. The Fathers of the SACRED HEARTS arrived in the Marquesas Islands in 1838; in ten years they converted only 216. While the baptism of the king and queen of the Marquesas in 1853 marked progress, missionaries continued to confront such issues as the adherence to pagan customs, alcoholism, tribal wars, and diseases such as that which decimated the population between 1838 and 1880. Persecution forced the missionaries to abandon the islands more than once, although by 1900 Catholicism began to take root. The Vicariate Apostolic of the Marquesas Islands (1848) became the Diocese of Taiohae in 1966. An overseas territory of France since 1946, the region is administered from Tahiti. By 2000 there were 85 parishes in the region, and the population of approximately 250,000 was 30 percent Catholic and 50 percent Protestant.

[EDS.]

New Britain. New Britain is the largest island in the Bismarck Archipelago, 13,000 square miles in area. Administratively it is part of Papua New Guinea. Following its discovery by the British in 1700, Wesleyan missioners were the first to arrive. MARIST FATHERS arrived in 1844 and were joined by the Milan Foreign Missions Institute. In 1882 the area was entrusted to the Sacred Heart Missionaries. The region was administered as New Pomerania after becoming a German colony in 1884. Louis Couppé, the first vicar apostolic, arrived in 1888 and developed the mission after abolishing the "religious districts." After being part of the Vicariate Apostolic of Central Oceania from 1836, and that of Melanesia from 1844, in 1889 New Britain joined the Solomon Islands as the Vicariate Apostolic of New Britain. Undeterred by catastrophes such as the murder of seven religious in the Baining Mountains in 1904, in 1912 Couppé founded the Daughters of the Immaculate Conception, a native sisterhood that had more than 70 members by the mid-1900s. In 1921 the region became part of the Trust Territory of New Guinea. Despite World War II, which resulted in a Japanese invasion and the deaths of 58 missioners, 23 of whom were murdered, growth caused the division of the Vicariate of Rabaul through the creation of Kavieng. The vicariate of Rabaul eventually advanced to the status of archdiocese.

[J. GLAZIK/EDS.]

New Caledonia. New Caledonia, 7,367 square miles in area, is a French overseas territory comprising the islands of New Caledonia and Île des Pins, the Loyalty Islands, and several other islet groups. Protestant evangelization in the region began in 1834, when Polynesian catechists came to the Loyalty Islands, and the London Missionary Society organized a mission two decades later. In 1843 Bishop Guillaume Douarre, together with four other Marist Fathers, founded a mission at Balade to evangelize the Melanesian natives. In 1847 the Vicariate Apostolic of New Caledonia was established, but its success was short-lived when Brother Blaise Marmoiton

was slain and the other missioners expelled. France's annexation of the region in 1853 preserved the safety of the mission but gradually changed its character. The main island became a penal colony, on which 11,000 *libérés* remained as settlers. French governors promoted colonization and exploited the islands' extensive mineral resources, supplanting the indigenous tribes. When successive vicars apostolic expressed distress at the ill effects of these changes on native life, they met anticlerical opposition in government circles and bowed finally to the inevitable. Missions were reorganized to care for growing numbers of Europeans, while also tending Melanesian converts and some 11,000 immigrants from Vietnam, Indonesia, the Wallis Islands, and elsewhere. By the late 1800s political and religious tensions led Protestants to entrust their mission to the *Société des Missions Évangéliques* of Paris, although the London Missionary Society did not completely withdraw until 1921. In 1966 New Caledonia came under the jurisdiction of the Archdiocese of Nouméa. By 2000 the region had a population of 201,816, over 60 percent Catholic. The region contained 28 parishes tended by nine secular and 35 religious priests. Other religious aided in the operation of the region's 34 primary and 22 secondary Catholic schools.

[J. E. BELL/EDS.]

Papua New Guinea. Sighted by the Portuguese in 1511, the island of New Guinea was discovered and claimed by Spain in 1527, and British explorers ventured into the eastern region in the 18th century. The Dutch annexed the western half in 1828, while the forbidding climate, dense forests, and difficult terrain in the east caused it to be left undeveloped until 1884, when England established a protectorate over Papua and Germany established the colony of Kaiser-Wilhelmsland in the northeast. New Guinea was included in the Vicariate Apostolic of Melanesia, created in 1844 and entrusted to the Marist Fathers, although slaughter and disease brought that mission to an end before it reached the island. The Milan Foreign Mission Society received the area in 1852 but suffered a similar fate. In 1881 the vicariate was entrusted to the Sacred Heart Missionaries, who founded a mission on Yule Island in 1885. Kaiser-Wilhelmsland was entrusted to the Divine Word Missionaries as a prefecture apostolic in 1896. In both regions, Catholics had been preceded by Protestant missions and both the German and British-Australian governments impeded normal development of the mission by creating exclusive territorial spheres of influence for the various Christian missionary groups. The missionaries laid out extensive coconut plantations and later added cocoa and coffee plantations that made the missions partially self-supporting. In 1904 Britain ceded Papua to Australia; during World War I the Australians captured Kaiser-

Wilhelmsland and administered it first as a mandate terri-tory of the League of Nations and then as a trust territory of the United Nations. During World War II more than 100 priests, brothers, and sisters were killed, and in the next few decades new vicariates apostolic were estab-lished in the region. In 1964 a regional major seminary was erected at Madang. Papua New Guinea achieved in-dependence in 1975, although the region was the site of violence throughout the 1990s as the island of Bougain-ville fought unsuccessfully for independence. By 2000 the region had four archdiocese: Manang, Mount Hagen, Port Moresby, and Rabaul, under which were adminis-tered the region's 374 parishes. The population of 4,926,984 was estimated to be 30 percent Catholic. Many of Papua New Guinea's priests continued to be foreign by the end of the 1990s.

[R. M. WILTGEN/EDS.]

New Ireland. New Ireland, at about 2,800 square miles in area the largest island after New Britain, is locat-ed in the Bismarck Archipelago to the northeast of Papua New Guinea. Mariners from the Netherlands were the first to explore this section of Melanesia. The Marquis de Rays established the colony of Port Breton, to which were sent over 500 colonists. Ecclesiastically it pertained successively to the Vicariates Apostolic of Western Oce-ania (1836–44), Melanesia (1844–89), New Britain (1889–1922), and Rabaul (1922–57). From 1884 until the end of World War I the island was a German colony named New Mecklenburg. Wesleyan missionaries arrived first, the first Catholic mission begun in 1902 by the Sa-cred Heart Missionaries. The mission survived World War I without serious damage, its members making sig-nificant scientific contributions to ethnology, botany, and linguistics. After 1921 the region became an Australian mandate, part of the trust Territory of New Guinea. World War II brought Japanese occupation and consider-able destruction to the missions. In 1957 the Vicariate Apostolic of Kavieng was created, and entrusted to the Sacred Heart Missionaries. Kavieng was later created a diocese.

[J. GLAZIK]

Solomon Islands. The Solomon Islands, which in-cludes several islands and totals 16,120 square miles in land area, is located east of New Guinea. With the moun-tainous, forested interior impassable except by foot, trav-el occurred mostly along the coasts by canoe or ship. The Melanesians native to the region speak a wide variety of languages, pidgin English being the lingua franca. Mis-sion work in the Solomons was begun by the Marist Fa-thers when Bishop Épalle landed on Santa Isabel and was immediately slain. Violence and disease cost the Marists two more bishops and five priests before they withdrew

temporarily. In 1898 Bishop Vidal, SM, resurrected the southern mission with more success. Bishop Broyer, SM, inaugurated the apostolate in the northern islands in 1899, but missioners were so enfeebled by malaria that they won only 353 converts in the next decade. The Vicariate Apostolic of the Southern Solomon Islands, erected in 1912, included the islands of Guadalcanal, San Cristobal, and Malaita, while the Vicariate Apostolic of the North-ern Solomon Islands, erected in 1930, included Bougain-ville. By 1942 Catholics numbered 27,000, but World War II brought devastation to these missions and caused missioners to be evacuated, interned, or killed by the Jap-anese. It also invigorated antiwhite, anti-Christian cults, which were active but localized two decades later, as the Catholic population grew. In 1959 the two apostolates were combined with the islands of Santa Isabel, New Georgia, and Choiseul as the Vicariate Apostolic of the Western Solomon Islands and entrusted to the Domini-cans. This vicariate was later raised to the archdiocese of Honiara. The region achieved independence in 1978 and by 2000 had a population of 466,194, 19 percent of whom were Catholic. The 29 parishes among the islands were tended by 51 priests, half native. The Church operated 28 primary and eight secondary schools on the Solomon Is-lands, most of which were subsidized by the state in lieu of a state-run education system.

[J. E. BELL/EDS.]

Tonga. Located in Polynesia, the Kingdom of Tonga contains about 200 islands, with a total land area of 259 square miles. The first attempts at evangelization were made by Protestant missionaries, who entered the region in 1797. Tonga was the first island group to be visited by Bishop POMPALLIER, who arrived in Vavau harbor in Oc-tober 1837. Though at first well received, Pompallier was later refused permission to remain because of the influ-ence of Wesleyan missionaries, established in Vavau since 1826. In 1842 Father Chevron and Brother Attale, members of the Marist Fathers, arrived at Nukualofa; they were allowed to land and reside with the pagans at Pea, although during the next few years the intermittent wars waged by Taufaahau in an effort to make himself king of Tonga created a dangerous environment for Cath-olics. Taufaahau, a Protestant, considered all Catholics enemies, and it was only the occasional intervention of French gunboats that obtained some toleration for Catho-lics. In 1842 Tonga became part of the Vicariate of Cen-tral Oceania; it became a separate vicariate in 1937. Tonga constituted the Vicariate Apostolic of Tonga and Niue Islands in 1957, and later broke with Niue to be-come in 1966 a diocese directly subject to the Holy See. Evangelization progressed steadily, and during the mid-20th century there was notable progress in Catholic edu-cation in the region. By 2000 the population of 102,320 was 16 percent Catholic, organized in 12 parishes. Diplomatic relations with the Holy See were established in 1994. At the beginning of the 21st century, Tonga was the last surviving monarchy in all of Oceania.

[S. J. BOURKE/EDS.]

Tuvalu. Tuvalu, the former Ellice Islands, encompasses a group of islands situated near Kiribati consisting of nine coral atolls and covering 14 square miles. Made part of the Vicariate Apostolic of the Gilbert Islands in 1897, and civilly, the Gilbert and Ellice Island Colony of the Western Pacific High Commission of the British Commonwealth, Tuvalu eventually became independent due to the fact that its native population was Polynesian and their languages dissimilar to those of the Micronesian natives of the former Gilbert Islands (now Kiribati). Protestants were the first to arrive in the region followed by French missionaries of the Sacred Heart in 1888. World War II brought heavy losses, after which time the missions were staffed by religious from Australia. A mission *sui juris* was established at Funafuti in 1997, the year after Tuvalu established diplomatic relations with the Holy See. In 2000 the population of 10,840 was estimated to contain approximately 120 Catholics.

[EDS.]

Vanuatu. Formerly the New Hebrides, Vanuatu is a rugged archipelago largely of volcanic origin located northeast of New Caledonia and west of the Fiji Islands, 5,700 square miles in land area. The natives are Melanesians. Protestant missioners entered the region in 1839, and evangelization came at the cost of many lives. Marist Fathers came from New Caledonia early in the 19th century, but concentrated Catholic efforts waited until 1887, when Bp. Hilarion Frayasse, SM, sent four missioners and several native helpers, with the urging and help of the French government. Progress was slow. In 1904 the Vicariate Apostolic of New Hebrides Islands was created, and by 1938 Catholics numbered 2,600; Protestants 10,000; and those following native faiths 30,000. The diocese of Port Vila was established at the capital city in 1966, and the region became politically independent in July of 1980. Protestant missionary groups remained mostly English-speaking and very influential through the 20th century. Catholic missions remained associated with the French language, which was taught in the region's Catholic-run schools. By 2000 the population of 190,000 was estimated to be 16 percent Catholic.

Wallis and Futuna Islands. Located 120 miles apart and with a total area of 100 square miles, the Territory of Wallis and Futuna Islands is located northeast of the Fiji Islands and west of Western Samoa. In 1836 Bp. Jean Pompallier sent the Marists Father Pierre Bataillon

and Brother Joseph Luzy to Wallis and Father Pierre CHANEL with Brother Nizier to Futuna. Bataillon's forceful character, charity, and integrity greatly impressed the Polynesian king of Wallis, and by 1840 conversion efforts were proving successful on that island. Chanel met with less success on Futuna; he was slain in 1841 and became the first canonized martyr of the Pacific Islands mission. Wallis, which strove to create a native clergy, became entirely Catholic with the baptism of all its 2,700 inhabitants in 1842, as did Futuna in 1843. Under French control since 1842, the islands were a protectorate administrated by New Caledonia until 1961, when they became part of the French Overseas Territories. In 1935 the Vicariate Apostolic of the Wallis and Futuna Islands was created as part of the Vicariate Apostolic of Central Oceania, and entrusted to the Marist Fathers; it was raised to a diocese in 1966. By 2000 the population of 15,280 was predominately Catholic, and its priests native Polynesians.

[J. E. BELL/EDS.]

Bibliography: J. B. F. POMPALLIER, *Early History of the Catholic Church in Oceania,* tr. A. HERMAN (Auckland 1888). J. ROMMERSKIRCHEN and J. DINDINGER, *Bibliografia missionaria* (Rome 1936–), annual. C. R. H. TAYLOR, *A Pacific Bibliography* (Wellington, N.Z. 1964). F. M. CAMMACK and SHIRO SAITO, *Pacific Island Bibliography* (New York 1962). J. VERSCHEUREN, ''A Growing World: Problems of the Catholic Missions in Oceania,'' *Carmelus* 7 (1960) 277–330. C. DESTABLE and L. M. SÉDÈS, *La Croix dans l'archipel Fidji* (Paris 1943). P. O'REILLY, *Caledoniens* (Paris 1953). A. BURNS, *Fiji* (London 1963). V. DOUCERÉ, *La Mission catholique aux Nouvelles-Hebrides* (Lyons 1934). H. LAVAL, *Mangareva* (Braine-le-Comte, Bel.). J. HÜSKES ed., *Pioniere der Südsee* (Hiltrup 1932). L. MCDOUGALL, *MSC Missions* (Sydney 1945). *Seventy-Five Glorious Years, 1882–1957* (Vunapope, New Guinea 1957). R. W. ROBSON, *Handbook of Papua and New Guinea* (2d ed. Sydney 1958). A. M. MANGERET, *Mgr. Bataillon et les missions de l'Oceanie,* 2 v. (2d ed. Lyon 1895). E. SABATIER, *Sous l'Équateur du Pacifique. Les Îles Gilbert et la Mission Catholique, 1888–1938* (Paris 1939). SOANE MALIA [J. F. BLANC], *Chez les Méridionaux du Pacifique* (Lyons 1910). A. GRIMBLE, *A Pattern of Islands* (London 1952). *The Official Year Book of the Catholic Church of Australasia* (Sydney), annual. A. DUPEYRAT, *Papouasie: Histoire de la mission, 1885–1935* (Paris 1936). A. FREITAG, *Glaubenssaat in Blut und Tränen* (Kaldenkirchen 1948). R. STREIT and J. DINDINGER, *Bibliotheca missionum* (Freiburg 1916–) 21. *Le missioni cattoliche: Storia, geographia, statistica* (Rome 1950). S. DELACROIX, ed., *Histoire universelle des missions catholiques,* 4 v. (Paris 1956–59) 3. K. S. LATOURETTE, *Christianity in a Revolutionary Age: A History of Christianity in the Nineteenth and Twentieth Centuries,* 5 v. (New York 1958–62) 5. *Bilan du Monde* (Tournai 1964). *Annuario Pontifica* has data on all diocese.

OCHINO, BERNARDINO

Renowned preacher; b. district dell' Oca, Siena (hence his surname), 1487; d. Slavkov, Moravia, *c.* 1564. Ochino entered the Observant Franciscans (*c.* 1504), and after broad studies, he rose to be provincial and finally vicar for the Cisalpine province of his order. Craving a yet stricter rule, he transferred in 1534 to the Capuchins, of whom he was vicar-general from 1538–42 (*see* FRANCISCANS, FIRST ORDER). As a Lenten preacher, the gaunt ascetic of resonant voice and terrifying directness was eagerly sought by competing towns and bishops. In 1536, while in Naples, he had become acquainted with Juan de VALDÉS and his circle. Several of his later sermons were popularizations of the works of Valdés, and his understanding of the atonement was Valdesian. In 1539 he delivered at Venice a remarkable course of *Prediche,* showing a Protestant tendency in the doctrine of justification, all under the guise of opposing it.

Suspected and cited to Rome in 1542, Ochino was deterred from presenting himself on the advice of PETER MARTYR VERMIGLI at Florence. He escaped across the Alps, settling in Geneva, where he was cordially received by Calvin. He married a lady of Tusca who had once heard him as the great Capuchin preacher. From 1542 till 1545 he preached to the Italian congregation and wrote, publishing in 1544 his *Apologhi,* a collection of reminiscences and satirical anecdotes about popes, cardinals, priests, and friars. He served as minister of the Italian Protestant congregation at Augsburg (1545–47). When the city was occupied by the imperial forces, he escaped by way of Basel and Strassburg to find asylum in England (1547–53). Here he was made a prebendary of Canterbury and preached to the Italians in London, receiving a royal pension. Here also he composed his *Dialogue of the injuste usurped primacie of the Bishop of Rome* and the *Labyrinth,* the latter opposing predestination.

At the accession of Mary Tudor he became pastor of the Italian congregation at Zurich, where he published his *Dialogo del Purgatorio,* in which he upheld the view that the true purgatory is Jesus himself, purifying man of his sins. In his *Syncerae et verae doctrinae de Coena Domini defensio* he described the Lord's Supper in a Zwinglian fashion. His *XXX Dialoghi,* brought together in 1563, occasioned his banishment. His Protestant adversaries maintained that he was weak on the doctrine of the Trinity and that he had justified polygamy under color of a pretended refutation.

He found refuge in Poland under the protection of Prince Nicolas Radziwiłł and preached in Cracow until the edict of August 1564 banished all foreign dissidents. After losing, during his wanderings, three of his children, he found asylum in Slavkov with Niccolò Paruto, an exiled Venetian nobleman who espoused antitrinitarian Anabaptism. He died of the plague.

Bibliography: R. H. BAINTON, *Bernardino Ochino* (Florence 1940). B. NICOLINI, *Il pensiero di Bernardino Ochino* (Naples 1939). G. MÜLLER, *Die Religion in Geschichte und Gegenwart* (Tübingen 1957–65) 4:1555–56.

[G. H. WILLIAMS]

OCKHAMISM

A philosophical and theological system of thought based on the teachings of WILLIAM OF OCKHAM that flourished in the universities of Europe during the fourteenth and fifteenth centuries.

Characteristics. This philosophical and theological movement has not been adequately characterized by historians, nor has the label "Ockhamist" a completely definite connotation. Even those upon whom the name is imposed exhibit great variety in their theological thinking and are not infrequently opposed to one another. There are, however, general trends that are characteristic of the movement and that have caused it to be referred to as the *via moderna* as opposed to the *via antiqua* of the earlier scholastics.

Conceptualism. The most basic notion is, perhaps, the note of CONCEPTUALISM that began to enter into explanations of knowledge. According to this theory, the terms in a proposition signify a CONCEPT that stands for some extramental reality. This concept is a SIGN that can refer to one thing or to many. As a sign it is a mental reality and, like any reality, is itself singular and unique. It is universal only insofar as it can stand for many. Hence, its universality is purely functional and does not in any sense refer to a common nature possessed by many things outside the mind. This makes necessary a whole new logic of SUPPOSITION, that is, the manner in which terms stand for things, and gives a new turn to the old Aristotelian logic.

Singulars. Reality itself is a collection of absolute singulars, the distinguishable units of which are things and qualities. All other modifications of things are reduced to the reality of the things themselves. Things are similar, for example, because they are themselves; quantity is indistinguishable from the thing in its magnitude. Such a universe of unique singulars cannot have any necessary connections between the beings that compose it. Furthermore, since singulars depend for their being on the will of God and since the will of God can accomplish anything that does not involve a contradiction, it is always possible to have one given singular without another. Since, for example, an effect is different from its cause, it is possible for God to sustain the effect without its proper cause.

Motion. Another characteristic distinctive of Ockhamism, worth mentioning because it can serve to differentiate this movement from other types of nominalism, is its attitude toward motion. Ockham denied the existence of motion as an entity separate from the moving body, holding that motion was merely a term replacing a series of statements that the body was now here, now there, and so on. Others who are commonly referred to as nominalists, such as JOHN BURIDAN, ALBERT OF SAXONY, and NICHOLAS ORESME, were not only convinced of the reality of motion but, through their attempts to discover its proper cause, contributed to the origin of modern science (see M. Clagett).

Divine Will. The theory of divine omnipotence based on what God can will without contradiction is one of the dominant themes in later Ockhamism. It is basically an attempt to overcome the necessitarianism of Greek philosophy, a necessitarianism that Ockham thought the whole theory of the divine ideas had failed to solve. In place of a universe conceived as an expression of divine intelligibility, there is posited a universe radically contingent upon the divine will, even to the natures of things themselves. The same notion appears in ethics and morality, in which sin comes to be equated with prohibition and good is determined by the will of God instead of by any intrinsic intelligibility. Most of the Ockhamists went so far as to assert that God could command someone to hate Him. And why not, if good and evil are completely determined by what God wills them to be?

Knowledge. The experience one has of such a universe of unique singulars can never be more than a *de facto* association of many such singulars. There is an intuitive grasp of the individual thing sensibly affecting one here and now. All other knowledge is abstract knowledge. Since, in the first place, there is no necessity in such a universe and since relationship is not a reality distinct from the things themselves, there is no hope of establishing the necessity of the causal proposition. As a result, the conclusions of the natural sciences and of the philosophy of nature became at best highly probable propositions. Neither do the traditional arguments for the existence of God based on efficient, formal, and final causality any longer provide a demonstration for such existence. The same can be said about the existence of the human soul and its immortality.

Role of Faith. Hence, many of the conclusions that previous scholastic theologians considered to be capable of rational demonstration were made matters of faith only. The result was an ever widening gap between philosophy and theology, or better, perhaps, the relegation of philosophy to the status of a quasi-science of predictability about the events in nature and a corresponding skepticism about the validity of metaphysics. H. Oberman is probably correct when he questions the retreat to faith as stemming entirely from the low opinion of knowledge prevalent among Ockhamistic thinkers [*The Harvest of Medieval Theology* (Cambridge, Mass. 1963) 35]. But neither are the alternatives he suggests completely satisfactory. There may be other reasons; but granting the Ockhamistic metaphysics and logic, there is little else that can be done except to restrict drastically the range of human reason.

Chief Proponents. The *via moderna* had its influence, and the main themes of the movement appear consistently in the works of such men as ROBERT HOLCOT, ADAM WODHAM, GREGORY OF RIMINI, PETER OF AILLY, and Ockham's commentator, Gabriel BIEL. The two men who seem to represent best the extremes of the position are JOHN OF MIRECOURT and NICHOLAS OF AUTRECOURT.

John of Mirecourt divides all knowledge into that which is evident and that which is held with fear of error. Evident knowledge in the strictest sense is that which can be reduced to the principle of CONTRADICTION. Experiential knowledge is also evident, but it is never capable of leading to a strict DEMONSTRATION. The proofs for God's existence and the causal proposition are classed under the knowledge that is held with fear of error. The theme of the divine omnipotent will shows up strongly also. God can cause any act, including the act of hatred of Himself. John also thought an act could be contrary to the natural law without being demeritorious.

Nicholas of Autrecourt held also that the only certain knowledge was that which could be reduced to the principle of contradiction. Experience provides certain knowledge, but in a universe of individuals the existence of one thing can never be inferred from the existence of another. It is impossible for logic to detect any necessary connections in nature. Nicholas also repeated John of Mirecourt's opinion that God could cause an act of hatred of Himself. In his philosophy of nature, Nicholas returned to the old Greek ATOMISM, preferring it to the hylomorphic theory of Aristotle. Besides, a universe of disparate atoms with no necessary connections between them was all the more dependent on God.

Others, such as John Buridan, MARSILIUS OF INGHEN, and Nicholas of Oresme, made use of Ockham's logic, although they differed from Ockham in their analyses of the world of nature.

Influence. The University of Paris issued condemnations against Ockham in 1339 and against John of Mirecourt in 1347. In 1346 the Holy See condemned Nicholas of Autrecourt. Nevertheless, the movement continued to flourish. Terminist logic became prevalent not only in Paris and Oxford, but also at the universities of Heidelberg, Vienna, Erfurt, and Leipzig.

It would be inaccurate to maintain a direct influence of John of Mirecourt or Nicholas of Autrecourt on modern and contemporary EMPIRICISM. Christian theologians such as these were logicians and philosophers only in a secondary way. Nevertheless, there are some striking resemblances between the philosophizing of the late Middle Ages and such modern empiricists as J. LOCKE and D. HUME. And the logic of supposition, with its emphasis on functionality, is not too far divorced from the approach of contemporary linguistic analysis.

Criticism. With its world of absolutely singular entities and its rejection of any necessary connection between them, Ockhamism effectively destroyed any certain knowledge of that world beyond the intuitive grasp of an immediately present sense object. Since all abstract knowledge had nothing to do with existence, such knowledge could be at best a logic of possibilities with only an indirect reference to the real order. These possibilities, moreover, were abstracted from sensible experience. Hence, metaphysics was reduced to a logic of concepts that could not transcend the material world from which such concepts were taken. The causal relationship became a way of thinking about experience, rather than an insight grounded in the actual relationships between things. The rejection of any proof for the existence of God based on efficient or final causality was simply a necessary conclusion from such premises.

There is little reason to be surprised, then, when revelation and faith began more and more to take over conclusions held as rationally demonstrable by the earlier scholastics. Along with this went a corresponding SKEPTICISM about the intellect's ability to achieve any certainty either in natural science or in philosophy. The God who was believed to have created such a world did so with an arbitrariness restricted only by the principle of contradiction. Instead of the divine essence as intelligible being the source and exemplar of the universe, it is the divine will that establishes all things even to their intelligible natures. Instead of right reason being the norm of morality, now the command to act in such a way alone determines moral good and evil. A universe so conceived cannot do without faith. Once that faith was lost, skepticism or a return to reason conceived as sufficient for itself were the only possible answers.

See Also: NOMINALISM; SCHOLASTICISM.

Bibliography: W. OCKHAM, *Quodlibetal Questions*, tr. A. FREDDOSO, and F. KELLEY (New Haven, Conn. 1991). M. BASTIT, *Les principes des choses en ontologie medievale: Thomas d'Aquin, Scot, Occam* (Bordeaux 1997). J. P. BECKMAN, *Wilhelm von Ockham* (Munich 1995); *Ockham-Bibliographie* (Hamburg 1992). G. LEFF, *The Dissolution of the Medieval Outlook: An Essay on Intellectual and Spiritual Change in the Fourteenth Century* (New York 1976). A. A. MAURER, *The Philosophy of William of Ockham in the Light of Its Principles* (Toronto 1999). K. B. OSBORNE, ed., *A History of Franciscan Theology* (St. Bonaventure 1994). C. PANACCIO, *Les mots, les concepts, et les choses: La semantique de Guillaume d'Occam et le nominalisme d'aujourd'hui* (Montreal 1992). P. V. SPADE, ed., *The Cambridge Companion to Ockham* (Cambridge 1999).

[H. R. KLOCKER]

O'CLERY, MICHAEL

Franciscan lay brother, scribe, hagiographer, and historian (in Gaelic Mícheál Ó Clérigh); b. Donegal, Ireland, *c.* 1590; d. Louvain, Netherlands, 1643. O'Clery studied in Irish schools before going to the Spanish Netherlands some time before 1621. He entered the Franciscan Order in about 1622 at Louvain, where the Irish Franciscans had established the College of St. Anthony in 1607. Many important scholars and writers were attached to the College and it became the center of a movement to provide the Irish people with religious literature in their own language. A printing press, installed at the College in 1611, turned out many books during the next 60 years. At the time of O'Clery's entrance, Fathers Hugh WARD, Patrick FLEMING, and others connected with Louvain, had formed a plan to publish the lives of the Irish saints. O'Clery was dispatched to Ireland in 1626 to collect hagiographical material and send it to Louvain. He remained in Ireland at this task for 11 years.

In addition to a great amount of transcription, O'Clery compiled works of his own—calendars of saints' feasts, and genealogies of saints and kings—and reedited some early historical documents. In collaboration with three other scholars he produced (1632–36) his greatest work, *The Annals of the Four Masters,* an annalistic compilation from many sources covering the history of Ireland from the earliest times to 1616. In 1637 he returned to Louvain, where he compiled his *Foclóir nó Sanasan Nua* (a glossary of obscure words), which was printed on the college press in the year of his death.

O'Clery's achievement lay in rescuing from destruction many Irish historical records. Some of his material was used by Father John COLGAN, successor to Fathers Ward and Fleming, in his *Acta sanctorum Hiberniae* (1645) and *Triadis thaumaturgae seu divorum Patricii, Columbae, et Brigidae acta* (1647). The plan to publish the Saints' lives fell through after the death (1673) of Colgan's successor, Father Thomas Sheerin, but most of the material in O'Clery's manuscripts was published during the nineteenth century.

Bibliography: B. JENNINGS, *Michael Ó Cléirigh, Chief of the Four Masters, and His Associates* (Dublin 1936). T. Ó CLÉIRIGH, *Aodh Mac Aingil agus an Scoil Nua-Ghaedhilge i Lobhain* (Dublin

1936). S. O'BRIEN, ed., *Measgra i gcuimhne Mhichíl Uí Chléirigh: Miscellany of Historical and Linguistic Studies in Honour of Brother Michael Ó Cléirigh* (Dublin 1944).

[G. S. MACEOIN]

O'CONNELL, ANTHONY, SISTER

Civil War nurse; b. Limerick, Ireland, Aug. 15, 1814; d. Cincinnati, Ohio, Dec. 8, 1897. Mary, the daughter of William and Catherine (Murphy) O'Connell, came to the United States as a child and attended the school conducted by the URSULINE Sisters in Charlestown, Mass. Through William Tyler, a convert and priest, she became acquainted with Mother Elizabeth SETON's foundation at Emmitsburg, Md., and joined the Sisters of Charity in 1835. Two years later, as Sister Anthony, she was sent to Cincinnati, Ohio, to care for orphans. During the next 17 years she was active in the administration of hospitals and homes for children, establishing St. John's Hotel for Invalids as the city's first modern medical institution. In 1852 she was one of the seven founders of the Sisters of Charity of Cincinnati, and she served twice as procuratrix-general of the new congregation. In 1861, in response to a government appeal for nurses, Sister Anthony labored in Cincinnati and at various military hospitals. For her work she was praised as "the Florence Nightingale of America." After the war, her congregation was presented with Cincinnati's former Marine Hospital, which was renamed the Good Samaritan. In 1873 St. Joseph's Infant Home, the first hospital for unmarried mothers and abandoned infants in the area, was opened by the congregation. Until 1882 Sister Anthony was administrator of the Good Samaritan Hospital and also of St. Joseph's Home, where she died.

Bibliography: Archives, Sister of Charity, Mount St. Joseph, Ohio. E. R. JOLLY, *Nuns of the Battlefield* (Providence 1927). M. A. MCCANN, *History of Mother Seton's Daughters,* 3 v. (New York 1917–23).

[L. C. FEIERTAG]

O'CONNELL, DANIEL

Irish statesman; b. Carhen, Cahirciveen, Co. Kerry, Aug. 6, 1775; d. Genoa, Italy, May 15, 1847. O'Connell was the eldest son of Morgan (1739–1809) and Catherine (O'Mullane) O'Connell. The O'Connells farmed and traded in Kerry, where their ancestors had held military and church offices before the wholesale confiscation of Irish land by Oliver Cromwell. On the advice of an uncle, Count Daniel Charles O'Connell (1745–1833), a distinguished French general, Daniel was sent for education to the Austrian Netherlands—first to the English College at St. Omer (1791) and, the following year, to the Douay English College. Early in 1793, the French overran this area and O'Connell went to London, where he studied law until 1797; he was called to the Irish bar in 1798. In 1802 he married his cousin Mary, daughter of Dr. Thomas O'Connell of Tralee.

Emancipation Advocate. O'Connell had been an able student. His diary reveals that he had grasped quite clearly the idea of the English common law, and particularly the concept of the rights of the subject. He was one of the first Catholic lawyers permitted to practice in Ireland after the first anti-Catholic penal laws were modified. O'Connell, one day to be called "the Liberator," was quickly drawn toward the defense of his coreligionists whose political ambitions were being frustrated by the refusal of EMANCIPATION. In 1797 he had been associated with the revolutionary society of United Irishmen and also had joined the volunteer artillery corps of the Dublin lawyers. Yet he took no part in the rebellion of 1798. From 1799 for at least ten years he was a freemason—the Irish bishops did not implement papal condemnations of FREEMASONRY until much later. O'Connell was instrumental in securing the reelection as grand master of Richard Hely-Hutchinson, Lord Donoughmore, (1756–1825), a man whose services in the cause of Catholic emancipation he greatly admired. O'Connell probably ended his connection with the freemasons before 1824, and apparently on the advice of Abp. John TROY (1739–1823).

A highly successful barrister who was earning nearly £8,000 a year by the late 1820s, he was particularly effective in cross-examination, and in defense. His aggressive technique gave courage to Catholics long exploited legally by the Protestant ascendancy. But his method, as in the John Magee case (1814), while it weakened the reputation of opponents, was not always fully effective; the loss of one of his cases could entail the imposition of heavy punishments on his clients. Magee, for example, was imprisoned and fined for publishing criminal libels against the government.

As early as 1800 O'Connell had spoken at a meeting of Dublin Catholics in opposition to the legislative union with Great Britain; his position was contrary to the views of many of the bishops and upperclass laymen. During his 30-year career as a lawyer he gave much time to the successive Catholic organizations that attempted to secure political and social equality. Until 1812 the most important of these was the Irish Catholic Committee on which O'Connell replaced John Keogh (1740–1817) in the year (1807) when the policy of petitioning Parliament for the abrogation of the penal laws was again taken up systematically. This committee was suppressed by the government in 1812 and was succeeded by the Irish Catholic Board, of which O'Connell was also made a member. In 1813 English members of Parliament, who were pro-Catholic and who believed emancipation could be secured, introduced relief measures. These empowered the government by arrangement with the Holy See to exercise a veto on nominees to bishoprics in Great Britain and Ireland. The proposal was acceptable to the papal secretary of Propaganda G. B. (later Cardinal) Quarantotti, but the bill was abandoned because of the opposition of Bp. John Milner (1752–1826) and of O'Connell, whose views were those of the majority of the board. O'Connell's objection was that if the veto power was thus conceded, the clergy would appear to be civil servants, and in that role would forfeit the people's confidence. For this same reason O'Connell later rejected several relief bills introduced by Henry Grattan (1746–1820). Furthermore, O'Connell had hopes that if Grattan's friends, the Whigs, failed in their purpose, he could secure it through pro-Catholic Tories such as William Conyngham Plunket (1764–1854). For these reasons, also, he avoided committing himself on the subject of parliamentary reform. This issue had become associated with the Whig opposition to the Tory government of Robert Banks Jenkinson, second Earl of Liverpool (1770–1828). At this point of history, however, the pro-Catholic Tories were too weak to be truly effective and, accordingly, on April 25, 1823, O'Connell and Richard Lalor Sheil (1791–1851) started the Catholic Association, which charged membership dues of one shilling a year. Within 12 months O'Connell had gained a nationwide support, which had been effectively organized by the diocesan clergy and by the Catholic professional classes.

Alarmed at this development, the government introduced an act to suppress all such societies (1825). O'Connell went to London to promote a Catholic petition; he was persuaded by Plunket and Sir Francis Burdett (1770–1844) to accept a relief bill balanced by provisions for state payment of Catholic clergy and for disfranchisement of 40-shilling freeholders. Despite support by a majority of government ministers in the House of Commons, the proposal was defeated in the House of Lords, a vote largely influenced by a speech of the prime minister Lord Liverpool. In July of the same year, O'Connell organized the New Catholic Association, which in the general election of 1826 achieved spectacular successes and which ended the monopoly of political control of the freeholders in Waterford, Louth, and Monaghan. The government now began to fear that O'Connell would make it impossible for them to win Irish elections.

It was in this atmosphere that Arthur Wellesley, Duke of Wellington (1769–1852), who succeeded as

Daniel O'Connell.

prime minister in 1828, now was obliged to give way on the emancipation issue, for O'Connell had himself defeated the government supporter, William Vesey-FitzGerald (1783–1843), at a by-election for Co. Clare. Since Wellington was in power, the Irish Catholic Association had decided to oppose the reelection of any member accepting office from the government. Although Vesey-FitzGerald had been favorable to Catholic emancipation, his defeat made it clear that the government risked losing supporters, and that it dare not risk a general election. Such an election in Ireland would almost certainly result in the return of a solid bloc of pro-Catholics hostile to the government's policy.

O'Connell's victory, by a vote of 2057 to 982, was regarded as the death knell of landlord control of freeholders' votes. The clergy had utilized every influence in stimulating their people to believe that the issue was essentially a religious one. Thus, to Wellington, emancipation became a necessary concession in a final effort to ensure "that the Irish nobility and gentry would recover their lost influence, the just influence of property." It was the great merit of O'Connell that his efforts helped to build for the Irish masses the growing power that led to eventual control of their elected representatives. The passage of the act of Catholic emancipation, however, was accompanied by the statutory abolition both of the Catholic Association and of the voting rights of the 40-shilling freeholders (1829). Only those Catholics who would take an oath of allegiance to the British king, and thereby deny the temporal power of the pope in the United Kingdom, might thus secure legal exemption from the penal laws. Future members of religious orders need not expect such protection. Even O'Connell himself, without reelection, could not take his seat in Parliament unless he first subscribed to the anti-Catholic oath and declaration made applicable to all members before the Clare election. That no one dared oppose his reelection was some indication that the center of political gravity in Ireland had changed permanently.

Further Political Struggles. For some years after 1829, O'Connell's connections with Catholic issues were peripheral. His attempt to organize a nondenominational movement to repeal the union of the British and Irish parliaments was unsuccessful. He was feared by the dominant Protestant ascendancy, which in any case was not prepared to share its power. Determined to break that power, O'Connell appealed to the parliamentary reformers and to the democracy. In November 1830, Wellington, convinced that he could no longer prevent reform, retired and was succeeded as prime minister by Charles Grey (Viscount Howick and Earl Grey, 1764–1845). With O'Connell's support, this Whig leader secured the passage of the great reform act of 1832, which abolished many unrepresentative boroughs and gave to the upper middle class some share in political power. The Irish act (1833), which maintained many of the unrepresentative bulwarks of Protestant ascendancy, was less satisfactory. Further, social equality was still denied to farming Catholics who now began to refuse to pay tithes to Protestant clergy. The result was that a new form of agrarian revolt, partly countenanced by the Catholic clergy, became common. After 1834, under Grey's successor, William Lamb, Viscount Melbourne (1779–1848), O'Connell made more progress in securing "justice for Ireland" and in particular for the Catholics. A reform administration in Dublin, one particularly influential among the police, abandoned the habit of equating loyalists and Protestants. Catholics were slowly admitted to government offices, but legislative reforms did not go beyond converting tithes into a rent charge upon lands (1838), and abolishing the more indefensible parliamentary boroughs (1840). Meanwhile, since 1830 the existence of a nondenominational system of elementary education was causing increased Catholic and Protestant resentment particularly on the part of Abp. John MACHALE] (1791–1881) of Tuam; his opposition led him to support O'Connell who had revived the repeal of the union question in the Precursor Society in 1838. O'Connell convinced MacHale that the Repeal Association, established

in 1839, would prevent the Tory government of Sir Robert Peel (1788–1850), Melbourne's successor (1841), from reestablishing Protestant ascendancy, or, at the least, from permanently obstructing further Catholic emancipation. With renewed clerical support in most parts of the country (Abp. Daniel MURRAY of Dublin almost alone held aloof) O'Connell organized an enthusiastic national following. Despite his confident predictions of success for this great moral movement in 1843, Peel secured O'Connell's imprisonment for seditious conspiracy (June 30, 1844). He was released, after a successful appeal, three months later. Catholic Ireland treated this event as an occasion for spiritual rejoicing; even Archbishop Murray took part by sanctioning a *Te Deum.* Meanwhile, Peel had endeavored to divert Catholics from the Repeal Association by supporting a more moderate policy, which featured the state endowment of nondenominational higher colleges and a substantially increased subsidization of St. Patrick's of Maynooth. Through a bequests act, Peel also offered improved facilities for Catholic charities. A simultaneous approach was made to Rome to discourage Irish ecclesiastical involvement in politics. This attempt boomeranged when MacHale insisted on the danger to Catholicism from the colleges and bequests bills. Unfairly, O'Connell argued that the bequests law would be used to bar charities to religious orders. Rome ultimately condemned the legislation for colleges but not the bequests act. Immediately afterward, O'Connell was able to influence the clergy against that more militant group in the Repeal Association, the Young Irelanders, who were opposed to a renewed Irish alliance with the Whigs who had returned to power under Prime Minister Lord John Russell in June 1846. Rather than deny the right to resort to force in any extremity, the Young Irelanders left the Repeal Association.

Thereafter O'Connell desired to persuade the state to take measures to counteract the potato blight, which had first appeared in the autumn of the preceding year. The attempt was unsuccessful; the Whig government proved incapable of arresting the catastrophe, now known as the "Great Famine." Within ten years, the resultant fever, starvation, and emigration reduced by 25 percent the population of Ireland, which had once been more than eight million.

After O'Connell's death from a sudden cerebral illness, suffered at Genoa while he was on a pilgrimage to Rome, his son Daniel was received by Pope Pius IX. Under that pope's auspices a two-day funeral oration for O'Connell was delivered by Gioacchino VENTURA DI RAULICA (1792–1861). The speech glorified the union of religion and liberty.

O'Connell's religious convictions, apparently weakened in his youth, had been reinforced during his maturity, and were quite strong in his last years. Those years were, however, somewhat darkened by what seems to have been almost an obsession with the possibility of his eternal damnation.

O'Connell's Significance. This Irish statesman was the greatest single influence in the emergence of Irish political nationalism. He linked the constitutional movement of Grattan and of the 18th-century Protestant patriots to the emancipated Catholics. In his appeal to the masses he was closer to Theobald Wolfe Tone (1763–98) and to the United Irishmen than to Grattan, though in his mature years he opposed both the use of physical force and of revolutionary methods. His substitution of the clergy for the landlords as the local leaders of the people strengthened their mutual ties even after clerical interference at the end of the career of Parnell had weakened the Church's relations with the nationalists. A friend to Catholic liberal Europe and a forceful supporter of the advocates of Negro emancipation in America, O'Connell's influence on Irish nationalism helped to shape the 20th-century Republic of Ireland.

Bibliography: R. D. EDWARDS, ''The Contribution of Young Ireland to the Development of the National Idea,'' in *Essays Presented to T. Ua Donnchadha,* ed. S. PENDER (Cork 1947). A. HOUSTON, ed., *D. O'Connell: His Early Life, and Journal, 1795 to 1802* (London 1906). D. O'CONNELL, *A Memoir on Ireland, Native and Saxon* (Dublin 1843; 2d ed. 1844). J. O'CONNELL, ed., *Life and Speeches of D. O'Connell,* 2 v. (Dublin 1846), by his son. W. J. FITZPATRICK, ed., *Correspondence of D. O'Connell,* 2 v. (London 1888). O'Connell MSS in National Library of Ireland, and University College Dublin. J. A. REYNOLDS, *The Catholic Emancipation Crisis in Ireland, 1823–1829* (New Haven 1954). J. F. BRODERICK, *The Holy See and the Irish Movement for the Repeal of the Union with England, 1829–1847* (Rome 1951). C. G. DUFFY, *Young Ireland, 1840–1849,* 2 v. (2d ed. Dublin 1884–87). G. S. LEFEVRE, *Peel and O'Connell, a Review of Irish Policy* (London 1887).

[R. D. EDWARDS]

O'CONNELL, DENIS JOSEPH

Bishop; b. Donoughmore, County Cork, Ireland, Jan. 28, 1849; d. Richmond, Va., Jan. 1, 1927. He was the son of Michael and Bridget (O'Connell) O'Connell. The family immigrated to the United States and settled in South Carolina, where two brothers of Michael, Jeremiah J. and Joseph P., were missionaries. When Bishop James Gibbons was looking for candidates to build up the clergy of his new Vicariate of North Carolina, he met young Denis O'Connell. A close friendship developed between Gibbons and O'Connell, one that extended over a long lifetime and major national and international issues of Catholicism in the late nineteenth century. After prelimi-

nary studies at St. Charles College, Ellicott City, Md., O'Connell was sent (1871) to the North American College, Rome, for theology courses at the Urban College of the Propagation of the Faith. He was ordained on May 26, 1877 and received a Roman doctorate in theology. After returning to Richmond, where Gibbons had been transferred, O'Connell began priestly work as assistant at St. Peter's cathedral there. He was back in Rome within a few months, a postulator for Gibbons's pallium as newly appointed coadjutor archbishop of Baltimore. For the next five years he worked in the Diocese of Richmond under the direction of Bishop John J. Keane.

In the fall of 1883 Gibbons called O'Connell to Baltimore to assist in the preliminary arrangements for the Third Plenary Council of BALTIMORE, at which he served as one of the four secretaries. After the council he returned to Rome with the American bishops' committee to secure ratification of the conciliar decrees. In 1885 he was appointed rector of the North American College in Rome, and for the next 18 years he served as liaison man and Roman agent for members of the American hierarchy. During his term as rector (1885–95), the student body was enlarged, the physical plant improved, and an honor system established at the college. He also served as a Roman agent for Gibbons, who was elevated to the cardinalate in 1886.

O'Connell, the Roman intermediary, was made a domestic prelate in 1887; he took active part in the Roman aspects of the controversies centered on such questions as the KNIGHTS OF LABOR, Cahenslyism, The CATHOLIC UNIVERSITY OF AMERICA, the coming of an apostolic delegate to the United States, Henry George and the single tax, Archbishop John Ireland's FARIBAULT school PLAN, and AMERICANISM. As the lines of difference developed between so-called liberal and conservative members of the American Church of that period, O'Connell became a symbol of the liberal wing's position. He identified himself unqualifiedly with the policies of Gibbons, Ireland, and Keane, and alienated conservative-minded American bishops, who held differing views on the burning issues of the developing Church in the United States. Criticisms of O'Connell's activities, apart from his rectorship, increased to the point that his resignation from the college was requested on the grounds that he did not have the full confidence of the body of American bishops. From 1895 to 1903 O'Connell served as rector of Cardinal Gibbons's titular church of Santa Maria in Trastevere in Rome.

On Jan. 12, 1903, through the influence of his friends, O'Connell was appointed third rector of The Catholic University of America, Washington, D.C., which was then badly in need of academic, organizational, promotional, and financial direction. From 1903 to 1910 he worked, with some success, to establish educational improvements at the university. An annual collection was inaugurated that was to be taken up in all the dioceses of the United States for the advancement of the pontifical university in Washington. Student enrollment was increased; several prominent and capable professors were engaged; and academic procedures were formalized according to accepted standards in the academic community. The base of the university's educational program was extended to include undergraduate training as well as graduate studies. But O'Connell found it difficult to adjust to the American system of educational operation through a board of trustees and with input from the faculty. A financial crisis almost destroyed the university in 1904, when the total endowment funds of the institution were endangered by the financial failure of Thomas E. Waggaman, treasurer of the university, who had invested the funds of the university in his enterprises. The university's endowment was reduced by two-thirds of its investment value; confidence in its financial management was severely weakened; and extensive and prolonged revival was slow to take place.

On Dec. 12, 1907, O'Connell was named a titular bishop, a move that advanced his growing desire to be relieved of the rectorship in Washington. After Archbishop Patrick W. Riordan of San Francisco, Calif., petitioned Rome for his old friend O'Connell to become auxiliary bishop, the appointment was made on Dec. 25, 1908. When O'Connell was transferred to the See of Richmond on Jan. 19, 1912, as a suffragan of Cardinal Gibbons, the old discussions began anew that O'Connell would be appointed coadjutor of Baltimore and succeed to the premier see. But he was too old for such a consideration when Cardinal Gibbons died in 1921, and the bishop of Richmond continued directing the activities of the diocese of his youth until Jan. 15, 1926, when he resigned because of failing health.

[C. J. BARRY]

O'CONNELL, JOHN PATRICK

Theologian, editor, actively involved in the liturgical apostolate; b. Chicago, Ill., Jan. 12, 1918; d. Chicago, Feb. 20, 1960. Educated at Quigley Seminary, Chicago, and St. Mary of the Lake Seminary, Mundelein, Ill., where he earned the degrees of M.A. and S.T.D., he was ordained on May 1, 1943. After serving as a parish priest and as a teacher at Barat College, Lake Forest, Ill., he was selected by Cardinal Samuel Stritch to be the editor for The Catholic Press, Inc., of Chicago, of the *Holy Bible* (Holy Family edition, 1950, and several subsequent edi-

tions); the *Sunday Missal*; the *Prayer Book* and the *Life of Christ*, issued as a set (1954); the *Bible Story* (1959); and *Christ and the Church* (1960). Under his direction, The Catholic Press also published the French *La Sainte Bible* (1956), the Spanish *Sagrada Biblia* (1958), and after delays extending beyond his death, Portuguese and Italian translations of Holy Scripture. O'Connell was a member of the Mariological Society and of the Catholic Biblical Association.

Influenced by his pastor, Joseph P. Morrison, O'Connell became a zealous promoter of the liturgical apostolate. He served the Liturgical Conference as secretary (1946–47); as treasurer (1949–52); as a member of its Board of Directors and Advisory Council; and as editor of the proceedings of the 1946, 1957, 1958, and 1959 Liturgical Weeks. During the last years of his life, he was engaged in the work of programming the annual Liturgical Weeks. O'Connell contributed many articles to publications and addressed many clerical and lay audiences in spreading knowledge of the Church's worship.

At the directive of Cardinal Stritch, Father O'Connell made preliminary surveys with a view to the publication of a new edition of the *Catholic Encyclopedia*. Shortly after he was named a papal chamberlain on Dec. 28, 1959, he fell prey to a fatal disease. Until the day of his untimely death, he continued working to complete many of the projects he had undertaken.

Bibliography: F. R. MCMANUS, *Yearbook of Liturgical Studies* 1 (1960) xi–xiv.

[N. RANDOLPH]

O'CONNELL, WILLIAM HENRY

Cardinal and second archbishop of Boston; b. Lowell, Mass., Dec. 8, 1859; d. Boston, Mass., April 22, 1944. He was the youngest of 11 children of John and Brigid O'Connell, natives of County Cavan, Ireland. His father died when he was five but family sacrifices enabled him to attend Lowell public schools and then to enter St. Charles College, Ellicott City, Maryland, to study for the priesthood. However, in 1879 he left the seminary and entered Boston College, from which he graduated in 1881 with first honors in philosophy and physics. He reapplied for the priesthood and was sent by Abp. John J. Williams to the North American College in Rome. Illness terminated O'Connell's studies at Rome before he could obtain a doctorate. He was ordained June 7, 1884, returned to the U.S. in December, and did pastoral work for the next ten years, first at St. Joseph's in Medford, then at St. Joseph's in Boston's West End.

Early Career. Late in 1895, when a conflict of opinion in the U.S. hierarchy led to the resignation of the rectors of the North American College in Rome and the Catholic University of America, Cardinal James Gibbons named O'Connell rector of the NORTH AMERICAN COLLEGE. During the next six years, O'Connell doubled the enrollment of the North American College, rehabilitated its finances, and purchased the Villa Santa Caterina at Castel Gandolfo for summer sessions. He was made a domestic prelate in 1897. His relations with Pope Leo XIII, Papal Secretary of State Cardinal Rampolla, and the future Cardinal Merry del Val were cordial. He also formed friendships in Roman society and diplomatic circles that resulted in the bequest to the North American College of the library of the bibliophile William Heyward, and in the decoration of the college refectory at the expense of the American theater magnate, Benjamin F. Keith. In 1918 O'Connell received from the Keith estate a personal bequest totalling almost $2.5 million. He devoted the entire sum to charities for various Catholic institutions, rendering the final account of these disbursements in 1936.

On May 19, 1901, in the Corsini Chapel of the Basilica of St. John Lateran, O'Connell was consecrated third bishop of Portland, Maine, by Cardinal Satolli. Taking possession of his see, which had been vacant for nearly a year, he visited every parish in the state. He redecorated the Cathedral of the Immaculate Conception, introduced a forerunner of the Catholic Youth Organization, and fostered retreats for the clergy. In 1903 he declined the Holy See's appointment to the Archdiocese of Manila in the Philippine Islands, which had recently been acquired by the U.S. Aware of the untrue reports that he had supported the Spanish cause against the U.S. in 1898, O'Connell frankly informed Rome that such gossip would impede his work in the Philippines and recommended that another choice be made.

After the Russo-Japanese War, O'Connell was named special papal envoy to Emperor Mutsuhito on Aug. 31, 1905. He had a personal audience with the emperor and empress and was decorated with the Grand Cordon of the Sacred Treasure. He made a thorough survey of the mission field in Japan, reporting to Pius X in Rome in January 1906. His recommendations, all adopted, included the introduction of many religious orders into Japan, the fostering of a native clergy, and the founding of a Catholic university at Tokyo, to be staffed by Jesuits.

Assignment to Boston. On Feb. 21, 1906, Pius X, disregarding the recommendations from the bishops of New England, named O'Connell titular bishop of Constantia, and coadjutor with right of succession to the aged Archbishop Williams of Boston. The news was not favorably received in Boston but O'Connell remained unperturbed. He concluded his affairs in Portland and went to Boston to be installed formally on April 3, 1906. At the death of Williams on Aug. 30, 1907, the 47-year-old O'Connell took up the reins that he would hold firmly for the next 37 years.

A born leader, O'Connell once said: "I have never hesitated to speak as plainly as possible . . . whenever direction was needed." He began at once to reorganize the large archdiocese in which he found many institutions debt ridden and run down. In 1908, when the apostolic constitution of Pius X, *Sapienti consilio,* removed the Church in the U.S. from mission supervision to full national status like that of the Church in older European countries, O'Connell was a leader in establishing diocesan administrative offices. His zeal for the missions, both foreign and home, was shown in his support of the Catholic Missionary Congress held at Chicago in 1908 and at Boston in 1913. He encouraged two Boston priests in the founding of new missionary congregations. James Anthony WALSH was released from the Boston archdiocese to become a cofounder of the Catholic Foreign Mission Society; the Vincentian Thomas JUDGE, born in Boston, was aided in his work for home missions in founding the MISSIONARY SERVANTS OF THE MOST HOLY TRINITY, a community of sisters, the MISSIONARY SERVANTS OF THE MOST BLESSED TRINITY, and the Missionary Cenacle Apostolate. O'Connell also pioneered in supporting (1917) the open-air preaching of the Jewish convert and lay apostle to the man in the street, David GOLDSTEIN.

O'Connell was created the first native cardinal of Boston on Nov. 26, 1911. A group of non-Catholics in Boston presented him with a purse of $25,000, which he used for improving his titular Church of San Clemente in Rome. In the Boston archdiocese he placed institutions on a sound financial basis, encouraged early and frequent Communion, and introduced retreats for the laity, bringing the Passionists, the Religious of the Cenacle, and the Franciscans to Boston to conduct retreat houses.

Other Contributions. On the national scene, O'Connell's diocese was outstanding in both World Wars in efforts for servicemen. Patriotism was a frequent theme in his sermons. When President Wilson first proposed his Fourteen Points, the Cardinal spoke at Madison Square Garden (Dec. 10, 1918), eloquently urging self-determination for Ireland as well as for other peoples. In 1924, he spoke out publicly against the proposed child labor amendment to the Constitution as infringing on the rights of parents and of the states. He also spoke against birth control and preached against graft in politics. O'Connell helped to convert the National Catholic War Council of World War I into the National Catholic Welfare Conference. He was prominent in bringing about the change that today enables cardinals from any part of the globe to participate in the election of a new pope. In 1914, and again in 1922, the old rule of convening the conclave ten days after the death of a pope had frustrated O'Connell's journeys across the Atlantic. He protested so strongly that Pius XI personally promised to extend the time to 18 days. Thus, in 1939, O'Connell was able to reach Rome in time for the election of Pius XII.

Despite his preoccupation with the administration of mundane matters, the cardinal was a man of prayer and a patron of letters. An amateur organist, he composed the music for *The Holy Cross Hymnal* (Boston 1915). His music for the Latin motet *Juravit Dominus,* written in 1882, was sung for many years at first Masses of priests at the North American College in Rome and in the Boston archdiocese. The Universalist Church of the Redemption in Boston, with its fine organ, was bought by the cardinal and was dedicated as St. Clement's Church on Dec. 8, 1935. He served from 1932 to 1936 as a trustee of the Boston Public Library. To encourage Lenten devotions he translated from the Italian *The Passion of Our Lord* by Cardinal Gaetano De Lai (Boston 1923). O'Connell's particular devotion throughout his life was to our Lady of Perpetual Help.

In 1937 he was awarded an honorary degree by Harvard University, the first native Catholic prelate to be so recognized. During his administration parishes in the archdiocese increased from 194 to 322, and clergy from 600 to more than 1,500. Admissions to St. John's Seminary tripled; a score of new religious congregations were introduced into the area; parochial elementary schools were doubled and high schools tripled—taught by a total of more than 3,000 priests, brothers, and sisters. Three colleges for women were founded under his auspices and he aided the establishment of Boston College on its Chestnut Hill campus. In 1908 he purchased as a diocesan organ, the weekly newspaper, the *Pilot;* in 1934 he laid the cornerstone of a diocesan center, a six-story building with presses and offices for the *Pilot,* offices for diocesan bureaus, and a meditation chapel. An archdiocesan residence, the Crehan Library, and the chancery were built; he also enlarged St. John's Seminary, staffing it with diocesan priest-scholars. Active and vigorous in the service of the Church to the last week of his life, O'Connell, at his death, was buried in the mausoleum he had built on the seminary grounds.

Bibliography: W. H. O'CONNELL, *Reminiscences of Twenty-Five Years* (Boston 1926); *Recollections of Seventy Years* (Boston 1934). R. H. LORD et al., *History of the Archdiocese of Boston . . . 1604 to 1943,* 3 v. (New York 1944). D. G. WAYMAN, *Cardinal O'Connell of Boston* (New York 1955).

[D. G. WAYMAN]

O'CONNOR, JOHN JOSEPH

Cardinal, archbishop of NEW YORK; b. Jan. 15, 1920, Philadelphia; d. May 3, 2000, New York. The fourth child of Thomas and Dorothy Gomple O'Connor, he grew up in a working-class neighborhood in southwest Philadelphia, where he attended local public elementary and junior high schools and West Catholic High School for Boys before entering St. Charles Borromeo Seminary in 1936. Ordained a priest of the Archdiocese of Philadelphia on Dec. 15, 1945, he spent the next seven years as a teacher and guidance counselor in archdiocesan high schools while also serving as a parish priest.

In 1952 O'Connor began a 27-year career as a navy chaplain. His service with the Marines during the Vietnam War earned him the Legion of Merit. He strongly defended American involvement in the Vietnam War in *A Chaplain Looks at Vietnam* (Cleveland 1968), but later he expressed regret for having done so. In 1972 O'Connor was appointed the first Catholic senior chaplain at the U.S. Naval Academy, and in 1975 he attained the highest position available to him when he became the U.S. Navy Chief of Chaplains with the rank of rear admiral. He retired in 1979. During his military career, he also earned a doctorate in political science from Georgetown University.

In 1979 O'Connor was appointed titular bishop of Curzola and auxiliary to the military vicar, Terence Cardinal COOKE. O'Connor first became well known nationally when he was appointed to the five-member episcopal committee that prepared "The Challenge of Peace," the pastoral letter issued by the U.S. hierarchy in 1983. One week after the publication of the pastoral letter, he was appointed the bishop of Scranton, Pa. He was installed in June of 1983, but he remained in Scranton for only another seven months; on Jan. 31, 1984, he was appointed archbishop of New York in succession to Cardinal Cooke, who had died the previous October. One year later, Pope John Paul II made him cardinal, with the titular church of Ss. Giovanni e Paolo. On the same day as his elevation, it was announced that the Military Ordinariate had been reorganized as the Archdiocese for the Military Services, U.S.A., severing the connection between the archbishop of New York and the Military Ordinariate that had existed since its inception in 1917.

Cardinal Cooke, a shy man who disliked confrontation, made no attempt to fill the national role of his predecessor, Francis Cardinal Spellman. By contrast, O'Connor seemed to welcome confrontation and clearly aimed at assuming a prominent role in the U.S. hierarchy. He liked to be compared to the feisty John Hughes, New York's first archbishop, and he favored a style of leadership that seemed to be modeled on that of John Paul II.

Although he was 64 years old when he became archbishop, O'Connor adopted a grueling schedule with heavy emphasis on preaching and public appearances, the frequent use of both the press and television, and numerous pastoral visits to parishes and institutions. He also enjoyed occupying center stage at large-scale special events, such as the annual Mass for the Disabled in St. Patrick's Cathedral and a youth rally at Yankee Stadium that drew 40,000 people. In deference to New York's large Hispanic population, he mastered Spanish sufficiently well to celebrate Mass and preach in that language.

As in Scranton, O'Connor gave high priority to right-to-life issues. At a press conference in June of 1984, he answered a question about Catholic politicians and abortion legislation with the statement: "I do not see how a Catholic in good conscience can vote for an individual expressing himself or herself as favoring abortion." The comment was widely interpreted as a criticism of Congresswoman Geraldine Ferraro, the Democratic candidate for vice-president, and it led to public sparring between O'Connor and Governor Mario Cuomo of New York.

O'Connor's well-attended weekly press conferences after Sunday Mass in St. Patrick's Cathedral gave him a forum to comment on public issues. He relished the publicity, but he discontinued the press conferences in 1990, candidly admitting that he had said "some dumb things."

Two groups with whom O'Connor established particularly warm relationships were organized labor and New York's large and influential Jewish community. The Service Employees International Union, grateful for his support of labor unions, publicly hailed him as "the patron saint of working people." Commenting on the award, Monsignor George G. Higgins said, "Few bishops in U.S. history have been as consistently supportive as Cardinal O'Connor of labor's basic rights." Dr. Ronald Sobel, senior rabbi of Temple Emanuel-El, said: "I know of no member of the American Catholic hierarchy who has been more consistently sensitive to the interests of the Jewish people." At the time of the Persian Gulf War in 1991, the former admiral tried to restrain widespread pro-war enthusiasm by declaring: "No war is good. Every war is at best the lesser of evils." Mario Cuomo, with whom he often clashed, paid tribute to O'Connor's commitment to social justice by saying, "His work should have earned the cardinal a reputation as one of the Vatican's favorite social progressives as well as one of its premier conservative dogmatists."

O'Connor committed the archdiocese to maintaining its network of parochial schools, especially in poor neighborhoods, despite the sharp decline in the number of

John Joseph Cardinal O'Connor. (Catholic News Service)

teaching sisters and brothers. The Catholic Church also remained a major provider of health care and social services to the poor in New York City. However, the staffing of parishes became increasingly difficult since O'Connor was reluctant to close or consolidate parishes even as the number of active diocesan priests fell from 777 in 1983 to 585 in 1999. The number of diocesan seminarians decreased even more precipitously, from 221 to 84, despite O'Connor's persistent personal efforts to promote vocations.

Cardinal O'Connor offered his resignation to Pope John Paul II on reaching the mandatory retirement age of 75, but the pope allowed him to remain in office. In October of that year O'Connor welcomed the pontiff to New York for a successful papal visit that included a Mass before 125,000 people in Central Park. In late August of 1999 O'Connor underwent surgery for a brain tumor from which he never fully recovered, although he continued to make limited public appearances until the following March. On the occasion of his 80th birthday, the U.S. Congress bestowed upon him its highest civilian award, the Congressional Gold Medal. He died on May 3, 2000. He was buried in the crypt of St. Patrick's Cathedral, next to Pierre TOUSSAINT, a Haitian born into slavery who worked as a barber in New York and whom John Paul II had declared "Venerable" in 1996. O'Connor had

Bishop Edward Michael Egan (left) at funeral Mass for John Cardinal O'Connor, St. Patrick's Cathedral, New York. (AP/ Wide World Photos)

brought Toussaint's remains to St. Patrick's from an abandoned cemetery for blacks in lower Manhattan, and he had requested that he be buried next to him.

Bibliography: J. O'CONNOR and E. KOCH, *His Eminence and Hizzoner* (New York 1989). N. HENTOFF, *John Cardinal O'Connor: At the Storm Center of a Changing Catholic Church* (New York 1988).

[T. J. SHELLEY]

O'CONNOR, MARTIN JOHN

Archbishop, rector of NORTH AMERICAN COLLEGE, nuncio, and president of the Papal Commission for Social Communications; b. Scranton, Pennsylvania, May 18, 1900; d. Wilkes-Barre, Pennsylvania, Dec. 1, 1986. The only child of John and Belinda Caffrey O'Connor. After graduation from St. Thomas College (now University of Scranton), O'Connor entered the North American College in Rome where he earned doctorates in theology and canon law; he was ordained in Rome in 1924. Returning to the diocese of Scranton, Father O'Connor served in various administrative offices, and in 1943 he was consecrated Auxiliary Bishop of Scranton.

In December of 1946, O'Connor was named rector of the North American College in Rome. He was responsible for restoring the Via dell' Umilta and Castel Gandolfo properties, abandoned during the war years, and for building the new college on the Janiculum. Pope Pius XII dedicated the new facility on Oct. 14, 1953. In all, O'Connor served as rector for 18 years. Pope John XXIII named him archbishop in September of 1959.

Role in the Media. In 1948 Pius XII directed that a commission for religious and didactic films be organized with O'Connor as president. This commission was replaced in 1952 by the Pontifical Commission for Motion Pictures and extended in 1954 to include radio and television. In 1961 John XXIII, laying down new rules, elevated the Pontifical Commission for Cinema, Radio, and Television to a permanent office of the Roman Curia. Pope Paul VI, at the mandate of the Fathers of Vatican Council II, established the Pontifical Commission for the Media of Social Communications and extended its competency to embrace all media, the press in particular, and appointed to it experts from various countries, including laypersons and members of the press. O'Connor was named president, a position he had held continuously from the inception of the various commissions until his retirement in 1971.

On June 5, 1960, John XXIII appointed O'Connor to the General Preparatory Commission for the Second Vatican Council. Ten days later, he appointed him president of the Preparatory Secretariat for Press and Entertainment. The Secretariat was charged with the preparation of a schema on the media of social communications which, after presentation to the Council Fathers and redrafting, was promulgated on Dec. 4, 1963, by a decree of the Council titled *Inter mirifica*. Paul VI, at the beginning of the second period of the council, appointed O'Connor chairman of the newly formed press committee that oversaw the accreditation of more than two thousand correspondents and the daily publication, in nine languages, of resumes of the council speeches.

O'Connor served as a member of the press committee at the First General Assembly of the Synod of Bishops in 1967. In 1969 Paul VI convoked an Extraordinary Assembly of the Synod of Bishops of which O'Connor was a member. He was appointed to the Second General Assembly in 1971.

Paul VI appointed him nuncio to Malta, a post he held from 1965 to 1969. In 1966 he was appointed vice president of the Post-Conciliar Commission for the Apostolate of the Laity. In 1968 he was named consultor to the Pontifical Commission for Latin America. O'Connor retired in 1971 after having served the Church in Rome during five Pontificates. He returned to the United States in 1979.

Bibliography: V. A. YZERMANS, *American Participation in the Second Vatican Council* (New York 1967).

[T. V. BANICK]

O'CONNOR, MARY FLANNERY

Novelist and short-story writer; b. Savannah, Ga., March 25, 1925; d. Milledgeville, Ga., Aug. 3, 1964. She was the daughter of Edward Francis and Regina (Cline) O'Connor, of a pioneer Georgia Catholic family. At the age of 12 she moved with her parents to the Cline family home at Milledgeville. There she attended Peabody High School and graduated (1945) from Georgia State College for Women. She later (1948) studied creative writing at the University of Iowa. The initial attack of an incurable malady brought her home from New York a year later to live with her mother on the farm near Milledgeville, where she spent her remaining years.

Quiet and kind-heartedly humorous, O'Connor was committed to a Christian iconoclasm against the fraudulence and pietism of a secular age. She sought to make "the distortions in modern life" apparent to those "used to seeing them as natural." She did this through an original use of humor, horrendous satire, and violence in two novels and a score of stories. Her work, first meeting with hostility and dismay, won wide literary acclaim in the United States and abroad, and within a decade she was accorded front rank and received many recognitions. Her first novel, *Wise Blood* (1952, reissued 1960), is the story of a lunatic-fringe preacher who tries to found a church without Christ. Preaching a progressive nihilism, he backs his way into the Cross. The novel parodies the atheistic existentialism then pervading the literary and philosophical scene. (*See* EXISTENTIALISM IN LITERATURE). In *A Good Man Is Hard To Find* (1955), a collection of ten of her stories, O'Connor created a new form of humor to bare "the distortions." She employed it perhaps nowhere with more impact than in the title story. There, what is apparently secular satire on the accidental encounter of a gabbling grandmother and her unlovely family with a psychotic criminal who calls himself the Misfit turns into a religious ordeal that brings the grandmother salvation, along with a bloody slaughter. The story of Jonas (with emphasis on the action at sea) provides the theme of her second novel, (*The Violent Bear It Away*, 1960) and, in variation, of a later story, *The Lame Shall Enter First*. These dramas probe deeply the theology of free will (which she viewed as a conflict of wills in the sinner) and freedom (which she called a mystery). Nine of her last stories appeared posthumously in *Everything That Rises Must Converge* (1965), confirming further that the violent themes of her works conceal an apocalypse for her time.

Bibliography: M. F. O'CONNOR, "The Lame Shall Enter First," *Sewanee Review* 70 (1962) 337–379. *Current Biography* (1958) 317–318. J. F. FARNHAM, "The Grotesque in the Novels of F. O'C.," *America* 105 (May 13, 1961).

[B. CHENEY]

O'CONNOR, MICHAEL

First bishop of Pittsburgh, Pa., diocese; b. Queenstown, Ireland, April 27, 1810; d. Woodstock, Md., Oct. 18, 1872. He was the eldest son of Charles and Ellen Kirk O'Connor and brother of Bp. James O'Connor, first bishop of Omaha, Nebr. Michael entered the College of Propaganda, Rome, in 1824, was ordained on June 1, 1833, and received his doctorate in 1834. He then became vice rector of the Irish College and professor of Scripture of the Propaganda College. His mother's death in 1834 led him to refuse the rectorship of St. Charles Seminary, Philadelphia, and he returned to Ireland to care for his family. While he was preparing for a professorship at the College of St. Patrick, Maynooth, the Philadelphia invitation was renewed in 1838. He accepted and was rector of St. Charles Seminary from 1839 until he went to Pittsburgh as vicar-general of the diocese in 1841. When his appointment as first bishop of Pittsburgh was pending in 1843, he hastened to Rome to ask permission to become a Jesuit. Pope Gregory XVI's answer was: "You will be a bishop first and a Jesuit afterwards." He was consecrated on Aug. 15, 1843.

During his episcopate the number of priests in Pittsburgh increased fivefold and the number of churches more than doubled. He opened a chapel for African Americans, founded the *Catholic,* a weekly diocesan newspaper, and built a cathedral. A number of religious communities, including the first Sisters of Mercy to establish a convent in the United States, were invited into the diocese. Two colleges and St. Michael's Seminary were opened. The bishop advocated the right of Catholic education to share in public funds and encouraged development of parish schools. In 1853 the diocese was divided and O'Connor was transferred to Erie, but a year later the Holy See, moved by petitions of the clergy and laity, restored him to Pittsburgh. His health began to fail, and he took long trips to Europe, the Near East, and the Caribbean.

He resigned his see in 1860 and entered the Jesuit novitiate at Gorheim, Sigmaringen, Germany. Two years later he made his solemn profession. At first assigned to Boston College in Massachusetts, O'Connor later became assistant to the Jesuit provincial of Maryland. As a Jesuit he was an active preacher, lecturer, and retreat master. In 1870 he went to London to consult physicians about his health and returned to the United States on the same ship that carried the future Cardinal Herbert Vaughan and the first Mill Hill missionaries to African Americans. His last public appearance was at the black church of St. Francis Xavier, Baltimore, which he had been instrumental in acquiring. He retired to Woodstock College, Maryland, six months before his death in 1872.

Although O'Connor excelled in theology and patristic studies, his busy life left little time for writing and he published nothing except some newspaper articles and printed lectures.

Bibliography: A. A. LAMBING, *A History of the Catholic Church in the Dioceses of Pittsburgh and Allegheny* (New York 1880). W. P. PURCELL, *Catholic Pittsburgh's One Hundred Years* (Chicago 1943).

[J. J. HENNESEY]

O'CONNOR, THOMAS FRANCIS

U.S. Catholic Church historian and bibliographer; b. Syracuse, N.Y., Aug. 14, 1899; d. St. Louis, Mo., Sept. 15, 1950. He received his B.A. (1922) from the College of the Holy Cross, Worcester, Massachusettes, and his M.A. (1927) from Syracuse University. He taught at Little Rock University, Arkansas (1928–30); St. Louis University, Missouri (1931–37, 1948–50); and St. Michael's College, Winooski Park, Vermont (1937–39). He served for a time after 1941 as historiographer of the Diocese of Syracuse and was historiographer of the Archdiocese of New York from 1944 to 1948. Although O'Connor had a vast store of knowledge of the bibliography and history of the church in the U.S., he left practically no notes. Vollmar's *Catholic Church in America* (2d ed. New York 1963) lists 24 titles published by O'Connor in various historical journals. He was active in various historical societies and was president of the American Catholic Historical Association (1946–47). His early and unexpected death was caused by a hemorrhage resulting from a longstanding tubercular condition.

[E. R. VOLLMAR]

OCTOECHOS

In Byzantine music the term Octoechos (Gr. ὀκτώ, eight, and ἦχος, mode) has two distinct though closely allied meanings. In general it refers to the system of eight modes that forms the compositional framework of Byzantine ecclesiastical music: four authentic and four plagal modes, as in Western chant. More particularly it designates a collection of proper hymns, chiefly for the Morning and Evening Services, providing an entire set of such pieces for each mode. The collection was designed for performance in cycles of eight weeks: in the 1st week (beginning after Easter) the hymns of Mode I Authentic would be used, in the second week the hymns of Mode II Authentic, and so on, until after the completion of the modal series the cycle recommenced with Mode I. Thus the Octoechos, taken in conjunction with the hymns of

feasts fixed by the calendar, and those of the Lenten and Easter seasons, made provision for music throughout the church year. In its earlier form it comprised pieces for the Sundays only; later additions supplied hymns for the weekdays as well, the whole compilation receiving the name of Great Octoechos (ἡ μεγάλη Ὀκτώηχος) or Parakletike (Παρακλητική).

Origins. The origins of the system, as of the collection based upon it, are obscure. It appears to owe little if anything directly to the classical and Hellenistic Greek tonal system, despite the assignation of classical names to modes of the Octoechos by some medieval Byzantine theorists. Attempts by modern scholars to trace it to the musical vestiges or cosmological beliefs of earlier Near Eastern peoples are speculative at best. Even the time of its appearance in Christian hymnody cannot be determined with any precision. An 11th-century text of the *Plerophoriai* of John of Maiuma (*c.* 515) contains an allusion to "music of the Octoechos," but its authenticity is questionable. Grave doubt attaches also to the oft-repeated assertion that a hymn collection of the same period, the work of SEVERUS OF ANTIOCH (512–19), was an Octoechos. The sole surviving MSS of this collection present it in Syriac translation, and the earliest of these MSS, more than a century and a half later than the presumed original, shows no sign of an arrangement according to mode; only in much later copies does such a categorization exist. In any case it seems that the eight-mode system had become established within the Greek liturgical world by the end of the 7th century. To cite one piece of evidence: a papyrus fragment no later than early 8th century gives a modal sign—though no other musical notation—for the hymns it preserves. Byzantine tradition ascribed the composition of the Octoechos, or at least a large part of its Sunday nucleus, to St. JOHN DAMASCENE (*c.* 750). In its generality the attribution is certainly dubious, but it may contain some element of historical fact. The very earliest musical MSS (10th century) have "John the Monk" as author of the canons of the Octoechos; and the initial letters of another set of Sunday hymns form the word Ἰωάννου (of John)—this sort of acrostic signature is traditional in Byzantine hymnology. But even if the identity of this "John" with the Damascene were assured, whether he was in any sense the composer of the music that the MSS convey would remain doubtful—and this is true generally of the poets to whom hymns are ascribed. In the 9th century, after the resolution of the iconoclastic controversy, the Octoechos was completed by the addition of the weekday hymns, the work of monks of the STUDION monastery in Constantinople—in particular Joseph the Hymnographer (883). The final canon in the series has as its acrostic τῆς Ὀκτωήχου τῆς νέας θεῖον τέλος (the divine conclusion of the New Oktoechos), perhaps the earliest known instance of the term's referring unambiguously to a corpus of hymns. Not until much later does the word occur as heading of a separate MS or section of a MS.

The Modes in Their Technical Aspects. As for the musical system itself, the songs from every particular mode are composed largely from a restricted set of melodic formulas characteristic of that mode. These formulas may be employed in many different combinations and variations; nevertheless, most of the phrases of any given hymn are reducible to one or another of this small number of basic melody-fragments. (For formulas of Mode I as they are exemplified in a selection of phrases from a number of hymns, see E. Wellesz, *A History of Byzantine Music and Hymnography* [2d ed. Oxford 1961] app. V.)

The church music belonging to various peoples, such as the Serbs, the Armenians, the Syrians, and the Copts, as found in our own times, exhibits analogous modal systems, depending in the same fashion on melodic formulae—the specific formulae, of course, differing from one musical culture to another. (No musical documentation from the Byzantine period exists for any of these peoples; there are, e.g., medieval Armenian musical MSS, but their notation is undecipherable.) Study of these modal systems has led some scholars to conclude that, in such a system, each mode is defined simply by its characteristic melody patterns, rather than by some abstract scale pattern: the latter sort of definition was the subsequent rationalization of theorists. Byzantine theory in its full development did provide such a rationalization; and the system thus defined appears to be essentially identical to that of Latin plainchant. This conclusion is suggested by the medieval Latin practice of assigning Greek number names to the Latin modes; it is confirmed by Wellesz' publication of a hymn whose Greek text had been translated into Latin, and whose music appears substantially the same in both kinds of notation. The total range of the system (with rare extensions) covers what is represented in modern transcription as the two-octave white-key gamut *a–a"*. Within this, Mode I Authentic has an approximate range of *d–d'*, with finalis on *a'* or *d*; Mode II Authentic, *e–e'*, with finalis on *b'* or *e*; Mode III Authentic, *f–f'*, with finalis on *c'* or *f*; Mode IV Authentic, *g–g'*, with finalis on *d'* or *g*. The plagal modes have ranges lying a fourth below the numerically corresponding authentic; they use only the lower finalis of the two found in the corresponding authentic modes. This diatonic system remained the basis of Byzantine music down to the 17th and 18th centuries, when it disappeared, along with the entire repertory embodying it, under the Turkish influence, leaving only the texts and the modal assignations as they had been in medieval times. For a categorization

of the contents of the Octoechos as a musical service-book, see Tillyard.

Bibliography: E. WELLESZ, *Eastern Elements in Western Chant* (Monumenta Musicae Byzantinae 1; Oxford 1947); "Die Struktur der servischen Oktoëchos," *Zeitschrift für Musikwissenschaft* 2 (1919) 140–48. H. J. W. TILLYARD, *The Hymns of the Octoechus*, 2 v. (Monumenta Musicae Byzantinae 3, 5; Oxford 1940, 1952). J. JEANNIN and J. PUYADE, "L'Octoëchos syrien," *Oriens Christianus* NS 3 (1913) 82–104, 277–98. A. BAUMSTARK, *Festbrevier und Kirchenjahr der syrischen Jakobiten* (Paderborn 1910). E. W. BROOKS, "The Hymns of Severus," *Patrologia orientalis*, ed. R. GRAFFIN and F. NAU (Paris 1903–) 6:1–179; 7:593–803. F. NAU, "Jean Rufus, évêque de Maïouma: Plérophories," ibid. 8:1–208. L. TARDO, *L'Ottoeco nei MSS. melurgici* (Grottaferrata 1955). Παρακλητικὴ ἤτοι Ὀκτώηχος ἡ μεγάλη (Rome 1885); Ὀκτώηχος (Rome 1886). O. STRUNK, "The Tonal System of Byzantine Music," *Musical Quarterly* 28 (1942) 190–204; "The Antiphons of the Oktoechos," *Journal of the American Musicological Society* 18 (1960) 50–67.

[I. THOMAS/EDS.]

O'CULLENAN, GELASIUS (GLAISNE)

Order of Cîteaux, abbot of Boyle, Co. Roscommon, Ireland; b. probably at Mullaghshee near Ballyshannon, Co. Donegal, 1554; d. Dublin, Nov. 21, 1580. He was the eldest of seven sons of whom six became ecclesiastics, five being Cistercians. At an early age Glaisne entered the monastery, completed his novitiate and theological studies at Paris, and eventually became a doctor of the Sorbonne. Having visited Rome, he returned to Ireland, where he was made abbot of the suppressed Abbey of Boyle. There he carried on his sacred ministry until his arrest in 1580 with Eoghan O Maoilchiarain, Premonstratensian abbot of Holy Trinity in Loch Cé. Imprisoned in Dublin Castle, they were tortured and, having refused to conform, were sentenced to death and executed. Glaisne's near-contemporary, the Cistercian Menologist Chrysostomus Henriquez, called O'Cullenan "the ornament of the Cistercian Order, the splendour of our age, and the glory of all Ireland." Glaisne's name is included in the list of Irish martyrs awaiting beatification.

See Also: IRISH CONFESSORS AND MARTYRS.

Bibliography: C. HENRIQUEZ, *Menologium Cisterciense* (Antwerp 1630). M. HARTRY, *Triumphalia chronologica Monasterii Sanctae Crucis in Hibernia*, ed. D. MURPHY (Dublin 1895). J. MACENLEAN, "Eoin Ó Cuileannáin . . . ," *Archivium Hibernicum* 1 (1912) 77–121.

[C. S. Ó CONBHUÍ]

O'DALY, DANIEL

Priest and diplomat; b. Kilsarkon, County Kerry, Ireland 1595; d. Lisbon, June 30, 1662. His father, Conchubhar, was a bard and soldier of Gerald, earl of Desmond, his mother an O'Keefe from Duhallow barony. He entered the Dominicans in his youth and because of the persecution in Ireland, he was educated in Spain, studying first in Lugo, then in Burgos, where he was ordained. After further studies he returned to Emly diocese as a "fugitive" priest. He was recalled to Louvain to teach in the newly erected college for Irish Dominicans and he became superior in 1624. While raising funds in Madrid, he obtained Philip IV's consent to begin the College of Corpo Santo at Lisbon, a foundation similar to that of Louvain. He later founded the convent of Bom Sucesso for Irish-born Dominican nuns at Belem in Lisbon, in return for which concession he recruited a body of Irish soldiery for Spanish service in the Low Countries. With the restoration of the Portuguese monarchy (1640), he was appointed confessor to Luiza de Guzman, wife of the new king, John of Braganza. Several diplomatic missions followed: in 1649, to Charles Stuart at Jersey; in 1650 a secret mission to Pope Innocent X concerning the nomination of Portuguese bishops then being blocked by Spain; in 1655 to France first as envoy, then as accredited ambassador to negotiate financial and military help. After King John's death (1656), O'Daly acted as chief adviser to the widow-regent. He also helped to negotiate a matrimonial alliance between Charles II of England and Catherine of Braganza. He refused nomination to the archbishopric of Goa, but he was eventually nominated bishop of Coimbra in 1662 by the regent who had previously endowed Corpo Santo when it needed expansion. He died as bishop-elect and was buried in Corpo Santo, where a slab bearing his inscription is preserved despite the 1755 earthquake. Both his foundations survive to the present day. His Latin history of the Geraldines was published in 1655, *Initium, incrementum et exitus Geraldinorum,* with an appendix on religious persecution in 17th-century Ireland. The work, though slight, has merit and was translated into French by Abbé Joubert in 1697 and into English by C. P. Meehan, Dublin, 1847.

Bibliography: D. O'DALY, *History of the Geraldines,* tr. C. P. MEEHAN (2d ed. Dublin 1878); MSS in Bom Sucesso Convent, and in National Archives, Lisbon. T. DE BURGO, *Hibernia Dominicana* (Kilkenny 1762). M. A. O'CONNELL, *For Faith and Fatherland* (Dublin 1888). E. PRESTAGE, *The Diplomatic Relations of Portugal with France, England, and Holland from 1640 to 1688* (Watford 1925); *Frei Domingos do Rosário (D. O'Daly) diplomata e politico* (Coimbra 1926).

[M. B. MACCURTAIN]

O'DANIEL, VICTOR FRANCIS

Educator, historian; b. Cecilville, Ky., Feb. 15, 1868; d. Washington, D.C., June 12, 1960. His parents, Richard Jefferson and Sarah Ann (Hamilton) O'Daniel, sent him to public and parochial schools near Cecilville. He then studied at St. Rose Priory, Springfield, Ky., where he entered the Order of Preachers on March 21, 1886, and at St. Joseph's Priory, Somerset, Ohio. After ordination on June 16, 1891, at Columbus, Ohio, he took further studies in theology (1893–95) at the Dominican house of studies at Louvain, Belgium, and received the lectorate in theology. Upon returning to the United States, he was professor of theology at St. Rose's and St. Joseph's priories (1895–1901), and at the Dominican houses of study in Benicia, Calif. (1901–06) and Washington, D.C. (1906–13). He held the office of novice master for various periods during his teaching career.

As first archivist of St. Joseph's province, a post he held from 1907 to 1960, O'Daniel organized the Dominican archives in Washington, assembling a valuable collection of materials, much of which would otherwise have been lost. In 1909, when the order awarded him a master's degree in theology, he did extensive research in Europe, especially in the Dominican archives in Rome. He devoted himself exclusively to historical work after 1913. In 1915, with Peter GUILDAY, he was cofounder of the *Catholic Historical Review* and was an associate editor from 1921 to 1927. In addition to the historical studies which he wrote for this journal, O'Daniel's works include *The Dominican Province of St. Joseph: Historical-Biographical Studies* (1930), *The Dominicans in Early Florida* (1942), and biographies of such Dominicans as Edward D. Fenwick, Charles H. McKenna, and Richard Pius Miles.

Bibliography: W. ROMIG, ed., *The Book of Catholic Authors* 4th ser. (Grosse Pointe, Mich. 1947). "V. F. O'Daniel," *Dominicana* 26 (1941) 111–112, 237–243; 45 (1960) 283–284.

[W. A. HINNEBUSCH]

ODDI, DIEGO, BL.

Baptized Giuseppe; Franciscan lay brother; b. June 6, 1839, Vallinfreda near Rome; d. June 3, 1919, Bellegra, Italy. Born into a poor family, Giuseppe Oddi labored in the fields rather than attend school. At age twenty, he felt a mysterious spiritual calling and responded by praying each evening before the Blessed Sacrament. Shortly thereafter (1860) he made a pilgrimage to the Bellegra (Rome) hermitage of St. Francis of Assisi, where he was deeply impressed by the prayer life of the brothers. He returned in 1864 and was met by Mariano da ROCCACASALE (1778–1866; beatified with Oddi), who helped Oddi discern his vocation. Overcoming his parents' objections, Oddi entered the friary at Bellegra as a tertiary oblate (1871), but later professed solemn vows

(1889). During his forty years as a brother, he begged alms throughout the Subiaco region. A miracle attributed to Brother Diego's intercession was approved April 6, 1998, leading to his beatification by Pope John Paul II on Oct. 3, 1999.

Feast: June 6 (Franciscans).

Bibliography: *Acta Apostolicae Sedis* 19 (1999): 965. *L'Osservatore Romano,* Eng. ed. 40 (1999): 1–3; 41 (1999): 2.

[K. I. RABENSTEIN]

ODERISIUS, BL.

Abbot and cardinal; d. Dec. 2, 1104. He was descended from the family of the counts of Marsi, educated at the Abbey of MONTE CASSINO under Abbot Richer (d. 1055), and created cardinal in 1059. He served as prior of Monte Cassino under Abbot Desiderius, later Pope VICTOR III, and succeeded him as abbot in 1087. Oderisius governed Monte Cassino in the same spirit as his predecessor and completed the great buildings that Desiderius had begun. He became involved in Byzantine-German politics, but apparently without prejudice to his primary loyalty to the apostolic see. An author himself, Oderisius was a friend of scholarship and encouraged LEO MARSICANUS to begin his chronicle.

Feast: Dec. 2.

Bibliography: *Monumenta Germaniae Historica: Scriptores* 7:912. L. TOSTI, *Storia della badia di Monte-Cassino,* 3 v. (Rome 1842–43) 2:4–23. A. M. ZIMMERMANN, *Kalendarium Benedictinum: Die Heiligen und Seligen des Benediktinerorderns und seiner Zweige* (Metten 1933–38) 3:384–385. A. M. ZIMMERMANN, *Lexikon für Theologie und Kirche* (Freiburg 1957–65) 7:1095–96.

[B. D. HILL]

O'DEVANY, CONOR, BL.

Bishop of Down and Connor, martyr; b. *c.* 1553; d. Dublin, Feb. 11, 1612. He entered the Franciscan Friary of Donegal (date unknown) and was consecrated bishop of Down and Connor Feb. 1, 1583. In 1587 O'Devany (or Conor) was one of the Irish prelates who met in the Diocese of Clogher, where the decrees of the Council of Trent were promulgated. In 1588 he was arrested and confined in Dublin Castle, but two years later he was released by W. Fitzwilliam, the lord deputy, since "the law at present does not authorize the execution of the prisoner and the only charge against him is the exercise of spiritual authority." In 1591 he was granted special ecclesiastical faculties by Cardinal William ALLEN because of his piety and zeal. He also collected materials on the lives of those who were persecuted for the faith. These were later included in the *Analecta nova et mira* by David Rothe, Bishop of Ossory from 1617 to 1619 (ed. P. Moran, Dublin 1884). In 1605 O'Devany was accused by spies of visiting the pope and the king of Spain at the request of Hugh O'Neill, and was again arrested and imprisoned. There he remained until his trial for high treason in 1611. Found guilty, he was sentenced to be hanged, drawn, and quartered. Two ministers accompanied the bishop to the scaffold, offering him bribes if he would renounce his faith. There he was executed together with a secular priest, Patrick O'Loughran (*see* IRISH CONFESSORS AND MARTYRS). O'Devany was beatified on Sept. 27, 1992.

Bibliography: J. T. GILBERT, *The Dictionary of National Biography from the Earliest Times to 1900,* 63 v. (London 1885–1900) 14:864–865. D. MURPHY, *Our Martyrs* (Dublin 1896), bibliog.

[L. MCKEOWN]

ODILIA, ST.

Abbess and patroness of Alsace, also called Adilia, Othilia, Ottilia; b. *c.* 660; d. *c.* 720. The daughter of Attich (d. *c.* 700), duke of Alsace, Odilia was first abbess of the convent of Hohenburg (MONT SAINTE-ODILE) and foundress of Niedermünster. According to a 10th–century vita of questionable reliability, written probably at Mont Sainte–Odile (Odilienberg), she was born blind and taken secretly to a convent, possibly Baume-les-Dames, to escape the wrath of her father. It is reported that she miraculously received her sight when St. ERHARD baptized her, and this extraordinary incident accounts for the portrayal of the saint holding a book on which two eyes are lying. Her cult is very old and widespread; her name was inserted into the Litany of All Saints as early as the ninth century. Odilia is invoked as the patroness of those afflicted with diseases of the eye, and the collect of the Mass for her feast day likewise recalls the saint's cure from blindness and prays that through Odilia's intercession the faithful may turn their eyes from earthly vanity to God.

Feast: Dec. 13.

Bibliography: *Monumenta Germaniae Historica Scriptores rerum Merovingicarum* (Berlin 1826–) 6:24–50. A. M. ZIMMERMANN, *Kalendarium Benedictinum: Die Heiligen und Seligen des Benediktinerorderns und seiner Zweige* (Metten 1933–38) 3:424–427. A. BUTLER, *The Lives of the Saints,* ed. H. THURSTON and D. ATTWATER (New York 1956) 4:551–553. M. COENS, *Analecta Bollandiana* 54 (1936) 20, 27; 55 (1937) 68. A. BURG, *Histoire de l'Église d'Alsace* (Colmar 1946). A. SCHÜTTE, *Handbuch der deutschen Heiligen* (Cologne 1941) 272. J. BILLING, *Die Heiligen der Diözese Strassburg* (Colmar 1957) 25–31. C. RIFFENACH and F. ALLEMANN, *Odile d'Alsace* (Strasbourg 1985). L. MANCINELLI, *Il* *miracolo di Santa Odilia* (Turin 1989). G. TRENDEL and M. VOGT, *Le Mont Sainte-Odile, trange et sacr.* (Strasbourg 1992). J. L. BAUDOT and L. CHAUSSIN, *Vies des saints et des bienheureux selon l'ordre du calendrier avec l'historique des fêtes* (Paris 1935–56) 12: 413–417. L. RÉAU, *Iconographie de l'art chrétien* (Paris 1955–59) 3:999–1003.

[H. DRESSLER]

ODILO OF CLUNY, ST.

Fifth abbot of Cluny; b. Auvergne, France, 962; d. Abbey of Souvigny, Jan. 1, 1049. He was a member of the Mercoeur family who became a cleric at Saint-Julien in Brioude and later requested the monastic habit at CLUNY, which at that time was governed by (St.) MAJOLUS OF CLUNY, fourth abbot there. Odilo, chosen by Majolus as coadjutor in 991, was the acting abbot by 994 and showed immediately his outstanding qualities of leadership and organization. His 50 years as abbot (999–1049) were characterized by an ever-growing number of Cluniac daughter houses and properties grouped into an ''order'' under his firm authority (*see* CLUNIAC REFORM). This formation of an ''order'' was one of the consequences of EXEMPTION, for Cluny centralized under itself all monasteries that had received the privilege of temporal immunity and exemption from episcopal power granted by GREGORY V in 998 or 999, and confirmed by Pope JOHN XIX in 1027. The papacy always upheld the monks of Cluny in any resulting conflicts of jurisdiction, for it recognized clearly the importance of monasticism in strengthening papal authority, in fighting SIMONY (*see* GREGORIAN REFORM), and in spreading Christianity, e.g., in Spain.

Odilo's diplomatic activity is well known. He received the imperial insignia from Emperor HENRY II, to whom he had been counselor since 1002. Cluny listed Henry in the necrology of the abbey after the emperor's death in 1024. Odilo was equally loyal to the Capetian monarchy; he was able to be the mediator between Emperor CONRAD II and the king of France, Robert II, in 1025. Such political activity shows that Cluny and its abbots were not basically opposed to seignorialism, even if relations between Odilo and Emperor Henry III were less than cordial.

About 1030 to 1031 the abbot established the commemoration of ALL SOULS' DAY for his own monastery and dependent houses. This was later adopted by the universal Church. In 1041 Odilo favored the extension of the Truce of God. He was always concerned with helping the poor, going so far as to sell the holy treasures of the monastery during a famine in 1033. Odilo pursued the building of Cluny to such an extent that his biographer

Jotsaldus [ed. F. Ermini, *Studi medievali* 1 (1928) 401–405] wrote that he had ''renewed everything at Cluny except the walls of the church'' (*see* CLUNIAC ART AND ARCHITECTURE). About 1042 the abbey was inhabited by about 75 religious.

His writings include *Vita S. Maioli* (Marrier-Duchesne, 279–290; *Patrologia Latina* 142:943–962), *Epitaphium Adalheidae* (Marrier-Duchesne, 353–369; *Monumenta Germaniae Historica Scriptores* 4:633–645), letters (Marrier-Duchesne, 349–354; *Patrologia Latina* 142: 939–944), sermons (Marrier-Duchesne, 371–408; *Patrologia Latina* 142: 991–1036), and *Medicina spiritualis contra temptationem concupiscentiae carnalis* (ed. G. Morin, *Revue Bénédictine* 16 [1899] 477–478). He wrote also a hymn in honor of St. Majolus, *Maiolus pater inclitus* (ed. G. Morin, *Revue Bénédictine* 38 [1926] 56). Other hymns are found in *Patrologia Latina* 142:961–964 and *Analecta hymnica* 50 (1907) 297–301; several fragments are in *Patrologia Latina* 142:1035–38.

Odilo died after one of his numerous trips to Italy, and was succeeded by HUGH OF CLUNY. He was canonized in 1063.

Feast: Jan. 1 (French Benedictines); April 29 (general).

Bibliography: Works. *Bibliotheca cluniacensis,* ed. M. MARRIER and A. DUCHESNE (Paris 1614; repr. Mâcon 1915). *Patrologia Latina,* ed. J. P. MIGNE, 217 v. (Paris 1878–90). A. BRUEL, ed., *Recueil des chartes de l'abbaye de Cluny,* 6 v. (Paris 1876–1903) 3:190–821; 4:1–174, 825–827. **Literature.** M. MANITIUS, *Geschichte der lateinischen Literatur des Mittelalters,* 3 v. (Munich 1911–13), 2:138–142. B. BLIGNY, *L'Église et les ordres religieux dans le royaume de Bourgogne aux XIᵉ et XIIᵉ siècles* (Grenoble 1960). J. HOURLIER, *Saint Odilon, abbé de Cluny* (Louvain 1964). P. CHAUDAGNE, *Saint Odilon* (Souvigny 1972).

[R. GRÉGOIRE]

ODIN, JOHN MARY

U.S. missionary bishop; b. Ambierle, France, Feb. 25, 1801; d. there, May 25, 1870. He was the seventh of ten children born of Jean and Claudine (Seyrol) Odin. After some preliminary schooling with a priest uncle in Nosilly, he pursued studies at the colleges of L'Argentière and Alix. While in the Seminary of Saint-Sulpice in Lyons, he heard of the need for priests in Louisiana from a missionary bishop, Louis William DUBOURG. At 22, as a subdeacon, he came to the Mississippi Valley, entered the seminary at the Barrens near St. Louis, Mo., and joined the Congregation of the Mission. Having completed his novitiate, he was ordained by Bishop Dubourg on May 4, 1823. The young priest engaged in missionary work in Missouri, Arkansas, and Texas. He also served as professor and president of the Barrens seminary, pastor at Cape Girardeau, and theologian at the Second Provincial Council of Baltimore. At 40, he was appointed vice prefect to Very Rev. John TIMON, CM, in Texas. Odin won the esteem of the Texans; during the first session of the fifth congress of the Texas Republic, the legislature requested him to act as chaplain of the senate. On April 16, 1841, he received a brief appointing him titular bishop of Claudiopolis and coadjutor-administrator of the American Northwest with see in Detroit. On the advice of Timon, he declined and returned the bulls to Rome. By briefs dated July 16, 1841, Gregory XVI raised Texas from prefecture to vicariate apostolic, confirmed Odin in the See of Claudiopolis, and named him vicar apostolic in Texas. Bishop Antoine Blanc consecrated him in St. Louis Cathedral, New Orleans. Following the Baltimore Council of 1846, the former Republic of Texas became a diocese with Galveston as the see city. Odin, the first bishop, consecrated St. Mary's Cathedral there on Nov. 26, 1848. In 1852 he reported that his diocese had 25 priests serving 30 churches and twice as many mission stations. Nine years later, before leaving for New Orleans, he showed on his inventory 46 churches and 46 priests, including the Oblates of Mary Immaculate whom he had brought to the diocese.

The Mexican War was fought while Odin was ordinary in Texas; the Civil War was raging when he arrived as archbishop in New Orleans (see NEW ORLEANS, ARCHDIOCESE OF). Despite war and Reconstruction, he managed to continue the work of his predecessor, Archbishop Blanc, and to expand it by inviting six communities of men and women to the archdiocese. He was particularly successful in recruiting clerics while he was on a trip to Europe during the height of the Civil War and, despite the blockade of New Orleans, personally escorted nearly 50 priests and seminarians who had volunteered to labor in Louisiana and Texas. Odin had chartered for their transportation a passenger ship, the *Ste. Genevieve,* which was nicknamed ''the floating seminary,'' and which landed at New Orleans on Good Friday, April 3, 1863. Although considerate of his priests in both Texas and Louisiana, he was regarded as a strict disciplinarian. He held synods in the two dioceses over which he presided. From the content of these synodal regulations and from the tenor of his pastoral letters, it is evident that he countenanced no abuses of ecclesiastical discipline and dealt promptly with infractions. During the Civil War, Odin was the Holy Father's contact in the South, as Abp. John Hughes was intermediary in the North. Odin's problems following the war were aggravated by the attitude of priests and people toward African Americans, who, as slaves, had been admitted to churches and the Sacraments

but who, once freed, were made to feel less than welcome at services. The archbishop promptly appealed to various religious communities to assign men and women religious for special ministration to blacks and for the education of their children, but antipathy was so intense that none heeded his request until 1867 when St. Joseph's School in Convent, La., was opened under the auspices of the Religious of the Sacred Heart. Another aftermath of the war was the closing of the diocesan seminary in Faubourg Bouligny because of lack of funds.

Odin accepted the invitation of Pius IX to attend the 18th centenary of the martyrdom of St. Peter in 1867 and in 1869–70 Vatican Council I. Prior to the latter event, the archbishop had asked for a coadjutor and on May 1, 1870, Napoleon Joseph Perché, his vicar-general, was consecrated in St. Louis Cathedral. Less than a month later, having left Rome because of the precarious condition of his health, Odin died.

Bibliography: J. D. G. SHEA, *A History of the Catholic Church within the Limits of the United States,* 4 v. (New York 1886–92) v.4. M. A. FITZMORRIS, *Four Decades of Catholicism in Texas, 1820–1860* (Washington 1926).

[H. C. BEZOU]

ODO OF CAMBRAI, BL.

Also known as Odo of Tournai, bishop, philosopher, and theologian whose teaching at Toul and Tournai gave a new impetus to realism; b. Orléans, France, 1050; d. Abbey of Anchin, near Arras, June 19, 1113. He was chosen bishop of Cambrai in 1095. He introduced the CLUNIAC REFORM into his monastery of SAINT-MARTIN at Tournai. His principal work, *De peccato originali,* used an exaggerated realism to explain the transmission of original sin. Other extant writings, theological in nature, include a treatise on the Canon of the Mass, a dialogue with a Jew adducing philosophical reasons for Christ's coming, a short treatise on final impenitence, and a Gospel harmony.

Feast: June 19.

Bibliography: F. LABIS, ''Le Bx. Odon, évêque de Cambrai . . . ,'' *Revue Catholique de Louvain* 14 (1856) 445–460, 519–526, 574–585. M. DE WULF, *Histoire de la philosophie en Belgique* (Brussels 1910) 24–32. É. AMANN, *Dictionnaire de théologie catholique,* ed. A. VACANT, 15 v. (Paris 1903–50; Tables générales 1951–) 11.1:931–935. C. DEREINE, ''O. de Tournai et la crise du cénobitisme au XIe siècle,'' *Revue du moyen-âge latin* 4 (1948) 137–154. T. GREGORY, ''La Dottrina del peccato originale e il realismo platonico: O. di T.,'' *Platonismo medievale: Studi e Richerche* (Rome 1958) 31–51.

[M. I. J. ROUSSEAU]

ODO (ODA) OF CANTERBURY, ST.

Archbishop of CANTERBURY; d. June 2, 958. Odo, called ''the Good,'' was born of pagan Danish parents but brought up by a thane of King ALFRED. King Athelstan made him bishop of Ramsbury in 927 and employed him as ambassador to Hugh Capet, duke of the Franks. In 942 King Edmund offered him the See of Canterbury, which he accepted only after receiving the Benedictine habit from Fleury. As archbishop he restored Elmham as a separate bishopric for East Anglia, ordered his bishops to make annual visitations of their dioceses, and made the building of parish churches part of his church reform. He ordered ten chapters dealing with morals and ecclesiastical discipline to be drawn up. Although not enacted by a synod, ''Odo's *Chapters* are the only 10th-century ordinances of the same category as synodal acts and related sources.'' The *Chapters* are drawn largely from the Legatine Councils of 786. Odo also encouraged Frithegode to write a metrical *Life of St. Wilfrid of York.* Odo's cult was observed at Canterbury, where his name appears in calendars of Christ Church (Henry Bradshaw Society 72: 175; 77:73).

Feast: July 4 (formerly June 2).

Bibliography: Sources. G. SCHOEBE, ''The Chapters of Archbishop Oda (942/6) and the Canons of the Legatine Councils of 786,'' *Bulletin of the Institute of Historical Research* 35 (1962) 75–83. EADMER OF CANTERBURY, *Vita sancti Odonis, Patrologia Latina* 133:933–944 (erroneously ascribed to Osbern of Canterbury). ''Vita sancti Oswaldi'' in *The Historians of the Church of York and Its Archbishops,* ed. J. RAINE (*Rerum Britannicarum medii aevi scriptores*) 71.1:399–475. WILLIAM OF MALMESBURY, *Gesta pontificum anglorum,* ed. N. E. S. A. HAMILTON (*Rerum Britannicarum medii aevi scriptores*) 52:20–24, 30, 248. Literature. W. HUNT, *The Dictionary of National Biography from the Earliest Times to 1900,* 14:866–868. R. R. DARLINGTON, ''Ecclesiastical Reform in the Late Old English Period,'' *English Historical Review* 51 (1936) 385–428. F. M. STENTON, *Anglo-Saxon England* (2d ed. Oxford 1947) 342, 352–353, 360–362, 431, 442. M. DEANESLY, *The Pre-Conquest Church in England* (New York 1961). R. W. SOUTHERN, *Saint Anselm and His Biographer* (New York 1963).

[B. W. SCHOLZ]

ODO OF CHÂTEAUROUX

French cardinal, known also as *Odo de Castro Radulphi;* b. Champagne *c.* 1208; d. Orvieto, Jan. 26, 1273. He studied at the University of Paris where he became a master in theology in 1230 and where he undoubtedly taught for some time. In 1234 he was a canon of Paris; in 1238 he was promoted to the chancellorship of the University, but resigned in order to enter the CISTERCIANS at Grandselve. Innocent IV named him to succeed JACQUES DE VITRY as cardinal bishop of Frascati in 1244,

and in October 1245 he went to France as papal legate to preach the Sixth CRUSADE. While there he condemned John of Brescia's theses on light (Dec. 21, 1247) and the Talmud (May 15, 1248). He was a great friend of King LOUIS IX and during the Crusade (1248–54) accompanied him to Egypt and Palestine where Odo was able to pacify the quarrels of the Frankish lords. Back in Italy by 1254 he presided at Anagni (July 1255) over the commission examining the *Liber introductorius in evangelium eternum* written by Gerard de Borgo San Donnino, a work subsequently condemned by Alexander IV. He was sent as legate to Limoges in 1264 but lived most of the rest of his life in Italy. Many sermons and theological works are attributed to Odo. Although it is doubtful that he wrote either a commentary on Jeremiah or the *Conciones et homiliae de tempore et de sanctis,* he is credited with a letter written at Cyprus in 1249, which is a kind of journal of the Crusade. Odo's fame derives more from his active life than from his writings.

Bibliography: Sources. *Chartularium universitatis Parisiensis* 1:202–211. J. B. PITRA, *Analecta novissima spicilegii Solesmensis,* 2 v. (Paris 1885–88) 2:188–343. F. GRATIEN, ''Sermons franciscains . . . ,'' *Études franciscaines* 29 (1913) 171–195, 647–655. A. WALZ, ''Odonis de Castro Radulphi . . . sermones sex . . . ,'' *Analecta Sacri Ordinis Praedicatorum* 17 (1925–26) 174–223. M. M. DAVY, ed., *Les Sermons universitaires . . .* (Paris 1931). J. LECLERCQ, ''Le Sermon sur la royauté . . . ,'' *Archives d'histoire doctrinale et littéraire du moyen-âge* 18 (1943) 143–180. Literature. P. C. F. DAUNOU, *Histoire littéraire de la France* 19:228–232. É. AMANN, *Dictionnaire de théologie catholique* 11.1:935–936. P. GLORIEUX, *Répertoire des maîtres en théologie de Paris au XIIIᵉ siècle* 1:304–311. M. M. LEBRETON, *Dictionnaire de spiritualité ascétique et mystique* 4.2:1675–78.

[É. BROUETTE]

ODO OF CLUNY, ST.

Second abbot of Cluny; b. Aquitaine, *c.* 879; d. Tours, Nov. 18, 942. He was the son of Ebbo I, Lord of Déols, who dedicated him to St. MARTIN OF TOURS. Odo received his early education at the court of Duke William of Aquitaine and then studied the liberal arts at Tours and at Paris under REMIGIUS OF AUXERRE. After having received the tonsure at 19, Odo lived an austere and industrious life as canon of St. Martin of Tours. Under the direction of Bl. BERNO, he became a monk at Baume, a Cluniac monastery, where he was a master at the age of 30. His humility won the confidence of Berno, first abbot of CLUNY, who had him ordained, and then in 927 elected as his successor as abbot of Cluny. While abbot, Odo received 188 deeds of donation. By March 931 Pope JOHN XI granted Cluny the privilege of exemption and authorized Odo to reform so many monasteries in Gaul and Italy that the medieval chronicler FLODOARD OF REIMS called Odo ''the restorer of monasteries and of the Holy Rule.'' Odo was the initiator of the Cluniac monastic observance, the *ordo cluniacensis* (*see* CLUNIAC REFORM). Struck by the deplorable state of the Church in his day, Odo insisted upon the value of the monastic life to the Church: the ''apostolic life'' of the monks was a continuation of the renewal and purification begun at Pentecost. Both LEO VII in 936 and 939, and STEPHEN VIII in 941, entrusted him with the peace negotiations in those Italian conflicts that involved the interest of the Roman Church. Odo fell sick in Rome and returned to Tours where he died, having already designated Aymard as his successor at Cluny. Odo's relics are kept at l'Isle-Jourdain (Gers). His literary work includes the *Moralia in Job*, a résumé of the *Moralia* of Gregory I the Great [*Patrologia Latina*, ed. J. P. Migne (Paris 1878–90) 133:107–152]; *Collationes*, conferences or lectures where Odo's patristic and humanistic culture is particularly apparent (*Patrologia Latina* 133:517–638); *Occupatio*, a poem in seven books, which is a meditation on sacred history (ed. A. Svoboda, Leipzig 1900); *Vita s. Geraldi Auriliacensis comitis* (*Patrologia Latina* 133:639–704); and the *Vita Gregorii Turonensis episcopi* (*Patrologia Latina* 133:513–516). He wrote 12 anthems and four hymns in honor of St. Martin, as well as the hymn *De corpore Christi* [*Patrologia Latina* 133:513–516, *Analecta Hymnica* 50 (Leipzig 1907) 265–270]. The musical works attributed to Odo (*Patrologia Latina* 133:755–816) are probably apocryphal.

Feast: Nov. 18 (French Benedictine Congregation), April 29 (Benedictine Order).

Bibliography: Sources. M. MARRIER and A. DUCHESNE, eds., *Bibliotheca cluniacensis* (Paris 1614; repr. 1915). *Patrologia Latina*, ed. J. P. MIGNE (Paris 1878–90) 133:9–816. A. BRUEL, ed., *Recueil des chartes de l'abbaye de Cluny*, 6 v. (Paris 1876–1903) 1:278–530; 5:844–845. F. STEGMÜLLER, *Repertorium biblicum medii aevi* (Madrid 1949–61) v.4 6117–20. Literature. J. H. PIGNOT, *Histoire de l'Ordre de Cluny*, 3 v. (Autun 1868) v.1. M. MANITIUS, *Geschichte der lateinischen Literatur des Mittelalters*, 3 v. (Munich 1911–31) 2:20–27. J. LECLERCQ, ''L'Idéal monastique de saint O. d'après ses oeuvres,'' *À Cluny: Congrès scientifique* (Dijon 1950) 227–232. P. THOMAS, ''Saint O. de Cluny et son oeuvre musicale,'' *ibid.* 171–180. J. LAPORTE, ''Saint O., disciple de saint Grégoire le Grand,'' *ibid.* 138–143. JOHN OF SALERNO, *St. O. of Cluny*, tr. and ed. G. SITWELL (New York 1958). J. SEMMLER, *Lexicon für Theologie und Kirche* 2 7:1100–01. M. HUGLO, ''Odo'' in *The New Grove Dictionary of Music and Musicians, vol. 13*, ed. S. SADIE, 503 (New York 1980). D. M. RANDEL, ed., *The Harvard Biographical Dictionary of Music* 647 (Cambridge 1996). N. SLONIMSKY, ed. *Baker's Biographical Dictionary of Musicians, Eighth Edition* 1329 (New York 1992).

[R. GRÉGOIRE]

Miniature of St. Odo of Cluny, 10th-century manuscript, Austrian National Library, Vienna (Cod. 51, fol. 45v.).

ODO RIGALDUS

Theologian; b. near Paris (date unknown); d. Rouen, July 2, 1275. He joined the Franciscan Order *c.* 1236, and studied at the University of Paris from 1240–41 to 1245; in this latter year on the death of John de la Rochelle he succeeded him as regent. Rigaldus commented on the *Sentences* of Peter Lombard and on at least 15 disputed theological questions. Only Books 1, 2, and 3 of the *Commentary* are authentic, *Bruxelles Bibl. Roy.* 1542 and *Troyes Bibl. Comm.* 1862 being spurious. As a student of theology he had collaborated with Alexander of Hales, John de la Rochelle, and Robert de la Basée on an exposition of the Franciscan Rule, which has become known as the *Expositio Regulae Quatuor Magistrorum.* His other writings remain substantially unedited.

Upon his election to the See of Rouen he was consecrated by Innocent IV at Lyons, April 26, 1248. He was a favorite of Louis, King of France, and was a collaborator on the Treaty with England in 1258. He worked actively with Bonaventure at the Council of Lyons (1274) for the return of the Greeks. An important document, the *Regestrum visitationum,* gives an account of his episcopal activity as metropolitan from July 17, 1248, to Dec. 15, 1269. His intellectual stature has become recognized recently as modern theologians rank him among the superior minds of the mid-13th century.

Bibliography: R. MÉNINDÈS, "Eudes Rigaud, Frère Mineur," *Revue d'histoire Franciscaine* 8 (1931) 157–178. P. ANDRIEU-GUITRANCOURT, *L'Archevêque Eudes Rigaud et la vie de l'Église aux XIIIᵉ siècle, d'après le Regestrum Visitationum* (Paris 1938). F. M. HENGUINET, "Les Manuscrits et l'influence des écrits théologiques d'Eudes Rigaud, O.F.M.," *Recherches de théologie ancienne et médiévale* 11 (Louvain 1939) 324–350. K. F. LYNCH, "The Alleged Fourth Book of Odo Rigaud on the Sentences and Related Documents," *Franciscan Studies* 9 (St. Bonaventure, N.Y. 1949) 87–145. S. BROWN, "Note biographique sur Eudes Rigaud," *Le moyen- âge* 41 (1931) 167–194. *The Register of Eudes of Rouen,* tr. S. BROWN, ed. J. O'SULLIVAN (New York 1964). C. CHENEY, *Episcopal Visitation* (Philadelphia 1983). O. G. DARLINGTON, *The Travels of Odo Rigaud* (Philadelphia 1940). J. BOUVY, "Les questions sur la grace dans le Commentaire des Sentences d'Odon Rigaud," *Recherches de théologie ancienne et médiévale* 27 (Louvain 1960) 291–343; "La necessite de la grace dans le Commentaire des Sentences d'Odon Rigaud," *Recherches de théologie ancienne et médiévale* 28 (Louvain 1961) 59–96. W. H. PRINCIPE, "O.R. as a Precursor of St. Bonaventure on the Holy Spirit as 'Effectus Formalis' in the Mutual Love of the Father and Son," *Medieval Studies* 39 (1977) 498–505. L SILEO, *Teoria della scienza teologica: Quaestio de scientia theologiae di Odo Rigaldi e altri testi inediti (1230–1250),* 2 v. (Studia Antoniana 27; Rome 1984).

[K. F. LYNCH]

O'DONNELL, EDMUND

First Jesuit martyred by the English government; b. Limerick, Ireland, 1542; d. Cork, Oct. 25, 1572. He entered the Society of Jesus in Rome in 1561. After studies in Loreto and Florence, he was sent to Flanders for his health. He returned to Limerick in 1564 to teach in the school established by David Woulfe, SJ. The school was dispersed in 1568, and O'Donnell stayed with his family until January of 1570, when he left for Madrid to raise funds for Woulfe's release from prison. In 1570 he returned to Ireland with the money but left again for the Iberian Peninsula sometime later. Although his journeys were undertaken in behalf of Woulfe, there is some evidence that he must also have acted as courier in bringing to James Fitzmaurice the bull of Pius V excommunicating Elizabeth. On his last return to Ireland, he was arrested on the warrant of Thomas FitzJohn Arthur, a Catholic, and was tried, condemned, and then executed with great barbarity on Oct. 25, 1572. That O'Donnell was in minor orders at the time of his death is clear from the appeal of Arthur to Rome for absolution from the censure he had incurred. Arthur also stated that O'Donnell was unjustly condemned.

See Also: IRISH CONFESSORS AND MARTYRS.

Bibliography: Archives, Society of Jesus, Rome. E. HOGAN, *Distinguished Irishmen of the 16th Century* (Dublin 1896). D. MURPHY, *Our Martyrs* (Dublin 1896).

[F. FINEGAN]

O'DONNELL, HUGH ROE

Ruler of the autonomous Irish state of Tír Chonaill and principal ally of Hugh O'NEILL in the Catholic Confederates' War (1594–1603); b. Ballyshannon?, Donegal, Oct. 29, 1572; d. Simancas, Spain, Sept. 10, 1602. He was kidnapped in an English stratagem in October of 1587, but he escaped from Dublin Castle Jan. 5, 1592 and was inaugurated as "Ó Domhnaill" on April 23, 1592. He ejected the English from the Franciscan Abbey of Donegal and maintained almost continual warfare against Elizabeth I. O'Neill joined him openly in 1595. His expeditions into Connacht in 1596 and 1597 opened communications with Western chiefs for conjunction with the Ulster insurgents and facilitated their joint victory of the Yellow Ford on Aug. 14, 1598; this victory encouraged the Southern chiefs to join the Confederation. His victory of the Curlews on Aug. 15, 1599 contributed to the frustration of Lord Deputy Essex's campaign. He preceded O'Neill in marching (November 1601) to support the Spaniards besieged in Kinsale. After the Irish defeat there (December 1601), he sailed to Spain to petition Philip III for reinforcements. Disappointed, he sickened and died at Simancas. His death hastened the end of Irish military resistance; his brother Ruaidhrí submitted in December of 1602, O'Neill, on March 23, 1603. However, the lengthy war deferred general persecution of Irish Catholics and allowed time for reinforcements to their clergy from their new continental seminaries.

Bibliography: L. Ó CLÉRIGH, *The Life of Aodh Ruadh Ó Domhnaill,* transcribed by P. WALSH, 2 v. (Irish Texts Society 42, 45; Dublin 1948–57).

[J. HURLEY]

ODORIC OF PORDENONE, BL.

Franciscan missionary also known as Odericus; b. Pordenone, Italy, *c.* 1265; d. Udine, Italy, Jan. 14, 1331. He entered the FRANCISCAN order at Udine *c.* 1280 and was ordained a priest some ten years later. In 1296 he began his remarkable career as a world missionary, which lasted about 35 years. For more than a decade and a half he was engaged in missionary work with other Franciscans in the MONGOL Khanate of Kipchak in southern Russia and probably also on the Balkan Peninsula. For a short time he returned to Italy, but in 1314 he set sail from Venice for the Near East. During the next eight years he did missionary work in the three Franciscan custodies of Constantinople, Trebizond (Asia Minor, present-day Turkey), and Tabriz (Persia, present-day Iran). From Sultani-yeh in northern Persia he set out in 1322 with an Irish confrere, Friar James, for the Far East in order to join Archbishop JOHN OF MONTE CORVINO in Cathay (northern China). After traveling through southern Persia, northern Arabia, and Chaldea (Iraq), he sailed from Hormuz in the Persian Gulf. At Thana, near Bombay, he recovered the relics of THOMAS OF TOLENTINO and his three companions, who had been martyred there about two years earlier. After visiting both the Malabar and the Coromandel coasts of India, he set sail from Quilon and stopped at the islands of Sumatra, Java, and probably Borneo, but by way of Cochin China and Great Nicobar Island. He had to return to Ceylon to get a ship to take him to Guangzhou, China. After arriving there in the latter part of 1324, he traveled overland to the capital in the north. At Zaitun (present Quanzhou) he stayed for a while with Bishop Andrew of Perugia (fl. 1307–26) and his Franciscan confreres, who had two churches in the city. On the northward journey he visited Fuzhou, Hangzhou, Nanjing, and Yangzhou, finding at Yangzhou another Franciscan mission center. In 1325 he finally reached Khanbaliq, or Cambaluc, (modern-day Beijing), and for three years he assisted Archbishop John of Monte Corvino and the other Franciscans working in the capital. Shortly before the archbishop's death in 1328, Odoric was commissioned to go back to Europe to recruit new missionaries for China. He made the return journey overland through the vassal kingdom of Tenduk (present-day provinces Shanxi, Shaanxi, and Gansu), where he found a church at T'o-k'o-t'o, built by King George, a convert of Monte Corvino. Though he mentions Tibet, he did not visit that country but continued through Almalyk, near Kuldja (present-day Yining) in Xinjiang, the western gateway of China, where seven Franciscans later died (1339) as the first martyrs of China. Then traveling through Chinese Turkestan and central Asia, around the Caspian Sea, to Persia, Iraq, Syria, and probably Palestine, he reached Venice at the end of 1329 or beginning of 1330. He set out for Avignon to see Pope JOHN XXII, but he fell ill in Pisa and returned to Udine by way of Padua, where he dictated his famous journal in May of 1330. The journal was one of the most famous travel books of the Middle Ages, and it was plagiarized by the author of *The Travels of Sir John Mandeville*. The cult of Bl. Odoric was approved by BENEDICT XIV on July 2, 1775. Odoric is venerated as the patron of the Chinese missions and also of long-distance travelers. The best edition of his journal is that published by A. Van den Wyngaert, OFM, in *Sinica Franciscana* (Quaracchi 1929)

1:413–495, and the best account of his life is in the accompanying introduction and notes.

Feast: Jan. 14 (formerly 12) (Conventual Franciscans).

Bibliography: Sources. Eng. tr. of journal in *Cathay and the Way Thither*, ed. and tr. H. YULE, 2 v. (London 1866); Ital. tr. *Relazione del viaggio in Oriente e in Cina*, ed. Camera di commercio, industria, artigianato e agricoltura, (Pordenone 1982); Germ. tr. *Der Bericht des Odoric da Pordenone über seine Reise nach Asien*, tr. R. JANDESEK (Bamberg 1987); Fr. tr. *Les merveilles de la terre d'outremer: traduction du XIVᵉ siècle du récit de voyage d'Odoric de Pordenone*, tr. J. DE VIGNAY, ed. D. A. TROTTER (Exeter, Eng. 1990). Literature. M. GNAUCK, *Odorich von Pordenone, ein Orientreisender des 14. Jahrhunderts* (Leisnig 1895). *Bibliotheca hagiographica latina antiquae et mediae aetatis*, 2 v. (Brussels 1898–1901) 6303–6316. H. CORDIER, *Les Voyages en Asie, au XIVᵉ siècle, du bienheureux frère O. de Pordenone* (Paris 1891). G. GOLUBOVICH, "Il B. Fr. Odorico da Pordenone, O.F.M.," *Archivum Franciscanum historicum* 10 (1917): 17–46. D. SCHILLING, "War der sel. Odorich von Pordenone in Japan?" *ibid.* 35 (1942): 153–176. G. PULLÉ, *Viaggio del beato Odorico da Pordenone* (Milan 1931). A. BUTLER, *The Lives of the Saints*, 4 v. (New York 1956) 1:88–89. M. A. HABIG, *In Journeyings Often* (St. Bonaventure, N.Y. 1953) 80–108. A. TEETAERT, *Dictionnaire de théologie catholique*, 15 v. (Paris 1903–50) 11.1:942–947.

[M. A. HÀBIG]

ODYSSEUS

Of all the characters created by Homer, Odysseus, or Ulysses, as he is called in the Latin tradition, has had the longest life and the most varied fortunes. From the 6th century B.C. the mental and moral flexibility of Odysseus was viewed unfavorably, and the tradition of Odysseus as a symbol of deceit was established. However, Stoic and Cynic emphasis on his manliness and resourcefulness in overcoming evil forces led to a restoration of his Homeric image and a recognition of his high moral qualities. Vergil reflects the first tradition (*Aeneid*, bk. 2); and Horace, the second (*Epist.* 1.2).

Early Christian writers were inclined to follow the second tradition, being impressed in particular, by the story of the meeting of Odysseus and the Phaeacian Princess Nausicaa and, above all, by that of his resistance to the temptations of the Sirens. The voyage of Odysseus became a symbol of the Christian's journey through life; the Sirens, the powers of evil to which he is exposed; his ship, the church; and its mast, the cross of Christ. In one of the stories of the medieval *Gesta Romanorum* [No. 156, *De subversione Troiae*, ed. H. Oesterley (Berlin 1872)], Paris represents the devil; Helen, the soul or all mankind held captive by the devil; Troy, hell; Ulysses, Christ; Achilles, the Holy Ghost. The temptation of Odysseus by the Sirens has been used as a theme also in Christian art.

Bibliography: W. B. STANFORD, *The Ulysses Theme: A Study in the Adaptability of a Traditional Hero* (Oxford 1954); "Studies in the Characterization of Ulysses IV: Ulysses in the Post-Classical Latin Tradition," *Hermathena* 77 (1951) 52–64. H. RAHNER, *Greek Myths and Christian Mystery*, tr. B. BATTERSHAW (New York 1963) esp. ch. VII, "Odysseus at the Mast," 328–386. E. WÜST, "Odysseus," *Paulys Realencyklopädie der klassischen Altertumswissenschaft* 17.2 (1937) 1905–96, esp. 1964–76.

[M. R. P. MCGUIRE]

OECOLAMPADIUS, JOHANNES

Originally Husschyn, Hussgen, or Heussgen, theologian and reformer of Basel; b. Weinsberg in the Palatinate, 1482; d. Basel, Nov. 24, 1531. By 1515, when he first came to Basel after years of education in Bologna, Heidelberg, Stuttgart, and Tübingen, his philological erudition in Latin, Greek, and Hebrew was prodigious. As a proofreader for the publisher Froben, he worked on Erasmus' editions of the New Testament and St. Jerome, and throughout his life he prepared numerous editions and translations of the Greek fathers. In 1520, weary of his ecclesiastical labors, he abruptly entered a Briggitine monastery in Bavaria, only to withdraw just as abruptly two years later. In November of 1522 he returned to Basel and was appointed a professor at the university in 1523. Thereafter, he ceaselessly promoted the cause of reform in the city through extensive lectures and sermons, in the Minster as well as in St. Martin's Church. Elsewhere in Switzerland he promoted it through his publications, notably in the Eucharistic controversy, and his participation in theological disputations such as those in Baden (1526) and Bern (1528), and the Colloquium in Marburg (1529), where he defended the Eucharistic doctrine of his close friend, Huldrych ZWINGLI. After the city council on Feb. 8, 1529, ordered the removal of images and the abolition of the Mass, Oecolampadius directed and supervised the reform of the Basel church until his death, employing the monumental reforming ordinance of April 1, which he prepared.

Bibliography: K. R. HAGENBACH, *Johann Oekolampad und Oswald Myconius* (Leben und ausgewählte Schriften der Väter und Begründer der reformirten Kirche 2; Elberfeld 1859) 3–306. E. STAEHELIN, *Das theologische Lebenswerk Johannes Oekolampads* (Quellen und Forschungen zur Reformation-geschichte 21; Leipzig 1939); ed., *Briefe und Akten zum Leben Oekolampads*, 2 v. (*ibid.* 10, 19; 1927–34); *Oekolampad-Bibliographie* (Nieuwkoop, Neth. 1963). L. CRISTIANI, *Dictionnaire de théologie catholique* (Paris 1903–50) 11.1:947–951. H. R. GUGGISBERG, *Die Religion in Geschichte und Gegenwart* (Tübingen 1957–65) 4:1567–68. E. ISERLOH, *Lexikon für Theologie und Kirche* (Freiburg 1957–65) 7:1125–26. F. L. CROSS, *The Oxford Dictionary of the Christian Church* (London 1957) 976.

[C. GARSIDÉ, JR.]

OERTEL, JOHN JAMES MAXIMILIAN

Editor; b. Ansbach, Bavaria, Germany, April 27, 1811; d. Jamaica, N.Y., Aug. 21, 1882. He was educated at the University of Erlangen, Germany, before his ordination as a Lutheran minister. Immigrating to New York City in 1837, he led 95 Prussian immigrants to join the Saxon congregations (now Lutheran Church—Missouri Synod) in St. Louis, Missouri, in 1839. Denominational quarrels led to his conversion to Catholicism the following year. He served as an instructor in German at St. John's College, Fordham, New York, before going to Cincinnati, Ohio, as editor of the *Wahrheitsfreund.* The German–language newspaper *Kirchenzeitung,* which he founded in Baltimore, Maryland, in 1846, was moved to New York City in 1851 and became the most influential German paper in the U.S. In 1875 Oertel was made a Knight of St. Gregory by Pius IX.

[J. L. MORRISON]

OESTERREICHER, JOHN M.

Pioneer in Catholic-Jewish relations, author, and editor; b. Stadt-Liebau, Moravia, Feb. 2, 1904; d. New Jersey, April 18, 1993. Oesterreicher's parents, both Jewish, died in the Holocaust, as did the priest who baptized him in 1924. Oesterreicher was ordained a priest in 1927 and was named professor of religion by the University of Vienna in 1935. From 1934 to 1938, he edited a Catholic journal, *Die Erfuellung* ("Fulfillment"), the purpose of which was to denounce Nazi persecution of Jews. When the Germans entered Vienna, Oesterreicher was interrogated by the Gestapo. He fled in April 1939, reaching Paris that September. There, he published *Racisme, Antisémitisme, Antichristianisme* (Paris 1939; New York 1943) and made weekly anti-Nazi radio broadcasts. He fled again in June 1940 across the border into Spain, and eventually arrived in the United States on the SS *Exeter* on November 12, 1940.

Along with parish work for the Archdiocese of New York, Oesterreicher taught at Manhattanville College from 1944 to 1953. Chief among his articles from that period is a study of the Good Friday prayer, "Pro perfidis Judaeis" [*Theological Studies* 8 (1947): 85–101], in which he suggested that the term *perfidis* be translated as "unbelieving" rather than the pejorative "perfidious." In 1948, the Sacred Congregation of Rites, under the signature of Pope Pius XII, mandated this change in translation [*Acta Apostolicae Sedis* 40:342]. In 1955 the same Congregation restored the rite of *flectamus genua* (kneeling) to the intercession for the Jewish people [*Acta Apostolicae Sedis* 47:838-47], another change for which

Oesterreicher had argued. In 1959, Pope John XXIII eliminated the term *perfidis* from the Good Friday prayer; following the Second Vatican Council, the prayer was completely revised.

Oesterreicher's book, *Walls Are Crumbling: Seven Jewish Philosophers Discover Christ* (New York and London 1952) was translated into Dutch (Haarlem 1954), French (Paris 1955), Spanish (Madrid 1961), and Japanese (1969).

On the feast of the Annunciation, March 25, 1953, Oesterreicher signed an agreement with Seton Hall University to establish an Institute of Judeo-Christian Studies, the first such at a major Catholic institution of higher learning. Five "yearbooks" of the Institute, titled *The Bridge* (New York 1955; 1956; 1958; 1962; 1970), chronicled Jewish-Christian relations before and after the Second Vatican Council.

In 1960, with fourteen other priests, Oesterreicher presented a petition to Augustin Cardinal Bea that the Second Vatican Council consider reconciliation with the Jewish people. In February 1961, he was appointed to the Subcommission for Jewish Questions, which drafted the text of what would become the Conciliar Declaration Nostra Aetate, "On the Church's Relationship to Non-Christian Religions" (Oct. 28, 1965). His "Introduction and Commentary" to the text in H. Vorgrimler, ed., *Commentary on the Documents of Vatican II* (New York 1969, vol. 3) is considered definitive.

Oesterreicher's prolific writings to 1978 are listed in the festschrift in his honor [A. Finkel and L. Frizzell, eds., *Standing before God: Studies on Prayer in Scriptures and Tradition* (New York 1981) 393-399] and updated to 1993 in *Experiences and Expectations: The Fortieth Anniversary of the Institute of Judeo-Christian Studies* (Seton Hall 1993). Major works since then include: *Martin Buber and the Christian Way* (New York 1986), *The New Encounter between Christians and Jews* (New York 1986), and *God at Auschwitz?* (Seton Hall 1993). He served for over two decades as advisor to the U.S. Bishops' Secretariat for Ecumenical and Interreligious Affairs. He died on *Yom ha-Shoah* 5753, Holocaust Remembrance Day.

Bibliography: E. L. EHRLICH, "In Memoriam John Oesterreicher (1904-1993)," *Orientierung* 10 (May 1993) 109-110. J. FILTEAU, "Msgr. Oesterreicher Dies: Pioneered Catholic-Jewish Relations," *Catholic News Service* (Washington, 20 April 1993) 12-13. L. FRIZZELL, ed., "Homilies and Tributes in Memory of Msgr. John M. Oesterreicher," *Institute of Judeo-Christian Studies, Seton Hall University* (South Orange 1993). "A Pioneer in Christian-Jewish Dialogue," *The Tablet* (London 1 May 1993) 557. F. WEINZIERL, "Beginnings of John M. Oesterreicher's Work," in A. FINKEL and L. FRIZZELL, eds., *Standing before God* (New York 1981) 13-19.

[E. J. FISHER]

OFFICE, ECCLESIASTICAL

According to *Lumen gentium* 5, the Church received from Jesus Christ the mission of announcing the kingdom of God and inaugurating it among all people. A variety of means exist by which the Church fulfills this mission; one fundamental means is through ecclesiastical office. Ecclesiastical office has existed from the beginning of the Church (see, e.g., von Campenhausen) but the concept has undergone a major transformation since the Second Vatican Council. This transformation, rooted in the theological, and particularly, ecclesiological, insights of Vatican II, allows for greater participation in the Church's mission by all the Christian faithful, ordained or lay.

Theology

The definition of ecclesiastical office as found in the *Code of Canon Law* (c.145.1) includes three elements: (1) a function—an ability or capacity to perform certain actions tending to a spiritual goal; (2) a stable determination of the range and limits of this function through divine or ecclesiastical ordinance; (3) a spiritual purpose.

First Element. That there must in the nature of things be found some distinction of activities in the Church follows from its constitution by Our Lord as a true society or people (*see* SOCIETY [THEOLOGY OF]). The Pauline description of the Church as Body of Christ was precisely invoked by him to justify functional differentiations found from the beginning within the community.

> Now there are varieties of gifts, but the same Spirit; and there are varieties of ministries, but the same Lord; and there are varieties of workings, but the same God, who works all things in all. Now the manifestation of the Spirit is given to everyone for profit. . . . For as the body is one and has many members, and all the members of the body, many as they are, form one body, so also is it with Christ. . . . For the body is not one member, but many. . . . Now if they were all one member, where would the body be? But as it is, there are indeed many members, yet but one body. . . . Now you are the body of Christ, member for member. And God indeed has placed some in the Church, first apostles, secondly prophets, thirdly teachers; after that miracles, then gifts of healing, services of help, power of administration, and the speaking of various tongues. (1 Cor 12.4–29; cf. Rom 12.4–8; Gal. 3.27–28; Eph 4.11–13)

Whether society or Body or vine and branches or kingdom or people or family or household, there must be distribution of activities for the good of the whole.

This division of functions is attested in the *Dogmatic Constitution on the Church* promulgated by Vatican II, when the council states: "As all the members of the human body, though they are many, form one body, so also are the faithful in Christ (cfr. 1 Cor. 12, 12). So in the building up of Christ's body a diversity of members and functions obtains. There is only one Spirit, who, according to His own richness and the needs of the ministries, gives His different gifts for the welfare of the Church (cfr. 1 Cor. 12, 1–11)'' (7; *Acta Apostolicae Sedis* 57 [1965] 10).

Second Element. If the first element found in the definition of ecclesiastical office is well attested by appeal to reason and to the sources of revelation, it is not perhaps clear that the second element is necessarily attested: the stable determination of the range and limits of these functions by divine or ecclesiastical ordinance. Could it not be that Our Lord intended to bestow functions on a quite temporary basis through a transitory energizing of one or other within the community so that he who today speaks in tongues tomorrow interprets, and he who today prophesies tomorrow is endowed with no special function at all? To the Catholic mind this question is answered not so much by an appeal to the unlikelihood or unnaturalness of such a disposition in an enduring group, or to the confusion and disorder that would so easily result, but by an appeal to the evident intention of Christ in creating the original apostolate. The Catholic view has always been that Christ selected and separated, prepared and instructed the TWELVE to bear His Person and continue His salvific action, not only through their lifetime but until He should come again.

The history of the first age portrays a community in which the permanent apostolic function is of paramount significance. The same Paul who readily enough admits the divine provenance, the legitimacy, of CHARISMS peremptorily by reason of his apostolic mandate regulates and restrains charismatic functioning:

> What then is to be done, brethren? When you come together each of you has a hymn, has an instruction, has a revelation, has a tongue, has an interpretation. Let all things be done unto edification. If anyone speaks in a tongue, let it be by twos or at most by threes, and let them speak in turn, and let one interpret. But if there is no interpreter let him keep silence in the church, and speak to himself and to God. Of the prophets, let two or three speak at a meeting, and let the rest act as judges. But if anything is revealed to another sitting by let the first keep silence. . . . Thus I likewise teach in all the churches of the saints. Let women keep silence in the churches, for it is not permitted them to speak, but let them be submissive, as the Law also says. . . . If anyone thinks that he is a prophet or spiritual, let him recognize that the things I am writing to you are the Lord's

> commandments. If anyone ignores this, he shall be ignored. (1 Cor 14.26–38)

Paul at least is not unaware that over and above the ephemeral gifts for community sanctification there stands a stable mission entrusted to the Twelve and to him.

So when in the very early days of the community at Jerusalem there arose a practical problem, the APOSTLES did not wait for nor seem to expect any charismatic solution but proceeded without delay to set up an institutional arrangement. To meet the complaints of the Hellenist group that their widows were being slighted in the distribution of alms, the Apostles directed the community to present to them seven suitable candidates, "that we [the Apostles] may put them in charge of this work" (Acts 6.3). In the selection and investiture of the seven one can reasonably discern the beginning and the prototype of subordinate ministries with determined functions. Though some special or charismatic endowments may have been expected of those presented as candidates ("select from among you seven men of good reputation, full of the Spirit and of wisdom" [Acts 6.37]), there can be no question that the determination of the function was made by the Apostles as the established representatives and plenipotentiaries of Christ. In the Pauline Churches as time went on there was through prayer and the IMPOSITION OF HANDS designation of those who in a permanent way functioned as bishops or PRESBYTERS (Acts 14.25; 20.28; Phil 1.1; 1 Tm 3.1–7; 5.17–19) and DEACONS (Phil 1.1; 1 Tm 3.8–13) of the individual communities.

Third Element. The third and final element in an ecclesiastical office is that of its spiritual purpose. The determined function is not merely a service, an accommodation to the needs of others, a labor for the benefit of others, as would be the ministrations of a waiter, an usher, a clerk, an attendant, but a ministration that brings life or helps to maintain life, that directs in the way of God. So the one who holds an office does truly serve, does truly benefit others, but as the father or the guardian who stands in the place of the father serves the family. The basis and justification for all this goes back directly to the role of Christ Himself in the economy of salvation. He came not to be the object of ministrations, but as a minister, a servant, to give His life as a ransom for many, without in the least hesitating to accept the designation of Lord and Master ("You call me Master and Lord, and you say well, for so I am. If, therefore, I the Lord and Master have washed your feet, you also ought to wash the feet of one another"—Jn 13.13–14). In the Christian scheme of things, paradoxical though it may seem, there is no incompatibility between service and power: it is not to "lord it over them" (Mt 20.25) that some are vested with authority in the community, but that they may more effectively serve by standing in His place to whom "all authority in heaven and on earth has been given" (Mt 28.18). From the days of the Apostles and at the level of the apostolic commission given them, those who hold office in virtue of a power received from on high (Acts 1.8) are to exercise a function that connotes a corresponding obligation on the part of the other members to receive this ministration. There is at once power and lowliness, authority and humility, modesty and majesty in one who says in Christ's name: "If I do not wash thee, thou shalt have no part with me" (Jn 13.8).

That offices in the Church connote at once power and service is the repeated teaching of Vatican Council II: "For those ministers, who are endowed with sacred power, serve their brethren in order that all who are of the people of God and therefore enjoy a true Christian dignity, working toward a common goal freely and in an orderly way, may arrive at salvation. . . . That function however which the Lord committed to the shepherds of His people is a true service, which in S. Scripture is significantly called 'diakonia.' or ministry. . . . Bishops govern the particular Churches . . . by their authority and sacred power, which they use only for the development of their flock in truth and holiness, remembering that he who is greater should become the lesser and he who is chief become as the servant. . . . A bishop . . . must keep before his eyes the example of the Good Shepherd, who came not to be ministered unto but to minister . . . and to lay down His life for His sheep (cfr. *Io.* 10, 11)" (*Dogmatic Constitution on the Church* 18, 24, 27; *Acta Apostolicae Sedis* 57 [1965] 21–22, 29, 32–33).

Finally, the existence of offices so described implies no denial of the fact that there will always be room and welcome in the Church for those who without participating in the ordinary, institutional authority of the Church are mysteriously and charismatically called to providential tasks of reformation, renewal, *aggiornamento.* Of these charismatic gifts Vatican Council II remarks, "whether they be the more outstanding or the more simple and widely diffused, they are to be received with thanksgiving and consolation, for they are especially suited to and useful for the needs of the Church. . . . Judgment however as to their genuineness and proper use belongs to those who are leaders of the Church and to whom in particular it belongs not, indeed, to extinguish the Spirit but to test all things and hold fast to that which is good" (*Dogmatic Constitution on the Church* 12; *Acta Apostolicae Sedis* 57 [1965] 16–17).

See Also: AUTHORITY, ECCLESIASTICAL; BISHOP (IN THE CHURCH); MYSTICAL BODY OF CHRIST; PRIMACY OF THE POPE.

Bibliography: R. NAZ, *Dictionnaire de droit canonique,* ed. R. NAZ, 7 v. (Paris 1935–65) 6:1074–1105. H. ZELLER et al., *Lexikon für Theologie und Kirche,* ed. J. HOFER and K. RAHNER, 10 v. (2d, new ed. Freiburg 1957–65) 1:451–457. M. SCHMAUS, ibid. 5:386–387. K. MÖRSDORF, ibid. 6:188–192. J. COLSON, *Les Fonctions ecclésiales aux deux premiers siècles* (Bruges 1956). H. VON CAMPENHAUSEN, *Kirchliches Amt und geistliche Vollmacht in den ersten drei Jahrhunderten* (Tübingen 1953). W. MICHAELIS, *Das Ältestenamt der christlichen Gemeinde im Licht der Heiligen Schrift* (Bern 1953). H. ASMUSSEN, *Die Kirche und das Amt* (Munich 1939). D. E. HEINTSCHEL, *The Mediaeval Concept of an Ecclesiastical Office* (Catholic University of America Canon Law Studies 363; Washington, D.C. 1956).

[S. E. DONLON/EDS.]

Canon Law

Current Comprehension. Canon 145, §1 offers the following succinct definition: "An ecclesiastical office is any function constituted in a stable manner by divine or ecclesiastical ordinance to be exercised for a spiritual purpose." Under the previous *Code of Canon Law,* an ecclesiastical office involved participation either in the power of governance (power of jurisdiction) or in the power of orders and, in as much as only clerics could receive these, clerics alone could hold an ecclesiastical office. Such participation in the power of governance or of orders is no longer required for all offices; as one consequence, therefore, lay men and women may acquire certain ecclesiastical offices for which they are capable.

The definition of office includes three elements: a function (*munus,* pl. *munera*), constituted in a stable manner by divine or ecclesiastical ordinance and serving a spiritual purpose. First and fundamentally, an office is a function, a *munus.* A variety of functions exist in the Church and all the baptized, in virtue of that sacrament and through their exercise of these functions, participate in the Church's mission. These functions have been understood in terms of the threefold *munera* (or functions) of Jesus Christ as priest, prophet, and ruler. Thus, an ecclesiastical office serves to fulfill the mission of the Church following the example of Jesus Christ in the exercise of the common and ministerial priesthoods; the proclamation of the Word of God; and in the governance of the People of God.

The second element concerns the recognition of a particular function as of particular importance or necessity for the Church: the function is constituted an office by divine or ecclesiastical ordinance. Church teaching has determined that certain offices derive from the intention of Jesus Christ—for example, the office of the bishop of Rome (the Petrine ministry), the college of bishops, and the office of diocesan bishop. Other offices are established by the competent Church authority—for example, the office of chancellor or finance officer in a diocese; the office of superior in an institute of consecrated life or a society of apostolic life. Determination of "competent authority" derives from an examination of the law or of the decree that establishes the office. For example, the diocesan bishop appoints an individual chancellor of the diocese, an office established by the code itself (see cc. 470 and 482). The bishop may establish particular offices for his own diocese. The approved constitutions of an institute of consecrated life determine the appointment of superiors.

The "stability" of an office needs to be understood from two perspectives. First, the function that is designated an office implies that this is an ongoing task, useful for the Church not just for one particular occasion or purpose but also for the foreseeable future. The office will have an incumbent who will exercise its functions and who will be replaced, when necessary and according to the appropriate norms, by another incumbent. Second, in order for an individual to fulfill the task appropriately, the person needs some assurance of personal stability in the office to assure its proper exercise. This stability applies even when an individual is appointed at the prudent discretion of a competent Church authority; the latter needs a just cause to remove an individual from an office (see c. 194, §3.). Two further points: first, an office requires a "job description," that is, a listing of the obligations and rights associated with that particular function. Second, an individual exercising an office does so not on personal initiative but rather in response to a request from some person or group in the Church (for example, a general chapter of an institute of consecrated life electing an individual as superior; a bishop appointing an individual finance officer for his diocese).

The third element is a spiritual purpose. Office as such aims at the service of the Christian faithful—the reason for its existence. Therefore, an individual accepts and exercises an office in the Church not for personal benefit but for service. The individual officeholder acts on behalf of the Church, participating in the mission that Jesus Christ entrusted to the Church.

Implications of Ecclesiastical Office. From the perspective of these constitutive elements of ecclesiastical office, specific implications need due emphasis. These implications reflect the importance of an office for the Church and for fulfilling her mission and are necessary for the valid exercise of the tasks associated with a specific office.

First, the competent ecclesiastical authority must provide for an office in writing—the individual does not simply assume the office acting alone. A variety of means exist for such provision—through free conferral by a competent authority; through installation by competent authority, when an individual or a group has a right to present a person for an office; through election—with confirmation by competent authority if necessary or through simple acceptance of the office if no confirmation is necessary (see cc. 146–156).

Second, an individual must be qualified for an office—fundamentally, the individual must be in communion with the Church (that is, at the minimum, the individual is a baptized Christian, not necessarily Catholic. Some commentators, however, hold that 'communion' here implies the individual is Catholic. See c. 205 which refers to "full communion"). In addition, the person must possess the qualities required for the specific office in question (see c.149). Certain offices entailing "the full care of souls" require that the incumbent have received priestly ordination (c. 150).

Third, an ecclesiastical office is lost through a variety of means: lapse of a specific period of time; reaching a specific age determined by law; resignation; transfer; removal; privation (see c. 184), and by death.

For the first two—term and age—the competent authority must communicate such loss of office to the incumbent in writing (c. 186). To resign an office an incumbent must be mentally competent as well as not subject to grave fear unjustly inflicted or as a result of malice, error, or simony. To effect a transfer, the competent authority must have the capacity to provide for both offices—the one being vacated and the one being assumed. If the incumbent is unwilling, the competent authority must have grave cause and follow proper procedure. The code provides one example of such a procedure in canons 1740–1752, which concern the transfer of pastors.

Privation refers to loss of office as a penalty; removal does not necessarily imply the incumbent has incurred a penalty.

Removal occurs either by decree of the competent authority or by the law itself. As already noted, the competent authority needs a just cause to replace an individual appointed at the authority's prudent discretion. More serious reasons are needed to replace an individual appointed either for an indefinite or determined time. The law itself, in canon 194, §1, removes from office a person who has lost the clerical state; one who has "publicly defected from the Catholic faith or from the communion of the Church"; and a cleric who has attempted marriage.

For privation, the competent authority must follow the norms of law. These norms include "The Application of Penalties" in canons 1341–1353 and canons 1717–1728 of "The Penal Process."

In order to maintain justice, the code requires that, in all these cases, competent authority must respect contractual obligations as well as to ensure the individual's decent support.

Bibliography: J. PROVOST, "Ecclesiastical Offices [cc. 145–196]," in *New Commentary on the Code of Canon Law,* ed. J. BEAL, J. CORIDEN, and T. GREEN (New York/Mahwah 2000) 195–229. H. VON CAMPENHAUSEN, *Ecclesiastical Authority and Spiritual Power in the Church of the First Three Centuries* (Peabody, Mass. 1997).

[R. J. KASLYN]

OFFICE FOR FILM AND BROADCASTING

Office within the United States Catholic Conference of Bishops, successor to the National Catholic Office of Motion Pictures (NCOMP), originally the National Legion of Decency (founded 1934). In 1980, the office merged with the National Catholic Office for Radio and Television and together they formed the present Department of Communications within the Bishops' Conference, under whose auspices the Office for Film and Broadcasting operates. It is based in New York City.

In the 1930s and 1940s, the Legion of Decency claimed a membership of over 11 million Americans, about one moviegoer in twelve. Its influence on the motion picture industry was decidedly adversarial because so many of Hollywood's projects were seen as possessing loose moral content. Bishops often put pressure on the Catholic financiers who backed such films, particularly Bishop John T. Cantwell of Los Angeles. He persuaded Archbishop McNicholas of Cincinnati to form an Episcopal Committee for Motion Pictures, Radio, and Television within the conference of bishops, a committee that McNicholas chaired from 1933–1944. Together with people like Martin P. Quigley, a devout Catholic and publisher of the film industry's leading trade paper throughout the 1940s and 1950s, the Legion exerted pressure on Hollywood to produce quality entertainment. Gradually, however, the Legion and later the NCOMP's influence waned. Its powerful ability to rate a film's moral value was supplanted by an increasingly well-formed lay opinion on what was acceptable viewing.

However, the bishops have seen fit to continue to guide audiences in making decisions on what they watch through capsule reviews and a rating system that departs from the standard film industry's G, PG, PG-13, NC-17, R, and X ratings. In 1971, NCOMP and National Council of Churches' Broadcasting and Film Commission withdrew support from the film industry's rating system. Currently, there are four subdivisions to the "A" or "morally unobjectionable" category: A-I, for general patronage; A-II, for adults and adolescents; A-III, for adults; and A-IV, for adults, but with reservations. The classification O is given to films that are found to be totally incompatible with Christian moral values or standards of decency.

Since 1995 the Office for Film and Broadcasting has issued a weekly movie review of select films. Reviews of certain television programs began in 1975 and video releases in 1992 when it became apparent that the video cassette recorder was influencing how Americans were selecting their entertainment.

See Also: EROTIC LITERATURE.

Bibliography: There is a compilation of some 8,000 movie reviews of virtually every feature length film since 1966 in *Our Sunday Visitor's Family Guide to Movies and Videos,* H. HERX, ed. (Huntington, Ind. 1999). G. D. BLACK, *The Catholic Crusade Against the Movies, 1940–1975* (New York 1997); *Hollywood Censored: Morality Codes, Catholics, and the Movies* (New York 1994). M. MCLAUGHLIN, *A Study of the National Catholic Office for Motion Pictures* (Ph.D. diss., University of Wisconsin, 1974). J. M. PHELAN, *The National Catholic Office for Motion Pictures: An Investigation of the Policy and Practice of Film Classification* (Ph.D. diss., New York University, 1968). J. M. SKINNER, *The Cross and the Cinema: The Legion of Decency and the National Catholic Office for Motion Pictures, 1933–1970* (Westport, Conn. 1993). F. WALSH, *Sin and Censorship: The Catholic Church and the Motion Picture Industry* (New Haven 1996). Archival material for the National Catholic Office for Film and Broadcasting (1966–1990) and its predecessor, the Episcopal Committee on Motion Pictures (1933–1944), is housed at the Catholic University of America. The papers of Martin P. Quigley are archived at Georgetown University.

[P. J. HAYES]

OFFICE OF THE DEAD

One of the oldest special Offices in the DIVINE OFFICE. It goes back at least to the 7th century and may even antedate GREGORY THE GREAT (d. 604), for this Office is purely Roman in the arrangement of its Psalms and bears no trace of monastic and Gallican elements, such as introductory prayers and hymns. Its schema is similar to the Office of the last three days of HOLY WEEK and these are known to be very primitive. Its original form had only MATINS, LAUDS, and VESPERS. Pius X (d. 1914) added the LITTLE HOURS. During the Middle Ages this Office was frequently recited in addition to the Divine Office. Although Pius V (d. 1572) did away with all obligation in the matter, he did leave a twofold Office for the Feast of ALL SOULS. Pius X removed this duplication by making the Office of the Dead the sole Office for November 2. The 1960 Code of Rubrics deleted the Vespers of the Dead formerly added to All Saints' Vespers. In addition to its use on All Souls, the Office of the Dead is prayed in whole or in part in connection with the funeral services of clerics and religious. From the 1970s onward, the practice of praying a portion of the Office at wakes for lay people has grown.

In the revised LITURGY OF THE HOURS (1971), the Office of the Dead comprises: the Office of Readings, Morning Prayer, Daytime Prayer, Midmorning Prayer, Midday Prayer, and—a new departure from tradition—Night Prayer. The psalmody, antiphons included, for the Office of Readings, Morning Prayer, 1st and 2d Evening Prayer, is proper. The psalmody for Midmorning, Midday, and Midafternoon Prayer is taken from the Complementary Psalmody used during the year, but the antiphons are proper. The Night Prayer is taken from the office of Sunday. The revised Order of Christian Funerals includes an abbreviated Office of the Dead.

The liturgical reforms of Vatican II introduced notable changes in the themes and tone of the Office of the Dead. Throughout there is a greater emphasis on the victory and joy of the resurrection, rather than on the fears and sorrows of death and judgment. The spirit of Christian joy is manifested especially in the hymns, with their reference to Christ as the Lord of the Resurrection. The exultant alleluia rings through many of the hymns, and the doxology, "Glory be to the Father, etc.," concludes each psalm rather than the austere and penitential "Eternal rest grant unto them, O Lord."

Bibliography: L. EISENHOFER and J. LECHNER, *The Liturgy of the Roman Rite*, tr. A. J. and E. F. PEELER from the 6th German ed., ed. H. E. WINSTONE (New York 1961) 474–475. J. H. MILLER, *Fundamentals of the Liturgy* (Notre Dame, Ind. 1960) 344. M. RIGHETTI, *Manuale di storia liturgica*, 4 v. (Milan): v.2 (2d ed. 1955) 2:218–219. H. LECLERCQ, *Dictionnaire d'archéologie chrétienne et de liturgie*, ed. F. CABROL, H. LECLERCQ, and H. I. MARROU, 15 v. (Paris 1907–53) 12.2:2006–09. C. CALLEWAERT, *Sacris erudiri* (Steenbrugge 1940) 169–177. *The Liturgy of the Hours* (New York 1976).

[G. E. SCHIDEL/P. F. MULHERN/EDS.]

O'FIHELY, MAURICE

Also known as Mauritius de Portu Fildaeo, Scotist Franciscan Conventual; b. Baltimore or Clonfert, Ireland, *c.* 1460; d. Galway, March 25, 1513. O'Fihely studied at Oxford, became regent of studies at the Franciscan friary in Milan by 1488, and regent at the Padua friary in 1491. Shortly thereafter he held the chair of Scotistic theology in the university. Julius II consecrated him archbishop of Tuam, Ireland, on June 26, 1506. In 1513, having attended the first two sessions of the Fifth Lateran Council, he left Italy to take possession of his diocese, but died on the way. The leading Scotist of his day, he is still one of the best interpreters of John DUNS SCOTUS, many of whose

works he edited. A number of his own theological and metaphysical works were included in the Wadding edition of Scotus's *Opera omnia*. To his contemporaries he was known as *Flos mundi*.

Bibliography: J. H. SBARALEA, *Supplementum et castigatio ad scriptores triium ordinum S. Francisci a Waddingo* (Rome 1906–36) 2:242–243. A. G. LITTLE, *The Grey Friars in Oxford* (Oxford 1892) 267–268. C. EUBEL, et al. *Hieraarchia Catholica medii (et recentioris) aevi* (Padua 1958) 3:340. E. LONGPRÉ, *Dictionnaire de théologie catholique*, ed. A. VACANT et al., (Paris 1903–50) 10.1:404–405.

[P. FEHLNER]

OGILVIE, JOHN, ST.

Jesuit martyr; b. Scotland, 1579–80; d. Glasgow Cross, March 10 (N.S.), 1615. In a deposition (Oct. 15, 1614) after his capture, Ogilvie gave his father's name as "Walter Ogilvie of Drum." As a Jesuit novice he described himself as "Strathilensis," "of Strathisla." His family may thus have been associated with Drum-na-Keith, in Strathisla, Banffshire. In the deposition he also noted his absence from Scotland for 22 years, i.e., from 1591–92. One of his name matriculated at Helmstedt on Aug. 19, 1592. Ogilvie was at the Scots College, Louvain (later established at Douai), in 1596; it was there that he, a Calvinist in his youth, became a Catholic. Because of the poverty of the college, he was sent (1598) to Regensburg; he moved to Olmutz while still a lay student. He finally became a Jesuit novice at Brno in 1599. He took his vows at the Jesuit College at Graz, Austria, Dec. 26, 1601. His five years there were later commemorated in a biography [in *Undeni Graecenses Academici,* by M. Bonbardi, SJ (Graz 1727)]. After an interval of teaching, he began theology at Olmutz. In 1610 he moved to Paris, where he was ordained.

Ogilvie was stationed at Rouen, but kept importuning the superior general to send him to Scotland. At last his request was granted, and in 1613 he began his short missionary career in Scotland, working mostly in Edinburgh, Renfrewshire, and Glasgow. He was betrayed in Glasgow, Oct. 14 (N. S.), 1614, and remained thereafter in captivity. His own account of his imprisonment was smuggled out of prison. He suffered extreme torture, but showed great courage and skill in defending the spiritual supremacy of the pope. He was ultimately sentenced to death, hanged at Glasgow Cross, and buried in the criminals' plot of an unidentified burial ground outside the city.

No relic of his body remains; however, centers of devotion exist at St. Thomas's, Keith, Banffshire; St. Aloysius's, Garnethill, Glasgow; Sacred Heart, Edinburgh;

and Craighead House, Bothwell. His cause was introduced under the rules drawn up by URBAN VIII in 1625. The first process opened at Würzburg in May of 1628; the following January a similar process began in Rome. Nearly three centuries later, the Apostolic Process opened in Glasgow, July 12, 1927. The beatification, by PIUS XI, took place on Dec. 22, 1929, and the canonization, by Paul VI, on Oct. 17, 1976. There are two main portraits: the ''Douai'' portrait, now at the church of S. Gilles, Pecquincourt, Nord, France; and the ''Roman'' portrait, now at the Gesù, Rome. An illustration (unrelated to either) is given in Bonbardi's *Undeni Graecenses Academici.*

Feast: March 10; Oct. 14 (Jesuits).

Bibliography: W. E. BROWN, *John Ogilvie . . .* (London 1925). T. COLLINS, *Martyr in Scotland . . .* (London 1955). A. BUTLER, *The Lives of the Saints,* rev. ed. H. THURSTON and D. ATTWATER (New York 1956) 1:552–556. L. MACFARLANE, *Lexikon für Theologie und Kirche,* ed. J. HOFER and K. RAHNER (Freiberg 1957–65) 7:1121. G. G. SMITH, *The Dictionary of National Biography from the Earliest Times to 1900* (London 1885–1900) 14:912–914. *Acta Apostolicae Sedis* 69 [1977] 305–311; *L'Osservatore Romano* English edition 1976, n. 43, 1–3. M. K. RICHARDSON, *Father John Ogilvie* (London 1976). B. A. MOORE, *John Ogilvie* (Melbourne 1977). D. HICKEY and G. SMITH, *Miracle* (London 1978). C. CARRELL and G. BOARDMAN, eds., *St. John Ogilvie; An Illustrated History of His Life, Martyrdom, and Canonisation* (Glasgow 1979).

[J. QUINN]

O'GORMAN, THOMAS

Bishop, educator; b. Boston, Mass., May 1, 1843; d. Sioux Falls, S. Dak., Sept. 18, 1921. He was the first of four children born to John and Margaret (O'Keefe) O'Gorman. The family moved west to Chicago, Ill. (1848); with John O'Gorman's childhood friend Richard Ireland and his family, among whom was the future Abp. John IRELAND, they resumed their westward trek to St. Paul, Minn. (1852). That same year Thomas O'Gorman and John Ireland enrolled among the first students of Bp. Joseph Cretin's Latin School on the upper floor of the frontier Cathedral of St. Paul—the first seminarians of the diocese. When O'Gorman was ten years old and Ireland 15, they were sent to the minor seminary of the Marists at Meximieux, France, and subsequently to the major seminary at Montbel. O'Gorman returned to St. Paul and was ordained by Bp. Thomas Grace on Nov. 5, 1865. He was first assigned to Rochester, Minn., where he built St. John's church and became known as a preacher and organizer. In 1877 he resigned to join the Society of St. Paul, continuing his preaching in the New York area and converting the financier Thomas Fortune Ryan to the Catholic Church. He was recalled (1882) to St. Paul by his friend, now Bp. John Ireland, and assigned to Faribault as pastor, and later (1885) as first rector of the newly established St. Paul Seminary and president of St. Thomas College there. After ten years he resigned to teach dogmatic theology, English, and French in the college. During these years he wrote several articles and deepened his knowledge of ecclesiastical history. In 1890 he was appointed professor of church history in The Catholic University of America, Washington, D.C., where he actively supported the liberal policies of the Americanists during the several controversies of the late 19th century in American Catholicism (*see* AMERICANISM). He wrote *A History of the Roman Catholic Church in the United States* (1895), a summary of the original research of John Gilmary SHEA.

On Jan. 24, 1896, O'Gorman was appointed bishop of Sioux Falls, a suffragan see of the Province of St. Paul, where his friend John Ireland was the first archbishop. The new bishop was consecrated by Abp. Francesco Satolli, first Apostolic Delegate to the U.S., in St. Patrick's Church, Washington, D.C., on April 19, 1896, and installed in the procathedral of his see on May 2, 1896. At that time the diocese had 51 diocesan and 14 regular clergy, 50 churches with resident priests, 61 missions with churches, 100 stations, ten chapels, 14 parochial schools, 61 Indian schools, two orphanages, and one hospital. There were three communities of religious men and six of women in the diocese; and the total Catholic population, both Indian and white, was estimated at 30,000.

O'Gorman, who began his active pastoral apostolate with energy, wrote to his friend Denis O'Connell from ''Avignon'': ''I fear I must resign myself to being the routine Bishop of an unknown Western diocese, and I assure you I find enough work to do as such.'' New hospitals were opened at Yankton and Pierre (1897), Aberdeen (1901), Sioux Falls (1910), and Mitchell and Milbank (1921). The vast extent of the diocese and growth in population encouraged an east-west division in South Dakota in 1902 between Sioux Falls and Lead (changed to Rapid City in 1930). During his administration in Sioux Falls, O'Gorman continued his Roman contacts and visits and was appointed (1902), through the offices of Archbishop Ireland, to the Taft Commission to deal with Rome regarding the friars' land problem in the Philippine Islands. St. Joseph's Cathedral in Sioux Falls was completed in 1919, and Columbus College was begun in 1909, first in Chamberlain and after 1921 in Sioux Falls, and continued until it was closed in 1939 because of financial difficulties. At the close of O'Gorman's 26 years as bishop of Sioux Falls, the Catholic population had doubled to 69,164 and there were 127 diocesan and 13 religious priests serving 114 churches and 83 missions in his jurisdiction.

[C. BARRY]

O'HARA, EDWIN VINCENT

Bishop, sociologist; b. Lanesboro, Minn., Sept. 6, 1881; d. Milan, Italy, Sept. 11, 1956. His parents, Owen and Margaret (Nugent) O'Hara, sent him to public schools for his early education. Later he entered St. Thomas College and the Seminary of St. Paul, St. Paul, Minn. He was accepted for the Archdiocese of Oregon City (later Portland), Ore., and was ordained on June 10, 1905, in St. Paul. His first assignment by Archbishop Alexander Christie was as assistant at the cathedral in Portland. In 1907 he formed the Summer Institute for Teachers and the Catholic Education Association of Oregon. Following a period of ill health in 1910, he spent a year of advanced study at The CATHOLIC UNIVERSITY OF AMERICA, Washington, D.C. Upon returning to Portland, he demonstrated a practical concern for social rights characteristic of the Progressive Movement of that period. His initial interest was in the struggle for minimum wages for women and a general minimum-wage law. Supported by the National Consumers League, he led a committee whose report was instrumental in the enactment in 1913 of the Oregon minimum-wage law, which was to be tested in the courts in the case of *Stettler v. O'Hara*. O'Hara's role in the making of this legislation was indicated when Governor Oswald West named him chairman of the new State Industrial Welfare Commission.

Apart from such achievements, however, it was in the area of rural sociology that O'Hara was to attain his greatest reputation. After his return from service as chaplain with the U.S. Army in France in 1918, he began to promote Catholic education in rural districts. In 1920 at the National Catholic Welfare Conference (NCWC), he proposed the establishment of the Rural Life Bureau and became its first chairman. After obtaining a transfer to the rural parish of Eugene, Ore., he devoted himself to the problems of country life, publishing *A Program of Catholic Rural Action* (1922) and *The Church and the Country Community* (1927) and convening the first National Catholic Rural Life Conference in St. Louis, Mo., in 1923. O'Hara's interest in rural welfare was combined with concern for education. In 1922 he had organized the first Catholic Religious Vacation School and, when the Oregon School Bill requiring compulsory attendance at public schools was proposed, he led the fight against it with the aid of many noted jurists. As archdiocesan superintendent of schools, he conducted litigation in state courts and the U.S. Supreme Court that resulted in the Oregon law being declared unconstitutional. From 1929 to 1930 O'Hara was directly engaged in teaching, offering courses in parish sociology at The Catholic University of America and, during the summer, at the University of Notre Dame, Ind.

On Nov. 5, 1930, O'Hara was consecrated as bishop of Great Falls, Mont. From the start of his episcopacy he sought to advance the Confraternity of Christian Doctrine. After establishing the confraternity in his diocese on Dec. 17, 1930, he helped to form a Rocky Mountain and Pacific Coast confraternity and to establish a national headquarters for the confraternity at The Catholic University of America. He secured the appointment of a committee of the hierarchy to study the question, and he was instrumental in obtaining a letter from the Congregation of the Council on Jan. 12, 1933, requiring the establishment of the confraternity in each diocese. Thereafter a national center for the confraternity was located at NCWC headquarters in Washington, D.C., and on Oct. 31, 1935, the first congress of the confraternity was held in Rochester, N.Y. Catechetical reform and biblical translation also received attention from Bishop O'Hara. He headed a committee of bishops who prepared a revision of the Baltimore Catechism, which had not been changed since its adoption by the Third Plenary Council in 1884. The revision was published on June 21, 1941, under the auspices of the confraternity. In January of 1936, O'Hara organized a committee of theologians and Scripture scholars to discuss a revised English translation of the Scriptures. Subsequently, the Catholic Biblical Association of America was formed on Oct. 3, 1936, and the *Catholic Biblical Quarterly* began publication in 1938. In 1952, the anniversary of the invention of printing and of the publication of the Gutenberg Bible, the Confraternity of Christian Doctrine published its first volume of the revised version of the Old Testament, containing eight historical books. At this time O'Hara received a special letter of commendation from Pius XII.

On April 16, 1939, O'Hara was appointed to the See of Kansas City, Mo. (changed on August 29, 1956, to Kansas City-St. Joseph). There he earned the title of "the building Bishop," adding, within 10 years, 42 churches, 14 convents, 16 grade schools, 6 high schools, and 2 colleges. In September of 1954 O'Hara was made personal archbishop. He died while on his way to the International Congress of the Restored Liturgy in Assisi, Italy.

Bibliography: J. G. SHAW, *Edwin Vincent O'Hara, American Prelate* (New York 1957). T. M. DOLAN, *Some Seed Fell on Good Ground* (Washington, D.C. 1992).

[T. T. MCAVOY]

O'HARA, JOHN FRANCIS

Cardinal; b. Ann Arbor, Mich., May 1, 1888; d. Philadelphia, Pa., Aug. 28, 1960. As the son of John and Eleanor (Thornton) O'Hara, he received his early education in the parochial grade school and public high school of Peru, Ind., where his father was a practicing lawyer. Later he studied at the Collegio de Sagrada Corazon in Montevideo, Uruguay, where his father served as American consul. On returning to the U.S., he entered the University of Notre Dame, Ind., where he taught Spanish while earning his bachelor of philosophy degree. He entered the novitiate of the Congregation of Holy Cross, Aug. 15, 1912, made his first profession Sept. 14, 1914, and was ordained in Indianapolis, Ind., on Sept. 9, 1916, by Bp. Joseph Chartrand. He spent the first year of his priesthood in historical studies at The Catholic University of America, Washington, D.C., followed by a summer at the Wharton School of Commerce at the University of Pennsylvania, Philadelphia. In September 1917 he returned to Notre Dame University and established a department of commerce in response to the increased enrollment of prospective businessmen in the university. With O'Hara as dean, this became the College of Commerce in 1920.

In his priestly activities, O'Hara began to manifest the same zeal in administering the Sacraments that he had shown as a builder of the business school. While acting as a counselor to the students, he urged them to take advantage of the possibility of frequent and even daily Holy Communion, which had been revived by the decrees of Pius X. He was made prefect of religion and gave up his deanship to devote his time to this work and to teaching some classes in religion. Despite the increasing enrollment in the university after World War I, he literally became acquainted with nearly every one of the 2,000 or more students. To reach them, he began to post and later to distribute a one-page religious bulletin in which he combined criticism of student weaknesses with strong inspiration. In 1933, when Rev. Charles O'Donnell, CSC, President of Notre Dame University, became fatally ill, O'Hara was appointed acting president. He was elected president the following year. His presidency was signalized by the increase and advancement of the faculty, the erection of new buildings, and the expansion of undergraduate work. On Dec. 11, 1939, Pius XII named him titular bishop of Milasa and military delegate to Abp. (later Cardinal) Francis Spellman of New York, Military Vicar of the Armed Forces of the U.S. O'Hara was consecrated Jan. 15, 1940, at Notre Dame by Spellman; he established headquarters in New York, where he was joined by Bp. William T. McCarty, CSSR.

Because of the draft law and the expansion of the army and navy after World War II began in Europe, the office of military delegate acquired a great importance that was increased when the U.S. entered the war in December 1941. O'Hara not only administered the central office in New York, but visited personally the camps and offices of the chaplains, administering the Sacrament of Confirmation and looking into the spiritual welfare of soldiers and sailors. He reorganized the military ordinariate, setting up eight military vicar delegates, and during the war he supervised nearly 5,000 priests who attended to the religious needs of Catholics in the Armed Forces.

On March 10, 1945, O'Hara was transferred to the See of Buffalo, N.Y., where he was installed by Spellman on May 8, 1945. During his episcopate, he renovated the cathedral church, established new parishes, introduced new religious communities, and held a National Eucharistic Congress in 1947. O'Hara was appointed to the See of Philadelphia, vacated by the death of Cardinal Dennis Dougherty on Dec. 28, 1951, and he was installed by Abp. Amleto Cicognani, Apostolic Delegate, on Jan. 9, 1952. O'Hara brought to his new position the same zeal for Catholic education and for frequent reception of the Sacraments that had characterized his work as chaplain at Notre Dame University, as military delegate, and as bishop of Buffalo. He established 55 new parishes and 14 new Catholic high schools, and reorganized the administration of the archdiocesan charities. He continued his efforts to have personal contact with both clergy and laity. John XXIII made him a member of the College of Cardinals Dec. 15, 1958. Already his active career as priest and administrator had begun to weaken his health. Although frequently hampered by arthritis and other infirmities, the cardinal endeavored to meet all his commitments. He died in Philadelphia, and his body was returned to Sacred Heart Church at Notre Dame for burial.

Bibliography: Articles by T. T. MCAVOY et al., in *Records of the American Catholic Historical Society of Philadelphia* 64.1 (1953) 3–56.

[T. T. MCAVOY]

O'HELY, PATRICK, BL.

Irish bishop of Mayo, martyr; b. west Ireland, probably Connacht (formerly Connaught), date unknown; d. Kilmallock, County Limerick, 1579. Little is known with certainty of his early career beyond his education in Spain and Italy by the Franciscans, his ordination, and his consecration as bishop of Mayo c. 1576. In this period of Irish history the Celtic clergy, and especially the hierarchy on the continent, were barred from relieving Irish Catholics at home of their shortage of priests and the Tudor government kept a constant vigil on all Irish harbors to prevent European-ordained clerics from returning. But Bishop O'Hely, with a number of clerical companions, slipped into Ireland by following a roundabout course through Dingle Bay into Kerry not far from Tralee. Although he eluded the royal guards who were assigned to search ships, he was turned over to the royal authorities by an informer a few weeks after his arrival. Following his arrest he was summoned before Sir William Drury, the king's representative at Kilmallock in County Limerick. O'Hely refused to deny his faith or recognize Queen Elizabeth I as head of the church. He and his close companion Father Cornelius O'Rorke (O'Rourke) were tortured, placed on the rack, their legs and arms broken with hammers, and sharp instruments wedged into the nails of their fingers and toes. After several days of torment both were hanged and their bodies suspended on the gallows for more than two weeks. O'Hely was beatified on Sept. 27, 1992.

Bibliography: W. M. BRADY, *The Episcopal Succession in England, Scotland, and Ireland, A. D. 1400 to 1875*, 3 v. (Rome 1876–77). J. S. CRONE, *Concise Dictionary of Irish Biography* (rev. ed. Dublin 1937). M. W. P. O'REILLY, *Memorials of Those Who Suffered for the Faith in Ireland* (London 1868). A. J. WEBB, *Compendium of Irish Biography* (Dublin 1878). A. F. POLLARD, *The Dictionary of National Biography from the Earliest Times to 1900*, 63 v. (London 1885–1900) 14:959.

[E. J. MURRAY]

OHIO, CATHOLIC CHURCH IN

The first state formed from the Northwest Territory, Ohio was admitted into the Union in 1803. Its prehistoric inhabitants were the Hopewell, also known as the Mound Builders because of their earthen mounds used for burial and, perhaps, ritual practices. There are many of these burial grounds and other unusual earthworks still preserved in the state, the most noteworthy being the Great Serpent Mound near Hillsboro, Ohio. The Seneca from Canada, Michigan, and New York also constituted a strong presence in Ohio as they followed the Allegheny and Ohio Rivers on long hunting forays in the winter months. The Miami and Wyandotte were also significant tribes within the geographical boundaries of the state.

Catholicism came to the territory with French explorers and missionaries who entered Ohio through Lake Erie and the Ohio River, but the first permanent settlement in Ohio was not established until 1788 at Marietta. From there the state grew rapidly. By 1800 the population exceeded 45,000, most of these coming from the eastern seaboard and Kentucky. Ethnically and religiously they were Protestant Ulster Irish accompanied later by a significant German immigration from Pennsylvania. Few of these early settlers were Catholic, but there was a settlement of French Catholics in Gallia County who founded

Archdiocese/Diocese	Year Created
Archdiocese of Cincinnati	1850
Diocese of Cleveland	1847
Diocese of Columbus	1868
Diocese of Steubenville	1944
Diocese of Toledo	1910
Diocese of Youngstown	1943

the city of Gallipolis, on the Ohio River, in the southeastern region of the state. Father Peter Joseph Didier, O.S.B., worked among these Catholics as early as 1791, but seems to have left in discouragement after a few years of hardship and failure.

Until 1785, the entire region was included in the jurisdiction of the Diocese of Quebec. There were several missionary journeys in the old territory and early missions were founded by French Jesuits. However, none of these became permanent, and Ohio remained mission territory into the 19th century. In 1789 the Diocese of Baltimore was established in the new republic, and Ohio became part of the first U.S. see.

About 1802 a small group of settlers from near the Maryland-Pennsylvania border moved into Somerset, Pennsylvania, and then went on to found a small community of Catholics called Somerset in southeastern Ohio. Mostly of Alsatian extraction and led by a devout Catholic, Jacob Dittoe, they petitioned Bishop John Carroll for priests to serve this new settlement. Jacob Dittoe, in fact, had written to Carroll twice, in 1805 and 1808, requesting priests for the isolated Catholic settlements of Ohio. It was not until 1818, after the founding of the Diocese of Bardstown in 1810 and the establishment of the Dominican Friars near Springfield, Kentucky, by Edward Fenwick, O.P. (1768–1832), that the first permanent parish in Ohio was founded. Fenwick and his nephew, Nicholas Young, O.P., came across the village of Somerset on one of their many missionary travels and authorized the construction of a church for the settlement. According to local lore, Father Fenwick heard an ax being wielded in the forest and veered from his route in order to discover the source of the sound. He found Dittoe at work clearing land. Eventually, the Dominicans were given 320 acres of cleared farmland, and Somerset became an important center for the friars. In 1830, the Dominican Sisters from Washington County, Kentucky, opened a girls' academy in Somerset. St. Joseph in Somerset remained an education and formation center for the eastern province of the Dominican Fathers until 1968. The priory remained standing until 1976. The Dominican Sisters moved to St. Mary of the Springs in Columbus in 1868, after struggling with the consequences of a disastrous fire in 1866, and have maintained the old St. Mary of the Springs College and Academy as Ohio Dominican College.

On June 19, 1824, Pope Pius VII responded to the expanding Catholic population in Ohio and created the Diocese of Cincinnati with Edward Fenwick as its first bishop. The bishop of Bardstown, Benedict Flaget, consecrated Fenwick in St. Rose Church, Washington County, Kentucky, on Jan. 14, 1822. Fenwick had immediate problems when he transferred his residence from the outskirts of Cincinnati to a location in the city on Sycamore Street. The laity challenged the merging of diocesan and Dominican property and brought the dispute before the Congregation for the Propagation of the Faith. The congregation ordered a separation of diocesan and Dominican property, and in 1828 established the policy that diocesan property was to be held by Fenwick in the name of the diocese and willed to his successor in the See of Cincinnati. This arrangement spread throughout the Northwest Territory and is credited with keeping trusteeism from becoming a major problem for the Church in these states.

Fenwick was not only a residential bishop but also an active missionary. He traveled extensively throughout Ohio. Fenwick was born of a large landholding family in Maryland and had joined the English province of the Dominicans in Belgium. He returned to Europe on fund raising missions and was aided by Pope Leo XIII's support in collecting significant funds in Belgium, Holland and England. During his absence, from 1823 to 1825, a new episcopal residence was constructed and a cathedral completed and dedicated on Dec. 17, 1826. Fenwick opened a theological seminary, St. Aloysius, in May 1829. Fenwick's intense labors and travels left him in poor health. He petitioned for a coadjutor but died on a missionary journey in Wooster, Ohio, on Sept. 26, 1832, before one was appointed. On May 12, 1833, Pope Gregory XVI named John Baptist PURCELL (1800–83) as the second bishop of Cincinnati. He had completed his studies for the priesthood at St. Sulpice in Paris and was ordained by the archbishop of Paris before returning as professor and president of Mt. St. Mary's in Emmitsburg, Maryland. He was consecrated in Baltimore on Oct. 13, 1833. Purcell's half century in office as bishop and later archbishop of Cincinnati was a period of enormous growth and expansion of the Church in the state of Ohio. He was a learned and expansive man with a flair for the dramatic.

During the early years of Purcell's reign, there was a significant social change underway in Cincinnati. The Catholic population was transformed from an Irish Catholic community into a predominantly German Catholic Church with a minimum of ethnic tensions. Purcell, in contrast to the situation in many other urban areas of the country, was able to manage the transition with a minimum of ethnic tension and conflict. This was unique in the American Church where newer ethnic groups often clashed with the increasingly numerous Irish American hierarchy.

Purcell's European experience gave him inroads into the Church in Europe where he received both financial assistance and personnel for his rapidly growing missionary diocese. A participant in the first VATICAN COUNCIL, he initially opposed the definition of papal infallibility for ecumenical reasons. He had clearly and articulately defended his position in a series of public debates in Ohio with Alexander CAMPBELL, founder of the Disciples of Christ, in 1836. Nevertheless, he accepted the conciliar definition and, while remaining seemingly intellectually unconvinced, offered his obedience to the Church and, personally, to Pope Pius IX. Edward FITZGERALD, a priest of the Archdiocese of Cincinnati who became bishop of Little Rock in 1867, actually voted against the definition at the council, though he too publicly acquiesced.

Purcell allowed great freedom to the German congregations in Cincinnati and accepted a moderate form of trusteeism for the German parishes. Because of the earlier arrangement between the Irish Catholics and Bishop Fenwick, the actual ownership of the German parishes remained in the hands of the local bishop. The extreme forms of trusteeism, therefore, were not realized in Cincinnati. Purcell, however, was careful not to extend this form of local government to the Irish congregations of Cincinnati. He accepted the assistance of the Tirolean province of the Franciscan Fathers, centered in Innsbruck, Austria, to work with the German population in the city of Cincinnati. He also secured the services of the Precious Blood Fathers and Brothers, under the leadership of Father Francis de Sales Brunner, to serve the rural German population of northwestern Ohio. Both of these religious communities became separate provinces centered in the diocese, the Franciscans in Cincinnati and the Precious Blood Fathers in Carthagena, Ohio.

In 1850, Pope Pius IX raised Cincinnati, along with New York and New Orleans, to the status of an archdiocese, and Purcell became the first archbishop of the new province of Ohio. One of his goals was to open a seminary to provide the necessary education for those called to the priesthood. After several attempts, he undertook the construction of a facility west of the city, on Price Hill. The new seminary opened in 1851 as Mt. St. Mary's of the West. The name was reminiscent of his days as rector of Mt. St. Mary's in Maryland. In 1924 the seminary was moved to Norwood, Ohio, and in the early 1980s to its present location on the eastside of Cincinnati. Religious sisters also came to serve the expanding Catholic population of the state. St. Elizabeth Ann Seton's Sisters of Charity had arrived from Emmitsburg in 1829 and undertook educational and charitable works throughout the diocese. When their congregation affiliated with the French Daughters of Charity, the sisters in Cincinnati chose to become a separate canonical community known as the Sisters of Charity of Cincinnati. In 1920 they established their College of Mt. St. Joseph's on the Ohio. Among the many notable women of the congregation, Sister Blandina Segale has a special place in the folklore of the American West as friend and teacher of Billy the Kid. In 1830, when Bishop Fenwick brought four Dominican Sisters from Kentucky to open a school in Somerset, they included Sister Benvin Sansbury, the sister of Sister Angela Sansbury, the first Dominican Sister professed in the United States. In 1839, Bishop Purcell obtained the services of the Sisters of Notre Dame, while visiting their motherhouse in Namur, Belgium, and in 1840, eight Notre Dame Sisters opened a school for girls at St. Xavier's Parish in Cincinnati, and in 1865, a school for Holy Cross and St. Patrick's parishes in Columbus.

The remarkable growth of the numbers of religious communities of women in the 19th century worked to the great benefit of the Church in Ohio. By mid-century the Sisters of Mercy from Kinsale, Ireland, the Franciscan Sisters of Stella Niagara, New York, the Ursulines, the Sisters of the Holy Humility of Mary, Sisters of Saint Joseph, the Good Shepherd Sisters, and many other congregations had come to serve the expanding Catholic population of the state. They worked not only in Cincinnati and the other early Catholic settlements, but also among the Catholics moving into the Ohio River valley, the industrially developing cities of Youngstown, Cleveland, Steubenville, and Toledo, and the German farmlands of northwest Ohio. The Sisters of the Precious Blood were an important part of the rural German communities of northwestern Ohio. Along with the Precious Blood Fathers, they were the most significant religious presence throughout that part of the state. Purcell's reign ended, sadly, in scandal and personal tragedy. His brother and chancellor, Father Edward Purcell, had tried to provide a safe banking service for the Catholics of Cincinnati and was successful during some of the financial crises of the mid-19th century. During the Panic of 1877–78, however, there was a run on Purcell's financial holdings and the funds to respond to the demands were simply not available. In fact, there were only a third of the funds demanded available. The legal battles were not finally resolved until 1905 when investors received a settlement based on their initial investments.

Archbishop Purcell publicly acknowledged the terrible situation and offered his resignation to Pope Leo XIII. The pope allowed Purcell to retain the title of archbishop,

but he retired, with his brother, to the Ursuline convent in St. Martin, Ohio. He died there, after suffering a series of strokes, on July 4, 1883. He was succeeded by the bishop of Natchez, Mississippi, William Henry Elder, who faced the task of managing a financially shattered archdiocese while at the same time attempting to maintain the growth and strength of the Catholic Church in the aftermath of disillusionment, anger, and loss of faith. The situation was so widely known and so severe that Bishops Edward Fitzgerald of Little Rock and Bernard McQuaid of Rochester had both refused the appointment to Cincinnati. Elder turned out to be an excellent choice. He was learned and cultured and a good reconciler of divergent opinions and conflicting movements. He held the position for 24 years and died Oct. 31, 1904. The courts dealt with the Purcell financial scandal during Elder's entire time as archbishop.

In addition to the strong European immigrant communities, there were also African American Catholics in Ohio in the 19th century. Daniel Rudd (1854–1903), who had been born a slave in Bardstown, Kentucky, published a black Catholic weekly newspaper, *American Catholic Tribune*, beginning in the late 1880s. Beginning in Springfield, Ohio, where he had migrated in order to attend high school, he eventually published the newspaper in Cincinnati, and then in Detroit, until the late 1890s. He was confident that the Catholic Church possessed the means, through its teaching and its structure, to overcome all forms of racism in the nation. Rudd was a principal organizer of the five black Catholic lay congresses, whose delegates were elected by parishes across the country, that were held between 1889 and 1894, including one in Cincinnati (1890). There was a continuing attraction for American blacks to convert to Catholicism through the mid-20th century. In several small southern Ohio cities, blacks were not welcome to pursue high school education in the public schools, and so many converted to Catholicism in order to attend Catholic high schools. Chillicothe, Ohio, the state's first capital, experienced this phenomenon, and families such as the Menefees, Mitchells, and Hairstons remain an important part of the black Catholic population of southern Ohio.

Cincinnati's jurisdiction had been divided twice during the reign of Archbishop Purcell. In 1847, Pope Pius IX created the Diocese of Cleveland, comprising the entire northern section of Ohio. The first bishop, Louis Amadeus Rappe, had come to America with three other French priests, John Baptist Lamy, Joseph Machebeuf and Louis de Groesbriand, all of whom had been recruited for the American missions by Archbishop Purcell. Lamy first went to Danville, Ohio, then known as Sapp Settlement, and served as a missionary priest in central Ohio, founding St. Vincent parish in Mt. Vernon, Ohio, and St. Francis de Sales in Newark, Ohio, before being named the archbishop of Santa Fe. He remains a significant figure in American literature as the archbishop in Willa Cather's *Death Comes for the Archbishop*. Groesbriand went on to become the bishop of Burlington, Vermont, and Machebeuf the bishop of the Diocese of Epiphany, later known as Denver.

Rappe had only one permanent church in his new diocese, St. Mary on the Flats. Within five years, Rappe had built a new cathedral dedicated to St. John the Evangelist. The Catholic population grew rapidly, and several synods were held to help guide the growing Church. Rappe faced great ethnic tensions when waves of immigration broke over the new diocese. The results were less fortuitous for Rappe in Cleveland than for Purcell in Cincinnati. Various ethnic groups in the new diocese were in great conflict with each other and the bishop. Rappe became increasingly disheartened by the intense conflict, and when he submitted his resignation to Pope Pius IX in 1870 while attending the Vatican Council, his enemies in Cleveland used the occasion to accuse him of scandalous behavior. The local newspaper, *The Leader*, took up the story, and Rappe was vilified throughout the city. No truth was ever ascertained concerning the charges of confessional solicitation, but Rappe happily took up missionary work in the Diocese of Burlington among the French-speaking population of northern New York and Vermont. He died on Grand Island in Lake Champlain in 1877, and was buried in the cathedral at Cleveland. On March 3, 1868, Cincinnati was further divided by the creation of the Diocese of Columbus. Sylvester Rosecrans, brother of the Civil War General William Rosecrans and auxiliary bishop of Cincinnati, was appointed the first bishop of Columbus. Rosecrans was converted to Catholicism while a student at Kenyon College in Gambier, Ohio. As a consequence of his conversion he had to withdraw from Kenyon, then an Episcopalian men's college founded by the Protestant Episcopal Bishop Philander Chase in 1824. By the time Rosecrans became bishop, Columbus had some 40,000 Catholics. Somerset, Ohio, site of the first permanent Catholic church in the state, was in the new diocese and remained under the Dominicans who had been there since 1818, and who still remained responsible for the church in Somerset into the year 2001. Rosecrans built a new cathedral for Columbus, neither wishing to choose the Irish church, St. Patrick's, nor the German church, Holy Cross (formerly St. Remigius parish), for his cathedral. He dedicated the new St. Joseph Cathedral on Oct. 20, 1878, and died the following day. He was succeeded by John Watterson, president of Mt. St. Mary's in Emmitsburg, Maryland.

Watterson paid off the cathedral debt but by expanding the number of parishes and schools, left the diocese heavily in debt. There was some consideration of suppressing the new diocese for financial reasons, but Watterson's death and the arrival of the financially adept former Cincinnati chancellor, Henry Moeller, ensured the continued existence of the Columbus diocese. In 1904, James J. Hartley was appointed bishop of Columbus. He reigned until 1944 and continued the expansion and building of the institutions which spread and supported the faith. In 1923 he opened a local seminary dedicated to St. Charles Borromeo, which remained in operation until 1969. It is now the only Catholic boys' high school in Columbus.

During the early 20th century, the industrial cities of Ohio grew so rapidly that new dioceses had to be created. In 1910 Toledo became a diocese. The first three bishops of Toledo were to move on to other sees: Joseph Schrembs to Cleveland, Samuel Stritch to Chicago, and Karl Alter to Cincinnati. The Toledo Cathedral of the Queen of the Most Holy Rosary was planned by Bishop Schrembs, begun by Bishop Stritch, and completed in 1940 by Bishop Alter. It is the finest example of Spanish Plateresque architecture in the country. Toledo, like the other Ohio industrial cities, was challenged to care for the great waves of immigrants pouring in from eastern and southern Europe. During the Second World War, the wartime economy with its demand for steel and other materials needed for the war effort provided ample opportunity for numerous Catholic immigrants to find work in the Ohio industrial belt. Two new dioceses were erected during these years of rapid wartime expansion: Youngstown, with James McFadden as bishop (1943–52), in 1943, and Steubenville, with John King Mussio as bishop (1945–77), in 1944. Schools, hospitals, colleges, and charitable institutions proliferated throughout the state. The sacrifice and hard work of religious sisters maintained most of these institutions.

Ohio became a center for Catholic higher education. Major colleges and universities were founded and sustained by religious congregations of men and women. The University of Dayton was founded in 1850 by the Marianist Fathers and Brothers who still provide the leadership of the university. Ohio's largest Catholic university, it draws students from across the United States and abroad. The Marian Institute of the university has the largest Marian library in the world and grants pontifical degrees in Marian theology through its affiliation with the Marianum University in Rome.

Xavier University in Cincinnati and John Carroll University in Cleveland were founded by the Society of Jesus, in 1831 and 1886 respectively. These Jesuit universities have provided the Catholic population of Ohio with the Jesuit educational tradition for well over a century and a half. Today they face the same Catholic identity issues that most Catholic colleges and universities face, but still maintain a significant number of priests and scholastics in administration and on the teaching faculty.

The Ursuline Sisters of Toledo and Cleveland were leaders in Catholic higher education for women in northern Ohio, as were the Sisters of Mercy in Toledo and the Holy Humility of Mary Sisters in Cleveland. The College of Mt. St. Joseph on the Ohio, founded by the Sisters of Charity of Cincinnati, has been a mainstay of Catholic women's education in the Archdiocese of Cincinnati. The funds for the establishment and development of these institutions and other institutions owned and operated by communities of women religious throughout the state and the country were acquired through the ability and skill of the sisters themselves, giving further testimony to the extraordinary ability and resourcefulness of American women religious. Few women in American society during the 19th and early part of the 20th centuries had such opportunities to develop and use their education and natural abilities in such public and professional ways. As the decline in vocations to the religious life accelerated and the costs of operation increased greatly, many of the smaller Catholic colleges merged, closed or secularized. Nevertheless many remained and continue to provide educational opportunities for the people of Ohio and across the country.

A unique phenomenon in Catholic higher education in Ohio is the Franciscan University of Steubenville. Founded in 1946 as the College of Steubenville by the Sacred Heart Province of the Third Order Regular of St. Francis with the cooperation of Bishop John King Mussio, the university floundered for many years until Father Michael Scanlan, T.O.R., was elected president in 1974. He led the university into the Charismatic movement and beyond. By the time Scanlan retired as president in 2000, after 26 years of service, the university had gained a national reputation by placing a strong emphasis on orthodoxy and youthful enthusiasm, and had won recognition as a source of church renewal and youth retreats.

Ohio is also the home of the Pontifical College Josephinum, a seminary that offers undergraduate, pretheology and theology degree programs. Founded originally as St. Joseph's Orphan Home in Pomeroy, Ohio, by German born Father Joseph J. Jessing, the institution became incorporated as a seminary in Columbus in 1888. Jessing sought to provide free seminary education for poor German boys to serve the needs of the German immigrant population of the United States, and at the founder's initiative, the seminary came under pontifical jurisdiction in 1892. With the Apostolic Nuncio to the United States as the Chancellor and also the Ordinary of the Josephinum, the seminary holds the unusual position of being the only such institution for the education of students for the priesthood outside of Italy. The state is also home to three diocesan seminaries, Mt. St. Mary's of the West in Cincinnati, as well as Borromeo and St. Mary Seminaries in Cleveland.

The hierarchy of Ohio has played a major role in the life of the Church of the United States. Cardinal Joseph Bernardin, as general secretary of the National Catholic Welfare Conference (NCWC), was instrumental in founding the United States Catholic Conference and the National Conference of Catholic Bishops (NCCB). He served there as general secretary and president. In 1972, he was named archbishop of Cincinnati and remained there until 1982, when he was transferred to the Archdiocese of Chicago. Bishop James Malone, bishop of Youngstown from 1966 to 1995, was also active in the NCWC and the NCCB, serving as its president from 1984 to 1986. Archbishop Daniel Pilarczyk of Cincinnati and Bishop Anthony Pilla of Cleveland have also served as presidents of the Conference, from 1990 to 1992, and from 1996 to 1998, respectively.

In addition to Cardinal Bernardin, Bishop Samuel Stritch of Toledo (1921–30) also became cardinal archbishop of Chicago. Bishop John J. Carberry of Columbus (1965–68) went on to become the cardinal archbishop of St. Louis. Bishop James Hickey of Cleveland (1974–80) became the cardinal archbishop of Washington and Auxiliary Bishop John Krol of Cleveland (1953–61) became the cardinal archbishop of Philadelphia. Other Ohio bishops have also had a significant impact on the life of the national Church. Most notable among these were Archbishops John T. McNicholas of Cincinnati (1925–50) and Karl J. Alter, also of Cincinnati (1950–69). Joseph Schrembs, Bishop of Cleveland (1921–45) and Edward F. Hoban, Bishop of Cleveland (1945–66) were both awarded the personal title of archbishop in recognition of their leadership roles within the Church in the United States.

The bishops of Ohio collaborate in the work of the Church in the state through the Ohio Catholic Conference. Founded in 1945 under the presidency of Archbishop McNicholas, it was known as the Ohio Catholic Welfare Conference. In 1967, in conformity with the change in the National Catholic Welfare Conference, it changed its name to the Ohio Catholic Conference. Meetings are usually held twice a year in Columbus under the presidency of the archbishop of Cincinnati. The conference identifies itself as "the official representative of the Catholic Church in public matters affecting the Church and the general welfare of the citizens of Ohio." It focuses on educational and health issues as well as social concerns, and it lobbies the state legislature on issues pertaining to Catholic interests and those of the general well-being of the citizens of the state.

The Catholic Church in Ohio rests on the institutions, leadership, and labor of earlier leaders; clerical, religious, and lay. From Jacob Dittoe of Somerset to the German trustees of Cincinnati to the newer forms of public presence, the faithful have built and sustained a strong community of believers. The Church in Ohio has positioned itself well to face the challenges of its next century.

Bibliography: The story is recorded by R. BRENNAN, O.P., in *Cradle of the Faith in Ohio,* published in 1968. F. F. BROWN, *A History of the Roman Catholic Diocese of Steubenville, Vol. I: The Mussio Years 1945–1977* (Lewiston/Queenston/Lampeter 1994). J. J. HARTLEY, ed., *A History of the Diocese of Columbus,* 2 v. (Columbus, Ohio 1918–43). Also see The Catholic Record Society, 197 East Gay St. Columbus, Ohio 43215. M. E. HUSSEY, *A History of the Archdiocese of Cincinnati* (Strasbourg, France 2000). M. J. HYNES, *History of the Diocese of Cleveland: Origin and Growth (1847–1952)* (Cleveland 1953). L. A. MOSSING, *History of the Diocese of Toledo,* 9 v. (Fremont, Ohio 1983).

[F. P. LANE]

O'HURLEY, DERMOT, BL.

Archbishop, listed among Irish martyrs proposed for canonization; b. Lycadoon, Limerick, 1519; d. Dublin, June 30, 1584. After graduating at Louvain in 1551, he taught philosophy there and subsequently canon and civil law at Reims. He was consecrated in Rome in 1581, and appointed archbishop of Cashel September 11, receiving the pallium November 27. Landing near Dublin in September 1583, he escaped capture in Drogheda and Slane and proceeded to his own province. Because of the government's threats to his host in Slane, he surrendered at Carrick–on–Suir and was imprisoned in Dublin Castle October 7. He was examined repeatedly by lord justices Loftus and Wallop and, on instructions of Elizabeth's secretary Walsingham, was tortured. Denying charges of treason but refusing religious conformity, he was, on Elizabeth's mandate, hanged after being condemned by martial law, there being no evidence for conviction by civil courts. According to tradition, he was buried in St. Kevin's churchyard, Dublin. O'Hurley was beatified on Sept. 27, 1992.

Bibliography: S. Ó MURTHUILE, *A Martyred Archbishop of Cashel* (Dublin 1935).

[J. HURLEY]

OKEGHEM, JAN VAN

Great Renaissance composer of the Flemish school (also Ockeghem, Okenghem); b. Hainaut?, Flanders, c. 1420; d. Tours, France, *c.* 1495. He began his musical career as a member of the polyphonic section of the Antwerp cathedral choir. In 1446 he joined the chapel of the Duke of Bourbon and seven years later transferred to the Royal Chapel, where he successively served as chaplain and composer to three French Kings, Charles VII, Louis XI, and Charles VIII. He was appointed treasurer of the Abbey of St. Martin, of which French monarchs were titular abbots. Fellow musicians wrote motets in his honor during his lifetime and elegies at his death. His stature and influence during the later 15th century were considerable, for his style both links and separates the era of DUFAY and that of DESPREZ.

Although he wrote some secular music, Okeghem's church music forms by far the larger and more important part of his output. Plainsong is used either as a *cantus firmus* or by way of paraphrase in several of his motets, which include magnificent settings of the antiphons AVE MARIA, SALVE REGINA, and ALMA REDEMPTORIS MATER. The responsory for Vespers of the Purification, *Gaude Maria,* is also a work of impressive proportions and noble polyphonic textures. Of his Masses, 11 survive in complete form. He was one of many composers who successfully transmuted the secular character of the *L'homme armé* melody into a contrapuntal mosaic of intensely religious fervor, and (like Dufay and J. OBRECHT) he employed the flowing final melisma of a Maundy Thursday antiphon in a notable *Missa Caput.* In the *Missa Fors seulement* he draws upon a rondeau of his own composition for highly diversified melodic material. Of his four-part Masses, the *Missa Mi-Mi* (so called for its bass voice motto) provides ready proof of his ability to write a straightforward and classical style. Both the *Missa Cuiusvis toni* and the *Missa Prolationum* are feats of almost unrivaled musical technique, the latter providing a veritable ''art of canon'' comparable to J. S. BACH's great *Art of Fugue.* The impressive Requiem qualifies as the earliest extant polyphonic setting of the *Missa pro Defunctis.*

Bibliography: *Collected Works,* ed. D. PLAMENAC (2d ed. Philadelphia 1959–). D. PLAMENAC, *Die Musik in Geschichte und Gegenwart,* ed. F. BLUME (Kassel-Basel 1949–) 9: 1826–38. G. REESE, *Music in the Renaissance* (rev. ed. New York 1959) F. FITCH, *Johannes Ockeghem: Masses and Models* (Paris 1997). A. MAGRO, '''Premièrement ma baronie de Chasteauneuf': Jean de Ockeghem, Treasurer of St. Martin's in Tours'' *Early Music History 18: Studies in Medieval and Early Modern Music,* ed. I. FENLON (Cambridge 1997) 165–258. M. J. RALEY, ''Johannes Ockeghem and the Motet *Gaude Maria Virgo,*'' *Anuario Musical* 46 (1991), 27–55. E. SCHREURS, ''Ockeghem in Tours herdacht,'' *Musica Antiqua* 14 (1997), 77–78. R. STEWART, ''. . .*Ita desiderat anima mea ad te, Deus* (Ps. 42:1), Johannes Ockeghem, a Most Medieval Composer,'' *Tidschrift van de Koninklijke Vereniging voor Nederlandse Muziekgeschiedenis* 47 (1997), 163–200. J. VAN BENTHEM, '''Prenez sur moy vostre exemple': *Signae,* Text and Cadences in Ockeghem's *Prenez sur moy* and *Missa Cuiusvis toni,*'' *Tidschrift van de Koninklijke Vereniging voor Nederlandse Muziekgeschiedenis*

47 (1997), 99–118. D. VAN OVERSTRAETEN, "Le lieu de naissance de Jean Ockeghem (ca 1420–1497), une énigme élucidée," *Revue Belge de Musicologie* 46 (1992), 23–32.

[D. STEVENS]

OKLAHOMA, CATHOLIC CHURCH IN

Located in the southwestern United States, Oklahoma was admitted to the Union in 1907 as the 46th state. It is bounded on the north by Kansas and Colorado, on the east by Missouri and Arkansas, on the south by the Red River and Texas, and on the west by New Mexico and the Texas Panhandle.

History. The area, traversed by Coronado in the 16th century and explored by the Spanish and French in the 17th and 18th centuries, became the property of the United States by the Louisiana Purchase of 1803. Federal policy very early designated it as a permanent home for the resettlement of various Native American tribes, and the Five Civilized Tribes of the southeastern United States were moved there (1830–45). Virtually the whole area was originally apportioned to these groups, but their tribal districts were later reduced, in part because of their support for the Confederacy during the Civil War. Many other tribes were then relocated within what became known as Indian Territory. One unassigned portion near the center, which became known as the Oklahoma Territory, was opened to white settlement by the famous run of April 22, 1889. Meanwhile the U.S. government directed the native peoples to give up tribal title to their reservation lands and to take allotments as individuals. The resulting "surplus" lands were opened to whites between 1891 and 1906. This made it possible for the Twin Territories to be granted statehood on Nov. 16, 1907.

In Oklahoma, a traditional stronghold of white Protestant culture, residents of foreign birth were few before 20th century. The Southern Baptists constitute the most numerous church group; the Methodists, Presbyterians, Church of Christ, and Disciples of Christ have sizable memberships. Numerous evangelical sects are very active, but the Jewish and Muslim populations are minimal. In the 2001 state population of 3,724,000, Catholics numbered 160,898, or about four percent of the total population of the state.

Missionary Activity. Although friars and priests had accompanied the Coronado and DeSoto expeditions when they passed through the region in 1541 and 1542, no Catholic missionary activity was seen again until 1830, when the Jesuit Charles Van Quickenborne offered Mass at three sites in the northeast portion of the present state. Nominally under the bishop of St. Louis, Missouri, from 1826 to 1843, this vast country was visited occasionally by Jesuits from the Osage Mission in St. Paul, Kansas, who ministered to the army camps and native tribes. When the Diocese of Little Rock, Arkansas, was erected in 1843, Oklahoma was included within its original boundaries. Priests from Fort Smith, Arkansas, made regular missionary tours through the western extension of the diocese.

Of the many tribes in the Oklahoma territory during the 19th century, only two were predominantly Catholic, the Osage and Potowatomi. The first Catholic church in Indian Territory was built in 1872 at Atoka, Choctaw Nation, by Rev. Michael Smyth of Ft. Smith, but he attended it irregularly. Permanent missionary activity began in 1875 with the arrival of French Benedictines from the Abbey of Pierre-que-Vire. Dom Isidore ROBOT, briefly taking up residence in Atoka, was appointed the first prefect apostolic of the Indian Territory in 1876. (This was the only prefecture apostolic ever established in a region that was then part of the United States.) Among the Potowatomi, Robot founded Sacred Heart Mission, termed "the cradle of Catholicity in Oklahoma," and built boarding schools for boys and girls, the latter in the care of Sisters of Mercy from Lacon, Illinois. He was named an abbot *honoris causa* by Pope Leo XIII in 1879.

The Benedictine prefecture under Robot and his successor, Ignatius Jean, continued until 1891, when the first bishop, Theophile Meerschaert, a Belgian-born priest working in Mississippi, took over the administration of the Twin Territories. Although Meerschaert's title at first was Vicar Apostolic of the Indian Territory (1891–1905), in fact the Church was too late on the scene to do much effective evangelization of Native Americans, who were too disheartened and disorganized to respond to the white man's religion. Growth of the Church in Oklahoma would come with the arrival of Irish railroad workers, Italian and Polish coal miners, and German farmers.

The seat of the vicariate was located at Guthrie, the territorial capital following the land run of 1889, but in 1905 when the vicariate was elevated to diocesan rank and, styled the Diocese of Oklahoma, Bishop Meerschaert moved the see city to Oklahoma City, which was shortly to become the state capital. Counting his time as vicar apostolic, Bishop Meerschaert served in Oklahoma for almost 33 years (1891–1924). Under Meerschaert there was a rapid growth in the number of churches and missions, and a large increase in priests and sisters. An incident that occurred during his episcopate was to have lasting significance on the national scene. In 1917 the state legislature passed the so-called Bone-Dry Law, which forbade the import of alcoholic spirits into Oklahoma. (Manufacture of wine and liquor within the state boundaries was already forbidden by the Oklahoma constitution.) The diocese went to court, charging infringement of religion, and the state supreme court upheld the complaint in 1918. Ironically, this paved the way for national Prohibition, once the precedent for an exception on religious grounds was established in the Oklahoma case.

When Meerschaert died in 1924, he was succeeded by Francis Clement Kelley (1924–1948). Bishop Kelley, recognizing the growing importance of Tulsa to the life the state and the Church in Oklahoma, took steps to have the diocese redesignated as Diocese of Oklahoma and Tulsa in 1930. Kelley's successor was his close friend, Bishop Eugene J. McGuinness (1948–1957), who had served as coadjutor with right of succession since 1944. McGuinness in turn was succeeded by an Oklahoman, the pastor of the co-cathedral in Tulsa, Victor J. Reed (1958–1971). Shortly before his sudden death Bishop Reed had initiated discussions about dividing the diocese. Bishop John R. Quinn, his successor, carried the effort forward. In December 1972, Rome created a new ecclesiastical province. The metropolitan see was to be the Archdiocese of Oklahoma City, with Quinn as the first archbishop (1972–1977). The suffragan sees were to be Diocese of Tulsa with Msgr. Bernard J. Ganter, chancellor of the Galveston-Houston diocese, as the first bishop (1972–1977), and the Diocese of Little Rock, Arkansas, which was transferred from the Province of New Orleans.

See Also: OKLAHOMA CITY, ARCHDIOCESE OF; TULSA, DIOCESE OF.

Bibliography: M. U. THOMAS, *The Catholic Church on the Oklahoma Frontier, 1824–1907* (St. Louis 1938). T. E. BROWN, *Bible-belt Catholicism: A History of the Roman Catholic Church in Oklahoma, 1905–1904*, vol. 33. (New York 1977). J. D. WHITE, *Diary of a Frontier Bishop: The Journals of Theophile Meerschaert* (Tulsa 1994). J. D.WHITE, *Getting Sense: The Osages and their Missionaries* (Tulsa 1997); *This Far by Faith: 125 Years of Catholic Life in Oklahoma, 1875–2000* (Strasbourg, France 2001). G. FOREMAN, *A History of Oklahoma* (Norman, Okla. 1942). R. GITTINGER, *The Formation of the State of Oklahoma, 1803–1906* (Norman, Okla. 1939). E. C. MCREYNOLDS, *A History of the Sooner State* (Norman, Okla. 1954). *Oklahoma Statutes, 1961*, 3 v. (St. Paul 1961). *Oklahoma Digest, 1890 to Date* (St. Paul 1934-).

[J. F. MURPHY/W.C. GARTHOEFFNER/J.D. WHITE]

OKLAHOMA CITY, ARCHDIOCESE OF

By reason of a bull of Pope Paul VI (Dec. 13, 1972), the Diocese of Oklahoma City and Tulsa was divided and Oklahoma City (*Oklahomapolitana*) was designated the metropolitan see (Feb. 6, 1973). The state of Oklahoma had been established as a vicariate apostolic in 1891 and as a diocese in 1905 with Oklahoma City as the diocesan seat. In 1930 the see was redesignated the Diocese of Oklahoma City and Tulsa. At the time that the Archdiocese of Oklahoma City was established (February 1971), Tulsa was made a diocese, and it together with the Diocese of Little Rock, AR, became suffragans of the new archdiocese. At the time when the Archdiocese of Oklahoma City was first established there were about 65,000 Catholics in a total population of 1.5 million; in 2001 the population of the area increased to 2.2 million and the number of Catholics to 98,000.

When the Diocese of Little Rock, AR was erected (1843) it included the Indian Territory (now Oklahoma). Priests from Fort Smith, AR made regular missionary tours through the western extension of the diocese. In 1872, through the efforts of Father Michael Smyth, the first Catholic Church in Oklahoma was built at Atoka, then the terminus of the Missouri, Kansas and Texas railroad. Three years later, Bp. Edward Fitzgerald of Little Rock assigned the whole Indian Territory to the Benedictine Isidore ROBOT, the first priest to take up permanent residence in Oklahoma. On July 9, 1876, Piux IX established the Territory as a prefecture apostolic and named Robot first prefect. When he resigned in 1886, he was succeeded by another Benedictine, Ignatius Jean (1886–1890).

Diocesan Development. After the opening of a large portion of the area to white settlers in 1889, the Holy See, on May 29, 1891, raised Oklahoma to the status of a vicariate apostolic and appointed Theophile Meerschaert, then vicar general of the Diocese of Natchez, MS, vicar apostolic with episcopal rank.

Forty-four years old at the time of his appointment, Meerschaert would serve in Oklahoma for 32 years. It was a period of rapid growth in the number of churches and missions and a large increase in the ranks of the clergy and religious. Originally his seat was at Guthrie, the territorial capital following the Land Run, but on Aug. 17, 1905, the Diocese of Oklahoma was erected and the bishop's headquarters was moved to the rapidly growing town of Oklahoma City—which would become the state capital in 1910, three years after Oklahoma achieved statehood.

Bishop Meerschaert died in 1924 and was succeeded by Monsignor Francis Clement Kelley, founder and president of the Catholic Church Extension Society. One of the most illustrious churchmen to work in Oklahoma, he was the author of 17 books on a wide variety of subjects. As bishop he managed the Church's transition from a predominately rural population to an urban one, opening parishes in Oklahoma City and Tulsa, and suppressing several dozen marginal country parishes across the state.

He recognized the growing importance of Tulsa to the Church's life. Early in his episcopate he considered moving the episcopal seat there, but in 1930 he settled for a redesignation: the Diocese of Oklahoma City and Tulsa, naming the Church of the Holy Family (built in 1914) in Tulsa as the co-cathedral.

During the Depression, Kelley managed to keep the diocese financially solvent through publishing and by giving retreats and lectures around the country. (He was jokingly known as the bishop *from* Oklahoma.) Although his first years were marked by energetic efforts at expansion, the economic crisis of the 1930s made further initiatives inadvisable. Meerschaert had despaired of attracting American vocations, choosing instead to bring in priests and seminarians from Europe, particularly his native Belgium. Kelley ordained the first two Oklahoma-born diocesan priests in 1928. Relatively few ordinations followed in succeeding years, although Kelley promoted postgraduate studies in Rome and Louvain, and this led to several innovations, such as street preaching, and the introduction of the Young Christian Worker and Christian Family movements, begun in Belgium under Joseph Cardijn. (The first American unit of the Young Christian Workers was at Ponca City, OK).

In 1942 Kelley suffered a series of strokes and was a semi-invalid until his death in 1948. In 1944 Rome appointed as apostolic administrator, Bishop Eugene J. McGuinness, until then the bishop of Raleigh, NC. McGuinness led the Oklahoma church during the expansive postwar years, opening many new hospitals, parishes, and schools. He also campaigned forcefully for vocations. "You have given me your money," he would tell parishioners, "now give me your blood!" The result was an astounding increase among seminarians and religious women. Kelley had begun a junior seminary in 1928, but by the time it was ready to open, he had no funds to operate it. McGuinness established a temporary institution near Oklahoma City, then made plans for a permanent complex, which opened in 1958, a few months after his death. When the bishop began his episcopate in Oklahoma, there were 11 seminarians. Within a few years of the new seminary's inauguration, it had an enrollment of 128. Ordination ceremonies for 10 or 11 priests were common during the McGuinness years.

On Dec. 5, 1957, Monsignor Victor J. Reed, rector of Holy Family Co-Cathedral in Tulsa, was appointed auxiliary bishop of the diocese. Soon afterward, on December 27, Bishop McGuinness suffered a fatal heart attack. The Holy See appointed Reed to succeed him and he was consecrated as the fourth diocesan ordinary on March 5, 1958.

The defining issues for his episcopate were the Second Vatican Council and the war in Vietnam. Bishop Kelley had bequeathed a rich intellectual heritage, and one result was that Catholics in Oklahoma were better prepared for the changes that ensued from the Council. In 1966, St. Gregory's in Shawnee was the scene of the first diocesan council held in the United States after Vatican II. At the same time, Bishop Reed was assailed from two fronts within the diocese. On the one hand were those enraged by what they viewed as the Church's betrayal of its traditions, while on the other there were priests and sisters who became disenchanted with the bishop because they were looking for change beyond what he could authorize. A sudden drop in vocations obliged him to close McGuinness's seminary after only ten years in operation. The manifold pressures may have contributed to his sudden death on Sept. 8, 1971, at the age of 65.

At the time he died, Reed had already begun meetings with a view to dividing the diocese. His successor, Bishop John R. Quinn, the former auxiliary of San Diego, CA, carried this effort forward, with the result that on Dec. 19, 1972, Rome announced the creation of the Archdiocese of Oklahoma City, the establishment of the Diocese of Tulsa, and the combining of these two with the Diocese of Little Rock to form a new ecclesiastical province. Quinn was named the first archbishop.

Even before the diocese was divided, Quinn had to resolve a difficult situation involving "experimental parishes" in Oklahoma City and Tulsa. He requested an evaluation from the Center for Applied Research in the Apostolate (CARA), Washington, DC. Informed that the two parishes were not serving the purposes for which they were formed, he terminated both communities. Another of his accomplishments was in 1974 to resurrect the diocesan newspaper that had been discontinued, as *The Sooner Catholic*. Subsequently, it went on to receive many awards for excellence from the Catholic Press Association.

When Archbishop Quinn was named archbishop of San Francisco early in 1977, he was replaced in Oklahoma by Archbishop Charles A. Salatka, the former bishop of Marquette, MI. Consecrated as auxiliary bishop of Grand Rapids in 1962, Salatka was among the youngest bishops at Vatican II. At his retirement 30 years later, he was the eldest surviving bishop who had seen service at the council. In his 15 years in Oklahoma City, he consolidated the archdiocese's fiscal holdings and developed its outreach to an expanding Hispanic population. Bishop Eusebius J. Beltran, who had served as bishop of the Tulsa diocese since 1978, was named to succeed Archbishop Salatka when he retired in 1992. Archbishop Beltran took office on Jan. 22, 1993. Since then he has continued the initiatives of his predecessor toward Hispanics, while extending the archdiocese's outreach toward youth.

Bibliography: M. U. THOMAS, *The Catholic Church on the Oklahoma Frontier, 1824–1907* (St. Louis 1938; Univ. microfilms 1940). J. D. WHITE, *This Far by Faith: 125 Years of Catholic Life in Oklahoma, 1875–2000.* (Strasbourg 2001).

[W. C. GARTHOEFFNER/J. D. WHITE]

OLAF I TRYGGVESSØN, KING OF NORWAY

Reigned 995 to September 9 (or 10), 1000; b. *c.* 968; d. Swold. Olaf (Tryggvasøn) was brought up in Novgorod and spent his youth as a Viking. From *c.* 991 he lived in the British Isles, where he was baptized. Only in 995 did he return to Norway, which he had left with his mother soon after his birth. He was the great-grandson of Harold Finehair, and thus the chieftains recognized him as the sovereign ruler of Norway without any serious opposition. Olaf was an ardent Christian who was determined to introduce Christianity throughout his country, and this led to minor struggles with the strong pagan chieftains. Christianity was legally introduced in Iceland *c.* 1000 at the instigation of Olaf. His methods of conversion were hardhanded and not very subtle. He is remembered as the apostle of Norway and Iceland, and he is the hero of several sagas of a hagiographic cast. He died in the naval battle of Swold, where he was fighting against an alliance of the Danish and Swedish kings and an exiled Norwegian chieftain.

Bibliography: B. ADALBJARNARSON, *Om de norske kongers sagaer* (Oslo 1937), with bibliog. S. UNDSET, *Saga of Saints,* tr. E. C. RAMSDEN (New York 1934). H. KOHT, *Norsk biografisk leksikon* (Oslo 1921–) 10:413–419. G. TURVILLE-PETRE, *The Heroic Age of Scandinavia* (London 1951) 130–139. H. HOLZAPFEL, *Lexikon für Theologie und Kirche,* ed. J. HOFER and K. RAHNER, 10 v. (2d, new ed. Freiburg 1957–65) 7:1138.

[H. BEKKER-NIELSEN]

OLAF II, KING OF NORWAY, ST.

Reigned 1015 to July 29, 1030; b. Oplandet, Norway, 995; d. Stiklestad, Norway. His father was a chieftain descended from Harold Finehair. Olaf Haraldsson's early career is not known in detail, but it seems that he was a Viking from his 12th year, the events of his youth being recorded in scaldic verse. Having been baptized in Rouen in 1014, he returned to Norway in 1015 to assert his royal claims. His rebellion against Danish and Swedish overlords in Norway had a strong popular appeal. Olaf was an ardent Christian and tried by every means to uproot the last traces of paganism in Norway; in this he was quite successful. When King Canute the Great was proclaimed king of all Norway in 1028, Olaf fled the

country and went into exile in Russia. In the spring of 1030 he returned to Norway, leaving his illegitimate son, the future King Magnus the Good, at the Russian court. He met his opponents in the battle of Stiklestad, where he was killed. Very soon after his death even his enemies came to recognize that they had killed a saint; his intercession was invoked and miracles were recorded. His body was moved to Trondheim, which became the center of the Olaf cult. He was the patron saint of Norway and was venerated also in England, Denmark, Sweden, Finland, and Iceland. He was the subject of medieval Scandinavian iconography, and his life is recorded in several legends, or sagas, both in Latin and in the vernacular.

Feast: July 29.

Bibliography: *Bibliotheca hagiographica latina antiquae et mediae aetatis,* 2 v. (Brussels 1898–1901; suppl. 1911) 2:6322–26; Suppl. 240. O. WIDDING et al., "The Lives of the Saints in Old Norse Prose: A Handlist," *Mediaeval Studies* 25 (1963) 294–337, esp. 327–328. S. UNDSET, *Saga of Saints,* tr. E. C. RAMSDEN (New York 1934); *Sankt Olav,* tr. M. NEUHAUSER (Vienna 1947). A. W. BRØGGER, *Norsk biografisk leksikon* (Oslo 1923–) 10:374–390. G. TURVILLE-PETRE, *The Heroic Age of Scandinavia* (New York 1951) 140–164. C. E. GIBSON, *The Two Olafs of Norway* (London 1968). V. HENRIKSEN, *Sverdet; Hellig Olav i Borg* (Oslo 1974); *Hellig Olav* (Oslo 1985). M. BLINDHEIM et al., *Olav, konge og helgen, myte og symbol* (Oslo 1981). E. LUTHEN, *I pilegrimenes fotspor til Nidaos* (Oslo 1992). *Gokstadhøvdingen og hans tid,* ed. T. FROST (Sandefjord 1997). *Helgonet i Nidaros: Olavskult och kristnande i Norden,* ed. L. RUMAR (Sweden 1997). M. KOLLANDSRUD, *Pilegrimsleden til Nidaros* (Oslo 1997). G. AXEL-NILSSON, "Sankt Olavs hjälm och sporrar": helgonreliker eller vapengarnityr? (Göteborg 1998).

[H. BEKKER-NIELSEN]

OLÁH, MIKLÓS (OLAHUS)

Archbishop of Gran (Esztergom), Primate of Hungary, humanist; b. Hermanstadt (Nagyszeben), Hungary, Jan. 10, 1493; d. Pressburg, Hungary (now Bratislava, Czechoslovakia), Jan. 14, 1568. Oláh, of Wallachian descent, was educated at the Chapter School of Varad and as a page at the court of Vladislav II. After ordination in 1516, he served as secretary to George Szatmáry, chancellor, and later archbishop, of Gran. He was also secretary to King Louis II and continued in this position after Louis's death at the battle of Mohács (1526), serving Queen Mary of Hungary. When Mary was appointed regent of the Netherlands by Charles V, Oláh accompanied her (1531) and engaged in diplomatic missions and humanistic studies until 1542, when he returned to Hungary. Oláh also won the friendship of Erasmus. As an official at the court of Ferdinand I, he became royal chancellor and bishop of Agram (1544), bishop of Erlau (1548), and eventually, archbishop of Gran (1553). Oláh, as primate of Hungary, vigorously encouraged Church

Olaf II, King of Norway, standing third from left. (©Bettmann/CORBIS)

reform and opposed Protestant encroachments in Hungary. By frequent visitations, provincial synods, and administrative decrees, Catholicism was strengthened and advanced. Catholic schools and the Jesuits, invited into Hungary (1561), were the principal means of inculcating Catholic beliefs. The decrees of Trent were also employed to revive devotion and zeal. An author of several theological and historical works, including the *Ordo et Ritus Ecclesiae Strigoniensis* (1560) and *Hungaria et Attila* (1562), Oláh combined religious conviction and humanist teachings.

Bibliography: T. VON BOGYAY, *Lexikon für Theologie und Kirche*, ed. J. HOFER and K. RAHNER, 10 v. (2d, new ed. Freiburg 1957–65) 7:1137–38. D. SINOR, *History of Hungary* (New York 1959).

[P. S. MCGARRY]

OLAVIDE Y JAUREGUI, PABLO DE

Peruvian scholar and Catholic apologist; b. Lima, 1725; d. Baeza, Spain, 1803. He was a symbol of the century of the Enlightenment, a leader in the movement against traditionalism, and one of those who prepared Spain to adjust to the modern world and come closer to the European intellectual current. In 1752 he went to Spain, occupying there a high position, owing to his intellectual compatibility with the Enlightened ministers of Charles III. Between 1757 and 1764 he spent long periods of time in France and Italy. In 1767 he was unexpectedly appointed chief officer of justice of Seville, intendant of Andalucía, and later superintendent of the colonization of Sierra Morena, an ambitious project for the conversion of vast desert areas into arable lands inhabited by a model rural society. In those positions Olavide's work had two facets: (1) the reform of the cultural regulations of the University of Seville through changing its scholastic orientation and secularizing the teaching system; and (2) the reform of the economic order through agrarian reform. These ideas aroused great opposition. In 1776 he became involved in an inquisitorial trial because of his imprudence in religious matters. In 1780 he escaped to France, where he remained for 18 years.

As a friend of the Encyclopedists (he translated various dramatic works, among them, Voltaire's *Zayre*), he was well received there, especially by Marmontel and by Diderot, who wrote a biographical sketch of him. While in exile he recovered his lost faith and piety after having survived Jacobine imprisonment. He became an apologist of the Catholic faith against the secular Enlightenment. He returned to Spain (1798) and remained there until his death. His most important work is *El evangelio en triunfo o historia de un filósofo desengañado* (1798). Autobiographical in nature, it reports the psychological drama in the conversion of an unbeliever and defends the divinity of Jesus and the authenticity of the sacred books. According to Menéndez y Pelayo, it was a precursor of *Le génie du christianisme* of Chateaubriand.

Bibliography: M. DEFOURNEAUX, *Pablo de Olavide ou l'Afrancesado* (Paris 1959).

[G. LOHMANN VILLENA]

OLD CATHOLICS

A loosely associated group of autonomous communities brought together in the Union of Utrecht (1889) under the presidency of the archbishop of Utrecht. The term Old Catholic implies that VATICAN COUNCIL I introduced into the Roman Catholic Church innovations that left Old Catholicism as the repository of traditional Catholic beliefs. The Old Catholic Church has been colored by many Protestant influences, but it is not a Protestant body. All Old Catholic Churches are strongly influenced by 19th-century nationalism; but none of them is an established state church.

History. The Schism of UTRECHT, which began early in the 18th century, anteceded the Old Catholic movement, which it later joined. Its following was very small by 1870 when a considerable number of Catholic priests and laymen in Germany refused to accept the definitions of Vatican Council I on papal infallibility and primacy. FEBRONIANISM and JOSEPHINISM, particularly as it was expounded by Ignaz von WESSENBURG, greatly influenced the thinking of these men. Ignaz von DÖLLINGER, Johann FRIEDRICH, Franz REUSCH, Johann von Schulte, and other scholars who opposed the Vatican Council's decrees on the papacy exerted still greater influence. Many laymen in these groups belonged to the upper middle class and were also strongly influenced by secularism and nationalism.

In September 1871 at Munich, 300 representatives met to organize the Old Catholic movement; a similar congress gathered in Cologne in 1872. Episcopal leadership was lacking because the entire Catholic hierarchy subscribed to the Vatican Council's decrees. To obtain a validly consecrated bishop, the Old Catholics chose Joseph Reinkens as bishop (June 1873). He was then consecrated by Bp. Heykamp of Deventer in the Netherlands, who belonged to the Little Church of Utrecht (OBC). Döllinger, whose relations with the Old Catholics were always ambiguous, refused to become involved in organized schism and eventually broke completely with the movement because of its innovations. The leaders of the KULTURKAMPF supported the Old Catholics. In Prussia and Baden the government granted them a subsidy and a share of Catholic Church property. In Switzerland the schismatics called themselves *Christ katholiken*; they were more influenced by secularism and theological liberalism than their associates in Germany, but they failed to gain a wide following. Austria likewise produced an inconsiderable number of Old Catholics.

Polish nationalism gave rise to the POLISH NATIONAL CATHOLIC CHURCH, which admits intercommunion with Old Catholics and Anglicans and subscribes to the Declaration of Utrecht. Inability to accomodate to a non-Polish priesthood and quarrels over education and the administration of church property led in 1897 to the establishment of a breakaway church in Scranton, Pa., that absorbed earlier Polish dissident groups and created a diocese under the jurisdiction of Francis Hodur. Hodur was consecrated bishop in 1907 by bishops of the OBC.

In Poland the mystical sect of MARIAVITES began in 1906 and spread rapidly. At the Old Catholic Congress in Vienna (1909), General Kiréev, a Russian religious enthusiast, presented three Mariavite priests. One of them, John Kowalski, was consecrated bishop in Utrecht by Old Catholic bishops.

Doctrine and Discipline. The autonomous episcopates constituting the Old Catholic community have as a common doctrinal basis the Declaration of Utrecht (1889). However, the Polish National Church and the Swiss *Christkatholisch* Church maintain beliefs out of harmony with this declaration. In accordance with this document Old Catholics accept the decrees of the first eight ecumenical councils. (Until 1889 some Old Catholics considered themselves bound by the Tridentine decrees.) They admit Sacred Scripture and tradition as sources of revelation; but their notion of tradition differs from the Roman Catholic one. The bishop of Rome is recognized as having merely a primacy of honor, but not a primacy of jurisdiction or infallibility as defined in Vatican Council I. On the one hand, Old Catholics reject both the dogmas of papal infallibility and the Immaculate Conception. On the other hand, they admit seven sacraments, acknowledge the Real Presence in the Eucharist, and recognize the apostolic succession. Auricular confession is optional; sins may be confessed before the congregation or a priest. Clerical celibacy has been abolished. The liturgy resembles the Roman one and is celebrated in the vernacular. Liturgical vestments are the same as the Roman ones.

Each bishopric is autonomous and is governed by a bishop, who in turn must abide by the canons enacted by clerical and lay members of synods, the highest authority. Synods also elect bishops. Since 1889 the Old Catholic archbishop of Utrecht has been president of the International Old Catholic Congress. As a result of an agreement reached in Bonn (1931), intercommunion with the Anglicans has since existed. Each group recognizes the catholicity and independence of the other and admits members of the other communion to participate in its sacraments.

Bibliography: C. B. MOSS, *The Old Catholic Movement: Its Origins and History* (2d ed. London 1964), by an Anglican. J. F. VON SCHULTE, *Der Altkatholizismus* (Giessen 1887), by an Old Catholic. J. TROXLER, *Die neuere Entwicklung des Altkatholizismus* (Cologne 1908). V. CONZEMIUS, ''Aspects ecclésiologiques de l'évolution de Döllinger et du vieux Catholicisme,'' *Revue des sciences religieuses* 34 (1960) 247–279. P. GSCHWIND, *Geschichte der Entstehung der christkatholischen Kirche der Schweiz,* 2 v. (Bern 1904–10). W. H. DE VOIL and H. D. WYNNE-BENNETT, *Old Catholic Eucharistic Worship* (New York 1936). P. ANSON, *Bishops at Large* (London 1964). K. PRUTER, *A History of the Old Catholic Church* (Scottsdale, Ariz. 1973). K. PRUTER and J. G. MELTON, *The Old Catholic Sourcebook* (New York 1983)

[S. J. TONSOR/EDS.]

OLD CHAPTER

A body of the English clergy; it was originated by William BISHOP, bishop of Chalcedon, who in 1623, as part of his plan to reorganize the missionary Church in England, instituted a chapter consisting of a dean and canons. Its functions, as he conceived them, were threefold: to act as an advisory body to the bishop; to preserve continuity of jurisdiction *sede vacante*; and when the bishop died, to submit to Rome nominations for his successor. Its author took this step, however, without prior reference to Rome, which refused to accord the chapter any official recognition, maintaining that Bishop had acted beyond his jurisdiction. Nevertheless, Rome refrained from any act of censure, chiefly, it seems, from fear of creating scandal. After the death of Richard SMITH, bishop of Chalcedon in 1655, the chapter made a somewhat exaggerated claim that it had the unofficial approval of both Innocent X and Alexander VII for assuming jurisdiction over the Church in England and issuing faculties *sede vacante*. Rome eventually decided to appoint another bishop, insisting that the chapter should cease to attempt to exercise jurisdiction: both Philip Howard, who was to have been appointed in 1672 if political circumstances had not prevented it, and John Leyburn, who was appointed in 1685, were made to promise to enforce this. Though after 1685 it never again tried to exercise jurisdiction, the chapter continued to claim canonical status and to perpetuate itself until the hierarchy was restored in 1850; its members then disbanded and reformed themselves into the Old Brotherhood of the Secular Clergy.

Bibliography: Archives of the Old Brotherhood, partly catalogued in 1876 (HMC. 5th Report. Appendix: 463–470.). Many documents were removed to Westminster Cathedral Archives (ser. A, v.17ff.; ser. B, v.25ff.). The rest remain with the Old Brotherhood. H. TOOTELL, *Dodd's Church History of England*, ed. M. A. TIERNEY, 5 v. (London 1839–43). E. H. BURTON, *Life and Times of Bishop Challoner*, 1691–1781, 2 v. (London 1909). B. HEMPHILL (pseud. for B. WHELAN), *The Early Vicars Apostolic of England,* 1685–1750 (London 1954) *passim.* J. SERGEANT, *An Account of the Chapter* . . . ed. W. TURNBULL (London 1853), based on Ward's MS history in the Old Brotherhood Archives. J. A. WILLIAMS, ''The Old Chapter and the Secular Clergy,'' *Catholic Recusancy in Wiltshire* (London 1968). G. V. ANSTRUTHER, *Cardinal of Norfolk* (in progress), ch. 4, 5. T. A. BIRRELL, ''English Catholics without a Bishop,'' *Recusant History* 4.4 (1957–58). A. F. ALLISON, ''Richard Smith, Richelieu and the French Marriage,'' *ibid.* 7.4 (1963–64).

[A. F. ALLISON]

OLD DELUDER SATAN ACT

The name given to the Massachusetts school ordinance of 1647, derived from its preamble, which begins, ''It being one of the chief projects of that old deluder Satan to keep men from the knowledge of the Scriptures.'' The legislation proper required that townships of 50 families or more appoint a common schoolmaster to teach reading and writing, his wages to be paid by either the parents or the town. Townships of 100 families were to establish a grammar school to prepare students for the university. Townships failing to comply with these demands were to pay a yearly fine of £5 to the nearest school until the order be carried out.

This ordinance is often quoted both as a measure to restrict Anglican and Catholic influence through the imposition of Puritan belief, and as the first Colonial legislative approval of the Calvinist principle of union of church and state in education with the latter given the authority to promote education as a public service. The preamble, however, seems rather an expression of religious belief offered as motivation to fulfill an obligation that had educational, social, and religious ramifications: the training of citizens who would be of service to church and state rather than a charge upon the community.

Although schools had been established by free initiative before the 1647 ordinance, they were few and not widely effective. The ordinance of 1642, the first Massachusetts educational legislation, had placed the responsibility for the literacy of children and indentured servants upon the heads of families. Since this legislation had proved insufficient, the 1647 ordinance required the establishment of an educational system and offered religious motivation and monetary sanctions to ensure its organization.

Bibliography: S. E. MORISON, *The Intellectual Life of Colonial New England* (New York 1956).

[F. F. BURCH]

OLD ROMAN CHANT

The chant of Rome exists in two versions: Gregorian, found especially in musical manuscripts copied in Carolingian domains beginning in the late 9th century, and Old Roman, known from a small group of musical manuscripts—three graduals, two antiphoners, and an orational—written in Rome between 1071 and *c.* 1250.

Comparison of Old Roman and Gregorian. Comparison of the two reveals essentially the same Mass and Office structure, calendar, and texts, though with minor differences, e.g., in the Old Roman, the absence of a Mass for the Fourth Sunday of Advent, a special Vespers for Easter week, the lack of hymns, the use of only eight responsories in Matins, and a "double" Matins Office for certain feasts. More striking are the musical differences, showing two distinct yet cognate melodic traditions. In general, one finds similar melodic shapes, confirming the common origin of both melodic repertories, but independent stylistic development, the Old Roman presenting a more ornate version of the repertory as the brief excerpt illustrates.

Many theories have been proposed to explain which is the older or original melodic version; to what the melodic and liturgical differences can be ascribed; when, how, and why the "split" into two traditions occurred; and why the Gregorian is not found in Rome before *c.* 1250 (the manuscript evidence suggests only the Old Roman was known in Rome before this time). Mocquereau focused attention on the Old Roman chant (which he called "Vatican") as early as 1891, concluding from a study of three of the sources that the Old Roman melodies constituted a post–Gregorian transformation. Andoyer's slightly later studies revealed a more ancient liturgical practice in the Old Roman and the ab-

sence of feasts known to have been added to the Gregorian after *c.* 800; he therefore classified the repertory as pre–Gregorian. A summary of more recent thinking follows.

Recent Theories. On the basis of historical–liturgical evidence [M. Andrieu, *Les 'Ordines Romani' du haut moyen–âge,* 5 v. 3 (Louvain 1951) 211–227], Bruno Stäblein believes that both chants are of Roman origin and that the Old Roman version is earlier, revised into the Gregorian in the late 7th century. Joseph Smits van Waesberghe points to certain veiled references in the *Liber Pontificalis* to a struggle for liturgical primacy between Roman monks and clergy in the 7th century as further testimony that two chants may have existed in Rome at this time, one for each group. Other such evidence has attracted still other scholars to this view. Nevertheless, caution must be exercised here for the historical testimony has been shown to be sometimes totally unreliable and often ambiguous. However probable this theory may seem, no unequivocal evidence for it has yet been found.

Other research has sought answers primarily from the music itself. Helmut Hucke, for example, comparing the gradual chants of both repertories, concludes that the more direct, less ornate Gregorian melodies are later transformations of the Old Roman, made not in Rome but in a different stylistic climate with different aesthetic preferences—in Carolingian France. Walther Lipphardt, however, sees the Old Roman as the later version, produced not by revision but as the result of a presumed oral tradition in Rome. Taking into account the appearance of Gregorian–chant manuscripts in the Carolingian empire beginning around the end of the 9th century, but the total lack of any musical manuscripts in Rome before 1071, he suggests the chant that accompanied the Roman liturgy into France in the 9th century was the Gregorian, known orally in Rome but written down and fixed in France. The Old Roman is the result of two more centuries of oral transmission of those same melodies in Rome. Hence, Lipphardt proposes that we have the Roman chant in two stages of development: in the 9th–century form as recorded in France, and in the 11th–century form as recorded in Rome.

The Old Roman manuscript evidence seems, at least for the present, to complicate rather than clarify the situation. The paucity of musical sources—only six—could be explained by presuming the Old Roman remained an orally transmitted tradition up to its demise in the second half of the 13th century. These few manuscripts, then, may have served primarily to help ensure conformity in the oral tradition, or to help aid memory, or even just to preserve this unique melodic repertory. Moreover, in certain places, e.g., the antiphons of the Psalter and the Office for the Dead, melodic divergencies among the sources containing these melodies are so great as to suggest manuscript redaction directly from oral tradition. Most often, however, the sources reveal virtual identity for pieces in common, indicating a uniform and well–established written tradition. Possibly, then, some interplay between oral and written forms of the Old Roman chant may have existed.

In any case, all theories advanced so far should be considered inconclusive. The historical–liturgical evidence is of doubtful value; the meaning of the manuscript evidence is unclear; and the musical studies are incomplete. At present, we are still unable to determine whether the melodic differences between Old Roman and Gregorian can be attributed to evolution in an oral tradition, to different stylistic developments, or to deliberate reform; or whether the general assumption, valid in other disciplines, that the more ornate version of something is necessarily later applies here. What is needed most now is a systematic, exhaustive musical comparison of the two melodic repertories. Perhaps then it will be possible to describe more exactly their relationship and to trace more clearly the development of each.

Bibliography: W. APEL, "The Central Problem of Gregorian Chant," *Journal of the American Musicological Society* 9 (1956) 118–127. P. F. CUTTER, "The Question of the 'Old–Roman' Chant: A Reappraisal," *Acta Musicologica* 39 (1967) 2–20. S. J. P. VAN DIJK, "The Urban and Papal Rites in Seventh– and Eighth–Century Rome," *Sacris eruditi,* xii (1961), 411–87; "The Old Roman Rite," *Studia patristica,* v (1962), 185–205; "Recent Developments in the Study of the Old–Roman Rite," *Studia patristica,* 8 (1966), 299–319. P. PEACOCK "The Problem of the Old Roman Chant," *Essays Presented to Egon Wellesz,* ed. J. WESTRUP (Oxford 1966), 43–7. P. F. CUTTER, "The Old–Roman Chant Tradition: Oral or Written?," *Journal of the American Musicological Society,* 20 (1967), 167–89. T. CONNOLLY, "Introits and Archetypes: Some Archaisms of the Old Roman Chant," *Journal of the American Musicological Society* 25 (1972), 157–74. P. F. CUTTER, "Oral Transmission of the Old–Roman Responsories?," *Musical Quarterly,* 62 (1976), 182–94. H. HUCKE, "Toward a New Historical View of Gregorian Chant," *Journal of the American Musicological Society* 33 (1980), 437–67. J. DYER, "Latin Psalters, Old Roman and Gregorian Chants," *Kirchenmusikalisches Jahrbuch* 67 (1984), 11–30. P. BERNARD, "Sur un aspect controversé de la réforme carolingienne: 'vieux–romain' et 'grégorien'," *Ecclesia orans,* vii (1990), 163–89. T. KARP, "Interrelationships between Old Roman and Gregorian Chant," *Cantus Planus IV: Pécs 1990,* 187–203. M. BEZUIDENHOUT, "The Old and New Historical Views of Gregorian Chant: Papal and Franciscan Plainchant in Thirteenth–Century Rome," *International Musicological Society: Congress Report* v. 15 (Madrid 1992). D. HILEY, *Western Plainchant: A Handbook* (Oxford 1993), 530–40. J. DYER, "Prolegomena to a History of Music and Liturgy at Rome during the Middle Ages," *Essays on Medieval Music in Honor of David G. Hughes,* ed. G. M. BOONE (Cambridge, Mass. 1995), 87–115. P. BERNARD, *Du chant romain au chant grégorien* (Paris 1996).

[P. CUTTER/EDS.]

OLDEGAR, ST.

Political counselor, crusader, and re-founder of Tarragona metropolitanate; b. Barcelona, 1060; d. Barcelona, March 1, 1137. A child canon of Barcelona where he became deacon (1089), dean (1094), and priest, Oldegar (or Oleguer) retired to Saint-Adrian in Provence where he became prior (1099), then to its motherhouse, Saint-Ruf in Avignon, where he became abbot (1113). In 1116 he was elected bishop of Barcelona, at that time the central see for the autonomous Count of Barcelona-Provence. In 1118 the pope and the count made him metropolitan in exile as well, with the task of restoring the metropolitanate of Tarragona, a step psychologically important to crusading Catalonia. Oldegar traveled to Rome and Palestine, to reform councils at Toulouse (1119) and REIMS (1119), to the first LATERAN COUNCIL (1123), and to Clermont (1130). As crusade legate in SPAIN, especially during the Tortosa and Lérida campaigns, Oldegar—in his position of peacemaker—helped remove Castilian armies from Aragon, thus preparing the way for the later union of Aragon and Catalonia.

Feast: March 6.

Bibliography: H. FLÓREZ et al., *España sagrada* (Madrid 1747–1957) 29:472–499, biog. A. BUTLER, *The Lives of the Saints,* rev. ed. H. THURSTON and D. ATTWATER (New York 1956) 1:503–504. F. SOLDEVILA, *Història de Catalunya,* 3 v. (Barcelona 1962). For additional bibliog., *see* BARCELONA.

[R. I. BURNS]

OLDMEADOW, ERNEST JAMES

Journalist and novelist; b. Chester, England, Oct. 31, 1867; d. London, Sept. 11, 1949. He was the son of Wesleyan parents and he embarked on the ministry in Nova Scotia. He was converted to Catholicism in 1897 and shortly after was appointed editor of the London *Musical Times.* Cardinal Francis BOURNE offered him the editorship of the *Tablet* on the death of James Milburn (1860–1923) who had served the paper for many years, the last three as editor. Oldmeadow accepted and was, from Bourne's point of view, a good choice: they agreed that the journal's primary purpose was to defend the Church against the Church of England. In his 13 years as editor Oldmeadow conducted the controversy with unremitting zest; he had a vigorous, pugnacious style, which he kept fresh, he said, by writing standing up and wearing a hat. After World War I, however, there was not the same public for the old controversy in the old way. Bourne expected to draw, as his predecessors had done, a substantial income for the archdiocese from two-thirds of the profits of the paper; the other portion went to Cardinal Herbert Vaughan's foundation for the MILL HILL MISSIONARIES. When the paper's circulation fell to less than 3,000, Cardinal Arthur HINSLEY, Bourne's successor, soon sold it and thus Oldmeadow's editorship was terminated (1936) in a manner he resented. But the paper had never absorbed all his interests. He had founded a wine business (1912) under the name Francis Downman, and had made some mark as a novelist of the romantic Edwardian school. He was versatile and warmly convivial, and his apparently belligerent manner did him less than justice. In 1933 Bourne made him, together with H. Belloc and G. K. Chesterton, a Knight Commander of St. Gregory. Oldmeadow remained vigorous until he was more than 80, but after leaving the *Tablet* he took little part in Catholic life beyond writing the two-volume *Francis Cardinal Bourne* (1940–44), and novels, among them *Susan* (1907), *The Scoundrel: A Romance* (1907), and *Antonio* (1909), the best-known of a long list that began with *Lady Lohengrin* in 1896. He wrote also studies of Schumann, Chopin, and Mozart.

[D. WOODRUFF]

O'LEARY, HENRY JOSEPH

Second archbishop of Edmonton, Alberta, Canada; b. Richibucto, New Brunswick, Canada, March 13, 1879; d. Victoria, British Columbia, Canada, March 5, 1938. He was ordained Sept. 1, 1901, and after a brief period of parish and chancery work, he was named bishop of Charlottetown, Prince Edward Island, and consecrated at Bath–hurst, New Brunswick, May 22, 1913. Zealous in promoting priestly and religious vocations, the young bishop proved himself also a capable administrator, undertaking a vast program of church and school development. On Sept. 7, 1920, he was transferred to the Edmonton archdiocese, where he continued his pastoral efforts, particularly in the field of education. Schools, churches, and hospitals were the special object of his solicitude. In spite of illness in his later years, O'Leary indefatigably strove to pave the way for the sound future development of the Edmonton archdiocese.

Bibliography: Archives, Archdiocese of Edmonton.

[C. DOZOIS]

OLGA, ST.

Also known as Helga, princess of Kiev; b. Pskov, Russia, *c.* 890; d. Kiev, Russia, July 11, 969. Probably of Slavic descent, Olga married Igor, the Varangian prince of Kiev in 903, and after his death on campaign in 945 she acted as regent for their son Svyatoslav (d.

972). Her revenge against the Drevlianians for her husband's death is described at length by Nestor in the *Primary Chronicle,* and the monastic historian has high praise for her courage and ability as a ruler. She instituted administrative and fiscal reforms throughout the realm and hastened its recovery from the destructive wars of Igor. Late in 957 she visited Constantinople; and although the Russian sources describe her baptism there, it appears from a careful reading of the Greek accounts that Olga had already been a Christian for several years when she visited the court of Emperor CONSTANTINE PORPHYROGENITUS. Although she might well have been received into the Latin rite in Kiev *c.* 955, the princess, in an effort to gain autonomy for the Russian church, was prepared to enter into relations with either Rome or Byzantium, and her visit to Constantine was followed by a letter to OTTO I, asking that missionaries be sent to her people. Her baptism was not followed by the conversion of the whole nation, for the pagan party rallied around her son Svyatoslav, who resisted all efforts of his mother to instruct him in the faith. After her son had come of age in 964, Olga again served as regent in Kiev while he was engaged in wars against the Bulgars, and on her death he gave her a Christian burial in that city. Olga was early recognized as a saint and is honored in the Russian and Ukrainian Churches, along with her grandson VLADIMIR, who effected the Christianization of his people *c.* 988.

Feast: July 11.

Bibliography: *The Russian Primary Chronicle,* ed. and tr. S. H. CROSS and O. P. SHERBOWITZ–WETZOR (Cambridge, Mass. 1953) 64–87, 111. CONSTANTINE, PORPHYROGENITUS, *De cerimoniis . . . ,* bk. 2, ch. 15 in *Patrologia Graeca,* ed. J. P. MIGNE, 161 v. (Paris 1857–66) 112:1107–12. E. GOLUBINSKY, *Istoriia russkoi tserkvi* (2d ed. Moscow 1900–01) 1.1:74–104, 241–242. G. LAEHR, *Die Anfänge des russischen Reiches* (Berlin 1930) 103–106. G. VERNADSKY, *Kievan Russia* (New Haven 1948) 32–47. A. BUTLER, *The Lives of the Saints,* rev. ed. H. THURSTON and D. ATTWATER, 4 v. (New York 1956) 3:72. B. DEL COLLE, *Olga e Gorbaciov: 1000 anni di cristianesimo in Russia* (2d ed. Turin 1988). *Kniaginia Kievskaia Olga* (Moscow 2000) anonymous author. A. S. KOROLEV, *Istoriia mezhdukniazheskikh otnoshenii na Rusi* (Moscow 2000).

[B. J. COMASKEY]

OLIER, JEAN JACQUES

Founder of the Seminary and the Society of Saint-Sulpice; b. Paris, Sept. 20, 1608; d. Issy, April 2, 1657. Olier was baptized in the church of St. Paul, Paris, on the day of his birth; he spent his childhood in Lyons, where his father had been assigned as administrator of justice. There he completed his classical education with the Jesuits. He made his philosophical studies at the College of Harcourt, Paris. After studying theology at the Sorbonne, he undertook further Hebrew study in Rome. Returning to France in 1631 on the occasion of his father's death, Olier placed himself under the spiritual direction of (St.) VINCENT DE PAUL and was subsequently ordained on May 21, 1633, by Bp. Étienne Puget, auxiliary bishop of Metz.

Although he remained a lifelong friend of (St.) Vincent, Olier came under the guidance of Père Charles de CONDREN, the superior of the Oratory, who had dedicated himself to the renovation of priestly life in France. When Olier was offered a bishopric, which his family urged him to accept, it was De Condren who prevailed upon him to refuse it. Before he died (Jan. 7, 1641), De Condren divulged his plans for implementing the Tridentine decrees concerning the preparation of candidates for the priesthood.

On Dec. 29, 1642, Olier and two priests rented a small house in Vaugirard, a suburb of Paris, not to initiate a religious community, but to establish a favorable environment for the training of priests. The experiment attracted attention, and soon six priests and eight seminarians shared a common schedule of work and prayer. On Aug. 10, 1642, Olier assumed charge of the parish church of Saint-Sulpice, Paris, and the community of Vaugirard joined him there. In 1643 Olier requested the government's approval for his society of priests. In November 1645, this petition was granted. In 1652 Olier relinquished his pastoral charge of the parish of Saint-Sulpice and devoted the rest of his life primarily to seminary work. He had the happiness of assigning priests of his community to four other seminaries: Nantes (1649), Viviers (1650), Le Puy (1652), and Clement (1653).

The last five years of his life were marked by great suffering and physical hardship caused by his intense labors. Olier is a leader of the "French School of Spirituality," and his writings have had a worldwide influence into the 20th century. Although he did not produce a systematic or scientific corpus of ascetical theology, his works show him to be a master of the spiritual life (*see* SULPICIANS).

Bibliography: *Oeuvres complètes*, ed. J. P. MIGNE (Paris 1857). E. M. FAILLON, *Vie de M. Olier*, 2 v. (4th ed. Paris 1873). P. POURRAT, *Father Olier, Founder of St. Sulpice*, tr. W. S. REILLY (Baltimore 1932). P. BOISARD, *La Compagnie de St. Sulpice, trois siècles d'histoire*, 2 v. (multigraphed; Paris 1962). E. A. WALSH, *The Priesthood in the Writings of the French School: Berulle, De Condren, Olier* (Washington 1949). F. MONIER, *Vie de Jean Jacques Olier, curé de la paroisse et fondateur du séminaire de Saint-Sulpice* (Paris 1914). E. LEVESQUE, *Dictionnaire de théologie catholique*, ed. A. VACANT et al. (Paris 1903–50) 11.1:963–982.

[C. J. NOONAN]

OLIGER, LIVARIUS

Franciscan historian; b. Schorbach (Diocese of Metz), France (Germany), Feb. 17, 1875; d. Rome, Jan. 29, 1951. He entered the FRANCISCAN order in 1892, was ordained in 1900, and from 1906 to 1950 held the chair of Franciscan history at the Antonianum in Rome. From 1911 to 1915 he also served as associate editor of the *Archivum Franciscanum historicum* at Quaracchi (near Florence) and during World War I (1915–18) returned to Germany, where he taught at St. Anna in Munich. Oliger held the post of professor of hagiography (from 1931) and historical method (from 1941) at the University of the Lateran and was cofounder of the Franciscan journal *Antonianum* (Rome 1926–). His writings—including critical editions and commentaries; pioneer work on the FRANCISCAN SPIRITUALS, FRATICELLI, and Brethren of the Free Spirit; mission history; biography; and hagiographical studies—were crowned by his *Expositio quattuor magistrorum super regulam fratrum minorum, 1241–1242* (Rome 1950).

Bibliography: *Miscellanea historica p. L. Oliger . . . oblata* Antonianum 20 (Rome 1945) with bibliog. L. SPÄTLING, *Franziskanische Studien* 32 (1950) 362–381, with bibliog. since 1945. *Antonianum* 26 (1951) 210–214.

[O. J. BLUM]

OLIVA, ABBEY OF

Cistercian monastery near Danzig, founded in 1174 by Subislaus I, a prince of Pomerania, colonized in 1186 from the abbey of Kolbatz. It became the center of the CISTERCIAN mission in Prussia. In 1224 pagan Prussians demolished the monastery, and it was after this that a three-aisled Romanesque basilica, based on the second plan of CLAIRVAUX (*see* CISTERCIAN ART AND ARCHITECTURE), was built. When this church was destroyed by fire in 1350, it was rebuilt in its present dimensions (more than 300 feet long) with the addition of a polygonal gallery choir. The star vaulting, built from 1577 to 1582, was patterned on English models. In the 18th century the church was remodeled along extravagant baroque lines; among other innovations, a famous organ with three manuals and 83 stops was installed. The abbey was secularized in 1831; the abbey church, converted into a parish church in 1835, became the cathedral of the newly established Diocese of Danzig in 1925. Since 1945 Oliva has been a Polish Cistercian priory.

Bibliography: *Die Ältere Chronik und die Schrifttafeln von Oliva*, ed. T. HIRSCH in *Scriptores rerum Prussicarum*, 5 v. (Leipzig 1861–74) v. 1. *Fontes Olivenses*, ed. W. KETRZYŃSKI in *Monumenta Poloniae historica*, 6 v. (Cracow 1864–93) 6:257–382. *Annales Olivenses aetate posteriores* (Thorn 1916–18). T. HIRSCH, *Das*

Kloster Oliva (Danzig 1850). H. J. SLEUMER, *Die Ursprüngliche Gestalt der Zisterzienser Abteikirche Oliva* (Heidelberg 1909). F. J. WOTHE, ''Die Kirchen der Diözese Danzig,'' *Festgabe für Bischof Carl M. Splett* (Hildesheim 1963) 14–22.

[A. SCHNEIDER]

OLIVAINT, PIERRE

Jesuit priest; b. Paris, Feb. 22, 1816; d. there, May 26, 1871. After studies at the Collège Charlemagne and the École normale, Olivaint gained an *agrégé* in history, taught in Paris and Grenoble, and then tutored the son of the Duc de Rochefoucauld-Liancourt. Although religiously indifferent as a youth, he entered the JESUITS (1845). After ordination (1850), he taught history (1852–57) in the newly opened Collège de Vaugirard in Paris. During his term there as rector (1857–65), the college became the leading private school in the capital. Olivaint was then named superior of the Jesuit Parisian residence at rue de Sèvres (1865–71). He was absorbed in retreat and sodality work until the outbreak of the Franco-Prussian War (1870). When his residence was designated an auxiliary hospital during the war, he showed an equal devotion to the wounded.

When the Commune revolted against Versailles, he sent his community from Paris but remained there himself with a priest and two brothers. He and Father Caubert were arrested (April 4, 1871), and sent to the Conciergerie prison where they found three other Jesuit priests, Ducoudray, Clerc, and de Bengy. Next day the Commune declared the prisoners ''hostages of the people of Paris.'' By April 13 more than 200 hostages had been gathered in the prison of Mazas. When the government reoccupied all Paris except the 11th *arrondissement,* the Commune ordered their execution, and had them transferred to the Rouquette prison. Six hostages, including two Jesuits, were shot on May 24. Two days later, 47 prisoners, including Olivaint and his fellow religious, were ordered to leave the Rouquette. Guarded by communards, they walked to Belleville through jeering crowds until, at 83 rue Haxo, the mob massacred them and threw their bodies into a cesspool. After the fall of the Commune (May 28), the remains of Olivaint and his Jesuit companions were returned to the rue de Sèvres. Their beatification process was introduced in Rome in 1937.

Bibliography: A. DE PONLEVOY, *Actes de la captivité et de la mort des RR. PP. P. Olivaint . . .* (Paris 1871; 17th ed. 1907). C. CLAIR, *Pierre Olivaint* (Paris 1878). É. LECANUET, *L'Église de France sous la Troisième République* 1: 99–126. L. KOCH, *Jesuiten-Lexikon* 1324–25.

[R. J. SEALY]

OLIVÉTAN, PIERRE ROBERT

Reformer and biblical scholar; b. Noyon, *c.* 1506; d. Ferarra, 1538. Olivétan was a relative of John Calvin, with whom he was associated at the University of Paris and in the publication of his French version of the Bible. A reformer, he fled from Paris to Orléans and in May of 1528 was studying Greek and Hebrew in Strassburg. He may have preceded Guillaume FAREL in teaching Reform doctrines in Geneva, but he was soon expelled (1532). At Neuchâtel he was employed by the sect of the WALDENSES in the Piedmont valley, for whom he prepared a French translation of the Bible. The work *La Bible qui est toute la Saint Escriture* appeared at Neuchâtel in June of 1535, with a preface by Calvin and a notable introduction by ''the humble little translator,'' who lays the book at the feet of Christ's body, the Church. Calvin credits Olivétan with a lively and penetrating mind; E. Doumergue calls him for his eloquence and humor ''un Rabelais évangelique''; H. Kunze pronounces him ''a rationalist philologian.'' He used Jacques Lefèvre d'Étaples's earlier translation with scholarly discretion.

Bibliography: É. DOUMERGUE, *Jean Calvin,* 7 v. (Lausanne 1899–1927) 1:117–125. H. KUNZE, *Die Bibelübersetzungen von Lefèvre d'Étaples und von P. R. Olivétan* (Leipzig 1935). J. COURVOISIER, *Die Religion in Geschichte und Gegenwart,* 7 v. (3d ed. Tübingen 1957–65) 4:1627.

[J. T MCNEILL]

OLLÉ-LAPRUNE, LÉON

French philosopher, b. Paris, July 25, 1839; d. there, Dec. 13, 1898. He came of a deeply Christian family. Ollé-Laprune studied at the Lycée Condorcet and the École Normale (1858). He was honored with the degree *agrégé des lettres* (1861), and taught successively at the *lycées* of Nice (1861), Douai (1864), Versailles (1868), and Henry IV in Paris (1871). From 1875 to his death he lectured at the École Normale.

Ollé-Laprune was a fervent Catholic; the example of his life as well as the sublimity of his thought had great influence on his students, especially at the École Normale. The essential characteristic of his teaching was the inauguration of a living philosophy whose duty it was to seek concrete certitude, at once solidly moral and intellectual. The true philosopher, he would say, thinks with his whole being, and is always ''attached to God as principle, support, light and rule of all thought.'' Some of his many works are *La Philosophie de Malebranche* (1870), *De la Certitude morale* (1880), *Le Prix de la vie* (1894), *La Vitalité chrétienne* (1901), and *La Raison et le rationalisme* (1906). Ollé-Laprune's greatest contribution was the inspiration he gave to a brilliant disciple, M. BLON-DEL. In his thesis on *L'Action* (1893), the pupil undertook to develop in a systematic manner the message of his master—a message calling for the establishment of an "integral realism" in thought, in action, and in being.

Bibliography: R. CRIPPA, *Enciclopedia filosofica,* 4 v. (Venice-Rome 1957) 3:1010–13.

[R. JOLIVET]

OLMOS, ANDRÉS DE

Franciscan missionary and linguist, early investigator of Native American lore in New Spain; b. near Oña, Burgos, Spain, *c.* 1491; d. Tampico, New Spain, buried there, August of 1570 (not Oct. 8, 1571, as some sources state). He spent some years in Olmos, near Valladolid, whence came the name he used. He studied at the University of Valladolid and at age 20 entered the Franciscan Order at Abrojo. When his superior, Juan de ZUMÁRRA-GA, was named bishop of Mexico, he took Andrés de Olmos to New Spain with him in 1528. According to the chronicler Vázquez, he was in Guatemala from 1529 to the middle of 1530, but it is probable that he was there after 1543. He spent some time in Tecamachalco, where he was superior in 1543; in Tlalmanalco; in Cuernavaca; and in Tlaxcala. In 1544 he tried to go to Florida and was at least instrumental in getting the expedition under way. He was chiefly responsible for spreading Christianity among the Huastec, Totonac, Tepehua, and Chichimec tribes, often with great sacrifice. From Hueytlalpan he evangelized the surrounding area and in the process learned Totonac and Tepehua. There, to assist in the work of conversion, he wrote his *Arte de la lengua mexicana* (1547) and prepared grammars in Totonac and Huastec. In 1557, or shortly thereafter, he penetrated the interior north of Tamaholipa and sought help in colonizing the area of the three rivers of Palmas (today Soto la Marina), Bravo, and Achiuse (today the Mississippi).

[J. MEADE]

OLSSON, ERIK (OLAI)

Theologian, historian; b. Sweden, *c.* 1422; d. Uppsala, Sweden, Dec. 24, 1486. Educated in Rostock, where he was *magister artium* in 1452, he became a canon in Uppsala as indicated by a document of 1459, and was a *magister in sacra theologia* of Siena in 1475. From 1477 to his death he was professor of theology at the University of Uppsala (founded 1477). Though he was a learned theologian and a writer of hymns, he is principally remembered as "the father of Swedish historiography."

His chief work, *Chronica regni Gothorum (Chronica Erici Olai),* is a chronicle with a fine patriotic spirit and a somewhat strong feeling of hatred toward Denmark. It was written probably in the late 1460s and the early 1470s, and compiled from a vast collection of sources, both in Latin and in the vernacular, among them the rhymed chronicles.

Bibliography: *Chronica Erici Olai* in *Scriptores rerum Svecicarum medii aevi,* 3 v. (Uppsala 1818–76) 2:1–165. H. ÖSTLUND in *Svenska män och kvinnor,* v. 2 (Stockholm 1944) 438–439. E. NYGREN, *in Svenskt biografiskt lexikon,* v. 14 (Stockholm 1953) 216–242, with bibliog.; *Kulturhistorisk leksikon for nordisk middelalder,* v. 2 (Copenhagen 1957) 603–604. H. JÄGERSTAD, *Lexikon für Theologie und Kirche,* ed. J. HOFER and K. RAHNER, 10 v. (2d, new ed. Freiburg 1957–65) 3:992–993.

[H. BEKKER-NIELSEN]

OLYMPIAS, ST.

Early Christian widow, deaconess, and devoted friend of St. JOHN CHRYSOSTOM; b. Constantinople, *c.* 361; d. Nicomedia, July 25, 408. Heiress to a fabulous fortune, Olympias was reared by her uncle, Procopius, an intimate friend of GREGORY OF NAZIANZUS. For her marriage to Nebridius, prefect of Constantinople (384), Gregory composed a poem, the earliest Christian Mirror for Women (*Patrologia Graeca* 37: 1541–50). After two unhappy years of marriage she was left a childless widow and devoted herself to God's service and a life of charity. She refused offers of remarriage and rejected a kinsman of Emperor Theodosius, who curtailed her association with ecclesiastics and impounded her property for five years. She devoted her time and wealth to charitable works and encouraged GREGORY OF NYSSA in his Scripture commentaries; and Bishop Nectarius made her a deaconess. When John Chrysostom succeeded Nectarius as patriarch in 398, she placed herself under his spiritual direction and founded a convent adjoining the cathedral. During the tragic events that led to Chrysostom's illegal deposition, she stood by him and refused to enter into communion with his unlawful successor. This led to her own persecution and exile, during which Chrysostom exhorted and consoled her in 17 letters (404–7). Under JUSTINIAN I her body was returned to Constantinople and buried in the convent that she had founded and that the emperor had rebuilt.

Feast: Dec. 17 (Roman MARTYROLOGY); July 24, 25, and 26 (Greek Church).

Bibliography: *Analecta Bollandiana* 15 (1896) 400–423; 16 (1897) 44–51, *Vita.* S. LE NAIN DE TILLEMONT, *Mémoires pour servir à l'histoire ecclésiastique des six premiers siècles* 11:416–440, 629–631. E. VENABLES, *Dictionary of Christian Biography* 4:73–75. H. LECLERCQ, *Dictionnaire d'archéologie chrétienne et de*

Father Edward Flanagan in Germany. (©Bettmann/CORBIS)

liturgie 12.2:2064–71. JOHN CHRYSOSTOM, *Lettres à Olympias,* ed. and tr. A. M. MALINGREY (*Sources Chrétiennes* 13; 1947, 2d ed. Paris 1968); *Lettre d'exil à Olympias et à tous les fidèles,* ed. and tr. A. M. MALINGREY (Paris 1964). C. BUTLER, ed., *The Lausiac History of Palladius,* 2 v. (Cambridge, Eng. 1898–1904) ch. 56. E. A. CLARK, *Jerome, Chrysostom, and Friends* (2d ed. New York 1982).

[P. W. HARKINS]

OMAHA, ARCHDIOCESE OF

Erected as the vicariate apostolic of Nebraska on Jan. 9, 1857; it was designated the Diocese of Omaha (*Omahensis*) on Oct. 2, 1885, and an archdiocese on Aug. 7, 1945, with suffragan sees at Grand Island and Lincoln, NE. In 2001 there were about 214,046 Catholics in a total population estimated at 830,522.

Early History. A Catholic settlement, made at St. John's City in Dakota County in 1856 by Rev. Jeremiah

F. TRECY of Dubuque, IA, was cut short by a destructive tornado after four years. When the first vicar apostolic, James M. O'Gorman, prior of the Trappist monastery at New Melleray, IA, arrived in Nebraska on June 3, 1859, he found several hundred Catholic families, principally in Omaha and along the Missouri River. O'Gorman brought the Sisters of Mercy (1864) and the Benedictine Sisters (1865), laying the foundations for a continuous history of Catholic education. He built a modest cathedral with money collected in the East and from workers constructing the Union Pacific and Burlington railroads. When he died in 1874, in addition to the Benedictines who had been laboring in southeastern Nebraska, O'Gorman had admitted approximately 30 secular priests, of whom about 18 continued to serve with some degree of permanence in the vicariate.

Two years later James O'Connor of Pittsburgh, PA was appointed second vicar apostolic and was consecrated on Aug. 20, 1876. He continued O'Gorman's work, launching the Sisters of Mercy on a program of secondary education and entrusting Creighton College (later University), built with a gift from the estate of Edward CREIGHTON to the Jesuits. The bishop also introduced the Poor Clares to Omaha, where, with financial assistance from John A. Creighton, they built their first permanent foundation in the U.S.; invited the Religious of the Sacred Heart to establish an academy, the now-defunct Duchesne College; and requested the Poor Sisters of St. Francis Seraph to inaugurate their extensive system of hospitals. Moreover, O'Connor personally supervised extensive Catholic colonization in the state, notably the Irish in Greeley County in the 1880s. He showed his solicitude for other national groups, which were similarly attracted by cheap farmland or railroad employment, by bringing the Franciscans and a group of Jesuits from Central Europe into the vicariate to work among the Bohemians and Poles. In addition, he directed the proliferation of parishes and schools that followed the heavy immigration.

Diocese. When the Diocese of Omaha, consisting of the states of Nebraska and Wyoming, was erected in 1885, O'Connor was appointed its first bishop. Among O'Connor's achievements was his spiritual direction of St. Katharine DREXEL, foundress of the Sisters of the BLESSED SACRAMENT. In Thurston County, NE in 1908, she founded St. Augustine's Indian School in Winnebago, a ministry which endured into the 21st century.

In 1887 the Omaha diocese was further reduced when all of Nebraska south of the Platte River was established as the Diocese of Lincoln. Wyoming, with its see at Cheyenne, became a distinct diocese. Under the watch of O'Connor and his immediate successors, the diocese, and especially the city of Omaha, welcomed Italian, Polish, Hungarian, and Ukrainian immigrants. O'Connor died in 1890 and was succeeded by Bp. Richard Scannell, who was transferred to Omaha from Concordia, KS on Jan. 30, 1891.

By temperament a scholarly recluse, Scannell, nevertheless, carried forward the work of building new churches and schools. The House of the Good Shepherd opened a home for girls in Omaha. In 1907, following Scannell's decision to raze the old cathedral, the cornerstone was laid for a new edifice in Spanish Renaissance style, which took more than 50 years to complete. St. Cecilia's Cathedral was consecrated in 1959; it contains an array of liturgical art including Albin Polasek's bronze *Crucifixus* on the high altar, his bronze stations of the cross, and wood sculptures. It was renovated extensively in 2000, in part to reflect Kimball's original designs for the ceiling. In 1912 the central and western counties of the state lying north of the Platte River were erected into a distinct diocese; the see, originally at Kearney, was transferred in 1917 to Grand Island following the annexation of four populous western counties from the Omaha diocese.

After Bishop Scannell's death in 1916, Jeremiah J. HARTY of St. Louis, MO, former archbishop of Manila, Philippine Islands, succeeded to the See of Omaha. Ill health marked the greater part of his 11 years there, preventing Harty from accomplishing any aggressive programs. Nevertheless, he did introduce new organization, diocesan in scope, and it was during his administration and with his encouragement that the world renowned institution of Boys' Town, a community founded to assist homeless and abandoned youth, was started by Rev. Edward FLANAGAN in 1917. Boys' Town, renamed Girls' and Boys' Town in 2000 to reflect the growing female population, continues to attract large numbers of visitors to its campus in West Omaha.

On May 29, 1928, Joseph Rummel, a New York priest, was consecrated to succeed Harty, who died on Oct. 29, 1927, but the Depression thwarted many of Rummel's plans. Circumstances forced him to divert funds from a successful campaign in 1930 to finance diocesan expansion for relief work among the faithful. During Rummel's episcopate, Omaha hosted the Sixth National Eucharistic Congress in September 1930. When Rummel was transferred to the Archdiocese of New Orleans, LA in 1935, Bp. James Hugh RYAN, rector of The Catholic University of America in Washington, DC, took his place. World War II similarly neutralized many of Ryan's efforts.

Archdiocese. Under Bishop Ryan, the growth of the Church in Nebraksa was recognized when, in 1945, Omaha was raised to an archdiocese. Ryan died in 1947 and his place was taken by Gerald T. Bergan of Des Moines, IA, under whom the archdiocese experienced phenomenal development. By 1963 more than $60 million had been spent on construction, including that of a home for the aged and a now-defunct minor seminary. Twenty-three religious orders of women with a total of 805 sisters, assisted by 562 lay teachers, were engaged in elementary and secondary teaching. Between 1950 and 1960, the number enrolled in Catholic elementary schools almost doubled, and the number enrolled in secondary schools grew by approximately 50 percent.

Bergan's auxiliary, Daniel Sheehan, was named the archbishop of Omaha in 1969, and endeavored to sustain the diocesan commitment to education in the years following the Second Vatican Council until his retirement in 1993. His successor, Elden Curtiss, focused on maintaining Omaha's relatively high number of archdiocesan seminarians, averaging seven ordinations to the priesthood per year throughout the 1990s.

In the 1990s, agribusiness, communication industries, and suburban expansion, led to the growth of megaparishes, which emerged on the southern and western sides of the metropolitan area. Hispanic immigrants, attracted by jobs in the meatpacking and other industries, created a new ministerial need. Ministries to Vietnamese, Hmong, and Sudanese refugee populations also grew at the close of the 20th century.

Jesuits, who direct Creighton University and Creighton Preparatory School in Omaha; Benedictines, who serve Mount Michael High School near Elkhorn; and the Columban Fathers, whose national headquarters are in Bellevue, are among the significant communities of men religious represented in the archdiocese. The Sisters of Mercy, who founded the College of St. Mary for women in Omaha in 1923; the Servants of Mary; the Poor Clares; the Notre Dame Sisters; and the Society of the Sacred Heart, who operated Duchesne College prior to its closing and maintain Duchesne High School, are among the women religious serving northeast Nebraska.

Bibliography: Archives, Archdiocese of Omaha. H. W. CASPER, *History of the Catholic Church in Nebraska*, 3 v. (Milwaukee 1960–1966). W. E. RAMSEY and B. DINEEN SHRIER, *A Gentle Shepherd: The Life and Times of Archbishop Daniel E. Sheehan* (Omaha, NE 1999). SISTER LORETTA, C.P.P.S., *History of the Catholic Church in the Diocese of Lincoln, Nebraska, 1887–1987* (Lincoln, NE 1986). S. SZMRECSANYI, *History of the Catholic Church in Northeast Nebraska* (Omaha, NE 1983).

[H. W. CASPER/S. A. WEIDNER]

OMAN, THE CATHOLIC CHURCH IN

The Sultanate of Oman ('Umân wa-Musqat in Arabic) comprises the Arabian peninsula of Musandam. It is bound on the north by the United Arab Emirates and the Gulf of Oman, on the east by the Gulf of Oman and the Arabian Sea, on the south by the Arabian Sea and on the west by Yemen, Saudi Arabia and the United Arab Emirates. A long, steep, semicircular mountain range protects the region's fertile coastal plain, while the western region becomes increasingly arid near its boundary with the "empty quarter," as the Rub 'al-Khali desert is known. Natural resources include petroleum, natural gas, copper, marble, asbestos, limestone, gypsum and chromium, while dates, limes, bananas and alfalfa are the predominant agricultural products.

Oman's economy is based on petroleum and natural gas exports, although the nation is not a member of OPEC; the country also benefits from its strategic position as a transit point for international crude oil trade. Other economic sectors include the sea trade and the export of dates, for which the region has been renowned

Capital: Musqat.
Size: 120,000 sq. miles.
Population: 2,533,388 in 2000.
Languages: Arabic; English, Baluchi, Urdu, and Indian dialects are spoken in various regions.
Religions: 63,300 Catholics (2.5%), 49,698 Protestants (2%), 2,052,940 Muslims (81%), 367,450 Hindus (14.5%).
Apostolic vicariate: Abu Dhabi, Arabia.

since ancient times; vines are cultivated in the more fertile mountain regions. Eighty percent of the population is literate.

Oman was established by Arabs in the first century as a trading outpost of Mesopotamia. Conquered by Muslims in the 7th century, it was ruled by independent IMĀMS, or emirs subservient to the caliphate of Abbasside at Baghdad. The region became a Portuguese possession in 1506, but the Portuguese withdrew by 1650 due to repeated attacks by Ottoman Turks, who reestablished their trading empire. A century later, in 1754, Ahmad ibn Said, a descendant of the imam of Yemen, claimed the region and his dynasty remained in power in 2000. Oman became a sultanate in 1793, and relations with Great Britain were established in 1798. Although Oman was the most powerful nation in Arabia in 1800, with control of Zanzibar and the coast of Iran and Pakistan, it suffered economic and political decline during the later 19th century, in part because of tribal warfare. Oman fell under British protection in 1913, its relationship strengthened by a series of treaties. Britain proved to be a benevolent ally to the sultanate: through British intervention, revolts against the repressive sultan Said bin Taimur were suppressed in 1953 and 1965, and in 1967 Great Britain ceded the Kuria Muria Islands to Oman. The discovery of oil in the region in 1964 boosted the country's economy, although it sparked a political upheaval that was resolved after the sultan was deposed by his British-educated son, Sultan Qaboos bin Said, during a bloodless palace coup in July of 1970. Taimur fled to England and ended his life in exile at a hotel in London. A revolution staged by a guerilla group called the Popular Front for the Liberation of Oman was put down in 1975, as Qaboos began his ambitious program of controlled modernization. He also maintained good relationships with Great Britain and Oman's mideast neighbors. By the close of the 20th century, the sultan exhibited signs of increasing liberalization, permitting women to run for election and legalizing political parties within Oman, as well as undertaking efforts to privatize the country's oil industry. On Nov. 6, 1996, Qaboos issued the Basic Charter, a decree granting basic civil liberties to all Omani citizens, including freedom of religion. In somewhat of a contrast, however, suffrage remained restricted to 50,000 voters in the 1997 election.

OMAN

By 2000 Oman had four parishes tended by one secular and six religious priests. Catholic missions existed at Shar and Salalah, and two churches were built on government-provided land in Muscat. As a religious minority in a predominately Muslim country, Catholics respected the tenets of shari'a (ISLAMIC LAW) by refraining from evangelization activities among Oman's Muslim population. All children of Omani citizens were required to receive education in Islam, although non-citizens were not required to follow suit. While publication of Catholic materials was not permitted in Oman, no prohibition was placed against their import. The government encouraged ecumenical dialogue. Most Omani were Ibadi Muslims, although a Shia Muslim population resided in Muscat.

Bibliography: *Bilan du Monde* (Paris 1964) 2:602. B. THOMAS, *Arab Rule under the Al Bu Sa'id Dynasty of Oman, 1741–1937* (London 1938). *Annuario Pontificio* has data on all diocese.

[A. JAMME/EDS.]

OMER OF THÉROUANNE, ST.

Bishop; b. Orval (*Aurea Vallis*), near Coutances, France; d. Thérouanne, Sept. 1, *c.* 670. Omer (or Otmar, whence the Latin, *Audomarus*) and his father Friulph, who were perhaps of Saxon origin, entered the Columban Abbey of LUXEUIL after the death of Omer's mother, Domitta. When named bishop of Thérouanne (*c.* 635–40), Omer took the suggestion of St. ACHARIUS OF NOYON and sent for three other Luxeuil monks, SS. Momelinus, BERTINUS, and Ebertramnus, to help him in his work of completing the conversion of the peoples of his diocese. Momelinus governed the original abbey they built near Sithiu until 660, when he was elevated to the episcopacy of Noyon-Tournai. Then Bertinus succeeded as abbot. Having received several properties from a certain Adroald, Omer gave Bertinus the island of Sithiu in the River Aa, as a new site for the abbey (later SAINT-BERTIN) and also the church of Sainte-Marie, which he had built on a neighboring hill. Omer was buried in this church, after granting Sithiu a privilege of immunity. The city of Saint-Omer was later built on the slopes of the hill between these two shrines.

Feast: Sept. 9.

Bibliography: *Acta Sanctorum* Sept. 3:384–417. *Monumenta Germaniae Historica: Scriptores rerum Merovingicarum* (Berlin 1826–) 5:729–764. O. BLED, ''Les Reliques . . . de St. Omer,'' *Mémoires de la Société des Antiquaires de la Morinie* 32 (1914–20) 1–112. G. COOLEN, ''Saint Colomban et Saint Omer,'' *Mélanges colombaniens* (Paris 1950) 361–375. A. BUTLER, *The Lives of the Saints,* rev. ed. H. THURSTON and D. ATTWATER, 4 v. (New York 1956) 3:516–517.

[G. COOLEN]

OMISSION

The nonperformance of some action; it is of concern to the moralist only when a person could and should do what he leaves undone. The omission of an act when its performance is impossible or is in no way a matter of obligation is of no moral significance. Similarly, if a person fails to do something through inculpable ignorance of or inadvertence to his obligation to act, the omission is not morally imputable, because if he is unconscious of an obligation to act, it cannot be said that he should, or ought to, act. When there is an obligation to act, the failure to perform the required act can be due either to simple nonchoice or to deliberate choice. It is due to nonchoice, and is negatively or indirectly voluntary, when a person, though conscious of an obligation to act, simply does not act or occupies himself with something incompatible with the fulfillment of his duty, but without reaching a positive decision not to do what he should. It is due to deliberate choice when a person reaches an explicit decision to omit what he should do (THOMAS AQUINAS, *Summa theologiae* 1a2ae, 71.5).

In all cases of voluntary omission, whether due to nonchoice or deliberate choice, one is responsible for his failure to act, and the morality of the omission is determined in accord with the same norms that are applied to a positive choice to do something. If there is advertence to the obligation to do something, the omission of the performance of the act is equatable with a positive sinful choice, and the result is a grave or venial sin as the gravity of the obligation and the circumstances of the case demand. It is to be noted, however, that choices of nonperformance are qualified by the same influences that affect choices to act. Accordingly, such subjective elements as fear and passion can, under certain conditions, lessen personal imputability.

Bibliography: THOMAS AQUINAS, *Summa theologiae* 1a2ae, 6.3. D. M. PRÜMMER, *Manuale theologiae moralis*, ed. E. M. MÜNCH (Freiburg-Barcelona 1955) 1:360. B. H. MERKELBACH, *Summa theologiae moralis* (Paris 1949) 1:60. H. NOLDIN, *Summa theologiae moralis*, rev. A. SCHMITT and G. HEINZEL (Innsbruck 1961–62) 1:92, 292–293.

[A. BURROUGHS]

OMNI DIE DIC MARIAE

The second section of a lengthy Marian hymn, or *Mariale*, whose first section begins with *Ut jucundas cervas undas*. The *Omni die*, shortest of all the parts, has 19 stanzas whose verse form is alternate acatalectic and catalectic trochaic dimeter with internal rhyme in the first and third verses (aa/b,cc/b). The meter and rhyme scheme are so intricate that their competent use in a lengthy poem demanded talent in Latin verse composition. It has been ascribed variously to BERNARD OF CLAIRVAUX (d. 1153), ANSELM OF CANTERBURY (d. 1109), CASIMIR of Poland (d. 1484), and others. But it is ascribed also to BERNARD OF CLUNY (fl. 1150), who in his *De contemptu mundi*, a 3,000-line poem of similar difficulty, proved his ability to use such a meter. And since no manuscript yet discovered precedes his time, the weight of greater probability

leads Julian and others to name him as the author. The text, together with a number of other stanzas found in various MSS, is given in *Analecta hymnica* 50:423–482.

Bibliography: U. CHEVALIER, *Repertorium hymnologicum* (Louvain-Brussels 1892–1921) 2:14070. J. JULIAN, ed., *A Dictionary of Hymnology* (New York 1957) 1200–02. J. DE GHELLINCK, *L'Essor de la littérature latine au XIIe siècle* (Brussels-Paris 1946) 2:223–226. F. J. E. RABY, *A History of Christian-Latin Poetry from the Beginnings to the Close of the Middle Ages* (Oxford 1953) 318–319.

[G. E. CONWAY]

OMNIBONUS (OMNEBENE)

Bishop and canonist; d. Verona, Oct. 22, 1185. Little is known of Omnibonus's early life other than that he was a student of Gratian. He taught Canon Law at Bologna during the pontificate of Pope Eugene III and also later at Verona. In 1157 he became bishop of Verona, a post he held until his death. As a canonist, he was one of the early members of the group later known as the DECRETISTS (i.e., those whose main concern was to comment on the *Decretum* of GRATIAN). He is very likely the author of the *Abbreviatio Decreti*, a reordered version of Gratian's *Decretum*. Omnibonus's *Abbreviatio* is divided into two parts, 26 distinctions and 37 *causae*. It was glossated upon by later canonists, but it does not appear to have played a very important role in the history of Canon Law. He is also most likely the same person as Omnibonus, the author of a theological treatise from about the same period. The theological treatise of Omnibonus shows the influence of the school of Abelard, Hugh of Saint-Victor, Roland, and, of course, Gratian.

Bibliography: A. VAN HOVE, *Commentarium Lovaniense in Codicem iuris canonici 1*, v. 1–5 (Mechlin 1928–); v.1, Prolegomena (2d ed 1945) 1:441–442. R. CHABANNE, *Dictionnaire de droit canonique*, ed. R. NAZ, 7 v. (Paris 1935–65) 6:1111–12.

[J. M. BUCKLEY]

OMNIPOTENCE

Omnipotence is derived From the Latin *omnis* (all) and *potens* (capable of making or producing). Divine omnipotence is a divine operative attribute, an active POTENCY, or power, for acting *ad extra*. As an active potency it is distinguished from a passive potency, or capacity for receiving ACT, which would be opposed to God's perfection. By this power God has dominion over all things outside Himself, which He has brought into existence and which He holds in existence.

Omnipotence extends, however, only to beings that have the inherent possibility of existence—that is, that do not include a contradiction. Thus, God cannot make a square circle or an infinite created being since the essential notes here cancel each other out. (For this reason it is impossible for God to commit a sin—that is, act in a way contrary to His own intrinsic goodness.) These hypothetical beings lie beyond God's power, not because God's power is limited, but because of the inherent limitation in the idea of the thing itself.

Similarly, God's power cannot reverse His own eternal decrees, for this implies change of intention or new knowledge, both of which are impossible in a perfect God.

Some actions are called impossible for God even though they themselves can exist, yet cannot coexist with God's other decrees. Thus, it is true to say that man's immortal soul could be destroyed by God's power, if one considers His power in itself. Yet granting God's design in making man's soul immortal by nature, it is not possible that He act against His own plan. Thus one may say that destroying man's soul is beyond God's ordered power (*potentia ordinata*—considering His power in conjunction with His divine decrees), but not beyond His absolute power (*potentia absoluta*—considering in itself His power over man's soul). The usefulness, however, and even the validity, of this distinction is generally called into question.

Omnipotence has been considered the attribute most proper to a deity by men of all times and places. The Bible in particular voices continually the theme of God's power in comparison with the limited power of alien gods or of temporal rulers of Egypt or Babylonia. God is always able to save His people from these enemies. If at times He chooses not to, it is only because His people have not observed His laws.

Most of the Biblical names of God imply power to act or make, though the exact meaning of these terms is often under dispute. Abraham worships '*ēl šaddai* (God the Almighty) in Gn 17.1 and '*ēl 'elyôn* (Most High God or God Eternal) in Gn 14.18; '*ēl* [*see* EL (GOD) Gn 46.3], and as found in '*ĕlōhîm* (*see* ELOHIM) throughout the Old Testament, means the Strong God. God is also called "the Mighty One of Jacob" (Gn 4, 9.24), "the creator of the heavens. . . the designer and maker of the earth" (Is 45.18), and "the Lord of the whole earth" (Jos 3.11, 13). This notion of omnipotent Lordship is intimately linked with Jesus' divinity throughout the Gospel of St. Mark.

Somewhat mysterious in meaning is the most proper name of God, *Yahweh* (*see* YAHWEH), probably originally meaning "He who causes all things to be," rather than the later, more common, rendering, "I am who am" (Ex 3.14).

In addition, many metaphors refer to Yahweh's hand or arm as symbolic of God's power to rule or guide or punish (cf. Jos 4.24; Ezr 7.28; Ex 15.16).

Omnipotence is not of merely speculative interest to Israel, for this attribute fosters faith's vision of the *mirabilia Dei:* the salvation acts of God for His people [cf. Dt 3.24; Ps 105(106).2]. It invites the believer to prayer of gratitude or petition; it is one of the motives held out to Israel to sanctify itself.

The doctrine that all things depend upon God appears in the opening chapters of Genesis, where God unfolds His plan of creation. (For treatment of the question whether or not creation out of nothing is to be found here, *see* CREATION.) By God's simple utterance things came to be, and as He wants them to be. Moon and sun, often worshiped by pagans, are here merely creatures. In Exodus, God's power is made manifest publicly before Egypt and its Pharaoh (cf. also Is 19.1). In such a way God has power over all nations (Nm 21.3; 1 Sm 14.12). The more marvelous is the work of God's omnipotence in that He selects an unworthy nation for His favors. Even evil is fitted into God's plan; Israel is often purified by it.

The culmination of God's power is found in the incarnation (cf. Rom 1.4). Jesus redeems man and even the physical world by becoming man, performing miracles, dying, and rising again. In the last times He will return, the Son of Man (Dn ch. 7), coming to judge all things as Lord and master.

These Biblical teachings have been interpreted by the magisterium of the Church (see H. Denzinger, *Enchiridion symbolorum,* Index syst. Blbc).

Scholastic theology considers a number of questions in this area. Omnipotence follows upon God's essence as PURE ACT, having within Himself His own fullness of actuality. Since one thing is able to cause another insofar as it is itself in act, God alone is capable of giving existence to created things. Of course, God's omnipotence is in reality completely identified with His essence, distinguished only by a virtual minor distinction. Other problems dealt with in systematic theology are God's freedom in creating (ibid. 3002) and man's freedom under God's causality (*see* OMNISCIENCE; PREDESTINATION).

See Also: GOD, ARTICLES ON.

Bibliography: *Dictionnaire de théologie catholique,* ed. A. VACANT et al., 15 v. (Paris 1903–50; Tables générales 1951-), Tables générales 1:975–993. C. SPICQ, *Lexikon für Theologie und Kirche* ed. J. HOFER and K. RAHNER, 10 v. (Freiburg 1957–65); suppl., *Das Zweite Vatikanische Konzil: Dokumente und Kommentare,* ed. H. S. BRECHTER et al., pt. 1 (1966) 1:353–355. T. AQUINAS, *Summa theologiae,* 1a, 25; *C. gent.* 2.7. F. SUÁREZ, *De Deo* 3.9. J. D. COLLINS, *God in Modern Philosophy* (Chicago 1959). R. GARRIGOULAGRANGE, *The One God,* tr. B. ROSE (St. Louis 1943). P. HEINISCH,

Theology of the Old Testament, tr. W. G. HEIDT (Collegeville, Minn. 1950).

[G. ROXBURGH]

OMNIPRESENCE

The infinite and omnipotent God is in all things everywhere. Such, briefly, is the teaching of Scripture and tradition. Omnipresence is an attribute of God, the infinite and first cause of all, who is actually present in all existing places and things. This presence is not to be interpreted as dimensional or spatial, since God is utterly simple and infinite and thus free of all spatial limitations. Rather He is present as an agent to His effects. So God is everywhere, for He is the source of the being and action in all places and things. Moreover, since in God power and action are one, He is substantially present in all existing things through His power and operation.

God's omnipresence has a relationship to divine immensity of actuality to aptitude. For immensity is the infinite plenitude of subsistent being that is free from all spatial limitations and, thus, is able to be present in all things. Immensity implies the power to be everywhere. Omnipresence is the actual exercise of the power to be everywhere. Whereas immensity is an essential, absolute, and eternal attribute in God, omnipresence is relative to created being.

Omnipresence is implicit in those scriptural texts that speak of God's immensity. But Scripture is explicit also. In earlier books the notion of omnipresence remains undefined, although God's presence is known not to be confined to one place (Gn 12.4–9; 14.20). Later, the idea of God's omnipresence is more definitely expressed: God is everywhere by His nature, for He transcends and permeates all things (Dt 4.39; Wis 8.1) and sees them as they are [Ps 112(113).5–9; 101(102).20–21; Prv 5.21; 15.3]; no one can escape His presence [Ps 138(139).7–12; Am 9.2; Is 43.2]. Christ calls attention to the presence of the "Father, who sees in secret" (Mt 6.6) and who is present in heaven and on earth (Mt 6.9–13; 5.35). God is everywhere, as St. Paul explains to the Athenians (Acts 17.24–28; cf. Eph. 4.6).

Patristic teaching distinguishes God's omnipresence from His immensity (e.g., St. Cyril of Alex., *In Jn.* 1.9) and explicitly states that God is everywhere and wholly everywhere (e.g., St. Hilary, *De Trin.* 2.6). Theologians maintain this patristic doctrine and commonly distinguish how God is present in all things: He is present to them by His essence and power, and all things are open to His knowledge; while in the just, God is present in a special way through His grace (St. Thomas, *Summa theologiae,*

1a, 8.3). The immensity of God is a defined dogma (H. Denzinger, *Enchiridion symbolorum,* 3001).

See Also: INDWELLING, DIVINE; JESUS CHRIST.

Bibliography: E. MANGENOT, *Dictionnaire de théologie catholique,* ed. A. VACANT et al., 15 v. (Paris 1903–50; Tables générales 1951) 4.1:948–1023. X. LE BACHELET, ibid. 1023–1152. M. CHOSSAT, ibid. 1152–1243. J. M. DALMAU, *Sacrae theologiae summa,* ed. Fathers of the Society of Jesus, Professors of the Theological Faculties in Spain, 4 v. (Madrid), v. 1 (1962), v. 2 (1958), v. 3 (1961), v. 4 (1962); *Biblioteca de autores cristianos* (Madrid 1945) 2.1:126–134. Y. M. J. CONGAR, *The Mystery of the Temple,* tr. R. F. TREVETT (Westminster, Md. 1962). J. DANIÉLOU, *The Presence of God,* tr. W. ROBERTS (Baltimore 1960). L. REYPENS, *Dictionnaire de spiritualité ascétique et mystique. Doctrine et histoire,* ed. M. VILLER et al. Paris (1932) 3:883–929.

[M. F. MORRY]

OMNISCIENCE

The term divine science might also be used here. It brings into focus the heated, lengthy, and continuing theological controversy on the relationship between the certitude of God's knowledge and human freedom. Taken from this standpoint, the attribution of divine science to God signifies that He possesses infinitely perfect science or certain knowledge of Himself. He also knows perfectly all that has existed, exists, or will exist in both the physical and moral order. This divine science extends to every free act, but this foreknowledge implies no necessity. The Catholic Church defined at the First Vatican Council that God is infinite in all His perfections and possessed of intellect and will (H. Denzinger, *Enchiridion symbolorum,* 3001). The council also stated that this knowledge whereby "all things are naked and open to his eyes" (Heb 4.13) is the foundation of the providential governance of all things, "even the future free actions of creatures" (*Enchiridion symbolorum* 3003; *see* FREE WILL AND PROVIDENCE).

Historical Considerations. Viewing historically man's understanding of God's omniscience is a useful prelude to the systematic treatment.

Old Testament. In Biblical theology the existence of knowledge in God is a necessary consequence of the fact that for Biblical revelation God is a personal God. In general, therefore, this divine knowledge as personal is at heart a knowledge of God's people (*see* PEOPLE OF GOD). And, frequently, God's knowledge designates acts of care, help, and succor [see Jb 31.6; Ps 1.6; 72 (73).11; 102(103).14; 143(144).3]. It is also this highly personalist note that gives to the Biblical affirmations of the divine knowledge their strongly religious character. There is no shadow of doubt in the Old Testament (OT) that

God knows all things, but the fundamental note is that He knows all that takes place on earth. All human existence is lived out in His sight and is known to Him. It is this fact that gives dramatic perspective to Job's sorrow (Jb 28.24). God knows the just and the unjust to the very roots of their being [Ps 10(11).4; 32(33).15; Prv 15.11; 16.2]. Knowing men, God knows their thoughts, their intentions, their most secret actions [Ps 93(94).1–2; Ps 138(139)]. It is this conviction that informs the moral dimension of the religious activity of God's people.

It is, moreover, the conviction of God's perfect knowledge of all things that engenders Israel's confidence in God's providential designs. The deeply personal character of God's knowledge is also emphasized by the fact that it is concrete and experiential. God knows His people as the husband his wife. All things that exist are the work of His hand. The Psalmist proclaims that God knows all that He has created and that He who made the eye does indeed see [Ps 93(94).9].

While this personal note is characteristic of the Biblical affirmation, there is another note that is peculiarly proper to the teaching on divine knowledge. For what gives to the OT teaching on God's knowledge an originality beyond merely natural theology is the note of wisdom. Not only does God know but He understands all these things. What is clear in the OT development is that the sapiential authors move from the idea of wisdom as a largely practical thing to the idea of wisdom being a kind of subsistent reality in God. It finally becomes a personal characteristic of such cosmic status that it is personified as the agent of God's creation and providential ordering of the universe (e.g., Prv 8.22–31).

It is also from this standpoint of wisdom that the OT conception of God's knowledge has some areas of equivalence to the scholastic concept of divine science; for it is something beyond all human knowing and quite proper to God (e.g., Is 28.29; 40.13). To the sages of Israel God's wisdom in terms of the knowledge of good and evil is far beyond man's—God alone is truly wise (Jb 28.12–28; Is 40.13). It is this approach that makes of wisdom "an aura of the might of God and a pure effusion of the glory of the Almighty" (Wis 7.25). What is of note in the whole sapiential approach in the OT is that only by implication does it involve itself with the great prophetic themes of covenant, election, and salvation [see WISDOM (IN THE BIBLE)].

New Testament. It is in the New Testament (NT) that the whole notion of God's knowledge and wisdom is synthesized with His saving work. The personal character of wisdom is revealed in Christ to correspond to a Person distinct from the Father—the WORD (Jn ch. 1). It is this transcendent and creative wisdom that is incarnated in Jesus Christ (Col 1.15–20). In Jesus Christ, the only Son of the Father, is revealed God's love for the world (Jn 3.16). Wisdom as divine understanding is seen to subsist in the Son: ". . . no one knows the Son except the Father; nor does anyone know the Father except the Son, and him to whom the Son chooses to reveal him" (Mt 11.27). It is the knowledge that God has of Himself that the Son reveals: "No one has at any time seen God. The only-begotten Son, who is in the bosom of the Father, he has revealed him" (Jn 1.18). St. Paul, writing to the Corinthians, tells them that the deep things of God known only by the Spirit (1 Cor 2.11–12) are the wisdom that is manifested in Christ: "From him you are in Christ Jesus, who has become for us God-given wisdom, and justice, and sanctification, and redemption" (1 Cor 1.30). The concern of the NT, like that of the OT, is not a natural theology but God's saving activity. Accordingly the divine knowledge to which they testify is essentially that which looks to SALVATION. Yet all these affirmations suppose and rest upon the fact: God truly knows.

Patristic Teaching. When one turns to the actual teaching of the gospel, he finds a new dimension with a radically new note not found in the Biblical affirmations. This dimension arises from the rational tradition that is so much a part of the Greco-Roman culture. Hence, from the beginning, the Greek Christian writers were called upon to make use of a variety of philosophical sources and elements in order to explain and defend the Christian revelation (*see* THEOLOGY, INFLUENCE OF GREEK PHILOSOPHY ON). Thus, along with an extensive use of symbolism to explain the meaning of Christian revelation there is a consistent effort to establish a Christian philosophical notion of God and His actions. It is therefore in this context that the patristic teaching on God's knowledge must be set. For these Christian writers sought to establish and safeguard the spiritual nature, the holiness, and, above all, the supremacy of God through concepts appropriate to men trained in the schools of Greek philosophy.

The first note stressed in this teaching, which in turn forms the foundation for the divine knowledge, is what might be called the total supernaturality of God. G. L. Prestige thinks that "philosophically, this idea was expressed by the [Greek] word ὑπεροχή, which may fairly be translated transcendence" [*God in Patristic Thought* (London 1952) 25]. He points out that the word occurs in Irenaeus (*Adversus. haereses* 5.2.3; *Patrologia Graeca* 7:1127) but that its use is best illustrated in the *Clementine Homilies:* "He who would worship God ought before all else to know what is peculiar to the nature of God alone, which cannot pertain to another . . . . This is peculiar to God, that He alone is, as the maker of all, so also the best of all. That which makes is indeed superior in power to that which is made; that which is boundless is superior in magnitude to that which is bounded; in respect of beauty, that which is comeliest; in respect of happiness, that which is most blessed; in respect of understanding, that which is most perfect. And in like manner in other respects He incomparably possesses transcendence'' (*Hom. clem.* 10.9; cf. Prestige, 25–26). This serves to illustrate the fundamental emphasis on the transcendent character of God's understanding and affirms the incomparable superiority of God over all that He has made.

The other general note in Greek Christian thought directly related to God's knowledge is the very heavy emphasis on His providence. For, while insisting on the divine transcendence, revelation also makes it clear that God is not remote from man but enters personally into his history. His nature, however, is revealed through His works and His providence (e.g., see Theophilus of Antioch, *Ad Autol.* 1.5; *Patrologia Graeca,* 6:1030–31). In the explanation of this providential ordering there is strong emphasis on the notion of planning or designing. It is in this connection that the Greek word οἰκονομία (economy) plays a somewhat striking role. It undergoes in the Christian writers a gradual transformation from the simple meaning of administering or overseeing to planning or designing (cf. Prestige, 57–62). Thus God economizes the affairs of the world, so that the man who realizes that God's providence rules the world knows that events come out for the best under the economy of the ruler (cf. *Hom. clem.* 2.36, *Patrologia Graeca,* 2:102; Clement of Alexandria, *Strom.* 3.17; *Patrologia Graeca,* 8:1205–08). In general, God's providence or economy involves His action in the world of nature, of human history, of salvation (*see* ECONOMY, DIVINE). It finds its supreme expression in the INCARNATION, ''for which, the word 'oekonomia,' without any verbal qualification, is the regular patristic term from the third century onwards'' (Prestige, 67). Here can be seen how closely the notion of God's knowledge corresponds to the NT teaching.

Specifically, with regard to the divine knowledge, the basic Biblical teaching is constantly affirmed. God knows all that is and will be, and the whole measure and order of things is disposed in accord with His wisdom (see, e.g., Irenaeus, *Adversus haereses* 2.26.3, *Patrologia Graeca,* 7:801–802; 2.30.9, *Patrologia Graeca,* 7:821–823; Origen, *Contra Celsum* 2.30, *Patrologia Graeca,* 11:850–851; Cyril of Jerusalem, *Catechism* 4.5, *Patrologia Graeca,* 33:459). However, in so affirming this, the Christian teachers were faced almost from the beginning by a problematic raised by the Gnostics. Some of the Gnostics would maintain that men are divided into different categories so that by their nature the spiritual will necessarily be saved, the earthly will necessarily be

reprobated, and the psychic, who alone are unnecessitated, are alone free. Marcion, who wrote within the Christian framework itself, maintained that the God of the OT was distinct from the God revealed in the NT. On this basis Marcion held that the God of the Mosaic dispensation was arbitrary and unjust in His treatment of men, taking no account of their merits. Celsus, whose thought is the object of a major work by Origen, taught that if God has certain knowledge of man's future acts, then human freedom is not possible (cf. H. D. Simonin, OP, ''La Prédestination d'après les pères grecs,'' *Dictionnaire de théologie catholique* 12.2:2815–32).

In the face of the issues raised by these heretical positions, there is found in the Fathers a constant defense both of God's foreknowledge of all human activity and of human freedom. Irenaeus sums up the basic problem: ''But that which He said, 'how often have I desired to gather your sons and you would not,' demonstrates the ancient law of liberty, because God made man free from the beginning, having his own power even as his own soul to accept God's commands freely and not by compulsion'' (*Adversus haereses* 4.37.1; *Patrologia Graeca* 7:1099). Scriptural texts in particular are interpreted to bring out this point. For example, Eusebius of Caesarea insists that the fact that God foreknew Judas would be a traitor does not force him to be such (*Praep. evang.* 6.11; *Patrologia Graeca* 21:491). John Chrysostom, interpreting the texts from Mt 18.7 and Lk 17.1 that it is necessary that scandals come, goes on to say that this does not take away free choice or liberty or subject life to necessity. For the fact that scandal is predicted is not what causes it to occur (see *In Matt. hom.* 59.1; *Patrologia Graeca* 58:573–575). Augustine, dealing with predestination when he is writing against the Pelagians and Semi-Pelagians, is forced to take up this point on a number of occasions. He affirms in general as well as in specific cases that what God foresees will be the future does not force that particular action to be done (*Lib. arb.* 3.4.11; *Patrologia Latina* 32:1276). In the case of Adam and Eve the cause of their fall is not the divine foreknowledge but their evil will (*General ad literature* 11.9.12; *Patrologia Latina* 34:434). God foresees, too, what is in our wills, but He does not take away free choice (*Civ.* 5.10.2; *Patrologia Latina* 41:153).

Carolingian Era. The whole question raised by Augustine comes to a head in the Carolingian era with the issues raised by Gottschalk (cf. É. Amman, *L'Époque carolingienne, Histoire de l'église depuis les origines jusqu'à nos jours* 6:320–344). In an age when Augustine is the teacher par excellence, Gottschalk takes his ideas on predestination and presents them without their author's nuances or flexibility. It is also true that the Augustinian conceptions have already begun to be harshened under the influence of Isidore of Seville, but they now become the focus of a major conflict in the Carolingian world [cf. H. Rondet, *Gratia Christi* (Paris 1948) 170–179]. For Gottschalk simply it is a fact that God predestines some to eternal life and they will not perish, and those not predestined to eternal life will perish; no question of merit or demerit or liberty appears to enter into his position.

In the controversy that follows upon this, all the great names of Carolingian theology are involved—Hincmar, Rabanus Maurus, John Scotus Erigena, Florus of Lyons, and many others. Two councils are held, one under Hincmar at the royal residence at Quiercy and the other at Valence. The statements of these councils on the issue have a large role in the theological tradition that develops after them; in fact, for a good many modern theologians they have been looked upon as normative. One statement from the Council of Valence is particularly notable. It is largely a quotation from Florus of Lyons: "[We faithfully hold that] God foresees and has foreseen eternally both the good works that the good would do and the evil works that the evil would do . . . . He has foreseen that the good would be good entirely through His grace and would receive their reward through that grace, so also that the evil would be evil by their own malice and would be condemned by His justice to eternal punishment. . . . But the foreknowledge of God has not placed on any evildoer a necessity whereby he could not be otherwise, but he was going to be by his own will just as God . . . has foreseen in His omnipotent and unchangeable majesty" (H. Denzinger, *Enchiridian symbolorum,* 626–627; cf. B. Lavaud, "La controverse sur la prédestination av XIIᵉ siècle," *Dictionnaire de théologie catholique,* 12.2: 2901–35). This statement may be taken as summing up the patristic response to the problematic that is so central to the whole matter of God's knowledge.

Systematic Theology. Revelation clearly affirms the fact that God knows. The task of systematic theology is to determine as far as it can what is to be understood by this revealed fact. It does this by bringing to bear on the revealed affirmation the psychological resources of a man who himself is able to know. It also employs the philosophic intelligence of the Church, since any treatment of knowledge and understanding implies a philosophic position. In the matter of divine knowledge, it should also be noted that the task is complex. For theology must show that God truly knows, but, in using man's knowledge as a resource in understanding, theology must not blur the explanation by excessive anthropomorphism [*see* ANTHROPOMORPHISM (IN THEOLOGY)]. Ultimately the act of divine knowledge must be reducible to the pure act of being.

Man's Knowing. Beginning with man's own experience of knowing, what stands out is the fact that in some way man as knower enters into a special relationship with objects other than himself. For the fact is that the KNOWLEDGE of an object is the presence of the object in thought. The act of knowing appears to grasp the very nature of the object without modifying that object in its own actuality. Yet, in comprehending the object thought does not cease to be thought. Intelligence grasps the idea of a tree or a stone but does not itself become a tree or stone in actuality. Moreover, while the object known and the concept and judgments about it determine the content of knowledge, they are not the only element of knowledge. For there are operations of the central reality that is intelligence itself in action. Thus there is the reflexive consciousness of this knowledge, whereby the knower understands that it is knowledge and is conscious of this central operation of understanding; hence the capacity to reflect upon what he knows and relate it to the rest of what he knows. Finally, this act of knowledge is immanent in the one knowing since it takes place only in the subject, for the act by which the object exists in his thought is the very act by which he knows—the understanding in act is the intelligible in act.

The root of this capacity to know is immateriality. In material things the coming of a new form means the disappearance of the previous form. It is the very possibility of this kind of change that is called matter, since change here means a loss of integrity. To know, on the other hand, means to be another in some way, yet retain integrity of being. St. Thomas, as the general scholastic tradition, explains this capacity by the use of the term species, which has been translated modernly as "knowledge-likeness" [cf. *Summa Theologiae,* v.4, *Knowledge in God,* tr. T. Gornall, SJ (New York 1964) 17]. This means that the object is present in thought "intentionally," that is, by reason of its form (that which makes it to be what it is) and with nothing of materiality. To know, therefore, means that the object known exists intentionally (as in contradistinction to actually) in the mind of the knower, or in an intelligible mode of existence. This is possible because intelligibility is present in all things; in the common Christian philosophical and theological tradition this follows from the very fact of creation. Because God has created all things, then the universe in its every part is a participation in God the supreme intelligible.

God's Knowing. It is in the light of this conception of knowledge that the general Catholic theological tradition stemming from St. Thomas has treated of the divine knowledge. It recognizes that in the created way in which man is knower and knows there is the knower not only in act but also in potency. It is also evident that the thing known is in potency as well as in act. Yet, it is maintained that this distinction arises not from the nature of knowing but because the act of knowing takes place in a creature, man. Knowing of itself is essentially act or perfection, and potency is not necessary to knowing. The more perfectly actualized, therefore, the more perfectly intelligible. The more potency is negated, the more closely identified are understanding and the thing understood. In God, as totally perfect and pure actuality, there is no potency; hence essence, intellect, understanding are all one and the same. "Since, therefore, God has no potentiality but is pure actuality, in Him intellect and what is known must be identical in every way" (*Summa Theologiae* 1a, 14.2). Further, since there is no form in God distinct from His existence, then it follows that His essence is the very way in which God knows. Necessarily, then, God's act of knowing is His essence and His very being ("ipsum eius intelligere sit eius essentia et eius esse"— *Summa Theologiae* 1a, 14.4). In sum, what is argued is that God is an infinite, eternal, and substantial act of understanding [cf. B. Lonergan, SJ, "The Concept of Verbum in the Writings of St. Thomas Aquinas," *Theological Studies* 10 (1949) 359–393].

Objects of Divine Knowledge. What traditionally have been called the secondary objects of divine knowledge may now be considered. By reason of the fact that God knows Himself perfectly (since His very being is His act of knowledge), then He knows His own power perfectly. This divine power, in turn, extends to other things by the very fact that it is the first efficient cause of all things. God, accordingly, knows things other than Himself, and He knows them immediately and specifically, not successively and generically. God also knows evil. While evil is a privation, an absence of good, yet because God knows all goods perfectly He knows that some of them will suffer corruption because of evils. So, through the very fact of knowing good, God also knows evil. God also knows individuals, and this again stems from His causality. For God's knowledge is coextensive with His causality. "He knows other things through His essence insofar as [His essence] is the likeness of all things as their productive principle; therefore, his essence must be the sufficient principle for knowing all things made through it not only in their universal nature but in their individuality" (*Summa Theologiae* 1a, 14.11). Finally God can know not only those things that actually exist or have existed but all that can be produced either by Himself or by creatures. Traditionally this is called the science of simple intelligence (*scientia simplicis intelligentiae*), i.e., the certain knowledge of all possible participations of the divine essence. Once again this is a consequence of the proposition that the divine essence, through which the divine intellect knows, is the adequate likeness of everything that is or can be, both with regard to common principles and what is proper to each individual.

Divine Knowledge of the Future. A distinct place has been given to this matter of God's knowledge of the future because of the extensive theological controversy that has centered on it since the 16th century. As was seen above, the Christian Fathers were quite conscious of the problem of God's knowledge of the future, predestination, and human liberty. By way of a solution, basically, they had simply insisted that there was no incompatibility. In the 16th century, however, as a result of the Calvinist preaching, the question of predestination and God's foreknowledge becomes a central issue. For what is involved is man's free participation in God's salutary activity. This Calvinist preaching is made particularly acute by the teaching of BAIUS (cf. H. Rondet, 287–293). The polemical exigencies, in the end, make inescapable the Catholic theological controversy. Any study of this Catholic controversy makes it clear that there is no question that God knows all future events. What is in question is the mode of knowing future contingents, and, in particular, future contingents that are dependent on the exercise of free choice by man. As the controversy originates, both sides rest their case on the interpretation of St. Thomas. The basic article (*Summa Theologiae* 1a, 14.13) looks to showing that the divine knowledge of the future contingents is quite different from man's. Man can only foresee these conjecturally because he only knows them in their causes. God, on the other hand, knows these future contingents not only in their causes but in their existence. Hence, while contingents come into existence for men successively, God, who transcends time, knows them at once because His knowledge is measured by eternity. "All things that are in time are eternally present to God . . . because He eternally surveys all things as they are in their presence to Him" (*Summa Theologiae* 1a, 14.13).

The problematic of the divine knowledge of the future as it came to the fore in the 16th century was in part the necessary consequence of a more immediate problem. The actual issue, as raised by the reformed preaching (and given immediacy by the teaching of Baius), was the relationship of divine GRACE and human liberty. Faced with this issue, the Dominican tradition had tended to respond by giving primacy to the omnipotence of the divine will. Contrariwise, directly confronted with the Calvinist preachers and the followers of Baius, the Jesuits had tended to stress human liberty.

It is these two basically related emphases that are brought into controversial confrontation by the ascendancy of Domingo Báñez to the leadership of the Dominican tradition at Salamanca in 1577. Basically, and at the risk of oversimplification, one may say that Báñez and the

Thomistic tradition he gives rise to understand St. Thomas as teaching that God knows all future contingents in their causes inasmuch as they are determined by Himself, the first cause [cf. D. Báñez, *Scholastica commentaria in primam partem Summae Theologiae s. Thomae* (Madrid 1934) 351]. It is in the light of this principle that the subsequent Báñezian interpretation would seek to interpret the key statement of St. Thomas: "The divine knowledge must be regarded as the cause of things when taken in conjunction with His will" (*Summa Theologiae* 1a, 14.8). In this statement Báñezians would see St. Thomas as maintaining that the divine will must intervene if the purely possible is, in any sense, to become a future. So viewed, there can be no science of vision, no knowledge of what will be or might be unless the divine will decrees it to be. This decree cannot be a mere matter of execution; it must be a matter of determination—i.e., a predetermining decree (*see* PREDETERMINATION). Only in this way can the merely possible become the future in any sense. In this framework liberty is preserved by making it have its source in man's judgment—the choice of means. The actuality or the efficacy of the act, however, must come from God; this is the physical PREMOTION. In this view, the unchangeable design of God does not bear on man's judgment and so does not destroy his liberty (*see* BÁÑEZ AND BAÑEZIANISM).

This basic position as formulated by Báñez very quickly was brought into direct confrontation with the Jesuit teaching in Spain. The first confrontation was at a public disputation in Valladolid in 1582. From this point on debates took place all over Spain. Louvain was involved, the Inquisition in both Portugal and Spain was called on, and finally the controversy was brought to Rome (cf. E. Vansteenberghe, "Molinisme," *Dictionnaire de théologie catholique*, 10.2: 2094–2101; 2154–66). In the midst of this theological turmoil the *Concordia* of Luis de MOLINA appeared after much opposition, particularly by Báñez. As a result, it contained an extensive appendix defending the author's work against the critique of Báñez.

Molina had been assigned to comment on the first part of St. Thomas's *Summa*. In this task he had concentrated on the endeavor to reconcile human liberty, divine foreknowledge, providence, and predestination. The key to his whole conception is what he calls middle science (*SCIENTIA MEDIA*). As does every Catholic theologian, Molina accepts as indisputable the fact that the FUTURIBLE (the hypothetical future) is an object of the divine knowledge. In the Báñezian conception these futuribles are a highly secondary issue to the future contingent. Molina, however, makes them a central element in his solution of the question since they are the object of the middle science. The question is: how are such hypothetical futures to be known by God? Molina is convinced that if these futuribles and future free contingents depend from a divine decree then human liberty is inconceivable. Consequently, he looks for another way, and this way is precisely signified by the term middle science. For Molina and those who follow him the divine knowledge of future contingents has, as it were, three stages, or moments. First, by natural science, or the science of simple intelligence, God knows all possibles. So He knows all that a given free agent placed in any possible condition will do. Second, by middle science God knows what any free agent would do if set in such and such a situation with such and such assistance, in a determined set of circumstances. These are the futuribles, the hypothetical futures. Finally, God decides to actualize a particular order of things. In this order are verified the circumstances and conditions already foreseen through the middle science. And so since God knows what this free agent would do, if placed in these circumstances, and then by a simple executive decree He actualizes a particular order, He knows infallibly what the free agent will do. This is free knowledge, or the science of vision. It is the contention of those who uphold this basic position that it preserves God's causal primacy since nothing in fact exists until God decrees it. Yet liberty is also safeguarded since the decree does not bear on man's free determination but only on the realization of a particular order and circumstances (*see* MOLINISM).

The length of this article allows only for a bare statement of each position. It forbids any lengthy discussion of the very rigorous criticism that has been leveled by each side in the controversy, as well as the vigorous, if sometimes violent, defenses that have been undertaken by the proponents of the positions. For a bibliography one may consult E. Vansteenberghe's article on Molinism noted above. To be noted also is the fact that within the general Báñezian and Molinistic positions there are divergences and many carefully nuanced variations. So, for example, Suárez does not accept a number of the conclusions put forth by Molina. Accepting the middle science, Suárez nonetheless differs very strongly on the presentiality of future contingents. He also demands much more of determination with regard to the future contingents than Molina allows and is sharply critical of Molina in this regard (cf. *Opuscula* 2.7.3). Within the Báñezian tradition divergences can also be found, as well as efforts, in the general Thomistic tradition, to reconcile—in such theologians as L. Billot and J. Van der Meersch in their tracts on the one God [J. Van der Meersch, *De Deo uno et trino* (2d ed. Bruges 1928); L. Billot, *De Deo uno et trino* (7th ed. Rome 1926)].

Contemporarily there has been a good deal of dissatisfaction with the focus of the controversy and its results.

There is a tendency to judge the elements of the controversy as sifting down from too rigid an approach and the controversy itself as having been conducted on too narrow and too unhistoric a level. The genetic study of the thought of St. Thomas set in its actual historical context has given rise to a critical reevaluation of both the issues and the answers traditionally formulated. And so, B. Lonergan, SJ, believes that the Bañezian system runs counter to a whole body of doctrine and texts in St. Thomas [cf. "St. Thomas's Theory of Operation," *Theological Studies* 3 (1942) 387–389; "St. Thomas's Thought on *Gratia operans*," *ibid.* 565]. Lonergan would also maintain that the synthesis of St. Thomas himself demands instrumental cooperation rather than predetermination. He argues ". . . the Molinist lacks the speculative acumen to make his grace leave the will instrumentally subordinate to divine activity. But the Bañezian has exactly the same speculative blind-spot: because he cannot grasp that the will is truly an instrument by the mere fact that God causes the will of the end . . ." (*ibid.* 577). As Lonergan sees it, there is a failure on both sides to understand properly the position of St. Thomas on the divine transcendence (cf. *ibid.* 578). It is criticisms such as this that have inclined a number of others to restudy the whole question and to reduce its proportionate importance in the theological study of the divine nature [e.g., J. Farrelly, OSB, *Predestination, Grace and Free Will* (Westminster MD 1964); W. G. Most, *Novum tentamen ad solutionem de gratia et praedestinatione* (Rome 1963)].

For the believing Christian divine knowledge also implies Trinitarian doctrine and theology. Only through revelation is it possible to see that while much of the fact of God's knowledge can be formulated in the natural light of reason, some understanding of the full meaning and depth of this knowledge requires a knowledge of the Trinity. Here, it is affirmed that while God is an eternal subsistent act of understanding and each of the Divine Persons is the same act of understanding, yet only the Father understands as uttering the Word, His only begotten Son (cf. *Summa Theologiae* 1a, 34.1 ad 3;34.2 ad 4).

See Also: CONGREGATIO DE AUXILIIS; FREE WILL; FREE WILL AND GRACE; GRACE, ARTICLES ON; GRACE, CONTROVERSIES ON; PROVIDENCE OF GOD (THEOLOGY OF); WILL OF GOD.

Bibliography: A. MICHEL, *Dictionnaire de théologie catholique,* ed. A. VACANT, 15 v. (Paris 1903–50; Tables générales 1951–) 14.2:1598–1620. O. SEMMELROTH, *Lexikon für Theologie und Kirche,* ed. J. HOFER and K. RAHNER, 10 v. (2d, new ed. Freiburg 1957–65) 1:356–358. P. DESCOQS, *Praelectiones theologiae naturalis,* 2 v. (Paris 1932–38). W. F. DEWAN, *The One God* (Englewood Cliffs, NJ 1963). P. DUMONT, *Liberté humaine concours divin d'après Suárez* (Paris 1936). R. GARRIGOU-LAGRANGE, *The One God,* tr. B. ROSE (St. Louis 1943); *Providence,* tr. B. ROSE (St. Louis 1937); *Predestination,* tr. B. ROSE (St. Louis 1939). F. GENUYT, *Le Mystère de Dieu* (Paris 1963). JOHN OF ST. THOMAS, *Cursus theologicus II* (Quebec 1948) 419–684. R. JOLIVET, *The God of Reason,* tr. M. PONTIFEX (New York 1958). B. G. MURCHLAND, ed. and tr., *God Among Men* (Notre Dame, IN 1960).

[E. M. BURKE]

ONAHAN, WILLIAM JAMES

Catholic lay leader; b. Leighlin Bridge, County Carlow, Ireland, Nov. 24, 1836; d. Chicago, Ill., Jan. 12, 1919. As the son of John and Johanna Onahan, he lived for a time in Liverpool, England, immigrated to New York in 1851, and joined his family in Chicago in 1854. From office boy and shipping clerk he rose through a flour commission brokerage to high status in the business and political life of Chicago. Onahan was actively interested in political affairs and supported Stephen A. Douglas's presidential aspirations. After marrying Margaret Duffy in 1860, he served during the Civil War as civilian secretary of the Irish Brigade, recruited for the Union Army, and subsequently supported the peace movement and engaged in Democratic ward politics. Business and politics did not preclude Church activities, and he performed countless services for Bp. James Duggan of Chicago, aided the Jesuits in purchasing real estate, assisted several sisters' orders, and engaged in debating at the Catholic Institute and Catholic Lyceum. He was a director of the Catholic Asylum and Reformatory, organized the St. Patrick's Society, and served Abp. John Ireland in promoting Irish Catholic colonization projects in Minnesota and Nebraska. Personal advancement came with his appointment as a member of the Chicago Board of Education in 1863, reform work as city collector, and service as city comptroller and as president of the public library and the Home Savings Bank. In opposing Chicago's socialists, arbitrating strikes, campaigning for temperance, and resisting immigration restrictionists, Onahan performed many civic and religious tasks; for these he received the Laetare medal from the University of Notre Dame, Ind., and was made honorary private chamberlain by Leo XIII in 1895.

Onahan was Chicago correspondent of the New York *Freeman's Journal* and author of articles in the *Catholic World, Illinois Catholic Historical Review, American Catholic Historical Researches,* and other journals. He also published in 1895 some of his lectures on the Jesuits, having previously (1891) published *The Religious Crisis in France, Our Rights and Duties as Catholics and Citizens, Our Faith and Our Flag,* and *The Influence of the Catholic Layman.* He was for four decades a corresponding member of the Chicago Historical Society and ended his career as president of the Illinois

Catholic Historical Society and honorary vice president of the Illinois State Historical Society. Onahan was considered by many the outstanding layman of the late 19th century, and was chosen to organize the Catholic Lay Congress in Baltimore, MD, in 1889. He proposed an international lay congress in Chicago in conjunction with the World's Fair, and also served as organizing chairman of the Columbian Catholic Congress, which met with the Parliament of Religions in 1893.

Bibliography: M. S. PAHOREZKI, *The Social and Political Activities of William James Onahan* (Washington 1942).

[J. R. BETTS]

ONANISM

In common usage often taken to mean improperly completed intercourse or even masturbation. The word is taken from the story of Onan in the Book of Genesis (38.1–10). Onan was commanded by his father, Judah, to take Tamar, the widow of his brother, Her, who had been slain by the Lord, and to perform his duty as brother-in-law and raise up descendants for his brother. This was in accordance with the custom of LEVIRATE MARRIAGE. Onan, however, to avoid raising up descendants for his brother, ''wasted his seed upon the ground'' whenever he had relations with Tamar. Because what he did was evil in the sight of the Lord, Onan was slain. Popular usage of the term onanism is based on the assumption that the evil for which the Lord took Onan's life was his unchastity. This, however, is by no means clear from the text, in which his refusal to conform to the prescribed marriage custom can be seen as the wickedness that brought vengeance upon him. Consequently, no certain argument can be based upon this text to prove the sinful character of either improperly completed intercourse or MASTURBATION. Evidence for this must be sought elsewhere.

See Also: CONTRACEPTION.

Bibliography: D. M. PRÜMMER, *Manuale theologiae moralis*, ed. E. M. MÜNCH, 3 v. (12th ed. Freiburg-Barcelona 1955) 3:699–704.

[J. D. FEARON]

O'NEILL, SARA BENEDICTA

Lay apostle; b. Chicago, Ill., March 17, 1869; d. Chicago, Jan. 11, 1954. She studied romance languages at Northwestern University in Evanston, Ill., and, much later, library science at the University of Chicago. She taught for 35 years at Tilden Public High School in Chicago. Through her friendship with Ellen Gates Starr, a convert and a coworker of Jane Addams of Hull House, she acquired an admiration for the Benedictines and the contributions they had made through their libraries. During her life she made five trips to the Benedictine monastery of Monte Cassino in Italy and also visited the monasteries of Maria Laach and Beuron in Germany.

She was professed as an oblate of St. Benedict at Monte Cassino on Aug. 4, 1902. At that time she conceived the idea of a library that would serve the cultural, religious, and intellectual interests of people in the Loop of Chicago. She spent the next 25 years interesting her friends and associates in the project. The St. Benedict Library, finally established on Oct. 30, 1931, became a rendezvous for writers and intellectuals and afforded them an opportunity to meet informally. She was also known as an apostle of the liturgical movement when the phrase was hardly known to most lay Catholics.

[E. V. CARDINAL]

ONTOLOGICAL ARGUMENT

The phrase ''ontological argument'' is generally understood by historians of philosophy to refer to an argument for the existence of GOD. The term ontological was used by Immanuel KANT to describe Descartes's version of the argument. Later historians, however, have applied the term to every form of the argument, but especially to that formulated by St. ANSELM OF CANTERBURY in his *Monologion* and *Proslogion*. The effect of such diversity of usage has tended to obscure essential differences in the assumptions on which various forms of the argument rest, as well as to ignore the different purposes for which the argument was employed.

St. Anselm and Descartes. The ontological argument has been used in both theological and philosophical contexts. The texts of St. Anselm and DESCARTES are the primary examples of these two uses. According to St. Anselm, the purpose of the argument is to help to understand ''in some degree Thy truth which my heart believes and loves.'' In contrast, Descartes's philosophical use of the argument is concerned with establishing an intellectual sanction for true judgments concerning ''the essence of material things.''

The direct consequence of locating the argument for the existence of God within a theological context is to see the argument as unique and applicable in only one instance. But Descartes, in formulating his version of the argument, says that he intends to show that the existence of God ''would pass with me for a truth at least as certain as I ever judged any truth of mathematics to be . . . .'' (*Meditation* 5). For him, mathematical proofs are the paradigms for all proofs concerned with material things. Consequently he regards the ontological argument as a most general and paradigmatic kind of proof.

The failure to distinguish between the ontological argument as a model for other arguments and as a unique argument has had unfortunate consequences in evaluating the argument, especially the version of St. Anselm. Post-Kantian and contemporary criticism have generally relied on criteria of proof that are indeed relevant to any argument serving as a paradigm for other proofs, but irrelevant to an argument intended to hold in only one instance. A summary of St. Anselm's arguments supports this notion.

Argument in the Monologion. St. Anselm describes the *Monologion* as a soliloquy, i.e., as "a meditation on the grounds of faith." He cautions the reader first to "read diligently Augustine's books on the Trinity, and then judge my treatise in the light of those" (*Monologion,* pref.). The subject of the meditation is the "essence of divinity" and includes the many things that we "necessarily believe regarding God and his creatures" (ch. 1). The stated purpose of the argument is to show by reason alone how far one can come toward an understanding of the truths of belief, even if one does not believe. St. Anselm adds one most important condition regarding the strength of his argument: The conclusions drawn should be understood as having a qualified, or quasi, necessity and not an absolute NECESSITY.

The term necessity, as St. Anselm uses it, means-"always either compulsion or restraint" (*Cur Deus Homo,* ch. 17). Moreover, necessity refers to the actions and operations of creatures, but is not predicable of the divine nature itself. For "when we say with regard to God that anything is necessary or not necessary, we do not mean that, as far as He is concerned, there is any necessity either coercive or prohibitory, but we mean that there is a necessity in everything else, restraining or driving them in a particular way" (*ibid.*).

Premises and Conclusion. Since the meditation is about God and His creation, St. Anselm proceeds from assumptions that he regards as most evident regarding creatures. All men seek to enjoy only those things that they consider GOOD. It is clear that every man sometime reflects on the cause of that phenomenon. St. Anselm's meditation on this resulted in the following argument, which he says has quasi-necessity: Every object of desire is regarded or conceived as good, where good is understood as either a useful or a noble object. Sense experience and intellectual reflection show that there are innumerable objects that vary in goodness and intensity of desirability. This multiplicity demands a single unifying PRINCIPLE OF EXPLANATION, which also serves as the principle of order among the degrees of goodness. Such a principle cannot have the same generic characteristics as do other objects of desire. Consequently, the good that is to be the principle of all goods that admit of a variation in degree of goodness must itself not admit of any variation in degree. Hence, the principle of order and explanation of the multiplicity of goods must be a supreme good. For any good that can be thought or perceived to vary in degree can be neither self-ordering nor self-explanatory.

The notion of a supreme good means that it is good in itself rather than by PARTICIPATION in or by comparison with any other good. Since all other goods are good because of the supreme good, the supreme good must also be the most noble or mighty good (*see* GOOD, THE SUPREME).

The objects of desire have natures that themselves vary in degree of worth or dignity. Hence, the supreme good too must have a nature or essence that is supreme. It follows that the supreme nature is the ordering principle of all other essences or natures. But the supreme nature, being the principle of all other natures, cannot itself have an ordering principle. Hence, the supreme nature is unqualifiedly autonomous or self-subsistent. As a corollary it follows that all other natures or essences proceed from the supreme nature. St. Anselm observes finally that the meaning of self-subsistence can be expressed only analogically, or more properly, through figurative speech, but this in no way vitiates the truth of what is understood.

Summary of the Reasoning. The argument of the *Monologion* can be reduced to four propositions: (1) Men desire objects they think to be good—objects that vary in degree of goodness. (2) Because the variance in degree is intelligible, there must exist an invariable principle of order, i.e., a supreme good that is the source of all goodness. (3) The objects of desire have natures that vary in worth and dignity. (St. Anselm says that whoever doubts this cannot be called a man.) (4) Because the worth of natures varies in degree there must exist a supreme nature that is invariable and does not admit of comparison, i.e., a self-subsistent nature that is the originative principle of all variable natures.

Argument in the Proslogion. Most commentators do not usually regard the argument of the *Monologion* as a version of the ontological argument, reserving that title to the proof in the *Proslogion.* One commonly held reason for making such a distinction is that the argument of the *Monologion* assumes causal principles and is analogous to the "fourth way" of St Thomas (*see* GOD, PROOFS FOR THE EXISTENCE OF). St. Anselm, however, seems to see the difference between the two to be in the number of arguments rather than in method or procedure. Whereas in his preface to the *Proslogion* he describes the

Monologion as bound together by a number of arguments, he aspires in the *Proslogion* to formulate a single argument that would prove the existence of God.

Difference in Intent. A possible explanation for the difference in the number of arguments may be found in the difference in aspect and intention between the two works. The *Monologion* treats of God and His creation, while the *Proslogion* reflects on God and His attributes. The *Monologion* begins with assumptions concerning the actions and nature of creatures that are evidently multiple, but the *Proslogion* begins with a single assumption about the meaning of the term God. Moreover, St. Anselm states that the *Proslogion* differs from the *Monologion* in being a discourse rather than a soliloquy; yet it is a discourse of the soul with itself, rather than a dialogue or scientific treatise on THEOLOGY. In the *Proslogion,* St. Anselm advises the reader to "Enter the inner chamber of thy mind; shut out all thoughts save that of God, and such as can aid thee in seeking Him; close thy door and seek Him" (ch. 1). The *Proslogion* is a matter of "faith seeking understanding."

The argument of the *Proslogion* has two distinct concerns. St. Anselm says: "And so, Lord, do Thou, who dost give understanding to faith, give me, so far as Thou knowest it to be profitable, to understand that Thou art as we believe; and that Thou art that which we believe" (ch. 2). The argument for the existence of God is restricted to the first of these concerns, i.e., understanding "that Thou art as we believe."

St. Anselm takes on faith that God is "a being than which nothing greater can be conceived" (*ibid.*). This verbal formula of the belief, he says, is understood by everyone who hears the words. But what is at issue is not that one understand the words, but that what the words signify does exist apart from the understanding of the hearer. St. Anselm argues that there is a difference between something existing both in fact and in the understanding, and something existing in the understanding only. He adds that to exist in both ways "is greater" than to exist in the understanding only. Consequently, he concludes that by understanding the meaning of the term God, one must also understand that God exists apart from the understanding. The corollary to the argument is that it is impossible both to understand the meaning of the term God and to conceive that God does not exist apart from the understanding. St. Anselm does say it is, of course, possible to articulate sentences that assert the nonexistence of God, for understanding in no way coerces the use of language. But this understanding does prohibit one from conceiving as true the assertion that God does not exist, even if one is unwilling to believe that God does exist.

Synopsis of the Argument. A paraphrase of the argument shows the extent of its claim and implicitly reveals the grounds of the continuing controversy about its validity. In effect St. Anselm says; (1) I hold on faith that God exists. (2) I hold on faith that He is "that than which nothing greater can be conceived." (3) I rationally examine the content of the concepts given by faith. (4) It is impossible that the *understanding* of those concepts totally encompasses, comprehends, or contains the meaning of "that than which nothing greater can be conceived." (5) Hence, the understanding can now truly affirm what was already held on faith, i.e., that God exists extramentally, and is that that we believe. (6) Given the meaning of God on faith, it is impossible for reason to conceive that He does not exist.

Evaluations of the Argument. St. Anselm's argument was first challenged by a monk named Gaunilon, whose first critical objection was that St. Anselm had begged the question by assuming the definition of God, and then constructing a proof based on the hypothetical character of the definition. St. Anselm in reply calls "on [his] faith and conscience" to deny the arbitrariness of the definition (Anselm, *Apologetic,* ch. 1). The second objection of Gaunilon was that St. Anselm's argument is invalid because it moves without warrant from ideas to realities; he cites as an example the concept of a perfect island, and argues that on St. Anselm's grounds such an island ought to exist. The charge is denied by asserting that the argument holds only in the case of God, and, hence, is incapable of refutation by a counter-example that does not depend on a movement from faith to reason, but only on REASONING.

Later scholastics are divided on the merits of the argument. St. THOMAS AQUINAS and RICHARD OF MIDDLETON reject the argument. St. Thomas's rejection of the argument invariably turns on the question,"Whether the existence of God is self-evident?" His reply is that St. Anselm's argument does not succeed in showing that the existence of God is self-evident to us (*Summa theologiae* 1a, 2.1. ad 2). Other scholastics such as ALEXANDER OF HALES, St. BONAVENTURE and DUNS SCOTUS accepted St. Anselm's argument with modification. Scotus was concerned to show that there is no contradiction in asserting that an infinite being is comprehensible to a finite mind. As part of his proof, Scotus says he will "touch up" St. Anselm's argument: "His description must be understood thus: 'God is a being than which'—when thought of without a contradiction—'a greater cannot be thought of' without a contradiction." The effect of that qualification is reflected in the conclusion Scotus draws: "It follows that there exists in reality such a highest thinkable as mentioned, through which God is described" (*De primo principio,* concl. 9).

After Descartes's use of the ontological argument for strictly philosophical purposes, new criteria of evaluation were introduced. Admitting his indebtedness to Duns Scotus and distinguishing between a priori and a posteriori proofs, LEIBNIZ argued that if God is possible, He exists. A version of the argument was used also by SPINOZA to show that God necessarily exists, while LOCKE rejected the argument for roughly the same reasons as those of St. Thomas. Kant's famous dictum that existence is not a predicate led him to attack Descartes's version of the argument—a rejection that was seconded by HEGEL, but only on the ground that St. Anselm's statement was faulty in form.

Recent discussion of the argument has been led by Norman Malcolm, who construes one form of St. Anselm's argument to conclude that God has necessary existence, a conclusion that Malcolm asserts follows from a valid argument. Critics of Malcolm's position have either found his use of the term necessity ambiguous, or have argued on formal logical grounds that the argument as presented is invalid.

The preponderance of contemporary secular scholarly opinion regards both the Anselmian and the Cartesian view of the ontological argument as logically invalid and metaphysically suspect. There is no consensus among Christian scholars about the proper interpretation and evaluation of St. Anselm's argument. Interpretations vary from seeing the argument as rigorously demonstrative to finding in it an adequate mystical theology, or regarding it as a rough but solid beginning of a systematic natural theology. Judgments concerning the validity of the argument are as varied as are the interpretations.

The position taken here is that the ontological argument of St. Anselm has nothing significant in common with the later versions of Descartes, *et al.* Because St. Anselm's argument is absolutely unique, it cannot be evaluated in the light of later criteria nor can it be criticized for its failure to accomplish purposes for which it was not intended. St. Anselm did not intend to make a formal proof for the existence of God. He was not concerned with making a scientific demonstration for the existence of a necessary being, or for the possibility of a necessary being, or for the non-contradictoriness of the existence of a necessary being. Instead, St. Anselm intended his argument to exemplify a method through which the understanding can find an expression for the certitude of FAITH or through which reason can find a way to articulate the "reasonable solidity of Truth." From this perspective the argument can be regarded as valid.

Bibliography: ANSELM OF CANTERBURY, *Proslogium; Monologium; An Appendix in Behalf of the Foot by Gaunilon; and Cur Deus Homo,* tr. S. N. DEAN (La Salle, IL 1954); *Opera Omnia,* ed. F. S. SCHMITT, 6 v. (Edinburgh 1946–) critical text. N. MALCOLM, "Anselm's Ontological Arguments," *Philosophical Review* 69 (1960) 41–62; articles in reply, *Philosophical Review* 70 (1961) 56–111. A. DANIELS, "Quellen, Beiträge und Untersuchungen zur Geschichte der Gottesbeweise im Dreizehnten Jahrhundert," *Beiträge zur Geschichte der Philosophie und Theologie des Mittelalters* 8.1–2 (1909). M. CAPPUYNS, "L'Argument de saint Anselme," *Recherches de théologie ancienne et médiévale* 6 (1934) 313–330. K. BARTH, *La Preuve de l'existence de Dieu d'après Anselme de Cantorbéry,* tr. J. CARRÈRE (Neuchâtel 1958). R. G. MILLER, "The Ontological Argument in St. Anselm and Descartes," *The Modern Schoolman* 32 (1955) 341–349; 33 (1955) 31–38. C. HARTSHORNE, "Logic of the Ontological Argument," *Journal of Philosophy* 58 (1961) 471–473.

[A. NEMETZ]

ONTOLOGISM

Essentially the affirmation that the idea of BEING, which is immediately and intuitively present to the human intellect, is God Himself. This description will be borne out and will serve as a general guide in the following historical, theological, and philosophical examination of ontologism.

Ontologism Viewed Historically. The word "ontologism" as a term generally used to describe a philosophic system is of nineteenth-century origin. It indicates one element of the basic tenet of the teaching in question, namely, that man has being (ὄν ὄντος, being) as the object of his intellect. From this fact, which ontologists take as axiomatic, another essential element of their theory is deduced: the being that is the object of the intellect is Being, God Himself. The principal defenders of this proposition in the nineteenth century were V. GIOBERTI in Italy, G. Ubaghs in Belgium, and, to a lesser extent, O. BROWNSON in the United States. Brownson, for example, castigates "the Christian peripatetics" for not admitting "that the universal, the necessary, the eternal, the immutable without the intuition of which the contingent and the particular are inconceivable, and no syllogism is possible, are identically the divine being, the *ens necessarium et reale,* or God himself" [*Boston Quarterly Review,* 2d New York series (Oct. 1860) 436]. A. ROSMINI-SERBATI, although often called an ontologist, states explicitly: "That which is shown to our mind when it sees being and nothing else is not the living and acting God, and consequently cannot receive in any way the personal denomination of God" [*Del divino nella natura,* v. 4 of *Teosophia* (5 v. Turin 1859–74) 11].

Although ontologism was formulated under a specific title only in the nineteenth century, the theory had been favored centuries earlier. In France its great master was N. MALEBRANCHE, ably expounded by H. Gerdil, who quotes also from Thomassin and Marcilio Ficino with approval. "Only He [God] can throw light upon the [human] spirit by His own substance. . . it is He who rules over our spirit, according to St. Augustine, without the mediation of any creature. . . . One cannot conceive that the infinite can be represented by anything created. . .it must be said that one knows God through Himself, although the knowledge one has of Him in this life is very imperfect" [Gerdil (quoting Malebranche), 170]. In other words, the knowledge one has of God, even on a natural plane, is dependent upon an immediate, although obscure, intuition of Him.

Malebranche's appeal to St. Augustine indicates sufficiently that the upholders of ontologistic teaching did not consider their theory as new. For them, its roots were deep in history, and, consequently, it drew its nourishment from the instinctive movement of the human spirit as expressed in the great minds of the ages. On a historical piano they appealed to Plato, to St. Augustine, and to St. Thomas Aquinas.

For St. Augustine "the forms—now ideas in the divine mind—yield their eternal truth to the mind in the light of a divine illumination in the mind. This is an exact replica of Plato's image of the sun: for Augustine, too, God is to the mind what the sun is to the things visible to the eye" [A. H. Armstrong and R. H. Markus, *Christian Faith and Greek Philosophy* (London 1960)]. From considerations of this kind, whose truth cannot be denied, ontologists went on to conclude that their teaching was based on that of the masters of antiquity. They found further support in St. Thomas Aquinas: ". . .we are said to see all things in God and to make our judgments according to Him, insofar as through a participation of His light we know and judge all things; for the natural light itself of reason is a certain participation of the divine light" (*Summa Theologiae* 1a, 12.11 ad 3). Although St. Thomas himself explicitly denies that the purely natural man sees God, ontologists maintain that this cannot follow from his dicta about man's participation in the divine light. According to them, being seen by the mind is either the Creator or a creature. If it is the divine light, it cannot be a creature. Therefore, it must be the Creator [cf. V. Gioberti, *Degli errori di Antonio Rosmini* (Brussels 1841) 37–38].

Ontologism Viewed Theologically. Among the propositions condemned by the Holy Office in 1861 as unsafe for teaching (*tuto tradi non possunt*) was the statement: "At least an habitual, immediate knowledge of God is essential to the human intellect in such a way that, without it, it cannot know anything: for it is the intellectual light itself" (H. Denzinger, *Enchiridion symbolorum*, [32d ed. Freiburg 1963] 2841). From a theological point of view, this condemnation was the culmination of a con-

troversy that had raged during the previous years between "traditionalists" who maintained in various ways that even a purely natural man has an essential need of revelation, and the extremists among those who upheld the natural autonomy of human reason. Although the particular reasons for the dangers inherent in ontologism were not expressed in the condemnatory decree, they may fairly be summarized under two headings of Catholic doctrine: the distinction between the Creator and the creature, and the distinction between nature and grace.

If, as Gioberti maintains, ideas are the real things themselves, there would seem to be no place for a distinction between God and His creatures. Basically, Gioberti's principle leaves no room for a distinction between act and potency or, consequently, between essence and existence. It follows that the essence of all beings is to exist. The way is thus open for the final step to pantheism: If the essence of all beings is to exist, there must be only one Being that embraces all existence.

There is an equal danger of confusing the natural with the SUPERNATURAL in the ontologistic way of regarding the nature of the object of man's natural intellect. If by nature, without reference to supernature, man is granted a direct, even if obscure, glimpse of God's reality, it is difficult to see how any grace given to him can differ in kind from the light of reason he receives in his natural creation. Moreover, if his human nature essentially demands the vision of God it would seem that the notion of grace as an altogether gratuitous gift of God to man is to be rejected. Brownson, for example, while avoiding the Scylla of pantheism, seems to be in danger from the Charybdis of naturalism. "Nothing remains [in order to avoid pantheism] but to admit that the soul has, by one and the same act, an intuition of God and itself. . .the Creator presents himself, in the act of creation, to the created spirit as the object of its activity" [*Boston Quarterly Review* (Jan. 1860) 49].

Ontologism Viewed Philosophically. Philosophically, ontologism takes its stand upon a fact open to observation, that is, the knowledge of being in general is that alone which enables man to know particular beings. Ontologists accept wholeheartedly St. Thomas's *ens communissimum* as the first thing known to the intellect. In order to say "the thing is something" (e.g., "the table is large"), one must first know what "is" means. Then they add: but "is" is the name of God. Therefore, one must know God to affirm anything of anything.

It is implicit in this argument that the fundamental knowledge of the human intellect cannot be abstracted from knowledge of material things or spring from the human spirit. It cannot be abstracted from material things because it is the prerequisite by which they are known, and also because being as such is not to be found in them. They are only the effects of being. Just as God precedes the creation, so knowledge of God precedes knowledge of His creatures.

It cannot spring from the human spirit because the spirit itself is created and cannot produce the infinite. According to the ontologists, consideration of material things and of the human spirit can only lead to the conclusion that the knowledge of Being, God Himself, is given to the spirit by the Creator at the first moment of its existence.

Ontologists saw their system as the only answer to the sensism of Locke and the subjectivism common to Kant and Descartes. Malebranche, by showing that the light of reason cannot itself come from the senses, intended to oppose the materialistic interpretation imparted by Locke to the adage: "Nihil est in intellectu quod non prius fuerit in sensu"; Gioberti, by upholding the reality of the object given to the spirit from outside itself, set himself against German idealism and French psychologism, both of which are essentially subjective.

Philosophical objections to ontologism are not hard to find. The chief difficulty springs from observation. While it is true that one must know being in general as a condition for knowing anything at all (for of anything known it must at least be said: "it *is* something"), experience shows that this being is not Being (God, the infinite reality). If it were, what need would there be to know any finite reality?

The key to the right understanding of the relationship between the limitless being known by man's intellect and the infinite reality is best found in St. Thomas's illustration, not in the ontologistic explanation. Just as one can see the light of the sun without seeing the sun itself, so the light of reason, which is immutable truth, can be seen by the intellect without its seeing God Himself (cf. *Summa Theologiae* 1a, 12.11; *C. gent.* 3.47). Ignoring this distinction means opting for ontologism.

See Also: BEATIFIC VISION; GOD, INTUITION OF; ILLUMINISM; KNOWLEDGE, THEORIES OF; LIGHT OF GLORY.

Bibliography: Sources. N. MALEBRANCHE, *De la recherche de la verité,* 2 v. (Paris 1674). H. S. GERDIL, *Défense du sentiment du P. Malebranche . . .* (Turin 1748). G. C. UBAGHS, *Du Problème ontologique des universaux* (Liège 1845). V. GIOBERTI, *Introduzione allo studio della filosofia* (Brussels 1844). Studies. A. FONCK, *Dictionnaire de théologie catholique,* 15 v. (Paris 1903–50) 11.1:1000–61, the most complete study available. L. LATOUR, *Lexikon für Theologie und Kirche,* 10 v. (2d, new ed. Freiburg 1967–65) 7:1161–64. P. BURGELIN, *Die Religion in Geschichte und Gegenwart,* 7 v. (3d ed. Tübingen 1957–65) 4:1635–36. L. FOUCHER, *La Philosophie catholique en France au XIXe siècle . . .* (Paris 1955). J. HENRY, *Le Traditionalisme et l'ontologisme à l'université de Louvain (1835–65)* (Louvain 1922). L. STEFANINI, *Gioberti* (Milan 1947).

[D. CLEARY]

ONTOLOGY

From the Greek *ontos* and *logos,* ontology refers to the investigation of being as such, or to the science of being as being. It may also consider what it means to be, what sorts of entities are countenanced, and what kinds of ultimate presuppositions or principles are held or obtained. The term "ontology" is usually traced to the early 17th century, but its significance for modern philosophical reflection is rooted in both ancient and medieval speculation about metaphysics. In the 17th century ontology was initially identified as a part of metaphysics, but today "metaphysics" and "ontology" are often used in popular speech as synonyms. This article traces the origin and development of the term from its inception in Aristotle's *Metaphysics,* its solidification as a single science in the Middle Ages, and its separation from metaphysics proper, under the influence of Wolff, during the modern period. The Wolffian tradition survives in modern philosophical usage and serves to explain the order of many scholastic manuals in which ontology is placed after logic and before tracts on special metaphysics.

Ancient and Medieval Origins. In a series of writings, later classified by Andronicus of Rhodes (*c.* 50 B.C.) as "the books after the physical ones" (*ta biblia meta ta physika*), Aristotle discusses a science of being simply as being and not as some particular class of beings or part of being. Though he acknowledges in the fourth book of the *Metaphysics* (1003a–1003b19) various senses of "being", he claims that there is one *primary* sense or character by virtue of which these many senses are understood, and that there is some primary science or first philosophy. In the sixth book (1026a16–32), Aristotle refers to a first philosophy that is concerned with being as being, but in contrast to physics and mathematics, precisely as the speculative science of what is separate from matter and motion. First philosophy in this context is labeled "theology" inasmuch as the divine would only be present in something of this nature, i.e., some immutable being (*ousia akinetos*). Aristotle adds further that this theology would be universal by virtue of the fact that it is first philosophy, i.e., by virtue of its consideration of being in the primary sense.

These references in Aristotle's *Metaphysics* to a science of being as being and to divine science, to "first philosophy" and to "theology," are not unambiguous, as subsequent thinkers repeatedly recognized. Is Aristotle referring to two distinct sciences or is he employing more than one name for the same science? If the latter, how can both being in general and a particular being be the subject of the same science?

In the 13th century, appropriating Aristotle's three-fold division of the speculative sciences (physics, mathematics, and what Aquinas variously calls "first philosophy" or "metaphysics" or "theology"), Aquinas argues that primary being and being in general are the subject of the same science (*eadem enim est scientia primi entis et entis communis*) inasmuch as primary being(s) are principles of the others (*nam prima entia sunt principia aliorum*; cf. Aquinas' *In Boeth. de Trin.* 5.1, *In 10 meta.* 6 and 11, and the *Proemium* to the latter). Nevertheless, given the potential for ambiguity in Aristotle's writings themselves, medieval philosophers before and after Aquinas debated the subject matter of metaphysics, as evidenced in the first of the questions raised by Duns Scotus regarding Aristotle's *Metaphysics*, viz., "Whether the subject of metaphysics is being insofar as it is being, as Avicenna posited being, or God and the Intelligences, as posited by the commentator Averroes?" In the 17th century what may be viewed as the equivalent to Avicenna's interpretation of the subject matter of Aristotle's *Metaphysics* is dubbed "ontology."

Modern Period. R. Göckel in his *Lexicon philosophicum* (1613) continues the Aristotelian tradition of distinguishing three progressively abstract "contemplative sciences." However, after physics and mathematics, Göckel accepts a further distinction, urged by Pererius, between divine science and the science of being. The former Göckel labels the transnatural science of God and angels, the latter "ontology," i.e., the science of being and transcendence. In another 17th century *Lexicon philosophicum*, authored by Micraelius and first published in 1653, a general metaphysics, apparently identified with ontology and concerned with being in the most abstract sense, is distinguished from a particular metaphysics which considers the types of beings separate from matter, viz., God, angels, and the departed souls. Also identifying ontology (or "ontosophy") as the study of *ens in genere*, although in a fashion much closer to Aristotle's descriptions of "first philosophy," is Clauberg in his *Elementa philosophiae sive Ontosophia* (1647) and in the *Prolegomena* to his *Metaphysica* (1656). In Du Hamel's *Philosophie vetus et nova* (1678) "ontology" is identified as the first or primary sort of metaphysics, the "scientia generalis" concerned with the nature of being itself, its principles, properties, and types. The two kinds of specialized metaphysics, derivative of this ontology, are the study of the causes of physical things (*physicae contemplationis caput*) and natural theology.

What these various 17th century thinkers commonly illustrate is a tendency to distinguish ontology from theology—a marked departure from the medieval view of metaphysics as a single science. Representing an even more radical departure within this context is Leibniz's tentative classification of ontology within the scientia generalis he outlines in his *Introductio ad Encyclopediam arcanam; sive initia et specimina scientiae generalis* (1679). *Scientia generalis*, "the science of the knowable in the universe inasmuch as it is such," is said to include, in addition to logic, gnoseology, and various other arts, "perhaps also ontology or the science of something and nothing, of being and not-being, of a thing and the mode of a thing, of substance and accident" (*forte etiam Ontologiam seu scientiam de Aliquo et Nihilo, Ente et Non Ente, Re et modo rei, Substantia et Accidente*). More influential than Leibniz for the modern use of the term "ontology" in general is the work of the systematizer of a Leibnizian metaphysics, Christian Wolff. According to Wolff's *Philosophia prima sive ontologia* (1729), "Ontology or first philosophy is the science of being in general or insofar as it is being" (*Ontologia seu Philosophia prima est scientia entis in genere, seu quatenus ens est*), a *metaphysica generalis* in contrast to the secondary *metaphysicis specialibus*: rational psychology, cosmology, and rational theology.

With Wolff, then, the dismemberment of what Aristotle apparently and Aquinas quite clearly construed as a single science (first philosophy, theology, metaphysics) is complete. For Wolff first philosophy is ontology, the study of being as being, and not to be confused with the particular metaphysical discipline of rational theology.

Enlightenment Era. Although sharply critical of Wolff's "dogmatic" metaphysics, Kant expressed appreciation for the "incontestable service" rendered by the clarity of Wolff's delineation of ontology. In the prize essay, "What is the actual progress made by metaphysics since the time of Leibniz and Wolff?" (1791) Kant in fact identifies ontology with transcendental philosophy [*see also "The Architectonic of Pure Reason"* at the end of the *Critique of Pure Reason* (1781; 1787)]. Ontology in this sense can be considered a propaedeutic to metaphysics and in that sense even a part of metaphysics, where "metaphysics" is precisely understood as the science of progressing from knowledge of the sensible to that of the supersensible.

> Ontology is that very science (as part of metaphysics) which constitutes a system of all concepts of understanding and fundamental principles, yet only insofar as the latter concern objects which can be given to the senses and thus can be corroborated by experience.

Wolff's conception of ontology as a science of being as being, apart from particular beings, resembles, at least formally, one of the meanings of "first philosophy" articulated in Aristotle's *Metaphysics*. By contrast, in Kant's transformation of ontology into a system of categories and principles of sensible, verifiable objects, the echo of the Aristotelian heritage may seem fainter, yet it is no less discernible. Kant's ontology is precisely that system of concepts and principles by virtue of which alone a sensible object can be judged to be. (Also resembling Aristotle's approach to "first philosophy" as well as Aquinas' account of the same, Kant ties this ontology to that which can be said to be in a primary sense, viz., the mode of being sensibly given.)

Not unlike Kant, Hegel employs a Wolffian notion of "ontology" in connection with his own discussion of categories in his "objective logic," constituted by the first half, i.e., the first two books of the *Science of Logic*. The objective logic is supposed to take the place of ontology in the traditional, i.e., Wolffian metaphysics, "the part of that metaphysics that is supposed to investigate the nature of *Ens* in general" (cf. the General Division of the Logic in the Introduction to Hegel's *Science of Logic*).

Scholastic Tradition. Towards the end of the 19th century and even up to the middle of the 20th century several authors in the scholastic tradition continue to determine the subject matter of ontology in terms of (sometimes critically refined) medieval and Aristotelian accounts of the degrees of abstraction. These writers also generally employ Wolff's terminological identification of "metaphysica generalis" and "ontology." See, for example, the opening page of Carolo Frick's *Ontologia sive Metaphysica Generalis* (1894): "Metaphysica generalis seu ontologia definitur: scientia rerum, prouti sub rationibus maxime abstractis et hinc communibus exhibentur" or VAN STEENBERGHEN'S *Ontology* (1946). The aim of Cardinal Mercier's *Metaphysique generale ou ontologie* (1910) is a demonstration of the sort of interpretation of metaphysics found in Aquinas. "We will show . . . why the science which has the divine being for its object does not differ formally from that which treats of being in general."

Contemporary Phenomenology. In Husserl's *Ideas for a Pure Phenomenology and Phenomenological Philosophy* (1913) he argues that every factual science has theoretical foundations in pure sciences of essential being. Husserl labels these sciences of essences "ontologies" and distinguishes *formal ontologies* concerned with the essence of objectivity in general from *regional or material ontologies* concerned with regional essences, those ultimate and concrete (in the sense of self-sustaining) generic unities in a hierarchy of essences, such as nature, human being, history. Formal ontology

here corresponds to what Husserl in his *Logical Investigations* (1901), following Meinong, called "a pure (apriori) theory of objects as such," the study of formal, objective categories (e.g., whole and part, genus and species), the correlates of categories of meaning (e.g., proposition, truth). *In Formal and Transcendental Logic* (1929) formal ontology is described as "a science of possible objects purely as possible" and thus as a theory of science by way of contrast with the correlative, thematic concern of formal logic for judgments alone. Although the aims and specifications are quite distinct, Husserl's "formal ontology" as the pure science of essences in the sense of possible objectivities bears a certain (and acknowledged) affinity to Kant's conception of ontology.

Perhaps the thinker most identified with ontology in the 20th century was Martin Heidegger (17:284b) who claimed indeed that "phenomenology, taken in terms of its content, is the science of the being of the particular being (*Sein des Seienden*)—ontology" and that "ontology is only possible as phenomenology." This identification of ontology and phenomenology proposed by Heidegger in *Being and Time* (1927) departs at once from Husserl's pure science of essences as well as from traditional ontologies in the history of Western philosophy. Precisely because they are rooted in largely unquestioned, pre-ontological modes of human existence, traditional interpretations of what it means to be take their bearings from theoretical inquiries into particular beings, thereby conflating quite distinctive ways of being (for example, the diverse modes of being proper to things, tools, theoretical objects, humans) and reducing being (or, literally, the sense of 'to be') to some particular sort of being. In Heidegger's telling if dramatic expression, traditional ontology betrays the forgottenness of being (*Seinsvergessenheit*). Posing the question of being at all accordingly requires the destruction of the traditional content of ontology by way of a *fundamental ontology*, that is, an interpretation of the fundamental structures of human existence as regards its own most intimate and everyday ways of being; in short, its being-in-the-world as such. The question of being remains the aim of this fundamental ontology, but precisely by way of opening up the horizon "in which something such as being in general becomes understandable," i.e., "the clarification of the possibility of the understanding of being in general, which belongs to the constitution of the particular being we call the human existent or being-there (*Dasein*)." Within this horizon time (though not the derivative, putatively endless time of clocks and measurement) discloses itself as the meaning of being.

Following World War II Heidegger began to turn from this phenomenological project of a fundamental ontology with its apparent pretensions to a scientific interpretation of what it means to be. Without denying the necessity of having gone down that path, Heidegger sought to bring into play a kind of thinking, more rigorous than science, in which what it means to be announces itself. In Heidegger's later thinking, then, "ontology" (and its synonyms in his early writings "phenomenology," "hermeneutics") was no longer part of his vocabulary for posing the question of being—nor, in his estimation, can it. "The question of the essence of being dies away, if it does not give up the language of metaphysics, since the metaphysical representing prevents it from thinking the question of the essence of being" (*On the Question of Being* 1955).

Linguistic Analysts. For other philosophers of the 20th century, especially those concerned with the development of logical languages and the foundations of the sciences, "ontology" signified a confused or at best irrelevant consideration. Thus, in "Logic without Ontology" (1944) Ernest Nagel urged a purely operational or contextual account of the role of logico-mathematical disciplines in inquiry, thereby effectively dismissing as "gratuitous and irrelevant" interpretations of their "ultimate meaning" or calls for the necessity of some "a priori insight into the most pervasive structure of things." So also in "Empiricism, Semantics, and Ontology" (1950) Rudolf Carnap distinguished questions of existence internal to a linguistic framework and thus answerable by logical or empirical methods from external questions "concerning the existence or reality *of the system of entities as a whole*." The latter sorts of questions of existence cannot be answered because they are framed in the wrong way, that is to say, they are incapable of theoretical resolution because they lie outside the theoretical framework itself. The question as to what sort of things a language will refer to is not a theoretical, but a *practical* question.

> For those who want to develop or use semantical methods, the decisive question is not the alleged ontological question of the existence of abstract entities but rather the question whether the use of abstract linguistic forms or, in technical terms, the use of variables beyond those for things (or phenomenal data) is expedient and fruitful for the purposes for which semantical analyses are made, viz., the analysis, interpretation, clarification, or construction of languages of communication, especially languages of science.

(An albeit strained, but nonetheless quite interesting parallel to Heidegger's criticism of the putatively theoretical approach of traditional ontology is patent, the difference is, of course, that Heidegger did not reduce nontheoretical questioning to matters of belief or pragmatic choice.)

Carnap's influential essay grapples with the problem that even highly formal languages, like those of mathematics and the physical sciences, seem unable to avoid referring to abstract entities such as properties, classes, relations, numbers, and propositions. Accordingly, in addition to the pejorative use just noted, "ontology" has come to designate the sorts of entities or theories about the sorts of entities countenanced by a linguistic system. Questions about the implications of a theory of reference or a semantics are ontological questions. Thus, in *Word and Object* (1960) Quine spoke of the philosopher's task of "clearing ontological slums." Ontology's job is precisely to scrutinize the uncritical acceptance of such realms as those of physical objects or of classes. By criticizing the tendency on the part of Carnap and others to embrace a sharp boundary between questions of meaning and questions of fact, Quine extended Carnap's own pragmatic approach to ontology (*Word and Object* was dedicated to Carnap), but in a manner that also called into question his distinction between the internal and external (ontological) questions.

Twentieth-Century Ontologies. Among U.S. and British philosophers during the 20th century there were attempts by thinkers such as Bradley and McTaggart, Whitehead (although he called his epic *Process and Reality* [1929] "an essay in cosmology"), and Hartshorne to construct ontologies in the tradition of speculative metaphysicians. Perhaps the most sustained such effort is to be found in the works of Paul Weiss. Beginning with *Reality* in 1938, followed by *Modes of Being* (1958), *Beyond All Appearances* (1974), *First Considerations* (1977), and *Privacy* (1983), Weiss developed a novel, pluralistic ontology or "study of realities," as he called it. These realities are the actualities (Weiss' "substitute for 'substances' with their supposed adventitious accidents"), finalities ("a plurality of subordinating and subordinated, but ultimately real conditions and sources of contexts which enable particulars to be together"), and the *dunamis* (an inexhaustible, creative ground, "an indeterminate maw out of which the actualities originate and into which they return").

See Also: PHILOSOPHY, HISTORY OF; METAPHYSICS.

[D. O. DAHLSTROM]

OPERATIONALISM

A method of defining concepts, mainly those of modern science, in terms of the measuring techniques and other operations associated with their use. It refers as well to the doctrine that the meaning of a statement or symbol is synonymous with a set of operations that enable an observer to decide whether or not the statement is true or the symbol is correctly applied. Where no such set of operations can be specified, the statement or symbol in question is said to be meaningless.

Basic notions. Operationalism was first enunciated by the American physicist P. W. Bridgman and in its subsequent development it is sometimes called operationism. It is a variation of POSITIVISM, which received its earliest systematic expression in the *Cours de philosophie positive* (Paris 1830–42) of Auguste COMTE. The key thesis of positivism, then as now, is that natural science should limit its concern to what is given in sense experience. Thus, definitions and theories in science should avoid reference to entities or causes whose existence is not experimentally verifiable. Bridgman, in broad agreement with this rule and with the later positivist principle that the meaning of a statement is expressed in the method by which it is verified, attempted a further analysis of verification procedures in terms of particular kinds of operation (*see* LOGICAL POSITIVISM, VERIFICATION).

As a proposal to purify the language of science, operationalism recommends that the terms used in natural science be defined by reference to the human actions associated with their use. For example, an operational definition of length in the context of measuring a straight metal bar might read: "the number obtained by placing one end of a yardstick at one end of the bar and then reading the numeral at the point where the yardstick meets the other end." In the field of thermodynamics Bridgman is celebrated for his efforts to define operationally such concepts as heat and temperature.

Critique. Many theorists in the social and behavioral sciences maintain that operational definitions give precision to their terminologies. However, considered as a blanket proposal for restyling all definitions in science, operationalism has met with criticism. One objection concerns the inclusiveness of the concept of operation. If operation includes everything done with deliberation in the furtherance of scientific inquiries, the term applies to such behavior as waiting for a chemical reaction to complete itself, looking for indications of handwork on a piece of flint, and keeping records of the various strata from which prehistoric relics are excavated. Since such behavior is closely interwoven with the uses of scientific terms, and is in fact learned along with those uses, the wholesale adoption of operational definitions would amount in most cases to spelling out what is already known to scientists and is inseparable from sound scientific practice. Related to this is the criticism that operationalism would multiply rather than clarify scientific concepts by requiring a different symbol for each set of operations associated with a concept. Distance, for exam-

ple, would splinter into as many separate concepts as there are techniques for measuring distances in optics, astronomy, geodesy, and so on.

It is possible to advocate the use of operational definitions in science without accepting the narrowed conception of meaning woven into Bridgman's discussions. There he sets limits to significant discourse by requiring that the operations needed for verifying a statement be specifiable; otherwise, the statement must be counted meaningless. Objections of two types have dogged Bridgman's position from the start. The first points out that the declared synonymity between "knowing the meaning of a statement *S*" and "knowing what operations would lead to the verification of *S*" is stipulated by Bridgman himself, and does not sum up what the term meaning conveys in the language from which he borrowed it. Those who appreciate the force of this objection take a relaxed view of the apparent threat posed by operationalism against the meaningfulness of ethical and metaphysical statements. A second objection proceeds in large part from critics who, though in sympathy with Bridgman's EMPIRICISM, argue that his criterion of meaningfulness needlessly puts in question a number of useful and trouble-free types of scientific proposition, such as contrary-to-fact conditional statements and those dealing with the remote past.

See Also: SEMANTICS.

Bibliography: P. W. BRIDGMAN, *The Logic of Modern Physics* (New York 1927); *The Nature of Some of Our Physical Concepts* (New York 1952). C. C. PRATT, *The Logic of Modern Psychology* (New York 1939; reprint 1948). R. B. LINDSAY, "A Critique of Operationalism in Physics," *Philosophy of Science* 4 (1937) 456–470. C. G. HEMPEL, "A Logical Appraisal of Operationism," *The Validation of Scientific Theories*, ed. P. FRANK (Boston, Mass. 1956) 52–58.

[H. A. NIELSEN]

OPINION

A state of mind that assents to a JUDGMENT, while realizing that the opposite, or another point of view, may be true. It is opposite is CERTITUDE, an objectively well-founded and firm assent. Opinion, including in it the possiblity of gradations of truth, may vary from mere surmise to the settled conviction of a prudential judgment, a range commonly experienced while conducting the practical affairs of life. In this sense opinion is equivalent to a practical certitude that is conscious of the possibility of error. Since opinion involves making a judgment, however sure, it differs from DOUBT, defined as the suspension of judgment.

Kinds of Opinion. While differences between kinds of opinion are not too marked, one can distinguish various degrees. Suspicion or surmise means an opinion that is held on very low probability, since there is little evidence to rely upon. Hypothesis is a conjecture or tentative explanation of a fact or situation that is used as a norm in making observations and experiments. Not purely arbitrary, it is a reasonably entertained general opinion, often of an expert in the field, proposed with the expectation of its being later proved true or false, adequate or inadequate, by testing the predictions derived from the hypothesis.

Theory. The term THEORY has many meanings, but all of them include a lack of certitude, so it is classed as opinion. In one sense, it can mean any hypothesis, unverified or verified to a degree. In another, it can be limited to those hypotheses that have been somewhat confirmed and are thereby generally accepted, such as electromagnetic theory. In this sense, a theory is the educated opinion of a learned man. In a given area, such as psychology, there may be, and often are, rival theories—depending on the selection of initial principles of explanation.

Public Opinion. This is collective judgment rendered by a given society relative to some fact or tenet. The term, coined at the end of the 18th century, is reminiscent of the *vox populi* of the Romans. Public opinion may assent to something false, such as polytheism in a pagan society, or to something true, such as monotheism, or to a given side of a proposition that is only probable. Some members—even a majority—may have certitude about the view expressed; others may not. In a democracy this can give rise to crucial questions on the freedom of expression in morality, religion, politics, and education.

Opinion and Knowledge. Despite varying views on the nature and object of KNOWLEDGE, philosophers have generally maintained a distinction between knowledge and opinion. For them the opposite of true knowledge is ERROR and so is untenable; whereas the opposite of an opinion may reasonably be held. Thus, for PLATO, the objects of knowledge are the immutable and intelligible forms; for ARISTOTLE, the essential and the necessary; for Hume, the relations between ideas that can be proved; for KANT, sensible presentations informed by the categories; for HEGEL, all of reality as one with Absolute Spirit. On the other hand, for Plato, the objects of opinion are sensible things that are always becoming and never truly are; for Aristotle, the accidental and contingent; for Hume, matters of fact; for Kant, the nonsensible, such as human freedom or the existence of God.

In each case the basic distinction is consistent with the view points of Plato and Aristotle: the man who knows not only asserts something to be true, but has adequate reasons for doing so; but the man who has opinion, even if it should happen to be true, cannot explain his stand, and so is insecure. Furthermore, in knowledge, the object itself compels the mind to assent; in opinion, some factor other than the object does this, for example, the will (Pascal, Thomas Aquinas, Hobbes), or sentiment or instinct (Hume).

Opinion and Dialectical Inquiry. In the *Topics,* Aristotle clearly distinguishes between DEMONSTRATION, which results in scientific knowledge, and dialectical reasoning, which results in opinion and probability. The dialectical process proceeds by way of drawing conclusions, "certain things being laid down" (*Topica* 100a 25). In this sense, from the opinions of experts, in science or philosophy, one draws conclusions. It may also proceed by INDUCTION, "a passage from individuals to universals" (*Topica* 105a 13). In either case one arrives only at probability. So, as viewed by Aristotle, this sort of reasoning serves as a source only for new opinions, and it is midway between RHETORIC and demonstration. DIALECTICS, at first meaning the art of dialogue or discussion, has taken on many usages from Zeno to the present day; it is most closely linked with opinion in the Aristotelian usage.

See Also: DIALECTICS; CERTITUDE, EPISTEMOLOGY; METHODOLOGY (PHILOSOPHY).

Bibliography: L. M. RÉGIS, *Epistemology* (New York 1959); *L'Opinion selon Aristote* (Ottawa 1935). J. OESTERLE, *Logic* (new ed., New York 1963). F. M. CORNFORD, tr., *Plato's Theory of Knowledge: The "Theaetetus" and the "Sophist"* (New York 1952).

[R. F. O'NEILL]

OPPENHEIM, PHILIPP

Liturgical scholar; b. at Olpe-Sauerland, Germany, Jan. 7, 1899; d. at Gerleve, Aug. 8, 1949. He became a Benedictine at Gerleve in 1919 and received his doctorate in theology at Breslau in 1928, having studied under F. J. Dölger (1879–1940). He lived in Rome from 1928, lecturing in patrology and liturgy at San Anselmo and was named professor of liturgy there in 1932. He became professor of liturgy at the Lateran University in 1945 and at the Propaganda in 1946. In 1942 he became censor for the Pontifical Academy of Liturgy and in 1947 was named consultor on the Congregation of Rites and a member of its Liturgical Commission. His most famous works are *Symbolik und religiöse Wertung des Mönchskleides im christlichen Atltertum* (Münster 1932); *Die Consecratio Virginum als geistesgeschichtliches Problem: Eine Studie zu ihrem Aufbau, ihrem Wert und ihrer Geschichte* (Rome 1943); and the *Institutiones Systematico-Historicae in Sacram Liturgiam* (Rome 1937).

Bibliography: H. ENGBERDING, *Ephemerides liturgicae* 64 (1950) 81–82.

[A. ROTH]

OPPOSITION

The formal relations between pairs of propositions having the same subjects and predicates, but varying in quality or quantity are called species of opposition. The four propositions so constituted are: the universal affirmative, called *A*; the particular affirmative, called *I*; the universal negative, called *E*; and the particular negative, called *O*. Of these, *A* and *O* are evidently contradictories, for *A*, affirming a predicate of everything subsumed under a subject, and *O*, denying the predicate of at least one instance of that subject, cannot both be true and cannot both be false. So also *I*, affirming the predicate of some instance of the subject, and *E*, denying it of everything the subject denotes, are contradictories. These relations hold, regardless of the existential import ascribed to categorical propositions.

Subalternation and Superalternation. Respecting existential import, one school understands particular propositions as asserting the EXISTENCE of what their subjects signify, and understands universals as leaving the question of existence open. On this interpretation, there are no other relations between these propositions: *A* and *E*, *A* and *I*, *E* and *O*, are independent of each other. Another school, however, interprets the affirmatives as existential, so that they are false whenever nothing corresponding to their subjects exists, their contradictories being therefore true. With this interpretation, another relation between these propositions comes to light: universals imply particulars of like quality. This relation, commonly called subalternation, is really twofold; unlike contradiction, it is not symmetrical. The truth of either contradictory implies the falsity of the other. By contrast, the truth of the universal implies the truth of the particular, but not vice versa. For precision's sake, therefore, it is well to call the relation of the universal to the particular, superalternation; that of the particular to the universal, subalternation. The universal is the superaltern; the particular, the subaltern.

Contrariety and Subcontrariety. Logicians have long employed the so-called "square of opposition" to illustrate these relations and others derived from them. At the upper corners of this square are the symbols for the universals, at the lower corners, those for the particulars. Each is connected by a diagonal with its contradictory. From the relations described, two others are deduced. Since *A* implies the falsity of *O*, and the falsity of *O* implies that of *E*, by the principle that implication is transitive, one infers that *A* implies that *E* is false, that is, that either *A* or *E* is false. The falsity of *A*, however, implies nothing about *E*, nor does the falsity of *E* imply anything about *A*. For from the falsity of *A* nothing follows but the truth of *O*, which implies nothing with regard to *E*; and

the falsity of *E* implies only the truth of *I*, which implies nothing about *A*. This relation, represented by the upper horizontal line, according to which either *A* or *E* or both are false, is called contrariety.

The relation between particulars is shown in a similar manner. The falsity of *I* implies the truth of *E*, which implies that of *O*. Again, since implication is transitive, one concludes that either *I* or *O* is true. But the truth of *I* implies only that *E* is false, from which fact nothing follows as regards *O*; and *O* implies nothing but the falsity of *A*, which determines nothing about *I*. Thus particulars may be both true, or one may be true while the other is false, but they cannot both be false. This relation, represented by the lower horizontal line, is called subcontrariety.

Implied Relationships. On the interpretation of categorical propositions first mentioned, there is no square of opposition for propositions of this kind, but only a "cross of contradiction," representing the relations of *A* and *O*, and of *I* and *E*. Nevertheless, the square is not without significance in illustrating the relationships between propositions of any kind; the principles of contradiction and of implication, which are its basis, are of universal validity. For example, if a proposition, *p*, implying another, *q*, replaces *A*, while *q*, not-*p*, and not-*q*, replace *I*, *O*, and *E*, respectively, the following conclusions result: not-*q* implies not-*p*; *p* and not-*q* are contraries; and *q* and not-*p* are subcontraries. Similar relations could be deduced on the supposition that *p* and *q* were contraries, or that they were subcontraries. Aristotle's discussion of the contraries, "Socrates is well" and "Socrates is ill," may be illustrated by this device (*Cat.* 13b 26–35). The square shows that "Socrates is well" implies its obverse, as does "Socrates is ill," but that neither is implied by its obverse; and that either "Socrates is not well" or "Socrates is not ill" must be true.

See Also: PROPOSITION; LOGIC.

Bibliography: M. GHIO, *Enciclopedia filosofica* (Venice-Rome 1957) 3:1055–56. J. A. OESTERLE, *Logic: The Art of Defining and Reasoning* (2d ed. Englewood Cliffs, N.J, 1963). E. D. SIMMONS, *The Scientific Art of Logic* (Milwaukee 1961). V. E. SMITH, *The Elements of Logic* (Milwaukee 1957). J. J. DOYLE, "The Square of Opposition in Action," *The New Scholasticism* 35 (1961) 41–75.

[J. J. DOYLE]

OPTATUS OF MILEVIS, ST.

Bishop and polemicist; d. *c.* 400. Optatus is known primarily as the author of a document written *c.* 363 to 376 against Parmenian, the Donatist bishop of Carthage.

The original title is lost and the work is now known as *Contra Parmenianum Donatistam.* The MS tradition indicates changes and additions in the original document to which Optatus added an incomplete seventh book in 385. Optatus sets himself to ease the return of the Donatists to the Catholic Church by a conciliatory presentation of the causes of the schism, which he shows to be no longer consequential in the actual problems under dispute. He calls the Donatists schismatics, not heretics (1:11–12), and refutes the objections of Parmenian with doctrinal and historical considerations, giving the history of the schism wherein the Donatists alone are responsible (b. 1); the Catholic Church is the only true Church of Christ in unity with the Cathedra Petri and spread throughout the world (b. 2). He contends that the Donatists are wrong in proclaiming themselves a martyr church and in accusing Catholics as persecutors. The Catholics did not enlist the civil power, which, however, Optatus defends as just (b. 3). He rejects the Donatist use of Isaiah 66.3 and Psalms 140.5 against Catholics and their Sacraments (b. 4), and condemns the Donatist rebaptism since the Sacraments are valid independently of the instrument (b. 5). He objects to the cruelty of the Donatists, and particularly the Circumcellions, against the Catholics (b. 6), and finally tries to judge the *traditores* of the Diocletian persecution as mildly as possible (b. 7).

For his historical argumentation, Optatus used a collection of acts that had been assembled as early as 330 and 347 in defense of Bishops Caecilianus and Felix. This collection is represented by a ten-piece appendix preserved in only one MS tradition, but it is generally recognized as authentic. G. Morin and A. Wilmart also credit him with five sermons of which only the Christmas sermon is genuine.

The theological doctrine of Optatus is particularly weighty, and AUGUSTINE, after 400, used much of it for his teaching on the Church and the Sacraments. Optatus distinguishes between person and office. The Sacraments are of themselves sanctifying agents, since the confectors are not the masters but the servants of the Sacraments (5.4, 7). Salvation brings with it faith and the Trinity (5.1). The unity of the visible Church is guaranteed by the bishop's office and the Sacraments; and the Cathedra Petri in Rome is the link of unity for the worldwide Church (2.2–4).

In contradistinction to the Donatists, Optatus is outspokenly friendly to the emperor and defends the imperial Church system prevailing since CONSTANTINE I. The Church can live securely in the Roman Empire and not among the barbarians. Above the emperor there is only God, hence loyalty is due to him particularly as a Christian ruler (3.3, with proof adduced from 1 Tm 2.2).

Feast: June 4.

Bibliography: *Libri VII (Contra Parmenianum) and Acta,* ed. C. ZIWSA (*Corpus scriptorum ecclesiasticorum latinorum* 26; 1893); *Sermones Patrologia Latina,* ed. J. P. MIGNE, 217 v., indexes 4 v. (Paris 1878–90), Suppl. 1:288–300. *The Work of Saint Optatus against the Donatists,* ed. and tr. O. R. VASSALL-PHILLIPS (London 1917). *Clavis Patrum latinorum,* ed. E. DEKKERS (2d ed. Streenbrugge 1961), 244–249. É. AMANN, *Dictionnaire de théologie catholique,* ed. A. VACANT et al., 15 v. (Paris 1903–50; Tables générales 1951–), 11.1:1077–84. P. MONCEAUX, *Histoire littéraire de l'Afrique chrétienne,* 7 v. (Paris 1901–23), 5:241–306. O. BARDENHEWER, *Geschichte der altkirchlichen Literatur,* 5 v. (Freiburg 1913–32), 3:491–495. E. DINKLER, *Paulys Realenzyklopädie der klassischen Altertumswissenschaft,* ed. G. WISSOWA et al. 18.1 (1939) 765–771. A. C. DE VEER, ''À propos de l'authenticité du livre VII d'Optat de Milev,'' *Revue des études augustiniennes* 7 (1961) 389–391. T. ŠAGI-BUNIĆ, ''Controversia de Baptismate,'' *Laurentianum* 3 (1962) 167–209. E. L. GRASMÜCK, *Coercitio: Staat und Kirche im Donatistenstreit* (Bonn 1964). C. MAZZUCCO, *Ottato di Milevi in un secolo di studi: problemi e prospettive* (Bologna 1993).

[A. STUIBER]

OPTIMISM

Optimism may be understood either as a general feeling and attitude of mind or as a philosophical system. The former is a habitual tendency to see the world, and all that happens in it, from the bright side and to look hopefully to the future. The latter teaches that the present world is essentially good and in practice assumes two forms, one absolute, the other relative. Absolute optimism holds that this is the best possible world, that it is either absolutely perfect or as perfect as it can be. Relative optimism admits that the world could be better, but maintains that the good it contains is of such value that its existence is preferable to its non-existence.

The term optimism is often taken in a broader sense, as in evolutional optimism or sociological optimism, or as in its cognate, meliorism. Evolutional optimism affirms that there is a slow but constant progress in the evolution of the universe (J. G. FICHTE, P. TEILHARD DE CHARDIN); sociological optimism expects a solution to the social question sometime in the future; and meliorism asserts that life possesses a real value, which man can increase by his personal efforts.

Forms of Optimism. All great religions are optimistic. They assure man that the evil that makes him suffer in the present life has no absolute power over him. Even BUDDHISM presents its faithful with a method by which they can escape the sorrows of life and the deceptive illusions of existence. Zoroastrianism similarly assures man that the malignant divinity responsible for evil in the world will be finally defeated by the supreme Good Principle (*see* ZOROASTER). MANICHAEISM, a synthesis of Zoroastrian, Gnostic, and Christian notions, maintains that man's final salvation can be easily accomplished by belief in Mani as the prophesied Paraclete and by leading an ascetic life. The Gnostics promise their faithful a happy immortality, provided that they adopt the teaching of psychic intermediaries (aeons) between God and man, and cultivate their spiritual and intuitive powers.

Greek philosophy is decidedly optimistic. For PLATO, the world is a product of God's providence, and therefore it is the most beautiful and the best (*Tim.* 30A). According to Aristotle, nature as well as God does nothing in vain; it foresees the future and implants in all things something divine (cf. *Cael.* 271a 33; *Eth. Nic.* 1153b 32). The fundamental principle of Stoic philosophy is that man can be happy regardless of his position in the world, for happiness is within and is obtained by mastering one's appetites and passions. According to PLOTINUS, the objects of intellectual knowledge are the Ideas in the Nous, and its climax is a mystical union with the One, itself the ultimate good.

Such thought exercised a notable influence on philosophers in the Middle Ages and in the Renaissance; in fact, the absolute optimism of NICHOLAS OF CUSA and Giordano BRUNO is clearly dependent upon Plotinus, as is the later optimism of B. SPINOZA. Pantheistic optimism, such as Spinoza's, starts from a gratuitously asserted identity of God with the world and terminates in a negation of evil in the world that is itself untenable.

More interesting and authentic is the optimism of G. W. LEIBNIZ. [In fact, the term optimism, used for the first time by the Jesuits (1737), designated Leibniz's theory that the world created by God is the best possible (Lat. *optimus,* best). The term was popularized by Voltaire in his novel *Candide ou l'Optimisme* (1759).] Attacking the Manichaean dualism of P. BAYLE, Leibniz strove to demonstrate his thesis. He argued that if the slightest evil that exists in the world were missing, it would no longer be this world, because, taking all things into consideration, this was judged best by the Creator who chose it. As there is an infinity of possible worlds in the divine ideas, and since only one can exist, there must be a sufficient reason for God's choice. This reason can only be found in the degrees of perfection these worlds contain, since each possibility can claim existence only in the measure of the perfection it possesses (cf. *Monadologie,* ch. 53–54).

Absolute optimism was taught also by N. MALEBRANCHE, who had some influence on Leibniz. "God, discovering in the infinite treasures of His Wisdom an infinity of possible worlds," he writes, "decided to create the one which could come to be and maintain itself in existence by the simplest laws." Such a world bears "to the highest degree the marks, the stamp, of His attributes," and glorifies Him best (*Traité de la nature et de la grâce,* 1.13).

Evaluation. Some maintain that optimism entails the negation of God's OMNIPOTENCE, and consequently of God Himself, because if the present world is the best of all possible worlds, God cannot produce anything better. This argument is of doubtful value. Just as no one can make a square circle, so no one (not even God) can create something better than the best.

Again, the notion of the best possible world is fictitious. It applies to a world whose perfection cannot be surpassed by any other world; consequently, a world that constitutes the last term in the series of possible worlds. Yet the series of possible worlds is infinite, and the last term in such a series is as unintelligible as, for example, a square circle. Moreover, no matter how perfect one imagines a world to be, its perfection will always be finite. Consequently an infinite chasm will always exist between it and absolute perfection. And so it will always be possible to interpolate other worlds that are more and more perfect.

Absolute Optimism. According to optimists such as Leibniz and Malebranche, the best world means a world that manifests the divine perfections to a degree that no other world could equal. How does one know that it is precisely this present world that manifests God's perfections in this way? Certainly not by experience. Here the optimists appeal to a priori considerations. Malebranche says that God "acts exactly according to what He is, and according to all He is" (*Entretiens* 9, ch. 11). Now in doing so, how could He fail to give all possible perfection to the world? Malebranche here confounds the divine action in its source with the divine action in its term. The former, being identical with God's essence, is the most perfect. But the latter essentially depends upon the free will of God, and for this very reason can be limited in different ways.

According to Leibniz, God's will always chooses the greatest good. Any theory that would claim the contrary, "would clash with the supreme principle of sufficient reason" (*Théodicée* 2, ch. 175). If one admits this reasoning, one must say that God's action is subject to necessity, that the present world emerged from competition with all possible worlds. Such absolute optimism, under pretension of exalting God, degrades Him. It is incompatible with true Christian belief.

Relative Optimism. For the Christian, the present world cannot be essentially evil. But the Catholic can go further and maintain, with the Fathers of the Church, scholastic philosophers, and many other thinkers, a moderate or relative optimism. Two features are discernible in the present world: (1) the beings that actually exist in it and (2) the relations that unite these beings to each other and produce in this way the admirable order existing in nature. Hypothetically, the present world could contain more perfect things than it does because God could create more perfect things, e.g., new species of living beings. But this would be a different world, not the present world, and thus the hypothesis involves a hidden contradiction. To the objection that things could be better ordered, it suffices to note that the order of this world is not the effect of CHANCE or of external NECESSITY. It is founded on the laws of NATURE, and the laws of nature have their basis in the natures of things. It must therefore be concluded that the present world cannot be better ordered; and, to this extent, it gives reason for entertaining a moderate or relative optimism.

See Also: PESSIMISM; UNIVERSE, ORDER OF; GOOD; EVIL.

Bibliography: P. FAGGIOTTO, *Enciclopedia filosofica,* 4 v. (Venice-Rome 1957) 3:1094–96. É. H. GILSON, *The Spirit of Medieval Philosophy,* tr. A. H. C. DOWNES (New York 1940) 108–27. L. STEFANINI, ''Ottimismo tomistico e pessimismo esistenzialistico,'' *Sapientia Aquinatis,* Congressus Thomisticus Internationalis, 4th (Bibliotheca Pontificiae Academiae Romanae S. Thom. Aquinatis 1; Rome 1955) 562–72. L. NUTRIMENTO, *La definizione del bene in relazione al problema dell'ottimismo* (Padua 1936). P. SIWEK, *The Philosophy of Evil* (New York 1950).

[P. SIWEK]

OPTIMISM (THEOLOGICAL ASPECT)

The Christian message supposes the existence, but also the contingency, of EVIL in the world: evil is present, but it would not be (at least in its actual extent) without mankind's free choice. Therefore, one can speak of an OPTIMISM in theology only in the sense that evil is not total (the various beings remain essentially good) and does not take the upper hand over good (evil will not only be subordinate to good, but has even now a function in the triumph of good).

Revelation shows the value not only of the spirit but also of matter (cosmological optimism). Christian faith is not compatible with that absolute dualism that makes matter the principle of evil (Plotinism, Gnosticism, Manichaeism, Catharism). The good God has created the whole world and found it good (Gn ch. 1–2): the world is the work of the divine wisdom (Prv ch. 8) and reflects the perfection of its author (Wis ch. 13; Romans ch. 1). This teaching was developed by Irenaeus against Gnosticism, by Tertullian against Marcion, and by Augustine against the Manichaeans. The goodness of the material world was also reaffirmed by the magisterium of the Church against Priscillianism (H. Denziger, *Enchiridion symboliorum,* 199, 207, 456, 458, 462) and against medieval Catharism (H. Denziger, *Enchiridion symboliorum,* 790, 800, 1333, 1336).

In opposition to the exaggerated optimism of the Pelagians, the Church teaches that man by ORIGINAL SIN was changed for the worse in body and soul (H. Denziger, *Enchiridion symboliorum,* 371, 1511). He cannot on his own observe the natural law for long (H. Denziger, *Enchiridion symboliorum,* 1541, 1572). To be converted he needs the assistance gratuitously given by God (H. Denziger, *Enchiridion symboliorum,* 374, 376, 1525, 1553). At the beginning, however, he was not in this state, and the corruption introduced by sin does not totally destroy his natural goodness (anthropological optimism). By means of human reason man can arrive at the knowledge of God, the principle and end of the world (Wis ch. 13; Rom 1.20; H. Denziger, *Enchiridion symboliorum,* 3004, 3026). The human will is capable of good acts, even without any supernatural help, and, above all, maintains its liberty, with which it can consent to the invitation of grace (H. Denziger, *Enchiridion symboliorum,* 1521, 1555). This is denied to no one, not even to the infidel (H. Denziger, *Enchiridion symboliorum,* 2305, 2426, 2439). Sacred Scripture in fact invites sinners to be converted and holds them responsible for not being converted (Mt 23.37; Rom 10.16; Acts 7.51–53).

Although there are individual creatures irremediably hostile to God who ensnare men (the fallen angels), these are not such by their nature, but, having been created good, they became evil through their free individual choice. This doctrine (which has a Biblical foundation in 2 Pt 2.4; Jude 6) was inculcated by Irenaeus, Justin, Athenagoras, Clement of Alexandria, Tertullian, Cyprian, etc. against the various kinds of absolute dualism and was defined by the Fourth Lateran Council (H. Denziger, *Enchiridion symboliorum,* 800). Not even the snares of the fallen angels constitute a completely negative aspect of the universe: diabolical temptation can never overcome the resistance of man assisted by grace (1 Cor 10.13) and is useful for the good of the elect (Rom 8.28). The end of time will mark the definite defeat of the rebel angels (Rv 20.9) and of those who have freely chosen to imitate them (angelogical optimism).

See Also: HAPPINESS; JUSTICE OF MEN; MAN; PROGRESS; TEMPORAL VALUES, THEOLOGY OF; WELTANSCHAUUNG.

Bibliography: On the problem of evil. C. JOURNET, *The Meaning of Evil,* tr. M. BARRY (New York 1963). J. MARITAIN, *Saint Thomas and the Problem of Evil,* tr. M. L. ANDISON (Milwaukee 1942). A. G. SERTILLANGES, *Le Problème du mal,* 2 v. (Paris 1948–51). **On the world.** S. PÉTREMENT, *Le Dualisme chez Platon, les gnostiques et les manichéens* (Paris 1947). J. H. WRIGHT, *The Order of the Universe in the Theology of St. Thomas Aquinas* (Rome 1957). *Il mondo nelle prospettive cosmologica, assiologica, religiosa* (Atti del XIV convegno di studi filosofici cristiani di Gallarate 1959; Brescia 1960). **On man.** J. MOUROUX, *The Meaning of Man,* tr. A. H. G. DOWNES (New York 1948). M. FLICK and Z. AL-

SZEGHY, *Il vangelo della grazia* (Florence 1964). **On eschatology**. T. F. GLASSON, *The Second Advent* (London 1945). R. W. GLEASON, *The World to Come* (New York 1958). E. C. RUST, *The Christian Understanding of History* (London 1947). J. H. WRIGHT, ''The Consummation of the Universe in Christ,'' *Gregorianum* 39 (1958) 285–294. **On angelology**. J. D. COLLINS, *The Thomistic Philosophy of the Angels* (Washington 1947). media>

[Z. ALSZEGHY]

OPTION FOR THE POOR

The meaning and intent of the phrase ''option for the poor'' is found in *Octogesimo adveniens* (1971), an apostolic letter of Pope Paul VI, which stated, ''In teaching us charity, the gospel instructs us in the preferential respect due to the poor and the special situation they have in society: the more fortunate should renounce some of their rights so as to place their goods more generously at the service of others'' (n. 23; cf. n. 42). The voluntary commitment to the cause of the socially deprived and solidarity with them in their problems and struggles was first given formal expression by the Latin American bishops at Medellin (1968), and was reaffirmed at their Conference in Puebla (Mexico), attended by Pope John Paul II in 1979.

In the Latin American framework the ''preferential option for the poor'' is inextricably associated with themes of liberation theology, and the struggle against oppression of every kind. During the period between Medellin and Puebla, considerable controversy surrounded the struggle for social justice that Medellin had affirmed and accelerated. As base communities began to organize and contend for the rights of the poor, individuals and groups with vested interests in the establishment used repressive methods to defend their power bases and privileges. Advocates of a new, more just social order were subjected to torture, imprisonment, murder and exile.

The document published by the Latin American bishops at the close of the Puebla meeting contains a chapter titled, ''A Preferential Option for the Poor'' (nn. 1134–1165). Although the document does not present a systematic analysis of the phrase, it clearly describes what is involved.

> . . . we are going to take up once again the position of . . . Medellin, which adopted a clear and prophetic option expressing preference for, and solidarity with, the poor. . . . We affirm the need for conversion on the part of the whole Church to a preferential option for the poor, an option aimed at their integral liberation (n. 1134).
>
> This option, demanded by the scandalous reality of economic imbalances in Latin America, should

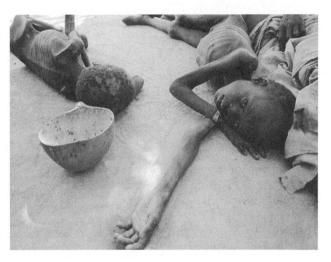

Sudanese girl (center), close to death from starvation, lying with her mother (right) and brother inside a compound run by Doctors without Borders (MSF), Ajiep, Sudan, 1998. (Associated Press/AP)

> lead us to establish a dignified, fraternal way of life together as human beings and to construct a just and free society (n. 1154).
>
> We will make every effort to understand and denounce the mechanisms that generate this poverty (n. 1160).

The Puebla Document (DP) identifies the poor as the indigenous peoples (DP 34), the peasants (DP 35), the workers (DP 29, 36), the marginalized urban dwellers (DP 38), the underemployed and the unemployed (DP 37, 50, 576, 838), children (DP 32) and the elderly (DP 39). It concerned the bishops that the marginalized were looked upon as second-class citizens whose rights could be crushed underfoot with impunity (DP 1291, DP 18). In a ''Message to the Peoples of Latin America'' the Puebla Conference stated very clearly that to opt for the poor means to take up their cause (n. 3).

Although Pope John Paul II in his address to the bishops at Puebla did not use the phrase ''option for the poor,'' he expressed a similar idea when he stated, the Church ''is prompted by an authentically evangelical commitment which, like that of Christ, is primarily (*sobre todo*) a commitment to those most in need.'' On other occasions during his visit to Mexico he expressed a preferential, though, he took pains to make it clear, not an exclusive love for the poor.

The option for the poor has been adopted as a formal principle by the Canadian and U.S. bishops in recent statements on the economies of their respective nations. This is an important acknowledgment by these hierarchies that the program of social reform that this axiom implies is relevant also in first-world contexts. The Canadian Conference of Catholic Bishops in its statement on the socioeconomic order mentioned "the preferential option for the poor," and then added:

> In a given economic order, the needs of the poor take priority over the wants of the rich. This does not, in turn, simply mean more handouts for the poor. It calls, instead, for an equitable redistribution of wealth and power among peoples and regions.

The U.S. bishops in their pastoral message *Economic Justice for All* (1986) do not speak of a *preferential*, but of a *fundamental* option for the poor.

> This "option for the poor" does not mean pitting one group against another, but rather, strengthening the whole community by assisting those who are most vulnerable. As Christians, we are called to respond to the needs of *all* our brothers and sisters, but those with the greatest needs require the greatest response (n. 16).

The American bishops introduce their reflection on the option for the poor with the assertion, "the justice of a society is tested by the treatment of the poor."

In his encyclical *Sollicitudo rei socialis* (On Social Concern, 1987) Pope John Paul II spoke of the "*option or love of preference* for the poor" and explained, "This is an option, or *special form* of primacy in the exercise of Christian charity, to which the whole tradition of the Church bears witness" (SRS 42). The pope goes on to emphasize the global dimensions of the social question and says:

> this love of preference for the poor, and the decisions which it inspires in us, cannot but embrace the immense multitudes of the hungry, the needy, the homeless, those without medical care and, above all, those without hope of a better future. It is impossible not to take account of these realities (SRS 42).

This same terminology, "a preferential love" for people oppressed by poverty, appears in the Catechism of the Catholic Church (2448). The CCC also quotes the Vatican II decree *Apostolicam actuositatem,* which makes the point that "the demands of justice" requires that we share our goods with the poor, and "that which is already due in justice is not to be offered as an act of charity" (2446). The Catechism, like *Sollicitudo rei socialis,* calls for structural reform at all levels to redress the inequitable distribution of the world's goods and the international economic imbalance.

In the years since the axiom was first formulated, the preferential option for the victims of social injustice has come to represent a short-hand description for a new kind of program aiming at integral liberation of all powerless, marginalized, economically deprived, despised and outcast persons. The elimination of starvation, disease, unemployment, unjust wages, homelessness, illiteracy, impoverishment, in brief, all manifestations of institutionalized violence or social sin is seen as a prophetic challenge to all people who yearn for peace founded on justice. And this agenda which uses a variety of descriptions to illustrate a sociology of oppression is seen as an inescapable consequence of fidelity to the gospel message which, according to the pastoral statements of bishops across several continents, itself gives priority to service of the poor and disadvantaged.

Bibliography: R. ANTONCICH, *Christians in the Face of Injustice. A Latin American Reading of Catholic Social Teaching* (Maryknoll, N.Y. 1987). G. BAUM, *The Priority of Labor: A Commentary on Laborem exercens Encyclical Letter of Pope John Paul II* (New York 1982). G. BAUM and D. CAMERON, *Ethics and Economics: Canada's Catholic Bishops on the Economic Crisis* (Toronto 1984). L. BOFF and V. ELIZONDO, eds., *Option for the Poor: Challenge to the Rich Countries* (Edinburgh 1986). L. BOFF, *Cry of the Earth, Cry of the Poor* (Maryknoll, N.Y. 1997). M. BYERS, ed., *Justice in the Marketplace: Collected Statements of the Vatican the United States Catholic Bishops on Economic Policy, 1891–1984* (Wash., D.C. 1985). D. DORR, *Option for the Poor: A Hundred Years of Vatican Social Teaching,* rev. ed. (Maryknoll, N.Y. 1992). I. ELLACURIA and J. SOBRINO, eds. *Mysterium Liberationis: Fundamental Concepts of Liberation Theology* (Maryknoll, N.Y. 1993). J. EAGLESON and P. SCHARPER, eds., *Puebla and Beyond: Documentation and Commentary* (New York 1979). G. GUTIERREZ, *The Power of the Poor in History* (New York 1983). NATIONAL CONFERENCE OF CATHOLIC BISHOPS, *Economic Justice for All: Pastoral Letter on Catholic Social Teaching and the U.S. Economy* (Wash., D.C. 1986).

[P. SURLIS]

OPUS DEI

The Prelature of the Holy Cross and Opus Dei is a personal prelature of the Roman Catholic Church, with its central offices located in Rome. The Second Vatican Council made provisions for the juridical format of personal prelatures to facilitate the carrying out of "specific apostolic tasks." Prelatures form part of the pastoral and hierarchical structure of the Church. They are dependent on the Congregation for Bishops.

The aim of the prelature of Opus Dei is to promote among Christians an awareness that all are called to seek holiness and to contribute to the evangelization of every sphere of society. The prelature provides for the pastoral and spiritual care of its members, extending this help to many other people, in accord with each one's situation and profession (cf. *Statutes of Opus Dei,* 2:1). The faithful of the prelature strive to put into practice the teachings of the Gospel by exercising the Christian virtues and sanctifying their ordinary work (cf. *Statutes of Opus Dei,* 2).

The tomb of Opus Dei founder, Josemaría Escrivá, in the Vatican. (©Vittoriano Rastelli/CORBIS)

Msgr. Josemaría ESCRIVÁ founded Opus Dei on Oct. 2, 1928. On Feb. 14, 1930, Blessed Josemaría understood by God's grace that Opus Dei was meant to develop its apostolate among women as well. From 1946 on, he resided in Rome. He died on June 26, 1975 and was beatified on June 26, 1992. From Rome he oversaw Opus Dei's apostolic expansion throughout the world, beginning with Portugal, England, Italy, France, Ireland, the United States, and Mexico. From the outset, he relied on the encouragement and stimulus of the episcopal hierarchy. From 1943, Opus Dei received all of the necessary approvals from the Holy See, culminating in its establishment as a personal prelature by Pope John Paul II on Nov. 28, 1982.

The prelature of Opus Dei spread throughout every continent, comprises the prelate, currently Bishop Javier Echevarría, 1,700 priests, and 90,000 laity who, with a divine vocation, are freely incorporated into the prelature. The clergy incardinated in the prelature come from among the laymen. "The laity incorporated in the Prelature do not alter their personal situation, either canonically or theologically. They continue to be ordinary lay faithful, and act accordingly in everything they do, specifically in their apostolate (Congregation for Bishops, Declaration concerning Opus Dei, Aug. 23, 1982, 2b).

The lay faithful of the prelature enjoy the same freedom as other Catholic citizens, their equals, in all professional, family, social, political, and financial activities. These activities do not fall under the prelature's jurisdiction, which extends only to the ascetical and apostolic commitments that each one freely assumes by means of a contractual bond. The prelature's lay faithful remain under the diocesan bishop's jurisdiction in everything established by common Church law for the Catholic faithful.

The Priestly Society of the Holy Cross, inseparably united to the Prelature of Opus Dei, is governed by the prelate of Opus Dei as its president general. The prelature's priests belong to the Priestly Society of the Holy Cross. In addition, diocesan priests who wish to seek holiness in the exercise of their ministry may be associated as well. Their tie to the priestly society in no way compromises their loyalty to their own bishop, who continues to be their only superior. The prelature of Opus Dei also relies on cooperators, some of whom are non-Catholics or even non-Christians. Although not incorporated into the prelature, cooperators collaborate in its apostolate by their prayer, work, and alms.

The prelature of Opus Dei directs the Pontifical University of the Holy Cross in Rome, as well as the University of Navarre in Spain. Other apostolic undertakings, including universities in Latin America, Italy, and the Philippines, student residences, cultural centers, technical and agricultural institutes, medical clinics, and a variety of centers for the development of disadvantaged areas, have the pastoral assistance of the prelature which takes on responsibility for their Christian orientation.

Opus Dei's most important contribution to the Church's mission, however, is not its corporate apostolates but rather the effort of each member to sanctify his or her ordinary, daily work and to bring those around them closer to God. The process for beatification is underway for several members of Opus Dei, among them the Argentine engineer Isidoro Zorzano (1902–1943) and the young Spanish woman Montserrat Grases (1941–1959).

Bibliography: P. BERGLAR, *Opus Dei. Life and Work of its Founder Josemaría Escrivá* (Princeton 1993). A. FUENMAYOR, F. OCARIZ, and J. L. ILLANES, *The Canonical Path of Opus Dei* (Princeton and Chicago 1994). J. L. ILLANES, *On the Theology of Work* (Dublin 1982). A. DEL PORTILLO, *Immersed in God: Blessed Josemaría Escrivá, Founder of Opus Dei* (Princeton 1996). P. RODRIGUEZ, *Particular Churches and Personal Prelatures* (Dublin 1986). P. RODRIGUEZ, F. OCARIZ, and J. L. ILLANES, *Opus Dei in the Church: An Ecclesiological Study of the Life and Apostolate of Opus Dei* (Dublin and Princeton 1994).

[R. PELLITERO]

ORACLE

In addition to that of Delphi, the most famous of Greek oracles (*see* DELPHI, ORACLE OF), a number of other oracles, especially those of Zeus and Apollo, enjoyed a wide reputation in the Greek world.

Oracles of Zeus. At Dodona, Zeus replaced a pre-Greek divinity. The priests, who followed an archaic manner of life, employed as oracular devices the rustling of ancient oaks and the murmurs of a spring in the sacred grove; a device attested for the 4th century, B.C. was a noise made by a brazen kettle when it was struck by a little chain hanging beside it, after it had been set in motion by a wind blowing in the proper direction. The oracle was at its zenith in the age of Pindar (518–438 B.C.), but had practically ceased to function by the beginning of the Christian Era.

The oracle of Zeus at the oasis of Siwa was really an oracle of the Egyptian god Ammon. It was already consulted by Greek statesmen in the 5th century B.C., but its reputation was enhanced by the visit of Alexander the Great, who was greeted by the priest of the shrine as the son of Ammon. Just how the oracle was delivered to Alexander is unknown. Ordinarily, the responses of Zeus Ammon were given in the Egyptian manner, i.e., by the manipulation of a statue of Ammon carried in procession. At Olympia, the cult of Zeus probably took the place of the earlier cult of the goddess Gea. The location of the oracle was a large altar, which was formed from the ashes of the sacrificed animals and was sprinkled with water from the river Alpheus. The response of Zeus was sought by means of haruspicy and empyromancy.

Oracles of Apollo. The most important oracle after Delphi, and probably the oldest, was that of Didyma near Miletus. A pre-Greek divinity of the place was gradually equated with Apollo. For a long period the oracle was under the control of the priestly family of the Branchidae. It possessed the right of asylum, and this right was reconfirmed by the Roman Emperor Tiberius. The responses were given by a priestess after preparation by fasting and prayer and after taking a foot bath in the spring, which bubbled beside the temple. The priestess sat on a tripod, and like the priestess of Delphi, she was probably in a state of ecstasy (Iamblichus, *De myst.* 3.2). The oracle lost its importance in the 2d century A.D. One of its last responses was heavy in consequences, for it led Diocletian to decide on his persecution of the Christians (Lactantius, *De morte pers.* 10).

The oracle of Apollo at Claros, near Colophon, was hardly less famous, and likewise possessed the right of asylum. The consultants assembled in a waiting-room and gave their names. The oracle chamber may originally have been a grotto in the mountainside, but later it was situated nearer the valley. The priest descended into the grotto, drank from the water of a spring, and then, without relying on orally expressed questions, but on telepathy, he gave his responses in verse (Tacitus, *Ann.* 2.54). From the 1st century A. D., questions could be presented also in writing. Even ''speaking'' statues of the god, which were sent into various regions, could be questioned directly. There is evidence that in the later imperial age, questions were presented at the oracle itself from places as far distant as northern Britain.

The island of Delos, the reputed birthplace of Apollo, also had an oracle. The voice of the god sounded from the fissures in Mt. Cynthus (Vergil, *Aen.* 3.90). In the age of the Seleucids, an oracle of Apollo, that of Daphne, was established near Antioch, and its procedure was modeled probably on that of Delphi.

Other Oracles. Oracles were often given through temple incubation. The healing hero-god Asclepius played a role in this kind of divination at his chief center, Epidaurus, and also in his temples at Athens, Rome, and elsewhere. Healing hero-gods, like Trophonius, delivered their oracles in the manner of oracles at Delphi or Claros. NECROMANCY was practiced for the sake of obtaining oracles, especially in those places that were regarded as entrances into the lower world—grottoes or subterranean passages, from which in many cases poisonous vapors were emitted. Such places and their vapors were thought of as means for receiving oracles. Among the best-known sites of this kind were Phigalia in Arcadia, and especially Cumae near Naples, the seat of the Cumaean sibyl, the most famous of all the sibyls.

Bibliography: J. E. FONTENROSE, *Oxford Clasical Dictionary,* ed. M. CARY et al. (Oxford 1949) 624, with cross ref. and bibliog. K. LATTE, ''Orakel,'' *Paulys Realenzyklopädie der klassischen Altertumswissenschaft,* ed. G. WISSOWA et al. (Stuttgart 1893) 18.1 (1942) 829–866. P. MONCEAUX, ''Oraculum,'' C. DAREMBERG and E. SAGLIO, *Dictionnaire des antiquités grecques et romaines d'après les testes et les monuments,* 5 v. in 9 (Paris 1877–1919) 4:214–223. A. BOUCHÉ-LECLERCQ, *Histoire de la divination dans l'Antiquité,* 3 v. (Paris 1879–82) old, but still basic.

[K. PRÜMM]

ORACLE (IN THE BIBLE)

The Israelites, like other ancient peoples, asked (Heb. *šā'al:* Nm 27.21; Jgs 1.1; 20.22; 1 Sm 10.22; 23.2; 30.8; 2 Sm 2.1; 5.19; or *dāraš:* Gn 25.22–23; 1 Sm 9.9; 1 Kgs 22.8, 14–23; 2 Kgs 22.18–19) their God for information about imminent matters of personal or national importance or about future events. Yahweh answered in most cases through officially recognized persons (priests, seers, prophets, etc.) and in different oracular ways that were dignified and worthy of His nature and revelation. He condemned practices that were too base or humanistic, or that placed Him as one among equals or even as the chief one of many gods.

One of the principal functions of the priests was to utter oracles (Dt 33.8), and this type of oracle was called *tōrāh,* ''instruction law'' (Jer 18.18). Thus, Moses was often approached to inquire of God for the people and make known His decisions (Ex 18.15–16; 33.7–11). The high priest through the URIM AND THUMMIM (Ex 28.30;

The Mouth of Truth in Santa Maria in Cosmedin, Italy. (©David Lees/CORBIS)

Lv 8.8) or the ephod (1 Sm 23.6–12; 30.7–8) gave divine answers. The Levite priest of Micah was consulted by the Danites for a divine decision (Jgs 18.5–6). Levitical priests were to try difficult cases at God's chosen sanctuary, and disobedience to their decisions carried the death penalty (Dr 17.8–12). There was also a common custom of casting lots, and this was regarded at times as indicating the divine will (1 Sm 14.38–42; Acts 1.26).

The seer (Heb. *rō'eh*) and the prophet (Heb. *nābî'*) also were consulted for divine decisions; e.g., the seer Samuel (1 Sm 9.9; 11.18–20), and the Prophets Nathan (2 Sm 7.17), Elijah (1 Kgs 18.36–39), Elisha (2 Kgs 8.7–15), Isaiah (Is 38.1–6), and Micaiah, son of Imlah (1 Kgs 22.7–28). Even without its being requested, their pronouncements and writings were regarded as words or oracles of Yahweh. The technical term for an oracle of a prophet is *ne'ūm yhwh,* literally ''pronouncement of Yahweh.'' It occurs 361 times in the Hebrew OT, mostly in the books of the ''writing'' Prophets, where it generally stands at the end of a short oracle given in Yahweh's name, traditionally rendered in English as ''Thus says the Lord.'' It serves as a sort of signature guaranteeing the authenticity of the oracle.

Bibliography: A. BARUCQ, *Dictionnaire de la Bible* supplement, ed. L. PIROT et al. (Paris 1928–) 6:775–787.

[J. E. STEINMUELLER]

ORANGE, COUNCILS OF

Two synods (441 and 529) held at ORANGE (Arausio), in what is now southern France (Dept. Vaucluse).

HILARY OF ARLES presided over the first, which 16 bishops attended. There 30 canons were enacted dealing with disciplinary matters.

Orange II was held under the presidency of CAESARIUS OF ARLES. AUGUSTINE's theology of grace, though wholeheartedly adopted by Rome, was held in suspicion by LÉRINS, a great intellectual and monastic center near Marseilles. Profoundly influenced by John CASSIAN, Lérins was also Semi-Pelagian. Cassian taught that there was some natural sanctity in man before baptism; he distinguished two modes of action in grace: salvific and tutelary. In the latter mode God only seconds and crowns man's efforts. VINCENT OF LÉRINS distorted Augustine, quoting him out of context to discredit him. PROSPER OF AQUITAINE emerged as Augustine's indefatigable champion, and Rome itself defended the memory of the illustrious theologian (H. Denzinger, *Enchiridion symbolorum* 237). FAUSTUS OF RIEZ (abbot of Lérins, 433–462; bishop of Riez, 462–485?), one of the greatest ecclesiastical figures of 5th-century Gaul, in his struggle against Lucidus, a predestinarian, wrote a treatise on grace which, while it categorically rejected Pelagianism, offered no satisfactory metaphysical alternative, thus emphasizing the fact that Augustinian metaphysics on the topic were hard to replace.

In the meantime Caesarius of Arles, a splendid example of the second generation of Lérins (490–497?), was consecrated bishop of Arles (503). In the continuing struggle against Semi-Pelagianism, Caesarius was the champion of pure Augustinian doctrine in regard to "prevenient and liberating grace as an absolute condition of the reintegration of the human will in its supernatural faculties and ends" (A. Fliche and V. Martin, *Histoire de l'élise depuis les origines jusqu' á nos jours* 4:416). Nineteen *capitula* to this effect were submitted by him to Rome (*c.* 528) but were rejected as too subtle. Maxims gathered by Prosper of Aquitaine from Augustine's writings were substituted by Felix IV. On July 3, 529, at the dedication in Orange of a church built by Liberius, the praetorian prefect, Caesarius submitted to 13 bishops a declaration on grace and free will, which all signed and sent to Rome. Boniface II, successor to Felix IV, approved them on Jan. 25, 531 (H. Denzinger, 398–400).

The statement of Caesarius has three parts: (1) *prooemium* (H. Denzinger, 370); (2) 25 canons, eight on original sin (H. Denzinger, 371–372) and grace (H. Denzinger, 373–378) and 17 *capitula* taken from Prosper's digest of Augustine (H. Denzinger, 379–395); and (3) the conclusion of Caesarius of Arles, which is really the heart of the declaration. In it he corrects the erroneous theories of Cassian and Faustus, emphasizes the need for grace, and condemns predestination to evil. Baptism restores man and strengthens the will. The declaration at Orange, a model of charity, condemns theories not persons. Orange II enjoyed great prestige; its canons, together with those of CARTHAGE (418), contributed to the theology of grace and were used by the Council of Trent. Orange II ended the Semi-Pelagian controversy in southern Gaul.

See Also: SEMI-PELAGIANISM; GRACE, CONTROVERSIES ON; FAITH, BEGINNING OF; FREE WILL AND GRACE; GRACE, ARTICLES ON.

Bibliography: Sources. J. D. MANSI, *Sacrorum Conciliorum nova et amplissima collectio* (Florence-Venice 1757–98) 6:433–452; 8:711–724. *Patrologia Latina*, ed. J. P. MIGNE (Paris 1878–90) 51:723–730. **Literature.** C. J. VON HEFELE, *Histoire des conciles d'après les documents originaux*, tr. and continued by H. LECLERQ (Paris 1907–38) 2.1:430–454; 2.2:1085–1110. L. DUCHESNE, *L'Église au VIᵉ siècle* (Paris 1925). F. H. WOODS, ed. and tr., *Canons of the Second Council of Orange* (Oxford 1882). M. CAPPUYNS, "L'Origine des *Capitula* d'Orange 529," *Recherches de théologie ancienne et médiévale* 6 (Louvain 1934) 121–142. G. DE PLINVAL, *Dictionnaire d'histoire et de géographie ecclésiastiques*, ed. A. BAUDRILLART. et al. (Paris 1912—) 12:186–196. G. FRITZ, *Dictionnaire de théologie catholique*, ed. A. VACANT et al. (Paris 1903–50) 11.1:1087–1103. A. FLICHE and V. MARTIN, eds., *Histoire de l'élise depuis les origines jusqu' à nos jours* (Paris 1935—) 4:397–419. P. FRANSEN, *Lexikon für Theologie und Kirche*, ed. J. HOFER and K. RAHNER (Freiburg 1957–65) 7:1188–89.

[C. M. AHERNE]

ORANGE, MARTYRS OF

The Martyrs of Orange is a group of 32 beatified religious women martyred at Orange, France, during the FRENCH REVOLUTION between July 6 and July 26, 1794. Two were CISTERCIAN nuns from Avignon; the others were from Bollène, near Avignon, and included 16 URSULINES, 13 SACRAMENTINE nuns, and one Benedictine nun. For refusing to take the oath *Liberté Égalité*, the nuns of Bollène were expelled from their convents (Oct. 13, 1793), arrested, and held in La Cure prison in Orange. There these and other nuns formed a kind of religious community, chose a superior, and spent several hours daily in prayer and pious exercises until condemned for fanaticism and superstition. The first to die by guillotine was the Benedictine Suzanne Deloye (July 6). On July 7 Marie Suzanne de Gaillard, a Sacramentine, followed.

The Ursulines Marie Anne de Guilhermier, Marie Anne de Rocher, Marie Gertrude de Ripert d'Alauzier, and Sylvie Agnès de Romillon died on July 9 and 10; and on July 11, three Sacramentines, Rosalie Clotilde Bès, Marie Elisabeth Pélissier, and Marie Claire Blanc, who were joined at the guillotine by Marie Marguerite d'Albarède, an Ursuline. Two more Sacramentines, Madeleine Talieu and Marie Cluse, died on July 12 with Marguerite de Justamond, a Cistercian, and Jeanne de Romillon, an Ursuline. The Ursulines Marie Anastasie de Roquard, Marie Anne Lambert, and Marie Anne Depeyre and the Sacramentines Elisabeth Verchière, Thérèse Faurie, and Anne Minutte suffered on July 13. On July 16 the guillotine claimed Marie Rose de Gordon, Marguerite Charransol, and Marie Anne Beguin-Royal, Sacramentines; Marie Anne Doux, Marie Rose Laye, and Dorothée de Justamont, Ursulines; and the Cistercian Madeleine de Justamont. On July 26 Marie-Madeleine de Justamont, Anne Cartier, Marie Claire du Bac, and Elisabeth Consolin, Ursulines, and Marie Marguerite Bonnet, a Sacramentine, died. The 32 were beatified on May 10, 1925.

Feast: July 9.

Bibliography: H. LECLERCQ, *Les Martyrs*, 15 v. (Paris 1902–27) v. 12. J. BAUDOT and L. CHAUSSIN, *Vies des saints et des bienheureux selon l'ordre du calendrier avec l'historique des fêtes,* ed. by the Benedictines of Paris, 12 v. (Paris 1935–56); v. 13, suppl. and table générales (1959) 7:209–215.

[M. LAWLOR]

ORANS

The figure of a person with arms extended and the palms of the hands open in a prayerful attitude prevalent in ancient pagan and early Christian art. This motif is found in bas-reliefs and sculpture in pagan cemeteries and on coins with the legend *pietas,* particularly of the Roman imperial period. It is seen in funerary monuments such as the late Egyptian stele representing the deceased. In the primitive Christian catacombs the earliest *orantes* are purely representational figures; but in the 2d century, they depict individuals marked with names or richly clothed, with or without an imprecatory legend, e.g., *Zoë in pace; In Deo vivas.* The 3d-century *orantes* are accompanied by petitions for the beholder, e.g., *In pace et pete pro nobis.* That they were considered related to the future life is seen in depictions with the Good Shepherd or with animals and plants being vivified by the Water of Life. In the 2d century OT figures such as Abraham, Noe, Isaac, and Susanna were likewise depicted as *orantes* and later, martyrs such as Mennas, Januarius, Thecla, Cecilia, and Agnes. In early Byzantine art Mary is pictured as an *orans;* this mode continued in the East, but the tradition disappeared in the West with the catacombs.

Considerable study has been devoted to deciphering the exact significance of the *orans* from G. B. de ROSSI'S conjecture of the Ecclesia Militans to Styger's symbol of heavenly glory and WILPERT'S prayer for those still on earth. The gesture is still used by clergy in the celebration of the Mass and other liturgical celebrations. In many places, the custom of the faithful praying the Lord's Prayer at Mass in the ancient orans posture has been revived in the wake of Vatican II.

Bibliography: T. KLAUSER, *Jahrbuch für Antike und Christentum* 2 (1959) 115–145; 3 (1960) 112–133. J. K. LEONARD and N.D. MITCHELL, *The Postures of the Assembly during the Eucharistic Prayer* (Chicago, 1994).

[J. BEAUDRY/EDS.]

ORATIO SUPER POPULUM

The presider's prayer of blessing over the assembly before the dismissal at the end of Mass. It is introduced by the words "Bow your heads and pray for God's blessing." (In Latin, "Humiliate capita vestra Deo"). The Sacramentary of Verona (Leonine Sacramentary) testifies to the *Oratio super populum* as a blessing given at the close of every Mass. It is evident from the contents of many of these prayers that this was primarily a blessing given to all. Little by little it was restricted until St. Gregory I confined it to the ferial days of Lent. In the Middle Ages, the *Oratio super populum* was supplanted (outside of Lent) by a general blessing at the end of Mass. The liturgical reforms initiated by Vatican II brought about a revival of this practice. The revised Sacramentary and other liturgical books provide a wide range of options for use on solemnities, feasts, and Sundays.

Bibliography: J. A. JUNGMANN, *The Mass of the Roman Rite,* tr. F. A. BRUNNER (rev. ed. New York 1959) 531–535. A. G. MARTIMORT, ed., *L'Église en prière* (Tournai 1961) 431–432.

[W. J. O'SHEA/EDS.]

ORATORIANS

The Confederation of the Oratory of St. Philip Neri (CO) was founded in 1575 at Rome, Italy, by Philip NERI; it was approved by the Holy See in 1612 and confederated and reapproved in 1942. The members live in common without vows and seek their own sanctification by following the evangelical counsels, community life, prayer, and the priestly and lay ministry.

General Organization. Each congregation of the Oratory, composed of priests and lay brothers, is completely autonomous. There is no central government in the Oratory, although in 1942, when the constitutions were reapproved, all Oratories were confederated into "The Institute of the Oratory of St. Philip Neri," with a procurator-general at Rome. His duty is to represent the individual congregations of the Oratory to the Holy See and to assist them when requested. He may also vindicate the rights of Oratories, revive defunct congregations, and aid those in crisis. In 1958 the Holy See provided a new office in the institute, that of visitor of the Oratory, also known as delegate of the Apostolic See. This visitor represents the Holy See to the individual congregations. There also exists in the institute the office of postulator general. Every six years delegates of the individual congregations assemble in Rome at the tomb of St. Philip to hold a congress. This is not ordinarily a legislative group; the continuance of its business is handled between congresses by a board of elected permanent deputies from the various national groups of the confederation.

It is, however, the individual congregations that constitute the confederation, and their form of life is unique in the Church. These congregations are composed of priests and brothers who freely practice the evangelical counsels. Oaths, vows, or promises that would bind one to the congregation are forbidden by the constitution. No congregation may have a second house or assume the task of ruling another congregation. The spirit of the Oratory is democratic and adapted to secular priests living in common. Besides novices there are two categories of priests: triennial members, who have only a consultative vote, and the sexennial members, who have a decisive vote. The superior of the Oratory, who is called provost, is elected triennially by the six-year members who have been admitted to active vote. This superior may be reelected every third year according to an ancient privilege and he is a major superior. He is assisted in the government of the congregation by four elected deputies. Without the consent of these deputies he may not make appointments or changes of officials. The provost and the deputies constitute the deputy congregation, which meets regularly to decide community affairs.

The general congregation is composed of all the members who have at least attained triennial status, and without the consent of this congregation no general law or regulation binding all the members may be made, nor may any business be initiated with the Holy See. The constitutions provide many checks and balances on the authority of its superiors and officials. Each congregation is commonly known by the name of the city wherein it is located. It is forbidden for two congregations to be located in the same city. The constitution admits of exceptions on this point for large modern cities. The lay brothers are supported by the congregation. The priests also are supported by the congregation but contribute to the congregation their earnings from ministries. The system of support for the members and for the congregation varies in each house in view of the circumstances of the times and the place in which a particular congregation is located. The principle is that Oratorians should, as much as possible, serve at their own expense and abstain from community funds.

Admission and Status. New congregations may come into existence either by being established from already existing Oratories, or, more commonly, by the invitation of ordinaries who wish a congregation in their diocese. A newly established Oratory must remain a diocesan congregation until all the elements required by the constitutions are fulfilled. At that time it is admitted by the Holy See to the Institute of the Oratory of St. Philip Neri as a congregation of pontifical right; only then does it become a genuine congregation of the Oratory. The autonomy of each congregation is complete, embracing apostolate, form of life, community exercises, finances, and education of its students. The constitutions and general statutes are observed by all congregations, but their nonpreceptive directives are left to further determination by particular statutes of the individual congregations and to decisions or decrees of the deputy or general congregations. There is no superior general or anyone, other than the Holy See, who may issue directives or rules for the autonomous houses.

The clerical members of each Oratory are ordained by their proper ordinary. The dimissorial letters permitting ordination are issued by the provost of the congregation. The Oratorians are incardinated into their own congregation with the reception of diaconate. In this case a priest may not depart from the congregation until he has found a bishop to receive him. The congregations of the Oratory are closely and fraternally linked to the clergy of their diocese. They are subject to the local ordinary except in those matters that are expressly excluded by force of law, i.e., in matters pertaining to their own institute and its constitutions and general statutes, internal government and discipline, economic administration, and episcopal visitation. Their close union with, and cooperation in, the program of the local ordinary flows from the nature of the congregation as a society of priests of the secular clergy. They cooperate in the bishop's labors and work for souls in their field, according to the command and program of the local ordinary. They do not enjoy the privilege of exemption from the jurisdiction of the local ordinary except in the four above-mentioned areas.

Foundations. Congregations of the Oratory of St. Philip Neri exist in the U.S. in Rock Hill, South Carolina; Monterey, California; Pittsburgh, Pennsylvania.; Pharr, Texas; Brooklyn, New York; Metuchen, New Jersey; and

Philadelphia, Pennsylvania. Three congregations exist in England: Birmingham, established by John Henry Cardinal NEWMAN; London, established by Frederich William FABER; and Oxford. There are congregations in Italy, France, Spain, Poland, Germany, Austria, Switzerland, the Netherlands, Mexico, Colombia, Costa Rica, Chile, Brazil, Canada, and South Africa.

The individual congregations of the institute of the Oratory are bound to each other by a bond of fraternal charity and by common constitutions and general statutes. They give to one another needed assistance, advice, labor, and materials and even lend members or transfer them when possible and necessary, although one's vocation is always to a specific congregation. They receive one another with fraternal hospitality into their houses and exchange information among houses. Beyond this they have a strong affection and respect for the autonomy of each house.

Bibliography: L. PONNELLE and L. BORDET, *St. Philip Neri and the Roman Society of His Times,* tr. R. F. KERR (New York 1933). A. CAPECELATRO, *The Life of Saint Philip Neri,* tr. T. A. POPE (new ed. New York 1926). V. J. MATTHEWS, *St. Philip Neri* (London 1934). M. JOUHANDEAU, *St. Philip Neri,* tr. G. LAMB (New York 1960). P. TURKS, *Philip Neri: The Fire of Joy,* tr. D. UTRECHT (New York 1995).

[E. V. WAHL]

ORBIS BOOKS

Orbis Books is the publishing arm of the Catholic Foreign Mission Society of America, popularly known as the MARYKNOLL FATHERS AND BROTHERS. Established in 1970, Orbis continues a tradition of book publishing initiated with the founding of the Society in 1911 by James A. WALSH (1867–1936) and Thomas F. PRICE (1860–1911). Editorial offices are located at the Society's headquarters at Maryknoll, N.Y., near Ossining, N.Y., 35 miles north of New York City.

Historically, the books published by the Maryknoll Society have focused on educating the public about missions and missionaries. Cofounder James A. Walsh, himself the author of the first three books published by Maryknoll, formulated the policy clearly: "Our book department has developed considerably. . . . Our principle, however, in the scale of mission literature, is to seek little or no direct profit. Our aim is to find readers. Substantial interest usually follows" (*Field Afar,* April 1921, p. 119). Orbis has consistently operated on the principle that "Maryknoll has never been afraid to publish a book that may not turn a profit, as long as that book has the potential to heal or enlighten or enoble" (*Maryknoll,* June 2000, p. 46).

Early Maryknoll books were popular accounts of people around the world and the work of missionaries among them. In the post-World War II period an increasing number of books focused on the deeper issues confronting peoples, their societies, and their churches. Directors of Maryknoll publishing at that time were Frs. John J. Considine and Albert J. Nevins, whose own works significantly advanced knowledge about the missionary world. Many of these books were contracted out to commercial publishers—Scribners, Longmans, Kenedy, and others—to assure a wide distribution.

The aftermath of the Second Vatican Council saw a rich production of theological and pastoral writing in Europe and North America. New voices soon emerged in Latin America, then in Asia and Africa. In 1970 the director of social communications for Maryknoll, Fr. Miguel d'Escoto, recently returned from service in Latin America, and Mr. Philip Scharper, the experienced former editor of Sheed and Ward, proposed that Maryknoll commit its efforts in the coming years to enabling these voices to be heard in English, thus to challenge and inspire as wide a world audience as possible. The Society endorsed the project under the new "Orbis" logo. Titles would carry the note: "Through Orbis Books, Maryknoll aims to foster the international dialogue that is essential to mission. The books published, however, reflect the opinions of their authors and are not meant to represent the official position of the society."

Among the earliest titles was *A Theology of Liberation* (1973) by Peruvian theologian Gustavo Gutierrez, later signaled by *Time* magazine as one of the most important books of the decade. Other authors included Juan Luis Segundo, Leonard BOFF, Jon Sobrino, from Latin America; C.S. Song, Kosuke Koyama, Michael Amaladoss and Aloysius Pieris from Asia; and Jean-Marc Ela, Lamin Sanneh, and Allan Boesak from Africa. Orbis soon became the leading publisher in English of the liberation theologies. There followed reflective studies in black and native American theology, and works by Hispanic and feminist authors. Scripture studies were abundant. A pioneering methodological study appeared with Robert Schreiter's *Constructing Local Theologies* (1985). The publication of David Bosch's *Transforming Mission* (1991) provided a comprehensive summary of the evolution of missiology and paradigm shifts in mission. Interreligious dialogue was served in studies by Jacques Dupuis and others. Historical studies have increased in recent years, including G. Gutierrez' *Las Casas* (1993) and the monumental *History of Vatican II,* five volumes, edited by Giussepe Alberigo and Joseph Komonchak (1995 ff.). Recent lists likewise reflect the current search for a deepened contemporary spirituality. Finally, Orbis has made available collections of key papal teachings, bishops' documents, and international synods along with the critical commentary of scholars. In all its publications, Orbis seeks "to examine the global dimensions of Christian faith, to invite dialogue with diverse cultures and religious traditions, and to serve the cause of reconciliation and peace."

Bibliography: G. G. HIGGINS, "Orbis Leads Its Chosen Field," *Maryknoll* (April 1981) 55–57. M. LEACH, "Impossible Dream Comes True," *Maryknoll* (June 2000) 42–46.

[W. D. MCCARTHY]

ORCHARD LAKE SCHOOLS

The Orchard Lake Schools is the general name for a complex of schools, centers, archives, museums and an art gallery located in Orchard Lake, Michigan, 35 miles northwest of downtown Detroit. The schools are: SS. Cyril and Methodius Seminary, Saint Mary's College of Ave Maria University and Saint Mary's Preparatory High School. Each school has its own Board of Trustees and its own head. The overall administration of buildings and grounds and the centers, archives, museums and art gallery as well as the coordination of the work of the three schools is vested in a Chancellor and a Board of Regents.

The Orchard Lake Schools were founded in 1885 by Father Jozef Dabrowski in Detroit in the center of the first Polish immigrant settlement. Father Dabrowski was born in Russian Poland in 1842. While a university student he became involved in revolutionary activity and was forced to flee abroad after the failure of the 1863–64 uprising. Ordained a priest in Rome in 1869, he took an assignment to serve Polish immigrants in rural Wisconsin. In 1874 he brought the Sisters of the Congregation of St. Felix of Cantilice to his parish, thus becoming their founder in the United States. He served as their chaplain until his death in 1903. The Felician Sisters moved their headquarters to Detroit in 1882. He transferred with them to the city and there began the Polish Seminary.

The Polish Seminary was born of the realization in the late 1870s that the growing Polish settlements in the United States were not attracting enough priests and educated laity from Europe to serve their needs. Father Leopold Moczygemba, a priest who had been serving Polish immigrants for more than two decades, went to Rome to petition the Pope for permission to raise funds for a school and seminary to educate immigrants and their sons for service to their community. His petition to Pope Leo XIII was approved on Jan. 14, 1879. The Pope wrote at the bottom of his letter: "Annuimus in omnibus juxta petita. Leo P.M. XIII," (We agree to everything according to your petition. Pope Leo XIII). Unable to implement the plan himself, the aged Father Moczygemba turned the papal permission over to Father Dabrowski. Father Dabrowski, who had been one of the leading proponents of the idea of the new educational institution, had already established a reputation in the new Polish community as a leading supporter of education at all levels. He is regarded as the Father of the Polish American parochial school system.

When Father Dabrowski chose Detroit as a suitable central location for the institution, the original idea of a site in rural Nebraska was abandoned. It was clear by the 1880s that the Poles would not follow the Germans and Czechs into prairie farming, but they would become workers in the new industrial heartland. The school, after beginning with three students in 1885, rapidly developed into a five-year classics program and a five-year seminary curriculum. From the outset, instruction was in Polish, English and Latin. It ordained its first priests on March 9, 1890. By the early 20th century it had over 300 students.

Administratively the school and its property were under the jurisdiction of the Ordinary of Detroit. In practice, the Bishops of Detroit allowed the school's administration wide latitude in managing its own affairs. In turn, the administration and clerical faculty strongly supported the authority of the hierarchy in its struggles with independentist tendencies in Polish American parishes before 1914. The schools were, from the beginning, also staffed by lay faculty including several distinguished scholars such as Professor Thomas Siemiradzki, the translator of Kant into Polish. Although begun for Polish immigrants, Father Dabrowski also opened the programs to students from other ethnic groups including Lithuanians, Ruthenians, Ukrainians, Czech and Slovaks. The school had a Lithuanian department and had plans for a "Bohemian" department at the time of Father Dabrowski's death. After World War I, when the lines of national identity were drawn more sharply, the number of non-Poles dwindled and the schools became more exclusively Polish American.

The growth in all the Seminary departments coincided with the growth of the Polish immigrant community in Detroit. By 1909, Father Witold Buchaczkowski, the second rector, unable to find property for expansion, purchased the campus of the recently closed Michigan Military Academy on the northeastern shore of Orchard Lake. The hundred-acre site, expanded to 120 acres by a later purchase, has remained the home of the schools since 1909.

Between 1927 and 1929, the Polish Seminary was reorganized into three schools on the basis of American models: a major theological seminary, now designated clearly as SS. Cyril and Methodius Seminary, a four-year college seminary named Saint Mary's and a four-year residential high school also called Saint Mary's. When the institution was founded it was dedicated to SS. Cyril and Methodius (1885 marked the millennial anniversary of their mission to the Slavs) and simultaneously to the Immaculate Conception. The reform divided these patrons, leaving the high school and college dedicated to the Virgin and the seminary to the Apostles to the Slavs. The college and high school in 1929 were incorporated together in the State of Michigan and received a charter to offer secondary and collegiate level courses without restriction. The seminary was added to the college and high school charter in 1941.

In 1941, the Archbishop of Detroit transferred the ownership of the Orchard Lake Schools to an independent lay and clerical Board of Trustees to avoid seizure of the property by creditors. The Archdiocese, as a result of the Depression, was on the verge of bankruptcy. In 1977, each of the schools received a separate administrative head and in 1983 the structure was reorganized to give each school a separate Board of Trustees. The Archbishop of Detroit was designated as the Chair of Seminary Board of Trustees.

For the half century after the reorganization, Saint Mary's High School prepared a significant percentage of the lay leaders of the Polish American community in Detroit and in the United States. Its graduates went on to major universities and professional schools, especially medical, dental and law schools. With the decline in interest in residential high schools and the wider opportunities available for third and later generations of Polish Americans, the enrollment showed a marked decline. A reform begun in 1989 ended mandatory residency, widened the academic curriculum and introduced a vigorous new sports program. It revitalized the high school as a major regional Catholic boys preparatory school serving the northwestern suburbs of Detroit. Its academic ratings and the success of its graduates have given it standing as one of the best preparatory schools in the Detroit area. Twenty percent of its students, including many from abroad, primarily the Far East, continue to reside on campus. In the 2000/2001 school year it enrolled 425 students, the highest total in its history.

Saint Mary's College remained largely a college seminary until 1965, although the majority of its students did not go on to a major seminary. It admitted laymen in 1965 and women in 1970 and broadened its educational program. By 1980 it had evolved into a regular Catholic liberal arts college. During the 1970s and early '80s, the college became a resource to third and fourth generation Polish Americans seeking to understand their Polish Catholic experience in America and the homeland of their ancestors. It also hosted the Polish-Jewish dialogue in the United States and the Black Polish Alliance of Detroit.

After the fall of the Soviet bloc, Saint Mary's College returned with renewed interest to its mission to serve as a bridge between Poland and east-central Europe and the United States. It sponsors biannual conferences on Polish affairs, publishes an annual *Periphery,* devoted to political and cultural topics, and recruits students from the region in large numbers. It has established ties with four Polish universities and has its own program in Kraków. In addition, faculty members with an academic specialty in Polish studies grew to ten. In 2000 there were more than 170 international students at the college with more than half from Poland. The expansion of Polish studies coincided with a similar effort in Polish American studies, as the college became the home of the Polish American Historical Association.

The end of the century also saw a concerted effort to reassert a strong Catholic identity. This thrust, as well as the new effort in Polish studies, was aided by an affiliation that brought new resources to the school. In 2000, the Orchard Lake Schools created Ave Maria University under its charter and made Saint Mary's College its first campus. The Board of Ave Maria College in Ypsilanti, Michigan then joined the new corporation of the Orchard Lake Schools as a second sponsor of the university. As of June 2000 Saint Mary's College is governed by a new Board chosen by the two affiliating sponsors: Ave Maria College and the Orchard Lake Schools. The enrollment of Saint Mary's College for 2000 was 492 students, the highest total in its history.

SS. Cyril and Methodius Seminary remains an interdiocesan seminary staffed by a faculty clergy from several United States dioceses and from Poland, as well as religious and laity. Most of its seminarians are recruited from minor seminaries in Poland. After a two-year course in English language and American culture, the seminarians embark on a four-year program of priestly formation and theological studies. During their seminary training they affiliate with a United States diocese and upon completion they are ordained for that diocese. The seminary offers masters degrees in divinity, theology and pastoral Ministry. In addition to the Priestly Formation program the seminary enrolls laymen and women seeking graduate training. At the fall 2000 registration the seminary enrolled 28 seminarians and 55 lay students. Over the course of its history the Orchard Lake Schools have educated 18,000 students and ordained over 2,600 priests for the American church. The seminary includes John Cardinal Król and Adam Cardinal Maida among its former students.

The Orchard Lake Schools are known widely for the Central Archive of Polonia which houses one of the largest collections of materials on the Polish Catholic experience in the United States and archival materials on the Polish Army in World War II. The College and Seminary Library has a valuable collection of Polish books including rare imprints published in the United States. A complex of museums documents the Polish World War II experience on all fronts. The Polish American Liturgical Center publishes a Polish-language missalette used in celebrating mass in Polish in North America and several other countries. The Art Gallery has the largest collection of Polish art in the United States in addition to fine examples of religious and secular paintings from elsewhere in Europe.

For its entire 116-year history, the Orchard Lake Schools have been supported by contributions primarily from Polish Americans throughout the United States.

Bibliography: J. SWASTEK, "The Formative Years of the Polish Seminary in the United States," in *Sacrum Poloniae Millenium* 6 (1959), 39–149, reprinted by the Center for Polish Studies and Culture of the Orchard Lake Schools in 1985. F. MOCHA, ed., "Polish American Institutions of Higher Learning," in *Poles in America: Bicentennial Essays* (Stevens Point, Wis. 1978), 461–496.

[T. RADZILOWSKI]

ORDEAL

A method of determining the guilt or innocence of a suspected or accused person by subjecting him to dangerous physical tests, the results of which are regarded as manifestations of divine judgment. It is essentially a form of divination. The practice is very old and has almost a universal distribution. It was widespread among the ancient Semitic and Indo-European peoples, especially among the Germans and the Slavs, and is found also in India, China, the Pacific islands, Australia, and Africa. While attested for the Americas, the practice is confined largely to Chile and Mexico.

Forms of the Ordeal. Among the numerous forms of the ordeal, several main types may be distinguished: ordeals by poison, by water, by hot iron, by fire, and by combat.

The poison ordeal is found principally among the peoples of West Africa. The accused must drink a concoction that produces vomiting or narcotic effects. If immediate vomiting results, and the accused suffers no ill effects, he is judged to be innocent. On the other hand, if he becomes dizzy and loses control of his faculties, he is thought to be guilty. Witch doctors play an important role in the poison ordeal, and the accused person often betrays his guilt through a fear that is heightened by the superstitious beliefs of his environment.

Ordeal by water is already mentioned in the Code of Hammurabi (Num 2, 132), and was widely practiced among the peoples of Europe. The accused person— often a woman accused of adultery—was required to plunge into deep water, preferably running water. If the person sank at once and did not rise immediately to the surface, he was adjudged to be innocent. If, however, he did not sink at once, or arose quickly to the surface and floated, it was thought that the water rejected him and that he was therefore guilty. Boiling water and boiling oil also were used in ordeals. The accused was required to plunge his hand and forearm into the hot liquid and his guilt or innocence was determined at once, or after three days, according to the greater or less degree of injury suffered by his hand or arm.

The hot iron ordeal was common among the ancient peoples of Europe and Asia and is still found in certain primitive cultures. The accused was required to grasp a heated ploughshare or to carry a piece of heated iron a prescribed number of steps. He was judged guilty or innocent either immediately, or after three days, according to the extent of injury suffered in this trial. An Irish ordeal requiring an accused woman to run her tongue across a red-hot adze is mentioned, but this practice does not seem to have been common.

The fire ordeal is found to have been practiced especially in Asia among the Hindus and other peoples within the orbit of their influence. The accused person was required to walk over burning charcoal or other material and, if unharmed, was judged to be innocent on the ground that the fire, a living force, refrained from injuring him.

Bibliography: A. E. CRAWLEY et al., J. HASTINGS, ed., *Encyclopedia of Religion and Ethics*, 13 v. (Edinburgh 1908–27) 9:507–33, a comprehensive world survey. L. LEITMAYER, *Lexikon für Theologie und Kirche*, ed. J. HOFER and K. RAHNER, 10 v. (2d, new ed. Freiburg 1957–65) 4:1130–32. R. THURSWALD, "Gottesurteil," *Reallexikon der Assyriologie*, ed. E. EBELING and B. MEISSNER (Berlin 1928–) 4.2:441–48.

[M. R. P. MCGUIRE]

In the Bible. The bitter-water ordeal of Numbers 5.11–31 is the only clear example of an ordeal in the Bible. The text appears to be a conflation of two separate but complementary forms of the ordeal ritual: that of the execratory oath [*see* OATHS (IN THE BIBLE)] and that of the drinking of the "bitter water." The results of both were interpreted as judgments of God. Although the latter aspect smacked somewhat of magic, its purpose was sacred: to appeal to God for a decision on the guilt or innocence of the accused. A woman accused of adultery, holding in her hand a cereal offering (without oil or frankincense), was presented to a priest. He then sprinkled some dust from the floor of the tent over a vessel of water and had her take an oath of execration (Num 5.21). After washing down the solution of ink in which the accompanying curses were written, the priest poured it into the now "bitter water," then waved a part of the cereal offering before the Lord, and had the woman drink the mixture. If the woman was innocent, no harm befell her and she remained fruitful. If she was guilty, the dreaded consequences of the curse took place, usually in the form of frequent miscarriages. If guilty, a woman would apparently prefer to confess and take her chances on a lesser punishment than to suffer the dire consequences of the oath. Even if the bitter-water ritual is ultimately traceable to pagan practices and betrays magical overtones, the Biblical writer has deliberately placed it into a sacral context by attributing its effectiveness to the powerful hand of God (Num 5.21). It is at least more humane than the corresponding prescription in the Code of Hammurabi.

One aspect of the golden calf episode in Exodus 32.1–24 also reflects the bitter-water ordeal; the idolatrous image is ground into powder and given to the Israelites to be drunk (20).

The ordeal was present to some extent also in the custom of seeking decisions by lot, as when Achan's offense was discovered (Jos 7.13–26) and Jonathan's breach of the *ḥērem* (1 Sam 14.36–45) was revealed. For this reason the high priest's breastplate containing the deciding lots URIM AND THUMMIM was called the "breastplate of judgment" (Exodus 28.15). Memory of the ordeal may also have influenced the Prophets to speak of "poisoned waters" of sinfulness contaminating the people of Israel (Jeremiah 8.14; 9.15; 23.14; Ez 23.31–34).

Bibliography: *Encyclopedic Dictionary of the Bible*, tr. and adap. by L. HARTMAN (New York 1963), from A. VAN DEN BORN, *Bijbels Woordenboek* (1676). E. KUTSCH, *Die Religion in Geschichte und Gegenwart*, 7 v. (3d ed. Tübingen 1957–65) 2:1808–09. R. PRESS, "Das Ordal im alten Israel," *Zeitschrift für die alttestamentliche Wissesnschaft* 51 (1933) 121–40. P. VAN IMSCHOOT, *Théologie d l'Ancien Testament*, 2 v. (Tournai 1954–56) 2:263–65.

[E. J. CIUBA]

The Medieval Ordeal. The ordeal in medieval Europe was a form of judicial trial whereby the innocence or guilt of accused persons was made to depend upon some feat of physical endurance. The result was regarded as definitive proof and as a judgment of God. Most forms of ordeal had the favor of the Church until 1215, and were preceded by certain religious acts.

Kinds of Ordeal. In general, medieval ordeals were bilateral or unilateral. In the former, the contending parties to a duel or single combat might be represented on occasion by proxies, for example, by one or more "champions." Thus in 1179, when the people of Rosny claimed

not to be serfs of the Abbey of Sainte-Geneviève in Paris, the case was decided "forever" in favor of the abbey by a judicial duel ordered by King Louis VII in which, on the day appointed, the men of Rosny failed in fact to accept the "repeated challenge" of the Abbot, Stephan of Tournai [A. Luchaire, *Études sur les Actes de Louis VII* (Paris 1885) 2:323]. The unilateral ordeal, on the other hand, tested an accused person as such, who, to prove his innocence, was required to carry a ball of hot iron in his hand for a certain distance, to plunge his arm to the wrist or elbow in a caldron of boiling water, to be submerged in cold water, to walk blindfolded between red-hot ploughshares, or to walk barefoot on glowing coals.

Church Attitudes. The attitude of secular and ecclesiastical authorities to ordeals varied. Although Constantine successfully prohibited gladiatorial combats (*Corpus iuris civilis* (Berlin): v.2 *Codex Iustinianus*, ed. P. Krueger 11.44.1), King Liutprand in 731 complained that he was powerless to abolish duels since they were part of Lombard tradition. And whereas popes Gregory the Great (590–604) and Martin I (649–53) confirmed for the monastery of Saint Peter at Rouen the right of holding "secular trials of cold water and the like" (Browe 2:3–4), Pope Nicholas I (858–67), in the famous case of King LOTHAIR II and Queen Theutberga, averred that a duel at least had "no divine sanction whatsoever" (*Corpus iuris canonici*, ed. E. Friedberg C.2 q.5 c.22); but in the same context, Hincmar of Reims defended hot and cold water ordeals. A celebrated precedent was set by Pope Stephan V (886–89) when, in reply to a query whether parents whose children had been smothered while sleeping with them should be made to prove by ordeal that death was accidental, he declared that ordeals of hot iron and cold water "had no canonical basis" (*Corpus iuris canonici* C.2 q.5 c.20; Browe 1:14).

On the whole the canonists were hostile to the idea, from IVO OF CHARTRES (1099) and GRATIAN (*c.* 1140) to HUGUCCIO (*c.* 1190), who regarded the practice as utterly unjustifiable and a form of "tempting God"; the aforementioned canonist-theologian Stephan of Tournai was somewhat confused; SICARDUS OF CREMONA (*c.* 1180) would allow it in cases involving the lower classes (Browe 2:88–104). With the notable exception of PETER CANTOR (d. *c.* 1196), who attacked it resoundingly, theologians of the period generally refrained from discussing it. However, possibly as a result of the opposition of Huguccio and Peter Cantor, the Fourth LATERAN COUNCIL in 1215 under Innocent III (who personally had allowed ordeals in civil though not ecclesiastical trials: Browe 1:30–36) prohibited the clergy from blessing or consecrating trials by ordeal (c.18; *Conciliorum oecumenicorum decrta* 220; *Corpus iuris canonici* X 3.50.9). Although it did not specifically disallow the use of ordeals in administering secular justice, this canon was a turning point in the disappearance of these customary practices (*purgationes vulgares,* as the canonists called them) from European law. England, Normandy, and Denmark at once followed the Council's lead, and justices in eyre were instructed in England in January 1219 to adopt other evidentiary procedures in the future. Trial by ordeal was further nullified by the development of merchant law, of inquest in ecclesiastical and secular law, and of juries in English law. That ordeals, particularly judicial duels, did not go out of vogue completely is evidenced by repeated papal prohibitions (Browe 1:38–47) and by writers such as Raymond of Peñafort, Thomas Aquinas, Dante, Suárez, and De Liguori. A celebrated survival of bilateral ordeal by fire was the proposal by a Franciscan that it be used by SAVONAROLA to test his prophecies. Savonarola rejected the proposal.

Bibliography: A. MICHEL, *Dictionnaire de théologie catholique,* ed. A. VACANT et al., 15 v. (Paris 1903–50) 11.1:1139–52. P. BROWE, ed., *De ordaliis,* 2 v. (Rome 1932–33). H. LECLERCQ, *Dictionnaire d'archéologie chrétienne et de liturgie,* ed. F. CABROL, H. LECLERCQ, and H. I. MARROU, 15 v. (Paris 1907–53) 12.2:2377–90. C. LEITMAIER, *Die Kirche und die Gottesurteile* (Vienna 1953). H. NOTTARP, *Gottesurteilstudien* (Munich 1956). J. W. BALDWIN, "The Intellectual Preparation for the Canon of 1215 against Ordeals," *Speculum. A Journal of Mediaeval Studies* 36 (1961) 613–36.

[L. E. BOYLE]

ORDER

Few notions have both so rich a heritage of meaning and so clear an application to all fields of knowledge as does order. There are many myths of cosmic order and its polar opposite, chaos, and there is no great religion without some PRINCIPLE of order. If men do not worship the transcendent God of Genesis, who imposes arrangement, then they have an immanent principle of law and of right relation of THING to thing and PERSON to person (*ṛta* in Sanskrit, *dhamma* in Pali, *tao* in Chinese, as well as the more familiar Greek notions associated with κόσμος, δίκη, μοῖρα, θέμις, and νοῦς). Until comparatively recent times order is not only always regularly associated with deity ("Order is Heaven's first law," A. Pope, *Essay on Man,* Ep. 4.49) but also always a virtue in man (according to W. Jaeger, cosmos "originally signifies right order in a state or other community"). As preserved in the expression "law and order," the orderly is the right way to behave, the disorderly is the wrong way. Order applies, then, not only to the lawful universe but to right action of man; order is also regularly associated with intelligibility. To order may mean to act regularly, or with system, i.e., to arrange acts by method. In the last

meaning, to order is to strive toward a goal, and those things that serve to achieve a goal are said to be ordered to it. Aristotle's favorite example of an order is an army, but St. THOMAS AQUINAS uses an example of another kind of order, a heap of stones. Stones can scarcely be said to be led, or to be under a leader; nevertheless, even when placed by chance, there is a gradation from the topmost to the lowermost (*In 5 meta.* 13.939). Order, then, has many senses, and things ordered in one way may yet not be ordered in another.

Formal Analysis. Exact definition of order seems only to have been achieved by scholastic philosophy, and the recent elaboration by symbolic logic, largely in the 20th century, has served to reduce the ambiguity of the term (*see* LOGIC, SYMBOLIC). The primitive notion, itself indefinable, is RELATION. Since relation is between things (in the most general sense, including terms of thought), order presupposes a plurality of things. A theorem common to both St. Thomas and such moderns as J. ROYCE, A. N. WHITEHEAD, and B. RUSSELL is that one thing cannot be ordered. The most general definition of order is to be related in some definite way. One definite way in which things are related is a series; that is, one thing is prior to another. In spite of the many senses in which "this" may be prior to "that," it follows immediately that "that" is posterior to "this." Logicians say of two symbols that they are well ordered when it makes a difference which is to the right of the other. "Before" and "after" are of this type. St. Thomas's defining statement is:

> The terms "before" and "after" are attributed according to the relation of some principle. Now order includes some mode of the "before" and "after." Hence, wherever there is a principle, it is necessary that there be also an order of some kind. [*Summa theologiae* 2a2ae, 26.1]

Order, then, is not meant absolutely, but always in some respect, or as Whitehead put it: "'Order' is a mere generic term: there can only be some definite specific 'order,' not merely 'order' in the vague" [*Process and Reality* (New York 1929) 128].

St. Thomas seems first to have made explicit what is shared by all serial orders and what differentiates one from another:

> . . .the notion of order includes the notion of the prior and the posterior. Thus there can be said to be an order of things according to all those modes, spatial, temporal and all like others, according to which a thing can be said to be before another. [*In one sent.* 20.1.3.1]

The modern way of expressing such a relation is to call it asymmetrical. That is, if *A* is larger than *B,* then

B cannot be larger than *A,* etc. In a familiar symbol, if *A* > *B,* then immediately it follows, *B* < *A* (in the example *B* is smaller than *A*). There are also symmetrical relations, in which the relation, r, is such that *ArB* implies *BrA.* The most obvious example of a symmetrical relation is equality. It makes no difference whether it is said that *A = B* or *B = A,* for one follows necessarily from the other.

"The notion of order includes the notion of the prior and the posterior," said St. Thomas. The modern says that asymmetry is necessary to an ordering relationship, but that it is not sufficient. For in a series, say the stones piled one atop the other, there is the same relation "on top of" holding between the top and the middle, and between the middle and the bottom stone. The relationship is called transitive when there are three things so related that when *ArB* and *BrC,* then *ArC.* This is certainly the case for "earlier than in time," or "to the right of in space," or "larger than in quantity," etc. Now although, as has been seen, serial relations are transitive and asymmetrical, there are also relations that are transitive and symmetrical. To use the former example of equality, it is obvious that when *A = B* and *B = C,* then it must follow that *A = C.* The common notion of Euclid is that things equal to the same thing are equal to each other. Those who have developed the theory of order here being expounded consider the principle of ordering relations no less fundamental in human thought. Consider such a relation as "heavier than," says William JAMES, and symbolizing the relation >, when *a > b > c > d,* then *a > d.* Evidently three terms are the minimal number for transitivity, and since there can be no maximum number of terms, the formal types of order are infinite.

> The principle of mediate comparison is only one form of a law which holds in many series of homogeneously related terms, the law that *skipping intermediary terms leaves relations the same.* This axiom of skipped intermediates or of transferred relations occurs, as we soon shall see, in logic as the fundamental principle of inference, in arithmetic as the fundamental property of the number-series, in geometry as that of the straight line, the plane and the parallel. *It seems to be on the whole the broadest and deepest law of man's thought.* [James, *Principles of Psychology* (New York 1890, 1950) 2:646]

Asymmetry and transitivity are not sufficient to define serial order. A third important factor to be made explicit, whether in the case of St. Thomas's rocks one atop another or James's objects of different weights, is that if any two are chosen, there is the relation "above" or the relation "heavier than," and either it or its opposite holds. Since by virtue of this property one can form a single system of the items, it is called connexity. It is found in the case of musical notes, where, because of the rela-

tion "higher than in pitch," one can construct scales. The beauty of this is obvious to anyone who reflects upon how he uses numbers, whether whole numbers or fractions. Of any two (different numbers, not equal one to the other), one is greater than the other, and occupies a unique place in the series called the order of magnitude.

The foregoing analyzes a common intuitive concept of order that is learned in the nursery: a place for everything and everything in its place. It would be false to argue that this is the only formal definition of order. One might, for example, define order as a relation that is aliorelative (or nonreflexive, i.e., not related to itself but to another), transitive, and connected, and deduce asymmetry. [A. N. Whitehead, "Mathematics," *Encyclopaedia Britannica,* 11th ed.; also in *Essays in Science and Philosophy* (London and New York 1948) 197]. It would be false to argue also that this definition fits all kinds of order. It applies only to series that are open, i.e., in which the same term does not recur. There are not only asymmetrical relations that are called orderly, but also all symmetrical relations, such as the many forms of balance in which an axis divides matching or balanced sides.

Historical Survey. The concrete kinds of order (as distinguished from the formal types of order) may best be sketched in terms of their exemplification in the history of thought.

To a great extent the Egyptians viewed their kingdom as an expression of an eternal and unchanging order. For the Babylonians there was a struggle to maintain order in the universe and in human affairs, and an element of risk. One way of reading history as reflected in men's concepts is to regard SOCIETY itself, and man's arts and sciences, as efforts to overcome confusion, to respond to the threat of chaos. Since contemporary human society lives in a period of vast uncertainty, it tends to smile at the complacency of the Egyptians and to feel sympathetically the anxiety of the Babylonians. The facts seem to be that there are periods when questioning the eternal order, or its goodness, rises to prominence. In contrast to the serenity of ARISTOTLE is the restlessness of St. AUGUSTINE (in the *Confessions*). In contrast to the serenity of St. Thomas and DANTE is the uncertainty of WILLIAM OF OCKHAM and his followers. Some of the Elizabethans express confidence in the hierarchical ordering, somewhat as conceived by St. Augustine in *The City of God* (*Civ.* 19.13), but the rise of mechanical science in the early 17th century is associated with the unrest of John DONNE ("'Tis all in peeces, all cohaerance gone"). Yet the mechanical order became itself the ground of confidence:

> All nature is but art unknown to thee; All chance direction, which thou canst not see; All discord,

harmony not understood; All partial evil, universal good. [A. Pope, *Essay on Man,* Ep. 1.10]

In contrast to the serenity of the post-Newtonian men of the Enlightenment is the emphasis on the arbitrary and willful ways of individual genius in the Romantic period. Man is most recently being deeply affected by the existentialists—S. A. KIERKEGAARD, F. W. NIETZSCHE, F. M. DOSTOEVSKIĬ, and their followers—who tend not only to question any knowledge of a divine order but also to belittle knowledge of an order of nature, to scoff at the law of human institutions, even to exalt chaos above order.

To trace the history of order is to go to the heart of Greco-Roman, medieval, and modern thought. It is also to discover those experiments that, in both their successes and failures, are most valuable in framing an adequate philosophy.

Greek Thought. The Greek achievement is fourfold. To the pre-Socratics man is indebted for the discovery that he inhabits a cosmos. The Ionian naturalists tend to stress mechanical order; particularly DEMOCRITUS (and later EPICURUS and LUCRETIUS) would account for all qualitative differences by changes in spatial order (τάξις). ANAXAGORAS counts this a failure to explain the "why" of order: the "how" alone lacks the purpose of intelligence (νοῦς). PYTHAGORAS and the Pythagoreans stress an intelligible order of forms to account for the sensuous harmony, especially as musical instruments produce sounds by simple proportions of the lengths of strings or vibrating columns of air. PLATO and Aristotle, however differing in their theories of form, both account for the GOOD and the beautiful as illustrations of order (*see* BEAUTY). Thus is born the concept of good order (εὐταξία) that the Stoics stress, and a problem is set for St. Augustine: if everything that is has an order, and some things are bad, how can there be bad order? (*See* EVIL.) Plato and Aristotle achieve concepts of the ordering of men in society and of the succession of the orders of constitutions.

Medieval Thought. The Christian achievement of a philosophy of order is best studied by St. Augustine, particularly in his brilliant dialogue *De ordine.* The plurality of orders is illustrated in nature, in the arts, in language, and above all in the moral life, seen in the light of divine providence. Christian philosophy surpasses its pagan predecessors in richness; problems of great depth are explored and solved, and without these achievements the modern world cannot be imagined. One is the conception of all peoples as part of an evolving pattern in time. History is a succession of orders: a concept developed centuries later by G. VICO and, most recently, by E. Voegelin's *Order and History* (Baton Rouge, LA 1956–). The second problem is that of the ultimate good of man. Salva-

tion belongs to what is commonly called "the order of grace," and Christian philosophies of order stress a sharp break between the methods by which one knows the natural order and the supernatural order. No modern philosopher of order has stated this better than B. PASCAL in his fragmentary *Pensées,* which are worth reading on the three orders, any one irreducible to any other (history is neither nature, nor supernature, and is studied in a unique fashion).

Modern Thought. A great modern achievement is the understanding of the world of nature as a unitary order. How the new science was made possible by the medieval theological framework, which itself grew out of the ancient movements, is shown by Whitehead in *Science and the Modern World* (New York 1925): "There can be no living science unless there is a widespread instinctive conviction in the existence of an *Order of Things,* and, in particular, of an *Order of Nature*"(5). The world ruled by power that is all-extensive, down to the least detail, yet in principle intelligible, is the living faith of Christianity. This was lacking, Whitehead argues, in those regions where science did not arise. Order is coupled by the founders of modern philosophy with method, that is, regular procedure in investigating nature. A crucial question, particularly for modern empiricists (D. HUME and his followers), is whether science can proceed without knowledge of an order of things and whether method is sufficient without metaphysical grounding. Modern metaphysics of order have been most various; doctrines of two orders ("order dualism"), an order of knowing and an order of being (R. DESCARTES); or reduction of all orders to one logical order ("order monism" of B. SPINOZA). There are other forms of "order monism": one mechanical order (T. HOBBES); one divine order (N. MALEBRANCHE); one order of the mind, without a real material order (G. BERKELEY). There is also the view of mind imposing categorial order on otherwise chaotic sensations (I. KANT), which might be called "order subjectivism." The later phases have stressed a recognition of change in species and CHANCE as a factor in their development (C. R. DARWIN). Thus, as argued by A. O. Lovejoy in *The Great Chain of Being* (Cambridge, MA 1936), the hierarchical order persisting from the ancients into the schemes of the Enlightenment has been displaced, and a temporal and dynamic ordering prevails.

The present crisis was prepared by H. BERGSON and the pragmatists, such as James. Bergson denied any real chaos: disorder was merely frustration in not finding the order one had expected (*Creative Evolution,* tr. A. Mitchell, New York 1911). James came to doubt any real order: the world has any order one chooses to recognize in it: it is as beans spilled on the table: a person can see whatever patterns are of interest to him (*Varieties of Religious Experience,* New York 1902, 1963, etc.).

Contemporary Thought. Contemporary philosophies of order—not only pragmatist but also existentialist, positivist, and Marxist—are all reacting against HEGELIANISM. The phrase that expresses "order-monism" in Royce is "one true Order of things" (*The World and the Individual,* New York 1900). Contemporary protests often take the form of extreme "order-dualism" or "order-pluralism." Philosophers who voice such protests assert confidently that there is no one final and eternal order; this ideal of one final order is mocked by L. WITTGENSTEIN as the search for a "crystal palace." The existentialists, following Dostoevskiĭ, who protested against cosmic order in the name of radical human freedom, tend toward acosmism: they tend to say that man alone is the only principle of order, and each individual man from moment to moment as his interests and tasks shift.

The great hope of some contemporaries (G. G. Grisez, I. Jenkins, and P. G. Kuntz, all somewhat close to Paul Weiss, *Modes of Being,* Carbondale, IL 1958) is that a new systematic understanding can be developed. The errors of the past have been the fallacious reduction of the cosmos to one mode of being or, on the other hand, the overstress on the discontinuity of orders. Stated positively, there are several modes of order. If the hope of these new systems is fulfilled, the universe can be understood as many orders together.

See Also: UNIVERSE, ORDER OF; RELATION.

Bibliography: M. J. ADLER, ed., *The Great Ideas: A Syntopicon of Great Books of the Western World,* 2 v. (Chicago 1952); v.2, 3 of *Great Books of the Western World,* see index. G. GIANNINI, *Enciclopedia filosofica,* 4 v. (Venice-Rome 1957) 3:1062–67. *Paulys Realenzyklopädie der klassischen Altertumswissenschaft,* ed. G. WISSOWA, et al. 18.1 (1931) 930–936. J. ROYCE, J. HASTINGS, ed., *Encyclopedia of Religion & Ethics,* 13 v. (Edinburgh 1908–27) 9:533–540. *American Catholic Philosophical Association. Proceedings of the Annual Meeting* 17 (1941) 1–52. E. CASSIRER, *Logos, Dike, Kosmos in der Entwicklung der griechischen Philosophie* (Göteborg 1941). W. W. JAEGER, *Paideia: The Ideals of Greek Culture,* tr. G. HIGHET, v.1 (2d ed. New York 1945). H. KRINGS, *Ordo: Philosophische-historische Grundlegung einer abendländischen Idee* (Halle 1941). AUGUSTINE, *Ordine,* ed. and tr. R. P. RUSSELL as *Divine Providence and the Problem of Evil* (New York 1942), also in *Writings of St. Augustine (The Fathers of the Church: A New Translation,* ed. R. J. DEFERRARI 1; 1948) 239–332. L. R. WARD, *God and World Order* (St. Louis 1961). J. M. RAMIREZ, *De ordine Placita quaedam Thomistica* (Salamanca 1963). H. MEYER, *Thomas von Aquinas: Sein System und seine geistesgeschichtliche Stellung* (2d ed. Paderborn 1961). B. COFFEY, "The Notion of Order according to St. Thomas Aquinas," *The Modern Schoolman* 27 (1949) 1–18. E. A. PACE, "The Concept of Order in the Philosophy of St. Thomas," *The New Scholasticism* 2 (1928) 51–72. H. A. ROMMEN, *The Natural Law: A Study in Legal and Social History,* tr. T. A. HANLEY (St. Louis 1947). C. I. LEWIS, *Mind and the World Order* (New York 1929; pa. 1956). W. D. OLIVER, *Theory of Order* (Yellow Springs, OH 1951). J. D. WILD, *Human Freedom and Social Order: An Essay in Christian Philosophy* (Durham, NC 1959). C. J. SCHNEER, *The Search for Order* (New York 1960). A. D. RITCHIE, *Studies in the History and Methods of the Sciences* (Edinburgh 1958). E. HEIMANN, *Freedom and Order* (New York 1947). H. KUHN, "Le Concept de l'ordre," *Greg* 43 (1962) 254–267. G. G. GRISEZ, "Sketch of a Future Metaphysics," *The New Scholasticism* 37 (1964) 310–340. I. JENKINS, "The Matrix of Positive Law," *Natural Law Forum* 6 (1961) 1–50. P. G. KUNTZ, "Modes of Order," *Review of Metaphysics* 16 (1962–63) 316–345; "Mythical, Cosmic, and Personal Order," *ibid.* 718–748; "Order in Language, Phenomena, and Reality: Notes on Linguistic Analysis, Phenomenology, and Metaphysics," *Monist* 49 (1965) 107–136.

[P. G. KUNTZ]

ORDER OF CHRIST

A military order established March 14, 1319, by John XXII, at the request of King Diniz of Portugal. The order received all the Portuguese properties of the suppressed Order of the TEMPLARS. Its chief seat was originally at Castro Marim, and later at THOMAR. The Order of Christ was bound to the observance of the customs of the Castilian Order of CALATRAVA and was subject to the visitation of the Cistercian abbot of Alcobaça. The pope appointed the first master, requiring him and his successors to take an oath of loyalty to the Holy See. In the future the abbot of Alcobaça was to preside at the election of the master. The Cistercian general chapter of 1320 consented to these arrangements and the first chapter of the Order of Christ was held at Lisbon in 1321. Until the 15th century the order was governed by a succession of masters; afterward princes of the royal family administered it. The most famous of these, Henry the Navigator (d. 1460), reformed the order and secured for it spiritual jurisdiction in the Atlantic islands and African regions, which were explored and colonized through his efforts. In 1542 Paul III revoked the right of the abbot of Alcobaça to visit the order. Nine years later Julius III annexed the mastership to the crown in perpetuity.

Bibliography: *Definições e estatutos dos cavalleiros e freires da Ordem de Nosso Senhor Jesu Christo* (Lisbon 1628, 1671, 1717, 1746). J. VIEIRA DA SILVA GUIMARÃES, *A Ordem de Christo* (Lisbon 1901). A. JANN, *Lexikon für Theologie und Kirche,* ed. J. HOFER and K. RAHNER (Freiberg 1957–65) 2:1183.

[J. F. O'CALLAGHAN]

ORDER OF THE SWAN

The Order of the Swan was a sodality whose goal was to further devotion to the Virgin Mary and to promote charity; originally membership was confined to princes, knights, and noble personages. Founded by Elector Frederick II of Brandenburg on Sept. 29, 1440, the order had its seat at Sankt Marien monastery on the Harlunger Berg, near Brandenburg, Germany. The brothers of the Order of the Swan vowed to say seven Our Fathers and seven Hail Marys daily—or to give seven pennies to the poor instead. Furthermore, they pledged to fast on the vigils of all feasts of the Virgin and to celebrate the feasts themselves with the greatest possible dignity. No adulterer, fornicator, traitor, robber, or drunkard could belong to the brotherhood. Members were obligated to make considerable contributions to the order, in return for which they gained all the spiritual benefits it earned. Membership in the order carried considerable prestige, not only in Germany, but elsewhere in Europe; it was originally restricted to 30 men (who had to furnish proofs of nobility) and seven women. The Elector Frederick II changed the statutes on Aug. 25, 1452, admitting commoners to the sodality. The badge of the order consisted of a gold or silver collar (called ''The Society''), from which was suspended a medallion showing the Virgin and Child supported by a crescent bearing the motto of the order, *Ave Mundi Domina.* Hanging from this medallion was an image of a swan, the proper titular of the order. The Reformation spelled the end of the order. It was, however, revived by King Frederick William IV of Prussia on Dec. 24, 1843, as a free association of men and women of all social classes, whose purpose was social welfare.

Bibliography: R. M. B. VON STILLFRIED–RATTONITZ, *Der Schwanenorden* (Halle 1845). S. HÄNLE, *Urkunden und Nachweise zur Geschichte des Schwanen–Ordens* (Ansbach 1876). R. M. B. VON STILLFRIED–RATTONITZ and S. HÄNLE, *Das Buch vom Schwanenorden* (Berlin 1881). C. MEYER, *Schwanenordens–Ritterkapelle* (Ansbach 1909). E. A. PRINZ ZUR LIPPE, *Orden und Auzeichnungen in Geschichte und Gegenwart* (Heidelberg–Munich 1958) 158.

[G. GROSSCHMID]

ORDERICUS VITALIS

Benedictine, the leading historian of France in the 12th century; b. Attingham, England, Feb. 16, 1075; d. Saint-Evroult, Normandy, Feb. 3, 1142. In 1085 he became an oblate in the abbey of SAINT-EVROULT-D'OUCHE in Normandy, where he received an excellent liberal education under John of Reims. He was ordained in 1108. In 1109 he adapted and enlarged the *Gesta Normannorum ducum* of William of Jumièges. In 1123, at the request of his abbot, Roger du Sap, he began his most important work, the *Historia ecclesiastica* in 13 books, completed in 1141. An especially important source for the period from 1125 to 1140, the *Historia* was originally planned as a history of his monastery. It soon grew into a universal history of the period, treating of persons and trends in the history of the Church; giving lists of popes, abbots, and rectors of churches; and recounting the history of the NORMANS in England, Southern Italy, Normandy, and the CRUSADER STATES. As an enthusiastic chronicler of the CRUSADES, Ordericus represents the best tradition of monastic HISTORIOGRAPHY, interested in events both religious and profane. Ordericus, little known in the Middle Ages, is appreciated today for his broad interest and accuracy in detail. His principal sources, carefully noted by him, were mainly oral. Among his informants were those who happened through the monastic guest-house: clerics, monks, pilgrims, knights, jongleurs, and merchants. Among earlier historians known to Ordericus were Pompeius Trogus, GREGORY OF TOURS, and BEDE. He also consulted monastic archives and the contemporary chronicles of Dudo of Saint-Quentin, William of Jumièges, and FULCHER OF CHARTRES.

Bibliography: Editions. *Historia ecclesiastica,* ed. A. LE PRÉVOST, 5 v. (Paris 1838–55); *Patrologia Latina* 188; *The Ecclesiastical History of England and Normandy,* tr. T. FORESTER, 4 v. (London 1853–56). Literature. *Geschichte der lateinischen Literatur des Mittelalters* 3:441–448, 522–528. H. WOLTER, *Ordericus Vitalis: Ein Beitrag zur kluniazensischen Geschichtsschreibung* (Wiesbaden 1955).

[B. LACROIX]

ORDINALS, ROMAN

In Latin, *Ordines Romani* (singular: *Ordo Romanus*). Medieval service books that described the customary (*consuetudines*) ordering (*Ordines, ordinarium*), or sequence of liturgical ceremonies.

Purpose. In the ancient Church, each minister performed only his part of the function. In fact, for each minister there was usually a special book containing only those texts pertaining to his role (*see* LITURGICAL BOOKS OF ROMAN RITE). To coordinate the activities of the various ministers and to ensure a smoothly organized service, someone comparable to a MASTER OF CEREMONIES was required. He had his own book, the ordinal. The first ordinals were very likely succinct personal notes of such a master, compiled by himself or the sacristan for local use. Written ordinals and their wide distribution filled a historical need; namely, that which arose when a local liturgy moved outside its own confines or when strangers replaced a native minister. There are also special official rubrical collections: the *Ordo* (*see* ORDO, ROMAN), designating the liturgical texts to be used for each day of the year, and the CEREMONIAL OF BISHOPS (*Caeremoniale Episcoporum,*) containing all the rubrics concerning episcopal functions.

History. The emergence of Carolingian Europe from chaos is in large part due to a program of borrowings from Rome (in organization and institutions, in culture and religion) which was in progress under Charlemagne. Having borrowed sacramentaries, lectionaries, graduals, etc., he needed also Roman ordinals. Members of monastic scriptoria copied prodigious numbers of MSS. Pure Roman manuscripts quickly acquired local elements, unintentional misreadings by copyists, or deliberate modifications by liturgical editors. Not only were collections of pure and altered ordinals amassed as reference works for libraries, but other collections, meant to supply actual norms for the living liturgy, were kept up to date and continuously developed. Still other ordinals were joined to didactic material for the theological training of the clerics. Key monastic centers throughout the Continent and the islands assured the survival of the ordinals.

Editions. Many had edited ordinals, for instance, Morin, Martène, Hittorp, Tommasi, De Rossi, Duchesne, and especially Mabillon, but none had worked on them critically until Michel ANDRIEU. Andrieu offers a highly scientific edition, and in texts that he has in common with other scholars, Andrieu must have preference. His lifetime work made available the pure Roman ordinals and their Gallican offspring. Andrieu culled 50 such ordinals from the manuscript libraries of Europe; by tedious line-by-line comparisons of myriad manuscripts, he retraced the genealogy of varied copies to their family homes, carefully dated them, and in the process revealed the slow evolution of the rites of Rome with the admixture of Gallican modifications that was to end in the 10th-century Romano-German pontifical. The liturgy embodied in this new ordinal entered Rome with Otto I (912–973), spread anew from the Lateran, and ultimately dominated the Western world.

In volume 1 Andrieu lists individually the titles of ordinals and under each gives reference to available editions and the known manuscripts in which they are found. Following this is a description of each manuscript consulted. A third section gives a history, and a valuable index ends the 631-page volume. Volume 2, after an introduction, takes up the text of the first 13 ordinals, each preceded by a chapter on the manuscript traditions, date and place of origin, and brilliant essays commenting on the text. A critical text with copious notes closes Andrieu's plan of work. Volume 3 covers ordinals 14–34; volume 4 ordinals 35–49; volume 5, the famed ordinal 50, covers Hittorp's *Ordo Romanus Antiquus*. This last tome is the work of Andrieu, but his untimely death left to A. van Roey and A. H. Thomas the task of preparing it for the press. In general ordinals 1–10 deal with the Mass; 12–19, the office; 20–33, principal functions of the liturgical year; 34–40, ordinations in their ember day set-

Roman Ordinal XVII, 9th-century manuscript page describing recital of monastic office (Bib, Vat. Cod. Pal. Lat. 574, fol. 152v).

ting; 41–44, dedication of churches and honors paid to relics; 45–48, the crowning of the emperor; 49, obsequies; and 50 deals with the liturgy of the whole liturgical year in 55 chapters. Along with these 50 ordinals, Andrieu points out the original Roman practice.

Bibliography: M. ANDRIEU, *Les ordines romani du haut moyen âge* (Louvain 1951). L. LARSON-MILLER, *Medieval liturgy : a book of essays* (New York 1997). E. PALAZZO, *A history of liturgical books from the beginning to the thirteenth century* (Collegeville, Minn. 1998).

[R. T. CALLAHAN/EDS.]

ORDINARIES, ECCLESIASTICAL

''Ordinary'' in Church law denotes those clerics listed in c. 134 of the Code of Canon Law. Ordinary jurisdiction is that power to govern which flows automatically from an office that a person holds (*Codex iuris canonici* c. 131 §1). This is distinguished from delegated jurisdiction, which is received by direct grant of one having authority without any essential relationship with an ecclesiastical office (*Codex iuris canonici* c. 131 §2).

Canon law does not define the term ordinary but simply enumerates those who are to be considered such. The

Code of Canon Law in c. 134 lists the following as ordinaries: (1) the Roman pontiff; (2) diocesan bishops; (3) others who are placed over some particular church or community equivalent to a particular church according to c. 368 (e.g., abbots *nullius* and prelates *nullius*); (4) the vicars general and episcopal vicars of those enumerated in (2) and (3); (5) for their own members, major superiors in clerical religious institutes of pontifical right and clerical societies of apostolic life of pontifical right who at least possess ordinary executive power. The code designates the following as major superiors: the supreme moderator of a religious institute or society of apostolic life; the provincial superior; the superior of an autonomous house; and the vicars of all those above mentioned (*Codex iuris canonici* cc. 620, 734).

Canon 134 makes the distinction between local ordinaries (those in groups 1 to 4 above) and other ordinaries (major superiors of clerical religious institutes of pontifical right and clerical societies of apostolic life of pontifical right who at least possess ordinary executive power). The local ordinary's jurisdiction extends over all those who are in the territory that he governs, whereas the jurisdiction of the religious ordinary is restricted to his own subjects.

In the Code of Canons of the Eastern Churches, the legislation on hierarchs is substantially the same as the Latin legislation on ordinaries (cf. *Codex Canonum Ecclesiarum Orientalium* c. 984).

Bibliography: U. BESTE, *Introductio in codicem* (5th ed., Naples 1961) 212–216, 312. M. J. KEENE, *Religious Ordinaries and Canon 198* (Catholic University of America CLS 135; Washington 1942).

[M. J. KEENE]

ORDINATIONS IN THE ROMAN RITE

The object of this entry is to discuss the particular form the Sacrament of Holy Orders has taken in the Roman rite. In order to do this it will be necessary to discuss the meaning of terms and then to investigate the historical evolution of each ordination ritual.

Meaning of Terms

Like many of the words used in the Roman liturgical books, *ordinato* and *ordo* have a civil origin, going back even to pre-Christian times.

Ordinatio. This was the technical term used at imperial Rome for the act of appointing civil functionaries to office. It was natural enough that the Roman Christians should borrow a familiar word to signify the appointment of ecclesiastical functionaries, of which the highest and most important are those involved in liturgical functions. So in time the word was limited to describe the rite of consecration to liturgical office or the sacred ministry.

"Ordination" is used by St. Jerome at the beginning of the 5th century as the Latin synonym for the Greek *cheirotonia*, the laying on of hands (*Commentarium in Isaiam* 16.58.10; *Patrologia Latina* 24:569); in time the word came to embrace all ordinations. Nowadays, the term simply means to ordain or promote to any order. *Ordinatio* became the term referring to the consecration of bishops as well as the promotion to priesthood and deaconship; the Roman Martyrology still speaks of "Ordinatio Sti Ambrosii Episcopi" for example. The Pontifical has substituted *Consecratio* for *ordinatio* in this case, but since the episcopate is the summit of Holy Orders and its source, we must include episcopal consecration in this study.

Ordo. Order is likewise a term that originally belonged to the Roman civil vocabulary, where it was used to designate a definite social body distinct from the *plebs*, or people—such as the Senate (*ordo clarissimus*), or the knights (*ordo equestrianus*), or the group that made up the governing body in any city (*ordo civicus*). Since the word had no pagan religious associations, Christians did not hesitate to adopt it to express the special place the clergy had within the people of God. Thus Tertullian uses it to describe the body of the clergy as set apart from the people (*De exhortianone casitatis* 7; *Patrologia Latina* 2:9222); the Theodosian code made it official by speaking of the *ordo ecclesiasticus* (*Cod. Theodosianus* 16.5.26).

The first step in the adaptation of the word to ecclesiastical use was to make it designate the whole body of the clergy. From that to using it to designate the different degrees into which the clergy was divided was a natural step. So we have the *ordo presbyterii* and the *ordo episcoporum*.

It is important that the word always had a collective sense in the usage of the ancient Church; a man did not so much receive an order as he was received into it and entered into it, as we say today that a man enters into the Society of Jesus, or is received into the Franciscan Order.

History of Ritual

In studying ordinations in the Roman rite different approaches are possible. The best seems to be to trace the historical origin and development and see how it took the form it has today, for the modern rite is the product of a long development in which a multiplicity of rites and formulas have accumulated around the original simple li-

New priests receive the Eucharist during their ordination at St. Vitus cathedral, Prague. (©Liba Taylor/CORBIS)

turgical action. To look into the history of this development is to make the meaning of the essential rite stand out in higher relief.

The modern ritual for the conferring of the Sacrament of Holy Orders is contained in the *Pontificale Romanum* (*see* PONTIFICAL, ROMAN). Until the 9th century the prayers and formulas to be used in conferring Holy Orders were found in the Sacramentaries, which contained the celebrant's prayers for Mass and other Sacraments and sacred rites. The ceremonies or actions that together with the words made up the sacred rites were contained in another book called the Ordinal. During the 9th and 10th centuries someone conceived the idea of putting both prayers and actions together in the one volume for greater convenience. The first compilation of this kind, or at any rate the most successful, originated at Mainz between 950 and 982. It became known as the *Pontificalis ordinis liber*, because of its content, and the Roman-Germanic Pontifical, because of its origin. This

book, with an ordination ritual already more developed than that in the Sacramentaries that preceded it, was accepted at Rome in the 11th century, where it was adapted to the use of the Roman court during the following centuries. William DURANTI the Elder (d. 1296), a civil lawyer who had become bishop of Mende, recast it and adapted it still more for his own use. This Pontifical was revised and approved for use at Rome in 1486; after further revision it was imposed on the Latin Church in 1596. The Roman Rite of Ordination emerged from the one in Duranti's Pontifical.

Consecration of a bishop. Since the episcopate is the fullness of the priesthood, we begin with it; then treat the other major orders—priesthood and diaconate, as well as a brief look at the now suppressed subdiaconate and other minor orders.

Ancient Roman Ritual: 3d to 5th Century. One of the oldest rites of episcopal consecration in existence is described in the *Apostolic Tradition* drawn up about the 3rd or 4th centuries (2–4; B. Botte, *La Tradition apostolique de saint Hippolyte: Essai de reconstitution* 4–16). The rite is simplicity itself. The neighboring bishops assemble with the local clergy and people on a Sunday. With the consent of those present these bishops impose their hands on the elect, while all pray silently, invoking the Holy Spirit. Then one of the bishops is asked to place his hands on the head of the elect and recite the consecratory prayer. These are, therefore, two distinct IMPOSITIONS OF HANDS: one in silence and once accompanied by the consecratory prayer. The prayer calls down the Holy Spirit upon the elect that he may shepherd the flock and fulfill the office of priesthood (*sacerdotium*) in a blameless manner, offering sacrifice, and forgiving sins. After the prayer all exchange the kiss of peace with him and ''salute him who has been made worthy.'' The deacons then place the offerings upon the altar and the newly ordained bishop celebrates the Eucharist at once.

The ritual described in the *Apostolic Tradition* has been maintained in the East with slight modifications; but at Rome it fell into disuse, and another more elaborate form was adopted perhaps as early as the middle of the 5th century. At any rate we encounter the main prayers of the present rite in slightly modified form in the LEONINE SACRAMENTARY (Veronense) (946, 947; Mohlberg 199).

Consecration at Rome: 6th to 9th Centuries. Two forms of episcopal consecration are described by the Roman Ordinal, and they differ considerably from one another. One is the form for the consecration of the bishop of Rome, the pope, by the bishops of the neighboring sees, the other is that conferred by the pope himself upon those chosen for these neighboring sees. The man chosen to be bishop of Rome in these early centuries was often not a bishop at the time of his election. He was therefore consecrated at St. Peter's, and his ordination was the joint action of the suburbicarian bishops; the bishop of Albano says the first prayer (the Collect *Adesto*), the bishop of Porto the second (*Propitiare*). Then the deacons hold the open book of Gospels on his head while the bishop of Ostia says the prayer of consecration. The archdeacon places the pallium upon the new bishop, who then ascends his throne, gives the kiss of peace to the priests, and intones the *Gloria* (*Ord. Romanus 40A and 40B*; M. Andrieu *Les 'Ordines Romani' du haut moyen-âge* 4:297, 307–308).

However, when the pope consecrated bishops for one of the dioceses of central Italy, he conferred the episcopate without the assistance of coconsecrators. The reason for this seems to be that the pope as chief bishop is considered to embody the *ordo episcopalis*, which in ordinary consecrations is symbolized by the presence of three bishops.

On the eve of his consecration the candidate for the episcopal office is examined by the pope in the presence of all the clergy. The consecration itself takes place on Sunday. During the Gradual of the Mass the elect goes to the sacristy, where he is vested in dalmatic, chasuble, and sandals by the archdeacon, the acolytes, and subdeacons. They then escort him back to the church, where the pope presents him to the people and invites all to join in a prayer for the elect. The Litany of the Saints is sung while the pope, the bishop-elect, and clergy lie prostrate before the altar. ''When the Litany is completed,'' Ordo 34 says, ''let them arise and let him [the pope] bless him'' (40; M. Andrieu, *Les 'Ordines Romani' du haut moyen-âge* 4:613). The blessing consists of the pope placing his hands on the elect and reciting the prayer of consecration given in the Sacramentaries. This prayer is already much longer than the one given in the *Apostolic Tradition* and completely different from it. Then the consecrator gives the kiss of peace to the new bishop, who in turn gives it to the other bishops and to the priests. When that is over, the pope seats him in the first rank of the bishops. At the Communion of the Mass he receives the manual of episcopal functions from the consecrator. The new bishop communicates by receiving a portion of the consecrated bread and at the same time sets aside enough for 40 days so that he may receive Communion during the time from the bread consecrated during the ordination Mass. By order of the pope he then gives Communion to the people.

Romano-Gallican Ritual: 9th to 15th Centuries. Between the ancient Roman rite of episcopal ordination, even in the somewhat developed form just described, and the modern episcopal consecration there is a vast difference. This is the result of the elaboration made by the Romano-Gallican ritual, an elaboration made by the Romano-Gallican ritual, an elaboration completed by the innovations of Duranti (M. Andrieu, *Le Pontifical Romain au moyen-âge* 3:311–320). The ritual of consecration underwent considerable development and addition both in the formularies used and in the individual rites that go to make up the whole. First of all the the name was changed from *ordinatio episcopi* to *consecratio electi in episcopatum*. It is beyond doubt that in time this contributed to thinking of the ordination of a bishop as in another class from that of a priest, instead of what it really is, the crowning and culmination of Holy Orders. An examination of the bishop-elect was introduced into the rite after the Collect and the ancient Roman consecration prayer expanded. In fact, the Romano-Germanic Pontifical transforms the ancient ordination prayer of the Roman rite into a consecratory Preface after the model of the Preface of the Mass, even to the dialogue at the beginning (*ibid.* 1:147).

The most striking innovation made in the Romano-Gallican ritual was the introduction of the anointings. While the old Roman rite was content to ask that God sanctify the elect with the dew of heaven by anointing, the new rite from beyond the Alps has the consecrator interrupt the prayer at this point to pour sacred chrism on the head of the elect, with the formula, "ungetur et consacretur caput tuum. . . ." This was obviously an attempt in true Gallican style to give visible expression to the words of the prayer (it was probably influenced by the contemporary practice of anointing the head of the king at his coronation). After the preface the new ritual also added the anointing of the thumbs; the 13th century papal Pontifical extended this to the whole hand (*ibid* 2:361). At first this anointing of the hands was done only when a man went directly from the diaconate to the episcopate; it was not repeated if the candidate was already a priest.

According to the ancient Roman tradition, the bishop-elect presented himself for ordination already invested in the insignia of his office. But outside of Rome the procedure was different; Isidore of Seville (d. 636) attests to the practice of giving the new bishop his ring and staff as symbols of his jurisdiction and his spiritual powers during the ceremony (*De ecclesiasticis offciis* 2.5.12; *Patrologia Latina* 83:783–784). The 12th-century papal Pontifical introduced the custom of handling the Gospel Book with the admonition to go and preach to the people committed to his care (*Le Pontifical Romain au moyen-âge* 1:150).

Duranti in his turn added the words *Accipe Spiritum Sanctum* to the imposition of hands, the singing of the *Veni Sancte Spiritus* during the anointing of the hands, enthronement of the bishop, and finally the singing of the *Te Deum* at the end of the rite (*ibid.* 3:382, 383, 389–391).

The ceremony of the placing of the opened Gospel Book upon the head of the bishop-elect makes its appearance for the first time in a 6th-century Ordinal (*Ordo Rom.* 40 A. 5; *Les 'Ordines Romani' du haut moyen-âge* 4:297). At first this was confined to the episcopal consecration of the pope, but in the Gallican lands it was extended to all consecrations. The custom itself is quite ancient; it came from the East, where it is mentioned in the ritual of the 4th century *Apostolic Constitutions* (8.4.6; F. X. Funk, ed., *Didascalia et constituiones apostolorum* 1:473).

Ordination of priests and deacons. The essential part of this ceremony, the imposition of hands accompanied by a variable but appropriate consecratory formula, has been a liturgical constant throughout history. However, the surrounding ceremony has passed through three stages of development just as the ritual for the consecration of bishops.

First Stage: The Primitive Roman Ritual. This is also contained in the *Apostolic Tradition* (7–8; *La Tradition apostolique de saint Hippolyte* 20–26). The ordination takes place in the presence of the presbyterium and the assembly of the faithful during the Sunday celebration of the Eucharist. It follows the Prayer of the Faithful. For both priests and deacons ordination consists of two elements: (1) the laying on of hands, and (2) the prayer of consecration.

The bishop and all the priests present lay hands on the man who is to be ordained to the priesthood. The bishop prays that God may impart the Holy Spirit to him so that he may help and govern God's people with a pure heart. Only the bishop lays hands on the candidates for deaconship because, as the Apostolic Tradition says, he is ordained not for the priestly office but to assist the bishop in a special way. The prayer said over the ordinand asks that God will give him the Holy Spirit "of grace, solicitude and industry" so that he may serve the Church and minister at the altar in such a way that he may deserve to be promoted to a higher rank, the priesthood. The bishop is still allowed considerable freedom in the formulas to be used. He may extemporize a formula using the given text as a model, "so long as the prayer is correct and orthodox."

Second Stage: 6th to 9th Centuries: The rite described in the 7th century Sacramentaries and Ordinals took form during the 6th century. The sources for this second stage are the earlier Sacramentaries and the *Ordo Romanus* 34 (M. ANDRIEU *Les 'Ordines Romani' du haut moyen-âge* 3:601–613).

First of all came the election of the ordinands by the clergy and the ratification of this choice by the people. Then on Monday in the Ember Week of December those to be ordained were called together by the pope; in his presence they swore an oath that they had not committed any of the crimes that would exclude them from ordination. On Wednesday they attended the pope's Mass. During the Mass a lector read the names of the candidates for priesthood and deaconship and then said the words still found substantially in the Roman Pontifical at the beginning of the ordination, only today they are spoken by the ordaining prelate: "If anyone has anything against these men, let him speak up" (*Ordo Rom.* 36.9; *Les 'Ordines Romani' du haut moyen-âge* 4:196). The same proclamation was made again on Friday.

The ordination began Saturday afternoon at St. Peter's. After the Gradual the pope called the ordinands to his throne and designated the church each priest and deacon was ready to serve. Then those to be ordained deacons, already dressed in the dalmatic, the sign of their future rank, stood with bowed heads before the pope; he invited all to prayer, and while the Litany of the Saints was sung, the ordinands prostrated on the floor. When the litany was finished, the pope placed his hands on the head of each one and blessed him (*Ordo Rom.* 36:18; *Les 'Ordines Romani' du haut moyen-âge* 4:198). This blessing included the prayer *Exaudi Domine* and the consecratory prayer *Deus honourum dator.* Then he vested the ordinands with the chasuble over the dalmatic and gave them the kiss of peace, which they in turn gave the others and then took their place beside him.

The ordination to the priesthood followed the same pattern except that the ordinands already wore the chasuble. The blessing was of course proper to the ordination to priesthood. When the pope ordained he alone imposed hands; if any other bishops ordained, the other priests present came forth and imposed hands after him. The new priests took their places in the first rank of the priests. At Communion they received the Eucharist first and, like the new bishops, had to set aside enough for 40 days' Communion.

What is immediately striking here is the extreme simplicity of the ancient Roman rite of ordinations, even though there has been some development over that recorded in the Apostolic Tradition. There is a minimum of signs (action and words), and those are extremely clear and well defined.

The Roman-Gallican Ordination Rite: 9th to 15th Centuries. The third and final stage represents a complete transformation from the ancient simplicity to an extreme complexity. This transformation was the result of the fusing of the Roman ritual with that of the Gallican ritual of ordination, a fusion reached in the 10th-century Mainz Romano-Germanic Pontifical. This new composite rite reached Rome about the year 1000 and in the course of the 13th century was further modified by the additions of Duranti. What we have today is therefore the Romano-Gallican ritual as amended by Duranti.

In the new ritual for the ordination of priests the bishop first enquired about the fitness of the candidate and tested his willingness to receive the priesthood and remain in it and obey the bishop. After the prayer of consecration, *Emitte quaesumus,* the new priest was clothed in priestly vestments (stole and chasuble) with appropriate formulas. The prayer *Deus sanctificationum* was added to the ancient Roman prayers. Some scholars believe that this added prayer was the essential formula of the older Gallican ritual before it was fused with the Roman rite. The new priest's hands were anointed with holy oil and he was presented with the chalice and paten containing the wine and the bread. The words *Accipe potestatem* accompanied this *traditio instrumentorum.* The ordination concluded with the special blessing *Ut sitis benedicti in ordine sacerdotali* now given at the end of Mass.

There is a different emphasis in this new rite. While the ancient Roman ordination prayer emphasized the fact that the newly ordained entered the *presbyterium* and became the coworker of the bishop, the new addition underscored the doctrine of the sacrificing priesthood and saw the priest primarily as celebrant of the Mass. While something could be said in favor of these innovations taken singly, the general effect in the eyes of discriminating people was to burden heavily a rite that had already departed considerably from the simplicity and sobriety of the ancient Roman ritual.

All these additions had entered into the Frankish service books in the course of the 9th century from various sources. The anointing of the hands, for example, appeared for the first time in the *Missale Francorum* (6th–7th century) that originated in Poitiers (8.33; Mohlberg 10). At first chrism was used for this anointing, but by the 13th century the oil of the catechumens had replaced the chrism, at least in Rome. The present custom was definitely fixed by Duranti. The presentation of chalice and paten containing unconsecrated bread and wine, which caused so much discussion among theologians in later times, arose during the 9th century in Gallican lands. It was accepted by the Mainz Pontifical in 950 and from that passed into all subsequent Roman books.

From Duranti come most of the rites added at the end of the present ordination Mass: the antiphon *Jam non dico vos,* the recitation of the Apostles' Creed, the final imposition of hands with *Accipe Spiritum Sanctum; quorum peccata retinueris . . .*, the unfolding of the chasuble, the promise of reverence and obedience, and the final admonition *Quia res quam tracturi estis.* Concelebration by the newly ordained with the bishop comes form the 13th century. Although Duranti spoke only of a silent optional concelebration, the present practice was already established in the 13th-century Pontifical of the Roman Curia.

The ordination to the diaconate underwent a parallel development to that of the priesthood in the medieval Romano-Gallican ritual. Like the priests, deacons were clothed in the vestments of their office after the prayer of consecration; they received the book of the Gospels as the symbol of their office as heralds of the Gospel. The ordination ended with the prayer *Domine sancte spei fidei . . .*, which is found originally in the *Missale Francorum* (7.26; Mohlberg 7); it may have been the consecration prayer of the old Gallican ordination rite.

In the modern ritual of ordination of deaconship is found once again the influence of Duranti. He added to what was in the Romano-Gallican ritual, modified it, and changed it in many details. He added the opening instruction on the duties of deacon. He made the already existing prayer of consecration into a preface like the Preface at Mass, with introductory dialogue and *Vere dignum*. Moreover, he introduced the formula *Accipe spritum sanctum*.

Subdiaconate. Here again we have a rite that from original simplicity reached great elaborateness, until its suppression by Pope Paul VI in 1972. Until the later part of the 12th century, in fact, the subdiaconate was considered a minor order, and so the ritual for the ordination of subdeacons was almost like that for minor orders. Thus, according to the *Apostolic Tradition* (13; *La Tradition apostolique de saint Hippolyte: Essai de reconstitution* 32) he received no imposition of hands but was simply nominated to assist the deacon. In the 6th century we find that there was a ritual for his ordination consisting of the delivery of an empty chalice (John the Deacon, *Epist. ad Senarium* 10; *Patrologia Latina* 59:405). Then the 8th-century Roman Ordinal 34 says that he first took an oath that he had not committed any crime that would bar him from orders. Upon this he received the chalice and the same blessing that was given to the acolytes (*Les 'Ordines Romani' du haut moyen-âge* 3:604).

Like the other ordination rituals, that for subdeacons was more fully developed in the Gallican lands. There the 6th-century apocryphal document known as the *Statutua Ecclesiae Antiqua* inspired the Frankish Sacramentaries and their ordination rituals. We find that in the Gallican rite the archdeacon presents the subdeacon with a cruet of water and towel, in addition to the challice presented by the bishop. The *Missale Francorum* (6.17; Mohlberg 5) is the first to provide a formula to go with the giving of the chalice; it is much longer than the modern form, though it begins with the same words *Vide cujus ministerium tibi traditur . . . .* The Romano-Germanic Pontifical has a developed rite similar to that for the ordination to minor orders.

The changes in the rite made during the 13th century had as their obvious purpose to give more dignity to the subdiaconate. Again most of these changes were the work of Duranti, who either invented or popularized the investiture with amice, tunic, and maniple; composed the instruction about the liturgical duties of the subdeacon; and inserted the delivery of the Epistle book. What is more, he advanced the singing of the Litany of the Saints so that it would include the candidates for subdeaconship as well as for deaconship and priesthood.

The effect of all this was to make the ordination of the subdeacon superficially similar to the ordination of priests and deacons. But a closer look at the rite reveals the absence of the imposition of hands and the consecratory preface, which, of course, is what really makes the difference. Strangely enough, Duranti did not include the admonition to observe celibacy. This was added only in the 15th-century Roman Pontifical, long after his time.

Minor orders. The ordination ritual for each of the historical minor orders, before Pope Paul VI suppressed them in 1972, was very simple in comparison with that of the major orders: (1) an admonition concerning the duties of that office, (2) the presentation of the instruments proper to each order together with a formula indicating the power thus conferred, and (3) a concluding prayer begging God's blessing. Nevertheless this ceremonial is a development of the original rite.

While the third prayer of the ancient form of the Solemn Prayers on Good Friday gives the full list of minor orders (with the addition of subdeaconship, which was considered a minor order until the 12th century), the medieval Roman Ordinals speak only of the ordination of lectors, acolytes, and subdeacons—an indication that the other minor orders had fallen into disuse by the middle ages.

Lectors were usually young boys. If a father wanted to offer one of his sons to be a lector, he had to instruct the lad in reading and then propose him to the pope as a candidate. On a prearranged day he was tested by being made to read a selection at the night vigil. If he passed the test he was then and there ordained a lector by what is surely the shortest ordination formula on record. The pope blessed him with the words "With Blessed Peter the Apostle the Blessed Paul the chosen vessel interceding for you, may the Lord save and protect you and bestow a learned tongue upon you" (*Ordo Rom.* 35.4; *Les 'Ordines Romani' du haut moyen-âge* 4.33).

Acolytes were ordained during Mass while bishops and priests were distributing Communion to the people. Since their principal function was to carry the Eucharist to the absent and present the consecrated bread to the priests for the fraction of the Host during Mass, the presentation of the *sacculum*, or little bag to carry the Eucharist, was an important part of the ordination rite. The candidate was first vested in chasuble and stole, then presented to the pope who gave him the *sacculum*. He received this in his hands, which were covered with the folds of the chasuble. Then he prostrated before the pope, who said the blessing over him (*Ordo Rom.* 35.8; *Les 'Ordines Romani' du haut moyen-âge* 4:34).

This ritual for the minor orders was much developed by the Romano-Germanic Pontifical, which also revived the other minor orders that had fallen into disuse, porter and exorcist. Already there was a tradition in the Frankish lands of such ordinations as in the *Missale Francorum* (2–5; Mohlberg 4). This Gallican ritual was in turn derived ultimately from the famous apocryphal work the

Statuta ecclesiae antiqua (Les 'Ordines Romani' du haut moyen-âge 3:615–619), which originated in southern France at the beginning of the 6th century. These Gallican practices found their way into the Romano-Germanic Pontifical and from that into the Roman Pontificals of the Middle Ages. Duranti's only contribution was to enlarge the admonition given at the beginning of the ordination to each order.

Impact of Vatican II. The main impetus for the current reform of ordination rites for bishop, priest, and deacon, as well as the new rites for the institution of readers and acolytes was given by Vatican II. The Constitution on the Sacred Liturgy, Dec. 4, 1963, stated (par. 76): ''Both the ceremonies and texts of the ordination rites are to be revised.'' This revision deals with reform of the Roman Pontifical of Pope Clement VIII (d. 1605), promulgated in 1596. As far as ordinations are concerned, this Pontifical remained basically unchanged until the recent reforms.

Prior to the more complete reform of the ordination rites in 1968 there were several intermediate steps. A revised Pontifical was issued by Pope John XXIII on Feb. 28, 1962, in which there were no *significant* changes. The next was the translation of the liturgical texts into the vernacular, approved by the U.S. National Conference of Catholic Bishops on Aug. 27, 1965, and confirmed by the Apostolic See on July 14, 1967. The vernacular rites of ordination and episcopal consecration were issued by the Bishops' Committee on the Liturgy, Sept. 12, 1967, in accord with the above authorization. This was simply a translation of the existing rites contained in the then current Pontifical. This edition also included several appendixes containing excerpts from the *Ritus Servandus in Celebratione Missae* (March 7, 1965), giving the rubrics for concelebration: a shortened Litany of the Saints, translations of the *Veni, Creator Spiritus* and *Te Deum,* and two additional *Hanc Igitur* for episcopal consecration in English translation.

On June 18, 1968, in the Apostolic Constitution *Pontificalis Romani Recognitio,* Pope Paul VI approved the new rites of ordination for bishop, priest, and deacon and decreed that these rites supercede the ordination rites in the Roman Pontifical. In this decree, Pope Paul stated that ''the greatest attention must be paid to the important teaching on the nature and effects of the sacrament of Order which was proclaimed by the Council.'' The Council document stated that the liturgy should express this doctrine in its own way: ''. . . the texts and rites should be drawn up so that they express more clearly the holy things which they signify; the Christian people, so far as possible, should be enabled to understand them with ease and to take part in them fully, actively, and as befits a community'' (Const. on Sacred Liturg. 21).

The accomplishment of this aim is evident in the introductory instructions for the ordination rites. In each instance, it is emphasized that the ordination should always take place at a time and place when a large number of the faithful can be present and participate, e.g., a Sunday or holyday. It is also suggested that the sanctuary be so arranged that the faithful may have a clear view of the liturgical rite and participate more fully.

The communal nature of the ordination rite is also highlighted by full participation by all in the exercise of their respective Order. All bishops and assisting priests are encouraged to concelebrate with the principal consecrator, and when a bishop is ordained in his own church the principal consecrator may invite the bishop-elect to preside over the Eucharistic liturgy. In the ordination of priests, the *ordinandi* are to concelebrate their ordination Mass with the bishop; deacons are also directed to exercise their office in the rite. In all instances, the people are encouraged to participate fully.

Ordination of a bishop. The Mass begins with the traditional procession into the church. The bishop-elect is vested in all the priestly vestments as well as pectoral cross and dalmatic. There is no administration of the oath of allegiance to the Holy See. After the Gospel, the bishop-elect is presented to the principal consecrator by one of the priests. The latter reads the Apostolic Mandate. At the conclusion of the reading, the assembly gives its consent according to local custom (usually applause). The principal consecrator then addresses an instruction to the people, clergy, and finally the bishop-elect. He may use the instruction in the rite or one of his own composition. This instruction, although similar to that found in the *Pontificale Romano-Germanicum,* is a new redaction reflecting the theology of Orders of Vatican II. Emphasis is given the Church as the people of God, as well as the hierarchal and collegial aspects of its nature. The bishop is to preach the word; form his flock in holiness; lead as one who serves; pray and offer sacrifice for his people; love as a father and brother the priests and deacons, his partners in the ministry, the poor and infirm, the strangers and aliens.

The examination of the bishop-elect is more radically altered. Greater emphasis is placed on the ancient practice of the bishop-elect being examined in the presence of the people. Much of the duplication is eliminated; its content is more scriptural than formerly. There is also greater emphasis upon collegiality and cooperation with the people and the presbyterate.

The litany is preceded by an invitation to prayer in bidding-prayer form. The shorter form of the revised litany is used and it is not interrupted for the special blessing of the bishop-elect formerly inserted in the litany. The litany is concluded with a collect of Gelasian origin.

The rite is further clarified by the introduction of the imposition of hands independently of the imposition of the book of Gospels. The principal consecrator and all the consecrating bishops impose their hands in silence. Only then is the book placed upon the head of the bishop-elect, where it is held by two deacons until the prayer of consecration is completed.

At this point the most radical of the changes takes place. The former prayer of consecration which is of Gallican origin gives way to the ancient prayer found in the Apostolic Tradition. This restores the most ancient of the known consecration prayers in the Church, one which has been maintained continuously in Coptic and West Syrian liturgies. As a result, a more primitive concept of the office of bishop emerges, placing greater emphasis on his role as shepherd-leader among his people.

Another feature of the reform of the consecratory prayer has to do with clarity and emphasis. No longer is there an introductory dialogue and preface; but, more importantly, there is no interruption of the consecratory prayer for the anointing of the head of the bishop-elect. The anointing is delayed until the prayer is concluded. The anointing of the hands of the bishop-elect is omitted entirely, and there is a considerable simplification of the presentation of the episcopal insignia.

After the newly ordained bishop is seated (in a considerably modified ceremony), the concelebration of Mass continues with the liturgy of the Eucharist at which the new bishop, if he be the ordinary, may be invited to preside. There is the traditional blessing of the assembly by the new bishop, a final blessing in the form of a solemn prayer over the people, and the procession from the church.

Ordination of a presbyter. The rationale for the reform of this rite is well stated in the decree *Pontificalis Romani Recognitio:* ''. . . it seemed necessary to restore the entire rite, . . . to greater unity and to express in sharper light the central part of the ordination . . . the imposition of hands and the consecratory prayer.''

The reformed rite is not unlike the ordination of a bishop through the liturgy of the word. The ordination per se begins, after the Gospel has been proclaimed, with the call and presentation of the candidates and the consent of the people.

The first change is found in the instruction to the people and candidates, and the examination of the candidates. Although both have structural origins in the *Pontificale Romano-Germanicum* and the *Pontificale Durandi,* they are updated to reflect the theology of the presbyterate enunciated at Vatican II. Clear emphasis is given to the unity of the presbyterate with Christ as teacher,

priest, and king in the building up of the Church as the people of God, the body of Christ, and the temple of the Holy Spirit. Emphasis is also given to the office to preach the Gospel, to shepherd the faithful, and to celebrate the worship of God as priests of the New Testament. A new element is inserted at this point requiring the examination of the candidate and exacting a promise of obedience. Both have their origin in the *Pontificale Romano-Germanicum* and the *Pontificale Durandi.*

The reformed litany is introduced and concluded with a type of bidding prayer and collect from the Gelasian and the Verona Sacramentaries. The imposition of hands by the ordaining bishop and the presbyters is done in silence and is followed by a revised prayer of consecration, also of Gelasian origin. Only the words of the conferral of the ''dignity of the presbyterate'' remain the same. Again, the dialogue and preface are omitted.

Following the consecratory prayer there is considerable simplification: investiture in stole and chasuble does not involve the ordaining bishop; the anointing of the hands is simplified and introduces a new prayer for the anointing, of Gallican origin; and there is no transmission of instruments.

The ordination Mass continues with the liturgy of the Eucharist. Other elements deleted from the reformed rite include the formal profession of faith, the ceremony extending the power to forgive, and the final admonition.

Ordination of a deacon. ''In the lower grade of the hierarchy are deacons on whom hands are imposed 'not for the priesthood, but for the ministry' [Constitution of the Church of Egypt, 3.2]. Strengthened by sacramental grace, they serve the People of God in the *diaconia* of liturgy, word, and charity, in communion with the bishop and his presbytery'' [*Lumen gentium* par. 29].

Few changes were made in the ordination rite for deacons. The format follows the changes noted in the rites for bishop and presbyter. Following the proclamation of the Gospel, there is the usual call and election followed by the instruction. This instruction is adapted from that of the *Pontificale Durandi* and incorporates elements from Vatican II documents. The examination of the candidates and the promise of obedience are new and quite similar to those found in the ordination of presbyters.

As in the other rites the litany is introduced and concluded with similar prayers of Gelasian origin. The laying on of hands is done in silence and separately from the consecratory prayer; apart from a few deletions, it remains practically the same as the former rite.

The investiture with the stole and dalmatic is simplified and done without accompanying prayers. Only the presentation of the book of Gospels retains a ceremonial action, but with a new prayer from the *Pontificale Romano-Germanicum.*

The ordination Mass is concluded with the liturgy of the Eucharist, the new deacons fulfilling their Order by assisting the ordaining bishop.

See Also: ACOLYTE; BISHOP (SACRAMENTAL THEOLOGY OF); DEACON; DEACONESS; LECTOR; PORTER; PRIESTHOOD; SUBDEACON; TONSURE.

Bibliography: M. ANDRIEU, "Les Ordres mineurs dans l'ancien rit romain," *Revue des sciences religieuses* 5 (1925) 232–274. B. KLEINHEYER, *Die Priestweihe im römischen Ritus* (Trier 1962). G. ELLARD, *Ordination Anointings in the Western Church before 1000 A.D.* (Cambrige, Mass. 1933). W. M. ABBOTT, ed., *The Documents of Vatican II* (New York 1966), Dogmatic Constitution on the Church *Lumen Gentium* pp. 14–96; Constitution on the Sacred Liturgy *Sacrosanctum Concilium* pp. 137–178. J. DESHUSSES, ed., *Le Sacramentaire Gregorien,* "Spicilegium Friburgense" v. 16 (Fribourg 1971); J. DESHUSSES, *Ephemerides liturgicae* v. 83 (1969) 3–98; *Maison-Dieu* 98 (1969) 63–142; 102 (1970). H. LIETZMANN, ed., *Das Sacramentarium Gregorianum,* Liturgewissenschaftliche Quellen und Forschungen, heft. 3 (Münster 1921). L. C. MOHLBERG, ed., *Liber Sacramentorum Romanae Aeclesiae Ordnis Anni Circuit,* Rerum Ecclesiasticarum Documenta, series major, fontes 4 (Rome 1960); *Missale Francorum,* Rerum Ecclesiasticarum Documenta, series maior, fontes 2 (Rome 1957). National Conference of Catholic Bishops, *The Rites of Ordination and Episcopal Consecration* (Washington, D.C. 1967); *The Ordination of Deacons, Priests, and Bishops,* provisional text (Washington, D.C. 1973). PAUL VI, "Constitution Apostolique 'Pontificalis Romani,'"; *Maison-Dieu* 94 (1968) 179–189; "Ad Pascendum," *Pope Speaks* 17 (1972) 234–240; "Ministeria Quaedam," *Pope Speaks* 17 (1972) 257–261. H. B. PORTER, *The Ordination Prayers of the Ancient Western Churches,* Alcuin Club Collections, no. 49 (London 1967). D. N. POWER, *Ministers of Christ and His Church* (London 1969). A. M. ROUGET, "Les nouveaux rituel d'ordination," *Maison-Dieu* 94 (1968) 63–142. P. F. BRADSHAW, *Ordination Rites of the Ancient Churches of East and West* (New York 1990). J. F. PUGLISI, *The Process of Admission to Ordained Ministry: A Comparative Study,* 2 vols. (Collegeville, Minn. 1996–99).

[W. J. O'SHEA/J. D. SHAUGHNESSY/EDS.]

ORDINES JUDICIARII

A type of legal literature that flourished from the 12th to the 16th century. The *ordines* were treatises that described procedure in courts. Although some dealt exclusively with procedure in ecclesiastical courts, it was more common, at least from the 13th century, for them to treat also of civil procedure, according to Roman law and Canon Law. The similarities between the two procedures were more significant than the differences.

Purpose. The *ordines* were practical in purpose and design. They described, sometimes in extraordinary detail, judicial procedure step by step, from initial citation to final sentence and appeal. Some *ordines* treated only specific parts of judicial procedure (e.g., the examination of witnesses). The medieval *ordines* varied considerably in length, from just a single folio to a large folio volume. The distinction between the *ordines* and other similar works, namely formularies and *consuetudines,* was not precise. Generally speaking, formularies were collections of forms of instruments used in a legal action. Yet many formularies arranged the forms according to the steps followed in court and, in addition, introduced the forms with rubrics; this made them not wholly unlike many *ordines* which contained examples of forms. The formularies, however, were of greatest utility to notaries; the *ordines,* to practicing lawyers. The *consuetudines* described the procedural practice actually in use in a specific court without references to laws, canons, and authors; the *ordines,* on the other hand, stated general procedural principles with the usual references, besides including frequent references to regional and local laws and customs.

Important Examples. The earliest extant *ordo* is probably the very short *Excerpta legum edita a Bulgarino causidico,* composed before 1140. The Anglo-Norman school of canonists in their notable production of canonical works of great variety during the 12th century was responsible for many *ordines* (e.g., Ulpianus, Otto of Paris). An anonymous *ordo* called *Ordo iudiciarius Causa II, quaestio I* was completed in 1171, probably at Amiens or Reims; and before the end of the same century there appeared the *Ordo iudiciarius Bambergensis (c.* 1182–85), the *Rhetorica ecclesiastica (c.* 1190), and other *ordines* by such canonists as Peter Blois, William Longchamp, Peter de Cadorna, Eilbertus of Bremen, and Ricardus Anglicus. The treatise *Actor et reus,* a procedural dialogue, was composed in England in the early years of Innocent III's pontificate. Another important and popular *ordo* was that of TANCRED (*c.* 1214–16). It underwent many redactions, was translated into French and German, and became the model for subsequent *ordines.*

Those *ordines* composed after 1234 took account of the procedural titles in the Decretals of GREGORY IX. Among the extant treatises from this period are those by Gratia of Arezzo (after 1234), Peter Penerchio (*Scientiam, c.* 1235–40), WILLIAM OF DROGHEDA (*Summa aurea,* 1239), Master Arnulph (*Summa minorum, c.* 1250–54), and the lay canonist GILES OF FOSCARARI (*c.* 1263–66).

This type of canonical treatise reached its highest peak with the *Speculum iudiciale* of William DURANTI THE ELDER, in 1272, which underwent redactions, acquired additions, and became the standard procedural treatise for the late Middle Ages. It exercised a commanding influence on the treatises written by John Ur-bach and John Berberius in the 15th century and by Ulrich Tenngler in the early 16th century.

Bibliography: *Tractatus universi juris duce et auspice Gregorio XIII,* 18 v. (Venice 1584–86). L. WAHRMUND, ed., *Quellen zur Geschichte des römisch-kanonischen Processes im Mittelalter,* 5 v. (Innsbruck-Heidelberg 1905–31). H. KANTOROWICZ and W. W. BUCKLAND, *Studies in the Glossators of the Roman Law* (Cambridge, Eng. 1938). S. KUTTNER, *Repertorium der Kanonistik* (Rome 1937). S. KUTTNER and E. RATHBONE, ''Anglo-Norman Canonists of the 12th Century,'' *Traditio* 7 (1949–51) 279–358. J. F. VON SCHULTE, *Die Geschichte der Quellen und der Oliteratur des kanonischen Rechts,* 3 v. in 4 pts. (Stuttgart 1875–80). A. VAN HOVE, *Commentarium Lovaniense in Codicem iuris canonici,* v. 1–5 (Mechlin 1928—), v.1. A. M. STICKLER, *Dictionnaire de droit canonique,* ed. R. NAZ, 7 v. (Paris 1935–65) 6:1132–43.

[F. D. LOGAN]

ORDO, ROMAN

Basically a calendar needed for the daily celebration of the proper Mass and Office in use throughout the Roman rite. In a ready, abbreviated format, it not only regulates the annual interplay of the temporal and sanctoral cycles, the fixed and moveable feasts, but it also notes any peculiar rubrics and gives seasonal pastoral reminders as needed. Because of special liturgical offices, local churches and monastic groups may vary from the Roman Ordo. The modern Ordo is but the development of local calendars and priests' rubrical and pastoral directories; it became a necessity after Trent decreed a uniform liturgy.

[R. T. CALLAHAN/EDS.]

ORÉ, LUIS GERÓNIMO DE

Franciscan linguist and bishop; b. Ayacucho, Peru, 1554; d. Concepción, Chile, Jan. 30, 1630. Oré was one of 11 children (four of the boys became Franciscan priests, five of the girls became Poor Clares, and one boy became a diocesan priest), who were educated at home with special instruction in music, both instrumental and vocal. He grew up speaking Spanish, Quechua, and Aymará. After being ordained in Lima on Dec. 31, 1582, Oré first labored in Lima, preaching on Sundays and holydays to the Amerindians gathered in the plaza before the cathedral. He also helped to translate into Quechua the catechism of the Third Council of Lima.

He spent the years 1584 to 1598 as a missionary among the Collaguas people of southern Peru. This experience enabled him to write *Símbolo católico indiano* (Lima 1598), a synthesis of the material taught to the Collaguas together with many hymns translated or composed by Oré, many of which are still sung today. In 1598 he was appointed vicar of the convent of Lima, and he taught courses in the native languages Quechua and Aymará. This work was interrupted by an invitation from Antonio de Raya, Bishop of Cuzco, to supervise the instruction of the native people in his diocese. Other bishops soon gave him similar powers in Arequipa, La Paz, and Charcas.

In 1604 he went to Rome to present the *ad limina* report of Bishop Raya to the pope. While in Rome he printed in Latin *Conciones per annum* (1606), a work that he had prepared earlier in Quechua and Aymará but had not received royal permission to print in those languages. He also published *Tratado de indulgentiis* (1606) and, perhaps his greatest work, *Rituale seu manuale peruanum* (Naples 1607). This was intended primarily for the missionary in Peru with a special catechism for confession and Communion. It was printed in Latin, Spanish, Quechua, Aymará, Mochica, Puquina, Guaraní, and Brazilian. The Puquina sections are probably the largest fragments of that language still extant.

Preparing to return home from Spain, Oré received news of the death of Francis Solano (1610) and was charged with the task of collecting information in Spain for his cause. By 1613 the task was finished and published as *Relación de la vida y milagros del Venerable P. Fray Francisco Solano* (Madrid 1614). It remains the best source on the life of Francis before he left Spain.

In 1614 Oré led a group of Franciscan missionaries to Florida to inspect the Franciscan missions there and in Cuba. He organized the Franciscan province of Florida and moved the provincial's residence and the novitiate from St. Augustine to Havana. This novitiate was probably the first institution of its kind within the present limits of the United States. On his return to Spain in 1618, Oré published *Relación de los mártires de la Florida.* Shortly thereafter the king named him bishop of Concepción (formerly La Imperial), Chile. He was consecrated in Lima in 1621, and arrived in his see the next year. His diocese was in a deplorable condition since it had been vacant for 14 years, and native rebels had dominated the region of Osorno and Valdivia for 20 years, cutting communications between the northern and southern parts of the diocese. Oré visited his diocese three times, began a seminary, and energetically promoted the conversion of the indigenous tribes while protecting their rights through laws drawn up in a diocesan synod. He willed his fine library to the Franciscan friary in Concepción.

Bibliography: L. G. DE ORÉ, *The Martyrs of Florida, 513–1616,* ed. and tr. J. M. GEIGER (New York 1937), also in *Franciscan Studies* 18 (1936), whole issue.

[A. S. TIBESAR]

Dedication of St. Mary's Church, Mount Angel, Oregon c. 1912.
(©CORBIS)

OREGON, CATHOLIC CHURCH IN

Oregon lies on the shores of the Pacific Ocean, surrounded by Washington, Idaho, Nevada, and California. Originally part of the Oregon Country, Oregon became a territory in 1849 and a state in 1859. Salem is the capital, and Portland the most populous city. Ecclesiastically, the state is divided, with the Archdiocese of PORTLAND (until 1928, Oregon City) in the western part of the state, covering 29,717 square miles, and the Diocese of Baker (until 1952 Diocese of Baker City) on the eastern side, covering 66,826 square miles.

Early History. Jointly occupied by Great Britain and the U.S. between 1818 and 1846, Oregon was the home of explorers and fur traders, most of whom were in the service of the Hudson's Bay Company. The Catholic French-Canadians, former employees of the company, who during the 1820s and 1830s settled in the Willamette Valley, south of the Columbia River in the area called French Prairie, desired priests to serve them. At the sug-

gestion of Dr. John McLoughlin, company director at Fort Vancouver, they petitioned Msgr. Joseph PROVENCHER, Vicar Apostolic of the Red River country in Canada, for Catholic missionaries, and on Feb. 28, 1836, the Holy See placed the Oregon Country under his care. Unable to accept, he forwarded the petition to the bishop of Quebec, and on April 17, 1838, Francis Norbert BLANCHET was named vicar-general to the ordinary of Quebec with jurisdiction over the vast Oregon territory. At the same time, another young priest of Quebec, Modeste Demers, was appointed to assist Blanchet.

The two priests arrived at Fort Vancouver on Nov. 24, 1838, and began their missionary activities among the French-Canadians and Native Americans. Pioneers at French Prairie had already constructed a small log church in 1836, in which Blanchet celebrated the first Mass on Jan. 6, 1839, after blessing it under the title of St. Paul the Apostle. This mission was Blanchet's most important one, and served as his headquarters during the formative years. Other missions established by Blanchet and Demers were Fort Vancouver, Cowlitz, Oregon City, and Fort Nesqually. In 1842 the missionaries were joined by two priests from Quebec, Anthony Langlois and John Bolduc, who labored for several years in Oregon.

Almost simultaneous with these beginnings was the activity of Pierre J. DE SMET, SJ, among the Native Americans in the Rocky Mountain area and the far eastern part of the Oregon Country. After his initial appearance there in 1840, he returned to St. Louis, Mo., to obtain help for the western missions. He then set out again for Oregon and arrived at Fort Vancouver on June 8, 1842, where he was welcomed by Blanchet and Demers. During De Smet's short stay at Vancouver, the three priests carefully surveyed the entire mission situation of the Pacific Northwest and decided that great possibilities existed, but that many coworkers, supplies, and finances were necessary. They further resolved to petition the bishops of Quebec, St. Louis, and Baltimore for the establishment of the hierarchy in the Oregon Country. De Smet, chosen to go East and then to Europe to procure all the help possible, departed June 30, 1842.

Beginning in 1842, a tide of American immigration flowed toward Oregon from the eastern states, increasing the population so rapidly between 1843 and 1845 that McLoughlin (who had become a Catholic in 1842) petitioned the bishop of Quebec to obtain English-speaking and American priests for Oregon. When a shortage of American priests prohibited this, it was left to European missionaries to care for Oregon. Meanwhile, De Smet reached Europe, recruited a small band of priests and nuns, and returned to Fort Vancouver in August of 1844 with five Jesuits and six Sisters of Notre Dame de Namur.

St. Francis Xavier Mission was established as Jesuit headquarters near the Willamette River adjacent to St. Paul, and the sisters opened schools at St. Paul and Oregon City.

First Ordinary, 1846–80. When the entire Oregon Country was erected a vicariate apostolic on Dec. 1, 1843, Blanchet was named vicar, but word did not reach him until November of 1844. The bishop-elect then departed for Montreal, where he was consecrated on July 25, 1845. Hoping to obtain more missionary help for Oregon, Blanchet spent the next years in Europe, seeking personnel and funds. During this time, he persuaded the Holy See to erect his vicariate into an ecclesiastical province, and on July 24, 1846, the Archdiocese of Oregon City and two suffragan sees, Walla Walla and Vancouver Island, were established. The creation of the U.S.'s second ecclesiastical province at this time and place was considered in some quarters to have been premature and unwise.

The new archbishop returned to his see in August of 1847 with the funds collected in Europe and with 21 missionaries, including eight priests and seven sisters. The future was promising, for the Native American missions were prospering and heavy American immigration to the area had prompted expansion of facilities at St. Paul, Oregon City, and other missions. During the next decades, however, governmental interference in the Native American missions, incessant wars with the tribes, and unfounded accusations against Catholic missionaries, practically ruined the mission work among the natives. Moreover, the discovery of gold in California prompted a mass exodus southward, including a majority of the Catholics at St. Paul and Oregon City. French Prairie almost became a ghost parish and the Jesuits and the Sisters of Notre Dame de Namur terminated their diocesan endeavors and went south, where the need was greater. The clergy dwindled to seven, arriving Americans were largely non-Catholic, and debts left from the building expansion remained to cripple the see for several years.

In the mid-1850s the situation improved somewhat when the archbishop's personal tour of South America for financial help aided in reducing the debt. The Sisters of the Holy Names of Jesus and Mary arrived in 1859 from Montreal and reestablished Catholic education; European volunteers increased the ranks of the clergy; and the city of Portland began to grow. The American Catholics strengthened the parish of the Immaculate Conception, founded by Rev. James Croke in 1851, and it became the center of the struggling archdiocese. In 1862 Blanchet transferred his episcopal residence from Oregon City to Portland. Immaculate Conception became the procathedral, remaining such until 1928, when it became the actual cathedral with the change in seat of the archdiocese. John F. Fierens succeeded Croke as rector, and Portland's Catholicity made noteworthy progress during his 30-year pastorate. The diocesan newspaper *Catholic Sentinel* was begun in 1869; more Catholic schools were opened and several Catholic societies were founded in the 1870s; and St. Vincent Hospital was established in 1875.

The size of the archdiocese was reduced considerably on March 3, 1868, when the Holy See created the Vicariate of Idaho, making the eastern boundary of Oregon the boundary of the archdiocese. In 1878 increasing disability led Blanchet to accept a coadjutor, Bp. Charles SEGHERS of Vancouver Island; in 1880 the archbishop resigned, and three years later died in Portland, after 64 years in the priesthood.

Seghers and Gross. Seghers succeeded to the see on Dec. 20, 1880, but directed its affairs for only a short time, resigning in 1884 to return to Vancouver Island. In his brief term, however, he had made many missionary journeys in Oregon and helped the Benedictines establish an abbey at Mount Angel. On Feb. 1, 1885, Bp. William GROSS, CSSR, of Savannah, Ga., succeeded Archbishop Seghers.

In his 13 years as metropolitan, Gross directed many efforts of Catholic expansion, especially in education. In 1886 he founded the Sisters of St. Mary for teaching in diocesan schools. Before his death on Nov. 4, 1898, he had succeeded in bringing to the archdiocese additional religious help, including the Christian Brothers, Dominican Sisters, Sisters of Mercy, and Sisters of the Good Shepherd. He directed the relocation in 1898 of St. Mary's Procathedral from the business section of Portland to a site in a residential area.

Twentieth-Century Developments. Alexander Christie, of Vancouver Island, was appointed Feb. 12, 1899, as fourth archbishop of Oregon City. His 25-year episcopate coincided with a revival of commerce and immigration in Oregon, and he met the challenge of increased population by establishing new parishes, churches, schools, and other institutions. Significant among these was Columbia University, later renamed the University of Portland, which opened in 1901. Another boundary change of the archdiocese came in 1903 when the Diocese of Baker City was erected with jurisdiction over Oregon territory east of the Cascade Mountains. Christie's last years were marked by the controversy over the so-called OREGON SCHOOL CASE involving a state law of 1922 designed to force all children up to 16 to attend public schools. The archbishop died on April 6, 1925, the same year that the U.S. Supreme Court declared the law unconstitutional.

On April 30, 1926, Bp. Edward D. Howard, auxiliary bishop in Davenport, Iowa, was appointed to succeed Christie. Since parishes, population, and religious and educational institutions had increased greatly during the period from 1875 to 1925, the new archbishop dedicated himself to organization and consolidation of diocesan functions. Although Bp. Blanchet had moved the episcopal residence to Portland in 1962, the diocese was still known officially as the Archdiocese of Oregon City. It was during the time of Archbishop Howard that it became officially designated as the Archdiocese of Portland. He supervised the erection of chancery offices, established new parishes, promoted the liturgical movement, centralized the school system under a superintendent's office, created the Catholic Charities organization to coordinate all social and charitable works, established new schools, notably Central Catholic High School in Portland, developed the catechetical ministry through the Confraternity of Christian Doctrine, and made a concerted effort to encourage vocations to the priesthood. Howard's administration was marked by a threefold increase in the Catholic population from 61,036 in 1926 to 186,560 in 1963, with the number of clergy increasing from 174 to 430, and the addition of 23 parishes.

In 1966 at the age of 89 Archbishop Howard retired (he died at the age of 105). Howard had attended all the sessions of the Second Vatican Council but it was the task of his successors to implement it. Some of the resistance that they encountered in the Archdiocese of Portland was also felt in the diocese of Baker. The two dioceses collaborated in a number of endeavors, and in the 1970s they formed the Oregon Catholic Conference as a Catholic public policy organization for the state.

Education. Catholic education in Oregon had its beginnings at St. Joseph's College, an elementary school for boys, in St. Paul on Oct. 17, 1843. The next year the Sisters of Notre Dame de Namur started a girls' school in St. Paul and later in Oregon City. Loss of population and teachers during the Gold Rush forced the discontinuance of all Catholic schools by 1853. Archbishop Blanchet personally went to Quebec in 1859 to recruit 12 volunteers from the Sisters of the Holy Names. With the advent of new religious groups in Portland during the Gross, Christie, and Howard administrations, both elementary and secondary schools increased. Catholic education developed more slowly and differently in the Baker because of the vast area and scattered population. The Baker diocese relies more on parish religious education programs rather than on a Catholic schools, in the years after Vatican II the number of schools declined in both dioceses.

Catholic higher education began when Gross convinced the Benedictine Monks to open Mount Angel College in 1887 and a seminary in 1889. The college was discontinued in 1946, but Mount Angel Seminary continued to serve dioceses and religious communities. The Holy Names school, St. Mary's Academy and College in Portland, empowered to grant degrees in 1893, became the first Northwest liberal arts college for women. In 1910 the school moved near Lake Oswego and in 1930 was renamed Marylhurst College. Closed in 1974, the college re-opened that fall as a private, nontraditional, co-educational college for adults, becoming a university in 1998. Columbia University opened in 1901 as a boys' prep school, and in 1902 the Holy Cross priests bought the campus. Fully collegiate in 1927, the institution became the University of Portland in 1935. The school became coeducational in 1951.

Although Catholics are the largest single religious group in Oregon, they are a distinct minority. In 2001 Catholics numbered 324,020, about 10 percent of the state's population of 3.2 million.

Bibliography: L. M. LYONS, *Francis Norbert Blanchet and the Founding of the Oregon Missions, 1838–1848,* Catholic University of America, *Studies in American Church History* 31, 1940. E. V. O'HARA, *Pioneer Catholic History of Oregon,* 4th ed. (Paterson 1939). W. B. BAUMAN, *Catholic Contributions to Oregon History* (Mt. Angel, Ore. 1959). C. B. BAGLEY, ed., *Early Catholic Missions in Old Oregon,* 2 v. (Seattle 1932).

[F. M. CAMPBELL/P. BRANDT]

OREGON SCHOOL CASE

The Oregon School case (*Pierce v. Society of Sisters,* 268 U.S. 510), handed down in 1925 by the U.S. Supreme Court, upheld the right of parents to control the education of their children when it declared unconstitutional a law that would have made attendance at public schools mandatory.

Background of the Oregon law. The attempt to divest parents of their right to control the education of their children grew out of the May 1920 resolution of the Masons of the Scottish rite of the southern jurisdiction advocating ". . . the free and compulsory education of the children of our nation in public primary schools. . . ." The procedural plan adopted by the proponents of this move bypassed legislative action. It was decided to have a direct vote of the people on the measure through use of the initiative procedure. Accordingly, in a spectacular one-day campaign under the direction of the Scottish-rite Masons of Oregon, sufficient signatures were obtained to place on the ballot for the general election in November of 1922 an initiative measure to compel children between the ages of eight and 16 to attend the public schools of Oregon.

Any doubt concerning the sponsorship of the initiative measure was dispelled by an advertisement in Oregon newspapers by P. S. Malcolm, Inspector General of Oregon Scottish-rite Masons, stating that the anti-private school measure was sponsored by the supreme council, Scottish rite for the southern jurisdiction of the U.S., the grand lodge of Oregon, and the imperial council of the nobles of the mystic shrine (*Catholic Sentinel,* Aug. 3, 1922).

Arguments against passage of the initiative measure were filed with the secretary of state by Catholic organizations, Seventh-day Adventists, Episcopalians, Lutherans, Presbyterians, principals of private schools, and a citizen taxpayer association. The lone argument in behalf of the measure was filed by the Scottish-rite Masons.

Those opposing the measure argued that: (1) The title was deceptive to the extent that the measure is described as a compulsory education law. Compulsory education was already a part of the law of the state together with the regulation of private schools. (2) The proposal would deprive the schools and teachers of their property rights under the 14th Amendment to the Federal Constitution. (3) Parents would be deprived of religious liberty, that is, the right to rear and educate their children in accordance with the dictates of conscience.

The Masonic argument was based on the following propositions: (1) "Our nation supports the public school for the sole purpose of self-preservation." (2) "The assimilation and education of our foreign-born citizens in the principles of our government, the hopes and inspiration of our people, are best secured by and through attendance of all children in our public schools." (3) "We must now halt those coming to our country from forming groups, establishing schools, and thereby bringing up their children in an environment, often antagonistic to the principles of our government." (4) "Mix the children of the foreign-born with the native-born, and the rich with the poor. Mix those with prejudices in the public school melting pot for a few years while their minds are plastic, and finally bring out the finished product—a true American." (5) "The permanency of this nation rests in the education of its youth in our public schools, where they will be correctly instructed in the history of our country and the aims of our government, and in those fundamental principles of freedom and democracy, reverence and righteousness, where all shall stand upon one common level." (6) "When every parent in our land has a child in our public schools, then and only then will there be united interest in the growth and higher efficiency of our public schools." (7) "Our children must not under any pretext, be it based upon money, creed or social status, be divided into antagonistic groups, there to absorb the narrow views of life as they are taught. If they are so divided, we will find our citizenship composed and made up of cliques, cults and factions each striving, not for the good of the whole, but for the supremacy of themselves. A divided school can no more succeed than a divided nation."

This attack on private schools was not limited to the state of Oregon. Similar legislation was pending in Michigan and California and threatened in Washington, Indiana, Nebraska, and several other states. Throughout the country, newspaper editorials alerted the people to the widespread nature of the proposed legislation.

In Oregon a bitter campaign ensued. Newspaper headlines shouted the divided and bitter feelings of the people. The *New York Post* underscored an important element in this controversy, namely, that the KU KLUX KLAN was actively supporting the initiative measure.

The combination of forces opposed to parochial schools was sufficient to give the proposal a 15,000 plurality and it became law. By its terms it would become operative in 1926.

Struggle in the courts. Opponents of compulsory attendance in public schools turned to the courts for redress. At this juncture the bishops of the U.S. entered the contest through the recently formed National Catholic Welfare Conference. The *St. Louis Progress* reported that the Bishops' Committee met in Chicago and the "outstanding result of the gathering was the unanimous decision to get behind a test of the Oregon school law in both State and Federal Courts with all of the moral, spiritual and financial aid necessary, and to use every legitimate means to secure the law's repeal" (Jan. 25, 1923).

In addition to financial aid, the NCWC, through its press department, gave wide coverage to all aspects of the Oregon law and created a national awareness of its implications. The education department and other departments of the NCWC prepared a series of pamphlets on the law, the rights of parents in the education of their children, and the traditional understanding of the Constitution. This material not only aroused the country but, in the words of Father John Burke, General Secretary of the NCWC, "intelligently guided it."

In 1923 legal action was initiated in the Federal District Court to test the constitutionality of the Oregon law. In the same year the Supreme Court rendered a decision in the case of *Meyer v. Nebraska* (262 U.S. 390), which had a very important bearing on the Oregon school law litigation. The Meyer case was an important precedent for the decision in the Pierce case.

Meyer v. Nebraska precedent. The Nebraska statute provided that no foreign language could be taught in the nonpublic schools of the state. It was enacted in an atmosphere of hostility to private schools—the same legislature having come within one vote of adopting a law that would have forced all children to attend public schools. The Supreme Court of Nebraska upheld the constitutionality of the law, and an appeal was taken to the Supreme Court of the U.S.

In the course of the oral argument an interesting colloquy took place between Mr. Arthur Mullen, attorney for the plaintiff, and Mr. Justice McReynolds. Mr. Mullen argued very forcefully that the Nebraska legislation involved more than a denial of the property right of the teachers. He indicated that in the last analysis the legislation was directed at the right of the parents to send their children to private schools. At this point Mr. Justice McReynolds interposed, saying: "How did they abolish private schools? Did the State prohibit private schools?" Replying, Mr. Mullen observed: "I say, your Honor, that they could no more abolish private schools than they could—" Mr. Justice McReynolds broke in: "I just wanted to see what you claim. What about the power of the State to require the children to attend the public schools? . . . You will admit that, will you not?" Mr. Mullen's reply was clear and definitive: "I do not admit that. *I deny that a State can, by a majority of the legislature, require me to send my child to the public schools.*"

He then proceeded to develop the proposition that the parental right is within the liberty guaranteed by the 14th Amendment. In conjunction with this argument, Mr. Mullen observed that there was a close connection between the exercise of the parental right and freedom of religion. In a colloquy with Chief Justice Taft, he argued that the liberty that is guaranteed by the 14th Amendment includes religious freedom. Mr. Mullen, in taking this position, laid the basis for the eventual argument that the right to send children to a parochial school rests not only on *parental right* but also upon *religious freedom.*

Paradoxically, the justice who intimated that the state had a right to ban all private schools wrote the opinion for the court invalidating the Nebraska statute. In the course of his opinion, he stated: "[Plaintiff's] right . . . to teach and the right of parents to engage him so to instruct their children, we think, are within the liberty of the [14th] Amendment."

He observed collaterally that, among other rights, the 14th Amendment includes the right to the free exercise of one's religion. Admittedly, this was not the primary basis for the decision. It rested on the property right of the teacher and the right of parents whose children attended the schools in question. Nevertheless, this was the first time in the history of the Supreme Court that the parental right to educate was even obliquely associated with reli-

gious freedom. It was a decision that broke new ground and provided a fertile field for the growth of principles establishing the right to educate.

The Court's recognition of the parental right and its association of religious liberty with this right represented a tremendous victory, for at the time of this decision private education had its back to the wall. Many states had adopted legislation similar to the Nebraska law. Others were considering or, as in the case of Oregon, had passed laws banning all private schools, and these laws were not originating in legislatures. Through initiatives and referendums the people themselves were waging a war against private schools. The decision of the Supreme Court in the Nebraska case was the beginning of the end of this movement. The Nebraska case had an immediate impact on the Oregon School case by establishing persuasive precedents for the legal arguments of the plaintiffs.

The Federal District Court. Judge John Kavanaugh, appearing for the Sisters of the Holy Names, called the Federal District Court's attention to the Nebraska case and said: "It leaves nothing, your Honors, to be said upon the question. They have recognized the private school, they have upheld its rights." In addition to developing the institution's rights, Judge Kavanaugh commented extensively on the parental right. For example, in his oral argument to the Court, he stated:

Now people in this country have certain natural and inherent rights. Those rights existed before constitutions were made, and those rights will exist after constitutions are dissolved. They are not created by the constitution, but they are secured by the constitution; and among these rights are the inherent and the natural right of a parent to direct the education of his own child in a private school that conforms to all of the regulations of the state.

The attorney who appeared as the representative of the Scottish-rite bodies, and Governor Walter M. Pierce, argued that the Oregon law was well within the police power of the state, since the state had the right to control education. He also contended that the corporations that brought the action could not rely on asserted rights of parents.

The Federal District Court ruled that the Oregon law was unconstitutional. In so holding it declared: "The absolute right of these schools to teach in the grammar grades, . . . and the right of the parents to engage them to instruct their children, we think, is within the liberty of the Fourteenth Amendment." And on the institutional right the court asserted:

Compulsory education being the paramount policy of the state, can it be said, with reason and justice, that the right and privilege of parochial and private schools to teach in the common school grades is inimical or detrimental to, or destructive of, that policy? Such schools and their patrons have the same interest in fostering primary education as the state, and appropriate regulation will place them under supervision of school authorities.

Governor Pierce of Oregon announced that the state would appeal the decision of the U.S. Supreme Court. The issue thereupon became a national one.

The U.S. Supreme Court. In order to ensure the best possible representation before the court the services of William Guthrie were retained. Associated with him in the defense of the parochial and private school interests were Judge Kavanaugh of Portland, Ore., and Garret McEnerney of San Francisco, Calif. In addition to the briefs filed by these attorneys, briefs *amicus curiae* were filed by the Episcopal Church, the Seventh-day Adventists, and the American Jewish Committee, all of whom argued that the Oregon law was unconstitutional. The general tenor of these briefs is reflected in the following excerpt from the brief of the Seventh-day Adventists: "These natural rights [of parents] have been protected by every Bill of Rights declared in any government at any time and are always spoken of as existing, but never as bestowed by government."

The brief of Mr. Guthrie effectively demonstrated that the issues at stake were the maintenance of religious liberty, the inviolability of the parental right against state encroachment, and the institutional right to the protection of its property. A strong brief emphasizing the property rights of private schools was filed by Mr. John C. Veatch on behalf of the Hill Military Academy, one of the plaintiffs in the action.

The attorneys for the state showed a keen appreciation of the arguments predicated on the parental right. An attempt was made to demonstrate that the rights of parents were not violated but that the law merely represented a harmonization of the respective interests of the state and parents. However, in the conclusion of the state's brief, its basic position was stated in the following words: "The necessity for any other kind of school than that provided by the state has ceased to exist. The public school is everywhere recognized as being an institution vital to the welfare of the individual citizen, and to that of the state and nation" (*Oregon School Cases, Complete Record,* p. 200).

At the outset of the oral argument before the Court, Justice McReynolds put the main issue in focus when he stated to the Attorney General, Mr. Willis S. Moore: "You understand that the sharp issue presented here is whether the State can require a child to go to the public school." Mr. Moore agreed that this was the critical question and then proceeded to argue that the people have the right, in the exercise of the police power, to enact laws requiring all children to attend public schools and that the "limitations of the power are primarily with the people." At this point the Chief Justice suggested that this power is subject to the limitations of the Constitution. The attorney general replied that, since education was a power reserved to the states under the 10th Amendment, the limits of law rest primarily with the people.

Guthrie, in his oral argument, stated that of all the interests invaded, "First and foremost, the law involves the sacred right of parents in the discharge of their duty to educate their children." He then proceeded to point out that manner in which rights of the children, the teachers, and the institutions were violated. All these issues, he stated, involved the maintenance of basic liberties to such an extent that if these rights were denied, the day would come when men would no longer be able to enjoy those "sacred rights which free men cherish and free governments are established to maintain and secure."

Judge Kavanaugh, in the concluding argument, demonstrated that the private schools had complied with all state regulations and that this law was not in the nature of regulation but of destruction. He emphasized that it deprived the institutions of valuable property rights without due process of law.

Within three months the Supreme Court rendered its decision, unanimously holding that the Oregon law was unconstitutional. Justice McReynolds, writing for the court, stated on June 1, 1925:

> Under the doctrine of *Meyer v. Nebraska,* 262 U.S. 390, we think it entirely plain that the act of 1922 unreasonably interferes with the liberty of parents and guardians to direct the upbringing and education of children under their control. As often heretofore pointed out, rights guaranteed by the Constitution may not be abridged by legislation which has no reasonable relation to some purpose within the competency of the state. The fundamental theory of liberty upon which all governments in this Union repose excludes any general power of the state to standardize its children by forcing them to accept instruction from public teachers only. The child is not the mere creature of the state; those who nurture him and direct his destiny have the right coupled with the high duty, to recognize and prepare him for additional obligations. [268 U.S. 534]

Continuing, he pointed out that the schools had been deprived of their property without due process of law. In this connection, Justice McReynolds observed that the appellee corporations ". . . have business and property for which they claim protection. These are threatened with destruction through the unwarranted compulsion which appellants are exercising over present and prospective patrons of their schools. And this Court has gone very far to protect against loss threatened by such action" (268 U.S. 535).

It is significant to observe that the Supreme Court's decision rested not merely on the property right of the plaintiff corporations. The most important aspect of this decision is the recognition and application of the right of parents to control the education of their children. From the beginning of the controversy to the final decision, this was the predominant argument of those opposing the Oregon school law. From the first arguments filed with the secretary of the state of Oregon challenging the initiative measure, up to and including the final oral argument, reference was constantly made to the proposition that the fundamental freedom at stake was the inalienable right of parents to oversee their children's education.

Reaction and influence. Within a few days, 490 major editorials were published in 44 states commenting favorably on the decision. Nor was this attitude sectional. The attitude of the press in the South, where the Klan had its origin and where Masonry was strong, was uniformly laudatory.

The articulation of the principle of the parental right in education has had a strong influence on the growth of the nonpublic school system in this country and has been cited in many countries throughout the world in defense of educational freedom. Pius XI in the encyclical *Christian Education of Youth* gave explicit approval to the Supreme Court's decision. It had more than a little influence on the formulation of Article 26(3) of the United Nations' Declaration of Human Rights providing that: "Parents have a prior right to choose the kind of education that shall be given to their children."

Bibliography: *Oregon School Cases: Complete Record* (Baltimore 1925). N. G. MCCLUSKEY, *Catholic Viewpoint on Education* (Garden City 1959). J. T. TINNELLY, "The Right to Educate: The Role of Parents, Church, State," *National Catholic Education Association Bulletin* 55 (1958) 35–46. L. PFEFFER, *Church, State and Freedom* (Boston 1953) 510–519. P. G. KAUPER, *Civil Liberties and the Constitution* (Ann Arbor 1962). J. C. BRUNNER *A Critical Analysis of the Development of Arguments Against Nonpublic Schools from the Oregon School Case to 1960* (Washington 1960). C. F. ZOLLMANN, *American Church Law* (St. Paul 1933).

[G. E. REED]

O'REILLY, BERNARD

Second bishop of Hartford, Conn.; b. Columkille, County Longford, Ireland, 1803; d. at sea, Jan. 23, 1856.

He studied at Grand Seminaire, Montreal, Canada, and St. Mary's College, Baltimore, Md., before his ordination in October of 1831. He did parish work in Brooklyn and Rochester, N.Y., until 1847, when he became vicar-general of the new Diocese of Buffalo, N.Y. In 1850 he was named to succeed William Tyler as bishop of Hartford. After his consecration at Rochester on November 10, the new bishop concentrated his efforts on obtaining more clergy for a territory served by only seven priests and five churches. In 1851 he brought the Sisters of Mercy into his diocese and courageously protected them from attack by a Know-Nothing mob. He went to Dublin, Ireland, the following year and brought back a number of priests. During his episcopate, he provided the diocese with 34 new churches, 14 new schools, three orphan asylums, and St. Mary's Seminary, Providence, R.I., which he founded in 1851. It was on a trip to Europe to seek the help of the Brothers of the Christian Schools that O'Reilly was drowned, when his ship, the *Pacific,* sank with all aboard.

[J. L. MORRISON]

O'REILLY, EDMUND

Archbishop of Armagh; b. Dublin, 1606; d. Saumur, France, March 1669. O'Reilly was educated and ordained (1629) in Dublin, where he also did parish work. In 1633 he went to the Louvain, where he studied under the Jesuits and Franciscans before his appointment as prefect of Irish secular priests and seminarians resident at the Louvain. O'Reilly returned to Ireland in 1641. He supported the Irish rebellion, serving as governor of Wicklow (1642). Archbishop Thomas Fleming of Dublin appointed him vicar-general and apostolic administrator (1642–48) while Fleming was at Kilkenny, seat of the Catholic Confederation. O'Reilly's sympathies were with the independence faction of the rebels, and he opposed any truce with the royalist James Butler, Marquis of Ormond, who sought Irish aid against the English parliamentary forces. Fleming replaced O'Reilly as vicar-general in 1649 but restored him in 1650. In 1653 O'Reilly was arrested, imprisoned, and charged with a murder that had occurred while he was governor of Wicklow. He was tried (Sept. 6–7, 1654), found guilty, and pardoned; finally, he left Ireland. O'Reilly fled to Lille, where he received his appointment as archbishop of Armagh, although he did not receive the pallium until 1657. He attempted to return to Ireland by way of London, but fearing possible arrest in England, O'Reilly returned to France. It was not until 1659 that he reached Ireland, where he remained until the Stuart restoration (1661). The Spanish ambassador in London accused O'Reilly of anti-Stuart activities, and for this Pope Alexander VII recalled the primate to Rome (1661–65), where he appears to have vindicated himself. In 1665 O'Reilly visited Ireland and attended the national synod held in Dublin (1666). His opposition to the pro-English activities and remonstrance of Father Peter WALSH angered Ormond, who imprisoned the primate for three months. O'Reilly, exiled once again, went to France, where he died.

Bibliography: A. F. POLLARD, *The Dictionary of National Biography from the Earliest Times to 1900*, 14:1140–41. R. BELLINGS, *History of the Irish Confederation and the War in Ireland. 1641–1649*, ed. J. T. GILBERT, 7 v. (Dublin 1882–91). E. CURTIS, *A History of Ireland* (6th ed. New York 1951). R. BAGWELL *Ireland under the Stuarts*, 3 v. (London 1909–16).

[P. S. MCGARRY]

OREMUS

Latin for "Let us pray." In the Roman rite it is commonly used by the officiating minister to invite the attention of the faithful to certain prayers of the Eucharist and the Liturgy of the Hours (e.g., the Collect, the Lord's Prayer), and other liturgical functions. Ordinarily in the Roman rite, the prayer of the officiating minister follows immediately upon the *Oremus;* and this rule is prescribed by the earlier Roman ordinals, such as the *Ordo Romanus I* (ed. M. Andrieu, no.53). Traditionally on Good Friday, the celebrant adds to the Oremus a clause specifying the intention for which he invites prayer. The *Oremus* was followed by *Flectamus genua* (Let us kneel) and a period of silent prayer. *Levate* (Rise) was then pronounced, and the celebrant recited his prayer in the name of all.

Bibliography: J. A. JUNGMANN, *The Mass of the Roman Rite,* tr. F. BRUNNER, 2 v. (New York 1951–55) 1:366–370. A. FORTESCUE, *The Mass* (New York 1912) 247–248.

[E. J. GRATSCH/EDS.]

ORGAN, LITURGICAL USE OF

While ancient writers clearly indicate that the organ played an important part in the ceremonial life of the people of the ancient world, little is known about the early form of the organ prior to the instrument known as the hydraulus, generally attributed to the Greek engineer Ctesibius, active in Alexandria *c.* 250 B.C. The organ pipe itself and a primitive form of wind-chest, in which the flow of air from the common supply to the pipes was controlled by a system of wooden slides, was known much earlier; the unique feature of the hydraulus was the system of maintaining steady wind through the use of hydraulic pressure. For its time the hydraulus was an

"Salve Regina," 1512, organ music from "Tabularuren etlicher Lobgesang," by Arnolt Schlick.

ingenious and almost perfect device. Complete details of its construction are given by Vitruvius (A.D. 60) and Hero of Alexandria (A.D. 120). Although the organ continued to increase in size during the first few centuries of the Christian era, we know very little else about the organ of this period except that its outstanding feature seems to have been its loudness. St. Jerome (400) mentions an organ in Jerusalem so loud that it could be heard nearly a mile away at the Mt. of Olives. By the 4th century, wind was being supplied by bellows. In 951 a very large organ was built for Bishop Elphege in the cathedral at Winchester. With its 400 pipes of bronze, 26 bellows, and two sets of 20 keys, each key controlling ten pipes, it is reputed to have taken 70 men to maintain the wind supply and two organists to play it.

Although it is not known exactly when the organ was first used for religious purposes, the writings of St. Julian of Toledo, a Spanish bishop, indicate that it was in common use in the churches of Spain by the year 450. We know that in the 7th century Pope St. Vitalian (666) introduced the organ in Rome in order to improve the singing of the congregation. As an aid to the introduction of Roman Rite into the churches of France, Pepin (714–768), the father of Charlemagne, ordered an organ from the Byzantine emperor Constantine Copronymus and had it installed in the church of St. Corneille at Compiègne (757). Charlemagne also received a similar instrument from the Eastern Emperor in the year 812, and a copy of the instrument at Compiègne placed at Aix-la-Chapelle *c.* 811 is reputed to have been the first organ in

Germany. Apparently the art of making and using organs developed rapidly in Germany in the latter half of the 9th century, for in the year 880 Pope John VIII requested Anno, Bishop of Friesingen, to send him a good organ and, along with it, a competent player to instruct Romans in the art.

Although the organ has never been prescribed for use in the Roman Catholic Church by canon law, it has apparently been used in the Church consistently since the 9th century. By the 13th century the organ was certainly in general use throughout the Latin Church and thus was deeply involved in the development of the musical and liturgical tradition of the Church. Many of the important liturgical books refer to the organ frequently, and the fact that, though never specifically prescribed, it is assumed to be present and an important aid to the liturgy is seen by the frequent instructions of the Church that direct that it shall be played at specific times. The high esteem in which the Church holds the organ is perhaps best summarized in the following excerpt from Vatican Council II: "The pipe organ adds a wonderful splendor to the Church's ceremonies, and powerfully lifts up men's mind to God and to higher things."

Bibliography: M. PRAETORIUS, *Syntagma musicum,* 3 v. (v.1 Wittenberg 1614–15; v.2, 3 Wolfenbüttel 1619), fac. ed. by W. Gurlitt (Kassel 1959–). M. MERSENNE, *Harmonie universelle,* 2 v. in 3 (Paris 1636–37), Eng. tr. R. E. CHAPMAN (The Hague 1957) v.3. F. BÉDOS DE CELLES, *L'Art du facteur d'orgues,* 4 pts. in 2 v. (Paris 1766–78) fac. ed. by C. MAHRENHOLZ, 4 v. (Kassel 1934–36). W. ELLERHORST, *Handbuch der Orgelkunde* (Einsiedeln 1936). W. L. SUMMER, *The Organ: Its Evolution, Principles of Construction and Use* (3d ed. London 1962). W. H. BARNES, *The Contemporary American Organ* (7th ed. Glen Rock, N.J. 1959). C. SACHS *The History of Musical Instruments* (New York 1940). D. J. TARRANT et al., eds., *Proceedings: Symposium Liturgy and Architecture* (Clarke College, Dubuque, Iowa 1964). J. E. BLANTON, *The Organ in Church Design* (Albany, Tex. 1957). B. SONNAILLON, *King of Instruments: A History of the Organ* (New York 1985). P. WILLIAMS, *The Organ in Western Culture, 750–1250* (Cambridge 1993).

[L. I. PHELPS/EDS.]

ORGANICISM

In general, organicism refers to the theory that everything is essentially organic, vital, dynamic, or processlike in character. More specifically, in medicine, organicism suggests that each bodily organ has its own dynamic unity, and consequently every disease is associated with a structural lesion of the organ. In biology, organicism states that the individual dynamic system running through the entire organ is equivalent to the life principle. The organicistic theory is meant to serve as a mediator between vitalism on one hand and MECHANISM on the other. Defenders of organicism insist that LIFE in general and all the specific life processes are manifestations of a basic function or operation made possible only because of the autonomous organization of the whole system. Negatively expressed, the individual components of the living system cannot explain life.

In social thought, organicism suggests that it is most fruitful to interpret societies, large and small, as individual, living, grouplike entities. Again the most significant feature of these organic groups is their dynamic, vital, processlike structure. A social group must be viewed as an intermingling process of ideas, beliefs, goals, drives, and wants. Like every other living being, a society goes through the processes of birth, growth, death, and decay. Each social entity has its own peculiar moods, patterns, likes, dislikes, passions, and attitudes.

Concerning theological matters, the organicists argue that all religious truths and beliefs must be seen as living, changing, and relative to the problems of the time. That is, while religious convictions grow and change, the more important ideas remain only relatively stable and of greater or lesser importance depending on the needs of the people and the entire social situation.

In contemporary philosophy, the theory of organicism has undergone rigid development and detailed application in the writings of A. N. WHITEHEAD. The impact of this concept on Whitehead's thinking can be seen in the fact that the word process plays a key role in the title and the development of his work *Process and Reality,* in which he sets out to explain the "philosophy of organicism." Many of the basic terms in his philosophy, such as experience, creativity, actual entity, concrescence, prehension, event, and ingression are indicative of the importance that the concept of organic process has in his philosophy.

Whitehead argues that an organicistic interpretation will give a clearer understanding of God, man, and the universe in general and will aid in repudiating some of the more serious contemporary philosophic inadequacies. Specifically, a philosophy of organicism will rekindle trust in speculative philosophy, help question the belief that language is an adequate expression of thought, enable man to see the errors in faculty psychology, encourage criticism of the subject–predicate form of expression, and aid in repudiating sensationalism as well as the Kantian idea that the world is a construct.

Bibliography: A. N. WHITEHEAD, *Process and Reality* (New York 1929).

[M. J. FAIRBANKS]

ORIGEN AND ORIGENISM

A distinction must be made between the life and teachings of Origen himself and the teachings, in part not strictly his, ascribed to him by later followers and opponents. Hence the first part of this article deals with Origen himself and the second with the influence of his teachings and of doctrines ascribed to him in the centuries following his death.

Origen

Surnamed Adamantius (man of steel or diamond), Origen was the principal theologian of the early Greek Church; b. probably Alexandria, 184 or 185; d. probably Tyre, 253 or 254.

Life. The main details of Origen's life are preserved in a panegyric by St. Gregory Thaumaturgus, in Eusebius of Caesarea (*Hist. eccl.* 6), and in several writings of St. Jerome. Of a Christian family, the oldest of seven children, Origen was taught profane and sacred literature by his father, LEONIDES, and may have been a student under CLEMENT OF ALEXANDRIA. Under Septimius Severus in 202 Leonides was decapitated as a martyr, but Origen, despite his desire for martyrdom, continued his studies; at 18 he opened a school of grammar to support his family. Demetrius, Bishop of Alexandria, entrusted him with the instruction of catechumens, and he courageously assisted many of his students who were martyred. He gave up his grammar school to concentrate on CATECHESIS and devoted himself to an austere life. With more zeal than wisdom he took Mt 19.12 literally and mutilated himself.

Entrusting his colleague Heraclas with the catechumens, Origen gradually gave his main attention to the Christian formation of the more advanced group; and in order to answer the objections of learned pagans and heretics, as well as for direction in the study of the Scriptures, he followed courses in philosophy given by Ammonius Saccas, the father of NEOPLATONISM. Porphyry witnesses this in his *Contra Christianos,* cited by Eusebius. But there is still some doubt whether it is the Christian Origen whom Porphyry calls a disciple of Ammonius Saccas in his *Life of Plotinus* and whom Proclus cites.

Origen did acquire a considerable philosophical education, which he utilized in his teaching. He began to write between 215 and 220, aided by a rich convert named Ambrose, who furnished him with secretaries and copyists; the *Peri Archon* was one of his first books. He also journeyed to Rome and to Arabia (Jordan) at the invitation of the governor. He left Alexandria in 215 during the reprisals visited on the city by Emperor Caracalla and apparently spent two years in hiding at CAESAREA IN CAP-

Origen. (©Bettmann/CORBIS)

PADOCIA, living at the expense of the virgin Juliana (Palladius, *Hist. Laus.* 64); he then visited Palestine, where Bps. Theoctistus of Caesarea and Alexander of Jerusalem invited him to preach, though he was still a layman. This action elicited the protest of his own bishop, Demetrius of Alexandria. Mammaea, the mother of the Emperor, had him sojourn in Antioch *c.* 224 to inform her about the Christian religion. Called to Greece in 230 for a discussion with heretics, he passed through Palestine and was ordained a priest by Bishop Theoctistus. On his return to Alexandria he was banished by Bishop Demetrius, who called two synods to censure his ordination as illicit.

Leaving his catechetical school to Heraclas, Origen began to teach at the school of CAESAREA IN PALESTINE (231 to 233), where one of his disciples was GREGORY THAUMATURGUS, who spent five years with him and wrote a panegyric (*On Gratitude to Origen*) in which he described Origen's program and pedagogical method. Origen preached frequently, and only toward the end of his life were his homilies, with his permission, taken down by stenographers and published. He also composed commentaries on the Scriptures and wrote his *Contra Celsum.* He journeyed to Arabia to bring Bp. BERYLLUS OF BOSTRA back to orthodoxy and to combat the Thnetopsychites, the sect that proclaimed the mortality of the soul before the Resurrection. It was probably there that he engaged in a dialogue with Heraclides, who was accused of MODALISM, the verbatim report of which was discovered in Egypt in 1941. He spent some time in Cappadocia with his disciple FIRMILIAN OF CAESAREA, stopped at Nicomedia and wrote a *Response* to JULIUS AFRICANUS, and was in Athens for several months in 240. The persecution of DECIUS put an end to his multifarious activities in 250, when he was imprisoned and tortured; but he confessed the faith with fortitude. He was cruelly kept alive in the hope that he could be forced to apostatize, but on the death of the Emperor he was set free. His health was broken, however, and he died at 69. His grave was still visible in the cathedral of Tyre during the 13th century.

Writings. A man of virtue and genius with prodigious capacity for work, Origen left a large corpus of writings of which only part has been preserved in Greek or in the Latin versions by RUFINUS OF AQUILEIA, JEROME, and others. The question of the exactitude of the translations, the authenticity of numerous fragments preserved in exegetical CATENAE, and citations in later writers have given rise to many literary problems. The most trustworthy quotations are preserved in the *Apologia* of PAMPHILUS of Caesarea and the *Philocalia of Origen,* the latter a selection of his thoughts published by SS. BASIL and GREGORY OF NAZIANZUS.

Scriptural Exegesis. Origen's ambition was to be an interpreter of the Scriptures. The majority of his works are exegetical, and the Bible holds a principal place in all his writings. To furnish Christians with a valid text of the Scriptures in their discussions with the Jews, he constructed his *Hexapla* of the Old Testament, a work composed in six columns containing the Hebrew text both in Hebrew and in Greek characters and the Greek versions of Aquila, Symmachus, the SEPTUAGINT, and Theodotion, in which he uses diacritical marks to indicate divergences in readings. For certain OT books he added three further translations and, in his *Tetrapla,* probably edited four versions without the Hebrew. Only fragments of this gigantic labor remain. In his letter to Julius Africanus he discusses the canonicity of the story of Susanna.

Kinds of Exegetical Works. Origen's exegetical works are of three kinds. (1) Scientific commentaries, of which four have been partially preserved: on John (in Greek), Matthew (in Greek and an anonymous Latin version), the Song of Songs, and the Epistle to the Romans (in Latin by Rufinus). Numerous fragments of his on Genesis, the Psalms, Lamentations, the Major and Minor Prophets, and the Pauline Epistles also have survived. (2) His homilies preached at Caesarea, Jerusalem, Athens, and elsewhere include those on Genesis, Exodus, Leviticus, Numbers, Joshua, Judges, and 1 Samuel (in the Latin

version by Rufinus); on the Song of Songs, Isaiah, Jeremiah, Ezekiel, and St. Luke (in Jerome's translation); a homily in Greek on the Pythoness of Endor; 20 homilies in Greek on Jeremiah, the majority translated by Jerome; and numerous fragments. (3) Finally, the scholia, or short exegetical notes, now lost in the mass of fragments. The most complete list of his works, without being exhaustive, however, was made by Jerome in his *Letter to Paula* (*Epist.* 33), which was omitted in many manuscripts and was unknown to earlier editors of Jerome's letters. It was rediscovered *c.* 1845.

Method of Exegesis. Origen's literary, critical, grammatical, and historical explanations of scriptural passages are innumerable, but the literal sense of a text is the basis for his spiritual interpretation; he believed in the historicity of a pericope even when he gave it an allegorical interpretation. Sometimes, however, he admitted that a "corporeal" meaning was nonexistent. At times Origen dealt with figurative or anthropomorphic passages and referred to the "materiality" of a metaphor as the literal meaning, in contradistinction to the modern practice of considering the literal meaning to be the sense intended by the original author. Sometimes he dealt with passages that were incoherent in the Greek text or that posed difficult exegetical problems of which he was fully aware but did not always have the means of resolving. Occasionally, he failed to consider the literal, literary, psychological, or historical context or displayed an exaggerated subtlety; but these instances are rare in relation to the whole of his works.

The literal sense, according to Origen, was not the reason for which the Holy Spirit had given the Scriptures to the Christians. The juridical and ceremonial prescriptions of the Law had been abolished by Christ, and the historical narratives in themselves are worthless for the spiritual director and pastor. The true sense willed by the Holy Spirit is the spiritual sense, which Origen found in the New Testament and earlier tradition and of which he is the great proponent.

Christ is the center of history. The Old Testament is revelation only insofar as it is a prophecy related to Christ. In each of the OT characters, narratives, and prescriptions, the interpreter will find the image of Christ or of the Church, the realities of the New Covenant, and particularly the Sacraments. The first coming of Christ still retains its prophetic character; it brought about an eschatological accomplishment that is as yet only incompletely possessed, "as in a mirror or an enigma," but the desire to possess it completely is felt by the Christian. The "gospel in time" is identical in substance (*hypostasis*) with the "eternal gospel" of beatitude; it only differs by reason of *epinoia,* or the imperfect manner in which men contemplate and possess it.

It is thus that Origen expresses the essential fact of Christian sacramentalism. The spiritual sense, then, foreshadows future blessings and determines for the faithful their comportment in the interval between the two *parousiai,* or comings, of Christ and brings them celestial gifts according to the measure of their spiritual ascension or development. In this vision of the world on two planes—that of symbol and that of mystery, which he borrowed from Platonism—Origen describes the sacramentalism of the New Covenant and the symbolism essential to any true knowledge of God.

Hardly understood by historians between the Renaissance and modern times, this type of exegesis is, except for certain bizarre developments and doubtful procedures, an essential element of Christian teaching. But Origen, along with the majority of Fathers, may be criticized on two points. Although they were correct in concluding that the Holy Spirit is the author of Scripture, they did not pay sufficient attention to the human author; accordingly, they could not resolve the difficulties arising on this score, although Origen himself was fully aware of them. In his opinion it did not become the Divine Dignity to have dictated even one useless word; hence under the most insignificant detail or pleonasm some intention of the Holy Spirit had to be discovered. It is thus that the artificiality of certain particular interpretations arose, despite the profundity or beauty of a commentary as a whole. They are frequently introduced by an etymology or an arithmetic symbolism, a procedure that is Biblical as well as Hellenic in origin. Origen's spiritual exegesis forms a complex whole; but from the schema outlined above, one can see that other influences—rabbinical, apocalyptic, Philonian, Hellenic, and Gnostic—were operative.

Spirituality. Origen's spiritual teaching, everywhere present in his exegesis, makes him the creator of a spiritual theology. Mystical theology occupies a large place in his commentaries on John and on the Song of Songs; but in his later works, written as a priest, he was more attentive to the practical aspects of the Christian life than he was in those written in Alexandria. The *Exhortation to Martyrdom,* addressed to Ambrosius during the persecution of Emperor Maximinus the Thracian, betrays one of the constants in the life of Origen, the spirituality of martyrdom. The *Treatise on Prayer,* which is preserved in Greek, contains, among other things, the first methodical explanation of the Our Father.

The moral and ascetical doctrine of Origen is worthy of careful study, for it can render service in the attempt to clarify the origins of MONASTICISM. A thesis regarding spiritual combat pervades his ANTHROPOLOGY and his ANGELOLOGY: the soul, the seat of free will and of the

personality, is fought over by the spirit (*pneuma, spiritus,* including grace and participation of the Holy Spirit) and the flesh. The soul is divided into a superior part, the organ of contemplation and virtue, which is called intelligence (*nous, mens*) or the dominant faculty (*hēgemonikon, principale cordis*), and an inferior part, which corresponds in a certain measure to concupiscence. In this battle man is solicited by both good and evil angels to follow Christ or Satan.

On many points Origen possessed an integral doctrine, which is not outlined in systematic fashion but is dispersed at the hazard of his exegesis: on martyrdom, virginity and chastity, mortification, etc. Virtues are the names (*epinoiai*) given to Christ and identified with him as pertaining to His very substance. He who possesses them participates in the divine nature. But human beings only receive them through the humanity of Christ, which is His ''Shadow''; here below man has only the ''shadows'' of virtue.

Mysticism and Mystery. Many of the great themes of mystical literature go back to Origen. In his commentary on the Song of Songs; instead of the traditional, ecclesial interpretation given to this allegory, he sees the soul of the Christian as the spouse of Christ and closely relates the individual with the collectivity of Christ's body, the Church. The Ascent of the Mountain prefigures a spiritual ascension through prayer and virtue: as on Mt. Thabor the divinity of Christ appeared more and more in His transfigured humanity.

In order for the Incarnation to produce its effects in an individual, Jesus has to be born in him by Baptism and grow there, as He will if the subject gives Him the opportunity by leading a virtuous life. Among those making progress five spiritual senses develop: sight, which uncovers divine realities; hearing, which lets the words of God be heard when He reveals the meaning of the Scriptures interiorly to the soul; touch, which allows one to examine the flesh of the Word; smell and taste, which express the delicacies of knowledge—a connaturality that increases with the ascension of a soul dedicated to perfecting its immediate knowledge of the divine. Such is the object of the charism of Wisdom, of which one effect is spiritual DISCERNMENT. The source of this connaturality is in the creation of the soul according to the IMAGE OF GOD, who is the Word; only the similar can know the similar.

The object of this knowledge is Mystery: the mysteries of visible and invisible realities, or of the relations in the Trinity, all of which are recapitulated in the person of the Son, the Image of the Father, containing the intelligible world, insofar as wisdom is concerned, the ideas and reasons for all things. Perceived in this light, which the divine Persons freely communicate, mystery is a nourishment, transforming the soul to the true nature of mystery, which is supernatural; it is a wine rejoicing in a "sober drunkenness," which exalts conscience and liberty. For understanding, which is an encounter of two liberties, includes at once passivity and activity: divine grace does not lay hold to man despite himself, in an ecstasy that would be a kind of divine folly; inconscience or lack of understanding is a sign of diabolic possession.

Knowledge is given in meditation on Scripture and requires the renouncement of sin and the world, as well as purity of heart. Faith is its necessary principle; but with faith the object becomes present; it is seen and touched without an intermediary: to comprehend and to love are confounded in union. The "esotericism" with which Origen is often reproached is common to all the mystics: it is not necessary to give someone something he can comprehend; otherwise revelation will be useless to him and could even prove to be an evil. To accuse him of spiritual snobbishness, one would have to ignore the continual exhortations contained in his homilies urging all Christians to make progress in their spiritual knowledge. It is necessary to call attention likewise to the profoundly affective devotion Origen has for the person of Christ, which is so similar to that of St. BERNARD OF CLAIRVAUX. Evidence of his own personal mystical experience is rare, for Origen speaks little of himself; but it is sufficiently explicit.

Speculative Theology. Origen's speculation, like his spiritual doctrine, is inseparable from his exegesis. He ignores distinctions into branches or categories in the knowledge of God. For this his commentaries and homilies are the sources, particularly his masterpiece, the *Commentary on John;* then the tract *On the Resurrection,* and the *Stromateis,* of which we have but fragments; the *Treatise on First Principles* (*Peri Archon*); and finally his last work, which is entirely preserved in Greek, the *Contra Celsum,* a vast, apologetic tract that refutes step by step the *True Discourse* of the philosopher Celsus. This discourse of Celsus was the most serious attack in the intellectual realm that Christianity had ever experienced; it was considered still pertinent by the freethinkers of the 19th century who discovered in it so many of their anti-Christian arguments. In Origen's rebuttal the essential proof for the divinity of Christianity is the profundity and multitude of the moral conversions it brought about.

Fidelity. The fidelity of Origen to the rule of faith as known in his day cannot be doubted; and if he is occasionally mistaken in his pursuits, it is on points that were clarified only later. But his work gives a handle to incomprehensions or obtuseness, for it is scarcely systematic, not even in the *Peri Archon.* Docile most frequently to the scriptural text on which he is commenting, he tries to

attain the unknowable mystery by many different approaches, some of them antithetic. This is why he should not be studied except in the totality of his work; one cannot draw a definite conclusion from a text isolated from the rest of his writings. His is a theology of research, modestly making use of hypotheses, suppositions, attempted explanations; and one is not fair to Origen if he transforms these into affirmations of dogmas of the faith.

Origen can be explained by the heresies he combats. Facing the Marcionites he sustains both the goodness of God the Creator, who is one with the Father of Jesus, and the agreement of the two Testaments, as well as the value of the Old Testament. Against the Valentinians he defends FREE WILL and personal responsibility, the refusal of recognition of a PREDESTINATION by nature. Against the Modalists he defends the personality of the LOGOS; and against the Adoptionists, His eternal GENERATION. Against the Docetists, he defends the true humanity of Christ as a condition for the Redemption. Against anthropomorphic tendencies, CHILIASM, and the literalists in the Church he defends the spirituality of God, the soul, and final beatitude, as well as the abolition of the Jewish law by Christ. One cannot reproach him for not having foreseen later heresies, as his detractors try to do; or for employing with an orthodox intention—as can be proved from other passages in his works—formulas that later came to have a heterodox sense.

The philosophy of Origen underlying his doctrines and his vocabulary is Middle PLATONISM, a mystical Platonism mixed with much STOICISM and some ARISTOTELIANISM. He makes use of it as a theologian, using it largely with a Christian end in view. Its defects have often been exaggerated in unconscious imitation of Protestant tendencies or a too scholastic mentality.

Origen's Theology. Theology, in almost all its divisions, made considerable progress with Origen, even if the results were not always perfect. His conception of the Trinity sought to safeguard the divine "monarchy" and to avoid modalist and adoptionist solutions. Thus in God he insists on a hierarchy of origin and speaks of the Father, because He is Father, as the source of divinity; hence He is the source of the divine nature that He shares with the other two Persons without diminution.

Origen refuses to consider the *probolē* (*prolatio*) of the Valentinians, who suppose a division of the divine substance similar to the process of human and animal generation; the Son and the Holy Spirit do not come forth from the bosom of the Father. The Trinitarian vocabulary was as yet not precise, and Origen did not always clearly distinguish the hierarchy of origin from the hierarchy of power; thence arose a SUBORDINATIONISM that betrays a theological insufficiency and not a dogmatic position.

The Son. Engendered from all eternity, mediator between God and the world, the Son possesses multiple *epinoiai* or names: His diverse scriptural titles that the Valentinians dissected into different Eons but that connote for Origen the relations of the Son with the world and with men. They have a real foundation in the simplicity of His hypostasis. The principal of these is Wisdom, who embraces the intelligible world of the principles of all beings (and here, Platonic ''forms'' are confounded with Stoic ''reasons''), and is the model for creation. Then comes the Word (*Logos*), who gives expression to this Wisdom and is the agent of Creation; then a great number of others, viz, virtues and diverse functions of the Son in the Redemption and in man's spiritual progress.

The union of the Son with human nature is anterior to the Incarnation. According to the Origenian hypothesis, His soul had been created with the preexistent intelligences. Finding itself ''under the form of God'' by its union with the Word, His soul was the spouse of the preexistent Church, that is to say, of the collectivity of intelligent being. It alone escaped the cosmic fall. The Son, agent of the theophanies of the Old Testament, appears in His soul, which has retained its primitive angelico-human state; thus He is an angel among angels, a man among men. For love of his fallen spouse, the soul of Christ took flesh in Mary, and the Word followed it in the KENOSIS, remaining mysteriously in the bosom of the Father, His proper ''place.'' He revealed the divine to man, expressing it in a human being.

On the cross Christ was delivered to diabolic powers as a ransom according to the scriptural image of the Redemption that Origen exploits with many other images. He descended into hell to deliver the captive souls whom He carried with Him in the Ascension. The lack of a precise concept of person saves this doctrine from NESTORIANISM, for in many of his other passages Origen affirms the equivalent of the HYPOSTATIC UNION and the COMMUNICATION OF IDIOMS. Against the Gnostics, Origen defended the reality of the flesh of Jesus, who, according to quite clear statements, ''subsists in glory.''

The Holy Spirit. The Holy Spirit proceeds from the Father through the Son, who communicates to Him His *epinoiai.* He is the Sanctifier and constitutes the ''material'' of the charisms which corresponds to our ''actual graces.'' But His role as inspirer of Scripture is not clearly distinguished from that of the Son.

Spirits and Man. Origen's angelology and demonology are strongly developed: good and evil angels are guardians of nations, provinces, dioceses, individuals; they are appointed to diverse parts of nature, to virtues or to vices. The stars, animated and intelligent, are not agents of man's destiny, which depends on grace and free will, but constitute the signs that the angels alone can read. The heavens are the Bible of the angels.

Man, like the angels, has been created according to the image of God, the Word. This participation in the existence and divinity of the Father and in the filiation and rationality of the Son, understood in a supernatural (sanctifying grace) rather than in a natural sense, to employ modern distinctions, is not destroyed by sin but obscured by diabolic and bestial images that the Redeemer alone can remove.

Origen often speculates on the nature of the risen body according to 1 Cor 15.35–44; a material substance, always fluent, cannot determine the identity of the body, made stable by a corporeal form (Platonism) or a seminal reason (Stoicism), the latter, present in the earthly body, germinating to endow the body with glory.

Mary, the Church, and the Sacraments. Describing Mary as the THEOTOKOS, according to the testimony of Socrates (*Hist. eccl.* 7.32), Origen is the first theologian to affirm clearly her perpetual virginity. Even though he did not believe her to be without fault, he sees in her a great spiritual type. He is very attentive to the mystical aspects of the Church rather than to its visible aspects, without, however, losing sight of them. He possessed a doctrine for Baptism, the Eucharist, Penance, Orders, and Matrimony. His Platonic and realistic notion of symbolism expresses very well the identity in substance between the ''temporal'' gospel and the ''eternal gospel'' mentioned above. But the essential ''sacrament'' for him is Scripture, an incarnation of the Logos in the written word, analogous to the flesh, preparing or announcing the unique Incarnation.

Origenism

The current of thought called Origenism is far from representing the complete heritage of the master: it comes from certain of his speculations separated from the whole, deprived of their hypothetical and antithetical character, and made into a system by posterity. The substance of Origen's theology nourished the Fathers of the 4th century and has become through them the anonymous common good of Christian thought.

The Peri Archon. These speculations are found particularly in the *Peri Archon,* or *Treatise on the First Principles,* one of his earliest works, written at Alexandria, and the cause of his posthumous difficulties. This book seems to be composed of two tracts placed end to end, following the same plan: Trinity, rational creatures, and the world; then, of an appendix on Scripture and a résumé. He desires to oppose to the ''principles'' of MARCION those of the Church. It seems to have originated in the oral teaching of Origen, which Gregory Thaumaturgus describes as following the Socratic manner: a discussion of opposing opinions and manners of research rather than a *summa theologica.* It is difficult to gauge how far Origen is involved in the opinions he discusses, which are in themselves at times contradictory.

The preface sets out the various matters that form part of the rule of faith; beyond them, the author engages in research with its risks and perils, making use of Scripture, reason, and his philosophic erudition. Of this work the only sections now available in Greek are the chapters on free will and on Scripture that are published in the *Philocalia.* The whole treatise is preserved in a Latin version made by Rufinus; but his adaptations are the subject of diverse judgments on the part of critics who consider them according to their evaluation of Origen. A number of Greek and Latin fragments are available, coming for the most part from decided adversaries of Origen, such as Jerome and Justinian. P. Koetschau, in his edition for the Berlin Corpus (*Die griechischen Christlichen Schriftsteller der ersten drei Jahrhunderte*), has added to the confusion by inserting in the text of Rufinus, as if he had consciously omitted them, the *Testimonia* that were collected in relation to Origenism or to the heresies that have no indisputable connection with Origen. Thus this edition must be used with caution.

The Preexistence of Souls. The preexistence of souls, including that of Christ, is a favorite hypothesis of Origen: in the beginning God created pure intelligences (*noes*), all equal, which were vested with ethereal bodies, since the Trinity alone is incorporeal; these spent their being in contemplation of God. All except that of Christ grew cold in their fervor and became souls (*psychē,* or soul; the word is derived by Origen from *psychos,* cold). The degree of their fall differentiated them into angels, men, and demons, categories that do not seem to be separated by impassable limits. God then created the sensible world and the grosser bodies to furnish men with a means for redemption. This Platonic doctrine offered Origen too easy a means of answering the Valentinian theory concerning the nature of souls and the Marcionite accusation of injustice on the part of the Creator by attributing the diversity of conditions among angels, men, and devils to free will and an original choice.

The Apocatastasis. It is not possible to prove that Origen's doctrine concerning the *APOCATASTASIS* or universal restoration at the end of time is heretical. It was drawn from Pauline texts and is not pantheistic. It does not entail the destruction of individual personalities, as the reproaches made by Origen to the Stoic final conflagration demonstrate. No precise text of his holds the salvation of the devil; in fact he expressly protested against

this idea in a letter to friends in Alexandria that is mentioned by both Jerome and Rufinus; and his speculations are susceptible of two interpretations. He certainly preferred to speak of purgatory, of a baptism of eschatological fire, of which he is one of the earliest proponents, rather than of the eternity of punishment. His reserve manifested a certain constraint, but one can affirm no more, and the rule of faith at the time did not yet have defined limits.

A categorical assertion of Origen regarding the *apocatastasis* would contradict his hypothesis of the perpetual return of things, which at times he presupposes, even when he criticizes the idea among the Stoics. It is certainly irreconcilable with one of his master ideas, namely, free will. It was no more than a great hope on his part.

Other Errors. Other errors imputed to Origen are contradicted by indisputable citations of his authentic works. His speculations concerning the divine *henad* have been exaggerated in a pantheistic sense, being unmindful of the Christian context that modifies them. Jerome thought he discovered in the *Peri Archon* the final disappearance of the "risen" bodies that were absorbed in this *henad* or unity. But this notion is not in the Greek texts or in Rufinus's translations; nor is it attested by METHODIUS OF OLYMPUS, who read this book and described Origen's conception of the glorious bodies, which he attacked vehemently.

According to Epiphanius of Constantia, Origen said that the Son does not see the Father; and this would underline His inferiority in the Godhead. Actually, Origen was intent on affirming merely His incorporeality; and there are any number of citations that affirm that the Son knows the Father. Methodius mentions a text from the *Peri Archon* according to which God is the creator from all eternity; but the text is not concerned with the creation of intelligent being, in spite of Methodius, for Origen shows that these have had their beginning. He has reference to Platonic ideas or Stoic "reasons," which are the principles of being, created in the eternal generation of the Word or Wisdom that contains them.

JEROME and JUSTINIAN I attribute to Origen the notion of METEMPSYCHOSIS, which certain Greek texts treat as absurdity, foreign to the thought of the Church. According to Jerome, again Origen held that in heaven there would be a renewal of the sacrifice of Christ for the demons; but in his *Commentary on John* (1.35) Origen affirms the unicity of Christ's sacrifice. Jerome did not comprehend Origen's insistence on the universal effect of the drama of the cross.

Certain misunderstandings come as a result of a later particularization of the Christian vocabulary. Origen seems to have made the Word and the Spirit creatures, because following Prv 8.22 and Col 1.15 he speaks of the first as *ktisma* (the created), reserving for the word *poiēma* (something made) the meaning of a creature; in this he is followed by Pope DIONYSIUS and he treats of both as *genētoi,* not distinguishing, as was later done, between this word in the sense of created and *gennētoi* (begotten).

Justinian said Origen thought the risen bodies were spherical in shape. The probable source of this absurdity is in the tract *On Prayer* (31.3), where Origen means the stars and not risen bodies when he speaks of "celestial bodies." Origen certainly uses expressions that are depreciatory in relation to the earthly body in keeping with his Platonic ideas and for an ascetical purpose; but the opposite is not lacking; and the whole complex of his ideas taken together show great equilibrium.

In brief, although statements that have given rise to Origenism are to be found in the works of Origen, all the arguments which serve for the refutation of Origenism can likewise be found there.

Later Origenism. The *Kephalaia gnostica* of EVAGRIUS PONTICUS (345–399), of which an unexpurgated Syrian version has recently been discovered, and a letter of Evagrius to MELANIA THE ELDER give us information regarding the opinions of a group of monks in Egypt and Palestine, admirers of Origen in the second half of the 4th century: Evagrius, Isidore of Pelusium, Palladius, Ammonius, and the three other TALL BROTHERS. Melania, Rufinus, and DIDYMUS THE BLIND were in relation with them. The ocean of Origenistic ideas, tumultuous, ever in flux and reflux, had become a river flowing down through banks that had been wisely reinforced. The different theses described above were developed in a grandiose system, cleared of all that was contradictory. While the master's synthesis, purified from its too bold speculations by theological progress and the experience of heresies, was anonymously preserved in the orthodox tradition, the heterodox character of these speculations, separated from their counterparts, was accentuated in this system.

Evagrius, who is above all a great spiritual author, underwent a systematization similar to the spiritual doctrine of Origen, an increasing of the Platonic and Gnostic elements and a taking of them over into a monastic context of pure contemplation; but in so doing he did not run counter to orthodoxy.

This doctrine brought about the first Origenistic crisis at the end of the 4th century. Origen was criticized; but he was read only one-sidedly, in accordance with the interpretation provided by his so-called disciples. The crisis passed, and it was Evagrius who was read rather than Origen.

The Origenist monks of the 6th century, whose turbulence provoked the second Origenistic quarrel, were divided into two factions. The moderates desired to preserve in Christ as man, distinguished from the Word, a certain superiority over other intelligent beings; but they thus brought the whole system into question. These were the Protoctists, called such because they saw in Christ as man the first created. Their adversaries accused them of introducing a fourth person into the Trinity, whence their nickname of Tetradites.

On the contrary, the Isochristes, faithful to Evagrius it would seem, made of Christ an intelligent being like others, whose sole superiority was temporary and consisted in having remained united to the Word when all the others fell; but in the end they too will become the "equals of Christ" in the reconstituted *henad* or unity.

If the "impious" Origen was spurned by the Syrians—and none of his works are preserved in that language—they paradoxically attested a great admiration for the "holy father" Evagrius, whom they knew through expurgated texts, such as the first Syrian version of the *Kephalaia gnostica.* But the second version, which was discovered recently, shows that the real Evagrius was not completely unknown. His thought has been found, reinforced with Gnostic influences, in STEPHEN BAR-SŪDHAILĒ, who was in Palestine during the second Origenistic quarrel. In the *Book of Hierotheus,* which is attributed to Stephen, this thought of Evagrius, mixed with PSEUDO-DIONYSIAN ideas, takes on a pantheistic aspect that Evagrius had wanted to avoid.

Origenistic Controversies. During his lifetime, Origen experienced contradictions. It is not certain that doctrinal difficulties were involved in his troubles with Bishop Demetrius, but it is not improbable (*Comm. in Jn 5; Epist. ad Fabianum.*). But he had the reputation of a defender of the faith, as his *Dialogue with Heraclides* indicates. During 150 years his admirers prevailed over his detractors. At the time of his death many of his disciples and friends occupied important episcopal sees and safeguarded his memory: Dionysius the Great at Alexandria, Theoctistus, then Theotecnus at Caesarea in Palestine, Firmilian in Caesarea of Cappadocia, Gregory Thaumaturgus, and his brother Athenodorus in Pontus. The processes against PAUL OF SAMOSATA, Bishop of Antioch, were in good part their doing.

Supporters. The schools of ALEXANDRIA (with Theognostus and Pierius) and of CAESAREA remained faithful to the doctrine of the master. In the latter, Pamphilus, aided by Eusebius, composed an *Apology for Ori-*

gen, refuting his accusers by citing his texts. His opponents were, above all: METHODIUS OF OLYMPUS, who, although dependent on Origen, fought against his ideas on the glorious bodies and the creation *ab aeterno;* PETER OF ALEXANDRIA, on subordinationism, preexistence, and the glorious bodies; and EUSTATHIUS OF ANTIOCH, on the interpretation of the *Pythoness of Endor.*

The opposition between the Antiochians and Alexandrians in scriptural exegesis continued. But the great doctors of the 4th century read his works assiduously, and their own writings attest to this fact. They had reservations about his ideas but still considered him as "the stone which sharpens all of us" (Gregory of Nazianzus) and "the second master of the Church after the Apostle" (Didymus the Blind, followed by Jerome).

ATHANASIUS OF ALEXANDRIA used his Trinitarian texts in the Arian controversy; Basil and Gregory of Nazianzus composed the *Philocalia* of Origen; GREGORY OF NYSSA is the most representative inheritor of his mysticism and accepted his *apocatastasis;* Eusebius of Caesarea gave him a most important place in his *Ecclesiastical History;* and Didymus wrote a commentary on the *Peri Archon.*

AMBROSE of Milan and other Latin Fathers used him constantly; EUSEBIUS OF VERCELLI and HILARY OF POITIERS translated some of his writings and were imitated by Rufinus of Aquileia and Jerome, still full of enthusiasm for him. Having an intimate knowledge of his writings, which would be much less read subsequently in the Orient, these 4th-century Fathers were capable of judging his boldnesses in relation to the whole of his thought.

Opponents. The Arians, however, took refuge behind him, and his Egyptian disciples compromised him. Epiphanius of Constantia denounced him in his *Ancoratus* and *Panarion* (ch. 64) and attacked JOHN OF JERUSALEM in 392 as a protector of the Origenists. He won over Jerome, who started a pamphlet war against his old friend Rufinus because the latter remained true to his master; their subsequent quarrel scandalized Augustine. Rufinus defended Origen and asserted that the *Peri Archon* had been interpolated by heretics (*De adult. librorum Origenis*). THEOPHILUS OF ALEXANDRIA, who had read Origen, changed camps in the interest of his patriarchal politics, chased Isidore and the Tall Brothers from Egypt, and was able to depose JOHN CHRYSOSTOM from the Patriarchate of Constantinople for having sheltered them. He condemned Origen in a synodal letter (400) and in three paschal letters (401, 402, 404), which were immediately translated into Latin by Jerome; and Pope ANASTASIUS I confirmed the condemnation in letters to Simplicianus and Venerius of Milan.

This was the first Origenistic crisis; it came to a close in 402 with the silence of Rufinus, whose death in 411 did not disarm his adversary, St. Jerome. (The questions that were raised in the course of the controversy have been discussed above.) He was reproached with having allegorized the scriptural narratives of Creation and of paradise. To the interpretations made by contemporary Origenists, Jerome and Theophilus did not hesitate to add their own conclusions. Epiphanius in particular, making use of a supposititious apostasy of Origen, widely spread unbelievable gossip, which weighed long and heavily on his reputation (see H. de Lubac, *Exégèse médiévale* 1:257–274).

6th Century. In the first half of the 6th century Origenistic monks provoked trouble in the Great Laura of St. SABAS and in the New Laura near Jerusalem. In 543 an edict of Justinian I appeared, which had been provoked by the papal apocrisiarius Pelagius (later pope), in the form of the *Liber adv. Origenem* or the *Letter to Mennas,* the patriarch of Constantinople [J. D. Mansi, *Sacrorum Conciliorum nova et amplissima collectio*, 31 v. (Florence-Venice 1757–98) 9:487–534]. It was approved apparently by the Pope and the four patriarchs. The text of this decree does not manifest a direct knowledge of Origen's writings; the accusation that he placed the image of God in the body of man confounds Origen with the Anthropomorphites, his constant adversaries, and directly contradicts all his teaching. The citations and the fragments of the *Peri Archon* that accompany it come from a dossier sent to Pelagius by the anti-Origenists of Palestine. The ten anathemas adjoined (H. Denzinger, *Enchiridion Symbolorum*, ed. A. Schönm [32d ed. Freiburg 1963] 203–211) are aimed at Origen and reproduce the complaints raised in the first controversy, concerning subordinationism and "the spherical-shaped glorious bodies."

But these troubles did not cease. On the death of their leader, Nonnus, the Origenists divided into two camps, and the Protoctists allied themselves with the anti-Origenists. The complicated history of the Council of CONSTANTINOPLE II in its relation to Origenism has been narrated by F. Diekamp. The council had been retarded by the resistance of Pope VIGILIUS, and during the interval Justinian had addressed a letter to the bishops (preserved by Georgius Monachus and by Cedrenus; Mansi 9:533–538) to which correspond the 15 anathemas, discovered by P. Lambeck in 1679, but which do not appear in the official acts of the council. They expressly concern the Origenistic monks. A. Guillaumont has shown that they reproduce the Christology of Evagrius.

Justinian opened the council without the agreement of Vigilius; and in its discussions little attention was paid to Origen, except to put his name in the list of heretics condemned in canon 11. He was not mentioned in the Emperor's opening discourse, which is the source of the council's anathemas, nor in the letter of Vigilius approving the council after the fact (Mansi 9:413–420). But later councils have repeated the condemnation. Following ordinary norms of interpretation, however, there is no question of holding that Origen was a formal heretic—the bishops were persuaded that he was a heretic through the belief of Epiphanius; nor is it necessary to admit that the errors with which he was charged are really his. Unfortunately, this condemnation occasioned the loss of the greater part of his works in their original language.

Present. The West continued to read Origen and to appreciate him as exegete and spiritual director until the end of the 12th century (Bernard of Clairvaux, William of St.-Thierry); but the rise of Aristotelianism caused his star to recede. Brought back to honor during the Renaissance (Pico de la Mirandola, Erasmus), he has been a sign of contradiction among his numerous historians ever since. At the end of the 19th and beginning of the 20th century he was considered more a Greek philosopher than a Christian theologian: he was accused of having preached Plato all during his life thinking he was preaching Christ. But in 1931 W. Völker raised his spiritual doctrine to its proper honor, and in 1950 H. de Lubac rediscovered the technique for understanding his exegesis. Despite variations in appreciation, modern critics can no longer ignore these two aspects of his teaching.

Bibliography: Works. *Patrologia Graeca* v.11–17, with *Hexapla*, ed. P. L. B. DRACH, v.15–16; *Die griechischen christlichen Schriftsteller der ersten drei Jahrhunderte* (1899–1955); *Entretien avec Héraclide*, ed. J. SCHERER (Cairo 1949; 2d ed. *Sources Chrétiennes* 67; 1960); *Commentary on St. John's Gospel*, ed. A. E. BROOKE, 2 v. (Cambridge, Eng. 1896); *Hexapla*, ed. F. FIELD, 2 v. (Oxford 1867–75); *Philocalia*, ed. J. A. ROBINSON (Cambridge, Eng. 1893), Eng. tr. G. LEWIS (Edinburgh 1911); *Prayer, Exhortation to Martyrdom*, tr. J. J. O'MEARA (Ancient Christian Writers 19; 1954); *The Song of Songs*, tr. R. P. LAWSON (ibid. 26; 1957); *Origen on First Principles*, tr. G. W. BUTTERWORTH (Society for Promoting Christian Knowledge, 1936), Eng. tr. of *De Principiis*; *Contra Celsum*, tr. H. CHADWICK (Cambridge, Eng. 1953); *Selections from the Commentaries and Homilies*, tr. R. B. TOLLINGTON (Society for Promoting Christian Knowledge, 1929). J. E. L. OULTON and H. CHADWICK, eds. and trs., *Alexandrian Christianity* (Philadelphia 1954), includes selections from Origen. Literature. R. CADIOU, *Origen: His Life at Alexandria*, tr. J. A. SOUTHWELL (St. Louis 1944). J. DANIÉLOU, *Origen*, tr. W. MITCHELL (New York 1955). E. DE FAYE, *Origen and His Work*, tr. F. ROTHWELL (London 1926). W. VÖLKER, *Das Vollkommenheitsideal des Origenes* (Tübingen 1931). R. GÖGLER, *Zur Theologie des biblischen Wortes bei Origenes* (Düsseldorf 1963). R. M. GRANT, *The Earliest Lives of Jesus* (Society for Promoting Christian Knowledge, 1961). R. P. C. HANSON, *Allegory and Event* (Richmond, Va. 1959); *Origen's Doctrine of Tradition* (Society for Promoting Christian Knowledge, 1954). H. DE LUBAC, *Histoire et espirit* (Paris 1950); *Exégèse médiévale*, 2 v. in 4 (Paris 1959–64) v. 1. M. F. WILES, *The Spiritual Gospel* (Cambridge, Eng.

1960). F. BERTRAND, *Mystique de Jésus chez Origène* (Paris 1951). S. BETTENCOURT, *Doctrina ascetica Origenis* (St Anselm 16; 1945). H. CROUZEL, *Théologie de l'image de Dieu chez Origène* (Paris 1956); *Origène et la "connaissance mystique"* (Paris 1961); *Origène et la philosophie* (Paris 1962); *Virginité et mariage selon Origène* (Bruges 1963). G. GRUBER, *Zōe. Wesen, Stufen, und Mitteilung des wahren Lebens bei Origenes* (Munich 1962). M. MARTINEZ, *Teologia de la luz en Origenes* (Comillas 1963). G. TEICHTWEIER, *Die Sündenlehre des Origenes* (Regensburg 1958). H. T. KERR, *The First Systematic Theologian: Origen of Alexandria* (Princeton 1958). P. NEMESHEGYI, *La Paternité de Dieu chez Origène* (Paris 1960). F. DIEKAMP, *Die origenistischen Streitigkeiten im 6. Jahrhundert* (Münster 1899). G. FRITZ, *Dictionnaire de théologie catholique*, 15 v. ed. A. VACANT et al (Paris 1903–50) 11.2:1565–88. A. GUILLAUMONT, *Les "Kephalaia gnostica" d'Évagre le Pontique* (Paris 1963). J. QUASTEN, *Patrology*, 3 v. (Westminster, Md.) 2:37–101.

[H. CROUZEL]

ORIGINAL JUSTICE

In the present study, two questions will be posed. The first and more important asks what the faith is that Catholics profess relative to original justice. The second is not dogmatic in the strict sense. It is theological, and inquires how and in what way this truth—like other mysteries—can be understood by man after divine revelation.

Dogmatic. It may be of assistance to present in diagram form what is under consideration here (see accompanying table). If one were to attempt to plot out on a time line the various states that form the religious-moral history of humanity in relation to God, the first, for Catholicism, would be innocence, or original justice. The dividing line *DBE* is that of ORIGINAL SIN. The period or duration signified by the segment *AB* is discussed subsequently. [Dogmatically it is possible that points *B* and *A* coincide with the first moment of humanity's conscious life.]

There is another way to consider the same phenomenon. In the life of the Christian on earth (falling into the segment *BC* above), there are two stages. The segment *A'B'* (see accompanying table) is his original religious-moral condition as he enters the world. This is designated as original sin and means the individual is debilitated with regard to leading a life that is worthy of a human being, let alone a son of God. Although this weakness affects his mind and will, he did not personally cause it. Baptism for the child (together with personal conversion in the adult) effects a transformation known as justification.

Christ's merits renew in fallen man the image of his Maker. That renewal, the result of divine initiative, involves at least a partial restoration of the individual to mankind's original condition or state. In a true sense, the

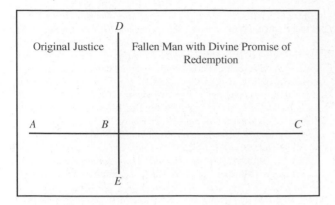

justified man today relives, or recapitulates, in himself the religious-moral history of the race—only in reverse order, as the diagrams indicate. All of this has further implications.

The first thing one must keep in mind is this. The justified man by God's GRACE through Christ is internally proportioned to living out a life as a son of God. He is not thus constituted when he first comes into the world. Even then, however, he is still absolutely called to do so despite his condition of personal inability to respond without Christ's assistance, which is from the first moment divinely assured him in view of his need and God's goodness. His state at birth or conception is that of Adam in ch. 3 of Genesis rather than that of Adam in ch. 1 or 2—fallen, but with divinely inspired hope of salvation already begun and already affecting him. The justified man, however, is in many, if by no means all, respects like humanity itself in its primordial religious-moral condition. Positive scientific method may not disclose a difference between the baptized and unbaptized, the justified and unjustified. This does not, however, exclude the fact that a difference is there, one perceptible only through divine revelation and its acceptance in faith. Similarly it may be that neither science nor secular history finds any traces of a change in humanity, now in a fallen state although once in a condition of original justice. That change, or difference, is no less real and impresses itself on man only as a result of God's interpretation of human religious history.

Even in divine revelation, however, the state of original justice is not in itself an object of direct, extended consideration. This does not imply that it is without foundation in the written word of God. It is there, but somewhat in the background. Even in the Old Testament, Genesis ch. 2 does not seem to have been written to spell out in detail what man was like before and without the sin and injustice only too evident to Israel beholding itself and other peoples. Together with the third chapter, it forms a divinely inspired account of the origin of evil—

tracing it to man and not to God, whose works are just, who made all things good, and who walked in peace, harmony, and friendship with man. Still it is the fact that man caused the central disharmony and injustice in the world that makes him unlike what he was before or what he would have been had he acted otherwise.

A pivotal theme of the New Testament is that God has called sinful man to sonship through Jesus Christ in Baptism. Through the latter, man is restored, renewed, and reformed in the image of his Maker (Eph 4.23–24; Col 3.10; Ti 3 4–5). The life that was once in the world before sin and death gained entrance is restored to men through Jesus Christ, the second Adam (Rom 5.10–21; 1 Cor 15.21–22). The precondition for this is man's existence in a similar state at one point of his religious-moral history.

The same phenomenon manifests itself in the teaching of the Church. It is not as if the Church were directly concerned with Adam's original condition. Its real mission to preach and teach is directed to fallen and redeemed man. Humanity in its state of innocence is relevant as a factor required for a less inadequate grasp of what Jesus Christ has done for historical, guilty man. To restore is to give back what was lost; to restore justice and holiness implies man's possession of both at one time.

In view of this, it is not surprising that the teaching Church prescinded from defining certain questions regarding original justice. One of these was whether man was created immediately in this condition or in one where by divine assistance he was to dispose himself for the latter. Another was whether man in justice and holiness possessed sanctifying grace prior to the Fall. It is dogmatically tenable as well to hold that man was faced with a choice in the first moment of his existence (his response being negative—original sin). In this way original justice is a real, historical divine offer, one with definite effects in man, effects proposed immediately for man's acceptance or rejection. Even in this conception of things, it is still a gratuitous gesture on the part of a loving God, whose generosity does not leave humanity unaffected. Implied is an irrevocable invitation to a rational creature to share in the fellowship or life of the Trinity. Acceptance would have signified man's willingness to be thus transformed, elevated, supernaturalized—in a word, deified, but without losing his human condition. However, there were other gifts as well. One was immortality, the promise of life with immunity from the necessity of undergoing the death man now experiences. Another was integrity; effective commitment to the truly good was not to be accompanied by the difficulty man now feels because of internal conflict within himself.

The Church taught, especially at the Council of Trent (H. Denzinger, *Enchiridion symbolorum* 1511), that Adam was constituted by God in holiness and justice. The latter signified a condition in which man was destined for personal union with God in the BEATIFIC VISION. This included provision of whatever man needs to live a life ordered to such a union. It is interesting to note that the Biblical expression with which St. Paul described the Christian was applied in retrospect to man in his original condition as related to God.

In reference to the above state, the term historical is rightly taken to mean real, factual, but not necessarily verifiable or detectable by positive scientific method. Consequently the prehistorian's inability to discover evidence from such a period in no way stands at odds with Catholic dogma. Catholic theologians can maintain that the condition, state, or period in question was momentary and no more. Thus the lack of any traces left behind would not be unintelligible, especially since science would find it even more difficult to deal with this religious-moral condition of primitive man than with many other factors of greater permanence in his existence. Why then has there been such insistence on such a state or condition?

The reason is that the Church considers it necessary to make faith in the redemptive act of Jesus Christ more integral (and, hence, also more intelligible). It fills in important details, gives nuances to what is otherwise a blunt fact. There is much to the Redemption-justification of man that transcends his power to understand. Only God could attest—since only He can make just—that the death of Jesus Christ, His Son, is redemptive for the latter's brothers and sisters. Only He could relate to man precisely to what extent humanity needed to be saved and redeemed, what the salvation brought by His Son entailed in terms of restoration. The Church, especially by reading and reflecting on His word, came under the inspiration of the Spirit to understand Redemption-justification as restoration to a prior state, at least under certain aspects; hence original justice in its profession of faith.

Theological. Further questions have arisen in the course of time regarding the intelligibility of this dogmatic truth. One of the foremost is the extent to which the details of Genesis ch. 2 are to be taken as a description of factual conditions realized in the state of original justice. Recognition that the history there related is of a very special type—accompanied by and embellished with many symbols—has helped considerably. Thus the degree of cultural attainment realized in Adam of Genesis appears less as a direct object of scriptural affirmation than as antithesis to the assertion that man's present state of ignorance, strife, etc., is humanly caused, consequent

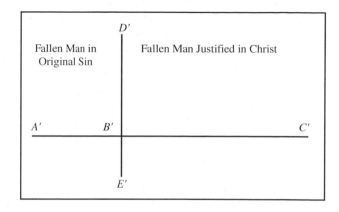

upon a misuse of freedom. The world is different for man in Genesis ch. 2 and 3; many theologians are beginning to regard this as a way of asserting that man's change for the worse in relation to God sets him in disaccord with the rest of nature as well. Such an interpretation has the obvious advantage of posing fewer difficulties in a confrontation with positive science, which finds only a primitive degree of development in men in their earliest states.

There was once a type of speculation current in Catholic theology that was often introduced with the question: What if Adam had not sinned? The exact, concrete details of a universe with man abiding in a state of original justice were not directly revealed by God. The fact—however long or short a period was entailed—is one thing; all the implications are another. The first is necessary to grasp the meaning of Christ's redemptive act. The latter is not. A fortiori one can only conjecture about the concrete mode of realization of what might have been. More and more Catholic theologians have come to wonder whether such a line of inquiry is likely to be conducive to further insights and truth. The proper and direct object of theology is the divinely revealed word of what the Triune God has done, does, and will do for man in salvation history—not the even more abstruse area of concrete detail in the realm of what He might have done.

This is not to say what might have been is always irrelevant to what is or has been. The scriptural description of original justice involves an intimacy between God and man surpassing, but not destroying that of Creator-creature. The dogmatic way of putting this is that in its original state humanity was deified, or endowed with gifts belonging properly to God alone or Divine Persons. Because of this, it is necessary to conclude that God could have produced man without this relation of sonship and merely with that of creaturehood. In this case, the "what might have been" is quite relevant to the gratuity of "what is." However, "what might have been" had original justice been preserved casts little light on what has been through divine intervention in Jesus Christ for restoration.

A final question that deals with the relation between sanctifying grace and original justice has also concerned Catholic theologians. In terms of causal theory, it has been asked whether the former acts as formal or efficient cause of the latter.

See Also: CONCUPISCENCE; DESTINY, SUPERNATURAL; ELEVATION OF MAN; JUSTICE OF MEN; MAN; OBEDIENTIAL POTENCY; PRETERNATURAL; SUPERNATURAL; SUPERNATURAL EXISTENTIAL.

Bibliography: A. MICHEL, *Dictionnaire de théologie catholique.* ed. A. VACANT et al. (Paris 1903—50) 8.2:2038–42. K. RAHNER, *Lexikon für Theologie und Kirche*, ed. J. HOFER and K. RAHNER (Freiberg 1957–65) 8:72. A. M. DUBARLE, *The Biblical Doctrine of Original Sin*, tr. E. M. STEWART (New York 1965). M. FLICK and Z. ALSZEGHY, *Il createre: L'inizio della salvezza* (2d ed. Florence 1961). J. DE FRAINE, *The Bible and the Origin of Man* (New York 1962), tr. from Dutch (Antwerp 1956). J. B. KORS, *La Justice primitive et le péché originel d'après s. Thomas* (Le Saulchoir, Kain 1922). H. DE LUBAC, *Le Mystère du surnaturel* (Paris 1965). S. LYONNET, *De peccato originall* (Rome 1960). H. RENCKENS, *Israel's Concept of the Beginning,* tr. C. NAPIER (New York 1964). W. A. VAN ROO, *Grace and Original Justice according to St. Thomas* (*Analecta Gregoriana* 75; Rome 1955). H. U. VON BALTHASAR and E. GUTWENGER, "Der Begriff der Natur in der Theologie," *Zeitschrift für katholische Theologie* 75 (1953) 452–464. J. BITTREMIEUX, "La Distinction entre justice originelle et la grâce sanctifiante d'apres s. Thomas d'Aquin," *Revue thomiste* 26 (1921) 121–150. P. J. DONNELLY, "The Gratuity of the Beatific Vision and the Possibility of a Natural Destiny," *Theological Studies* 11 (1950) 374–404. C. J. PETER, "The Position of Karl Rahner regarding the Supernatural: A Comparative Study of Nature and Grace," *Catholic Theological Society* 20 (1965). L. RENWART, "La Nature pure à la lumière de l'encyclique *Humani generis,*" *Nouvelle revue théologique* 74 (1952) 337–354. A. HULSBOSCH, *God in Creation and Evolution,* tr. M. VERSFELD (New York 1965). P. SCHOONENBERG, *Man and Sin,* tr. from the Dutch J. DONCEEL (Notre Dame, Ind. 1965). R. FRANCOEUR, *Perspectives in Evolution* (Baltimore 1965).

[C. J. PETER]

ORIGINAL SIN

The hereditary sin incurred at conception by every human being as a result of the original sinful choice of the first man, ADAM. Before treating theologically of original sin, this article considers the Biblical data.

IN THE BIBLE

First the possible evidence for original sin in the Old Testament is considered, then the New Testament teaching.

Possible Evidence in the Old Testament. The Old Testament makes no explicit or formal statement regarding the transmission of hereditary guilt from the first man to the entire human race; but such a doctrine harmonizes with the general atmosphere of the Old Testament and is hinted at in some passages. Thus, the story of the fall of man in Genesis ch. 3 explains the human condition, and this is marked by a universal tendency toward sin. Chapter 4 of Genesis (from the YAHWIST tradition, like ch. 3) illustrates, by a series of anecdotes, how sin has invaded mankind. Chapter 5 (of the Pentateuchal PRIESTLY WRITERS) may show the same thing through its reduction of life spans (see also Gn 11.10–26, also of the priestly tradition), even though this would be a more subtle method. In Gn 6.5 a strong indictment is presented against man's universal inclination to sin, and the "justice" of Noe (Noah) is qualified by 8.21—a kind of divine resignation to man's sinfulness. Solomon's prayer (1 Kgs 8.46) implies the same, and Ecclesiastes is aware of some evil having entered into mankind (Eccl 7.20). The words of Ps 50(51) 7 may be no more than a personal outcry, but many good scholars have seen a universal condition reflected in its words. Of dubious value is Jb 14.4 in the Masoretic Text, even if the Vulgate, perhaps through Christian influence, is most expressive. However, Wis 2.24 is significant: "By the envy of the devil death entered into the world." In strict exegesis one may not call the doctrine of original sin, as defined by the Council of Trent, a teaching of the Old Testament; but the foundations for it are there, strong and undeniable.

Teaching of the New Testament. It should be remarked that the New Testament seldom, if ever, formulates theological definitions such as are currently used. Its doctrine is set forth mostly in a descriptive manner. While one may gather, here and there in the New Testament, hints at the universality of sin, it is only St. Paul, in Eph 2.3 ("We were by nature children of wrath even as the rest") and especially in Rom 5.12–19, who forcefully brings out the doctrine. Through an extended series of contrasts Paul's doctrine gains great power: sin and death have entered into all men (Rom 5.12); in the transgression of the one, the rest died (5.15); consequent upon the judgment passed on one man, all men were condemned (5.18); and through the disobedience of one man the rest were constituted sinners (5.19). Only one inclined to quibble could deny Paul's general thought. Still it is true that Paul does not explicitly say all that will be said by the Council of Trent. This, of course, is quite a normal phenomenon in the development of doctrine. Paul lays a strong foundation from which details may be drgawn harmoniously and legitimately.

Bibliography: J. BLINZLIBR, *Lexikon für Theologie und Kirche*, ed. J. HOFER and K. RAHNER (Freiburg 1957–65) 3:965–967. *Encyclopedic Dictionary of the Bible,* tr. and adap. by L. HARTMAN (New York 1963) 1677–78. A. M. DUBARLE, *Le Péché originel dans*

"Adam and Eve in Paradise," 13th-century Norwegian painting. (©Archivo Iconografico, S.A./CORBIS)

l'écriture (Paris 1958). T. BARROSSE, "Death and Sin in St. Paul's Epistle to the Romans," *Catholic Biblical Quarterly* 15 (1953) 438–458. S. LYONNET, "Le Péché originel en Rom 5,12: L'Exégèse des pères grecs et les décrets du concile de Trente," *Biblica* 41 (1960) 325–355; "Le Péché originel et l'exégèse de Rom 5,12–14," *Revue des Sciences Religieuses* 44 (1956) 63–84; "Le Sens de ἐφῷ en Rein 5,12 . . . ," *Biblica* 36 (1955) 436–456. A. HULSBOSCH, *God in Creation and Evolution,* tr. M. VERSFELD (New York 1965) ch.2. A. VANNESTE, "La Préhistoire du décret du Concile de Trente sur le Péché originel," *Nouvelle revue théologique* 86 (1964) 355–368, 490–510.

[I. HUNT]

IN CATHOLIC FAITH AND THEOLOGY

The term original sin designates a number of things. One is a condition of GUILT, weakness, or debility found in human beings historically (or in which they are personally situated), prior to their own free option for good or evil (*peccatum originale originatum*). This is a state of being rather than a human act or its consequence. The other meaning has to deal with the origin of that state: its cause or source (*peccatum originale origbzans*). In what follows, both meanings will be treated from a dogmatic and from a strictly theological point of view.

Dogmatic: Sin of Adam. It is first of all imperative to understand the motivation behind the Church's concern with this issue. The Church saw it closely connected with something very central to the Christian's profession of faith: that the Father has sent His Son Jesus as Savior. This was present in the earliest apostolic preaching and creeds (Acts 2.38–40; 3.26; 4.12; H. Denzinger, *Enchridion symbolorum,* ed. A. Schönmetzer 1, 3, 4, 40, 42). Similarities notwithstanding, it was not just another human confrontation with the problem of evil or a purely philosophical stand relative to the same issue. Faith in Jesus as redeemer implied that God had offered a solution of His own. If man was in a state of real need, it was one his Creator took into account and sought to remedy. To the adults who heard Peter on Pentecost, the need of salvation was not one that required a great deal of elabora-

Illustration of large apple lifted to reveal Redeemer, Pennsylvania German fraktur, 19th century.

tion. They might inquire about ways and means, but they accepted the fact itself without undue question (Acts 2.36–41). Then and later the preaching-believing Church radiated the conviction that through divine condescension in Christ, man could reach God's own interpretation-solution of the evil present in the human situation.

It is not surprising, however, that questions soon arose concerning the further implications of that evil. These had a significance at once soteriological and sacramental. To what extent is Christ really the savior of all men—only after their personal sins, or even before? To what degree is Baptism conducive to the forgiveness of sins—only for those who have offended God on their own initiative?

These questions led to an explicitation of the Church's faith and understanding of man's need for Christ in terms of sin and death. A scriptural basis for such a development existed (Eph 2.10; Rom 5.12–21; 1 Cor 15.22). It is quite another matter, however, to ask whether the Church in this matter proceeded from the Bible by making use of purely scientific, positive criteria to determine its meaning. There is no indication that it did; the Church relied on the Spirit of Truth who guides its faith throughout the ages (cf. *Enchridion symbolorum* 1514 relative to Rom 5.12). This is not to say that its interpretations, authentically formulated, have been contrary to sound exegetical determination of the literal sense. It is only to assert that the believer contends the Church had other aids as well in expressing the latent significance of God's written word.

Question of Origins. One of the Church's earliest confrontations with problems of this nature dealt with the question of origins. The Marcionists and Manichaeans tended to see in human history a struggle between the good God—father of Jesus Christ and author of the New Testament—and the evil god, who manifested his severity and justice in the Old. Equivalently the question was, when did God begin to save. The Church asserted the strict unity of the redeeming God, the maker of all things who directs all to man's salvation from the earliest beginnings to culmination in His Son, Jesus.

This is an element that is often overlooked, though it is of considerable significance in the NICENE CREED. There Jesus the Savior in time is said to have preexisted in the realm of invisible realities before becoming incarnate. He is begotten but not made; this by the Father, who is, however, the maker of all other realities, visible and invisible (*Enchridion symbolorum* 125–126). This distinction between the Son as invisible though not made and other invisible realities that are made by the Father through the same Son has soteriological as well as strictly Christological import. As Son and Savior, He stands related to the Father in a manner different from that of other invisible realities, which are made. Although the Holy Spirit was not directly taken into account in this context at Nicaea I, the twofold distinction just enumerated was expanded at the First Council of Constantinople and later (*Enchridion symbolorum* 75, 150, 800,1300). As proceeding, the Holy Spirit is neither Father nor Son; as Lord and life-giver, He shares their creative-salvific work. God three-in-one is thus presented as distinct from all other realities, both visible and invisible.

Satan and Adam. The same invisible world became again the object of concern in the Middle Ages at the instance of the Albigenses. What was at issue was not philosophical dualism as such or even a mere denial of universal divine providence, or government, of human affairs. Again the question was intimately related to a central Christian truth. though the technical terms in which it was answered might at first seem to indicate otherwise.

The Jewish people had once asked themselves: When did Yahweh begin His saving action in history—at the Exodus or before, with the Patriarchs or earlier? The Christian, who professed belief in the same saving God, had a similar difficulty. The God who so commended His love for man in the work of His only Son Jesus, how much did He love? How strong was His love? St. Paul had written that neither death nor life nor any creature could separate the Christian from the love of God in Jesus Christ (Rein 8.31–39). What then of the principle hostile to man's salvation?

In the Fourth Lateran Council, the Church proclaimed more than the universal origin of all realities from the same good God. It went further and pronounced that the principle opposed to man in working out his salvation is not only dependent on that God but was originally created good and chose evil personally. It was at his instigation that man gave sin and death admission to the world (*Enchridion symbolorum* 800). Thus the origin of the evil situation in which the world is found came not from God but from man himself at the instigation of a created, invisible power. Dualism in salvation history is therefore different from the philosophical dualism encountered elsewhere. For an interpretation that makes the decree *Firmiter* of this Council at once more symbolic and philosophical, see Peter Schoonenberg, *God's World in the Making* (Duquesne Studies, Theological Series 2; Pittsburgh 1964) 8–9.

Monogenism. Even though it is treated in a separate encyclopedia article, mention must be made of MONOGENISM in this context. In *Hurnani gertefts* Pills XII. warned:

> For Christ's faithful cannot embrace that opinion which maintains either that after Adam there existed on this earth true men who did not take their origin through natural generation from him as from the first parent of all, or that Adam represents a certain number of first parents; since it is in no way apparent how such an opinion can be reconciled with that which the sources of revealed truth and the documents of the teaching authority of the Church propose with regard to original sin, which proceeds from a sin actually committed by an individual Adam and which through generation is passed on to all and is in everyone as his own. [*Enchridion symbolorum* 3897.]

It is well to note the intentional precision with which this was expressed. Monogenism is not described as an article of faith or even unequivocally as a theological conclusion following necessarily from the dogma of Adam's sin. Still the question of polygenism, at least in certain forms, is proposed as one affecting original sin as the faith of the Church professes it. According to the document carefully interpreted, certain polygenistic hypotheses *appear* to offer insoluble difficulties with regard to

the dogma of original sin as proceeding from one Adam, but this does not rule out the possibility that the incompatibility may be seen in the future to have been only apparent. It must be added that *Humani generis* does not offer positive justification for the hope of any who may think this will be the case. For a further discussion of the question, e.g., from the point of view of the possibility of preadamites, see K. Rahner, *Theological Investigations,* v.1, tr. C. Ernst (Baltimore 1961) 231–239.

Fact. The precise nature of the sin of Adam in Genesis ch. 3, as well as the time and circumstances of its commission, have not been the objects of explicit definition by the Church. As is the case with original justice, it is more the fact than the details surrounding it that has concerned the Church in teaching (*Enchridion symbolorum* 3514, 3862–64).

Dogmatic: Consequences in Progeny. First of all the Church professes belief that Adam of Genesis by his sin brought about a change of religious-moral condition in relation to God not only for himself (*see* ORIGINAL JUSTICE) but also for subsequent men. This the Catholic episcopate expressed most clearly in the Council of Trent. The change in question is there described as involving loss of justice and holiness, incurrence of divine wrath, death of soul as well as of body (*Enchridion symbolorum* 1512). Men may and do imitate Adam in his sin; they may personally set up obstacles to a state of FRIENDSHIP WITH GOD. Even prior to so doing, however, they are, for the reason that they are human beings descended historically from him, affected by the sin and guilt he brought into the world—a condition or state at least in its most extended ramifications their more immediate ancestors may have aggravated or helped to perpetuate through personal sins (*Enchridion symbolorum* 1513). Exaggerated humanism at the time of the Renaissance had particular difficulty in accepting the fact that one's religious-moral state could be so affected by something prior to his own free choice. A similar tendency at the time of Pelagius and St. Augustine had occasioned a much earlier determination of Adam's influence on his progeny (cf. *Enchridion symbolorum* 222–224, 231, 237, 239, 371–372, 398–400). In both instances the Church reacted by seeing in the assertion of man's autonomy in self-determination, both for good and for evil, a direct challenge to the saviorship of Jesus Christ.

Capacity for Good. If, on the one hand, there has been insistence that man in his religious-moral life depends on Christ, that without Christ he has no religious-moral significance (cf. Council of Orange; *Enchridion symbolorum* 392), still another truth has been present in the Church's teaching as well. Affected though he is by the sin of Adam, man is nevertheless a being possessed of the capacity for good; he has free will. This does not mean that he will ever exercise that power without Christ, or even that his possession of it to begin with is without Christ, in whom all things are created. This simply means that historical man, affected by Adam's sin, is not so corrupted as to be without a radical power for choosing good (*Enchridion symbolorum* 1555).

At this point it may be well to note the fact that insistence on a humanity that remains truly human though affected by original sin is by no means out of accord with the Scriptures. The New Testament speaks of the community of Christ and other men, His brothers, in humanity despite humanity's sinfulness in them and sinlessness in Him (Heb 4.15; 7.26–27). An observation similar to this has been made by Karl Barth (*Kirchliche Dogmatik* 4.1:480–481).

Role of Christ. The Church has forcefully asserted Adam's evil influence on his progeny and has simultaneously taught that Christ exerts a contrary and superior influence for good. To speak solely and exclusively of man as under the sway of sin and evil caused by the first human sin is therefore to make use of an abstraction. It is a useful one and corresponds to a portion of a complex reality. Man in his relations with God is historically subjected to the most varied influences. From the start he is created in Jesus Christ, called to God through the latter, and aided in attaining such union; but he is affected also by the evil introduced into the world by the first Adam. An age that has come to recognize the major influence of heredity and environment on man may not find it difficult to understand that man, even from a religious-moral point of view, can be affected both adversely by human evil that he did not perpetrate and favorably by good for which he was not ultimately responsible. The Church itself has tried to make clear that for all its insistence on the reality of the adverse moral condition that man is born into because of Adam, still it is not the same as a situation of personal sin (recall the distinction made in this regard at the Councils of Lyons II and Florence, and in later ecclesiastical documents; *Enchridion symbolorum* 858, 1306, 1946–48, 2003).

Specifically, Catholic faith includes the assertion that because of man's first offense against God, human beings now enter this world in special need of the redeeming assistance-grace of Jesus Christ. Called to live as a son of God, man cannot do so without special reliance on the natural Son—this due to the original ingratitude of the first human beings to whom adopted sonship was offered. As to death, this much is likewise certain from the teaching of the Church: the death that man now dies he undergoes because of the sin of Adam. [For disputed interpretations of the implications this has, see further M. Flick and Z. Alszeghy, *Il Creatore: L'Inizio della salvezza* (2d ed. Florence 1961) 319; R. Troisfontaines, *I Do Not Die,* tr. F. E. Albert (New York 1963); K. Rahner, *On the Theology of Death,* tr. C. H. Henkey (Quaestiones Disputatae 2; New York 1962) 54–57.] What is more, the difficulty man now experiences in applying himself effectively to accomplishing real, religious good is there because of Adam historically. For all the natural character of CONCUPISCENCE, it is not what God intended or what He offered man in his original religious-moral condition. As a result, according to Catholic teaching, the lack of justice-holiness, immortality, and integrity in historical man is a real privation and not a mere absence. The reasoning leading to this is that because their restoration through Jesus Christ (at least in its state of consummation) is a real deification of sinful man, it follows that justice-holiness, etc., were a deification in relation to innocent man as well, there by divine offer and intent but absent subsequently (save through Jesus Christ), because of human sin, which sets man in discord with himself, the world, and God.

Theological. In what follows, it is proposed to give special attention to the theological hypotheses proposed to understand, within the limits open to man after revelation, the mystery involved in *peccatum originale originatum.* There can be no question that the nexus between a personal sin of a remote ancestor and a condition of guilt in a descendant has received different nuances of understanding in the history of Christian thought. St. Augustine was hesitant when it came to deciding whether parents passed on merely a body or a body and soul both directly affected by Adam's sin (*C. Iulian.* 5.4.17; *Patrologia Latina*, ed. J. P. Migne 44:794). Nevertheless, the connection between original sin in offspring and concupiscence in parents is something he asserted as well (*C. Iulian. op. imperf.* 2.45, *Patrologia Latina* 45:1161; cf. *Nupt. et concup.* 1.24.27, *Patrologia Latina* 44:429). One can hold with Trent for transmission "generatione, non imitatione" without being constrained to accept such a view of marital relations. The assertion that the sin of Adam affects man before his own personal sin is by no means coincident with stating that he contracts it by a sin his parents commit at his generation or by some result of sin present therein though his parents may not actually be guilty.

Theories concerning Transmission. In this precise area a number of theories have been put forward by Catholic theologians. They attempt to explain how a truly guilty condition can affect man historically prior to his own choice and due to a misuse of liberty on the part of previously deceased humanity. One of these theories accords Adam a type of moral or juridical headship over the human race. In this conception of the matter, God by an inscrutable decree established Adam of Genesis as the legal representative of all Humanity, which would descend from him. His exercise of free choice would be taken as theirs; he would act in their name, for better or worse. The consequence of his conduct would affect all. As a matter of fact he rejected God's offer of friendship and passed on to his descendants a heritage of enmity with God. All men can be said to have acted in him and through him because of the fact that he was their head, so constituted not by them but by their Creator in His good pleasure. This theory has at least the advantage of appealing directly to the free choice of God. Cardinal Juan de Lugo (1583–1660) expounded it at some length; for this reason it is often associated with his name (see *De poenitentia* 7.7; *De incarnatione* 7.3–4). What remains extremely difficult to understand in the explanation is the analogy made between the sinfulness of a state in subsequent men and an act of choice in Adam. Still it has proponents, at least in its mitigated form, among Catholic theologians today (see J. F. Sagues, *De Deo creante et elevante, Sacrae theologiae summa*, ed. Fathers of the Society of Jesus, Professors of the Theological Faculties in Spain 2.2).

Since the theory of Adam's moral headship involves the problem of understanding how each man's will can be presumed (even by God) to have coincided with that of Adam, certain Catholics proposed an alternative theory according to which Adam is to be considered as the physical, not the moral, head of the human race. This was the position, for example of Cardinal L. Billot [*De peccato originali* (Rome 1912)].

Their assumption is that Adam could pass on his humanity only as he possessed it. Having rejected divine friendship, he found that humanity affected by sin in himself, and he generated children similarly disposed. His descendants come from him in this condition: they are deprived of the wherewithal to live out their ineradicable call to divine sonship, save through Jesus as head in a redemptive as well as a creative order.

One major difficulty with this theory is that it has often in the past looked as if man received from Adam a humanity that in its own line was fully intact. One must try to see this in comparison with the tradition that man was, if not corrupted, nevertheless really wounded even in his humanity. When original justice and the gifts it involved are conceived as an accident affecting human nature, it is only too simple to imagine its loss with the nature remaining not only intact but in equilibrium in its own right. Still the Church maintains that man historically without Christ (a state he never totally experiences but one that merits consideration to see the primacy and necessity of Christ) is incapable of living an entire life wor-

thy of a human being and much less of a son of God. How is it that because of Adam, even if he does pass on a humanity that is deprived of the wherewithal to live as son, man cannot even live as long as befits a human being? How can the lack of what in themselves were gifts cause anything even approximating a condition of sin or guilt, particularly in those whose wills have not yet ratified the act that caused the loss?

Other attempts to formulate theories have been made with questions such as these in mind. An aspect of physical headship has been retained: Adam as progenitor did pass on his humanity as he possessed it after his sin, that is, in a truly weakened condition. How? The divine offer of friendship entailed as well a possibility of living without the difficulty injected into life by concupiscence. With concupiscence, selfishness is an obstacle to leading a truly human life. To do so requires at times a recognition and acceptance of the fact that sacrifice of personal convenience and preference is required for the glory of God and the good of man. To love God above all else and to love all creatures as He loves them are imperative for man; selflessness often is required to achieve this. Whatever there is to be said for the possibility of other orders in which man might have been, there is no reason to hold or even think tenable that man in this present order can make that option other than through Jesus Christ. His aid is always at least remotely ordered to man's living as a son and not as a mere human being. And even so, the value found in the old theological distinction between *gratia sanans* and *elevans* may still be recognized. To pass on a humanity subject to concupiscence, in an order where purely natural aids against concupiscence are not offered, is to pass on a humanity that is in a weakened condition morally even before it acts. Prior to its option for good or evil, it is so disposed that without aid in the order of humanity itself it is going to fall freely. But to avoid failure requires divine assistance, an assistance that is given only in ultimate relation to living a life worthy of a son of God. For an extended treatment of this opinion, see M. Flick and Z. Alszeghy, 455–470.

Related Questions. There are many other questions that are raised by the dogma of original sin. Some of these are connected with a particular conception of the state from which Adam fell. Some presuppose more than divine revelation has offered in telling man about that state and what would have been had it lasted or been initially accepted by Adam. Others are peculiarly modern and ask, for example, just what the implications are for the doctrine of original sin in the evolutionist assumption that the present human race did have more than one pair of ultimate ancestors in the remote past.

Whatever answer is offered to such a question, the defectibility that follows necessarily as a consequence of creaturehood is not sufficient to explain the present evil in the human situation. Philosophy might well conclude with probability to the opposite; empirical sciences similarly. The Church, starting with its experience of Christ as redeemer and revealer, has concluded that He offered gifts that were at once a restoration and a deification. As a restoration, they were at least really available to man previously through God's goodness; as a deification, their loss involved more than the exercise of liberty that is present and a necessary condition of defectibility in every creature that is human. One cannot, in the light of revelation, start with the assumption that original sin has been satisfactorily accounted for if an explanation is given of how each of a number of remote ancestors sinned as men. That would indeed explain evil, but not the evil God Himself has indicated to be present in the world. Misuse of human liberty is one thing; it is involved in original sin. But the misuse revealed is one that brings with it a privation of godliness, which is not identical with defective creaturehood. A truly superhuman, or God-like, condition was present in humanity originally, at least by divine offer; it was lost, possibly in the first moment of truly human existence, only to be reoffered in restoration to all men by Christ.

Recent Church Teaching. The documents of Vatican II made scant reference to the first sin. The *Pastoral Constitution on the Church in the Modern World* (*Gaudium et spes*, 13) briefly asserted that humanity (*homo*), made by God in a condition of righteousness (*iustitia*), violated its freedom "at the outset of history" (*ab exordio historiae*), and thereby fell into a state of both internal and external disorder, and of susceptibility to death (*Gaudium et spes* 18). Paul VI, however, cited Trent and recalled Rom 5:12, the seminal text in the tradition, when in his *Credo of the People of God* (1968) he stated that "all have sinned in Adam," such that now all suffer the consequences of that man's sin (*originalem culpam ab illo commissam*). Because of this sin, the nature passed on to us by our protoparents (*protoparentibus nostris*) is destitute of grace and wounded in its natural powers. Also instructive was the revision in 1969, under the direction of a papal commission established by Paul VI, of the discussion of original sin in the Dutch Catechism of 1966 (*Het Nieuwe Katechismus*) so that it would accord more closely with the Tridentine teaching of an inherited nature injured by sin. John Paul II spoke of the death introduced into the world by "the disobedience of Adam" (*Evangelium vitae*, n. 36), and he made awareness of the effect the first sin has had on the human condition an important part of his analysis of the moral life in *Veritatis splendor*.

The most thorough statement of the Church's continued view on original sin is that found in the *Catechism of the Catholic Church* (1992). The *Catechism* expressly affirms each of the elements that have belonged to the doctrine in the west since the time of Augustine's commentaries on St. Paul: that the physical, psychological, and spiritual condition of each human being, the relation of human beings to one another, their relation to visible creation, and even the state of the physical world itself, have been fragmented by virtue of an act committed by man (variously referred to as "Adam" or "Adam and Eve" or "our first parents") at the beginning of human history despite his (or their) having been created by God in holiness. In consequence, we are burdened with a nature inclined to sin (concupiscence) and destined for death. The one element not explicitly referred to is the idea that all share in the guilt (*reatus*, to use Trent's term) of that first act. Instead, the Catechism speaks of the passing on to us of "Adam's sin" which, in the words of Trent, is the "death of the soul," and because of which even infants are baptized "for the remission of sins" (n. 403). The Catechism maintains, with a sharpness lacking perhaps in the documents of Vatican II, the event character of the first sin as a personal act that affected the whole of history and each person within it. Even more significantly, however, it situates this sin within what it claims is a more fundamental event, the event that has defined history from its beginning, namely the event of Christ's atoning Incarnation (nn. 385–89, 402). Hence, the Catechism provides the doctrine of original sin with a Christological setting that is absent in the decree of Trent, but which one may find in the work of Vatican II, and which reflects the Christological focus that characterized the entire twentieth century.

Developments in Theology. The twentieth-century writer who exerted the greatest influence on the theology of original sin was Pierre Teilhard de Chardin. Teilhard's abiding concern was to reconcile the teaching on original sin with the evidence of science, and thereby demonstrate the credibility of the faith to an educated, contemporary audience. The majority of theologians over the last 40 years have adopted at least the broad outline of his approach, which is to place the history of human sin within the evolutionary progress of the world. Whether one views the sin of a first individual or first group in the earliest human period as having lost for all of us the grace of God (Rahner) or, as Teilhard himself believed and which has become more common, one regards sin as the necessary failure of a species that is still in the process of maturing, lying at the heart of this approach is the picture of Christ as active in the world since the moment of creation, unifying, integrating, and ultimately drawing all into the presence of the Father (Segundo, Duffy, Mooney, Korsmeyer). The difficulty is that this amounts to a denial of the Fall, the teaching that, as Trent put it, a first human decision changed the human condition "for the worse" (*in deterius*). Physical death (or for Rahner, our experience of it) and suffering, the inclination to self and hence our alienation from ourselves, each other and from God, are said to be natural to us as finite and physical, even though they are certain to be overcome, by virtue of the grace of Christ, in the eschaton. It was out of concern for this trend that the Catechism warned against taking sin "as merely a developmental flaw, a psychological weakness, a mistake, or the necessary consequence of an inadequate social structure, etc." (*Catechism of the Catholic Church* 387). For their part, however, theologians have been frustrated by what they regard as a blind insistence on taking biblical "myth" as historical fact (Daly). Yet to a great extent, Church authorities and theologians seem to have been talking past each other. The latter consider the doctrine of original sin as addressing the same questions about human origins as do the natural sciences, e.g., how and why did the species arise, under what circumstances, whether from a single couple, a single group, or a variety of groups in a variety of locations, etc. Church teaching, on the other hand, has proposed the doctrine as an explanation, based on revelation, of the human person as free and self-transcendent, belonging to a single community generated from the mutuality of man and woman, the subject of a divine vocation which nevertheless required purchase in the blood of Christ (John Paul II, "Message to the Pontifical Academy of Sciences," 1996). If this doctrine establishes a standard against which may be measured certain empirical extrapolations that refer to the nature of the person, it nonetheless does not propose a kind of rival natural history. The task presently facing theology is the investigation of ways that will lead beyond the impasse, which requires a reconsideration of the doctrine on its own terms. Meriting fuller notice is the suggestion by D. Keefe that the first sin be understood as lying neither before nor beyond our history, nor as still another event lying within the flow of history, but as an exercise of human freedom that is constitutive of history.

See Also: DEATH (THEOLOGY OF); DESTINY, SUPERNATURAL; ELEVATION OF MAN; GRACE, ARTICLES ON; IMMACULATE CONCEPTION; MAN; NATURAL ORDER; OPTIMISM (THEOLOGICAL ASPECT); MONOGENISM AND POLYGENISM; PRETERNATURAL; SALVATION; SUPERNATURAL; SUPERNATURAL ORDER.

Bibliography: A. GAUDEL, *Dictionnaire de théologie catholique,* ed. A. VACANT et al. (Paris 1903–50) 12.1:275–606. J. BLINZLER et al., *Lexicon für Theologie und Kirche,* ed. J. HOFER and K. RAHNER (Freiburg 1957–65) 3:965–973. S. LYONNET, *Dictionnaire de la Bible* supplement ed. L. PIROT et al. (Paris 1928–) 7:481–567; *De peccato originali* (Rome 1960). A. M. DUBARLE, *The Biblical Doctrine of Original Sin,* tr. E. M. STEWART (New York 1965). J. DE FRAINE, *The Bible and the Origin of Man* (New York 1962), tr. from Dutch. V. J. PETER, *The Doctrine of Ruard Tapper Regarding Original Sin and Justification* (Rome 1965). H. RENCKENS, *Israel's Concept of the Beginning,* tr. C. NAPIER (New York 1964). M. SECKLER, *Instinkt und Glaubenswille nach Thomas von Aquino* (Mainz 1961). M. FLICK, "Lo stato di peccato originale," *Gregorianum* 38 (1957) 299–309; "Problemi teologici sull' 'ominazione,'" *ibid.* 44 (1963) 62–70. R. J. PENDERGAST, "The Supernatural Existential, Human Generation, and Original Sin," *Downside Review* 82 (1964) 1–24. C. J. PETER, "The Position of Karl Rahner regarding the Supernatural: A Comparative Study of Nature and Grace," *Catholic Theological Society of America Proceedings* 20 (1965). E. SCHILLEBEECKX, "L'Instinct de la foi selon s. Thomas d'Aquin," *Revue des sciences philosophiques et théoligiques* 48 (1964) 377–408. J. DE FRAINE, *Adam and the Family of Man,* tr. D. RAIBLE (New York 1965). A. HULSBOSCH, *God in Creation and Evolution,* tr. M. VERSFELD (New York 1965). H. DE LUBAC, *La Pensée religieuse du Père Teilhard de Chardin* (Paris 1962). P. SMULDERS, *La Vision de Teilhard de Chardin,* tr. from the Dutch C. D'ARMAGNAC (Paris 1964). P. SCHOONENBERG, *Man and Sin* (Notre Dame, Indiana 1965). PAUL VI, "Original Sin and Modern Science," *The Pope Speaks* 11 (1966) 229–235. JOHN PAUL II, "Address to Pontifical Academy of Sciences," *The Pope Speaks* 42 (1997) 118–121. U. BAUMANN, *Erbsünde? Ihr traditionelles Verständnis in der Krise heutiger Theologie* (Freiburg 1970). C. BAUMGARTNER, *Le péché originel* (Paris 1969). P. BURKE, "Man Without Christ: An Approach to Hereditary Sin," *Theological Studies* 29 (1968) 4–18. J. L. CONNOR, "Original Sin: Contemporary Approaches," *Theological Studies* 29 (1968) 215–240. G. A. DALY, *Creation and Redemption* (Wilmington 1989); "Original Sin," in *Commentary on the Catechism of the Catholic Church,* ed. M. J. WALSH (Collegeville, Minnesota 1994), 97–111. S. J. DUFFY, "Our Hearts of Darkness: Original Sin Revisted," *Theological Studies* 89 (1988) 597–622. M. FLICK and Z. ALSZEGHY, *Il peccato originale* (Brescia 1972). P. GRELOT, *Péché originel et la rédemption, à partir de l'épître aux Romains* (Paris 1973). H. HAAG, "The Original Sin Discussion, 1966–1971," *Journal of Ecumenical Studies* 10 (1973) 259–289. D. J. KEEFE, *Covenantal Theology: The Eucharistic Order of History,* 2 v. (Lanham 1991). J. D. KORSMEYER, *Evolution and Eden: Balancing Original Sin and Contemporary Science* (New York 1998). P. LENGSFELD, *Adam et le Christ: La typologie Adam-Christ dans le Nouveau Testament et son utilization dogmatique par M. J. Scheeben et K. Barth* (Paris 1970). S. MACISAAC, *Freud and Original Sin* (New York 1974). G. MARTELET, *Libre réponse à un scandale: La faute originelle, la souffrance et la mort* (Paris 1986). B. MCDERMOTT, "The Theology of Original Sin: Recent Developments," *Theological Studies* 38 (1977) 478–512. C. F. MOONEY, "Theology and Science: A New Commitment to Dialogue," *Studia Theologica* 52 (1991) 289–329. K. RAHNER, "Evolution and Original Sin," *Concilium* 26 (New York 1967); "Monogenism," *Sacramentum Mundi* 4:105–107; "Original Sin," *ibid.* 4:328–334; "Erbsünde und Monogenismus" in K.-H. WEGER, *Theologie der Erbsünde* (Freiburg 1970); "The Sin of Adam," *Theological Investigations* 11 (New York 1974) 247–262; "Natural Science and Reasonable Faith," *Theological Investigations* 21 (1988) 16–55. P. RICOEUR, *The Symbolism of Evil* (Boston 1969); "Guilt, Ethics and Religion" in *The Conflict of Interpretations* (Evanston 1974) 425–439; "'Original Sin': A Study in Meaning," *ibid.* 269–286. H. RONDET, *Original Sin: The Patristic and Theological Background* (Staten Island 1972). L. SABOURIN, "Original Sin Reappraised," *Biblical Theology Bulletin* 3 (1973) 41–81. A. SCHMIED, "Konvergenzen in der Diskussion um die Erbsünde," *Theologie der Gengenwart* 17 (1974) 144–156. K. SCHMITZ-MOORMANN, *Die Erbsünde: Überholte Vorstellungbleibender*

Glaube (Freiburg 1969). J. SEGUNDO, *Evolution and Guilt* (Maryknoll, New York 1974). M. J. SUCHOCKI, *The Fall to Violence: Original Sin in Relational Theology* (New York 1994). P. TEILHARD DE CHARDIN, *The Phenomenon of Man* (New York 1959); *Christianity and Evolution* (New York 1971). G. VANDERVELDE, *Original Sin: Two Contemporary Roman Catholic Approaches* (Amsterdam 1975). A. VANNESTE, *The Dogma of Original Sin* (Brussels 1975).

[C. J. PETER/K. MCMAHON]

ORIOL, JOSEPH, ST.

Miracle-worker; b. Vich (Barcelona), Spain, Nov. 23, 1650; d. Barcelona, March 23, 1702. Oriol's father died when he was a child and his mother worked hard to bring up her family. With the help of friends, he was able to reach ordination and obtain a doctorate in theology. He lived humbly, did penance, and adhered strictly to the demands of his priestly life. He was not an extraordinary preacher, but his evangelical simplicity inspired his hearers. Impelled by a strong desire to go to the foreign missions, he journeyed to Rome, but fell ill, and Our Lady, in a vision, directed him to return to Barcelona. He predicted the day and hour of his death, and distributed his few possessions to the poor without revealing the reason. He was beatified in 1806 and canonized by PIUS X on May 20, 1909.

Feast: March 23.

Bibliography: *Acta Apostolicae Sedis* 1 (1909) 605–621. J. BALLESTER DE CLARAMUNT, *Vida de San José Oriol* (Barcelona 1909). *Enciclopedia de la Religión Católica,* 7 v. (Barcelona 1951–56) 4.2: 838–840. T. VERGÈS I FORNS, *Sant Josep Oriol i l'Església del Pi* (Barcelona 1975), art.

[S. A. JANTO]

ORIONE, LUIGI, BL.

Founder of the Congregation of the *Piccola Opera della Divina Providenza* (Little Work of Divine Providence); b. June 23, 1872, Pontecurone (Alessandria), Italy; d. March 12, 1940, San Remo (Imperia), Italy. Orione joined the Franciscans at Voghera at an early age but left because of poor health. St. John BOSCO accepted him into the Salesian Oratory in Turin (1886). In 1890 Orione entered the seminary in Tortona in his native diocese and began what was to be his main work in life by caring for poor boys.

After ordination (April 13, 1895) he opened a lodging house for needy seminarians. As the work expanded he accepted orphans and elderly and needy persons. His Little Work of Divine Providence, a network of laity and religious dedicated to charitable works and prayer, was modeled on the foundation of St. Giuseppe COTTOLENGO. To attain the goals of the Piccola Opera, Don Orione founded a number of religious congregations: the SONS OF DIVINE PROVIDENCE; the LITTLE MISSIONARY SISTERS OF CHARITY; the Hermits of Divine Providence; the Brothers of Divine Providence, who wear lay dress, but follow a common rule of life; and the blind Sacramentine Sisters, who dedicate themselves to prayer. By 2000 Orione's disciples in these related institutes had spread to 30 countries and were found on five continents. One hundred sixteen volumes of his writings, as well as voice recordings, are preserved in the Archives of the Piccola Opera della Divina Providenza in Rome.

Worn out from his labors, he died. His remains repose in Tortona. The *Decretum super scripta* in his beatification cause was issued in 1956. Pope John Paul II declared Orione blessed on Oct. 26, 1980, presenting him to the Church as a "marvelous and genial expression of Christian charity." The pope described him as "having the character and heart of the Apostle Paul, tender and sensitive, indefatigable and courageous, tenacious, and dynamic."

Feast: March 12.

Bibliography: *A Priceless Treasure Don Orione. Letters & Writings,* 2 v. (London 1995). *Acta Apostolicae Sedis* 72 (1981): 477–480. *L'Osservatore Romano,* English edition, no. 44 (1980). G. BARRA, *Don Orione* (Turin 1970). E. A. CUONO, *Don Orione* (Victoria, Argentina 1967). *Don Orione. L'apostolo tortonese a 100 anni dalla nascita* (Turin 1972). A. GEMMA, *Don Orione: un cuore senza confini* (Gorle, Italy 1989); *I fioretti di Don Orione* (Rome 1994). A. GEMMA, ed., *La scelta dei poveri più poveri: scritti spirituali* (Rome 1979). *The Restless Apostle. From the Writings of Don Orione* (London 1981). D. A. HYDE, *God's Bandit, The Story of Don Orione, "Father of the Poor"* (Westminster, MD 1957). G. PAPÀSOGLI, *Vita di don Orione,* fourth ed. (Turin 1994). G. PICCININI, *Luce dai colli* (Boston 1958).

[T. F. CASEY]

ORLÉANS-LONGUEVILLE, ANTOINETTE D'

Foundress of the Benedictines of Notre-Dame du Calvaire; b. Trie, near Rouen, 1572; d. Poitiers, April 25, 1618. Having been married in 1588 and widowed in 1596, she entered the Feuillantines of Toulouse in 1599 and became prioress in 1604. In 1605 her aunt Éléonore de Bourbon, abbess of FONTEVRAULT, used papal and royal influence to bring the unwilling Antoinette to be her vicar for reform of the abbey and its priories. The pope first allowed her to remain a Feuillantine in this post, but in 1607 he made her assume the habit and rule of Fontevrault. Meeting constant resistance to her reforms, she sought, and in 1609 obtained, permission to resign; this she did in 1611 after her aunt's death. Guided always by Father Joseph LE CLERC DU TREMBLAY, she went to Lencloître, a priory of the order, and successfully reformed it, but interference by the jealous new abbess of Fontevrault led her to get permission in 1617 to found the independent community of Notre-Dame du Calvaire. For this Antoinette established primitive Benedictine observance in a new monastery in Poitiers, where she died. Papal approbation in 1622 assured the future of the still-flourishing congregation.

Bibliography: *La Fondatrice de la Congrégation des Bénédictines de Notre-Dame du Calvaire, Madame Antoinette d'Orléans-Longueville,* by a nun of Notre-Dame du Calvaire (Poitiers 1932). T. CIVRAYS, *Dictionnaire d'histoire et de géographie ecclésiastiques,* ed. A. BAUDRILLART (Paris 1912–) 3:826–829. J. CHAUSSEY, *Catholicisme* 1:674–675.

[W. H. PRINCIPE]

ORONA MADRIGAL, JUSTINO, ST.

Martyr, pastor, b. April 14, 1877, Atoyac, Jalisco, Diocese of Ciudad Guzmán, Mexico; d. July 1, 1928, Guadalajara. Justino was the son of an extremely poor family. He completed his initial studies at Zapotlán, then entered Guadalajara's seminary (1894). After his ordination (1904), he served as a parish priest at Poncitlán, Encarnación, Jalisco, and Cuquío. Despite an atmosphere of anticlericalism and religious indifference, he was an exemplary priest. While he was pastor of Cuquío (Archdiocese of Guadalajara), he founded the Congregation of Claretian Brothers of the Sacred Heart to care for orphans and poor children. When the persecution intensified, he and his pastor, (St.) Atilano CRUZ, decided to remain with their flock despite the danger, but hid themselves on the nearby ranch of Las Cruces with Justino's brother José María and Toribio Ayala (June 28, 1928). Federal forces arrived there at dawn with the mayor of Cuquío. Justino opened the door, shouted "Viva Cristo Rey!," and was shot. His body was deposited in the Cuquío's town square. His mortal remains were moved to San Felipe Church in Cuquío. Fr. Orona was both beatified (Nov. 22, 1992) and canonized (May 21, 2000) with Cristobal MAGALLANES [*see* GUADALAJARA (MEXICO), MARTYRS OF, SS.] by Pope John Paul II.

Feast: May 25 (Mexico).

Bibliography: J. CARDOSO, *Los mártires mexicanos* (Mexico City 1953). J. DÍAZ ESTRELLA, *El movimiento cristero: sociedad y conflicto en los Altos de Jalisco* (Mexico, D.F. 1979).

[K. I. RABENSTEIN]

OROSIUS

Ancient Church historian; b. Spain, *c.* 390; d. after 418, place unknown. Paul Orosius first appeared in history at Hippo, Africa, in 414 as a young priest consulting AUGUSTINE about a book on the origin of the human soul, *Commonitorium de errore Priscillianistarum et Origenistarum.* Augustine gave him his written opinion in 415; but meanwhile he had instructed Orosius about the new and dangerous heresy of Pelagianism and sent him to the Holy Land, where Pelagius himself was residing (*see* PELAGIUS AND PELAGIANISM). Orosius and Pelagius met in Jerusalem in July of 415, before a synod of the bishops of Palestine. After listening to both sides, Bishop JOHN OF JERUSALEM referred the matter to Rome and insinuated that Orosius's teaching was not entirely orthodox. In his *Liber apologeticus* Orosius indignantly refuted this accusation and explained why the bishops should have condemned Pelagius. Upon Orosius's return to Hippo in 416, Augustine requested him to write a book proving that greater calamities had occurred in pagan than in Christian times. This would serve as a historical supplement to his own monumental *City of God.*

Orosius completed this task in two years (418) and disappeared from history. He had divided the history of mankind from the creation to his own day into seven distinct periods. His work, called *Historiarum adversus paganos libri VII,* is dependent for its information on previous writers, except for the events from 377 to 417 about which he provides contemporary information. Orosius proved conclusively what Augustine had asked him to do, and DANTE therefore called him "the advocate of the Christian centuries" (*Paradiso* 10.119).

This first history of the world by a Christian writer enjoyed an immense prestige for many centuries, and over 200 MSS have been found in the medieval libraries. BOSSUET in his *Universal History* is indebted to Orosius. Modern historians regard it as one-sided and superficial; but even they admire the author's literary style, his appreciation of what *Romania*—his favorite word for Roman culture—meant to the world, his hope of a better civilization from a commingling of the Roman and Germanic people, and his sublime faith that a wise, omnipotent, and merciful God governs the affairs of men.

Bibliography: OROSIUS, *Historiarum adversum paganos libri VII,* ed. C. ZANGEMEISTER (*Corpus scriptorum ecclesiasticorum latinorum* 5; 1882), Eng. *Seven Books of History Against the Pagans,* tr. and ed. I. W. RAYMOND (New York 1936). É. AMANN, *Dictionnaire de théologie catholique,* ed. A. VACANT et al., 15 v. (Paris 1903–50; Tables Générales 1951–) 11.2:1602–11. P. GUILDAY, ed., *Church Historians* (New York 1926). G. DE PLINVAL, A. FLICHE and V. MARTIN eds., *Histoire de l'église depuis les origines jusqu'à nos jours* (Paris 1935–) 4:96–97. J. MARTIN, *Lexikon für Theologie und*

Kirche, ed. J. HOFER and K. RAHNER, 10 v. (2d, new ed. Freiburg 1957–65) 7:1238–39.

[S. J. MCKENNA]

OROZCO, ALFONSO DE, BL.

Augustinian ascetical writer; b. Oropesa (Toledo), October 17, 1500; d. Madrid, Sept. 19, 1591. He studied first at home, then in Salamanca, and followed the lead of his elder brother Francis by entering the Augustinians in 1521. From 1530 to 1554 he was superior, successively, at Soria, Medina, Seville, Granada, and Valladolid. He was appointed court preacher and counselor to Charles V in 1554. Later he was adviser to Philip II, son of Charles. His intense apostolate merited him the good will of all. King and people alike were edified by his zeal, penitential life, and works of charity. He was beatified by Leo XIII on Oct. 1, 1881. Orozco wrote and edited many spiritual and apologetical works. His first and most important work was *Vergel de oración y monte de contemplación* (Seville 1544). He wrote also *Desposorio espiritual* (Seville 1551); *Regimiento del alma* (Valladolid 1551); *Las siete palabras de la Virgen* (Valladolid 1556); *Victoria de mundo* (Valladolid 1565); *Arte de amar a Dios y al projimo* (Valladolid 1568); *De la suavidad de Dios* (Valladolid 1588); *Bonum certamen* (Valladolid 1562); and *Regalis institutio* (Alcalá 1565).

Bibliography: LEO XIII, ''Quod Paulus Apostolus aiebat'' (Apostolic letter, October 1, 1881) *Leonis XIII Acta,* 23 v. (Rome 1881–1905) 2:374–384. M. DEL PRADO GONZALEZ, ''Teologia de la cruz en el beato Alfonso de Orozco,'' *Nova et Vetera* 19 (1994) 327–344. L. RUBIO CALZON, *El beato Alonso de Orozco hombre de letras: Indice de sus escritos y su significación como autor* (Madrid 1992). F. LANG, *Dictionnaire de spiritualité ascétique et mystique. Doctrine et histoire,* ed., M. VILLER et al. (Paris 1932) 1:392–395.

[B. CAVANAUGH]

OROZCO Y JIMÉNEZ, FRANCISCO

Mexican archbishop and educator; b. Zamora, Michoacán, Nov. 19, 1864; d. Guadalajara, Feb. 18, 1936. After entering the seminary in Mexico, he was sent to the South American College in Rome, an institution for which he had great affection and whose benefactor he remained all his life. He studied in the Gregorian University, from which he received the licentiate in theology and the doctorate in philosophy. Years later he earned another doctorate in the newly restored Pontifical University in Mexico. On his return from Rome he became professor and then vice rector of the College of Arts in Zamora, held the same post in the Clerical College of Tacuba, and again in the Seminary of Mexico. Consecrated bishop of Chiapas (1902), he devoted himself to caring for the hitherto neglected flock. Among his achievements in the diocese were the following: he founded five schools for girls and one for boys staffed with professors trained in Europe; he brought electricity to San Cristóbal de las Casas; and he helped to pacify the warring Chamulas and to lead them to a peaceful Christian existence. He became archbishop of Guadalajara in 1913, just as the years of persecution and social and political upheaval were beginning in Mexico. By 1914 he had to go into hiding, living disguised for many months, as he again had to do under President Calles in 1925. Three times he was forced into exile because of the desperate conditions. Nevertheless, Archbishop Orozco managed to increase the number of schools and bring about social improvements among his flock. Orozco y Jiménez was a great admirer of the Society of Jesus and helped it in many ways, even with financial aid during the years of persecution and exile. To him the Jesuits owed the construction of the Colegio of Ysleta where their novices and scholastics were trained from 1925 to 1951. The archbishop favored giving the Jesuits charge of the projected Montezuma Seminary. He was responsible for the publishing of various collections of documents on the history of the Church in Chiapas and Guadalajara and even paid personally for the publication of important historical works.

Bibliography: J. I. DÁVILA GARIBI, *Serie cronológica de los prelados que a través de cuatro siglos ha tenido la antigua diócesis, hoy arquidiócesis de Guadalajara, 1548–1948* (Mexico City 1948); *Labor científica y literaria del Excmo y Rvo. Sr. Dr. y Mtr. D. Francisco Orozco y Jiménez* (Guadalajara 1937). E. VALVERDE TÉLLEZ, *Bio-bibliografía eclesiástica mexicana, 1821–1943,* 3 v. (Mexico City 1949).

[D. OLMEDO]

ORPHAN (IN THE EARLY CHURCH)

In the primitive Church, the local Christian community took into its care any child who had lost one or both parents. This attitude set the Church clearly apart from the pagan world, which was ''without affection.'' Actually, except in Athens, where the law said that the state must educate the children of citizens killed in war until age 18, orphans among the pagans could count on no other assistance except that of their near relatives or the rare individual who was moved by their misery.

From the Jews of the OT the Christians inherited the conviction that God is the Father of orphans (Ps 67.6) and that the surplus of the harvests granted by God accrue by right to the orphan (Dt 24.21). But it was chiefly their ''faith which works through charity'' (Gal 5.6) that provided Christians with the bases and motives for their attitude toward orphans.

At Rome in the 2d century JUSTIN MARTYR declared explicitly that every Sunday, at the end of the apostolic assembly, "those who have in abundance . . . give freely, each as he wills, and what is collected is given over to him who presides, and he aids the orphans and widows" (*Apol.* 67). In 197 at Carthage, Tertullian wrote in the same vein and said that Christians had a common treasury into which each placed his contribution freely according to his means "to aid the boys and girls who have neither fortune nor parents" (*Apol.* 39). In the more important communities the deacons kept up-to-date books of the persons assisted, and the Christian orphans were officially inscribed in these. Even though the non-Christian orphans were not listed here, they were not discriminated against in the distribution of alms. The Church especially urged the faithful to adopt orphans or to give the girls dowries so that they could marry and to set the boys up as apprentices (*Const. Apost.* 4.1–2).

Only after the official recognition of the Church (*c.* 313), when the emperor aided charitable institutions by according them legal protection and financial assistance, did the Church inaugurate a new form of aid to orphans by founding, especially in the East and later in the West, homes for orphans, called *orphanotrophia.* St. Ephrem, St. Basil, and St. John Chrysostom distinguished themselves especially by such foundations. These houses were built not only in the shadow of the cathedrals together with other hospices, but also close to monasteries when they began to spread. Steps were taken simultaneously to educate and instruct orphan children and to use their talents for chant and liturgical ceremonies, bringing about an identification of the *orphanotrophion* and the *schola cantorum*; in some cases priests and monks were recruited from among them. About the end of the 6th century such recruitment gave rise in Rome to a type of junior seminary that provided the Church in the 7th century with four popes: Deusdedit, Leo II, Benedict II, and Sergius II.

Bibliography: L. LALLEMAND, *Histoire des enfants abandonnés* (Paris 1885); *Histoire de la charité,* 4 v. in 5 (Paris 1902–12). R. HERRMANN, *La Charité de l'Église* (Mulhouse 1961) 19–53. H. LECLERCQ, *Dictionnaire d'archéologie chrétienne et de liturgie,* ed. F. CARROLL, H. LECLERQ, and H. I. MARROU, 15 v. (Paris 1907–53) 1.1:1301–06.

[J. BEAUDRY]

ORPHISM

A modern term for the complex of beliefs and religious practices associated with the name of Orpheus, the legendary "sweet singer" of Thrace. Contemporary scholarship is by no means in accord on the content and nature of Orphism, or even, in any meaningful sense, on its existence. Some scholars admit as evidence virtually all that is atypical of Greek religion (such as the "Orphic" grave tablets and the Pindaric passages on metempsychosis); others reject whatever is not specifically designated as Orphic.

Classical Greece recognized Orpheus as not only a poet, but also the culture hero who first instituted Greek mystery cults and rites (τελεταί). Any and all mysteries, therefore, including the Eleusinian, might be called "Orphic." In addition, Athens in the fifth and fourth centuries B.C. knew of sectarian groups who called themselves Orphics, regarded Orpheus as their "lord," reverenced sacred books, and lived an "Orphic life," in which vegetarianism and a taboo on the use of wool were conspicuous features. There were also Orphic practitioners who preyed on men's superstitious fears of the afterlife, professed the ability to perform salutary rites of purification, and even dabbled in magic. There is little archeological or literary evidence to suggest that these groups represented a stable and continuing movement.

In support of the claim that Orphism was possessed of a lofty spiritual content, it is customary to cite the myth of the Titans, who dismembered the infant Dionysus and were then blasted by the thunderbolt of Zeus. From their ashes or soot man was created. Thus, in the alleged Orphic interpretation, man's nature is primarily Titanic and evil, but also, since the Titans had tasted the god's flesh, it contains a divine element. The corollary is that man should so live as to free his divine soul from the "tomb" or "prison" of the body, and so realize his potential immortality.

The primary purpose of the myth was evidently to account for the σπαραγμός, the rending ritual of the Dionysiac cult; it enjoyed a certain currency, and, with or without the sequel of man's creation, appears in several variant forms. Some of these may have been "Orphic," in the sense that speculative theological writings were often sealed with his name. Yet if this was the "cardinal myth" of historic Orphism, it is strange that the inference as to man's divine nature was explicitly drawn only once, by the late Neoplatonist, Olympiodorus (fl. sixth century. A.D.). Pending proof that the doctrine was specifically Orphic and early, the precise nature and influence of Orphism must remain problematical.

Bibliography: M. P. NILSSON, *Geschichte der griechischen Religion* (Munich 1955–61) 1:678–699; 2:246–431. W. K. C. GUTHRIE, *Die Religion in Geschichte und Gegenwart* (Tübingen 1957–65) 4:1703–05, with bibliog. K. PRÜMM, *Dictionnaire de la Bible,* suppl. ed. L. PIROT, et al. (Paris 1928–) 6:55–86; "Die Orphik im Spiegel der neueren Forschung," *Zeitschrift für katholische Theologie* 78 (1956) 1–40.

[F. R. WALTON]

ORSI, GIUSEPPE AGOSTINO

Dominican theologian and cardinal; b. Florence, Italy, May 9,1692; d. Rome, Italy, June 12, 1761. He taught philosophy and theology first in the convent of San Marco, FLORENCE, where he was also prior, and then after 1732 at the Casanatense Library in Rome. In 1738 he was appointed secretary to the Congregation of the INDEX; in 1749, master of the Sacred Palace; and in 1759, cardinal priest with the title of San Sisto. A man of wide learning and deep piety, he was a controversialist, theologian, and historian of high merit. His chief work is the *Istoria ecclesiastica* in 21 volumes (Rome 1749–62, the last volume, posthumously), which he wrote to counteract the obvious tendencies toward GALLICANISM in Claude FLEURY's *Histoire ecclésiastique* (Paris 1691–1723). His work goes only as far as the end of the seventh century, but it was continued to 1529 by Filippo Becchetti, OP, and republished several times. One of the best editions is that of Venice in 1822, which with its continuation runs to 42 volumes. Noteworthy among his other numerous works is the *De irreformabili Romani pontificis in definiendis fidei controversiis iudicio* (Rome 1739) in three volumes, written in defense of the papacy against Gallican theories.

Bibliography: G. G. BOTTARI, who edited the posthumous ed. of v.21 of the *Istoria,* wrote a life of Orsi as an introd. to be found in all eds. of the work. A. FABRONI, *Vitae Italorum doctrina excellentium,* 18 v. (Pisa 1778–99) 11:6–36. M. M. GORCE, *Dictionnaire de théologie catholique,* ed. A. VACANT, 15 v. (Paris 1903–50; Tables générales 1951–) 11.2:1612–19. G. MORONI, *Dizionario de erudizone storico-ecclesiastica,* 103 v. in 53 (Venice 1840–61) 49:144–145.

[S. OLIVIERI]

ORSINI

Important noble family of Rome, leader of the Guelfs, the supporters of the papacy in the long struggle against the empire and the Ghibellines from the twelfth to the sixteenth century. The Orsini, Colonna, SAVELLI, and Conti were among the oldest Roman families. These four families had the greatest prestige in the centuries after 1100; the Orsini and Colonna gradually became the leaders and outlived the Savelli and Conti. All depended on legends and tradition to some extent for their early history. One Orsini legend told of a widow in Flanders whose son was nursed by a domestic bear; this boy, *Orso* (bear), who gave the family its name, arrived in Rome *c.* 425 and was given land in Umbria. The Orsini claimed relationship with two medieval popes, STEPHEN II and St. PAUL I, and with 17 other saints and blessed persons who lived between 222 and 1330, among them the brothers SS. JOHN and Paul, martyred in 362, St. BENEDICT, and his sister St. Scholastica.

Bl. *John Orsini,* b. Rome, 1032; d. Trogir (Yugoslavia), 1110–11 (feast, Nov. 14). Before 1073 he was sent with others by Pope Alexander II to prevent a schism in Trogir. Orsini became bishop there in 1100 and kept the see united with Rome. His interest in both the spiritual and civic welfare of the city was recognized by his being declared its patron.

Anti-Ghibelline Activity. The years from *c.* 1100 to 1562 were of high importance for the papacy-Orsini alliance. Pitted against them were the empire and the COLONNA. Often the cries resounded in Rome: "Orsi and Holy Church," "The People and Colonna" (*see* GUELFS AND GHIBELLINES). From 1144 to 1280 the prestige of the Orsini increased and was higher than that of the Colonna. The first of the Orsini cardinals became Pope CELESTINE III (1191–98), and he rewarded the family with fiefs for their assistance in defeating the Colonna. From a few villages the possessions of both families had grown to a dozen or more in the thirteenth century, requiring the maintenance of more retainers. Then in 1241 Senator *Matteo Rosso Orsini* (d. 1246) inflicted a severe defeat on the Colonna. Their houses were destroyed and their fortified mausoleum of Augustus was captured, and Matteo remained powerful in Rome (1241–43). One of his sons, *Giovanni Gaetano,* became cardinal and later Pope NICHOLAS III (1277–80). But between 1288 and 1431 the Orsini during three periods were forced to play a secondary role while their rivals dominated the city. First, Pope NICHOLAS IV (1288–92), who had been bishop of Palestrina, the principal Colonna possession, favored the Colonna. They exercised great influence over him; then having become bolder, they dared to challenge Pope BONIFACE VIII. The Orsini assisted Boniface in capturing Palestrina, and several Colonna fled to France; but the triumph of the Orsini lasted only until 1303, when Sciarra and Stefano Colonna returned to Rome and were powers there for about 25 years. They made a truce with the Orsini in 1306, but fighting broke out again, and the Orsini achieved no important gains except for a brief interval after Sciarra left Rome in 1328. However, the family did not lose prestige. During the AVIGNON PAPACY and the WESTERN SCHISM (1305–1417) eight members were created cardinals. In the fourteenth century the Orsini added to their holdings Bracciano, a most valued possession for 300 years and the seat of the major branch of the family until it became extinct. With the election of a Colonna as Pope MARTIN V (1417–31), the Colonna family again became powerful. Alarmed by the position of their rival, the Orsini persuaded Martin's successor, Pope EUGENE IV, to curb the Colonna and helped to destroy Palestrina. Again in the pontificate of SIXTUS IV, the Orsini family assisted papal troops in defeating the Colonna (1481–84). There were other evidences of the importance of the Orsini:

they contracted marriages in 1444 and 1487 with two future kings of Naples, Ferdinand of Aragon and Frederick of Aragon; in 1469, with Lorenzo de' MEDICI; and in 1488, with his son Piero. During these years the Orsini built the great castle at Bracciano.

Cesare BORGIA's defeat of the Colonna seemed a victory for the Orsini; then he turned on them, and they too lost possessions. Pope JULIUS II (1503–13) restored properties to both families and brought about a brief reconciliation between them. There were times between 1523 and 1557 when the Orsini were overshadowed or defeated by the Colonna, and the Guelf cause seemed lost. The Ghibellines did not succeed, however, in overthrowing or limiting the temporal power of the papacy. The Orsini and other Guelfs were on the winning side, and they were rewarded for their support. In 1560 Pius IV promoted the Bracciano branch to the rank of duke and bestowed the honor of being one of the two princes in attendance at the papal throne. The Colonna was the other. Another service of the Orsini to the Church was the governing of the STATES OF THE CHURCH, Orsini bishops and laymen performing the required duties.

Orsini Cardinals. A study of the Orsini cardinals is another way of measuring the importance of the family to the Church. It was natural for the popes to reward their allies; accordingly, the Orsini had more cardinals than the Colonna did during the centuries of conflict; between 1144 and 1562, there were 22 Orsini and only 11 Colonna cardinals. Several times there were two or three Orsini in the college of cardinals at the same time; only twice were there two Colonna. The Orsini had a pope and three cardinals before the first Colonna was created cardinal in 1192 or 1193, and even then the Colonna had to share his honor with an Orsini simultaneously created cardinal. During the Avignon papacy and the Western Schism, eight Orsini and only four Colonna became cardinals. None of the Orsini cardinals was ever so independent as Cardinals Giacomo and Pietro Colonna in Pope Boniface VIII's pontificate, or so aggressive as Cardinal Pompeo Colonna in Pope Clement VII's pontificate. There were two Orsini popes before a Colonna was elected pope, and Martin V proved to be the only Colonna ever to achieve that honor. After the Guelf-Ghibelline conflict became passé c. 1562 and before 1789, another Orsini became Pope BENEDICT XIII; twelve Colonna but only five Orsini became cardinals. The Orsini cardinals (the first date indicates appointment) included *Giacinto,* 1144, who later became Pope Celestine III; *Giordano,* 1145 (d. 1165); *Pietro,* 1181 (d. 1181); *Bobone,* 1182 (d. 1189); perhaps another *Bobone,* 1192 or 1193; *Giovanni Gaetano,* 1244, later Pope Nicholas III; *Matteo Rosso,* 1261–63? (d. 1305); *Giordano,* 1278 (d. 1287), brother of Nicholas III; *Latino Frangipane Malabranca,* 1278 (d. 1294), nephew of Nicholas

Virginio Orsini, one of the commanders of the papal army of Pope Sixtus IV, in a detail of the "Crossing of the Red Sea" fresco in the Sistine Chapel, Vatican.

III; *Napoleone,* 1288 (d. 1342), another nephew of Nicholas III. Matteo Rosso was the grandson of Senator Matteo Rosso; he participated in 13 election conclaves, including the one that elected his uncle, Pope Nicholas III. He supported Pope Boniface VIII and opposed the French influence that lured the papacy to Avignon. Latino was a student in Paris and prior of the Dominican friary in Rome. Popes Martin IV, Honorius IV, and Nicholas IV consulted him on important questions; Dominican writers call him blessed. Napoleone also studied in Paris. He restored Orvieto and Gubbio to papal obedience under Boniface VIII. In contrast with his cousin Cardinal Matteo Rosso, he worked for the election of Pope CLEMENT V, the first pope in Avignon. Philip IV of France gave him a pension.

The fourteenth century numbered other Orsini cardinals, including *Francesco,* 1295 (d. 1312); *Gian Gaetano,* or *Giovanni,* 1316 (d. 1335), a legate in several provinces, opposed the Ghibellines who invited Emperor Louis IV the Bavarian to Rome, withdrew from Rome, and then brought Rome back to papal obedience after Louis's departure—Pope JOHN XXII did not approve of the cardinal's war against the Colonna and ordered him to return to Tuscany. *Matteo,* 1327 (d. 1340), a nephew of Cardinal Gian Gaetano, a Dominican who taught in Florence, Rome, and Paris (Dominicans call him blessed); *Rinaldo,* 1350 (d. 1374); *Giacomo,* or *Jacopo,* 1371 (d. 1379); *Poncello,* 1378 (d. 1395); *Tommaso,* 1379? (d. 1390); and *Raimondello,* 1381, marked the latter half of the turbulent century. *Giordano,* 1405 (d. 1438), attended the councils of PISA and CONSTANCE; served as legate in France, England, Hungary-Bohemia for Pope Martin V; visited churches and religious houses in Rome to reform abuses; and as legate at BASEL supported Pope Eugene IV. *Latino,* 1448 (d. 1477), was pious and well educated in law; in 1472 he commanded the fleet against the Turks; during an illness Pope Sixtus IV and the college of cardinals visited him; he established a library that was destroyed in the sacking of Rome, 1527. *Giambattista,* 1483 (d. 1503); *Franciotto,* 1517 (d. 1533?); and *Flavio,* 1565 (d. 1581), spanned the sixteenth century. *Alessandro,* 1615 (d. 1626), spent his youth in Florence at the court of Ferdinand I, his maternal grandfather; served as legate in Ravenna, where he relieved distress during a time of poor harvests and paid peasants for their losses during the delay of court procedures; in Rome he was the patron of G. GALILEI, engaged in many charitable works, and led an ascetical life. *Virginio,* 1641 (d. 1676), who gave up his right of inheritance as the firstborn son in order to be a religious, became a KNIGHT OF MALTA and won reknown in war against the Turks. *Vincenzo Maria* (his name in the Dominican Order), 1672, later became Pope Benedict XIII. *Domenico,* 1743 (d. 1789), a great nephew of Benedict XIII, was made a grandee of Spain by Charles III and served as Ferdinand IV's ambassador from Naples to Rome.

Conclusion. A present-day map of Rome reflects the importance of the family in four place names, three of them streets. One of the streets refers to a palace on Monte Giordano, the site of the Taverna palace today. A few years after the Savelli family became extinct, the Orsini purchased their palace (1717) at the theater of Marcellus. Later it was sold, but it is still called the Orsini palace. In 1834 Pope Gregory XVI confirmed the honor of being princes in attendance at papal functions as the exclusive right of the Orsini and Colonna families. (Special circumstances have on occasion modified this declaration.) It has been exercised by both families into the twentieth century.

Bibliography: P. LITTA et al., *Famiglie celebri italiane,* 14 v. (Milan 1819–1923) v. 10. G. MORONI, *Dizionario de erudizione storico-ecclesiastica,* 103 v. in 53 (Venice 1840–61) 27:147; 49:145–172; 55:233–243. L. PASTOR, *The History of the Popes From the Close of the Middle Ages,* 40 v. (London-St. Louis 1938–61) 1:293–297; 4:379–384; 5:247–248; 6:125–127, 218; 9: 275–276. L. CÀLLARI, *I palazzi di Roma* (3d ed. Rome 1944). G. B. COLONNA, *Gli Orsini* (Milan 1955). F. BOCK, *Lexikon für Theologie und Kirche,* 10 v. (2d, new ed. Freiburg 1957–65) 7:1241–44.

[M. L. SHAY]

ORTEGA Y GASSET, JOSÉ

Spanish philosopher; b. Madrid, May 9, 1883, d. there, Oct. 18, 1955. Ortega obtained his doctorate in philosophy and letters at the Central University, Madrid (1904), and subsequently attended the universities of Leipzig, Berlin, and Marburg. From 1910 to 1936 he was professor of metaphysics at the University of Madrid. He was a prolific writer; his complete works, including those published posthumously, fill nine volumes.

From his first writings, Ortega preferred the vitalistic philosophy of the turn of the century to the IDEALISM of his professors at Marburg, and he focused his attention on the individual within a concrete "circumstance." The influence of F. W. NIETZSCHE and W. DILTHEY is apparent in Ortega's writings, although he defends the originality and superiority of his philosophy over the empiricist thought of Dilthey. Several of his themes on human existence are also found in M. Heidegger, but Ortega is careful to point out the priority of his own publications.

In interpreting Ortega's thought, the chronology of his works (especially those published posthumously) must be kept in mind. The main ideas of his "metaphysics" and epistemology, substantially unchanged since about 1932, are the following. The radical reality is life, "my life." All other realities are rooted, in the sense that they must appear in one way or another, in my life. Life can be described as what "I" do with the "circumstance," or as the effort for "my" realization within a given "circumstance." The "I" or the ego is a project, a program. "Circumstance" means everything else, including my body and soul. Independently of my interpretations, the circumstance (i.e., things) consists in mere facilities and difficulties.

The "instrument" by which one can capture radical reality is the vital reason that, in the last analysis, is identical with life itself. My life, a continuous making and not something already made, must constantly consider and weigh the facilities and difficulties of the situation; it must choose—"we are necessarily free"—between the different possibilities or alternatives, and it must reason. This is the meaning of vital reason, and since life is essentially time or history, vital reason is also historical reason. Its method is narration. It does not use Eleatic, universal, and identical concepts, but concrete and "occasional" concepts of variable content.

Since every individual is a project, the circumstance or the facilities and difficulties each one faces are different. Hence each man has a different point of view vis-à-vis the universe. What one sees, another cannot see; what is true for one may not be true for another. All points of view are necessary for seeing the whole truth. The truth of ideas, as distinct from truth as authenticity, consists in their correspondence with one's idea of reality; it is "a matter of internal policy."

In spite of his perspectivism and his definition of truth, Ortega rejects RELATIVISM in the traditional sense of the term. A few texts in Ortega's earlier writings explicitly affirm the existence of a transcendent, absolute reality, whereas later expressions seem to preclude its truly transcendent and absolute character. The later position, which can hardly be interpreted from a purely phenomenological point of view, seems more in harmony with his final philosophy. Ortega wrote also, with genial insights, on philosophy of history, psychology, literature, art, sports, technology, and above all on social and political philosophy.

Ortega contributed immensely to the philosophical awakening of his countrymen; his writings, encompassing in masterful style all realms of culture, and the *Revista de Occidente,* which he founded and edited, introduced their readers to the whole of European and world thought. His own philosophy has influenced, in greater or less degree, contemporary Spanish laymen and thinkers in other lands. The deficiencies of his philosophy stem from his de-essentialized ideas concerning the "I" and life; his idealistic and, in spite of his protests, relativistic concept of truth; the inability of his vitalistic conception to reach transcendence; his radical historicism; and the exclusion of universal moral norms.

See Also: LIFE PHILOSOPHIES.

Bibliography: *Obras completas,* 9 v. (4th ed. Madrid 1957–63). J. MARÍAS, AGUILERA, *Ortega y la idea de la razón vital* (2d ed. Madrid 1948); *La escuela de Madrid* (Buenos Aires 1959). J. FERRATER MORA, *Ortega y Gasset: An Outline of His Philosophy* (New Haven 1957). S. M. RAMÍREZ, *La filosofía de Ortega y Gasset* (Barcelona 1958). F. ALLUNTIS, "The Vital and Historical Reason of José Ortega y Gasset," *Franciscan Studies* 15 (1955): 60–78.

[F. ALLUNTIS]

ORTHODOX AND ORIENTAL ORTHODOX CHURCHES

The word Orthodox is derived from the Greek words ὀρθός (right) and δόξα (belief).

Orthodox Churches

The term "Orthodox Churches" in its conventional historical sense designates those Churches of the Christian East that: (a) accepted and have maintained the teachings of the Council of Chalcedon, (b) hold on to the historic ecclesial and liturgical traditions of Byzantium, and (c) are in communion with the Ecumenical Patriarch of Constantinople. The Orthodox Churches comprise three categories: (1) autocephalous churches that are self-governing, but in communion with each other and with the Ecumenical Patriarch of Constantinople, (2) autonomous churches that have internal autonomy but remain dependent on an autocephalous church; and (3) dependent churches. A fourth category exists, comprising those churches that hold on to (a) and (b), but are separated from communion because of political exigencies (e.g., Russian Church Abroad) or theological controversies (e.g., Old Believers and Old Calendarists), are presently not in communion with Constantinople or Moscow. These churches are:

Autocephalous Churches (in order of precedence and honor):
Ecumenical Patriarchate of Constantinople
Patriarchate of Alexandria
Patriarchate of Antioch
Patriarchate of Jerusalem
Orthodox Church of Russia
Orthodox Church of Serbia
Orthodox Church of Romania
Orthodox Church of Bulgaria
Orthodox Church of Georgia
Orthodox Church of Cyprus
Orthodox Church of Greece
Orthodox Church of Poland
Orthodox Church of Albania
Orthodox Church in the Czech and Slovak Republics
Orthodox Church in America**—The autocephaly status of the Orthodox Church in America is recognized by all other autocephalous Orthodox Churches except the Ecumenical Patriarchate, which insists that the Moscow Patriarchate has no right to grant autocephaly without its agreement.

Autonomous Churches:
Orthodox Church of Mount Sinai
Orthodox Church of Finland
Orthodox Church of Japan
Orthodox Church of China
Estonian Apostolic Orthodox Church

Churches Dependent on the Ecumenical Patriarchate:
American Carpatho-Russian Orthodox Greek Catholic Church
Ukrainian Orthodox Church of the USA and Diaspora
Russian Orthodox Archdiocese in Western Europe
Albanian Orthodox Diocese of America

Patriarch Filaret, giving sacraments to child, Ukrainian Orthodox church, Kiev, Ukraine. (AP/Wide World Photos)

Belarusan Council of Orthodox Churches in North America
Ukrainian Orthodox Church of Canada

Orthodox Churches of Irregular Status:
Old Believers (Old Ritualists)
Russian Orthodox Church Outside Russia
Ukrainian Orthodox Church Kiev Patriarchate
Ukrainian Autocephalous Orthodox Church
Macedonian Orthodox Church
Old Calendar Orthodox Churches

Characteristic Features of the Orthodox Churches. Centralization of Church government was never developed in the East as was the case in the Latin West; therefore the stress has been on the autonomous action of each local bishop in his diocese, guided by the concerted actions of a Holy Synod or collegiality type of government. In all the Orthodox Churches, the bishop of the capital city, whether he is a patriarch, metropolitan, or archbishop, is considered the chief among all the other bishops of that given nation, but he has no jurisdiction in the strict sense over other bishops. All Church decisions are made by the episcopal council or synod at which the chief prelate presides, but as an equal among equals. Not only is there a supreme synod gathered around the chief prelate, but there are also lesser synods and councils for each diocese and parish. Ordinarily there are two such councils: one, an ecclesiastical tribunal, passes judgments on marriage cases, dispensations, and the granting of divorces; the other deals with the financial administration of ecclesiastical property. Orthodox Churches hold Sacred Scripture and tradition as the two fonts of Christian revelation. These two sources are presented to the faithful mainly in a setting of strongly liturgical emphasis. Orthodox fidelity to tradition is revealed in its scrupulous fidelity to the teachings of the first seven ecumenical councils and the writings of the early Fathers.

Oriental Orthodox Churches

The term "Oriental Orthodox Churches" refers to those six Churches that are identified by their non-reception of the Council of Chalcedon (451), and are not in communion with the Ecumenical Patriarch. In the past, these churches were called Monophysite Churches by their opponents, although the reality was far more complex and nuanced. The term "Oriental Orthodox" is preferred, as none of these churches ever held on to the strict monophysite position of Eutychus and Dioscorus. Through ecumenical dialogues and joint statements that have emerged since the 1970s, the dispute over Chalcedon has been acknowledged as essentially one of semantics and terminology rather than substantial theology, viz., the Oriental Orthodox Churches hold on to the same christological understanding as the Orthodox and Catholic Churches. The six Oriental Orthodox Churches are:

Armenian Apostolic Church
Coptic Orthodox Church
Ethiopian Orthodox Church
Syrian Orthodox Church
Malankara Orthodox Syrian Church
Eritrean Orthodox Church

For further information about these churches, see under their separate headings in this encyclopedia.

Strictly speaking, the Assyrian Church of the East (erroneously known as the "Nestorian Church") is neither Orthodox nor Oriental Orthodox, as a result of its unique christological tradition.

See Also: ASSYRIAN CHURCH OF THE EAST.

Bibliography: A. ATIYA, *A History of Eastern Christianity* (London 1968). S. BULGAKOV, *The Orthodox Church* (Crestwood, NY 1988). D. CONSTANTELOS, *Understanding the Greek Orthodox Church: Its Faith, History and Practice* (New York 1982). N. DAVIS, *A Long Walk to Church: A Contemporary History of Russian Orthodoxy* (Boulder, Co. 1995). M. EFTHIMIOU and G. CHRISTOPOULOS, *A History of the Greek Orthodox Church in America* (New York 1984). J. ELLIS, *The Russian Orthodox Church: A Contemporary History* (London 1986). D. GEANAKOPLOS, *A Short History of the Ecumenical Patriarchate of Constantinople* (330-1990) (Brookline, Mass. 1990). P. GREGORIOS, W. LAZARETH, and N. NISSIOTIS, eds., *Does Chalcedon Divide or Unite? Towards Convergence in Orthodox Christology* (Geneva 1981). H. HILL, ed, *Light from the East: A Symposium on the Oriental Orthodox and Assyrian Churches* (Toronto 1988). J. MEYENDORFF, *The Orthodox Church* (Crestwood, NY 1981). R. ROBERSON, *The Eastern Christian Churches: A Brief Survey*, 6th ed (Rome 1999). K. WARE, *The Orthodox Church*, rev. ed. (New York 1997).

[G. A. MALONEY/EDS.]

ORTHODOX CHURCH IN AMERICA (OCA)

The Orthodox Church in America is an autocephalous church of the Eastern Orthodox communion, formerly known as "The Russian Orthodox Greek Catholic Church of America," or "the Metropolia." Its "autocephaly" was officially granted on April 10, 1970, by the patriarch of Moscow. The Orthodox Church in America was proclaimed an autocephalous Church on Oct. 19, 1970, during the All-American Council meeting at St. Tikhon's Monastery in South Canaan, Pa. The Metropolia adopted a new name—"Orthodox Church in America" (OCA). The OCA is a member of the World Council of Churches and the National Council of Churches in the U.S.A. Governed by a council of bishops, clergy, and laity, the OCA includes over 650 parishes and other institutions. English is the primary language of worship. Twenty Orthodox monasteries (eight female, twelve male) have been established throughout the United States and Canada under OCA jurisdiction. St. Vladimir's Seminary, in Crestwood, N.Y., is OCA's seminary and school of theology, while St. Tikhon Monastery in South Canaan, Pa., offers seminary studies. There is also a seminary for the training of indigenous clergy in Kodiak, Alaska. Various Orthodox groups in the United States such as Albanian, Bulgarian, Rumanian, Russian, Serbian, Ukrainian, etc., have parishes that are part of the OCA.

The first official Orthodox mission to America was launched on Dec. 21, 1793, when a group of volunteers from the monasteries Valaam and Konevitsa (located on the Russo-Finnish border) left St. Petersburg for Alaska, then a Russian territory. This missionary group included one Archimandrite; three priest-monks; one deacon-monk; one lay monk, Herman (d. 1837, canonized as Saint in 1970), famous for his ascetic life and efforts to defend Alaskan natives from ruthless Russian traders; and several staff members. Guided by Shelikov, a Russian businessman, the group traveled for 293 days and a distance of 7,300 miles before arriving at its destination.

The arrival of the first official Orthodox missionary to Kodiak on Sept. 24, 1794, occurred almost a century after the first Russian-Siberian entrepreneurs had permanently settled in Alaska. The Orthodox faith in North America is believed to have had been brought first by Orthodox laity, primarily men who baptized their indigenous wives, offspring and servants. Mass baptisms took place only after the first official Orthodox mission arrived; Juvenal, one of the missionary priest-monks, is reported as baptizing several thousand natives. Despite its relatively sensitive approach to the pre-Christian spirituality of the Aleuts (in which Orthodox Christianity was presented not as the abolition, but as the fulfillment, of the Aleut's ancient religious heritage), the Alaskan mission had several martyrs. One of them was Juvenal himself, killed by indigenous people in 1796. After the sale of Alaska to the United States (1867), the Orthodox mission spread to other parts of the North American continent.

The permanent establishment of the North American mission owes much to the person of John Veniaminov, a priest (d. 1879 as Metropolitan Innocent of Moscow, canonized by the Russian Orthodox Church in 1977 as a Saint, "Enlightener of the Aleuts, Apostle to America and Siberia") who arrived in Unalaska in 1824 with his family. By translating the Gospel of St. Matthew into the Unangan Aleut vernacular, then inaugurating a parish school in Unalaska in 1828, Veniaminov opened a new chapter in the story of the Alaskan Mission. Years later, when he was consecrated a bishop, Veniaminov appointed Jacob Netsvetov, a priest of Aleut and Russian ancestry who graduated from Irkutsk Seminary, (canonized by the OCA on Oct. 15 and 16, 1994 as "St Jacob, Enlightener of the Peoples of Alaska"), to conduct missionary work in the Yukon River delta. Netsvetov preached Christianity for almost 20 years among the Yup'ik Eskimo and Athabascan Native tribes, baptizing hundreds of their people in the Innoko River. Netsvetov's headquarters was at Ikogmiut (a village known today as "Russian Mission").

By 1867, when Alaska became an American territory, the Alaskan mission, demonstrating extraordinary linguistic adaptability and cultural sensitivity, had grown to nine Orthodox parishes having 12,000 indigenous Christians organized into 35 chapels with 17 schools and 3 orphanages. The sale of Alaska to the United States, however, altered the Orthodox church's situation. In its effort to "Americanize" Orthodox native peoples, the new territorial authorities preferred to cooperate with proselytizing Protestant missionary groups. Under Protestant influence, Orthodox prayers, icons, and native languages were forbidden in Alaska's American schools. This development caused the Russian Holy Synod to elevate, in 1870, the Alaskan mission to become a diocese "of the Aleutian Islands and Alaska." The new diocesan bishop (John Mitropolsky, 1870–1876) decided to relocate to San Francisco. Mitropolsky saw San Francisco as both a city from which the Alaskan mission could best be defended and as a base for the mission's expansion in the continental United States. In subsequent years, the diocese was transferred two times: first in 1872, when it was moved from Sitka, Alaska, to San Francisco after becoming the diocese "of the Aleutian Islands and North America" (1900); then in 1905, after incorporating a large number of "Uniate" immigrant parishes from Galicia and Carpatho-Russia, the diocesan headquarters was transferred to New York. The intention of the missionary diocese was to extend its ministry to the entire North American continent and to establish a united, culturally and linguistically pluralistic Orthodox Church in Ameri-

ca while providing each of the Orthodox communities with a bishop of its respective nationality.

Tikhon (Belavin) (d. 1925, canonized Oct. 9, 1989) was appointed bishop of Alaska in 1898. A future patriarch of Moscow (1918), he became Archbishop of the American diocese of the Russian Orthodox Church of North America, residing in New York City from 1905 to 1907. In 1905, in keeping with the initial plan of the mission, Tikhon submitted a proposal for an *autocephalous* church in America to the Russian Synod of St. Petersburg. Foreseeing the inevitable Americanization of his flock, Tikhon believed that only an autonomous ecclesiastic structure, governed in America, would best reflect and help to accommodate the ethnic pluralism of its membership. From 1905 to 1907, Tikhon decentralized ecclesiastical control, adapting Russian ecclesiastical structure and worship to the local cultural environment. Tikhon encouraged services in English and published the necessary liturgical books containing translations of the liturgy into English.

Extremely rapid expansion of the missionary diocese in North America encouraged Tikhon to establish several Russian Orthodox theological schools, among them a seminary and women's college. Such establishment allowed the missionary diocese to grow into a multi-ethnic American diocese, becoming the foundation for a new autonomous immigrant Church. By 1917, the Orthodox mission in North America included more than 350 parishes and chapels, with monasteries, orphanages, fraternal societies, and schools. It was also publishing its own printed materials.

The Russian Revolution (1917) and subsequent anti-ecclesiastical legislation in the new Soviet state hampered Tikhon's project of establishing an autonomous American Orthodox Church. During 1918 and 1919 when The Third "All-American Council" took place, the missionary diocese attempted to defend its canonical jurisdiction over the Orthodox community in North America, but it was unsuccessful. Unable to maintain canonical unity in an increasingly polarized ethnic situation, the missionary diocese lost a substantial number of its Carpatho-Russian parishes. In 1922, these formed their own national jurisdiction. Neither could the American diocese react effectively to the establishment of a "Greek Archdiocese of North and South America" by the ecumenical patriarch, Meletios IV Metaxakis, in 1921. Intended to bring together numerous immigrant (600,000 Greek immigrants came to the United States between 1890 and 1920) Greek independent "trustee" parishes, the new Greek archdiocese became the largest Orthodox body in America; yet it was politically divided until 1931. In the same period the American missionary diocese began to decline. In 1924, after refusing to offer a statement of loyalty to the Soviet atheist government, the diocese proclaimed its self-government in cooperation (until 1926) with "the Synod in Exile," also known as "the Karlovtsy Synod," now known as the Russian Orthodox Church Abroad or the Russian Orthodox Church outside Russia. Due to internal divisions, the American diocese lost much of its influence as a multi-ethnic American diocese, increasingly becoming more a Russian "Metropolia," the name by which it eventually became known. The older, typically multi-ethnic *parish* that had previously characterized the missionary diocese fragmented into smaller, ethnic *parishes* that sought to change the church's jurisdiction. The appearance of the Greek Orthodox diocese in America plus the lack of regular canonical status for the old missionary archdiocese (metropolia) caused new non-Russian groups of immigrants to affiliate with their mother churches abroad by inviting priests directly from those countries. This process contributed to continuing division of the Orthodox community in America into a number of national dioceses and archdioceses, each of which was designated by its ethnic origin. Since the early 1920s, the majority of Orthodox parishioners in America have belonged to the denominational family of "ethnic churches" rather than to one "missionary Orthodox immigrant church."

Currently, the Orthodox in North America remain divided into 32 distinct administrative "jurisdictions," divisions based principally on ethnic origin. However, OCA's proclamation of autocephaly in 1970 opened a new chapter for Orthodox Americans, who have begun to emphasize anew the unity of Orthodoxy in America, regardless of ethnic origin and independent of foreign interests. OCA, in its call to all Orthodox Christians in America, including bishops, clergy, and laity, extended an invitation to every Orthodox body in America to unite so as to constitute visibly one Church. This remains the official position of the Orthodox Church in America, although OCA's autocephaly has not been recognized by the Ecumenical Patriarchate which, being "first among equals," claims that it alone among Orthodox Churches has the authority to grant autocephaly. Recent meetings between the Ecumenical Patriarch and the primate of the Orthodox Church in America, Metropolitan Theodosius, and more specifically the Ecumenical Partiarch's historic visit to St. Nicholas OCA's Cathedral in Washington, D.C., on July 4, 1990, indicate the concerns of both churches for unity of the Orthodox Church and for Orthodoxy in America. Relations between OCA and the Greek archdiocese, previously strained at times, improved during the 1990s.

The OCA appears to be the principal church claiming a direct continuation of efforts begun by the first Orthodox missionaries to North America in 1794. The OCA has about 1,000,000 members of Russian, Ukrainian, Bulgarian, Macedonian, Serbian, Romanian, Mexican, and Albanian backgrounds, who represent half of an almost 2,000,000 American population identifying itself as Orthodox Christian. These numbers are based on independent national religious surveys from 1970 to 1993 and on U.S. Census data from 1990, as quoted by OCA's sources.

Bibliography: BISHOP GREGORY (AFONSKY), *History of the Orthodox Church in Alaska, 1774–1914* (Kodiak, AK 1977). P. GARRETT, *St. Innocent: Apostle to America* (Crestwood, NY 1979). M. OLEKSA, *Alaskan Missionary Spirituality* (Crestwood, NY 1992). *Orthodox America 1794–1976: Development of the Orthodox Church in America*, C. J. TARASAR and J. H. ERICKSON, eds. (Syosset, NY 1975). R. PIERCE, *The Russian Orthodox Religious Mission in America, 1794–1837* (Kingston, ONT 1978). W. SPERRY, *Religion in America, Orthodox Christians in North America, 1794–1994* (Orthodox Christian Publications Center 1995). M. STOKOE, in collaboration with L. KISHKOVSKY, *Orthodox Christians in North America 1794–1994* (Oyster Bay Cove, NY 1994). *Historical Dictionary of the Orthodox Church*, M. PROKURAT, A. GOLITIZIN, & M. D. PETERSON, eds. (Lantham, MD 1996).

[M. YOUROUKOV/R. B. MILLER]

ORTHODOX CHURCH OF BULGARIA

An autocephalous Orthodox Church and national church of Bulgaria that is in communion with the Ecumenical Patriarchate of CONSTANTINOPLE.

Early history. In 679, the Bulgars, led by Asparukh [or Isperikh (643–701)] had defeated a Byzantine army led by Emperor CONSTANTINE IV, forcing Byzantium to accept a peace treaty in 681. Moving south, the Bulgarians settled in territories where Christianity had been flourishing for several centuries. The Church Council of Serdica (modern-day Sofia) in 342 A.D. gave evidence of Christianity's popularity and the importance of that territory for its development in the early fourth century. Contacts between Bulgarians and Christians increased, especially after rapid expansion of the Bulgarian state during the reign of Krum (802–814), but it was not until 865, under Khan (Tsar) BORIS (852–889) that Christianity became the official religion in Bulgaria. The peace treaty of 863 between Byzantium and Bulgaria required, among other things, that Boris permit Byzantine missionary activity in Bulgaria.

Boris' baptism in 865, followed by mass baptisms of Bulgarians, opened the door to the establishment of Orthodox Christianity in Bulgaria. But in 866, when PHOTIUS, the patriarch of Constantinople rejected Boris' request to establish a national hierarchy, Boris switched his allegiance to Pope NICHOLAS I. That same year, Boris sent emissaries to Rome, requesting Latin missionaries, Latin liturgical books, and a civil code to replace those of the Byzantine missionaries. Encouraged by Pope Nicholas I's positive response in his famous letter to the Bulgarians, by which the pope revealed his intention for the institution of a Bulgarian hierarchy, Boris gave his full support to the work of Latin missionaries. The Bulgarian drift toward Rome was evidenced by intensive Latin missionary activity, and by the preaching and celebration of Latin liturgy. In 868 Boris wrote to Pope ADRIAN II, reminding him of his predecessor's (Pope Nicholas I) support for a Bulgarian autocephalous church. However, he was frustrated by Rome's slowness to his request, and disappointed when the pope refused to name Marinus (whom Boris favored) as head of the Bulgarian hierarchy. Expressing his displeasure with the pope's replacement of Formosus (a bishop of Porto and a head of the Latin mission to Bulgaria) by the subdeacon Sylvester, Boris seized the opportunity to turn, once again, toward Constantinople.

The issue of the jurisdiction of the Bulgarian Church became a contentious point between Rome and Constantinople at the Fourth Council of Constantinople (870). Over the protests of the Roman legates, the Byzantines, with the approval of Ignatius, Patriarch of Constantinople, sent an archbishop and several bishops to Bulgaria. Despite Byzantine attempts to reintroduce their rite into Bulgaria, neither Byzantine nor Latin rites succeeded. Rather, the newly introduced Byzantine-Slav rite appeared more suitable for the needs of the Slavs. Institution of the Slav rite resulted from efforts of SS. Cyril and Methodius and their disciples, who developed the Slavic alphabet and translated the Holy Scriptures and Byzantine liturgical books into Slavic (a language contemporarily known as Old Bulgarian or Old Church Slavonic). This new rite accelerated the Christianizing of Bulgaria. The arrival in Bulgaria in 886 of Clement, Naum, Angelar, and other disciples of Methodius, who had been expelled from Moravia after Pope Stephen V's prohibition of Slavic liturgy there, constituted an event of signal importance for efforts to Christianize Bulgarians and Slavs.

In Bulgaria, Cyril's and Methodius' disciples undertook translations of church books and the training of priests. St. Clement and St. Naum established influential church and educational centers in Pliska, Preslav, and Ohrid (on the shores of Lake Ohrid, in Macedonian territory today), where more than 3,000 priests were educated to conduct religious services in Old Bulgarian (Slavonic). During the next two decades, Christianity in Bulgaria developed into a full-scale national Church headed by an archbishop approved by Constantinople, the first of whom was Joseph, appointed on March 4, 870. Consequently, Boris' waverings between Rome and Constantinople eventually resulted in the establishment of an autonomous Bulgarian church. But it was not until 893 that Christianity was proclaimed as the state religion by the national assembly, after which the Slavic language was officially adopted and Byzantine books were replaced by Slavic texts.

An important political dimension of the Bulgarian conversion to Christianity was the centralization of authority, as evidenced during the reign of Boris' younger son, Simeon (893–927). To further his efforts at reorganizing the ecclesiastical hierarchy and replacing Greek bishops with bishops of Slavic origin, Simeon appointed two new bishops. Clement was consecrated bishop of Velika and Dragovitya (today's Macedonia), while Constantine was named bishop of Preslav. Simeon's dream of Bulgaria having a national hierarchy, indigenous clergy, a unique liturgy and religious practices of its own was for a time fulfilled. John Exarch became the first Bulgarian archbishop appointed to the town of Preslav (904). Ecclesiastical development progressed even further when the National Synod of Preslav (918) proclaimed Leontius, the archbishop there, ''Patriarch of Bulgaria,'' thereby establishing the Bulgarian Patriarchate. But it was not until the last year of Simeon's reign (927), when Damian, successor of Leontius, was formally recognized as patriarch by both Rome and Constantinople. By the end of Simeon's reign, the Bulgarian Patriarchate (by then relocated to Dorostol—today the town of Silistra) had as many as forty dioceses and metropolitans under its jurisdiction.

Under Simeon's successors, Byzantium invaded and gained control of Bulgaria. In 1018 Bulgaria and the Bulgarian Church completely lost their independence, remaining under the control of Byzantium until 1185. The Greek hierarchy took control of the Patriarchate of Ohrid in an attempt to replace the Bulgarian Slavic rites with liturgy in the Greek language. The archbishop of Ohrid was a Greek, appointed by Constantinople, as were all the bishops under his jurisdiction. The See of Ohrid, which had arisen as a most important center of Slavic Christianization, after 1018 became a bastion for the Hellenization of Bulgaria. It was from Ohrid in 1054, that Bulgaria became mired in the Schism between Rome and Constantinople (the archbishop of Ohrid, Leo was a supporter of Michael Cerularius, patriarch of Constantinople). For the Bulgarian church, the century and a half of Hellenic domination had been devastating. The resultant lack of communication between a Greek hierarchy imposed by Constantinople and the church's lower clergy, most of whom were of Bulgarian origin, permitted resurgence of the PAULICIAN and BOGOMIL sects.

During the reign of Ivan's and Peter's brother and successor Kaloyan (1197–1207), primacy of Rome in

Bulgarian church affairs was reasserted. Pope INNOCENT III granted Kaloyan the title of king. He also reaffirmed Archbishop Basil of Bulgaria as primate of the Bulgarian Church (1204), encouraging the latter to retain the church's well-established Slavic rites. But the fall of Constantinople under the crusaders on April 13, 1204, accompanied with an extreme cruelty with which the crusaders treated the local population, some of Bulgarian descent, seemed to have cooled Kaloyan's feelings toward Rome. Unwilling to surrender to the crusaders, who had already been looking for Bulgaria's submission, Kaloyan sought Pope Innocent III's intercession for a peaceful outcome, but to no avail. Alienated, Bulgaria returned to the Byzantine sphere of influence, especially after Byzantium's new recognition of the Bulgarian church's independence. But the final break with Rome did not come officially until 1235, when the Bulgaro-Byzantine Council of Blasherna proclaimed autonomy of the Bulgarian Church, in communion with Nicaea, while reaffirming the title of patriarch for the head of the Bulgarian church in the capital of Turnovo.

Bulgaria under the Turks. The period from 1396 to 1878 witnessed the end of the Bulgarian kingdom and the beginning of five centuries of Turkish political domination in Bulgaria. For the Bulgarian church, this was a period of Greek ecclesiastical domination which came into effect in 1416. Proclaimed by the Ottomans to be the Father of all Christians (or the "Roman nation," *Rum millet*), the Patriarchate of Constantinople was established in Phanar as a vehicle for mediation between the Sublime Portal (Turkish government) and the Christian population dwelling in the Ottoman empire. Greeks gradually replaced Bulgarian bishops while the Greek language was substituted for Bulgarian in churches. This led to a forceful Hellenization of the Slavic population and ecclesiastical domination of the Bulgarian church, which actually ceased to exist for almost five hundred years. The archbishops of Ochrid were the only exceptions, as they temporarily retained the titles of primates or patriarchs of Bulgaria. This situation remained until 1767, when the archbishop of Ochrid became a subject of Constantinople. The liturgy was celebrated in Bulgarian only in monasteries hidden among remote mountains.

In 1870 Makaripolski succeeded in creating an Orthodox exarchate recognized by the Turkish Sublime Portal, which issued a decree establishing an autocephalous Bulgarian church. Headed by an EXARCH with jurisdiction over the 15 dioceses of Bulgaria and Macedonia, the church again became a moving force in Bulgarian life. The exarchate represented Bulgarian interests to the Sublime Portal and sponsored subsequent expansion of Bulgarian churches and schools. The national synod of the Bulgarian exarchate in Constantinople approved the first ecclesiastical constitution in 1871, although the Greek patriarch based there refused to recognize this independent church and subsequently excommunicated its adherents (1872). But the exarchate reorganized and consolidated after the Russian-Turkish war (1878), when Bulgaria achieved a measure of political independence.

The Church Stands against Jewish Deportation. After election of Ferdinand Saxe-Coburg-Gotha, a grandson of Louis-Philippe of France, as a prince of Bulgaria by the Grand National Assembly in July of 1887, Bulgaria officially became a monarchy. Boosted by the 19th century national revival which was reflected in church life, education, and monasticism, the Church nevertheless began showing some signs of decline by the mid-20th century. The period between the two world wars was difficult for Bulgarians. In an effort to maintain a de facto neutrality, positioned as it was between Hitler's Germany and Stalin's USSR, Bulgaria allied with Germany and adhered to Hitler's treaty of 1939 promising not to invade the Soviet Union. Bulgaria's alliance with Germany brought the most difficult modern challenge to the Bulgarian nation and church: how to boycott Nazi plans for deporting Bulgarian Jews to Poland for eventual extermination in concentration camps. The official reaction of the Bulgarian Orthodox Church against state-sustained anti-Semitism opened a chapter of Bulgarian modern church history known as "the rescue of the Bulgarian Jews in 1943." Bulgarian church resistance to anti-Jewish legislation began as soon as the government announced a project to establish a "Law for a Defense of the Nation (1940)." In his memorandum dated Nov. 15, 1940, Archbishop Neofit of Vidin countered that any persecution of individuals belonging to ethnic or religious minorities would impede the Church's divine mission of salvation.

In 1943 the Bulgarian Orthodox Church then initiated its rescue effort. Two metropolitans played a significant roles in defending Jews: Stefan, archbishop of Sofia, and Kiril, archbishop of Plovdiv (and future patriach of Bulgaria). Kiril became noteworthy for his successful effort to release 1,500 Plovdiv Jews who had been arrested and prepared for deportation. Kiril sent a telegram to King Boris and the Bulgarian government informing them of the church's intention to stop, "by any means," the anti-Jewish action. He declared that he would lie down on the rails in front of the train transporting the Jews rather than allow this to happen. The success of his campaign became evident on March 10, when orders were issued to release imprisoned Jews in Plovdiv. Some members of the Bulgarian National Assembly supported Kiril's action, and Peshev, a congressman, together with 42 members belonging to the majority of the assembly, on March 17 signed a letter of protest to the prime minister against Jewish deportations.

In later stages of the Jewish deportation campaign, the church harbored many Jews, hiding them from the police. Dr. Hananel, the chief rabbi in Bulgaria, found temporary refuge in Archbishop Stefan's house on May 24, 1943. Stefan assured the rabbi that the Holy Synod of the Bulgarian Orthodox Church would do everything possible to halt Jewish deportations. In correspondence with the king and top government officials, Stefan warned that he would open the doors of all Bulgarian churches and turn them "into fortresses in defense of . . . the Jews" if anti-Jewish persecutions continued. King Boris himself resisted Nazi imposition of the deportation campaign. By this solid resistance of the Bulgarian Church, the king and some members of the National Assembly, many Jews from Bulgaria (around 50,000) were saved.

The Church under Communism. The new communist regime which came into power at the end of World War II showed an anti-religious orientation almost immediately after its establishment. Between 1944 and 1947, several influential events involving the Bulgarian Orthodox Church took place. First, Metropolitan of Sofia Stefan was elected exarch of Bulgaria on Jan. 21, 1945. On February 22 of the same year, the schism imposed on the Bulgarian Orthodox Church by Constantinople in 1872 was lifted. Under the new regime, the Church lost not only its international connections but also its relevance to Bulgarian society. Overall reduction of the Church's role in Bulgarian society had a predictably negative impact on Orthodox clergy. Despite the Holy Synod's decision of Dec. 14, 1945, to organize parish schools in all parishes, the process of decline in religious education proved irreversible. Eventually, Orthodox Christian seminaries in Plovdiv and Sofia were closed down, at first under pretext of accommodating Soviet troops. New legislation that came into effect on June 27, 1947, authorized the expropriation of two-thirds of the Church's extensive property holdings.

As head of the Bulgarian Orthodox Church, Exarch Stefan attempted to adapt to the new political regime, but he resisted efforts of the Bulgarian Communist Party to control church affairs directly. Such resistance was futile, and many Bulgarian Orthodox bishops and clergy, together with their Catholic and Protestant counterparts, were executed or imprisoned during the persecutions that followed. In its effort to dominate church affairs, the communist government fomented internal dissension in the Bulgarian Orthodox Church by establishing a priests' union, which challenged the church's constitution. Stefan resigned his office, allegedly under pressure, and retired to a monastery on Sept. 6, 1948. Legislation adopted on Feb. 24, 1949, subjected all religious denominations to strict state supervision. Kiril, Stephan's successor, did not offer effective resistance as the new state restrictions

on religious associations brought church activities under complete state control.

The reestablishment of the Bulgarian patriarchate in 1953, without approval of the Patriarchate in Constantinople (this approval did not come until 1961 under the Ecumenical Patriarch Athenagoras), completed the process of the Bulgarian Orthodox Church's consolidation under the communist regime (1944–1987). Kiril, Metropolitan of Plovdiv, was elected as new patriarch of Bulgaria.

The situation of the Bulgarian Orthodox Church did not significantly change after Kiril's death, which was followed by Maximus' election as the new patriarch of Bulgaria in 1971. The church remained under state restrictions and continued its decline in numbers of clergy, religious, and laity. It was during this period when many worship places fell into disuse for lack of priests and monastic vocation, while a few smaller monasteries were quietly taken over by the state and converted into medical facilities and other state establishments. Isolated from society and from Bulgarian youth, who were then engaged in forceful participation in the Young Communists League (*komsomol*), the Church barely managed to survive.

The situation did not change significantly until the late 1980s, when reforms launched by Soviet President Mikhail Gorbachev began to have some impact in Bulgaria. Among various dissident groups organized in Bulgaria, one named the "Committee for Defense of the Religious Rights, Freedom of the Conscience and Spiritual Values" was lead by Christophor Sabev, an Orthodox hieromonk residing in Veliko Tarnovo. Founded on Dec. 15, 1988, the group had several objectives: primarily liberation of the hierarchy of the Bulgarian Orthodox Church from communist influence; reestablishment of religious education in state schools; and guaranteeing freedom to conduct religious rites and ceremonies in public places. The organization also demanded changes to previous denominational law and abrogation of restrictions applying to religious publications.

The movement conducted its campaign by organizing peaceful candlelight processions of icons (called *litias*) in which several hundred people participated. The organization was persecuted and its leader, Christophor Sabev, was arrested and briefly jailed. Under pressure from the regime, on March 28, 1989, the Church's Holy Synod denounced Christophor Sabev's movement, claiming that such establishment contradicted canons of the Orthodox Church and its Constitution. But the eventual fall of communism in Bulgaria, following Zhivkov's resignation on Nov. 10, 1989, marked the beginning of a post-communist era, when Christophor Sabev's movement became a central element of the democratic opposition to the old regime.

The Post-Communist Era Schism. After elections in the autumn of 1991, Sabev became a member of the opposition in Parliament, then led by the Union of Democratic Forces (UDF). With UDF's help, Sabev decided to launch a campaign for purging the Bulgarian Orthodox Church of communist element and influences. The process of church "decommunization" was intended to begin with the head of Bulgarian Orthodox Church, Patriarch Maxim. Primarily this was because Maxim's election had taken place under communist rule and he had the support of the communist regime. Furthermore, Maxim and his synod were not widely believed to have reacted effectively on issues of human rights and religious freedom during the communist regime. In an effort to purge the Bulgarian Orthodox Church and compel Patriarch Maxim to resign, Sabev and his allies applied political pressure, which apparently had a negative effect on the Bulgarian Orthodox Church's ecclesiastical life. Sabev's subsequent struggle for the Church's decommunization, in which other members of its hierarchy were involved, precipitated a major ecclesiastical crisis by publicly challenging both the Church's integrity and its moral authority.

The process of decommunization began when four metropolitans influenced by Sabev's political power (among them Pankratiy and Kalinik, who had occupied two of the most important administrative positions during the communist period: those of the Church's internal and external affairs) decided to abandon Maxim and the synod over which he presided. The group established an alternative synod (May 19, 1992) under the presidency of Metropolitan Pimen, who was afterward elected as the alternative patriarch of Bulgaria. Intended to be a promoter of renewal within the Bulgarian Orthodox Church, the alternative synod was envisioned as lasting until a subsequent national church council provided conditions for new elections. Sabev's incorporation into the new ecclesiastical structure and his elevation to the episcopate was intended to be the most significant symbol of church renovation.

Fulfillment of the plan began with Sabev's direct intervention into the Council of Ministers, through the Department of Religious Denominations that had been created by the communist regime to control all religious institutions from one centralized political entity. The same department then declared illegal Maxim's position as patriarch, an office he had occupied for twenty-two years. Metody Spasov, at that time head of the Religious Denominations Department, announced the decision on the basis of the Council of Minister's edict #92 from May 25, 1992. One day after the Council of Ministers announced Maxim's deposal, Sabev was consecrated as a bishop by the metropolitans Pankratiy, Kalinik, and Stefan in the presence of bishops Antoniy and Galaction.

Regarding this announcement as political interference in church affairs, the majority of Bulgarian Orthodox Church's metropolitans and bishops who had supported Maxim decided to file an official protest against the decision. But with government approval Sabev and his supporters occupied the office building of the Holy Synod on May 31, 1992, paralyzing the operation of Maxim's synod. Maxim lodged a criminal complaint "for breaking in" against Subev, Pimen, and their supporters, but without any effect. Instead, instructions came from the prosecutor's office of the Republic of Bulgaria on July 10, 1992, confirming the government's support for Pimen and his new synod. Maxim, in turn, convoked a National Archbishop Council, which on July 22, 1992, condemned the new schism and what the council called "the illegal consecration of Sabev" into the episcopacy. The council unfrocked the four participating metropolitans as well as the bishops who had joined them.

There were efforts from the side of the Bulgarian society and Bulgarian Orthodox Church's lower clergy to reconcile the two rival groups within the church. On Sept. 3, 1992, an alternative clerical organization called the Movement for Reunion of the Bulgarian Orthodox Church met with Prime Minister Philip Dimitrov and other representatives of his government in an effort to solve the problem, but they met with no evident success. A Bulgarian High Court decree on Nov. 5, 1992 confirmed the Council of Ministers Department of Religious Denominations' decision, thereby sanctioning the alternative Holy Synod with Metropolitan Pimen as its recognized presiding bishop. The UDF's government supported the High Court's decision.

Events occurring between May 19 and Nov. 5, 1992 denoted a process of gradual separation (schism) that took place first within Bulgarian Orthodox Church's hierarchy and clergy, then within the laity. Both sides of the divided synod claimed to be the ruling body within the Church. The majority of parishes and parish priests within the Church, as well as two-thirds of the metropolitans and bishops, defended Patriarch Maxim and his synod while some leaders of the Priest Union, and UDF's government headed by Philip Dimitrov, seemed to support Pimen's side. Ongoing government intervention in the Bulgarian Orthodox Church's affairs apparently contributed to subsequent widening of the schism, resulting in further deterioration of ecclesiastical life and an increase in civil disorder.

After he became a bishop, Sabev gradually separated from the group which had consecrated him. He gave as his reason Pankratiy's and Kalinik's participation in ecumenical services, of which the more conservative Sabev disapproved. Not seeing "signs of repentance" from the side of metropolitans Kalinik and Pankratiy, Sabev separated from them and founded a new archbishopric in Ternovo. Subsequently, he lost much of his personal political influence; the ecclesiastical body he founded exists today, but with diminished influence. Several attempts at reuniting the two synods have not succeed. Most notable among these was an attempt in 1988, when the Panorthodox Council was convoked in Sofia. Orthodox patriarchs and archbishops from all over the world gathered in Sofia to try and resolve the schism within the Bulgarian Orthodox Church. The council recognized all of the consecrations effected by the alternative synod, invited all of the bishops to join Maxim's synod and declared the schism to be over. Metropolitans Pancratiy and Kalinik repented and returned to the earlier synod under Maxim, but Pimen remained in the schism until his death in 1999. Pimen's alternative synod continues to exist, although only a small group of clergy remain involved. After decisions of the State High Court, currently two different bodies under the name of Bulgarian Orthodox Church exist juridically. A third ecclesiastical body, known as "The Bulgarian Orthodox Church of the Old Calendar" also exists, but it is not in communion with either of the other two recognized church bodies.

Bibliography: I. BOICHEV, "Varkovniat sud osadi tzerkovnite dela kakto Pilat xristovite," *Duma* 158 (June 3, 1992). I. BORISLAVOV, "Archiereisky sabor smukna rasoto na Sabev I go otlachi ot tzerkvata," *Duma* 175 (July 23, 1992). C. BOYADJUEFF, *Saving the Bulgarian Jews in World War II* (Ottawa 1989). P. DIMOV, "Zashto ne varviat rabotite v Tzerkavata," *Democrazia* 215 (791) (Sept. 9, 1992). I. DUIYCHEV, *Balgarsko Srednovekovie. Prouchvaniya Varhu Politicheskata I Kuturna Istoriya* (Sofia 1972). C. B. FREDERICK, *The Bulgarian Jews and the Final Solution 1940–1944*, (Pittsburgh 1972). D. KALKANDZIEVA, *Balgarskata Pravoslavna Tsarkva I Darzhava 1944–1953* (Sofia 1977). N. MAKOV, "Ot tzerkovnia spor gubiat mirianite," *Democrazia* 211 (787) (Sept. 4, 1992). C. SABEV, *Svetlina za Bulgaria* (Veliko Tarnovo 1994). T. SABEV, et al., "Church Life and Ecumenical Relations under the Communist Rule," *History of the Ecumenical Movement* (World Council of Churches, 2002). T. SABEV, *Samostoyna Narodnostna Tsarkva v Srednovekovna Balgaria* (Sofia 1987). I. SNEGAROV, *1100 godini ot Pokrastyvaneto na Balgarskiya narod* (Sofia 1966). V. N. ZLATARSKI, *Istoriya na Balgarskata Darzhava Prez Srednite Vekove* (Sofia /v tri Toma 1970–1972).

[M. YOUROUKOV]

ORTHODOX CHURCH OF CYPRUS

This church received its status as an autocephalous church in the Council of EPHESUS (431) with an archbishop as its head. It is ruled today by the constitution of 1914 and other synodal rulings made in 1917–18. Supreme authority belongs to its Holy Synod, which includes the archbishop and three metropolitans who make up the entire hierarchy of the four eparchies. The archbishop resides in Nicosia, and, according to the Orthodox precedence, holds fifth place among the Orthodox leaders; but this is disputed by the Russian Orthodox Patriarch.

Bibliography: R. ROBERSON, *The Eastern Christian Churches: A Brief Survey*, 6th ed (Rome 1999).

[G.A. MALONEY/EDS.]

ORTHODOX CHURCH OF GEORGIA

The Republic of Georgia, called in early times Iberia, is located in the region commonly known as Central Asia. A part of the Soviet empire for much of the 20th century, it gained its independence in the aftermath of the collapse of Soviet communism. This entry treats of the Orthodox Church of Georgia. For the historical development of the Georgian Church, *see* GEORGIA, CHURCH IN ANCIENT.

Organization. The Georgian Orthodox Church came under the Russian Moscow patriarchate when Czar Alexander annexed Georgia in 1801. The Georgian catholicos was forced to resign and was replaced by a Russian exarch nominated by the Holy Synod of Saint Petersburg. From that time until the Russian revolution of 1917 the Georgian Church was under the domination of the Russian Orthodox Church, which sought at every turn to suppress all native elements in the Georgian hierarchy and liturgy, making both conform to the centralization of Moscow. But when the Russian czar fell and along with him the Russian Orthodox Church as the state religion, the Georgian Church seized the opportunity to establish once again under a native catholicos. The Communists annexed Georgia as a republic of the Soviet Union in 1921, but the Georgian Church clung to its autocephalous status, and was finally recognized as independent of the Moscow patriarchate by Patriarch Sergius on Oct. 31, 1943.

The supreme head of the Georgian Church is the catholicos-patriarch, elected and consecrated by the assembly of bishops. The country is divided into eparchies (dioceses). Traditional Georgian law granted the catholicos-patriarch the same power as that of a king. In exceptional cases, the kings intervened in the affairs of the Church. On the other hand, by tradition the clergy participated in the life of the state. Thus the highest representatives of the Church sat at the Council of State (*Darbazi*) next to high officials and representatives of the country.

In the hierarchy of the state, the second rank (prime minister) was reserved to a bishop, who at the same time retained the episcopal See of Tshkondidi (Chqondidi); so the prime minister was also called *Tshkondideli* (of Tshkondidi). Thus Church and State were in accord.

Liturgy. Archbishop John, the original head of the Georgian Church, introduced the Greek liturgy and performed the ceremonies in Greek, which was subsequently replaced by the Georgian language. The first version of the liturgy in the Georgian tongue was that of Saint James. Translated in the Georgian convent of Jerusalem, it remained in use until the 10th or 11th century. The manuscripts of this version are preserved in the Library of Mount Sinai, at Gaza, at the Vatican, and at Tiflis (Tbilissi). In the 10th or 11th century, following a translation by Euthime and George of Mthatsminda, the liturgy of Saint Basil and Saint Chrysostom replaced the previous one. In the 12th century, the ''Typicon'' of Saint Saba was translated and widely used. The liturgy, as revised by Philatoes (XIV), was celebrated in Georgia from the 18th century on. At the same time, Catholicos-Patriarch Antony I made it correspond more closely with Slavic texts.

The Georgian Euchlogion is divided into ''Kondaki,'' or various liturgical texts, used in the liturgy and Divine Office and ''kurthkhevani,'' or various benedictions for stated occasions.

Mass was always accompanied by chants. Nine collections of liturgical hymns are known: five are in Georgia, three at Mount Sinai and one at Mount Athos. The most ancient chant is dated about the 8th century. The more important ones were composed by Michael Modrekili, a monk composer, and were accompanied by musical notes that remained undecipherable because they resembled no existing sign. The enigma was finally solved in 1962 by the Georgian scholar Paul Ingorokva.

Like the notes, the Georgian ecclesiastical chants also are of Georgian origin. They were based on a very old form; only the words were changed. Even when translation was necessary, care was taken to adapt them to the Georgian form and style.

Monastic Life. Because the life of the Georgian people was often agitated within the country, their monastic life found its expansion on foreign soil. The first Georgian convent was founded in Jerusalem by Peter the Iberian; it was later restored by Emperor Justinian. This was the Convent of the Cross, at present possessed by the Greeks. In Palestine the Georgians possessed other convents: Saint Nicholas, Saint Saba, Saint John, the Grotto of Bethlehem, Saint Abraham, and Saint Basil. To these should be added the convents of Saint Samuel in the basin of the Jordan, of Kranie, of Saints Cosmas and Damian, of the cavern near Antioch, of Mount Sinai, of Ezra and of Kastana on Mount Black. All these monasteries and others were founded between the 5th and the 9th century.

The second period of monastic life abroad coincided with the foundation of the famous convent of Iviron on Mount Athos in Greece, now (1965) possessed by the Greeks. This monastery was founded in the 10th century, by John, a former officer of King David the Couropalate, who embraced the monastic life. His example was followed by his only son, Euthine, who became a famous Doctor of the Church, a new Chrysostom, as he was called. He had worthy successors, the most important of whom was George of Mthatsminda.

In the 11th century, another Georgian lord, this time the great domesticos of the Byzantine Empire, Gregorii Bakouriani, founded a monastery at Batchkovo (Bulgaria). He endowed it with an extraordinary amount of goods and presented it with a typicon whose original Georgian version and Latin translation were published by Father Tarchnichvili at Louvain in 1954. From the beginning of the 12th century, this convent was governed by the great Doctor of the Church, John Petritzi, who later became rector of the academy of Guelathi.

In all these convents, the Georgian monks conducted cultural activity on a large scale. In order to provide Georgian churches with necessary books, they produced manuscripts, many of which have universal value.

In Georgia itself, monastic life began a little later. However, by the 5th century some convents had been already erected, and in the 6th century the Syrian Fathers established a great number of them. The first ones were founded by John at Zedazeni and by David at Garedja; Shio, called the Troglodite, chose a grotto where he established his residence. Others followed their example. At the same time (6th century) were built the episcopal church of Mtskhetha, the cathedral of Sion at Tiflis, the monasteries of Ananouri and Alaverdi, and others.

Famous was the monastic movement in Tao-Klardjethie, from the 8th to the 10th century, initiated by the celebrated Gregory of Khandztha. The 12 better-known monasteries were Daba, Opiza, Mere, Parekhi, Khandztha, Shatberdi, Miznazori, Tskarosthavi, Baratheltha, Bertha, Djmerki, and Doliskana. They were subsequently followed by the famous churches of Koutaisi and Ateni and by the monasteries of Zarzma, Safara, Khakhouli, and others.

Consequently, the 10th century was a time of splendor for Georgian Christian literature. Three great centers rivaled one another: that of Syria and Palestine, of the Balkans, and of Tao-Klardjethie. In addition to literature, these centers formed the leaders of the Georgian Church. It was they who directed Georgia's academies, which in turn formed the leaders of the state.

Thus Christianity embraced the whole life of the Georgian people. Among the great personages, first place belongs to Peter of Iberia, son of a Georgian king and bishop of Gaza, who became one of the most celebrated heads of Christianity in the East. He had been educated at the court of Byzantium for a career of state, but became a cleric instead. He was believed to be the author of the Areopagitic books. Among the great Doctors of the Church, Gregory of Khandztha (9th century), John and Euthime (10th century), George of Mthatsminda, George Khoutses-Monazoni, Ephrem the Minor (11th century), and philosophers Petritzi and Arsen of Ikaltho (12th century) deserve mention.

Holy Books. Holy Books were translated in Georgia from the very beginning of Christianity. Some fragments of the Bible, translated in the 5th century, have been preserved. However, according to all indications, translation had already begun at the end of the 4th century. First to be translated were the "Epistles of the Apostles," which have been preserved in a manuscript of the 9th century and which report the date of their translation as 397 to 398.

Later followed the translation of the New Testament, from Greek and Syrian, and perhaps even from Hebrew. Translations, as well as original works of the 7th and 8th centuries, were numerous. Most of the texts have been preserved in several translations, since, for the purpose of improvement, they were translated a second and even a third time. The last edition of the Bible, in its definitive form, was elaborated by the Monastery of Iviron in the 10th and 11th centuries. It has been used until the present time.

In 1709 King Vakhtang established a printing press, and the New Testament was the first book to be published. However, the entire Bible was printed for the first time in Moscow in 1743 by order of the Royal Princess of Georgia. The last edition, a partial one, completed for scientific purposes, and with very limited printing, was published after World War II.

Bibliography: M. F. BROSSET, comp. and tr. *Histoire de Georgie: Depuis l'antiquité jusqu'au XIXᵉ siècle*, 5 v. (Leningrad 1849–58), containing chronicles and hist. annals of Georgia. G. D. DZHAVAKHISHVIL, *Kharthelvi eris istoria*, v.1 (Tiflis 1960). W. E. D. ALLEN, *A History of the Georgian People* (London 1932). A. MANVELICHVILI, *Histoire de Géorgie* (Paris 1951). P. PEETERS, "Les débuts du Christianisme en Géorgie d'après les sources hagiographiques," *Analecta Bollandiana* 50 (1932) 5–58. M. TARCHNIŠVILI, "Sources arméno géorgiennes de l'histoire ancienne de l'Église de Georgie," *Le Muséon* 60 (1947) 29–50. R. P. BLACKE, "Georgian Theological Literature," *Journal of Theologi- cal Studies* 26 (1924–25) 50–64. J. VON ASSFLAG, "Zum Kirchenjahr und zur neuesten Geschichte der georischen Kirche," *Bedi Kharthlisa: Revue de Kharthvélologie* no. 34–35 (1960). P. INGOROKVA, *Giorgi merchule* (Tiflis 1954), the monumental work on the Georgian monastic life and Christian literature of the 8th to 10th centuries. R. ROBERSON, *The Eastern Christian Churches: A Brief Survey* (6th ed. Rome 1999).

[A. S. MANVEL/EDS.]

ORTHODOX CHURCH OF GREECE

The Orthodox Church in Greece considered itself liberated from the yoke of the Turks only when it had obtained both its political freedom and its status as an autocephalous church. The patriarchate of Constantinople recognized it as an autocephalous church in 1850. Today it forms the only Orthodox church that is officially the accepted church of the nation. A synodal type of ecclesiastical administration was accepted. The Permanent Synod comprises 13 bishops, including the leader of the Greek Church, the Archbishop of Athens and All Greece.

See Also: GREECE, THE CHURCH IN, 2. THE MODERN CHURCH; ORTHODOX AND ORIENTAL CHURCHES.

Bibliography: D. CONSTANTELOS, *Understanding the Greek Orthodox Church: Its Faith, History and Practice* (New York 1982). F. LITSAS, ed. *A Companion to the Greek Orthodox Church* (New York 1984). R. ROBERSON, *The Eastern Christian Churches: A Brief Survey*, 6th ed (Rome 1999).

[G. A. MALONEY/EDS.]

ORTHODOX CHURCH OF ROMANIA

Romanians represent the residue of the Thraco-Daco-Bessian peoples from the Balko-Danubian provinces of the Roman Empire. Their language is Romance, having been formed from the rustic Latin spoken by the populations of those provinces under Roman control. Nevertheless, a considerable Slavic influence is found in their lexicon and phonetics, owing to their intermingling with Slav populations that had moved there in the 6th and 7th centuries. They always called themselves *Rumâni*, but non-Roman peoples (Germans, Slavs) called them Walachians, that is, Romans or Latins (Volcae, Welsch, Volochi). Although Romanians are a Latin people, most of them belong to the autocephalous Romanian Orthodox Church.

The beginnings of Christianity are not clear in Romanian history, but it seems that in the early centuries the first work of evangelization was done by Latin missionaries. The form that Christianity took was linked intimately with political developments and divisions. From the 2d to the 4th century, the three civil districts of Illyricum, Dacia, and Macedonia belonged to the praetorian prefecture of Illyricum, located at Sirmium. The other two provinces of Moesia Inferior and Scythia Minor (Dobrodgea) belonged to the civil district of Thracia, that is, to the praetorian prefecture of the East, located at Heraclea. Thus Christian evangelization of the Balko-Danubian provinces came from the East and the West. In 389 Gratian, Emperor of the West, ceded to his brother Theodosius I, Emperor of the East, Dacia and Macedonia, now called Oriental Illyricum. In 421 Theodosius I made the provinces of Oriental Illyricum subject to the tribunal appeal of the bishop of Constantinople. Notwithstanding the strong protest of Pope Boniface II in 438, the decree of Theodosius was inserted into the Code of imperial laws. In 424 or 437, under Theodosius II, Western Illyricum was annexed to the Byzantine Empire. Thus the patriarch of Constantinople had jurisdiction of all the Illyrian provinces. He sent his missionaries and bishops into the area establishing the Orthodox Church and the canonical discipline of Byzantium.

When the Bulgars embraced Christianity from Byzantium, they also brought to the *Rumâni* the Byzantine liturgy in the Old Slavonic language. Instrumental in introducing the Byzantine-Slav rite into the kingdom of Great Moravia, which bordered on Bulgaria, were the Greek brothers Saints CYRIL and Methodius. With their activity in Moravia (863–85) and that of their disciples in Bulgaria the Slav-Bulgarian liturgical usages were introduced among the Walacho-Romanians, who, with their dukedoms of Banat and Transylvania, were subject to the first Bulgarian Empire.

After the withdrawal of the Tartars in the 13th century, the first Walacho-Romanian state, called Walachia, was formed in 1330. Moldavia was formed shortly after, in 1363. The rulers of Walachia and Moldavia petitioned the Patriarch of Constantinople to erect a metropolis in their kingdoms. A metropolitan was appointed in 1359 for Walachia with residence in Arges; and another, for Moldavia in 1393 with residence at Suceava, later changed to Jassy. Transylvania was under the Hungarian Empire from 1004. Thus through the centuries these three principalities of Walachia, Moldavia, and Transylvania existed separately one from another. Finally in 1881 Romania was united into a single kingdom of Walachia and Moldavia, whose religion was Byzantine Orthodoxy.

Organization of the Orthodox Romanian Church.

The Orthodox Church in the independent provinces of modern Romania began to unify into one church in the 19th century. The two assemblies of the independent principalities of Walachia and Moldavia elected Colonial Alexander Ion Cuza (1859–66) as prince for both princi-

palities. This union was recognized by Turkey and the other great powers in 1861 when the two united principalities were called Romania for the first time. The new Prince enacted laws concerning the Church that were in contrast with its traditional spirit. He made civil marriage compulsory, allowed divorce, and secularized the large estates of monasteries. He organized the church in an autocephalous way with a central synod answerable to the state.

After a jurisdictional quarrel with the Patriarch of Constantinople, the autocephaly of the Romanian Church was acknowledged in 1885. On Feb. 4, 1925, the Holy Synod decreed the primate of the Romanian Church (the archbishop of Bucharest) to be Patriarch. The decision was approved by the state and recognized by both the Ecumenical Patriarch of Constantinople and the other Orthodox Churches of the Near East and Europe. Thus was formed the Orthodox Church of Romania.

[L. TAUTU/R. ROBERSON/EDS.]

Romanian Orthodox Church in the Communist and Post-Communist Years

The declaration of a Communist People's Democracy in Romania on Dec. 30, 1947, was followed on May 24, 1948, by the election of Justinian Marina (Feb. 22, 1901 to Mar. 26, 1977) as patriarch of the Romanian Orthodox Church. Justinian had well-known socialist political views and was said to be a personal friend of the newly-installed first secretary of the Romanian Communist Party, Gheorghe Gheorghiu-Dej. Thus, he was well placed during his 29 years in office to guide the church through an initial period of vicious Stalinist persecution (including the nationalization of church property, the imprisonment of thousands of clergy, and a reduction of the numbers of monks and nuns in the monasteries from over 7,000 in 1956 to 2,200 by 1975), and later to establish with the regime a *modus vivendi* known as "The Romanian Solution."

Patriarch Justinian essentially accepted the narrow boundaries drawn around his church by the state in return for the government's toleration of a certain level of ecclesial activity. The patriarch was able to oversee an improvement in the level of education of the clergy, a notable monastic reform, and the restoration of many important historic churches, monasteries, and other monuments. Under Nicolae Ceaușescu it became possible for Justinian to guide the church toward an accommodation with the regime because it was adopting a nationalist form of Communism that envisaged a certain role for the church in the life of the nation. Many Communist officials considered themselves Orthodox Christians.

Justin Moisescu was elected fourth patriarch of the Romanian Orthodox Church in June 1977. More an academic than politician, Justin had to deal with criticism for not sufficiently resisting the government's decision to demolish some 24 churches and three monasteries in central Bucharest and for his handling of the defrocking and imprisonment of certain Orthodox priests opposed to the regime. The most well known of these was Gheorghe Calciu Dumitreasa, who was sentenced to ten years in prison in 1978 for preaching a series of Lenten sermons at the Bucharest seminary in which he characterized atheism as a philosophy of despair. He was released and sent into exile in the United States in 1984.

Even so, by 1985 the Romanian Orthodox was the most vigorous church in Eastern Europe. Church sources stated that there were about 17,000,000 faithful (80 percent of the population), 8,165 parishes served by 8,545 priests, and 1,500 nuns and 1,000 monks living in 122 monasteries. There were six seminaries and two theological institutes, one in Bucharest and one in Sibiu. High quality theological journals were published, including three by the patriarchate itself and one by each of the five metropolitanates. In addition, the patriarchate was able to make use of limited resources to carry out an ambitious publication program that brought to light six more volumes in a series of Romanian translations of the *Philokalia*, more than 30 in a projected series of 90 volumes of translations of patristic writings, and an assortment of Bibles and other liturgical and theological works. In addition, the church was able to publish the theological contribution of Dumitru Stăniloae (1903–93), one of the most prominent Orthodox theologians of the century.

Justin died on July 31, 1986. On November 9, the metropolitan of Iaşi, Teoctist Arăpaşu, was elected patriarch. He also had to contend with the destruction of more churches in Bucharest and even the government's rumored desire (later confirmed) to demolish the patriarchal complex in the capital and transfer the see to Iaşi. Teoctist was able to direct the republication of the 1688 Bucharest Bible, an event that illustrated the central role the church played in the standardization of the Romanian language and the evolution of Romanian culture. The patriarch was also able to take several trips abroad. He visited Ecumenical Patriarch Dimitrios I in Istanbul in May 1987, and became the first Romanian patriarch in history to visit a Roman pontiff when he met John Paul II in Rome on Jan. 5, 1989. It was later revealed that Teoctist had acted against the wishes of the government in meeting with the pope.

End of Ceauşescu Regime. The downfall of the Ceauşescu regime on Dec. 22, 1989, triggered a crisis in the Romanian Orthodox Church, which was strongly criticized for having publicly supported the Communist government. The Holy Synod met on Jan. 10, 1990, apologized for those "who did not always have the courage of the martyrs," and expressed regret that it had been "necessary to pay the tribute of obligatory and artificial praises addressed to the dictator" to ensure certain liberties. It also annulled all the ecclesiastical sanctions that it had been compelled to impose on members of the clergy for political reasons. In the face of harsh criticism for alleged collaboration with the Communist regime, Patriarch Teoctist resigned his office on Jan. 18, 1990. However, in early April Teoctist resumed his duties as patriarch by unanimous decision of the Holy Synod. Although this move was criticized in Romanian intellectual circles, the Synod decided that it was more important to maintain continuity in the face of political change, and to acknowledge the views of the other Orthodox churches, which had continued to re-cognize Teoctist as patriarch.

A few days after the fall of the Ceauşescu regime, a "Reflection Group for the Renewal of the Church" was established in Bucharest. Its seven clerical and lay members set out to interpret what they perceived to be the growing desire among the Orthodox faithful for change and renewal in the life of the church, and to initiate a dialogue with the church leadership to help it overcome the current "spiritual impasse."

On June 7, 1990, a member of this group, the 38-year-old auxiliary bishop of Timişoara, Daniel Ciobotea, was elected metropolitan archbishop of Iaşi, the second-ranking post in the Romanian Orthodox hierarchy. Ciobotea had studied in the West and had taught from 1981 to 1988 at the Ecumenical Institute of the World Council of Churches at Bossey, Switzerland. His election to the see from which all previous Romanian patriarchs had been taken was part of an effort to reform the church and provide it with new and more vigorous leadership.

In September 1990 the Holy Synod approved important modifications to the basic statutes of the Patriarchate. It removed those sections providing for state interference in the church's affairs and declared the full autonomy of the church from the state.

On June 21, 1992 the Holy Synod declared canonizations for the second time in its history. Nineteen new Romanian saints were proclaimed, and the "Sunday of the Romanian Saints" was inserted into the liturgical calendar on the second Sunday after Pentecost.

At a meeting in January 1993 the Holy Synod re-established two jurisdictions in areas that were part of Romania in the interwar period: in northern Bukovina (now in Ukraine) and in Bessarabia, most of which is in the independent republic of Moldova. This move sparked a confrontation with the Moscow patriarchate to which the Orthodox dioceses in those regions had belonged since World War II. Most Orthodox in those areas remained in newly established autonomous jurisdictions associated with the Russian Orthodox Church.

A census carried out by the Romanian government in January 1992 revealed that 87 percent of the population (19.8 million) considered itself to belong to the Romanian Orthodox Church. It is interesting to note that after four decades of antireligious propaganda, the census uncovered only 11,000 atheists and 25,000 who said they were not affiliated with any faith community.

By early 1993 the number of Orthodox seminaries in the country had risen to 18 with a total of 2,811 students. The two higher-level theological institutes that had been allowed to function in Bucharest and Sibiu were reintegrated into the university faculties they had belonged to before the advent of the Communist regime, and ten other theology faculties were set up at universities in Iaşi, Cluj-Napoca, Craiova, Arad, Oradea, Piteşti, Alba Iulia, Baia Mare, Constanţa, and Tîrgovişte. The students in these numbered 2,890, including significant numbers of laypeople and nuns. Monastic life thrived, with 192 monasteries (111 female and 81 male) and 75 sketes (63 female and 12 male) with a total of 5,179 monks and nuns in 1992. At that time there was a total of 8,452 priests and 12,397 places of worship. There was also a proliferation of theological journals (9), periodicals (10) and newspapers (5). For the first time since 1948 the church also began to engage in organized charitable activity, such as administering orphanages, hospitals, and retirement homes.

Another important development was the reactivation of Orthodox lay movements, all of which had been banned by the Communists. By the end of 1992 there were eight such organizations, the most important being the Oastea Domnului (The Army of the Lord). Founded by Josif Trifa in 1923, this renewal movement emphasized evangelization, personal morality, an experiential relationship with God, and Bible study. It grew quickly, and in the 1930s was absorbed into the structures of the Orthodox Church. During the Communist years the movement maintained a secret membership of perhaps as many as 500,000. The organization resurfaced after December 1989 and again received the blessing of the Orthodox Church. However, some of its members have connections with Protestant evangelical groups and are ambivalent about these links to institutional church structures.

In spite of the problems it now faces, the Romanian Orthodox Church has emerged from several decades of Communist persecution having preserved the close links that have long existed between it and the great majority of the Romanian people. Although its activity has been hindered by the catastrophic economic conditions that followed the fall of Ceauşescu, the new freedoms it has enjoyed since December 1989 have allowed it to begin to reassert its prominent role in the country and to explore the kind of relationship with the state and other churches that is appropriate for a postcommunist and increasingly westernized society.

Romanian Orthodox Christians in the United States. Historically, the Romanian Orthodox diaspora in the United States the Romanian Orthodox are divided into three different jurisdictions. The Romanian Orthodox Church and the Canonical Episcopate of America, in communion with the Orthodox Church of Romania has its see in Detroit. The Romania Orthodox Episcopate of America, with its see at Detroit, Michigan, is under the jurisdiction of the Orthodox Church in America. In 1993, these two groups agreed to establish full ties, ending the hostile atmosphere between them. The third, and smallest group is the Romanian Orthodox Episcopate of Eastern Hemisphere, under the jurisdiction of the Russian Synodal Church in Exile. Its see is also in Detroit.

Bibliography: M. PACURARIU, *Istoria Bisericii Ortodoxe Române,* 3 v. (Bucharest 1980–1981). A. SCARFE, ''The Romanian Orthodox Church,'' in P. RAMET, ed., *Eastern Christianity and Politics in the Twentieth Century* (Durham, N.C. 1988) 208–31. M. PACURARIU, *Geschichte der Rumänischen Orthodoxen Kirche* (Erlangen 1994). I. BRIA, *Romania: Orthodox Identity at a Crossroads of Europe* (Geneva 1995). R. ROBERSON, *The Eastern Catholic Churches: A Brief Survey* (6th ed. Rome 1999).

[R. ROBERSON]

ORTHODOX CHURCH OF RUSSIA

The Russians are an East Slavic people whose ancestors moved into the vast plain between the Baltic and Black Seas in the sixth century. Initially the East Slavic tribes formed a large number of warring city-states, but in the ninth century political power began to consiolidate first at Novgorod and later at Kiev (882). Christianity became the official religion under the Grand Prince Vladimir I (d. 1015) who married Anna, sister of Byzantine Emperor Basil II. Prince Vladimir was baptized along with many of his followers in the waters of the Dnieper river in 988 A.D. according to the Greek rite. Thus, Byzantine Christianity became the faith of the three peoples who trace their origins to Rus' of Kiev: the Ukrainians, Belarussians, and Russians.

The Russian Church became semi-autonomous in 1037 when the patriarch of Constantinople consecrated

St. Basil's on Red Square, Moscow. Photograph by Susan D. Rock. (Reproduced by permission.)

Theopemptus metropolitan of Kiev. When the city was destroyed during the Mongol invasions (1237–40), large numbers of people moved northward. By the fourteenth century a new center grew up around the principality of Moscow, and the metropolitans of Kiev took up residence there. In 1448 Metropolitan Isidore was deposed for having accepted, on behalf of his Church, the union with Rome that had been ratified at the Council of Florence. His successor changed the primatial title to metropolitan of Moscow.

Third Rome. About the time that Constantinople fell to the Turks in 1453, Russia was throwing off Mongol rule and becoming an independent state. Because the old Rome was said to have fallen into heresy, and the New Rome, Constantinople, had fallen under control of the Turks, some Russians began to speak of Moscow as the "Third Rome" that would carry on the traditions of Orthodoxy and Roman civilization. The czar (caesar) was now the champion and protector of Orthodoxy just as the

Byzantine emperor once had been. The Russian Church had already begun to develop its own style of iconography and church architecture and its own theological and spiritual traditions.

A Russian Orthodox patriarchate was officially established by Constantinople in 1589, but it was abolished by Peter the Great in 1721. The Church was then administered by a HOLY SYNOD under regulations that brought the Church under close state supervision. During this period, especially in the nineteenth century, a great revival of Russian Orthodox theology, spirituality, and monasticism took place.

In August 1917, after the abdication of the czar but before the Bolshevik Revolution, a synod of the Russian Orthodox Church began in Moscow. It reestablished the Russian patriarchate and elected Metropolitan Tikhon of Moscow to that office. But before the synod ended, it was learned that the metropolitan of Kiev had been murdered and that persecutions had begun. Patriarch Tikhon was outspoken in his criticism of the Communists in his early years as patriarch, but moderated his public position after a year in prison.

Patriarch Tikhon and his successor Patriarch Sergius worked out a modus vivendi with the government that set the tone of church-state relations under Communism. In 1927 Patriarch Sergius declared loyalty to the Soviet government and promised the support of the Russian Orthodox Church on all issues. In return, the state allowed the Church a very restricted sphere of activity, limited in practice to liturgical worship. Persecution and repression of religion in the U.S.S.R. took different forms in different periods: virtually all the theologians and leaders of the Orthodox Church were either exiled in the 1920s or executed in the 1930s. Conditions improved somewhat during World War II and in Stalin's later years, but Khrushchev, intent on "abolishing" religion by 1980, began to intensify the persecutions in 1959.

Many churches were closed after the revolution, and another massive wave of church closings took place under Khrushchev in 1959 to 1962. In 1914, 54,457 churches were registered, but in the late 1970s there were only about 6,800. The number of functioning monasteries (1,498 in 1914) was down to 12, and the 57 theological seminaries operating in 1914 had been reduced to three in Moscow, Leningrad (Saint Petersburg), and Odessa, with theological academies of higher studies in the first two cities.

Perestroika and Glasnost. With the rise of Mikhail Gorbachev to power in 1985 the situation of the Russian Orthodox Church began to improve dramatically. His policies of perestroika ("restructuring") and glasnost ("openness") gave the Church greater freedom and recognition. Early in 1988 Gorbachev received the leaders of the Orthodox Church in the Kremlin on the eve of the millennium celebrations commemorating the baptism of Prince Vladimir in 988. Patriarch Pimen of Moscow and All Russia presided over the Divine Liturgy, surrounded by members of the Russian Orthodox hierarchy and witnessed by Agostino Cardinal Casaroli, Vatican secretary of state who represented Pope John Paul II, Robert Runcie, the archbishop of Canterbury, and representatives of other Christian bodies. When aged and ailing Patriarch Pimen died May 3, 1990, the Church moved rapidly to name his successor. A council composed of bishops and elected priests and laity, using secret ballots for the first time since 1918, selected the 61-year-old metropolitan of Leningrad and Novgorod as Patriarch Aleksy II of Moscow and All Russia.

In October 1992 the Saint Tikhon of Moscow Theological Institute opened in Moscow for training Orthodox

laity. The students, more or less evenly divided between women and men, numbered some 650 in the first year. On Feb. 24, 1993, the Russian Orthodox Church established Saint John the Theologian University in Moscow to continue the Russian humanist educational tradition and to offer an in-depth study of the theological disciplines as well. In 1994, Patriarch Aleksy II stated that there were 15,985 churches in the territory of the former Soviet Union, served by 12,841 priests and 1,402 deacons. His Church now had three theological academies (Moscow, Saint Petersburg, and Kiev), 14 seminaries, and a total of 47 schools with about 4,000 students. Two hundred eighty-one monastic communities existed or were being formed.

The membership of the Orthodox Church of Russia is estimated at 60 million. In December 1993, the University of Chicago's National Opinion Research Center released the results of a poll that documented an extraordinary growth of religious faith in Russia. It showed that between one half and three quarters of the Russian people believed in God, depending on how the question was worded. Although 11 percent; said they were Orthodox when growing up, 28 percent reported themselves as Orthodox now, indicating that the Russian Orthodox Church had more than doubled its membership. The trend towards theism was strongest in the 17 to 24 age group, where 30 percent had converted from atheism to belief in God. An astonishing 75 percent of those surveyed reported having "a great deal of confidence in the Church." But another survey conducted by the All-Russian Center of Public Opinion Studies in August 1994 revealed that while 52 percent of those surveyed considered themselves believers, only 2 percent attended Church services at least once a week.

New Freedom, New Challenges. The Russian Church is struggling to adapt to the rapid changes taking place in Russian society. The Church has strictly enforced a ban on the participation of clergy in politics and seems to be developing a closer relationship with the Russian military. The patriarchate has vigorously opposed proselytizing activities of other religious groups in the country and supported a bill passed by the parliament but unsigned by President Yeltsin restricting the activity of such groups. In the fall of 1994 the Russian government agreed to help finance the reconstruction of the Cathedral of Christ the Savior, a massive nineteenth-century structure leveled by Stalin in 1931 that once dominated the Moscow skyline. Patriarch Aleksy laid the new cornerstone on Jan. 7, 1995.

An assembly of the entire Russian Orthodox episcopate took place in Moscow from Nov. 29 to Dec. 2, 1994. Patriarch Aleksy told the bishops that the Church had gone through a very difficult period since their last meeting in 1992, having had to deal with problems relating to liturgical practice, proper theological and pastoral formation, and ecclesial service to society. The assembly turned down a call from conservative elements for the Moscow patriarchate to withdraw from all ecumenical organizations, but it condemned the missionary activity being carried out in Russia by American Methodist, Evangelical, and Presbyterian groups and by certain South Korean Protestants. The bishops sanctioned the beginning of a vast effort to catechize and evangelize the Russian population and set up a special commission to review liturgical practice and texts to make the liturgy more easily understood by the faithful.

The gradual disintegration of the Communist system and the Soviet Union created centrifugal forces that threatened the unity of the Moscow patriarchate. In January 1990, when conditions were already changing, the Bishops' Council of the Russian Orthodox Church met in Moscow and decided to grant a certain measure of autonomy to the Orthodox Churches in Ukraine and Byelorussia (now Belarus). Each of these were made exarchates of the Moscow patriarchate, with the optional names "The Ukrainian Orthodox Church" and "The Byelorussian (now Belarussian) Orthodox Church." Following the dissolution of the Soviet Union on Dec. 25, 1991, and the independence of the various successor states, the patriarchate granted similar autonomous status to the Orthodox Churches in Estonia, Latvia, and Moldova.

But because the Orthodox Church in Ukraine was demanding greater freedom, on Oct. 27, 1990, another session of the Bishops' Council granted "independence and self-government" to the Ukrainian Orthodox Church and abolished the title "Ukrainian Exarchate." The Church remained autonomous, with the metropolitan of Kiev still a member of the Holy Synod of the Moscow Patriarchate. After Ukraine declared its independence on Aug. 24, 1991, Metropolitan Filaret of Kiev began to seek complete separation of his Church from the Moscow patriarchate. This, however, was refused at a meeting of the Russian Orthodox Bishop's Council in April 1992. Matters came to a head in May 1992 when the Moscow patriarchate deposed Filaret and appointed Metropolitan Vladimir (Volodymyr) (Sabodan) of Rostov as new metropolitan of Kiev. Subsequently, Filaret joined the non-canonical Ukrainian Autocephalous Church.

Another problem arose in the newly-independent ex-Soviet republic of Moldova. Before 1812 and again from 1918 to 1944, Moldova (then known as Bessarabia) had been part of Romania. In spite of the fact that the Moscow patriarchate had granted autonomous status to its Mol-

dovan diocese, the Holy Synod of the Romanian Orthodox Church decided in December 1992 to reconstitute its own metropolitanate of Bessarabia in the same territory. Thus, the Orthodox in Moldova split between the two rival jurisdictions, but the great majority of parishes remain loyal to the jurisdiction linked to the Moscow patriarchate.

In Estonia, an autonomous Orthodox Church under the patriarchate of Constantinople existed from 1923 until it was absorbed into the Moscow patriarchate in 1945 after the country was annexed by the Soviet Union. In the wake of Estonian independence in 1991, there were calls for the reestablishment of this Church, which had maintained its headquarters in Stockholm in exile. Later the Estonian government officially recognized it as the legal continuation of the Estonian Orthodox Church that existed in the interwar period. But on Oct. 5, 1994, the Holy Synod of the Moscow patriarchate expressed support for its autonomous Estonian diocese and protested that it was in danger of losing ownership of its parish churches and the large Piukhtitsy Convent of the Assumption. Altogether there are eighty Orthodox parishes with about 40,000 faithful in the country, half of them Estonian-language, eight bilingual, and the rest Russian-language. Fifty of the parishes support the reestablishment of the autonomous church under Constantinople. In February 1995 a delegation from the patriarchate of Constantinople visited both Estonia and the Moscow patriarchate in an effort to facilitate a solution to the problem.

Bibliography: N. DAVIS, *A Long Walk to Church: A Contemporary History of Russian Orthodoxy* (Boulder, Colorado 1995). J. ELLIS, *The Russian Orthodox Church: A Contemporary History* (London 1986). D. POSPIELOVSKY, *The Russian Church Under the Soviet Regime 1917–1982,* 2 v. (Crestwood, New York 1984). R. G. ROBERSON, *The Eastern Christian Churches* (revised 6th ed. Rome 1999).

[R. G. ROBERSON]

ORTHODOX CHURCH OF SERBIA

The Serbs belong to the Southern Slavs. They have a common language with the Croats, from whom they were distinguished and separated even before both settled in the 7th century in the Balkan Peninsula. The territory settled by the Serbs belonged to various provinces of the Roman Empire.

Religious influences from the Western Church entered during the reign of Emperor Heracleus (610–641) through Dalmatia and Albania, but reached only the Slavs that were close to the cities along the coast. The Serbs in the center of the Balkan Peninsula, isolated by almost impassable mountains, were only sporadically affected. The dominance of the Byzantine culture, radiating from Salonika and Ohrid, had a more enduring effect, especially after the Slavic dialect was elevated by SS. Cyril and Methodius to a literary language. The sending out of missionaries by the Emperor Basil I the Macedonian (867–886) and the return of the disciples of the apostles of the Slavs to Macedonia and Bulgaria following their expulsion from Moravia (886), must have had consequences also among the Serbs, although information concerning the ecclesiastical situation before the time of St. Sava is scant. In a document of Stevan Nemanja, Sava's father, ''*his* bishop'' is mentioned, with the title of Rasa. According to a chrysobull of the Byzantine Emperor MICHAEL VIII Palaeologus this sole bishopric was erected in 950 as a suffragan of the autocephalous archiepiscopate of Ohrid.

The Serbian Archiepiscopate. The movements of the Crusades and the struggle for Constantinople brought the Balkan region into prominence. In the second half of the 12th century political independence from the Byzantine emperor was achieved (1183), and a strong Serbian state was formed by the Grand Župan Stevan Nemanja (1159–95). His youngest son, Rastko, as a monk named Sava, received his education in the monasteries of Mount Athos, where he had gone against the wishes of the father. The latter followed him, erected the monastery of Chilandar and took the habit under the name of Simeon (1196). Sava's elder brother, Stevan II Prvovenčani (First-Crowned), received in 1217 from Pope Honorius III the crown and recognition as king, which he had been unable to secure from Innocent III because of the opposition of the Hungarian King Emmerich. But the orientation toward the West was of short duration. Sava received from both the Byzantine Emperor and the Orthodox patriarch of Constantinople permission for the erection of an archiepiscopate, with the right to administer independently all internal affairs of the Serbian Church, especially the appointment of the archbishop and the bishops (1219). Sava was consecrated their first archbishop.

The nine dioceses established during St. Sava's government were situated in what today is the Macedonian Republic and the Autonomous Region of Kosovo-Metohija, and the southernmost part of Serbia proper. After having erected several monasteries with schools, and having established the Serbian Church on a solid hierarchical foundation, St. Sava resigned (1233), and went on a pilgrimage to the Holy Land. On his return trip he died in Trnovo (Bulgaria) in 1236. While the political organization of the Serbs throughout history collapsed several times, his work, the Serbian Orthodox Church, survived the most adverse vicissitudes, and is still in existence.

Serbian Orthodox priest celebrates Mass in Gracanica monastery. The ceremony commemorates Serbian battles against Ottoman Turks, their subsequent defeat, and the foundation of Serbian nationalism. (AP/Wide World Photos)

The Serbian Patriarchate. The zenith in the development of Serbia was reached under Stevan Dušan (1331–55). Taking advantage of the civil wars within the Byzantine Empire, he added to his domains Macedonia, Albania, Epirus, and Thessaly; his predecessors had already extended their rule toward the north, up to the Danube and Sava. In 1346 Dušan was crowned ''Emperor of the Serbs and the Greeks'' in Skopjei, and, in imitation of the Byzantine model, the archbishop was elevated to the dignity of patriarch. The erection of the patriarchate, in the presence of the Bulgarian patriarch and the archbishop of Ohrid, was necessitated by other considerations too. Only a hierarch with this highest dignity could incorporate into the church of Dušan's empire the autocephalous Church of Ohrid and the dioceses of the Patriarchate of Constantinople in Macedonia, Epirus and Thessaly. The patriarch's residence was at Peć since Arsenije I, the successor of St. Sava. The dioceses were now distributed into metropolitan districts. The ecumenical patriarch protested and then excommunicated the new patriarchate, as well as the entire Serbian State and people (1352). However, the increased danger from the Turks after their victory at the Maritza (1371) forced Constantinople as well as the Serbs to seek friends, and the excommunication was retracted and the patriarchate recognized (1376).

Domination of the Turks. The arrival of the Turks had a far reaching influence on the destiny of the Serbian Church. The Orthodox patriarchs were recognized as supreme heads of their people even in civil matters, and the Turks ruled their Christian subjects not directly, but mediately through their religious superiors, the patriarchs and bishops.

As for the Serbian patriarch, it seems that the Turks did not recognize him as head of his nation, probably because they had no effective contacts with him, but regarded the autocephalous archbishop of Ohrid as responsible for the Serbs. No Serbian patriarch is mentioned after 1500 until the Serbian Patriarchate was reestablished in 1557 by the Grand Vizier Mehmed Sokolović, a Serb who had embraced Islam when as a child he was forcibly drafted into the Janizaries. A relative of the Grand Vizier, the monk Makarije, became the first patriarch. The Serbian Church, now an administrative part of the Turkish political organization, was expected to unite all the Slavs up to the Carpathian Mountains, bring them under Turkish control, and lure them away from the Christians in western Europe. The patriach was spiritual and temporal head of all the Serbs and other Orthodox under his jurisdiction from the Adriatic to Rumania, and from the Carpathian Mountains to Macedonia, governing them through 22 bishops.

The ceaseless unrest caused by the wars of the Turks in the 17th and 18th centuries led to continued migrations of the Serbs toward the north and west. Their original region was settled by Albanians. The Serbs migrated in large numbers toward areas north of the Danube, into Syrmium, Bosnia and Hercegovina, Dalmatia, and into Croatia-Slavonia. The Hungarian King Mathias Corvinus (1458–90) conferred upon the Serbian leader Vuk Branković the title of despot, which was taken from the Byzantine administrative hierarchy, and acknowledged him as commander of the Serbs, whom Hungary needed for the protection of the southern boundaries against the advancing Turks. Whenever the Turks ceded a territory to the Austrian emperor, all citizens of the Islamic faith, although of Croatian or Serbian nationality and language, were obliged according to the tenets of Islam to leave the country of the Christian ruler. The vase void spaces were accordingly settled by the Serbs, who had thus over the centuries almost completely evacuated their original seats, and transferred their center to the Danube, Sava, and Drina Rivers. Especially memorable were the great treks of 1690 under Patriarch Arsenije III Crnojević, of 30,000 families, in response to the proclamation of Emperor Leopold I, by which he promised to grant them national and religious liberty under his scepter; and that of 1739 under Patriarch Arsenije IV Jovanović-šakabent, in flight from the vengeance of the Turks who had been angered by their support of Austria.

The chief bishop of the migrants established their final residence in Karlovci, a small town on the Danube, close to the numerous monasteries previously erected in the Fruška Gora, an isolated mountain range in Syrmium. The patriarchs continued to reside in Peć until the abolition of the patriarchate (1766). The archbishops of Karlovci were considered exarchs of the patriarchal throne of Peć. The jurisdiction of the migrating Serbian patriarchs was not affected by the move to the new regions, since they had, as true ethnarchs, considered and styled themselves as patriarchs of the people, ''the Serbs,'' and not as of a certain city or country.

The Third Serbian Patriarchate. The collapse of the Austro-Hungarian Monarchy (1918) led to the establishment of the Kingdom of the Serbs, Croats, and Slovenes, later called Yugoslavia. The Serbs were again politically united for the first time since the Middle Ages. The sectional Churches were dissolved and the Serbian Patriarchate was reestablished (1920). In Yugoslavia between the two world wars, the Serbian Orthodox Church enjoyed a privileged position for several reasons: the Serbs, although not constituting a majority, were the numerically largest nationality in the state, and the chief beneficiary from the advantages accruing from a larger political unit. The reigning family was Serbian, and to be successful in the civil or military service it was advantageous to be of the Orthodox faith. Although so close a relationship between politics and Church had its corruptive effect upon a spiritual organization, the Serbian Orthodox Church made every effort to repair the wounds caused by the centuries of Islamic oppression and the continuous wars. This evolution was interrupted by World War II, which was fought in the Balkans by the various nationalities, split among themselves.

The coming of the Communist regime under Josip Broz Tito severed the bonds between the Serbian Church and the State, gravely damaged the Church by confiscations and curtailment of liberty, but involuntarily enhanced the prestige of the patriarch and the meaning of the Church for the Serbian nation. The collapse of communism in the Eastern European bloc paved the way for a renaissance of the Serbian Orthodox Church in public life.

Monastic Life. Monasteries, under Greek direction, existed in the territory of the Serbian Church before the time of St. Sava, some probably going back to that of the disciples of SS. Cyrillus and Methodius. They received a great increase under Sava's government. He reestablished in 1196 the former Greek monastery of Chilandar on the Holy Mount Athos, which remained the spiritual center of Serbian monasticism for centuries, along with the new convents of Žiča, Studenica, Visoki Dečani, Mileševo, Sopočani, and numerous others.

The medieval Serbian Church was one of monasteries, and the importance of the monks and nuns can be compared with that in the early Church of Scotland and Ireland. In the absence of cities as cultural centers, the monasteries were the residences of all the bishops, the only schools, centers of art, depositories of public and private documents, etc. The copying of books for the needs of the Serbian Church as well as that of other Slavic nations prospered in such close proximity to Greek sources. Monasteries sometimes contained up to 200 subjects. They were divided into classes: imperial lavras, subject solely to the monarch; archiepiscopal, and later stauropegial convents, under the direct authority of the patriarch; and eparchial monasteries, under the supervision of the diocesan bishops. The bishop's own residence was always a monastery of which he was the superior.

The Serbs established in the 15th century in the Fruška Gora in Syrmium a new, Serbian Holy Mountain, with several monasteries: Krušedol, Hopovo, Šišatovac, Vrdnik (Ravanica), Kuveždin, Beoćin, Bešenovo, Grgetek, and Fenek. From the 17th century these convents performed a valuable service to the Serbian Church when the nation migrated to the north.

Church Art. Over the many centuries, the Serbian Orthodox Church developed a mixed architectural style, being at the point at which Italian influences from across the Adriatic meet the Byzantine influences from the South.

In respect to painting, particularly fresco, Serbia holds its own even if compared with the abundance of Italian monuments of art. Matejić, Nagoričino, Chilander, Gračanica, Dečani (with more than 1,000 compositions), and numerous other convents and churches, dispersed all over the country, usually away from the main routes of communication, are a testimony that painting was nurtured in the Serbia of the kings and czars at a degree of excellence somewhat higher than that existing at the same time in western Europe. The loss of political independence under the Turks brought to a nearly complete and abrupt stop the further development of artistic manifestations.

The Serbian Orthodox Church Today. The Serbian Orthodox Church is headed by His Holiness, the Arch-

bishop of Peé, Metropolitan of Beograd-Karlovci, and Serbian Patriarch. The patriarch is elected from the number of those Serbian bishops who have administered a diocese at least five years. The Council of the Bishops presents three candidates to the electoral assembly composed of all bishops, certain other secular and regular clergy, and lay representatives from the various eparchies.

The patriarch enjoys the privilege of performing the consecration of all bishops, either in person or through a delegate, of consecrating the Holy Myro (Chrism) for the entire Serbian Church, of wearing the white *panakamilavka,* a white veil that covers the cylindrical headgear and falls down upon the shoulders.

The Serbian Orthodox Church is administered by the patriarch with the assistance of two synods. The Holy Council of the Bishops, *Sveti Arhijerejski Sabor,* is composed of all diocesan bishops. It is the legislator and supreme authority of the Church, to be called together whenever the patriarch with the Holy Synod of Bishops decides, especially for the election of bishops. The Holy Synod of Bishops, *Sveti Arhijejski Sinod,* is the executive organ of the Council of Bishops. It is composed of the patriarch and four bishops. For all decisions of the patriarch the assent of a majority of the members of the Holy Synod of Bishops is required.

The High Tribunal of the Church is a court of appeal from diocesan tribunals, although the Synod and the Council of Bishops also have judicial power in major causes, especially those concerning transgressions of bishops and of the patriarch himself. The Patriarchal Council is entrusted with legislation and supervision in the sphere of temporal administration, and has a number of laymen among its members. Its executive organ is the Patriarchal Administrative Board, composed of the patriarch and six clerical and seven lay members.

The diocesan bishop is assisted by a vicar-general, *arhijerejski zamenik,* of his choice. The Eparchial Church Tribunal has a twofold competence: it is the diocesan administrative office (chancery), and also a court of first instance under the presidency of the bishop or his deputy, assisted by two other priests, secretaries-reporters, and other personnel. The Eparchial Council is in charge of the temporal management of the diocesan property, and supervises the same activity in the parishes. Its executive organ is the Eparchial Administrative Board.

The diocese, *eparhija,* is divided into districts, composed of a number of parishes, each headed by the episcopal vicar, *arhijerejski namesnik.* His official duty is to represent the bishop in his district, and to decide matters of lesser importance. Every parish has but one priest for

300 to 500 families, but several parishes can be centered in the same church. The Congregational Meeting is charged with the management of the temporal affairs of the parish or parishes. All the parishes of municipalities with up to 50,000 faithful are united in one Congregational Meeting. Its executive organ is the Congregational Committee. Membership in these bodies belongs to all priests of the parish or parishes and to lay members, elected by all parishioners. Their number varies with the number of the parishioners, varying from 24 to 60 in the Congregational Meeting, and six to twelve in the Congregational Committee.

Bishops are taken only from monks or from among widowed priests who have taken monastic vows. In addition, they are required to be graduates of a higher school of theology. Sometimes laymen with a higher education, e.g., lawyers, college teachers, join the rank of the regular clergy, having become widowers, and are, after theological preparation, advanced to the hierarchy.

Liturgical Worship. The liturgical rite of the Serbian Orthodox Church is that of Constantinople, called also BYZANTINE LITURGY. With the acceptance of the liturgical books from the Ukraine and Russia, where Patriarch NIKON (1652–67) had them reformed according to the usage of the Greeks, uniformity was established with the Common Byzantine Liturgy. The liturgical language of the Serbian Church is the Church Slavonic, originally the Slavic dialect from the surroundings of Saloniki, adapted to the use of the Church under the influence of the Serbian language. Liturgical books were printed in *Srbulj,* a form of the Church-Slavonic, as early as 1494, and in 1495 the *Psaltir* of Cetinje appeared. Under the Turks, and later because of the opposition of popes and Catholic bishops, it became increasingly difficult to continue the printing of liturgical books, whereas good editions, prepared in Kiev and Moscow, became available at the end of the 17th century. The acceptance of these books displaced the Serbian versions and introduced the Ukrainized form of the Church-Slavonic. Voices were raised repeatedly, advocating the return to the *Srbulj,* while others suggested the introduction of the modern Serbian language. English is now employed extensively in the U.S. and in Canada in the celebration of the Divine Liturgy and other services.

A peculiarity of the Serbians is the *krsna slava* of pre-Christian origin, a memorial rite to honor ancestors. Each family has a certain patron saint, or a certain feast of the liturgical calendar, on the day of which the *krsna slava* is to be celebrated. It is assumed that this day is identical either with the day when the ancestor accepted Christianity by baptism, or with the day of the patron saint adopted by the ancestor. The *krsna slava* is inherited in the male line. It is celebrated by an elaborate religious rite, often with the intervention of the priest, who visits the home to bless and cut the *slavski kolač* or cake.

Bibliography: D. SLIJEPČEVIĆ, *Istorija Srpske Pravoslavne crkve,* v.1: *Od pokrštavanja srba do kraja XVII veka* (Munich 1962), contains a systematic survey and bibliog. of all previous histories of the Serbian Church. A. HUDAL, *Die serbisch-orthodoxe Nationalkirche* (Graz 1922). C. S. DRAŠKOVIĆ, ''Die Lage der Orthodoxen Kirche in Jugoslavien,'' in F. POPAN and Č. S. DRAŠKOVIĆ, *Orthodoxie heute in Rumänien und Jugoslawien,* ed. K. RUDOLF (Vienna 1960) 137–176. A. PRINETTO, *L'organizzazzione della Chiesa Serba Ortodossa in base alla nuova costituzione del 1931 e legge statale del 1929* (Dissertation unpublished. Pontificia U. Gregoriana, no. 913; Rome 1941). V. J. POSPISHIL, *Der Patriarch im Rechte der Serbisch-Pravoslavischen Kirche* (Diss. unpub. Pontificia U. Gregoriana; Rome 1949). ''The Sixth Centenary of the Serbian Patriarch,'' (in Serbian) *Glasnik, Srpske' Pravoslavne Crkve* no. 9 (Belgrade, Sept. 1, 1946) 129–207. *Oriente Cattolico: Cenni storici e statistiche* (Vatican City 1962) 235–245. R. ROBERSON, *The Eastern Christian Churches: A Brief Survey,* 6th ed (Rome 1999).

[V. J. POSPISHIL/EDS.]

ORTHODOX SYMBOLIC BOOKS

The Orthodox Churches follow the Nicaean-Constantinopolitan Creed as the symbol or statement of their faith; but as they admit the ecumenicity of the decisions of only the first seven ecumenical councils [*see* COUNCILS, GENERAL (ECUMENICAL), THEOLOGY OF; COUNCILS, GENERAL (ECUMENICAL), HISTORY OF], they have been constrained in modern times to formulate their own statement of faith particularly in dealing with Catholicism and Protestantism. This has been done in a concise and definite form by a number of prelates and theologians in their Symbolic Books (symbolon or creed) whose statements and definitions, however, do not have an obligatory or infallible status as do the decisions of the ancient Church. They are authoritative, but depend for acceptance on the approbation of various authorities.

The principal confessions are: (1) The Confession of the Patriarch GENNADIUS II Scholarius of Constantinople, made after the fall of Constantinople in 1453 for the Sultan Mohammed II. It dealt primarily with the Trinity, the Incarnation, immortality, and the Resurrection. (2) The three answers given by the Patriarch Jeremiah II of Constantinople to the German Protestant theologians in 1576, 1579, and 1581. (3) The Confession of METROPHANES CRITOPOULOS (1625), who became patriarch of Alexandria in 1636. This confession is orthodox in content, but of Protestant inspiration. (4) The Confession of Peter Moghila, Metropolitan of Kiev (1633–47), which was called the Great Catechism and was aimed at neutralizing the Protestant influence of the Confession of the Patriarch of Constantinople, Cyril Lukaris. The Great Catechism, written originally in Slavic and in Latin (before 1640), was then translated into Greek by Meletius Syrigus; it was approved, with some corrections, by the patriarch of Constantinople in 1643 as well as by the other Oriental patriarchs. It was published in Greek for the first time only in 1667, however. It went through numerous editions and translations into different languages. As is evident from his Small Catechism (1645), Moghila himself refused to approve the corrected translations, which had an anti-Catholic bias. (5) The Confession of the Patriarch Dositheus of Jerusalem, which was approved by the Synod of Jerusalem in 1672, and was composed with definite Catholic influence in an anti-Protestant sense. (6) The Catechism of the Metropolitan Philaret of Moscow, which in its third edition (1839) was modified in accord with the anti-Protestant reform of 1836. It went through many editions. (7) The Encyclical of the four Oriental Patriarchs, headed by the Patriarch Anthimus VI of Constantinople in 1848. This letter was a negative response to the invitation of Pope Pius IX for union with the Catholic Church. (8) The Encyclical of the Patriarch Anthimus VII of Constantinople (1895) in answer to a letter from Pope LEO XIII.

The authority of the Symbolic Books among the Orthodox varies. The Confession of Peter Moghila and that of Dositheus are accepted for the most part by the Greeks and Slavs, while the Catechism of Philaret is considered as a Symbolic Book only by the Russians and Slavs and is ignored by the Greeks. The significance of the Encyclical of 1848 was increased by Khomiakov who considered it as the foundation for his ecclesiology. In former times the Symbolic Books were greatly esteemed; during the last few decades, however, critical voices have been raised against them because of either the Catholic or the Protestant influences under which they were proposed. The Confession of Gennadius II was never accepted by all the Orthodox churches as an authentic expression of orthodoxy. The Confession of Metrophanes Critopoulos, even though a private work, enjoys considerable authority among many Greek Orthodox today. According to the Orthodox leaders it will be the obligation of a future pan-orthodox council to decide what kind of obligatory authority should be given to the Symbolic Books.

Bibliography: E. J. KIMMEL, *Monumenta fidei Ecclesiae Orientalis*, 2 v. (Jena 1843–50). J. MICHALCESCU, *Die Bekenntnisse und die wichtigsten Glaubenszeugnisse der griechisch-orientalischen Kirche* (Leipzig 1904). A. MALVY and M. VILLER, eds., *La Confession orthodoxe de Pierre Moghila* (Orientalia Christiana 39; Rome 1927). J. N. KARMIRES, Τὰ δογματικὰ καὶ συμβολικὰ μνημεῖα τῆς Ὀρθοδόξου Καθολικῆ Ἐκκλησίας 2 v. (Athens 1952–53). A. PALMIERI, *Theologia dogmatica orthodoxa*, 2 v. (Florence 1911–13). M. JUGIE, *Theologia dogmatica christianorum orientalium ab ecclesia catholica dissendentium*, 5 v. (Paris 1926–35) 1:671–682. S. ZANKOW, *Das orthodoxe Christentum des Ostens* (Berlin 1928). M. JUGIE, *Échos d'Orient* (Paris 1897–) 28 (1929) 423–430. M. GORDILLO, *Compendium theologiae orientalis* (3d ed. Rome 1950). H. MULERT, *Konfessionskunde*, ed. E. SCHOTT and K. ONASCH (3d ed. Berlin 1956) 72–153. K. ALGERMISSEN, *Konfessionskunde* (7th ed. Celle 1957) 465–469. B. SCHULTZE, *Lexikon für Theologie und Kirche*, ed. J. HOFER and K. RAHNER, 10 v. (2d, new ed. Freiburg 1957–65); suppl., *Das ZweiteVatikanische Konzil: Dokumente und kommentare*, ed. H. S. BRECHTER et al., pt. 1 (1966) 2:148–149.

[B. SCHULTZE]

ORTHODOXY

The word orthodoxy, derived from the Greek, means ὀρθός (right) and δόξα (belief). This word is primarily used in connection with those churches of the Christian East. The title itself is ancient and was not used by the Orthodox Churches to express their position in reference to Rome so much as to indicate their fidelity to the first seven ecumenical councils. Unlike the Oriental Orthodox Churches and the Assyrian Church of the East, the Orthodox Churches insist upon their orthodoxy by their reception of the christology of the Council of Chalcedon (451). In using the term ''orthodoxy'' to describe themselves, the Orthodox Churches speak of not only preserving true belief about God and Christ but also preserve right worship; they glorify God in the true way in the liturgy. This extension of the term orthodoxy to embrace not only right belief (ortho-dogma) but also right glory (ortho-doxa) indicates the importance of the Church as a worshiping community, revealing the deep liturgical foundations of the Christian East.

Bibliography: S. BULGAKOV, *The Orthodox Church* (Crestwood, NY 1988) V. LOSSKY, *The Mystical Theology of the Eastern Church* (Cambridge 1957) J. MEYENDORFF, *The Orthodox Church* (Crestwood, NY 1981) A. SCHMEMANN, *For the Life of the World: Sacraments and Orthodoxy* (Crestwood, NY 1973). A. SCHMEMANN, *The Historical Road of Eastern Orthodoxy* (Crestwood, NY 1977). K. WARE, *The Orthodox Church*, rev. ed. (New York 1997)

[M. E. WILLIAMS/EDS.]

ORTIZ DE ZÁRATE, PEDRO, VEN.

Argentine martyr; b. Jujuy, 1622; d. in the Chaco, Oct. 27, 1683. He was the grandson of one of the founders of the early settlements in Jujuy and inherited a fortune in land and money. In 1644 he married Petronila de Ibarra, a member of another of the founding families; they had two sons. After the death of his wife in 1653, Ortiz de Zárate studied with the Jesuits; he was ordained in 1659. He was then appointed pastor in Jujuy. However, his great ambition was to convert the natives of the Chaco

Father Anatoly prays while believers listen during Orthodox Easter service at Orthodox church, Kiev, Ukraine. (AP/Wide World)

and to civilize them through preaching the gospel. He sought permission from the royal authorities and from the bishop of Tucumán to organize a missionary expedition into the region with two Jesuits. They left Jujuy on Oct. 18, 1682, with Ortiz de Zárate paying all the expenses of the expedition. Within the forests of the Chaco he founded two settlements: Santa Maráa and San Rafael. The natives gave the appearance of being friendly but the next year they killed Ortiz de Zárate and the Jesuit Father Salinas. All the existing documents that refer to Ortiz de Zárate assert that he led a holy life of mortification. His reputation for saintliness has grown since his death. A bone from his arm is preserved in the House of the Good Shepherd in Jujuy.

Bibliography: M. A. VERGARA, *Estudios sobre historia ecclesiástica de Jujuy* (Tucumán, Argen. 1942).

[M. A. VERGARA]

ORTLIBARII

A strongly ascetic movement, known also as Ortlibenses, that owed its name to Ortlieb of Strasbourg (*c.* 1200). An example of lay protest against institutional religion, they are mentioned in 13th-century documents with the Cathari and WALDENSES, and lesser sects as well, thus underscoring the confusion about their teaching in the minds of their contemporaries. For example, a constitution issued by Emperor FREDERICK II on May 14, 1238, proscribed the *Ortolevos* with a number of other heresies (*Monumenta Germanica Historica* [Berlin 1826—] *Leges* 4: Const. 2:284–285). According to ALBERT THE GREAT's judgment of the heretics of the Swabian district of Ries (Diocese of Augsburg) *c.* 1270, the Ortlibarii had been condemned by Innocent III for holding ''that man must abstain from externals and follow the spirit that is in him.'' They were reminiscent, on the one hand, of the pantheism of the AMALRICIANS centered in Paris (according to Jundt and Preger), and on the other, of the dualism of the widespread Gnostic-Manichaean stream (Haupt). However, significant differences set them apart from these movements as well as from the Waldenses with whom Müller was anxious to establish a relationship. The Ortlibarii espoused a cause that not only aimed to dissolve the visible Church but sought also to undermine essential tenets of the Christian tradition. The principal source for their teachings is the so-called Passau Anonymus (*Pseudo-Rainer*), begun *c.* 1260. The sect did not accept divine creation of the world, which they considered eternal. Its members reopened the Christological question with an attack on Trinitarian doctrine. Turning to the Sacraments, they rejected the Eucharist and adjudged infant Baptism useless since conscious adherence to their movement alone was efficacious. To the Catholic hierarchy they opposed their own Perfect Ones who, they claimed, could bind and loose. They recognized no obligation to pay TITHES, asserting that the clergy ought to earn its livelihood by manual labor. The papacy was identified with the harlot of the Apocalypse. Once the pope and emperor were converted to the sect, the Last Judgment would be imminent. Failure to be numbered among the sectaries merited damnation. Although they denied the resurrection of the body, they assumed the perfection of the spirit. Of particular interest to civil government was their rejection of oaths and capital punishment. While unlike the Cathari they countenanced marriage, they enjoined continence. The Ortlibarii did not survive the 13th century; presumably they were absorbed by the Brothers and Sisters of the Free Spirit of the 14th century.

Bibliography: S. M. DEUTSCH, J. J. HERZOG and A. HAUCK, eds., *Realenzyklopädie für protestantische Theologie,* 24 v. (3d ed. Lepzig 1896–1913) 14:498–501. W. PREGER, *Geschichte der deutschen Mystik im Mittelalter,* 3 v. (1874–93) 1:191–196. A. JUNDT, *Histoire du panthéisme populaire au moyen âge et au seizième siècle* (Strasburg 1875) 36–41. H. HAUPT, ''Waldensia,'' *Zeitschrift für Kirchengeschte* 10 (1888) 316–328. K. MÜLLER, *Die Waldenser und ihre einzelnen Gruppen* (Gotha 1886) 130–132, 169–171. H. GRUNDMANN, *Religiöse Bewegungen im Mittelalter* (2d ed. Hildesheim 1961). J. J. I. VON DÖLLINGER, *Beiträge zur Sektengeschichte des Mittelalters,* 2 v. in 1 (Munich 1890; repr. New York 1960) 2:299, 301, 317, 330, 400, 703.

[E. W. MCDONNELL]

ORTOLANA (HORTULANA), BL.

Wife and mother; d. before 1238. A descendant of the noble Fiumi family, she grew up to be a very devout young woman. She made several pilgrimages to Monte Gargano and to Rome, and *c.* 1192 she undertook the hazardous journey to the Holy Land. On her return she married Count Favarone di Offreduccio of Assisi. She was the mother of four children, including St. CLARE OF ASSISI and St. Agnes of Assisi. After the death of her husband, who had at first strongly opposed the religious vocation of their children, Ortolana joined the POOR CLARES at the convent of San Damiano at Monticelli near Florence, where her third daughter, Beatrice, was also a nun. She was buried close to her daughters in the church of St. Clare at Assisi, and she is honored by the FRANCISCANS with the title of blessed.

Feast: Jan. 2.

Bibliography: CIRO DA PESARO, *La beata Ortolana d'Assisi* (Rome 1904). Z. LAZZERI, ''Il processo di canonizzazione di S. Chiara d'Assissi,'' *Archivum Franciscanum historicum* 13 (1920) 403–507. A. FORTINI, ''Nuove notizie intorno a S. Chiara di Assisi,'' *ibid.* 46 (1953) 3–43. L. BRACALONI, S. *Chiara d'Assisi* (2d ed. Milan 1949), *passim.* O. ENGLEBERT, *St. Francis of Assisi: A Biography,* tr. E. M. COOPER, 2d augm. ed. by I. BRADY and R. BROWN.

[B. J. COMASKEY]

ORTON, WILLIAM AYLOTT

Philosopher, economist; b. Bromley, England, Feb. 9, 1889; d. Northampton, Mass., Aug. 13, 1952. He was the son of William Amor and Emma (Aylott) Orton. During World War I he served in the British army at Gallipoli, and in Egypt and France. He was wounded at the Battle of the Somme and later joined the intelligence staff of the British War Office. In 1917 he married Olmen Marlais Moment. Orton received the B.A. degree from Cambridge University, England, in 1919, and then entered the industrial relations department of the Ministry of Labour. Later, while studying at the University of London, he won the London *Athenaeum's* essay contest and published essays and articles in the *Westminster Review* and the *New Age.* After receiving the M.A. degree from Cambridge University, he went to the United States to join the faculty of Smith College, Northampton, Mass.; Bryn Mawr College, Bryn Mawr, Pa.; and the University of California at Berkeley. He was awarded honorary degrees by the University of London; Boston College, Boston, Mass.; and Georgetown University, Washington, D.C. He published articles in popular magazines and in the *American Journal of Sociology, International Journal of Ethics, American Economic Review,* and *Encyclopaedia of the Social Sciences.* Among his books were *America in Search of Culture* (1933), *Prelude to Economics* (1933), *The Economic Role of the State* (1949), and *The Liberal Tradition* (1945). In his writings Orton often referred to Catholic history and to classic literature. In his public lectures he frequently urged the people of the United States to accept the role of leadership in the modern world. Although aware of the value of conservative philosophy, he believed that the liberal viewpoint alone assumed responsibility for the future and was based on the confident outlook of Christianity.

[J. R. BETTS]

ORVAL, ABBEY OF

A Cistercian abbey in Luxembourg province, Belgium, founded in 1070 by Count Arnulf II of Chiny for some Benedictine monks from Calabria. Orval (Aureavallis, Güldenthal) passed into the possession of the Clerks Regular in 1110 and eventually was taken over by Cistercians from the Abbey of TRE FONTANE in 1132. The first Cistercian abbot was Constantine (d. 1145), a disciple of St. Bernard of Clairvaux, who was noted for holiness. In 1251 or 1252 Orval was burned, and the monks dispersed. Under succeeding abbots it flourished and was well governed except during the decline following the Reformation in the Netherlands in the 16th century. Its spirit was restored by Abbot Bernard de Montgaillard (d. 1628), but the buildings were again destroyed by Huguenots in 1637. Abbot Carl von Benzeradt (d. 1707) drew up new statutes of strict observance for Orval. During the rule of Abbot E. Henrion (d. 1729), it was a focal point of Jansenism, but in 1750 those monks infected with the heresy were removed. Orval prospered and in 1750 it owned 300 towns, from which it derived a rich income. It fell victim to the French Revolutionists and was suppressed in 1796. In 1926 Trappists from the Abbey of SEPT-FONS built a priory upon its ruins.

Bibliography: L. H. COTTINEAU, *Répertoire topobibliographique des abbayes et prieurés,* 2 v. (Mâcon 1935–39) 2:2148–49. N. TILLIÈRE, *Histoire de l'abbaye d'Orval* (6th ed. Gembloux 1958). C. GRÉGOIRE, *Lexikon für Theologie und Kirche,* ed. J. HOFER and K. RAHNER, 10 v. (2d, new ed. Freiburg 1957–65) 7:1258.

[E. D. MC SHANE]

OSBALDESTON, EDWARD, BL.

Priest, martyr; b. ca. 1560 at Osbaldeston, Lancashire, England; hanged, drawn, and quartered at York, Nov. 16, 1594. Edward studied at Douai, then at Rheims, where he was ordained (Sept. 21, 1585). He worked on the Continent until he was sent to Yorkshire in April 1589. Betrayed by an apostate priest, he was apprehended on Sept. 30, 1594. Following his trial at York, Osbaldeston was convicted of high treason for being a priest. Challoner prints a portion of a still extant letter from Osbaldeston to his fellow-prisoners in York Castle, which reveals the martyr's humility and the serene trust in God with which he anticipated his death. He was beatified by Pope John Paul II on Nov. 22, 1987 with George Haydock and Companions.

Feast of the English Martyrs: May 4 (England).

See Also: ENGLAND, SCOTLAND, AND WALES, MARTYRS OF.

Bibliography: R. CHALLONER, *Memoirs of Missionary Priests,* ed. J. H. POLLEN (rev. ed. London 1924), I, no. 106. J. H. POLLEN, *Acts of English Martyrs* (London 1891).

[K. I. RABENSTEIN]

OSBERN OF GLOUCESTER

Lexicographer, exegete; fl. *c.* 1150. Little is known about his life beyond the fact that he was born probably in the township of Pinnock in Gloucestershire, England, that he was a Benedictine at Gloucester under Abbot Hamelin (1148–79), and that he dedicated his commentary on Judges to Gilbert Foliot, who was then bishop of Hereford (1148–63). Although Osbern also wrote commentaries on Genesis, Exodus, Deuteronomy, and Numbers and treatises on the Incarnation, Nativity, Passion, and Resurrection (none published), his most influential work remained his *Liber derivationum* (sometimes called *Panormia*), which is to be assigned to the third quarter of the 12th century when Osbern was an old man. Set in an allegorical framework and arranged alphabetically with two sections to each letter, this dictionary of derivations, well equipped with *testimonia* from both ancient and medieval writers, entered the main stream of European learning, appearing in Bavaria and Austria before the end of the 12th century and becoming the main source for the glossary of HUGUCCIO OF PISA (d. 1210).

Bibliography: Works. *Liber derivationum,* ed. A. MAI, in *Classicorum auctorum e Vaticanis codicibus editorum,* 10 v. (Rome 1828–38), v.8. G. LOEWE, *Corpus Glossariorum latinorum,* ed. G. GOETZ, 7 v. (Leipzig 1888–1923) 1:196–215, for description of work and reproduction of preface. Preface also in R. W. HUNT, ''The 'Lost' Preface to the *Liber derivationum* of Osbern of Gloucester,'' *Mediaeval and Renaissance Studies* 4 (1958) 267–282. British Museum MS Bibl. Reg. 6DIX, for exegetical works. Biography. W. MEYER, ''Ueber Mai's Thesaurus novus latinitatis,'' *Rheinisches Museum für Philologie* 29 (1874) 179–183, G. GOETZ, ''Beiträge zur Geschichte der lateinischen Studien im Mittelalter,'' *Berichte über die Verhandlungen der Königlich-Sächsischen Gesellschaft der Wissenschaften zu Leipzig, Philologisch-Historische Klasse* 55 (1903) 121–154. *Geschichte der lateinischen Literatur des Mittelalters* 3:187–190. É. PELLEGRIN, ''Un Manuscrit des *Derivationes* d'Osbern de Gloucester annoté par Pétrarque (Paris BN cod. lat. 7492),'' *Italia medioevale e umanistica* 3 (1960) 263–266.

[R. B. PALMER]

OSIANDER, ANDREAS

Nuremberg reformer; b. Gunzenhausen in Frankish Brandenburg, Dec. 19, 1498; d. Königsberg, Oct. 17,

1552. Osiander was a classical student at Leipzig, Altenburg, and Ingolstadt, and became an accomplished linguist, but did not obtain a degree. He was ordained in 1520, taught Hebrew in the Augustinian Cloister at Nuremberg, and was later identified with Lazarus Spengler (1479–1534), Wenceslaus Linck (1483–1547), and Willibald PIRKHEIMER as a Nuremberg reformer. In 1522 he published his *Biblia sacra,* a version of the Vulgate based on original texts. A Lutheran, he married in 1525.

Osiander opposed Zwingli's view of the Lord's Supper. He was invited to the Marburg Colloquy (1529) and to Augsburg (1530). He assisted in church visitations in lands of Markgrave George of Brandenburg-Ansbach and, with Johann BRENZ, drafted the Brandenburg-Nuremberg Church Ordinance (1532). He was a discussant at Schmalkalden (1537), Hagenau, Worms (1540), and Regensburg (1541), where his criticism of Melanchthon brought about his recall.

Although he was unusually gifted, Osiander's haughty, overbearing, disputatious, and unrestrained manner irritated his enemies and alienated his friends. Although adept at pointing out error, he rarely contributed constructive solutions. He could not forego polemics. When asked by Rhäticus (Georg Joachim von Lauchen 1514–76) to edit and publish Copernicus's *De revolutionibus orbium coelestium* (1543), Osiander added his own preface in which he claimed the work was based on hypotheses. Although Copernicus's adherents were furious, the claim kept the book off the Index until the 17th century.

Although he was nominally Lutheran, Osiander's teachings, because of certain mystical assumptions, had a strange twist on sin, grace, and, particularly, justification, which he regarded not as a forensic act, as did Luther, but a gradual process resulting from Christ's indwelling in the sinner. He differed also with Luther's teaching on church discipline and private confession.

After his abrupt departure from Nuremberg (1548), Osiander remained in Königsberg in the service of Duke Albert of Prussia, first as pastor of the *Altstädtische Kirche,* and later, as professor *primarius* at Königsberg. His lack of academic degrees aroused the jealousy of older professors, and his dissident views caused friction with the orthodox younger men who had studied under Luther and Melanchthon. Particularly divisive was Osiander's strange view of justification, an argument in which Melanchthon and Flacius were eventually embroiled; but Duke Albert continued his confidence in Osiander and even elevated him in 1551 to president of the bishopric of Samland. At Osiander's death the duke honored him with a royal funeral.

Bibliography: W. MÖLLER, *Andreas Osianders Leben und ausgewählte Schriften (Väter und Begründer der Lutherischen Kirche* 5; Elberfeld 1870); *Allgemeine deutsche Bilgraphie* (Leipzig 1875–1910) 24:473–483. W. MÖLLER and P. TSCHACKERT, J. J. HERZOG and A. HAUCK, eds. *Realencyklopädie für protestantische Theologie* (Leipzig 1896–1913) 14: 501–509. E. BIZER, *Die Religion in Geschichte und Gegenwart* (Tübingen 1957–65) 4:1730–31. P. MEINHOLD, *Lexikon für Theologie und Kirche,* ed. J. HOFER and K. RAHNER (Freiberg 1957–65) 7:1261–63.

[E. G. SCHWIEBERT]

OSMUND OF SALISBURY, ST.

Bishop, chancellor; d. Dec. 3–4, 1099. Osmund, or Osmer, was a Norman noble who went to England with his uncle, WILLIAM I the Conqueror, for whom he served as chaplain and then chancellor (*c.* 1072–78). He was consecrated bishop of Salisbury in 1078. Prominent in civil as well as ecclesiastical affairs of the realm, he is believed to have directed a large portion of the Domesday survey. As bishop he completed the cathedral of Old Sarum (not the present cathedral of Salisbury) and established there a cathedral chapter of secular canons. Emulation of this example gradually brought the English cathedral system into conformity with Continental practice. He also organized the liturgical services for his diocese and the compilation provided the basis of the later "Sarum Use" that was widely adopted throughout the British Isles. He was canonized by Pope CALLISTUS III, Jan. 1, 1457, the last canonization of a saint from England until that of Sir Thomas MORE in 1935. On July 23, 1457, his remains were translated from Old Sarum to the Lady Chapel in Salisbury.

Feast: Dec. 4.

Bibliography: WILLIAM OF MALMESBURY, *Gesta pontificum Anglorum,* ed. N. E. S. A. HAMILTON (*Rerum Britannicarum medii aevi scriptores* 52; 1870) 183–184, 424–431. *The Register of S. Osmund,* ed. W. H. R. JONES, 2 v. (*ibid.* 78; 1883–84). *The Canonization of Saint Osmund,* ed. A. R. MALDEN (Salisbury, Eng. 1901). C. L. KINGSFORD, *The Dictionary of National Biography From the Earliest Times to 1900* (London 1885–1900) 14:1207–09. W. J. TORRANCE, *The Story of Saint Osmund, Bishop of Salisbury* (Salisbury, Wiltshire 1978).

[R. D. WARE]

OSRHOENE

Osrhoene is a region between the Euphrates and Tigris rivers whose capital was EDESSA. During the first two Christian centuries it was a small kingdom under the dynasty of Abgar. In 216 the Emperor Caracalla incorporated it into the Roman Empire as a province. Christianity had been introduced into Osrhoene early, most probably from Antioch by Jewish Christians. There is no historical foundation for the legends of ABGAR, King of Osrhoene, recorded by Eusebius (*Hist. eccl.* 1.12–13) to the effect that the king begged Jesus to come and heal his daughter. To this request Jesus was alleged to have sent a written reply saying that he was going to send his disciple, Thaddeus (Thaddai), to heal the girl and preach the Gospel. However, according to trustworthy sources, there were Christians in Osrhoene as early as the latter half of the 2nd century.

The Epitaph of ABERCIUS and information in Eusebius (*Ecclesiastical History* 5.24) witness to the fact that counsel was sought from the Diocese of Osrhoene in the matter of the fixing of the date for Easter. At the beginning of the 3rd century JULIUS AFRICANUS found the heretic BARDESANES in the court of King Abgar IX. There is no conclusive evidence for A. von HARNACK'S contention that this king embraced Christianity and that Osrhoene was the first Christian kingdom. The Christians of Osrhoene wrote in Syriac; their greatest glory was St. EPHREM.

Bibliography: J. P. MARTIN, *Les Origines de l'Église d'Édesse et des églises syriennes* (Paris 1889). I. ORTIZ DE URBINA, "Le origini del cristianesimo in Edessa," *Gregorianum,* 15 (1934) 82–91.

[I. ORTIZ DE URBINA]

OSSÓ Y CERVELLÓ, ENRIQUE (HENRY) DE, ST.

Priest and founder of the Society of Saint Teresa of Jesus (*Compañia de Santa Teresa de Jesús*); b. Vinebre (village near Tarragona), Spain, Oct. 15 or 16, 1840; d. Gilet near Valencia, Spain, Jan. 27, 1896.

The youngest of the three children of Jaime de Ossó and his wife Micaela Cervelló, Enrique was apprenticed at age twelve to his uncle, a Barcelona merchant, when he fell gravely ill and was sent home. Upon his recovery he was apprenticed to a businessman in Reus, Don Ortal, but Enrique left everything behind following his mother's death (Sept. 15, 1854).

He began to study for the priesthood at Tortosa's seminary (1854–60), and then at Barcelona (1860–61, 1863–66), where he completed spiritual exercises for the subdiaconate (May 1866) under the direction of Saint Anthony Mary CLARET. He was still a seminarian when he returned to the Tortosa seminary to teach in 1862. There he was ordained in 1867. In June 1870, Enrique made a pilgrimage to Rome in the company of two other later saints, Claret and Emmanuel DOMINGO Y SOL. He began his catechetical work and offered popular missions in Tortosa in 1871, while continuing to teach mathematics in Tortosa's seminary until the bishop relieved him from his faculty duties.

Ossó y Cervelló founded several associations for lay people: the Association of the Immaculate Conception for farmers (1870); Association of the Daughters of Immaculate Mary and Saint Teresa of Jesus for youth (approved 1873); Brotherhood of Saint Joseph for men (1876); and Little Flock of the Child Jesus (*Rebañito del Niño Jesús,* 1876) for children.

The inspiration for his greatest work came during his prayer in April 1876, and was realized several months later (June 23) when eight young women committed to help him found the Society of Saint Teresa of Jesus for Christian education. In 1878 the cornerstone was laid in Tortosa for the first house and the following year the eight founders pronounced their vows in the chapel of St. Paul in Tarragona (Jan. 1, 1879). The foundation quickly spread to Portugal and Latin America, and, in 1885, to Algeria, but was not without difficulties.

Ossó used modern methods to communicate the Gospel message. The weekly *El amigo del puebla* (*The People's Friend,* founded in 1871), which responded to the prevailing anticlerical attitudes, was censured. In October 1872, he published the first edition of the monthly magazine *Santa Teresa de Jesús* as well as his first book, *Guía práctica del catequista* (*Practical Guide for Catechists*). In 1874, he produced the first edition of *El cuarto de hora de oración* (*Fifteen Minutes of Prayer*). He also published *Handbook of the Friends of Jesus, Treasure Chest for Children, Novena to Saint Joseph, The Spirit of Saint Teresa, Tribute to Saint Francis de Sales, Novena to the Holy Spirit,* and *Novena to the Immaculate Conception,* as well as textbooks used by the sisters and many other publications.

On Jan. 2, 1896, Enrique retired to the Franciscan convent of Santo Espiritu at Gilet, where he suffered a stroke and died. Initially he was buried in Gilet; in July 1908 his body was translated to the chapel of the Company of Saint Teresa in Tortosa, Spain. Ossó's cause for beatification was introduced in 1923, but suspended from 1927 until 1957, when it was reintroduced. He was declared venerable in 1976. Pope John Paul II both beatified (Oct. 14, 1979) and canonized him (June 16, 1993, at Madrid, Spain).

Feast: Jan. 27 (Carmelites).

Bibliography: M. GONZÁLEZ MARTÍN, *The Power of the Priesthood: A Life of Father Henry de Ossó,* tr. by L. BONNECARRÈRE (Barcelona 1971). M. V. MOLINS, *Así era Enrique de Ossó: biografía del fundador de la Compañía de Santa Teresa* (Burgos 1993); *Henry de Osso, priest and teacher,* tr. O. DAIGLE, ed. J. ROXBOROUGH (Covington, La. 1993). *Acta Apostolicae Sedis* (1982): 673–76. *L'Osservatore Romano,* Eng. ed. 43 (1979): 13–14.

[K. I. RABENSTEIN]

OSSUARIES

Rectangular containers of limestone, baked clay, or wood, used to store the bones of bodies deposited in the *loculi* of tombs or caves, to make room there for new burials. Several hundred ossuaries, some plain, many decorated on one side with matching rosettes in a paneled framework, have been found near Jerusalem, Nablus, and other places in Palestine. Their size (20-to-32 by 12-to-20 by 10-to-16 inches) was dictated by the measurements of skull and femur bone. The lids, often fitted in grooves, were flat, rounded, or gabled. The chief interest of these caskets lies in the graffiti found on many of them; written, probably by the one who transferred the bones, in Aramaic, Greek, or both, they give, usually, only the name of the person whose bones the box contained. Many of the names are known from the Bible, Josephus, or the Murabba' āt finds; some are new. The Aramaic inscription *yhwš' br ywsp* (Jesus son of Joseph) on a 1st-century ossuary has no bearing on the Resurrection; both names were very common among Jews of the period. Cross marks, not certainly of Christian origin, on the lids or sides of ossuaries, may have been inspired by Ez 9.4–6 or placed there to ward off demonic influence.

Bibliography: N. AVIGAD, "A Depository of Inscribed Ossuaries in the Kidron Valley," *Israel Exploration Journal* 12 (1962) 1–12. D. FISHWICK, "The Talpioth Ossuaries Again," *New Testament Studies* 10 (1963–64) 49–61. B. BAGATTI and J. MILIK, *Gli Scavi del "Dominus Flevit,"* v.1 (Jerusalem 1958). C. H. KRAELING, "Christian Burial Urns?" *The Biblical Archeologist* 9 (1946) 16–20. E. M. MEYERS, *Jewish Ossuaries: Reburial and Rebirth* (Rome 1971). R. H. SMITH, "Cross Marks on Jewish Ossuaries," *Palestine Exploration Quarterly* 106 (1974) 53–66. J. P. KANE, "Ossuary Inscriptions of Jerusalem," *Journal of Semitic Studies* 23 (1978) 268–282. P. FIGUERAS, *Decorated Jewish Ossuaries* (Leiden 1983). P. FIGUERAS, "Jewish Ossuaries and Secondary Burial: Their Significance for Early Christianity," *Immanuel* 19 (1984–85) 41–57. B. R. MCCANE, "Bones of Contention: Ossuaries and Reliquaries in Early Judaism and Christianity," *Second Century* 8 (1991) 235–246.

[M. A. HOFER/EDS.]

OSTRACON

An inscribed potsherd. Since papyrus or leather often proved expensive for ordinary writing chores such as memoranda, letters, and receipts or even at times for official communications, the ancients resorted to potsherds as a writing material. Such material was readily available, required no preparation, and could be reused if necessary. The writing was sometimes scratched on the surface but was normally inscribed with pen and ink. Such a surface, however, was not practical for writing in cuneiform. Some inscribed potsherds (ostraca) have been found in Palestine and have thrown light on the biblical period.

St. Oswald and King Aidan seated at dinner, illumination from the "Berthold Missal" of the Abbey of Weingarten in Swabia, 1200–1232 (Morgan MS 710, folio 101v).

The most famous are the Lachis letters and the Samarian ostraca.

See Also: EPIGRAPHY, HEBREW.

[T. H. WEBER]

OSWALD, KING OF NORTHUMBRIA, ST.

Martyr; b. 604; d. Aug. 5, 642. The son of King Aethelfrith, he lived in exile after his father's death in 616, and was brought up in the monastery of IONA. His cousin, King EDWIN OF NORTHUMBRIA, was slain in battle in 633 fighting against Penda, the heathen King of Mercia, and Cadwallon, Penda's British ally. A year later Oswald attacked Cadwallon at Heavenfield, near Hexham, and won a great victory. The wooden cross Oswald erected before the battle long enjoyed fame for its miraculous powers. After Edwin's death Northumbria had lapsed into heathenism, but Oswald, with the help of AIDAN OF LINDISFARNE, sent as bishop from Iona at his request, set about its reconversion. He often accompanied Aidan on evangelizing tours from his see in LINDISFARNE, sometimes acting as interpreter since Aidan spoke but little English. So Christianity, in its Celtic form, was restored.

BEDE recounted many tales about the king's humility and generosity. For some time he was overlord of all the English kingdoms, but in 642 he was killed fighting against Penda. His last words, "May God have mercy on their souls," a prayer for his soldiers, later became a proverb. Bede is the source for several stories about cures that took place on the spot where Oswald fell. His body was later discovered and brought by his niece, Queen Osthryth, to a monastery at Bardney in Mercia; but the brethren were unwilling to receive the bones of a former foe. At length the monks were convinced by a column of light above the bier that these were the relics of a saint and gladly received them. From then on the monastery doors were kept continually open. Oswald's head was placed in the coffin of St. CUTHBERT OF LINDISFARNE and is still in Durham. The arms, long incorrupt, were deposited at Bamborough. The body was translated to Gloucester when Bardney was destroyed in 909 by the Danes; later WILLIBRORD took some of the relics to Frisia, and many continental churches still claim them. He is venerated as a martyr, and churches were dedicated to him in France, Belgium, Switzerland, Germany, and northern Italy.

Feast: Aug. 9 (formerly 5).

Bibliography: BEDE, *Historia ecclesiastica* 2.5, 20; 3.1–3, 5, 6, 9, 11–13; 5.24. *Acta Sanctorum* Aug. 2:83–103. AELFRIC OF EYNSHAM, *Lives of Three English Saints*, ed. G. I. NEEDHAM (London 1966, rev. ed. Exeter 1976). W. HUNT, in *The Dictionary of National Biography from the Earliest Times to 1900,* 63 v. (London 1885–1900; reprinted with corrections, 21 v., 1908–09, 1921–22, 1938; supplement 1901–) 14:1215–17. A. H. THOMPSON, ed., *Bede, His Life, Times, and Writings* (Oxford 1935) 217–220. J. OSWALD, in *Lexikon für Theologie und Kirche*, ed. J. HOFER and K. RAHNER, 10 v. (2d new ed. Freiburg 1957–65) 7:1296. R. BRÄUER, *Das Problem des "Spielmännischen" aus der Sicht der St.-Oswald- Überlieferung* (Berlin 1969), legends. *Der Münchner Oswald: mit e. Anh., Die ostschwäbische Prosabearbeitung,* ed. M. CURSCHMANN (Tübingen 1974). C. M. FANDREY, *Das Oswald-Reliquiar im Hildesheimer Domschatz* (Göppingen 1987).

[B. COLGRAVE]

OSWALD OF YORK, ST.

Archbishop; d. Worcester, Feb. 29, 992. As bishop of Worcester (961) and archbishop of York (972), Oswald shared with DUNSTAN and ETHELWOLD the glory of establishing the 10th-century Anglo-Saxon monastic revival. A Dane by birth, he was brought up by his uncle, Archbishop ODO OF CANTERBURY. Ordained deacon and priest at Fleury, he introduced its reformed practices into England, founding a small Benedictine monastery at Westbury (c. 962), an influential house at RAMSEY (c. 971), and communities at Winchcombe, Pershore, and perhaps Deerhurst, Ripon, and Evesham. Unlike Ethel-

wold, Oswald avoided violent reform, monasticizing the See of WORCESTER gradually and by example (c. 974–977). With Dunstan, he helped to crown Kings EDGAR, EDWARD THE MARTYR, and Ethelred II. Sources about his life include the *Vita sancti Oswaldi auctore anonymo* (ed. J. RAINE, *Historians . . . York, Rerum Britannicarum medii aevi scriptores.* [London 1858–96]), EADMER's *Vita sancti Oswaldi,* as well as the *Chronicon abbatiae Rameseiensis,* and the works of FLORENCE OF WORCESTER and WILLIAM OF MALMESBURY.

Feast: Feb. 28.

Bibliography: *Acta Sanctorum* Feb. 3:755–762. W. HUNT, *The Dictionary of National Biography From the Earliest Times to 1900* (London 1885–1900) 14:1217–19. J. A. ROBINSON, *The Times of Saint Dunstan* (Oxford 1923). E. S. DUCKETT, *Saint Dunstan of Canterbury* (New York 1955). E. JOHN, "St. Oswald and the Tenth Century Reformation," *The Journal of Ecclesiastical History* 9 (1958) 159–172. D. KNOWLES, *The Monastic Order in England, 943–1216* (Cambridge, England 1962). *St. Oswald of Worcester: Life and Influence*, ed. N. BROOKS and C. CUBITT (London 1996).

[W. A. CHANEY]

OTEIZA SEGURA, FAUSTINO, BL.

Martyr, priest of the Order of Poor Clerics Regular of the Mother of God of the Pious Schools (Piarists); b. Feb. 14, 1890, in Ayegui, Navarre, Spain; d. Aug. 9, 1936. Faustino was professed in 1907 and ordained in 1913. Thereafter he was assigned to Peralta where he taught in the elementary school and later served as novice master. He witnessed the martyrdoms of Dionisio PAMPLONA, Manuel SEGURA LÓPEZ, and Brother David MARAÑÓN and chronicled them in a letter to the provincial written on Aug. 1, 1936. He lived piously in the prison house, sustained by his devotions to the Blessed Mother, until his execution with Florentín Felipe NAYA on a roadside near Peralta. He was beatified on Oct. 1, 1995 by Pope John Paul II together with 12 other Piarists (*see* PAMPLONA, DIONISIO AND COMPANIONS, BB.).

Feast: Sept. 22.

Bibliography: "Decreto Super Martyrio," *Acta Apostolicae Sedis* (1995): 651–656. *La Documentation Catholique* 2125 (Nov. 5, 1995): 924.

[L. GENDERNALIK/EDS.]

OTHLO OF SANKT EMMERAM

Benedictine scholar; b. near Freising, Germany *c.* 1010; d. Sankt Emmeram Abbey, Regensburg, Nov. 23, *c.* 1070. A precocious child, Othlo received his early education at TEGERNSEE and HERSFELD ABBEYS. Finding the secular clerical life unsatisfactory, he entered SANKT EMMERAM in 1032. A sensitive, gifted, and imaginative monk, Othlo experienced various spiritual trials and worried especially about his enthusiasm for classical literature. Such concern reveals the early influence of those CLUNIAC REFORM ideals that led him into serious patristic and scriptural studies. At Sankt Emmeram, where he taught WILLIAM OF HIRSAU, he was encouraged to write. His first major composition, the *De doctrina spirituali*, was a long poetic exhortation to virtue, with criticism of pagan classical studies. His *Dialogus de tribus quaestionibus* (*c.* 1053) expounds various theological themes: it rests on St. Augustine and attacks the new dialectical approach to theology.

Because of disagreements that he had with the bishop of Regensburg, Othlo left Sankt Emmeram and lived at FULDA (1062–66), where he composed a biography of St. BONIFACE and probably the life of St. WOLFGANG OF REGENSBURG, the *Liber visionum*, describing divine manifestations including some he himself received, and the *Libellus manualis*, a powerful harangue to clergy and laity to reform and return to proper respect for religion—a realistic commentary on the age. At Fulda he also began the *Proverbia* (ed. C. G. Korfmacher, Chicago 1936), an extensive collection of memorable sayings culled for pedagogical purposes from Christian and classical sources. Leaving Fulda, Othlo visited Amorbach Abbey, where he wrote the *Quomodo legendum sit in rebus visibilibus*, on Christian education. Having returned to Sankt Emmeram (*c.* 1068) and feeling the weight of years, Othlo composed the *De cursu spirituali*, a homiletic work using St. Paul's figure of speech. It displays a thorough familiarity with Scripture and skill in the allegorical method of exegesis. His final work, the *Libellus de suis temptationibus, varia fortuna et scriptis*, is autobiographical. Among Othlo's minor works, difficult to date, are lives of SS. ALTO, Nicholas, and Magnus, some religious poetry, sermons, and his puzzling *Translatio s. Dionysii*. He also produced counterfeit charters on behalf of Sankt Emmeram.

Bibliography: Works. *Patrologia latina* (Paris 1878–90) 146:9–434. *Monumenta Germaniae Historica: Poetae* (Berlin 1926–) 4:521–542; 11:376–393; 15.2:843–846; 30.2:823–837. *Monumenta Germaniae Historica: Scriptores rerum Germanicarum* (ibid.) 53:111–217. *Acta Sanctorum* Nov. 2:565–597. Literature. M. MANITIUS, *Geschichte der lateinischen Literatur des Mittelalters* (Munich 1911–31) 2:83–103. G. MISCH, *Geschichte der Autobiographie* (3d ed. Bern 1949–) 3.1:57–107. B. BISCHOFF, *Die deutsche Literatur des Mittelalters* 3:658–670; 5:831; *Lexikon für Theologie und Kirche* (Freiburg 1957–65) 7:1298–99.

[R. H. SCHMANDT]

OTHMAR, ST.

Abbot; b. *c.* 689; d. Werd near Stein am Rhein, Switzerland, Nov. 16, 759. Othmar (Otmar, Audemar, Audomar) was educated for the priesthood at the imperial court. In 719 he was invited to assume the direction of a colony of monks who had settled near the grave of St. GALL. Othmar built them a monastery to be governed by the BENEDICTINE RULE. He also established the first house for lepers in Switzerland. In his defense of the autonomy of the Abbey of SANKT GALLEN, he suffered imprisonment and exile. In 769 his remains were returned to Sankt Gallen, and in 867 they were buried in the church named for him. He is represented in art as an abbot with a staff and sometimes with a small cask for the refreshment of pilgrims.

Feast: Nov. 16.

Bibliography: J. DUFT, *Sankt Otmar in Kult und Kunst* (St. Gallen 1966). *Monumenta Germaniae Historica: Scriptores* (Berlin 1826-) 2:41–47. J. DUFT, ed., *St. Otmar: Die Quellen zu seinem Leben* (Zurich 1959). L. RÉAU, *Iconographie de l'art chrétien* (Paris 1955–59) 3.2:1014–15. J. M. CLARK, *The Abbey of St. Gall as a Centre of Literature and Art* (Cambridge, Eng. 1926). A. M. ZIMMERMANN, *Kalendarium Benedictinum: Die Heiligen und Seligen des Benediktinerordens und seiner Zweige* (Metten 1933–38) 3:312–315.

[B. D. HILL]

O'TOOLE, GEORGE BARRY

Educator, author, cofounder of the Catholic University of Beijing, China; b. Toledo, Ohio, Dec. 11, 1886; d. Washington, D.C., March 26, 1944. He studied at St. John's University, Toledo, and received doctorates in philosophy and theology from the Urban University, Rome. After ordination in Rome (Nov. 1, 1911), he served as secretary to Joseph Schrembs, Bishop of Toledo (1912–15); diocesan canonist (1913–15); pastor of St. Aloysius, Bowling Green, Ohio (1915–17); professor of philosophy, St. Vincent Seminary, Latrobe, Pa. (1917–18); U.S. Army chaplain (1918–19); professor of philosophy (1919–20) and dogmatic theology (1923–24) again at St. Vincent's; professor of animal biology, Seton Hill College, Greensburg, Pa. (1919–20, 1923–24); rector of the Catholic University of Peking (1925–33); professor and head of department of philosophy, Duquesne University, Pittsburgh, Pa. (1934–37), professor of philosophy, The Catholic University of America, Washington, D.C. (1937–44); and editor in chief of the *China Monthly* (1939–44). With Archabbot Aurelius Stehle, OSB, he established the Catholic (*Fu Jen*) University of Beijing (relocated at Taipei, Formosa, 1962); at the time of his departure from China in 1933, it included schools of arts, sciences, and education, with approximately 100 faculty members and 1,100 students. O'Toole was made a domestic prelate in 1934. A detailed list of his writings is included in D. D. Runes, ed., *Who's Who in Philosophy* (New York 1942) 348.

Bibliography: Archives, The Catholic University of America, unpub. biog. of Rt. Rev. Msgr. George Barry O'Toole. M. HOEHN, ed., *Catholic Authors: Contemporary biographical sketches, 1930–47* (Newark 1948) 603–605.

[J. F. WIPPEL]

OTT, MICHAEL

Abbot; b. Neustad am Main, Bavaria, March 18, 1870; d. Crookston, Minn., Feb. 15, 1948. He pursued classical studies at St. John's University, Collegeville, Minn., and there joined the Benedictine Order in 1889. He was sent to the International College of Sant' Anselmo in Rome, where he received his doctorate in philosophy and was ordained on June 29, 1894. Upon returning to St. John's University, he taught commercial subjects and supervised the student publication, the library, and the print shop. He was secretary of the university's board of administration and subprior of the abbey when he was elected abbot of St. Peter's Abbey, Muenster, Saskatchewan, Canada. The abbatial blessing took place in St. Peter's Church at Muenster on Oct. 28, 1919. Two years later St. Peter's Abbey became an abbey *nullius,* subject directly to the Holy See, and Ott was designated as the first abbot ordinary. One of his first decisions after becoming abbot was to establish a secondary school at Muenster. In 1921 a new building was completed and classes began in St. Peter's College, which was soon recognized as a junior college affiliated with the University of Saskatchewan at Saskatoon. From 1931 until his death in 1948, he served as chaplain to the Benedictine convent in Crookston, Minn.

[J. WEBER]

OTTAVIANI, ALFREDO

Cardinal; b. in the Trastevere sector of Rome, Oct. 29, 1890; d. at the Vatican, Aug. 3, 1979. Ottaviani came from a poor family of six children. He was ordained a priest March 18, 1916, and studied at the Athaneum of St. Apollinaris (now the Pontifical Lateran University) where he completed doctorates in philosophy, theology, and canon and Roman law ("utriusque iuris"). He taught public ecclesiastical law there and, at the same time, philosophy at the Athaneum of the Sacred Congregation of the "Propaganda Fide" (now the Pontifical Urban University). He also worked in the same dicastery as a "minutante." While teaching at St. Apollinaris he collaborated with his colleagues (later Cardinals) Cicognani, Roberti and Larraona and founded the canon law journal "Apollinaris."

In 1926 Ottaviani became rector of the Pontifical Bohemian College (Nepomucene) and two years later he was appointed Under Secretary of the Sacred Congregation of Extraordinary Affairs (currently the Council for Public Affairs of the Church). As Under Secretary he collaborated in the preparation of numerous concordats (e.g., with Romania and Poland) and the Lateran Treaty of 1929. When he became the "Sostituto" of the Secretariat of State in 1929, it was necessary to resign his teaching positions.

His work at the Supreme Sacred Congregation of the Holy Office (now called the Congregation for the Doctrine of the Faith) began in 1935 when he was named Assessor. Later, he became Secretary of the Congregation and then its Prefect. Eventually, because of age, he became Prefect Emeritus, though he continued to participate in the work of the congregation and its commissions until his death. He was created a cardinal in the Consistory of Jan. 12, 1953, by Pope Pius XII. Almost ten years later he was nominated archbishop to the titular see of Berea and consecrated bishop on April 19, 1962. In his capacity as Secretary of the Holy Office, he was named President of the Preparatory and then Conciliar Commission for Theology at the Second Vatican Council. This commission was responsible for drafting the conciliar decrees on the church, *Lumen gentium*, and on divine revelation, *Dei Verbum*.

His writings include: *Institutiones Iuris Publici Ecclesiastici* (2 v.), used as a standard text for many years at the Pontifical Lateran Athaneum; *Compendium Iuris Publici Ecclesiastici*, used as a text for students of theology; *Il Baluardo* (1961), a collection of talks and writings; *Arma Veritatis* (1947), an introduction to an edition of the encyclicals "Immortale Dei" of Leo XIII and "Divini Redemptoris" of Pius XI; *Luce di Roma Cristiana nel Diritto; Doveri dello Stato cattolico verso la Chiesa*; and *Un seminarista esemplare*.

In his activities as a professor and member of the Roman Curia, Ottaviani never failed to maintain an active priestly ministry, especially for youth at the Oratorio San Pietro. In his daily ministry to these youths, "Don Alfredo" was always organizing a wide variety of activities in which he was an active participant. For these children each Sunday from 1928 to 1952, he was "l'ignorante" in a catechesis dramatically presented through the medium of comic theater with Cardinal Borgongini, who played the educated Catholic who responded to questions about the faith proposed by the "ignorant" Catholic. During WWII, there were always six to eight children whom he sheltered in his own home. The "Oasis of Saint Rita" in Frascati, near Rome, was founded by him as a home for orphans and abandoned children. He would visit them frequently, helping with schoolwork and enlisting the interest and active participation of his friends and associates.

[J. E. FOX]

OTTERBEIN, PHILIP WILLIAM

Cofounder and first bishop of the Church of the UNITED BRETHREN IN CHRIST; b. Dillenburg, Germany, June 3, 1726; d. Baltimore, Md., Nov. 17, 1813. He studied for the ministry at Herborn and was ordained (1749) a minister of the German Reformed Church. In 1753, Rev. Michael Schlatter encouraged him to immigrate to America. Otterbein was the pastor of Reformed churches in York and Lancaster, Pa., and Frederick, Md., before accepting a call to Baltimore in 1774. The origin of the Church of the United Brethren is traced to his meeting with the Mennonite preacher Martin BOEHM in 1767. Although Otterbein commissioned lay preachers and held the first conference of the Brethren in 1789, he continued to attend the Reformed synods until 1800. The consecration of Methodist Bishop Francis Asbury took place in 1785 in Otterbein's Baltimore church, and he maintained close ties with other early Methodist leaders.

Bibliography: A. W. DRURY, *The Life of Rev. Philip William Otterbein* (Dayton 1894). F. ASBURY, *Journal and Letters*, ed. E. T. CLARK et al., 3 v. (Nashville 1958).

[R. K. MACMASTER]

OTTO, RUDOLF

Protestant theologian and scholar; b. Peine, Germany, Sept. 25, 1869; d. Marburg an der Lahn, March 6, 1937. He was a professor at Göttingen (1897–1914), at Breslau (1914–1917), and at Marburg (1917–1929). Otto was influenced especially by Kant, J. F. Fries, (1773–1843), and F. D. E. SCHLEIERMACHER, and became prominent as a philosopher of religion. As opposed to Neo-Kantian ideas, he developed his concept of "the Holy," as a religious a priori, in his own independent attitude toward the good, the true, the beautiful. His book, *Das Heilige* (The Holy) appeared (Breslau 1917) at the so-called turning point in the philosophy of religion in Germany that is associated especially with the name of M. SCHELER (1874–1928). The latter was one of the first to recognize the importance of Otto's work. In his analy-

sis, which now has a permanent place in the science of religion, Otto defined the Holy as "the Numinous," which expresses itself in feeling or consciousness as the "contrasting harmony" of the *fascinans* (the attracting element) and the *tremendum* (the awe-inspiring element). On the epistemological side, however, he was not able ultimately to win conviction for his position.

His chief works are *Das Heilige* (Breslau 1917; 35th ed. Munich 1963); English translation, *The Idea of the Holy*, tr. J. W. Harvey (New York 1958); *Aufsätze, das Numinose betreffend* (Stuttgart 1923; 4th ed. 1929); *West-Oestliche Mystik* (Gotha 1926); *Die Gnadenreligion Indiens und das Christentum* (Gotha 1930); and *Das Gefühl des Ueberweltlichen* (Munich 1932).

See Also: SACRED AND PROFANE.

Bibliography: G. WÜNSCH, *Die Religion in Geschichte und Gegenwart* (Tübingen 1957–65) 4:1749–50 with bibliog. J. HESSEN, *Religionsphilosophie*, 2 v. (2d ed. Munich 1955) 1:269–297. R. F. DAVIDSON, *Rudolf Otto's Interpretation of Religion* (Princeton 1947). F. K. FEIGEL, *Das Heilige: Kritische Abhandlung über Rudolf Ottos gleichnamiges Buch* (2d ed. Tübingen 1948).

[A. HOLL]

OTTO I (THE GREAT), EMPEROR

Reigned as German king 936–973; emperor 962–973; b. 912; d. Memleben (buried in the cathedral at Magdeburg). Son of King Henry I and Queen Mathilda. Henry I appears to have designated his eldest son, Otto, as heir to the throne in 929 as part of his so-called *Hausordnung*. Around the same time (929–930), Otto married Edith, sister of King Athelstan of Wessex (England) and a descendent of St. Oswald. Otto's status as heir apparent was confirmed during an assembly at Erfurt, in 935. Following King Henry's death, the nobility elected, enthroned, and did homage to Otto at Aachen, where he was consecrated by Archbishop Hildebert of Mainz. Whether or not Henry was conscious of the implications, his designation of Otto as sole heir to the throne represented a significant departure from the Carolingian practice of dividing the realm among a king's sons. From this point on, the German realm would be considered indivisible. Otto's ecclesiastical consecration at Aachen, in contrast, represented a return to Carolingian practice and a departure from the model of his father's succession. Henry I had rejected the offer of an ecclesiastical sacring, according to the common view, to indicate that he would not set himself above or try to dominate the German dukes, as his predecessor King Conrad I had done. In accepting an ecclesiastical consecration, Otto sent the opposite message. Subsequently, Otto would reject his father's practice of entering into mutually obligatory

Otto I.

agreements with magnates and make little effort to present himself as first among equals.

It is commonly asserted, though not unequivocally, that tension generated by the more limited options available to members of the royal house and by a new more autocratic style of kingship lay behind the revolts that marked the early years of Otto's reign. In any case, there is no question that these revolts arose when disaffected members of the aristocracy coalesced around equally disaffected members of the ruling house. Between 937 and 941, Otto's half-brother Thankmar and brother Henry, each aggrieved for somewhat different reasons, appeared at the center of uprisings. Thankmar's revolt ended with his own death, but Henry was reconciled and, in 947, was installed as duke of Bavaria with powers similar to those of a king. There was some thought that Henry had a valid claim to the throne, having been born while his father was actually king, and the unusual settlement may have constituted implicit recognition that his revolt was justified. In 953–954, another revolt crystalized around Duke Liudolf of Swabia, Otto's son by Edith and, at least initially, the monarch's designated successor. In this case, the chief source of disaffection appears to have been Otto's second marriage (to Adelheid), which appeared to threaten both Liudolf's position at court and his inheritance. Liudolf was soon joined by other magnates, most notably

Duke Conrad of Lotharingia and Archbishop Frederick of Mainz. The revolt was initially successful, but effectively came to an end with the invasion of the Magyars (954), which caused all parties to close ranks around the king. Otto's victory over the Magyars at the Lechfeld (955), even if the threat from which it freed Christendom and the Reich was not as severe as some Ottonian sources suggest, clearly increased Otto's prestige and strengthened his hand against enemies and rivals. It may also have caused at least some of Otto's contemporaries to attribute to him a position comparable to that of an emperor.

The acquisition of the emperorship in 962, part of the titulature of German rulers until 1806, represents one of the most long lasting of Otto I's accomplishments. Otto made an initial effort to acquire the imperial crown during his first expedition to Italy in 951. This expedition was instigated by an appeal for help from the widowed queen of the LOMBARDS, Adelheid, who had fallen into the clutches of Berengar II of Ivrea. Marriage to Adelheid would convey a claim to the throne of the Lombards and this, presumably, figured among the German monarch's incentives. Otto succeeded in rescuing the queen and, after marrying her, celebrated his coronation at Pavia in October of 951. Tentative approaches to Pope AGAPETUS II regarding an imperial coronation met with refusal, however, probably because neither the popes nor the Roman aristocracy had any interest in acquiring an overlord. By 959, the situation had changed. As part of his settlement of the political situation in northern Italy, Otto had allowed Berengar II to rule as a sub-king under Ottonian hegemony. Nevertheless, after Otto's return to Germany, he was able to behave as if his rulership was independent and unchallenged. Faced with the threat of Berengar's power, Pope JOHN XII appealed to Otto to rescue the papacy. Before setting out for Italy, Otto secured the succession to the throne by having his son, OTTO II, elected and crowned at Aachen. On Feb. 2, 962, Otto was crowned by the pope in the basilica of St Peter. In return, Otto issued the privilege known as the *Ottonianum* which confirmed Carolingian donations to the papacy. Otto also secured for himself the right to a promise of fidelity from the pope prior to the latter's consecration. Later he extracted from the Romans an oath that they would never elect and consecrate a pope without Otto's permission. Acquisition of the imperial title also affected Otto's relations with Byzantium, since he now acquired an interest in southern Italy, a Byzantine sphere of influence. Tension between the two empires rose perceptibly during Otto's third Italian campaign (966–972), as Otto assumed a more active stance in that region. The result, after a period of warfare, was a compromise whereby Otto retained control of Benevento and Capua and had his imperial title recognized by the Constantinople. He also secured a Byzantine princess, Theophanu, as a bride for his son, Otto II.

Otto's ecclesiastical polices centered on his efforts to exploit the material and personal resources of the church in the interest of government. The result, sometimes referred to as the Imperial Church System, reflected a remarkable degree of cooperation between church and monarchy. In return for protection, immunity, and access to royal patronage, royal churches and monasteries were expected to contribute to military campaigns and offer hospitality to the king during his travels through the realm. Personnel recruited from these churches also staffed the royal chapel, the community of churchmen who tended to the liturgical needs of the royal court and performed a variety of administrative and diplomatic tasks.

Perhaps the most spectacular evidence of Otto's alliance with the church can be seen in his efforts to reorganize the ecclesiastical structure of the eastern frontier and further the Christianization of tributary populations among the Slavs. This process may have already begun with the foundation of the monastery of St. Maurice at Magdeburg (937), but certainly lay behind his efforts, from 955 on, to elevate that church to the status of an archbishopric. The foundation of bishoprics at Brandenburg, Havelburg, Merseburg, Meissen, and Zeitz as suffragans of Magdeburg, and of Oldenburg as suffragan of Hamburg-Bremen, figured in this plan as each incorporated a significant Slavic population.

Bibliography: K.J. LEYSER, *Rule and Conflict in an Early Medieval Society: Ottonian Saxony* (London 1979) passim. H. BEUMANN, *Die Ottonen* (2d ed. Stuttgart 1991) 42–44, 53–112. T. REUETER, *Germany in the Early Middle Ages, 800–1056* (London 1991) 148–180. E. MUELLER-MERTENS, "The Ottonians as Kings and Emperors," in *The New Cambridge Medieval History,* v.3., ed. T. REUTER (Cambridge 1999) 233–266.

[D.A. WARNER]

OTTO II, EMPEROR

Reign: German King 961–983, Emperor 967–983. d. Rome, Italy. Buried in the Basilica of St Peter. Son of Emperor OTTO I and Empress Adelheid. Husband of Theophanu. Otto was elected king at the age of six years in 961 and crowned at Aachen. Following his father's death in 973, he succeeded to the throne, barely eighteen years old and unopposed. He had already acquired the title of emperor some years earlier (967), having been crowned as his father's co-emperor by Pope John XIII. Through his marriage to Theophanu, a Byzantine princess, Otto II had also secured recognition of his title by the Byzantine court. Although his succession was uncontested, Otto II, like his father, encountered opposition soon afterwards. In the south of the realm, Otto's efforts to arrange the succession to the Duchy of Swabia instigated his cousin, Duke Henry "the Quarrelsome" of Bavaria to rebel. Henry's uprising (974–978) is noteworthy, among other things, because it attracted the support of Duke Boleslav II of Bohemia and Duke Mieszko I of Poland. Following his defeat, Duke Henry lost his duchy and was imprisoned at Utrecht. Otto used the occasion to reorganize the southern duchies, granting Bavaria to Duke Otto of Swabia and combining the formerly Bavarian region of Carinthia with the Italian marches to form an independent duchy of Carinthia.

Another conflict emerged in the west, where Otto's efforts to exert his influence over the Duchy of Lotharingia incited the west Frankish ruler, Lothar, who also had a claim to the area. In 977, Otto appointed Lothar's estranged brother, Charles, as duke in lower Lotharingia. Lothar responded with a surprise attack on Aachen in 978, nearly capturing the emperor himself. Otto's counter attack, on the city of Paris, yielded little in the way of concrete results, but presumably satisfied the emperor's honor. In 980, a meeting between the two monarchs resulted in the Frankish king's surrender of any claim to Lotharingia.

In Italy, Ottonian rule appeared secure, though in Rome itself aristocratic factions such as the Crescentii continued to struggle for power and for control of the papacy, the prize that power customarily bestowed. Otto II is generally thought to have pursued the claims of the imperial office with far greater intensity that his father had. From the beginning, he apparently aimed to conquer and actually rule in southern Italy, thereby bringing the entire peninsula under his authority. This plan was reflected in a new title, *Imperator Romanorum augustus,* that suggested his intent to rule over all of Italy and much more clearly set his claims against those of Byzantium. Such a policy clearly would have to encounter opposition not only from the Byzantines but also from the Saracens, each of which had not only claims but also possession of actual territory in the area. In 981, Otto launched a campaign in south Italy and was initially successful. Nevertheless, an encounter with a Saracen army on the Calabrian coast ended in a complete and disastrous defeat for Otto's forces (July 13, 982). Otto managed to escape. Thereafter, an assembly of German and north Italian magnates met at Verona (May 983) and agreed to send reinforcements and also to elect the emperor's three year old son Otto III king. Clearly, Otto had by no means given up his hopes for victory, but elsewhere, the empire was encountering even more serious challenges. In the summer of 983, as Otto made plans for a new expedition

Otto III, the Holy Roman Emperor (at Charlemagne's Tomb), engraving. (Archive Photos)

to the Italian south, the Slavic confederation of the Liutizi staged a massive uprising against German hegemony. It obliterated the results of several decades of missionary work and effectively ended German expansion in the east, at least for several generations. The emperor's death from malaria (Dec. 7, 983) brought his plans for Italy to an abrupt end and apparently left the empire's problems in the hands of his young son and his wife, the dowager empress Theophanu.

Bibliography: H. BEUMANN, *Die Ottonen* 2d. ed. (Stuttgart 1991) 113–126. T. REUTER, *Germany in the Early Middle Ages, 800–1056* (London 1991) 174–180. E. MUELLER-MERTENS, ''The Ottonians as Kings and Emperors,'' in *The New Cambridge Medieval History* vol. 3. ed. T. REUTER (Cambridge 1999) 233–266, at 254–257.

[D. A. WARNER]

OTTO III, EMPEROR

Reign: German King 983–1002, Emperor 996–1002. b. 980. d. Paterno, Italy. Buried St. Mary, Aachen. Otto III was the son of Emperor Otto II and Theophanu. Otto ascended the throne at the age of three and, though legally king, clearly required guidance in the business of government. Since the standards concerning rule by minors and the formation of regencies were as yet ill defined, the immediate result of the young king's succession was a battle for control among his relatives. Otto's uncle, Henry ''the Quarrelsome'' seized the young king and declared himself the boy's guardian. Henry had just been freed from captivity, his punishment for rebellion against Otto's father (Otto II). Since Henry was Otto's oldest male relative, he had a valid claim, and as Theophanu was still in Italy, he had the advantage of surprise. Initially, Henry gave the impression that his ambitions went no farther than the guardianship. Gradually, however, it became clear that he intended to exercise power in his own right or perhaps to rule alongside Otto as a dominant co-ruler, on the Byzantine model. Public opinion, divided to this point, now began to rally around Otto, who may have benefited from the fact that he had already been anointed and crowned. On June 29, 984, Duke Henry was forced to surrender the king to a regency that was dominated by the boy's mother, Theophanu, until her death in 991, and afterwards by Otto's grandmother Adelheid. The two women continued the patterns of government established by Otto I, especially the alliance with the church. In the west, Theophanu's skillful diplomacy ensured that Lotharingia remained within the boundaries of the Empire. In the East, campaigns continued to be launched against the trans-Elbian Slavs, though without reversing the results of the great uprising of 983. In Italy, the support of powerful magnates and the presence of Adelheid, erstwhile queen of the LOMBARDS, insured the stability of Ottonian interests.

Otto reached his majority in 994. In spite of vigorous scholarly debate regarding the significance of specific aspects of Otto's reign, there is little doubt regarding his concern to redefine the political order in Italy and on the Empire's eastern frontier. In 996, Otto launched his first expedition to Italy. This visit is noteworthy, among other things, because it marked the advent of the first German pope. Upon hearing of Pope John XV's death, Otto had his cousin Bruno installed on the papal throne. The new pope took the name GREGORY V (996–999) and repaid Otto's generosity by crowning him emperor on May 21, 996. Subsequently, Otto issued diplomata in which he referred to himself as ''Emperor of the Romans,'' and demonstrated his role as leader of Christendom by presiding over a synod together with the pope. Although this point remains very much in dispute, it is possible that Otto also used this occasion to denounce as a forgery the *Constitutum Constantini* (DONATION OF CONSTANTINE). It was on this occasion, as well, that Otto met and was deeply impressed by Gerbert of Reims and ADALBERT OF PRAGUE, two men, one a great intellectual and visionary, the other a saint and martyr, who would significantly influence the emperor's imperial vision. It is indicative of the limits of

Otto's power that Pope Gregory encountered difficulties as soon as his imperial protector left Italy. Under the leadership of Crescenzio (Crescentius), the Romans expelled Gregory from the city and elevated in his place John Philagathos as Pope John XVI. This act of rebellion incited Otto to launch a second expedition to Italy which, among other things, resulted in the execution of Crezenzio and the degradation of his anti-pope.

Upon the death of Gregory V, Otto appointed Gerbert of Aurillac as Pope Silvester II (999–1003). Silvester's reign was marked by continued cooperation between pope and emperor. This cooperation was evident, in particular, on the Empire's eastern frontier, where Otto and Silvester collaborated in the establishment of a Polish archbishopic at Gniezno (1000). Gniezno was the burial place of Adalbert of Prague, and contemporary sources portray the emperor's progress from Rome as a kind of pilgrimage. Modern scholars have seen in it yet another example of Otto's concern to represent himself as the leader of Christendom. Diplomata issued along the way described Otto as "servant of the Apostles" and "servant of Jesus Christ." On the way back to Rome, Otto stopped at Aachen, where he apparently had the tomb of Charlemagne opened so that he could view the emperor's corpse. The meeting at Gniezno also appears to have substantially altered political relations between the Empire and Poland, and may have affected relations with other eastern neighbors as well. The establishment of an archbishopric at Gniezno marked the beginning of an independent ecclesiastical organization for the Polish duchy and hence, an important stage in its consolidation as a medieval state. Otto clearly intended to elevate the prestige of the Polish duke, Boleslav "Chrobry," whom he declared an "ally and friend of the Roman people." Although this point too is controversial, he may also have elevated Boleslav to the rank of king through the bestowal of a crown. If this latter point can be accepted, Otto's regulation of the Empire's relations with Poland may be seen, in conjunction with the foundation of a Hungarian archbishopric at Gran, as part of an overall imperial strategy.

Among modern scholars, that strategy is commonly identified as having the goal of creating a renovated Roman empire based on the city of Rome. This plan or program found its most striking manifestation in the phrase *Renovatio Romanorum imperii,* which appears on a lead seal attached to one of Otto's diplomata. In his classic definition of Otto's *Renovatio,* P. E. Schramm declared that Otto had constructed the policies of his government around an ideal vision of Rome that was unique in being specifically secular, political, and universal. Recent scholarship has cast doubt on Schramm's definition without necessarily replacing it. In any case, Otto's un-

timely death, at the age of twenty-one, ensured that whatever plan he may have had remained incomplete.

Bibliography: P. E. SCHRAMM, *Kaiser Rom und Renovatio* (Berlin 1929, reprint Darmstadt 1984). H. BEUMANN, *Die Ottonen* 2nd. ed. (Stuttgart 1991) 127–156. D. A. WARNER, "Ideals and Action in the Reign of Otto III." *Journal of Medieval History* 29: 1–18. E. MÜLLER-MERTENS, "The Ottonians as Kings and Emperors," in *The New Cambridge Medieval History,* ed. T. REUTER (Cambridge 1999) 3:233–266

[D. A. WARNER]

OTTO OF BAMBERG, ST.

Bishop, Apostle of Pomerania; b. Swabia, Germany, 1060–62; d. Bamberg, June 30, 1139. Born of a noble family, Otto received a thorough education. In 1088 he was appointed chaplain to the court of Duchess Judith of Poland, the sister of Emperor HENRY IV. He was sent on diplomatic missions to the court of the emperor and was given the task of supervising the construction of the cathedral of SPEYER.

Early in 1102 he was made chancellor to Henry IV, and on Dec. 25, 1102, was appointed bishop of Bamberg. Because of controversies between Henry IV, HENRY V, and the metropolitans of Mainz, Otto was not consecrated bishop until May 13, 1106, at Anagni by Pope PASCHAL II. He prudently avoided taking sides in the continuing political and ecclesiastical conflicts in the empire and tried to act as mediator between the groups. When Henry V went to Rome to be crowned emperor in 1110–11, Otto accompanied him and received the PALLIUM on April 15, 1111, probably because of his success as a mediator. He also took an essential part in preparing the Concordat of WORMS (1122). For many years he directed a great number of activities in his diocese: he rebuilt the cathedral, which had been destroyed by fire; he improved the cathedral school, founded new parishes, and built many churches and hospitals. In a well-balanced policy, he fortified the territory of the Diocese of Bamberg (by building castles) and enlarged it through new acquisitions.

He especially favored monasticism, founding or renovating about 30 monasteries and giving them to Benedictines of the Hirsau Congregation, to PREMONSTRATENSIANS, and to CISTERCIANS. He limited the power of the district rulers. Otto's two missions to Pomerania (1124–25 and 1128), where he established and organized the Church, won for him the title of Apostle of the Pomeranians. He is buried in the abbey of Michelsberg near Bamberg. Canonized in 1189 by Pope CLEMENT III, he is venerated especially in the territory and monasteries of the Diocese of Bamberg.

Feast: July 2 (Roman MARTYROLOGY), Sept. 30 (Bamberg), Oct. 1 (Pomerania).

Bibliography: E. VON GUTTENBERG, ed., *Das Bistum Bamberg,* v. 1.1 of *Die Bistümer der Kirchenprovinz Mainz* (Germania Sacra 2; Berlin 1937) 115–138. J. BRAUN, *Tracht und Attribute der Heiligen in der deutschen Kunst* (Stuttgart 1943). J. KIST, *Fürst- und Erzbistum Bamberg* (Bamberg 1962). H. CHRIST, in *900 Jahre Speyerer Dom* (Speyer 1961) 110–122. J. PETERSOHN, *Baltische Studien* NF 49 (1962–63) 19–38. D. ANDERNACHT, *Die Biographien Ottos von Bamberg* (Unpub. diss., Frankfurt a. M. 1950). W. DZIE-WULSKI, ''Stasunek Ottona Bamberskiego . . . ,'' in *Zapiski historyczne* 23 (Toruń) 119–140. K. LIMAN, *Dialog Herborda: ze studiów historycznoliterackich nad biografia lacinska XII wieku* (Poznan 1975); *Studia historyczno-literackie nad zywotami biskupa Ottona z Bambergu* (Poznan 1966). *Bischof Otto I. von Bamberg: Beginn der Christianisierung des Peenegebietes,* ed. N. BUSKE, G. OTT and J. WÄCHTER (Greifswald 1977). G. BOJAR-FIJALKOWSKI, *Swiety Otton z Bambergu* (Warsaw 1986).

[F. DRESSLER]

OTTO OF CAPPENBERG, BL.

Premonstratensian; d. Feb. 23, 1171. The sons of Count Godfrey of Cappenberg and Beatrice, Otto and his brother Bl. Godfrey of Cappenberg, a devout layman, gave their ancestral lands to NORBERT OF XANTEN for the foundation of the first abbey of PREMONSTRATENSIAN canons in Germany in 1122. Otto entered the community and served as the fourth prior of Cappenberg Abbey from 1156 until his death. Godfrey died (1127) at Ilbenstadt Abbey, which he had founded, and Otto had some of his relics brought back to Cappenberg.

Bibliography: *Monumenta Germaniae Historica: Scriptores* (Berlin 1826) 12:513–530. M. ERENS, *Dictionnaire d'histoire et de géographie ecclésiastiques* (Paris 1912) 11:917–927. N. BACK-MUND, *Monasticon Praemonstratense* (Straubing 1949–56) 1:101, 158. S. SCHNEIDER, *Cappenberg* (Münster 1949). H. GRUNDMANN, *Der Cappenberger Barbarossakopf . . . Stiftes Cappenberg* (Cologne 1959).

[C. DAVIS]

OTTO OF FREISING

Bishop and historian; b. Neuburg? near Vienna *c.* 1111–12; d. Morimond, Sept. 22, 1158. Otto, the son of Margrave LEOPOLD III of Austria and Agnes, daughter of Emperor HENRY IV, studied at Paris, perhaps under Abelard, Gilbert de la Porrée, and Hugh of St. Victor. He entered the Cistercians at the Abbey of MORIMOND, was elected abbot (1137), and shortly after, was made bishop of the Bavarian See of Freising. Under his stepbrother, Emperor Conrad III, he joined the Second Crusade as a military commander. Otto served as political adviser and diplomat at the German court under Conrad and his successor, the Emperor Frederick I Barbarossa.

Otto's great interest in the intellectual pursuits of his time led him to be the first to acquaint his countrymen with the New Logic of Aristotle. His main historical work, the *Historia de duabus civitatibus,* a world chronicle in eight books, is the most noteworthy attempt at a philosophical interpretation of world history in the Middle Ages. Unlike earlier and contemporary world chroniclers Otto selected his facts in accordance with certain leading ideas that he discussed at length in the prefaces. He was influenced especially by St. Augustine's *City of God* and fully endorsed the saint's concept of the *Civitas Dei* as the community of all saints living and dead (*see* HISTORY, THEOLOGY OF). Otto began his account with man. Like Augustine, he saw one city deriving from Cain, the other from Abel. Unlike Augustine, Otto did not tend to identify completely the pagan empires or *regna* with the City of Satan, but rather saw them as a sphere where his ''two cities'' met and intermingled. Otto believed that by God's providence the Roman Empire was selected to be the world organization that would prepare mankind for the coming of the City of God. At first, this task fell on the Church of the early Christians. But under Constantine and still more completely under Charlemagne, emperor and pope, those ''two persons in the Church,'' each acting as a vicar of Christ in his own sphere, achieved that unity and peace on earth that paved the way to the City of God in a transcendental future. Insight into the ever deepening conflict between *regnum* and *sacerdotium* that marked the history of the West after the collapse of the Carolingian Empire (*see* CAROLINGIAN DYNASTY)—a conflict in which Otto hesitated to take sides—tinged his account with a deep pessimism. This was especially apparent in the seventh book, which described contemporary events. To Otto history had become the story of human misery. As his hope for the realization of the City of God on earth faded, he turned, in the last chapters of the seventh book, to the Cistercians, which in turn led to the description of the eschatological events that would herald the appearance of the Heavenly Jerusalem after history, *post praesentem vitam* (book 8). Otto finished his chronicle in 1146, in the midst of the confusions and wars of the reign of Conrad III.

When Otto's nephew, Frederick Barbarossa, ascended the German throne (1152) a new era of peace and good government seemed to augur well for a renewal of the empire. Otto began another historical work, the *Gesta Friderici imperatoris* or *Deeds of Frederick Barbarossa,* in a more optimistic vein. Otto died after finishing only the two first books. His clerk, Rahewin of Freising, continued the work.

Bibliography: Editions. *Ottonis episcopi Frisingensis chronica sive historia de duabus civitatibus,* ed. A. HOFMEISTER, *Monumenta Germaniae Historica: Scriptores rerum Germanicarum* (Berlin 1826–); *Ottonis et Rahewini gesta Friderici imperatoris,* ed. G. WAITZ, *Monumenta Germaniae Historica: Scriptores rerum Germanicarum*; *The Two Cities,* tr. C. C. MIEROW (New York

1928); *The Deeds of Frederick Barbarossa,* tr. C. C. MIEROW (New York 1953). Literature. W. WATTENBACH, *Deutschlands Geschichtsquellen im Mittelalter bis zur Mitte des 13. Jh.,* v.1 (7th ed. Stuttgart-Berlin 1904), v.2 (6th ed. Berlin 1894) 2:271–279. J. HASHAGEN, *Otto von Freising als Geschichtsphilosoph und Kirchenpolitiker* (Leipzig 1900). A. HAUCK, *Kirchengeschichte Deutschlands,* 5 v. (9th ed. Berlin-Leipzig 1958) 4:476–485. A. HOFMEISTER, ''Studien über Otto von Freising,'' *Neues Archiv der Gesellschaft für ältere deutsche Geschichtskunde* 37 (1912) 99–161, 633–768. M. MANITIUS, *Geschichte der lateinischen Literatur des Mittelalters,* 3 v. (Munich 1911–31) 3:376–388. F. FELLNER, ''The Two Cities of Otto of Freising,'' *American Catholic Historical Review* 20 (1934–35) 154–174. J. SPÖRL, *Lexikon für Theologie und Kirche,* ed. J. HOFER and K. RAHNER, 10 v. (2d, new ed. Freiburg 1957–65) 7:1307–09; *Grundformen hochmittelalterlicher Geschichtsanschauung* (Munich 1935) 31–50. P. BREZZI, ''Ottone di Frisinga,'' *Bullettino dell'Istituto storico Italiano* 54 (1939) 129–328. *Otto von Freising: Gedenkgabe zu seinem 800. Todesjahr,* ed. J. A. FISCHER (Freising 1958).

[H. WIERUSZOWSKI]

OTTOBEUREN, ABBEY OF

Benedictine monastery in the Diocese of AUGSBURG, Germany. Founded perhaps in 764, it became important under Abbot Rupert J. (1102–45), who introduced the HIRSAU *Consuetudines,* reformed Irsee and ELLWANGEN, founded MARIENBERG and one of the abbey's convents, completed the building of Ottobeuren's abbey and church, and instituted a scriptorium that flourished under his successor Isingrim. After a gradual decline until 1477, the abbey revived with reform from MELK. Prior N. Ellenbog (d. 1543) roused an interest in scholarship, and Abbot L. Wiedemann (1508–46) instituted a printing press in 1509. In 1617 Ottobeuren furnished almost the whole staff of professors (six priests) for the new University of Salzburg. Priests from Ottobeuren later taught in Rottweil, Freising, and Fulda, and in the abbey's own school. Abbot Rupert II Ness (1710–40) completely rebuilt the church and cloister in a masterpiece of south German baroque. Of the 19 out of 45 priests who maintained the monastic life after the secularization of 1802, only one lived to see the restoration in 1834. Ottobeuren then remained a priory under St. Stephen in Augsburg until it again became an independent abbey (July 2, 1918). The Bavarian Concordat of 1817 gave permission for educational and pastoral work to the house; the abbey, which cares for the parish of Ottobeuren, has maintained a boys' boarding school since 1855, an agricultural school (1920–36), and a Gymnasium for liberal arts (1922–38, and since 1946).

Bibliography: *Ottobeuren: Festschrift zur 120-Jahrfeier der Abtei* (Augsburg 1964). *Ottobeuren 764–1964: Beiträge zur Geschichte der Abtei* (Augsburg 1964), special issue of *Studien und Mitteilungen zur Geschichte des Benediktinerordens und seiner Zweige,* v.73 (1962). B. KUEN, *Lexikon für Theologie und Kirche,* ed. J. HOFER and K. RAHNER, 10 v. (2d, new ed. Freiburg 1957–65) 7:1310–11.

Abbey of Ottobeuren. (©Vanni Archive/CORBIS)

[B. KUEN]

OTTOMAN TURKS

A militant dynasty of Anatolian Turks who created an Islamic state in the Balkans, the Near East, and North Africa, threatening western Europe and assuming leadership of the Muslim world. This empire, which arose in the later Middle Ages, survived until modern times, when it disintegrated into nation states.

Rise to Power. The Ottoman state, founded in Bithynia *c.* 1299, was one of many petty principalities that sprang up in the ruin of the Seljuk Sultanate of Konya after that state was forced to become a vassal of the Mongol Il-Khans (*see* SELJUKS). Weakened by the Turcoman invasions of Asia Minor and by the Fourth Crusade (1202–04), the Byzantine Empire could not prevent the

Suleyman I, Ottoman Sultan, 1520–1566 Venetian portrait. (©Ali Meyer/CORBIS)

Islamic expansion westward. The Ottoman state was created by warriors, who refused to become peaceful citizens, on the Byzantine-Islamic frontier. Its location and the vigor of its ruling family helped the principality to grow rapidly at Byzantine expense, and by 1353 it had reached the European side of the Hellespont. In 1389 the power of Serbia was broken at the battle of Kosovo, and in 1396 Western Europe's attempt to meet the swiftly growing threat failed with the ill-fated Crusade of Nicopolis. The fortress city of Constantinople on the Bosphorus became a free enclave in the Ottoman state. At the same time, by marriage and political pressure, the Anatolian Turkish principalities were being absorbed. Reasons for this astonishing expansion must be sought in the comparative weakness of the Balkan Byzantine successor-states, the military and political efficiency of the Ottomans, and the post-Crusade hostility of the Greeks and Slavs to the Franks and the Latin Church. Given a choice of domination by Western Europe or the sultan, popular sentiment favored the sultan.

Ottoman civilization, which arose on the frontier between Byzantine civilization and the Persian-Islamic Seljuk culture, borrowed freely from both in its formative stage and took its final form only around the beginning of the 16th century A.D. The defeat of Sultan Bayazid by

TIMUR (Tamerlane) in 1402 was only a temporary setback to Ottoman expansion. In 1453 Constantinople was taken after a heroic defense, to become the Ottoman capital.

Subject Peoples. While the ruling class were Muslims, Eastern Orthodox Christians were governed through their bishops and clergy subject to the patriarch of Constantinople, appointed by the sultan. The Greek clergy thus had far more real power than they had had in the Byzantine period, particularly over the Slavs in Ottoman territory. Jews and Armenians also were governed as separate communities through their own clergy, and this arrangement (*see* DHIMMI) seems to have been highly acceptable to the subject peoples until the 18th and 19th centuries, when internal Ottoman decline brought oppressive fiscality and interference.

Religious practice at the folk level in Anatolia and the Balkans, among Christians and Muslims, was strikingly similar, and equally distant from either orthodox Christianity or orthodox Islam; this situation together with the tax benefits of conversion explains why many subjects became Muslims despite the absence of forced conversion.

The talents of the subject peoples were channeled into the ruling class by the peculiar system of *devshirme*. Promising Balkan Christian boys were taken in levies, nominally converted to Islam, and educated as the sultan's private property. The ablest of them could rise to the highest offices of the state, frequently benefiting their Christian relatives, and forming an elite dependent on neither birth nor wealth. The rest were enrolled in the Janissaries, the sultan's private army. The Muslims opposed their own exclusion from the fruits of power, hence the *devshirme* was discontinued *c.* 1700.

Consolidation and Decline. State theory depended on an absolute autocracy, hereditary in the male Ottoman line, and the first ten sultans were long-lived, able soldier-statesmen. The last of these, Süleyman I, "The Magnificent," (1520–66) took Hungary, invaded Austria, and besieged imperial Vienna. Since each Ottoman prince was a candidate for the throne, state security demanded that the successful candidate put his brothers to death. In theory the sultan was subject to the Law of Islam, but since he controlled the conditions by which it was interpreted he was bound only insofar as he chose.

With the rise of the dynasty of the SAFAVIDS in Western Iran in 1502, its theocratic Islamic heresy, preached by the Safavi brotherhood (SHĪ'ITES) had a deep appeal for the Turcomans of Anatolia. Largely in self-defense, the Ottomans became officially, militantly, SUNNITES. This was intensified after 1517, when the kingdom of the Mamelukes in Syria and Egypt was annexed. Soon North

Africa, except for Morocco, came under Ottoman rule. Without continuing the shadowy 'ABBĀSID caliphate of Cairo, the sultans could truly claim to be the leaders of Sunnite Islam. Western Christendom, torn by wars and heresies, was kept from being overrun only by the fact that the Ottomans were also at war with Persia.

The internal decline of the Ottomans coincided with the growth and transformation of Europe; but, blinded largely by its own early military success, the still medieval Ottoman state found no reason to transform itself as Europe was doing. With a more formidable West in the 17th century and several defeats from Western armies, together with an aggressively expanding Russia entertaining Balkan ambitions in the 18th, xenophobia and anti-Christian fanaticism grew in Ottoman society, estranging the subject peoples. The sultans sought alliances with Europe against Russia, but had to pay a heavy price in concessions and capitulations, chiefly to England and France. Whereas it had been once the terror and fascination of Europe, the empire became the "sick man" of Europe.

The spread of nationalist ideologies among the Balkan peoples in the 19th century, abetted by foreign powers, led to continual losses of territory; in World War I even the predominantly Moslem Arabs rebelled. Tardy and inconclusive efforts at internal modernization from 1839 to 1922 led to no lasting gains. Finally, in a rejection of the whole imperial system, a revolt headed by Kamal Ataturk in 1922 put an end to the Ottoman state and set up a national Turkish republic in Anatolia.

See Also: TURKEY, THE CATHOLIC CHURCH IN.

Bibliography: P. WITTEK, *The Rise of the Ottoman Empire* (London 1938). G. J. S.-L. EVERSLEY and V. CHIROL, *The Turkish Empire (1288–1922)* (London 1923). H. A. R. GIBB and H. BOWEN, *Islamic Society and the West* (New York 1950). B. LEWIS, *The Emergence of Modern Turkey* (London 1961). J. H. KRAMERS et al., *Encyclopedia of Islam*, ed. M. T. HOUTSMA et al., 4 v. (Leiden 1913–38) 3:965–1024.

[J. A. WILLIAMS]

OTTONIAN RENAISSANCE

The popular name for the cultural surge experienced throughout the HOLY ROMAN EMPIRE under the Roman emperors OTTO I the Great, OTTO II, and OTTO III; that is, during the years 936 to 1002. If this renaissance is to be understood, it must be linked with the intellectual movement initiated by CHARLEMAGNE and his successors, the so-called CAROLINGIAN RENAISSANCE, when scholars tried to preserve and revitalize the culture of the late classical and early Christian period. The most distinctive characteristic of the Ottonian as opposed to the earlier

"Ottoman Sultan Mohammed II," portrait by Gentile Bellini, 1479.

Carolingian Renaissance was the greater part played by indigenous northern and eastern European influences in the cultural flowering of the 10th century.

Furthermore, the Ottonian Renaissance profited from the increased trade and communication with the older and more cultivated areas to the south, such as the Lombard kingdom, Venice, and Còrdoba, and from its continued relations with Byzantium. Although the Ottonian, like the Carolingian, Renaissance attempted essentially to revive classical antiquity, it was able to imbue its work with a more personal touch and greater depth. Especially effective in creating the new intellectual atmosphere were the currents emanating from the imperial court of the Ottos, especially from such men as Archbishop BRUNO OF COLOGNE, NOTKER OF LIÈGE, and ADALDAG OF BREMEN. This new intellectualism spread as the missionary efforts of the Archdiocese of Salzburg and the dioceses of Freising, Passau, and Regensburg were directed southeastward; the cathedral school in Magdeburg, directed by Ohtric, one of the most famous scholars of his time, became both recipient and disseminator of the new Christian learning. Monasteries, reinvigorated by the CLUNIAC REFORM and the "strict observance" movement initiated at GORZE (Brogne), roused themselves to special spiritual and intellectual endeavors. Works of historical impor-

Eleventh-century Ottonian chalice. (©Elio Ciol/CORBIS)

tance and literary worth were written in both Italy and Germany (LIUTPRAND OF CREMONA, WIDUKIND OF COR-VEY, and ROSWITHA OF GANDERSHEIM)—works outstanding both for the knowledge of classical culture they displayed and for their rhetorical skill. Works of architecture, such as the abbey church of the nuns of Gernrode, the narthex and crypt of Oberzell monastery at Reichenau date from the period.

The Ottonian renaissance is sometimes designated as a renaissance of Carolingian culture; but, in continuing the work of the Carolingians, it produced much that was peculiar to itself. It undoubtedly reached its peak under Otto III (983–1002), both in its cultural efforts and in its maturity of religious thought; it was an era marked by the desire to evangelize peoples considered heathen (an endeavor that entirely consumed Otto III) and by enthusiasm for the arts and learning. While there are only meager remains of this artistic and intellectual activity, it is known to have been the developmental period of guilds of builders and artisans. It is clear also that the Emperor himself attempted with some success to write poetry. There is well-documented evidence to his collaborations in more than one literary venture, e.g., when his friend Bishop ADALBERT OF PRAGUE was martyred, he personally took part in the composition of a poetic life and paean in honor of his martyrdom. Contemporaries saw the emperor, even while he was still very young, as the center of the intellectual and artistic life of his era. His almost impassioned participation in such endeavors increased considerably in his mature years, and through his tutors, who were also the most brilliant men at court, viz,

Gerbert of Aurillac, the future Pope SYLVESTER II, whom the Emperor personally invited to his service, accompanying the summons with a poem, and Archchancellor HERIBERT OF COLOGNE, he provided the empire with effective intellectual leadership.

In view of Otto III's commanding personality, it is understandable that during his reign sculpture, miniatures, and book illuminations all served the glorification of the ruler. An example is found in those pages produced by the REICHENAU school of art after the imperial coronation on May 21, 996, including the famous double page of the Otto III Gospel Book (in Munich), the undisputed masterpiece, as well as similar pages in the Musée Condé in Chantilly, and in the Bamberg Josephus MS. These illuminated pages, which undoubtedly were produced after the coronation and which seem to have been products of competition among the most distinguished master miniaturists of the day (K. and M. Uhlirz, *Jahrbücher . . . Otto III*), show the influence of lands to the east (Sclavinia, that is, southern Slav and Polish territories, Hungary, and the Balkans). In charming contrast to these artistically arranged representations in which every detail (the color of hair, the stance, the weapons, etc.) is expressive in its political significance, is the simple work of a cleric from Ivrea who naïvely represented the emperor in his ordinary winter clothes, receiving from the hands of the Blessed Virgin a crown that has pediments like the crown of St. Stephen. Although sculptured likenesses of the emperor are rare, he is represented by a carving on the ivory holy-water font in Aachen and on the fountain at St. Bartholomew-in-the-Island, Rome, which shows the likeness of St. Adalbert on the reverse side of the column. It may be expected that future archeological discoveries will extend the knowledge of the Ottonian period.

See Also: MEDIEVAL LATIN LITERATURE.

Bibliography: J. DE GHELLINCK, *Littérature latine au môyen-age* (Paris 1939) 2:9–43. P. E. SCHRAM, *Kaiser, Rom und Renovatio* (2d ed. Darmstadt 1957). E. R. CURTIUS, *European Literature and the Latin Middle Ages,* tr. W. R. TRASK (New York 1953). F. J. E. RABY, *A History of Secular Latin Poetry in the Middle Ages* (2d ed. Oxford 1957) 1:252–306. F. J. E. RABY, *A History of Christian-Latin Poetry from the Beginnings to the Close of the Middle Ages* (Oxford 1953) 202–229. K. and M. UHLIRZ, *Jahrbücher des Deutschen Reiches unter Otto III* (Berlin 1954). J. F. BÖHMER, *Die Regesten des Kaiserreiches unter Otto III, 980–1002,* ed. M. UHLIRZ (*Regesta imperii* 2.3; Graz-Cologne 1956–57). M. UHLIRZ, "Das deutsche Gefolge Ottos III in Italien," *Gesamtdeutsche Vergangenheit: Festgabe für H. v. Srbik* (Munich 1938) 21–38; "Aus dem Kunstleben der Zeit Ottos III," *Festschrift Schramm* (Weisbaden 1964) 51–56. L. GRODECKI et al., *Le Siècle de l'an Mil* (Paris 1973). *The Plays of Hrotsvit of Gandersheim,* tr. K. WILSON (New York 1989). H. MAYR-HARTING, *Ottonian Book Illumination: An Historical Study* (2d ed. London 1999).

[M. UHLIRZ]

OUEN OF ROUEN, ST.

Bishop also known as Owen, Audoin, Dado, or Audo(e)nus; b. near Soissons, France; d. Clichy, Aug. 24, 684. Ouen came from a wealthy family and was the longest-lived of several distinguished men educated at the court of Chlothar II (d. 629), who served Dagobert I (629–639) and ultimately became bishops. While referendary (chancellor) to Dagobert, he founded the monastery of Rebais near Meaux and obtained for it a famous privilege (635). Consecrated bishop of Rouen (May 13, 641), he promoted monasticism (notably at FONTENELLE) and built many churches. His support of the palace mayor Ebroïn illustrates a continued interest in public affairs. Late in life he undertook a pilgrimage to Rome. His remains were translated to Rouen and accorded a public cult (May 7, 685).

Feast: Aug. 24.

Bibliography: DESIDERIUS CADURCENSIS, *Epistulae,* 1:9–10; 2:6. *Monumenta Germaniae Historica: Epistolae* (Berlin 1826–) 3:198–199, 206. *Vita Audoini,* ed. W. LEVISON, *Monumenta Germaniae Historica: Scriptores rerum Merovingicarum* (Berlin 1826–) 5:536–567. E. VACANDARD, *Vie de saint Ouen, évêque de Rouen* (Paris 1902); also in *Revue des questions historiques* (Paris 1866–) 63 (1898) 5–50; 69 (1901) 5–58; 71 (1902) 5–71. F. BEYERLE, ''Das Formelbuch des westfränkischen Mönchs Markulf und Dagoberts Urkunde für Rebais, a 635,'' *Deutsches Archiv für Erforschung des Mittelalters* (Cologne-Graz 1950–); supersedes *Deutsches Archiv für Geschichte des Mittelalters* (Weimar 1937–43) and *Neues Archiv der Gesellschaft für ältere deutsche Geschichtskunde* (Hanover 1876–1936) 9 (1952) 43–58.

[W. GOFFART]

OULTREMONT, EMILIE D', BL.

In religion, Mother Mary of Jesus, also called Baroness Emilie Olympe Marie Antoinette van der Linden d'Hooghvorst, married woman, missionary, and foundress of the Society of Mary Reparatrix; b. Wégimont, Liège, Belgium, Oct. 11, 1818; d. Florence, Tuscany, Italy, Feb. 22, 1878. Emilie was the daughter of Count d'Oultremont of Liège, who was later (1840) the Belgian minister to the Holy See. At age nineteen she was married to Baron Victor van der Linden d'Hooghvorst and bore him four children before his early death ten years later (1847). Her family wanted her to remarry, but the baroness made a vow of chastity. Two of her daughters—Mother Mary of St. Victor (1843–72) and Mother Mary of St. Julienne (1846–67)—assisted her in the foundation of the Society of Mary Reparatrix. Under the spiritual direction of the JESUITS, particularly that of Paul Ginhac (1824–95), the society was canonically established in Strasbourg, Alsace-Lorraine, in 1857. The following year she took the name Mary of Jesus and made her first vows

Former Abbey Church of Saint-Ouen, Rouen. (©Vanni Archive/ CORBIS)

together with her daughters and eight other companions. The mission of the society is ''to make known the tenderness of God's love for the world, to follow Jesus as Mary did, and to collaborate with Him in His mission of Redemption-Reparation.'' Her relics are enshrined in the Church of Santa Croce e San Bonaventura in Rome. She was beatified on Oct. 12, 1997 by Pope John Paul II.

Feast: Oct. 11

Bibliography: *Acta Apostolicae Sedis,* no. 20 (1997): 999. *L'Osservatore Romano,* English edition, no. 42 (1997): 1–2, 12. *Emilie d'Oultremont, Baroness d'Hooghvorst, Foundress of the Society of Mary Reparatrix and Her Two Daughters* (London 1932). *In the Silence of Mary: The Life of Mother Mary of Jesus* (London 1964). C. COUVREUR, *Témoignage pour tous les temps, vie, esprit, oeuvre d'Emilie d'Oultremont, fondatrice de la Société de Marie Réparatrice* (Toulouse 1967). V. DELAPORTE, *The Society of Marie Reparatrice* (Montreal 1919). P. SUAU, *The life of Mother Mary of Jesus, Emilia d'Oultremont, Baroness d'Hooghvorst* (London 1913).

[K. I. RABENSTEIN]

OUR LADY MOTHER OF MERCY, BROTHERS OF

Popularly known as the Brothers of Tilburg, *Congregatio Fratrum Beatae Mariae Virginis, Matris Miseri-*

cordiae (CFMM, Official Catholic Directory #0980), founded in 1844 by Joannes Zwijsen (1794–1877), then a parish priest in Tilburg, and from 1854 archbishop of Utrecht. Its principal purpose is teaching. Members included priests and brothers until 1916. Since then all members have been brothers, because of the limited scope for priestly activities and the extension of educational work. In its modified form the institute received papal approval in 1927. By 1864 the congregation had many primary schools in the Netherlands and some boarding schools, notably St. Henricus Institute for blind boys at Grave. A school for deaf mute boys was opened in Maaseik, Belgium, in 1851. In the 1880s the brothers erected schools in the West Indies. After World War I they started schools in Indonesia. The most important recent foundation in Belgium is a school for deaf mute boys in Hasselt. Since 1939 houses have been established in Africa and South America. In 1963, the brothers established their first house in the U.S., in Oxnard, Calif. The generalate is in Tilburg, The Netherlands.

Bibliography: T. HORSTEN, *De Fraters van Tilburg, 1844–1944*, 3 v. (Tilburg 1946–52). *In de voortuin der Congregatie der Fraters van O. L. Vrouw Moeder van Barmhartigheid* (Tilburg 1950). *Ontmoetingen,* 17 v. (1957–64).

[P. N. BROEDERS/EDS.]

OUR LADY OF CHARITY, NORTH AMERICAN UNION SISTERS OF

The North American Union Sisters of Our Lady of Charity (NAU-OLC, Official Catholic Directory #3070) traces its origins to the Sisters of Our Lady of Charity of Refuge, a congregation of religious women founded in Caen, France (1641), by St. John EUDES. Preliminary papal approbation was granted Jan. 2, 1666, and complete approval in 1741. The seven Houses of Refuge in existence at the time of the French Revolution were dispersed, but the work was resumed again at Tours and spread through France as circumstances permitted. The original purpose of the congregation was to provide a shelter for women of dissolute behavior, but it was later modified to include the care and training of neglected, dependent teenage girls. In the 19th century a separate branch developed as the Sisters of Our Lady of Charity of the GOOD SHEPHERD.

The first American foundation was established in 1855 at Buffalo, N.Y., by Mother Mary of St. Jerome, from Rennes, France. Although each house of the order is autonomous, the U.S. communities established a federation in 1944 for the purpose of strengthening the contemplative and apostolic life of the sisters. Similar federations were organized in Europe. In 1979, Rome granted permission for the establishment of the North American Union of the Sisters of Our Lady of Charity, with its administrative offices in Wheeling, W.V. Within the union are the congregations of Our Lady of Charity of Green Bay, Wis.; Buffalo, N.Y.; El Paso, Texas; Erie, Pa.; Pittsburgh, Pa.; Rochester, N.Y.; San Antonio, Texas; Walden, N.Y.; and Wheeling, W.V. In the U.S., the sisters run residential homes for women, nursing homes, day care centers, pastoral ministries, outreach programs, and the care of immigrants.

[M. GRABIAK/EDS.]

OUR LADY OF GOOD COUNSEL

The church that enshrines the original fresco of Our Lady of Good Counsel is located in the small town of Genazzano about 30 miles southeast of Rome in the Diocese of Palestrina. According to the still current legend, this church stood unfinished and roofless when, on April 25, 1467, the image of the Madonna was miraculously transported there from its former home in Scutari, Albania. Coming to rest precariously on a narrow stone ledge in the wall inside the church, the legend continues, the picture has remained in that position to the present day.

Careful investigations undertaken between 1957 and 1959 for the purpose of restoration have revealed something of the true origin of the fresco. The image of the Madonna—about 12 inches wide and 17 inches high—that the viewer sees encased in its elaborate glass, metal, and marble framework, is part of a larger fresco that once covered a portion of the wall now hidden by the baroque shrine altar. Art experts consulted during the restoration suggest that the fresco, and therefore the Madonna as well, is the work of the early 15th-century artist, Gentile da Fabriano. On the site of the present church once stood a small chapel within which Gentile painted his fresco around the time of Martin V (1417–31). At some subsequent date, but before 1467, the fresco, so it is surmised on the basis of the evidence, was covered over with plaster, and on the wall was hung a terra cotta Madonna, which was known as Our Lady of Good Counsel.

In 1467 the AUGUSTINIANS (in whose custody the shrine still remains) undertook to build a church on the site, enclosing within the structure the wall on which the then covered fresco was painted. This work was sponsored by a widow named Petruccia, who exhausted her means on the project and was unable to continue the construction. At that point the image of the Madonna appeared and was taken to be a token of divine favor. The unexpected appearance was perhaps brought about by the construction work in this way: when the stone ledge referred to above was being inserted into the wall, the plaster covering cracked and separated from the wall, revealing the fresco beneath. The image was immediately hailed as the Madonna of Paradise, an allusion to its apparently heavenly origin; but soon it came to be known by the former title of the shrine, Madonna of Good Counsel. One striking aspect of the fresco, which has lent a certain credence to the legends surrounding it, is that the upper portion of the image is separated from the wall and leans slightly forward. The fresco, nothing more than a thin layer of plaster, has survived for centuries in this precarious state, even through the aerial bombardment of Genazzano during World War II. Because of this condition, the restoration undertaken in 1957 was a delicate task.

The unfinished church was completed soon after the event of April 1467 and became the center of continuous pilgrimage. The numerous cures recorded as having occurred since then have caused the Madonna to be called miraculous. Many honors have been granted to the shrine by the Holy See, especially in more recent times. The initial approval of the devotion to Our Lady of Good Counsel was apparently given by Paul II. Although the record of his approval is not extant, there is abundant evidence of recognition by later popes: Sixtus IV, Alexander VI, Pius V, Gregory XIII, and Urban VIII. In 1682 Innocent XI approved the placing of a golden crown over the image, and in 1753 Benedict XIV established the Pious Union of Our Lady of Good Counsel, a spiritual society to which many indulgences were attached. Pius VI granted to the Augustinian Order, in 1779, a proper Mass and Office for the feast day. Pius IX had a personal devotion to the Mother of God under this title; he made a pilgrimage to Genazzano in 1864.

More than any other pope, Leo XIII was deeply attached to this devotion, which had associations with his childhood in Carpineto, a town not far from Genazzano. He instituted the white scapular of Good Counsel, inserted the title Mother of Good Counsel into the Litany of Loreto, declared the shrine a minor basilica, and installed a copy of the image over the altar in the Pauline chapel in the Vatican. Pius XII dedicated his reign to the Madonna of Good Counsel, and John XXIII made a visit to her shrine on Aug. 25, 1959. The present church, which replaced the former one about 1628, has been renovated in recent years, and elaborate mosaics have been added to the facade. A noteworthy 19th-century pastor of this church, Bl. Stefano Bellesini, is buried beneath the main altar. The feast day of Our Lady of Good Counsel is celebrated on April 26.

Bibliography: *Acta ordinis e. S. Augustini: Commentarium officiale* (1961) 25–33. A. F. ADDEO, "Apparitionis imaginis B.V.M. a Bono Consilio documenta," *Analecta augustiniana* 20 (1946) 3–140. G. MALIZIA, "Il santuario del Buon Consiglio a Genazzano," *Lunario Romano* 21 (1992).

[A. J. ENNIS]

OUR LADY OF PERPETUAL HELP (SUCCOUR)

A title given to the Blessed Virgin Mary, emphasizing her unfailing eagerness to pray for the welfare of human beings, especially those who seek her intercession. The original picture of Mary under this title is venerated in the Redemptorist church of Sant'Alfonso in Rome.

History. This picture, painted by an unknown artist in Crete in the 14th or 15th century, was brought to Rome *c.* 1495 by a merchant who apparently had stolen it from some church in Crete. In Rome he contracted a mortal illness, but before his death he consigned the painting to the friend in whose house he had been lodging, with the request that it be placed in some church, as a form of restitution. The friend promised, but later changed his mind at the request of his wife, who wished to keep the picture. Then Mary herself was seen in a vision by the little daughter of the family, and commanded that her picture be placed in a church dedicated to St. Matthew between the basilicas of St. Mary Major and St. John Lateran. To this child Our Lady also revealed herself as "Holy Mary of Perpetual Help."

Accordingly, on March 27, 1499, the picture of Our Lady of Perpetual Help was solemnly enthroned on the high altar of St. Matthew's church, cared for by the Augustinians. A tablet narrating the history of the painting was affixed nearby. For the next three centuries Our Lady of Perpetual Help was venerated there, and many miracles were ascribed to her intercession. However, in 1798 the French army seized Rome and led Pius VI into captivity. Shortly afterward, the church of St. Matthew, together with 30 other churches of Rome, was leveled to the ground at the order of the French commander. The picture of Our Lady of Perpetual Help was removed by the Augustinians from the church before its destruction and after being kept for a short while in the church of St. Eusebius, was transferred to the private chapel of the Irish Augustinians at their monastery of Santa Maria in Posterula, where it remained in comparative obscurity for many years.

In 1863 Francis Blosi, SJ, preaching at the church of the Gesù on the Roman shrines of Mary, related the history of Our Lady of Perpetual Help at St. Matthew's and expressed the desire that the picture be found and again placed in a church between St. Mary Major's and St. John

Lateran's. This came to the attention of Michael Marchi, a Redemptorist, who knew the whereabouts of the picture because as a boy he had served Mass in the private chapel of the Augustinians. In 1855 the Redemptorists had purchased land for their motherhouse and a church on the Via Merulana, including the site on which St. Matthew's had stood. When Pius IX heard the story, he commanded that the picture be given to the Redemptorists for their church, since it fulfilled the condition laid down in the vision—"between the basilicas of St. Mary Major and St. John Lateran." The superior general of the Redemptorists was told to give the Augustinians another picture in compensation.

The picture of Our Lady of Perpetual Help was exposed for public veneration above the high altar of the church of Sant'Alfonso on April 26, 1866. The feast of Mary under the title of Perpetual Help (though restricted to certain churches and not in the calendar of the universal Church) is June 27.

Iconography. The original picture of Our Lady of Perpetual Help is painted on wood, and it measures about 17 by 21 inches. It is distinctly Byzantine in style, and many similar portrayals of Our Lady are found throughout the East and in Russia. This manner of portraying Mary is a further development of the famous Hodegetria, an icon of Mary (painted by St. Luke, according to some) venerated for centuries in Constantinople but destroyed in 1453 when that city fell to the Turks.

In addition to Mary, the picture represents her divine Son as a child of two or three years old, seated on his Mother's left hand, with his hands clasping her right hand. On either side are the angels Michael and Gabriel, bearing the instruments of the Passion. In Greek characters the abbreviated names of the four figures are added. The artist wished to depict the mental anguish of Christ as He gazes at the cross, and with a touching stroke painted the left sandal falling off His foot as He winces in terror. This portrayal of the Passion of Christ in an image of Mary classifies the picture as a "Passion Madonna." Such pictures are found today in many Orthodox churches, such as the cathedral of Rethymnon on the island of Crete.

The title "Our Lady of Perpetual Help," originally derived from Mary's own apparition to the little girl, is also most appropriately symbolized by this picture. For, although the sufferings awaiting her Son are so vividly portrayed, Mary's face is turned, not to Him but to those who gaze on the picture. Though she is indeed saddened by the vision of the instruments of the Passion, her sympathy goes out primarily to the children of men.

Bibliography: C. M. HENZE, *Mater de Perpetuo Succurso* (Bonn 1926), first scientific monograph, extract; *Our Lady of Perpetual Help,* tr. F. J. CONNELL (New York 1940). J. F. BYRNE, *The Glories of Mary in Boston* (Boston, Mass. 1921).

[C. HENZE]

OUR LADY OF THE GARDEN, SISTERS OF

(OLG); also known as *Gianelline,* or *Hortus Conclusus*; a papal religious congregation founded by St. Anthony GIANELLI, Jan. 12, 1829, at Chiavari, in Liguria, Italy, with the collaboration of Sister Caterina Podestà, who succeeded Gianelli upon his death in 1846 as superior general, and gave a vigorous impulse to the institute. Sister Podestà went to Rome (1864) to obtain papal approval of the institute and of the rules (1882). During the plague in Liguria (1835–37) the sisters became distinguished for such heroic charity that they were awarded medals of merit by King Charles Albert. The impulse of social charity has directed their activities to hospitals, schools for girls, homes for the aged, and orphanages. In 1856 the first members went to South America and undertook hospital work in Montevideo. From there they spread to Argentina (1859), Brazil (1908), Chile (1929), and Paraguay (1945). They also began work in Jordan (1901), Spain (1949), and the U.S. (1962). The generalate is in Rome.

Bibliography: L. RODINO, *Istoria del religioso istituto delle Figlie di Maria SS. dell'Orto* (Genoa 1889).

[A. FERRAIRONI]

OUR LADY OF THE MISSIONS, SISTERS OF

(RNDM); a religious congregation founded in 1861 at Lyons, France, by Mother Mary of the Heart of Jesus (Euphrasie Barbier, 1829–93). The institute, established primarily for educational, social and pastoral work in mission lands, received papal approval in 1906. By 1890, houses existed on three continents. In 1920 the congregation reopened its French houses, which had been suppressed in 1902 by the laic laws. The generalate is in Rome. At the beginning of the 21st century, there were more than 900 sisters serving in Australia, Bangladesh, British Isles, Canada, France, India, Italy, Kenya, Latin America, Myanmar, New Zealand, Papua New Guinea, Philippines, Samoa, Senegal and Vietnam.

Bibliography: A. COULOMB, *Life of the Very Reverend Mother Marie du Coeur de Jésus* (Mechlin 1914). R. RIOS, *A Heroine of the Mission Field* (London 1944). *Teaching Nations 100 Years* (Regina, Can. 1961).

[I. ROSS]

OUR LADY OF THE SACRED HEART, DAUGHTERS OF

(FDNSC; Official Catholic Directory #0900); a congregation of religious women founded in 1882 at Issoudun, France, by Jules Chevalier and Marie Louise HARTZER (1837–1908). The institute developed from a small group that Father Chevalier united into a congregation in 1874, but that languished until the arrival of Madam Hartzer, a widow born in Wissembourg (now in the Bas-Rhin department) in northeastern France. Following the Franco-Prussian War she came to France with her father and two sons, settled in Issoudun after her sons joined the Sacred Heart Missionaries, and became associated with Chevalier's followers. Under her leadership, the Daughters grew into the present congregation. The Holy See granted its decree of praise in 1908 and approved the constitutions in 1928. In their apostolate the Daughters engage in educational and hospital work. The congregation spread first to Australia (1884), then to Belgium, Switzerland, Netherlands, Brazil, Italy, Ireland, England, and Spain. In 1955 it entered the U.S., in the Diocese of Camden, N.J. The motherhouse is in Rome. The U.S. provincialate is in Bellmawr, N.J.

Bibliography: F. and L. HARTZER, *La Réverende Mère Marie-Louise Hartzer* (Paris 1913).

[L. F. PETIT/EDS.]

OUR LADY OF THE SNOW

The legend that gives this name to the feast (August 5, also called the Dedication of the Basilica of St. Mary Major) is that in the pontificate of Liberius (352–366) a childless Roman couple promised their wealth to the Virgin Mother of God. Her approval of their vow was indicated by a miraculous midsummer snowfall on the Esquiline Hill; by her appearance the same night in a dream to the patrician John and his wife, instructing them to build a church on the site; and by her confirmation of these instructions in the dream of Pope Liberius. The church was built, and later rebuilt during the pontificate of St. Sixtus III (432–440). It has been called by various titles and is now known as the Basilica of St. Mary Major.

No mention of the legend is found before the 10th century, and the prevailing attitude toward it is one of disbelief. It has been noted, for example, that in tracing the site for the church the snowfall untraditionally oriented the basilica to the west rather than the east. The congregation that Benedict XIV appointed in 1741 to reform the Breviary recommended that the lessons proper to the feast be omitted, on the grounds that it seemed unlikely that such an extraordinary occurrence would have gone unmentioned for so long. However, the feast had been extended to the universal Church during the pontificate of St. Pius V (1566–72), who is buried in the basilica, and the feast remains in the liturgical calendar.

Devotion to Our Lady of the Snow in the U.S. was introduced in 1941 by the Missionary Oblates of Mary Immaculate (OMI). As interest in the devotion grew, the Oblates established the National Shrine of Our Lady of the Snows in Belleville, Illinois to promote the devotion and accommodate the increasing number of pilgrims. Originally opened as an outdoor shrine 1962, further expansion of the Shrine resulted in the completion of the Church of Our Lady of the Snows for indoor liturgies in 1991, and the Millennium Spire in 1998.

Bibliography: *Liber pontificalis*, ed. L. DUCHESNE, v.1–2 (Paris 1886–92) 1:207–208, 232. H. GRISAR, *History of Rome and the Popes in the Middle Ages*, ed. L. CAPPADELTA, 3 v. (London 1911–12) 1:140, para 2. H. LECLERCQ, *Dictionnaire d'archéologie chrétienne et de liturgie*, ed. F. CABROL, H. LECLERCQ, and H. I. MARROU, 15 v. (Paris 1907–53) 10.2:2091–2119.

[M. S. CONLAN/EDS.]

OUR LADY OF THE WAY, SOCIETY OF

An international secular institute of pontifical right, founded 1936 by Karl Dinkhauser, S.J. and Maria Elisabeth von Strachotinsky. Originally established as a pious union in 1936, Pope Pius XII reorganized it as a secular institute in 1947. In 1953, it became a secular institute of pontifical right. The members vow to follow the evangelical counsels of chastity, poverty, and obedience; but they remain integrated in their social and occupational groups. They follow various occupations, live wherever appropriate for their apostolate, and do not wear a distinctive garb. The society does not have works of its own; its apostolate is accomplished by the immersion of its members into their own local and occupational fields. The spirit of the society and its constitution stem from the *Spiritual Exercises* of St. Ignatius: to work for the glory of God; to develop an alert conscience and a strong sense of responsibility; to be ready for self-sacrifice; and to be aware of the call to apostolic ministry in each and all encounters. The society has members worldwide in Europe, North America, the Caribbean, India, Japan and the Philippines.

[A. EMERY/EDS.]

OUR LADY OF VICTORY MISSIONARY SISTERS

(OLVM, Official Catholic Directory #3130); a pontifical institute of religious women founded in 1922 at Chicago, Ill., by Rev. John J. Sigstein; its members devote themselves to religious education and social work. Bp. John F. Noll, of Fort Wayne, Ind., built Victory Noll, the congregation's motherhouse, at Huntington, Ind. Our Lady of Victory Missionary Sisters, commonly known as Victory Noll sisters, teach religion on the elementary and secondary levels for Catholic children who attend public schools. The congregation are also engaged in youth ministries, counseling, and parish ministries.

[E. A. CLIFFORD/EDS.]

OVALLE, ALFONSO DE

Chilean Jesuit priest and historian; b. Santiago, Chile, 1601; d. Lima, Peru, March 16, 1651. He entered the Jesuits in 1618 and studied at Córdoba de Tucumán. In 1625 he returned to Chile, where he became famous as a preacher. He taught philosophy and theology and was rector of San Francisco Javier Seminary. In 1640 he was elected procurator for Rome and Madrid. He went to Europe via Lima and Panama and arrived at Cádiz at the beginning of 1642. While in Madrid he persuaded the king and the Council of the Indies to finance a large Jesuit expedition to accompany him upon his return. He also obtained tax exemptions and other benefits for the many victims of the earthquake of Santiago in 1647. He spent two or three months with the Chilean missionary Luis de Valdivia in Valladolid, and their conversations contributed to his historical publications of those years. At the end of 1643 he arrived in Rome. After consulting, among others, the general of the order, Muzio Vitelleschi, he wrote *Histórica relación del reino de Chile* (Rome 1646, in two editions, Spanish and Italian), which has been reprinted many times and translated into the principal European languages. This work is the basis of Ovalle's reputation. Because of its sound historical information and its elegant classical diction, it is considered the outstanding literary monument of colonial Chile.

[F. MATEOS]

OVARIOTOMY

Literally means the cutting of an ovary. Ovariotomy is a term often used loosely to signify the removal of one or both ovaries of a female (ovariectomy). Oophorectomy is considered by many a preferable term for this procedure.

[T. J. O'DONNELL]

OVERBERG, BERNARD

Educator; b. Höckel bei Voltlage, northwest of Osnabrück, May 1, 1754; d. Münster, Nov. 9, 1826. Overberg began studies for the priesthood in 1774 and was ordained at Rheine on Dec. 20, 1779. He was chaplain in Everswinkel (1780–83), director of the Münster normal school (1783), synodal examiner (1786), rector of the diocesan seminary and dean of Liebfrauenkirche (1809), Konsistorialrat (1816), honorary canon (1823), and Oberkonsistorialrat (1826).

In 1783 Franz von FÜRSTENBERG, the vicar-general, entrusted Overberg with the direction of the newly organized normal school in Münster. Overberg completely transformed the Catholic educational system in Münster, bringing it to a high degree of excellence. His pedagogical system was based on religious and moral education stressed equally with the development of teaching skills and complete mastery of subject matter. Foreseeing difficulties for the teaching religious orders in Germany, he encouraged the education of laywomen, inspiring them to regard the vocation of teaching as a true apostolate. When appointed rector of the seminary in Münster, he concerned himself especially with the moral formation of the clergy, at the same time continuing to exercise a strong influence on diocesan education through books and lectures, notably in the field of Christian doctrine.

Overberg was also a successful confessor and spiritual guide. He won the confidence of Amalia GALLITZIN and was instrumental in her return to the Church, remaining her lifelong friend and advisor. He also guided the priestly career of her son, Demetrius Augustine GALLITZIN. He influenced many contemporaries, including the convert Graf Friedrich Leopold von Stolberg; the stigmatized mystic Anna Katharina EMMERICH; foundresses of religious institutes: Clara FEY, Franziska SCHERVIER, Pauline von Mallinckrodt; and the poets Luisa Hensel and Annette Elisabeth von Droste-Hülshoff.

Overberg's most important work is his *Anweisung zum zweckmässigen Schulunterricht für die Schullehrer im Fürstentum Münster* (Münster 1793, 1835; Joseph Esterhues, ed, Paderborn 1957), in which he sets forth his pedagogical aims, methods, and principles. He also wrote *Die Geschichte des alten und neuen Testamentes* (Münster 1799, 1889), *Christkatholisches Religions-Handbuch* (Münster 1804, 1827), *Katechismus der christkatholischen Lehre zum Gebrauche der grösseren Schüler* (Münster 1804, 1852), *Katechismus der christkatholischen Lehre zum Gebrauche der kleineren Schüler* (Münster 1804–48), and *Kleiner Haussegen* (Münster 1807, 1836).

Bibliography: B. OVERBERG, *Aus dem Tagebuche einer grossen Seele: Die Tagebücher Bernard Overbergs,* ed. P. KRÜGER

(Kavelaer 1937). R. STAPPER, *Bernard Overberg als pädagogischer Führer seiner Zeit* (Münster 1926). H. M. HEUVELDOP, *Leben und Wirken Overbergs* (Münster 1933). H. HOFFMANN, *Bernard Overberg* (2d ed. Augsburg 1949). W. SAHNER, *Overberg als Pädagoge und Katechet und das Arbeitsschulprinzip* (Gelsenkirchen 1949). S. SUDHOF, *Lexikon für Theologie und Kirche*, ed. J. HOFER and K. RAHNER (Freiberg 1957–65) 7:1319.

[M. F. LAUGHLIN]

OVID IN CHRISTIAN CULTURE

Publius Ovidius Naso (43 B.C.–A.D. 17), one of the most gifted of Roman poets, exercised an influence on Christian and secular poetry in the Middle Ages and the Renaissance second only to that of Vergil. Within a few years of his death his *Metamorphoses* became the standard work of reference for Greek and Roman mythology and legend, a position it has never lost. For painters, poets, and preachers, it became the greatest single source of myth, although the *Heroides* and *Fasti* were much used also. Similarly, Ovid's treatment of love is the most significant single literary formulation of erotic experience in the Latin tradition. When Augustine (*Conf.* 3.1) says, "I was not yet in love, but in love with loving" (*nondum amabam sed amare amabam*), he uses the word "love" (*amare*) with just that shade of meaning given it by Ovid. In the tradition before Ovid, love was usually treated as an aberration, madness, or sickness (*furor, uesania, morbus,* etc.) affecting the individual lover. Ovid extended and deepened this conception to emphasize his view that love is essentially a mutual experience between two persons who are equally involved. His Pyramus and Thisbe, Ceyx and Halcyone, Philemon and Baucis, and many others become typical examples for the Latin tradition after him. One always thinks of these lovers in pairs, whereas the typical lover of Greek epigram, the new comedy, or earlier Latin elegy is usually thought of by himself.

In technical matters, such as metrics, prosody, and poetic diction, Ovid's usage became the classical standard. Later writers admired Vergil but wrote in the language of Ovid. Ovid's influence became so dominant in the 12th and 13th centuries, especially as the patron of the wandering scholars, that the great medievalist L. Traube called this period the *Aetas Ovidiana* in Latin poetry. In the Middle Ages Ovid was widely interpreted in an allegorical manner and so ingeniously construed as to be found an authority on moral conduct. His works were an important source of the tradition of courtly love. E. K. Rand says that Chaucer owed to Ovid "a greater debt than to any other poet, old or new." He was much used by Dante and Boccaccio and had a great vogue in Neo-Latin poetry in general.

Poets tend like other craftsmen to learn their trade from earlier masters; in this sense Ovid has been one of the great masters, not only in the Latin tradition, but in modern European languages also. The English authors Dryden, Pope, and Milton, among many others, were his pupils. The Romantic revolt in poetry may be understood as a rebellion against the too dominant and restrictive influence of those standards of classicism that Ovid seems best to represent.

Bibliography: M. SCHANZ, C. HOSIUS, and G. KRÜGER, *Geschichte der römischen Literatur* 4 v. in 5 (Munich 1914–35) 2:206–264. E. K. RAND, *Ovid and His Influence* (Boston 1925). R. R. BOLGAR, *The Classical Heritage and Its Beneficiaries* (Cambridge, Eng. 1954). H. F. FRÄNKEL, *Ovid: A Poet between Two Worlds* (Berkeley 1945). F. MUNARI, *Ovid im Mittelalter* (Zürich 1960). *Geschichte der lateinischen Literatur des Mittelalters,* v.1–3, indexes s.v. Ovidius. L. K. BORN, "O. and Allegory," *Speculum* 9 (1934) 362–379. J. SEZNEC, *The Survival of the Pagan Gods: The Mythological Tradition and Its Place in Renaissance Humanism and Art,* tr. B. F. SESSIONS (New York 1953).

[M. P. CUNNINGHAM]

OWEN, NICHOLAS, ST.

Called "Little John," English martyr and Jesuit lay brother; b. Oxfordshire, date unknown; d. London, March 2, 1606. Owen probably was the son of Walter Owen of Oxford, and the brother of Henry, a Catholic printer, and Walter and John, priests. Nicholas first appears in Catholic history as a prisoner in London in 1582. He was the open champion of the innocence of Edmund CAMPION, whose servant he is said to have been. Soon after the arrival of Henry GARNET in England (July 1586) Owen, then at liberty, entered his service, in which he remained for the next 18 years.

He was employed principally in the construction of hiding places in Catholic centers established by his master, since he was a superb carpenter, mason, and architect. A few authentic examples survive, e.g., at Sawston Hall near Cambridge; Huddington Court, Worcestershire; Coughton Hall, Warwickshire, which point to his limitless ingenuity. The fullest contemporary appreciation of his character and work was written by John GERARD: "I verily think no man can be said to have done more good of all those that laboured in the English vineyard. For first, he was the immediate occasion of saving many hundreds of persons, both ecclesiastical and secular, and of the estates also of these seculars, which had been lost and forfeited many times over if the priests had been taken in their houses." Since he knew the hiding places of most priests in England, he was certain to receive very severe treatment if captured.

He was finally taken at Hinlip Hall, near Worcester, on Jan. 23, 1605. With Ralph Ashley he was forced out of hiding by starvation, and tried to pass himself off as a priest to save Garnet. The ruse failed. Taken to London, Owen was mercilessly tortured in the Tower. As a result of a fall from a horse he had a rupture, which legally exempted him from racking, but this was ignored by the Council. When he gave no information injurious to any Catholic, the torture became more violent. On March 2 while Owen was on the rack, his entrails burst out; he survived some hours in agony. On his death the Council gave out that he had committed suicide, but few believed it. He was beatified by Pius XI on Dec. 15, 1929, and canonized by Paul VI in 1970 as one of the Forty Martyrs of England and Wales.

See Also: ENGLAND, SCOTLAND, AND WALES, MARTYRS OF.

Feast: March 12; October 25 (Feast of the 40 Martyrs of England and Wales); December 1 (Jesuits).

Bibliography: A. BUTLER, *The Lives of the Saints*, rev. ed. H. THURSTON and D. ATTWATER (New York 1956) 1:579–581. H. FOLEY, ed., *Records of the English Province of the Society of Jesus*, 7 v. (London 1877–82) 4.1:245–267. J. GERARD, *The Autobiography of a Hunted Priest*, tr. P. CARAMAN (New York 1952); *The Condition of Catholics under James I. Fr. Gerard's Narrative of the Gunpowder Plot*, ed. J. MORRIS (2d ed. London 1872). J. N. TYLENDA, *Jesuit Saints and Martyrs* (Loyola Press, Chicago 1998), 67–69. M. WAUGH, *Blessed Nicholas Owen* (Postulation pamphlet; London 1961).

[G. FITZHERBERT]

OWENSBORO, DIOCESE OF

The diocese of Owensboro (Owensburgensis), comprising 32 counties in western Kentucky, was established Dec. 9, 1937, from territory taken from LOUISVILLE, which became a metropolitan see at that time. Owensboro is Kentucky's third most populous city.

The first bishop, Francis R. Cotton, known for his piety, ruled the diocese strictly until his death, Sept. 25, 1960. Cotton made early preparations for a diocesan synod, which in its final session in Feb. 1943 adopted 114 statutes, later approved by Rome and promulgated. His successor was Henry J. Soenneker who, consecrated in 1961, served until 1982. Soenneker in turn was succeeded by John J. McRaith who was consecrated late in 1982.

From its earliest years, the new diocese attracted several religious communities to labor among its people, the GLENMARY HOME MISSIONERS being among the first (1941). The Ursuline Sisters of Mount Saint Joseph, founded in 1874 by the Ursuline Sisters of Louisville, are an autonomous community with a motherhouse at Maple Mount, a few miles southwest of Owensboro. Mount Saint Joseph Academy which had its beginning in 1874, continued until 1983. In 1925, the Ursuline Sisters began a junior college for women on the motherhouse grounds. In 1950, the school moved to Owensboro, today's Brescia University.

A diocesan Marian shrine, under the title "Mary Mother of the Church: Mary Model of All Christians" was dedicated in 1989. The Office of Hispanic Ministry was created in 1997 to better serve an Hispanic population estimated at 8,000. The Great Jubilee 2000 was celebrated in western Kentucky, at the invitation of Bishop John McRaith, as a joint effort of Christians throughout the area. A large candle, representing Christ, began its pilgrimage throughout the 32 counties on Reformation Sunday 1999, that concluded on Pentecost, 2000, at the Owensboro Sports Center. There, in a gathering of prayer and celebration, Christian leaders from many denominations signed an accord to work together for justice. The Owensboro diocese in 2000 reported 79 parishes serving a Catholic population of 50,000.

Bibliography: *The First Synod* (Owensboro 1943). *First Review & Year Book* (Owensboro 1952). J. HAYDEN, ed. *This Far by Faith: The Story of Catholicity in Western Kentucky* (Owensboro 1987). J. A. BOONE, ed. *The Roman Catholic Diocese of Owensboro, Kentucky* (Owensboro 1995).

[M. E. NAHSTOLL/C. F. CREWS]

OWL AND THE NIGHTINGALE, THE

The Owl and the Nightingale is a 12th-century poem generally regarded as one of the outstanding works in Middle English. It takes the form of a debate between the two birds as to which excels the other. The birds are well trained in the medieval *débat* tradition, and as their arguments develop, they range over many of the central intellectual questions of the century. The author never forgets, however, that the antagonists are birds, and they speak in character as they attack each other's personal habits, singing ability, and nest–building skill, as well as philosophical and moral outlooks. The poem is as noted for its liveliness and wit as for its rhetorical accomplishment.

It is clear, however, that the owl and the nightingale are more than mere representatives of two species of birds. Though scholars disagree upon any specific interpretation of their characters, or of their debate, the nightingale clearly stands for a joyous, the owl for a sober, approach to life. Among the most important of their topics is man's attitude toward his religion: should it be penitential or celebratory?

The birds are unable to convince one another, and agree to take their quarrel to one Nicholas of Guilford, who, we are told, is preeminent for both learning and able judgment. But the reader is left simply with the debate: the author appears to suggest that either view of life alone is partial, that both the sober owl on its stump and the playful nightingale on its branch have important things to say and make mistakes, which need correction, and that a proper tension of their attitudes contributes balance to life; resolution of the argument is less important than practical truth.

The author and the exact provenance of the 2,000-line, octosyllabic poem are unknown. It is not now generally supposed that Nicholas was the author, or that the poem was written at Guilford. The dialect is that of the southwestern part of England, and the work has importance as a philological document, as well as for its literary qualities.

Bibliography: *The Owl and the Nightingale,* ed. E. G. STANLEY (London 1960). R. M. WILSON, *Early Middle English Literature* (London 1939) ch. 7. H. HÄSSLER, *"The Owl and the Nightingale" und die literarischen Bestrebungen des 12. und 13. Jahrhunderts* (Frankfurt a. M. 1942). H. WALTHER, *Das Streitgedicht in der lateinischen Literatur des Mittelalters* (Quellen und Untersuchungen zur lateinischen Philologie des Mittelalters 5.2; Munich 1920).

[N. D. HINTON]

OXFORD, UNIVERSITY OF

One of two ancient English universities, in Oxford, the county seat of Oxfordshire, England.

City of Oxford. Situated between the upper Thames and the Cherwell, this ancient "ford of oxen" was fortified against the Danes in 912 by Edward the Elder, King of the West Saxons. By 1000, Oxenford was one of the principal towns of the country. After the Conquest, Norman earls built a massive castle, city walls, and many churches. In the 12th century the ancient nunnery of St. Frideswide was given to the Austin Canons. The growth of the University in the 13th century brought Dominicans (1221), Franciscans (1224), Carmelites (1256), Friars of the Sack (*c.* 1262), Cistercians (1280), Benedictines (1283), Trinitarians (1293), and other religious orders. From the 13th to the 16th century the privileged position of the University repressed growth of the town, particularly after the riots of St. Scholastica's Day, 1355. Formerly a township in the Diocese of Lincoln, it became a cathedral city under Henry VIII. During the Reformation religious houses were suppressed or turned into secular colleges. National divisions of sympathy were reflected in the perennial feud between city and University, which was not reconciled until the visit of George III in 1785. The 20th century brought great growth and change. Many ancient religious orders have returned, and some newer congregations share in the activity of the city and the University. Since the reestablishment of the Catholic hierarchy, Oxford has been in the Diocese of Birmingham.

University. The origin of this oldest university in England is lost in obscurity, even after all legend has been discounted. Individual masters, like Theobald of Étampes, are known to have taught clerks (clerics) in Oxford before 1117; around 1150 some masters held their own schools there. It was not until Henry II checked the flow of English scholars to Paris, however, that English masters and students flocked to Oxford. By 1180 "a large number of scholars" from different faculties resided there (GERARD OF CAMBRAI), but probably without much formal organization until the legatine ordinance of 1214. ROBERT GROSSETESTE was appointed chancellor (*c.* 1215 21), representing the bishop of Lincoln; curricula in theology, law, medicine, and arts were modeled on University of Paris practice. The arrival of mendicant orders proved beneficial. In 1254 Innocent IV confirmed all immunities, liberties, and customs of the University and as at Paris, no clerk could enroll in theology unless he had first been a regent master in arts. The congregation of regents and nonregents of all faculties (*congregatio magna*), later called the convocation, was the supreme governing body; the congregation of all regent masters of all faculties (*congregatio minor*) governed ordinary affairs. To govern the arts faculty, regent masters in arts formed their own congregation (*congregatio nigra*), presided over by two proctors, one *Australis* and the other *Borealis,* who were the original University executives. Lectures were always given in the schools, and scholars lived wherever they could. Riots and disorders between "town and gown" induced Bp. Walter de Merton in 1264 to found a residence for secular students of theology, mainly his relatives, similar to the college founded by Robert de SORBON in Paris. Two earlier residential halls, University College (1249) and Balliol (1263), were soon reorganized to conform to Merton's statutes. Originally these colleges merely provided good lodging and company for a select group of fellows. Only later did the colleges become the self-contained, autonomous units that, grouped together, make up the University of Oxford as it exists today.

As a corporate body, the University dates only from the reign of Elizabeth I, when an act of Parliament, passed in 1571, incorporated "the chancellor, masters and scholars" of Oxford, and imposed the oath of supremacy and the 39 Articles. In 1634 the ancient, scattered statutes of the University were codified by Abp. William Laud and ratified by royal charter. The Laudian Code is still the basis of the existing statutes, although many modern provisions have been added. In 1850 the first royal commission was appointed to reform and mod-

Oriel College, Oxford. (©Historical Picture Archive/CORBIS)

ernize the University. Since 1854 continued organizational reform has been accompanied by the introduction of modern subjects: natural science, economics, modern and Oriental languages, social studies, fine arts, agriculture and forestry. In 1920 women were admitted to full membership in the University.

Organization. The chancellor, masters, and scholars form a corporate body within which the colleges are individual corporations. The highest officer is the chancellor, usually a man of distinction, elected by convocation. In practice the head is the vice-chancellor, a head of one of the colleges, who is nominated annually by the chancellor for a total of three years. Two proctors are appointed annually by two of the colleges in rotation. University business is initiated by the Hebdomadal council and decided upon by the congregation (all resident M.A.'s). The council consists of five ex officio members (chancellor, vice-chancellor, two proctors, and either the outgoing or incoming vice-chancellor) and 18 M.A.'s elected by the

congregation. Since 1926 the power of convocation (resident and nonresident M.A.'s) has become nominal. The administrative work is delegated to academic bodies, supervised by the general board of faculties, and nonacademic bodies, such as curators.

No one can study for a degree or be a member of the University unless he is a member of one of the 26 colleges for men: University (founded 1249), Balliol (1263), Merton (1264), St. Edmund's Hall (*c.*1278), Exeter (1314), Oriel (1326), Queen's (1340), New College (1379), Lincoln (1427), All Souls (1438, no undergraduates), Magdalen (1458), Brasenose (1509), Corpus Christi (1517), Christ Church (1546), Trinity (1554, formerly Benedictine, Durham), St. John's (1555, formerly Cistercian, St. Bernard), Jesus (1571), Wadham (1612), Pembroke (1624), Worcester (1714, formerly OSB, Gloucester), Keble (1870, only for Anglicans), Hertford (1874), St. Antony's (1951), Nuffield (1958, for doctorate candidates), St. Catherine's (1868, reorganized 1962), and St. Peter's (1929, reorganized 1962); or the five colleges for women: Lady Margaret Hall (1878), Somerville (1879), St. Hugh's (1886), St. Hilda's (1893), and St. Anne's (1952). Besides innumerable authorized lodgings, there are five permanent private halls: Mansfield College, Campion Hall (Jesuit), St. Benet's Hall (Benedictine), Regent's Park College, and Greyfriars (Franciscan). Since 1954 Queen Elizabeth House has been a center for commonwealth studies.

Studies for degrees are of three kinds: (1) the normal undergraduate studies for the B.A. in any set subject; (2) undergraduate studies in one of the higher faculties, normally taken after the B.A., for the B.D., in theology, B.C.L. in law, the B.M. and B.Ch. (Surgery) in medicine, and B.Mus. in music; (3) original research under a supervisor for the degrees of B.Litt., B.Sc., B Phil., and D.Phil. Higher doctorates are awarded for published work containing an original contribution to the advancement of learning.

There are 16 faculties and one department in which one may study: theology, law, medicine, litterae humaniores ("greats," the ancient arts faculty), modern history, English, modern European languages, Oriental studies, physical science (including mathematics), biological sciences, social studies (philosophy, politics, and economics, or "modern greats"), anthropology and geography, music, agriculture and forestry, psychology, fine arts, and a department of education.

Examinations for the B.A., the basic Oxford degree, are: (1) responsions—entrance examination taken before coming up to the University or its equivalent; (2) first public examination, which may be an honors examination (moderations), taken between the 3d and 6th term after matriculation, in Greek and Latin, mathematics, natural science or law, or a pass examination designed as a preliminary to one of the final honor schools; (3) final schools examination, generally an honors examination, in a single subject or in two or three closely related subjects, taken between the 8th and 12th term after matriculation. Having passed the final schools examination, a B.A. graduate may retain his name on the books of his college for a total of 21 terms (seven years) and supplicate for the degree of M.A. without any further examination, and thus become a member of the convocation.

Oxford uses two educational systems: the university lecture system, which centers on the lecturer's current interest or university needs, and the tutorial system, which centers on the needs of the undergraduate. The undergraduate is not obliged to attend any lectures, but he usually attends those pertinent to the final schools examination or those recommended by his tutor. The tutorial system, perfected in the 19th century, is the basic

educational technique at Oxford. A freshman on his arrival at the beginning of his first term is introduced to the college tutor in charge of the subject that he intends to study. This college tutor determines the immediate needs of the individual and assigns one or more tutors who will be responsible for the intellectual development of the undergraduate. The precise form of the tutorial, or weekly session with the tutor, varies with the subject. Basically it is the presentation of some exercise, essay, or experiment, read or performed, singly or in small groups, for the tutor to criticize, query, or explain. The weekly tutorial is based on a heavy reading course, including the list published by the board of faculty concerned. The tutor's primary function is to instruct and to develop the critical abilities of the undergraduate.

The academic year at Oxford consists of three full terms of eight weeks each, fixed by the Hebdomadal council: Michaelmas, beginning on the second Sunday in October; Hilary, beginning on the first Sunday after January 14; and Trinity, beginning on the last or next to last Sunday in April, depending on the date of Easter. Specified terms of residence, usually nine and never less than six, are a condition of admission to any degree. These terms, each of which must be at least 42 days long, must be kept by residence within the walls of a college, hall, or in licensed lodgings. During the two short vacations of six weeks each and during the long summer vacation the student is expected to complete the heavy reading program set by the board of faculty and his tutor.

Strictly speaking, Oxford offers no graduate courses. Since 1895, however, certain faculties have established research degrees, particularly for graduates of other universities. The first research degree established was the B.Litt. The candidate must be accepted by a college or society, and through the college by the appropriate board of faculty for the area of research. The subject proposed for a thesis must be approved and a supervisor appointed. The examination for the degree is based solely on the written dissertation, which can be submitted after one year (if he is a graduate of Oxford) or two years of research, but not later than the third.

Application for admission as an advanced student in the technical sense for the D.Phil. degree is similar to the B.Litt. and B.Phil. However, much more is expected and a longer time is allowed (between two and five years, with possible extensions). A successful dissertation for the D.Phil. degree is "an original contribution to knowledge set forth in such a manner as to be fit for publication." When the original statute establishing the degree of D.Phil. was passed in 1917, advanced studies at Oxford secured a definite position subject to systematic control by the University.

In recent decades, through the work of the royal commission the University has come to assume a greater responsibility in the advancement of learning. Nuffield College, founded in 1937, was unique in being a University institution and not an independent corporation. It is a postgraduate college intended "to encourage research especially but not exclusively in the field of social studies." St. Catherine's was reconstituted as a full college in 1962 to promote study of the technological sciences. The University museum, the University laboratory of physical chemistry, erected in 1939–40, the Clarendon laboratory, completed in 1940, and more recent science buildings are under the direct control of the University and not of any particular college, although many of the colleges have their own laboratories.

Oxford is particularly blessed with good libraries. Besides college libraries, there is a central University library consisting of more than six separate collections in various buildings. The most famous is the Bodleian, founded in 1602 by Thomas Bodley, and its extensions, the Radcliffe Camera and the New Library, opened in 1946. The Bodleian is particularly rich in manuscripts and books. The Radcliffe science library contains the scientific section of the University library. The library of Rhodes House specializes in African and colonial history; the Indian Institute contains books dealing with India and Pakistan; Taylor Institute specializes in modern European languages and literature; and the Ashmolean Museum contains a number of specialist libraries in fine arts, archeology, antiquities, classics, and papyrology. Besides these there are smaller faculty libraries specializing in English, modern history, China and Chinese books, geography, and mathematics.

Details of the various fees, grants, prizes, and scholarships, notably the Rhodes scholarship, are given in *Handbook to the University of Oxford,* published and revised periodically by the Oxford University Press. The Rhodes scholarships, established under the last will (1899–1901) of the South African statesman, Cecil Rhodes, are for students from the British Empire, the U.S., and Germany. The great majority of American Oxonians have been Rhodes scholars.

Bibliography: A. G. LITTLE, *The Grey Friars in Oxford* (Oxford 1892). C.E. MALLET, *A History of the University of Oxford,* 3.v. (London 1924–27). J. WELLS, *Oxford and Its Colleges* (9th ed. London 1910). S. GIBSON, ed., *Statuta antiqua universitatis Oxoniensis* (Oxford 1931). A. G. LITTLE and F. PELSTER, *Oxford Theology and Theologians, c. A.D. 1282–1302* (Oxford 1935). H. RASHDALL, *The Universities of Europe in the Middle Ages,* ed. F. M. POWICKE and A. B. EMDEN, 3 v. (new ed. Oxford 1936). D. A. CALLUS, "Introduction of Aristotelian Learning to Oxford," *Proceedings of the British Academy* 29 (1943) 229–281. W. A. HINNEBUSCH, *The Early English Friars Preachers* (Rome 1951). E. CRASTER, *History of the Bodleian Library, 1845–1945* (Oxford 1952). A. B. EMDEN, *A Biographical Register of the University of Oxford to A.D. 1500,* 3 v. (Oxford 1957–59). M. H. CURTIS, *Oxford and Cambridge in Transition, 1558–1642* (Oxford 1959). F. PELSTER and D. A. CALLUS, *Lexikon für Theologie und Kirche,* ed. J. HOFER and K. RAHNER, 10 v. (2d, new ed. Freiburg 1957–65) 7:1320–23. Publications. *Oxford University Calendar* (1810–) yearly. *University of Oxford Examination Statutes* (1883–) yearly. *Oxford University Gazette* (1870–), regularly. *Oxford Historical Society Publications* (1884–1936; N.S. 1939–). *Handbook to the University of Oxford* (1932–) esp. 1962 and periodic revisions. *Oxford Studies Presented to Daniel Callus* (Oxford 1960).

[J. A. WEISHEIPL/EDS.]

OXFORD MOVEMENT

An effort by Anglican clergymen of Oxford University between 1833 and 1845 to renew the Church of England by a revival of Catholic doctrine and practice. The following phases of the movement are discernible: (1) rise and progress (1833–39), (2) crisis (1839–41), (3) Tract 90 and its aftermath (1841–45), and (4) the period after Newman.

Background. The Church of England (*see* ANGLICANISM) emerged from the Reformation as an amalgamation of Catholic and Protestant doctrine and practice. These two disparate elements were welded together in the interest of national unity, mainly during the reign of Elizabeth I. The Catholic tradition, or HIGH CHURCH element, triumphed over the Protestant element during the period of such famous Anglo-Catholic divines as Lancelot ANDREWES and William LAUD. The REVOLUTION OF 1688 enabled the Protestant party to gain the ascendancy. LATITUDINARIANISM, which minimized doctrine, represented a third party.

By 1800 the English Church greatly needed reform. With its deep internal divisions, worldly prelates, and ineffectual clergy, however, it was hardly prepared to undertake this task itself. Hence it was faced with the prospect of having unwelcome reforms imposed upon it by secularist and liberal members of Parliament. The first such reform occurred in 1833 when ten Anglican bishoprics were suppressed in Ireland. To many loyal churchmen this was an omen of more drastic changes, perhaps even of disestablishment.

Rise and Progress (1833–39). A fear of such drastic moves motivated John KEBLE's sermon entitled "National Apostasy" (July 14, 1833), which John Henry NEWMAN considered the beginning of the Oxford Movement. The sermon was followed by a meeting held from July 25 to July 29 at Hadleigh, Suffolk, attended by a number of prominent clergymen, including Hugh Rose, William Palmer, and Richard Hurrell FROUDE. They decided to organize a defense of the Church through the formation of committees and the issuance of joint manifestoes.

Newman, Keble, and Froude, however, believed that the only true remedy for the evil condition of the Church lay in a theological and spiritual renewal. They held that the Catholic heritage of the Book of COMMON PRAYER and of the 17th-century divines had to be recovered. The English Church had to reaffirm her commitment to the almost forgotten Catholic truths, namely: she held divine authority as part of God's visible kingdom; her sacraments were indispensable channels of grace; and her bishops were successors of the Apostles. This message they decided to communicate to the clergy in brief pamphlets, subsequently named *Tracts for the Times,* an expedient originated by Newman, who wrote the first one (*see* TRACTARIANISM).

Keble, "the true and primary author" of the movement according to Newman, was a gentle poet and scholarly pastor who had imbibed the Catholic tradition in his father's rectory. Froude, an ardent disciple of Keble, burned with an impatient zeal to restore the Church of England to its medieval spiritual power. Newman, a bold, searching thinker, was a patristic scholar who had moved from an Evangelical to a Catholic position through his reading and personal contacts at Oxford, especially his friendship with Froude and Keble.

One of the first important conquests of the movement occurred at the end of 1833 when Edward B. PUSEY signed his initials to *Tract 18.* Regius professor of Hebrew, canon of Christ Church, and an aristocrat with friends in high places, he already enjoyed a reputation for great learning and holiness. His adherence to the cause was of invaluable assistance in establishing the movement as a serious contender for influence in the Church.

Newman, with his natural gifts, his acute, sensitive mind, his great capacity for friendship, and his insight into the minds of others, was destined to be the movement's natural leader. It was a leadership he exercised in many ways. His sermons at St. Mary's, Oxford, where he was vicar, were a powerful means of attracting many to the movement's ideals. Published as *Parochial and Plain Sermons* (1834–42), they reveal the essence of the Oxford reformation, its unworldliness, uncompromising quest for holiness, and unflinching asceticism. The sermons' psychological penetration, scriptural wisdom, and matchless beauty of language have made them enduring masterpieces.

Newman also did the most to establish a theoretical basis for the movement This was the object of a series of lectures delivered between 1834 and 1836 and published as *The Prophetical Office of the Church* (1837). Drawing on the 17th–century Anglican divines, he argued that the Church of England held an intermediate position, a *via media* between the extremes of Roman infallibility and Protestant private judgment. Her rule of faith was simple fidelity to the teaching of the Fathers. He confessed, however, that Anglo-Catholicism was still merely a religion on paper. There was a great need of theological investigation of the Anglican tradition to make it one, intelligible, and consistent. To this end Newman, Keble, and Pusey began to edit the 45-volume *Library of the Fathers* (1838–88), a series of English translations of patristic writings, and the 83-volume *Library of Anglo-Catholic Theology* (1841–63).

In his *Apologia* Newman revealed that the *via media* was based on three fundamental principles—dogma, the sacramental system, and anti-Romanism. The chief opponents of dogma, he said, were the Liberals, who viewed religion as a mere matter of opinion. His anti-Romanism at the time was evident in his reference to the pope as anti-Christ and in his accusations against Rome of corrupting the Gospel truths.

Valuable recruits were soon gained, especially among the younger fellows of Oriel and Trinity. Such talented scholars as Charles Marriott, Robert Wilberforce, Frederick Rogers, Richard W. Church, and Isaac Williams rallied to the reform banner. As Newman remarked (*Apologia,* 76) "the Anglo-Catholic party suddenly became a power in the National Church and an object of alarm to her rulers and friends."

Latent hostility erupted with the publication in 1838 of the private papers of Froude, who died in 1836. These *Remains* offended great numbers by their strong anti-Protestant character and confirmed a growing suspicion that the movement was pro-Roman.

Crisis (1839–41). Newman considered the year 1839 as the zenith of the movement. The revival of Catholicism seemed to answer definite spiritual needs of many members of the Church of England. Several developments, however, marked this year as the beginning of a crisis. There was, first, the formation of a new party of eager, acute, resolute minds with definite sympathies for Rome. Such men as William G. WARD, Frederick Oakeley, F. W. FABER, and J. D. DALGAIRNS "cut into the original movement at an angle, fell across its line of thought, and then set about turning that line in its own direction" (*Apologia,* 164).

A more fateful development occurred when doubts suddenly arose in Newman's mind about his *via media.* He found in his study of early history that MONOPHYSITISM had upheld a *via media* similar to the Anglican one. At the same time he saw in St. Augustine's phrase *"securus judicat orbis terrarum"* a rule of faith that seemed to invalidate the Anglo-Catholic's rule of fidelity to the Fathers. As he put it, "the deliberate judgment, in which the whole Church at length rests and acquiesces, is an infallible prescription . . . against such portions of it as protest and secede.'' Catholicity, or communion with the whole Church, was the essential mark of the true Church, not fidelity to antiquity.

> While the history of St. Leo showed me that the deliberate and eventual consent of the great body of the Church ratified a doctrinal decision as a part of revealed truth, it also showed that the rule of Antiquity was not infringed, though a doctrine had not been publicly recognized as so revealed till centuries after the time of the Apostles. Thus, whereas the Creeds tell us that the Church is One, Holy, Catholic, and Apostolic, I could not prove that the Anglican communion was an integral part of the One Church, on the ground of its teaching being Apostolic or Catholic, without reasoning in favour of what are commonly called the Roman corruptions; and I could not defend our separation from Rome and her faith without using arguments prejudicial to these great doctrines concerning our Lord, which are the very foundation of the Christian religion. The Via Media was an impossible idea! [*Apologia,* 149]

Still Newman tried to meet his own difficulty in an article in the *British Critic* (January 1840), in which he argued that jurisdictional or other forms of visible intercommunion were not necessary between the parts of the one visible Church. The English Church, although separated from Rome, was still the Catholic Church in England since it was still in possession of ''the Succession, the Episcopal form, the Apostolic faith, and the use of the Sacraments'' (*Essays Critical and Historical,* 20).

Tract 90 and Aftermath. However, Ward and others in the party leaning toward Rome cited the THIRTY-NINE ARTICLES to disprove Newman's contention that the Anglican Church held its common faith with Rome. The Articles were drawn up to exclude Roman doctrines from the English Church, they said. In reply Newman undertook a commentary on the Articles in *Tract 90,* which he published in February 1841. It was a crucial experiment, he recognized. He tried to prove that the Articles implied a distinction between Catholic teaching and Roman dogma; that they definitely did not condemn the former and did not even condemn the latter entirely. Rather the historical circumstances of their composition show that they were deliberately made general and vague in order to pacify those in the national Church with Catholic tendencies, as well as those with Protestant ones. Thus, although Article 21 simply states that ''General Councils . . . forasmuch as they be an Assembly of men may err . . . ,'' Newman claimed that this did not rule out their inerrancy ''when they are a thing of heaven.'' Despite the extreme subtlety of some of his distinctions, subsequent study has verified Newman's main contention.

The tract was not answered with argument, however. Panic and wrath ensued at this denial of the Protestant character of the Articles. All the resentment stored up against the ''Oxford Malignants'' now burst out in full fury. The heads of houses at Oxford, notorious for their ignorance of theology, publicly censured *Tract 90* as an evasion. Newman's bishop demanded the cessation of the tracts.

Newman retreated to a mission church he had built at Littlemore, his position in the established Church seriously compromised. Then three more blows fell, all but destroying his belief in the Anglican Church. A further study of ARIANISM showed him again the existence of another heretical *via media* in early Church history, i.e., Semi-Arianism. Second, the bishops one by one disowned Newman's interpretation of the Articles. Finally, the establishment of an Anglican bishopric in Jerusalem embracing Lutherans and other Protestants indicated a formal recognition of Protestant doctrines. This was the ultimate condemnation of the *via media* for Newman.

Meanwhile Pusey was suspended from preaching for two years after delivering a moderate Tractarian sermon on the Holy Eucharist. Then Ward entered the conflict. With remorseless logic he defended the thesis that since Rome alone fulfilled ''the ideal of a Christian Church'' (the title of his book), the Anglican Church must humbly sue for readmission to her communion. Official Oxford was outraged. His book was censured, and he was deprived of his master's degree in the Oxford convocation (Feb. 13, 1845).

Newman despaired of the Anglican Church and withdrew into lay communion after preaching his last sermon, ''The Parting of Friends'' (Sept. 25, 1843). He was kept back from Rome for two years by difficulties over Tridentine doctrines, transubstantiation, and Catholic devotion to the Blessed Mother and the saints. Further study led him to favor the view that a principle of development was at work in the Church from earlier times. After writing his *Essay on Development* (1845) to prove this point to his own satisfaction, he made his profession of Catholic faith to Father Dominic BARBERI (Oct. 9, 1845).

After Newman. Ward, Faber, Oakeley, Dalgairns, and many others left Anglicanism with Newman. Pusey and Keble assumed leadership of the faltering party. Oxford ceased to be its headquarters. Pastoral and liturgical matters overshadowed doctrinal ones.

Another wave of secessions to Rome occurred in 1851 over the case of Rev. George C. Gorham. The bishop of Exeter had refused a parish to Gorham because of his questionable views on Baptismal regeneration. The bishop's decision, however, was reversed by the Privy

Council in an unprecedented intervention in doctrinal matters. The impotence of the teaching authority of the Church appeared manifest to a number of clergymen, including Henry MANNING (later cardinal), who thereupon made their submission to Rome.

A long struggle was waged within the Church of England by Pusey, Keble, and their associates to revive the Catholic Sacraments, particularly the Eucharist and Penance. Puseyites were condemned by the archbishop of Canterbury and were brought to court for advocating the Catholic doctrinal interpretation of these Sacraments, but their patience and perseverance gradually won partial acceptance of this doctrine in the Church of England.

The revival of Catholic ceremonial, the use of altar lights, Eucharistic vestments, etc., was another result of work by Pusey and his friends. Although these practices were sanctioned by the Prayer Book, their advocates had to contend with furious mobs that wrecked churches where the reforms were introduced and with hostile bishops who condemned them as popish innovations. The revival of religious orders in the Church of England was another outcome of the Oxford Movement. Pusey's foundation of a sisterhood in 1845 was followed by the foundation of other communities of men or women. *See* RELIGIOUS ORDERS, ANGLICAN-EPISCOPALIAN.

The Oxford Movement failed to revive Catholic orthodoxy or to check the rising Liberalism in the Church of England. Its successful revival of Anglo-Catholic sacramental and liturgical practice, however, has greatly influenced the spirit and form of contemporary Anglican worship (*see* ANGLO-CATHOLICS).

Bibliography: J. H. NEWMAN, *Apologia pro vita sua* (1st ed. London 1864). J. R. GRIFFIN, *John Keble, Saint of Anglicanism* (Macon, GA 1987). M.R. O'CONNELL, *The Oxford Conspirators: A History of the Oxford Movement, 1833–1845* (Lanham, MD 1991). O. CHADWICK, *The Spirit of the Oxford Movement: Tractarian Essays* (Cambridge, England 1990). P.B. NOCKLES, *The Oxford Movement in Context: Anglican High Churchmanship, 1760–1857* (Cambridge, England 1994).

[T. S. BOKENKOTTER/EDS.]

OXYRHYNCHUS

A provincial capital (Coptic, Pemdije), about 200 kilometers south of Cairo, which became a large and important city during the Hellenistic period. In about A.D. 380 it was listed as a diocese with at least 10 churches, in addition to many monasteries in the surrounding region. During the Byzantine period it was the metropolis and commercial center of the province of Arcadia, but it gradually declined under Muslim rule and is now in ruins. Its chief importance lies in the immense collection of papyri discovered there, beginning with the excavations of B. Grenfell and A. Hunt (1897–1907), W. F. Petrie (1922), and Breccia (1927–28). They unearthed thousands of unknown and very important pagan and Christian documents: fragments of classical literature, gospels, apocrypha, Greek and Hebrew hymns, patristic texts, calendars, and inventories of churches, as well as civil and commercial items.

Bibliography: B. P. GRENFELL et al., eds., *The Oxyrhynchus Papyri* (London 1898—). K. PREISENDANZ, *Papyrusfunde und Papyrusforschung* (Leipzig 1933). H. GERSTINGER, *Lexikon für Theologie und Kirche*, ed. J. HOFER and K. RAHNER, 10 v. (2d new ed. Freiburg 1957–65) 7:1324–35. H. DELEHAYE, *Analecta Bollandiana* (Brussels 1882—) 42 (1924) 83–99.

[G. T. DENNIS]

OZANAM, ANTOINE FRÉDÉRIC, BL.

Married layman, French historian and literary scholar, and founder of the Society of St. Vincent de Paul; b. Milan, Italy, April 23, 1813; d. Marseilles, France, September 8, 1853.

A tradition of the Ozanam family traced its descent from a seventh-century Jew, Samuel Hosannam, converted by St. DESIDERIUS OF CAHORS, whom he sheltered from persecution. Frédéric was brought up and educated in Lyons. In 1829 he underwent a "crisis of doubt," which he overcame with the assistance of his teacher, Abbé Noirot. This experience consolidated the intellectual basis of his faith and imbued him with deep charity in controversy with unbelievers.

In 1831 he published his first work, a refutation of the socialist theories of the Saint-Simonians. In the same year he went to Paris to study law and made the acquaintance of the leaders of the Catholic revival—Chateaubriand, Montalembert, Lacordaire, Ampère, and others. He was concerned to refute the attacks on Catholicism that were widespread in the Sorbonne. It was in May of 1833 that he and a few fellow students formed a "Conference of Charity" to undertake practical work among the poor. This is accepted as the foundation date of the Society of St. Vincent de Paul, although its formal title and rules were not adopted until 1835. Ozanam insisted that the Society should not restrict its charity to Catholics and that countries should assist each other; thus, the Paris Society aided Dublin during the Irish famine and Dublin reciprocated during the Revolution of 1848.

Ozanam completed his first degree in law in 1834, and was called to the bar in Lyons. However, his true bent was for literature and history. He returned to Paris, where he took his first degree in literature in 1835, his doctorate

Pope John Paul II at a Mass celebrated at Notre Dame for the beautification of Antoine Frédéric Ozanam, Paris, 1997. (Bassignac-Deville-Vioujard-Quidu-Ribeiro/Gamma)

in law in 1836, and his doctorate in literature in 1839. During this period he was active in the Society of St. Vincent de Paul, the Society for the Propagation of the Faith, Catholic journalism, and many Catholic causes. He was instrumental in bringing about the first of Lacordaire's famous series of Lenten sermons in Notre Dame.

Ozanam became the first to hold a chair as professor of commercial law at Lyons in 1839, but returned to Paris the following year to teach foreign literature at the Sorbonne. He was elected professor in 1844. His studies of Dante, beginning with his doctoral thesis, revolutionized critical work on the poet. Although Ozanam is a neglected figure in nineteenth-century historiography, his research in the development of Christian Latin, literature, and art showed an acquaintance with the original texts and contemporary critical research in the major European languages that was remarkable in the French scholarship of his day.

Ozanam advocated that Catholics should play their part in the evolution of the democratic state and unsuccessfully stood for election to the National Assembly in 1848. He denounced economic liberalism and any form of socialism. Lecture 24 in his course of commercial law is a brilliant exposition of Catholic social doctrine, foreshadowing RERUM NOVARUM and antedating the *Communist Manifesto* in its attention to the social question. Ozanam's personal visitations to the poor and his reports of the St. Vincent de Paul Society antedated even Villermé's pioneer social investigation published in 1840.

Ozanam may justly be regarded as an exemplar of the lay apostolate in family, social, and intellectual life. His marriage (June 23, 1841) to Amelie Soulacroix produced one daughter, Marie (b. 1845). Without neglecting family duties he worked for social justice.

At his request, Ozanam was buried in the church crypt of Saint-Joseph-des-Carmes at the Catholic Institute of Paris, among the students to whom he gave the best of himself. His cause for beatification, introduced in 1925, was followed by the declaration of his heroic virtues (July 6, 1993) and the approval of a miracle attributed to his intercession (June 25, 1996). Pope John Paul II beatified Ozanam, August 22, 1997, in Notre Dame Cathedral at Paris during the World Youth Day celebrations.

Feast: Sept. 8.

Bibliography: Works by Frédéric Ozanam: *Oeuvres complètes,* 11 v. (Paris 1859–65). *Dante et la philosophie catholique au 13e siècle* (Paris 1839); *Études germaniques,* 2 v. (Paris 1847–49); *Les poètes franciscains en Italie au 13e siècle* (Paris 1852). *Lettres de Frédéric Ozanam. édition critique,* 5 v., ed. D. OZANAM (Paris 1961–97). Literature about Frédéric Ozanam: C. A. OZANAM, *Vie de Frédéric Ozanam* (Paris 1879). T. E. AUGE, *Frederic Ozanam and His World* (Milwaukee, Wisc. 1966). L. BAUNARD, *Ozanam d'après sa correspondance* (Paris 1912), a standard work published by the Catholic Truth Society of Ireland as *Ozanam in his Correspondence.* B. CATTANÉO, *Frédéric Ozanam le bienheureux* (Paris 1997). V. CONZEMIUS, *Frédéric Ozanam* (Freiburg, Switz. 1985). G. FORSANS, *Frédéric Ozanam 1813–53. Un précurseur de notre temps dans la fidélité à l'évangile* (Chambray-les-Tours 1991). I. GOBRY, *Frédéric Ozanam ou la foi opérante* (Paris 1983). G. GOYAU, *Frédéric Ozanam* (Paris 1925); et al., *Ozanam: Livre du centenaire,* rev. ed. (Paris 1931). H. GUILLEMIN, *La bataille de Dieu* (Geneva 1944). H. L. HUGHES, *Frederick Ozanam* (London 1933). J.-A. LAMARCHE, *Frédéric Ozanam: fondateur de la Société Saint-Vincent-de-Paul* (Montréal 1997). F. MÉJECAZE, *Fr. Ozanam et l'église catholique* (Paris 1932). L. MEZZADRI, *Federico Ozanam: se non ho la carità non sono niente* (Cinisello Balsamo (Milano) 2000). K. O'MEARA, *Frederic Ozanam, Professor at the Sorbonne; His Life and Works* (Edinburgh 1876). E. RENNER, *The Historical Thought of Frédéric Ozanam* (Washington 1960). M. DES RIVIÈRES, *Ozanam. Un savant chez les pauvres* (Montréal 1984). A. P. SCHIMBERG, *The Great Friend: Frederick Ozanam* (Milwaukee, Wisc. 1946). M. VINCENT, *Ozanam. Une jeunesse romantique* (Paris 1994).

[F. MACMILLAN]

P

PACCA, BARTOLOMEO

Cardinal, papal diplomat; b. Benevento (Campania), Italy, Dec. 25, 1756; d. Rome, April 19, 1844. Of noble birth, he studied in Naples under the Jesuits and in Rome at the Collegio Clementino and the Accademia dei Nobili Ecclesiastici. In 1785 he received minor and major orders, becoming titular archbishop of Damietta and nuncio to Cologne, where he met the opposition of the bishop-electors of Mainz and Cologne, who were incensed against the Holy See because of the erection of the nunciature in Munich. These bishops, who were hostile to interventions in spiritual matters by nuncios, were impregnated with FEBRONIANISM and were defenders of the Congress of EMS. The repercussions of the French Revolution did more to improve the situation than did Pacca's firmness and ability. He was named nuncio extraordinary to Louis XVI, whose flight Pius VI believed successful, but the king's capture at Varenne made Pacca's mission pointless. As nuncio to Lisbon from 1794 to 1801, he had to struggle against the regalianism inherited from POMBAL and upheld at the University of Coimbra. Created cardinal (1801), Pacca became one of the most influential *zelanti*. He opposed the French CONCORDAT OF 1801 and remained in contact with the bishops of the Ancien Régime who refused submission to it. His nomination as prosecretary of state on June 18, 1808, after the occupation of Rome by Miollis and the expulsion of Cardinals Consalvi and Giulio Gabrielli by the French, indicated PIUS VII's will to resist. For impeding Pacca's arrest, the pope was also seized and carried off from Rome (July 1809). Pacca was imprisoned in the stronghold of San Carlo di Fenestrelle in Piedmont from July of 1809 until the CONCORDAT OF FONTAINEBLEAU (February 1813), after which he was permitted to rejoin Pius VII.

Contrary to what Pacca wrote in his memoirs (*Memorie storiche del Ministero*), neither he nor the cardinals around the Holy Father were responsible for the pope's decision to withdraw the concessions to Napoleon I in this so-called concordat, only the basis of a definite arrangement. On January 28 Pius VII made his own decision and annulled these agreements in a secret declaration. Pacca's role consisted in counseling the best procedure to minimize the consequences of the pope's act. For this, Pacca incurred Napoleon's wrath and was deported to Uzès in southern France. He reentered Rome with Pius VII on May 24, 1814. During the Hundred Days he fled with the pope to Genoa to escape Murat, who invaded the States of the Church (March 1815).

As prosecretary of state from May 19, 1814 to July 2, 1815, during the sojourn of the secretary of state CONSALVI at Paris and the Congress of Vienna, Pacca practiced a policy of restoring the old order, contrary to Consalvi's broader views. During the latter part of Pius VII's pontificate, Pacca allied with the *zelanti* and ceaselessly opposed the reforms judged necessary by the pope. At the conclave in 1823 Pacca actively participated in the reaction which resulted in Consalvi's disgrace. Pacca became bishop successively of Frascati (1818), Porto and Santa Rufina (1821), and Ostia and Velletri (1829). Under Leo XII, Pius VIII, and Gregory XVI he was prodatary and a member of important congregations in the Curia.

Pacca was a true churchman, solidly pious, courageous in upholding the Church's rights, cultured, a patron of artists, and promoter of the first archeological excavations at Ostia; but his outlook was that of the Ancien Régime and lacked open-mindness. He failed to understand Pius VII and Consalvi and passed severe judgments on them. His volumes of memoirs, published under various titles, are valuable historical sources, but they must be utilized with caution because later he substantially altered the section concerning Pius VII's captivity. To know his real sentiments it is necessary to refer to the original text.

Bibliography: G. BRIGANTE COLONIA, *Bartolomeo Pacca, 1756–1844* (Bologna 1931). A. DURANTE, *Tre papi e un cardinale* (Rome 1940). J. LEFLON and C. PERRAT, ''Les Suppressions et édulcorations qu'a fait subir à ses *Mémoires* le cardinal P,'' *Chiesa e stato nell'ottocento: Miscellanea in onore di P. Pirri*, ed. R. AUBERT et al., 2 v. (Padua 1962), 2:355–381. L. PASZTOR, ''Per la storia del *Concordato* di Fontainebleau,'' *ibid.* 597–606.

[J. LEFLON]

PACCANARISTS

Popular title of the Society of the Faith of Jesus, a religious institute that followed the rule of the JESUITS, dedicated itself to carry on their work, and above all sought the restoration of this order, suppressed in 1773. Its founder, Niccolò Paccanari (1773–?), was an enthusiastic and eloquent Italian, born at Valsugana near Trent; he was, however, deficient in formal education, humility, and prudence. Business and soldiery occupied him until a serious illness, (1795) followed by the influence of a pious Roman confraternity called the Oratory of Caravita and 14 months of prayerful retirement, led him to establish in Rome a religious congregation (Aug. 15, 1797). His four companions, one a former Jesuit priest, chose him superior, although he had only the tonsure. Members took the three vows of religion plus a fourth vow of special obedience to the pope, whose formulation proved a stumbling block to many former Jesuits. The garb was the one once worn by Italian Jesuits. Early in 1798 Pius VI approved the new institute, selected its name, permitted it to recite the Breviary with Jesuit supplements, and to admit former Jesuits.

With papal encouragement Paccanari arranged a union with the Society of the SACRED HEART OF JESUS (April 18, 1799), almost identical in rule and purpose with his own institute. Paccanari, not a priest until 1800, became superior of the merged groups that bore the title of his original foundation, although his had but 19 members, whereas the other had 50, far superior in caliber, education, influence, and material resources.

For a few years the society increased rapidly in numbers as it spread from Italy and Austria into Germany, Switzerland, France, Holland, and England. It gained a good reputation for varied pastoral and educational activities. When Pius VII confirmed the Jesuits in White Russia (1801) and in parts of Italy (1804) and allowed them to accept recruits from elsewhere, many Paccanarists joined them. Paccanari discontented his subjects by his worldly outlook, ambition to retain authority, and disinclination to restore the Society of Jesus or to affiliate with it. All the 70 or so members in France won the nuncio's approval to form an independent body. After a papal investigation, Paccanari received a ten-year prison sentence (August 1808). Released by the French (1809), he returned to prison for another offense (1810). No further reliable record of him exists. When the Jesuits were completely restored (1814), most of the few remaining Paccanarists joined them.

Bibliography: O. PFÜLF, *Die Anfänge der deutschen Provinz der neu erstandenen Gesellschaft Jesu* (Freiburg 1922). J. BURNICHON, *La Compagnie de Jésus en France, 1814–1914* (Paris 1914–) v.1. A. GUIDÉE, *Vie du R. P. Joseph Varin* (2d ed. Paris 1860). H. CHADWICK, "Paccanarists in England," *Archivum historicum Societatis Jesu* 20 (1951) 143–166. A. RAYEZ, "Clorivière et les Pères de la Foi," *ibid.* 21 (1952) 300–328. L. KOCH, *Jesuiten-Lexikon: Die Gesellschaft Jesu einst und jetzt* (Paderborn 1934) 1763–64. L. DERIÈS, *Les Congregations religieuses au temps de Napoléon* (Paris 1929).

[J. F. BRODERICK]

PACE, EDWARD ALOYSIUS

Educator, author; b. Starke, FL, July 3, 1861; d. Washington, D.C., April 26, 1938. As the son of George Edward and Margaret (Kelly) Pace, he was descended on his father's side from 17th-century English colonists in Virginia; his maternal grandfather was Owen Kelly, comptroller of ports of Halifax, Nova Scotia. He attended public school in Starke, and Duval High School, Jacksonville, before studying for the priesthood at St. Charles College, Ellicott City, MD (1876–80), and the North American College (with classes at the Propaganda University), Rome, where he was ordained on May 30, 1885.

After being awarded the S.T.D. degree in 1886, he returned to the Diocese of St. Augustine, FL, and served for two years as rector of the cathedral and chancellor. In 1888, following his selection for the faculty of the projected Catholic University of America, Washington, D.C., he returned to Europe for graduate studies in psychology. After a year at Louvain and Paris, he transferred to Leipzig, where he studied under Wilhelm Wundt, and received the Ph.D. magna cum laude in 1891. Thereafter he served at the Catholic University of America as professor of psychology (1891–94) and of philosophy (1894–1935), dean of the School of Philosophy (1895–99, 1906–14, 1934–35), general secretary (1917–25), vice rector (1925–36), and founder (1899) and first director of the Institute of Pedagogy, which developed into the department of education. In 1936 he was named vice rector emeritus and professor of philosophy emeritus. The psychological laboratory that he established in 1891 was the second in America and the first in a Catholic university. As an editor of the *Catholic Encyclopedia* (1907–14), Pace took a leading part in planning and bringing it to a successful conclusion. At the international Congress of Arts and Sciences held in St. Louis, MO, in 1904, Pace served as chairman of the section of experimental psychology. He became first editor of *Studies in Psychology and Psychiatry* (1926), and with Thomas Edward Shields he founded and edited the *Catholic Educational Review* (1911). He was founder and first president of the American Catholic Philosophical Association, which was established at the Catholic University of America in 1926, and with James Hugh RYAN he first edited its journal, *New Scholasticism*. In 1925 he was elected president of the American Council on Education and in 1929 was appointed by President Herbert Hoover to the National Advisory Committee on Education. He received the medal Pro Ecclesia et Pontifice (1914), was named a prothonotary apostolic (1920), and received various honorary degrees.

Pace's publications include his doctoral dissertation, *Das Relativitaets-prinzip in Herbert Spencer's psychologischer Entwicklungslehre;* many articles in philosophy, religion, and education; and *The Mass for Every Day in the Year* (1916), one of the first modern translations of the Missal, which he prepared with John J. Wynne, SJ. A pioneer in experimental psychology, Pace's teaching and writing were characterized by depth and originality of thought, careful reasoning, and clarity of expression. In 1919, the American bishops commissioned him to compose a national pastoral letter; his notable document analyzing issues then facing the Church and the nation was signed by Cardinal James Gibbons ''in his own name and in the name of the hierarchy.''

Bibliography: Pace Papers, Catholic University of America Archives, Washington, D.C. J. K. RYAN, ''In Memory of Edward Aloysius Pace,'' *New Scholasticism* 35 (1961) 141–151. H. MISIAK and V. M. STAUDT, *Catholics in Psychology: A Historical Survey* (New York 1954). C. A. HART, ed., *Aspects of the New Scholastic Philosophy* (New York 1932), festschrift.

[J. K. RYAN]

PACEM IN TERRIS

Eighth encyclical of JOHN XXIII, issued April 11, 1963. Although widely hailed as an encyclical on international peace, in the narrow sense, its scope covers the whole range of order in human affairs, for it identifies peace with that unity of order that is based on respect for the law of God. To this end it expounds, in a more comprehensive manner than any previous papal document, the order that should prevail between man and man, between man and the community, and between communities *inter se* and the world community.

Because of the immense scope of the encyclical, it is not surprising that different interests welcomed it for different reasons. In one respect it appealed to all, namely, in its sincere desire for brotherhood between men. Western newspapers welcomed the encyclical for its humanitarian vision and boundless confidence in man's capacity for peace. Soviet news agencies gave it the favor of relatively extensive summary. In certain respects its welcome was selective. Some socialist sources praised it vaguely for positions already advocated by socialists, particularly internationalism, while the Communist press headlined its plea for disarmament to the extent that

Autographed copy of ''Pacem in terris,'' signed by Pope John XXII, willed to John F. Kennedy, preserved in Kennedy Memorial Museum, Boston, Massachusetts.

Radio Vatican felt it necessary to issue a reminder that insistence on human freedom and dignity rather than advocacy of disarmament was at the core of the document.

The first part of *Pacem in terris* is built on the truth that order between individual men must be founded on the fact that man is a person. Such order consists essentially in respect for rights and duties that pertain to man entirely in virtue of his personality. The encyclical is a veritable charter of human rights, which it lists in specific detail, and is in a way reminiscent of the UN Universal Declaration of Human Rights.

In its second part the encyclical presents the relationship between the individual and the state as basically one of subjection to authority—not, however, as an authority rooted simply in physical force, but rather one representing the coercive power of a moral entity. For this reason the ordinances of human authority must be in accordance with the order of God's law. The encyclical launches into an important exposition of the philosophy of law that is diametrically opposed to all forms of legal positivism.

In its third part the encyclical argues that states, just as individuals, are the subjects of rights and duties. These rights and duties are translated into practical action by the persons who govern the state, for through these alone can the state be subjected to the moral law. Among the many things that this entails is a practical recognition of the equality of all states in dignity, whatever their racial backgrounds or their political or cultural stages of development. Recognition of solidarity implies in the concrete, not only that individual states should pursue their ends without hurting one another, but also that they should join forces whenever the efforts of an individual government cannot achieve its desired goals. The encyclical insists that trust rather than fear should be the vivifying factor in relationships between states. In place of the law of fear, which has prevailed for so long, the law of love should be substituted. Here there is a direct reference to war and peace, in the form of a plea that the arms race cease, that the stockpiles that exist be reduced equally and simultaneously by the countries concerned, and that nuclear weapons be banned and eventually a general disarmament reached.

The fourth part of the encyclical urges the importance of interdependence between states. Greater today than ever before, the collaboration that such interdependence stimulates puts an end to former ideas about absolute sovereignty and absolute national self-determination. The conclusion of the encyclical is devoted to pastoral exhortations. Catholics are urged to cooperate both individually and corporately with non-Catholics and even non-Christians for the advancement of praiseworthy social and political ends.

Bibliography: Official Latin text in *Acta Apostolicae Sedis* 55 (1963) 257–304. English translation in D. J. O'BRIEN and T.A. SHANNON, eds., *Catholic Social Thought: The Documentary Heritage* (Maryknoll, NY, 1992) 131–162. J. NEWMAN, *Principles of Peace: A Commentary on John XXIII's "Pacem in Terris"* (Oxford, 1964). D. J. O'BRIEN, "A Century of Catholic Social Teaching: Contexts and Comments," in J. A. COLEMAN, ed., *One Hundred Years of Catholic Social Thought* (Maryknoll, NY, 1991) 13–24.

[J. NEWMAN]

PACHER, MICHAEL

A leading late-Gothic painter and woodcarver in the Tyrol; b. near Brixen, *c.* 1435; d. Bruneck?, 1498. Pacher's workshop in Bruneck was on an important alpine road, and Pacher himself seems to have traveled to northern Italy, first as a young painter in the 1450s and again about 1475. His art shows a synthesis between the north Italian style of Mantegna's frescoes in the Eremitani church, Padua, and the widespread early Netherlandish style of Rogier van der Weyden. Pacher's most important work is the "St. Wolfgang Altarpiece" (1471–81, St. Wolfgang, Austria), which has a carved wooden shrine with life-size colored figures in a "Coro-

nation of the Virgin" and a predella forming the center for two pairs of double-tiered painted wings. The spiky, carved pinnacles of the frame contain painted and gilded wooden figures; the sharp, angular folds of their drapery can be paralleled in Pacher's paintings. Scenes from the life of Christ and of the Virgin are depicted with detailed realism in spatially roomy surroundings in which the "worm's-eye view" perspective has been derived from Mantegna. His "Altarpiece of the Four Latin Fathers" (*c.* 1483, Pinakothek, Munich) shows a further development. Instead of a series of independent pictures, there is a central perspective construction for the four panels, and the elaborately carved frame of the "St. Wolfgang Altarpiece" is here painted illusionistically. The monumental figures under ornate painted canopies carry on a lively dialogue with their foreshortened symbols.

Bibliography: E. HEMPEL, *Das Werk Michael Pachers* (4th ed. Vienna 1941).

[M. M. SCHAEFER]

PACHOMIUS, ST.

Founder of CENOBITISM, one of the greatest of the monastic fathers; b. Esneh, Egypt, *c.* 290; d. Egypt, 346. Pachomius founded nine monasteries for men and two for women in the THEBAÏD, of which he was a native, and gave them a written rule that is still extant. Born and raised a pagan, he met some Christians in his youth while serving in the army. Their charity so edified him that he became a Christian and, eventually, a solitary (*c.* 314) at Schenesit under the direction of the hermit St. Palaemon. About six years later he moved a short distance away to TABENNISI and there began to develop what later became the first *coenobium* or monastery of the full communal life. His contemporaries, as well as present-day scholars, viewed him as a man of vision and purpose who from the beginning of monasticism saw the need for a development that would provide against the spiritual and physical hazards of the solitary life, by centering the movement on the communal charity inherent in Christianity from its start. He began with a few monks, who promised to obey him and to share in common the fruits of the employment that they had secured for themselves.

As the number of his disciples increased, Pachomius gradually developed a concept of mortification based on total obedience to superiors and subordinate officers, under whom all work was organized, and complete common ownership of goods and the fruits of labor. By the time he died, his monasteries formed a great and closely knit congregation, in which thousands of monks were organized for work in many trades and for common morning and evening prayer and meals. Throughout his lifetime Pachomius presided as superior general. He established Pabou, his second foundation, as his motherhouse and held there at Easter and in August of each year a general gathering of his superiors. The style and contents of his rule indicate that it was composed over a long period of time and not dictated by an angel according to the legend recorded by PALLADIUS (*Historia Lausiaca* 32.1). Its achievement was to provide an adequate economic and spiritual basis for the common life, legislating with discretion for what was of common obligation and allowing freedom for greater austerity on the part of the individual monk.

Six biographies of Pachomius by contemporaries survive; and also several of his instructions to his monks and the instructions and letters of his two great successors, Horsiesi (d. 380) and Theodore (d. 368). The two ruled jointly after a schism threatened the congregation in 350. Their writings, especially Horsiesi's *De doctrina institutione monachorum*, reveal a deep understanding and development of the Pachomian ideal. Within Horsiesi's lifetime the influence of Pachomius's rule had extended beyond the Pachomian monasteries and affected the cenobitic foundations and Rule of BASIL of Caesarea.

In 404 JEROME responded to a request to provide a Latin translation of the rule for the Latins who were entering the Pachomian monasteries. This text is the only one that has survived; it was the means by which Pachomian influence advanced in the West. The *Regula Vigilii* (or *Regula Orientalis*) written in Gaul *c.* 420 depends much on Pachomius's rule, borrowing about a quarter of its text. The sixth- or seventh-century *Regula Tarnatensis* also shows significant dependence. The Rule of St. BENEDICT (*c.* 540), and the rules of CAESARIUS OF ARLES and of his successor Aurelian (written *c.* 512–550) show less but unmistakable dependence. BENEDICT OF ANIANE (d. 821) includes the Latin version of Pachomius's rule in his collection of rules and refers to it frequently in his *Concordia regularum*. Besides the direct influence of his rule, Pachomius's influence must be estimated to some extent in terms of the total influence of cenobitism as the prevailing form of monasticism in Christian civilization.

Feast: May 9 (Roman martyrology and Coptic Church).

Bibliography: H. QUECKE, ed., *Die Briefe Pachoms* (Regensburg 1975). J. QUASTEN, *Patrology*, 3 v. (Westminster, Md. 1950–) 3:154–160. *Vitae.* Gr. ed. F. HALKIN (*Subsidia Hagiographica* 19; Brussels 1932). Syriac. P. BEDJAN, ed., *Acta martyrum et sanctorum*, 7 v. (Paris 1890–97) 5:122–176. Arabic. E. AMÉLINEAU, ed., *Histoire de S. Pakhôme et de ses communautés* (Annales de Musée Guimet 17) 337–711. L. T. LEFORT, tr., *Les Vies coptes de S. Pachôme et de ses premiers successeurs* (Louvain 1943); ed. and tr., *Oeuvres de S. Pachôme et de ses disciples*, 2 v. (*Corpus scriptorum Christianorum orientalium* [Paris-Louvain 1903] 159–160, Scriptores Coptici 23–24; 1956). A. BOON and L. T. LEFORT, eds., *Pachomiana latina* (Louvain 1932). *The Life of Pachomius: vita prima Graeca*, tr. A. N. ATHANASSAKIS (Missoula, Mont. 1975) with Greek text. *The Life of Saint Pachomius and His Disciples*, tr. A. VEILLEUX (Kalamazoo, Mich. 1980). E. A. T. BUDGE, *Coptic Apocrypha in the Dialect of Upper Egypt* (London 1913) 352–382. P. LADEUZE, *Étude sur le cénobitisme pakhomien* (Louvain 1898). H. BACHT, "L'Importance de l'idéal monastique de S. P. pour l'histoire du monachisme chrétien," *Revue d'ascétique et de mystique* 26: (1950) 308–326; in *Antonius Magnus Eremita*, ed. B. STEIDLE (*Studia anselmiana* 38) 66–107. C. DE CLERCQ, *Mélanges L. Halphen* (Paris 1951) 169–176. A. J. FESTUGIÈRE, *Les moines d'Orient*, v. 4 (Paris 1964). *Pachomian koinonia*, tr. A. VEILLEUX, 3 v. (Kalamazoo, Mich. 1980-1982). P. ROUSSEAU, *Pachomius: The Making of a Community in Fourth-Century Egypt* (Berkeley 1985). A. DE VOGÜÉ, *De Saint Pachôme à Jean Cassien: études littéraires et doctrinales sur le monachisme égyptien à ses débuts* (Rome 1996).

[M. C. MCCARTHY]

PACHYMERES, GEORGE

Byzantine historian; b. Nicaea, 1242; d. Constantinople, *c.* 1310. In 1261 he moved to Constantinople, where he held high positions in both state and Church. He was well educated, and his interests and writings covered a wide range of topics; but his most important work is his Συγγραφικαὶ ἱστορίαι, a history of the reigns of the Emperors MICHAEL VIII PALAEOLOGUS and ANDRONICUS II PALAEOLOGUS (1261–1308). An eyewitness of many of the events he narrates, he is noted for his impartiality, even when writing of Michael's policy of ecclesiastical union with Rome, to which he was strongly opposed. He enters into detail on doctrinal matters, and his style is often difficult because of his fondness for archaisms. He also composed a short treatise on the Procession of the Holy Spirit, in which he accepted the Damascene formula, "through the Son," some works on ARISTOTLE, and several others on Dionysius the Areopagite (*see* PSEUDO-DIONYSIUS).

Bibliography: G. PACHYMERES, *De Michaele et Andronico Palaeologis libri XIII*, ed. I. BEKKER, 2 v. (Bonn 1835), repr. PG v.143–144; *Quadrivium*, ed. P. TANNERY, rev. E. STEPHANOU (St-Test 94; 1940). G. MORAVCSIK, *Byzantinoturcica*, 2 v. (2d ed. Berlin 1958) 1:280–282. V. LAURENT, *Dictionnaire de théologie catholique*, ed. A. VACANT et al. (Paris 1903–50) 11.2:1713–18. F. DÖLGER, *Lexikon für Theologie und Kirche*, ed. J. HOFER and K. RAHNER (Freiburg 1957–65) 7:1332. H. G. BECK, *Kirche und theologische Literatur im byzantinischen Reich* (Munich 1959) 679.

[G. T. DENNIS]

PACIAN OF BARCELONA, ST.

Bishop; b. Spain, *c.* 310; d. Barcelona, Spain, before 392. Though married, and the father of the praetorian prefect, Dexter, Pacian became bishop of Barcelona and was praised by JEROME for his learning, sanctity, and pastoral zeal (*De vir. illus.* 106). Of his writings, only three works are certainly authentic: *De Baptismo* or sermon to catechumens, which speaks of the spiritual renewal and purification effected by baptism and describes the effects of ORIGINAL SIN with a clarity that was rare before the time of AUGUSTINE; a *Contra Novatianos,* in three letters to Sympronian, a rigorist propagating the condemned doctrines of NOVATIAN; and a *Paraenesis sive exhortatorius libellus,* an earnest plea in favor of penance, and a stern reminder of the far more severe punishments awaiting those who die without having fulfilled the penances imposed on them. This work presents invaluable source material for the study of the penitential system then in vogue throughout Spain. Pacian's other writings have disappeared, and the treatises attributed to him by Dom G. MORIN are of doubtful authenticity.

Pacian's doctrine on penance elaborated the teaching of Scripture and tradition—particularly as set forth by TERTULLIAN and CYPRIAN—to assert that the Church has the power from God to forgive all sins committed after baptism. In his first letter to Sympronian occurs the famous phrase ''My name is Christian; but my surname, Catholic.'' By Catholic he meant the worldwide expansion of the Church, the unity of faith among all its members, and their submission to one supreme head.

Feast: March 9.

Bibliography: *Obras,* tr. and ed. L. RUBIO FERNÁNDEZ (Barcelona 1958). B. ALTANER, *Patrology,* tr. H. GRAEF from 5th German ed. (New York 1960) (Span. ed. 1949) appendix. É. AMANN, *Dictionnaire de théologie catholique,* ed. A. VACANT et al., 15 v. (Paris 1903–50; Tables générales 1951–) 11.2:1718–21. G. MORIN, ''Traité inédit de Pacien de Barcelone,'' *Revue Bénédictine* 29 (1912) 1–28; ''Un nouvel opuscule de Saint Pacien'' *ibid.,* 30 (1913) 286–293. *Revue d'histoire ecclésiastique* 38 (1942) 414–417.

[S. J. MCKENNA]

PACIFICO OF SAN SEVERINO, ST.

Franciscan administrator and mystic; b. San Severino in the Marches of Ancona, Italy, March 1, 1653; d. there, Sept. 24, 1721. A member of the distinguished family of the Divini, he was orphaned at an early age and brought up by an uncle who treated him very harshly. He entered the Observant Franciscans at Forano when he was 17 and was ordained to the priesthood in 1678. He taught philosophy for two years before beginning his preaching career. For eight years he worked with marked success among the poor inhabitants of the Apennine villages. When he was 35, he contracted an illness that left him deaf, blind, and crippled. These infirmities, which he bore with resignation for more than 30 years, did not prevent him from ably performing the duties of vicar and guardian at the Friary of Our Lady of Grace in San Severino where he resided continuously after 1705. He frequently experienced prolonged ecstasies while celebrating Mass, on several occasions displayed the gift of prophecy, and many times miraculously cured the sick. He was beatified by PIUS VI in 1786 and canonized by GREGORY XVI in 1839.

Feast: Sept. 24.

Bibliography: LÉON DE CLARY, *Lives of the Saints and Blessed of the Three Orders of St. Francis,* 4 v. (Taunton, Eng. 1885–87) 3:224–229. S. MELCHIORRI, *Vita di San Pacifico da San Severino* (Rome 1839), C. ORTOLANI, *San Pacificio da San Severino* (Rome 1929).

[C. J. LYNCH]

PACIFICUS OF NOVARA, BL.

Also known as Pacific of Cerano (Ceredano), Franciscan Observant preacher; b. Ceredano, province of Novara, Italy, *c.* 1420; d. Sassari, Sardinia, June 4, 1482. After the death of his parents, he was educated by BENEDICTINES in his native city. In 1445 he joined the FRANCISCAN Order. He was engaged in preaching popular missions in most of the provinces of Italy (1452–71). Appointed apostolic nuncio to Sardinia, he preached the crusade, announced by SIXTUS IV, against Muḥammad II (1480). Shortly after, at the instance of the general chapter of the Observants in Ferrara (1481), he conducted the visitation of the Sardinian friars. In 1473 he prepared a *Somma morale,* a casuistic manual for confessors, known also as the *Somma Pacifica;* it was printed in Milan in 1479 and frequently thereafter. His cult was confirmed in 1745.

Feast: June 9; June 8 (Franciscans).

Bibliography: *Acta Sanctorum* June 1:406–407. L. WADDING, *Scriptores Ordinis Minorum* (3d ed. Quaracchi-Florence 1931–) 14:190, 306, 375–376. M. CAZZOLA, *Il b. Pacifico Ramati* (Novara 1882). J. H. SBARALEA, *Supplementum et castigatio ad scriptores trium ordinum S. Francisci a Waddingo,* 2 v. (Rome 1806; new ed. in 4 v. 1906–36) 2:302. A. BUTLER, *The Lives of the Saints,* ed. H. THURSTON and D. ATTWATER, 4 v. (New York 1956) 2:506. E. GRAU, *Lexikon für Theologie und Kirche,* ed. J. HOFER and K. RAHNER, 10 v. (2d, new ed. Freiburg 1957–65) 7:1333. A. L. STOPPA, *Il beato fra Pacifico da Cerano* (Cerano 1974).

[O. J. BLUM]

PACIFISM

This term admits of no single definition. It can denote a political movement that seeks to eliminate war by inducing all nations to settle their disputes peacefully, but more commonly nowadays it denotes an ideology based on a personal conviction that war is morally unjustifiable. Absolute or doctrinal pacifism condemns all war as immoral; relative or practical pacifism limits its objection to particular wars or forms of war.

Pre-Christian Attitude. The ancient pagan world seems to have regarded war as a natural phenomenon or necessary evil entailed by the struggle for existence, and military service as a duty of citizenship or a burden owed to the sovereign that might bring gain or glory. Buddhism was exceptional among pagan religions in preaching a creed of nonviolence. The historical books of the OT echo with the clash of battles fought in the conquest or defense of the Promised Land, always with the conviction that they were a sacred duty willed by the God of Israel, Lord of Hosts. Jeremiah (27–29) might condemn particular wars, and Isaiah (11.1–9) foretell the reign of the Prince of Peace, but none of the prophets condemned all war as such. The ESSENES, an ascetical Jewish sect dating probably from the 2d century B.C., are said to have repudiated violence, but they were unrepresentative of Israel and are not mentioned in the Bible.

New Testament. The NT message is fundamentally one of peace among men of good will (Lk 2.14), based on brotherhood in Christ and sonship of His Father. Christ indeed warned His disciples that His Gospel would set men at variance: ''I have come to bring a sword, not peace'' (Mt 10.34); but He Himself blessed the peacemakers, rejected the *lex talionis* of an eye for an eye, and urged His followers not to resist evildoers, but to turn the other cheek, love their enemies, do good to them that hated them, and pray for them that persecuted and calumniated them (Mt 5.9, 38–39, 44).

That He did not condemn all use of physical force is clear from His use of a whip in driving the merchants from the Temple (Jn 2.14–16). Nor, to judge from his warm commendation of the faith of the centurion (Lk 3.14), did He regard the military profession as an impediment to discipleship. Nevertheless, though He had warned His disciples that they would need swords (Lk 22.36), He would not let them be used to save Him from arrest, and He ordered Peter to sheath the sword with which he had struck the High Priest's servant, ''for all those who take the sword will perish by the sword'' (Mt 26.52).

The subsequent attitude of the Apostles to the use of force was similarly qualified. St. Paul wrote: ''If it be possible, as far as in you lies, be at peace with all men'' (Rom 12.18); yet he acknowledged the right and duty of rulers to wield the sword, as God's ministers, in defense of the public good (Rom 13.4). So too St. Peter preached

LE PRÉSIDENT DU REICH ALLEMAND, LE PRÉSIDENT DES ÉTATS-UNIS D'AMÉRIQUE, SA MAJESTÉ LE ROI DES BELGES, LE PRÉSIDENT DE LA RÉPUBLIQUE FRANÇAISE, SA MAJESTÉ LE ROI DE GRANDE-BRETAGNE, D'IRLANDE ET DES TERRI-TOIRES BRITANNIQUES AU DELÀ DES MERS, EMPEREUR DES INDES, SA MAJESTÉ LE ROI D'ITALIE, SA MAJESTÉ L'EMPEREUR DU JAPON, LE PRÉSIDENT DE LA RÉPUBLIQUE DE POLOGNE, LE PRÉSIDENT DE LA RÉPUBLIQUE TCHÉCOSLOVAQUE,

Ayant le sentiment profond du devoir solennel qui leur incombe de développer le bien-être de l'humanité;

Persuadés que le moment est venu de procéder à une franche renonciation à la guerre comme instrument de politique nationale afin que les relations pacifiques et amicales existant actuellement entre leurs peuples puissent être perpétuées;

Convaincus que tous changements dans leurs relations mutuelles ne doivent être recherchés que par des procédés pacifiques et être réalisés dans l'ordre et dans la paix, et que toute Puissance signataire qui chercherait désormais à développer ses intérêts nationaux en recourant à la guerre devra être privée du bénéfice du présent Traité;

Espérant que, encouragées par leur exemple, toutes les autres nations du monde se joindront à ces efforts humanitaires et, en adhérant au présent Traité dès qu'il entrera en vigueur, mettront leurs peuples à même de profiter de ses bienfaisantes stipulations, unissant ainsi les nations civilisées du monde dans

The Kellogg-Briand Pact was an agreement originally signed in 1928 by 15 nations whose leaders renounced war as an instrument of national policy. (CORBIS)

peace (1 Pt 3.8–11), but he baptized the centurion Cornelius without apparently requiring him to seek another profession (Acts 10.47).

Early Christian Position. For the first three centuries of the Christian era, the general exclusion of Christians from public life removed the moral problem of war from the area of their immediate responsibility and concern. Only in regard to service in the imperial forces did a practical case of conscience arise. Many converts continued in fact to serve, and those who left the army seem to have done so in order to avoid being involved in idolatrous practices, or to devote themselves more directly to the service of God, rather than from any conscientious objection to war as such. The problem was never officially solved. Some, like St. Hippolytus (*c.* 170-*c.* 236), condemned voluntary military service by Christians (F. Funk, *Didascalia et Constitutiones Apostolorum,* Paderborn 1905, 2:97); and, a century later, after the Emperor Licinius had imposed idolatry on all his forces, canon 12 of the First Council of Nicea (325) enacted a severe penalty against Christians who reenlisted in the imperial army; but only Tertullian, writing as a Montanist *c.* 202 A.D. (*De Idololatria,* 19), and Lactantius (*Divinae Institutiones* 6.20) condemned military service outright. None

Quakers read a list of names of those who have died in Vietnam as a protest against America's involvement in the war. (©Hulton-Deutsch Collection/CORBIS)

of the accepted Fathers of the Church ever adopted this extreme position; and although the episcopate generally discouraged the military career while it involved religious and moral dangers, it ceased to do so after the conversion of Constantine, when these religious and moral dangers were largely removed.

Post-Constantine Tradition. What eventually became the accepted Christian attitude toward war was first established by St. Augustine. His doctrine, as contained in *Civ.* (19.7, 12, 13, 15), can be summarized as follows: peace is a supreme social good, indispensable to the proper development of man and human institutions; true peace consists, however, not in the mere absence of war, but in the tranquillity of order. It presupposes a just, equitable, and harmonious order of things like and unlike that secures to everyone and everything its due place. War cannot be justified except as a necessary means to the establishment or restoration of this order and of the peace that is its fruit; but it can so be justified because just men may be forced into war by the injustice of others. Nevertheless, war is so monstrous a means to just order that no public authority has the right to undertake it, even for a just cause, unless all peaceful means to an equitable settlement have first been tried in vain.

The conclusion that war can be justified was accepted by subsequent Christian writers of the early Middle Ages, notably by St. Isidore of Seville (*Etymologiae,* 18.1; *Patrologia Latina,* 82:639) and by Gratian (*Decretum,* 23, 1–3); St. Thomas Aquinas was himself content

merely to enumerate and to analyse the necessary, conditions, viz, legitimate authority, just cause, and right intention (*Summa Theologiae* 2a2ae, 40.1). The outstanding Catholic authorities of later days, Francisco de Vitoria, OP (*c.* 1485–1546), Francisco de Suárez, SJ (1548–1617), and Louis Taparelli d'Azeglio (1793–1862), underlined or developed certain aspects of this traditional doctrine, but kept its substance intact. Vitoria, by arguing that the right of princes to make war on unjust aggressors was necessary to world order (*Relectiones Theologicae* 6; *De Iure Belli* 19; Lyons 1587, 234), implicitly made the exercise of the right dependent on the interests of world order. Taparelli enlarged on this point and drew the conclusion that the right of war of individual states would cease if and when an international society capable of imposing justice came into being (*Saggio Teoretico di Diritto Naturale,* Prato 1883, 2:198). Suárez rejected the notion that princes have the right to punish injustice anywhere in the universe (*De Charitate* 13.4.3; *Opera Omnia* 12, Paris 1858, 744).

Pacifist Sects. Denial of the right of war was limited in effect to a few heretical sects of relatively later date and minor influence. The WALDENSES, who originated in the 12th century, initially condemned all war or taking of human life, but eventually fought in their own self-defense. Certain groups of the 16th-century ANABAPTIST sect, notably the Swiss Brethren and the MENNONITES, likewise advocated pacifism and nonresistance. John Smyth, from whom the English Baptists derive, came under Mennonite influence, but not a few of his religious descendants fought in Cromwell's army. More consistent in their religious opposition to war and military service were and are the Quakers, founded by George Fox in 1668 and established in Pennsylvania by William Penn in 1682. Most of these sects, like the later PLYMOUTH BRETHREN and CHRISTADELPHIANS, were inspired primarily by the desire to return to what they believed to have been the primitive and true form of Christianity, or else to withdraw from a world which they believed to be irretrievably bad; pacifism was a consequence of their religious creed rather than one of its basic tenets.

Modern Developments. Modern pacifism is less closely associated with religious belief. Its adherents are to be found in all the major religious denominations and may belong to none. Some, like Tolstoy (1820–1910), base their philosophy of absolute pacifism on the Sermon on the Mount but without necessarily accepting the divinity of Christ. Others have been inspired by the success of Gandhi's policy of nonviolent resistance in India. With others, pacifism is a matter merely of personal conviction, either in regard to the will of God or in regard to the futility of war as a means to justice. Others see it as a practical policy, either in the form of nonviolence, which will convert aggressors by benevolence, or in the form of passive resistance, which will finally break their will. Others still are pacifist only in the sense that they work unceasingly for an international order in which war will be replaced by arbitration, judicial decision, or, failing these, by international police action. Fruits of their activity may be seen in the international peace congresses that led up to the Hague Convention (1899), the Hague Court (1907), or even the Kellogg Pact (1928), by which the signatory nations formally renounced war as a means of settling international differences.

Since the Second World War, Catholic reflection on pacifism, absolute and relative, has developed in three stages. First, with the advent of the threat of nuclear war, many Catholics adopted a position of relative pacifism. They admitted that a war of national defense against unjust aggression could be justified if the traditionally required conditions were fulfilled, but denied that these could in fact be fulfilled in the modern world, because war had become so violent and indiscriminate that its evil consequences, moral and physical, were bound to outweigh the intended good. Cardinal Ottaviani came close to accepting this position, when he insisted that not even a defensive war may be waged unless the responsible authority is *sure* of victory and even more sure that the good accruing to the nation outweighs the monstrous evils that will result for itself and the world (*Institutiones Iuris Publici Ecclesiastici,* Rome 1947, 1.86). Vatican II did not go so far as this, but simply condemned the idea that an act of war, nuclear or not, directed to "the indiscriminate destruction of whole cities or vast areas with their inhabitants" could be acceptable (*Gaudium et spes* 80). With the decrease in likelihood of nuclear war and the rise of terrorism at the beginning of the third millennium, Catholic thinking about war came to be less dominated by the prospect of "total war."

Second, the council extended its recognition of pacifism as a legitimate public stance in saying that "it seems just that laws should make humane provision for the case of conscientious objectors who refuse to carry arms, provided they accept some other form of community service" (*GS* 79; also *Catechism of the Catholic Church* 2311).

Third, nonviolence has increasingly been promoted not as a simple negative (the absence of violence) but as a positive, practical program that can address some of the causes of war. At the time of Vatican II a number of Catholics, encouraged by John XXIII's encyclical *PACEM IN TERRIS*, saw this hope embodied in calls for the development of international structures of cooperation and development: the community of nations organizing itself to address global needs, rather than individual nations pursuing a narrow conception of their own concerns. More generally, the teachers of the Church have highlighted the connection between peace and social justice. In a message, "To Reach Peace, Teach Peace," issued on the World Day of Peace in 1979, Pope John Paul II outlined seven principles which are fundamental to world peace: human affairs must be dealt with humanely, not with violence; tensions, rivalries and conflicts must be settled by reasonable negotiations; opposing ideologies must confront each other in a climate of dialogue and free discussion; the legitimate interests of particular groups must also take into account the legitimate interest of the other groups involved and of the demands of the higher common good; recourse to arms cannot be considered the right means for settling conflicts; the inalienable human rights must be safeguarded in every circumstance; it is not permissible to kill in order to impose a solution. The pope's statement reflects a deepened appreciation for the practice of nonviolence both as a method of achieving justice and as a spiritual practice. Vatican II had both recognized and praised those "who renounce the use of violence in the vindication of their rights and who resort to methods of defense which are otherwise available to weaker parties too, provided that this can be done without injury to the rights and duties of others of the community itself" (*GS* 33). Such statements are not an endorsement of absolute pacifism; however, they call for the development of a form of pacifism that matches the just-war theorist's concern for the need to protect those threatened by an aggressor.

Moral Appraisal. Despite the legitimacy that has been accorded to pacifism in recent decades, absolute pacifism is still judged irreconcilable with Catholic doctrine. Catholic exegetes likewise commonly reject the pacifist interpretation of Christ's teaching. His pronouncement on nonresistance to evil is taken as a counsel rather than as a precept, and for private individuals rather than for public authorities, since these latter would fail in an essential duty were they to offer no forceful resistance to violent aggressors from within or without. His warning to those who "take the sword" is commonly understood, as by St. Augustine (*Contra Faustum* 22.70), to refer to those who usurp the function of rulers, for rulers alone bear the sword as God's ministers (Rom 13.14). Nor is there any intrinsic contradiction between a just war and Christ's command that we love our enemies. A just war expresses hatred of the evil deed rather than of the evildoer.

On the other hand, the chief contention of relative pacifism is deduced from accepted Catholic principles. It is the logic of the conclusion that is disputed. No one can deny that the fulfillment of one of the essential conditions of just war (that the intended good shall outweigh the evil entailed) becomes less likely with every increase in the violence and indiscriminate destruction of modern war. Indeed, it is almost impossible to conceive of any merely temporal good that could outweigh the evil consequences of a total nuclear war; and though experience since 1945 has shown that not every modern war need be either total or nuclear, such a conflict remains a serious possibility. It was this consideration that led Pius XII to declare that nothing less than the absolute necessity of self-defense against an unjust aggression threatening the very life or integrity of a state or the essential and inalienable rights of its members can nowadays provide a just cause for war (address, Sept. 30, 1954, *Acta Apostolicae Sedis* 46:589). But Pius XII was equally insistent that ''the right to stand on the defensive cannot be denied to any State even today'' (address Oct. 3, 1953, *Acta Apostolicae Sedis* 45:733) and that a situation can arise in which it can legitimately be exercised even against nuclear attack (Christmas message 1956, *Acta Apostolicae Sedis* 49:19). The immense evils liable to result from it are not demonstrably greater than those that would afflict mankind if force could no longer be used to repel the armed aggression of tyranny.

Whether the repeated calls of Pope John Paul II, the writings of the U.S. bishops (esp. *The Challenge of Peace*) and the efforts of peace-groups from all traditions can transcend the impasse of the endless argument between pacifists and just-war advocates, between the concerns of justice and those of peace, remains to be seen. A justice-seeking form of nonviolence is less easily accused of naivete toward the reality of sin in this ''in between'' time of history straining toward the eschaton. The development of such a form of pacifism remains partial at best. And absent an effective proposal for protecting the COMMON GOOD in a nonviolent way, a nation's recourse to military action against an aggressor must be recognized as legitimate, if the criteria of a just war are met.

See Also: WAR, MORALITY OF; CONSCIENTIOUS OBJECTION; EPIKEIA.

Bibliography: In addition to the works already cited, R. COSTE, *Le problème du droit de guerre dans la pensée de Pie XII* (Paris 1962). M. F. SCHELER, *L'Idée de paix et le pacifisme* (Paris 1953). J. NEWMAN, *Studies in Political Morality* (Chicago 1963) 69–118. W. J. NAGLE, ed., *Morality and Modern Warfare* (Baltimore 1960) contains an article by a practical pacifist, G. C. ZAHN, and an excellent bibliography by W. J. BROWN. C. J. CADOUX, *The Early Christian Attitude to War* (London 1940) non-Catholic pacifist. J. LEWIS, *The Case Against Pacifism* (London 1940). E. A. RYAN, ''Rejection of Military Service by the Early Christians,'' *Theological Studies* 13 (1952) 1–32. J. CHILDRESS, ''Moral Discourse About War in the Early Church,'' *Journal of Religious Ethics* 12:1 (1984). J. DWYER, ed., *The Catholic Bishops and Nuclear War* (Wash. D.C. 1984). S. HAUERWAS, *The Peaceable Kingdom* (Notre Dame, Ind. 1983). R HEYER, *Nuclear Disarmament: Key Statements of Popes,*

Luca Pacioli with mathematical instruments, painting by Jaco Bar, late 15th century. (Archivo Iconografico, S.A./CORBIS)

Bishops, Councils and Churches (Mahwah, N.J). NCCB, *The Challenge of Peace: God's Promise and Our Response* (Wash. D.C. 1983). G. SHARP, *The Politics of Nonviolent Action* (Boston, Mass. 1973). G. A. VANDERHAAR, *Christians and Nonviolence in the Nuclear Age* (Mystic, Conn. 1982). J. H. YODER, *Nevertheless: The Varieties and Shortcomings of Religious Pacifism* (Scottsdale, Pa. 1976).

[L. L. MCREAVY/F. X. MEEHAN/EDS.]

PACIOLI, LUCA

Mathematician, Franciscan friar, the great teacher of mathematics in the courts and universities of Renaissance Italy; b. Borgo San Sepolcro, Tuscany, 1445; d. after 1514. His education was provided by the Franciscan Friars, and his writings show that his life was shaped by the reading of his early years. The force and influence of the Humanistic movement also are apparent in his works, into which he introduced theological moralizing, literary reminiscences, scholarly anecdotes, and practical hints. He brought the mathematics of the universities into close relation with that of artists and architects. Pacioli's great contribution to civilization consisted in unearthing old material on mathematics and systematizing and formulating it with reference to the discovery of general truths and the operation of general laws.

The *Summa de arithmetica, geometrica, proportioni et proportionalita* (Venice 1494) is the first known published book of Pacioli. The *Summa* was influenced in a great measure by the *Liber Abaci* of Leonard of Pisa (1202) and is an extension of the works of JORDANUS DE NEMORE (1236) and JOHN DE SACROBOSCO (1256). The *Divina Proportione* (Venice 1509) was written in collaboration with Leonardo da Vinci, and is of interest to both artists and mathematicians.

Bibliography: L. PACIOLI, *Divine Proportion* (Norwalk, CT 2001). R. E. TAYLOR, *No Royal Road: Luca Pacioli and His Times* (North Stratford, NH 1981). T. A. LEE, A. BISHOP, and R. H. PARKER, eds., *Accounting History from the Renaissance to the Present: A Remembrance of Luca Pacioli* (New York 1996).

[M. C. ZELLER]

PADEREWSKI, IGNACY JAN

Foremost pianist of his time, composer, premier of Poland (1919–20), signer of the Versailles Treaty (1919); b. Kurylówka, Poland, Nov. 6, 1860; d. New York City, June 29, 1941. Both his parents, Jan Paderewski, estate administrator, and Polixena (Nowicka) Paderewska, had musical backgrounds. His first wife, Antonia Korsak, died in childbirth, leaving him with an invalid son, Alfred. He married Mme. Helena de Rosen Gorska in 1899. He studied piano and composition privately, at the Warsaw Conservatory (1872–78), and in Berlin, and piano with Leschetizky in Vienna. His pianistic debuts were in Vienna (1887) and in the U.S. (1891) at Carnegie Hall with the New York Symphony Orchestra under Walter Damrosch. He was noted for his performance of music by his compatriot Chopin, whose works he was editing before his death. His compositions include two operas, a symphony, a cantata, three works for solo instrument and orchestra, a violin and piano sonata, 22 songs, and more than 54 piano pieces.

Paderewski donated generously to Polish relief during World War I, and was an architect of Poland's independence at the war's end. After its reenslavement by Hitler he vowed never to return until Poland was again free. In life he was honored by many nations and universities; at his death his body lay in state in St. Patrick's Cathedral, New York, and was interred in Arlington National Cemetery, a temporary haven granted by President Roosevelt. A bronze marker was placed at the site in 1963 at the instance of President Kennedy.

Bibliography: R. LANDAU, *Ignace Paderewski: Musician and Statesman* (New York 1934). A. STRAKACZ, *Paderewski As I Knew Him*, tr. H. CHYBOWSKA (New Brunswick, N.J. 1949). C. R. HALSKI, *Grove Dictionary of Music and Musicians*, ed. E. BLOM, 9 v. (5th ed. London 1954) 6:482–484. J. W. HOSKINS, *Ignacy Jan Paderewski, 1860–1941: A Biographical Sketch and a Selective List of Reading Materials* (Washington D.C. 1984). J. JASIENSKI, ed., *Ignacy Jan Paderewski: antologia* (Poznan 1996). E. SLIVINSKI LISANDRELLI, *Ignacy Jan Paderewski: Polish Pianist and Patriot* (Greensboro 1999). M. PERKOWSKA, "Ignacy Jan Paderewski" in *The New Grove Dictionary of Music and Musicians, vol. 14*, ed. S. SADIE, (New York 1980) 73–75. D. M. RANDEL, ed., *The Harvard Biographical Dictionary of Music* (Cambridge 1996) 660–661. N. SLONIMSKY, ed., *Baker's Biographical Dictionary of Musicians, Eighth Edition* (New York 1992) 1352–1353.

[H. E. MEYERS]

Ignacy Jan Paderewski.

PADILLA, DIEGO FRANCISCO

Colombian priest, patriot, and pamphleteer; b. Bogotá, Colombia, *c.* 1754; d. Bojacá, Colombia, April 9, 1829. His parents were Alejo Padilla and Juana Francisca Rico. Diego, who joined the AUGUSTINIANS about 1770, had two brothers in the same order, in addition to four other brothers and three sisters who entered the religious life. Of the ten, Diego was the most gifted; he gained a reputation for erudition, eloquence, and literary skill. A contemporary reported that by 1809 Padilla had published 49 pamphlets (the majority of them anonymous) in defense of religion and of the movement for independence in New Granada. In 1810 he was one of the leading spokesmen for independence and he became a member of the first junta of the revolutionary government. With Manuel Bernardo Álvarez he published a weekly political journal, *El aviso al público,* that lasted for five months beginning on Sept. 19, 1810. He also founded a similar publication called *El sabatino.* In 1816, convicted of revolutionary activity by the Spanish authorities, Padilla was sent into exile in Spain. Pardoned on Jan.15, 1820, he was released from prison and, some months later, at his request, granted permission to return to Colombia. His remaining years were spent in Bojacá where he had previously served as pastor.

Bibliography: M. G. ROMERO, "Participación del clero en la lucha por la independencia," *Boletín de historia y antigüedades* 49 (1962) 325–344. L. MONROY, "Los Agustinos en el pueblo de Bojacá, Colombia," *Archivo agustiniano* 56 (1962) 348–397.

[A. J. ENNIS]

PADILLA, JUAN DE

Martyr, missionary; b. Andalusia, Spain, *c.* 1500; d. *c.* 1542. He arrived in Mexico in 1528. Little is known of his background, but he had reportedly been a soldier in his youth and had joined the Order of Friars Minor in Spain. He accompanied the expedition of Nuño de Guzmán to New Galicia in 1529 and 1530. He went to Tehuantepec in 1533 to join an expedition that Hernando Cortez planned to send to the Orient. When the expedition did not materialize, he served in the Indian missions of Poncitlan and Tuchpán and founded the Franciscan friaries of Zapotlan and Tamazula. He also was superior at Tulantzingo. In 1540 Padilla joined Francisco Vázquez de Coronado's expedition to New Mexico. On the way north he was in the vanguard of the expedition with the exploratory groups. He went with Capt. Pedro de Tovar to the Hopi pueblos in July and August 1540; with Capt. Pedro de Alvarado across western New Mexico to the Rio Grande pueblos in August and September 1540; with Don Lope de Urrea to Pecos in the summer of 1541; and with Coronado's select team in the final dash to Quivira. When Coronado returned to Mexico in 1542, Padilla stayed behind to work among the Indians. In the spring of 1542 he set out for Quivira, accompanied by two Indian assistants, a Portuguese named Andrés do Campo, a few personal servants, and some Wichita braves from Quivira. He was well received among the Quivirans, but during a visit to another tribe he was attacked and killed by strange Indians. Do Campo and the two Indian assistants escaped and, after several years of wandering, reached Mexico to tell their story. The first priest to be martyred on what became U.S. soil, Padilla is commemorated on November 30.

[F. WARREN]

PADILLA Y ESTRADA, IGNACIO DE

Augustinian bishop; b. Mexico City, 1695; d. Mérida, Yucatán, July 20, 1760. His family held high social position; his grandparents were the Oidor Juan de Padilla Guardiola y Guzmán and Jerónima Cisneros; his parents, Juan Ildefonso Padilla Cisneros and Micaela Gregoria Estrada. Apparently he used various combinations of these names during his lifetime. After joining the Augustinians, he dedicated his life to study and preparation for an ascetic life. He received the doctorate in theology at the University of Mexico, then taught philosophy and theology at the Colegio of San Pablo, where he soon became rector. He held a number of offices: secretary of the province, visitor of the convents of Guadalajara and Havana, and prior of the convent in Mexico City. He was sent to Rome as a representative of the province, and was in Spain in 1743 on his way back to America when he was nominated archbishop of Santo Domingo. After consecration in Madrid, he arrived in Santo Domingo in 1745, where he undertook the reformation of the clergy and the rebuilding of churches, restoring the cathedral and opposing the destruction of the Jesuit college. He refused the bishopric of Guatemala in 1751 and that of Popayán in 1752, but finally accepted that of Mérida, Yucatán, in 1753. There he reformed the seminary, providing it with a new constitution and with an enlarged building; he endowed three chairs and brought in professors from Mexico to fill them. At his own expense he set up ten scholarships in the seminary for children of the poor and of the indigenous people. He stressed the welfare of the indigenous people in many ways and supported, with his interest and his money, hospitals for them.

[E. RODRÍGUEZ-DEMORIZI]

PADRE PIO (FRANCESCO FORGIONE), ST.

Capuchin-Franciscan priest, stigmatic; b. Pietrelcina, Italy, May 25, 1887; d. San Giovanni Rotondo, Italy, Sept. 23, 1968.

From early childhood he exhibited a spiritual sensitivity bordering on mysticism. Later, he confided to his spiritual director that at the age of five he thought of consecrating himself to God forever, a desire that he felt materialized when he entered the Capuchin-Franciscan Order. In his formative years as a Capuchin, physical ill-health and encounters with the devil plagued the quiet, gentle, and reserved friar.

After his ordination to the priesthood in 1910, his life was relatively uneventful, except for a brief stint—six weeks—in the medical corps of the Italian Army during World War I. He received a medical discharge after mistakenly being considered a deserter.

In 1918, he was officially assigned to the friary at San Giovanni Rotondo and in September of that year he was first gifted with the visible phenomenon of the stigmata. When the Vatican and the Capuchin Order intervened to ascertain the facts concerning the stigmata, Padre Pio had to face suspicion, embarrassment, and disciplinary action in addition to his crosses of ill-health and demonic affliction. Considerable controversy arose among doctors and the clergy over the natural and supernatural aspects of his stigmata.

The Vatican began its investigation by forbidding Padre Pio to say Mass publicly. This action by the Holy See combined with rumors that Padre Pio would be transferred from San Giovanni Rotondo stirred violent riots by the townspeople resulting in 14 deaths and 80 injuries. As a result, in 1920 Church authorities imposed restrictions that were to last 13 years on his public activities. Through it all Padre Pio remained obedient and compliant. Finally in 1933, Pius XI lifted the ban telling the friar's archbishop: "I have not been badly disposed toward Padre Pio, but I have been badly informed about Padre Pio."

For 50 years Padre Pio never left San Giovanni Rotondo; yet his influence was felt everywhere as the world flocked to him for spiritual favors. Aside from saying Mass, preaching, hearing confessions, and being a victim of Christ's suffering, he did nothing extraordinary except for the creation of one mighty monument: Padre Pio's hospital, *Casa Sollievo della Sofferenza*, which was the result of his zeal and inspiration. After his death in 1968, the impact of his life, sanctity, and spirituality remained a powerful influence on the faithful and on the Church.

On the occasion of the centenary of Padre Pio's birth (1987), Pope John Paul II visited the tomb of the Capuchin stigmatic and paid him this tribute: ". . . as a religious he generously lived out the ideal of the Capuchin friars, just as he lived out the ideal of the priest. . . . Were not the altar and the confessional the two poles of his life? This priestly witness contains a message as valid as it is timely."

Padre Pio was beatified by Pope John Paul II on May 2, 1999, and canonized on June 16, 2002. His legacy includes nearly 3,000 prayer groups comprised of about 500,000 members.

Feast: May 25.

Bibliography: PADRE PIO DA PIETRELCINA, *Epistolario-Corrispondeza con le Figlie Spirituali (1915–1922)* (San Giovanni Rotondo 1977); *Epistolario-Corrispondenza con i Direttori Spirituali (1910–1922)* (San Giovanni Rotondo 1971); *Vita di Padre Pio attraverso le lettere*, ed. A. MOTTA (Milan 1995). P. TREECE, *Meet Padre Pio* (Ann Arbor, Mich. 2001). G. PREZIUSO, *The Life of Padre Pio*, tr. and ed. J. AUMANN (New York 2000). F. CONTESSA, *Padre Pio: Venerable—December 18, 1997, Blessed—May 2, 1999, Saint* (New York 1999). FRANCISCAN FRIARS OF THE IMMACULATE, *Padre Pio: The Wonder Worker* (New Bedford, Mass. 1999). E. MALATESTA, *La vera storia di Padre Pio: l'unica biografia completa con i documenti segreti esclusi nel processo di beatificazione* (Casale Monferrato 1999); *I miracoli che hanno fatto santo Padre Pio*, with A. AMATI (Casale Monferrato 1998). S. M. MANELLI, *Padre Pio of Pietrelcina* (New Bedford, Mass. 1999). A. PRONZATO, *Padre Pio da Pietrelcina: mistero glorioso* (Milan 1999). R. ALLEGRI, *Padre Pio: un santo tra noi* (Milan 1998); *Il catechismo di Padre Pio* (Milan 1996); *A tu per tu con Padre Pio* (Milan 1995), Eng. tr. *Padre Pio: A Man of Hope* (Ann Arbor, Mich. 2000); *I miracoli di padre Pio* (Milan 1993). G. SCARALE, *Padre Pio nel cuore* (Milan 1998). D. M. GAUDIOSE, *Mary's House: Mary Pyle, Under the Spiritual Guidance of Padre Pio* (New York 1993); *Prophet of the People* (New York 1974). J. A. SCHUG, *A Padre Pio Profile* (Petersham, Mass. 1987); *Padre Pio* (Huntington, Ind. 1976). C. RUFFIN, *Padre Pio: The True Story* (Huntington, Ind. 1982). J. MCCAFFERY, *The Friar of San Giovanni* (London 1978; Garden City, N.Y. 1981); *Tales of Padre Pio* (Kansas City 1979). G. PAGNOSSIN, *Il Calvario di Padre Pio*, 2 v. (Padova 1978). G.

Padre Pio celebrating Mass, San Giovanni Rotondo, Italy, 1964. (AFP/CORBIS)

A statuette of a woman used in pagan ceremonies. (©Phil Schermeister/CORBIS)

FESTA, *Misteri di Scienza e Luci di Fede, le Stigmate Padre Pio da Pietrelcina* (Rome 1938).

[S. F. MIKLAS]

PAGAN

A term now used in a religious sense to designate a person who is not a Christian, Jew, or Muslim. How the Latin word *paganus*, from which it comes, acquired the meaning of non-Christian is still not entirely settled. In profane Latin of the 1st century A.D., *paganus* was used in two senses: first, in the meaning of "rural" to describe the inhabitant of a *pagus*, or country district; second, in the sense of "civil" or "civilian," in contrast to the "military." It was long assumed that the Christians eventually adopted the term *paganus* to designate a non-Christian, either because the inhabitants of country districts resisted conversion to Christianity or because the Christian was a *miles Christi*, "a soldier of Christ," and therefore to be distinguished in a religious sense from the non-Christian civilian. It is significant, however, that the Christians did not adopt the term *paganus* in the meaning of non-Christian before the age of Constantine. They commonly employed the terms of scriptural origin—

nationes, gentilis, and *ethnicus*. With paganism still so strong in urban centers, especially in the West, there was no reason for making a sharp distinction between urban and rural conditions and for adopting a term for non-Christian that would apply primarily, if not exclusively, to rural areas. However when, in the course of the 4th century, Christians became more numerous and increasingly conscious of their own solidarity and social and religious prestige, the analogy of the contrast between *paganus* and *militaris* undoubtedly suggested the employment of the word as an appropriate designation, but not necessarily a derogatory one, for non-Christians as profane persons, outsiders, not members of the Christian community. The term, incidentally, seems to have had a history of popular usage before it was given literary and official sanction, for St. Augustine speaks of "*gentiles vel iam vulgo usitato vocabulo paganos*" (*Epist.* 184 *bis* 3, 5). It is first employed officially in a rescript of Valentinian I of the year A.D. 370 (*Codex Theodosianus* 14.2.18).

Bibliography: J. ZEILLER, *Paganus: Étude de terminologie historique* (Paris 1917); "Paganus: Sur l'origine de l'acceptation religieuse du mot," *Comptes rendus de l'Acad. des Insc. et Belles Lettres* (Paris 1940) 526–543. C. MOHRMANN, "Encore une fois: 'Paganus,'" *Vigiliae christianae* 6 (Amsterdam 1952) 109–121, the best treatment, and with pertinent bibliography. E. BICKEL, "'Pagani': Kaiseranbeter in den Laren-Kapellen der 'pagi urbani' im Rom Neros und des Apostels Petrus," *Rheinisches Museum für Philologie* 97 (1954) 1–47.

[M. R. P. MCGUIRE]

PAGE, ANTHONY, BL.

Priest, martyr; b. ca. 1563 at Harrow-on-the-Hill, Middlesex, England; hanged, drawn, and quartered at York, April 20, 1593. The well-born Anthony Page studied at Christ College at Oxford (1581–1584) and the English College at Rheims (1584–91), where he was ordained, Sept. 21, 1591. He was sent on the English Mission, but immediately arrested and condemned for being a priest. He was beatified by Pope John Paul II on Nov. 22, 1987 with George Haydock and Companions.

Feast of the English Martyrs: May 4 (England).

See Also: ENGLAND, SCOTLAND, AND WALES, MARTYRS OF.

Bibliography: R. CHALLONER, *Memoirs of Missionary Priests,* ed. J. H. POLLEN (rev. ed. London 1924), I, no. 98. J. H. POLLEN, *Acts of English Martyrs* (London 1891).

[K. I. RABENSTEIN]

Ruins of Temples of Jupiter and Bacchus, ca. 10–249 A.D., Baalbek, Lebanon. (©Roger Wood/CORBIS)

PAGNINI, SANTES

Also known as Pagninus or Pagnino, philologist and biblical scholar; b. Lucca, Tuscany, Oct. 18, 1470; d. Lyons, France, Aug. 24, 1536. He entered the Dominican order on Feb. 16, 1487, at Fiesole (near Florence), where one of his early masters was Girolamo SAVONAROLA. Florence at that time was a center for Oriental studies, and Pagnini displayed a facility in this field. He was elected prior several times (e.g., at Pistoia 1502, Florence 1504, Lucca 1508) and gained a reputation for sanctity as well as for learning. Called to Rome by Leo X, he taught Oriental studies there until 1521. Adrian VI named him apostolic preacher and master of sacred theology. In 1524 he went to Lyons, where he fought successfully against the Waldensian and Lutheran heresies, and where appeared the most important of his several publications, the *Veteris et Novi Testamenti nova translatio* (1528), a Latin translation of the Bible from the original texts. The fruit of 25 years of labor, it was the first Latin translation

of the Hebrew Bible since that of St. Jerome and the first Bible in which all the verses were numbered, chapter by chapter, a notation still in use in modern Bibles. Whatever the translation's defects, all admit its faithfulness in rendering the original idiom, and many concede that it influenced the English versions of the OT through the use made of it by the early Protestants.

Bibliography: J. D. GAUTHIER, "Santes Pagninus, O.P.," *The Catholic Biblical Quarterly* 7 (1945) 175–190. *Dictionnaire de la Bible,* ed. F. VIGOUROUX, 5 v. (Paris 1895–1912) 4.2:1949–50.

[A. SMITH]

PAIDEIA, CHRISTIAN

The system of education in the faith that the early Christians created through a combination of the Biblical revelation and the cultural patterns suggested by Hellenistic literature and philosophy. It had as its objective the

The weathered stones of a fifth-century Christian basilica are scattered among the ruins of Dodona, an ancient Greek site dedicated to the god Zeus. (©Wolfgang Kaehler/CORBIS)

achieving of the wisdom of God, through a spiritual formation under the divine Pedagogue, the Logos, or the Word of God. The paideia looked to the formation of character and appreciation of values as much as it did to imparting knowledge or information. Its final aim was the true GNOSIS, or Christian philosophy, whose end was the imitation of Christ.

Development to Clement of Alexandria. The early Church provided detailed instruction for catechumens and clergy but did not think of creating a separate educational system for children. In the secular schools the Christian child pursued the *enkyklios paideia,* the all-round culture of Hellenism that the Romans called *humanitas* and studied in the *trivium* and *quadrivium.* Religious development was provided, outside this classical training, mainly in the family circle and in the Church.

The expression Christian paideia was first used in the Epistle of CLEMENT I of Rome (*1 Cor.* 21.6, 8; cf. 16.5;

35.8; 56.2, 16). Like St. Paul, the author stressed that the young should be subject to parental formation and discipline. POLYCARP bade husbands teach their wives "to train their children in the knowledge and fear of God" (*Ad Phil.* 4.2). The Shepherd of HERMAS also insisted on family sanctification through discipline and training (*Vis.* 1.3.1–2; 2.3.1).

Since Homer and pagan mythology formed the basis of secular paideia, it presented dangers to the faith of Christians. But to shun the schools was impossible, as even TERTULLIAN admitted: "How can we reject profane studies, without which religious studies are impossible?" (*De idol.* 10.4). But he banned Christians from teaching in the schools, and his basic opposition to Hellenism was expressed in his frequently quoted: "What has Athens to do with Jerusalem; the Academy with the Church?" (*Praescrip.* 7). TATIAN, the Syrian, was even more uncompromising in regard to pagan learning. For him the grammarians were idle prattlers (*Orat.* 26), and he turned his back on Greek paideia to become a professor of the philosophy of the barbarians. He found the Scriptures unpretentious in their language but too old and divine to be compared with the erroneous opinions of the Greeks (*Orat.* 29). Tatian had been a pupil of the more liberal JUSTIN MARTYR at the latter's school in Rome, where Christianity was offered as the true philosophy.

By the end of the 2nd century the catechumenal schools seem to have taken final form. Here the bishop or his delegate gave elaborate instructions preceding baptism; examples of these courses of instruction survive in the *Great Catechism* of GREGORY OF NYSSA, the *Catecheses* of CYRIL OF JERUSALEM and of THEODORE OF MOPSUESTIA, and in the *De catechizandis rudibus* of St. AUGUSTINE. These schools contributed to the intellectual formation of candidates for Baptism, but their main function was to impart doctrinal, ascetical, and liturgical training, with the Scriptures as the basic text.

The catechetical schools offered more advanced instruction in the Christian way of life; provided protection against the immorality and persecutional attacks of pagan adversaries; and deepened the knowledge of the faith for the neophytes. The most famous of these was the school of Alexandria. While Pantaenus and Clement of Alexandria evidently lectured on the Christian doctrines, it is only with Origen that the school acquired its official, ecclesiastical standing. Its pupils were adults in the process of conversion; and under Origen's direction the elementary catechesis came to be delegated to Heraclas, and Origen devoted himself to advanced philosophy and exegesis.

The Major Roles of Clement and Origen. For CLEMENT OF ALEXANDRIA (*c.* 200), paideia was the most excellent and perfect possession in life, a useful propaedeutic for the appreciation of the word of the Lord (*Paid.* 1.5.16; *Strom.* 1.5). His indebtedness to Greek classical authors, poets, and philosophers is obvious on every page. He had a decided predilection for Plato but was actually eclectic, regarding all of Greek philosophy as a guide to Christ, the best of educators (*Strom.* 2.2). His *Paidagogos* is the first complete educational treatise that combines pagan learning and cultural patterns with Christian theological thought and the sacramental way of life. It gives a minute description of the Christian's day, beginning with the main meal in the evening, and discusses every phase of his life.

Origen urged GREGORY THAUMATURGUS "to extract from the philosophy of the Greeks what may serve as a course of study or a preparation for Christianity, and even from geometry and astronomy what would serve to explain the Sacred Scriptures, in order that all that the sons

of philosophy are wont to say about geometry and music, grammar, rhetoric, and astronomy, as fellow helpers of philosophy, may be said about philosophy itself in relation to Christianity." Thus he regarded all secular subjects as "ladders to reach the sky"; and his students were expected to be familiar with every aspect of Hellenic knowledge as a preparation for their study of Scripture. Origen taught at Alexandria from 212 to 231 and thereafter at Caesarea until his death. During the 4th century the Church Fathers in the various areas where the Church was well established used their secular education as a background for developing the Church's understanding of divine revelation.

The Golden Age of Christian Paideia in the East. The Cappadocian Fathers made important contributions. GREGORY OF NAZIANZUS, in his *Panegyric on Basil,* spoke for both of them when he said: "As we have compounded healthful drugs from reptiles, so from secular literature we have received principles of inquiry and speculation, while we have rejected their idolatry, terror, and pit of destruction." BASIL of Caesarea, a friend of the pagan orator Libanius and an impeccable Greek stylist, elaborated on the utility of Greek literature properly used for the educated Christian in his *To Young Men, on How They Might Profit from Pagan Literature.* His *Monastic Rules* also was important in shaping an erudite monasticism. Gregory of Nazianzus in his *Invective Orations against Julian* [the Apostate] severely castigated that Emperor for his efforts to exclude Christians from higher education. In virtue of a decree of Julian on June 17, 362 (*CodTheod* 13.3.5), Christian teachers had either to abandon Christianity and return to belief in the pagan gods or cease to teach. MARIUS VICTORINUS had to quit his professorship of rhetoric at Rome, and many grammarians, rhetors, and even professors of medicine were affected; but the decree was rescinded by Julian's successor (364).

JOHN CHRYSOSTOM is the outstanding writer on pedagogy among the Fathers. Of especial importance is his *De inani gloria et de educandis liberis,* which deplores the lack of religious and moral training in an age that devoted so much energy to training in the arts, in literature, and in rhetoric. He reminded parents that they were bringing up "a philosopher, and a champion, and a citizen of Heaven."

Christian Paideia in the West. In the West the study of Greek declined in the 4th century; but the great Christian writers, such as LACTANTIUS, HILARY OF POITIERS, AMBROSE, JEROME, and Augustine, were masters of the rhetorical culture of their time. They derived their knowledge of Greek philosophy mainly from Latin sources, especially Cicero. Ausonius, however, spoke of "Greek grammarians" in his native Bordeaux, who used Homer as the first text (5.46) in their instruction.

Jerome studied under the famed *grammaticus* Donatus, and he himself expounded Vergil, the comedians, lyric poets, and historians during his sojourn in Bethlehem. Two of his letters (*Epist.* 107, 128) deal with the education of girls dedicated to God's service. Letter 22 gives an account of his famous dream in which he heard the Judge's condemnation, *Ciceronianus es, non Christianus,* and he asked rhetorically, *Quid facit cum psalterio Horatius? Cum evangeliis Maro? Cum apostolo Cicero?* But it is clear from his subsequent writings that his studies of the sacred writers did not exclude a continued interest in the classical.

According to St. Augustine, the Christian writer should despoil pagan literature as the Jews despoiled the Egyptians when they were leaving Egypt; the gold and silver in the writings of pagans are not their own but are dug out of the mines of God's providence and more properly belong to the follower of Christ when he has abandoned paganism. The arts in secular learning are a help in understanding the Scriptures (*Doct. Christ.* 2.16.28). His *De beata vita* ushered in the birth of Western Christian philosophy and a renewal of paideia under Christian auspices. Among later writers, Boethius, with his *Consolation of Philosophy,* integrated a wealth of classical learning and pagan philosophy with an apparently orthodox Christianity; Cassiodorus's *Institutes* was devoted to an encyclopedic treatment of sacred and profane knowledge; GREGORY I the Great scorned literary niceties and endorsed monastic education and a new, specifically Christian education that rejected the classical and emphasized home training and moral formation; Martianus Capella and ISIDORE OF SEVILLE handed on the tradition of paideia to the Middle Ages.

Bibliography: H. FUCHS, *Reallexikon für Antike und Christentum,* ed. T. KLAUSER (Stuttgart 1970) 2:350–362, with bibliog. F. X. PORTMANN, *Die göttliche Paidagogia bei Gregor von Nazianz* (St. Ottilien 1954). P. PETIT, *Les Étudiants de Libanius* (Paris 1956). H. HAGENDAHL, *Latin Fathers and the Classics* (Göteborg 1958). M. L. W. LAISTNER, *Christianity and Pagan Culture in the Later Roman Empire* (Ithaca, N.Y. 1951). M. TESTARD, *Saint Augustin et Cicéron,* 2 v. (Paris 1958). A. J. FESTUGIÈRE, *Antioch païenne et chrétienne* (Paris 1959). J. FONTAINE, *Isidore de Séville et la culture classique dans l'Espagne wisigothique,* 2 v. (Paris 1959). E. L. FORTIN, *Christianisme et culture philosophique au V(e) siècle* (Paris 1959). H. I. MARROU, *A History of Education in Antiquity,* tr. G. LAMB from 3d Fr. ed. (New York 1956); ed. and tr., *Clément d'Alexandrie: Le Pédagogue,* v.1 (Sources Chrétiennes 70; 1960). W. BARCLAY, *Educational Ideals in the Ancient World* (London 1959). W. W. JAEGER, *Early Christianity and Greek Paideia* (Cambridge, Mass. 1961). P. RICHÉ, *Éducation et culture dans l'Occident barbare,* VI(e)–VIII(e) *siècles* (Paris 1962). E. KEVANE, *Augustine the Educator* (Westminster, Md. 1964).

[T. P. HALTON]

PAINE, JOHN, ST.

English martyr; b. Peterborough, date unknown; d. Chelmsford, Essex, April 2, 1582. His family was probably Protestant, but the time and circumstances of his conversion are unchronicled. He entered Douai College in 1574 to study for the priesthood and was for a time made bursar of the college; this indicates that he had some experience in stewardship, probably as a servant of the Shelley family at Stondon Hall in Essex. While he was at Douai, he saw a vision of the figure of Christ rising from the Sacrament during the Elevation. This vision was the subject of the Bosworth Burse now in Leicester Museum. On April 7, 1576, Paine was ordained, and a few days later he set out for England with (St.) Cuthbert MAYNE. Paine made his way to Ingatestone Hall in Essex, where the old, widowed Lady Petre lived, an uncompromising Catholic. Here he remained in the guise of a steward until about February 1577 or earlier, when he was arrested and, for a brief time, imprisoned. After a visit to Douai he returned to Ingatestone some time before June 1578. He continued to work there until the middle of July 1581, when he was betrayed into the hands of George (Judas) Elliot, Edmund CAMPION's captor, at Haddon in Oxfordshire. He was examined before Walsingham at Greenwich, then sent to the Tower and racked several times. In March 1582 he was taken to the dungeons of Colchester castle to await trial. He was charged with conspiracy against Queen Elizabeth and was sentenced to be hanged, drawn, and quartered. When offered his liberty if he would change his religion, he told the officials "to stop their foolish babbling." The sentence was carried out at Chelmsford on April 2, 1582. After praying, he protested that "his feet did never tread, his hands did never write, nor did his wit ever invent any treason against her majesty." Since he was so well known and loved in the district, the crowd would not allow the hangman to cut him down and disembowel him until he was dead. He was beatified by Leo XIII on Dec. 29, 1886 and canonized on Oct. 25, 1970 (*see* ENGLAND, SCOTLAND, AND WALES, MARTYRS OF).

Feast: April 2; May 4; Oct. 25.

Bibliography: W. ALLEN, *A Briefe Historie of the Glorious Martyrdom of Twelve Reverend Priests,* ed. J. H. POLLEN, 2 v. (St. Louis 1908). B. C. FOLEY, *Blessed John Paine* (Postulation pamphlet; London 1961). A. BUTLER, *The Lives of the Saints* (New York 1956) 2:16–17. B. CAMM, *Lives of the English Martyrs,* 2 v. (New York 1904–05).

[G. FITZHERBERT]

PAINE, THOMAS

Journalist and pamphleteer whose political writings influenced American opinion in favor of independence, and whose popular tracts on Deism attacked organized religion; b. Thetford, Norfolk, England, Jan. 29, 1737; d. New York City, June 8, 1809. His early religious training was in his mother's Anglican faith; his father was a Quaker artisan, and young Paine served his apprenticeship in his shop. He was later employed as a staymaker, opened his own shop (1759), and became a customs officer (1764). Paine found his true calling in 1772, when he wrote *The Case of the Officers of Excise,* a plea for higher wages printed for distribution to Parliament by a subscription raised among his fellow customs officers. Discharged from his post, he immigrated to Philadelphia, Pa., in 1774; there he edited the *Pennsylvania Magazine,* contributing articles to its columns. He published a plea for the abolition of the slave trade and joined an antislavery society (1775), but his political views did not find expression until *Common Sense* (1776) issued a spirited demand for independence from Great Britain. Although the ideas he expressed were in no sense original, the influence of *Common Sense* in shaping public opinion was immense. Unlike earlier pamphleteers, Paine did not argue abstract truths but struck at George III and the whole British constitution. Paine's Hobbesian view of government was modified by a Lockean approach to society, but his isolationist view of America's role in world affairs owed little to literary sources. He served briefly as brigade major with Gen. G. Washington's army and began to write *The American Crisis* on a drumhead during the retreat across New Jersey. *The Crisis* appeared in 13 numbered pamphlets issued between 1776 and 1783.

In 1781 he visited France as secretary to an American mission and in 1782 was formally hired as a publicist for the Continental Congress; he later served the French embassy in the same capacity. Always interested in practical science, Paine invented an improved bridge and visited France again in 1787 to promote it. The French foreign office subsidized his *Prospects on the Rubicon* (1787) on Anglo-French relations, while he divided his time between London and Paris. As a reply to Edmund Burke's *Reflections on the French Revolution,* he issued *The Rights of Man,* rejecting theories of rule by a priesthood or an aristocracy as based on superstition or force and arguing in favor of democracy with its basis in reason and the free consent of individual citizens. Any theory looking to the past is to be rejected, since every generation must act for itself and has no power to bind posterity. His positive suggestions for reform appeared in the second part of *The Rights of Man* (1792).

The French Assembly made him an honorary citizen in 1792 and shortly thereafter he was elected to the Convention. He took his seat, but his opposition to the execution of Louis XVI and his association with the Girondists led to his arrest and imprisonment in 1793. With the help

Thomas Paine, photograph of painting by Romney.

of James Monroe he was released in 1794 and restored to his post as a deputy. *The Age of Reason* was still in manuscript at Paine's arrest; it appeared in 1794, offering the classic explanation of Deism and attacking the Bible and Christianity. Stating his belief in God and humanity, he argued that Christ did not found a religion, but called men to the practice of moral virtues and belief in one God; thus for him Christianity was the invention of mythmakers. Large segments of the work dealt with rather pedestrian scriptural criticism. Bishop Richard Watson of Llandaff wrote a refutation in 1796, and Paine was engaged in writing a lengthy reply until shortly before his return to America in 1802. He was closely associated with Elihu Palmer in promoting Deism and wrote articles for Palmer's monthly, the *Prospect,* from 1804 to 1805. In 1807 he published a critical pamphlet on the New Testament.

Bibliography: *Complete Writings,* ed. P. S. FONER, 2 v. (New York 1945), with biog. essay. G. VALE, *The Life of Thomas Paine* (New York 1841). M. D. CONWAY, *Life of Thomas Paine,* 2 v. (New York 1892). A. O. ALDRIDGE, *Man of Reason* (Philadelphia 1959). H. M. MORAIS, *Deism in 18th Century America* (New York 1960). G. A. KOCH, *Republican Religion: The American Revolution and the Cult of Reason* (New York 1933).

[R. K. MACMASTER]

Music manuscript page from "Duetto Comico," by Giovanni Paisiello, 1774. (©Archivo Iconografico, S.A./CORBIS)

PAISIELLO, GIOVANNI

Church and opera composer of early classical style; b. Taranto, Italy, May 9, 1740; d. Naples, June 5, 1816. As a youth he studied at the conservatory of S. Onofrio in Naples; he then taught there while composing his first music. At first he wrote only sacred music, but later he became extremely successful in opera, composing more than 100 works in this form. He spent eight years (1776–84) at the court of Catherine II at St. Petersburg, Russia, producing there his most famous opera, *The Barber of Seville* (1782). He later held the post of *maestro di cappella* at the court of Naples until he left in 1799 for political reasons. He was Napoleon's favorite composer and became his *maître de chapelle* in Paris 1802; but after an unsuccessful struggle to please the Paris public, he resumed his position at Naples under Joseph Bonaparte a year later. His sacred music includes, among other works, 30 Masses with orchestra; several Masses for varying combinations; a Requiem scored for two choruses, orchestra, and organ; 40 motets; a Miserere; a Magnificat; and an oratorio on the Passion. Like his operas, these have the florid arias and grandiose choruses of the period, but also reveal the natural melodic beauty that characterizes his best work.

Bibliography: A. LOEWENBERG, "Paisiello's and Rossini's Barbiere di Siviglia," *Music and Letters* 10 (London 1939) 157–167. H. V. F. SOMERSET, "Giovanni Paisiello," *ibid.* 18 (1937) 20–35. A. MONDOLFI, *Die Musik in Geschichte und Gegenwart*, ed. F. BLUME (Kassel-Basel 1949–) 10:639–647. J. L. HUNT, "The Life and Keyboard Works of Giovanni Paisiello (1740–1816)" (Ph.D. diss. University of Michigan, 1973). K. B. MOHR, "Giovanni Paisiello's Gli astrologi immaginari: An Urtext Edition" (Ph.D. diss. Florida State University, 1969). D. POULTNEY, "Giovanni Paisiello" in *International Dictionary of Opera*, 2 v. ed. C. S. LARUE (Detroit 1993) 979–982. S. WILLIER, "*Nina, ossia La Pazza per amore (Nina, or Mad for Love)*" *ibid.*, 936–37. D. M. RANDEL, ed., *The Harvard Biographical Dictionary of Music* (Cambridge 1996). M. F. ROBINSON, "Giovanni Paisiello" in *The New Grove Dictionary of Music and Musicians*, ed. S. SADIE (New York 1980)14:97–102. M. F. ROBINSON and U. HOFMANN, *Giovanni Paisiello (1740–1816), A Thematic Catalogue of His Music, Vol. 1: The Dramatic Works*

(Hillsboro 1991). N. SLONIMSKY, ed., *Baker's Biographical Dictionary of Musicians* (8th ed. New York 1992).

[W. C. HOLMES]

PAKISTAN, THE CATHOLIC CHURCH IN

Pakistan is located in South Asia, bordered by India on the east, Iran and Afghanistan on the west, and China on the north. The population consists of five principal ethnic communities: Punjabi (55 percent of the population); Sindhi (20 percent); Pashtun (Pathan) (10 percent); Mujahir (immigrants from India at the time of the 1947 partition of India and Pakistan) (10 percent); and Baloch (5 percent). Pakistan attained independence from British rule on August 14, 1947, when the predominantly Muslim areas of India— West Punjab, Sindh, Baluchistan, the Northwest Frontier and East Bengal—were united to form the new country. Conceived as a homeland for Muslims of India, with non-Muslims equal citizens, the secular vision of the founder, Muhammad Ali Jinnah, was altered soon after his death. In 1956 the country was proclaimed an Islamic republic and Islam became the state religion. Continuing ethnic and civil strife between West and East Pakistan developed into a full-blown civil war in 1971, resulting in the independence of Bangladesh, the former East Pakistan. Islam has been promoted by successive martial law regimes as a way of legitimating their rule. In recent years this has led to ethnic and sectarian violence among Muslims and discriminatory and repressive laws against minorities.

Early Christian Presence. Pakistan is the site of the ancient Indus civilization (2,600 BC) and the northern areas formed part of the ancient Silk Route, which gave birth to the Buddhist Gandhara civilization in Swat (200 BC–200 AD). St. Thomas the Apostle was reputed to have passed through Taxila, near present-day Rawalpindi on his way to India. Though this cannot be verified, the presence of Christian communities in the area as early as the third century does witness to early activities. Along the Silk Route, two Assyrian Church of the East (Nestorian) crosses have been discovered and the Gilgit cross was found in a place (Kunodas) known to be an ancient burial place. A 7th century cross has been found near Chilas.

No permanent work resulted from the visits of these early Christians. In 1569 Jesuit missionaries from GOA, Frs. Monserrat and Acquaviva, arrived at the court of Akbar in Lahore. They were favored and accompanied the emperor to his residence at Fatehpur Sikri. After fourteen years of unsuccessful endeavors, they left the Moghul court in 1583. A second mission in 1583 and a

Capital: Islamabad.
Size: 310,403 sq. miles.
Population: 141,553,775 in 2000.
Religions: Sunni Islam (76%), Shi'a Islam (20%), Christians (2%), Hindus (1%). The remaining 1% consists of small communities of Parsee, Baha'i, Buddhists, Sikh and tribal religionists.
Metropolitan Sees: Karachi, with suffragan Hyderabad; Lahore, with suffragans Faisalabad, Islamabad-Rawalpindi, and Multan.

third in 1594 were both fruitful. By 1597 there was a large church in Lahore and in 1604 the emperor allowed all his subjects to embrace Christianity. More priests arrived from Goa and began publishing in Persian books on the history and teaching of Christianity. Akbar's grandson, Shahjahan, proved less friendly and, in 1650, ordered the destruction of the Lahore church. The Catholic population of Lahore at that time comprised three distinct communities: the Europeans (mostly Portuguese), the Armenians and Indian converts. In 1606 they numbered about 50. By 1714, quite a number of the soldiers were Christian. During this time, Lahore was the center for various missionary expeditions to Kafiristan (present day Chitral in Pakistan and Nuristan in Afghanistan). These lasted from 1587 until 1700. After this the number of Jesuits began to decrease. By 1750 the Christian soldiers had no resident priest and by 1752 the soldiers themselves were deported to Kabul by the invading king, Ahmed Shah. In this same period of the sixteenth and seventeenth centuries some Augustinians and Carmelites from Bombay and Goa evangelized Sindh near the Portuguese factories of Thatta but little is known of their activities and work ceased with the persecution of 1672. It was not begun again until after the conquest of Sindh by the British in 1842.

The Beginnings of the Modern Church. The beginnings of the present-day Catholic Church in Pakistan can be traced to the annexation of the Punjab by the British in 1846 and to services provided to those Christians who were British citizens, civil and military, as well as to immigrants from the southern provinces of India. To meet this need, Capuchins came from Agra to Lahore, and Carmelites and Jesuits from Bombay to Sindh and Baluchistan. To this day many important administrative and railway centers have as a colonial legacy at least three churches in every military cantonment, one Anglican, one Presbyterian and one Catholic. Lahore became an apostolic vicariate in 1855 and in 1886 a diocese. The northwestern provinces of Kashmir and Kafiristan were constituted into an apostolic prefecture entrusted to the Mill Hill Fathers, headquartered in Rawalpindi, in 1887.

Sindh and Baluchistan remained under the jurisdiction of Bombay.

Until 1890, the Church restricted itself mostly to the service of foreigners. Subsequently, demands from mainly lower-caste Hindus desiring closer contact with the Church in the Lahore-Sialkot area led to the development of the Pakistani Catholic Church. Over 80 percent of all Pakistani Catholics trace their roots to this ethnic group. In the Punjab the diocese of Lahore stretched from Jullundur to Bahawalpur. Direct mission work began from Sialkot in 1889–1890 and spread to the districts of Gujrat, Jhelum, Gujranwala and Sheikhupura and especially in villages established in the newly irrigated areas of the Doab. These Catholic agricultural colonies and villages

became centers for evangelization in the surrounding areas.

A growing Catholic community and responsibility for a vast area dictated the need of ceding the eastern districts of Lahore diocese to the newly formed archdiocese of Simla-Delhi in 1910. In 1936 the entire division of Multan was formed into a prefecture and entrusted to the Dominicans of the Roman province, who had arrived five years earlier. In the North, the districts of Sargodha and Gujrat were attached in 1938 to the apostolic prefecture of Rawalpindi. The territory entrusted to Mill Hill was enlarged and included the civil divisions of Peshawar, Dera Ismail Khan, Rawalpindi and Sargodha. In 1947 this prefecture was raised to the status of a diocese. Sindh and Baluchistan remained part of the archdiocese of Bombay, where Jesuits, mostly Spanish, worked. Centres were established in the more important towns but there was little direct evangelization. In 1934 the whole territory was detached from Bombay to form the independent mission of Karachi under the care of the Dutch Franciscans.

In this pre-partition period, charitable and educational institutions were established in towns and villages throughout the area. Pioneers in the field in Lahore were the Religious of Jesus and Mary from Lyons (1856), and in Karachi, the Daughters of the Cross from Liege (1862). Two local congregations were formed during this time: the Franciscan Tertiary Sisters of Lahore (1922) and the Franciscan Missionaries of Christ the King in Karachi (1937).

The Church in Independent Pakistan. Independence in 1947 found the Catholic Church still part of two distinct ecclesiastical units with Sindh, Khairpur and Baluchistan belonging to the ecclesiastical province of Bombay, while the Punjab, Bahawalpur and the Northwest depended on the archdiocese of Delhi. Changes were made to accommodate the new political reality. The diocese of Karachi was created on May 28, 1948 for Sindh and Baluchistan, and was raised to the status of an archdiocese two years later. In 1958 the archdiocese was divided to form the new diocese of Hyderabad entrusted to the Franciscans. In 1960, after the arrival, in 1956, of Dominicans from New York, the diocese of Multan was entrusted to the Americans and the districts of Lyallpur (present-day Faisalabad), Jhang and Sahiwal were separated to form the new diocese of Faisalabad, entrusted to the Italian Dominicans. In 1973 Pope Paul VI raised the archbishop of Karachi, Joseph Cordeiro, to the rank of cardinal. Lahore was erected an archdiocese on April 23, 1994, and Armando Trindade named the first archbishop. There are also two monasteries: one Carmelite monastery in Lahore and one of Dominican nuns in Karachi. Many religious formation houses were established in Lahore. St. Francis Xavier Seminary in Lahore is affiliated with the Urbanianum in Rome, while the National Catholic Institute of Theology in Karachi has sought affiliation with Yarra Theological Union (Melbourne).

Roughly half the Christian population belongs to different Protestant churches. The Church of Pakistan, inaugurated in 1970 through a union of Anglicans, Methodists, Lutherans and Presbyterians, claims the largest number of adherents. Other groups include the Salvation Army, Adventist, Baptist, Full Gospel and many smaller pentecostal and evangelical bodies. Relations between churches are generally friendly, especially when the welfare and survival of the tiny Christian minority is seen at risk. The bishops of the Church of Pakistan and the Catholic Bishops Conference of Pakistan meet occasionally and have made joint representations to the government. Ecumenical and interfaith cooperation is active on the national level in the Christian Study Centre in Rawalpindi, founded in 1967 to promote understanding between Muslims and Christians, the Idara-e-Aman-o-Insaf, the center for Peace and Justice in Karachi, and the Pastoral Institute in Multan, where regular ministerial meetings are held.

Church and Society. It would be hard to calculate the influence the Church has had on society but one witness to the presence and efficiency of church work is the frequent encouragement by leaders to government officials to work with "missionary zeal." For years, the only quality education and health care was that offered by missionary institutions. There are over 600 Catholic educational institutions, providing instruction in the national and provincial languages and in English, to Christian, Muslim and Hindu students. Since 1969 the government has exercised increasing control over Christian institutions and the activities of foreign missionaries. Most private schools and colleges were nationalized between 1972 and 1974. Although this law affected Muslim schools as well, its main purpose was perceived as weakening the Christian influence in Pakistan. Ownership, however, remained with the churches. In Sindh and in several dioceses of the Punjab, many of these schools have since been returned.

Besides traditional hospital care, the Church has always had a medical presence in the rural areas, where 80 percent of the population lives. It has done pioneering work in the care and eradication of Hansens disease, and in care for the disabled, the elderly and the destitute. Many centers have been opened recently for the awareness and cure of drug addiction. Low-cost housing schemes, sponsored by diocesan agencies, have benefitted many. Organizations like Catholic Relief Service (CRS) and Caritas have collaborated with the government in rehabilitation and health projects for refugees and displaced persons.

With Pakistani leadership in the dioceses and in many of the religious congregations, and with an active and educated laity, what was not possible before has now become possible. Forty years ago, there were only two national publications, one an English weekly from Karachi, the other a monthly in Urdu from Lahore. Now there are theological journals in English (*Focus from Multan*) and in English and Urdu (*Al Mushir* from Rawalpindi). National and diocesan commissions and centers publish regular magazines and newsletters. Evidence of this coming of age is also seen in the small but growing number of Pakistani women religious on mission in Asia, Africa and Latin America, and in the involvement of lay men and women in the field of catechetics, education and in the different commissions for justice and peace. This involvement has led to close cooperation with non-governmental organizations and human rights groups, out of which working alliances, deeper understanding and genuine friendship with Muslims have developed. The role of the Justice and Peace Commission of the Major Superiors Leadership Conference was crucial in organizing non-governmental organizations (NGOs) in the Jubilee 2000 campaign for cancellation of debt.

The martial law regime of General Zia-ul-Haq (1976–1988) introduced the system of separate electorates, where minorities (Christian, Hindu, Ahmadi, Parsee) vote only for candidates of their own religion. This effectively reduced minorities to second class citizens. In his attempt to create an Islamic society, Zia-ul-Haq introduced ordinances changing the laws of evidence (making the testimony of a non-Muslim witness equal to only half the value of a Muslim's), curtailing the civil rights of minorities and women, and introducing into the penal code mandatory death sentences for derogatory remarks against the Prophet Muhammad or desecration of the Qur'an. This led to street protests by women and the formation of many activist women's groups. It also led to the beginnings of the modern dialogue between Muslims and Christians. In most instances, particularly in Lahore and Multan, this began as the initiative of Muslims who wished to present a more tolerant and pluralist face of Islam, different from the monochromatic vision of Zia-ul-Haq. Since then, Christians and Muslims (the Muslims often at great risk to their own life) have defended those accused of blasphemy, worked together for the repeal of the amendments to the penal code regarding blasphemy and for the restoration of the joint electorate. Active centers for Muslim-Christian dialogue are the ecumenical Christian Study Centre in Rawalpindi, the Pakistan Association for Interreligious Dialogue based in Lahore and several groups in Karachi.

A continuing issue for Christians in Pakistan is one of identity as minority in a Muslim country. The Christian is not dhimmi, a member of a conquered race, nor is the Christian because of separate electorates and discrimination a citizen with equal rights. There were difficulties for Christians and Hindus during the wars with India in 1965 and 1971, when churches, temples and homes were attacked and Hindu and Christian loyalty suspect. Despite occasional flurries of violence after the Salman Rushdie affair and the Gulf War, Christians felt things were getting better. A defining moment came in 1992 when the government announced the addition of a column for religion in the national identity card. This was seen as discriminatory and led to mass protests, hunger strikes, press conferences and sit-ins with Christians joined by Hindus and Muslims. The government was forced to back down. The more lasting effect was the minority awareness and experience of power. They succeeded because the protests began at the grass-roots: they were united, had the support of many Muslims, and effective use was made of the media.

Christians and other minorities continue to face discrimination in civil society. They are especially vulnerable if they live in the vicinity of a mosque, where a loudspeaker could rouse a mob in minutes. The Christian community has been able to live with these things but was completely unprepared for a ferocious attack on Christian settlements in the Khanwal area near Multan on February 5–6, 1997. Churches and homes were attacked and burnt. The results of the government inquiry have not been released but it appeared that religion was used for political purposes. The aftermath was important for several reasons. The government was embarrassed by the international attention, many Muslims apologized to their Christian neighbors, and official and unofficial delegations visited the area. One of them comprised Muslim religious leaders, who themselves washed the floors of the desecrated churches and begged pardon from those who had been rendered homeless.

Bibliography: *The Catholic Church in Pakistan Directory* (Islamabad 1998). J. C. ENGLAND, *The Hidden History of Christianity in Asia: The Churches of the East before 1500* (Delhi and Hong Kong 1996). J. ROONEY, MHM, *A History of Christianity in Pakistan* (Rawalpindi 1984–89). B. MENDES, "Looking Back at the ID Card Issue," *Focus* Supplement no. 1(1993). F. E. STOCK *People Movements in the Punjab* (Pasadena CA 1968). "The Shantinagar Story," *Focus* vol. 17, no. 1.

[T. C. MCVEY]

PALACE SCHOOLS

Palace schools is a name applied to education given in the courts of kings and emperors at the end of the Merovingian and all through the Carolingian periods.

Historical development. When Charlemagne reorganized education, which had been sorely neglected during the long period of military campaigns, churches and monasteries were in almost exclusive control of schools. Palace schools (*schola palatii*), however, which Charlemagne, taking advantage of an ancient tradition of royal patronage, had established for members of the court, boy lectors at the royal chapel, children of the nobility, and laymen, were an exception.

In fact, although there were no schools properly so-called in the Merovingian palaces, many young nobles and future bishops spent some years in the *contubernium* (residence) of the prince, often after having previously attended some school, as we see in the 7th century in the case of St. Ermenland, if we can believe his biographers, who was "withdrawn from school to be placed in a royal palace." Even at the time of the early Carolingians, where, as among the Merovingians, the term *schola palatii* is found, this *schola* does not seem to be a school, as the word is generally understood, but rather a group of clergy and laymen who surrounded the king in his palace; for example, Benoît d'Arlane, who, though ranked *inter scholares,* was appointed cup-bearer, a duty that seems incompatible with the pursuit of serious literary studies. Nevertheless, constant association with palace officials did not fail to afford the young people some insight into state affairs, which explains the passage from *Vita Adalardi:* "Adalard, Charlemagne's cousin, was instructed at the palace in the *prudentia* (wisdom) of the world by the same teachers as the prince of the land." This prince of the land was Charlemagne, whose early education was incidental and who, only in later years when he came into power, received any formal intellectual training.

Organization. Whatever doubt may exist about the Merovingian school, it is certain that Charlemagne's palace was an active center of serious study. Charlemagne took a personal interest in the restoration of arts and letters. In 774, on his return from the campaign in Italy that established the papal state, he brought back with him the grammarian Pierre de Pise and Paul Warnefield, also called Paul the Deacon; and in 776 he called in Pauline d'Aquilée. Charlemagne's truly great teacher, however, the head of the palace school, was the renowned ALCUIN, former pupil at the episcopal school at York, who after several short visits to the court, established his residence there in 793. Even though Alcuin later withdrew to Tours, he never lost interest in his first mission, where he continued to wield a strong influence. The Irish monk Dungal and Theodulf d'Orléans were among other famous teachers at the court for short periods. The school continued its activity under Charlemagne's successors, when from 845 to his death in 875, John the Scot (Joannes Scotus) was one of its most representative masters.

At the end of the 9th century, the most renowned palace school was that established by Alfred the Great, considered in English literature as the first translator. Having heard of the great learning and virtue of GRIMBALD, abbot of Saint-Bertin in France, Alfred invited him to Great Britain to restore the teaching of letters. Like the Carolingians, he gathered at his court the children of high birth to teach them to read both Latin and their native Anglo–Saxon tongue.

Objectives. Education in the palace school was intended first of all for the emperor and his court who formed, it seems, an academy, since Alcuin in a letter to Charlemagne referred to his academicians. The women of the Carolingian family also took part—reading poetry, solving problems, discussing theological and grammatical questions, and the like. The academicians took assumed names: Charlemagne called himself David; Angilbert, Homer; Eginhard, an artist, Beseleel; and the Abbess Gisela, Charlemagne's sister, Lucy. Mingled with these scholars were children who followed more elementary and no doubt more formative courses. The monk St. Gall, in his *Gestis Caroli Magni,* tells us that the children were entrusted to the special care of the Irishman Clement.

Curriculum. It would be a mistake to place the academicians of either Charlemagne's or Alfred the Great's palace school and the children of the *schola* on the same plane as that of the students in the later medieval universities. The subject matter taught was, in comparison, very elementary, based on German common sense and subtlety and adapted to minds barely familiar with the most rudimentary notions of early science.

The education given at the Carolingian palace school has come down to us through the works left by Alcuin. Like Cassiodorus, 6th-century Roman monk, author, and educator, he divided the courses among the seven LIBERAL ARTS: the *trivium*—grammar, rhetoric, and logic, which constituted the first step—and the *quadrivium*—arithmetic, geometry, music, and astronomy, which made up the second step. On each of the subjects Alcuin wrote a small tract summarizing his teaching methods in which the oral exchange (dialogue) between teacher and student played an important part. Although Alcuin compared the seven liberal arts to the seven pillars of the house of wisdom, his teaching seems to have been elementary and not devoid of mistakes; for example, in his pamphlet on spelling he gives *hippocrita* (*hypocrita*), synonym for *simulator,* as a derivative of *hippo-falsum,* and *chrisis-judicium.*

Educational influence. It is evident that the educational influence of the *scholae palatii* was not so extensive as the vast program drawn up by Alcuin and theoretically adopted by his successors. This rather tenuous influence was felt principally on the grammatical plane since all the schools, from the end of the 11th century, devoted more time to grammar, considered the most necessary of all the arts. The palace school also contributed to the development of oratory. Charlemagne in Alcuin's *Rhetorica* remarks that since this art was of major importance in civil affairs, it would be absurd "to ignore the precepts of the art in which they are constantly involved." A prominent place was also given to logic, which, wrote Rabanus Maurus, "is the discipline of disciplines that teaches how to teach, and to learn how to learn; and in which reason discovers and shows what it is, what it wishes, what it sees.'' The four other liberal arts, on the contrary, seem to have been somewhat neglected and wielded little educational influence.

Finally, while other schools founded by Charlemagne and Alfred were devoted to the education of priests only, the palace schools contributed considerably to the literary and administrative formation of great laymen. At a time when culture was at its lowest ebb, the palace schools restored ancient disciplines—the liberal arts—and kept alive the legacy of classical antiquity, particularly by the interpretation of Sacred Scripture and the use of commentaries made by the Fathers of the Church. This dependence on ancient learning, both pagan and Christian, deeply influenced curricular orientation until the end of the 12th century.

Bibliography: J. B. WEISS, *Geschichte Alfreds des Grossen* (Schaffhausen 1852). J. E. SANDYS, *History of Classical Scholarship,* 3 v. (Cambridge, Eng.), v. 1 (3d ed. 1921), v. 2, 3 (2d ed. 1906–08); repr. (New York 1958). C. PLUMMER, *The Life and Time of Alfred the Great* (Oxford 1902). L. MAÎTRE, *Les Écoles épiscopales et monastiques en Occident avant les universités* (2d ed. Paris 1924). M. L. W. LAISTNER, *Thought and Letters in Western Europe, A.D. 500 to 900* (2d ed. New York 1957). P. RICHÉ, *Éducation et culture dans l'Occident barbare, VIᵉ–VIIIᵉ siècles* (Paris 1962). H. LECLERCQ, *Dictionnaire d'archéologie chrétienne et de liturgie,* ed. F. CABROL, H. LECLERCQ, and H. I. MARROU, 15 v. (Paris 1907–53) 4.2:1805–13, 1872–76.

[J. IMBERT]

PALACIOS, MANUEL ANTONIO

Paraguayan bishop, executed for his supposed involvement in a conspiracy against the republic; b. Luque, near Asunción, July 1824; d. Lomas Valentinas, Dec. 21, 1868. He attended the literary academy where he was a brilliant student. In September 1848 he was ordained by Bishop López. When he was curate of Villeta, he was proposed, on Nov. 20, 1862, as auxiliary bishop by the president of the republic, Francisco Solano López. He was consecrated in the Cathedral of Asunción on Aug. 30, 1863, by Bishop Urbieta, whom he succeeded on Jan. 29, 1865. From the beginning of the Paraguayan War, he served as first chaplain of the army, accompanying Marshal López as friend and confidant. However, by order of López, he was taken prisoner in San Fernando, along with several other persons accused of treason to Paraguay and its government. In 1868 he was condemned to death in a summary judgment at Lomas Valentinas and was executed by firing squad in company with Benigno López, the marshal's brother; Gen. Vicente Barrios, the marshal's brother-in-law; José Berjes, Minister of Foreign

Affairs; Eugenio Bogado, Vicar General; José María Leite Pereira, Consul of Portugal; Capt. Simón Fidanza of the Italian Navy in the service of Paraguay; Col. Paulino Alem, former commandant of Humaitá; Juan Bautista Zalduondo, nephew of Palacios; and three distinguished ladies from Asunción.

The cause and manner of Palacios's death have given an unhappy fame to his episcopate, although the truth of the San Fernando conspiracy has been much discussed. The prosecutor himself, a relative of Palacios, later referred to it as a "supposed" plot. Further, the accused were denied the right of defense; the trials were secret; and the confessions were extracted by whippings, by an old form of military punishment known as "cepo," and by crushing the fingers with a hammer. Scholars now believe that the plot never existed, that the sentencing and execution of a group of prominent men and women was simply a desperate attempt by Marshal López to maintain the morale of a decimated population whose total destruction was increasingly imminent. According to the most reliable documents and the statements of some survivors, it had become clear that the Paraguayan cause in the war was definitely lost when Paraguayan resistance on the southern frontier was broken with the fall of Humaitá. Two opposing factions resulted: those who believed it preferable to risk total destruction of their country rather than see it submit to an iniquitous tyranny and become the victim of injustice; and those who believed that such an extreme position was inhuman and useless, that no people should be obliged to sacrifice itself completely. Bishop Palacios and the others who were executed held the second opinion, as the statements of the prosecutor of the trial indicated.

Bibliography: S. GAONA, *El clero en la guerra del 70* (2d ed. Asunción 1961).

[A. N. ACHA DUARTE]

PALAFOX Y MENDOZA, JUAN DE

Spanish bishop of Puebla, Mexico; b. Fitero, Navarre, Spain, 1600; d. Osma, Spain, 1659. Even in recent times Palafox has been a subject of controversy and heated discussion. The illegitimate son of Jaime Palafox, Marquesa of Ariza, he studied in Salamanca and was ordained after having served as fiscal to the Councils of War and the Indies. As chaplain he accompanied Empress María to Germany. In 1610 he arrived in Mexico, in the same group that included the new viceroy López Pacheco, Duke of Escalona, to assume his duties as bishop of Puebla de los Angeles. Along with his appointment as bishop, Palafox had been designated Visitor of the *audiencia* and of the University of Mexico. The viceroy, a first cousin of the Duke of Braganza in Portugal, became suspect during the war for Portuguese independence and was recalled to Spain. Palafox, who had also suspected López of sympathy for the Portuguese cause, took over the post of viceroy for a few months but later, recognizing the viceroy's loyalty to the King, returned to his diocese.

The bishop's ecclesiastical policies brought him into conflict with several religious orders, particularly the Jesuits, with whom he had a famous lawsuit that originated when Palafox denied the Jesuits the right to hear confessions and preach. The dispute lasted several years and was eventually settled in favor of the bishop. A cultured and enthusiastic person, Palafox worked zealously. He supported education, enlarging the existing institutions such as the Tridentine College, and founding new ones, such as a girls' school and a literary academy to which he gave a library of 6,000 volumes, known today as the Biblioteca Palafoxiana de Puebla. In 1644 he inspected the University of Mexico and the next year drafted a new constitution for it. It was not well received by some members of the faculty, especially the religious, who had been excluded from the rectorship. At their request the viceroy suspended the constitution. It was not confirmed by the king until 1649, after Innocent X settled the case between Bishop Palafox and the Jesuits, and through a series of complications it did not become effective until 1671.

On his return to Spain in 1649, Palafox was minister of the Council of Aragon and later became bishop of Osma. His fame as a holy man brought the introduction of his cause for beatification. In 1767 the pope confirmed his "reputation for sanctity, virtue, and miracles *in genere.*" Palafox wrote many works—canonical, religious, moral, political, historical, and literary—which were published in 15 volumes after his death. His political writings reflect a great concern for the decline of Spanish power, and in *Juicio político de los daños y reparos de cualquiera monarquía* he analyzed the foreign and national policies that contributed to the decline. Although he was essentially a Hispanist, Palafox was able to see the importance of the various nations, that is, of the multiple nationality of the monarchy. He pleaded for the recognition of the individuality of each group and its equality with Castile and decried the distrust that prevented the full use of the monarchy's resources and energy.

Bibliography: G. GARCÍA, *Don Juan Palafox y Mendoza, obispo de Puebla y Osma, visitador y virrey de la Nueva España* (Mexico City 1918). J. L. BECERRA LÓPEZ, *La organización de los estudios en la Nueva España* (Mexico City 1963).

[H. PEREÑA]

PALAMAS, GREGORY

Byzantine mystical theologian, defender of HESYCHASM, bishop and saint in the Orthodox Church; b. Constantinople, *c.* 1296; d. Thessalonica, Nov. 14, 1359. Of a well-to-do family from Asia Minor, Gregory received a liberal education at the imperial university, came under the influence of the mystically minded metropolitan of Philadelphia, Theolytus, and at 22 entered a monastery on Mt. Athos with his two younger brothers. When the Turkish invasions of 1325 threatened the monastic life there, Palamas migrated to Thessalonica, where in 1326 he was ordained a priest and with ten companions retired to a hermitage on a mountain near Beroea. For five years he lived the life of the Hesychastic monk: five days of solitude and silence; then, on Saturday and Sunday, meeting with the others to celebrate the Eucharist and engage in spiritual conversation. He returned to Mt. Athos in 1331, fleeing Serbian incursions, and lived in the hermitage of St. Sabas, where he followed the same regime as at Beroea. In 1335 or 1336 he was appointed hegumen (abbot) of the Grand Laura, but he returned after a short while to St. Sabas.

Controversy with Barlaam. At St. Sabas Palamas became acquainted with the theology of BARLAAM, a Greek Orthodox monk from Calabria who was employing the syllogistic method in his attempt to refute the doctrine of the Latin Church regarding the procession of the Holy Spirit. Palamas wrote two letters to Barlaam (1332–33) in which he defended the position that apodictic arguments were possible in theology and rejected the agnosticism implied in the extreme apophatic, or negative, theology of Barlaam.

Barlaam, meanwhile, had begun to criticize the Hesychastic monks. He sarcastically impugned their psychophysical prayer practices, calling the monks *omphalopsychoi* (men-with-their-soul-in-their-navel) because of the prayer posture adopted by the monk, who was to focus his eyes on a spot below his chest for concentration (*see* JESUS PRAYER). Barlaam attacked in particular the explanation of the monks' goal of meditative contemplation (*hesychia*). The Hesychasts claimed that the saints as "the pure of heart" have the vision of God promised them in this life (Mt 5.8). They can see within themselves the working of the Holy Spirit as an uncreated grace. The Spirit is seen as a white light, the same light that shone about the Lord during the Transfiguration on Mt. Tabor. Barlaam accused the monks of Messalianism, a fourth-century dualistic heresy apparently adopted by the PAULICIANS in their claim that God was visible to human eyes. Barlaam prepared a work against this Hesychastic doctrine; but before its publication, Isidore, the future Patriarch of Constantinople, called Palamas from

Mt. Athos to aid in the refutation of Barlaam's charges (1338). Palamas prepared a threefold work (Triad) on the Hesychasts. He followed this with a second Triad, in which he described his famous distinction between God's being and His energy or operation. This became a distinctive characteristic of his theology. Later he defended the bodily prayer practices of the monks by insisting on the unity of the engraced man and rejected an extreme Platonic division of body and soul that would not see grace influencing and elevating the body of man to actual participation in the divine life of grace.

Elaboration of Palamas's Theology. In defending the presence of the Holy Spirit as uncreated GRACE within the saints, Palamas rejected Western explanations based on the idea of grace as created *and* supernatural. Such a concept of grace, Palamas argued, did not sufficiently explain the deification of the engraced man. A created entity is not the divinity, and man must somehow be deified by grace and thus participate in the very divinity. Only uncreated grace, the Spirit of God, can truly elevate the Christian to the divine life.

Palamas further sought to justify the Athonite monks and maintained that the action of God within the soul is a visible light, although not visible in the Messalian, heretical way, but visible to eyes elevated by grace. This light is the same as the light of the Transfiguration, which was not, as Barlaam claimed, a material light, but rather the divinity of the Lord, a divine energy. However, Palamas admitted that the Apostles did not see the essence or the nature of the divinity, which is invisible and incomprehensible, but rather this divine ''energy'' or activity. So too the saint sees a divine energy and not the essence of the Godhead. Even in the eternal life the blessed will not see the essence of God, which is incomprehensible, but rather the divine energy. The Holy Spirit, who sanctifies the saint, is seen as an uncreated divine energy present in the saint and deifying him. Barlaam rejected Palamas' explanations as unsatisfactory because they divided the Godhead into nature and energies. In 1341 Palamas accepted the theology of the *Hagiorite Tome* of PHILOTHEUS COCCINUS which became a fundamental manual for the monks of Mt. Athos.

Continued Controversy and Last Years. At a synod held in the Hagia Sophia in Constantinople (June 10, 1341) his position was examined; but despite Barlaam's representations, the theological question was left open, and both monks were forbidden to engage in further polemic. A former student of Palamas, GREGORIUS AKINDYNOS (d. 1349), led an opposition party of anti-Palamites who unsuccessfully attempted to have the *Tome* of 1341 repudiated. In August, however, a second synod was held without the patriarch; and JOHN VI CAN-

TACUZENUS, who was eventually to seize the imperial throne, upheld the Palamite theology. However, Palamas was banished to Heraclea a short while later. In 1344 the anti-Palamite party led by Akindynos had Palamas condemned and excommunicated; but this action was colored by a mixture of motives that were both political and ecclesiastical in nature.

In 1347 Cantacuzenus overthrew the Emperor and selected the former monk Isidore as patriarch. He set about the vindication of Palamas, who was named archbishop of Thessalonica but could not take possession of his see until 1350 when the city came under the control of the new emperor. In July 1351 at a new synod in Constantinople Palamas's doctrines were declared orthodox, while Akindynos and Barlaam were condemned and Nicephorus Gregoras was banished. The *Tome* published by this synod was signed by the Patriarch Callistus, and the actions of the synod established Palamas as a teacher of orthodoxy. In a journey between Constantinople and Thessalonica, Palamas was captured by the Turks and was released only after several years upon the payment of a ransom. Meanwhile, in 1354 John V Palaeologus had regained the throne. He arranged a confrontation between Palamas and Nicephorus Gregoras, but was so badly impressed by the two disputants that he lost all interest in their quarrel. Palamas spent his last years as archbishop of Thessalonica, engaged mainly in refuting the charges of Gregoras and composing mystical treatises. He died of an intestinal paralysis, and was canonized in 1368 by the synod under the Patriarch Philotheus Coccinus of Constantinople. He has a special commemoration on the second Sunday in Lent.

Critical Evaluation. Several Western theologians, such as D. Pétau, M. Jugie, and E. Candal, have regarded the teachings of Palamas as at variance with the doctrines of the Western Church, particularly his distinction between the divine nature and the divine operation, which they maintain destroys the simplicity of God's nature. The teaching of Palamas that the blessed in heaven do not see the divine nature but a divine energy seems to be in contradiction with the teaching of Pope BENEDICT XII (Denz 1000) that the blessed enjoy a face-to-face vision of the divine essence.

Palamite doctrine on the divine nature of the light of Mt. Tabor and the visible presence of uncreated grace in the pure of heart has been an obstacle for Western theologians in accepting Palamas as a teacher of orthodoxy. On the other hand, Palamas's insistence that the whole man is engraced, body and soul, and the stress that he placed on the role of the body in prayer has been adopted in the West by theologians such as I. Hausherr.

The majority of Palamas's literary productions were devoted to defending his Hesychast doctrine by using a combination of Platonic and Aristotelian philosophy as foundation. Besides nine tracts in defense of the Hesychasm of the monks, ten treatises against Akindynos and five against Gregoras, he wrote small tracts, letters, and a poem of 618 iambic verses. He published six writings against the Latin theology, two of which (in 1355 and 1356) were directed against a papal legation in Constantinople, and a third against JOHN XI BECCUS. He also wrote apologetic tracts on his captivity in Islam; 150 chapters on spiritual practices, ethics, and theology; prayers; sermons, of which a homiliarium with 63 pieces was published soon after his death; and a commentary on the Ten Commandments.

Bibliography: J. P. MIGNE ed. *Patrologia Graeca* v. 150–151. H. G. BECK, *Kirche und theologische Literatur im byzantinischen Reich* (Munich 1959) 364–368, 712–715. J. MEYENDORFF, *A Study of Gregory Palamas,* tr. G. LAWRENCE (London 1964); θεολογία 25 (1954) 602–613; ed. and tr., *Défense de saints hésychastes,* 2 v. (*Spicilegium sacrum Lovaniense* 1959). R. JANIN, *Lexicon für Theologie und Kirche,* 10 v. 4:1214. M. JUGIE, A. VACANT, et al., ed. *Dictionnaire de théologie catholique,* 15 v. (Paris 1903–50) 11.2:1735–76. I. HAUSHERR, ''L'Hésychasme,'' *Orientalia Christiana periodica* 22 (1956) 5–40, 241–285. B. KRIVOSHEIN, *The Eastern Churches Quarterly* 3 (1938–39) 26–33, 71–84, 138–156, 193–214. V. LOSSKY, *The Vision of God,* tr. A. MOORHOUSE (London 1963). G. G. ARNAKIS, *Speculum* 26 (1951) 104–118; *Byzantion* 22 (1952) 305–312. P. WITTEK, *ibid.* 21 (1951) 421–423.

[H. D. HUNTER]

PALASER, THOMAS, BL.

Priest, martyr; b. ca. 1570 at Ellerton-upon-Swale (near Boulton), North Riding, Yorkshire, England; hanged, drawn, and quartered Aug. 9, 1600 at Durham. He studied in the English College at Valladolid (1592–96) where he was ordained (1596). Upon returning to England, he was arrested almost immediately in the home of Bl. John NORTON with Norton, his wife Margaret, and Bl. John TALBOT. All four were tried at Durham and sentenced to death: Palaser for his priesthood and the others for assisting him. Margaret Norton, who was pregnant, and another gentleman, who was condemned at the same time but apostatized, were reprieved. The attempted poisoning of Palaser and his companions by the jailer's wife resulted in the conversion of Mary Day, her servant. Palaser, Norton, and Talbot were beatified by Pope John Paul II on Nov. 22, 1987 with George Haydock and Companions.

Feast of the English Martyrs: May 4 (England).

See Also: ENGLAND, SCOTLAND, AND WALES, MARTYRS OF.

Bibliography: R. CHALLONER, *Memoirs of Missionary Priests,* ed. J. H. POLLEN (rev. ed. London 1924). J. H. POLLEN, *Acts of English Martyrs* (London 1891).

[K. I. RABENSTEIN]

PALAU Y QUER, FRANCISCO, BL.

Also called Francis of Jesus Mary Joseph; Discalced Carmelite (OCD), mystic priest, thaumaturge, and founder of the Theresian Missionary Carmelite Sisters and the Missionary Carmelite Sisters; b. Aytona, Lérida (Lleida) Province of Catalonia, Spain, Dec. 29, 1811; d. Tarragona, March 20, 1872. Born into a poor but devout family, Francis Palau entered the seminary at Lérida in 1828. After studying philosophy and completing one year of theology, he joined the Discalced Carmelites (1832). He made his religious profession on Nov. 14, 1833 and was ordained a priest on April 2, 1836.

Upheaval in Spain at the time caused him to live outside the cloister in France from 1840 to 1851. Upon returning to Spain, he preached and gave missions in the Balearic Islands and in Barcelona, where he founded his ''School of Virtue,'' a model for catechetical instruction. The school was suppressed upon the accusation that it was being used to foment labor strikes, and Francis was forced into exile, from 1854 to 1860, on the small barren island of Vedrá, off the coast of Ibiza.

When Francis was allowed to return to the mainland following the intervention of Queen Isabella II, he organized small communities of women (1860–61) in the Balearic Islands that later became the Theresian Missionary Carmelite Sisters and the Missionary Carmelite Sisters. He also founded the now-defunct Brothers of Charity. Fr. Palau traveled to Rome to present his concerns to the pope (1866) and to serve as consultor to the bishops gathered for Vatican Council I (1870). He died peacefully at age 60 and was beatified by John Paul II on April 24, 1988.

Feast: Nov. 7 (Carmelites).

Bibliography: *L'Osservatore Romano,* English edition, no. 16 (1988). GREGORIO DE JESÚS CRUCIFICADO, *Braza entre cenizas: Biografía del R. P. Francisco Palau y Quer* (Bilbao, Spain 1956).

[K. I. RABENSTEIN]

PALEOGRAPHY, GREEK

The philological discipline dealing with Greek writings on papyrus, parchment, and paper from the 4th century B.C. to the 16th century A.D.

The Epigraphical Style of the Papyri and the Formation of the Ptolemaic Literary and Documentary

Epigraphical style: "Curse of Artemisia," 4th century B.C.

Hands. Before the copious finds of papyri in the second half of the 19th century, inscriptions were almost the sole evidence for the form of Greek writing before the 4th century A.D. (*see* PAPYROLOGY). The earliest Greek papyri from the second half of the 4th century B.C., such as the Vienna Papyrus, the *Curse of Artemisia,* the Berlin papyrus containing the *Persians* of Timotheus, and the Orphic text on a charred papyrus found in a Hellenistic grave near Thessalonica in 1962 and not yet published, all exhibit in their writing close connections with inscriptions incised on stone. It is surprising to note that there are no ligatures in these earliest examples of Greek handwriting. The letters follow each other without connection, and word and sentence divisions are absent. Round forms are avoided, Epsilon and Sigma are written in angular form as in inscriptions, and Phi shows a triangle in place of a circle or ellipse. This form of writing, which may be called the "Epigraphical style" (Hunger), falls regularly within the space of two lines (majuscule writing) with only individual letters (e. g., Epsilon, Rho, or Nu) rising above or going below these boundaries.

On the basis of the few examples so far known from this early period, it appears that the Greeks did not have a cursive hand before the Hellenistic Age. The investigation of early Ptolemaic papyri has shown that both the literary hand, i.e., the calligraphic script employed for literary texts and books, and the documentary hand, i.e., the cursive or common form of writing, of the last centuries B.C., developed from the epigraphical style (*see* EPIGRAPHY, CHRISTIAN). While the literary hand in principle avoids ligatures, the cursive tries constantly to combine two, three, or more letters, and often employs numerous time and space saving abbreviations, without, however, obscuring the meaning of the text for the addressee familiar with the circumstances or allusions. The literary hand always remained essentially a majuscule script running between two lines. The cursive, on the contrary, soon broke through the two-line system and, from the Late Empire, became a typical four-line form of writing.

Development of the Greek Literary Hand to the End of the Uncial. During the more than 1,000 years during which the Greek literary hand flourished in a majuscule form, few stylistic tendencies can be noted, and they are limited to a few centuries. In the 1st century B.C. and the 1st century A.D. the so-called Hook style was in vogue, but its antecedents are to be traced to a much earlier period. The most famous example of this type of writing is the Florentine papyrus containing the *Lock of Berenice* of Callimachus (*Papiri greci e latini* 1092). The rounded forms predominate not only in the case of Epsilon and Sigma, but also in that of Alpha, Mu, and Pi. In the way of ornament many letters standing on the line are furnished with little horizontal hooks or serifs—so Eta, Iota, Mu, Nu, Pi, Rho, Upsilon, and Phi. Occasionally such hooks are found on the upper line as well. The two-line system is strictly maintained, and there are no ligatures. The famous rolls of Herculaneum, which were already discovered in the 18th century, fall largely within this stylistic category.

Many papyri of the 2d and 3d centuries A.D. exhibit another stylistic form that, since W. Schubart, is called the Strict style. Marked regularity in the composition of the individual letters and of the whole line gives the script an aesthetically pleasing character. While some papyri of the Strict style observe regularly the vertical position in their letters, and others admit a slight slope to the right, all show in common a contrast between unusually broad and especially small letters. Eta, Mu, Nu, Pi, and Omega are broadened to a marked degree, and Delta, Kappa, Lambda, and Chi are flattened. On the other hand, letters such as Beta, Theta, Epsilon, and Sigma are kept extremely small. Omicron, Sigma, and Omega are frequently written in such small and cramped form that they cannot fill the interval between the two lines, which in other cases is well occupied. True letter connections (ligatures) are lacking. Through the writing of two letters close together (juxtaposition), however, there are frequent examples of apparent ligatures. As reading aids, accents, apostrophes, and punctuation marks are found in papyri of the Strict style, especially in those containing poetic texts. They are to be explained by the contemporary interest in the theory and use of accents (see Herodian, Καθολικὴ προσῳδία, 2d century A.D.). Subsequently, this usage declined until a full accentual system was de-

Byzantine minuscule: 10th century A.D.

veloped in the Middle Byzantine minuscule. Characteristic representatives of the Strict style are the Bacchylides Papyrus (British Museum), the Alcaeus Papyrus (Oxyrhynchus Papyri 1234), the Vienna Xenophon (G.24568), and the Phaedrus Papyrus (Oxyr. Pap.1016).

The "Biblical style" developed out of the Strict style in the course of the 3d century A.D. It takes its name from the famous biblical MSS of the 4th and 5th centuries, namely, the *Codex Sinaiticus* (London), *Codex Vaticanus* (Vat. Gr. 1209), and *Codex Alexandrinus* (London). The conventional designation "uncial" for this stylistic form is rightly questioned, but, in any case, to avoid misunderstandings the term should not be used for other types of writing. To the early precursors of the Biblical style in the 2d and 3d century A.D., a London Homer Papyrus (Pap. Lit. Lond. 7) and a Berlin Homer Papyrus (Pap. Berol. 7499), must now be added the earliest witness for the Gospel of St. John, known only since 1956 (Pap.[66] = Pap. Bodmer II). The most important

characteristic feature of the Biblical style is the tendency to equalize the divergent sizes of small and broad letters. In this style most letters can be reduced to a basic square form or inscribed in a square. Iota, Rho, Phi, and Omega are the only exceptions. Full, rounded forms dominate, and the two-line system is strictly observed. Narrow or "emaciated" letters are avoided except at the ends of lines.

After the century of the great Biblical MSS this style developed only very gradually. The uncials of the famous Dioscorides MS at Vienna, which was written *c*. 512, exhibit thickenings at the extremities of Epsilon and Sigma, heavy dots on the top of the upper line in the case of Kappa, Pi, and Tau, and knoblike feet on the extended base of the Delta. Kappa frequently appears in two parts, a phenomenon that leads to popular confusion of EK and EIC. The length of the lower parts of Phi, Rho, and Upsilon is marked. Besides the uncial MSS showing vertical letters, others are found with a significant slope. This

Metochites style: 14th century A.D.

slope, however, should not be employed as a criterion for dating. In the Middle Byzantine period the uncial was used beside the newly introduced minuscule, especially in liturgical texts, well into the 12th century. Characteristic features of this late and so-called liturgical uncial are pointed oval forms of the earlier round letters, long trunnions on the crossbars of the Gamma, Delta, Theta, Pi, and Tau, and a marked contrast between light upstrokes and heavy downstrokes.

A special development of the uncial in the 6th to the 10th centuries has recently been called the Coptic style (by J. Irigoin). The Copts adopted the Greek uncial as the literary hand for committing their own literature to written form, but they stylized it probably under the influence of the chancery of the Alexandrian Patriarchate—in the direction of the chancery hand. The Coptic style exhibits unusually large individual letters, a small Alpha, and a deep-saddle form of Mu. Good examples are the Papyrus Codex of CYRIL OF ALEXANDRIA in Dublin, Paris, and Vienna, and the *Paschal Letter* from Alexandria of 719, now in Berlin. The Biblical Style, as an ornamental script for superscriptions, colophons, lemmata, and marginalia lived on for centuries in the form of a small uncial influenced by the chancery hand.

The Cursive from the Early Empire to the Arab Domination in Egypt. The Greek cursive of the Imperial

Age developed without marked transitional features from the Ptolemaic documentary hand. The papyrus documents of the Early Empire are often written in a small, narrow script that consciously ignores stylization and constantly permits interchange in the *ductus* of its letters. The same letters are often written by the same hand in two or three different ways. The possibilities of confusion between various letters, as between Mu and Nu, Eta and Upsilon, multiply. In the 2d and 3d centuries, Beta usually rests on a broad horizontal base, and the bipartite Epsilon rises above the upper line. In the 3d century the lower extremities of letters increase in length to such a degree that they extend into the next line or even beyond it. The neglect of style, *ductus,* and alignment, and the deterioration of regular letter forms in documents written in this script increased steadily from the 4th century. As opposed to this kind of writing, the chanceries of high officials clung to their markedly characteristic style (the Chancery style). The vertical is emphasized, and the letters are regularly formed, but they are always taller than they are broad, so that the script reminds one of a trellis or lattice (Lattice Script). Individual "emaciated" forms (Alpha, Omicron, and also Delta and Omega), marked lower extensions, and ornamental hooks at the foot of many letters distinguish the Chancery style.

After the establishment of CONSTANTINOPLE as the new imperial residence and the foundation of the Byzantine Empire, the field belonged to the so-called Byzantine cursive, which is preserved in many thousands of papyrus documents and letters of the 4th to the 7th century. This new script of everyday use was strongly influenced by the Chancery style. Through numerous extensions of its letters upward and downward it became, toward the end of the 4th century, a true four-line system of writing. The most striking upward extensions are shown by Beta, Epsilon, Eta, Iota, and Kappa, and by Delta also in the shape of the Latin D. Extensions downward appear in Beta, Gamma, Iota, Rho, Phi, Chi, Psi, and especially in Lambda, which sinks completely below the line. Large and small letters are set off clearly from one another. The Byzantine cursive, with its many gradations and its frequent baroque ostentation, is the living image of the Byzantine spirit and outlook, characterized by its predilection for orders of rank and ceremonial in all phases of life.

Following the Arab conquest of Egypt (641) the Byzantine cursive deteriorated, and the difference between large and small letters increased even more. In a parallel development, however, there should be noted the gradual consolidation of letter forms that later—from the second half of the 8th century—were to constitute the elements of the new Byzantine minuscule. Hence many documents of the 7th and 8th centuries exhibit side by side in their colophons uncial and half-cursive letter forms that point to the coming of the minuscule.

The Byzantine Minuscule from Its Beginning to the 16th Century. The greater number of some 60,000 extant Greek MSS from the Byzantine period are written in the consciously created script that is customarily called book minuscule, calligraphic minuscule, or simply minuscule. The beginnings of this script, which developed out of the Byzantine cursive, may be traced back to *c.* 800. Clearly an attempt was made to combine the beauty and clarity of the uncial with the fluidity and practical utility of the cursive. The so-called *Codex Uspensky,* an *evangeliarium* written in 835, is the oldest dated MS to show pure minuscule. The transfer of the extant works of ancient literature from uncial MSS to MSS written in the new minuscule was a process of decisive importance for the history of the transmission of texts. It was carried out in the age of the Macedonian dynasty (9th and 10th centuries).

The minuscule, like the Byzantine cursive, is a four-line system of writing: the elements of many letters rise above or sink below the lines. It exhibits a tendency to combine two to ten, or even more, letters into a continuous unit—often without regard for separation of words. The following features are valuable for dating in the first centuries of the minuscule: writing above the line—the letters standing on the pre-drawn or impressed line (mostly in the 9th century); a slight slope to the left (likewise in the 9th century); and the form of the rough breathing—a half-Eta in the 9th and 10th centuries, an angular form in the 10th and 11th centuries, and a round form predominating from the late 10th century and gaining ground steadily in subsequent centuries. The entrance of uncial letter forms into later MSS (from the 10th century) can also be observed, but not everywhere with the same regularity.

The older division of minuscule MSS into three or four periods has been abandoned. It seems preferable to make only two major divisions: (1) the period from the 9th to the 12th century, characterized by a predominantly conservative script retaining symmetrical forms and exhibiting gradual introduction of changes; (2) the period from the end of the 12th century, characterized by marked changes in the form of writing and a pronounced deterioration of order or regularity in *ductus.*

From the 9th to the 12th Century. In general, the minuscule MSS of the 9th and 10th centuries present a fairly symmetrical aspect, with an austere to reserved character that results from a certain angularity of forms. In the 11th century the scribes in the scriptoria of the capital overcame this harshness or primness by using regular round forms, avoiding points and angles, and eliminating uncial

letters and abbreviations. Because of the resemblance of many groups of letters in which the elements of this script, especially the circular Omicron and the fanlike round Upsilon similar to a string of pearls, predominate, this form of writing has been christened ''Pearl script'' (Hunger).

The changes in the aspect of writing that appear in many MSS of the 12th century resulted from the enlargement and cruder formation of many letters, new ligatures, and abbreviations, and from the piling up of letters on one another. The circumflex is extended in use and spans three or more letters, and the boundaries of the writing area are broken by lines running into the margin, or by letters with excessively large upper and lower extremities in beginning and closing lines. A glance at the originals of imperial documents of the 10th and 11th centuries shows that the script of the imperial chancery reveals in especially pronounced forms the characteristic features mentioned above. In all probability, therefore, the chancery may have exercised its influence on the minuscule.

From the End of the 12th to the 16th Century. The majority of minuscule MSS experienced marked changes in the course of the 13th century. The phenomena noted above increased in a much more extensive manner. The ligatures Epsilon-Rho and Epsilon-Xi pass from the pointed to the rounded form. The syllable μεν is written in a single character with a high, drawn-out and hooklike Epsilon. The prepositions ἐπὶ and μετὰ appear in cursive abbreviation, and Iota subscript and the modern Epsilon (sloping to the left) are frequent. Accents are connected not only with abbreviations, but also with letters and tachygraphic signs. Neglect of alignment and *ductus,* and abandonment of aesthetic considerations, often transform the calligraphic minuscule into a purely utilitarian hand.

The influence of political events is closely connected with the history of writing. The establishment of the LATIN EMPIRE by the Venetians and the crusaders (1204) forced many Byzantines to leave Constantinople. From new centers (Nicaea and Epirus) they planned restoration of the Byzantine state. During this period, following the dissolution of the Byzantine imperial chancery in the capital, it was possible to employ the large ornamental letters and flourishes and the extended extremities of letter forms that had hitherto been restricted to the imperial chancery. It should not be overlooked, however, that in addition to such degenerate and undisciplined hands of the 13th century, there were others that, in a consciously archaizing tendency, attempted to continue an approximation of the Pearl script of the 11th century. In most such cases there is question of biblical texts or liturgical MSS. A closer examination indicates that the archaizing scribes from the 13th to the 15th centuries sooner or later betrayed themselves by the use of modern elements in their writing.

In the late 13th and in the first half of the 14th century two further styles of Greek writing may be noted. Many MSS from the period 1275 to 1325 are characterized by the fact that some of their rounded letters, such as Omicron, Sigma, Omega, Alpha, and the ligature Epsilon-Iota are written especially large. These closed, round forms float over the jumble of the rest of the script after the manner of blobs of fat in a soup (the "Blob style").

The imperial chancery under ANDRONICUS II (ruled 1282–1328) and his grandson, ANDRONICUS III (ruled 1328–41), employed another distinctive style. Archaizing and calligraphic elements were used to create a new and aesthetically satisfying minuscule that, to its advantage, turned away from the examples of the unpretentious common script described above. Its limited use of abbreviations and large letters with long upper and lower extremities, its reduction of the large accent marks to small form, and its moderation in the employment of ligatures, all bear witness to the work of disciplined scribes. Since this style, in addition to its use in imperial documents of the age, appears especially in MSS containing the works of Theodore Metochites, Grand Logothete and friend of Andronicus II, it may be called the Metochites style (Hunger). It is found—in somewhat modified form—until the end of the 14th century.

In the early 15th century the Byzantines, in an effort that parallels that of the Western humanists in Italy, attempted to go back to the minuscule forms of the 9th to the 12th centuries, thus improving the contemporary script and putting a brake on further deterioration. By the use of separation of letters and words, punctuation, and free standing accents, the MSS written in the revised style—often containing classical authors—were made much more legible.

Following the invention of printing by Johann GUTENBERG, the first book set wholly in Greek type, namely, the *Greek Grammar* of Constantine Lascaris, was published at Milan in 1476. The cutting of Greek type fonts, difficult as it was at first, reached its maturity by the 1490s at the presses of Zacharias Calliergis, but especially in the outstanding productions of Aldus MANUTIUS. At this time, and far into the 16th century, a reciprocal influence may be noted in MSS and printed books. Many letter forms of the "Press Minuscule" betray their origin by a certain rigidity and lack of adaptability. The single-stroke Tau with handlelike crossbar; the elongated Gamma with a similar handle; the ugly, squashed majuscule Theta; and the angular Phi, all characterize the Press Minuscule.

Bibliography: B. A. VAN GRONINGEN, *Short Manual of Greek Palaeography* (3d ed. Leiden 1963). E. M. THOMPSON, *An Introduction to Greek and Latin Palaeography* (Oxford 1912). A. DAIN, *Les Manuscrits* (rev. ed. Paris 1964). W. SCHUBART, *Griechische Paläographie* (Munich 1925). R. DEVREESSE, *Introduction à l'étude des manuscrits grecs* (Paris 1954). A. SIGALAS, Ἱστορία τῆς Ἑλλενικῆς Γραφῆς (Salonika 1934). V. GARDTHAUSEN, *Griechische Paläographie*, 2 v. (2d ed. Leipzig 1911–13). H. HUNGER, *Studien zur griechischen Paläographie* (Vienna 1954); "Antikes und mittelalterliches Buch- und Schriftwesen," in *Geschichte der Textüberlieferung der antiken und mittelalterlichen Literatur*, ed. H. HUNGER et al. (Zurich 1961–) 1:25–147, esp. 72–107. J. IRIGOIN, "Pour une étude des centres de copie byzantins," *Scriptorium* 12 (1958) 208–227; 13 (1959) 177–209; "L'Onciale grecque de type copte," *Jahrbuch der österreichischen byzantinischen Gesellschaft* 8 (1959) 29–51. C. H. ROBERTS, *Greek Literary Hands, 350 B.C.–A.D. 400* (Oxford 1956). K. and S. LAKE, eds., *Monumenta palaeographica vetera. First Series: Dated Greek Minuscule Manuscripts to the Year 1200,* 10 v. (Boston 1934–39), indexes to v.1–10 (1945). E. MIONI, *Introduzione alla paleografia greca* (Padua 1973). E. GAMILLSCHEG and D. HARLFINGER, *Repertorium der griechischen Kopisten 800–1600* (Vienna 1981–97). E. FOLLIERI, *Codices graeca Bibliothecae Vaticanae selecti, temporum locorumque ordine digesti commentariis et transcriptionibus instructi* (Vatican City 1969).

[H. HUNGER]

PALEOGRAPHY, LATIN

The object of Latin paleography is the study of the various forms of handwriting in which Latin texts were written and of the forms of writing derived from them. Like all alphabets used in ancient Italy, the Latin alphabet represents a Western type of Greek alphabet, that is, an alphabet in which the Γ, Δ, Λ, Π, Ρ, Σ, and Υ of the Eastern and classical Greek alphabet have forms that are quite similar to C, D, L, P, R, S, and V (U), but in which the X was pronounced *ks* and not *kh*, the H indicated aspiration, and the Digamma and Koppa were still in use. The Latins, however, did not borrow their alphabet directly from the Greeks, according to most authorities, but took it from the Etruscans. This would explain why their C had the value of a voiceless guttural, which gave it the same value as K and Q, and why there was no symbol to denote the voiced guttural (ModE G). Their G was created only in 312 B.C. by modifying the letter C.

Rise and Spread of Latin Writing. The oldest Latin text is that engraved on the mutilated stele found in 1899 on the site of the old *Forum Romanum*. It dates from either the end of the 7th century B.C. or the beginning of the 6th. Latin writing was used by Roman soldiers, merchants, and officials throughout the empire. In the East, however, as well as in other areas where Greek was used as a means of communication, neither the Latin language nor the Latin script took root. In the Eastern areas of the empire various native linguistic groups, such as the Copts, the Goths, and later some of the Slavs, used alphabets derived essentially from the Greek alphabet. As a result, after the fall of the empire, Latin handwriting, like the Latin language, survived only in the West.

After the 3d century, Latin writing became that of the Roman Church, and from the 6th to the 12th century, in the course of the Christianization of the pagan peoples of northern Europe, it became the writing of Ireland, Germany, Norway, and Sweden. At various times Latin writing was adopted for the vernacular languages (even for non-Indo-European ones): for Celtic in the 1st century; in the 8th century for Welsh, English, and German; for French in the 9th century; for Provençal, Catalan, Spanish, Portuguese, Norwegian, and Icelandic in the 12th century; for Italian, Hungarian, Czech, Danish, and Swedish in the 13th century; for Old Prussian in the 14th century and for Polish and Croatian in the 15th century. Basque, Breton, Lithuanian, Lettish, Estonian, and Finnish adopted Latin writing in the 16th century; Albanian and Romanian, in the 19th century.

Through the influence of printing, Latin writing became widely disseminated and received a fixed form during the 15th century, and it has since become the writing of Western civilization. During the 19th century, Catholic and Protestant missionaries adapted the Latin alphabet to many native languages, among others, those of Vietnam and Madagascar. Some of the nationalistic and revolutionary movements of the 20th century, in an attempt to fight illiteracy and to promote modernization, abandoned traditional writing in favor of the Latin form of writing. Even though Russia and many other nations in the former U.S.S.R. still retain their Cyrillic alphabet, other nations have adopted the Latin hand. Since 1926 it has been used by the Islamic-Turkish republic of the former U.S.S.R; and since 1928, by Turkey. China officially adopted the Latin alphabet in 1958 but was faced with a tremendous task of adjustment, which it has still hardly begun.

The Science of Paleography. The first scientific treatise on Latin paleography is found in the last four chapters of Book I of the *De re diplomatica* (1681) by Dom Jean MABILLON. A contemporary of the first naturalists, among them J. P. de Tournefort, whose *Éléments de Botanique* (1694) contained the first modern classification of plants, Mabillon attempted to classify the scripts known to him on the basis of their distinctive characteristics. He thus distinguished three types of Roman script—the uncial, or capital; the *minuta*, or minuscule; and the *minuta forensis*—as well as four types of national hands that he believed to be original creations, Gothic, Lombard, Frankish, and Anglo-Saxon.

This classification was refuted and rejected by Scipione Maffei in his *Istoria diplomatica* (1727). Maffei was the first to advance the thesis of the original unity of Latin writing. He maintained that the so-called national hands were only ''degenerate'' forms of Roman writing.

The six-volume *Nouveau traité de diplomatique* (1750–65) by R. P. Tassin and C. F. Toustain, Benedic-

tines of the congregation of Saint-Maur (*see* MAURISTS), is the masterpiece of the ''Nomenclature School,'' or, as their members would be called today by the naturalists, the ''taxonomists.'' To some extent the *Nouveau traité* is to the *De re diplomatica* of Mabillon what the *Systema naturae* (1735) of C. Linnaeus is to the *Éléments de botanique* of Tournefort. The paleographic section of the *Nouveau traité* is an ''abecedarian history'' in which the authors strove to teach ''the art of determining the age and the country of origin of the letters by studying the variety of their forms and characteristics, acquired between their origin and the 18th century'' (2.2). One can only admire the work of the two Maurists. Unfortunately, however, their classifications were not based on such obvious and fundamental characteristics as those selected by the genius of Linnaeus. Script is neither a living organism, the product of natural growth, nor even a system of self-developing forms. The ordering of hands on the basis of external characteristics can lead only to arbitrary and extremely complicated classifications. In fact the classification of the Maurists is recognized today as completely inadequate, and frequently incomprehensible.

In the latter half of the 19th century, W. Wattenbach in his *Anleitung zur lateinischen Paläographie* (1866) and Léopold Delisle in his works after 1875 found a new and more fruitful approach. Both Wattenbach and Delisle studied the letters in relation to their formation in writing. Botanists might describe their approach as that of the ''geneticists,'' for they tried to reconstitute the *ductus*, i.e., the movement of the pen in forming the letter, and to establish a genealogy of writing based on the historical development of its forms. The latter approach resembled that of their contemporaries the comparative philologists, who sought to establish families of languages. Delisle and Wattenbach succeeded in separating paleography from diplomatics and in definitively making paleography an autonomous discipline. At the same time L. Traube assigned paleography its true place among the historical sciences by viewing the scripts it studies as the expression or reflection of a civilization.

Latin Writing from the 1st to the 6th Century. Although in principle the ''science of handwriting'' does not need to concern itself with the material on which the letters are written, the very fact that scholars turned their attention to the *ductus* led them to neglect the fixed forms of writing, which are characteristic of engraved letters. Latin inscriptions on stone and bronze were, even as late as 1850, almost the only known specimens of Roman writing and the only ''documents'' preserved—as opposed to narrative sources and juridical codifications. The study of these inscriptions was established as an autonomous discipline under the name of epigraphy. Paleography, accordingly, abandoned inscriptions to devote itself solely to the study of official documents and books written by hand and in ink. Since the oldest manuscripts then known could be dated no earlier than the 4th or 5th century, paleographers ignored the preceding centuries. Epigraphists, however, showed little or no interest in the form of the letters. As a result, scholars began the history of Latin writing only with the 5th century. So complete was the ignorance of earlier scripts that Natalis de Wailly attempted to prove that the wax tablets found in 1841 in the gold mines of Transylvania, and dated between A.D. 139 and 162, were forgeries. In 1889 M. Prou expressed the same opinion in the first edition of his *Manuel de paléographie* (24).

Meanwhile, the excavations at Pompeii had revealed the cursive Latin hand of the 1st century. The first graffiti were discovered in 1765 but were not published until 1792 and 1793 in Nuremberg (cf. R. Garucci, *Graffiti de Pompei*, 2d ed. Paris 1856). Their publication was barely noticed, and it was not until 1837 that the *Inscriptiones Pompeianae* of J. Wordsworth brought them to the attention of the scholarly world. In 1849 the first edition of the *Graffiti* of Garucci contained a thoroughly satisfactory study of cursive writing, but it too was scarcely noticed by paleographers. Finally, some slight interest was shown in the publication of C. Zangemeister's *Inscriptiones parietariae Pompeianae* (*Corpus inscriptionum latinarum* 4; Berlin 1871).

Four years after Zangemeister's publication, the tables of the banker Jucundus were discovered at Pompeii, but they did not become common knowledge until Zangemeister in 1898 devoted the *Supplementi pars prior* of *Corpus inscriptionum latinarum* v. 4 to their publication. The first ancient Latin papyrus to be unearthed in modern times, the *Carmen de bello Actiaco,* had been found during the excavations at Herculaneum in 1730 and was reproduced as an engraving in 1793 in the first volume of the *Herculanensium voluminum quae supersunt* (*see* PAPYROLOGY). Zangemeister and Wattenbach in their *Exempla codicum latinorum litteris maiusculis scriptorum* (Heidelberg 1876) plates 1, 2, 3, reproduced two others in part. From 1895 Egypt began to furnish literary as well as documentary Latin papyri but in very small numbers—approximately 200 between 1895 and 1914—of which only half were published at the time; and only about 50 were reproduced by 1915. A young American papyrologist, H. B. Van Hoesen, studied their script (*Roman Cursive Writing*, Princeton 1915) and traced the history of the Roman cursive hand from the 1st to the 6th century. But the study of all forms of writing used prior to the 5th century was not definitively included in Latin paleography until the publication in 1921 of Luigi Schiaparelli's *Scrittura latina nell'eta romana.*

All the above-mentioned works were remarkable; yet they were not as perfect and precise as their authors might have made them had the available documentation been less rudimentary.

The Use of Photography and Electronic Digitalization. Photography was first introduced into paleography in 1858 by T. von Sickel, who later used photoengraving as well in his *Monumenta graphica medii aevi ex archivis et bibliothecis imperii Austriaci collecta* (10 fasc. 1858–82). Paleographers were rather slow in recognizing the potential role of photomechanical reproduction. The imperfections of the first processes, the high cost of the stereotype plates, and the unsatisfactory lighting apparatus were no doubt the cause of their slowness. In 1871 Zangemeister failed in his attempts to reproduce photographically the graffiti (*Corpus inscriptionum latinarum* 4:11.39), and E. Hübner decided against employing photoengraving in his *Exempla scripturae epigraphicae latinae* (Berlin 1885). In fact, the photography of graffiti and inscriptions continues to present particular difficulties (cf. J. S. and A. E. Gordon, *Contributions to the Paleography of Latin Inscriptions,* Berkeley 1957; repr. Milan 1977). The most adequate process for photographing graffiti and wax tablets involves the use of sodium lamps, but this is extremely difficult outside a well-organized laboratory. The paleographical study of inscriptions is therefore still in its infancy, and this has inhibited the study of the Latin calligraphy of the first four centuries. Even as late as 1953 there were barely three or four photographs of the graffiti of Pompeii, and scholars were content to use copies. The first photographs of the Latin papyri of Herculaneum were published by E. A. Lowe in *Codices latini antiquiores* (v. 3 Oxford 1938, Nos. 385–387).

There have been numerous reproductions of medieval manuscripts, and starting in the late 19th century several large collections appeared in which the photography leaves nothing to be desired. These collections, however, had no preestablished design and were arranged by chance, depending on findings and research. As a result they contributed only a fragmentary documentation on which no exhaustive study could be based. These insufficiencies were partially remedied by the prodigious development of microfilm technique, but a more effective remedy would come through a series of systematic and massive facsimile collections.

The first, *Codices Latini Antiquiores* (= CLA), conceived and carried to completion by E. A. Lowe, began to appear in 1934. In twelve volumes (1–11 + Supplement) (Oxford 1934–1971) and two series of Addenda in *Mediaeval Studies* (47 and 54, Toronto 1985 and 1992) a paleographical description and a sample facsimile from one or more pages are furnished for every known extant Latin literary manuscript copied before the 9th century (1884 items in all). Starting in 1954, A. Bruckner and R. Marichal and eventually many other collaborators did something similar for official documents. Their *Chartae latinae antiquiores* (= ChLA), in 49 volumes (1–4: Olten-Lausanne; 5–49: Dietikon-Zurich; 1954–98), provides a complete facsimile edition with transcription of all known extant Latin charters copied before the 9th century (1468 items in all). With some exceptions (a few papyri, graffiti, wax tablets, and inscriptions) all the extant writing evidence of the first eight centuries of the Christian era is now available for study in published facsimiles.

The same, however, cannot be said, and almost certainly will never be able to be said, for the period from the 9th century onward, because of the sheer mass of the surviving material (hundreds of thousands of manuscripts and documents). Just the same, for the 9th century itself some systematic projects are underway. All of its Latin literary manuscripts from the Continent are being systematically described, though unfortunately without facsimiles, in B. Bischoff's *Katalog der festländischen Handschriften des neunten Jahrhunderts* (*mit Ausnahme der wisigotischen*) (Wiesbaden 1998–). Part I deals in alphabetical order by place of preservation with the manuscripts from Aachen to Lambach. The documents of the 9th century have begun to be published in a facsimile edition in a second series of *Chartae latinae antiquiores*, edited by G. Cavallo and G. Nicolaj (Dietikon-Zurich, 1998–). Seven volumes (50–56) were published by 2000 (181 items, all from Italy).

But long before these two 9th-century projects began to see the light of day another approach had already been taken to the massive numbers of manuscripts from the later period. At an international conference held in Paris in 1953 at the instigation of C. Samaran most of the leading Latin paleographers of the time decided to support a plan to publish catalogues with sample facsimiles of all the objectively dated manuscripts copied before 1600 (or at least 1550), i.e., up to a time by which the codex was definitively replaced by the printed book. The international committee, under whose aegis each nation would publish its own dated, and if it so desired also its objectively placed, manuscripts, became in 1957 the Comité International de Paléographie (Latine, added to its name in 1985 = CIPL) and henceforth provided permanent patronage and direction for paleographical studies.

The first volume of the *Catalogue des manuscrits datés* (= CMD), issued in two parts for the descriptions and the facsimiles respectively, appeared in 1959 and dealt with the Musée Condé and Parisian libraries other than the Bibliothéque Nationale. By 2000 42 volumes

had been published, mostly also in two parts, treating the dated manuscripts in Austria, Belgium, France, Germany, Great Britain, Holland, Italy, Sweden, Switzerland, and Vatican City. Even though most of these national catalogues are still not wholly complete, there are now facsimiles of almost 25,000 dated manuscripts available for comparison by anyone who wishes to date an undated manuscript, and also available of course for anyone interested in tracing the history of Latin scripts. This is certainly one of the greatest accomplishments in the whole history of paleography. That no analogous project has yet been undertaken for the publication of dated documents (charters, etc.) down to modern times, however desirable this would be, is undoubtedly due to its enormity, since most documents are dated and would therefore have to be included.

If photography marked a new era in the history of paleography by making a generic advance over hand-drawn facsimiles and by giving in its further developments—enlargement, ultraviolet and infrared lights, color filters, x-rays, beta-radiography, etc.—an image of a manuscript often more clear and legible than the original itself, a still greater era may have been introduced with the invention of the computer and of digitalized reproduction or electronic ''photography.'' Enlargement can now be pushed far beyond the possibilities of traditional photography without a loss of precision. Data can be manipulated to enhance or deemphasize any element one chooses, with an obvious advantage for the reading of palimpsests. The application of computerization to the study of scripts is still in its infancy, but the use of digitalized images, eventually of thousands and thousands of manuscripts, promises to make paleographical study enormously easier, cheaper, and more thorough, and to make all of these advantages accessible even in the privacy of the paleographer's own home.

Modern Trends in Paleography. In England and in Austria at the beginning of the 20th century two calligraphers, Edward Johnston and Rudolph von Larisch, as a result of their researches in Latin manuscripts, began to study the writing technique and the shape and holding of the pen best adapted for forming the ancient letters (see E. Johnston, *Writing and Illuminating and Lettering*, London 1906; and the work of a student of Larisch, Otto Hurm, *Schriftform im Schreibwerkzeug*, Vienna 1928). In France in the 1930s and 1940s, Jean Mallon and R. Marichal sought to find in the technical modifications of ancient writing the origin of the considerable changes that Latin writing had undergone during the first four centuries of the Christian era. Their research was independent of that of Johnston and Larisch but led to similar conclusions. In Germany many scholars working in fields touching paleography tried, with considerable temerity, to explain the variations of script in the light of similar changes in architecture and the other arts; at the same time others applied graphology to the history of writing (see H. Fichtenau, *Mensch und Schrift im Mittelalter*, Vienna 1946). As paleography became conscious of its true object, it was more able to clarify its relationship to neighboring disciplines. The study of book scripts was no longer isolated from that of the book itself; and, in fact, a new name, "codicology," was invented for this specialized discipline. This new tendency, advocated particularly in Belgium by F. Masai, led to the creation in Brussels in 1946 of the review *Scriptorium* and in Paris in 1982 of the *Gazette du livre médiéval* which has since become the organ for the CIPL and its companion organization, the Association Paléographique Internationale Culture-Écriture- Société (= APICES). Finally, greater knowledge of the Latin papyri of Egypt has given greater urgency to the question of the relationship between Greek and Latin writing, even though J. Mallon's wish to establish a distinct field of "Greco-Roman" paleography has not come to fruition.

These various developments have resulted in some new theories regarding the history of Latin script. Originally the Greek, Etruscan, and Latin alphabets consisted of "capitals," i.e., generally their form was similar to the letters that are still used in the titles of most books and signs; hence their name. Over a long period the capital, more or less carelessly employed, had been the only form of Latin writing, and at the beginning of the Christian era it was still the only bookscript. The script that became the printers' Roman type font of today, the minuscule, was the humanistic round hand that had been revived at the beginning of the 15th century by the humanists of Florence from the Caroline minuscule of the Carolingian renaissance. To be sure, the Caroline minuscule underwent many changes after the 9th century. Toward the end of the 12th century it assumed angular forms that made the humanists disdainfully call it "Gothic," a name that it still retains but without the pejorative connotations. As writing developed, this Gothic minuscule, while continuing in a formal textual or textura mode, was also debased into various cursive forms, which during the 16th century became extremely difficult to read. These cursive hands continued to be used throughout the 17th century especially by notaries, bailiffs, and lawyers. But at Florence, in the first half of the 15th century, a humanistic cursive hand, the model for the later Italic type font, had been created, paralleling the humanistic round hand and influenced by it. The humanistic cursive had its beginning in the chanceries. Meanwhile in France the normal Gothic cursive hand, known as bastard Gothic, became the book hand, particularly for books written in the vernacular. Modern forms of handwriting were born of both the hu-

manistic cursive and the bastard hands. Therefore, since the 14th century at the latest, all Latin forms of writing have been derived, at least in part or indirectly, from the Caroline minuscule.

Where the Caroline minuscule came from thus becomes the obvious question, to which, basically, two answers have been given. One claims that it comes ultimately out of the later Roman cursive as this was modified in Merovingian Gaul and gradually through a number of pre-Caroline stages made more simple and written more deliberately. This answer can explain all the letter forms in Caroline minuscule except its uncial *a*. The other answer derives it from half-uncial, which can explain all its letter forms except *a, g,* and *n*. The two answers, however, are not as incompatible as they might seem. The scribes who first produced a recognizable Caroline minuscule had undoubtedly earlier been writing a more cursive pre- Caroline minuscule and the new script retained the proportions and something of the vitality of their earlier script. At the same time the models towards which the pre-Caroline letters were moving came, except for *a, g,* and *n*, from half-uncial. But they did not become quite identical with the half-uncial forms—they were less broad and more supple—and the Caroline minuscule scribes continued to make a clear distinction between their script and half-uncial, using the latter mainly for special purposes such as prefaces or first lines of new texts.

If one wants to trace the origins of Caroline minuscule back beyond the later Roman cursive or half-uncial, there is now available, thanks to the excavations of archaeologists since the late 19th century, a considerable amount of new material to compare from the first centuries, including older or earlier Roman cursive and early half-uncial or primitive minuscule. Even the new material, however, is still too sparse, particularly from the crucial second and third centuries, to bring about a unanimous answer. Those who see Caroline minuscule deriving from further developments in the later Roman cursive tend to find the origin of this cursive in the earlier Roman cursive, thanks to changes in the direction of the strokes and to writing dynamics (cf. Bischoff 1990, 65). The earlier Roman cursive would derive from capital script. The later Roman cursive would also be the source of both primitive minuscule and half-uncial. Those who see Caroline minuscule deriving directly from half-uncial tend to find the origin of half-uncial in early half-uncial or primitive minuscule. This latter script would derive in turn from the capital script under the influence of a changed angle of the writing material with respect to the scribe, the result of the change from the papyrus roll to the codex form of the book and possibly also of a different manner of holding the pen. The later Roman cursive would derive from the primitive minuscule (cf. Marichal).

To the paleographer the broad lines in the development of Latin writing appear to have been surely drawn: they follow closely the outline of the intellectual evolution of Western civilization. Yet one very challenging task remains: to determine—with greater or lesser certainty, depending on the degree to which the various types of Gothic and humanistic scripts have been "canonized"—the geographical and chronological characteristics of the last three centuries of the Middle Ages, thereby permitting the localizing and dating of all the documents of that period. With this achievement, rendered immensely more feasible by the many series of *Manuscrits Datés* now available, paleography will have made a valuable contribution to the history of culture and to the history of the diffusion of ideas, a contribution which it alone can supply.

Bibliography: G. BATTELLI, *Lezioni di paleografia latina* (4th ed. Vatican City 1999). B. BISCHOFF, *Latin Palaeography: Antiquity and the Middle Ages*, trans. by D. Ó CRÓINÍN and D. GANZ (Cambridge-New York 1990) from *Paläographie des römischen Altertums und des abendländischen Mittelalters* (2nd ed. Berlin 1986). B. BISCHOFF et al., *Nomenclature des écritures livresques du IXe au XVIe siécle* (Paris 1954). G. CENCETTI, *Lineamenti di storia della scrittura latina* (Bologna 1954; reprinted with bibliographical update 1997). J. J. JOHN, "Latin Paleography" in *Medieval Studies: An Introduction*, ed. by J. M. POWELL (2nd ed. Syracuse 1992) 3–81. J. MALLON, *Paléographie romaine* (Madrid 1952). R. MARICHAL, "L'Écriture latine et la civilisation occidentale du Ier au XVIe siécle," in *L'Écriture et la psychologie des peuples* (Paris 1963) 199–247. M. B. PARKES, *English Cursive Book Hands 1250–1500* (Oxford 1969). A. M. PIAZZONI, "Vers une paléographie électronique?" in *Gazette du livre médiéval* 33 (1998) 11–19. F. STEFFENS, *Lateinische Paläographie* (2nd ed. Trier 1909, and 3rd unaltered ed. Berlin 1929, reprinted 1964), still the best general collection of facsimiles. B. L. ULLMAN, *The Origin and Development of Humanistic Script* (Rome 1960). C. E. WRIGHT, *English Vernacular Hands* (Oxford 1960). Current bibliography in *Gazette du livre médiéval* (Paris 1982–) and the "Bulletin codicologique," in *Scriptorium* (Brussels 1959–).

[R. MARICHAL/J. J. JOHN]

PALESTINE

This article treats the topic of Palestine under the following headings: (1) The Name, (2) Physical Geography, (3) Political Geography, (4) Natural History, (5) Archeology, (6) Pre-Israelite Ethnology, and (7) Holy Places.

1. The Name

The term Palestine is derived from the PHILISTINES who invaded and settled the central and southern coastal area of the Holy Land about the same time that the Israel-

Stele depicting lion and dog fights, 14th century, Palestine.

ites were invading the central highlands from the eastern and southern deserts (*c.* 1200 B.C.). In early Christian terminology Palestine included the territory that extended from the foothills of the Lebanon Mountains in the north to the edge of the desert, the Negeb, in the south, and from the Mediterranean Sea eastward to the Transjordan Plateau, a usage derived from the Roman designation *Syria Palaestina* for this area, the southern section of the Roman province of Syria. This usage prevails today.

Biblical Names for Palestine. The writers of the pentateuch called this territory CANAAN and its inhabitants Canaanites (Gn 12.5; Ex 15.15). The Hebrews, after their gradual conquest of it during the 12th and 11th centuries B.C., called it the land of Israel, the name that they used to refer to their confederation of 12 tribes descended from the patriarch Israel (Jacob). They considered it to be the land promised them by God as part of His covenant blessing (Heb 11.9; Gn 12.6–7; Ex 12.25). After the Exile, Zechariah termed it the Holy Land, the land of Yahweh's holy people, ruled by Him as their King (Zec 2.16; 2 Mc 1.7; Ex 19.5–8). In Hellenistic and Roman times it was known as Judea from JUDAH, the tribe that dwelt in the hill country from JERUSALEM south to Beersheba. To this greatly reduced territory the Jewish exiles

Nazareth and Church of Annunciation, Israel. (©Richard T. Nowitz/CORBIS)

returned from Babylon and there established an ethnarchy that became the Hasmonaean Kingdom.

More generally, localities that were frequently mentioned or that played an important part in the Bible have been given the name Lands of the Bible. These extended much beyond the confines of Israel at the time of its greatest expansion in the reigns of David and Solomon (10th century B.C.). The OT Bible Lands included what is known today as the Fertile Crescent going from UR, an ancient city of Sumer, near the Persian Gulf, through the fertile lands of Mesopotamia, North Syria, Lebanon, and Palestine, to the lands made fruitful by the Nile River. They also included, in late books of the OT, Persia, Asia Minor, Greece and its islands, and Rome. In the NT the geographical outlook spread with the carrying of the gospel "to the ends of the earth" (Acts 1.8) and became centered more to the west, on Asia Minor, Greece, and Italy, mainly because of the Pauline literature and the Acts. This general area is of interest to all serious Biblical students, but this article restricts itself to the much smaller territory known as Palestine.

The Area of Modern Palestine. Palestine lies between the Arabian Desert and the Great Sea, the Mediterranean, as east and west boundaries; its north and south limits are the Lebanon and Anti-Lebanon massif and the southern desert, approximately from the 33rd to the 29th degree north latitude (roughly the latitude of Alabama). This north to south expanse corresponds generally to that of the Biblical description, from Dan to Beer-sheba (Jgs 20.1; 1 Sm 3.20), a distance of about 145 air miles. The

greatest extent from east to west is close to 100 miles in the southern area when one includes the Transjordan region. The territory's total area therefore is only about 10,000 square miles, 4,000 of them east of the Jordan. Palestine is smaller than Belgium, hardly larger than Sicily, and approximately the same size as Vermont.

2. Physical Geography

Palestine's position on a land bridge between the ancient civilizations of the Tigris-Euphrates and Nile Valleys gave it a special importance as a highway for caravans and rival armies. It also was the only easy land passage from Egypt to the Phoenician coast and on to Asia Minor; the Transjordan route to the Red Sea and southern Arabia ran along its eastern boundary. By its physical surroundings, therefore, it was one of the main crossroads of the Near East. Israel's economic, political, and cultural life was always greatly influenced by this fact.

Topography of Palestine. Three of the four main regions of Palestine are mentioned in Nm 13.29: the highlands, the seacoast, and the Jordan Valley. Add to these the Transjordan Plateau, and one obtains four zones, running north and south, parallel to the sea, which may be considered separately in their physical and topographical characteristics. Here only three will be described, the coastal plain, the hill country, and Transjordan

The Coastal Plain. Most of Palestine's littoral is flat and without natural shelter except for the smallest boats. The eastbound currents that run along the north coast of Africa have banked the shores with sand as far north as Mt. Carmel, leaving a straight coastline without natural harbors. In fact, the two seaports that had any importance, Joppa and CAESAREA, were mainly artificial. North of Palestine the irregular coast of Phoenicia provided many harbors suitable for ancient ships, the most important being Tyre and Sidon whence ships sailed southwest to Egypt and Carthage and northwest to the Aegean and Italy. The best harbor along Palestine's coast was Acco, the Greek Ptolemais (Acts 21.7), and St. Jean d'Acre of the crusaders, a port that remained throughout the biblical period in other than Israelite possession. Acco's function as a port has now passed to Haifa at the foot of Mt. Carmel, southward across the Bay of Acco.

The limestone hills of Upper Galilee reach all the way to the coast a short distance south of Tyre and form a headland separating the Phoenician plain from that of Acco or Asher, thus protecting the southern approach to Tyre. Southward, beyond the Plain of Asher (very fertile, except for the sand dunes along the shore) and the interruption of Mt. Carmel projecting its head into the sea, the narrow plain of Dor (Jos 12.23;1 Mc 15.11–14) widens into the marshy, luxuriant plain of Sharon, in biblical times thickly covered with an oak forest (Is 33.9; 35.2) and now famous for its citrus groves. The plain of Sharon extends to the valley of Aijalon, which joins the Brook of Cana to enter the sea a little north of Joppa. The rich plain of Philistia, the ancient land of the Philistines, lies to the south of this main entrance into the hill country of Judea and Ephraim, occupying a section of the coast that is likewise very fertile except for the sand dunes along the shore. The area's fertility was exploited by Palestinian Arabs who cultivated extensive citrus groves there, now the possession of the Israelis. Farther south the annual rainfall diminishes rapidly and the plain gradually becomes desert in the western reaches of the Negeb. The width of the coastal plain varies from five miles at Acco, and two miles around Dor, to the maximum of 20 miles inland from Gaza.

This coastland provided the main route northward from Egypt, "the way of the Philistines' land" (Ex 13.17). It terminated its desert journey across the base of the Sinai triangle at Gaza, where it met the road leading east to Beer-sheba. The next main junction was just outside Askelon, where it crossed the road going inland to Lachish, thence to Jerusalem and JERICHO. It then passed before the walls of Ashdod at the confluence of three valleys coming down from the east, then on to Jabneel, crossing the road to Jerusalem through the Valley of Sorek. Farther north it met at Beth-Dagon, the main road between Joppa and Lydda that continued eastward to Aijalon, the Beth-Horons, and Ramah. A caravan having business in the western Plain of Sharon, Caesarea, Dor, Acco, and the Phoenician coast would have veered west to Joppa here and then north along the coast, but one whose destination was Damascus or the Plain of Esdraelon with its many important cities would have continued directly north until it came to the western end of the pass of MEGIDDO, whence it would veer northeastward toward the Sea of Galilee, passing many junctions with east-west roads. The coastal plain was therefore a funnel for almost all traffic toward Egypt. The only other route was the more difficult Road to Shur from Beer-sheba southwestward through the Negeb and the Desert of Shur to Lake Timsah, a way that the Israelites would have had to follow whenever enemies occupied the Philistine Plain.

The Hill Country. East of the coastal plain the highland ridge of Judea and Ephraim does not begin immediately, but some foothills of more recent formation interpose a barrier to direct entrance to the hill country. Along this minor ridge important frontier cities were placed, such as Aijalon, Gezer, Lachish, and Debir, guarding the various valleys leading farther inland. This region was called the Shephelah, the foothills of Dt 1.7. To its east and forming another natural barrier lay a nar-

Tel Hazor, Israel. (©Richard T. Nowitz/CORBIS)

row chalkstone valley or moat sometimes referred to as the Moat of Judah. One easily sees why the Israelites and the Philistines were continually vying to control this territory.

The central highlands of Palestine are the backbone of the country, formed by the ridge of Judah and Ephraim that, with only the interruption of the Plain of Esdraelon, runs from the Negeb to join, through Lower and Upper Galilee, the Lebanon ranges. The Lebanons rise 6,000 feet above the sea level, while in the Anti-Lebanon range Mt. Hermon towers at 9,232 feet. Palestine's highest peak is Mt. Jarmak in Upper Galilee at almost 4,000 feet. Compared to these heights Mt. Tabor, five miles east of NAZARETH in Lower Galilee, is not much more than a prominent hill rising out of the Esdraelon Plain to less than 2,000 feet.

Upper Galilee is a lofty plateau, rugged and wild, forming the foothills of the Lebanons, with Safad as its principal modern town. The waters of Merom (Jos 11.5, 7) were probably those of the Wadi Meiron east of Safad. The ancient Hyksos and Canaanite city of Hazor (Jos 11.10; 1 Kgs 9.15) and its plain lie on the eastern slope of the central ridge, a short distance southwest of Lake Huleh.

Lower Galilee is a series of transverse, east-to-west ridges alternating with enclosed valleys and picturesque wooded defiles. This was the more populated and cultivated part of northern Palestine, the "District of the Gentiles" and "the seaward road," i.e., the main trunk route past the Sea of Galilee and Hazor to Damascus (Is 8.23;

Ancient center of the tribe of Dan in the plain at the foot of Mt. Hebron near the northeast border of Palestine. (©Shai Ginott/ CORBIS)

see also Mt 4.15). Bethsaida, the home town of the Apostles Peter, Andrew, and Philip, at the northern end of the Sea of Galilee, CAPERNAUM, the headquarters of Jesus during the first part of His public ministry (Mt 4.13), and Tiberias, built in honor of the Roman Emperor Tiberius by HEROD ANTIPAS during the life of Jesus, were really in the Jordan Valley but can be considered as Galilean cities. Sepphoris was the capital of Herod's tetrarchy of Galilee (Lk 3.1) before he built Tiberias. Some other important cities of Galilee were Arbela (1 Mc 9.2), CANA (Jn 2.1), Endor (1 Sm 28.7–8), Nain (Lk 7.11–17), and Shunem (2 Kgs 4.8). Gabaath-Hammore (Jgs 7.1), an ancient volcano a few miles south of Tabor, is responsible for the fertility of the surrounding valleys and was called at one time "Little Hermon." NAZARETH is a pleasant spot nestling on the side of a steep hill a few miles south of Sepphoris. The Horns of Hattin, a pass along the main trunk route as it descended to the Sea of Galilee, was a strategic spot and the site of many battles, including SALADIN's victory over the crusaders in 1187.

The plains of Megiddo and Jezreel form an important break in the central highlands and an easy passage from the Mediterranean to the Jordan Valley. The water parting near Jezreel marks the division between the two val-

leys. The Plain of Megiddo, "the great plain" (1 Mc 12.49), and the coastal Plain of Acco are drained to the west by the Kishon River, which in the rainy season becomes a torrent (Jgs 5.21). In the Hellenistic period the Plain of Megiddo was called the Plain of Esdraelon, from the Greek name for Jezreel, a town guarding its eastern boundary. From Jezreel a more narrow plain drops off quickly eastward to below sea level and merges into the plain of Beth-shan, part of the Jordan Valley. These plains formed a zone of great agricultural wealth and strategic importance, as is clear from the many fortified cities guarding their gates, from west to east, Jokneam, Megiddo, Taanach, Ibleam, Jezreel, and Beth-Shan. Megiddo, already occupied in the 4th millennium B.C., was where King Josiah was killed in battle while trying to stop the northward march of the Egyptian army under Neco (2 Kgs 23.29). Since so many battles were fought at this pass, it became in Revelation (16.14–16), under the form Armageddon, the scene of the last great battle between the forces of good and evil. Beth-Shan (1 Sm 31.10) was known in the Hellenistic period as Scythopolis (2 Mc 12.29–30), a city of the DECAPOLIS. Mt. Gilboa, just west of Beth-Shan and the site of Saul's death (2 Sm 1.21), forms the northeast end of the mountain ridge of Ephraim.

The highlands of Ephraim or Samaria, rising to the maximum height of 3,332 feet at Baal-Hazor just northeast of Bethel (2 Sm 13.23), have several fertile valleys and small plains, those of Dothan, SHECHEM, and Lebona. The Judean section of the range is more uniformly hill country and less fertile, although adequate for olive groves and vineyards. No well-defined geographical feature, however, marks the boundary between the regions of Ephraim and Judah.

Ascending from the plain of Esdraelon, the highland road passed the cities of Dothan, Samaria, and Shechem, which controlled the important defile between Mt. Gerizim and Mt. Ebal, the mounts of cursing and blessing (Dt 27.11–13). Farther south the road followed the water parting most of the time, passing near Lebona, Shiloh, BETHEL, Mizpeh, Machmas, Gibeah, Jerusalem, BETHLEHEM, and reaching its highest point just north of Hebron, whence it descended to Beer-sheba. At Hebron another road branched off to the southeast, passing Carmel of Judah, Maon, Arad, and joining the road from Beer-sheba that led to the Araba and the mining and smelting area of Eziongeber.

East of the divide the land falls rapidly to the Jordan Valley, forming an eroded wilderness that is much more desolate in the southern Judean section. From Shechem a road along the Wadi Fara leads gradually down to the Jordan Valley and was possibly the way used by Abraham and his family to ascend to Shechem (Gn 12.6). More arduous canyon roads link Bethel and Jerusalem with Jericho. South of Jerusalem the paths leading down to the Dead Sea along canyon walls were used only by shepherds or fugitives, for they terminated in the wilderness of Judah, useful only for winter grazing and seclusion from the inhabited lands.

The central and southern hill country of Palestine has the aspect of a pocket cut off from the surrounding regions by the narrowness of its transverse valleys and canyons. Although it was close to the main trunk route of the Middle East, it was not astride it, as was the Plain of the Philistines and the Esdraelon Valley. It looked down upon the crossroads of the world and the caravans laden with treasures from Egypt and Mesopotamia, but it was by its physical nature aloof in its heights. Passing armies could ignore it on their way to Egypt or to Syria and Iraq and would slash back at it only when it provoked or hindered them in their main purpose. This physical aloofness has always been an important factor in the hill country's history.

Transjordan. The great plateau east of the Jordan Valley, with its lofty and precipitous bluffs facing toward the west and its gradual merging with the Arabian Desert to the east, is commonly known as the Transjordan. The lowest level on the plateau is 1,500 feet, but to the south in Edom it rises to 5,000 feet. Its principal peaks in the central region range in height from 3,500 to 4,000 feet.

Four important river valleys, the Yarmuk, the Jabbok, the Arnon, and the Zered cut this tableland in a westerly direction and form boundaries of well-known regions. North and east of the Yarmuk lay Bashan and the plain of Hauran. Gilead with its fertile highland valley lay between the Yarmuk and the Arnon, and at the eastern headwaters of the Jabbok the kingdom of Ammon flourished. Sihon's Amorrite kingdom once possessed all of the region from the Arnon to the Jabbok but was conquered by the Israelites and surrendered its territory to the tribes of Gad and Reuben. Moab (*see* MOABITES) was originally situated between the Arnon and the Zered (Nm 21.13) but later extended its territory northward to include the eastern bank of the Jordan River just north of the Dead Sea, thus giving its name to this region, the Plains of Moab. South of the Zered lay Edom in the highest part of the Transjordan. Farther south the Midianites, a seminomadic people, dwelt along the shores of the Gulf of Aqaba.

The King's Highway (Nm 20.17) was the main route running north and south along this plateau from Damascus to Aqaba. In Roman times it was Trajan's Road, and under Turkish rule, the Sultan's Highway. By it the Damascus market had access to the exotic products of South Arabia. Some of the most important towns along the route were Theman, Sela, and Bozrah in Edom; Kirhareseth (the capital), Aroer, and Dibon in Moab; Madeba and Heshebon in land constantly contested between Moabites and Israelites; Rabbah, the capital of Ammon, conquered by Joab and David (Philadelphia, now Amman, the capital of the Hashemite Kingdom of Jordan); Gerasa, a city of Gilead, captured by Alexander Jannaeus, one of the HASMONAEANS, in 83 B.C.; Ramoth in Gilead, Arbela; and finally, in Bashan, Ashtaroth and Karnaim (Gn 14.5; Am 6.13).

The fertile region of Transjordan was much wider in the north (in Bashan and Hauran) than in the south. Gilead was also very fertile, producing oil, wine, and grain, the staples of the Near East, and was famous for its timber.

Hydrography of Palestine. In Dt 8.7 Palestine is described as a land highly favored by water courses and springs, and other texts mention numerous wells. A land's water resources depend on its climate, especially its rainfall, and on its geological nature.

Climate. In no such small area of the world are there such differences in rainfall and climate as are found in Palestine. This is due to a complex of causes: its situation between the southeastern angle of the Mediterranean and the vast Arabian Desert, its hill country immediately falling off to the world's lowest and hottest valley, and its high plateau in the Transjordan. Whatever the causes, the effects are startling.

The climate's main feature is its two seasons: the long, completely dry summer, and the comparatively short rainy season when cyclonic storms come blowing off the sea. The rainy season has a quite variable beginning and ending, the early and late rains of the Bible (Dt 11.14) both of great importance. The early rains are necessary for plowing and planting, the late rains for bringing the grain to full ear. The early rains should begin in late October, and when they are delayed until late November or even early January the crops suffer from a tardy germination. The heaviest rains arrive in January, February, and early March, not the steady, soaking rain of more northern regions, but heavy showers, continuous on the first day of the storm, followed by intermittent showers for two or three days. Once the storm has passed, the atmosphere becomes extremely clear, and one may look from Jerusalem and see to the east every crag of the mountains of Moab more than 30 miles away. This is the time for collecting as much water as possible in pools and cisterns for the long dry season ahead. The late rains, ripening the harvest, occur in late March and early April, but when they come much later and are violent hail storms, the crops and the frail blossoms on the fruit trees may suffer irreparable damage.

May and early June on the one hand and late September and October on the other are transitional periods during which the dry, scorching desert wind, the sirocco, may descend on Palestine without warning and with dire results for all living things. The heat and dryness are oppressive; verdure quickly withers; the air becomes opaque with fine sand that magnifies the sun's heat; and man and beast grow irritable. Fortunately, the sirocco usually last for no more than two or three days—in autumn, blown away by the rain-burdened westerly winds, and in June, by the summer westerlies that become a constant feature of every day when the land heat of late morning grows intense enough to draw them from the sea.

From mid-June to mid-September the weather pattern remains the same, the heat of the late morning gives way to the cooling sea breeze of the afternoon, which gradually moves inland, reaching the edge of Transjordan by about 4 P.M. Along the coast the humidity is higher; the breeze, less refreshing; and the discomfort of the day, prolonged into the night. In the hill country the nights are cool and the shade during the day is always refreshing compared to the coast's humid shade. In the Jordan Rift even the sea air rushing down its steep slopes is so heated that it becomes only an afternoon annoyance. The wind's effect on the eastern plateau is refreshing, but it arrives too late to lower the day's heat very much.

The amount of rainfall diminishes greatly from north to south, from west to east, and from higher to lower altitudes. The annual rainfall of Jerusalem is almost 24 inches, while only five miles to the east it decreases rapidly; and in Jericho, 17 miles away, it measures only about five inches. At Beer-sheba, 50 miles south of Jerusalem, the annual rainfall measures only eight to nine inches, but at the same altitude and distance to the north it measures more than 20. In the highlands of Upper Galilee it reaches more than 35 inches; on the summit of Mt. Hermon, the source of the Jordan River's water, the annual precipitation is more than 60 inches. The coastal region, because of its low altitude, receives less rain than the hills; thus Transjordan, higher than the central ridge, sometimes receives more rainfall than Jerusalem, although it is much farther from the sea. One must remember that Palestine's annual rainfall is crowded into a five-month period, a fact that is important in understanding its reliance on springs, wells, and cisterns, and the formation of its wadis or torrent canyons.

Springs and Wells. The absorbent limestone structure of Palestine's rock bed provides storage for the heavy winter rains. The sources of the subterranean water occur sporadically throughout most of the land and afford places for human habitation. The main towns usually were built near an important spring or well, and intricate subterranean passages were devised to bring the well's water within the city walls so that in times of siege a supply would always be available. Such a tunnel to the fountain of Gihon in Jerusalem was repaired and extended by Hezekiah in preparation for the onslaught of the Assyrians (2 Kgs 20.20). Similar constructions have been found at Megiddo, Lachish, Gibeon, etc. The spring at Jericho is one of the main reasons why this is the site of the oldest-known town in the world.

Where well water was insufficient, or simply to supply a greater abundance of water, cisterns were built to store the winter rains. Samaria, built by Israel's King Omri, had no natural spring and depended solely on its vast cisterns.

Rivers and Wadis. The only copious perennial watercourse in Palestine that merits comparison with even a minor American river is the Jordan. The few perennial rivers are rushing torrents during the rainy season, quickly draining the highlands and causing marshes in the low-lying plains, but, as summer advances, they become quiet rivulets whose courses may be discovered only by the vegetation along their narrow banks. Most of the watercourses, however, flow only during the rainy season, becoming dry beds or washes soon after its end.

The wadis of Palestine have scarred the domelike hill country with deep canyons, especially on the eastern and western slopes of the Jordan rift. One of the most impressive wadis is the canyon of the River Arnon, which rivals the rugged beauty of the canyons of the southwestern U.S. Though they are beautiful, these torrents have been the main source of erosion of the hill country. They also are impediments to travelers and the cause of many a tortuous road.

Bibliography: F. M. ABEL, *Géographie de la Palestine,* 2 v. (Paris 1933–38). L. H. GROLLENBERG, *Atlas of the Bible,* tr. J. M. REID and H. H. ROWLEY (New York 1956). M. DU BUIT, *Géographie de la Terre Sainte* (Paris 1958). *Oxford Bible Atlas,* ed. H. G. MAY et al. (New York 1962). D. BALY, *The Geography of the Bible* (New York 1957); *Geographical Companion to the Bible* (New York 1963).

[E. LUSSIER]

3. Political Geography

"This is a list of the kings whom Joshua and the Israelites conquered west of the Jordan . . . thirty-one kings in all" (Jos 12.7–24). A statement such as this gives a good indication of conditions in Palestine prior to the Israelite invasion. It was a land divided, a country of mixed population and independent city-states. (For the pre-Israelite ethnology of the country, see section 6 below.) However, this feature is characteristic of Palestine throughout its long history. Rarely was there ever one single united country, and when, on occasion, such a union was achieved, it was of relatively short duration.

Period of Joshua and the Judges. A picture of the division of the land among the twelve tribes of Israel is given in Joshua ch. 13–21. (*See* JOSHUA, BOOK OF). Despite the apparent details that are presented, it is, nevertheless, difficult to determine the precise boundaries of each of the tribal allotments. East of the Jordan, half of the tribe of Manasseh (specifically, the clan of Machir) occupied the districts of Bashan and part of Gilead (Jos 13.8–14); Gad, the rest of Gilead between the Jabbok and Heshbon (13.24–28); and Reuben, the land between Heshbon and the Arnon (13.15–23). West of the Jordan, JUDAH received the greatest portion—from the Valley of Hinnom (*see* GEHENNA) at Jerusalem to Kadesh-Barnea) and the Wadi of Egypt in the Negeb (15.1–63). Part of this territory was alloted to Simeon—cities in the general vicinity of Beer-sheba (19.1–9). North of Judah were the smaller possessions of BENJAMIN (18.11–28) and Dan (19.40–48). Central Palestine was occupied by EPHRAIM (16.4–10) and the other half of Manasseh (17.1–13). In the district of Galilee, Naphtali (19.32–39) was in the north, Zebulun (19.10–16) and Issachar (19.17–23) in the south, and Asher (19.24–31) along the coast.

The division of the land is presented as the outcome of the Israelite conquest under the leadership of JOSHUA, son of Nun. But the Book of JUDGES gives a different story (Jgs 1.1–36). The two accounts seem to be but two aspects of a much more complicated history. Probably some of the tribes had been there since the time of Jacob and were already in possession of land. In the course of time these tribes made attempts to increase their territorial possessions. With the coming of Joshua and the tribes under his command, the conquest reached its full proportions. The complete picture, therefore, would be one of occupation and settlement in different stages over a long period of time culminating in the invasion led by Joshua. The land thus became the possession of tribes who were related by common ancestry and eventually united by the bond of a religious COVENANT with YAHWEH, the God of their fathers, Abraham, Isaac, and Jacob, the God who had brought deliverance to those Israelites who had been enslaved in Egypt. But this bond was a very loose one, and there was little lasting unity. It was only when a common danger, the extension of PHILISTINE power, threatened all the tribes that unity was achieved by the establishment of the monarchy (1 Sm 4.2–10.27). But even this would turn out to be of relatively short duration.

Period of the Monarchy. With the establishment of the monarchy the tribes in fact gained control of the land to which they had laid claim. Israel's first king, Saul, began the offensive and began well, but in the end was far from successful (1 Sm 11.1–15.9; 31.1–6).

It was up to DAVID to lead a united Israel to victory. This warrior king began by reducing the Philistines to subjection, so that they were never again troublesome to Israel (2 Sm 5.17–25; 8.1). He continued the conquest by subduing the Canaanite city-states of the land and taking Jerusalem, making it the political and religious capital of the kingdom (5.6–10). His dominion eventually included the ARAMAEANS in the north and the Ammonites, MOABITES, and EDOMITES in the east and southeast (8.2–14; 10.6–19; 12.26–31). Thus the kingdom reached its greatest limits, the extent of which was never again to be seen by any subsequent king of Israel. From the frontier of Hamath in the north to the Gulf of Aqabah in the south, from the Mediterranean Sea to the desert—all the land was subject to Jerusalem.

This was the inheritance of SOLOMON, a kingdom of peace and prosperity. His task was to keep it intact. It was, indeed, the golden age. However, while the royal court grew in size and splendor, the condition of the people grew worse. To maintain his court Solomon divided the country into 12 administrative districts (1 Kgs 4.7–19), the boundaries of which ignored the old tribal divisions. Moreover, in all of this, Judah seemed to have enjoyed a privileged position. The result was a widespread dissatisfaction that eventually, after the death of the king, brought about the dissolution of the empire and the division of the kingdom.

Two independent kingdoms emerged: Israel in the north and Judah in the south, with the border between the two of them in the tribal territory of Benjamin. During their joint existence they were sometimes hostile, sometimes friendly, and at times even allied in a common cause. But whatever the internal problems, the greatest dangers were from without.

Israel remained in existence a little more than 200 years before the power of Assyria brought about its destruction. An initial Assyrian conquest (734–732 B.C.) resulted only in a reduction of territory to central Palestine; the districts of Dor, Megiddo and Gilead became provinces of Assyria (2 Kgs 15.29). However, ten years later (722 B.C.) Samaria was invested and annexed to the Assyrian kingdom as a province, and Israel ceased to exist.

Judah alone remained, by choice, a vassal of Assyria. With the rise of Babylonian power, the might of Assyria was crushed, and the end of the southern kingdom was near. The first Babylonian capture of Jerusalem (597 B.C.) was accompanied by deportations (2 Kgs 24.10–16), but the kingdom was permitted to survive. A second onslaught (587 B.C.), however, ended it; and a governor was put in charge of the territory (2 Kgs 25.1–22).

From the Exilic to the Roman Period. Little is known about events during the exilic period. In the 6th century the Nabataeans occupied the land of Edom, forcing the Edomites to move into the Negeb, subsequently known as Idumea. From there they caused trouble for the people remaining in the land of Judah and left bitter memories of these years. In Babylon the exiles cherished the hope of returning, a hope that was fulfilled with the rise of Persian power.

The Persian conquest freed the exiles and permitted them to return to their own land (538 B.C.; Ezr 1.1–4). It also saw the organization of the empire into satrapies. Palestine was in the fifth satrapy, called Abar Nahara (Beyond the River, i.e., west of the Euphrates). It was composed of various provinces, each under the jurisdiction of a local governor. The province of Judah was called Yehud, and its people Yehudim (Jews). The other provinces of Palestine were: Idumea, to the south of Judah; Samaria, Galilee, Dor, and Ashdod, to the north and along the coast; Gilead, Ammon, and Moab in Transjordan.

The conquest by Alexander the Great (333 B.C.) brought Palestine under his dominion. But after his death, it changed hands five times during the struggle of the Diadochi (323–301 B.C.). Eventually the kingdom of the Ptolemies in Egypt and that of the Seleucid dynasty comprising Asia Minor, Syria, and Babylonia were established. Palestine at first fell to the Ptolemies, but in fact it remained a bone of contention and the cause of conflicts for a century (301–198 B.C.). In the end it fell to the Seleucids.

Seleucid policy of Hellenization caused the Maccabean uprising (166–135 B.C.), resulting in independence for Palestine [see MACCABEES, HISTORY OF THE]. A kingdom came into existence, ruled by the descendants of the Maccabees, the HASMONAEANS. The extent of this kingdom reached proportions almost as great as that of the time of David; it included Idumea, Judah, Samaria, Galilee, and Transjordan. But internal affairs brought its downfall, and in 63 B.C., Pompey, who had already annexed Syria as a Roman province, intervened and annexed most of Palestine in the same way, Judah, Galilee, Perea, and Idumea alone remaining semi-independent vassal states.

For a brief period Palestine was reunited under HEROD THE GREAT (40–4 B.C.). At his death it was divided among his sons. Archelaus received Judea, Samaria, and Idumea; HEROD ANTIPAS, Galilee and Perea; and Philip the Tetrarch, the northern districts of Transjordan. In A.D. 6 the territory of Archelaus was added to the imperial province of Syria and a procurator was put in charge; in A.D. 34 the same fate befell the territory of Philip. In A.D. 37 Herod AGRIPPA I was given the territory of Philip. To this was added the territory of Herod Antipas in A.D. 40, and shortly thereafter, Judea, Samaria, and Idumea—initiating another short period of unity until A.D. 44, when Palestine once more became a Roman province under a procurator. Northern Transjordan and parts of Galilee and Perea formed the kingdom of Herod AGRIPPA II. But after the turbulent uprising of A.D. 70, which saw the destruction of Jerusalem, all of Palestine passed under Roman rule, to remain so for more than half a millennium. During this time Palestine enjoyed a period of relative peace and prosperity, undisturbed by outside aggression. Internally the revolt of BAR KOKHBA (132–135) caused some disturbance, but it was quickly suppressed by the Romans with widespread destruction. Jerusalem was rebuilt as a Roman provincial city by the emperor Hadrian, who called it Aelia Capitolina. Then in 313 CONSTANTINE I, the Great, having embraced Christianity, proclaimed its liberty, and his mother, HELENA, converted it into a Christian city and restored its name.

From the Byzantine Period to Modern Times. With the division of the Roman Empire into West (Rome) and East (Constantinople) toward the end of the 4th century, the welfare of Palestine was bound to Byzantine rule. It was a time for pilgrimages, and the years that followed were tranquil.

This period of internal development was shattered in 611 when the Persians under Chosroes swept through Palestine, wrought havoc, and established themselves there for about 15 years. Byzantine rule came to a definitive end with the coming of the followers of Muḥammad in 636. By 640 the Arab conquest was complete. Palestine was divided into two provinces: Al-Urdunn in the north and Filistin in the south. It was ruled successively by the UMAYYAD, 'ABBĀSID, and Fatimid Caliphs.

The devastation caused in the Holy Land by the SELJUK Turks in 1071 was followed by the turbulent era of the CRUSADES beginning in 1099. Under crusader rule, Palestine became the Kingdom of Jerusalem, and the country was divided into various baronies. The crusaders were followed by the Mamelukes of Egypt in 1250. Then, in 1517, the conquest of Palestine by the OTTOMAN TURKS brought it under Turkish rule until the 20th century.

The beginning of the 20th century saw the growth of Arab nationalism, the rise of Zionism, and World War I. When the allied troops led by General Allenby entered Palestine in 1917, Turkish rule came to an end, and Palestine was under British mandate until 1948. It was indeed the modern period, but the events were only a repetition of past history. It was a time of warfare and territorial division, hardly a new occurrence for the land of Palestine.

Bibliography: H. HAAG, *Lexikon für Theologie und Kirche*, ed. J. HOFER and K. RAHNER (Freiburg 1957–65) 7:1362–63. G. E. WRIGHT and F. V. FILSON, eds., *The Westminster Historical Atlas to the Bible* (rev. ed., Philadelphia 1956). J. BRIGHT, *A History of Israel* (Philadelphia 1959), good bibliog. J. W. PARKES, *A History of Palestine from 135 A.D. to Modern Times* (New York 1949), excellent bibliog. S. RUNCIMAN, *A History of the Crusades*, 3 v. (Cambridge, England 1951–54), excellent bibliog.

[F. SEPER]

4. Natural History

The study of the natural history of Palestine is limited here to botany and zoology of the Holy Land, therefore, to a description and classification of its flora (or plant life) and its fauna (or animal life).

FLORA

After a description of the plant life of the Holy Land in the biblical period, an account is given of the flora of modern Palestine according to its phytogeographic areas.

Plant Life in the Biblical Period. It is accepted by most modern scholars that no radical change has occurred in the climate of the Holy Land since the beginnings of recorded history. This conclusion is based upon evidence from many sources. In the literary realm, the descriptions of the land found in the Bible, the MISHNAH, and the TALMUD show that the seasons and agricultural variations were identical then with those of the present day.

Forests. Contrary to the commonly accepted theory, studies have shown that the forest was not an important factor in the biblical landscape. Even before the conquest by JOSHUA, son of Nun, the land was settled in noticeable density, and the major portion of the regions suitable for agriculture was seeded or planted and cultivated intensively. These conditions precluded the existence of forests. In the rocky mountainous regions there were, indeed, woods, but these were not protected from man or beast. In the Biblical and Talmudic descriptions of the land there is very little mention of forests. Individual trees that served cultic purposes or had been associated with important events are noted. Yet, since the Bible mentions the existence of wild animals, it can be deduced that the land of Israel was forested to some extent. These animals inhabited the deserts, the Jordan Valley, and the forests of Bashan and Mt. Hermon, and from these regions they came out to the settlements. Widespread forests existed principally in Bashan and in Lebanon, and these regions supplied lumber for palaces, temples, and other large buildings. Extensive woods called the Forest of Ephraim existed in Gilead, where the war between David and Absalom took place (2 Sm 18.8). Perhaps this was the forest referred to by Joshua when he advised the landless sons of Joseph to clear the forest and settle there

(Jos 17.15). The accepted interpretation, however, is that the reference is to the forest on the mountains of Ephraim in Samaria.

The development of a forest in a region of sufficient rainfall usually follows the destruction of agriculture there. This idea is expressed several times in the Scriptures (e.g., Hos 2.14; Mi 3.12; Jer 26.18), and actually, during all the periods of settlement on the land, there was continual struggle between the sown and cultivated tracts on the one hand and the forest and wasteland on the other. During periods of war and postwar destruction the cultivated areas were deserted, and wild grasses, bushes, and trees thrived; but in peacetime these areas were reclaimed by agricultural settlement.

Grazing Lands. Following Joshua's conquest of Canaan and during the period of the early Judges, the cultivation of the terraced hills was destroyed, and in its place the wild flora flourished, as the Bible had warned (Dt 7.22; see also Is 17.9), and as a result of the destruction of agriculture, the grazing lands were extended (see also Is 7.28). This process recurred repeatedly during the various periods of peace and war in biblical times. The major wealth of the Holy Lands consisted of fruits and grains. Although it was described as a "land of milk and honey," one cannot assume from this that the pasture land ("milk") exceeded in extent the land used for cultivation. From the Scriptures it is evident that, while extensive pasture lands existed on the east side of the Jordan and in Bashan, on the west side of the Jordan livestock-raising existed only on a small scale, and the herds were fed mostly from the stubble of the grain fields.

Dependence on Rainfall. The agriculture of the Holy Land depended on natural rainfall; this fact is emphasized in the Bible by comparing the land of Israel (at the south of Mt. Hermon), of the Yarkon (at Aphek, which "drinks in rain from the heavens,") with Egypt, which is completely dependent on irrigation (Dt 11.10–12). In this connection came the warning regarding the withholding of rain as a consequence of sin (Dt 11.17). Years of famine caused by lack of rain are often noted in the Bible. One verse describes Israel as a "land of streams of water, with springs and fountains welling up in the hills and valleys" (Dt 8.7). From this some might conclude that there have been changes in the land since those days, but there is no basis for such a conclusion. There are still many springs there (about 800 of them having been counted), but most of them have a very limited flow. Only the sources of the Dan Rās el-'Ain, and of the Na'aman (at 'Ayūn el-Baṣṣ seven miles southeast of Acco) supply in normal years more than a cubic meter of water a second. Some 40 others supply between 100 to 1,000 liters per second (the majority of them being in the Huleh and in the Beisan Valley); all the others are minor. The author of the Letter of ARISTEAS exaggerates in evaluating the Jordan as the most important factor in the agriculture of the Land of Israel. Flavius Josephus heaps praise on the irrigation of Jericho (*Bell.Jud.* 4.8.3) and the Plain of Genasar (*ibid.* 3.10.6), but he is correct in his conclusion that the most fertile part of the land of Israel is the "land of thirst [for rain] according to its nature" (*ibid.* 3.3.4). Indeed, farming that depends on rainfall has to a large extent determined the landscape of Israel.

The cultivated areas in ancient times were not different from those of today. The deserts described in the Bible include in their boundaries the areas of desert and wasteland of the present day. The Negeb was a grazing land, though in rainy years its northern parts could be seeded (Gn 26.12). Here and there in the Bible is mentioned the growth of certain wild trees in specific localities: sycamore trees in the foothills (1 Kgs 10.27); willows along the brooks (Is 44.4); tamarisks in the desert (Jer 17.6); wild jujubes in swampy jungles (Jb 40.21); etc. Of forest trees, mention is made especially of the oak, the terebinth, and the storax. The conifers grew especially in Bashan and Lebanon; cedar, juniper, pine, and cypress are mentioned in Isaiah as species that will bloom in the desert and wasteland in the time to come (Is 41.19; 60.13).

The praise of Israel in Dt 8.8 refers to its seven basic farm products: it is a "land of wheat and barley, of vines and fig trees and pomegranates, of olive oil and of honey." Three groups are included: of the grains are wheat and barley, of the fruits are grapes, figs, and pomegranates, and of important produce from trees are oil from olives and honey (i.e., syrup) from dates.

Plants of the Bible. The Bible mentions about 100 names of plants, most of which grew in Israel, and it is relatively easy to identify almost all of them by studying the descriptions of them as given in the Scriptures, the Mishnah, and the Talmud, as well as by philology, etymology, and a comparison with the flora of modern Palestine. There are names of flora in the Bible that identify whole groups, *šāmîr wešayit* (thorn bushes of all kinds: Is 5.6; 9.17) and *qôṣ wedardar* (thistles of all kinds: Gn 3.18; Hos 10.8). The Bible mentions mainly plants that either have economic importance or that suitably illustrate a parable. Doubtless there were other important plants and trees that the Bible had no occasion to mention, such as the carob, which is referred to only in Lk 15.16.

Flora of Modern Israel according to Phytogeographic Areas. Israel is very rich in plant species, their number reaching to more than 2,000. The abundance of species is due to several causes: the variegated history of

the flora, dating back to early geologic periods, the variation in topography, and, above all, the fact that the country provides a meeting ground for three vegetation belts—the Mediterranean, the Irano-Turanic, and the Saharo-Sindic.

Mediterranean Vegetation. Included are areas on both sides of the Jordan, where the amount of rainfall is more than 350 millimeters (13.8 inches), which makes cultivation of the land possible either summer or winter. In this zone the flora of the mountain areas differs from that of the seashore.

The mountain area was the most important for ancient agriculture. Cultivation of the land pushed back the forests that had abounded there in prehistoric times. At present there still remain forests and groves containing such trees as the Aleppo pine (*Pinus halepensis*) and its oft-associated species, the common oak (*Quercus calliprinos*), and the Palestine terebinth (*Pistacia palaestina*), several other species of trees, as well as many bushes and shrubs. This type of forest is still widespread in Gilead, and its traces remain in Upper Galilee, the Carmel Range, Samaria, and Judah. Such forests develop well on soil developed from Cenomanian and Eocene limestone.

Another type of Mediterranean forest is that of the Thabor oak (*Quercus ithaburensis*), with which is associated the Atlantic terebinth (*Pistacia atlantica*). This type is found in the western part of Lower Galilee, in Golan, and in the Huleh Valley. Such a forest was formerly in Sharon, but it was destroyed to make way for agriculture and pasture land.

Most of the groves in the land consist of the common oak (*Quercus calliprinos*) and the Palestine terebinth (*Pistacia palaestina*). As a result of the cutting of timber and the gnawing of goats, the trees are in the form of bushes. Such woods are spread on the mountains at an altitude of 1,000 to 4,000 feet.

On the foothills at the west range of the mountains of Galilee and on Mt. Carmel are spread the carob (*Ceratonia siliqua*) and the mastic (*Pistacia lentiscus*). Occasionally this type of flora is found on the sandy limestone hills near Caesarea and on the sands near Netanya. All these types of flora are accompanied by many types of bushes, perennial and annual. Another type of flora is that of the so-called garigue, scrubland with bushes not above the height of a man. Here the *Calycotome* thorn bush and various species of rockroses (*Cistus*) and salvia predominate.

On the unforested Mediterranean shore is found a distinctive group of low plants, wooded or grassy. Very prevalent is the Poterium thorn bush (*Poterium spinosum*), which is important in the prevention of soil erosion on the slopes of the hills. In the places where this flora has been destroyed, the land has been swept away by the winds and the rain.

Along the Mediterranean shore are sandy soil, mixtures of sandy clay and sandy chalk. Such soils are not favorable to plant development because of their poor organic composition and meager ability to hold rain water. Here grow deep-rooted plants, those of the steppe and the desert that can thrive on a small amount of water, as well as annuals that have a short period of growth. These plants are in constant danger of being covered by shifting dunes or undercut by winds. But there are species here that have developed means of defense against the force of the wind, particularly the Retama broom plant (*Retama roetam*) and the Gallic tamarisk (*Tamarix gallica*). Here grow species that are not sensitive to the salty spray of the sea or to the saline sand. There are also tropical trees such as the sycamore fig (*Ficus sycomorus*) and the wild jujube (*Zizyphus spina-Christi*).

Irano-Turanic Vegetation. This is centered in the northern Negeb, the Judean Desert, and the highlands of Transjordan. The climate is dry and the amount of rainfall 200 to 300 millimeters (8–12 inches), within the limits for stable growth. In this area there are almost no natural woodlands. Its soils are semiarid or loess. One finds sparse groups of trees or bushes; the common type is wormwood (*Artemisia herba-alba*).

Saharo-Sindic Vegetation. This type covers the largest territory, but it is poorest in species. It includes the southern Negeb, the Araba, and the desert regions of Edom and Moab. The amount of rainfall is less than 200 millimeters (eight inches) and is usually far below this level. The rains are concentrated in a very short winter. The soil is not fertile. It is comprised mainly of gravel and rocks; trees are found only in the bottom of the wadies, and the plant cover is very sparse, the typical type being the *Zygophyllum dumosum* bush. In the sandy regions plants are more plentiful, with species of *Haloxylon* and *Retama* predominating. In this area there are large salt deposits, especially in the lower Jordan Valley and in the Araba. There are dense growths of saline flora, including species of *Atriplex* and *Salicornia*. Near freshwater springs are oases where a tropical flora thrives, of which acacia and wild jujube are typical.

Hydrophilic Vegetation. Throughout the country plants are found that grow alongside bodies of water, swamps, river banks, and springs. Among the trees in this category are the poplar (*Populus euphratica*), tamarisk (*Tamarix jordanis*), Oriental plane (*Platanus orientalis*), and willow. At the side of every body of water are reeds and cattails, and in the Huleh swamps (which have now been drained) the papyrus was formerly common.

Cultivated Plants and Associated Species. In modern times essentially the same crops are being raised as in the ancient era; but in fruits the emphasis has moved away from the sweet fruits that are rich in calories, such as figs and dates, which were highly valued in ancient times, to the juicy fruits, especially the fruit trees of the *Rosaceae* family, such as the apple, pear, plum, and peach. Hundreds of new species, such as the orange, have been brought in; many of them originated in the New World. Especially numerous are the kinds of ornamental flora that have been brought to the land from countries all over the world.

Hundreds of species of weeds are associated with the cultivated plants. These are more closely connected with the plants that they accompany than to any specific locale. Among them are species established in the country from antiquity, whose seeds are found in archeological excavations along with the seeds of cultivated plants, and others that have been introduced in recent times along with the new plants.

FAUNA

After a brief description of the Palestinian fauna in the prehistoric period, lists of the biblical fauna are given; the changes in the Holy Land from biblical to modern times are then discussed, with an account of the zoogeography of modern Palestine, and finally a few words are said on the domestic animals of ancient Israel.

Palestinian Fauna in the Prehistoric Period. The natural history of Israel reaches far back in time. The most important and dynamic period was the Pleistocene era, when changes appeared in the fauna of the area, especially as a result of invasions from other areas. This fauna was similar to that which is now found on the savannas of East Africa. Bones of the wart hog, hippopotamus, rhinoceros, striped hyena, and many different species of gazelles other than those currently found in Palestine have been discovered. Bones also of elephants and mastodons have been found in the Lower Pleistocene. Later there occurred a migration of animals from India and Central Asia, among which were wild cattle, wild horses, wild asses, gazelles, wolves, and badgers. There was only limited migration of northern animals following the Ice Age in Europe. During the Upper Pleistocene a tropical climate prevailed in Palestine. After this there occurred a period of drought, which brought about the disappearance of the tropical fauna. By the end of the Stone Age, the Holy Land was already the habitat of the fauna that is described in the Bible and has persisted to recent times. This is supporting evidence for the theory that since the Stone Age there have not been radical climatic changes in the country.

Biblical Fauna. About 120 animal names appear in the Bible (not including synonyms). They may be grouped systematically as follows. Mammals (39 names) may be subdivided according to cloven-hoofed and ruminating (13), cloven-hoofed nonruminating (3), single-hoofed (4), carnivora (8), rodents (4), and other orders (7). Birds (38 names) may be divided according to ritually clean fowl (9), birds of prey (diurnal) (5), vulturine birds (4), birds of prey (nocturnal) (11), and birds of other orders (9). Other fauna includes reptiles and similar creatures (13) and insects and other small creatures (20).

From this list it can be seen that mammals, birds, and reptiles are the most adequately represented in the Bible. Of the 75 species of mammals in modern Palestine (including domestic cattle), about half are mentioned. Of the 350 species of birds, 38 are mentioned, and of the 80 species of reptiles, 12 are mentioned in the Bible. It must be stressed that the references to these animals (as also to the flora) are incidental, and they are cited to illustrate laws of ritual cleanliness or are used symbolically or allegorically. The occurrence of so many names demonstrates the highly developed perception of the scriptural writers in their understanding of the phenomena of nature. It is thought possible to identify in a majority of cases the names of the biblical fauna with established species.

Changes in Fauna from Biblical to Modern Times. Although no great changes have transpired in the fauna of the Holy Land since biblical times, the last few generations have witnessed the disappearance from the country and the surrounding regions of some of the animals that are mentioned in the Bible. The depredations have been especially severe in the case of the ruminants and cloven-hoofed, for of the ten mentioned in the Bible, only the gazelle and the Nubian ibex are left today. The wild ox (*Bos primigenius*) had already disappeared from the region at a rather early period. The others continued to inhabit the country or region up to the beginning of the 20th century. As previously noted, this does not imply a change in climate or plant cover. The main reason for the disappearance of these animals, whose flesh is eaten, is the improvement of hunting weapons. To the gun must be ascribed, as well, the destruction of the large predators, such as the lion, the bear, the leopard, and the cheetah in the confines of the country. Some think that the existence of these predatory animals in the Holy Land in the time of the Bible is proof that the land was sparsely settled at that time. But these animals inhabited the country in the Roman and Byzantine periods, when the land was, undoubtedly, densely populated. We may infer from the Scriptures that even in biblical times these beasts of prey did not inhabit the cis-Jordanian area; their habitat was the thickets of the Jordan (Jer 49.19), the forests of Bashan (Dt 33.22), and the mountains of Lebanon and

Hermon (Sg 4.5). From these places they invaded settled areas, and in times of destruction and famine they would remain there for awhile.

The lion was still found in the Negeb during the Crusades. The Syrian bear ranged down to the northern borders of Palestine until the beginning of the 20th century, and scattered traces of it have recently come to light in the mountains of Lebanon. The leopard still reaches Upper Galilee from Lebanon occasionally. Until only a few decades ago the cheetah (*Acinonyx jubata*) still survived in the Negeb, and some of its traces have recently been found at Yotvata in the Araba. Of the big animals that are now completely extinct in the country, the hippopotamus (*hippopotamus amphibius*)—the behemoth of Jb 40.15–24—may be mentioned. The crocodile—called the tannîn [the "dragon" of Ps 90(91).13; Is 27.1; etc.] and the Leviathan (Jb 40.25–41.26)—inhabited the western streams of Palestine until the end of the 19th century. The ostrich (*Struthio camelus*)—mentioned in Lam 4.3; Jb 39.13—disappeared from the area in the 19th century, although some effort has been made in recent years to bring it back. At the end of the 19th century the last survivors of the Syrian wild ass (*Equus hemionus hemihippus*) and the Arabian wild ass (*Equus hemionus onager*) were exterminated in the Syrian desert.

The expansion of Jewish settlement in the country, especially modern agricultural settlement, has altered the populations of various animals. There has been an increase in those species that have been able to adapt themselves to the new conditions. The increased number of fishponds has brought an increase in waterfowl. Also the swamp cat (*Catolynx chaus chrysomelo notis*) is spreading. All the means employed against the jackals have not deterred them from multiplying. The poisonous bait laid out to exterminate the jackals and rodents have caused the destruction of the vulturine birds that have eaten the poisoned carrion. Thus, for example, of the griffon vulture (*Gyps fulvus*), which ranged over the country until the early 20th century and is often mentioned in the Bible as the *nešer* (commonly mistranslated as "eagle"), only a few pairs still survive. Laws for the protection of wildlife that were enacted in the state of Israel have prevented the annihilation of certain creatures that had been in danger of complete extinction. The gazelle has noticeably increased throughout the country, and the Nubian ibex, too, has spread into the hills of Ein Gedi and Eilat.

The Zoogeography of Modern Palestine. The animal ranges coincide with the vegetation zones in Palestine (see above). To the Mediterranean group belong the hare, the chuckar partridge, the swallow, the agama, and others. To the Saharo-Sindic group belong various species of desert mice, the desert lark, the sandgrouse, the gecko, the cobra, and many other species. To the Irano-Turanic group belong the creatures that inhabit the northern Negeb and the desert of Judah, for instance, the tiger weasel (*Vormela*), the bustard, the *isolepis* agama, and others. To the Sudano-Decanic group belong the creatures that inhabit the lower Jordan Valley, especially the oasis areas of the desert and the vicinity of the Dead Sea. To the tropical groups belong the cheetah, the honey badger, the tropical cuckoo, the carpet viper, and others. To the holarctic group belong the northern creatures, for instance, the shrew, and the meadow pipit.

Palestine, at the juncture of three continents, is a meeting place of creatures of many different regions, and it has a rich variety of species. Currently known are 68 species of mammals, about 350 species of birds, about 80 species of reptiles, about 40 species of fresh-water fishes, and 8 species of amphibia. According to F. S. Bodenheimer, the number of recognized insect species is about 8,000 and, in his opinion the total reaches about 22,000. According to this scholar, the Arthropoda number about 900 known species and possibly total about 2,000. As for the invertebrates, there are about 300 recognized species, with the possible total of about 2,750.

Domestic Animals. Domestication of animals began at a very early period in Palestine. On the rocks of Kilwa in Transjordan prehistoric carvings of camels and cattle have been found. Jericho has yielded clay statues of a herd of goats, lambs, and pigs from *c.* 5000 B.C. Inside an Egyptian temple at Beth-shan figurines of cats have been found. (Cats are not mentioned in the Bible.) There have been found in the Holy Land paintings of dogs of at least four different breeds. The cattle are of uncertain breed. In paintings of the Roman and Byzantine period, hunchback cattle, such as the zebu, are depicted. The black, long-eared goat was a very early inhabitant, and it is pictured as early as 1500 B.C. This is also the case in regard to the broad-tailed sheep. The horse was not an important domestic animal; more important were the ass and the mule. In addition to the dove, chickens were raised as early as the period of the Israelite monarchy; a cock is depicted on a seal found at Tell en-Nasbeh, probable site of ancient Mizpeh. To the royal courts were brought decorative tropical birds, such as the peacock; and the courts received monkeys also (1 Kgs 10.22).

Bibliography: Flora. H. BALFOUR, *The Plants of the Bible* (new ed. London 1885). O. CELSIUS, *Hierobotanicon*, 2 v. (Amsterdam 1748). P. CULTRERA, *Flora Biblica* (Palermo 1861). G. H. DALMAN, *Arbeit und Sitte in Palästina*, 7 v. in 8 (Gütersloh 1928–42). I. LÖW, *Die Flora der Juden*, 4 v. in 5 (Vienna-Leipzig 1924–34). H. N. and A. L. MOLDENKE, *Plants of the Bible* (Waltham, Mass. 1952). In Hebrew. B. CHIZIK, *Otsar ha-Tsemahim* (Herzlia 1952). M. ZOHARY, *Olam ha-Tsemahim* (Tel Aviv 1954); *Geobotanikah* (Merhavya 1955). J. FELIKS, *Olam ha-Tsomeah ha-Mikrai* (Tel Aviv 1957); *Ha-Haklaut be-Eretz Yisrael bi-tekufat ha-Mishnah*

veha-Talmud (Jerusalem 1963). Fauna. F. HASSELQUIST, *Iter palaestinum*, ed. C. VON LINNÉ (Stockholm 1757). H. B. TRISTAM, *The Fauna and Flora of Palestine* (London 1884); *Natural History of the Bible* (10th ed. New York 1911). L. LEWYSOHN, *Die Zoologie des Talmuds* (Frankfurt 1858). F. S. BODENHEIMER, *Tierwelt Palästinas*, 2 v. (Leipzig 1920); *Prodromus faunae palaestinae* (Cairo 1937); *Animal and Man in Bible Lands* (Leiden 1960). J. FELIKS, *The Animal World of the Bible*, tr. P. IRSAI (Tel Aviv 1962). In Hebrew. I. AHARONI, *Torat ha-Hai*, 3 v. (Tel Aviv 1927–49); *Zikhronot Zoolog Ivri* (Tel Aviv 1942–43). Y. MARGOLIN, *Zoologia* (Tel Aviv 1959). F. S. BODENHEIMER, *Ha-Hai be-Artsot ha-Mikra*, 2 v. (Jerusalem 1949–56); *Ha-Hai be-Eretz Yisrael* (Tel Aviv 1953). J. FELIKS, *Ha-Hai shel ha-Tanakh* (Tel Aviv 1954).

[J. FELIKS]

5. Archeology

Palestine, as used here, embraces the lands not only to the west but also to the east of the River Jordan. After World War I both territories were under British mandate. Under the mandatory power a Department of Antiquities was organized to protect and promote the study of the antiquities of the country. According to the norms of this department an antiquity is "an object which has been constructed, shaped, inscribed, erected, excavated or otherwise produced or modified by human agency earlier than the year 1700 A.D." To preserve the movable antiquities, John D. Rockefeller, Jr., provided funds for the construction of an appropriate museum in Jerusalem; it was opened to the public in 1938. The Department of Antiquities established its headquarters here also. At that time the files of the department contained records of about 4,000 archeological sites [see R. W. Hamilton, "Schedule of Historical Monuments and Sites," *Palestine Gazette Extraordinary* 1375, suppl. 2 (Nov. 24, 1944)] and about 40,000 objects, all of which were made accessible to scholars. Typical objects of all periods have been arranged in chronological order in the visitors' galleries. The *Palestine Archaeological Museum Gallery Book* (hereafter *PAMGB*) aids the visitor in studying those objects and gives him a good survey of all the periods. The Department published its own periodical *Quarterly of the Department of Antiquities in Palestine* (hereafter *QDAP*) and a number of books and pamphlets on special places and themes. Since the termination of the mandate in 1948 the museum has been administered by an international board of trustees, under whose direction it has become the center for the study of the so-called Dead Sea Scrolls. The museum continues to be a valuable aid for study, although now both Jordan and Israel have their own Departments of Antiquities with their own museums and publications.

Both before and after 1948 the departments of antiquities have been assisted in their work by numerous foreign individuals, schools, and organizations. Thus, for example, N. Glueck alone, in his surface surveys, has added more than 1,400 names of archeological sites to the registers, and numerous excavations by others have greatly augmented the number of objects in the museums.

Summaries of the results achieved have been published by such scholars as C. Watzinger, W. F. Albright, K. Kenyon, and G. E. Wright. These have followed an ascending chronological order which will be followed also in the present article.

The earliest periods are named for the most effective materials available for tools: thus Stone, Bronze, and Iron Ages. Later periods are named for the political rulers of the area—the Persians, Greeks, Romans, Byzantines, Arabs, Crusaders, and Turks. Each such period is subdivided by archeologists using chronological (early, middle, late) or stratigraphical terms (lower, middle, upper); these are then often reduced to numbers or subdivided (e.g., Late Bronze III). Great strides have been made in refining the methods used, but much still remains vague and uncertain.

STONE AGE

Palestine is remarkable for the profusion of informative evidences that it has provided bearing on human existence in all phases of this long, essentially prehistoric period from *c.* 500,000 to *c.* 3100 B.C. After a long Early Stone Age (Paleolithic) period, rapid development in the Mesolithic and following (Neolithic, Chalcolithic, Proto-Urban) periods leads up to the historical times.

Paleolithic or Early Stone Age. This period extends from *c.* 500,000 B.C. to *c.* 10,000 B.C. The names of its subdivisions have been derived from similar cultures discovered in European countries: Chellean, Tayacian, Acheulean, Levalloiso-Mousterian, and Aurignacian. Animal remains suggest that the people of this entire period were primarily hunters and fishers. Such remains have turned up both in open-air sites and in caves.

Open-air Sites. The principal stations of this sort known until now are in the neighborhood of Jerusalem and near the lakes in the north. The oldest of these sites is near the southern end of the Sea of Tiberias at a place called Afiqim. It was discovered in 1960. Regarding it, M. Stekelis [*Israel Exploration Journal* (hereafter *IEJ*) 10 (1960) 118] reports: "The finds prove that the site was inhabited by men in the Lower Pleistocene Age, half a million years ago. These finds include few human remains: two fragments of a human skull, four times as thick as that of modern man, and one incisor tooth, the most ancient human remains ever discovered in the Near East. . . . Fossil bones of some forty different species of animals, most of them now extinct, were found. . . . Other finds consisted of flint tools and chopping instru-

ments belonging to what is known as the 'pebble culture.'" The relation of this find to other Lower Paleolithic levels in Galilee and Lebanon is discussed by E. de Vaumas ["Chronologie des dépôts paléolithiques stratifiés," *IEJ* 13 (1963) 195–207, with bibliography].

Caves. Near the northwestern shore of the Sea of Tiberias, near Nazareth, south of Mount Carmel, and in the Judean Desert, caves containing Early Stone Age deposits were excavated by F. Turville-Petre, R. Neuville, M. Stekelis, D. A. E. Garrod, and others. As a result of the work carried out in these caves, D. A. E. Garrod writes: "In the caves of Wady el-Mughara, for the first time, the Stone Age industries hitherto known only from isolated deposits, or as part of a very incomplete series, were found in place in a long and apparently continuous sequence extending from the Tayacian to the end of the Mesolithic" [D. A. E. Garrod and D. M. A. Bate, *The Stone Age of Mount Carmel: Excavations at the Wady el-Mughara* (hereafter *SAMC*) v.1 (Oxford 1937) 114]. The oldest industry found in the caves, the Tayacian, is characterized by small irregular flakes (see *SAMC* 114). The Acheulean level comes next; its flint industry is highly developed and consists chiefly of flakes. In this period human beings seem first to have been buried in or near caves. The minimum date suggested for such burials is about 50,000 years ago. The Galilee Skull, the first of these human remains in caves to be found, was excavated in 1925 by F. Turville-Petre in Mugharet ez-Zuttiyeh, northwest of the Sea of Galilee [see F. Turville-Petre et al., *Researches in Prehistoric Galilee 1925–1926* (London 1927) 15–106]. It is now on exhibit in the Palestine Archeological Museum. According to *PAMGB* No. 33, "the skull belongs to a type of man closely related to the Neanderthal race," which is "distinguished by strongly protruding eye-brow ridges, and by a low, receding forehead which indicates incomplete development of the brain" [see also *The Biblical Archaeologist* 26 (1963) 73–91].

The Lower Aurignacian industry marks an advanced flint culture; the hand axes disappear completely. It is followed by the Middle Aurignacian, the Athlitian and the Kebaran, the latest Palaeolithic industry. This industry belongs to a society of food-gatherers, leaving no buildings [see *SAMC* 116–117; *IEJ* 10 (1960) 259].

Mesolithic Period. During this time people lived in caves, near caves, or in structures out in the open. The first cave in which this culture was found was the Shukba cave in Wadi Natūf, northwest of Jerusalem. The excavations were made in 1928 by Garrod, who named the industry Natufian (see *SAMC* 114). Later, in her work in the Wadi el-Mughara, she found two layers of this industry in the Mugharet el-Wad: the lower (B 2) she called Lower

Natufian; the upper (B 1) Upper Natufian. The former was also found by F. Turville-Petre in layer B of el-Kebara; it was particularly rich in worked and carved bone (*SAMC* 113, 117). R. Neuville found the same culture in various caves of the Judean Desert [R. Neuville et al., *Le Paléolithique et le Mésolithique du Désert de Judée* (hereafter *PMDJ*) (Paris 1951)]. The upper Natufian was found at Khiam on a terrace out in the open [see *SAMC* 113; *PMDJ* 135, 155; *Revue biblique* 70 (1963) 106–110].

Typical of the Mesolithic Period are blades and tools of minute size, called pygmy flints or microliths. Harpoons and fishhooks suggest that the people were fishers; sickles may indicate the beginning of agriculture; heads of animals carved on bone handles mark the beginnings of art; a carving of a human head is the oldest representation of a human being hitherto discovered in Palestine; and figures of deer or gazelles carved on or out of stone or bone illustrate high artistic skill. Pendants worn as charms or amulets suggest religious views [see *PAMGB* No. 150–249; *Eretz Israel* 6 (1956) 21–24, 27]. The shrine found beneath the tell near the spring of Jericho also suggests that the people were religious [see K. Kenyon, *Archaeology of the Holy Land* (hereafter *AHL*) 41–42]. This shrine preserved wood that made a carbon-14 test possible, and for the first time yielded an absolute date near the 9th millennium B.C. for this period. Other objects associated with this shrine made it possible to link it with the Lower Natufian of Mughâret el-Wad and thus fix the absolute chronology of that well-stratified site.

Mesolithic remains outside of caves have been found both at Eynan and Oren. They consist at present of stone foundations of both dwellings and tombs, close together. The dwellings are supposed to represent the first colony living outside of caves known in Palestine. The burial of the dead near their habitations continues an older custom [see *IEJ* 10 (1960) 14–22; *Antiquity and Survival* 2:2–3, 91–110; *IEJ* 7 (1957) 125, 8 (1958) 131, 10 (1960) 118–119; *The Biblical Archaeologist* 26 (1963) 76–77; *PAMGB* No. 249].

Neolithic Period. Between the Mesolithic and the Neolithic periods at JERICHO there were transitional settlements, which K. Kenyon called Proto-Neolithic; they produced 13 vertical feet of deposit without any substantial structure. The deposit was made up of innumerable floors bounded by slight humps, which were all that remained of slight hutlike structures. The same flint and bone industry, allied to the Lower Natufian of Mount Carmel, extended through the transitional Proto-Neolithic state to the large-scale settlement that followed. Jericho has, therefore, provided evidence of the transition from man as a hunter to man as a member of a settled community (see *AHL* 42–43).

Prepottery-Neolithic Period. This period is represented in the next two stages in the development of Jericho. In the earlier of these stages (Prepottery Neolithic A) Jericho had a solid, free-standing, stone town wall. A great stone tower was built against the inside of the western sector of the wall. Against the wall and its tower, curvilinear houses were built. The third series, successively constructed, of these houses produced charcoal timbers that gave a carbon-14 dating of 6850 B.C. plus or minus 210. The walls and tower were older (see *AHL* 43–47). According to D. Kirkbride [*Palestine Exploration Quarterly* (1960) 117–119] the flint instruments of this period resembled the Natufian flints of the two preceding periods.

The Prepottery-Neolithic B stage at Jericho had a flint industry that is called Tahunian and is considered the classic Neolithic industry of Palestine. It is not certain whether it developed from the Natufian or was superimposed on it; the latter seems to have been the case at Jericho, where there are new city walls and rectangular buildings, several of which were places of worship. The floors were covered with plaster, beneath which were found human burials. The heads were separated from the bodies and covered with plaster; the lifesize clay figures found by J. Garstang and later by K. Kenyon most probably came from this stage. Carbon-14 tests gave the following dates: 6250 B.C. plus or minus 200; 5850 B.C. plus or minus 160 (see *AHL* 47–57).

Evidence of this same period was discovered by Kirkbride in excavations carried out by her in 1956, 1958, 1959, and 1961 at Seyl Aqlat, in Beida, north of ancient Petra. Carbon-14 tests yielded dates in the 7th millennium B.C. [see *Palestine Exploration Quarterly* (1960) 136–145].

Pottery-Neolithic A and B Periods. These two periods are distinguished from all the preceding periods by the presence of fired-clay vessels. In the A stage some of the ware is coarse, other ware is fine and decorated. The chief difference is the finish. The finer ware has a comparatively smooth surface and is covered as a rule by a cream-colored slip. This slip in turn is partially covered by a red slip, so that the reserve portions of the cream slip form a pattern, usually in some combinations of chevrons or triangles. To heighten the contrast, the red slip is finely burnished with a beautifully lustrous finish. Altogether, it is a most attractive ware and contrasts strongly with the coarse pottery (see *AHL* 61, 62, and Fig. 4 in that source).

The Pottery-Neolithic-A material was discovered by Garstang in a level at Jericho that is known as Jericho IX and by Kenyon in numerous pits that served as habitations all over the site; in the next level there is a slight improvement in the habitations, as in the objects used in them.

In the B stage many of the vessels are covered with a deep-red slip, sometimes burnished, sometimes matte. The most characteristic decoration, found on both jars and bowls, is bands of herringbone incisions. The bands are usually delineated by grooves, and very often they are covered by a band of cream slip, with the rest of the vessel covered by a red slip (see *AHL* 65).

J. Kaplan ["The Neolithic Pottery of Palestine," *Bulletin of the American Schools of Oriental Research* 156 (December 1959) 15–22] asserts that Miss Kenyon's B stage is mixed, consisting of both Neolithic and Chalcolithic wares; the former he calls Yarmukian, the latter Jericho VIII or Ghassulian. In both phases the herringbone bands occur, but they differ from one another: "in the Yarmukian phase the pattern is part of the filling between the lines which create the zigzag band, whereas at Jericho VIII or Ghassul it is independent ornamentation surrounding the vessel in a band or bands and not in a zigzag pattern." Kaplan's conclusions are that only two main Neolithic phases have become known in the pottery of Palestine up to now: the "Yarmukian" and the older Jericho IX; the latter can be subdivided into two secondary phases based on a related site, Batashi IVa (upper) and Batashi IVb (lower). He asserts that Jericho VIII should not be combined with the Yarmukian Neolithic, nor is the Wadi Rabah material to be so combined, as seems to have occurred at Byblos in Lebanon (Byblos A). "Jericho VIII" and "Wadi Rabah" constitute distinct Chalcolithic phases.

Jericho was the first site in which the earliest pottery of Palestine was found in a stratified context. In 1959 Kaplan knew of seven such sites: besides Jericho, also Abu Usba', Sha'ar ha-Golan, Tell-Aviv, Teluliyot Batashi in the Vale of Sorek, Khirbet Sheikh 'Ali in the Jordan Valley south of Tiberias, and Kfar Gil'adi in the extreme north of Palestine. More recent explorations are rapidly increasing the number of sites in which this period is represented. The Pottery Neolithic Periods fall in the 5th millennium B.C.

Chalcolithic Period. In Palestine, this period, roughly the 4th millennium B.C., is characterized by the manufacture and use of copper objects, while stone implements continued to be used. It first became known through the work that the Pontifical Biblical Institute carried out from 1929 to 1938 at Tulaylat el-Ghassūl, a site east of the Jordan and a little north of the Dead Sea. Since that time this culture has been noted in many other places throughout Palestine. Details are given by R. North in *Ghassul 1960, Excavation Report* [*Analecta biblica* 14 (1961)]. As a result of his own work at Ghassul (1959–60), North confirmed the existence of four levels or strata there, but he was not able to detect any change in culture in those strata. The same is said regarding the Chalcolithic sites explored in the neighborhood of Beersheba (see S. Yeivin, 13–19). The houses at Ghassul were rectangular and their interiors were often painted; in the Beer-sheba region the inhabitants lived partly underground, partly in pits sunk beneath the surface, and partly in rectangular buildings above ground. Ossuaries in the form of buildings, animals, or jars, found especially at Hedera, Azor, and Bne Beraq in the plain adjacent to the Mediterranean, suggest the form of the houses in that region.

At Ein Gedi, near the Dead Sea, a sacred enclosure of this period was found high up a mountain above the spring there. It consists of a wide open court, with a high place and three houses in the center; one, of the "broad house" type, was certainly used for ritual purposes; it is very well preserved, with a fireplace and benches inside [see *Christian News from Israel* (hereafter *CNI*) 14 (1963) 2:16; *Revue biblique* 70 (1963) 575–576, Pl. 23a]. In a cave in the Judean Desert a hoard of bronze and ivory cult objects of this period was discovered [see *IEJ* 11 (1961) 78–79, 12 (1962) 156].

According to J. A. Callaway [*The Biblical Archaeologist* 26 (1963) 78–82], the first intimations of SHEOL (the abode of the dead) go back to this period, when the dead began to be buried away from the habitations of the living. The chronological relations of the different phases of this culture are not yet clear. This holds true especially with reference to the gray burnished ware first found in Esdraelon sites. Carbon-14 tests yield dates toward the end of the 4th millennium for this culture (see *AHL* 82).

Proto-Urban Period. This is a new term invented by K. Kenyon (explained in *AHL* 84–100). It deals with three groups of pottery in use at about the same time and interlocking. These point to three different groups of people who are known principally from their tombs, not from their towns; they do not seem to have had any fortified towns, but seem to have been mere villagers living in poor dwellings. Some of the sites on which they lived were subsequently abandoned and remained so for a long time; such are Tell en-Nasbeh, a little north of Jerusalem, and Samaria; others were later to develop into towns, such as MEGIDDO, Jericho, Beth-shan, and Tell Far'ah (northeast of Nablus). The tombs are peculiar; they are the earliest to be cut into rock and to contain multiple burials. Their date has been fixed in the latter part of the 4th millennium. A central point has been fixed by a carbon-14 test made on material from Jericho; it is around 3200 B.C. and is confirmed by sealings on jars. Originally, some of these finds were assigned to the latter part of the Chalcolithic Period (the gray burnished ware, generally known as Esdraelon ware) and others (red painted ware) to the Early Bronze Age.

BRONZE AGE

In Palestine, as in other areas of ancient occupation, the term Bronze Age was intended originally as a designation of the period between the earliest use of nonprecious metals and the spread of iron tools. Today, the name is largely conventional, and includes three well-known periods (Early, Middle, and Late Bronze) extending from *c.* 3100 to *c.* 1200 B.C.

Early Bronze Age. This age (EB) is characterized by the development of villages into towns or cities that were protected by walls, of which good examples have been found at various places. At Jericho the walls were built of unbaked bricks made in molds. On the western side of the city 17 phases of building and rebuilding of the walls were traced. The walls were protected by round and rectangular towers and by an external ditch. The defenses of Tell el-Far'ah (northeast of Nablus) date from the fourth phase of its existence at the beginning of EB II; at the north they are of stone protected by a glacis of beaten earth; on the west they are of brick; this brick section collapsed at the end of the fifth period of occupation, before the beginning of EB III. The massive wall found at Megiddo was considered a city wall by the excavators, but Kenyon considers it a terrace wall because of the houses built against its exterior. The fortifications of Khirbet Kerak were built of brick either in EB I or in EB II. Those of Ai were constructed of stone, and consist of either three or two lines at various points; their date, however, remains uncertain. The so-called citadel was still in use in EB III. The town wall of Ras el-'Ain may go back to EB I.

Buildings inside the fortifications show a marked change in the course of this period. The earliest houses are the best; some have rounded ends; others are completely round. Timber was common. Associated with the houses are brick-built silos. From Tell el-Far'ah there is evidence that a new type of pottery kiln was introduced during the period; it continued in use down to the Roman Period. A conical stone altar with steps originated in EB III at Megiddo. V. M. Seton-Williams [*Iraq* 11 (1949) 79–83] distinguishes two types of temples in the EB Age, each with its distinctive ground plan. One is a single-chambered type, as at Jericho VII; the other is a more complex structure that contains at least three rooms, as at Hai. The sanctuary at Tell el-Far'ah has two rooms [see *Revue biblique* 68 (1961) Pl. 33, No. 671]. A remarkable building at Khirbet Kerak may have been either a shrine or a granary. The tombs were large rock-cut chambers with multiple burials. The pottery is characterized by a burnished slip, usually red, but occasionally black; it forms the basis for distinguishing three phases known as EB I, II, and III, beginning *c.* 3100 and ending *c.* 2300 B.C. The period is conventionally known as the EB Age,

but in fact there is no certain evidence that bronze was used, and even copper was not very common (see *AHL* 101–134).

The Middle Bronze Age. This period (MB) begins with a subperiod characterized as intermediate (EB/MB) by K. Kenyon [*AHL* 135–161; K. Kenyon, *Excavation at Jericho I: The Tombs Excavated in 1952–54* (Jerusalem 1960) 180–262, hereafter *EJ I*]. Others insist on calling it MB I, which term is retained in this article.

Middle Bronze Age I. In this period (2250–1850/1800 B.C.) the inhabited places were without walls and the houses were few in number. The three temples of stratum 15 at Megiddo probably belong to it. Tombs are numerous and characterized by individual burials. Much of the pottery is peculiar; R. Amiran endeavored to arrange it in three groups which she called A, B, and C [see *IEJ* 10 (1960) 204–225]. Albright, however, prefers a different sequence; he thinks that Amiran's A should come after C [*Bulletin of the American Schools of Oriental Research* 168 (1962) 36–42]. Both Albright and Glueck think that this is the period during which Abraham came to Palestine [see *Bulletin of the American Schools of Oriental Research* 163 (1961) 38–40; Glueck, *Rivers in the Desert,* 60–105].

Middle Bronze Age II. In this period (*c.* 1850/1800–1550/1500 B.C.) the cities were defended by walls. All those that have been excavated reveal a number of phases and can be illustrated by the walls of Jericho. In the earlier stages the single-wall type was used; this was replaced in the later phases by massive ramparts that consisted of three or four sections: an enormous fill, revetted below by a stone wall and crowned on top by the actual defensive wall. It is doubtful whether there was a ditch. All or some of these elements (the ditch, the revetment, the bank, and the wall) have been found at Tell ed-Duweir (Lachish), Tell Jeriseh, Tell el-'Ajjūl, Tell Far'ah (Beth-pelet), Tell Beit Mirsim, Megiddo, Hazor, and SHE-CHEM. At several places the gateways also were preserved; they consisted of a passage with three pairs of buttresses between which the actual gates were probably placed; this was the case at Megiddo X, Shechem, Tell Beit Mirsim, and Tell Far'ah (in the south).

The eastern side of the mound of Jericho reveals several streets and the houses flanking them. On the lower floor there were shops and storage places; on the upper floor habitations. In one group of chambers J. Garstang [*The Story of Jericho* (London 1940) 97–98] found vases of such fine quality that they seemed to represent temple offerings and furniture. One vase was decorated with a molded snake, "a terrestrial emblem of the Mother-goddess, symbolizing Life within the earth." Modeled serpents on cult objects of this period are very numerous (see *PAMGB* No. 773 and *passim*). Temples and cult objects of this period are known from Nahariya [see *QDAP* 14 (1950) 1–41; *IEJ* 6 (1956) 14–25]; from Shechem [see *Bulletin of the American Schools of Oriental Research* 169 (Feb. 1963) 5–32; *The Biblical Archaeologist* 16 (1963) 129–130], both a temenos (1800–1650) and a fortress-temple (1650–1550); probably from Megiddo VIII; and from Tell el-Far'ah in the north [see *Revue biblique* 64 (1957) 559–567].

The tombs of Jericho in this period are noteworthy because they preserved till modern excavation not only the usual objects of clay and metal, but also objects of wood. The clay vessels found at Jericho provided Kenyon with a basis for distinguishing five phases of MB II. Regarding the MB II Period, see *AHL* 170–194; *EJ I* 263–518.

Late Bronze Age. Archeology reveals that in the Late Bronze (LB) period (16th–13th centuries B.C.) numerous cities were destroyed; good examples are Jericho, which fell twice, and Tell Beit Mirsim, both of which were restored only after long intervals. From those that survived or were rebuilt there is evidence that the art of fortification changed but little; both vertical and battered city walls remained in use. The city gates at Megiddo and Beth-shemesh were a continuation or a development of the type in use in the MB Period. The better houses consisted of rooms built around a courtyard. The palace near the gate at Mageddo contained a large number of ivories; an inscription dated one ivory object to the time of Ramses III (1175–1144 B.C.).

The discoveries of temples and objects used in them have been reported from Megiddo, Shechem, Tell Abu Hawam near Haifa, Beth-shan, Hazor, and Tell ed-Duweir. A stele of the god Mekal was found in the 14th-century temple at Beth-shan; it contained also a panel representing a struggle between a lion and a dog. In one of several temples at Hazor was found a stele with two hands raised in prayer, along with many other stelae without representations. For the burial of prominent persons shaft tombs continued to be used. For the first time in history plastered cisterns began to be used; this made it possible to build homes and towns at places where there was no natural water supply.

Written sources from Palestine are now quite numerous. From Beth-shan come royal and private stelae dating from the 14th and 13th centuries; their inscriptions are in Egyptian hieroglyphs and reveal something about the political and religious conditions in Palestine at that time. A fragment of another stele of Thutmose III or Amenophis II was discovered at Tell el-'Oreimeh near the northwestern part of the Sea of Tiberias. Inscribed statues of Ramses III (1175–1144 B.C.) were found at Beth-shan

and Megiddo. At Tell el-Amarna in Egypt were found more than 350 cuneiform tablets, mostly official letters sent from Palestine between 1364 and 1347 B.C. Other cuneiform tablets turned up in Palestine itself at Taanach (12 tablets), Tell el-Hesi, Shechem, Lachish, and Beth-shemesh. The art of the period is illustrated by stelae, statues, figurines, ivories, etc. Peculiar to this period are bichrome ware, base ring ware, and stirrup vessels. The first group is characteristic of the beginning of the period, the second of the whole period, and the third of the end of the period. The first is a local product; the other two come from Cyprus and Mycenae, respectively. They indicate the country's extensive trade contacts with the Mediterranean. See *AHL* 195–220; Albright, *Archaeology of Palestine* (hereafter *AP*) 96–109.

BIBLICAL PERIOD AND LATER

The Israelite settlement in Palestine coincides roughly with the beginning of the Iron Age (*c.* 1200 B.C.); later periods are identified by archeologists with the name of the occupying power of the moment, beginning with the Persians.

Iron Age. Towns and fortresses of the Iron Age (12th to 6th centuries B.C.) were protected by casemate walls, though solid walls with projections and recesses also are found, for example, at Megiddo. Their gates continued older traditions with slight modifications. The use of Proto-Aeolic capitals is now known from Jerusalem, Ramet Rachel, Samaria, Megiddo, and Hazor. Tunnels supplied water to Jerusalem, Gibeon, Megiddo, and Saidiyeh. Temples are reported from Beth-shan, Megiddo, Hazor, Arad, Ashdod, etc. Palaces, storerooms, and vast stables are reported from Megiddo and elsewhere. For the burial of the dead divan-shaped tombs were used; coffins made of clay have been recovered at Tell el-Far'ah in the Negeb, at Beth-shan, and at Sahab; they have anthropoidal lids (see Galling BR 448–449). At Tell el-Kheleifeh, ancient Eziongeber, a copper refinery has been excavated (see N. Glueck, *The Other Side of the Jordan,* 89–113).

Inscriptions are numerous. D. Diringer in *Le iscrizioni antico-ebraiche palestinesi* (Florence 1934) and S. Moscati in *L'epigraphia ebraica antica* (Rome 1951) have collected most of the Hebrew inscriptions known up to 1951. To these we may now add a Canaanite tablet of the 12th century B.C. from Taanach [*The Biblical Archaeologist* 26 (1963) 125]; new material from the 7th century B.C. [*Bulletin of the American Schools of Oriental Research* 165 (February 1962) 34–46]; numerous inscriptions from Arad since 1961; stamped jar handles from Jib; the LACHIS (LACHISH) Letters, etc. Ivories, especially from Samaria [see J. W. and G. M. Crowfoot, *Samaria-Sebaste, II: Early Ivories from Samaria* (London 1938)] illustrate the art of the period. Religious practices are illustrated by numerous Astarte figurines and stands for burning incense or making offerings; they are often decorated with human figures or with animals such as doves and snakes (see *AHL* 221–297; *AP* 112–142).

Persian Period. In this period (6th to 4th centuries B.C.) administrative buildings existed principally at Lachish, Tell Jemmeh, and Ramet Rachel. Tombs of the shaft type are reported from Tell el-Far'ah in the Negeb, from Gezer, and from 'Athlit. Coins put in their appearance for the first time in the Persian period. Astarte figurines, numerous in earlier periods, still continued to be in use, though their style was already influenced by Greek art (see *PAMGB* No. 710). From Lachish alone over 150 crude incense altars are reported [see O. Tufnell et al., *Lachish III: The Iron Age* (London, New York, and Toronto 1953) 226; *PAMGB,* No. 720, 721]. Glass began to be used for seals (see *PAMGB* No. 766). Amulets had representations of Egyptian gods. Inscriptions occur on many small objects. Most interesting, however, are the papyri found in 1962 and 1963; they come from Samaria, and deal with legal and administrative matters; they are written in Aramaic and date from the time between Artaxerxes III (358–338) and 335 B.C. [see *The Biblical Archaeologist* 26 (1963) 110–121; *Bulletin of the American Schools of Oriental Research* 171 (1963) 2].

Greek Period. This period (4th to 1st centuries B.C.) is also commonly referred to as the Hellenistic period. Greek culture had been introduced into Palestine long before Alexander the Great had conquered it (332 B.C.) and subjected it to his rule and that of his successors, the Ptolemies of Egypt (down to 198 B.C.) and the Seleucids of Syria. For a description of the round towers and the fort of the Greek period at Samaria, see J. W. Crowfoot et al., *Samaria-Sebaste, I: The Buildings of Samaria* (London 1942) 24–31 (hereafter *SS I*); the fortifications and buildings of Tell Sandahannah are treated by F. J. Bliss and R. A. S. Macalister, *Excavations in Palestine 1898–1900* (London 1902) 52–57. In Tell Sandahannah are the earliest tombs of the *kôkîm* (oven-shaped) type found in Palestine; the walls are painted and have numerous inscriptions [see J. P. Peters and H. Thiersch, *Painted Tombs in the Necropolis of Marissa* (London 1905)]. Rhodian jar handles with stamped inscriptions characterize this period. Moreover, coins are now a very important means for dating the monuments. The discovery of the Samaria papyri has convinced F. M. Cross that his dates of "the old Exodus manuscript from Cave 4, Qumran (*c.* 250 B.C.) and the archaic Samuel manuscript (*c.* 225 B.C.) now appear to be minimal, and it is clear in turn that the so-called Hasmonean hands of Qumran cannot be reduced in date" [*The Biblical Archaeologist* 26 (1963) 120]. New light has been shed on this period by work at 'Araq el-Emir [see *Bulletin of the American Schools of Oriental Research* 171 (October 1963) 8–55; see also C. Watzinger, *Denkmäler Palästina II* (hereafter *DP II*) 10–30; *AP* 146–154].

Roman Period. Jerash in Transjordan and Samaria west of the Jordan (see *SS I,* 31–37) were typical Roman cities of this period (1st century B.C. to 4th Christian century). Walls, gates, columned streets, forums, stadia, theaters, nymphaea, baths, and temples were some of their chief features; the palaces were noteworthy for their architecture, paintings, mosaics, and baths. As places of worship the pagans had their temples, dedicated to many deities, and also Semitic-style high places; the Jews had not only their famous temple in Jerusalem but also numerous synagogues, especially in Galilee. For burial purposes there were mausoleums built of stone containing sarcophagi; rock-cut chambers with graves in the form of *kôkîm* or arcosolia also contained sarcophagi or ossuaries, often with decorations and inscriptions carved on them; in a few cases the chambers were painted [see Annual of the Department of Antiquities of Jordan (hereafter *ADAJ*) 4–5 (1960) 116]. Most of the Qumran manuscripts and those which have been and are being found more to the south belong to this period (*see* DEAD SEA SCROLLS). For more details regarding this period one can consult *AP* 154–176; *DP II* 31–116. The excavations at Herodium, *Liber Annuus Studii Biblici Franciscani* (hereafter *LA*) 13 (1963) 219–277; Masada, *IEJ* 7 (1957) 1–65; Caesarea, *CNI* 14:3–4 (1963) 20–24; Jerash, *ADAJ* 4–5 (1960) 123–127; Petra, *ADAJ* 5–6 (1960) 119–122; 6–7 (1962) 13–54, and other sites, are constantly shedding new light on this period.

Byzantine Period. This period (4th to 7th century A.D.) was characterized by the public use of the cross on churches, monasteries, private homes, and burial places. All these monuments were generally quite plain on their exteriors, but inside they were beautified by the extensive use of marble, mosaics, and paintings. The decorative elements now took on a Christian character; their inspiration was generally derived from the Scriptures and the liturgy. The same holds true regarding the numerous inscriptions, which, however, contain much historical information as well. The dead continued to be buried in rock-cut tombs like those of earlier periods, especially the arcosolia type; a new practice was that of interment in shaft tombs inside churches and monasteries or in nearby cemeteries [see *DP II,* 117–164; B. Bagatti, *L'Archeologia Cristiana in Palestina* (Florence 1962)]. SYNAGOGUES of this period closely resembled churches in their form and decorations, though their distinctive character was generally indicated by candelabra and inscriptions. See *LA* 4 (1954) 219–246.

First Arab Period. At the beginning of this period (7th–11th centuries), i.e., up to about the middle of the 8th century, synagogues, churches and mosques, as well as new palaces, flourished; after that almost all began to be neglected and to fall into ruins. The palaces at Khirbet el-Minyeh, at the northwestern part of the Sea of Tiberias (see *IEJ* 10 (1960) 226–243), and at Khirbat al Mafjar, north of Jericho [see *QDAP* 5–14; D. C. Baramki, *Guide to the Umayyad Palace at Khirbat Mafjar* (Jerusalem 1947); R. W. Hamilton and O. Grabar, *Khirbat al Mafjar: An Arabian Mansion in the Jordan Valley* (Oxford 1959)] have been excavated. The latter consisted not only of a royal palace, but also of baths, mosques, colonnaded courtyards, pools, gardens, groves, etc. For some of the floors, beautiful mosaics were used; for the walls and ceilings, geometrical motifs, human beings, and animals were executed in stucco.

Period of the Crusades and After. Palestine is still dotted with the castles, churches, and monasteries built by the Crusaders (11th and 12th centuries); some are well preserved. The location of these monuments is indicated on a map published by the Palestine Government in 1937 (*Palestine of the Crusaders: A Map of the Country*); an accompanying text was prepared by C. N. Johns, who himself carried on work at the castle at 'Athlit (see *QDAP* 1–4). On pages 20–21 of the brochure he indicates other sources dealing with these monuments. In the period after the Crusades (late 12th to 16th centuries) Saladin and his successors generally adapted older buildings to their purposes and repaired them. See R. W. Hamilton, *The Structural History of the Aqsa Mosque* (Jerusalem 1949); H. Luke and E. Keith-Roach, *The Handbook of Palestine and Transjordan* (London 1934) 85–89.

Bibliography: W. F. ALBRIGHT, *The Archaeology of Palestine* (Baltimore 1960). K. M. KENYON, *Archaeology in the Holy Land* (New York 1960). G. E. WRIGHT, *Biblical Archaeology* (rev. ed. Philadelphia 1963). S. YEIVIN, *A Decade of Archaeology in Israel 1948–1958* (Istanbul 1960). C. WATZINGER, *Denkmäler Palästinas,* 2 v. (Leipzig 1933–35). H. C. J. LUKE and E. KEITH-ROACH, eds., *The Handbook of Palestine and Transjordan* (3rd ed. London 1934). N. GLUECK, *Rivers in the Desert* (New York 1959); *The River Jordan* (Philadelphia 1946); *The Other Side of the Jordan* (New Haven 1940). *The Holy Land: New Light on the Prehistory and Early History of Israel* (Antiquity and Survival 2.2–3; The Hague 1957).

[S. J. SALLER]

6. Pre-Israelite Ethnology

References to the pre-Israelite population of Palestine are far from lacking in the Bible. They are to be found in the lists of peoples dispossessed by the invading tribes of Israel and in incidental statements about the earlier inhabitants of the land or of particular localities. About some of these people very little is known. They have left little more than their names on the pages of the Bible. Such, for example, are the so-called giants of the land: the Emim who are said to have dwelt in Moab (Dt 2.10–11); the Anakim, found in the vicinity of Hebron (Nm 13.22, 32–33; Dt 2.10,21); and the Rephaim, inhabitants of Bashan and the environs of Jerusalem (Gn 14.5; Dt 3.13; 2 Sm 21.16, 18). Other enigmatic names are those of the Avvim who lived in villages near Gaza (Dt 2.22); the Zuzim (Gn 14.5) in Gilead; and the Zamzummim, found in Ammon (Dt 2.20). Girgashites are named without any locality (Gn 10.16; 15.21; Dt 7.1). The Amalekites were a primitive people of the Negeb (Ex 17.8–16; Nm 13.29).

Other groups, however, have left their mark on the pages of history. They are known not only from biblical references, but can be found in extra-biblical literature as well—in such texts as those coming from Mari, Amarna, etc. First and foremost are the two Semitic groups, the Canaanites and the Amorrites. In addition, the non-Semitic elements are represented by the Hurrians, Hittites, Hivites, Jebusites, and Perizzites.

Canaanites and Amorrites. Canaanites (Channanites) occupied the whole area west of the Jordan (*see* CANAAN AND CANAANITES). The land of Canaan, later known in part as Phoenicia (*see* PHOENICIANS), is the oldest designation for the land of Palestine. Historically the Canaanites were apparently in Palestine as early as the 4th millennium B.C. Biblically this term has both a geographical and an ethnic meaning. Geographically it can refer to any and all the inhabitants of the territory west of the Jordan, whatever their ethnic origin may be. More precisely, however, it is used to refer to that ethnic group of peoples who were dispossessed by the Israelites (Ex 3.8, 17; 13.5; 33.2) and who are said to have inhabited the coastal regions and the plains (Nm 13.29).

AMORRITES appear in northern Syria, the land of Amurru, toward the beginning of the 2nd millennium B.C. Thence they spread out through the fertile crescent, founding such dynasties as those of Mari and Babylon. Biblically they are found on both sides of the Jordan and are said to have preferred the mountainous regions (Nm 13.29). They dwelt particularly in Judah (Jos 10.5) and in the areas of Bashan (Nm 21.33–34) and Heshbon (Nm 21.26). As a geographic term Amorrite is used to refer to the pre-Israelite population of Palestine in general, regardless of ethnic affiliation (Am 2.9–10).

Hurrians and Hittites. Of the non-Semitic population, Hurrians, Hittites, and Hevites deserve special considerations. The Hurrians were a non-Indo-European Armenoid people who settled especially in northern Mesopotamia, particularly in the land subsequently known as Mitanni, and in eastern Mesopotamia, e.g., at Nuzi. They were among the Hyksos who invaded Egypt. According to the Bible, where they are called Horites, the Hurrians were among the ancient inhabitants of central Palestine [Gn 34.2 (Septuagint)] and Seir (Edom: Gn 14.6; Dt 2.12, 22). Ethnically, it would seem that the Jebusites, the early inhabitants of Jerusalem, belonged to Hurrian stock (Ez 16.45). Despite the prominence of Hurrians in extrabiblical literature they receive only scant attention in the Bible.

On the other hand Hivites are found at Shechem (Gn 34.2), Gibeon (Jos 9.7), Mt. Lebanon (Jgs 3.3), Mt. Hermon (Jos 11.3), and in the vicinity of Sidon (2 Sm 24.7), but they receive no mention whatever in any of the extrabiblical literature. It has been suggested that Hivite is a local name for Hurrian. Another attractive theory is that the Hurrians of Seir (Edom) were really Hivites and that the Hivites mentioned in the biblical narratives were in fact Hurrians.

More enigmatic still are the references to the Hittites of the Bible, where they are called Hethites. Historically, three groups called HITTITES are known: the Proto-Hittites or Hattians, the Hittites of the 2nd millennium B.C. or Nesians who used mostly cuneiform for their writings, and the Hittites of the 1st millennium B.C. whose inscriptions are in hieroglyphics. Who the Hittites of Palestine might have been remains a historical problem. They are said to have dwelt in the vicinity of Hebron (Gn 23.2–4; 25.10) and Beer-sheba and in the hill country of southern Palestine (Gn 26.34). It is possible, though not probable, that Hurrian should be substituted for Hittite in the biblical narratives. All three of these terms—Hurrian, Hevite, Hittite—differ only in the middle letter in the Hebrew consonantal text: *ḥry, ḥwy,* and *ḥty.* Confusion, therefore, could easily have resulted in the transmission of the text.

Receiving frequent mention, usually in conjunction with other dispossessed peoples, are the Perizzites. They are found at Bethel, at Shechem, and in the hill country of Judah (Gn 15.20; Ex 3.8, 17; Dt 7.1; Jos 17.15; etc.). However, not much can be said about them. Judging from the above name alone, the Perizzites could have been of Hurrian origin. Names ending in "-izzi" are known from extra-biblical Hurrian references. Whatever the case may be, they were a distinct ethnic group in the pre-Israelite population of Palestine.

Bibliography: J. BRIGHT, *A History of Israel* (Philadelphia 1959) 106–107. J. C. L. GIBSON, "Observations on Some Important Ethnic Terms in the Pentateuch," *Journal of Near Eastern Studies* 20 (1961) 217–238.

[F. SEPER]

7. Holy Places

For Christians the term "holy places of Palestine" designates the sites in the Holy Land that have been made sacred by the presence of Jesus or His blessed Mother or the Apostles. From the viewpoint of relative importance, the holy places are either primary or secondary. In the former class are the cave where Jesus was born, the tomb in which He was buried, etc.; in the latter class are the Pool of Shiloh, the place where St. Stephen was stoned, etc. The holy places may be connected either with private houses, as the home of Mary at Nazareth, the Cenacle, etc., or with sites in the open, such as the Mount of the Beatitudes, the place at the Jordan where Jesus was baptized, the Garden of Gethsemani, etc. On the basis of scholarly certitude the holy places may be regarded either as authentic or as based on pious legend. To the former class belong the site of the Annunciation, the cave of Christ's Nativity, the tomb of Lazarus at Bethany, etc.; to the latter belong the STATIONS OF THE CROSS, the site where Mary and Joseph found Jesus in the temple, etc.

Nature. Shrines or sanctuaries were erected at the holy places at different times. The reasons for building them were various: to honor the place as a king is honored by giving him a crown, to preserve them from profanation, and especially to have a proper edifice for the celebration of the sacred liturgy. Bad weather or, in certain periods of history, the interference of unbelievers would have prevented Christians from celebrating the Eucharist there in peace, and since the Eucharist was considered the best means of being united with Christ at these venerated sites, sacred edifices were erected there.

In regard to the architectural form, at the holy places the churches are or have been of five naves (the basilica at Bethlehem and the former basilica at Calvary), of three naves (at Gethsemani, Tabor, Bethany, etc.), and of one nave (the ancient chapel of the Multiplication of the Loaves and of the BEATITUDES at et-Tabga), or churches with the ground plan of a Greek cross (formerly at Jacob's Well), or of a circle (the rotunda of the Ascension), or octagonal (over the house of Peter at Capernaum). The present owners are either Muslims (the church of the Ascension), or Israeli (the Cenacle), or Latin-rite Catholics (Tabor, Nazareth, Capernaum, Ain Karem, etc.), or Greek Orthodox (Jacob's Well, Jebel Quaranṭāl, i.e., the site of our Lord's 40-day fast), or the three communities jointly of Latin Catholics, Greek Orthodox, and Armenians (the Holy Sepulcher and the Basilica of Bethlehem, in both places the *status quo* going back to 1852, when a Turkish decree ordained that these three Christian communities should henceforth retain what rights they had there as of that year).

History. The sanctuaries at the holy places date almost exclusively from the 4th century, when Christians of Gentile origin first came in numbers to the Holy Land. At first the Judeo-Christians of Palestine regarded the holy places as memorials, and they left most of them in their pristine state. Such were the tombs of Jesus, of the Blessed Virgin, of St. Joseph, and of LAZARUS. But a few of the holy places they adapted, in simple fashion, for Christian worship, such as the house of the Holy Family at Nazareth and the upper room on "Christian Zion." The first important period for the building of Christian sanctuaries at the holy places in Palestine was that of the 4th and 5th centuries, when construction proceeded chiefly under the patronage of the Byzantine emperors. The second such period was in the 12th century, when the crusaders had control of the Holy Land, and the third was from the middle of the 19th century to the present. Between these periods of construction there were periods of destruction: in 614, when Palestine was devastated by the Persians; from 638 to 1099, during which time the Muslims on several occasions destroyed certain Christian sanctuaries, and from 1187 to the present, when the Muslims, though not actively destructive, have often interfered with Christian worship at the holy places.

Authenticity. To evaluate the authenticity of any of the holy places of Palestine, two main conditions must be fulfilled if the site is to be considered authentic: its localization must not contradict the data of the Bible, and the tradition connected with it must go back to Apostolic times. If either of these requirements is missing, the place must be regarded as having merely devotional value. Thus, the localization of Emmaus at modern Amwas has, in its favor, a tradition going back at least to Byzantine times; but the site does not seem to agree with the Gospel data, since its distance from Jerusalem is much greater than the 60 stadia given in the best manuscripts of Lk 24.13. The location of Emmaus at modern el-Qubeibeh agrees with the Gospel data of 60 stadia, but the tradition connected with this site does not seem to be older than crusader times.

Since almost all the sanctuaries in the Holy Land date from the 4th and later centuries, and consequently the earliest descriptions left by pilgrims date from these centuries, one may wonder how it is possible to show that there is any tradition in regard to them going back to the time of the Apostles. However, for a certain group of the holy places it is possible to suppose that throughout the early centuries of Christianity there were Judeo-Christians in these places who would have been as interested in these sacred sites as modern Christians are. Until not long ago such continuous presence of Judeo-Christians in the Holy Land was not suspected. But recent discoveries at NAZARETH and at Dominus Flevit, as well as a more careful study of the Talmudic sources, of certain statements of the Fathers, and of the sparse data col-

lected by Eusebius, have shown that during the first few Christian centuries a certain number of Judeo-Christians continued to live in Palestine, especially in its mountain regions.

Judeo-Christian Traditions. To mention a few cases in particular, it is known, for instance, that "the brethren [relatives] of the Lord" lived at Nazareth at least until 250 as leaders of the local Christian community, and precisely at the present traditional site of the Annunciation, archeological excavations have brought to light a religious edifice resembling a synagogue that was built not later than the 3rd century, together with certain caves that were venerated at even an earlier date. Many graffiti here with the words "holy place" or with such an invocation as X[AIP]E MAPIA ("Hail, Mary!") show, not only the continuous veneration of the place, but also the Judeo-Christian character of its possessors and visitors, which had already been surmised from the literary sources.

The presence of *Mînîm* (Judeo-Christians) at Capernaum during the early Christian centuries is well known from the Talmud. The tradition locating the CENACLE on Christian Zion is witnessed to by a retrospective passage in Epiphanius and especially by the so-called "Tomb of David" there, which is to be related with the Christian synagogues at Nazareth. The tomb of the blessed Virgin at JERUSALEM, which is mentioned in Judeo-Christian sources, was held to be connected with "very ancient" tradition when the sanctuary there was erected by Gentile Christians. At the cave of Gethsemani there was preserved, even after the Constantinian peace, the remembrance of a sacred supper that had been held there formerly by the Judeo-Christians. The cave of the Eleona (ἐλαιών, olive grove) on the MOUNT OF OLIVES, regarded as the site where Jesus taught His disciples the LORD'S PRAYER, is mentioned in the apocryphal sources and is spoken of as a venerated site by Eusebius five years before Constantine began his program of building sanctuaries in the Holy Land. The same is true of the tomb of Lazarus and the cave of the Nativity at BETHLEHEM. The latter site was known also to Origen and even St. Justin. When the site of the Holy SEPULCHER was recovered in 326, the Gentile Christians took pains to verify its authenticity by establishing its agreement with the Gospel data, such as the earthquake fissure in the rock of CALVARY and the single burial niche in the tomb chamber there, so that the tradition that had been maintained by the Judeo-Christians for this site was relegated to a subordinate position.

The Evangelists did not think it opportune to refer to everything that concerned the holy places. But other points of information were transmitted by the apocryphal Gospels; thus, the Gospel of the Hebrews places the fasting of Jesus on Mount Tabor, and the Proto-Evangelium of James has the beginning of the Annunciation take place at the fountain in Nazareth. This does not mean that such extra-evangelical traditions are always historical. Rather, they give evidence of a difference, going back to a very early period, between Galilean traditions and Judean ones, e.g., regarding the place of the 40-day fast of Jesus after His Baptism (*see* TEMPTATIONS OF JESUS).

Despite the many vicissitudes that Palestine has suffered in the course of its long history, most of the place names throughout the country have been preserved from remote antiquity to the present with remarkable fidelity. Therefore, there is no reason to doubt the local traditions that preserved the biblical names, not only of such villages as Nazareth and Nain, but also also of such localities as Gethsemani and Shiloh.

From the examples just cited, as well as from others that could be given, it can be seen that, in order to establish the authenticity of the holy places, it is necessary to study each case by itself against its historical background. To reject all of them as spurious or to accept all of them as authentic without further ado is an easy way out, but it does not lead to the truth.

Exegetical Value. The scientific study of the holy places can contribute much to general biblical studies, whether this confirms the authenticity of the places or whether it establishes their value more precisely. Thus, for instance, the excavation and study of the Pool of BETHESDA both confirm and explain the statement in Jn 5.2 that this pool had "five porticoes"; the location of the Garden of Gethsemani shows how far from Jerusalem Jesus was when arrested (Mt 26.36, 47); Jacob's Well at Shechem shows what the Samaritan woman meant when she told Jesus that "the well is deep" (Jn 4.6.11); the sanctuary of the Nativity at Bethlehem shows that the manger in which the infant Jesus was bedded was in a cave that was used for a stable, as many caves still are so used in Palestine (Lk 2.7); the rustic character of Nazareth at the time of Christ, as shown by the archeological excavations there, throws light on Nathanael's question, "Can anything good come out of Nazareth?" (Jn 1.46).

Bibliography: C. KOPP, *The Holy Places of the Gospels,* tr. R. WALLS (New York 1963). E. HOADE, *Guide to the Holy Land* (Jerusalem 1942 and later eds.); *Marian Shrines in Mary's Land* (Ottawa 1958). B. BAGATTI, *L'archeologia cristiana in Palestina* (Florence 1962). D. BALDI, *Enchiridion locorum sanctorum* (2nd ed. Jerusalem 1955). G. PERELLA, *I Luoghi Santi* (Piacenza 1936). A. OLIVAN, *Maria nella sua terra* (Milan 1958). Authenticity of the Holy Places. B. BAGATTI, "Sguardo storico (ai giudeo-cristiani)," *Il simbolismo dei giudeo-cristiani,* ed. E. TESTA (Jerusalem 1962) 19–33; "Sainte Sion," *Saint Jacques le Mineur* (Jerusalem 1962) 13–22; "Le origini della 'tomba della Vergine' in Getsemani," *Revista Biblica Italiana* 11 (1963) 38–52; "Autenticità del S. Sepolcro," *La Terra Santa* 38 (1962) 299–302; "Origine dei Luoghi santi di Palestina," *Liber Annuus* 14 (1963–64) 32–64. E. TESTA, "Le Grotte dei misteri giudeo-cristiane," *ibid.* 65–144. B. BAGATTI, *L'Église de la circoncision* (Jerusalem 1965) 93–113.

[B. BAGATTI]

PALESTINE, EARLY CHURCH IN

Since the time of Diocletian, it was customary to distinguish (1) Palestina prima, or the middle section of West Jordania, with Caesarea as capital; (2) Palestina secunda, or Galilee and Peraea, with its capital at Scythopolis; (3) Palestina tertia, or salutaris, the southern part of Judaea and Peraea, with capital at Petra.

Early Palestinian Christianity. With the Palestinian revolt against Rome in 66, the Christian community left Jerusalem for Pella in Transjordan. Their bishop was Simeon, relative of Jesus and successor of James. By this gesture the Jewish Christians separated themselves from the Temple, which was destroyed in 70 by Titus. Some Christians returned from Pella, and Eusebius (*Ecclesiastical History* 4.5) states that 15 bishops succeeded one another at Jerusalem up to the revolt under Hadrian, all of Hebrew descent. This large number probably includes the *presbyteroi,* one of whom was chosen as bishop. The Christians of Jerusalem adhered to Jewish practices, and the Epistle of Jude and the Apocryphal Gospel of James seem to come from this group. They were not favored by the Jews, and BAR KOKHBA persecuted them during his revolt of 132 to 135. Suppressed by Hadrian, Jerusalem was rebuilt as Aelia Capitolina, and only a few Christians returned. Others migrated to Kokaba in Transjordania, to Nazareth, and to Aleppo. In Jerusalem itself, pagan statues were erected on the site of the Temple, and on Golgotha, the mount of the Crucifixion, a temple was erected to the Capitoline Triad.

Palestinian Bishoprics. Christian missionaries were sent from Palestine to the churches of Egypt, Osrhoene, and Adiabene. Though it was the land where Christianity originated, Palestine was not the scene of its most rapid diffusion and remained considerably behind the Greek-speaking cities of Syria. Palestinian towns with bishops before 325 were, besides Jerusalem and Caesarea (which had a bishop *c.* 190), Maximianopolis; Scythopolis; Sebaste; Flavia Neapolis; Ascalon; Diospolis, or Lydda; Nicopolis; Gadara; Azotus; Ascalon; Eleutheropolis; Jericho; Capitolias; Aila; and Gaza. Jaffa became an episcopal see after the time of Constantine. Pella seems to have become a permanent episcopal see only in the 5th century.

As early as the reign of Domitian, Gnostic tendencies appeared among the Palestinian Christians. As Vespasian before him, Domitian sought out relatives of Jesus, fearing a renewed Messianism. When Christians were martyred under Trajan, Simeon, bishop of Jerusalem and son of Cleophas, was among them. Lucian's satire in his *Life of Peregrinus* gives a garbled picture of a Palestinian community of the 2d century. When synods were held under Pope Victor concerning the date of Easter, the assembled bishops of Palestine (*c.* 190) wrote a letter acknowledging agreement with the Western usage. Two Palestinian bishops are known to have attended this synod: Theophilus of Caesarea and Narcissus of Jerusalem. Bishops of Syria also were present, a fact that indicates that they did not belong to distinct ecclesiastical provinces at this time. Under Marcus Aurelius, Jerusalem had bishops of gentile descent, e.g., Narcissus and Alexander. Little by little, this community adapted itself to the universal Church, while a minority tended to sectarianism. Virginity was highly honored, and there are indications of a renewed Christian messianism, contemporary with a similar Jewish movement that inspired Septimius Severus, during a journey through Palestine in 202, to forbid further proselytism.

Origen at Caesarea. In 231, Theoctistus, bishop of Caesarea, ordained ORIGEN a priest, and made him head of the school which achieved considerable renown. Origen was active as lecturer and preacher, so that the city became an intellectual center for the Christians. The persecution of Valerian produced martyrs in Palestine in 257 to 258, but in spite of the emperor's hostility the majority of the region had been Christianized by the end of the 3d century.

As early as 260, Theotecnus, a student of Origen, was bishop of Caesarea, and under his successor the school was directed by PAMPHILUS who continued the tradition established by Origen and developed the famous library, which contained many Christian texts, including the Hexapla. Its intellectual direction reflected Alexandrian rather than Antiochene thought. When Arius was condemned, however, he took refuge with EUSEBIUS OF CAESAREA and was declared innocent by a local council in Palestine, even though the bishop of Jerusalem, Macarius, opposed him. A certain number of Palestinian bishops, including Maximus and Saint CYRIL OF JERUSALEM, agreed with the condemnation of Arius at Nicaea, but Eusebius of Caesarea led the attack against the Nicaean bishops that culminated in the council of Tyre-Jerusalem of 335. This assembly deposed Athanasius and repudiated the term HOMOOUSIOS. The successor of Eusebius, Acacius of Caesarea, became the head of the homoean faction and with imperial help in 360 reversed ecclesiastical power in the East. But even the support of the Emperor Valens (364–78) could not prevent the victory of orthodoxy. In 379, 153 Eastern bishops expressed their agreement with Rome.

Palestinian Monasticism. Monasticism began in Palestine during the first years of the 4th century with Hilarion of Gaza, who settled near Maiuma and whose fame attracted disciples. The Laura of Pharan on the Dead Sea was founded by Saint Chariton of Iconium about 320, and the coenobitic form of monastic life flourished. Other foundations were those of Saint EPIPHANIUS OF CONSTANTIA (*c.* 335) at Besanduk near Eleutheropolis; of Saints EUTHYMIUS and Theoctistus near Jericho; of Saint GERASIMUS on the Jordan; and of Saint THEODOSIUS near Bethlehem. Particularly important and lasting to our own times is the Great Laura founded near Jerusalem by Saint Sabas (d. 532). Latin monks were located at Bethlehem under Saint JEROME (386), while nuns dwelt nearby under Paula. MELANIA THE ELDER and RUFINUS OF AQUILEIA founded a double monastery on Mount Olivet in Jerusalem (*c.* 376). MELANIA THE YOUNGER took up her abode there early in the 5th century and erected two monasteries, as she had previously done at Tagaste in Africa.

In the 4th century Jerusalem entered into dispute with Caesarea over possession of the metropolitan see. The Council of Nicaea (*c.* 7) admitted a special position of honor for Jerusalem. But its bishops, particularly John (386–417) desired metropolitan status, and in 451 the Council of CHALCEDON declared Juvenal (421–458) patriarch and head of the three provinces of Palestine at the expense of Antioch.

Jerusalem further owed its growing importance to pilgrimages, which became progressively popular in the 4th century. CONSTANTINE I and HELENA erected several magnificent buildings in Jerusalem and Bethlehem. The liturgy of Jerusalem, described by Aetheria, exercised a great influence in the whole church, by reason of the pilgrims who witnessed it (*see* ITINERARIA).

Monophysitism and Origenism. Palestine had a strong anti-Chalcedonian party, though weaker than in Syria and Egypt. Juvenal, the patriarch, was ejected and replaced by an opponent of the council of Chalcedon and was not restored until the Byzantine army had defeated hordes of fanatical monks in 453. Though the monks generally favored orthodoxy, especially under Euthymius and Sabas, the Monophysite leaders, and particularly the intruder Theodosius, installed anti-Chalcedonians in many sees, and the opposition was kept alive especially from the monastery of Maiuma. In 513 the monk Severus succeeded in having Elias, the patriarch of Jerusalem, exiled, even though he was defended by the great abbots, Theodosius and Sabas. The Patriarch John (d. 524) was hostile to the Monophysites, so that Jerusalem was the only patriarchate not in the hands of the Monophysites when Justin became emperor in 519. Since Jerusalem relied upon the powerful patriarchate of Constantinople for protection against its rivals, Antioch and Alexandria, it was involved on the side of this see in the ACACIAN SCHISM. In the 6th century, it was considered to hold fourth place among the patriarchates of the East, after Constantinople, Alexandria, and Antioch.

PELAGIANISM was dealt with by a provincial council at Diospolis (or Lydda) in 415, which was misinformed by Pelagius and declared him innocent. A dispute over Origenism lead to a heated controversy at the end of the 4th century between Bishop John of Jerusalem and Rufinus on the one side, and Saints Jerome and Epiphanius on the other. The problem became acute in the 6th century when the monks of the New Laura of Thecue defended Origen's orthodoxy, whereas the outstanding monk of Palestine, Saint Sabas, head of the old or Great Laura, led his opponents. When two Origenist monks, Domitian and THEODORE ASCIDAS, were named bishops by Justinian and enlisted the support of THEODORA in their cause, a strong anti-Origenist movement was begun by the Patriarch Peter of Jerusalem. This led to a Synod at Gaza (539) and an edict of Justinian in 542, condemning nine propositions of Origen. Several Palestinian monks, headed by Theodore Ascidas, in the desire to avenge themselves and to avoid further persecution, persuaded Justinian to devote himself to another problem, that of the THREE CHAPTERS.

In addition to the earliest Judeo-Christian writers of Palestine, several early apologists and propagandists are considered Palestinian by birth or activity: Ariston of Pella, JUSTIN MARTYR, JULIUS AFRICANUS, Pamphilus and Eusebius of Caesarea, Cyril of Jerusalem, Epiphanius of Constantia, and CYRIL OF SCYTHOPOLIS. The end of the 6th and the beginning of the 7th centuries constituted a period of prosperity, but the Persian invasion of 614 proved catastrophic: thousands of Christians were slaughtered, many churches and monasteries were destroyed or damaged, and the patriarch Zacharias was exiled. At this time the true cross was captured. Even though the victory of the Emperor HERACLIUS forced the Persians to restore the cross, the dispute over MONOTHELITISM brought new troubles, and the Patriarch Saint SOPHRONIUS (634–38) sharply attacked this heresy. But he was forced to arrange the surrender of Jerusalem to the Arabs under the Caliph Omar in 637; and although Christianity survived under Muslim rule, the distrust of the Arabs for the orthodox patriarchs made it impossible to give him a successor for 68 years.

Bibliography: M. LE QUIEN, *Oriens Christianus*, 3 v. (Paris 1740; rpre. Graz 1958). F. M. ABEL, *Histoire de la Palestine*, 2 v. (Paris 1952). A. VON HARNACK, *The Mission and Expansion of*

Giovanni Pierluigi Da Palestrina. (Bettmann/CORBIS)

Christianity in the First Three Centuries, tr. and ed. J. MOFFATT, 2 v. (2d ed. New York 1908). H. JEDIN, *Handbuch der Kirchengeschichte,* 6 v. (Freiburg 1962–): v. 1., K. BAUS, ed., *Von der Urgemeinde zur frühchristlichen Grosskirche,* with "Einleitung zur Kirchengeschichte" by H. JEDIN. J. DANIÉLOU and H. I. MARROU, *The First Six Hundred Years,* tr. V. CRONIN, v. 1 of *The Christian Centuries* (New York 1964–). J. A. FITZMEYER, "The Bar Cochba Period," in *The Bible in Current Catholic Thought,* ed. J. L. MCKENZIE (New York 1962) 133–68. F. VAN DER MEER and C. MOHRMANN, *Altas of the Early Christian World,* ed. and tr. M. F. HEDLUND and H. H. ROWLEY (New York 1958). L. DUCHESNE, *L'Église au VIe siècle* (Paris 1925). A. FLICHEM and V. MARTIN, eds., *Histoire de l'église depuis les origines jusqu'à nos jours* (Paris 1935–) v. 1–4. E. STEIN, *Histoire du Bas-Empire,* tr. J. R. PALANQUE, 2 v. in 3 (Paris 1949–59) v. 1–2.

[J. J. GAVIGAN]

PALESTRINA, GIOVANNI PIERLUIGI DA

Foremost composer of Renaissance vocal polyphony of the Roman school; b. Palestrina, Italy (whence the name by which he has been known ever since), probably at the end of 1525; d. Rome, Feb. 2, 1594. He may have been a chorister of the Palestrina cathedral, for after its bishop, Cardinal della Valle, had been made archpriest of the basilica of St. Mary Major, Rome (1534), the young boy was transferred to that choir and was singing as a full member in 1537. He returned home when his voice changed in 1539 but began his higher musical education in Rome in 1540. At that time the new St. Peter's was being built, and the city was full of great Renaissance artists, architects, and sculptors—a stimulating environment for the rising musician. In 1544, his training finished, he was appointed *organista e maestro di canto* of the cathedral of Palestrina, a post that lasted seven years, during which time he married a fairly wealthy girl. When the reigning bishop of Palestrina, Cardinal del Monte, became Pope Julius III (1551), the young composer returned to Rome, this time as master of the Julian choir.

The Early Phase of His Work. His first volume of Masses, dedicated to Julius and containing the famous engraving of the Pope receiving the music from Palestrina's hands, was published in 1554. Four of these Masses are earlier compositions, but the fifth *Ecce Sacerdos Magnus,* was a new work in the Pope's honor. Julius' ill-advised reward was to appoint him to the pontifical choir, an exclusive and proud body of singers, who were not pleased to have the newcomer forced upon them. This appointment, moreover, meant that Palestrina had to give up his Julian choirmastership. Even more unluckily, Julius III died within three months, and his successor, Marcellus, within 23 days of election. The next pope, Paul IV, a reformer, soon found two reasons to dismiss Palestrina from his new position: he was married, and he had recently published a book of madrigals—both were against the rules for Church musicians. The young man, however, had the perspicacity to obtain a papal pension that was to last for the rest of his life, even though he had been a member of the choir for only a few months.

The music at the Lateran Basilica had deteriorated since the departure of LASSO for Antwerp in 1555, and in October of the same year Palestrina easily obtained this post (his impressive *Lamentations* setting was composed there; *see* TENEBRAE). Although the pay was small, he had his pension and also a wine-selling business. Indeed, so sure was he of his financial position that he could afford to leave the Lateran over a monetary squabble concerning his eldest son; he did not accept another position until March 1561, when he became choirmaster at St. Mary Major, the basilica of his childhood. A few years later, restlessness overtook him, and an opportunity to direct music in the fabulous Villa d'Este during the summer of 1564 turned his thoughts to court employment. Also, the new Roman seminary had offered him the directorship of music with free living, education for his family, and leisure to pursue his courtly career; not surprisingly, that he relinquished the position at St. Mary Major. These years, however, remained indecisive, and after an offer from Emperor Maximilian of Vienna had been lost through Pa-

lestrina's own cupidity, he turned his attention to ecclesiastical work. His one friend during all these courtly contacts was the Duke of Mantua, to whom he sent many compositions during 20 years. In 1571 he again accepted the mastership of the Julian choir, and from this time on he was exclusively a church musician. His good fortune, however, was darkened by a series of personal sorrows. The ever-present Roman plagues and pestilences killed his son Rodolfo in 1572, his brother Silla a year later, his second son Angelo in 1575, and finally his wife, whom he had deeply loved, in 1580.

During this long, checkered period, Palestrina published several collections: the first book of motets in 1563, the second book of Masses (which included the *Missa di Papa Marcello*), in 1567, and more motets in 1569.

The Later Phase. His style changed notably at this time: the number of vocal parts began to increase. In 1572 he increased the number of vocal parts in the motets from the usual four and five to between five and seven parts. In 1575 he increased the number again to eight vocal parts. The style of composition, too, rapidly matured. The early canonic writing which featured Netherlandish technique gave way to a more serene style where contrapuntal and homophonic writing were integrated into a unique fluency, and the madrigalism of the earlier works almost disappeared. His sorrows had enabled him to produce some of his more poignant works, such as the *Improperia* and some of the *Lamentations* as well as many of the larger motets. From 1577 he was engaged partly in an abortive effort to revise the Gradual, whose plainsong had become so full of errors that it was impossible to construct a unified liturgy. This herculean task was abandoned after a few years, and nothing more was done about it for another four decades. The Medicean edition, as it was called when finally published, had little or no connection with Palestrina's work (*see* CHANT BOOKS, PRINTED EDITIONS OF).

Depressed by his losses of both family and fortune, Palestrina turned to religion and offered himself for the priesthood. He received the tonsure and even a benefice, but within a few months he was quietly married to a rich widow who brought with her a prosperous furrier's business. Palestrina, ever a resourceful businessman, switched comfortably from the wine trade to furs, and life began afresh. Whereas publication of his works had been sporadic between 1563 and 1575, three volumes were produced in the year 1581 and another in 1582. Indeed, these last 13 years saw the publication of 16 different collections, comprising more than 400 compositions. After his death, his son Iginio published many volumes of Masses and motets, but some of the finest works, because of changing musical fashion, remained in manuscript. Glorious Masses like *Assumpta Est Maria* and *Ecce Ego Joannes,* and motets, such as *Salve Regina* and *O Sacrum Convivium,* had to wait for three centuries before gaining wide currency.

Evaluation. Palestrina's position at the end of his century was rather like that of Bach after his death. Both composers used a conservative technique, a style virtually reflecting a past age, although in a strikingly individual and compelling manner. But the new music was already emerging, and it is small wonder that their music was abandoned as being old-fashioned. There is no doubt that Palestrina deliberately adopted a restrained manner of composing in order to produce a more remote and less modern style than that of his contemporaries. Even the madrigals, both secular and spiritual, are restrained to a point where they may be compared unfavorably with those of lesser contemporaries, although they contain much good music. Some of the early church music is a little unsure and derivative, but the works of his middle period, and certainly his later compositions are ideal for liturgical use. They possess those qualities of serenity and impersonality that are essential for divine worship.

Palestrina's coffin bore the title *Princeps Musicae.* It could be argued that composers such as MORALES, Lasso, and VICTORIA were perhaps more adventurous, and that Lasso and many others were more effective in the secular field. No one, however, would seriously deny Palestrina the title *Princeps Musicae Sacrae.*

Bibliography: *Opera omnia,* ed. F. X. HABERL, 33 v. (Leipzig 1862–1903), see pref. by Haberl; *Le Opere complete,* ed. R. CASIMIRI et al. (Rome 1939–), there are innumerable performing editions of his most popular items. Biography. G. BAINI, *Memorie Storico-critiche della vita e delle opere. . . ,* 2 v. (Rome 1828), a curiosity. M. BOBILLIER, *Palestrina,* 2 v. in 1 (Paris 1906). F. RAUGEL, *Palestrina* (Paris 1930). H. COATES, *Palestrina* (New York 1938; repr. 1949), best biog. Technical. A. CAMETTI, "Le case di G. P. da Palestrina in Roma," *Rivista musicale italiana* 28 (1921) 419–432; "Rubino Mallapert, maestro di G. P. da Palestrina," *ibid.* 29 (1922) 335–347; "G. P. da Palestrina e le sue alleanze matrimoniali," *ibid.* 30 (1923) 489–510. R. CASIMIRI, *Giovanni Pierluigi da Palestrina Nuovi documenti biografici,* 2 pts. (Rome 1918–22), pamphlet; *Il codice 59 del'archivio musicale lateranense, autografo di inedite e dieci tavole fototipiche* (Rome 1919), pamphlet. H. K. ANDREWS, *An Introduction to the Technique of Palestine* (London 1958), the only complete study of Palestrina's technique of composition. K. G. FELLERER, *Palestrina* (Regensburg 1930). K. JEPPESEN, *The Style of Palestrina and the Dissonance,* tr. M. W. HAMERIK (New York 1927). G. REESE, *Music in the Renaissance* (rev. ed. New York 1959). P. H. LÁNG, *Music in Western Civilization* (New York 1941). L. BIANCHI and G. ROSTIROLLA, *Iconografia palestriniana* (Lucca 1994). B. BUJIC, "Palestrina, Willaert, Arcadelt, and the Art of Imitation," *Recercare* 10 (1998) 105–131. J. ROCHE, "*The Praise of it Endureth For Ever:* The Posthumous Publication of Palestrina's Music," *Early Music* 22 (1994) 631–639. N. O'REGAN, "The Performance of Palestrina: Some Further Observations," *Early Music* 24 (1996) 144–154.

[P. E. PEACOCK]

PALEY, WILLIAM

English divine and philosopher; b. Peterborough, July 1743; d. Lincoln, May 25, 1805. Educated at Christ's College, Cambridge, he served there as a successful lecturer and tutor until 1776, when he became rector of Musgrave in Westmorland. In 1782 he was made archdeacon of Carlisle. *The Principles of Moral and Political Philosophy* (London 1785), based on his lectures at Cambridge, went through 15 editions in his lifetime and was used at Cambridge as a standard textbook. His most original work, *Horae Paulinae, or the Truth of the Scripture History of St. Paul Evinced by a Comparison of the Epistles Which Bear His Name and the Acts of the Apostles and with One Another,* appeared in 1790. The most famous of his books are *A View of the Evidences of Christianity* (2 v. London 1794), and *Natural Theology, or Evidences of the Existence and Attributes of the Deity collected from the Appearances of Nature* (London 1802), in which he set forth his fully developed argument from design for the existence of God. He changed the ground of the argument from astronomy to anatomy in order to argue to God from the evidences of design in animal and human organisms. One of the most successful apologists of his time, Paley was a guiding light of the "evidential school" of rationalist theologians who were very influential in the Church of England, especially at Oxford, during the early 19th century, and against whose ideas the leaders of the OXFORD MOVEMENT reacted.

Bibliography: *Works,* ed. E. PALEY, 7 v. (London 1825). F. C. COPLESTON, *History of Philosophy* (Westminster MD 1946–63) 5:195–199. L. STEPHEN, *History of English Thought in the 18th Century,* 2 v. (London 1927).

[E. SILLEM]

PALI CANON

The main body of the Buddhist canonical texts developed in the period between Buddha's death (483 B.C.) and Asoka's reign (273–231 B.C.), though its oral tradition was committed to writing in the Pāli language only in the reign of Vattāgamani Abhaya (29–17 B.C.), in Ceylon. The *Tipiṭaka* (Skt. *Tripiṭaka*), The Three Baskets of Theravāda tradition, consists of three main divisions.

The first is the *Vinaya Piṭaka,* The Basket of Rules for the orders of monks, nuns, and lay people, subdivided into three collections: (1) *Suttavibha·aga,* under 15 headings grouping the rules for individual discipline and the disciplinary action required in case of infringement; (2) *Khandhaka*, in 22 chapters outlining the norms for the organization of the orders; (3) *Parivāra*, containing 19 supplementary sections on the foundation of the order of nuns and the sacred councils, which were convoked at Rājagṛha and Vaiśālī.

The second is the *Sutta Piṭaka*, The Basket of Discourses, attributed to Buddha, divided into five sections (*nikāya*): (1) *Dīgha Nikāya*, a series of 34 long lectures on points of doctrine (reward of asceticism, attitude to caste, points of contact and contrast with Brahmanism), including the *Mahāparinibbānasuttanta* (The Great Chapter of Complete Nirvāna), an account of the last days of Buddha; (2) *Majjhima Nikāya*, a series of 152 medium-length sermons and dialogues on points of Buddhist religion; (3) *Saṃyutta Nikāya*, a series of more than 2,700 short statements on related topics, including the *Dhammacakkapavattanavagga*, the so-called Sermon of Benares on setting in motion the wheel of the law; (4) *A·aguttara Nikāya*, a progressive series of 11 sections arranged according to the number of topics expounded in each; (5) *Khuddaka Nikāya*, ''minor series'' of 15 works including the exquisite and ancient stanzas of the *Dhammapada* (Way of the Law), the *Theragāthā*, and *Therīgāthā*, psalms for choir recitation, and the *Jātaka* containing 547 stories of former lives of Buddha, along with the *Nidānakathā*, the oldest connected biography of Buddha in three parts.

The third is the *Abhidhamma Piṭaka*, The Basket of Supplementary Doctrines, treating in systematic fashion doctrinal questions evidently raised at a later epoch in debates among rival schools and comprising seven works: *Puggalapaññatti; Dhātukathāpakarana; Dhammasaṃgani; Vibhaṇga; Patthānapakaraṇa; Yamaka;* and *Kathāvatthu.*

See Also: BUDDHISM.

Bibliography: B. C. LAW, *A History of Pāli Literature*, 2 v. (London 1933). M. WINTERNITZ, *A History of Indian Literature*, tr. S. KATKAR (London 1927–34) v. 2. G. BORSANI, *Prospetti e Indice del Tipiṭaka* (Milan 1942). A. S. ROSSO, ''Buddhism in India, Ceylon and Burma,'' *Worldmission* 3 (1952) 62–82. A. BAREAU, *Les Premiers conciles bouddhiques* (Paris 1956). W. RAHULA, *The History of Buddhism in Ceylon: The Anuradhapura Period, 3d Century, B.C.–l0th Century A.D.* (Colombo, Ceylon 1956). W. T. DE BARY et al., comps., *Sources of Indian Tradition* (*Records of Civilization* 56; New York 1958). G. F. ALLEN, ed. and tr., *The Buddha's Philosophy: Selections from the Pāli Canon and an Introductory Essay* (New York 1959). A. B. GOVINDA, *The Psychological Attitude of Early Buddhist Philosophy and Its Systematic Representation according to Abhidhamma Tradition* (London 1961). C. H. PHILIPS, ed., *Historians of India, Pakistan and Ceylon* (New York 1961).

[A. S. ROSSO]

PALIMPSEST

A technical term of paleography, used to designate a MS of leather or parchment that was used more than once. Since such materials were scarce and expensive, the writing was often erased from an old codex by washing and/or scraping, so that the surface could be used again. The term refers only to leather or parchment MSS, since papyrus and paper would not permit such rough treatment. If the MS was erased twice, it was called a double palimpsest. The original writing was seldom completely destroyed and can frequently be read, at least in part. As a result, some palimpsests have great value for the scholar. Chemical agents such as ammonium hydrosulfide once proved useful in making the text readable, but today ultraviolet lamps and especially infrared photography aid in deciphering a text. The most famous palimpsests of the Bible are the Codex Ephraemi Rescriptus (C), Codex Nitriensis (R), and Codex Syrus-Sinaiticus.

[T. H. WEBER]

PALLADINO, LAWRENCE BENEDICT

Missionary; b. Tiglieto, Italy, Aug. 15, 1837; d. Missoula, Montana, Aug. 19, 1927. Lawrence was the youngest boy of Giulio and Maddalena (Rizzi) Palladino's seven children. After attending Genoa's minor seminary, he became a Jesuit novice at Querciuoli in the Duchy of Modena, Italy, Nov. 18, 1855. The anti-clericalism of Italian nationalists explains his training in Austria and France before he was ordained on May 30, 1863, at Nice, France. Early in 1864 he went to California, where he studied and taught at St. Ignatius College, San Francisco, until 1867. He then began missionary service in the Pacific Northwest. During the next 60 years he worked among settlers and Indians in Washington, Idaho, and Montana. He is usually associated with Montana where he spent 44 years (at St. Ignatius Mission, at Helena, and at Missoula). He purchased property in Helena that was later transferred to John B. Brondel, first Bishop of Helena, when the see was established in 1884. Palladino served at different times as the new bishop's secretary, counselor, director of education, and vicar-general. He spent many years, also, as pastor of St. Francis Xavier's Church, Missoula. His civic activities during Montana's formative years and his role as regional historian gave his works lasting value. Because of the disappearance of many of the materials he used, his *Indian and White in the Northwest: A History of Catholicity in Montana* (1894) became a primary source for Montana history.

Bibliography: W. N. BISCHOFF, *The Jesuits in Old Oregon* (Caldwell, Idaho 1945). W. P. SCHOENBERG, *Jesuits in Montana, 1840–1960* (Portland, Ore. 1960).

[W. N. BISCHOFF]

PALLADIUS, ST.

Bishop of Ireland; d. probably in Brittany, after 432. According to the *Chronicon* of PROSPER OF AQUITAINE, Pope CELESTINE I sent Palladius, a Roman deacon "ad Scottos in Christum credentes" to the Christians of Ireland, where he labored to combat PELAGIANISM and reorganize the Church. His history is complicated by the legends that accompany the diverse lives of St. PATRICK. Palladius seems to have settled near a Christian center (the port of Inber De, south of Dublin?) and he had to battle against Pelagianism. The details concerning his departure from Ireland in 432 and the possible lack of success that caused it, as well as his death in Britain, are not certain. Upon learning of the death of Palladius, Patrick, then in Gaul, is supposed to have received permission from Germain of Auxerre to continue the work of Palladius in Ireland. The *Chronicon* of Prosper of Aquitaine alleges that Palladius was still in Ireland in 433 and 434, but this interpretation is not widely held.

Feast: July 7.

Bibliography: *Acta Sanctorum* July 2:286–290. L. GOUGAUD, *Christianity in Celtic Lands,* tr. M. JOYNT (London 1932). J. L. G. MEISSNER, *Proceedings of the Royal Irish Academy* 40 (1931–32) 371. P. GROSJEAN, *Analecta Bollandiana* 63 (1945) 73–86, 112–119. J. CARNEY, *The Problem of St. Patrick* (Dublin 1961).

[P. ROCHE]

Palimpsest folio from "Codex Ephraemi Rescriptus (Cod. Gr. 9, fol. 60v).

PALLADIUS OF HELENOPOLIS

Fourth-century monk, bishop, and writer; b. Galatia, 363 or 364; d. probably Aspuna, before 431. At 23, a pupil of EVAGRIUS PONTICUS, he embraced the monastic life on the Mount of Olives in Jerusalem. Later he became acquainted with the Egyptian ascetics, spent some time in Alexandria, and retired to the Nitrian Desert about 390. He remained there for nine years, became ill, and at the advice of an Alexandrian physician returned to Palestine (399). The next year he journeyed to Bithynia and was consecrated bishop of Helenopolis by (St.) JOHN CHRYSOSTOM.

When sent to Ephesus to investigate charges brought against Bp. Antoninus by Eusebius of Valentinopolis, Palladius appeared with John Chrysostom at the Synod of the OAK near Chalcedon in 403. The Synod banished John, and Palladius went to Rome to lay the case before Pope INNOCENT I (405). The Western Emperor HONORIUS sent him to Constantinople with a decision in favor of John, but the Eastern Emperor Arcadius exiled him to Egypt, where, at Syene (406–408), he wrote his *Dialogus de vita Sancti Joannis Chrysostomi,* a principal source for the life of John Chrysostom.

Palladius spent four years in the Thebaid of Egypt at Antinoë and returned to his diocese only after opposition to John Chrysostom ceased in 412. In Galatia he lived with a priest named Philoramus, and in 417 he was transferred to the Diocese of Aspuna, where he wrote the *Lausiac History* (419–420). The *Epistola de Indicis gentibus et de Bragmannibus* attributed to Palladius suggests a trip to India; but is actually a report he seems to have received from a Theban advocate. The Palladian authorship is suggested by similarities in style and diction with his other works.

The writings of Palladius have a moral purpose. His *Dialogus* seeks to edify by the example of a saintly bishop and shows how John Chrysostom's enemies fell victims to greed and pride in planning his downfall. In the *Historia Lausiaca* he portrays the life of good monks but does not develop a theory of ascetical theology. He used the example of those who had fallen from grace to show how temptations to pride and vainglory must be expelled. The *Epistola* describes the gymnosophists of India as dedicated to an ascetical ideal. This work was read and copied frequently during the Middle Ages.

The Palladian authorship of these works has been contested. In antiquity, however, there was no doubt that the interlocutors in the *Dialogus* are Palladius and Bishop

John. The exordium is strongly reminiscent of the opening passage in Plato's *Republic*.

The *Lausiac History* of Palladius is a work of the highest importance for the history of early monasticism. In the 19th century his veracity was questioned; but today the work is accepted as reliable in the sections where Palladius had spoken to the people involved or had seen the events he describes. His account falters when he depends upon hearsay.

The *Epistola de Indicis* was known in Europe during the Middle Ages in a garbled Latin translation as the *Commonitorium Palladii* supposedly translated by St. Ambrose. Actually, only the first part of the work belongs to Palladius; and thus far no satisfactory proof has been offered against his authorship.

Bibliography: PALLADIUS OF HELENOPOLIS, *Dialogus de vita S. Joannis Chrysostomi,* ed. P. R. COLEMAN-NORTON (Cambridge, Eng. 1928), Eng. tr. H. MOORE (London 1921); *The Lausiac History,* ed. C. BUTLER, 2 v. (Cambridge, Eng. 1898–1904); ed. and tr. R. T. MEYER (*Ancient Christian Writers*; 1965). H. RAHNER, *Lexicon für Theologie und Kirche,* ed. J. HOFER and K. RAHNER (Freiburg 1957–65) 8:6. H. LECLERCQ, *Dictionnaire d'archéologie chrétienne et de liturgie,* ed. F. CABROL, H. LECLERCQ, and H. I. MARROU (Paris 1907–53) 13.1:912–930. A. KURFESS, *Paulys Realenzyklopädie der klassischen Altertumswissenschaft,* ed. G. WISSOWA et al. (Stuttgart 1893)18.3 (1949) 203–207. J. QUASTEN, *Patrology* (Westminster MD 1950) 3:176–180. J. D. M. DERRETT, ''The History of *Palladius on the Races of India and the Brahmans,*'' *Classica et Mediaevalia* 21 (1960) 64–99. E. SCHWARTZ, ''Palladiana,'' *Zeitschrift für die neutestamentliche Wissenschaft und die Kunde der älteren Kirche* 36 (1937) 161–204. F. X. MURPHY, *Rufinus of Aquileia* (Washington 1945) 175–179. R. DRAQUET, *Revue d'histoire ecclésiastique* 41 (1946) 321–364; 42 (1947) 5–49.

[R. T. MEYER]

PALLAVICINO, PIETRO SFORZA

Cardinal, historian, and theologian; b. Rome, Nov. 28, 1607; d. Rome, June 5, 1667. Although he was a descendant of the Parma line of the noble Pallavicini family, he renounced his rights as first-born to become a cleric. He studied letters, philosophy, and theology at the Roman College, and law at the Sapienza. He became a doctor of theology (1628), and on June 21, 1637, he entered the Society of Jesus, becoming a professor of philosophy and then of theology at the Roman College. In the spring of 1652 he took up his greatest work, the history of the Council of Trent. His friend Alexander VII proclaimed him a cardinal on Nov. 10, 1659. In his earlier years he was strongly inclined toward purely literary pursuits, publishing works on literary style and a tragedy, *Ermenegildo martire*. In his later theological writings, *Del bene* (4 v. Rome 1644), *Assertiones theologicae* (Rome 1649–52), and *Disputationes in primam secundae D.*

Thomas (Rome 1653), he was a faithful disciple of Cardinal Juan de Lugo and not an original thinker. Pallavicino proved his loyalty to his order by his *Vindicationes Societatis Jesus* (Rome 1649) and his last published work *Arte della perfezione cristiana* (Rome 1665). His greatest fame rests on his historical works. His *Vita di Alessandro VII,* which remained in manuscript till 1839, is a careful work of high value. Since the appearance of the antipapal *Historia del Concilio Tridentino* by Paolo SARPI in 1619 there had been need for a refutation based on a thorough study of available documents. Terenzio Alciati, SJ, who had been gathering materials for such a work for 25 years, died in 1651. Pallavicino was given the task and the work appeared during 1656 and 1657 and in further improved editions. For centuries it was a reliable source, though heavy with polemical tone.

Bibliography: I. AFFÒ, *Memorie della vita e degli studi del Cardinale Sforza Pallavicino* (Faenza 1792). *Bibliothèque de la Compagnie de Jésus* 6: 120–143. J. DUHR, *Dictionnaire de théologie catholique* 11.2:1831–34. L. KOCH, *Jesuiten-Lexikon* 1362–63. H. JEDIN, *Der Quellenapparat der Konzilsgeschichte Pallavicinos* (Rome 1940). H. JEDIN, *History of the Council of Trent,* tr. E. GRAF, v. 1–2 (St. Louis 1957–60). I. MACCHIA, *Relazioni fra il padre gesuita Sforza Pallavicino e Fabio Chigi* (Turin 1907).

[A. C. WAND]

PALLEN, CONDÉ BENOIST

Editor; b. St. Louis, Mo., Dec. 5, 1858; d. New York City, May 26, 1929. His parents were Montrose A., a physician and teacher of medicine, and Anne (Benoist) Pallen, daughter of a St. Louis banker and a descendant of the Chevalier Benoist who served with Montcalm in the French and Indian War. After graduating from Georgetown University, Washington, D.C., Pallen received a doctorate (1885) from St. Louis University and taught there briefly before continuing his studies in Rome. After his return to St. Louis he was editor of *Church Progress* (1887–97) and served as Catholic revisory editor for two general encyclopedias. He joined a small group of scholars to project the first comprehensive Catholic encyclopedia in the English language, serving as an organizer of the board of editors (1904–05) and as managing editor (1905–13); *The Catholic Encyclopedia* (16 v., 1907–14; supplement, 1922) became the authoritative international work of reference on the constitution, discipline, and history of the Catholic Church. As president of Encyclopedia Press, Inc. (1913–20), he was later associated with other publishing ventures, including the *New Catholic Dictionary* (1929).

Pallen was an advocate of conservative economic and social views and served as chairman of the department of subversive movements of the National Civic

Pope John Paul II being vested with Pallium. (Bettmann/CORBIS)

Federation. Leo XIII honored him with the medal *pro ec-clesia et pontifice* and Pius XI named him a Knight of St. Gregory. His published works include numerous articles and *The Philosophy of Literature* (1897), *New Rubaiyat* (1898), *Epochs of Literature* (1898), *The Feast of Thalar-chus* (1901), *Death of Sir Launcelot and Other Poems* (1902), *The Meaning of the Idylls of the King* (1904), *Collected Poems* (1915), *Education of Boys* (1916), *The Story of Literature* (1917), *Crucible Island* (1919), *As Man to Man*: *The Adventures of a Commuter* (1927), *Ghost House* (1928), and *The King's Coil* (1928).

[F. X. GERRITY]

PALLIUM

The pallium is a circular band about two inches wide, made of white wool, and worn over the chasuble about the neck, breast, and shoulders. It has two pendants, one hanging down in front, the other in back. It is set with six black crosses of silk, one each on the breast and back, one on each shoulder, and one on each of the pendants.

In the Eastern Churches the pallium is a longer and wider cloth, marked by four red crosses and given by the Oriental patriarchs to their metropolitans and other distin-guished bishops.

The pallium is made (at least partially) from the wool of two lambs that are blessed each year at the Basilica of St. John Lateran on Jan. 21, the feast of St. Agnes. The new pallia is blessed by the pope in the crypt of St. Peter at vespers on June 28, the vigil of the feast of SS. Peter and Paul. The blessed pallia are kept overnight at the crypt and conferred on the newly appointed metropoli-tans on the feast.

Origin and Symbolism. The pallium began to be worn in the 4th century by bishops of the Eastern Church-es and by the Bishop of Rome to emphasize the episcopal dignity and pastoral office. One cannot say definitely whence it derived. In the 6th century, the pallium was conferred by the pope on bishops of the Latin Church, es-pecially metropolitans, until it gradually became the sym-bol of the metropolitan office. In the 9th century, John VIII commanded all metropolitans to petition the pope for the pallium within three months of their appointment or confirmation. Since then the pallium has been the sym-bol of the jurisdiction conferred upon metropolitans by the Roman pontiff and it signifies a certain participation in the pope's supreme pastoral office. It also represents their close union with the See of Rome. When worn by the pope, the pallium signifies the fullness of pontifical power.

Petition and Use in the Latin Church. In the Latin Church, a metropolitan is obliged, either in person or by proxy, to ask the Roman pontiff (*instanter, instantius, instantissime*) for the pallium within three months of his consecration or, if already consecrated, of his canonical promotion in the consistory [*Codex iuris canonici* c.437, §1]. By a decree dated May 11, 1978, Pope Paul VI ordered that the pallium was to be conferred only on metropolitans and on the Latin Patriarch of Jerusalem (see AAS 70 [1978] 442).

The pope may use the pallium at any time. A metropolitan in the Latin Church may use the pallium in every church of his province according to the norm of liturgical laws, but not outside his province even with the consent of the local ordinary [*Codex iuris canonici* c.437, §2]. The reason for this restriction arises from the fact that since the pallium is a symbol of metropolitan authority, it does not make sense for a metropolitan to wear the pallium in places where he is unable to exercise that authority. There are two exceptions to this general rule: the Latin Patriarch of Jerusalem and the Patriarch of Lisbon are endowed with the privilege of wearing their pallia even outside their provinces (see *Communicationes* 14 [1982] 190). If a metropolitan is transferred to another metropolitan see, he must obtain another pallium [*Codex iuris canonici* c.437, §3].

Bibliography: L. TROMBETTA, *De pallio archiepiscopali: Elucubratio canonico–liturgico–historica* (Sorrento 1923). R. LESAGE, *Vestments and Church Furniture,* tr. F. MURPHY (New York 1960) 139–142. F. J. WEBER, ''The Sacred Pallium and Its History,'' *Liturgical Arts* 30 (1962) 91, 106. J.C. NOONAN, JR., *The Church Visible: The Ceremonial Life and Protocol of the Roman Catholic Church* (New York 1996) 359–363.

[J. A. ABBO/EDS.]

PALLOTA, MARIA ASSUNTA, BL.

Missionary; b. Force, in the Marches of Ancona, Italy, Aug. 20, 1878; d. Tong-Eul-Koo, China, April 7, 1905. From her early years Pallota worked to help support her poor family. She acquired only enough formal schooling to read and write. In 1898 in Rome, she joined the Franciscan Missionaries of Mary (*see* FRANCISCAN SISTERS). During the next few years she dwelt in the congregation's convents in Rome, Grottaferrata, and Florence, working about the house and in the garden and infirmary, and teaching catechism. She sailed for China (1904), and there in the orphanage at Tong-Eul-Koo, she continued her humble tasks. While caring for the plague-

stricken during a typhus epidemic she fell victim to the disease. Humility, kindness; obedience, and prayerfulness distinguished her life. Her remains, which were incorrupt when exhumed in 1913, are in China. She was beatified Nov. 7, 1954.

Feast: April 7.

Bibliography: E. FEDERICI, *Bienheureuse Maria Assunta* (Rome 1954). *Acta Sanctae Sedis* 47 (1955) 28–33. J. L. BAUDOT and L. CHAUSSIN, *Vies des saints et des bienheureux selon l'ordre du calendrier avec l'historique des fêtes,* ed. THE BENEDICTINES OF PARIS (Paris 1935–56) 13:205–208.

[M. F. S. CONDON]

PALLOTTI, VINCENT, ST.

Religious founder; b. Rome, April 21, 1795; d. there, Jan. 22, 1850. He was the son of a prosperous grocer. From his early years he developed a special devotion to the Blessed Virgin and an intense compassion for the poor. After studying in Rome at the Roman College and at the Sapienza, he was ordained (1818). He taught theology at the Sapienza for ten years before he devoted himself completely to spiritual guidance and preaching. In 1827 he became spiritual director at the Roman College and often acted as confessor at various national colleges for future priests. He was intimately acquainted with St. Gaspare del BUFALO and Nicholas WISEMAN. As rector of the church of Santo Spirito dei Neapolitani, he suffered for more than a decade from slanders by the other priests there, who were jealous of his promotion and resentful of his zeal. Vincent interested himself also in projects to revive artisan guilds and to establish schools for young workers and farm boys. During the cholera epidemic of 1837 he organized relief for the plague-stricken. His spiritual and charitable ministrations so impressed the Romans that they referred to him as a second St. Philip NERI. In 1835 he founded the PALLOTTINES, and later, the Sisters of the Catholic Apostolate, from whom developed the PALLOTTINE MISSIONARY SISTERS. Vincent shared Rome's hopes for the conversion of England arising out of the OXFORD Movement and sent priests to assist Frederick William FABER. His inspiration was instrumental in the founding of the MILL HILL MISSIONARIES and of several mission colleges. His fame for sanctity was increased by his reputation as a thaumaturge and prophet. Pius XI called him a forerunner of CATHOLIC ACTION. His body lies incorrupt in the church of San Salvatore in Onda, Rome. Vincent Pallotti was beatified on Jan. 22, 1950, by Pope Pius XII, and he was canonized on Jan. 20, 1963, by Pope John XXIII.

Feast: Jan. 22

Bibliography: E. WEBER, *Vincent Pallotti: Apostle and Mystic,* tr. from the Ger. (New York 1964). J. FRANK, *Vincenz Pallotti,*

2 v. (Friedberg 1952–63). F. BONIFAZI, *Soul of a Saint* (Staten Island NY 1963); *Yearning of a Soul* (Boston 1979).

[H. E. SCHAAK]

PALLOTTINE MISSIONARY SISTERS

(SAC, Official Catholic Directory# 3150); a congregation founded in Rome, Italy, in 1843, by St. Vincent PALLOTTI, to care for children, especially orphans. When, in 1890, the Pallottine Fathers began a mission in the German colony in the Cameroons, Africa, the help of sisters also was required. Since the Italian sisters were not interested in mission work, it was decided to invite candidates from Germany to enter the novitiate in Rome. Those who answered this call were trained there and sent to Africa. When it became evident that the Pallottine Missionary Sisters should have their own motherhouse in Germany, a plan that was realized in 1895, a new branch of the Pallottine family came into existence. From Limburg, Germany, these sisters spread to England, Switzerland, Central America, Poland, South Africa, and in 1912 to the U.S. In the U.S., the sisters engage in education, catechetics, healthcare, daycare, retreats, counseling, parish ministries, pastoral and social outreach. When papal approval was granted to the congregation in 1964, its official title was established as Missionary Sisters of the Catholic Apostolate. The generalate is in Rome. The U.S. provincialate is in Florissant, Mo.

[M. B. KURTH/EDS.]

PALLOTTINE SISTERS OF THE CATHOLIC APOSTOLATE

(CSAC, Official Catholic Directory # 3140); a pontifical institute founded in 1843 by St. Vincent PALLOTTI in Rome, Italy, to care for children orphaned by the cholera plague. Benedetta Gabrielli was the first sister to receive the habit at the Pia Casa di Carità, Rome. The first general chapter, held in 1886, elected Mother Raphael Castellani as superior general. Mother Raphael sent five sisters to the U.S. in 1889 to work among the Italian immigrants. In 1911 the congregation was approved by the Holy See, and in 1933 missions were begun in South America, in Brazil and Argentina. The charism of the order prompts them to engage in any work that corresponds to the needs of the places where they serve; the sisters are engaged in teaching, healthcare, pastoral ministries and social outreach. The generalate is in Rome. The U.S. provincialate is in Harriman, N.Y.

[M. E. ZIEGLER/EDS.]

PALLOTTINES

The Society of the Catholic Apostolate (SAC, Official Catholic Directory #0990), popularly known as Pallottine Fathers, was founded by St. Vincent PALLOTTI in 1835 at Rome, Italy. Under his direction, a group of clerics and lay people formed the Pious Union of the Catholic Apostolate, which received formal approbation in 1835. Its objective was to revive faith and charity in all Catholics and to diffuse these virtues throughout the entire world by prayers, labors, or other contributions.

As the membership increased and activities expanded, Pallotti saw the need for a group of priests who would devote their energies entirely to the work. Those who with him assumed this task, soon evolved into a society entitled Congregation of the Catholic Apostolate; it was to function as a connecting bond between the secular and religious priests, both of whom Pallotti desired to see labor side by side in all apostolic activities. Thus the society assumed a secular and a religious character: the secular was expressed by the absence of vows; the religious, by the observance of common life and promises. At first Pallotti did not favor constitutions or rules other than the Gospels, but he was constrained by experience to introduce them.

Despite papal approval, Pallotti's work was seriously threatened. The Lyons Society for the Propagation of the Faith claimed that Pallotti's work was merely duplicating its own program on behalf of foreign missions and had his society suppressed in 1838. When Pallotti clarified the situation for Gregory XVI, the decree of suppression was revoked. The words Catholic Apostolate raised objection from some who believed that the apostolate was reserved to the hierarchy. Four years after Pallotti's death the controversy was settled by a decree (1854) that changed the name to Pious Society of Missions. The original title was restored in 1947, when the concept of the universal apostolate was better understood.

Because of the Roman Revolution, Pallotti's death in 1850, and the change in title that obscured its nature, the society's development was slow until 1880. However, by the turn of the century there were 30 houses in eight countries. In 1890 the Pallottines accepted a request to evangelize the African Cameroons, where by 1914 they had baptized 25,000 converts and were instructing 40,000 catechumens. By 1909 the society had over 500 members and was divided into four provinces. After World War I, it continued to flourish, and created in Germany the Schoenstatt movement, a Marian apostolic movement that implements Pallotti's program.

The first Pallottines arrived in the U.S. to minister to New York's Italians; this was the beginning of the Immaculate Conception Province of the eastern states. The foundations for a midwestern province, the Mother of God Province, were laid when, in 1921, a house was established in Milwaukee, Wis. Two other provinces, the Irish and the Italian, have established their foundations in the U.S. In the U.S., the Pallottines are engaged in parish administration, chaplaincies, retreats, missions, hospitals, immigrant care, schools, and social outreach. The generalate is in Rome.

Bibliography: J. GAYNOR, *Life of St. Vincent Pallotti* (Rome 1963). E. WEBER, *Vincent Pallotti: Apostle and Mystic* (New York 1964).

[H. E. SCHAAK/EDS.]

PALLU, FRANÇOIS

Vicar apostolic in southwest China and a founder of the Paris Foreign Mission Society; b. Tours, France, Aug. 30, 1626; d. Moyang, China, Oct. 29, 1684. His father was a lawyer and mayor. During his youth, Pallu was made a canon of St. Martin's. In Paris, he met Father De Rhodes, SJ, who was coming from Tongking to obtain from Rome the appointment of native bishops in the Far East. Pallu and his friends agreed to support De Rhodes and went to Rome, aided by the Assembly of the Clergy and the Company of the Blessed Sacrament. In 1658 Pallu was appointed titular bishop of Heliopolis, and vicar apostolic of Tongking, Laos, and southwest China. He wanted helpers and money, and this led him to start a society of priests without vows who would go to the missions. With the help of Pierre LAMBERT DE LA MOTTE, his first fellow-worker, he wrote instructions for the benefit of missioners. Throughout his life he traveled from the East to Rome to further mission work and to obtain the approval and help of the Holy See. He had to struggle against the governments of Spain and Portugal, and a number of religious who were opposed to the setting up of native churches. He is recognized as the main founder of the PARIS FOREIGN MISSION SOCIETY. Pallu was a man of great gifts, kindly, and with sound judgment and strong willpower. He gave himself zealously to spread the Church in the Far East.

Bibliography: F. PALLU, *Lettres,* ed. A. LAUNAY, 2 v. (Angoulême 1905). A. LAUNAY, *Histoire générale de la Société des Missions Étrangères,* 3 v. (Paris 1894). L. BAUDIMENT, *François Pallu* (Paris 1934). J. GUENNOU, *Les Missions Étrangères* (Paris 1963). J. GLAZIK, *Lexikon für Theologie und Kirche,* ed. J. HOFER and K. RAHNER (Freiburg 1957–65) 8:11.

[H. PROUVOST]

PALM SUNDAY

The solemnity of "Palm Sunday" marks the beginning of Holy Week in the Roman liturgical calendar. The feast appears as early as the Gelasian and Gregorian Sacramentaries. The procession of the Palms gives this Sunday its distinctive character.

The annual procession of the palms originated in Jerusalem as a commemoration of the entry of Christ into the Holy City to consummate the great work of the Redemption. According to Egeria's 4th century account of the Holy Week celebrations in Jerusalem, the people of Jerusalem were led to reenact this event at the spot where it had actually happened. The faithful of Jerusalem gathered around their bishop on the Mount of Olives. There they sang hymns and listened to readings from the Old Testament and to the Gospel account of our Savior's entry. Then at five o'clock they set out carrying olive or palm branches in their hands, accompanying the bishop, who was seated on a mule, to the Church of the Resurrection. During this procession they sang psalms and hymns with the constant refrain: "Blessed is He who comes in the Name of the Lord." Upon arriving at the church they sang Vespers.

From Jerusalem this custom made its way to the churches of the Gallican rite in the West. In turn, the entire rite came to Rome from the Gallican lands through the Romano-Germanic Pontifical of the 10th century.

By the Middle Ages the rite of the palms had acquired a distinctly dramatic form. The procession would go from one church to another, usually one outside the city walls. The presence of Christ was symbolized in various ways: in some parts of France by the gospel book, in northern Italy by a large cross decorated with green foliage, in Germany by an image of Christ borne on the back of a wooden donkey, in England and Normandy by the Blessed Sacrament itself. Upon returning to the gate of the city or to the door of the principal church, the faithful would cast their garments and their palm or olive branches before the symbol of Christ and repeat the same acclamations the Jews had used to greet the coming of the Messiah King. There too the hymn *Gloria Laus, et honor* (All glory, laud and honor) was sung, a choir within the gates alternating with those outside. Then one of the clerics knocked at the door and all entered singing the antiphon *Ingrediente Domino in Sanctam Civitatem.*

In the beginning there was no blessing provided for the palms. The earliest blessing is found in the *Liber Ordinum* of the Mozarabic Rite (6th century). By the end of the Middle Ages this had become a very elaborate ceremonial. Such emphasis was laid upon the blessing and upon the palm itself as a sacramental that the real purpose

Palm Sunday Procession. (©Jeremy Horner/CORBIS)

of the whole ceremony was obscured. In time the procession became secondary, and often was not observed at all. That is why Pius XII's Holy Week Ordinal (promulgated in 1955) simplified the blessing and restored the procession of the palms. Thus the triumphal procession in honor of Christ the King once more occupies the central place that belongs to it. Like all the Holy Week rites, it is not a mere commemoration, but a mysterium in which not only the historical event is recalled to mind but Christ's own victory is reenacted in the Church. We celebrate this event only by living it. Hence all are invited to take part in it by carrying palms and singing the acclamations to the King. Because of the festive nature of the procession the priest and the sacred ministers wear red—the royal color, the color of victory—instead of the penitential purple; and the cross, the standard of victory, is carried unveiled.

Bibliography: W. J. O'SHEA, *The Meaning of Holy Week* (Collegeville, Minn. 1958). T. J. TALLEY, *Origins of the Liturgical Year*, 2nd emended edition (Collegeville 1991). T. J. TALLEY, "The Entry into Jerusalem in Liturgical Tradition," in *With Ever Joyful Hearts: Essays on Liturgy and Music: Honoring Marion J. Hatchett*, ed. J. N. ALEXANDER (New York 1999) 211–226. J. M. PIERCE, "Holy Week and Easter in the Middle Ages," in *Passover and Easter: Origin and History to Modern Times*, eds. P. F. BRADSHAW and L. A. HOFFMAN (Notre Dame, Ind 1999) 161–185.

[W. J. O'SHEA/EDS.]

PALMENTIERI, LUDOVICO DA CASORIA, BL.

Baptized Arcángelo; Franciscan priest; founder of the Brothers of Charity (Grey Franciscan Friars of Charity or *Frati Bigi*) and Sisters of St. Elizabeth (*Suore Bigie*); b. Mar. 11, 1814, Casoria (near Naples), Campania, Italy; d. Mar. 30, 1885, Pausilippo near Naples, Italy.

Arcángelo was a cabinetmaker in his youth. Attracted by the Franciscans at the nearby friary in Naples, Arcángelo entered the order at Avellino (June 17, 1832) and took the name Ludovico (Louis). Shortly after the completion of the year's novitiate, he was appointed to study and teach philosophy, chemistry, and mathematics in San Pietro Convent, Naples. His affinity for science led him later to found a meteorological observatory, an academy of religion and science, and five magazines. Other literary accomplishments included an Italian translation of the works of Saint BONAVENTURE and a pocket edition of the Bible.

Following the advice of his superiors, he instituted a branch of the Third Order at San Pietro from which he formed (1859) a religious institute, commonly known as the *Frati Bigi* because of their grayish-colored habits. In 1862, Ludovico instituted a congregation of religious women, known as the *Suore Bigie*, whom he placed under the protection of Saint ELIZABETH OF HUNGARY. These congregations made his many charitable works possible.

Ludovico was ordained to the priesthood on June 4, 1837. In 1847, during a mystical experience in prayer, he discerned a vocation to serve the poor actively. He opened a pharmacy in the friary and, later, infirmaries for the elderly and sick friars of the province. Additionally, he founded care centers for children; institutes for the blind, and deaf and dumb; hospices for travelers; agricultural colonies; and savings and loan societies for the poor. About 1852, he opened the first of two schools for the children of emancipated African slaves with the intention that they would return home to evangelize Africa. He later entrusted the continuance of this work to Anna Maria Fiorelli Lapini and her Stigmatine Sisters.

Ten years before his death, he was attacked with a serious and painful illness, from which he never completely recovered. He died in the Marine Hospital he had established for elderly sailors. The numerous charitable institutions in Naples, Rome, Assisi, and Florence that owe their origin to Ludovico of Casoria, as well as his fame for sanctity even during his lifetime, account for the veneration in which he was held by all classes. His mortal remains were entrusted to his spiritual daughters, the *Suore Bigie*, in 1887. The cause for Ludovico's beatification was introduced in Rome in 1907. He was declared venerable on Feb. 13, 1964, and beatified by John Paul II on April 18, 1993.

Feast: March 30.

Bibliography: *Epistolario*, ed. G. D'ANDREA (Naples 1989). A. CAPECELATRO, *La vita del p. Lodovico da Casoria* (Naples 1887).

[K. I. RABENSTEIN]

PALMER, WILLIAM

Theologian and archaeologist; b. Mixbury, Oxfordshire, England, 1811; d. Rome, 1879. Palmer was educated at Rugby School and Oxford University, and was ordained deacon in the Church of England in 1832. From 1834 to 1843 he was tutor at Durham University and then classical examiner and tutor at Oxford, where he had been elected a fellow of his college, Magdalen. He was a high churchman, and in 1840 and again in 1842 went to Russia to learn about the Orthodox Church there and investigate the possibility of intercommunion between it and the Anglicans. This led to his best-known written work, *Notes on a Visit to the Russian Church,* edited by Cardinal Newman and published in 1882. Palmer was disturbed by certain aspects of the Church of England and for a time seriously considered joining the Orthodox, but in 1855 he was received into the Catholic Church and spent the rest of his life in Rome studying archaeology. Among his other published writings on ecclesiastical and archaeological topics were a *Harmony of Anglican Doctrine with the Doctrine of the Eastern Church* (1846) and an *Introduction to Early Christian Symbolism* (1859). In his later years he wrote, in Latin, a commentary on the book of Daniel (1874) and translated from the Russian *The Patriarch Nicon and the Tsar,* 6 v. (1871–76). His learning was highly respected by Newman, Perrone, and Dölinger.

He must be distinguished from his contemporary, another William Palmer (1803–85), an Anglican theologian of repute who in 1846 published a reply to Newman's *Essay on the Development of Christian Doctrine.*

[D. ATTWATER]

PALMIERI, AURELIO

Italian Orientalist; b. Savona, May 4, 1870; d. Rome, Oct. 18, 1926. After joining the AUGUSTINIANS (1885) he transferred to the ASSUMPTIONISTS (1890) and then returned to the Augustinians (1902). He resided at the Italian Augustinian Holy Rosary parish in Lawrence, Massachusettes, from 1913 to 1916. During the First World War his knowledge of European languages led to work supported by the American government. Because of his private conduct and erroneous ideas, he fell into difficulties with ecclesiastical authorities and was laicized. During 20 years devoted to Oriental, especially Byzantine, studies, he published 15 scholarly books, notably *Die Polemik des Islam* (Salzburg 1902), *La Chiesa Russa* (Florence 1908), *Dositeo patriarcha greco di Gerusalemme, 1647–1707* (Florence 1909), and *Theologia dogmatica orthodoxa* (2 v. Florence 1911–13). Besides editing *Bessarione,* the Italian journal devoted to Byzantine studies, he wrote 130 articles for it between 1896 and 1923. Between 1917 and 1923 he also wrote six articles on the relationship between Italian immigrants and religion in the United States. In some of these articles he elaborated on the question of the "Italian problem" in the Catholic Church in America. Together with his writings for other Italian and foreign periodicals and for the *Dictionnaire de théologie catholique,* the total of his articles exceeded 300. During his last years he headed the Institute for Eastern Europe.

Bibliography: *Studi Bizantini* 1 (1925): 261–269, lists all Palmieri's writings. E. LO GATTO, *"Bibliografia essenziale degli* scritti di A. P.," *L'Europe orientale* 6 (1926): 519–532. D. A. PERINI, *Bibliographia Augustiniana*, v. 3 (Florence 1935) 45–48. E. C. STABILI, "Palmeiro, Aurelio (1870 1925)," in *The Italian American Experience: An Encyclopedia*, ed. S. J. LA GUMINA, et al. (New York 2000).

[G. A. MALONEY]

PALMIERI, DOMENICO

Jesuit philosopher, theologian; b. Piacenza, Italy, July 4, 1829; d. Rome, May 29, 1909. He was ordained and entered the Society of Jesus in 1852. After teaching philosophy, theology, and Scripture at the seminary of Fermo and the college at Spoleto, he became professor of philosophy (1861–67) and of dogma (1867–78) at the Gregorian University. He espoused a kind of dynamism, claiming that HYLOMORPHISM was incompatible with the findings of natural science. His position in Rome became precarious during the Thomistic revival under Leo XIII. After transfer to Maastricht in Holland in 1878, he taught exegesis there until 1894. In that year he returned to Rome as theologian to the Sacred Penitentiary and consultor to the Holy Office and was later on the Commission for the Code of Canon Law. He was among the first to attack the Modernist error of LOISY. The publication of his works extends from 1874 to 1910. Noteworthy are his *Institutiones Philosophiae,* his reedition of Gury's and Ballerini's moral works, and his commentary on Dante's *Divina Comedia.*

[J. FLYNN]

PALMS, LITURGICAL USE OF

A liturgical palm is a branch of the palm tree, in Greek φοίνιξ, in Latin, *dactylifera,* or date-bearing palm. The palm tree was considered in Biblical times as a princely tree and was used as a symbol of victory and well-being and also as temple decoration. Because of the tree's height and graceful trunk, with its crown of serrated branches and shade-providing leaves, it served as a shelter and provided food in desert borderlands and was highly prized among Egyptians, Babylonians, Assyrians, and Jews. The palm tree was considered holy in Babylon and later was sacred to the Greek god Apollo at Delos. Several cities were referred to specifically as the Palm City: Thamar (Ez 47.19), Jericho (Dt 34.3), and En–Gedi (Pliny, *Hist. nat.* 5.17). The palm tree supplied figures and similes for poets (Ps 92.13) and was used as a name for girls (Gn 38.6; 2 Sm 13.1). It provided decor for the ornamentation of temples among the Phoenicians, Assyrians, and Egyptians (1 Kgs 6.29; Ez 40.16, 22).

Among both the Romans and the Jews it was carried in joyful or triumphant processions. In 293 B.C. victorious Roman soldiers bore palm branches when parading in Rome; and the palm was given as a victory emblem at public games. Of earlier date was its usage among the Israelites; people carried palm branches during the Feast of Tabernacles (Lv 23.40; Neh 8.15); and it was part of the bouquet, or *lulab,* offered on festive occasions as a sign of homage or to celebrate a victory (1 Mc 13.37; Jn 12.13).

Christ's triumphal entry into Jerusalem, when the people strew palm branches in his path and greeted him with Hosannas (Jn 12.12–13), became a liturgical function on PALM SUNDAY in the 4th century. But already in the New Testament the palm was connected with martyrdom (Rv 7.9) and was used to decorate grave markers and tombs in the catacombs as a sign of the triumphal death of the martyr (Paul of Nola, *Epist.,* 32.10). On mosaics and on sarcophagi it usually stands for paradise, and Christ is frequently portrayed amid palms in heaven. So also in ancient church decorations the Lamb of God and the Apostles are depicted amid palms. In the Middle Ages palms served as a symbol of Sunday; and in the Renaissance, under humanist influence, they came to stand for virtues or an augury for a good marriage and length of years.

The palm blessed at Mass on Palm Sunday is carried home by the faithful as a sacramental and symbol of Christ's presence among them. It is usually placed over the bed, entwined on a crucifix, or displayed near some holy picture or statue. Often it is decorated with ribbons or worked into an artistic pattern, such as a cross. In Western countries this has been the custom since at least the 11th century, and both palm and olive tree branches are so employed. Before Ash Wednesday the blessed palm is burned, and its residue is used in the distribution of ashes as a symbol of penance during Lent.

Bibliography: H. I. MARROU, *Mélanges d'archéologie et d'histoire,* 58 (1941–46) 109–113. J. E. HARRISON, *Prolegomena to the Study of Greek Religion* (3d ed. Cambridge, Eng. 1922) 78–82.

[F. X. MURPHY/EDS.]

PALMYRA

Ancient and modern caravan center of the Syrian Desert between Damascus (150 miles SW) or Homs (100 miles W) and Deir ez-Zor (130 miles E). "Palmyra" is apparently (Greek via Latin) from the Semitic "date palm" (Hebrew *tāmār;* Aramaic *tamrā';* Arabic *tamrun*); the modern name Tadmor may be a variant (or another Semitic root with common prefix *t-*); but it is scarcely SOLOMON's Tadmor that is mentioned in 2 Chr 8.4, where the reading should be Tamar (Thamar), a town in southern Juda (Ez 47.9; 48.28), as in 1 Kgs 9.18 [see J. Starcky, *Dictionnaire de la Bible*, suppl. ed. L. Pirot, 5:1068]. The only mention of a pre-Hellenistic Tadmor may be in Mari documents (*c.*1750 B.C.) or in inscriptions of Tiglath-Pileser I (1116–1078 B.C.); see P. Dhorme, *Revue biblique* 53 (1924) 106.

The far-flung surviving ruins, cleared by T. Wiegand's German expedition, come from a period beginning *c.* 200 B.C.. In 44 a.d. the settlement was already "monumental" as known from the visit of Tiberius' nephew Germanicus and from a Bel temple inscription of 32 (Stoneman, p. 52), but still with a mostly unstable nomadic population (Browning, p. 28). But colonnaded Palmyra's magnificence is chiefly due to Hadrian's visit (A.D. 129)—especially the major temple of Bel (BAAL), distinct from a smaller temple of Belšamin (Baal-šamayim); see A. Collart, *Annales archéologiques de Syrie* 7 (1957) 67–94. Several hundred of the original 750 sandstone columns are still erect, stretching 1,240 yards from a monumental gateway (now partly reconstructed) past a theater (built *c.* A.D. 140) in the heart of the city—unlike most Roman-Syrian parallels; see E. Frezouls, *Syria* 36 (1959) 202.

Palmyra's most characteristic contribution to world culture is its funerary sculpture, showing the whole family of the deceased reunited around a festive banquet table, framed by rows of busts of near relatives that seal their respective burials [see Parlasca; E. Ruprechtsberger, *Ausstellung Linz 1987*; H. Ingholt, *Studier* (Copenhagen 1928)]. These sculptured burials were arranged either in several stories of a tower, of which a good number survive, notably those of Elahbel (A.D. 103) and Jamblichus (A.D. 80)—see E. Will, *Syria* 26 (1949) 87–116, 258–312; cf. 34 (1957) 262–277—or in underground chambers, most of which have been transferred to museums, especially Yarhai's (A.D. 108), reconstructed in Damascus [see R. Amy and H. Seyrig, *Syria* 17 (1936) 229; *Annales archéologiques de Syrie* 1 (1951) 32–40]. Some of the tombs contain inscriptions in the Palmyrene language (see bibliography), closely related to Nabataean and the Aramaic of the DEAD SEA SCROLLS (*see* ARAMAIC LANGUAGE, 1).

Rome built up Palmyra's strength to a maximum under the local ruler Odeinat; but after his death (A.D. 268) his widow Zenobia declared her independence and successfully resisted sporadic attacks by the Roman legions until a strong army was sent against her. She was captured and made to grace Aurelian's triumph in Rome (thus earning him the bad name of "general who conquered a woman"), then comfortably ended her days in a villa at Tivoli.

The desert ruins of Palmyra are now dominated by a castle named for Ibn Ma'an but really built by Fakhr-al-Dīn II al-Ma'nī (*c.* A.D. 1600).

See Also: ARABIA, 3

Bibliography: R. STONEMAN, *Palmyra and Its Empire: Zenobia's Revolt against Rome* (Ann Arbor 1992). I. BROWNING, *Palmyra* (1979). M. GAWLIKOWSKI, "Palmyra," *Anchor Bible Dictionary* 5 (1992) 136–137. P. PARLASCA, "Die palmyrenische Grabkunst," *Mitteilungen der archäologischen Gesellschaft Steyermark* 94 (1989–90) 112–136. M. COLLEDGE, *The Art of Palmyra* (1976). H. J. W. DRIJVERS and M. VERSTEEGH, "Palmyra," *Aufstieg und Niedergang der Römische Welt* 2.8 (1977) 837–863; H. DRIJVERS, *The Religion of Palmyra* (Leiden 1976). J. TEIXIDOR, *The Pantheon of Palmyra* (Leiden 1974). W. MACDONALD, *Architecture of the Roman Empire* (New Haven 1965). E. WILL, *Les Palmyreniens* (Paris 1992). J. STARCKY, *Palmyre* (Paris 1952); *Dictionnaire de la Bible*, suppl. ed. L. PIROT, et al. (Paris 1928–) 6:1066–1103. H. LECLERCQ, *Dictionnaire d'archéololgie chrétienne et de liturgie* 13 (1957) 962. T. WIEGAND, ed., *Palmyra: Ergebnisse der Expedition von 1902–1917*, 2 v. (Berlin 1932). M. I. ROSTOVTSEV, *Caravan Cities*, tr. D. and T. TALBOT RICE (Oxford 1932) 91–152. Palmyrene language. D. HILLERS, *Zeitschrift für Althebraistik* 8 (1995) 55–62. J. CANTINEAU, *Grammaire du palmyrénien épigraphique* (Cairo 1935). F. ROSENTHAL, *Die Sprache der palmyrenischen Inschriften . . .* (Leipzig 1936).

[R. NORTH]

PALOMAR, JOHN OF

Spanish theologian; fl. 1431–43. Although he was one of the leading figures at the Council of BASEL, very little is known of his early life. He served successively as archdeacon of Barcelona, chaplain to Pope EUGENE IV, and auditor of the Sacred Palace. With John of RAGUSA he presided briefly over the Council of Basel from July 1431 until the return of Cardinal CESARINI from Bohemia. After 1433 Palomar was engaged in debate with the Hussites at the council over the Church's right to possess goods and temporal jurisdiction. He was also one of a small group led by Cesarini who defended the principle of papal supremacy against the proponents of CONCILIARISM, defending the basic dictum that the See of Peter may be judged by no one. His *Scriptum contra Basileense concilium* (MS Paris, B.N. lat. 1442) was a bitter rejection of the council's decrees and claims to superiority.

Bibliography: J. D. MANSI, *Sacrorum Conciliorum nova et amplissima collectio* (Graz 1960) 29:1105–68. J. J. I. VON DÖLLINGER, *Beiträge zur Politischen, Kirchlichen, und Kulturgeschichte . . .*, 3 v. (Regensburg 1862–82) 2:414–441. N. VALOIS, *Le pape et le concile, 1418–50*, 2 v. (Paris 1909) 1:116–129; 2:53–56. É. AMANN, *Dictionnaire de théologie catholique*, ed. A. VACANT et al. (Paris 1903–50) 8.1:796–797. *Enciclopedia de la religión Católica*, ed. R. D. FERRERES et al. (Barcelona 1950–56) 4:895.

[D. S. BUCZEK]

PALÓU, FRANCISCO

Missionary; b. Palma, Majorca, Jan. 22, 1723; d. Querétaro, Mexico, April 6, 1789. He entered the Franciscan Order in 1739 and studied under Junípero SERRA. Palóu was ordained in 1747, and two years later went to Mexico as a missionary. He and Serra were assigned to the missionary Apostolic College of San Fernando, Mexico City. From 1750 to 1760 he served in the Indian missions of the Sierra Gorda, north of Querétaro. In 1767 he went to Lower California to work in the missions left vacant by the expulsion of the Jesuits, and he eventually became missionary president of that area. Palóu remained in charge of the missions of the Lower California Peninsula until the region was transferred to the Dominicans in 1773. In that year he went to the newly opened mission field of Upper California, where he became temporary superior because of Serra's absence in Mexico. During this period he began his *Noticias de la Nueva California* (1874), a history of the first years of California's colonization. He also accompanied two expeditions to the San Francisco Bay area, acting as diarist. In 1776 Palóu founded Mission San Francisco, where he served during most of his years in California. He assisted the dying Serra at the latter's Mission San Carlos in 1784. Upon the president's death, Palóu again assumed temporary charge of the upper California area and began his classic biography of Serra, the *Relación histórica de la vida y apostólicas tareas del Venerable Padre Fray Junípero Serra* (1787). Recalled to San Fernando College in 1785, he was elected superior in 1786 and held office until he died.

Bibliography: F. PALÓU, *Life of Fray Junípero Serra,* tr. and annot. M. J. GEIGER (Washington 1955). H. E. BOLTON, *Palóu and His Writings* (Berkeley 1926).

[E. D. BURNETT]

PAMMACHIUS, ST.

Roman senator; b. *c.* 340 of the Furian family; d. Rome, 409–10. He was a friend and fellow student of St. JEROME in their youth, and Jerome's extant correspondence of later years includes a number of letters addressed to Pammachius, who was intensely interested in theological controversy, as well as one (*Ep.* 83) addressed to Jerome from Pammachius and Oceanus. Pammachius was married to Paulina, the second daughter of St. PAULA of Rome. After Paulina's death, near the end of the fourth century, Pammachius turned to the religious life and used his wealth for the care of the poor. In conjunction with St. FABIOLA he founded a hospice at Ostia, and he may have been a founder of the church of SS. John and Paul on the Caelius in Rome. He was termed *ecclesiae munerarius* by St. PAULINUS OF NOLA (*Ep.* 13). St. AUGUSTINE's *Ep.* 58 is addressed to Pammachius.

Feast: Aug. 30.

Bibliography: *Sancti Eusebii Hieronymi epistulae,* ed. I. HILBERG, 3 v. (*Corpus scriptorum ecclesiasticorum latinorum* 54–56; 1910–18) 48, 49, 57, 66, 83, 84, 97. *Acta Sanctorum* Aug. 6:555–563. F. CAVALLERA, *Saint Jérôme,* 2 v. (*Spicilegium sacrum Lovaniense* 1, 2; 1922).

[T. C. LAWLER]

PAMPHILUS, ST.

Martyr; b. Berytus, Phoenicia (modern Beirut, Lebanon); d. Caesarea, Palestine, February 16, 310. The two early biographies, one written by his master Pierius, according to Philip of Side, and the other by his disciple EUSEBIUS OF CAESAREA, have been lost. Eusebius took his name (Eusebius Pamphili) to display the spiritual filiation between them and speaks of him with admiration in his *Ecclesiastical History* and in his *On the Martyrs of Palestine,* where he gives a résumé of his career, imprisonment, and martyrdom (ch. 11.1).

Pamphilus, of a noble family of Berytus, received a careful education and exercised public office there, then became, at the Didaskaleion of Alexandria (Photius, *Bibliotheca* 118–119), a student of Pierius, head of the school under Bishop Theonas after 281 (Jerome, *De vir. ill.* 76). Pierius was called Origen the Younger because of his talents and the admiration he had for that great theologian; he communicated this conviction to Pamphilus, who later reopened the School of CAESAREA founded by ORIGEN. Ordained by Bishop Agapius (*c.* 290), Pamphilus was renowned for his asceticism and charity as well as for his knowledge.

Speaking of his disciples, the brothers Apphianus and Aedesius, Eusebius described the spiritual and scriptural orientation of the teaching of Pamphilus (*De mart. Palest.* 4.6; 5.2). He reorganized the Christian library attached to the school at Caesarea and employed a band of copyists. Arrested in 307, he was held in prison for two years and then decapitated during the persecution of Maximinus Daia.

The only known writing of Pamphilus is his *Apology for Origen,* composed while in prison with the assistance of Eusebius of Caesarea, who was the author of the work's sixth book (Eusebius, *Hist. eccl.* 6.33, 36; Photius, *Bibl.* 118). JEROME testifies to Pamphilus's authorship (*De vir. ill.* 75). But after Jerome became an anti-Origenist, he attributed the *Apology* to Eusebius, whom he described as a semi-Arian to discredit the work. Only book 1 in the translation of RUFINUS OF AQUILEIA exists. It begins with a letter to the Palestinian confessors condemned to the mines and indicates the proper manner of judging the difficulties in Origen's thought: the hypothetical and doubtful character of his speculations, which are not dogmatic affirmations and frequently are self-contradictory. Pamphilus bears witness to Origen's fidelity to orthodoxy. By numerous citations of Origen's works, some of which are otherwise unknown, he refutes the accusations made against Origen's doctrine on the Trinity, the Incarnation, the historicity of the Scriptures, the Resurrection, the soul, metempsychosis, and eternal damnation.

Feast: June 1.

Bibliography: *Patrologica Graeca,* ed. J. P. MIGNE, 161 v. (Paris 1857–66). 17:541–616. E. VENABLES, in *A Dictionary of Christian Biography,* ed. W. SMITH and H. WACE, 4 v. (London 1877–87) 4:178–179. G. BARDY, *Dictionnaire de théologie catholique,* ed. A. VACANT et al., 15 v. (Paris 1903–50; Tables générales 1951–). 11.2:1839–41. J. QUASTEN, *Patrology,* 3 v. (Westminster, Md. 1950–60) 2:144–146. F. X. MURPHY, *Rufinus of Aquileia* (Washington 1945).

[H. CROUZEL]

PAMPLONA, DIONISIO AND COMPANIONS, BB.

Martyrs; Religious of the Order of Poor Clerics Regular of the Mother of God of the Pious Schools (PIARISTS); d. June-December 1936; beatified Oct. 1, 1995 by Pope John Paul II.

Dionisio Pamplona, born Oct. 11, 1868 in Calamocha, Teruel, Spain; d. July 25. Pamplona made his solemn profession in 1889 and was ordained a priest in 1893. He taught in several Piarist schools in Spain and then Argentina. In 1934 he was appointed rector of the novitiate house in Peralta, Huesca, Spain, where he also served as pastor of the local church. He was devoted to the Piarist rule and allowed the love of God to animate all he did. The religious persecution marking the Spanish Civil War intensified in 1936. On July 23, 1936 the Revolutionary Committee placed the Piarist community under house arrest in a secluded home away from the church and school. The next day at dawn, Pamplona left the house unnoticed by the guards and returned to the church to celebrate Mass. As he was locking the church to leave, armed men seized him and later took him to the prison in Monzón. On June 25 around eleven o'clock in the evening, the soldiers removed Pamplona with several other prisoners, led them to the main square, and lined them up for execution. Pamplona was singled out and shot to death.

Other members of the Piarist community martyred during the Civil War were beatified with Pamplona. Each is listed below by the date of his death in 1936. Further details may be found in the individual entries.

July 28: Manuel SEGURA LÓPEZ, priest (age 55) and David Carlos MARAÑÓN, lay brother (age 28).

August 9: Faustino OTEIZA SEGURA, priest (age 46) and Florentín Felipe NAYA, lay brother (age 79).

August 14: Juan AGRAMUNT RIERA, priest (age 29).

August 17–18 (night of): Enrique CANADELL QUINTANA (age 46).

August 20: Matias CARDONA MESEGUER, priest (age 33).

September 16: Ignacio CASANOVAS PERRAMÓN, priest (age 43).

September 22: Carlo NAVARRO MIGUEL, priest (age 25).

October 2: Francisco CARCELLER GALINDO, priest (age 35).

December 9: José FERRER ESTEVE, priest (age 32).

December 27: Alfredo PARTE SAIZ, priest (age 37).

At their beatification Pope John Paul II observed, "They are not heroes of an inhuman war but teachers of youth who, as both religious and teachers, faced up to their tragic fate by authentic witness to the faith, giving by their martyrdom, the ultimate lesson of their life."

Feast: Sept. 22.

Bibliography: "Decreto Super Martyrio," *Acta Apostolicae Sedis* (1995) 651–656. *La Documentation Catholique* 2125 (Nov. 5, 1995) 924.

[L. GENDERNALIK/EDS.]

PAMPLONA, FRANCIS OF

Capuchin lay brother and missionary; b. Pamplona, Spain, Aug. 11, 1597; d. La Guaira, Venezuela, Aug. 31, 1651. He was born Tiburcio de Redin, of a noble family, and first followed a career in the military, holding high offices and distinguishing himself for his skill and courage. In 1637, however, he was converted to a life of penance as a Capuchin and dedicated his efforts to the foreign missions. He joined Bonaventure of Allesano in founding a Capuchin mission in the Congo in 1645. Returning to Europe, he solicited support for the missions in London, Rome, and Madrid. After 1647 he went to the missions in Spanish America, where he spent his remaining years laboring in Panama and Venezuela.

Bibliography: C. DA TERZORIO, *Le missioni dei Minori Cappuccini,* v. 10 (Rome 1938) 370–398. *Documentos históricos: Fray Francisco de Pamplona,* v.3 (1948) 67–73.

[J. C. WILLKE]

PAMPURI, RICCARDO, ST.

Baptized Erminio Filippo (Herman Philip), physician, lay brother of the Hospitallers of St. John of God; b. Aug. 2, 1897, Trivolizi (near Pavia), Lombardy, Italy; d. May 1, 1930, Milan. The second youngest of the eleven children of wine merchants Innocente Pampuri and Angela Campari, who died of tuberculosis when Erminio was three, Erminio was raised by his uncle Carlo Campari in Turin following his father's death (1907). There, Erminio became involved in CATHOLIC ACTION. He studied medicine at the University of Pavia (1915–21) with an interruption for military service in the Italian Army Medical Corps (1917–18). In 1921, he joined his uncle Carlo's practice in Morimondo (Milan) as a general physician. He became an active member of the St. Vincent de Paul Society, joined the Third Order of Franciscans (1922), fostered the growth of a parish Catholic Action youth group, and organized spiritual exercises in preparation for the 1925 Jubilee. Under the spiritual direction of Fr. Riccardo Beretta, he entered the HOSPITALLERS OF ST. JOHN OF GOD (June 22, 1927). After receiving the habit and name Brother Riccardo (Richard; Oct. 21, 1927), he completed his novitiate and began his work as director of the dental clinic at St. Ursula's Hospital in Brescia (Oct. 24, 1928). Following his death at age 33 from bronchial pneumonia, his remains have been venerated in a chapel dedicated to him in Trivolzio. Pampuri's beatification process was opened in 1949. Pope John Paul II both beatified (Oct. 4, 1981) and canonized (Nov. 1, 1989) him in Rome.

Feast: May 1.

Bibliography: *Acta Apostolicae Sedis* 74 (1982): 376–379. *L'Osservatore Romano,* English Edition, no. 41: 1, 12. Comune di Trivolzio, *Trivolzio: il paese di San Riccardo Pampuri nel centenario della sua nascita* (Pavia 1997). L. CIONI, *Il santo semplice: vita di san Riccardo Pampuri* (Genoa 1996). N. MUTSCHLECHNER, *Ein Arzt wählt Gott—Der Heilige Frater Richard Pampuri aus dem Orden der Barmherzigen Brüder* (Munich 1991).

[K. I. RABENSTEIN]

PANAMA, THE CATHOLIC CHURCH IN

The Republic of Panama is, geographically, the narrowest part of Central America and unites North and South America. It is situated between the Republics of Colombia on the east and Costa Rica on the west. On the north is the Atlantic Ocean and on the south the Pacific Ocean. Rugged mountains run the length of the interior, falling to plains and rolling hills near the coast. The climate is hot and humid, marked by a rainy season from

> **Capital:** Panama City.
> **Size:** 28,576 sq. miles.
> **Population:** 2,808,270 in 2000.
> **Languages:** Spanish, English.
> **Religions:** 2,302,780 Catholics (82%), 140,500 Muslims (5%), 196,590 Protestants (7%), 168,400 without religious affiliation.
> **Archdiocese:** Panama City, with suffragans Chitré, Colón-Kuna Yala, Davíd, Penonomé, and Santiago de Veraguas. A prelature is located at Bocas del Toro, and an apostolic vicariate is located in Darién.

May to January. Natural resources include copper, mahogany timber and shrimp; agricultural products consist of bananas, rice, corn, coffee and sugarcane.

Panama is an isthmus with the 47 mile-long interoceanic Panama Canal located at its narrowest point. Begun by the French in 1882, the canal was completed by the U.S. Army Corps of Engineers between 1904 and 1914. The canal was placed at the service of worldwide maritime trade and governed by the United States under the authorization of the Republic of Panama until 1999, when the entire canal zone (553 sq. miles) was turned over to the republic.

A Spanish colony until 1821, Panama broke its ties to Gran Columbia and became independent as a U.S. protectorate in 1903. The region, controlled by a succession of volatile administrations, required repeated intervention by the U.S. in order to preserve its interest in the canal zone. From 1988 to 1989 General Manuel Noriega seized control; he was deposed, with U.S. backing in favor of a civilian regime, and was convicted of drug trafficking in 1992. Most Panamanians are ethnic mestizo, with Amerindian, European (Spanish) and West Indian minorities. Indigenous people live in the mountainous regions, while others reside in the country's more populous areas. During the 1980s and 1990s the region's rainforests were severely diminished through deforestation.

The Early Church. Both Spanish explorer Rodrigo de Bastidas in 1501 and Christopher Columbus, on his fourth voyage to the New World in 1502, traveled portions of Panama, although neither perceived it was an isthmus. This was left to Vasco Núñez de Balboa, who crossed from one ocean to the other in 1513. The Holy See, by petition of the catholic King Ferdinand of Spain, created the bishopric of Darién, the oldest on the American continent and the fourth in the New World. In 1514 Franciscans led by Bishop Juan de QUEVEDO, and six years later Dominicans led by Bishop Vicente Peraza, entered the region to convert the indigenous tribes of Darién. With the support of the Spanish crown, these first missionaries staked out settlements in the mountains, val-

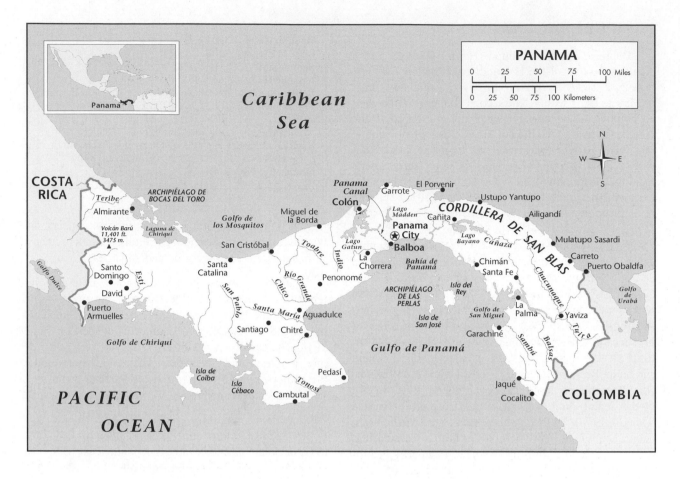

leys and plains, many of which grew into major cities in the centuries that followed.

Jesuits began their residence in the isthmus in the middle of the 16th century, and, in addition to missionary work, devoted their efforts to education. Some of their native students were inspired to enter the Society of Jesus, among them theologian Pedro Ignacio de Cáceres, educator Juan Antonio Giraldo and Agustín Hurtado, a zealous missionary, who in 1677 was martyred by natives to whom he was preaching the gospel. Dominican General Adriano Ufelde de Santo Tomás was among the most noted evangelist of the colonial period, and his written works provided historians with a valuable source of historical information.

The Panamanian curia was suffragan of the archdiocese of Seville till 1546, of Lima until 1836, of Bogotá till 1901 and finally of Cartagena de Indias till 1925, at which time, by disposition of Pius XI, the Republic of Panama became an archdiocese. In 1749 the University of St. Xavier was founded by the native priest Francisco Javier de Luna Victoria. Many native Panamanians also reached the high honor of the episcopate, among them Francisco Javier de Luna, bishop of Chuquisaca, Bolivia

(d. *c.* 1778) and Manuel Joaquín González de Acuña y Sanz Merino, bishop of Panama (1797–1813).

An Independent Panama. Led by Bishop José Higinio Durán, the Church took a leadership role in the independence movement, and in 1821 Panama gained independence from Spain. Under the new government, the Church enjoyed independence from civil government while maintaining cordial relations. Freedom of religion was granted to all faiths by the new constitution, and this attracted a number of evangelical Protestant groups. The constitution, promulgated following independence from Columbia on Nov. 3, 1903, recognizing that the Catholic faith predominated, extended it special protection, financing its missions and granting subsidies for the construction of churches and the development of charitable foundations, especially in the field of education and scholarships for parochial schools. The Church had no other properties or income apart from donations. Under a new constitution dated Oct. 11, 1972, freedom of religion was continued. In addition, Catholicism continued to be taught in state-run schools, although parents could exempt their children from this curriculum. Clerics were prohibited from holding public office.

Iglesia del Carmen (Church of Carmen), Panama City. (©Danny Lehman/CORBIS)

In the middle of the 20th century a shortage of priests required that men's vocations be supplemented by Spanish clergy; vocations continued to be adequate among women. Religious communities active in the region included Jesuits, Augustinians, Paulists, Franciscans, Salesians, Christian Brothers, Benedictines, Sisters of Charity, Maryknoll, Discalced Carmelites, Franciscans, Dominicans, Mercedarians and Servants of Mary. Despite the inroads made by foreign evangelical Protestant groups during the second half of the century, the Church participated enthusiastically in ecumenical conferences, through which it effected positive social change in Panama.

Through the leadership of General Omar Torrijos from 1968 to 1981, Panama gained economic autonomy, and in 1977 a treaty was signed under which the canal would revert to Panama by the end of the century. Torrijos was killed in 1981. Seven years later General Manuel Noriega took control. Following elections in May of 1989 during which president-elect Guillermo Endara was forced into hiding and charges of corruption abounded, Church leaders accused Noriega of fraudulent election practices. Over 20,000 U.S. troops descended on the Panamanian capital to depose Noriega, who was suspected of drug trafficking on a large scale. Ten days later Noriega surrendered Panama's high office, his relinquishment of power aided by Church mediation. In 1990 Endara abolished the country's standing military. During the 1990s the government of Ernesto Balladares encouraged a strong economy based on banking, international trade and tourism. Government corruption, perhaps caused by Panama's position as a distribution point for illegal drugs, however continued to be a problem. Remarking on Panama's acquisition of all rights to the Panama Canal on Dec. 31, 1999, Pope John Paul II called it a "magnificent opportunity" for the government to improve the quality of life for all Panamanians.

Into the 21st Century. By 2000 there were 161 parishes tended by 166 diocesan and 230 religious priests. Other religious included approximately 55 brothers and 560 sisters, many of whom aided the Panamanian people through their work in the nation's 41 primary and 39 secondary Catholic schools. In 1999 Church leaders participated in a peace initiative near the Colombian-Panama border in an effort to end confrontations between Marxist and other guerilla groups, engaged in fighting, that endangered and impoverished local populations.

Bibliography: E. J. CASTILLERO REYES, *Historia de Panamá* (6th ed. Panama 1959). G. RUDOLF, *Panama's Poor: Victims,*

Agents, and Historymakers (Miami 1999). *Annuario Pontificio* has information on all diocese.

[E. J. CASTILLERO/EDS.]

PANBABYLONISM

A theory of interpretation of history advanced in Germany at the beginning of the 20th century that claimed to find traces of an essential Babylonian influence in all the cultures and religions of the world. The theory was proposed in several forms, the most notable being those of Hugo Winckler, *Himmels- und Weltenbild der Babylonier als Grundlage der Weltanschauung und Mythologie aller Völker* (1903), and Alfred Jeremias, *Die Panbabylonisten* (1907). These men observed that the cosmogonies of the various nations were permeated with astral motifs and concluded that this worldwide similarity in mythological types argued for a common cultural heritage that had its roots in Babylonia, the birthplace of both astronomy and astrological religion. Some of the ramifications of their theory were to picture Israelite history and tradition as a shadowy borrowing from Mesopotamia and to portray Christ as a fictional reincarnation of the Babylonian god, Bel-Marduk. Another variety of Panbabylonism was exemplified in P. Jensen's *Das Gilgamesch-Epos in der Welt-literatur* (1906), which found that Babylonian hero under different guises in the literature of almost all nations and viewed Christ as a solar-myth figure modeled on Gilgamesh. The extravagant claims of the school were effectively dismissed from serious consideration after the scientific investigations of the astronomer-Assyriologist F. X. Kugler in his *Auf den Trümmern des Panbabylonismus* (1909) and *Im Bannkreis Babels* (1910).

Bibliography: A. DEIMEL, *Pantheon Babylonicum* (Rome 1914) 35–39. C. M. EDSMAN, *Die Religion in Geschichte und Gegenwart* (Tübingen 1957–65) 5:35–36. P. SCHEBASTA, *Christus und die Religionen der Erde* (Vienna 1961) 1:548–550. F. M. TH. DE LIAGRE BÖHL, *Christus und die Religionen der Erde* 2:447–448. F. KÖNIG, *Christus und die Religionen der Erde* 3:745–746.

[J. A. BRINKMAN]

PANENTHEISM

Panentheism, (Gr. παν, all; εν, in; θεος, God) in its simplest form, is the view that the world is in God, but God is not the world. In metaphysics, it utilizes a real distinction between the essence of God and God's existence, or considers God as having accidents really distinct from God's nature. Panentheism stands as a kind of surrelativism holding for a mutuality in relationship between God and the world not only is the world dependent upon God, but God also is to some extent dependent upon the world. It regards the world as an actual fulfillment of God's creative possibility.

The term panentheism seems to have been introduced by Karl C. F. Krause (1781–1832) to distinguish his doctrine from contemporary forms of PANTHEISM and EMANATIONISM. The term was used also by Friedrich Jacobi and by a few members of the theological faculty at Tübingen, though not so pointedly. Today it describes the views of those who introduce a polarity in the notion of God as both eternal and temporal, and as including yet transcending the world.

Panentheism is rooted in a conviction that the world as possible in the mind of God becomes actualized and thereby adds to God's actuality. It opposes the Thomistic view of God as PURE ACT. Panentheists give special importance to what they call a logic of polarity, which has a close affinity to Hegelian dialectics, as the only means of escaping ultimate dilemmas arising from the use of categories.

Historical Survey. In one sense, the present forms of panentheism can be traced to PLATO, who discussed both being and becoming in a manner that could imply a dipolar view of ultimate reality. His "One" seems to have contained individual beings even as it remained indivisible.

Medieval Thought. JOHN SCOTUS ERIUGENA viewed creation as the production of Ideas in the World, and designated a stage of completion for such productivity in quite the same manner as do present-day panentheists. Moreover, his distinction of God as Creator and God as the End of all things implies fulfillment, and reads much like Whitehead's primordial and consequent natures of God.

Ramanuja (1017–1137) tempered the impersonal Hindu panentheism of his day with a personalistic notion of BRAHMAN as cause of all things, but he also maintained that all the things of this world formed the body of Brahma. His doctrine of nonduality with differences (*vishistadvaita*) seems more in line with modern polaristic views than with either panentheistic MONISM or theistic DUALISM.

Although John DUNS SCOTUS insisted on freedom in the act of creation, traces of panentheism may be seen in his view of God as being necessitated to will the ideas of things, and in his doctrine of the univocity of being. Further, his ideas of infinity and his insistence upon the limitations of metaphysics imply a polarity.

Meister ECKHART emphasized the transcendence of God and maintained that one could not affirm anything of God in such a way as to rule out its opposite—an idea similar to the later notion of polarity.

Renaissance and Modern Thinkers. NICHOLAS OF CUSA leaned even further towards panentheism. He held that the world is explication of what is implication in God and conceived of the infinite as including and reconciling all opposites. Such ideas not only established ground for the doctrine of dipolarity, but also emphasized the theme of fulfillment that was presented by later panentheists.

Friedrich SCHELLING described the ABSOLUTE as the identity of all differences. For Schelling, God will ''be'' only when the Absolute has fully revealed itself. His God is in process in somewhat the same manner as Whitehead's consequent God.

Accepting the complexity of the concept of God, Gustav Fechner (1801–87) proposed the view of an inclusive eternal-temporal deity. He maintained that such opposing descriptions are partial truths that can be reconciled through proper re-interpretation or completion, thus harmonizing them with the more general conception of God.

The triadic doctrine of the Absolute Spirit proposed by Hegel considers nature as an externalization of the Absolute, and portrays the Absolute itself as a never-ending process that implies eternity and temporality.

Two Russian thinkers, Vladimir SOLOV'EV and Nikolai BERDYAEV, emphasized the incarnational aspect of panentheism. Solov'ev presented God as polarized and developed this view through the notions of man-Godhood and God-manhood. Berdyaev looked to a transfigured world as the ultimate expression of God and wrote, in a rather mystical fashion, of a divine history, a divine becoming, a divine need, and above all, a divine suffering. For Berdyaev we are creatively responsive to God, and we enrich God's life.

Contemporary Directions. Alfred N. WHITEHEAD offered a dipolar God by distinguishing between the so-called primordial and consequent aspects of the divine nature: the primordial aspect is God considered as the first cause of all things; the consequent aspect is God as the end of all things. Arguing from the relativity of all things, he held for a reaction of the world upon God to the extent that the whole of the created order stands as a fulfillment of God's concrete actuality, though not of God's abstract nature.

Muhammad Iqbal (1875–1938) described God's creative life as an organic whole existing as an open possibility, so that God is ever being completed by the world without changing God's essential nature.

The interpretation of participated being given by Pierre TEILHARD DE CHARDIN seems to have concluded with the placement of all things in God by what he calls a unitive transformation. While insisting that this infusion of the one and the many does not add anything essential to God, he implied that it does add something accidental to the divine being.

Paul TILLICH's approach to ultimate reality through symbolization used the notion of polarity to overcome the tendency to impose limitations upon God. It fit in well with the basic approach of panentheism.

Sarvepalli Radhakrishnan (1888–1975) made a distinction between divine being and divine action, rejecting the idea of confining the illimitable to a single form or perfection. He held that abstract possibility and concrete realization are both contained in the one reality, which he identified as the Absolute-God. Although he said that this distinction is only logical, he seemed to use it as a real distinction; thus it gave his thought a panentheistic polarity.

Charles HARTSHORNE did the most to give panentheism formal expression as a view of God. He developed a dipolar concept of God, resting on a fundamental distinction between his concrete actuality and his abstract existence. He attributed the traditional categories of absoluteness, infinity, immutability, and so on to God's abstractness while maintaining that his concreteness makes God truly related, finite, mutable, and so on, just like any other actuality. Hartshorne explained what it means to say that God is truly in the world and yet is not identical with it. He developed more fully than the other panentheists the logic of panentheism, arguing that the predication of contrary predicates of God makes better philosophical and religious sense than classical theism.

Critical Evaluation. Critics of panentheism have charged that it involves erroneous understandings of logic, CAUSALITY, and ANALOGY. The focal point of criticism has been the logic of dipolarity, on which panentheism rests. Hartshorne consistently argued that, despite attributing contrary predicates of God (e.g., transcendent-immanent, absolute-relative, infinite-finite), panentheism does not violate the principle of non-contradiction since these are predicated of God under different aspects. Furthermore the relationship between the pairs of contraries is asymmetrical: one set includes the other but not the other way around. Contrary to traditional philosophies of being, Hartshorne maintained that God's absoluteness is explainable as contained in God's relativity rather than vice versa.

Critics have also questioned whether the distinction between God and the world is really sufficiently delineated since panentheists deny the doctrine of *creatio ex nihilo*. In panentheism, God's being Supreme Cause does not require that he have the kind of independence of the world reflected in the traditional doctrine of creation.

For Christian theists panentheism needs to be developed further if it is to be reconcilable with the doctrine of the Trinity. While dipolarity can be useful in explaining how God can be transcendent and immanent in the world or in shaping a new kind of Christology, it still remains unclear as to how it can support the doctrine of a triune God.

Bibliography: C. HARTSHORNE and W. L. REESE, eds. *Philosophers Speak of God* (Chicago 1953). C. HARTSHORNE, *Man's Vision of God and the Logic of Theism* (Chicago 1941).

[E. R. NAUGHTON/S. SIA]

PANGE LINGUA GLORIOSI

The opening words of two liturgical hymns. (1) *Pange lingua gloriosi lauream certaminis,* a hymn of the holy cross by Venantius FORTUNATUS, written *c.* 569 for the reception of a relic of the cross, sent by Emperor JUSTIN II to Queen RADEGUNDA, in Poitiers. One of the most famous Passiontide hymns of all times, it was traditionally used in the GOOD FRIDAY ceremony of the veneration of the cross since the ninth century. At one time, it was also sung at MATINS and LAUDS of Passiontide, as well as for the Feast of the Triumph of the Cross. The original text consists of ten stanzas, each having three lines in trochaic tetrameter, a form once used in marching songs of the Roman soldiers. The hymn briefly recounts Christ's earthly life, embedded in the history of the Redemption, beginning with humanity's fall, and makes passing allusions to the instruments of the Passion. Christ's cross appears as the tree of life, especially selected for the glorious task of bearing Christ. This holy cross hymn later became the model for many compositions, among them the not less famous Eucharistic hymn, (2) *Pange lingua gloriosi corporis mysterium,* which was traditionally sung at Vespers and during procession on Corpus Christi and HOLY THURSDAY. It has five three-line stanzas and a doxology, in catalectic and accentual trochaic tetrameter. This masterpiece of medieval poetry was written probably by St. THOMAS AQUINAS (or by someone in his entourage) *c.* 1264. Written to a preexisting melody (that of the holy cross sequence *Laudes crucis attollamus*), by the Goliardic poet Hugh Primas of Orléans, it contains many echoes and reminiscences from earlier hymns; still it is an original piece of work, with highly poetic inspiration and doctrinal exactitude. Its fifth stanza, *Tantum ergo,* is sung (to various melodies) at the BENEDICTION OF THE BLESSED SACRAMENT.

Bibliography: J. CONNELLY, *Hymns of the Roman Liturgy* (Westminster MD 1957) 118–120, the Eucharistic Sequence, 82–84, the holy cross, etc., hymn. *Analecta hymnica* 50:71, 585–586. J. SZÖVÉRFFY, *Die Annalen der lateinischen Hymnendichtung* (Berlin 1964–65) 1:129–135; 2:251–252. F. J. E. RABY, *A History of Christian-Latin Poetry from the Beginnings to the Close of the Middle Ages* (Oxford 1953) 90, Venantius Fortunatus; 408, Thomas Aquinas. B. FISCHER, *Lexikon für Theologie und Kirche,* ed. J. HOFER and K. RAHNER (Freiburg 1957–65) 8:21, cf. H. VANDERHOVEN, *Paroisse et Liturgie* 33 (1951) 168–173.

[J. SZÖVÉRFFY]

PANIGAROLA, FRANCESCO

Franciscan Observant preacher and theologian; b. Milan, June 6, 1548; d. Asti, May 31, 1594. He was born of the noble Panigarola family and baptized Jerome. He began his studies at Pavia in 1561 and continued them later at Bologna. He led a very dissipated life, but was suddenly converted and entered the Friars Minor Observant in Florence on May 15, 1567. There he took the name Francesco to distinguish himself from an uncle Jerome, a member of the same province. He made his regular ecclesiastical studies at Padua and Pisa. It was said of him that he became as devout in religion as he had been dissipated in the world.

After his ordination, he began to preach in the large cities of Italy and gained great renown. St. Pius V was so impressed by his eloquence that he sent him to Paris for two years to study the Fathers.

In 1579 Panigarola refused the generalate of his order, but was elected a general definitor and was appointed visitator for all the Italian provinces. In 1583 he was commissioned by St. Charles Borromeo to preach against Lutheranism and Calvinism, which were gaining a foothold in the Tyrol. He became celebrated as a controversialist and is credited with saving the Rhaetian provinces from the Reformation. His sermons on Calvinism, *Lettioni sopra dogmi dette calviniche* (Milan 1582), were translated into several languages and were many times reprinted.

In 1586 Sixtus V named him bishop of Grisopolis and the next year transferred him to Asti, where Calvinism was active. In 1587 he was sent by Sixtus V as part of a diplomatic mission to Paris; he did not return to his diocese until 1590. In Asti he spent his few remaining years in energetic action, especially preaching and combatting the doctrines of the Reformation.

Panigarola's published works number 33, and there are at least as many in manuscript form. Most of his writings are in the field of sacred eloquence, and include especially his philosophical and theological polemics against the teachings of Luther and Calvin. Notable among his printed works are *Rhetorica ecclesiastica* (Cologne 1605) and *Conciones 100 supra Christi passionem coram D. Carlo Borromeo recitatae* (Venice 1585).

Bibliography: A. TEETAERT, *Dictionnaire de théologie catholique,* ed. A. VACANT et al. (Paris 1903–50) 11.2:1850–53. O. BONMANN, *Lexikon für Theologie und Kirche,* ed. J. HOFER and K. RAHNER (Freiburg 1957–65) 8:22. H. HURTER, *Nomenclator literarius theologiae catholicae* (Innsbruck 1903–13) 3:249.

[P. F. MULHERN]

PANNONHALMA, ABBEY OF

Archabbey and center of the Hungarian BENEDICTINES (Mártonhegy, Martinsberg, *Mons sacer Pannoniae*). The foundation, near Györ (Raab), was initiated by Duke Géza in 996 and completed in 1101 under King St. STEPHEN by monks from Brevnov in Bohemia. An abbey *nullius* with all the privileges of MONTE CASSINO, it was the chief agent of Hungary's conversion to Christianity and throughout the Middle Ages was a center of learning and culture, as well as the scene of political events. After organizing the Hungarian Benedictine Congregation in 1512 and becoming an archabbey in 1514, it was for a century a bastion that resisted the Turkish invasion. JOSEPH II secularized it (1786) but Francis I restored it (1802). From then until World War II it was engaged in secondary education and headed the congregation, which, incorporating the abbeys of Bakonybél, Tihany, Dömölk, and Zalavár and administering 25 parishes and 8 gymnasia, had about 300 priest monks. In 1948 the Communist government secularized the possessions of the congregation. The monastery has a valuable library and is rich in cultural monuments. Hungarian Benedictines have settled in Brazil and California.

Bibliography: L. ERDÉLYI, *A Pannonhalmi Szent-Benedek-rend története,* 14 v. (Budapest 1902–16). T. VON BOGYAY, *Lexikon für Theologie und Kirche,* ed. J. HOFER and K. RAHNER, 10 v. (2d, new ed. Freiburg 1957–65) 7:125.

[L. J. LEKAI]

PANPSYCHISM

From the Greek πᾶν meaning all, and ψυχή meaning soul, a philosophical theory that all reality, including inorganic matter, is animated and possesses a psychic nature similar to that of the human soul. It is to be distinguished from HYLOZOISM, the doctrine that all matter is endowed with life but possesses no psychic element.

Old Forms. Panpsychism can be traced back to early Greek philosophers, such as HERACLITUS and EMPEDOCLES, but it is only in the Renaissance that it assumed a concrete and systematic form. Thus in his *Nova de universes philosophia* (Venice 1593), Francesco Patrizi

Pannonhalma Benedictine Monastery. (©Carmen Redondo/ CORBIS)

(1529–97) developed the Neoplatonic theme of an eternal divine light pervading the whole universe, and described knowledge in terms that indicated a similarity of nature between knower and object known. Likewise, Geronimo Cardano (1501–76) defended the doctrine of a WORLD SOUL informing the universe as a psychic principle and Giordano BRUNO (1548–1600) stated even more clearly that the world soul is ''the formal constitutive principle of the universe and all that is contained in it'' [*De la causa, principio et uno,* Venice (London): 1584]. The doctrine of a world soul was defended also by Tommaso CAMPANELLA (1568–1639), who accepted the theory of universal sensation propounded by Bernardino TELESIO and developed it into a metaphysical theory that being is essentially composed of power, knowledge and love.

Modern Forms. In modern times panpsychism has found supporters among philosophers of different trends of thought, principally in Germany, but also in England, the United States, Italy and France.

Germany. The theory of G. W. LEIBNIZ that all reality is made up of monads considered as conscious units reflecting the entire universe is clearly of a panpsychic nature. More recently G. T. Fechner (1801–87) revived the Renaissance theme of an animated universe, which he held to be a unitary system penetrated by the spirit of God and including all other minor ''systems'' as sentient subjects. Among such systems he classed not only animals, but plants, the earth and the heavenly bodies. Rudolph LOTZE (1817–81) restated Leibniz's theory of unextended and conscious monads, and Friedrich Paulsen (1846–1908) presented physical reality as a manifestation of a supreme psychic unit, God, conceived essentially as Will, a doctrine that has many elements in common with the systems of A. SCHOPENHAUER and W. Wundt. This monistic conception of reality was shared also by Ernst Haeckel (1834–1919), for whom God was the sum total of the infinite psychic realities that compose the universe.

England and the United States. Like Haeckel in Germany, William K. Clifford (1845–79) in England arrived at panpsychism from his theory of evolution. If man evolves from inorganic matter, matter must contain the elements of consciousness as this is known to exist in man. Hence the entire universe consists of ''mind stuff.'' Another British philosopher whose conception of reality was impregnated with panpsychic motives was Alfred N. WHITEHEAD (1861–1947), who, with Leibniz, is believed to be ''one of two great artificers of the panpsychic philosophy in its present form'' (*A History of Philosophical Systems*, 450). He pictured the world as a process of events rather than of things. Each event contains within itself its own past, anticipates its future and represents all other events by their effects on it. Thus an event is the synthetic unity of the universe comprehended as oneness, as well as the mirror of the entire universe. It is also an organism in which each part affects the whole and, in turn, is determined by the whole as to its role within it.

In the United States also panpsychism had a few followers. Charles S. PEIRCE (1839–1914) maintained that mind and matter are but different aspects of a single feeling process. When something is considered in its relations and reactions, it is regarded as matter; when understood as feeling, it appears as consciousness. Josiah ROYCE (1855–1916) shared Fechner's basic view of the psychic aspect of all beings. However he defended the peculiar theory that in addition to individual animals, each species of animal as a whole is a single conscious unit. A more recent American exponent of the panpsychic doctrine was Charles A. Strong (1862–1940), whose attempt to solve the problem of interaction between body and mind led him to the denial of their essential difference and to the conception of matter as a psychic reality.

Italy and France. In Italy and France panpsychism was found chiefly among philosophers of spiritualistic tendencies. Thus, in Italy, Vincenzo GIOBERTI (1801–52) not only held the doctrine of an animated universe but also claimed that the principle of animation is of an intellectual nature. In France the spiritualistic movement started by MAINE DE BIRAN and developed by J. G. F. Ravaisson (1813–1900) reached its climax in the theory of vital impulse (*élan vital*) as the immanent principle directive of all organic evolution, a doctrine proposed by H. BERGSON. By P. TEILHARD DE CHARDIN (1881–1955) the process of integral evolution was conceived to extend from elemental matter to reflex consciousness and to attain to its final stage in the ''Omega Point.''

Evaluation. Panpsychism is untenable both as a scientific theory and as a philosophical doctrine. Living beings differ from inanimate matter because of their structural organization and their activities. They are composed of cells or combination of cells forming organs and they are characterized by metabolism, growth, reproduction and internal power of adaptation to environment. This distinction becomes even more evident in animals, which, in addition to vegetative powers, have the capacity for sensation, and in man, who alone among all corporeal creatures is endowed with the power of reasoning. By attributing to matter vital and psychic forces that are proper to plants and animals respectively, panpsychists fail to take into account the essential distinction that separates one order of being from another.

See Also: SOUL; SOUL, HUMAN; SPIRIT.

Bibliography: C. HARTSHORNE, ''Panpsychism,'' *A History of Philosophical Systems*, ed. V. T. A. FERM (New York 1950). G. MARTANO, *Enciclopedia filosofica*, 4 v. (Venice-Rome 1957) 3:1127–29. R. EISLER, *Wörterbuch der philosophischen Begriffe*, 3 v. (4th ed. Berlin 1927–30) 2:372–374. P. TEILHARD DE CHARDIN, *The Phenomenon of Man*, tr. B. WALL (New York 1959). C. A. STRONG, *Essays on the Natural Origin of the Mind* (London 1930).

[B. M. BONANSEA]

PANTAENUS, ST.

Second-century Christian author. The scanty knowledge about Pantaenus comes primarily from EUSEBIUS, who stated (*Hist. Eccl.* 5.10) that he had been trained in the Stoic philosophy and was head of a private school of philosophy at Alexandria about 180. Previously, although Eusebius reported this only as tradition, he had been a zealous missionary and had reached India (i.e., probably South Arabia), where he had found Christians who knew the Gospel of St. Matthew in Hebrew (Aramaic) which they had received from St. BARTHOLOMEW. He was still alive in 194 (Eusebius, *Chron.* 2210) and died probably in that decade, being succeeded by CLEMENT OF ALEXANDRIA.

In the *Hypotyposes,* Clement mentioned Pantaenus as his teacher and quoted "his opinions and traditions" (*Hist. Eccl.* 6.13). Eusebius thought that he also alluded to him in the *Stromateis* (1.11.2; particularly quoted *Hist. Eccl.* 5.11); where after mentioning certain unnamed teachers Clement concluded: "I found rest when I came upon the last (he was the first in power), after tracking him to where he was in Egypt. He the true Sicilian bee, gathering the flowers of the prophetic and apostolic meadow, engendered in the soul of his hearers an unfading element of knowledge."

Possibly Pantaenus came originally from Sicily. He seems to have promoted liberal studies, for ORIGEN (*Hist. Eccl.* 6.14) defended his own study of philosophy by reference to his example. He also wrote scriptural commentaries that were extant in JEROME's time (*De vir. ill.* 36), but nothing has survived. His importance lies in his contribution to the scholarly tradition of Alexandrian Christianity.

Feast: July 7 (Roman MARTYROLOGY), June 22 (Coptic Church).

Bibliography: J. QUASTEN, *Patrology* 2:4–5. J. MUNCK, *Untersuchungen über Klemens von Alexandria* (Stuttgart 1933) 151–204. G. BARDY, *Recherches de science religeuse* 27 (1937) 65–90, school. M. HORNSCHUH, *Zeitschrift Kirchengeschichte* 71 (1960) 1–5, 19–25. H. I. MARROU, ed. and tr., *À Diognète* (*Sources Chrétiennes* 33; 1951) 266–268.

[M. WHITTAKER]

PANTHEISM

Pantheism, from παν, all, and θεός, god, is a view of reality that tends to identify the world with God or God with the world. Pantheism is not so much a doctrine as it is the implication of views expressed in terms of the world, GOD, the ABSOLUTE, or infinity. It generally emphasizes the IMMANENCE of God in the world and deemphasizes, or ignores, His TRANSCENDENCE over the world. Since no one has as yet failed to make some distinction between transcendent and immanent aspects of infinite being, there never has been a complete and utter pantheism.

Scholastics tend to reduce pantheism to a form of ATHEISM on the ground that identification of God with the world implies the denial of Him as transcendent and really distinct from the world—a view fundamental to all forms of THEISM. However, the majority of those who are labeled pantheists manifest a strong religious commitment to God in one way or another; in fact, many of them are properly classified as religious thinkers. Again, views of reality termed pantheistic usually embody some limitation that effectively negates complete identification between God and the world. One such limitation now identifies itself as PANENTHEISM and claims many earlier thinkers as proponents. Beyond this, a more general element of restriction is found in MONISM, which distinguishes between absolute and FINITE BEING, but reduces one to an illusion or appearance of the other. Interpretations of such reductions, of course, differ widely.

Origins in the East. Throughout ancient Indian philosophy, with its direction toward self, themes occur that are clearly pantheistic. The general current of Vedic literature conveys the notion of a purely immanent deity (Purusa), frequently described as the whole of reality (*see* VEDAS). In the UPANISHADS, the notions of Brahman and Ātman are proposed as manifestations of the Absolute, Brahma being the objective evolutionary manifestation and Ātman the conscious or subjective manifestation. In idealistic interpretations of Upanishadic literature, the world is appearance or illusion (*see* MAYA RELIGION). In materialistic interpretations, the world is the reality; deity is impersonal, mythical, a manifestation of the world. Even the lofty Bhagavadgītā presents the Absolute as equally present in all things. Since JAINISM and BUDDHISM fully identify the Absolute with the world, their pantheism is at root atheistic.

In ancient Chinese thought, TAOISM, especially in doctrines of LAO-TZŬ, reflects a certain pantheism in that the Tao is said to have produced all things out of itself.

Greek and Roman Thought. Among the ancient Greeks, Xenophanes denounced the polytheism of his day but made God the totality of being. PARMENIDES extended this pantheism to an extreme monism expressed in terms of being and paralleling some of the ancient Hindu notions of the Absolute. This doctrine of Parmenides was developed by Melissus to include the notion of infinity. For these monists, changing reality was an illusion, much as it was for the idealistic interpreters of the Upanishads. On the other hand, HERACLITUS offered a monism in which permanence was the illusion and change the only reality. He called his primal fire Zeus, Logos, or Deity, and developed a doctrine similar to the almost contemporary Buddhist theory of "momentariness" (Kṣaṇabhangavāda). [*See* GREEK PHILOSOPHY (RELIGIOUS ASPECTS).] Both Platonism and NEOPLATONISM evidence tendencies toward pantheism that derive from foundations in Plato's thought. The relation between the doctrine of the One and that of Ideas suggests a similarity to the Hindu doctrine of Maya, where the only reality is God and everything else is merely an appearance. Centuries later, PLOTINUS reinforced this Platonic implication of pantheism with his own doctrine of EMANATIONISM, which gave inspiration to many later pantheists.

The STOICISM of Greece and Rome tried to overcome polytheism but seems have fallen short of theism and to have settled for pantheism. The Stoics maintained that the material alone was real, yet they looked upon God as the author of the world. For most of them God was the WORLD soul, and they described Him as fire, ether, air, mind, or combinations of these; in this sense the Stoic God was part of this world.

Non-Christian Medievals. Among the Hindus of the Middle Ages, Shaṅkara (788–820) tried to maintain the transcendence as well as the immanence of God, but his doctrines imply a limited variety of pantheism (panentheism) that accepts the Upanishadic notion of God as the lower Brahma (Īshvara) and immanent in the world. In the 12th century, Ramanuja also perceived the inadequacy of pure pantheism, identified Brahma as God and individual, but then regarded God as qualified by matter with souls constituting His body. A limiting factor in Ramanuja's thought is his notion that identity includes difference and unity includes diversity, much as this was later proposed by Hegel.

The Islamic philosopher ALFARABI, under the influence of the Neoplatonic *Theologia Aristotelis* and *LIBER DE CAUSIS,* combined the Aristotelian spheres with emanationism to maintain the existence of a supreme agent intellect from which all substantial forms were derived. No Arabian philosopher went further than Alfarabi, and most of them, including AVICENNA and AVERROËS, were saved from the pantheistic implications of their views by their concern for religious truth and the transcendence of God. (*See* ARABIAN PHILOSOPHY.)

While relatively little pantheism is found in Jewish thinkers of the time, one man stands out for his leanings in this direction, viz, AVICEBRON (ibn-Gabirol). He seems to have identified the matter of this world with God and to have reduced the doctrine of CREATION to a theory of emanation. Yet his attempt to unite the world and God in terms of Divine Wisdom or the Divine Word led many European scholars to regard him as a Christian. Avicebron exerted a strong influence also on the cabalists, a 13th-century group of mystics (*see* CABALA).

Christian Thinkers. Four distinct tendencies are apparent among the Christians of the Middle Ages. First there is that of the controversial JOHN SCOTUS ERIUGENA, the 9th-century Neoplatonist. In his *Division of Nature,* he made what seems to be a real distinction between God as the Creator and God as the end of all things—a distinction similar to Whitehead's antecedent and consequent God. For Eriugena, creation was a "theophany," a mani-

festation of God. Although this strongly resembles the Hindu doctrine of Maya, Eriugena clearly accepted the reality of both God and the world, and his pantheism (a matter of prolonged controversy) may be more a consequence of inadequate language than an attempt to identify the world with God.

Then, at the beginning of the 13th century, AMALRIC OF BÈNE made God the formal principle in all things by his notion that the Holy Spirit was the soul of the world, while DAVID OF DINANT presented a monistic and materialistic view of the world by identifying primary matter, mind, and God in the ancient Hindu tradition.

Thirdly, the thought of Meister ECKHART shows the influence of Neoplatonism on the highest levels of religious thought. For Eckhart, God transcends all concepts, even that of being, so that strictly He cannot be called a being. Yet Eckhart held that being flows eternally from God, and this led him to identify being with the Holy Spirit. Thus he tended to confuse ideas in the mind of God with the world itself, much as did Erigena.

Finally NICHOLAS OF CUSA, the leading Platonist of his day and a staunch believer in the orthodoxy of both Erigena and Eckhart, held that the world is explication of what is implication in God; God is infinitely one so that, in Him, all opposites are reconciled or overcome. Although Nicholas does mark God off from the world, his expressions have implications similiar to the views of the ancient Hindus on the Absolute and of Plotinus on the One.

Renaissance and Reformation. Giordano BRUNO anticipated Spinoza in his monistic concept of substance: God is substantial nature. For him, God (*natura naturans*) is transcendent and beyond our knowledge; yet the world (*natura naturata*) is that into which the Infinite divides itself and is likewise infinite. Consequently there is a recurrent identification of God, as Nature, with the world, with God being the immanent principle as well as external cause of the universe.

In the 17th century, the Protestant mystic Jakob BÖHME exerted wide influence, especially on later German and Russian MYSTICISM. While his doctrine of external dualism suggests panentheism more than pure pantheism, Böhme viewed God as an evolutionary figure, sometimes nothing more than a divinity in man or his spiritual force.

Later in the same century, SPINOZA formulated his pantheism. His monistic approach to the notion of substance made the world attributes or modes of God. While he did use the term "creation", he also spoke of *natura naturans* and *natura naturata* in the same way as Bruno, with the same suggestion of emanationism. Thus, while

Spinoza looked upon God as the cause of the world, immanent cause and nature are for him one in essence and identical with God.

It was during the 18th-century debate over religion that Toland actually introduced the terms "pantheism" and "pantheist". Toland's final view seems to have reduced God to the material universe and to have made Him little more than a mechanistic law of nature.

Transcendentalism and Idealism. Although KANT was not a pantheist, his idealistic IMMANENTISM did occasion in many of his followers a tendency toward pantheism. An interesting aspect of this development of transcendental IDEALISM was the great outpouring of ideas about God in the end of the 18th and beginning of the 19th centuries (*see* KANTIANISM; NEO-KANTIANISM).

Within the 19th century, SCHOPENHAUER distinctively and consciously took direction from Indian thinkers, principally from Buddhism. Although his philosophy tends toward atheistic Buddhism, Schopenhauer makes the world and man momentary reflections of a transcendent Will. His views of this absolute Will imply something more personal than mere force, even though he considered his pantheism as an atheism. Later FECHNER held that God is the totality of things as the infinite consciousness of the universe and a kind of world soul.

The transcendental EGOISM of FICHTE reduced God to moral order and an expression of the self. SCHELLING developed a bipolar approach like that used later by Whitehead and identified both the real and the ideal in the Absolute in a manner reflecting Böhme's influence and the Upanishadic approach. While Hegelian monism—qualified by dialectical logic—seems more panentheistic than pantheistic, HEGEL regarded the Absolute as totally immanent to, and constantly developing in, human consciousness. Later FEUERBACH reduced the Absolute to a mere abstraction in his atheistic philosophy. The Russian mystic SOLOV'EV reflected the influence of Spinoza, Schopenhauer, and Buddhism; he proposed a spiritualistic personalism that drifted toward pantheism through its emphasis on the unity of all beings with the Divinity and its relatively uncritical notion of Godmanhood.

Recent Directions. Among significant contemporary thinkers, Spencer viewed God as some kind of physical force and the ground of evolution. Haeckel, while attempting to find some middle position between making God either extrinsic or intrinsic to the world, identified God with nature. For E. von HARTMANN, the Absolute was the Unconscious but also the principle of vitality in all things. H. Höffding offered a critical monism in which reality was one; yet for him the One is immanent in the many, although it transcends the many. Although PEIRCE

admits a doctrine of creation, he seems to have looked upon God as a primordial element of the universe, an evolutionary principle within the world. William JAMES described his position as a kind of pantheism, not absolute and monistic, but rather a "finite pluralism" that provided for God's being in the world but not as the only existing substance. For F. H. BRADLEY, the Absolute was the reality of things in their psychical existence. Josiah ROYCE considered God the absolute experience of which our minds were fragments; this absolute was infinite and all comprehensive.

Although BERGSON denied any suggestions of pantheism in his ideas, his doctrine of creative evolution is open to such implications. Samuel ALEXANDER identifies Deity as a quality of the world and goes on to consider the world as God's body and Deity as God's mind in much the same way as Upanishadic Hinduism. Because WHITEHEAD deliberately limited his pantheism through the instrumentality of Hegelian dialectics, he is more properly classified as a panentheist. BRIGHTMAN tried to limit his own tendency toward pantheism by negating absolute unity in God and by having God achieve his goals gradually. Weiss presents God as one of his modes of being; yet, in offering four coordinate and irreducible modes of being, he insists that each mode enters as part of the others.

Catholic Doctrine. Catholic teaching has always opposed the basic notions of pantheism. A personalistic religion, Catholicism upholds metaphysical reality of the individual, the spirituality but finitude of the human SOUL, and personal fulfillment through immortal union with God as an infinite and distinct personal being. All such ideas are suppressed or negated by pantheism.

From the Middle Ages to the present, the Church has concerned itself with pantheistic implications in the writings of individual thinkers such as Erigena, Eckhart, and Bruno. Yet a formal condemnation of pantheism as such was not made until Pius IX condemned pantheism by a decree of the Holy Office (1861), in his allocation *Maxima quidem* (1862), and in his "Syllabus of Errors" (1864) [H. Denzinger, *Enchiridion symolorum,* ed. A. Schönmetzer (32d ed. Freiburg 1963) 2843, 2845, 2846, 2901]. Vatican Council I condemned it formally also (*ibid.* 3023–25). Under LEO XIII, the Holy Office again condemned such ideas as those implied in the works of ROSMINI-SERBATI (*ibid.* 3206, 3209, 3212–15). PIUS X, in his encyclical *Pascendi,* further warned against the implications of pantheism (*ibid.* 3477, 3486).

The fact that pantheistic leanings are found primarily among Catholic thinkers who are more mystical than doctrinal, and whose religious sincerity can hardly be questioned, may serve to explain why other views with pantheistic overtones have never been formally condemned.

Critical Evaluation. In criticizing pantheism, one should first acknowledge the religious fervor manifested in the works of most pantheists, their dislike of distinctions and abstract analysis, and a basic difficulty in their subject matter, viz, that it is impossible for finite minds to comprehend the infinity of God.

As a general criticism, pantheism negates or limits the excellence of God to the point where He does not seem to be a special and distinct being. The confusing element is that all pantheists use special terms, usually capitalized, such as God, the Absolute, the One, or the Infinite, and seemingly intend to denote a special being or, at least, a special mode of being that transcends other beings. Nevertheless, atheistic implications are almost always present, if only because the thinkers involved, in their religious enthusiasm, do not concern themselves with the theoretical implications of their statements.

Pantheists further fail to distinguish between cause and effect. They often speak of God as the cause of the world, but not as the efficient, extrinsic cause; rather they tend to reduce God to some kind of a material source of the universe. Such thinkers frequently substitute a doctrine of emanationism for creation, ignoring the notion of EFFICIENT causality—itself basic to our understanding of the world.

Ignoring fundamental metaphysical distinctions, pantheists approach or discuss reality in a univocal, rather than an analogical, manner that does not take into account difference as well as sameness (*see* ANALOGY). In this respect, pantheism is too limited in its treatment of ultimate values. This limitation of viewpoint is reflected in the monism that is either explicit or implicit in pantheism. Where DUALISM seems to be accepted, one aspect is actually reduced to the other, considered as a mere manifestation of the other, or treated as an illusion.

Another confusion arises from the notion of transcendence, reduced by some pantheists to the potentiality of the world or of man. This view seems to contradict itself by establishing transcendence, which stands for perfection, as a mere extension of this world or finite beings in this world: both notions involve imperfection. Other pantheists look upon transcendence as the negation of all finite being to the degree that all perfections of finite being, such as PERSONALITY, immortality, and FREEDOM, become ultimately meaningless. Such reductions of transcendence to either superimmanence or negation cannot be accepted as reasonable.

Lastly, pantheism does not seem to grant the infinite positive value except as a mere quantitative inclusion of all things. It makes no distinction between actual infinity, which must be looked upon as pure perfection, and potential infinity, which involves incompleteness or imperfection. Reason demands that a superlative being—and the Infinite is presented by pantheists as superlative—be judged as actually and absolutely infinite.

Bibliography: C. N. BITTLE, *God and His Creatures* (Milwaukee 1953). F. J. THONNARD, *A Short History of Philosophy,* tr. E. A. MAZIARZ (rev. and correc. New York 1955). J. F. ANDERSON, *The Bond of Being* (St. Louis 1949). J. D. COLLINS, *God in Modern Philosophy* (Chicago 1959). C. SHARMA, *A Critical Survey of Indian Philosophy* (London 1960). E. H. GILSON, *Being and Some Philosophers* (Toronto 1949). N. A. BERDÎAEV, *The Russian Idea;* tr. R. M. FRENCH (New York 1948; repr. pa. Boston 1962). C. HARTSHORNE and W. L. REESE, eds. *Philosophers Speak of God* (Chicago 1953). F. CLARK, ''Pantheism and Analogy,'' *The Irish Theological Quarterly* 20 (1953) 24–38. J. BAYART, ''Hindu Pantheism,'' *Clergy Monthly Supplement* 3 (1956) 102–108. E. A. PACE, *The Catholic Encyclopedia,* ed. C. G. HERBERMANN, 16 v. (New York 1907–14; suppl. 1922) 11:447–450. F. A. SCHALCK, *Dictionnaire de théologie catholique,* ed. A. VACANT, 15 v. (Paris 1903–50) 11.2:1855–74.

[E. R. NAUGHTON]

PANVINIO, ONOFRIO

Antiquarian and historian; b. Verona, February 24, 1530; d. Palermo, April 7, 1568. Pavinio entered the Augustinian Order in his native city in 1541. In 1547 he was sent to Naples for studies, and in 1549, to Rome. While his first research was concerned with Roman antiquity, he also began to study church history. At the request of the Augustinian prior general, SERIPANDO, he compiled a chronicle of the order's history, published anonymously with the Augustinian *Constitutions* (Rome 1551). From 1554 until his death he was employed in the service of Cardinal Alessandro Farnese.

His *Romani Pontifices et Cardinales* (Venice 1557) aligned the sequence of the popes and cardinals. Among his works on Roman themes, the *Fastorum Libri V* (Venice 1558), which set in order the Roman consuls and emperors, was the most significant. He revised and updated Platina's *Lives of the Popes* (Venice and Cologne 1562; and Venice 1568). This work, accompanied by his ecclesiastical chronicle, was reissued in the original Latin and in translation up to the 18th century. A book of portraits of 27 popes from Urban VI to Pius V (Rome 1568) set the pattern for similar works. Major works, found only in manuscript, include a history of papal elections in ten volumes and the lives of the popes and cardinals, richly illustrated with portraits, coats-of-arms, and seals. At his premature death he left many incomplete works, including a history of the Church, intended to refute the CENTURIATORS OF MAGDEBURG, and a projected work on Roman antiquities in 100 volumes. His defense of the primacy of the papacy (Verona 1589) and other works have been edited posthumously up to recent times.

With the authorization of Pius IV, Panvinio visited sites throughout Italy to collect documents, inscriptions, and illustrations. Among his correspondents he counted leading scholars of the day: Antonio Agustín, Carlo Sigonio, Ottavio Pantagatho, Piero Vettori, and Vincenzio Borghini. Angelo Massarelli, secretary of the Council of Trent, supplied him with material derived from the papal archives. Although some writings betray hasty composition and lack of mature judgment, they preserve important sources. His descriptions of Roman churches remain valuable for art historians. His indefatigable labors in unearthing and organizing vast amounts of historical material have merited the admiration of later scholars, and Paul Fridolin Kehr notes that the history of papal diplomatics begins with Panvinio and Massarelli.

Bibliography: *Biographisch-Bibliographisches Kirchenlexikon,* 7: 1486–1489. K. A. GERSBACH, "Onofrio Panvinio's *De comitiis imperatoriis* and Its Successive Revisions: Biographical Background and Manuscripts," *Analecta Augustiniana* 53 (1990): 410–452; "Onofrio Panvinio and Cybo Family Pride in His Treatment of Innocent VIII and in the *XXVII Pontificum Maximorum Elogia et Imagines,*" *Analecta Augustiniana* 54 (1991): 117–141; "Onofrio Panvinio, OSA, and His Florentine Correspondents Vincenzio Borghini, OSB, Pietro Vettori, Francesco de' Medici," *Analecta Agustiniana* 60 (1997): 207–280. J.-L. FERRARY, *Onofrio Panvinio et les Antiquités Romaines* (Rome 1996). D. A. PERINI, *Onofrio Panvinio e le sue opere* (Rome, 1899); *Bibliographia Augustiniana,* 4 vols. (Florence 1929–1938) 3:53–65.

[K. A. GERSBACH]

PANZANI, GREGORIO

Secret papal agent in England (1634–36), Bishop of Mileto; b. date unknown; d. Mileto, Italy, 1662. When Henrietta Maria married Charles I in 1625, her godfather, previously nuncio in Paris, had become Pope Urban VIII. Urban sent a personal emissary to Henrietta, primarily to assess the papist situation in England. For this delicate mission, the pope's nephew and secretary of state Francesco Barberini, who was also Cardinal Protector of England, chose Panzani, a former Oratorian. Panzani's instructions were to try to settle sharp differences among the English Catholics, particularly between the secular and regular clergy (most of all, the Jesuits) on the need or expediency of having a bishop and on the lawfulness of taking the oath of allegiance to the king. Panzani was to look for signs, at court and among the Anglican clergy, of good will towards Rome. With this in mind he formed a close friendship with Sir Francis Windebank, secretary of state and a Crypto-Catholic enthusiastic for reunion. Both worked to establish an official exchange of agents

between pope and queen. The latter's first two candidates, Sir Robert Douglas and Sir Arthur Brett, both Catholics and approved by King Charles, died before taking up their appointments. Eventually, Sir William Hamilton, a distant relative of the king, was sent to Rome (June 1636). A month later George Con, a Scot long resident in Rome, arrived in London as Pope Urban's agent to the queen. He was well received by Charles I and at once became popular in court and clerical circles. Panzani, who remained with him for six months, had meanwhile been sending fortnightly dispatches to Cardinal Barberini, reporting every sign of friendliness: the general esteem in which Pope Urban was held, particularly by the king; sermons preached by Anglican clergy attacking the Puritans or deploring the break with the Holy See; reunion talks with the Bishop of Chichester, who expressed his readiness to acknowledge the pope as Vicar of Christ; and suggestions for discussions in France between "moderate" Catholics and Anglicans. Panzani also sent Barberini a dossier on the two archbishops and 25 bishops of the Church of England, classifying the theological and personal attitude of each. Con's dispatches after Panzani's departure show that the Church of England would never reunite with the Holy See except on a basis of parity of rights, which Con at once made clear could never be. On his return to Rome, early in 1637, Panzani was made a canon of San Lorenzo in Damaso and a court judge. In August 1640, he became bishop of Mileto, where he remained until his death in 1662.

Bibliography: G. PANZANI, *Memoirs,* tr. J. BERINGTON (Birmingham, Eng. 1793). G. ALBION, *Charles I and the Court of Rome* (London 1935).

[G. ALBION]

PAPACY

This article treats of the development of the papacy (*papatus*) and the office of pope in five historical divisions: (1) the early period, to 590, (2) the medieval period, (3) the Renaissance and early modern period, (4) the modern period (1789–1958), and (5) the contemporary period (1958–2001).

1. Early Period.

At the earliest stage of the papacy's development, two elements will be discussed: its Biblical foundations and its juristic complexion.

Biblical Foundations. The title deed of the papacy as an institution in its claim to universality in the spiritual sphere of government is found in two crucial passages of the New Testament. The one is the text of St. Matthew

Courtyard within the Pope's Palace (Palais des Papes), which was used by French popes during the Great Schism, Avignon, France. (©Angelo Hornak/CORBIS)

(Mt 16.18–19), which traditional exegesis understands to have been a promise made by Christ to St. Peter; the other is the fulfillment of the promise contained in Christ's words to Peter: "Feed my sheep" (Jn 21.17). Both passages gave rise to the claim of two kinds of primacy (*primatus*) in the Roman Church: a magisterial and a jurisdictional primacy; the former is concerned with the final definition of doctrine and teaching; the latter, with government in the sense of a final decision. This article deals mainly with the jurisdictional aspect of the Roman Church, for it is in this function that the popes themselves saw the true nature and character of the papacy, and from the outset they considered that it was part of their duty to direct the path of organized Christianity. The essential point, which was invariably stressed by the papacy, was that in the Biblical passages, notably in the Matthean verses, Christ founded a new society, namely, the Church, and provided a government for the Church by conferring on Peter a fullness of power. It was a unique,

creative act of Christ Himself. Further, since the Church was never, from the papal point of view, a merely spiritual or sacramental body, but an organized, visible, juristic, and corporate society that needed constant guidance for the realization of its aims, the conferment of governmental powers on Peter implicitly and necessarily contained the provision for a succession into these powers, specifically bestowed as they were on the Prince of the Apostles. In the consideration, therefore, of the governmental work of the papacy, the character of the body over which government was to be exercised and the divine establishment of that government must always be given due attention.

Juristic Complexion. That in the primitive Christian period the Roman Church was credited with an authority superior to that of any other patriarchal see, can be gathered from the letter written by Pope CLEMENT I (*c.* 92) to the Corinthians in which he made important statements

The large statue of St. Peter above a crowd of 350,000 people who came to receive the papal benediction of Easter Sunday. Photo by Massimo Ascani. (©Bettmann/CORBIS)

Illuminated manuscript from an Italian church depicting a papal scene. (©David Lees/CORBIS)

concerning the nature of the Church and laid down principles that in embryonic form contained maxims of government. That in view of its location, the Roman Church was in actual fact credited with preeminence over other sees is a matter of history. Perhaps the most telling witness to this preeminence is Irenaeus (*c.* 180), who clearly stated that the Roman Church possessed *potentior principalitas* and that special importance attaches to the apostolicity of that Church. Numerous testimonies could be cited to prove the factual preeminence of the Roman Church. It is similarly a matter of history that in the early centuries of the Christian era there was no doctrinal elaboration of the jurisdictional position of the Roman Church. Its function as the supreme jurisdictional authority, though operative, did not become the subject of reflective thought before the end of the 4th century; at least there is no evidence to suggest the contrary. Actual proof of the function of the Roman Church as the institution charged with making Christian doctrine part of the social fabric is contained in the first extant decretal letter of a pope—that of Siricius, dispatched in 385 to Spain—which is an important legal document. It may be said that the period between Siricius and LEO I (440–461) was the period of gestation in the conceptual development of the Roman primacy. The juristic complexion of the papacy as an institution of government similarly finds a ready explana-

tion in the location of the Roman Church. The form in which government was exercised was Roman, i.e., the Roman law and constitution served as models on which to formulate governmental principles and to transact governmental affairs. The matter was Biblical, i.e., the substance of the papal government principles and measures was derived from the Bible. It is therefore noteworthy that at exactly the time when Jerome took on the enormous task of rendering the Hebrew text of the Bible into Latin, the Roman Church had begun the process of entering fully into the life of contemporary society. Moreover, it was the legislation of THEODOSIUS the Great that made Christianity the official religion of the Roman Empire. There was a steady accumulation of papal decrees in the early fifth century; there was also a rapid development of concept and actions that, under Leo I, gave shape to a system culminating in the properly juristic function of the pope as successor of Peter. Nor should one underestimate in this historical process the factual, primatial position of the Roman Church, endorsed by the Roman synod of 380, which clearly stated the "double apostolicity" of this Church, i.e., the one Church that had been founded by the two Apostles, Peter and Paul. The Councils of Ephesus and Chalcedon confirmed this development. Leo I's supreme mastery of Roman law enabled him to construct the thesis of Peter's function, and therefore that of the pope, in so satisfactory a way that it stood the test of time. The Roman Church had by right the primacy (*principatus*) because, according to Leo, the head of this Church was, though personally unworthy, the heir of St. Peter (*indignus haeres beati Petri*). In these two terms, coined by Leo, the whole papal program is epitomized. It was the merit of Peter, the Prince of the Apostles, to have recognized Christ at Caesarea Philippi, and because of this recognition Christ had distinguished him by conferring plenary powers on him. This was a special merit that belonged to Peter, personally, which meant that it could not be transmitted or conveyed to anyone else. But the functions, i.e., the powers given by Christ, were purely objective, and could be transmitted.

To explain this theme Leo utilized the Roman law of inheritance according to which the heir inherits all the deceased person's assets and liabilities, though not his personal qualifications, distinctions, and merits. The powers given by Christ to Peter constituted an office that was indeed capable of being inherited. Hence, although the pope was heir to the full Petrine powers—the office of Peter as builder of the Church—he was unworthy as a person to wield the powers contained in that office. Leo's doctrine therefore clearly distinguished between the person of the pope and the office itself—a distinction with far-reaching consequences. What mattered for purposes of government was the office, and not the personal character of the individual pope. He may personally have been a saint, a mediocrity, or even a scoundrel; all this was of no interest, as many popes pointed out. The essential point was that the pope succeeded into the powers of Peter, and the totality of powers constituted, according to Leo, a fullness of power—*plenitudo potestatis*. Consequently, there was, as far as the scope and extent of powers went, identity between Peter and the pope. This identity placed a great burden of responsibility upon the pope, because his verdicts, judgments, and pronouncements took effect in this world as well as in the next; hence the frequently stated *gravissimum pondus* of responsibility upon papal shoulders. The so-called automatism of papal plenitude of power, as conceived by Leo, was to be a hallmark of papal thought throughout the Middle Ages. There was no tribunal and no higher court that could subject papal rulings to a revision; nor did an appeal lie from a papal decision to any other authority or court. This explains the later emergence of the view that the decrees of general COUNCILS acquire their validity through papal sanction, either in the convocation of the council or in posterior approval. It explains also why in the Middle Ages an appeal from the papacy's judgment to a general council was branded as a sign of heresy. In short, the pope was the point of intersection between heaven and earth. There is no intermediary between pope and Peter: no pope *qua* pope succeeds his predecessor, but succeeds Peter directly, again a principle of the papacy that has stood the test of time.

The Leonine thesis brings into clear relief the properly conceived monarchic institution of the papacy according to which the sum total of powers is in the hands of the pope. Therefore, one can speak of a vertical or descending concept of government, because whatever power is found in the Church, in the congregation of the faithful, is conceptually derived from the pope: hence the early pictorial representation of the Roman Church as the source of a river. This theme has particular relevance for episcopal power, which only later was formally held to have been dependent on the pope for its exercise of jurisdiction. In other words, the bishop was called upon to participate in the papal solicitude for all Christians, but not in the papal plenitude of power. The *principatus Romanae ecclesiae* was the usual designation for this monarchic conception. The exercise of this papal *principatus* had, however, exclusive reference to government, i.e., to jurisdiction, the final verdict arrived at by the law and exhibiting effects solely by means of the law. Correctly understood, the pope as monarchic governor (*gubernator*), and in his function as pope, stands outside and above the Church that was entrusted to him, and this idea was expressed by the maxim *papa a nemine judicatur*. Although this statement was made at the beginning

A portion of "The Line of Popes," a series of woodcut figures by Anton Koberger, appearing on the borders of the pages of "World Chronicle" by Hartmann Schedel, 1493, printed in Nuremberg, Germany.

of the sixth century in a spurious document, the idea itself was considerably older, as is proved by a similar statement of Pope ZOSIMUS. In modern terminology this concept is called absolute sovereignty (*superioritas*), a notion that can likewise be found in the medieval concept of kingship. Further, because the pope in his official capacity is identical with Peter, the principle of the infallibility of certain papal pronouncements finds its ready explanation. As heir to Petrine powers, a pope cannot pronounce erroneously in matters of faith and morals. Therefore, no pope could or did say that any of his predecessors had erred in doctrine, because the consequence would have been that Peter himself had been the victim of error. A further consequence of the fundamental Leonine position was that the pope claimed, by virtue of his function, to be endowed with an *auctoritas sacrata*, i.e., a supreme and final authority, in which concept a number of charismatic qualities are discernible. The secular power, on the other hand, possessed a regal power (*potestas regalis*). As a result of the spread of Christianity amongst the barbarian nations, the papacy thus became the primary instrument in propagating the idea that civilized government could be conducted solely by means of law. In other words, the papacy, itself the heir of the ancient Roman principle of the superiority of law, utilized this idea in the interests of the whole Christian community while pursuing its evangelical mission. In this lies one of the great historic achievements of the papacy.

In order to understand the full import of the terms *auctoritas* and *potestas*, adapted to ecclesiastical usage by Leo I, then by GELASIUS I, one should realize that the second half of the fifth century witnessed an acceleration of the monarchic program by the imperial government at CONSTANTINOPLE. At the same time the papacy, as a result of Leo's clear exposition of the Petrine function of the pope, acquired the means, i.e., the legal principles with which to combat the ever-increasing claims of the imperial government. The papacy was now faced with the necessity of challenging the validity and legality of imperial measures that, in its opinion, fell outside the scope of imperial functions. In so doing, the papacy was forced to declare itself on certain vital governmental points; and throughout its long and checkered history in the Middle Ages it never deviated from them. The imperial government had gone so far as to decree the faith and doctrine of Christians and to intervene drastically in the ecclesiastical organism by appointing and dismissing prelates. Armed with the primatial doctrine of Leo, the papacy issued its serious challenge to the imperial government and raised the question whether the emperor was suitably qualified to direct the body under his control in the manner in which he did, and by what authority he did so. Although the emperors acted in the belief that it was their duty as divinely appointed rulers to direct the Empire in all its vital aspects, the papacy maintained that the direction of the body of Christians, i.e., the Church, must be in the hands of those who were specially qualified to carry out this function. The definition of dogma, fixing the purpose and aim of Christian life, and the organization of the Church were the right and duty of the papacy, and not of the imperial government. The papal position, arrived at in the late fifth century and adhered to throughout subsequent centuries, was that the overall direction, the final authority in matters that affected the vital interests and the structural fabric of the Church—in short the *auctoritas sacrata*—belonged by virtue of his function solely to the pope. He was instituted as the ''builder of the Church'' and had to lead the faithful to their end, and the means to this was the law. The emperor, though clearly also instituted by God, had different functions in Christian society, and as a Christian actually belonged to the body entrusted by Christ to Peter's successor. He had a *potestas regalis*, i.e., power to act within the framework of his divine trust, or as Gelasius I said, the emperor's duty was to learn (*discere*), not to teach (*docere*), in the religious sphere. What the papacy here laid down was nothing less than the principle of division of labor and of respective spheres of power. This Leonine-Gelasian program received precision in the subsequent development, notably through ISIDORE OF SEVILLE and above all through GREGORY VII, according to whom the *potestas regalis* existed to supplement the word of the *sacerdotium* by regal power so as to eradicate evil. But since evil (sin) was prompted by the devil, God Himself had instituted secular government for the purpose of exterminating evil. It is thus clear that from the fifth century onward the papacy adhered to a teleologically conceived system of government.

The firm stand taken by FELIX III and Gelasius I in the matter of the imperially imposed HENOTICON, dealing with a doctrinal matter, led to the first serious schism between East and West (*see* ACACIAN SCHISM), lasting some 30 years. A settlement was reached between the Emperor JUSTIN I and Pope HORMISDAS in 519.

Subsequent development was to show that the theory of government in Constantinople culminated in the concept of the emperor as priest and king, the former admittedly only in an external sense, yet in a manner that seriously infringed the exercise of papal primatial rights. This was especially true during the reign of JUSTINIAN I, which brought so-called CAESAROPAPISM to its apogee. The position of the papacy was difficult: the city of Rome and the whole of Italy were parts of the Empire and the popes themselves civil subjects of the emperor. Though fundamentally Constantinople recognized the primacy of the pope, the imperial government left no doubt about the final direction of the Christian body politic. The dilemma was most serious: if the popes remonstrated against the regal-sacerdotal decrees of the imperial government and insisted upon the exercise of Roman primacy, they ran the risk of committing the *crimen laesae majestatis* against the emperor. If they acquiesced, they became unfaithful to their own vocation and duty. (In this connection *see* VIGILIUS, POPE.) It is at this juncture in the late sixth century that the truly historic significance of GREGORY I emerges.

2. Medieval Period

The medieval papacy logically built on the premises inherited from its immediate past.

Gregory I to Gregory VII. Gregory I had been papal representative (*apocrisiarius*) to the imperial court for a number of years before his election to the papacy. While at Constantinople he reached the conclusion that the regal-sacerdotal idea of government was so firmly entrenched there that, however regrettable this state of affairs, it would be futile and dangerous to press the Roman primatial claim against the East. As long as the popes were subjects of the Empire, they were exposed to serious charges if they insisted upon the exercise of their primatial rights because in their civil capacity they were under the emperor. But if they were to act as popes in regions where the imperial writ did not run, they could press the primatial claim to its fullest extent. In this realization lies Gregory I's historic importance: he never acquiesced in or approved of the imperial theory, but accepted reality and, with the history of the sixth century before his eyes, logically concluded that the future held no promise for the papacy in the East. Gregory I opened up the West to the papacy by his missions to Gaul and England. In these areas, from the outset, papal jurisdiction was exercised without reference to Constantinople. It was, in actual fact, from the farthest corner of medieval Europe, the British Isles, that the historic conversion of the Germans took place. Anglo-Saxon missionaries not only established close relations between England and the papacy, but they also were instrumental in forging the strong links between the FRANKS and the papacy, links that were to give medieval Europe its specific character. It cannot be said that the papacy in the seventh century inherited Gregory's vision and appreciation of the historical situation, since it was difficult for the popes in this century to break with established traditions. Of these none was stronger than the ubiquity of *Romanitas:* Rome was Roman, the papacy was Roman, and the Empire was Roman. And yet the imperial government advanced more and more on the road that had so alarmed the papacy. The period was indeed a heroic age of the papacy, which suffered for its principles in the face of imperial encroachment upon religious and ecclesiastical policy. When after the turn of the century the imperial government promoted ICONOCLASM by legislation, GREGORY II openly challenged Constantinople. Indeed, if the papacy wished to live up to its vocation, two alternatives were open. The pope would have to remove himself physically from Rome and reside among ''the barbarians,'' or the city of Rome with its surrounding districts would have to be withdrawn from imperial control. The first alternative was certainly in the mind of Gregory II when he issued in 729 his challenge to the Emperor LEO III. But it was abandoned for excellent reasons. As later events were to show, the papacy, deprived of its historic and natural surroundings, would become the pawn of contending territorial factions. There remained the other alternative that was adopted by STEPHEN II (III). When Rome was threatened by the Lombards, he appealed to PEPIN, King of the Franks. The background of this crucial step was the sanction given by Pope ZACHARY to the deposition of the last Merovingian king, Childeric III. The papal sanction was based on the principle that only he should be effective king who was useful—and about the uselessness of Childeric there was no doubt. Later GREGORY VII was to utilize this principle fully. Stephen's appeal culminated in his journey to Ponthion in Gaul (Epiphany 754) where he made clear to Pepin that the Lombards had conquered and stolen territory that by right belonged to St. Peter and hence to the pope. The document that was to support this papal claim of ownership was the DONATION OF CONSTANTINE. Although the ostensible reason for this appeal was the restitution of stolen property, a real motive was the establishment of a territorial entity in central Italy, independent of Constantinople. In two campaigns (754 and 756) Pepin drove the LOMBARDS out and made over the territories to the pope. The document was deposited at the Confession of St. Peter and established the STATES OF THE CHURCH (*Patrimonium beati Petri*), which were to last until 1870. A most powerful link was forged between the new and virile Frankish dynasty and the papacy, a link that was to endure through the Middle Ages and beyond. The emergence of the papacy as an independent entity gave rise to a number of institutional changes: the regulation of papal elections (769), confining this function to the Roman clergy; notice of the elections was no longer to be sent to Constantinople, but to the Frankish court; papal coins were now struck; and the popes abandoned the dating of their documents according to imperial years.

The papacy had won freedom of action and was, so to speak, master in its house. The last chapter in the direct relations between Constantinople and the papacy in the eighth century was the coronation of Pepin's son, CHARLEMAGNE, upon whom Pope LEO III conferred the imperial crown, making him thereby emperor of the Romans.

This coronation had far-reaching results. It set a precedent for the papacy insofar as no pope had ever crowned an emperor in Rome; the title deed for the pope's action was at least implied in the Donation of Constantine. And as there could not be two emperors of the Romans, the Eastern emperor was degraded to a mere "king of the Greeks" whose orthodoxy was in any case rather suspect; the Roman imperial crown was where the pope wished it to be. Although Charlemagne himself had reservations regarding this papal notion, it subsequently came to be accepted in the West, though never in the East. What is remarkable and what explains the eventual victory of the papacy is the dynamic initiative that the papacy in the earlier Middle Ages had firmly kept in its hands. Throughout the ninth century small but significant elements were added, e.g., the combination of coronation and anointing in one ceremony when STEPHEN IV crowned Louis I emperor of the Romans at Reims in 816; and the subsequent coronation in 823, which was performed in St. Peter's basilica, henceforth the rightful place for imperial coronations, and at which for the first time a sword was conferred on the emperor as part of the coronation ceremonial. It was in the ninth century that the pope appeared as the constituent organ of Roman emperorship, a function that enormously added to the prestige of the papacy. Other factors not of its own making, but nevertheless potently assisting the papacy in its growth, were the troubles of succession during Louis I's reign, the FALSE DECRETALS, the brisk conciliar activity in the Frankish domains, and the general unrest in the Frankish empire—all of which likewise served to make the papacy the rallying point of Christian civilization in the ninth century. The papacy was in a position to state or to restate and define its fundamental principles in numerous letters and decrees, notably those of NICHOLAS I and JOHN VIII. The papacy's relations with the East, especially as a result of PHOTIUS' attitude, worsened considerably when Nicholas I had opportunity to elaborate the primatial function of the papacy vis-à-vis the recalcitrant Eastern patriarch. But precisely because the papacy had established closest links with the Frankish dynasty, the collapse of that power had repercussions on the papal institution itself. The history of the papacy in the tenth century proves that it was still partly in the hands of the Roman nobility and partly in the hands of the newly risen Saxon dynasty in Germany. OTTO I, though humbly supplicating for the imperial crown, treated the Roman Church as if it were a German PROPRIETARY CHURCH. The essence of this system was lay patronage exercised to a degree that violated basic principles of Church government, above all, those relating to the conferment of the ecclesiastical office itself. Otto I applied this even to the papacy itself in his so-called *Ottonianum* (963) and imposed severe restrictions on the freedom of the papal electors, with equal severity circumscribing the governmental activity of the papacy. At the same time, however, the personalities and lives of the popes in the tenth century inspired little reverence and still less respect for the successors of Peter. Nevertheless, the papacy, despite the low moral standard of individual popes, kept the program alive. In this period the coronation rites were greatly improved and embodied the traditional papal theme of the emperor as the organ of government specifically created on a universal scale and charged with specific tasks mentioned in the ceremony. However low the virtues of the popes, the papacy as an institution was none the worse for it; it continued to develop internally and to promote its principles, at least programmatically. Perhaps at no other time in its long history has the papacy so much profited from the Leonine distinction between person and office.

Hildebrandine Era. The overbearing power of the Saxon and early Salian emperors had prevented the papacy from translating its principles into reality. During this period popes were made and unmade by the emperors, who, inspired as they were by the CLUNIAC REFORM, certainly were convinced that they acted in the interests of Christendom and of the papacy. The premature death of HENRY III (1056) and the minority of his son, HENRY IV, provided the papacy with the long-sought opportunity for implementing basic principles of government. The Papal CURIA was assisted in this process by the influx of a number of outstanding men from beyond the Alps, who were mainly responsible for the cosmopolitan outlook characteristic of the papacy in the eleventh century. Perhaps nothing reflects better the new attitude of the papacy than the numerous institutional measures initiated, developed, or modified in the second half of the eleventh century. One of the first measures was the passing of the PAPAL ELECTION DECREE in April 1059. The significance of this decree lies partly in its adoption and refinement of the procedure envisaged in 769 and partly in the abolition of the obnoxious *Ottonianum*. With this decree the college of CARDINALS came into being as the advisory body of the pope. The same year witnessed the first coronation of the pope (NICHOLAS II), which, though not an essential element in his assumption of power, was nevertheless a symbolic means of presenting the pope in his monarchic status, and was readily understood by contemporaries. The wide-flung policy of the pre-Gregorian papacy necessitated the institution of the legatine system, since the legates functioned as the prolonged arms of the pope and could be in constant touch with faraway bishops, princes, and governments. The legates were also a guarantee that papal instructions were carried out. Because of the papacy's wide European connections a number of new departments came into being, and old ones were adapted to the exigencies of the time. Of these departments, none was more important than the chancery, which became the very nerve center of the Christian body politic. The residence of the pope, the Lateran, was reconstituted and here a number of new departments came to be greatly developed, especially the financial and judicial. From this time onward the papacy also began to harness FEUDALISM to its governmental scheme. The enfeoffment of the Normans in 1059 started the long line of papal feudal contracts, so that by the end of the following century the Papal Curia had more feudal vassals than any other European court. In strictest theory the feudal lord was not the pope, but St. Peter himself, on whose behalf the pope acted. Some of the feudal services could be rendered by money payment (*feodum censuale*) in the place of the usual military service. The governmental scheme of the papacy was above all in need of a law. Hitherto there was no single law of the Church, and it was the acute realization of Gregory VII, when he was still Archdeacon Hildebrand, that the Roman Church as a governmental institution needed a legal code that was specifically related to the papacy. His impetuous demand to some of his colleagues in the Curia resulted in a spate of canonical collections of which the common feature was the emphasis on the primatial position of the Roman Church. This was the beginning of the legal development that culminated in the *Decretum* of Gratian in the twelfth century. It should be pointed out, however, that all these collections of Canon Law were private efforts and did not receive official papal sanction.

The pontificate of Gregory VII demonstrated for the first time the practical application of papal principles of government: the papacy had now entered upon the path of effective rulership by means of the law. Although there was at first not much tangible success for the papacy, a number of important principles were clearly reformulated and restated and came to be subsequently the pillars of the papal government: the exaction of the episcopal oath of obedience, the enforcement of episcopal visits to Rome (*visitatio liminum apostolorum*), stern prohibition of SIMONY and lay INVESTITURE, the enforcement of celibacy, and appeals to the Roman Curia. In the exercise of its governmental functions the papacy made known and acted upon the principle that the life of a Christian on earth determined his life in the other world, i.e., obedience to papal law was an indispensable condition for salvation, and that the material things of this world had merely auxiliary value insofar as they assisted the realization of the Christian's true aim—salvation. Resting upon this basic principle, amply supported as it was by the Bible, patristic lore, and earlier papal doctrine, the papacy could not and did not attribute inherent value to matter (the temporal) as such, but merely recognized its function as a means to an end. From this arose the claim, again pursued and acted upon by the papacy, that the end determined the use of material things—from the Christian teleological standpoint a perfectly understandable thesis. Precisely because the papacy was the divinely instituted government of the Christian world, its opponents, especially kings and emperors, could make little headway against it; they had little with which to answer the papal arguments of governing a Christian world. For the papal principles of government were basically rooted in the concept of the Church as the congregation of the faithful, entrusted by Christ to the pope through St. Peter and ruled by Peter's successor. Its end was otherworldly, and none other than the holder of the keys of the kingdom of heaven knew by virtue of his special qualification how to achieve this end. Kings and emperors were indubitably members of the Church and as such were subject to papal jurisdiction. They had, moreover, as their title "king by the grace of God" made clear, received their kingdom as a trust from God for the sake of actualizing Christian principles. Who else but the pope was the proper organ to watch over the discharge of this trust? From the medieval-historical point of view these papal principles of government exhibited extraordinary consistency and logical coherence. Nonetheless, censorious criticism has often been directed against both the principles themselves and their application by contemporaries as well as by modern critics. Their observations culminate in the assertion that the papacy, by dealing with temporal matters, became oblivious of its primary function as a spiritual organ. The point, however, to which insufficient attention and importance is attached by the critics of the papal government at work, is that the Church was an earthly society held together by faith in Christ as well as a society that by virtue of the same faith pursued otherworldly aims. This dual nature of the Church—an organic, visible, and juristic body, as well as a sacramental society—makes understandable the exercise of governing powers by the papacy. But there is no statement or action by any medieval pope that justified papal jurisdiction solely on grounds that were or could be considered purely temporal. What the medieval papacy at all times insisted upon was the application of the teleological principle. No criterion has ever been formulated according to which the spiritual could be separated from the temporal. Indeed, in a Christocentric society this separation could not conceptually come about: the categorization of human activities into religious, moral, or political is of post-medieval origin, while in the Middle Ages the Christian was viewed from no other standpoint than that of Christianity.

The schism between East and West (*see* EASTERN SCHISM) had already moved Gregory VII to issue an appeal for a crusade. URBAN II succeeded in bringing about the CRUSADE, in itself a major undertaking, which released the first large-scale mass movement in the Middle Ages. The resistance to Islam and the liberation of the holy places from Seljuk oppressions were most pressing and urgent motives. Meanwhile the problem of lay investiture by king or emperor was settled on a somewhat pragmatic basis, first in France, shortly followed by the compromise reached with England, and lastly with the German Emperor in the Concordat of WORMS (1122). The principles for which Gregory VII had fought gradually received recognition: the subsequent period saw the highest ascendancy of the medieval papacy. The so-called First LATERAN COUNCIL of 1123 is counted as the first general council of the Middle Ages, soon to be followed by the second in 1139 and the third in 1179. Each was held under the presidency of the pope and issued numerous and fundamental decrees regulating virtually all aspects of public and social life. Now that canonistic scholarship also had come into being at the University of BOLOGNA, the papacy was in a position to call upon well-trained jurists for all its essential departments, and with ALEXANDER III the long and distinguished line of jurist-popes began. The outstanding features of the twelfth-century papacy were its considerable legal output in decretals and its successful fight against the new and overbearing Staufen dynasty in Germany as well as against other kings, notably HENRY II of England, who resisted the full implementation of papal principles of government. Another feature of the twelfth century was the stand taken against emerging heresies, notably those of the Waldenses and the Cathari, who showed a keen spirit of resistance to papal law and order. These successes of the papacy are all the more remarkable as a considerable period of Alexander III's pontificate was marred by a pernicious schism, engineered and sustained by the Staufen Frederick I. The work of the papacy in the twelfth century also entailed institutional changes: the systematization of the legatine machinery, the chancery, and appellate jurisdiction; the emergence of new papal documents to cope with the increased output; the regulation of the papal election procedure and the introduction of the two-thirds majority for a valid election; the introduction of regular meetings of pope and cardinals (the consistory) in which fundamental questions were discussed and decided; the reorganization of the financial departments of the Curia by outstanding chamberlains.

Zenith of the Medieval Papacy. With the accession of INNOCENT III in 1198, the papacy entered upon its most splendid period. A man of great learning and vision, a first-class jurist with an enormous working capacity, he reconstituted the papal state and clarified the vital relations between the papacy and Sicily. His dealings with the disputed succession in Germany are a model of astute diplomacy; he made kingdoms (such as Bulgaria, England, and Portugal) fiefs of the papacy; he was highly successful in bringing back to the fold a number of heretical sects; he witnessed the fall of Constantinople in 1204 and became instrumental in establishing a Latin ecclesiastical organization in the Near East; in the regular consistory meetings his legal acumen shone forth; he prevented tension between the episcopacy and the papacy from deteriorating into rebellion. Almost all the PAPAL REGISTERS of his pontificate have been preserved. The Fourth Lateran Council in 1215 under his presidency marked the zenith of papal power in the Middle Ages. More than 1,200 participants attended this assembly, and its legislation was to exercise an influence beyond the medieval period. During this pontificate, the first official collection of CANON LAW was published by Innocent himself (1209). In short, the papacy had reached the status of a universal power, not only in name but also in fact, taking an active part in every department of public life.

In many respects the history of the papacy in the thirteenth century is an appendix to the Innocentian pontificate. Under HONORIUS III the new MENDICANT ORDERS were established and emerged as great civilizing and pastoral agencies in medieval Europe and beyond. In this pontificate the Staufen king, FREDERICK II, was crowned emperor (November 1220), and on this occasion Frederick issued a number of laws dealing with the menace of heresy. Throughout the thirteenth century the papacy refined and expanded its principles and institutions. New institutions developed in this period had a significant bearing upon the making of modern international law, e.g., the protection of legates and their safe conduct; the sanctity of treaties; proper treatment of hostages, prisoners, and exiles. As a universal power the papacy was in a position to command kings and other secular princes to take steps against heretics, to allot territory to a victorious belligerent party, to depose rulers and establish others in their place, and to take (especially in Eastern Europe) effective steps in organizing diocesan structures. The papacy, now ruled by some of its ablest lawyer-popes, such as INNOCENT IV, had to face the full rigor of the conflict with Frederick II. In the First Council of LYONS (1245) Innocent excommunicated and deposed the emperor; this step resulted in an anarchic interregnum in Germany, lasting some 30 years. The same Council also promulgated disciplinary decrees that remained in force until 1918. The Second Council of Lyons (1274) under GREGORY X witnessed the temporary union between the Eastern and the Latin Churches (*see* ECUMENICAL MOVEMENT), and among other decrees issued an important one on papal elections: the practice hitherto observed in holding elections in CONCLAVE was turned into law. Among the institutional measures developed in the 13th century were those concerned with papal PROVISIONS, reservations, expectancies, collations, and the regularization of papal taxation. In its attempt to combat HERESY, the papacy under GREGORY IX instituted the INQUISITION, a special tribunal directly subordinated to the pope. There are many explanations for the increase of heresy throughout Europe, but as far as the papacy itself was concerned, one measure that seems to have engendered most opposition was the ready exercise of papal plenitude of power through ecclesiastical censures, which, though not misused nor abused, was certainly over used and thus became blunted. The theme of papal plenitude of power was not a problem of theology or law, but one concerned with handling power wisely and prudently.

The papacy was at all times, if not the begetter, at any rate a strong supporter of the universities. Toulouse and Rome saw the establishment of seats of learning by the papacy, which had always entertained amicable relations with the older universities, such as Bologna and Paris, and with the more recent foundations as well. Nevertheless, the spirit of inquiry promoted in the universities released forces that in their full maturity contributed to the diminution of papal authority in the following decades. Above all, the rediscovery of ARISTOTLE and of his corpus of thought and the awakening of a national spirit in the individual kingdoms, notably in France, brought about a considerable estrangement between the papacy and the faithful in general. By virtue of its commanding governing position in Europe, the papacy had perforce to deal with a number of issues that were not always properly explained nor adequately understood by the faithful. Unwittingly thereby the papacy aroused antagonism and resistance in quarters that were basically by no means antipapal. Moreover, in the conflict between the papacy under BONIFACE VIII and the French king, Philip IV, the former had failed to realize the strength and influence of the new forces. Instead, he relied for his arguments almost exclusively on traditional (Roman) doctrine which was largely conceived within the framework of the imperial government, but which made little impression on national kingdoms, such as France. That the papacy suffered defeat in this conflict was not the fault of Boniface VIII (who brought forth no argument that had not been advanced before), but arose partly from the loss of dynamic initiative by the papacy throughout the second half of the thirteenth century and partly from its underestimating the power and strength of ''mere'' kings. Precisely because the papacy concentrated so much on the Empire, European kings had been able to strengthen their position, virtually unimpeded by the papacy. It would be erroneous, nevertheless, to say that the papacy after Boniface became virtually a French satellite because it took up residence at Avignon for the following 70 years (*see*

AVIGNON PAPACY). That the papacy under CLEMENT V assisted in the suppression of the TEMPLARS in France was due to papal timidity and to a number of circumstances over which the papacy had no control.

Decline of Papal Authority. It is worth pointing out that by the middle of the thirteenth century the papacy had reached its apogee of authority, influence, and prestige in Europe. There can be no doubt that the secret of its success had been an unyielding adherence to its program and the pursuit of dynamic and constructive policies that contributed to the welding of Europe into one more or less coherent whole. Apart from the factors already mentioned as contributing to the papacy's decline, there were others, such as opportunism; the *ad hoc* adjustment of some vital principles to emerging situations; the frequently questionable conferment of benefices by way of reservation, collation, and postulation; the incidence of very high taxation; the underestimation of new forces; and the blunting of papal censures through overuse. More and more Europe disintegrated into its national component parts, and the role of the papacy as a suprare-gal governmental organ was considerably modified: what came to count more and more was the law of the national kingdoms and less and less the law of the papacy. The development of political thought proper—one of the by-products of the renewed study of Aristotle and of the revival of Roman law—also must be reckoned as a contributory factor in the decline of papal authority. For this development led to the conceptual elaboration of a dualism of public bodies, i.e., the State as a product of nature and the Church as a supranatural product. This dualism found its reflection in the view—advocated particularly by MARSILIUS OF PADUA—that only the laws of the State were true, enforceable laws, while the laws of the Church were not, strictly speaking, laws, but statements to which a merely persuasive force could be attributed. Law was, according to this thesis, the expression of the will of the people, and because the pope was said to be the head of a divinely instituted society, his decrees could assume the character of law only if the people (or the State) so willed it. The Avignon papacy was very much overshadowed by these and similar doctrines, which to some extent influenced even the Curia itself; the monarchic function of the pope came to be questioned, with the consequence that the college of cardinals assumed greater powers. Electoral CAPITULATIONS were a clear symptom of the tension between pope and cardinals. Similarly, the WESTERN SCHISM was a symptom of unresolved constitutional conflicts resulting in the emergence of conciliarism, which saw its victory in the Council of Constance.

Eve of the Reformation. The election of MARTIN V meant not only the end of the schism, but also the beginning of an era in which the papacy was to recoup a good deal of its lost prestige. The reestablishment of the papal state, which had sunk into anarchy, was taken in hand, and so was the fight against the HUSSITES. As all traces of conciliarism had not been wiped out, Martin, in implementing the decrees of Constance, convoked a new synod at Pavia for April 1423, but shortly afterward transferred it to Siena. This council produced none of the necessary reform decrees, and a new council was summoned to BASEL in 1431. Meanwhile the new pope, EUGENE IV, showed little taste for bowing to conciliarism. The much desired *reformatio in capite* as well as the reforms of the clergy, of papal taxation, elections, reservations, etc., brought about such serious tension that an open breach resulted. One part of the council was transferred to Ferrara in 1437, while the other remained at Basel. The Council of Ferrara was recognized as the legitimate continuation of the original Council of Basel and counts as the seventeenth general council of the Church. Its great success, however temporary, was the union between the Latin and Greek Churches, eventually achieved at FLORENCE in 1439. The papacy also provided a great stimulus to the revival of Greek studies and thus in a way assisted in the birth of the RENAISSANCE. A great preoccupation of the fifteenth-century papacy was the threat to the West by the advance of the Turks, who, since the fall of Constantinople in 1453, were justifiably considered a menace to Christianity. In the second half of the century, the papacy became very active in the promotion of a crusade against Islam, though circumstances were no longer propitious for its execution. A further notable achievement was the arrangement of concordats with secular governments; in fact, since the fifteenth century, this form of treaty came to be the *modus* by which the relations between the papacy and states were regulated on an international scale. A good part of the city of Rome was rebuilt during this century under the aegis of the papacy, and above all, plans of rebuilding St. Peter's, the papal library, and the Vatican were actively taken in hand, though the moving spirit behind these plans, NICHOLAS V, did not live to see the fruit of his planning. The vision of the papacy had nevertheless become restricted: it was Rome and to a certain extent Italy that almost exclusively preoccupied papal interest, and far less the universal tasks in which the papacy traditionally saw its foremost mission. Moreover, the personal character of some of these popes was far from approaching the customary bearing of St. Peter's successors, and it is understandable that the institution of the papacy should have suffered from them, although the cataclysm into which Europe was thrown after the turn of the century was due only to a very small degree, if at all, to the personal bearing of these popes. What they made abundantly clear on an objective level was that the office of the supreme pontiff must be separated from his personality, as indeed Leo I had proclaimed

exactly a millennium earlier. It was on this distinction between office and person that the papacy had actively entered the historic scene in that age, and it was on that distinction that the papacy as an institution successfully recovered from the depth into which it had been plunged by the popes of the late fifteenth century.

Bibliography: H. VON SCHUBERT, *Geschichte der christlichen Kirche im Frühmittelalter* (Tübingen 1921). L. NINA, *Le finanze pontificie nel medioevo,* 3 v. (Milan 1929–32). H. K. MANN, *The Lives of the Popes in the Early Middle Ages from 590 to 1304,* 18 v. (London 102–32). E. CASPAR, *Geschichte de Papsttums von den anfängen bis zur höhe der Weltherrschaft,* 2 v. (Tübingen 1930–33). W. E. LUNT, ed. and tr., *Papal Revenues in the Middle Ages,* 2 v. (New York 1934). H. LECLERCQ, *Dictionnaire d'archéologie chrétienne et de liturgie,* ed. F. CABOL, H. LECLERCQ, and H. I. MARROU, 15 v. (Paris 1907–53) 13.1:1111–1345. V. MARTIN, *Dictionnaire de théologie catholique,* ed. A. VACANT et al., 15 v. (Paris 1903–50) 11.2:1877–1944. G. GLEZ, *ibid.* 13.1:247–344. F. COPPA, ed. *Encyclopedia of the Vatican and Papacy* (London 1999). E. EICHMANN, *Die Kaiserkrönung im Abendland,* 2 v. (Würzburg 1942); *Weihe und Krönung des Papstes im Mittelalter* (Munich 1951). R. ENO, *The Rise of the Papacy* (Wilmington, Delaware 1990). A. FORTESCUE, *The Early Papacy: To the Synod of Chalcedon in 451,* 3rd ed. by S. REID (Southampton 1997). J. GAUDEMET, *La Formation du droit séculier et du droit de l'église aux IVe et Ve siècles* (Paris 1957). P. GRELOT, ''Pierre et Paul, fondateurs de la 'primaute' romaine,'' *Istina* 27 (1982) 228–68. L. HERTLING, *Communio: Church and Papacy in Early Christianity* (Chicago 1972). P. JOHNSON, *The Papacy* (New York 1997). W. LADUE, *The Chair of St. Peter: A History of the Papacy* (New York 1999). J. LORTZ, *Geschichte der Kirche in ideengeschichtlicher Betrachtung* (21st ed. Münster 1962–) v.1. H. RAHNER, *Kirche und Staat im frühen Christentum: Dokumente aus acht Jahrhunderten und ihre Deutung* (Munich 1961). B. SCHIMMELPFENNIG, *The Papacy* (New York 1992). W. ULLMANN, *Principles of Government and Politics in the Middle Ages* (New York 1961); *The Growth of Papal Government in the Middle Ages* (2d ed. New York 1962); *Gelasius I: (492–496). Das Papsttum an der Wende der Spatantike zum Mittelalter* (Stuttgart 1981). H. BARION, *Die Religion in Geschichte und Gegenwart,* 7 v. (3d ed. Tübingen 1957–65) 5:44–47. K. ALAND et al., *ibid.* 5:51–71. G. SCHWAIGER and K. RAHNER, *Lexikon für Theologie und Kirche,* ed. J. HOFER and K. RAHNER, 10 v. (2d, new ed. Freiburg 1957–65) 8:36–48. H. E. A. FEINE, *Kirchliche Rechtsgeschichte* (4th ed. Cologne 1964–). J. CANNING, *A History of Medieval Political Thought 300–1450* (London-New York 1996). C. MORRIS, *The Papal Monarchy: The Western Church from 1050 to 1250: Oxford History of the Christian Church* (Oxford Press 1989). A. PARAVICINI-BAGLIANI, *The Pope's Body,* tr. D. S. PETERSON (Chicago and London 2000). K. PENNINGTON, *Pope and Bishops: The Papal Monarchy in the Twelfth and Thirteenth Centuries* (Philadelphia 1984). B. TIERNEY, *Origins of Papal Infallibility 1150–1350: A Study on the Concepts of Infallibility, Sovereignty and Tradition in the Middle Ages* (Studies in the History of Christian Thought 6; Leiden 1972).

[W. ULLMANN]

3. Renaissance and Early Modern Period

This section of the history of the papacy extends from the period of cultural transition known as the RENAISSANCE (c. 1450) to the great political, social, and religious upheaval of the FRENCH REVOLUTION (1789).

The Renaissance Papacy. The bitter conciliar quarrels of the fourteenth and fifteenth centuries had shown that the most dangerous crisis of the Church of the late Middle Ages was a constitutional one: its background was the impassioned demand for a reform *"in capite et membris."* Attempts for a stronger democratization of the Church had failed with the fateful ending of the Council of Basel, although the conciliar ideas reaffirmed there remained powerful for centuries. After the experience of Constance and Basel, the strengthened papacy resisted the summoning of a general council, thereby abandoning its most powerful court for proposing reform measures. As the needed self-reform did not come about, the multicolored "autumn of the Middle Ages" was the forerunner of a religious revolution in the Church. With the highly cultured Nicholas V (1447–55), under whom the last antipope, FELIX V, resigned there began that close connection between the papacy, humanism, and the Renaissance which would endure well into the sixteenth century. After the evident decline of the political power of the Holy See, Nicholas and many of his successors aimed at regaining esteem for the papacy and Church by making them the leading centers of culture. Renaissance Rome became a focal point of arts and sciences, while at the same time the religious character of the papacy declined. With a few exceptions, the Renaissance popes became embroiled in secular affairs, wars, money-making, nepotism, and sensual passion. Nicholas V, the first and most high-minded pope of this epoch, concluded with the German King Frederick III, as ruler of the realm, the Vienna Concordat, which remained in force till the end of the Holy Roman Empire in 1803. But since the "gravamina of the German nation" was not heeded, the anticurial opposition in the Empire grew. In 1452 Frederick III was crowned emperor in St. Peter's; it represented the last imperial coronation ceremony in Rome. In 1453 Constantinople fell to the Turks—not without the fault of the popes and of the Occident, neither of whom had given efficient aid.

The pontificates of the Spaniard CALLISTUS III (1455–58) and of the cultured humanist Enea Silvio Piccolomini, PIUS II (1458–64), were dominated by the thought of a crusade against the Turks. But everywhere in Europe national interest prevailed, so that notwithstanding all papal efforts, a common undertaking did not come about. The sense of spiritual responsibility increasingly receded during the pontificate of Sixtus IV (1471–84), under whom the Spanish Inquistion was expanded; INNOCENT VIII (1484–92), who issued the fateful "Witches Bull" (*Summis desiderantes*, Dec. 5, 1484), was gravely compromised by his role as guardian of the Turkish Prince Dschem; finally, under the impetuous Borgia (Borja), ALEXANDER VI (1492–1503), the papacy

further declined. Unrestricted nepotism and unscrupulous money-making involved the popes more and more in unseemly political quarrels. While Alexander VI showed political foresight in drawing a demarcation line between the Spanish and Portuguese empires of the New World, his anti-French policy in Italy and his plans for making the papal state a permanent fief of the Borgias came to naught. His successor was the high-minded PIUS III (1503), whose reign lasted less than a month. The bitter foe of the Borgias, JULIUS II (1503–13), physically and intellectually a powerful character ("il terrible"), was one of the most capable popes, though far more an Italian Renaissance prince and general than a priest. Using diplomatic and military means he sought to establish a strong, independent papacy in an Italy free from foreign domination; the League of Cambrai (1509) and the Holy League (1511) were formed to serve this purpose. A schism in France was prevented only with difficulty when King Louis XII reinforced the PRAGMATIC SANCTION and, with the aid of several cardinals, caused a general Church council to convene at Pisa in 1511. Julius II countered the move by calling together the Fifth Lateran Council (1512–17). Under his princely protection, Rome became the center of the Italian High Renaissance, where Bramante, Micheangelo, and Rafael created masterpieces to the glorification of Church and papacy. His successor of the house of Medici, LEO X (1513–21), greatly disappointed the expectations of reformists. His secular, extravagant mode of life, as well as his whole manner of Church government, indicated a lack of spiritual responsibility.

With the inglorious end of the Fifth Lateran Council vanished the last possibility of an internal reform (*see* LATERAN COUNCILS). Thus, when, in 1517, Martin LUTHER launched his open challenge, a catastrophe for papacy and Church was at hand. The occasion was given by the promulgation of an indulgence stipulating a money offering in connection with the building of the new basilica of St. Peter. Neither Pope nor Curia was aware of the religious motives of Luther, nor did they foresee the weighty consequences of his action. They also underestimated the anti-Roman state of mind of much of Europe. Thus, in a short time large sections of central and eastern Europe, as well as the whole Germanic North (England, Scotland, Scandanavia), went over to PROTESTANTISM. After 1520, Luther looked upon the pope as an Antichrist. John CALVIN opened up an even deeper chasm with the papacy. Although the Protestant Reformation of the sixteenth century represented an attempt to restore the purity of an original Christianity, the resultant split in Christendom became the greatest misfortune in Church history.

In 1516 Leo X and Francis I of France signed a concordat in which, in exchange for the abolition of the Pragmatic Sanction, the Pope had to recognize a nearly complete supremacy of State over Church. The pious and moral Netherlander ADRIAN VI (1522–23), the last German and last non-Italian pope prior to John Paul II initiated the reform of the Church *in capite*. At the Imperial Diet at Nuremberg (1522) he had the legate Francesco Chiergati pronounce the papal acknowledgment of guilt and assert the Pope's firm intention to achieve Church reform. The Pope's early death ended these hopes. The Medici pope CLEMENT VII (1522–34) followed the old ways. Besides, he allowed himself to come into fateful opposition to Emperor Charles V (1519–56), whose lifelong efforts to restore the unity of faith were rather hindered than supported by papal policy. Under Clement VII the great defection from papacy and Church advanced rapidly, especially in Germany and in the Nordic kingdoms. England separated from the papacy following the marriage scandals of King HENRY VIII. And from the 1530s on, a militant CALVINISM spread from Geneva to France, the Netherlands, Scotland, Hungary, and Poland, and became with LUTHERANISM and ANGLICANISM the third main branch of a reformed Christendom (*see* REFORMED CHURCHES).

Catholic Reform and Counter Reformation. The Protestant Reformation of the sixteenth century curbed the power of the papacy. Yet, the immense shock at last caused the Curia to join the movement of reform that had been growing for decades in Spain and in small circles of Italy. After the early failure of Adrian VI, the pontificate of PAUL III (1534–49) signified a turn of events. Though his way of life still followed wholly the traditions of the Renaissance popes, his wide education and political sense convinced him that the real strength of papal policy lay in following spiritual and ecclesiastical principles. But he seems to have had no clear ideas about the extent of necessary measures, and since he shrank from radial steps, his pontificate is characterized by hesitation. Of great importance for the Catholic reform was the thorough renewal of the college of cardinals, the appointment of the commission for Church reform in 1536 (*Consilium de emendanda ecclesia*), the promotion of new orders (THEATRINES, BARNABITES, SOMASCHI), especially the approval of the Society of Jesus in 1540, the renewal of the Roman Inquisition (*Sanctum Officium*, 1542), and most of all the Council of TRENT in session with interruptions from 1545 to 1563. The council could not restore the lost unity of faith, but it laid the broad basis for a thorough internal renewal by determining the most important articles of faith and by issuing sweeping decrees of reform. Notwithstanding the episcopalian tendencies, especially from the Spaniards and French, the popes remained masters of the council. Although showing serious weaknesses, JULIUS III (1550–55) had a pronounced sense of

his spiritual office. PAUL IV (1555–59) tried with passionate energy to hurry the reform without the council, thereby involving himself in a series of catastrophes through political ineptitude and uncompromising severity. Under PIUS IV (1559–65) the Council of Trent completed its labors, having successfully overcome several threatening crises. A whole series of unfinished topics (the Roman Catechism, Missal, and Breviary, the edition of the Vulgate) were expressly entrusted to the Pope. The new edition of liturgical books, appearing for the most part under PIUS V (1566–72), resulted in the acceptance of the Roman rite by nearly the whole Church. The Council of Trent and active new religious orders, such as the JESUITS, were among the most important factors in strengthening the Church.

Since the defection of nearly all the Germanic nations, post-Tridentine Catholicism has been characterized by a preponderance of Romanic nations. The radical attacks on the papacy by Protestant reformers made the Catholic reaction stress the importance of the priestly office in the Church, especially in the office of the pope. Their pitiless judgements, however, also made even well meaning and necessary criticism in the Church difficult. All attempts at reunion with Protestants, the aim of some of the most generous minds on both sides, proved unsuccessful. The most difficult problem, then as now, proved to be the position of the pope in the Church. Although the mentality and character of some post-Tridentine popes showed serious defects, there can be no further question of "unworthy" popes. The great popes Pius V, GREGORY XIII (1572–85), and SIXTUS V (1585–90) energetically and successfully assumed leadership of Catholic reform. In 1570 Pius V declared ELIZABETH I of England excommunicated and deposed—the last and unsuccessful papal deposition of an important ruler. The naval victory at LEPANTO over the Turks (1571) also was caused by his efforts. Gregory XIII supported Counter-Reformation forces, especially in Germany, France, England, Poland, and Sweden, although these were sometimes ill advised. Existing diplomatic representatives of the Holy See at Vienna, Paris, Madrid, and Lisbon were expanded by permanent nunciatures at Lucerne in Switzerland, at Graz in Inner Austria, at Cologne for Lower Germany, and at Brussels. These nunciatures assumed an important ecclesiastical and political role in preventing innovations, giving effect to the Tridentine reform, supervising bishops and the Church organization, and promoting Counter-Reformation forces.

Conflicts with state power and with the individual metropolitans and bishops developed, especially in the eighteenth century. The Jesuits, besides gaining leadership in a rapidly developing new educational system, became the most important helpers of a strengthened papacy. Sixtus V, combining a tremendous capacity for work with political wisdom, continued the reconstruction of the Church. His reorganization of the Curia and of the general government of the Church by setting up 15 Cardinal Congregations in 1588 and limiting the number of cardinals to 70, a number that remained unchanged until the twentieth century. He made Rome a baroque city and—less felicitously—ordered a new edition of the Vulgate. This period clearly demonstrated the trend toward greater centralization in Church government around papacy and Curia. It also reveals that the restrengthened papacy's most significant Protestant adversary was well-organized Calvinism, while Lutheranism and Anglicanism had noticeably declined as foes, the former by splitting up into numerous national churches, the latter though its isolation.

Catholic reform and the reconquest of lost territory, once started, were continued by CLEMENT VIII (1592–1605), PAUL V (1605–21), GREGORY XV (1621–23), and, to a lesser degree, URBAN VIII (1623–44). They found the strongest political backing for their plans from the Spanish and Austrian Hapsburgs and the Bavarian Wittelsbachs. France at last found peace when, after the end of the destructive wars with HUGUENOTS, the Bourbon King HENRY IV turned Roman Catholic in 1593. In the seventeenth century France rapidly advanced to the position of a great European power, thanks to the statesmanship of RICHELIEU. Paul V attempted to revive medieval claims of a supremacy of the Church in political matters, although everywhere, even in the Catholic national states, a tendency toward national churches was acquiring new strength, especially in the GALLICANISM expressed by Edmond RICHER. His policy led to serious political conflicts and failures in particular with the republic of Venice (1605–07, excommunication of the Senate, interdict over the Republic) and with England (prohibition of the loyalty oath of Catholics to the king after the Gunpowder Plot of 1605). In the Thirty Years' War Paul V and Gregory XV supported Emperor Ferdinand II and the Catholic League under Maxmillian I of Bavaria. The reintroduction of Catholicism into Bohemia after the victory of 1620 and in the Upper Palatinate was greeted in Rome with joy. The transfer of the electoral office to Maximilian of Bavaria was vigorously supported by the papal diplomacy in order to safeguard the election of a Catholic emperor.

The establishment of the Congregation of the Propagation of the Faith in 1622 indicated that the papacy intended to take over the leadership of the expanding world missionary movement. Under the Baberini Pope Urban VIII, a patron of arts, stately baroque buildings were erected in Rome. As in the Renaissance period, this building was accompanied by the destruction of many monuments of antiquity and the Middle Ages. Nepotism, never quite extinct, flared up again in Urban's pontificate. The Pope, deceived by Richelieu, leaned, toward the French's side during the Thirty Years' War, thereby harming indirectly the Catholic party in Germany, although he strove sincerely for peace. The Peace of WESTPHALIA, which caused great damage to the Catholic Church, was concluded in 1648 under INNOCENT X (1644–55) after long negotiations. During the war and at the time of the peace the political weakness of the papacy had become painfully apparent. It was noted that often political thought and action were determined by simple reasons of state rather than by religious and ethical principles.

From the Peace of Westphalia to the French Revolution. In this period princely absolutism became firmly established in nearly all European states. The progressive secularization of the West forced the papacy, now internally strengthened and of high moral caliber, to accept not only the increasing loss of political influence but even the control of its internal affairs. It had to fight absolutism, an Enlightenment that too often was anti-papal and anti-ecclesiastical, JANSENISM, Gallicanism in France, Episcopalianism (FEBRONIANISM) in Germany, and JOSEPHINISM in the Hapsburg lands. All these phenomena were evident to a greater or lesser degree in all Catholic countries. Probably wishing to avoid political conflicts, the cardinals in this period elected honest but undistinguished popes; none were strong personalities, with the exception of Innocent XI and BENEDICT XIV.

The greatest political difficulties for the Holy See arose from France. Through the labors of Cardinals Richelieu and Mazarin and during the long reign of Louis XIV (1643–1715) that country had its "great century" when it stood at the top of its political power and spread its cultural influence over the whole Europeanized world. After a painful confrontation during the pontificate of the peaceable and restrained ALEXANDER VII (1655–67), the incorruptible and deeply religious INNOCENT XI (1676–89) lived to see bitter quarrels with the unscrupulous absolutism of Louis XIV regarding the *régale*, rights of diplomatic immunity of the French ambassador in Rome, and papal condemnation of the four Gallican articles of 1682 (*see* REGALIA; ASSEMBLIES OF FRENCH CLERGY). An open schism was prevented probably only by the intervention of François FÉNELON and the change of government in England brought on by the Glorious REVOLUTION OF 1688.

In international politics, also, Innocent XI found the King of France his greatest opponent, a fact especially fateful in view of the mortal Turkish danger. Considerable aid from the Pope made possible the decisive victory at Vienna in 1683 that relieved Europe from Turkish pressure on its eastern boundaries. Purity of aims and means gained Innocent XI high repute even with non-Catholics. Under Innocent XII (1691–1700) the quarrel with France could finally be settled in view of the imminent extinction of the Spanish Hapsburgs because of the death on Nov. 1, 1700, of Charles II, King of Spain, without a son. A long war for the rich Spanish inheritance was not settled until the Treaty of Utrecht (1713) recognized Phillip of Anjou as Phillip V of Spain. Fearing a Hapsburg hegemony, CLEMENT XI (1700–21) took the side of the French Bourbons, which led to a short war with Emperor Joseph I in 1708.

The teachings of Luther, Calvin, and their followers on grace and justification led Catholic theologians to focus on the doctrine of the original state of man in paradise, to the Fall, and to the relation of divine grace and man's freedom. The Council of Trent had left the central problem of cooperation grace and free will undecided. As in late antiquity, this gave rise to long and violent debates, in which the papacy repeatedly intervened. The old distinction between the theological schools of Thomists and Scotists emerged vividly in a modern form. In 1567 Pius V rejected 79 theses of Michel de Bay, professor at Louvain, and his adherents (see BAIUS AND BAIANISM). The aftermath of this quarrel was seen in the discussion about the doctrine of grace of the Jesuit Leonard LESSIUS. Sixtus V forbade both parties to censure each other. At the end of the sixteenth century another severe conflict broke out between Dominicans and Jesuits (Domingo BÁÑEZ, OP; Luis de MOLINA, SJ). After long deliberations of the papal commission of inquiry (see CONGREGATIO DE AUXILIS), neither Clement VIII nor Paul V gave a decision. A similar situation existed in the 200-year dispute over systems of moral theology. Both extremes were condemned: LAXISM by ALEXANDER VII (1665–66) and Innocent XI (1679), RIGORISM by ALEXANDER VIII (1690). Theological contention came to a pitch in the century-long quarrel over the interpretation of the AUGUSTINUS, written by bishop Cornelius JANSEN and printed posthumously (1640). Jansenism, which started in Louvain, soon took hold of France and influenced the Catholic lands of Europe. Jansenistic doctrines were first condemned by Urban VIII (1642), later by Innocent X (1653); after the inheritance of Alexander VII (1644), the charitable CLEMENT IX brought about a temporary truce in 1669 (Clementine peace). The hostile activity of Louis XIV made the quarrel in France flare up again c. 1700 and occasioned Clement XI's two great bulls of condemnation, Vineam Domini (1705) and UNIGENITUS (1715). In the end the bishops of France submitted, but not so in the Netherlands, where Utrecht became the seat of the schism (1723). The papal condemnation of Jansenism made the latter movement often an ally of the opponents of Roman centralization, as in the Gallican and Josephinist movements and the Synod of PISTOIA (1786). Quietism also received papal condemnation, first by Innocent XI, who after long hesitation proscribed propositions found in the Guía espiritual of Miguel de MOLINOS (1687), then by Innocent XII, who was pressured by the French crown to censure the Explication des Maximes des Saints of Fénelon (1699).

The ENLIGHTENMENT period brought a great turning away from the acknowledgement of Christianity as revealed religion. The Catholic Church and the papacy especially were mercilessly attacked by many enlightened philosophers in France, Portugal, Spain, and Naples-Sicily. Increasing difficulties were overcome for the time being by the capable and learned Benedict XIV (1740–58), whose measures for internal reform of the Church and whose wise and timely policy of compromise in external affairs testify to his deliberate moderation, prudent compliance, and sincere love of peace, without surrender of essential rights of the Church. The pontificates of CLEMENT XIII (1758–69) and CLEMENT XIV (1769–74) were completely overshadowed by discussion about the dissolution of the Society of Jesus. Long demanded by the Bourbon states, which unilaterally had already effected it in their respective dominions, the suppression of the order was decreed in 1773 by Clement XIV, after deep reflection. The long antecedents of this affair, the brutal states, and also the unsuccessful petitionary journey of PIUS VI (1775–99) to Emperor Joseph II in Vienna (1782), revealed the political impotence of the papacy in the period of Enlightenment. The end of the eighteenth century witnessed the deepest humiliation of the modern papacy in the wake of the FRENCH REVOLUTION.

Bibliography: For extensive sources and literature see: L. PASTOR, *The History of Popes From the Close of the Middle Ages*, 40 v. (London 1938–61). F. X. SEPPELT, *Geschichte der Päpste von den Anfängen biz zur Mitte des 20.Jh.*, v.4–5 (Leipzig 1931–41). K. BIHLMEYER and H. TÜCHLE, *Kirchengeschichte*, 3 v. (17th ed. Paderborn 1962). A. FLICHE and V. MARTIN, eds., *Histoire de l'église depuis les origines jusqu'à nos jours* (Paris 1935–). P. PASCHINI and V. MONACHINO, eds., *I papi nella storia*, 2 v. (Rome 1961). J. W. O'MALLEY, ed. *Catholicism in Early Modern History* (St. Louis, Missouri 1988). A. D. WRIGHT, *The Early Modern Papacy: >From the Council of Trent to the French Revolution 1564–1789* (London 2000). J. A. F. THOMSON, *Popes and Princes, 1417–1517* (London 1980). H. M. VAUGHN, *The Medici Popes* (Port Washington, New York 1971). P. PARTNER, *Renaissance Rome, 1500–1559* (Berkeley 1976). R. BIRELEY, *The Refashioning of Catholicism: A Reassment of the Counter-Reformation* (Washington, D.C. 1999). M. R. O'CONNELL, *The Counter-Reformation, 1559–1610* (New York 1974). R. PO-CHIA HSIA, *The World of Catholic Renewal, 1540–1700* (New York 1996). J. DULUMEAU, *Catholicism between Luther and Voltaire* (London 1977). W. J. CALLAHAN and D. HIGGS, eds., *Church and State in Catholic Europe of the Eighteenth Century* (Cambridge 1979). H. DANIEL-ROPS, *The*

Church in the Eighteenth Century (Garden City, New York 1966). H. GROSS, *Rome in the Age of Enlightenment* (Cambridge 1990).

[G. SCHWAIGER]

4. The Modern Period (1789–1958)

The history of the papacy in this period extends from the tumultuous impact of the French Revolution of 1789 upon the Church and its leadership through the papacy's involvement in the early Cold War.

The main lines of historical development in the institution of the papacy during the period 1789 to 1958 are clear-cut. The quarter century between the outbreak of the French Revolution and Napoleon's downfall witnessed determined and violent assaults against the papal spiritual and temporal power that seriously menaced the very existence of the office; yet it also registered gains of long-term significance. Then followed a reversal of fortune almost unparalleled in suddenness and importance. Since 1815 the prestige and effective spiritual powers of succeeding popes have continued to mount, even after 1870. More than ever Rome became the vital center of the Church throughout the world. Particularly since mid-nineteenth century, ecclesiastical administration has been centralized in the Eternal City to an unprecedented degree. Clergy and laity have become accustomed to turn to the popes for doctrinal and pastoral guidance regularly, not merely in periods of crisis; and they have entertained for recent pontiffs a personal reverence that earlier centuries rarely knew. Papal temporal power nevertheless suffered mounting difficulties from its restoration in 1815 to its disappearance in 1870; its revival in 1929 was on a very limited scale.

From 1789 to 1815. Events in France gave direction to the history of the Church and of the papacy during these years.

Losses. From the beginning of his pontificate, Pius VI, like his predecessors, had to contend with Catholic governments imbued with the tenets of monarchical absolutism and regalism that viewed with suspicion or hostility any exercise of papal authority within their borders and defied or disregarded Rome save when it suited their interests to do otherwise. These states utilized the *exequatur* and *placet,* the appeal as from an abuse, and the menace of schism as standard devices to maintain as much national spiritual autonomy as possible within a universal Church. Gallicanism, allied with Jansenism, continued to oppose the full hierarchical supremacy of the papacy. In Germanic lands Febronianism and Josephinism, with similar aims, reached their peak during this pontificate. All four of these antipapal tendencies converged close to Rome at the synod of Pistoia (1784),

convoked by Bishop Scipione de' RICCI, whose decrees merited the solemn papal condemnation, *Auctorem fidei* (1794). Protestant rulers preserved their antipapal traditions and displayed more intolerance toward Rome than toward their Catholic subjects. After engineering the suppression of the Jesuits in 1773, the more radical champions of the Enlightenment envisioned the abolition of the papal office.

As the French Revolution (1789–99) progressed, leaders intent on de-Christianizing France gained control. Their antipapal predispositions were intensified by Pius VI's opposition to the principles of 1789, and still more by his condemnation of the CIVIL CONSTITUTION OF THE CLERGY and the oaths of civil disobedience demanded of the clergy, and by his aversion to the whole body of ecclesiastical legislation of the French Assembly. When the Pope supported the first coalition of European powers arrayed against France, the revolutionaries retaliated by annexing papal territories in southern France, invading Italy, seizing the States of the Church, and establishing a republic in Rome. After stripping Pius VI of his temporal power, the French deprived him of his liberty. His death while a prisoner marked a low point in the papacy's fortune and gave rise to a prophecy that the apostolic succession had come to a close with the demise of ''Pius the Last.''

The next pope's humiliation surpassed those of his predecessor. After election at a conclave which convened in Venice, PIUS VII (1800–23) quickly revealed his independence by spurning Austrian enticements to reside in Vienna and by returning to his own capital. The first part of his pontificate was linked with the career of Napoleon I. As Bonaparte's military prowess extended his political sway and religious system over most of western Europe, including Italy, danger mounted that the Holy See would become a French vassal, the Pope an imperial chaplain, and Paris the center of the Church. Pius VII could not decline an invitation to attend the coronation in Paris, where he sat among the onlookers as Napoleon crowned himself emperor (1804). When the Pope refused to ally with France in the Continental Blockade, Napoleon seized Rome, deprived Pius VII of his temporal power, and held him prisoner in Savonna and Fontainbleau (1809–14). So close was the Pope's confinement that he could scarcely function even in his spiritual capacity.

Gains. An audit confined to adversities would be incomplete and misleading. The revolutionary era brought gains for the papacy that at least balanced the losses and prepared the way unwittingly for still greater advances. Badly as the two popes fared, their traditional foes fared worse. In the collapse of the monarchy and *ancien régime,* Gallicanism, particularly Political Gallicanism, received a serious wound from which it never fully recovered. Parlement, long a stronghold of Gallicanism, did not survive the Revolution. Although the Civil Constitution of Clergy started a schism in France, it caused also a noticeable rift in the façade of ecclesiastical Gallicanism. After the Constituent Assembly, without consulting the Church, passed (July 12, 1790) and promulgated this law (August 24), it prevented the French hierarchy from meeting in a national synod to chart a course through the crisis. Thereupon 30 of the 32 bishops among the Assembly's delegates drew up an *Exposition des principes sur la Constitution civile* (October 30) and with the almost unanimous approval of their fellow bishops submitted it to Pius VI seeking his guidance in applying the Civil Constitution. In the *Exposition* the Gallican bishops referred to the "successor of St. Peter, placed in the center of Catholic unity, who must be the interpreter and organ of the will of the universal Church." Pius VI delayed his formal condemnation of the law until the following March.

The CONCORDAT OF 1801, arranged between Napoleon and Pius VII without the concurrence of the French hierarchy, dealt a blow to the ecclesiastical Gallicanism, It was a recognition by the First Consul that the Pope held the key to restoring religious peace to France. In redrawing the ecclesiastical map of France and reducing the number of dioceses from 85 to 60, the Concordat permitted an unprecedented exercise of papal power requiring that the entire French hierarchy, whether Constitutional prelates or ordinaries in office previous to 1789, resign their sees. The 45 bishops who refused to resign were summarily removed from office. Twelve Constitutional bishops were named to the new sees, but they had to sign a submission to papal decisions concerning French religious affairs. Thereby they implicitly retracted their adherence to the Civil Constitution.

Napoleon's secularization of ecclesiastical principalities in Germany served to impoverish a group of wealthy, powerful, traditionally anti-Roman Rhenish bishops, weakened their Febronianism, and forced them and German Catholics in general to look to Rome for support.

From 1815 to 1878. Waterloo proved helpful for the noncombatant papacy. After Napoleon's downfall it became a principle beneficiary of the widespread disillusionment with the bloodshed and political and social upheaval in France, where democracy had quickly given way to military dictatorship. The statesmen who assembled at the Congress of Vienna (1814–15) sought a restoration of the *ancien régime* as far as possible. In their plans to stabilize a conservative, monarchical, legitimist system of law and order throughout Europe, they recog-

nized the altar as the sturdiest support of thrones. The allied powers that had displayed slight concern for the Pope's welfare when he was despoiled of his territories and his liberty, returned to him the States of the Church, save for the land in France. For the future of the papacy it was significant that no other ecclesiastic regained his confiscated principality. Governments that had expelled the Jesuits in the third quarter of the previous century and browbeaten the popes until the order was completely suppressed did not object when in 1814 Pius VII restored the Society of Jesus worldwide, proving strong support for the papacy as it had previous to 1773.

Reorganization of the Church. The second part of Pius VII's pontificate stands in marked contrast to the first. Events since 1789 had disorganized religious as well as secular society throughout Europe. Pius VII utilized his newly won influence and assumed leadership in rebuilding the Church. States that in the previous century had insisted on controlling internal religious affairs were eager to cooperate in arranging with Rome concordats or less formal agreements. The Holy See's policy in Germany took advantage of the fact that this region emerged from the Congress of Vienna as a loose confederation of political units. Dalberg, Wessenberg, and others favored a single German concordat in the hope of unifying the Church there with minimal dependence on Rome. Pius VII forestalled them by making separate arrangements with individual rulers, notably the Protestant King of Prussia, who found this an advantageous way of keeping formerly independent prelates civilly obedient. Succeeding decades witnessed the Cologne mixed marriage dispute and other Church-State disagreements that caused extended vacancies in several German sees, placed Catholics on the defensive, and nurtured the growth of ULTRAMONTANISM.

New Political Developments. Following the French Revolution there emerged a trend toward constitutional governments, secular in aim, officially indifferent or hostile toward religion, unwilling to favor one creed over another or to help any creed. Many states have followed the United States in separating Church and State. The material support, privileges, social and political status that the clergy enjoyed under the *ancien régime* greatly diminished or disappeared. The ties that once bound the clergy to so closely to the civil power and kept alive Gallicanism and other forms of ecclesiastical particularism no longer held. Political factors were very important in diverting the clergy en masse toward Rome as the one source willing and able to help them. The best example is France, particularly after 1830. What had long been the main center of Catholic opposition to the papacy assumed the lead in ultramontanism. Secular nationalism swelled to excessive proportions throughout the world during the nineteenth century, but ecclesiastical nationalism greatly declined.

The increasing menace of secularism, laicism, anticlericalism, materialism, and communism on an international scale also impelled Catholics to solidify their own ranks under the common leadership that Rome alone could provide.

Ultramontanism. Doctrinal and, even more, practical considerations promoted a remarkable growth of ultramontanism, which began early in the nineteenth century and developed into a well-organized, aggressive, and irresistible movement by mid-century. Ultramontanism was a complex movement, but in general it favored an authoritarian, highly centralized ecclesiastical government with the pope exerting his primacy of jurisdiction in all domains of the entire Church. This, the ultramontanes were convinced, was essential for the effectiveness of the Church and even for the salvation of society. Ultramontanism advocated also freeing the Church from all State tutelage and unifying liturgy, discipline, devotion, and customs according to the Roman model. Like most important movements in the life of the Church, this one grew from humble origins and won wide popular support among the lower clergy and laity. Until mid-century the popes remained somewhat aloof from it, partly because of its connection with Hugues Félicité de Lamennais and partly from a papal fear of alienating the French government. However, Pius IX favored it and placed himself at its head. The three most prominent literary champions of ultramontanism were not theologians but publicists and apologists: Joseph de MAISTRE, LAMENNAIS, and Louis VEUILLOT. Ultramontanism won followers in many countries, but chiefly in France, Germany, and Belgium. It proved a major force in preparing the way for the solemn definition of papal prerogatives in 1870 and in undermining the vestiges of Gallicanism, Febronianism, and Josephinism. Some ultramontanes allowed their enthusiastic adulation for the papacy to carry them to theologically unsound extremes, but this was not characteristic of the movement as a whole.

Action of the Popes (1823–46). LEO XII (1823–29) and PIUS VIII (1829–30) continued the centralizing tendencies of Pius VII. Most important in this regard was GREGORY XVI (1831–46). As pope he retained his keen interest in theology and in the missions. His principle theological work, *Il trionfo della Santa Sede e della Chiesa* (1799), strongly upheld the Church's independence of the civil power and papal primacy and infallibility, and it foretold the ultimate triumph of the Holy See and the Church. Gregory XVI put his teachings into effect by withstanding the secularizing aims of several governments and their encroachments on the spiritual power in Prussia and elsewhere. He was insistent on Rome's right to name bishops, particularly in Latin America, where he came into conflict with some of the newly independent republics. Despite growing unrest in the States of the Church, he determined to retain his temporal power. As a teacher he took the lead in condemning the doctrines of Lamennais and HERMES.

The papal control of Catholic missions throughout the world dates from this pontificate. Civil rulers, with little counsel from Rome, had often been responsible for spreading Christianity during the Middle Ages. The great missionary expansion of the sixteenth and seventeenth centuries after the era of geographical discoveries was accomplished largely by the Spanish and Portuguese governments, which interpreted the PATRONATO REAL and *padroado* in such a way as to monopolize control of the missions in their far-flung colonies. A combination of factors made the eighteenth century one of such precipitous decline that scarcely 300 missionaries were active by 1800. Penury of personnel and other reasons did not allow this situation to improve much during the following three decades. Circumstances became more favorable under the Gregory XVI, whose preoccupation with evangelization won him a reputation as the mission pope of his century. Since Spain and Portugal had by then ceased to be major powers and were unable to supply their former material support, they could not effectively resume their old *patronato* and *padroado* pretensions. Gradually Rome gained exclusive control. The Congregation for the PROPAGATION OF THE FAITH (Propaganda), which Napoleon I had abolished in 1808, was reorganized in 1817. Barolomeo Capellari acted as its prefect from 1826 until his election as Pope Gregory XVI in 1831. The Propaganda soon played the important role designed for it at its foundation in 1622. Its jurisdiction included Asia, Africa, Oceania, Australia, and the entire Western Hemisphere, as well as Prussia, Scandinavia, the Netherlands, and the British Isles. Acting through the Congregation, Gregory XVI assigned mission territories to religious institutes, decided the status of all missions, and appointed, promoted, and transferred the vicars and prefects who headed them. The Pope worked out the guiding principles and methods for the missioners. Gregory XVI and his successors took the lead in trying to eliminate colonialism and nationalism, particularly European nationalism, from the missions and in developing native clergies. Gone were the interminable negotiations among the Propaganda, the *patronato* powers, and religious orders with a quasi-monopoly in certain areas. Save for very limited territories remaining under the *patronato real* and *padroado*, all missions depended directly on the Propaganda, except for those under the Congregation for the Oriental Church since 1917 and the few subjected to the Consistorial Congregation.

The extraordinary mission development after 1831 received slight financial support from governments. Gregory XVI and later popes have promoted the organizations to raise by private charity the huge sums needed; they have exhorted the faithful to contribute and in the twentieth century brought the headquarters of many of these societies to Rome.demonstrate its intent to keep them under its personal direction and to obtain firsthand information about them.

Pius IX (1846–78). In the development of the papacy one of the most important pontificates in modern times is that of PIUS IX. He was the first pope to assume active leadership of ultramontanism, which he helped build almost into a ''party.'' To undermine Gallicanism still further, the Pope placed several well-known works on the Index. Some of them had been textbooks in French seminaries, and one by them, by Louis Bailly, had been taught at Maynooth. Pius IX also promoted liturgical unification by substituting Roman practices for a variety of local liturgies, particularly French ones. A concentrated effort was made to standardize ecclesiastical usages according to norms established in Rome. Even before 1870, centralization of authority and administration made such strides that it stands out as one of the most notable features of this pontificate. The Roman Curia emerged as the Church's administrative nerve center. Its functionaries served the Pope in ever more effective exercise of his jurisdictional primacy throughout the world. Accompanying this growth in the Roman Congregations was a marked improvement in the spiritual earnestness, intellectual caliber, professional competence, and industry of their staffs. But they did not always have a thorough grasp of contemporary needs and trends. Although the Curial cardinals were of high quality, Pius IX reduced their spiritual and temporal influence and consulted them rarely on broader issues, save for ANTONELLI and a few others.

Individual bishops came into more direct contact with papal authority. More so than his predecessors, Pius IX named bishops himself, regardless of local preferences, and in doing so revealed his inclination for ultramontanes. (By 1869 only 81 bishops chosen by Gregory XVI remained in a total of 739). Papal initiative was responsible for an increasing number of national seminaries in Rome, where promising future priests and bishops received ultramontane training and a preference for Roman usages. *AD LIMINA* VISITS became more frequent. Refractory bishops were beckoned to Rome. Appeals to the Curia from diocesan decisions, even in minor matters, were countenanced. The Holy See frowned on national synods but approved provincial councils. The large number of these provincial gatherings between 1846 and 1869 demonstrated the progress of ultramontanism among the bishops. The same trend was evident in the large episcopal assemblages in Rome in 1854, 1862, and 1867. Papal nuncios were more active than before in the internal affairs of local churches; they intervened regularly between Rome and bishops and between bishops and local clegy. The work of Fornari in Paris provides the most memorable example of a nuncio utilizing every circumstance to promote ultramontnaism.

As a teacher for the entire Church Pius IX was more active than his predecessor. It is especially noteworthy in the present context that the solemn definition of the IMMACULATE CONCEPTION, pronounced by Pius IX (Dec. 8, 1854) in the presence of a great international gathering of his bishops, made no mention of episcopal approbation, although this had been sought and received. The manner of defining this doctrine was intended as a practical demonstration of papal infallibility. The bishops attended the ceremony as spectators. It was during this pontificate above all that the Catholic world developed a strong personal devotion to each incumbent in the chair of St. Peter. Pius IX's winning personality and his conduct during very troubled years won him immense popularity.

VATICAN COUNCIL I marked the climax of this pontificate with a solemn definition of papal INFALLIBILITY and PRIMACY of jurisdiction. It brought to completion centuries of doctrinal development and removed permanently from serious consideration conciliarist or episcopalist arguments about the pope's position in the Church. When the final decision came, there was no energetic opposition from governments. Within the Council the minority based its case mainly on the inopportuneness of defining these matters at this time. Most of the Catholic world rejoiced in the definitions. Those irreconcilables who started the schism of the OLD CATHOLICS represented the insignificant minority.

Temporal Power. If alterations in society benefited the papal spiritual position, they weakened and finally destroyed the temporal power. Economic backwardness made the States of the Church a financial burden instead of a source of income for the Holy See. As the forces unleashed by the French Revolution permeated Italy, the Papal States ceased to provide independence for the popes, who were compelled to rely on military aid from France and Austria to restrain domestic unrest that was fomented by the drive to unify the Italian peninsula politically. Almost simultaneously in 1870 Vatican Council I established the pope permanently at the pinnacle of spiritual power, and an invading Italian army ended the papal temporal power. Rome feared that the loss of the States of the Church would eventually entail the sacrifice of papal spiritual independence; but matters turned out otherwise. Pius IX and his successors until Pius XI retired behind the walls of the Vatican as voluntary prisoners protesting against the seizure of their state and against the Law of GUARANTEES and awaited the solution of the ROMAN QUESTION. Meanwhile the papacy's international diplomatic standing remained intact and its spiritual power continued to increase.

1878 to 1958. LEO XIII (1878–1903), PIUS X (1903–14), BENEDICT XV (1914–22), PIUS XI (1922–39), and PIUS XII (1939–58) were all zealous men of high spiritual and intellectual caliber and both esteemed and influential. In 1917 the promulgation by Benedict XV of the Code of CANON LAW terminated a long process of growth in ecclesiastical law and exalted the position of the papacy in the Church's legal structure, just as Vatican Council I did in a doctrinal way. To Heiler the Code marked "the victory of papalism, the completion of centralization, the conclusion of centuries of development of the primacy of jurisdiction." Never was the papal magisterial power more in evidence than after 1878. As teachers in matters of faith and morals these five popes were prodigiously active. Heterodox doctrines were rare in Catholic ranks; but when they appeared, they served to reveal the enormous influence of the papal magisterium. Thus MODERNISM subsided quickly after Pius X's condemnation. Pius XII's *HUMANI GENERIS* nipped in the bud several novel doctrines. The contrast is striking between the effectiveness of those pronouncements and those issued by seventeenth- and eighteenth-century popes during the Jansenist disputes. For topical variety and volume of teachings, the writings, allocutions, and broadcasts of Pius XII surpassed anything in papal history. This extremely conscientious and industrious supreme pontiff kept in the closest possible touch with all sections of the Church, familiarized himself with current problems, and considered it his duty to provide solutions for all of them. It is doubtful that any pope made more extensive use of his position as spiritual monarch. After Cardinal Maglione's death in 1944, for example, Pius XII dispensed with even a secretary of state.

Administrative centralization in Rome continued to increase, although this is not a necessary corollary of the definitions in 1870. Primacy of jurisdiction does not require limitless centralization of administration any more than it compels the absorption of all episcopal jurisdiction. Burgeoning bureaucracy and its effects roused criticisms in the ranks of the hierarchy and elsewhere. Doctrinally the popes remained within their rights. In the practical order each pope must endeavor to conciliate his powers and obligations with those of the bishops, according to changing circumstances. The tendency toward centralization and uniformity was not the same everywhere. Thus the Eastern Churches in union with Rome long enjoyed autonomy in their liturgy, law, and discipline. After Pius IX, this autonomy was considerably reduced, notably in disciplinary matters, but not to the same extent as in the West.

Papal relations with bishops were harmonious and close. Detailed quinquennial reports, which had to be sent to Rome from all dioceses, enabled twentieth-century popes to maintain over all episcopal administrations careful surveillance and methodical control. Vatican Council I did not pronounce on the relationship between the pope and the bishops, but this was addressed during the course of the Second Vatican Council (1962–65).

Bibliography: H. MARC-BONNET, *La Papauté contemporaine, 1878–1945* (Paris 1946). P. BREZZI, *The Papacy: Its Origins and Historical Evolution,* tr. H. J. YANNONE (Westminister, Maryland 1958). W. BERTRAMS, *The Papacy, the Episcopacy, and Collegiality* tr. P. T. BRANNAN (Westminister, Maryland 1964). H. C. KOENIG, ed., *Principles for Peace: Selections from Papal Documents from Leo XIII to Pius XII* (Washington, D.C. 1943) R. AUBERT, *The Church in a Secularized Society* (New York 1978). F. J. COPPA, *The Modern Papacy Since 1789* (London 1998). E. E. Y. HALES, *The Catholic Church in the Modern World* (Garden City, New York 1958). M. GIACOMO, *La Chiesa nell' eta del liberalismo* (Brescia 1978). *Church and Society: Catholic Social and Political Thoughts and Movements, 1789–1950,* ed. J. N. MOODY et. al. 21–92. (New York 1953). O. CHADWICK, *A History of the Popes, 1830–1914* (Oxford 1998). E. E. Y. HALES, *Revolution and Papacy, 1769–1816* (Notre Dame, Indiana 1966). J. MCMANNERS, *The French Revolution and the Church* (New York 1970). M. M. O'DWYER, *The Papacy in the Age of Napoleon and the Restoration, Pius VII, 1800–1823* (New York 1985). N. BLAKISTON, ed. *Extracts from the Dispatches of Odo Russel from Rome 1858–1870* (London 1962). C. BUTLER, *The Vatican Council: The Story Told From Inside in Bishop Ulathorne's Letters* (New York 1930). F. J. COPPA, *Pope Pius IX: Crusader in Secular Age* (Boston 1979). M. GIACOMO, *Pio IX (1846–1850)* (Rome 1974). F. J. COPPA, *Pio IX (1851–1866)* (Rome 1986). F. J. COPPA, *Pio IX (1867–1878)* (Rome 1990). I. GIORDANI, *Pius X: A Country Priest* tr. T. J. TOBIN (Milwaukee 1954). G. P. FOGARTY, *The Vatican and the Americanist Crisis: Denis J. O'Connell, American Agent in Rome, 1885–1903* (Rome 1974). P. GRANFIELD, *The Papacy in Transition* (New York 1980). J.F. POLLARD, *The Unknown Pope: Benedict XV (1914–1922) and the Pursuit of Peace* (London and New York 1999). R. ANDERSON, *Between Two Wars: The Story of Pope Pius XI (Achille Ratti) 1922–1939* (Chicago 1977). G. PASSELECQ, and B. SUCHECKY, *The Hidden Encyclical of Pius XI* (New York 1998). P. BLET, *Pius XII and the Second World War According to the Archives of Vatican* (New York 1999). F. J. COPPA, ed., *Controversial Concordats: The Vatican's Relations with Napoleon, Mussolini and Hitler* (Washington, D.C. 1999). A. RHODES, *The Vatican in the Age of Dictators, 1922–1945* (New York 1973). R. RYCHLAK, *Hitler, the War, and the Pope* (Huntington, Indiana 2000).

[J. F. BRODERICK/EDS.]

5. The Contemporary Papacy (1958–2001)

This section of the history of the papacy extends from the election of JOHN XXIII (1958) to the opening of the third millennium.

Following the death of Pius XII, 51 Cardinals entered the conclave on Oct 25, 1958, to select a successor. Some considered the age of the 77-year-old Angelo Roncalli an advantage, convinced that the Church needed a transitional pope who would not have time to introduce innovations. He was elected on October 28. Immediately, John XXIII recognized the need for some updating or *aggiornamento* of the Church as well as an *aperturismo* or opening up of the institution as he sought an accommodation with the contemporary world.

John referred to *aggiornamento* in November 1957, and it was to become his trademark. Early on, he conceived of calling a Council, the twenty-first of the Church, announcing his intention in January 1959. He perceived it as the Church's response to modernity. On Oct. 11, 1962, the Council officially opened.

Among the themes of his pontificate was a concern for the persecuted Church where pastors could not perform their duties in freedom, encouraging the so-called *Ostpolitik* or opening to the eastern bloc and particularly Moscow.

Rather than continuing Piux XII's anticommunist crusade, John was prepared to adopt a pragmatic approach to the communist regimes, letting Moscow know that the Vatican sought improved relations. He utilized Agostino CASAROLI, his new secretary of state, to reach accommodation with a series of communist governments, securing the liberation of a number of ecclesiastics from eastern Europe and enabling him to fill vacant bishoprics there. Assured the Council would not condemn communism, Khruschev gave permission for Russian Orthodox observers to attend and allowed some 90 bishops from the communist countries of Eastern Europe to participate.

John did not neglect the social question. On May 15, 1961, he issued MATER ET MAGISTRA, on the Church as mother and teacher of all nations, stressing the role of Christianity and social progress. John claimed that Leo's RERUM NOVARUM initiated a process by which the Church made itself the champion of the rights of the working class. John concurred with Leo that private property was a right that entailed social obligations, adding that the state could not remain aloof from economic matters. He decried the sums squandered on ill-conceived national prestige and armaments to the detriment of workers.

Like Pius XI, who issued QUADRAGESIMO ANNO, John believed that the relationship between wages and profits must take into consideration the common good. John, too, was not prepared to accept communism or socialism, whose objectives did not transcend material-well being. However, he argued that that COMMON GOOD required that the public authority broaden its scope, keeping in mind that the world's goods were intended for the support of the entire human race. John's *Mater et magistra* accepted the welfare state as an expression of the common good. His call for social and international peace was repeated in his last encyclical *PACEM IN TERRIS* (On Universal Peace) of April 11, 1963. In it, the papacy came to terms with individual rights introduced by the revolutionary movement, but within a Christian context.

In November 1959, Pope John issued *Princeps pastorum* on the missions and the native clergy. The pope warned that the missionary contribution must be carefully attuned to local needs, expressing the hope that the local clergy would be able to select from among its ranks those capable of governing, forming, and educating their own seminarians.

When John closed the first session of the Council on Dec. 8, 1962, the expectations aroused had not been fulfilled. During its two crowded months no decrees had been approved. John, who had cancer, would not be able to see the Council to its conclusion. John's popularity stemmed from his personal warmth and his willingness to take risks.

The conclave of June 19, 1963, elected as pope the 65-year-old Giovanni Battista Montini, the Cardinal Archbishop of Milan, who was considered John's choice. He assumed the name PAUL VI. Following his election to the papacy, Paul announced that the Council would reopen on Sept. 29, 1963. *Aggiornamento* remained one of his goals, as well as the need to revise the canon law and reform the curia, while he continued the commitment to social justice enunciated in his predecessor's encyclicals. Paul outlined new directives for the Council, including the admission of lay Catholics, the extension of invitations to non-Catholic observers, and the appointment cardinal moderators. At the opening of this second session he called for renewal, Christian unity, and dialogue with the contemporary world. Paul wanted to the bishops to exercise their rights to govern the Church with him, while seeking conditions for ecumenical encounters with non-Catholics.

In December 1963, Paul announced his pilgrimage to the Holy Land the next year. The first pope to fly in an airplane, and first to visit the Holy Land, Paul met the Ecumenical Patriarch of Constantinople there, as well as the Armenian Patriarch and the Anglican Archbishop of Jerusalem. As Paul prepared for the third session of the Council scheduled to convene in mid-September 1964, he stressed the need for unity, which had moved him to visit the Holy Land. In August he issued the first encyclical letter *ECCLESIAM SUAM* which continued the dialogue within the Church, with non-Catholic Christians, with non-Christians, and even non-believers. Indeed, it called for a dialogue with the entire, contemporary world. In September 1964, Paul prepared for the opening of the third session of the Council, making provisions to have some women attend as auditors without the right to speak or vote during the debates.

At year's end, Pope Paul ventured to Bombay, India, where he expressed his desire to narrow the gap between the world's Christians and non-Christians. Returning to Rome, Paul planned for the fourth and final session of the Council. In January 1965, he revealed his decision to name 27 new cardinals, stressing the need to make the college more universal and appointing the four major Eastern patriarchs to it. In June 1965, when Paul addressed the College of Cardinals, he surveyed the problems confronting the Church, including collegiality, the reform of canon law, mixed marriages, birth control, world peace, and the Council. Pope Paul also addressed the problems confronting the global community. He supported the United Nations quest for disarmament and fight against hunger, addressing it on the twentieth anniversary of its organization. His message was "no more war, war never again." The pope's plan had four major elements. First, relations between states should be governed by reason, justice, law and negotiation rather than by fear, violence, deceit or war. This, in turn, required disarmament. The money saved from the stockpiling of weapons should be utilized to assist the developing nations and solving the problems of hunger and poverty. Finally, the Pope saw the need to protect fundamental human rights, and above all, religious liberty.

As the council came to a close on December 7, a joint declaration by Paul VI and Patriarch ATHENOGORAS I, read at Rome and Istanbul simultaneously, nullified the Catholic-Orthodox exchange of excommunications issued in 1054. On Dec. 8, 1965, Pope Paul declared the Council closed.

The decade following the Council was dominated by a continuing discussion of the need to implement its decisions. Paul established commissions to continue its work, as well as yearly meetings in Rome to further the dialogue. His social encyclical on the development of peoples, POPULORUM PROGRESSIO, was issued on March 26, 1967. Deemed by some the *magna carta* for justice and peace, Paul showed his concern for those attempting to escape the ravages of hunger, poverty, endemic disease, and ignorance as he made a plea for social justice and fundamental improvement for the impoverished masses of the third world. Citing Leo's *Rerum novarum*, Pius XI's *Quadragesimo anno*, John XXIII's *Mater et magistra* and *Pacem in terris*, as well as his own trips to Latin America (1960) and Africa (1962), he addressed the perplexing problems of these continents. In August 1968,

Pope Paul flew to Bogota and Medellín, Columbia, the first visit of a pope to Latin America. Here *Populorum progressio* was appreciated for its support of the third world, as was the condemnation of the unequal distribution of the world's goods cataloged in *Humanae vitae*.

Paul pursued a *via media*, encouraging the Extraordinary Synod at the end of 1969 to explore the relationship between papal primacy and episcopal collegiality. In 1970, he ruled that bishops should submit their resignation when they reached 75, and that cardinals after their eightieth year could no longer participate in a conclave. Some suggested that the Pope himself should retire, but Paul continued to preside over the Church and travel on behalf of peace and social justice. In 1969, he visited Africa, again the first Pope to do so, while in 1970 he visited the Philippines where the Bolivian painter Benjamin Mendoza made an attempt against his life in Manila. Undaunted, the Pope continued his *Ostpolitik* by seeking a reconciliation with the communist regimes of Eastern Europe, establishing diplomatic relations with Yugoslavia in 1971 and improving relations with Hungary.

Paul continued to inject the Vatican in international affairs, supporting peace in Vietnam, and upholding the cause of the United Nations. In July 1972, the Holy See participated in the Conference on Security and Co-Operation in Europe at Helsinki as a participant and not simply as an observer, marking the first full participation in an international conference since the Congress of Vienna of 1815. Casaroli, who was at Helsinki, followed this by a visit to Moscow in 1972, the first Vatican official to travel there in an official capacity. Subsequently, he traveled to Castro's Cuba. In 1973 Paul established a "Study Commission on the Role of Women in Church and Society." On Aug. 6, 1978, Paul died at Castel Gandolfo, following a heart attack.

Among his achievements, he brought John's Council to a successful conclusion and continued his work of *aggiornamento* and reconciliation with the contemporary world. He dismantled the papal court and reformed the Roman curia without alienating either, and introduced collegiality in the Church without undermining papal primacy. He internationalized the Vatican and visited the Holy Land, India, Turkey, the United Nations in New York, Latin America, the Philippines, Australia and Portugal among other places. He helped to make the Church in Africa an African Church, and implemented the use of modern languages in the liturgy. For conservatives he had gone too far, for liberals his reformism remained incomplete.

Cardinal Albino Luciani, the Patriarch of Venice, was elected pope at the end of August 1978 under the name JOHN PAUL. Determined to continue the work of his two predecessors, he did not have time to do so, dying some 33 days following his election—one of the shortest pontificates in modern times.

On October 16, 1978, during the second conclave of that year, Cardinal Karol Wojtyła, archbishop of Kraków, was elected and took the name JOHN PAUL II. He was the first Slav pope and the first non-Italian since Hadrian VI of Utrecht in 1522. Only 58, Wojtyła, the 264th pope, was the youngest since Pius IX in 1846. The new pope quickly embarked on a series of travels that covered more territory than those of all of his predecessors combined. The most significant of the early travels was to Poland (June 2-10, 1979), the first of three visits there before the opening of Eastern Europe. The triumphant papal tour altered the mentality of fear that prevailed in Poland and much of the Eastern bloc. On display even at this early stage were two factors that marked John Paul II's pontificate: his personal popularity, which heightened public perception of the pope as the voice of the Church; and a new engagement of the Church in the world.

The themes for John Paul II's pontificate were set forth in his first encyclical, *REDEMPTOR HOMINIS* (1979): Christian unity, the preparation for the Great Jubilee of the Year 2000, the implementation of the Second Vatican Council, evangelization and mission. Most notable was the pope's emphasis on the Church's message to the world, based on *Gaudium et spes* 22, "The truth is that only in the mystery of the Incarnate Word does the mystery of man take on light" (cited in *RH* 8). Christian personalism, seeing the human person in the light of revelation, emerged as the basis for much of John Paul II's teaching. The engagement with the world proposed here had been prepared by the fate of the papacy since the loss of the States of the Church. As noted in the previous section of this article, the teaching authority of the papacy grew immensely concurrently with the papacy's loss of temporal power. Nor was this teaching confined to inner-Church matters, as can be seen, for example, in the rise of papal social teaching. Yet the Church's proclamations on matters of concern to all men were often based in a conception of the social order (society being under the direction of a legislator/governor obedient to the natural law) that was not shared by those countries whose constitutions emerged from the age of revolution. Vatican II had attempted to speak the truth of Christ to the world in a language that it could understand; John Paul II's personalism developed this further. The dignity of the person—the calling of each person to eternal union with God in Christ, and what is necessary to foster that vocation—became the basis for papal teaching on the evils of socialism's subordination of the person to the State (*LABOREM EXERCENS*), of consumerism (*CENTESIMUS ANNUS*), of the denigration of women (*Mulieris digni-*

tatem), and of all assaults on human life (*EVANGELIUM VITAE*). It also grounded the pope's teaching that moral theology ought to be concerned primarily with the call of every person to beatitude (*VERITATIS SPLENDOR*); that human reason, rightly understood, is an indispensable part of the Christian life (*FIDES ET RATIO*); and that Christians are called to manifest to the world the transformative power of suffering in love (*Salvifici doloris*; *DIVES IN MISERICORDIA*).

In 1983, in an address to the Latin American bishops assembled in Haiti, the pope called for a new evangelization, "new in its ardor, its methods, and its expression," in keeping with a recognition of the dignity and ultimate destiny of the human person. Thus, for example, this evangelization emphasizes dialogue and respect for existing cultures, at the same time as it calls for a transformation of all cultures. The missionary work of the Church at the end of the twentieth century, hampered in part by declining numbers in missionary religious orders, received a great boost from the pope himself. In his travels, from Poland to the Philippines, from Nicaragua to the United States, he routinely drew huge, enthusiastic crowds, receptive to his personal, pastoral presence. Especially noteworthy in this regard were the WORLD YOUTH DAYS, celebrated every other year, beginning in 1987.

The implementation of Vatican II required not only the renewal of the Church's mission to the world, but also the practical implementation of the council's vision of the Church as *COMMUNIO*. The relationship of the bishops to the pope and the role of the Roman Curia in the governance of the Church were two decisive issues. The SYNOD OF BISHOPS, established by Paul VI in 1965, had met approximately every three years in general assemblies. They continued to do so under John Paul II, treating themes of the Christian family (1980), reconciliation and penance (1983), laity (1987), priests (1990), consecrated life (1994), and the role of the bishop (2001). An extraordinary assembly was called in 1985 to reflect on the Second Vatican Council, twenty years later. In 1991 the pope began calling special assemblies of the synod, gathering bishops of distinct areas of the world (Europe, Asia, the Americas, Oceania, Africa, Lebanon). A consistent theme of these assemblies was evangelization.

Despite the prominence given to the bishops through the assemblies of the Synod and the development of national episcopal conferences, the Roman Curia remained the administrative nerve center of the Church. This was evident in the question of the authority of episcopal conferences, a matter of some dispute following the council. The apostolic letter *Apostolos suos*, issued *motu proprio* by John Paul II in 1998, clarified that a doctrinal declaration of a conference is binding only if the members approve it unanimously or it receives a *recognitio* from the Apostolic See after receiving the approval of at least two-thirds of the conference. The authority of Rome was emphasized also by the promulgation of several key documents for the universal Church: e.g., a revised Code of Canon Law; the *Code of Canons for the Eastern Churches*; the *Catechism of the Catholic Church*; the *General Directory for Catechesis*; and the *Directory for the Application of Principles and Norms on Ecumenism.* The Curia took a proactive role in teaching and governing the universal Church. Preeminent in this respect was the CON-GREGATION FOR THE DOCTRINE OF THE FAITH, under the direction of Cardinal Joseph Ratzinger. Disciplinary action was taken against several theologians and prelates. Most significant of these was Archbishop Marcel LEFEB-VRE, who had denounced the changes in the Church arising from Vatican II. Lefebvre was excommunicated in 1988 after he ordained four bishops without papal permission. A papal commission, *Ecclesia Dei,* was established to facilitate the reconciliation of the members of Lefebvre's movement with the Church.

Though the administration of the Church continued to be centralized, the composition of that administration was changing substantially. In 1988 the pope reorganized the Curia via the apostolic letter *Pastor bonus.* More importantly, the internationalization of the college of cardinals (and indirectly of the Curia) begun by Paul VI was expanded greatly by John Paul II. In 2001, only one of the nine curial congregations and one of the eleven pontifical councils was headed by an Italian; most were headed by non-European cardinals.

One congregation whose importance increased greatly during this time was the Congregation for the Causes of Saints. By the year 2000, John Paul II had celebrated over 300 canonizations and almost 1000 beatifications. His twentieth-century predecessors had, all together, celebrated 98 and 79, respectively. The theme of the "universal call to holiness" of the Second Vatican Council thus received extraordinary emphasis. Previously, local impetus toward canonization had been met by a cautious attitude from Rome; now, it was evident that Rome encouraged local churches to recognize models of holiness in their midst.

The role of the papacy on the world political stage was most obvious in Eastern Europe and the fall of communism. It was also evident in various interventions with the United Nations (Cairo Conference on Population [1994]; Beijing Conference on the Status of Women [1995]) in support of the Christian understanding of human rights and especially the good of the family. The Vatican criticized the "contraceptive imperialism" of the modernized world vis-a- vis the third world. Vatican diplomacy played a key role in shifting the focus of the Cairo conference from controlling population through birth control to an emphasis on increased education, job opportunities, and full civil rights for women. Another striking development was the establishment of diplomatic relations between the Vatican and the State of Israel in 1993. Pope John Paul was a credible spokesman against anti-Semitism, having suffered under Nazi occupation in his youth in Poland and having been active in protecting Jews at that time. He repeatedly denounced the outbursts of anti-Semitism in Europe. In 1998 a Vatican document entitled "We Remember: A Reflection on the Shoah" recognized that anti-Judaism among Christians facilitated the genocidal anti-Semitism of the Nazis. Regret for anti-Judaism was repeated by the pope during his March 2000 visit to the Holocaust Museum in Jerusalem.

The ecumenical efforts begun by a variety of movements in the nineteenth and twentieth centuries were taken up by the council and grew throughout the late twentieth century. John Paul II issued an encyclical on the subject (*UT UNUM SINT*) and promoted extensive ecumenical discussions with Protestant and Anglican communions as well as numerous Orthodox Churches. No visible union arose from these efforts, but the principle of ecumenical dialogue as a normative part of the Church's mission was enshrined. Particularly difficult for the papacy was the approach to take to the Orthodox Churches. After the fall of communism and the restoration of much religious liberty in Eastern Europe, old feuds between Orthodox Churches and Eastern Churches in union with Rome flared up again, the former refusing to recognize the latter, the latter appealing to Rome to support their rights. The pope's wish to make a fraternal visit to the patriarch of Moscow was frustrated time and again. Interreligious dialogue achieved greater success. In *Redemptor hominis*, the pope laid down the principle that the Church must be attentive to the work of the Spirit in followers of non-Christian religions (*RH* 6). Dialogue with the great cultures and religions of the world thus became a part of papal ministry to a degree that it never had been before. The pope himself met with a variety of religious leaders, most famously the Dalai Lama, and personally overrode some objections from the Curia in order to call for a World Day of Prayer for Peace in Assisi in 1986. More than sixty religious leaders, most of them non-Christian, joined the pope in Assisi to pray in the presence of one another.

A century and more of popes of exemplary character, fine intelligence, and, frequently, enormous popular appeal had raised the prestige of the papacy to an exalted height. Entering the third millennium, the pope had become the world's most significant, internationally recognized moral authority.

Bibliography: L. ACCATOLI, *Man of the Millennium: John Paul II* (Boston 2000). A. ALEXIEV, ''The Kremlin and the Vatican'' *Orbis* (Fall 1983) 554–65. R. AUBERT, *The Church in a Secularized Society* (New York 1978). F. J. COPPA, *The Modern Papacy 1789, The Longman History of the Papacy* (London 1988). A. FLANNERY, ed., *Vatican Council II: The Conciliar and Post Conciliar Documents* (Grand Rapids, Michigan 1992). M. E. DE FRANCISCUS, *Italy and the Vatican: The 1984 Concordat Between Church and State, Studies in Modern European History*, ed. F. J. COPPA (New York 1989). A. FROSSARD, *Be Not Afraid: Pope John Paul Speaks Out on his Life, his Beliefs, and his Inspiring Vision for Humanity*, tr. J. R. FOSTER (New York 1984). V. GORRESIO, *The New Mission of Pope John XXIII*, tr. C. L. MARKMANN (New York 1969). M. HABIGER, *Papal Teaching on Private Property, 1891–1981* (Lanham, Maryland 1990). P. HEBBLETHWAITE, *Pope John XXIII: Shepherd of the Modern World* (Garden City, New York 1985). P. HEBBLETHWAITE, *Paul VI: The First Modern Pope* (New York 1993). D. J. HOLMES, *The Papacy in the Modern World, 1914–1978* (New York 1981). M. MALINSKI, *Pope John Paul II: The Life of Karol Wojityla*, tr. P. S. FALL (New York 1979). M. MALACHI, *The Keys of this Blood: The Struggle for World Dominion Between Pope John Paul II, Mikail Gorbachev, and the Capitalist West* (New York 1990). M. B. MELADY, *The Rhetoric of Pope John Paul II* (Westport, Connecticut 1999). M. MILLER, ed., *The Encyclicals of John Paul II* (Huntington, Indiana 1999). J. E. SMITH, *Humanae Vitae, A Generation Later* (Washington D.C. 1991). H. STEHLE, *Eastern Politics of the Vatican*, tr. S. SMITH (Athens, Ohio 1981). T. SZULC, *John Paul II: The Biography* (New York 1995). G. WEIGEL, ed., *A New Wordly Order: John Paul II and Human Freedom* (Lanham, Maryland 1992).

[F. J. COPPA/EDS.]

PAPADOPOULOS, CHRYSOSTOMOS

Orthodox archbishop, ecclesiastical historian; b. Madytos, eastern Thrace, July 1, 1868; d. Athens, Oct. 28, 1938. After earlier training at Constantinople, Jerusalem, and Smyrna he studied theology at the University of Athens (1889–91) and at the ecclesiastical academies of Kiev (1891–93) and St. Petersburg (1893–95). From 1895 until 1909 he taught at the theological School of the Cross in Jerusalem, where he was ordained and was made an archimandrite (1900). After two years spent in parish work in Alexandria (1909–11), he acted as director of the Rizarion Seminary in Athens (1911–23) and also as professor of ecclesiastical history at the University (1914–23). The Holy Synod elected him archbishop of Athens and of all Greece (1923). Papadopoulos published numerous articles on ecclesiastical history, his principal scholarly interest, and also many on ethics. He wrote also a history of the Oriental patriarchates and a history of the Greek and Slavic Orthodox Churches. He influenced deeply the cultural and political life of Greece between World Wars I and II. He favored the ecumenical movement, but showed slight sympathy for Catholics of the Greek rite.

Bibliography: Biography and complete list of his works in *Enaisima* (miscellanea in his honor), ed. G. PAPAMICHAIL (Athens 1931); and in *Theologia* 16 (1938) 369–408; 17 (1939) 257–272. H. PIERRE, ''L'union de l'Orient avec Rome,'' *Orientalia Christiana* 18.1 (1930) 5–165, correspondence between P. Ch. and the Catholic exarch of Greece, George Calavassy. J. SALAVILLE, *Catholicisme* 2:1116—17.

[J. KRAJCAR]

PAPAL ARBITRATION

International arbitration, of which papal arbitration is an aspect, evoked a vast literature between 1870 and 1920. These writings mirrored quite perfectly the assumption of civilized society that rational juridical forms might be substituted for irrational military methods to resolve conflicting claims of sovereign states. Since 1929 and the abandonment of the assumption that *ratio* can control *vis*, arbitration as a juridical form has its greatest utility in cases of private law and labor negotiations and is scarcely noticed in international legal literature save in its historical aspects. Arbitration, a method of adjudication developed in classical Greece and refined by Roman usage and jurisprudence, depends on several assumptions common to the contenders and the arbitrator. Some of these assumptions are good faith, equality, and a belief in some kind of punitive sanction. The contenders assume, first, that the losses incurred in arbitration are substantially less than would occur were they to resort to a trial of strength and, second, that the arbitrator is as much concerned with equity, as they understand the term, as are they themselves.

Medieval Development. Papal arbitration was one aspect of that subtle process by which the Roman Catholic Church in the West became in the Middle Ages the veritable heir of the Roman Empire. The process had already begun in the NT period, when Church members were exhorted to settle their differences without recourse to pagan courts (1 Cor 6.1–9). Among the privileges extended to bishops by the Constantinian peace was imperial recognition (*Codex Theodosianus*, ed. T. Mommsen and P. Meyer, 2 v. in 3 [Berlin 1905] 1:27.1) of the validity of decisions rendered by the bishop in his capacity either of *iudex* (judge) or *arbiter* (arbitrator), and the obligation of the state to enforce the decisions rendered by an ecclesiastical person. As the internal cohesion of the Empire dissolved especially in the 5th and 6th centuries, not only did all bishops assume greater administrative and judicial responsibility, but the bishops of the patriarchical sees, except Constantinople, became shadowy proconsuls.

From the time of the Lombard invasions into Italy, the bishops of Rome became steadily the sole Roman, political, and judicial power of the West. After freeing itself first from Byzantine and, later, Carolingian domination, the papacy of the 11th century rose to a position of leadership based solidly on written law in contrast with Germanic contention for headship based on custom of relatively brief duration. The great popes of the 12th and 13th centuries, many of them former professors of law—both Canon and Roman—appointed Roman law forms of arbitration for many classes of difficulties arising between two juridical persons. "It is in the collection of GREGORY IX (1234) that one must seek out the Canon Law doctrine on arbitration and its codification. This doctrine is taken from Roman law, which it reproduced almost completely and without change, except in those areas peculiarly inspired by Christian ideas or which the dictates of practice necessitated. The doctrine remained without notable change up to the Code of Canon Law of 1917'' (Amanieu).

However, as the feudal monarchs of the 13th century developed greater awareness of their own juridical personalities (*Rex est imperator in regno suo*), the popes, who became more deeply involved in European power politics and were recognized for this reason to be of the same power stature as the secular monarchs, were more and more often called upon to act as arbitrators. BONIFACE VIII arbitrating the dispute between King PHILIP IV the Fair and EDWARD I of England (1297); ALEXANDER VI, between Portugal and Spain (1493); and GREGORY XIII, between Poland and Russia (1572–83), exemplified successful papal adjudication of international disputes. Whereas textbooks often refer to popes as arbitrators, they seldom note that the Holy See itself not infrequently employed the method of arbitration to resolve its own political differences with Italian states and combinations of states, a fact that underscores the grave responsibilities which devolved on the pope as a territorial sovereign.

Modern Era. The religious and political upheavals of the 16th and 17th centuries diminished the possibility of arbitration but by no means ended the need for it. With J. BODIN's definition of sovereignty and the growth of the modern state with its large and absolute authority, the peacelovers of the civilized nations began to seek juridical mechanisms for the promotion of peace; and in the early writers, such as Hugo GROTIUS, one finds recourse to the Roman law doctrine of arbitration. The congress system of making and maintaining peace, begun in the 18th century and developed in the years that followed, recognized arbitration and finally set up at The Hague a panel of jurists to be employed for arbitration of disputed claims. But only rarely did secular rulers employ the good offices of the Holy See in arbitration. In 1885 Pope LEO XIII was selected to arbitrate the claims of the German Empire and Spain in the Caroline Islands. The overtures of BENEDICT XV (July 28, 1915, and especially Aug.

1, 1917) to serve as mediator between the belligerents in World War I met with no success. More cautiously, PIUS XII fashioned his public reactions during World War II to the prospective role of peacemaker—to which, however, he was not invited. In his first encyclical, *ECCLESIAM SUAM*, PAUL VI, by offering his services in the cause of peace, maintained the traditional attitude of the papacy toward international arbitration.

It may be concluded that the prevailing ethical standard of European society has been gauged by its view of papal arbitration. The Church preserved the Roman law of arbitration and the great legist popes of the Middle Ages disseminated that equitable form. Since secular governments began to replace Romano-canonical methods, they have sought, particularly from the 17th century, to devise universally acceptable systems of arbitration. But lacking a common ethic and a common religious orientation, modern nations can act in concert only *ad hoc* and on the basis of the balance of power, best described by St. Augustine as a *latrocinium*, or robbers' treaty.

Bibliography: J. H. RALSTON, *International Arbitration from Athens to Locarno* (Palo Alto 1929). J. EPPSTEIN, *The Catholic Tradition of the Law of Nations* (London 1935). A. AMANIEU, *Dictionnaire de droit canonique*, ed. R. NAZ, 7 v. (Paris 1935–65) 1:862–895. G. BALLADORE PALLIERI and G. VISMARA, *Acta pontificia juris gentium* (Milan 1946). C. PHARR et al., eds. and trs., *The Theodosian Code and Novels* (Princeton 1952). A. BERGER, *Encyclopedic Dictionary of Roman Law* (Transactions of the American Philosophical Society NS 43.2; Philadelphia 1953).

[S. WILLIAMS]

PAPAL CEREMONY AND VESTURE

As supreme head of the universal Church, the pope can officiate in any existing liturgical rite, Eastern or Western. However, as bishop of Rome, he regularly celebrates according to the Roman Rite.

Ceremonial. While the ritual he observes is that followed by all archbishops, there are nonetheless many ceremonies special to the pope.

The Papal Pontifical Mass. In a pontifical mass, the pope wears several vestments, as explained below; the college of cardinals and bishops or abbots attending Mass are vested in cope or chasuble (the cardinal deacons in dalmatics), and all wear the white miter. Historically, the first part of the papal mass was the solemn entry of the pope, carried on the *sedes gestatoria* and wearing his great mantle and the TIARA, both of which have fallen into disuse. The Liturgy of the Word of the papal mass closely follows closely the rite of a bishop's pontifical Mass in his own cathedral. The special rite in this part of the Mass is the chanting of the Gospel in Latin and Greek.

The coronation ceremony of Pope Paul VI outside St Peter's in July 1963. (©David Lees/CORBIS)

During the papal mass, there is one very particular rite, which has never been allowed in any other diocese or rite, that is, the pope's Communion at his throne.

Canonization. Until the time of Pius XII the ceremony was quite long. The *Ave Maris Stella* was sung during the procession into St. Peter's Basilica behind the banner of the servant of God. Upon arrival before the papal throne, the postulator of the cause knelt before the pontiff and asked *instanter* (urgently) the canonization; the Litany of the Saints followed. Again the postulator approached the throne and requested *instantius* (more urgently) for the glorification of the servant of God; the *Veni Creator* was then sung. For a third time the postulator went to the pope and begged *instantissime* (most urgently). At this the pontiff read the declaration of canonization. The *Te Deum* concluded this part of the rite.

However, in order to abbreviate the ceremony Pius XII had the Litany of the Saints chanted during the procession into the basilica; the three petitions were joined into one followed by the *Veni Creator* and the declaration. In the Mass that follows there is a solemn procession with offerings of candles, wine, bread, and doves. The first report of such an offertory procession comes from

the canonization of St. Bridget of Sweden, which took place in 1391.

Other Rites. The pope also reserves to himself the opening and closing of ecumenical councils, the opening of the Holy Doors in JUBILEE YEARS, the blessing of the archbishop's PALLIUM, the blessing of the GOLDEN ROSE that he offers from time to time as a gift to some personality or sanctuary.

Vesture. The pope has two kinds of vesture: the prelatial, or nonliturgical, and liturgical.

Prelatial Dress. This is very simple. In his daily life he wears a white cassock or simar, with the small humeral cape and oversleeves that go with it; a white silk sash; and a zucchetto to match. In cold weather the pope wears a long cloak of red wool, called a *mantello,* and a red hat with gold trimmings. For receptions the pope wears a long linen rochet, usually ornamented with lace, and over it the mozzetta or humeral cape, which, in summer is of red satin, and in winter of red velvet, with ermine trimmings. During Eastertide the mozzetta and shoes are of white satin. With the red velvet mozzetta the pope wears, instead of the white skull cap, a papal biretta, called *camauro,* made to match the mozzetta. According to the best traditions, when wearing the mozzetta, the pope wears the pectoral cross under it and over the rochet. Although the use of a white cassock goes back many centuries, the papal color is red and that is the reason mozzetta, *camauro,* shoes, *mantello,* and hat are always red, except during Eastertide.

Liturgical Vestments. Besides the pontifical vestments worn by all archbishops, historically the pope has two vestments that are proper, or reserved, to him, viz, the FANON and the *subcinctorium* (below the girdle).

The *subcinctorium* took the form of a maniple of the same width from top to bottom and is ornamented with an *Agnus Dei* at the lower end. It is attached to a special girdle and hangs on the pope's right side. The *subcinctorium* has now no practical meaning. Up to the 13th century it was commonly worn by all bishops, and St. Charles Borromeo tried to reintroduce its use in the AMBROSIAN RITE as a pontifical vestment. The *subcinctorium* is closely related also to the Greek epigonation: a lozenge-shaped piece of stiff, embroidered material attached to the girdle and worn as part of pontifical dress. Both the vestments were originally related to the MANIPLE, which was a towel or handkerchief, usually attached to the waist of the garment, and for hygienic use.

The falda, worn by some popes and fallen into disuse, is not strictly a vestment, but a white flowing robe with a train that falls around the feet. When used, it is placed over the rochet. Since the falda is so long, it must be lifted by assistants whenever the pope walks during ceremonies. The diaries of Alexander VI (d. 1503) speak of it as a papal ornament, but there is no agreement regarding its origin or significance.

The pope's cope or great mantle is like any other cope, except that it is either white or red. He wears the cope at solemn entries, before he vests for Mass, and when he is present, vested, at his throne.

Bibliography: P. SALMON, *Étude sur les insignes du pontife dans le rit romain* (Rome 1955). R. LESAGE, *Vestments and Church Furniture,* tr. F. MURPHY (New York 1960). T. KLAUSER, *Der Ursprung der bischöflichen Insignien und Ehrenrechte* (2d ed. Krefeld 1953). M. DYKMANS, *Le cérémonial papal de la fin du Moyen Age à la Renaissance* (Brussels, 1977). J.-C. NOONAN, *The Church Visible: The Ceremonial Life and Protocol of the Roman Catholic Church* (New York 1996). S. TWYMAN, *Papal Ceremonial at Rome in the Twelfth Century* (London 2002).

[J. NABUCO/EDS.]

PAPAL ELECTION DECREE (1059)

A judgment issued by the Roman Synod in April 1059, under the presidency of Pope NICHOLAS II, to regularize the procedure of papal elections.

Background. Earlier attempts had been made to avert uncanonical accession and the civil disorders that normally attended elections: the synodal decree of 816, the oath that Louis the Pious and LOTHAIR I required of the Romans (824), and the cession of Pope LEO VIII to OTTO I (963). All had tried to ensure orderly and canonical accessions by guaranteeing the emperor's role as arbiter in the elections. The decree of 1059, however, was the first effort to establish administrative machinery within the Church for that purpose. Prepared for by the development of the college of cardinals under the reformed papacy, the burden of the decree was anticipated early in 1059 when Nicholas II became the liege lord of Robert Guiscard, Duke of Apulia and Calabria, receiving Robert's promise in future to assist the "better" cardinals, the clergy, and the laity of Rome in electing and consecrating suitable men as popes.

Content. The framers of the decree began by recalling that the Roman Church had been endangered by SIMONY after the death of STEPHEN IX and stating their hope that the subsequent provisions would provide against the recurrence of such peril. They specified that on the death of a bishop of Rome the cardinal bishops should consider the succession among themselves, then admit the cardinal priests to their deliberations, and finally take counsel with the rest of the Roman clergy and with the Roman laity. Scholars interpret these rules to mean that the cardinal bishops were to nominate a candidate, that the lesser cardinal clergy were to approve him, and that the other clergy and the people were formally to accept him. The decree then quotes a passage from the letter of Pope LEO I to Rusticus saying that no one could be truly a bishop unless he were elected by the clergy of his church, accepted by his people, and consecrated by the bishops of his province on the approval of their metropolitan. It adds that, since the Roman Church had no metropolitan superior, the cardinal bishops discharged the office of the metropolitan in the case of papal elections.

In accord with a decree of STEPHEN III, the 1059 decree required that the pope be elected from the Roman Church itself, and that to HENRY IV of Germany and his successors must be reserved the "honor" (i.e., the formal privileges) that Rome had already granted Henry in accepting him as emperor-designate, which his successors must personally request of the apostolic see. This provision is commonly understood to refer to the right of approval that Byzantine emperors from JUSTINIAN I onward had demanded in papal elections and that the earlier regulations about accessions to the Roman See had guaranteed. The decree added that if civil conditions in Rome were too disturbed to allow the immediate enthronement of the bishop-elect, he might exercise the full authority of the papacy even before his formal installation, and it concluded by cursing those who would work to subvert its provisions and blessing those who observed them. The subscriptions of witnesses, led by the signature of Nicholas II, ended the text.

Significance. The appraisal of the decree's intent and importance is one of the most vexed problems of medieval history, and it has been complicated by the presence of a deliberately corrupted version of the decree written within 40 years after the issuance of the original. The earliest students of the problem distinguished the original as the "papal" version and the corrupted reading as the "imperial" and tended to judge the two documents outside their historical context. Scholars at the end of the 19th and the beginning of the 20th century generally accepted the distinction of "papal" and "imperial"; but they argued that the original decree was the first major effort of the GREGORIAN REFORM to free papal elections from lay influence, especially from imperial intervention, and that, to achieve their goal, its authors ascribed the effectual act of election to the cardinals, leaving only ceremonial rights to the German king.

The decree was, scholars judged, the true cause of the repudiation of Nicholas II by German bishops in 1061 and of the schism that followed. In 1936 A. Michel brought this interpretation into doubt, setting the decree into the ecclesiological context of the Gregorian reform rather than into the conventional setting of the struggle between the Church and the temporal power; and H. G. Krause has recently developed and convincingly modified Michel's thought. Michel argued on textual grounds, and Krause has since confirmed, that the distinctions of "papal" and "imperial" were erroneous, and that the corrupt reading came not from the imperial chancery but from among the schismatic cardinals who abandoned GREGORY VII in 1084. Michel dated the false version for 1084, but Krause assigned it generally to the period 1085–1100. They both pointed out that the later version is much the same as the original and that such changes as it contains enhance, on balance, the powers of the lesser cardinal clergy, rather than those of the German king. This version, however, had only slight effect. Krause particularly contested the view that the original decree was designed to free papal elections from imperial control. He suggested rather that the authors of the decree intended to free the papacy from the schism and local conflict that attended Nicholas's accession in 1058 by confirming precisely those powers of arbitration that the earlier enactments on papal elections had described and that HENRY III had vigorously exercised. In this way they hoped to subject local interests to the superior juridical competence of the Empire and to give the earlier process canonical force through synodal approval. Krause further maintained that the repudiation of Nicholas II by the German bishops and the schism of 1061 resulted, not from displeasure at the curtailment of imperial prerogatives by the decree, but from the quite unrelated animosity of Abp. ANNO OF COLOGNE toward Nicholas. In addition to its critical importance in polemical works of the INVESTITURE STRUGGLE, the decree has significance as the basis of modern procedure in papal elections.

Bibliography: Editions. *Monumenta Germaniae Historica* (Berlin 1826–): Constitutiones 1:537–551. H. G. KRAUSE, *Das Papstwahldekret von 1059 und seine Rolle im Investitursteit* (Studi gregoriani 7; 1960). Literature. A. MICHEL, *Papstwahl und Königsrecht oder das Papstwahl-Konkordat von 1059* (Munich 1936); "Das Papstwahlpaktum von 1059," *Historisches Jahrbuch der Görres-Gesellschaft* 59 (1939) 291–351. R. HOLTZMANN, "Zum Papstwahldekret von 1059," *Zeitschrift der Savigny-Stiftung für Rechtsgeschichte, Romanistische Abteilung* 27 (1938) 135–153. B. SCHMEIDLER, "Zum Wahldekret Papst Nikolaus II. vom Jahre 1059," *Historische Vierteljahrschrift* 31 (1937–39) 554–560.

[K. F. MORRISON]

PAPAL ELECTIONS, VETO POWER IN

The *jus exclusivae,* or secular veto, in papal elections was a device used by the Catholic powers of Spain, Austria, and France to prevent the election of a candidate thought unfriendly to their interests. Although secular rulers tried to influence papal elections earlier, the Emperor Charles V is the first known to have drawn up lists of acceptable and nonacceptable candidates, which he gave to cardinals friendly to Spain. Philip II allowed such names to be made public. These procedures developed slowly into the "immemorial right" of exclusion (also known as the veto, or *Ausschliessungsrecht*). Only in the late 17th and, more clearly, in the 18th century was a formal claim made by France, Austria, and Spain to exclude one candidate each during a CONCLAVE.

The wishes of the ruler were made known to a cardinal chosen for the purpose. The cardinal had to exercise his judgment as to the necessity of making the exclusion known in a formal session of the conclave, or of attaining the desired end by hints or warnings in private conversation. Timing was a critical concern because the exclusion should be pronounced only when a cardinal was near attaining the two-thirds vote necessary to elect a pope. Because several candidates might be undesirable in the sovereign's view, the cardinal would wish to hold back the use of his single veto as long as possible. On the other hand, after the election itself the veto would be meaningless. Sometimes the opportunity was lost: an unforeseen shift in the vote would result in election; in 1846 the cardinal bearing the Austrian veto arrived after the election.

St. Pius X in *Commissum nobis* (Jan. 20, 1904) abolished the veto absolutely.

See Also: POPES, ELECTION OF.

Bibliography: T. ORTOLAN, *Dictionnaire de théologie catholique*, ed. A. VACANT et al., (Paris 1903–50) 3.1:720–727. A. MOLIEN, *Dictionnaire de droit canonique*, ed. R. NAZ (Paris 1935–65) 3:1319–42. J. B. SÄGMÜLLER, *The Catholic Encyclopedia*, ed. C. G. HERBERMANN et al. (New York 1904–14; suppl. 1922) 5:677–678. L. LECTOR, *Le Conclave* (Paris 1894). H. THURSTON, "State Interference in Papal Elections," *Month* 102 (1903) 337–348.

[M. O'CALLAGHAN]

PAPAL REGISTERS

Papal registers (*regesta, regestra, registra*) are bound volumes containing copies of official papal letters and documents, today preserved in the VATICAN ARCHIVES (with a few exceptions). They represent a fairly continuous series from INNOCENT III (1198–1216) onward, but there is evidence that registers were kept as early as the 4th century, and probably earlier. They followed the Roman imperial model of the *commentarii,* and were the work of the papal notaries, whose office eventually became the chancery by the 11th century. Such records were essential, for the Roman pontiff ruled largely by promulgation and written acts and decrees. However, apart from the reconstructed register of GREGORY I (590–604), based on 9th-century and later materials, a late excerpt of JOHN VIII (872–882), the first contemporary register of GREGORY VII (1073–85), and some partial transcripts of the 12th century, e.g., of the antipope ANACLETUS II (1030–38; *see* PIERLEONI), none of the early registers have survived. We deduce their existence from various CANONICAL COLLECTIONS, e.g., the *DIONYSIANA*, *QUESNELLIANA*, and *Britannica*, and the testimony of such canonists as Deusdedit (*see* DEUSDEDIT, COLLECTION OF) and ANSELM OF LUCCA. The order of registration was generally chronological (by indictions, and from Gregory VII onward by pontifical years). No attempt was made to classify matter until the 13th century, when, e.g., Innocent III ordered a *Regestum super negotio Romani imperii*. With the growth of papal administration and the problems created by the AVIGNON PAPACY and the WESTERN SCHISM came an increasingly complicated system of registers.

There are several series of papal registers. (1) Vatican Registers are the oldest and the most important. There are 2,042 items, mostly on parchment, opening properly with Innocent III (Reg. Vat. 4) in 1198 and extending to CLEMENT VIII (1592–1605). (2) Avignonese Registers were compiled at Avignon between 1316 and 1415, and remained there until the 18th century. There are 349 volumes on paper. The majority were transcribed into the Vatican Registers. They contain *Litterae communes* and *Litterae secretae*. (3) Lateran Registers constitute 2,467 volumes, kept in the lateran palace until 1892. They cover the period between 1389 and 1897, but their contents concern only ecclesiastical and administrative matters, i.e., copies of *Litterae communes* (favor and justice). Many volumes are missing, especially as a result of the Napoleonic Wars.

The opening of the Vatican Archives to the scholarly world in 1881 fulfilled a long-felt need. The archives constitute a major source for European history, especially that of the Middle Ages. Many of the documents are of outstanding importance. Thus Gregory VII Reg. 2.55a is the famous DICTATUS PAPAE and 3.10a is the deposition of the Emperor HENRY IV. Finally, there is a continuing discussion among historians as to the method and form of compiling the registers, e.g., whether the corrected draft or the finished letter was the model, and also how far the registers are themselves original or merely transcripts of the original Chancery Registers. The likely solution is that no single system prevailed throughout.

(4) The papal Penitentiary, the central office for dispensations, absolutions, and licences, kept registers of its own. These registers, which were begun in the early 15th and continued until well into the 19th century, are now deposited in the Vatican Archives and have been accessible to scholars since 1983 upon special permission. (5) From 1334 all incoming petitions to the pope were registered in the *Registra supplicationum* (see Boyle and Diener). (6) From ca. 1470 a new abbreviated form of papal letter came into use, the littera brevis (i.e. shorter letters), which were registered as Brevia (see Gualdo). (7) The Papal Chamber kept several registers concerning the financial affairs of the Holy See, such as the Introitus et Exitus registers or the Annate registers (see Diener and Boyle).

Bibliography: Sources: *Registra Vaticana 1–136. Iohannes VIII-Benedictus XII (876–1342)*, 136 CD-ROMs (Archivio Segreto Vaticano, Vatican City) [photographic reproduction of the Vatican Registers]. *Die Register Innozenz' III.*, ed. by O. HAGENEDER, A. HAIDACHER et al. for the Österreichisches Kulturinstitut in Rom, 7 v. to date (Graz-Cologne-Vienna 1964ff). *Registres et lettres des Papes du XIIIᵉ et du XIVᵉ siècle*, ed. École française de Rome, 80 v. (Rome 1883ff); also published on 3 CD-ROMs (Turnhout, Belgium). *Calendar of Entries in the Papal Registers relating to Great Britain and Ireland*, 18 v. to date (London 1893ff). *Repertorium Germanicum*, ed. German Historical Institute in Rome, 9 v. to date (Berlin and Tübingen 1916ff). *Repertorium Poenitentiariae Germanicum*, ed. L. SCHMUGGE et al. for the German Historical Institute in Rome, 4 v. to date (Tübingen 1996ff). Studies: L. BOYLE, *A Survey of the Vatican Archives and of Its Medieval Holdings* (Subsidia mediaevalia 1; Toronto 1972). H. DIENER, *Die grossen Registerserien im Vatikanischen Archiv (1378–1523)* (Tübingen 1972). T. FRENZ, *Die Kanzlei der Päpste der Hochrenaissance (1471–1527)* (Bibliothek des Deutschen Historischen Instituts in Rom 63; Tübingen 1986). G. GUALDO, *Sussidi per la consultazione dell' Archivio Vaticano* (Collectanea Archivi Vaticani 17; Vatican City 1989).

[J. GILCHRIST/L. SCHMUGGE]

PAPAL VOLUNTEERS FOR LATIN AMERICA

The Papal Volunteers for Latin America (PAVLA) were volunteer Catholic lay missionaries committed to pastoral and social work in Latin America for short-term service, usually three years. Consistent with the stress on Catholic Action found in papal encyclicals (e.g., Pius XI's *Non Abbiamo Bisogno* in 1931, and Pius XII's *Mystici Corporis* in 1943) and with the orientation of the National Catholic Welfare Conference (NCWC), the Pontifical Commission for Latin America (CAL) approved PAVLA on April 20, 1960. Monsignor Paul Tanner, General Secretary of the NCWC wrote to the U.S. bishops, asking them to establish the program in their dioceses. Michael Lies, a diocesan priest of Wichita, Kansas, was named the first national director in 1961, and served one year in that capacity. The national office, established in Chicago, was placed under the Bishop's Committee for Latin America, and administered by the

NCWC's Latin America Bureau, whose director from 1959 to 1968 was John J. Considine, M.M., a Maryknoll priest. The office was meant to function as an umbrella agency, coordinating the requests of Latin American bishops for assistance within their dioceses and other ecclesiastical jurisdictions, and the diocesan directors, religious communities, lay mission societies, and even individual volunteers that wanted to participate.

Independent language schools in Cuernavaca, Mexico; Petropolis, Brazil; and Ponce, Puerto Rico, as well as a few domestic Catholic colleges and universities provided varying degrees of language, theological, pastoral, and cultural formation for candidates. In the first year, 112 volunteers were sent to Latin America. They and subsequent lay missionaries were primarily engaged in various forms of teaching, medicine, social work, community development, and the creation of credit unions.

A series of problems plagued the program from its inception, including an initial lack of financial support, tension between many diocesan directors and the national office over questions of coordination and control, and deep disagreements among various parties over the screening, formation, and assignment of candidates. Many volunteers, once in Latin America, experienced little local support for their apostolates. By 1967, the number of active PAVLA volunteers began to decline. When Louis Michael Colonnese, a priest of Davenport, Iowa, became director of the Latin America Bureau in 1968, he initiated the process that resulted in the closing of the national office in 1971.

Bibliography: A. DRIES, *The Missionary Movement in American Catholic History* (Maryknoll, N.Y. 1998). G. M. COSTELLO, *Mission to Latin America: The Successes and Failures of a Twentieth-Century Crusade* (Maryknoll, N.Y. 1979).

[J. F. GARNEAU]

PAPCZYŃSKI, STANISLAUS

Founder of the MARIAN FATHERS; b. Podegrodzie, near Stary Sacz, Poland, May 18, 1631; d. Góra Kalwaria, Sept. 17, 1701. His baptismal name was John Baptist. He studied in the Piarist college in Podoliniec (Spicz) and in Jesuit colleges in Lvov and in Rawa Mazowiecka. In 1654 he entered the Piarist novitiate in Podoliniec, receiving the religious name Stanislaus of Jesus-Mary. In 1656, in Warsaw, at the close of his second novitiate combined with a theology course, he took his simple vows and became a subdeacon. In 1661 he was ordained at the Piarist college of Rzeszów. Transferred to Warsaw in 1663, he became renowned as a teacher of eloquence, a preacher, and confessor. In 1669 he was secularized,

but in the act of his release from vows and the oath of perseverance in the Piarist Institute on Dec. 2, 1670, he solemnly promised God to continue in the religious life through the "Society of the Marian Clerics of the Immaculate Conception," which he planned to found. This new Marian Congregation received its first ecclesiastical approval in 1673, and he was appointed superior of a small hermitage at Korabiew (Puscza Mariańska), near Zyradów. In 1677 he fixed his residence in Nowa Jerozolima (Góra Kalwaria) near Warsaw and devoted the rest of his life to the government and canonical establishment of the Marians in the strict observance of the *Norma Vitae,* the constitutions he had written for them. Upon the approval of the Marians by the Holy See in 1701, Papczyński made his solemn profession, and he died a few months later. His body rests in the "Cenacle" Chapel of Góra Kalwaria. His beatification process, begun in 1769, was interrupted in 1775 and resumed in 1953. His principal writings are *Prodromus Reginae Artium* (Cracow 1669), *Templum Dei Mysticum* (Cracow 1675), and *Norma Vitae* (Warsaw 1687).

Bibliography: G. A. NAVIKEVIČIUS, *Stanislao di Gesù Maria Papczyński 1631–1701* (Doctoral diss. Gregorian U. Rome 1960). C. KRZYŻANOWSKI, *Stanislaus a Jesu Maria Papczyński, . . . Magister studii perfectionis* (Rome 1963).

[M. RZESZUTEK]

PAPHNUTIUS

The name of many monks in the Egyptian desert, among whom the more important were:

Paphnutius the Bishop, St., a bishop of the Upper THEBAID; d. *c.* 356. He attended the Council of NICAEA, 325, and the Synod of Tyre, 335. His left knee had been mutilated and his right eye torn out in the persecution of Maximinus. He was esteemed by CONSTANTINE I and by the prelates at Nicaea. It was perhaps due to his influence that the council left the question of continence to the discretion of those clergy who had been married before ordination. If this Paphnutius is the "confessor and monk" to whom a miracle is attributed in the *Vita Antonii* (58; *see* R. MEYER, tr., *Ancient Christian Writers* 10:69, 122, n. 198), he may also be the "anchorite . . . of the desert about Heracleos . . . in the Thebaid" mentioned in the *Historia Monachorum* (16).

Feast: Sept. 11 (Roman MARTYROLOGY).

Paphnutius the Buffalo, anchorite and priest of the desert of Scete. He was 90 years old when visited by John CASSIAN in 395, and was the only monastic leader in Scete to hold a public reading of the letter of the Patriarch THEOPHILUS OF ALEXANDRIA condemning anthropomorphism (397).

Paphnutius the Anchorite, St., martyr; d. *c.* 303; who suffered martyrdom under Diocletian, according to the Roman Martyrology.

Feast: Sept. 24.

Paphnutius the Abbot, St.; d. *c.* 480; the reputed father of St. Euphrosyne. He is highly venerated in the East.

Feast: Sept. 25.

Bibliography: H. DELEHAYE, ed., "Passio," *Analecta Bollandiana* 40 (1922) 328–343, Gr. *Acta Sanctorum* Sept. 6:681–688, Lat. SOCRATES, *Ecclesiastical History* 1:11 in *Patrologia Graeca,* ed. J. P. MIGNE, 161 v. (Paris 1857–66) 67:102–106. SOZOMEN, *Ecclesiastical History* 1:23 *ibid.* 67:925–926. C. J. VON HEFELE, *Histoire des conciles d'après les documents originaux,* tr. and continued by H. LECLERCQ, 10 v. in 19 (Paris 1907–38) v. 1.1. J. CASSIAN, *Conlationes,* ed. M. PETSCHENIG (*Corpus scriptorum ecclesiasticorum latinorum* 13; 1886) 3:4.1, 10.2–3. "Paphnutius the Buffalo," H. LECLERCQ, *Dictionnaire d'archéologie chrétienne et de liturgie,* ed. F. CABROL, H. LECLERCQ, and H. I. MARROU, 15 v. (Paris 1907–53) 13.1:1358–61.

[M. C. MCCARTHY]

PAPIAS OF HIERAPOLIS

Bishop and chronicler of primitive Christianity; b. *c.* A.D. 60 or 70; d. *c.* 125. Information on Papias is supplied by EUSEBIUS OF CAESAREA (*Hist. Eccl.* 2.15.2, 3.39.13) and IRENAEUS OF LYONS (*Adv. haer.* 5.33.4). Irenaeus testifies that Papias heard the Apostle John preach and was acquainted with Polycarp; Eusebius makes mention of his *Explanation of the Sayings of the Lord* (in 5 bks.). In the preface to this work, Papias asserts that his main endeavor is to record the truth, and that he had made a collection of the *logia* (sayings that included both words and deeds) of the Apostles that were reported to him by a presbyter. Irenaeus took this to mean that Papias was quoting the Evangelist John, whereas Eusebius maintains that Papias spoke of two Johns, indicating the Evangelist as one, and the other as the companion of Aristion, one of the presbyters, or elders, of the primitive Church (*Hist. Eccl.* 3.39.7). Eusebius further believed that the second John was the author of the Apocalypse and accused Papias of transmitting the heretical doctrine of CHILIASM to Irenaeus and other early churchmen (*ibid.* 3.39.12–13).

Papias stated that Mark the Evangelist was the interpreter of Peter, that Mark had never heard Christ, but that he had carefully recorded everything he remembered from Peter's preaching (*ibid.* 3.39.15). Of Matthew, Papias maintained that he "wrote down the *logia* of the Savior in the Hebrew *dialektikos* [language or dialect], and each one interpreted them as best he could" (3.39.16). Irenaeus took this to refer to the Hebraisms that appear frequently in Matthew's Gospel. Origen, howev-

er, thought it meant that Matthew had originally written his Gospel in Hebrew. Papias also witnessed to the existence of the apocryphal Gospel according to the Hebrews, out of which he reported a story of the woman taken in adultery that differs from the disputed pericope in John's Gospel (7.53–8.11). Papias refers to the daughters of the Apostle Philip, who told him of a miracle concerning a certain Justus Barsabbas, as well as, in Eusebius's judgment, several bizarre parables attributed to the Savior (*Hist. Eccl.* 3.39.9–13).

Papias's exegesis was used not merely by Irenaeus, but by Origen and Western theologians down to VICTORINUS OF PETTAU. His testimony, however, has raised many problems in regard to the formation of the Gospel texts, an Aramaic version of Matthew, the identity of the two Johns, and other questions about the history of the primitive Church. According to a late legend he died a martyr.

Bibliography: J. QUASTEN, *Patrology* (Westminster, Maryland 1950–) 1:82–85. G. BARDY, *Dictionnaire de théologie catholique,* ed. A. VACANT et al. (Paris 1903–50) 11.2:1944–47. M. JOURJON, *Dictionnaire de la Bible,* suppl. ed. L. PIROT, et al. (Paris 1928–) 6:1104–1109. J. KÜRZINGER, *Lexikon für Theologie und Kirche,* ed. J. HOFER and K. RAHNER (Freiberg 1957–65) 8:34–36. E. PREUSCHEN, ed. and tr., *Antilegomena* (2d ed. Giessen 1905) 91–99, 195–202. K. BIHLMEYER, ed., *Die Apostolischen Väter* (2d ed. Tübingen 1956–) 133–140. F. WOTKE, *Paulys Realenzyklopädie der klassischen Altertumswissenschaft,* ed. G. WISSOWA et al. 18.2 (1949) 966–976. J. F. BLIGH, *Theological Studies* 13 (1952 234–240. J. MUNCK, *Harvard Theological Review* 52 (1959) 223–243; *Neotestamentica et Patristica* (Leiden 1962) 249–260. K. BEYSCHLAG, *Studia patristica,* v.4 (TU 79; 1961) 268–280.

[F. X. MURPHY]

PAPINI TARTAGNI, NICCOLÒ

Historian, b. San Giovanni Valdarno, Italy, 1751; d. Terni, Dec. 16, 1834. He served as minister general of the Franciscan Conventuals (1803–09). He was a contemporary and successor of Giovanni Giacinto SBARAGLIA in the historical research on the FRANCISCANS, and his published works are all in the area of Franciscan history. These include *Etruria francescana* (part 1a, Siena 1787; part 2a, unpublished), *Notizie sicure della morte, sepoltura, canonizzazione e traslazione di s. Francesco e del ritrovamento del di lui corpo* (Florence 1822; Foligno 1824), *Storia del Perdono di Assisi* (Florence 1824), *Storia di S. Francesco d' Assisi* (2 v. Foligno 1825–27, 3d unedited) and "Index Fratrum Minorum Conventualium qui scientias et artes, conducti, publice tradiderunt," *Miscellanea Francescana* 31 (1931); 32 (1932). His unpublished bibliographical works can be found in the archives of the general curia of the Franciscan Conventuals in Rome. They are in a folio volume, Cod.c. 128, *Appen-*

Papyrus fragment, text of Book of Hebrews 12.1–11, 4th Century.

dix ad supplementum scriptorum Franciscanorum P. M. Hyacinthi Sbaraglia; scriptores ordinis minorum conventualium ab anno 1650 ad annum 1820, which also includes a supplementary appendix and a second essay continuing the list to the year 1830. A manuscript, *I et II Index onomasticus scriptorum universae Franciscanae familiae seu trium ordinum S. Francisci ab origine usque ad annum MCDL,* dated 1828, is in the collections of the National Library of Florence, No. II ii, 181.

Bibliography: D. SPARACIO, ''Gli studi di storia e i minori conventuali,'' *Miscellanea Francescana* 20 (1919) 56–64.

[J. J. SMITH]

PAPYROLOGY

The study of ancient documents written on papyri (plural of papyrus). Papyrus (Greek ὁ or ἡ πάπυρος, ἡ βίβλος; Latin *papyrus;* as writing material also Greek ὁ

χάρτης, Latin *charta*) was the name given to a certain plant (*Cyperus papyrus,* Latin) and to a writing material made from it in antiquity. The papyrus plant, which was cultivated especially in the delta of the Nile, was put to various practical uses, e.g., for the making of rafts and boats in Egypt.

Writing Material. The most important use of papyrus, however, was in the manufacture of a writing material that was employed by the Egyptians from the 3d millennium B.C., by the Greeks from the 6th century B.C., and by the Romans from the 3d century B.C. until well into the Middle Ages, when it was supplanted by paper. (Although the word ''paper'' is derived from the word ''papyrus'', paper is made by an entirely different process.) On the ancient use of papyrus, see Herodotus, *Hist.* 2.92; Theophrastes, *Hist. plant.* 4.8, 3; Pliny, *Hist. nat.* 13.11 (68)–12(83); S. N. Lewis, *L'Industrie du papyrus dans l'Égypte Greco-Romaine* (Paris 1934). According to Pliny (*ibid.* 13.12[74]), for the making of the writing material the pith of papyrus stalks was sliced into thin strips (called σχίζαι in Greek and *scissurae* or *philyrae* in Latin), a number of the strips were laid vertically side by side, over these a number of strips were laid horizontally side by side, and the two layers were pressed together, dried out, and rubbed smooth, to form oblong leaves. The finished leaves were called σελίδες in Greek and *plagulae* in Latin. Several such leaves (20 of them according to Pliny, *ibid.*) were then pasted side by side (hence the word κόλλημα, literally "a glueing," came to mean page or column) in such a way that the sides of the leaves with the horizontal fibers were all kept on the same (upper or recto) side of the long sheet. Sheets were made in different lengths and heights. A finished sheet was rolled around a narrow cylinder (*scapus*) with the recto on the inside, and so it was offered for sale. The sheet itself was often called a *scapus* ("roll" of papyrus). The long sheet either served as a SCROLL (*volumen*) on which lengthy documents, especially literary works, were written, or the individual pages were cut from it for the writing of short documents, letters, etc. Writing was put ordinarily only on the recto with its horizontal fibers, seldom on the back or verso with its vertical fibers. A papyrus written on the verso was called an ὀπισθόγραφον.

The earliest instrument used for writing on papyrus was a sedge stalk cut off at an angle at one end or frayed at the end into a sort of small brush. After the 3d century B.C. a thin reed (κάλαμος, *calamus*) sharpened to a point and split at one end was used as a pen. The ordinary ink used for writing was black (μέλαν, *atramentum*), made from soot; but other colors, such as brown (sepia) and crimson (ἔγκαυστον, *encaustum*) were employed. Pictorial additions were in cinnabar (vermillion) or other colors.

In pharaonic times the Egyptian manufacture of papyrus was a monopoly of the individual temples and their priests; in Ptolemaic times it was a state monopoly. In the Byzantine and Arabic periods the first leaf (πρωτόκολλον, whence the word "protocol") of a papyrus roll was impressed with a government stamp stating where and when the roll was made. According to its quality there were various kinds of papyrus, from the fine *charta hieratica* or *regia* (*Augusta, Livia*) down to ordinary wrapping material (*charta emporetica*); see Pliny, *Hist. nat.* 13.74–79; Isidorus, *Orig.* 6.9. Writing was done on other material also, such as potsherds (*see* OSTRACON), wax tablets, and parchment. In the early imperial period literary texts began, apparently in Christian circles, to be written on separate leaves that were bound in a codex (modern book form). Parchment was more suitable for this purpose and soon was the only material used for codices. Smaller documents, however, continued to be writ-

ten on papyrus for many centuries, e.g., in the papal chancery until the 11th century.

Papyrus Manuscripts, Papyri. Outside of Egypt, where the climate was kind to them, ancient and medieval papyrus MSS have almost entirely fallen victims to the destructive forces of time. Only by accident have a few Latin papyrus codices or fragments of them and some papyrus documents been preserved in European libraries and archives. Thus in papyrus there are a codex of Josephus's *Jewish Antiquities* in Milan; a codex of some of St. Hilary's works in Vienna; individual leaves of a codex containing some sermons and letters of St. Augustine in Paris, Geneva, and Leningrad; a codex containing extracts from St. Isidore's *Synonyma* and a homily of St. Eucherius in St. Gall, Switzerland; and a codex containing some of the writings of St. Avitus of Vienne in Paris. Some of the other preserved papyrus documents are a few dozen papal bulls in French, Italian, German, and Spanish archives, in addition to some 800 mostly Greek scrolls containing philosophical works recovered in 1572 from the ruins of the city of Herculaneum that was covered with lava from Mt. Vesuvius in A.D. 79. A few papyrus documents have been found also at DURA-EUROPOS on the Euphrates, at Nessana in the Negeb of Palestine, and at some other places (see Preisendanz, *Papyrusfunde* 18–66; *Handbuch* 166–170).

Papyri from Egypt. Large masses of papyrus MSS written in ancient Egyptian, Coptic, Arabic, Persian, Aramaic, Hebrew, Latin, and especially Greek have been found only in the sand-covered graves, ruins, and rubbish piles of the ancient settlements of the native land of the papyrus plant, rain-poor Egypt. As early as the end of the 18th century and the beginning of the 19th the learned world became aware of Egyptian papyri through accidental finds. But it was only in 1877 that the interests of scholars was fully aroused by the discovery of an immense amount of papyrus MSS at El Faiyûm (site of the ancient city of Arsinoë), and impetus was thereby given to organized excavations by European and American scholars, especially in the ruins of the Faiyûm regions (at Arsinoë, Soknopaiu Nēsos, Theadelphia, Tebtynis, and Philadelphia) and in Heracleopolis Magna, Oxyrhynchus, Hermopolis Magna, El iba, Thebes (NO-AMON), Panopolis, Syene, Elephantine, and other places. (For the location of these places on a map, *see* EGYPT.)

Some of the papyri that were discovered in these excavations have been kept in Egyptian museums (in Alexandria and Cairo). But most of the papyri entered public or private collections in Europe or America, especially in England (London, Oxford, and Manchester), Ireland (Dublin), France (Paris, Lille, and Strasbourg), Italy (Milan, Turin, Florence, and Naples), Germany (Berlin,

Munich, Heidelberg, Giessen, Marburg, Jena, and Würzburg), Holland (Leiden), Norway, Denmark, Russia (Tiflis), Switzerland (Basel, Geneva, and Zurich), and the United States (Ann Arbor, Chicago, Princeton, New York, Berkeley, and other cities). In these collections the papyri, which were usually found in a damaged and soiled condition, have been restored, preserved, and scientifically studied by specialists in papyrology, a discipline that has been developed for this purpose. By the 1960s about 7,000 papyri had been published, and the number of those still unedited in the collections and still hidden in the sands of Egypt is no doubt several times that amount.

Contents. The papyri have thrown lasting light on all branches of the study of antiquity: not only Egyptology and Arabic studies, but especially classic philology and the history of Greek and Roman law, economics, sociology, and religion. Classical philology has been enriched by the discovery of many literary papyri, mostly from the 1st to the 3d century, containing fragmentary or even complete classical works that previously had either been preserved in much more recent parchment MSS or been considered entirely lost, e.g., Aristotle's Ἀθηναίων Πολιτεία (*Constitution of Athens*), Sophocles's Ἰχνευταί (*The Investigators*), Herondas's *Mimes,* Bacchylides's *Choral Odes,* and Menander's Δύσκολοσ (*The Discontented Man*), and other comedies. Not only classical studies, however, but other disciplines also have been greatly benefited by the many thousands of papyrus MSS that have been discovered, such as official edicts and decrees, business documents, financial accounts, invoices, receipts, last wills, contracts (for sales, rents, loans, hiring, teaching, and marriage), and letters. Such papyri give a faithful and impressive picture of all public and private life in Egypt until the Arabic period.

The study of the script and language of these records has made it possible to obtain for the first time an accurate knowledge of the development both of Greek handwriting from the 4th century B.C. to the 10th Christian century and of the colloquial Greek language (Κοινή) throughout the same period, so that the biblical GREEK LANGUAGE, which previously had been a rather isolated phenomenon, can now be assigned its rightful place in this development.

Biblical and Christian Papyri. The papyri are of immense importance for all branches of theological studies, but especially for biblical studies, since many of the papyri contain fragments of OT and NT books (such as some in the Chester Beatty Papyri, the Freer Collection, the Bodmer Collection, and others) that go back, at least in part (e.g., P⁵² of the Fourth Gospel from A.D. 125), to the 2d century. They are therefore much older than the oldest parchment MSS and consequently of inestimable value for biblical textual criticism. At least fragments of every book of the NT except 1 and 2 Timothy and 2 and 3 John are preserved in the papyri.

Of scarcely less value are the Greek and Coptic papyri that contain liturgical or patristic texts, e.g., those of the 1941 find at Tura of writings of Origen and Didymus, the menologies (liturgical calendars), the *libelli* (documents certifying that the persons named in them have offered sacrifice to the gods) from the Decian persecution (middle of the 3d century), certain Gnostic apocrypha (as the *Gospel of Thomas* and the *Gospel of Truth* found at Nag' Hammâdi) and other heretical writings, and last but not least, numerous incantation and other magical texts. All these religious texts, together with the secular documents, bring to life for modern man the world in which the gospel was first preached and offer him a vivid picture of Egypt's early Christian life, of its flourishing monasticism, of the turbulence of its religious quarrels and schisms, and even of the continuance, in the Christian era, of its ancient pagan superstitions, concepts, and customs.

Bibliography: Manuals and introductions. L. MITTEIS and U. WILCKEN, *Grundzüge und Chrestomathie der Papyruskunde,* 4 v. (Leipzig-Berlin 1912). W. SCHUBART, *Einführung in die Papyruskunde* (Berlin 1918). A. CALDERINI, *Papyri: Guida allo studio della papirologia antica Greca e Romana* (Milan 1944). W. PEREMANS and V. VERGOTE, *Papyrologisch Handboek* (Louvain 1942). F. G. KENYON, *Books and Readers in Ancient Greece and Rome* (2d ed. Oxford 1951). K. PREISENDANZ, *Papyrusfunde und Papyrusforschung* (Leipzig 1933); "Papyruskunde," *Handbuch der Bibliothekswissenschaft,* ed. G. LEYH, v. 1 (2d ed. Wiesbaden 1952) 163–248, extensive history of the discoveries and collections, with bibliog. of the whole pertinent literature. A. BATAILLE, *Les Papyrus* (Paris 1955), with extensive bibliog. also for the language and script and a list of the *religionsgeschichtlich* papyrus literature, 58–66. H. HUNGER et al., eds., *Geschichte der Textüberlieferung der antiken und mittelalterlichen Literatur,* v. 1 (Zurich 1961) 29–50, 72–113, 168–170. H. METZGER, *Wege und Probleme der Papyrusforschung,* v. 2 *Die frühchristliche Welt im Lichte der Papyri* (Schweizer Beiträge zur Allgemeinen Geschichte 10; 1952) 199–208. C. H. ROBERTS, *Greek Literary Hands, 350* B.C.– A.D. *400* (Oxford 1956). **Encyclopedia articles.** H. LECLERCQ, *Dictionnaire d'archéologie chrétienne et de liturgie,* ed. F. CABROL, H. LECLERCQ, and H. I. MARROU, 15 v. (Paris 1907–53) 13.1:1370–1520, with extensive bibliog. and many illustrations. E. LEVESQUE and F. PRAT, *Dictionnaire de la Bible,* ed. F. VIGOUROUX, 5 v. (Paris 1895–1912) 4:2079–94. B. BOTTE, *Dictionnaire de la Bible,* suppl. ed. L. PIROT et al. (Paris 1928–) 6:1109–20. *Encyclopaedia biblica,* ed. T. K. CHEYNE and J. S. BLACK, 4 v. (London 1899–1903) 5:3556–63. H. GERSTINGER, *Lexikon für Theologie und Kirche,* ed. J. HOFER and K. RAHNER, 10 v. (2d, new ed. Freiburg 1957–65) 8:63–65. A. DEISSMANN, *Realencyklopädie für protestantische Theologie,* ed. J. J. HERZOG and A. HAUCK, 24 v. (3d ed. Leipzig 1896–1913) 14:667–675. K. TREU, *Die Religion in Geschichte und Gegenwart,* 7 v. (3d ed. Tübingen 1957–65) 5:91–93. *Encyclopedic Dictionary of the Bible,* tr. and adap. by L. HARTMAN (New York 1963), from A. VAN DEN BORN, *Bijbels Woordenboek* 1704–13. Publications of papyri. These are listed in most of the works mentioned above under Manuals and introductions, esp. those of Preisendanz and Bataille; current pubs. are given in the periodicals mentioned below under Periodicals, with current reports and bibliogs.; among the more recent pubs. are the following: J. O. TJAEDER, *Die nichtliterarischen lateinischen Papyri Italiens aus der Zeit* (Lund 1955) 445–700. R. CAVENAILE, ed., *Corpus papyrorum latinorum* (Vienna 1956–). V. A. TCHERIKOVER et al., eds., *Corpus papyrorum Judaicorum*, 3 v. (Cambridge, Mass. 1957–64). Selections and special eds. E. J. GOODSPEED and E. C. COLWELL, *A Greek Papyrus Reader* (Chicago 1935). A. S. HUNT et al., *Select Papyri*, 3 v. (New York 1932–50). W. SCHUBART, *Ein Jahrtausend am Nil: Briefe aus dem Altertum verdeutscht und erklärt* (2d ed. Berlin 1923). J. G. WINTER, *Life and Letters in the Papyri* (Ann Arbor 1933). H. THIERFELDER, *Unbekannte antike Welt: Eine Darstellung nach Papyrusurkunden* (Gütersloh 1963). A. DEISSMANN, *Light from the Ancient East*, tr. L. R. M. STRACHAN (rev. ed. New York 1927). G. GHEDINI, *Lettere cristiane dai papiri greci del III e IV secolo* (Milan 1923). C. DEL GRANDE, ed., *Liturgiae, preces, hymni christianorum e papyris collecti* (Naples 1938). R. KNIPFING, "The Libelli of the Decian Persecution," *Harvard Theological Review* 16 (1923) 345–390. A. BLUDAU, "Dieägyptischen Libelli und die Christenverfolgungen des Kaiser Decius," *Römische Quartalschrift für christliche Altertumskunde und für Kirchengeschichte* (Freiburg 1887–) 27 (1913), suppl. K. PREISENDANZ, et al., eds., *Papyri graecae magicae*, 2 v. (Leipzig 1928–31). Periodicals, with current reports and bibliog. *Aegyptus: Revista italiana di egittologia e papirologia* (Milan 1920–). *Archiv für Papyrusforschung und verwandte Gebiete* (Leipzig 1900–). *Chronique d'Égypte* (Brussels 1925–). *Études de papyrologie* (Cairo 1932–). *Journal of Egyptian Archaeology* (London 1914–). *Journal of Juristic Papyrology* (New York 1946–). *Mizraim: Journal of Papyrology* (Philadelphia 1933–). *Revue des études grecques* (Paris 1888–). *Recherches de papyrologie: Travaux de l'Institut de papyrologie de Paris* (Paris 1961–). *Studia papyrologica: Revista española de papirologia* (Barcelona 1962–). Lists of published papyri. R. A. PACK, *The Greek and Latin Literary Texts from Greco-Roman Egypt* (2d ed. Ann Arbor1965). Biblical papyri. A. RAHLFS, *Verzeichnis der griechischen Handschriften des AT* (Berlin 1914). M. M. PARVIS and A. P. WIKGREN, eds., *NT Manuscript Studies* (Chicago 1950). G. MALDFELD and B. M. METZGER, "Detailed List of the Greek Papyri of the NT," *Journal of Biblical Literature* 68 (1949) 359–370. G. MALDFELD, "Die griechischen Handschriften des NT auf Papyrus," *Zeitschrift für die neutestamentliche Wissenschaft und die Kunde der älteren Kirche* 42 (1949) 228–253; 43 (1950–51) 260–261. F. G. KENYON, *Our Bible and the Ancient Manuscripts*, 5th ed. rev. A. W. ADAMS (New York 1958) 113–119, 185–190. W. C. VAN UNNIK, *Evangelien aus dem Nilsand* (Frankfurt 1960). O. PARET, *Die Bibel: Ihre Überlieferung in Druck und Schrift* (Stuttgart 1949) 50–52.

[H. GERSTINGER]

PARABLES OF JESUS

The English word parable is from the Greek παραβολή, whose root connotation involves the placing of things side by side for the sake of comparison; it was a technical term for a figure of speech in ancient oratory. Before undertaking to describe the characteristics of Jesus' parables and their place in the Gospel context, this article, by way of background, outlines some relevant points about figures of speech as they pertain to parables and reviews the history of parable exegesis. At the end, as kind of postscript, it discusses the relation of the parables reported in the canonical Gospels to those found in the *Gospel of Thomas*.

Simile, Metaphor and Allegory. The most basic forms of illustration are the simile and the metaphor. In a simile one thing is likened or compared to another thing of a different kind for illustrative purposes (often with the words "like" or "as"); for example, "Woe to you, scribes and Pharisees, hypocrites! because you are like whitewashed tombs" (Mt 23.27). This colorful method of description is common in ordinary speech. A metaphor is a compressed simile in which one thing is identified or equated with another, or the qualities of one thing are directly ascribed to another; for example, "You are the salt of the earth" (Mt 5.13); "Beware of the leaven of the Pharisees" (Mk 8.15). This figure is more literary than the simile and is frequent in poetry.

The more elaborate forms of illustration, the parable and the allegory, are really expansions of the basic figures. A parable is a developed simile in which the story, while fictitious, is true to life. The latter feature differentiates a parable from a fable. Parables are frequently used today in speeches and sermons in which the speaker tells a story whose moral or punch line illustrates his topic. An ALLEGORY is a developed metaphor prolonged into continuous narrative. Ideally, in the technical and classical usage, the parable is distinct from allegory. In the parable the details and characters have no hidden meaning; the important thing is the lesson of the story. Details serve only to bring out the principal point. Another mark of differentiation is that the parable, like the simile, is a popular and less literary figure of speech. But in practice the traits of allegory are often present in a parable. The story may have one principal point (parable), but some of the characters may have a significance of their own. Already Quintilian, the 1st-century Latin authority on oratory, recognized such intermingling.

History of Parable Exegesis. In the exegesis of the Church Fathers the parables of Jesus were treated as allegories, and the Fathers were greatly concerned with the significance of all the details of the parables. They indulged in an exegesis that at times seems rather fanciful, although beneath their allegorizing the Fathers often came to a valid basic interpretation of the parable involved.

In modern times there was a violent reaction to the long centuries of allegorizing the parables initiated by the German Protestant scholar A. Jülicher. In his work *Die Gleichnisreden Jesu* (2 v. Freiburg 1888–89) he rejected 18 centuries of allegorizing and insisted that the parables of Jesus were simple, moralizing stories. The parables

Illumination from "Codex Aureus," depicting parable of Laborers in Vineyard, from Ecternach, written at Trier ca. 983–993, preserved in Stiftung für Kunst und Wissenschaft, Coburg, Germany.

Former Abbey Church of Saint-Pierre in Moissac; bas-relief depicting the parable of Dives and Lazarus in the South Porch, France. (©Ruggero Vanni/CORBIS)

had one point, and no one should seek hidden meaning in the details or characters of the parables; allegory is a literary figure, and Jesus was a simple preacher.

The wide implications of this popular position were very serious. As they are reported in the Gospels, some of the parables of Jesus have obvious allegorical characteristics, e.g., the parable of the Tenants in the Vineyard (Mk 12.1–11), where the characters are identifiable. If one were to follow Jülicher's principle strictly, the allegorical features would indicate that the parable could not be attributed to Jesus but would have to be regarded as a literary creation of the early Church. Again, three other parables receive an explanation in the Gospels: the Sower (Mk 4.13–20), the Weeds (Mt 13.36–43), and the Fish Net (Mt 13.49–50). These explanations are somewhat allegorical, for they interpret the individual details and characters. Here too, according to Jülicher's principle, the explanation of these parables could not be attributed to Jesus.

In time scholars challenged Jülicher's principle as being too doctrinaire. It is clear that, while the parables have one principal point, many of them are not free from allegorical features. This is evident if one approaches the parables of Jesus from a Semitic viewpoint rather than from the technical distinctions of classical oratory. Hebrew has one word for these figures of speech, *māšāl,* which covers all the Greek divisions and more. Under *māšāl* are grouped, in the Old Testament and the rabbinical writings, proverbs, maxims, symbols, riddles, parables, allegories, and fables. The παραβολή of the Greek New Testament is the equivalent of *māšāl.* Subsumed under it are proverbs (Lk 4.23), maxims (Lk 14.7–11), riddles (Mk 7.15–17), examples (Lk 12.15–21), figurative speech (Mk 4.33), similes (Mt 13.33), metaphors (Mt 5.14), and, finally, parables, and parables with simple al-

"Christ Explaining a Parable to the Disciples," manuscript illumination by Cristoforo de Predis from the *"Predis Codex."*
(©Archivo Iconografico, S.A./CORBIS)

legorical characteristics. Thus, ''parable'' can cover a range from a single-line metaphor or simile to a long narrative. The distinctions that underlie Jülicher's theory would have been strange to Jesus and cannot be used mechanically to interpret His parables. Finally, it should be noted that the word παραβολή does not occur in the Fourth Gospel; there, as a synonym, another Greek word, παροιμία, is used, which also covers a range of figurative speech (16.25).

Literary Dimension. Subsequent to the seminal work of Joachim Jeremias, who traced the development of the parables from their earliest stages to their final redaction in the Gospels, and who reconstructed the main aspects of the teaching of Jesus from the parables, a major shift in parable study occurred in the mid-1960s. Amos Wilder and Robert Funk, in proposing that parables be treated as poetic language, broke with the tradition which had been predominant since Jülicher of viewing the para-

bles primarily as rhetorical forms with a single meaning or focus. At the heart of both poetry and parable, they argued, is a metaphor which, by the surprising equation of dissimilar elements (e.g., ''The eye is the lamp of the body,'' Mt 6.22), produces an impact on the imagination that cannot be conveyed by discursive speech. Metaphor leads beyond the expressive power of language so that logically, ''interpretation of parables should take place in parables'' (Funk, *Language,* p. 196).

The parables tell us in image and symbol what God and God's reign is ''like,'' but their open-ended and often enigmatic quality prevent us from finding one-to-one correspondences between the nature or action of God and the situation in the parables. As metaphors, the parables use concrete and familiar images which touch people in their everyday lives, but which point to a reality which transcends definition or literal description. Metaphor has thus moved from the status of a literary trope or figure of speech to a theological and hermeneutical category which characterizes all religious speech. The parables of Jesus become themselves paradigms for language about God.

Paul RICOEUR stressed that the parables of Jesus are more properly ''metaphoric'' than metaphors since they comprise extended narratives which combine the narrative form and metaphorical process (''Biblical Hermeneutics,'' p. 33). As narratives they continue the narrative legacy of the Biblical tradition, and those who read the stories told by Jesus realize that life itself is ''a pilgrimage, a race, in short, a history'' (Wilder, *Rhetoric,* 65). The narrative potential of the parables was pursued by Dan Otto Via who offered a ''dramatic'' reading of the longer parables. From study of their plot and interaction of characters Via divided the parables into ''tragic'' and ''comic'' parables, understood in the classic sense as a sudden reversal of fortune from good to evil or the reverse. He argued that the parables confront their readers with the same tragic or salvific possibilities as those confronted by their characters. Readers can, like the Unmerciful Servant (Mt 18.23–35), remain untouched by unmerited forgiveness and continue to live in a world of strict justice which ultimately destroys them. They can look at the ''salvation'' of a picaresque or roguish Unjust Steward (Lk 16.1–8) and realize that God summons us to live by our wits when faced with a crisis.

Parables are not only metaphoric, they contain novel twists or paradoxes (i.e., apparent incongruities which convey a deeper truth). Generous vineyard owners about to give equal pay for unequal work generally do not make those who worked all day stand around while they first pay those hired at the seventh hour (Mt 20.8). Fathers in a first-century Near Eastern culture generally do not ''run'' (Lk 15.20). A major key to the ''meaning'' of a given parable is where the realism begins to break down.

Ricoeur and later J. Dominic Crossan stress the paradoxical quality of parables. Their fundamental message is that things are not as they seem; you must have your tidy image of reality shattered. The Good Samaritan (Lk 10.29–37) is not primarily an illustration of compassion toward those suffering, but a challenge to see the enemy (i.e., the Samaritan) as ''good.'' The paradox of the parables corresponds to the paradox of Jesus' action in associating with tax collectors and sinners. The parables operate, according to Ricoeur, by a pattern of orientation, disorientation, and reorientation. Their hyperbolic and paradoxical language embodies an extravagance which shocks our normal perceptions, so that we are drawn to the extraordinary within the ordinary. The parables dislocate our project of trying to fit our lives into a tight pattern, which Ricoeur feels is equivalent to Paul's criticism of ''justification by works.'' The parables offer a poetics

of faith by summoning us to openness and trust in the face of the unexpected (''Biblical Hermeneutics,'' p. 122–128).

Characteristics of Jesus' Parables. Jesus took illustrations from daily life that attracted the hearers' attention by vividness and narrative color. While these illustrations enabled the hearers to understand His message better, they often had a strange or novel twist that left enough doubt to challenge the hearers into active thought and inquiry. These characteristics are worthy of detailed study.

Illustrations from Daily Life. Jesus was familiar with a rural Galilean milieu: outdoor scenes of farming and shepherding, and domestic scenes in a simple one-room house (Lk 11.5–8). The homes of the rich were seen only through the kitchen door—the view of servants and slaves. The farming was hill-country farming, done in small patches with stone fences and briars (Mk 4.5–7), not in the broad lowland plains. There were donkeys, sheep, wolves, and birds; seeds, wheat, and harvest; lilies of the field and fruit trees; patches and wineskins and lamps; children in the market place, laborers and merchants. Now, even for those readers who know something of rural life the ancient techniques described in the Gospels are somewhat puzzling, and special knowledge is required. For instance, the careless broadcasting of seed in the parable of the Sower is explained by the fact that in Palestinian farming sowing sometimes took place before plowing.

Storytelling Techniques. Among the Gospel parables are found vivid narratives employing all the techniques of storytelling. One of these would be the rule of three, namely, that in popular stories it is customary to have three characters with the point of illustration lying in the third. Thus, in the parables, three servants are entrusted with the talents, and three men pass the man who fell among robbers. Another technique of storytelling is direct discourse: rarely is it told in the third person what a character is thinking. Rather, the characters talk aloud to themselves so that the hearer may find out what is in their minds, e.g., in the parable of the Pharisee and the Publican (Lk 18.9–14) and in that of the Rich Fool (Lk 12.16–21). Only one conversation can hold the stage at a time; and consequently, when three characters are involved, as in the Talents, the direct confrontation is repeated three times (Mt 25.14–28). Thinking of the parables as stories will also help to make understandable the peculiarities and inconsistencies that appear in them. ''That is for the sake of the story'' is the answer to many a difficulty that arises if one is too logical, e.g., why a dishonest steward should be allowed to make an inventory (Lk 16.1), or why workers should be paid in inverse order (Mt 20).

Novel Twists and Challenging Points. In the stories told by Jesus there is often a novel twist that must have made his hearers take notice. Who would have expected the scapegrace prodigal son to emerge as a more sympathetic character than the elder son who stayed at home? At times, as one may suspect from the similarity of Jesus' parables to those of the rabbis, Jesus may have used well-known stories or characters and have supplied new endings. The priest, the Levite, and the layman may have been stock characters in religious tales; but in Jesus' story, the third character was a hated Samaritan, and it was he who was the most sympathetic of the three.

Frequently there was a challenge in the parables of Jesus, the challenge of the kingdom of God. In evaluating the parables as moral lessons Jülicher made the mistake, so common in the liberal theology of the late 19th century, of reducing Jesus to a preacher of good morals. Some of the parables, such as that of the Good Samaritan, were a blistering attack on the established religious policy of the time. Others, such as the parable of the Tenants in the Vineyard and that of the Talents, were threats of imminent judgment on the leaders of Judaism. Still others, such as the Sower and the Mustard Seed, were an apologia for the slowness and insignificance of the results of His own ministry in Galilee. Jesus sought constantly to involve His hearers personally in the challenge of the parables. Many times He asked them, ''What do you think?'' (see Mt 21.31; Lk 7.42) and made them pass judgment on the outcome of the parabolic story. The Matthean version of the parable of the Tenants in the Vineyard has the audience itself pass judgment on the Jewish leaders who rejected Jesus (Mt 21.41; but cf. Mk 12.9). Throughout the Gospel is heard the personal appeal of Jesus: ''He who has ears to hear, let him hear.''

Purpose of the Parables. The fact that some of the parables had to be explained by Jesus to the disciples who had not understood them (Mk 4.10, 34; Mt 13.36; Jn 16.29) raises the question of the purpose of the parables. The overwhelming evidence of the Gospels is that the parables made Jesus' message intelligible. Yet in a passage that separates the parable of the Sower from its explanation (Mk 4.11–12) the disciples are told: ''. . . to those outside, all things are treated in parables, that 'Seeing they may see but not perceive; and hearing they may hear but not understand.''' Was the purpose of the parables, then, to confuse and obfuscate?

Today many authors recognize that this passage is really a summation, not of the purpose, but of the result of preaching the kingdom of God in parables. The challenge of the parables was rejected by the majority of hearers who saw and heard but refused to perceive and understand. The parables were a sword of judgment. The

passage cited above as part of Mk 4 is an adaptation of Is 6.10, which is quoted several times in the New Testament and became the standard Christian explanation of why Jesus' ministry had not been received by Israel (Jn 12..7–41; Acts 28.26–27).

Therefore, if the parables blinded men's minds and hearts, it was more because men refused their piercing challenge than because men could not intellectually understand them. This does not mean that the parables were always clear to all. Jesus' picture of the kingdom of God was quite different from that of the political kingdom of David that was popularly expected, and so his parabolic exposition of the kingdom often had to be explained. Also, Jesus was chary of detailed descriptions of the future action of God in definitively establishing the kingdom (Mt 24.36; Acts 1.6–7). The parables could unfold the true nature and destiny of the kingdom without arousing vain speculation about the future. Thus, the vagueness, which is of the nature of symbolic language, served Jesus' purpose. Well does Mark say of the parable: ''And in many such parables he spoke the word to them according as they were able to understand it'' (Mk 4.33).

Parables in the Gospel Context. The evangelists not only transmit the parables, but each stamps them with his own theological perspective through editorial changes, by locating them in a definite context (e.g., the three parables of Lk 15; the eschatological parables of Mt 24 and 25), and by addition of material from their own sources. The parables simultaneously influence and reflect the different theologies of the Synoptic Gospels.

The world of Mark's parables is that of the village, farming, and the processes of nature, and he has only one long dramatic parable (Mk 12.1–11). His parables lead the readers into the mystery of the KINGDOM (Mk 4.11), and serve the two major motifs of his theology, christology and discipleship. In contrast to Mark, Matthew has a great number. He takes over all of Mark's except for the Seed Growing Secretly (Mk 4.26–29), and incorporates extensive parabolic sayings and longer parables from Q, e.g., the Lost Sheep (18.12–14), the Marriage Feast (22.1–14), the Wise and Faithful Servants (24.45–51), and the Talents (25.14–30). Matthew's theology assumes its distinctive shape from parables found only in his Gospel, such as the Wheat and the Tares (13.24–30), the Unmerciful Servant (18.23–35), the Laborers in the Vineyard (20.1–16), the Ten Bridesmaids (25.1–13), and the Sheep and the Goats (25.31–46).

Matthew's parables manifest common literary and theological traits. Matthew loves extravagance. Mark's shrub (4.32) becomes a tree (Mt 13.32) and the debt of the servant (Mt 18.24) exceeds the taxes of Syria, Phoenicia, Judaea, and Samaria. His parables contain many allegorical features and he is fond of APOCALYPTIC imagery to underscore the crisis occasioned by the teaching of Jesus (eternal fire; outer darkness; weeping and gnashing of teeth; see 13.42, 50; 22.13; 24.51; 25.30). Matthew changes the parable of the Lost Sheep (18.12–14) from a defense of Jesus' fellowship with tax collectors (cf. Lk 15.1–7), to concern for the "little ones" in the community—a major theme of chapter 18. In editing parables received from Mark and parables only in his Gospel, Matthew also reflects the conflict with the Judaism of his time (see 21.28–43; 22.1–14). The parables which conclude the eschatological discourse (24.45–25.31) all deal with responsible ethical action in the face of coming judgment, a theme which reverberates throughout the discourse and the Gospel.

The Gospel of Luke contains the most extensive collection of parables in the New Testament, including those which are seen as classic statements of the teaching of Jesus, such as the Good Samaritan (10.29–37) and the Prodigal Son (15.11–32). Luke's parables eschew allegory; they offer stories which are true to life and by the frequent use of soliloquy (12.17; 15.17–19; 16.3–4) they invite us into the world of the characters. They occur for the most part in the "travel narrative" (Lk 9.51–19.27) and reflect distinct Lukan themes such as the importance of compassion and mercy (1.78; 7.13; 10.33; 15.20), the dangers of wealth (12.13–21; 16.19–31) and the importance of prayer (11.5–10; 18.1–14). More than any evangelist Luke presents the demands of *daily* Christian life, so that the parables become paradigms of Christian existence.

Parables in the Fourth Gospel. John differs markedly from the Synoptics in the use of figurative language. However, if one recalls the scope of the term *māšāl* and that in the Biblical mentality there is no emphatic distinction between the various types of figurative language, then what is found in John can certainly come under the designation παραβολή (as the equivalent of *māšāl*), even though John does not use that word.

Jesus is found citing proverbs in John 4.35, 37. More often Johannine figurative language is applied to Jesus Himself, e.g., metaphors wherein Jesus is the bread of life (6.35), the source of living water (7.38), the light of the world (8.12). In the Synoptics, figurative language is frequently used for the kingdom of God, a term which does not loom large in Johannine thought. Actually, the emphasis that the Synoptics put on the coming and acceptance of the KINGDOM OF GOD, John puts on the sending of Jesus by the Father. The challenge to men presented in the Synoptic tradition by the kingdom of God is presented in John (e.g., 3.16–21) by the person of Jesus. The uses of figurative language in the two traditions are quite

analogous, then, to their theological emphases. (*See* JOHN, GOSPEL ACCORDING TO ST.)

There are more elaborate instances of figurative language in John that border on allegory. On the basis of Jülicher's theory, some use Johannine allegory as an indication of the lateness of the Gospel and its lack of authentic tradition. Jesus, however, was just as capable of speaking in simple allegories as were the rabbis of his time. Moreover, the proposed Johannine allegories must be analyzed. Taking the figure of the shepherd and the sheep in John 10.1–13 as an example, one may suggest that in 10.1–3a and 3b–5 there really are two short parables. Then, in 10.6 there is a failure to understand the parables, just as there is in Mark 4.10; and in 10.7–13 there is a somewhat allegorical explanation of the parables, just as in Mark 4.13–20. Again, an analysis of the simple allegory of the vine and branches in John 15.1–8 would show Old Testament and Synoptic parallels. Thus, the Johannine tradition in relation to parables is not as startlingly different as it might seem at first sight.

Gospel of Thomas and Synoptic Parables. The discovery in 1945 of the Coptic *Gospel of Thomas* (not to be confused with the apocryphal *Infancy Gospel of Thomas*) among the 13 Coptic manuscripts at Nag Hammadi and its subsequent publication, as well as the realization that the texts found in the late 19th century at Oxyrhynchus in Egypt were also from the *Gospel of Thomas*, precipitated a lively discussion on the relation of its 114 sayings to similar sayings in the Synoptic Gospels. Roughly 25 percent are virtually identical with parallel sayings in the Synoptic Gospels. The others represent variants of Synoptic sayings, sayings of Jesus known from the Church Fathers and Apocryphal Gospels, as well as sayings found only in the *Gospel of Thomas*.

Especially important are those parables and parabolic sayings which are parallel to similar sayings in the Synoptic Gospels (principally, *Gos. Thom.* #8=Mt 13.47–50; #9=Mk 4.2–9, *et par.*; #20=Mk 30–32, *et par.*; #21=Mk 3.27; 4.26–29; #35=Mk 3.23–27, *et par.*; #57=Mt 13.24–30; #63=Lk 12.13–21; #64=Mt 22.1–14; Lk 14.15–24; #65=Mk 12.1–12, *et par.*; #76=Mt 13.45–46; #96=Mt 13.33, Lk 13.20–21; #107=Mt 18.12–14; Lk 15.3–7; #109=Mt 13.44). Two parables (#97–98) have no parallels in the Synoptics. The parables of the *Gospel of Thomas* show a strong affinity with those in Q and lack those which are often seen as distinctive of the teaching of Jesus, e.g., the Unmerciful Servant (Mt 18.23–35), the Sheep and the Goats (Mt 25.31–46), the Good Samaritan (Lk 10.29–37), and the Prodigal Son (Lk 15.11–32).

As in the Synoptic parables the introductory formula is "like"; unlike them the formula is often "The Kingdom of the Father is like.'' While the Synoptic parables are addressed often to the crowds or to Jesus' disciples, the parables of the *Gospel of Thomas* are directed exclusively to the disciples. The parables of the *Gospel of Thomas* lack references to the Old Testament found in the Synoptic parables and the work is negative toward the Old Testament (see #52).

Three principal theories have emerged on the relationship of the *Gospel of Thomas* to the Synoptics: dependence on the Synoptic Gospels; essential independence of the Synoptics; and partial dependence and partial independence. Since the parables of the *Gospel of Thomas* appear in a different order than in the Synoptics and in a simpler form (i.e., without allegorical additions), and since they do not reflect the distinctive theology of the Gospels, the majority opinion rejects direct literary dependence on the Synoptics, and favors use of a common or similar primitive tradition. In specific cases the parables of the *Gospel Of Thomas* may be closer than the Synoptics to the original words of Jesus.

Earlier commentators on the *Gospel of Thomas* often described it as ''Gnostic,'' but recent studies question this by arguing that, while stressing asceticism and wisdom, it is on the borderline between Gnosticism and orthodoxy (Crossan, Davies, and Quispel). While much remains unsettled about the *Gospel of Thomas,* such as its original language, its provenance and date (speculations range from mid-first century A.D. until late second), its literary structure, and the relation of tradition and redaction within the text, it remains an important resource for the study of the history and development of the sayings of the Gospels (especially the parables), as well as for the religious history of early Christianity.

Bibliography: General and Literary Dimension of Parables. R. E. BROWN, ''Parable and Allegory Reconsidered,'' *Novum Testamentum* 5 (1962) 36–45. J. JEREMIAS, *The Parables of Jesus* (rev. ed. New York 1963). M. BOUCHER, *The Parables* (Wilmington, Delaware 1981), J. E. BREECH, *The Silence of Jesus* (Philadelphia 1983). J. D. CROSSAN. *In Parables: The Challenge of the Historical Jesus* (New York 1973). J. DRURY, *The Parables in the Gospels* (New York 1985). R. FUNK, *Language, Hermeneutic and the Word of God* (New York 1966). W. S. KISSINGER, *The Parables of Jesus: A History of Interpretation and Bibliography* (Metuchen, New Jersey 1979). H.-J. KLAUCK, *Allegorie and Allegorese in synoptischen Gleichnistexten* (Münster 1978). J. LAMBRECHT, *Once More Astonished: The Parables of Jesus* (New York 1981). S. MCFAGUE, *Metaphorical Theology* (Philadelphia 1982). P. PERKINS, *Hearing the Parables of Jesus* (New York 1981). N. PERRIN, *Jesus and the Language of the Kingdom* (Philadelphia 1976). P. RICOEUR, ''Biblical Hermeneutics,'' *Semeia* 4 (1975) 27–148. M. A. TOLBERT, *Perspectives on the Parables: An Approach to Multiple Interpretations* (Philadelphia 1979). D. O. VIA, *The Parables: Their Literary and Existential Dimension* (Philadelphia 1967). H. WEDER, *Die Gleichnisse Jesu als Metaphern* (Göttingen 1978). A. WILDER, *Early Christian Rhetoric: The Language of the Gospel,* (2d ed. New York 1971). Parables in Context of Gospels. K. E. BAILEY, *Poet and Peasant* and *Through Peasant Eyes,* 2 v. in 1 (Grand Rapids 1984) [on Luke]. M. BOUCHER, *The Mysterious Parable* (Washington 1977) [on Mark]. C. E. CARLSTON, *The Parables of the Triple Tradition* (Philadelphia 1975). J. R. DONAHUE, *The Gospel in Parable* (Philadelphia 1988). M. GOULDER, ''Characteristics of the Parables in the Several Gospels,'' *Journal of Theological Studies* 19 (1968) 51–69. J. KINGSBURY, *The Parables of Jesus in Matthew 13* (London and St. Louis 1977). Parables and the Gospel of Thomas. *Text. The Facsimile Edition of the Nag Hammadi Codices,* 12 v. (Leiden 1972–), v. 3 (=Codex II) contains *The Gospel of Thomas.* A. GUILLAUMONT, et al., *The Gospel According to Thomas,* Coptic text and Eng. tr. (New York 1959). Translations, J. ROBINSON, ed., *The Nag Hammadi Library in English* (San Francisco 1977) 117–130; also in R. FUNK, ed., *New Gospel Parallels,* v. 2 (Philadelphia 1985) 93–187. Studies. S. DAVIES, *The Gospel of Thomas and Christian Wisdom* (New York 1983). J. D. CROSSAN, *Four Other Gospels* (Minneapolis 1985). H. MONTEFIORE, ''A Comparison of the Parables of the Gospel according to Thomas and of the Synoptic Gospels,'' H. MONTEFIORE and H. E. W. TURNER, eds., *Thomas and the Evangelists* (Naperville 1962) 40–78. G. QUISPEL, ''The Gospel of Thomas Revisited,'' B. BARC, ed., *Colloque International sur Les Textes de Nag Hammadi* (Québec; Louvain 1981) 218–266.

[R. E. BROWN/ J. R. DONAHUE/EDS.]

PARACLETE

The word *Paraclete,* peculiar in the Bible to the Gospel of St. John, directly denotes the role of the Holy Spirit as intercessor, consoler, teacher, and defender of Christ's disciples; yet implicit in the fourth Gospel (Jn 14.26) is the fundamental thought that Jesus Himself is the primary Paraclete, a thought that John clearly enunciates elsewhere (1 Jn 1.2).

Extra-Biblical Use of the Term. The English word Paraclete comes, through the Latin *Paracletus,* from the Greek Παράκλητοσ. The verb παρακαλειν means ''to call to one's side''; hence it has various derived meanings depending on the function for which one is called, such as to defend, to intercede, to console. Morphologically, as a verbal adjective ending in τοσ, the word Παράκλητοσ would normally have a passive meaning, ''one called to another''; yet in usage, the meaning derives primarily from the function of the one called, so that the few examples of this word in extra-Biblical Greek show rather the active meaning, ''helper, defender, mediator, consoler.'' In Jb 16.2 the Hebrew active (hiph'îl) participle *menaḥămîm,* ''comforters,'' was translated as παράκλητοι by Aquila and Theodotion. The term appears also in Philo in an active sense, ''helper'' or ''mediator'' (*De Specialibus Legibus* 1.237; *De Opificio Mundi* 23). In rabbinical Judaism this Greek term was taken over into Mishnaic Hebrew as a transliterated loanword, *peraqlît.* As such, it was used for both human and angelic mediators or intercessors, and especially for the ''advocate'' (the one called) who pleads the cause of another in a judicial process.

Johannine Usage. The word Paraclete occurs only five times in the Bible, and all five occurrences are in the writings of St. John: 1 Jn 2.1; Jn 14.16, 26; 15.26; 16.7.

Christ, the Paraclete. In 1 Jn 2.1 it is Jesus Christ who is termed the paraclete. The active sense of the word is clear in this case; Jesus is our defender, our intercessor before the Father. If Christians commit sin, they should not despair; they have Christ, who is Himself "just" (i.e., innocent), as their advocate to plead their case before God's supreme tribunal. This concept of Jesus Christ as the heavenly Paraclete, or Advocate, leads naturally to the use of the term in the farewell discourse of Jesus at the LAST SUPPER (Jn 14–16).

The Holy Spirit, the Paraclete-Advocate. In His discourse at the Last Supper Jesus announces His imminent departure from this earth (Jn 13.33, 14.2; 16.5), but He also tells His disciples of a return that is to follow very shortly after this absence (14.18, 28). This return is then explained in terms of the abiding presence of the Spirit of the glorified Lord who will be sent from the Father and the Son after the Son's glorification (16.7–11; see also 7.39). When the HOLY SPIRIT is first mentioned in this context, He is described as "another Paraclete" (14.16). Jesus is the primary and, in a certain sense, even the unique Paraclete; the Holy Spirit is "another" only in the sense that through Him Jesus will remain forever present with the Apostles and with all who through them come to believe in Him. They and their spiritual descendants in the Church will not be left like defenseless orphans to become the prey of an evil world; they will have a permanent advocate to plead their cause before the just tribunal of God against all the evil tribunals of this world (14.16–18). The usage of the term here is similar to, but broader than, that in 1 Jn 2.1. The Paraclete who is the Spirit of the glorified Christ, in defending the Church, must condemn the world that has wrongfully accused it. Here the defender is also a prosecutor. This activity of the Spirit-Paraclete can be perceived only by faith; even though this divine Advocate is the very "Spirit of truth" (14.16; 15.26; 16.13), the world will not listen to Him (14.17).

The Holy Spirit, the Paraclete-Defender. The next passage where the Spirit-Paraclete appears is Jn 14.26. This time only one aspect of His dual role as defender-prosecutor is stressed. He must keep the Apostles ever mindful of all that Jesus has taught them and make plain to them what they have not yet fully understood (see also 16.12–15), for only insofar as they remain faithful to His teaching can their divine Advocate prove them blameless before the judgment seat of God against all the accusations of this world (16.1–4). In these two Paraclete passages in John ch. 14, the Spirit appears primarily as the Advocate defending the Apostles and the Church.

The Spirit-Paraclete, Witness of the Truth. In Jn 15.1–8 the absolute need of the Apostles to remain united with Jesus is described under the symbolism of the vine. Then in 15.18–25 the Apostles are warned that they, in their union with Christ, will share in the world's hatred and persecution of Him. Therefore, the Spirit-Paraclete will also have to come to the defense of Christ; He will bear witness to the truth of what Jesus did and said and was (15.26). It is in the Spirit's defense of the mission of Jesus that the truth of the Apostles' mission is guaranteed (15.27; see also Mk 13.11; Mt 10.20; Lk 12.12).

Judicial Role of the Spirit-Paraclete. The exact meaning of Jn 15.26 is made clearer in the final and climatic use of the term Paraclete in Jn 16.7. Once again Jesus reiterates that His departure is but the condition and prelude to His return in the Spirit (16.5–6). Moreover, when the Spirit-Paraclete of Jesus comes, He will do three things: first, He will prove that the world is guilty of sin because it acted unjustly in refusing to believe in Jesus, as well as in condemning Him "without cause" (15.25) to death before its human tribunal; secondly, He will prove that Jesus was "just," i.e., innocent, by bearing witness to the fact that His death was not a defeat but a glorious return to the Father; thirdly, having established both the guilt of the world and the innocence of Jesus, He will pass sentence of condemnation on "the prince of this world," i.e., Satan. Human tribunals may condemn Jesus and His followers (15.18–25; 16.1–4; 17.16), but before the solemn tribunal of God, the Paraclete overturns and reverses these judgments—on Jesus (15.26; 16.7) and on those who are faithful to Him (14.16, 26).

Bibliography: *Encyclopedic Dictionary of the Bible*, tr. and adap. by L. HARTMAN (New York 1963) 1717–20. J. BEHM, G. KITTEL, *Theologisches Wörterbuch zum Neuen Testament* (Stuttgart 1935–) 5:798–812. X. LÉON-DUFOUR, ed., *Vocabulaire de théologie biblique* (Paris 1962). L. J. LUTKEMEYER, "The Role of the Paraclete (Jn. 16:7–15)," *The Catholic Biblical Quarterly* 8 (1946) 220–229. O. BETZ, *Der Paraklet: Fürsprecher im häretischen Spätjudentum, im Johannes-Evangelium und in neu gefundenen gnostischen Schriften* (Leiden 1963). R. E. BROWN, *The Gospel According to John* (Anchor Bible 29 and 29A; Garden City 1966). *passim.*

[D. M. CROSSAN]

PARACLETE, SERVANTS OF THE

(SP, Official Catholic Directory, #1230); a clerical congregation, was founded by Gerald M. C. Fitzgerald at Jemez Springs, New Mexico, in January 1947. Father Fitzgerald considered Cardinal Francis Spellman, of New York; Abp. Edwin V. Byrne, of Santa Fe; and Abp. William D. O'Brien, of the Extension Society, as cofounders because of their vital interest and support. The specific purpose of the congregation is the care of priests, especially those on temporary retirement from active duty. At Jemez Springs, where the first monastery, Via Coeli, was opened in what had formerly been a mountain inn, priests quickly gave support to the work in a spirit epitomized by the motto of the congregation: "For Christ in His priests." The constitutions were approved in May of 1952, and the congregation was formally erected by Archbishop Byrne on June 1, 1952. The generalate is Jemez Springs, N.M.

[G. FITZGERALD/EDS.]

PARADIS, MARIE-LÉONIE, BL.

Baptized Alodie Virginie, foundress of the Little Sisters of the Holy Family; b. May 12, 1840, at L'Acadie (Sainte Marguerite de Blairfindie, a suburb of Montréal), Québec, Canada; d. May 3, 1912, at Sherbrooke, Québec.

She was the daughter of a miller, who sent her to a boarding school run by the Sisters of Notre Dame at Saint-Laurent. Paradis entered the religious life at age thirteen, taking vows in 1857 as a Holy Cross sister. She was sent to St. Vincent's Orphanage in New York City. For sometime she taught in various schools. In 1864, she was given charge of the domestic work in an Indiana household. Later she had the same responsibilities at St. Joseph's College, Memramcook, New Brunswick.

Finding many young women eager to join her in this vocation, she formed a new community, Little Sisters of the Holy Family (1880), which received canonical approval in 1896 and papal approbation in 1905. The sisters work in the kitchens, laundries, and sacristies of colleges, seminaries, episcopal residences, and retirement homes for priests. They began with the household management of the apostolic delegations in Canada and Washington, DC. In 1885, the novitiate was transferred to Sherbrooke, Québec, where the motherhouse was later established. Although Mother Marie-Léonie was frail and often ill, she continued her service until a few hours before her peaceful death.

At her beatification in Montréal, Sept. 11, 1984, John Paul II declared that Marie-Léonie "never shied away from the various forms of manual labor which is the lot of so many people today and which held a special place in the Holy Family and in the life of Jesus of Nazareth himself."

Feast: May 4 (Canada).

Bibliography: *Acta Apostolicae Sedis* 78 (1986): 13–15. *L'Osservatore Romano,* English edition, no. 39 (1984): 9.

[K. I. RABENSTEIN]

PARADISE

Paradise is a place or state of bliss and immortality. This concept has its roots in the description and conditions of the Garden of Eden in Genesis, but appears in other places in the Old Testament and the New Testament and in extra–Biblical writings, in all of which it has undergone considerable development. This article will discuss first the terminology and then the concept of paradise as related to the primeval age, the eschatological age, and the present age.

Terminology. The word paradise comes to us through the Greek παράδεισος, which in turn derives from the ancient Persian *pairi–daēza,* meaning an enclosure wall, the space enclosed, and finally a park. This Persian term was taken over by late Hebrew in the form of *pardēs* and is found in Neh 2.8; Eccl 2.5; and Sg 4.12. The Septuagint uses παράδεισος to translate both *pardēs* and the more classical Hebrew word for garden, *gan,* whether there be reference to a garden in the ordinary sense (e.g., Nm 24.6; Is 1.30; Jer 29.5) or to the Garden of EDEN (Gn 2.8–3.24 *passim;* Jl 2.3), which is elsewhere called the Garden of God (e.g., Gn 13.10; Is 51.3; Ez 28.13; 31.8–9) or simply Eden (e.g., Ez 31.9, 16, 18; Sir 40.27). In later Jewish writings and in the New Testament, Paradise takes on a special and at times intricate religious significance.

Paradise of Primeval Age. The Yahwist narrative of Gn 2.4b–3.24 states that after creation man was placed in a garden (*gan*) where trees of all kinds grew (including the TREE OF LIFE and the TREE OF KNOWLEDGE), where there was copious water and a wide assortment of natural life. References to the Garden of Eden or the Garden of God are found in Gn 13.10; Is 51.3; Ez 31.8–9; 36.35; Jl 2.3; and Sir 40.27, with slightly varying terminology being used. The enigmatic Ez 28.13–19 not only speaks of Eden, the Garden of God, but also gives a kind of parallel and variant tradition of the Fall; in this text there is reference to a richly clad royal figure, a mountain, a cherub, and a fall from pristine innocence through trafficking and haughtiness (to mention some obvious features that differentiate it from the Genesis account).

In Genesis one may note several discordant features within the account, e.g., the probable reference to a kind of artesian well in 2.6 stands in contrast with the river system in 2.10–14, from both of which the ground or earth (Heb. 'ădāmâ) is watered (the 'ădāmâ being understood for the moment as outside the Garden). In 2.9 the reference to the Tree of Knowledge seems to be added to the verse, and 3.3 bears out the suggestion. In 3.22–23 only the man is spoken of as being driven out of the Garden, although the narrative has involved the woman very intimately. These examples point to various elements having been brought together from different sources with clever, but not perfect, literary skill.

From these and other disharmonies, it appears that there are various teachings in this account. One teaching is sin's influence on the earth's poverty (3.17–19), although one is free to suggest that the real cause is man's lack of industry and resourcefulness in his fallen condition. The Garden, too, is depicted as a place of blessedness and of closeness to God. One may note here, as in the case of Utnapishtim's dwelling in the GILGAMESH epic, the idea of remoteness: "far away at the mouth of the rivers" [J. B. Pritchard, *Ancient Near Eastern Texts Relating to the Old Testament*[2] (2d, rev. ed. Princeton 1955) 95b]. Thus Gn 2.8 speaks of the Garden "out in the steppe" ("Eden" presupposing the Sumerian e d i n, via the Akkadian *edinu,* which means steppe), "off towards the East"—the terms that are both vague and somewhat mysterious. The Hebrew *'ēden* (delight) is a clever and significant wordplay. The parallel use of terms in Is 51.3 brings out the same idea.

The possible location of Paradise has long intrigued men, especially those of fundamentalist outlook who have little knowledge of and concern for literary forms. Since two of the four rivers in 2.10–14 can be identified, the *p^erāt* and the *ḥiddeqel* being the Euphrates and the Tigris respectively, while the other two remain difficult to identify, many have thought of some location near the headwaters of the above named rivers. It is, however, extremely doubtful that the Yahwist had scientific geography in mind. He more likely borrowed famous names out of the past, thus adding to the luster of the Garden—which was not the site where earliest man actually lived. The emphasis is on man's primitive state and his lost opportunity for immortality. The number four elicits a note of universality (cf. "four corners of the earth" in Is 11.12 and the "four winds" in Mt 24.31).

Paradise in the Eschatological Age. In the writings of the Old Testament Prophets man's future happiness— vaguely situated in the "latter times"—is often depicted in terms reminiscent of Paradise. The peace and ideal justice to be procured by the messianic king will be like those of Paradise in Is 11.6–11. The same image is found in Hos 2.20, where peace in the animal kingdom and cessation of war are depicted. References to Eden are found in descriptions of the Promised Land in Is 51.3 and Ez 36.35, while the promise of longevity reminiscent of the immortality proffered to man in Eden is found in Is 65.17–25.

According to the Apocrypha and some rabbinical writings, Paradise will be the place of reward and bliss following upon judgment (e.g., Enoch 61.1–13; Testament of Levi 18.10–14; Apocalypse of Baruch 4). In

Adam and Eve Expelled From Paradise and the Birth of Death, from Saint Augustine's "City of God," 1486–1587. (©Gianni Dagli Orti/CORBIS)

these descriptions one finds the most varied ideas, e.g., Paradise is to be established in Jerusalem; the Tree of Life will flourish once more. The eschatological Paradise is often identified with the primeval Paradise. The Testament of Levi 18.10 tells how the high priest of the messianic age will open the gates of Paradise and remove the flaming sword mentioned in Gn 3.24. On the other hand, Paradise was described by some rabbis as close to GEHENNA or as associated with SHEOL, the latter term now being taken as one form of reference to future bliss [for many references, see R. H. Charles, *The Apocrypha and Pseudepigrapha of the Old Testament* (Oxford 1913) 1:861 s.v. "Paradise"].

In the New Testament Paradise is described with more restraint, and only three times by name. Of these references only Rv 2.7 is of interest. In this text the conquerors are promised the fruit of the Tree of Life that is in the Paradise of God. This fruit, symbolizing a very real spiritual value, is already available. Such a notion is common to New Testament thought, where union with Christ anticipates eschatological benefits. Revelation ch. 22 is filled with imagery drawn from Genesis ch. 2 and 3, although Paradise is not specifically named.

Paradise in the Present Age. If one makes the identification of the primeval Paradise with that to come, one might presuppose that Paradise has never ceased to exist. Such a notion could be derived from Gn 3.23–24, understood in a crassly literal sense. On the other hand, as the doctrine on RETRIBUTION after death developed, and a separate lot for the good and the wicked was postulated, speculation regarding entrance into Paradise quite normally increased. Some of the apocryphal writings state that after death and prior to resurrection the elect (and especially the Patriarchs) will be placed in Paradise (see Jubilees 4.23). The location of Paradise was likewise discussed. Some situated it, with Gn 2.8, in the East (e.g., Jubilees 8.16); others placed it in the North (Enoch 61.1–4; cf. 77.3; IS 14.13); and still others placed it in the West (reported by Josephus as Essene doctrine in *Bell. Jud.* 2.155–158; 4 Esdras 14.9). Still others assumed, seemingly, that after the Fall of Man, Paradise was removed from the earth and taken up to heaven with God (Life of Adam and Eve 25.3; Apocalypse of Baruch 4.6; 4 Esdras 4.7–8) and is, more precisely, in the "third heaven" (Apocalypse of Moses 37.5; Slavonic Enoch 8.1).

In the New Testament in Lk 23.43 Our Lord refers to the then already existing temporary abode of the just after their death. The notion is linked to that of ABRAHAM'S BOSOM, mentioned in Lk 16.23. In 2 Cor 12.2–4 Paradise is situated in the "third heaven" (an identification found in Slavonic Enoch 8.1), God's abode being the "seventh heaven." Underlying the "great chasm" of Lk 16.26 is the same notion of temporary beatitude, opposed in this instance to HADES. With our present knowledge of the universe it is impossible to point toward Paradise, i.e., heaven, as a distinctive place, though it would seem preferable to conceive of it as a place distinct from the earth.

See Also: AFTERLIFE, 2.

Bibliography: C. COTHENET, *Dictionnaire de la Bible,* suppl. ed. L. PIROT, et al. (Paris 1928–) 6:1177–1220. *Encyclopedic Dictionary of the Bible,* tr. and adap. by L. HARTMAN (New York 1963), from A. VAN DEN BORN, *Bijbels Woordenboek* 1720–25. P. HOFFMANN, *Lexikon für Theologie und Kirche,* ed. J. HOFER and K. RAHNER, 10 v (2d, new ed. Freiburg 1957–65) 8:69–72. A. JEPSEN and F. HESSE, *Die Religion in Geschichte und Gegenwart,* 7 v. (ed ed. Tübingen 1957–65) 5:96–100. J. JEREMIAS, G. KITTEL *Theologisches Wöterbuch zum Neuen Testament* (Stuttgart 1935–) 5:763–771. J. L. MCKENZIE, "The Literary Characteristics of Gn 2–3," *Theological Studies* 15 (1954) 541–572. H. RENCKENS, *Israel's Concept of the Beginning,* tr. C. NAPIER (New York 1964) 204–213. J. DANIÉLOU, *From Shadows to Reality,* tr. W. HIBBERD (Westminster, Md. 1960) 11–65. J. WEISENGOFF, "Paradise and St. Luke 23:43," *American Ecclesiastical Review* 103 (1940) 163–167.

[I. HUNT]

PARADOX

A statement that seems at first to defy ordinary understanding, even to the point of self-contradiction, but that may, on closer examination, prove to be well founded. The term has been applied to certain religious teachings, e.g., God at one time took on the identity of a particular man, and to antithetical sayings found in Scripture, such as St. Paul's description of the ministers of God, "As sorrowful yet always rejoicing; as poor yet enriching many; as having nothing yet possessing all things" (2 Cor 6.10). For paradoxical constructions arising in sciences such as metaphysics, logic, and mathematics, *see* ANTINOMY.

[H. A. NIELSEN]

PARAGUAY, JESUIT MARTYRS OF, SS.

Jesuit missionaries and martyrs; d. Rio Grande do Sul, Brazil, Nov. 15 and 17, 1628; canonized at Asunción, Paraguay, by John Paul II, May 16, 1988.

Roch González de Santa Cruz, b. Asunción, Paraguay, 1576; d. Caaró, November 17; he dedicated his life to the evangelization of the native peoples. He was appointed priest of the cathedral and, in 1609, vicar-general of the diocese. On May 9, 1609, he entered the Society of Jesus. In 1615 he began his missionary work by founding the *Reducción* of Itapúa and in subsequent years other such settlements. In 1620 he was appointed by his superiors to give religious instruction to the inhabitants of the area that is now the Brazilian state of Rio Grande do Sul. There he was martyred at the *Reducción* of Todos los Santos, the last one he founded. He had two companions in his martyrdom.

Alonso Rodríguez, b. Zamora, Spain, March 10, 1598; d. Caaró, November 15. He entered the Society of Jesus on March 25, 1614, and arrived in Buenos Aires on Feb. 15, 1617. After completing his studies, he gave religious instruction to the native peoples for four years.

Juan del Castillo, b. Belmonte, Spain, Sept. 14, 1596; d. Iyuí in the *Reducción* of La Asunción, two days later (November 17). He entered the Society of Jesus on March 22, 1614. Assigned to Paraguay, he arrived in Buenos Aires with Rodríguez and worked among the native peoples there for three years.

Their bodies were taken first to the *Reducción* of Candeleria and later transferred to that of the Immaculate Conception. These Jesuits became the first American martyrs to be beatified (Jan. 28, 1934, by Pius XI).

Pope John Paul II praised the Paraguayan martyrs because "neither the obstacles of the wilderness, the misunderstanding of people, nor the attacks of those who saw their evangelizing activity as a threat to personal interests could intimidate these champions of the faith'' (canonization homily). They are patrons of native traditions.

Feast: Nov. 16.

Bibliography: L. G. JAEGER, *Os-bem aventurados Roque González, Alfonso Rodríquez e João del Castillo: Mártires do Caaró e Pirapó,* 2d ed. (Pôrto Alegre 1951). L. KOHLER, *Los tres héroes de Caaró y Pirapó* (Posadas, Argentina 1978). G. MÁRKUS, *The Radical Tradition: Revolutionary Saints in the Battle for Justice and Human Rights* (New York 1993) 143–50. C. J. MCNASPY, *Conquistador without Sword: The Life of Roque González* (Chicago 1984), tr. of *Roque González de Santacruz, un conquistador sin espada* (Asunción, Paraguay 1983). H. THURSTON, ''The First Beatified Martyr of Spanish America,'' *Catholic Historical Review* 20 (1934–35): 371–83. J. N. TYLENDA, *Jesuit Saints & Martyrs* (Chicago 1998) 387–92. R. F. VELÁZQUEZ, *Roque González de Santa Cruz, colonia y reducciones en el Paraguay de 1600* (Asunción, Paraguay 1975).

[H. STORNI]

PARAGUAY, THE CATHOLIC CHURCH IN

A landlocked country in the heart of South America, joined to the sea by the great Paraguay and Paraná rivers, the Republic of Paraguay is bordered on the north and northwest by Bolivia, on the northeast, east and southeast by Brazil, and on the southwest and west by Argentina. A predominately agricultural nation, Paraguay benefits from the Gran Chaco, an area of black, fertile pastureland and forest in its west; the eastern landscape rises to grass-covered plains and rolling hills, with marshes and shallow lakes to the south. The Paraguay River runs south through the center of the country on its way to the Atlantic Ocean. Natural resources include hydropower, timber, iron ore and manganese; agricultural products consist of cotton, sugarcane, soybeans, corn, wheat, tobacco, tapioca and fruits and vegetables.

Since becoming an independent republic in 1811, Paraguay has been involved in two international wars: that of the Triple Alliance against Brazil, Argentina and Uruguay (1865–70), during which most of its adult male population was killed, and the Chaco War against Bolivia (1932–35), during which it gained territorially. A military dictatorship was overthrown in 1989, ushering in a series of freely elected, democratic governments. The population of Paraguay was overwhelmingly mestizo by 2000. Deforestation—the result of employing slash and burn methods to render farmland—resulted in a loss of five million acres of rain forest by 2000.

The Early Church. The area was originally inhabited by the Cario people and was discovered by Alejo Gar-

Capital: Asunción.
Size: 157,000 sq. miles.
Population: 5,585,830 in 2000.
Languages: Spanish; Guarani is spoken in rural areas.
Religions: 5,470,200 Catholics (90%), 276,330 Protestants (5%), 3,500 Jews (.06%), 2,000 Muslims (.03%), 256,800 without religious affiliation.
Archdiocese: Asunción, with suffragans Alto Paraná, Benjamin Aceval, Caacupé, Carapeguá, Concepción, Coronel Oviedo, Encarnación, San Juan Bautista de Las Misiones, San Lorenzo, San Pedro, and Villarrica del Espiritu Santo. Apostolic vicariates are located in Chaco Paraguayano and Pilcomaya, and a military ordinariate is also located in the country.

cía in 1524, after which colonization was begun. During the colonial period Spain provided an ample number of priests for the area and protected the religious orders in order to evangelize the Cario and multiply the subjects of the Crown. The Franciscans arrived in 1537, and from Asunción carried on missions in interior regions. Among the early missionaries were Alonso Lebrón, Alonso de San Buenaventura, Luis de BOLAÑOS, Bernardo de Armenta and the natives Gabriel de la Anunciación and Francisco de Guzmán. The first bishop to arrive was Pedro Fernández de la Torre. Mercedarians, Hieronymites and Dominicans preceded the Jesuits, each orders with schools and convents. The most famous Jesuits in colonial Paraguay were Manuel de Lorenzana, Antonio RUÍZ DE MONTOYA, Nicolás del TECHO, Pedro LOZANO, Francisco Xavier de Charlevoix, Nicolás Yapuguai, José Guevara, Simón Bandini, José CARDIEL, José Insaurralde, Diego de Boroa, Manuel Paramás, Nicolás Mastrilli, Alonso Barzana, Martin DOBRIZHOFFER, Pablo Restivo, José Sánchez Labrador, Pedro Montenegro, Roque Gonzáles de Santa Cruz, Domingo Muriel and José Quiroga. The principal obstacles for the propagation of the faith were learning of languages, the nomadic character of the native Cario, the ravages of the Portuguese *bandeirantes,* and the conflicts between political and religious authorities. The first missionaries used music and gifts to attract the Cario, and after learning their language they used songs and prayers to gain participants in their *doctrinas* and oratories, the foundations of the REDUCTIONS that were large communal centers of learning and enterprise. The success of the reductions became of concern to the government, which successfully dismantled them in 1768 by removing the Jesuits from Paraguay.

As the Catholic population grew, so did the need for a hierarchy. The Church of Asunción was erected in 1547, and the canonical founder of the see of Paraguay was the Spaniard Juan de Barrios, although he never reached his bishopric but was succeeded by Pedro Fer-

nández de la Torre (1556–72). During the first four centuries of its existence, the see was governed for only 200 years and was otherwise vacant or abandoned. Of the first 40 bishops, only 20 came to Paraguay. In 1929 the ecclesiastical Province of Paraguay was erected.

The Church and an Independent State. The most important institute founded in Asunción during the colonial period was the Colegio Seminario Conciliar de San Carlos, which was inaugurated on April 12, 1783 and educated almost all the leaders of the independence movement. During the colonial period the Church was very rich, and held ranches on government lands. During the independence period the Church was sympathetic toward the revolution and some priests worked for its success. No major reform touched the Church as a result of independence, which was gained on May 14, 1811, although relations between Church and State became relatively tense because of the right of patronage that the new state assumed and that influenced the election of bishops. In 1822 the dictator José Gaspar de Francia confiscated all Church properties and transformed its convents into barracks. During the War of the Triple Alliance the most serious crisis occurred between Church and State as a result of the execution of Bishop Manuel Antonio PALACIOS in 1868.

There was no lack of priests until the War of the Triple Alliance. At that point, Isidro Gavilán reorganized the Church due to a lack of clergy, and the Church was leaderless for 11 years. The first postwar priests were ordained in 1886 by Bishop Pedro Juan Aponte. They included Juan Sinforiano BOGARÍN, who later became the first archbishop of Asunción. Their funds came from the foreign mission bureaus of each order and the contributions of the faithful, and their work supplemented the social work of the state.

The Modern Church. Following the War of the Triple Alliance, Paraguay went into an economic decline, due predominately to the lack of its adult male workforce, most of whom had been killed or maimed during the war. In 1932 the country found itself at war again, this time with Bolivia, from which it won several large areas of land in the Chaco by 1935. This fertile region, believed to contain oil reserves, sparked an improvement in Paraguay's economic outlook. In 1954 Gen. Alfredo Stroessner took power in a coup backed by the U. S. government. While some efforts were made to aid landless peasants, the declining economy forced the government to become increasingly repressive.

During the mid-20th century, the Church was still under the protection of the state and was supported by the contributions of the faithful. Absolute divorce was not recognized; only physical and financial separation was legal under Paraguayan law. The Universidad Católica Nuestra Señora de la Asunción, founded in 1960, was the first private university officially recognized by the Paraguayan government. In addition there were primary and secondary schools conducted by religious throughout the republic. In spite of these schools, the influence of Catholic teaching in the country was not high, and this trend continued into the next few decades as the forces of liberalism and anticlericalism collided with the region's increasing economic decline and the resultant poverty and unemployment. The dictatorship of President Alfredo Stroessner, which had by now lost U.S. backing, drew increasing ire from Church leaders, who blamed his mismanagement for the nation's economy. Due to the increase in evangelical missionaries, Protestant activity grew in the region, its influence spreading through the rural areas in particular.

In 1989 a military coup led by General Andrés Rodrígez deposed Stroessner, in part in defense of the Church. Under the civilian presidency of Juan Carlos Wasmosy, who gained power in democratic elections in 1993, the economic crisis continued, forcing the unem-

Photograph of a Paraguan at the Roman Catholic mission of Santa Teresa, in the Chaco. (©Richard Bailey/CORBIS)

ployed into protest marches by mid-decade. An election later in the decade was followed by upheaval as President Raul Cubas was implicated in the March of 1999 murder of vice president Luis Maria Argana and forced to resign. While attempting to prevent the collapse of democracy against such upheaval, Church leaders remained outspoken in the political arena, particularly in regard to issues of social welfare, and denounced the corruption that had pervaded both society and government. In 1997 the government initiated a training program, to be run by the Catholic Church, to train the nation's military in "the respect of human dignity and in a culture of social peace and reconcilliation."

Into the 21st Century. By 2000 there were 323 parishes tended by 250 diocesan and 441 religions priests. Other religious, which included approximately 180 brothers and 1,300 sisters, dedicated themselves to the propagation of the faith, teaching at the 160 primary and 131 secondary schools and assisting in hospitals, at missions established in the interior of the country, homeless shelters and other centers of social assistance. In 1998 the apostolic nunciature opened a hospital for HIV-positive children to be administered by the Vincentian Sisters, at Tablada Nueva, in honor of the 20th anniversary of Pope John Paul II's pontificate. Despite the fact that the government had no state religion, the Church often performed Mass at state functions. Paraguay's traditional pilgrimage was to the Sanctuary of the Virgin of the Miracles in Caacupé, near Asunción, which had a legendary origin.

Bibliography: A. N. ACHÁ DUARTE, *Anuario eclesiástico del Paraguay* (Asunción 1963). *Registro oficial de la República del Paraguay* (1869). H. FERREIRA GUBETICH, *Geografía del Paraguay* (4th ed. Asunción 1960). G. FURLONG CÁRDIFF, *Misiones y sus pueblos guaraníes* (Buenos Aires 1956). C. R. CENTURIÓN, *Historia de las letras paraguayas,* 3 v. (Buenos Aires 1947–51); *Historia de la cultura paraguaya,* 2 v. (2d ed. Buenos Aires 1961).

[C. R. CENTURIÓN/EDS.]

PARALIPOMENON (CHRONICLES), BOOKS OF

Paralipomenon, or, first and second Chronicles, are the names given to the two books, originally one, that recount the history of the chosen people from a postexilic viewpoint, tracing it from Adam to the Edict of Cyrus in 538 B.C., but concentrating mostly on the history of the Judean monarchy. Palestinian Jews (and Hebrew printed Bibles) called these books (*sēper*) *dibrê hayyāmîm,* a title idiomatically equivalent to "annals" or "happenings of the times." Greek-speaking Jews in their Septuagint (followed by the Vulgate and some modern editions) referred to these books by the name παραλειπόμενα, which the Fathers of the Church understood as designating the books' content, "things omitted" (from previous Biblical histories). Some scholars, however, prefer to translate παραλειπόμενα as "things transmitted." St. Jerome, in his *Prologus galeatus,* says that these books are a "chronicle of the whole of divine history," with which phrase the modern appellation of these books, Chronicles, agrees. For these books themselves, *see* CHRONICLER, BIBLICAL.

[N. J. MCELENEY]

PARAY-LE-MONIAL

City in Saône-et-Loire department, Diocese of AUTUN, Burgundy, east central France. Next to LOURDES, it is the most popular pilgrimage center in France (since 1865). The rural parish Paray became le-Monial when CLUNIAC monks were sent there by St. MAJOLUS at the request of Count Lambert of Chalon (973), who endowed the foundation and gave a charter to the people. As the population increased, the monastery became a priory under Cluny and continued so, the prior being lord of the town, until 1789. The monastery church, dedicated to Our Lady in 977 and consecrated in 1004 by Bp. Hugh of AUXERRE, Lambert's son, was replaced *c.* 1100 by the present model of Burgundian Romanesque (with a semicircular choir beneath an octagonal tower 184 feet high and a 14th-century fresco of Christ Pantocrator, discovered in 1935). In 1794 the city purchased the church, which revolutionaries were about to destroy. Following the revelations of the Sacred Heart to St. Margaret Mary ALACOQUE (1673–75), the church became the Basilica of the Sacred Heart (1875). The shrine of the revelations and the saint's relics are in the Visitation monastery founded through the efforts of Jesuits (1626), who had established a mission in Paray to combat Calvinism (1619). The relics of Bl. Claude de LA COLOMBIÈRE were translated from the monastery to the Jesuit chapel (1930). The hospital of Paray, originally under Benedictines, is now staffed by Sisters of St. Marthe. Other monuments in Paray include the Chapel of Notre Dame de Romay, the tower of St. Nicholas, the hôtel de ville, and Hiéron (a Eucharistic museum founded in 1893).

Bibliography: É. LECANUET, *L'Église de France sous la Troisième République,* 4 v. (Paris 1930–31) v.1. A. GAUDILLIÈRE, *Lumières de Paray* (St. Léger-Vauban 1955). J. VIREY, *Paray-le-Monial et les églises du Brionnais* (new ed. Paris 1962).

[M. L. LYNN]

PAREDES Y FLORES, MARIANA DE JESÚS, ST.

Also known as Mariana of Quito, the "Lily of Ecuador"; b. Quito, Ecuador, Oct. 31, 1618; d. there, May 26, 1645. The eighth child of Jerónimo Zenel Paredes y Flores and Mariana Jaramillo de Granobles, Mariana upon her parents' death was left to the care of her sister, Jerónima, and brother-in-law, Cosme de Caso. Since the child had already begun her life of prayer, fasting, and penance, her guardians found a religious adviser for her in the Jesuit priest, Juan Camacho. She had a series of Jesuit confessors, but her most influential spiritual adviser was the Jesuit lay brother, Hernando de la Cruz. As models for her spiritual life she chose St. CATHERINE OF SIENA, St. ROSE OF LIMA, and St. TERESA OF ÁVILA. Mariana did not enter a convent, but spent most of her time in an austerely furnished upper room in her sister's house. She wore a black garment modeled on the Jesuit cassock. Tradition holds that she joined the Third Order of St. Francis at age 21 and wore its cord; though she never wore the habit while she was alive, she was buried with it over her black "Jesuit dress." While continuing her life of personal mortification, she encouraged the poor, hungry, and ill to come to her for help. In her sister's house she developed a kind of free clinic and a school room in which she

Sacre-Coeur Basilica in Paray-le-Monial. (©Vanni Archive/CORBIS)

taught native children. A number of times she predicted that the house would eventually become a Carmelite convent. In 1645, when Lima was visited with a number of calamaties—earthquakes, epidemics, volcanic eruptions—Mariana publicly offered her life for the benefit of the city. Within the generation after her death the process for beatification was begun, but it was beset with mishaps to the documents and the sponsors. She was finally canonized by PIUS XII on July 9, 1950.

Feast: May 26.

Bibliography: C. M. LARREA, *Las biografías de Santa Mariana de Jesús* (Quito 1970). F. P. KEYES, *The Rose and the Lily* (New York 1961). A. ESPINOSA PÓLIT, *Santa Mariana de Jesús hija de la Compañía de Jesús* (Quito 1957).

[J. M. VARGAS]

PAREJA, FRANCISCO

Mercedarian chronicler; place and date of birth unknown; d. Sept. 9, 1688. Nothing is known of his early years, not even his parents' names. He probably studied at the Mercedarian convent in Mexico City. In 1652 he was in Spain. He was the first rector of the San Ramón Nonato College in Mexico City (1654); professor of theology at the University of Mexico (1656); provincial twice (1655 and 1668); and provincial chronicler (1671). His main literary work was *Crónica de la provincia de la Visitación de Ntra. Sra. de la Merced redención de cautivos, de Nueva España,* which was completed Nov. 4, 1687. It remained unedited for two centuries. Cristobal de Aldana published a compendium of it about 1770; this edition was poorly printed and lacked a press signature. Juan Rodríguez Puebla (1798–1848), Mexican educator, made a manuscript copy of Pareja's *Crónica.* This copy was taken to Europe in 1869 and sold to a London bookseller, but was not published. The original manuscript, signed by Pareja, was discovered in Mexico and then published in two volumes in 1882–83. The unsigned preface contains historical information on Pareja and the vicissitudes the manuscript had gone through. The *Crónica* has three distinct parts: the first is an account of the Mercedarian pioneers in Mexico; the second is concerned with the Mercedarians who came to Mexico in 1576 to found a permanent community and carries the history to 1687; the third part is a collection of documents, added by editors, bringing the history of the order up to 1844. Pareja's purpose was to support his claim that the Mercedarians came to Mexico before the Franciscans, Dominicans, or Augustinians. The *Crónica* is very useful for the history of the Mercedarian Order. Two copies are extant: one in the library of the Museo de Antropología e Historia in Mexico City; the other in the Library of Congress, Washington, D.C.

[E. GÓMEZ TAGLE]

PAREJA, FRANCISCO DE

Franciscan missionary in Florida; dates of birth and death unknown. He was a native of Auñon, Spain, and joined the Franciscan Order in the Province of Castile. Pareja went to Florida as an Indian missionary in 1595 and served at San Juan del Puerto (in the area of modern Jacksonville) until 1616. He was then elected provincial of the Province of Santa Elena, which comprised Cuba, Florida, and Georgia. According to Fray Luis Gerónimo de Oré, visitor general to Florida in 1616, Pareja was a missionary of great sanctity and incredible zeal; he had expert knowledge of the Timucuan language. He wrote valuable mission reports and made frequent trips into the interior. Pareja composed the following works, all of which were printed in Mexico: *Cathecismo en lengua castellana y timuquana* (1612), *Cathecismo y breve exposición de la doctrina Christiana* (1612), *Confessionario en lengua castellana y timuquana* (1613), *Arte y pronunciación en lengua timuquana y castellana* (1614), and *Cathecismo y examen para los que comulgan en lengua castellana y timuquana* (1627).

Bibliography: L. J. DE ORÉ, *Relación histórica de la Florida, escrita en el siglo XVII,* ed. A. LÓPEZ, 2 v. (Madrid 1931–33); *The Martyrs of Florida (1513–1616),* tr. M. J. GEIGER (Franc Studies 18; New York 1936). M. J. GEIGER, *The Franciscan Conquest of Florida (1573–1618)* (Washington 1937).

[M. GEIGER]

PARENESIS

Parenesis (also spelled paraenesis) is derived from the Greek *parainesis,* advice, or *paraineō,* advise, recommend, urge, exhort. The word has been taken over from Greek rhetorical vocabulary by Biblical scholars as a technical description for passages with an exhortatory content concerned with proper moral or religious living. In the NT the term is found twice, both times in verbal form (Acts 27.9, 22). Passages judged to be parenetic often contain the similarly used *parakaleō,* exhort (e.g., Rom 12.1; 1 Thes 4.1; 1 Pt 2.11; 5.1).

Parenesis tends to be expressed briefly by using a succession of imperative statements. It gives personal counsel on moral and spiritual matters, practical advice for the listener or reader. A dominant feature of such exhortation is the use of traditional materials, especially popular maxims of wisdom passed on from generation to generation. Parenetic writing is characterized by the author's selection of a *topos,* i.e., focus upon a particular topic of moral concern. The development of the *topos* often uses such figures as similes, metaphors, parables, allegories, fables, and myths. The parenetic teaching may also be set forth in antitheses, i.e., expressed in the distinctive dualistic motif of the "two ways." Finally, parenesis is inclined to use catalogues of virtues and vices, groups of sayings, and, in some instances, *Haustafeln,* tables of household duties.

Biblical Instances. While parenesis is easily recognizable in the OT (e.g., in the wisdom literature in Prv 10.1–22.16, the "Proverbs of Solomon," and throughout Sir), most attention has been directed to its presence in the NT. Major sections of Paul's writings are considered to be parenetic (1 Thes 4–5; Gal 5–6; 1 Cor 6–7; Rom 6, 12–15). Various other epistles have parenetic sections throughout (Heb, 1 Pt) or are entirely so (Jas).

Twentieth-century assessments by A. Malherbe and S. Stowers warn, however, that parenesis has been generally understood too narrowly in New Testament studies as the stringing together of traditional precepts and exhortations usually placed before the conclusion of a letter. In their judgment parenesis includes not only precepts but also such things as advice, supporting argumentation, various modes of encouragement and dissuasion, the use of examples, models of conduct, etc. Thus, it is argued, for example that 1 Thessalonians as a whole is a parenetic letter using such rhetoric. In this approach the pastoral epistles would also be termed parenetic insofar as they compare well with fictitious letters of exhortation written in the names of various philosophers. Romans is the letter of Paul that comes closest to having a discrete parenetic section (chs. 12–15), but this is deemed misleading because the earlier part of the letter also has exhortatory materials (ch. 6).

Patristic Literature and Moral Theology. Parenesis is also frequently found in patristic writings (*see* e.g., *Didache; Epistle of Barnabas; 1 Clement*; Polycarp, *Philippians*; Basil, *Letter* 2; Augustine, *Letters* 19, 112, 210). The most outstanding example of the "two ways" motif in all of early Christian exhortation is that found in the beginning of the *Didache:* "There are two ways: a way of life and a way of death; and the difference between these two ways is great."

The early Christian proclamation of Christ, the kerygma, is related by many to parenesis analogously as gift and task, indicative and imperative, and from the perspective of theological reflection as dogmatics and ethics.

Thus the good news of the gospel is seen as the basis for the claims of parenesis. At the same time, it has been observed that parenesis draws attention to an essential element in the preaching of God's word: "It does not merely instruct, but paves the way for and reveals the blessed reality that is preached, liberating, consoling, fortifying its hearers and enabling them to accept it: a law which gives to them the power they need to fulfill it" (Rahner-Vorgrimler, p. 336).

Parenesis has moved also into the vocabulary of some moral theologians (e.g., B. Schüller and R. McCormick) as a term designating a supposedly distinct type of moral discourse. These moralists stress a difference between, and the perils of confusing, normative ethics with exhortatory moralizing, i.e., parenesis. Parenesis is understood to be a kind of verbal or exemplary persuasion to behave in a way that is already conceded to be the right way of behaving; the parenetic discourse is basically motivational, while the normative ethical formulation is mainly declarative. It has been argued in response (e.g., by J. Gaffney), however, that such a distinction is too sharply drawn and that the exhortation these theologians call parenesis is in fact integrally part and parcel of the moral norms to which it refers.

Bibliography: J. GAFFNEY, "On Parenesis and Fundamental Moral Theology," *Journal of Religious Ethics* 11 (1983) 23–34. A. J. MALHERBE, "Exhortation in First Thessalonians," *Novum Testamentum* 25 (1983) 238–256. J. I. H. MCDONALD, *Kerygma and Didache. The Articulation and Structure of the Earliest Christian Message,* Society for New Testament Studies, Monograph 37 (Cambridge 1980). K. RAHNER and H. VORGRIMLER, "Parenesis," *Theological Dictionary* (Freiburg 1965) 335–336. D. SCHROEDER, "Parenesis," *The Interpreters Dictionary of the Bible* supplement, ed. K. CRIM et al. (Nashville 1976) 643. S. K. STOWERS, *Letter Writing in Greco-Roman Antiquity,* Library of Early Christianity 5 (Philadelphia 1986).

[F. M. GILLMAN]

PARIS, INSTITUT CATHOLIQUE DE

An institution of higher learning, the Catholic university of Paris.

History. In 1845 Denis Auguste Affre, Archbishop of Paris, opened an ecclesiastical school of higher learning in a former Carmelite convent. It was an old building situated in a large park where, in the 17th century, the Carmelites, desirous of introducing St. Teresa's reform into France, had established residence. It was in this house and park that in September 1792 the priests and bishops (240 in number) imprisoned in the convent were massacred. Their remains were buried in the crypt of the church. J. B. LACORDAIRE, OP, lived in the same house for several years and F. Ozanam is interred there (1853).

In 1875 the French parliament passed a law granting freedom to higher education and permitting the establishment of private universities. That same year 22 bishops meeting in Paris decided to found a Catholic university in the capital. The three Faculties of Law, Letters, and Science were thereupon established and the Catholic University of Paris inaugurated July 16, 1876. It lacked only a Faculty of Theology, which was difficult to found since there already existed a state Faculty of Theology at the Sorbonne. This, however, was suppressed in 1886 and another one established at the Catholic University in 1889.

In the meantime, the law of 1880 curtailed freedom of higher education by denying private institutions the power to grant degrees and the right to use the title university. Thenceforth the Catholic University of Paris had to be satisfied with the title Catholic Institute of Paris, which it still bears.

The years 1893 to 1910 were very trying ones for the Catholic Institute, which had to cope with serious financial difficulties (1893–95) and problems arising from what was later known as Modernism, a movement precipitated by theories on the inspiration of Sacred Scripture and its historical value proposed by Alfred LOISY, whom Maurice d' Hulst, the rector, and Louis DUCHESNE had appointed to the Catholic Institute in 1893. Following the Modernist crisis, the Faculty of Theology was reorganized and the major chairs of dogma, apologetics, and moral philosophy were entrusted to the Society of Jesus. In 1906, acting on the law of separation, the state confiscated the property and buildings of the Catholic Institute. They were not bought back until 1923. The importance of the canonical Faculties (Theology, Philosophy, and Canon Law) was established in 1935 when the Catholic Institute, having adopted the constitution *Deus scientiarum Dominus,* was named a pontifical university.

Development. The Catholic Institute witnessed much growth after World War I. It has witnessed the multiplication of affiliated institutes and schools which, because of their specialization, have succeeded in eliminating the rigid programs imposed in the Faculties and in opening up its instruction to newly emerging disciplines. The Institute is composed of three Faculties of Religious Sciences (Theology, Canon Law, and Philosophy) and three of Humanities (Law, Literature and Natural Sciences). There are schools of liturgy, Oriental languages, social sciences, Christian Greek and Latin, French language and culture, and numerous affiliated research centers and institutes. Each Faculty, Institute, or School has its own program, examinations, and diplomas, the most common of which are the licentiate and the doctorate. Each has its own dean (Faculties), director, or president (Schools and Institutes), assisted by a council that determines internal affairs and elects the professors. The decisions of these councils are approved by the rectoral council.

Faculties, Schools, and Institutes all enjoy administrative, but not financial, autonomy; the recruitment and titles of professors vary according to each Faculty, School, or Institute. Chaplains are responsible for the students' religious instruction and formation. Representatives chosen by the students assure rapport between teachers and pupils. The latter have their own autonomous organizations.

Bibliography: *Annuaire de l'Institut catholique de Paris. Nouvelles de l'Institut catholique,* periodical. A. BAUDRILLART, *Vie de Monseigneur d'Hulst,* v. (Paris 1912–14); *L'Institut catholique* (Paris 1930); *Vingt-cinq ans de rectorat: L'Institut catholique de Paris (1907–1932)* (Paris 1932). J. BRUGERETTE, *Le Prêtre français et la société contemporaine,* 3 v. (Paris 1933–38) v.2 *Vers la séparation* J. CALVET, "L'Institut catholique de Paris" in L. HALPHEN et al., *Aspects de l'Université de Paris* (Paris 1949) 251–266.

[E. JARRY/EDS.]

PARIS, MARTYRS OF

This term refers to a group of 191 men who were beatified after being put to death in various Parisian prisons during the FRENCH REVOLUTION. They are sometimes called the September Martyrs because their execution occurred on Sept. 2 or 3, 1792, as part of the September massacres during the first Reign of Terror. The catalogue of beatified martyrs includes 2 archbishops, 1 bishop, 176 priests, 1 lay brother, 5 deacons, 1 tonsured cleric, and 5 laymen. The martyrdoms occurred in 4 places: 95 executed in the Carmelite convent, 72 in the Vincentian seminary of St. Firmin, 21 in the Abbey of SAINT-GERMAIN-DES-PRÉS, and 3 in the prison of La Force.

The Circumstances. Two sets of circumstances led up to the massacres. The first was the strong opposition of a large part of the French clergy to the CIVIL CONSTITUTION OF THE CLERGY, resulting in their refusal to take the required oath to support it. The second was the critical situation that developed from the military reverses of the revolutionary armies and that permitted bitterly antireligious groups to operate freely. Following the manifesto (July 11, 1792) of the Duke of Brunswick, leader of the Prussian forces, threatening vengeance on the French for mistreating their rulers, the Parisian mob stormed the Tuileries (August 10), massacred the Swiss guards, and imprisoned King Louis XVI and the Queen in the Temple. Effective power in the capital passed from the Legislative Assembly to the Commune and the Jacobin clubs. Municipalities received authorization (August 11) to arrest suspects, including nonjuring priests. Most priests in the provinces went into exile following the decree of August 11 that banished them. In Paris ecclesiastics and other suspects were herded into Bicêtre, Châtelet, the Conciergerie, La Force, and other prisons, or into the jails improvised in the Carmelite convent, St. Firmin, and Saint-Germain-des-Prés. Panic spread as fears of invasion grew. When false rumors circulated (September 2) that Verdun had surrendered and that the prisoners were preparing an uprising, mobs invaded the prisons and executed hundreds after summary trials. About three-fourths of the victims, totaling between 1,100 and 1,400, were criminals. Some were political prisoners, but the clerics had been incarcerated for religious reasons. Beatification occurred only in cases where it was proved that death was inflicted for reasons of faith. Almost all the beatified martyrs were massacred for their refusal to support by oath the Civil Constitution. In 1926 the Congregation of Rites deferred action on 22 other persons who were put to death in the last three of the above-named prisons. None of those who were put to death in other prisons during the September massacres have been beatified.

The Martyrs. The list of beatified martyrs follows (with year of birth noted when known).

At the Carmelite convent perished Jean Marie du Lau d'Alleman (b. 1738), Archbishop of Arles; François Joseph de LA ROCHEFOUCAULD MAUMONT (1736), Bishop of Beauvais; and his brother Pierre Louis de la Rouchefoucauld Bayers (1744), Bishop of Saintes.

Most of the martyred priests belonged to the Archdiocese of PARIS. Several of them, who came from other French dioceses, were residing in the capital. About one-third of the secular priests had been stationed in one or another of 26 dioceses throughout the country. Their occupations were diversified. The majority were engaged in pastoral work as pastors, curates, or chaplains; several served in seminaries as superiors, professors, or librarians; and some were vicars general of dioceses or held other equally important administrative posts.

The following were secular priests: Vincent Abraham (1740), André Alricy (1712), Daniel André Des Pommerayes (1756), André Angar, Jean Aubert, Pierre Balzac (1750), Jean Bangue (1744), Louis Barret (1753), Joseph Bécavin (1767), Louis Remi Benoist (1740), his brother Louis Remi Nicolas Benoist (1755), Michel Binard (1742), Robert le Bis (1719), Nicolas Bize (1737), Pierre Bonsé (1719), Jean Bottex (1749), Jean Bousquet (1751), Antoine du Bouzet (1739), Pierre Briquet, Pierre Brisse (1733), Jean Capeau, Charles Carnus (1749), Jean Caron (1730), Bertrand de Caupenne (1753), Armand Chapt de Rastignac (1727), Claude Chaudet, Antoine Boucharenc de Chaumeils (1738), Nicolas Clairet

(1726), Claude Colin (1728), Nicolas Colin (1750), Louis le Danois (1741), François Dardan (1733), Mathurin Deruelle, Gabriel Desprez de Roche (1751, vicar general of the Archdiocese of Paris), Thomas Dubuisson (1737), Jacques Dufour, François Dumasrambaud de Calandelle (1754), Denis Duval (1740), Henri Ermès, Joseph Falcoz (1726), Gilbert Fautrel (1730), Claude Fontaine (1749), Armand de Foucauld de Pontbriand (1751), Philibert Fougères (1742), Michel de la Gardette (1744), Pierre Garrigues (1725), Nicolas Gaudreau (1744), Louis Gaultier (1717), Pierre Gervais (1753), Étienne Gillet (1758), Georges Girous (1765), Jean Goizet (1742), André Grasset de Saint-Sauveur (born in Canada 1758), Joseph Gros (1742), Jean Guilleminet (1738), Yves Guillon de Keranrum (1748, vice chancellor of the University of Paris), Julien Hédouin (1760), Pierre Hénocq (1749), Saintin Huré (1765), Jean Jannin (1754), Pierre Joret (1761), Jean Le Laisant (1753) and his brother Julien (1761), Gilbert Lanchon (1754), Jacques de la Lande (1735), Pierre Landry (1762), Jean Lanier (1753), Laurent, Jean de Lavèze Belay (1742), Michel Leber (1731), Jean Lecan, Pierre Leclerq (or Clerq, 1744), Olivier Lefebvre (1728), Jean Legrand (1745), Jacques Lejardinier des Landes (1750), Jean Lemaitre (1767), Jean Leroy (1738), François Londiveau (1764), Louis Longuet (1757), Martin Loublier (1733), Jacques de Lubersac (1729), Louis Mauduit (1763), Gaspard Maignien (1752), Jean Marchand (1765), Claude Marmotant (1748), Claude Mayneaud de Bisefranc (1750), François Méallet de Fargues (1764), Jacques Menuret (1734), Jacques Le Meunier (1747), Henri Millet (1760), François Monnier (1763), Thomas Monsaint (1725), Marie François Mouffle (1754), Jean Baptiste Nativelle (1743) and his brother René (1751), Mathias Nogier (1764), Joseph Oviefve (1748), Joseph Pazery de Thorame (1751), his brother Jules (1763) and uncle Pierre (1735), François Pey (1759), Jean Philippot (1743), Pierre Ploquin (1762), René Poret (1732), Julien Poulain de Launay (1744), Jean Quéneau (1758), Jacques Rabé (1750), Jean Rateau (1758), Pierre Régnet (1755), Yves Rey de Kervisic (1761), Nicholas Roussel (1730), Marc Royer (1720), Jean de Saint Clair (1734), Pierre Saint James (1742), Urbain Salin de Niart (1760), Henri Samson (1754), Jacques Schmid (1752), Jean Séguin (1754), Jean Simon, Pierre de Turmenyes (1744), René Urvoy (1766), Pierre Verrier (1722), and Pierre Vitalis (1759).

Priests belonging to the regular clergy included three Maurists: Louis Barreau de La Touche (1758), René Massey (1732), and Ambroise Chevreux (1728), the superior general. Jean Bonnel de Pradal (1738) and Claude Ponse (1729) belonged to the Canons Regular of St. Genevieve; Jean Bernard (1759), to the Canons Regular of St. Victor. Jean Burté (1740) was a Conventual Franciscan;

Jean Morel (Père Apollinaire, 1739), a Capuchin; and Georges Girault (Père Severin, 1728), a Third Order Franciscan. Charles Hurtrel (1760) was a Minim. Claude Bochot (1720) and Eustache Félix (1735) were Doctrinarians. François Hébert (1735), Pierre Pottier (1743), and François Lefranc (1739), assistant to the superior general, were Eudists. Urbain Lefebvre (1725) was a member of the Paris Foreign Mission Society. The Vincentians numbered Jean Gruyer (1734) and Louis François (1751), head of the Parisian seminary of St. Firmin.

The Sulpicians supplied 12 martyred priests: Bernard Cucsac (1728), Thomas Dubray, Jacques Galais (1754), Pierre Gaugain (1725), Pierre Guérin (1759), Jacques Hourrier (1751), Henri Luzeau de la Mulonnière (1762), Jean Pontus, Pierre Psalmon (1749), Claude Rousseau (1751), Jean Savine (1760), and Jean Tessier. Six of them had been in charge of seminaries.

Twenty-three priests had been JESUITS until the suppression of the order. They were: René Andrieux (1742), François Balmain (1733), Jean Benoît (1731), Charles Béraud du Pérou (1737), Jacques Bonnaud (1740), Claude Cayx-Dumas (1724), Jean Charton de Millou (1736), Guillaume Delfaut (1733), Jacques Friteyre-Durvé (1725), Claude Cagnières des Granges (1722), Charles Le Gué (1724), Pierre Guérin du Rocher (1759) and his brother Robert (1736), Éloy Herque du Roule (1741), Anne Alexandre Lanfant (1726), Claude Laporte (1734), François Le Livec de Tresurin (1726), Thomas Loup (called Bonnotte, 1719), Vincent le Rousseau (1726), Jean Seconds (1734), François Vareilhe-Duteil (1734), Nicolas Verron (1740), and Mathurin de la Villecrohain le Bous de Villeneuve (1731).

Louis Boubert (1766), Louis Hurtrel (brother of Bl. Charles Hurtrel, the Minim), Jacques Robert de Lezardière (1768), Étienne de Ravinel (1769), and Charles Veret (1763) were seminarians who had received the deaconate. Nezel, a tonsured cleric, was a professor at the Sulpician seminary in Issy, near Paris. Guillaume Nicolas Leclercq (Brother Solomon, 1745) was general secretary of the Christian Brothers.

Five laymen complete the catalogue. Sebastien Desbrielles (1739) and Jean Duval had been teachers, and Louis Rigot (1751), a sacristan. Jean de Villette (1731) and Charles Régis de la Calmette, Count of Valfons, were former army officers.

The entire group was beatified Oct. 17, 1926.

Feast: Sept. 2 or 4.

Bibliography: *Acta Apostolicae Sedis* 18 (Rome 1926) 415–425, 439–447. G. LENÔTRE, *Les Massacres de Septembre* (Paris 1907); *La Maison des Carmes* (Paris 1933). H. WELSCHINGER, *Les Martyrs de Septembre* (Paris 1927). P. CARON, *Les Mas-*

sacres de Septembre (Paris 1935). J. HÉRISSAY, *Les Journées de Septembre* (Paris 1946). H. FOUQUERAY, *Un Groupe des Martyrs de Septembre 1792: Vingt-trois anciens Jésuites* (Paris 1926). W. J. BATTERSBY, *Brother Solomon, Martyr of the French Revolution* (New York 1960). J. L. BAUDOT and L. CHAUSSIN, *Vies des saints et des bienheureux selon l'ordre du calendrier avec l'histroique des fêtes,* 12 v. (Paris 1935–56) 9:53–71, good bibliog.

[W. J. BATTERSBY]

PARIS, UNIVERSITY OF

One of the oldest and most influential universities of Europe, founded as a voluntary association of teaching masters in the 13th century.

Origin and Early Development Before 1500

At the turn of the 12th century, such masters as Anselm of Laon, William of Champeaux, Peter Abelard, William of Conches, Adam du Petit Pont, Gilbert de la Porrée, Alan of Lille, and Richard and Hugh of Saint-Victor had attracted to Paris large numbers of masters and students from all parts of Europe. As a result of the influx, many of the teaching masters, especially those attached to the School of Notre Dame Cathedral, found it necessary to teach outside the cathedral cloister. They lectured in the open streets, particularly in the Rue du Fouarre, in the schools of the Abbey of Mont Ste. Geneviève; on the Petit Pont, and, in the vicinity of Saint Germain-des-Prés, on the left bank of the Seine, henceforth known as the Latin quarter. The masters thus removed from the immediate control of the cathedral organized themselves, in accord with the contemporary guild movement, into a corporate association bound together by oath.

The masters' association was formally approved in 1200 when King Philip Augustus accorded the masters the charter of privileges that guaranteed them exemptions and immunity from the civil and criminal jurisdiction of the local provost and his magistrates, and recognized that as clerics they were subject to their own elected officials and to the bishop of Paris. Between 1208 and 1215 the university obtained papal sanction as a corporate association with the right to representation at the papal court, to have a seal of its own, and to regulate the dress, method of teaching, and the funerals of its deceased masters. It also affirmed the university's independence from the jurisdiction and control of the cathedral chancellor. Although the chancellor retained the power to confer the license to teach (*licentia docendi*), he could not withhold it from anyone judged competent or qualified by a majority of the teaching masters. As a result of another revolt against local authorities, Gregory IX reinforced the uni-

versity's autonomous rights in the bull *Parens scientiarum* (April 13, 1231), often referred to as the Magna Carta of the university. The provisions of this bull reaffirmed the university's right to make its own rules and regulations regarding the curriculum, the individual members of the association, and the rents of hospices, and to call a cessation of lectures whenever any of these rights were violated or abrogated.

Organization. By the early 13th century the teaching masters were differentiated into four Faculties: Arts, Medicine, Canon Law, and Theology.

Nations. The Faculty of Arts, the most numerous of the Faculties and the stepping stone to the others, was at an early period divided into four nations: French, Picard, Norman, and English (English-German). These nations, representing primarily geographical regions rather than states or localities, were probably based on an earlier voluntary grouping of the masters and students according to the land from which they had come or in which they were born. Masters in the French nation came not only from France but also from southern and eastern Europe and from Asia Minor; in the Picard, from Flanders and the Walloon country; in the Norman, from Normandy and Brittany; and in the English (English-German), from the British Isles, Holland, the Germanies, and Scandinavia, as well as from Hungary and the Slavic lands. Each nation had its own elected officers: a proctor who headed the nation, a treasurer or receptor, and its own bedels and messengers to serve the nation and its members; its own chapel, patron saint and feast days, places of assembly, and revenues. Moreover, each nation drew up its own rules and regulations in the assemblies called by the proctors. The four nations, through their proctors and other officers, also maintained matriculation rolls, looked after the schools in which masters of the nations taught, and took care of members who fell ill or died. The proctors or other delegates of the nations elected the rector, who served as head of the Faculty of Arts and eventually as head of the university association as a whole.

Each of the four Faculties had its own similar officers, statutes, and schools: in the Faculty of Arts the executive officer was the rector; in the three Faculties of Medicine, Canon Law, and Theology, a dean was chosen by the members of his Faculty. The deans, like the rector, presided over the Faculty congregations that discussed and drew up measures relating to the Faculty as a whole: curriculum, qualifications for matriculation and for obtaining the baccalaureate or other degrees, and the rules governing the determination or defense of the thesis by candidates for the degree or license to teach.

University Council. The other administrative agencies of the university were the council and the general university congregation. The council, which met at stated intervals and was made up of the rector, the three deans, and the four proctors of the nations, examined and acted upon matters relating to the university association and its members. It was at the university congregation, however, to which were summoned all the teaching masters, that measures affecting the teaching, the relations of the university to the outer world, and other matters, were drawn up, debated, and voted upon. At these congregations, and in accordance with specified rules, other officers elected to assist the rector in carrying out university measures were the bedels, treasurer, messengers, *peciarii* (supervisors of texts), parchment dealers, booksellers, and copyists or scribes.

Colleges. Since the University of Paris was a masters' association, the students were attached to it only through the masters and therefore at first lacked discipline and supervision outside the schools. To fill this need, as well as to provide for the basic necessities of food, lodging, and a small stipend for poor scholars, from an early date philanthropists and other benefactors endowed hostels or colleges. Provision was thus made for poor scholars and for those coming from specified localities. Examples of the former are the College of Eighteen (Collège des dix-huits); the College of the Good Children of St. Honoré, founded by Étienne Belot and his wife; and Ave Maria College. Illustrative of the latter are the Colleges of Bayeux and Narbonne, France, and of Linkoping and Skara, Sweden. The Collège de Sorbonne was founded by Robert de SORBON to accommodate poor scholars who were already masters of arts but who were studying in the Faculty of Theology. In time several colleges became places of instruction as well as of lodging.

Curriculum. The curriculum of the university was administered under the four Faculties. In the Faculty of Arts, instruction was based on the LIBERAL ARTS, the mastery of which was to serve as the foundation and stepping stone for higher Faculties. The course of study in medicine comprised lectures on the Latin translations of the works of the Greek physicians Hippocrates and Galen, of the Arabic physicians Rasis and Avicenna, and of some Latin authors, with practical experience under the direction of a doctor of medicine for six months in Paris and for one year outside the city. In Canon Law the principal texts studied were the *Decretum* of Gratian, together with several additions, namely, the Decretals of Gregory IX, the *Liber Sextus* of Boniface VIII, the Constitutions of Clement V, and the Extravagantes or collection of papal laws. In theology instruction was centered upon the Bible, the works of the Church Fathers, Peter Lombard's *Sentences,* and compilations of Thomas Aquinas's *Questiones* and *Summae,* as well as upon some works of other medieval authors.

Method of Instruction. In general use was the lecture or commentary and gloss on a specific text, followed by the repetition or review and the *collatio* or discussion and conference. The lectures were usually divided into the ordinary, those given in the morning by the members of the Faculty, and the extraordinary or cursory, usually given in the late-afternoons or on feast days by guest lecturers or bachelors in the Faculty. In addition, there were disputations that applied the rational method of inquiry in the presentation, explanation, and proving of a specific proposition and the answering of objections raised against it. Frequent references were made to the Bible, the Fathers, Aristotle, and other standard authors. There were also the *Quodlibeta* disputations and the disputed questions. In the former, at a public session, the professor in charge was asked questions at random from the leading topics of the day. A bachelor closely associated with the professor then gave tentative replies; at a later session the professor made a formal reply in the form of a disputation. In the disputed questions, the professor set his own question and then proceeded in the form of the disputation.

Examinations: Determination and Inception. At Paris, after following a prescribed course of studies, the candidate for a degree or license to teach underwent a series of examinations: (1) a private interrogation or *responsion* conducted by his own professor to ascertain whether he was ready for the examination for the determination; (2) after a careful scrutiny of the candidate's qualifications and fitness, the examination for determination, conducted by a committee of professors chosen for the purpose; (3) the determination, consisting of a series of disputations carried on for several weeks by the candidate himself. If judged successful, he was accorded the license to teach anywhere (*Licentia ubique docendi*). The final step was the initiation or inception (*inceptio*) into the Faculty.

Rights, Privileges, Immunities. The University of Paris and its members, through the grants and support of the French monarchs and the papacy, held a highly privileged position. It enjoyed, among other exemptions, immunity from the civil and criminal jurisdiction of the local magistrates, from the disciplinary ban of excommunication by the local bishop, from all tolls and taxes as well as from military and other levies except under very unusual circumstances, and freedom from the obligation to respond to summons to civil or ecclesiastical courts outside the city of Paris except under the direct will of the pope. The university had the right to make and enforce rules and regulations for its own members; to set up courses and examinations; to regulate the time, content, and method of teaching; and to determine the rent of houses occupied by its members. University members also enjoyed the right to be named to vacant benefices, to be preferred to all others for appointment whenever such vacancies occurred, and to enjoy the returns of their benefices while they were studying at Paris for a period of from five to seven years. In the 13th century, moreover, they could call a cessation of lectures whenever their rights were violated. The provost of Paris served as the conservator of royal privileges; one of the bishops outside Paris, but in its vicinity, acted as the conservator of apostolic privileges.

Influence. The fame and importance of the University of Paris between the 13th and 15th centuries attracted many famous European scholars and theologians: ROGER BACON, ALEXANDER OF HALES, ALBERT THE GREAT, THOMAS AQUINAS, BONAVENTURE, DUNS SCOTUS, Jean Buridan, WILLIAM OF OCKHAM, Nicole Oresme, Jean GERSON, PETER OF AILLY, and others. The university's influence was far-reaching. Not only did it provide a model for the universities of northern Europe founded before 1500, but through its professors and graduates, bound to it in perpetuity by an oath, it made a strong impression upon contemporary thought and action. Many of its graduates were leaders in affairs of church and state: Innocent III, Gregory IX, Urban IV, and other popes as well as bishops, archbishops, and others who served as royal and ecclesiastical judges, counselors, and administrators. Doctors on the Medical Faculty, moreover, served as royal and papal physicians; other members of the university gave aid and counsel to the French monarchs, participated in the theological and doctrinal discussions of the time, served in the peace commissions during the Hundred Years' War, and played an important role in the Council of CONSTANCE, which healed the papal schism.

Bibliography: H. RASHDALL, *The Universities of Europe in the Middle Ages,* ed. F. M. POWICKE and A. B. EMDEN, 3 v. (new ed. Oxford 1936). L. J. DALY, *The Medieval University,* 1200–1400 (New York 1961). P. KIBRE, *The Nations in the Mediaeval Universities* (Cambridge, Mass. 1948); *Scholarly Privileges in the Middle Ages* (Cambridge, Mass. 1962). L. HALPHEN et al., *Aspects de l'Université de Paris* (Paris 1949). J. BONNEROT, *L'Université de Paris du moyen âge à nos jours* (Paris 1933). A. L. GABRIEL, *Student Life in Ave Maria College, Mediaeval Paris* (Notre Dame, Ind. 1955); *Skara House at the Mediaeval University of Paris* (Notre Dame, Ind. 1960); "The College System in the Fourteenth Century Universities," *The Forward Movement of the Fourteenth Century,* ed. F. L. UTLEY (Columbus, Ohio 1961). P. GLORIEUX, *Les Origines du Collège de Sorbonne* (Notre Dame, Ind. 1959).

[P. KIBRE]

Later History

Although the university's prestige was not enhanced throughout the 14th century, its numbers increased regularly (almost 800 master regents in the Faculty of Arts alone in 1408). It was "Milady the University, daughter of the king of France," and its members were conscious of its importance. The intellectual vigor of the 13th century, however, was lacking during the 14th and 15th centuries when minds went astray in subtle and often futile discussions. In 1400 Gerson said of his colleagues: "The theologians are the laughing stock of the other Faculties."

The WESTERN SCHISM, in which the university took sides, dealt it a heavy blow. It not only turned certain students away, but what was still more serious, it provoked the departure of certain masters for Prague, Vienna, Cologne, or Heidelberg. Finally, the English conquest and occupation of Paris, to which the university rallied, and the establishment in the 15th century of several universities in France (Caen, Poitiers, Bordeaux) dimmed its radiance. Its renown was sustained, nevertheless, by such masters as Pierre d'Ailly (1350–1420) and Gerson (1363–1420).

The university, moreover, greatly impaired its intellectual prestige by allowing itself to become deeply involved in the Western Schism. After having rallied under pressure from Charles V of France to the French antipope, Clement VII (Robert of Geneva), the university decided in an assembly of the four Faculties to submit the matter of allegiance to the council (1381), thus following the teaching of its two illustrious masters, Conrad of Gelnhausen and Henry of Langenstein. It henceforth adhered to the resolution of the council, from which it did not swerve except when obliged by force to propose the abdication of the rival popes (1394) or the withdrawal of obedience (1398 and 1406–08). At the Council of Constance (1415–18), it was the Parisian masters Pierre d'Ailly, Guillaume Fillastre, and Gerson who were the leading spokesmen.

The university was no less engaged in political controversy than in religious disputes. In 1413 it condemned the theories justifying tyrannicide; but in 1418 the duke of Burgundy forced it to reverse its decision. Likewise, in February of 1413, the university joined the people of Paris in asking the king for reforms; in May it took part in the preparation of the *ordonnances cabochiennes* that prescribed the reforms.

Soon overcome by popular violence (of which Gerson was personally a victim), the university broke with the Cabochians and by its presence approved the session of the Parlement in which the king dissolved the *ordonnances cabochiennes* (September of 1413).

These political entanglements and the reversal of loyalty that often accompanied them could not enhance the authority of the university. The deterioration of scholastic methods also dimmed its scientific brilliance. Faced with growing humanism, the University of Paris could not recover its pristine vigor. When it became evident that a new body of teaching was necessary, the crown created it outside the aged body of the university, which had fought against registration of the concordat of 1516 in the name of Gallican liberty and thereby opposed both pope and king. In 1530 Francis I established royal lectors to answer the intellectual needs of the new age; the lectors later separated from the university to become the COLLÈGE DE FRANCE (built in 1610 on its present site). During the religious crises of the 16th century, the Faculty of Theology aligned itself against the reformers, while the university as a whole opposed the admission of Jesuits into France.

In 1598 Henry IV (whom the university had recognized the day following his entry into Paris) reformed the university, determining the discipline, the living arrangements of the students, and the curriculum. For the first time, university regulations were established without the intervention of ecclesiastical authority.

Development in the 17th and 18th Centuries. The university continued its educational function of training lawyers, physicians, and jurists. Just as it had been untouched by the spirit of the Renaissance, it remained insensitive to the great philosophical currents and the first signs of a modern scientific spirit.

At the beginning of the 17th century the Sorbonne became the center of the Faculty of Theology not only because of the quality of its teachers but also because of the number of its students. Cardinal Armand Jean du Plessis Richelieu, elected headmaster of the Sorbonne in 1622, restored and enlarged its buildings. Since then the Sorbonne has been the center of theological activity and of Parisian university life. By its approval or disapproval, it exercises a kind of spiritual magistracy that reaches beyond the limits of the Ile-de-France.

The Edict of April 1679 reformed all French universities into four Faculties: Theology, Décret (which in 1679, with the reintroduction of Roman law in Paris, became the Faculty of Law), Medicine, and Arts (which gave access to the other three). The rector, elected by the proctors of the four nations of the Faculty of Arts, administered the entire corporate body. He was admitted to the Parlement of Paris and to the king's council whenever the interests of the university were in question. Each Faculty was headed by a dean, elected by the regent doctors. The master and student personnel was increased by the addition of registrars, collectors, lawyers, and attorneys who defended the university's interests in Parlement and at the *Chatelet* (law court) of Paris; and by bedels, booksellers, illustrators, and writers. Mendicant monks (Franciscans, Carmelites, Augustinians), as well as Dominicans, regular canons of St. Victor, Trinitarians, and monks of Cluny and of Saint Germain-des-Prés were also affiliated with the university. All enjoyed important privileges (tax exemption, jurisdictional privileges, etc.).

As in the preceding period, the concerns of the university extended beyond the strict framework of teaching. Several times the Sorbonne interfered in political debates under pretext of juridical or theological questions (e.g., condemnation in 1616 of the theses of the Jesuit Anton Santarelli, who taught that the pope could remove incompetent princes; the attack on ecclesiastical competence in the matter of marriage apropos the annulment of Gaston of Orléan's marriage in 1634).

These political involvements were proof of the university's prestige without, however, increasing its influence. Concerned mainly with professional preparation, the university left new research to the academies. In the period following the expulsion of the Jesuits (1762) and the closing of their colleges, diverse projects were published on national education (La Chalotais in 1763, and also others in Parlement) that contained requests for the introduction of subjects ignored by the university: modern languages, modern history, geography, physics, etc. Renewing the heritage of the dissolved Jesuit colleges, the university changed the Collège Louis le Grand into a training school for teachers. The enterprise, however, was not successful. On the eve of the Revolution, the Faculty of Theology had ten professors; Law had seven in addition to 12 doctors; Medicine had 152 doctors, of whom seven were teachers; Arts combined the principals and regents of the colleges; there were 5,000 students. A doctoral examination for recruiting teachers for the Faculty of Arts was inaugurated in 1766.

From 1789 to 1896. The University of Paris disappeared together with the other universities during the revolutionary years, without being formally dissolved. The law of the three Brumaire year IV instituting central schools reestablished an outline for higher education. Medical schools were founded in the year XI (1804). The term university reappeared with the law of May 10, 1806, establishing a national university for the whole empire. In fact, an Imperial University was organized by the decree of March 17, 1808. Within this university, and according to territorial distribution, were Faculties of Catholic Theology, Law, Medicine, Sciences, and Literature. The entire organization was subject to strict control by the emperor. Isolated one from the other, these Faculties were not federated into universities. It was not until the laws of April 28, 1893 (art. 71) and July 10, 1896 (art. 1) that Faculties were regrouped into universities. Juridically the University of Paris was reborn (the system of French universities is actually ruled by the decree of July 31, 1920).

In fact, the Faculties of Paris had resumed work as early as 1808. In 1821 Theology, Sciences, and Literature had set themselves up in the "old house of the Sorbonne." The Faculty of Law remained in the buildings that were planned by J. Soufflot and constructed for it between 1764 and 1772. After the suppression of Theology in March of 1885, the university became fully secular in orientation.

20th Century Developments. The beginning of the 20th century witnessed a renaissance of the University of Paris as a center for education and research comprising the five Faculties—Law and Economics, Medicine, Sciences, Literature and Human Sciences, and Pharmacy. After World War II, the University of Paris continued the expansion begun at the turn of the century. This increase in enrollment had been accompanied by the multiplication of new educational subjects and the ever-broadening horizons in exact and human sciences, in all of which the university has shown great interest. The influx of students and educational developments necessitated additional space for new laboratories, amphitheaters, libraries, and study halls. In a saturated city where one university alone must meet the needs of eight million inhabitants, it was necessary to consider a dispersion of educational and research centers toward the suburbs. By the 1960s the Faculty of Sciences had already acquired a very important center at Orsay, followed by further expansion to the west and north of Paris. Student protests and riots led to the national crisis of May of 1968 and the resulting restructuring of the university into decentralized schools.

Bibliography: P. GLORIEUX, "La Faculté de théologie de Paris et ses principaux docteurs au XIIIᵉ siècle," *Revue d'histoire de l'Église de France* 32 (1946) 241–264. L. HALPHEN and P. GLORIEUX, *L'Université de Paris au XIIIᵉ siècle* (Paris 1949). A. LUCHAIRE, *L'Université de Paris sous Philippe-Auguste* (Paris 1899). P. MICHAUDQUANTIN, "Le Droit universitaire dans le conflit parisien de 1252–1257," *Studia Gratiana* 8 (1962) 579–599. G. POST, "Parisian Masters as a Corporation, 1200–1246," *Speculum* 9 (1934) 421–445. M. TOULOUSE, *La Nation anglaise-allemande de l'Université de Paris, des origines a la fin du XVᵉ siècle* (Paris 1939). A. DOUARCHE, *L'Université de Paris et les Jésuites (XVIᵉ et XVIIᵉ siècles)* (Paris 1888). C. M. JOURDAIN, *Histoire de l'Université de Paris aux XVIIᵉ et XVIIIᵉ siècles*, 2 v. (Paris 1888). A. J. M. LEFRANCE, *Histoire du Collège de France, depuis ses origines jusqu'à la fin du premier Empire* (Paris 1893).

[J. GAUDEMET/EDS.]

PARIS FOREIGN MISSION SOCIETY

A religious institute of secular priests, the first one devoted exclusively to foreign missions (Société des Missions Etrangères de Paris, Societas Parisiensis Missionum ad exteras gentes, MEP).

It began *c.* 1660 as a result of the following conjunction of circumstances: (1) the French clergy and laity, es-

pecially the members of a piouss apostolic association calle the COMPAGNIE DU SAINT-SACREMENT, were eager to participate in missions hitherto reserved to religious; (2) some missionaries, notably Alexandre de RHODES, SJ, wished to form a native clergy in the Far East; (3) the Congregation for the PROPAGATION OF THE FAITH (Propaganda), founded in 1622, wanted to gain effective control of missions up to then dominated by the Spanish and Portuguese governments with their claims of *PATRONATO REAL* and *padroado*. The efforts of the Compagnie du Saint-Sacrement, begun in 1646, led to the naming in various missions of a VICAR APOSTOLIC dependent on Propaganda and charged with the formation of a native clergy in Tonkin, Cochinchina, and China. Before departing for the East, Bps. François PALLU, Pierre LAMBERT DE LA MOTTE, and Ignace Cotolendi ordered their procurators to establish a seminary. King Louis XIV and the local ordinary approved the Paris Mission Seminary in 1663; the Holy See approved it in 1664.

One hundred missionaries, including many laymen, embarked for Asia between 1660 and 1700; but only 62 went between 1700 and 1822, for the 18th century lacked fervor, and the seminary, closed by the French Revolution in 1792, was unable to open until the fall of Napoleon I (1815). Between 1822 and 1963 there were 3,816 departures for the missions. Bishop François Laval confided to the MEP his seminary in Quebec and the missions dependent on him, in Acadia, Ill., and elsewhere. This situation lasted from 1665 to the Treaty of Paris (1763). From its start the society centered its activities in the Far East, and labored in Tonkin, Cochinchina, Siam, and western China. In 1776 it assumed responsibility for evangelizing southern India, until the Jesuits took over part of this region (1836). As MEP missioners became more numerous, Propaganda assigned them new territories: Japan and Korea (1831); Manchuria (1838); Tibet (1846); the Chinese provinces of Guangdong, Guangxi the Hainan (1848); Burma (1855); and Malaysia, detached from the mission of Siam (1899). By 1920 the society had relinquished three of these fields, but its 1,139 members, aided by 1,109 native priests, were still entrusted with regions populated by 250 millions. Since 1920 the society has ceded 30 mission fields to various religious congregations, and 41 to native clergies formed by it. After the closing of China to missionaries, the MEP was assigned Hwalien in Taiwan (1952); Madagascar, for work among the Chinese (1953); and the mission of Mananjary (1961).

To develop a native clergy the society founded a general seminary in Siam (1665), which has since been transferred to Penang, Malaysia. Other seminaries were opened in Cochinchina (1665), Tonkin (1666), and China (1703). The original Chinese one lasted only a short time, but reopened in Jiuquan (1777). In 1909 membership reached its highest total, with 38 bishops, 1,377 priests, and six lay auxiliaries or brothers. Since its inception, about 200 of its members have sacrificed their lives for the faith. Among the 23 martyrs that have been beatified, 20 were canonized by Pope John Paul II.

In its government the MEP followed a collegiate form until 1921. Since then it has had a superior general, who since 1950 has been elected by a general assembly, along with his assistants. Members do not take religious vows, but promise to serve for life in the missions while receiving temporal support from the MEP.

Bibliography: J. GUENNOU, *Les Missions étrangères* (Paris 1963). G. GOYAU, *Les Prêtres des Missions Étrangères* (Paris 1932). A. LAUNAY, *La Société des missions étrangères, 1658–1913,* 2 v. (Paris 1912–16); *Histoire générale de la Société des Missions Étrangères,* 3 v. (Paris 1894). H. HEIMBUCHER, *Die Orden und Kongregation der katholischen Kirche,* 2 v. (3d ed. Paderborn 1932–34) 2:600–606. J. GUENNOU, "La fondation de la Société des Missions Étrangères de Paris," *Sacrae Congregationis de Propaganda Fide, 1/1: memoria rerum 1622–1700* (Freiburg 1971) 523–537. J. P. WIEST, "Catholic Mission Theory and Practice: Lessons of the Paris Foreign Mission Society and Maryknoll," *Missiology* 10 (1982) 171–184. G. M. OURY, *Mgr François Pallu, ou les missions étrangères en Asie au 17ue siècle* (Paris 1985).

[J. GUENNOU]

PARISH VISITORS OF MARY IMMACULATE

(PVMI; Official Catholic Directory #3160); a contemplative missionary congregation of women, founded, 1920, in New York City by Mother Mary Teresa Tallon with the approval of Archbishop (later Cardinal) Patrick Hayes. The congregation was canonically erected on April 25, 1927. At a time when Christian family life was rapidly declining, the foundress conceived the idea of sisters engaging in family visitation to restore the spirit of the Holy Family to the home. The sisters engage in family visitations, counseling, missionary outreach and religious education, focusing on person-to-person evangelization. The motherhouse is at Monroe, N.Y.

[M. L. COONEY]

PARK (LE PARC), MONASTERY OF

Premonstratensian abbey at Heverlee, Louvain, Belgium, Diocese of Mechelen, circary (province) of Brabant. It was founded as a double monastery *c.* 1128 by Duke Godfrey I of Lorraine, and itself founded in 1137 the Abbey of Ninove on the Dendre (suppressed in 1796). The nuns of Park soon transferred, probably to the Augustinian Parc-les-Dames (Cistercian 1215–1796). The nuns of Gempe and 19 churches were under the rule of the abbot of Park, which became a flourishing monastery. The *Annales Parchenses* (1148–1458) were compiled in the abbey. Abbot T. van Tuldel, mitred in 1462, resisted the commendatory system energetically. In the 17th century Park was a center of Tridentine reform in the order. Abbots J. Druys and J. Maes in 1630 drew up new statutes and the *ordinarius* of the order. Suppressed in 1789–90 by JOSEPH II and in 1797 by the French, Park was restored in 1836 and became an abbey again in 1872. In 1896 it undertook a mission in Montes Claros, Brazil. Until 1914 it published the scientific periodical *Analectes de l'ordre de Prémontré.* The abbey is one of the most charming in Belgium. The Romanesque church was extensively remodeled in the 17th and 18th centuries; the style of the monastery is Renaissance and baroque. Park has always been a center of learning; its monks included the historian R. van Wafelghem and the Vatican expert in Coptic sciences F. A. van Lantschoot. Its archives are extensive and valuable.

Bibliography: C. L. HUGO, *S. Ordinis Praemonstratensis annales,* 2 v. (Nancy 1734–36) v. 2. J. E. JANSEN, *L'Abbaye norbertine de Parc-le Duc* (Malines 1929). N. BACKMUND, *Monasticon Praemonstratense,* 3 v. (Straubing 1949–56) 2:317–322.

[N. BACKMUND]

PARKER, MATTHEW

Scholar and archbishop of Canterbury who helped shape the Elizabethan religious settlement; b. Norwich, Aug. 6, 1504; d. London, May 17, 1575. Parker entered Corpus Christi College, Cambridge, in 1522 and took his B.A. degree in 1525. In 1527 he was ordained, and in 1528 he became associated with the Cambridge Reformers, a student group with Lutheran sympathies. When Anne Boleyn became queen, Parker was made her chaplain, and in 1537 he became chaplain to Henry VIII. In 1544, on the king's recommendation, he became master of his old college and in 1545, vice chancellor of Cambridge. At the accession of Edward VI in 1547 Parker married Margaret Harlestone of Norfolk. Parker's Protestant sympathies were avowed with increasing openness as the successive regencies of Somerset and Northumberland drew England steadily in a Protestant direction. Upon Edward's death in 1553 Parker espoused the cause of Northumberland's unfortunate pawn, Lady Jane Grey. For this and for his marriage he was deprived of his offices by Catholic Queen Mary. Having no taste for martyrdom, he spent the five years of her reign in hiding, devoting his time to translating the Psalms and writing in defense of the marriage of priests.

Following the accession of Elizabeth I, Parker was elected Archbishop of Canterbury in 1559 and was consecrated by four Henrician and Edwardian bishops. Since the Ordinal employed had been repealed in the reign of Mary, the consecration was valid only if royal supremacy was also accepted. Parker's consecration thus became a key problem in the later controversy over Anglican Orders. The most important among Archbishop Parker's hundreds of appointments were to ten sees that Mary and Cardinal Pole had left vacant. He furthered the English Reformation by filling them with Protestants.

Parker, a modest, pious, reserved man, was always a moderate. In 1545 he saved Cambridge's colleges from dissolution during the Henrician confiscations. Years later, he strove to limit further spoliation of the church by Elizabethan courtiers. Always interested in scholarship and antiquities, Parker tried to revive the Saxon language, founded the Society of Antiquaries, and collected ancient manuscripts at a time when learning was being plundered. His magnificent manuscript collection was the most important of many gifts he bequeathed to Cambridge. As archbishop, Parker sought a middle way between Catholics and Puritans. Significantly, the worst Elizabethan persecution of Catholics commenced only after his death. With the Puritans, Parker ordered an end to ''prophesyings'' and enforced a compromise between the queen's desire for elaborate vestments and the Puritans' insistence upon none at all, depriving those Puritans who refused to comply.

Bibliography: J. STRYPE, *The Life and Acts of Matthew Parker*, 3 v. (Oxford 1821). H. GEE, *The Elizabethan Clergy and the Settlement of Religion, 1558–1564* (Oxford 1898). H. N. BIRT, *The Elizabethan Religious Settlement* (London 1907). B. M. H. THOMPSON, *The Consecration of Archbishop Parker* (London 1934). J. B. MULLINGER, *The Dictionary of National Biography from the Earliest Times to 1900* (London 1885–1900) 15:254–264. V. J. K. BROOK, *A Life of Archbishop Parker* (Oxford 1962). E. W. PERRY, *Under Four Tudors* (London 1940). P. HUGHES, *The Reformation of England* (New York 1963).

[B. NORLING]

PARKER, THEODORE

Unitarian minister; b. Lexington, Mass., Aug. 24, 1810; d. Florence, Italy, May 10, 1860. Parker was a child prodigy, but poverty prevented his receiving any formal education. He taught school for some years to finance his studies at Harvard Divinity School; he was ordained in 1837 as pastor at West Roxbury, Mass. He stressed the immanence of God in nature and the human mind, and rejected many traditional Christian teachings. Parker became the center of controversy with the publication of *The Transient and Permanent in Christianity*

(1841) and *Discourse of Matters Pertaining to Religion* (1842). After resigning his pastorate, he organized his own Boston, Mass., congregation in 1845. Parker was active in reform movements, particularly the antislavery cause. He wrote abolitionist tracts and participated in the rescue of fugitive slaves.

Bibliography: *Collected Works,* ed. F. P. COBBE, 14 v. (London 1863–71). H. S. COMMAGER, *Theodore Parker* (Boston 1936). J. E. DIRKS, *Critical Theology of Theodore Parker* (New York 1948).

[R. K. MACMASTER]

PARKINSON, ANTHONY

English Franciscan historian; b. Cuthbert, Lancashire, England, 1667; d. East Hendred, Berkshire, Jan. 30, 1728. Professed as a Franciscan at Douai, he was appointed philosophy professor at the Franciscan college there in 1692. After being assigned to the English mission two years later, he served as superior of the Franciscans at Warwick (1698–1701) and at Birmingham (1701–10), as guardian at Oxford (1710–13), and as provincial (1713–16, 1722–25). In this last post, he participated in the Franciscan general chapter at Rome in 1723. His principal work is the *Collectanea Anglo-Minoritica, or a Collection of the Antiquities of the English Franciscans or Friars Minors Commonly Called Gray Friars* (London 1726). He spent his remaining years as guardian of Coventry and as chaplain to the Eyston family of Berkshire.

Bibliography: FATHER THADDEUS, *The Franciscans in England 1600–1850* (London 1898).

[P. S. MC GARRY]

PARKMINSTER (CHARTERHOUSE)

St. Hugh's Charterhouse, Partridge Green, Horsham, Sussex, England; Southwark diocese. This CARTHUSIAN MONASTERY was founded in 1873 from La Grande Chartreuse as a refuge in anticipation of the possible expulsion of religious orders from France. This need coincided with the desire of the English Catholic hierarchy to restore the Carthusians to England, and a property in Sussex called Parknowle (changed to Parkminster) was chosen. Building commenced in 1876, using local and Bath stone and paving stones from Belgium for the cloisters. More than 600 workmen of different nationalities were employed, and the foundation stone was laid in October of 1877. In 1883, the first prior was appointed, the novitiate opened, and the church consecrated. The spire has become a well-known landmark. There are 4,000 feet of cloisters, the main garth being one of the largest of its kind in the world. A fine library houses 30,000 volumes, including valuable MSS dating from the earliest days of the order. Parkminster is the only charterhouse in England today and continues the tradition of the nine English charterhouses (from WITHAM to SHEEN) prior to the Reformation.

Bibliography: A MONK OF PARKMINSTER, ''The Return of the Carthusians to England,'' *The Southwark Record* (Sept.–Oct. 1939). *St. Hugh's Charterhouse* (Marseille 1963), guidebook.

[A. GRAY]

PARMENIDES

Parmenides of Elea inaugurated Western metaphysical thinking; b. probably in the middle of the latter half of the sixth century B.C. He is reported to have been introduced to philosophy by a Pythagorean named Ameinias, and his cultural background at Elea, a Phocaean colony on the west coast of Italy, was Ionian. His philosophy was expressed in a poem of which considerable fragments, as quoted by ancient writers, survive.

Content of the Poem. Although this was composed as a literary unit, it is divided by commentators into three parts: a proem or apocalyptic introduction, a section on truth, and a section on opinion (δόξα) or things as they appear. Textual difficulties and ambiguities in key passages, as well as the poetic form, often leave the meaning highly controversial.

Introduction. In the proem, in imagery found to a large extent in Hesiod (*Theog.* 744–761), Parmenides is borne from the dwellings of night aloft toward light on a chariot guided by sun maidens. Beyond the portals of the ways of night and day he is ushered into the presence of an unnamed goddess, there to be instructed in the knowledge of all things, first of the convincing truth, then of the unreliable ''opinions of mortals,'' in the sense of being shown how things had to appear as they do (H. Diels, *Die Fragmente der Vorsokratiker: Griechisch und Deutsch* 3 v. [10th ed. Berlin 1960–61] 28B 1).

Truth. The way of inquiry following upon truth asserts that there is being—for there not to be is not possible. The directly opposite way, namely, that there is no being and cannot be any, cannot even be entered by human thought (*Frg.* 2). But Parmenides is also barred by the goddess from another way, the way actually traveled by mortals. This is two-headed, reverberating, perplexed, unseeing, undiscerning; for it gives nonbeing the same status as being and yet distinguishes them, setting up for everything a way that goes simultaneously in opposite directions. It is the way of sense perception and hearsay, and has to be superseded by difficult reasoning.

The signposts identifying the legitimate way are as follows: being cannot become or perish, it is a whole, without motion or change, without end, without past or future, all together, indivisible, continuous, finite, lacking nothing, perfectly self-identical, entirely homogeneous, and unique—for, since there is no nonbeing, there is nothing that could in any way come to be or cease to be, or divide or multiply being, or cause defect or difference in it. All apparent changes in the cosmos, and distinctions between being and nonbeing, are but conventional names for the one all-embracing reality.

Opinion. From the goddess, Parmenides then learns why things appear to mortals differently from the way they are. By custom, mortals set up two basic and opposite forms, light and night, one of which it is not legitimate to posit. Each is entirely self-identical and in no way the same as the other. Given equal status by human cognition, they fill everything and differentiate things from one another according to their relative predominance in each thing (*Frgs.* 6–9). Even individual cognition, with all conscious identity in a man, is but an ever-varying combination of the two basic forms, light and darkness (*Frg.* 16). In this framework cosmogony is taught Parmenides by the goddess (*Frgs.* 10–15; 17–19). Complete predominance of darkness in an individual's constitution is death (*Frg.* A 46), while full predominance of light, as the proem makes clear, allowed Parmenides during special inspiration to see things solely under the aspect of being.

Influence and Interpretation. Parmenides's teaching had wide influence in GREEK PHILOSOPHY. His formal (in contrast to existential) notion of being, passed on through Aristotle and Neoplatonism, deeply impregnated scholastic, classical, and neoscholastic metaphysics, with the notable exception of that of St. Thomas Aquinas.

Interpreters differ widely over Parmenides. His doctrine of being, isolated from its poetic setting, is variously regarded as an abstract dialectic, a mystical experience, a philosophical monotone, or a sediment from preceding philosophies. His way of seeming, likewise isolated, has been viewed as a report of teachings rejected by him, or as tenets impossible to reconcile with his doctrine of being. Yet the contrast between light and night in the proem seems explained in terms of being and then carried through to the concluding section. No rational link between the sections is possible. In this cast the whole poem gives a consistent and penetrating account of both the way things are and the way they appear. Aristotle (*Meta.* 986b 31–33; 1010a 2–3) is almost certainly right in reporting that for Parmenides beings meant sensible things only, and that the same reality known as one by reason appears multiple through sensation.

Bibliography: K. REINHARDT, *Parmenides und die Geschichte der griechischen Philosophie* (2d ed. Frankfurt am Main 1959). W. J. VERDENIUS, *Parmenides: Some Comments on His Poem* (Groningen 1942). G. VLASTOS, "Parmenides' Theory of Knowledge," *American Philological Association, Transactions and Proceedings* 77 (1946): 66–77. J. H. M. LOENEN, *Parmenides, Melissus, Gorgias* (Assen 1959).

[J. OWENS]

PAROUSIA

The coming of the glorified Christ as the climax of SALVATION HISTORY. This article treats first the biblical data on the Parousia and then the Parousia from a theological viewpoint.

In the Bible

For a better understanding of the scriptural data on the Parousia, it is well to begin by considering the general questions of the terminology, the meaning of the doctrine, and the time of the Parousia, particularly as presented in the writings of St. Paul. The doctrine as contained in the individual books of the NT is then examined, and the solution of the problem of the delay of the Parousia is briefly considered.

Terminology. The term "Parousia" is a transliteration of the Greek word παρουσία. In classical Greek the word had the meaning of "presence" or "arrival." St. Paul used the word to speak of his own presence among the Corinthians (2 Cor 10.10) and the Philippians (Phil 2.12), of the presence of Stephanas, Fortunatus, and Achaicus among the Corinthians (1 Cor 16.17), of his future arrival at Philippi (Phil 1.26), and of the arrival of Titus at Corinth (2 Cor 7.6–7). In Hellenistic Greek παρουσία had acquired two technical meanings: (1) the public arrival of officials, which was accompanied by appropriate ceremony; and (2) the presence of the gods, manifested in acts of power, or assumed to be an invisible reality in the cult. Before A.D. 51, the approximate date of 1 Thessalonians, the Church borrowed this technical usage to express its doctrine of the presence of the risen Christ to conclude salvation history. After the biblical period, the doctrine came to be known as the Coming (*adventus*) or the Second Coming of Christ. The word παρουσία in the sense of the presence of the risen Christ at the conclusion of history is found in 1 Thes 2.19; 3.13; 4.15; 5.23; 2 Thes 2.1, 8; Jas 5.7–8; 2 Pt 1.16; 3.4, 12; 1 Jn 2.28. An exceptional usage occurs in 2 Thes 2.9, where παρουσία refers to the presence of "the lawless one," the Pauline opponent of Christ at the end of history.

The primitive Church understood the Parousia event as the time of God's final judgment upon all people (1 Thes 1.10). For this reason scriptural authors made use of the term "the day of the Lord" in reference to the Parousia. In the Hebrew Scriptures the DAY OF THE LORD (Yahweh) is a technical term for God's saving acts in history. Before the time of Amos, the day of Yahweh was understood as a time of blessings and happiness; but Amos taught that the day of Yahweh was also a time of punishment. The term and its meaning were borrowed by Christian writers, who substituted Christ's title LORD for the name YAHWEH. Clear examples of the usage of "the day" or "the day of the Lord" to designate the Parousia as the time of the final judgment to be rendered by Christ on humankind are in Rom 2.16; 13.12; 1 Cor 1.8; 3.13; 5.5; Eph 4.30; Phil 1.6; 1 Thes 5.2, 4; 2 Thes 1.10; 2.2; 2 Tm 1.12; 4.8; 2 Pt 3.10; Acts 17.31 [*see* JUDGMENT, DIVINE (IN THE BIBLE)].

In the Pastoral Epistles ἐπιφάνεια (EPIPHANY, manifestation) is the term used for the Parousia (1 Tm 6.14; 2 Tm 4.1, 8; Ti 2.13). Some authors consider ἐπιφάνεια to be synonymous with παρουσία, but this opinion may be questioned. It is certainly not true for 2 Tm 1.10, where ἐπιφάνεια is used of the Incarnation. In 2 Thes 2.8 Paul combines the two terms: "by the manifestation [ἐπιφάνεια] of his coming [παρουσία]." While some scholars consider this phrase to be a pleonasm, i.e., the repetition of the same idea in different terms, it is probable that Paul intends a particular nuance of meaning here (indicated below). Although the word ἐπιφάνεια is employed in classical Greek in the meaning of outward appearance, only in later Greek is it used to mean the visible (not necessarily corporeal) manifestation of a hidden divinity. Finally, the NT designates the παρουσία with the word ἀποκάλυψις (1 Cor 1.7; 2 Thes 1.7; 1 Pt 1.7, 13; 4.13). In ordinary Greek ἀποκάλυψις meant the uncovering of something hidden. In the Greek of late Judaism and the Jewish apocalyptic literature, the word meant the revelation of divine secrets.

Meaning of the doctrine. In the NT, Parousia is an eschatological concept, i.e., it expresses faith in a final act of God that is to occur when human history has reached its divinely determined goal. This act of God will usher in a life in which all humanity is completely under the rule of God. The doctrine presupposes the RESURRECTION OF THE DEAD (1 Thes 4.16), whose eternal condition and new existence (1 Cor 15.51) are under the direction and dominion of the risen Christ, mysteriously present to effect and to govern the lot of humanity (in His παρουσία). The initial effect of the presence of the risen Christ, with which all humanity will be confronted, is the final judgment rendered by Christ (the day of the Lord). The just are to be "with the Lord" (1 Thes 4.17), while the unjust are to be banished from Him (2 Thes 1.9). Thus the Parousia will make known the significance of Christ for all humanity (ἐπιφάνεια), and at the same time it will disclose God's design for the eternal destiny of humankind (ἀποκάλυψις). The language in which Paul describes the Parousia event in 1 Thes 4.16–17 and 2 Thes 2.3–10 is taken mainly from Jewish APOCALYPTIC. It is not to be understood as a literal historical description. The NT does not indicate how the presence of the risen Christ is to occur at the end of history or how this presence will be recognized by humankind.

Time of the Parousia. Once the doctrine of the Parousia is presented to faith, the question naturally arises regarding the time when the event is to occur. The teaching of Christ and of St. Paul on the time of the Parousia is one of the most celebrated questions in the field of biblical scholarship. Many scholars have argued that in the teaching of Jesus the Parousia is certainly proximate, i.e., it is to occur within the lifetime of the Twelve or within a single generation. Other scholars have attributed a similar teaching to St. Paul. Some Catholic scholars have believed that Paul was personally convinced of a proximate Parousia, which he himself would live to witness, though he did not actually teach this personal opinion as a certitude of faith. At an opposite extreme are the opinions of those scholars who attempt to prove that there was no thought at all of a proximate Parousia in the Church of early period, and a fortiori in the teaching of Jesus. The early Church anticipated the imminent destruction of the Temple, prophesied by Jesus, and a union with Him through personal death. The Parousia was expected only in the remote future.

In 1 and 2 Thessalonians. The study of early Christian thought on the time of the Parousia has its natural point of departure in the Epistles to the THESSALONIANS, which are certainly among the earliest and probably the earliest of the Pauline Epistles (written *c.* A.D. 51). These Epistles and 2 Pt 3.3–14 are the only documents in the NT to speak expressly (and not simply by allusion) of the doctrine of the Parousia. In 1 Thes 4.12–18, Paul addresses himself to the question of mourning for the Christian dead in Thessalonica. He considers that some among the Thessalonians are guilty of an undesirable manifestation of grief over their dead (v. 13). His response is to stress (1) the certainty from faith of the resurrection of these dead (v. 14), and (2) the time of their resurrection as an occurrence before the Parousia (v. 16), so that (3) death itself will not place these believers in Christ at a disadvantage when the Parousia occurs (v. 15). Paul's main doctrinal objective in this passage is quite clear. He wishes to state the chronological relationship between the Parousia and the resurrection of the dead: first the resurrection, then the Parousia. The Thessalonians, therefore, are not justified in understanding the doctrine of the Parousia to imply that death deprives the Christian of the

joys to be anticipated from the event itself. Paul concludes his remarks with the observation that the Thessalonians should "comfort one another with these words" (v. 18), i.e., with the doctrine he has presented to them: resurrection first, then the Parousia. Here he envisions the possibility of further deaths among these Christians. On these occasions, the living should remind the bereaved of the doctrine he has here taught.

This concluding advice of Paul was of practical relevance only on the supposition that the Thessalonian Christians made a direct connection between their faith in Christ as Savior and the Parousia of Christ; they considered it undesirable that death should intervene between the time of their conversion to Christ and the Parousia of Christ. This sentiment indicates that they were in anticipation of a proximate Parousia, i.e., the presence of Christ as the concluding event of salvation history within their own lifetimes. In framing his doctrine so as to point up the chronology—resurrection first, then the Parousia—Paul wrote to them exactly in terms of this proximate expectancy: "we who live, who survive until the coming of the Lord" (v. 15). Thereby he included himself in their hope of escaping death because of an early occurrence of the Parousia. Analysis of 1 Thes 4.12–18 makes it impossible to avoid the conclusion that both Paul and the Thessalonians had in view a proximate Parousia. The Paul felt bound to write as if the Parousia-event were, at the least, a real possibility within the lifetime of the Thessalonians and himself. Further, he ascribed his teaching that the resurrection precedes the Parousia to the "word of the Lord," i.e., the teaching of Jesus. Mindful as he was of the "word of the Lord," he did not appeal to it to disabuse the Thessalonians of their expectancy of a proximate Parousia. Instead, he wrote from this very standpoint. This fact suggests that Paul knew of nothing in the teaching of Jesus that required him to fix the Parousia in the distant future.

In 2 Thes 2.1–12 (2 Thessalonians was written about six months after 1 Thessalonians) Paul again concerned himself with the Thessalonians' expectancy of the Parousia. On this occasion, however, he rejected an idea being spread among them: that the "day of the Lord is already here" (v. 2), i.e., that the time of the final judgment by Christ has actually arrived. Paul flatly denied that such is the case, characterizing this opinion as a deception (v. 3). He reminded them of his previous teaching concerning the occurrence of a religious apostasy and the appearance of a "man of lawlessness" before the Parousia (v. 3–5). Since in his judgment there was no evidence that these events were occurring, he declared that the day of the Lord was not a process that had begun. In effect, he denied that the Parousia was imminent, i.e., an event to be anticipated from day to day; but he said nothing in this passage in 2 Thessalonians to modify the position on the proximity of the Parousia that he had taken in 1 Thessalonians. In 2 Thessalonians he stated categorically that the Parousia was not about to occur; but in neither epistle did he state categorically that the Parousia would not occur within the lifetime of some of the Thessalonian Christians.

In Other Epistles. There is no evidence in the NT that other Christian communities underwent similar crises of faith over the doctrine of the Parousia as occurred in Thessalonica. There is abundant testimony, however, that Christian communities in general entertained the same proximate expectancy as the Thessalonians. In Jas 5.7–8 (the Epistle of St. JAMES may have been written as early as the mid-40s or as late as 90–100) the hope of the Parousia is held out as a motive for patience in trials. In 1 Jn 2.28 (probably to be dated before 98) the possibility of the occurrence of the Parousia in the near future is still left open (see also 1 Jn 2.18). In 1 Pt 1.7, 13 (probably in the early 60s, but possibly 90–95), as in James, the thought of the Parousia is presented as a consolation in the midst of persecutions. The passage in Jude 14–24 (datable from the early 60s to 100) also seems to have been composed in a thought context of the proximate Parousia. In 1 Cor 1.7–8 Paul can appeal to the Corinthians' expectancy of the revelation (ἀποκάλυψις) of Christ for which the gifts of Christ have prepared them. In 1 Cor 4.5 he warns them against rendering condemnatory judgments "until the Lord comes," when judgment will be rendered by Christ. In 1 Cor 6.1–7, he criticizes them for appealing against one another to pagan lawcourts, and he asks why they are not willing to accept injustice. The latter question appears a plausible one only in view of the proximate Parousia, a possibility that, in the view of Paul, depresses the importance of the things of this world.

Paul's observations on marriage in 1 Cor 7.28–31 are couched in the framework of the proximate Parousia, to which he expressly alludes in the phrase "the time is short" (v. 29). He reminds the Corinthian Christians, lately converted from paganism, that preparation for the final judgment is the main factor that should influence their decision on marriage. He recommends virginity as a more desirable state than marriage, provided this choice is motivated by the desire to prepare for the judgment of Christ at the Parousia (1 Cor 7.32–35) and provided it is freely made by those Christians who see in virginity the opportunity for a fuller dedication to the Christian life (1 Cor 7.36–38) (*see* CORINTHIANS, EPISTLES TO THE).

Parousia in the books of the New Testament. The teaching of St. Paul on the Parousia has been considered above. Other NT literature is here discussed on the basis of the commonly accepted chronology, Mark (A.D. 65–70), Luke (*c.* 75), Matthew (75–85), 2 Peter (probably 80–100). The Johannine writings and Revelation are discussed separately.

In Mark. Although actual data on the Parousia is slight in Mark's Gospel, the conception is undeniably present (Mk 8.38; 13.26; 14.62). Its setting in the discourse on the destruction of the Temple (Mk 13.26) has provoked extensive discussion among scholars on the origin of the discourse as a whole and in particular on the authenticity of Mk 13.24–27, a series of verses apocalyptic in style. It is generally agreed that Mark ch. 13 is a composition that incorporates words spoken by Jesus on different occasions into a unit centering on the theme of the destruction of the Temple. All that is said in the discourse on this point is stated to be proximate in time (13.28–31), i.e., it is to occur within the period of the first Christian generation. It is this clear assertion that has produced the question concerning the authenticity of Mk 13.24–27, since these verses can be understood to forecast the occurrence of the Parousia immediately upon the destruction of the Temple.

Beginning with the work of Timothée Colani (1824–88), *Jésus Christ et les croyances messianiques de son temps* (1864), many scholars (including the Catholic M. J. Lagrange) have sided with Colani in judging Mk 13.24–27 to be of Judaeo-Christian origin rather than a record of the teaching of Jesus. Two arguments are advanced for this opinion, namely, that Jesus was not guilty of error and that He never spoke in apocalyptic language. Recent scholars, however, have recognized the arbitrary character of the opinion that Jesus never employed apocalyptic language. There is in fact nothing in Mk 13.24–27 that could not have been uttered by Jesus Himself. Apart from the problem of attributing error to Him when Mk 13.24–27 is understood in the sense of chronological time, it is necessary to question the assumption that the passage is concerned solely with chronological time. Like all biblical writers, Mark proposes salvation history, i.e., the salvific acts of God within history. When Mk 13.24–27 is interpreted from this standpoint, the evangelist must be understood to say that after the fulfillment of Jesus' prophecy on the destruction of the Temple, Christians are not to anticipate another messianic intervention into history until the Parousia. Mark's passage, to be sure, does not exclude the possibility of the Parousia in the chronological sense as an immediate occurrence after the destruction; the evangelist leaves this possibility distinctly open. But his position on the proximity of the Parousia is no stronger than that of St. Paul in 1 Thes 4.12–18. The evidence of the Pauline epistles, outlined above, shows clearly enough that the early Church commonly entertained the possibility of a proximate Parousia. The Gospel of Mark remains within this tradition. Whereas St.

Paul had occasion to inculcate the time sequence—resurrection first and then the Parousia—Mark advances the sequence—the destruction first, and then, as the next messianic intervention of God, the (possibly proximate) Parousia. (For further consideration of the position of Mark, see below on the teaching of Jesus and the Parousia.)

In Luke. Luke's eschatological discourse (Luke ch. 21) closely parallels Mark ch. 13 both in material content and in sequence of thought. Nonetheless, it contains certain ideas that show that Luke was in a position to offer some degree of clarification to the Church of his time on the relationship between the destruction of the Temple and the Parousia. As in Mark, the Lucan discourse answers two questions raised by the prophecy of Christ concerning the destruction of the Temple: the first question inquires when the destruction is to occur; and the second requests the sign by which the imminence of the event will be recognizable (cf. Lk 21.5–7 with Mk 13.1–4). The Lucan answer to the question on the sign (Lk 21.20–24) differs from Mark's (Mk 13.14–20) in four significant respects: (1) the sign itself, a siege by armies, is on the historical level in contrast to the indeterminate biblical phrase of Mark-Matthew, "the ABOMINATION OF DESOLATION" (Dn 9.27); (2) the destruction of Jerusalem, not simply that of the Temple, is the point at issue; (3) the destruction is presented as a divine judgment against the Holy City, a conception that follows the Jewish understanding of Israel's catastrophes (2 Kgs 9.6–9; Hos 9.7; Jer 5.29); (4) a period of time is envisioned after the destruction, described by Luke as "the times of the nations," during which the teachings of Christ are to be offered to the Gentiles.

Luke's counterpart (Lk 21.25–28) to the apocalyptic passage in Mk 13.24–27, expanding upon the Parousia, is set in the context of "the times of the nations" instead of the context of the destruction, as in Mark. Amid distress and fear upon the earth, the Parousia of the Son of Man occurs. During this period, the Christian is not to be disturbed; rather, he is to reflect that the fullness of the Redemption to come with the Parousia. Luke thus removes the possible relationship in time between the destruction and the Parousia that is so conspicuous in Mark. Although it is perhaps too much to say with some modern scholars that Luke eliminates the proximity of the Parousia altogether, he does disassociate it in time from the destruction of Jerusalem.

In accordance with his chronological disassociation of the destruction and the Parousia, Luke, by comparison to Mark, modifies the response of Jesus to the question on the time of the destruction (cf. Lk 21.29–33 with Mk 13.28–31). Although "all things" prophesied by Jesus

are to occur before His generation has passed away (Lk 21.32), the fulfillment of the prophecies in Luke consists in the knowledge that the reign of God is near (Lk 21.31). Thus, in Luke the destruction of Jerusalem is understood as a sign of the Parousia of Christ: the fulfillment of His prophecy on the doom of Jerusalem indicates the fulfillment of His prophecy on the Parousia. Those who witness the fulfillment of the first prophecy should look to the fulfillment of the second (Lk 21.32–36). In this sense of the gradual revelation in history of God's salvific plan, Jesus' words are fulfilled within a single generation.

In Matthew. Matthew's is the only one of the four Gospels to use the term παρουσία (Mt 24.3, 27, 37, 39). His use of it gives his discourse on the destruction of the Temple (Matthew ch. 24) a different orientation of thought from its parallels in Mark ch. 13 and Luke ch. 21. In Mark and Luke, Jesus is asked concerning the time of the destruction and for a sign by which the imminence of the event will be recognizable. In Matthew the question on the time of the destruction remains. However, the request of the disciples for a sign pertains, not to the destruction, but to "your Parousia and the end of the age [τοῦ αἰῶνος, AEON]" (Mt 24.3b). Unlike the discourse in Mark ch. 13 and Luke ch. 21, Matthew ch. 24 treats explicitly a question that is only implicit in Mark and Luke: whether or not the proximity of the Parousia, and therefore of the end of natural human history, is to be recognized by a sign.

Although the question of the time of the end is the main one for Matthew ch. 24, the evangelist has retained the traditional question on the time of the destruction of the Temple (Mt 24.3a) as well as the traditional material that responds to it (Mt 24.4–26). This material has substantially the same meaning as in Mk 13.5–23: it pertains to the destruction of the Temple, warning against false messiahs and false signs, forecasting persecution, demanding perseverance, and advising flight upon the appearance of the "abomination of desolation." However, to the Marcan warnings against false messiahs and false prophets (cf. Mk 13.21–23 with Mt 24.23–26), Matthew adds two sayings of Jesus (Mt 24.27–28) to the effect that the Parousia will be unannounced (v. 27) and will be inevitably recognized by all people (v. 28). He thereby strengthens the teaching of Mk 13.21–23 that after the destruction, no messianic intervention other than the Parousia is to be expected.

Matthew's apocalyptic passage (Mt 24.29–31) parallel to Mk 13.24–27, elaborating upon the Parousia, is introduced by the word εὐθέως (immediately). As in Mark, the evangelist's thought is best comprehended in terms of salvation history: in the divine, salvific plan the Parousia is the only messianic intervention to be anticipated as following upon the destruction. The entire human race is to recognize the presence of the Son of Man, and the last judgment is to occur.

Up to this point in the discourse (Mt 24.4–31), Matthew, as Mark, asserts the destruction of the Temple and the Parousia, but does not address himself to the questions concerning the time of the destruction and the sign of the Parousia. He now does so (Mt 24.32–36), utilizing, however, traditional material, found also in Mk 13.28–32: as the fig tree in bloom indicates the nearness of summer, so the fulfillment in history of the prophecies of Jesus (Mt 24.33) is "the sign of [His] parousia and of the end of the age" (Mt 24.3b). The fulfillment in history can only refer to the destruction of the Temple, since the day and the hour of the Parousia itself is a secret held by the Father alone (Mt 24.36). For Matthew the destruction of the Temple is the theological sign of the Parousia, but not its chronological sign. The time of the Parousia is a divine secret that the Father did not reveal even to the Son. Whereas in Mark the Parousia is left in possible chronological proximity to the destruction of the Temple, and whereas in Luke it is chronologically separated from the destruction of Jerusalem, in Matthew the stress is on the mystery enshrouding the time of the event.

Historical Teaching of Jesus. Scholars of the Gospels are not in agreement that Jesus actually taught the Parousia during His lifetime. Numerous passages in the Gospels attribute sayings to Him concerning "the coming [ἔρχομαι]" of the Son of Man (Mk 8.38; 13.26; 14.26; Lk 9.26; 12.40; 18.8; 21.27; Mt 10.23; 16.27; 24.30, 44; 25.31; 26.64). The interpretation of these sayings is rendered difficult by the fact that the Gospel tradition has not always conserved their original historical context. Either the evangelists or the tradition before them have, to a degree, reinterpreted some of these sayings in the light of the early Church's fuller understanding of Jesus' mission. From the critical standpoint, two sound points of departure for the interpretation of these sayings can be indicated: (1) in 1 Thes 4.15 St. Paul asserts that he bases his statements about the Parousia on "the word of the Lord," i.e., on the historical teaching of Jesus; (2) the passages indicated in the parenthesis above have in common the doctrine of the "coming [ἔρχομαι]" of the Son of Man. These facts reveal that there is no ground to deny a priori that the Parousia originated in the historical teaching of Jesus. On the other hand, one must ascertain carefully whether Jesus taught this doctrine explicitly or merely contented Himself with providing a foundation for the Church's later comprehension of it.

The most significant passage for the understanding of Jesus' historical teaching on the Parousia is the state-

ment He made at His trial before the Sanhedrin as quoted in Mk 14.62 (see also Mt 26.64): "You will see the Son of Man seated at the right hand of the Power and coming with the clouds of heaven." Although scholars of the Gospels concede that the saying is substantially historical, they are not in accord on the meaning Jesus intended to convey. For some scholars Jesus here declared not only His Resurrection, but also His Parousia. For others He simply affirmed that He would be vindicated by being brought to God upon His execution. Interpretation of the saying must take into consideration its prophetic character. Prophecy is frequently obscure in its content at the time it is uttered. Only through the development of events and the evaluation of the prophecy in the light of other religious doctrines is its true significance comprehended. Thus the RESURRECTION and ASCENSION OF JESUS CHRIST (cf. the exaltation of Jesus in Phil 2.9), as well as His headship of the new messianic community (cf. Acts 2.36), provide a fuller comprehension of His saying in Mk 14.62 than was possible when He made the statement historically. St. Paul's allusion in 1 Thes 4.15 to the historical teaching of Jesus on the Parousia finds its minimal justification in the fact that Jesus spoke of the "coming" of the Son of Man that would have future and final relevance, not only to His own disciples, but also to the entire world. The recollection of such sayings is embodied in Mk 8.38 and Mt 25.31–32.

Jesus' historical teaching insisted upon vigilance in preparation for "that day" (Mk 13.33–37; Mt 24.42–51; Lk 21.34–36), i.e., the time of final judgment, and He declared His own ignorance of the time of the event (cf. Mk 13.32 with Mt 24.36). St. Paul sets forth the same doctrine (1 Thes 5.1–2) as well known to the Thessalonians. It would seem, then, that the historical teaching of Jesus Himself compelled the early Church to entertain the possibility of an imminent Parousia, since nothing in the Lord's teaching excluded this possibility. Such an orientation of thought in the primitive Church forced it to focus its attention on the person of Jesus and His teaching, and to a considerable degree it was responsible for the development of the material on Jesus and His teaching that made possible the composition of the four Gospels.

In the Johannine Literature and Revelation. The only explicit reference to the Parousia in the Johannine literature (1, 2, 3 John and John) lies in 1 Jn 2.28, which expresses a Christian hope concerning the presence of Christ as judge not unsimilar to 1 Thes 2.10. Elsewhere in 1 John the doctrine of the Parousia seems clearly to be assumed (1 Jn 3.2) or can be inferred from statements about the ANTICHRIST (2.18; 4.3). No mention is made of the doctrine in 2 and 3 John, but 2 John does speak of the Antichrist (2 Jn 7).

The Fourth Gospel does not employ the term πα-ρουσία. Neither does it utilize the figure of the Son of Man to depict a presence of the risen Christ in history that will terminate the course of human events. The Gospel begins and ends by placing its central figure, "the Anointed One, the Son of God" (Jn 20.31), within the Godhead. The prologue (1.1–18) names Him the LOGOS, eternally preexistent, who entered the world by becoming Incarnate (1.14). The remainder of the Gospel conceives His life as a passage through suffering, death, and Resurrection to the realm of the Father (12.32; 20.17). The significance of the divine origin, earthly career, and final glorification of Jesus for Christians is not spelled out in the Fourth Gospel in terms of the Parousia, but rather in terms of a union with Christ that has its beginning in the Christian's earthly existence (3.3; 4.10; 6.53; 15.1) and its terminus in a life that will transcend the bonds of human mortality (3.15; 4.14; 6.54; 14.2). This presentation of Christian faith as a supernatural union with Christ, the Son of God, that begins in mortal human existence and ends in a superterrestrial sharing in the divine life draws out the ultimate significance of the doctrine of the Parousia. The Parousia is the logical presupposition of such Johannine statements as the following: "The Father loves the Son and has handed all things over to him. Whoever believes in the Son has life eternal. Whoever disobeys the Son will not see life, but must endure God's wrath" (3.35–36); "I solemnly assure you, an hour is coming and is now here when the dead shall hear the voice of God's Son, and those who have listened shall live" (Jn 5.25); "And when I do go and prepare a place for you, I am coming back to take you along with me so that where I am, you may also be" (Jn 14.3). In these passages, the Christian life is conceived as an anticipation of the Parousia.

Revelation, like the Fourth Gospel, rather presupposes the doctrine of the Parousia than inculcates it. At the outset of the work, the risen and ascended Jesus is described symbolically as existing within the Godhead (Rv 1.13–16). From this position, He addresses messages to the seven churches (2.1–3.22), in the course of which perseverance in the Christian faith is urged until His coming (2.25). The coming is directed especially against persecutors of Christians (6.10) and is described in 6.15–17 in terms reminiscent of Lk 23.30. The coming on behalf of the just is taken up from Rv 19.11 to the conclusion of the work. Here the Parousia is explicitly announced as part of the divine irrevocable plan: "And behold, I am coming quickly" (22.7). This assertion is repeated at the end of the book, together with the author's prayer affirming his firm conviction of the coming and requesting that it take place in accordance with God's design: "Amen. Come, Lord Jesus" (22.20). Revelation is clearly the product of the persecutions experienced by the early Church, especially under Nero (A.D. 54–68) and Domitian (A.D. 81–96). Its author, writing probably during the reign of Domitian, utilized the Church's doctrine of the Parousia to encourage the faith of Christians in these dire circumstances.

Delay of the Parousia. Criticism of the Christian doctrine of the Parousia is reflected in 2 Pt 3.3–10, a late epistle dating probably after A.D. 80. The criticism consists in ridicule of the doctrine on the ground that the Parousia has not materialized (3.4). The objection presupposes a Christian expectancy of an early Parousia. However, neither the source of the criticism nor the concrete circumstances of it is ascertainable. The author of the Epistle responds by invoking the creative power of the word of God (3.5), the punitive power of His word (3.6), and the difference between the human conception of time and the working out of God's design in history (3.7–8). He reassures his Christian readers that the nonoccurrence of the Parousia is not evidence against the truth of the doctrine but rather an indication of the divine mercy still bent on the repentance of humankind (3.9). Finally, he reasserts the doctrine, stressing that the occurrence of the Parousia will be unanticipated because of its suddenness and that this event will terminate human history as humans have known it (3.10).

Some scholars have urged that the Gospel of Luke is preoccupied with the question of the so-called delay of the Parousia. They appeal to such passages as Lk 12.45, which speaks of a delay in the return of a householder, and 19.12, which describes a man embarking upon a long journey (see also 20.9). It remains possible that the Gospel of Luke anticipated a problem that arose among some early Christians when the Parousia failed to materialize; but these passages can be understood also as parabolic detail that has no intentional reference to the Christian expectancy of a proximate Parousia.

See Also: ESCHATOLOGY (IN THE BIBLE).

Bibliography: A. FEUILLET, *Dictionnaire de la Bible*, suppl. ed., ed. L. PIROT (Paris 1928–) 6:1331–1419. H. CONZELMANN, *Die Religion in Geschichte und Gegenwart* (Tübingen 1957–65) 5:130–132. *Encyclopedic Dictionary of the Bible*, tr. and adap. L. HARTMAN (New York 1963) 1728–39. G. R. BEASLEY-MURRAY, *Jesus and the Future* (New York 1954), with extensive bibliog.; *A Commentary on Mark Thirteen* (London 1957). H. CONZELMANN, *Theology of St. Luke*, tr. G. BUSWELL (New York 1960). A. CORELL, *Consummatum est: Eschatology and Church in the Gospel of St. John* (New York 1958). T. F. GLASSON, *The Second Advent* (3d ed. London 1963). W. G. KÜMMEL, *Promise and Fulfillment*, tr. D. M. BARTON (Naperville, Ill. 1957). B. RIGAUX, *Saint Paul: Les Épîtres aux Thessaloniciens Études bibliques* (1956). J. A. T. ROBINSON, *Jesus and His Coming* (Nashville, Tenn. 1958). J. P. MEIER *A Marginal Jew* (New York, 1991, 1994).

[C. P. CEROKE/EDS.]

In Theology

Early symbols professing the great Christian mysteries place the Second Coming (always an essential truth of faith) side by side with the Incarnation, death and Resurrection of Christ [see the apostolic, Athanasian, Nicene, and Nicene-Constantinopolitan creedal formulations (H. Denzinger, *Enchiridion symbolorum* 11, 30, 41, 76, 125–126, 150)]. The patristic tradition witnessing to the importance of the Parousia in the Christian mind is clear and constant. The writings of the Apostolic Fathers, reflecting a lingering Jewish apocalyptic spirit, as well as the teaching of Christ on the seeming imminence of His eschatological predictions, are strongly eschatological. Clement of Rome, in his letter to the Corinthians (96–97), affirms the proximity of the Parousia and reproves the skeptical (23.3–5). The Didache concludes facing the Parousia and the duties of Christians arising from its approach (16.1). Widespread yearning for the return of Christ in glory attests to an intense parousial faith in the early Church. Any misunderstanding of the proximity of the Second Coming was born of obscurity inherent in the prophetico-apocalyptic message of Christ and Paul.

Millenarianism. Many in the first two centuries interpreted 2 Pt 3.8–9 and Rv 20.4–5 literally and looked to a future messianic kingdom prior to the Parousia. Thus MILLENARIANISM was born. A residue of Jewish speculation on the duration of the intermediary messianic reign was probably at work here [cf. J. Bonsirven, *Le Judaïsme palestinien au temps de Jésus-Christ, sa théologie* (Paris 1934–35) 427]. Papias of Hierapolis in the 2d century paints a vivid picture of the millennial era (*Patrologia Graeca* 7:1213–15). Among its early adherents Millenarianism numbered Pseudo-Barnabas, Irenaeus, Justin, Tertullian, Lactantius, and Hippolytus. Never universally held as part of apostolic tradition, chiliasm did tend to replace in the 2d century what previously had been the expectation of an imminent Parousia. Such excess indicates the force of eschatological hope in the early Church. An unfortunately inept way of affirming that history is the expectation of Christ, chiliastic dreams revive from time to time [cf. decree of Holy Office, *Acta Apostolicae Sedis* 36 (1944) 212 (H. Denzinger, *Enchiridion symbolorum* 3839)].

Kingdom and empire. As the Church expanded through the Roman world in the 3d and 4th centuries and won state recognition, Millenarianism waned. Persecution lessened; the present time seemed less provisory; the Parousia less imminent. Wed to Rome, many considered the messianic kingdom as realized in the spread of the empire (see, e.g., Eusebius, *Hist. eccl.* 10.4). Others, by solitude and virginity, renounced identification of the eschatological kingdom with the world and saw the establishment of the true kingdom in the Parousia (see, e.g., tracts on virginity by Methodius, Ambrose, Basil of Ancyra, Gregory of Nyssa). It was Augustine who dealt the death blow to both the chiliasts and those identifying Christ's reign with temporal society (*Civ.* 20.6–13). The fall of Rome in 410 further stifled such deviations. Like people in every other age, faced with the fragility and radical impermanence of the world's institutions, many saw the empire's demise as presaging the end.

Particular judgment, purgatory, beatific vision. The vivacity of early belief in the Parousia left its stamp on patristic theologizing about the particular judgment, purgatory, and the beatific vision. At the outset, it was thought that departed souls lived in a state of parousial expectancy. The evident delay of the Second Coming gradually gave rise to closer study of the lot of the soul after death, and a marked doctrinal development took place. It was only in the 4th century that particular judgment was generally received into the mainstream of patristic thought, without, however, usurping the primacy of the parousial judgment. Similarly, since retribution immediately after death hinges upon particular judgment, patristic teaching on purgatory developed slowly and was first conceived in function of the Parousia. For Origen and others, purification of the just commences with the Parousia (see A. Michel, "Purgatoire," *Dictionnaire de théologie catholique* 13.1:1193–96). The Greek Fathers of the 4th century fell heir to Origen's thought and with but rare exception viewed the dead as awaiting definitive parousial judgment and purgation in the final conflagration. In the 9th century, this parousial orientation perdured in Photius (*Ad Amphil* 6.15) and survived to the beginning of the 15th century and the Council of Florence. In the West it was Augustine especially who insisted on purification immediately after death (*Civ.* 21.46). In the ante-Nicene period, beatitude was likewise so closely bound up with the return of Christ that it was generally considered delayed until the parousial resurrection. From the 4th to the 9th century, the lot of the elect was gradually though not wholly separated from the Parousia. Following the 9th-century cleavage between East and West, enjoyment of the beatific vision by the elect immediately after death was common doctrine in the West, whose tradition culminated in 1336 with the constitution *BENEDICTUS DEUS* of Benedict XII (H. Denzinger, *Enchiridion symbolorum* 1000–02). Though the doctrine was not yet in possession in the East, it had numerous and weighty partisans there.

Perspective. Doctrinal development concerning retribution was slow and faltering precisely because patristic theologians, like the New Testament itself, focused primarily on the perfection of creation, history and humanity redeemed in Christ and glorified with Him at the term of this earthly economy, and only secondarily on the fate of the individual. Recall the New Testament images of the meal, the wedding, the holy city. In this perspective all converges upon the Parousia: judgment, retribution, consummation of life inaugurated by Christ's Resurrection, definitive constitution of His kingdom. Though time corroded the urgency of parousial hope, the Parousia always remained a key mystery [see the conciliar teaching of Lateran IV, 1215 (H. Denzinger, *Enchiridion symbolorum* 801), Lyons II, 1274 (*ibid.* 852), Florence, 1442 (*ibid.* 1338), the Tridentine profession of faith, 1564 (*ibid.* 1862)]. The impact of the doctrine in the medieval period, an age not of printed word but of artistic image, is felt in the painting and sculpture of the era, as well as in the popular preaching. With time, joyous hope for the return of Christ was colored with pessimistic desire for the last day, when Christ's justice would pronounce vengeful judgment on this world's injustice. With the rise of rationalistic theology and the decline of historical sensitivity, the Parousia lost much of its larger significance and became little more than doomsday.

In the rediscovery of eschatology by contemporary theology, the Parousia is restored to its rightful place as final event of salvation history. The glorious return of Christ and the ensemble of eschatological events He will then effect mark the consummation of God's redemptive plan. As such the Parousia is certain and promised, yet a reality already at the heart of the present world. Salvation is now present, though not yet unveiled in full cosmic dimension (Rom 8.17–23). While the kingdom of God is essentially a kingdom to come, it is presently realized in those who share by grace in the redemptive work of Christ (Jn 12.31; 2 Cor 5.17; 6.2; Col 1.22; 1 Jn 1.7). The present is the future anticipated. For in this realized Redemption are sewn new promises. The Parousia will harvest in final, perfect form what already is (1 Jn 3.2). Dead with Christ by Baptism and already risen to a new life (Rom 6.1–11), through adhesion to Christ Christians anticipate final judgment (Jn 3.17; 5.24). This in no way implies that the Parousia brings with it nothing new. Christ's emergence from His secret presence in His Church, His resurrection of the dead, His definitive judgment and situation of each person within the divine plan, His transfiguration of non-rational creation, His enthronement as center of creation, all are new events giving the personal *eschata,* death and particular judgment, their full significance. Yet these final events now exist hiddenly in Christ's KINGDOM, as Christ Himself lives hiddenly in glory to be manifested only at His return (Col 3.1–4). Hence the Parousia is not simply another item in an array of last things. As God's final loving intervention, it is the plenitude of Redemption, the crowning triumph of Christ as SAVIOR.

The central, decisive event of history is neither at the beginning nor at the end; it is the Resurrection of Christ. What preceded was preparation; what follows is the "end time" (cf. 1 Cor 10.11), the time of the Church in and through which Christ incorporates into Himself all comprised in His eternal decree, communicates to them divine life, and reveals His power to bring to its ultimate state the kingdom predestined. The appearance of Christ at the end of ages will close this period of growth. Then He will present to the Father His kingdom finally established as the perfect, unfailing realization of divine wisdom, power, and love (1 Cor 15.20–28). The glory of Christ will be extended by Him to the members of His kingdom who by faith and baptismal REBIRTH are associated to His paschal mystery (1 Thes 4.14–18; 2 Thes 1.10; Phil 3.20–21). The root of the parousial mystery is men's solidarity with Christ (1 Jn 2.28). Thus Redemption is actualized in history now hastening to fulfillment in the parousial theophany, wherein the ultimate defeat of Satan will be realized in the completion of the Trinity's saving work.

Sacraments. It is not difficult to see why the early Church did not fear the end of time but yearned for it, as Tertullian says, as the farmer for the harvest, the soldier for the definitive end of struggle (*De orat.* 5). The Christian is turned to the future with tranquil assurance that the Parousia will perfect and manifest what has already been wrought in him inchoatively and is possessed in pledge (2 Cor 1.22; 5.5). In the present stage of the redemptive process, intermediary between the two comings of Christ, creation possesses in the obscurity of faith the glory now perfectly possessed by the "Firstborn" (Col 1.15) and awaits the definitive reality in the final stage ushered in by the Parousia. Meanwhile, it is especially in its Sacraments that the Church meets in veiled contact the Christ to come. Each Sacrament mysteriously renders accessible the mystery of Christ and associates the Christian to Him. Commemorating the past, introducing the Christian presently to an ultratemporal and ultraterrestrial life, the Sacraments are pregnant with future reality and announce the return of Christ to reveal and crown His victory now hidden in Himself and those united to Him. Parousial dimension is found above all in the Eucharist, the food of immortality (Jn 6.54), which heralds the death of Christ "until He come" (1 Cor 11.26) and is a foretaste of the heavenly banquet (Mt 8.11). By sacramental insertion into the mystery of Christ, the Christian knows a double-track existence: he lives now in the era of the Parousia, yet remains in the era of history.

For schools of Protestant theology holding a "consequent" and wholly supratemporal eschatology, no eschatological transformation has penetrated history. Hiddenly accomplished only in Christ, it is extrinsically appropriated to the Christian by faith. The kingdom is present only insofar as Christ, who brings it, is present. Wholly future, the kingdom has not begun its realization in us. The Parousia, far from being the maturation and culmination that Catholic theology views it to be, will be a commencement.

Expectation of Parousia. If anything is clearly affirmed by Christ, it is that we remain ignorant to the end concerning the day of the Parousia (cf., e.g., Mt 24.36; Lk 12.40). Theologians follow the healthy skepticism of Aquinas (*Summa theologiae* 3a, suppl., 73) relative to any literal interpretation of scriptural signs. Perturbations in nature and society are foretold not to date the Parousia but to kindle and orientate human hopes. The definitive theophany cannot be determined by any cosmic catastrophe or by human PROGRESS. What is relevant for Christians, living now in the paratemporal, is the theological, rather than the chronological, imminence of Christ's return. This parousial hope gives meaning and consistency to history and manifests God's immanence to its linear development. If Redemption works in and through historical evolution, only when the redemptive decree of God has run its divinely plotted course will Christ come forth from His abiding presence in His Church. The expectancy of the Church, however, is not directed merely to history's term, but to encounter with the Bridegroom, who will show time to have been a history of salvation, and subject all things to Himself. Through the Word all things were made at the beginning (Col 1.16); through the Word Incarnate all things will be remade at the end. The seed of glory in man will be brought to fruition; the universe, far from being annihilated, will be gloriously transfigured into a suitable habitat for glorified humanity and a luminous reflection of Christ's glory (Rom 8.19–23; 2 Pt 3.7–13). Aside from the fact of transformation, Scripture and patristic tradition provide little detail on the extent and mode of this re-creation. Linked with humanity in sin, the cosmos will be linked to the human race in Redemption (*C. gent.* 4.97; *Comp. theol.* 169–171). The new Adam will create a new Eden, where the cosmic integrity destroyed by sin will be restored and God will be "all in all" (1 Cor 15.28).

See Also: DEATH (THEOLOGY OF); END OF THE WORLD; ESCHATOLOGISM; ESCHATOLOGY (IN THEOLOGY); ESCHATOLOGY, ARTICLES ON; FIRE OF JUDGMENT; INCORPORATION IN CHRIST; JUDGMENT, DIVINE (IN THEOLOGY); JUDGMENT, DIVINE (IN THE BIBLE); MYSTERY THEOLOGY; PURGATORY; RESURRECTION OF CHRIST, 2; RESURRECTION OF THE DEAD, 2.

Bibliography: E. PAX and K. RAHNER, *Lexikon für Theologie und Kirche,* ed. J. HOFER and K. RAHNER (Freiburg 1957–65) 8:120–124. A. WINKLHOFER, *Handbuch theologischer Grundbegriffe,* ed. H. FRIES (Munich 1962–63) 1:327–336; *The Coming of His Kingdom,* tr. A. V. LITTLEDALE (New York 1963). J. GALOT, "Eschatologie," *Dictionnaire de spiritualité ascétique et mystique,* ed. M. VILLER et al. (Paris 1932–) 4:1020–59. A. FEUILLET, *Dictionnaire de la Bible,* suppl., ed. L. PIROT (Paris 1928–) 6:1331–1419. L. BILLOT, *La Parousie* (Paris 1920). O. CULLMANN, *Le Retour du Christ* (Neuchâtel 1943); *Christ and Time,* tr. F. V. FILSON (rev. ed. Philadelphia, Pa. 1964). R. SCHNACKENBURG, *God's Rule and Kingdom,* tr. J. MURRAY (New York 1963). H. U. VON BALTHASAR, "Eschatology," in *Theology Today: Renewal in Dogma,* v. 1, ed. J. FEINER et al., tr. P. WHITE and R. H. KELLY (Milwaukee, Wis. 1965) 222–244. L. BEAUDUIN, "Ciel et résurrection," in H. M. FÉRET, ed., *Le Mystère de la mort et sa célébration* (*Lex orandi* 12; Paris 1956). A. M. HENRY, ed., "The Return of Christ," *The Historical and Mystical Christ,* tr. A. BOUCHARD (*Theology Library* 5; Chicago 1958). P. HUMBERT et al., "La Fin du monde," *Lumière et vie* 11 (Sept. 1953), whole issue. A. JANSSENS, "La Signification sotériologique de la parousie," *Divus Thomas* 36 (1933) 25–38. A. MICHEL, "La Doctrine de la parousie et son incidence dans le dogme et la théologie," *Divinitas* 3 (1959) 397–437. M. SCHMAUS, "Das Eschatologische im Christentum," in *Aus der Theologie der Zeit,* ed. G. SÖHNGEN (Regensburg 1948). J. WRIGHT, "The Consummation of the Universe in Christ," *Gregorianum* 39 (1958) 285–294. J. A. T. ROBINSON, *Jesus and His Coming* (Nashville, Tenn. 1958). O. CULLMANN, *Immortality of the Soul or Resurrection of the Dead?* (New York 1958). J. P. MARTIN, *Last Judgment in Protestant Theology from Orthodoxy to Ritschl* (Grand Rapids, Mich. 1963). J. DANIÉLOU, "Christologie et Eschatologie," *Das Konzil von Chalkedon: Geschichte und Gegenwart,* ed. A. GRILLMEIER and H. BACHT (Würzburg 1951–54) 3:269–286.

[S. J. DUFFY/EDS.]

PARRAS, PEDRO JOSÉ

Franciscan missionary and writer; b. Pancrudo, near Teruel, Spain, *c.* 1710; d. Córdoba, Argentina, Sept. 7, 1784. Parras joined the Franciscan Order in Aragon and was being trained to teach when he volunteered for the missions of Río de la Plata. In 1748 his expedition was in Cádiz at the same time as that of Junípero SERRA. After arriving in Buenos Aires, Parras traveled to Paraguay as visitator of the Franciscan province. His learning and moderate tendencies were valued by Manuel Antonio de la Torre, bishop of Paraguay, who chose him as his adviser on his official visit to the Jesuit Reductions in 1759, and also by Pedro de Cevallos, the governor of Paraguay. Parras was not a member of the anti-Jesuit group, and his attitude was reflected in the objective position of Cevallos. Both Cevallos and Parras returned to Spain in 1766, where Parras attended the General Chapter of the Order (Valencia 1768) as delegate of the Argentine Province and remained to become guardian of the Franciscan house in Zaragoza. When the Portuguese threat again increased in La Plata, Cevallos was sent back, and he requested Parras to accompany him. Grateful for his services, Cevallos frequently recommended him for a bishopric, but this was opposed by the Commissary General of the Indies, Manuel de Vega. Parras was named rector of the University of Córdoba, Argentina, in 1778, a post he filled with great success and tact until his death. He published two works of permanent merit: *Diario y derrotero de sus viajes* (1749–52), a delightful travel account of his trip from Valencia to Paraguay, together with an appendix of his report on the Jesuit Reductions in 1759; and *Gobierno de los regulares de la América* (2 v. Madrid 1783), a masterful account of the legal position of religious in Spanish America at that time; it is clear, reasonable, and often marked by a touch of humor.

Bibliography: P. J. PARRAS, *Fray Pedro José de Parras: Diario y derrotero de sus viajes, 1749–1753* (Buenos Aires 1943). P. PASTELLS, ed., *Historia de la Compañía de Jesús en la provincia del Paraguay,* 8 v. in 9 (Madrid 1912–49).

[L. G. CANEDO]

PARRENIN, DOMINIQUE

Missionary and sinologist; b. Russey, near Besançon, France, Sept. 1, 1665; d. Peking, Sept. 29, 1741. He was admitted into the Society of Jesus on Sept. 1, 1685, and left for the China mission in 1697. At the court of Peking he pleased Emperor K'ang-hi with his extensive knowledge and his familiarity with the Chinese and Tatar-Manchu languages. With this advantage he discussed physics, history, and the place of Christianity in producing the culture of the West. His great service to China was in making maps, especially the great map of China. His popularity at court was greatly responsible for preventing the total destruction of the Christian mission during the hostile reign of Yong-tsching (1723–35), son of K'ang-hi. Many of his letters were published by J. B. du Halde in *Lettres édifiantes et curieuses* (Paris 1711) and *Description de la Chine et de la Tartarie Chinoise* (Paris 1735, Eng. tr. E. Cave, 2 v. London 1738–41). Others are found in the Bibliothèque Nationale, Paris.

Bibliography: C. SOMMERVOGEL et al., *Bibliothèque de la Compagnie de Jésus* (Brussels-Paris 1890–1932) 6:284–290. L. KOCH, *Jesuiten-Lexicon: Die Gesellschaft Jesu einst und jetzt* (Louvain-Heverlee 1962) 1383–84. S. DELACROIX, ed. *Histoire universelle des missions catholiques* (Paris 1956–59) 2:177, 360. B. H. WILLEKE, *Lexicon für Theologie und Kirche*, ed. J. HOFER and K. RAHNER (Freiburg 1957–65) 8:110.

[J. S. SCHWARZ]

PARSCH, PIUS

Leading Austrian liturgist and biblicist; b. Olmütz, Moravia, May 18, 1884; d. Klosterneuburg, Austria, March 11, 1954. Parsch became a Canon of St. Augustine at Klosterneuburg in 1904 and studied there until his ordination in 1909. He taught pastoral theology for a while, then served as a military chaplain during World War I.

Upon entering the order, he took the name Pius in honor of Pius X with whom he shared a love of Holy Scripture. Parsch not only taught Scripture, he also devoted his writings to it, including his doctoral dissertation and his best efforts after World War II, especially in the periodical he founded, *Bibel und Liturgie.* He shared Pius X's concern for bringing the liturgy to the people and making it understood by them. To this purpose, he devoted himself to the many editions of liturgical texts and numerous published explanations of the liturgy that made his monastery a liturgical center of Austria, and indeed of all the German-speaking countries.

The name he gave his work, "Popular Liturgical Apostolate," is noteworthy. It pinpointed his main concern; it was not for research, nor for monastic or academic liturgical forms, much less for liturgical reform. His energy was spent in an apostolate for the Christian people, to bring them to both interior and exterior participation in the liturgy. He aimed at vanquishing liberalism in Austria by unfolding the mysteries of faith and grace. He sought these goals by means of an ideal form of worship celebrated daily in the little Church of St. Gertrude in Klosterneuburg. Because he concentrated on the popular aspects of the liturgical revival, he occasionally risked superficiality in his explanations, which in part have been brought up to date by later research. Parsch was a pioneer in his insistence on an intimate connection between liturgy and Scripture. He came upon this not only through his own scriptural training and teaching, but also through his realization that the people can be brought to an understanding of the liturgy only by a knowledge of Scripture.

His spirit and work have been a major influence on popular liturgical movement throughout the world. Chief among his works are *The Church's Year of Grace* (Collegeville, Minn. 1953–58; first in German in 1929); *The Liturgy of the Mass* (St. Louis 1936; rev. ed. 1957); *The Breviary Explained* (St. Louis 1952; first in German in 1940); *Seasons of Grace* (New York 1963); and *Volksliturgie* (Klosterneuburg 1940).

Bibliography: *Ephemerides liturgicae* 68 (1954) 256–257. T. WARNUNG and T. SCHNITZLER, "In memoriam Pii Parsch," *Liturgisches Jahrbuch* 4 (1954) 230–236. G. ZUNINI, "Apostolato liturgico in azione; le conquiste del P. Parsch," *Ambrosius* 5 (1929) 26–32.

[T. SCHNITZLER]

PARSEES

As their name indicates, are descendants of Persian immigrants who settled in Bombay and its vicinity and who brought their Iranian religion with them. To the 130,000 who now live in India should be added about

20,000 "cousins" who remain in Iran, in the regions of Kerman and Yazd. The Parsees of India have adopted the Gujerati language of the Bombay area. All claim allegiance to the god Mazda or Ormazd and to his prophet Zardusht or Zoroaster. However, under the influence of Hinduism, Islam, and Christianity, their religion has lost much of its original dualism. Ahriman has for the most part been reduced to a symbol of man's evil tendencies.

The most striking features of the Parsees' religion are fire worship and the exposure of corpses in "Towers of Silence." During their fire worship, which is carried out in fire temples, the priest, holding a ritual staff, covers his mouth with a veil which is intended to protect the fire from any possible impurity. The ceremony is completed by a continuous reading of a large portion of the Avesta. The Parsees are not a caste, but they remain a closed community. They never marry outside their group and they make no attempt to convert non-Parsees to their religion. They are antiascetic and have little interest in astrology and mysticism. They are conspicuous for their generosity and interest in education as well as for their wealth, their desire to alleviate misery without distinction of race or religion, and their founding of hospitals, orphanages, and schools. Under Western influence they have changed their dress and abolished infant marriage.

Bibliography: D. MENANT, J. HASTINGS, ed., *Encyclopedia of Religion & Ethics,* 13 v. (Edinburgh 1908–27) 9:640–650. J. DU-CHESNE-GUILLEMIN, *La Religion de l'Iran ancien* (Paris 1962).

[J. DUCHESNE-GUILLEMIN]

PARSONS, WILFRID

Editor, author, educator; b. Philadelphia, Penn., March 17, 1887; d. Washington, DC, Oct. 28, 1958. He was the son of Paul Julian and Alice (Avery) Parsons. After attending high school in New York, he entered the Society of Jesus in 1903. He studied at the Jesuit seminary in Louvain, Belgium (1907–09), and at Woodstock, Maryland, where he obtained his Ph.D. (1910) and was ordained (1918). He went to Rome, received a doctorate in theology from the Gregorian University (1921), and then returned to Woodstock as professor of theology (1922–24). From 1925 to 1936 he served as editor of the Jesuit weekly, *America,* tending to support New Deal reforms and to oppose Republican economic policies; he was also a sharp critic of Rev. Charles E. COUGHLIN, a bitter opponent of F. D. Roosevelt's administration. After 1936 Parsons was engaged in teaching political science at Georgetown University (1936–37, 1948–50, 1954–58) and the Catholic University of America (1938–47), both in Washington, D.C. He contributed articles to several Catholic journals, including *Thought,* which he founded

in 1926. His books include *The Pope and Italy* (1929), *Mexican Martyrdom* (1936), *Early Catholic Americana* (1939), *Which Way Democracy?* (1939), and *The First Freedom* (1948).

[J. L. MORRISON]

PART

A part is related to a WHOLE as something into which a whole is divisible and of which it is constituted. Thus a whole is prior to its parts in the order of being and of understanding, but in the order of becoming the parts are prior to the whole that is made from them by process of change.

Quantitative and Integral Parts. In the clearest case, a part is something into which a QUANTITY is divisible. A quantitative part is smaller in comparison with the larger whole of which it is a part when both whole and part are finite and actual. A part that can measure the whole without remainder is called an aliquot part, as two is of four or three of nine. A continuous quantity is always divisible into parts that in turn are also divisibles, not indivisibles. A quantitative point can be the beginning or end of a line or of a segment of a line, but it is indivisible and so is not a part of a line. A whole or cardinal number is a discrete quantity composed of units. The unit is both part and measure of numbers, but in the order of discrete quantity it is without parts and is indivisible. The parts of which a quantity is composed or integrated and into which it is divisible are called integral parts. A natural body has integral parts that exhibit qualitative differences and are called heterogeneous parts, as the various organs of plant or animal and the parts of molecules or atoms. Integral parts that are required for the whole to be, without which it cannot be, or that are regularly present in the whole, are called proper parts, as the head or hand in man.

Physical, Entitative, and Virtual Parts. In a sensible thing composed of matter and form, both the matter and the form are called physical parts. The wood of which a chair is made is part of the chair, namely, the MATTER, and the figure of a statue is part of the statue, namely, the FORM. When both matter and form are extended or quantified, they are likewise divisible into parts, as this or that part of the wood or part of the figure. The primary principles, or natures, of which natural bodies are made and composed are also called physical parts, as the material nature, or proper matter, of a chemical compound or of an organism and its formal nature, or specifying form. The parts of which any created being, as such, is composed are called entitative parts, namely essence and existence.

Parts that do not include the full perfection of the whole, as the vegetative and sensitive parts of the animal, are said to be virtual, or potential. Such parts are distinguishable by human reason even though they are not distinct in the whole, which is one and undivided in itself, and when made distinct by mental precising they include the whole but not wholly. Thus the animal is an organism; moreover, it is a sensitive organism.

Logical Parts. The parts signified by terms expressed in a definition are called logical parts, because they express man's understanding of an essence, or essential nature. In a DEFINITION composed of terms that signify the GENUS and the specific difference, the genus is part of the SPECIES because the species expresses the whole essence, whereas the genus expresses the virtual part that is determinable by the difference. Thus if man is defined as a tool-making animal, the term ''animal'' signifies the determinable part of the essence, or essential nature, of man, and the term ''tool-making'', understood radically, signifies the determining part, or specific difference in man. However, the species that are included in a genus are parts of the genus, called subjective parts, because the genus is the whole that includes the species, whether these are actual or merely in potency.

See Also: DISTINCTION, KINDS OF; DIVISION (LOGIC); ELEMENT; ATOMISM.

Bibliography: ARISTOTLE, *Metaphysics* 1023b 12–25. THOMAS AQUINAS, *Summa contra Gentiles* 2.72. V. MATHIEU, *Enciclopedia filosofica* (Venice-Rome 1957) 3:1171–72.

[W. H. KANE]

PARTE SAIZ, ALFREDO, BL.

Martyr, priest of the Order of Poor Clerics Regular of the Mother of God of the Pious Schools (Piarists); b June 1, 1899 in Cilleruelo de Bricia, Burgos, Spain; d. Dec. 27, 1936. Alfredo Parte was a priest from the Collegio Villacarriedo. In mid-August 1936, he fled to his uncle's home in Santander. On November 15 he was seized. He consoled his fellow prisoners and endured his suffering with patience until he was executed by gunfire. He was beatified on Oct. 1, 1995 by Pope John Paul II together with 12 other Piarists (*see* PAMPLONA, DIONISIO AND COMPANIONS, BB.).

Feast: Sept. 22.

Bibliography: ''Decreto Super Martyrio,'' *Acta Apostolicae Sedis* (1995): 651–656. *La Documentation Catholique* 2125 (5 November 1995): 924.

[L. GENDERNALIK/EDS.]

PARTICIPATION

In the Platonic tradition, where the notion was first systematically developed, participation (μέθεξις) signifies the derivation of temporal diversity from eternal unity, and the structural dependence of the many on the One. In Christian thought it means the complete dependence of creatures on the Creator in the order of efficient, exemplary, and final causality. Not only was the word commonly used by the Fathers and schoolmen, but the notion is fundamental to their entire thought.

Various Usages. In ordinary usage the word signifies a sharing or taking part in a common effort, glory, nature, or movement; thus in every order of causality one may ''share'' or ''take part'' in some whole (*pars,* part; and *capere,* take). As a transitive verb, it signifies the act of giving or communicating something to others, as when we say that God shares or participates His life, goodness, and truth with creatures. Ordinarily it is used in the intransitive sense of a subject ''having a part'' or ''taking part'' in some reality (physical, moral, or spiritual), as though a whole were somehow divided among many. In this sense it is said that Christ ''deigned to become partaker of our humanity'' (*Sacram. Leon.,* 159). The postclassical abstract noun designates the active and passive reality of sharing or communicating. In grammar the adjectival form of a verb called a participle similarly signifies a subject sharing some quality or situation (cf. Isidore, *Etymol.* 1.21.11; *Patrologia Latina* [Paris 1878–90] 82:88).

In philosophical usage the word is analogical, always involving a reference of many to one or one to many. ''To participate is to take a *quasi* part; thus when something receives a part of what belongs to another fully, it is said 'to share' it, just as man is said to share animality because he does not have the whole of animality exclusively; for the same reason Socrates shares humanity; similarly even a subject shares accidents, and matter shares form, because substantial or accidental form, which of its very nature is common, is limited to this or that subject; likewise an effect is said to participate in its cause, particularly when it does not equal the cause, as when we say that the air shares the light of the sun, because it does not receive light with the same brilliance that exists in the sun'' (St. Thomas, *In Boeth. de hebdom.* 2.24).

Origins with the Greeks. The philosophical notion of participation was used by PLATO to explain the relation between the contingent, individual forms and the eternal, unchangeable Ideas. ARISTOTLE attributes the origin of this doctrine to the Pythagoreans, who taught that all things exist by imitation (μίμησις) of numbers; for him, Plato simply introduced the new term participation (μέθεξις) and said that all things exist by participation, changing only the name. According to Aristotle, both the Pythagoreans and Plato left undecided what this participation or imitation of Forms could be (*Meta.* 987b 10–14). It is true that the doctrine of participation in the writings of Plato is undeveloped and includes all types of being involving any kind of dependence, likeness, coexistence, and the like.

History of the Concept

Already in the *Phaedo* things are said "to participate" (μετάσχεσις: 100C, 101C), "to receive" (μετάληψις: 102B), to be what they are by a "presence or communion" (παρουσία, κοινωνία: 100D; also *Rep.* 437E; *Soph.* 247A, 248C, E) or even by an "appertaining" (ἐπεῖναι, παραγιγνεσθαι: 103D, 105C; cf. *Symp.* 211B) of the "model" in which many participate (*Phaedo* 78D; cf. *Rep.* 476A, D; 496A; 507B). In this doctrine Plato saw the answer to Zeno's problem: if many things exist, they must simultaneously be similar and dissimilar, one and many, in motion and in rest (*Parm.* 127E); Plato's answer is that the "Ideas" do not combine with sensible things but exist per se "apart" (καθ'αὑτά: *Phaedo* 129D–130A).

Plato and Aristotle. According to Aristotle, who apparently is reporting the oral teaching of the master, between sensible things and separated Forms Plato placed mathematical beings, "which occupy an intermediate position, differing from sensible things in being eternal and unchangeable, from Forms in that there are many alike, while the Form itself is in each case unique" (*Meta.* 987b 15–18). For Plato the object of wisdom is the Idea as Exemplar (παράδειγμα), the Idea as "that which completely is" (τὸ παντελῶς ὄν) and therefore "perfectly knowable" (τὸ παντελῶς γνωστόν) as "the One among many" (τὸ ἓν ἐπὶ τῶν πολλῶν), thus permitting knowledge transcending the perception of transitory and corruptible things (τὸ νοεῖν τι φθαρίντος: *Soph.* 248E). In the *Dialogues* of his maturity Plato presents two orders of participation: that of sensible objects in ideal Forms, and that of Forms among themselves. This extension of the notion of participation to the ideal Forms themselves was important for the later development of philosophy, for it allows for various kinds of participation [μετέχειν δὲ πολλῶν οὐδέν κωλύει: *Parm.* 161A; cf. P. Natorp, *Platos Ideenlehre* (2d ed., Leipzig 1921) 231, 469–470].

One of the major difficulties inherent in the Platonic notion of participation, based as it is on the logico-mathematical relation of the universal to the particular, is the famous problem of the "third man" (τρίτος ἄνθρωπος) discussed by Plato (*Parm.* 132A, B) and urged by Aristotle (*Meta.* 990b 17 and 1059b 8): If similarity among many individuals presupposed a "form in itself,"

then the similarity of the many to the one presupposes another form, and so on (see the detailed argument in Alexander of Aphrodisia, *In meta.* 990a 15, ed. Hayduck, 83–85). For this and other reasons, Aristotle firmly and contemptuously rejected Platonic participation: "To say that they are patterns and that other things share them is to use empty words (κενολογεῖν) and poetical metaphors" (μεταφορὰς λέγειν ποιητικάς: *Meta.* 991a 20; cf. 1079a 4–13, 1079b 24–26).

In opposition to the Platonic imitation of a transcendent ideal, Aristotle insisted on the IMMANENCE of concrete forms and on the true CAUSALITY of particular causes on particular effects. Aristotle did not deny the existence of spiritual substances, intelligences, or souls in celestial bodies (*Cael.* 285a 29–30), but his insistence on physical causality distinguished his doctrine from Platonic participation. The apparent impasse was solved in two ways. Pure Aristotelians such as Alexander of Aphrodisias explained participation by means of causality, while Neoplatonists admitted the necessity of causality within the framework of participation. This latter approach was more influential in Christian thought.

Neoplatonic Teaching. The distinctive aim of NEOPLATONISM was to show the basic harmony between Plato and Aristotle, blaming Aristotle's critique on Plato's faulty expression through "poetic metaphors," "myths," etc. For pagan Neoplatonists it was important to demonstrate the overall harmony between the two outstanding Greek philosophers in order to defend the Greek ideal of wisdom against what they regarded as a barbaric religion founded on expiation for sin by the Crucifixion of Christ.

While faithful to the basic principle of Platonic participation, Neoplatonism transformed it in such a way as to make Aristotle's critique and principles its own. This harmony between Plato and Aristotle was already proclaimed by Ammonius, the teacher of Plotinus, who transcended apparent differences by his "intensive method" (Photius, *Bibl.* cod. 214; PG 103: 701A–708B). For the Latin West BOETHIUS proclaimed this same harmony (*In Arist. de interp.* 2, prol.; *Patrologia Latina* 64:433). In Arabic Neoplatonism the theme of agreement pervaded the whole of philosophy; for ALFARABI the difference between the two philosophers was simply one of method—Plato chose analysis, Aristotle synthesis—and Aristotle was seen as "the follower and perfecter, the help and consultor of Plato" [F. Dieterici, *Alfarabis philosophische Abhandlungen* (Leiden 1892) 3, 17–21].

Plotinus. PLOTINUS, the most eminent representative of Neoplatonism, clearly absorbs Aristotelian notions in his Platonic synthesis. In his celebrated doctrine of the three Hypostases (Mind, Soul, Life), Plotinus tried desperately to reduce the distance between transcendence and immanence. For him the νοῦς of Aristotle coincided with the ὄντως ὄν of Plato since the Mind, the supreme principle of the world, cogitates a multiplicity of Ideas, which are the eternal exemplars of all reality and true knowledge. This multiplicity of Ideas cannot be derived from the sensible world, but from Mind itself. Thus Plato's world of Ideas is localized by Plotinus in the νοῦς of Aristotle. The crucial problem of causality is solved by the doctrine of emanation (πρόοδος) by means of the WORLD soul, which fashions the world and everything in it according to the separated Ideas in Mind. Since for Plotinus the separated Ideas are endowed with specific quantities, qualities, movements, and rest, all sensible realities depend on the Ideas and derive from them their individual movements and appropriate changes of quantity and quality [cf. A. Covotti, *Da Aristotele ai Bizantini* (Naples 1935) 226–228]. *See* EMANATIONISM.

Proclus. More profoundly, the syncretist, Neoplatonic notion of participation revived the pre-Socratic notion of "dialectical method," which reached its widest application in PROCLUS. The novelty of this dialectic, explicitly introduced into the doctrine of participation, is the importance given to negation as the momentum of change, and consequently as the foundation of dialectics itself [cf. G. W. F. Hegel, *Geschichte der Philosphie*, ed. Michelet (Berlin 1833) 2.66]. These negations (ἀποφάσεις) were not considered privations of being, but productions of opposite determinations, as sketched in Plato's *Parmenides*. Proclus maintained that "the method of negations (τρέπος τῶν ἀποφάσεων) has an unusual character; it conforms to the dignity of the One; its function is primary; it far transcends all things in the unknowable and ineffable excellence of simplicity" (*Theologia Platonis*, 2.10). The work of Proclus marks the high point in the speculative synthesis of Plato and Aristotle, replacing the negative attitude of Alexander (see the explicit statement of Simplicius, *In 3 de caelo*, 7.306a 1).

In general it can be said that Arabic Neoplatonism and AUGUSTINIANISM developed the common, intuitive notion of participation ascending toward the One; it stemmed from the traditions of Plotinus and Porphyry. The Thomistic notion of participation, on the other hand, is directly inspired by the more rigorous dialectical method, which stemmed from IAMBLICHUS and Proclus through PSEUDO-DIONYSIUS and the small Arabic work entitled *LIBER DE CAUSIS* .

Thomistic Notion

From the beginning St. THOMAS AQUINAS appreciated the radical difference between Platonic and Aristotelian principles. Rejecting the Neoplatonic concordism prevalent in medieval Augustinianism and Arabic writers, he developed a precise notion of participation based upon a new concept of *esse* as the *actus essendi*, not to be confused with the *existentia* of Augustinianism and RATIONALISM. It is from the concept of *esse* as the ultimate act that St. Thomas developed his notion of participation and his entire metaphysics (*see* EXISTENCE).

Basic Elements. The most important elements in the Thomistic notion of participation include the concepts of act, of the unicity of the substantial form, of the personal individuality of the human soul, and of the real distinction between essence and *esse,* or act of being, in creatures.

Concept of Act. Aquinas's starting point is the Aristotelian concept of ACT as perfection *in se* and *per se.* Thus by its very nature act is prior to POTENCY, whether it is understood as activity or as FORM. St. Thomas accepted this "primacy of act" without reservation, and rejected the attempt of AVICEBRON to reduce everything to potency instead of to act. Because of this new concept of act as perfection, the affirmation of BEING, there arose a new and wider concept of potency as capacity to receive perfection, i.e., negation as PRIVATION. Two important consequences follow from this for St. Thomas: (1) Potency is not a univocal concept signifying prime matter alone, but an analogical concept embracing all the ways a thing can be a subject of act: "Being a subject is not peculiar to the matter that is part of substance, but is a universal property of all potentiality" (*De subs. sep.* 8). (2) Prime matter, being exclusively a "subject," can have no act whatever of its own; all its actuality stems from form so that not even God can make matter exist without form (*Quodl.* 3.1.1). (*See* MATTER AND FORM).

Unicity of Substantial Form. The second element in the Thomistic metaphysics of participation follows from this new concept of act and potency: the unicity of substantial form in all bodies, living and nonliving. In man this unique substantial form is his intellectual soul. For St. Thomas a "plurality of forms," even hierarchically ordered from lowest (*forma corporeitatis*) to the highest (*forma intellectiva*), would destroy the essential unity of act in man; all acts after the first could be nothing but accidental forms. This view was fiercely contested during St. Thomas's lifetime, because it seemed to deny that Christ's dead body continued to be divine when separated from a permanent form; but for St. Thomas divinity and identity were due not to form, but to the Person of the Word who continued to be united hypostatically to both body and soul (*Quodl.* 2.2.1 and ad 1). In St. Thomas's view, the single form in man is responsible not only for the spiritual functions of thinking and willing, but also for the lower functions of sensation, nutrition, and natural motions (*Summa Theologiae* 1a, 76.3–5). Thus the higher form is said to contain the lower forms virtually. (*See* FORMS, UNICITY AND PLURALITY OF.)

Individuality of the Soul. The third element in the Thomistic metaphysics of participation is the personal individuality of the human SOUL and its functions. This rejection of the principal Averroist tenet is developed under two aspects: (1) Phenomenologically, one's consciousness, thoughts, aspirations, desires, and loves are seen to be personal functions, belonging to a concrete, individual person. (2) Metaphysically, the ground of this phenomenon is seen to be none other than the personal intellectual soul (first act), which is the root of human activity (second act). The immateriality of certain personal functions, such as thinking and aspiring, indicates that the personal soul has an immaterial *esse* proper to it and inseparable from it: "*Esse* properly belongs to the form, which is act . . . . But it is impossible that a form be separated from itself; therefore it is impossible that a subsistent form should cease to be" (*Summa Theologiae* 1a, 75.6; 50.5).

Essence and Esse. The fourth element in the Thomistic metaphysics of participation is the real distinction in all created things between essence and the act of being (*esse*). This fundamental Thomistic insight, originally derived from Boethius and AVICENNA, was eventually seen as a consequence of the primacy of act in participation. This is seen in two stages: (1) Being (*esse*) is the first perfection and the act of all acts (*ibid.* 1a, 4.1 ad 3, 2); pure perfection (*perfectio separata*) cannot be anything but unique; subsisting being must be one, namely God, whose essence is to be. (2) All creatures, whose essence is not to be, must participate or share existence as a gift; thus all creatures are beings (*entia*) by participation. In this view essence is a subject, a potentiality for *esse,* which is the sublime reality shared by many as a gift from God. With this view of participation, St. Thomas could reject Augustinianism, which made matter essential for creatures, and Averroism, which made immaterial substances (intelligences) independent of God's creative and sustaining act. Finally, this participation is the basis for the Thomistic doctrine of ANALOGY between God and creatures, for just as God is being by essence (*per essentiam*), so creatures are being by participation (*per participationem:* see *Summa Theologiae* 1a, 4.3 ad 3). In St. Thomas's conception, *esse* is no longer an accident, as Avicenna thought, but the immanent act of substance, and the proper effect of God alone (*Quodl.* 12.5.1).

Kinds of Participation. Some Thomists (e.g., L. B. Geiger) believe that St. Thomas developed two notions of participation, each distinct: (1) Participation by similitude (*secundum similitudinem*), in which participated beings diversely reflect, mirror, or symbolize the reality

participated. (2) Participation by composition (*secundum compositionem*), in which a subject shares, or has, the participated characteristic, e.g., *esse*. In this view creatures not only participate in *esse* by composition, but the very composite is a "similitude" reflecting God.

Static Structure of Being. Other Thomists, rejecting this interpretation of the Thomistic synthesis, prefer to see in St. Thomas's doctrine of participation a complete dissolution (the Hegelian *Aufhebung*) of the Platonic-Aristotelian tension. For these, *esse* as the act of all acts must be distinguished not only from essence, but also from existence in the Kantian sense. In order to preserve the theory of *actus essendi,* they prefer to divide participation initially into transcendental and predicamental: the first type concerns *esse* and its transcendental attributes; the second concerns univocal formalities of GENUS with respect to SPECIES, and species with respect to individuals. Transcendental participation of *esse* has already been mentioned; it is the second that needs special consideration because of its Aristotelian roots. It is true, as Aristotle says, that genera and species are predicated of subjects essentially (*per essentiam*) and not by participation (*per participationem*). However, a genus is differently realized and actualized in the various species according to different degrees of participated perfection (cf. Fabro, *La nozione metafisica di participazione,* 161). Thus while genera and species may be logically predicated as univocal and essential attributes, in the physical order they must be considered as potestative wholes, capable of being shared unequally according to different degrees of perfection. Predicamentally even individual men participate in human nature (see text of *In Boeth. de hebdom.* 2.24, quoted above). St. Thomas speaks about predicamental participation when he says, "Just as this individual man participates in human nature, so every created being participates, if I may say so, in the nature of being (*naturam essendi*), since only God is His *esse*" (*Summa Theologiae* 1a, 45.5 ad 1; cf. *C. gent.* 1.32; *Quodl.* 2.2.1). Thus in a static or structural consideration of beings, transcendental participation is the real composition of subject and *esse,* while predicamental participation is the real composition of matter and form in essence, and substance and accident in general.

Causal Participation. Parallel to this static consideration of being, one must consider the dynamic or causal order. Causal participation is likewise twofold: transcendental and predicamental. Causal transcendental participation is the production of the common *esse* of all creatures by creation (*De pot.* 3.5 ad 1–2; *De ver.* 21.5 ad 5–6). *Esse* is the proper effect of divine causality (CREATION and divine CONSERVATION), and it is in virtue of this direct production of *esse* that God works immediately on every created cause. Causality as predicamental participation, on the other hand, is concerned with *fieri* or BECOMING in the order of genera and species. Here the pertinent principle is "form gives *esse*" (*forma dat esse*), which seems to invert the causal relationship discovered in the transcendental order. However, the principle has two meanings: (1) substantial form bestows formal and constitutive *esse*, inasmuch as it confers a specific kind of being; (2) substantial form as formal act of the essence is the true subject of the *actus essendi* (*C. gent.* 2.54). Thus form is the predicamental mediator between God and the existing finite being (cf. Fabro, *Participation et causalité*, 344–362). From this it follows that in all the actions of creatures, even the free actions of men, God intimately operates in all things as the universal First Cause of all being and all activity. Creatures, however, participate in this causality only on condition that they likewise remain true and responsible causes of action.

Extension of Participation. To the extent that participation allows one to conceive the universe as a reflection of divine ideas or exemplars, one may speak of participation by similitude. The EXEMPLARY causality of immaterial forms on material forms is expressed by Boethius (*De trin.* 2), while Pseudo-Dionysius refers to the exemplars of all existing things as preexisting in the mind of God (*De div. nom.* 5.8; *Patrolgia Graeca* 3:824). But here again participation by similitude must be considered in both the transcendental and the predicamental orders. Transcendentally this similitude exists in the relation of dependence of FINITE being on the Infinite (*see* INFINITY). In the predicamental order this similitude can be seen in the universal affinity all beings have for each other. Thus lower beings tend to approach the more perfect as though they participated in their perfections. This ontological affinity, which orders the entire cosmos, can be expressed as the principle of the metaphysical continuity of beings, which St. Thomas borrows directly from Pseudo-Dionysius: "Divine wisdom joins the highest of the lower to the lowest of the higher" (*De div. nom.* 7.3; *Patrologia Graeca* 3:872; cf. Proclus, *Elem. theol.*, prop. 147, ed. Dodds, 128).

In view of this principle, all created knowledge can be seen in terms of participation. Thus angelic intuitive knowledge of itself resembles (by participation) divine intuition, while through infused species it participates in all other things (*Summa Theologiae* 1a, 56.2; *De subs. sep.* 13). Similarly, human intuitive knowledge of FIRST PRINCIPLES resembles angelic "intellection," while man's more characteristic knowledge is REASONING, whereby he reaches out to all other reality. Even the highest of the sense faculties, the COGITATIVE POWER, participates in rationality and in a certain freedom (*ibid.* 1a, 78.4 ad 5; *In 3 anim.* 13.397). Likewise, sense appetites participate in rationality and freedom when they obey the order of right reason (*In 3 sent.* 35.1.1.4; *Summa Theologiae* 2a2ae, 47.5 ad 1); this participation is realized through moral VIRTUE.

From this principle of the metaphysical continuity of all being also emerges a conception of the world as an orderly solidarity of all things (*De ver.* 16.1). This continuity, imperfectly realized in the static structure of being, reaches its fullness when beings reach their ultimate goals through activity. For man this ultimate goal is the dynamic, supernatural union with God that is possible only through GRACE, which is a participation in the life and powers of God as He is in Himself. "Only a rational creature is capable of God (*capax Dei*) in this way, because he alone can know and love God explicitly" (*De ver.* 22.2 ad 5); for this reason "only rational creatures have an immediate directedness to God" (*Summa Theologiae* 2a2ae, 2.3). Consequently, because man's spirit is infinitely receptive, he cannot find complete happiness in anything that is good only by participation, but can find it only in Him who is goodness *per essentiam* (*ibid.* 1a2ae, 3.7). This is eternal beatitude. The highest and most sublime participation ever willed by God is the personal union of the Word with human nature in Christ. As "a partaker of our human nature" God not only renewed the whole human race (ἀνακεφαλαίωρις), but He also gave men the power to become partakers of divinity through the grace of Christ.

Participation and Analogy. The Platonic theory of vertical imitation and the Aristotelian theory of horizontal causality of universals on particulars tend to emphasize formal univocity, while the true language of participation is necessarily that of analogy. The Thomistic notion of participation, founded in *esse* as supreme intensive act, makes it possible to pass from finite to Infinite Being through analogical discourse. Since the foundation of all analogical language is participation, the three basic types of analogy are discussed here in terms of participation.

Analogy of Proportionality. Basically this analogy, whether proper or metaphorical, is a proportion of two or more proportions, for example, accidents are to their being proportionately what substance is to its being. Despite the radical difference between SUBSTANCE and ACCIDENT, there is a certain proportional similarity that allows us to use one predicate of both analogically. The basis of this proportional similarity is the fact that all accidents participate in the being (*esse*) of substance. Thus while the formal, logical structure of this kind of analogy is simply relations of SIMILARITY, its root is actual dependence and participation. In the wider, transcendental order, all creatures have their *esse* by participation from God, *Ipsum Esse Subsistens*. Consequently the analogical proportionality between the goodness of God and the goodness of creatures, the wisdom of God and the wisdom of creatures, and the like, is based on the fact of transcendental participation, which is the basis also for predicamental participation (composition of substance and accidents, matter and form). It is this static analogy of proportionality that is expressed in the tension of similarity-dissimilarity according to the Platonic view of the vertical "fall" of beings. Moreover, it is precisely through this static analogy of proportionality that beings obtain the proper consistency of *esse,* each in its own way, since each being is actuated by the proper act of participated *esse.* For St. Thomas—in keeping with the demands of Heidegger—the difference between to be and to exist is founded on being, as intensive emergent act, that is diversely shared by each being.

Analogy of Attribution. In contrast to static analogy of proportions, analogy of intrinsic attribution is dynamic in that it is based on causality and dependency. In analogy of attribution, a term that properly belongs to one subject, for example, healthy in body, is attributed to other subjects because of some causal dependence, for example, healthy apples, healthy medicine, and so on. In the analogy of being, *esse* properly belongs to God alone, but it is predicated of creatures because God creates and conserves the *esse* of each creature. This analogy is called intrinsic attribution because each creature really does have being intrinsically, even though it is from another. Analogy of attribution emphasizes the "otherness" of the characteristic participated. Thus creatures are being only by participation (*ens per participationem*), and accidents are being only by participation. In this way analogy of proportionality presupposes analogy of attribution in the existential order. For this reason analogy of attribution culminates metaphysical investigation in resolving the many to the One, the diverse to the All. While PANTHEISM denies the TRANSCENDENCE of God, either by reducing God to creatures or by identifying creatures with God, the metaphysics of St. Thomas maintains the transcendence of God above all creatures and at the same time recognizes His IMMANENCE in participated being. In fact, only a doctrine of participation can maintain both His transcendence and His immanence.

Analogy of Inequality. The analogy of inequality within genera and species, as has been explained, is founded on predicamental participation. While the logician considers genera and species to be univocal abstractions, the realist sees that a genus is differently realized in the various species; that is, the perfection of the genus is unequally shared by the various species within a given genus. This inequality of participation is the indispensable condition for multiplicity of species, just as the indispensable condition for multiplicity of individuals is the divisibility of matter. Thus from the formal point of view, a generic definition is univocally predicated of various subjects, but from the existential point of view, these subjects participate unequally in the full perfection (cf. *Summa Theologiae* 1a2ae, 88.1 ad 1; *C. gent.* 1.32).

See Also: BEING; EXISTENCE; EMANATIONISM; IMMANENCE; TRANSCENDENCE; ACT; CAUSALITY; ANALOGY.

Bibliography: C. FABRO, *La nozione metafisica di partecipazione secondo S. Tomaso d'Aquino* (3d ed. rev. and enl. Turin 1964); *Participation et causalité selon S. Thomas d'Aquin* (Louvain 1961). L. B. GEIGER, *La Participation dans la philosophie de S. Thomas d'Aquin* (Paris 1942). R. J. HENLE, *Saint Thomas and Platonism* (The Hague 1956). *De Thomistische Participatienleeren* (Nijmegen 1944). J. DE FINANCE, *Être et agir dans la philosophie de saint Thomas* (Paris 1945). P. KLUBERTANZ, *St. Thomas Aquinas on Analogy* (Chicago, Ill. 1960). J. MUNDHENK, *Die Begriffe der "Teilhabe" und des "Lichts" in der Psychologie und Erkenntnislehre des Thomas von Aquin* (Würzburg 1935). G. SÖHNGEN, "Thomas von Aquin über Teilhabe durch Berührung," *Die Einheit in der Theologie* (Munich 1952). K. KRENN, *Vermittlung und Differenz?* (Rome 1962). F. ULRICH, *Homo Abyssus* (Einsiedeln 1961). L. OEING-HANHOFF, *Ens et unum convertuntur* (Münster 1953). A. HAYEN, *L'Intentionnel dans la philosophie de saint Thomas* (Brussels 1942). G. SIEWERTH, *Der Thomismus als Identitätsystem* (2d ed. Frankfurt 1961). E. J. SCHELLER, *Das Priestertum Christi im Anschluss an den hl. Thomas von Aquin* (Paderborn 1934).

[C. FABRO]

PASCAL, BLAISE

Mathematician, Christian apologist; b. Clermont-en-Auvergne, June 19, 1623; d. Paris, Aug. 19, 1662. Despite his brief life and incomplete work, Pascal was one of the most universal geniuses of modern France and a singularly novel and profound interpreter of the Christian conscience. In him life and thought were intimately commingled: the witness of the man is no less significant than the message of his work.

Pascal's life can be thought of as a drama in which three principles confront each other: science, the world, and God. His genius first became apparent through science. Deprived of maternal care at the age of three, he was brought up with admirable devotion and competence by his father, Etienne, a mathematician of genuine ability, who, in order to devote himself more fully to the education of this son and two daughters, Gilberte and Jacqueline, gave up his post as magistrate of Clermont-Ferrand to move to Paris in 1631. In the capital, Blaise, whose mathematical genius manifested itself at an early age, was soon able to take part in the discussions of those savants who gathered around Father Mersenne. In 1639 Pascal wrote his *Essai pour les coniques,* a widely acclaimed treatise in which he demonstrated a remarkable new property of conic sections.

From 1640 to 1647 Pascal lived at Rouen, where Richelieu had appointed his father administrator. Here Pascal invented his famous arithmetical machine, the first known mechanical calculator, an achievement by which he showed himself as competent in technical matters as he was in pure science. His machine enjoyed considerable success, not only among the savants, but with the general public as well, and made him famous.

First Conversion. From his father Blaise had received a thorough, though not very fervent, religious education. In 1646 the young man was exposed to the revelation of a much more demanding Christianity. Several disciples of Jean du Vergier, Abbé of Saint Cyran (d. 1643), lived in the vicinity of Rouen, and Pascal became acquainted with their austere doctrine which advocated, primarily, the necessity of "conversion"—an abandonment of the world and submission to God. He accepted this demand enthusiastically, became a convert himself, and won his family over to his point of view. He woke to the fact that he genuinely relished one of the most dangerous of worldly enticements, fame, and resolved forthwith to abandon the sciences, the means by which he had won renown.

This resolution, however, was not immediately reduced to practice. Pascal continued his research and plunged into physics in an effort to interpret the famous experiment of Torricelli. Through some original, most ingenious experiments, he demonstrated the existence of the vacuum and the weight of air. At the same time he advanced the principles of a truly modern scientific philosophy based on primary reliance on the experiment; through him came the final break between true science and metaphysics.

Meanwhile, stricken by a serious illness, the young savant returned to Paris in 1647. His doctors had recommended diversions—advice which was, indirectly, the cause of some relaxation of his religious discipline. Worldliness again gained ground in his mind, and he began again to frequent the "world." He attached himself principally to a nobleman, the Duc de Roannez, through whom he made the acquaintance of two very charming men, the Chevalier de Méré and Mitton. They became the models for his "emancipated free-thinker" of the *Pensées*, and though he turned away from them, they had taught him much—they made him taste of MONTAIGNE, and they convinced him that the science of man was of far greater importance than the science of things.

During this time Pascal continued his scientific labors and established the foundations of the calculus of probabilities. But neither science nor the world could satisfy this soul so enamored of the absolute. In 1654 his sister Jacqueline, who had become a religious in the

Blaise Pascal.

Convent at PORT-ROYAL, privately heard him confess his confusion and understood immediately that, for the second time, he had become a convert. The famous and brilliantly written *Mémorial* recalls the intense religious experience that resulted, during the night of November 23, 1654, in the revelation of the living God.

Second Conversion and Port-Royal. Through this second conversion Pascal found himself intimately linked with the theologians and recluses of Port-Royal. He traveled there repeatedly for retreats, and the one of January 1655 gave rise to the *Entretien avec M. de Sacy sur Epictète et Montaigne*. A similar period of prayer the following year made him decide to embark on *Les Provinciales* (*Lettres écrites par Louis de Montalte à un provincial*), the masterpiece of the great mass of pamphlet literature brought out by the Jansenist controversies. (*See* JANSENISM.) At the same time Pascal remained in touch with his fashionable friends, trying to win them over to his views. He succeeded in the case of the Duc de Roannez, and addressed some remarkable letters to the duke's sister, Mlle. de Roannez (1656). It was in thinking about Méré and Mitton that Pascal conceived his project of an apologetic for the Christian religion, to be directed toward the unbelievers, for which the *Pensées* form the rough draft.

Although he had given up the sciences on his conversion in 1654, Pascal returned to them in 1658 at the urgent request of friends who persuaded him that publication of a worthwhile discovery would add weight to the arguments of his apologetic. Thus it was that he published (1658) some investigations on the curve called *roulette,* or cycloid, that provided the foundations for differential and integral calculus. But this episode was unique; following it Pascal withdraw from all lay activity. His illness, which returned in 1659 and from which he would never again be free, prohibited from that moment on any mental effort. His only writing of this period, a "Prayer asking God to make good use of his illness," expresses an ardent desire for a conversion still more perfect. In his last years Pascal accomplished one final spiritual ascension, which, reaching its culmination during the course of a terrible agony, brought him to a sort of sainthood.

Significance of his Work. He left a diversified life's work touching on the sciences, philosophy, theology, and spirituality, but at the same time extending beyond them because it was the work of neither a savant nor a specialist, but of a man gifted with a winning personality and a mind of profound insight. He owed to science his rigorous regard for truth, based on geometric reasoning or the experimental method, but he had come quickly to the conclusion that science was powerless to discern the condition of humanity, to fix the objectives of human life—in a word, powerless to attain those truths essential to man. One may properly say that the two fundamental traits of Pascal's mind were the strict demands of the absolute and the need of a living truth.

It is not surprising that he fervently embraced the Christian message, especially in the form in which it was made known to him. A devout Catholic, Pascal at the same time adhered to the thought of Port-Royal, that one need not be too rigid in the formulation of theological propositions, and as a fervent Augustinian, he believed that in the domain of religion knowledge is inseparable from love. The certainties of faith are not grasped through reason, but through the heart, the mainspring of love, which submits to revealed truth and fosters its manifestation. (*See* AUGUSTINIANISM.)

From this conviction springs the deep feeling of the *Provinciales.* If Pascal grappled with the "casuistry" of the Jesuits, it was not because he was ignorant of certain difficulties and the necessity of resolving them, but because he wished to use only the light of revelation and not that of a reason corrupted by the Fall, which tends, understandably, to define duty as a function of self-interest. He was hostile to any compromise between humanism and Christianity, and refused to place any faith in a human nature sustained only by its own strength.

The impotence of man's reason is no less clearly set forth in the Pensées. Granted that impotence, how can the verities of Christianity be demonstrated? As a matter of fact, Pascal does not propose a rational demonstration. If the reason is too weak to achieve the absolute, it is at least strong enough to prove "that there are an infinite number of things which surpass it." It can realize the contradiction of man—his weakness and his nobility—but it cannot explain them; only revelation can resolve the problems imposed by the reason. In addition, reason can grasp revelation as a historical fact surrounded by certain wonderful events that guarantee its supernatural character. The method of the physician, who from some facts arrives at an explanatory hypothesis, is equally applicable to apologetics.

Through his sensitivity to the human drama, and the exalted ideal he propounded of a religion that rejects any compromise with worldly standards of value, Pascal impregnated his work with a ferment whose power is far from being exhausted.

Bibliography: *Oeuvres complètes,* ed. L. BRUNSCHVICG and P. L. BOUTROUX, 14 v. (Paris 1904–14); *Pensées,* ed. L. LAFUMA, 3 v. (Paris 1951). J. MESNARD, *Pascal: His Life and Works,* tr. G. S. FRASER (London 1952). M. L. HUBERT, *Pascal's Unfinished Apology: A Study of His Plan* (New Haven 1952). A. MAIRE, *Bibliographie générale des oeuvres de Blaise Pascal,* 5 v. (Paris 1925–27).

[J. MESNARD]

PASCENDI

Encyclical letter of PIUS X (Sept. 8, 1907), which, along with the Holy Office's decree *LAMENTABILI* and the Oath against MODERNISM, forms the basis of the Church's condemnation of Modernism. Presenting a logical synthesis, not found wholly in any one Modernist's work, *Pascendi* emphasized root tendencies and principles. Successively it considered various roles of the Modernist.

As philosopher the Modernist proposed an agnosticism that limited all knowledge to phenomena and a vital immanence that made religion, revelation, and faith simply a sense springing from the collective subconscious and the Church its product apart from historical events. As believer he resorted to an intuition of the heart to find the divine reality. DOGMA he considered a series of secondary symbolic formulas that must be continually adjusted to the religious sense. As theologian he postulated an immanence that often savored of pantheism. As historical critic he based his work on a concealed philosophy of vital immanence. *Pascendi* termed Modernism "the synthesis of all heresies." The encyclical concluded with a list of disciplinary measures to be taken in the training of priests and in the censoring of written works.

The various statements of the encyclical should be interpreted in the context of its major preoccupation, which is to condemn (1) agnosticism, both in natural theology and in the symbolic, nonobjective approach to dogmatic content; (2) vital immanence, an exclusive immanence of the divine and a consequent natural, vital evolution of revelation; (3) total emancipation of exegesis from dogma and of political-religious movements from ecclesiastical authority.

Bibliography: PIUS X, ''Pascendi dominici gregis'' (encyclical, Sept. 8, 1907) *Acta Sanctorum Sedis* 40 (1907) 593–650, Eng. *All Things in Christ*, ed. V. A. YZERMANS (Westminster, Md. 1954). J. RIVIÉRE, *Le Modernisme dans l'Église* (Paris 1929). A. FARGES and J. LEBRETON, *Dictionnaire apologétique de la foi catholique*, ed. A. P. ALÈS (Paris 1911–22) 3:637–695. H. STIRNIMANN, *Lexicon für Theologie und Kirche*, ed. J. HOFER and K. RAHNER (Freiburg 1957–65) 8:126–127.

[J. J. HEANEY]

PASCHAL, ANTIPOPE

Pontificate: 687. Nothing is known of archdeacon Paschal until he attempts to bribe the imperial exarch at Ravenna into confirming his election as successor to Pope Conon (686–7). At this time, since the Roman church was still part of the empire, it was customary for papal elections to be ratified by the emperor's administrator in Ravenna. This exarch, John Platyn, agreed to support Paschal, but the election was contested by the military aristocracy, which put forward the archpriest Theodore (Antipope, 687) as its candidate. Both rivals occupied the Lateran palace between October and December 687. The stalemate was ended after a meeting of city officials, clergy, and leaders of the militia. They elected Sergius I (687–701) as a compromise candidate, and he was forcibly installed in the Lateran. Theodore recognized the new pope (who would eventually be named a saint), but Paschal remained obstinate and complained to the exarch. John Platyn soon appeared in Rome, but seeing the broad support for Sergius, he ratified his election. For his part, Paschal continued to oppose Sergius, attempting to replace him. Soon Paschal was tried and imprisoned in a monastery, where he died in 692.

Bibliography: L. DUCHESNE, ed. *Liber Pontificalis* (Paris 1886–92; repr. 1955–57) 1.369–72, 377; 3.343. P. JAFFÉ, *Regesta pontificum Romanorum* (Leipzig 1885–88; repr. Graz 1956) 1.243. J. RICHARDS, *The Popes and the Papacy in the Early Middle Ages, 476–752* (London 1979) 206–8, 266, 274. J. N. D. KELLY, *The Oxford Dictionary of Popes* (New York 1986) 82. G. SCHWAIGER, *Lexikon des Mittelalters* (Munich 1993) 6.1753.

[P. M. SAVAGE]

PASCHAL I, POPE, ST.

Pontificate: Jan. 24, 817 to Feb. 11, 824. Little is known of Paschal's life before he became Pope, except that he was of Roman origin, was educated at the papal curia, was ordained to the priesthood, and was appointed abbot of the monastery of St. Stephen Major. Perhaps during part of his early career he played a role in papal administration. The surviving evidence suggests that his election to the papal office had general support in Rome.

At the time of Paschal I's election there remained a variety of unanswered questions about the relationship between the Pope and the Papal States and the recently created western Roman emperor and his empire. During the last years of his reign CHARLEMAGNE (768–814) had done little to clarify that issue; neither had the tumultuous pontificate of Pope LEO III (795–816) contributed to a solution. Apparently concerned about his relationship with the Franks, one of Paschal's first actions as Pope was to establish communications with Emperor LOUIS I THE PIOUS (814–840), who had assumed the imperial office less that three years earlier and had already shown signs of moving in new directions in his political and religious policy. Paschal dispatched two letters to Louis. The first sought to explain the circumstances surrounding his election and consecration, which had occurred without the involvement of the emperor. This enigmatic letter seems to reflect uncertainty about the role of the western emperor in papal elections and a strong desire on the part of Paschal to avoid any sign of impropriety with respect to the emperor. The second requested that Louis renew the friendship pact that had existed between the papacy and the Carolingian rulers since the time of King PEPIN III (751–768) and reconfirm the territorial concessions granted to the papacy by Pepin III and Charlemagne. Again the pope seemed anxious to define the boundaries of the Papal States and to clarify its role in the Carolinian empire. Louis responded promptly by issuing in 817 a document called the *Pactum Ludovicianum* which set forth in writing the terms that Louis and Pope STEPHEN IV (V) (816–817), Paschal's immediate predecessor, had agreed upon during their meeting in 816. Although the authenticity of this important document has been challenged many times by modern historians, it is now generally accepted as authentic in its main provisions. The *Pactum* renewed the friendship pact between the papacy and the Franks and confirmed the exact territories and patrimonies that pertained to the papacy in a way that sanctioned papal claims to a large part of Italy. Louis recognized papal sovereignty in administrative and judicial functions in the Papal States, except in cases where the Pope asked for imperial assistance or where inhabitants of the Papal States who claimed to be oppressed sought justice from the emperor. The emperor pledged to protect

Christic with Saints by the Jordan River, Church of St. Prassede, Rome. Pope Paschal I, the donor of the mosaic and restorer of the 5th century church is at left holding model of the church.

the Papal State and to allow complete freedom of papal elections. The generous terms of the *Pactum Ludovicianum* have sometimes been interpreted as an instance where Louis' misdirected piety led to undue concessions to the Church at the expense of the secular authority. In reality, the *Pactum* represented an important step in formally integrating the Papal States into the structure of the Carolingian Empire in a manner that gave to that entity and its ruler, the Pope, a privileged place, immune for the most part from outside interference.

During most of Paschal I's pontificate the *Pactum Ludovicianum* served as a workable arrangement governing papal-Frankish relationships. When Louis the Pious enacted his famous *Ordinatio imperii* of 817, which arranged for his succession in terms aimed at preserving the unity of the Carolingian empire rather than observing the Frankish tradition of dividing the realm among all male heirs, Paschal I gave his approval. Paschal I responded

to Louis I's request that he lend papal support to the missionary effort of EBBO, archbishop of Reims, in Denmark by providing Ebbo with a letter that designated him papal legate to the mission field in the North. In 821 Paschal sent legates bearing gifts to celebrate the marriage of LO-THAIR I, heir to the imperial title. In 823 the Pope welcomed Lothair I to Rome and bestowed on him the crown of the kingdom of Italy and the title emperor; although Louis I had already designated Lothair I as co-emperor in 817, Paschal's act reinforced the idea that papal participation was necessary to legitimate assumption of the imperial crown.

During most of his pontificate Paschal was in full control of affairs in the Papal States with little interference from either Emperor Louis I or his surrogate in Italy, Lothair I. Little is known about papal activity during these years. Paschal I gave some attention to the renewal of ICONOCLASM by the eastern emperor, LEO V

(813–820), a matter drawn to his attention chiefly by the appeals of THEODORE THE STUDITE, the leader of the considerable anti-iconoclastic forces opposing Emperor Leo V in the East. Theodore's appeals were couched in terms that recognized the Pope as the ultimate source of orthodox doctrine. Aside from welcoming victims of persecution in the eastern empire, Paschal wrote letters denouncing the iconoclasm of Leo V and his successor, Michael II (820–829). Papal condemnation was a factor in sustaining the opposition within the Eastern empire. Paschal also gave considerable attention to rebuilding and redecorating churches in Rome, continuing the policy of transforming the physical appearance of the city begun by his predecessors during the eighth century.

Despite the appearance of calm surrounding affairs during most of Paschal I's pontificate, all was not well. Bits of information scattered through the record suggest a rising tide of opposition to his administration of the Papal States. The opposition came chiefly from the Roman secular nobility, who were increasingly unhappy with the clerical control of the Papal States. In 822 the appearance of co-emperor Lothair I in Italy triggered a crisis, which came to a head in 823 when two high officials in the papal administration were put to death, apparently because they headed a faction in Rome favorable to Lothair I. Their pro-Frankish position raised doubts about their loyalty to Paschal I. Although Paschal sent a letter to Louis claiming his innocence, supporters of the victims brought him a version of events in Rome that implicated Paschal I in the murders. The emperor decided to send envoys to investigate, but before the imperial inquest could be completed the Pope appeared before the imperial envoys and many bishops and swore an oath of purgation vowing he was innocent of any wrongdoing. He was following the example set by Pope Leo III in 800 in a similar situation. Louis was momentarily satisfied with Paschal I's denial of culpability; the Pope's death soon after ended further inquiry into his conduct. But apparently Louis I soon became convinced that the situation in Rome required a closer examination of the relationship between Pope and emperor. It was redefined during the pontificate of Paul I's successor, Pope Eugenius II (824–827), in the *Constitutio Romana* of 824, which provided for more imperial control over papal administration and papal elections than had prevailed before. In a sense, the end result of Paschal I's pontificate was tighter integration of the Papal States into the Carolingian empire through the imposition of severe limitations on the independence of the Pope as ruler of the Papal States. This consequence probably should not be construed as an antipapal action on the part of Louis the Pious. Rather, it was another facet of the emperor's effort to unify the Christian community into a single *imperium Christianum* in which spiritual and secular leaders could act in accord to realize God's will.

Feast: May 14.

See Also: CAROLINGIAN DYNASTY; CAROLINGIAN REFORM; STATES OF THE CHURCH.

Bibliography: *Le Liber Pontificalis*, ed. L. DUCHESNE, 3 v., 2nd ed. (Paris 1955–1957) 2:52–68, English translation as *The Lives of the Ninth-Century Popes (Liber Pontificalis). The Ancient Biographies of Ten Popes from A.D. 817–891*, trans. with intro. and notes by R. DAVIS, Translated Texts for Historians 20 (Liverpool 1995) 1–30. *Regesta Pontificum Romanorum ab condita ecclesia ad annum post Christum MCXCVIII*, ed. P. JAFFÉ, 2 v., 2nd ed. (Leipzig 1885–1888) 1:318–320. *Annales regni Francorum*, a. 817–824, ed. F. KURZE, Monumenta Germaniae Historica, Scriptores rerum Germanicarum in usum scholarum (Hannover 1895; reprinted, 1989) 145–164, English translation in *Carolingian Chronicles: Royal Frankish Annals and Nithard's Histories*, trans. B. W. SCHOLZ (Ann Arbor, Mich. 1970) 101–115. *Theganus, Gesta Hludowici Imperatoris*, chs. 18 and 30, and *Astronomus, Vita Hludowici Imperatoris*, chs. 27, 34, 36, and 37, both in *Thegan, Die Taten Kaiser Ludwigs; Astronomus, Das Leben Kaiser Ludwigs*, ed. and trans. E. TREMP, Monumenta Germaniae Historica, Scriptores rerum Germanicarum in usum scholarum 64 (Hannover 1995) 200, 218, 372, 402, 414, 418–420, an English translation of the passage from the Astronomer in *Son of Charlemagne. A Contemporary Life of Louis the Pious*, chs. 27, 34, 36, 37, trans. with intro. and notes A. CABANISS (Syracuse, N.Y. 1964) 62, 71, 75, 76–77. *Capitularia regum Francorum*, ed. A. BORETIUS and V. KRAUSE, 2 v., Monumenta Germaniae Historica, Leges, Sectio II (Hannover 1893–1897; reprinted, 1980–1984) 1:352–355 (text of the *Pactum Ludowicianum*). *Epistolae selectae pontificum Romanorum Carlo Magno et Ludowico Pio regnantibus scriptae*, ed. K. HAMPE, Monumenta Germaniae Historica, vol. 5: Epistolae Karolini Aevi, vol. 3 (Berlin 1899; reprinted, 1995). 68–71.

[R. E. SULLIVAN]

PASCHAL II, POPE

Pontificate: Aug. 13, 1099, to Jan. 21, 1118; Benedictine; b. Rainerius, at Bieda, in central Italy. He entered a monastery as a boy (not Cluny as commonly supposed, but probably a dependent house of Vallombrosa), became cardinal priest of San Clemente under GREGORY VII, served as legate in Spain under URBAN II, and was subsequently abbot of ST. PAUL-OUTSIDE-THE-WALLS. His personal sanctity helped determine his election to succeed Urban II. His pontificate did not prove an easy one. The main problems he faced were (1) the existence of antipopes; (2) the conflict with the secular powers, especially in Germany, France, and England; (3) the need to further the reform of the Church. Underlying them all was one theme—the struggle for control of episcopal elections.

His reign opened well. Emperor HENRY IV, after the death of Guibert of Ravenna (CLEMENT III, ANTIPOPE) in 1100, withdrew support from subsequent antipopes, Th-

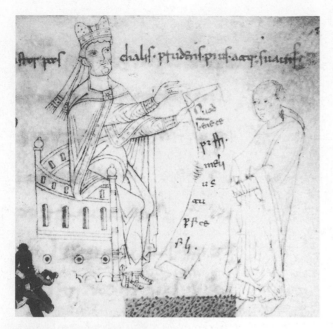

Pope Paschal II inviting the monk John to continue the "Chronicon Vulturnense."

eoderic (1100–02), Albert (1102), and Sylvester IV (1105–11); these no longer proved a serious threat to Paschal. Both Henry and the pope hoped to settle their differences, but neither of them would give way on the investiture issue. Paschal renewed the ban against Henry and prohibited lay investiture at the Roman synod in 1102. Subsequently he favored the revolt of Henry's son (1105). The son made a large number of promises, but as HENRY V he proved just as determined to retain control over investiture.

Despite meetings with the royal legates in 1106, 1107, and 1110, Paschal was disillusioned, and he condemned Henry V at the Synods of Guastalla (1106), Troyes (1107), Benevento (1108), and the Lateran (1110). Polemic literature on both sides aggravated the dispute. Henry finally marched on Rome, for he was determined to obtain imperial coronation and the right of investiture. The outcome was the fiercely debated concordat at Sutri (Feb. 9, 1111), by which, in return for free elections, Paschal granted church property in the Empire to Henry and agreed to crown him as emperor.

Both papal and imperial supporters condemned the agreement. Henry then took Paschal prisoner and forced him to recognize lay investiture (Privilege of Ponte Mammolo, Apr. 12, 1111). These actions seriously damaged the unity of the papal party. Ultimately Paschal repudiated the privilege (1112) and explicitly condemned lay investiture in 1116. He finally left Rome and returned only on Jan. 14, 1118, to die there a few days later. During this long struggle with Henry V, Paschal had also intervened

to settle the dispute of ANSELM, Archbishop of Canterbury, with HENRY I OF ENGLAND (1107). The interest of that settlement lies in its departure from the strict principles of the GREGORIAN REFORM, thus providing a basis for subsequent settlements with France (also in 1107) and with Henry V (Concordat of WORMS, 1122).

Paschal has generally been criticized for his failure, and little has been said of his work for the Church in other regions, e.g., in the Latin Kingdom of JERUSALEM. Even his contemporaries—enemies and friends alike—condemned his actions (see the *Liber de honore ecclesiae* of Placidus of Nonantula, *Monumenta Germaniae Historica: Libelli de lite* 2:568). He did not solve the conflict with the Empire; but if success be the guiding principle, it may be asked how much he differed from the example of his more able predecessors. His attitude toward temporal possessions was ideally the right one. He certainly contributed toward depriving the *REGALIA* of their sacramental character, making the concordat of 1122 possible. His pontificate was one more step in the direction of sharply distinguishing lay and clerical powers and offices.

See Also: INVESTITURE STRUGGLE.

Bibliography: F. X. SEPPELT, *Geschichte der Päpste von den Anfängen bis zur Mitte des 20. Jh.* 3:134–151. C. MARCORA, *Storia dei papi* (Milan 1961) 2:346–358. A. STACPOOLE, "Hildebrand, Cluny and the Papacy," *Downside Review* 81 (1963) 142–164, 254–272. J. G. ROWE, "Paschal II and the Relation Between the Spiritual and Temporal Powers in the Kingdom of Jerusalem," *Speculum* 32 (1957) 470–501. P. JAFFÉ, *Regesta pontificum romanorum ab condita ecclesia ad annum post Christum natum 1198,* ed. S. LÖWENFELD 1:702–772. *Monumenta Germaniae Historica: Constitutiones* 1:134–152, 564–574. A. FLICHE and V. MARTIN, eds., *Histoire de l'église depuis les origines jusqu'à nos jours* 8:338–375. H. SEIBERT, "Paschalis II," *Lexikon für Theologie und Kirche* (Freiburg, Basel, Rome, Vienna 1993) 7:1409–1410. G.M. CANTARELLA, *Pasquale II e il suo tempo* (Naples 1997). I. M. RESNICK, "Odo of Cambrai and the Investiture Crisis of the Early Twelfth Century," *Viator* 28 (1997) 83–98. J. N. D. KELLY, *Oxford Dictionary of Popes* (New York 1986) 160.

[J. GILCHRIST]

PASCHAL III, ANTIPOPE

Pontificate: April 22, 1164 to Sept. 20, 1168. Born into a noble family, Guido of Crema was a prominent member of the papal curia as cardinal priest of St. Callisto, and was arguably the strongest supporter of antipope Victor IV (1159–64) among the curia. Guido was elected successor to Victor after the latter died suddenly at Lucca. His election (April 22, 1164) was highly irregular because only two schismatic cardinals, two bishops, and the prefect of Rome participated. Nonetheless, Paschal was consecrated at Lucca by the bishop of Liège on April

26, 1164. His election and consecration were instigated by one of Frederick I Barbarossa's (1152–90) most trusted advisors: Rainald of Dassel, the emperor's chancellor for Italy and the archbishop of Cologne (1159–67). For this reason Frederick soon ratified Paschal's election, even though it was done without his advice.

At this time Frederick was losing support among the German clergy. Archbishop Eberhard of Salzburg had long opposed imperial policy toward the papacy, but upon the death of Victor IV the archbishops of Mainz, Trèves, and Magdeburg also came out against Frederick. These were influential prelates who believed that an important opportunity to end the schism had been quashed by the emperor's support of Paschal. Yet the emperor managed to turn this opposition to his advantage. He took an oath at the diet of Würzburg (May 22, 1165) never to recognize Alexander III (1159–81) and then demanded that all German clergy do the same. Those clergy who were present followed Frederick in his oath; other clergy who continued to recognize Alexander had their lands confiscated by the emperor and given to laymen. Thus by the end of 1167, Frederick had replaced in his territories (i.e., most of Germany, northern Italy, and Burgundy) virtually every churchman who had sided with Alexander with supporters of Paschal.

For his part, Paschal was forced to reside in Viterbo, since he could not remain in Rome because of local pressure from the communes and others who opposed imperial control of the papacy. He appears to have approved Frederick's request for the canonization of Charlemagne, who was elevated to sainthood by Rainald of Dassel on Jan. 8, 1166. In July 1167, after a difficult campaign through Lombardy, Frederick entered Rome and marched on St. Peter's with Paschal at his side. Pope Alexander was forced to flee for another part of Rome, and eventually to Benevento. On July 22 Paschal was formally enthroned in St. Peter's and actively assumed his role as pope. On July 30 he consecrated over a dozen bishops and patriarchs, and on August 1 solemnly crowned Frederick and Beatrice as emperor and empress. Yet, Paschal's usefulness to the emperor had passed and Frederick was already discussing the possibility of both pope and antipope stepping aside in favor of a new election.

But a few weeks later when an outbreak of malaria in Rome decimated Frederick's army, he was forced to break camp and march north to the German frontier. Rainald of Dassel, Frederick's trusted advisor and Paschal's great supporter, was among the two thousand who perished. Paschal was forced to go north with Frederick and did not return to Italy until early 1168. At that time the Romans only accepted him grudgingly, probably because

the city was negotiating for the release of many citizens held captive by the emperor. Furthermore, the Lombards were challenging the imperial presence more effectively than ever before. He died on Sept. 20, 1168, a few weeks after retiring to a secure part of the city because of fear of a future Roman senate election that might favor Pope Alexander. Although the force of the schism had largely been spent, Frederick still found an imperial antipope useful in dealing with Alexander and so allowed Callistus III (1168–78) to be named Paschal's successor.

Bibliography: L. DUCHESNE, ed. *Liber Pontificalis* (Paris 1886–92; repr. 1955–57) 2.410–20. P. JAFFÉ, *Regesta pontificum Romanorum* (Leipzig 1885–88; repr. Graz 1956) 2.426–29. F. X. SEPPELT, *Geschichte der Päpste von den Anfängen bis zur Mitte des zwanzigsten Jahrhunderts* (Munich 1954–59) 248–58, 273–78, 608ff. M. BALDWIN, *Alexander III and the Twelfth Century* (Glen Rock, NJ 1968). W. ULLMANN, *A Short History of the Papacy in the Middle Ages* (London 1972). T. REUTER, *The Papal Schism, the Empire and the West, 1159–69* (Diss. Exeter 1975). J. N. D. KELLY, *The Oxford Dictionary of Popes* (New York 1986) 178–79. C. MORRIS, *The Papal Monarchy: The Western Church from 1050–1250* (Oxford 1989). I. S. ROBINSON, *The Papacy 1073–1198: Continuity and Innovation* (Cambridge 1990). G. SCHWAIGER, *Lexikon des Mittelalters* (Munich 1993) 6.1753-4.

[P. M. SAVAGE]

PASCHAL BAYLON, ST.

Franciscan monk; b. Torre-Hermosa, Aragon, Spain, May 24, 1540; d. Villareal in Castellon, Spain, May 15, 1592. He was a shepherd, the son of Martin Baylon and Elizabeth Jubeira, peasants of lowly origins, and he taught himself to read and write. In 1564 he was received into the Alcantarine Franciscans at Monteforte. His superiors urged him to study for the priesthood, but he chose to become a lay brother. During most of his religious life he served as porter. In this office he showed remarkable kindness to the poor who came to the friary door. His personal austerities surpassed the severe demands of the Alcantarine constitutions. He was granted marvelous insights into the mysteries of religion, and his counsel was sought by learned and saintly persons. But it was his devotion to the Eucharist that emerged as the dominant theme of his life. In this connection numerous miracles are reported by his early biographers, but it is not always easy to distinguish fact from legend.

His writings consist of two books of prayers and reflections that he jotted down on scraps of paper. One of these volumes was edited by Jaime Sala and published at Toledo in 1911 under the title *Opúsculos de San Pascual Bailón.* Because of the number of cures worked through his intercession, PAUL V beatified Paschal in 1618, 26 years after the saint's death. He was canonized by ALEXANDER VIII in 1690, and, in 1897 LEO XIII designated him patron of all Eucharistic congresses and societies.

Feast: May 17.

Bibliography: *Acta sanctorum* May 4:48–131. O. ENGLEBERT, *Saint Pascal Baylon* (Paris 1942). V. FACCHINETTI, *Pasquale Baylon, frate minore: Il santo dell'Eucaristia* (Milan 1922). A. GROETEKEN, *Paschalis Baylon: Ein Heiligenbild aus Spaniens Goldenem Jahrhundert* (Cincinnati 1912). L. GUIM CASTRO, *San Pascual Bailón: Celestial patrono de los Congresos Eucarísticos* (Vich, Spain 1953). C. NAVARRETE, *San Pascualito Rey y el culto a la muerte en Chiapas* (Mexico City 1982). L. A. PORRENTRUY, *The Saint of the Eucharist,* tr. O. STANIFORTH (San Francisco 1905). L. PRINCIPE, *Pasquale Baylón, santo, ieri e oggi* (Naples 1973). I. A. RUSSO, *San Pasquale Baylon* (3d ed. Naples 1968). J. XIMENEZ, *Chrónica del beato Fr. Pascual Bailón* (Valencia 1601).

[C. J. LYNCH]

PASCHASIUS RADBERTUS, ST.

Abbot, theologian of the Eucharist; b. Soissons, *c.* 785; d. *c.* 860. He entered the Benedictine abbey of COR-BIE under Abbot ADALARD the Elder (814–821) whose life he was to write (*Patrologia Latina,* 120:1507–56). Though only a deacon, he was elected abbot of Corbie *c.* 843 but later resigned (before 853) because of opposition to his plans for reform. In 831 Paschasius wrote his treatise *Concerning the Lord's Body and Blood* (*Patrologia Latina,* 120:1267–1351), the first monograph ever written on the Eucharist. Revised by Paschasius in 844, it was severely criticized by RATRAMNUS and RABANUS MAURUS. Toward the end of his life Paschasius answered his critics in his famous letter to Frudegard (*Patrologia Latina,* 120:1351–66). In addition to commentaries on Psalms 44, Jeremiah, and Matthew (*Patrologia Latina,* 120:31–1256), he wrote works dealing with the three theological virtues (*Patrologia Latina,* 120:1387–90), the Virginal Birth (*Patrologia Latina,* 120:1367–86), the martyrdom of Rufinus and Valerius (*Patrologia Latina,* 120:1489–1508), the life of Abbot WALA (*Patrologia Latina,* 120:1559–1650), and a number of poems and letters. His letter on the Assumption of the Blessed Virgin, formerly attributed to St. Jerome (*Patrologia Latina,* 30:122–142), was often cited in Christological treatises of the Middle Ages. Paschasius is known to have attended the synods of Paris (847) and Quierzy (849), but the date of his death is uncertain.

Concerning the Eucharist, Paschasius taught that "the substance of bread and wine is changed into Christ's Body and Blood" (*De Corp.,* 8.2). In dealing with the Real Presence of Christ in the Eucharist he described it as the very flesh of Mary, which had suffered on the Cross, was buried, and rose again (*De Corp.,* 4.3 and 7.2). He held that by the omnipotence of God it is miraculously created or multiplied daily at each Consecration (*De Corp.,* 4.1 and 12.1). His opponents rejected this doctrinal presentation as too crude and materialistic. In his letter to Frudegard, Paschasius reaffirmed his view and tried to show that it was in complete accord with the teaching of the Fathers. Modern historians of theology agree that Paschasius overstressed the identity of the historical and the Eucharistic body and that the manner in which he had recourse to legends was not commendable. Paschasius's great influence was partly due to the fact that at the end of the 11th century a number of passages copied from his work began to be circulated under the name of St. Augustine.

Feast: April 26.

Bibliography: Works. Collection of his works, ed. J. SIRMOND (Paris 1618), MABILLON (Paris 1677), and MARTÈNE (Paris 1733), reprinted in *Patrologia Latina,* ed. J. P. MIGNE, 271 v., indexes 4 v. (Paris 1878–90) 120; *Poems,* ed. L. TRAUBE, *Monumenta Germaniae Historica: Poetae* (Berlin 1826–) 3.1:38–53; *Letters,* ed. E. DUEMMLER, *Monumenta Germaniae Historica: Epistolae* (Berlin 1826–) 6.1:133–149, critical eds. A. RIPBERGER, *Der Pseudo-Hieronymus-Brief IX "Cogitis me"* (Spicilegium Friburgense 9: Fribourg 1962), with bibliog. Literature. E. CHOISY, *Paschase Radbert* (Geneva 1888). D. STONE, *A History of the Doctrine of the Holy Eucharist,* 2 v. (New York 1909) 1:216–220. J. GEISELMANN, *Die Eucharistielehre der Vorscholastik* (Paderborn 1926). H. PELTIER, *Pascase Radbert* (Amiens 1938). K. VIELHABER, *Lexikon für Theologie und Kirche,* ed. J. HOFER and K. RAHNER, 10 v. (2d, new ed. Freiburg 1957–65) 8:130–131. C. CHAZELLE, "Figure, Character, and the Glorified Body in the Carolingian Eucharistic Controversy," *Traditio,* 47 (1992) 1–36. W. COLE, "Theology in Paschasius Radbertus' Liturgy-Oriented Marian Works," in *De Cultu Mariano Saeculis VI–XI,* v. 3 (Rome 1972) 395–431.

[N. M. HARING]

PASSAGLIA, CARLO

Theologian; b. Pieve S. Carlo, Lucca, Italy, May 2, 1812; d. Turin, March 12, 1887. In 1827 he became a Jesuit. From 1840 to 1844 he was prefect of studies at the Germanicum in Rome, and in 1844 professor of dogma at the Roman College. He became professor at the papal Sapienza University in Rome in 1858, left the Jesuits in 1859, and in 1860 was named a member of the papal commission for the theological investigation of the *Causa italica.* In 1860 he wrote *Il pontifice ed il principe.* He was Cavour's mediator, and in 1861 he published, anonymously, *Pro causa italica ad episcopos catholicos,* which was placed on the Index. He fled Rome in October of the same year and accepted a professorship in moral philosophy at the state university of Turin. In 1862 he directed to Pius IX a petition on behalf of about 9,000 Italian priests and was suspended. He was the editor of the weekly *Il mediatore* (1862–66), the daily *La pace*

(1863–64), and *Il gerdil* (1864). In 1863 and 1864 he was a member of Parliament. He had been seeking reconciliation with the Church since 1868, and on March 8, 1887, a few days before his death, he obtained it.

Passaglia was a patristically oriented theologian with strong leanings toward Petavius and Thomassin. He published the first book of Petavius's *Dogmatics* in 1857. He showed a mastery of theology, and together with G. PER-RONE and his two disciples, K. SCHRADER and J. B. FRAN-ZELIN, he renewed the study of it at the Roman College. There he was the teacher of renowned German theologians, including H. J. DENZINGER, F. HETTINGER, B. JUNGMANN, H. von HURTER, and M. SCHEEBEN. Passaglia took part in the preparatory work that led to the definition of the Immaculate Conception of Mary, and to the wording of the bull *Ineffabilis Deus*. Yet at Vatican I, Passaglia's view of the mediate papal power of jurisdiction was rejected. His theological works are of lasting value, for example: *Commentarium theologicorum,* 3 v. (Rome 1850–51), *De ecclesia Christi,* 2 v. (Regensburg 1853–56), and *De immaculata deiparae semper virginis conceptu,* 3 v. (Rome 1854, Naples 1855). From his unpublished material H. Schauf edited *De conciliis oecumenicis, theses* (Rome 1961).

Bibliography: C. SOMMERVOGEL et al., *Bibliothèque de la compagnie de Jésus* (Brussels-Paris 1890–1932) 6:332–336. C. BOYER, *Dictionnaire de théologie catholique,* ed. A. VACANT et al. (Paris 1903–50) 11.2:2207–10. H. HURTER, *Nomenclator literarius theologiae catholicae* (Innsbruck 1903–13) 5.2:1499–1500. L. BIGI-NELLI, *Biografia del Sac. Prof. Carlo Passaglia con documenti* (Turin 1887). P. D'ERCOLE, *Carlo Passaglia: cenno biobibliografico e ricordo* (Turin 1888). C. G. AREVALO, *Some Aspects of the Theology of the Mystical Body of Christ in the Ecclesiology of G. Perrone, C. Passaglia, and Cl. Schrader* (Rome 1959). W. KASPER, *Die Lehre von der Tradition in der römischen Schule* (Freiburg 1962).

[H. SCHAUF]

PASSERINI, PIETRO MARIA

b. Cremona, 1597; d. Rome, 1677. Passerini, a canonist, became procurator general of the Dominican Order. For 20 years he was a professor at the Sapienza in Rome and was renowned for his work on the Roman Curia. His principal writings are the *De electione canonica tractatus* (Rome 1661), *De hominum statibus et officiis* (1665), and the *Regulare Tribunale* (1677).

Bibliography: M. M. GORCE, *Dictionnaire de théologie catholique,* ed. A. VACANT et al. (Paris 1903–50) 11.2:2210–11. H. HURTER, *Nomenclator literarius theologiae catholicae* (Innsbruck 1903–13) 4:253–254.

[L. R. KOZLOWSKI]

PASSIO

Passio was originally the account of suffering of a martyr written by Christians and based on the testimony of eyewitnesses. In the earliest type of *passio,* the miraculous element plays a restricted part, as in the accounts of the martyrdoms of St. POLYCARP and SS. PERPETUA and Felicity, or in the *passio* of the Scillitan Martyrs (*c.* 180). Later authors embellished this type of narrative with fanciful and miraculous happenings to edify, or to satisfy, popular tastes. This was done in the case of the *passiones* of SS. HIPPOLYTUS, SEBASTIAN, CECILIA, AGNES, and the FOUR CROWNED MARTYRS, making the task of discovering the authentic ones difficult for modern hagiographers. Another type of *passio* that became popular from the 5th century onward was a completely legendary account of a martyr's or saint's life and death, which usually had nothing more than a name and possibly a location as foundation. The *passio* of St. CATHERINE OF ALEXANDRIA and that of St. GEORGE are without historical foundation. The *passio* even in its most authentic form is to be distinguished from an authentic Act of the martyrdom, which is the official shorthand report of the trial and death of a martyr. Only a few of these have survived. (*See* ACTS OF THE MARTYRS.)

The *passio* was used by the APOLOGISTS as a subsidiary proof of the divine origin of the Christian religion; but its specific purpose was to encourage Christians to honor and imitate the martyrs. In theology the *passio* as an account of the sufferings of a martyr points to the relevance of the faith as an absolute factor in the life of the early Church. The martyr was challenged to forswear his faith or die for it. Likewise, the confessions of faith frequently put into the mouth of the martyr, whether authentic or not, witness to belief in a living, triune God, the Resurrection of Christ, and Christian belief in final glory.

Bibliography: A. HAMMAN, *Lexikon für Theologie und Kirche,* ed. J. HOFER and K. RAHNER (Freiburg 1957–67) 7:133–134; *Theologie und Glaube* 45 (1955) 35–43. G. LAZZATI, *Gli sviluppi della letteratura sui martiri nei primi quattro secoli* (Turin 1956). *Acta Sanctorum,* (Paris 1863–). *Analecta Bollandiana* (Brussels 1882–). *Bibliotheca hagiographica latina antiquae et mediae aetatis,* 2 v. (Brussels, 1898–1901; suppl. 1911). *Bibliotheca hagiographica Graeca,* ed. F. HALKIN, 3 v. (Brussels 1957). R. AIGRAIN, *L'Hagiographie* (Paris 1953). H. DELEHAYE, *Les Passions des martyrs et les genres littéraires* (Brussels 1921).

[F. X. MURPHY]

PASSION

From the Latin *passio* (Gr. πάθος), meaning something suffered or undergone, has a variety of significations. In its etymological sense it refers to physical suffering, particularly that associated with the martyrdom of early Christians (*see* PASSIO). In a broader philosophical meaning, as opposed to action it signifies the reception of the activity of some extrinsic agent or mover, and as such is enumerated among the CATEGORIES of being (*see* ACTION AND PASSION). It is used also to designate the species of QUALITY according to which there can be alteration (*see* MOTION), and, by extension, to signify any attribute, affection, or PROPERTY of a subject. In psychology, Cartesian usage identifies passions with states of the soul resulting from the action of "animal spirits"; Aristotelian and scholastic usage, on the other hand, refers to all types of emotional activity as passions (*see* EMOTION). More commonly accepted usages refer to any violent or intense emotion, particularly an ardent affection for one of the opposite sex, as passion (*see* LOVE; SEX). Among Christians, the word is frequently used to indicate the sufferings of Christ.

[W. A. WALLACE]

PASSION OF CHRIST, I (IN THE BIBLE)

This article, concerned primarily with the story of Christ's Passion and death as told in the four Gospels, is composed of four main sections: the ancient, common basis of a Passion narrative prior to the four written Gospels; the development of the Gospel tradition about the Passion; characteristics of the four canonical Passion narratives; the use of the OT in the Passion accounts. A specific treatment of the Resurrection is not included in this article, although the realization of the unity of the one redemptive mystery, Passion-death-Exaltation, is basic to the discussion (*see* RESURRECTION OF CHRIST, 1). For the theological significance of Christ's Passion, *see* EXPIATION (IN THE BIBLE); REDEMPTION (IN THE BIBLE); SALVATION.

Pre-Gospel Passion Narrative. The Passion narratives in the present Gospels (Mark ch. 14–15; Matthew ch. 26–27; Luke ch. 22–23; John ch. 18–19) differ from the rest of the Gospel material in that they seem not to have been compiled from individual, self-contained units or stories, but present a unified, sequential account of the final events in Jesus' life and ministry. Recognizing the very different character of these stories as continuous narratives, the adherents of the form-critical school have acknowledged the very ancient tradition upon which they are based. Modern Biblical scholarship agrees that there was a primitive narrative; but there are divergent opinions on the genre, content, and milieu of the formation of that narrative. Only as a whole could the story answer the question, "How could Jesus have been brought to the cross by the people who were blessed by His signs and wonders?" To counter this scandal of the cross, individual incidents from the Passion would not do; the entire purposeful narrative, giving exact geographical and temporal data, was seen to be necessary. (*See* FORM CRITICISM, BIBLICAL.)

Several arguments from literary criticism support the hypothesis of such a primitive narrative. More than any other part of the Gospels, this section has the nature of a connected historical account. Although the first ten chapters of Mark, for example, comprise separate blocks of material loosely connected and without continuous chronological or topographical coherence, with the beginning of the Passion story, we find a definitely sequential account. Among all four Gospels there is substantial agreement regarding the course of events of the Passion. Although chronological arrangements in earlier parts of the Gospels reflect more freely the particular interests of the writers, the events of Holy Week seem to have been so fixed in the tradition and so respected as the record of the climax of Jesus' life that the order could not be freely changed; it might be abridged, expanded, or supplemented, but its general order was retained. J. Jeremias observes that John's Gospel rarely shows parallels to Mark's account in the description of Jesus' ministry, but beginning with the entrance into Jerusalem, the Johannine narrative agrees with the Marcan rather broadly until the arrest, and then quite strictly after that. These parallels are striking, for the substance of the narrative is the same, even though details and wording may differ and even though religious and doctrinal interests are more obviously present in John than in Mark. This similarity of structure in the Passion accounts of all four Gospels has a natural explanation if there was such a basic narrative, traditional before the written Gospels.

At present critics do not express complete agreement about what the pre-Gospel narrative comprised, but most include the following incidents, which can be distinguished more easily in Mark: the plot of the priests (Mk 14.1–2); JUDAS' treason (14.10–11); the LAST SUPPER (14.17–25); the arrest of Jesus (14.43–52); the trial before the CHIEF PRIESTS (14.53–72—not admitted by all as part of the primitive narrative) and before PILATE (15.1–15); the CRUCIFIXION with some of its concomitant events (15.21–41); and the burial (15.42–47). These episodes are the ones referred to in Christ's own prophecies of the Passion (Mk 8.31; 9.29–30; 10.33) and in the earliest apostolic preaching (e.g., Acts 3.13–16; 13.27–31). From an analysis of Semitic expressions in Mark, V. Taylor proposes that Mark utilized the Greek Passion narrative current in Rome and that he expanded this with certain personal reminiscences of Peter. X. Léon-Dufour, however, maintains that an examination of Semitisms in Matthew indicates that the first Gospel also witnesses to an

Scenes of the Last Supper and of Jesus Christ washing the feet of a disciple are depicted in a stained glass window of the Chartres Cathedral, France. (©Adam Woolfitt/CORBIS)

older, more primitive narrative, of which Matthew and Mark would represent two recensions, the one Semitic (Matthew), the other Roman (Mark).

Development of the Gospel Tradition. While there is essential agreement among the four Gospels on the important events of the Passion, each of the accounts is a unique composition with its own literary characteristics and theological viewpoint. Even Mark's presentation, though barely more than an outline, has singular features and theological interests. Present-day understanding of the NT emphasizes the benefits to be gained by appreciating the differences for what they are: signs of the individual view of the Evangelist, the needs of the particular audience addressed, and the literary style of the author. The passion narratives can best be understood as SALVATION HISTORY (*Heilsgeschichte*), i.e., history with a theological intent. In order to appreciate the narratives fully,

one must be alert to the theological, missionary, and liturgical factors that influenced their formation.

In Acts and in the Pauline Epistles evidence is found of the focus on Jesus' death and Resurrection in the early preaching and doctrinal development. Christ's death on the cross determined the conception not only of messianic salvation, but also of God's entire revelation through the OT. In Paul's early Epistles it can be seen how the first missionaries overcame the tremendous stumbling block of the cross by their Christological interpretation of the OT. The apologetic necessity of answering objections to a crucified Messiah led them to seek and achieve profound religious and theological insights into the meaning of the event. From saying that Jesus was Messiah despite the Crucifixion (Acts 2.23,36; 3.13–15, 17–18; etc.), they came to say that He was Messiah in virtue of the Crucifixion because this was the fulfillment of the will of God (Gal 3.10–13; 6.14; Rom 4.25). Liturgical influences on the Passion narratives include the celebration of the Eucharist, the administration of the Sacraments, and what may be called the "liturgy of the word."

While the kerygma (preaching) is the core of the apostolic preaching, the Passion narrative based on it is chiefly didache (instruction); that is, it is an illustration and an elucidation of the basic proclamation of salvation (*see* KERYGMA). To retain all the many deeds and sayings of Jesus was not possible (Jn 21.25); so the primitive community and the Evangelists preserved certain ones by a selective operation. Evidence of this is seen in the preservation of incidents from the Passion that prove that Jesus, Messiah and God's Son, foreknew His Passion and freely chose to suffer for our Redemption. The three Synoptic writers stress Christ's prophecies of the Passion, and John underlines the same truth in the parable of the Good Shepherd (Jn 10.11–18). To stress the innocence of Jesus, the tradition emphasizes the guilt of the Jews, while in comparison it seems to mitigate the responsibility of Pilate. The Evangelists achieve this emphasis, however, only by leaving out some things that would tend to exonerate the Jews and not by inventing anti-Jewish stories; at the same time, they present the Passion as the fulfillment of God's will, so that both the Jews and Pilate are but instruments in God's redemptive design (Lk 24.45–47).

Particular Characteristics of the Gospel Narratives. A study of similarities and differences among the four Gospel Passion narratives deepens appreciation of their significance and also reveals much about the way in which the early Christian community and the Evangelists understood them. Mark may be taken as the basis for comparison because it is simplest and earliest. Mark presents a historical view of Jesus' ministry and emphasizes the themes of hiddenness, secrecy, and lack of understanding about Jesus and His mission. The narrative of the Passion itself makes up a substantial part, approximately one-fifth, of the entire Gospel. For this reason, some critics have described Mark's Gospel as simply a Passion narrative with an introduction. Its purpose is more comprehensive than this, however; it seeks to elucidate the doctrine of Jesus Christ as Redeemer and Son of God. This basic theme is highlighted in three key places: in the opening statement (1.1); at Caesarea Philippi, the turning point of the Gospel (8.29); and at Jesus' death (15.39). The Passion narrative is an integral part of this total plan; as Peter's confession prepares the way for the narrative of the Passion, so the words of the pagan centurion (15.39) provide the final comment on it. Immediately after Peter's confession (8.29), Jesus' new teaching on the necessity of suffering is introduced.

In their account of the trial of Jesus, the Synoptic writers imply what John states explicitly: that the issue for which Jesus is condemned by the Sanhedrin is His teaching of His divinity (Mk 14.61–62; Mt 26.63–64; Lk 22.66–71; Jn 18.19–21). Before Pilate, however, the Sanhedrin attempts to indict Jesus on political charges, knowing well that blasphemy is not a charge that will win a death sentence from the Roman governor. The religious issue central to the trial is evident when the Jews insist: "We have a Law, and according to that Law he must die, because he has made himself Son of God" (Jn 19.7). Under pressure from the chief priests and the mob, Pilate fears an insurrection, so he delivers Jesus to be crucified (Mk 15.15). The connotation of παραδιδόναι (to deliver, to hand over), so frequently used in the accounts, is that ultimately it is God's will that is being fulfilled, the human agents being but instruments (cf. Rom 8.32; Acts 2.23; Is 53.4). Significant of the restraint of the Gospel accounts is the fact that the cruel torture of the scourging is described with a single Greek word (Mk 15.15).

Like John, both Mark and Matthew associate a mocking and spitting scene with that of the scourging (Mk 15.15–19; Mt 27.26–30); and like the fourth Evangelist, also, they emphasize the royal caricature of the "King of the Jews." Luke, on the other hand, in a scene proper to his Gospel, separates the mocking and scourging; he attributes the mocking to the court of HEROD ANTIPAS, where Jesus is treated with contempt because of His claim to royalty (Lk 23.11). In the third Gospel the scourging alternative proposed by Pilate follows closely upon this scene at Herod's court. Luke's special source has apparently given him information about the dealings between Herod and Pilate, for the other Evangelists do not seem to know of Jesus' appearance before the Tetrarch of Galilee (see also Acts 4.24–30). As the mercenaries of Pilate took their cue from the official accusations at the trial and mocked Jesus as a political pretender, so also earlier, the attendants at the court of the Sanhedrin had taken their cue from the charges of that court, ridiculing and maltreating Jesus as a religious pretender, taunting Him to exercise now His powers of prophecy (Mk 14.65). John associates maltreatment of Jesus with the questioning before Caiaphas (Jn 18.22–23); indeed, this unofficial hearing is more likely than the official meeting of the Sanhedrin.

Mark, followed by Matthew and Luke, tells of Simon of Cyrene's part in carrying the cross. For John's theological purpose, the incident of Simon's help seems unimportant, and he chooses instead to emphasize that Jesus goes freely to His death carrying the cross Himself and fully in charge of His destiny (Jn 19.17). In keeping with the Roman custom, the plaque announcing the deed for which He was being executed was posted on the cross above Jesus' head. All four accounts report this, but in four slightly different wordings, an interesting example of the way in which the primitive tradition preserved the substance, but not necessarily the exact details, of the events.

Old Testament in Passion Narratives. In Jesus' own teaching regarding His Passion, one of the most striking elements is His use of OT allusions and His interpretation of the Scriptures in function of His own person and mission: in God's salvific plan, He is the climax toward which all of Israel's history has been moving. His doctrine is so firmly rooted in scriptural thought that one can have little understanding of it unless one knows the significance of the OT references made. Especially in the Servant of the Lord oracles in Deutero-Isaiah and in Psalms 21(22) and 68(69), the early Church and the Evangelists saw delineated clearly the prefiguring of the Just One who suffered vicariously for His people (Mk 15.23, 34, 36; Mt 27.42–43; Lk 23.34, 35–37; Jn 19.24, 28, 29). Jesus Himself had consistently taught that He was the fulfillment of the Scriptures and had identified Himself with the Isaiah Servant. The Apostles and first Christians, meditating upon these passages, were impressed with the great similarities between the sufferings of the Isaian Servant and of Christ. Their desire to stress prophetic fulfillment was an important influence upon the formation, selection of events, and manner of narration of the Passion story. In the tradition we find preserved especially those things that show the fulfillment of prophecy, while more profane information may be omitted. Not merely the Passion as a whole, but also many individual happenings are seen as the fulfillment of Scripture and God's foreordained will, e.g., the betrayal by Judas, the arrest of Jesus, the flight of His disciples, His being raised up on the wood of the cross, and His shameful death as a criminal. The use of the OT by each of the Evangelists provides some unique insights into the meaning of the Passion.

Mark. The chief OT theme developed by Mark is that of Christ as Suffering Servant (cf. Is 52.13–53.12). In Mk 14.21 the Gospel points out that Jesus, the Son of Man, "goes his way" to death "as it is written." Mark seems to allude to Is 53.7 in his description of Jesus' silence before the high priest and before Pilate (Mk 14.61; 15.5). The description of the mistreatment of Jesus before the Sanhedrin (Mk 14.65) recalls the language of Is 50.6. On Calvary, Jesus' Crucifixion between the two thieves (Mk 15.27) recalls a passage from Isaia (53.12).

Matthew. The account in Matthew likewise emphasizes Jesus' role as Servant of Yahweh, but it reveals a particular interest in showing a literal accomplishment of prophecy. The language of Matthew is noticeably Biblical, e.g., in 26.3–5, 14–16, describing the plot of the Jewish council against Jesus and perhaps recalling Ps 30(31).14 and Ps 2.1–2. His account of Judas' betrayal of Jesus for 30 pieces of silver recalls Zec 11.12–13, which he later cites explicitly in telling of Judas' fate (Mt 27.9–10). The derision by those standing about the cross recalls the words of Ps 21(22).9, and their resemblance to the words of Wis 2.12–20 is even more striking.

Luke. For his Passion narrative, Luke uses not only the Mark-Matthew tradition, but other sources as well. He includes incidents and OT allusions that contribute to the themes of his Gospel, including Jesus as the Chosen One of God, the Messiah (Lk 23.35). Luke's stress upon Jesus' fulfillment of the Servant prophecy is apparent, for he includes the allusions of the other Synoptics; and he makes a special point of emphasizing the realization of Is 53.12, "And he was counted among the wicked," by alluding to it in three different verses (Lk 22.37; 23.32–33). On Calvary Jesus' last words as recorded in Luke express the filial obedience of the Redeemer, the Chosen One, as He cries in the words of Ps 30(31).6, "Father, into thy hands I commend my spirit" (Lk 23.46).

John. In his use of OT allusions, the fourth Evangelist presents a developed, refined theology of Jesus' redemptive death. John omits many of the Synoptic details (e.g., Simon of Cyrene, the weeping women, the jeering of the onlookers, the darkness, the tearing of the Temple veil) and selects other incidents in which he sees special significance. Deep reflection on the meaning of Jesus' life and mission enabled John to see profound and sometimes subtle symbolism in the circumstances of the Passion. He conceives of Jesus' Passion as the beginning of His Exaltation, the supreme revelation to the world of His universal kingship and His divinity. John alone mentions the seamless tunic; his intention here may be to stress that Jesus dies as high priest of the New Covenant; for according to the Jewish historian Josephus, the robe of the Jewish high priest was a seamless one, described by Ben Sirach as a "glorious robe" (Sir 50.11). John concludes the description with another citation of Psalm 21(22); here is an interesting example of the personal way in which John employs data from the apostolic tradition. Matthew and Mark cite the opening words of this Psalm in their description of the Crucifixion; John, however, sees Jesus' Passion primarily as the beginning of His glory, so he omits this seeming cry of desperation and prefers to point out (Jn 19.24) the fulfillment of those other words in the same Psalm: "They divided up my garments among them, and for my vesture they cast lots" [Ps 21(22).19].

The typology of the Paschal Lamb is paramount in John's account. John stresses that Jesus' sacrifice takes place at the same time as that of the paschal lambs in the

Temple (Jn 13.1; 18.28; 19.14, 31). When the sacrifice has been accomplished, and the Divine Lamb hangs dead upon the cross, John points out the significance of the piercing of His side (19.34–37). The meaning of this event is explained by two texts of Scripture: the blood attests to the reality of the sacrifice, and the water, symbol of the Spirit (Jn 7.39), its spiritual fecundity. Many Fathers of the Church, with accurate insight into John's teaching, have seen in the water the symbol of Baptism, in the blood that of the Eucharist, and thus in the two Sacraments, the sign of the Church, the New Eve being born from the side of the New Adam. John's citation (19.36), "Not a bone of him shall you break," presents a composite picture of the Savior as Servant of Yahweh and Paschal Lamb [cf. Ex 12.46; Ps 33(34).21]. Thus John sees the consummation of Jesus' Exaltation realized even at His death. He applies the citation of Zec 12.10, "They shall look on him whom they have pierced," not only to the piercing there on Calvary but also to the compelling, attracting power of the crucified, exalted Jesus (Jn 19.37; see also 3.14; 8.28; 12.32). His sacrifice accomplished, Jesus, the Paschal Lamb whose sacrifice wins universal redemption, draws all men to Himself so that with Him and through Him, all return to the Father.

See Also: TRIAL OF JESUS.

Bibliography: X. LÉON-DUFOUR, *Dictionnaire de la Bible,* suppl. ed. L. PIROT, et al. (Paris 1928–) 6:1419–92, with detailed bibliog.; "Mt et Mc dans le récit de la Passion," *Biblica* 40 (1959) 684–696; "Autour des récits de la Passion," *Recherches de science religieuse* 48 (1960) 489–507. K. H. SCHELKLE, *Die Passion Jesu in der Verkündigung des N.T.: Ein Beitrag zur Formgeschichte und zur Theologie des N.T.* (Heidelberg 1949). A. M. RAMSEY, *The Narratives of the Passion* (Contemporary Studies in Theology 1; London 1962). V. TAYLOR, "The Narrative of the Crucifixion," *New Testament Studies* 8 (1961–62) 333–334. M. JUDGE, *The Passion Narratives in the College Sacred Doctrine Courses* (Doctoral diss. microfilm; CUA 1963), bibliog. 267–280.

[M. JUDGE]

PASSION OF CHRIST, II (DEVOTION TO)

In the strict sense DEVOTION is an act of the will giving oneself with fervor to the service of God or divine cult. The Passion is the suffering both interior and exterior endured by Jesus Christ from the Last Supper until His death on the cross. Further, the earliest Latin use of the term *passio* refers to the entirety of the paschal mystery, and this includes the Resurrection and the Ascension, as well as the sufferings of Good Friday.

From apostolic times these events have been looked on as an integrated action on the part of the Savior of mankind and, aside from the actual NT Passion narratives, are generally mentioned as a whole in the writings of the early Church. Thus are they referred to in the Acts of the Apostles (1.3), where St. Luke wrote of Christ alive "after His Passion." St. Paul, using the same unification, preferred the personification in "Christ Crucified" (1 Cor 1.23) or the instrumentality in "the Cross" (Gal 6.14). St. Peter referred to the totality of His "sufferings" (1 Pt 2.21, 23) and exhorted his hearers to follow in Christ's steps. In the carrying out of this exhortation the lives and the martyrdom of the Apostles show the intensity of their devotion to to the service of God and His Son. But from the early Church, in a period close to the Passion, when the Second Coming was thought of as imminent, there is little literature specifically concerned with devotion to Christ's Passion, but rather a group of human, individual, joyous passions patterned on Christ's action and reported sometimes by the sufferers, sometimes by their pagan onlookers.

Moreover, there is also the hypothesis that the emphasis on the Resurrection rather than the suffering came about through the desire on the part of the Church to combat misunderstandings of the two natures of Christ that overemphasized His humanity. Special attention to the Passion sufferings may have been deliberately avoided in order to prevent adding to the imbalance.

From the East there came, on the one hand, most of the early heresies concerning Christ's nature, and on the other hand, outstanding devotion to Christ's Passion.

The Syrian Church, although lacking Rome's influence, had a certain aura because it was centered in the Holy Land and possessed the relics of the Passion, which it concealed and revealed in turn. The personalized and intense devotion to Christ's Passion that the Syrian Church nurtured was typified by St. Ignatius of Antioch, who, on his way to Rome to his own martyrdom, wrote in glowing terms of the triumph of Christ's Passion and Resurrection, "Him I seek who died on our behalf; Him I desire who rose again for our sake . . . . Permit me to be an imitator of the Passion of my God" (*Epist. ad Rom.* 4, 9).

St. Melito of Sardis (2d century), in a homily on the Passion, referred to the "Passover" and Christ in His mission to the world and His Resurrection, ending: "Listen while you tremble! He that suspended the earth was hanged up; He that fixed the heavens was fixed with nails; He that supported the earth was supported upon a tree; the Lord was exposed to ignomity with a naked body; God put to death!" [W. Cureton, *Spicilegium Syriacum* (London 1861) 55]. St. Ephraem—who used to interrupt his own sermons from time to time to exclaim, "Glory be to Him, how much He suffered!"—gives this vignette:

"Let the heavens and earth stand awestruck to behold Him who swayeth the rod of fire, Himself smitten with scourges, to behold Him who spread over the earth the veil of the skies and who set fast the foundations of the mountains, who poised the earth over the waters and sent down the blazing lightning-flash, now beaten by wretches over a stone pillar that His own word had created'' [T. J. Lamy, *S. Ephraemi Syri Hymni et Sermones* (4 v. Louvain 1882–1902) 1.511].

It was in Jerusalem, part of the Syrian Church, that the relics of the Passion were rediscovered; and in the 4th century the pilgrim Aetheria reported the veneration of the true cross on Good Friday and the reading of the Gospel of the Agony in Gethsemane during Holy Week. The veneration of the true cross was the precursor of adoration of the wood in the Good Friday liturgy.

Development in the West. In the period of the expansion of the Church from the 5th century, there are the teachings of the Fathers regarding the Passion. St. Augustine, bearing in mind Christ's tremendous sacrifice and the men for whom He died, prayed, "Look, O loving Father, on thy most loving Son suffering so many outrages for me: See, most loving Ruler, who it is that suffers and remember to be kind to him for whom He suffered . . . . Note His innocent hands dripping with holy blood and being placated forgive the sins which my hands have done'' [*Meditationes S. Augustini* (pseudo.) ch. 6]. St. Anselm wrote: "I, myself am the wound of your sorrow, I am to blame for your murder. I have merited that you should die, I am the scourge of vengeance upon you. I am the real malice in your Passion, the real suffering in your Crucifixion'' (*Meditations* 7). St. Bernard advised: "As much as we can, let us love our wounded Lord, let us give love for love, and embrace Him whose hands and feet and side wicked ploughmen have furrowed'' (*Omnia Opera S. Bern.* 3:3). These three quotations span five centuries. The Church passed from an age of persecution into one of missionary zeal and from a time of adult Baptism into one when infant Baptism was general. The necessity of replacing the catechesis of those who learned, accepted, and were baptized with one for those who were baptized and then learned and had to be led to acceptance produced a new emphasis on compassion, the actual feeling with the suffering of Christ. The development of a concept of sin as something that man must put off anew every day after baptism also contributed to the idea of a personal wounding of Christ by each man's sin.

St. Francis of Assisi introduced a new element into devotion to the Passion. Through the use of crib scenes and crucifixes, he began to bring to the people a human Christ with whom to suffer. Francis bore the signs of his own devotion to the Passion in the stigmata, the wounds

The Passion of Christ, devotional image. (©Elio Ciol/CORBIS)

of Christ in man's flesh, of which Francis is the first known example. From Francis we have the invocation "We adore The, O Christ, and we bless The, because by Thy Holy Cross Thou hast redeemed the world.'' St. Thomas Aquinas and St. Bonaventure excelled in their teachings concerning the dignity and effects of devotion to the Passion. All of this devotion was strengthened among the laity by the practices the Crusaders brought back from the Holy Land and by the instructive devices that mendicant preachers had developed, such as the STATIONS OF THE CROSS, miracle plays, Passion tropes, hymns, prayers, and Books of Hours, replete with Passion references.

The Devotio Moderna, which is crystallized in the *Imitation of Christ*, and in a similar way the *Spiritual Exercises* of St. Ignatius of Loyola, stressed the Passion as a means of daily perfection, the support of every virtue, and the means to endure every affliction.

Among the outstanding missionary preachers who moved the masses by their emphasis on the Passion of Our Lord were SS. Vincent de Paul, John Eudes, Alphonsus Liguori, Paul of the Cross (who founded the Passionists), and Leonard of Port Maurice (who preached the Way of the Cross). The love of the crucified Christ was promoted by such pulpit orators of the 18th and 19th centuries as Bossuet, Bourdaloue, Fénelon, and Lacordaire. Through these periods there was a steady increase in the number and type of devotion accorded not only the Passion itself but also the individual phases and even the instruments of Christ's suffering. Among these subsidiary devotions are numbered the cult of Holy Relics, reaffirmed by Vatican Council II, devotion to the Holy Infancy, the Holy Face, the Precious Blood, and the instruments of the Passion, as well as to the Sacred Hearts of Jesus and Mary and the Sorrows of Mary. Passion feasts and Offices also developed, and the practices of the Holy Hour, the Three Hours Agony, and the Forty Hours devotion became common.

The Mass and the Sacraments. St. Francis of Assisi was followed in the stigmata by many mystics of the Passion, and every age has produced new writers to develop the theme of Christ's Passion in ways pertinent to that age. In every age, however, it is the Mass that is the major source and the prime mover of devotion to the Passion. The Mass, as the perfect reenactment of all the events of Christ's Passion, His suffering, death, and Resurrection, forever present to man, is also the perfect act of devotion to those events for man. All the Sacraments commemorate the Passion, most especially, of course, the Holy Eucharist, but in Baptism man is called upon to be baptized "into Christ Jesus . . . into His death. For we were buried with Him by means of Baptism into death, in order that, just as Christ has risen from the dead. . . so we also may walk in newness of life" (Rom 6.3–5). In Confirmation we have become "the temple of the Holy Spirit . . . for you have been bought at a great price. Glorify God and bear Him in your body" (1 Cor 6.19–20). And in the other four Sacraments there are equal reminders that it is in Christ and His Church through the Passion in all its fullness that we receive the abundance of God's life. In a like manner the sacramentals of the Church, and in a special way the Sign of the Cross, draw efficacy from Christ's Passion. But it is the restored rites of Holy Week that have brought the Passion into prominence so that Christians may appreciate the words of Pope St. Leo I: "Our Lord's Passion is being continually reenacted until the end of the world; for just as, in the person of His saints, it is Christ Himself who is honored, it is Christ Himself who is loved; just as in the person of His poor, it is Christ Himself who is fed and clothed, so, in the person of all who suffer wrongs for justice' sake, it is Christ Himself who suffers" (*Sermo* 7.5).

Bibliography: P. POURRAT, *Christian Spirituality*, tr. W. H. MITCHELL et al., 4 v. (New York 1922–27; Westminster, Md. 1953–55). M. J. OLLIVIER, *The Passion*, tr. E. LEAHY (Boston 1901). R. PLUS, *Folly of the Cross* (New York 1927). J. MEAD, *Hours of the Passion* (Milwaukee 1956). C. MARMION, *Christ in His Mysteries* (St. Louis 1926). J. DANIÉLOU, *The Bible and the Liturgy* (Notre Dame, Ind. 1956). F. X. DURRWELL, *The Resurrection: A Biblical Study*, tr. R. SHEED (New York 1960). W. F. HOGAN, *Christ's Redemptive Sacrifice* (Englewood Cliffs, N.J. 1963). J. A. JUNGMANN, *Pastoral Liturgy* (New York 1962).

[J. MEAD]

PASSION PLAYS

The Passion play was a genre of medieval religious drama, of relatively late and slow development, which concentrated on the suffering, death, and Resurrection of Christ, and was thus distinguished from the Corpus Christi cycles narrating the entire Biblical story from Creation to Judgment (*see* DRAMA, MEDIEVAL).

Origins. A survey of the origins and primitive forms of Passion drama reveals the liturgical background and lyrical character of these cautious and tentative experiments and will disclose the pattern of the more elaborate plays staged in Germany and France during the late Middle Ages. The absence of any dramatic representation of Christ's death until the early 13th century, when all other types of liturgical play had long been performed, may very well mean a reluctance to imitate in a fictive manner the awesome mystery of Christ's sacrifice, especially since the Mass as the central act of the liturgy was itself the actual continuation of that sacrifice.

During the 12th century, however, the custom of chanting a long, lyrical *planctus*, or lament, of the Blessed Virgin became attached to the Good Friday veneration of the cross. The latter ceremony already included the choral singing of the Savior's reproaches (the *IMPROPERIA*) and the uncovering of a veiled crucifix with the words "Ecce lignum crucis." A cleric would then stand before this cross and sing the lament of the Sorrowful Mother in stanzas of Latin verse marked by the literary and musical artistry characteristic of the great Sequences and hymns (*see* SEQUENCE). Some texts contained lines of reply in the voice of Christ or of St. John, and, as impersonation of these voices probably accompanied the chanting, real drama was present. Rubrics calling for solemn, stylized gestures eventually appeared (e.g., in the text from Cividale, Italy). Karl Young regarded such activity as genuine Passion drama. When incidents from Christ's trial, journey to Calvary, and Crucifixion were included in the plays of the 13th century, the *planctus* of Mary was structured into the complex design, the texts often using the two best known of the earlier lyrical compositions, the "Planctus ante nescia" and the "Flete, fideles animae."

Further Influences. Other formative influences on these plays have been suggested. One was the dramatic homily on the Passion, in which the preacher often came close to impersonation of characters through quoted speech and imitated gesture. Important, too, was the long narrative poem on the death of Christ, the most important being the so-called *Passion des jongleurs*, written *c.* 1200, which is said to underlie a whole group of Burgundian dramas of about a century later. The only extant texts of Passion plays in Latin, however, are the two in the Benediktbeuern MS from the 13th century, and their form suggests a development rather by elaboration of already existing liturgical plays than by accretion to dramatic lyric, sermon, or narrative poem.

The first of these Benediktbeuern plays, the *Ludus breviter de Passione*, was meant to be followed by a Resurrection scene, as the rubric directs, and therefore can be regarded as a prologue to the Easter play. It covers the events from the Last Supper to the burial of Christ, but much of its action was left to be performed in pantomime, e.g., the nailing to the cross. Hardin Craig, who regards this short text as an expansion backward of an Easter play, believes also that the longer Passion dramatization in the same MS was built around an already existing and highly embellished play of Mary Magdalene and her brother Lazarus. Such a hypothesis about the origin of the Passion play in earlier liturgical drama, rather than in any extrinsic source, is supported by the difference in literary maturity between the prose of the Passion incidents (which often reads like mere stage direction) and the mature poetry of the Magdalene performance, some of it in Latin and some in German. Both of these Benediktbeuern plays reveal lyrical associations, however, for they contain the *planctus Mariae*, the shorter text using the "Planctus ante nescia" and the longer one the "Flete, fideles animae." Although these texts from Germany are the only surviving ones, records of nonextant plays of the same nature are to be found in Siena, Padua, and Sulmona in Italy.

Vernacular Plays. The early vernacular Passion plays belong to the turn of the 14th century in both Germany and France. It is clear that this stage of development for the dramas on the death of Christ was reached more slowly than the parallel elaboration of the Christmas plays, which had probably achieved cyclic proportions in the 13th century. In any case, it is important to regard the Passion play as an integral unit separate from the Christmas plays and also from the Corpus Christi plays. The typical plan of the vernacular Passion drama is a threefold design: the Fall (of the angels and of man), the suffering of Christ, and finally the Resurrection. This plan omits virtually all of the Old Testament history except the original sin of Adam and Eve and ordinarily does not include the Nativity of the Savior. The life of Christ may be taken up at the beginning of His public ministry or at His triumphal entry into Jerusalem.

German Plays. The oldest surviving German Passion play is found in a St. Gall MS, undated but probably of the early 14th century. Its span of sacred history extends from the marriage feast of Cana to the Resurrection. Of comparable date is the Vienna play, which adds to the St. Gall pattern the narrative of Adam's Fall, thus presenting

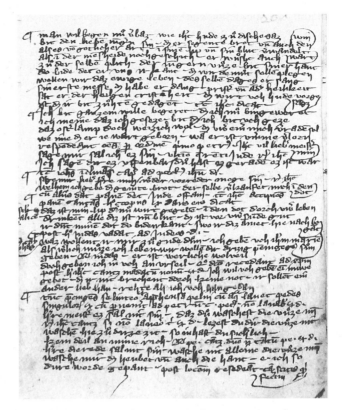

Manuscript page from oldest surviving German Passion Play (St. Gallen Codex 919, fol. 205v), describing Jesus washing the Apostles feet.

for the first time the triptych effect of the usual Passion play. Perhaps the most notable feature of the St. Gall text is the presence of a prologue in the voice of St. Augustine, a trace thus appearing of the famous Prophet plays, in which the Church Father summoned a procession of witnesses to the Messiah. This prophetic prologue was a common feature of the Christmas plays, but Creizenach regards the abridged form of it in the St. Gall text as an indication that it fulfilled the same function for the Passion plays. Augustine serves also as a commentator here, at times interrupting to give a brief outline of coming action and at other times to give a little homily based on a scene just concluded. After Christ washes the feet of the Disciples, for example, Augustine gives an exhortation to humility, and after the Crucifixion he offers a meditation on the sorrows of Mary.

The flowering of German Passion plays occurred in the 15th and 16th centuries, which witnessed the expansion of the texts to many thousands of lines and thus to an action requiring three days for performance. Among those surviving, two groups of plays call for special mention, the Frankfurt and the Tyrol texts.

The nucleus of the first group of plays is the Frankfurt *Dirigierrolle*, that is, an outline or register of the characters, incidents, and cues for a Passion play. It reveals in skeletal form a very extensive undertaking, from a Prophet play to an Ascension scene, with an epilogue debate between the allegorical figures Ecclesia and Synagoga. This is a director's manual, but it is rich enough in detail to reveal indebtedness to a long narrative poem on the Redemption entitled *Die Erlösung* and to simpler plays of the St. Gall type. In its turn it has served as a point of departure for other Passion plays performed in the same general area, of which the best known are the Alsfeld and the Heidelberg texts. These come to us in MSS written shortly after 1500, and the latter in its present form is really a library version rather than an actors' copy. The great length of the scenes is due to the loquacity of the characters, immeasurably changed and grown from the cryptic speeches in the early plays, and to the lavish use of comic motifs.

The presence of buffoonery is quite marked in these southwestern German plays, notably in the scenes of merry devils, of Mary Magdalene's worldly life, and even of the counting out and quarreling over Judas's 30 silver coins. Allegory is used sparingly, but effectively, e.g., in the Heidelberg personification of Death as summoner of Lazarus; Death boasts ironically of his unlimited power and then suffers humiliation in his defeat by Christ's miracle at Lazarus's tomb (Jn 11.1–46). Also noteworthy in this text is the juxtaposition of prefigurative scenes from the Old Testament immediately before the corresponding events of the New Testament related typologically to them. Thus, the acquittal of Susanna by Daniel (Daniel ch. 13) is staged as a prelude to Christ's encounter with the woman taken in adultery (Jn 8.1–11). This method of structuring type and antitype in sacred history is not widespread in drama. The much later Oberammergau play has something akin to this arrangement in a series of *tableaux vivants* from prefigurative Old Testament events preceding each New Testament scene.

The Tyrol Passion plays from the eastern Alpine region are, like the Frankfurt group, related one to another and are presumed to have a common origin. They are distinguished from other German specimens by a greater selectivity of incident and by a uniformly elevated tone. Omitting Old Testament material, they begin late in the life of the Redeemer, with the council of the Jews plotting His death. They cover a three-day division of performance: the arrest and trials of Christ, the Crucifixion, and the Resurrection. On the first two days, comic intrusion into the solemn scenes is virtually absent, but on the third day there is a notable amount of it. It is highly probable that the first and second divisions were actually performed on Holy Thursday and Good Friday, when the buffoonery would have been regarded as unacceptable; the third day's action, given on Easter or shortly afterward, would have a context of returning joy capable of supporting the comic dimension.

French Plays. French Passion plays reveal much the same history as do those in Germany. The early vernacular texts are of Burgundian provenance and are all related ultimately to the nondramatic narrative poem *Passion des jongleurs,* mentioned above. The oldest play in this group is called *La Passion du Palatinus.* Although it has many dramatic and interesting touches—such as the forging of the nails for the Crucifixion by the wife of the blacksmith, who himself refuses the odious task—this play is still clumsy and awkward in many ways. G. Cohen has even expressed doubt that it was actually performed, since it lacks rubrics that can be regarded as stage directions. There is a closely related *Passion d'Autun,* existing in two versions; and a much later and more elaborate *Passion de Semur* associated with the Burgundian area.

The really great French Passion plays are those of Eustache Mercadé and Arnoul Greban, both 15th-century dramatists whose gigantic plays were subjected to revision and adaptation by later writers, most skilfully by Jean Michel. These French *mystères* show divergence from the standard German design; although they omit most of the Old Testament narrative, they do include the Nativity and early life of Christ. Moreover, they envelope the titanic serial narrative in a unifying framework known as the *Procès de Paradis,* quite different from the German forms of prophetic prologue and Augustinian commentary. The *Procès* is a dramatization of the debate among Righteousness, Mercy, Truth, and Peace at the throne of God, allegorizing the conflict between His justice and His mercy. The allegorized virtues, known in homiletic literature as the Four Daughters of God, are reconciled only when the Second Person of the Trinity undertakes to expiate man's sin; they reappear at intervals in the long cycle, most notably at the return of Christ to heaven when Justice (Righteousness) at first sulks in a corner, but then, in a dramatic and thrilling capitulation, accepts the satisfaction made by the Redeemer.

Mercadé's *Passion d'Arras,* as it is called, surpasses Greban's in the theological profundity of its material, but is in turn excelled by the latter's skill in poetry and music. The position held by Greban as organist and choirmaster at Notre Dame Cathedral in Paris developed in him the technical mastery that he displayed in versification, dialogue, lyric forms, and musical pieces. His *Passion* has been well termed a melodrama, not in the modern sense, but in the original concept of a play rich in musical melody. Closely associated with this technical achievement and inseparable from it is Greban's mastery of emotional language, especially that of tenderness and pity. He could thus express in moving fashion the anguish of Christ in thc Garden and His plea to the Father; above all he could imaginatively represent the role of the Sorrowful Mother pleading with her Son to evade the Passion and cross, then lamenting in her traditional *planctus Mariae* the actualization of her worst fears for His welfare.

Modern Survival. Performances of Passion plays continued long into modern times. One of the German dramas is still flourishing in a regular presentation at Oberammergau every tenth year. The origin of this custom is a well-known series of events related to the Thirty Years' War of the early 17th century. During the devastation of the Bavarian countryside by Swedish troops in 1632, a severe outbreak of the plague occurred, first in the lowlands, spreading gradually to the upland villages, including Oberammergau. After months of such disaster, the town council of this devout Catholic village decided upon a vow: they would sacrifice a year in every decade to the presentation of a Passion play. This promise was made by all the villagers for themselves and their descendants as an act of penance and petition for deliverance; it is the Oberammergau tradition that no one died of the plague after this solemn religious act. The most famous actors to play the role of the "Christus" in the 20th century have been members of the Lang family, Anton and a distant relative, Alois.

From the 12th-century *planctus Mariae* and the simple Latin plays of the Benediktbeuern MS to the gigantic spectacles of the German and French cycles, the Passion play has been a paraliturgical expression of popular devotion to the suffering of the Redeemer and has engaged the talents of innumerable craftsmen, poets, musicians, and actors, who have coveted an opportunity to take part in it by designing its scenes, singing in its chorus, or being chosen to act in the great role of the "Christus."

Bibliography: G. COHEN, *Le Théâtre en France au moyen âge* (rev. ed. Paris 1948). H. CRAIG, *English Religious Drama of the Middle Ages* (Oxford 1955). W. M. A. CREIZENACH, *Geschichte des neueren Dramas*, 5 v. (Halle 1893–1916; v. 2, rev. ed. 1918). G. FRANK, *The Medieval French Drama* (Oxford 1954). C. J. STRATMAN, *Bibliography of the Medieval Drama* (Berkeley 1954). K. YOUNG, *The Drama of the Medieval Church*, 2 v. (Oxford 1933). E. H. CORATHIEL, *Oberammergau and Its Passion Play* (Westminster, Md. 1960). R. FRONING, ed., *Das Drama des Mittelalters*, 3 v. (Stuttgart 1891–92). F. MONE, ed., *Schauspiele des Mittelalters* (Karlsruhe 1846). *Le Mystère de la Passion d'Arnoul Greban*, ed. G. PARIS and G. RAYNAUD (Paris 1878). E. ROY, *Le Mystère de la Passion en France du XIVᵉ au XVIᵉ siècle*, 2 v. (Dijon 1903–04), still a classic, but corrected by later studies. J. E. WACKERNELL, *Altdeutsche Passionsspiele aus Tirol* (Graz 1897).

[E. C. DUNN]

PASSIONEI, DOMENICO

Cardinal, statesman, and man of letters; b. Fossombrone, Italy, Dec. 4, 1682; d. Camaldoli di Frascati, Italy, July 5, 1761. When 13 years old he attended the Clementine College at Rome, conducted by the SOMASCAN FATHERS. Under the guidance of his uncle Msgr. Guido Passionei he completed his studies with distinction and won the friendship of the scholars Antonio Magliabechi and Giusto Fontanini and the Cardinals Henry NORIS and Tommaso Ferrari. Through them he was introduced to the MAURISTS and the highest cultural circles. Family tradition more than vocation (so he writes in a letter to Cardinal Neri Corsini) initiated him into an ecclesiastical career, and he studied dogmatic theology and Church history under the direction of Giuseppe TOMAS. Clement XI commissioned him to take the cardinal's hat to Ludovico Gualtieri, nuncio to France; Passionei remained in France from 1706 to 1708.

From his friends Jean MABILLON, Bernard de MONTFAUCON, Eusèbe Renaudot, and Cardinals Cesar d'Estrées and Louis Antoine de NOAILLES, he learned a great love of books and with them he frequented the Abbey of Saint-Germain-des-Prés, which had become the meeting place of French intellectuals. His initiative and desire to excel annoyed Msgr. Agostino Cusani, the new nuncio to France. He was ordered to leave, and with resentment went first to Brussels, then to Holland, where he remained from 1708 to 1713. As the representative of Clement XI, he showed diplomatic skill at the Treaty of Utrecht (1713–14) and the Congress of Baden (1714), which ended the conflict between France and Spain over the Spanish succession. At Solette he presided at the renewal of the alliance between France and the Catholic Swiss cantons, and in 1715 he returned to Fossombrone.

Passionei became secretary of the Propagation of the Faith in 1720 and played a notable role in the conversion to Catholicism of the Protestant historian Johann Georg von Eckart. He was made bishop of Ephesus in *partibus* by Innocent XIII (1721) and sent to Switzerland as nuncio. Transferred to the nunciature of Vienna (1730), he became the friend of Eugene of Savoy; Prince Ludwig von Würtenburg, whom he converted to Catholicism; and the Venetian ambassador, Marco Foscarini. Later, in Rome, Foscarini stole from him the MSS *Arcana Papatus* of Paolo Sarpi and a dossier of Sarpi's letters. At Vienna Passionei tutored the daughters of Charles VI; he also blessed the marriage of Francis of Lorraine with Archduchess Maria Theresa of Austria. In 1738 he was appointed to the secretariate of briefs by Clement XII and created cardinal, first of S. Bernardo alle Terme and later of S. Lorenzo in Lucina. In 1755 Benedict XIV named him prefect of the Vatican Library. In the palace of the Consulta on the Quirinal Passionei amassed a rich private library of 40,000 volumes. After his death this library was bought by the Augustinians, and later added to the Angelica Library in Rome, except for about 6,000 volumes that made up the first nucleus of the Civic Library of Fossombrone (April 19, 1784). Among his writings are *Universae philosophiae studia* (Rome 1701) and *Acta legationis helveticae ab anno 1723 ad annum 1729* (Zug 1729; 2d ed. Rome 1738).

Passionei remains a figure of controversy. He has been considered an enemy of the Jesuits because he rejected Molinism and probabilism; and because he opposed the beatification of Robert Bellarmine, but voted for that of Juan de Palafox. This antipathy is alleged as the chief cause of his failure to win the papal election in the conclave of 1758. He is also censured as a Roman Jansenist because of his association with scholars, themselves suspected of Jansenistic sympathies, who gathered at the "Hermitage" at Camaldoli da Frascati. Here he presided, seated beneath a portrait of Antoine Arnauld and holding the *Lettres provinciales* of Blaise Pascal. G. V. Vella calls him a bibliophile with "library kleptomania," who used his position as papal nuncio to visit monasteries with the intent of finding and receiving as gifts precious MSS and rare books. His critics seem in agreement, however, on his skills in his various diplomatic posts. Regarding his alleged Jansenistic sympathies, it can be said that Passionei shared the anti-Jesuitism of the transalpine Jansenists, but remained substantially orthodox in his theology and loyalty to Rome.

Bibliography: M. RIOLLET, *Correspondance, 1724–1727 de Valbonnais avec Mgr. Passionei* (Grenoble 1933). P. L. GALLETTI, *Memorie per servir alla storia della vita del Card. Domenico Passionei* (Rome 1762). F. M. TORRICELLI, comp., *Antologia,* 4 v. (Fossombrone, Italy 1842–46). A. VERNARECCI, *Fossombrone dai tempi antichissimi ai nostri,* 2 v. (Fossombrone 1907–14). E. ROSA, "La causa del ven. card. Bellarmino e l'oppozione del card. Passionei," *La civiltá cattolica* 69, (1918) 2:336–346; "Carteggio inedito del card. de Tencin a Benedetto XIV intorno al ven. card. Bellarmino" *ibid.* 4:48–55; "Le *Memorie* della città di Fossombrone e il card. Domenico Passionei," *ibid.* 2: 254–261. M. COSTELBARCO-ALBANI, *Della Somaglia, un grande bibliofilo del secolo XVIII* (Florence 1937). E. DAMMIG, *Il movimento giansenista a Roma nella seconda metà del secolo XVIII* (Vatican City 1945). A. MERCATI, *Note per la storia di alcune biblioteche romane nei secoli XVI–XIX* (Vatican City 1952). G. V. VELLA, "L'abate Domenico Passionei e le sue missioni diplomatiche dal 1708–1716," *Nuova Rivista Storica* 33, 302–341; 34 (1950) 197–234; *Il Passionei e la politica di Clemente XI, 1708–1716* (Biblioteca della Nuova Rivista Storica 19). E. SGRECCIA, *Il fondo card. Passionei della Biblioteca civica di Fossombrone* (Fano, Italy 1963), extract from *Studia Picena,* v. 31.

[R. BELVEDERI]

PASSIONIST NUNS

Also known as Religious of the Passion of Jesus Christ (CP, Official Catholic Directory, #3170). A cloistered contemplative community of women founded by Saint PAUL OF THE CROSS. On May 3, 1771, the first superior, Mother Mary Crucified, born Faustina Constantini (1713–1787) and nine other women donned the Passionist habit, took the customary vows of poverty, chastity, obedience and enclosure as well as a fourth vow, also taken by their Passionist brothers, to promote devotion to the Passion of Christ. The nuns fulfill this unique vow through their lives of prayer and penance, as stipulated in the Rule written by Paul of the Cross in 1769 and approved by the Holy See on Sept. 30, 1770.

Mother Mary Crucified first met Paul of the Cross in 1738, when he preached a retreat for her cloistered Benedictine community. She remained in regular contact with him through the intervening years, while he worked to bring to fruition his dream of the Passionist Congregation for men and the cloistered community for women.

For over 100 years the nuns' only monastery was the original foundation in Corneto, Italy, but in 1872 a second foundation was established in Mamers, France. In 1910 the first monastery was established in the United States. Today, the Passionist nuns are present throughout the world.

Each monastery is autonomous and develops, within the contemplative lifestyle, its own means of financial support. All monasteries continue a close spiritual affiliation with the larger Congregation of the Passion.

Bibliography: P. F. SPENCER, CP, *As a Seal Upon Your Heart: The Life of St. Paul of the Cross, Founder of the Passionists* (Middlegreen, England 1994). R. MECURIO, CP, *The Passionists* (Collegeville 1992). J. MEAD, *St. Paul of the Cross* (New Rochelle, NY 1983).

[E. RINERE]

PASSIONIST SISTERS

Also known as Sisters of the Cross and Passion (CP, Official Catholic Directory, #3180). Founded in Manchester, England, March 25, 1851 by Elizabeth Prout (1820–1864) with guidance from Passionist priests Gaudentius Rossi and Ignatius Spencer (1799–1864), from whom the first sisters received their spiritual heritage. The institute, originally known as the "Catholic Sisters of the Holy Family," formally affiliated with the Congregation of the Passion in 1874, and adopted the title "Sisters of the Cross and Passion" (CP). Initial approbation of the rule was received from the Holy See in 1863.

Nineteenth-century Manchester was in the process of developing into one of England's first industrial centers and was also the subject of a Catholic revival, or "second spring." Under this dual influence, the new institute brought Passionist spirituality as well as education and basic social services to those disenfranchised by the industrialization process. Unique for its time, the institute was itself open to the poor since it did not require dowries from women who sought membership. By the beginning of the 20th century, it was one of the largest apostolic communities in England and exerted great influence in the development of national educational plans.

From these roots, the congregation expanded to Ireland, Scotland and Wales, as well as to South America (Chile, Peru, Argentina), the United States, Africa (Botswana), the West Indies (Jamaica), and Eastern Europe. Its focus remains response to the needs of the poor through education or other social outreach.

Bibliography: A. M. REYNOLDS, CP, *Heralds of Hope: The Sisters of the Cross and Passion* (Strasbourg 1988). E. HAMER, *Elizabeth Prout, 1820–1864: A Religious Life for Industrial England* (Bath 1994).

[E. RINERE]

John Dominic Tarlattini, first provincial and associate founder of the Passionists in the United States.

PASSIONISTS

(Official Catholic Directory, #1000). A religious institute professing simple perpetual vows and officially entitled the Congregation of the Passion of Jesus Christ, for which the initials are "C. P." The habit is a black tunic with a leather belt. The heart-shaped emblem with a cross mounted on the heart with the inscription *Jesu XPI Passio* "The Passion of Jesus Christ" in Greek, Hebrew, and Latin is the official seal of the Passionists and is worn on the tunic.

Origin. The Passionists were founded in Italy in 1720 by Paul Francis Danei (now St. PAUL OF THE CROSS), who, at the age of 26, after a retreat of 40 days, wrote the *Rule* and *Constitutions* for his Passionist Community. The following year he took a vow to promote the memory of the Passion; this particular vow accounts for the Congregation's distinctive spirituality and its specific apostolate. In 1725 Benedict XIII permitted Paul to recruit members, but it was not until 1737 that the first foundation was completed on Monte Argentario near Orbetello.

Papal approval was granted for the *Rule* in 1741 and again in 1769, following two revisions. The reasons for the delay in approval were: (1) the severity of the original *Rule*, which had to be tempered so as to make it livable; (2) Paul had extensive correspondence with the Holy See to convince them the purpose of the Community was to keep alive the "*memory* of the Passion" rather than simply to promote "*devotion* to the Passion." After the *Rule* was approved for the first time, Paul sought to obtain permission for solemn vows for his brethren. The reason for this is that it would allow him more authority in presenting candidates for ordination, rather than making him dependent on the local bishop for such permissions. It would also allow him to establish a Community of PASSIONIST NUNS. On November 16, 1769, Clement XIV's bull *Supremi Apostolatus* praised and approved the Passionist Congregation. Soon after, the pope entrusted to the Passionists the perpetual custody of the ancient Basilica of SS. John and Paul on the Coelian Hill in Rome that became the General Headquarters of the Congregation. By the time of his death, October 18, 1775, Paul had established 12 houses, two provinces, and in Rome, one hospice; he presided over six General Chapters; his members numbered 114 priests and 62 brothers. He also founded a second community, the cloistered Passionists Nuns.

Spirituality. The spirituality of the Passionists is identical with that of its founder. The cross dominated Paul's life. He desired to participate as intimately and absolutely as possible in the sufferings and death of the Redeemer to effect the complete transformation of his soul in God. The establishment of an Institute whose members would perpetually carry out this ideal and bring its fruits to countless souls was the single object of all his labors. The *Rule* and the way of life he bequeathed his followers aimed at removing every obstacle to participation in

Bernard Mary Silvestrelli.

Christ's Passion and at providing every means to render it efficacious. Hence, the spirit of the Congregation, emphasized in its official documents, is one of prayer, penance, and solitude.

Rule. St. Paul of the Cross' *Rule* for the Passionists has had only three revisions in over 200 years. In 1917 a minor revision was occasioned by the new *Code of Canon Law*. The second was completed in 1958 after a study was carried out according to the desires and norms of the Holy See. The *Rule* and *Constitutions* were again given papal approval by John XXIII in the brief *Salutiferos Cruciatus*. The *Rule* and *Constitutions* were revised again in 1984 after the Second Vatican Council, which exhorted religious communities to rediscover their founders and charism. The Passionist *Rule* states that the specific purpose of the Congregation is "to recall and promote the memory of the Passion of Christ by its way of life and its apostolate, especially its ministry of preaching."

Passionists take the traditional vows of poverty, chastity, and obedience, as well as a special vow to keep alive in the hearts of the people of God the memory of the sufferings and passion of Christ. The members of this Congregation are called to a contemplative-apostolic spirituality. This is attained through a serious commitment to prayer, community living, and a vigorous apostolic ministry. This latter is especially attained through the preaching of the word of God, in retreats and parochial missions, and by teaching people to pray.

Apostolate. The Second Vatican Council had a profound influence on the life and ministry of the Congregation. The decrees of the 42nd (1988), 43rd (1994), and 44th (2000) General Chapters of the Congregation have researched the founder and the charism of the Community. As a result, the Community has developed a rich understanding of the "memory of the Passion," which in turn has driven the members to identify with and embrace the "crucified of the world" today. These Chapters have motivated its members to have "a passion for life, and a life for the Passion" in contemporary society.

History. For the first 35 years after the death of its founder, the Congregation progressed slowly but steadily, with emphasis on the contemplative and penitential aspects of the life. The first crisis occurred in 1810, when religious communities in Italy were forced to disperse by the Napoleonic suppression of religious communities. Reestablished by Pius VII in 1814, the Passionists were among the first communities reconstituted in Rome. It would take several years for the Community to regain its original vitality before considering any further growth. Before 1840, the Congregation limited itself to Italy, where it had two provinces. The 60 following years, however, were years of increase and expansion during which houses were founded in 13 countries in Europe and America; ten new provinces were formed; a mission in Bulgaria was increased; and a mission to the Australian aborigines was undertaken. The membership rose from 371 in 1840 to 1,475 in 1905.

The man credited for this new growth, Anthony Testa, was well prepared to direct the progress of the Community. After 12 years as provincial of a northern Italian province, he was chosen to be the Superior General of the Congregation. As Superior General he governed for 23 years (1830–62) and is regarded as the second founder. Bernard Silvestrelli guided the Institute from 1875 until his death in 1911. His reputation for holiness and the favors obtained through his intercession led to the introduction of his cause before the Holy See.

In 2001, the total membership of the Passionists was 2,326 religious: 13 bishops, 1,779 priests, 274 brothers, five permanent deacons, and 255 students. There were approximately 400 communities of Passionists throughout the world, spread over 55 countries on the five continents, organized into 23 provinces, four Vice Provinces, and one General Vicariate, with various Provincial Vicariates in mission areas.

Outstanding Members. Besides St. Paul of the Cross, other members of the Congregation have been canonized: St. Eugene BOSSILKOV (1900–1952), St. Innocent Canoura Arnau (1887–1934), St. Gabriel POSSENTI (1838–1862), and St. Vincent STRAMBI (1745–1824). St. Gemma GALGANI (1878–1903) and St. Maria GORETTI (1890–1902) were also sponsored by the Passionists. Fourteen other causes are in various degrees of advancement before the Holy See. Most notable among these causes are: Blessed Dominic BARBERI (1792–1849), who received John Henry NEWMAN into the Church; Blessed Pius CAMPIDELLI (1868–1889), Blessed Isidore De Loor (1881–1916) from Belgium, Blessed Nicephorous Díez-Tejerina (1893–1936) and 27 martyred Passionists (priests, brothers, and students) in the Spanish Civil War, Blessed Charles HOUBEN (1821–1893), a Hollander in Dublin, Ireland, Blessed Grimaldo SANTAMARIA (1883–1902), Blessed Bernard Mary SILVESTRELLI (1840–1921), and Blessed Lawrence SALVI (1782–1856). About 50 other Passionist religious are listed in postulation archives.

Work in the United States. The Passionists established the first house of their Congregation in the U. S. at Pittsburgh, Pa., in 1852 at the invitation of Bishop Michael O'Connor. In 2001 they had 35 communities in the U. S., one in Canada, and two in Jamaica, West Indies. There are 366 religious in two provinces: the eastern with the headquarters at South River, New Jersey, and the western with headquarters in Chicago, Illinois. Foremost among the preaching communities, Passionists pioneered in the retreat movement; they conducted retreats for the laity, priests, and religious, and preached parish missions and renewal programs throughout the United States and Canada. The Passionists in the United States established independent vicariates and are still staffing missions in China, Haiti, Honduras, India, Jamaica, West Indies, Japan, Korea, and the Philippines, as well as, parishes in African-American communities in Alabama, Georgia, and North Carolina. In the past, they published *The Sign,* a monthly magazine of national interest, and are highly involved in television ministries.

Bibliography: C. YUHAUS, *Compelled to Speak: the Passionists in America, Origin and Apostolate* (Westminster, MD 1967). R. MERCURIO, C. P., *The Passionists* (Collegeville, MN 1991). F. WARD, *The Passionists: Sketches Historical and Personal* (New York 1923). F. GIORGINI, *History of the Passionists* (Rome 1987–1988).

[K. O'MALLEY/C. J. YUHAUS]

PASSOVER, FEAST OF

From later Biblical times the Passover, formerly sometimes called the Pasch (Heb. *happesaḥ,* Gr. τὸ πάσχα), celebrated on the night of the 14th to the 15th of Nisan (March or April), has been the principal feast of the Jewish calendar. In the Bible it is combined with the Feast of Unleavened Bread, which is kept from the 15th to the 21st of Nisan. Passover commemorates the Israelites' exodus from Egypt and is observed with great solemnity as well as rejoicing. From the many Biblical references to it, both legislative and historical, no completely clear picture of its origin and evolution is apparent, but there is a widespread consensus of scholarly opinion.

The Sources. The Old Testament texts that contain laws for the observance of the Passover are the passages in the ancient festival calendars of Ex 23.15; 34.18 (see also 34.25); Dt 16.1–8; Lv 23.5–8; Nm 28.16–25 (see also 9.9–14), besides Ex ch. 12, which gives the feast a historical setting. Celebrations of the Passover are described or referred to in Nm 9.1–14; Jos 5.10–12; 4 Kgs 23.21–23 (see also 2 Chr 35.1–19); 2 Chr 30.127; Ezr 6.19–22. In addition to the principal Old Testament texts, important witnesses to the antiquity of the feast are found in a papyrus and two ostraca of the 5th century B.C. from the Jewish settlement at Elephantine in Egypt. In the New Testament, the Passion narratives of all four Gospels mention details of the Passover. Moreover, the intertestamental *Book of Jubilees,* the writings of Philo Judaeus and Flavius Josephus, and other ancient works describe the feast. The Mishnah tractate *Pesahim* contains details of the later mode of observance.

Name. The Old Testament derives the name *pesah* from a Hebrew verb meaning to limp or to jump and hence to jump over or to pass over (e.g., Ex 12.27), referring to Yahweh's "passing over" the houses of the Israelites during the 10th PLAGUE OF EGYPT. But this historical explanation is secondary, and it is not clear that the etymology in it is the original one. Attempts to derive the word from Akkadian or Egyptian roots have not won general acceptance.

In this article the name Passover will be understood to refer to the combined Feast of Passover and Unleavened Bread except where otherwise indicated.

Origin. The oldest Biblical allusions to the festival (Ex 23.15; 34.18) do not mention the name Passover but enjoin the keeping of the Feast of Unleavened Bread for seven days in the spring month of Abib (the old name for Nisan). Since in the later texts this observance forms part of the Passover festival, it is generally held that two originally distinct feasts were combined into one. Probable origins of both can be reconstructed.

The Feast of Unleavened Bread or Feast of Azymes (Heb. *ḥag hammaṣṣôt,* Gr. ἡ ἑορτὴ τῶν ἀζύμων) was one of the three great agricultural pilgrimage feasts, along with the Hebrew Feasts of PENTECOST and BOOTHS (Tabernacles), that the Israelites, after their entry into the Promised Land, adopted from the Canaanites. It was celebrated at the beginning of the barley harvest but at no fixed date; the fact that it extended from Sabbath to Sabbath may have been an Israelite innovation. The avoidance of leaven was probably a symbol of the new beginning being made with the new harvest; nothing from the old year was to be retained when the new season began. Though the calendars give as the reason for the feast, "For in the month of Abib you came out of Egypt," this theme was not original; the Feast of Unleavened Bread, like the other *ḥaggîm,* or pilgrimage feasts, was originally a harvest festival. (*see* UNLEAVENED BREAD (IN THE BIBLE).

Passover in the restricted sense appears in the oldest allusions as a sacrifice and sacrificial meal of quite different significance and background. A lamb was sacrificed on the evening of the full moon in the month later called Nisan, and its blood was spread around the doorframes of homes. The meat was roasted and consumed that night with bitter herbs and unleavened bread. Apparently the rite was conducted privately by families or small groups at home, although one cannot exclude the possibility that at some early epoch whole tribes gathered for it at local sanctuaries. In any event, it appears to be very ancient in the history of Israel, even though the oldest festival calendars do not mention it, perhaps because it was not at the time a public celebration.

Passover seems to be the spring festival of nomadic peoples when they sacrificed one of the firstlings of the flock in petition for an ensuing year of prosperity. Analogies for it have been pointed out among ancient and modern Arab tribes, and all of its details can be accounted for among the customs of a shepherd people. For example, the bitter herbs were a natural seasoning, the unleavened bread the normal fare of nomads, and the blood upon the doorframes an apotropaic rite, i.e., one performed to ward off evil spirits. The "destroyer" mentioned in Ex 12.23 is regarded as a trace of this last element. The Israelites had been seminomads prior to their settlement in Canaan, and they may have celebrated this feast even in Egypt before the Exodus. But sometime after that event they altered its meaning radically.

Evolution. The description of the "first Passover" in Ex ch. 12 (a late text embodying several traditions) relates the familiar story of the slaughter of the firstborn of Egypt and the destroying angel's "passing over" of the Israelites as they feasted within their homes. Moses enjoins observing the feast and explains all its rites as growing out of and commemorating the events of that historic night. In this passage, the seven days of Unleavened Bread are said to commemorate the going out of Egypt, and all references to either feast in the festival calendars make the same association. It is not a natural association, however, and the very probable origin of the feasts lies elsewhere. What is found in these texts is evidence of the process of historicizing by which the three great pilgrimage festivals of the Israelite year were invested with a role in reliving the drama of SALVATION HISTORY. In the case of Unleavened Bread this process took place earlier than for Pentecost and Booths, since it is only for Unleavened Bread that the earliest calendars (i.e., those of the YAHWIST and the ELOHIST) mention the historical connotation. How early the nomadic Passover was cast in the historical mold of Ex ch. 12 it is impossible to say, but it is not unlikely that it happened in the time of Moses himself. The intervention in Israel's history portrayed as the Exodus may in fact have occurred at the spring sacrificial celebration.

One can be somewhat more precise in estimating the time when the feasts of Passover and Unleavened Bread were combined into one festival. This event is connected with the centralization of the Israelite cult under Josiah, King of Judah (*c.* 640–609 B.C.), that is reflected in the Deuteronomic tradition of the Pentateuch. Josiah's Passover (2 Kgs 23.21–23; 2 Chr 35.1–19) is described as unique since the most ancient times, and the Deuteronomic ordinances (Dt 16.1–8) insist that the feast must be celebrated at the Jerusalem Temple. Josiah had made the shepherd Passover a pilgrimage festival as well, and since it nearly coincided in time with the Feast of Unleavened Bread—and also in its connotations, the latter recalling the hardships of the Israelites' flight—the two were eventually held to be parts of one festival. Unleavened Bread thus received a specific date (Nisan 15–21), and although it could no longer be observed from Sabbath to Sabbath, the first and last days were still kept as days of rest from work.

That this combining of the feasts was preexilic is confirmed by the fact that they are joined in Ezekiel's ideal festival calendar (Ez 45.21). Several texts seem to suggest that the combining took place even earlier, but the evidence of the calendars must be preferred. The Passover of Joshua (Jos 5.10–11) does not clearly mention the eating of unleavened bread as a festival rite; the account of King Hezekiah's Passover (2 Chronicles ch. 30), purportedly celebrated at the Temple in the 2d month because it had not been done properly in Nisan, is probably not historical, at least in its details. The "Passover Papyrus" from Elephantine, which may be dated 419 B.C., confirms the union of the two feasts.

Ancient Rites. It is the passages of the Priestly tradition (see PRIESTLY WRITERS, PENTATEUCHAL), especially Ex 12.1–20, 43–49; Nm 28.16–25, that provide the most detailed picture of the Passover celebration. The rites began on the 10th day of the 1st month (with the year reckoned as beginning in spring) when the sacrificial victim was chosen, a spotless male lamb, one-year old, for each family or group of families. In the early evening of the 14th day of the month the people assembled at the Temple, and the lambs were slaughtered; previously this had taken place privately at home or at local shrines. Immediately afterward, the blood of the PASSOVER LAMB was daubed upon the doorposts and lintel of the house where the meal was to be consumed, in memory of the sign used to protect the Israelites in Egypt. The lamb was then roasted and had to be consumed that night, along with bitter herbs and unleavened bread, which recalled the haste and the rigors of the flight from Egypt. No bone of the sacrificial victim could be broken and no leftovers kept; all remains had to be burned by the next morning.

The participants were to eat the Passover meal "in haste," with loins girded, sandals on, and staff in hand, i.e., dressed for traveling in remembrance of the suddenness of Israel's departure from Egypt. All the members of the household participated in the meal, even slaves and strangers, provided they were circumcised. The observance was of obligation for all, and ritual uncleanness in certain circumstances or the fact of being on a journey did not excuse from it (Nm 9.9–13), although in general, later texts imply the need for ritual purity (e.g., Ezr 6.20–21).

For the following seven days all were required to eat only unleavened bread and to be certain that no leaven was found in the home under penalty of being "cut off from Israel." The strictness of this obligation seems more a consequence of the agricultural origin of the custom than of the symbolic meaning attached to it. On the 1st and 7th days (i.e., the 15th and the 21st of Nisan) there was to be rest from work, an assembly at the Temple, and special sacrifices. In Lv 23.9–14 it was prescribed that "on the day after the sabbath" (an ambiguous dating that was to be the subject of controversy in later Judaism) a sheaf of the first fruits of the harvest should be waved before Yahweh (i.e., offered as a quasi sacrifice of the new harvest). Special sacrifices accompanied this ceremony, and from this day were calculated the seven weeks to Pentecost.

At the time of the New Testament, Passover was observed according to the general lines of the Priestly tradition, with strict adherence to the Deuteronomic insistence that the sacrifice itself take place at the Temple; people brought their lambs to be killed and then returned home or to some nearby house to eat the ritual meal. The atmo-sphere of familial joy surrounding the feast had by that time been considerably heightened. In the Gospels themselves the Passover plays an important role, historically and symbolically, but the Synoptics and the Fourth Gospel disagree about whether or not the Last Supper was a paschal meal. There is some evidence that the QUMRAN COMMUNITY observed the feast, perhaps even quite independently of the Temple ritual and following their own calendar, which assigned the Passover annually to the same day of the week. Tuesday. After the destruction of the Temple at the fall of Jerusalem (A.D. 70), the sacrifice of the paschal lamb disappeared, along with all Temple rites, from the festival observance, and the rite for the Passover meal was embellished to preserve the symbolism of the feast. It is disputed whether this rite, to be described below, may not have come into existence even before the destruction of the Temple.

The slaughter of the Passover lamb survives even today in the practice of the Samaritan community centered about Nablus. It is sometimes argued that, since the destruction of their temple on Mt. Gerizim (129 B.C.) did not destroy this ritual, the ritual must have been performed privately in a family festival and not merely as a temple sacrifice. Indeed, many aspects of the Samaritan Passover celebration recall what it must have been like in the time of the Israelite kingdom. In Samaritan usage, for example, the feasts of Passover and of Unleavened Bread are still regarded as separate.

Modern Passover Meal. The ritual paschal meal, held privately in the home and sometimes conducted for groups, especially of travelers away from home, is commonly called the Seder (Heb. *sēder*, order, arrangement). The present-day Seder is substantially the same as the ceremony outlined in the Mishnah (*Pes.* 10). The narrative text followed during the meal is called the Passover HAGGADAH (story), and both terms Seder and Haggadah are used to designate the booklet containing text and ceremonies.

Two preliminary rites are closely linked with the Seder. One is the formal searching of the home on the night before Passover for any form of leaven or leavened food, which is set aside and later destroyed or given away. No leaven may remain in the home during the festival, and utensils used for leavened foods must be replaced or purified. The other preliminary ceremony is the so-called Fast of the Firstborn observed prior to the Passover meal.

A table set for the Seder contains the following special items: three cakes of unleavened bread (*maṣṣôt*, matzos) placed on a Seder dish and covered, a roasted shank bone symbolizing the paschal lamb, a roasted egg as an offering for the feast, bitter herbs (*mārôr*, usually horseradish), some parsley and salted water, a mixture of nuts and fruit (*ḥărōset*) used to sweeten the bitter herbs, enough wine for four cups each, and a cup at each place with an extra one for Elijah, who is expected to announce the redemption on Passover night.

The ceremony begins with the blessing (*qiddûš*) over the first cup of wine. Parsley dipped in water is eaten in memory of the hardships of the Israelites' life in Egypt. The master of the house breaks the middle cake of *maṣṣâ* and conceals half of it to be eaten at the end of the meal (the *'ăpîqômān*). Then the youngest one present asks the dramatic question, "Why is this night different from other nights?" There follow four specific questions regarding the unleavened bread, the bitter herbs, reclining on cushions, and eating parsley. In answer, the master of the house reads the main narrative of the Haggadah, recounting the events of the Exodus (fulfilling the command of Ex 13.8 to teach the children on Passover night). There are also several rabbinic explanations, including a commentary on Dt 26.5–8, "A wandering Aramean was my father. . . ." The Hallel is then begun [Ps 112(113)–113A(114)], the second cup is drunk with a blessing, and all wash their hands in preparation for the meal. This begins with handing around and eating first *maṣṣôt*, then bitter herbs dipped in *ḥărōset,* and these again served on pieces of unleavened bread. Then the main body of the meal is taken, and the *'ăpîqômān* is eaten last to retain the taste of *maṣṣâ*. Grace is said, and the third cup is drunk. Finally the Hallel is completed [Ps 113B(115)–117(118)], the Great Hallel [Ps 135(136)] sung, and the last cup taken with a blessing.

At various times and in various regions additions have been made to this basic structure. The most familiar of these is the addition in the Ashkenazic (German-Jewish rite) Seder of five medieval folk songs or poems at the end of the meal, including the *"Eḥād mî yôdēa"* (Who knows one?) and the *Had gadyā'* (An only kid).

Bibliography: *Encyclopedic Dictionary of the Bible,* tr. and adap. by L. HARTMAN (New York 1963), from A. VAN DEN BORN, *Bijbels Woordenboek* 1746–51. H. HAAG, *Lexikon für Theologie und Kirche,* ed. J. HOFER and K. RAHNER, 10 v. (2d, new ed. Freiburg 1957–65) 8:133–37; *Dictionnaire de la Bible,* suppl. ed. L. PIROT, et al. (Paris 1928–) 6:1120–49. R. DE VAUX, *Ancient Israel, Its Life and Institutions,* tr. J. MCHUGH (New York 1961) 484–93. E. G. HIRSCH, *The Jewish Encyclopedia,* ed. J. SINGER, 13 v. (New York 1901–06) 9:548–56. T. H. GASTER, *Passover, Its History and Traditions* (New York 1949). J. B. SEGAL, *The Hebrew Passover from the Earliest Times to A.D 70* (London Oriental Series 12; London 1963), review in *The Catholic Biblical Quarterly* 26 (1964) 123–26. P. GRELOT, "Études sur le 'Papyrus Pascal' d'Éléphantine," *Vetus Testamentum* 4 (1954) 349–84. C. W. ATKINSON, "The Ordinances of Passover-Unleavened Bread," *Anglican Theological Review* 44 (1962) 70–85. N. FÜGLISTER, *Die Heilsbedeutung des Pascha* (Studien zum Alten und Neuen Testament 8; Munich 1963). J. JEREMIAS, *Die Passahfeier der Samaritaner,*

Zeitschrift für die alttestamentliche Wissenschaft Beiheft 59 (Giessen 1932). "Pesahim," *The Mishnah,* tr. H. DANBY (Oxford 1933) 136–51. *The Haggadah,* tr. C. ROTH (London 1934). L. N. DEMBITZ, *The Jewish Encyclopedia* 11:142–47. A. Z. IDELSOHN, *Jewish Liturgy and Its Development* (New York 1932) 173–87.

[G. W. MACRAE]

PASSOVER LAMB

The animal sacrificed annually at Passover and consumed in the ritual meal.

In the Old Testament, the ancient Priestly law of Ex 12.3–10 probably reflects an earlier custom of sacrifice among shepherd peoples. The victim, taken from the flock, could be either a lamb or a kid, male, unblemished, and born within the preceding year, hence the first fruits representing the whole flock. It was to be separated from the flock in advance to mark it as a sacred victim set apart for the divinity. The animal was immolated by having its throat cut at twilight, then roasted whole over an open fire. None of its bones could be broken (Ex 12.46). Its flesh was consumed in a ritual Passover meal during the night. Since Passover was a family feast, the sacrificial slaying was originally performed by the father of the family.

The Deuteronomic law, which transformed the Feast of PASSOVER into a pilgrimage feast, permitted the use of the young of oxen as well as of smaller animals (Dt 16.2), an updating resulting from the change from a pastoral to an agrarian economy. The ritual sacrifice thenceforth had to be performed at the Jerusalem Temple and was eventually assimilated to the regulations of Leviticus ch. 3 for communion sacrifices: the immolation could be performed only by priests, and the fat pieces were burned on the altar (2 Chr 35.10–14). The immolation was performed at sunset.

In New Testament times, the evening sacrifice was anticipated by an hour to provide time for the immolation of the lambs, which had to be completed by sunset. The owner of the lamb slew it himself, but the priests dashed the blood at the foot of the altar and burned the fat, to the sound of trumpets and the singing of the Hallel. Then each Israelite took his lamb home and roasted it whole on a spit made of pomegranate wood (*Pesaḥim* 5.1–7). Since the destruction of the Temple, the Jews celebrate Passover without the lamb; only the Samaritans retain the ancient usage.

The comparison of Jesus to the Passover lamb is the result of the reflection of the early Christian community upon the circumstances of His death at Passover. Paul is the first to express it, in 1 Cor 5.7: as the sacrifice of the lamb is a memorial of the deliverance from Egypt and in later times was regarded as expiatory, so Christ's sacrificial death at Passover has redeemed mankind from the slavery of sin. The theme occurs also in Jn 19.36, where the prohibition against breaking a bone is applied to Jesus on the cross, and also in the Johannine chronology, which places the Crucifixion on the preparation day, when the lambs were sacrificed in the Temple.

See Also: LAMB OF GOD.

Bibliography: *Encyclopedic Dictionary of the Bible*, tr. and adap. by L. HARTMAN (New York 1963) 1751. J. BLINZLER, *Lexikon für Theologie und Kirche*, ed. J. HOFER and K. RAHNER (Freiburg 1957–65) 8:137. G. WALTHER, *Jesus, das Passalamm des Neuen Bundes* (Gütersloh 1950).

[C. J. PEIFER]

PASTOR, LUDWIG VON

Historian; b. Aachen, Jan. 31, 1854; d. Innsbruck, Sept. 30, 1928. Pastor is known as the "Historian of the Popes" and is remembered for his monumental history of the papacy from Martin V (1417) to Pius VI (1799). His use of the Vatican archives, in an age when methods of scientific research were greatly influencing historical exposition, made his study the first thoroughly documented history of the papacy, surpassing the works of Leopold von RANKE and Mandell CREIGHTON. Born to a Lutheran father and a Catholic mother, Pastor was converted to Catholicism after his father's death (1864). Johannes Janssen, famed Catholic historian, influenced Pastor in his youth, and he pursued his natural inclination for historical studies. As Janssen's protégé and friend, he received a solid education, graduating from a gymnasium (1875) and studying at the universities of Louvain, Bonn, Berlin, and Vienna. He earned his doctorate in history at the University of Graz (1878). Interested in Church history, he investigated various archives in Italy, and sought permission to inspect the secret papal archives, which had been open to scholars only on a limited basis before 1870 and closed thereafter. Pastor, determined to gain access to the undisclosed treasure of Vatican documents, wrote petitions and appealed to high-ranking churchmen. His persistence was rewarded (1879) with the granting of limited privileges. In 1883, however, Pope LEO XIII unexpectedly removed all research restrictions for all scholars. At a special audience of historians, Leo XIII stated: "True history must be written from the original sources. . . . We have nothing to fear from the publication of these documents." To Pastor personally, who was then engaged in research on the papacy, the Pontiff said: "Owing to this decree [*Saepenumero considerantes*] you have a good advantage over Ranke. . . . The fact that

Samaritans gather on Mount Gerizim in the spring at Passover to slay lambs and roast them over a fire as an offering to God. Near Nabulus, Samaria, Jordan. 1965. (©Dean Conger/ CORBIS)

many of these writings have never been used and some not even known, must increase the value of your work considerably. Naturally it will spread your fame as an historian." Pastor is generally credited with influencing this new Vatican policy.

He spent his remaining years engaged in research, writing, and teaching. As professor at the University of Innsbruck (1881–1901) Pastor became a popular teacher with an enthusiastic student following. He received numerous honorary degrees and decorations and was eventually raised to the rank of hereditary nobility by the Austrian emperor. He was appointed director of the Austrian Historical Institute in Rome (1901) and Austrian ambassador to the Holy See (1920). Pastor died eight weeks after the death of the other renowned Catholic historian of the popes, Msgr. Horace K. Mann.

Pastor was a prolific writer of books and articles: his principal work was *History of the Popes from the Close of the Middle Ages* (16 v. 1886–1933; Eng. ed. 40 v. 1891–1953). This massive study aims at describing the forces of the Reformation era as reflected in the history of 55 popes. Pastor skillfully blended the inner life of the papacy with political and cultural tendencies. Certain interpretations and his criteria for selecting documents have been questioned by historians. Pastor's belief that only a Catholic can adequately understand and interpret the papacy has also been challenged. In general, however, the tone of his magnum opus is moderate and far from apologetic. That he provides a wealth of unused sources and presents an erudite, comprehensive account of the popes of the 15th through 18th centuries makes this study indispensable. His other major work is J. Janssen and L. Pastor, *Geschichte des deutschen Volkes* (8 v. 1893–1926), a cultural history of Germany during the Reformation begun by Janssen and completed by Pastor who wrote the last two volumes after his friend's death. Pastor also wrote a biography, *Johannes Janssen, ein Lebensbild* (1892), as well as biographies of others, e.g., August Reichensperger, Max von Gagern, and Viktor Dankl. Among his Church histories are *Die Korrespondenz des Kardinals Contarini während seiner deutschen Legation 1541* (1880), *Allgemeine Dekrete der Römischen Inquisition aus den Jahren 1555–1597* (1912), and *Katholische Reformatoren* (1924).

Bibliography: L. VON PASTOR, *Tagebücher, Briefe, Erinnerungen*, ed. W. WÜHR (Heidelberg 1950); autobiography in *Die Geschichtswissenschaft der Gegenwart in Selbstdarstellungen*, ed. S. STEINBERG, 2 v. (Leipzig 1925–26) 2:169–198. F. FELLNER, "Ludwig von Pastor," *Church Historians*, ed. P. GUILDAY (New York 1926) 373–415. J. W. THOMPSON and B. J. HOLM, *History of Historical Writing*, 2 v. (New York 1942) 2:546–549.

[J. T. COVERT]

PASTORAL EPISTLES

Three New Testament texts, 1–2 Timothy and Titus, have been collectively known as the Pastoral Epistles since the mid-nineteenth century. The Canon of Muratori said that they were written "for the ordering of ecclesiastical discipline." Used by Polycarp of Smyrna, these epistles were assumed to have been written by the apostle Paul until the advent of historical criticism in the early nineteenth century. Over the course of two centuries scholars advanced a number of arguments against their authenticity so that by the end of the twentieth century biblical scholarship reached almost universal consensus that these texts had not been written by Paul. A small number of scholars continue to hold that some of Paul's personal notes have been incorporated into 2 Timothy (the so-called fragment hypothesis).

Authenticity. Detailed study of the epistles' vocabulary and style has been one of the major factors leading to the scholarly consensus. One of every five words in the Pastorals do not appear elsewhere in the New Testament, another one of every five do not appear in any of the other

"epistles of Paul." Several of Paul's characteristic words and phrases, "body," for example, are absent from these epistles. Several other words are used in the Pastorals, but with a meaning different from their meaning in Paul's own writings, for example "faith" (1 Tm 1.5, etc.) and "rulers" (Ti 3.1).

The Pastorals are relatively silent about some of Paul's most important ideas, the resurrection, the Holy Spirit, and, according to some scholars, justification. The epistles' way of dealing with opponents also differs from that of Paul. Opponents are dispatched with conventional idiom — they are deceivers and impostors (2 Tm 3.13), whose minds and consciences have been corrupted (Ti 1.15). Little attempt is made to refute their ideas (with the exception of 1 Tm 4.3–5). Titus is urged to avoid stupid controversies, genealogies, dissensions, and quarrels because they are unprofitable and worthless (Ti 3.9). Attempts to create a specific profile of these opponents have been largely doomed to failure because of the paucity of real data about them. They seemed to have practiced some forms of sexual and dietary abstinence (1 Tm 4.3) and espoused some form of elitism. Many scholars consider that the Pastorals were dealing with some form of early gnosticism, perhaps even a Jewish form of gnosticism (Ti 1.14), a kind of popular philosophy but not the Christian heresy of the second century.

Almost all study of the Pastorals demonstrate the "historical" information about Paul's life and ministry gleaned from these letters does not fit in with the data that can be garnered from Paul's own letters and the Acts of the Apostles. Many of the individuals mentioned in the Pastorals, especially in 2 Timothy, Hermogenes and Onesiphorus, for example, are otherwise unknown in the New Testament but reappear in the second-century apocryphal *Acts of Paul*.

While the literary genre of 2 Timothy is different from that of 1 Timothy and Titus, it is clear that the three Pastorals constitute a mini-corpus within the New Testament. They share similar ideas, a common vocabulary, and a remarkable stylized image of the Apostle Paul. In the Pastoral Epistles, Paul is portrayed as the apostle par excellence. There is no mention of any other apostle. Timothy and Titus are not presented as Paul's co-workers; rather they are portrayed as Paul's "sons," men who have learned from Paul and will carry on his work. Paul is presented as the norm for the "full knowledge of the truth," an example to be followed, and the source of church discipline.

Late twentieth-century studies of Hellenistic epistolography have led to an evaluation of the Pastorals, whose canonicity is not at issue, as attempts to actualize the Pauline tradition. That disciples would write a piece of epistolary literature in the name of a revered teacher was not an unknown practice in the Hellenistic world. By so doing they honored the memory of the teacher and showed the relevance of his teaching to subsequent generations. The Pastoral Epistles came into being in this way. Their anonymous author, most likely a single author for all three epistles, adopted Paul's apostolic letter form in attempt to show how Paul's legacy was to be adapted to the situation of local churches in the late first century C. E. The three epistles were probably composed in Asia between 90 and 100 C. E. The epistles' circumstances of composition imply that they must be viewed in a positive light, not as the work of a dying Paul or as New Testament texts of lesser value.

1 Timothy. First Timothy is the longest of the three epistles. It is an ecclesial text whose literary form makes it one of the oldest examples of Christian "congregational rules," of which the 1983 Code of Canon Law is a more recent example. Sections are devoted to overseers (3.1–7), servers (3.8–13), including female servers (3.11), widows (5.3–16), and the elder's bill of rights (5.17–19). Some commentators speak of "bishops," "deacons," "women deacons," "an order of widows," and the rights of "priests" but the use of such terms is anachronistic. 1 Timothy is an early attempt to organize the "household of God" (1 Tm 3.15); roles within the church have not yet reached the definition that they will later attain in later centuries when the terms are used to designate specific offices in the church.

In addition to the organization of the church, 1 Timothy is also concerned with the way that believers behave in the household of God. Accordingly the qualifications stipulated for those who function as overseers and servers were qualities that should be had by every Hellenistic householder. Women were expected to have "modesty" (2.15), the epitome of the Hellenistic woman's domestic virtues. The pursuit of wealth is presented as a derogation of godliness and a source of all kinds of evil (6.5–10, 17–19).

2 Timothy. The epistolary structure of 2 Timothy tends to cloak the reality of its being a kind of farewell discourse. An imprisoned and isolated Paul is about to die (4.6–8). The epistle "reminisces" about Paul's life and mentions a whole series of people with whom Paul was associated in one way or another. Timothy is constantly encouraged to learn from Paul and to carry on Paul's work (2.8–14; 4.1–2; etc.). He appears to have been virtually "ordained" by Paul through the ritual gesture of the imposition of hands (1.6–7).

Titus. The Epistle to Titus is the shortest of the three texts and arguably the oldest. Its literary genre is similar to 1 Timothy; its foci are the same, church order and

St. Paul handing Gospel to youth, representing possibly either Titus or Timothy.

proper behavior. Its epistolary opening offers an image of Paul's apostolate that is rich in theology and wide in focus. With regard to church order, Titus appears to speak of elders and the overseer almost interchangeably. He does not speak about widows nor specifically mention female servers. Titus' moral exhortation principally takes the form of a household code in which are spelled out the qualities of older men, older women, younger women, younger men, and slaves (2.1–10).

Teaching. The Pastorals speak about Christian behavior in in much the same way as contemporary philosophic moralists. "Godliness" or "piety" was a virtue for which everyone is to strive. Some describe the ethics of the Pastorals as an "ideal of good citizenship." The description may not be apt but there is no doubt that the Pastorals foster the conventional moral values of the time, including respect and prayer for civil authority (1 Tm 2.2; Ti 3.1). To some extent their encouragement of a conventional ethic stems from a desire that the church be accepted in Greco-Roman society of the late first century. The ethos of the times expected young women to bear children, raise them, and be subservient to their husbands (1 Tm 2.12, 15; Ti 2.4–5). The Pastorals' support of conventional ethical values represents an accommodation to the times. The expectation of an imminent Parousia is no longer on the horizon, so the church was required to settle into the world in which it existed.

The emphasis on church structures and ethics is accompanied by a number of rich theological insights that have been wrongly and unfortunately neglected in some writing on the Pastorals. In the Pastorals, "faith" means the content of faith. Descriptive phrases talk about faith as "the full knowledge of tthe truth," "soun teaching," "trustworthy sayings," and "these things," i.e. the things that Timothy and Titus have received from Paul. Church structures are important; no less important are the considerations that the church is an assembly and the place where God dwells and that it is a pillar of truth (1 Tm 3.15).

The "theology" or understanding of God in the Pastorals is celebrated in doxologies and the multiplication of God's attributes. The theological statement in 1 Tm 6.15–16 appears to be an apologetic profession of faith in the One God (1 Tm 2.5) in the Greco-Roman world that recognized some emperors as gods. The Pastorals remind their readers that God is the Creator (1 Tm 4.4) and the One who inspired the scriptures (2 Tm 3.16).

Although the Pastorals have little to say about the Holy Spirit (1 Tm 3.16; 4.1; 2 Tm 1.14; Ti 3.5) and therefore lack a developed pneumatology, they provide their readers with elements of a rich christology. A christological hymn appears in 1 Tm 3.16. An "epiphany" or "appearance" motif is the key element in the christology of the Pastorals. Christ appeared in time as Savior (2 Tm 1.10; Ti 3.4–5); he will appear again as Savior and judge (1 Tm 6.14; 2 Tm 4.1–8). Believers exist and live their lives between these epiphanies. The man Jesus is the one mediator (1 Tm 2.5–6). He has destroyed death and revealed life and immortality (2 Tm 1.10). The Pastorals' use of the epiphany motif was borrowed from the Greco-Roman world where emperors were revered as saviors and occasionally considered to be god made manifest.

Bibliography: R. F. COLLINS, "The Image of Paul in the Pastorals," *LTP* 31 (1975) 147–173. R. F. COLLINS, "The Pastoral Epistles" in *Letters That Paul Did Not Write: The Epistle to the Hebrews and the Pauline Pseudepigrapha* (Wilmington 1988) 88–131. B. FIORE, *The Function of Personal Example in the Socratic and Pastoral Epistles* (Rome 1986). M. HARDING, *What Are They Saying about the Pastoral Epistles?* (New York 2001). G. W. KNIGHT, III, *Commentary on the Pastoral Epistles* (Grand Rapids 1992). I. H. MARSHALL, *The Pastoral Epistles* (Edinburgh 1999). L. OBERLINNER, *Die Pastoralbriefe,* HTKNT 11/2. 3 vols. (Freiburg, Basel, Vienna, 1994–1996). J. D. QUINN, *The Letter to Titus* (New York 1990). J. ROLOFF, *Der Erste Brief an Timotheus* (Zurich 1988). M. WOLTER, *Die Pastoralbriefe als Paulustradition* (Göttingen 1988).

[R. F. COLLINS]

PASTOUREAUX, CRUSADE OF THE

The *Pastoureaux* were bands of peasants and laborers who swept through France in 1251 in a popular uprising similar to the Children's Crusade. Their aim was to free the king of France, LOUIS IX, who was then a captive of the Muslims, and to reconquer Jerusalem. The *Pastoureaux* were led by a mysterious "Master of Hungary," a powerful and persuasive preacher about 60 years old. The "Master" also sent an emissary to England in an effort to raise other bands there, but his representative was torn to pieces by a mob. The movement was accompanied by violent attacks upon feudal lords and upon the clergy, particularly the FRANCISCANS and DOMINICANS, who were held in some way responsible for the disasters that befell St. Louis's crusade in Egypt. The queen-regent, Blanche of Castile, was at first inclined to assist the *Pastoureaux,* but when news of their more violent outbreaks reached her, she ordered their suppression. The "Master of Hungary" was killed in battle near Villeneuve-sur-Cher and the main bands quickly broke up. Only a few of the *Pastoureaux* ever reached the Holy Land.

Bibliography: MATTHEW PARIS, *Chronica majora,* ed. H. R. LUARD, 7 v. (*Rolls Series* 57; 1872–83) 5:246–254. É. BERGER, *Histoire de Blanche de Castille* (Paris 1895). J. DELALANDE, *Les Extraordinaires croisades d'enfants et de pastoureaux au moyen âge* (Paris 1962).

[J. A. BRUNDAGE]

PATARINES

Constituents of a religious movement with social overtones originating among the laity and certain sections of the clergy, especially the lower clergy, in northern Italy in the early part of the second half of the 11th century.

Origin. The derivation of the term is unclear, but it probably has its origin in *Pataria,* a quarter of Milan where the group was particularly active. The earliest known "Patarine" preaching was that of the deacon of Milan, ARIALDO, at Varese (early 1057), and later in Milan. He was soon joined by Landulph Cotta, the notary of the church in Milan. Initially Patarine preaching was directed against priests' concubinage or marriage (*see* CELIBACY, HISTORY OF). However, it soon came to condemn, with equal vehemence, every kind of SIMONY, attacking specifically the archbishop of Milan, Guido of Velate, but by extension, implicating the greater part of the clergy, most of whom were guilty of some personal simony or had, at least, been ordained by simoniac bishops. This antisimony movement struck also at the vested interests of the upper classes of the laity, for they had insinuated their own members into the ranks of the higher clergy precisely by means of simoniac practices.

The Patarine movement signified a more intense participation by the laity in the life of the Church, and the ethical standards demanded by that laity resulted in an active campaign to reform the morals of the clergy. In an age that drew its spiritual values from the evangelical counsels of perfection, i.e., apostolic poverty and virginity, it was natural that the laity demanded chastity of its clergy and condemned any traffic in sacred objects, as well as excessive wealth or power for clergymen. The Patarine movement was, in fact, but one facet of an age that produced at one and the same time the heretical CATHARI and the GREGORIAN REFORM, new eremitical groups such as the CAMALDOLESE and VALLOMBROSANS, and the reform of both monks and canons. Thus, the Patarines of Florence were much influenced by the Vallombrosans, and Arialdo himself founded a reformed chapter of canons regular.

Milan remained the head of the Patarine movement, and after the death of Landulph Cotta, his brother ERLEMBALD, a layman, assumed its leadership. To the bishops, to the supporters of the Church's diocesan hierarchy, and to those faithful to local church traditions, the Patarines appeared to be a dangerous lay movement subversive of the sacramental hierarchy and of Holy Orders itself. It *was* such, in its extreme forms; for certain lay Patarines took upon themselves the duty of preaching, especially against corrupt clergy. Nor did they limit themselves to abstaining, as directed by decrees of the councils, from participation in rites celebrated by priests guilty of simony; they would even use force to prevent any of the other faithful from participating and would forcibly remove an unworthy cleric from the altar, from the church, and from his benefices, which he, as a simonist, had legally forfeited. The Patarines often did not act as the executors of a regular canonical sentence of condemnation of an unworthy churchman, but on their own initiative proclaimed to the people the cleric's guilt. Pope ALEXANDER II, even though he was a fellow townsman and supporter, reproved the Milanese Patarines for taking matters into their own hands in this way.

The Patarine movement did not go so far as to deny the special character and indispensable function of the priesthood. The Milanes Patarines, however, refused to attend rites celebrated by contumacious priests or to receive the Sacraments from such clerics, and they sought out priests and bishops free of every taint so that they might "freely" receive the Sacraments from them (*mente libera,* as one source puts it). To find such men they dispatched a mission to Vallombrosa and gladly welcomed a bishop, Rudolph, sent from the Vallombrosan area to minister to their needs in Milan. When the Patarines considered simonist ordinations as invalid and the Sacraments administered by such priests and bishops as sacrilegious, they were simply following the common teaching in the Church of the day, supported by Cardinal HUMBERT OF SILVA CANDIDA, who was not without Val-

lombrosan connections. PETER DAMIAN himself had allowed and promoted lay preaching, although he limited it to "earnest exhortation" and excluded doctrinal preaching.

Crisis in Milan. When the Milanese Patarines appealed to the Holy See against the diocesan bishop and clergy, Rome dispatched an exploratory mission in 1057. Two years later, a second mission composed of Peter Damian and the Milanese Bishop of Lucca, Anselm I of Baggio, later Pope Alexander II, reconciled Archbishop Guido to the Church along with any guilty priests who declared themselves willing to amend their ways and to do penance. But the traditionalist Ambrosian clergy was irritated by the Patarines' appeals to Rome, and Archbishop Guido soon reverted to his old ways, sided with antipope Cadalus of Parma, and persecuted the Patarines. Alexander II thereupon granted Erlembald the gonfalon of Saint Peter, entrusting this layman with exercising the physical coercive power of the Church; the pope then excommunicated Guido (March 9, 1066), touching off a violent anti-Patarine reaction that led to the murder of Arialdo (June 28).

The Patarine movement spread to other Italian cities, notably Cremona, Piacenza, Lodi, and later Brescia. A religious movement in Florence had the essential characteristics of the Patarines if not their name; it united the laity and the lower clergy under JOHN GUALBERT and his Vallombrosans against corrupt ecclesiastics and the simonist Bishop Peter Mezzabarba, a Pavian nobleman. The faithful appealed to the pope, who sent Peter Damian to attempt a reconciliation: by the victory of their representative in an ordeal by fire, the insurgents convicted Mezzabarba of simony and persuaded him to resign.

In Milan itself the ephemeral reconciliation and futile reform effected by a third pontifical mission in 1067 were swept away by the schism that broke out after the resignation of Archbishop Guido in 1070, a schism between Godfrey, appointed and invested by the German king (Henry IV), and ATTO OF MILAN, elected by the Patarines and recognized by the Holy See. Thus the campaign of the Patarines for Church reform became part of the vaster arena of the imperial-papal INVESTITURE STRUGGLE. Pope GREGORY VII naturally gave strong support to Erlembald and to the Patarines in their fight against the corrupt clergy and the schismatic archbishop, who had received lay INVESTITURE.

Erlembald was killed in a tumult triggered by his trampling on holy chrism that had been consecrated by a simoniac bishop. His death marked the end of Patarine agitations (1075). The Ambrosian Archbishop Anselm III submitted to Pope URBAN II, whose conciliatory policy toward the bishops of central and northern Italy smoothed the way for rooting out some of the worst evils of the Church in that area. And thus the chief cause of Patarine complaints disappeared in the atmosphere of the new enthusiasm for the Crusades. An important social result of the Patarine movement was the destruction of the network of vested interests and family contacts that had enabled a few powerful Lombard families to keep the most important sees of central and northern Italy, especially Tuscany, for their own members. However, there remained in Lombardy, especially in Milan, a small group of Patarine extremists, dissatisfied with the compromise of a moderate and orderly reform. These smoldering resentments and the deluded aspirations for radical religious renewal later found expression in other reform movements or in new heretical currents.

Bibliography: Sources. *Arnulphi gesta archiepiscoporum mediolanensium,* in *Monumenta Germaniae Historica: Scriptores* (Berlin 1826–) 8:17–25. *Landulphi Senioris Mediolanensis historiae libri quatuor,* in L. A. MURATORI, *Rerum italicarum scriptores, 500–1500,* 25 v. in 28 (Milan 1723–51); continued by G. M. TARTINI and N. G. MITTARELLI (1748–71) 4:81–128. *Vita sancti Arialdi auctore Andrea abbate Strumensi,* in *Monumenta Germaniae Historica: Scriptores* 30.2:1047–75. Literature. C. PELLEGRINI, *I ss. Arialdo ed Erlenbaldo* (Milan 1897). S. M. BROWN, ''Movimenti politico-religiosi a Milano ai tempi della pataria,'' *Archivo-storico italiano,* 58 (Florence 1931) 227–78. C. VIOLANTE, *La pataria milanese e la riforma ecclesiastica,* v. 1 *Le premesse, 1045–1057* (Rome 1955); ''I movimenti patarini e la riforma ecclesiastica,'' *Annuario dell' Università Cattolica del S. Cuore . . . 1955–57* (Milan 1957) 209–23. E. WERNER, ''Παταρηνοί—Patarini: Ein Beitrag zur Kirchen- und Sektengeschichte des 11. Jahrhunderts,'' *Vom Mittelalter zur Neuzeit* (Berlin 1956) 404–19. G. MICCOLI, ''Per la storia della pataria milanese,'' *Bullettino dell' Istituto storico italiano per il medioevo e Archivio Muratoriano* 70 (1958) 43–123.

[C. VIOLANTE]

PATENSON, WILLIAM, BL.

Priest and martyr; b. Durham, England; d. hanged, drawn, and quartered at Tyburn (London), Jan. 22, 1592. Following his seminary studies (1584–87) at Rheims, France, Patenson was ordained (1587) and returned to England (1589). There he ministered in the western counties until his arrest while dining in the home of Lawrence Mompesson at Clerkenwell on the Third Sunday of Advent 1591. He was condemned at the Old Bailey shortly after Christmas. During his imprisonment, Patenson reconciled several convicts imprisoned with him. He was beatified by Pius XI on Dec. 15, 1929.

Feast of the English Martyrs: May 4 (England).

See Also: ENGLAND, SCOTLAND, AND WALES, MARTYRS OF.

Bibliography: R. CHALLONER, *Memoirs of Missionary Priests,* ed. J. H. POLLEN (rev. ed. London 1924; repr. Farnborough 1969), I, no. 94. J. H. POLLEN, *Acts of English Martyrs* (London 1891), 115–17.

[K. I. RABENSTEIN]

PATERNITY, DIVINE

What is designated in contemporary theological literature under the title divine paternity is perhaps a little ambiguous. On first glance, *paternity* would be simply the Latin derivative (from *paternitas*) corresponding to the more familiar Anglo-Saxon *fatherhood.* Thus, one might expect to see treated under the rubric divine paternity the entire Old and New Testament revelation bearing upon the fatherhood of God and the way this became assimilated and interpreted in the Judeo-Christian community ever since. Actually, however, such a wide and biblically oriented use of *paternity* is rarely, if ever, encountered. Centuries of theological, and ultimately scholastic, convention have reserved this Latinism for the Father's unique relation to the eternal Son as grasped and expressed in the technicalities of Trinitarian doctrine and theology.

Historically, this technical usage grew out of a theological insight that can be traced back at least as far as the Cappadocian Fathers—Basil, Gregory of Nazianzus, and Gregory of Nyssa. This was the understanding that plurality within the Godhead was not a contradiction, because the three—Father, Son, and Holy Spirit—differed from one another not in respect to Godhead as such but in respect solely to what was proper to each, and this property (ἰδιότης) was something purely relative. Even earlier, Athanasius had written (*Or. 3 c. Arian.* 4; *De syn.* 49) that whatever is said of the Father is said likewise of the Son, excepting only the very name Father. Subsequently, with the schoolmen and especially Aquinas, the idea of the relative property first appearing with Athanasius and the Cappadocians was still further developed and refined by means of a carefully worked out doctrine of relations. The whole meaning of paternity is simply ''to be with reference, or respect, to'' son. There is no question, therefore, of the Father being more God than the Son or of having some perfection not shared by the Son. For Father and Son differ in no absolute way, but only in what is exclusively relative.

See Also: GOD (FATHER); AGENNĒTOS; PERSON (IN THEOLOGY); PERSON, DIVINE; RELATIONS, TRINITARIAN; TRINITY, HOLY; TRINITY, HOLY, ARTICLES ON.

Bibliography: B. LONERGAN, *De Deo Trino,* v. 2, *Pars systematica* (3d ed. Rome 1964), esp. 115–185. For the historical origins of the notion, see the same author's companion volume *De Deo Trino,* v. 1, *Pars dogmatica* (2d ed. Rome 1964) 195–204. J. N. D.

KELLY, *Early Christian Doctrines* (2d ed. New York 1960) 263–269.

[R. L. RICHARD]

PATIENCE

Patience is a moral virtue that disposes and inclines a man to suffer and endure present evils without unreasonable dejection. Patience is a perfection of the concupiscible appetite that disposes it to submit to the control of reason so that the difficulties of life will not overwhelm a man with sadness. The primary action that flows from this virtue is to endure; thus patience is annexed to the virtue of fortitude as a potential part. Since the acquisition of any virtue requires the endurance of some sorrow, generally on the sense level, patience is said to prepare the way for the acquisition of all of the other virtues.

Patience does not require the endurance of all present evils. Some can reasonably be avoided or mitigated, and to fail to take action to this end could be culpable. A mother, for example, with a family of small children to control cannot endure unlimited chaos and disorder with apathetic serenity; not infrequently she will be obliged to feel and express some measure of indignation and irritation.

Patience, motivated by man's willingness to endure unpleasant things in order to attain natural virtue and natural goods, is an acquired virtue. Beyond this there is infused into man's soul with sanctifying grace a supernatural virtue of patience that is motivated by a supernatural willingness to endure trouble and affliction in order to attain sanctity and union with God. This supernatural patience can be a joyous thing—suffering for love of God is a source of joy.

True patience possesses three special characteristics: it must be universal, humble, and supernatural. Patience endures every type of evil that should be borne, no matter what may be its kind, cause, or consequences. Patience is humble when it does not complain unduly or seek attention, sympathy, or compassion. Patience is supernatural when it is motivated by charity. St. Paul said: "Charity is patient" (1 Cor 13.4).

Two vices are opposed to the virtue of patience: insensibility and impatience. Insensibility is a lack of feeling that leaves a person stoical and unmoved by his own suffering or by that of others. Impatience is an unreasonable refusal to endure sorrow from present troubles necessary for the accomplishment of works of virtue. Impatience manifests itself externally by unreasonable anger, complaints, and evidences of depression or discouragement; internally, it shows itself in feelings of antipathy to trials and suffering, and in an excessive inclination to protect oneself against all discomfort. The vice of impatience leads a man to the feeling that there is no joy in loving and serving God; it inclines man to avoid the difficulties and the sorrows that often are the prelude to great joy and happiness.

Bibliography: THOMAS AQUINAS, *Summa theologiae*, 2a2ae, 136. E. VANSTEENBERGHE, *Dictionnaire de théologie catholique*, ed. A. VACANT et al., 15 v. (Paris 1903–50; Tables générales 1951–) 12.1:2247–51. AUGUSTINE, *Patientia.* TERTULLIAN, "Patience," *Disciplinary, Moral, and Ascetical Works*, tr. R. ARBESMANN et al. (New York 1959). A. ROYO, *The Theology of Christian Perfection*, tr. and ed. J. AUMANN (Dubuque 1962). *Encyclopedic Dictionary of the Bible*, tr. and adap. by L. HARTMAN (New York 1963), from A. VAN DEN BORN, *Bijbels Woordenboek* 1758–60. FRANCIS DE SALES, *Introduction to the Devout Life*, tr. M. DAY (Westminster, Md 1959).

[R. DOHERTY]

PATIENCE (IN THE BIBLE)

The quality or virtue of patience is presented as either forbearance or endurance. In the former sense it is a quality of self-restraint or of not giving way to anger, even in the face of provocation; it is attributed to both God and man and is closely related to mercy and compassion. In the latter sense it is a virtue by which one bears the trials of this life with resignation to God's will, and is therefore associated with hope [*see* HOPE (IN THE BIBLE)]; obviously in this sense it is predicated only of man. This article discusses patience as forbearance, patience as endurance, and continues with a discussion on the eschatological aspect of patience.

Patience as Forbearance. God's patience with men is one of His most frequently stressed attributes in the Old Testament; compare especially the use of the Hebrew roots *rḥm* and *ḥnn*. He is called upon as "a merciful [*rāḥûm*] and gracious [*ḥannûn*] God, slow to anger and rich in kindness and fidelity" (Ex 34.6; see also Nm 14.18; Wis 11.24–12.1; Jl 2.13; Neh 9.17). The psalmists praise Him because He does not punish men harshly, but is patient with them [Ps 77(78). 38–39; 85(86).15; 102(103).8; 144(145).8–9]. The greatness of His patience exceeds that of man (Sir 18.8–13) and therefore is not easily understood by impatient man (e.g., Jer 15.15; Jon 4.2). The purpose of this patience is to bring man to repentance (Wis 11.23; 12.8–10); man remains free to abuse it—but he does so to his own detriment (Is 5.18; 57.11–13). The New Testament reflects the same doctrine; cf. especially the use of the Greek μακροθυμία. God "endures with great patience vessels of wrath" (Rom 9.22), and has shown his forbearance in condoning former sins in the vicarious death of Christ (Rom 3.25–26). Therefore, man should not misuse God's patience (Rom 2.4–5), but rather should come to repentance (1 Pt 3.9).

The Old Testament praises the patient man because he possesses much good sense (Prv 14.29), allays discord (Prv 15.18), and is stronger than a warrior (Prv 16.32). According to the New Testament, patience purifies faith (1 Pt 1.6), fosters hope (Rom 8.25; 15.4), leads to perfection (Jas 1.4), and pertains to charity (1 Cor 13.4, 5, 7). Thus, it is a fruit of the Holy Spirit (Gal 5.22), deriving its power from God (Col 1.11). It is, moreover, God's own patience that Christians must imitate in dealing with others (Mt 5.45; 18.23–35). Therefore their patience must be universal (1 Thes 5.14) and prudent (2 Cor 11.19), and must pervade their daily conduct (Eph 4.2; Col 3.12). There should be no complaining against one another (Jas 5.8), because by bearing one another's burdens they can fulfill the law of Christ (Gal 6.2). Such patience is especially necessary for those who would spread the kingdom of God. St. Paul performed his apostolic work ''in all patience'' (2 Cor 12.12) in order not to give offense and in order to prove himself a worthy minister of God (2 Cor 6.4–6). He wished his patience to be an example to Timothy (2 Tm 3.10) and urged him to work patiently (1 Tm 6.11; 2 Tm 4.2) and to be a ''forbearing teacher'' in instructing others (2 Tm 2.24). Writing to Titus, he recommended the same virtue for the elders of the Church (Ti 2.2).

Patience as Endurance. The Christian's bearing of suffering (expressed especially in the Greek term ὑπομονέ) has its precedent in the Old Testament where the afflicted put all their trust in God [e.g., Ps 24(25).3; 26(27).14; 32(33).20] and where the Prophets call Yahweh ''the Hope of Israel'' (Jer 14.8; 17.13). Christ tells us that it is only through this patient endurance of suffering that our life will bear fruit (Lk 8.15). St. Peter exhorts the Christians to endure unjust suffering because it is of great value in the eyes of God (1 Pt 2.19–20). St. Paul, too, recommends patience in affliction (Rom 12.12), rejoices in his own sufferings (Rom 5.3; 1 Cor 4.12; 2 Cor 1.6), and praises the endurance of his recent converts (2 Thes 1.4) because through such endurance they will enter the kingdom of God (Acts 14.21).

Eschatological Aspect. The Christian's patience is also eschatological. Although the coming of Christ is certain, the day and the hour are not (cf. Mt 24.1–51; Mk 13.1–37; Lk 21.5–38; 1 Thes 4.13–5.11; 2 Thes 2.1–12). Hence, the life of Christians here on earth consists in ''looking for the blessed hope and coming of the great God and our Savior Jesus Christ'' (Ti 2.13). They should not be easily shaken from their right minds (2 Thes 2.2), but should patiently wait (Jas 5.7–8; Heb 10.36; 12.1), for only those who persevere until the end will be saved (Mt 10.22).

See Also: PAROUSIA; SUFFERING.

Bibliography: *Encyclopedic Dictionary of the Bible*, tr. and adap. by L. HARTMAN (New York 1963) 1758–60. X. LÉON-DUFOUR, ed., *Vocabulaire de théologie biblique* (Paris 1962) 764–767. C. SPICQ, ''Patientia,'' *Revue des sciences philosophiques et théologiques* 19 (1930) 95–106. J. HORST, G. KITTEL, *Theologisches Wörterbuch zum Neuen Testament* (Stuttgart 1935–) 4:377–390. R. BULTMANN, *ibid.* 4:585–595.

[J. BUKOVSKY]

PATRIARCHATE

Part I: Historical Developments

A patriarchate (Gr. πατριαρχεία, Lat. *Patriarchatus*) is a patriarch's office, see, reign, or, most often, the territory he governs. The number of patriarchates was in the course of time enlarged from the original three to five, and subsequent historical factors caused a multiplication of patriarchates.

The Three Patriarchs. The oldest Canon Law admitted only three bishops as having what later ages called patriarchal rights—the bishops of Rome, Alexandria, and Antioch. The successor of St. Peter held the patriarchate of Rome, or patriarchate of the West. Before the Council of Nicaea I (325) two bishops in the East had the same patriarchal authority over large territories, those of Alexandria and Antioch. It is difficult to say exactly how they obtained this position. The organization of provinces under metropolitans followed, as a matter of obvious convenience, the reorganization of the Empire made by Diocletian. In the new system the most important cities in the East were Alexandria in Egypt and Antioch in Syria. Consequently the bishop of Alexandria became the chief of all Egyptian bishops and metropolitans; the bishop of Antioch held the same place over Syria and at the same time extended his sway over Asia Minor, Greece, and the rest of the East. Diocletian had divided the Empire into four great prefectures. Three of these (Italy, Gaul, and Illyricum) made up the Roman patriarchate; the other, the East (*Praefectura Orientis*), had five (civil) ''dioceses''—Thrace, Asia, Pontus, the Diocese of the East, and Egypt. Egypt was the Alexandrine patriarchate. The Antiochene patriarchate embraced the civil Diocese of the East. The other three civil divisions of Thrace, Asia, and Pontus would probably have developed into separate patriarchates but for the rise of Constantinople.

Later it became popular to connect all three patriarchates with the Prince of the Apostles. St. Peter had also reigned at Antioch, and he had founded the Church of Alexandria through his disciple St. Mark. At any rate the Council of Nicaea in 325 recognized the supreme place of the bishops of these three cities as related to an "ancient custom" (c.6). Rome, Alexandria, and Antioch are the three old patriarchates, whose unique position and order were disturbed by later developments.

The Pentarchy: Five Patriarchates. When pilgrims began to flock to the Holy City, the bishop of Jerusalem, the guardian of the sacred shrines, began to be considered the head of more than a mere suffragan of Caesarea. The Council of Nicaea (325) gave him an honorary primacy, saving, however, the metropolitical rights of Caesarea (c.7). Juvenal of Jerusalem (420–458) succeeded finally, after much dispute, in changing this honorary position into official rule over a patriarchate. The Council of Chalcedon (451) severed Palestine and Arabia (Sinai) from Antioch and formed the Patriarchate of Jerusalem (sess. 7 and 8). Since that time Jerusalem has always been counted among the patriarchal sees.

The greatest change, the one that met most opposition, was the rise of Constantinople to patriarchal rank. Because Constantine had made Byzantium the "New Rome," its bishop, once the humble suffragan bishop of Heraclea, thought that he should become second only, if not almost equal, to the bishop of old Rome. For many centuries the popes opposed this ambition, not because any of them thought of disputing their first place, but because they were unwilling to change the old order of the hierarchy. In 381 the Council of Constantinople declared that "the Bishop of Constantinople shall have the primacy of honor after the Bishop of Rome, because it is New Rome" (c.3). The popes (Damasus, Gregory the Great) refused to confirm this canon. Nevertheless Constantinople grew by favor of the emperor, whose centralizing policy found a ready help in the authority of his court bishop. The Council of Chalcedon (451) established Constantinople as a patriarchate with jurisdiction over Asia Minor and Thrace and gave it the second place after Rome (c.28). Pope Leo I (440–461) refused to admit this canon, which was made in the absence of his legates; for centuries Rome still refused to give the second place to Constantinople. It was not until the Fourth Lateran Council (1215) that the Latin patriarch of Constantinople would be allowed this place; in 1439 the Council of Florence was to give it to the Greek patriarch. Meanwhile, however, in the East the emperor's wish was powerful enough to obtain recognition for his patriarch; from the time of the Council of Chalcedon Constantinople was practically, if not legally, the second patriarchate. The new order of five patriarchs—Rome, Constantinople, Alexandria, Antioch, Jerusalem—known as the *pentarchy*, became in Orthodox ecclesiology an essential element of the consti-

tution of the Church. (*See* ROME, PATRIARCHATE OF; CONSTANTINOPLE, PATRIARCHATE OF; ALEXANDRIA, PATRIARCHATE OF; ANTIOCH, PATRIARCHATE OF; JERUSALEM, PATRIARCHATE OF.)

Multiplication of Patriarchates. At the time of the Great Schism (1054) the great Church of the Empire knew practically these five patriarchs only, though "minor" patriarchates had already begun in the West. The Council of Constantinople IV (869) had solemnly affirmed their position (c.11). The schism, and further distinctions that would not have existed but for it, considerably augmented the number of bishops who claimed the title of patriarch. But even before the great schism, the earlier Oriental Orthodox Churches that separated from Constantinople on their non-reception of Chalcedon had resulted in the appearance of patriarchs as leaders of these churches.

Developments in the five traditional patriarchates occasioned by nationalist tendencies and schism have resulted in new patriarchates emerging. To be under a patriarch had come to be the normal, and apparently necessary, condition for any Church. Instead of being merely an honorable title for the occupants of the five ancient sees of Christendom (pentarchy), the name patriarch was looked upon as denoting the leader of a national church.

Bibliography: T. A. KANE, *The Jurisdiction of the Patriarchs of the Major Sees in Antiquity and in the Middle Age* (Catholic University of America, CLS 276; Washington 1949). D. GEANAKOPLOS, *A Short History of the Ecumenical Patriarchate of Constantinople* (330–1990) (Brookline, MA 1990). K. WARE, *The Orthodox Church*, rev. ed. (New York 1997).

[J. J. MCGRATH/EDS.]

Part II: Ecumenical Patriarchate of Constantinople

This entry deals with the origins, historical developments and nature of the office of Ecumenical Patriarchate of Constantinople, the territory of the patriarchate, the *synodos endēmousa*, the subordinate officials and their duties.

Ecumenical Patriarch. Patriarch was a title of honor given at first to any bishop of advanced years or special dignity. In Justinian's legislation, patriarch takes on its technical sense, connoting a definite rank in the hierarchy, that of a chief bishop ruling over an extensive territory and subject only to the Patriarch of Rome. The designation "ecumenical" was employed in isolated cases in addressing Dioscurus of Alexandria, Pope St. Leo, and Acacius of Constantinople, but became the customary designation of the patriarchs of Constantinople after the Acacian schism. Scholars have reached no agreement on its meaning or original importance. It can be said only that as applied to the patriarch of Constantinople, it met with no objection until Popes Pelagius II (579–590) and Gregory the Great (590–604), who opposed it strongly and persistently; and it remained a bone of contention between Rome and Byzantium for centuries afterward. It was not made strict etiquette in communicating with a patriarch until the reign of the Patriarch PHOTIUS (858–867; 877–886). The title was never used by the patriarch of himself, but only by others speaking to him or of him, until Michael I Cerularius (1043–58) placed it on his seal; and it finally became part of the official title under Manuel I (1217–22).

Synodos Endēmousa. The patriarch's rights were always intimately associated with the *synodos endēmousa*, and rested not on legislation either ecclesiastical or civil but on custom, to which according to Roman theory law was but the servant and supplement. During semi-Arian times the emperor would refer ecclesiastical matters to a synod of the many bishops in his retinue gathered under the presidency of the local ordinary. That this procedure would continue seems to have been taken for granted as something perfectly natural, e.g., by St. Gregory of Nazianzus and St. Ambrose, even after 381 when Theodosius the Great restored orthodoxy in the East and Constantinople became the permanent residence. Hence, from the very beginning we see St. John Chrysostom convoking the *synodos endēmousa* (literally, ''stopping-over synod''). The bishops who were stopping over on business at Constantinople were called together into a synod by and under the patriarch to decide appeals either made directly to it or referred to it by the emperor from any part of the East regardless of patriarchal boundaries. About the 9th century membership in the synod was restricted to the metropolitans and autocephalous (i.e., exempt from the metropolitan) archbishops of the patriarchate, to whom were added the synod's five highest administrative officials.

Canonical Requirements and Other Formalities. Since the time of Theodosius the Great, patriarchs were appointed by the emperor, but canonical traditions required certain formalities. In the earlier period, the patriarch was elected like any other bishop, but from about the end of the 9th century only the synod had the right of election; it nominated three candidates from whom the emperor chose one, or, if none pleased him, he selected another for the (automatic) approval of the synod. The successful candidate then received the same investiture as lay dignitaries from the emperor and was consecrated the following Sunday, always by the metropolitan of Heraclea. He held office for life and could be canonically deposed only by the synod; treason automatically terminated his tenure.

Once enthroned, the patriarch became the head of the Orthodox Church of Byzantium. In time, his powers developed in connection with his presidency of the synod, and it is impossible to distinguish his personal rights from those exercised conjointly with it. Furthermore, the emperor had greater authority in all matters not requiring orders, though he always consulted the patriarch before publishing any ordinance affecting religion and always addressed it to him. Actually, the patriarch could at times wield tremendous influence, e.g., one of strong character, particularly a monk, confronting a weak ruler, especially if the Church was in a position to throw its weight to either of two evenly balanced political parties. In general, the emperor kept nearly complete control of ecclesiastical geography and the rank of sees (which determined the precedence of bishops), usually by suggestion to the synod and with the consent of the patriarch. After the quarrel over the tetragamy, marriage legislation was more and more reserved to the Church. The spiritual head enjoyed most independence in the liturgy and in the maintaining of ecclesiastical discipline. He also had the final say in the choice of metropolitans, picking from three candidates presented by the synod. From the 9th century he possessed the very important privilege of *stauropegia* (planting of the cross), i.e., the canonical establishment of a religious house; this also entitled him to approve of a proposed abbot and to collect the *kanonikon*, a sort of tribute. At about the same time he acquired the exclusive right to consecrate the chrism.

Officials. The officials of the Church of Hagia Sophia in Constantinople were the officials of the patriarchate. In the middle and late periods, they were five: (1) *megas oikonomos* (grand manager), who controlled the entire property of the patriarchate, both cash and real estate; (2) *megas sakkelarius* and (3) *ho sakkeliou*, of whom the one had charge of all monastic establishments and the other, of all parish churches throughout the patriarchate, but their functions were frequently interchanged; (4) *megas skeuophylax* (grand sacristan), who took care of all precious possessions of the Church and acted as sacristan of Holy Wisdom with general supervision of the lands that furnished materials used in the liturgy (wheat, wine, oil, wax, etc.); (5) *megas chartophylax* (grand archivist), who, though he ranked fourth and was always only a deacon, had by far the greatest power, since he was the vice-patriarch and the real ecclesiastical governor of Constantinople; he controlled all access personal or by mail to the patriarch, determined the worthiness of all candidates for priesthood or episcopacy, tried all clergy (not bishops) guilty of any offense, determined freedom to marry, and, as archivist, also acted as chief canonist, issuing interpretations, in the name of the synod, that had force of law. These five highest dignitaries were known as the *Exokatakoiloi* and were comparable to the Roman Cardinals; they were members of the synod outranking the metropolitans. Originally they were all deacons, but subsequently many were priests. Another important functionary often mentioned in the sources was the APOCRISIARIUS (Nuncio), a permanent representative that the patriarch kept at each of the other patriarchates. Metropolitans had permanent or temporary *apocrisiarii* in Constantinople, and each bishop with his metropolitan. From the earlier Byzantine period two offices ought to be mentioned: that of the archdeacon, head of the administration when all officials were deacons, later reduced to his purely liturgical duties, and the *synkellos* (cell-mate), second in rank to the patriarch and successor designate; later on, the term became a purely honorary title of bishops. All of these dignitaries had many minor officials under them and office help at their disposal.

Bibliography: L. BRÉHIER, *Les Institutions de l'Empire byzantin* (*Le Monde byzantin* 2; Paris 1949). F. DVORNIK, *Byzance et la primauté romaine* (Paris 1964); *Idea of Apostolicity in Byzantium and the Legend of the Apostle Andrew* (Cambridge, MA 1958). J. HAJJAR, *Le Synode permanent dans l'Église byzantine des origines au XIe siècle* (Orientalia Christiana Analecta 164; 1962). D. GEANAKOPLOS, *A Short History of the Ecumenical Patriarchate of Constantinople (330–1990)* (Brookline, MA 1990). K. WARE, *The Orthodox Church*, rev. ed. (New York 1997).

[M. J. HIGGINS/EDS.]

Part III: Patriarchate in the Eastern Catholic Churches

Of the twenty-one Eastern Catholic Churches *sui juris* in communion with the See of Rome, six are patriarchal churches, i.e., they possess the ancient patriarchal form of ecclesial government with the highest and most comprehensive expression of self-government. These six Eastern Catholic Patriarch churches are, in order of precedence, dignity and honor:

(1) the Patriarch of Antioch and all the East for the Maronite Church,

(2) the Coptic Catholic Patriarch of Alexandria,

(3) the Patriarch of Antioch and all the East, Alexandria and Jerusalem for the Melkite Greek Catholic Church,

(4) the Patriarch of Antioch and all the East for the Syrian Catholic Church,

(5) the Patriarch of Babylon for the Chaldean Catholic Church,

(6) the Patriarch of Cilicia for the Armenian Catholic Church.

Appointment and Request for Communion with Rome. The appointment, jurisdiction, power and prerogatives of Eastern Catholic Patriarchs are determined by the CODE OF CANONS OF THE EASTERN CHURCHES, title IV, "The Patriarchal Churches," canons 51–150. The synod of bishops of a patriarchal church elects the new patriarch (*Codex Canonum Ecclesiarium Orientalium* c. 63), who, if he has been previously ordained a bishop, is enthroned upon the synod's acceptance of the election results (*Codex Canonum Ecclesiarium Orientalium* c. 75). The enthronement confers the office of patriarch on the successful candidate (*Codex Canonum Ecclesiarium Orientalium* c. 77 §1). He then sends a formal notification of his election to the Pope of Rome and the other five patriarchs of his election, and formally requesting ecclesiastical communion with their churches. As the highest form of self-government within the Eastern Catholic Churches, the appointment of a new patriarch does not require the confirmation of the Holy See, merely the notification of the election and a request for communion. However, until he receives the testimonial of ecclesial communion from the Pope of Rome, the newly enthroned patriarch can neither convene a synod nor ordain a bishop (*Codex Canonum Ecclesiarium Orientalium* c. 77 §2).

Governance of a Patriarchal Church. Following ancient canonical practice of the Christian East, all patriarchal churches, whether in communion with Rome or Constantinople, are not monarchical in leadership structure. Rather, in the spirit of ecclesial collegiality, leadership in all patriarchal churches is synodal, viz., a patriarch governing a patriarchal church together with a holy synod. Thus, the *Codex Canonum Ecclesiarium Orientalium* stipulates that the patriarch presides over his church together with the *patriarchal synod*, which holds the highest legislative, judicial and electoral power within a patriarchal church (*Codex Canonum Ecclesiarium Orientalium* c. 110). In addition to the patriarchal synod, there is also a *permanent synod* comprising the patriarch and four bishops that functions as an executive committee of the larger *patriarchal synod* (see *Codex Canonum Ecclesiarium Orientalium* c. 115–121). The *Codex Canonum Ecclesiarium Orientalium* also provides for a *patriarchal convocation* of all bishops and representatives from the clergy, all religious communities of men and women, institutions of learning and laity that is convoked every five years (*Codex Canonum Ecclesiarium Orientalium* cc. 140–145).

Territorial Jurisdiction. Every patriarch exercises supra-metropolitan authority (*Codex Canonum Ecclesiarium Orientalium* c. 56), but only within the territorial boundaries of the patriarchal church (*Codex Canonum Ecclesiarium Orientalium* c. 78 §2). Chapter 7 of title IV (*Codex Canonum Ecclesiarium Orientalium* cc. 146–150) regulates the jurisdiction of the patriarch and his patriarchal synod outside the traditional territorial limits of the patriarchal church. To illustrate: within the territorial boundaries of the patriarchal church, a patriarch has the power to ordain bishops without having to obtain the approval of the Pope of Rome. However, with respect to the appointment of bishops outside of patriarchal territory, the patriarch forwards a slate of three names to the Pope of Rome, who reserves to himself the power to appoint the bishop (*Codex Canonum Ecclesiarium Orientalium* c. 149).

As a rule, all legislation promulgated by a patriarchal synod has force of law only within the territorial limits of the patriarchal church (*Codex Canonum Ecclesiarium Orientalium* c. 150). There are three exceptions to this rule: (1) Liturgical legislation binds all members of a patriarchal church wherever they may be; (2) All legislation endowed with the force of law by the eparchial bishop becomes eparchial law, and (3) the Pope of Rome approves the legislation and grants it force of law throughout the world (see *Codex Canonum Ecclesiarium Orientalium* c. 150 pp. 2–3).

See Also: COUNCIL OF CATHOLIC PATRIARCHS OF THE ORIENT; CODE OF CANONS OF THE EASTERN CHURCHES.

Bibliography: *Code of Canons of the Eastern Churches,* Latin-English ed. (Washington, DC 2001). J. CHIRAMEL, *The Patriarchal Churches in the Oriental Code* (Alwaye, India 1992). J. HAJJAR, "Patriarchal Synods in the New Eastern Code of Canon Law," *Concilium* 26 (1990) 88–97. J. D. FARIS, *The Eastern Catholic Churches: Constitution and Governance According to the "Code of Canons of the Eastern Churches"* (Brooklyn, NY 1992). J. ABBAS, "Canonical Dispositions for the Care of Eastern Catholics Outside Their Territory," *Periodica de re Canonica* 86 (1997) 321–362.

[G. SALEM/EDS.]

Part IV: Patriarchates in the Latin Church

Within the Latin Church, there is only one true patriarch who is vested with powers of governance and jurisdiction—the Roman Pontiff as Patriarch of the West. Indeed, the Patriarchate of Rome was one of the five historical patriarchates of the pentarchy.

Apart from the Roman Pontiff, all other patriarchates within the Latin Church are purely honorific, without any prerogative of power or jurisdiction (*Codex iuris canonici* c. 438). At present, the following Latin prelates hold the honorific title of patriarch with respect to their Sees:

> Latin Patriarch of Jerusalem
> Patriarch of Venice
> Patriarch of Lisbon
> Patriarch of the East Indies
> Patriarch of the West Indies

Canon 438 of the 1983 Code of Canon Law does make provision for the possibility of the Roman Pontiff granting special powers to a patriarch as "apostolic privilege," or that a patriarch may acquire such power by "approved custom."

[G. SALEM/EDS.]

PATRIARCHS, BIBLICAL

A condensed study of the Biblical patriarchs warrants the following plan: origin and uses of the word "patriarch," the pre-Abrahamic patriarchs, the structure of the genealogies, the problem of their long lives, and the similar lists in ancient Mesopotamia.

Origin of "Patriarch." In the Septuagint (LXX) version, πατριάρχης, from which patriarch is derived, first appears in Chronicles, where it is used for translating several Hebrew expressions. Some of its significations are: the heads of Israelite families (2 Chr 19.8; 26.12); in many Greek manuscripts, the priestly and Levitical family chiefs (1 Chr 24.31); the chiefs over the tribes of Israel (1 Chr 27.22); the captains of companies of 100 men (2 Chr 23.20; cf. 2 Kings 11.19). It has a more restricted use in the apocryphal 4 Maccabees 16.25, where it apparently refers to the 12 sons of Jacob. The same book, however, speaks of "our patriarchs, Abraham, Isaac, and Jacob" (7.19). The word also appears in the New Testament where it refers to the 12 sons of Jacob (Acts 7.8–9); to David (Acts 2.29); to Abraham (Heb 7.4).

In present-day exegesis "patriarch" properly refers to ABRAHAM, ISAAC, and JACOB, although two other acceptations are acknowledged: the eponymous ancestors of the 12 tribes of Israel, Joseph and his brothers; and the ten antediluvian and ten postdiluvian celebrities listed by the Pentateuchal PRIESTLY WRITERS in Genesis 5.1–32 and 11.10–26, respectively. In the last case, one would not speak of "patriarchal times," which comprise only the period of Abraham, Isaac, and Jacob. In this article the term patriarchs is used only in the last acceptation signifying the pre-Abrahamic patriarchs.

Pre-Abrahamic Patriarchs. The list of antediluvian patriarchs from Adam to Noah is attributed to the Priestly Writers. The YAHWIST too handed down parallel but incomplete lists (Gn 4.17–22, 25–26) containing only six generations after Cain and only one after Seth. The Priestly genealogy proceeds from Adam through Seth, while the Yahwist proceeds from Adam through Cain in its major genealogy. Notwithstanding the variants, it can be established that the same names appear in both lists.

Structure of the Genealogies. The two Priestly lists of Genesis 5.1–32 and 11.10–26 are almost identical in form. Stereotyped formulas, typical of this tradition, are used for each patriarch in both lists and include the name

The Sacrifice of Isaac, grisaille painting by Andrea Mantegna, 15th century. (©Archivo Iconografico, S.A./CORBIS)

of the patriarch, his age when he begot his first son, and the number of years he lived after the birth of that son. The lists are only slightly divergent; chapter 5 totals the duration of the lifetime of each patriarch, while chapter 11 does not.

The fact that each genealogy contains ten generations is not mere coincidence. It reveals the author's desire for symmetry in the periods that preceded and followed the deluge. This is all the more apparent when one considers the divergence between the Masoretic Text and the LXX. In the Masoretic Text, one finds ten patriarchs in each period provided that Noah figures in both periods. The LXX adds Cainan from Gn 5.9–14 to the second list in Gn 11.12–13, thus eliminating the necessity of counting Noah twice. The Greek interpolater of the addition sacrificed accuracy for perfect symmetry. His preference for literary perfection and his grasp of the original author's intentions are thus apparent.

Extraordinary Ages. The didactic rather than historical nature of the lists is further confirmed by the amazingly long lives of the patriarchs. All procreated at, and lived to, an age that today, despite our highly superior medical knowledge, would be preposterous. Among the antediluvian patriarchs, according to the Masoretic Text, the shortest life span was 365 years and the earliest procreation age, 65 years. Most of them exceeded 900 years or were not far removed from that age at death except Enoch, 365 years, and Lamech, 777 years, both figures being symbols of perfection in Hebrew numerology. On the average, the postdiluvian patriarchs had a shorter life. Their ages range downward from 950 for Noah, and 600 for Shem, to 148 for Nahor.

Literal Interpretation. The historicity of the genealogies used to be a trying problem for scholars. One of the attempts at a solution was to ignore the problem and accept the strict historical character of the passages and the figures. Modern scholars unhesitatingly reject this position because it pays no attention to historical or literary criticism. Its advocates would be accused of Biblical FUNDAMENTALISM today, since they considered that anything contained in the Bible must be interpreted literally and is of necessity historically accurate. They also referred to the legends of other cultures that assert the great longevity of their early ancestors and concluded that the common accord implies a one-time reality. There is no scientific evidence, however, to corroborate this stand. On the contrary, the findings of science show that the life span of primitive man was shorter than ours today. Many favored a modified position but still inflexibly adhered to the historical accuracy of the figures. The year, they conjectured, lasted only one month or more—an erroneous assumption, since, in the Bible, the word "year" always

means a span of 12 months and is clearly distinguished from shorter periods.

Didactic Literary Device. The solution admitted by most modern scholars takes the figures as didactic literary artifices without strict historical intent. The genealogies and the ages of the patriarchs reflect ancient traditions and a system of computation for which a completely satisfactory explanation has not yet been found. Modern interpretation stresses the texts' etiological character as a function of religious teaching. Why is man's life span so limited' A long, fruitful life was considered an incomparable blessing, the reward of faithful service to God. The gradual shortening of man's life span was in keeping with the progress of evil in the world. In Noah's day, evil was so rampant that God said to Noah, "The end of all creatures of flesh is in my mind; . . . I will destroy them" (Gn 6.13). As a result, God punished man by the Deluge and reduced his life expectancy by hunderds of years (cf. Noah's, Shem's, Arphaxad's, and Peleg's ages). This chastisement showed God's hatred of sin and gave a reason for the evil of man's short lifetime. The extraordinary ages of the patriarchs, therefore, have religious implications and are to be taken as didactic symbols.

Textual Discrepancies. There are notable discrepancies in the numbers of the lists in the Masoretic Text, the Samaritan Pentateuch (the original Hebrew text of the first five books of the Bible handed down by the Samaritans and quite different in places from the Masoretic Text; it dates, in its first form, from *c.* 300 B.C.), and the LXX. The freedom with which the figures were altered indicates that they were known to be symbolic and could be modified to bring out more clearly the religious lesson. A comparison shows that the Samaritan Pentateuch agrees with the Masoretic Text down to the fifth patriarch Mahalaleel but keeps to a decreasing amount of years for the following names, in contrast to the Masoretic Text, which has the sixth and eighth patriarchs living longer than Adam. A corresponding lessening of the ages at which the patriarchs first generated a son leads to a discrepancy of 349 years less than the period between Adam and the Flood in the Samaritan Pentateuch.

The LXX adds 100 years to the first five names and to the seventh for the procreation age and thus lengthens the antediluvian period by 606 years and 955 years more than the Masoretic Text and Samaritan versions. All three agree on the perfect age of Enoch, 365 years, but neither of the other two agrees with the Masoretic Text on the perfect 777 years of Lamech. The LXX agrees with the Masoretic Text on the age of the longest-lived patriarch, Methuselah, both as to generating age and age at death, 187 and 969.

These variants are interesting but not very enlightening. The reason that procreation was delayed so long in all three, but especially in the LXX, is most puzzling. It may merely have been to underline the extraordinary characteristics of the men of old, who were closer to God and His original act of creation and who, therefore, could not have been like the ordinary men of the ancient writers' experience.

The case of Enoch is significant. He is described by a Hebrew idiom meaning that he was an extremely holy man. "Enoch walked with God; and he was seen no more because God took him" (Gn 5.24). One would expect him to have lived much longer than the other patriarchs, but his lifetime was only 365 years. However, this figure is a perfect number, the exact duration of the solar year. His mysterious disappearance without the mention of his death is also indicative of his unique position. Later Judaism did not miss these significant details; it made him a messianic figure comparable to Elijah, who was also "taken up by God," and attributed to him apocryphal books that inspired at least one New Testament writer, Jude 14–15 (*see* ENOCH).

Mesopotamian Genealogies. The Babylonians had similar lists of antediluvian kings. Two cuneiform texts, W.B. 444 and W.B. 62 (*The Weld-Blundell Collection, Oxford Editions of Cuneiform Inscriptions,* v. 2, p. 8f and plate VI), and the Greek text of BEROSSUS, a Chaldaean priest of the time of Alexander the Great, are well known. Only eight names (given in J. B. Pritchard, *Ancient Near Eastern Texts Relating tothe Old Testament* 265) are contained in W.B. 444, whereas W.B. 62 and the text of Berossus, like the Genesis genealogy of the antediluvian patriarchs, contain ten names. The names in the two cuneiform lists are nearly identical, though they do not appear in the same order; those of the Greek text can be identified with the kings in the cuneiform texts. The last name in W.B. 444 is UbarTutu of Shuruppak, the father of the Deluge hero, Utnapishtim (in Akkadian), but the other two lists end with the hero himself, Ziusudra (in Sumerian), Xisouthros (in Greek). The life span of the antediluvian kings is very much longer than that of the biblical patriarchs. Again the figures vary from one list to another and thus reveal the authors' indifference to historical chronology. A look at the list of W.B. 444 will exemplify the grossly exaggerated ages of the Mesopotamian kings: A-lulim of Eridu, 28,800 years; Alalgar of Eridu, 36,000 years; En-men-lu-Anna of Badtibira, 43,200 years, etc., with a total of 241,000 years for the eight kings before the Flood. In this list, the 241,000 years from the monarchy's institution, identified with Creation, to the death of the last antediluvian king contrasts with the 456,000 years of W.B. 62 and the 432,000 years of the Berossus text (the two last include the hero of the Flood plus another previous king). The figures, therefore, were subjected to alterations from one text to another.

Many critics have studied the resemblances and the differences between these lists and the Genesis genealogies. The differences are more striking. The Babylonian lists speak of kings and intend to show the unbroken succession of monarchs from the Creation onward; their perspective is decidedly national. The Biblical genealogies consider the patriarchs as the ancestors of all the races and nations; their perspective is universal and manifests God's supremacy over all of mankind. The chronological computations are very dissimilar, and it is unlikely that the Biblical system is based on the Babylonian. Efforts to identify the patriarchs' names with those of the antediluvian kings have been futile, save for that of Noah, which may possibly have the same meaning as Utnapishtim and its Sumerian equivalent Ziusudra. There may also be some relationship between Enoch's 365 years, as a solar year symbol, and the seventh king of W.B. 62 and the text of Berossus, the king of Sippar, the city of the sun. It appears, therefore, that the Priestly traditions concerning the antediluvian and postdiluvian patriarchs are only remotely non-Israelite traditions.

Bibliography: J. CHAINE, *Le Livre de la Genèse* (Paris 1951). J. SCHILDENBERGER, *Vom Geheimnis des Gotteswortes* (Heidelberg 1950) 261–303. H. CAZELLES, *Dictionnaire de la Bible,* suppl. ed. L. PIROT et al. (Paris 1928–) 1:745–54; 7:81–82. *Encyclopedic Dictionary of the Bible,* tr. and adap. by L. HARTMANS (New York 1963), from A. VAN DEN BORN, *Bijbels Woordenboek* 855–56, 1342, 1760, 1920–26.

[N. VAILLANCOURT]

PATRICIAN BROTHERS

Popular name for the Congregation of the Brothers of St. Patrick (FSP, Official Catholic Directory #1160), founded at Tullow, County Carlow, Ireland, in 1808 by Bp. Daniel Delany (1747–1814) of the Diocese of Kildare and Leighlin. The congregation, approved by Rome in 1893, engages in the apostolate of Christian education. The U.S. foundation was established in 1948, and headquartered in Midway City, Calif. The brothers work in the Archdiocese of Los Angeles and Diocese of Orange.

Bibliography: *Dr. Delany and the Patrician Brothers* (Tullow, Ire. 1955).

[D. LOMASNEY/EDS.]

PATRICIUS ROMANORUM

Patrician of the Romans, an honorary title instituted by Emperor CONSTANTINE I (306–37) as a personal distinction for his principal juridical and military officers. The emperors of the fifth and sixth centuries conferred it, with other honors such as the consulate, upon barbarian chieftains, as well as upon high imperial officials; individual kings of the Visigoths, Ostrogoths, Franks, and Burgundians all held the title. The patriciate remained honorific. In the West, it survived the imperial collapse of the seventh and eighth centuries only in Italy, where the fact that the effective imperial representative, the exarch of RAVENNA, was also *patricius* gave the title genuine political content. After the LOMBARDS suppressed the exarchate in the eighth century, the patriciate assumed a new character, which it retained until its extinction. In their search for a ruler to assume the duties of defense that the exarchs had formerly owed to the bishops of Rome, the popes of the late eighth century granted the patriciate to their chosen defenders, the Frankish kings. Pope STEPHEN II conferred the title upon PEPIN III the Short and his sons CHARLEMAGNE and CARLOMAN in 754, when he also anointed and crowned them as kings of the Franks, specifically designating them as protectors of the Roman Church. In 781 Charlemagne likewise saw Pope ADRIAN I anoint and crown his sons Pepin and Louis as kings and proclaim them *patricii*. The title thus came to be an ancillary distinction of the Frankish kings peculiarly expressive of their political and military obligations in Italy, and after the coronation of Charlemagne as emperor (800), it became an attribute of the imperial office itself. Some scholars have maintained that in bestowing the patriciate, Stephen II and Adrian I deliberately usurped prerogatives of the Byzantine emperors and moved to adapt to papal direction what had been the most powerful imperial office in Italy. The patriciate, however, retained the institutional independence of papal authority that it had held in the time of the exarchate, and, though it was frequently bestowed by medieval popes to secure temporal defenders, it was also assumed in other ways by persons hostile to the papacy. Thus, heads of the great Roman family the CRESCENTII, claimed the patriciate by popular election late in the tenth century, and turned the official powers they attributed to the office toward undermining the alliance between the papacy and the Ottonian rulers at the same time that the emperors themselves used the title "by apostolic benediction." Likewise, Emperor Henry IV, who wore the golden circlet of the *patricius* at least as early as 1061, commanded Pope Gregory VII to descend from the throne of St. Peter by virtue of the patriciate he held "through the bestowal of God and the sworn assent of the Romans" (1076). Still, because of its close association with papal prerogatives, the insurgent Roman commune abolished the office (1144–45).

Bibliography: L. VON HEINEMANN, *Der Patriziat der deutschen Könige: ein Beitrag zur Geschichte der Beziehungen zwischen Staat und Kirche im Mittelalter* (Wolfenbüttel 1888). F. GREGOROVIUS, *History of the City of Rome in the Middle Ages*, tr. A. HAMILTON, 8 v. in 13 (London 1894–1902). L. HALPHEN, *Charlemagne et l'empire carolingien* (Paris 1947). L. BRÉHIER, *Le monde byzantine* (Paris 1947–50) v.2, *Les institutions de l'empire byzantine*. R. FOLZ, *L'idée d'empire en occident du Ve au XIVe siècle* (Paris 1953); *Le couronnement impérial de Charlemagne* (Paris 1964). P. E. SCHRAMM, *Herrschaftszeichen und Staatssymbolik*, 3 v. (Schriften der Monumenta Germaniae historica 13; Stuttgart 1954–56). O. TREITINGER, *Die oströmische Kaiser-und Reichsidee nach ihrer Gestaltung im höfischen Zeremoniell* (2d ed. Darmstadt 1956). J. DEÉR, "Die Vorrechte des Kaisers im Rom (772–800)," *Schweizerische Beiträge zur allgemeinen Geschichte* 15 (1957) 5–63. W. ULLMANN, *The Growth of Papal Government in the Middle Ages* (2d ed. New York 1962).

[K. F. MORRISON]

PATRICK, ST.

Apostle of Ireland; b. *c.* 389; d. *c.* 461? (feast, March 17). Patrick (Patricius), as he himself relates, was born in Roman Britain, son of the *decurio* (alderman), and later deacon, Calporn(i)us. The dates of his birth and death are disputed, as is his chronology generally. At the age of 16, while staying on his father's country estate (probably near Ravenglass), he was seized by Irish raiders and sold as a slave in Ireland. After six years' servitude as a shepherd, and encouraged by a voice in his sleep, he escaped, found a ship to take him on board, and eventually reached home. For the worldly youth that he had been, though a nominal Christian, captivity had become a means of spiritual conversion. A desire to preach the Christian faith to the Irish grew within him to the certainty of a vocation. Once in a dream he even heard the "voice of the Irish" calling him back. He went to the Continent to train for the priesthood and probably stayed for some time as disciple of St. GERMAIN at Auxerre. Perhaps he visited colonies of monks at Lérins and on the islands of the Tyrrhene Sea.

His desire for converting the Irish did not find favor with his superiors, mainly because of his defective education, for which he had never been able to compensate properly. Upon the death of Palladius, whom Pope CELESTINE I had sent to the Irish as their first bishop in 431, Patrick was appointed his successor. His mission concentrated on the west and north of Ireland, where nobody had preached the gospel before. Having secured the protection of the local kings, he toured the country extensively and made numerous converts. Church organization had to be adapted to the political and social conditions of Ireland. Since there were no towns on the Roman pattern, Patrick established episcopal churches with quasi-monastic chapters as were found not infrequently on the Continent, especially in Gaul. Although he never mentions his own see, the claim of Armagh to be Patrick's church, though not recorded before the 7th century, seems to represent a genuine tradition. The clergy was

Saint Patrick. (Bettmann/CORBIS)

originally recruited on the Continent (Gaul) and in Britain, but later increasingly from among the native converts. Patrick also propagated monasticism in the primitive form as practiced in the islands off the Mediterranean coast of Gaul.

In his missionary work he had to face frequent dangers to his freedom and even to his life. The Druids were probably his chief opponents. Patrick's conduct of the mission was severely criticized by the British clergy and also, it seems, by some persons in Ireland. Things would appear to have come to an issue when Patrick demanded the excommunication of the British Prince Coroticus, who during a retaliatory raid on Ireland had killed some of Patrick's converts and sold others into slavery. To his critics Patrick replied with his *Confessio,* written in his old age.

Writings. Of the writings that go under Patrick's name, his *Confessio* and the letter (*Epistola*) concerning the raid of Coroticus are commonly accepted as genuine. The *Confessio* is an account of Patrick's spiritual development and a justification of his mission, but above all it is a homage to God and thanksgiving for His grace, for having called Patrick, an unworthy sinner, to the apostolate. Autobiographical and historical detail are merely incidental and often difficult to interpret.

The letter is directed partly against the raiders and Coroticus, their leader, partly against the higher clergy of Britain and their scornful attitude toward the Irish bishop. Both works are written in an unusual mixture of Biblical and Vulgar Latin, which often results in strained and obscure language.

Opinion is divided about the authenticity of the *Dicta* (Sayings) of Patrick in the Book of Armagh, especially the first one, which refers to a sojourn on the Tyrrhene Islands, and the last one, which urges the chanting of *Kyrie eleison, Christe eleison* at all canonical hours. The canons of a circular letter issued by Bishops Patricius, Auxilius, and Iserninus after the so-called synod of St. Patrick, are probably substantially genuine. Ecclesiastical life as implied in this document, and in particular the frequent references to diocesan jurisdiction of bishops and to canonical discipline, are consistent with a 5th-century date and would not fit into the pattern of the Irish monastic Church of later times. A number of these canons are quoted under Patrick's name in the *Collectio Hibernensis* alongside others that are spurious. The beautiful Old Irish morning prayer known as "The Breastplate of St. Patrick" is of later date than the saint's lifetime.

Doctrine. Patrick was a man of action, with little inclination for learning. His writings are proof of his firm belief in his vocation, of his devotion to his cause, and of his courage and humility. His "voices"—foretelling his escape from captivity, calling him to the Irish apostolate, comforting him when in disgrace—are for the most part capable of a perfectly natural explanation; only the experiences related in the *Confessio* (ch. 24, 25) have the characteristics of mystical prayer.

Of his doctrine, little can be stated beyond its orthodoxy. A certain emphasis in his teaching regarding grace might possibly be interpreted as anti-Pelagian. The credal statements in his *Confessio* (ch. 4) echo a formal creed of Gallican type. Patrick's Biblical text, as far as can be judged, is also Gallican.

Chronology. The only contemporary sources for Patrick's life are his genuine writings and the entries concerning St. Germain and Palladius in the Chronicle of PROSPER OF AQUITAINE. The former are, unfortunately, not precise enough for even approximation of an absolute chronology of the events referred to; they merely place Patrick within the 5th century. The *Confessio* does contain elements of a relative chronology: capture at the age of 16; escape from slavery at 22; some form of ecclesiastical censure because of a sin he had committed when barely 15 years old, disclosed "after 30 years"—but the date upon which they are reckoned is not clear. On the other hand, the precise dates given by Prosper (delegation of St. Germain to Britain in 429, mission of Palladius to Ireland in 431) bear on the chronology of Patrick only on the assumption that a document from the church of Auxerre, embedded in some lives of St. Patrick, is a genuine record of the saint's life, which some scholars doubt. According to this document, Patrick succeeded Palladius after a very short time; this would bear out the Irish annals, which date the beginning of his mission as of 432. These annals, however, record the death of a *Patricius senex* in 457 or 461, and the death of the "apostle" Patrick in 493 or thereabouts. However, the value of the Irish annals as sources for the early Christian period has been questioned by J. V. Kelleher of Harvard.

The Latin and Irish Lives of St. Patrick from the 7th century onward are written mainly with a view to promoting the territorial and juridical claims of the See of ARMAGH. They portray a powerful miracle worker, in the manner of Irish hagiographical legend, who has little in common with the author of the *Confessio.* How much genuine tradition in regard to persons and places they may contain is largely a matter of speculation. It has been observed that most of the persons with whom they bring Patrick into contact belong to the late rather than the middle decades of the 5th century and that the annalistic obits of many of Patrick's disciples fall in the first decades of the 6th century.

This conflicting evidence has been differently interpreted. J. Bury accepted 432 as the initial year of Patrick's mission and 461 as the date of his death. He was followed, in the main, by E. MacNeill, P. Grosjean, and L. Bieler. T. F. O'Rahilly believed that the mission of Palladius, whom he identified with *Patricius senex,* lasted from 432 to 461 and was continued by the British Patrick from 461 to *c.* 490. J. Carney allows for only one Patrick, whose mission he dates from 457 to 493. Accordingly, he maintains that Palladius was sent to Scotland, not to Ireland, and the first mission to Ireland, including the foundation of Armagh, was the work of St. Secundinus (annalistic date of arrival: 439), to whom an early hymn on St. Patrick is ascribed in later manuscripts. M. Esposito would make Patrick precede rather than succeed Palladius. D. Binchy, weighing carefully the arguments on all sides, concludes that the balance of probability favors the opinion of O'Rahilly. C. Mohrmann, analyzing Patrick's Latin, inclines to accept the chronology of Bury. It does seem possible, without forcing the evidence, to vindicate the chronology of Bury in all essentials, except that 432 as the initial year of Patrick's mission is probably a little too early.

Cult and Relics. A cult of St. Patrick is attested in the 6th century. The day of his death is first recorded in the 7th-century Life of St. Gertrud, who died on March 17, 659. In the 9th century Ferdomnach, scribe of Armagh, testified to the celebration of St. Patrick's feast as a triduum. The cult of St. Patrick and some of his relics were brought to Péronne in Picardy by St. Fursa (middle of 7th century); the cult soon spread over France, Italy, and Germany. When the Anglo-Normans established themselves in Ireland, they took over the cult of St. Patrick and of other Irish saints. In 1186 relics of SS. Patrick, Brigid, and Columcille were solemnly deposited in the cathedral of Down under the patronage of John de Courcy and Bishop Malachy. An English Cistercian of De Courcy's entourage, Jocelin of Furness, was commissioned to write a life of St. Patrick, and this became the standard text of later times. With the recent Irish emigration the cult has spread over many parts of the New World.

St. Patrick's Purgatory in Lough Derg, a place of penitential pilgrimages since the 12th century, has probably no connection with the saint. The earliest pictorial representation of St. Patrick dates from *c.* 900. The two most common ones—Patrick's expelling all poisonous snakes from Ireland and his symbolizing the Holy Trinity by the shamrock leaf—are based on legend.

Feast: March 17.

Bibliography: St. Patrick's *Confessio,* the 7th-century Life by Muirchú, and the *Breviarum* by Tírechán have been collected in the Book of Armagh, an early 9th-century manuscript, now in Trinity College, Dublin. Editions. J. GWYNN, ed., *Liber Ardmachanus* (Dublin 1913). L. BIELER, ed., *Libri Epistolarum s. Patricii Episcopi in Classica et mediaevalia* 11 (1950) 1–150; 12 (1951) 79–214; repr. in 2 v. (Dublin 1952); *The Irish Penitentials* (Scriptores Latini Hiberniae 5; Dublin 1963), the canons; *The Works of St. Patrick* (Ancient Christian Writers 17; Westminster, Md.–London 1953), *Confessio,* letter, sayings, canons, hymn attributed to St. Secundus, Breastplate. E. I. HOGAN, ed., *Documenta de s. Patricio* (Brussels 1884). J. COLGAN, ed., *Trias thaumaturga* (Louvain 1647) 11–116; new eds. are being prepared by L. BIELER. W. STOKES, ed., *Tripartite Life of St. Patrick,* 2 v. (*Rerum Britannicarum medii aevi scriptores* 89; London 1888; repr. New York 1965), critical ed. and tr. K. MULCHRONE (Dublin 1939–). Literature. J. B. BURY, *The Life of St. Patrick* (New York 1905). J. F. KENNEY, *The Sources for the Early History of Ireland:* v. 1, *Ecclesiastical* (New York 1929) 319–356. E. MACNEILL, *St. Patrick, Apostle of Ireland* (London 1934; 2d ed., J. RYAN, 1964). T. F. O'RAHILLY, *The Two Patricks* (Dublin 1942). L. BIELER, *The Life and Legend of St. Patrick* (Dublin 1949). J. CARNEY, *The Problem of St. Patrick* (Dublin 1961). C. MOHRMANN, *The Latin of St. Patrick* (Dublin 1961). D. A. BINCHY, ''Patrick and His Biographers,'' *Studia Hibernica* 2 (1962) 7–173. R. E. MCNALLY, *American Catholic Historical Review* 47 (Washington 1961–62) 305–324. J. B. BURY, *The Life of St. Patrick and His Place in History* (Mineola, N.Y. 1998). D. N. DUMVILLE et al, eds. L. ABRAMS, *Saint Patrick, A.D. 493–1993* (Woodbridge, UK ; Rochester, N.Y. 1993). N. D. O'DONOGHUE, *Aristocracy of Soul: Patrick of Ireland* (Wilmington, Del. 1987). R. P. C. HANSON, *The Life and Writings of the Historical Saint Patrick* (New York 1983). L. DE PAOR, *Saint Patrick's World: The Christian Culture of Ireland's Apostolic Age* ([S.l] 1993).

[L. BIELER]

PATRIOTISM

The love of and devotion to one's country, having as its moral foundation the virtue of PIETY. Benedict XV considered it a twin virtue with religion itself and a tie between the human person and his roots in nature.

Basis and Notion. Its social foundation is community. Man is bound to act in accordance with the divinely revealed and humanly confirmed truth that it is not good for him to be alone. Genesis attributes the statement of this truth to the Lord God before Eve's creation; it can be understood in an even stronger sense after the fact: given his social nature, it is impossible for man to be alone, and any pretension to independence from the human community must be disastrous because it is unrealistic and inhuman. Each man is compelled by nature to live in society for the attainment of his personal good, which good in turn provides the basis for society's growth and development toward a common good, ordered in love and justice. To live humanly is to live in community; and to live morally, as a creature under God, is to love that community of which one forms a part.

Patriotism in the sense of the love of one's community is therefore a duty of man flowing from intelligent recognition and moral acceptance of the very form of creation: the creation not of the individual, man, who existed alone only long enough for God to confirm the fact of his incompleteness, but of the human family, mankind, which provides the social principle of the person's being and the necessary context for his truly personal growth.

But patriotism as a form of charity, or love, has a more specific object in its actuation than mankind or the human family as such. According to St. Thomas Aquinas, the particular love of one's fatherland is an important aspect of that preferential form of charity that is called *pietas* (*Summa theologiae* 2a2ae, 101.1). Through piety the person has an obligation of love to God, parents and fatherland. Each is in some sense a principle of man's being: God through creation; parents through procreation and education; fatherland through a formation of one's cultural and historical identity.

Patriotism, in its specific sense of love of fatherland, or of one's people, is a historical corollary of a natural demand of community. The love of community that is an imperative of man's created being gains only a vague and illusory existence if it is directed finally at nothing more specific than mankind. And again, love-in-community, when confined to family and friends, or even a local community, becomes a confinement, or limitation, of the person, if not even a "passion against" when it meets the larger communities of nation and world. To the love of hearth and of mankind, a love of country is the psychological and moral, as well as historical, mediacy.

Patriotism can therefore be defined descriptively as the reverent acknowledgment of community as it is expressed in history in a form intermediate to home and world, a response in love to the people and milieu in which man exists because he is created not only as a member of a family or species but is bound to a particular cultural group in space, time and tradition. Put more concisely, patriotism is a special form of piety binding a person to his historical and cultural sources. As such, it makes certain practical demands of the person: loyalty to his nation, collaboration in its political order and the will to seek the moral perfection of his people.

Traditional Catholic teaching, notably as it is synthesized doctrinally and in practical applications by the modern popes, has insisted especially on the profoundly moral basis of rightly ordered patriotism. Pius XI reminded Christian citizens in *Ubi arcano Dei* that "it is never lawful, nor even wise, to dissociate morality from the affairs of practical life," so that "in the last analysis, it is 'justice which exalteth a nation: but sin maketh nations miserable'" (Proverbs 14.34). The citizen must seek the good of his nation according to the norms of a moral order rooted in nature itself, though confirmed by Old Testament precepts and New Testament counsels. The Catholic acknowledgment of natural law is nowhere more explicit or normative than in moral questions connected with the *ius gentium,* nationalism and internationalism, civic loyalty and patriotism.

National and International Dimensions. The understanding of this natural moral order in practical affairs, though often difficult and obscure, admits no concessions from political expediency or in the name of "moral ambiguity" to violations of justice. Thus, within a moral context, an act of civil disobedience may conceivably be the patriot's deepest expression of love, when other actions would only pass over or strengthen a process of injustice corroding the community. The Christian citizen is bound to his nation in a loyal but intelligent union, accepting gladly his national identity but freeing himself and his nation, by a continual reference to the supranational values of charity and justice, for constant growth and reformation. For patriotism is love, and love wills the good of the other—in the case of a nation, a good dependent on its united response to the just claims of its citizens and, to whatever extent possible, to the human needs beyond its borders.

There is no contradiction in seeing a nation's own common good dependent on its contribution to the common good of other peoples in an international community, since, as Pius XII pointed out in *Summi pontificatus,* "legitimate and well-ordered love of our native country should not make us close our eyes to the all-embracing nature of Christian charity." This is so true that patriotism rightly understood, far from obstructing a love of mankind, becomes itself in modern papal teaching one of the bases for sane and salutary internationalism.

The charity of patriotism, while being preferential in its practical object, is at the same time universal in its ultimate aim. It is directed at the exaltation of one's nation under God and thus at its fulfillment in justice of the moral principles governing the relations among states. The devout patriot fears nothing so much for his nation as its following a course of injustices that, however "politically realistic," he recognizes as a way of self-destruction. Since patriotism is a form of charity directed toward a social order whose goal and perfection is justice, its concern for the nation's good extends naturally and harmoniously into the international order, where the nation's drive for global justice is its own exaltation. The aggressive character of political nationalism, the "immoderate nationalism" that Pius XI repeatedly distinguished from patriotism, is, on the other hand, the kind of sin that "maketh nations miserable."

The flowering of a rightly ordered patriotism is therefore wider than one's own fatherland alone and seeks relations of that land to the wider human community and world—hence the manner in which modern papal teaching emphasizes at every turn the balance between a sane nationalism and a humane internationalism. Recent popes base this integration of patriotic piety with international loyalty on the fact that the preferential love that finds its object in the nation wills the good of that nation as realizable through its pursuit of a justice greater than itself and extending beyond its borders. Furthermore, since patriotism is a species of charity, its development involves the deepening of an unspecified power at its source in the human will. Man widens his family through love. Just as the father's deepening love for his family increases his capacity for love, so must the true patriot's love for his country grow naturally until it simultaneously embraces the world while yet remaining, alive and effective within the symphony of human loves and social loyalties, the special preferential piety that is patriotism.

Bibliography: General. J. C. BENNETT, *The Christian as Citizen* (New York 1955). M. CURTI, *The Roots of American Loyalty* (New York 1946). C. DAWSON, *Religion and the Modern State* (New York 1935). C. J. H. HAYES, *Essays on Nationalism* (New York 1926); *Christianity and Western Civilization* (Stanford 1954). J. L. SPALDING, *Things of the Mind* (Chicago 1894; 4th ed. 1901); *Socialism and Labor and other Arguments, Social, Political and Patriotic* (Chicago 1902) ch. 8, essay on "Patriotism." C. VAN DOREN, *Patriotic Anthology* (New York 1941). J. J. WRIGHT, *National Patriotism in Papal Teaching* (Westminster, Md. 1956). Encyclicals. LEO XIII, "Sapientiae christianae" (Jan. 10, 1890) *Acta Sanctorum,* 22 (1890) 385–404; Eng., *Tablet,* 75 (Jan. 25, 1890) 121–126; "Immortale Dei" (Nov. 1, 1885) *Acta Sanctorum,* 18 (1885) 161–180; Eng., *Catholic Mind,* 34 (Nov. 8, 1936) 425–429. PIUS XI, "Caritate Christi compulsi" (May 3, 1932) *Acta Apostolicae Sedis,* 24 (1932) 177–194; Eng. *ibid.* 30 (June 22, 1932) 228–243. JOHN XXIII, *Mater et Magistra.* JOHN XXIII *Pacem in terris.*

[J. J. WRIGHT]

PATRIPASSIANISM

A Trinitarian heresy that denied that the Logos, Jesus Christ, possessed subsistence and implied that God the Father Himself suffered and died on the cross in the guise of the Son. This term is thus synonymous with SABELLIANISM and was invented by the Latin Fathers who called the propagators of MONARCHIANISM *patripassiani* (attributors of suffering to the Father) while the Greeks called them Sabellians. TERTULLIAN, in his *Treatise Against Praxeas 1,* first insisted on this implication of Sabellianism, taking Praxeas to task not only for his monarchianism, but also for his opposition to MONTANISM, which Praxeas persuaded the pope (apparently Victor I) to condemn: *Duo negotia diaboli Praxeas Romae procuravit: . . . Paracletum fugavit et Patrem crucifixit* (Praxeas achieved two works of the devil in Rome: . . . he put the Holy Spirit to flight and crucified the Father). Some scholars think that Tertullian misrepresented Praxeas's

archaic Trinitarian formulations to make him the father of MODALISM, and so discredit him, for the name Praxeas does not appear elsewhere in contemporary sources; others suggest that Tertullian is using the word Praxeas (busybody) as a nickname for Pope Callistus.

Bibliography: TERTULLIAN, *Treatise Against Praxeas,* ed. and tr. E. EVANS (Society for Promoting Christian Knowledge; 1949). J. DANIÉLOU and H. MARROU, *Des origines à saint Grégoire le Grand,* v.1 of *Nouvelle histoire de l'Église* (Paris 1963–) 1:138. G. BARDY, *Dictionnaire de théologie catholique,* ed. A. VACANT et al., (Paris 1903–50) 10.2:2196–2200.

[P. LEBEAU]

PATRISTIC PHILOSOPHY

Patristic philosophy can be considered from the point of view of the history of Christianity—and it is then part of the science of PATRISTIC STUDIES—or from the point of view of the history of philosophy that began outside, and before, the Christian community. The point of view of this article is the history of philosophy.

The history of Western philosophy has three periods: ancient, medieval, and modern. The medieval is the period of the religious philosophies: Jewish, Christian, and Mohammedan. Though "medieval" designates the European period of the 11th to the 14th centuries A.D., the history of CHRISTIAN PHILOSOPHY comprises the two periods of patristic and SCHOLASTIC PHILOSOPHY. The patristic period extends from the beginnings of Christianity to the 8th century (or from St. JUSTIN MARTYR, *c.* 100–164, to St. JOHN DAMASCENE, d. *c.* 749) and is limited to the Mediterranean basin. The development of patristic thought begins with the apostolic Fathers and continues with the Apologists and the beginnings of theology and philosophy to the golden age of the 4th century (Nicaea, 325 to Chalcedon, 451); the final period concludes with Damascene.

The idea that patristic thought belongs to the history of philosophy except for its extrinsic influence has been challenged. The rationalist philosophers (E. Bréhier) maintained that patristic thought is not philosophy because it depends upon a revelation that cannot be questioned. Scholastic theologians have said that the Fathers did not adequately distinguish philosophy and theology and consequently their work was properly theology (P. Mandonnet). In response, some have admitted the actual fusion of philosophy and theology in the Fathers, but have maintained that the distinction was made in principle and that true philosophical work was done that prepared the way for scholastic philosophy (B. Geyer). Others have defended an intermediate concept of "Christian philosophy" and argued that though precisions were

"St. Augustine (of Hippo) Dictating His Works to a Scribe," 13th century fresco, Upper Church, Basilica of S. Francesco, Assisi, Italy.

made later, there was a properly Christian philosophy in the Fathers as well as in the scholastics (É. Gilson).

On the other hand, rationalist historians have argued that the more philosophical of the Fathers (Origen, Gregory of Nyssa, Augustine) were not authentic Christians but really Gnostics or Neoplatonists. There is as a result an extensive literature studying the question, and in each case it has been resolved in favor of the Christianity of the patristic writer.

General Movements of Patristic Philosophy

Not all the patristic writers were philosophers. Some were exegetes, preachers, poets, or theologians in the technical sense. Though there were some elements of philosophy in the apostolic Fathers, Justin was the first Christian "philosopher"—not only because he professed philosophy before his conversion and called himself a philosopher as a Christian, but especially because he made the basic distinction between the logos of revelation and the logos of Greek philosophy or of reason.

Greek. But the dominant and almost exclusive philosophical tradition among the Greek writers is that

which originated with the school of CLEMENT OF ALEXANDRIA (*c.* 150–219) and ORIGEN (*c.* 185–254). In the 4th century it moved to Cappadocia principally in GREGORY OF NYSSA (*c.* 335–395), and then to Athens(?) with PSEUDO-DIONYSIUS the Areopagite (*c.* 500). There are other figures of philosophical importance—such as NEMESIUS OF EMESA (*c.* 400), whose *De natura hominis* was mistakenly attributed to Gregory of Nyssa in the Middle Ages, and Damascene, who is important principally as a summit and transmitter of patristic teaching to the scholastics—but the Alexandrian tradition is the mainline of Greek patristic philosophy.

Latin. In the beginning Greek was the language of the writers in the Roman world also, but Latin began to be used toward the end of the 2d century by MINUCIUS FELIX (*c.* 180) and TERTULLIAN (*c.* 155–245). However, though a certain amount of philosophy came to the Christians by way of Cicero and Varro, for the most part the development of philosophy among the Latin Fathers was the result of the influence of the Greek writers, both Christian and pagan. In the Roman spirit Tertullian and St. AMBROSE contributed to the development of moral philosophy, and Tertullian made some important beginnings in the definition of theologico-philosophical concepts. By far the most important Latin Father philosophically, however, was St. AUGUSTINE. Augustine was an original thinker and the history of his doctrine followed the itinerary of his development from Manichaeism, through skepticism and Neoplatonism, to Christianity. But since the strongest philosophical influence on him was that of PORPHYRY, PLOTINUS, and the Greek Fathers, he may be assimilated to the Alexandrian tradition in philosophy.

Second in importance to Augustine is BOETHIUS, a layman. Though Augustinian and Neoplatonic at base, his thought is not as mystical and spiritual. His *Consolation of Philosophy* presents an example of lay philosophy, though he also wrote theological treatises that are philosophically important. He is especially significant for his effort to make both Plato and Aristotle available to the Latin world, and particularly for introducing Aristotelian logic into European philosophy. The work of translation of the Neoplatonists into Latin had been begun much earlier by MARIUS VICTORINUS.

Nature of Philosophy in the Fathers

In the Western world philosophy means the type of rational understanding developed by the Greeks. For this reason the history of philosophy is in large part the history of the influence of Greek philosophy.

Influence of the Greeks. The influence of Hellenism on Christian origins is discernible in the Old Testament, e.g., in the Book of Wisdom. Greek influences are recognizable also in the New Testament, in John and Paul. But the first major effort to unite Greek speculation with the Bible was made by PHILO JUDAEUS (*c.* A.D. 40). GNOSTICISM likewise had much to do with initiating the movement among the Christians, since it professed to be able to discern in the Scriptures a secret, saving doctrine that had large elements of Greek philosophy in it. One of the motives of the Alexandrian school was to develop a true Christian Gnosticism, though Origen was undoubtedly stimulated also by the beginnings of Neoplatonism in which he seems to have taken part.

The history of pagan philosophy at the time of the beginning of Christianity is not very well known. It was a period of syncretism, not only between philosophies but also between religions, and there was no dominant school. Plotinus (d. A.D. 270) presented the first strong new philosophy since Stoicism and Epicureanism. The first Christians therefore tended to be eclectic. Plato (*Timaeus*), however, seemed closer to Moses (Genesis) than the others, while Epicurus and Aristotle were considered the most incompatible with Christianity. Even skepticism was significant, not only in the development of Augustine's thought, but also in provoking arguments for the

necessity of faith. Once Neoplatonism developed, however, it had a preponderant influence on the Christians (Plotinus and Porphyry on Augustine, Proclus on Dionysius).

Concept of Philosophy. The distinction and meanings of theology and philosophy as used in the post-scholastic world were not operative in the patristic period. Among the pagans philosophy was a general term for the doctrine and way of life of a particular group of men. Theology meant simply the part of philosophy that treated of God. The patristic philosophers compared Christianity to the pagan philosophies, much as Christianity and communism might be contrasted. They distinguished between "our philosophy" and the philosophy of "those outside." Thus, philosophy could be considered as a way of human beatitude (Augustine), or a way of salvation through higher, speculative knowledge (Gnosticism), or a way of Christian perfection by the elevation of the mind of God (Alexandrians).

Thus the movement of philosophy among both the pagans and the Christians was toward beatifying knowledge. The Christians, however, insisted that the goal could not be achieved by finite reason alone. Faith is necessary from beginning to end. Thus the process goes from simple faith in revelation, through the hierarchy of human and divine sciences, to mystical contemplation and union with God. This process involves a dialectic of faith and reason that recognizes the validity of human reason proceeding from an analysis of creatures to the Creator (Wis 13; Rom 1.20; Greek philosophy) but considers this insufficient. Faith and reason are interrelated as teacher and pupil in the natural process of human learning (Augustine).

The desire for God did not exhaust all the causes of philosophical reasoning among the Christians. Philosophy was needed to meet the challenge of the pagans (e.g., CELSUS) and to clarify the meaning of the Christian revelation in the face of heretical views within. Moreover, philosophers such as Justin, when converted, could not resist philosophizing within Christianity. Neither did the intellectual mystical tradition present the only view of Christian perfection. There were those such as Basil and Ambrose who stressed the Biblical service of God and the life of the moral virtues.

General Synthesis Of Patristic Philosophy

A catalogue of the philosophical opinions of the individual patristic writers taken chronologically can be found in the Catholic histories of Christian or medieval philosophy (Gilson, Copleston). Some general lines of doctrine are sketched here.

When patristic philosophy is seen from the viewpoint of the history of philosophy, it is generally considered as a correction and development of Greek philosophy. Though there are merits in this procedure, it gives a false perspective. Patristic philosophy began with the Hebrew tradition and the Bible. Greek philosophy entered this tradition and taught the patristic philosophers how to develop the philosophical elements in revelation rationally (cf. C. Tresmontant). But the patristic philosophers also saw themselves as different from the Jews, who held strictly to the Old Testament. The difference, of course, was Christ, and though the mystery of Christ took them beyond the realm of rational understanding, nevertheless the theology of Christ forced a reconstruction of philosophy that can be called specifically Christian, at least in the historical sense.

Trinitarian Doctrine. Christ meant first of all the doctrine of the Trinity, the mystery of one divine nature but three Persons. This was anathema to the Jews, who saw it as a species of polytheism; but philosophically speaking, it forced against the Arians a distinction between generation (the Son) and creation that sharpened appreciably the notion of creation out of nothing derived from the Old Testament.

Creation and Divine Ideas. The Fathers found it easy to adapt the myth of Plato's *Timaeus* and understood God as an omnipotent artist who freely willed the world in time out of nothing according to patterns that He contemplates in His divine mind. But the break was made with Greek philosophy both by denying any kind of dualism of matter that is coeternal with the Creator and is shaped by Him, and by denying any kind of generationism whereby creatures proceed from God's substance in some way. To the Platonic division between the intelligible and the sensible a more embracing and radical division was added—between Creator and creature—in such a way that the division of creature contained the division of spiritual and material.

The nature of this last division was not always clear to the Fathers, and a certain reality was sometimes attributed to the divine ideas distinct from the being of God, as though God first created the intelligible world that the material world imitated, in a Platonic fashion. The Platonic myth of the fall of man into the body was also sometimes used, as in Gregory of Nyssa. But the ultimate pattern that prevailed was that of Dionysius, who made every creature apart from God a substance and made the intelligible creation the orders of the angels (as against the hypostases of Plotinus and Proclus). The question whether the angels were able to contribute to the creative process was asked but not definitely answered. They were granted some gubernatorial functions in the universe, which was conceived as one whole under God.

After Origen's thesis of multiple worlds, the patristic doctrine settled in the direction of one single creation in time, which, however, went through gradual stages of development until man appeared and the history of civilization began. Here the harmonization between Genesis and the *Timaeus* is again apparent. Augustine followed Gregory of Nyssa in making use of the theory of SEMINAL reasons to explain how it was possible that the whole of creation was produced "at once" (as they understood Sir 18.1 to teach) but nevertheless went through the stages of the six days. The theory of an eternal world was constantly rejected as contrary not only to revelation but also to Plato. The possibility of distinguishing between the conclusions of reason (which might leave the question of eternity open) and the affirmations of revelation (which does not) did not occur to the Christian world before MAIMONIDES suggested it in the 12th century. Hence, time and history were primary categories of patristic thought, and the world scheme of the Fathers came closer to the 20th-century evolutionary and historical world view than did that of the scholastics.

Psychology of Person. Another great influence of the Trinitarian doctrine on philosophy came in the development of the psychology of the PERSON. It was principally Augustine who reconstructed the Greek psychology into a new Christian synthesis. Christ is the Word of God. This teaching enabled the Fathers to join the Platonic and Stoic theories of the logos. In Augustine the interior word became the middle term of a process that came out of memory and completed itself in love. Plato's theory of reminiscence was changed into a doctrine of divine ILLUMINATION, which formed at once the basis for absolute knowledge and the ascent of the mind to God. Taken objectively as being, truth, and goodness, the triad joined the ontology of the Greeks and became a Christian doctrine of PARTICIPATION whereby all things descend from, and exist by, the One Being who is the cause of all.

In patristic philosophy there are, then, two forms of participation, that of EXEMPLARISM, or participation in the creative ideas by imitation, and an ontological participation whereby creatures derive from the Creator in descending grades of perfection. At the heart of this philosophy is the principle enunciated by Boethius that the imperfect presupposes the perfect (*Consol. phil.* 3.10).

Knowledge of God. The mystery of the Trinity brought forth yet another theme of patristic philosophy, the knowability yet incomprehensibility of God. The Arian, EUNOMIUS OF CONSTANTINOPLE, had attempted to apply univocally to God the Aristotelian categories taken from the sensible world. It became clear in the debate that this could not be done, and the beginnings of the doctrine of ANALOGY were shaped. Moreover, though it is true that reason can apply names from creatures to the Creator in a transcendent manner, nevertheless God still remains incomprehensible and a mystery. This is the constant theme of the Greek Fathers. The negative theology of Dionysius is perhaps their strongest statement about God, though it is mitigated by Damascene's position that God is naturally and readily known by a kind of instinctive ascent from creatures to the Creator.

Teaching on the Incarnation. Christ also means the INCARNATION, that is, the mystery of the assumption of human nature by a divine Person so that the Second Person of the Trinity is both God and man. This forced the Fathers to establish their understanding of the human nature that the Word assumed. Christ did not assume a soul without a body, or a body without a soul; He had all the powers and faculties of man. In terms of the division of creatures into spiritual and material, it became clear that man was a composite of both "natures" and mediated between both worlds. It was possible, then, with Gregory of Nyssa, to define him both as a rational animal and as a corporeal spirit.

Spirit. The notion of SPIRIT and of the spirituality of the human soul did not come easy for the early Fathers. Stoicism and Manichaeism had a developed materialism that included God and held thinkers such as Tertullian and Augustine in its grasp for a while. Scripture itself, especially the Old Testament, was not clear and forceful on this point. Thus it was probably Neoplatonism—in part a reaction to the materialism of Hellenistic philosophy—that did most to clarify the spiritual nature of the soul. But this left the Fathers with a certain dualism in man of soul and body that was not completely overcome. The soul was not conceived in a simple undifferentiated way, however, but rather as a hierarchy of powers and functions that stretched between the poles of spirit and matter. As the soul became more interior, it became more spiritual and also the center wherein God dwelt. This psychology was intimately connected with the theory of mystical contemplation, itself the Christian response to the immanentist doctrine of Plotinus. Within the Alexandrian tradition, at least, the ascetical and moral teaching of the Fathers was worked out from the point of view of this mystical psychology. Thus the life of virtue was structured toward union with God. The view of man's nature as composite made it relatively easy to defend the immortality of the human soul, though it was not as helpful regarding the question of the resurrection of the body.

Person and Nature. The Incarnation and the doctrine of the Trinity both forced a distinction between person and nature, though from opposite directions. The Incarnation presented an instance of one Person but two natures;

the Trinity of one nature but three Persons. This led to new precisions about the Aristotelian category of SUBSTANCE, but particularly it made important the problem of UNIVERSALS and individuals. The question that Boethius bequeathed to the Middle Ages in his commentary on Porphyry's *Isagoge* was not merely a speculative question that intrigued the scholastics; it was very closely bound up with the doctrines of the Trinity and the Incarnation. The solutions of the Fathers tended to be a modification of Platonism and Stoicism and to stress the unity of a nature in all men that was nevertheless possessed by different individuals or persons. When their views were repeated in the early Middle Ages, they came under the sharp criticism of ABELARD, and the problem came into greater prominence.

Role of the Redemption. Christ finally also means redemption. This immediately engages the problem of EVIL, which was probably the most absorbing problem in the syncretic period of the beginning of the patristic age. All the dualistic religions of the East and the Hellenistic philosophies revolved around the mystery of GOOD and evil, the freedom and determinism of man, the providence of God. It is in this context that the historical significance of Christianity can best be understood. Because of the patristic doctrine of creation of all beings by God, who is Being, any kind of absolute DUALISM had to be rejected. There is nothing that did not proceed from God. In this there was a parallelism with the Plotinian doctrine of the emanation of all from the One. Because God is good only, everything He made was good, even matter, and in this the Plotinian doctrine was modified. But perhaps the greatest impulse toward the recognition of the goodness of matter came from the doctrine of the Incarnation; for it was early established against DOCETISM that matter was assumed also by the Son.

Freedom. Consequently, the Christians moved in the direction of explaining evil metaphysically in the Platonic sense of nonbeing, but morally as having its possibility in the FREEDOM and finitude of man. The Fathers worked hard, therefore, to defend human freedom against Manichaeism. On the other hand, the mission of Christ as redeemer also taught them to fend off Pelagian optimism. Man's freedom, then, was seen in an ambivalent position, as drawn to determinism in the physical world and as elevated to freedom by the grace of Christ. The same dialectic that was mentioned above regarding faith and reason was operative also between grace and freedom. These questions absorbed much of Augustine's time, but Nemesius, and especially Damascene, worked to clarify the psychology of choice. In this area the positive help of Aristotle was finally apparent.

Image of God. The doctrine of redemption in patristic thought is closely related also to the doctrine of man as the IMAGE OF GOD. This doctrine was derived from Genesis, but it also fitted well with the Platonic scheme. For the Christians, however, the image of God meant the image of the Creator, and so it was the freedom of man and his position as lord of the world that characterized man's likeness to God. This position, developed by Gregory of Nyssa and others, was to be repeated by St. THOMAS AQUINAS. It is this image that was dimmed by the Fall, that was brought back to its original intention by the redemptive grace of Christ, and that was given a new goal by the new reality of the Son of God made man. Thus, though the Christian doctrine of the Fall and Redemption resembles the Platonic cycle, the patristic doctrine of image also lays the theoretical foundations for man's creative and productive function in history and civilization. He is to be a second creator.

But because men are ultimately free, they are divided into two camps: those who struggle with Christ to redeem the world and those who do not. There is then a dualism of spirits in history, but it is the result of the freedom of creatures and not of two absolute and independent sources. This is the theme of Augustine's great *City of God,* which furnished the blueprint for the Christian Middle Ages.

Conclusion

Patristic philosophy is not a single tradition, nor is it a separate science apart from the totality of developing Christian life. It did not answer definitively all the questions it raised, but it did explore most of them and set themes and directions that formed the bases not only for medieval philosophy but for much of modern philosophy as well.

Bibliography: É. BRÉHIER, *Période Héllenistique et Romaine,* v.1.2 of *Histoire de la philosophie,* 2 v. (Paris 1926–32). F. C. COPLESTON, *History of Philosophy* (Westminster, MD 1946–) v.2. F. UEBERWEG*Grundriss der Geschichte der Philosophie,* 5 v. (Berlin 1923–28) v.2. E. H. GILSON, *History of Christian Philosophy in the Middle Ages* (New York 1955). B. ROMEYER, *La Philosophie chrétienne jusqu'à Descartes,* 3 v. (Paris 1935–37) C. TRESMONTANT, *The Origins of Christian Philosophy,* tr. M. PONTIFEX (New York 1963); *A Study of Hebrew Thought,* tr M. F. GIBSON (New York 1960); *La Métaphysique du christianisme et la naissance de la philosophie chrétienne* (Paris 1961). R. ARNOU, *Dictionnaire de théologie catholique,* ed. A. VACANT, 15 v. (Paris 1903–50; Tables générales 1951–) 12.2:2258–2392. J. DANIÉLOU, *Message évangélique et culture hellénistique aux IIe et IIIe siècles,* v.2 of *Histoire des doctrines chrétiennes avant Nicée* (Tournai 1961). M. SPANNEUT, *Le Stoïcisme des Pères de l'Église de Clément de Rome à Clément d'Alexandrie* (Paris 1957). H. A. WOLFSON, *Philo,* 2 v. (Cambridge, MA 1947). A. J. FESTUGIÈRE, *L'Idéal religieux des Grecs et l'Évangile* (Paris 1932).

[R. F. HARVANEK]

PATRISTIC STUDIES

The study of the FATHERS OF THE CHURCH. Also referred to as patrology, a term first used by the Lutheran theologian Johannes Gerhard as the title of a posthumous work (1653). Although the terms patrology, patristics, and the history of ancient Christian literature are sometimes employed interchangeably, it seems advisable to distinguish three scholarly disciplines, covering on broad lines the same period of history and much the same authors, but eyeing their material from distinctive standpoints. Patrology normally has a more historical cast, setting forth the life, writings (genuine, doubtful, spurious), and significant doctrines (or doctrinal significance) of the various authors. Patristics concentrates on the content, primarily theological, of the writings of the Fathers and implies a systematic exposition of their doctrine in whole or in part. The term stems from the 17th century and was first used in Lutheran circles, where theology was divided into Biblical, positive, scholastic, symbolic, and speculative. (*See* PATRISTIC THEOLOGY.) The history of ancient Christian literature is more in conformity with the philological development and outlook of the 19th and 20th centuries; it puts the Fathers in the framework of the general history of literature, gives more play to the literary aspect of the works involved, and has legitimately introduced (as patrology itself has been compelled to do) a number of writers who are not technically Fathers or even orthodox Christians, but deserve a place in the treatment of the literature of the time. The controversy over the scope and character of early Christian literature initiated early in the 20th century by A. von HARNACK, O. Bardenhewer, and others has long since been resolved, and "ancient Christian literature" is now universally recognized as a satisfactory expression.

Patristic Studies through Trent. The history of patristics goes back to the *Church History* of EUSEBIUS OF CAESAREA (early 4th century) and JEROME's *De viris illustribus* (392). The latter was continued in the patristic era by GENNADIUS OF MARSEILLES, ISIDORE OF SEVILLE, and ILDEFONSUS OF TOLEDO. In the Middle Ages the most significant "patrology" was PHOTIUS's *Myriobiblon* or *Bibliotheca* (858). The catalogue (*c.* 1317–18) of the last great Nestorian writer 'ABDISHO BAR BERĪKĀ is important for early Syriac literature. Other medieval compilers, such as SIGEBERT OF GEMBLOUX, HONORIUS OF AUTUN, and Johannes TRITHEMIUS, were content to rely on Jerome and Gennadius. Fresh impetus for patristic study came from the discovery of early Christian texts during the Renaissance, the return to antiquity sparked by the humanists, the Reformation thesis of a gradual deterioration of primitive Christianity, and theological discussions at the Council of TRENT.

Seventeenth and Eighteenth Centuries The studies of the 17th century and the first half of the 18th constitute a first flowering of high-level patristic scholarship on a vast expanse, with remarkable editions (preeminently by the MAURISTS) distinguished for prolegomena and critical apparatus, the painstaking *De scriptoribus ecclesiasticis* of Robert BELLARMINE, comprehensive historical productions such as L. S. le Nain de TILLEMONT's 16-volume *Mémoires pour servir a l'histoire ecclésiastique des six premiers siècles* (1693–1712) and R. CEILLIER's 23-volume *Histoire générale des auteurs sacrés et ecclésiastiques* (1729–63), and the research of Denis PETAU, who gave to positive theology its rightful place in sacred science (notably in his 4-volume *Dogmata theologica*, 1644–50).

Nineteenth Century. Stimulated in part by A. MAI, J. A. MÖHLER, and J. D. PITRA, the 19th century inaugurated another productive period of patristic scholarship, marked by new discoveries, especially in the Oriental field; the establishment of university chairs of patrology; J. P. MIGNE's comprehensive *Patrologiae cursus completus* (1844–66); the critical editions of the Latin Fathers (*Corpus scriptorum ecclesiasticorum latinorum*, 1866–) and the Greek (*Die griechischen christlichen Schriftsteller der ersten drei Jahrhunderte*, 1897–) undertaken with philological competence by the Vienna and the Prussian Academies of Sciences respectively; and the passage from vast histories to treatises, monographs, and manuals. This fluorescence produced, toward the end of the century, the extraordinary patristic research initiated by A. von Harnack and O. Bardenhewer, accompanied by scholars such as F. Loofs and L. DUCHESNE, F. X. von FUNK and P. BATIFFOL—whose research was continued and intensified by F. J. DÖLGER, H. LIETZMANN, A. BAUMSTARK, G. MORIN, G. BARDY, B. ALTANER, and a host of others.

Twentieth Century. Twentieth-century patrologists have shown a predilection for exploring more profoundly the doctrinal content of the Fathers, investigating the evolution of words and ideas, and plumbing the patristic stress on history and mystery. Since World War II, new interest in patristic study has been stimulated by striking discoveries (Tura, Nag' Hammâdi, Bodmer papyri) Of unparalleled importance is the long-delayed publication of the texts and translations of the Gnostic writings of Nag' Hammâdi in Egypt, providing firsthand evidence of the range of Gnostic ideas opposed by so many Church Fathers, and now allowing some of the material to be seen more accurately as a development of traditions to be found in the NT and earlier (e.g. the collections of the "sayings" of Jesus). Interest has also been stimulated by the prolific production of texts and translations (cf. *Corpus christianorum*, 1953–, ultimately to replace Migne;

A. Hamman's *Supplementum* to *Patrologia Latina*, ed. J. P. Migne, [Paris 1878–90] v.1–96, 1958– ; *Sources chrétiennes*, 1942– ; *Corpus scriptorum christianorum orientalium*, 1903–, but esp. since 1949; *Ancient Christian Writers*, 1946– ; *Corpus christianorum: Series graeca*; *Oxford Early Christian Texts*). Readily accessible research tools are also available (e.g. G. W. H. Lampe, ed., *Patristic Greek Lexicon*, the Strasbourg Centre's *Biblia patristica*, indexing biblical citations and allusions in early Christian writers). This renewed interest has been quickened by the quadrennial Oxford International Conference on Patristic Studies, the ecumenical movement, and an increasing awareness of the significance of doctrinal development.

Among the emphases of recent historical scholarship have been: less interest in using the Fathers as supports for particular theological or ecclesiological positions; greater concern for understanding than for the application of such categories as "orthodox" and "heretical"; increased sophistication in the exploratory use of philosophical, psychological, and sociological analytical tools to deepen and freshen that understanding; heightened sensitivity to and appreciation of the rich diversity revealed in early Christian literature, not only among the Fathers but also between them and their opponents (many of whose writings have not been preserved); broadened interest in the concrete ways of being human and of being religious of the men and women who produced, read, and preserved (and sometimes destroyed) the writings of the Church of the first few centuries.

Vatican Council II has endorsed the study of the Fathers, pointing to our gaining a deepened sense of how the Scriptures have been used in the Church (*Dei Verbum* 23) and our retrieving a more inclusive, more "ecumenical" spirituality (*Unitatis redintegratio* 15). But Christians have also become more aware of certain other fairly common positions of the patristic era which have contributed to an unfortunate heritage, demanding serious reexamination today. These positions or attitudes of many of the Fathers would include: a pervasive anti-Judaism; an ambivalence toward sexuality and toward the human body; an antifeminism, understandable but regrettable nonetheless; a Christology which only infrequently took adequate account of the humanity of Jesus; and, especially after Constantine, a political and ecclesiastical "triumphalism" of a kind which, since Vatican II, can be more readily acknowledged and transcended.

Bibliography: Bibliographical aids. K. SCHAFERDIEK, ed. *Bibliographia Patristica* XXVI–XXVII, 1981–82 (Berlin 1986). J. LIÉBAERT, "Patrologie," *Catholicisme* 10 (1985) 829–858 T. P. HALTON and R. D. SIDER, "A Decade of Patristic Scholarship, 1970–79," *Classical World* 76 (1982–83) 65–127, 313–383. AUGUSTINIAN PATRISTIC INSTITUTE OF ROME, *Patrology*, A. DI BE-

RARDINO, ed., with intro. by J. QUASTEN, *The Golden Age of Latin Patristic Literature from the Council of Nicea to the Council of Chalcedon,* tr. P. SOLARI (Westminster 1986). ASSOCIATION INTERNATIONALE D'ÉTUDES PATRISTIQUES, *Bulletin d'information et de liaison, No. 11. (1985) Annuaire* (Turnhout 1985). F. M. YOUNG, *From Nicaea to Chalcedon: A Guide to the Literature and its Background* (London/Philadelphia 1983). H. CROUZEL, *Bibliographie critique d'Origène* (La Haye 1971), with *Supplément 1* (1983), Fichier augustinien. *Augustine bibliography,* prémier supplément (Boston 1981). S. P. BROCK, ''Syriac Studies 1971–1980. A Classified Bibliography,'' *Patrologia orientalis* (1981–82) 291–404. Series. W. J. BURGHARDT, ''Literature of Christian Antiquity: 1975–1979,'' *Theological Studies* 41 (1980) 151–180; ''1979–1983,'' *Theological Studies* 45 (1984) 275–306. P. JACQUEMENT, ''Les Pères de l'Église pour tous,'' *Revue des sciences philosophiques et théologiques* 65 (1981) 365–370. C. MONDÉSERT, ed., *Le Monde grec ancien et la Bible* (Bible de tous les temps 1, Paris 1984). J. FONTAINE and C. PIETRI, eds., *Le Monde latin antique et la Bible* (Bible de tous les temps 2; Paris 1985). A.-M. LA BONNARDIRE, ed., *Saint Augustin et la Bible* (Bible de tous les temps 3; Paris 1986). E. DEKKERS, ''Corpus Christianorum,'' *Epemerides theologicae Lovanienses LX* (Bruges 1984) 190–193. R. M. GRANT, *Gods and the One God,* Library of Early Christianity 1 (Philadelphia 1986). Other Works. J. QUASTEN, *Patrology,* (Westminster, Md. 1950–). F. L. CROSS, *The Early Christian Fathers* (London 1960). B. ALTANER, *Miscellanea Giovanni Mercati* (Rome 1946) 1:483–520. W. BAUER, *Orthodoxy and Heresy in Earliest Christianity,* R. KRAFT and G. KRODEL, eds. (Philadelphia 1971). J. DANIÉLOU, *History of Early Christianity,* 3 v., tr. J. BOWDEN (London and Chicago 1964–1977). A. GRILLMEIER, *Christ in Christian Tradition,* tr. J. BOWDEN (2d rev. ed. Atlanta 1976). E. HENNECKE, W. SCHNEEMELCHER, and R. MCL. WILSON, eds., *New Testament Apocrypha* 2 v., tr. A. J. B. HIGGINS, et al. (Philadelphia 1963–64). J. J. PELIKAN, *The Christian Tradition,* v. 1, *The Emergence of the Catholic Tradition* (Chicago 1971). J. M. ROBINSON, ed., *The Nag Hammadi Library* (Claremont, Cal. 1977). J. M. ROBINSON and H. KOESTER, *Trajectories through Early Christianity* (Philadelphia 1971). E. A. LIVINGSTONE, ed., *Studia Patristica,* XVIII. Papers of the 1983 Patristic Conference, 4 v. (Kalamazoo 1985–87). B. LAYTON, ed., *The Rediscovery of Gnosticism.* Proceedings of International Conference on Gnosticism at Yale University, 2 v. (Leiden 1981). E. P. SANDERS, ed., *Jewish and Christian Self-Definition,* v. 1. *The Shaping of Christianity in the Second and Third Centuries* (Philadelphia 1980). C. HEDRICK and R. HODGSON, eds., *Nag Hammadi, Gnosticism and Early Christianity* (Peabody, Mass. 1986). M. AUBINEAU, ''Textes nouveaux d'Hésychius de Jérusalem. Bilan et méthodes,'' *Studia Patristica,* XVIII, 345–351. J. DIVIAK, *Sancti Aurelii Augustini opera. Sect. 2 Pars 6. Epistolae ex duobus codicibus nuper in lucem prolatae, Corpus Scriptorum ecclesiasticorum latinorum,* 88 (Vienna 1981). G. H. R. HORSLEY, *New Documents Illustrating Early Christianity: A Review of the Greek Inscriptions and Papyri published in 1978* (North Ryde, NSW 1983). B. A. PEARSON and J. E. GOEHRING, eds., *The Roots of Egyptian Christianity* (Philadelphia 1986). H. CHADWICK, *History and Thought of the Early Church* (London 1982). G. C. STEAD, *Substance and Illusion in the Christian Fathers* (London 1985). S. BROCK, *Syriac Perspectives on Late Antiquity* (London 1984). H. J. W. DRIJVERS, *East of Antioch: Studies in Early Syriac Christianity* (London 1984). R. M. GRANT, *Christian Beginnings: Apocalypse to History* (London 1983). R. A. MARKUS, *From Augustine to Gregory the Great* (London 1983).

[W. J. BURGHARDT/D. P. EFROYMSON/T. HALTON]

PATRISTIC THEOLOGY

The development of Christian thought about God and the mystery of man's destiny in the writings of the Fathers of the Church during the first seven centuries A.D. constitutes patristic theology. It differs from Biblical theology in that it consciously reflects the philosophical and religious thought of the Hellenistic world, while its emphasis on a positive approach to Scripture and the Church's tradition and its lack of systematization distinguish it from scholastic and post-Tridentine theology.

Coincident with the Biblical approach, patristic theology is concerned primarily with an event: man's meeting with Christ, the Son of God, who suffered under Pontius Pilate, died, and rose again from the dead. This was the essential consideration of Christian thought, and from time to time threatened to be the Christian's sole interest. However in the annunciation and explanation of this event the Church's teachers were constrained to utilize contemporary philosophy, religious concepts, and cultural patterns in order to defend and clarify their message. Thus patristic theology is an amalgam of Judeo-Christian, Hellenistic, and some Oriental thought adapted to the singular facts enunciated in the Old and New Testaments about God, and enacted by Christ in His own life, and in the life of the Church, His Mystical Body.

It was EUSEBIUS OF CAESAREA, the great Church historian, who in the 4th century certified the legitimacy of the word theology for Christian usage. He described the Evangelist St. John as ''The Theologian,'' since his Gospel is concerned primarily with the divinity of Christ (*De eccl. theol.* 1.20; 2.12), and announced the purpose of his Church history as a demonstration of the ''theology and economy of salvation according to Christ'' (*Ecclesiastical History* 1.1.7; *prol.* 2).

THE BEGINNINGS

Earlier Christian thinkers had hesitated to use the words *theologos, theologia, theologein* because, as St. Augustine, quoting the naturalist Varro, remarked, there were three kinds of pagan theology: rational, or an explanation of the gods in their myths; physical, or the explanation of the world in its causes; and civil, devoted to the essentially political religion and cult of the city-state or imperial dynasty (*Civ.* 6.5; Tertullian, *Ad nat.* 2.1, 2).

Greek thought associated theology with the theogonies of the poets, particularly Orpheus, Homer, and Hesiod. Aristotle contrasted these theologians with Thales and Anaximander who sought a physical explanation of things, while in his *Metaphysics* (bk. 12) he supplied a philosophy about God that is a solid natural theology. The Neoplatonists and some Church Fathers considered Plato a theologian, although he used the word theology to designate the educative value of mythology (*Rep.* 379A).

CLEMENT OF ALEXANDRIA gave Christian recognition to theology as the knowledge of divine things. While Clement recognized the poetical function of ancient pagan theology, he credited the philosophers with a desire to achieve knowledge of the true God (*Strom.* 1.13; 5.9). Origen spoke of the "ancient theologians among the Greeks" and the "theology of the Persians" as devoted to an explanation of religion and the divinity; but gradually he limited *theologia* and *theologein* to the Christian sense of a true knowledge of God (*Cont. Cel.* 6.18; *Comm. in Jn* 2.34) and particularly of Christ the Savior (*ibid.* 1.24).

Despite the warnings of early Christians such as Tatian, Tertullian, and Lactantius against a speculative consideration of faith, an explanation of the fact of Christ's activities, and the mystery embodied in the CHRISTIAN WAY OF LIFE in the Church early proved a necessity. This was apparent to St. Paul, who experienced the shock caused by the preaching of "Christ crucified, a scandal to the Greeks, a stumbling block to the Jews." While he warned against "philosophy" and human deceit controlled by the demons (Col 2.8–20), he illustrated his teaching with parallels in nature and in Judeo-Hellenistic thought.

Jewish Theology. Jewish theological speculation embodied in the Apocalypses, Haggadah, Pescherim, and liturgical writings greatly influenced both the New Testament and the Judeo-Christian thought concerned with the nature of God, angelology, eschatology, and dualistic considerations of the problem of evil. These influences are apparent in the so-called APOSTOLIC FATHERS from Clement and the Didache to the Pseudo-Barnabas and Ignatius of Antioch. But it was with the Apologists that true theological thinking began.

Converts from philosophy, convinced that in Christ the Logos they had finally achieved truth, they utilized the arguments and *topoi* in the handbooks and florilegia of the current Stoic, Pythagorean, and Platonic schools to ridicule the gods and counter the anti-Christian charges. While they addressed the public authorities in protest against persecution of the Christians, their primary function was a missionary effort aimed at converting their contemporaries. In this they had as precedent a considerable Judeo-Hellenistic literature in the *Letter of Aristeas,* the Judeo-Christian *Sibylline Books,* and PHILO JUDAEUS. They admitted that the philosophers had achieved some appreciation of truth which, since it was one, had to be homogeneous. Following Philo they claimed that Plato and the earlier thinkers had read Moses and the Prophets for their knowledge of monotheism or

had retained a kernel of truth given in an original revelation and preserved among both Greeks and barbarians. But in any case the Christians now possessed the fullness of truth in Christ (Theophilus of Antioch, *Ad Autol.* 2.12; Justin, *1 Apol.* 20; Athenagoras, *Suppl.* 1.6).

The Apologists. The late 2d-century writers confronted their audience with the "unique, eternal, invisible God" (Athenagoras, *Resur.* 10), "Creator of the universe" (Justin, *2 Apol* 12.1), manifest in his works (Theophilus of Antioch, 1.6) and reminded them of the judgment facing all mankind (Justin, *ibid.*). Though differing in method, they presented the doctrine of the Resurrection with considerable argument following St. Paul (1 Cor) and St. John (Jn 12.24). They contrasted the purity of the Christian life with the immorality of the pagan (Justin *1 Apol.* 14.1–4), utilizing the technique of the early catechesis in the DIDACHE and Letter of Barnabas.

Athenagoras stressed the Christian doctrine of love of neighbor, sanctity of marriage, and virginity (*Suppl.* 32–33); and the *Epistle to Diognetus* maintained that the Christians lived like their neighbors but kept the laws of God and man, serving as a leaven for society, giving it life as the soul does the body (5.6–13).

What the Christians took from the Greeks was a manner of explaining both monotheism and the divinity of Christ, leaning on amalgams of Platonic philosophy to establish God's oneness, and on Stoicism for speculation on the Logos. Later they turned to Middle Platonism and Neoplatonism. The danger in this process was illustrated by the Gnostics, who employed the Platonic philosophies to speculate about God and Christ, but without the Judaic insistence on the historical actuality of Christ and His eschatological setting. Their idealist concept of the divinity gave Him no concrete place in history, and only an apparent piercing of time and space in the salvationary work of Christ. Despising the material world, they called for an absolute spiritualizing of man. The Church rejected this teaching with its parallels in Manichaeism and Marcionism, which were combatted by Irenaeus of Lyons, Hippolytus of Rome, and Tertullian.

THEOLOGICAL SPECULATION

Theological advancement began with Justin and Irenaeus who spoke of the *oikonomia,* or economy of salvation, to designate the events in the life of Christ, "the Son of God who existed before the morning star and the moon, who consented to become flesh in order that by this economy, the serpent who from the beginning had acted evilly, and the angels who imitated him, might be destroyed" (Justin, *Dialogue* 45.4).

Justin embodied the mysteries of Christ, particularly His virgin birth and His Passion, in the economy, comparing these glories to the Parousia, or second coming (*Dialogue* 30.3). He included the events of the Old Testament, which he maintains are a typology of the things accomplished by Christ (*Dialogue* 134.2). They are thus part of his theology of the Word, who carries out the will of His Father (*Dialogue* 67.6) in the theophanies of the Old Testament (*Dialogue* 126.3, 5; 127.1) and operates through the Church in the Eucharist and the sacraments of His power (*1 Apol.* 66.2), which will be visible in the second coming (*Dialogue* 54.1).

These fundamental ideas are developed by Irenaeus, who considered the Incarnation of Christ as the key to the history of salvation wherein God has approached man to bring man to God (*Adversus haereses* 4.20.1), an idea that will be emphasized by St. ATHANASIUS (*De Incarn.* 53). Again it is Christ who carried out His Father's will in the Old Testament encounters (*Demonst.* 45), and who is the Beginning and the Law, the Resurrection and the Life. He saw the two Testaments as two steps in the reeducation by grace of man who sinned from ignorance as a child (*nepios*), and portrayed Christ as the recapitulation of man, submitting to human experience, but conquering sin and the devil and effecting a recapitulation of all things in His Church by sending man the Holy Spirit in preparation for the final restoration of all things in God (*Adversus haereses* 3–5; *Demonst.* 31–33).

Development of Speculative Theology. True theological speculation began with the 3d-century Fathers, particularly Clement of Alexandria, Origen, Methodius of Olympus, Hippolytus of Rome, and Tertullian. The doctrine of ideas in the mind of God had been accepted by Philo Judaeus and combined with Jewish thought expressed in the Books of Wisdom, which saw God's wisdom not merely as an attribute, but as a mysterious entity, possibly personal, who in the beginning assisted God in creation. First-century Jewish speculation had concentrated further on powers, the names of God, and the angel of God, through whom He worked in dealing with the universe. Philo translated the Hebrew word *dabar* (the power, or word, of God) by the Greek word Logos, thus identifying the notion of knowledge or wisdom with the Hebrew idea of God's power. The Stoics employed logos for the fiery rational principle that formed the universe, while the Neoplatonists defined logos as "a power (*dynamis*) that represents a higher principle in action on a lower plane."

When St. John in the prologue of his Gospel named Christ the Logos who was with God and is God, he was reflecting common usage in both the Diasporic Jewish and Hellenistic milieu. But John gave the Logos a definite meaning: He is a person; and Heb 1.3 further identified Christ with God's wisdom, calling him the "shining

out of His glory." In contrast to the cyclical concept of history based on the material world as merely a reflection of ideas in the divine mind, the Christian thinkers of the 3d century followed the Judaic unilinear concept of history, and insisted on the historical reality of Christ, a beginning to the universe, man's destiny with creation, the history of the Fall, Redemption through the Incarnation, and the Church as an eschatological setting.

The Alexandrians were able to locate speculation about the essence of divinity within the Biblical perspective. Hence in considering Neoplatonic doctrine of the One-in-Many—the transcendent being, from whom proceeds the first mind, or Demiurge, who in turn brings into existence the intelligent soul of the universe—they had at least a similitude for the doctrine of the Trinity. But it was a dangerous similitude, and caused some of the Christian thinkers to subordinate the Logos to the Father, and the Holy Spirit to the Logos.

Arius and Eunomius later made the Father the transcendent One; the Logos-Son, the Divine Mind; and the Holy Spirit, something equivalent to the world soul. In reaction to this tendency, the Monarchians (*see* MONARCHIANISM) denied a real distinction in the persons of the Trinity, seeing them as single phases in the divine life, or modes (*see* MODALISM) of the divine being. The latter were likewise influenced by Stoicism, which postulates an expanding and contracting Divinity who produces the universe out of His divine substance and periodically reabsorbs it into Himself.

Conciliar Definitions. Athanasius of Alexandria and the Council of NICAEA I (325) clarified the issue of the Trinity by denying that there could be degrees of divinity, and defining the Son as HOMOOUSIOS or consubstantial with the Father, thus likewise eliminating any idea of inferiority of the Son in relation to the Father. The definition of the consubstantiality of the Holy Spirit with Father and Son was the result of subsequent discussion led by DIDYMUS THE BLIND, HILARY OF POITIERS, Basil of Caesarea, and the Cappadocian fathers and consummated by the Council of CONSTANTINOPLE I in 381.

SCRIPTURAL FOUNDATIONS AND INFLUENCE

The greater portion of this early Christian theology was represented by scriptural exegesis. Justin and Irenaeus had engaged in a typological explanation of the Old Testament in relation to the New, and Clement of Alexandria stressed the fact that the Old Testament was a preparation for the New. He utilized a collection of texts called *Testimonia* that were a continuation of the Jewish technique, to supply a series of types such as the tree of life planted in the world which represented the Divine Wisdom for Moses and Solomon (*Strom.* 5.2.75).

In the East: Clement and Origen. Clement's theology stemmed from his conception of the Logos as the divine reason and teacher of the world, and is developed in his exegesis by an insistence on Christ's activities as the mysteries or sacraments whose salvific effects originated before the creation of the universe, and are extended through time in the Church, in which the hierarchy is established on the pattern of the angelic choirs.

Origen most consciously used the allegorical techniques employed by the pagan teachers in the explanation of Homer and the poets. He worked out a threefold interpretation of the Scriptures: the literal or historical meaning, the moral, and the typological. This methodology was reflected in both Western and Eastern exegesis, rising to a fourfold interpretation—literal, allegorical, typological, and anagogic—with Hilary of Poitiers and RUFINUS OF AQUILEIA (*De bened. patriarch.*).

Origen's *Peri Archon,* or First Principles, is actually an attempt at theological speculation rather than a systematic treatise. Its four books dealt with God, the world, freedom, and revelation, and were explicitly intended as ''an examination into the reasons behind'' the unalterable truths of the faith revealed by Christ and preached by the Apostles. Aided by the Holy Spirit, he desired ''to form a connected series and a body of truths based on the Scriptures and deduced by drawing correct conclusions from those truths'' (*Preface* 10). His errors regarding the preexistence of souls, a possible metempsychosis, and the *anakephalaiosis* or recapitulation arose from Neoplatonist influence in a realm of thought he felt was open to speculation.

The typological approach to theology is furthered by Hippolytus, who developed the relation between Joseph, David, Susanna, and Christ, and the Church. He is the first Father to compose a consecutive explanation of a book of Scripture—his Commentary on the Canticle of Canticles. His contribution to the catechesis of the Resurrection and the mystagogic significance of the Church and Sacraments influenced AMBROSE of Milan and CYRIL OF JERUSALEM, particularly in regard to the triple parousia of Christ in his Christology, ecclesiology and eschatology. METHODIUS OF OLYMPUS pursued the typology of Christ as the new Adam, and of the Church as the new Eve. He gave a mystical explanation of the relation between Christ and the Virgin in an ecclesial sense, and indulged in number speculation certainly influenced by the Pythagoreans.

In the West: Tertullian and His Successors. In the West Tertullian, despite his disjoinder ''What has Athens to do with Jerusalem?'' (*De Idol.* 19), witnessed at once to the Church's theological tradition concerning the nature of God, the relationship between the two Testaments (*Adv. Marc.*), the Christology, and sacramental mysteries of the faith. He helped determine the Church's terminology, and more particularly the development of moral concepts based on free will and God's law, influenced at once by his legal background, the Stoic attitude toward nature, and the Church as an institution in competition with the imperial organization surrounding it.

The law of God and the law of the Gospel were explained as the guide to the Church's tradition and deposit of faith; the bishops were the official dispensers of the divine mysteries, and the Church was the Ark without which no one could be sanctified. In his soteriological thought, sin was a crime against God's sovereignty calling for satisfaction, and words such as debt, guilt, and merit are often employed. The redemption is seen as an intervention of God to vindicate His law through One who took man's sin upon Himself to achieve man's forgiveness.

In order to be the Mediator between God and man, Christ had to be both true God and true man (*Adv. Marc.* 2, 3; *De Resur.* 63). Thus soteriological thought gave rise to Christological precisions, and this is true of Novatian's *De Trinitate,* Ambrose's *De fide,* and Augustine's *De Trinitate,* and led directly to Leo's *Tome to Flavian* accepted at the Council of CHALCEDON, which ''recognized the difference of the natures'' united without admixture or confusion in the One Person of the Son of God.

The Problem of Grace. Western preoccupation with man's moral obligations brought about the problems of the nature of grace and its efficacy posed by the Pelagians (*see* PELAGIUS AND PELAGIANISM) and settled by Jerome, Augustine, and the Roman See; and, while the doctrine of man's deification was brought to the West by Irenaeus and echoes through Tertullian (*Adv. Marc.* 2.27) and Cyprian (*Epist.* 58.6), its appearance in Hilary of Poiters and Leo I is due to their contact with later Eastern ideas. This is likewise true of concern for freedom of the will, which Origen found necessary to assert against the astrologers of his day, and Tertullian defended against the Stoics and Marcion.

Cyprian of Carthage was involved in the controversy over penance and the rebaptism of heretics, problems that forced him to reconsider his doctrine on the unity of the Church, and which led in the 4th and 5th centuries to a development of the Roman understanding of the papal primacy that grew obviously from Siricius and Innocent I to Leo I and Gelasius, and was full-fledged with Gregory the Great.

There was a constant interchange of Western and Eastern ideas all during this period, aided by the exile of Hilary in the East and Athanasius in the West and a constant going back and forth of bishops, scholars, and monks. Athanasius was responsible for the flowering of a vast cenobitic and monastic movement in Italy and Gaul during the 4th century, stimulated by his *Life of St. Anthony the Hermit* (*see* ANTHONY OF EGYPT, ST.). Ambrose of Milan, Rufinus of Aquileia, and Jerome contributed to the furtherance of ascetical thought based upon the writings and experiences of St. Basil, St. PACHOMIUS, and the DESERT FATHERS; they stressed the value of virginity and continence as well as the practice of austere virtue that is a consequence of participation in the mysteries of salvation.

THE GOLDEN AGE OF PATRISTIC THEOLOGY

In the East, theological speculation continued with the mystical tendencies embodied in the Alexandrian doctrine of man made in the image of God and called to the imitation of Christ, as it was developed particularly in GREGORY OF NYSSA, EVAGRIUS PONTICUS, and EPHREM THE SYRIAN. At the same time, Antiochene preoccupation with the literal approach toward the Scriptures and a more Aristotelian anthropology represented by Diodore of Tarsus (d. 394), Flavian of Antioch (d. 404), THEODORE OF MOPSUESTIA (d. 428), and THEODORET OF CYR (d. *c.* 466) made them wary of the allegorical exegesis favored at Alexandria. In their Christology, they insisted upon the human factors in Christ's constitution, leading their Alexandrian opponents to accuse them of dividing Christ into "two sons" when Nestorius refused to apply the term THEOTOKOS to Mary, preferring to call her the *Christotokos,* or Mother of Christ.

Christology. The Christological problem arose in good part from the attempt to apply the Trinitarian concepts of substance and person directly to the person and natures in Christ. It was also the result of the Alexandrian ontological approach, seeing man's deification as his final goal, whereas the Antiocheans had a fear of breaking down the impassable distinction between the finite and the infinite and saw man's destiny in moral perfection that would be realized in the resurrection.

The quarrel came to a climax at the Council of EPHESUS in 431, when the Church defined the doctrine of the Theotokos; it reached a second climax at the Council of Chalcedon (451), when Antiochene, Alexandrian, and Western thought were amalgamated on the basis of Leo's *Tome to Flavian* and the *Letter of Union* signed by both Cyril of Alexandria and John of Antioch in 433. No great progress was made at Justinian's Council of CONSTANTINOPLE II in 553, and as a consequence questions regarding Christ's human faculties returned to bother the Church down to modern times, though the question of two wills was settled at the Council of CONSTANTINOPLE III in 681.

Heretical Views. The controversies during the later patristic period occasioned the rise of two separate heretical churches, the Monophysite and the Nestorian (*see* MONOPHYSITISM; NESTORIANISM), and involved the ecclesiastical and imperial authorities in a series of struggles that resulted in the domination of the Eastern Church by the State, with the emperors taking an active part in the theological controversies. Some of the emperors, such as THEODOSIUS II and JUSTINIAN I, demonstrated considerable theological ability.

The Monophysites, with SEVERUS OF ANTIOCH, PHILOXENUS OF MABBUGH, and their supporters, produced an enormous theological literature and were able to influence clergy, monks, and laity by their insistence on man's vocation to deification with a definite mystical tendency. Their opponents were equally productive, from JOHN THE GRAMMARIAN and FACUNDUS OF HERMIANE, whose *Defense of the Three Chapters* was one of the finer theological productions of the 6th century, to JOHN OF SCYTHOPOLIS, the Chalcedonian who wrote the first commentary on the writings of the Pseudo-Dionysius, and LEONTIUS OF BYZANTIUM, who wrote against both the Nestorians and the Eutychians, employing Aristotelian logic and Neoplatonist psychology.

The two men who dominate the great productive period of patristic theology are JOHN CHRYSOSTOM in the East, and Augustine in the West. Chrysostom exhibited a reluctance to enter the intricacies of theological disputation, saying that the two natures in Christ are conjoined "by a union ineffable and past understanding; ask not how" (*Hom. in Joh.* 11.2). He devoted himself to a practical explanation of the whole of Scripture in his homilies and pastoral instruction that is unsurpassed in breadth of interest, social and psychological understanding, and witness to the traditional teaching of the Church.

Augustinian Theology. St. AUGUSTINE insisted that the understanding of the faith (*intellectus*) is not merely a knowledge of the truths of revelation, but an encounter with God as an end to be loved. It is the *pia fides* that purifies the soul. He refused to separate knowledge from its moral obligations. The Augustinian theology of contemplation implies the use of all man's resources in soul and spirit, and the vision at Ostia was an immortal example of this experience.

In the *De Trinitate* he offered a systematic explanation: the movement toward God constituted by an exercise of wisdom forces the soul to use corporeal objects, then the memory for previous acquisitions, to find God in the superior portion of the mind. The use of sensible similitudes and the resources of science and the arts open the mind to a comprehension of divine things enhanced by faith and elevated by grace. Thus the first seven books of the *De Trinitate* were devoted to the process of *credere:* he established the existence of the Trinity, studied the divine attributes, and answered objections on evidence in the Scriptures and Church Fathers. In books 8 to 15 he proceeded *modo interiore,* by analogies taken from nature, man's moral life, and divine wisdom, to give an insight into the mystery. He thus justified the employment of profane studies and the technique of theology based on pagan disciplines.

In his numerous treatises Augustine covered the whole ambit of theological interest from grace and Christology to the intricacies of the ascetico-mystical life, incorporating the liberal arts, free will and concupiscence, marriage and virginity, and the Church and the Sacraments in a vast synthesis of life in Christ.

Patristic Heritage. The heritage of patristic theology was preserved through the effort of John CASSIAN for the monks of the West, and of CASSIODORUS, ISIDORE OF SEVILLE, and BEDE for the Western Church more generally. In the East, the return to the negative theology of the 1st-century Neoplatonist Albinus, combined with the emphasis of a hierarchical ascension toward mystical union with God, was propagated by the 6th-century mitigated Monophysite writer, PSEUDO-DIONYSIUS the Areopagite. Eastern thought was summed up in the anonymous *De Sectis* and in the writings of the 7th-century Sophronius of Damascus, MAXIMUS THE CONFESSOR, and particularly St. JOHN DAMASCENE, whose *De fide orthodoxa* is a remarkable summary of Greek thought on the principle Christian doctrines and was taken over by the Western scholastics.

Whereas a polemical spirit characterized much of the patristic theological writings, equanimity had been practiced by Clement of Alexandria and Origen; in his five theological orations, Gregory of Nazianzus called for justice and charity in dealing with opponents, while St. Leo the Great insisted on moderation.

The scholastics made considerable use of the patristic writings, particularly in florilegia, or collections of texts that go back to the 3d and 4th centuries and are the continuations of the Biblical *Testimonia.* Their witness to the Church's tradition has never been unheeded; but a tendency to rationalize their teachings and theology generally prevailed in the late scholastic and post-Tridentine period, despite the call of Melchior CANO, and above all PETAU, for a return to the Fathers, and the great work of rediscovery and edition that was undertaken by the humanist Churchmen of the 15th and early 16th century, and pursued assiduously by the MAURISTS.

Since the middle of the 19th century there has been a reflowering of patristic thought, made possible by the comprehensive reprinting effort of J. P. MIGNE, the critical editions of the Berlin and Vienna corpora, the more recent *Corpus Christianorum,* and translations such as the *Sources chrétiennes,* the *Ancient Christian Writers,* and others. The turn of the 20th century saw a reflowering of patristic theology in both Catholic and non-Catholic circles, which seems to have taken on new proportions in the post-World War II period and is a substantial factor in the ecumenical progress resulting from Vatican Council II.

Bibliography: A. H. ARMSTRONG and R. A. MARKUS, *Christian Faith and Greek Philosophy* (New York 1964). J. DANIÉLOU, *Message évangélique et culture hellénistique aux IIe et IIIe siècles* (Tournai 1961); *History of Early Christianity,* 3 v., tr. J. BOWDEN (London and Chicago 1964–77). J. DE GHELLINICK, *Patristique et moyenâge: Études d'histoire littéraire et doctrinale,* v.1 (2d ed. Paris 1949), v.2, 3 (Brussels 1947–48) v.1–3. J. QUASTEN, *Patrology,* 3 v. (Westminster, Maryland 1950–) v.1–3. B. ALTANER, *Patrology,* tr. H. GRAEF from 5th German ed. (New York 1960). A. VON HARNACK, *History of Dogma,* tr. N. BUCHANAN et al., 7 v. (London 1896–99). J. TIXERONT, *History of Dogmas,* tr. H. L. BRIANCEAU, 3 v. (St. Louis 1910–16). AUGUSTINIAN PATRISTIC INSTITUTE OF ROME, *Patrology,* A. DI BERARDINO, ed., with introduction by J. QUASTEN, *The Golden Age of Latin Patristic Literature from the Council of Nicea to the Council of Chalcedon,* tr. P. SOLARI (Westminster 1986). A. GRILLMEIER, *Christ in Christian Tradition,* tr. J. BOWDEN (2d rev. ed. Atlanta 1976). J. J. PELIKAN, *The Christian Tradition,* v. 1, *The Emergence of the Catholic Tradition* (Chicago 1971).

[F. X. MURPHY]

PATRON SAINTS

INTRODUCTION

The custom of designating patron saints arose from the practice of building churches over the tombs of martyrs. Constantine was responsible for the great Roman basilicas of St. Peter and St. Paul-Outside-the-Walls. Similarly the basilicas of St. Lawrence in Agro Verano, St. Sebastian, St. Agnes on the Via Nomentana, among others, were built on sites where their bodies were buried. The saints came to be regarded as the special advocates and intercessors for the churches and the people who assembled in them. Dedication of churches to saints and angels followed. The reference to the seven angels of the seven churches the Book of Revelation (1:20 ff) may have provided a precedent for the practice of churches seeking the patronage of angels. A church in Ravenna was dedicated to St. Michael the Archangel as early as 545.

Over time the choice of a particular patron has depended upon many factors. In summary, patrons have been chosen for one or more of the following reasons: (1) a church or chapel is the burial place of a martyr or con-

Saint Benardo, Patron Saint of Climbers, Valle d'Aosta, Italy. (©Sandro Vannini/CORBIS)

fessor; (2) a church or chapel is the repository of an important relic of the saint; (3) saints who were the first to bring the Gospel message to a region or a people as, for example, St. Patrick in Ireland, St. Ansgar in Scandinavia; (4) the cult of a saint fostered by national pride and tradition; (5) the popularity of a saint at a given time, e.g. St. Thérèse of Lisieux in the 20th century; (6) the personal devotion and priorities of a pastor or important benefactor; (7) the identification of a saint with a particular situation or condition in his lifetime or heritage.

The 1917 Code of Canon Law spoke of *titles,* that is, the permanent names assigned to churches to distinguish one from another. If the title was the name of a saint, the person was called a *patron,* an advocate (1917 CIC c. 1168), and the titular feast was to be celebrated annually in the church. Blessed were able to be named patrons only with permission of the Holy See, generally granted to places and groups associated with the individual. The 1983 code is silent on the matter of titular patrons.

Patrons found their greatest popularity in the high Middle Ages. Towns were named after saints and nearly every institution and circumstance of life had its heavenly protector. The choice of heavenly patrons by guilds of artisans and craftsmen was dictated by some attribute or legend associated with the name of saint that linked their members to him or her. St. Vitus who was said to have been martyred in a caldron appealed to kettle-makers. Archers venerated St. Sebastian. Wagon-makers chose St. Catherine of Alexandria because a wheel was the means of her martyrdom. Tailors sought the patronage of St. Martin of Tours because he was said to have cut his mantle in half, giving one part to a beggar who turned out to be Christ. The intercession of other saints was implored for particular illnesses because they themselves had suffered from a particular malady or they ministered to those who had.

The practice of giving a child a Christian name at baptism is of medieval origin. As late as the ninth century, children in Germany were customarily given old Teutonic names, but gradually the sentiments of the people led to the custom of conferring the name of saints at baptism. The name of John the Baptist was very widely invoked in the 11th century, then the names of the apostles, and eventually the names were taken from litanies of the saints and the liturgical calendar. The importance given in medieval times to patron saints is reflected a decree of the Council of Benevento in 1374 that forbade the practice of repeating the baptismal rite in a case where a name had been omitted in the original administration. The Catechism of the Council of Trent strongly urged that the name given at baptism be from the catalogue of saints.

The saint after whom one is named is held up as a model for imitation as well as being one's guardian and advocate (II, s.v., Baptism, n. 76). The 1917 Code of Canon Law encouraged parents to choose a saint's name and, if they refused, the pastor was to enter both the given name and the name of a saint in the baptismal register (c. 761). The 1983 Code states that "parents, sponsors, and the pastor are to see that a name is not given which is foreign to Christian sentiment" (CIC c. 855).

The patron serves as a model of holiness and charity for the neophyte. The *Catechism of the Catholic Church* explains at baptism that people are sanctified by the Lord's name, and Christians receive their name in the Church. "This can be the name of a saint, that is, of a disciple who has lived a life of exemplary fidelity to the Lord. The patron saint provides a model of charity; we are assured of his intercession" (no. 2156).

Dates in parentheses represent the date that an individual was declared to be patron; most patronages have developed in a less formal manner.

PATRONS

Academics: Thomas Aquinas

Actors: Genesius

Adopted children: Clotilde, Thomas More

Advertisers: Bernardine of Siena (May 20, 1960)

Alpinists: Bernard of Montjoux (or Menthon) (August 20, 1923)

Altar servers: John Berchmans

Anesthetists: René Goupil

Animals: Francis of Assisi

Archaeologists: Damasus

Archers: Sebastian

Architects: Thomas Apostle

Art: Catherine de Virgi of Bologna

Artists: Luke, Catherine of Bologna, Bl. Fra Angelico (February 21, 1984)

Astronomers: Dominic

Athletes: Sebastian

Authors/Writers: Francis de Sales (April 26, 1923), Lucy

Aviators: Our Lady of Loreto (1920), Joseph of Cupertino

Bachelors: Giuseppe Mario Carolo Alphonse Moscati

Bakers: Elizabeth of Hungary, Nicholas

Bankers: Matthew, Bl. Joseph Tardini

Barbers: Cosmas and Damian, Louis

Basket-makers: Anthony, Abbot

Bees: Ambrose

Beggars: Martin of Tours

Blacksmiths: Dunstan

Blood banks: Januarius

Bookbinders: Peter Celestine

Bookkeepers: Matthew
Booksellers: John of God
Boy Scouts: George
Brewers: Luke, Nicholas of Myra
Bricklayers: Stephen
Brides: Nicholas of Myra
Bridges: John Nepomucene, Bénézet
Broadcasters: Gabriel
Builders: Vincent Ferrer
Butlers: Adelelm

Cabdrivers: Fiacre of Breuil
Canonists: Raymond of Peñafort
Carpenters: Joseph
Catechists: Angela Merici, Charles Borromeo, Peter Canisius, Robert Bellarmine
Catechumens: Ambrose of Milan, Augustine of Hippo
Catholic Action: Francis of Assisi (1916)
Catholic Press: Francis de Sales
Charitable societies: Vincent de Paul (May 12, 1885)
Chastity: Thomas Aquinas
Chefs (Italian): Francis Caracciolo (1996)
Chefs (Pastry): Honoratus
Childbirth: Felicity, Raymond Nonnatus, Gerard Majella, Margaret of Antioch, Bl. Marie d'Oignies
Children: Nicholas of Myra
Choirboys: Dominic Savio (June 8, 1956)
Church Universal: Joseph (December 8, 1870)
Circus people: Julian the Hospitaller
Civil Disorder/Riots: Andrew Corsini
Colleges and Universities: Thomas Aquinas, Bl. Contardo Ferrini
Comedians: Vitus
Communications personnel: Gabriel
Computer Users: Isidore of Seville
Confessors: Alphonsus Liguori (April 26, 1950)
Converts: Justin, Elizabeth Seton
Cooks: Martha
Coppersmiths: Maurus

Dairy workers: Brigid of Ireland
Dancers: Vitus
Dentists: Apollonia
Desperate situations: Gregory Thaumaturgist, Jude Thaddeus, Rita of Cascia
Difficulties: Eustace
Divorce: Helena
Dyers: Maurice, Lydia

Ecologists, Environmentalists: Francis of Assisi (November 29, 1979)
Ecumenists: Cyril and Methodius, Bl. Elizabeth Hesselblad, Bl. María Gabriella Sagheddu
Editors: John Bosco
Educators, Catholic: Bl. Karolina Gerhardinger

Emigrants: Frances Xavier Cabrini (September 8, 1950)
Engineers: Ferdinand Ill
Epidemics and Pestilence: Christopher and Giles
Epilepsy: Vitus, Willibrord
Eucharistic Devotion: Pierre Julien Eymard, Paschal Baylon (November 28, 1897)
Expectant mothers: Raymond Nonnatus, Gerard Majella

Falsely accused: Raymond Nonnatus
Families: Bl. Gianna Beretta Molla, Bl. Giuseppina Bonino, Bl. Giovanni Piamarta
Farmers: George, Isidore
Fathers: Joseph (1899)
Firemen: Florian
Fire prevention: Catherine of Siena
First communicants: Tarcisius
Fishermen: Andrew
Flight Attendants: Bona of Pisa (March 2, 1962)
Florists: Thérèse of Lisieux
Forest workers: John Gualbert
Foundlings: Holy Innocents
Friendship: John the Divine, Aelred of Rievaulx
Funeral directors: Joseph of Arimathea, Dismas

Gardeners: Adelard, Tryphon, Fiacre, Phocas
Glassworkers: Luke
Goldsmiths: Dunstan, Anastasius
Gravediggers: Anthony, Abbot
Gypsies: Bl. Zeferino Jimenez

Hagiographers: Athanasius, Gregory the Great
Hairdressers: Martin de Porres
Homeless: Margaret of Cortona, Benedict Joseph Labré
Home Missions: Katharine Drexel
Horses: Giles
Hospital administrators: Basil the Great, Frances X Cabrini
Hospitality/Lodgings: Gertrude of Nivelles, Julian the Hospitaller
Hospitals: Camillus de Lellis and John of God (June 22, 1886)
Housekeepers: Zita
Hunters: Hubert, Eustachius

Infantrymen: Maurice
Innkeepers: Amand, Julian the Hospitaller

Janitors: Theobald
Jewelers: Eligius, Dunstan
Journalists: Francis de Sales (April 26, 1923), Bl. Titus Brandsma
Jurists: John Capistrano

Laborers: Isidore, James, John Bosco
Lawyers: Ivo (Yves Helory), Genesius, Thomas More
Librarians: Jerome
Lighthouse Keepers: Venerius of Milan (March 10,

1961)
Linguists: Gottschalk
Locksmiths: Dunstan
Lost Articles: Anthony of Padua, Arnulf of Metz, Daniel of Padua
Lovers: Raphael, Valentine

Maids: Zita
Mariners: Michael, Nicholas of Tolentino
Marriage: John Francis Regis, Bl. Otto Neururer, Ursula of Cologne, Bl. Benedetta Frassinello, Bl. Elizabeth Canori-Mora, Bl. Giuseppe Tovini
Married Couples: Joachim and Anne, Bl. Luchesius and Buona of Poggibonsi
Merchants: Francis of Assisi, Nicholas of Myra
Messengers: Gabriel
Metal workers: Eligius of Noyon
Military chaplains: John Capistrano (February 10, 1984)
Millers: Arnulph, Victor
Missionaries: Francis Xavier (March 25, 1904), Thérèse of Lisieux (December 14, 1927), Peter Claver (1896, Leo XIII), Benedict the Moor
Missions, parish: Leonard of Port Maurice (March 17, 1923)
Mothers: Monica
Motorists: Frances of Rome
Music: Arnulf of Metz, Cecilia of Rome, Dunstan of Canterbury, Philip Neri
Musicians: Gregory the Great, Cecilia, Dunstan
Mystics: John of the Cross, Teresa of Avila, Bl. Rafqa

Native Americans: Bl. Kateri Tekakwitha
Notaries: Luke, Mark
Nurses and Nursing: Agatha, Catherine of Siena, Elizabeth of Hungary, John of God (1930, Pius XI), Camillus de Lellis, Raphael

Orators: John Chrysostom (July 8, 1908)
Organ builders: Cecilia
Orphans, Abandoned Children: Jerome Emiliani (1928), Bl. Daniel Brottier

Painters: Bl. Fra Angelico
Parenthood: Adelaide of Burgundy, Rita of Cascia
Pharmacists: Cosmas and Damian, Gemma Galgani
Philosophers: Justin, Edith Stein
Physicians: Pantaleon, Cosmas and Damian
Pilgrims: James the Greater
Poets: Brigid of Ireland, John of the Cross
Poor: Lawrence, Anthony of Padua, Bl. Giacomo Cusmano, Bl. Maria Bernardina Jablonska
Poor souls: Nicholas of Tolentino
Possessed: Bruno, Denis
Postal employees: Gabriel
Priests: Jean-Baptiste Vianney (April 23, 1929)
Printers: John of God

Prisoners: Dismas, Joseph Cafasso
Public relations: Bernardine of Siena (May 20, 1960)
Publishers: Bl. Timothy Giaccardo, Bl. Joseph Tardini

Race relations: Martin de Porres
Radiologists: Michael (January 15, 1941)
Refugees: Bl. Angela Truszkowska, Bl. Kateri Tekakwitha
Retreats: Ignatius Loyola (July 25, 1922)

Sailors: Cuthbert, Brendan, Eulalia, Christopher, Peter González, Erasmus, Nicholas
Scholars: Bede the Venerable
Schools, Catholic: Thomas Aquinas (August 4, 1880), Joseph Calasanz (August 13, 1948)
Scientists: Albert the Great (August 13, 1948), Bl. Niels Stensen
Sculptors: Four Crowned Martyrs
Seamen: Francis of Paola
Searchers of lost articles: Anthony of Padua
Secretaries: Genesius
Secular Franciscans: Louis of France, Elizabeth of Hungary
Seminarians: Charles Borromeo
Senior Citizens: Polycarp, Marie Poussepin
Shepherds: Drogo
Shoemakers: Crispin and Crispinian
Sick: John of God and Camillus de Lellis (June 22, 1886)
Silversmiths: Andronicus
Single mothers: Margaret of Cortona
Skaters: Lydwina
Skiers: Bernard of Montjoux (or Menthon)
Social workers: Louise de Marillac (February 12, 1960), John Francis Regis
Soldiers: Hadrian, George, Ignatius, Sebastian, Martin of Tours, Joan of Arc
Spelunkers: Benedict
Stenographers: Genesius, Cassian
Stonecutters: Clement
Stonemasons: Stephen
Students: Thomas Aquinas
Surgeons: Cosmas and Damian, Luke
Swordsmiths: Maurice

Tax collectors: Matthew
Teachers: John Baptist de la Salle (May 15, 1950)
Telecommunications workers: Gabriel (January 12, 1951)
Television: Clare of Assisi (February 14, 1958)
Theologians: Augustine, Alphonsus Liguori, Thomas Aquinas
Thieves, Repentant: Dismas
Tour Guides: Bona of Pisa
Toymakers: Claude
Translators: Jerome

Travelers: Nicholas of Myra, Christopher, Raphael, Julian the Hospitaller

Unborn Children: Bl. Gianna Beretta Molla

Vocations: Alphonsus Liguori, Bl. Annibale Francia

Watchmen: Peter of Alcántara
Weavers: Paul the Hermit, Anastasius the Fuller
Wine merchants and Bar Keepers: Amand of Maestricht
Workers: Joseph

Youth: Aloysius Gonzaga (1729, 1926), John Berchmans, Bl. Pier Giorgio Frassati

INTERCESSORS IN TIMES OF PERIL AND ILLNESS

Abdominal pain: Erasmus
Abuse, Child: Bl. Laura Vicuña, Bl. Maríam Baouardy
Abuse, Wife: Bl. Elisabetta Canori-Mora, Bl. Victoria Rasoamanarivo
AIDS and Incurable Diseases: Bl. Damian de Veuster, Thérèse of Lisieux
Alcoholism: John of God, Monica, Venerable Matthew Talbot
Barren women: Elizabeth
Blindness: Odilia, Raphael, Bl. Rafqa al-Rayes
Cancer: Peregrine, Ezequiel Moreno y Díaz
Deafness: Francis de Sales, Bl. Pierre-François Jamet
Disabled: Bl. Kateri Tekawitha, Bl. Maria Bernardina Jablonska
Dying: Joseph
Earthquakes: Eustochia Calafato
Epilepsy: Albanus of Mainz, Vincent Ferrer, Vitus of Sicily
Eye disease: Lucy, Raphael, Leodogar of Autun
Fever: Antoninus of Florence, Albert of Trapani, Barbara
Glandular conditions: Cadoc of Llancarfan
Gout: Bl. Emilia Bicchieri, Erconwald of London, Gerebernus of Sonsbeck, Gregory the Great, Idesbald of Flanders
Headaches: Teresa of Jesus (Avila), Denis
Heart disease: John of God
Imprisonment: Maximilian Kolbe, Bl. Jacinta Marto, Bl. Maríam Baouardy
Insomnia: Modestus and Crescentia MM, Vitus of Sicily
Invalids: Roch
Liver Disease: Albert of Trapani, Gerard of Brogne, Odilo of Cluny
Lung disease: Bernardino of Siena
Mental Illness: Dymphna of Gheel, Christina Mirabilis
Nervous Disorders: Bartholomew the Apostle
Paralysis: Osmund of Salisbury
Rheumatism: James the Greater
Stomach problems: Brice of Tours, Emeritiana of Rome, Timothy the Apostle

Stress: Walter of Pontoise
Strokes: Andrew Avellino
Throat ailments: Blase
Tuberculosis: Gemma Galgani, Thérèse of Lisieux
Ulcers: Martin of Tours
Wounds: Adelgondes of Maubeuge, Marciana of Mauritania

PLACES

Africa: Moses the African, Our Lady Queen of Africa (declared by Cardinal Lavigerie, 1876)
Algeria: Cyprian of Carthage
Angola: Immaculate Heart of Mary (November 21, 1984)
Central Africa: Most Pure Heart of Mary
Congo, Democratic Republic of: Immaculate Conception
Equatorial Guinea: Immaculate Conception of Mary (May 25, 1986)
Ethiopia: Frumentius
Lesotho: Immaculate Heart of Mary
Madagascar: Vincent de Paul
Nigeria: Our Lady Queen of Nigeria
North Africa: Cyprian of Carthage
South Africa: Our Lady of the Assumption (March 15, 1952)
Tanzania: Immaculate Conception (December 8, 1964)
Tunisia: Immaculate Conception

Central, North and South America
Argentina: Bl. Laura Vicuña, Francis Solano, Immaculate Conception, Our Lady of Lujan
Bolivia: Francis Solano, Our Lady of Candelaria, Our Lady of Copacabana, Our Lady of Mount Carmel
Brazil: Immaculate Conception, Nossa Senhora de Aparecida, Peter of Alcántara
Canada: Anne, John de Brébeuf, Isaac Jogues & Companions, Joseph Québec, John the Baptist
Central America: Our Lady of Guadalupe, Rose of Lima
Chile: Francis Solano, James the Greater, Our Lady of Mount Carmel
Colombia: Louis Bertrand, Peter Claver, Our Lady of Chiquinquira, Our Lady of the Rosary
Costa Rica: Our Lady of the Angels
Cuba: Our Lady of Charity (1605), Virgen de Regla
Dominican Republic: Dominic de Guzmán, Our Lady of High Grace
Ecuador: Sacred Heart of Jesus, Most Pure Heart of Mary
El Salvador: Our Lady of Peace (October 10, 1966)
Guatemala: James the Greater
Haiti: Our Lady of Perpetual Help
Honduras: Our Lady of Suyapa
Jamaica: Mary of the Assumption
Latin America: Rose of Lima
Mexico: Bl. Elías Nieves, Joseph, Our Lady of Guadalupe Cuautitlán, Bonaventure

Mexico City: Philip de las Casas (first native-born saint)
Nicaragua: James the Greater
North America: Isaac Jogues & Companions, Our Lady of Guadalupe
Paraguay: Francis Solano, Our Lady of the Assumption (July 13, 1951), Our Lady of Lujan
Peru: Francis Solano, Joseph (March 19, 1957), Rose of Lima, Turibius of Mongrovejo
Puerto Rico: Our Lady of Divine Providence
Santo Domingo: Our Lady of Ransom
South America: Rose of Lima
United States: Immaculate Conception (1846), Our Lady of Guadalupe
Uruguay: James the Greater, Our Lady of Lujan, Philip the Apostle, Virgen de los Treinte y Tres (November 21, 1963)
Venezuela: Our Lady of Comotomo
West Indies: Gertrude of Helfta

Asia

Borneo: Francis Xavier
China: Joseph, Mary, Queen of China
East Indies: Francis Xavier, Thomas the Apostle
India: Francis Xavier, Our Lady of the Assumption, Rose of Lima, Thomas Didymus, Goa, Bl. Joseph Vaz
Indonesia: Bl. Virgin Mary
Japan: Francis Xavier, Peter Baptist
Korea: Joseph, Bl. Virgin Mary
Mongolia (Inner): Immaculate Conception of Mary
Mongolia (Outer): Francis Xavier
Pakistan: Francis Xavier, Thomas Didymus
Philippines: Pudentiana, Our Lady of the Immaculate Conception, Rose of Lima, Sacred Heart of Mary
Sri Lanka: Lawrence the Deacon, Our Lady of Lanka
Thailand: Bl. Nicholas Bunkerd Kitbamrung
Vietnam: Joseph

Asia Minor: John the Evangelist
Alexandria: Cyril of Alexandria
Arabia: Mary, Our Lady of Arabia
Egypt: Mark the Evangelist
Iran: Addai and Mari, Maruthas
Jordan: John the Baptist
Palestine: Mary, Queen of Palestine
Syria: Addai, Mari
Turkey: John Chrysostom, John the Evangelist

Europe: Benedict of Nursia (declared 1964 by Paul VI), Pope Benedict III, Cyril and Methodius (declared December 31, 1981, by John Paul II), Bridget of Sweden (declared October 1, 1999 by John Paul II), Catherine of Siena (declared October 1, 1999 by John Paul II), Edith Stein (declared October 1, 1999 by John Paul II)
Albania: Our Lady of Good Counsel
Alps: Bernard of Menthon

Armenia: Bartholomew the Apostle, Gregory the Illuminator (apostle)
Austria: Colman of Stockerau, Florian of Noricum, Joseph, Leopold the Good, Maurice of the Theban Legion, Our Lady of Mariazell, Severino
Belgium: Columbanus of Ghent, Joseph, Our Lady of Banneux, Our Lady of Baeuraing
Bosnia: (Banja Luka) Bonaventure
Bulgaria: Cyril and Methodius, Demetrius
Croatia: (Dubrovnik) Blaise of Sebaste
Cyprus: Barnabas the Apostle
Czech Republic: Adalbert, Cyril and Methodius, John of Nepomuk, Ludmilla, Procopius, Wenceslaus of Bohemia
Denmark: Ansgar (apostle of Denmark), King Canute
England: Augustine of Canterbury, George the Great, Gregory the Great, Michael the Archangel
Finland: Henry of Uppsala (apostle)
France: Denis, Joan of Arc, Laurent, Martin of Tours, Our Lady of the Assumption, Remigius, Thérèse of Lisieux (May 3, 1944), Vincent the Deacon
Georgia: Nino
Germany: Boniface
Gibraltar: Bernard of Clairvaux, Our Lady of Europe (May 31, 1979)
Greece: Andrew the Apostle, Nicholas of Myra, Paul of Tarsus
Hungary: Bl. Astericus (Anastasius), Gerard, Stephen of Hungary, Bl. Virgin Mary
Iceland: Ansgar, Thorlac Thorhallsson (January 14, 1984)
Ireland: Brigid of Kildare, Columbanus of Bangor, Patrick of Ireland, Our Lady of Knock, Our Lady of Limerick
Italy: Bernardino of Siena, Catherine of Siena, Francis of Assisi, Our Lady of Loreto, Our Lady of Perpetual Help, Our Lady of Pompeii, Our Lady of Tears, Our Lady of the Snow
Lithuania: Casimir, Cunegund (Kinga, 1695), Hyacinth, John Cantius, John of Dukla, John of Kanty (1737)
Luxembourg: Cunegund, Our Lady of Comfort, Willibrord
Malta: Agatha of Catania, Devota of Corsica, Our Lady of the Assumption, Paul of Tarsus
Monaco: Devota of Corsica
Netherlands: Plechelm, Willibrord
Norway: Olaf of Norway, Magnus of Orkney
Poland: Adalbert of Prague, Casimir, Cunegund (Kinga, 1695), Florian of Noricum, Hedwig of Anjou, Hyacinth, John Cantius (1737), John of Dukla, Our Lady of Częstochowa, Our Lady of Jasna Góra, Stanislaus of Kraków, Stanislaus Kostka
Portugal: Antony of Padua, Francis Borgia, George the Great, Immaculate Conception, Vincent
Romania: Cyril and Methodius, Nicetas

Russia: Andrew the Apostle, Basil the Great, Boris, Casimir, Joseph, Nicholas of Myra, Thérèse of Lisieux, Sergius of Radonez, Vladimir I of Kiev

Scandinavia: Ansgar

Scotland: Andrew the Apostle, Columba, Margaret of Scotland (1673), Palladius

Serbia: Sava

Slovakia: John of Nepomuk, Our Lady of the Assumption, Our Lady of Sorrows

Slovenia: George the Great

Spain: Euphrasius, Felix, Immaculate Conception, James the Greater, John of Avila, John of Nepomuk, Raymond Nonnato, Teresa of Avila, Vincent the Deacon

Sweden: Ansgar, Birgitta of Sweden, Eric, Gall, Sigfrid

Switzerland: Gall, Bl. Nicholas of Flüe

Ukraine: Josaphat, Vladimir

Wales: David (Dewi) of Wales

Oceania: Peter Mary Chanel

Australia: Our Lady Help of Christians (1964), Bl. Mary MacKillop

New Caledonia: Our Lady of the Assumption

New Zealand: Our Lady Help of Christians (1964)

Papua New Guinea: Michael the Archangel (May 31, 1979)

Solomon Islands: Michael the Archangel, Most Holy Name of Mary (September 4, 1991)

Bibliography: D. ATTWATER, *A New Dictionary of Saints*, ed. J. CUMMINGS (rev. ed. Collegeville, Minn. 1993). *Catholic Almanac,* ed. OUR SUNDAY VISITOR (Indiana 1999). *Penguin Dictionary of Saints* (3d ed. London 1995). *Butler's Lives of the Saints*, ed. M. WALSH (San Francisco 1991). H. DELEHAYE, *Sanctus* (Brussels 1954). D. FARMER, *The Oxford Dictionary of Saints* (4th ed. New York 1997). S. KELLY and R. ROGERS, *Saints Preserve Us* (New York 1993). J. C. J. METFORD, *Dictionary of Christian Lore and Legend* (London 1983). H. ROEDER, *Saints and Their Attributes* (Chicago 1955). A. SANDOVAL, *The Directory of Saints* (New York 1996).

[K. I. RABENSTEIN/EDS.]

PATRONATO REAL

Royal patronage, a form of Church-State relationship in which the State played an active role in the administration and support of the Church, developed extensively in the colonial empires of Portugal and Spain. Papal grants were its foundation but it was extended through the centuries by the unilateral action of the State.

Padroado of Portugal

Padroado or patronage is a form of ecclesiastical benefice.

Origin. From the fifth century, laymen were called upon by the Church to help in the building of churches and in the establishment of other pious foundations. In return they were offered several privileges. The Council of Trent was very outspoken on this matter. Two kinds of rights were assigned to the patron: *jus praesentandi* and *jura honorifica.* The first entitled him to appoint the person to the ecclesiastical benefice, whether bishop, parish priest, abbot, etc. Rights and duties of the patrons were summarized in the following Latin verses: *Patrono debetur honos, onus, emolumentum, Praesentet, praesit, defendat, alatur egenus.* Patronage was thus both binding and useful to the patron. In case of need he could even avail himself of the revenues of his church or ecclesiastical foundation.

Christianity developed throughout Europe by means of this system of patronage. Portugal was no exception. Kings and nobles were patrons to many churches, chapels, and other pious foundations. In the 15th century the popes extended Portuguese patronage overseas, as the building of churches and the formation and maintenance of missionaries entailed enormous expenses. It was the Order of Christ, established in Portugal in 1319 to replace the Order of the Temple, then about to be suppressed, which received this right of patronage. As the administrators of the Order of Christ were members of the royal family, the overseas patronage became known as the Royal Patronage. The Church realized that, although there were many misuses and complaints about European patronage, it was necessary to encourage the Portuguese to carry their Christian faith overseas. From then on patronage decayed in Europe, but flourished in Africa, India, Brazil, China, Japan, etc. The reaction of the popes, from the beginning of the Portuguese expansion, was most enthusiastic. MARTIN V in 1418 started a long list of graces and privileges granted by the Church to the Portuguese overseas patronage.

The system was duly carried out with good results. Bishops were presented by the kings of Portugal, as administrators of the Order of Christ and later nominated by the Holy See. In 1580 Portugal fell under the Spanish crown and remained thus up to 1640, when a national revolution reestablished a Portuguese dynasty on the throne. During this period (1580–1640) something new had happened in Church organization. The Congregation for the PROPAGATION OF THE FAITH (Propaganda Fide) was established in 1622, and it immediately took command of all mission work. Its first "Instructions" ordered Propaganda missionaries to carry the gospel to regions other than those already under padroado personnel. From 1622 to 1640 Portuguese patronage cooperated with the Propaganda Fide. In 1640, however, after the victory of the Portuguese revolution, relations between the two missionary bodies were seriously undermined. Spain did not at once recognize Portuguese independence and influenced the Holy See to take the same position. Portuguese bishops died one after the other, both in Europe and in the East, and were not replaced by the normal appointment of others. It was only in 1668, when both Spain and the Holy See recognized Lusitanian independence, that this sad state of affairs could be duly redressed.

Padroado versus Propaganda Fide. During this critical period of 28 years (1640–68) the long, drawn-out clashes began between missionaries sent by the Propaganda and those under the padroado. They took place mainly in Cochin China, Tonkin, Siam, and India. The padroado missionaries had several flourishing missions in these regions that had been entrusted by pontifical bulls to padroado dioceses. Taking advantage of the political situation then prevailing in Europe, Propaganda missionaries, instead of establishing themselves in other places, preferred to occupy positions close to the ones belonging to the padroado dioceses. In France, under Louis XIV, the Société des Missions Etrangères de Paris (*see* PARIS FOREIGN MISSION SOCIETY) was founded in this period.

The Jesuit Alexander de RHODES, after an extensive tour of the East, came to the conclusion that the Church could not depend altogether on the decadent padroado dioceses. According to his opinion, the Holy See should appoint titular bishops or vicars apostolic, sent directly by Rome and independent from Lisbon. Portugal held the opinion that since the dioceses had been duly created and their boundaries properly marked in their respective bulls, any change would have to be agreed upon after mutual consultation. Besides, according to Portuguese officials, the vicars apostolic would be welcome in territories not assigned to the padroado dioceses; once within diocesan boundaries, such vicars apostolic would automatically fall under diocesan jurisdiction.

In 1658 the Holy See appointed the first two vicars apostolic, FRANÇOIS PALLU, Bishop of Heliopolis and Pierre LAMBERT DE LA MOTTE, Bishop of Berith. They received from the Holy See the task of exercising their jurisdiction not only in Tonkin and Cochin China, but also over all adjoining territories. Tonkin and Cochin China belonged to the padroado. A similar occurrence took place in Siam. The missionaries sent by the Société des Missions Etrangères de Paris built a church only four or five miles away from the one under the padroado priests. In 1668 the Holy See declared that Siam belonged indeed to the Diocese of Malacca, but later on, in 1669, came a new statement from Rome to the effect that the French missionaries could hold jurisdiction over their own Christians. Thus originated the famous double jurisdiction. Clashes occurred and in 1673 Siam was definitely taken out of the Malacca diocese. Tonkin belonged to the MACAU diocese, but was also taken over by the Propaganda in 1696, as was Cochin China.

India, however, was the scene of the most deplorable misunderstanding between padroado and Propaganda missionaries. Portuguese padroado had the following dioceses in Indian territory: GOA, Cochin, Mylapur and Cranganor. Bombay became an object of dispute between the Goanese clergy (padroado) and the Propaganda missionaries. Bombay had been given to the English as part of the dowry of the Portuguese Princess Catherine, when she married Charles II of England. The Bombay Catholic population, mainly composed of Goans, remained sympathetic toward their own missionaries (the Goan clergy), who were appointed by their ordinary, the archbishop of Goa. The new Protestant political authorities of Bombay did not rely on such priests and managed to have new missionaries sent them by the Vicar Apostolic of the Great Mogul, recently appointed, Father Mauritius of St. Theresa, an Italian Carmelite. In spite of Portuguese remonstrances, the Holy See agreed to the change and in 1720 the Goan fathers had to leave. As time went on, relations between Goa and Bombay authorities improved and in 1789 the vicar apostolic of the Great Mogul, Father Victory of St. Mary, received official notification to quit Bombay, which by then was the official residence of the same vicars apostolic. Thus the Goan priests came back, but the Bombay Catholics were already deeply divided. The East India Company, in order to avoid any further breaches of the peace, decided to divide the then existent churches between the two groups: two for the padroado and two for the Propaganda missionaries.

Between 1834 and 1836, when Portugal had broken off her diplomatic relations with Rome, the Holy See under Gregory XVI reorganized the Indian missions. Three eminent theologians were consulted as to whether the Holy See could extinguish the Portuguese padroado outside non-Portuguese territories without consulting the patron. Gregory XVI acted immediately and published the brief *Multa praeclare* on April 24, 1838, in which it was solemnly stated that the padroado was to be exercised only in the archdiocese of Goa and in the diocese of Macau. All the other Indian territories would belong to the Propaganda. Although Bombay belonged to the archdiocese of Goa, apparently in Rome it was taken for granted that it did not. It was this geographical error that was at the root of all future clashes. As there was no official new statement from the Holy See regarding Bombay, the padroado missionaries defended their presence in Bombay to their utmost. It was, in fact, during these years that the Church in India was shaken by most regrettable disputes. In 1841 diplomatic relations between Lisbon and Rome were renewed.

In the meantime, however, things went so far that three bishops became involved in the imbroglio: J. da Silva Torres, Archbishop of Goa; J. da Mata, Bishop of Macao; and A. Hartmann, Vicar Apostolic of Patna. Bombay was always the crucial question. While the padroado bishops maintained that until a new official decision by the Holy See was published, Bombay would continue to belong to the archdiocese of Goa, Propaganda circles asserted that by the *Multa praeclare* it had ceased to belong to the padroado and there was no need for further official pronouncement. The Holy See came to the conclusion that the best solution was to conclude a concordat with Portugal.

Conclusion. The concordat was duly signed in 1857. In 1886 a new concordat was negotiated and remained valid until 1928. Portuguese padroado maintained in India, besides the archdiocese of Goa, the diocese of Damão (later attached to Goa), the titular diocese of Cranganor, the diocese of Cochin, and that of St. Thomas of Mylapur. Bombay remained under double jurisdiction. Other agreements were afterward signed with the effect of reducing more and more the field of the padroado missions. In 1950, after the independence of India and upon negotiations with the Holy See, Portugal renounced the padroado in Indian territory, but the archdiocese of Goa kept some mission posts outside Portuguese Goa. A final agreement signed on Oct. 25, 1953, put an end to the padroado in India. In 1974, the Portuguese renounced their padroado privileges over the Archdiocese of Macau, putting an end to the padroado system.

In Africa and in Brazil, the padroado system had no difficulties at all, for the Propaganda missionaries did not try to work in those territories. Conflicts burst out only in territories given first to the padroado but claimed afterward by the Propaganda. As other missionaries stepped in and as Portugal had lost influence in such territories, the padroado had to adapt itself to the new circumstances.

[A. DA SILVA REGO]

Patronato of Spain

The origin, theories, operation, and effects of the patronato of Spain are similar to those of the Portuguese padroado.

Origin and Theories. Upon the return of Columbus from his first trip to America, the rulers of Spain, Ferdinand and Isabella, immediately asked Pope Alexander VI for documents affirming their right to the recently discovered territory (*see* ALEXANDRINE BULLS). Through letters issued in 1493, the Holy Father charged these rulers with the spiritual conquest of the natives of the New World, making concessions so broad and vague that they lent themselves to differing interpretations.

The first of these documents was the confidential *Inter caetera* (May 3) in which a grant was made, with exclusive rights to all the islands and land (the rights of the Portuguese rulers being respected) and with concession of apostolic privileges for the Christianizing enterprise to which the Spanish monarchs were obligated. Others followed: *Piis fidelium* (June 25), granting vicarial power to appoint the missionaries who were to go to the Indies and various privileges to these and to the natives of the lands discovered; *Inter caetera* (probably June 28), broader than the bull of the same name, with some variations but with the same intent; *Eximiae devotionis* (probably July 2), granting *pleno jure* all the privileges that the Portuguese enjoyed; and *Dudum siquidem* (September 25), which annulled the previous concessions and made a new general grant, unconditional and unlimited, and broader so as to include India.

Since the rights acquired by the king over the territories of the Indies were not clarified, the grant of general patronage was issued again during the papacy of Julius II. On July 28, 1508, the bull *Universalis ecclesiae* was issued; it gave the rulers of Castile and León the right in perpetuity to grant permission for the construction of "large churches" and to propose proper persons for the offices and benefices of the cathedrals, collegiate churches, monasteries and other pious places. It stipulated that presentations for benefices decreed in consistory were to be made to the pope and all the rest of the bishops.

From the papal documents, Spanish authors arrived at various theories as to the juridical nature of the royal right, which evolved historically as follows: (1) During the 16th century, patronage, properly speaking, was considered an ecclesiastical juridical right that the king exercised by virtue of specific apostolic concession. (2) In the 17th century it was held that the royal vicariate that made the king a delegate of the pope for the Church in the Indies originated in the Church, but once granted, it was irrevocable, properly and exclusively the monarch's in full right (juridically it could be classified as a mixed right, ecclesiastical and civil). (3) The regalism of the 18th century maintained that it was the right of the monarch, inherent in the crown and as such juridically a purely civil right, which the monarch exercised over some ecclesiastical affairs. The reaction of the Church to the doctrines these theories proclaimed was to put the works of their authors on the Index of Prohibited Books, as was done with the *De indiarum iure* (Madrid 1641) of Juan de Solórzano Pereira, and the *Tractatus de regio patronata* (Madrid 1677) of Pedro Frasso.

Operation. In spite of theoretical distinctions, in practice the right of patronage was exercised in almost the same manner throughout the centuries of viceregal government in the Americas. Since presentation was the essential right of patronage, this aspect is most interesting to examine. Whenever the king had notice of a vacant see, he sent an order to the Cámara of the Council of the Indies to propose candidates. From all the information that had been accumulated on the ecclesiastics, the Cámara selected three names and suggested them to the king, who consulted the father confessor. The latter chose one, which the king invariably proposed to the Holy See for papal approval. The appointment of capitular prebendaries was made in the same way, without the intervention of the Roman Curia.

According to the legislative system of the Indies, the viceroys, the presidents of the *audiencias* and the provincial governors were vice patrons; they were charged with proposing candidates for offices and benefices. In the case of vacancies in benefices held by secular clergy, the bishop or the *cabildo* of the vacant see if the benefice was a bishopric, called the candidates together within a set time. When the examinations had been taken and the candidates approved, the three most suitable ones were proposed to the vice patron; he chose one and proposed him to the bishop for canonical bestowal of the benefice. For benefices held by the regular clergy, the religious superiors selected three of their subjects, in accord with their rights and proposed them to the vice patron. The latter chose one and proposed him to the bishop, who had the right to examine the candidate before approving him for the appointment.

In spite of strict limitation of the right of patronage to the presentation of candidates, the kings arrogated to themselves derivative rights. These involved not only the bureaucratic procedures to which the nominees were subjected (the same as those applying to civil public officials), but also limitations on the autonomy of the Church and of the hierarchy. The Council of the Indies was given the right to examine all documents issued by the Holy See and to allow their free circulation (*regium exequatur*), to hold back those that it did not want to reach the Church in America, or to change their content in order that the king's right of patronage might not be infringed upon. The bishops were prohibited from making visits *ad limina* and from sending information about their dioceses to Rome; they were required to send it to the Council of the Indies. Through these measures the Church in the Indies was kept completely isolated from the Roman Curia during the three centuries of the colonial period.

The king also maintained the right to send the bishop-elect to govern the diocese while procedures were under way to obtain papal approval, as well as the right of being represented in provincial councils and among the applicants for benefices by a royal delegate, who defended patronage. The holders of benefices did not receive inalienable possession of them; they were subject to removal *ad nutum* by the vice patron and the bishop, by common agreement, for just cause. In practice the patronato regulated the qualifications of candidates for the priesthood and for the religious life, as well as the erection of monasteries and the destruction of those built without royal permission. There was even legislation as to the place that the ecclesiastic judge and vicar-general of the diocese, not being prebendary, was to occupy in the meetings of the ecclesiastic chapter inside and outside the choir.

Effects. The methods of control established by the king—many of them not canonical—limited the action of the Church in America and hindered its full development during the viceregal period. The dioceses kept their original limits, which made spiritual government difficult. Permission was denied for building monasteries and other pious establishments; the ordination and profession of mestizos was prohibited (during the 17th century), contributing to the scarcity of secular and regular clergy and of nuns, which deprived the faithful of proper training. The anticanonical subjection of the religious orders to juridic decree and diocesan law limited the privileges and the autonomy which the Church grants to the orders to enable them to develop their apostleship in the most suitable manner; it made them virtually officials of the State.

Because of this system, which prevailed for three centuries, when independence was achieved in the American provinces the Church lacked the training necessary for establishing autonomy within the State. The new governments tried to obtain from the Holy See the same privileges of patronage that the rulers of Castile had enjoyed. Ferdinand VII prevented this through his representative to the Vatican, alleging his right of presentation, which he claimed had been granted to the person of the king, not because of his political bonds with the American people. The new republics systematically rejected nominees who arrived from Rome. In order to reconcile the interests of the various parties, the Holy See tried to provide bishops *in partibus* while the problem was being solved, but this effort met with protest and resistance on the part of the American hierarchy. Pius VII, Leo XII and Pius VIII finally stopped making nominations. In Mexico all the bishoprics were vacant in April 1829.

The Spanish government continued to exercise the right of patronage in Cuba, Puerto Rico and the Philippines during the 19th century.

Bibliography: Portugal. A. DA SILVA REGO, *Le Patronage portugais de l'Orient: Aperçu historique* (Lisbon 1957). J. GODINHO, *The Padroado of Portugal in the Orient, 1454–1860* (Bombay

1924). E. HULL, *Bombay Mission History and the Padroado Question,* 2 v. (Bombay 1927–30). A. LOURENÇO, *Utrum fuerit Schisma Goanum post Breve "Multa praeclare" usque ad annum 1849* (Goa 1947). Spain. J. GARCÍA GUTIÉRREZ, *Apuntes para la historia del origen y desenvolvimiento del regio patronato indiano hasta 1857* (Mexico City 1941). A. DE LA HERA, *El regalismo borbónico en su proyección indiana* (Madrid 1963). P. DE LETURIA, *Relaciones entre la Santa Sede e Hispanoamérica,* 3 v. (*Analecta Gregoriana,* 101–103; 1959–60).

[W. M. PORRAS]

ISBN 0-7876-4014-X

90000

COALINGA REFERENCE
31965000029964
REF. 282.03 NEW V.10

West Hills College Coalinga
Fitch Library
300 Cherry Lane
Coalinga, CA 93210

Coalinga Reference Collecti
31965 0029956
New Catholic encyclopedia